INDEX OF ECONOMIC ARTICLES
In Journals and Collective Volumes

Index of
Economic Articles

IN JOURNALS AND COLLECTIVE VOLUMES

Volume XXX · 1988

Part Two—Author Index

Prepared under the auspices of

THE JOURNAL OF ECONOMIC LITERATURE

of the

AMERICAN ECONOMIC ASSOCIATION

JOHN PENCAVEL

Editor

MOSES ABRAMOVITZ

Associate Editor

DRUCILLA EKWURZEL

Associate Editor

ASATOSHI MAESHIRO

Editorial Consultant

MARY KAY AKERMAN

Assistant Editor

NASHVILLE, TENNESSEE
AMERICAN ECONOMIC ASSOCIATION
1992

Student Classifiers: Ruben Berrios, Shailendra Gajanan, Chang-ky Lee, Simran Sahi, Robert Sinclair, and Walter Smith-Villavicencio.

Library of Congress Catalog Card Number: 61–8020
International Standard Book Number: 0–917290–19–4
International Standard Serial Number: 0536–647X
Printed in the United States of America

TABLE OF CONTENTS

INTRODUCTORY DISCUSSION

This volume of the *Index* lists, both by subject category and by author, articles in major economic journals and in collective volumes published during the year 1988. The articles listed include all articles published in English or with English summaries in the journals and books identified in the following sections. Part One includes the Subject Index of Articles in Journals and Collective Volumes, and Part Two consists of an alphabetical Author Index of all the articles indexed in Part One.

Relationship to JEL

This *Index* is prepared largely as an adjunct to the bibliographic activities of the *Journal of Economic Literature (JEL)*. Economies of joint production are pursued throughout the production process. Journals included are those indexed in the *JEL* quarterly; collective volumes are selected from the annotated 1988 books; the classification system is a more detailed version of the *JEL* system.

Journals Included

The 314 journals listed represent, in general, those journals that we believe will be most helpful to research workers and teachers of economics. These journals are listed below on page x.

Generally, articles, notes, communications, comments, replies, rejoinders, as well as papers and formal discussions in proceedings and review articles have been indexed. There are some exceptions; only articles in English or with English summaries are included—this practice results in a slightly reduced coverage compared with the *JEL* quarterly. Articles lacking author identification are omitted, as are articles without economic content. Identical articles appearing in two different journals in 1988 are listed from both sources. The journal issues included usually fall within a single volume. When a volume of a journal overlaps two calendar years, for example, Fall 1987 to Summer 1988, we include the issues from the two volumes relating to 1988 as best we can determine.

Collective Volumes

The collective volumes consist of the following:
1. *Festschriften*
2. Conference publications with individual papers
3. Collected essays, original, by one or more authors
4. Collected essays, reprinted, by one or more authors
5. Proceedings volumes
6. Books of readings

All original articles in English are indexed with the exception of unsigned articles or articles without economic content. Reprinted articles are included on the basis that a researcher would be interested in knowing about another source of the article. The original publication dates are shown in italics on the citations of reprinted articles. Excerpts are not included. The same article appearing for the first time in different collective volumes in the same year is cited from both publications.

In the article citation, reference to the book in which the article appears is by author or editor of the volume. If the same person or persons wrote or edited more than one book included in the 1988 *Index*, it is indicated by a I or II appearing in both the source given in the article citation and the bibliographic reference in the book listing. If the same person wrote one book and edited another in 1988, the specification of "ed." in the reference indicates which book is being cited.

The collective volumes are listed alphabetically by author or editor beginning on page xvi and include a full bibliographic reference. If there is more than one edition, the publisher cited is the one on the copy the *JEL* received, usually the American publisher.

Arrangement

The *Index* consists of two parts:
1. A Subject Index in which the articles are arranged by subject.
2. An Author Index.

Part One—Subject Index

In Part One, all articles are listed alphabetically by first author under each 4-digit subject category. Joint authors are listed up to three; beyond that, only the first author is listed, followed by *et al.*

There is one exception to the alphabetical author arrangement. In the 0322 category, a subdivision of **History of Thought** entitled **Individuals,** the arrangement is first alphabetical by the individual discussed in the article and then alphabetical by the article's author.

Articles with empirical content or discussing a particular geographic area carry a geographic descriptor (see discussion below).

Classification System

The classification system is an expansion of the 3-digit classification system used in the *Journal of Economic Literature* to a 4-digit system with slightly over 300 subcategories. The classification system, itself, is shown beginning on page xxxvi (Part One). In most cases, the classification heading is self-explanatory; however, in some cases, notes have been added to clarify the coverage or indicate alternative subject classifications. The basic approach in classification is from the point of view of the researcher rather than the teacher; course content does not necessarily coincide with subfields of our classification system. In all cases where there are two or more 4-digit classifications under a 3-digit category, there is a zero classification; in most instances this is labeled "General." The zero or general category has been used both as an inclusive and a residual category. For example, an article discussing *all* aspects of international trade theory appears in the general category. There are also some articles that do not fall in any of the individual subcategories and these, too, are classified in the general or zero category.

The criterion used in the classifying process is whether persons interested in this topic would wish to have the article drawn to their attention. With the advent of our online ECONOMIC LITERATURE INDEX on Dialog and our compact disc EconLit available from SilverPlatter, the interpretation of "interest" has broadened slightly to include cross-classifications that indicate the subject matter, particularly in such categories as industry studies or occupational designations. Over half of the articles are classified in more than one subcategory. From time to time, we find it desirable to add subject classifications as particular topics become prominent or to change subject headings to make them more descriptive of the contents of the category.

Geographic Descriptors

Geographic descriptors appear in brackets at the end of any article entry in the Subject Index where the article cites data from or refers to a particular country or area. Research workers interested in these countries, thus, are made aware of the empirical content in the article. The descriptors used are countries or broader areas, such as Southeast Asia (S.E. Asia); articles referring to cities or regions within a country are classified under the country. In general, the country name is written out in full with some adaptations and abbreviations, *e.g.*, U.S. is used for United States, U.K. for United Kingdom, and U.S.S.R. for Union of Soviet Socialist Republics. Abbreviations include: W. for West, E. for East, S. for South, N. for North. A shortened name such as W. Germany is used rather than the correct, but longer, Federal Republic of Germany. When broader regions are used as descriptors, the article may or may not refer to the full unit. For example, OECD has been used at times when most, but not all, of the OECD member countries are referred to.

Index volumes prior to 1979 sometimes did not include geographic descriptors on articles listed under subject categories 1210, 1211, 1220, 1221, 1230, 1240, and 1241, involving general or comparative economic country studies. In the 1979 *Index* and later volumes, these articles carry geographic descriptors in order to facilitate identification in the ECONOMIC LITERATURE INDEX and on EconLit. Because the descriptor fields are limited to five, very general descriptors, such as LDCs (developing countries) and MDCs (developed countries), are often used on articles.

The fact that an article carries a geographic descriptor does not necessarily preclude its being primarily theoretical in nature. Any theoretical article drawing on empirical data to demonstrate its findings will carry a geographic descriptor.

Topical Guide to the Classification System

There is an alphabetical listing of standard economic terms and concepts at the end of Part One. References are to the appropriate 4-digit classification numbers, not to page numbers.

Part Two—Author Index

Part two consists of an alphabetical Author Index in which citations appear under each author (up to three) of an article. Wherever possible, the full first name and middle initial or middle name(s) are used. Wherever it could be definitely ascertained, articles by the same person are grouped together with only one listing of the name. Authors' first names and initials are listed differently in various journals and books; for example, an individual may be identified as John L. Smith, J. L. Smith, or John Smith. Thus, despite our best efforts, we were left in doubt in several instances. Joint authors are listed up to three; beyond that, only the first author is listed, followed by *et al.* Under each author, articles are listed alphabetically. Names carrying prefixes are alphabetized according to the first *capitalized* letter, with occasional exceptions following national practices; thus, van Arkadie would appear under A and D'Alabro under D.

LIST OF JOURNALS INDEXED 1988

Accounting Review, Vol. 63, Issue nos. 2–4.

Acta Oeconomica, Vol. 39.

L'Actualité Economique, Vol. 64.

African Economic History, Issue no. 17.

American Economic Review, Vol. 78.

American Economist, Vol. 32.

American Historical Review, Vol. 93.

American Journal of Agricultural Economics, Vol. 70.
Title changed from Journal of Farm Economics in 1968.

American Journal of Economics and Sociology, Vol. 47.

American Real Estate and Urban Economics Association Journal, Vol. 16.

Annales d'Economie et de Statistique, Issue nos. 9–12, 1988.
Title changed from Annales de l'INSEE in 1986.

Annals of Public and Co-operative Economy, Vol. 59.

Annals of Regional Science, Vol. 22.

Antitrust Bulletin, Vol. 33.

Applied Economics, Vol. 20.

Asian-Pacific Economic Literature, Vol. 2.

Atlantic Economic Journal, Vol. 16.

Aussenwirtschaft, Vol. 43.

Australian Bulletin of Labour, Vol. 14, Issue nos. 2–4; Vol. 15, Issue no. 1.

Australian Economic History Review, Vol. 28.
Title changed from Business Archives and History in 1967; entitled Bulletin of the Business Archives Council of Australia prior to 1962.

Australian Economic Papers, Vol. 27.

Australian Economic Review, Issue nos. 81–84.

Australian Journal of Agricultural Economics, Vol. 32.

Australian Tax Forum, Vol. 5.

Banca Nazionale del Lavoro—Quarterly Review, Issue nos. 164–167.

Bangladesh Development Studies, Vol. 16.

British Journal of Industrial Relations, Vol. 26.

British Review of Economic Issues, Vol. 10.

Brookings Papers on Economic Activity, Issue nos. 1–2, 1988.

Bulletin for International Fiscal Documentation, Vol. 42.

Bulletin of Economic Research, Vol. 40.
Title changed from Yorkshire Bulletin of Economic and Social Research in 1971.

Bulletin of Indonesian Economic Studies, Vol. 24.

Business Economics, Vol. 23.

Business History Review, Vol. 62.
Title changed from Bulletin of the Business Historical Society in 1954.

Cahiers Économiques de Bruxelles, Issue nos. 117–120.

Cambridge Journal of Economics, Vol. 12.

Canadian Journal of Agricultural Economics, Vol. 36.

Canadian Journal of Development Studies, Vol. 9.

Canadian Journal of Economics, Vol. 21.

Canadian Public Policy, Vol. 14.

Carnegie–Rochester Conference Series on Public Policy, Vols. 28–29.
Vols. 1–17 were listed as supplements to the Journal of Monetary Economics.

Cato Journal, Vol. 7, Issue no. 3; Vol. 8, Issue nos. 1–2.

Cepal Review, Issue nos. 34–36.

Challenge, Vol. 31.

Chinese Economic Studies, Vol. 21, Issue nos. 2–4; Vol. 22, Issue no. 1.

Colección Estudios CIEPLAN, Issue nos. 23–25.

Comparative Economic Studies, Vol. 30.
Title changed from ACES Bulletin in 1985.

Contemporary Policy Issues, Vol. 6.

Cuadernos de Economia, Vol. 25.

Czechoslovak Economic Digest, Issue nos. 1–8, 1988.

Czechoslovak Economic Papers, Issue no. 25.

Demography, Vol. 25.

Desarrollo Económico, Vol. 27, Issue no. 108; Vol. 28, Issue nos. 109–111.

Developing Economies, Vol. 26.

Eastern Africa Economic Review, Vol. 4.

Eastern Economic Journal, Vol. 14.

Eastern European Economics, Vol. 26, Issue nos. 3–4; Vol. 27, Issue nos. 1–2.

Econometric Reviews, Vol. 7.

Econometrica, Vol. 56.

Economia (Portuguese Catholic University), Vol. 12.

Economia Internazionale, Vol. 41.

Economia e Lavoro, Vol. 22.

Economia Politica, Vol. 5, Issue nos. 2–3.

Economia delle Scelte Pubbliche/Journal of Public Finance and Public Choice, Vol. 6.

Economic Analysis and Workers' Management, Vol. 22.

Economic Computation and Economic Cybernetics Studies and Research, Vol. 23.
   Title changed from Studii şi Cercetǎri Economicè in 1974. Changed from issue numbers to volume numbers in 1978.

Economic Development and Cultural Change, Vol. 36, Issue nos. 2–4; Vol. 37, Issue no. 1.

Economic Geography, Vol. 64.

Economic Inquiry, Vol. 26.
   Title changed from Western Economic Journal in 1974.

Economic Journal, Vol. 98.

Economic Modelling, Vol. 5.

Economic Notes, Issue nos. 1–3, 1988.

Economic Record, Vol. 64.

Economic Review (Keizai Kenkyu), Vol. 39.

Economic and Social Review, Vol. 19, Issue nos. 2–4; Vol. 20, Issue no. 1.

Economic Studies Quarterly, Vol. 39.

Economica, Vol. 55.
   Title changed from Economica, N.S. in 1974.

Económica, Vol. 34.

Economics of Education Review, Vol. 7.

Economics Letters, Vols. 26–28.

Economics and Philosophy, Vol. 4.

Economics of Planning, Vol. 22.

Économie Appliquée, Vol. 41.

Économies et Sociétés, Vol. 22.

De Economist, Vol. 136.

Ekonomiska Samfundets Tidskrift, Vol. 41.

Empirica, Vol. 15.

Empirical Economics, Vol. 13.

Energy Economics, Vol. 10.

Energy Journal, Vol. 9, Issue nos. 1, 3–4; Special Electricity Reliability Issue; Special South and Southeast Asia Pricing Issue.

Environment and Planning A, Vol. 20.

Estudios Económico, Vol. 3.

European Economic Review, Vol. 32.

European Review of Agricultural Economics, Vol. 15.

Explorations in Economic History, Vol. 25.
   Title changed from Explorations in Entrepreneurial History in 1969–70.

Federal Reserve Bank of Atlanta Economic Review, Vol. 73.

Federal Reserve Bank of Dallas Economic Review, January, March, May, July, September, November, 1988.

Federal Reserve Bank of Minneapolis Quarterly Review, Vol. 12.

Federal Reserve Bank of New York Quarterly Review, Vol. 13, Issue nos. 1–3.

Federal Reserve Bank of Richmond Economic Review, Vol. 74.

Federal Reserve Bank of San Francisco Economic Review, Issue nos. 1–4, 1988.

Federal Reserve Bank of St. Louis Review, Vol. 70.

Journal of Econometrics, Vols. 37–39.

Journal of Economic Behavior and Organization, Vols. 9–10.

Journal of Economic Development, Vol. 13.

Journal of Economic Dynamics and Control, Vol. 12.

Journal of Economic Education, Vol. 19.

Journal of Economic History, Vol. 48.

Journal of Economic Issues, Vol. 22.

Journal of Economic Literature, Vol. 26.

Journal of Economic Perspectives, Vol. 2

Journal of Economic Psychology, Vol. 9.

Journal of Economic Studies, Vol. 15.

Journal of Economic Surveys, Vol. 2.

Journal of Economic Theory, Vols. 44–46.

Journal of Economics (Zeitschrift für Nationalökonomie), Vol. 48.
Title changed from **Zeitschrift für Nationalökonomie** in 1986.

Journal of Economics and Business, Vol. 40.
Title changed from **Economics and Business Bulletin** in 1972–73.

Journal of Energy and Development, Vol. 13, Issue no. 2; Vol. 14, Issue no. 1.

Journal of Environmental Economics and Management, Vol. 15.

Journal of European Economic History, Vol. 17.

Journal of Finance, Vol. 43.

Journal of Financial Economics, Vols. 20–22.

Journal of Financial and Quantitative Analysis, Vol. 23.

Journal of Financial Research, Vol. 11.

Journal of Financial Services Research, Vol. 1, nos. 2–4.

Journal of Futures Markets, Vol. 8.

Journal of Health Economics, Vol. 7.

Journal of Human Resources, Vol. 23.

Journal of Industrial Economics, Vol. 36, Issue nos. 3–4; Vol. 37, Issue nos. 1–2.

Journal of Institutional and Theoretical Economics, Vol. 144.
Title changed from **Zeitschrift für die gesamte Staatswissenchaft** in 1986.

Journal of International Economics, Vols. 24–25.

Journal of International Money and Finance, Vol. 7.

Journal of the Japanese and International Economies, Vol. 2.

Journal of Labor Economics, Vol. 6.

Journal of Labor Research, Vol. 9.

Journal of Law and Economics, Vol. 31.

Journal of Law, Economics, and Organization, Vol. 4.

Journal of Legal Studies, Vol. 17.

Journal of Macroeconomics, Vol. 10.

Journal of Mathematical Economics, Vol. 17.

Journal of Monetary Economics, Vols. 21–22.

Journal of Money, Credit and Banking, Vol. 20.

Journal of Policy Analysis and Management, Vol. 7, Issue nos. 2–4.

Journal of Policy Modeling, Vol. 10.

Journal of Political Economy, Vol. 96.

Journal of Portfolio Management, Vol. 14, Issue nos. 2–4; Vol. 15, Issue no. 1.

Journal of Post Keynesian Economics, Vol. 10, Issue nos. 2–4; Vol. 11, Issue no. 1.

Journal of Public Economics, Vols. 35–37.

Journal of Quantitative Economics, Vol. 4.

Journal of Regional Science, Vol. 28.

Journal of Risk and Insurance, Vol. 55.

Journal of Risk and Uncertainty, Vol. 1.

Journal of the Royal Statistical Society, Series A, Vol. 151.

Journal for Studies in Economics and Econometrics, Vol. 12.

Journal of Transport Economics and Policy, Vol. 22.

Journal of Urban Economics, Vols. 23–24.

Recherches Economiques de Louvain, Vol. 54.

Regional Science Perspectives, Vol. 18.

Regional Science and Urban Economics, Vol. 18.

Regional Studies, Vol. 22, Issue nos. 2–6.

Resources and Energy, Vol. 10.

Review of Black Political Economy, Vol. 16, Issue nos. 3–4; Vol. 17, Issue nos. 1–2.

Review of Economic Conditions in Italy, Issue nos. 1–3, 1988.

Review of Economic Studies, Vol. 55.

Review of Economics and Statistics, Vol. 70.
Title changed from The Review of Economic Statistics in 1948.

Review of Income and Wealth, Vol. 34.

Review of Industrial Organization, Vol. 3, Issue nos. 3–4.

Review of Marketing and Agricultural Economics, Vol. 56.

Review of Radical Political Economics, Vol. 20.

Review of Regional Studies, Vol. 18.

Review of Social Economy, Vol. 46.

Revue d'Economie Politique, Vol. 98.

Revue Économique, Vol. 39.

Ricerche Economiche, Vol. 42, Issue nos. 2–4.

Rivista Internazionale di Scienze Economiche e Commerciali, Vol. 35.

Rivista di Storia Economica, Vol. 5.

Scandinavian Economic History Review, Vol. 36.

Scandinavian Journal of Economics, Vol. 90.
Title changed from Swedish Journal of Economics in 1976; entitled Ekonomisk Tidskrift prior to 1965.

Schweizerische Zeitschrift für Volkswirtschaft und Statistik, Vol. 124.

Science and Society, Vol. 52.

Scottish Journal of Political Economy, Vol. 35.

Singapore Economic Review, Vol. 33.
Title changed from Malayan Economic Review in 1983.

Social Choice and Welfare, Vol. 5.

Social and Economic Studies, Vol. 37.

Social Science Quarterly, Vol. 69.

Social Security Bulletin, Vol. 51.

South African Journal of Economics, Vol. 56.

Southern Economic Journal, Vol. 54, Issue nos. 3–4; Vol. 55, Issue nos. 1–2.

Southern Journal of Agricultural Economics, Vol. 20.

Soviet and Eastern European Foreign Trade, Vol. 24.

Soviet Economy, Vol. 4.

Statistical Journal, Vol. 5, Issue nos. 2–4.

Studi Economici, Vol. 43.

Survey of Current Business, Vol. 68.

Tijdschrift voor Economie en Management, Vol. 33.
Title changed from Tijdschrift voor Economie in 1975.

Urban Studies, Vol. 25.

Water Resources Research, Vol. 24.

Weltwirtschaftliches Archiv, Vol. 124.

Western Journal of Agricultural Economics, Vol. 13.

World Bank Economic Review, Vol. 2.

World Bank Research Observer, Vol. 3.

World Development, Vol. 16.

World Economy, Vol. 11.

Yale Journal on Regulation, Vol. 5.

Yale Law Journal, Vol. 97, Issue nos. 3–8; Vol. 98, Issue nos. 1–2.

Zeitschrift für Betriebswirtschaft, Vol. 58.

Zeitschrift für Wirtschafts- und Socialwissenschaften, Vol. 108.

LIST OF COLLECTIVE VOLUMES INDEXED 1988

AARON, HENRY J.; GALPER, HARVEY AND PECHMAN, JOSEPH A., eds. *Uneasy compromise: Problems of a hybrid income–consumption tax.* Studies of Government Finance: Second Series. Washington, D.C.: Brookings Institution, 1988.

ABED, GEORGE T., ed. *The Palestinian economy: Studies in development under prolonged occupation.* London and New York: Routledge, 1988.

ADLER, NANCY J. AND IZRAELI, DAFNA, eds. *Women in management worldwide.* Armonk, N.Y. and London: Sharpe, 1988.

AGANBEGYAN, ABEL AND TIMOFEYEV, TIMOR. *The new stage of perestroika.* Special Report series. New York: Institute for East–West Security Studies, 1988.

AHO, C. MICHAEL AND LEVINSON, MARC. *After Reagan: Confronting the changed world economy.* New York: Council on Foreign Relations, 1988.

ALBANESE, PAUL J., ed. *Psychological foundations of economic behavior.* With a foreword by TIBOR SCITOVSKY. New York and London: Greenwood Press, Praeger, 1988.

ALBERT, BILL AND GRAVES, ADRIAN, eds. *The world sugar economy in war and depression, 1914–40.* New York and London: Routledge, 1988.

ALLEN, JOHN AND MASSEY, DOREEN, eds. *The economy in question.* Restructuring Britain series. Newbury Park, Calif.; London and New Delhi: Sage in association with the Open University, 1988.

ALLEN, KRISTEN AND MACMILLAN, KATIE, eds. *U.S.–Canadian agricultural trade challenges: Developing common approaches: Proceedings of a Symposium held at Spring Hill Conference Center, Wayzata, Minnesota, July 22–24, 1987.* Washington, D.C.: Resources for the Future, 1988.

ALPER, NEIL O. AND HELLMAN, DARYL A., eds. *Economics of crime: A reader.* Needham Heights, Mass.: Simon and Schuster, Ginn Press, 1988.

AMBROSETTI, ANTONIO; GORI, FRANCO AND LUCCHETTI, ROBERTO, eds. *Mathematical economics: Lectures given at the 2nd 1986 Session of the Centro Internazionale Matematico Estivo (C.I.M.E.) held at Montecatini Terme, Italy, June 25–July 3, 1986.* Lecture Notes in Mathematics series, vol. 1330. New York; Berlin; London and Tokyo: Springer, 1988.

ANDERSON, ANNELISE AND BARK, DENNIS L., eds. *Thinking about America: The United States in the 1990s.* Stanford, Calif.: Hoover Institution Press; distributed by National Book Network, Lanham, Md., 1988.

ANDERSON, PHILIP W.; ARROW, KENNETH J. AND PINES, DAVID, eds. *The economy as an evolving complex system: The proceedings of the Evolutionary Paths of the Global Economy Workshop, held September, 1987, in Santa Fe, New Mexico.* Santa Fe Institute Studies in the Sciences of Complexity, vol. 5. Redwood City, Calif.; Don Mills, Ontario; Wokingham, U.K. and Sydney: Addison-Wesley, 1988.

ANNIS, SHELDON AND HAKIM, PETER, eds. *Direct to the poor: Grassroots development in Latin America.* Boulder, Colo. and London: Rienner, 1988.

ANTONELLI, GILBERTO AND QUADRIO-CURZIO, ALBERTO, eds. *The agro-technological system towards 2000: A European perspective.* Contributions to Economic Analysis series, no. 174. Amsterdam; New York; Oxford and Tokyo: North-Holland; distributed in the U.S. and Canada by Elsevier Science, New York, 1988.

ARCHER, LEONIE J., ed. *Slavery and other forms of unfree labour.* History Workshop Series. London and New York: Routledge, 1988.

ARESTIS, PHILIP, ed. *Post-Keynesian monetary economics: New approaches to financial modelling.* New Directions in Modern Economics series. Aldershot, U.K.: Elgar; distributed in the U.S. by Gower, Brookfield, Vt., 1988.

ARROW, KENNETH J., ed. *The balance between industry and agriculture in economic development: Proceedings of the Eighth World Congress of the International Economic Association, Delhi,*

India. Volume 1. *Basic issues*. New York: St. Martin's Press in association with the International Economic Association, 1988.

ARROW, KENNETH J. AND BOSKIN, MICHAEL J., eds. *The economics of public debt: Proceedings of a conference held by the International Economic Association at Stanford, California*. New York: St. Martin's Press, 1988.

ASEFA, SISAY. ed. *World food and agriculture: Some problems and issues*. Kalamazoo, Mich.: W. E. Upjohn Institute for Employment Research, 1988.

ASIMAKOPULOS, ATHANASIOS. *Investment, employment and income distribution*. Aspects of Political Economy series. Boulder, Colo.: Westview Press; Cambridge: Polity Press in association with Blackwell, 1988.

ASIMAKOPULOS, ATHANASIOS, ed. *Theories of income distribution*. Recent Economic Thought Series. Norwell, Mass.; Lancaster and Dordrecht: Kluwer Academic, 1988.

ASSOCIATION OF PRIVATE EDUCATION. *Journal of Private Enterprise*. Vol. 6, no. 1. *Proceedings of the Thirteenth Annual Conference, Cleveland, Ohio, April 24–26, 1988*. Waco, Tex.: Author, 1988.

ATTWOOD, D. W. AND BAVISKAR, B. S., eds. *Who shares? Co-operatives and rural development*. Oxford; New York; Toronto and Delhi: Oxford University Press, 1988.

AUERBACH, ALAN J., ed. *Corporate takeovers: Causes and consequences*. National Bureau of Economic Research Project Report series. Chicago and London: University of Chicago Press, 1988. (I)

AUERBACH, ALAN J., ed. *Mergers and acquisitions*. National Bureau of Economic Research Project Report series. Chicago and London: University of Chicago Press, 1988. (II)

AUSUBEL, JESSE H. AND HERMAN, ROBERT, eds. *Cities and their vital systems: Infrastructure past, present, and future*. National Academy of Engineering Series on Technology and Social Priorities. Washington, D.C.: National Academy Press, 1988.

AYDALOT, PHILIPPE AND KEEBLE, DAVID, eds. *High technology industry and innovative environments: The European experience*. New York and London: Routledge, 1988.

BAILEY, DEREK T., ed. *Accounting in socialist countries*. London and New York: Routledge, Chapman and Hall; Routledge, 1988.

BAILEY, STEPHEN JAMES AND PADDISON, RONAN, eds. *The reform of local government finance in Britain*. London and New York: Routledge, 1988.

BALDWIN, ROBERT E., ed. *Trade policy in a changing world economy*. Chicago: University of Chicago Press, 1988. (I)

BALDWIN, ROBERT E., ed. *Trade policy issues and empirical analysis*. National Bureau of Economic Research Conference Report series. Chicago and London: University of Chicago Press, 1988. (II)

BALDWIN, ROBERT E.; HAMILTON, CARL B. AND SAPIR, ANDRÉ, eds. *Issues in U.S.–EC trade relations*. National Bureau of Economic Research Conference Report series. Chicago and London: University of Chicago Press, 1988.

BARBER, WILLIAM J., ed. *Breaking the academic mould: Economists and American higher learning in the nineteenth century*. Middletown, Conn.: Wesleyan University Press; distributed by Harper and Row, Scranton, Pa., 1988.

BARKER, TERRY AND DUNNE, PAUL, eds. *The British economy after oil: Manufacturing or services?* London; New York and Sydney: Croom Helm in association with Methuen, 1988.

BARNETT, WILLIAM A.; BERNDT, ERNST R. AND WHITE, HALBERT, eds. *Dynamic econometric modeling: Proceedings of the Third International Symposium in Economic Theory and Econometrics*. International Symposia in Economic Theory and Econometrics series. Cambridge; New York and Melbourne: Cambridge University Press, 1988.

BARRÈRE, ALAIN, ed. *The foundations of Keynesian analysis: Proceedings of a conference held at the University of Paris I—Pantheon-Sorbonne*, New York: St. Martin's Press, 1988.

BATES, ROBERT H., ed. *Toward a political economy of development: A rational choice perspective*. California Series on Social Choice and Political Economy, no. 14. Berkeley and London: University of California Press, 1988.

and wealth distribution. Brighton, United Kingdom: Simon and Schuster International Group, Wheatsheaf Books; New York: St. Martin's Press, 1988.

BROWN, ELEANOR, ed. *Readings, issues, and questions in public finance.* Irwin Series in Economics. Homewood, Ill.: Irwin, 1988.

BROWN, ROY CHAMBERLAIN, ed. *Quantity and quality in economic research.* Volume 2. Lanham, Md. and London: University Press of America; Santa Rosa, Calif.: International Society of Statistical Science in Economics, 1988.

BROWNE, LYNN E. AND ROSENGREN, ERIC S., eds. *The merger boom: Proceedings of a conference held at Melvin Village, New Hampshire, October 1987.* Conference Series, no. 31. Boston: Federal Reserve Bank of Boston, 1988.

BRUNO, MICHAEL, ET AL., eds. *Inflation stabilization: The experience of Israel, Argentina, Brazil, Bolivia, and Mexico.* Cambridge, Mass. and London: MIT Press, 1988.

BRYANT, RALPH C., ET AL., eds. *Empirical macroeconomics for interdependent economies.* Washington, D.C.: Brookings Institution, 1988.

BRYANT, RALPH C.; HOLTHAM, GERALD AND HOOPER, PETER, eds. *External deficits and the dollar: The pit and the pendulum.* Washington, D.C.: Brookings Institution, 1988.

BULMER-THOMAS, VICTOR. *Studies in the economics of Central America.* New York: St. Martin's Press, 1988.

BURKE, EDMUND, III, ed. *Global crises and social movements: Artisans, peasants, populists, and the world economy.* Boulder, Colo. and London: Westview Press, 1988.

BURSTEIN, MEYER LOUIS. *Studies in banking theory, financial history and vertical control.* New York: St. Martin's Press, 1988.

BURTON, JOHN F., JR., ed. *New perspectives in workers' compensation.* Frank W. Pierce Memorial Lectureship and Conference Series, no. 7. Ithaca: ILR Press, 1988.

BUTLER, JAMES R. G. AND DOESSEL, DARREL P., eds. *Economics and Health: 1987 Proceedings of the Ninth Australian Conference of Health Economists.* Australian Studies in Health Service Administration series, no. 63. Kensington: University of New South Wales, School of Health Administration, 1988.

BYRNE, JOHN AND RICH, DANIEL, eds. *Planning for changing energy conditions.* Energy Policy Studies series, vol. 4. New Brunswick, N.J. and Oxford: Transaction Books, 1988.

CAMPBELL, DONALD T. *Methodology and epistemology for social science: Selected papers.* Edited by E. SAMUEL OVERMAN. Chicago and London: University of Chicago Press, 1988.

CANADIAN TAX FOUNDATION. *Income tax enforcement, compliance, and administration: Corporate management tax conference, 1988.* Toronto: Author, 1988.

CANDILIS, WRAY O., ed. *United States service industries handbook.* Foreword by SENATOR WILLIAM PROXMIRE. Westport, Conn. and London: Praeger, 1988.

CANTO, VICTOR A. AND LAFFER, ARTHUR B., eds. *Supply-side portfolio strategies.* Westport, Conn. and London: Greenwood Press, Quorum Books, 1988.

CARLSSON, JERKER AND SHAW, TIMOTHY M., eds. *Newly industrializing countries and the political economy of South–South relations.* New York: St. Martin's Press, 1988.

CARTER, COLIN A. AND GARDINER, WALTER H., eds. *Elasticities in international agricultural trade.* Westview Special Studies in International Economics and Business series. Boulder, Colo. and London: Westview Press, 1988.

CARTER, DONALD D., ET AL. *Labour law under the charter: Proceedings of a conference sponsored by Industrial Relations Centre/School of Industrial Relations and Faculty of Law, Queen's University at Kingston, 24–26 September 1987.* Kingston, Ontario: Queen's University, *Queen's Law Journal* and Industrial Relations Centre, 1988.

CASSING, JAMES H. AND HUSTED, STEVEN L., eds. *Capital, technology, and labor in the new global economy.* AEI Studies, no. 480. Washington, D.C.: American Enterprise Institute for Public Policy Research; distributed by University Press of America, Lanham, Md. and London, 1988.

CAVACIOCCHI, SIMONETTA, ed. *I porti come impresa economica.* Instituto Internazionale di Storia Economica, "F. Datini"—Prato, Serie II, no. 19. Florence: Le Monnier, 1988.

CREASEY, PAULINE AND MAY, SIMON, eds. *The European armaments market and procurement cooperation.* With contributions by FRANÇOIS HEISBOURG AND KEITH HARTLEY. New York: St. Martin's Press, 1988.

CROSS, ROD, ed. *Unemployment, hysteresis and the natural rate hypothesis.* Oxford and New York: Blackwell, 1988.

CROW, BEN AND THORPE, MARY, ET AL. *Survival and change in the third world.* New York: Oxford University Press, 1988.

CURRIE, DAVID AND VINES, DAVID, eds. *Macroeconomic interactions between North and South.* Cambridge; New York and Melbourne: Cambridge University Press, 1988.

CURTIS, DONALD; HUBBARD, MICHAEL AND SHEPHERD, ANDREW. *Preventing famine: Policies and prospects for Africa.* With contributions from EDWARD CLAY ET AL. New York and London: Routledge, 1988.

CYERT, RICHARD M. *The economic theory of organization and the firm.* New York: New York University Press; distributed by Columbia University Press, 1988.

CYERT, RICHARD M. AND MOWERY, DAVID C., eds. *The impact of technological change on employment and economic growth: Papers commissioned by the Panel on Technology and Employment.* Cambridge, Mass.: Harper and Row, Ballinger, 1988.

DADUNA, JOACHIM R. AND WREN, ANTHONY, eds. *Computer-aided transit scheduling: Proceedings of the Fourth International Workshop on Computer-Aided Scheduling of Public Transport.* Lecture Notes in Economics and Mathematical Systems series, vol. 308. New York; Berlin; London and Tokyo: Springer, 1988.

DANZIGER, SHELDON H. AND PORTNEY, KENT E., eds. *The distributional impacts of public policies.* Policy Studies Organization Series. New York: St. Martin's Press in association with the Policy Studies Organization, 1988.

DANZIGER, SHELDON H. AND WITTE, JOHN F., eds. *State policy choices: The Wisconsin experience.* La Follette Public Policy Series. Madison: University of Wisconsin Press, 1988.

DARNELL, ADRIAN AND EVANS, LYNNE, eds. *Contemporary economics: A teacher's update.* Oxford and Atlantic Highlands, N.J.: Allan, 1988.

DAUGHETY, ANDREW F., ed. *Cournot oligopoly: Characterization and applications.* Cambridge; New York and Melbourne: Cambridge University Press, 1988.

DEMSETZ, HAROLD. *Ownership, control and the firm.* The Organization of Economic Activity series, vol. 1. Oxford and New York: Blackwell, 1988.

DERNBERGER, ROBERT F. AND ECKAUS, RICHARD S. *Financing Asian development 2: China and India.* Asian Agenda Report series, no. 8. Lanham, Md. and London: University Press of America; New York: The Asia Society, 1988.

DEVINNEY, TIMOTHY M., ed. *Issues in pricing: Theory and research.* Lexington, Mass. and Toronto: Heath, Lexington Books, 1988.

DÍAZ-ALEJANDRO, CARLOS F. *Trade, development and the world economy: Selected essays of Carlos F. Díaz-Alejandro.* Edited by ANDRÉS VELASCO. Oxford and New York: Blackwell, 1988.

DICKE, DETLEV C. AND PETERSMANN, ERNST-ULRICH, eds. *Foreign trade in the present and a New International Economic Order.* Progress and Undercurrents in Public International Law series, vol. 4. Fribourg, Switzerland: University Press in cooperation with the International Law Association's Committee on Legal Aspects of a New International Economic Order; distributed by Westview Press, Boulder, Colo., 1988.

DICKSON, MICHAEL G.; ROSENER, WOLFGANG AND STORM, PAUL M., eds. *Security on movable property and receivables in Europe: The principal forms of security in the European Community (except Greece) and Switzerland.* Oxford: ESC for the Association Européenne d'Etudes Juridiques et Fiscales, 1988.

DIEBOLD, WILLIAM, JR., ed. *Bilateralism, multilateralism and Canada in U.S. trade policy.* Council on Foreign Relations Series on International Trade. Cambridge, Mass.: Harper and Row, Ballinger, 1988.

DIJKSTRA, THEO K., ed. *On model uncertainty and its statistical implications: Proceedings of a workshop, held in Groningen, the Netherlands, September 25–26, 1986.* Lecture Notes in Economics and Mathematical Systems series, vol. 307. New York; Berlin; London and Tokyo: Springer, 1988.

DIMSON, ELROY, ed. *Stock market anomalies*. Cambridge; New York and Melbourne: Cambridge University Press, 1988.

DLUGOS, GÜNTER; DOROW, WOLFGANG AND WEIERMAIR, KLAUS, eds. *Management under differing labour market and employment systems*. In collaboration with FRANK C. DANESY. Berlin and New York: de Gruyter, 1988.

DOGRAMACI, ALI AND FÄRE, ROLF, eds. *Applications of modern production theory: Efficiency and productivity*. Studies in Productivity Analysis series. Norwell, Mass.; Dordrecht and Lancaster: Kluwer Academic, 1988.

DORIAN, JAMES P. AND FRIDLEY, DAVID G., eds. *China's energy and mineral industries: Current perspectives*. Westview Special Studies in Natural Resources and Energy Management series. Boulder, Colo. and London: Westview Press in cooperation with the East–West Center Resources Systems Institute, 1988.

DORNBUSCH, RUDIGER. *Exchange rates and inflation*. Cambridge, Mass. and London: MIT Press, 1988.

DOSI, GIOVANNI, ET AL., eds. *Technical change and economic theory*. Edited and compiled by the MAASTRICHT ECONOMIC RESEARCH INSTITUTE ON INNOVATION AND TECHNOLOGY. International Federation of Institutes for Advanced Study (IFIAS) Research Series, no. 6. London and New York: Pinter; distributed by Columbia University Press, New York, 1988.

DRIEHUIS, W.; FASE, M. M. G. AND DEN HARTOG, H., eds. *Challenges for macroeconomic modelling*. Contributions to Economic Analysis series, no. 178. Amsterdam; Oxford and Tokyo: North-Holland; distributed in the U.S. and Canada by Elsevier Science, New York, 1988.

DUNNING, JOHN AND ROBSON, PETER, eds. *Multinationals and the European Community*. Oxford and New York: Blackwell, 1988.

DUUS, PETER, ed. *The Cambridge history of Japan*. Volume 6. *The twentieth century*. Cambridge; New York and Melbourne: Cambridge University Press, 1988.

EARL, PETER E., ed. *Behavioural economics*. Volume 1. Schools of Thought in Economics series, no. 6. Aldershot, U.K.: Elgar; Brookfield, Vt.: Gower, 1988.

EARL, PETER E., ed. *Behavioural economics*. Volume 2. Schools of Thought in Economics series, no. 6. Aldershot, U.K.: Elgar; Brookfield, Vt.: Gower, 1988.

EARL, PETER E., ed. *Psychological economics: Development, tensions, prospects*. Recent Economic Thought Series. Norwell, Mass.; Lancaster and Dordrecht: Kluwer Academic, 1988.

EBERSTADT, NICHOLAS. *Foreign aid and American purpose*. With a foreword by THEODORE W. SCHULTZ. AEI Studies, no. 474. Washington, D.C.: American Enterprise Institute for Public Policy Research; distributed by National Book Network, Lanham, Md., 1988.

EDWARDS, D. AND RAUN, N. E., eds. *COMPSTAT: Proceedings in computational statistics, 8th symposium held in Copenhagen 1988*. Heidelberg: Physica; New York: Springer, 1988.

EGAN, JOHN J., ET AL. *Space commerce: Proceedings of the Second International Conference and Exhibition on the Commercial and Industrial Uses of Outer Space, Montreux, Switzerland, 21–25 February 1988*. New York; London; Tokyo and Camberwell, Australia: Gordon and Breach Science, 1988.

EHRENBERG, RONALD G., ed. *Research in labor economics*. Volume 9. A Research Annual. Greenwich, Conn. and London: JAI Press, 1988.

EHRLICH, PAUL R. AND HOLDREN, JOHN P., eds. *The Cassandra Conference: Resources and the human predicament*. College Station: Texas A&M University Press, 1988.

EICHENGREEN, BARRY AND HATTON, T. J., eds. *Interwar unemployment in international perspective*. NATO Advanced Science Institute Series. Norwell, Mass. and Dordrecht: Kluwer Academic in cooperation with NATO Scientific Affairs Division, 1988.

EICHHORN, WOLFGANG, ed. *Measurement in economics: Theory and applications of economic indices*. In cooperation with W. ERWIN DIEWERT ET AL. Heidelberg: Physica, 1988.

EISELT, H. A. AND PEDERZOLI, G., eds. *Advances in optimization and control: Proceedings of the Conference "Optimization Days 86," held in Montreal, Canada, April 30–May 2, 1986*.

Lecture Notes in Economics and Mathematical Systems series, no. 302. New York; Berlin; London and Tokyo: Springer, 1988.

ELLIOTT, KIMBERLY ANN AND WILLIAMSON, JOHN, eds. *World economic problems.* Special Report series, no. 7. Washington, D.C.: Institute for International Economics, 1988.

ELTIS, WALTER AND SINCLAIR, PETER J. N., eds. *Keynes and economic policy: The relevanace of* The General Theory *after fifty years.* Reprint. Introduced by NIGEL LAWSON. London: Macmillan in association with the National Economic Development Office; distributed by International Specialized Book Services, Portland, Oreg., 1988.

ENGLAND, CATHERINE AND HUERTAS, THOMAS, eds. *The financial services revolution: Policy directions for the future.* Innovations in Financial Markets and Institutions series. Norwell, Mass.; Lancaster and Dordrecht: Kluwer Academic, 1988.

FABOZZI, FRANK J., ed. *Advances in futures and options research.* Volume 3. A Research Annual. Greenwich, Conn. and London: JAI Press, 1988.

FARKAS, GEORGE AND ENGLAND, PAULA, eds. *Industries, firms, and jobs: Sociological and economic approaches.* With a foreword by MICHAEL PIORE. Plenum Studies in Work and Industry series. New York and London: Plenum Press, 1988.

FARMER, RICHARD N. AND MCGOUN, ELTON G., eds. *Advances in international comparative management.* Volume 3. A Research Annual. Greenwich, Conn. and London: JAI Press, 1988.

FEDERAL HOME LOAN BANK OF SAN FRANCISCO. *Expanded competitive markets and the thrift industry: Proceedings of the Thirteenth Annual Conference, December 10–11, 1987, San Francisco, California.* San Francisco: Author, 1988.

FEDERAL RESERVE BANK OF KANSAS CITY. *Financial market volatility: A symposium sponsored by the Federal Reserve Bank of Kansas City, Jackson Hole, Wyoming, August 17–19, 1988.* Federal Reserve Bank of Kansas City Symposium Series. Kansas City, Mo.: Author, 1988.

FEDOROV, VALERI AND LAUTER, HENNING, eds. *Model-oriented data analysis: Proceedings of an IIASA (International Institute for Applied Systems Analysis) workshop on data analysis held at Eisenach, GDR, March 9–13, 1987.* Lecture Notes in Economics and Mathematical Systems series, vol. 297. New York; Berlin; London and Tokyo: Springer, 1988.

FEENSTRA, ROBERT C., ed. *Empirical methods for international trade.* Cambridge, Mass. and London: MIT Press, 1988.

FEINBERG, RICHARD E. AND FFRENCH-DAVIS, RICARDO, eds. *Development and external debt in Latin America: Bases for a new consensus.* Notre Dame, Indiana: University of Notre Dame Press, 1988.

FEINSTEIN, CHARLES H. AND POLLARD, SIDNEY, eds. *Studies in capital formation in the United Kingdom, 1750–1920.* Oxford; New York; Toronto and Melbourne: Oxford University Press, Clarendon Press, 1988.

FELDSTEIN, MARTIN, ed. *International economic cooperation.* National Bureau of Economic Research Conference Report series. Chicago and London: University of Chicago Press, 1988. (I)

FELDSTEIN, MARTIN, ed. *The United States in the world economy.* National Bureau of Economic Research Conference Report series. Chicago and London: University of Chicago Press, 1988. (II)

FERRIS, GERALD R. AND ROWLAND, KENDRITH M., eds. *Research in personnel and human resources management.* Volume 6. A Research Annual. Greenwich, Conn. and London: JAI Press, 1988.

FEUCHTWANG, STEPHAN; HUSSAIN, ATHAR AND PAIRAULT, THIERRY, eds. *Transforming China's economy in the eighties.* Volume 1. *The rural sector, welfare and employment.* Boulder, Colo.: Westview Press; London: Zed Books; Bombay: Oxford University Press, 1988.

FEUCHTWANG, STEPHAN; HUSSAIN, ATHAR AND PAIRAULT, THIERRY, eds. *Transforming China's economy in the eighties.* Volume 2. *Management, industry and the urban economy.* Boulder, Colo.: Westview Press; London: Zed Books; Bombay: Oxford University Press, 1988.

FIELEKE, NORMAN S., ed. *International payments imbalances in the 1980s: Proceedings of a conference held at Melvin Village, New Hampshire, October 1988.* Conference Series, no. 32. Boston: Federal Reserve Bank of Boston, 1988.

GOMEZ FERNANDEZ, JUAN ALFREDO, ET AL., eds. *Approximation and optimization: Proceedings of the International Seminar held in Havana, Cuba, Jan. 12–16, 1987.* Lecture Notes in Mathematics, no. 1354. New York; Berlin; London and Tokyo: Springer, 1988.

GOODALL, BRIAN AND ASHWORTH, GREGORY, eds. *Marketing in the tourism industry: The promotion of destination regions.* London and Sydney: Croom Helm; distributed by Methuen, New York, 1988.

GOODHART, CHARLES, ET AL. *Financial regulation—or over-regulation?* Introduced by CENTO VELJANOVSKI. Edited by ARTHUR SELDON. IEA Readings series, no. 27. London: Institute of Economic Affairs, 1988.

[GOODWIN, RICHARD M.] *Growth cycles and multisectoral economics: The Goodwin tradition. Proceedings of the Workshop in Honour of R. M. Goodwin.* Edited by GIANNI RICCI AND KUMARASWAMY VELUPILLAI. Lecture Notes in Economics and Mathematical Systems series, no. 309. New York; Berlin; London and Tokyo: Springer, 1988.

GRAHAM, JOHN D., ed. *Preventing automobile injury: New findings from evaluation research.* Dover, Mass.: Auburn House, 1988.

GRANDMONT, JEAN-MICHEL, ed. *Temporary equilibrium: Selected readings.* Economic Theory, Econometrics, and Mathematical Economics series. San Diego; London; Sydney and Toronto: Harcourt Brace Jovanovich, Academic Press, 1988.

GRANT, JOHN H., ed. *Strategic management frontiers.* Monographs in Organizational Behavior and Industrial Relations series, vol. 10. Greenwich, Conn. and London: JAI Press, 1988.

GRAY, S. J. AND COENENBERG, A. G., eds. *International group accounting: International Harmonisation and the Seventh EEC Directive.* Croom Helm Series on International Accounting and Finance. London and Sydney: Croom Helm in association with Methuen, 1988.

GREENAWAY, DAVID, ed. *Economic development and international trade.* New York: St. Martin's Press, 1988.

GREENBERG, WARREN, ed. *Competition in the health care sector: Ten years later.* Durham, N.C. and London: Duke University Press, 1988.

GREGORY, ROBERT GEORGE AND BUTLIN, NOEL GEORGE, eds. *Recovery from the depression: Australia and the world economy in the 1930s.* Cambridge; New York and Melbourne: Cambridge University Press, 1988.

GRIFFITH-JONES, STEPHANY, ed. *Managing world debt.* Hemel Hempstead, U.K.: Simon and Schuster International, Harvester-Wheatsheaf; New York: St. Martin's Press, 1988.

GRILICHES, ZVI. *Technology, education, and productivity: Early papers with notes to subsequent literature.* Oxford and New York: Blackwell, 1988.

GRØNHAUG, KJELL AND KAUFMANN, GEIR, eds. *Innovation: A cross-disciplinary perspective.* Oslo: Norwegian University Press; distributed by Oxford University Press, New York, 1988.

GUARDUCCI, ANNALISA, ed. *Prodotto lordo e finanza pubblica secoli XIII–XIX.* Istituto Internazionale di Storia Economica, "F. Datini"—Prato, Serie II, no. 8. Florence: Le Monnier, 1988.

GUERRIERI, PAOLO AND PADOAN, PIER CARLO, eds. *The political economy of international co-operation.* London and Sydney: Croom Helm in association with Methuen, 1988.

GUILE, BRUCE R. AND QUINN, JAMES BRIAN, eds. *Managing innovation: Cases from the services industries.* National Academy of Engineering Series on Technology and Social Priorities. Washington, D.C.: National Academy Press, 1988. (I)

GUILE, BRUCE R. AND QUINN, JAMES BRIAN, eds. *Technology in services: Policies for growth, trade, and employment.* National Academy of Engineering, Series on Technology and Social Priorities. Washington, D.C.: National Academy Press, 1988. (II)

GUTH, WILFRIED, ed. *Economic policy coordination: Proceedings of an international seminar held in Hamburg.* Washington, D.C.: International Monetary Fund; Hamburg: HWWA-Institut für Wirtschaftsforschung, 1988.

GUTOWSKI, ARMIN AND HOLTHUS, MANFRED, eds. *Limits to international indebtedness.* Revised edition. New Brunswick, N.J. and Oxford: Transaction Books, [1986] 1988.

GWARTNEY, JAMES D. AND WAGNER, RICHARD E., eds. *Public choice and constitutional economics.*

[HOLLANDER, STANLEY C.] *Historical perspectives in marketing: Essays in honor of Stanley C. Hollander.* Edited by TERRENCE NEVETT AND RONALD A. FULLERTON. Lexington, Mass. and Toronto: Heath, Lexington Books, 1988.

[HOLZMAN, FRANKLYN D.] *Economic adjustment and reform in Eastern Europe and the Soviet Union: Essays in honor of Franklyn D. Holzman.* Edited by JOSEF C. BRADA, ED A. HEWETT, AND THOMAS A. WOLF. Duke Press Policy Studies series. Durham and London: Duke University Press, 1988.

HOOD, NEIL AND VAHLNE, JAN-ERIK, eds. *Strategies in global competition: Selected papers from the Prince Bertil Symposium at the Institute of International Business, Stockholm School of Economics.* London and Sydney: Croom Helm; distributed by Methuen, New York, 1988.

HOPKINS, MICHAEL J. D., ed. *Employment forecasting: The employment problem in industrialised countries.* London and New York: Pinter; distributed by Columbia University Press, New York, 1988.

HORWICH, GEORGE AND WEIMER, DAVID LEO, eds. *Responding to international oil crises.* Foreword by SENATOR BILL BRADLEY. AEI Studies series, no. 464. Washington, D.C.: American Enterprise Institute for Public Policy Research; distributed by University Press of America, Lanham, Md. 1988.

HOSIER, RICHARD H., ed. *Energy for rural development in Zimbabwe.* Energy, Environment and Development in Africa series, no. 11. Stockholm: Royal Swedish Academy of Sciences, Beijer Institute; Uppsala: Scandinavian Institute of African Studies, 1988. (I)

HOSIER, RICHARD H., ed. *Zimbabwe: Industrial and commercial energy use.* Energy, Environment and Development in Africa series, no. 10. Stockholm: Royal Swedish Academy of Sciences, Beijer Institute; Uppsala: Scandinavian Institute of African Studies, 1988. (II)

HUGHES, HELEN, ed. *Achieving industrialization in East Asia.* Trade and Development series. Cambridge; New York and Melbourne: Cambridge University Press, 1988.

HULA, RICHARD C., ed. *Market-based public policy.* Policy Studies Organization series. New York: St. Martin's Press in association with the Policies Studies Organization, 1988.

HUNT, AUDREY, ed. *Women and paid work: Issues of equality.* New York: St. Martin's Press, 1988.

IKENBERRY, G. JOHN; LAKE, DAVID A. AND MASTANDUNO, MICHAEL, eds. *The state and American foreign economic policy.* Cornell Studies in Political Economy series. Ithaca and London: Cornell University Press, 1988.

INOGUCHI, TAKASHI AND OKIMOTO, DANIEL I., eds. *The political economy of Japan.* Volume 2. *The changing international context.* Stanford, Calif.: Stanford University Press, 1988.

INTERNATIONAL FISCAL ASSOCIATION, ed. *Recognition of foreign enterprises as taxable entities.* Studies on International Fiscal Law series, vol. 73a. Deventer, the Netherlands and Norwell, Mass.: Kluwer Law and Taxation for the International Fiscal Association, 1988. (I)

INTERNATIONAL FISCAL ASSOCIATION, ed. *Tax treatment of computer software.* Studies on International Fiscal Law series, vol. 73b. Deventer, the Netherlands and Norwell, Mass.: Kluwer Law and Taxation for the International Fiscal Association, 1988. (II)

INTERNATIONAL MONETARY FUND RESEARCH DEPARTMENT. *Staff studies for the World Economic Outlook, July 1988.* World Economic and Financial Surveys series. Washington, D.C.: International Monetary Fund, 1988.

IRI, MASAO AND YAJIMA, KEIJI, eds. *System modelling and optimization: Proceedings of the 13th IFIP Conference, Tokyo, Japan, August 31–September 4, 1987.* Lecture Notes in Control and Information Sciences series, vol. 113. New York; Berlin; London and Tokyo: Springer, 1988.

IVES, J. AND PITT, D. C., eds. *Deforestation: Social dynamics in watersheds and mountain ecosystems.* European Year of the Environment series. New York and London: Routledge, 1988.

JAMES, KENNETH AND AKRASANEE, NARONGCHAI, eds. *Small and medium business improvement in the ASEAN region: Production management.* ISEAS Field Report Series, no. 21. Singapore: Institute of Southeast Asian Studies, ASEAN Economic Research Unit, 1988.

JAPAN INSTITUTE OF LABOUR, ed. *Highlights in Japanese industrial relations.* Volume 2. *A selection of articles from the* Japan Labor Bulletin. Tokyo: Editor, 1988.

JENSON, JANE; HAGEN, ELISABETH AND REDDY, CEALLAIGH, eds. *Feminization of the labor force:*

Paradoxes and promises. Europe and the International Order series. New York: Oxford University Press, 1988.

JEPMA, CATRINUS J., ed. *North–South co-operation in retrospect and prospect*. New York and London: Routledge, 1988.

JOHNSON, CHRISTOPHER, ed. *Privatization and ownership*. Lloyds Bank Annual Review series, vol. 1. London and New York: Pinter, 1988.

JOHNSON, THOMAS G.; DEATON, BRADY J. AND SEGARRA, EDUARDO, eds. *Local infrastructure investment in rural America*. Westview Special Study series. Boulder, Colo. and London: Westview Press, 1988.

JOHNSTON, GEORGE M.; FRESHWATER, DAVID AND FAVERO, PHILIP, eds. *Natural resource and environmental policy analysis: Cases in applied economics*. Boulder and London: Westview Press, 1988.

JONES, DEREK C. AND SVEJNAR, JAN, eds. *Advances in the economic analysis of participatory and labor-managed firms*. Volume 3. A Research Annual. Greenwich, Conn. and London: JAI Press, 1988.

JONES, STUART, ed. *Banking and business in South Africa*. New York: St. Martin's Press, 1988.

DE JONG, H. W., ed. *The structure of European industry*. Second Revised Edition. Studies in Industrial Organization, vol. 8. Norwell, Mass. and Dordrecht: Kluwer Academic, [1981] 1988.

JORGE, ANTONIO AND SALAZAR-CARRILLO, JORGE, eds. *Foreign investment, debt and economic growth in Latin America*. New York: St. Martin's Press, 1988.

JUVILER, PETER AND KIMURA, HIROSHI, eds. *Gorbachev's reforms: U.S. and Japanese assessments*. Hawthorne, N.Y.: de Gruyter, Aldine de Gruyter, 1988.

KACPRZYK, JANUSZ AND FEDRIZZI, MARIO, eds. *Combining fuzzy imprecision with probabilistic uncertainty in decision making*. Lecture Notes in Economics and Mathematical Systems series, vol. 310. New York; Berlin; London and Tokyo: Springer, 1988.

KACPRZYK, JANUSZ AND ROUBENS, MARC, eds. *Non-conventional preference relations in decision making*. Lecture Notes in Economics and Mathematical Systems series, no. 301. New York; Berlin; London and Tokyo: Springer, 1988.

KATHURIA, SANJAY; MIRALAO, VIRGINIA AND JOSEPH, REBECCA. *Artisan industries in Asia: Four case studies*. Technical Study series, no. 60e. Ottawa: International Development Research Centre, 1988.

KAUFMAN, BRUCE E., ed. *How labor markets work: Reflections on theory and practice*. Lexington, Mass. and Toronto: Heath, Lexington Books, 1988.

KAYNAK, ERDENER, ed. *Transnational retailing*. New York and Berlin: de Gruyter, 1988.

KEILMAN, NICO; KUIJSTEN, ANTON AND VOSSEN, AD, eds. *Modelling household formation and dissolution*. Oxford; New York; Toronto and Melbourne: Oxford University Press, Clarendon Press, 1988.

KELLY, RITA MAE, ed. *Promoting productivity in the public sector: Problems, strategies and prospects*. Policy Studies Organization Series. New York: St. Martin's Press in association with the Policy Studies Organization, 1988.

KEMPER, ROBERT L., ed. *Financial services yearbook*. Volume 1. Berkeley: University of California Press, 1988.

KESSLER, DENIS AND MASSON, ANDRÉ, eds. *Modelling the accumulation and distribution of wealth*. Oxford; New York; Toronto and Melbourne: Oxford University Press, Clarendon Press, 1988.

KHOURY, SARKIS J. AND GHOSH, ALO, eds. *Recent developments in international banking and finance*. Volume 2. Lexington, Mass. and Toronto: Heath, Lexington Books, 1988.

KIM, YONG H., ed. *Advances in working capital management*. Volume 1. VENKAT SRINIVASAN, collaborator. A Research Annual. Greenwich, Conn. and London: JAI Press, 1988.

KINDLEBERGER, CHARLES P. *The international economic order: Essays on financial crisis and international public goods*. Cambridge, Mass.: MIT Press, 1988.

KIRCHHOFF, BRUCE A., ET AL., eds. *Frontiers of entrepreneurship research, 1988: Proceedings of the Eighth Annual Babson College Entrepreneurship Research Conference*. Wellesley, Mass.: Center for Entrepreneurial Studies, Babson College, 1988.

KLAMER, ARJO; McCLOSKEY, DONALD N. AND SOLOW, ROBERT M., eds. *The consequences of economic rhetoric.* Cambridge; New York and Melbourne: Cambridge University Press, 1988.

KNIGHTS, DAVID AND WILLMOTT, HUGH, eds. *New technology and the labour process.* Studies in the Labour Process series. London: Macmillan Press; distributed by Sheridan House, Dobbs Ferry, N.Y., 1988.

KOHLI, UDDESH AND GAUTAM, VINAYSHIL, eds. *Human resources development and the planning process in India.* New Delhi: Vikas; distributed in N. America by Advent Books, New York, 1988.

KOHN, MEIR AND TSIANG, SHO-CHIEH, eds. *Finance constraints, expectations, and macroeconomics.* Oxford; New York; Toronto and Melbourne: Oxford University Press, Clarendon Press, 1988.

KOZMETSKY, GEORGE; MATSUMOTO, HIROSHI AND SMILOR, RAYMOND W., eds. *Pacific cooperation and development.* Westport, Conn. and London: Greenwood Press, Praeger, 1988.

KREGEL, J. A.; MATZNER, EGON AND RONCAGLIA, ALESSANDRO, eds. *Barriers to full employment: Papers from a conference sponsored by the Labour Market Policy Section of the International Institute of Management of the Wissenschaftszentrum of Berlin.* New York: St. Martin's Press, 1988.

KUMCU, ERDOĞAN AND FIRAT, A. FUAT, eds. *Marketing and development: Toward broader dimensions.* Research in Marketing series, supplement 4. Greenwich, Conn. and London: JAI Press, 1988.

KURZHANSKI, A.; NEUMANN, K. AND PALLASCHKE, D., eds. *Optimization, parallel processing and applications: Proceedings of the Oberwolfach Conference on Operations Research, February 16–21, 1987 and the Workshop on Advanced Computation Techniques, Parallel Processing and Optimization held at Karlsruhe, West Germany, February 22–25, 1987.* Lecture Notes in Economics and Mathematical Systems series, vol. 304. New York; Heidelberg; London and Tokyo: Springer, 1988.

LAMB, ROBERT AND SHRIVASTAVA, PAUL, eds. *Advances in strategic management.* Volume 5. A Research Annual. Greenwich, Conn. and London: JAI Press, 1988.

LAMPE, DAVID, ed. *The Massachusetts miracle: High technology and economic revitalization.* Cambridge, Mass. and London: MIT Press, 1988.

LANGHAMMER, ROLF J. AND RIEGER, HANS CHRISTOPH, eds. *ASEAN and the EC: Trade in tropical agricultural products.* Singapore: Institute of Southeast Asian Studies, ASEAN Economic Research Unit, 1988.

LAVIGNE, MARIE, ed. *East–South relations in the world economy.* Boulder, Colo. and London: Westview Press in cooperation with the Commissariat Général du Plan, 1988.

LAWLER, EDWARD J. AND MARKOVSKY, BARRY, eds. *Advances in group processes.* Volume 5. A Research Annual. Greenwich, Conn. and London: JAI Press, 1988.

[LECOMBER, RICHARD] *Economics, growth and sustainable environments: Essays in memory of Richard Lecomber.* Edited by DAVID COLLARD, DAVID PEARCE, AND DAVID ULPH. New York: St. Martin's Press, 1988.

LEE, CHUNG H. AND NAYA, SEIJI, eds. *Trade and investment in services in the Asia–Pacific region.* Pacific and World Studies series, no. 1. Inchon, Korea: Inha University, Center for International Studies; Boulder, Colo.: Westview Press, 1988.

LEE, RONALD D.; ARTHUR, W. BRIAN AND RODGERS, GERRY, eds. *Economics of changing age distributions in developed countries.* International Studies in Demography series. Oxford; New York; Toronto and Melbourne: Oxford University Press, Clarendon Press, 1988.

LEE, RONALD D., ET AL., eds. *Population, food and rural development.* International Studies in Demography. Oxford; New York; Toronto and Melbourne: Oxford University Press, Clarendon Press, 1988.

LEVINE, MARC V., ET AL. *The state and democracy: Revitalizing America's government.* Alternative Policies for America series. New York and London: Routledge, 1988.

LEWIN, DAVID, ET AL., eds. *Public sector labor relations: Analysis and readings.* Third edition. Lexington, Mass. and Toronto: Heath, Lexington, [1977, 1981] 1988.

LEWIS, JOHN P., ET AL. *Strengthening the poor: What have we learned?* Overseas Development

Council, U.S.–Third World Policy Perspectives series, no. 10. New Brunswick, N.J. and Oxford: Transaction Books, 1988.

LIBECAP, GARY, ed. *Corporate reorganization through mergers, acquisitions, and leveraged buyouts.* Advances in the Study of Entrepreneurship, Innovation, and Economic Growth series, supplement 1. Greenwich, Conn. and London: JAI Press, 1988. (I)

LIBECAP, GARY, ed. *Innovation in new markets: The impact of deregulation on airlines, financial markets, and telecommunications.* Advances in the Study of Entrepreneurship, Innovation, and Economic Growth series, vol. 2. Greenwich, Conn. and London: JAI Press, 1988. (II)

LIEBOWITZ, RONALD D., ed. *Gorbachev's new thinking: Prospects for joint ventures.* Cambridge, Mass.: Harper and Row, Ballinger, 1988.

LINDBLOM, CHARLES E. *Democracy and market system.* Scandinavian Library series. Oslo: Norwegian University Press; distributed by Oxford University Press, New York, 1988.

LINZ, SUSAN J. AND MOSKOFF, WILLIAM, eds. *Reorganization and reform in the Soviet economy.* Armonk, N.Y. and London: Sharpe, 1988.

LITAN, ROBERT E; LAWRENCE, ROBERT Z. AND SCHULTZE, CHARLES L., eds. *American living standards: Threats and challenges.* Washington, D.C.: Brookings Institution, 1988.

LITAN, ROBERT E. AND WINSTON, CLIFFORD, eds. *Liability: Perspectives and policy.* Washington, D.C.: Brookings Institution, 1988.

LITTLE, JO; PEAKE, LINDA AND RICHARDSON, PAT, eds. *Women in cities: Gender and the urban environment.* New York: New York University Press; distributed by Columbia University Press, 1988.

LIU, SHU-HSIEN AND ALLINSON, ROBERT E., eds. *Harmony and strife: Contemporary perspectives, East and West.* Hong Kong: Chinese University Press, 1988.

LUCAS, ROBERT E. B. AND PAPANEK, GUSTAV F., eds. *The Indian economy: Recent development and future prospects.* Westview Special Studies on South and Southeast Asia series. Boulder, Colo. and London: Westview Press in cooperation with the Boston University Center for Asian Development Studies, 1988.

LYBECK, J. A. AND HENREKSON, M., eds. *Explaining the growth of government.* Contributions to Economic Analysis series, no. 171. Amsterdam; Oxford and Tokyo: North-Holland; distributed in the U.S. and Canada by Elsevier Science, New York, 1988.

MABRO, ROBERT, ed. *The 1986 oil price crisis: Economic effects and policy responses. Proceedings of the Eighth Oxford Energy Seminar (September 1986).* Oxford; New York; Toronto and Melbourne: Oxford University Press for the Oxford Institute for Energy Studies; distributed in the U.S. and Canada by PennWell Books, Tulsa, 1988.

MACKAY, ROBERT J., ed. *After the crash: Linkages between stocks and futures.* AEI Studies, no. 477. Washington, D.C.: American Enterprise Institute for Public Policy Research; distributed by University Press of America, Lanham, Md., 1988.

MAITAL, SHLOMO, ed. *Applied behavioural economics.* Volume 1. New York: New York University Press; distributed by Columbia University Press, 1988.

MAITAL, SHLOMO, ed. *Applied behavioural economics.* Volume 2. New York: New York University Press; distributed by Columbia University Press, 1988.

MANGUM, GARTH AND PHILIPS, PETER, eds. *Three worlds of labor economics.* Armonk, N.Y. and London: Sharpe, 1988.

MARCH, JAMES G. *Decisions and organizations.* New York and Oxford: Blackwell, 1988.

DE MARCHI, NEIL, ed. *The Popperian legacy in economics: Papers presented at a symposium in Amsterdam, December 1985.* Cambridge; New York and Melbourne: Cambridge University Press, 1988.

MARER, PAUL AND SIWIŃSKI, WŁODZIMIERZ, eds. *Creditworthiness and reform in Poland: Western and Polish perspectives.* Bloomington: Indiana University Press in association with the Indiana Center for Global Business and the Polish Studies Center, Indiana University, 1988.

MARGINSON, PAUL, ET AL. *Beyond the workplace: Managing industrial relations in the multi-establishment enterprise.* Warwick Studies in Industrial Relations. Oxford and New York: Blackwell, 1988.

MARSTON, RICHARD C., ed. *Misalignment of exchange rates: Effects on trade and industry.* National Bureau of Economic Research Project Report series. Chicago and London: University of Chicago Press, 1988.

MAYNES, E. SCOTT AND ACCI RESEARCH COMMITTEE, eds. *The frontier of research in the consumer interest: Proceedings of the International Conference on Research in the Consumer Interest.* Columbia, Mo.: American Council on Consumer Interests, 1988.

MAYNTZ, RENATE AND HUGHES, THOMAS P., eds. *The development of large technical systems.* Max Planck Institute for Social Research series. Boulder, Colo.: Westview Press; Frankfurt am Main: Campus, 1988.

MCKERN, BRUCE AND KOOMSUP, PRAIPOL, eds. *The minerals industries of ASEAN and Australia: Problems and prospects.* Winchester, Mass.; London; Sydney and Wellington; Unwin Hyman, Allen and Unwin, 1988.

MEADE, JAMES. *The collected papers of James Meade.* Volume 1. *Employment and inflation.* Edited by SUSAN HOWSON. Winchester, Mass.; London and Sydney: Unwin Hyman, Allen & Unwin; 1988.

MEADE, JAMES. *The collected papers of James Meade.* Volume 2. *Value, distribution and growth.* Edited by SUSAN HOWSON. Winchester, Mass.; London and Sydney: Unwin Hyman, 1988.

MEADE, JAMES. *The collected papers of James Meade.* Volume 3. *International economics.* Edited by SUSAN HOWSON. Winchester, Mass. and London: Unwin Hyman, 1988.

MELAMED, LEO, ed. *The merits of flexible exchange rates: An anthology.* Fairfax, Va.: George Mason University Press; distributed by University Publishing Associates, Lanham, Md., 1988.

MELLOR, JOHN W. AND AHMED, RAISUDDIN, eds. *Agricultural price policy for developing countries.* Baltimore and London: Johns Hopkins University Press for the International Food Policy Research Institute, 1988.

MESA-LAGO, CARMELO, ed. *Cuban Studies.* Volume 18. Pitt Latin American Series. Pittsburgh: University of Pittsburgh Press for the Center for Latin American Studies, 1988.

MÉTIVIER, MICHEL AND WATANABE, SHINZO, eds. *Stochastic analysis: Proceedings of the Japanese–French Seminar held in Paris, France, June 16–19, 1987.* Lecture Notes in Mathematics series, vol. 1322. New York; Berlin; London and Tokyo: Springer, 1988.

MEYER, JOHN R. AND GUSTAFSON, JAMES M., eds. *The U.S. business corporation: An institution in transition.* Cambridge, Mass.: Harper and Row, Ballinger, 1988.

MIKDASHI, ZUHAYR, ed. *International banking: Innovations and new policies. Proceedings of a colloquium held by the École des Hautes Études Commerciales de l'Université de Lausanne.* Introduced by CHARLES IFFLAND AND PIERRE LANGUETIN. New York: St. Martin's Press, 1988.

MINER, WILLIAM M. AND HATHAWAY, DALE E., eds. *World agricultural trade: Building a consensus.* Halifax, Nova Scotia: Institute for Research on Public Policy; Washington, D.C.: Institute for International Economics, 1988.

MIROWSKI, PHILIP. *Against mechanism: Protecting economics from science.* Totowa, N.J.: Littlefield, Adams; Rowman and Littlefield, 1988.

MISSOURI VALLEY ECONOMIC ASSOCIATION. *The Journal of Economics.* Volume 14. Cape Girardeau, Mo.: Author, 1988.

MITCHISON, ROSALIND AND ROEBUCK, PETER, eds. *Economy and society in Scotland and Ireland, 1500–1939.* Edinburgh: Donald; distributed in the U.S. and Canada by Humanities Press, Atlantic Highlands, N.J., 1988.

MITRA, ASHOK, ed. *China: Issues in development.* New Delhi: Tulika Print Communication Services; distributed in North America by Advent Books, New York, 1988.

MOGGRIDGE, D. E., ed. *Editing modern economists: Papers given at the Twenty-Second Annual Conference on Editorial Problems, University of Toronto, 7–8 November 1986.* New York: AMS Press, 1988.

MOST, KENNETH S., ed. *Advances in international accounting.* Volume 2. A Research Annual. Greenwich, Conn. and London: JAI Press, 1988.

MOTAMEN, HOMA, ed. *Economic modelling in the OECD countries*. International Studies in Economic Modelling series. London and New York: Routledge, 1988.

MUNIER, BERTRAND R., ed. *Risk, decision and rationality*. Theory and Decision Library, Series B: Mathematical and Statistical Methods. Norwell, Mass.; Lancaster; Dordrecht and Tokyo: Kluwer Academic, Reidel, 1988.

MURDOCK, STEVE H. AND LEISTRITZ, F. LARRY, eds. *The farm financial crisis: Socioeconomic dimensions and implications for producers and rural areas*. Westview Special Studies in Agricultural Science and Policy series. Boulder, Colo. and London: Westview Press, 1988.

MUROYAMA, JANET H. AND STEVER, H. GUYFORD, eds. *Globalization of technology: International perspectives*. *Proceedings of the Sixth Convocation of the Council of Academics of Engineering and Technological Sciences*. Washington, D.C.: National Academy Press, 1988.

NAS, TEVFIK F. AND ODEKON, MEHMET, eds. *Liberalization and the Turkish economy*. Contributions in Economics and Economic History series, no. 86. Westport, Conn. and London: Greenwood Press, 1988.

NASH, GERALD D.; PUGACH, NOEL H. AND TOMASSON, RICHARD F., eds. *Social Security: The first half-century*. Albuquerque: University of New Mexico Press, 1988.

NEIMARK, MARILYN, ed. *Advances in public interest accounting*. Volume 2. A Research Annual. Greenwich, Conn. and London: JAI Press, 1988.

NICHOLAS, STEPHEN, ed. *Convict workers: Reinterpreting Australia's past*. Studies in Australian History. Cambridge; New York and Melbourne: Cambridge University Press, 1988.

[NOVE, ALEC] *The Soviet economy on the brink of reform: Essays in honor of Alec Nove*. Edited by PETER WILES. Winchester, Mass. and London: Unwin Hyman; Sydney: Allen and Unwin, 1988.

[NUTTER, G. WARREN] *Ideas, their origins, and their consequences: Lectures to commemorate the life and work of G. Warren Nutter*. Edited by the THOMAS JEFFERSON CENTER FOUNDATION. G. Warren Nutter Lectures in Political Economy series. Washington, D.C.: American Enterprise Institute for Public Policy Research; distributed by University Press of America, Lanham, Md., 1988.

OKIMOTO, DANIEL I. AND ROHLEN, THOMAS P., eds. *Inside the Japanese system: Readings on contemporary society and political economy*. Stanford, Calif.: Stanford University Press, 1988.

O'MARA, GERALD T., ed. *Efficiency in irrigation: The conjunctive use of surface and groundwater resources*. A World Bank Symposium. Washington, D.C.: World Bank, 1988.

ONIDA, FABRIZIO AND VIESTI, GIANFRANCO, eds. *The Italian multinationals*. Croom Helm Series in International Business. London and Sydney: Croom Helm in association with Methuen, 1988.

ORISHIMO, ISAO; HEWINGS, GEOFFREY J. D. AND NIJKAMP, PETER, eds. *Information technology: Social and spatial perspectives*. *Proceedings of an international conference on information technology and its impact on the urban-environmental system held at the Toyohashi University of Technology, Toyohashi, Japan, November 1986*. Lecture Notes in Economics and Mathematical Systems series, vol. 315. New York; Berlin; London and Tokyo: Springer, 1988.

PADDISON, RONAN AND BAILEY, STEPHEN, eds. *Local government finance: International perspectives*. London and New York: Routledge, 1988.

PALMER, JOHN L.; SMEEDING, TIMOTHY AND TORREY, BARBARA BOYLE, eds. *The vulnerable*. Changing Domestic Priorities Series. Washington, D.C.: Urban Institute Press; distributed by University Press of America, Lanham, Md., 1988.

PANG, ENG FONG, ed. *Labour market developments and structural change: The experience of ASEAN and Australia*. Singapore: Singapore University Press, 1988.

PARIKH, JYOTI K., ed. *Sustainable development in agriculture*. Norwell, Mass.; Lancaster and Dordrecht: Kluwer Academic, Martinus Nijhoff; Laxenburg: International Institute for Applied Systems Analysis, 1988.

PARK, UNGSUH K. *Korea and her neighboring economies*. Seoul National University, Institute of Social Sciences, Korean Studies Series, no. 11. Seoul: Seoul National University Press, 1988.

PAUS, EVA, ed. *Struggle against dependence: Nontraditional export growth in Central America and the Caribbean.* Series in Political Economy and Economic Development in Latin America. Boulder, Colo. and London: Westview Press, 1988.

PECHMAN, JOSEPH A., ed. *World tax reform: A progress report. Report of a conference held in Washington, D.C., on November 12–13, 1987, sponsored by the Brookings Institution.* Brookings Dialogues on Public Policy series. Washington, D.C.: Brookings Institution, 1988.

PENNSYLVANIA ECONOMIC ASSOCIATION. *Proceedings of the Third Annual Meeting, May 27 and 28, 1988.* University Park: Pennsylvania State University, 1988.

PERKINS, EDWIN J., ed. *Essays in economic and business history: Selected papers from the economic and business historical society, 1987.* Volume VI. With the editorial assistance of BRENDA JOHNSON AND MARTHA ROTHERMEL. Los Angeles: University of Southern California, History Department for the Economic and Business Historical Society, 1988.

[PERROUX, FRANÇOIS] *Regional economic development: Essays in honour of François Perroux.* Edited by BENJAMIN HIGGINS AND DONALD J. SAVOIE. Boston; London; Sydney and Wellington: Unwin Hyman, 1988.

PESEK, BORIS P. *Microeconomics of money and banking and other essays.* New York: New York University Press; distributed by Columbia University Press, 1988.

PETERSON, WALLACE C., ed. *Market power and the economy: Industrial, corporate, governmental, and political aspects.* Recent Economic Thought Series. Norwell, Mass.; Dordrecht and Lancaster: Kluwer Academic, 1988.

PICARD, ROBERT G., ET AL., eds. *Press concentration and monopoly: New perspectives on newspaper ownership and operation.* Communication and Information Science series. Norwood, N.J.: Ablex, 1988.

PINSTRUP-ANDERSEN, PER, ed. *Food subsidies in developing countries: Costs, benefits, and policy options.* Baltimore and London: Johns Hopkins University Press for the International Food Policy Research Institute, 1988.

PITT, JOSEPH C., ed. *Theories of explanation.* New York and Oxford: Oxford University Press, 1988.

PIZZORUSSO, ALESSANDRO, ed. *Law in the making: A comparative survey.* Contributions by FRANCESCO CAPOTORTI ET AL. Foreword by STIG STROMHOLM. European Science Foundation Research on the Legislative Process series. New York; Berlin; London and Tokyo: Springer, 1988.

POHL, HANS AND RUDOLPH, BERND, eds. *German yearbook on business history, 1987.* Berlin; New York; London and Tokyo: Springer, 1988.

POTICHNYJ, PETER J., ed. *The Soviet Union party and society.* Cambridge; New York and Melbourne: Cambridge University Press, 1988.

POWERS, DAVID R., ET AL. *Higher education in partnership with industry: Opportunities and strategies for training, research, and economic development.* Jossey-Bass Higher Education Series. San Francisco and London: Jossey-Bass, 1988.

PRESTON, LEE E., ed. *International and comparative studies.* Research in Corporate Social Performance and Policy series, vol. 10. Greenwich, Conn. and London: JAI Press, 1988.

VAN RAAIJ, W. FRED; VAN VELDHOVEN, GERY M. AND WÄRNERYD, KARL-ERIK, eds. *Handbook of economic psychology.* Dordrecht and Norwell, Mass.: Kluwer Academic, 1988.

RAIKHY, P. S. AND GILL, SUCHA SINGH, eds. *Resource mobilisation and economic development: A regional perspective.* Amritsar, India: Guru Nanak Dev University, Punjab School of Economics, 1988.

RAPPING, LEONARD A. *International reorganization and American economic policy.* New York: New York University Press; distributed by Columbia University Press, 1988.

RESEARCH AND INFORMATION SYSTEM FOR THE NON-ALIGNED AND OTHER DEVELOPING COUNTRIES. *Biotechnology revolution and the third world: Challenges and policy options.* New Delhi: Author, 1988.

REYNOLDS, BRUCE L., ed. *Chinese economic reform: How far, how fast?* San Diego; London; Sydney and Toronto: Harcourt Brace Jovanovich, Academic Press, 1988.

RHODES, GEORGE F., JR. AND FOMBY, THOMAS B., eds. *Nonparametric and robust inference.* Advances in Econometrics series, vol. 7. Greenwich, Conn. and London: JAI Press, 1988.

FREEMAN. ISEAS Research Notes and Discussions Paper, no. 63. Singapore: Institute of Southeast Asian Studies, ASEAN Economic Research Unit, 1988.

SCHEFFLER, RICHARD M. AND ROSSITER, LOUIS F., eds. *Advances in health economics and health services research.* Volume 9. *Private-sector involvement in health care: Implications for access, cost, and quality.* A Research Annual. Greenwich, Conn. and London: JAI Press, 1988.

SCHIEFER, GERHARD, ed. *Videotex, information and communication in European agriculture: Proceedings of the 15th Symposium of the European Association of Agricultural Economists (EAAE) February 16th–18th, 1987, Kiel, Germany.* Kiel: Wissenschaftsverlag Vauk, 1988.

SCHIEHLEN, WERNER AND WEDIG, WALTER, eds. *Analysis and estimation of stochastic mechanical systems.* International Centre for Mechanical Sciences Courses and Lectures series, no. 303. New York and Vienna: Springer, 1988.

SCHMANDT, JURGEN; CLARKSON, JUDITH AND RODERICK, HILLIARD, eds. *Acid rain and friendly neighbors: The policy dispute between Canada and the United States.* Revised edition. Duke Press Policy Studies series. Durham, N.C.: Duke University Press, [1985] 1988.

SCHOTT, JEFFREY J. AND SMITH, MURRAY G., eds. *The Canada–United States Free Trade Agreement: The global impact.* Washington, D.C.: Institute for International Economics, 1988.

SCHULTZ, T. PAUL, ed. *Research in population economics.* Volume 6. A Research Annual. Greenwich, Conn. and London: JAI Press, 1988.

SCHWARTZ, BILL N., ed. *Advances in accounting.* Volume 6. A Research Annual. Greenwich, Conn. and London: JAI Press, 1988.

SCHWARZ, F. H., ed. *Soy protein and national food policy.* Boulder, Colo. and London: Westview Press in cooperation with Protein Technologies International, 1988.

SELDEN, MARK. *The political economy of Chinese socialism.* An East Gate Book. The Political Economy of Socialism series. Armonk, N.Y. and London: Sharpe, 1988.

SENGUPTA, JATI K. AND KADEKODI, GOPAL K., eds. *Econometrics of planning and efficiency.* Advanced Studies in Theoretical and Applied Econometrics series. vol. 11. Norwell, Mass.; Dordrecht and Lancaster: Kluwer Academic, 1988.

SEWELL, JOHN W. AND TUCKER, STUART K., eds. *Growth, exports, and jobs in a changing world economy: Agenda 1988.* Overseas Development Council U.S.–Third World Policy Perspectives series, no. 9. New Brunswick, N.J. and London: Transaction Books, 1988.

[SHAPLEY, LLOYD S.] *The Shapley value: Essays in honor of Lloyd S. Shapley.* Edited by ALVIN E. ROTH. Cambridge; New York and Melbourne: Cambridge University Press, 1988.

SHAW, G. K., ed. *The Keynesian heritage.* Volume 1. Schools of Thought in Economics series, no. 1. Aldershot, U.K.: Elgar; Brookfield, Vt.: Gower, 1988.

SHAW, G. K., ed. *The Keynesian heritage.* Volume 2. Schools of Thought in Economics series, no. 1. Aldershot, U.K.: Elgar; Brookfield, Vt.: Gower, 1988.

SHOVEN, JOHN B., ed. *Government policy towards industry in the United States and Japan.* Cambridge; New York and Melbourne: Cambridge University Press, 1988.

SIMCOX, DAVID E., ed. *U.S. immigration in the 1980s: Reappraisal and reform.* Boulder, Colo. and London: Westview Press in cooperation with the Center for Immigration Studies, Washington, D.C., 1988.

SIMMS, MARGARET C. AND MYERS, SAMUEL L., JR., eds. *The economics of race and crime.* New Brunswick, N.J. and Oxford: Transaction Books, 1988.

SINDELAR, H. RICHARD, III AND PETERSON, J. E., eds. *Crosscurrents in the Gulf: Arab, regional and global interests.* London and New York: Routledge, 1988.

SIRAGELDIN, ISMAIL AND SORKIN, ALAN, eds. *Public health and development.* Research in Human Capital and Development series, vol. 5. Greenwich, Conn. and London: JAI Press, 1988.

SMITH, C. SELBY, ed. *Economics and health: 1988.* Proceedings of the Tenth Australian Conference of Health Economists. Clayton, Australia: Monash University, Faculty of Economics and Politics, Public Sector Management Institute, 1988.

SMITH, THOMAS C. *Native sources of Japanese industrialization, 1750–1920.* A Philip E. Lilienthal Book. Berkeley and London: University of California Press, 1988.

SOPIEE, NOORDIN; HAMZAH, B. A. AND LEONG, CHOON HENG, eds. *Crisis and response: The challenge to South–South economic co-operation.* Kuala Lumpur: Institute of Strategic and International Studies; distributed by Routledge, New York, 1988.

SOUTHALL, ROGER, ed. *Labour and unions in Asia and Africa: Contemporary issues.* New York: St. Martin's Press, 1988.

SPENCE, A. MICHAEL AND HAZARD, HEATHER A., eds. *International competitiveness.* Cambridge, Mass.: Harper and Row, Ballinger, 1988.

SRINIVASAN, T. N. AND BARDHAN, PRANAB K., eds. *Rural poverty in South Asia.* New York: Columbia University Press, 1988.

STARR, MARTIN K., ed. *Global competitiveness: Getting the U.S. back on track.* American Assembly series. New York and London: Norton; Markham, Ontario: Penguin Books, 1988.

STAW, BARRY M. AND CUMMINGS, L. L., eds. *Research in organizational behavior.* Volume 10. Annual Series of Analytical Essays and Critical Reviews. Greenwich, Conn. and London: JAI Press, 1988.

STEEDMAN, IAN, ed. *Sraffian economics.* Volume 1. Schools of Thought in Economics series, no. 4. Aldershot, U.K.: Elgar; Brookfield, Vt.: Gower, 1988.

STEEDMAN, IAN, ed. *Sraffian economics.* Volume 2. Schools of Thought in Economics series, no. 4. Aldershot, U.K.: Elgar; Brookfield, Vt.: Gower, 1988.

STIGLER, GEORGE J., ed. *Chicago studies in political economy.* Chicago and London: University of Chicago Press, 1988.

STRASSMANN, W. PAUL AND WELLS, JILL, eds. *The global construction industry: Strategies for entry, growth and survival.* World Industry Studies, no. 7. Winchester, Mass. and London: Unwin Hyman; Sydney: Allen and Unwin, 1988.

STREETEN, PAUL, ed. *Beyond adjustment: The Asian experience.* Washington, D.C.: International Monetary Fund, 1988.

SUGIYAMA, CHŪHEI AND MIZUTA, HIROSHI, eds. *Enlightenment and beyond: Political economy comes to Japan.* Tokyo: University of Tokyo Press; distributed by Columbia University Press, New York, 1988.

SULLIVAN, SEAN AND LEWIN, MARION EIN, eds. *The economics and ethics of long-term care and disability.* AEI Studies, no. 467. Washington, D.C.: American Enterprise Institute for Public Policy Research; distributed by University Press of America, Lanham, Md., 1988.

SUMMERS, LAWRENCE H., ed. *Tax policy and the economy.* Volume 2. Cambridge, Mass.: National Bureau of Economic Research; 1988.

SUMNER, DANIEL A., ed. *Agricultural stability and farm programs: Concepts, evidence, and implications.* Westview Special Studies in Agriculture Science and Policy series. Boulder, Colo. and London: Westview Press, 1988.

TAN, LOONG-HOE AND AKRASANEE, NARONGCHAI, eds. *ASEAN–U.S. economic relations: Changes in the economic environment and opportunities.* Singapore: Institute of Southeast Asian Studies, ASEAN Economic Research Unit; San Francisco: Asia Foundation, Center for Asian Pacific Affairs, 1988.

TAVIS, LEE A., ed. *Rekindling development: Multinational firms and world debt.* Multinational Managers and Developing Country Concerns series. Notre Dame, Ind.: University of Notre Dame Press, 1988.

TENG, WEIZAO AND WANG, N. T., eds. *Transnational corporations and China's open door policy.* Lexington, Mass. and Toronto: Heath, Lexington Books, 1988.

THORNTON, ROBERT J.; HYCLAK, THOMAS AND ARONSON, J. RICHARD, eds. *Canada at the crossroads: Essays on Canadian political economy.* Contemporary Studies in Economic and Financial Analysis series, vol. 64. Greenwich, Conn. and London: JAI Press, 1988.

THWEATT, WILLIAM O., ed. *Classical political economy: A survey of recent literature.* Norwell, Mass.; Dordrecht and Lancaster: Kluwer Academic, 1988.

TIETZ, REINHARD; ALBERS, WULF AND SELTEN, REINHARD, eds. *Bounded rational behavior in experimental games and markets: Proceedings of the Fourth Conference on Experimental Economics, Bielefeld, West Germany, September 21–25, 1986.* Lecture Notes in Economics and Mathematical Systems series, vol. 314. New York; Berlin; London and Tokyo: Springer, 1988.

TILTON, JOHN E.; EGGERT, RODERICK G. AND LANDSBERG, HANS H., eds. *World mineral exploration: Trends and economic issues*. Washington, D.C.: Resources for the Future, 1988.

TIMPE, A. DALE, ed. *Managing people*. The Art and Science of Business Management series, vol. 6. New York and Oxford: Facts on File, 1988.

TISDELL, CLEM AND MAITRA, PRIYATOSH, eds. *Technological change, development and the environment: Socio-economic perspectives*. New York and London: Routledge, 1988.

TONIOLO, GIANNI, ed. *Central banks' independence in historical perspective*. Berlin and New York: de Gruyter, 1988.

TOOL, MARC R., ed. *Evolutionary economics*. Volume 1. *Foundations of institutional thought*. Armonk, N.Y. and London: Sharpe, 1988.

TOOL, MARC R., ed. *Evolutionary economics*. Volume 2. *Institutional theory and policy*. Armonk, N.Y. and London: Sharpe, 1988.

TSURUMI, E. PATRICIA, ed. *The other Japan: Postwar realities*. An East Gate Book. Armonk, N.Y. and London: Sharpe for the *Bulletin of Concerned Asian Scholars*, 1988.

TULLOCK, GORDON. *Wealth, poverty, and politics*. Oxford and New York: Blackwell, 1988.

TURNER, R. KERRY, ed. *Sustainable environmental management: Principles and practice*. London: Pinter, Belhaven Press in association with the Economic and Social Research Council (ESRC); Boulder, Colo.: Westview Press, 1988.

TYSON, LAURA D'ANDREA; DICKENS, WILLIAM T. AND ZYSMAN, JOHN, eds. *The dynamics of trade and employment*. Cambridge, Mass.: Harper & Row, Ballinger, 1988.

UNITED NATIONS. *Sanctions against South Africa: The peaceful alternative to violent change*. U.N. Sales No. E.88.I.5. New York: Author, 1988.

UNO, KIMIO AND SHISHIDO, SHUNTARO, eds. *Statistical data bank systems: Socio-economic database and model building in Japan*. Amsterdam; Oxford and Tokyo: North-Holland; distributed in the U.S. and Canada by Elsevier Science, New York, 1988.

URABE, KUNIYOSHI; CHILD, JOHN AND KAGONO, TADAO, eds. *Innovation and management: International comparisons*. De Gruyter Studies in Organization series, vol. 13. New York and Berlin: de Gruyter, 1988.

URRUTIA, MIGUEL, ed. *Financial liberalization and the internal structure of capital markets in Asia and Latin America*. U.N. Sales No. E.88.III.A.7. Tokyo: United Nations University, 1988.

URRUTIA, MIGUEL AND YUKAWA, SETSUKO, eds. *Development planning in mixed economies*. U.N. Sales No. E.88.III.A.6. Tokyo: United Nations University, 1988. (I)

URRUTIA, MIGUEL AND YUKAWA, SETSUKO, eds. *Economic development policies in resource-rich countries*. Tokyo: United Nations University, 1988. (II)

USELDING, PAUL J., ed. *Research in economic history*. Volume 11. A Research Annual. Greenwich, Conn. and London: JAI Press, 1988.

UYEHARA, CECIL H., ed. *U.S.–Japan science and technology exchange: Patterns of interdependence*. Westview Special Studies in International Economics and Business series. Boulder and London: Westview Press in cooperation with the Japan–America Society of Washington, 1988.

UZAWA, HIROFUMI. *Preference, production, and capital: Selected papers of Hirofumi Uzawa*. Cambridge; New York and Melbourne: Cambridge University Press, 1988.

VERNON, RAYMOND, ed. *The promise of privatization: A challenge for U.S. policy*. New York: Council on Foreign Relations, 1988.

VIVEKANANDA, FRANKLIN, ed. *Premises and process of maldevelopment*. Stockholm: Bethany Books, 1988.

VLASSOFF, CAROL AND BARKAT-E-KHUDA, eds. *Impact of modernization on development and demographic behaviour: Case studies in seven third world countries*. IDRC series, no. 260e. Ottawa: International Development Research Centre, 1988.

WACHTER, SUSAN M., ed. *Social Security and private pensions: Providing for retirement in the twenty-first century*. Lexington, Mass. and Toronto: Heath, Lexington Books, 1988.

WALKER, CHARLS E. AND BLOOMFIELD, MARK A., eds. *Intellectual property rights and capital formation in the next decade*. Lanham, Md.: University Press of America; Washington, D.C.: American Council for Capital Formation Center for Policy Research, 1988.

WOODSIDE, ARCH G., ed. *Advances in business marketing.* Volume 3. A Research Annual. Greenwich, Conn. and London: JAI Press, 1988.

WRIGLEY, NEIL, ed. *Store choice, store location and market analysis.* New York and London: Routledge, Chapman and Hall; Routledge, 1988.

YAMAZAKI, HIROAKI AND MIYAMOTO, MATAO, eds. *Trade associations in business history: Proceedings of the Fuji Conference.* International Conference on Business History series, no. 14. Tokyo: University of Tokyo Press; distributed by Columbia University Press, New York, 1988.

YANNOPOULOS, G. N. *Customs unions and trade conflicts: The enlargement of the European Community.* New York and London: Routledge, 1988.

YOCHELSON, JOHN, ed. *Keeping pace: U.S. policies and global economic change.* Center for Strategic and International Studies Book series. Cambridge, Mass.: Harper and Row, Ballinger, 1988.

ZAREMBKA, PAUL, ed. *Research in political economy.* Volume 11. A Research Annual. Greenwich, Conn. and London: JAI Press, 1988.

ZERBE, RICHARD O., JR., ed. *Research in law and economics.* Volume 11. Greenwich, Conn. and London: JAI Press, 1988.

ZIMBALIST, ANDREW, ed. *Cuban political economy: Controversies in Cubanology.* Series in Political Economy and Economic Development in Latin America. Boulder, Colo. and London: Westview Press, 1988.

ZSCHOCK, DIETER K., ed. *Health care in Peru: Resources and policy.* Westview Special Studies on Latin America and the Caribbean. Boulder, Colo. and London: Westview Press, 1988.

Author Index of Articles
in Current Periodicals and Collective Volumes

Abbreviated titles for journals are the same as those used in the *Journal of Economic Literature*. Full titles of journals may be found on pages x–xv.

Books have been identified by author or editor (noted *ed.*). In rare cases where two books by the same author appear, volumes are distinguished by I or II after the name. In some cases there appear two books by the same person, once as author, once as editor. These are distinguished by *ed.* noted for the edited volume. Full titles and bibliographic references for books may be found on pages xvi–xxxix.

Aage, Hans. A Small, Open Share Economy. *Cambridge J. Econ.*, December 1988, *12*(4), pp. 471–79.

Aaker, David A. and Stayman, Douglas M. Are All the Effects of Ad-Induced Feelings Mediated by A_{Ad}? *J. Cons. Res.*, December 1988, *15*(3), pp. 368–733.

Aanestad, James M. Statistical Data on Services. In *Candilis, W. O., ed.*, 1988, pp. 155–71.

Aaron, Henry J.; Galper, Harvey and Pechman, Joseph A. Uneasy Compromise: Problems of a Hybrid Income–Consumption Tax: Introduction. In *Aaron, H. J.; Galper, H. and Pechman, J. A., eds.*, 1988, pp. 1–13.

_____ **and Schwartz, William.** The Painful Prescription: Rationing Hospital Care. In *Brown, E., ed.*, 1988, pp. 97–104.

Aasland, Dag. Humanistic Economics: The Money Circuit as a Language. *Écon. Soc.*, September 1988, *22*(9), pp. 187–88.

_____. A Short Note on the Abstraction of Economic Life. *Écon. Soc.*, September 1988, *22*(9), pp. 21–27.

Abadía, Antonio. An Index of Prices and Taxes: Spain, 1981–1987. *Econ. Letters*, 1988, *28*(3), pp. 243–46.

Abalkin, Leonid I. Relying on the Lessons of the Past. *Prob. Econ.*, June 1988, *31*(2), pp. 6–18.

_____. Restructuring the Management of the Economy: A Continuation of the Work of the October Revolution. *Prob. Econ.*, August 1988, *31*(4), pp. 6–23.

_____. Restructuring the System and Methods of Planned Management. *Prob. Econ.*, January 1988, *30*(9), pp. 6–18.

Abbate, F. Development Lending and Conditionality: Comment. In *Jepma, C. J., ed.*, 1988, pp. 161–64.

Abbott, George C. Scotland as a Case Study in Development. *Can. J. Devel. Stud.*, 1988, *9*(1), pp. 137–54.

Abbott, Jacky and Gerritsen, Rolf. Shifting to Certainty? Australian Rural Policy in 1987: Review. *Rev. Marketing Agr. Econ.*, April 1988, *56*(1), pp. 9–26.

Abbott, Philip C. Estimating U.S. Agricultural Export Demand Elasticities: Econometric and Economic Issues. In *Carter, C. A. and Gardiner, W. H., eds.*, 1988, pp. 53–85.

_____; **Habeck, M. and Brown, Deborah J.** Sources of Export Earnings Instability: The Role of Agriculture. *J. Agr. Econ.*, January 1988, *39*(1), pp. 69–79.

_____; **Paarlberg, Philip L. and Patterson, Paul M.** Supplier Substitutability by Importers: Implications for Assessing the 1980 U.S. Grain Embargo. *Southern J. Agr. Econ.*, December 1988, *20*(2), pp. 1–14.

Abdalla, Adil E. A. A Characterization of Employment Distortions in Labor Contracts with Asymmetric Information. *Econ. Letters*, 1988, *27*(1), pp. 15–21.

Abdel-Khalek, Gouda. Income and Price Elasticities of Energy Consumption in Egypt: A Time-Series Analysis. *Energy Econ.*, January 1988, *10*(1), pp. 47–58.

Abdel-Khalik, A. Rashad. Incentives for Accruing Costs and Efficiency in Regulated Monopolies Subject to ROE Constraint. *J. Acc. Res.*, Supplement, 1988, *26*, pp. 144–74.

Abdel-Rahman, A.-M. M. Optimality and Production Efficiency of Some Cropsharing Systems. *J. Econ. Stud.*, 1988, *15*(1), pp. 53–70.

Abdel-Rahman, H. M. Product Differentiation, Monopolistic Competition and City Size. *Reg. Sci. Urban Econ.*, February 1988, *18*(1), pp. 69–86.

Abderrezak, Ali and Thomas, Lloyd B., Jr. Anticipated Future Budget Deficits and the Term Structure of Interest Rates. *Southern Econ. J.*, July 1988, *55*(1), pp. 150–61.

_____ **and Thomas, Lloyd B., Jr.** Long-term Interest Rates: The Role of Expected Budget Deficits. *Public Finance Quart.*, July 1988, *16*(3), pp. 341–56.

Abdolmohammadi, M., et al. Factors Motivating Academic Research in Accounting. In *Schwartz, B. N., ed.*, 1988, pp. 159–73.

Abdou, J. Neutral Veto Correspondences with a Continuum of Alternatives. *Int. J. Game Theory*, 1988, *17*(2), pp. 135–64.

Abdullah, Dewan A. and Rangazas, Peter C. Money and the Business Cycle: Another Look. *Rev. Econ. Statist.*, November 1988, *70*(4), pp. 680–85.

_____ **and Rangazas, Peter C.** Testing Some Monetarist Propositions. *Rev. Econ. Statist.*, February 1988, *70*(1), pp. 173–77.

Abdullah, Tahira. Employment Situation and Economic Exploitation of Poor Earning Women in Rawalpindi: Comments. *Pakistan*

Devel. Rev., Part 2, Winter 1988, *27*(4), pp. 799–801.

Abe, H. and Alden, J. D. Regional Development Planning in Japan. *Reg. Stud.*, October 1988, *22*(5), pp. 429–38.

Abe, Kenzo. Anatomy of Tax Incidence in the Initially Distorted Economy of Variable Returns to Scale. *J. Public Econ.*, October 1988, *37*(1), pp. 113–20.

_____ **and Tawada, Makoto.** Public Production and the Incidence of a Corporate Income Tax. *Econ. Stud. Quart.*, September 1988, *39*(3), pp. 233–45.

Abed, George T. The Palestinian Economy: Summary and Conclusions. In *Abed, G. T., ed.*, 1988, pp. 329–41.

_____ . The Palestinian Economy under Occupation: Introduction and Overview. In *Abed, G. T., ed.*, 1988, pp. 1–12.

Abedin, Joynal and Bose, G. K. Farm Size and Productivity Difference—A Decomposition Analysis. *Bangladesh Devel. Stud.*, September 1988, *16*(3), pp. 71–79.

Abeele, Piet Vanden. Economic Agents' Expectations in a Psychological Perspective. In *van Raaij, W. F.; van Veldhoven, G. M. and Wärneryd, K.-E., eds.*, 1988, pp. 479–515.

Abel, Andrew B. An Analysis of Fiscal Policy under Operative and Inoperative Bequest Motives. In *Helpman, E.; Razin, A. and Sadka, E., eds.*, 1988, pp. 91–106.

_____ . Fiscal Policies and International Financial Markets: Comment. In *Frenkel, J. A., ed.*, 1988, pp. 217–21.

_____ . The Implications of Insurance for the Efficacy of Fiscal Policy. *J. Risk Ins.*, June 1988, *55*(2), pp. 339–78.

_____ . Stock Prices under Time-Varying Dividend Risk: An Exact Solution in an Infinite-Horizon General Equilibrium Model. *J. Monet. Econ.*, November 1988, *22*(3), pp. 375–93.

_____ . Why Is the Government in the Pension Business? Comment. In *Wachter, S. M., ed.*, 1988, pp. 35–40.

_____ **and Blanchard, Olivier Jean.** Investment and Sales: Some Empirical Evidence. In *Barnett, W. A.; Berndt, E. R. and White, H., eds.*, 1988, pp. 269–96.

_____ **and Warshawsky, Mark J.** Specification of the Joy of Giving: Insights from Altruism. *Rev. Econ. Statist.*, February 1988, *70*(1), pp. 145–49.

Abell, John D. Unanticipated Deficits and Interest Rates. *Amer. Econ.*, Fall 1988, *32*(2), pp. 11–19.

Abernethy, Margaret A.; Magnus, Anne and Stoelwinder, Johannes U. An Assessment of Alternative Models for Costing Nursing Services: A Measurement Theory Perspective. In *Smith, C. S., ed.*, 1988, pp. 127–44.

_____ **and Stoelwinder, Johannes U.** Management Information Systems in Public Hospitals: The Queen Victoria Medical Centre Experience. In *Butler, J. R. G. and Doessel, D. P., eds.*, 1988, pp. 3–19.

Abetti, Pier A. and Stuart, Robert W. Field Study of Technical Ventures—Part III: The Impact of Entrepreneurial and Management Experience on Early Performance. In *Kirchhoff, B. A., et al., eds.*, 1988, pp. 177–93.

Abiru, Masahiro. Vertical Integration, Variable Proportions and Successive Oligopolies. *J. Ind. Econ.*, March 1988, *36*(3), pp. 315–25.

Abizadeh, Fay and Arthur, Louise M. Potential Effects of Climate Change on Agriculture in the Prairie Region of Canada. *Western J. Agr. Econ.*, December 1988, *13*(2), pp. 216–24.

_____ ; **Arthur, Louise M. and Carter, Colin A.** Arbitrage Pricing, Capital Asset Pricing, and Agricultural Assets. *Amer. J. Agr. Econ.*, May 1988, *70*(2), pp. 359–65.

Abizadeh, Sohrab and Yousefi, Mahmood. An Empirical Re-examination of Wagner's Law. *Econ. Letters*, 1988, *26*(2), pp. 169–73.

_____ **and Yousefi, Mahmood.** Growth of Government Expenditure: The Case of Canada. *Public Finance Quart.*, January 1988, *16*(1), pp. 78–100.

Abouchar, Alan. Keynesian Microeconomics and the Microeconomics of Keynes in Public Sector Investment Decisions. In *Hamouda, O. F. and Smithin, J. N., eds.*, Vol. 2, 1988, pp. 49–57.

Abowd, John M. Public Sector Union Growth and Bargaining Laws: A Proportional Hazards Approach with Time-Varying Treatments: Comment. In *Freeman, R. B. and Ichniowski, C., eds.*, 1988, pp. 38–40.

_____ **and Vroman, Wayne.** Disaggregated Wage Developments. *Brookings Pap. Econ. Act.*, 1988, (1), pp. 313–38.

Abraham, Filip; Deardorff, Alan V. and Stern, Robert M. The Impact of Tariffs on Profits in the United States and Other Major Trading Countries. *Weltwirtsch. Arch.*, 1988, *124*(4), pp. 623–34.

Abraham, Fred J. Chief Executive Officer Compensation: Comment [Executive Salaries and Their Justification]. *J. Post Keynesian Econ.*, Spring 1988, *10*(3), pp. 474–78.

Abraham-Frois, Gilbert and Berrebi, Edmond. Optimisation et prix de production. (With English summary.) *Revue Écon. Polit.*, Jan.–Feb. 1988, *98*(1), pp. 66–77.

Abraham, H. Do Markets Clear or Not? The Contribution of Modern General Equilibrium Theory. *J. Stud. Econ. Econometrics*, July 1988, *12*(2), pp. 1–5.

_____ . Non-Walrasian Equilibria and Involuntary Unemployment: Comment. *S. Afr. J. Econ.*, June–Sept. 1988, *56*(2–3), pp. 196–200.

Abraham, Katharine G. Flexible Staffing Arrangements and Employers' Short-term Adjustment Strategies. In *Hart, R. A., ed.*, 1988, pp. 288–311.

_____ **and Farber, Henry S.** Returns to Seniority in Union and Nonunion Jobs: A New Look at the Evidence. *Ind. Lab. Relat. Rev.*, October 1988, *42*(1), pp. 3–19.

Abramovitz, Moses. Following and Leading. In *Hanusch, H., ed.*, 1988, pp. 323–41.

Abreu, Dilip. On the Theory of Infinitely Repeated Games with Discounting. *Econometrica*, March 1988, *56*(2), pp. 383–96.

———— **and Rubinstein, Ariel.** The Structure of Nash Equilibrium in Repeated Games with Finite Automata. *Econometrica*, November 1988, *56*(6), pp. 1259–81.

Abu-Amr, Ziad. The Gaza Economy: 1948–1984. In *Abed, G. T., ed.*, 1988, pp. 101–20.

Abu Kishk, Bakir. Industrial Development and Policies in the West Bank and Gaza. In *Abed, G. T., ed.*, 1988, pp. 165–89.

Acharya, B. P. The Instruments of Urban Land Policy in India: Opportunities for Future Direction. *Environ. Planning A*, November 1988, *20*(11), pp. 1427–47.

Acharya, Sankarshan. A Generalized Econometric Model and Tests of a Signalling Hypothesis with Two Discrete Signals. *J. Finance*, June 1988, *43*(2), pp. 413–29.

Acharya, Shankar. India's Fiscal Policy. In *Lucas, R. E. B. and Papanek, G. F., eds.*, 1988, pp. 287–318.

Achebe, Ifeanyi. Indigenization: An Examination of the Legal Problems within Nigeria's Experience. In *Pennsylvania Economic Association*, 1988, pp. 196–224.

Achenbaum, W. Andrew. Social Security's Three R's. In *Nash, G. D.; Pugach, N. H. and Tomasson, R. F., eds.*, 1988, pp. 113–44.

Achinstein, Peter. The Illocutionary Theory of Explanation. In *Pitt, J. C., ed.*, 1988, pp. 199–222.

Ackermann, Nancy. Just Compensation, Land-Use Regulation, and the Compensable Temporary Taking: *First English Evangelical Lutheran Church of Glendale v County of Los Angeles*, — U.S. —, 107 S. CT. 2378 (1987): Comment. *Natural Res. J.*, Spring 1988, *28*(2), pp. 393–416.

Ackrill, Margaret. Britain's Managers and the British Economy, 1870s to the 1980s. *Oxford Rev. Econ. Policy*, Spring 1988, *4*(1), pp. 59–73.

Acs, Zoltan J. and Audretsch, David B. Innovation in Large and Small Firms: An Empirical Analysis. *Amer. Econ. Rev.*, September 1988, *78*(4), pp. 678–90.

———— **and Audretsch, David B.** Small-Firm Mobility: A First Report. *Econ. Letters*, 1988, *26*(3), pp. 281–84.

———— **and Audretsch, David B.** Testing the Schumpeterian Hypothesis. *Eastern Econ. J.*, April–June 1988, *14*(2), pp. 129–40.

Aczél, J. 'Cheaper by the Dozen': Twelve Functional Equations and Their Applications to the 'Laws of Science' and to Measurement in Economics. In *Eichhorn, W., ed.*, 1988, pp. 3–17.

Adair, John J. and Simmons, Rex. From Voucher Auditing to Junkyard Dogs: The Evolution of Federal Inspectors General. *Public Budg. Finance*, Summer 1988, *8*(2), pp. 91–110.

Adam, Dietrich. Die Eignung der belastungsorientierten Auftragsfreigabe für die Steuerung von Fertigungsprozessen mit diskontinuierlichem Materialfluss. (With English summary.) *Z. Betriebswirtshaft*, January 1988, *58*(1), pp. 98–115.

Adam, M. C. and Farber, A. Le financement de l'innovation technoligique. Deuxième partie: L'apport de la théorie finanacière. (With English summary.) *Cah. Écon. Bruxelles*, First Trimester 1988, (117), pp. 3–36.

Adamowicz, Wiktor L. Behavioral Implications of Nonmarket Valuation Models. *Can. J. Agr. Econ.*, Part 2, December 1988, *36*(4), pp. 929–39.

————; **Higginson, Nancy and Hawkins, Murray.** Pricing Relationships in Interdependent North American Hog Markets: The Impact of the Countervailing Duty. *Can. J. Agr. Econ.*, November 1988, *36*(3), pp. 501–18.

Adams, Barry J. and Ponnambalam, Kumaraswamy. Comment on "Error Analysis of Conventional Discrete and Gradient Dynamic Programming." *Water Resources Res.*, June 1988, *24*(6), pp. 888–89.

Adams, C. D.; Baum, A. E. and MacGregor, B. D. The Availability of Land for Inner City Development: A Case Study of Inner Manchester. *Urban Stud.*, February 1988, *25*(1), pp. 62–76.

Adams, Dale W. The Conundrum of Successful Credit Projects in Floundering Rural Financial Markets. *Econ. Develop. Cult. Change*, January 1988, *36*(2), pp. 355–67.

Adams, F. Charles. Hysteresis Effects and Unemployment. In *Cross, R., ed.*, 1988, pp. 392–96.

———— **and Boyer, Russell S.** Forward Premia and Risk Premia in a Simple Model of Exchange Rate Determination. *J. Money, Credit, Banking*, November 1988, *20*(4), pp. 633–44.

Adams, George W. Remedial and Procedural Issues Arising from the Charter of Rights and Freedoms. In *Carter, D. D., et al.*, 1988, pp. 301–30.

Adams, John. Trade and Payments as Instituted Process: The Institutional Theory of the External Sector. In *Tool, M. R., ed., Vol. 2*, 1988, *1987*, pp. 421–42.

Adams, John S. Growth of U.S. Cities and Recent Trends in Urban Real Estate Values. In *Ausubel, J. H. and Herman, R., eds.*, 1988, pp. 108–45.

Adams, Michael. Franchising—A Case of Long-term Contracts: Comment. *J. Inst. Theoretical Econ.*, February 1988, *144*(1), pp. 145–48.

Adams, Philip D. Some Comparisons of Recent Estimates of Agricultural Supply Elasticities for the Australian Economy. *Rev. Marketing Agr. Econ.*, December 1988, *56*(3), pp. 352–60.

Adams, Richard M. and Johnson, Neal S. Benefits of Increased Streamflow: The Case of the John Day River Steelhead Fishery. *Water Resources Res.*, November 1988, *24*(11), pp. 1839–46.

————, **et al.** Implications of Global Climate Change for Western Agriculture. *Western J. Agr. Econ.*, December 1988, *13*(2), pp. 348–56.

Adams, Richard N. Evolution and Development.

In *Bennett, J. W. and Bowen, J. R., eds.*, 1988, pp. 33–60.

Adams, Roy J. The Role of Management in a Political Conception of Industrial Relation Level of the Enterprise. In *Dlugos, G.; Dorow, W. and Weiermair, K., eds.*, 1988, pp. 177–91.

Adams, Walter and Brock, James W. Reaganomics and the Transmogrification of Merger Policy. *Antitrust Bull.*, Summer 1988, *33*(2), pp. 309–59.

Adams, William James. Should Merger Policy be Changed? An Antitrust Perspective. In *Browne, L. E. and Rosengren, E. S., eds.*, 1988, pp. 173–94.

_____ and Sappington, David E. M. Profiting from 'Countervailing' Power: An Effect of Government Control. *Int. J. Ind. Organ.*, 1988, *6*(3), pp. 323–33.

Adamson, R. Review of W. S. Jevons's 'Studies in Deductive Logic.' In *Wood, J. C., ed., Vol. 1*, 1988, *1881*, pp. 30–36.

Adamson, Rolf. Economic History Research in Sweden since the Mid-1970s. *Scand. Econ. Hist. Rev.*, 1988, *36*(3), pp. 51–66.

Adas, Michael. Market Demand versus Imperial Control: Colonial Contradictions and the Origins of Agrarian Protest in South and Southeast Asia. In *Burke, E., III, ed.*, 1988, pp. 89–116.

Addams, H. Lon. Up to Speed in 90 Days: An Orientation Plan. In *Timpe, A. D., ed.*, 1988, *1985*, pp. 124–28.

Addison, John T. The Demand for Workers and Hours and the Effects of Job Security Policies: Theory and Evidence: Comment. In *Hart, R. A., ed.*, 1988, pp. 33–38.

_____ and Chilton, John B. Wage Patterns: An Evolutionary Perspective. *J. Lab. Res.*, Summer 1988, *9*(3), pp. 207–19.

Adelaja, Adesoji O.; Andrews, Margaret S. and Lopez, Rigoberto A. The Effects of Suburbanization on Agriculture. *Amer. J. Agr. Econ.*, May 1988, *70*(2), pp. 346–58.

Adell, Bernard. Law and Industrial Relations: The State of the Art in Common Law Canada. In *Hébert, G.; Jain, H. C. and Meltz, N. M., eds.*, 1988, pp. 107–46.

_____. The Queen's University Conference on Labour Law under the Charter: An Introduction to the Proceedings. In *Carter, D. D., et al.*, 1988, pp. 2–16.

Adelman, Irma. Confessions of an Incurable Romantic. *Banca Naz. Lavoro Quart. Rev.*, September 1988, (166), pp. 243–62.

_____. A Poverty-Focused Approach to Development Policy. In *Wilber, C. K., ed.*, 1988, pp. 493–507.

_____ and Morris, Cynthia. Interactions between Agriculture and Industry during the Nineteenth Century. In *Antonelli, G. and Quadrio-Curzio, A., eds.*, 1988, pp. 23–31.

_____ and Robinson, Sherman. Macroeconomic Adjustment and Income Distribution: Alternative Models Applied to Two Economies. *J. Devel. Econ.*, July 1988, *29*(1), pp. 23–44.

_____ and Robinson, Sherman. Macroeconomic Shocks, Foreign Trade, and Structural Adjust-

ment: A General Equilibrium Analysis of the U.S. Economy, 1982–1986. In *Carter, C. A. and Gardiner, W. H., eds.*, 1988, pp. 137–62.

_____ and Sunding, David. Economic Policy and Income Distribution in China. In *Reynolds, B. L., ed.*, 1988, *1987*, pp. 154–71.

_____; Taylor, J. Edward and Vogel, Stephen. Life in a Mexican Village: A SAM Perspective. *J. Devel. Stud.*, October 1988, *25*(1), pp. 7–24.

Adelstein, Richard P. Mind and Hand: Economics and Engineering at the Massachusetts Institute of Technology. In *Barber, W. J., ed.*, 1988, pp. 290–317.

Adeniyi, E. O.; Ayodele, A. I. and Diejomaoh, V. P. The Development Planning Experience in Nigeria: Effectiveness, Problems, and Prospects. In *Urrutia, M. and Yukawa, S., eds. (I)*, 1988, pp. 227–62.

Aderhold, Robert; Cumming, Christine and Harwood, Alison. International Linkages among Equities Markets and the October 1987 Market Break. *Fed. Res. Bank New York Quart. Rev.*, Summer 1988, *13*(2), pp. 34–46.

Adikibi, Owen T. The Multinational Corporation and Monopoly of Patents in Nigeria. *World Devel.*, April 1988, *16*(4), pp. 511–26.

Adler, Hans J. and Wolfson, Michael C. A Prototype Micro–Macro Link for the Canadian Household Sector. *Rev. Income Wealth*, December 1988, *34*(4), pp. 371–92.

Adler, Michael and Detemple, Jérôme B. Hedging with Futures in an Intertemporal Portfolio Context. *J. Futures Markets*, June 1988, *8*(3), pp. 249–69.

_____ and Detemple, Jérôme B. On the Optimal Hedge of a Nontraded Cash Position. *J. Finance*, March 1988, *43*(1), pp. 143–53.

Adler, Moshe. The American Dream and Central City Blight Are American. *J. Econ. Behav. Organ.*, June 1988, *9*(4), pp. 381–92.

Adler, Nancy J. Pacific Basin Managers: A *Gaijin*, Not a Woman. In *Adler, N. J. and Izraeli, D., eds.*, 1988, pp. 226–49.

_____ and Izraeli, Dafna N. Women in Management Worldwide. In *Adler, N. J. and Izraeli, D., eds.*, 1988, pp. 3–16.

Adler, Sy. A Comparative Analysis of Rail Transit Politics, Policy and Planning in Canada and the United States. *Logist. Transp. Rev.*, September 1988, *24*(3), pp. 265–79.

Admati, Anat R. and Pfleiderer, Paul. Selling and Trading on Information in Financial Markets. *Amer. Econ. Rev.*, May 1988, *78*(2), pp. 96–103.

Adolph, Brigitte and Wolfstetter, Elmar. Lohnindexierung und Geldpolitik bei informativen Preisen. (Wage Indexation and Monetary Policy if Prices Are Informative. With English summary.) *Z. Wirtschaft. Sozialwissen.*, 1988, *108*(3), pp. 335–53.

Adorf, H.-M. and Murtagh, F. Clustering Based on Neural Network Processing. In *Edwards, D. and Raun, N. E., eds.*, 1988, pp. 239–44.

Aerts, Walter and Theunisse, Hilda. Belgium and

the Seventh Directive. In *Gray, S. J. and Coenenberg, A. G., eds.*, 1988, pp. 41–75.

Afexentiou, P. C. Displacement Effect: An Econometric Test for Cyprus 1960–1982. *Soc. Econ. Stud.*, September 1988, 37(3), pp. 237–52.

Afriat, Sydney N. Efficiency in Production and Consumption. In *Dogramaci, A. and Färe, R., eds.*, 1988, pp. 251–68.

Afriyie, Kofi. A Technology-Transfer Methodology for Developing Joint Production Strategies in Varying Technological Systems. In *Contractor, F. J. and Lorange, P.*, 1988, pp. 81–95.

Afxentiou, Panayiotis C. Opportunity Costs: Some Issues. *S. Afr. J. Econ.*, March 1988, 56(1), pp. 94–99.

Afzal, Mohammad; Raja, Tariq Aslam and Mohammad, Ali. Some Differentials in Infant and Child Mortality Risks in Pakistan 1962–1986. *Pakistan Devel. Rev.*, Part 2, Winter 1988, 27(4), pp. 635–42.

Aganbegyan, Abel G. Acceleration and Perestroika. In *Aganbegyan, A. and Timofeyev, T.*, 1988, pp. 25–43.

———. The Program of Radical Restructuring. *Prob. Econ.*, September 1988, 31(5), pp. 6–22.

Agapos, A. M. and Beatty, Warren. A Study of Comparative Air Fares in the Southeast United States. *Logist. Transp. Rev.*, September 1988, 24(3), pp. 249–64.

Agarwal, Manmohan. A Comparative Analysis of India's Export Performance, 1965–80. *Indian Econ. Rev.*, July–Dec. 1988, 23(2), pp. 231–62.

Agbeyegbe, Terence D. An Exact Discrete Analog of an Open Linear Non-stationary First-Order Continuous-Time System with Mixed Sample. *J. Econometrics*, November 1988, 39(3), pp. 237–50.

Aggarwal, R. N. Indian Automobile Industry: Problems and Prospects. *Indian Econ. J.*, Oct.–Dec. 1988, 36(2), pp. 50–61.

Aggarwal, Raj and Soenen, Luc A. The Nature and Efficiency of the Gold Market. *J. Portfol. Manage.*, Spring 1988, 14(3), pp. 18–21.

——— and Soenen, Luc A. Private Use of Official Currency Cocktails: The Relative Success of the ECU and the SDR. *Banca Naz. Lavoro Quart. Rev.*, December 1988, (167), pp. 425–40.

Aghevli, Bijan B.; Kim, Insu and Neiss, Hubert. Growth and Adjustment: Experiences of Selected Subcontinent Countries. In *Streeten, P., ed.*, 1988, pp. 30–53.

Agliardi, Elettra. Microeconomic Foundations of Macroeconomics in the Post-Keynesian Approach. *Metroecon.*, October 1988, 39(3), pp. 275–97.

———. On the Trade-off between Technological Efficiency and Allocative Efficiency. A Model of Contestable Markets in Terms of Game Theory. *Econ. Notes*, 1988, (2), pp. 110–36.

Agrawal, Jagdish; Kamakura, Wagner A. and Ratchford, Brian T. Measuring Market Efficiency and Welfare Loss. *J. Cons. Res.*, December 1988, 15(3), pp. 289–302.

Agrawal, Nisha. The Economic Effects of Public Housing in Australia. *Econ. Rec.*, December 1988, 64(187), pp. 254–67.

———. Sources of Inequality between Male and Female Wages in Australia. *Australian Econ. Rev.*, Summer 1988, (84), pp. 26–36.

——— and Meagher, G. A. Structural Reform, Macro Policies and Income Distribution. *Australian Econ. Rev.*, Spring 1988, (83), pp. 42–52.

Aguigneir, P. Regional Disparities since 1978. In *Feuchtwang, S.; Hussain, A. and Pairault, T., eds., Vol. 2*, 1988, pp. 93–106.

Aguilar, Renato and Sandelin, Bo. Qualitative Response Estimations of the Selling Behaviour in the Swedish Market for Owner-Occupied Houses. *Urban Stud.*, February 1988, 25(1), pp. 77–84.

Aguirre, Carlos A. and Shome, Parthasarathi. The Mexican Value-Added Tax (VAT): Methodology for Calculating the Base. *Nat. Tax J.*, December 1988, 41(4), pp. 543–54.

Agyemang, Augustus Asante. The Suitability of Arbitration for Settling "Political" Investment Disputes Involving African States. *J. World Trade*, December 1988, 22(6), pp. 123–27.

Aharoni, Yair. The United Kingdom: Transforming Attitudes. In *Vernon, R., ed.*, 1988, pp. 23–56.

Aharony, Joseph; Saunders, Anthony and Swary, Itzhak. The Effects of DIDMCA on Bank Stockholders' Returns and Risk. *J. Banking Finance*, September 1988, 12(3), pp. 317–31.

Ahking, Francis W. and Miller, Stephen M. Models of Business Cycles: A Review Essay. *Eastern Econ. J.*, April–June 1988, 14(2), pp. 197–202.

Ahkong, Alain. Changes to the Income Tax Act: Singapore. *Bull. Int. Fiscal Doc.*, May 1988, 42(5), pp. 217–22.

Ahlheim, Michael. A Reconsideration of Debreu's "Coefficient of Resource Utilization." In *Bös, D.; Rose, M. and Seidl, C., eds.*, 1988, pp. 21–48.

——— and Wagenhals, Gerhard. Exakte Wohlfahrtsmasse in der Nutzen-Kosten-Analyse. (Exact Welfare Measurement in Cost Benefit Analysis. With English summary.) *Z. Wirtschaft. Sozialwissen.*, 1988, 108(2), pp. 169–93.

Ahlström, Krister. Den europeiska ekonomiska integrationen ur finsk industri synvinkel. (European Economic Integration from the Point of Finnish Industries. With English summary.) *Ekon. Samfundets Tidskr.*, 1988, 41(3), pp. 135–45.

Ahluwalia, Isher Judge. Industrial Policy and Industrial Performance in India. In *Lucas, R. E. B. and Papanek, G. F., eds.*, 1988, pp. 151–162.

Ahluwalia, Montek S. India's Economic Performance, Policies and Prospects. In *Lucas, R. E. B. and Papanek, G. F., eds.*, 1988, pp. 345–60.

Ahmad, Eatzaz. Combining Yearly and Quarterly Data in Regression Analysis. *Pakistan Devel. Rev.*, Part 2, Winter 1988, 27(4), pp. 715–22.

_____. Determinants of Debt Problem in Pakistan and Its Debt-Servicing Capacity: Comments. *Pakistan Devel. Rev.*, Part 2, Winter 1988, 27(4), pp. 817–18.

Ahmad, Ehtisham. Trade Regimes and Export Strategies with Reference to South Asia. In *Streeten, P., ed.*, 1988, pp. 117–59.

_____; **Coady, David and Stern, Nicholas.** A Complete Set of Shadow Prices for Pakistan: Illustrations for 1975–76. *Pakistan Devel. Rev.*, Spring 1988, 27(1), pp. 7–43.

_____; **Ludlow, Stephen and Stern, Nicholas.** Demand Response in Pakistan: A Modification of the Linear Expenditure System for 1976. *Pakistan Devel. Rev.*, Autumn 1988, 27(3), pp. 293–308.

Ahmad, Muzaffer. Structural Adaptation and Public Enterprise Performance: Comments. In *Streeten, P., ed.*, 1988, pp. 203–07.

Ahmad, Sultan. International Real Income Comparisons with Reduced Information. In *Salazar-Carrillo, J. and Rao, D. S. P., eds.*, 1988, pp. 75–92.

Ahmadian, Majid. Pricing Policies of an Oil Cartel with Expectation of Substitute Producers. *Energy J.*, January 1988, 9(1), pp. 115–20.

Ahmed, Ehsan; Rosser, J. Barkley, Jr. and Sheehan, Richard G. A Global Model of OECD Aggregate Supply and Demand Using Vector Autoregressive Techniques. *Europ. Econ. Rev.*, November 1988, 32(9), pp. 1711–29.

Ahmed, Iftikhar. The Bio-revolution in Agriculture: Key to Poverty Alleviation in the Third World? *Int. Lab. Rev.*, 1988, 127(1), pp. 53–72.

_____. Pro-poor Potential. In *Research and Info. System for the Non-aligned and Other Developing Countries*, 1988, pp. 134–49.

Ahmed, Mohammad. Financial Repression in the LDCs: A Survey of Issues and Reappraisal. *Pakistan J. Appl. Econ.*, Summer 1988, 7(1), pp. 19–41.

Ahmed, Qazi Masood. Comparative Analysis of Agricultural Income Tax with USHR: A Case Study of Nawabshah. *Pakistan Econ. Soc. Rev.*, Winter 1988, 26(2), pp. 109–26.

_____. The Discrepancies in the Government Policies and Their Influence on Set Target: A Case Study of Education Sector Sixth Five Year Plan. *Pakistan Econ. Soc. Rev.*, Summer 1988, 26(1), pp. 21–40.

Ahmed, Raisuddin. Pricing Principles and Public Intervention in Domestic Markets. In *Mellor, J. W. and Ahmed, R., eds.*, 1988, pp. 55–80.

_____. Rice Price Stabilization and Food Security in Bangladesh. *World Devel.*, September 1988, 16(9), pp. 1035–50.

_____. Structure, Costs, and Benefits of Food Subsidies in Bangladesh. In *Pinstrup-Andersen, P., ed.*, 1988, pp. 219–28.

_____ **and Mellor, John W.** Agricultural Price Policy for Accelerating Growth: Conclusions. In *Mellor, J. W. and Ahmed, R., eds.*, 1988, pp. 265–91.

_____ **and Mellor, John W.** Agricultural Price Policy—The Context and the Approach. In *Mellor, J. W. and Ahmed, R., eds.*, 1988, pp. 1–10.

Ahmed, Sadiq and Alamgir, Mohiuddin. Poverty and Income Distribution in Bangladesh. In *Srinivasan, T. N. and Bardhan, P. K., eds.*, 1988, pp. 11–38.

Ahmed, Ziaul Z. and Brand, Horst. Productivity in Industrial Inorganic Chemicals. *Mon. Lab. Rev.*, March 1988, 111(3), pp. 33–40.

Ahn, Chang Mo and Thompson, Howard E. Jump-Diffusion Processes and the Term Structure of Interest Rates. *J. Finance*, March 1988, 43(1), pp. 155–74.

Ahn, Choong Yong. Foreign Investment and Trade Promotion Schemes: With Some Comparisons between Korea and Latin American Countries. *J. Econ. Devel.*, December 1988, 13(2), pp. 163–79.

Ahn, Jeong Keun and Nourse, Hugh O. Spatial Economic Interdependence in an Urban Hierarchy System. *J. Reg. Sci.*, August 1988, 28(3), pp. 421–32.

Ahn, Sung K. and Reinsel, Gregory C. Nested Reduced-Rank Autoregressive Models for Multiple Time Series. *J. Amer. Statist. Assoc.*, September 1988, 83(403), pp. 849–56.

Ahn, T.; Charnes, A. and Cooper, W. W. Using Data Envelopment Analysis to Measure the Efficiency of Not-for-Profit Organizations: A Critical Evaluation—A Comment. *Managerial Dec. Econ.*, September 1988, 9(3), pp. 251–53.

Aho, C. Michael. Bilateralism, Multilateralism and Canada in U.S. Trade Policy: Foreword. In *Diebold, W., Jr., ed.*, 1988, pp. vii–xiii.

_____. Technology, Structural Change, and Trade. In *Cyert, R. M. and Mowery, D. C., eds.*, 1988, pp. 419–42.

_____ **and Levinson, Marc.** The Economy after Reagan. *Foreign Aff.*, Winter 1988–89, 67(2), pp. 10–25.

Ahwireng-Obeng, F. Entrepreneurial Revolution for the African Third World: The Case of Ghana. *Can. J. Devel. Stud.*, 1988, 9(1), pp. 19–34.

Aiello, Robert J. They Hear You . . . But They're Not Listening. In *Timpe, A. D., ed.*, 1988, 1983, pp. 164–68.

Aiginger, Karl. A New Dichotomization for Uncertainty Models. In *Munier, B. R., ed.*, 1988, pp. 575–93.

_____ **and Breuss, Fritz.** Some Doubts on the Current Paradigma of Intra-industry Trade. *Empirica*, 1988, 15(1), pp. 27–50.

Aigner, Dennis J. On Econometric Methodology and the Search for Causal Laws. *Econ. Rec.*, December 1988, 64(187), pp. 323–26.

_____ **and Balestra, Pietro.** Optimal Experimental Design for Error Components Models. *Econometrica*, July 1988, 56(4), pp. 955–71.

_____; **Schneider, Friedrich and Ghosh, Damayanti.** Me and My Shadow: Estimating the Size of the U.S. Hidden Economy from Time Series Data. In *Barnett, W. A.; Berndt, E. R. and White, H., eds.*, 1988, pp. 297–334.

Aigrain, Pierre R. Advances in Materials Science.

In *Muroyama, J. H. and Stever, H. G., eds.*, 1988, pp. 41–44.

Aislabie, Colin J. Economic Incentives and the Pattern of the Australian Tariff. *Australian Econ. Pap.*, June 1988, *27*(50), pp. 20–32.

———— **and Tisdell, Clem A.** Profit Maximization and Marketing Strategies: Demand Rotation and Social Influences [A Note on Price-Advertising Reaction Function]. *Managerial Dec. Econ.*, March 1988, *9*(1), pp. 77–82.

Aït-Laoussine, Nordine and Gault, John C. The 1986 Oil Price War: An Economic Fiasco. In *Mabro, R., ed.*, 1988, pp. 81–103.

Aiuppa, Thomas A. Evaluation of Pearson Curves as an Approximation of the Maximum Probable Annual Aggregate Loss. *J. Risk Ins.*, September 1988, *55*(3), pp. 425–41.

Aivazyan, S. A. Model- and Method-Oriented Intelligent Software for Statistical Data Analysis. In *Fedorov, V. and Lauter, H., eds.*, 1988, pp. 153–57.

Aiyagari, S. Rao. Economic Fluctuations without Shocks to Fundamentals; or, Does the Stock Market Dance to Its Own Music? *Fed. Res. Bank Minn. Rev.*, Winter 1988, *12*(1), pp. 8–24.

————. Nonmonetary Steady States in Stationary Overlapping Generations Models with Long Lived Agents and Discounting: Multiplicity, Optimality, and Consumption Smoothing. *J. Econ. Theory*, June 1988, *45*(1), pp. 102–27.

Aizenman, Joshua. Monopolistic Competition and Labor Market Adjustment in the Open Economy. In *Marston, R. C., ed.*, 1988, pp. 169–89.

————. Optimal Tax Policy for Balance of Payments Objectives: Comment. In *Frenkel, J. A., ed.*, 1988, pp. 338–44.

————. Successful Adjustment in a Multi-sectorial Economy. *Int. Econ. J.*, Spring 1988, *2*(1), pp. 85–99.

———— **and Borensztein, Eduardo R.** Debt and Conditionality under Endogenous Terms of Trade Adjustment. *Int. Monet. Fund Staff Pap.*, December 1988, *35*(4), pp. 686–713.

———— **and Frenkel, Jacob A.** Sectorial Wages and the Real Exchange Rate. *J. Int. Econ.*, February 1988, *24*(1–2), pp. 69–91.

Akaishi, Giselda; Tison, Elisabeth and Zumaran Paz, Jorge. Latin and Central America: The Challenge to the United States. In *Lavigne, M., ed.*, 1988, pp. 182–211.

Akella, Srinivas R. and Greenbaum, Stuart I. Savings and Loan Ownership Structure and Expense-Preference. *J. Banking Finance*, September 1988, *12*(3), pp. 419–37.

Aker, Ugur. Imaginary Transactions in Turkish Foreign Trade. In *Pennsylvania Economic Association*, 1988, pp. 346–61.

Akerlof, George A. Irving Fisher on His Head: The Consequences of Constant Threshold-Target Monitoring of Money Holdings. In *Shaw, G. K., ed., Vol. 2*, 1988, *1979*, pp. 156–74.

————. The Market for "Lemons": Quality Uncertainty and the Market Mechanisms. In *Ricketts, M., ed., Vol. 1*, 1988, *1970*, pp. 207–19.

————; **Rose, Andrew Kenan and Yellen, Janet L.** Job Switching and Job Satisfaction in the U.S. Labor Market. *Brookings Pap. Econ. Act.*, 1988, (2), pp. 495–582.

————; **Rose, Andrew Kenan and Yellen, Janet L.** The New Keynesian Economics and the Output–Inflation Trade-off: Comment. *Brookings Pap. Econ. Act.*, 1988, (1), pp. 66–75.

———— **and Yellen, Janet L.** Fairness and Unemployment. *Amer. Econ. Rev.*, May 1988, *78*(2), pp. 44–49.

Akgiray, Vedat and Booth, G. Geoffrey. Mixed Diffusion-Jump Process Modeling of Exchange Rate Movements. *Rev. Econ. Statist.*, November 1988, *70*(4), pp. 631–37.

———— **and Booth, G. Geoffrey.** The Stable-Law Model of Stock Returns. *J. Bus. Econ. Statist.*, January 1988, *6*(1), pp. 51–57.

————; **Booth, G. Geoffrey and Seifert, Bruce.** Distribution Properties of Latin American Black Market Exchange Rates. *J. Int. Money Finance*, March 1988, *7*(1), pp. 37–48.

Akgür, Teoman. Cumhuriyet Dönemi (1924–1986) Mevduat, Kredi ve Para Serilerinin Oluşturulmasi. (Construction of Monetary Time Series of the Republican Era [1924–1986]. With English summary.) *METU*, 1988, *15*(3–4), pp. 181–211.

Akhtar, Afifa and Sathar, Zeba A. Evidence of Fertility Decline in Karachi. *Pakistan Devel. Rev.*, Part 2, Winter 1988, *27*(4), pp. 659–68.

Akimaru, Harou. Assessment of New Information Services in Japan. In *Orishimo, I.; Hewings, G. J. D. and Nijkamp, P., eds.*, 1988, pp. 47–65.

Akin, John S.; Popkin, Barry M. and Schwartz, J. Brad. Price and Income Elasticities of Demand for Modern Health Care: The Case of Infant Delivery in the Philippines. *World Bank Econ. Rev.*, January 1988, *2*(1), pp. 49–76.

———— **and Schwartz, J. Brad.** The Effect of Economic Factors on Contraceptive Choice in Jamaica and Thailand: A Comparison of Mixed Multinomial Logit Results. *Econ. Develop. Cult. Change*, April 1988, *36*(3), pp. 503–27.

van den Akker, Piet A. M. and Nelissen, Jan H. M. Are Demographic Developments Influenced by Social Security. *J. Econ. Psych.*, March 1988, *9*(1), pp. 81–114.

Akkina, Krishna and Varamini, Hossein. Rational Expectations and the Term Structure of Interest Rates: An Empirical Study of Group Ten Countries. In *Missouri Valley Economic Assoc.*, 1988, pp. 128–34.

Akrasanee, Narongchai and James, Kenneth. Small and Medium Business Improvement in the ASEAN Region: Production Management: Preface. In *James, K. and Akrasanee, N., eds.*, 1988, pp. ix–x.

———— **and Kaosa-ard, Mingsarn Santikarn.** U.S.–Thai Relations: Selected Case Studies in Agribusiness. In *Tan, L.-H. and Akrasanee, N., eds.*, 1988, pp. 177–99.

————; **Sestakupt, Pharadorn and Kultravut, Sunee.** Technical Efficiency and Production Management: The Thai Experience. In *James, K. and Akrasanee, N.*, eds., 1988, pp. 164–207.

_____ and Tan, Loong-Hoe. Changes in the ASEAN–U.S. Economic Environment and Opportunities: An Introductory Overview. In *Tan, L.-H. and Akrasanee, N.*, eds., 1988, pp. xv–xxii.

Al-Haj, Majid. The Changing Arab Kinship Structure: The Effect of Modernization in an Urban Community. *Econ. Develop. Cult. Change*, January 1988, *36*(2), pp. 237–58.

Al Hamad, Abdlatif Y. The Impact of the Oil Price Decline on the Economic Development of Arab Countries. In *Mabro, R.*, ed., 1988, pp. 259–72.

Al Husseini, Mohammad Farouk. Some Aspects of the Saudi Arabian Oil Supply Policy. In *Mabro, R.*, ed., 1988, pp. 105–17.

Al, Pieter G. and van Bochove, Cornelis A. A Synoptic Structure of the System of National Accounts. *Rev. Income Wealth*, March 1988, *34*(1), pp. 45–70.

Al-Sahlawi, Mohammed A. Gasoline Demand: The Case of Saudi Arabia. *Energy Econ.*, October 1988, *10*(4), pp. 271–75.

_____. GCC Energy Demand Outlook to 2000. *Energy Econ.*, January 1988, *10*(1), pp. 42–46.

Alada, A. Dinç. Iktisatta Belirsizlik Anlayişi Üzerine Notlar. (On the Concept of Uncertainty in Economics. With English summary.) *METU*, 1988, *15*(1–2), pp. 183–90.

Alagh, Yoginder K. Regional Dimension of Indian Agriculture. In *Lucas, R. E. B. and Papanek, G. F.*, eds., 1988, pp. 29–52.

Alaluf, Mateo and Vanheerswynghels, Adinda. Local Employment, Training Structures and New Technologies in Traditional Industrial Regions: European Comparisons. In *Aydalot, P. and Keeble, D.*, eds., 1988, pp. 184–96.

Alam, M. Shahid. Domestic Monopoly, Quotas, Two-Way Trade and Tariff Equivalence. *Southern Econ. J.*, July 1988, *55*(1), pp. 202–05.

Alamgir, Mohiuddin. Some Lessons from IFAD's Approach to Rural Poverty Alleviation. In *Lewis, J. P., et al.*, 1988, pp. 93–109.

_____ and Ahmed, Sadiq. Poverty and Income Distribution in Bangladesh. In *Srinivasan, T. N. and Bardhan, P. K.*, eds., 1988, pp. 11–38.

Alänge, Sverker and Scheinberg, Sari. Swedish Entrepreneurship in a Cross-Cultural Perspective. In *Kirchhoff, B. A., et al.*, eds., 1988, pp. 1–15.

Alaouze, Chris M. The Probability Distribution of the Average Marginal Products of Cobb–Douglas Factors with Applications. *Australian J. Agr. Econ.*, Aug.–Dec. 1988, *32*(2–3), pp. 153–61.

Alatanand Xingwu, Liu. China's Policy Towards Her Minority Nationalities. In *Mitra, A.*, ed., 1988, pp. 136–59.

Alatas, Secha; Tjiptoherijanto, Prijono and Ananta, Aris. Labour Market Developments and Structural Change in Indonesia. In *Pang, E. F.*, ed., 1988, pp. 66–99.

Alauddin, Mohammad and Tisdell, Clem A. Has

the Green Revolution Destabilized Food Production?: Some Evidence from Bangladesh. *Devel. Econ.*, June 1988, *26*(2), pp. 141–60.

_____ and Tisdell, Clem A. Impact of New Agricultural Technology on the Instability of Foodgrain Production and Yield: Data Analysis for Bangladesh and Its Districts. *J. Devel. Econ.*, September 1988, *29*(2), pp. 199–227.

_____ and Tisdell, Clem A. New Agricultural Technology and Sustainable Food Production: Bangladesh's Achievements, Predicament and Prospects. In *Tisdell, C. and Maitra, P.*, eds., 1988, pp. 35–62.

_____ and Tisdell, Clem A. Patterns and Determinants of Adoption of High Yielding Varieties: Farm-Level Evidence from Bangladesh. *Pakistan Devel. Rev.*, Summer 1988, *27*(2), pp. 183–210.

_____ and Tisdell, Clem A. The Use of Input–Output Analysis to Determine the Appropriateness of Technology and Industries: Evidence from Bangladesh. *Econ. Develop. Cult. Change*, January 1988, *36*(2), pp. 369–91.

de Alba, Enrique. Disaggregation and Forecasting: A Bayesian Analysis. *J. Bus. Econ. Statist.*, April 1988, *6*(2), pp. 197–206.

Alba, Joseph W. and Chattopadhyay, Amitava. The Situational Importance of Recall and Inference in Consumer Decision Making. *J. Cons. Res.*, June 1988, *15*(1), pp. 1–12.

Albach, Horst. Kosten, Transaktionen und externe Effekte im betrieblichen Rechnungswesen. (With English summary.) *Z. Betriebswirtshaft*, November 1988, *58*(11), pp. 1143–70.

_____. Management of Change in the Firm—Theoretical Analysis and Empirical Evidence. In *Urabe, K.; Child, J. and Kagono, T.*, eds., 1988, pp. 197–224.

_____. Praxisorientierte Unternehmenstheorie und theoriegeleitete Unternehmenspraxis. Zum Gedenken an Wolfgang Kilger. (With English summary.) *Z. Betriebswirtshaft*, May–June 1988, *58*(5–6), pp. 630–47.

Albalkin, Leonid. A New Conception of Centralism. *Prob. Econ.*, May 1988, *31*(1), pp. 6–13.

Albanese, Paul J. The Changing Motivation for Having Children. In *Maital, S.*, ed., *Vol. 1*, 1988, pp. 255–68.

_____. The Formation and Change of Fertility Preferences: A Case Study of the Generational Change in the Size of the Italian Family in the United States. *J. Behav. Econ.*, Spring 1988, *17*(1), pp. 35–55.

_____. The Intimate Relations of the Consistent Consumer: Psychoanalytic Object Relations Theory Applied to Economics. In *Albanese, P. J.*, ed., 1988, pp. 59–79.

_____. Psychological Foundations of Economic Behavior: Introduction. In *Albanese, P. J.*, ed., 1988, pp. ix–xii.

Albegov, M. M.; Volkonskii, V. A. and Gofman, K. G. Optimization Realism or Economic Nihilism? *Matekon*, Summer 1988, *24*(4), pp. 61–71.

Albelda, Randy and Mann, Cindy. Jobs, Fathers

and the States: Welfare Policy and the New Federalism. *Rev. Radical Polit. Econ.*, Summer–Fall 1988, *20*(2–3), pp. 61–67.

Albers, Wulf. Revealed Aspirations and Reciprocal Loyalty in Apex Games. In *Tietz, R.; Albers, W. and Selten, R.*, eds., 1988, pp. 333–50.

_____ **and Brunwinkel, Andrea.** Equal Share Analysis for Location Games. In *Tietz, R.; Albers, W. and Selten, R.*, eds., 1988, pp. 303–16.

Albert, Bill. The Peruvian Sugar Industry 1918–1939: Response to the World Crisis. In *Albert, B. and Graves, A.*, eds., 1988, pp. 71–84.

_____ **and Graves, Adrian.** The World Sugar Economy in War and Depression: 1914–40: Introduction. In *Albert, B. and Graves, A.*, eds., 1988, pp. 1–25.

Albert, Hans. Hermeneutics and Economics: A Criticism of Hermeneutical Thinking in the Social Sciences. *Kyklos*, 1988, *41*(4), pp. 573–602.

Albert, James H. Computational Methods Using a Bayesian Hierarchical Generalized Linear Model. *J. Amer. Statist. Assoc.*, December 1988, *83*(404), pp. 1037–44.

Albin, Peter S. and Appelbaum, Eileen. The Computer Rationalization of Work: Implications for Women Workers. In *Jenson, J.; Hagen, E. and Reddy, C.*, eds., 1988, pp. 137–52.

Albin, Tom and Paulson, Steve. Environmental and Economic Interests in Canada and the United States. In *Schmandt, J.; Clarkson, J. and Roderick, H.*, eds., 1988, pp. 107–36.

_____; **Paulson, Steve and Britton, Barbara.** The U.S. Policy Response to Acid Rain. In *Schmandt, J.; Clarkson, J. and Roderick, H.*, eds., 1988, pp. 159–84.

Albinowski, Stanisław. Logic and Principles of the System: Discussion: The Second Stage of the Reform. *Eastern Europ. Econ.*, Spring 1988, *26*(3), pp. 61–71.

Albon, Robert. Liberalization of the Post Office. In *Johnson, C.*, ed., 1988, pp. 111–23.

_____. The Welfare Costs of the Australian Telecommunications Pricing Structure. *Econ. Rec.*, June 1988, *64*(185), pp. 102–12.

Albornoz, Mario G. Centenario de la Pontificia Universidad Católica de Chile y Breve Historia de la Escuela de Economía. (With English summary.) *Cuadernos Econ.*, December 1988, *25*(76), pp. 325–29.

Albrecht, Don E. and Murdock, Steve H. The Effects of the Farm Crisis on Rural Communities and Community Residents. In *Beaulieu, L. J.*, ed., 1988, pp. 198–210.

_____ **and Murdock, Steve H.** The Structural Characteristics of U.S. Agriculture: Historical Patterns and Precursors of Producers' Adaptations to the Crisis. In *Murdock, S. H. and Leistritz, F. L.*, eds., 1988, pp. 29–44.

d'Alcantara, G. A Comparative Analysis of Actual Dutch Macroeconomic Models. In *Driehuis, W.; Fase, M. M. G. and den Hartog, H.*, eds., 1988, pp. 151–205.

Alchian, Armen A. Information Costs, Pricing, and Resource Unemployment. In *Shaw, G. K.*, ed., *Vol. 1*, 1988, *1969*, pp. 263–82.

_____. Promotions, Elections and Other Contests: Comment. *J. Inst. Theoretical Econ.*, February 1988, *144*(1), pp. 91–93.

_____. Some Economics of Property Rights. In *Ricketts, M.*, ed., *Vol. 1*, 1988, *1965*, pp. 289–311.

_____ **and Demsetz, Harold.** Production, Information Costs, and Economic Organization. In *Demsetz, H.*, 1988, *1972*, pp. 119–43.

_____ **and Demsetz, Harold.** Production, Information Costs, and Economic Organization. In *Ricketts, M.*, ed., *Vol. 1*, 1988, *1972*, pp. 312–30.

_____ **and Woodward, Susan L.** The Firm is Dead; Long Live the Firm: A Review of Oliver E. Williamson's *The Economic Institutions of Capitalism. J. Econ. Lit.*, March 1988, *26*(1), pp. 65–79.

Alcorn, John; Gleicher, David and Swanson, Paul A. Toward a General Model of Price, Choice of Technique and Distribution in a Centrally-Planned, Socialist Economy. *Econ. Planning*, 1988, *22*(3), pp. 117–35.

Alden, J. D. and Abe, H. Regional Development Planning in Japan. *Reg. Stud.*, October 1988, *22*(5), pp. 429–38.

Alderman, Harold. Estimates of Consumer Price Response in Pakistan Using Market Prices as Data. *Pakistan Devel. Rev.*, Summer 1988, *27*(2), pp. 89–107.

_____. Food Subsidies in Egypt: Benefit Distribution and Nutritional Effects. In *Pinstrup-Andersen, P.*, ed., 1988, pp. 171–82.

_____ **and Kumar, Shubh K.** Food Consumption and Nutritional Effects of Consumer-Oriented Food Subsidies. In *Pinstrup-Andersen, P.*, ed., 1988, pp. 36–48.

_____ **and Pinstrup-Andersen, Per.** The Effectiveness of Consumer-Oriented Food Subsidies in Reaching Rationing and Income Transfer Goals. In *Pinstrup-Andersen, P.*, ed., 1988, pp. 21–35.

_____ **and Sahn, David E.** The Effects of Human Capital on Wages, and the Determinants of Labor Supply in a Developing Country. *J. Devel. Econ.*, September 1988, *29*(2), pp. 157–83.

Alderson, Michael J. and Lee, Cheng F. Corporate Pension Policy and Capital Structure Decisions. *J. Econ. Bus.*, August 1988, *40*(3), pp. 209–28.

Aldrich, Howard and Staber, Udo. An Evolutionary View on Changes in Employment Relationships: The Evolution of Organizational Control in the United States. In *Dlugos, G.; Dorow, W. and Weiermair, K.*, eds., 1988, pp. 63–78.

Aldrich, Mark. OSHA Fines and the Value of Saving a Life. *J. Policy Anal. Manage.*, Winter 1988, *7*(2), pp. 356–62.

Aleinikoff, T. Alexander. Updating Statutory Interpretation. *Mich. Law Rev.*, October 1988, *87*(1), pp. 20–66.

Alesina, Alberto. Alternative Monetary Regimes: A Review Essay. *J. Monet. Econ.*, January 1988, *21*(1), pp. 175–83.

———. Can Speculative Attacks on EMS Currencies Be Avoided? *Giorn. Econ.*, Nov.–Dec. 1988, 47(11–12), pp. 537–43.

———. Credibility and Policy Convergence in a Two-Party System with Rational Voters. *Amer. Econ. Rev.*, September 1988, 78(4), pp. 496–805.

———. The End of Large Public Debts. In *Giavazzi, F. and Spaventa, L., eds.*, 1988, pp. 34–79.

——— and Sachs, Jeffrey D. Political Parties and the Business Cycle in the United States, 1948–1984. *J. Money, Credit, Banking*, February 1988, 20(1), pp. 63–82.

——— and Spear, Stephen E. An Overlapping Generations Model of Electoral Competition. *J. Public Econ.*, December 1988, 37(3), pp. 359–79.

——— and Tabellini, Guido. Credibility and Politics. *Europ. Econ. Rev.*, March 1988, 32(2–3), pp. 542–50.

Alessie, Rob J. M. and Kapteyn, Arie. Preference Formation, Incomes, and the Distribution of Welfare. *J. Behav. Econ.*, Spring 1988, 17(1), pp. 77–96.

———; Melenberg, Bertrand and Weber, Guglielmo. Consumption, Leisure and Earnings-Related Liquidity Constraints: A Note. *Econ. Letters*, 1988, 27(1), pp. 101–04.

Alexander, Donald L. An Empirical Test of Monopoly Behaviour: An Application to the Hardwood Case. *Appl. Econ.*, August 1988, 20(8), pp. 1115–27.

———. The Oligopoly Solution Tested. *Econ. Letters*, 1988, 28(4), pp. 361–64.

Alexander, Gordon J.; Eun, Cheol S. and Janakiramanan, S. International Listings and Stock Returns: Some Empirical Evidence. *J. Finan. Quant. Anal.*, June 1988, 23(2), pp. 135–51.

Alexander, J. N. and Trivedi, Pravin K. Incorporating International Competitiveness into the Demand for Labour Function: Some Issues of Specification and Interpretation. *Econ. Rec.*, September 1988, 64(186), pp. 196–208.

Alexander, Jeffrey A. and Morrisey, Michael A. Hospital–Physician Integration and Hospital Costs. *Inquiry*, Fall 1988, 25(3), pp. 388–401.

Alexander, William P. and Shumway, C. Richard. Agricultural Product Supplies and Input Demands: Regional Comparisons. *Amer. J. Agr. Econ.*, February 1988, 70(1), pp. 153–61.

Alexeev, Michael. Are Soviet Consumers Forced to Save? *Comp. Econ. Stud.*, Winter 1988, 30(4), pp. 17–23.

———. The Effect of Housing Allocation on Social Inequality: A Soviet Perspective. *J. Compar. Econ.*, June 1988, 12(2), pp. 228–34.

———. Market vs. Rationing: The Case of Soviet Housing. *Rev. Econ. Statist.*, August 1988, 70(3), pp. 414–20.

———. Microeconomic Modeling of Parallel Markets: Reply. *J. Compar. Econ.*, December 1988, 12(4), pp. 610–13.

———. The Underground Market for Gasoline in the USSR. *Comp. Econ. Stud.*, Summer 1988, 30(2), pp. 47–68.

Alfriend, Malcolm C. International Risk-Based Capital Standard: History and Explanation. *Fed. Res. Bank Richmond Econ. Rev.*, Nov.–Dec. 1988, 74(6), pp. 28–34.

Ali, Abbas. A Cross-National Perspective of Managerial Work Value Systems. In *Farmer, R. N. and McGoun, E. G., eds.*, 1988, pp. 151–69.

Ali, Anuwar. The Quest for Technology Transfer. In *Sopiee, N.; Hamzah, B. A. and Leong, C. H., eds.*, 1988, 1986, pp. 309–26.

Ali, Rasheed A. Domestic and International Constraints on Market Development. In *Kozmetsky, G.; Matsumoto, H. and Smilor, R. W., eds.*, 1988, pp. 59–65.

Ali, Syed Mubashir and Nasir, Zafar Mueen. Gains in Life Expectancy by Elimination of Specified Causes of Death in Pakistan. *Pakistan Devel. Rev.*, Part 2, Winter 1988, 27(4), pp. 645–51.

Ali, Syed Zahid and Khan, Shahrukh Rafi. Some Findings on Higher Educated Unemployment in Pakistan. *Can. J. Devel. Stud.*, 1988, 9(2), pp. 261–78.

Alidi, Abdulaziz S. An Optimization Model for the Utilization of Wood Residues as an Energy Source. *Resources & Energy*, March 1988, 10(1), pp. 79–94.

Aliprantis, C. D. and Burkinshaw, O. The Fundamental Theorems of Welfare Economics without Proper Preferences. *J. Math. Econ.*, 1988, 17(1), pp. 41–54.

Alkan, Ahmet. Nonexistence of Stable Threesome Matchings: Note. *Math. Soc. Sci.*, October 1988, 16(2), pp. 207–09.

Allain, Jean-Pierre. Consumer Organization and Representation in Developing Countries. In *Maynes, E. S. and ACCI Research Committee, eds.*, 1988, pp. 506–09.

———. International Trade: Boon or Bane for Third World Consumers? In *Maynes, E. S. and ACCI Research Committee, eds.*, 1988, pp. 397–404.

Allais, Maurice. The General Theory of Random Choices in Relation to the Invariant Cardinal Utility Function and the Specific Probability Function: The (U, θ) Model: A General Overview. In *Munier, B. R., ed.*, 1988, pp. 231–89.

———. La théorie des choix dans l'œuvre de René Roy une analyse critique. (With English summary.) *Revue Écon. Polit.*, May–June 1988, 98(3), pp. 315–57.

———. A New Neo-Bernoullian Theory: The Machina Theory: A Critical Analysis. In *Munier, B. R., ed.*, 1988, pp. 345–403.

———. Some Remarkable Properties of the Determination of a Bounded Continuous Distribution by Its Moments. In *Munier, B. R., ed.*, 1988, pp. 557–61.

Allan, Andrew and Cross, Rod. On the History of Hysteresis. In *Cross, R., ed.*, 1988, pp. 26–38.

Allard, Richard J. Rent-Seeking with Non-identical Players. *Public Choice*, April 1988, 57(1), pp. 3–14.

Allen, Beth. Using Trembling-Hand Perfection to

Alleviate the Interlinked Principal–Agent Problem. *Scand. J. Econ.*, 1988, *90*(3), pp. 373–82.

_____ **and Azariadis, Costas.** Informational Theories of Employment. *Amer. Econ. Rev.*, May 1988, *78*(2), pp. 104–09.

Allen, Franklin. A Theory of Price Rigidities when Quality is Unobservable. *Rev. Econ. Stud.*, January 1988, *55*(1), pp. 139–51.

_____ **and Faulhaber, Gerald R.** Optimism Invites Deception. *Quart. J. Econ.*, May 1988, *103*(2), pp. 397–407.

Allen, Jacqueline F. and Berger, Mark C. Black–White Earnings Ratios: The Role of Cohort Size Effects. *Econ. Letters*, 1988, *26*(3), pp. 285–90.

Allen, John. Fragmented Firms, Disorganized Labour? In *Allen, J. and Massey, D., eds.*, 1988, pp. 184–228.

_____. Towards a Post-industrial Economy? In *Allen, J. and Massey, D., eds.*, 1988, pp. 91–135.

_____ **and Massey, Doreen.** Restructuring Britain: The Economy in Question: Introduction. In *Allen, J. and Massey, D., eds.*, 1988, pp. 1–6.

Allen, Joseph P. Industrial Space Facility. In *Egan, J. J., et al.*, 1988, pp. 181–200.

Allen, Kristen and Smith, Murray G. An Overview of Agricultural Issues in the U.S.–Canadian Free Trade Agreement. In *Allen, K. and Macmillan, K., eds.*, 1988, pp. 1–8.

Allen, Linda. The Determinants of Bank Interest Margins: A Note. *J. Finan. Quant. Anal.*, June 1988, *23*(2), pp. 231–35.

_____ **and Thurston, Thom.** Cash-Futures Arbitrage and Forward-Futures Spreads in the Treasury Bill Market. *J. Futures Markets*, October 1988, *8*(5), pp. 563–73.

Allen, Paul R. and Wilhelm, William J. The Impact of the 1980 Depository Institutions Deregulation and Monetary Control Act on Market Value and Risk: Evidence from the Capital Markets. *J. Money, Credit, Banking*, Part 1, August 1988, *20*(3), pp. 364–80.

Allen, Peter M. Evolution, Innovation and Economics. In *Dosi, G., et al., eds.*, 1988, pp. 95–119.

Allen, R. G. D. Professor Slutsky's Theory of Consumers' Choice. In *Ricketts, M., ed., Vol. 1*, 1988, *1936*, pp. 9–18.

Allen, Ralph C. and Stone, Jack H. Managerial Productivity and Firm Size: A Comment on Oi's Managerial Time Allocation Model. *Econ. Inquiry*, January 1988, *26*(1), pp. 171–73.

Allen, Richard V. Foreign Policy and National Security: The Pacific Basin. In *Anderson, A. and Bark, D. L., eds.*, 1988, pp. 127–38.

Allen, Robert C. The Growth of Labor Productivity in Early Modern English Agriculture. *Exploration Econ. Hist.*, April 1988, *25*(2), pp. 117–46.

_____. Inferring Yields from Probate Inventories. *J. Econ. Hist.*, March 1988, *48*(1), pp. 117–25.

_____ **and ÓGráda, Cormac.** On the Road Again

with Arthur Young: English, Irish, and French Agriculture during the Industrial Revolution. *J. Econ. Hist.*, March 1988, *48*(1), pp. 93–116.

Allen, Steven G. Declining Unionization in Construction: The Facts and the Reasons. *Ind. Lab. Relat. Rev.*, April 1988, *41*(3), pp. 343–59.

_____. Further Evidence on Union Efficiency in Construction. *Ind. Relat.*, Spring 1988, *27*(2), pp. 232–40.

_____. Productivity Levels and Productivity Change under Unionism. *Ind. Relat.*, Winter 1988, *27*(1), pp. 94–113.

_____. The Retirement Decision in Cross-National Perspective: Discussion. In *Ricardo-Campbell, R. and Lazear, E. P., eds.*, 1988, pp. 297–311.

_____. Unions and Job Security in the Public Sector. In *Freeman, R. B. and Ichniowski, C., eds.*, 1988, pp. 271–96.

Allen, Stuart D. and McCrickard, Donald L. Deficits and Monetary Growth in the United States: A Comment. *J. Monet. Econ.*, January 1988, *21*(1), pp. 143–53.

_____, **et al.** The Use of Inputs by the Federal Reserve System: An Extended Model. *Public Choice*, December 1988, *59*(3), pp. 205–14.

Allgeier, Peter F. Korean Trade Policy in the Next Decade: Dealing with Reciprocity. *World Devel.*, January 1988, *16*(1), pp. 85–97.

Allingham, Michael G. and Sandmo, Agnar. Income Tax Evasion: A Theoretical Analysis. In *Ricketts, M., ed., Vol. 1*, 1988, *1972*, pp. 359–74.

Allison, Scott T.; Samuelson, Charles D. and Messick, David M. Framing and Communication Effects on Group Members' Responses to Environmental and Social Uncertainty. In *Maital, S., ed., Vol. 2*, 1988, pp. 677–700.

Allsbrook, O. O., Jr. and Gilliam, K. P. A Cyclical Interpretation of Money. *Kredit Kapital*, 1988, *21*(2), pp. 243–52.

Alm, James. Compliance Costs and the Tax Avoidance–Tax Evasion Decision. *Public Finance Quart.*, January 1988, *16*(1), pp. 31–66.

_____. Noncompliance and Payroll Taxation in Jamaica. *J. Devel. Areas*, July 1988, *22*(4), pp. 477–95.

_____. Uncertain Tax Policies, Individual Behavior, and Welfare. *Amer. Econ. Rev.*, March 1988, *78*(1), pp. 237–45.

Almy, Susan W. Vertical Societies and Co-operative Structures: Problems of Fit in North-eastern Brazil. In *Attwood, D. W. and Baviskar, B. S., eds.*, 1988, pp. 46–68.

Alogoskoufis, George and Manning, Alan. Wage Setting and Unemployment Persistence in Europe, Japan and the USA. *Europ. Econ. Rev.*, March 1988, *32*(2–3), pp. 698–706.

de Alonso, Irma Tirado and Salazar-Carrillo, Jorge. Real Product and Price Comparisons between Latin America and the Rest of the World. *Rev. Income Wealth*, March 1988, *34*(1), pp. 27–43.

Alonso, William. Population and Regional Development. In *[Perroux, F.]*, 1988, pp. 131–41.

Alpern, Steve and Snower, Dennis J. "High–Low

Search" in Product and Labor Markets. *Amer. Econ. Rev.*, May 1988, 78(2), pp. 356–62.

Alperovich, Gershon. A New Testing Procedure of the Rank Size Distribution. *J. Urban Econ.*, March 1988, 23(2), pp. 251–59.

_____ **and Katz, Eliakim.** The Location Decision and Employment Suburbanization. *Urban Stud.*, June 1988, 25(3), pp. 243–47.

Alpert, William T. and Guerard, John B., Jr. Employment, Unemployment and the Minimum Wage: A Causality Model. *Appl. Econ.*, November 1988, 20(11), pp. 1453–64.

Als, Georges. The Nightmare of Economic Accounts in a Small Country with a Large International Banking Sector. *Rev. Income Wealth*, March 1988, 34(1), pp. 101–10.

Alschuler, Lawrence R. Multinationals and Maldevelopment Alternative Development Strategies in Argentina, the Ivory Coast, and Korea. In *Vivekananda, F., ed.*, 1988, pp. 144–63.

Alsters, Theo; Nijkamp, Peter and van der Mark, Ronald. Evaluation of Regional Incubator Profiles for Small and Medium Sized Enterprises. *Reg. Stud.*, April 1988, 22(2), pp. 95–105.

Alston, Julian M. Economic Theology and the Consumer Interest. *Rev. Marketing Agr. Econ.*, April 1988, 56(1), pp. 7–8.

_____ **and Chalfant, James A.** Accounting for Changes in Tastes. *J. Polit. Econ.*, April 1988, 96(2), pp. 391–410.

_____ **; Edwards, Geoff W. and Freebairn, John W.** Market Distortions and Benefits from Research. *Amer. J. Agr. Econ.*, May 1988, 70(2), pp. 281–88.

_____ **and Freebairn, John W.** Producer Price Equalization. *Rev. Marketing Agr. Econ.*, December 1988, 56(3), pp. 306–40.

_____ **and Johnson, Paul R.** Factor Price Equalisation among International Farmland Markets. *Australian J. Agr. Econ.*, Aug.–Dec. 1988, 32(2–3), pp. 142–52.

Alt, Raimund; Krämer, Walter and Ploberger, Werner. Testing for Structural Change in Dynamic Models. *Econometrica*, November 1988, 56(6), pp. 1355–69.

Altaev, V. I., et al. On the Analytical Approach to the Study of Simulation Models of Economic Systems. *Matekon*, Spring 1988, 24(3), pp. 32–51.

Altăr, M. Considerations on Economic Cybernetics. *Econ. Computat. Cybern. Stud. Res.*, 1988, 23(1), pp. 83–87.

Alter, George C. and Becker, William E. Estimating Lost Future Earnings Using the New Worklife Tables: Authors' Reply. *J. Risk Ins.*, September 1988, 55(3), pp. 545–47.

Alter, Theodore R. Institutions and Agricultural Economics in the Twenty-first Century: A Discussion. In *Hildreth, R. J., et al., eds.*, 1988, pp. 335–39.

_____. New Directions and Challenges for Modeling of Community Infrastructure Analysis. In *Johnson, T. G.; Deaton, B. J. and Segarra, E., eds.*, 1988, pp. 117–20.

Alterman, William. BLS to Produce Monthly In-

dexes of Export and Import Prices. *Mon. Lab. Rev.*, December 1988, 111(12), pp. 36–40.

Althöfer, Ingo. Nim Games with Arbitrary Periodic Moving Orders. *Int. J. Game Theory*, 1988, 17(3), pp. 165–75.

Altig, David. Econometric Analysis of Consumption Behavior and Fiscal Policy: A Review Essay. *J. Monet. Econ.*, July 1988, 22(1), pp. 155–64.

Altinkemer, Melike and Rusek, Antonin. Determination of the Spot Exchange Rate: Japanese Yen per U.S. Dollar. In *Pennsylvania Economic Association*, 1988, pp. 377–86.

Altman, Morris. Economic Development with High Wages: An Historical Perspective. *Exploration Econ. Hist.*, April 1988, 25(2), pp. 198–224.

Altman, Stuart H.; Beatrice, Dennis F. and Bachman, Sara S. What Influences a State's Approach to Medicaid Reform? *Inquiry*, Summer 1988, 25(2), pp. 243–50.

_____ **and Rodwin, Marc A.** Halfway Competitive Markets and Ineffective Regulation: The American Health Care System. In *Greenberg, W., ed.*, 1988, pp. 101–17.

Altonji, Joseph G. Unions and Job Security in the Public Sector: Comment. In *Freeman, R. B. and Ichniowski, C., eds.*, 1988, pp. 296–303.

_____ **and Paxson, Christina H.** Labor Supply Preferences, Hours Constraints, and Hours–Wage Trade-Offs. *J. Lab. Econ.*, April 1988, 6(2), pp. 254–76.

Altshuler, Alan A. Management by Groping Along: A Comment. *J. Policy Anal. Manage.*, Fall 1988, 7(4), pp. 664–67.

Altshuler, Rosanne. A Dynamic Analysis of the Research and Experimentation Credit. *Nat. Tax J.*, December 1988, 41(4), pp. 453–66.

Alvarez de Stella, Ana Maria. Economic Crisis and Foreign Debt Management in Venezuela. In *Griffith-Jones, S., ed.*, 1988, pp. 211–44.

Alvarez, Yvette. External Debt and Adjustment: The Case of Belize 1980–1986. *Soc. Econ. Stud.*, December 1988, 37(4), pp. 39–56.

Alvey, J. Stanley Jevons: A Centennial Assessment. In *Wood, J. C., ed., Vol. 1*, 1988, 1982, pp. 351–68.

Alvi, Eskander. Information Revelation and Principal–Agent Contracts. *J. Lab. Econ.*, January 1988, 6(1), pp. 132–46.

Alvoni, Elisabetta. An Algorithm for Time Series Decomposition Using State-Space Models with Singular Transition Matrix. In *Edwards, D. and Raun, N. E., eds.*, 1988, pp. 369–74.

Alwan, Layth C. and Roberts, Harry V. Time-Series Modeling for Statistical Process Control. *J. Bus. Econ. Statist.*, January 1988, 6(1), pp. 87–95.

Aly, Hassan Y. and Grabowski, Richard. Technical Change, Technical Efficiency, and Input Usage in Taiwanese Agricultural Growth. *Appl. Econ.*, July 1988, 20(7), pp. 889–99.

Amabile, Teresa M. From Individual Creativity to Organizational Innovation. In *Grønhaug, K. and Kaufmann, G., eds.*, 1988, pp. 139–66.

_____. A Model of Creativity and Innovation in Organizations. In *Staw, B. M. and Cummings, L. L., eds.*, 1988, pp. 123–67.

Amacher, Ryan C. The Principles of Economics from Now until Then: A Comment. *J. Econ. Educ.*, Spring 1988, *19*(2), pp. 152–55.

Amano, Akihiro. Japan's External Imbalance and Exchange Rates. In *Uno, K. and Shishido, S., eds.*, 1988, pp. 31–51.

Amanuma, Takahiko. A Comparison from a Japanese Point of View. In *Holl, U. and Trevor, M., eds.*, 1988, pp. 93–94.

Amariglio, Jack L. The Body, Economic Discourse, and Power: An Economist's Introduction to Foucault. *Hist. Polit. Econ.*, Winter 1988, *20*(4), pp. 583–613.

Amato, Louis and Wilder, Ronald P. Market Concentration, Efficiency, and Antitrust Policy: Demsetz Revisited. *Quart. J. Bus. Econ.*, Autumn 1988, *27*(4), pp. 3–19.

Amaziane, Brahim and Bourgeat, Alain. Effective Behavior of Two-Phase Flow in Heterogeneous Reservoir. In *Wheeler, M. F., ed.*, 1988, pp. 1–22.

Ambler, Steve. Fiscal and Monetary Policy in an Open Economy with Staggered Wages. *Weltwirtsch. Arch.*, 1988, *124*(1), pp. 58–73.

_____ **and Phaneuf, Louis.** Interest Rate Innovations and the Business Cycle. *Econ. Letters*, 1988, *26*(4), pp. 305–09.

Ambrose, Jan Mills and Seward, J. Allen. Best's Ratings, Financial Ratios and Prior Probabilities in Insolvency Prediction. *J. Risk Ins.*, June 1988, *55*(2), pp. 229–44.

Ambrosi, Gerhard Michael. Adam Smith's Labour Command Values: A Post Keynesian Interpretation. *Écon. Soc.*, March 1988, *22*(3), pp. 17–33.

Amel, Dean F. and Rhoades, Stephen A. Strategic Groups in Banking. *Rev. Econ. Statist.*, November 1988, *70*(4), pp. 685–89.

American Assembly. Final Report of the Seventy-fourth American Assembly. In *Starr, M. K., ed.*, 1988, pp. 299–315.

Amerkhail, Valerie L.; Spooner, Gillian M. and Sunley, Emil M. The Fall and Rise of the U.S. Corporate Tax Burden. *Nat. Tax J.*, September 1988, *41*(3), pp. 273–84.

Ames, Glenn C. W.; Hammett, A. Lawton and Chen, Nen-Jing. Implications of a Tariff on Imported Canadian Softwood Lumber. *Can. J. Agr. Econ.*, March 1988, *36*(1), pp. 69–81.

_____ **and Haniotis, Tassos.** The 'Oilseed Tax' and U.S. Soyabean Exports to the Enlarged European Community. *Europ. Rev. Agr. Econ.*, 1988, *15*(1), pp. 39–54.

_____**; Haniotis, Tassos and Baffes, John.** The Demand and Supply of U.S. Agricultural Exports: The Case of Wheat, Corn, and Soybeans. *Southern J. Agr. Econ.*, December 1988, *20*(2), pp. 45–55.

Amha, Wolday. Personal Earnings in Ethiopian State-Owned Manufacturing: The Case of Edi-get Cotton Factory. *Eastern Afr. Econ. Rev.*, December 1988, *4*(2), pp. 59–64.

Amigues, Jean-Pierre; Moreaux, Michel and

Gaudet, Gérard. Bertrand and Cournot Equilibrium Price Paths in a Nonrenewable Resource Differentiated Product Duopoly. In *Eiselt, H. A. and Pederzoli, G., eds.*, 1988, pp. 343–57.

Amin, Aloysius Ajab. Supply Response Estimation for Perennials under 'Distorted' Price Regime. In *Pennsylvania Economic Association*, 1988, pp. 642–49.

Amin, Shahid. Sugar Mills and Peasants in Northern India, 1914–40. In *Albert, B. and Graves, A., eds.*, 1988, pp. 182–93.

Amirkhalkhali, Saleh and Jamieson, Barbara. Provincial Public Finance in the Atlantic Region, 1965–1984. *Can. Public Policy*, June 1988, *14*(2), pp. 197–203.

Ammons, David N. and Molta, David J. Productivity Emphasis in Local Government: An Assessment of the Impact of Selected Policy Environment Factors. In *Kelly, R. M., ed.*, 1988, pp. 69–83.

Amoako-Tuffour, Joe and McMillan, Melville L. An Examination of Preferences for Local Public Sector Outputs. *Rev. Econ. Statist.*, February 1988, *70*(1), pp. 45–54.

Amos, Orley M., Jr. Unbalanced Regional Growth and Regional Income Inequality in the Latter Stages of Development. *Reg. Sci. Urban Econ.*, November 1988, *18*(4), pp. 549–66.

Amranand, Piyasvasti and Chongpeerapien, Tienchai. Petroleum Product Pricing in Thailand. *Energy J.*, Special Issue, 1988, *9*, pp. 15–43.

Amrhein, Carl G. and Harrington, James W., Jr. Location, Technical Change and Labour Migration in a Heterogeneous Industry. *Reg. Stud.*, December 1988, *22*(6), pp. 515–29.

Amsden, Alice H. Taiwan's Economic History: A Case of *Etatisme* and a Challenge to Dependency Theory. In *Bates, R. H., ed.*, 1988, *1979*, pp. 142–75.

Amundsen, Rolf and Kristensen, Kai. En vurdering af den danske punktafgiftsstruktur. (Is the Danish Commodity Tax Structure Optimal? With English summary.) *Nationaløkon. Tidsskr.*, 1988, *126*(3), pp. 323–34.

Amuzegar, Jahangir. The U.S. External Debt in Perspective. *Finance Develop.*, June 1988, *25*(2), pp. 18–19.

Anam, Mahmudul. On the Policy Intervention in the Harris–Todaro Model with Intersectoral Capital Mobility. *Economica*, August 1988, *55*(219), pp. 403–07.

_____. Quota-Induced Rent Seeking, Terms of Trade and National Welfare: A Paradox. *J. Devel. Econ.*, May 1988, *28*(3), pp. 389–95.

_____. The Welfare Effects of Capital Inflow in the Presence of a Tariff (Quota) with Revenue (Premium) Seeking. *Econ. Letters*, 1988, *26*(1), pp. 69–72.

_____ **and Katz, Eliakim.** Rent-Seeking and Second Best Economics. *Public Choice*, December 1988, *59*(3), pp. 215–24.

Anan'ich, Boris V. The Russian Private Banking Houses, 1870–1914. *J. Econ. Hist.*, June 1988, *48*(2), pp. 401–07.

Anand, Punam; Holbrook, Morris B. and Stephens, Debra. The Formation of Affective Judgments: The Cognitive–Affective Model versus the Independence Hypothesis. *J. Cons. Res.*, December 1988, *15*(3), pp. 386–91.

Anandakrishnan, Munirathna, et al. Microcomputers in Schools in Developing Countries. In *Bhalla, A. S. and James, D.*, eds., 1988, pp. 112–26.

Anania, Giovanni and Bohman, Mary. Domestic Farm Policy and the Gains from Trade: Comment. *Amer. J. Agr. Econ.*, August 1988, *70*(3), pp. 735–39.

Ananta, Aris; Alatas, Secha and Tjiptoherijanto, Prijono. Labour Market Developments and Structural Change in Indonesia. In *Pang, E. F.*, ed., 1988, pp. 66–99.

Ananthan, C. S. Pacific Cooperation & Development: Introduction. In *Kozmetsky, G.; Matsumoto, H. and Smilor, R. W.*, eds., 1988, pp. 1–10.

Anas, Alex. Agglomeration and Taste Heterogeneity. *Reg. Sci. Urban Econ.*, February 1988, *18*(1), pp. 7–35.

_____. Optimal Preservation and Pricing of Natural Public Lands in General Equilibrium. *J. Environ. Econ. Manage.*, June 1988, *15*(2), pp. 158–72.

_____. Statistical Properties of Mathematical Programming Models of Stochastic Network Equilibrium. *J. Reg. Sci.*, November 1988, *28*(4), pp. 511–30.

_____ and Cho, Joong Rae. A Dynamic, Policy Oriented Model of the Regulated Housing Market. *Reg. Sci. Urban Econ.*, May 1988, *18*(2), pp. 201–31.

_____ and Feng, Cheng Min. Invariance of Expected Utilities in Logit Models. *Econ. Letters*, 1988, *27*(1), pp. 41–45.

Anchordoguy, Marie. Mastering the Market: Japanese Government Targeting of the Computer Industry. *Int. Organ.*, Summer 1988, *42*(3), pp. 509–43.

Andernacht, Dieter. The Goldstein Project: Two Ways to Affordable Housing in the 1920s. In *Friedrichs, J.*, ed., 1988, pp. 115–25.

Andersen, Esben Sloth and Lundvall, Bengt-Åke. Small National Systems of Innovation Facing Technological Revolutions: An Analytical Framework. In *Freeman, C. and Lundvall, B.-A.*, eds., 1988, pp. 9–36.

Andersen, Jay C. and Snyder, Donald L. Competition for Water: The Issue of Native American Water Rights. *Ann. Reg. Sci.*, February 1988, *22*, pp. 54–64.

Andersen, Ronald M.; Mullner, Ross M. and Young, Gaylen W. Health Care Coalitions: Continuity and Change. In *Scheffler, R. M. and Rossiter, L. F.*, eds., 1988, pp. 165–85.

Andersen, Torben M. Coordination and Business Cycles. *Europ. Econ. Rev.*, March 1988, *32*(2–3), pp. 398–407.

_____. Det danske opsparingsproblem og pensionsreformdebatten. (The Savings Deficit of the Danish Economy and the Debate on Pension Schemes. With English summary.) *Nationaløkon. Tidsskr.*, 1988, *126*(2), pp. 144–58.

_____. Rules or Discretion in Public Sector Decision-Making. *Scand. J. Econ.*, 1988, *90*(3), pp. 291–303.

_____ and Risager, Ole. Indkomstpolitikken under firkløverregeringen. (Danish Incomes Policy 1982–87. With English summary.) *Nationaløkon. Tidsskr.*, 1988, *126*(3), pp. 286–302.

_____ and Risager, Ole. Stabilization Policies, Credibility, and Interest Rate Determination in a Small Open Economy. *Europ. Econ. Rev.*, March 1988, *32*(2–3), pp. 669–79.

_____ and Sørensen, Jan Rose. Exchange Rate Variability and Wage Formation in Open Economies. *Econ. Letters*, 1988, *28*(3), pp. 263–68.

Anderson, Annelise. Domestic Policy and National Purpose: Immigration Policy. In *Anderson, A. and Bark, D. L.*, eds., 1988, pp. 391–400.

_____ and Bark, Dennis L. Thinking about America: The United States in the 1990s: An Introductory Overview. In *Anderson, A. and Bark, D. L.*, eds., 1988, pp. xxiii–xlvii.

Anderson, Barbara A. and Haines, Michael R. Essays in Exploration: New Demographic History of the Late 19th-Century United States. *Exploration Econ. Hist.*, October 1988, *25*(4), pp. 341–65.

_____ and Silver, Brian D. The Effects of the Registration System on the Seasonality of Births: The Case of the Soviet Union. *Population Stud.*, July 1988, *42*(2), pp. 303–20.

Anderson, Curt L., et al. The Economic Value of Derby Fishing: An Application of Travel-Cost Methodology in Lake Superior. *Reg. Sci. Persp.*, 1988, *18*(1), pp. 3–18.

Anderson, Eric E. Relative Efficiency of Charges and Quantity Controls in Fisheries with Continuous Stock Growth and Periodically Fixed Instrument Levels. *Marine Resource Econ.*, 1988, *5*(3), pp. 215–30.

Anderson, Erin. Transaction Costs as Determinants of Opportunism in Integrated and Independent Sales Forces. *J. Econ. Behav. Organ.*, April 1988, *9*(3), pp. 247–64.

_____ and Gatignon, Hubert. The Multinational Corporation's Degree of Control over Foreign Subsidiaries: An Empirical Test of a Transaction Cost Explanation. *J. Law, Econ., Organ.*, Fall 1988, *4*(2), pp. 305–36.

Anderson, F. J. and Cairns, Robert D. The Softwood Lumber Agreement and Resource Politics. *Can. Public Policy*, June 1988, *14*(2), pp. 186–96.

Anderson, Gary Michael. Mr. Smith and the Preachers: The Economics of Religion in the *Wealth of Nations*. *J. Polit. Econ.*, October 1988, *96*(5), pp. 1066–88.

_____. Public Finance in Autocratic Process: An Empirical Note. *Public Choice*, April 1988, *57*(1), pp. 25–37.

_____; Rowley, Charles K. and Tollison, Robert D. Rent Seeking and the Restriction of Human Exchange. *J. Legal Stud.*, January 1988, *17*(1), pp. 83–100.

———; **Shughart, William F., II and Tollison, Robert D.** A Public Choice Theory of the Great Contraction. *Public Choice,* October 1988, *59*(1), pp. 3–23.

——— **and Tollison, Robert D.** Democracy, Interest Groups, and the Price of Votes. *Cato J.,* Spring–Summer 1988, *8*(1), pp. 53–70.

——— **and Tollison, Robert D.** Legislative Monopoly and the Size of Government. *Southern Econ. J.,* January 1988, *54*(3), pp. 529–45.

Anderson, Gerard and Hay, Joel W. The Hospital Services Market: A Disequilibrium Analysis. *Southern Econ. J.,* January 1988, *54*(3), pp. 656–65.

Anderson, J. L. and Jones, E. L. Natural Disasters and the Historical Response. *Australian Econ. Hist. Rev.,* March 1988, *28*(1), pp. 3–20.

Anderson, J. R., et al. Changing Variability in Cereal Production in Australia. *Rev. Marketing Agr. Econ.,* December 1988, *56*(3), pp. 270–86.

Anderson, James E. Cross-Section Estimation of the Effects of Trade Barriers: Comment. In *Feenstra, R. C., ed.,* 1988, pp. 83–87.

———. Empirics of Taxes on Differentiated Products: The Case of Tariffs in the U.S. Automobile Industry: Comment. In *Baldwin, R. E., ed. (II),* 1988, pp. 42–44.

———. The Relative Inefficiency of Quotas. *J. Econ. Educ.,* Winter 1988, *19*(1), pp. 65–81.

Anderson, Joan B. and Colombo, J. A. Christian Base Communities and Grass-Roots Development. *J. Behav. Econ.,* Summer 1988, *17*(2), pp. 97–112.

Anderson, John C. Bargaining Outcomes: An IR Systems Approach. In *Lewin, D., et al., eds.,* 1988, *1979,* pp. 524–41.

Anderson, Joseph M. Empirical Analysis of World Oil Trade, 1967–1984. In *Horwich, G. and Weimer, D. L., eds.,* 1988, pp. 218–64.

Anderson, Kevin. Raya Dunayevskaya, 1910 to 1987, Marxist Economist and Philosopher. *Rev. Radical Polit. Econ.,* Spring 1988, *20*(1), pp. 62–74.

Anderson, Kym and Tyers, Rod. Imperfect Price Transmission and Implied Trade Elasticities in a Multi-commodity World. In *Carter, C. A. and Gardiner, W. H., eds.,* 1988, pp. 255–95.

——— **and Tyers, Rod.** Liberalising OECD Agricultural Policies in the Uruguay Round: Effects on Trade and Welfare. *J. Agr. Econ.,* May 1988, *39*(2), pp. 197–216.

Anderson, Lacelles. Rates of Return of Education for Females in El Salvador. *Soc. Econ. Stud.,* September 1988, *37*(3), pp. 279–87.

Anderson, P. W. A Physicist Looks at Economics: An Overview of the Workshop. In *Anderson, P. W.; Arrow, K. J. and Pines, D., eds.,* 1988, pp. 265–73.

Anderson, Paul F. Relative to What—That Is the Question: A Reply [On Method in Consumer Research: A Critical Relativist Perspective]. *J. Cons. Res.,* June 1988, *15*(1), pp. 133–37.

———. Relativism Revidivus: In Defense of Critical Relativism. *J. Cons. Res.,* December 1988, *15*(3), pp. 403–06.

Anderson, Philip. Economic Policy Considerations in the Taxation of Foreign Source Income. *Australian Tax Forum,* 1988, *5*(4), pp. 395–417.

Anderson, Richard G.; Dewald, William G. and Thursby, Jerry G. Replication in Empirical Economics: *The Journal of Money, Credit and Banking Project:* Reply. *Amer. Econ. Rev.,* December 1988, *78*(5), pp. 1162–63.

Anderson, Robert. Space Business: The Next Industrial Frontier. In *Egan, J. J., et al.,* 1988, pp. 75–83.

Anderson, Robert B.; Bomberger, William A. and Makinen, Gail E. The Demand for Money, the "Reform Effect," and the Money Supply Process in Hyperinflations: The Evidence from Greece and Hungary II Reexamined. *J. Money, Credit, Banking,* November 1988, *20*(4), pp. 653–72.

Anderson, Robert M. The Second Welfare Theorem with Nonconvex Preferences. *Econometrica,* March 1988, *56*(2), pp. 361–82.

Anderson, Ronald W. and Gilbert, Christopher L. Commodity Agreements and Commodity Markets: Lessons from Tin. *Econ. J.,* March 1988, *98*(389), pp. 1–15.

Anderson, Seth and Bos, Theodore. Consumer Sentiments and Share Price Behavior. *J. Behav. Econ.,* Summer 1988, *17*(2), pp. 113–18.

Anderson, Simon P. Equilibrium Existence in the Linear Model of Spatial Competition. *Economica,* November 1988, *55*(220), pp. 479–91.

——— **and Devereux, Michael.** Trade Unions and the Choice of Capital Stock. *Scand. J. Econ.,* 1988, *90*(1), pp. 27–44.

——— **and de Palma, André.** Spatial Price Discrimination with Heterogeneous Products. *Rev. Econ. Stud.,* October 1988, *55*(4), pp. 573–92.

———; **de Palma, André and Thisse, Jacques-François.** The CES and the Logit: Two Related Models of Heterogeneity. *Reg. Sci. Urban Econ.,* February 1988, *18*(1), pp. 155–64.

———; **de Palma, André and Thisse, Jacques-François.** A Representative Consumer Theory of the Logit Model. *Int. Econ. Rev.,* August 1988, *29*(3), pp. 461–66.

——— **and Thisse, Jacques-François.** Price Discrimination in Spatial Competitive Markets. *Europ. Econ. Rev.,* March 1988, *32*(2–3), pp. 578–90.

Anderson, Stephen H. and Ingraham, Patricia W. Assessing the Relationships between Program Design and Productivity: A Framework for Analysis. In *Kelly, R. M., ed.,* 1988, pp. 85–98.

Anderson, Terry L. and Hill, Peter J. Constitutional Constraints, Entrepreneurship, and the Evolution of Property Rights. In *Gwartney, J. D. and Wagner, R. E., eds.,* 1988, pp. 207–27.

Anderson, W. H. Locke and Thompson, Frank W. Neoclassical Marxism. *Sci. Soc.,* Summer 1988, *52*(2), pp. 215–28.

Anderson, William A. A Pedagogical Note on the Open Economy *IS–LM* Model. *J. Econ. Educ.*, Winter 1988, *19*(1), pp. 82–86.

Andersson, Åke E. Comparative Analysis of Population Evolution Models. In *Weidlich, W. and Haag, G., eds.*, 1988, pp. 265–84.

_____. Research, Technological Development and Structural Change. In *Orishimo, I.; Hewings, G. J. D. and Nijkamp, P., eds.*, 1988, pp. 9–20.

_____ and **Zhang, Wei-Bin.** The Two-Dimensional Continuous Spatial Input–Output System. *Ricerche Econ.*, April–June 1988, *42*(2), pp. 222–42.

Andersson, Edward. Företagsskattereformen. (Reform of Business Taxation. With English summary.) *Ekon. Samfundets Tidskr.*, 1988, *41*(4), pp. 223–31.

Andersson, Roland. Evaluation of School Closings: A Case Study from Västerås, Sweden. *J. Urban Econ.*, March 1988, *23*(2), pp. 150–61.

Anderton, R. and Desai, Meghnad. Modelling Manufacturing Imports. *Nat. Inst. Econ. Rev.*, February 1988, (123), pp. 80–86.

Andjiga, Nicolas G. and Moulen, Joël. Binary Games in Constitutional Form and Collective Choice. *Math. Soc. Sci.*, October 1988, *16*(2), pp. 189–201.

Ando, Albert and Auerbach, Alan J. The Corporate Cost of Capital in Japan and the United States: A Comparison. In *Shoven, J. B., ed.*, 1988, pp. 21–49.

_____ and **Auerbach, Alan J.** The Cost of Capital in the United States and Japan: A Comparison. *J. Japanese Int. Economies*, June 1988, *2*(2), pp. 134–58.

_____; **Ferris, Richard and Hayashi, Fumio.** Life Cycle and Bequest Savings: A Study of Japanese and U.S. Households Based on Data from the 1984 NSFIE and the 1983 Survey of Consumer Finances. *J. Japanese Int. Economies*, December 1988, *2*(4), pp. 450–91.

Ando, Faith H. Capital Issues and the Minority-Owned Business. *Rev. Black Polit. Econ.*, Spring 1988, *16*(4), pp. 77–109.

Andorka, Rudolf. Economic Difficulties—Economic Reform—Social Effects and Preconditions. *Acta Oecon.*, 1988, *39*(3–4), pp. 291–302.

Andreasen, Alan R. Consumer Complaints and Redress: What We Know and What We Don't Know. In *Maynes, E. S. and ACCI Research Committee, eds.*, 1988, pp. 675–722.

Andreff, Wladimir and Brunat, Eric. La notion de modernisation industrielle dans les economies socialistes, et son analyse. (The Concept of Modernizing the Industry in Socialist Economies. With English summary.) *Écon. Soc.*, February 1988, *22*(2), pp. 7–45.

Andrei, Anca and Oprescu, G. Optimizing the Physical Production Plan at the Level of Economic Units. *Econ. Computat. Cybern. Stud. Res.*, 1988, *23*(3), pp. 75–85.

Andreoni, James. Privately Provided Public Goods in a Large Economy: The Limits of Altruism. *J. Public Econ.*, February 1988, *35*(1), pp. 57–73.

_____. Why Free Ride? Strategies and Learning in Public Goods Experiments. *J. Public Econ.*, December 1988, *37*(3), pp. 291–304.

Andrew, Caroline; Coderre, Cécile and Denis, Ann. Women in Management: The Canadian Experience: The Relationship of Professional and Personal Lives. In *Adler, N. J. and Izraeli, D., eds.*, 1988, pp. 250–64.

Andrews, Donald R. and Tate, Uday S. An Application of the Stock Adjustment Model in Estimating Employment Multipliers for the South Central Louisiana Petroleum Economy, 1964–84: Note. *Growth Change*, Summer 1988, *19*(3), pp. 94–105.

Andrews, Donald W. K. Chi-Square Diagnostic Tests for Econometric Models: Introduction and Applications. *J. Econometrics*, January 1988, *37*(1), pp. 135–56.

_____. Chi-Square Diagnostic Tests for Econometric Models: Theory. *Econometrica*, November 1988, *56*(6), pp. 1419–53.

_____. Robust Estimation of Location in a Gaussian Parametric Model. In *Rhodes, G. F., Jr. and Fomby, T. B., eds.*, 1988, pp. 3–44.

_____ and **Fair, Ray C.** Inference in Nonlinear Econometric Models with Structural Change. *Rev. Econ. Stud.*, October 1988, *55*(4), pp. 615–39.

Andrews, Elizabeth J. and Wilen, James E. Angler Response to Success in the California Salmon Sportfishery: Evidence and Management Implications. *Marine Resource Econ.*, 1988, *5*(2), pp. 125–38.

Andrews, Emily S. and Chollet, Deborah J. Future Sources of Retirement Income: Whither the Baby Boom. In *Wachter, S. M., ed.*, 1988, pp. 71–95.

Andrews, Margaret S.; Lopez, Rigoberto A. and Adelaja, Adesoji O. The Effects of Suburbanization on Agriculture. *Amer. J. Agr. Econ.*, May 1988, *70*(2), pp. 346–58.

Andrews, Martyn. An International Perspective. In *Beenstock, M., ed.*, 1988, pp. 169–97.

_____. Some Formal Models of the Aggregate Labour Market. In *Beenstock, M., ed.*, 1988, pp. 25–48.

Andrews, Nicholas G. The Effectiveness of U.S. Sanctions against Poland. In *Marer, P. and Siwinski, W., eds.*, 1988, pp. 323–33.

_____. Political and Ideological Factors in Agricultural Policy. In *Marer, P. and Siwinski, W., eds.*, 1988, pp. 37–43.

Andrews, P. W. S. A Reconsideration of the Theory of the Individual Business. In *Earl, P. E., ed., Vol. 1*, 1988, *1949*, pp. 285–320.

_____ and **Meade, James.** Summary of Replies to Questions on Effects of Interest Rates. In *Meade, J., Vol. 1*, 1988, *1938*, pp. 91–105.

Andrews, William D. and Bradford, David F. Savings Incentives in a Hybrid Income Tax. In *Aaron, H. J.; Galper, H. and Pechman, J. A., eds.*, 1988, pp. 269–300.

Andrieu, J. N. and Le Gall, J. P. Reconnaissance de la personnalité fiscale des entreprises entreprises étrangères: France. (Recognition of Foreign Enterprises as Taxable Entities: France.

With English summary.) In *International Fiscal Association, ed. (I)*, 1988, pp. 411–29.

Andvig, Jens Christopher. From Macrodynamics to Macroeconomic Planning: A Basic Shift in Ragnar Frisch's Thinking? *Europ. Econ. Rev.*, March 1988, *32*(2–3), pp. 495–502.

Ang, B. W. Oil Substitution and the Changing Structure of Energy Demand in Southeast Asia: A Case Study. *J. Energy Devel.*, Autumn 1988, *14*(1), pp. 55–77.

Ang, James S. and Lai, Tsong-Yue. Functional Forms of the Capital Asset Pricing Model under Different Market Risk Regimes. *Financial Rev.*, August 1988, *23*(3), pp. 345–50.

—— **and Lai, Tsong-Yue.** On Optimal Pension Funding Policy. *J. Econ. Bus.*, August 1988, *40*(3), pp. 229–38.

—— **and Tucker, Alan L.** The Shareholder Wealth Effects of Corporate Greenmail. *J. Finan. Res.*, Winter 1988, *11*(4), pp. 265–80.

Angel, D. P. and Scott, Allen J. The Global Assembly-Operations of U.S. Semiconductor Firms: A Geographical Analysis. *Environ. Planning A*, August 1988, *20*(8), pp. 1047–67.

Angell, Wayne D. Statement to the U.S. House Subcommittee on Domestic Monetary Policy of the Committee on Banking, Finance and Urban Affairs, May 25, 1988. *Fed. Res. Bull.*, July 1988, *74*(7), pp. 453–57.

—— **and Kelley, Edward W., Jr.** Statement to the U.S. House Subcommittee on Domestic Monetary Policy of the Committee on Banking, Finance and Urban Affairs, May 3, 1988. *Fed. Res. Bull.*, July 1988, *74*(7), pp. 437–45.

Angermueller, Hans H. The Evolution of Banking Strategies and Services: The Dilemma Facing Today's Bankers. In *Mikdashi, Z., ed.*, 1988, pp. 25–43.

Anglard, Patrick; Gendreau, Francoise and Rault, A. Model Building for Decision Aid in the Agri-economic Field. In *Motamen, H., ed.*, 1988, pp. 283–311.

Angle, Harold L. and Perry, James L. Union Member Attitudes and Bargaining Unit Stability in Urban Transit. In *Lewin, D., et al., eds.*, 1988, *1984*, pp. 152–62.

Anglin, Paul M. The Sensitivity of Consumer Search to Wages. *Econ. Letters*, 1988, *28*(3), pp. 209–13.

—— **and Baye, Michael R.** Information Gathering and Cost of Living Differences among Searchers. *Econ. Letters*, 1988, *28*(3), pp. 247–50.

Angoff, Jay. Insurance against Competition: How the McCarran–Ferguson Act Raises Prices and Profits in the Property–Casualty Insurance Industry. *Yale J. Regul.*, Summer 1988, *5*(2), pp. 397–415.

Angotti, Thomas. The Stalin Period: Opening Up History. *Sci. Soc.*, Spring 1988, *52*(1), pp. 5–34.

Annable, James. Another Auctioneer Is Missing. *J. Macroecon.*, Winter 1988, *10*(1), pp. 1–26.

Annis, Sheldon. Can Small-Scale Development

Be Large-Scale Policy? In *Annis, S. and Hakim, P., eds.*, 1988, *1987*, pp. 209–18.

——. What Is Not the Same about the Urban Poor: The Case of Mexico City. In *Lewis, J. P., et al.*, 1988, pp. 133–48.

—— **and Cox, Stephen.** Community Participation in Rural Water Supply. In *Annis, S. and Hakim, P., eds.*, 1988, pp. 65–72.

Anselin, Luc. Model Validation in Spatial Econometrics: A Review and Evaluation of Alternative Approaches. *Int. Reg. Sci. Rev.*, 1988, *11*(3), pp. 279–316.

——. A Test for Spatial Autocorrelation in Seemingly Unrelated Regressions. *Econ. Letters*, 1988, *28*(4), pp. 335–41.

Antal, Araine Berthoin and Krebsbach-Gnath, Camilla. Women in Management: Unused Resources in the Federal Republic of Germany. In *Adler, N. J. and Izraeli, D., eds.*, 1988, pp. 141–56.

Antal, László, et al. Turning Point and Reform. *Eastern Europ. Econ.*, Summer 1988, *26*(4), pp. 5–44.

Antel, John J. Interrelated Quits: An Empirical Analysis of the Utility Maximizing Mobility Hypothesis. *Rev. Econ. Statist.*, February 1988, *70*(1), pp. 17–22.

Anthony, John Duke. The Gulf Cooperation Council: A New Framework for Policy Coordination. In *Sindelar, H. R., III and Peterson, J. E., eds.*, 1988, pp. 38–60.

Anthony, Joseph H. The Interrelation of Stock and Options Market Trading-Volume Data. *J. Finance*, September 1988, *43*(4), pp. 949–64.

Antille, Gabrielle and Fontela, Emilio. Origine et distribution de la productivité globale. (The Origin and the Distribution of Total Productivity. With English summary.) *Schweiz. Z. Volkswirtsch. Statist.*, September 1988, *124*(3), pp. 277–88.

Antle, John M. and Crissman, Charles C. The Market for Innovations and Short-run Technological Change: Evidence from Egypt. *Econ. Develop. Cult. Change*, July 1988, *36*(4), pp. 669–90.

Antle, Rick and Demski, Joel S. The Controllability Principle in Responsible Accounting. *Accounting Rev.*, October 1988, *63*(4), pp. 700–718.

Antoine, Guy C. IFC's Initiatives in Sub-Saharan Africa. *Finance Develop.*, December 1988, *25*(4), pp. 37–38.

Anton, James J. and Gertler, Paul J. External Markets and Regulation. *J. Public Econ.*, November 1988, *37*(2), pp. 243–60.

Antonelli, Gilberto and Quadrio-Curzio, Alberto. The Development of an Agro-technological System between Market Pulls and Structural Pushes. In *Antonelli, G. and Quadrio-Curzio, A., eds.*, 1988, pp. 1–16.

Antoniou, Andréas. A Measure of the Effect of Diversification, through External Growth, on Industrial Concentration: Some Illustrations. *Antitrust Bull.*, Spring 1988, *33*(1), pp. 161–83.

Antonov, Ventsislav. A Structural Analysis of Foreign Trade from the Standpoint of the National Economy. *Soviet E. Europ. Foreign Trade*, Summer 1988, *24*(2), pp. 38–54.

Antonovitz, Frances and Nelson, Ray D. Forward and Futures Markets and the Competitive Firm under Price Uncertainty. *Southern Econ. J.*, July 1988, *55*(1), pp. 182–95.

———— **and Roe, Terry L.** A Theoretical and Empirical Approach to the Value of Information in Risky Markets: A Reply. *Rev. Econ. Statist.*, August 1988, *70*(3), pp. 545–47.

Anvari, Mohsen. Corporate Cash Management in Canada: A Comparison with the United States. In *Kim, Y. H., ed.*, 1988, pp. 79–95.

Anwaruzzaman, Chowdhury. Determinants of Currency Ratio—Some Preliminary Evidence. *Bangladesh Devel. Stud.*, September 1988, *16*(3), pp. 99–106.

Aoki, Masahiko. The Japanese Bureaucracy in Economic Administration: A Rational Regulator or Pluralist Agent? In *Shoven, J. B., ed.*, 1988, pp. 265–300.

Aoki, Masanao. Cointegration, Error Correction, and Aggregation in Dynamic Models: A Comment. *Oxford Bull. Econ. Statist.*, February 1988, *50*(1), pp. 89–95.

————. Nonstationarity, Cointegration, and Error Correction in Economic Modeling: Introduction and Overview. *J. Econ. Dynam. Control*, June–Sept. 1988, *12*(2–3), pp. 199–201.

————. On Alternative State Space Representations of Time Series Models. *J. Econ. Dynam. Control*, June–Sept. 1988, *12*(2–3), pp. 595–607.

———— **and Havenner, Arthur.** An Instrumental Variables Interpretation of Linear Systems Theory Estimation. *J. Econ. Dynam. Control*, March 1988, *12*(1), pp. 49–54.

———— **and Leijonhufvud, Axel.** The Stock-Flow Analysis of Investment. In *Kohn, M. and Tsiang, S.-C., eds.*, 1988, pp. 206–29.

Aoki, Torao. Tax Reform in Japan. *Bull. Int. Fiscal Doc.*, March 1988, *42*(3), pp. 131–35.

Apedaile, L. P. and Li, Y. A Simulation of Economic Effects of Technology Transfer in Cereal Production. *Can. J. Agr. Econ.*, November 1988, *36*(3), pp. 473–88.

Apostolakis, Bobby E. Imports and Production of Food in India: An Econometric Approach, 1947–1986. *Singapore Econ. Rev.*, October 1988, *33*(2), pp. 21–39.

————. Imports as a Factor Input: A Study Based on U.K. Data, 1953–1984. *Rivista Int. Sci. Econ. Com.*, January 1988, *35*(1), pp. 43–58.

————. Imports Demand and Food Production in India: A Flexible Cost Function Approach, 1950–1986. *Ricerche Econ.*, July–Sept. 1988, *42*(3), pp. 470–88.

————. The Role of Technology Transfer in Soviet Development. *Rev. Radical Polit. Econ.*, Winter 1988, *20*(4), pp. 57–73.

————. Translogarithmic Production and Cost Functions: A Synopsis. *Econ. Stud. Quart.*, March 1988, *39*(1), pp. 41–63.

Apostolou, N. and Baltas, N. C. A Rational Expectations Model for the Poultry Sector in Greece. *Appl. Econ.*, July 1988, *20*(7), pp. 917–27.

Appel, David and Borba, Philip S. Costs and Prices of Workers' Compensation Insurance. In *Borba, P. S. and Appel, D., eds.*, 1988, pp. 1–17.

Appelbaum, Eileen and Albin, Peter S. The Computer Rationalization of Work: Implications for Women Workers. In *Jenson, J.; Hagen, E. and Reddy, C., eds.*, 1988, pp. 137–52.

Appelbaum, Elie and Katz, Eliakim. Portfolio Diversification and Taxation. *Econ. Letters*, 1988, *26*(2), pp. 189–95.

Appelbe, T. W., et al. Point-to-Point Modelling: An Application to Canada–Canada and Canada–United States Long Distance Calling. *Info. Econ. Policy*, 1988, *3*(4), pp. 311–31.

Appleby, Colin and Twigg, David. Computer Aided Design in the United Kingdom Car Industry. *Nat. Westminster Bank Quart. Rev.*, August 1988, pp. 39–52.

Apps, Patricia F. and Rees, Ray. Taxation and the Household. *J. Public Econ.*, April 1988, *35*(3), pp. 355–69.

Apte, D. P. The Role of Co-operative Dairy Schemes in Rural Development in India. In *Attwood, D. W. and Baviskar, B. S., eds.*, 1988, pp. 378–93.

Apuzzo, A.; Kerr, William A. and McLachlan, D. L. The Canada–U.S. Free Trade Agreement: A Canadian Perspective. *J. World Trade*, August 1988, *22*(4), pp. 9–34.

Arabie, P.; De Soete, G. and Hubert, L. On the Use of Simulated Annealing for Combinatorial Data Analysis. In *Gaul, W. and Schader, M., eds.*, 1988, pp. 329–40.

————, et al. Marketing Applications of Sequencing and Partitioning of Nonsymmetric and/or Two-Mode Matrices. In *Gaul, W. and Schader, M., eds.*, 1988, pp. 215–24.

Aradhyula, Satheesh V. and Holt, Matthew T. GARCH Time-Series Models: An Application to Retail Livestock Prices. *Western J. Agr. Econ.*, December 1988, *13*(2), pp. 365–74.

———— **and Sharma, B. M.** Farming Systems: Income Potential and Credit Requirements of Non-viable Farmers in Pithapuram Block, India. *J. Econ. Devel.*, June 1988, *13*(1), pp. 21–37.

Arafa, Salah. Community Cooperatives for Development: The Basaisa Village Experiment. In *Hedlund, H., ed.*, 1988, pp. 207–19.

Aragon, Yves; Laffont, Jean-Jacques and Le Pottier, Jacques. Testing the Democratic Hypothesis in the Provision of Local Public Goods. *J. Public Econ.*, July 1988, *36*(2), pp. 139–51.

————; **Laffont, Jean-Jacques and Le Pottier, Jacques.** Test de l'hypothèse démocratique dans le décisions budgétaires communales. (Test of the Democratic Hypothesis in French Communities. With English summary.) *Revue Écon.*, March 1988, *39*(2), pp. 405–20.

Arai, Kazuhiro. The Causes and Degree of Employment Internalization. *Hitotsubashi J. Econ.*, December 1988, *29*(2), pp. 201–17.

_____. The Cost of Living and the Seniority-Based Wage System in Japan. *Hitotsubashi J. Econ.*, June 1988, 29(1), pp. 21–35.

Aral, Mustafa M. and Tang, Yi. A New Boundary Element Formulation for Time-Dependent Confined and Unconfined Aquifer Problems. *Water Resources Res.*, June 1988, 24(6), pp. 831–42.

Aramburú, Carlos E. Family and Labour in Rural Peru: New Interpretations. In *Vlassoff, C. and Barkat-e-Khuda, eds.*, 1988, pp. 83–106.

Aranson, Peter H. Procedural and Substantive Constitutional Protection of Economic Liberties. In *Gwartney, J. D. and Wagner, R. E., eds.*, 1988, 1987, pp. 285–313.

Araquém da Silva, Ednaldo. Errata [Wage–Profit Trade-Offs in Brazil: An Input/Output Analysis, 1970–1975]. *Sci. Soc.*, Summer 1988, 52(2), pp. 132.

_____. Preços e distribuição de renda no Brasil: Uma análise de insumo-produto—1975. (With English summary.) *Pesquisa Planejamento Econ.*, August 1988, 18(2), pp. 361–77.

Arat, Zehra F. Can Democracy Survive Where There Is a Gap between Political and Economic Rights? In *Cingranelli, D. L., ed.*, 1988, pp. 221–35.

Araujo, A. The Non-existence of Smooth Demand in General Banach Spaces. *J. Math. Econ.*, 1988, 17(4), pp. 309–19.

Arbogast, Todd. The Double Porosity Model for Single Phase Flow in Naturally Fractured Reservoirs. In *Wheeler, M. F., ed.*, 1988, pp. 23–45.

_____; **Douglas, Jim, Jr. and Santos, Juan E.** Two-Phase Immiscible Flow in Naturally Fractured Reservoirs. In *Wheeler, M. F., ed.*, 1988, pp. 47–66.

Arcelus, F. J. and Levine, A. L. Merit Goods and Public Choice: The Case of Higher Education—Reply. *Public Finance*, 1988, 43(3), pp. 471–72.

Archer, R. and Rous, P. Peut-on desagreger la vitesse de circulation de la monnaie? (How to Disaggregate the Velocity of Money? With English summary.) *Écon. Soc.*, January 1988, 22(1), pp. 179–203.

Archer, R. W. Land Pooling for Resubdivision and New Subdivision in Western Australia. *Amer. J. Econ. Soc.*, April 1988, 47(2), pp. 207–21.

Archetti, Eduardo P. Ideologia y organizacion sindical: Las Ligas Agrarias del norte de Sante Fe. (With English summary.) *Desarrollo Econ.*, Oct.–Dec. 1988, 28(111), pp. 447–61.

Archibald, Robert B. and Baker, Samuel H. Aggregate Business Failures and Federal Credit Activity. *Public Finance Quart.*, April 1988, 16(2), pp. 219–43.

Ardito-Barletta, Nicolas. A Time for Adjustment with Growth. In *Tavis, L. A., ed.*, 1988, pp. 61–66.

Ardy, Brian. The National Incidence of the European Community Budget. *J. Common Market Stud.*, June 1988, 26(4), pp. 401–29.

Arellano, José Pablo. Crisis y recuperación econó-mica en Chile en los años 80. (Crisis and Economic Recovery in Chile in the Eighties. With English summary.) *Colección Estud. CIEPLAN*, June 1988, (24), pp. 63–84.

Arena, Richard; Froeschle, Claude and Torre, Dominique. Formation des prix et équilibre classique. Un examen préliminaire. (Price Formation and Classical Equilibrium: A Preliminary Investigation. With English summary.) *Revue Écon.*, November 1988, 39(6), pp. 1097–1117.

Arestis, Philip. The Credit Segment of a UK Post Keynesian Model. *J. Post Keynesian Econ.*, Winter 1987–88, 10(2), pp. 250–69.

_____. The Demand for Money in Small Developing Economies: An Application of the Error Correction Mechanism. In *[Frowen, S.]*, 1988, pp. 184–205.

_____. Post-Keynesian Monetary Economics: Introduction. In *Arestis, P., ed.*, 1988, pp. 1–10.

_____. Post-Keynesian Theory of Money, Credit and Finance. In *Arestis, P., ed.*, 1988, pp. 41–71.

_____. Wages and Prices in the UK: The Post Keynesian View. In *Sawyer, M. C., ed.*, 1988, 1986, pp. 456–75.

_____ **and Driver, Ciaran.** The Endogeneity of the UK Money Supply: A Political Economy Perspective. *Écon. Soc.*, September 1988, 22(9), pp. 121–38.

_____ **and Driver, Ciaran.** The Macrodynamics of the U.S. and U.K. Economies through Two Post-Keynesian Models. In *Arestis, P., ed.*, 1988, pp. 11–40.

_____ **and Eichner, Alfred S.** The Post-Keynesian and Institutionalist Theory of Money and Credit. *J. Econ. Issues*, December 1988, 22(4), pp. 1003–21.

_____; **Tool, Marc R. and Street, James H.** In Memoriam: Alfred S. Eichner 1937–1988. *J. Econ. Issues*, December 1988, 22(4), pp. 1239–42.

Argüden, R. Yilmaz. There is No Free Lunch: Unintended Effects of the New Military Retirement System. *J. Policy Anal. Manage.*, Spring 1988, 7(3), pp. 529–41.

Argy, Fred. Outlook for Interest Rates and the Exchange Rate. *Rev. Marketing Agr. Econ.*, April 1988, 56(1), pp. 68–74.

Argy, Victor. Policy Analysis with the MSG Model: Comment. *Australian Econ. Pap.*, Supplement, June 1988, 27, pp. 151–54.

_____. A Post-war History of the Rules *vs* Discretion Debate. *Banca Naz. Lavoro Quart. Rev.*, June 1988, (165), pp. 147–77.

Argyris, Chris. Problems in Producing Usable Knowledge for Implementing Liberating Alternatives. In *Bell, D. E.; Raiffa, H. and Tversky, A., eds.*, 1988, pp. 540–61.

Arida, Persio and Lara-Resende, André. Inflationary Inertia and Monetary Reform: Brazil. In *Chacel, J. M.; Falk, P. S. and Fleischer, D. V., eds.*, 1988, pp. 27–41.

Ariel, Robert A. Evidence on Intra-month Seasonality in Stock Returns. In *Dimson, E., ed.*, 1988, pp. 109–19.

Arif, Ghulam Mohammad and Irfan, Mohammad. Landlessness in Rural Areas of Pakistan and Policy Options: A Preliminary Investigation. *Pakistan Devel. Rev.*, Part 2, Winter 1988, 27(4), pp. 567–74.

Ariff, Mohamed. Islamic Banking. *Asian-Pacific Econ. Lit.*, September 1988, 2(2), pp. 48–64.

Ariyo, Ademola. Economic Considerations in the Choice of Depreciation Methods: Some Additional Evidence from Nigeria. In *Most, K. S., ed.*, 1988, pp. 87–97.

Ariyoshi, Akira. Japanese Capital Flows. *Finance Develop.*, September 1988, 25(3), pp. 28–30.

Arize, Augustine. The Demand and Supply for Exports in Nigeria in a Simultaneous Model. *Indian Econ. J.*, April–June 1988, 35(4), pp. 33–43.

————. Modelling Export Prices and Quantities in Selected Developing Economies. *Atlantic Econ. J.*, March 1988, 16(1), pp. 19–24.

van Ark, Bart. The Volume and Price of Indonesian Exports, 1823 to 1940: The Long-term Trend and Its Measurement. *Bull. Indonesian Econ. Stud.*, December 1988, 24(3), pp. 87–120.

———— **and Maddison, Angus.** Comparison of Real Output and Purchasing Power—Brazil/USA and Mexico/USA. In *Salazar-Carrillo, J. and Rao, D. S. P., eds.*, 1988, pp. 153–77.

Armani, Pietro. Considerations and Prospects on the Opening Up of Credit Markets from the Point of View of IRI. *Rev. Econ. Cond. Italy*, Sept.–Dec. 1988, (3), pp. 275–82.

Armentano, Dominick T. Rothbardian Monopoly Theory and Antitrust Policy. In *[Rothbard, M. N.]*, 1988, pp. 3–11.

Arminana, Ruben; Auvert, Bertran and Bertrand, William E. Microcomputer Applications in the Health and Social Service Sectors of Developing Countries. In *Bhalla, A. S. and James, D., eds.*, 1988, pp. 127–36.

Armington, Paul. North–South Interactions: A General-Equilibrium Framework for the Study of Strategic Issues: Discussion. In *Currie, D. and Vines, D., eds.*, 1988, pp. 101–05.

Armour, Leslie. Perestroika, Economics and Morality. *Int. J. Soc. Econ.*, 1988, 15(9), pp. 39–50.

Armstrong, Gary M.; Goldberg, Marvin E. and Brucks, Merrie. Children's Use of Cognitive Defenses against Television Advertising: A Cognitive Response Approach. *J. Cons. Res.*, March 1988, 14(4), pp. 471–82.

Armstrong, Harvey W. Estimating the Degree of Central Control of Spatial Industrial Policy: Great Britain, 1983/84. *Ann. Reg. Sci.*, March 1988, 22(1), pp. 17–35.

Armstrong, Hugh and Armstrong, Pat. Taking Women into Account: Redefining and Intensifying Employment in Canada. In *Jenson, J.; Hagen, E. and Reddy, C., eds.*, 1988, pp. 65–84.

Armstrong, J. Scott. Research Needs in Forecasting. *Int. J. Forecasting*, 1988, 4(3), pp. 449–65.

Armstrong, Kathleen M. and Lewis, Jacqueline A. Technological Innovation and Labour Market Adjustments. *Scot. J. Polit. Econ.*, May 1988, 35(2), pp. 162–70.

Armstrong, Pat and Armstrong, Hugh. Taking Women into Account: Redefining and Intensifying Employment in Canada. In *Jenson, J.; Hagen, E. and Reddy, C., eds.*, 1988, pp. 65–84.

Arndt, Heinz W. Colin Clark. In *[Clark, C.]*, 1988, pp. 1–7.

————. Comparative Advantage in Trade in Financial Services. *Banca Naz. Lavoro Quart. Rev.*, March 1988, (164), pp. 61–78.

————. "Market Failure" and Underdevelopment. *World Devel.*, February 1988, 16(2), pp. 219–29.

————. The Valuation Effect of Changes in Exchange Rates. *Banca Naz. Lavoro Quart. Rev.*, December 1988, (167), pp. 411–24.

Arnell, Nigel W. and Gabriele, Salvatore. The Performance of the Two-Component Extreme Value Distribution in Regional Flood Frequency Analysis. *Water Resources Res.*, June 1988, 24(6), pp. 879–87.

Arnold, Brian J. Future Directions in International Tax Reform. *Australian Tax Forum*, 1988, 5(4), pp. 451–69.

Arnold, J. T.; Dunn, James E. and Fryar, Edward O., Jr. Bayesian Evaluation of a Specific Hypothesis. *Amer. J. Agr. Econ.*, August 1988, 70(3), pp. 685–92.

Arnold, M. I. B. and Bronckers, M. C. E. J. The EEC New Trade Policy Instrument: Some Comments on Its Application (Reg. 2641/84). *J. World Trade*, December 1988, 22(6), pp. 19–38.

Arnold, N. Scott. Marx and Disequilibrium in Market Socialist Relations of Production: Reply. *Econ. Philos.*, October 1988, 4(2), pp. 337–40.

Arnold, Roger A. Prisoner's Dilemma, Transaction Costs, and Rothbard. In *[Rothbard, M. N.]*, 1988, pp. 12–23.

Arnon, Arie and Sternberg, Menachem. Forward Credit Commitments and Bank Behavior under Uncertainty: Implications for Monetary Control. *J. Macroecon.*, Fall 1988, 10(4), pp. 591–612.

Arnott, Richard J.; Hosios, Arthur J. and Stiglitz, Joseph E. Implicit Contracts, Labor Mobility, and Unemployment. *Amer. Econ. Rev.*, December 1988, 78(5), pp. 1046–66.

———— **and Stiglitz, Joseph E.** The Basic Analytics of Moral Hazard. *Scand. J. Econ.*, 1988, 90(3), pp. 383–413.

———— **and Stiglitz, Joseph E.** Randomization with Asymmetric Information. *Rand J. Econ.*, Autumn 1988, 19(3), pp. 344–62.

Arnott, Robert D. The Future for Quantitative Investment Products. *J. Portfol. Manage.*, Winter 1988, 14(2), pp. 52–56.

———— **and Sorensen, Eric H.** The Risk Premium and Stock Market Performance. *J. Portfol. Manage.*, Summer 1988, 14(4), pp. 50–55.

Aron, Debra J. Ability, Moral Hazard, Firm Size,

and Diversification. *Rand J. Econ.*, Spring 1988, *19*(1), pp. 72–87.

Aron, Joan L. Disease Control and Mortality Reduction. In *Sirageldin, I. and Sorkin, A., eds.,* 1988, pp. 43–56.

Aronovitch, Hilliard. The Mystique of Stock Market Wisdom. *Écon. Soc.,* September 1988, *22*(9), pp. 29–34.

Aronson, Jonathan D. The Service Industries: Growth, Trade, and Development Prospects. In *Sewell, J. W. and Tucker, S. K., eds.,* 1988, pp. 97–118.

Arora, Harjit K. Crowding Out in the Context of a Developed Country. *Indian J. Quant. Econ.,* 1988, *4*(1), pp. 1–20.

——— **and Mohtadi, Hamid.** Stagflation and Monetary Stabilization Policies in a Disequilibrium Framework: The Case of South Korea. *J. Post Keynesian Econ.,* Summer 1988, *10*(4), pp. 602–17.

Arora, S. K. Human Resources Development in Cooperatives. In *Kohli, U. and Gautam, V., eds.,* 1988, pp. 49–62.

Arrow, Kenneth J. The Balance between Industry and Agriculture in Economic Development: Introduction. In *Arrow, K. J., ed.,* 1988, pp. xvii–xxii.

———. Behavior under Uncertainty and Its Implications for Policy. In *Bell, D. E.; Raiffa, H. and Tversky, A., eds.,* 1988, *1983,* pp. 497–507.

———. International Finance and Trade in a Polycentric World: Overview of the Conference. In *Borner, S., ed.,* 1988, pp. 392–96.

———. Presidential Address: General Economic Theory and the Emergence of Theories of Economic Development. In *Arrow, K. J., ed.,* 1988, pp. 22–32.

———. Uncertainty and the Welfare Economics of Medical Care. In *Ricketts, M., ed., Vol. 2,* 1988, *1963,* pp. 277–309.

———. Workshop on the Economy as an Evolving Complex System: Summary. In *Anderson, P. W.; Arrow, K. J. and Pines, D., eds.,* 1988, pp. 275–81.

——— **and Fisher, Anthony C.** Environmental Preservation, Uncertainty, and Irreversibility. In *Ricketts, M., ed., Vol. 2,* 1988, *1974,* pp. 226–33.

——— **and Lind, Robert C.** Uncertainty and the Evaluation of Public Investment Decisions. In *Ricketts, M., ed., Vol. 2,* 1988, *1970,* pp. 211–25.

Arrufat, José Luis and Zabalza, Antonio. Efficiency and Equity Effects of Reforming the British System of Direct Taxation: A Utility-Based Simulation Methodology. *Economica,* February 1988, *55*(217), pp. 21–45.

Arshadi, Nasser and Lawrence, Edward C. The Distributional Impact of Foreign Deposits on Federal Deposit Insurance Premia. *J. Banking Finance,* 1988, *12*(1), pp. 105–15.

Arshanapalli, Gangadha; Skeels, Jack W. and McGrath, Paul. The Importance of Strike Size in Strike Research. *Ind. Lab. Relat. Rev.,* July 1988, *41*(4), pp. 582–91.

Arthur, C. J. Hegel's Theory of Value. In *Williams, M., ed.,* 1988, pp. 21–41.

Arthur, Louise M. The Greenhouse Effect and the Canadian Prairies: Simulation of Future Economic Impacts. In *Johnston, G. M.; Freshwater, D. and Favero, P., eds.,* 1988, pp. 226–43.

——— **and Abizadeh, Fay.** Potential Effects of Climate Change on Agriculture in the Prairie Region of Canada. *Western J. Agr. Econ.,* December 1988, *13*(2), pp. 216–24.

———; **Carter, Colin A. and Abizadeh, Fay.** Arbitrage Pricing, Capital Asset Pricing, and Agricultural Assets. *Amer. J. Agr. Econ.,* May 1988, *70*(2), pp. 359–65.

——— **and Kraft, Daryl F.** The Effects of Technological Change on the Economic Impact of Agricultural Drought in Manitoba. *Can. J. Agr. Econ.,* July 1988, *36*(2), pp. 221–37.

———; **Smith, M. and MacMillan, J. A.** Economic Evaluation Methodology for an Alberta Agro-energy Project. *Can. J. Agr. Econ.,* Part 2, December 1988, *36*(4), pp. 905–13.

Arthur, W. Brian. Competing Technologies: An Overview. In *Dosi, G., et al., eds.,* 1988, pp. 590–607.

———. Self-reinforcing Mechanisms in Economics. In *Anderson, P. W.; Arrow, K. J. and Pines, D., eds.,* 1988, pp. 9–31.

———. Urban Systems and Historical Path Dependence. In *Ausubel, J. H. and Herman, R., eds.,* 1988, pp. 85–97.

——— **and Espenshade, Thomas J.** Immigration Policy and Immigrants' Ages. *Population Devel. Rev.,* June 1988, *14*(2), pp. 315–26.

Arthurs, H. W. "The Right to Golf": Reflections on the Future of Workers, Unions and the Rest of Us under the *Charter.* In *Carter, D. D., et al.,* 1988, pp. 17–31.

Artis, Michael J. Are Market Forces Adequate to Maintain Full Employment? If Not, Can Demand Management Policies Be Relied upon to Fill the Gap? In *Eltis, W. and Sinclair, P. J. N., eds.,* 1988, pp. 3–24.

———. The EMS in the Face of New Challenges. In *[Frowen, S.],* 1988, pp. 114–25.

———. How Accurate Is the World Economic Outlook? A Post Mortem on Short-Term Forecasting at the International Monetary Fund. In *International Monetary Fund Research Department,* 1988, pp. 1–49.

———. The 1988 Budget and the MTFS. *Fisc. Stud.,* May 1988, *9*(2), pp. 14–29.

Artisien, Patrick and Buckley, Peter J. Policy Issues of Intra-EC Direct Investment: British, French and German Multinationals in Greece, Portugal and Spain, with Special Reference to Employment Effects. In *Dunning, J. and Robson, P., eds.,* 1988, pp. 105–28.

Artle, Roland and Carruthers, Norman. Location and Market Power: Hotelling Revisited. *J. Reg. Sci.,* February 1988, *28*(1), pp. 15–27.

Artus, Patrick. Dynamique des actifs financiers et dévaluations avec endettement extérieur. (Dynamic Evolution of Financial Assets and Devaluations in an Economy with Foreign

Debt Interest Rate Control and Uncertainty on the Time of Devaluation. With English summary.) *Revue Écon.*, September 1988, *39*(5), pp. 973–98.

_____. La création d'une marché à terme peu-telle être déstabilisante? L'effet de la qualité des arbitrages et du mode de formation des anticipations. (Can Opening a Futures Market Be Destabilizing? The Effects of Imperfect Arbitrage and of the Way Expectations Are Formed. With English summary.) *Rech. Écon. Louvain*, 1988, *54*(4), pp. 385–408.

_____. La structure du commerce extérieur de produits manufacturés de la France. (With English summary.) *Revue Écon. Polit.*, May–June 1988, *98*(3), pp. 382–400.

_____. Le partage du profit: fondements micro-économiques et effets macroéconomiques. (Profit Sharing: Microeconomic Grounds and Macroeconomic Effects. With English summary.) *Ann. Écon. Statist.*, April–June 1988, (10), pp. 45–73.

_____. Sur quelle base fixer le taux de croissance de la masse monetaire. (How Should We Target the Growth of the Money Stock? With English summary.) *Écon. Soc.*, January 1988, *22*(1), pp. 155–77.

_____. Transmission internationale des chocs quels sont les canaux importants? (With English summary.) *Revue Écon. Polit.*, Sept.–Oct. 1988, *98*(5), pp. 655–71.

_____ and de Boissieu, Christian. The Process of Financial Innovation: Causes, Forms, and Consequences. In *Heertje, A., ed.*, 1988, pp. 101–26.

Aruga, Natsuki. "An' Finish School": Child Labor during World War II. *Labor Hist.*, Fall 1988, *29*(4), pp. 498–530.

Arvan, Lanny. Symmetric Equilibrium with Random Entry. *Math. Soc. Sci.*, December 1988, *16*(3), pp. 289–303.

Asam, P.-M. Corporate Requirements for Public Technology Policy: The Siemens Experience. *Aussenwirtschaft*, June 1988, *43*(1/2), pp. 191–99.

Asami, Yasushi. A Game-Theoretic Approach to the Division of Profits from Economic Land Development. *Reg. Sci. Urban Econ.*, May 1988, *18*(2), pp. 233–46.

Asamoah, Yaw A. Discussion of Prof. Chowd-hury's "Monetary Models of the IMF" In *Pennsylvania Economic Association*, 1988, pp. 725–26.

_____. The State and Agricultural Backwardness in West Africa. In *Pennsylvania Economic Association*, 1988, pp. 151–62.

Asbury, Penny L. and Barsky, Carl. Evaluation of Mean Wage Estimates in the Industry Wage Survey Program. *Mon. Lab. Rev.*, October 1988, *111*(10), pp. 24–29.

Asch, Peter and Quandt, Richard E. Betting Bias in 'Exotic' Bets. *Econ. Letters*, 1988, *28*(3), pp. 215–19.

Aschauer, David Alan. The Equilibrium Approach to Fiscal Policy. *J. Money, Credit, Banking*, February 1988, *20*(1), pp. 41–62.

_____. Tax Rates, Deficits, and Intertemporal Efficiency. *Public Finance Quart.*, July 1988, *16*(3), pp. 374–84.

Aschheim, Joseph and Tavlas, George S. Econometric Modelling of Partial Adjustment: The Cochrane–Orcutt Procedure, Flaws and Remedies. *Econ. Modelling*, January 1988, *5*(1), pp. 2–8.

Asefa, Sisay. World Food and Agriculture: Economic Problems and Issues: Introduction. In *Asefa, S., ed.*, 1988, pp. 1–8.

Asencio, Diego C. Brazil and the United States: Friendly Competitors. In *Chacel, J. M.; Falk, P. S. and Fleischer, D. V., eds.*, 1988, pp. 247–51.

Ashburn, Anderson. The Machine Tool Industry: The Crumbling Foundation. In *Hicks, D. A., ed.*, 1988, pp. 19–85.

Ashcroft, Brian K. External Takeovers in Scottish Manufacturing: The Effect on Local Linkages and Corporate Functions. *Scot. J. Polit. Econ.*, May 1988, *35*(2), pp. 129–48.

_____ and Love, J. H. The Regional Interest in UK Mergers Policy. *Reg. Stud.*, August 1988, *22*(4), pp. 341–44.

Asheghian, Parviz. Currency Devaluation: A Comparative Analysis of Advanced Countries and Less Developed Countries. *Quart. Rev. Econ. Bus.*, Summer 1988, *28*(2), pp. 61–70.

_____ and Foote, William G. Exchange Rate Devaluation: A Monetary Model and Empirical Investigation. *Eastern Econ. J.*, April–June 1988, *14*(2), pp. 181–87.

Asheim, Geir B. Rawlsian Intergenerational Justice as a Markov-Perfect Equilibrium in a Resource Technology. *Rev. Econ. Stud.*, July 1988, *55*(3), pp. 469–83.

Asher, Cheryl C. The Impact of Market Structure and Hospital Ownership on Price Competition among Hospitals. In *Pennsylvania Economic Association*, 1988, pp. 574–90.

Asher, Martin A. Saving Propensities and the Functional Distribution of Income. In *Pennsylvania Economic Association*, 1988, pp. 8–18.

Ashley, Richard. On the Relative Worth of Recent Macroeconomic Forecasts. *Int. J. Forecasting*, 1988, *4*(3), pp. 363–76.

Ashmead, Ralph. The Impact of Financial Stress on Agricultural Financial Intermediation: Performance and Opportunity. *Can. J. Agr. Econ.*, Part 2, December 1988, *36*(4), pp. 813–19.

Ashmore, P. E. and Day, T. J. Effective Discharge for Suspended Sediment Transport in Streams of the Saskatchewan River Basin. *Water Resources Res.*, June 1988, *24*(6), pp. 864–70.

Ashton, Alison Hubbard and Ashton, Robert H. Sequential Belief Revision in Auditing. *Accounting Rev.*, October 1988, *63*(4), pp. 623–41.

Ashton, D. J. Brokers' Recommendations—A Significant Result. *Econ. J.*, September 1988, *98*(392), pp. 844–50.

Ashton, Paul; Peel, Michael and Minford, Patrick. The Effects of Housing Distortions on Unemployment. *Oxford Econ. Pap.*, June 1988, *40*(2), pp. 322–45.

Ashton, Robert H. and Ashton, Alison Hubbard. Sequential Belief Revision in Auditing. *Accounting Rev.*, October 1988, *63*(4), pp. 623–41.

Ashtor, E. Catalan Cloth on the Late Medieval Mediterranean Markets. *J. Europ. Econ. Hist.*, Fall 1988, *17*(2), pp. 227–57.

Ashworth, Gregory. Marketing the Historic City for Tourism. In *Goodall, B. and Ashworth, G., eds.*, 1988, pp. 162–75.

_____ **and Goodall, Brian.** Tourist Images: Marketing Considerations. In *Goodall, B. and Ashworth, G., eds.*, 1988, pp. 213–38.

_____ **and Stabler, Michael J.** Tourism Development Planning in Languedoc: Le Mission Impossible? In *Goodall, B. and Ashworth, G., eds.*, 1988, pp. 187–97.

Ashworth, John. Local Government Finance. In *Darnell, A. and Evans, L., eds.*, 1988, pp. 118–34.

Asimakopulos, Athanasios. The Aggregate Supply Function and the Share Economy: Some Early Drafts of the *General Theory*. In *Hamouda, O. F. and Smithin, J. N., eds., Vol. 2*, 1988, pp. 70–80.

_____. Anticipations of Keynes's *General Theory*. In *Asimakopulos, A.*, 1988, *1983*, pp. 167–85.

_____. Investment, Employment and Income Distribution: Introduction: Kalecki, Keynes and Robinson. In *Asimakopulos, A.*, 1988, pp. 1–22.

_____. Joan Robinson and Economic Theory. In *Asimakopulos, A.*, 1988, *1984*, pp. 186–215.

_____. Kalecki and Keynes on Finance, Investment and Saving. In *Asimakopulos, A.*, 1988, *1983*, pp. 147–66.

_____. Kalecki on the Determinants of Profits. In *Asimakopulos, A.*, 1988, *1987*, pp. 77–99.

_____. A Kaleckian Theory of Income Distribution. In *Sawyer, M. C., ed.*, 1988, *1975*, pp. 377–97.

_____. A Kaleckian Theory of Income Distribution. In *Asimakopulos, A.*, 1988, *1975*, pp. 23–46.

_____. Keynes and Sraffa: Visions and Perspectives. In *Asimakopulos, A.*, 1988, *1985*, pp. 127–46.

_____. Keynes's Theory of Effective Demand Revisited. In *Asimakopulos, A.*, 1988, *1982*, pp. 100–126.

_____. Post-Keynesian Theories of Distribution. In *Asimakopulos, A., ed.*, 1988, pp. 133–57.

_____. Technical Progress, Market Forms and Unemployment. *Banca Naz. Lavoro Quart. Rev.*, September 1988, (166), pp. 293–310.

_____. Theories of Income Distribution: Introduction. In *Asimakopulos, A., ed.*, 1988, pp. 1–13.

_____ **and Burbidge, John B.** The Short-Period Incidence of Taxation. In *Asimakopulos, A.*, 1988, *1974*, pp. 47–76.

Askildsen, Jan Erik. Allocation of Capital and Labor in a Labor-Owned Firm Consisting of Het-

erogeneous Workers. *Scand. J. Econ.*, 1988, *90*(4), pp. 603–18.

_____; **Ireland, Norman J. and Law, Peter J.** Some Consequences of Differential Shareholdings among Members in a Labor-Managed and Labor-Owned Firm. In *Jones, D. C. and Svejnar, J., eds.*, 1988, pp. 65–81.

Aslanian, Carol B. Identifying Clients and Developing Program Contracts. In *Powers, D. R., et al.*, 1988, pp. 259–78.

_____. Providing Contract Training to Organizations. In *Powers, D. R., et al.*, 1988, pp. 243–58.

d'Aspremont, Claude and Jacquemin, Alexis. Cooperative and Noncooperative R&D in Duopoly with Spillovers. *Amer. Econ. Rev.*, December 1988, *78*(5), pp. 1133–37.

_____ **and Peleg, Bezalel.** Ordinal Bayesian Incentive Compatible Representations of Committees. *Soc. Choice Welfare*, November 1988, *5*(4), pp. 261–79.

Aspromourgos, Tony. The Life of William Petty in Relation to His Economics: A Tercentenary Interpretation. *Hist. Polit. Econ.*, Fall 1988, *20*(3), pp. 337–56.

Assemien, Alexandre. On Public Expenditure and Private Capital Accumulation: A Welfare Approach Using Sensitivity Analysis. *Metroecon.*, June 1988, *39*(2), pp. 141–59.

Asso, Pier Francesco and Barucci, Emilio. Ricardo on the National Debt and Its Redemption: Some Notes on an Unpublished Ricardian Manuscript. *Econ. Notes*, 1988, (2), pp. 5–36.

Assogba, Yao. Le paradigme interactionniste et le processus du développement communautaire: L'exemple des ONG en Afrique. (With English summary.) *Can. J. Devel. Stud.*, 1988, *9*(2), pp. 201–18.

Astakhov, Alexander S.; Denisov, Michail N. and Pavlov, Vladimir K. Prospecting and Exploration in the Soviet Union. In *Tilton, J. E.; Eggert, R. G. and Landsberg, H. H., eds.*, 1988, pp. 199–225.

Asteris, Michael. Britain's Seaports: Competition and Trans-shipment. *Nat. Westminster Bank Quart. Rev.*, February 1988, pp. 30–48.

Astin, Alexander W. and Inouye, Carolyn J. How Public Policy at the State Level Affects Private Higher Education Institutions. *Econ. Educ. Rev.*, 1988, *7*(1), pp. 47–63.

Atchabahian, Adolfo. Tax Reform Process: 1983–1987: Argentina. *Bull. Int. Fiscal Doc.*, February 1988, *42*(2), pp. 65–73, 77.

Aten, Robert H. The Effect of Federal, State and Local Tax Rates on Capital Gains: New York State's Experience: Discussion. *Nat. Tax J.*, September 1988, *41*(3), pp. 439–44.

Atesoglu, H. Sonmez. A Rational Expectations Model of Price and Wage Inflation for West Germany. *Weltwirtsch. Arch.*, 1988, *124*(3), pp. 480–89.

Athreya, M. B. Human Resource Development in the Service Sector. In *Kohli, U. and Gautam, V., eds.*, 1988, pp. 201–12.

Athukorala, Premachandra and Hazari, Bharat R. Market Penetration of Manufactured Imports from Developing Countries: The Australian Experience. *J. World Trade*, October 1988, 22(5), pp. 49–65.

_____ and Jayasuriya, Sisira K. Parentage and Factor Proportions: A Comparative Study of Third-World Multinationals in Sri Lankan Manufacturing. *Oxford Bull. Econ. Statist.*, November 1988, 50(4), pp. 409–23.

Atkins, Fiona. Land Reform: A Failure of Neoclassical Theorization? *World Devel.*, August 1988, 16(8), pp. 935–46.

Atkins, Frank and Serletis, Apostolos. The Low-Frequency Relationship between Money, Prices and Income. *Appl. Econ.*, July 1988, 20(7), pp. 877–87.

Atkinson, A. C. Least Median of Squares for Unmasking in Transformations and Multiple Regression. In *Fedorov, V. and Lauter, H., eds.*, 1988, pp. 97–105.

Atkinson, Anthony B. The Institute and the Microeconomics of Public Policy. *Nat. Inst. Econ. Rev.*, May 1988, (124), pp. 74–77.

_____. Redistribution, Inheritance, and Inequality: An Analysis of Transitions: Comments. In *Kessler, D. and Masson, A., eds.*, 1988, pp. 144–45.

_____; Bourguignon, François and Chiappori, Pierre-André. Fiscalité et transferts: Une comparaison franco–britannique. (Taxes and Benefits: A Franco–British Comparison. With English summary.) *Ann. Écon. Statist.*, July–Sept. 1988, (11), pp. 117–40.

_____; Bourguignon, François and Chiappori, Pierre André. What Do We Learn about Tax Reform from International Comparisons? France and Britain. *Europ. Econ. Rev.*, March 1988, 32(2–3), pp. 343–52.

_____; Bourguignon, François and Morrisson, Christian. Earnings Mobility. *Europ. Econ. Rev.*, March 1988, 32(2–3), pp. 619–32.

_____ and Leape, J. I. The Economic Analysis of Tax Reform: Introduction. *Europ. Econ. Rev.*, March 1988, 32(2–3), pp. 319–24.

Atkinson, Scott E.; Stanley, Linda R. and Tschirhart, John. Revenue Sharing as an Incentive in an Agency Problem: An Example from the National Football League. *Rand J. Econ.*, Spring 1988, 19(1), pp. 27–43.

Atoda, Naosumi; Suruga, Terukazu and Tachibanaki, Toshiaki. Statistical Inference of Functional Forms for Income Distribution. *Econ. Stud. Quart.*, March 1988, 39(1), pp. 14–40.

Attali, Jacques. The Costs of Changing the International Monetary System. In *Feldstein, M., ed. (I)*, 1988, pp. 147–51.

Attanasio, Orazio P. and Marini, Giancarlo. Countercyclical Policy and the Phillips Curve. Some Evidence for OECD Countries. *Econ. Notes*, 1988, (3), pp. 51–68.

_____ and van der Ploeg, Frederick. Real Effects of Demand- and Supply-Side Policies in Interdependent Economies. *Econ. Modelling*, April 1988, 5(2), pp. 151–64.

Attaran, Mohsen and Saghafi, Massoud M. Concentration Trends and Profitability in the U.S.

Manufacturing Sector: 1970–84. *Appl. Econ.*, November 1988, 20(11), pp. 1497–1510.

Attiga, Ali A. The Role of Energy in South–South Co-operation. In *Sopiee, N.; Hamzah, B. A. and Leong, C. H., eds.*, 1988, 1983, pp. 349–71.

Attwood, Donald W. Social and Political Pre-conditions for Successful Co-operatives: The Co-operative Sugar Factories of Western India. In *Attwood, D. W. and Baviskar, B. S., eds.*, 1988, pp. 69–90.

_____ and Baviskar, B. S. Who Shares? Co-operatives and Rural Development: Introduction. In *Attwood, D. W. and Baviskar, B. S., eds.*, 1988, pp. 1–20.

Atwater, H. B., Jr. From the Club of Rome to Agricultural Surplus: The Dramatic Reversal in World Agricultural Trade. In *Feldstein, M., ed. (II)*, 1988, pp. 460–68.

Atwood, Joseph A.; Watts, Myles J. and Helmers, Glenn A. Chance-Constrained Financing as a Response to Financial Risk. *Amer. J. Agr. Econ.*, February 1988, 70(1), pp. 79–89.

_____, et al. Incorporating Safety-First Constraints in Linear Programming Production Models. *Western J. Agr. Econ.*, July 1988, 13(1), pp. 29–36.

Aubert, Claude. China's Food Take-Off. In *Feuchtwang, S.; Hussain, A. and Pairault, T., eds., Vol. 1*, 1988, pp. 101–36.

_____. The New Economic Policy in the Chinese Countryside. In *Brada, J. C. and Wadekin, K.-E., eds.*, 1988, pp. 271–97.

Aubin, Christian, et al. The Growth of Public Expenditure in France. In *Lybeck, J. A. and Henrekson, M., eds.*, 1988, pp. 201–30.

Auburn, Jill Shore; Watt, Kenneth E. F. and Craig, Paul. World Economic Modeling. In *Ehrlich, P. R. and Holdren, J. P., eds.*, 1988, pp. 233–55.

Audretsch, David B. An Evaluation of Japanese R&D and Industrial Policies. *Aussenwirtschaft*, June 1988, 43(1/2), pp. 231–58.

_____. Divergent Views in Antitrust Economics. *Antitrust Bull.*, Spring 1988, 33(1), pp. 135–60.

_____ and Acs, Zoltan J. Innovation in Large and Small Firms: An Empirical Analysis. *Amer. Econ. Rev.*, September 1988, 78(4), pp. 678–90.

_____ and Acs, Zoltan J. Small-Firm Mobility: A First Report. *Econ. Letters*, 1988, 26(3), pp. 281–84.

_____ and Acs, Zoltan J. Testing the Schumpeterian Hypothesis. *Eastern Econ. J.*, April–June 1988, 14(2), pp. 129–40.

_____ and Yamawaki, Hideki. Import Share under International Oligopoly with Differentiated Products: Japanese Imports in U.S. Manufacturing. *Rev. Econ. Statist.*, November 1988, 70(4), pp. 569–79.

_____ and Yamawaki, Hideki. R&D Rivalry, Industrial Policy, and U.S.–Japanese Trade. *Rev. Econ. Statist.*, August 1988, 70(3), pp. 438–47.

Auerbach, Alan J. Capital Gains Taxation in the

United States: Realizations, Revenue, and Rhetoric. *Brookings Pap. Econ. Act.*, 1988, (2), pp. 595–631.

_____. Corporate Takeovers: Causes and Consequences: Introduction. In *Auerbach, A. J., ed. (I)*, 1988, pp. 1–7.

_____. The Effects of Jurisdiction Types and Numbers on Local Public Finance: Comment. In *Rosen, H. S., ed.*, 1988, pp. 103–06.

_____. Mergers and Acquisitions: Introduction. In *Auerbach, A. J., ed. (II)*, 1988, pp. 1–3.

_____. Should Interest Deductions Be Limited? In *Aaron, H. J.; Galper, H. and Pechman, J. A., eds.*, 1988, pp. 195–221.

_____ and Ando, Albert. The Corporate Cost of Capital in Japan and the United States: A Comparison. In *Shoven, J. B., ed.*, 1988, pp. 21–49.

_____ and Ando, Albert. The Cost of Capital in the United States and Japan: A Comparison. *J. Japanese Int. Economies*, June 1988, 2(2), pp. 134–58.

_____ and Hines, James R., Jr. Investment Tax Incentives and Frequent Tax Reforms. *Amer. Econ. Rev.*, May 1988, 78(2), pp. 211–16.

_____ and Poterba, James M. Why Have Corporate Tax Revenues Declined? In *Helpman, E.; Razin, A. and Sadka, E., eds.*, 1988, pp. 33–49.

_____ and Reishus, David. The Effects of Taxation on the Merger Decision. In *Auerbach, A. J., ed. (I)*, 1988, pp. 157–83.

_____ and Reishus, David. The Impact of Taxation on Mergers and Acquisitions. In *Auerbach, A. J., ed. (II)*, 1988, pp. 69–85.

_____ and Reishus, David. Taxes and the Merger Decision. In *Coffee, J. C., Jr.; Lowenstein, L. and Rose-Ackerman, S., eds.*, 1988, pp. 300–313.

Auerbach, P. and Rostowski, Jacek. Intra-year Fluctuations in Production and Sales: East and West. In *[Nove, A.]*, 1988, pp. 82–111.

Aukes, Robert G. Double Counting Agricultural Income: A Reply. *Can. J. Agr. Econ.*, July 1988, 36(2), pp. 357–58.

Auld, Douglas A. L. and Wilton, David A. The Impact of Progressive Income Tax Rates on Canadian Negotiated Wage Rates. *Can. J. Econ.*, May 1988, 21(2), pp. 279–84.

Ault, D. E. and Rutman, G. L. The 'Tragedy of the Commons' and Livestock Farming in Southern Africa: A Comment. *S. Afr. J. Econ.*, June–Sept. 1988, 56(2–3), pp. 212–17.

Ault, Eric B. CPCS's Voluntary Standards: An Assessment and a Paradox. In *Maynes, E. S. and ACCI Research Committee, eds.*, 1988, pp. 77–81.

Ault, Richard W. and Ekelund, Robert B., Jr. Habits in Economic Analysis: Veblen and the Neoclassicals. *Hist. Polit. Econ.*, Fall 1988, 20(3), pp. 431–45.

_____ and Ekelund, Robert B., Jr. Rent Seeking in a Static Model of Zoning. *Amer. Real Estate Urban Econ. Assoc. J.*, Spring 1988, 16(1), pp. 69–76.

_____; Kaserman, David L. and Barnett, Andy

H. The Rising Incidence of Co-authorship in Economics: Further Evidence. *Rev. Econ. Statist.*, August 1988, 70(3), pp. 539–43.

_____ and Saba, Richard P. Portfolio Choice with Investor Specific Transaction Costs. *Southern Econ. J.*, April 1988, 54(4), pp. 1012–19.

Aumann, Robert J. and Myerson, Roger B. Endogenous Formation of Links between Players and of Coalitions: An Application of the Shapley Value. In *[Shapley, L. S.]*, 1988, pp. 175–91.

Aura, Matti. Kan Skattereformen genmföras? (Can the Tax Reform Be Realized? With English summary.) *Ekon. Samfundets Tidskr.*, 1988, 41(1), pp. 23–24.

Auster, Ellen R. Owner and Organizational Characteristics of Black- and White-Owned Businesses: Self-Employed Blacks Had Less Training, Fewer Resources, Less Profits, but Had Similar Survival Rates. *Amer. J. Econ. Soc.*, July 1988, 47(3), pp. 331–44.

Ausubel, Jesse H. and Herman, Robert. Cities and Infrastructure: Synthesis and Perspectives. In *Ausubel, J. H. and Herman, R., eds.*, 1988, pp. 1–21.

Autenne, Jacques and de Lame, Jean. Traitement fiscal du logiciel dans l'informatique: Belgique. (Tax Treatment of Computer Software: Belgium. With English summary.) In *International Fiscal Association, ed. (II)*, 1988, pp. 221–40.

d'Autume, Antoine. La production jointe: Le point de vue de la théorie de l'équilibre général. (Joint Production and General Equilibrium Theory. With English summary.) *Revue Écon.*, March 1988, 39(2), pp. 325–47.

_____. Non-Walrasian Equilibria and Macroeconomics. In *Barrère, A., ed.*, 1988, pp. 66–92.

Auty, Richard M. The Economic Stimulus from Resource-Based Industry in Developing Countries: Saudi Arabia and Bahrain. *Econ. Geogr.*, July 1988, 64(3), pp. 209–25.

Auvert, Bertran; Bertrand, William E. and Arminana, Ruben. Microcomputer Applications in the Health and Social Service Sectors of Developing Countries. In *Bhalla, A. S. and James, D., eds.*, 1988, pp. 127–36.

Avdoulos, A.; Locker, H. Krijnse and Gerardi, D. Some Experiments with Phase IV ICP-Data. In *Salazar-Carrillo, J. and Rao, D. S. P., eds.*, 1988, pp. 93–112.

Aven, Petr O. The Distribution Mechanism and Social Justice. *Prob. Econ.*, April 1988, 30(12), pp. 43–58.

_____ and Shironin, V. M. The Reform of the Economic Mechanism. *Prob. Econ.*, June 1988, 31(2), pp. 33–48.

Averitt, Robert T. The Prospects for Economic Dualism: A Historical Perspective. In *Farkas, G. and England, P., eds.*, 1988, pp. 23–42.

Avery, David and King, B. Frank. A Tale of Two Georgias. *Fed. Res. Bank Atlanta Econ. Rev.*, Jan.–Feb. 1988, 73(1), pp. 24–35.

Avery, Robert B.; Belton, Terrence M. and Goldberg, Michael A. Market Discipline in Regulating Bank Risk: New Evidence from the Capital Markets. *J. Money, Credit, Banking*, November 1988, *20*(4), pp. 597–610.

_____; **Elliehausen, Gregory E. and Kennickell, Arthur B.** Measuring Wealth with Survey Data: An Evaluation of the 1983 Survey of Consumer Finances. *Rev. Income Wealth*, December 1988, *34*(4), pp. 339–69.

Avio, Kenneth L. Measurement Errors and Capital Punishment. *Appl. Econ.*, September 1988, *20*(9), pp. 1253–62.

Avramovic, Dragoslav. Debt and Development: Developing-Country Debt Revisited: Facts, Theory, and Policy. In *Elliott, K. A. and Williamson, J., eds.*, 1988, pp. 107–48.

_____. The Debt Problem of Developing Countries and Proposed Solutions: Rejoinder. In *Elliott, K. A. and Williamson, J., eds.*, 1988, pp. 168–71.

_____. Financial Co-operation among Developing Countries: Issues and Opportunities. In *Sopiee, N.; Hamzah, B. A. and Leong, C. H., eds.*, 1988, *1983*, pp. 215–31.

_____. The Role of Primary Commodities in Economic Co-operation among Developing Countries. In *Sopiee, N.; Hamzah, B. A. and Leong, C. H., eds.*, 1988, pp. 167–82.

_____. South–South Co-operation: Challenges and Opportunities. In *Sopiee, N.; Hamzah, B. A. and Leong, C. H., eds.*, 1988, pp. 39–58.

Aw, Bee Yan and Roberts, Mark J. Price and Quality Level Comparisons for U.S. Footwear Imports: An Application of Multilateral Index Numbers. In *Feenstra, R. C., ed.*, 1988, pp. 257–75.

Awad, M. Hashim. State, Foreign Aid and Cooperatives: The Sudanese Cooperative Development Bank Approach. In *Hedlund, H., ed.*, 1988, pp. 93–108.

Awartani, Hisham. Agricultural Development and Policies in the West Bank and Gaza. In *Abed, G. T., ed.*, 1988, pp. 139–64.

Awerbuch, Patricia; Makarim, Wajdi and Verzilli, Andrew G. Frustration Equilibrium and Disequilibrium Positions: Has Anything Changed in Eight Years? In *Pennsylvania Economic Association*, 1988, pp. 32–43.

Awerbuch, Shimon. Accounting Rates of Return: Comment. *Amer. Econ. Rev.*, June 1988, *78*(3), pp. 581–87.

Awusabo-Asare, Kofi. Interpretations of Demographic Concepts: The Case of Ghana. *Population Devel. Rev.*, December 1988, *14*(4), pp. 675–87.

Axelrod, Robert. The Problem of Cooperation. In *Cowen, T., ed.*, 1988, *1984*, pp. 237–54.

Axline, Larry L. Strategic People Planning. In *Timpe, A. D., ed.*, 1988, *1984*, pp. 29–32.

Axline, W. Andrew. Regional Co-operation and National Security: External Forces in Caribbean Integration. *J. Common Market Stud.*, September 1988, *27*(1), pp. 1–25.

Ayadi, Mohamed. Choix entre diverses spécifications pour l'étude de la demande agrégée des produits agro-alimentaires en Tunisie. (With English summary.) *L'Actual. Econ.*, June 1988, *64*(2), pp. 157–77.

Ayal, Eliezer B. Behavioural Variability in Migration. In *Maital, S., ed., Vol. 1*, 1988, pp. 303–16.

Ayanian, Robert. Political Risk, National Defense and the Dollar. *Econ. Inquiry*, April 1988, *26*(2), pp. 345–51.

Ayata, Sencer. Kasabada Zenaat Üretimi ve Toplumsal Tabakalaşma (Buldan). (Hand-Loom Cloth-Weaving Industry and Social Stratification in Buldan. With English summary.) *METU*, 1988, *15*(1–2), pp. 49–72.

Aydalot, Philippe. Technological Trajectories and Regional Innovation in Europe. In *Aydalot, P. and Keeble, D., eds.*, 1988, pp. 22–47.

_____ **and Keeble, David.** High-Technology Industry and Innovative Environments in Europe: An Overview. In *Aydalot, P. and Keeble, D., eds.*, 1988, pp. 1–21.

Aydogan, Kursat and Booth, G. Geoffrey. Are There Long Cycles in Common Stock Returns? *Southern Econ. J.*, July 1988, *55*(1), pp. 141–49.

Aylen, Jonathan. Privatisation of the British Steel Corporation. *Fisc. Stud.*, August 1988, *9*(3), pp. 1–25.

_____. Privatization in Developing Countries. In *Johnson, C., ed.*, 1988, *1987*, pp. 124–38.

Ayodele, A. I.; Diejomaoh, V. P. and Adeniyi, E. O. The Development Planning Experience in Nigeria: Effectiveness, Problems, and Prospects. In *Urrutia, M. and Yukawa, S., eds. (I)*, 1988, pp. 227–62.

Ayres, Clarence E. The Co-ordinates of Institutionalism. In *Samuels, W. J., ed., Vol. 1*, 1988, *1951*, pp. 9–17.

_____. Moral Confusion in Economics. In *Samuels, W. J., ed., Vol. 2*, 1988, *1934*, pp. 20–49.

_____. A New Look at Institutionalism: Discussion. In *Samuels, W. J., ed., Vol. 1*, 1988, *1957*, pp. 51–52.

Ayres, Ian. Determinants of Airline Carrier Conduct. *Int. Rev. Law Econ.*, December 1988, *8*(2), pp. 187–202.

Ayres, Robert U. Optimal Investment Policies with Exhaustible Resources: An Information-Based Model. *J. Environ. Econ. Manage.*, December 1988, *15*(4), pp. 439–61.

Ayuk, Elias T. and Ruppel, Fred J. Cotton Exports: Analysis of the Relationships between Sales and Shipments. *Southern J. Agr. Econ.*, July 1988, *20*(1), pp. 159–69.

Azabou, Mongi and Nugent, Jeffrey B. Contractual Choice in Tax Collection Activities: Some Implications of the Experience with Tax Farming. *J. Inst. Theoretical Econ.*, September 1988, *144*(4), pp. 684–705.

Azam, Jean-Paul. Un modèle néo-structuraliste d'inflation et chômage. (With English summary.) *Revue Écon. Polit.*, Jan.–Feb. 1988, *98*(1), pp. 78–89.

Azariadis, Costas. Human Capital and Self-Enforcing Contracts. *Scand. J. Econ.*, 1988, *90*(4), pp. 507–28.

_____. Imperfect Markets in Macroeconomics.

Econ. Stud. Quart., September 1988, *39*(3), pp. 193–207.

_____ and Allen, Beth. Informational Theories of Employment. *Amer. Econ. Rev.*, May 1988, *78*(2), pp. 104–09.

Azcarraga, Alvaro. The Two Way Street: How Earth Based Technologies Are Put to Work for Space Research. In *Egan, J. J., et al.*, 1988, pp. 331–45.

Azhar, Rauf A. The Economic Rate of Return in Small and Household Manufacturing Industries: Comments. *Pakistan Devel. Rev.*, Part 2, Winter 1988, *27*(4), pp. 884–85.

_____. Education and Technical Efficiency in Pakistan's Agriculture. *Pakistan Devel. Rev.*, Part 2, Winter 1988, *27*(4), pp. 687–95.

Aziz, Naheed. Households Headed by Women: Income, Employment and Household Organization: Comments. *Pakistan Devel. Rev.*, Part 2, Winter 1988, *27*(4), pp. 788–90.

Aziz, Sartaj. A Turning Point in Pakistan's Rural Development Strategy. In *Lewis, J. P., et al.*, 1988, pp. 111–20.

Azpiazú, Daniel and Kosacoff, Bernardo. Exports and Industrialization in Argentina, 1973–1986. *CEPAL Rev.*, December 1988, (36), pp. 61–81.

Baack, Ben and Ray, Edward John. Federal Transfer Payments in America: Veterans' Pensions and the Rise of Social Security. *Econ. Inquiry*, October 1988, *26*(4), pp. 687–702.

_____ and Ray, Edward John. Special Interests and the Nineteenth-Century Roots of the U.S. Military–Industrial Complex. In *Uselding, P. J., ed.*, 1988, pp. 153–69.

Baade, Robert A. and Dye, Richard F. An Analysis of the Economic Rationale for Public Subsidization of Sports Stadiums. *Ann. Reg. Sci.*, July 1988, *22*(2), pp. 37–47.

Babai, Don. The World Bank and the IMF: Rolling Back the State or Backing Its Role? In *Vernon, R., ed.*, 1988, pp. 254–85.

Babb, Emerson M. Assessing Opportunities in Food and Fiber Processing and Distribution: Discussion. *Amer. J. Agr. Econ.*, May 1988, *70*(2), pp. 480–81.

_____ and Long, Burl F. Alternative Enterprises for Strengthening Southern Agriculture. In *Beaulieu, L. J., ed.*, 1988, pp. 344–57.

Babb, Florence E. "From the Field to the Cooking Pot": Economic Crisis and the Threat to Marketers in Peru. In *Clark, G., ed.*, 1988, pp. 17–40.

Babbel, David F. Interest Rate Dynamics and the Term Structure: Note. *J. Banking Finance*, September 1988, *12*(3), pp. 401–17.

_____ and Klock, David R. Insurance Pedagogy: Executive Opinions and Priorities. *J. Risk Ins.*, December 1988, *55*(4), pp. 701–12.

Babula, Ronald A. and Penson, John B., Jr. Japanese Monetary Policies and U.S. Agricultural Exports. *J. Agr. Econ. Res.*, Winter 1988, *40*(1), pp. 11–18.

Baccouche, Rafiq and Laisney, François. Évaluation de six propositions de réforme de la TVA sur données microéconomiques. (With English summary.) *L'Actual. Econ.*, June 1988, *64*(2), pp. 178–208.

Băcescu, M. and Tamaş, I. An Efficient Method of Carrying Out Data Bases. *Econ. Computat. Cybern. Stud. Res.*, 1988, *23*(3), pp. 63–74.

Bach, Christopher L. U.S. International Transactions, Fourth Quarter and Year 1987. *Surv. Curr. Bus.*, March 1988, *68*(3), pp. 27–59.

Bacha, Edmar L. The Debt Problem of Developing Countries and Proposed Solutions: Comments. In *Elliott, K. A. and Williamson, J., eds.*, 1988, pp. 172–75.

_____. Escaping Confrontation: Latin America's Debt Crisis in the Late 1980s. In *Borner, S., ed.*, 1988, pp. 38–51.

_____. Latin America's Debt: A Reform Proposal. In *Chacel, J. M.; Falk, P. S. and Fleischer, D. V., eds.*, 1988, pp. 21–26.

_____. Moeda, inércia e conflito: Reflexões sobre políticas de estabilização no Brasil. (With English summary.) *Pesquisa Planejamento Econ.*, April 1988, *18*(1), pp. 1–15.

Bachar, Vladislav. The Internationalization of Production and Economic Relations between the Two Systems. *Czech. Econ. Digest.*, April 1988, (2), pp. 30–46.

Bachman, Sara S.; Altman, Stuart H. and Beatrice, Dennis F. What Influences a State's Approach to Medicaid Reform? *Inquiry*, Summer 1988, *25*(2), pp. 243–50.

Bachmann, Laurie McGavin; von Stumm, Michael and Lawrence, William. Tracking Recent Trends in the International Market for Art Theft. *J. Cult. Econ.*, June 1988, *12*(1), pp. 51–71.

Back, Kerry. Structure of Consumption Sets and Existence of Equilibria in Infinite-Dimensional Spaces. *J. Math. Econ.*, 1988, *17*(1), pp. 89–99.

Backhaus, Jürgen G. and Krabbe, Jacob J. Henry George's Theory and an Application to Industrial Siting. *Int. J. Soc. Econ.*, 1988, *15*(3–4), pp. 103–19.

Backhouse, Roger E. The Value of Post Keynesian Economics: A Neoclassical Response to Harcourt and Hamouda. *Bull. Econ. Res.*, January 1988, *40*(1), pp. 35–41.

Backus, David; Devereux, Michael and Purvis, Douglas. A Positive Theory of Fiscal Policy in Open Economies. In *Frenkel, J. A., ed.*, 1988, pp. 173–91.

Badaracco, Joseph L., Jr. Changing Forms of the Corporation. In *Meyer, J. R. and Gustafson, J. M., eds.*, 1988, pp. 67–91.

Baden-Fuller, Charles and Stopford, John M. Regional-Level Competition in a Mature Industry: The Case of European Domestic Appliances. In *Dunning, J. and Robson, P., eds.*, 1988, pp. 71–90.

_____ and Stopford, John M. Restructuring Mature Industries: The Challenge for Europe. In *Urabe, K.; Child, J. and Kagono, T., eds.*, 1988, pp. 225–41.

Badger, Daniel B., Jr. International Cooperation during Oil Supply Disruptions: The Role of the International Energy Agency. In *Horwich, G. and Weimer, D. L., eds.*, 1988, pp. 1–16.

Bădin, V. and Baz, Dragomira. Acceptance Control of Production Homogeneity in a Nonsteady Manufacturing Process. *Econ. Computat. Cybern. Stud. Res.*, 1988, 23(3), pp. 87–94.

Badrinath, S. G. and Chatterjee, Sangit. On Measuring Skewness and Elongation in Common Stock Return Distributions: The Case of the Market Index. *J. Bus.*, October 1988, 61(4), pp. 451–72.

Bae, Hyung. Strategic Investment Determining Time of Entry. *Int. Econ. J.*, Spring 1988, 2(1), pp. 21–28.

Baecher, Charlotte M. The Role of Consumer Union (CU). In *Maynes, E. S. and ACCI Research Committee, eds.*, 1988, pp. 843–48.

Baeck, Louis. Political Economy as a Science. *Tijdschrift Econ. Manage.*, 1988, 33(1), pp. 35–54.

_____. Spanish Economic Thought: The School of Salamanca and the *Arbitristas. Hist. Polit. Econ.*, Fall 1988, 20(3), pp. 381–408.

Baer, Walt. Employee-Managed Work Redesign—New Quality of Work Life Developments. In *Timpe, A. D., ed.*, 1988, 1986, pp. 207–12.

Baesel, Jerome B. and McMillan, Henry. The Role of Demographic Factors in Interest Rate Forecasting. *Managerial Dec. Econ.*, September 1988, 9(3), pp. 187–95.

Baffes, John; Ames, Glenn C. W. and Haniotis, Tassos. The Demand and Supply of U.S. Agricultural Exports: The Case of Wheat, Corn, and Soybeans. *Southern J. Agr. Econ.*, December 1988, 20(2), pp. 45–55.

Bagai, O. P. Logical and Methodological Improvements in Statistical Education with Special Reference to India. In *Brown, R. C., ed.*, 1988, pp. 1–14.

Baggarly, A. L. and Embry, Olice H. The History and Genealogy of Georgia Federal Bank, FSB. In *Perkins, E. J., ed.*, 1988, pp. 256–72.

Baghestani, Hamid and Mott, Tracy. The Money Supply Process under Alternative Federal Reserve Operating Procedures: An Empirical Examination. *Southern Econ. J.*, October 1988, 55(2), pp. 485–93.

_____ **and Noori, Esmail.** On the Rationality of the Michigan Monthly Survey of Inflationary Expectations. *Econ. Letters*, 1988, 27(4), pp. 333–35.

Bagley, Bruce M. Colombia and the War on Drugs. *Foreign Aff.*, Fall 1988, 67(1), pp. 70–92.

Bagliano, Fabio-Cesare. Structural Stability, Short-run Dynamics and Long-run Solutions in Feedback Models. The Case of the Money Demand Function for Italy: 1964–1986. *Giorn. Econ.*, Nov.–Dec. 1988, 47(11–12), pp. 575–99.

Bagozzi, Richard P. and Silk, Alvin J. Reply [Recall, Recognition and the Measurement of Memory for Print Advertisements]. *Marketing Sci.*, Winter 1988, 7(1), pp. 99–102.

Bagwell, Kyle and Bernheim, B. Douglas. Is Everything Neutral? *J. Polit. Econ.*, April 1988, 96(2), pp. 308–38.

_____ **and Ramey, Garey.** Advertising and Limit Pricing. *Rand J. Econ.*, Spring 1988, 19(1), pp. 59–71.

Bagwell, Laurie Simon and Shoven, John B. Share Repurchases and Acquisitions: An Analysis of Which Firms Participate. In *Auerbach, A. J., ed. (I)*, 1988, pp. 191–213.

Bahl, Roy. The New Urban Fiscal Economics. In *Bell, M. E., ed.*, 1988, pp. 1–40.

_____ **and Duncombe, William.** State and Local Government Finances: Was There a Structural Break in the Reagan Years? *Growth Change*, Fall 1988, 19(4), pp. 30–48.

Bahmani-Oskooee, Mohsen. Exchange Rate Flexibility and the Speed of Adjustment. *Kyklos*, 1988, 41(1), pp. 35–49.

_____. Oil Price Shocks and Stability of the Demand for International Reserves. *J. Macroecon.*, Fall 1988, 10(4), pp. 633–41.

_____ **and Malixi, Margaret.** Exchange Rate Flexibility and the LDCs Demand for International Reserves. *J. Quant. Econ.*, July 1988, 4(2), pp. 317–28.

_____ **and Niroomand, Farhang.** On the Exchange-Rate Elasticity of the Demand for International Reserves: Some Evidence from Industrial Countries. *Weltwirtsch. Arch.*, 1988, 124(1), pp. 161–68.

Bahri, Sonia. Economic Relations with OPEC Countries: Not Only Oil. In *Lavigne, M., ed.*, 1988, pp. 145–69.

Baier, Vicki Eaton; March, James G. and Sætren, Harald. Implementation and Ambiguity. In *March, J. G.*, 1988, 1986, pp. 150–64.

Bailar, Barbara A. Statistical Practice and Research: The Essential Interactions. *J. Amer. Statist. Assoc.*, March 1988, 83(401), pp. 1–8.

Bailey, Derek T. Accounting in Socialist Countries: Introduction. In *Bailey, D. T., ed.*, 1988, pp. 1–18.

_____. Accounting in the USSR. In *Bailey, D. T., ed.*, 1988, pp. 133–56.

_____. Accounting under Socialism: An Overview. In *Bailey, D. T., ed.*, 1988, pp. 173–84.

_____. The Business of Accounting: East and West. In *Bailey, D. T., ed.*, 1988, pp. 19–40.

Bailey, Elizabeth E. Price–Service–Quality Diversity in Deregulated Airline Markets. In *Libecap, G., ed. (II)*, 1988, pp. 13–46.

_____ **and Williams, Jeffrey R.** Sources of Economic Rent in the Deregulated Airline Industry. *J. Law Econ.*, April 1988, 31(1), pp. 173–202.

Bailey, Martin J. Distortions, Incentives and Growth. In *Giersch, H., ed.*, 1988, pp. 226–34.

_____ **and Tavlas, George S.** Trade and Investment under Floating Rates: The U.S. Experience. *Cato J.*, Fall 1988, 8(2), pp. 421–42.

Bailey, R. E. and Hatton, T. J. Female Labour Force Participation in Interwar Britain. *Oxford*

Econ. Pap., December 1988, *40*(4), pp. 695–718.

Bailey, Ralph E. The Impact of Low Oil Prices on U.S. Energy Markets. In *Mabro, R., ed.,* 1988, pp. 61–68.

Bailey, Richard. Privatising Electricity in the United Kingdom—Problems in Store. *Nat. Westminster Bank Quart. Rev.*, November 1988, pp. 38–52.

_____. Third World Fisheries: Prospects and Problems. *World Devel.*, June 1988, *16*(6), pp. 751–57.

Bailey, Stephen J. Local Government Finance in Britain. In *Paddison, R. and Bailey, S., eds.,* 1988, pp. 230–53.

_____ **and Martlew, Clive.** A Poll Tax for Britain? In *Bailey, S. J. and Paddison, R., eds.,* 1988, pp. 75–91.

_____ **and Paddison, Ronan.** Local Government Finance: International Perspectives: Introduction. In *Paddison, R. and Bailey, S., eds.,* 1988, pp. 1–5.

_____ **and Paddison, Ronan.** Local Government Finance: International Perspectives: Conclusions. In *Paddison, R. and Bailey, S., eds.,* 1988, pp. 254–64.

_____ **and Paddison, Ronan.** The Reform of Local Government Finance in Britain: Conclusion. In *Bailey, S. J. and Paddison, R., eds.,* 1988, pp. 205–18.

_____ **and Paddison, Ronan.** The Reform of Local Government Finance in Britain: Introduction. In *Bailey, S. J. and Paddison, R., eds.,* 1988, pp. 1–5.

Bailey, Thomas R. Market Forces and Private Sector Processes in Government Policy: The Job Training Partnership Act. *J. Policy Anal. Manage.*, Winter 1988, *7*(2), pp. 300–15.

Bailey, Warren Bernard. Canada's Dual Class Shares: Further Evidence on the Market Value of Cash Dividends. *J. Finance*, December 1988, *43*(5), pp. 1143–60.

_____. Money Supply Announcements and the Ex Ante Volatility of Asset Prices. *J. Money, Credit, Banking*, November 1988, *20*(4), pp. 611–20.

Baily, Martin Neil and Blair, Margaret M. Productivity and American Management. In *Litan, R. E; Lawrence, R. Z. and Schultze, C. L., eds.,* 1988, pp. 178–214.

_____ **and Gordon, Robert J.** The Productivity Slowdown, Measurement Issues, and the Explosion of Computer Power. *Brookings Pap. Econ. Act.*, 1988, (2), pp. 347–420.

Bain, George Sayers and Edwards, P. K. Why Are Trade Unions Becoming More Popular? Unions and Public Opinion in Britain. *Brit. J. Ind. Relat.*, November 1988, *26*(3), pp. 311–26.

_____ **and Price, Robert.** British Social Trends since 1900: The Labour Force. In *Halsey, A. H., ed.,* 1988, pp. 162–201.

Bain, Keith and Howells, Peter. The Teaching of Money. *Brit. Rev. Econ. Issues*, Spring 1988, *10*(22), pp. 55–79.

Bairam, Erkin. Balance of Payments, the Harrod Foreign Trade Multiplier and Economic

Growth: The European and North American Experience, 1970–85. *Appl. Econ.*, December 1988, *20*(12), pp. 1635–42.

_____. Government Expenditure and Economic Growth: Reflections on Professor Ram's Approach, a New Framework and Some Evidence from New Zealand Time-Series Data. *Keio Econ. Stud.*, 1988, *25*(1), pp. 59–66.

_____. Technical Progress, Elasticity of Substitution and Returns to Scale in Branches of Soviet Industry: Some New Empirical Evidence Using Soviet Republic Data, 1961–74. *Manchester Sch. Econ. Soc. Stud.*, June 1988, *56*(2), pp. 103–17.

_____. The Variability of Inflation: A New Approach and Some New Empirical Evidence. *Econ. Letters*, 1988, *28*(4), pp. 327–29.

_____. Variable Elasticity of Substitution, Technical Change and Industrial Growth: The Rumanian Experience. *J. Quant. Econ.*, January 1988, *4*(1), pp. 123–31.

_____. Verdoorn's Law Once Again: Its Specification and Interpretation. *Indian Econ. J.*, Jan.–March 1988, *35*(3), pp. 30–38.

Baird, Charles W. The Varieties of 'Right to Work'. An Essay in Honor of W. H. Hutt. *Managerial Dec. Econ.*, Special Issue, Winter 1988, pp. 33–43.

Bajekal, Madhavi. The State and the Rural Grain Market in Eighteenth Century Eastern Rajasthan. *Indian Econ. Soc. Hist. Rev.*, Oct.–Dec. 1988, *25*(4), pp. 443–73.

Bajic, Vladimir. Market Shares and Price–Quality Relationships: An Econometric Investigation of the U.S. Automobile Market. *Southern Econ. J.*, April 1988, *54*(4), pp. 888–900.

Bakar, Kamuruddin Abu and Tottle, Graham P. Microcomputer Use by the Malaysian Rubber Industry Smallholders Development Authority. In *Bhalla, A. S. and James, D., eds.,* 1988, pp. 85–96.

Baker, George P.; Jensen, Michael C. and Murphy, Kevin J. Compensation and Incentives: Practice vs. Theory. *J. Finance*, July 1988, *43*(3), pp. 593–616.

Baker, James A. James Baker on a New Trade Policy Strategy for the United States. *World Econ.*, June 1988, *11*(2), pp. 215–16.

Baker, Jonathan B. The Antitrust Analysis of Hospital Mergers and the Transformation of the Hospital Industry. *Law Contemp. Probl.*, Spring 1988, *51*(2), pp. 93–164.

_____. Private Information and the Deterrent Effect of Antitrust Damage Remedies. *J. Law, Econ., Organ.*, Fall 1988, *4*(2), pp. 385–408.

_____ **and Bresnahan, Timothy F.** Estimating the Residual Demand Curve Facing a Single Firm. *Int. J. Ind. Organ.*, 1988, *6*(3), pp. 283–300.

Baker, Laurie and Thomassin, Paul J. Farm Ownership and Financial Stress. *Can. J. Agr. Econ.*, Part 2, December 1988, *36*(4), pp. 799–811.

Baker, Meredith and Dawkins, Peter. The Economic Effects of Shorter Standard Working Hours in the Construction Industry: Some

Case Study Evidence. *Australian Bull. Lab.*, June 1988, *14*(3), pp. 492–506.

Baker, Ralph E. and Meyer, Fred A., Jr. Neighbourhood Co-production of Protection: A Private Sector Response to Crime. In *Hula, R. C., ed.*, 1988, pp. 111–20.

Baker, Samuel H. and Archibald, Robert B. Aggregate Business Failures and Federal Credit Activity. *Public Finance Quart.*, April 1988, *16*(2), pp. 219–43.

Baker, Stuart G. and Laird, Nan M. Regression Analysis for Categorical Variables with Outcome Subject to Nonignorable Nonresponse. *J. Amer. Statist. Assoc.*, March 1988, *83*(401), pp. 62–69.

Baker, Timothy D.; Schumann, Debra and deCodes, Jose. The Hidden Costs of Illness in Developing Countries. In *Sirageldin, I. and Sorkin, A., eds.*, 1988, pp. 127–45.

Baker, Timothy G. and Leatham, David J. Farmers' Choice of Fixed and Adjustable Interest Rate Loans. *Amer. J. Agr. Econ.*, November 1988, *70*(4), pp. 803–12.

———; **Turvey, Calum Greig and Driver, H. C.** Systematic and Nonsystematic Risk in Farm Portfolio Selection. *Amer. J. Agr. Econ.*, November 1988, *70*(4), pp. 831–36.

Bakker, B. B. and Sterks, C. G. M. Optimal Legal Standards in Negligence-Based Liability Rules. *De Economist*, 1988, *136*(3), pp. 383–400.

Bakker, Isabella. Women's Employment in Comparative Perspective. In *Jenson, J.; Hagen, E. and Reddy, C., eds.*, 1988, pp. 17–44.

Bakshi, Heena R. and Saxena, R. B. IMF Conditionality—A Third World Perspective. *J. World Trade*, October 1988, *22*(5), pp. 67–79.

Bakx, Keith. From Proletarian to Peasant: Rural Transformation in the State of Acre, 1870–1986. *J. Devel. Stud.*, January 1988, *24*(2), pp. 141–60.

Balabkins, Nicholas Wolfgang. Factors Which Have Influenced Nigeria's Industrial Development. *Rivista Int. Sci. Econ. Com.*, January 1988, *35*(1), pp. 29–42.

———. Gunnar Myrdal (1898–1987): A Memorial Tribute. *Eastern Econ. J.*, Jan.–March 1988, *14*(1), pp. 99–106.

———. Schmoller in Tsarist Turssia. *J. Inst. Theoretical Econ.*, June 1988, *144*(3), pp. 581–90.

Balachandran, Kashi R. and Ronen, Joshua. An Approach to Transfer Pricing under Uncertainty. *J. Acc. Res.*, Autumn 1988, *26*(2), pp. 300–314.

Balassa, Bela. Agricultural Policies and International Resource Allocation. *Europ. Rev. Agr. Econ.*, 1988, *15*(2–3), pp. 159–71.

———. Agricultural Policies and International Resource Allocation. *J. Policy Modeling*, Summer 1988, *10*(2), pp. 249–63.

———. China's Economic Reforms in a Comparative Perspective. In *Reynolds, B. L., ed.*, 1988, *1987*, pp. 120–36.

———. The Debt Problem of Developing Countries and Proposed Solutions. In *Elliott, K. A. and Williamson, J., eds.*, 1988, pp. 149–68.

———. The Interaction of Factor and Product

Market Distortions in Developing Countries. *World Devel.*, April 1988, *16*(4), pp. 449–63.

———. Interest of Developing Countries in the Uruguay Round. *World Econ.*, March 1988, *11*(1), pp. 39–54.

———. The Lessons of East Asian Development: An Overview. *Econ. Develop. Cult. Change*, Supplement, April 1988, *36*(3), pp. S273–90.

———. The "New Growth Path" in Hungary. In *Brada, J. C. and Dobozi, I., eds.*, 1988, pp. 3–32.

———. Policy Choices for Developing Countries. *Indian Econ. Rev.*, Jan.–June 1988, *23*(1), pp. 27–43.

——— **and Bauwens, Luc.** The Determinants of Intra-European Trade in Manufactured Goods. *Europ. Econ. Rev.*, September 1988, *32*(7), pp. 1421–37.

——— **and Bauwens, Luc.** Inter-industry and Intra-industry Specialization in Manufactured Goods. *Weltwirtsch. Arch.*, 1988, *124*(1), pp. 1–13.

Balasubramanyam, V. N. Export Processing Zones in Developing Countries: Theory and Empirical Evidence. In *Greenaway, D., ed.*, 1988, pp. 157–65.

Balázs, Katalin. Market-Oriented Scientific Research and Development after the Economic Reform. *Acta Oecon.*, 1988, *39*(3–4), pp. 271–90.

Balcet, Giovanni. Italian Non-equity Ventures Abroad: Evidence from Field Interviews. In *Onida, F. and Viesti, G., eds.*, 1988, pp. 96–109.

Baldessari, Bruno and Gallo, Francesca. A Robustness Property of the Projection Pursuit Methods in Sampling from Separably Dependent Random Vectors. In *Edwards, D. and Raun, N. E., eds.*, 1988, pp. 65–70.

Baldone, Salvatore. From Surrogate to Pseudo Production Functions. In *Steedman, I., ed.*, Vol. 1, 1988, *1984*, pp. 91–108.

Baldry, Jonathan C. Wealth Effects and the Valuation of Common Access Facilities: Some Calculations. *Econ. Rec.*, June 1988, *64*(185), pp. 128–32.

Balducci, Renato. Frammentazione della rappresentanza sindacale ed efficacia delle politiche di spesa. (With English summary.) *Stud. Econ.*, 1988, *43*(35), pp. 33–64.

Baldwin, Carliss Y. and Mason, Scott P. Evaluation of Government Subsidies to Large-Scale Energy Projects: A Contingent Claims Approach. In *Fabozzi, F. J., ed.*, 1988, pp. 169–81.

Baldwin, Nick and Prosser, Richard. World Oil Market Simulation. *Energy Econ.*, July 1988, *10*(3), pp. 185–98.

Baldwin, Richard E. Evaluating Strategic Trade Policies. *Aussenwirtschaft*, June 1988, *43*(1/2), pp. 207–30.

———. Hyteresis in Import Prices: The Beachhead Effect. *Amer. Econ. Rev.*, September 1988, *78*(4), pp. 773–85.

——— **and Krugman, Paul R.** Industrial Policy and International Competition in Wide-Bodied

Jet Aircraft. **In** *Baldwin, R. E., ed. (II)*, 1988, pp. 45–71.

_____ **and Krugman, Paul R.** Market Access and International Competition: A Simulation Study of 16K Random Access Memories. **In** *Feenstra, R. C., ed.*, 1988, pp. 171–97.

Baldwin, Robert E. Alternative Liberalization Strategies. **In** *Baldwin, R. E., ed. (I)*, 1988, *1987*, pp. 245–64.

_____. An Introduction to the Issues and Analyses. **In** *Baldwin, R. E.; Hamilton, C. B. and Sapir, A., eds.*, 1988, pp. 1–13.

_____. The Case against Infant-Industry Tariff Protection. **In** *Baldwin, R. E., ed. (I)*, 1988, *1969*, pp. 148–59.

_____. The Changing Nature of US Trade Policy since World War II. **In** *Baldwin, R. E., ed. (I)*, 1988, *1984*, pp. 19–41.

_____. The Economics of the GATT. **In** *Baldwin, R. E., ed. (I)*, 1988, *1980*, pp. 137–47.

_____. The Inefficacy of Trade Policy. **In** *Baldwin, R. E., ed. (I)*, 1988, *1982*, pp. 160–78.

_____. The New Protectionism: A Response to Shifts in National Economic Power. **In** *Baldwin, R. E., ed. (I)*, 1988, *1986*, pp. 207–23.

_____. The Political Economy of Postwar U.S. Trade Policy. **In** *Baldwin, R. E., ed. (I)*, 1988, *1976*, pp. 42–72.

_____. The Political Economy of Protectionism. **In** *Baldwin, R. E., ed. (I)*, 1988, *1982*, pp. 97–120.

_____. Rent Seeking and Trade Policy: An Industry Approach. **In** *Baldwin, R. E., ed. (I)*, 1988, *1984*, pp. 121–36.

_____. Responding to Trade-Distorting Policies of Other Countries. **In** *Baldwin, R. E., ed. (I)*, 1988, *1984*, pp. 224–32.

_____. Toward More Efficient Procedures for Multilateral Trade Negotiations. **In** *Baldwin, R. E., ed. (I)*, 1988, *1986*, pp. 190–203.

_____. Trade and Employment Effects in the United States of Multilateral Tariff Reductions. **In** *Baldwin, R. E., ed. (I)*, 1988, *1976*, pp. 181–89.

_____. Trade Policies under the Reagan Administration. **In** *Baldwin, R. E., ed. (I)*, 1988, *1984*, pp. 73–94.

_____. Trade Policy in a Changing World Economy: Autobiographical Introduction. **In** *Baldwin, R. E., ed. (I)*, 1988, pp. 3–15.

_____. Trade Policy Issues and Empirical Analysis: Introduction. **In** *Baldwin, R. E., ed. (II)*, 1988, pp. 1–8.

_____. U.S. and Foreign Competition in the Developing Countries of the Asian Pacific Rim. **In** *Feldstein, M., ed. (II)*, 1988, pp. 79–141.

_____ **and Green, Richard K.** The Effects of Protection on Domestic Output. **In** *Baldwin, R. E., ed. (II)*, 1988, pp. 205–26.

Bale, Harvey E., Jr. A Computer and Electronics Industry Perspective. **In** *Walker, C. E. and Bloomfield, M. A., eds.*, 1988, pp. 119–25.

Bale, Malcolm and Conway, Patrick. Approximating the Effective Protection Coefficient without Reference to Technological Data. *World Bank Econ. Rev.*, September 1988, *2*(3), pp. 349–63.

Balestra, Pietro and Aigner, Dennis J. Optimal Experimental Design for Error Components Models. *Econometrica*, July 1988, *56*(4), pp. 955–71.

Balk, B. M. and Kersten, H. M. P. The Precision of Consumer Price Indices Caused by the Sampling Variability of Budget Surveys; An Example. **In** *Eichhorn, W., ed.*, 1988, pp. 49–58.

Balkan, Erol and Kahn, James R. The Value of Changes in Deer Hunting Quality: A Travel Cost Approach. *Appl. Econ.*, April 1988, *20*(4), pp. 533–39.

Ball, Clifford A. Estimation Bias Induced by Discrete Security Prices. *J. Finance*, September 1988, *43*(4), pp. 841–65.

_____ **and Torous, Walter N.** Investigating Security-Price Performance in the Presence of Event-Date Uncertainty. *J. Finan. Econ.*, October 1988, *22*(1), pp. 123–53.

Ball, Laurence. Is Equilibrium Indexation Efficient? *Quart. J. Econ.*, May 1988, *103*(2), pp. 299–311.

_____. Job Switching and Job Satisfaction in the U.S. Labor Market: Comment. *Brookings Pap. Econ. Act.*, 1988, (2), pp. 583–87.

_____ **and Cecchetti, Stephen G.** Imperfect Information and Staggered Price Setting. *Amer. Econ. Rev.*, December 1988, *78*(5), pp. 999–1018.

_____; **Mankiw, N. Gregory and Romer, David.** The New Keynesian Economics and the Output–Inflation Trade-off. *Brookings Pap. Econ. Act.*, 1988, (1), pp. 1–65.

Ball, Michael O. and Benoit-Thompson, Huguette. A Lagrangian Relaxation Based Heuristic for the Urban Transit Crew Scheduling Problem. **In** *Daduna, J. R. and Wren, A., eds.*, 1988, pp. 54–67.

Ball, Ray and Bowers, John. Daily Seasonals in Equity and Fixed-Interest Returns: Australian Evidence and Tests of Plausible Hypotheses. **In** *Dimson, E., ed.*, 1988, pp. 74–90.

Ball, Robert M. Future Sources of Retirement Income: Whither the Baby Boom: Comment. **In** *Wachter, S. M., ed.*, 1988, pp. 103–07.

Ball, V. Eldon. Modeling Supply Response in a Multiproduct Framework. *Amer. J. Agr. Econ.*, November 1988, *70*(4), pp. 813–25.

Ballance, Robert H. Trade Performance as an Indicator of Comparative Advantage. **In** *Greenaway, D., ed.*, 1988, pp. 6–24.

Ballantine, John W.; Cleveland, Frederick W. and Koeller, C. Timothy. Corporate Profitability and Competitive Circumstance. *Eastern Econ. J.*, Jan.–March 1988, *14*(1), pp. 7–18.

Ballantyne, Harry C. Actuarial Status of the OASI and DI Trust Funds. *Soc. Sec. Bull.*, June 1988, *51*(6), pp. 4–9.

Ballard, Charles L. The Marginal Efficiency Cost of Redistribution: *Amer. Econ. Rev.*, December 1988, *78*(5), pp. 1019–33.

Ballard, K. P. and Moghadam, K. Small Area Modeling of the Industrial Sector (SAMIS): An

Integrated Econometric–Interindustry Approach. *Environ. Planning A*, May 1988, *20*(5), pp. 655–68.

Balleau, W. P. Water Appropriation and Transfer in a General Hydrogeologic System. *Natural Res. J.*, Spring 1988, *28*(2), pp. 269–91.

Ballentine, J. Gregory. Should Interest Deductions Be Limited? Comments. In *Aaron, H. J.; Galper, H. and Pechman, J. A., eds.*, 1988, pp. 221–30.

Ballestero, Florencio and Thoumi, Francisco. The Instability of Intra-Latin American and Caribbean Exports and Exchange Rates. In *Jorge, A. and Salazar-Carrillo, J., eds.*, 1988, pp. 59–81.

Balmer, Pamela W.; Hill, Bette S. and Blaser, C. Jean. Practical Issues in Developing Competitive Contracting for Home Care Services. In *Hula, R. C., ed.*, 1988, pp. 84–95.

Balmert, Neil P. A Different Look at Deposit Insurance. In *Kemper, R. L., ed.*, 1988, pp. 35–75.

Balough, Robert S. Inflation and Related Misperceptions: Comments. In *Pennsylvania Economic Association*, 1988, pp. 103–04.

_____. Testing the Stability of Investment Expenditures Models. In *Pennsylvania Economic Association*, 1988, pp. 60–75.

Baltagi, Badi H. On the Efficiency of Two-Stage and Three-Stage Least Squares Estimators. *Econometric Rev.*, 1988–89, *7*(2), pp. 165–69.

_____ **and Griffin, James M.** A General Index of Technical Change. *J. Polit. Econ.*, February 1988, *96*(1), pp. 20–41.

_____ **and Griffin, James M.** A Generalized Error Component Model with Heteroscedastic Disturbances. *Int. Econ. Rev.*, November 1988, *29*(4), pp. 745–53.

Baltas, N. C. and Apostolou, N. A Rational Expectations Model for the Poultry Sector in Greece. *Appl. Econ.*, July 1988, *20*(7), pp. 917–27.

Baltensperger, Max. Integration der nationalen Geld- und Kapitalmärkte. (Integration of Financial Markets. With English summary.) *Aussenwirtschaft*, September 1988, *43*(3), pp. 385–97.

Balvany, Iris. Hungary and the Thirld World: A Specific Approach. In *Lavigne, M., ed.*, 1988, pp. 225–35.

Balvers, Ronald J. Money Supply Variability in a Macro Model of Monopolistic Competition. *Econ. Inquiry*, October 1988, *26*(4), pp. 661–85.

_____. Monopoly Power and Downward Price Rigidity under Costly Price Adjustment. *Bull. Econ. Res.*, April 1988, *40*(2), pp. 115–31.

_____; **McDonald, Bill and Miller, Robert E.** Underpricing of New Issues and the Choice of Auditor as a Signal of Investment Banker Reputation. *Accounting Rev.*, October 1988, *63*(4), pp. 605–22.

Balzer, Harley D. The Soviet Union Today: Education, Science, and Technology. In *Cracraft, J., ed.*, 1988, pp. 245–57.

Bamber, E. Michael and Snowball, Doug. An Experimental Study of the Effects of Audit Structure in Uncertain Task Environments. *Accounting Rev.*, July 1988, *63*(3), pp. 490–504.

Bamberg, Günter and Richter, Wolfram F. Risk-Taking under Progressive Taxation: Three Partial Effects. In *Eichhorn, W., ed.*, 1988, pp. 479–97.

Bamberger, Ingolf. Stratégies et structures: Une analyse de leurs relations dans la perspective des nouveaux développements en théorie stratégique. (Strategy and Structure. A Study of Their Relationships from the Perspective of New Developments in Strategic Theory. With English summary.) *Écon. Soc.*, August 1988, *22*(8), pp. 7–23.

Bamfield, Joshua. Competition and Change in British Retailing. *Nat. Westminster Bank Quart. Rev.*, February 1988, pp. 15–29.

Banai-Kashani, Reza. A Note on the Subregional Employment Impact of Urban Revitalization. *Rev. Reg. Stud.*, Fall 1988, *18*(3), pp. 41–46.

Banaian, King. Models of the Political Process and Their Implications for Stagflation: A Public Choice Perspective: Appendix: An Overview of Political Business Cycle Models. In *Willett, T. D., ed.*, 1988, pp. 116–28.

_____ **and Willett, Thomas D.** Explaining the Great Stagflation: Toward a Political Economy Framework. In *Willett, T. D., ed.*, 1988, pp. 35–62.

_____ **and Willett, Thomas D.** Legislation and Political Business Cycles: Comment. *Kyklos*, 1988, *41*(3), pp. 507–11.

_____ **and Willett, Thomas D.** Models of the Political Process and Their Implications for Stagflation: A Public Choice Perspective. In *Willett, T. D., ed.*, 1988, pp. 100–116.

_____, **et al.** Subordinating the Fed to Political Authorities Will Not Control Inflationary Tendencies. In *Willett, T. D., ed.*, 1988, pp. 491–505.

Bance, Philippe. Approche méthodologique de l'économie mixte. Propriétés et comportements. (A Methodological Approach to the Mixed Economy: Properties and Behavior. With English summary.) *Ann. Pub. Co-op. Econ.*, Oct.–Dec. 1988, *59*(4), pp. 411–54.

_____. Sur l'approche matricielle des rapports de propriété et la thé orie du contrôle. (On the Matrix Approach of Property Relations and the Control Theory. With English summary.) *Revue Écon.*, March 1988, *39*(2), pp. 421–40.

Bandow, Doug. Making Friends in the Third World. In *Boaz, D., ed.*, 1988, pp. 143–54.

de Bandt, Jacques and Boussemart, Benoît. The European Textile Industries: Widely Varying Structures. In *de Jong, H. W., ed.*, 1988, pp. 183–209.

Bandyopadhyay, J. and Shiva, V. The Chipko Movement. In *Ives, J. and Pitt, D. C., eds.*, 1988, pp. 224–41.

Bandyopadhyay, Suraj and Von Eschen, Donald. Villager Failure to Co-operate: Some Evidence from West Bengal, India. In *Attwood, D. W. and Baviskar, B. S., eds.*, 1988, pp. 112–45.

Bandyopadhyay, Taradas. Extension of an Order

on a Set to the Power Set: Some Further Observations. *Math. Soc. Sci.*, February 1988, *15*(1), pp. 81–85.

_____. Revealed Preference Theory, Ordering and the Axiom of Sequential Path Independence. *Rev. Econ. Stud.*, April 1988, *55*(2), pp. 343–51.

Banerjee, Anindya and Dolado, Juan. Tests of the Life Cycle-Permanent Income Hypothesis in the Presence of Random Walks: Asymptotic Theory and Small-Sample Interpretations. *Oxford Econ. Pap.*, December 1988, *40*(4), pp. 610–33.

Banerjee, K. S. On the Factorial Approach to Index Number Problems, Consumption Analysis and Orthogonal Decomposition of National Income: A Review. In *Eichhorn, W., ed.*, 1988, pp. 59–66.

Banister, Judith and Hardee-Cleaveland, Karen. Fertility Policy and Implementation in China, 1986–88. *Population Devel. Rev.*, June 1988, *14*(2), pp. 245–86.

Bank, B. and Mandel, R. Quantitative Stability of (Mixed-) Integer Linear Optimization Problems. In *Kurzhanski, A.; Neumann, K. and Pallaschke, D., eds.*, 1988, pp. 3–15.

Banker, Rajiv D.; Datar, Srikant M. and Kekre, Sunder. Relevant Costs, Congestion and Stochasticity in Production Environments. *J. Acc. Econ.*, July 1988, *10*(3), pp. 171–97.

_____ and Maindiratta, Ajay. Nonparametric Analysis of Technical and Allocative Efficiencies in Production. *Econometrica*, November 1988, *56*(6), pp. 1315–32.

_____, et al. A Comparison of DEA and Translog Estimates of Production Frontiers Using Simulated Observations from a Known Technology. In *Dogramaci, A. and Färe, R., eds.*, 1988, pp. 33–55.

Banks, Jeffrey S. and Bordes, G. A. Voting Games, Indifference, and Consistent Sequential Choice Rules. *Soc. Choice Welfare*, 1988, *5*(1), pp. 31–44.

_____; Plott, Charles R. and Porter, David P. An Experimental Analysis of Unanimity in Public Goods Provision Mechanisms. *Rev. Econ. Stud.*, April 1988, *55*(2), pp. 301–22.

Bansal, Ashok K. and Chakravarti, Sangeeta. Effect of Nonnormal Prior for Regression Parameter on Bayes Decisions and Forecasts. *J. Quant. Econ.*, July 1988, *4*(2), pp. 247–59.

Banting, Keith G. Federalism, Social Reform and the Spending Power. *Can. Public Policy*, Supplement, September 1988, *14*, pp. S81–92.

Baoping, Guo. Macroeconomic Dynamic Input–Output Control Model with Time-Delay Investment. *Econ. Computat. Cybern. Stud. Res.*, 1988, *23*(2), pp. 75–84.

Baptiste, Fitzroy André. The Exploitation of Caribbean Bauxite and Petroleum, 1914–1945. *Soc. Econ. Stud.*, March–June 1988, *37*(1–2), pp. 107–42.

Bar-Haim, Aviad. Workers' Participation and Personnel Policies in Israel. *Int. Lab. Rev.*, 1988, *127*(3), pp. 381–97.

Bar-Ilan, Avner and Blinder, Alan S. The Life Cycle Permanent-Income Model and Consumer Durables. *Ann. Écon. Statist.*, Jan.–March 1988, (9), pp. 71–91.

Bar-On, Dan and Niv, Amittai. The Transition from a "Simple" Industry to a "Sophisticated" One in the Future Kibbutz. In *Maital, S., ed., Vol. 1*, 1988, pp. 357–75.

Bar-Yosef, Sasson and Landskroner, Yoram. Government Subsidies and the Value of the Firm. *Managerial Dec. Econ.*, March 1988, *9*(1), pp. 41–47.

Barahona, Pablo; Valdés, Alberto and Quiroz, Jorge. Reformas económicas en la agricultura y respuesta de la producción agregada: Chile 1960–1987. (With English summary.) *Cuadernos Econ.*, December 1988, *25*(76), pp. 389–403.

Baran, Paul A. On the Political Economy of Backwardness. In *Wilber, C. K., ed.*, 1988, pp. 96–108.

Baranzini, Andrea and Pillet, Gonzague. Procédure d'évaluation de la part de l'environnement dans un produit économique. (Evaluation Procedure of the Role of Environment at the Interface with Economic Systems. With English summary.) *Écon. Appl.*, 1988, *41*(1), pp. 129–50.

Barau, A. D. and Clark, J. H. Evaluating Alternative Mortgage Instruments for Low-equity Ontario Farms: A Correction. *Can. J. Agr. Econ.*, July 1988, *36*(2), pp. 359–60.

Barbarà, Salvador and Jackson, Matthew O. Maximin, Leximin, and the Protective Criterion: Characterizations and Comparisons. *J. Econ. Theory*, October 1988, *46*(1), pp. 34–44.

Barbarika, Alexander, Jr. and Dicks, Michael R. Estimating the Costs of Conservation Compliance. *J. Agr. Econ. Res.*, Summer 1988, *40*(3), pp. 12–20.

Barbash, Jack. A Department to Protect Workers' Equity. *Mon. Lab. Rev.*, February 1988, *111*(2), pp. 3–9.

Barber, Clarence L. Keynes's View of Investment. In *Hamouda, O. F. and Smithin, J. N., eds., Vol. 2*, 1988, pp. 35–40.

Barber, G. M. and Milne, W. J. Modelling Internal Migration in Kenya: An Econometric Analysis with Limited Data. *Environ. Planning A*, September 1988, *20*(9), pp. 1185–96.

Barber, John. Manufacturing and Services: Some International Comparisons. In *Barker, T. and Dunne, P., eds.*, 1988, pp. 63–82.

Barber, Linda J. and Herbert, John H. Regional Residential Natural Gas Demand: Comments. *Resources & Energy*, December 1988, *10*(4), pp. 387–91.

Barber, William J. The Fortunes of Political Economy in an Environment of Academic Conservatism: Yale University. In *Barber, W. J., ed.*, 1988, pp. 132–68.

_____. Political Economy and the Academic Setting before 1900: An Introduction. In *Barber, W. J., ed.*, 1988, pp. 3–14.

_____. Political Economy from the Top Down: Brown University. In *Barber, W. J., ed.*, 1988, pp. 72–94.

_____. Political Economy in an Atmosphere of Academic Entrepreneurship: The University of Chicago. In *Barber, W. J., ed.*, 1988, pp. 241–65.

_____. Political Economy in the Flagship of Postgraduate Studies: The Johns Hopkins University. In *Barber, W. J., ed.*, 1988, pp. 203–24.

Barbieri, William M.; Smith, Robert J. and Rehnfeldt, Maria. Indian Colonization in Paraguay: What Is Success? In *Annis, S. and Hakim, P., eds.*, 1988, pp. 58–64.

Barbiero, Tom P. A Reassessment of Agricultural Production in Italy, 1861–1914: The Case of Lombardy. *J. Europ. Econ. Hist.*, Spring 1988, *17*(1), pp. 103–16.

Barbone, Luca. Import Barriers: An Analysis of Time-Series Cross-section Data. *OECD Econ. Stud.*, Autumn 1988, (11), pp. 155–68.

Barclay, Michael J. and Litzenberger, Robert H. Announcement Effects of New Equity Issues and the Use of Intraday Price Data. *J. Finan. Econ.*, May 1988, *21*(1), pp. 71–99.

_____ **and Smith, Clifford W., Jr.** Corporate Payout Policy: Cash Dividends versus Open-Market Repurchases. *J. Finan. Econ.*, October 1988, *22*(1), pp. 61–82.

Bardhan, Pranab K. Agrarian Class Formation in India. In *Srinivasan, T. N. and Bardhan, P. K., eds.*, 1988, pp. 501–25.

_____. Demographic Effects on Agricultural Proletarianization: The Evidence from India. In *Lee, R. D., et al., eds.*, 1988, pp. 175–83.

_____. Sex Disparity in Child Survival in Rural India. In *Srinivasan, T. N. and Bardhan, P. K., eds.*, 1988, pp. 473–80.

_____ **and Srinivasan, T. N.** Rural Poverty in South Asia: Introduction. In *Srinivasan, T. N. and Bardhan, P. K., eds.*, 1988, pp. 1–8.

Barff, Richard A. and Knight, Prentice L., III. Dynamic Shift-Share Analysis. *Growth Change*, Spring 1988, *19*(2), pp. 1–10.

Barghouti, Shawki; Frederiksen, Harald D. and Perry, Christopher. Irrigation: Issues, Policies and Lending Strategies. In *Roberts, C., ed.*, 1988, pp. 71–78.

_____ **and Schuh, G. Edward.** Agricultural Diversification in Asia. *Finance Develop.*, June 1988, *25*(2), pp. 41–44.

Bark, Dennis L. and Anderson, Annelise. Thinking about America: The United States in the 1990s: An Introductory Overview. In *Anderson, A. and Bark, D. L., eds.*, 1988, pp. xxiii–xlvii.

Bark, Taeho and de Melo, Jaime. Export Quota Allocations, Export Earnings, and Market Diversification. *World Bank Econ. Rev.*, September 1988, *2*(3), pp. 341–48.

_____ **and Tybout, James R.** Macro Shocks and Industrial Portfolio Responses: An Econometric Model for LDCs. *Rev. Econ. Statist.*, November 1988, *70*(4), pp. 559–68.

Barkat-e-Khuda. Demographic Impact of Rural Development in Bangladesh. In *Vlassoff, C. and Barkat-e-Khuda, eds.*, 1988, pp. 36–48.

_____ **and Vlassoff, Carol.** Impact of Modernization on Development and Demographic Beha-

viour: Introduction. In *Vlassoff, C. and Barkat-e-Khuda, eds.*, 1988, pp. 1–4.

Barker, Terry. The Cambridge Multisectoral Dynamic Model and Alternative Strategies for Full Employment in the United Kingdom. In *Hopkins, M. J. D., ed.*, 1988, pp. 10–42.

_____. The Economic Consequences of Monetarism: A Keynesian View of the British Economy 1980–90. In *Shaw, G. K., ed.*, Vol. 2, 1988, *1980*, pp. 221–38.

_____. International Trade and the British Economy. In *Barker, T. and Dunne, P., eds.*, 1988, pp. 15–38.

Barkin, David. Fuga internacional de capitales, contrabando y financiamiento del desarrollo. (International Capital Flight, Smuggling, and Development Finance. With English summary.) *Estud. Econ.*, July–Dec. 1988, *3*(2), pp. 205–30.

Barkley, David L. The Decentralization of High-Technology Manufacturing to Nonmetropolitan Areas. *Growth Change*, Winter 1988, *19*(1), pp. 13–30.

_____; **Dahlgran, Roger A. and Smith, Stephen M.** High-Technology Manufacturing in the Nonmetropolitan West: Gold or Just Glitter. *Amer. J. Agr. Econ.*, August 1988, *70*(3), pp. 560–71.

Barkley, Paul W. Institutions, Institutionalism, and Agricultural Economics in the Twenty-first Century. In *Hildreth, R. J., et al., eds.*, 1988, pp. 313–35.

Barksdale, Hiram C., Jr. and Bello, Daniel C. Exporting Industrial Products at American Trade Shows. In *Woodside, A. G., ed.*, 1988, pp. 1–25.

Barlev, Benzion; Denny, Wanda and Levy, Haim. Using Accounting Data for Portfolio Management. *J. Portfol. Manage.*, Spring 1988, *14*(3), pp. 70–77.

Barmby, Tim. Models for Analysing Trip-Level Data. *Environ. Planning A*, January 1988, *20*(1), pp. 119–123.

_____. Testing the Negativity Condition for Labour Supply Functions Derived from a Stone-Geary Utility Function. *Bull. Econ. Res.*, January 1988, *40*(1), pp. 73–77.

Barnard, Jerald R. and Krautmann, Anthony C. Population Growth among U.S. Regions and Metropolitan Areas: A Test for Causality. *J. Reg. Sci.*, February 1988, *28*(1), pp. 103–18.

Barnard, Peter O.; Truong, Truong P. and Hensher, David A. The Role of Stated Preference Methods in Studies of Travel Choice. *J. Transp. Econ. Policy*, January 1988, *22*(1), pp. 45–58.

Barnas, D. J. and Harrington, James W., Jr. Foreign-Owned Firms and Regional–Functional Specialization. *Environ. Planning A*, July 1988, *20*(7), pp. 937–52.

Barnes, David W. Antitrust Dialogue on Social Science, Cultural Values, and Merger Law. *Antitrust Bull.*, Winter 1988, *33*(4), pp. 623–53.

_____. Revolution and Counterrevolution in Antitrust Law. *Antitrust Bull.*, Winter 1988, 33(4), pp. 655–76.

Barnes, James H., Jr. and Dant, Rajiv P. Methodological Concerns in Cross-Cultural Research: Implications for Economic Development. In *Kumcu, E. and Firat, A. F., eds.,* 1988, pp. 149–71.

Barnes, T. and Curry, M. Time and Narrative in Economic Geography. *Environ. Planning A,* February 1988, 20(2), pp. 141–49.

Barnett, Andy H.; Ault, Richard W. and Kaserman, David L. The Rising Incidence of Coauthorship in Economics: Further Evidence. *Rev. Econ. Statist.,* August 1988, 70(3), pp. 539–43.

Barnett, Donald F. The U.S. Steel Industry: Strategic Choices in a Basic Industry. In *Hicks, D. A., ed.,* 1988, pp. 162–208.

Barnett, Donald W. The Minerals Industry in Australia. In *McKern, B. and Koomsup, P., eds.,* 1988, pp. 116–60.

Barnett, Marguerite R. and Hefner, James. Implications of Revenue Sharing for Black Political and Economic Goals. *Rev. Black Polit. Econ.,* Fall 1988, 17(2), pp. 45–63.

Barnett, Randy E. One Cheer for the Reagan Years: Economic Liberties and the Constitution. In *Boaz, D., ed.,* 1988, pp. 379–90.

Barnett, William A. and Chen, Ping. The Aggregation-Theoretic Monetary Aggregates Are Chaotic and Have Strange Attractors: An Econometric Application of Mathematical Chaos. In *Barnett, W. A.; Berndt, E. R. and White, H., eds.,* 1988, pp. 199–245.

_____ **and Yue, Piyu.** Semiparametric Estimation of the Asymptotically Ideal Model: The Aim Demand System. In *Rhodes, G. F., Jr. and Fomby, T. B., eds.,* 1988, pp. 229–51.

Barney, G. O. and Jenner, M. G. Development, Security and North–South Relations: A Look into the Future. In *Jepma, C. J., ed.,* 1988, pp. 41–55.

Barney, L. Dwayne and Reynolds, R. Larry. Economics of Organ Procurement and Allocation. *J. Econ. Issues,* June 1988, 22(2), pp. 571–79.

Barnhart, Scott W. Commodity Futures Prices and Economic News: An Examination under Alternative Monetary Regimes. *J. Futures Markets,* August 1988, 8(4), pp. 483–510.

_____ **and Darrat, Ali F.** Budget Deficits, Money Growth and Causality: Further OECD Evidence. *J. Int. Money Finance,* June 1988, 7(2), pp. 231–42.

_____ **and Whitney, Gerald A.** Nonparametric Analysis in Parametric Estimation: An Application to Translog Demand Systems. *Rev. Econ. Statist.,* February 1988, 70(1), pp. 149–53.

Barnhill, Theodore M. The Delivery Option on Forward Contracts: A Comment. *J. Finan. Quant. Anal.,* September 1988, 23(3), pp. 343–49.

_____ **and Seale, William E.** Optimal Exercise of the Switching Option in Treasury Bond Arbitrages. *J. Futures Markets,* October 1988, 8(5), pp. 517–32.

Barniv, Ran and Bulmash, Samuel B. New Public Stock Issues by Seasoned and Unseasoned Firms: A Comparative Analysis in a Turbulent Environment—The Case of Israel. *Managerial Dec. Econ.,* March 1988, 9(1), pp. 27–34.

Baron, David P. Procurement Contracting: Efficiency, Renegotiation and Performance Evaluation. *Info. Econ. Policy,* 1988, 3(2), pp. 109–42.

_____. Regulation and Legislative Choice. *Rand J. Econ.,* Autumn 1988, 19(3), pp. 467–77.

_____ **and Besanko, David.** Monitoring of Performance in Organizational Contracting: The Case of Defense Procurement. *Scand. J. Econ.,* 1988, 90(3), pp. 329–56.

Baron, James N. The Employment Relation as a Social Relation. *J. Japanese Int. Economies,* December 1988, 2(4), pp. 492–525.

_____ **and Pfeffer, Jeffrey.** Taking the Workers Back Out: Recent Trends in the Structuring of Employment. In *Staw, B. M. and Cummings, L. L., eds.,* 1988, pp. 257–303.

Baron, T. and Bran, P. The Outlook of President Nicolae Ceuşescu, Party General Secretary, on the Impact of the Qualitative Transformations in the Economy on the Development of Economic Higher Education. *Econ. Computat. Cybern. Stud. Res.,* 1988, 23(4), pp. 15–23.

_____; **Ivan, I. and Goga, A.** Modelling the Cost of the Quality of Programme Systems. *Econ. Computat. Cybern. Stud. Res.,* 1988, 23(2), pp. 21–31.

Barone-Adesi, Giovanni and Tinic, Seha M. Stock Return Seasonality and the Tests of Asset Pricing Models: Canadian Evidence. In *Dimson, E., ed.,* 1988, pp. 129–46.

_____ **and Whaley, Robert E.** On the Valuation of American Put Options on Dividend-Paying Stocks. In *Fabozzi, F. J., ed.,* 1988, pp. 1–13.

Barr, Brenton M. Perspectives on Deforestation in the U.S.S.R. In *Richards, J. F. and Tucker, R. P., eds.,* 1988, pp. 230–61.

Barr, Graham D. I. and Bradfield, David J. Portfolio Selection in Thinly Traded Environments—A Case Study. *Managerial Dec. Econ.,* December 1988, 9(4), pp. 287–90.

_____ **and van den Honert, R. C.** Diversifying Mergers and Risk: A Comment. *J. Econ. Stud.,* 1988, 15(5), pp. 53–64.

Barrantes Hidalgo, Álvaro and de Sousa, Maria de Conceição Sampaio. Um modelo de equilíbrio geral computável para o estudo de políticas de comércio exterior no Brasil. (With English summary.) *Pesquisa Planejamento Econ.,* August 1988, 18(2), pp. 379–400.

Barrell, R. J. and Eastwood, Fiona. The World Economy. *Nat. Inst. Econ. Rev.,* February 1988, (123), pp. 20–33.

_____ **and Eastwood, Fiona.** The World Economy. *Nat. Inst. Econ. Rev.,* May 1988, (124), pp. 21–35.

_____ **and Eastwood, Fiona.** The World Economy. *Nat. Inst. Econ. Rev.,* August 1988, (125), pp. 23–39.

_____ **and Gurney, Andrew.** The World Economy. *Nat. Inst. Econ. Rev.*, November 1988, (126), pp. 18–31.

Barrère, Alain. The Foundations of Keynesian Analysis: Introduction. In *Barrère, A., ed., 1988*, pp. 1–12.

_____. The Foundations of Monetary Production Economy. In *Barrère, A., ed.*, 1988, pp. 15–48.

_____. The Keynesian Project. In *Barrère, A., ed.*, 1988, pp. xiii–xlvi.

_____. La généralisation de la théorie de la monnaie en économie monétaire de production. (The Generalization of the Theory of Money in a Monetary Economy of Production. With English summary.) *Écon. Appl.*, 1988, *41*(2), pp. 185–222.

Barrett, Brendan; Glasson, John and van Der Wee, Dominique. A Local Income and Employment Multiplier Analysis of a Proposed Nuclear Power Station Development at Hinkley Point in Somerset. *Urban Stud.*, June 1988, *25*(3), pp. 248–61.

Barrett, Richard E. Autonomy and Diversity in the American State on Taiwan. In *Winckler, E. A. and Greenhalgh, S., eds.*, 1988, pp. 121–37.

Barrett, W. Brian and Slovin, Myron B. Economic Volatility and the Demand for Consumer Durables. *Appl. Econ.*, June 1988, *20*(6), pp. 731–38.

_____; **Slovin, Myron B. and Sushka, Marie E.** Reserve Regulation and Recourse as a Source of Risk Premia in the Federal Funds Market. *J. Banking Finance*, December 1988, *12*(4), pp. 575–84.

Barro, Robert J. The Persistence of Unemployment. *Amer. Econ. Rev.*, May 1988, *78*(2), pp. 32–37.

_____ **and Becker, Gary S.** A Reformulation of the Economic Theory of Fertility. *Quart. J. Econ.*, February 1988, *103*(1), pp. 1–25.

Barrocas, Manuel P. Security on Movable Property and Receivables in Europe: Portugal. In *Dickson, M. G.; Rosener, W. and Storm, P. M., eds.*, 1988, pp. 142–52.

Barroux, Yves. New Issues in Corporate Finance: Comments. *Europ. Econ. Rev.*, June 1988, *32*(5), pp. 1187–89.

Barrows, Richard. Institutions, Incentives, and Agricultural Land Policy. In *Johnston, G. M.; Freshwater, D. and Favero, P., eds.*, 1988, pp. 21–42.

_____ **and Bonderud, Kendra.** The Distribution of Tax Relief under Farm Circuit-Breakers: Some Empirical Evidence. *Land Econ.*, February 1988, *64*(1), pp. 15–27.

Barry, Lynn M. District Bank Performance in 1987: Bigger Is Not Necessarily Better. *Fed. Res. Bank St. Louis Rev.*, March–April 1988, *70*(2), pp. 39–48.

Barry, Peter J. Double Counting Agricultural Income: A Comment. *Can. J. Agr. Econ.*, July 1988, *36*(2), pp. 353–56.

_____ **and Collins, Robert A.** Beta-Adjusted Hurdle Rates for Proprietary Firms. *J. Econ. Bus.*, May 1988, *40*(2), pp. 139–45.

_____; **Sonka, Steven T. and Gustafson, Cole R.** Machinery Investment Decisions: A Simulated Analysis for Cash Grain Farms. *Western J. Agr. Econ.*, December 1988, *13*(2), pp. 244–53.

Barsky, Carl and Asbury, Penny L. Evaluation of Mean Wage Estimates in the Industry Wage Survey Program. *Mon. Lab. Rev.*, October 1988, *111*(10), pp. 24–29.

Barsky, Robert B. and Summers, Lawrence H. Gibson's Paradox and the Gold Standard. *J. Polit. Econ.*, June 1988, *96*(3), pp. 528–50.

_____, **et al.** The Worldwide Change in the Behavior of Interest Rates and Prices in 1914. *Europ. Econ. Rev.*, June 1988, *32*(5), pp. 1123–47.

Bartel, Ann and Lewin, David. Wages and Unionism in the Public Sector: The Case of Police. In *Lewin, D., et al., eds.*, 1988, *1981*, pp. 494–506.

Bartels, Robert; Murray, Jane and Weiss, Andrew A. The Role of Consumer and Business Sentiment in Forecasting Telecommunications Traffic. *J. Econ. Psych.*, June 1988, *9*(2), pp. 215–32.

Barten, A. P. The History of Dutch Macroeconomic Modelling (1936–1986) In *Driehuis, W.; Fase, M. M. G. and den Hartog, H., eds.*, 1988, pp. 39–88.

Barth, James R. and Bradley, Michael D. On Interest Rates, Inflationary Expectations and Tax Rates. *J. Banking Finance*, June 1988, *12*(2), pp. 215–20.

_____ **and Regalia, Martin A.** The Evolving Role of Regulation in the Savings and Loan Industry. In *England, C. and Huertas, T., eds.*, 1988, pp. 113–61.

_____ **and Swamy, P. A. V. B.** An Application of Operational-Subjective Statistical Methods to Rational Expectations: Comment. *J. Bus. Econ. Statist.*, October 1988, *6*(4), pp. 473–74.

Barthelemy, Philippe. The Macroeconomic Estimates of the Hidden Economy: A Critical Analysis. *Rev. Income Wealth*, June 1988, *34*(2), pp. 183–208.

Barthold, Thomas A. and Boyd, Roy. A Note on Resource Value and Marketability. *Energy Econ.*, January 1988, *10*(1), pp. 79–83.

_____ **and Hochman, Harold M.** Addiction as Extreme-Seeking. *Econ. Inquiry*, January 1988, *26*(1), pp. 89–106.

Bartik, Timothy J. The Effects of Environmental Regulation on Business Location in the United States. *Growth Change*, Summer 1988, *19*(3), pp. 22–44.

_____. Evaluating the Benefits of Non-marginal Reductions in Pollution Using Information on Defensive Expenditures. *J. Environ. Econ. Manage.*, March 1988, *15*(1), pp. 111–27.

_____. Measuring the Benefits of Amenity Improvements in Hedonic Price Models. *Land Econ.*, May 1988, *64*(2), pp. 72–83.

_____. The New Economic Role of American States: Tennessee. In *Fosler, R. S., ed.*, 1988, pp. 139–200.

Bartlema, J. and Vossen, A. Reflections on Household Modelling. In *Keilman, N.; Kuijsten, A. and Vossen, A., eds.*, 1988, pp. 243–53.

Bartlett, Robin L. and Miller, Timothy I. Executive Earnings by Gender: A Case Study. *Soc. Sci. Quart.*, December 1988, *69*(4), pp. 892–909.

―――― **and Weidenaar, Dennis J.** An Introduction to the Proceedings of the 1987 Invitational Conference on the Principles of Economics Textbook. *J. Econ. Educ.*, Spring 1988, *19*(2), pp. 109–12.

Bartocci, Enzo. Le relazioni industriali in italia negli anni 1983–87. (Industrial Relations in Italy; 1983–87. With English summary.) *Econ. Lavoro*, Oct.–Dec. 1988, *22*(4), pp. 119–40.

Bartolini, Paolo; Salas, Jose D. and Obeysekera, J. T. B. Multivariate Periodic ARMA (1, 1) Processes. *Water Resources Res.*, August 1988, *24*(8), pp. 1237–46.

Bartolucci, Antonio and Silvestrelli, Maria. The Matching of Transport Demand with Supply in Italy. In *Bianco, L. and La Bella, A., eds.*, 1988, pp. 50–78.

Barton, David R. Selected Data Sources. In *Candilis, W. O., ed.*, 1988, pp. 173–217.

Barton, H. Arnold. The Danish Agrarian Reforms, 1784–1814, and the Historians. *Scand. Econ. Hist. Rev.*, 1988, *36*(1), pp. 46–61.

Barton, Margaret; Farkas, George and England, Paula. Structural Effects on Wages: Sociological and Economic Views. In *Farkas, G. and England, P., eds.*, 1988, pp. 93–112.

Bartrip, P. W. J. and Fenn, P. T. Factory Fatalities and Regulation in Britain, 1878–1913. *Exploration Econ. Hist.*, January 1988, *25*(1), pp. 60–74.

Bartusch, M.; Möhring, R. H. and Radermacher, F. J. M-Machine Unit Time Scheduling: A Report on Ongoing Research. In *Kurzhanski, A.; Neumann, K. and Pallaschke, D., eds.*, 1988, pp. 165–212.

Barucci, Emilio and Asso, Pier Francesco. Ricardo on the National Debt and Its Redemption: Some Notes on an Unpublished Ricardian Manuscript. *Econ. Notes*, 1988, (2), pp. 5–36.

de Bary, Brett. Sanya: Japan's Internal Colony. In *Tsurumi, E. P., ed.*, 1988, pp. 112–18.

Bas, Daniel. Cost-Effectiveness of Training in Developing Countries. *Int. Lab. Rev.*, 1988, *127*(3), pp. 355–69.

Başar, Tamer. Asynchronous Algorithms in Noncooperative Games. *J. Econ. Dynam. Control*, March 1988, *12*(1), pp. 167–72.

―――― **; d'Orey, Vasco and Turnovsky, Stephen J.** Dynamic Strategic Monetary Policies and Coordination in Interdependent Economies. *Amer. Econ. Rev.*, June 1988, *78*(3), pp. 341–61.

Basarrate Urizar, Begoña. El effecto tamaño y la imposición sobre dividendos y ganancias de capital. (With English summary.) *Invest. Econ.*, May 1988, *12*(2), pp. 225–42.

Basberg, Bjørn L. Patent Statistics as a Measure of Technological Change: Views on a Doctoral Dissertation. *Scand. Econ. Hist. Rev.*, 1988, *36*(1), pp. 62–75.

――――. Patents and the Measurement of Technological Change. In *Grønhaug, K. and Kaufmann, G., eds.*, 1988, pp. 457–73.

Bascom, Jonathan; Samatar, Abdi and Salisbury, Lance. The Political Economy of Livestock Marketing in Northern Somalia. *African Econ. Hist.*, 1988, (17), pp. 81–97.

Basevi, Giorgio. Monetary Cooperation and Liberalization of Capital Movements in the European Monetary System. *Europ. Econ. Rev.*, March 1988, *32*(2–3), pp. 372–81.

――――. The Worldwide Change in the Behavior of Interest Rates and Prices in 1914: Comments. *Europ. Econ. Rev.*, June 1988, *32*(5), pp. 1147–50.

――――; **Kind, Paolo and Poli, Giorgio.** Economic Cooperation and Confrontation between Europe and the U.S.A.: A Game-Theoretic Approach to the Analysis of International Monetary and Trade Policies. In *Baldwin, R. E.; Hamilton, C. B. and Sapir, A., eds.*, 1988, pp. 369–88.

Baskin, A. and Lagutkin, V. Economic Ties, Plan, and Contract. *Prob. Econ.*, April 1988, *30*(12), pp. 73–87.

Baskin, Jonathan Barron. The Development of Corporate Financial Markets in Britain and the United States, 1600–1914: Overcoming Asymmetric Information. *Bus. Hist. Rev.*, Summer 1988, *62*(2), pp. 199–237.

Basmann, Robert L. Causality Tests and Observationally Equivalent Representations of Econometric Models. *J. Econometrics*, Sept.–Oct. 1988, *39*(1–2), pp. 69–104.

――――; **Molina, David J. and Slottje, Daniel J.** A Note on Measuring Veblen's Theory of Conspicuous Consumption. *Rev. Econ. Statist.*, August 1988, *70*(3), pp. 531–35.

―――― **and Slottje, Daniel J.** Errata [A New Index of Income Inequality: The *B* Measure]. *Econ. Letters*, 1988, *26*(3), pp. 295–97.

Bassi, Laurie J. Poverty among Women and Children: What Accounts for the Change? *Amer. Econ. Rev.*, May 1988, *78*(2), pp. 91–95.

Bastani, Sharokh and Krzyzaniak, Marian. The Incidence of the U.S. Corporation Income Tax: An Old Problem Revisited. *Public Finance*, 1988, *43*(2), pp. 165–94.

Baston, V. J. and Bostock, F. A. Deception Games. *Int. J. Game Theory*, 1988, *17*(2), pp. 129–34.

Basu, Alaka Malwade. How Economic Development Can Overcome Culture: Demographic Change in Punjab, India. *Population Res. Policy Rev.*, 1988, *7*(1), pp. 29–48.

Basu, D. N. Estimating the Externalities of Groundwater Use in Western Argentina: Comment. In *O'Mara, G. T., ed.*, 1988, pp. 154.

―――― **and Ljung, Per.** Irrigation Management and Scheduling: Study of an Irrigation System in India. In *O'Mara, G. T., ed.*, 1988, pp. 178–94.

Basu, Kaushik. Notes on Nonlinear Pricing and Monopoly with a Comment on Backward

Agrarian Markets. *J. Quant. Econ.*, January 1988, *4*(1), pp. 33–43.

_____. Project Evaluation and the Shadow Wage: Accounting for Regional Disparities and Inequality. *Public Finance*, 1988, *43*(2), pp. 212–22.

_____. Strategic Irrationality in Extensive Games. *Math. Soc. Sci.*, June 1988, *15*(3), pp. 247–60.

Batchelor, Roy A. and Orr, Adrian B. Inflation Expectations Revisited. *Economica*, August 1988, *55*(219), pp. 317–31.

Bateman, Bradley W. G. E. Moore and J. M. Keynes: A Missing Chapter in the History of the Expected Utility Model. *Amer. Econ. Rev.*, December 1988, *78*(5), pp. 1098–1106.

Bateman, Deborah A.; Nishimizu, Mieko and Page, John M., Jr. Regional Productivity Differentials and Development Policy in Yugoslavia, 1965–1978. *J. Compar. Econ.*, March 1988, *12*(1), pp. 24–42.

Bates, Charles and White, Halbert. Efficient Instrumental Variables Estimation of Systems of Implicit Heterogeneous Nonlinear Dynamic Equations with Nonspherical Errors. In *Barnett, W. A.; Berndt, E. R. and White, H.*, eds., 1988, pp. 3–25.

Bates, Douglas M. and Lindstrom, Mary J. Newton–Raphson and EM Algorithms for Linear Mixed-Effects Models for Repeated-Measures Data. *J. Amer. Statist. Assoc.*, December 1988, *83*(404), pp. 1014–22.

Bates, J. M. and Günlük-Şenesen, Gülük. Some Experiments with Methods of Adjusting Unbalanced Data Matrices. *J. Roy. Statist. Soc.*, 1988, *151*(3), pp. 473–90.

Bates, John. Economic Issues in Stated Preference Analysis. *J. Transp. Econ. Policy*, January 1988, *22*(1), pp. 59–69.

_____. Papers on Stated Preference Methods in Transport Research. *J. Transp. Econ. Policy*, January 1988, *22*(1), pp. 7–9.

Bates, John J. Stated Preference Techniques and the Analysis of Consumer Choice. In *Wrigley, N.*, ed., 1988, pp. 187–202.

Bates, Robert H. Anthropology and Development: A Note on the Structure of the Field. In *Bennett, J. W. and Bowen, J. R.*, eds., 1988, pp. 81–84.

_____. Governments and Agricultural Markets in Africa. In *Bates, R. H.*, ed., 1988, pp. 331–58.

_____. The Political Economy of International Capital Markets. In *Bates, R. H.*, ed., 1988, pp. 7–11.

_____. The State and Development: Taiwan, Argentina, and Central America. In *Bates, R. H.*, ed., 1988, pp. 133–41.

_____. Toward a Political Economy of Development. In *Bates, R. H.*, ed., 1988, pp. 239–44.

Bates, Timothy. Do Black-Owned Businesses Employ Minority Workers? New Evidence. *Rev. Black Polit. Econ.*, Spring 1988, *16*(4), pp. 51–64.

Bateson, John E. G.; Boulding, William and

Reibstein, David. Conjoint Analysis Reliability: Empirical Findings. *Marketing Sci.*, Summer 1988, *7*(3), pp. 271–86.

Bateson, Patrick. The Biological Evolution of Cooperation and Trust. In *Gambetta, D.*, ed., 1988, pp. 14–30.

Batey, Peter W. J. and Madden, Moss. The Treatment of Migration in an Extended Input–Output Modelling Framework. *Ricerche Econ.*, April–June 1988, *42*(2), pp. 344–66.

Batie, Sandra S. Agriculture as the Problem: New Agendas and New Opportunities. *Southern J. Agr. Econ.*, July 1988, *20*(1), pp. 1–11.

Bator, Francis M. The Anatomy of Market Failure. In *Cowen, T.*, ed., 1988, *1958*, pp. 35–66.

Batra, Raveendra N. and Beladi, Hamid. Specific Factors, Unemployment and Trade Theory. *Weltwirtsch. Arch.*, 1988, *124*(3), pp. 435–44.

_____ **and Lahiri, Sajal.** Labour Turnover Cost and the Curious Properties of the Mobile Capital Harris–Todaro Model. *Europ. Econ. Rev.*, July 1988, *32*(6), pp. 1369–74.

Batra, S. M. Agrarian Relations and Sugar Cooperatives in North India. In *Attwood, D. W. and Baviskar, B. S.*, eds., 1988, pp. 91–111.

Batten, David F. On the Variable Shape of the Free Spatial Demand Function. *J. Reg. Sci.*, May 1988, *28*(2), pp. 219–30.

_____. Studies of Metropolitan Development: An Overview. *Ann. Reg. Sci.*, November 1988, *22*(3), pp. 1–10.

_____ **and Martellato, Dino.** Modelling Interregional Trade within Input–Output Systems. *Ricerche Econ.*, April–June 1988, *42*(2), pp. 204–21.

Battese, George E. and Coelli, Tim J. Prediction of Firm-Level Technical Efficiencies with a Generalized Frontier Production Function and Panel Data. *J. Econometrics*, July 1988, *38*(3), pp. 387–99.

_____**; Harter, Rachel M. and Fuller, Wayne A.** An Error-Components Model for Prediction of County Crop Areas Using Survey and Satellite Data. *J. Amer. Statist. Assoc.*, March 1988, *83*(401), pp. 28–36.

_____ **and Malik, Sohail J.** Estimation of Elasticities of Substitution for CES and VES Production Functions using Firm-Level Data for Food-Processing Industries in Pakistan. *Pakistan Devel. Rev.*, Spring 1988, *27*(1), pp. 59–71.

Battigalli, Paolo. Il concetto di equilibrio nei modelli strategici e parametrici. (On the Concept of Equilibrium in Strategic and Parametric Models. With English summary.) *Giorn. Econ.*, Jan.–Feb. 1988, *47*(1–2), pp. 99–118.

Battigalli, Pierpaolo. Implementable Strategies, Prior Information and the Problem of Credibility in Extensive Games. *Rivista Int. Sci. Econ. Com.*, August 1988, *35*(8), pp. 705–33.

Bau, Kaushik. Why Monopolists Prefer to Make Their Goods Less Durable. *Economica*, November 1988 , *55*(220), pp. 541–46.

Baudelot, Christian. La jeunesse n'est plus ce qu'elle était: Les difficultés d'une description.

(The Youth Is No Longer What It Used to Be: The Difficulties of a Description. With English summary.) *Revue Écon.*, January 1988, *39*(1), pp. 189–224.

Bauer, G. H. and Wendt, H. Water-Splitting Methods. In *Winter, C.-J. and Nitsch, J., eds.*, 1988, pp. 166–208.

Bauer, Hans H. Marktstagnation als Herausforderung für das Marketing. (With English summary.) *Z. Betriebswirtshaft*, October 1988, *58*(10), pp. 1052–71.

Bauer, Johannes M. and Latzer, Michael. Telecommunications in Austria. In *Foreman-Peck, J. and Müller, J., eds.*, 1988, pp. 53–85.

Bauer, Peter T. [Lord]. Aid Evaluation—Its Scope and Limits: Comment. In *Jepma, C. J., ed.*, 1988, pp. 182–86.

_____. Black Africa: Free or Oppressed? In *Walker, M. A., ed. (I)*, 1988, pp. 213–23.

Bauer, S. Agriculture—Economics and Ecology: Report. *Europ. Rev. Agr. Econ.*, 1988, *15*(2–3), pp. 299–300.

Bauer, Tamás. Deceleration, Dependency and 'Depaternalization': Some Considerations Concerning the Chances of the Soviet Union and Eastern Europe in the Coming Decades. *Acta Oecon.*, 1988, *39*(1–2), pp. 155–69.

_____. Economic Reforms within and beyond the State Sector. *Amer. Econ. Rev.*, May 1988, *78*(2), pp. 452–56.

_____. From Cycles to Crisis? *Eastern Europ. Econ.*, Fall 1988, *27*(1), pp. 5–44.

Baughman, Laura Megna. Auctioning of Quotas: Lots of Pain for Little Gain. *World Econ.*, September 1988, *11*(3), pp. 397–415.

Baum, A. E.; MacGregor, B. D. and Adams, C. D. The Availability of Land for Inner City Development: A Case Study of Inner Manchester. *Urban Stud.*, February 1988, *25*(1), pp. 62–76.

Baum, Christopher F. and Doyle, Joanne M. Dynamic Adjustment of Firms' Capital Structures in a Varying-Risk Environment. *J. Econ. Dynam. Control*, March 1988, *12*(1), pp. 127–33.

Baum, Donald N. Consumption, Wealth, and the Real Rate of Interest: A Reexamination. *J. Macroecon.*, Winter 1988, *10*(1), pp. 83–102.

Baum, Eric B. Neural Nets for Economists. In *Anderson, P. W.; Arrow, K. J. and Pines, D., eds.*, 1988, pp. 33–48.

Baum, Kenneth and Johnson, James D. Improving the Socioeconomic Data Base: A Discussion. In *Hildreth, R. J., et al., eds.*, 1988, pp. 484–89.

Baum, Sandra R. and Schwartz, Saul. Merit Aid to College Students. *Econ. Educ. Rev.*, 1988, *7*(1), pp. 127–34.

_____ and Sjogren, Jane. Cost-of-Living Adjustments for Social Security Benefits: Their Impact on the Incomes of the Elderly. In *Danziger, S. H. and Portney, K. E., eds.*, 1988, pp. 87–115.

Baumann, J.; Fischer, Manfred M. and Schubert, U. A Choice-Theoretical Labour-Market Model: Empirical Tests at the Mesolevel. *Envi-*

ron. Planning A, August 1988, *20*(8), pp. 1085–1102.

Baumann, Michael G. and Schwartz, Marius. Entry-Deterrence Externalities and Relative Firm Size. *Int. J. Ind. Organ.*, June 1988, *6*(2), pp. 181–97.

_____ and Williams, Michael A. Output–Inflation Tradeoffs in 34 Countries: Comment. *J. Econ. Bus.*, February 1988, *40*(1), pp. 97–101.

Baumann, Renato and Braga, Helson C. Export Financing in LDCs: The Role of Subsidies for Export Performance in Brazil. *World Devel.*, July 1988, *16*(7), pp. 821–33.

Baumel, C. Phillip; Lee, Tenpao and Kim, Tae-Kyun. Impact of Deregulation on the Financial Performance of the Class I Railroads: Heuristic Models of Pooled Time-Series and Cross-Sectional Data. *Logist. Transp. Rev.*, September 1988, *24*(3), pp. 281–96.

Baumgardner, James R. The Division of Labor, Local Markets, and Worker Organization. *J. Polit. Econ.*, June 1988, *96*(3), pp. 509–27.

_____. Physicians' Services and the Division of Labor across Local Markets. *J. Polit. Econ.*, October 1988, *96*(5), pp. 948–82.

Baumgratz, Delauro de Oliveira. A Developing Country's Case: The Brazilian Financial System. In *Mikdashi, Z., ed.*, 1988, pp. 45–53.

Baumol, William J. Economic Education and the Critics of Mainstream Economics. *J. Econ. Educ.*, Fall 1988, *19*(4), pp. 323–30.

_____. On Taxation and the Control of Externalities. In *Ricketts, M., ed., Vol. 2, 1988, 1972*, pp. 237–52.

_____ and Bradford, David F. Optimal Departures from Marginal Cost Pricing. In *Ricketts, M., ed., Vol. 2, 1988, 1970*, pp. 143–61.

_____; Dollar, David and Wolff, Edward N. The Factor-Price Equalization Model and Industry Labor Productivity: An Empirical Test across Countries. In *Feenstra, R. C., ed.*, 1988, pp. 23–47.

_____ and Faulhaber, Gerald R. Economists as Innovators: Practical Products of Theoretical Research. *J. Econ. Lit.*, June 1988, *26*(2), pp. 577–600.

_____ and Highsmith, Robert J. Variables Affecting Success in Economic Education: Preliminary Findings from a New Data Base. *Amer. Econ. Rev.*, May 1988, *78*(2), pp. 257–62.

_____ and Ordover, Janusz A. Antitrust Policy and High-Technology Industries. *Oxford Rev. Econ. Policy*, Winter 1988, *4*(4), pp. 13–34.

_____ and Wolff, Edward N. Productivity Growth, Convergence, and Welfare: Reply. *Amer. Econ. Rev.*, December 1988, *78*(5), pp. 1155–59.

Bausch, Thomas A. Harnessing Competition. In *Tavis, L. A., ed.*, 1988, pp. 284–87.

Bausor, Randall. Human Adaptability and Economic Surprise. In *Earl, P. E., ed.*, 1988, pp. 11–33.

_____ and Brown-Collier, Elba. The Epistemological Foundations of *The General Theory*. *Scot. J. Polit. Econ.*, August 1988, *35*(3), pp. 227–41.

Bautista, Romeo M. Foreign Borrowing as Dutch Disease: A Quantitative Analysis for the Philippines. *Int. Econ. J.*, Autumn 1988, *2*(3), pp. 35–49.

_____. Macroeconomic Models for East Asian Developing Countries. *Asian-Pacific Econ. Lit.*, September 1988, *2*(2), pp. 1–25.

Bauwens, Luc and Balassa, Bela. The Determinants of Intra-European Trade in Manufactured Goods. *Europ. Econ. Rev.*, September 1988, *32*(7), pp. 1421–37.

_____ **and Balassa, Bela.** Inter-industry and Intra-industry Specialization in Manufactured Goods. *Weltwirtsch. Arch.*, 1988, *124*(1), pp. 1–13.

_____; **van Dijk, Herman K. and Zellner, Arnold.** Bayesian Specification Analysis and Estimation of Simultaneous Equation Models Using Monte Carlo Methods. *J. Econometrics*, May–June 1988, *38*(1–2), pp. 39–72.

Baviskar, B. S. Dairy Co-operatives and Rural Development in Gujarat. In *Attwood, D. W. and Baviskar, B. S., eds.*, 1988, pp. 345–61.

_____ **and Attwood, Donald W.** Who Shares? Co-operatives and Rural Development: Introduction. In *Attwood, D. W. and Baviskar, B. S., eds.*, 1988, pp. 1–20.

Bawa, R. S. and Gill, Rajiv. Tax Effort in India— An Inter-state Analysis. In *Raikhy, P. S. and Gill, S. S., eds.*, 1988, pp. 114–26.

Baxter, John L. A General Model of Wage Determination. In *Earl, P. E., ed., Vol. 2*, 1988, *1980*, pp. 333–47.

_____. Intervening Variables in Economics: An Explanation of Wage Behavior. In *Earl, P. E., ed.*, 1988, pp. 125–46.

Baxter, Marianne. Toward an Empirical Assessment of Game-Theoretic Models of Policymaking: A Comment. *Carnegie–Rochester Conf. Ser. Public Policy*, Spring 1988, *28*, pp. 141–51.

Baxter, Scott and Vaughan, Michael B. Tuition, Unemployment and the Demand for Education: A Case Study for Classroom Use. In *Missouri Valley Economic Assoc.*, 1988, pp. 135–40.

Baxter, William F. Private Antitrust Litigation: New Evidence, New Learning: Comment: The Policy Implications of the Georgetown Data Set. In *White, L. J., ed.*, 1988, pp. 410–11.

Baye, Michael R. and Anglin, Paul M. Information Gathering and Cost of Living Differences among Searchers. *Econ. Letters*, 1988, *28*(3), pp. 247–50.

_____ **and Black, Dan A.** The Microeconomic Foundations of Measuring Bracket Creep and Other Tax Changes. *Econ. Inquiry*, July 1988, *26*(3), pp. 471–84.

Bayes, Jane. Labor Markets and the Feminization of Poverty. In *Rodgers, H. R., Jr., ed.*, 1988, pp. 86–113.

Bayliss, Peter. Toshiba's Approach to Purchasing. In *Holl, U. and Trevor, M., eds.*, 1988, pp. 27–45.

Bayly, C. A. and Subrahmanyam, Sanjay. Portfolio Capitalists and the Political Economy of

Early Modern India. *Indian Econ. Soc. Hist. Rev.*, Oct.–Dec. 1988, *25*(4), pp. 401–24.

Baysinger, Barry D.; Zeithaml, Carl P. and Keim, Gerald D. Toward an Integrated Strategic Management Process: An Empirical Review of Corporate Political Strategy. In *Grant, J. H., ed.*, 1988, pp. 377–93.

Baz, Dragomira and Bädin, V. Acceptance Control of Production Homogeneity in a Nonsteady Manufacturing Process. *Econ. Computat. Cybern. Stud. Res.*, 1988, *23*(3), pp. 87–94.

Bazerman, Max H.; Mannix, Elizabeth A. and Thompson, Leigh L. Groups as Mixed-Motive Negotiations. In *Lawler, E. J. and Markovsky, B., eds.*, 1988, pp. 195–216.

Bazler-Madžar, Marta. Regional Differentiation of Development Level and Efficiency of Growth. *Econ. Anal. Workers' Manage.*, 1988, *22*(4), pp. 271–87.

Beach, Charles M. and Finnie, Ross E. Family Background in an Extended Earnings-Generation Model: Further Evidence. *Eastern Econ. J.*, Jan.–March 1988, *14*(1), pp. 39–49.

Beamish, Paul W. and Schaan, Jean-Louis. Joint Venture General Managers in LDCs. In *Contractor, F. J. and Lorange, P.*, 1988, pp. 279–99.

Bean, Charles R. Real Wage Rigidity and the Effect of an Oil Discovery. *Oxford Econ. Pap.*, September 1988, *40*(3), pp. 451–62.

_____. Sterling Misalignment and British Trade Performance. In *Marston, R. C., ed.*, 1988, pp. 39–69.

_____ **and Turnbull, Peter J.** Employment in the British Coal Industry: A Test of the Labour Demand Model. *Econ. J.*, December 1988, *98*(393), pp. 1092–1104.

Bean, Frank D.; Lowell, B. Lindsay and Taylor, Lowell J. Undocumented Mexican Immigrants and the Earnings of Other Workers in the United States. *Demography*, February 1988, *25*(1), pp. 35–52.

_____; **Stephen, Elizabeth Hervey and Rindfuss, Ronald R.** Racial Differences in Contraceptive Choice: Complexity and Implications. *Demography*, February 1988, *25*(1), pp. 53–70.

Beard, Thomas R. and McMillin, W. Douglas. Do Budget Deficits Matter? Some Pre–World War II Evidence. *J. Econ. Bus.*, November 1988, *40*(4), pp. 295–308.

Bearden, William O.; Teel, Jesse E. and Mobley, Mary F. An Investigation of Individual Responses to Tensile Price Claims. *J. Cons. Res.*, September 1988, *15*(2), pp. 273–79.

_____; **Weilbaker, Dan C. and Urbany, Joel E.** The Effect of Plausible and Exaggerated Reference Prices on Consumer Perceptions and Price Search. *J. Cons. Res.*, June 1988, *15*(1), pp. 95–110.

Beare, John B. and Thakkar, Rasesh B. Optimal Government Bond Finance. *J. Macroecon.*, Spring 1988, *10*(2), pp. 217–29.

Bearman, Toni Carbo. Changes in International Marketing Techniques: Commentary. In *Cass-*

ing, J. H. and Husted, S. L., eds., 1988, pp. 138–41.

Beath, John A.; Katsoulacos, Yannis and Ulph, David T. R&D Rivalry vs R&D Cooperation under Uncertainty. *Rech. Écon. Louvain*, 1988, 54(4), pp. 373–84.

———; **Lewis, Geoffrey W. and Ulph, David T.** Policy Targeting in a New Welfare Framework with Poverty. In *Hare, P. G., ed.*, 1988, pp. 161–85.

Beatrice, Dennis F.; Bachman, Sara S. and Altman, Stuart H. What Influences a State's Approach to Medicaid Reform? *Inquiry*, Summer 1988, 25(2), pp. 243–50.

Beattie, Bruce R. Asymmetric Stages, Ridgelines and the Economic Region for the Two-Variable-Factor Production Function Model. *Southern Econ. J.*, January 1988, 54(3), pp. 562–71.

Beatty, David and Kennett, Steve. Striking Back: Fighting Words, Social Protest and Political Participation in Free and Democratic Societies. In *Carter, D. D., et al.*, 1988, pp. 214–66.

Beatty, Randolph P.; Lee, Cheng F. and Chen, K. C. On the Nonstationarity of Convertible Bond Betas: Theory and Evidence. *Quart. Rev. Econ. Bus.*, Autumn 1988, 28(3), pp. 15–27.

Beatty, Warren and Agapos, A. M. A Study of Comparative Air Fares in the Southeast United States. *Logist. Transp. Rev.*, September 1988, 24(3), pp. 249–64.

Beauchamp, J. J. and Mitchell, T. J. Bayesian Variable Selection in Linear Regression. *J. Amer. Statist. Assoc.*, December 1988, 83(404), pp. 1023–32.

——— **and Mitchell, T. J.** Bayesian Variable Selection in Linear Regression: Rejoinder. *J. Amer. Statist. Assoc.*, December 1988, 83(404), pp. 1035–36.

Beaucourt, Chantal. East European Agricultural Trade Policy. In *Brada, J. C. and Wadekin, K.-E., eds.*, 1988, pp. 422–39.

Beauford, E. Yvonne and Nelson, Mack C. Social and Economic Conditions of Black Farm Households: Status and Prospects. In *Beaulieu, L. J., ed.*, 1988, pp. 99–119.

Beaulieu, Lionel J. The Rural South in Crisis: An Introduction. In *Beaulieu, L. J., ed.*, 1988, pp. 1–12.

———; **Miller, Michael K. and Mulkey, David.** Community Forces and Their Influence on Farm Structure. In *Beaulieu, L. J., ed.*, 1988, pp. 211–32.

Beaumont, John R. Information Handling and Model Awareness: Towards a Research and Training Agenda. *Environ. Planning A*, September 1988, 20(9), pp. 1141–44.

———. Research and Policy Review 21. Britain's Future Wealth: The Need for Strategic Discussions on Research and Development. *Environ. Planning A*, February 1988, 20(2), pp. 195–201.

———. Store Location Analysis: Problems and Progress. In *Wrigley, N., ed.*, 1988, pp. 87–105.

Beaumont, P. B. and Harris, Richard I. D. Sub-

systems of Industrial Relations: The Spatial Dimension in Britain. *Brit. J. Ind. Relat.*, November 1988, 26(3), pp. 397–407.

Beaumont, Paul and Rose, Adam. Interrelational Income-Distribution Multipliers for the West Virginia Economy. *J. Reg. Sci.*, November 1988, 28(4), pp. 461–75.

Bebchuk, Lucian Arye. The Pressure to Tender: An Analysis and a Proposed Remedy. In *Coffee, J. C., Jr.; Lowenstein, L. and Rose-Ackerman, S., eds.*, 1988, 1987, pp. 371–97.

———. The Sole Owner Standard for Takeover Policy. *J. Legal Stud.*, January 1988, 17(1), pp. 197–229.

———. Suing Solely to Extract a Settlement Offer. *J. Legal Stud.*, June 1988, 17(2), pp. 437–50.

Beccaria, Luis and Yoguel, Gabriel. Apuntes sobre la evolución del empleo industrial en el período 1973–1984. (With English summary.) *Desarrollo Econ.*, Jan.–March 1988, 27(108), pp. 589–605.

Bechter, Dan M.; Chmura, Christine and Ko, Richard K. Fifth District Indexes of Manufacturing Output. *Fed. Res. Bank Richmond Econ. Rev.*, May–June 1988, 74(3), pp. 23–33.

Beck, E. M. and Colclough, Glenna S. Schooling and Capitalism: The Effect of Urban Economic Structure on the Value of Education. In *Farkas, G. and England, P., eds.*, 1988, pp. 113–39.

Beck, H. S.; Upton, M. and Wise, W. S. Is Publicly Funded Agricultural Research Excessive? A Comment. *J. Agr. Econ.*, September 1988, 39(3), pp. 453–55.

Beck, K. and Zweifel, Peter. Warum eine Grenzkostentarifierung für Elektrizität? (Why Marginal Cost Pricing of Electricity? With English summary.) *Schweiz. Z. Volkswirtsch. Statist.*, December 1988, 124(4), pp. 543–58.

Beck, Nathaniel. Politics and Monetary Policy. In *Willett, T. D., ed.*, 1988, pp. 366–95.

Beck, Peter. Recent Developments in Planning and Decision-Taking in Large Corporations. In *Saunders, C. T., ed.*, 1988, pp. 295–314.

Becker, Charles M. and Morrison, Andrew R. The Determinants of Urban Population Growth in Sub-Saharan Africa. *Econ. Develop. Cult. Change*, January 1988, 36(2), pp. 259–78.

Becker, Gary S. Crime and Punishment: An Economic Approach. In *Alper, N. O. and Hellman, D. A., eds.*, 1988, pp. 136–42.

———. Crime and Punishment: An Economic Approach. In *Stigler, G. J., ed.*, 1988, 1968, pp. 537–92.

———. Family Economics and Macro Behavior. *Amer. Econ. Rev.*, March 1988, 78(1), pp. 1–13.

———. Public Policies, Pressure Groups, and Dead Weight Costs. In *Stigler, G. J., ed.*, 1988, 1985, pp. 85–105.

———. A Theory of the Allocation of Time. In *Ricketts, M., ed., Vol. 1*, 1988, 1965, pp. 45–69.

——— **and Barro, Robert J.** A Reformulation of

the Economic Theory of Fertility. *Quart. J. Econ.*, February 1988, *103*(1), pp. 1–25.

_____ and Murphy, Kevin M. The Family and the State. *J. Law Econ.*, April 1988, *31*(1), pp. 1–18.

_____ and Murphy, Kevin M. A Theory of Rational Addiction. *J. Polit. Econ.*, August 1988, *96*(4), pp. 675–700.

_____ and Stigler, George J. Law Enforcement, Malfeasance, and Compensation of Enforcers. In *Stigler, G. J., ed.*, 1988, *1974*, pp. 593–611.

Becker, James F. Toward a "Real" Value Accounting. In *Neimark, M., ed.*, 1988, pp. 143–55.

Becker, L. Videotex Technology in Europe Similarities and Differences. In *Schiefer, G., ed.*, 1988, pp. 27–32.

Becker, Otwin and Huschens, Stefan. Bounded Rational Strategies in Sequential Bargaining: An Experiment and a Learning by Evolution Strategy. In *Tietz, R.; Albers, W. and Selten, R., eds.*, 1988, pp. 129–41.

Becker, William E. Assessing Personnel Practices in Higher Education: A Misleading Note of Caution. *Econ. Educ. Rev.*, 1988, *7*(4), pp. 445–49.

_____ and Alter, George C. Estimating Lost Future Earnings Using the New Worklife Tables: Authors' Reply. *J. Risk Ins.*, September 1988, *55*(3), pp. 545–47.

Beckerman, Wilfred and Jenkinson, Tim J. What Stopped the Inflation? Unemployment or Commodity Prices? In *Shaw, G. K., ed., Vol. 2*, 1988, *1986*, pp. 250–65.

Beckers, Harry L. Technological Cooperation in Europe. In *Muroyama, J. H. and Stever, H. G., eds.*, 1988, pp. 34–36.

Beckers, Stan. Performance Measurement and Performance Attribution in Less than Efficient Markets: A Case Study. In *Dimson, E., ed.*, 1988, pp. 240–53.

Becketti, Sean, et al. The Panel Study of Income Dynamics after Fourteen Years: An Evaluation. *J. Lab. Econ.*, October 1988, *6*(4), pp. 472–92.

Beckford, George L. Planning in the Caribbean under Capitalism and Socialism. *Soc. Econ. Stud.*, September 1988, *37*(3), pp. 289–301.

Beckman, Steven R. and Foreman, Joshua N. An Experimental Test of the Baumol–Tobin Transactions Demand for Money. *J. Money, Credit, Banking*, Part 1, August 1988, *20*(3), pp. 291–305.

Beckmann, Dennis G. A Note on Estimating the Static Effects of the GSP. *Weltwirtsch. Arch.*, 1988, *124*(3), pp. 566–69.

Beckmann, Martin J. An Economic Model of Urban Growth. In *Ausubel, J. H. and Herman, R., eds.*, 1988, pp. 98–107.

_____. Information Technology and Location. In *Orishimo, I.; Hewings, G. J. D. and Nijkamp, P., eds.*, 1988, pp. 153–60.

_____. Spatial Price Policy and the Distribution of Scientific Journals. *Ann. Reg. Sci.*, February 1988, *22*, pp. 1–7.

Bedrossian, Arakel and Moschos, Demetrios. In

dustrial Structure, Concentration and the Speed of Price Adjustment. *J. Ind. Econ.*, June 1988, *36*(4), pp. 459–76.

Beechert, Edward D. Technology and the Plantation Labour Supply: The Case of Queensland, Hawaii, Louisiana and Cuba. In *Albert, B. and Graves, A., eds.*, 1988, pp. 131–41.

Beechey, Veronica. Rethinking the Definition of Work: Gender and Work. In *Jenson, J.; Hagen, E. and Reddy, C., eds.*, 1988, pp. 45–62.

Beeghley, Leonard. Individual and Structural Explanations of Poverty. *Population Res. Policy Rev.*, 1988, *7*(3), pp. 201–22.

Beenstock, Michael. An Aggregate Model of Output, Inflation and Interest Rates for Industrialised Countries. *Weltwirtsch. Arch.*, 1988, *124*(3), pp. 403–19.

_____. An Econometric Investigation of North–South Interdependence. In *Currie, D. and Vines, D., eds.*, 1988, pp. 32–62.

_____. Regret and Jubilation in Union Wage Bargaining. *Oxford Econ. Pap.*, June 1988, *40*(2), pp. 296–301.

_____ and Blake, David. The Stochastic Analysis of Competitive Unemployment Insurance Premiums. *Europ. Econ. Rev.*, January 1988, *32*(1), pp. 7–25.

_____ and Chan, Kam-Fai. Economic Forces in the London Stock Market. *Oxford Bull. Econ. Statist.*, February 1988, *50*(1), pp. 27–39.

_____; Dickinson, Gerry and Khajuria, Sajay. The Relationship between Property-Liability Insurance Premiums and Income: An International Analysis. *J. Risk Ins.*, June 1988, *55*(2), pp. 259–72.

_____ and Lewington, Paul. Macroeconomic Policy and Aggregate Supply in the UK. In *Motamen, H., ed.*, 1988, pp. 327–52.

_____ and Warburton, Peter. A Neoclassical Model of the UK Labour Market. In *Beenstock, M., ed.*, 1988, pp. 71–104.

_____ and Whitbread, Chris. Explaining Changes in the Union Mark-Up for Male Manual Workers in Great Britain, 1953–1983. *Brit. J. Ind. Relat.*, November 1988, *26*(3), pp. 327–38.

Beer, Michael and Spector, Bert A. Managing Human Assets—It's Time for New Thinking. In *Timpe, A. D., ed.*, 1988, *1985*, pp. 232–37.

van Beers, Cees and Linnemann, Hans. Measures of Export–Import Similarity, and the Linder Hypothesis Once Again. *Weltwirtsch. Arch.*, 1988, *124*(3), pp. 445–57.

Beesley, Michael and Littlechild, Stephen C. Privatization: Principles, Problems and Priorities. In *Johnson, C., ed.*, 1988, *1983*, pp. 11–29.

Begg, David K. H. The Advantage of Tying One's Hands: EMS Discipline and Central Bank Credibility: Comments. *Europ. Econ. Rev.*, June 1988, *32*(5), pp. 1075–77.

_____. Hysteresis, Market Forces, and the Role of Policy in a Dynamic Game with Insiders and Outsiders. *Oxford Econ. Pap.*, December 1988, *40*(4), pp. 587–609.

Begg, Iain G. and Cameron, Gordon C. High

Technology Location and the Urban Areas of Great Britain. *Urban Stud.*, October 1988, 25(5), pp. 361–79.

Beggs, John J. Diagnostic Testing in Applied Econometrics. *Econ. Rec.*, June 1988, 64(185), pp. 81–101.

_____. A Simple Model for Heterogeneity in Binary Logit Models. *Econ. Letters*, 1988, 27(3), pp. 245–49.

_____ **and Chapman, Bruce J.** Immigrant Wage Adjustment in Australia: Cross Section and Time-Series Estimates. *Econ. Rec.*, September 1988, 64(186), pp. 161–67.

_____ **and Chapman, Bruce J.** Labor Turnover Bias in Estimating Wages. *Rev. Econ. Statist.*, February 1988, 70(1), pp. 117–23.

_____ **and Nerlove, Marc.** Biases in Dynamic Models with Fixed Effects. *Econ. Letters*, 1988, 26(1), pp. 29–31.

Begumisa, Gregory; Coughlin, Peter and Mwau, Geoffrey. Tied Aid, Industrial Dependence and New Tactics for Negotiations: Observations from Kenya. In *Coughlin, P. and Ikiara, G. K., eds.*, 1988, pp. 126–42.

Behn, Robert D. Management by Groping Along. *J. Policy Anal. Manage.*, Fall 1988, 7(4), pp. 643–63.

Behnia, Kamran. L'endettement des Etats-Unis. (The United States Indebtedness. With English summary.) *Écon. Appl.*, 1988, 41(4), pp. 913–21.

Behrend, Hilde. Price Images, Inflation and National Incomes Policy. In *Earl, P. E., ed., Vol. 2*, 1988, 1966, pp. 348–71.

_____. The Wage–Work Bargain. *Managerial Dec. Econ.*, Special Issue, Winter 1988, pp. 51–57.

Behrman, Jack N. Orientations and Organization of Transnational Corporations. In *Teng, W. and Wang, N. T., eds.*, 1988, pp. 61–73.

Behrman, Jere R. The Impact of Economic Adjustment Programs. In *Bell, D. E. and Reich, M. R., eds.*, 1988, pp. 103–44.

_____. Intrahousehold Allocation of Nutrients in Rural India: Are Boys Favored? Do Parents Exhibit Inequality Aversion? *Oxford Econ. Pap.*, March 1988, 40(1), pp. 32–54.

_____. Nutrition, Health, Birth Order and Seasonality: Intrahousehold Allocation among Children in Rural India. *J. Devel. Econ.*, February 1988, 28(1), pp. 43–62.

_____. Supply and Demand Variations and Export Earnings Instability: Response to a Further Comment. *Econ. Develop. Cult. Change*, April 1988, 36(3), pp. 577–79.

_____ **and Birdsall, Nancy M.** The Equity–Productivity Tradeoff: Public School Resources in Brazil. *Europ. Econ. Rev.*, October 1988, 32(8), pp. 1585–1601.

_____ **and Birdsall, Nancy M.** The Reward for Good Timing: Cohort Effects and Earnings Functions for Brazilian Males. *Rev. Econ. Statist.*, February 1988, 70(1), pp. 129–35.

_____; **Deolalikar, Anil B. and Wolfe, Barbara L.** Nutrients: Impacts and Determinants. *World Bank Econ. Rev.*, September 1988, 2(3), pp. 299–320.

_____; **Sickles, Robin C. and Taubman, Paul.** Age-Specific Death Rates. In *Ricardo-Campbell, R. and Lazear, E. P., eds.*, 1988, pp. 162–83.

_____; **Wolfe, Barbara L. and Blau, David M.** Schooling and Earnings Distributions with Endogenous Labour Force Participation, Marital Status and Family Size. *Economica*, August 1988, 55(219), pp. 297–316.

Beider, Perry B., et al. Comparable Worth in a General Equilibrium Model of the U.S. Economy. In *Ehrenberg, R. G., ed.*, 1988, pp. 1–52.

Beierlein, James G. and Gillis, William R. The Pennsylvania Agricultural-Access Program. In *Johnson, T. G.; Deaton, B. J. and Segarra, E., eds.*, 1988, pp. 131–34.

Beigie, Carl. Economic Trends in Canada. In *Thornton, R. J.; Hyclak, T. and Aronson, J. R., eds.*, 1988, pp. 49–59.

Beilock, Richard and Polopolus, Leo. Ranking of Agricultural Economics Departments: Influence of Regional Journals, Joint Authorship, and Self-Citations. *Amer. J. Agr. Econ.*, May 1988, 70(2), pp. 403–09.

Beirne, Martin and Ramsay, Harvie. Computer Redesign and 'Labour Process' Theory: Towards a Critical Appraisal. In *Knights, D. and Willmott, H., eds.*, 1988, pp. 197–229.

Beissinger, Mark R. The Soviet Union Today: The Leadership and the Political Elite. In *Cracraft, J., ed.*, 1988, pp. 37–52.

Bej, Emil. U.S. Trade with Centrally-Planned Economies: Prospects and Realities. *Rivista Int. Sci. Econ. Com.*, July 1988, 35(7), pp. 639–62.

op de Beke, J. M. J. Endogenous Extrapolation of Labor Force Participation Rates of Married Women. *De Economist*, March 1988, 136(1), pp. 118–35.

Bekemans, Léonce. Restructuring Labour Markets in the European Community. Recent Measures in Labour Market Adaptability. *Econ. Lavoro*, Oct.–Dec. 1988, 22(4), pp. 141–60.

Bekerman, Marta. Los flujos de capital hacia América Latina y la reestructuración de las economías centrales. (With English summary.) *Desarrollo Econ.*, Oct.–Dec. 1988, 28(111), pp. 425–45.

Beladi, Hamid. Variable Returns to Scale, Urban Unemployment and Welfare. *Southern Econ. J.*, October 1988, 55(2), pp. 412–23.

_____ **and Batra, Raveendra N.** Specific Factors, Unemployment and Trade Theory. *Weltwirtsch. Arch.*, 1988, 124(3), pp. 435–44.

_____; **Biswas, Basudeb and Tribedy, Gopal.** A Two Sector Analysis of Protection and Negative Value-Added. *Indian Econ. J.*, April–June 1988, 35(4), pp. 25–32.

_____ **and Naqvi, Nadeem.** Urban Unemployment and Non-immiserizing Growth. *J. Devel. Econ.*, May 1988, 28(3), pp. 365–76.

_____ **and Samanta, Subarna K.** Factor Market Distortions and Backward Incidence of Pollution Control. *Ann. Reg. Sci.*, March 1988, 22(1), pp. 75–83.

_____ **and Samanta, Subarna K.** Unanticipated Monetary Policy and Real Output—Some Evidence from the UK Economy. *Appl. Econ.*, June 1988, 20(6), pp. 721–29.

_____ **and Samanta, Subarna K.** Unanticipated Monetary Policy: Another Look for a Developing Country. *J. Macroecon.*, Spring 1988, 10(2), pp. 297–307.

_____ **and Zuberi, Habib A.** Environmental Constraints and a Dynamic Model for Energy Development. *Energy Econ.*, January 1988, 10(1), pp. 18–28.

Belenky, V. Z. and Belostotsky, A. M. Control of Economic Systems under the Process of Data Improvement. *J. Econ. Dynam. Control*, November 1988, 12(4), pp. 609–33.

Belgrano, Nestor J. Argentina: Rescheduling and Consolidation of the External Debt. *Bull. Int. Fiscal Doc.*, March 1988, 42(3), pp. 136–37.

Belisle, Sylvain and Dionne, Georges. Accessibilité aux ressources et demande de revascularisation du myocarde. (Accessibility to Resources and Demand of Heart Revascularization. With English summary.) *Can. J. Econ.*, February 1988, 21(1), pp. 129–45.

Belk, Russell W. Possessions and the Extended Self. *J. Cons. Res.*, September 1988, 15(2), pp. 139–68.

_____. Third World Consumer Culture. In *Kumcu, E. and Firat, A. F., eds.*, 1988, pp. 103–27.

_____; **Sherry, John F., Jr. and Wallendorf, Melanie.** A Naturalistic Inquiry into Buyer and Seller Behavior at a Swap Meet. *J. Cons. Res.*, March 1988, 14(4), pp. 449–70.

Belkaoui, Ahmed and Chan, James L. Professional Value System of Academic Accountants: An Empirical Inquiry. In *Neimark, M., ed.*, 1988, pp. 1–28.

Belkin, V. D. Myth and Reality about Socialist Price Formation. *Prob. Econ.*, September 1988, 31(5), pp. 56–66.

_____ **and Perevedentsev, Viktor I.** The Food Problem and the Lessons of Akchi. *Prob. Econ.*, April 1988, 30(12), pp. 18–42.

Bell, Carolyn Shaw. The Principles of Economics from Now until Then. *J. Econ. Educ.*, Spring 1988, 19(2), pp. 133–47.

Bell, Christopher Ross. The Assignment of Fiscal Responsibility in a Federal State: An Empirical Assessment. *Nat. Tax J.*, June 1988, 41(2), pp. 191–207.

_____. Economies of, versus Returns to, Scale: A Clarification. *J. Econ. Educ.*, Fall 1988, 19(4), pp. 331–35.

Bell, Clive and Sussangkarn, Chalongphob. Rationing and Adjustment in the Market for Tenancies: The Behavior of Landowning Households in Thanjavur District. *Amer. J. Agr. Econ.*, November 1988, 70(4), pp. 779–89.

Bell, David E. Disappointment in Decision Making under Uncertainty. In *Bell, D. E.; Raiffa, H. and Tversky, A., eds.*, 1988, 1985, pp. 358–83.

_____ **and Raiffa, Howard.** Marginal Value and Intrinsic Risk Aversion. In *Bell, D. E.; Raiffa, H. and Tversky, A., eds.*, 1988, pp. 384–97.

_____ **and Raiffa, Howard.** Risky Choice Revisited. In *Bell, D. E.; Raiffa, H. and Tversky, A., eds.*, 1988, pp. 99–112.

_____; **Raiffa, Howard and Tversky, Amos.** Descriptive, Normative, and Prescriptive Interactions in Decision Making. In *Bell, D. E.; Raiffa, H. and Tversky, A., eds.*, 1988, pp. 9–30.

_____ **and Reich, Michael R.** Health, Nutrition, and Economic Crises: Approaches to Policy in the Third World: Introduction and Overview. In *Bell, D. E. and Reich, M. R., eds.*, 1988, pp. 1–13.

Bell, David N. F. Implications of the Non-homogeneity of Standard and Overtime Hours on the Structure and Cyclical Adjustment of Labor Input: Comment. In *Hart, R. A., ed.*, 1988, pp. 107–11.

Bell, Edwina and Watts, Peter. Building a Statistical Knowledge Base: A Discussion of the Approach Used in the Development of THESEUS, a Statistical Expert System. In *Edwards, D. and Raun, N. E., eds.*, 1988, pp. 143–48.

Bell, Joe A. The Disinterest in Deregulation: Comment. *Amer. Econ. Rev.*, March 1988, 78(1), pp. 282–83.

Bell, Linda A.; Ceglowski, Janet and Hickok, Susan. The Competitiveness of U.S. Manufactured Goods: Recent Changes and Prospects. *Fed. Res. Bank New York Quart. Rev.*, Spring 1988, 13(1), pp. 7–22.

Bell, Michael E. and Bowman, John H. The State Role in Local Finance. In *Bell, M. E., ed.*, 1988, pp. 191–227.

Bell, Trevor. International Competition and Decentralization in South Africa: A Reply. *World Devel.*, December 1988, 16(12), pp. 1551–53.

Bellante, Don and Garrison, Roger W. Phillips Curves and Hayekian Triangles: Two Perspectives on Monetary Dynamics. *Hist. Polit. Econ.*, Summer 1988, 20(2), pp. 207–34.

Beller, Andrea H. and Blau, Francine D. Trends in Earnings Differentials by Gender, 1971–1981. *Ind. Lab. Relat. Rev.*, July 1988, 41(4), pp. 513–29.

_____ **and Graham, John W.** Child Support Payments: Evidence from Repeated Cross Sections. *Amer. Econ. Rev.*, May 1988, 78(2), pp. 81–85.

_____ **and Krein, Sheila Fitzgerald.** Educational Attainment of Children from Single-Parent Families: Differences by Exposure, Gender, and Race. *Demography*, May 1988, 25(2), pp. 221–34.

Bellettini, Giorgio. Unificazione del doppio mercato dei cambi. (On the Unification of the Double Exchange Market. With English summary.) *Giorn. Econ.*, May–June 1988, 47(5–6), pp. 293–308.

Bellis, Jean-François; Vermulst, Edwin and Musquar, Philippe. The New EEC Regulation on Unfair Pricing Practices in Maritime Transport: A Forerunner of the Extension of Unfair Trade Concepts to Services? *J. World Trade*, February 1988, *22*(1), pp. 47–65.

Bellmann, Lutz. Employment-at-Will, Job Security, and Work Incentives: Comment. In *Hart, R. A., ed.*, 1988, pp. 62–63.

Bello, Daniel C. and Barksdale, Hiram C., Jr. Exporting Industrial Products at American Trade Shows. In *Woodside, A. G., ed.*, 1988, pp. 1–25.

Bellofiore, Riccardo. Retorica ed economia. Su alcuni sviluppi recenti della filosofia della scienza economica e il loro rapporto con il metodo di Keynes. (Rhetoric and Economics. Some Recent Developments in Economic Methodology and Their Relationship with Keynes' Method. With English summary.) *Econ. Polit.*, December 1988, *5*(3), pp. 417–63.

Bellu, Renato R. Entrepreneurs and Managers: Are They Different? In *Kirchhoff, B. A., et al., eds.*, 1988, pp. 16–30.

Belman, Dale L. Concentration, Unionism, and Labor Earnings: A Sample Selection Approach. *Rev. Econ. Statist.*, August 1988, *70*(3), pp. 391–97.

_____ **and Heywood, John S.** Incentive Schemes and Racial Wage Discrimination. *Rev. Black Polit. Econ.*, Summer 1988, *17*(1), pp. 47–56.

_____ **and Heywood, John S.** Public Wage Differentials and the Public Administration "Industry." *Ind. Relat.*, Fall 1988, *27*(3), pp. 385–93.

Belongia, Michael T. Are Economic Forecasts by Government Agencies Biased? Accurate? *Fed. Res. Bank St. Louis Rev.*, Nov.–Dec. 1988, *70*(6), pp. 15–23.

_____. Prospects for International Policy Coordination: Some Lessons from the EMS. *Fed. Res. Bank St. Louis Rev.*, July–Aug. 1988, *70*(4), pp. 19–29.

_____ **and Gilbert, R. Alton.** The Effects of Affiliation with Large Bank Holding Companies on Commercial Bank Lending to Agriculture. *Amer. J. Agr. Econ.*, February 1988, *70*(1), pp. 69–78.

_____; **Hafer, R. W. and Sheehan, Richard G.** On the Temporal Stability of the Interest Rate–Weekly Money Relationship. *Rev. Econ. Statist.*, August 1988, *70*(3), pp. 516–20.

_____ **and Koedijk, Kees G.** Testing the Expectations Model of the Term Structure: Some Conjectures on the Effects of Institutional Changes. *Fed. Res. Bank St. Louis Rev.*, Sept.–Oct. 1988, *70*(5), pp. 37–45.

Belostotsky, A. M. and Belenky, V. Z. Control of Economic Systems under the Process of Data Improvement. *J. Econ. Dynam. Control*, November 1988, *12*(4), pp. 609–33.

Belova, Natalya Fedorovna and Dmitrichev, Igor Ivanovich. Statistics of Time Use in the USSR. *Statist. J.*, December 1988, *5*(4), pp. 393–402.

Belsley, David A. Conditioning in Models with Logs. *J. Econometrics*, May–June 1988, *38*(1–2), pp. 127–43.

_____. Modelling and Forecasting Reliability. *Int. J. Forecasting*, 1988, *4*(3), pp. 427–47.

_____; **Venetoulias, Aachilles and Welsch, Roy E.** Computer Guided Diagnostics. In *Edwards, D. and Raun, N. E., eds.*, 1988, pp. 99–104.

_____ **and Welsch, Roy E.** Modeling Energy Consumption—Using and Abusing Regression Diagnostics: Comment [Combining Robust and Traditional Least Squares Methods: A Critical Evaluation]. *J. Bus. Econ. Statist.*, October 1988, *6*(4), pp. 442–47.

Belton, Terrence M.; Goldberg, Michael A. and Avery, Robert B. Market Discipline in Regulating Bank Risk: New Evidence from the Capital Markets. *J. Money, Credit, Banking*, November 1988, *20*(4), pp. 597–610.

Beltratti, Andrea. La volatilita' del tasso di cambio e del prezzo dei titoli azionari. (With English summary.) *Econ. Int.*, Aug.–Nov. 1988, *41*(3–4), pp. 167–80.

Bemmels, Brian. The Effect of Grievants' Gender on Arbitrators' Decisions. *Ind. Lab. Relat. Rev.*, January 1988, *41*(2), pp. 251–62.

_____. Gender Effects in Discharge Arbitration. *Ind. Lab. Relat. Rev.*, October 1988, *42*(1), pp. 63–76.

Ben-Barak, Shalvia. Abortion in the Soviet Union: Why It Is So Widely Practiced. In *Potichnyj, P. J., ed.*, 1988, pp. 201–17.

Ben David, Moshe; Meissner, Frank and Berman, Brian W. Export Marketing for Off-Season Fresh Produce: The Case of Agrexco, Israel. In *Kumcu, E. and Firat, A. F., eds.*, 1988, pp. 253–83.

Ben-Horim, Moshe and Sivakumar, Narayanaswamy. Evaluating Capital Investment Projects. *Managerial Dec. Econ.*, December 1988, *9*(4), pp. 263–68.

Ben-Ner, Avner. Comparative Empirical Observations on Worker-Owned and Capitalist Firms. *Int. J. Ind. Organ.*, March 1988, *6*(1), pp. 7–31.

_____. The Life Cycle of Worker-Owned Firms in Market Economies: A Theoretical Analysis. *J. Econ. Behav. Organ.*, October 1988, *10*(3), pp. 287–313.

_____ **and Neuberger, Egon.** Towards an Economic Theory of the Firm in the Centrally Planned Economy: Transaction Costs: Internalization and Externalization. *J. Inst. Theoretical Econ.*, December 1988, *144*(5), pp. 839–48.

Ben-Porath, Yoram. Market, Government, and Israel's Muted Baby Boom. In *Lee, R. D.; Arthur, W. B. and Rodgers, G., eds.*, 1988, pp. 12–38.

_____. Simon Kuznets in Person and in Writing. *Econ. Develop. Cult. Change*, April 1988, *36*(3), pp. 435–47.

Ben-Ur, Joseph and Simon, Julian L. Demand, Cost and Prices in Duopoly. *Energy Econ.*, April 1988, *10*(2), pp. 117–24.

Ben Zion, Uri; Gradstein, Mark and Spiegel, Uriel. Financing of Public Goods and Noncooperative Theory of Bargaining. *J. Public Econ.*, December 1988, *37*(3), pp. 345–57.

Benabou, Roland. Search, Price Setting and Inflation. *Rev. Econ. Stud.*, July 1988, *55*(3), pp. 353–76.

Bénard, Jean. Les réglementations publiques de l'activité économique. (With English summary.) *Revue Écon. Polit.*, Jan.–Feb. 1988, *98*(1), pp. 1–59.

Benari, Yoav. An Asset Allocation Paradigm. *J. Portfol. Manage.*, Winter 1988, *14*(2), pp. 47–51.

_____. A Bond Market Timing Model. *J. Portfol. Manage.*, Fall 1988, *15*(1), pp. 45–48.

Benassi, Corrado. Asymmetric Information and Equilibrium Credit Rationing. A Survey. *Rivista Int. Sci. Econ. Com.*, Oct.–Nov. 1988, *35*(10–11), pp. 993–1020.

Benassy, Jean-Pascal. Neo-Keynesian Disequilibrium Theory in a Monetary Economy. In *Grandmont, J.-M., ed.,* 1988, pp. 383–403.

_____. The Objective Demand Curve in General Equilibrium with Price Makers. *Econ. J.*, Supplement, 1988, *98*(390), pp. 37–49.

Benavie, Arthur and Froyen, Richard T. The Impact of Monetary and Fiscal Policy on Aggregate Demand: Fixed versus Flexible Deposit Rates. *Quart. Rev. Econ. Bus.*, Summer 1988, *28*(2), pp. 71–87.

_____ and Froyen, Richard T. Price Level Determinacy and Nominal Interest Rate Pegging. *Oxford Econ. Pap.*, December 1988, *40*(4), pp. 634–45.

Benda, Peter M. and Levine, Charles H. The Assignment and Institutionalization of Functions at OMB: Lessons from Two Cases in Work Force Management. In *Rubin, I. S., ed.,* 1988, pp. 70–99.

Bendeck, Yvette and Sushka, Marie E. Bank Acquisitions and Stockholders' Wealth. *J. Banking Finance*, December 1988, *12*(4), pp. 551–62.

Bendeković, Jadranko and Teodorović, Ivan. Investment Decision-Making in Yugoslavia. In *Saunders, C. T., ed.,* 1988, pp. 255–67.

Bender, Bruce. An Analysis of Congressional Voting on Legislation Limiting Congressional Campaign Expenditures. *J. Polit. Econ.*, October 1988, *96*(5), pp. 1005–21.

Bender, Filmore E. Domestic Food and Agricultural Policy Research Directions: A Discussion. In *Hildreth, R. J., et al., eds.,* 1988, pp. 145–48.

Benedek, Wolfgang. Preferential Treatment of Developing Countries in International Trade—Past Experiences and Future Perspectives. In *Dicke, D. C. and Petersmann, E.-U., eds.,* 1988, pp. 71–109.

Benedick, Richard Elliot. A Landmark Global Treaty at Montreal. *Natural Res. J.*, Summer 1988, *28*(3), pp. 427–29.

Benencia, Roberto and Forni, Floreal H. Asalariados y campesinos pobres: El recurso familiar y la produccion de mano de obra. Estudios de casos en la provincia de Santiago del Estero. (With English summary.) *Desarrollo Econ.*, July–Sept. 1988, *28*(110), pp. 245–79.

_____ and Forni, Floreal H. Demographic Strategies in an Underdeveloped Region of a Modern Country: The Case of Santiago del Estero, Argentina. In *Vlassoff, C. and Barkat-e-Khuda, eds.,* 1988, pp. 73–82.

Benesh, Gary A.; Peterson, David R. and Fehrs, Donald H. Evidence of a Relation between Stock Price Reactions around Cash Dividend Changes and Yields. *J. Finan. Res.*, Summer 1988, *11*(2), pp. 111–23.

Benet, Ivan. Hungarian Agriculture in the 1970s and 1980s. In *Brada, J. C. and Wadekin, K.-E., eds.,* 1988, pp. 183–95.

Bengelsdorf, Carollee. Cubanology and Crises: The Mainstream Looks at Institutionalization. In *Zimbalist, A., ed.,* 1988, pp. 212–26.

_____. On the Problem of Studying Women in Cuba. In *Zimbalist, A., ed.,* 1988, pp. 119–36.

Benhabib, Jess; Jafarey, Saqib and Nishimura, Kazuo. The Dynamics of Efficient Intertemporal Allocations with Many Agents, Recursive Preferences, and Production. *J. Econ. Theory,* April 1988, *44*(2), pp. 301–20.

_____ and Laroque, Guy. On Competitive Cycles in Productive Economies. *J. Econ. Theory,* June 1988, *45*(1), pp. 145–70.

Benham, William; Parsons, Patrick R. and Finnegan, John, Jr. Editors and Their Roles. In *Picard, R. G., et al., eds.,* 1988, pp. 91–103.

Benjamin, Elisabeth R. and Shepard, Donald S. User Fees and Health Financing in Developing Countries: Mobilizing Financial Resources for Health. In *Bell, D. E. and Reich, M. R., eds.,* 1988, pp. 401–24.

Benjamini, Yael and Benjamini, Yoav. The Choice Among Medical Insurance Plans: Reply. *Amer. Econ. Rev.*, March 1988, *78*(1), pp. 281.

Benjamini, Yoav and Benjamini, Yael. The Choice Among Medical Insurance Plans: Reply. *Amer. Econ. Rev.*, March 1988, *78*(1), pp. 281.

Benko, Robert P. Intellectual Property Rights and New Technologies. In *Walker, C. E. and Bloomfield, M. A., eds.,* 1988, pp. 27–33.

_____. Intellectual Property Rights and the Uruguay Round. *World Econ.*, June 1988, *11*(2), pp. 217–31.

Bennati, Eleonora. Un metodo di simulazione statistica per l'analisi della distribuzione del reddito. (A Method of Statistic Simulation Applied to the Analysis of Income Distribution. With English summary.) *Rivista Int. Sci. Econ. Com.*, August 1988, *35*(8), pp. 735–56.

Bennett, Barbara A. and Zimmerman, Gary C. U.S. Banks' Exposure to Developing Countries: An Examination of Recent Trends. *Fed. Res. Bank San Francisco Econ. Rev.*, Spring 1988, (2), pp. 14–29.

Bennett, Elaine. Consistent Bargaining Conjectures in Marriage and Matching. *J. Econ. Theory,* August 1988, *45*(2), pp. 392–407.

_____ and Zame, William R. Bargaining in Cooperative Games. *Int. J. Game Theory,* 1988, *17*(4), pp. 279–300.

Bennett, John S. Optimal Wage Rates and Profit

Sharing in a Firm. In *Jones, D. C. and Svejnar, J., eds.*, 1988, pp. 149–65.

_____ **and Phelps, Michael.** The Supply Multiplier with a Self-Employed Private Sector. *Econ. Planning*, 1988, 22(3), pp. 101–08.

Bennett, John W. Anthropology and Development: The Ambiguous Engagement: Introductory Essay. In *Bennett, J. W. and Bowen, J. R., eds.*, 1988, pp. 1–29.

_____; **Cole, William and Sellers, Stephen G.** The Importance of Traditional Quality for Foods Containing Vegetable Protein Ingredients. In *Schwarz, F. H., ed.*, 1988, pp. 273–339.

Bennett, Karl M. External Debt, Capital Flight and Stabilization Policy: The Experiences of Barbados, Guyana, Jamaica and Trinidad and Tobago. *Soc. Econ. Stud.*, December 1988, 37(4), pp. 57–77.

Bennett, Paul and Kelleher, Jeanette. The International Transmission of Stock Price Disruption in October 1987. *Fed. Res. Bank New York Quart. Rev.*, Summer 1988, 13(2), pp. 17–33.

Bennett, Robert J. Local Government Finance: The Inevitable Day of Reckoning. *Reg. Stud.*, June 1988, 22(3), pp. 233–35.

_____. Non-domestic Rates and Local Taxation of Business. In *Bailey, S. J. and Paddison, R., eds.*, 1988, pp. 150–71.

Bennett, Stephen J. and Rapping, Leonard A. The Causes of High Real Interest Rates in the 1980s. In *Rapping, L. A.*, 1988, pp. 113–25.

Benninga, Simon and Possen, Uri M. Fiscal Policy and the Term Structure of Interest Rates. *J. Public Econ.*, December 1988, 37(3), pp. 331–44.

_____ **and Protopapadakis, Aris A.** The Equilibrium Pricing of Exchange Rates and Assets when Trade Takes Time. *J. Int. Money Finance*, June 1988, 7(2), pp. 129–49.

_____ **and Talmor, Eli.** The Interaction of Corporate and Government Financing in General Equilibrium. *J. Bus.*, April 1988, 61(2), pp. 233–58.

_____ **and Talmor, Eli.** Revenue-Neutral Changes in Corporate and Personal Income Taxes and Government Debt. In *Helpman, E.; Razin, A. and Sadka, E., eds.*, 1988, pp. 50–64.

Bennington, Gerald E. Assessing Market Potential. In *West, R. E. and Kreith, F., eds.*, 1988, pp. 125–66.

Benoit, Jean-Pierre. A Non-equilibrium Analysis of the Finitely-Repeated Prisoner's Dilemma. *Math. Soc. Sci.*, December 1988, 16(3), pp. 281–87.

Benoit-Thompson, Huguette and Ball, Michael O. A Lagrangian Relaxation Based Heuristic for the Urban Transit Crew Scheduling Problem. In *Daduna, J. R. and Wren, A., eds.*, 1988, pp. 54–67.

Benson, Bruce L. An Institutional Explanation for Corruption of Criminal Justice Officials. *Cato J.*, Spring–Summer 1988, 8(1), pp. 139–63.

_____. Corruption in Law Enforcement: One Consequence of "The Tragedy of the Commons" Arising with Public Allocation Processes. *Int. Rev. Law Econ.*, June 1988, 8(1), pp. 73–84.

_____. Legal Evolution in Primitive Societies. *J. Inst. Theoretical Econ.*, December 1988, 144(5), pp. 772–88.

_____ **and Engen, Eric M.** The Market for Laws: An Economic Analysis of Legislation. *Southern Econ. J.*, January 1988, 54(3), pp. 732–45.

_____ **and Faminow, M. D.** The Impact of Experience on Prices and Profits in Experimental Duopoly Markets. *J. Econ. Behav. Organ.*, June 1988, 9(4), pp. 345–65.

_____ **and Faminow, M. D.** Location Choice and Urban Growth in a Rent-Seeking Society. *Public Finance Quart.*, April 1988, 16(2), pp. 158–77.

_____ **and Feinberg, Robert M.** An Experimental Investigation of Equilibria Impacts of Information. *Southern Econ. J.*, January 1988, 54(3), pp. 546–61.

_____ **and Mitchell, Jean M.** Rent Seekers Who Demand Government Production: Bureaucratic Output and the Price of Complements. *Public Choice*, January 1988, 56(1), pp. 3–16.

Benson, Earl D.; Marks, Barry R. and Raman, K. K. Tax Effort as an Indicator of Fiscal Stress. *Public Finance Quart.*, April 1988, 16(2), pp. 203–18.

Benson, J. F.; Saunders, Caroline M. and Willis, K. G. The Impact of Agricultural Policy on the Costs of Nature Conservation. *Land Econ.*, May 1988, 64(2), pp. 147–57.

_____ **and Willis, K. G.** A Comparison of User Benefits and Costs of Nature Conservation at Three Nature Reserves. *Reg. Stud.*, October 1988, 22(5), pp. 417–28.

_____ **and Willis, K. G.** Valuation of Wildlife: A Case Study on the Upper Teesdale Site of Special Scientific Interest and Comparison of Methods in Environmental Economics. In *Turner, R. K., ed.*, 1988, pp. 243–64.

Benston, George J. A Comprehensive Analysis of the Determinants of Private Antitrust Litigation, with Particular Emphasis on Class Action Suits and the Rule of Joint and Several Damages. In *White, L. J., ed.*, 1988, pp. 271–328.

_____ **and Kaufman, George G.** Regulating Bank Safety and Performance. In *Haraf, W. S. and Kushmeider, R. M., eds.*, 1988, pp. 63–99.

Bental, Benjamin and Eckstein, Zvi. Inflation, Deficit, and Seignorage with Expected Stabilization. In *Helpman, E.; Razin, A. and Sadka, E., eds.*, 1988, pp. 238–53.

_____ **and Fixler, Dennis.** Firm Behavior and the Externalities of Technological Leadership. *Europ. Econ. Rev.*, November 1988, 32(9), pp. 1731–46.

Bentick, Brian L. and Pogue, Thomas F. The Impact on Development Timing of Property and Profit Taxation. *Land Econ.*, November 1988, 64(4), pp. 317–24.

Bentley, Orville G. The Changing Role of Agricultural Economics. In *Hildreth, R. J., et al., eds.*, 1988, pp. 14–20.

Benton, W. C. and Johnston, Wesley J. Bargaining, Negotiations, and Personal Selling. In *van Raaij, W. F.; van Veldhoven, G. M. and Wärneryd, K.-E., eds.*, 1988, pp. 449–71.

Benzing, Cynthia. A Reexamination of Money in the Aggregate Production Function. In *Pennsylvania Economic Association*, 1988, pp. 19–31.

Benzoni, Laurent. Sur la portée de la théorie hotellinienne des ressources épuisables. (With English summary.) *Revue Écon. Polit.*, Jan.–Feb. 1988, *98*(1), pp. 159–73.

Bequele, Assefa and Boyden, Jo. Working Children: Current Trends and Policy Responses. *Int. Lab. Rev.*, 1988, *127*(2), pp. 153–72.

Bera, Anil K.; Bubnys, Edward and Park, Hun Y. Conditional Heteroscedasticity in the Market Model and Efficient Estimates of Betas. *Financial Rev.*, May 1988, *23*(2), pp. 201–14.

_____ **and Higgins, M. L.** A Joint Test for Arch and Bilinearity in the Regression Model. *Econometric Rev.*, 1988–89, *7*(2), pp. 171–81.

_____ **and Newbold, Paul.** Checks of Model Adequacy for Univariate Time Series Models and Their Applications to Econometric Relationships: Comment. *Econometric Rev.*, 1988, *7*(1), pp. 43–48.

Beran, Rudolf. Balanced Simultaneous Confidence Sets. *J. Amer. Statist. Assoc.*, September 1988, *83*(403), pp. 679–86.

Beranek, William. A Historical Perspective of Research and Practice in Working-Capital Management. In *Kim, Y. H., ed.*, 1988, pp. 3–15.

_____ **and Forbes, Shawn M.** The Tax-Clientele CAPM and Firm-Size Effects: The Evidence. *Quart. J. Bus. Econ.*, Autumn 1988, *27*(4), pp. 87–112.

_____ **and Miles, James A.** The Excess Return Argument and Double Leverage. *Financial Rev.*, May 1988, *23*(2), pp. 143–50.

Berbel, J. Target Returns within Risk Programming Models: A Multi-objective Approach. *J. Agr. Econ.*, May 1988, *39*(2), pp. 263–70.

Berck, Peter and Perloff, Jeffrey M. The Dynamic Annihilation of a Rational Competitive Fringe by a Low-Cost Dominant Firm. *J. Econ. Dynam. Control*, November 1988, *12*(4), pp. 659–78.

Bercovich, Néstor and Katz, Jorge. Innovación genética, esfuerzos públicos de investigación y desarrollo y la frontera tecnológica internacional: nuevos híbridos en el inta. (With English summary.) *Desarrollo Econ.*, July–Sept. 1988, *28*(110), pp. 209–43.

Berechman, J. and Small, Kenneth A. Research Policy and Review 25. Modeling Land Use and Transportation: An Interpretive Review for Growth Areas. *Environ. Planning A*, October 1988, *20*(10), pp. 1285–1309.

_____ **and Werczberger, E.** Incorporating Neighborhood Effects into Spatial Allocation Models. *Environ. Planning A*, May 1988, *20*(5), pp. 595–607.

Berend, Iván. Growth Path and Capital Intensity. *Eastern Europ. Econ.*, Winter 1988–89, *27*(2), pp. 44–74.

Berenson, Stephen A.; Lane, Walter F. and Randolph, William C. Adjusting the CPI Shelter Index to Compensate for Effect of Depreciation. *Mon. Lab. Rev.*, October 1988, *111*(10), pp. 34–37.

Berg, Andrew and Sachs, Jeffrey D. The Debt Crisis: Structural Explanations of Country Performance. *J. Devel. Econ.*, November 1988, *29*(3), pp. 271–306.

Berg, Daniel and Mechlin, George F. Evaluating Research—ROI is Not Enough. In *Grønhaug, K. and Kaufmann, G., eds.*, 1988, *1980*, pp. 433–42.

van den Berg, G. M.; Duijsens, I. J., et al. and Duijkers, Thomas J. PRINCE: An Expert System for Nonlinear Principal Components Analysis. In *Edwards, D. and Raun, N. E., eds.*, 1988, pp. 149–53.

Berg, Gerald C. The Effects of the External Debts of Mexico, Brazil, Argentina, Venezuela, and the Philippines on the United States. *Appl. Econ.*, July 1988, *20*(7), pp. 939–56.

Berg, Hartmut. Motor-Cars: Between Growth and Protectionism. In *de Jong, H. W., ed.*, 1988, pp. 245–67.

Berg, Ivar and Kalleberg, Arne L. Work Structures and Markets: An Analytic Framework. In *Farkas, G. and England, P., eds.*, 1988, pp. 3–17.

van den Berg, L. and van der Meer, J. Dynamics of Urban Systems: General Trends and Dutch Experiences. *Environ. Planning A*, November 1988, *20*(11), pp. 1471–86.

Berg, Sanford V. Duopoly Compatibility Standards with Partial Cooperation and Standards Leadership. *Info. Econ. Policy*, 1988, *3*(1), pp. 35–53.

_____ **and Hoekman, Jacob M.** Entrepreneurship over the Product Life Cycle: Joint Venture Strategies in the Netherlands. In *Contractor, F. J. and Lorange, P.*, 1988, pp. 145–67.

Berg, Sven and Nurmi, Hannu. Making Choices in the Old-Fashioned Way. *Econ. Scelte Pubbliche/J. Public Finance Public Choice*, May–Aug. 1988, *6*(2), pp. 95–113.

Bergad, Laird W. Land Tenure, Slave Ownership, and Income Distribution in Nineteenth Century Cuba: Colón and Cárdenas, 1859–1876. *Soc. Econ. Stud.*, March–June 1988, *37*(1–2), pp. 301–40.

Berge, E. Some Comments on C. Hamnett's Reading of the Data on Sociotenurial Polarisation in South East England. *Environ. Planning A*, July 1988, *20*(7), pp. 973–77.

Bergendahl, Göran. Efficient Strategies for Natural Gas Expansion under Uncertainty: The Case of Sweden. *Energy Econ.*, April 1988, *10*(2), pp. 100–106.

Berger, Allen N. and Humphrey, David B. Interstate Banking and the Payments System. *J. Finan. Services Res.*, January 1988, *1*(2), pp. 131–45.

Berger, Bernard B. The Urban Wastewater Infrastructure. In *Ausubel, J. H. and Herman, R., eds.*, 1988, pp. 278–93.

Berger, Gordon M. Politics and Mobilization in

Japan, 1931–1945. In *Duus, P., ed.*, 1988, pp. 97–153.

Berger, James O. Bayesian Variable Selection in Linear Regression: Comment. *J. Amer. Statist. Assoc.*, December 1988, *83*(404), pp. 1033–34.

———— **and Deely, John.** A Bayesian Approach to Ranking and Selection of Related Means with Alternatives to Analysis-of-Variance Methodology. *J. Amer. Statist. Assoc.*, June 1988, *83*(402), pp. 364–73.

Berger, Kjell, et al. Effects of a Fall in the Price of Oil: The Case of a Small Oil-Exporting Country. In *Motamen, H., ed.*, 1988, pp. 457–71.

Berger, Lawrence A. A Model of the Underwriting Cycle in the Property/Liability Insurance Industry. *J. Risk Ins.*, June 1988, *55*(2), pp. 298–306.

————. Word-of-Mouth Reputations in Auto Insurance Markets. *J. Econ. Behav. Organ.*, September 1988, *10*(2), pp. 225–34.

Berger, Mark C. Cohort Size Effects on Earnings: Differences by College Major. *Econ. Educ. Rev.*, 1988, *7*(4), pp. 375–83.

————. Predicted Future Earnings and Choice of College Major. *Ind. Lab. Relat. Rev.*, April 1988, *41*(3), pp. 418–29.

———— **and Allen, Jacqueline F.** Black–White Earnings Ratios: The Role of Cohort Size Effects. *Econ. Letters*, 1988, *26*(3), pp. 285–90.

————; **Blomquist, Glenn C. and Scott, Frank A., Jr.** Impacts of Air Pollution Control Strategies in Kentucky. *Growth Change*, Spring 1988, *19*(2), pp. 40–55.

————; **Hoehn, John P. and Blomquist, Glenn C.** New Estimates of Quality of Life in Urban Areas. *Amer. Econ. Rev.*, March 1988, *78*(1), pp. 89–107.

———— **and Leigh, J. Paul.** The Effect of Alcohol Use on Wages. *Appl. Econ.*, October 1988, *20*(10), pp. 1343–51.

Berger, Thomas R. Conflict in Alaska. *Natural Res. J.*, Winter 1988, *28*(1), pp. 37–62.

Berges, Angel and Viñals, José M. Financial Innovation and Capital Formation. In *Heertje, A., ed.*, 1988, pp. 158–202.

van den Bergh, Willem Max; Wessels, Roberto E. and Wijmenga, Roel T. Two Tests of the Tax-Loss Selling Hypothesis. In *Dimson, E., ed.*, 1988, pp. 147–54.

Berglund, Tom. Bör statsägda företag privatiseras? (Should State Companies Be Privatized? With English summary.) *Ekon. Samfundets Tidskr.*, 1988, *41*(2), pp. 75–76.

———— **and Liljeblom, Eva.** Market Serial Correlation on a Small Security Market: A Note. *J. Finance*, December 1988, *43*(5), pp. 1265–74.

Bergman, Bruce J. Occupational Pay in Structural Clay Products Industries. *Mon. Lab. Rev.*, May 1988, *111*(5), pp. 47–50.

Bergman, Lars. Energy Policy Modeling: A Survey of General Equilibrium Approaches. *J. Policy Modeling*, Fall 1988, *10*(3), pp. 377–99.

Bergmann, Barbara R. An Experiment on the Formation of Expectations. *J. Econ. Behav. Organ.*, March 1988, *9*(2), pp. 137–51.

————. A Fresh Start Defended: Response. *Challenge*, May–June 1988, *31*(3), pp. 51–52.

Bergmann, Burckhard. Natural Gas in Western Europe: Facing the Oil Price Uncertainties. In *Mabro, R., ed.*, 1988, pp. 165–76.

Bergmann, Denis R. The Transition to an Overlapping Agricultural System in Europe: An Economic and Institutional Analysis. In *Antonelli, G. and Quadrio-Curzio, A., eds.*, 1988, pp. 53–72.

v. Bergmann-Winberg, Marie-Louise. Jämförelse av välfärd och samhällsststem. (Comparison of Welfare and Social Systems. With English summary.) *Ekon. Samfundets Tidskr.*, 1988, *41*(1), pp. 55–60.

Bergsma, Jan R. Planning of Tourists Routes: The Green Coast Road in the Northern Netherlands. In *Goodall, B. and Ashworth, G., eds.*, 1988, pp. 89–100.

Bergsten, C. Fred. The U.S. Economy at a Turning Point. *Challenge*, Nov.–Dec. 1988, *31*(6), pp. 17–25.

———— **and Dobell, Rod.** The Canada–United States Free Trade Agreement: The Global Impact: Preface. In *Schott, J. J. and Smith, M. G., eds.*, 1988, pp. vii–ix.

Bergstrom, Theodore C., et al. A Test for Efficiency in the Supply of Public Education. *J. Public Econ.*, April 1988, *35*(3), pp. 289–307.

Berkowitz, Edward D. The Cost–Benefit Tradition in Vocational Rehabilitation. In *Berkowitz, M., ed.*, 1988, pp. 10–28.

————. Disability Insurance and the Social Security Tradition. In *Nash, G. D.; Pugach, N. H. and Tomasson, R. F., eds.*, 1988, pp. 279–98.

Berkowitz, Marvin. End Users and Technical Staff as Influencers in Buying New Industrial Products: High Stakes, but Do They Really Matter? In *Woodside, A. G., ed.*, 1988, pp. 27–48.

Berkowitz, Monroe. Measuring the Efficiency of Public Programs: Costs and Benefits in Vocational Rehabilitation: Introduction. In *Berkowitz, M., ed.*, 1988, pp. 1–6.

————. Measuring the Efficiency of Public Programs: Costs and Benefits in Vocational Rehabilitation: Conclusion. In *Berkowitz, M., ed.*, 1988, pp. 257–63.

Berkowitz, S. D. Market and Market-Areas: Some Preliminary Formulations. In *Wellman, B. and Berkowitz, S. D., eds.*, 1988, pp. 261–303.

———— **and Wellman, Barry.** Introduction: Studying Social Structures. In *Wellman, B. and Berkowitz, S. D., eds.*, 1988, pp. 1–14.

Berkowitz, Stephen A.; Logue, Dennis E. and Noser, Eugene A., Jr. The Total Cost of Transactions on the NYSE. *J. Finance*, March 1988, *43*(1), pp. 97–112.

Berlage, Lodewijk and Terweduwe, Dirk. The Classification of Countries by Cluster and by Factor Analysis. *World Devel.*, December 1988, *16*(12), pp. 1527–45.

Berliant, Marcus and ten Raa, Thijs. A Foundation of Location Theory: Consumer Preferences and Demand. *J. Econ. Theory*, April 1988, *44*(2), pp. 336–53.

Berlin, Mitchell and Loeys, Jan. Bond Covenants

and Delegated Monitoring. *J. Finance*, June 1988, *43*(2), pp. 397–412.

Berliner, Joseph S. Bureaucratic Conservatism and Creativity in the Soviet Economy. In *Berliner, J. S.*, 1988, *1971*, pp. 188–211.

_____. Continuities in Management from Stalin to Gorbachev. In *Berliner, J. S.*, 1988, pp. 269–97.

_____. The Economics of Overtaking and Surpassing. In *Berliner, J. S.*, 1988, *1966*, pp. 159–87.

_____. The Informal Organization of the Soviet Firm. In *Berliner, J. S.*, 1988, *1952*, pp. 21–46.

_____. Monetary Planning in the USSR. In *Berliner, J. S.*, 1988, *1950*, pp. 1–20.

_____. Planning and Management. In *Berliner, J. S.*, 1988, *1983*, pp. 97–143.

_____. A Problem in Soviet Business Administration. In *Berliner, J. S.*, 1988, *1956*, pp. 47–60.

_____. Some International Aspects of Soviet Technological Progress. In *Berliner, J. S.*, 1988, *1973*, pp. 212–21.

_____. The Static Efficiency of the Soviet Economy. In *Berliner, J. S.*, 1988, *1964*, pp. 147–58.

_____. Technological Progress and the Evolution of Soviet Pricing Policy. In *Berliner, J. S.*, 1988, *1981*, pp. 222–45.

Berman, Brian W.; Ben David, Moshe and Meissner, Frank. Export Marketing for Off-Season Fresh Produce: The Case of Agrexco, Israel. In *Kumcu, E. and Firat, A. F., eds.*, 1988, pp. 253–83.

Berman, Peter and Ormond, Barbara A. Changes in Health Care Demand and Supply Accompanying Economic Development. In *Sirageldin, I. and Sorkin, A., eds.*, 1988, pp. 147–72.

Bernal, Richard L. Default as a Negotiating Tactic in Debt Rescheduling Strategies of Developing Countries: A Preliminary Note. In *Jorge, A. and Salazar-Carrillo, J., eds.*, 1988, pp. 41–58.

_____. The Great Depression, Colonial Policy and Industrialization in Jamaica. *Soc. Econ. Stud.*, March–June 1988, *37*(1–2), pp. 33–64.

Bernanke, Ben S. and Blinder, Alan S. Credit, Money, and Aggregate Demand. *Amer. Econ. Rev.*, May 1988, *78*(2), pp. 435–39.

_____; **Bohn, Henning and Reiss, Peter C.** Alternative Non-nested Specification Tests of Time-Series Investment Models. *J. Econometrics*, March 1988, *37*(3), pp. 293–326.

_____ **and Campbell, John Y.** Is There a Corporate Debt Crisis? *Brookings Pap. Econ. Act.*, 1988, (1), pp. 83–125.

Bernard, Georges. Probability in Quantum Mechanics and in Utility Theory. In *Munier, B. R., ed.*, 1988, pp. 545–56.

Bernard, Jean-Thomas. Canadian Electricity. *Energy J.*, October 1988, *9*(4), pp. 127–30.

_____ **and Thivierge, Simon.** Les politiques fiscales et financiéres des services d'électricité: Le cas d'Hydro-Québec. (With English summary.) *Can. Public Policy*, September 1988, *14*(3), pp. 239–44.

Bernardi, Luigi and Gerelli, Emilio. World Tax Reform: A Progress Report: Italy: Comment. In *Pechman, J. A., ed.*, 1988, pp. 147–53.

Bernardino, Adriana Teixeira and de Castro, Newton. A escolha de conteinerizaçao na exportaçao de manufaturados. (With English summary.) *Pesquisa Planejamento Econ.*, December 1988, *18*(3), pp. 709–40.

Bernardo, Daniel J. The Effect of Spatial Variability of Irrigation Applications on Risk-Efficient Irrigation Strategies. *Southern J. Agr. Econ.*, July 1988, *20*(1), pp. 77–86.

Berndt, Ernst R. Envelope Consistent Functional Separability. In *Barnett, W. A.; Berndt, E. R. and White, H., eds.*, 1988, pp. 27–41.

Bernheim, B. Douglas. Budget Deficits and the Balance of Trade. In *Summers, L. H., ed.*, 1988, pp. 1–31.

_____. Social Security Benefits: An Empirical Study of Expectations and Realizations. In *Ricardo-Campbell, R. and Lazear, E. P., eds.*, 1988, pp. 312–45.

_____ **and Bagwell, Kyle.** Is Everything Neutral? *J. Polit. Econ.*, April 1988, *96*(2), pp. 308–38.

_____ **and Shoven, John B.** Fiscalité et coût du capital: Une comparaison internationale. (Tax Systems and the Cost of Capital: An International Comparison. With English summary.) *Ann. Écon. Statist.*, July–Sept. 1988, (11), pp. 93–116.

_____ **and Shoven, John B.** Pension Funding and Saving. In *Bodie, Z.; Shoven, J. B. and Wise, D. A., eds.*, 1988, pp. 85–111.

_____ **and Stark, Oded.** Altruism within the Family Reconsidered: Do Nice Guys Finish Last? *Amer. Econ. Rev.*, December 1988, *78*(5), pp. 1034–45.

Bernholz, Peter. Hyperinflation and Currency Reform in Bolivia: Studied from a General Perspective. *J. Inst. Theoretical Econ.*, December 1988, *144*(5), pp. 747–71.

_____. Inflation, Monetary Regime and the Financial Asset Theory of Money. *Kyklos*, 1988, *41*(1), pp. 5–34.

_____. The New Institutional Economics Applied to Monetary Economics: Comment. *J. Inst. Theoretical Econ.*, February 1988, *144*(1), pp. 225–30.

_____ **and Faber, Malte.** Reflections on a Normative Economic Theory of the Unification of Law. In *Gwartney, J. D. and Wagner, R. E., eds.*, 1988, pp. 229–49.

Bernier, André and Fortin, Bernard. The Welfare Cost of Unemployment in Quebec: Harberger's Triangle Meets Okun's Gap. *Can. J. Econ.*, February 1988, *21*(1), pp. 161–81.

Bernier, Bernard. The Japanese Peasantry and Economic Growth Since the Land Reform of 1946–47. In *Tsurumi, E. P., ed.*, 1988, pp. 78–90.

Bernier, Gilles and Nguyen, The-Hiep. Beta and q in a Simultaneous Framework with Pooled Data. *Rev. Econ. Statist.*, August 1988, *70*(3), pp. 520–24.

de Bernis, Gérard. Endettement et développement?: Quelques leçons de la crise actuelle. (Indebtedness and Development: Some Lessons of Current Crisis. With English summary.) *Écon. Appl.*, 1988, *41*(4), pp. 679–708.

_____. Les contraditions des relations financieres internationales dans la crise. (The Contradictions in the International Financial Relationships during the Present Crisis. With English summary.) *Écon. Soc.*, May 1988, *22*(5), pp. 101–32.

Bernknopf, R. L., et al. An Economic and Geographic Appraisal of a Spatial Natural Hazard Risk: A Study of Landslide Mitigation Rules. *Environ. Planning A*, May 1988, *20*(5), pp. 621–31.

Bernstein, Henry. Development I: Variations on Capitalism. In *Crow, B. and Thorpe, M., et al.*, 1988, pp. 67–82.

_____. Development II: Variations on Socialism and Nationalism. In *Crow, B. and Thorpe, M., et al.*, 1988, pp. 83–99.

_____. Labour Regimes and Social Change under Colonialism. In *Crow, B. and Thorpe, M., et al.*, 1988, pp. 30–49.

_____. National Economies: Diversity and Integration. In *Crow, B. and Thorpe, M., et al.*, 1988, pp. 100–121.

_____. Production and Producers. In *Crow, B. and Thorpe, M., et al.*, 1988, pp. 54–66.

_____ **and Crow, Ben.** The Expansion of Europe. In *Crow, B. and Thorpe, M., et al.*, 1988, pp. 9–29.

Bernstein, Jeffrey I. Costs of Production, Intra- and Interindustry R&D Spillovers: Canadian Evidence. *Can. J. Econ.*, May 1988, *21*(2), pp. 324–47.

_____. Dynamic Factor Demands and Adjustment Costs: An Analysis of Bell Canada's Technology. *Info. Econ. Policy*, 1988, *3*(1), pp. 5–24.

_____. Multiple Outputs, Adjustment Costs and the Structure of Production for Bell Canada. *Int. J. Forecasting*, 1988, *4*(2), pp. 207–19.

_____ **and Nadiri, M. Ishaq.** Interindustry R&D Spillovers, Rates of Return, and Production in High-Tech Industries. *Amer. Econ. Rev.*, May 1988, *78*(2), pp. 429–34.

Bernstein, Mark Allen and Hegazy, Youseff. The Economic Costs of Electricity Shortages: A Case Study of Egypt. *Energy J.*, Special Issue, 1988, *9*, pp. 173–89.

Bernstein, Peter L. Financial Markets and Real Economies in the 1980s: What Really Happened? *Bus. Econ.*, July 1988, *23*(3), pp. 7–13.

_____. How Speculative Was the Bull Market? *J. Portfol. Manage.*, Fall 1988, *15*(1), pp. 1.

Beron, Kurt J. Applying the Economic Model of Crime to Child Support Enforcement: A Theoretical and Empirical Analysis. *Rev. Econ. Statist.*, August 1988, *70*(3), pp. 382–90.

Berrebi, Edmond and Abraham-Frois, Gilbert. Optimisation et prix de production. (With English summary.) *Revue Écon. Polit.*, Jan.–Feb. 1988, *98*(1), pp. 66–77.

Berrebi, Z. M. and Silber, Jacques G. Distance Functions and the Comparison of Development Levels. *Econ. Letters*, 1988, *27*(2), pp. 195–200.

Berridge, John. The Politicisation of Local Government. In *Bailey, S. J. and Paddison, R., eds.*, 1988, pp. 42–59.

_____ **and Goodman, John.** The British Universities Industrial Relations Association: The First 35 Years. *Brit. J. Ind. Relat.*, July 1988, *26*(2), pp. 155–77.

Berry, Brian J. L. Migration Reversals in Perspective: The Long-Wave Evidence. *Int. Reg. Sci. Rev.*, 1988, *11*(3), pp. 245–51.

Berry, S. Keith. The Allocation of Risk between Stockholders and Ratepayers in Regulated Utilities. *Land Econ.*, May 1988, *64*(2), pp. 114–24.

Berry, Sara. Property Rights and Rural Resource Management: The Case of Tree Crops in West Africa. In *Bennett, J. W. and Bowen, J. R., eds.*, 1988, pp. 143–61.

Berry, Steven and Briggs, Hugh. A Non-parametric Test of a First-Order Markov Process for Regimes in a Non-cooperatively Collusive Industry. *Econ. Letters*, 1988, *27*(1), pp. 73–77.

_____; **Gottschalk, Peter and Wissoker, Doug.** An Error Components Model of the Impact of Plant Closing on Earnings. *Rev. Econ. Statist.*, November 1988, *70*(4), pp. 701–07.

Bertelè, Umberto. The Agro-food Filière: A Microeconomic Study on the Evolution of the Industrial Apparatus under the Impact of Structural Changes. In *Antonelli, G. and Quadrio-Curzio, A., eds.*, 1988, pp. 209–30.

Berthélemy, Jean-Claude. The Transfer Paradox in a Non-Walrasian Context. *Weltwirtsch. Arch.*, 1988, *124*(3), pp. 420–34.

Bertho-Lavenir, Catherine. The Telephone in France 1879–1979: National Characteristics and International Influences. In *Mayntz, R. and Hughes, T. P., eds.*, 1988, pp. 155–77.

Berthoud, Arnaud. Economie politique et morale chez Walras. (Political and Moral Economy: Walras. With English summary.) *Écon. Soc.*, March 1988, *22*(3), pp. 65–93.

_____. Morale et enrichissement monétaire chez J. Locke. Réponse. (Morals and Monetary Enrichment in J. Locke: Response. With English summary.) *Écon. Soc.*, October 1988, *22*(10), pp. 3–19.

Bertonèche, Marc. International Financial Innovation and Stability of Capital Markets: A Case of Trade-Off. *Rev. Econ. Cond. Italy*, Sept.–Dec. 1988, (3), pp. 399–410.

Bertram, Hans-Henning and Winckler, Joachim. Scheduling on Microcomputers Using MICROBUS. In *Daduna, J. R. and Wren, A., eds.*, 1988, pp. 188–99.

Bertrand, Joseph. Review of Walras's *Théorie Mathématique de la richesse sociale* and Cournot's *Recherches sur les principes mathématiques de la théorie des richesses*. In *Daughety, A. F., ed.*, 1988, pp. 73–81.

Bertrand, William E.; Arminana, Ruben and Auvert, Bertran. Microcomputer Applications in the Health and Social Service Sectors of Developing Countries. In *Bhalla, A. S. and James, D., eds.*, 1988, pp. 127–36.

Berzuini, Carlo. Generating Rules by Means of Regression Analysis. In *Edwards, D. and Raun, N. E., eds.*, 1988, pp. 273–78.

Bes, C. and Sethi, S. Prakash. Dynamic Stochastic Optimization Problems in the Framework of Forecast and Decision Horizons. In *Eiselt, H. A. and Pederzoli, G., eds.*, 1988, pp. 230–46.

Besada, Manuel; Estevez, Margarita and Hervés, Carlos. Equilibria in Economies with Countably Many Commodities. *Econ. Letters*, 1988, 26(3), pp. 203–07.

_____; **Estévez, Margarita and Hervés, Carlos.** Existencia de equilibrio en una economía con producción e infinitas mercancias. (With English summary.) *Invest. Econ.*, January 1988, 12(1), pp. 69–81.

_____; **Estévez, Margarita and Hervés, Carlos.** Núcleo de una economía con infinitas mercancias. (With English summary.) *Invest. Econ.*, September 1988, 12(3), pp. 445–53.

Besanko, David and Baron, David P. Monitoring of Performance in Organizational Contracting: The Case of Defense Procurement. *Scand. J. Econ.*, 1988, 90(3), pp. 329–56.

_____ **and Donnenfeld, Shabtai.** The Impact of Buyers' Expectations on Entry Deterrence. *Econ. Letters*, 1988, 26(4), pp. 375–80.

_____ **and Donnenfeld, Shabtai.** Rate of Return Regulation and Product Variety. *J. Public Econ.*, August 1988, 36(3), pp. 293–304.

_____; **Donnenfeld, Shabtai and White, Lawrence J.** The Multiproduct Firm, Quality Choice, and Regulation. *J. Ind. Econ.*, June 1988, 36(4), pp. 411–29.

Besley, Timothy J. Optimal Reimbursement Health Insurance and the Theory of Ramsey Taxation. *J. Health Econ.*, December 1988, 7(4), pp. 321–36.

_____. Rationing, Income Effects and Supply Response: A Theoretical Note. *Oxford Econ. Pap.*, June 1988, 40(2), pp. 378–89.

_____. A Simple Model for Merit Good Arguments. *J. Public Econ.*, April 1988, 35(3), pp. 371–83.

_____. Tied-in Credit with a Monopoly Product Market. *Econ. Letters*, 1988, 28(2), pp. 105–08.

_____ **and Kanbur, S. M. Ravi.** Food Subsidies and Poverty Alleviation. *Econ. J.*, September 1988, 98(392), pp. 701–19.

_____ **and Preston, I. P.** Invariance and the Axiomatics of Income Tax Progression: A Comment. *Bull. Econ. Res.*, April 1988, 40(2), pp. 159–63.

Besomi, Daniele. Michal Kalecki: La dinamica economica tra materialismo e meccanicismo. (Economic Dynamics between Materialism and Mechanism: The Case of Michal Kalecki. With English summary.) *Econ. Polit.*, December 1988, 5(3), pp. 343–68.

Bessler, David A. Quantitative Techniques: A Discussion. In *Hildreth, R. J., et al., eds.*, 1988, pp. 199–204.

_____ **and McIntosh, Christopher S.** Forecasting Agricultural Prices Using a Bayesian Composite Approach. *Southern J. Agr. Econ.*, December 1988, 20(2), pp. 73–80.

_____ **and VanTassell, Larry W.** Dynamic Price and Adjustments between Commercial and Purebred Cattle Markets. *Southern J. Agr. Econ.*, December 1988, 20(2), pp. 137–43.

Bester, Helmut. Bargaining, Search Costs and Equilibrium Price Distributions. *Rev. Econ. Stud.*, April 1988, 55(2), pp. 201–14.

_____. Qualitative Uncertainty in a Market with Bilateral Trading. *Scand. J. Econ.*, 1988, 90(3), pp. 415–34.

Betancourt, Roger and Gautschi, David. The Economics of Retail Firms. *Managerial Dec. Econ.*, June 1988, 9(2), pp. 133–44.

Betge, Peter. Planung und Kontrolle von Betriebsmittelkosten. (With English summary.) *Z. Betriebswirtshaft*, November 1988, 58(11), pp. 1259–72.

Bethenod, Jean-Marie. La stabilité de la demande de monnaie en France, 1964–1985: l'apport d'une reformulation du revenu permanent. (With English summary.) *Revue Écon. Polit.*, July–Aug. 1988, 98(4), pp. 508–29.

_____ **and Prat, Georges.** Reformulation de la demande de monnaie et dynamique monetaire: France, 1964–1983. (A New Formulation of the "Standard" Model of Demand for Money. With English summary.) *Écon. Soc.*, January 1988, 22(1), pp. 205–47.

Bethlehem, Jelke G. and Keller, Wouter J. New Perspectives in Computer Assisted Survey Processing. In *Edwards, D. and Raun, N. E., eds.*, 1988, pp. 377–88.

Betson, David M.; Warlick, Jennifer L. and Smeeding, Timothy M. The Effects of Taxing Unemployment Insurance Benefits Accounting For Induced Labor Supply Responses. In *Danziger, S. H. and Portney, K. E., eds.*, 1988, pp. 149–67.

Bettelheim, Charles. Economic Reform in China. *J. Devel. Stud.*, July 1988, 24(4), pp. 15–49.

Bettio, Francesca. Sex-Typing of Occupations, the Cycle and Restructuring in Italy. In *Rubery, J., ed.*, 1988, pp. 74–99.

_____. Women, the State and the Family in Italy: Problems of Female Participation in Historical Perspective. In *Rubery, J., ed.*, 1988, pp. 191–217.

Betz, Frederick. The Nature of Cooperative Research: Reaching Agreement on Process, Uses, and Ownership. In *Powers, D. R., et al.*, 1988, pp. 281–98.

_____. Organizing and Managing a Cooperative Research Center. In *Powers, D. R., et al.*, 1988, pp. 299–327.

Betz, H. K. How Does the German Historical School Fit? *Hist. Polit. Econ.*, Fall 1988, 20(3), pp. 409–30.

Beukes, Theo E. Mineral Exploration in South Africa. In *Tilton, J. E.; Eggert, R. G. and Landsberg, H. H., eds.*, 1988, pp. 179–97.

Bevan, D. L., et al. Incomes in the United Republic of Tanzania during the "Nyerere Experiment." In *van Ginneken, W., ed.*, 1988, pp. 61–83.

Bewley, Ronald. AUTOBOX: A Review. *J. Appl. Econometrics*, July–Sept. 1988, *3*(3), pp. 240–44.

_____ **and Fiebig, Denzil G.** Estimation of Price Elasticities for an International Telephone Demand Model. *J. Ind. Econ.*, June 1988, *36*(4), pp. 393–409.

_____ **and Fiebig, Denzil G.** A Flexible Logistic Growth Model with Applications in Telecommunications. *Int. J. Forecasting*, 1988, *4*(2), pp. 177–92.

Bey, Roger P. and Burgess, Richard C. Optimal Portfolios: Markowitz Full Covariance versus Simple Selection Rules. *J. Finan. Res.*, Summer 1988, *11*(2), pp. 153–63.

_____ **and Collins, J. Markham.** The Relationship between Before- and After-Tax Yields on Financial Assets. *Financial Rev.*, August 1988, *23*(3), pp. 313–31.

Bezdek, Roger H. and Jones, Jonathan D. Federal Categorical Grants-in-Aid and State–Local Government Expenditures. *Public Finance*, 1988, *43*(1), pp. 39–55.

Bezucha, Robert. The French Revolution of 1848 and the Social History of Work. In *Burke, E., III, ed.*, 1988, *1983*, pp. 25–39.

Bezuneh, Mesfin; Deaton, Brady J. and Norton, George W. Food Aid Impacts in Rural Kenya. *Amer. J. Agr. Econ.*, February 1988, *70*(1), pp. 181–91.

Bhaduri, Amit. Comparative Advantage, External Finance and the Vulnerability of Industrialization. *Industry Devel.*, January 1988, (23), pp. 45–56.

_____. The Concept of the Marginal Productivity of Capital and the Wicksell Effect. In *Steedman, I., ed., Vol. 1*, 1988, *1966*, pp. 109–13.

_____. On the Significance of Recent Controversies on Capital Theory: A Marxian View. In *Steedman, I., ed., Vol. 2*, 1988, *1969*, pp. 369–76.

Bhagwati, Jagdish N. Export-Promoting Protection: Endogenous Monopoly and Price Disparity. *Pakistan Devel. Rev.*, Spring 1988, *27*(1), pp. 1–5.

_____. Export-Promoting Trade Strategy: Issues and Evidence. *World Bank Res. Observer*, January 1988, *3*(1), pp. 27–57.

_____. Global Interdependence and International Migration. In *Cassing, J. H. and Husted, S. L., eds.*, 1988, pp. 149–83.

_____. International Migration and Income Taxation. In *Helpman, E.; Razin, A. and Sadka, E., eds.*, 1988, pp. 13–32.

_____. Poverty and Public Policy. *World Devel.*, May 1988, *16*(5), pp. 539–55.

Bhalla, Ajit S. Microelectronics Use for Small-Scale Production in Developing Countries. In *Bhalla, A. S. and James, D., eds.*, 1988, pp. 53–64.

_____ **and James, Dilmus.** New Technologies and Development: Experiences in "Technology Blending": Introduction. In *Bhalla, A. S. and James, D., eds.*, 1988, pp. 1–9.

_____ **and James, Dilmus.** New Technologies and Development: Experiences in "Technology Blending": Conclusions and Lessons. In *Bhalla, A. S. and James, D., eds.*, 1988, pp. 287–305.

_____ **and James, Dilmus.** Some Conceptual and Policy Issues. In *Bhalla, A. S. and James, D., eds.*, 1988, pp. 28–37.

_____ **and Jéquier, Nicolas.** Telecommunications for Rural Development. In *Bhalla, A. S. and James, D., eds.*, 1988, pp. 269–83.

Bhalla, G. S. Agrarian Change in India since Independence. In *Kohli, U. and Gautam, V., eds.*, 1988, pp. 39–48.

Bhalla, Surjit S. Does Land Quality Matter? Theory and Measurement. *J. Devel. Econ.*, July 1988, *29*(1), pp. 45–62.

_____. Is Sri Lanka an Exception? A Comparative Study of Living Standards. In *Srinivasan, T. N. and Bardhan, P. K., eds.*, 1988, pp. 89–117.

_____. Sri Lanka's Achievements: Fact and Fancy. In *Srinivasan, T. N. and Bardhan, P. K., eds.*, 1988, pp. 557–65.

_____ **and Roy, Prannoy L.** Mis-specification in Farm Productivity Analysis: The Role of Land Quality. *Oxford Econ. Pap.*, March 1988, *40*(1), pp. 55–73.

_____ **and Vashistha, Prem.** Income Distribution in India—A Re-examination. In *Srinivasan, T. N. and Bardhan, P. K., eds.*, 1988, pp. 39–68.

Bhandari, Jagdeep S.; Driskill, Robert and Frenkel, Jacob A. Capital Mobility and Exchange Rate Overshooting: Reply. *Europ. Econ. Rev.*, January 1988, *32*(1), pp. 203–06.

Bhandari, Labdhi; Dholakia, Ruby Roy and Sharif, Mohammed. Consumption in the Third World: Challenges for Marketing and Development. In *Kumcu, E. and Firat, A. F., eds.*, 1988, pp. 129–47.

Bhandari, Laxmi Chand. Debt/Equity Ratio and Expected Common Stock Returns: Empirical Evidence. *J. Finance*, June 1988, *43*(2), pp. 507–28.

Bhangoo, K. S. and Singh, Lakhwinder. Changes in the Structure of Industrial Work Force in Punjab. *Margin*, Jan.–March 1988, *20*(2), pp. 54–64.

Bharadwaj, Krishna R. The Analytics of the Agriculture–Industry Relation. In *Arrow, K. J., ed.*, 1988, pp. 198–217.

_____. On the Maximum Number of Switches between Two Production Systems. In *Steedman, I., ed., Vol. 2*, 1988, *1970*, pp. 141–61.

_____. Sraffa's Ricardo. *Cambridge J. Econ.*, March 1988, *12*(1), pp. 67–84.

_____. Value through Exogenous Distribution. In *Steedman, I., ed., Vol. 1*, 1988, *1963*, pp. 11–14.

Bhargava, Alok and Sargan, John Denis. Estimating Dynamic Random Effects Models from Panel Data Covering Short Time Periods. In *Sargan, J. D., Vol. 2*, 1988, *1983*, pp. 270–96.

_____ **and Sargan, John Denis.** Maximum Likelihood Estimation of Regression Models with First Order Moving Average Errors When the Root Lies on the Unit Circles. In *Sargan, J. D., Vol. 2,* 1988, *1983,* pp. 182–203.

Bhasin, Vijay K. Demand for Money, Foreign Aid and the Non-neutrality of Money. *Indian Econ. J.,* July–September 1988, *36*(1), pp. 76–92.

_____. Supply of Money, Non-neutrality of Money and the Comparative Dynamics. *Keio Econ. Stud.,* 1988, *25*(2), pp. 49–65.

Bhaskar, V. The Kinked Demand Curve: A Game-Theoretic Approach. *Int. J. Ind. Organ.,* 1988, *6*(3), pp. 373–84.

Bhatia, Kul B. Tax Incidence in a Hierarchical Model. *J. Public Econ.,* November 1988, *37*(2), pp. 221–42.

Bhatia, Ramesh. Energy Pricing and Household Energy Consumption in India. *Energy J.,* Special Issue, 1988, *9,* pp. 71–105.

_____. Photovoltaic Lighting in Fiji. In *Bhalla, A. S. and James, D., eds.,* 1988, pp. 191–201.

_____. Photovoltaic Street Lighting in India. In *Bhalla, A. S. and James, D., eds.,* 1988, pp. 171–90.

Bhatt, V. V. Growth and Income Distribution in India: A Review. *World Devel.,* May 1988, *16*(5), pp. 641–47.

_____. On Financial Innovations and Credit Market Evolution. *World Devel.,* February 1988, *16*(2), pp. 281–92.

_____. Structural Adaptation and Public Enterprise Performance. In *Streeten, P., ed.,* 1988, pp. 174–202.

Bhattacharya, Malini. Experiments in Socialist Practice: Some Impressions of the People's Republic of China. In *Mitra, A., ed.,* 1988, pp. 169–81.

Bhattacharya, N.; Chatterjee, G. S. and Pal, Padmaja. Variations in Level of Living across Regions and Social Groups in Rural India, 1963/1964 and 1973/1974. In *Srinivasan, T. N. and Bardhan, P. K., eds.,* 1988, pp. 154–218.

Bhattacharya, Sudipto. Corporate Finance and the Legacy of Miller and Modigliani. *J. Econ. Perspectives,* Fall 1988, *2*(4), pp. 135–47.

_____ **and Guasch, J. Luis.** Heterogeneity, Tournaments, and Hierarchies. *J. Polit. Econ.,* August 1988, *96*(4), pp. 867–81.

_____ **and Jacklin, Charles J.** Distinguishing Panics and Information-Based Bank Runs: Welfare and Policy Implications. *J. Polit. Econ.,* June 1988, *96*(3), pp. 568–92.

Bhattacharyya, Amit K. and Hayes, Adrian C. Cottage Industry and Fertility in a Village in West Bengal, India. In *Vlassoff, C. and Barkat-e-Khuda, eds.,* 1988, pp. 49–57.

Bhattacherjee, Debashish. Unions, State and Capital in Western India: Structural Determinants of the 1982 Bombay Textile Strike. In *Southall, R., ed.,* 1988, pp. 211–37.

Bhatty, I. Z., et al. Some Thoughts after the Drought. *Margin,* April–June 1988, *20*(3), pp. 31–50.

Bhole, L. M. and Sundararajan, S. Impacts of

Devaluation on the Trade Balance. *Margin,* July–Sept. 1988, *20*(4), pp. 48–59.

Bhowmik, Sharit. Producers' Co-operatives in the Indian Tea Industry. In *Attwood, D. W. and Baviskar, B. S., eds.,* 1988, pp. 172–87.

Bhushan, Bharat and Raikhy, P. S. Role of Financial Institutions—An Inter State Analysis. In *Raikhy, P. S. and Gill, S. S., eds.,* 1988, pp. 152–68.

Bialer, Seweryn. Gorbachev's Program of Change: Sources, Significance, Prospects. In *Bialer, S. and Mandelbaum, M., eds.,* 1988, pp. 231–99.

Bianchi, Andrés. Latin America 1981–1984: Crisis, Adjustment, and Recovery. In *Urrutia, M., ed.,* 1988, pp. 17–42.

Bianchi, Carluccio and Rampa, Lorenzo. Financial Assets and the Short-run Dynamics of a Capitalist Economy. *Econ. Notes,* 1988, (3), pp. 29–50.

Bianchi, Patrizio and Forlai, Luigi. The European Domestic Appliance Industry, 1945–1987. In *de Jong, H. W., ed.,* 1988, pp. 269–96.

Bianco, Lucien and Hua, Chang-ming. Implementation and Resistance: The Single-Child Family Policy. In *Feuchtwang, S.; Hussain, A. and Pairault, T., eds., Vol. 1,* 1988, pp. 147–68.

Bianco, Lucio. Mathematical Models in Logistic System Design. In *Bianco, L. and La Bella, A., eds.,* 1988, pp. 210–57.

Biasco, Salvatore. Dynamic and Incapsulating Processes in the Generation of the World Demand. *Banca Naz. Lavoro Quart. Rev.,* June 1988, (165), pp. 179–215.

_____. Financial Markets, Investment and Employment: Comment. In *Kregel, J. A.; Matzner, E. and Roncaglia, A., eds.,* 1988, pp. 93–99.

Bibikov, Michael. The Comparative Study of the Medieval Ports of the Northern Pontos. 12th–15th Centuries. In *Cavaciocchi, S., ed.,* 1988, pp. 937–60.

Bible, Thomas D. and McMullen, B. Starr. Sources of Profit Risk for Small Wood Product Manufacturing Firms in the Pacific Northwest. *Land Econ.,* May 1988, *64*(2), pp. 184–95.

Bicchieri, Christina. Should a Scientist Abstain from Metaphor? In *Klamer, A.; McCloskey, D. N. and Solow, R. M., eds.,* 1988, pp. 100–114.

Bick, Avi. Producing Derivative Assets with Forward Contracts. *J. Finan. Quant. Anal.,* June 1988, *23*(2), pp. 153–60.

Bickel, Peter J. and Yahav, Joseph A. Richardson Extrapolation and the Bootstrap. *J. Amer. Statist. Assoc.,* June 1988, *83*(402), pp. 387–93.

Bidard, Christian. The Falling Rate of Profit and Joint Production. *Cambridge J. Econ.,* September 1988, *12*(3), pp. 355–60.

Biddle, Gary C. and Ricks, William E. Analyst Forecast Errors and Stock Price Behavior Near the Earnings Announcement Dates of LIFO Adopters. *J. Acc. Res.,* Autumn 1988, *26*(2), pp. 169–94.

Biddle, Jeff E. Intertemporal Substitution and Hours Restrictions. *Rev. Econ. Statist.*, May 1988, *70*(2), pp. 347–51.

_____ **and Zarkin, Gary A.** Worker Preferences and Market Compensation for Job Risk. *Rev. Econ. Statist.*, November 1988, *70*(4), pp. 660–67.

Bidkar, I. R. An Economic Analysis of R and D in Indian Firms: A Case Study. *Margin*, July–Sept. 1988, *20*(4), pp. 60–71.

_____. The Paradox of Indian Economic Development: A Schumpeterian Perspective. *Indian Econ. J.*, Jan.–March 1988, *35*(3), pp. 47–60.

Bieg, Hartmut and Rübel, Markus. Ausweis und Bewertung von Devisen- und Zinstermingeschäften in Bankbilanzen—Teil I. (Showing and Valuating Forward Exchange and Interest Rate Futures Deals on Bank Balance Sheets—Part I. With English summary.) *Kredit Kapital*, 1988, *21*(2), pp. 253–77.

_____ **and Rübel, Markus.** Ausweis und Bewertung von Devisen- und Zinstermingeschäften in Bankbilanzen—Teil II. (Showing and Valuating Forward Exchange and Interest Rate Futures Deals in Bank Balance Sheets—Part II. With English summary.) *Kredit Kapital*, 1988, *21*(3), pp. 422–50.

_____ **and Rübel, Markus.** Ausweis und Bewertung von Devisen- und Zinstermingeschäften in Bankbilanzen—Teil III. (Showing and Valuation of Forward Exchange and Interest Rate Futures Deals in Bank Balance Sheets—Part III. With English summary.) *Kredit Kapital*, 1988, *21*(4), pp. 592–624.

Biegeleisen, J. Alan and Sjoquist, David L. Rational Voting Applied to Choice of Taxes. *Public Choice*, April 1988, *57*(1), pp. 39–47.

Biehler, Hermann and Liepmann, Peter. Personelle Verbindungen und intersektorale Finanzbeziehungen zwischen den grössten deutschen. (Interlocking Directorates and Intersectoral Financial Relations between Large-scale Enterprises in Germany. With English summary.) *Jahr. Nationalökon. Statist.*, January 1988, *204*(1), pp. 48–68.

Bielasiak, Jack. Economic Reform versus Political Normalization. In *Marer, P. and Siwinski, W.*, eds., 1988, pp. 103–13.

Bienayme, Alain. Technologie et nature de la firme. (With English summary.) *Revue Écon. Polit.*, Nov.–Dec. 1988, *98*(6), pp. 823–49.

Bienenfeld, Mel. Regularity in Price Changes as an Effect of Changes in Distribution. *Cambridge J. Econ.*, June 1988, *12*(2), pp. 247–55.

Bienkowski, Wojciech. The Applicability of Western Measurement Methods to Assess East European Competitiveness. *Comp. Econ. Stud.*, Fall 1988, *30*(3), pp. 33–50.

Bier, Amaury G.; Paulani, Leda Maria and Messenberg, Roberto P. A crise do saneamento no Brasil: Reforma tributária, uma falsa resposta. (With English summary.) *Pesquisa Planejamento Econ.*, April 1988, *18*(1), pp. 161–96.

Biere, Arlo W. Involvement of Agricultural Economics in Graduate Agribusiness Programs: An Uncomfortable Linkage. *Western J. Agr. Econ.*, July 1988, *13*(1), pp. 128–33.

Bierens, Herman J. and Hartog, Joop. Estimating a Hedonic Earnings Function with a Nonparametric Method. *Empirical Econ.*, 1988, *13*(3–4), pp. 267–94.

_____ **and Hartog, Joop.** Non-linear Regression with Discrete Explanatory Variables, with an Application to the Earnings Function. *J. Econometrics*, July 1988, *38*(3), pp. 269–99.

Bierma, Thomas J. and Walbert, Mark S. The Permits Game: Conveying the Logic of Marketable Pollution Permits. *J. Econ. Educ.*, Fall 1988, *19*(4), pp. 383–89.

Bierman, Harold, Jr. The Dow Jones Industrials: Do You Get What You See? *J. Portfol. Manage.*, Fall 1988, *15*(1), pp. 58–63.

Bierwag, Gerald O. Deregulation of the Financial Services Industry and Depository Institutions. In *Libecap, G.*, ed. (*II*), 1988, pp. 193–219.

_____; **Kaufman, George G. and Latta, Cynthia M.** Duration Models: A Taxonomy. *J. Portfol. Manage.*, Fall 1988, *15*(1), pp. 50–54.

Bierwagen, Rainer M. and Hailbronner, Kay. Input, Downstream, Upstream, Secondary, Diversionary and Components or Subassembly Dumping. *J. World Trade*, June 1988, *22*(3), pp. 27–59.

Biewener, Carole. Keynesian Economics and Socialist Politics in France: A Marxist Critique. *Rev. Radical Polit. Econ.*, Summer–Fall 1988, *20*(2–3), pp. 149–55.

Bifani, Pablo. New Biotechnologies for Food Production in Developing Countries with Special Reference to Cuba and Mexico. In *Bhalla, A. S. and James, D.*, eds., 1988, pp. 241–57.

Biger, N. The Pricing of the SATS Bull and Bear Stocks. *J. Stud. Econ. Econometrics*, November 1988, *12*(3), pp. 1–9.

Biggart, Nicole Woolsey and Hamilton, Gary G. Market, Culture, and Authority: A Comparative Analysis of Management and Organization in the Far East. In *Winship, C. and Rosen, S.*, eds., 1988, pp. 52–94.

Bigler, Max. Eine längerfristige Interpretation der schweizerischen Aktienkursbewegungen. (A Long-term Interpretation of the Swiss Stock Price Movements. With English summary.) *Schweiz. Z. Volkswirtsch. Statist.*, June 1988, *124*(2), pp. 175–92.

_____. Finanzinnovationen und Geldpolitik. Schlussfolgerungen aus einem erweiterten Finanzmarktmodell. (Financial Innovation and Monetary Policy—Conclusions from an Extended Portfolio Model. With English summary.) *Kredit Kapital*, 1988, *21*(2), pp. 221–42.

Bigler, William R., Jr. and Kedia, Banwari L. Environment, Strategy, and Performance: An Empirical Analysis in Two Service Industries. In *Grant, J. H.*, ed., 1988, pp. 181–217.

Bigman, David and McNelis, Paul D. Inventory Mangement and Economic Instability in High Inflation Economies: A Macrodynamic Simulation. *J. Policy Modeling*, Summer 1988, *10*(2), pp. 229–47.

_____; **Newbery, David M. and Zilberman, David.** New Approaches in Agricultural Policy Research: Discussion. *Amer. J. Agr. Econ.*, May 1988, *70*(2), pp. 460–61.

Bigsten, Arne. A Note on the Modelling of Circular Smallholder Migration. *Econ. Letters*, 1988, *28*(1), pp. 87–91.

_____. Race and Inequality in Kenya, 1914–1976. *Eastern Afr. Econ. Rev.*, June 1988, *4*(1), pp. 1–11.

Bikales, Gerda and Imhoff, Gary. A Kind of Discordant Harmony: Issues in Assimilation. **In** *Simcox, D. E., ed.*, 1988, *1985*, pp. 137–50.

Bikhchandani, Sushil. Reputation in Repeated Second-Price Auctions. *J. Econ. Theory*, October 1988, *46*(1), pp. 97–119.

Billings, Dwight B. The Rural South in Crisis: A Historical Perspective. **In** *Beaulieu, L. J., ed.*, 1988, pp. 13–29.

Billingsley, Randall S. and Chance, Don M. The Pricing and Performance of Stock Index Futures Spreads. *J. Futures Markets*, June 1988, *8*(3), pp. 303–18.

_____ **and Chance, Don M.** Put–Call Ratios and Market Timing Effectiveness. *J. Portfol. Manage.*, Fall 1988, *15*(1), pp. 25–28.

_____ **and Lamy, Robert E.** The Regulation of International Lending: IMF Support, the Debt Crisis, and Bank Stockholder Wealth. *J. Banking Finance*, June 1988, *12*(2), pp. 255–74.

_____; **Lamy, Robert E. and Thompson, G. Rodney.** The Choice among Debt, Equity, and Convertible Bonds. *J. Finan. Res.*, Spring 1988, *11*(1), pp. 43–55.

Bilquees, Faiz. Inflation In Pakistan: Empirical Evidence on the Monetarist and Structuralist Hypotheses. *Pakistan Devel. Rev.*, Summer 1988, *27*(2), pp. 109–29.

_____ **and Hamid, Shahnaz.** Employment Situation and Economic Exploitation of Poor Earning Women in Rawalpindi. *Pakistan Devel. Rev.*, Part 2, Winter 1988, *27*(4), pp. 791–98.

Bina, Cyrus and Yaghmaian, Behzad. Import Substitution and Export Promotion within the Context of the Internationalization of Capital. *Rev. Radical Polit. Econ.*, Summer–Fall 1988, *20*(2–3), pp. 234–40.

Binder, John J. The Sherman Antitrust Act and the Railroad Cartels. *J. Law Econ.*, October 1988, *31*(2), pp. 443–68.

Bing, Jon and Thommessen, Gunnar. Tax Treatment of Computer Software: Norway. **In** *International Fiscal Association, ed. (II)*, 1988, pp. 439–52.

Bingen, R. James; Hall, A. E. and Ndoye, Mbaye. California Cowpeas and Food Policy in Senegal. *World Devel.*, July 1988, *16*(7), pp. 857–65.

Bingham, Barbara and Huffstutler, Clyde. Productivity Growth Slows in the Organic Chemicals Industry. *Mon. Lab. Rev.*, June 1988, *111*(6), pp. 44–51.

Bini Smaghi, L. and Vona, S. La coesione dello SME e il ruolo dei fattori esterni: Un'analisi in termini di commercio estero. (Economic Growth and Exchange Rates in the European Monetary System: Their Trade Effects in a Changing External Environment. With English summary.) *Giorn. Econ.*, Jan.–Feb. 1988, *47*(1–2), pp. 3–43.

Binkin, Martin. Technology and Skills: Lessons from the Military. **In** *Cyert, R. M. and Mowery, D. C., eds.*, 1988, pp. 185–222.

Binmore, Ken G. Modeling Rational Players: Part II. *Econ. Philos.*, April 1988, *4*(1), pp. 9–55.

_____ **and Herrero, M. J.** Matching and Bargaining in Dynamic Markets. *Rev. Econ. Stud.*, January 1988, *55*(1), pp. 17–31.

_____ **and Herrero, M. J.** Security Equilibrium. *Rev. Econ. Stud.*, January 1988, *55*(1), pp. 33–48.

_____; **Shaked, Avner and Sutton, John.** A Further Test of Noncooperative Bargaining Theory: Reply. *Amer. Econ. Rev.*, September 1988, *78*(4), pp. 837–39.

Binswanger, Hans Christoph and Meiners, Hubert. Von der Wirtschafgemeinschaft (EWG) zur Wirtschafts- und Umweltgemeinschaft (EWUG). (The Expansion of the European Economic Community into a European Economic and Environmental Community. With English summary.) *Aussenwirtschaft*, September 1988, *43*(3), pp. 399–421.

Binswanger, Hans P.; McIntire, John and Rosenzweig, Mark R. From Land Abundance to Land Scarcity: The Effects of Population Growth on Production Relations in Agrarian Economies. **In** *Lee, R. D., et al., eds.*, 1988, pp. 77–100.

_____ **and Pingali, Prabhu L.** Population Density and Farming Systems: The Changing Locus of Innovations and Technical Change. **In** *Salvatore, D., ed.*, 1988, pp. 165–86.

_____ **and Pingali, Prabhu L.** Population Density and Farming Systems: The Changing Locus of Innovations and Technical Change. **In** *Lee, R. D., et al., eds.*, 1988, pp. 51–76.

_____ **and Pingali, Prabhu L.** Technological Priorities for Farming in Sub-Saharan Africa. *World Bank Res. Observer*, January 1988, *3*(1), pp. 81–98.

_____ **and Quizon, Jaime B.** Distributional Consequences of Alternative Food Policies in India. **In** *Pinstrup-Andersen, P., ed.*, 1988, pp. 301–19.

Birch, David L. The Role of Small Business in New England. **In** *Lampe, D., ed.*, 1988, pp. 225–39.

Birch, Melissa H. Institution Building: Multilateral Development Banks and State-Owned Enterprises. *World Devel.*, February 1988, *16*(2), pp. 255–70.

Birch, Stephen. The Identification of Supplier-Inducement in a Fixed Price System of Health Care Provision: The Case of Dentistry in the United Kingdom. *J. Health Econ.*, June 1988, *7*(2), pp. 129–50.

Birch, Thomas D. Justice in Taxation: An Appraisal of Normative Tax Theory. *Soc. Sci. Quart.*, December 1988, *69*(4), pp. 1005–13.

Bird, Graham. An Analysis of Drawings on the International Monetary Fund by Developing Countries. In *Bird, G.*, 1988, *1981*, pp. 104–12.

_____. An Analysis of the Welfare Gains from Special Drawing Rights. In *Bird, G.*, 1988, *1978*, pp. 115–23.

_____. Balance of Payments Policy in Developing Countries. In *Bird, G.*, 1988, *1984*, pp. 18–60.

_____. Beyond the Brandt Report: A Strategy for World Economic Development. In *Bird, G.*, 1988, *1980*, pp. 254–68.

_____. The Changing International Economic Order and the Interests of Developing Countries. In *Bird, G.*, 1988, pp. 201–22.

_____. Debt Swapping in Developing Countries: A Preliminary Investigation. *J. Devel. Stud.*, April 1988, *24*(3), pp. 293–309.

_____. Developing Country Borrowing from Private Markets: Key Aspects and Prospects for the Future. In *Bird, G.*, 1988, pp. 147–82.

_____. Fund Financing and Financing the Fund. In *Bird, G.*, 1988, pp. 84–103.

_____. Low-Income Countries and International Financial Reform. In *Bird, G.*, 1988, *1983*, pp. 223–53.

_____. The Mix between Adjustment and Financing. In *Bird, G.*, 1988, *1980*, pp. 7–17.

_____. Oil Prices and Debt. In *Bird, G.*, 1988, *1987*, pp. 183–98.

_____. A Role for the International Monetary Fund in Economic Development. In *Bird, G.*, 1988, *1982*, pp. 63–83.

_____. The Role of SDRs in Financing Commodity Stabilisation. In *Bird, G.*, 1988, *1976*, pp. 134–44.

_____. SDR Distribution, Interest Rates and Aid Flows. In *Bird, G.*, 1988, *1981*, pp. 124–33.

Bird, Peter J. W. N. One More Externality Article: Reply. *J. Environ. Econ. Manage.*, September 1988, *15*(3), pp. 382–83.

Bird, Richard M. A Note on the Fragility of International Tax Comparisons. *Bull. Int. Fiscal Doc.*, May 1988, *42*(5), pp. 199–201.

_____. Shaping a New International Tax Order. *Bull. Int. Fiscal Doc.*, July 1988, *42*(7), pp. 292–99, 303.

Bird, Ron; Dennis, David and Tippett, Mark. A Stop Loss Approach to Portfolio Insurance. *J. Portfol. Manage.*, Fall 1988, *15*(1), pp. 35–40.

Birdsall, Nancy M. and Behrman, Jere R. The Equity–Productivity Tradeoff: Public School Resources in Brazil. *Europ. Econ. Rev.*, October 1988, *32*(8), pp. 1585–1601.

_____ **and Behrman, Jere R.** The Reward for Good Timing: Cohort Effects and Earnings Functions for Brazilian Males. *Rev. Econ. Statist.*, February 1988, *70*(1), pp. 129–35.

_____ **and Griffin, Charles C.** Fertility and Poverty in Developing Countries. *J. Policy Modeling*, April 1988, *10*(1), pp. 29–55.

_____ **and Sai, Frederick T.** Family Planning Services in Sub-Saharan Africa. *Finance Develop.*, March 1988, *25*(1), pp. 28–31.

Birecree, Adrienne M. Academic Freedom in the Academic Factory. *Challenge*, July–August 1988, *31*(4), pp. 53–56.

Birken, Lawrence. From Macroeconomics to Microeconomics: The Marginalist Revolution in Sociocultural Perspective. *Hist. Polit. Econ.*, Summer 1988, *20*(2), pp. 251–64.

Birkin, M. and Clarke, M. SYNTHESIS—A Synthetic Spatial Information System for Urban and Regional Analysis: Methods and Examples. *Environ. Planning A*, December 1988, *20*(12), pp. 1645–71.

Birley, Sue; Manning, Kingsley and Norburn, David. Implementing Corporate Venturing. In *Lamb, R. and Shrivastava, P., eds.*, 1988, pp. 165–79.

Birnie, David A. G. Living with GAAR: The Effect on Tax Practice. In *Canadian Tax Foundation*, 1988, pp. 5.1–16.

Bisaliah, S. and Sreenivasamurthy, D. Technological Innovations and Productivity Change in Agriculture. *Margin*, April–June 1988, *20*(3), pp. 51–56.

Bish, Robert L. Federalism: A Market Economics Perspective. In *Gwartney, J. D. and Wagner, R. E., eds.*, 1988, *1987*, pp. 351–68.

Bishop, Christine E. Competition in the Market for Nursing Home Care. In *Greenberg, W., ed.*, 1988, pp. 119–38.

_____. Use of Nursing Care in Continuing Care Retirement Communities. In *Scheffler, R. M. and Rossiter, L. F., eds.*, 1988, pp. 149–62.

Bishop, John A. Pigovian Taxes and "Full" Property Rights. *Eastern Econ. J.*, April–June 1988, *14*(2), pp. 193–96.

_____; **Chakraborti, S. and Thistle, Paul D.** Large Sample Tests for Absolute Lorenz Dominance. *Econ. Letters*, 1988, *26*(3), pp. 291–94.

_____ **and Yoo, Jang H.** Cigarette "Health Scare," Excise Taxes and Advertising Ban: Reply. *Southern Econ. J.*, January 1988, *54*(3), pp. 777–79.

Bishop, Paul. Academic–Industry Links and Firm Size in South West England. *Reg. Stud.*, April 1988, *22*(2), pp. 160–62.

Bishop, Richard C. Option Value: Reply. *Land Econ.*, February 1988, *64*(1), pp. 88–93.

_____ **and Boyle, Kevin J.** Welfare Measurements Using Contingent Valuation: A Comparison of Techniques. *Amer. J. Agr. Econ.*, February 1988, *70*(1), pp. 20–28.

_____; **Boyle, Kevin J. and Welsh, Michael P.** Validation of Empirical Measures of Welfare Change: Comment. *Land Econ.*, February 1988, *64*(1), pp. 94–98.

Bissaro, Gianantonio and Hamaui, Rony. The Choice of Invoice Currency in an Inter-temporal Model of Price Setting. *Giorn. Econ.*, March–April 1988, *47*(3–4), pp. 139–61.

Biswas, Basudeb; Tribedy, Gopal and Beladi, Hamid. A Two Sector Analysis of Protection and Negative Value-Added. *Indian Econ. J.*, April–June 1988, *35*(4), pp. 25–32.

Biswas, D. K. and Ramachandran, S. Infrastructure Development: The Indian Perspective. In *Research and Info. System for the Non-aligned* and *Other Developing Countries*, 1988, pp. 443–51.

Bitar, Sergio. External Trade and Foreign Investment: Comments. In *Feinberg, R. E. and Ffrench-Davis, R., eds.*, 1988, pp. 175–80.

———. Neo-conservatism versus Neo-structuralism in Latin America. *CEPAL Rev.*, April 1988, (34), pp. 45–62.

Bitros, George C. and Panas, Epaminondas E. Measuring Product Prices under Conditions of Quality Change: The Case of Passenger Cars in Greece. *J. Ind. Econ.*, December 1988, 37(2), pp. 167–86.

Bittlingmayer, George. Property Rights, Progress, and the Aircraft Patent Agreement. *J. Law Econ.*, April 1988, 31(1), pp. 227–48.

———. Resale Price Maintenance in the Book Trade with an Application to Germany. *J. Inst. Theoretical Econ.*, December 1988, 144(5), pp. 789–812.

———. Shorter Working Time and Job Security: Labor Adjustment in the Steel Industry: Comment. In *Hart, R. A., ed.*, 1988, pp. 86–89.

Bivens, Gordon E. A College Course in Consumer Education: Comments and Extensions. In *Maynes, E. S. and ACCI Research Committee, eds.*, 1988, pp. 875–78.

Bivin, David. The Behavior of Manufacturers' Inventories: 1967–1986. *J. Macroecon.*, Winter 1988, 10(1), pp. 63–81.

Bixby, Ann Kallman. Benefits and Beneficiaries under Public Employee Retirement Systems, Calendar Year 1985. *Soc. Sec. Bull.*, May 1988, 51(5), pp. 29–32.

———. Measuring Expenditures for Social Welfare Programs: Commentary. *Soc. Sec. Bull.*, June 1988, 51(6), pp. 20, 63–64.

———. Overview of Public Social Welfare Expenditures, Fiscal Year 1986. *Soc. Sec. Bull.*, November 1988, 51(11), pp. 27–28.

———. Public Social Welfare Expenditures, Fiscal Year 1985: Overview. *Soc. Sec. Bull.*, January 1988, 51(1), pp. 10–11.

———. Public Social Welfare Expenditures, Fiscal Year 1985. *Soc. Sec. Bull.*, April 1988, 51(4), pp. 21–31.

Bixley, Brian. Keynesian Economics, or *Plus ça change*. In *Hamouda, O. F. and Smithin, J. N., eds., Vol. 1*, 1988, pp. 131–38.

Björklund, Anders. What Experiments Are Needed for Manpower Policy? *J. Human Res.*, Spring 1988, 23(2), pp. 267–79.

Björkman, Ingmar. Japanskt företagande och företagande i Japan. En översikt. (Japanese Management and Management in Japan. A Survey. With English summary.) *Ekon. Samfundets Tidskr.*, 1988, 41(3), pp. 181–99.

Björkman, James Warner. Comparative Health Policies: A World of Difference. *Pakistan Devel. Rev.*, Part 1, Winter 1988, 27(4), pp. 473–92.

———. Indigenous Technological Capability in Developing Countries: A Preliminary Approach to Identification: Comments. *Pakistan Devel. Rev.*, Part 2, Winter 1988, 27(4), pp. 526–27.

Bjørndal, Trond. Optimal Harvesting of Farmed Fish. *Marine Resource Econ.*, 1988, 5(2), pp. 139–59.

———. The Optimal Management of North Sea Herring. *J. Environ. Econ. Manage.*, March 1988, 15(1), pp. 9–29.

———; Gordon, Daniel V. and Singh, Balbir. Economies of Scale in the Norwegian Fish-Meal Industry: Implications for Policy Decisions. *Appl. Econ.*, October 1988, 20(10), pp. 1321–32.

Black, Dan A. and Baye, Michael R. The Microeconomic Foundations of Measuring Bracket Creep and Other Tax Changes. *Econ. Inquiry*, July 1988, 26(3), pp. 471–84.

Black, Fischer and Jones, Robert. Simplifying Portfolio Insurance for Corporate Pension Plans. *J. Portfol. Manage.*, Summer 1988, 14(4), pp. 33–37.

Black, Jane M. and Bulkley, I. George. The Role of Strategic Information Transmission in a Bargaining Model. *Econ. J.*, Supplement, 1988, 98(390), pp. 50–57.

Black, P. A. and Cooper, J. H. Government Financing Requirement: Short and Long-run Consequences. *S. Afr. J. Econ.*, December 1988, 56(4), pp. 292–97.

Black, R. D. Collison. Classical Reassessments: Commentary. In *Thweatt, W. O., ed.*, 1988, pp. 221–25.

———. Editing the Papers of W. S. Jevons. In *Moggridge, D. E., ed.*, 1988, pp. 19–42.

———. Jevons and Cairnes. In *Wood, J. C., ed., Vol. 3*, 1988, 1960, pp. 61–81.

———. Jevons, Bentham and De Morgan. In *Wood, J. C., ed., Vol. 1*, 1988, 1972, pp. 280–97.

———. Jevons, Marginalism and Manchester. In *Wood, J. C., ed., Vol. 2*, 1988, 1972, pp. 63–69.

———. The Papers and Correspondence of William Stanley Jevons: A Supplementary Note. In *Wood, J. C., ed., Vol. 3*, 1988, 1982, pp. 266–76.

———. W. S. Jevons and the Economists of His Time. In *Wood, J. C., ed., Vol. 1*, 1988, 1962, pp. 197–211.

———. W. S. Jevons and the Foundation of Modern Economics. In *Wood, J. C., ed., Vol. 1*, 1988, 1972, pp. 298–310.

Black, Renee Allee. State Control of Mining on Federal Land: Environmental or Land Use Regulation? *Natural Res. J.*, Fall 1988, 28(4), pp. 873–81.

Black, Robert A. Recent Behavior of M1 Velocity, the Link Between Real-Balances Growth and Inflation, and Choice of Monetary Aggregate. In *Pennsylvania Economic Association*, 1988, pp. 116–24.

——— and Kreider, Rosalie. Critical Legal Studies and Economic Analysis: A Survey. In *Pennsylvania Economic Association*, 1988, pp. 492–506.

Black, Stanley W. Roundtable on Exchange Rate Policy. In *Marston, R. C., ed.*, 1988, pp. 149–56.

_____ and Salemi, Michael K. FIML Estimation of the Dollar–Deutschemark Risk Premium in a Portfolio Model. *J. Int. Econ.*, November 1988, *25*(3–4), pp. 205–24.

Black, William C.; Lichtenstein, Donald R. and Bloch, Peter H. Correlates of Price Acceptability. *J. Cons. Res.*, September 1988, *15*(2), pp. 243–52.

Blackburn, Keith. Collapsing Exchange Rate Regimes and Exchange Rate Dynamics: Some Further Examples. *J. Int. Money Finance*, December 1988, *7*(4), pp. 373–85.

Blackburn, McKinley L. and Bloom, David E. The Effects of Technological Change on Earnings and Income Inequality in the United States. In *Cyert, R. M. and Mowery, D. C.*, eds., 1988, pp. 223–63.

Blackburn, Robin. Defining Slavery—Its Special Features and Social Role. In *Archer, L. J.*, ed., 1988, pp. 262–79.

Blackley, Paul R. Explaining Relative Incomes of Low-Income Families in U.S. Cities. *Soc. Sci. Quart.*, December 1988, *69*(4), pp. 835–52.

_____ and Ondrich, Jan. A Limited Joint-Choice Model for Discrete and Continuous Housing Characteristics. *Rev. Econ. Statist.*, May 1988, *70*(2), pp. 266–74.

Blackorby, Charles. Consistent Commodity Aggregates in Market Demand Equations. In *Eichhorn, W.*, ed., 1988, pp. 577–606.

_____ and Donaldson, David. Cash versus Kind, Self-selection, and Efficient Transfers. *Amer. Econ. Rev.*, September 1988, *78*(4), pp. 691–700.

_____ and Donaldson, David. Money Metric Utility: Harmless Normalization? *J. Econ. Theory*, October 1988, *46*(1), pp. 120–29.

_____ and Schworm, William. The Existence of Input and Output Aggregates in Aggregate Production Functions. *Econometrica*, May 1988, *56*(3), pp. 613–43.

Blackwell, David W. and Kidwell, David S. An Investigation of Cost Differences between Public Sales and Private Placements of Debt. *J. Finan. Econ.*, December 1988, *22*(2), pp. 253–78.

Blackwell, Michael and Nocera, Simon. The Impact of Debt to Equity Conversion. *Finance Develop.*, June 1988, *25*(2), pp. 15–17.

Blackwood, Julian. World Bank Experience with Rural Development. *Finance Develop.*, December 1988, *25*(4), pp. 12–15.

Blaesius, Stefan. Zur Rentabilität von Lebensversicherungen. Helmut Diederich zum 60. Geburtstag. (With English summary.) *Z. Betriebswirtschaft*, July 1988, *58*(7), pp. 708–23.

Blaha, Jaroslav. Czechoslovak Science and Research in the Service of Integration. *Soviet E. Europ. Foreign Trade*, Fall 1988, *24*(3), pp. 54–70.

_____. La modernisation en tchecoslovaquie. (The Modernization in Czechoslovakia. With English summary.) *Écon. Soc.*, February 1988, *22*(2), pp. 79–106.

Blaikie, P. The Explanation of Land Degradation. In *Ives, J. and Pitt, D. C.*, eds., 1988, pp. 132–58.

Blair, Dudley W. and Placone, Dennis L. Expense-Preference Behavior, Agency Costs, and Firm Organization: The Savings and Loan Industry. *J. Econ. Bus.*, February 1988, *40*(1), pp. 1–15.

Blair, Margaret M. and Baily, Martin Neil. Productivity and American Management. In *Litan, R. E; Lawrence, R. Z. and Schultze, C. L.*, eds., 1988, pp. 178–214.

Blair, Peter D. and Miller, Ronald E. Measuring Spatial Linkages. *Ricerche Econ.*, April–June 1988, *42*(2), pp. 288–310.

Blair, Roger D. and Dewar, Marvin. How to End the Crisis in Medical Malpractice Insurance. *Challenge*, March–April 1988, *31*(2), pp. 36–41.

_____ and Makar, Scott D. The Structure of Florida's Medical Malpractice Insurance Market: If It Ain't Broke, Don't Fix It. *Yale J. Regul.*, Summer 1988, *5*(2), pp. 427–53.

_____ and Romano, Richard E. The Influence of Attitudes toward Risk on the Value of Forecasting. *Quart. J. Econ.*, May 1988, *103*(2), pp. 387–96.

Blais, André and Vaillancourt, François. The Political Economy of Taxation: Some Evidence for Canada. *Public Finance Quart.*, July 1988, *16*(3), pp. 315–29.

Blais, J. Y. and Rousseau, Jean-Marc. Overview of HASTUS Current and Future Versions. In *Daduna, J. R. and Wren, A.*, eds., 1988, pp. 175–87.

Blake, Andrew and Weale, Martin. Exchange-Rate Targets and Wage Formation. *Nat. Inst. Econ. Rev.*, February 1988, (123), pp. 48–64.

Blake, David and Beenstock, Michael. The Stochastic Analysis of Competitive Unemployment Insurance Premiums. *Europ. Econ. Rev.*, January 1988, *32*(1), pp. 7–25.

Blake, Robert W., et al. Profit-Maximizing Dairy Sire Selection Package. *Southern J. Agr. Econ.*, July 1988, *20*(1), pp. 141–44.

Blanchard, Olivier Jean. The Supply Side and Macroeconomic Modeling: Comment. In *Bryant, R. C., et al.*, eds., 1988, pp. 218–19.

_____ and Abel, Andrew B. Investment and Sales: Some Empirical Evidence. In *Barnett, W. A.; Berndt, E. R. and White, H.*, eds., 1988, pp. 269–96.

_____ and Mankiw, N. Gregory. Consumption: Beyond Certainty Equivalence. *Amer. Econ. Rev.*, May 1988, *78*(2), pp. 173–77.

_____ and Summers, Lawrence H. Beyond the Natural Rate Hypothesis. *Amer. Econ. Rev.*, May 1988, *78*(2), pp. 182–87.

_____ and Summers, Lawrence H. Hysteresis and the European Unemployment Problem. In *Cross, R.*, ed., 1988, pp. 306–64.

_____ and Summers, Lawrence H. Hysteresis in Unemployment. In *Shaw, G. K.*, ed., Vol. 1, 1988, 1987, pp. 313–20.

Blanchfield, Robert and Marsteller, William. Rising Export and Import Prices in 1987 Reversed the Trend of Recent Years. *Mon. Lab. Rev.*, June 1988, *111*(6), pp. 3–19.

Blanchflower, David G. and Millward, Neil. Trade Unions and Employment Change: An Analysis of British Establishment Data. *Europ. Econ. Rev.*, March 1988, *32*(2–3), pp. 717–26.

_____ **and Oswald, Andrew J.** Internal and External Influences upon Pay Settlements. *Brit. J. Ind. Relat.*, November 1988, *26*(3), pp. 363–70.

_____ **and Oswald, Andrew J.** Profit-Related Pay: Prose Discovered. *Econ. J.*, September 1988, *98*(392), pp. 720–30.

Blanchon, D. and Ferrandier, R. L'evolution recente du systeme financier francais: Les mots et les choses. (The Recent Evolution of the French Financial System: Words and Things. With English summary.) *Écon. Soc.*, January 1988, *22*(1), pp. 7–30.

Blanco, Herminio. Global Competition and the Special Challenges of Developing Countries: The Perspective of Developing Countries. In *Furino, A., ed.*, 1988, pp. 245–54.

_____. Lessons from Mexico: Comment. In *Bruno, M., et al., eds.*, 1988, pp. 391–92.

Blanco, José Antonio and Müller, Heinz H. Put-Optionen als Instrumente der Portfolioinsurance: Investitionsstrategien für institutionelle Anleger? (Puts as Instruments of Portfolio Insurance: Investment Strategies for Institutional Investors? With English summary.) *Schweiz. Z. Volkswirtsch. Statist.*, September 1988, *124*(3), pp. 391–404.

Blandford, David. Instability in World Grain Markets: A Reply. *J. Agr. Econ.*, January 1988, *39*(1), pp. 147–48.

_____. Market Share Models and the Elasticity of Demand for U.S. Agricultural Exports. In *Carter, C. A. and Gardiner, W. H., eds.*, 1988, pp. 195–24.

_____. A U.S. Perspective on Measuring Trade Effects of Domestic Agricultural Policies in the United States and Canada. In *Allen, K. and Macmillan, K., eds.*, 1988, pp. 81–99.

Blandy, Richard. Efficiency and Productivity in the Workplace—Where to Now? *Australian Bull. Lab.*, December 1988, *15*(1), pp. 20–28.

_____ **and Hancock, Susan.** The Australian Labour Market, September 1988. *Australian Bull. Lab.*, September 1988, *14*(4), pp. 535–63.

Blank, Emily C. The Effect of Current Hours of Work on the Future Wage Rate. *Atlantic Econ. J.*, June 1988, *16*(2), pp. 86.

_____. Layoffs and Wage Growth of Male Household Heads. *Eastern Econ. J.*, July–Sept. 1988, *14*(3), pp. 239–50.

Blank, Rebecca M. The Effect of Welfare and Wage Levels on the Location Decisions of Female-Headed Households. *J. Urban Econ.*, September 1988, *24*(2), pp. 186–211.

_____. Simultaneously Modeling the Supply of Weeks and Hours of Work among Female Household Heads. *J. Lab. Econ.*, April 1988, *6*(2), pp. 177–204.

_____. Welfare Payment Levels and the Migration of Female-Headed Families. In *Brown, E., ed.*, 1988, pp. 47–52.

Blaser, C. Jean; Balmer, Pamela W. and Hill, Bette S. Practical Issues in Developing Competitive Contracting for Home Care Services. In *Hula, R. C., ed.*, 1988, pp. 84–95.

Blattenberger, Gail and Lad, Frank. An Application of Operational-Subjective Statistical Methods to Rational Expectations. *J. Bus. Econ. Statist.*, October 1988, *6*(4), pp. 453–64.

_____ **and Lad, Frank.** An Application of Operational-Subjective Statistical Methods to Rational Expectations: Reply. *J. Bus. Econ. Statist.*, October 1988, *6*(4), pp. 475–77.

Blau, David M.; Behrman, Jere R. and Wolfe, Barbara L. Schooling and Earnings Distributions with Endogenous Labour Force Participation, Marital Status and Family Size. *Economica*, August 1988, *55*(219), pp. 297–316.

_____ **and Robins, Philip K.** Child-Care Costs and Family Labor Supply. *Rev. Econ. Statist.*, August 1988, *70*(3), pp. 374–81.

Blau, Francine D. Trends in Earnings of Women and Minorities: Discussion [Trends in Earnings Differentials by Gender, 1971–1981] [The Earnings of Women and Ethnic Minorities, 1959–1979]. *Ind. Lab. Relat. Rev.*, July 1988, *41*(4), pp. 547–52.

_____ **and Beller, Andrea H.** Trends in Earnings Differentials by Gender, 1971–1981. *Ind. Lab. Relat. Rev.*, July 1988, *41*(4), pp. 513–29.

Blaug, Mark. David Ricardo: A Review of Some Interpretative Issues: Commentary. In *Thweatt, W. O., ed.*, 1988, pp. 132–37.

_____. John Hicks and the Methodology of Economics. In *de Marchi, N., ed.*, 1988, pp. 183–95.

Blauwens, G. and Van de Voorde, E. The Valuation of Time Savings in Commodity Transport. *Int. J. Transport Econ.*, February 1988, *15*(1), pp. 77–87.

Blazar, William A. and Kolderie, Ted. The New Economic Role of American States: Minnesota. In *Fosler, R. S., ed.*, 1988, pp. 291–308.

Bleaney, Michael. The Consistency of Alternative Estimates of Growth in Centrally Planned Economies. *METU*, 1988, *15*(3–4), pp. 89–102.

Bleicher, Knut. Technology as a Basic Element of Corporate Strategy—A Conceptional Approach. *Aussenwirtschaft*, June 1988, *43*(1/2), pp. 155–73.

Blejer, Mario I. Growth, Investments, and the Specific Role of Fiscal Policies in Very Small Developing Economies. In *Jorge, A. and Salazar-Carrillo, J., eds.*, 1988, pp. 82–98.

_____ **and Cheasty, Adrienne.** High Inflation, Heterodox Stabilization, and Fiscal Policy. *World Devel.*, August 1988, *16*(8), pp. 867–81.

_____ **and Cheasty, Adrienne.** Some Lessons from "Heterodox" Stabilization Programs. *Finance Develop.*, September 1988, *25*(3), pp. 16–19.

_____ **and Guerrero, Isabel.** Stabilization Policies and Income Distribution in the Philippines. *Finance Develop.*, December 1988, *25*(4), pp. 6–8.

_____ **and Leiderman, Leonardo.** Modeling and

Testing Ricardian Equivalence: A Survey. *Int. Monet. Fund Staff Pap.*, March 1988, 35(1), pp. 1–35.

_____ and Sagari, Silvia B. Sequencing the Liberalization of Financial Markets. *Finance Develop.*, March 1988, 25(1), pp. 18–20.

_____ and Tanzi, Vito. Public Debt and Fiscal Policy in Developing Countries. In *Arrow, K. J. and Boskin, M. J., eds.*, 1988, pp. 230–63.

_____; Teijeiro, Mario O. and Tanzi, Vito. The Effects of Inflation on the Measurement of Fiscal Deficits. In *Blejer, M. I. and Chu, K.-Y., eds.*, 1988, pp. 4–19.

_____, et al. Fiscal Policies, Adjustment, and Stabilization. *Finance Develop.*, September 1988, 25(3), pp. 9–11.

Blessing, Helmut; Grote, Gerhard and Luft, Christa. Foreign Trade, Growth of the Socialist National Economy, and Comprehensive Intensification. *Soviet E. Europ. Foreign Trade*, Fall 1988, 24(3), pp. 71–95.

Bleuze, Eric and Sterdyniak, Henri. L'interdépendance des économies en change flexible: Les apports d'une maquette dynamique. (Interdependence of Economies under Flexible Exchange Rates: The Contributions of Dynamic Model. With English summary.) *Revue Écon.*, September 1988, 39(5), pp. 999–1033.

Blewett, Robert A. Hidden Tax Preferences and the Real Costs of Tuition Tax Credits. *Public Finance Quart.*, July 1988, 16(3), pp. 330–40.

_____ and Lane, Julia I. Development Rights and the Differential Assessment of Agricultural Land: Fractional Valuation of Farmland Is Ineffective for Preserving Open Space and Subsidizes Speculation. *Amer. J. Econ. Soc.*, April 1988, 47(2), pp. 195–205.

Blinder, Alan S. The Challenge of High Unemployment. *Amer. Econ. Rev.*, May 1988, 78(2), pp. 1–15.

_____. The Fall and Rise of Keynesian Economics. *Econ. Rec.*, December 1988, 64(187), pp. 278–94.

_____. Financing Constraints and Corporate Investment: Comment. *Brookings Pap. Econ. Act.*, 1988, (1), pp. 196–200.

_____. Life Cycle Saving vs. Intergenerational Transfers: Comments. In *Kessler, D. and Masson, A., eds.*, 1988, pp. 68–76.

_____. The Rules-versus-Discretion Debate in the Light of Recent Experience. In *Giersch, H., ed.*, 1988, pp. 45–63.

_____. Why Is the Government in the Pension Business? In *Wachter, S. M., ed.*, 1988, pp. 17–34.

_____ and Bar-Ilan, Avner. The Life Cycle Permanent-Income Model and Consumer Durables. *Ann. Écon. Statist.*, Jan.–March 1988, (9), pp. 71–91.

_____ and Bernanke, Ben S. Credit, Money, and Aggregate Demand. *Amer. Econ. Rev.*, May 1988, 78(2), pp. 435–39.

_____ and Solow, Robert M. Does Fiscal Policy Matter? In *Shaw, G. K., ed., Vol. 2*, 1988, 1973, pp. 317–37.

Bliss, Christopher. The Labour Market: Theory

and Experience. In *Beenstock, M., ed.*, 1988, pp. 1–23.

_____. A Theory of Retail Pricing. *J. Ind. Econ.*, June 1988, 36(4), pp. 375–91.

_____ and Joshi, Vijay. Exchange Rate Protection and Exchange Rate Conflict. *Oxford Econ. Pap.*, June 1988, 40(2), pp. 365–77.

Bloch, Erich. A National Research Strategy. In *Furino, A., ed.*, 1988, pp. 85–100.

Bloch, Peter H.; Black, William C. and Lichtenstein, Donald R. Correlates of Price Acceptability. *J. Cons. Res.*, September 1988, 15(2), pp. 243–52.

Blochet-Bardet, Anne, et al. Swiss Women in Management: The Quest for Professional Equality. In *Adler, N. J. and Israeli, D., eds.*, 1988, pp. 157–67.

Block, John R. Food Policy in an Evolving World Marketplace. In *Feldstein, M., ed. (II)*, 1988, pp. 468–72.

Block, Stanley B. and Gallagher, Timothy J. How Much Do Bank Trust Departments Use Derivatives? *J. Portfol. Manage.*, Fall 1988, 15(1), pp. 12–15.

Block, Walter. Economics of the Canadian Bishops. *Contemp. Policy Issues*, January 1988, 6(1), pp. 56–68.

_____. Fractional Reserve Banking: An Interdisciplinary Perspective. In *[Rothbard, M. N.]*, 1988, pp. 24–31.

_____. On Yeager's "Why Subjectivism?" In *Rothbard, M. N. and Block, W., eds.*, 1988, pp. 199–208.

_____ and Rockwell, Llewellyn H., Jr. Man, Economy, and Liberty: Essays in Honor of Murray N. Rothbard: Introduction. In *[Rothbard, M. N.]*, 1988, pp. ix–xviii.

_____ and Walker, Michael A. Entropy in the Canadian Economics Profession: Sampling Consensus on the Major Issues. *Can. Public Policy*, June 1988, 14(2), pp. 137–50.

Bloech, Jürgen. Werkstoffpreise und Gewinnfunktionen. (With English summary.) *Z. Betriebswirtshaft*, January 1988, 58(1), pp. 84–97.

Bloem, Adriaan M. Micro–Macro Link for Government. *Rev. Income Wealth*, September 1988, 34(3), pp. 289–311.

Blomeyer, Edward C. and Boyd, James C. Empirical Tests of Boundary Conditions for Options on Treasury Bond Futures Contracts. *J. Futures Markets*, April 1988, 8(2), pp. 185–98.

_____ and Johnson, Herb. An Empirical Examination of the Pricing of American Put Options. *J. Finan. Quant. Anal.*, March 1988, 23(1), pp. 13–22.

Blomo, Vito J. Dynamic and Spatial Welfare Changes from the Impact of Menhaden Fishery Conservation Plans on the U.S. Atlantic Coast. *Environ. Planning A*, January 1988, 20(1), pp. 111–118.

_____; Orbach, Michael and Maiolo, John R. Competition and Conflict in the U.S. Atlantic Coast Menhaden Industry. *Amer. J. Econ. Soc.*, January 1988, 47(1), pp. 41–60.

Blomquist, Glenn C. Valuing Urban Lakeview Amenities Using Implicit and Contingent Markets. *Urban Stud.*, August 1988, *25*(4), pp. 333–40.

_____; Berger, Mark C. and Hoehn, John P. New Estimates of Quality of Life in Urban Areas. *Amer. Econ. Rev.*, March 1988, *78*(1), pp. 89–107.

_____; Scott, Frank A., Jr. and Berger, Mark C. Impacts of Air Pollution Control Strategies in Kentucky. *Growth Change*, Spring 1988, *19*(2), pp. 40–55.

Blomquist, N. Sören. Nonlinear Taxes and Labor Supply. *Europ. Econ. Rev.*, July 1988, *32*(6), pp. 1213–26.

Blomqvist, Hans C. Some Problems in Estimating the "Natural" Rate of Unemployment from the Expectations-Augmented Phillips Curve. *Scand. J. Econ.*, 1988, *90*(1), pp. 113–20.

_____. Uncertainty and Predictive Accuracy: An Empirical Study. *J. Econ. Psych.*, December 1988, *9*(4), pp. 525–32.

Blomström, Magnus. Labor Productivity Differences between Foreign and Domestic Firms in Mexico. *World Devel.*, November 1988, *16*(11), pp. 1295–98.

_____; Lipsey, Robert E. and Kulchycky, Ksenia. U.S. and Swedish Direct Investment and Exports. In *Baldwin, R. E., ed. (II)*, 1988, pp. 259–97.

Blöndal, Gísli. Government Financial Reporting Systems in LDCs. *Finance Develop.*, September 1988, *25*(3), pp. 12–15.

Bloom, David E. Arbitrator Behavior in Public Sector Wage Disputes. In *Freeman, R. B. and Ichniowski, C., eds.*, 1988, pp. 107–24.

_____ and Blackburn, McKinley L. The Effects of Technological Change on Earnings and Income Inequality in the United States. In *Cyert, R. M. and Mowery, D. C., eds.*, 1988, pp. 223–63.

_____ and Freeman, Richard B. Economic Development and the Timing and Components of Population Growth. *J. Policy Modeling*, April 1988, *10*(1), pp. 57–81.

Bloom, Justin L. A New Era for U.S.–Japanese Technical Relations? A Cloudy Vision. In *Uyehara, C. H., ed.*, 1988, pp. 219–54.

Bloom, Robert and Naciri, M. Ahmed. An Analysis of the Accounting Standard-Setting Framework in Two European Countries: France and the Netherlands. In *Most, K. S., ed.*, 1988, pp. 69–85.

Bloomquist, Kim M. A Comparison of Alternative Methods of Generating Economic Base Multipliers. *Reg. Sci. Persp.*, 1988, *18*(1), pp. 58–99.

Blostin, Allan P.; Burke, Thomas P. and Lovejoy, Lora Mills. Disability and Insurance Plans in the Public and Private Sector. *Mon. Lab. Rev.*, December 1988, *111*(12), pp. 9–17.

Bluck, Susan and Suedfeld, Peter. Changes in Integrative Complexity Prior to Surprise Attacks. *J. Conflict Resolution*, December 1988, *32*(4), pp. 626–35.

Bluestone, Barry. Deindustrialization and Unem-

ployment in America. *Rev. Black Polit. Econ.*, Fall 1988, *17*(2), pp. 29–44.

_____. Time and the New Industrial State: Discussion. *Amer. Econ. Rev.*, May 1988, *78*(2), pp. 377–78.

_____ and Harrison, Bennett. The Growth of Low-Wage Employment: 1963–86. *Amer. Econ. Rev.*, May 1988, *78*(2), pp. 124–28.

Bluestone, Herman and Miller, James P. Prospects for Service Sector Employment Growth in Non-metropolitan America. *Rev. Reg. Stud.*, Winter 1988, *18*(1), pp. 28–41.

Blum, Reinhard. Enterprise Ownership and Managerial Behavior: Discussion. In *Hanusch, H., ed.*, 1988, pp. 145–50.

_____. Labour as Factor of Production or Yardstick for Distribution. In *Dlugos, G.; Dorow, W. and Weiermair, K., eds.*, 1988, pp. 11–25.

Blum, Ulrich C. H. and Guadry, Marc J. I. An Example of Correlation among Residuals in Directly Ordered Data. *Econ. Letters*, 1988, *26*(4), pp. 335–40.

Blume, Lawrence E. New Techniques for the Study of Stochastic Equilibrium Processes. In *Grandmont, J.-M., ed.*, 1988, *1982*, pp. 339–48.

Blumenthal, Marsha A. Auctions with Constrained Information: Blind Bidding for Motion Pictures. *Rev. Econ. Statist.*, May 1988, *70*(2), pp. 191–98.

Blumenthal, W. Michael. Two Perspectives on International Macroeconomic Policy Coordination. In *Feldstein, M., ed. (I)*, 1988, pp. 43–49.

_____. The World Economy and Technological Change. *Foreign Aff.*, 1987–88, *66*(3), pp. 529–50.

Blumstein, James F. and Sloan, Frank A. Antitrust and Hospital Peer Review. *Law Contemp. Probl.*, Spring 1988, *51*(2), pp. 7–92.

Blundell, Richard. Consumer Behaviour: Theory and Empirical Evidence—A Survey. *Econ. J.*, March 1988, *98*(389), pp. 16–65.

_____. Econometric Issues in Public Sector Economics. In *Hare, P. G., ed.*, 1988, pp. 219–47.

_____; Fry, Vanessa and Walker, Ian. Modelling the Take-up of Means-tested Benefits: the Case of Housing Benefits in the United Kingdom. *Econ. J.*, Supplement, 1988, *98*(390), pp. 58–74.

_____ and Laisney, François. A Labour Supply Model for Married Women in France: Taxation, Hours Constraints and Job Seekers. *Ann. Écon. Statist.*, July–Sept. 1988, (11), pp. 41–71.

_____, et al. Labour Supply Specification and the Evaluation of Tax Reforms. *J. Public Econ.*, June 1988, *36*(1), pp. 23–52.

Blustain, Harvey and Polishuk, Paul. Fiber Optics: Technology Diffusion and Industrial Competitiveness. In *Hicks, D. A., ed.*, 1988, pp. 308–42.

Boadway, Robin W. Measuring Marginal Effective Tax Rates: Theory and Application to Canada. *Ann. Écon. Statist.*, July–Sept. 1988, (11), pp. 73–92.

_____ and Townley, Peter G. C. Social Security and the Failure of Annuity Markets. *J. Public Econ.*, February 1988, 35(1), pp. 75–96.

Boamah, Daniel O. Short-Term Forecasting of Wages, Employment and Output in Barbados. In *Motamen, H., ed.*, 1988, pp. 539–59.

_____. Some Macroeconomic Implications of External Debt for Barbados. *Soc. Econ. Stud.*, December 1988, 37(4), pp. 171–91.

Board, John and Sutcliffe, Charles. Forced Diversification. *Quart. Rev. Econ. Bus.*, Autumn 1988, 28(3), pp. 43–52.

Boaz, David. Assessing the Reagan Years: Introduction. In *Boaz, D., ed.*, 1988, pp. 1–5.

_____. Educational Schizophrenia. In *Boaz, D., ed.*, 1988, pp. 291–303.

Bober, Stanley. Alternative Views of the Monetary Sector in the Macroeconomics Course. *Eastern Econ. J.*, Oct.–Dec. 1988, 14(4), pp. 381–88.

Bober, Wolfgang; Evsiukov, Evgenii and Kriuchkov, Nikolai. Scientific-Technological Cooperation in Chemistry. *Soviet E. Europ. Foreign Trade*, Spring 1988, 24(1), pp. 54–62.

van Bochove, Cornelis A. and Al, Pieter G. A Synoptic Structure of the System of National Accounts. *Rev. Income Wealth*, March 1988, 34(1), pp. 45–70.

Bock, David R. The Bank's Role in Resolving the Debt Crisis. *Finance Develop.*, June 1988, 25(2), pp. 6–8.

Böckenholt, I.; Both, M. and Gaul, W. PROLOG-Based Decision Support for Data Analysis in Marketing. In *Gaul, W. and Schader, M., eds.*, 1988, pp. 19–34.

Böckle, Franz. Verlangen Wirtschaft und Technik eine "neue Ethik"? (With English summary.) *Z. Betriebswirtshaft*, September 1988, 58(9), pp. 898–907.

Bockstael, Nancy E. and Kling, Catherine L. Valuing Environmental Quality: Weak Complementarity with Sets of Goods. *Amer. J. Agr. Econ.*, August 1988, 70(3), pp. 654–62.

Boddy, Raford. Basic Justice and Macropolicy. *Contemp. Policy Issues*, January 1988, 6(1), pp. 84–88.

Bodea, Constanţa; Diaconescu, G. and Velicanu, M. A Relational Operator for Sorted Join. *Econ. Computat. Cybern. Stud. Res.*, 1988, 23(2), pp. 33–36.

Bodie, Zvi; Marcus, Alan J. and Merton, Robert C. Defined Benefit versus Defined Contribution Pension Plans: What Are the Real Trade-offs? In *Bodie, Z.; Shoven, J. B. and Wise, D. A., eds.*, 1988, pp. 139–60.

_____; Shoven, John B. and Wise, David A. Pensions in the U.S. Economy: Introduction. In *Bodie, Z.; Shoven, J. B. and Wise, D. A., eds.*, 1988, pp. 1–8.

Bodin de Moraes, Pedro. Keynes, Sargent e o papel da política monetária em um plano de estabilização. (With English summary.) *Pesquisa Planejamento Econ.*, April 1988, 18(1), pp. 145–60.

Bodkin, Ronald G. A Survey of Non-Dutch European Macroeconometric Models: Some International Perspective. In *Driehuis, W.; Fase, M. M. G. and den Hartog, H., eds.*, 1988, pp. 221–50.

_____; Klein, Lawrence R. and Marwah, Kanta. Keynes and the Origins of Macroeconometric Modelling. In *Hamouda, O. F. and Smithin, J. N., eds., Vol. 2*, 1988, pp. 3–11.

_____ and Marwah, Kanta. Trends in Macroeconomic Modeling: The Past Quarter Century. *J. Policy Modeling*, Summer 1988, 10(2), pp. 299–315.

Bodnar, Judith; Dilworth, Peter and Iacono, Salvatore. Cross-sectional Analysis of Residential Telephone Subscription in Canada. *Info. Econ. Policy*, 1988, 3(4), pp. 359–78.

Bodurtha, James N., Jr. and Valnet, Frederique. Innovation in the International Money and Bond Markets: A Source of Lower Borrowing Costs? In *Khoury, S. J. and Ghosh, A., eds.*, 1988, pp. 45–86.

Boehlje, Michael D. The Macroeconomics of Agriculture and Rural America: A Discussion. In *Hildreth, R. J., et al., eds.*, 1988, pp. 400–402.

Boekhoudt, André H. Recognition of Foreign Enterprises as Taxable Entities: Netherlands. In *International Fiscal Association, ed. (I)*, 1988, pp. 511–34.

Boer, M. Vanden. Unemployment, Employment and Forecasting Models: The Belgian Experience. In *Hopkins, M. J. D., ed.*, 1988, pp. 78–102.

Boeri, Tito. Cost–Benefit Analysis: Credibility and Feasibility. *Econ. Scelte Pubbliche/J. Public Finance Public Choice*, May–Aug. 1988, 6(2), pp. 115–34.

Boertje, Bert and Kuipers, Simon K. On the Causes of the Rise in the Liquidity Ratio in the Netherlands during the Early Eighties. *De Economist*, March 1988, 136(1), pp. 50–90.

Boffito, Carlo. La riforma del sistema creditizio e finanziario nell'Unione Sovietica. (The Reform of the Banking and Financial System in the USSR. With English summary.) *Rivista Int. Sci. Econ. Com.*, Oct.–Nov. 1988, 35(10–11), pp. 897–924.

_____. Reforms and Export Promotion. In *Marer, P. and Siwinski, W., eds.*, 1988, pp. 151–62.

Bofinger, Peter. Das Europäische Währungssystem und die geldpolitische Koordination in Europa. (The European Monetary System and Monetary Policy Coordination in Europe. With English summary.) *Kredit Kapital*, 1988, 21(3), pp. 317–45.

Bogaert, Michael M. V. D., et al. Human Resources Development for Rural Development with Social Justice. In *Kohli, U. and Gautam, V., eds.*, 1988, pp. 26–38.

Boggess, William G. and Reichelderfer, Katherine. Government Decision Making and Program Performance: The Case of the Conservation Reserve Program. *Amer. J. Agr. Econ.*, February 1988, 70(1), pp. 1–11.

Boggio, Luciano. Export Expansion and Economic Growth: An "Empirical Regularity" and Its Explanation. *Empirica*, 1988, *15*(1), pp. 205–26.

Boggs, Paul T., et al. A Computational Examination of Orthogonal Distance Regression. *J. Econometrics*, May–June 1988, *38*(1–2), pp. 169–201.

Bognár, József. Decision-Making and Instruments for Socialist Foreign Trade. In *Saunders, C. T., ed.*, 1988, pp. 101–09.

Bogomolov, Oleg T. Prospects for the World Economy: An Overall View to West and East. In *Saunders, C. T., ed.*, 1988, pp. 19–32.

_____. Relationships between Rural and Industrial Development. In *Arrow, K. J., ed.*, 1988, pp. 76–84.

_____. The Socialist World on the Path of Restructuring. *Prob. Econ.*, July 1988, *31*(3), pp. 6–23.

Bohara, Alok K. An Analysis of the Effects of Oil Price Shocks on the Colorado Economy Using Vector Autoregression. *Rev. Reg. Stud.*, Fall 1988, *18*(3), pp. 23–30.

_____. Responses of Monetary Targets to Changes in Federal Reserve Operating Procedures: An Intervention Analysis Approach. *Amer. Econ.*, Fall 1988, *32*(2), pp. 45–50.

Bohi, Douglas R. and Toman, Michael A. Restructuring the IEA Crisis Management Program to Serve Members' Interests Better. In *Horwich, G. and Weimer, D. L., eds.*, 1988, pp. 200–217.

Böhm, Volker. Returns to Size vs Returns to Scale: The Core with Production Revisited. *J. Econ. Theory*, October 1988, *46*(1), pp. 215–19.

_____ **and Puhakka, Mikko.** Rationing and Optimality in Overlapping Generations Models. *Scand. J. Econ.*, 1988, *90*(2), pp. 225–32.

Bohman, Mary and Anania, Giovanni. Domestic Farm Policy and the Gains from Trade: Comment. *Amer. J. Agr. Econ.*, August 1988, *70*(3), pp. 735–39.

Bohn, Henning. Why Do We Have Nominal Government Debt? *J. Monet. Econ.*, January 1988, *21*(1), pp. 127–40.

_____; **Reiss, Peter C. and Bernanke, Ben S.** Alternative Non-nested Specification Tests of Time-Series Investment Models. *J. Econometrics*, March 1988, *37*(3), pp. 293–326.

Böhnisch, Wolf, et al. Predicting Austrian Leader Behavior from a Measure of Behavioral Intent: A Cross-Cultural Replication. In *Dlugos, G.; Dorow, W. and Weiermair, K., eds.*, 1988, pp. 313–22.

Bohr, Kurt. Zum Verhältnis von klassischer Investitions- und entscheidungsorientierter Kostenrechnung. (With English summary.) *Z. Betriebswirtshaft*, November 1988, *58*(11), pp. 1171–80.

Boidman, Nathan. An Offshore Transshipment Company Case: Indalex v. the Queen. *Bull. Int. Fiscal Doc.*, May 1988, *42*(5), pp. 202–12.

Boisier, Sergio. Regions as the Product of Social Construction. *CEPAL Rev.*, August 1988, (35), pp. 41–56.

de Boissieu, Christian and Artus, Patrick. The Process of Financial Innovation: Causes, Forms, and Consequences. In *Heertje, A., ed.*, 1988, pp. 101–26.

Bojadzeiv, G. Behavioural Strategy of Some Controlled Predator–Prey Systems. In *Eiselt, H. A. and Pederzoli, G., eds.*, 1988, pp. 283–92.

Bokemeier, Janet L. and Garkovich, Lorraine E. Factors Associated with Women's Attitudes toward Farming. In *Beaulieu, L. J., ed.*, 1988, pp. 120–40.

Bokemeier, L. Charles. Revenue Recognition Criteria for State and Local Governments. In *Chan, J. L. and Rowan, H. J., eds.*, 1988, pp. 129–57.

Bol, Georg. On the Definition of Efficiency Measures: A Note. In *Eichhorn, W., ed.*, 1988, pp. 167–69.

Boland, Lawrence A. Individualist Economics without Psychology. In *Earl, P. E., ed.*, 1988, pp. 163–68.

Bolch, Ben W. and Damon, William W. Modeling Divorcement in the Retail Petroleum Industry. *Quart. Rev. Econ. Bus.*, Summer 1988, *28*(2), pp. 46–60.

_____; **Damon, William W. and Hinshaw, C. Elton.** Visual Artists' Rights Act of 1987: A Case of Misguided Legislation. *Cato J.*, Spring–Summer 1988, *8*(1), pp. 71–78.

Boldrin, Michele. Persistent Oscillations and Chaos in Dynamic Economic Models: Notes for a Survey. In *Anderson, P. W.; Arrow, K. J. and Pines, D., eds.*, 1988, pp. 49–75.

_____ **and Montrucchio, Luigi.** Acyclicity and Stability for Intertemporal Optimization Models. *Int. Econ. Rev.*, February 1988, *29*(1), pp. 137–46.

_____ **and Scheinkman, José A.** Learning-by-Doing, International Trade and Growth: A Note. In *Anderson, P. W.; Arrow, K. J. and Pines, D., eds.*, 1988, pp. 285–300.

Boldt, David and McDonald, Brian. Review: Aremos Data Management and Econometric Software, Version 1.0. *Econ. Inquiry*, April 1988, *26*(2), pp. 365–67.

Boldur-Lătescu, G. The Complex Prospect for the Problem of Cybernetic–Economic Systems Control. *Econ. Computat. Cybern. Stud. Res.*, 1988, *23*(2), pp. 5–13.

Bolino, August C. British and American Horology: A Comment. *J. Econ. Hist.*, September 1988, *48*(3), pp. 665–67.

Bolle, Friedel. Learning to Make Good Predictions in Time Series. In *Tietz, R.; Albers, W. and Selten, R., eds.*, 1988, pp. 37–50.

_____. The Significance of Motivational Variables in International Public Welfare Expenditures: A Comment. *Econ. Develop. Cult. Change*, January 1988, *36*(2), pp. 393–96.

_____. Testing for Rational Expectations in Experimental Predictions. In *Maital, S., ed., Vol. 1*, 1988, pp. 319–34.

Bollens, Scott A. Municipal Decline and Inequality in American Suburban Rings, 1960–1980. *Reg. Stud.*, August 1988, *22*(4), pp. 277–85.

Bollerslev, Tim; Engle, Robert F. and Wooldridge, Jeffrey M. A Capital Asset Pricing Model with Time-Varying Covariances. *J. Polit. Econ.*, February 1988, *96*(1), pp. 116–31.

Bolling, Christine. Price and Exchange Rate Transmission Revisited: The Latin America Case. In *Carter, C. A. and Gardiner, W. H., eds.*, 1988, pp. 163–94.

Bollino, C. Andrea and Rossi, Nicola. Public Debt and Households' Demand for Monetary Assets in Italy: 1970–86. In *Giavazzi, F. and Spaventa, L., eds.*, 1988, pp. 222–43.

Bollino, Carlo; Ceriani, Vieri and Violi, Roberto. Il mercato unico europeo e l'armonizzazione dell'iva e delle accise. (With English summary.) *Polit. Econ.*, December 1988, *4*(3), pp. 315–59.

Bollman, Ray D. and Tomiak, Monica. Decoupled Agricultural Policy and the Lack of Production Alternatives. *Can. J. Agr. Econ.*, July 1988, *36*(2), pp. 349–52.

Bolnick, Bruce R. Evaluating Loan Collection Performance: An Indonesian Example. *World Devel.*, April 1988, *16*(4), pp. 501–10.

Boltho, Andrea. International Economic Cooperation: Some Lessons from History. *Rivista Storia Econ.*, S.S., June 1988, *5*(2), pp. 173–92.

_____. Is There a Future for Resource Transfers to the LDCs? *World Devel.*, October 1988, *16*(10), pp. 1159–66.

_____. Prospects for the World Economy: Comments. In *Saunders, C. T., ed.*, 1988, pp. 61–63.

Bolton, Patrick and Bonanno, Giacomo. Vertical Restraints in a Model of Vertical Differentiation. *Quart. J. Econ.*, August 1988, *103*(3), pp. 555–70.

Boltuck, Richard D. An Economic Analysis of Dumping: Reply. *J. World Trade*, December 1988, *22*(6), pp. 129–31.

Bombau, Marcelo E. and Bomchil, Maximo, Jr. Argentine Foreign Debt to Equity Conversion Programme. *Bull. Int. Fiscal Doc.*, October 1988, *42*(10), pp. 434–40.

Bomberger, William A.; Makinen, Gail E. and Anderson, Robert B. The Demand for Money, the "Reform Effect," and the Money Supply Process in Hyperinflations: The Evidence from Greece and Hungary II Reexamined. *J. Money, Credit, Banking*, November 1988, *20*(4), pp. 653–72.

Bomchil, Maximo, Jr. and Bombau, Marcelo E. Argentine Foreign Debt to Equity Conversion Programme. *Bull. Int. Fiscal Doc.*, October 1988, *42*(10), pp. 434–40.

Bomhoff, Eduard J. and Koedijk, Kees G. Bilateral Exchange Rates and Risk Premia. *J. Int. Money Finance*, June 1988, *7*(2), pp. 205–20.

_____ **and Schotman, Peter C.** The Term Structure in the United States, Japan, and West Germany. *Carnegie–Rochester Conf. Ser. Public Policy*, Spring 1988, *28*, pp. 269–313.

Bommer, Michael R. W. and O'Neil, Brian F. Analysis of Alternative Distribution Strategies.

Logist. Transp. Rev., September 1988, *24*(3), pp. 237–47.

Bomsel, Olivier. L'oligopole comme mode de croissance des industries minières et métallurgiques et les raisons de son dépassement. (The Oligopoly as a Mode of Growth of Mineral and Metal Industries and the Reasons for its Passing. With English summary.) *Écon. Soc.*, Nov.–Dec. 1988, *22*(11–12), pp. 35–55.

Bomze, Immanuel M. A Note on Aspirations in Non-transferable Utility Games. *Int. J. Game Theory*, 1988, *17*(3), pp. 193–200.

Bon, Ranko. Supply-Side Multiregional Input–Output Models. *J. Reg. Sci.*, February 1988, *28*(1), pp. 41–50.

Bonanno, Giacomo. Entry Deterrence with Uncertain Entry and Uncertain Observability of Commitment. *Int. J. Ind. Organ.*, 1988, *6*(3), pp. 351–62.

_____. Oligopoly Equilibria When Firms Have Local Knowledge of Demand. *Int. Econ. Rev.*, February 1988, *29*(1), pp. 45–55.

_____ **and Bolton, Patrick.** Vertical Restraints in a Model of Vertical Differentiation. *Quart. J. Econ.*, August 1988, *103*(3), pp. 555–70.

_____ **and Vickers, John.** Vertical Separation. *J. Ind. Econ.*, March 1988, *36*(3), pp. 257–65.

Bond, Andrew R. and Micklin, Philip P. Reflections on Environmentalism and the River Diversion Projects. *Soviet Econ.*, July–Sept. 1988, *4*(3), pp. 253–74.

Bond, Daniel L. and Klein, Lawrence R. The Medium-Term Outlook for the World Economy and the Implications for East–West Economic Relations. In *Saunders, C. T., ed.*, 1988, pp. 33–46.

Bond, Eric W. Optimal Commercial Policy with Quality-Differentiated Products. *J. Int. Econ.*, November 1988, *25*(3–4), pp. 271–90.

Bond, Gary E. and Thompson, Stanley R. Offshore Commodity Hedging under Floating Exchange Rates: Reply. *Amer. J. Agr. Econ.*, August 1988, *70*(3), pp. 727–28.

Bond, Stephen R. Stabilization Policy, Expected Output and Employment. *Oxford Bull. Econ. Statist.*, May 1988, *50*(2), pp. 139–58.

_____ **and Devereux, Michael.** Financial Volatility, the Stock Market Crash and Corporate Investment. *Fisc. Stud.*, May 1988, *9*(2), pp. 72–80.

Bondar, Joseph. Effects of the Social Security Benefit Increase, December 1987. *Soc. Sec. Bull.*, July 1988, *51*(7), pp. 32–35.

_____. Social Security Beneficiaries Enrolled in the Direct Deposit Program, December 1986. *Soc. Sec. Bull.*, February 1988, *51*(2), pp. 31–37.

Bonderud, Kendra and Barrows, Richard. The Distribution of Tax Relief under Farm Circuit-Breakers: Some Empirical Evidence. *Land Econ.*, February 1988, *64*(1), pp. 15–27.

Bondi, Liz and Peake, Linda. Gender and the City: Urban Politics Revisited. In *Little, J.; Peake, L. and Richardson, P., eds.*, 1988, pp. 21–40.

de Bondt, Raymond; Sleuwaegen, Leo and Veu-

gelers, Reinhilde. Innovative Strategic Groups in Multinational Industries. *Europ. Econ. Rev.*, April 1988, *32*(4), pp. 905–25.

Bonelli, Regis; Rios, Sandra Maria Polónia and Reis, Eustáquio José. Dívidas e déficits: Projeções para o médio prazo. (With English summary.) *Pesquisa Planejamento Econ.*, August 1988, *18*(2), pp. 239–70.

Bongaarts, John. Does Family Planning Reduce Infant Mortality? Reply. *Population Devel. Rev.*, March 1988, *14*(1), pp. 188–90.

Bonin, John P. The Share Economy: Taxation without Representation? In *Jones, D. C. and Svejnar, J., eds.*, 1988, pp. 185–200.

Bonnell, Sheila Mary and Rimmer, R. J. Trends and Cyclical Changes in Real Wages, Productivity and Distribution of Income during the 1930s. In *Brenner, Y. S.; Reijnders, J. P. G. and Spithoven, A. H. G. M., eds.*, 1988, pp. 89–116.

Bonnen, James T. Improving the Socioeconomic Data Base. In *Hildreth, R. J., et al., eds.*, 1988, pp. 452–83.

_____. Institutions, Instruments, and Driving Forces Behind U.S. National Agricultural Policies. In *Allen, K. and Macmillan, K., eds.*, 1988, pp. 21–39.

Bonnieux, F. and Rainelli, P. Agricultural Policy and Environment in Developed Countries. *Europ. Rev. Agr. Econ.*, 1988, *15*(2–3), pp. 263–81.

Bonnin, Michel and Cartier, Michel. Urban Employment in Post-Maoist China. In *Feuchtwang, S.; Hussain, A. and Pairault, T., eds., Vol. 1*, 1988, pp. 198–226.

Bonnisseau, Jean-Marc. On Two Existence Results of Equilibria in Economies with Increasing Returns. *J. Math. Econ.*, 1988, *17*(2–3), pp. 193–207.

_____ and Cornet, Bernard. Existence of Equilibria When Firms Follow Bounded Losses Pricing Rules. *J. Math. Econ.*, 1988, *17*(2–3), pp. 119–47.

_____ and Cornet, Bernard. Valuation Equilibrium and Pareto Optimum in Non-convex Economies. *J. Math. Econ.*, 1988, *17*(2–3), pp. 293–308.

Bonoma, Thomas V.; Crittenden, Victoria L. and Dolan, Robert J. Can We Have Rigor and Relevance in Pricing Research? In *Devinney, T. M., ed.*, 1988, pp. 337–59.

Bonte, J. and van Son, P. Health Statistics in the Netherlands for Health Policy and Evaluation: Experience and Developments. *Statist. J.*, August 1988, *5*(2), pp. 123–33.

Bontempo, Hélio Cézar. Transferências externas e financiamento do governo federal e autoridades monetárias. (With English summary.) *Pesquisa Planejamento Econ.*, April 1988, *18*(1), pp. 101–30.

Bookbinder, James H. and Ulengin, Fusun. Models for Improving Grain Transportation in Western Canada. *Logist. Transp. Rev.*, December 1988, *24*(4), pp. 349–67.

Bookstaber, Richard and Langsam, Joseph A. Portfolio Insurance Trading Rules. *J. Futures Markets*, February 1988, *8*(1), pp. 15–31.

Boomgaard, Peter. Treacherous Cane: The Java Sugar Industry between 1914 and 1940. In *Albert, B. and Graves, A., eds.*, 1988, pp. 157–69.

Boomsma, Anne; Molenaar, Ivo W. and Luijben, Thom. Modification of Factor Analysis Models in Covariance Structure Analysis: A Monte Carlo Study. In *Dijkstra, T. K., ed.*, 1988, pp. 70–101.

Boon, Martin; Kool, Clemens J. M. and de Vries, Casper G. Simulating Currency Substitution Bias. *Econ. Letters*, 1988, *28*(3), pp. 269–72.

Boone, Jean F. and Hardt, John P. A New U.S. Economic Policy toward Poland. In *Marer, P. and Siwinski, W., eds.*, 1988, pp. 335–44.

Boone, Louis E.; Gibson, Donald R. and Kurtz, David L. Rating Logistics and Transportation Faculties on the Basis of Editorial Review Board Memberships. *Logist. Transp. Rev.*, December 1988, *24*(4), pp. 684–90.

Boone, Peter and Sachs, Jeffrey D. Japanese Structural Adjustment and the Balance of Payments. *J. Japanese Int. Economies*, September 1988, *2*(3), pp. 286–327.

Boot, H. M. Debts, Drought, and Foreclosure: Wool-Producers in Queensland and New South Wales, 1870–1905. *Australian Econ. Hist. Rev.*, September 1988, *28*(2), pp. 33–52.

Booth, Alison and Schiantarelli, Fabio. Reductions in Hours and Employment: What Do Union Models Tell Us? In *Hart, R. A., ed.*, 1988, pp. 142–57.

Booth, Anne. Survey of Recent Developments. *Bull. Indonesian Econ. Stud.*, April 1988, *24*(1), pp. 3–35.

Booth, Douglas E. Urban Growth and Decline, Budgetary Incrementalism, and Municipal Finances: Milwaukee, 1870–1977. *Exploration Econ. Hist.*, January 1988, *25*(1), pp. 20–41.

Booth, G. Geoffrey and Akgiray, Vedat. Mixed Diffusion-Jump Process Modeling of Exchange Rate Movements. *Rev. Econ. Statist.*, November 1988, *70*(4), pp. 631–37.

_____ and Akgiray, Vedat. The Stable-Law Model of Stock Returns. *J. Bus. Econ. Statist.*, January 1988, *6*(1), pp. 51–57.

_____ and Aydogan, Kursat. Are There Long Cycles in Common Stock Returns? *Southern Econ. J.*, July 1988, *55*(1), pp. 141–49.

_____; Seifert, Bruce and Akgiray, Vedat. Distribution Properties of Latin American Black Market Exchange Rates. *J. Int. Money Finance*, March 1988, *7*(1), pp. 37–48.

Booth, James R.; Tehranian, Hassan and Trennepohl, Gary L. An Empirical Analysis of Insured Portfolio Strategies Using Listing Options. *J. Finan. Res.*, Spring 1988, *11*(1), pp. 1–12.

Booth, Richard A. The Promise of State Takeover Statutes. *Mich. Law Rev.*, June 1988, *86*(7), pp. 1635–1702.

Boothe, Paul M. Exchange Rate Risk and the Bid–Ask Spread: A Seven Country Comparison. *Econ. Inquiry*, July 1988, *26*(3), pp. 485–92.

_____ **and Poloz, Stephen S.** Unstable Money Demand and the Monetary Model of the Exchange Rate. *Can. J. Econ.*, November 1988, *21*(4), pp. 785–98.

Boots, Barry N. and Kanaroglou, Pavlos S. Incorporating the Effects of Spatial Structure in Discrete Choice Models of Migration. *J. Reg. Sci.*, November 1988, *28*(4), pp. 495–509.

Bopp, Anthony E. and Sitzer, Scott. On the 'Efficiency' of Futures Markets: Another View. *Energy Econ.*, July 1988, *10*(3), pp. 199–205.

Borba, Philip S. and Appel, David. Costs and Prices of Workers' Compensation Insurance. In *Borba, P. S. and Appel, D., eds.*, 1988, pp. 1–17.

Borchardt, Knut. Keynes' "Nationale Selbstgenügsamkeit" von 1933. Ein Fall von kooperativer Selbstzensur. (Keynes' "Nationale Selbstgenügsamkeit" in Gemany 1933. A Case of Cooperative Self-censorship. With English summary.) *Z. Wirtschaft. Sozialwissen.*, 1988, *108*(2), pp. 271–84.

Borchert, Manfred. Money, Debt and Developing Country Borrowing. In *[Frowen, S.]*, 1988, pp. 167–83.

Bordes, C. and Strauss-Kahn, M.-O. Dispositif de controle monetaire en France et chocs sur la vitesse dans un environnement en mutation. (The French Experience with Targeting and Velocity Shocks in a Changing Environment. With English summary.) *Écon. Soc.*, January 1988, *22*(1), pp. 105–53.

_____, **et al.** Tests économétriques de l'hypothèse de rationalité et de l'hypothèse de neutralité structurelle: le cas de la France. (With English summary.) *Revue Écon. Polit.*, May–June 1988, *98*(3), pp. 363–81.

Bordes, G. A. and Banks, Jeffery S. Voting Games, Indifference, and Consistent Sequential Choice Rules. *Soc. Choice Welfare*, 1988, *5*(1), pp. 31–44.

Bordo, Michael D. Central Banking under the Gold Standard: Comment. *Carnegie–Rochester Conf. Ser. Public Policy*, Autumn 1988, *29*, pp. 125–35.

_____ **and Jonung, Lars.** Some Qualms about the Test of the Institutionalist Hypothesis of the Long-run Behavior of Velocity: Reply. *Econ. Inquiry*, July 1988, *26*(3), pp. 547–49.

_____ **and Phillips, William H.** Faithful Index to the Ambitions and Fortunes of the State: The Development of Political Economy at South Carolina College. In *Barber, W. J., ed.*, 1988, pp. 42–71.

_____ **and Redish, Angela.** Costs and Benefits of Exchange Rate Stability: Canada's Interwar Experience. *Contemp. Policy Issues*, April 1988, *6*(2), pp. 115–30.

_____ **and Redish, Angela.** Was the Establishment of a Canadian Central Bank in 1935 Necessary? In *England, C. and Huertas, T., eds.*, 1988, pp. 69–86.

_____ **and Schwartz, Anna J.** Transmission of Real and Monetary Disturbances under Fixed and Floating Exchange Rates. *Cato J.*, Fall 1988, *8*(2), pp. 451–72.

Borenstein, Severin. On the Efficiency of Competitive Markets for Operating Licenses. *Quart. J. Econ.*, May 1988, *103*(2), pp. 357–85.

_____ **and Zimmerman, Martin B.** Market Incentives for Safe Commercial Airline Operation. *Amer. Econ. Rev.*, December 1988, *78*(5), pp. 913–35.

Borensztein, Eduardo R. and Aizenman, Joshua. Debt and Conditionality under Endogenous Terms of Trade Adjustment. *Int. Monet. Fund Staff Pap.*, December 1988, *35*(4), pp. 686–713.

Borg, Mary O. and Mason, Paul M. The Budgetary Incidence of a Lottery to Support Education. *Nat. Tax J.*, March 1988, *41*(1), pp. 75–85.

Borgan, Ørnulf and Hoem, Jan M. Demographic Reproduction Rates and the Estimation of an Expected Total Count per Person in an Open Population. *J. Amer. Statist. Assoc.*, September 1988, *83*(403), pp. 886–91.

Boris, Eileen. Homework in the Past, Its Meaning for the Future. In *Christensen, K. E., ed.*, 1988, pp. 15–29.

_____ **and Honey, Michael.** Gender, Race, and the Policies of the Labor Department. *Mon. Lab. Rev.*, February 1988, *111*(2), pp. 26–36.

Borisov, A. N. and Slyadz, N. N. Decision Making Based on Fuzzy Stochastic and Statistical Dominance. In *Kacprzyk, J. and Fedrizzi, M., eds.*, 1988, pp. 197–214.

Borjas, George J. Discrimination in HEW: Is the Doctor Sick or Are the Patients Healthy? In *Stigler, G. J., ed.*, 1988, *1978*, pp. 426–40.

_____. Earnings Determination: A Survey of the Neoclassical Approach. In *Mangum, G. and Philips, P., eds.*, 1988, pp. 21–50.

Born, Jeffery A.; Eisenbeis, Robert A. and Harris, Robert S. The Benefits of Geographical and Product Expansion in the Financial Service Industries. *J. Finan. Services Res.*, January 1988, *1*(2), pp. 161–82.

_____ **and Moser, James T.** An Investigation into the Role of the Market Portfolio in the Arbitrage Pricing Theory. *Financial Rev.*, August 1988, *23*(3), pp. 287–99.

_____; **Moser, James T. and Officer, Dennis T.** Changes in Dividend Policy and Subsequent Earnings. *J. Portfol. Manage.*, Summer 1988, *14*(4), pp. 56–62.

Borner, Silvio. The International Debt Problem: Concluding Remarks. In *Borner, S., ed.*, 1988, pp. 373–76.

Bornet, Vaughn Davis. RAND Brainpower in the National Interest, 1946 to 1986. In *Perkins, E. J., ed.*, 1988, pp. 289–302.

Bornstein, Morris. Price Reform in the USSR: Comment. *Soviet Econ.*, Oct.–Dec. 1988, *4*(4), pp. 328–37.

Borooah, Vani K. The Growth of Public Expenditure in the United Kingdom, 1960–86. In *Lybeck, J. A. and Henrekson, M., eds.*, 1988, pp. 299–326.

_____. Permanent Income, Rational Expectations and Government Consumption: A Multicountry Study. In *Lybeck, J. A. and Henrekson, M., eds.*, 1988, pp. 49–58.

_____ **and Lee, K. C.** The Effect of Changes in Britain's Industrial Structure on Female Relative Pay and Employment. *Econ. J.*, September 1988, *98*(392), pp. 818–32.

Börsch-Supan, Axel and Pitkin, John. On Discrete Choice Models of Housing Demand. *J. Urban Econ.*, September 1988, *24*(2), pp. 153–72.

Borth, D. and Graham, J. D. An Inventory Evaluation Approach for Common Use Stock Range Units in British Columbia. *Can. J. Agr. Econ.*, July 1988, *36*(2), pp. 279–94.

Borum, Joan D.; Conley, James R. and Wasilewski, Edward J. The Outlook for Collective Bargaining in 1988. *Mon. Lab. Rev.*, January 1988, *111*(1), pp. 10–23.

Borzeix, Anni and Maruani, Margaret. When a Strike Comes Marching Home. In *Jenson, J.; Hagen, E. and Reddy, C., eds.*, 1988, pp. 245–59.

Borzutzky, Silvia and Singh, Vijai P. The State of the Mature Industrial Region in Western Europe and North America. *Urban Stud.*, June 1988, *25*(3), pp. 212–27.

Bös, Dieter. Introduction: Recent Theories on Public Enterprise Economics. *Europ. Econ. Rev.*, March 1988, *32*(2–3), pp. 409–14.

_____. Welfare Effects of Privatizing Public Enterprises. In *Bös, D.; Rose, M. and Seidl, C., eds.*, 1988, pp. 339–62.

_____ **and Peters, Wolfgang.** Privatization, Internal Control, and Internal Regulation. *J. Public Econ.*, July 1988, *36*(2), pp. 231–58.

Bos, Marko and Nelson, Hans. Indirect Taxation and the Completion of the Internal Market of the EC. *J. Common Market Stud.*, September 1988, *27*(1), pp. 27–44.

Bos, Theodore and Anderson, Seth. Consumer Sentiments and Share Price Behavior. *J. Behav. Econ.*, Summer 1988, *17*(2), pp. 113–18.

Bosch, Darrell J. and Lee, Katherine L. The Farm Level Effects of Better Access to Information: The Case of Dart. *Southern J. Agr. Econ.*, December 1988, *20*(2), pp. 109–18.

Bosch, Deborah K.; Weyant, John P. and Peck, Stephen C. Industrial Energy Demand: A Simple Structural Approach. *Resources & Energy*, June 1988, *10*(2), pp. 111–33.

Bosch-Domènech, C. Escribano and Escribano, C. Regional Allocation of Public Funds: An Evaluation Index. *Environ. Planning A*, October 1988, *20*(10), pp. 1323–33.

Boscheck, Ralf. Cooperative R&D as Institutional Choice Implications for Antitrust Analysis. *Aussenwirtschaft*, June 1988, *43*(1/2), pp. 97–139.

Boschen, John F. Monetary Policy and the Information Content of Indexed Bonds. *J. Macroecon.*, Spring 1988, *10*(2), pp. 163–82.

_____ **and Mills, Leonard O.** Tests of the Relation between Money and Output in the Real Business Cycle Model. *J. Monet. Econ.*, November 1988, *22*(3), pp. 355–74.

Bose, Arun. The "Labour Approach" and the

"Commodity Approach" in Mr. Sraffa's Price Theory. In *Steedman, I., ed., Vol. 1*, 1988, *1964*, pp. 15–19.

Bose, G. K. and Abedin, Joynal. Farm Size and Productivity Difference—A Decomposition Analysis. *Bangladesh Devel. Stud.*, September 1988, *16*(3), pp. 71–79.

Bosi, Paolo; Golinelli, Roberto and Stagni, Anna. Effetti macroeconomici e settoriali dell'armonizzazione dell'Iva e delle accise: la valutazione del modello Hermes-Italia. (With English summary.) *Polit. Econ.*, December 1988, *4*(3), pp. 361–84.

Boske, Leigh B. Alternative Formulations of the Federal Highway Administration's Bid Price Index for Highway Construction. *Logist. Transp. Rev.*, June 1988, *24*(2), pp. 165–74.

Boskin, Michael J. Altering the Public/Private Mix of Retirement Incomes: Comment. In *Wachter, S. M., ed.*, 1988, pp. 227–30.

_____. Concepts and Measures of Federal Deficits and Debt and Their Impact on Economic Activity. In *Arrow, K. J. and Boskin, M. J., eds.*, 1988, pp. 77–112.

_____. Consumption, Saving, and Fiscal Policy. *Amer. Econ. Rev.*, May 1988, *78*(2), pp. 401–07.

_____. Future Social Security Financing Alternatives and National Saving. In *Wachter, S. M., ed.*, 1988, pp. 111–43.

_____. Observations on the Use of Textbooks in the Teaching of Principles of Economics. *J. Econ. Educ.*, Spring 1988, *19*(2), pp. 157–64.

_____. Tax Policy and Economic Growth: Lessons from the 1980s. *J. Econ. Perspectives*, Fall 1988, *2*(4), pp. 71–97.

_____; **Kotlikoff, Laurence J. and Shoven, John B.** Personal Security Accounts: A Proposal for Fundamental Social Security Reform. In *Wachter, S. M., ed.*, 1988, pp. 179–206.

_____ **and Puffert, Douglas J.** The Financial Impact of Social Security by Cohort under Alternative Financing Assumptions. In *Ricardo-Campbell, R. and Lazear, E. P., eds.*, 1988, pp. 207–32.

_____ **and Roberts, John.** A Closer Look at Saving Rates in the United States and Japan. In *Shoven, J. B., ed.*, 1988, pp. 121–43.

_____ **and Shoven, John B.** Poverty among the Elderly: Where Are the Holes in the Safety Net? In *Bodie, Z.; Shoven, J. B. and Wise, D. A., eds.*, 1988, pp. 115–34.

Bosman, H. W. J. The Separation of Nedbank, South Africa, from the Parent Institution in the Netherlands. In *Jones, S., ed.*, 1988, pp. 69–79.

Bossaerts, Peter. Common Nonstationary Components of Asset Prices. *J. Econ. Dynam. Control*, June–Sept. 1988, *12*(2–3), pp. 347–64.

Bossert, Walter and Buhl, Hans Ulrich. More on Sufficiency Conditions for Interior Location in the Triangle Space. *J. Reg. Sci.*, February 1988, *28*(1), pp. 127.

Bosshard, Rudolf. Perspectives after Punta del Este. In *Dicke, D. C. and Petersmann, E.-U., eds.*, 1988, pp. 39–41.

Bosso, Christopher J. Transforming Adversaries into Collaborators: Interest Groups and the Regulation of Chemical Pesticides. *Policy Sci.*, 1988, *21*(1), pp. 3–22.

Bossons, John. International Tax Competition: The Foreign Government Response in Canada and Other Countries. *Nat. Tax J.*, September 1988, *41*(3), pp. 347–55.

_____. World Tax Reform: A Progress Report: Canada: Comment. In *Pechman, J. A., ed.*, 1988, pp. 69–77.

Bostaph, S. and Shieh, Yeung-Nan. W. S. Jevons and Lardner's 'Railway Economy' In *Wood, J. C., ed., Vol. 3*, 1988, *1986*, pp. 316–32.

Bostock, F. A. and Baston, V. J. Deception Games. *Int. J. Game Theory*, 1988, *17*(2), pp. 129–34.

Bosworth, Barry. Effects of Taxes on Saving: Comments. In *Aaron, H. J.; Galper, H. and Pechman, J. A., eds.*, 1988, pp. 265–68.

Both, M.; Gaul, W. and Böckenholt, I. PROLOG-Based Decision Support for Data Analysis in Marketing. In *Gaul, W. and Schader, M., eds.*, 1988, pp. 19–34.

Botha, D. J. J. The Dollar and Floating Rates in the 'Seventies: Note. *S. Afr. J. Econ.*, June–Sept. 1988, *56*(2–3), pp. 201–11.

Botos, Balázs. The Structure of Our Industrial Foreign Trade and the Process of Internationalization. *Soviet E. Europ. Foreign Trade*, Summer 1988, *24*(2), pp. 55–72.

Bottomley, P. and Thirtle, C. Is Publicly Funded Agricultural Research Excessive? *J. Agr. Econ.*, January 1988, *39*(1), pp. 99–111.

Boucher, Michel. Considérations empiriques sur la technologie de l'industrie québécoise du camionnage public. (With English summary.) *L'Actual. Econ.*, September 1988, *64*(3), pp. 361–79.

Bouchon, Bernadette. Questionnaires with Fuzzy and Probabilistic Elements. In *Kacprzyk, J. and Fedrizzi, M., eds.*, 1988, pp. 322–30.

Boudreaux, Don. Rent Seeking and Legal Barriers to Entry. *Econ. Scelte Pubbliche/J. Public Finance Public Choice*, Jan.–April 1988, *6*(1), pp. 63–68.

_____ **and Ekelund, Robert B., Jr.** The Semantic Imp and Regulation: Reply. *J. Inst. Theoretical Econ.*, December 1988, *144*(5), pp. 889–90.

Boughton, James M. Exchange Rates and the Term Structure of Interest Rates. *Int. Monet. Fund Staff Pap.*, March 1988, *35*(1), pp. 36–62.

Bouillaguet-Bernard, Patricia and Gauvin, Annie. Female Labour Reserves and the Restructuring of Employment in Booms and Slumps in France. In *Rubery, J., ed.*, 1988, pp. 48–73.

_____ **and Gauvin, Annie.** Women's Employment, the State and the Family in France: Contradiction of State Policy for Women's Employment. In *Rubery, J., ed.*, 1988, pp. 163–90.

Bouillon, Marvin L. and Kleiner, Morris M. Providing Business Information to Production Workers: Correlates of Compensation and

Profitability. *Ind. Lab. Relat. Rev.*, July 1988, *41*(4), pp. 605–17.

Bouis, Howarth E. and Chern, Wen S. Structural Changes in Residential Electricity Demand. *Energy Econ.*, July 1988, *10*(3), pp. 213–22.

Boulding, Kenneth E. Population Factors in Development Economics. *Population Devel. Rev.*, Supplement, 1988, *14*, pp. 262–80.

_____. What Do We Want in an Economics Textbook? *J. Econ. Educ.*, Spring 1988, *19*(2), pp. 113–32.

Boulding, William; Reibstein, David and Bateson, John E. G. Conjoint Analysis Reliability: Empirical Findings. *Marketing Sci.*, Summer 1988, *7*(3), pp. 271–86.

Boulier, Bryan L. and Paqueo, Vicente B. On the Theory and Measurement of the Determinants of Mortality. *Demography*, May 1988, *25*(2), pp. 249–63.

Bouman, F. J. A. and Houtman, R. Pawnbroking as an Instrument of Rural Banking in the Third World. *Econ. Develop. Cult. Change*, October 1988, *37*(1), pp. 69–89.

Bourdaire, J. M. and Charreton, R. Industrial Practice of Decision Theory. In *Munier, B. R., ed.*, 1988, pp. 657–77.

Bourgeat, Alain and Amaziane, Brahim. Effective Behavior of Two-Phase Flow in Heterogeneous Reservoir. In *Wheeler, M. F., ed.*, 1988, pp. 1–22.

Bourgeois, Bernard; Criqui, Patrick and Percebois, Jacques. Energy Conservation versus Supply Strategies: Implications for Industrial Policy. *Energy J.*, July 1988, *9*(3), pp. 99–111.

Bourgoignie, Thierry. Product Liability: Old Arguments for a New Debate? In *Maynes, E. S. and ACCI Research Committee, eds.*, 1988, pp. 800–815.

Bourguignon, François. Wealth Holdings and Entrepreneurial Activity: Comments. In *Kessler, D. and Masson, A., eds.*, 1988, pp. 257–58.

_____; **Chiappori, Pierre-André and Atkinson, Anthony B.** Fiscalité et transferts: Une comparaison franco–britannique. (Taxes and Benefits: A Franco–British Comparison. With English summary.) *Ann. Écon. Statist.*, July–Sept. 1988, (11), pp. 117–40.

_____; **Chiappori, Pierre André and Atkinson, Anthony B.** What Do We Learn about Tax Reform from International Comparisons? France and Britain. *Europ. Econ. Rev.*, March 1988, *32*(2–3), pp. 343–52.

_____; **Morrisson, Christian and Atkinson, Anthony B.** Earnings Mobility. *Europ. Econ. Rev.*, March 1988, *32*(2–3), pp. 619–32.

Bourguinat, Henri. The European Monetary System (EMS): First Lessons and New Challenges. In *Saunders, C. T., ed.*, 1988, pp. 133–53.

Bourlange, Danielle and Doz, Catherine. Pseudo-maximum de vraisemblance: Expériences de simulations dans le cadre d'un modèle de Poisson. (Pseudo-maximum Likelihood Estimators: Monte-Carlo Experimentation in the Case of a Poisson Model. With English summary.) *Ann. Écon. Statist.*, April–June 1988, (10), pp. 139–76.

Bourles, Marie-Ange Moreau. Analysis of Recruitment and Dismissal System Based on French Experience. *Econ. Lavoro*, Apr.–June 1988, *22*(2), pp. 115–25.

Bourmeyster, Alexandre. Soviet Political Discourse, Narrative Program and the "Skaz" Theory. In *Potichnyj, P. J., ed.*, 1988, pp. 107–20.

Bourne, Compton. Financial Deepening, Domestic Resource Mobilisation and Economic Growth: Jamaica 1955–82. In *Jorge, A. and Salazar-Carrillo, J., eds.*, 1988, pp. 165–79.

_____ **and Singh, R. Oumade.** External Debt and Adjustment in Caribbean Countries. *Soc. Econ. Stud.*, December 1988, *37*(4), pp. 107–36.

Boussard, J. M. A French Perspective on Supply Control and Management. *J. Agr. Econ.*, September 1988, *39*(3), pp. 326–39.

Boussemart, Benoît and de Bandt, Jacques. The European Textile Industries: Widely Varying Structures. In *de Jong, H. W., ed.*, 1988, pp. 183–209.

Boutillier, Michel; Gabrielli, Daniel and Plihon, Dominique. La baisse des taux d'intérêt en France: Quels effets en attendre? (Consequences of the Decrease in the Level of Interest Rates in France. With English summary.) *Revue Écon.*, July 1988, *39*(4), pp. 841–76.

Bouton, Marshall M. Financing Asian Development 2: China and India: Foreword. In *Dernberger, R. F. and Eckaus, R. S.*, 1988, pp. xi–xiii.

Bouvier, Jean. The Banque de France and the State from 1850 to the Present Day. In *Toniolo, G., ed.*, 1988, pp. 73–104.

Bouvier, Leon. Immigration, Population Change and California's Future. In *Simcox, D. E., ed.*, 1988, pp. 153–74.

Bouxsein, Peter. Standards of Care in Medicine: Commentary. *Inquiry*, Winter 1988, *25*(4), pp. 450–51.

Bouyssou, Denis and Vansnick, Jean-Claude. A Note on the Relationships Between Utility and Value Functions. In *Munier, B. R., ed.*, 1988, pp. 103–14.

Bovarnick, Murray E. Human-Resources Policies for Transnational Corporations in China. In *Teng, W. and Wang, N. T., eds.*, 1988, pp. 233–49.

Bovenberg, Arij Lans. The Corporate Income Tax in an Intertemporal Equilibrium Model with Imperfectly Mobil Capitla. *Int. Econ. Rev.*, May 1988, *29*(2), pp. 321–40.

_____. Long-term Interest Rates in the United States: An Empirical Analysis. *Int. Monet. Fund Staff Pap.*, June 1988, *35*(2), pp. 382–90.

Bowden, Julian. "That's the Spirit!": Russian Oil Products Ltd. (ROP) and the British Oil Market, 1924–39. *J. Europ. Econ. Hist.*, Winter 1988, *17*(3), pp. 641–63.

Bowden, R. J. and Turkington, D. A. Identification Information and Instruments in Linear Econometric Models with Rational Expecta-tions. *J. Econometrics*, July 1988, *38*(3), pp. 361–73.

Bowden, Sue M. The Consumer Durables Revolution in England 1932–1938; a Regional Analysis. *Exploration Econ. Hist.*, January 1988, *25*(1), pp. 42–59.

Bowen, Alex and Matthews, Robin C. O. Keynesian and Other Explanations of Post-war Macroeconomic Trends. In *Eltis, W. and Sinclair, P. J. N., eds.*, 1988, pp. 354–88.

Bowen, David E. and Scheider, Benjamin. Services Marketing and Management: Implications for Organizational Behavior. In *Staw, B. M. and Cummings, L. L., eds.*, 1988, pp. 43–80.

Bowen, H. Kent and Kenney, George B. New Materials. In *Uyehara, C. H., ed.*, 1988, pp. 62–89.

Bowen, Harry P. Imperfect Competition, Scale Economies, and Trade Policy in Developing Countries: Comment. In *Baldwin, R. E., ed. (II)*, 1988, pp. 137–41.

_____. Protection and Welfare in the Presence of Dynamic Learning. *Weltwirtsch. Arch.*, 1988, *124*(4), pp. 607–22.

Bowen, John R. Power and Meaning in Economic Change: What Does Anthropology Learn from Development Studies? Concluding Essay. In *Bennett, J. W. and Bowen, J. R., eds.*, 1988, pp. 411–30.

Bowen, Richard L. and Leung, PingSun. Using Input–Output Analysis to Estimate Tax Exporting and Tax Pyramiding in Hawaii. *Ann. Reg. Sci.*, March 1988, *22*(1), pp. 49–62.

Bowen, William M. Tests on a Theory of Risk and Culture. *Reg. Sci. Persp.*, 1988, *18*(1), pp. 19–42.

Bower, Joseph L. The Managerial Estate. In *Meyer, J. R. and Gustafson, J. M., eds.*, 1988, pp. 149–68.

_____. Managing in a Politicized World. In *Grant, J. H., ed.*, 1988, pp. 73–86.

Bowers, John. Cost–Benefit Analysis in Theory and Practice: Agricultural Land Drainage Projects. In *Turner, R. K., ed.*, 1988, pp. 265–89.

_____. Farm Incomes and the Benefits of Environmental Protection. In *[Lecomber, R.]*, 1988, pp. 161–71.

_____ **and Nash, Christopher A.** Alternative Approaches to the Valuation of Environmental Resources. In *Turner, R. K., ed.*, 1988, pp. 118–42.

Bowers, John and Ball, Ray. Daily Seasonals in Equity and Fixed-Interest Returns: Australian Evidence and Tests of Plausible Hypotheses. In *Dimson, E., ed.*, 1988, pp. 74–90.

_____ **and Dimson, Elroy.** Stock Market Anomalies: Introduction. In *Dimson, E., ed.*, 1988, pp. 3–15.

Bowers, William J. and Pierce, Glenn L. Arbitrariness and Discrimination under Post-*Furman* Capital Statutes. In *Alper, N. O. and Hellman, D. A., eds.*, 1988, pp. 150–71.

_____ **and Pierce, Glenn L.** The Bartley–Fox Gun Law's Short-term Impact on Crime in Boston. In *Alper, N. O. and Hellman, D. A., eds.*, 1988, pp. 201–24.

_____ **and Pierce, Glenn L.** Deterrence or Brutalization: What Is the Effect of Executions? In *Alper, N. O. and Hellman, D. A., eds.*, 1988, pp. 172–200.

Bowes, Stan. The Role of the Tourist Board. In *Goodall, B. and Ashworth, G., eds.*, 1988, pp. 75–88.

Bowker, J. M. and Stoll, John R. Use of Dichotomous Choice Nonmarket Methods to Value the Whooping Crane Resource. *Amer. J. Agr. Econ.*, May 1988, 70(2), pp. 372–81.

Bowlby, Sophie. From Corner Shop to Hypermarket: Women and Food Retailing. In *Little, J.; Peake, L. and Richardson, P., eds.*, 1988, pp. 61–83.

Bowles, David C.; Ulbrich, Holley H. and Wallace, Myles S. Default Risk and the Effects of Fiscal Policy on Interest Rates: 1929–1945. *Public Finance Quart.*, July 1988, 16(3), pp. 357–73.

_____ **and Wang, Leonard F. S.** Risk Aversion, Forward Markets and the Competitive Labor-Managed Firm under Price Uncertainty. *Managerial Dec. Econ.*, December 1988, 9(4), pp. 275–78.

Bowles, Paul and White, Gordon. China's Banking Reforms: Aims, Methods and Problems. *Nat. Westminster Bank Quart. Rev.*, November 1988, pp. 28–37.

Bowles, Samuel. Profits and Wages in an Open Economy. In *Mangum, G. and Philips, P., eds.*, 1988, pp. 64–81.

_____ **and Boyer, Robert.** Labor Discipline and Aggregate Demand: A Macroeconomic Model. *Amer. Econ. Rev.*, May 1988, 78(2), pp. 395–400.

_____ **and Gintis, Herbert.** Contested Exchange: Political Economy and Modern Economic Theory. *Amer. Econ. Rev.*, May 1988, 78(2), pp. 145–50.

Bowley, M. The Predecessors of Jevons—The Revolution That Wasn't. In *Wood, J. C., ed.*, Vol. 3, 1988, 1972, pp. 86–104.

Bowman, Adrian W. and Härdle, Wolfgang. Bootstrapping in Nonparametric Regression: Local Adaptive Smoothing and Confidence Bands. *J. Amer. Statist. Assoc.*, March 1988, 83(401), pp. 102–10.

Bowman, John H. and Bell, Michael E. The State Role in Local Finance. In *Bell, M. E., ed.*, 1988, pp. 191–227.

_____ **and Mikesell, John L.** Uniform Assessment of Agricultural Property for Taxation: Improvements from System Reform. *Land Econ.*, February 1988, 64(1), pp. 28–36.

Bowman, Stephen W. Collections in the Insolvency Context. In *Canadian Tax Foundation*, 1988, pp. 12.1–66.

Bown, Lalage. The Nature and Role of Development Studies in Present-Day Britain. *World Devel.*, May 1988, 16(5), pp. 631–37.

Bowonder, B.; Prasad, S. S. R. and Unni, N. V. M. Dynamics of Fuelwood Prices in In-

dia: Policy Implications. *World Devel.*, October 1988, 16(10), pp. 1213–29.

Bowsher, Charles A. Federal Financial Management: Evolution, Challenges and the Role of the Accounting Profession. In *Chan, J. L. and Jones, R. H., eds.*, 1988, 1987, pp. 29–51.

Boyadjieva, L. N. and Vuchkov, I. N. Errors in the Factor Level: Parameter Estimation of Heteroscedastic Model and Robustness of the Experimental Designs. In *Fedorov, V. and Lauter, H., eds.*, 1988, pp. 134–43.

Boyce, David E. Combining Communication and Transport Technology to Improve Urban Travel Choices. In *Orishimo, I.; Hewings, G. J. D. and Nijkamp, P., eds.*, 1988, pp. 141–52.

_____ **; LeBlanc, Larry J. and Chon, Kyung S.** Network Equilibrium Models of Urban Location and Travel Choices: A Retrospective Survey. *J. Reg. Sci.*, May 1988, 28(2), pp. 159–83.

Boyce, Gordon. Steelmaking in Atlantic Canada. In *Choudhury, M. A., ed.*, 1988, pp. 159–70.

Boyce, P . M. and Butlin, M. W. Monetary Policy in Depression and Recovery. In *Gregory, R. G. and Butlin, N. G., eds.*, 1988, pp. 193–215.

Boyd, Derick. The Impact of Adjustment Policies on Vulnerable Groups: The Case of Jamaica, 1973–1985. In *Cornia, G. A.; Jolly, R. and Stewart, F., eds.*, 1988, pp. 126–55.

Boyd, Gale A.; Hanson, Donald A. and Sterner, Thomas. Decomposition of Changes in Energy Intensity. *Energy Econ.*, October 1988, 10(4), pp. 309–12.

Boyd, James C. and Blomeyer, Edward C. Empirical Tests of Boundary Conditions for Options on Treasury Bond Futures Contracts. *J. Futures Markets*, April 1988, 8(2), pp. 185–98.

Boyd, James W. and Jackson, John D. A Statistical Approach to Modeling the Behavior of Bond Raters. *J. Behav. Econ.*, Fall 1988, 17(3), pp. 173–93.

Boyd, John H. and Graham, Stanley L. The Profitability and Risk Effects of Allowing Bank Holding Companies to Merge with Other Financial Firms: A Simulation Study. *Fed. Res. Bank Minn. Rev.*, Spring 1988, 12(2), pp. 3–20.

_____ **; Prescott, Edward C. and Smith, Bruce D.** Organizations in Economic Analysis. *Can. J. Econ.*, August 1988, 21(3), pp. 477–91.

Boyd, Losana E. Why "Talking It Out" Almost Never Works Out. In *Timpe, A. D., ed.*, 1988, 1984, pp. 189–92.

Boyd, Michael L. Agriculture and the Debt Crisis. In *Marer, P. and Siwinski, W., eds.*, 1988, pp. 33–35.

_____. The Performance of Private and Socialist Agriculture in Poland: The Effects of Policy and Organization. *J. Compar. Econ.*, March 1988, 12(1), pp. 61–73.

Boyd, Neil T. and Jackson, Margaret A. Reducing the Risks of Pleasure: Responding to AIDS in

Canada. *Can. Public Policy*, December 1988, *14*(4), pp. 347–60.

Boyd, Robert L. Government Involvement in the Economy and the Distribution of Income: A Cross-national Study. *Population Res. Policy Rev.*, 1988, *7*(3), pp. 223–38.

Boyd, Roy and Barthold, Thomas A. A Note on Resource Value and Marketability. *Energy Econ.*, January 1988, *10*(1), pp. 79–83.

_____ **and Krutilla, Kerry.** The Politics and Consequences of Protectionism: A Case Study in the North American Lumber Market. *J. Policy Modeling*, Winter 1988, *10*(4), pp. 601–09.

Boyden, Jo and Bequele, Assefa. Working Children: Current Trends and Policy Responses. *Int. Lab. Rev.*, 1988, *127*(2), pp. 153–72.

Boyer, George R. What Did Unions Do in Nineteenth-Century Britain? *J. Econ. Hist.*, June 1988, *48*(2), pp. 319–32.

Boyer, Marcel and Moreaux, Michel. Rational Rationing in Stackelberg Equilibria. *Quart. J. Econ.*, May 1988, *103*(2), pp. 409–14.

Boyer, Robert. Defensive or Offensive Flexibility? In *Boyer, R., ed.*, 1988, pp. 222–51.

_____. Division or Unity? Decline or Recovery? In *Boyer, R., ed.*, 1988, pp. 194–221.

_____. Europe at the Crossroads. In *Boyer, R., ed.*, 1988, pp. 274–90.

_____. Formalizing Growth Regimes. In *Dosi, G., et al., eds.*, 1988, pp. 608–30.

_____. New Technologies and Employment in the 1980s: From Science and Technology to Macroeconomic Modelling. In *Kregel, J. A.; Matzner, E. and Roncaglia, A., eds.*, 1988, pp. 233–68.

_____. The Search for New Wage/Labour Relations: Complex and Contradictory, but Crucial. In *Boyer, R., ed.*, 1988, pp. 252–73.

_____. Technical Change and the Theory of 'Régulation.' In *Dosi, G., et al., eds.*, 1988, pp. 67–94.

_____. Wage/Labour Relations, Growth, and Crisis: A Hidden Dialectic. In *Boyer, R., ed.*, 1988, pp. 3–25.

_____ **and Bowles, Samuel.** Labor Discipline and Aggregate Demand: A Macroeconomic Model. *Amer. Econ. Rev.*, May 1988, *78*(2), pp. 395–400.

Boyer, Russell S. and Adams, F. Charles. Forward Premia and Risk Premia in a Simple Model of Exchange Rate Determination. *J. Money, Credit, Banking*, November 1988, *20*(4), pp. 633–44.

Boyes, William J.; Mounts, William Stewart and Sowell, Clifford. The Federal Reserve as a Bureaucracy: An Examination of Expense-Preference Behavior. *J. Money, Credit, Banking*, May 1988, *20*(2), pp. 181–90.

Boyko, Olga and Hamman, Robert L. Effect of Environmental Regulation on the Ability of Business Firms in the United States and Japan to Compete in International Trade. In *Pennsylvania Economic Association*, 1988, pp. 428–38.

Boyle, G. E. The Economic Theory of Index Numbers: Empirical Tests for Volume Indices of Agricultural Output. *Irish J. Agr. Econ. Rural Soc.*, 1988, *13*, pp. 1–20.

_____. The Measurement of Fertiliser Use in Ireland: A Note. *Irish J. Agr. Econ. Rural Soc.*, 1988, *13*, pp. 73–78.

Boyle, Glenn W. and Rao, Ramesh K. S. The Mean-Generalized Coefficient of Variation Selection Rule and Expected Utility Maximization. *Southern Econ. J.*, July 1988, *55*(1), pp. 1–18.

_____ **and Young, Leslie.** Asset Prices, Commodity Prices, and Money: A General Equilibrium, Rational Expectations Model. *Amer. Econ. Rev.*, March 1988, *78*(1), pp. 24–45.

Boyle, Kevin J. and Bishop, Richard C. Welfare Measurements Using Contingent Valuation: A Comparison of Techniques. *Amer. J. Agr. Econ.*, February 1988, *70*(1), pp. 20–28.

_____; **Welsh, Michael P. and Bishop, Richard C.** Validation of Empirical Measures of Welfare Change: Comment. *Land Econ.*, February 1988, *64*(1), pp. 94–98.

Boyle, Maureen. BLS to Publish Quarterly Data from Consumer Expenditure Survey. *Mon. Lab. Rev.*, July 1988, *111*(7), pp. 27–32.

Boyle, Phelim P. A Lattice Framework for Option Pricing with Two State Variables. *J. Finan. Quant. Anal.*, March 1988, *23*(1), pp. 1–12.

Boyne, George A. Politics, Unemployment and Local Economic Policies. *Urban Stud.*, December 1988, *25*(6), pp. 474–86.

van Brabant, Jozef M. CMEA Institutions and Policies versus Structural Adjustment: Comments. In *[Holzman, F. D.]*, 1988, pp. 170–84.

_____. Planned Economies in the GATT Framework: The Soviet Case. *Soviet Econ.*, Jan.–March 1988, *4*(1), pp. 3–35.

_____. Production Specialization in the CMEA—Concepts and Empirical Evidence. *J. Common Market Stud.*, March 1988, *26*(3), pp. 287–315.

Brac de La Perrière, Gilles and de Nayer, Marie-Christine. Le matif et la gestion du risque. (With English summary.) *Revue Écon. Polit.*, Sept.–Oct. 1988, *98*(5), pp. 701–12.

Brackman, Harold; Erie, Steven P. and Rein, Martin. Wedded to the Welfare State: Women against Reaganite Retrenchment. In *Jenson, J.; Hagen, E. and Reddy, C., eds.*, 1988, pp. 214–30.

Brada, Josef C. Industrial Policy in Eastern Europe. In *[Holzman, F. D.]*, 1988, pp. 109–46.

_____. Interpreting the Soviet Subsidization of Eastern Europe. *Int. Organ.*, Autumn 1988, *42*(4), pp. 639–58.

_____ **and Graves, Ronald L.** The Slowdown in Soviet Defense Expenditures. *Southern Econ. J.*, April 1988, *54*(4), pp. 969–84.

_____; **Hewett, Ed A. and Wolf, Thomas A.** Economic Stabilization, Structural Adjustment, and Economic Reform. In *[Holzman, F. D.]*, 1988, pp. 3–36.

_____; **Hey, Jeanne C. and King, Arthur E.** Inter-regional and Inter-organizational Differences in Agricultural Efficiency in Czechoslovakia. In *Brada, J. C. and Wadekin, K.-E., eds.*, 1988, pp. 334–43.

_____ **and Méndez, José A.** An Estimate of the

Dynamic Effects of Economic Integration. *Rev. Econ. Statist.*, February 1988, *70*(1), pp. 163–68.

_____ and Méndez, José A. Exchange Rate Risk, Exchange Rate Regime and the Volume of International Trade. *Kyklos*, 1988, *41*(2), pp. 263–80.

_____ and Méndez, José A. How Effective Is the CMEA? An International Comparison. In *Brada, J. C. and Dobozi, I., eds.*, 1988, pp. 171–95.

Bradbrook, Adrian J. Australian and American Perspectives on the Protection of Solar and Wind Access. *Natural Res. J.*, Spring 1988, *28*(2), pp. 229–67.

Bradburd, Ralph M. and Caves, Richard E. The Empirical Determinants of Vertical Integration. *J. Econ. Behav. Organ.*, April 1988, *9*(3), pp. 265–79.

_____ and Ross, David R. A General Measure of Multidimensional Inequality. *Oxford Bull. Econ. Statist.*, November 1988, *50*(4), pp. 429–33.

Bradbury, Katharine L. Shifting Property Tax Burdens in Massachusetts. *New Eng. Econ. Rev.*, Sept.–Oct. 1988, pp. 36–48.

_____ and Browne, Lynn E. New England Approaches the 1990s. *New Eng. Econ. Rev.*, Jan.–Feb. 1988, pp. 31–45.

_____ and Ladd, Helen F. City Taxes and Property Tax Bases. *Nat. Tax J.*, December 1988, *41*(4), pp. 503–23.

Bradbury, Michael E. and Calderwood, Shirley C. Equity Accounting for Reciprocal Stockholdings. *Accounting Rev.*, April 1988, *63*(2), pp. 330–47.

Braden, Bradley R. Increases in Employer Costs for Employee Benefits Dampen Dramatically. *Mon. Lab. Rev.*, July 1988, *111*(7), pp. 3–7.

Braden, J. B.; Johnson, G. V. and Miltz, D. Standards versus Prices Revisited: The Case of Agricultural Non-point Source Pollution. *J. Agr. Econ.*, September 1988, *39*(3), pp. 360–68.

Bradfield, David J. and Barr, Graham D. I. Portfolio Selection in Thinly Traded Environments—A Case Study. *Managerial Dec. Econ.*, December 1988, *9*(4), pp. 287–90.

Bradfield, Michael. Chasing the Tales that Wag the Dog. In *Choudhury, M. A., ed.*, 1988, pp. 84–93.

_____. Statement to the U.S. House Committee on Banking, Finance and Urban Affairs, May 24, 1988. *Fed. Res. Bull.*, July 1988, *74*(7), pp. 450–53.

Bradford, Colin I., Jr. Changes in the Structure of Trade and New Forms of Adjustment Policies. In *Guerrieri, P. and Padoan, P. C., eds.*, 1988, pp. 203–28.

Bradford, David F. Share Repurchases and Acquisitions: An Analysis of Which Firms Participate: Comment. In *Auerbach, A. J., ed. (I)*, 1988, pp. 213–77.

_____ and Andrews, William D. Savings Incentives in a Hybrid Income Tax. In *Aaron, H. J.; Galper, H. and Pechman, J. A., eds.*, 1988, pp. 269–300.

_____ and Baumol, William J. Optimal Departures from Marginal Cost Pricing. In *Ricketts, M., ed., Vol. 2*, 1988, *1970*, pp. 143–61.

Bradley, Ian and Price, Catherine. The Economic Regulation of Private Industries by Price Constraints. *J. Ind. Econ.*, September 1988, *37*(1), pp. 99–106.

Bradley, John and Fitzgerald, John. Industrial Output and Factor Input Determination in an Econometric Model of a Small Open Economy. *Europ. Econ. Rev.*, July 1988, *32*(6), pp. 1227–41.

Bradley, Mark. Realism and Adaptation in Designing Hypothetical Travel Choice Concepts. *J. Transp. Econ. Policy*, January 1988, *22*(1), pp. 121–37.

Bradley, Michael. Effects of Mergers and Acquisitions on the Economy: An Industrial Organization Perspective: Discussion. In *Browne, L. E. and Rosengren, E. S., eds.*, 1988, pp. 162–72.

_____; Desai, Anand and Kim, E. Han. Synergistic Gains from Corporate Acquisitions and Their Division between the Stockholders of Target and Acquiring Firms. *J. Finan. Econ.*, May 1988, *21*(1), pp. 3–40.

_____ and Jarrell, Gregg A. Evidence on the Gains from Mergers and Takeovers: Comment. In *Coffee, J. C., Jr.; Lowenstein, L. and Rose-Ackerman, S., eds.*, 1988, pp. 253–59.

Bradley, Michael D. and Barth, James R. On Interest Rates, Inflationary Expectations and Tax Rates. *J. Banking Finance*, June 1988, *12*(2), pp. 215–20.

_____ and Jansen, Dennis W. Informational Implications of Money, Interest Rate, and Price Rules. *Econ. Inquiry*, July 1988, *26*(3), pp. 437–48.

_____ and Jansen, Dennis W. New Classical Models, Policy Effectiveness and the Money Rule/Interest Rule Debate. In *Missouri Valley Economic Assoc.*, 1988, pp. 39–45.

_____ and Jansen, Dennis W. Price Rules, Wage Indexing, and Optimal Monetary Policy. *J. Macroecon.*, Fall 1988, *10*(4), pp. 515–37.

_____ and Smith, Stephen C. Employment, Prices, and Money in the Share Economy: An Alternative View. In *Jones, D. C. and Svejnar, J., eds.*, 1988, pp. 201–08.

_____ and Smith, Stephen C. On Illyrian Macroeconomics. *Economica*, May 1988, *55*(218), pp. 249–59.

Bradley, Michael G. and Graham, John W. Education and Asset Composition. *Econ. Educ. Rev.*, 1988, *7*(2), pp. 209–20.

Bradley, R. and Rees, John. State Science Policy and Economic Development in the United States: A Critical Perspective. *Environ. Planning A*, August 1988, *20*(8), pp. 999–1012.

Bradley, Robert L., Jr. Energy Policies: A Few Bright Spots. In *Boaz, D., ed.*, 1988, pp. 305–19.

Bradshaw, Benjamin S. and Rosenwaike, Ira. The Status of Death Statistics for the Hispanic Population of the Southwest. *Soc. Sci. Quart.*, September 1988, *69*(3), pp. 722–36.

Bradshaw, Michael J. Japan and the Economic Development of the Soviet Far East. In *Liebowitz, R. D., ed.*, 1988, pp. 189–203.

Brady, Gordon L. and Maloney, Michael T. Capital Turnover and Marketable Pollution Rights. *J. Law Econ.*, April 1988, *31*(1), pp. 203–26.

Braendgaar, Asger. International Technology Programmes and National Systems of Production: ESPRIT and the Danish Electronics Industry. In *Freeman, C. and Lundvall, B.-A., eds.*, 1988, pp. 184–200.

Braeuer, Walter. Das fehlende letzte Kapitel bei Galiani. (Galiani's Missing Last Chapter. With English summary.) *Rivista Int. Sci. Econ. Com.*, January 1988, *35*(1), pp. 7–10.

Braff, Allan J. Distribution: Neo-classical. In *Asimakopulos, A., ed.*, 1988, pp. 75–103.

Braga, Helson C. The Role of Foreign Direct Investment in Economic Growth: The Brazilian Case. In *Jorge, A. and Salazar-Carrillo, J., eds.*, 1988, pp. 210–32.

_____ and Baumann, Renato. Export Financing in LDCs: The Role of Subsidies for Export Performance in Brazil. *World Devel.*, July 1988, *16*(7), pp. 821–33.

_____; Santiago, Gilda Maria C. and Ferro, Luiz César M. Estrutura da proteçao efetiva no Brasil: 1985. (With English summary.) *Pesquisa Planejamento Econ.*, December 1988, *18*(3), pp. 663–84.

Brager, Bruce L. The Energy Monster Sleeps. *Challenge*, Sept.–Oct. 1988, *31*(5), pp. 58–59.

Braguinsky, Serguey. A Criticism of Monetarism—With Some Points from the Japanese Experience. *Keio Econ. Stud.*, 1988, *25*(2), pp. 41–48.

Brahmananda, P. R. Jevons's 'Theory of Political Economy'—A Centennial Appraisal. In *Wood, J. C., ed., Vol. 2*, 1988, *1971*, pp. 116–28.

Braid, Ralph M. Heterogeneous Preferences and Non-central Agglomeration of Firms. *Reg. Sci. Urban Econ.*, February 1988, *18*(1), pp. 57–68.

_____. Optimal Spatial Growth of Employment and Residences. *J. Urban Econ.*, September 1988, *24*(2), pp. 227–40.

_____. Uniform Spatial Growth with Perfect Foresight and Durable Housing. *J. Urban Econ.*, January 1988, *23*(1), pp. 41–59.

Brainard, Lawrence J. Trade, Debt, and National Security. In *Anderson, A. and Bark, D. L., eds.*, 1988, pp. 215–23.

Bråkenhielm, Sven. Vegetation and Air Pollution. Spatial and Temporal Aspects of Sampling in Environmental Monitoring. *Statist. J.*, November 1988, *5*(3), pp. 239–47.

Brakke, David F. and Loranger, Thomas J. The Extent of Snowpack Influence on Water Chemistry in a North Cascades Lake. *Water Resources Res.*, May 1988, *24*(5), pp. 723–26.

Brakman, Steven; Gigengack, Richard and Jepma, Catrinus J. The Speed of Adjustment as a Measure for Competitiveness. *Empirica*, 1988, *15*(1), pp. 161–78.

Brams, Steven J.; Fishburn, Peter C. and Merrill, Samuel, III. The Problem of Indeterminacy in Approval, Multiple, and Truncated Voting Systems: Rejoinder. *Public Choice*, November 1988, *59*(2), pp. 149.

_____; Fishburn, Peter C. and Merrill, Samuel, III. The Responsiveness of Approval Voting: Comments [The Problem of Indeterminacy in Approval, Multiple, and Truncated Voting Systems]. *Public Choice*, November 1988, *59*(2), pp. 121–31.

Bran, P. and Baron, T. The Outlook of President Nicolae Ceuşescu, Party General Secretary, on the Impact of the Qualitative Transformations in the Economy on the Development of Economic Higher Education. *Econ. Computat. Cybern. Stud. Res.*, 1988, *23*(4), pp. 15–23.

Branch, Ben and Geman, Donald. The Valuation of Stochastic Cash Flows. *Quart. J. Bus. Econ.*, Winter 1988, *27*(1), pp. 148–78.

Branco, I. M. and Paixão, J. Bus Scheduling with a Fixed Number of Vehicles. In *Daduna, J. R. and Wren, A., eds.*, 1988, pp. 28–40.

Branco, Kenneth J. and Williamson, John B. Economic Development and Income Distribution: A Cross-National Analysis. *Amer. J. Econ. Soc.*, July 1988, *47*(3), pp. 277–97.

Brand, Horst and Ahmed, Ziaul Z. Productivity in Industrial Inorganic Chemicals. *Mon. Lab. Rev.*, March 1988, *111*(3), pp. 33–40.

Brand, S. S. Privatization: An Economist's View. *S. Afr. J. Econ.*, December 1988, *56*(4), pp. 235–50.

Brander, James A. and Lewis, Tracy R. Bankruptcy Costs and the Theory of Oligopoly. *Can. J. Econ.*, May 1988, *21*(2), pp. 221–43.

_____ and Lewis, Tracy R. Oligopoly and Financial Structure: The Limited Liability Effect. In *Daughety, A. F., ed.*, 1988, *1986*, pp. 421–43.

_____ and Spencer, Barbara J. Unionized Oligopoly and International Trade Policy. *J. Int. Econ.*, May 1988, *24*(3–4), pp. 217–34.

Brandl, John. On Politics and Policy Analysis as the Design and Assessment of Institutions. *J. Policy Anal. Manage.*, Spring 1988, *7*(3), pp. 419–24.

Brandner, Walter. Steuerliche Behandlung von 'Computer Software': Osterreich. (Tax Treatment of Computer Software: Austria. With English summary.) In *International Fiscal Association, ed. (II)*, 1988, pp. 203–220.

Brandon, William P. Why Government Cannot Contain Health Care Costs: An Interpretation of the U.S. Health Care System. In *Kelly, R. M., ed.*, 1988, pp. 141–59.

Brandsma, A. S., et al. Retracing the Preferences behind Macroeconomic Policy: The Dutch Experience. *De Economist*, 1988, *136*(4), pp. 468–90.

Brandt, Jon A. and Kaylen, Michael S. A Note on Qualitative Forecast Evaluation: Comment. *Amer. J. Agr. Econ.*, May 1988, *70*(2), pp. 415–16.

Brandt, Karl. Dogmengeschichtliche Betrachtungen zur Stagnationsthese. (The Theory of Secular Stagnation: A Historical View. With English summary.) *Jahr. Nationalökon. Statist.*, December 1988, *205*(6), pp. 465–79.

Brandt, S. A., et al. Extensão rural e pesquisa agrícola: Uma avaliação cos problemas de não-homoteticidade e viés tecnológico. (With English summary.) *Pesquisa Planejamento Econ.*, April 1988, *18*(1), pp. 131–43.

Brannick, Teresa and Kelly, Aidan. Explaining the Strike-Proneness of British Companies in Ireland. *Brit. J. Ind. Relat.*, March 1988, *26*(1), pp. 37–55.

Branscomb, Lewis M. Technological Change and Its International Diffusion. In *Cassing, J. H. and Husted, S. L., eds.*, 1988, pp. 103–13.

Branson, William H. Coordination of Monetary and Fiscal Policies in the Industrial Economies: Comment. In *Frenkel, J. A., ed.*, 1988, pp. 113–18.

_____. Economic Structure and Policy for External Balance. In *Melamed, L., ed.*, 1988, *1983*, pp. 361–86.

_____. International Adjustment and the Dollar: Policy Illusions and Economic Constraints. In *Guth, W., ed.*, 1988, pp. 44–84.

_____. Political vs. Currency Premia in International Real Interest Rate Differentials: Comments. *Europ. Econ. Rev.*, June 1988, *32*(5), pp. 1119–21.

_____. Sources of Misalignment in the 1980s. In *Marston, R. C., ed.*, 1988, pp. 9–31.

_____ **and Love, James P.** U.S. Manufacturing and the Real Exchange Rate. In *Marston, R. C., ed.*, 1988, pp. 241–70.

_____ **and Marchese, Grazia.** International Payments Imbalances in Japan, Germany, and the United States. In *Fieleke, N. S., ed.*, 1988, pp. 19–50.

Brar, Jagjit S. and Hsing, Yu. Estimation of Flexible Elasticities of Demand for Seafood. In *Missouri Valley Economic Assoc.*, 1988, pp. 122–27.

Brase, Matthias. Sind die Zinsprognosen von Finanzmarktexperten rational? (Are Interest Rate Prognoses of Financial Market Experts Rational? With English summary.) *Kredit Kapital*, 1988, *21*(2), pp. 288–303.

Brashares, Edith; Speyrer, Janet Furman and Carlson, George N. Distributional Aspects of a Federal Value-Added Tax. *Nat. Tax J.*, June 1988, *41*(2), pp. 155–74.

Brastow, Raymond and Rystrom, David. Wealth Effects of the Drug Price Competition and Patent Term Restoration Act of 1984. *Amer. Econ.*, Fall 1988, *32*(2), pp. 59–65.

Brauchlin, Emil. Discussion to Session 2: Technology Initiatives and Corporate Policy. *Aussenwirtschaft*, June 1988, *43*(1/2), pp. 201–05.

Brauer, Greggory A. Closed-End Fund Shares' Abnormal Returns and the Information Content of Discounts and Premiums. *J. Finance*, March 1988, *43*(1), pp. 113–127.

Braulke, Michael. How to Retrieve the Lorenz Curve from Sparse Data. In *Eichhorn, W., ed.*, 1988, pp. 373–82.

Braun, Bradley M. Measuring Tax Revenue Stability with Implications for Stabilization Policy:

A Note. *Nat. Tax J.*, December 1988, *41*(4), pp. 595–98.

Braun, Denny. Multiple Measurements of U.S. Income Inequality. *Rev. Econ. Statist.*, August 1988, *70*(3), pp. 398–405.

Braun, Ernest and Polt, Wolfgang. High Technology and Competitiveness: An Austrian Perspective. In *Freeman, C. and Lundvall, B.-A., eds.*, 1988, pp. 203–25.

von Braun, Joachim. Effects of Technological Change in Agriculture on Food Consumption and Nutrition: Rice in a West African Setting. *World Devel.*, September 1988, *16*(9), pp. 1083–98.

_____. Food Subsidies in Egypt: Implications for the Agricultural Sector. In *Pinstrup-Andersen, P., ed.*, 1988, pp. 183–95.

_____. Implications of Consumer-Oriented Food Subsidies for Domestic Agriculture. In *Pinstrup-Andersen, P., ed.*, 1988, pp. 92–106.

_____ **and Huddleston, Barbara.** Implications of Food Aid for Price Policy in Recipient Countries. In *Mellor, J. W. and Ahmed, R., eds.*, 1988, pp. 253–63.

Braunstein, Yale M.; Jussawalla, Meheroo and Snow, Marcellus S. Major Issues in Information Services Trade. In *Lee, C. H. and Naya, S., eds.*, 1988, pp. 77–95.

Braverman, Avishay. Depressed Agricultural Prices and World Bank Operations. In *Roberts, C., ed.*, 1988, pp. 13–24.

_____ **and Hammer, Jeffrey S.** Computer Models for Agricultural Policy Analysis. *Finance Develop.*, June 1988, *25*(2), pp. 34–37.

Bravo, Giuliano Ferrari. J. M. Keynes al Tesoro durante la seconda guerra mondiale. (J. M. Keynes at the Treasury during the Second World War. With English summary.) *Rivista Storia Econ.*, *S.S.*, October 1988, *5*(3), pp. 365–96.

Brayton, Flint and Clark, Peter B. The Macroeconomic and Sectoral Effects of the Economic Recovery Tax Act: Some Simulation Results. In *Motamen, H., ed.*, 1988, pp. 141–64.

Brazil, Larry E.; Hendrickson, Jene' D. and Soroohian, Soroosh. Comparison of Newton-Type and Direct Search Algorithms for Calibration of Conceptual Rainfall–Runoff Models. *Water Resources Res.*, May 1988, *24*(5), pp. 691–700.

Brea, Jorge A.; Goetz, Andrew R. and Brown, Lawrence A. Policy Aspects of Development and Individual Mobility: Migration and Circulation from Ecuador's Rural Sierra. *Econ. Geogr.*, April 1988, *64*(2), pp. 147–70.

Brean, Donald J. S. International Influences on Canadian Tax Policy: The Free Trade Agreement and U.S. Tax Reform. In *Canadian Tax Foundation*, 1988, pp. 13.1–10.

Brecher, Charles and Horton, Raymond D. Community Power and Municipal Budgets. In *Rubin, I. S., ed.*, 1988, pp. 148–64.

Brecher, Michael and James, Patrick. Patterns of Crisis Management. *J. Conflict Resolution*, September 1988, *32*(3), pp. 426–56.

Brecher, Richard A. and Choudhri, Ehsan U.

The Factor Content of Consumption in Canada and the United States: A Two-Country Test of the Heckscher–Ohlin–Vanek Model. In *Feenstra, R. C.*, ed., 1988, pp. 5–17.

Brechin, Steven R. and Ness, Gayl D. Bridging the Gap: International Organizations as Organizations. *Int. Organ.*, Spring 1988, *42*(2), pp. 245–73.

Bredehoeft, John D. and Young, Robert A. Risk Aversion in Conjunctive Water Use. In *O'Mara, G. T.*, ed., 1988, pp. 155–67.

Breece, James H. and Coulson, N. Edward. Dynamics of the Transmission of Employment Effects across Metropolitan Areas. *Urban Stud.*, April 1988, *25*(2), pp. 145–49.

Breedon, Francis, et al. The Effect of Fiscal Reflation upon Employment. In *Eltis, W. and Sinclair, P. J. N.*, eds., 1988, pp. 79–101.

Breen, Richard. The Work Experience Programme in Ireland. *Int. Lab. Rev.*, 1988, *127*(4), pp. 429–44.

Breen, William J. The Labor Market, the Reform Impetus, and the Great War: The Reorganization of the State–City Employment Exchanges in Ohio, 1914–1918. *Labor Hist.*, Fall 1988, *29*(4), pp. 475–97.

Breheny, Michael J. Practical Methods of Retail Location Analysis: A Review. In *Wrigley, N.*, ed., 1988, pp. 39–86.

Breidbach, Hans-Josef. Just-in-Time Systems and Euro–Japanese Industrial Collaboration: Foreword. In *Holl, U. and Trevor, M.*, eds., 1988, pp. 7–9.

Breiger, Ronald L. and Jacobs, Jerry A. Careers, Industries, and Occupations: Industrial Segmentation Reconsidered. In *Farkas, G. and England, P.*, eds., 1988, pp. 43–63.

Breimyer, Harold F. Reflections on Communication in Agricultural Economics. *J. Agr. Econ. Res.*, Winter 1988, *40*(1), pp. 46–47.

Breit, William. The Development of Clarence Ayres's Theoretical Institutionalism. In *Samuels, W. J.*, ed., Vol. 1, 1988, 1973, pp. 178–91.

Brems, Hans. Time and Interest: Böhm–Bawerk and Åkerman–Wicksell. *Hist. Polit. Econ.*, Winter 1988, *20*(4), pp. 565–81.

———. Vi misstog oss ofta men tvivlade sällan. Randanmärkningar till nationalekonomins historia. (Frequently Wrong but Rarely in Doubt: Some Reflections on the History of Economic Analysis. With English summary.) *Ekon. Samfundets Tidskr.*, 1988, *41*(1), pp. 7–19.

Brennan, Michael J. and Copeland, Thomas E. Beta Changes around Stock Splits: A Note. *J. Finance*, September 1988, *43*(4), pp. 1009–13.

——— and Copeland, Thomas E. Stock Splits, Stock Prices, and Transaction Costs. *J. Finan. Econ.*, October 1988, *22*(1), pp. 83–101.

———; Maksimovic, Vojislav and Zechner, Josef. Vendor Financing. *J. Finance*, December 1988, *43*(5), pp. 1127–41.

——— and Schwartz, Eduardo S. Time-Invariant Portfolio Insurance Strategies. *J. Finance*, June 1988, *43*(2), pp. 283–99.

Brennan, Timothy J. Understanding "Raising Rivals' Costs." *Antitrust Bull.*, Spring 1988, *33*(1), pp. 95–113.

Brenneke, Judith S., et al. A Research and Evaluation Agenda for DEEP and Precollege Economic Education. *J. Econ. Educ.*, Winter 1988, *19*(1), pp. 5–13.

Brenner, Y. S. The Tricky Problem of Distribution. In *Brenner, Y. S.; Reijnders, J. P. G. and Spithoven, A. H. G. M.*, eds., 1988, pp. 11–53.

Brero, Andrea and Catalani, Mario S. Le ombre cinesi: Modelli stocastici per l'analisi dei comportamenti di impresa in ambiente di incertezza. (The Chinese Shadows: Stochastic Models for the Analysis of Firm Behavior under Uncertainty. With English summary.) *Rivista Int. Sci. Econ. Com.*, June 1988, *35*(6), pp. 539–62.

Breslaw, Jon A. Does Economic Theory Play a Role in Regulatory Decisions? The CRTC Cost Inquiry. *Land Econ.*, November 1988, *64*(4), pp. 372–76.

Breslin, Patrick and Chapin, Mac. Conservation Kuna-Style. In *Annis, S. and Hakim, P.*, eds., 1988, pp. 73–82.

Bresnahan, Timothy F. and Baker, Jonathan B. Estimating the Residual Demand Curve Facing a Single Firm. *Int. J. Ind. Organ.*, 1988, *6*(3), pp. 283–300.

Bressers, Hans and Klok, Pieter-Jan. Fundamentals for a Theory of Policy Instruments. *Int. J. Soc. Econ.*, 1988, *15*(3–4), pp. 22–41.

Breton, Michèle and L'Ecuyer, Pierre. On the Existence of Sequential Equilibria in Markov Renewal Games. In *Eiselt, H. A. and Pederzoli, G.*, eds., 1988, pp. 200–213.

Bretschneider, Stuart and Schroeder, Larry. Evaluation of Commercial Economic Forecasts for Use in Local Government Budgeting. *Int. J. Forecasting*, 1988, *4*(1), pp. 33–43.

———; Straussman, Jeffrey D. and Mullins, Daniel. Do Revenue Forecasts Influence Budget Setting? A Small Group Experiment. *Policy Sci.*, 1988, *21*(4), pp. 305–25.

Brett, E. A. States, Markets and Private Power: Problems and Possibilities. In *Cook, P. and Kirkpatrick, C.*, eds., 1988, pp. 47–67.

Breusch, T. S. and Wickens, M. R. Dynamic Specification, the Long-run and the Estimation of Transformed Regression Models. *Econ. J.*, Supplement, 1988, *98*(390), pp. 189–205.

Breuss, Fritz. Domestic and External Macro-policies: Comments. In *Saunders, C. T.*, ed., 1988, pp. 223–25.

———. Generalized Robinson and Marshall–Lerner Conditions When Exports Have an Import Content and Imports an Export Content. *Empirica*, 1988, *15*(2), pp. 351–63.

——— and Aiginger, Karl. Some Doubts on the Current Paradigma of Intra-industry Trade. *Empirica*, 1988, *15*(1), pp. 27–50.

Brewer, Anthony A. Cantillon and Mercantilism. *Hist. Polit. Econ.*, Fall 1988, *20*(3), pp. 447–60.

———. Cantillon and the Land Theory of Value. *Hist. Polit. Econ.*, Spring 1988, *20*(1), pp. 1–14.

_____. Edward West and the Classical Theory of Distribution and Growth. *Economica*, November 1988, *55*(220), pp. 505–15.

_____. On Ricardo and All That: A Rejoinder. *Rev. Radical Polit. Econ.*, Winter 1988, *20*(4), pp. 93–94.

_____. Technical Change in Illyria. *J. Compar. Econ.*, September 1988, *12*(3), pp. 401–15.

Brewer, Elijah, III. The Impact of Deregulation on the True Cost of Savings Deposits: Evidence from Illinois and Wisconsin Savings and Loan Associations. *J. Econ. Bus.*, February 1988, *40*(1), pp. 79–95.

Brewer, K. R. W.; Hanif, Muhammad and Tam, S. M. How Nearly Can Model-Based Prediction and Design-Based Estimation Be Reconciled? *J. Amer. Statist. Assoc.*, March 1988, *83*(401), pp. 129–32.

Brewin, Christopher and McAllister, Richard. Annual Review of the Activities of the European Communities in 1987. *J. Common Market Stud.*, June 1988, *26*(4), pp. 431–67.

Breyer, Friedrich. Hospital Finance and the Behavior of American For-Profit and Not-for-Profit Hospitals: Comment. In *Furubotn, E. G. and Richter, R., eds.*, 1988, pp. 45–50.

_____. Krankenhausfinanzierung in Selbstverwaltung. Kommentar. (With English summary.) *J. Inst. Theoretical Econ.*, April 1988, *144*(2), pp. 412–17.

_____ **and Wodopoia, Franz-Josef.** The Concept of "Scale" and Related Topics in the Specification of Econometric Cost Functions: Theory and Application to Hospitals. In *Eichhorn, W., ed.*, 1988, pp. 707–23.

Brickley, James A.; Lease, Ronald C. and Smith, Clifford W., Jr. Ownership Structure and Voting on Antitakeover Amendments. *J. Finan. Econ.*, Jan.–March 1988, *20*(1–2), pp. 267–91.

_____; **Netter, Jeffry M. and Jarrell, Gregg A.** The Market for Corporate Control: The Empirical Evidence Since 1980. *J. Econ. Perspectives*, Winter 1988, *2*(1), pp. 49–68.

Bridges, Douglas S. The Euclidean Distance Construction of Order Homomorphisms. *Math. Soc. Sci.*, April 1988, *15*(2), pp. 179–88.

Brierley, Peter. British Social trends since 1900: Religion. In *Halsey, A. H., ed.*, 1988, pp. 518–60.

Briffault, Richard. The New York Agency Shop Fee and the Constitution after *Ellis* and *Hudson*. *Ind. Lab. Relat. Rev.*, January 1988, *41*(2), pp. 279–93.

Brigante, John B. The Revolt against the Sandwich. *Challenge*, March–April 1988, *31*(2), pp. 52–57.

Briggs, A. Review of 'Papers and Correspondence of William Stanley Jevons, Volumes I and II.' In *Wood, J. C., ed., Vol. 3*, 1988, *1973*, pp. 127–29.

Briggs, Hugh and Berry, Steven. A Non-parametric Test of a First-Order Markov Process for Regimes in a Non-cooperatively Collusive Industry. *Econ. Letters*, 1988, *27*(1), pp. 73–77.

Briggs, John De Q. Comments on the Operation of the Antitrust System. In *White, L. J., ed.*, 1988, pp. 246–51.

Briggs, John, et al. The Decline of Gold as a Source of U.S. Monetary Discipline. In *Willett, T. D., ed.*, 1988, pp. 186–99.

Briggs, Vernon M., Jr. Human Resource Development and the Formulation of National Economic Policy. In *Tool, M. R., ed., Vol. 1*, 1988, *1987*, pp. 257–90.

Briguglio, Lino. Equilibrium and Disequilibrium Labour Market Models. *Econ. Anal. Workers' Manage.*, 1988, *22*(3), pp. 177–96.

Brillet, Jean-Louis. Model-Building on Microcomputers: Spreadsheets or Specific Software. In *Edwards, D. and Raun, N. E., eds.*, 1988, pp. 417–22.

_____ **and Laurent, Jean-Paul.** The Reliability of Control Experiments: Comparison of the Sources of Error. *J. Econ. Dynam. Control*, March 1988, *12*(1), pp. 173–79.

Brimelow, Peter. Canada: Rich by Nature, Poor by Policy. *Contemp. Policy Issues*, January 1988, *6*(1), pp. 28–38.

Brimmer, Andrew F. Income, Wealth, and Investment Behavior in the Black Community. *Amer. Econ. Rev.*, May 1988, *78*(2), pp. 151–55.

Brinkerhoff, Derick W. Implementing Integrated Rural Development in Haiti: The World Bank's Experience in the Northern Region. *Can. J. Devel. Stud.*, 1988, *9*(1), pp. 63–79.

Brinkman, George L.; Horbasz, Chris N. and Fox, Glenn. A Comparison of *Ex Post* and *Ex Ante* Measures of Producers' Surplus in Estimating the Returns to Canadian Federal Sheep Research. *Can. J. Agr. Econ.*, November 1988, *36*(3), pp. 489–500.

_____; **Widmer, Lorne and Fox, Glenn.** The Rate of Return to Agricultural Research in a Small Country: The Case of Beef Cattle Research in Canada. *Can. J. Agr. Econ.*, March 1988, *36*(1), pp. 23–35.

Brinkman, Henk Jan; Drukker, J. W. and Slot, Brigitte. Height and Income: A New Method for the Estimation of Historical National Income Series. *Exploration Econ. Hist.*, July 1988, *25*(3), pp. 227–64.

Brittan, Samuel and Riley, Barry. A People's Stake in North Sea Oil. In *Johnson, C., ed.*, 1988, *1978*, pp. 141–56.

Britton, Andrew; Gurney, Andrew and Joyce, Michael. The Home Economy. *Nat. Inst. Econ. Rev.*, May 1988, (124), pp. 7–20.

_____; **Gurney, Andrew and Joyce, Michael.** The Home Economy. *Nat. Inst. Econ. Rev.*, February 1988, (123), pp. 6–19.

_____; **Joyce, Michael and Gregg, Paul A.** The Home Economy. *Nat. Inst. Econ. Rev.*, November 1988, (126), pp. 6–17.

_____; **Joyce, Michael and Gregg, Paul A.** The Home Economy. *Nat. Inst. Econ. Rev.*, August 1988, (125), pp. 6–22.

Britton, Barbara; Albin, Tom and Paulson, Steve. The U.S. Policy Response to Acid Rain. **In**

Schmandt, J.; Clarkson, J. and Roderick, H., eds., 1988, pp. 159–84.

Briys, Eric; Kahane, Yehuda and Kroll, Yoram. Voluntary Insurance Coverage, Compulsory Insurance, and Risky–Riskless Portfolio Opportunities. *J. Risk Ins.*, December 1988, *55*(4), pp. 713–22.

Broadberry, Stephen N. The Impact of the World Wars on the Long Run Performance of the British Economy. *Oxford Rev. Econ. Policy*, Spring 1988, *4*(1), pp. 25–37.

_____. Perspectives on Consumption in Interwar Britain. *Appl. Econ.*, November 1988, *20*(11), pp. 1465–79.

Broadhead, Peter and Duckett, Stephen J. Death to the Oxymoron: The Introduction of 'Rational Hospital Budgeting' in Victoria, or Perhaps More Accurately, an Account of Progress towards That Goal. In *Butler, J. R. G. and Doessel, D. P.*, eds., 1988, pp. 22–33.

Broadhurst, David G. Issues in Withholding. In *Canadian Tax Foundation*, 1988, pp. 11.1–18.

Broadman, Harry G. and Hogan, William W. Is an Oil Tariff Justified? An American Debate: The Numbers Say Yes. *Energy J.*, July 1988, *9*(3), pp. 7–29.

Broadus, James M. Seabed Materials. In *Forester, T.*, ed., 1988, *1987*, pp. 338–60.

Brobeck, Stephen. Academics and Advocates: The Role of Consumer Researchers in Public Policy-Making. *J. Cons. Aff.*, Winter 1988, *22*(2), pp. 187–200.

Brochier, Hubert. Fondements idéologiques et visée scientifique en économie. (Ideological Foundations and Scientific Purpose in Economics. With English summary.) *Écon. Soc.*, October 1988, *22*(10), pp. 169–88.

Brock, Horace Wood. Environmental Impacts on Strategically Positioned Thrifts. In *Federal Home Loan Bank of San Francisco.*, 1988, pp. 123–38.

Brock, James W. and Adams, Walter. Reaganomics and the Transmogrification of Merger Policy. *Antitrust Bull.*, Summer 1988, *33*(2), pp. 309–59.

Brock, Philip L. Investment, the Current Account, and the Relative Price of Non-traded Goods in a Small Open Economy. *J. Int. Econ.*, May 1988, *24*(3–4), pp. 235–53.

Brock, William A. Nonlinearity and Complex Dynamics in Economics and Finance. In *Anderson, P. W.; Arrow, K. J. and Pines, D.*, eds., 1988, pp. 77–97.

_____ and **Dechert, W. D.** Theorems on Distinguishing Deterministic from Random Systems. In *Barnett, W. A.; Berndt, E. R. and White, H.*, eds., 1988, pp. 247–65.

_____ and **Majumdar, Mukul.** On Characterizing Optimal Competitive Programs in Terms of Decentralizable Conditions. *J. Econ. Theory*, August 1988, *45*(2), pp. 262–73.

_____ and **Sayers, Chera L.** Is the Business Cycle Characterized by Deterministic Chaos? *J. Monet. Econ.*, July 1988, *22*(1), pp. 71–90.

Bröcker, Johannes. Interregional Trade and Economic Integration. *Reg. Sci. Urban Econ.*, May 1988, *18*(2), pp. 261–81.

Brockett, Patrick L.; Hinich, Melvin J. and Patterson, Douglas. Bispectral-Based Tests for the Detection of Gaussianity and Linearity in Time Series. *J. Amer. Statist. Assoc.*, September 1988, *83*(403), pp. 657–64.

Brockhoff, Klaus. Die Bewährung von Gutenbergs Preis-Absatz-Funktion im Zigarettenmarkt. (With English summary.) *Z. Betriebswirtschaft*, August 1988, *58*(8), pp. 828–38.

Brockner, Joel. The Effects of Work Layoffs on Survivors: Research, Theory, and Practice. In *Staw, B. M. and Cummings, L. L.*, eds., 1988, pp. 213–55.

_____; **Delaney, John Thomas and Sockell, Donna.** Bargaining Effects of the Mandatory–Permissive Distinction. *Ind. Relat.*, Winter 1988, *27*(1), pp. 21–36.

Brockway, George P. Executive Salaries and Their Justification: Reply. *J. Post Keynesian Econ.*, Spring 1988, *10*(3), pp. 479–81.

_____. What Cost Us Was the Bull Market, Not the Crash. *Challenge*, Sept.–Oct. 1988, *31*(5), pp. 55–58.

Brodley, Joseph F. The Operation of the Litigation System: Comment: Critical Factual Assumptions Underlying Public Policy. In *White, L. J.*, ed., 1988, pp. 252–67.

Brodsky, William J. After the Crash: Linkages between Stocks and Futures: A Futures Perspective. In *MacKay, R. J.*, ed., 1988, pp. 55–62.

Brodt, Abraham I. Optimal Bank Asset and Liability Management with Financial Futures. *J. Futures Markets*, August 1988, *8*(4), pp. 457–81.

van den Broeck, Julien. Stochastic Frontier Inefficiency and Firm Size for Selected Industries of the Belgian Manufacturing Sector: Some New Evidence. In *Dogramaci, A. and Färe, R.*, eds.,, 1988, pp. 59–101.

van den Broek, Jan M. M. Earth Observation and Information Management. In *Egan, J. J., et al.*, 1988, pp. 47–54.

Broll, Udo and Gilroy, Bernard Michael. Intra-industry Trade and Differences in Technology. *Scot. J. Polit. Econ.*, November 1988, *35*(4), pp. 399–403.

Bromiley, Philip and Marcus, Alfred. The Rationale for Regulation: Shareholder Losses under Various Assumptions about Managerial Cognition. *J. Law, Econ., Organ.*, Fall 1988, *4*(2), pp. 357–72.

Bromley, Daniel W. Resource and Enviromental Economics: Knowledge, Discipline, and Problems. In *Hildreth, R. J., et al.*, eds., 1988, pp. 208–30.

_____ and **Segerson, Kathleen.** State Policy Choices: The Wisconsin Experience: Natural Resource Policy. In *Danziger, S. H. and Witte, J. F.*, eds., 1988, pp. 250–76.

Bromley, Rosemary D. F. and Rees, Joan C. M. The First Five Years of the Swansea Enterprise Zone: An Assessment of Change. *Reg. Stud.*, August 1988, *22*(4), pp. 263–75.

Bronckers, J. H. J. M. and Heuts, R. M. J. Forecasting the Dutch Heavy Truck Market: A Multivariate Approach. *Int. J. Forecasting*, 1988, *4*(1), pp. 57–79.

Bronckers, M. C. E. J. and Arnold, M. I. B. The EEC New Trade Policy Instrument: Some Comments on Its Application (Reg. 2641/84). *J. World Trade*, December 1988, *22*(6), pp. 19–38.

Bronfenbrenner, Martin. Instead of a Philosophy of Life. *Amer. Econ.*, Fall 1988, *32*(2), pp. 3–10.

_____. Reply to Martin and Mayhew on "Early American Leaders." *J. Econ. Issues*, March 1988, *22*(1), pp. 232–33.

Bronisz, Piotr and Krus, Lech. Application of Generalized Raiffa Solution to Multicriteria Bargaining Support. In *Iri, M. and Yajima, K.*, eds., 1988, pp. 207–11.

Brønn, Carl and Whalen, Thomas. Essentials of Decision Making under Generalized Uncertainty. In *Kacprzyk, J. and Fedrizzi, M.*, eds., 1988, pp. 26–47.

Bronsard, Camille and Salvas-Bronsard, Lise. Anticipations rationnelles, fonctions d'anticipations et structure locale de Slutsky. (Rational Expectations, Expectation Functions, and Slutsky Local Structure. With English summary.) *Can. J. Econ.*, November 1988, *21*(4), pp. 846–56.

_____ **and Salvas-Bronsard, Lise.** Sur trois contributions d'Allais. (With English summary.) *L'Actual. Econ.*, December 1988, *64*(4), pp. 481–92.

Brood, Edgar A. Netherlands: The Participation Exemption: Present and Future. *Bull. Int. Fiscal Doc.*, Aug.–Sept. 1988, *42*(8–9), pp. 369–73.

Brook, Robert H. and Dubois, Robert W. Assessing Clinical Decision Making: Is the Ideal System Feasible? *Inquiry*, Spring 1988, *25*(1), pp. 59–64.

Brooker, John R.; Terry, Danny E. and Eastwood, David B. Household Demand for Food Attributes. *J. Behav. Econ.*, Fall 1988, *17*(3), pp. 219–27.

Brooker, R. J. An Overview of the Murphy Model: Comment. *Australian Econ. Pap.*, Supplement, June 1988, *27*, pp. 200–202.

Brooker, Robert F. Empirical Estimation of a Homogeneous Non-homothetic Production Function for Milk Components Using California Data. In *Pennsylvania Economic Association*, 1988, pp. 745–52.

Brookfield, Harold. 'Sustainable Development' and the Environment: Review Article. *J. Devel. Stud.*, October 1988, *25*(1), pp. 126–35.

Brooks, Harvey. Reflections on the Telecommunications Infrastructure. In *Ausubel, J. H. and Herman, R.*, eds., 1988, pp. 249–57.

_____ **and Maccoby, Michael.** Corporations and the Work Force. In *Meyer, J. R. and Gustafson, J. M.*, eds., 1988, pp. 113–31.

Brooks, Karen. Soviet Union: The Anomaly of Private-cum-Socialist Agriculture: Discussion. *Amer. J. Agr. Econ.*, May 1988, *70*(2), pp. 437–38.

Brooks, Michael A. Toward a Behavioral Analysis of Public Economics. In *Earl, P. E.*, ed., 1988, pp. 169–88.

Brooks, Robert and Hand, John. Evaluating the Performance of Stock Portfolios with Index Futures Contracts. *J. Futures Markets*, February 1988, *8*(1), pp. 33–46.

Broom, David and Penny, Nicholas J. The Tesco Approach to Store Location. In *Wrigley, N.*, ed., 1988, pp. 106–19.

Broome, Benjamin J.; Korper, Susan H. and Druckman, Daniel. Value Differences and Conflict Resolution: Facilitation or Delinking? *J. Conflict Resolution*, September 1988, *32*(3), pp. 489–510.

Broome, John. Some Principles of Population. In *[Lecomber, R.]*, 1988, pp. 85–96.

Brooten, Dorothy; Brown, Linda and Finkler, Steven A. Utilization of Inpatient Services under Shortened Lengths of Stay: A Neonatal Care Example. *Inquiry*, Summer 1988, *25*(2), pp. 271–80.

Brorsen, B. Wade; Grant, Warren R. and Rister, M. Edward. Some Effects of Rice Quality on Rough Rice Prices. *Southern J. Agr. Econ.*, July 1988, *20*(1), pp. 131–40.

_____**; Irwin, Scott H. and Lukac, Louis P.** Similarity of Computer Guided Technical Trading Systems. *J. Futures Markets*, February 1988, *8*(1), pp. 1–13.

_____**; Irwin, Scott H. and Lukac, Louis P.** A Test of Futures Market Disequilibrium Using Twelve Different Technical Trading Systems. *Appl. Econ.*, May 1988, *20*(5), pp. 623–39.

Brosio, Giorgio and Marchese, Carla. The Growth of Government under Different Redistributive Rules: A Long Term Study of the Italian Case. *Public Finance Quart.*, October 1988, *16*(4), pp. 439–63.

_____ **and Marchese, Carla.** The Growth of Public Expenditure in Italy since the Second World War. In *Lybeck, J. A. and Henrekson, M.*, eds., 1988, pp. 187–200.

Brotherton, D. I. Grant-Aided Agricultural Activity in National Parks. *J. Agr. Econ.*, September 1988, *39*(3), pp. 376–81.

Brothwell, John. *The General Theory* after Fifty Years—Why Are We Not All Keynesians Now? In *Hillard, J.*, ed., 1988, pp. 45–63.

Brotman, Billie Ann and Fox, Pauline. The Impact of Economic Conditions on the Incidence of Arson: Comment. *J. Risk Ins.*, December 1988, *55*(4), pp. 751–54.

Broughton, John B. and Chance, Don M. Market Index Depository Liabilities: Analysis, Interpretation, and Performance. *J. Finan. Services Res.*, December 1988, *1*(4), pp. 335–52.

Brouwer, Floor and Nijkamp, Peter. Design and Structure Analysis of Integrated Environmental Planning Models. *Europ. Rev. Agr. Econ.*, 1988, *15*(1), pp. 19–38.

_____**; Nijkamp, Peter and Scholten, H.** Hybrid Log-Linear Models for Spatial Interaction and

Stability Analysis. *Metroecon.*, February 1988, 39(1), pp. 43–65.

Brouwer, J. Application of Household Models in Housing Policy. In *Keilman, N.; Kuijsten, A. and Vossen, A., eds.*, 1988, pp. 225–39.

Brouwer, Maria. Evolutionary Aspects of the European Brewing Industry. In *de Jong, H. W., ed.*, 1988, pp. 157–82.

Brown, A.; Murphy, M. and Sullivan, O. Sources of Data for Modelling Household Change with Special Reference to the OPCS 1% Longitudinal Study. In *Keilman, N.; Kuijsten, A. and Vossen, A., eds.*, 1988, pp. 56–66.

Brown, Arthur J. World Depression and the Price Level. *Nat. Inst. Econ. Rev.*, February 1988, (123), pp. 65–79.

_____. A Worm's Eye View of the Keynesian Revolution. In *Hillard, J., ed.*, 1988, pp. 18–44.

Brown, Bruce L. *Amaco v. Gambell:* Aboriginal Rights on the Outer Continental Shelf: Reopening Alaska Native Claims. *Natural Res. J.*, Summer 1988, 28(3), pp. 623–36.

Brown, Bryan J. H. Developments in the Promotion of Major Seaside Resorts: How to Effect a Transition by Really Making an Effort. In *Goodall, B. and Ashworth, G., eds.*, 1988, pp. 176–86.

Brown, Charles C. The Effect of Takeover Activity on Corporate Research and Development: Comment. In *Auerbach, A. J., ed. (I)*, 1988, pp. 96–97.

_____. Minimum Wage Laws: Are They Overrated? *J. Econ. Perspectives*, Summer 1988, 2(3), pp. 133–45.

_____ and Medoff, James L. Employer Size, Pay, and the Ability to Pay in the Public Sector. In *Freeman, R. B. and Ichniowski, C., eds.*, 1988, pp. 195–213.

_____ and Medoff, James L. The Impact of Firm Acquisitions on Labor. In *Auerbach, A. J., ed. (I)*, 1988, pp. 9–25.

Brown, Chuck. Will the 1988 Income Tax Cuts Either Increase Work Incentives or Raise More Revenue? *Fisc. Stud.*, November 1988, 9(4), pp. 93–107.

Brown, Clair. Income Distribution in an Institutional World. In *Mangum, G. and Philips, P., eds.*, 1988, pp. 51–63.

Brown-Collier, Elba and Bausor, Randall. The Epistemological Foundations of *The General Theory. Scot. J. Polit. Econ.*, August 1988, 35(3), pp. 227–41.

Brown, David P. The Implications of Nonmarketable Income for Consumption-Based Models of Asset Pricing. *J. Finance*, September 1988, 43(4), pp. 867–80.

Brown, David T. The Construction of Tender Offers: Capital Gains Taxes and the Free Rider Problem. *J. Bus.*, April 1988, 61(2), pp. 183–96.

Brown, Deborah J.; Abbott, Philip C. and Habeck, M. Sources of Export Earnings Instability: The Role of Agriculture. *J. Agr. Econ.*, January 1988, 39(1), pp. 69–79.

Brown, Douglas M. Do Physicians Underutilize

Aides? *J. Human Res.*, Summer 1988, 23(3), pp. 342–55.

_____ and Lapan, Harvey E. Utility Maximization, Individual Production, and Market Equilibrium. *Southern Econ. J.*, October 1988, 55(2), pp. 374–89.

Brown, Drusilla K. Measures of Openness: Comment. In *Baldwin, R. E., ed. (II)*, 1988, pp. 200–204.

_____. Trade Preferences for Developing Countries: A Survey of Results. *J. Devel. Stud.*, April 1988, 24(3), pp. 335–63.

Brown, Earl H.; Rosson, C. Parr and Levins, Richard A. Soybean Trader: A Microcomputer Simulation of International Agricultural Trade. *Southern J. Agr. Econ.*, July 1988, 20(1), pp. 153–57.

Brown, Eleanor and Kaufold, Howard. Human Capital Accumulation and the Optimal Level of Unemployment Insurance Provision. *J. Lab. Econ.*, October 1988, 6(4), pp. 493–514.

Brown, Gregory M. End of Purchase Requirements Fails to Change Food Stamp Participation. *Mon. Lab. Rev.*, July 1988, 111(7), pp. 14–18.

Brown, H. G. Opportunity Cost: Marshall's Criticism of Jevons. In *Wood, J. C., ed., Vol. 2*, 1988, *1931*, pp. 109–11.

Brown, John C. Coping with Crisis? The Diffusion of Waterworks in Late Nineteenth-Century German Towns. *J. Econ. Hist.*, June 1988, 48(2), pp. 307–18.

Brown, Kaye. Does Accessability to Health Services Improve Health? Commentary. In *Smith, C. S., ed.*, 1988, pp. 249–52.

_____ and Burrows, Colin. Health Insurance Decision-Making: A Literature Survey, Some Conclusions and a Few Suggestions. In *Smith, C. S., ed.*, 1988, pp. 165–88.

Brown, Keith C. and Harlow, W. V. Market Overreaction: Magnitude and Intensity. *J. Portfol. Manage.*, Winter 1988, 14(2), pp. 6–13.

_____; Harlow, W. V. and Tinic, Seha M. Risk Aversion, Uncertain Information, and Market Efficiency. *J. Finan. Econ.*, December 1988, 22(2), pp. 355–85.

Brown, Kenneth C. End-Use Matching and Applications Analysis Methodologies. In *West, R. E. and Kreith, F., eds.*, 1988, pp. 205–54.

Brown, Kristopher J. and Riddle, Dorothy I. From Complacency to Strategy: Retaining World Class Competitiveness in Services. In *Starr, M. K., ed.*, 1988, pp. 239–70.

Brown, Lawrence A. Reflections on Third World Development: Ground Level Reality, Exogenous Forces, and Conventional Paradigms. *Econ. Geogr.*, July 1988, 64(3), pp. 255–78.

_____; Brea, Jorge A. and Goetz, Andrew R. Policy Aspects of Development and Individual Mobility: Migration and Circulation from Ecuador's Rural Sierra. *Econ. Geogr.*, April 1988, 64(2), pp. 147–70.

Brown, Lawrence D. Comparing Judgmental to Extrapolative Forecasts: It's Time to Ask Why and When. *Int. J. Forecasting*, 1988, *4*(2), pp. 171–73.

———. Competition in the Health Care Sector: Ten Years Later: Afterword. In *Greenberg, W., ed.*, 1988, pp. 139–41.

——— **and McLaughlin, Catherine G.** 'May the Third Force Be With You': Community Programs for Affordable Health Care. In *Scheffler, R. M. and Rossiter, L. F., eds.*, 1988, pp. 187–211.

Brown, Linda; Finkler, Steven A. and Brooten, Dorothy. Utilization of Inpatient Services under Shortened Lengths of Stay: A Neonatal Care Example. *Inquiry*, Summer 1988, *25*(2), pp. 271–80.

Brown, Lorenzo. Modelling Diversified Utilities and Cross-Subsidization. *Resources & Energy*, September 1988, *10*(3), pp. 213–24.

Brown, M. A. and White, D. L. Stimulating Energy Conservation by Sharing the Savings: A Community-Based Approach. *Environ. Planning A*, April 1988, *20*(4), pp. 517–34.

Brown, Martin. Comparable Worth vs. Affirmative Action: Experience from the California Canning Industry. In *Mangum, G. and Philips, P., eds.*, 1988, pp. 241–46.

Brown, Murray and Wolfstetter, Elmar. Optimal Unemployment Insurance and Experience Rating. *Scand. J. Econ.*, 1988, *90*(4), pp. 529–47.

Brown, Peter G. Policy Analysis, Welfare Economics, and the Greenhouse Effect. *J. Policy Anal. Manage.*, Spring 1988, *7*(3), pp. 471–75.

Brown, Philip; Payne, Clive and Cleave, Nancy. Adding New Statistical Techniques to Standard Software Systems: A Review. In *Edwards, D. and Raun, N. E., eds.*, 1988, pp. 207–11.

Brown, Randall S. and Langwell, Kathryn. Enrollment Patterns in Medicare HMOs: Implications for Access to Care. In *Scheffler, R. M. and Rossiter, L. F., eds.*, 1988, pp. 69–96.

Brown, Stephen J. Joint Estimation of Factor Sensitivities and Risk Premia for the Arbitrage Pricing Theory: Discussion. *J. Finance*, July 1988, *43*(3), pp. 734–35.

———. Stable Factors in Security Returns: Identification Using Cross-Validation: Comment. *J. Bus. Econ. Statist.*, January 1988, *6*(1), pp. 21–23.

Brown, Stephen P. A. The New Fiscal Environment in Texas: What It Means for State Economic Growth. *Fed. Res. Bank Dallas Econ. Rev.*, January 1988, pp. 1–9.

——— **and Hill, John K.** Lower Oil Prices and State Employment. *Contemp. Policy Issues*, July 1988, *6*(3), pp. 60–68.

Brown, Stuart S. The People's Republic of China and the U.S. Unfair Trade Laws. *J. World Trade*, August 1988, *22*(4), pp. 79–94.

Brown, William and Nolan, Peter. Wages and Labour Productivity: The Contribution of Industrial Relations Research to the Understanding of Pay Determination. *Brit. J. Ind. Relat.*, November 1988, *26*(3), pp. 339–61.

Brown, William S. Institutional Structure and Deindustrialization. *J. Econ. Issues*, June 1988, *22*(2), pp. 589–97.

Browne, B. M. and Johnson, D. S. Infant Mortality in Inter-war Northern Ireland. In *Mitchison, R. and Roebuck, P., eds.*, 1988, pp. 277–87.

Browne, F. X. Interest and Non-interest Terms in the Process of Mortgage Market Clearing. *Econ. Soc. Rev.*, January 1988, *19*(2), pp. 71–97.

——— **and Honohan, Patrick.** Portfolio Choice in Irish Financial Markets. *Econ. Modelling*, January 1988, *5*(1), pp. 9–18.

Browne, Lynn E. Defense Spending and High Technology Development: National and State Issues. *New Eng. Econ. Rev.*, Sept.–Oct. 1988, pp. 3–22.

———. High Technology and Business Services. In *Lampe, D., ed.*, 1988, *1983*, pp. 201–24.

——— **and Bradbury, Katharine L.** New England Approaches the 1990s. *New Eng. Econ. Rev.*, Jan.–Feb. 1988, pp. 31–45.

——— **and Hekman, John S.** New England's Economy in the 1980s. In *Lampe, D., ed.*, 1988, *1981*, pp. 169–87.

——— **and Rosengren, Eric S.** Are Hostile Takeovers Different? In *Browne, L. E. and Rosengren, E. S., eds.*, 1988, pp. 199–229.

——— **and Rosengren, Eric S.** The Merger Boom: An Overview. In *Browne, L. E. and Rosengren, E. S., eds.*, 1988, pp. 1–16.

——— **and Rosengren, Eric S.** The Merger Boom: An Overview. *New Eng. Econ. Rev.*, March–April 1988, pp. 22–31.

Browne, M. Neil and Powers, Brian. Henry George and Comparable Worth: Hypothetical Markets as a Stimulus for Reforming the Labor Market. *Amer. J. Econ. Soc.*, October 1988, *47*(4), pp. 461–71.

———; **Wheeler, Mark and Hoag, John H.** Does a Professor's Reputation Affect Course Selection? In *Missouri Valley Economic Assoc.*, 1988, pp. 182–91.

Browne, Robert S. and Ellison, Julian. Impact of the 1975 Tax Cut on Income and Employment in the Black Community. *Rev. Black Polit. Econ.*, Fall 1988, *17*(2), pp. 5–9.

Browning, Edgar K. and Browning, Jacquelene M. Why Not a True Flat Rate Tax? In *Brown, E., ed.*, 1988, *1985*, pp. 127–42.

Browning, Jacquelene M. and Browning, Edgar K. Why Not a True Flat Rate Tax? In *Brown, E., ed.*, 1988, *1985*, pp. 127–42.

Browning, Robert X. Priorities, Programs, and Presidents: Assessing Patterns of Growth in U.S. Social Welfare Programs, 1950–1985. In *Danziger, S. H. and Portney, K. E., eds.*, 1988, pp. 13–32.

Brownstone, David; Englund, Peter and Persson, Mats. A Microsimulation Model of Swedish Housing Demand. *J. Urban Econ.*, March 1988, *23*(2), pp. 179–98.

———; **Englund, Peter and Persson, Mats.** Tax Reform and Housing Demand: The Distribution of Welfare Gains and Losses. *Europ. Econ. Rev.*, April 1988, *32*(4), pp. 819–40.

Brox, James; Carvalho, Emanuel and Lusetti, Dino. Input Substitution in Canadian Manufacturing: An Application of the CES-Translog Production Function. *Atlantic Econ. J.*, June 1988, *16*(2), pp. 22–46.

Brubaker, Earl R. Free Ride, Free Revelation, or Golden Rule. In *Cowen, T., ed.*, 1988, *1975*, pp. 93–109.

Bruce, Christopher J. The Adjudication of Labor Disputes as a Private Good. *Int. Rev. Law Econ.*, June 1988, *8*(1), pp. 3–19.

Bruce, Robert R. Telecommunications: The Need for a Policy Framework. In *Yochelson, J., ed.*, 1988, pp. 51–74.

Bruchey, Stuart. Fiscal Policy and Economic Growth in the Thought of Alexander Hamilton. In *Guarducci, A., ed.*, 1988, pp. 21–50.

Bruchis, Michael. The Nationality Policy of the CPSU and Its Reflection in Soviet Socio-political Terminology. In *Potichnyj, P. J., ed.*, 1988, pp. 121–41.

Brucker, Peter. Die Planung des Fertigungsablaufs mit Methoden der algorithmischen Geometrie. (With English summary.) *Z. Betriebswirtshaft*, January 1988, *58*(1), pp. 51–60.

Brucks, Merrie. Search Monitor: An Approach for Computer-Controlled Experiments Involving Consumer Information Search. *J. Cons. Res.*, June 1988, *15*(1), pp. 117–21.

_____; **Armstrong, Gary M. and Goldberg, Marvin E.** Children's Use of Cognitive Defenses against Television Advertising: A Cognitive Response Approach. *J. Cons. Res.*, March 1988, *14*(4), pp. 471–82.

Brüderl, J.; Diekmann, A. and Ziegler, R. Stellensuchdauer und Anfangseinkommen bei Hochschulabsolventen. Ein empirischer Beitrag zur Job-Search-Theorie. (Duration of Job Search and First Income of University Graduates: An Empirical Contribution to Job Search Theory. With English summary.) *Z. Wirtschaft. Sozialwissen.*, 1988, *108*(2), pp. 247–70.

Brudney, Jeffrey L. and Morgan, David R. Local Government Productivity: Efficiency and Equity. In *Kelly, R. M., ed.*, 1988, pp. 163–75.

Brudney, Victor. Shareholders versus Managers: The Strain in the Corporate Web: Comment. In *Coffee, J. C., Jr.; Lowenstein, L. and Rose-Ackerman, S., eds.*, 1988, pp. 150–54.

Brueckner, Jan K. and Follain, James R. The Rise and Fall of the ARM: An Econometric Analysis of Mortgage Choice. *Rev. Econ. Statist.*, February 1988, *70*(1), pp. 93–102.

Brufman, Juana J. Acerca del problema de la multicolinealidad en la estimación del modelo lineal. (About the Problem of Multicollinearity in the Estimation of the Linear Model. With English summary.) *Económica (La Plata)*, Jan.–June 1988, *34*(1), pp. 3–23.

Brugiavini, Agar and Weber, Guglielmo. L'armonizzazione delle imposte indirette: Effetti sul benessere dei consumatori italiani. (With English summary.) *Polit. Econ.*, December 1988, *4*(3), pp. 385–408.

Brumfield, William C. The Soviet Union Today: Architecture and Urban Planning. In *Cracraft, J., ed.*, 1988, pp. 164–74.

Brunat, Eric and Andreff, Wladimir. La notion de modernisation industrielle dans les economies socialistes, et son analyse. (The Concept of Modernizing the Industry in Socialist Economies. With English summary.) *Écon. Soc.*, February 1988, *22*(2), pp. 7–45.

Brundenius, Claes and Zimbalist, Andrew. Cubanology and Cuban Economic Performance. In *Zimbalist, A., ed.*, 1988, pp. 39–65.

Brunello, Giorgio. The Economic Implications of Liberalizing Japanese Financial Markets. *Rivista Int. Sci. Econ. Com.*, April–May 1988, *35*(4–5), pp. 409–35.

_____. Organizational Adjustment and Institutional Factors in Japanese Labour Market Adjustment: An Empirical Evaluation. *Europ. Econ. Rev.*, April 1988, *32*(4), pp. 841–60.

_____. Reverse Seniority Rules and the Responsiveness of Wages and Employment to External Shocks: A Note on the Japanese Experience. *Econ. Stud. Quart.*, September 1988, *39*(3), pp. 208–15.

_____. Rising Productivity and Rules for Layoffs: Should the Senior Go First? *Giorn. Econ.*, May–June 1988, *47*(5–6), pp. 277–92.

_____. Transfers of Employees between Japanese Manufacturing Enterprises: Some Results from an Enquiry on a Small Sample of Large Firms. *Brit. J. Ind. Relat.*, March 1988, *26*(1), pp. 119–32.

Bruner, Robert F. The Use of Excess Cash and Debt Capacity as a Motive for Merger. *J. Finan. Quant. Anal.*, June 1988, *23*(2), pp. 199–217.

Brunetta, Renato and Turatto, Renzo. Dall'equilibrio marginalista al paradigma generazionale. Comportamenti microeconomici in un modello dinamico di equilibrio sociale. (From the Classical Equilibrium to the Generational Paradigm. Microeconomic Behavior in a Dynamic Model of Social Equilibrium. With English summary.) *Econ. Lavoro*, Apr.–June 1988, *22*(2), pp. 13–36.

Bruni, Michele. Baby Booom e mercato del Lavoro. (Baby Boom and the Labour Market. With English summary.) *Econ. Lavoro*, Jan.–Mar. 1988, *22*(1), pp. 25–39.

_____. La domanda di flusso e le sue componenti: Alcune note esplicative. (Flow Demand and Its Components: A Few Explanatory Notes. With English summary.) *Econ. Lavoro*, Oct.–Dec. 1988, *22*(4), pp. 93–102.

Bruning, Edward R. and Hu, Michael Y. Profitability, Firm Size, Efficiency and Flexibility in the U.S. Domestic Airline Industry. *Int. J. Transport Econ.*, October 1988, *15*(3), pp. 313–27.

_____ **and Tehranian, Hassan.** Stock Market Reactions to Motor Carrier Regulatory Reform. *Int. J. Transport Econ.*, February 1988, *15*(1), pp. 7–27.

Brüninghaus, Beate. A Review of the New Literature on Business History. In *Pohl, H. and Rudolph, B., eds.*, 1988, pp. 94–120.

Brunk, Gregory G. The Major Factors of American Inventive Activity. *Soc. Sci. Quart.*, June 1988, *69*(2), pp. 491–500.

Brunn, Stanley D.; Webster, Gerald R. and Lowery, David. The Spatial Impact of Reaganomics: A Test of Six Models. *Growth Change*, Fall 1988, *19*(4), pp. 49–67.

Brunner, Karl. Allan H. Meltzer. *Carnegie–Rochester Conf. Ser. Public Policy*, Autumn 1988, *29*, pp. 3–9.

————— **and Meltzer, Allan H.** Money and Credit in the Monetary Transmission Process. *Amer. Econ. Rev.*, May 1988, *78*(2), pp. 446–51.

————— **and Meltzer, Allan H.** Stabilization Policies and Labor Markets. *Carnegie–Rochester Conf. Ser. Public Policy*, Spring 1988, *28*, pp. 1–8.

Bruno, Albert V. and Wildt, Albert R. Toward Understanding Attitude Structure: A Study of the Complimentarity of Multi-attribute Models. In *Earl, P. E., ed., Vol. 2*, 1988, *1975*, pp. 208–16.

Bruno, Michael and Piterman, Sylvia. Israel's Stabilization: A Two-Year Review. In *Bruno, M., et al., eds.*, 1988, pp. 3–47.

Bruno, Sergio. Muddling Through: American Interests in a Changing International Economy: Perspective. In *Guerrieri, P. and Padoan, P. C., eds.*, 1988, pp. 199–202.

—————. The Secret Story of the Rediscovery of Classical Unemployment and of Its Consequences on Economic Advisors. *Stud. Econ.*, 1988, *43*(36), pp. 3–37.

van Brunschot, Frank. Netherlands: "Fraus Legis" and Multinational Enterprises. *Bull. Int. Fiscal Doc.*, Aug.–Sept. 1988, *42*(8–9), pp. 355–59.

Brunton, Bruce G. Institutional Origins of the Military–Industrial Complex. *J. Econ. Issues*, June 1988, *22*(2), pp. 599–606.

Brunwinkel, Andrea and Albers, Wulf. Equal Share Analysis for Location Games. In *Tietz, R.; Albers, W. and Selten, R., eds.*, 1988, pp. 303–16.

Brus, Wlodzimierz. The Political Economy of Reforms. In *Marer, P. and Siwinski, W., eds.*, 1988, pp. 65–79.

Brusco, Sandro. Distribuzione eterogenea delle informazioni e convergenza all'equilibrio di aspettative razionali in un modello di equilibrio parziale. (Heterogeneous Distribution of Information and Convergence to Rational Expectations Equilibrium in a Partial Equilibrium Model. With English summary.) *Rivista Int. Sci. Econ. Com.*, July 1988, *35*(7), pp. 625–38.

—————. Heterogeneous Distribution of Information and Convergence to Rational Expectations Equilibrium in a Partial Equilibrium Model. *Econ. Letters*, 1988, *28*(1), pp. 21–25.

Brush, Candida G. and Hisrich, Robert D. Women Entrepreneurs: Strategic Origins Impact on Growth. In *Kirchhoff, B. A., et al., eds.*, 1988, pp. 612–25.

van Brussel, P. and Janssen, J. Classification of Microcomputers and Marketing Interpreta-

tion. In *Gaul, W. and Schader, M., eds.*, 1988, pp. 355–67.

Brust, Peter. Inventory Investment under Rising Cost and Demand Conditions. *Amer. Econ.*, Fall 1988, *32*(2), pp. 51–54.

Bryan, Greyson. Some Observations on Relationships between Tax and International Trade Law. *Bull. Int. Fiscal Doc.*, March 1988, *42*(3), pp. 110–15.

Bryan, Patrick. Agriculture: Comments. *Soc. Econ. Stud.*, March–June 1988, *37*(1–2), pp. 405–11.

Bryan, William R. and Linke, Charles M. Estimating Present Value of Future Earnings: Experience with Dedicated Portfolios. *J. Risk Ins.*, June 1988, *55*(2), pp. 273–86.

————— **and Linke, Charles M.** The Estimation of the Age/Earnings Profiles in Wrongful Death and Injury Cases: Comment. *J. Risk Ins.*, March 1988, *55*(1), pp. 168–73.

Bryant, Ralph C. Commodities, Debt and North–South Cooperation: A Cautionary Tale from the Structuralist Camp: Discussion. In *Currie, D. and Vines, D., eds.*, 1988, pp. 141–46.

—————; **Henderson, Dale W. and Symansky, Steven A.** Estimates of the Consequences of Policy Actions Derived from Model Simulations. In *Bryant, R. C., et al., eds.*, 1988, pp. 63–91.

————— **and Holtham, Gerald.** The U.S. External Deficit: Diagnosis, Prognosis, and Cure. In *Bryant, R. C.; Holtham, G. and Hooper, P., eds.*, 1988, pp. 57–81.

—————; **Holtham, Gerald and Hooper, Peter.** Consensus and Diversity in the Model Simulations. In *Bryant, R. C., et al., eds.*, 1988, pp. 27–62.

—————; **Holtham, Gerald and Hooper, Peter.** External Deficits and the Dollar: The Pit and the Pendulum: Introduction. In *Bryant, R. C.; Holtham, G. and Hooper, P., eds.*, 1988, pp. 1–9.

—————, **et al.** The Brookings Model Comparison Project: An Overview. In *Bryant, R. C., et al., eds.*, 1988, pp. 3–14.

Bryant, W. Keith. Consumer Complaints and Redress: Some Directions for Future Research. In *Maynes, E. S. and ACCI Research Committee, eds.*, 1988, pp. 723–26.

—————. Durables and Wives' Employment Yet Again. *J. Cons. Res.*, June 1988, *15*(1), pp. 37–47.

Bryce, Robert B. Keynes during the Great Depression and World War II. In *Hamouda, O. F. and Smithin, J. N., eds., Vol. 1*, 1988, pp. 146–50.

Brzezin, W. and Jaruga, Alicja. Accounting Evolution in a Planned Economy. In *Bailey, D. T., ed.*, 1988, pp. 41–58.

Brzezinski, Zbigniew. After the Carter Doctrine: Geostrategic Stakes and Turbulent Crosscurrents in the Gulf. In *Sindelar, H. R., III and Peterson, J. E., eds.*, 1988, pp. 1–9.

—————. America's New Geostrategy. *Foreign Aff.*, Spring 1988, *66*(4), pp. 680–99.

—————. U.S. Policy toward Poland in a Global Perspective. In *Marer, P. and Siwinski, W., eds.*, 1988, pp. 315–21.

Bublitz, Bruce O. and Zuckerman, Gilroy J. Discounting Deferred Taxes: A New Approach. In *Schwartz, B. N., ed.,* 1988, pp. 55–69.

Bubnys, Edward; Park, Hun Y. and Bera, Anil K. Conditional Heteroscedasticity in the Market Model and Efficient Estimates of Betas. *Financial Rev.,* May 1988, *23*(2), pp. 201–14.

Buc, Nancy L. Products Liability: The Views of a Practicing Attorney. In *Maynes, E. S. and ACCI Research Committee, eds.,* 1988, pp. 793–96.

Bucalo, John P., Jr. Successful Employee Relations. In *Timpe, A. D., ed.,* 1988, *1986,* pp. 169–88.

Buccola, Steven T. Social Welfare and Interpersonal Utility Comparisons in Applied Policy Research. *Amer. J. Agr. Econ.,* May 1988, *70*(2), pp. 454–58.

_____ **and Sukume, Chrispen.** Optimal Grain Pricing and Storage Policy in Controlled Agricultural Economies: Application to Zimbabwe. *World Devel.,* March 1988, *16*(3), pp. 361–71.

Buchanan, James M. An Economic Theory of Clubs. In *Cowen, T., ed.,* 1988, *1965,* pp. 193–208.

_____. An Economic Theory of Clubs. In *Ricketts, M., ed., Vol. 2,* 1988, *1965,* pp. 86–99.

_____. The Constitution of Economic Policy. In *Gwartney, J. D. and Wagner, R. E., eds.,* 1988, pp. 103–14.

_____. Constitutional Imperatives for the 1990s: The Legal Order for a Free and Productive Economy. In *Anderson, A. and Bark, D. L., eds.,* 1988, pp. 253–63.

_____. Contractarian Political Economy and Constitutional Interpretation. *Amer. Econ. Rev.,* May 1988, *78*(2), pp. 135–39.

_____. A Defense of Organized Crime? In *Alper, N. O. and Hellman, D. A., eds.,* 1988, pp. 258–75.

_____. The Economic Theory of Politics Reborn. *Challenge,* March–April 1988, *31*(2), pp. 4–10.

_____. Economists and the Gains from Trade. *Managerial Dec. Econ.,* Special Issue, Winter 1988, pp. 5–12.

_____. Justification of the Compound Republic: The *Calculus* in Retrospect. In *Gwartney, J. D. and Wagner, R. E., eds.,* 1988, *1987,* pp. 131–37.

_____. Market Failure and Political Failure. *Cato J.,* Spring–Summer 1988, *8*(1), pp. 1–13.

_____. Political Economy: 1957–1982. In *[Nutter, G. W.],* 1988, pp. 119–30.

_____ **and Vanberg, Viktor J.** The Politicization of Market Failure. *Public Choice,* May 1988, *57*(2), pp. 101–13.

Buchanan, W. Wary; Hoy, Frank and Vaught, Bobby C. Any Development Program Can Work. In *Timpe, A. D., ed.,* 1988, *1985,* pp. 307–15.

Buchholz, Todd G. Revolution, Reputation Effects, and Time Horizons. *Cato J.,* Spring–Summer 1988, *8*(1), pp. 185–97.

Buchholz, Wolfgang. Neutral Taxation of Risky Investment. In *Bös, D.; Rose, M. and Seidl, C., eds.,* 1988, pp. 297–316.

_____; **Richter, Wolfram F. and Schwaiger, J.** Distributional Implications of Equal Sacrifice Rules. *Soc. Choice Welfare,* 1988, *5*(2/3), pp. 223–26.

_____; **Richter, Wolfram F. and Schwaiger, J.** Distributional Implications of Equal Sacrifice Rules. In *Gaertner, W. and Pattanaik, P. K., eds.,* 1988, *1988,* pp. 135–38.

Büchtemann, Christoph F. Part-time Employment in the United States: Comment. In *Hart, R. A., ed.,* 1988, pp. 282–87.

_____ **and Vobruba, Georg.** The Welfare State and Jobs: Comment. In *Kregel, J. A.; Matzner, E. and Roncaglia, A., eds.,* 1988, pp. 208–11.

Buck, Andrew J. and FitzRoy, Felix R. Inflation and Productivity Growth in the Federal Republic of Germany. *J. Post Keynesian Econ.,* Spring 1988, *10*(3), pp. 428–44.

Buck, Maurice. The Role of Travel Agent and Tour Operator. In *Goodall, B. and Ashworth, G., eds.,* 1988, pp. 67–74.

Buck, Nick. Service Industries and Local Labour Markets: Towards 'An Anatomy of Service Job Loss.' *Urban Stud.,* August 1988, *25*(4), pp. 319–32.

Buck, Roland. Liquidity-Preference and Loanable-Funds in Patinkin's Full Employment Model—A Critique. In *Missouri Valley Economic Assoc.,* 1988, pp. 168–76.

Buck, Trevor W. Soft Budgets and Administration. *Comp. Econ. Stud.,* Fall 1988, *30*(3), pp. 51–70.

Buckler, Warren. Commentary: Continuous Work History Sample. *Soc. Sec. Bull.,* April 1988, *51*(4), pp. 12, 56.

Buckles, Stephen and Morton, John S. The Effects of Advanced Placement on College Introductory Economics Courses. *Amer. Econ. Rev.,* May 1988, *78*(2), pp. 263–68.

Buckley, M. Ronald and Cote, Joseph A. Measurement Error and Theory Testing in Consumer Research: An Illustration of the Importance of Construct Validation. *J. Cons. Res.,* March 1988, *14*(4), pp. 579–82.

_____ **and Eder, Robert W.** The Employment Interview: An Interactionist Perspective. In *Ferris, G. R. and Rowland, K. M., eds.,* 1988, pp. 75–107.

Buckley, Peter J. and Artisien, Patrick. Policy Issues of Intra-EC Direct Investment: British, French and German Multinationals in Greece, Portugal and Spain, with Special Reference to Employment Effects. In *Dunning, J. and Robson, P., eds.,* 1988, pp. 105–28.

_____ **and Casson, Mark.** A Theory of Cooperation in International Business. In *Contractor, F. J. and Lorange, P.,* 1988, pp. 31–53.

Budavari, Laszlo. Hesitating Steps Towards Self-government in Hungary. *Econ. Planning,* 1988, *22*(1–2), pp. 88–99.

Budd, Alan. Macro-economic Aspects of the 1988 Budget. *Fisc. Stud.,* May 1988, *9*(2), pp. 1–13.

_____; **Levine, Paul and Smith, Peter.** Real Wage Adjustment and Long-term Unemployment. In *Cross, R., ed.,* 1988, pp. 41–64.

———; **Levine, Paul and Smith, Peter.** Unemployment, Vacancies and the Long-term Unemployed. *Econ. J.*, December 1988, *98*(393), pp. 1071–91.

Budd, William; Rosenman, Robert and Fort, Rodney D. Perceptions, Fear, and Economic Loss: An Application of Prospect Theory to Environmental Decision Making. *Policy Sci.*, 1988, *21*(4), pp. 327–50.

Budeiri, Priscilla and Correia, Eddie. Antitrust Legislation in the Reagan Era. *Antitrust Bull.*, Summer 1988, *33*(2), pp. 361–93.

Bueno, Gerardo M. A Mexican View. In *Diebold, W., Jr., ed.*, 1988, pp. 105–27.

Buhl, Hans Ulrich and Bossert, Walter. More on Sufficiency Conditions for Interior Location in the Triangle Space. *J. Reg. Sci.*, February 1988, *28*(1), pp. 127.

Buhmann, Brigitte, et al. Equivalence Scales, Well-Being, Inequality, and Poverty: Sensitivity Estimates across Ten Countries Using the Luxembourg Income Study (LIS) Database. *Rev. Income Wealth*, June 1988, *34*(2), pp. 115–42.

Bühner, Rolf. Kapitalmarktbeurteilung von Technologiestrategie. (With English summary.) *Z. Betriebswirtshaft*, December 1988, *58*(12), pp. 1323–39.

Buhofer, Heinz and Frey, Bruno S. Prisoners and Property Rights. *J. Law Econ.*, April 1988, *31*(1), pp. 19–46.

Bui, Tung and Schenker-Wicki, Andrea. Co-oP: Un système d'aide à la décision de groupe pour les décisions stratégiques de l'entreprise. (Co-oP: A Group Decision Support System for Multiple Criteria Group Decision Making. With English summary.) *Schweiz. Z. Volkswirtsch. Statist.*, September 1988, *124*(3), pp. 445–54.

Buira, Ariel. International Payments Imbalances in Heavily Indebted Developing Countries: Discussion. In *Fieleke, N. S., ed.*, 1988, pp. 90–97.

Buiter, Willem H. 'Crowding Out' and the Effectiveness of Fiscal Policy. In *Shaw, G. K., ed.*, Vol. 2, 1988, *1977*, pp. 338–57.

———. Death, Birth, Productivity Growth and Debt Neutrality. *Econ. J.*, June 1988, *98*(391), pp. 279–93.

———. Macroeconomic Modelling for Economic Policy: Comments. In *Driehuis, W.; Fase, M. M. G. and den Hartog, H., eds.*, 1988, pp. 137–45.

———. Macroeconomic Policy Design in an Interdependent World Economy: An Analysis of Three Contingencies. In *Frenkel, J. A., ed.*, 1988, pp. 121–55.

———. The Right Combination of Demand and Supply Policies: The Case for a Two-Handed Approach. In *Giersch, H., ed.*, 1988, pp. 305–45.

———. Sterling Misalignment and British Trade Performance: Comment. In *Marston, R. C., ed.*, 1988, pp. 69–75.

———. Structural and Stabilization Aspects of Fiscal and Financial Policy in the Dependent Economy. *Oxford Econ. Pap.*, June 1988, *40*(2), pp. 220–45.

Bukman, P. Opening Address to the Conference by the Minister for Development Co-operation of the Netherlands: Development Policy in Retrospect and Prospect. In *Jepma, C. J., ed.*, 1988, pp. 25–38.

Bulajic, Milan. Protection of Intellectual Property Rights and Foreign Trade (Uruguay Round). In *Dicke, D. C. and Petersmann, E.-U., eds.*, 1988, pp. 292–300.

Bulgaru, M.; Stroe, R. and Ionescu, C. Turning to Account the Results of the Scientific Research of Economic Cybernetics and Economic Informatics in the Instructional–Educational Process. *Econ. Computat. Cybern. Stud. Res.*, 1988, *23*(4), pp. 25–36.

Bulkley, I. George and Black, Jane M. The Role of Strategic Information Transmission in a Bargaining Model. *Econ. J.*, Supplement, 1988, *98*(390), pp. 50–57.

Bull, Clive and Jovanovic, Boyan. Mismatch versus Derived-Demand Shift as Causes of Labour Mobility. *Rev. Econ. Stud.*, January 1988, *55*(1), pp. 169–75.

Bullard, Clark W. and Sebald, Anthony V. Monte Carlo Sensitivity Analysis of Input–Output Models. *Rev. Econ. Statist.*, November 1988, *70*(4), pp. 708–12.

Bullock, J. Bruce. Domestic Food and Agricultural Policy Research Directions: A Discussion. In *Hildreth, R. J., et al., eds.*, 1988, pp. 149–54.

Bulmash, Samuel B. and Barniv, Ran. New Public Stock Issues by Seasoned and Unseasoned Firms: A Comparative Analysis in a Turbulent Environment—The Case of Israel. *Managerial Dec. Econ.*, March 1988, *9*(1), pp. 27–34.

Bulmer-Thomas, Victor. The Balance-of-Payments Crisis and Adjustment Programmes in Central America. In *Bulmer-Thomas, V.*, 1988, *1987*, pp. 139–86.

———. Central America in the Inter-war Period. In *Bulmer-Thomas, V.*, 1988, *1984*, pp. 44–71.

———. The Central American Common Market. In *Bulmer-Thomas, V.*, 1988, *1988*, pp. 75–104.

———. Economic Development over the Long Run—Central America since 1920. In *Bulmer-Thomas, V.*, 1988, *1983*, pp. 19–43.

———. Economic Relations between Central America and Western Europe. In *Bulmer-Thomas, V.*, 1988, pp. 121–36.

———. The Kissinger Report. In *Bulmer-Thomas, V.*, 1988, pp. 208–15.

———. The New Model of Development in Costa Rica. In *Bulmer-Thomas, V.*, 1988, pp. 216–34.

———. Regional Integration within a Policy Regime of Openness. In *Bulmer-Thomas, V.*, 1988, pp. 105–20.

———. Studies in the Economics of Central America: Introduction. In *Bulmer-Thomas, V.*, 1988, pp. 1–15.

———. World Recession and Central American

Depression: Lessons from the 1930s for the 1980s. In *Bulmer-Thomas, V.*, 1988, *1985*, pp. 187–207.

Bulow, Jeremy and Rogoff, Kenneth. The Buyback Boondoggle. *Brookings Pap. Econ. Act.*, 1988, (2), pp. 645–98.

_____ **and Rogoff, Kenneth.** Comprehensive Debt Retirement: The Bolivian Example: Comment. *Brookings Pap. Econ. Act.*, 1988, (2), pp. 714–15.

_____ **and Rogoff, Kenneth.** Multilateral Negotiations for Rescheduling Developing Country Debt: A Bargaining-Theoretic Framework. *Int. Monet. Fund Staff Pap.*, December 1988, *35*(4), pp. 644–57.

Bultez, Alain and Naert, Philippe. SH.A.R.P.: SHelf Allocation for Retailers' Profit. *Marketing Sci.*, Summer 1988, *7*(3), pp. 211–31.

Bunch, David S. A Comparison of Algorithms for Maximum Likelihood Estimation of Choice Models. *J. Econometrics*, May–June 1988, *38*(1–2), pp. 145–67.

Bunders, Joske. Biotechnology and Appropriate Farming Systems. In *Research and Info. System for the Non-aligned and Other Developing Countries*, 1988, pp. 102–33.

Bundrick, Charles M.; Cuzán, Alfred G. and Moussalli, Stephanie D. Fiscal Expansion and Political Instability in the Iberic–Latin Region. *Public Choice*, December 1988, *59*(3), pp. 225–38.

Bundt, Thomas and Keating, Barry. Depository Institution Competition in the Deregulated Environment: The Case of the Large Credit Union. *Appl. Econ.*, October 1988, *20*(10), pp. 1333–42.

_____ **and Solocha, Andrew.** Debt, Deficits and the Dollar. *J. Policy Modeling*, Winter 1988, *10*(4), pp. 581–600.

Bunich, Pavel G. The Mechanism of Self-financing. *Prob. Econ.*, March 1988, *30*(11), pp. 60–77.

_____. The New Economic Mechanism and Credit Reform. *Prob. Econ.*, December 1988, *31*(8), pp. 80–94.

Bunke, Olaf. Assessing the Performance of Estimates without Knowledge on the Regression Function, the Variances and the Distributions. In *Fedorov, V. and Lauter, H.*, eds., 1988, pp. 158–64.

Bunker, John P. Is Efficacy the Gold Standard for Quality Assessment? *Inquiry*, Spring 1988, *25*(1), pp. 51–58.

Bunn, Julie Ann and David, Paul A. The Economics of Gateway Technologies and Network Evolution: Lessons from Electricity Supply History. *Info. Econ. Policy*, 1988, *3*(2), pp. 165–202.

Buongiorno, Joseph; Thompson, Howard E. and Farimani, Mehrdad. A Financial Model of Investment, with an Application to the Paper Industry. *Appl. Econ.*, June 1988, *20*(6), pp. 767–83.

Buras, Nathan. Irrigation Management and Scheduling: Study of Irrigation System in In-dia: Comment. In *O'Mara, G. T.*, ed., 1988, pp. 195–96.

_____. New Approaches to Using Mathematical Programming for Resource Allocation: Comment. In *O'Mara, G. T.*, ed., 1988, pp. 126–27.

Burbee, Clark R.; McNiel, Douglas W. and Foshee, Andrew W. Superfund Taxes and Expenditures: Regional Redistributions. *Rev. Reg. Stud.*, Winter 1988, *18*(1), pp. 4–9.

Burbidge, John B. and Asimakopulos, Athanasios. The Short-Period Incidence of Taxation. In *Asimakopulos, A.*, 1988, *1974*, pp. 47–76.

_____; **Magee, Lonnie and Robb, A. Leslie.** Alternative Transformations to Handle Extreme Values of the Dependent Variable. *J. Amer. Statist. Assoc.*, March 1988, *83*(401), pp. 123–27.

Burbridge, John J., Jr. Strategic Implications of Logistics Information Systems. *Logist. Transp. Rev.*, December 1988, *24*(4), pp. 368–83.

Burch, Philip H., Jr. The Alignment of Economic Forces Involved in Three Key Presidential Elections: 1896, 1912, and 1932. In *Zarembka, P.*, ed., 1988, pp. 125–204.

Burchardt, Michael. Vom homo oeconomicus zum homo portofolicus. (From Homo Oeconomicus to Homo Portfolicus. With English summary.) *Kredit Kapital*, 1988, *21*(4), pp. 532–55.

Burda, Michael C. Is There a Capital Shortage in Europe? *Weltwirtsch. Arch.*, 1988, *124*(1), pp. 38–57.

_____ **and Sachs, Jeffrey D.** Assessing High Unemployment in West Germany. *World Econ.*, December 1988, *11*(4), pp. 543–63.

Burdakov, O. and Richter, C. Parallel Hybrid Optimization Methods. In *Kurzhanski, A.; Neumann, K. and Pallaschke, D.*, eds., 1988, pp. 16–23.

Burdekin, Richard C. K. Economic Performance and the Determination of Presidential Elections in the U.S. *Amer. Econ.*, Fall 1988, *32*(2), pp. 71–75.

_____. Interaction between Central Bank Behaviour and Fiscal Policy: The U.S. Case. *Appl. Econ.*, January 1988, *20*(1), pp. 97–111.

_____ **and Burkett, Paul.** Monetary Accommodation of Income Claims and the Expectations-Augmented Phillips Curve: In Search of a Stable Policy Rule. *Weltwirtsch. Arch.*, 1988, *124*(1), pp. 169–77.

_____ **and Laney, Leroy O.** Fiscal Policymaking and the Central Bank Institutional Constraint. *Kyklos*, 1988, *41*(4), pp. 647–62.

Burdett, Kenneth and Vishwanath, Tara. Balanced Matching and Labor Market Equilibrium. *J. Polit. Econ.*, October 1988, *96*(5), pp. 1048–65.

_____ **and Vishwanath, Tara.** Declining Reservation Wages and Learning. *Rev. Econ. Stud.*, October 1988, *55*(4), pp. 655–65.

Burdon, Joan. Slavery as a Punishment in Roman Criminal Law. In *Archer, L. J.*, ed., 1988, pp. 68–85.

Bureau, Dominique and Formery, Zoé. Quand

peut-on justifier des aides aux exportations? (When Can Export Subsidies Be Justified? With English summary.) *Ann. Écon. Statist.*, Oct.–Dec. 1988, (12), pp. 109–26.

Burgelman, Robert A. A Comparative Evolutionary Perspective on Strategy-Making: Advantages and Limitations of the Japanese Approach. In *Urabe, K.; Child, J. and Kagono, T., eds.*, 1988, pp. 63–80.

_____. A Process Model of Internal Corporate Venturing in the Diversified Major Firm. In *Grønhaug, K. and Kaufmann, G., eds.*, 1988, *1983*, pp. 279–309.

Burger, Albert E. The Puzzling Growth of the Monetary Aggregates in the 1980s. *Fed. Res. Bank St. Louis Rev.*, Sept.–Oct. 1988, 70(5), pp. 46–60.

Burgess, David F. Complementarity and the Discount Rate for Public Investment. *Quart. J. Econ.*, August 1988, 103(3), pp. 527–41.

_____. On the Relevance of Export Demand Conditions for Capital Income Taxation in Open Economies. *Can. J. Econ.*, May 1988, 21(2), pp. 285–311.

Burgess, Jacquelin; Harrison, Carolyn M. and Limb, Melanie. People, Parks and the Urban Green: A Study of Popular Meanings and Values for Open Spaces in the City. *Urban Stud.*, December 1988, 25(6), pp. 455–73.

_____; Limb, Melanie and Harrison, Carolyn M. Exploring Environmental Values Through the Medium of Small Groups: 2. Illustrations of a Group at Work. *Environ. Planning A*, April 1988, 20(4), pp. 457–76.

_____; Limb, Melanie and Harrison, Carolyn M. Exploring Environmental Values through the Medium of Small Groups: 1. Theory and Practice. *Environ. Planning A*, March 1988, 20(3), pp. 309–26.

Burgess, Richard C. and Bey, Roger P. Optimal Portfolios: Markowitz Full Covariance versus Simple Selection Rules. *J. Finan. Res.*, Summer 1988, 11(2), pp. 153–63.

Burgess, Simon M. Employment Adjustment in UK Manufacturing. *Econ. J.*, March 1988, 98(389), pp. 81–103.

_____. Wage Rigidity and Information: Relativities and Target Rates of Wage Growth. *Oxford Econ. Pap.*, September 1988, 40(3), pp. 523–34.

Büring, O. and Schader, Martin. KREDIT: KEE-Based Support for Credit Decisions in a Mail-Order Firm. In *Gaul, W. and Schader, M., eds.*, 1988, pp. 83–92.

Burke, I. Australia's First Pictorialist. In *Wood, J. C., ed., Vol. 1*, 1988, *1955*, pp. 188–96.

Burke, Jonathan. On the Existence of Price Equilibria in Dynamic Economies. *J. Econ. Theory*, April 1988, 44(2), pp. 281–300.

Burke, Raymond R. and Srull, Thomas K. Competitive Interference and Consumer Memory for Advertising. *J. Cons. Res.*, June 1988, 15(1), pp. 55–68.

_____, et al. Deception by Implication: An Experimental Investigation. *J. Cons. Res.*, March 1988, 14(4), pp. 483–94.

Burke, Thomas P.; Lovejoy, Lora Mills and Blostin, Allan P. Disability and Insurance Plans in the Public and Private Sector. *Mon. Lab. Rev.*, December 1988, 111(12), pp. 9–17.

Burkett, John P. Slack, Shortage, and Discouraged Consumers in Eastern Europe: Estimates Based on Smoothing by Aggregation. *Rev. Econ. Stud.*, July 1988, 55(3), pp. 493–505.

Burkett, Paul. Informal Finance in Developing Countries: Lessons for the Development of Formal Financial Intermediaries. *J. Econ. Devel.*, December 1988, 13(2), pp. 81–110.

_____. Investment Fund Money and the Reproduction of Capitalism: A Marxian Approach. *Rev. Radical Polit. Econ.*, Summer–Fall 1988, 20(2–3), pp. 48–54.

_____ and Burdekin, Richard C. K. Monetary Accomodation of Income Claims and the Expectations-Augmented Phillips Curve: In Search of a Stable Policy Rule. *Weltwirtsch. Arch.*, 1988, 124(1), pp. 169–77.

Burkhauser, Richard V. Age-Specific Death Rates: Discussion. In *Ricardo-Campbell, R. and Lazear, E. P., eds.*, 1988, pp. 184–90.

_____ and Duncan, Greg J. Life Events, Public Policy, and the Economic Vulnerability of Children and the Elderly. In *Palmer, J. L.; Smeeding, T. and Torrey, B. B., eds.*, 1988, pp. 55–88.

_____; Feaster, Daniel J. and Holden, Karen C. The Timing of Falls into Poverty after Retirement and Widowhood. *Demography*, August 1988, 25(3), pp. 405–14.

Burki, Shahid Javed. Poverty in Pakistan: Myth or Reality? In *Srinivasan, T. N. and Bardhan, P. K., eds.*, 1988, pp. 69–88.

_____. Reform and Growth in China. *Finance Develop.*, December 1988, 25(4), pp. 46–49.

Burkinshaw, O. and Aliprantis, C. D. The Fundamental Theorems of Welfare Economics without Proper Preferences. *J. Math. Econ.*, 1988, 17(1), pp. 41–54.

Burlacu, Veronica and Cenuşă, G. N Random Functions—Almost Periodical in Probability. *Econ. Computat. Cybern. Stud. Res.*, 1988, 23(2), pp. 37–42.

Burmeister, Edwin and McElroy, Marjorie B. Arbitrage Pricing Theory as a Restricted Nonlinear Multivariate Regression Model: Iterated Nonlinear Seemingly Unrelated Regression Estimates. *J. Bus. Econ. Statist.*, January 1988, 6(1), pp. 29–42.

_____ and McElroy, Marjorie B. Joint Estimation of Factor Sensitivities and Risk Premia for the Arbitrage Pricing Theory. *J. Finance*, July 1988, 43(3), pp. 721–33.

Burnell, James D. Crime and Racial Composition in Contiguous Communities as Negative Externalities: Prejudiced Households' Evaluation of Crime Rate and Segregation Nearby Reduces Housing Values and Tax Revenues. *Amer. J. Econ. Soc.*, April 1988, 47(2), pp. 177–93.

Burnes, Bernard; Knights, David and Willmott, Hugh. New Technology and the Labour Process: Introduction. In *Knights, D. and Willmott, H., eds.*, 1988, pp. 1–19.

Burnett, John J. and Wood, Van R. A Proposed Model of the Donation Decision Process. In *Hirschman, E. and Sheth, J. N., eds.*, 1988, pp. 1–47.

Burney, Nadeem A. Combining Yearly and Quarterly Data in Regression Analysis: Comments. *Pakistan Devel. Rev.*, Part 2, Winter 1988, 27(4), pp. 723.

_____. Determinants of Debt Problem in Pakistan and Its Debt-Servicing Capacity. *Pakistan Devel. Rev.*, Part 2, Winter 1988, 27(4), pp. 805–16.

_____. The Rybczynski and Stolper–Samuelson Theorems in the Presence of External Economies of Scale. *Australian Econ. Pap.*, June 1988, 27(50), pp. 111–27.

Burniaux, Jean-Marc and Waelbroeck, Jean. Agricultural Protection in Europe: Its Impact on Developing Countries. In *Langhammer, R. J. and Rieger, H. C., eds.*, 1988, pp. 129–54.

Burns, Arthur F. The Ongoing Revolution in American Banking. In *Cassing, J. H. and Husted, S. L., eds.*, 1988, pp. 3–90.

Burns, E. Bradford. The Modernization of Underdevelopment: El Salvador, 1858–1931. In *Wilber, C. K., ed.*, 1988, pp. 174–202.

Burns, Michael C. Considerations in Privatizing a Large Crown Corporation. In *Walker, M. A., ed. (II)*, 1988, pp. 171–80.

Burns, Michael E. Macroeconomic Modelling in Australia: Foreword. *Australian Econ. Pap.*, Supplement, June 1988, 27, pp. 1–6.

Burns, Richard M.; Jordan, Bradford D. and Verbrugge, James A. Returns to Initial Shareholders in Savings Institution Conversions: Evidence and Regulatory Implications. *J. Finan. Res.*, Summer 1988, 11(2), pp. 125–36.

Burns, Terence. The UK Government's Financial Strategy. In *Eltis, W. and Sinclair, P. J. N., eds.*, 1988, pp. 428–47.

Burns, Thomas G. Present Trends and Outlook for Energy Markets on the Pacific Rim. In *Dorian, J. P. and Fridley, D. G., eds.*, 1988, pp. 3–36.

Burr, Deborah. On Errors-in-Variables in Binary Regression—Berkson Case. *J. Amer. Statist. Assoc.*, September 1988, 83(403), pp. 739–43.

Burridge, Peter and Wallis, Kenneth F. Prediction Theory for Autoregressive–Moving Average Processes. *Econometric Rev.*, 1988, 7(1), pp. 65–95.

Burrows, Colin. An Assessment of Alternative Models for Costing Nursing Services: A Measurement Theory Perspective: Commentary. In *Smith, C. S., ed.*, 1988, pp. 145–47.

_____ and Brown, Kaye. Health Insurance Decision-Making: A Literature Survey, Some Conclusions and a Few Suggestions. In *Smith, C. S., ed.*, 1988, pp. 165–88.

Burstein, Meyer Louis. Beyond the Banking Principle. In *Burstein, M. L.*, 1988, pp. 63–84.

_____. Colonial Currency and Contemporary Monetary Theory. In *Burstein, M. L.*, 1988, pp. 87–98.

_____. Diffusion of Knowledge-based Products. In *Burstein, M. L.*, 1988, pp. 210–31.

_____. The Economics of Tie-in Sales. In *Burstein, M. L.*, 1988, 1960, pp. 145–55.

_____. Homer on the History of Interest Rates. In *Burstein, M. L.*, 1988, pp. 99–109.

_____. Keynes and Money: A Comment. In *Hamouda, O. F. and Smithin, J. N., eds., Vol. 2*, 1988, pp. 162–65.

_____. Knut Wicksell and the Closure of His System: Critique and Reconstruction of the Cumulative Process. In *Burstein, M. L.*, 1988, pp. 48–62.

_____. Macro Foundations of Microeconomics. In *Burstein, M. L.*, 1988, pp. 11–22.

_____. Measurement of Quality Changes in Consumer Durables. In *Burstein, M. L.*, 1988, pp. 256–67.

_____. Optimal Diffusion of Innovated Durable Goods Subject to Technical Progress: The Rôle of Property Rights Régimes. In *Burstein, M. L.*, 1988, pp. 232–46.

_____. The Political Economy of Alexander Hamilton. In *Burstein, M. L.*, 1988, pp. 110–42.

_____. Some More Keynesian Economics. In *Burstein, M. L.*, 1988, 1975, pp. 23–40.

_____. Some Theory of Vertical Integration. In *Burstein, M. L.*, 1988, pp. 193–209.

_____. Still More Keynesian Economics. In *Burstein, M. L.*, 1988, pp. 41–47.

_____. A Theory of Full-line Forcing. In *Burstein, M. L.*, 1988, 1960, pp. 156–92.

_____ and Clower, Robert W. On the Invariance of Demand for Cash and Other Assets. In *Burstein, M. L.*, 1988, 1960, pp. 3–10.

_____ and Oi, Walter Y. Monopoly, Competition and Variability of Market Prices. In *Burstein, M. L.*, 1988, pp. 249–55.

Burt, Oscar R. and Worthington, Virginia E. Wheat Acreage Supply Response in the United States. *Western J. Agr. Econ.*, July 1988, 13(1), pp. 100–111.

Burtless, Gary. The Determinants of IRA Contributions and the Effect of Limit Changes: Comment. In *Bodie, Z.; Shoven, J. B. and Wise, D. A., eds.*, 1988, pp. 48–52.

_____. Disaggregated Wage Developments: Comment. *Brookings Pap. Econ. Act.*, 1988, (1), pp. 339–44.

Burton, David R. Constructive State and Local Tax Policy. In *Gold, S. D., ed.*, 1988, pp. 219–26.

Burton, John F., Jr. New Perspectives in Workers' Compensation: Introduction. In *Burton, J. F., Jr., ed.*, 1988, pp. 1–20.

_____; Hunt, H. Allan and Krueger, Alan B. The Impact of Open Competition in Michigan on the Employers' Costs of Workers' Compensation. In *Borba, P. S. and Appel, D., eds.*, 1988, pp. 109–44.

Burton, Lloyd. Negotiating the Cleanup of Toxic Groundwater Contamination: Strategy and Legitimacy. *Natural Res. J.*, Winter 1988, 28(1), pp. 105–43.

Burton, M. P. Irreversible Supply Functions Revisited. *J. Agr. Econ.*, January 1988, 39(1), pp. 113–20.

Burton, Richard M. and Obel, Børge. Opportunism, Incentives, and the M-Form Hypothesis: A Laboratory Study. *J. Econ. Behav. Organ.*, July 1988, *10*(1), pp. 99–119.

Burton, Robert O., Jr.; Featherstone, Allen M. and Schroeder, Ted C. Allocation of Farm Financial Stress among Income, Leverage, and Interest Rate Components: A Kansas Example. *Southern J. Agr. Econ.*, December 1988, *20*(2), pp. 15–24.

Burton, Steven J. Judge Posner's Jurisprudence of Skepticism. *Mich. Law Rev.*, December 1988, *87*(3), pp. 710–23.

Busche, Kelly and Hall, Christopher D. An Exception to the Risk Preference Anomaly. *J. Bus.*, July 1988, *61*(3), pp. 337–46.

Bush, Paul D. The Theory of Institutional Change. In *Tool, M. R., ed., Vol. 1,* 1988, *1987*, pp. 125–66.

Busse Von Colbe, Walther. Foreign Currency Translation. In *Gray, S. J. and Coenenberg, A. G., eds.,* 1988, pp. 223–43.

Bussmann, W. V. The Trade Deficit in Autos with Japan: How Much Improvement? *Bus. Econ.*, April 1988, *23*(2), pp. 20–25.

Bustamante, Blanca; Coloma, Fernando and Williamson, Carlos. El precio social de la mano de obra. (With English summary.) *Cuadernos Econ.*, April 1988, *25*(74), pp. 81–124.

Busterna, John C. Concentration and the Industrial Organization Model. In *Picard, R. G., et al., eds.,* 1988, pp. 35–53.

Butcher, Paul and Erdos, Joseph. International Social Security Agreements: The U.S. Experience. *Soc. Sec. Bull.*, September 1988, *51*(9), pp. 4–12.

Butenko, A. P. On the Nature of Property under the Conditions of Real Socialism. *Prob. Econ.*, December 1988, *31*(8), pp. 25–42.

Butler, Alison and Ellis, Christopher J. Ranking Alternative Share Contracts under Rational Expectations. *Europ. Econ. Rev.*, July 1988, *32*(6), pp. 1243–59.

Butler, Chris. Avoidance, Evasion or Illusion. *Australian Tax Forum,* 1988, *5*(2), pp. 257–64.

Butler, David. British Social Trends since 1900: Electors and Elected. In *Halsey, A. H., ed.,* 1988, pp. 297–321.

Butler, J. R. G. The Effect of Teaching on Public Hospital Costs: Evidence from Queensland. In *Butler, J. R. G. and Doessel, D. P., eds.,* 1988, pp. 38–75.

_____. The Geographic Distribution of Doctors: Does the Market Fail?: Commentary. In *Smith, C. S., ed.,* 1988, pp. 96–97.

_____. Management Information Systems in Public Hospitals: The Queen Victoria Medical Centre Experience: Discussion. In *Butler, J. R. G. and Doessel, D. P., eds.,* 1988, pp. 20–21.

_____. Specific Purpose Payments and the Commonwealth Grants Commission. In *Smith, C. S., ed.,* 1988, pp. 24–38.

_____ **and Doessel, D. P.** Alternative Schemes for Distributing Transfers to Natural Disaster Victims: Analysis and Implementation. *Econ. Rec.*, March 1988, *64*(184), pp. 47–54.

Butler, J. S.; Quddus, Munir and Liu, Jin-Tan. Variability of Inflation and the Dispersion of Relative Prices: Evidence from the Chinese Hyperinflation of 1946–1949. *Econ. Letters,* 1988, *27*(3), pp. 239–44.

Butler, JoAnn C. Local Zoning Ordinances Governing Home Occupations. In *Christensen, K. E., ed.,* 1988, pp. 189–200.

Butler, Richard J. Racial Wage Gaps: Comments. In *Mangum, G. and Philips, P., eds.,* 1988, pp. 175–79.

_____ **and Worrall, John D.** Experience Rating Matters. In *Borba, P. S. and Appel, D., eds.,* 1988, pp. 81–94.

_____ **and Worrall, John D.** Labor Market Theory and the Distribution of Workers' Compensation Losses. In *Borba, P. S. and Appel, D., eds.,* 1988, pp. 19–34.

Butler, Richard V. and Huston, John H. The Effects of Fortress Hubs on Airline Fares and Service: The Early Returns. *Logist. Transp. Rev.*, September 1988, *24*(3), pp. 203–15.

Butlin, M. W. and Boyce, P. M. Monetary Policy in Depression and Recovery. In *Gregory, R. G. and Butlin, N. G., eds.,* 1988, pp. 193–215.

Butrica, Andrew J. and Nier, Keith A. Telegraphy Becomes a World System: Paradox and Progress in Technology and Management. In *Perkins, E. J., ed.,* 1988, pp. 211–26.

Butsch, Jean-Louis. Les banques face à l'instabilité financière: Le rôle des Autorités de contrôle des établissements de crédit. (With English summary.) *Revue Écon. Polit.*, Sept.–Oct. 1988, *98*(5), pp. 731–45.

Butt, Abdul Rauf and Sheikh, Mohammad Amjad. An Analysis of Gap between Demand for and Supply of Higher Education in Pakistan. *Pakistan Econ. Soc. Rev.*, Summer 1988, *26*(1), pp. 41–55.

Butt, Jane L. Frequency Judgments in an Auditing-Related Task. *J. Acc. Res.*, Autumn 1988, *26*(2), pp. 315–30.

Butt, John and Chapman, Stanley D. Studies in Capital Formation in the United Kingdom, 1750–1920: The Cotton Industry, 1775–1856. In *Feinstein, C. H. and Pollard, S., eds.,* 1988, pp. 105–25.

Butt, Mohammed Sabihuddin and Jamal, Haroon. A Monetarist Approach to Inflation for Pakistan. *Pakistan Econ. Soc. Rev.*, Winter 1988, *26*(2), pp. 69–88.

Buttel, Frederick H. and Kenney, Martin. Prospects and Strategies for Overcoming Dependence. In *Research and Info. System for the Non-aligned and Other Developing Countries.,* 1988, pp. 315–48.

_____ **and Vandergeest, Peter.** Marx, Weber, and Development Sociology: Beyond the Impasse. *World Devel.*, June 1988, *16*(6), pp. 683–95.

den Butter, F. A. G. The DNB Econometric Model of the Netherlands Economy (Morkmon) In *Driehuis, W.; Fase, M. M. G. and den Hartog, H., eds.,* 1988, pp. 405–31.

Butterfield, D. W. and Kubursi, Atif A. Banker's

Preferences and Monetary Control. *Écon. Appl.*, 1988, *41*(1), pp. 109–27.

Büttner, Ulrich, et al. Expertensysteme zur Jahresabschlussanalyse für mittlere und kleine Unternehmen. (With English summary.) *Z. Betriebswirtschaft*, February 1988, *58*(2), pp. 229–51.

Buvinić, Mayra; Leslie, Joanne and Lycette, Margaret A. Weathering Economic Crises: The Crucial Role of Women in Health. In *Bell, D. E. and Reich, M. R., eds.*, 1988, pp. 307–48.

_____ **and Lycette, Margaret A.** Women, Poverty, and Development in the Third World. In *Lewis, J. P., et al.*, 1988, pp. 149–62.

Buzdalov, I. Cooperation and Democratic Reforms in the Economy. *Prob. Econ.*, August 1988, *31*(4), pp. 42–56.

Buzgalin, A. V. and Kolganov, A. I. Methods of State Management of the Economy. *Prob. Econ.*, April 1988, *30*(12), pp. 6–17.

Byatt, Ian C. R. World Tax Reform: A Progress Report: United Kingdom. In *Pechman, J. A., ed.*, 1988, pp. 219–36.

Bye, Barry V. Commentary: Disability Research. *Soc. Sec. Bull.*, May 1988, *51*(5), pp. 10, 54–55.

_____ **and Gallicchio, Salvatore J.** A Note on Sampling Variance Estimates for Social Security Program Participants: From the Survey of Income and Program Participation. *Soc. Sec. Bull.*, October 1988, *51*(10), pp. 4–21.

Byers, David. Data-FIT. *J. Econ. Surveys*, 1988, *2*(3), pp. 265–72.

Bygrave, William D. and Shulman, Joel M. Capital Gains Tax: Bane or Boon for Venture Capital? In *Kirchhoff, B. A., et al., eds.*, 1988, pp. 324–38.

_____, **et al.** Rates of Return of Venture Capital Investing: A Study of 131 Funds. In *Kirchhoff, B. A., et al., eds.*, 1988, pp. 275–89.

Bylinsky, Gene. What's Sexier and Speedier Than Silicon? In *Forester, T., ed.*, 1988, *1985*, pp. 193–202.

Byrd, William A. The Impact of the Two-Tier Plan/Market System in Chinese Industry. In *Reynolds, B. L., ed.*, 1988, *1987*, pp. 5–18.

Byres, Terry and Crow, Ben. New Technology and New Masters for the Indian Countryside. In *Crow, B. and Thorpe, M., et al.*, 1988, pp. 163–81.

Byrne, Daniel J. and Newhouse, Joseph P. Did Medicare's Prospective Payment System Cause Length of Stay to Fall? *J. Health Econ.*, December 1988, *7*(4), pp. 413–16.

Byrne, John and Rich, Daniel. Planning for Changing Energy Conditions: Introduction. In *Byrne, J. and Rich, D., eds.*, 1988, pp. 1–8.

Byron, Neil and Waugh, Geoffrey. Forestry and Fisheries in the Asian–Pacific Region: Issues in Natural Resource Management. *Asian-Pacific Econ. Lit.*, March 1988, *2*(1), pp. 46–80.

Caballero, M. A. G. Income Tax Reform: Assessment of the Income Tax on Employees for the Tax Period 1988 and Other Relevant Measures:

Costa Rica. *Bull. Int. Fiscal Doc.*, December 1988, *42*(12), pp. 532–33.

Cabestan, Jean-Pierre. The Modernization of Élites: The Evolution of Leadership Recruitment in the Central State Administration of the People's Republic of China from 1965 to 1985. In *Feuchtwang, S.; Hussain, A. and Pairault, T., eds., Vol. 2*, 1988, pp. 67–92.

Cable, John R. Is Profit-Sharing Participation? Evidence on Alternative Firm Types from West Germany. *Int. J. Ind. Organ.*, March 1988, *6*(1), pp. 121–37.

_____. A Model and Measure of Employee Participation: Guttman Scale Tests of the Espinosa–Zimbalist Hypothesis. In *Jones, D. C. and Svejnar, J., eds.*, 1988, pp. 313–26.

Cabral, Luis M. B. Asymmetric Equilibria in Symmetric Games with Many Players. *Econ. Letters*, 1988, *27*(3), pp. 205–08.

Cabrera, Alberto F. and Stampen, Jacob O. The Targeting and Packaging of Student Aid and Its Effect on Attrition. *Econ. Educ. Rev.*, 1988, *7*(1), pp. 29–46.

Cachon, Jean-Charles. Venture Creators and Firm Buyers: A Comparison of Attitudes towards Government Help and Locus of Control. In *Kirchhoff, B. A., et al., eds.*, 1988, pp. 568–79.

Cadsby, Charles Bram. Investment Performance of Canadian Real Estate Stocks using Sharpe's Performance Index: A Comment. *Managerial Dec. Econ.*, March 1988, *9*(1), pp. 75–76.

Cagan, Phillip. Financial Deregulation, Monetary Policy, and Central Banking: Commentary. In *Haraf, W. S. and Kushmeider, R. M., eds.*, 1988, pp. 254–60.

Cahuc, Pierre. Équilibres non walrasiens et négociations salariales. (Wage Bargaining with Non Walrasian Equilibria. With English summary.) *Revue Écon.*, July 1988, *39*(4), pp. 705–24.

_____. Incitations, prise de parole et négociations salariales. (Exit, Voice and Wage Bargaining. With English summary.) *Écon. Appl.*, 1988, *41*(3), pp. 571–93.

_____ **and Laurent, Thierry.** Emploi et négociations salariales en concurrence monopolistique: théorie et estimation. (Bargaining under Monopolistic Competition: Theory and Evidence. With English summary.) *Écon. Appl.*, 1988, *41*(3), pp. 543–69.

Caiden, Naomi. The Executive Budget—An Idea Whose Time Has Passed: Comments. *Public Budg. Finance*, Spring 1988, *8*(1), pp. 95–99.

_____. From the Summit: The President's Budget for 1989. *Public Budg. Finance*, Summer 1988, *8*(2), pp. 3–20.

_____. Shaping Things to Come: Super-Budgeters as Heroes (and Heroines) in the Late-Twentieth Century. In *Rubin, I. S., ed.*, 1988, pp. 43–58.

Caillaud, B., et al. Government Intervention in Production and Incentives Theory: A Review of Recent Contributions. *Rand J. Econ.*, Spring 1988, *19*(1), pp. 1–26.

Cain, Louis P. A Brief History of an Acquisition that Failed: The Kent Manufacturing Corporation. In *Hausman, W. J., ed.*, 1988, pp. 179–88.

Cain, Mead and McNicoll, Geoffrey. Population Growth and Agrarian Outcomes. In *Lee, R. D., et al., eds.*, 1988, pp. 101–17.

Cainarca, Gian Carlo; Colombo, Massimo G. and Mariotti, Sergio. La dinamica diffusiva dell'automazione flessibile. (The Diffusion Pattern of Flexible Automation. With English summary.) *Econ. Lavoro*, Jan.–Mar. 1988, *22*(1), pp. 41–63.

Caire, Guy. Le F.M.I. et la B.I.R.D. tels qu'ils se voient et tels qu'ils se donnent à voir. (I.R.D.B. and I.M.F.: How They See Them and How They Like to Be Seen. With English summary.) *Écon. Appl.*, 1988, *41*(4), pp. 775–819.

Cairncross, Alec. The Bank of England: Relationships with the Government, the Civil Service, and Parliament. In *Toniolo, G., ed.*, 1988, pp. 39–72.

———. The Development of Economic Statistics as an Influence on Theory and Policy. In *[Clark, C.]*, 1988, pp. 11–20.

Cairnes, J. E. New Theories in Political Economy. In *Wood, J. C., ed., Vol. 2*, 1988, *1872*, pp. 11–16.

Cairns, J. A. and Harris, A. H. Firm Location and Differential Barriers to Entry in the Offshore Oil Supply Industry. *Reg. Stud.*, December 1988, *22*(6), pp. 499–506.

Cairns, Robert D. and Anderson, F. J. The Softwood Lumber Agreement and Resource Politics. *Can. Public Policy*, June 1988, *14*(2), pp. 186–96.

——— and **Mahabir, Dhanayshar.** Contestability: A Revisionist View. *Economica*, May 1988, *55*(218), pp. 269–76.

Cakici, Nusret; Eytan, T. Hanan and Harpaz, Giora. American vs. European Options on the Value Line Index. *J. Futures Markets*, June 1988, *8*(3), pp. 373–88.

Caks, John and Pari, Robert. A Note on Bond Defeasance. *Financial Rev.*, May 1988, *23*(2), pp. 233–36.

Calabrese, Michael R. and Griffin, Joseph P. Coping with Extraterritoriality Disputes. *J. World Trade*, June 1988, *22*(3), pp. 5–25.

Calderwood, Shirley C. and Bradbury, Michael E. Equity Accounting for Reciprocal Stockholdings. *Accounting Rev.*, April 1988, *63*(2), pp. 330–47.

Caldwell, Bruce J. The Case for Pluralism. In *de Marchi, N., ed.*, 1988, pp. 231–44.

———. Hayek's "The Trend of Economic Thinking." In *Rothbard, M. N. and Block, W., eds.*, 1988, pp. 175–78.

———. Hayek's Transformation. *Hist. Polit. Econ.*, Winter 1988, *20*(4), pp. 513–41.

Caldwell, Philip. U.S. Competitiveness in a Global Environment. In *Feldstein, M., ed. (II)*, 1988, pp. 358–62.

Calegar, Geraldo M. and Schuh, G. Edward. Effects of Brazilian Wheat Subsidies on Income Distribution and Trade. In *Pinstrup-Andersen, P., ed.*, 1988, pp. 267–76.

Calem, Paul S. Entry and Entry Deterrence in Penetrable Markets. *Economica*, May 1988, *55*(218), pp. 171–83.

Calfee, John E. and Winston, Clifford. Economic Aspects of Liability Rules and Liability Insurance. In *Litan, R. E. and Winston, C., eds.*, 1988, pp. 16–41.

Calhoun, Charles A. and Espenshade, Thomas J. Childbearing and Wives' Foregone Earnings. *Population Stud.*, March 1988, *42*(1), pp. 5–37.

Calhoun, Craig. The "Retardation" of French Economic Development and Social Radicalism during the Second Republic: New Lessons from the Old Comparison with Britain. In *Burke, E., III, ed.*, 1988, pp. 40–72.

Calitz, E. Public Expenditure in South Africa: An Assessment of Trends and the Process of Determining Priorities. *J. Stud. Econ. Econometrics*, July 1988, *12*(2), pp. 25–35.

——— and **Döckel, J. A.** Die bestaansreg van buitebegrotingsfondse. (With English summary.) *J. Stud. Econ. Econometrics*, November 1988, *12*(3), pp. 31–39.

Calkins, Stephen. Equilibrating Tendencies in the Antitrust System, with Special Attention to Summary Judgment and to Motions to Dismiss. In *White, L. J., ed.*, 1988, pp. 185–239.

Callaghan, Bill. Keynes and the TUC in the 1930s and the 1980s. In *Eltis, W. and Sinclair, P. J. N., eds.*, 1988, pp. 340–53.

Callaghy, Thomas M. and Wilson, Ernest J., III. Africa: Policy, Reality or Ritual? In *Vernon, R., ed.*, 1988, pp. 179–230.

Callan, Scott J. Productivity, Scale Economies and Technical Change: Reconsidered. *Southern Econ. J.*, January 1988, *54*(3), pp. 715–24.

Callari, Antonio. Some Developments in Marxian Theory since Schumpeter. In *Thweatt, W. O., ed.*, 1988, pp. 227–58.

Callen, Jeffrey L. Management Bonus Plans in a Multiple-Agent Environment. *Managerial Dec. Econ.*, June 1988, *9*(2), pp. 127–31.

Calleo, David P.; Cleveland, Harold van B. and Silk, Leonard. The Dollar and the Defense of the West. *Foreign Aff.*, Spring 1988, *66*(4), pp. 846–62.

Callesen, Per. Budgetdepartementets anvendelse og udbygning af ADAM. (The Danish Macroeconomic Model as Applied to the Work in the Ministry of Finance. With English summary.) *Nationaløkon. Tidsskr.*, 1988, *126*(2), pp. 229–43.

Calliari, Sergio and Sartore, Domenico. La validità empirica della teoria neoclassica della domanda: Una verifica con i dati italiani 1960–1983. (An Empirical Assessment of the Neoclassical Theory of Demand: The Italian Case 1960–1983. With English summary.) *Rivista Int. Sci. Econ. Com.*, April–May 1988, *35*(4–5), pp. 313–44.

Calmfors, Lars and Hoel, Michael. Work Sharing and Overtime. *Scand. J. Econ.*, 1988, *90*(1), pp. 45–62.

Calomiris, Charles W. The Depreciation of the

Continental: A Reply. *J. Econ. Hist.*, September 1988, *48*(3), pp. 693–98.

_____. Institutional Failure, Monetary Scarcity, and the Depreciation of the Continental. *J. Econ. Hist.*, March 1988, *48*(1), pp. 47–68.

_____. Price and Exchange Rate Determination during the Greenback Suspension. *Oxford Econ. Pap.*, December 1988, *40*(4), pp. 719–50.

Calvo, Guillermo A. Costly Trade Liberalizations: Durable Goods and Capital Mobility. *Int. Monet. Fund Staff Pap.*, September 1988, *35*(3), pp. 461–73.

_____. Fiscal Policy, Trade Intervention, and World Interest Rates: Comment. In *Frenkel, J. A., ed.*, 1988, pp. 300–303.

_____. Servicing the Public Debt: The Role of Expectations. *Amer. Econ. Rev.*, September 1988, *78*(4), pp. 647–61.

_____ **and Obstfeld, Maurice.** Optimal Time-Consistent Fiscal Policy with Finite Lifetimes: Analysis and Extensions. In *Helpman, E.; Razin, A. and Sadka, E., eds.*, 1988, pp. 163–98.

_____ **and Obstfeld, Maurice.** Optimal Time-Consistent Fiscal Policy with Finite Lifetimes. *Econometrica*, March 1988, *56*(2), pp. 411–32.

Calvo, José Luis. Rendimientos del capital humano en educación en España. (With English summary.) *Invest. Econ.*, September 1988, *12*(3), pp. 473–82.

Calzolari, Giorgio and Panattoni, Lorenzo. Alternative Estimators of FIML Covariance Matrix: A Monte Carlo Study. *Econometrica*, May 1988, *56*(3), pp. 701–14.

_____ **and Panattoni, Lorenzo.** Finite Sample Performance of the Robust Wald Test in Simultaneous Equation Systems. In *Rhodes, G. F., Jr. and Fomby, T. B., eds.*, 1988, pp. 163–91.

Camacho, Antonio and Persky, Joseph J. The Internal Organization of Complex Teams: Bounded Rationality and the Logic of Hierarchies. *J. Econ. Behav. Organ.*, June 1988, *9*(4), pp. 367–80.

Camagni, Roberto. Functional Integration and Locational Shifts in New Technology Industry. In *Aydalot, P. and Keeble, D., eds.*, 1988, pp. 48–64.

Camdessus, Michel. The IMF: Facing New Challenges. *Finance Develop.*, June 1988, *25*(2), pp. 2–5.

Camerer, Colin. Gifts as Economic Signals and Social Symbols. In *Winship, C. and Rosen, S., eds.*, 1988, pp. 180–214.

_____ **and Fahey, Liam.** The Regression Paradigm: A Critical Appraisal and Suggested Directions. In *Grant, J. H., ed.*, 1988, pp. 443–59.

_____ **and Weigelt, Keith.** Experimental Tests of a Sequential Equilibrium Reputation Model. *Econometrica*, January 1988, *56*(1), pp. 1–36.

Cameron, A. C., et al. A Microeconometric Model of the Demand for Health Care and Health Insurance in Australia. *Rev. Econ. Stud.*, January 1988, *55*(1), pp. 85–106.

Cameron, Dan. The When, Why and How of Discipline. In *Timpe, A. D., ed.*, 1988, *1984*, pp. 334–40.

Cameron, David R. Distributional Coalitions and Other Sources of Economic Stagnation: On Olson's *Rise and Decline of Nations*. *Int. Organ.*, Autumn 1988, *42*(4), pp. 561–603.

Cameron, Gordon C. and Begg, Iain G. High Technology Location and the Urban Areas of Great Britain. *Urban Stud.*, October 1988, *25*(5), pp. 361–79.

Cameron, Samuel. The Economics of Crime Deterrence: A Survey of Theory and Evidence. *Kyklos*, 1988, *41*(2), pp. 301–23.

_____. The Impact of Video Recorders on Cinema Attendance. *J. Cult. Econ.*, June 1988, *12*(1), pp. 73–80.

_____. Strike Frequency and Legislative Change: Some U.K. Evidence. *Atlantic Econ. J.*, September 1988, *16*(3), pp. 89.

Cameron, Trudy Ann. A New Pardigm for Valuing Non-market Goods Using Referendum Data: Maximum Likelihood Estimation by Censored Logistic Regression. *J. Environ. Econ. Manage.*, September 1988, *15*(3), pp. 355–79.

Campano, Fred and Salvatore, Dominick. Economic Development, Income Inequality and Kuznets' *U*-shaped Hypothesis. *J. Policy Modeling*, Summer 1988, *10*(2), pp. 265–80.

Campbell, B. J. and Campbell, Frances A. Injury Reduction and Belt Use Associated with Occupant Restraint Laws. In *Graham, J. D., ed.*, 1988, pp. 24–50.

Campbell, Burnham O. and DeRosa, Dean A. Increasing Protectionism and Its Implications for ASEAN–U.S. Economic Relations. In *Tan, L.-H. and Akrasanee, N., eds.*, 1988, pp. 24–63.

Campbell, Donald E. A Characterization of Simple Majority Rule for Restricted Domains. *Econ. Letters*, 1988, *28*(4), pp. 307–10.

_____. A Generalization of the Second Theorem of Welfare Economics for Nonconvex Economies. *Int. Econ. Rev.*, May 1988, *29*(2), pp. 201–15.

_____. Redistribution of Wealth When Knowledge is Dispersed. *Soc. Choice Welfare*, November 1988, *5*(4), pp. 281–86.

_____ **and Truchon, Michel.** Boundary Optima and the Theory of Public Goods Supply. *J. Public Econ.*, March 1988, *35*(2), pp. 241–49.

Campbell, Donald T. Approximations to Knowledge. In *Campbell, D. T.*, 1988, pp. 62–93.

_____. Can We Be Scientific in Applied Social Science? In *Campbell, D. T.*, 1988, *1984*, pp. 315–33.

_____. Definitional versus Multiple Operationism. In *Campbell, D. T.*, 1988, pp. 31–36.

_____. "Degrees of Freedom" and the Case Study. In *Campbell, D. T.*, 1988, *1975*, pp. 377–88.

_____. Evolutionary Epistemology. In *Campbell, D. T.*, 1988, *1974*, pp. 393–434.

_____. The Experimenting Society. In *Campbell, D. T.*, 1988, pp. 290–314.

_____. Factors Relevant to the Validity of Experiments in Social Settings. In *Campbell, D. T.,* 1988, *1957,* pp. 151–66.

_____. Prospective: Artifact and Control. In *Campbell, D. T.,* 1988, *1969,* pp. 167–90.

_____. Qualitative Knowing in Action Research. In *Campbell, D. T.,* 1988, *1978,* pp. 360–76.

_____. Reforms as Experiments. In *Campbell, D. T.,* 1988, *1969,* pp. 261–89.

_____. Science's Social System of Validity-Enchancing Collective Belief Change and the Problems of the Social Sciences. In *Campbell, D. T.,* 1988, *1986,* pp. 504–23.

_____ **and Ross, H. Laurence.** The Connecticut Crackdown on Speeding: Time-Series Data in Quasi-experimental Analysis. In *Campbell, D. T.,* 1988, *1968,* pp. 222–37.

_____, **et al.** Quasi-experimental Designs. In *Campbell, D. T.,* 1988, *1974,* pp. 191–221.

Campbell, Duncan C.; Slowinski, Betty J. and Northrup, Herbert R. Multinational Union–Management Consultation in Europe: Resurgence in the 1980s? *Int. Lab. Rev.,* 1988, *127*(5), pp. 525–43.

Campbell, Frances A. and Campbell, B. J. Injury Reduction and Belt Use Associated with Occupant Restraint Laws. In *Graham, J. D., ed.,* 1988, pp. 24–50.

Campbell, Gwyn. Gold Mining and the French Takeover of Madagascar, 1883–1914. *African Econ. Hist.,* 1988, (17), pp. 95–126.

Campbell, John Y. and Bernanke, Ben S. Is There a Corporate Debt Crisis? *Brookings Pap. Econ. Act.,* 1988, (1), pp. 83–125.

_____ **and Clarida, Richard H.** Saving and Permanent Income in Canada and the United Kingdom. In *Helpman, E.; Razin, A. and Sadka, E., eds.,* 1988, pp. 122–41.

_____ **and Shiller, Robert J.** Interpreting Cointegrated Models. *J. Econ. Dynam. Control,* June–Sept. 1988, *12*(2–3), pp. 505–22.

_____ **and Shiller, Robert J.** Stock Prices, Earnings, and Expected Dividends. *J. Finance,* July 1988, *43*(3), pp. 661–76.

Campbell, Les. International Aspects of Accounting for Goodwill and Mergers. In *Gray, S. J. and Coenenberg, A. G., eds.,* 1988, pp. 191–222.

Campbell, Randolph B. Slave Hiring in Texas: Research Note. *Amer. Hist. Rev.,* February 1988, *93*(1), pp. 107–14.

Campbell, Robert L. The SEMTA Experience with Computer-Aided Scheduling. In *Daduna, J. R. and Wren, A., eds.,* 1988, pp. 279–87.

_____. The Soviet Economic Model. In *Bialer, S. and Mandelbaum, M., eds.,* 1988, pp. 65–95.

Campbell, Steven K. and Tilley, Daniel S. Performance of the Weekly Gulf –Kansas City Hard-Red Winter Wheat Basis. *Amer. J. Agr. Econ.,* November 1988, *70*(4), pp. 929–35.

Campbell, Terry L., et al. Job Satisfaction of Academic Accountants in Southern Business Administration Association Schools. In *Schwartz, B. N., ed.,* 1988, pp. 175–90.

Campbell, Thomas J. Commentary on the Data Base of the Georgetown Study. In *White, L. J., ed.,* 1988, pp. 82–86.

Campen, James T. and Mayhew, Anne. The National Banking System and Southern Economic Growth: Evidence from One Southern City, 1870–1900. *J. Econ. Hist.,* March 1988, *48*(1), pp. 127–37.

Campisi, Domenico and La Bella, Agostino. Evaluating the Economic Impact of Transportation Investment: An Input–Output Approach. In *Bianco, L. and La Bella, A., eds.,* 1988, pp. 443–62.

_____ **and La Bella, Agostino.** Transportation Investment and Dynamic Equilibrium in a Multiregional Input–Output System. In *Iri, M. and Yajima, K., eds.,* 1988, pp. 416–25.

_____ **and La Bella, Agostino.** Transportation Supply and Economic Growth in a Multiregional System. *Environ. Planning A,* July 1988, *20*(7), pp. 925–36,

Campos e Cunha, Luís. Transport Costs, Trade and Comparative Advantage. *Economia (Portugal),* May 1988, *12*(2), pp. 143–59.

Canarella, Giorgio and Pollard, Stephen K. Efficiency in Foreign Exchange Markets: A Vector Autoregression Approach. *J. Int. Money Finance,* September 1988, *7*(3), pp. 331–46.

Canavese, Alfredo J. and Di Tella, Guido. Inflation Stabilization or Hyperinflation Avoidance? The Case of the Austral Plan in Argentina: 1985–87. In *Bruno, M., et al., eds.,* 1988, pp. 153–90.

Candussi, Dores A. and Winter, James P. Monopoly and Content in Winnipeg. In *Picard, R. G., et al., eds.,* 1988, pp. 139–45.

Caniglia, Alan S. The Economic Evaluation of Food Stamps: An Intertemporal Analysis with Nonlinear Budget Constraints. *Public Finance Quart.,* January 1988, *16*(1), pp. 3–29.

Canner, Glenn B.; Fergus, James T. and Luckett, Charles A. Home Equity Lines of Credit. *Fed. Res. Bull.,* June 1988, *74*(6), pp. 361–73.

Canning, David J. Increasing Returns in Industry and the Role of Agriculture in Growth. *Oxford Econ. Pap.,* September 1988, *40*(3), pp. 463–76.

_____. Monetary Policy versus Wage Adjustment as a Response to Demand Shocks. *Econ. J.,* Supplement, 1988, *98*(390), pp. 75–82.

Cannings, Kathy. The Earnings of Female and Male Middle Managers: A Canadian Case Study. *J. Human Res.,* Winter 1988, *23*(1), pp. 34–56.

_____. Managerial Promotion: The Effects of Socialization, Specialization, and Gender. *Ind. Lab. Relat. Rev.,* October 1988, *42*(1), pp. 77–88.

Cansier, Dieter. Die amerikanischen Budgetdefizite und der Dolllarkurs. (The U.S. Budget Deficit and the Dollar Rate. With English summary.) *Kredit Kapital,* 1988, *21*(3), pp. 363–82.

Canto, Victor A. Exchange Rate Changes and the Stock Market: The Ps and Qs Meet the CATS. In *Canto, V. A. and Laffer, A. B., eds.,* 1988, pp. 143–64.

_____ and Laffer, Arthur B. Conclusions on Supply-Side Portfolio Strategies. In *Canto, V. A. and Laffer, A. B., eds.*, 1988, pp. 165–74.

_____ and Laffer, Arthur B. The Fat Cats Portfolio Strategy. In *Canto, V. A. and Laffer, A. B., eds.*, 1988, pp. 121–41.

_____ and Laffer, Arthur B. The State Competitive Environment: 1986–1987 Update. In *Canto, V. A. and Laffer, A. B., eds.*, 1988, pp. 103–19.

_____, et al. Protectionism and the Stock Market: The Determinants and Consequences of Trade Restrictions on the U.S. Economy. In *Canto, V. A. and Laffer, A. B., eds.*, 1988, *1986*, pp. 77–101.

Cantor, Joel C.; Monheit, Alan C. and Short, Pamela Farley. The Dynamics of Medicaid Enrollment. *Inquiry*, Winter 1988, *25*(4), pp. 504–16.

Cantor, Paul. Nationalization and Economic Growth. *Rev. Radical Polit. Econ.*, Winter 1988, *20*(4), pp. 81–84.

Cantor, Richard M. Work Effort and Contract Length. *Economica*, August 1988, *55*(219), pp. 343–53.

_____ and Driskill, Robert. Open-Economy Macro Policies and the Micro Foundation of Labor Market Arrangements. *J. Int. Econ.*, February 1988, *24*(1–2), pp. 159–72.

_____ and Mark, Nelson C. The International Transmission of Real Business Cycles. *Int. Econ. Rev.*, August 1988, *29*(3), pp. 493–507.

Cantor, Robin and Hewlett, James. The Economics of Nuclear Power: Further Evidence on Learning, Economies of Scale, and Regulatory Effects. *Resources & Energy*, December 1988, *10*(4), pp. 315–35.

Cantus, H. Hollister. Timely Transfer of Technology to the Marketplace. In *Egan, J. J., et al.*, 1988, pp. 301–08.

Cantwell, John. The Reorganization of European Industries after Integration: Selected Evidence on the Role of Multinational Enterprise Activities. In *Dunning, J. and Robson, P., eds.*, 1988, pp. 25–49.

Canziani, Arnaldo. Italy and the Seventh Directive. In *Gray, S. J. and Coenenberg, A. G., eds.*, 1988, pp. 105–16.

Canzoneri, Matthew B. and Henderson, Dale W. Is Sovereign Policymaking Bad? *Carnegie–Rochester Conf. Ser. Public Policy*, Spring 1988, *28*, pp. 93–140.

_____ and Henderson, Dale W. Time Consistency and Trigger Mechanisms in Open-Economy Monetary Policy Games. In *Borner, S., ed.*, 1988, pp. 338–55.

_____ and Minford, Patrick. When International Policy Coordination Matters: An Empirical Analysis. *Appl. Econ.*, September 1988, *20*(9), pp. 1137–54.

Cao, Shuzhen and Hua, Ying. Over Three Hundred People Apply for Jobs with the Hilton Hotel. *Chinese Econ. Stud.*, Summer 1988, *21*(4), pp. 26–28.

Capalbo, Susan M. Measuring the Components of Aggregate Productivity Growth in U.S. Agriculture. *Western J. Agr. Econ.*, July 1988, *13*(1), pp. 53–62.

Capdevielle, Patricia. International Differences in Employers' Compensation Costs. *Mon. Lab. Rev.*, May 1988, *111*(5), pp. 44–46.

Caplan, Arthur L. Is Medical Care the Right Prescription for Chronic Illness? In *Sullivan, S. and Lewin, M. E., eds.*, 1988, pp. 73–89.

Caplin, Andrew S. and Nalebuff, Barry J. On 64%–Majority Rule. *Econometrica*, July 1988, *56*(4), pp. 787–814.

Capotorti, F. The Law-Making Process in the European Communities. In *Pizzorusso, A., ed.*, 1988, pp. 275–305.

Cappelli, Peter and Sherer, Peter D. Satisfaction, Market Wages, and Labor Relations: An Airline Study. *Ind. Relat.*, Winter 1988, *27*(1), pp. 57–73.

_____ and Sterling, W. P. Union Bargaining Decisions and Contract Ratifications: The 1982 and 1984 Auto Agreements. *Ind. Lab. Relat. Rev.*, January 1988, *41*(2), pp. 195–209.

Capps, Oral, Jr. and Cheng, Hsiang-tai. Demand Analysis of Fresh and Frozen Finfish and Shellfish in the United States. *Amer. J. Agr. Econ.*, August 1988, *70*(3), pp. 533–42.

_____; Fuller, Stephen W. and Nichols, John P. Assessing Opportunities in Food and Fiber Processing and Distribution. *Amer. J. Agr. Econ.*, May 1988, *70*(2), pp. 462–68.

Capron, Henri and Kruseman, Jean-Louis. Is Political Rivalry an Incentive to Vote? *Public Choice*, January 1988, *56*(1), pp. 31–43.

Caravale, Giovanni. The Notion of Natural Wage and Its Rôle in Classical Economics. *Rivista Int. Sci. Econ. Com.*, July 1988, *35*(7), pp. 599–624.

Carbajo, Jose C. The Economics of Travel Passes. *J. Transp. Econ. Policy*, May 1988, *22*(2), pp. 153–73.

Carbaugh, Robert and Wassink, Darwin. International Economic Sanctions and Economic Theory. *Rivista Int. Sci. Econ. Com.*, March 1988, *35*(3), pp. 217–25.

Card, David. Empirical Tests of Labor-Market Equilibrium: An Evaluation: A Comment. *Carnegie–Rochester Conf. Ser. Public Policy*, Spring 1988, *28*, pp. 259–67.

_____. Longitudinal Analysis of Strike Activity. *J. Lab. Econ.*, April 1988, *6*(2), pp. 147–76.

_____ and Sullivan, Daniel G. Measuring the Effect of Subsidized Training Programs on Movements in and out of Employment. *Econometrica*, May 1988, *56*(3), pp. 497–530.

Cardarelli, Aldo and del Giudice, Michele. World Tax Reform: A Progress Report: Italy. In *Pechman, J. A., ed.*, 1988, pp. 141–46.

Cardim de Carvalho, Fernando J. Keynes on Probability, Uncertainty, and Decision Making. *J. Post Keynesian Econ.*, Fall 1988, *11*(1), pp. 66–81.

Cardoso, Eliana A. Inflation Stabilization: Brazil: Comment. In *Bruno, M., et al., eds.*, 1988, pp. 287–94.

_____ and Dornbusch, Rudiger. Dívida brasileira: Réquiem para a política de *Muddling*

Through. (With English summary.) *Pesquisa Planejamento Econ.*, August 1988, *18*(2), pp. 211–38.

Cardoso, Fernando Henrique. The Brazilian Democratic Movement Party (PMDB) after the Cruzado Plan. In *Chacel, J. M.; Falk, P. S. and Fleischer, D. V., eds.*, 1988, pp. 107–09.

Caretti, P. and Cheli, E. Statute and Statutory Instrument in the Evolution of European Constitutional Systems. In *Pizzorusso, A., ed.*, 1988, pp. 131–55.

Carey, Max L. Occupational Tenure in 1987: Many Workers Have Remained in Their Fields. *Mon. Lab. Rev.*, October 1988, *111*(10), pp. 3–12.

Cargill, Thomas F. Competition and the Transition of Finance in Japan and the United States. *J. Compar. Econ.*, September 1988, *12*(3), pp. 380–400.

————. Glass–Steagall Is Still Needed. *Challenge*, Nov.–Dec. 1988, *31*(6), pp. 26–30.

———— **and Hutchison, Michael M.** The Response of the Bank of Japan to Macroeconomic and Financial Change. In *Cheng, H.-S., ed.*, 1988, pp. 227–46.

———— **and Morus, Steven A.** A Vector Autoregression Model of the Nevada Economy. *Fed. Res. Bank San Francisco Econ. Rev.*, Winter 1988, (1), pp. 21–32.

Cariou, Bruno. Décisions de stockage, risque et cot du capital. Essai de formalisation. (Inventory Decisions, Risk and Cost of Capital. With English summary.) *Revue Écon.*, March 1988, *39*(2), pp. 349–67.

Carle, Susan D. A Hazardous Mix: Discretion to Disclose and Incentives to Suppress under OSHA's Hazard Communication Standard. *Yale Law J.*, March 1988, *97*(4), pp. 581–601.

Carleton, Willard T. and Chambers, Donald R. A Generalized Approach to Duration. In *Chen, A. H., ed.*, 1988, pp. 163–81.

————; **McEnally, Richard W. and Chambers, Donald R.** Immunizing Default-free Bond Portfolios with a Duration Vector. *J. Finan. Quant. Anal.*, March 1988, *23*(1), pp. 89–104.

———— **and Vander Weide, James H.** Investor Growth Expectations: Analysts vs. History. *J. Portfol. Manage.*, Spring 1988, *14*(3), pp. 78–82.

Carli, Guido. International Financial Policies. In *Feldstein, M., ed. (I)*, 1988, pp. 136–47.

————. The Return to Convertibility of the European Currencies. *Giorn. Econ.*, Nov.–Dec. 1988, *47*(11–12), pp. 525–36.

Carliner, Geoffrey. The Impact of Firm Acquisitions on Labor: Comment. In *Auerbach, A. J., ed. (I)*, 1988, pp. 26–28.

Carlos, Ann M. Land Use, Supply, and Welfare Distortions Induced by Inefficient Freight Rates. *Can. J. Econ.*, November 1988, *21*(4), pp. 835–45.

———— **and Hoffman, Elizabeth.** Game Theory and the North American Fur Trade: A Reply. *J. Econ. Hist.*, September 1988, *48*(3), pp. 681.

———— **and Nicholas, Stephen.** "Giants of an Earlier Capitalism": The Chartered Trading Com-

panies as Modern Multinationals. *Bus. Hist. Rev.*, Autumn 1988, *62*(3), pp. 398–419.

Carlotti, Paolo. Parabole, paradossi e interpretazioni alternative dell'approccio di analisi in termini di flusso. (Parables, Paradoxes and Alternative Interpretations for an Approach to Flow Analyses. With English summary.) *Econ. Lavoro*, Oct.–Dec. 1988, *22*(4), pp. 71–92.

Carlson, Benny. Lindahl, Dynamics and Death. *Scand. Econ. Hist. Rev.*, 1988, *36*(1), pp. 76–86.

Carlson, Dean A. Sufficient Conditions for Optimality and Supported Trajectories for Optimal Control Problems Governed by Volterra Integral Equations. In *Eiselt, H. A. and Pederzoli, G., eds.*, 1988, pp. 274–82.

Carlson, George N.; Brashares, Edith and Speyrer, Janet Furman. Distributional Aspects of a Federal Value-Added Tax. *Nat. Tax J.*, June 1988, *41*(2), pp. 155–74.

Carlson, John E. The Soviet Union Today: The KGB. In *Cracraft, J., ed.*, 1988, pp. 77–86.

Carlson, Keith M. How Much Lower Can the Unemployment Rate Go? *Fed. Res. Bank St. Louis Rev.*, July–Aug. 1988, *70*(4), pp. 44–57.

Carlson, Leonard A. and Swartz, Caroline. The Earnings of Women and Ethnic Minorities, 1959–1979. *Ind. Lab. Relat. Rev.*, July 1988, *41*(4), pp. 530–46.

Carlson, Les and Grossbart, Sanford. Parental Style and Consumer Socialization of Children. *J. Cons. Res.*, June 1988, *15*(1), pp. 77–94.

———— **and Kangun, Norman.** Demographic Discontinuity: Another Explanation for Consumerism? *J. Cons. Aff.*, Summer 1988, *22*(1), pp. 55–73.

Carlsson, Bo. Public Industrial Enterprises in Norway: A Comparison with Sweden. *Ann. Pub. Co-op. Econ.*, April–June 1988, *59*(2), pp. 197–213.

————. Public Industrial Enterprises in Sweden: Searching for a Viable Structure. *Ann. Pub. Co-op. Econ.*, April–June 1988, *59*(2), pp. 175–95.

Carlsson, Jerker. The Brazilian Penetration of Nigeria through Trade: A Case Study of South–South Trade Relations, 1965–79. In *Carlsson, J. and Shaw, T. M., eds.*, 1988, pp. 184–203.

————. Brazilian Trade with West Africa and Angola within the Portuguese Colonial Empire, 1500–1850: The Dialectics of South–South Exchange. In *Carlsson, J. and Shaw, T. M., eds.*, 1988, pp. 151–83.

———— **and Shaw, Timothy M.** Newly Industrializing Countries and South–South: Concepts, Correlates, Controversies and Cases. In *Carlsson, J. and Shaw, T. M., eds.*, 1988, pp. 1–22.

Carman, Gary. President Hoover's Historical Image. In *Perkins, E. J., ed.*, 1988, pp. 157–65.

Carman, Hoy F. Agricultural and Rural Areas Approaching the Twenty-first Century: A Synthesis of Teaching Issues. In *Hildreth, R. J., et al., eds.*, 1988, pp. 526–36.

———— **and Innes, Robert.** Tax Reform and Beef

Cow Replacement Strategy. *Western J. Agr. Econ.*, December 1988, *13*(2), pp. 254–66.

Carmichael, H. Lorne. Incentives in Academics: Why Is There Tenure? *J. Polit. Econ.*, June 1988, *96*(3), pp. 453–72.

Carmone, F. J., Jr.; Schaffer, C. M. and Green, Paul E. An Individual Importance Weights Model for Conjoint Analysis. In *Gaul, W. and Schader, M., eds.*, 1988, pp. 250–57.

Carneiro, Dionisio Días. Brazil and the IMF: Logic and Story of a Stalemate. In *Griffith-Jones, S., ed.*, 1988, pp. 141–69.

_____. Brazil's External Debt Outlook, 1986–1990. In *Feinberg, R. E. and Ffrench-Davis, R., eds.*, 1988, pp. 183–205.

Carnes, Richard B. and Olsen, John G. Productivity Shows a Decline in Automotive Repair Shops. *Mon. Lab. Rev.*, March 1988, *111*(3), pp. 22–26.

Carnevale, John T. Recent Trends in the Finances of the State and Local Sector. *Public Budg. Finance,* Summer 1988, *8*(2), pp. 33–48.

_____ and **Huckins, Larry E.** Federal Grants-in-Aid: Theoretical Concerns, Design Issues, and Implementation Strategy. In *Bell, M. E., ed.*, 1988, pp. 41–62.

Carnevale, Peter J. D., et al. Modeling Mediator Behavior in Experimental Games. In *Tietz, R.; Albers, W. and Selten, R., eds.*, 1988, pp. 160–69.

Caro, Jean-Yves and Kopp, Pierre. Quelques repères sur les services publics de radio et télévision en Europe. (An International Comparison of the Public Services of Radio and Television in 17 European Countries. With English summary.) *Revue Écon.*, May 1988, *39*(3), pp. 573–86.

Caron, François. The Evolution of the Technical System of Railways in France from 1832 to 1937. In *Mayntz, R. and Hughes, T. P., eds.*, 1988, pp. 69–103.

Caron, John B. Entrepreneurs Go Where the Opportunity Is. In *Tavis, L. A., ed.*, 1988, pp. 321–23.

Carpenter, Edwin H.; Cory, Dennis C. and Colby, Bonnie G. Uncertain Recreation Quality and Wildlife Valuation: Are Conventional Benefit Measures Adequate? *Western J. Agr. Econ.*, December 1988, *13*(2), pp. 153–62.

Carpenter, Frances H. The Impact of Financial Reporting Requirements on Municipal Officials' Fixed Asset Acquisition Decisions. In *Chan, J. L. and Rowan, H. J., eds.*, 1988, pp. 49–77.

Carpenter, Gregory S., et al. Modeling Asymmetric Competition. *Marketing Sci.*, Fall 1988, *7*(4), pp. 393–412.

Carpenter, Susan L. and Kennedy, W. J. D. The Denver Metropolitan Water Roundtable: A Case Study in Researching Agreements. *Natural Res. J.*, Winter 1988, *28*(1), pp. 21–35.

Carpenter, W. W.; Postma, H. and Soderstrom, E. J. "Profiting" from Technology Transfer: A Novel Approach. In *Furino, A., ed.*, 1988, pp. 211–24.

Carr, Barry, et al. A North American Perspective on Decoupling. In *Miner, W. M. and Hathaway, D. E., eds.*, 1988, pp. 113–40.

Carr, Jack L. and Mathewson, G. Frank. Unlimited Liability as a Barrier to Entry. *J. Polit. Econ.*, August 1988, *96*(4), pp. 766–84.

Carr, Peter P. The Valuation of Sequential Exchange Opportunities. *J. Finance,* December 1988, *43*(5), pp. 1235–56.

Carraresi, Paolo, et al. BDS: A System for the Bus Drivers' Scheduling Problem Integrating Combinatorial Optimization and Logic Programming. In *Daduna, J. R. and Wren, A., eds.*, 1988, pp. 68–82.

Carraro, Kenneth C. Farm Policy and Mandatory Supply Controls—The Case of Tobacco. *Fed. Res. Bank St. Louis Rev.*, Jan.–Feb. 1988, *70*(1), pp. 55–64.

_____. The 1987 Agricultural Recovery: A District Perspective. *Fed. Res. Bank St. Louis Rev.*, March–April 1988, *70*(2), pp. 29–38.

_____ and **Coughlin, Cletus C.** The Dubious Success of Export Subsidies for Wheat. *Fed. Res. Bank St. Louis Rev.*, Nov.–Dec. 1988, *70*(6), pp. 38–47.

Carrera, Cármen and Richmond, James. Investment Decisions under Majority Rule. *Economica,* August 1988, *55*(219), pp. 365–78.

Carreras, Francesc and Owen, Guillermo. Evaluation of the Catalonian Parliament, 1980–1984. *Math. Soc. Sci.*, February 1988, *15*(1), pp. 87–92.

Carrère, Marie-Odile. L'analyse marginale: une aide à la décision pour les entrepreneurs individuels: Les médicins libéraux et le choix de la liberté des prix. (Margin Analysis: A Help to Decision Making for Professionals: Private Practitioners and Deregulated Prices. With English summary.) *Écon. Soc.*, August 1988, *22*(8), pp. 63–79.

Carrick, Paul M. New Evidence on Government Efficiency. *J. Policy Anal. Manage.*, Spring 1988, *7*(3), pp. 518–28.

Carriker, Roy R. State Water Management Policy. In *Johnston, G. M.; Freshwater, D. and Favero, P., eds.*, 1988, pp. 43–70.

Carrillo, Ethel R. Distribution of Health Care Facilities. In *Zschock, D. K., ed.*, 1988, pp. 101–32.

Carrillo Gamboa, Emilio. Globalization of Industry through Production Sharing. In *Muroyama, J. H. and Stever, H. G., eds.*, 1988, pp. 86–105.

Carrington, Paul D. The Scientific Study of Legal Institutions: Foreword. *Law Contemp. Probl.*, Summer 1988, *51*(3), pp. 1–11.

Carrington, Selwyn H. H. The United States and Canada: The Struggle for the British West Indian Trade. *Soc. Econ. Stud.*, March–June 1988, *37*(1–2), pp. 69–105.

Carroll, Barbara Wake. Market Concentration in a Geographically Segmented Market: Housebuilding in Ontario, 1978–1984. *Can. Public Policy,* September 1988, *14*(3), pp. 295–306.

Carroll, Carolyn and Wei, K. C. John. Risk, Return, and Equilibrium: An Extension. *J. Bus.*, October 1988, *61*(4), pp. 485–99.

Carroll, Glenn R.; Delacroix, Jacques and Goodstein, Jerry. The Political Environments of Organizations: An Ecological View. In *Staw, B. M. and Cummings, L. L., eds.*, 1988, pp. 359–92.

Carroll, J. D., et al. Multidimensional Scaling in Marketing Research: An Illustrative Application to a Telecommunications Pricing Problem. In *Gaul, W. and Schader, M., eds.*, 1988, pp. 225–39.

Carroll, Raymond J.; Wu, C. F. Jeff and Ruppert, David. The Effect of Estimating Weights in Weighted Least Squares. *J. Amer. Statist. Assoc.*, December 1988, *83*(404), pp. 1045–54.

Carrozza, P. Central Law and Peripheral Law. In *Pizzorusso, A., ed.*, 1988, pp. 238–74.

Carruth, Alan A. and Disney, Richard F. Where Have Two Million Trade Union Members Gone? *Economica*, February 1988, *55*(217), pp. 1–19.

_____ **and Oswald, Andrew J.** Testing for Multiple Natural Rates of Unemployment in the British Economy: A Preliminary Investigation. In *Cross, R., ed.*, 1988, pp. 232–55.

Carruthers, Norman and Artle, Roland. Location and Market Power: Hotelling Revisited. *J. Reg. Sci.*, February 1988, *28*(1), pp. 15–27.

Carsel, Robert F. and Parrish, Rudolph. Developing Joint Probability Distributions of Soil Water Retention Characteristics. *Water Resources Res.*, May 1988, *24*(5), pp. 755–69.

Carslaw, Charles A. P. N. Anomalies in Income Numbers: Evidence of Goal Oriented Behavior. *Accounting Rev.*, April 1988, *63*(2), pp. 321–27.

Carson, Richard T. and Navarro, Peter. A Seller's (and Buyer's) Guide to the Job Market for Beginning Academic Economists. *J. Econ. Perspectives*, Spring 1988, *2*(2), pp. 137–48.

_____ **and Navarro, Peter.** Fundamental Issues in Natural Resource Damage Assessment. *Natural Res. J.*, Fall 1988, *28*(4), pp. 815–36.

_____ **and Subramanian, Shankar.** Robust Regression in the Presence of Heteroscedasticity. In *Rhodes, G. F., Jr. and Fomby, T. B., eds.*, 1988, pp. 85–138.

Carstensen, Peter C. Explaining Tort Law: The Economic Theory of Landes and Posner. *Mich. Law Rev.*, May 1988, *86*(6), pp. 1161–84.

Cartelier, Jean. Keynes's *General Theory:* Foundations for a Heterodox Political Economy? In *Barrère, A., ed.*, 1988, pp. 128–49.

Carter, C. F. Expectation in Economics. In *Earl, P. E., ed., Vol. 1*, 1988, *1950*, pp. 229–42.

_____. A Revised Theory of Expectations. In *Earl, P. E., ed., Vol. 1*, 1988, *1953*, pp. 243–52.

Carter, Colin A. Trade Liberalization in the Grain Markets. *Can. J. Agr. Econ.*, Part 1, December 1988, *36*(4), pp. 633–41.

_____; **Abizadeh, Fay and Arthur, Louise M.** Arbitrage Pricing, Capital Asset Pricing, and Agricultural Assets. *Amer. J. Agr. Econ.*, May 1988, *70*(2), pp. 359–65.

_____; **Gallini, Nancy T. and Schmitz, Andrew.** Producer–Consumer Trade-offs in Export Cartels: The Wheat Cartel Case: Reply. *Amer. J. Agr. Econ.*, November 1988, *70*(4), pp. 946.

_____ **and Gardiner, Walter H.** Issues Associated with Elasticities in International Agricultural Trade. In *Carter, C. A. and Gardiner, W. H., eds.*, 1988, pp. 1–16.

Carter, Grace M.; Trude, Sally and Keeler, Emmett B. Insurance Aspects of DRG Outlier Payments. *J. Health Econ.*, September 1988, *7*(3), pp. 193–214.

Carter, Jimmy. Philosophical Perspectives: Peace, Prosperity, Liberty: Challenges Old and New. In *Anderson, A. and Bark, D. L., eds.*, 1988, pp. 545–54.

Carter, Michael R. Equilibrium Credit Rationing of Small Farm Agriculture. *J. Devel. Econ.*, February 1988, *28*(1), pp. 83–103.

Carter, Richard. Some Implications of Beliefs for the Public and Private Sectors. *Can. J. Econ.*, November 1988, *21*(4), pp. 775–84.

Carter, Robert A. Innovation in Urban Systems: The Interrelationships between Urban and National Economic Development. *Ann. Reg. Sci.*, November 1988, *22*(3), pp. 66–79.

Carter, Robert L. The NAACP's Legal Strategy against Segregated Education. *Mich. Law Rev.*, May 1988, *86*(6), pp. 1083–95.

Carter, Stephen L. When Victims Happen to Be Black. *Yale Law J.*, February 1988, *97*(3), pp. 420–47.

Carter, Susan B. The Changing Importance of Lifetime Jobs, 1892–1978. *Ind. Relat.*, Fall 1988, *27*(3), pp. 287–300.

Cartier-Bresson, Jean. L'industrialisation brésilienne et la gestion de la contrainte externe. (With English summary.) *Can. J. Devel. Stud.*, 1988, *9*(1), pp. 35–62.

Cartier, Michel and Bonnin, Michel. Urban Employment in Post-Maoist China. In *Feuchtwang, S.; Hussain, A. and Pairault, T., eds., Vol. 1*, 1988, pp. 198–226.

Cartier, William and Murillo, Gabriel. Urbanization, the Informal Sector and Migration: Issues for Research and Cooperation. *Can. J. Devel. Stud.*, 1988, *9*(1), pp. 7–17.

Cartledge, Paul A. Serfdom in Classical Greece. In *Archer, L. J., ed.*, 1988, pp. 33–41.

Cartosio, Bruno. Herbert Gutman in Italy: History and Politics. *Labor Hist.*, Summer 1988, *29*(3), pp. 356–62.

Cartwright, David W. and Smith, Scott D. Deflators for Purchases of Computers in GNP: Revised and Extended Estimates, 1983–88. *Surv. Curr. Bus.*, November 1988, *68*(11), pp. 22–23.

Cartwright, Phillip A.; Kespohl, Elke and DeLorme, Charles D., Jr. The Effect of Temporal Aggregation on the Test of Wagner's Law. *Public Finance*, 1988, *43*(3), pp. 373–87.

Caruso, Andrea. Satellite Communications Open New Opportunities to the Industrial Sector. In *Egan, J. J., et al.*, 1988, pp. 119–24.

Carvalho, Emanuel; Lusetti, Dino and Brox, James. Input Substitution in Canadian Manufacturing: An Application of the CES-Translog Production Function. *Atlantic Econ. J.*, June 1988, *16*(2), pp. 22–46.

de Carvalho, Fernando J. Cardim. Keynes, a instabilidade do capitalismo e a teoria dos ciclos econômicos. (With English summary.) *Pesquisa Planejamento Econ.*, December 1988, *18*(3), pp. 741–63.

Cas, Alexandra; Diewert, W. Erwin and Ostensoe, Lawrence A. Productivity Growth and Changes in the Terms of Trade in Canada. **In** *Feenstra, R. C., ed.*, 1988, pp. 279–94.

Casas, Francois R. and Han, Jae-Dong. Achieving Pareto Superiority under Free Trade: An Alternative to the Dixit–Norman Scheme. *Int. Econ. J.*, Winter 1988, *2*(4), pp. 1–7.

Case, Karl E. Observations on the Use of Textbooks in the Teaching of Principles of Economics: A Comment. *J. Econ. Educ.*, Spring 1988, *19*(2), pp. 165–68.

—— **and Shiller, Robert J.** The Behavior of Home Buyers in Boom and Post-boom Markets. *New Eng. Econ. Rev.*, Nov.–Dec. 1988, pp. 29–46.

Casetti, Emilio and Krakover, Shaul. Directionally Biased Metropolitan Growth: A Model and a Case Study. *Econ. Geogr.*, January 1988, *64*(1), pp. 17–28.

Casey, Bernard. The Extent and Nature of Temporary Employment in Britain. *Cambridge J. Econ.*, December 1988, *12*(4), pp. 487–509.

Caskie, Donald B. Security on Movable Property and Receivables in Europe: Supplement for Scotland. **In** *Dickson, M. G.; Rosener, W. and Storm, P. M., eds.*, 1988, pp. 206–08.

Caspar, M.-L. Employment-cum-Training Contracts in France: The 1975–85 Record. *Int. Lab. Rev.*, 1988, *127*(4), pp. 445–61.

Cassedy, Edward S. and Meier, Peter M. Planning for Electric Power in Developing Countries in the Face of Change. **In** *Byrne, J. and Rich, D., eds.*, 1988, pp. 53–100.

Cassen, R. H. Aid Evaluation—Its Scope and Limits. **In** *Jepma, C. J., ed.*, 1988, pp. 167–81.

Cassing, James H. The Ongoing Revolution in American Banking: Commentary. **In** *Cassing, J. H. and Husted, S. L., eds.*, 1988, pp. 93–96.

—— **and Husted, Steven L.** Capital, Technology, and Labor in the New Global Economy: Introduction. **In** *Cassing, J. H. and Husted, S. L., eds.*, 1988, pp. xvii–xxvii.

Casson, Mark. Contractual Arrangements for Technology Transfer: New Evidence from Business History. **In** *Earl, P. E., ed., Vol. 2*, 1988, *1986*, pp. 88–118.

——. Recent Trends in International Business: A New Analysis. **In** *Borner, S., ed.*, 1988, pp. 215–40.

—— **and Buckley, Peter J.** A Theory of Cooperation in International Business. **In** *Contractor, F. J. and Lorange, P.*, 1988, pp. 31–53.

—— **and Pearce, Robert D.** Intra-firm Trade and the Developing Countries. **In** *Greenaway, D., ed.*, 1988, pp. 132–56.

Cassone, Alberto and Tasgian, Astrig. Growth and Decline of a Metropolitan Area: The Case of Torino. *Ann. Reg. Sci.*, November 1988, *22*(3), pp. 34–47.

Castagnoli, Erio and Mazzoleni, Piera. From an Oriental Market to the European Monetary System: Some Fuzzy-Sets-Related Ideas. **In** *Kacprzyk, J. and Fedrizzi, M., eds.*, 1988, pp. 389–99.

Castanias, Rick; Chung, Ki-Young and Johnson, Herb. Dividend Spreads. *J. Bus.*, July 1988, *61*(3), pp. 299–319.

Castelino, Mark and Chatterjee, Sris. T-Bond Futures Prices: Cheapest to Deliver versus the Index. **In** *Fabozzi, F. J., ed.*, 1988, pp. 291–300.

Castells, Manuel and Tyson, Laura D'Andrea. High-Technology Choices Ahead: Restructuring Interdependence. **In** *Sewell, J. W. and Tucker, S. K., eds.*, 1988, pp. 55–95.

Castillo, Carlos Manuel. The Costa Rican Experience with the International Debt Crisis. **In** *Feinberg, R. E. and French-Davis, R., eds.*, 1988, pp. 210–31.

Castillo, Mario and Cortellese, Claudio. Small and Medium-Scale Industry in the Development of Latin America. *CEPAL Rev.*, April 1988, (34), pp. 127–51.

Castle, Emery N. and Hildreth, R. J. Agricultural Economics at a Crossroads: An Overview. **In** *Hildreth, R. J., et al., eds.*, 1988, pp. 3–13.

Castro, Alfonso Peter. Southern Mount Kenya and Colonial Forest Conflicts. **In** *Richards, J. F. and Tucker, R. P., eds.*, 1988, pp. 33–55.

de Castro, Newton. Estrutura e desempenho do setor de transporte rodoviário de carga. (With English summary.) *Pesquisa Planejamento Econ.*, April 1988, *18*(1), pp. 55–82.

—— **and Bernardino, Adriana Teixeira.** A escolha de conteinerizaçao na exportaçao de manufaturados. (With English summary.) *Pesquisa Planejamento Econ.*, December 1988, *18*(3), pp. 709–40.

Catalani, Mario S. and Brero, Andrea. Le ombre cinesi: Modelli stocastici per l'analisi dei comportamenti di impresa in ambiente di incertezza. (The Chinese Shadows: Stochastic Models for the Analysis of Firm Behavior under Uncertainty. With English summary.) *Rivista Int. Sci. Econ. Com.*, June 1988, *35*(6), pp. 539–62.

Catarci, Tiziana and Santucci, Giuseppe. GRASP: A Complete Graphical Conceptual Language for Definition and Manipulation of Statistical Databases. **In** *Edwards, D. and Raun, N. E., eds.*, 1988, pp. 401–06.

Catephores, George and Morishima, Michio. Anti-Say's Law versus Say's Law: A Change in Paradigm. **In** *Hanusch, H., ed.*, 1988, pp. 23–53.

—— **and Morishima, Michio.** Anti-Say's Law versus Say's Law: A Change in Paradigm: Reply. **In** *Hanusch, H., ed.*, 1988, pp. 68–70.

Cater, Erlet. The Development of Tourism in

the Least Developed Countries. In *Goodall, B. and Ashworth, G., eds.*, 1988, pp. 39–66.

Cathie, John and Herrmann, Roland. The Southern African Customs Union, Cereal Price Policy in South Africa, and Food Security in Botswana. *J. Devel. Stud.*, April 1988, *24*(3), pp. 394–414.

Catinat, Michel, et al. Investment Behaviour in Europe: A Comparative Analysis. *Rech. Écon. Louvain*, 1988, *54*(3), pp. 277–324.

Cattan, Peter. The Growing Presence of Hispanics in the U.S. Work Force. *Mon. Lab. Rev.*, August 1988, *111*(8), pp. 9–14.

Caudill, Steven B. An Advantage of the Linear Probability Model over Probit or Logit. *Oxford Bull. Econ. Statist.*, November 1988, *50*(4), pp. 425–27.

_____. The Necessity of Mining Data. *Atlantic Econ. J.*, September 1988, *16*(3), pp. 11–18.

Cauley, Jon and Im, Eric Iksoon. Intervention Policy Analysis of Skyjackings and Other Terrorist Incidents. *Amer. Econ. Rev.*, May 1988, *78*(2), pp. 27–31.

Cavallo, Domingo. Three Views on Restoring Growth: Comment. In *Bruno, M., et al., eds.*, 1988, pp. 395–99.

_____ **and Domenech, Roberto.** Las políticas macroeconómicas y el tipo de cambio real. Argentina, 1913–1984. (With English summary.) *Desarrollo Econ.*, Oct.–Dec. 1988, *28*(111), pp. 375–400.

Cavalluzzo, Paul J. J. Freedom of Association—Its Effect upon Collective Bargaining and Trade Unions. In *Carter, D. D., et al.*, 1988, pp. 267–300.

Cavanagh, Ralph. Responsible Power Marketing in an Increasingly Competitive Era. *Yale J. Regul.*, Summer 1988, *5*(2), pp. 331–66.

Caveny, Regina and Nissan, Edward. Regional Population Growth Rate Differences: Note. *Growth Change*, Winter 1988, *19*(1), pp. 67–74.

_____ **and Nissan, Edward.** Relative Concentration of Sales and Assets in American Business. *Southern Econ. J.*, April 1988, *54*(4), pp. 928–33.

_____ **and Nissan, Edward.** Relative Welfare Improvements of Low Income versus High Income Countries. *World Devel.*, May 1988, *16*(5), pp. 607–14.

Caves, Douglas W. and Christensen, Laurits R. The Importance of Economies of Scale, Capacity Utilization, and Density in Explaining Interindustry Differences in Productivity Growth. *Logist. Transp. Rev.*, March 1988, *24*(1), pp. 3–32.

Caves, Richard E. Effects of Mergers and Acquisitions on the Economy: An Industrial Organization Perspective. In *Browne, L. E. and Rosengren, E. S., eds.*, 1988, pp. 149–68.

_____. Trade Exposure and Changing Structures of U.S. Manufacturing Industries. In *Spence, A. M. and Hazard, H. A., eds.*, 1988, pp. 1–26.

_____ **and Bradburd, Ralph M.** The Empirical

Determinants of Vertical Integration. *J. Econ. Behav. Organ.*, April 1988, *9*(3), pp. 265–79.

_____ **and Hurwitz, Mark A.** Persuasion or Information? Promotion and the Shares of Brand Name and Generic Pharmaceuticals. *J. Law Econ.*, October 1988, *31*(2), pp. 299–320.

Cebenoyan, A. Sinan. Multiproduct Cost Functions and Scale Economies in Banking. *Financial Rev.*, November 1988, *23*(4), pp. 499–512.

Cebotarev, E. A. Women, Human Rights and the Family in Development Theory and Practice (with Reference to Latin America and the Caribbean). *Can. J. Devel. Stud.*, 1988, *9*(2), pp. 187–200.

Cebula, Richard J. Crowding Out, Deficits, and Interest Rates: Reply. *Public Choice*, July 1988, *58*(1), pp. 95–97.

_____. Federal Government Budget Deficits and Interest Rates: An Empirical Analysis for the United States, 1955–1984. *Public Finance*, 1988, *43*(3), pp. 337–48.

_____. Federal Government Budget Deficits and Interest Rates: A Brief Note. *Southern Econ. J.*, July 1988, *55*(1), pp. 206–10.

_____, **et al.** Federal Government Budget Deficits and Interest Rates in the United States: An Empirical Analysis. *Econ. Int.*, Feb.–March 1988, *41*(1–2), pp. 1–7.

_____, **et al.** Financial-Market Effects of Federal Government Budget Deficits. *Weltwirtsch. Arch.*, 1988, *124*(4), pp. 729–33.

Ceccatelli, Ercola. Risks and Opportunities for the Major Italian Banks in a Climate of Closely Integrated Financial Markets. *Rev. Econ. Cond. Italy*, Sept.–Dec. 1988, (3), pp. 411–24.

Cecchetti, Stephen G. The Case of the Negative Nominal Interest Rates: New Estimates of the Term Structure of Interest Rates during the Great Depression. *J. Polit. Econ.*, December 1988, *96*(6), pp. 1111–41.

_____ **and Ball, Laurence.** Imperfect Information and Staggered Price Setting. *Amer. Econ. Rev.*, December 1988, *78*(5), pp. 999–1018.

_____; **Cumby, Robert E. and Figlewski, Stephen.** Estimation of the Optimal Futures Hedge. *Rev. Econ. Statist.*, November 1988, *70*(4), pp. 623–30.

de Cecco, Marcello. The End of Large Public Debts: Discussion. In *Giavazzi, F. and Spaventa, L., eds.*, 1988, pp. 85–89.

Cecutti, Albert and Harris, Beverly. Quality of Working Life: The Challenge of Occupational Health and Safety. In *Richardson, P. R. and Gesing, R., eds.*, 1988, pp. 105–09.

Ceder, Avishai. Designing Transit Short-Turn Trips with the Elimination of Imbalanced Loads. In *Daduna, J. R. and Wren, A., eds.*, 1988, pp. 288–303.

_____; **Fjornes, Bjoern and Stern, Helman I.** OPTIBUS: A Scheduling Package. In *Daduna, J. R. and Wren, A., eds.*, 1988, pp. 212–25.

Ceglowski, Janet; Hickok, Susan and Bell, Linda A. The Competitiveness of U.S. Manufactured Goods: Recent Changes and Prospects. *Fed.*

Res. Bank New York Quart. Rev., Spring 1988, *13*(1), pp. 7–22.

Cekota, Jaromir. The Contemporary Relevance of Marx's Economics: Theory and Evidence. *Eastern Econ. J.*, Jan.–March 1988, *14*(1), pp. 73–80.

_____. Technological Change in Canada (1961–80): An Application of the Surrogate Wage Function. *Can. J. Econ.*, May 1988, *21*(2), pp. 348–58.

Cella, Guido. Errata [The Supply Side Approaches to Input–Output Analysis: An Assessment]. *Ricerche Econ.*, Oct.–Dec. 1988, *42*(4), pp. 700.

_____. The Measurement of Interindustry Linkages: A Comment. *Ricerche Econ.*, Oct.–Dec. 1988, *42*(4), pp. 695–98.

_____. The Supply Side Approaches to Input–Output Analysis: An Assessment. *Ricerche Econ.*, July–Sept. 1988, *42*(3), pp. 433–51.

Celsi, Richard L. and Olson, Jerry C. The Role of Involvement in Attention and Comprehension Processes. *J. Cons. Res.*, September 1988, *15*(2), pp. 210–24.

Centeno, Lourdes. The Expected Utility Applied to Reinsurance. In *Munier, B. R., ed.*, 1988, pp. 679–89.

Centner, Terence J. and Wetzstein, Michael E. Reducing Moral Hazard Associated with Implied Warranties of Animal Health: Reply. *Amer. J. Agr. Econ.*, May 1988, *70*(2), pp. 413–14.

Cenuşă, G. and Burlacu, Veronica. *N* Random Functions—Almost Periodical in Probability. *Econ. Computat. Cybern. Stud. Res.*, 1988, *23*(2), pp. 37–42.

Cerchi, Marlene and Havenner, Arthur. Cointegration and Stock Prices: The Random Walk on Wall Street Revisited. *J. Econ. Dynam. Control*, June–Sept. 1988, *12*(2–3), pp. 333–46.

Ceriani, Vieri; Violi, Roberto and Bollino, Carlo. Il mercato unico europeo e l'armonizzazione dell'iva e delle accise. (With English summary.) *Polit. Econ.*, December 1988, *4*(3), pp. 315–59.

Černý, Rudolf. The Restructuring of the Economic Mechanism in Agriculture. *Czech. Econ. Digest.*, June 1988, (4), pp. 51–58.

Cernea, Michael M. Alternative Social Forestry Development Strategies. In *Ives, J. and Pitt, D. C., eds.*, 1988, pp. 159–90.

_____. Involuntary Resettlement and Development. *Finance Develop.*, September 1988, *25*(3), pp. 44–46.

Cerrito, Elio. Territorio, demani, comunità: per una interpretazione della questione demaniale. Il caso di Principato Citra nel XIX secolo. (Public Domain and Community: Towards an Interpretation of the History of Property in the Public Domain. The Case of *Principato Citra* in the 19th Century. With English summary.) *Rivista Storia Econ.*, S.S., October 1988, *5*(3), pp. 319–64.

Cervero, Robert. Revitalizing Urban Transit. In *Weicher, J. C., ed.*, 1988, pp. 71–81.

Češka, Jaroslav. Annual and Multi-annual Statistical Plans and Programmes in Czechoslovakia. *Statist. J.*, December 1988, *5*(4), pp. 429–37.

Cette, Gilbert and Taddei, Dominque. Chômage mixte et politiques économiques. Un modèle de déséquilbre. (Mixed Unemployment and Economic Policies: A Disequilibrium Model. With English summary.) *Revue Écon.*, November 1988, *39*(6), pp. 1119–41.

Ceuppens, P. R.; Peel, David A. and Lane, J. A. Critical Bounds for MA(2) and MA(3) Processes. *Econ. Letters*, 1988, *27*(2), pp. 133–40.

Ch'ng, Hak Kee; Chang, Zeph-Yun and Yeong, Wee Yong. Production Management Practices of Small and Medium Businesses in Singapore. In *James, K. and Akrasanee, N., eds.*, 1988, pp. 126–63.

Chacel, Julian M. Foreign Debt Servicing and Economic Growth. In *Chacel, J. M.; Falk, P. S. and Fleischer, D. V., eds.*, 1988, pp. 60–66.

Chadam, J. and Ortoleva, P. Reaction-Infiltration Instabilities. In *Wheeler, M. F., ed.*, 1988, pp. 67–76.

Chadee, D.; Saint-Louis, R. and Gilson, J. C. U.S. CVDs and Canadian Hog Exports: Methodological and Measurement Issues. *Can. J. Agr. Econ.*, Part 1, December 1988, *36*(4), pp. 669–87.

Chadha, V. and Singh, Gurjeet. An Analysis of Tax Evasion in Punjab. In *Raikhy, P. S. and Gill, S. S., eds.*, 1988, pp. 140–51.

Chae, Suchan. Existence of Competitive Equilibrium with Incomplete Markets. *J. Econ. Theory*, February 1988, *44*(1), pp. 179–88.

_____ and Yang, Jeong-Ae. The Unique Perfect Equilibrium of an *N*-Person Bargaining Game. *Econ. Letters*, 1988, *28*(3), pp. 221–23.

Chakrabarti, Alok K.; Chiang, Thomas C. and Clark, John J. Stock Prices and Merger Movements: Interactive Relations. *Weltwirtsch. Arch.*, 1988, *124*(2), pp. 287–300.

_____; Chiang, Thomas C. and Clark, John J. Trend and Stochastic Movements in U.S. Merger Activity. *Quart. Rev. Econ. Bus.*, Summer 1988, *28*(2), pp. 6–19.

Chakrabarti, Subir K. Refinements of the β-Core and the Strong Equilibrium and the Aumann Proposition. *Int. J. Game Theory*, 1988, *17*(3), pp. 205–24.

Chakraborti, S.; Thistle, Paul D. and Bishop, John A. Large Sample Tests for Absolute Lorenz Dominance. *Econ. Letters*, 1988, *26*(3), pp. 291–94.

Chakraborty, Debasish and Kulkarni, Kishore. Effects of Output Growth on Balance of Payments. *Margin*, Oct.–Dec. 1988, *21*(1), pp. 41–53.

_____ and Miller, Norman C. Economic Growth and the Balance of Payments. *J. Econ. Devel.*, December 1988, *13*(2), pp. 57–79.

Chakravarti, Sangeeta and Bansal, Ashok K. Effect of Nonnormal Prior for Regression Parameter on Bayes Decisions and Forecasts. *J. Quant. Econ.*, July 1988, *4*(2), pp. 247–59.

Chakravarty, Satya R. Extended Gini Indices of

Inequality. *Int. Econ. Rev.*, February 1988, 29(1), pp. 147–56.

──────. On the Separable Industry Performance Evaluation Function. *Econ. Letters*, 1988, 27(2), pp. 179–82.

────── **and Weymark, John A.** Axiomatizations of the Entropy Numbers Equivalent Index of Industrial Concentration. In *Eichhorn, W., ed.*, 1988, pp. 383–97.

Chakravarty, Sukhamoy. Reflections on the Use of Mathematical Reasoning in Economics. *J. Quant. Econ.*, January 1988, 4(1), pp. 1–10.

Chalamwong, Yongyuth and Feder, Gershon. The Impact of Landownership Security: Theory and Evidence from Thailand. *World Bank Econ. Rev.*, May 1988, 2(2), pp. 187–204.

──────; **Feder, Gershon and Onchan, Tongroj.** Land Policies and Farm Performance in Thailand's Forest Reserve Areas. *Econ. Develop. Cult. Change*, April 1988, 36(3), pp. 483–501.

Chalfant, James A. and Alston, Julian M. Accounting for Changes in Tastes. *J. Polit. Econ.*, April 1988, 96(2), pp. 391–410.

Chalk, Andrew J. Competition in the Brewing Industry: Does Further Concentration Imply Collusion? *Managerial Dec. Econ.*, March 1988, 9(1), pp. 49–58.

Chaloner, Kathryn. An Approach to Experimental Design for Generalized Linear Models. In *Fedorov, V. and Lauter, H., eds.*, 1988, pp. 3–12.

Chaloner, W. H. Jevons in Manchester: 1863–1876. In *Wood, J. C., ed., Vol. 1*, 1988, 1972, pp. 268–79.

Chaloupka, Frank J. and Marty, Alvin L. Optimal Inflation Rates: A Generalization. *J. Money, Credit, Banking*, February 1988, 20(1), pp. 141–44.

Chalupa, Svatopluk. Agriculture on the Starting Line. *Czech. Econ. Digest.*, November 1988, (7), pp. 3–20.

──────. The Restructuring of the Economic Mechanism in Agriculture. *Czech. Econ. Digest.*, August 1988, (5), pp. 44–50.

Chamberlain, Gary. Asset Pricing in Multiperiod Securities Markets. *Econometrica*, November 1988, 56(6), pp. 1283–1300.

Chamberlain, Mark and Wren, Anthony. The Development of Micro-BUSMAN: Scheduling on Micro-computers. In *Daduna, J. R. and Wren, A., eds.*, 1988, pp. 160–74.

Chamberlain, P. J. An Empirical Bayes Approach to Modeling Drought. *Western J. Agr. Econ.*, July 1988, 13(1), pp. 92–99.

Chamberlain, Trevor W.; Cheung, C. Sherman and Kwan, Clarence C. Y. Cash versus Futures Prices and the Weekend Effect: The Canadian Evidence. In *Fabozzi, F. J., ed.*, 1988, pp. 329–39.

Chambers, Brian R.; Hart, Stuart L. and Denison, Daniel R. Founding Team Experience and New Firm Performance. In *Kirchhoff, B. A., et al., eds.*, 1988, pp. 106–18.

Chambers, Donald R. and Carleton, Willard T. A Generalized Approach to Duration. In *Chen, A. H., ed.*, 1988, pp. 163–81.

──────; **Carleton, Willard T. and McEnally, Richard W.** Immunizing Default-free Bond Portfolios with a Duration Vector. *J. Finan. Quant. Anal.*, March 1988, 23(1), pp. 89–104.

Chambers, Robert G. and Lee, Hyunok. Expenditure Constraints and Profit Maximization in U.S. Agriculture: Reply. *Amer. J. Agr. Econ.*, November 1988, 70(4), pp. 955–56.

────── **and Phipps, Tim T.** Accumulation and Rental Behavior in the Market for Farmland. *Western J. Agr. Econ.*, December 1988, 13(2), pp. 294–306.

Chamot, Dennis. Blue-Collar, White-Collar: Homeworker Problems. In *Christensen, K. E., ed.*, 1988, pp. 168–176.

Champernowne, D. G.; Meade, James and Stone, Richard. The Precision of National Income Estimates. In *Meade, J., Vol. 1*, 1988, 1942, pp. 136–51.

Champion, Anthony G. The Reversal of the Migration Turnaround: Resumption of Traditional Trends? *Int. Reg. Sci. Rev.*, 1988, 11(3), pp. 253–60.

Chamratrithirong, Aphichat and Cherlin, Andrew. Variations in Marriage Patterns in Central Thailand. *Demography*, August 1988, 25(3), pp. 337–53.

Chan, Arthur H. Adapting Natural Resources Management to Changing Societal Needs through Evolving Property Rights. *Rev. Soc. Econ.*, April 1988, 46(1), pp. 46–60.

──────. Policy Impacts of *Sporhase v. Nebraska*. *J. Econ. Issues*, December 1988, 22(4), pp. 1153–67.

Chan, Audrey. Women Managers in Singapore: Citizens for Tomorrow's Economy. In *Adler, N. J. and Izraeli, D., eds.*, 1988, pp. 54–73.

Chan, James L. and Belkaoui, Ahmed. Professional Value System of Academic Accountants: An Empirical Inquiry. In *Neimark, M., ed.*, 1988, pp. 1–28.

────── **and Jones, Rowan H.** Comparative Governmental Accounting: An Introductory Note. In *Chan, J. L. and Jones, R. H., eds.*, 1988, pp. 3–10.

Chan, K. C. On the Contrarian Investment Strategy. *J. Bus.*, April 1988, 61(2), pp. 147–63.

────── **and Chen, Nai-Fu.** An Unconditional Asset-Pricing Test and the Role of Firm Size as an Instrumental Variable for Risk. *J. Finance*, June 1988, 43(2), pp. 309–25.

Chan, Kam-Fai and Beenstock, Michael. Economic Forces in the London Stock Market. *Oxford Bull. Econ. Statist.*, February 1988, 50(1), pp. 27–39.

Chan, Kenneth S. Optimum Trade Policies and Retaliation. *Can. J. Econ.*, May 1988, 21(2), pp. 427–33.

──────. Trade Negotiations in a Nash Bargaining Model. *J. Int. Econ.*, November 1988, 25(3–4), pp. 353–363.

────── **and Mestelman, Stuart.** Institutions, Efficiency and the Strategic Behaviour of Sponsors and Bureaus. *J. Public Econ.*, October 1988, 37(1), pp. 91–102.

Chan, Louis K. C. Unanticipated Monetary Policy

and Real Economic Activity: Some Cross-Regime Evidence. *J. Monet. Econ.*, November 1988, *22*(3), pp. 439–59.

Chan, M. W. Luke and Krinsky, Itzhak. Expectation Formation and Portfolio Models for Life Insurers. *J. Risk Ins.*, December 1988, *55*(4), pp. 682–91.

_____ **and Mountain, Dean C.** The Interactive and Causal Relationships Involving Precious Metal Price Movements: An Analysis of the Gold and Silver Markets. *J. Bus. Econ. Statist.*, January 1988, *6*(1), pp. 69–77.

_____ **and Rotenberg, Wendy D.** Financial Distress in the Canadian Agricultural Sector: A Macro Analysis. *Can. J. Agr. Econ.*, November 1988, *36*(3), pp. 531–38.

Chan, Ngai Hang. The Parameter Inference for Nearly Nonstationary Time Series. *J. Amer. Statist. Assoc.*, September 1988, *83*(403), pp. 857–62.

Chan, Pingfai and Koray, Faik. Fiscal Policy and Stabilization of Exchange Rates under Alternative Criteria. *Can. J. Econ.*, February 1988, *21*(1), pp. 96–114.

Chan, Y. and Yi, P. Bifurcation and Disaggregation in Lowry–Garin Derivative Models: Theory, Calibration, and Case Study. *Environ. Planning A*, September 1988, *20*(9), pp. 1253–67.

Chanas, Stefan and Nowakowski, Marek. From Fuzzy Data to a Single Action—A Simulation Approach. In *Kacprzyk, J. and Fedrizzi, M., eds.*, 1988, pp. 331–41.

Chance, Don M. Boundary Condition Tests of Bid and Ask Prices of Index Call Options. *J. Finan. Res.*, Spring 1988, *11*(1), pp. 21–31.

_____ **and Billingsley, Randall S.** The Pricing and Performance of Stock Index Futures Spreads. *J. Futures Markets*, June 1988, *8*(3), pp. 303–18.

_____ **and Billingsley, Randall S.** Put–Call Ratios and Market Timing Effectiveness. *J. Portfol. Manage.*, Fall 1988, *15*(1), pp. 25–28.

_____ **and Broughton, John B.** Market Index Depository Liabilities: Analysis, Interpretation, and Performance. *J. Finan. Services Res.*, December 1988, *1*(4), pp. 335–52.

_____ **and Ferris, Stephen P.** Margin Requirements and Stock Market Volatility. *Econ. Letters*, 1988, *28*(3), pp. 251–54.

Chand, Sheetal K. and van Til, Reinold. Ghana: Toward Successful Stabilization and Recovery. *Finance Develop.*, March 1988, *25*(1), pp. 32–35.

Chandavarkar, Anand. The Informal Sector: Empty Box or Portmanteau Concept? Comment. *World Devel.*, October 1988, *16*(10), pp. 1259–61.

Chander, Subhash. Professional Manpower Development in Irrigation Sector in India. In *Kohli, U. and Gautam, V., eds.*, 1988, pp. 89–93.

Chandiwana, D. Q., et al. Energy for Rural Development in Zimbabwe: Concepts and Issues for Growth with Equity. In *Hosier, R. H., ed. (I)*, 1988, pp. 1–19.

Chandler, Colby H. Competition in the World Economy. In *Rosow, J. M., ed.*, 1988, pp. 165–74.

Chandler, Ralph Clark. The Commercial Republic Re-examined: A Critique of the Economization Model of Public Policy Making. In *Hula, R. C., ed.*, 1988, pp. 181–203.

Chandler, Susan M. and Doktor, Robert H. Limits of Predictability in Forecasting in the Behavioral Sciences. *Int. J. Forecasting*, 1988, *4*(1), pp. 5–14.

Chandler, William U. Planning for Energy Efficiency. In *Byrne, J. and Rich, D., eds.*, 1988, pp. 9–52.

Chandra, Ashok. Some Observations on HRD for Services. In *Kohli, U. and Gautam, V., eds.*, 1988, pp. 270–79.

Chandra, N. K. National and Local Level Planning: China, the USSR, India. In *Mitra, A., ed.*, 1988, pp. 115–35.

Chandra, Shailaja. Human Resources Development for Women in India. In *Kohli, U. and Gautam, V., eds.*, 1988, pp. 213–23.

Chang, Chih. A Note on the von Neumann–Morgenstern Solution [Cooperative Games with Coalition Structures]. *Int. J. Game Theory*, 1988, *17*(4), pp. 311–14.

Chang, Ching-Cheng and Stefanou, Spiro E. Specification and Estimation of Asymmetric Adjustment Rates for Quasi-Fixed Factors of Production. *J. Econ. Dynam. Control*, March 1988, *12*(1), pp. 145–51.

Chang, Ching-huei. Optimal Taxation of Business and Individual Incomes. *J. Public Econ.*, March 1988, *35*(2), pp. 251–63.

Chang, Ching-Meei. A Hazard Rate Analysis of Fertility Using Duration Data from Malaysia. In *Schultz, T. Paul, ed.*, 1988, pp. 137–59.

Chang, Chung-Sik and Lee, Ki-Young. Anomalies in the Stock Returns over Trading and Nontrading Periods: Further Evidence in the Korean Stock Market. *Quart. J. Bus. Econ.*, Spring 1988, *27*(2), pp. 139–61.

Chang, Cyril F. and Tuckman, Howard P. Cost Convergence between For-Profit and Not-for-Profit Nursing Homes: Does Competition Matter? *Quart. Rev. Econ. Bus.*, Winter 1988, *28*(4), pp. 50–65.

Chang, Dae W. The Global Construction Industry: The Republic of Korea. In *Strassmann, W. P. and Wells, J., eds.*, 1988, pp. 141–59.

Chang, Eric C. A Monthly Effect in Commodity Price Changes: A Note. *J. Futures Markets*, December 1988, *8*(6), pp. 717–22.

_____ **and Kim, Chan-Wung.** Day of the Week Effects and Commodity Price Changes. *J. Futures Markets*, April 1988, *8*(2), pp. 229–41.

_____ **and Pinegar, J. Michael.** Does the Market Reward Risk in Non-January Months? *J. Portfol. Manage.*, Fall 1988, *15*(1), pp. 55–57.

_____ **and Pinegar, J. Michael.** A Fundamental Study of the Seasonal Risk–Return Relationship: A Note. *J. Finance*, September 1988, *43*(4), pp. 1035–39.

Chang, Fwu-Ranq. The Inverse Optimal Problem: A Dynamic Programming Approach. *Econometrica*, January 1988, *56*(1), pp. 147–72.

Chang, Myong-Hun and Harrington, Joseph E., Jr. The Effects of Irreversible Investment in Durable Capacity on the Incentive for Horizontal Merger. *Southern Econ. J.*, October 1988, *55*(2), pp. 443–53.

Chang, Philip C. Economies of Scope, Synergy, and the CAPM. *J. Finan. Res.*, Fall 1988, *11*(3), pp. 255–63.

——. A Measure of the Synergy in Mergers under a Competitive Market for Corporate Control. *Atlantic Econ. J.*, June 1988, *16*(2), pp. 59–62.

Chang, Se-Won. Tax Treatment of Computer Software: Republic of Korea. In *International Fiscal Association, ed. (II)*, 1988, pp. 485–92.

Chang, Sea Jin and Choi, Unghwan. Strategy, Structure and Performance of Korean Business Groups: A Transactions Cost Approach. *J. Ind. Econ.*, December 1988, *37*(2), pp. 141–58.

Chang, Sokan. Proposals for Reforming the GATT-Antidumping Code. In *Dicke, D. C. and Petersmann, E.-U., eds.*, 1988, pp. 187–96.

Chang, Wen-Ya and Lai, Ching-chong. Fixed Exchange Rates and Capital Mobility Regulations. *Indian Econ. J.*, April–June 1988, *35*(4), pp. 18–24.

—— **and Lai, Ching-chong.** Tax Evasion and Tax Collections: An Aggregate Demand–Aggregate Supply Analysis. *Public Finance*, 1988, *43*(1), pp. 138–46.

Chang, Winston W. and Michael, Michael S. Optimum Tariff and Its Optimum Revenue Distribution. *Econ. Letters*, 1988, *28*(4), pp. 369–74.

Chang, Zeph-Yun; Yeong, Wee Yong and Ch'ng, Hak Kee. Production Management Practices of Small and Medium Businesses in Singapore. In *James, K. and Akrasanee, N., eds.*, 1988, pp. 126–63.

Channon, Derek F. Strategic Evolution and Portfolio Management Techniques. In *Grant, J. H., ed.*, 1988, pp. 219–36.

Channon, Geoffrey. Railroad Competition and Its Management in the United States and Britain before 1914. In *Hausman, W. J., ed.*, 1988, pp. 189–97.

——. Railway Pooling in Britain before 1900: The Anglo-Scottish Traffic. *Bus. Hist. Rev.*, Spring 1988, *62*(1), pp. 74–92.

Chant, Elizabeth M. and Walker, David A. Small Business Demand for Trade Credit. *Appl. Econ.*, July 1988, *20*(7), pp. 861–76.

Chantrel, Laure. Représentations sociales et croissance économique: Riches et pauvres dans les écrits des publicistes français du XVIIᵉ siècle. (With English summary.) *Revue Écon. Polit.*, March–April 1988, *98*(2), pp. 189–208.

Chao, Chi-chur and Takayama, Akira. Product Differentiation, Heterogeneous Labor, and Non-homotheticity: Statics and Dynamics. *Southern Econ. J.*, October 1988, *55*(2), pp. 263–78.

Chao, Hung-po, et al. Priority Service: Market

Structure and Competition. *Energy J.*, Special Issue, 1988, *9*, pp. 77–104.

Chao, Shu-Wen and Lee, Maw Lin. Effects of Social Security on Personal Saving. *Econ. Letters*, 1988, *28*(4), pp. 365–68.

Chapin, Mac and Breslin, Patrick. Conservation Kuna-Style. In *Annis, S. and Hakim, P., eds.*, 1988, pp. 73–82.

Chapman, Bruce J. and Beggs, John J. Immigrant Wage Adjustment in Australia: Cross Section and Time-Series Estimates. *Econ. Rec.*, September 1988, *64*(186), pp. 161–67.

—— **and Beggs, John J.** Labor Turnover Bias in Estimating Wages. *Rev. Econ. Statist.*, February 1988, *70*(1), pp. 117–23.

Chapman, Guillermo O., Jr. Interlocking Time Frames: Adjustment, Structural Change, and Strategies. In *Tavis, L. A., ed.*, 1988, pp. 142–49.

Chapman, Janet G. Gorbachev's Wage Reform. *Soviet Econ.*, Oct.–Dec. 1988, *4*(4), pp. 338–65.

Chapman, John N. and Strier, Leonid. Five-Year Plans for Soviet Agricultural Industries: Are They Relevant as Production Indicators? *Comp. Econ. Stud.*, Fall 1988, *30*(3), pp. 71–93.

Chapman, Stanley D. Venture Capital and Financial Organisation: London and South Africa in the Nineteenth Century. In *Jones, S., ed.*, 1988, pp. 27–45.

—— **and Butt, John.** Studies in Capital Formation in the United Kingdom, 1750–1920: The Cotton Industry, 1775–1856. In *Feinstein, C. H. and Pollard, S., eds.*, 1988, pp. 105–25.

Chappell, Henry W., Jr. and Keech, William R. The Unemployment Rate Consequences of Partisan Monetary Policies. *Southern Econ. J.*, July 1988, *55*(1), pp. 107–22.

Chapple, Simon. The Price Equation, Excess Demand, and Normal Cost Pricing: A Comment. *Appl. Econ.*, December 1988, *20*(12), pp. 1689–91.

Chapuis, Christine. Nuclear Energy After Chernobyl: Views from Four Countries: France. *Energy J.*, January 1988, *9*(1), pp. 31–34.

Charemza, Wojciech; Gronicki, Miroslaw and Quandt, Richard E. Modelling Parallel Markets in Centrally Planned Economies: The Case of the Automobile Market in Poland. *Europ. Econ. Rev.*, April 1988, *32*(4), pp. 861–83.

Chari, V. V. Time Consistency and Optimal Policy Design. *Fed. Res. Bank Minn. Rev.*, Fall 1988, *12*(4), pp. 17–31.

—— **and Jagannathan, Ravi.** Banking Panics, Information, and Rational Expectations Equilibrium. *J. Finance*, July 1988, *43*(3), pp. 749–61.

——; **Jagannathan, Ravi and Ofer, Aharon R.** Seasonalities in Security Returns: The Case of Earnings Announcements. *J. Finan. Econ.*, May 1988, *21*(1), pp. 101–21.

Charles, Anthony T. Fishery Socioeconomics: A Survey. *Land Econ.*, August 1988, *64*(3), pp. 276–95.

Charmant, Alain, et al. Productivité des facteurs

de production et prix de l'énergie. (Embodied Technical Change and Energy Prices. With English summary.) *Écon. Soc.*, April 1988, 22(4), pp. 219–45.

Charnes, A.; Cooper, W. W. and Ahn, T. Using Data Envelopment Analysis to Measure the Efficiency of Not-for-Profit Organizations: A Critical Evaluation—A Comment. *Managerial Dec. Econ.*, September 1988, 9(3), pp. 251–53.

———, **et al.** Extremal Principle Solutions of Games in Characteristic Function Form: Core, Chebychev and Shapley Value Generalizations. In *Sengupta, J. K. and Kadekodi, G. K., eds.*, 1988, pp. 123–33.

Charney, Alberta H.; Oxford, Thomas P. and Taylor, Carol A. A Recursive Conjoint Modeling Approach to State Severance Tax Analysis: Mining Florida Phosphates. *Resources & Energy*, December 1988, 10(4), pp. 355–86.

Charnsupharindr, Pichai. Growth and Utilization of Labor in Thailand. *Philippine Rev. Econ. Bus.*, March–June 1988, 25(1–2), pp. 101–49.

Charos, Evangelos N. and Simos, Evangelos O. The Effects of Human Capital and R&D upon International Trade Flows: Evidence from a Multi-input, Multi-output Model for the United States. *Weltwirtsch. Arch.*, 1988, 124(4), pp. 701–12.

Charreton, R. and Bourdaire, J. M. Industrial Practice of Decision Theory. In *Munier, B. R., ed.*, 1988, pp. 657–77.

Chartrand, Harry Hillman. The Crafts in the Post-modern Economy. *J. Cult. Econ.*, December 1988, 12(2), pp. 39–66.

Chase, Darren; Ross, Carlyle and Kaliel, Dale. Economics of Cow-Calf Production in Alberta. *Can. J. Agr. Econ.*, Part 2, December 1988, 36(4), pp. 821–36.

Chase, Robert. Commodity Aid for Agricultural Development. In *Roberts, C., ed.*, 1988, pp. 199–204.

Chassin, Mark R. Standards of Care in Medicine. *Inquiry*, Winter 1988, 25(4), pp. 437–50.

Chateauneuf, Alain. Uncertainty Aversion and Risk Aversion in Models with Nonadditive Probabilities. In *Munier, B. R., ed.*, 1988, pp. 615–27.

Chatfield, Chris. Apples, Oranges and Mean Square Error: Editorial. *Int. J. Forecasting*, 1988, 4(4), pp. 515–18.

———. The Future of Time-Series Forecasting. *Int. J. Forecasting*, 1988, 4(3), pp. 411–19.

Chatterjee, G. S.; Pal, Padmaja and Bhattacharya, N. Variations in Level of Living across Regions and Social Groups in Rural India, 1963/1964 and 1973/1974. In *Srinivasan, T. N. and Bardhan, P. K., eds.*, 1988, pp. 154–218.

Chatterjee, Sangit and Badrinath, S. G. On Measuring Skewness and Elongation in Common Stock Return Distributions: The Case of the Market Index. *J. Bus.*, October 1988, 61(4), pp. 451–72.

Chatterjee, Sris and Castelino, Mark. T-Bond Futures Prices: Cheapest to Deliver versus the

Index. In *Fabozzi, F. J., ed.*, 1988, pp. 291–300.

Chatterji, Manas. Role of Information in Technology Transfer. In *Orishimo, I.; Hewings, G. J. D. and Nijkamp, P., eds.*, 1988, pp. 71–88.

Chatterji, Monojit. Economic Growth, Productivity Growth and Economic Structure in India, 1961–1982. *J. Quant. Econ.*, January 1988, 4(1), pp. 107–22.

——— **and Price, Simon.** Unions, Dutch Disease and Unemployment. *Oxford Econ. Pap.*, June 1988, 40(2), pp. 302–21.

Chatterji, Sukanta. Norway-Aided Kerala Fishery Project: An Example of Maldevelopment. Will the Planned Orissa Fishery Project Be a Real Development Project? In *Vivekananda, F., ed.*, 1988, pp. 134–43.

Chattopadhyay, Amitava and Alba, Joseph W. The Situational Importance of Recall and Inference in Consumer Decision Making. *J. Cons. Res.*, June 1988, 15(1), pp. 1–12.

Chaturvedi, A. and Van Hoa, Tran. The Necessary and Sufficient Conditions for the Uniform Dominance of the Two-Stage Stein Estimators. *Econ. Letters*, 1988, 28(4), pp. 351–55.

Chaubey, P. K. On Choice of Money Stock Measures—A Reaction. *Indian Econ. J.*, July–September 1988, 36(1), pp. 93–94.

Chaudhary, M. Aslam. International Debt and Foreign Dependency: Policy Options for Pakistan. *Pakistan Devel. Rev.*, Part 2, Winter 1988, 27(4), pp. 829–34.

Chaudhry, M. Ghaffar and Iqbal, Zafar. Regional Distribution of Agricultural Incomes in Pakistan: An Intertemporal Analysis. *Pakistan Devel. Rev.*, Part 2, Winter 1988, 27(4), pp. 537–46.

Chaudry-Shah, Anwar. Capitalization and the Theory of Local Public Finance: An Interpretive Essay. *J. Econ. Surveys*, 1988, 2(3), pp. 209–43.

Chauveau, Jean-Marie and Gordon, Kathryn M. World Price Uncertainty and Agricultural Policy Formulation under Rational Expectations. *Europ. Rev. Agr. Econ.*, 1988, 15(4), pp. 437–56.

Chavas, Jean-Paul. Developments in Economics of Importance to Agricultural Economics: A Discussion. In *Hildreth, R. J., et al., eds.*, 1988, pp. 264–65.

———. On Competitive Speculation under Uncertainty: An Alternative View of the Inverse-Carrying Charge. *J. Econ. Bus.*, May 1988, 40(2), pp. 117–28.

——— **and Citzler, Annette M.** On the Economics of Household Composition. *Appl. Econ.*, October 1988, 20(10), pp. 1401–18.

——— **and Cox, Thomas L.** A Nonparametric Analysis of Agricultural Technology. *Amer. J. Agr. Econ.*, May 1988, 70(2), pp. 303–10.

———; **Pope, Rulon D. and Leathers, Howard.** Competitive Industry Equilibrium under Uncertainty and Free Entry. *Econ. Inquiry*, April 1988, 26(2), pp. 331–44.

Chaykowski, Richard P.; Ehrenberg, Randy A. and Ehrenberg, Ronald G. Determinants of the Compensation and Mobility of School Superintendents. *Ind. Lab. Relat. Rev.*, April 1988, *41*(3), pp. 386–401.

———— and Ehrenberg, Ronald G. On Estimating the Effects of Increased Aid to Education. In *Freeman, R. B. and Ichniowski, C., eds.*, 1988, pp. 245–62.

Chazan, Willy. French Mineral Exploration, 1973–82. In *Tilton, J. E.; Eggert, R. G. and Landsberg, H. H., eds.*, 1988, pp. 261–81.

Cheah, C.-W. Voluntary Health Insurance and Providers' Price Discounting Behaviour in Korea: Discussion. In *Butler, J. R. G. and Doessel, D. P., eds.*, 1988, pp. 207–09.

———— and Doessel, D. P. Technology and Health Expenditures in Australia: Results from the Residual Approach. In *Smith, C. S., ed.*, 1988, pp. 1–18.

———— and Doessel, D. P. A Theoretical Note on the Measurement of the Welfare Cost of Health Insurance. In *Butler, J. R. G. and Doessel, D. P., eds.*, 1988, pp. 170–88.

Cheape, Charles. Not Politicians but Sound Businessmen: Norton Company and the Third Reich. *Bus. Hist. Rev.*, Autumn 1988, *62*(3), pp. 444–66.

Cheasty, Adrienne and Blejer, Mario I. High Inflation, Heterodox Stabilization, and Fiscal Policy. *World Devel.*, August 1988, *16*(8), pp. 867–81.

———— and Blejer, Mario I. Some Lessons from "Heterodox" Stabilization Programs. *Finance Develop.*, September 1988, *25*(3), pp. 16–19.

Checchi, Daniele. Il coordinamento internazionale delle politiche economiche. Una rassegna della letteratura recente. (International Economic Policy Coordination. A Survey on Recent Literature. With English summary.) *Ricerche Econ.*, Oct.–Dec. 1988, *42*(4), pp. 652–77.

———— and Opromolla, Paolo. The Role of Financial Sectors in Business Cycle Analysis. *Rivista Int. Sci. Econ. Com.*, March 1988, *35*(3), pp. 269–94.

Checkland, Olive. 'Vain' Learning and the Advent of Political Economy in Meiji Japan. In *Sugiyama, C. and Mizuta, H., eds.*, 1988, pp. 257–71.

Checkland, S. G. Economic Opinion in England as Jevons Found It. In *Wood, J. C., ed., Vol. 1*, 1988, *1951*, pp. 125–45.

Chege, Michael. The State and Labour: Industrial Relations in Independent Kenya. In *Coughlin, P. and Ikiara, G. K., eds.*, 1988, pp. 169–89.

Cheli, E. and Caretti, P. Statute and Statutory Instrument in the Evolution of European Constitutional Systems. In *Pizzorusso, A., ed.*, 1988, pp. 131–55.

Chelius, James R. and Extejt, Marian M. The Narcotic Effect of Impasse Resolution Procedures. In *Lewin, D., et al., eds.*, 1988, *1985*, pp. 399–411.

———— and Kavanaugh, Karen. Workers' Compensation and the Level of Occupational Injuries. *J. Risk Ins.*, June 1988, *55*(2), pp. 315–23.

Chen, Andrew H.; Doherty, Neil A. and Park, Hun Y. The Optimal Capital Structure Decision of Depository Financial Intermediaries. In *Chen, A. H., ed.*, 1988, pp. 91–111.

———— and Kang, Hyosuk. Financial Implications of ERISA: Theory and Evidence. *J. Econ. Bus.*, August 1988, *40*(3), pp. 193–208.

———— and Lee, Cheng F. Special Issue on Pensions: Introduction. *J. Econ. Bus.*, August 1988, *40*(3), pp. 191.

Chen, Chau-nan and Lai, Ching-chong. Capital Mobility, Trade-Balance Elasticity, and Exchange Rate Dynamics. *Southern Econ. J.*, July 1988, *55*(1), pp. 211–14.

————; Lai, Ching-chong and Tsaur, Tien-wang. The Loanable Funds Theory and the Dynamics of Exchange Rates: The Mundell Model Revisited. *J. Int. Money Finance*, June 1988, *7*(2), pp. 221–29.

Chen, David M. and Welch, Robert L. On the Properties of the Valuation Formula for an Unprotected American Call Option with Known Dividends and the Computation of Its Implied Standard Deviation. In *Fabozzi, F. J., ed.*, 1988, pp. 237–56.

Chen, Gavin M. A Note on Emerging Issues in Minority Business Research. *Rev. Black Polit. Econ.*, Spring 1988, *16*(4), pp. 5–9.

———— and Cole, John A. The Myths, Facts, and Theories of Ethnic, Small-Scale Enterprise Financing. *Rev. Black Polit. Econ.*, Spring 1988, *16*(4), pp. 111–23.

Chen, K. C.; Beatty, Randolph P. and Lee, Cheng F. On the Nonstationarity of Convertible Bond Betas: Theory and Evidence. *Quart. Rev. Econ. Bus.*, Autumn 1988, *28*(3), pp. 15–27.

———— and D'Arcy, Stephen P. The Effect of Changes in Pension Plan Interest Rate Assumptions on Security Prices. *J. Econ. Bus.*, August 1988, *40*(3), pp. 243–52.

Chen, Kuan, et al. Productivity Change in Chinese Industry: 1953–1985. *J. Compar. Econ.*, December 1988, *12*(4), pp. 570–91.

Chen, Lincoln C. Health Policy Responses: An Approach Derived from the China and India Experiences. In *Bell, D. E. and Reich, M. R., eds.*, 1988, pp. 279–305.

Chen, Nai-Fu. Equilibrium Asset Pricing Models and the Firm Size Effect. In *Dimson, E., ed.*, 1988, pp. 179–96.

————. Stable Factors in Security Returns: Identification Using Cross-Validation: Comment. *J. Bus. Econ. Statist.*, January 1988, *6*(1), pp. 16.

———— and Chan, K. C. An Unconditional Asset-Pricing Test and the Role of Firm Size as an Instrumental Variable for Risk. *J. Finance*, June 1988, *43*(2), pp. 309–25.

————; Copeland, Thomas E. and Mayers, David. A Comparison of Single and Multifactor Portfolio Performance Methodologies. In *Dimson, E., ed.*, 1988, pp. 254–71.

Chen, Nen-Jing; Ames, Glenn C. W. and Hammett, A. Lawton. Implications of a Tariff on Imported Canadian Softwood Lumber. *Can. J. Agr. Econ.*, March 1988, *36*(1), pp. 69–81.

Chen, Paul. Wage Changes in Long-Term Labor Contracts. In *Ehrenberg, R. G., ed.*, 1988, pp. 133–86.

Chen, Ping and Barnett, William A. The Aggregation-Theoretic Monetary Aggregates Are Chaotic and Have Strange Attractors: An Econometric Application of Mathematical Chaos. In *Barnett, W. A.; Berndt, E. R. and White, H., eds.*, 1988, pp. 199–245.

Chen, Son-Nan. Estimation Risk and the Demand for Risky Assets under Uncertain Inflation: Heterogeneous versus Homogeneous Expectations. *Quart. Rev. Econ. Bus.*, Summer 1988, 28(2), pp. 30–45.

Chen, Wen-Kuei and Ritchken, Peter H. Downside Risk Option Pricing Models. In *Khoury, S. J. and Ghosh, A., eds.*, 1988, pp. 205–25.

Chen, Yin-fang. Transnational Corporations and World Development: An Evolutionary View. In *Teng, W. and Wang, N. T., eds.*, 1988, pp. 33–46.

Chen, Yizi and Wang, Xiaoqiang. Reform: Results and Lessons from the 1985 CESRRI Survey. In *Reynolds, B. L., ed.*, 1988, *1987*, pp. 172–88.

Chenery, Hollis. Industrialization and Growth: Alternative Views of East Asia. In *Hughes, H., ed.*, 1988, pp. 39–63.

Cheng, C. S. Agnes; Smith, James L. and Siegel, Daniel R. Failure of the Net Profit Share Leasing Experiment for Offshore Petroleum Resources. *Rev. Econ. Statist.*, May 1988, 70(2), pp. 199–206.

Cheng, Hang-Sheng. Monetary Policy and Inflation in China. In *Cheng, H.-S., ed.*, 1988, pp. 401–29.

_____ **and Glick, Reuven.** Monetary Policy Changes in Pacific Basin Countries. In *Cheng, H.-S., ed.*, 1988, pp. 3–14.

Cheng, Hsiang-tai and Capps, Oral, Jr. Demand Analysis of Fresh and Frozen Finfish and Shellfish in the United States. *Amer. J. Agr. Econ.*, August 1988, 70(3), pp. 533–42.

Cheng, Leonard K. Assisting Domestic Industries under International Oligopoly: The Relevance of the Nature of Competition to Optimal Policies. *Amer. Econ. Rev.*, September 1988, 78(4), pp. 746–58.

Cherin, Antony C. and Melicher, Ronald W. Impact of Branch Banking on Bank Firm Risk via Geographic Market Diversification. *Quart. J. Bus. Econ.*, Spring 1988, 27(2), pp. 73–95.

Cherkes, Martin and Yaari, Uzi. Unions, Default Risk, and Pension Underfunding. *J. Econ. Bus.*, August 1988, 40(3), pp. 239–42.

Cherlin, Andrew and Chamratrithirong, Aphichat. Variations in Marriage Patterns in Central Thailand. *Demography*, August 1988, 25(3), pp. 337–53.

Chern, Wen S. and Bouis, Howarth E. Structural Changes in Residential Electricity Demand. *Energy Econ.*, July 1988, 10(3), pp. 213–22.

_____ **and Hama, Mary Y.** Food Expenditure and Nutrient Availability in Elderly Households. *J. Cons. Aff.*, Summer 1988, 22(1), pp. 3–19.

Chernichovsky, Dov and Meesook, Oey Astra. Urban-Rural Food and Nutrition Consumption Patterns in Indonesia. In *Sirageldin, I. and Sorkin, A., eds.*, 1988, pp. 193–205.

Cherry, Robert. Shifts in Radical Theories of Inequality. *Rev. Radical Polit. Econ.*, Summer–Fall 1988, 20(2–3), pp. 184–89.

_____ **and Goldberg, Gertrude S.** Fresh Start of False Start? *Challenge*, May–June 1988, 31(3), pp. 48–51.

Chesi, Marco. Tasso di attivitë della popolazione italiana e sviluppo economico nel secondo dopoguerra. (The Activity Rate of the Italian Population and Economic Development after World War II. With English summary.) *Rivista Int. Sci. Econ. Com.*, September 1988, 35(9), pp. 853–89.

Chesnais, François. Multinational Enterprises and the International Diffusion of Technology. In *Dosi, G., et al., eds.*, 1988, pp. 496–527.

Chesney, James; Fleming, Steven and DesHarnais, Susan. Trends and Regional Variations in Hospital Utilization and Quality during the First Two Years of the Prospective Payment System. *Inquiry*, Fall 1988, 25(3), pp. 374–82.

Chesney, Marc and Loubergé, Henri. Les options sur devises: une revue des modèles théoriques et des travaux empiriques. (Currency Options: A Survey of Theoretical and Empirical Work. With English summary.) *Finance*, December 1988, 9(2), pp. 7–33.

Chesterman, Esther. Demand for Treatment and Choice of Provider: General Practitioner or Accident and Emergency Unit. In *Smith, C. S., ed.*, 1988, pp. 98–124.

Cheung, C. Sherman and Kwan, Clarence C. Y. A Note on Simple Criteria for Optimal Portfolio Selection. *J. Finance*, March 1988, 43(1), pp. 241–45.

_____ **; Kwan, Clarence C. Y. and Chamberlain, Trevor W.** Cash versus Futures Prices and the Weekend Effect: The Canadian Evidence. In *Fabozzi, F. J., ed.*, 1988, pp. 329–39.

Cheung, Paul P. L.; Sulak, Donna B. and Montgomery, Mark R. Rates of Courtship and First Marriage in Thailand. *Population Stud.*, November 1988, 42(3), pp. 375–88.

Cheung, Steven N. S. The Fable of the Bees: An Economic Investigation. In *Cowen, T., ed.*, 1988, *1973*, pp. 279–304.

Chevalier, Jean-Marie. De l'oligopole pétrolier à l'oligopole énergétique. (From Oil Oligopoly to Energy Oligopoly. With English summary.) *Écon. Soc.*, Nov.–Dec. 1988, 22(11–12), pp. 87–103.

Chevallier-Farat, Thérèse. Le rôle du marché interbancaire international. (With English summary.) *Revue Écon. Polit.*, Sept.–Oct. 1988, 98(5), pp. 673–99.

Chevallier, Jean-Yves; Legendre, François and Morin, Pierre. L'investissement dans un contexte de faible croissance et de taux d'intérêt élevés. Une étude sur données individuelles du comportement des entreprises industrielles françaises. (With English summary.) *Rech. Écon. Louvain*, 1988, 54(2), pp. 221–49.

Chevrier, Yves. NEP and Beyond: The Transition to 'Modernization' in China (1978–85). In *Feuchtwang, S.; Hussain, A. and Pairault, T., eds., Vol. 1,* 1988, pp. 7–35.

Chew, David C. E. Effective Occupational Safety Activities: Findings in Three Asian Developing Countries. *Int. Lab. Rev.,* 1988, *127*(1), pp. 111–24.

Chew, Soo Hong; Epstein, Larry G. and Zilcha, Itzhak. A Correspondence Theorem between Expected Utility and Smooth Utility. *J. Econ. Theory,* October 1988, *46*(1), pp. 186–93.

_____ **and Epstein, Larry G.** The Law of Large Numbers and the Attractiveness of Compound Gambles. *J. Risk Uncertainty,* March 1988, *1*(1), pp. 125–32.

Chhibber, Ajay. Raising Agricultural Output: Price and Nonprice Factors. *Finance Develop.,* June 1988, *25*(2), pp. 44–47.

Chi, Schive. An Intra-firm Study of X-Efficiency of Taiwan's Sugar Industry. *Devel. Econ.,* June 1988, *26*(2), pp. 161–71.

Chiang, Alpha C. and Miller, Stephen M. Inflation Expectations, Wealth Perception, and Consumption Expenditure. *Eastern Econ. J.,* Jan.–March 1988, *14*(1), pp. 27–38.

Chiang, Raymond and Venkatesh, P. C. Insider Holdings and Perceptions of Information Asymmetry: A Note. *J. Finance,* September 1988, *43*(4), pp. 1041–48.

Chiang, Shih-Chen and Masson, Robert T. Domestic Industrial Structure and Export Quality. *Int. Econ. Rev.,* May 1988, *29*(2), pp. 261–70.

Chiang, Thomas C. The Forward Rate as a Predictor of the Future Spot Rate—A Stochastic Coefficient Approach. *J. Money, Credit, Banking,* May 1988, *20*(2), pp. 212–32.

_____ **; Clark, John J. and Chakrabarti, Alok K.** Stock Prices and Merger Movements: Interactive Relations. *Weltwirtsch. Arch.,* 1988, *124*(2), pp. 287–300.

_____ **; Clark, John J. and Chakrabarti, Alok K.** Trend and Stochastic Movements in U.S. Merger Activity. *Quart. Rev. Econ. Bus.,* Summer 1988, *28*(2), pp. 6–19.

_____ **and Hindelang, Thomas J.** Forward Rate, Spot Rate and Risk Premium: An Empirical Analysis. *Weltwirtsch. Arch.,* 1988, *124*(1), pp. 74–88.

Chiappori, Pierre-André. Nash-Bargained Households Decisions: A Comment. *Int. Econ. Rev.,* November 1988, *29*(4), pp. 791–96.

_____ . Rational Household Labor Supply. *Econometrica,* January 1988, *56*(1), pp. 63–90.

_____ . World Tax Reform: A Progress Report: France: Comment. In *Pechman, J. A., ed.,* 1988, pp. 113–18.

_____ **; Atkinson, Anthony B. and Bourguignon, François.** Fiscalité et transferts: Une comparaison franco–britannique. (Taxes and Benefits: A Franco–British Comparison. With English summary.) *Ann. Écon. Statist.,* July–Sept. 1988, (11), pp. 117–40.

_____ **; Atkinson, Anthony B. and Bourguignon, François.** What Do We Learn about Tax Reform from International Comparisons? France and Britain. *Europ. Econ. Rev.,* March 1988, *32*(2–3), pp. 343–52.

_____ **and Guesnerie, Roger.** Endogenous Fluctuations under Rational Expectations. *Europ. Econ. Rev.,* March 1988, *32*(2–3), pp. 389–97.

Chiarella, Carl. The Cobweb Model: Its Instability and the Onset of Chaos. *Econ. Modelling,* October 1988, *5*(4), pp. 377–84.

Chiarini, Bruno. Macroeconomic Policy in a Coalition System. *Giorn. Econ.,* July–Aug. 1988, *47*(7–8), pp. 401–26.

_____ . A Note on the Control Theory Framework for Policy Analysis. *Stud. Econ.,* 1988, *43*(35), pp. 93–104.

Chib, Siddhartha; Tiwari, Ram C. and Jammalamadaka, S. Rao. Bayes Prediction Density and Regression Estimation—A Semiparametric Approach. *Empirical Econ.,* 1988, *13*(3–4), pp. 209–22.

_____ **; Tiwari, Ram C. and Jammalamadaka, S. Rao.** Bayes Prediction in Regressions with Elliptical Errors. *J. Econometrics,* July 1988, *38*(3), pp. 349–60.

Chick, Victoria. Sources of Finance, Recent Changes in Bank Behaviour and the Theory of Investment and Interest. In *[Frowen, S.],* 1988, pp. 30–48.

_____ **and Dow, Sheila C.** A Post-Keynesian Perspective on the Relation between Banking and Regional Development. In *Arestis, P., ed.,* 1988, pp. 219–50.

Chicoine, David L. and Deller, Steven C. Representative Versus Direct Democracy: A Tiebout Test of Relative Performance: Comment. *Public Choice,* January 1988, *56*(1), pp. 69–72.

_____ **and Giertz, J. Fred.** Uniformity in a Dual Assessment System. *Nat. Tax J.,* June 1988, *41*(2), pp. 247–55.

_____ **; Walzer, Norman and Deller, Steven C.** Economies of Size and Scope in Rural Low-Volume Roads. *Rev. Econ. Statist.,* August 1988, *70*(3), pp. 459–65.

Chidiya, Charles; Weiner, Dan and Moyo, Sam. Energy Use in Zimbabwe's Agricultural Sector. In *Hosier, R. H., ed. (I),* 1988, pp. 20–59.

Chiesa, Gabriella. Government Deficit, Real Exchange Rate and International Transmission. *Bull. Econ. Res.,* June 1988, *40*(3), pp. 207–16.

Child, John. Information Technology and Organization. In *Urabe, K.; Child, J. and Kagono, T., eds.,* 1988, pp. 255–301.

Childers, Thomas. Big Business, Weimar Democracy, and Nazism: Henry Turner's *German Big Business and the Rise of Hitler. Bus. Hist. Rev.,* Spring 1988, *62*(1), pp. 128–33.

Childers, Victor E. Managing in the Third World. In *Farmer, R. N. and McGoun, E. G., eds.,* 1988, pp. 61–74.

Chilton, John B. and Addison, John T. Wage Patterns: An Evolutionary Perspective. *J. Lab. Res.,* Summer 1988, *9*(3), pp. 207–19.

Chilton, Kenneth W. and Weidenbaum, Murray L. Public Policy toward Corporate Takeovers:

Introduction. In *Weidenbaum, M. L. and Chilton, K. W., eds.*, 1988, pp. vii–xvi.

Chinapah, Vinayagum; Fägerlind, Ingemar and Tuijnman, Albert. Adult Education and Earnings: A 45-Year Longitudinal Study of 834 Swedish Men. *Econ. Educ. Rev.*, 1988, 7(4), pp. 423–37.

Ching, Chauncey T. K.; Hsu, George J. Y. and Leung, PingSun. Energy Planning in Taiwan: An Alternative Approach Using a Multiobjective Programming and Input–Output Model. *Energy J.*, January 1988, 9(1), pp. 53–72.

Chinloy, Peter. The Effect of Shifts in the Composition of Employment on Labor Productivity Growth: Canada 1971–1979. In *Dogramaci, A. and Färe, R., eds.*, 1988, pp. 195–220.

Chiorazzi, Michael, et al. Empirical Studies in Civil Procedure: A Selected Annotated Bibliography. *Law Contemp. Probl.*, Summer 1988, 51(3), pp. 87–207.

Chipande, Graham. The Impact of Demographic Changes on Rural Development in Malawi. In *Lee, R. D., et al., eds.*, 1988, pp. 162–74.

Chiplin, B. and Sloane, P. J. The Effect of Britain's Anti-discrimination Legislation on Relative Pay and Employment: A Comment. *Econ. J.*, September 1988, 98(392), pp. 833–38.

Chipman, Ralph and Jasentuliyana, Nandasiri. Satellite Remote Sensing in Developing Countries: The Experience of West Africa. In *Bhalla, A. S. and James, D., eds.*, 1988, pp. 223–40.

Chirinko, Robert S. Business Tax Policy, the Lucas Critique, and Lessons from the 1980's. *Amer. Econ. Rev.*, May 1988, 78(2), pp. 206–10.

————— **and Fazzari, Steven M.** Tobin's Q, Nonconstant Returns to Scale, and Imperfectly Competitive Product Markets. *Rech. Écon. Louvain*, 1988, 54(3), pp. 259–75.

Chisari, Omar O. A Comment on the Positivity Constraint in Olech's Theorem. *Econ. Notes*, 1988, (1), pp. 143–44.

————— **and Cristini, Marcela.** El impuesto a la tierra: una discusión de sus efectos económicos para el caso argentino. (Land Tax: A Discussion of Its Economic Effects in the Argentine Case. With English summary.) *Económica (La Plata)*, July–Dec. 1988, 34(2), pp. 155–84.

Chisholm, Anthony H. Sustainable Resource Use and Development: Uncertainty, Irreversibility and Rational Choice. In *Tisdell, C. and Maitra, P., eds.*, 1988, pp. 188–216.

—————. Teaching Agricultural Economics. *Rev. Marketing Agr. Econ.*, August 1988, 56(2), pp. 212–17.

Chishti, Salim and Mahmud, S. Fakhre. Energy Substitution in Pakistan's Manufacturing. *Pakistan Econ. Soc. Rev.*, Summer 1988, 26(1), pp. 57–64.

Chiswick, Barry R. Differences in Education and Earnings across Racial and Ethnic Groups: Tastes, Discrimination, and Investments in Child Quality. *Quart. J. Econ.*, August 1988, 103(3), pp. 571–97.

—————. Hispanic Men: Divergent Paths in the U.S. Labor Market. *Mon. Lab. Rev.*, November 1988, 111(11), pp. 32–34.

—————. Illegal Immigration and Immigration Control. *J. Econ. Perspectives*, Summer 1988, 2(3), pp. 101–15.

————— **and Miller, Paul W.** Earnings in Canada: The Roles of Immigrant Generation, French Ethnicity, and Language. In *Schultz, T. Paul, ed.*, 1988, pp. 183–228.

Chmura, Christine; Ko, Richard K. and Bechter, Dan M. Fifth District Indexes of Manufacturing Output. *Fed. Res. Bank Richmond Econ. Rev.*, May–June 1988, 74(3), pp. 23–33.

Cho, David Chinhyung and Frees, Edward W. Estimating the Volatility of Discrete Stock Prices. *J. Finance*, June 1988, 43(2), pp. 451–66.

Cho, Dong W. and McDougall, Gerald S. Demand Estimates for New General Aviation Aircraft: A User-Cost Approach. *Appl. Econ.*, March 1988, 20(3), pp. 315–24.

————— **and McDougall, Gerald S.** Explaining General Aviation Turbine Utilization. *Logist. Transp. Rev.*, March 1988, 24(1), pp. 68–83.

Cho, Dongsae. The Impact of Risk Management Decisions on Firm Value: Gordon's Growth Model Approach. *J. Risk Ins.*, March 1988, 55(1), pp. 118–31.

—————. Some Evidence of Scale Economies in Workers' Compensation Insurance. *J. Risk Ins.*, June 1988, 55(2), pp. 324–30.

Cho, Jang-Ok and Rogerson, Richard. Family Labor Supply and Aggregate Fluctuations. *J. Monet. Econ.*, March–May 1988, 21(2–3), pp. 233–45.

Cho, Joong Rae and Anas, Alex. A Dynamic, Policy Oriented Model of the Regulated Housing Market. *Reg. Sci. Urban Econ.*, May 1988, 18(2), pp. 201–31.

Cho, Lee-Jay and Luther, Norman Y. Reconstruction of Birth Histories from Census and Household Survey Data. *Population Stud.*, November 1988, 42(3), pp. 451–72.

Cho, Yoon Je. The Effect of Financial Liberalization on the Efficiency of Credit Allocation: Some Evidence from South Korea. *J. Devel. Econ.*, July 1988, 29(1), pp. 101–10.

—————. Some Policy Lessons from the Opening of the Korean Insurance Market. *World Bank Econ. Rev.*, May 1988, 2(2), pp. 239–54.

Choate, G. Marc and Thompson, Fred. Budget Makers as Agents: A Preliminary Investigation of Discretionary Behavior under State-Contingent Rewards. *Public Choice*, July 1988, 58(1), pp. 3–20.

Choate, Pat and Linger, Juyne. Meeting the Technology Challenge: Toward a U.S. Agenda. In *Yochelson, J., ed.*, 1988, pp. 19–32.

Choffray, Jean-Marie; Lilien, Gary L. and Yoon, Eunsang. New Industrial Product Performance: Models and Empirical Analysis. In *Woodside, A. G., ed.*, 1988, pp. 49–77.

Choi, Dosoung; Defusco, Richard A. and Philippatos, George C. Risk, Return and International Investment by U.S. Corporations. *Appl. Econ.*, September 1988, 20(9), pp. 1199–1209.

Choi, E. Kwan and Lapan, Harvey E. Tariffs versus Quotas under Uncertainty: Restricting Imports and the Role of Preference. *Int. Econ. J.*, Winter 1988, 2(4), pp. 35–55.

Choi, J. Y.; Salandro, Dan and Shastri, Kuldeep. On the Estimation of Bid–Ask Spreads: Theory and Evidence. *J. Finan. Quant. Anal.*, June 1988, 23(2), pp. 219–30.

Choi, Jongmoo Jay. Debt Financing and the Cost of Capital in the Neoclassical Investment Model. *Amer. Econ.*, Spring 1988, 32(1), pp. 19–23.

Choi, Thomas Y. and Nesbitt, Dale M. Is an Oil Tariff Justified? An American Debate: The Numbers Say No. *Energy J.*, July 1988, 9(3), pp. 31–59.

Choi, Unghwan and Chang, Sea Jin. Strategy, Structure and Performance of Korean Business Groups: A Transactions Cost Approach. *J. Ind. Econ.*, December 1988, 37(2), pp. 141–58.

Chokor, B. A. Research Policy and Review 22. Environment–Behaviour–Design Research: An Agenda for the Third World. *Environ. Planning A*, April 1988, 20(4), pp. 425–34.

Choldin, Harvey M. Government Statistics: The Conflict Between Research and Privacy. *Demography*, February 1988, 25(1), pp. 145–54.

Chollet, Deborah J. and Andrews, Emily S. Future Sources of Retirement Income: Whither the Baby Boom. In *Wachter, S. M., ed.*, 1988, pp. 71–95.

_____ and Friedland, Robert B. Employer Financing of Long-term Care. In *Scheffler, R. M. and Rossiter, L. F., eds.*, 1988, pp. 3–22.

Chomát, Jiří and Zeman, Karel. The Fuels and Energy Balance. *Czech. Econ. Digest.*, June 1988, (4), pp. 71–86.

Chon, Kyung S.; Boyce, David E. and LeBlanc, Larry J. Network Equilibrium Models of Urban Location and Travel Choices: A Retrospective Survey. *J. Reg. Sci.*, May 1988, 28(2), pp. 159–83.

Chongpeerapien, Tienchai and Amranand, Piyasvasti. Petroleum Product Pricing in Thailand. *Energy J.*, Special Issue, 1988, 9, pp. 15–43.

Chossudovsky, Michel. World Unemployment and China's Labour Reserves. In *Southall, R., ed.*, 1988, pp. 32–48.

Chotiner, Barbara Ann. Soviet Local Party Organs and the RAPOs. In *Potichnyj, P. J., ed.*, 1988, pp. 48–64.

Chou, Ray Yeutien. Volatility Persistence and Stock Valuations: Some Empirical Evidence Using Garch. *J. Appl. Econometrics*, Oct.–Dec. 1988, 3(4), pp. 279–94.

Chou, Shuh S.; Grandstaff, Peter J. and Ferris, Mark E. Forecasting Competitive Behavior: An Assessment of AT&T's Incentive to Extend Its U.S. Network. *Int. J. Forecasting*, 1988, 4(4), pp. 521–33.

Chou, Tein-Chen. American and Japanese Direct Foreign Investment in Taiwan: A Comparative Study. *Hitotsubashi J. Econ.*, December 1988, 29(2), pp. 165–79.

_____. Concentration and Profitability in a Dichotomous Economy: The Case of Taiwan. *Int.*

J. Ind. Organ., December 1988, 6(4), pp. 409–28.

_____. The Evolution of Market Structure in Taiwan. *Rivista Int. Sci. Econ. Com.*, February 1988, 35(2), pp. 171–94.

Chou, W. L. and Shih, Y.C. Trade, Determinants, and Causality: A Case of Hong Kong's Exports to the United States. *Int. Econ. J.*, Winter 1988, 2(4), pp. 21–33.

Choudhri, Ehsan U. and Brecher, Richard A. The Factor Content of Consumption in Canada and the United States: A Two-Country Test of the Heckscher–Ohlin–Vanek Model. In *Feenstra, R. C., ed.*, 1988, pp. 5–17.

Choudhury, Masudul Alam. Service Sector Diversification as an Alternative Prescription for Cape Breton Development. In *Choudhury, M. A., ed.*, 1988, pp. 171–79.

_____. Some Concepts and Goals of Regional Economic Development. In *Choudhury, M. A., ed.*, 1988, pp. 1–12.

Chouraqui, Jean-Claude. Public Sector Deficits in OECD Countries: Causes, Consequences and Policy Reaction. In *Cavanna, H., ed.*, 1988, pp. 1–40.

Chow, Gregory C. Economic Analysis of the People's Republic of China. *J. Econ. Educ.*, Winter 1988, 19(1), pp. 53–64.

_____. Money and Price Level Determination in China. In *Reynolds, B. L., ed.*, 1988, 1987, pp. 29–43.

Chow, Peter C. Y. and Kellman, Mitchell. Anti-LDC Bias in the U.S. Tariff Structure: A Test of Source versus Product Characteristics. *Rev. Econ. Statist.*, November 1988, 70(4), pp. 648–53.

Chowdhury, Abdur R. Expenditures and Receipts in State and Local Government Finances: Comment. *Public Choice*, December 1988, 59(3), pp. 277–85.

_____. The Infant Mortality–Fertility Debate: Some International Evidence. *Southern Econ. J.*, January 1988, 54(3), pp. 666–74.

_____. Monetary Policy, Fiscal Policy and Aggregate Economic Activity: Some Further Evidence. *Appl. Econ.*, January 1988, 20(1), pp. 63–71.

_____. Velocity and the Variability of Money Growth: Some International Evidence. *Econ. Letters*, 1988, 27(4), pp. 355–60.

Chowdhury, Nuimuddin. Accounting for Subsidized Food Resources Distributed in Statutory Rationing in Bangladesh. *Bangladesh Devel. Stud.*, December 1988, 16(4), pp. 41–64.

_____. Farmers' Participation in the Paddy Markets, Their Marketed Surplus and Factors Affecting It in Bangladesh: A Comment. *Bangladesh Devel. Stud.*, March 1988, 16(1), pp. 99–107.

_____. Income Tax Incidence in Bangladesh, 1980–84. *Bangladesh Devel. Stud.*, September 1988, 16(3), pp. 81–97.

_____. Where the Poor Come Last: The Case of Modified Rationing in Bangladesh. *Bangladesh Devel. Stud.*, March 1988, 16(1), pp. 27–54.

Chowdhury, Omar Haider. Effective Tax Rates for Bangladesh: 1984–85. *Bangladesh Devel. Stud.*, June 1988, 16(2), pp. 57–80.

———— **and Hossain, Mahabub.** Tax Structure of Bangladesh: An Overview. *Bangladesh Devel. Stud.*, December 1988, 16(4), pp. 65–91.

Christainsen, Gregory B. Fiat Money and the Constitution: A Historical Review. In *Willett, T. D., ed.*, 1988, pp. 424–34.

————. Gold and the Constitution: Retrospect and Prospect. In *[Rothbard, M. N.]*, 1988, pp. 32–43.

————. James Buchanan and the Revival of Classical Political Economy. *Challenge*, March–April 1988, 31(2), pp. 11–15.

————. The Natural Environment and Economic Education. *J. Econ. Educ.*, Spring 1988, 19(2), pp. 185–97.

Christensen, Kathleen E. Independent Contracting. In *Christensen, K. E., ed.*, 1988, pp. 79–91.

————. The New Era of Home-Based Work: Conclusion: Directions for the Future. In *Christensen, K. E., ed.*, 1988, pp. 201–06.

————. White-Collar Home-Based Work—The Changing U.S. Economy and Family. In *Christensen, K. E., ed.*, 1988, pp. 1–11.

Christensen, Laurits R. and Caves, Douglas W. The Importance of Economies of Scale, Capacity Utilization, and Density in Explaining Interindustry Differences in Productivity Growth. *Logist. Transp. Rev.*, March 1988, 24(1), pp. 3–32.

Christiano, Lawrence J. Why Does Inventory Investment Fluctuate So Much? *J. Monet. Econ.*, March–May 1988, 21(2–3), pp. 247–80.

———— **and Ljungqvist, Lars.** Money Does Granger-Cause Output in the Bivariate Money–Output Relation. *J. Monet. Econ.*, September 1988, 22(2), pp. 217–35.

Christiansen, M. Organization and Focus of a Farm-Oriented Regional Videotex Service. In *Schiefer, G., ed.*, 1988, pp. 165–72.

———— **and Graumann, U.** Current Developments: Closed User Group Plant Production: A New Service of TELE AGRAR. In *Schiefer, G., ed.*, 1988, pp. 173–76.

Christiansen, Robert E. and Tower, Edward. Effect of a Fertilizer Subsidy on Income Distribution and Efficiency in Malawi. *Eastern Afr. Econ. Rev.*, December 1988, 4(2), pp. 49–58.

Christiansen, Vidar. Choice of Occupation, Tax Incidence and Piecemeal Tax Revision. *Scand. J. Econ.*, 1988, 90(2), pp. 141–59.

Christie, Ian. The Soviet Union Today: The Cinema. In *Cracraft, J., ed.*, 1988, pp. 284–92.

Christl, Josef. An Empirical Analysis of the Austrian Beveridge Curve. *Empirica*, 1988, 15(2), pp. 327–50.

Christoffersen, René M. and Jensen, Flemming Dalby. Pensionsreform og den finansielle sektor. (Pension Savings and the Financial Sector. With English summary.) *Nationaløkon. Tidsskr.*, 1988, 126(2), pp. 205–16.

Christy, Craig V. and Ironside, R. G. Performance of High-Technology Firms in a Periph-eral Resource-Based Economy: Alberta, Canada. *Growth Change*, Fall 1988, 19(4), pp. 88–100.

Chrystal, K. Alec and Thornton, Daniel L. The Macroeconomic Effects of Deficit Spending: A Review. *Fed. Res. Bank St. Louis Rev.*, Nov.–Dec. 1988, 70(6), pp. 48–60.

———— **and Thornton, Daniel L.** On the Informational Content of Spot and Forward Exchange Rates. *J. Int. Money Finance*, September 1988, 7(3), pp. 321–30.

———— **and Wood, Geoffrey E.** Are Trade Deficits a Problem? *Fed. Res. Bank St. Louis Rev.*, Jan.–Feb. 1988, 70(1), pp. 3–12.

————; **Wood, Geoffrey E. and Coughlin, Cletus C.** Protectionist Trade Policies: A Survey of Theory, Evidence and Rationale. *Fed. Res. Bank St. Louis Rev.*, Jan.–Feb. 1988, 70(1), pp. 12–29.

Chu, C. W. and Ignatiev, Alex. Epitaxial Thin Film Growth in Outer Space. In *Egan, J. J., et al.*, 1988, pp. 283–97.

Chu, Chen-Chin. A Risk Premium under Uncertain Inflation: The Inflation Futures Evidence. *J. Futures Markets*, June 1988, 8(3), pp. 353–63.

Chu, Chin-Yi. An Income-Specific Stable Population Model: Theory and Potential Applications. In *Schultz, T. Paul, ed.*, 1988, pp. 337–66.

Chu, David K. W. Welfare Management in Free Enterprise and Socialist Economic Systems: A Study of Six Countries. In *Farmer, R. N. and McGoun, E. G., eds.*, 1988, pp. 21–45.

Chu, Flora and Perry, Seymour. Selecting Medical Technologies in Developing Countries. In *Bell, D. E. and Reich, M. R., eds.*, 1988, pp. 379–99.

Chu, Ke-young. External Shocks and Fiscal Policy in LDCs. *Finance Develop.*, June 1988, 25(2), pp. 28–30.

———— **and Morrison, Thomas K.** World Non-oil Primary Commodity Markets: Reply [A Medium-term Framework of Analysis]. *Int. Monet. Fund Staff Pap.*, March 1988, 35(1), pp. 204.

Chu, Wan-wen. The Effect of Learning on Market Structure. *Southern Econ. J.*, July 1988, 55(1), pp. 196–201.

————. Export-Led Growth and Import Dependence: The Case of Taiwan, 1969–1981. *J. Devel. Econ.*, March 1988, 28(2), pp. 265–76.

Chua, Wai Fong. Of Gods and Demons, Science and Ideology. In *Neimark, M., ed.*, 1988, pp. 29–46.

Chudnovsky, Daniel. The Diffusion and Production of Numerically Controlled Machine Tools with Special Reference to Argentina. *World Devel.*, June 1988, 16(6), pp. 723–32.

Chun, Youngsub. The Equal-Loss Principle for Bargaining Problems. *Econ. Letters*, 1988, 26(2), pp. 103–06.

————. Nash Solution and Timing of Bargaining. *Econ. Letters*, 1988, 28(1), pp. 27–31.

————. The Proportional Solution for Rights Problems. *Math. Soc. Sci.*, June 1988, 15(3), pp. 231–46.

_____ **and Thomson, William.** Monotonicity Properties of Bargaining Solutions when Applied to Economics. *Math. Soc. Sci.*, February 1988, *15*(1), pp. 11–27.

Chung, Ching-Fan and Lopez, Elena. A Regional Analysis of Food Consumption in Spain. *Econ. Letters*, 1988, *26*(3), pp. 209–13.

_____**; Theil, Henri and Lopez, Elena.** Tracing the Composition Changes of Japan's Consumer Budget, 1920–1980. *Empirical Econ.*, 1988, *13*(1), pp. 59–64.

Chung, Jae Wan. International Monetary Flows and Stability in Foreign Exchange Markets. *Appl. Econ.*, May 1988, *20*(5), pp. 611–22.

Chung, Ki-Young; Johnson, Herb and Castanias, Rick. Dividend Spreads. *J. Bus.*, July 1988, *61*(3), pp. 299–319.

Chung, Un-Chan. Capital Liberalization in Korea. In *Lee, C. H. and Naya, S., eds.*, 1988, pp. 181–93.

Churakov, V. Iakov. Jobs and Labor Resources. *Prob. Econ.*, January 1988, *30*(9), pp. 70–86.

Chye, Tan Eu and Semudram, M. The Monetarist versus Neo-Keynesian Controversy over Inflation: The Malaysian Evidence. *Indian Econ. J.*, July–September 1988, *36*(1), pp. 48–54.

Ciaschini, Maurizio. Input–Output Analysis: An Introduction. In *Ciaschini, M., ed.*, 1988, pp. 1–16.

Cichocki, Krzysztof and Wojciechowski, Waldemar. Investment Coefficient Matrix in Dynamic Input–Output Models: An Analysis and Prognosis. In *Ciaschini, M., ed.*, 1988, pp. 231–52.

Čičin-Šain, Ante. Domestic and External Macropolicies: Comments. In *Saunders, C. T., ed.*, 1988, pp. 225–27.

Ciesielski, Z. Nonparametric Polynominal Density Estimation in the L^p Norm. In *Gomez Fernandez, J. A., et al., eds.*, 1988, pp. 1–10.

Cigler, Beverly A. Political and Organizational Considerations in Infrastructure Investment Decision-Making. In *Johnson, T. G.; Deaton, B. J. and Segarra, E., eds.*, 1988, pp. 201–13.

_____. Rural Infrastructure Research Needs. In *Johnson, T. G.; Deaton, B. J. and Segarra, E., eds.*, 1988, pp. 233–44.

Cigno, Alessandro. Macroeconomic Consequences of the 'New Home Economics.' In *Lee, R. D.; Arthur, W. B. and Rodgers, G., eds.*, 1988, pp. 139–50.

Cimoli, M. Technological Gaps and Institutional Asymmetries in a North–South Model with a Continuum of Goods. *Metroecon.*, October 1988, *39*(3), pp. 245–74.

Cinar, E. Mine and Vu, Joseph D. The Effect of Individual Stock Option Expirations on Stock Returns before and after the Introduction of SP 100 Index Options. In *Fabozzi, F. J., ed.*, 1988, pp. 341–56.

Cingranelli, David Louis and Wright, Kevin N. Correlates of Due Process. In *Cingranelli, D. L., ed.*, 1988, pp. 154–72.

Cipolletta, Innocenzo. Muddling Through: Amer-

ican Interests in a Changing International Economy: Perspective. In *Guerrieri, P. and Padoan, P. C., eds.*, 1988, pp. 195–98.

Ciriacono, Salvatore. *Datini Reconsidered:* Vent'anni di storiografia economica a Prato. ("Datini Reconsidered": Twenty Years of Economic Historiography in Prato. With English summary.) *Rivista Storia Econ., S.S.*, October 1988, *5*(3), pp. 405–17.

Ciscel, David H. and Heath, Julia A. Patriarchy, Family Structure and the Exploitation of Women's Labor. *J. Econ. Issues*, September 1988, *22*(3), pp. 781–94.

Citzler, Annette M. and Chavas, Jean-Paul. On the Economics of Household Composition. *Appl. Econ.*, October 1988, *20*(10), pp. 1401–18.

Civardi, Marisa Bottiroli and Lenti, Renata Targetti. The Distribution of Personal Income at the Sectoral Level in Italy: A SAM Model. *J. Policy Modeling*, Fall 1988, *10*(3), pp. 453–68.

Čížkovský, Milan. Direct Relations between Organizations of CMEA Member Countries. *Czech. Econ. Digest.*, May 1988, (3), pp. 56–60.

Claassen, Emil-Maria. Comments [Labor Market Barriers to More Employment: Causes for an Increase of the Natural Rate? The Case of West Germany] [Distortions, Incentives, and Growth]. In *Giersch, H., ed.*, 1988, pp. 235–37.

Claessens, Stijn. Balance-of-Payments Crises in a Perfect Foresight Optimizing Model. *J. Int. Money Finance*, December 1988, *7*(4), pp. 363–72.

Claeys, Gregory. Lewis Masquerier and the Later Development of American Owenism, 1835–1845. *Labor Hist.*, Spring 1988, *29*(2), pp. 230–40.

Clague, Christopher K. Explanations of National Price Levels. In *Salazar-Carrillo, J. and Rao, D. S. P., eds.*, 1988, pp. 237–62.

_____. Purchasing-Power Parities and Exchange Rates in Latin America. *Econ. Develop. Cult. Change*, April 1988, *36*(3), pp. 529–41.

Clain, Suzanne Heller and Leppel, Karen. The Growth in Involuntary Part-Time Employment of Men and Women. *Appl. Econ.*, September 1988, *20*(9), pp. 1155–66.

Clair, Robert T. The Performance of Black-Owned Banks in Their Primary Market Areas. *Fed. Res. Bank Dallas Econ. Rev.*, November 1988, pp. 11–20.

Clancy, Donald K.; Freeman, Robert J. and Willits, Stephen D. Public Employee Retirement System Reports: A Study of Knowledgeable User Information Processing Ability. In *Chan, J. L. and Rowan, H. J., eds.*, 1988, pp. 3–48.

Clarence-Smith, Gervase. Protectionism and Sugar Production in Central and Equatorial Africa, 1910–1945. In *Albert, B. and Graves, A., eds.*, 1988, pp. 209–20.

Clarete, Ramon L. and Whalley, John. Interactions between Trade Policies and Domestic Distortions in a Small Open Developing Country. *J. Int. Econ.*, May 1988, *24*(3–4), pp. 345–58.

Clarida, Richard H. and Campbell, John Y. Saving and Permanent Income in Canada and the United Kingdom. In *Helpman, E.; Razin, A. and Sadka, E., eds.*, 1988, pp. 122–41.

Clark, Allen L. and Johnson, Charles J. Mineral Exploration in Developing Countries: Botswana and Papua New Guinea Case Studies. In *Tilton, J. E.; Eggert, R. G. and Landsberg, H. H., eds.*, 1988, pp. 145–78.

Clark, C. J.; Lawler, K. A. and Seddighi, H. R. The Structure of the Charity Sector in England and Wales: A Statistical Analysis. *Appl. Econ.*, March 1988, *20*(3), pp. 335–50.

Clark, Charles M. A. Equilibrium, Market Process, and Historical Time. *J. Post Keynesian Econ.*, Winter 1987–88, *10*(2), pp. 270–81.

Clark, David E.; Kahn, James R. and Ofek, Haim. City Size, Quality of Life, and the Urbanization Deflator of the GNP: 1910–1984. *Southern Econ. J.*, January 1988, *54*(3), pp. 701–14.

_____ **and Kahn, James R.** The Social Benefits of Urban Cultural Amenities. *J. Reg. Sci.*, August 1988, *28*(3), pp. 363–77.

Clark, Don P. U.S. Production in Foreign-Trade Zones: Potential for Reducing Tariff Liability. *J. World Trade*, December 1988, *22*(6), pp. 107–15.

_____; **Hofler, Richard and Thompson, Henry.** Separability of Capital and Labor in U.S. Manufacturing. *Econ. Letters*, 1988, *26*(2), pp. 197–201.

Clark, Gordon L. Time, Events, and Places: Reflections on Economic Analysis. *Environ. Planning A*, February 1988, *20*(2), pp. 187–94.

_____ **and Johnston, K.** The Geography of U.S. Union Elections: Addenda. *Environ. Planning A*, July 1988, *20*(7), pp. 979–82.

Clark, Gracia. Price Control of Local Foodstuffs in Kumasi, Ghana, 1979. In *Clark, G., ed.*, 1988, pp. 57–79.

_____. Traders versus the State: Introduction. In *Clark, G., ed.*, 1988, pp. 1–16.

Clark, Gregory. Can Management Develop the World? Reply. *J. Econ. Hist.*, March 1988, *48*(1), pp. 143–48.

_____. The Cost of Capital and Medieval Agricultural Technique. *Exploration Econ. Hist.*, July 1988, *25*(3), pp. 265–94.

Clark, Ian N.; Major, Philip J. and Mollett, Nina. Development and Implementation of New Zealand's ITQ Management System. *Marine Resource Econ.*, 1988, *5*(4), pp. 325–49.

Clark, J. H. and Barau, A. D. Evaluating Alternative Mortgage Instruments for Low-equity Ontario Farms: A Correction. *Can. J. Agr. Econ.*, July 1988, *36*(2), pp. 359–60.

Clark, Joel P. and Flemings, Merton C. Advanced Materials and the Economy. In *Forester, T., ed.*, 1988, *1986*, pp. 163–78.

_____, **et al.** How Critical are Critical Materials? In *Forester, T., ed.*, 1988, *1985*, pp. 273–86.

Clark, John J.; Chakrabarti, Alok K. and Chiang, Thomas C. Stock Prices and Merger Move-

ments: Interactive Relations. *Weltwirtsch. Arch.*, 1988, *124*(2), pp. 287–300.

_____; **Chakrabarti, Alok K. and Chiang, Thomas C.** Trend and Stochastic Movements in U.S. Merger Activity. *Quart. Rev. Econ. Bus.*, Summer 1988, *28*(2), pp. 6–19.

Clark, Kim B. Managing Technology in International Competition: The Case of Product Development in Response to Foreign Entry. In *Spence, A. M. and Hazard, H. A., eds.*, 1988, pp. 27–74.

_____ **and Summers, Lawrence H.** Labour Force Participation: Timing and Persistence. In *Cross, R., ed.*, 1988, pp. 203–31.

Clark, Norman G. Some New Approaches to Evolutionary Economics. *J. Econ. Issues*, June 1988, *22*(2), pp. 511–31.

_____ **and Juma, Calestous.** Evolutionary Theories in Economic Thought. In *Dosi, G., et al., eds.*, 1988, pp. 197–218.

Clark, Peter B. Empirical Macroeconomics for Interdependent Economies: Comparison and Evaluation of Model Simulations: Comment. In *Bryant, R. C., et al., eds.*, 1988, pp. 149–51.

_____ **and Brayton, Flint.** The Macroeconomic and Sectoral Effects of the Economic Recovery Tax Act: Some Simulation Results. In *Motamen, H., ed.*, 1988, pp. 141–64.

Clark, Peter K. Nearly Redundant Parameters and Measures of Persistence in Economic Time Series. *J. Econ. Dynam. Control*, June–Sept. 1988, *12*(2–3), pp. 447–61.

_____. Postwar Developments in Business Cycle Theory: A Moderately Classical Perspective: Comment. *J. Money, Credit, Banking*, Part 2, August 1988, *20*(3), pp. 476–78.

Clark, Robert M. and Kim, H. Youn. Economies of Scale and Scope in Water Supply. *Reg. Sci. Urban Econ.*, November 1988, *18*(4), pp. 479–502.

Clark, Roger D. The Primate and the Elephant City: A Tale of Two Theses. *Soc. Sci. Quart.*, March 1988, *69*(1), pp. 40–52.

Clark, Stephen A. An Extension Theorem for Rational Choice Functions. *Rev. Econ. Stud.*, July 1988, *55*(3), pp. 485–92.

_____. Revealed Independence and Quasi-linear Choice. *Oxford Econ. Pap.*, September 1988, *40*(3), pp. 550–59.

Clark, Truman A.; Joines, Douglas H. and Phillips, G. Michael. Social Security Payments, Money Supply Announcements, and Interest Rates. *J. Monet. Econ.*, September 1988, *22*(2), pp. 257–78.

_____ **and Laffer, Arthur B.** Are Small Cap Stocks Still Alive? In *Canto, V. A. and Laffer, A. B., eds.*, 1988, pp. 9–24.

_____ **and Laffer, Arthur B.** The Impact of Tax Reform on Income-Producing Real Estate. In *Canto, V. A. and Laffer, A. B., eds.*, 1988, pp. 25–53.

Clark, W. A. V. Understanding Residential Segregation in American Cities: Interpreting the Evidence: A Reply. *Population Res. Policy Rev.*, 1988, *7*(2), pp. 113–21.

_____; **Deurloo, M. C. and Dieleman, F. M.** Generalized Log-linear Models of Housing Choice. *Environ. Planning A,* January 1988, *20*(1), pp. 55–69.

_____ **and Mueller, Milan.** Hispanic Relocation and Spatial Assimilation: A Case Study. *Soc. Sci. Quart.,* June 1988, *69*(2), pp. 468–75.

Clark, William. Production Costs and Output Qualities in Public and Private Employment Agencies. *J. Law Econ.,* October 1988, *31*(2), pp. 379–93.

Clarke, Harry R. and Reed, William J. A Stochastic Analysis of Land Development Timing and Property Valuation. *Reg. Sci. Urban Econ.,* August 1988, *18*(3), pp. 357–81.

Clarke, M. and Birkin, M. SYNTHESIS—A Synthetic Spatial Information System for Urban and Regional Analysis: Methods and Examples. *Environ. Planning A,* December 1988, *20*(12), pp. 1645–71.

Clarke, Malcolm. Forestry Development in Upland Britain. In *[Lecomber, R.],* 1988, pp. 97–120.

Clarke, Michael and Tilman, Rick. C. B. Macpherson's Contributions to Democratic Theory. *J. Econ. Issues,* March 1988, *22*(1), pp. 181–96.

Clarke, Richard N., et al. Sources of the Crisis in Liability Insurance: An Economic Analysis. *Yale J. Regul.,* Summer 1988, *5*(2), pp. 367–95.

Clarke, Roger. Revenue Maximising Sales Taxes in Oligopolistic Equilibrium When Costs Vary between Firms. *Bull. Econ. Res.,* January 1988, *40*(1), pp. 79–82.

Clarke, Sally. Farmers as Entrepreneurs: Regulation and Innovation in American Agriculture during the Twentieth Century. In *Hausman, W. J., ed.,* 1988, pp. 207–11.

Clarke, Stephen V. O. Have We Caught the British Disease? *Challenge,* Jan.–Feb. 1988, *31*(1), pp. 29–36.

Clarkson, Judith; Roderick, Hilliard and Schmandt, Jurgen. Acid Rain and Friendly Neighbors: The Policy Dispute between Canada and the United States: Preface. In *Schmandt, J.; Clarkson, J. and Roderick, H., eds.,* 1988, pp. xiii–xv.

_____ **and Schmandt, Jurgen.** Acid Rain and Friendly Neighbors: The Policy Dispute between Canada and the United States: Conclusions. In *Schmandt, J.; Clarkson, J. and Roderick, H., eds.,* 1988, pp. 253–302.

Clarkson, Kenneth W. Panel: The Issues in Regulation and Deregulation: The Case for Minimizing Regulation. In *Maynes, E. S. and ACCI Research Committee, eds.,* 1988, pp. 441–45.

Clarkson, L. A. and Crawford, E. Margaret. Dietary Directions: A Topographical Survey of Irish Diet, 1836. In *Mitchison, R. and Roebuck, P., eds.,* 1988, pp. 171–92.

Clarkson, Max B. E. Corporate Social Performance in Canada, 1976–86. In *Preston, L. E., ed.,* 1988, pp. 241–65.

Claus of the Netherlands [Prince]. The Human Dimension of Economic Models. In *Driehuis,*

W.; Fase, M. M. G. and den Hartog, H., eds., 1988, pp. 1–6.

Clauser, Steven B. and Cooper, Barbara S. The Champus Reform Initiative: Tailoring Private-Sector Innovations to Public-Sector Needs. In *Scheffler, R. M. and Rossiter, L. F., eds.,* 1988, pp. 247–65.

Clavijo, Sergio. Macroeconometría de una economía pequeña y abierta asando análisis de vectores autorregresivos. (Macroeconometrics of a Small Open Economy Using Vector Autoregression Analysis. With English summary.) *Estud. Econ.,* Jan.–June 1988, *3*(1), pp. 3–25.

Clay, Edward. Assessment of Food-Entitlement Interventions in South Asia. In *Curtis, D.; Hubbard, M. and Shepherd, A.,* 1988, pp. 141–56.

_____. Floods in Bangladesh, 1974 and 1984: From Famine to Flood-Crisis Management. In *Curtis, D.; Hubbard, M. and Shepherd, A.,* 1988, pp. 131–37.

Clayton, Elizabeth. Rural Infrastructure in the Soviet Union: Roads and Other Priorities. In *Brada, J. C. and Wadekin, K.-E., eds.,* 1988, pp. 361–69.

Clayton, Kenneth C. United States Perspective: Southern Agriculture and the World Economy: The Multilateral Trade Negotiations. *Southern J. Agr. Econ.,* July 1988, *20*(1), pp. 73–76.

Cleare, Anthony and Furnham, Adrian. School Children's Conceptions of Economics: Prices, Wages, Investments and Strikes. *J. Econ. Psych.,* December 1988, *9*(4), pp. 467–79.

Cleary, Paul D. and McNeil, Barbara J. Patient Satisfaction as an Indicator of Quality Care. *Inquiry,* Spring 1988, *25*(1), pp. 25–36.

Cleave, John. Environmental Assessments. *Finance Develop.,* March 1988, *25*(1), pp. 44–47.

Cleave, Nancy; Brown, Philip and Payne, Clive. Adding New Statistical Techniques to Standard Software Systems: A Review. In *Edwards, D. and Raun, N. E., eds.,* 1988, pp. 207–11.

Cleaver, Kevin M. The Use of Price Policy to Stimulate Agricultural Growth in Sub-Saharan Africa. In *Roberts, C., ed.,* 1988, pp. 81–91.

de Cleene, T. A. and Douglas, R. O. Final Report of the Consultative Committee on Full Imputation and International Tax Reform: Statement. *Bull. Int. Fiscal Doc.,* October 1988, *42*(10), pp. 442–47.

Cleland, John and Rodríguez, Germán. The Effect of Parental Education on Marital Fertility in Developing Countries. *Population Stud.,* November 1988, *42*(3), pp. 419–42.

_____ **and Rodríguez, Germán.** Modelling Marital Fertility by Age and Duration: An Empirical Appraisal of the Page Model. *Population Stud.,* July 1988, *42*(2), pp. 241–57.

Clem, Andrew; Kuemmerling, Robert A. and Howell, Craig. Domestic Price Rise during 1987 Reflects Swing of Energy Prices. *Mon. Lab. Rev.,* June 1988, *111*(6), pp. 20–26.

Clem, Ralph S. The Soviet Union Today: Ethnicity. In *Cracraft, J., ed.,* 1988, pp. 303–14.

_____. *Perestroika:* The Social Context of Reform

in the Soviet Union. **In** *Liebowitz, R. D., ed.*, 1988, pp. 9–22.

Clement, Hermann. Changes in the Soviet Foreign Trade System. *Soviet E. Europ. Foreign Trade*, Winter 1988–89, *24*(4), pp. 1–94.

Clement, Rainer. Divergent or Convergent Growth within the European Community? Answers from a Macro-economic Point of View. *Jahr. Nationalökon. Statist.*, December 1988, *205*(6), pp. 480–91.

_____. Zur Notwendigkeit entwicklungspolitischer Massnahmen in der Europäischen Gemeinschaft. (Notes on the Necessity of Development Policies within the European Community. With English summary.) *Konjunkturpolitik*, 1988, *34*(2), pp. 85–103.

Clemente, C. L. A Pharmaceutical Industry Perspective. **In** *Walker, C. E. and Bloomfield, M. A., eds.*, 1988, pp. 127–34.

Clements, Benedict J. and Kim, Kwan S. Comércio exterior e distribuiçâo de renda: O caso brasileiro. (With English summary.) *Pesquisa Planejamento Econ.*, April 1988, *18*(1), pp. 17–36.

Clements, Kenneth W. and Selvanathan, E. Antony. The Rotterdam Demand Model and Its Application in Marketing. *Marketing Sci.*, Winter 1988, *7*(1), pp. 60–75.

Clements, R. T.; Hansen, C. D. and Hames, M. J. The Reserve Bank Econometric Model of the New Zealand Economy. *Econ. Modelling*, April 1988, *5*(2), pp. 83–132.

Clemenz, Gerhard. Comparative Advantage and Gains from Trade in the Presence of Random Preferences. *J. Inst. Theoretical Econ.*, September 1988, *144*(4), pp. 706–20.

Clemhout, Simone and Wan, Henry Y., Jr. A General Dynamic Model of Bargaining—The Perfect Information Case. **In** *Eiselt, H. A. and Pederzoli, G., eds.*, 1988, pp. 293–305.

Cleveland, Frederick W.; Koeller, C. Timothy and Ballantine, John W. Corporate Profitability and Competitive Circumstance. *Eastern Econ. J.*, Jan.–March 1988, *14*(1), pp. 7–18.

Cleveland, Harold van B.; Silk, Leonard and Calleo, David P. The Dollar and the Defense of the West. *Foreign Aff.*, Spring 1988, *66*(4), pp. 846–62.

Cleveland, William S. and Devlin, Susan J. Locally Weighted Regression: An Approach to Regression Analysis by Local Fitting. *J. Amer. Statist. Assoc.*, September 1988, *83*(403), pp. 596–610.

_____; **Devlin, Susan J. and Grosse, Eric.** Regression By Local Fitting: Methods, Properties, and Computational Algorithms. *J. Econometrics*, January 1988, *37*(1), pp. 87–114.

Cline, Robert J. Should States Adopt a Value-Added Tax? **In** *Gold, S. D., ed.*, 1988, pp. 235–54.

Cline, William R. Can the East Asian Model of Development Be Generalized? **In** *Wilber, C. K., ed.*, 1988, pp. 282–97.

_____. The Debt Problem of Developing Countries and Proposed Solutions: Comments. **In**

Elliott, K. A. and Williamson, J., eds., 1988, pp. 175–84.

_____. International Debt: Progress and Strategy. *Finance Develop.*, June 1988, *25*(2), pp. 9–11.

Clinton, Kevin. Transactions Costs and Covered Interest Arbitrage: Theory and Evidence. *J. Polit. Econ.*, April 1988, *96*(2), pp. 358–70.

Closs, M. J. Canada: The Neighbouring Auto Industry. **In** *Thornton, R. J.; Hyclak, T. and Aronson, J. R., eds.*, 1988, pp. 131–44.

Cloutier, Norman R. Pareto Extrapolation Using Grouped Income Data. *J. Reg. Sci.*, August 1988, *28*(3), pp. 415–19.

Clovis. Jevons and the Establishment. **In** *Wood, J. C., ed., Vol. 3*, 1988, *1964-5*, pp. 82–85.

Clower, Robert W. The Consequences of Economic Rhetoric: The Ideas of Economists. **In** *Klamer, A.; McCloskey, D. N. and Solow, R. M., eds.*, 1988, pp. 85–99.

_____. Keynes and the Classics Revisited. **In** *Hamouda, O. F. and Smithin, J. N., eds., Vol. 1*, 1988, pp. 81–91.

_____. The Keynesian Counter-revolution: A Theoretical Appraisal. **In** *Shaw, G. K., ed., Vol. 1*, 1988, *1965*, pp. 235–62.

_____ **and Burstein, Meyer Louis.** On the Invariance of Demand for Cash and Other Assets. **In** *Burstein, M. L.*, 1988, *1960*, pp. 3–10.

Clutterbuck, John B. Karl Llewellyn and the Intellectual Foundations of Enterprise Liability Theory. *Yale Law J.*, May 1988, *97*(6), pp. 1131–51.

Cnossen, Sijbren. Discussion [Issues in Integration of Federal and Provincial Sales Taxes: A Canadian Perspective] [The (Apparent) Demise of Sales Tax Deductibility: Issues for Analysis and Policy]. *Nat. Tax J.*, September 1988, *41*(3), pp. 391–94.

_____. World Tax Reform: A Progress Report: Overview. **In** *Pechman, J. A., ed.*, 1988, pp. 261–68.

Coady, David; Stern, Nicholas and Ahmad, Ehtisham. A Complete Set of Shadow Prices for Pakistan: Illustrations for 1975–76. *Pakistan Devel. Rev.*, Spring 1988, *27*(1), pp. 7–43.

Coakley, Jerry. American Banks' Credit to UK Industry. **In** *Harris, L., et al., eds.*, 1988, pp. 190–213.

_____. Bank Lending and the Control of Industry: An Empirical Study. **In** *Harris, L., et al., eds.*, 1988, pp. 170–89.

_____. The Internationalisation of Bank Capital. **In** *Harris, L., et al., eds.*, 1988, pp. 69–87.

_____ **and Harris, Laurence.** Evaluating the Role of the Financial System. **In** *Harris, L., et al., eds.*, 1988, pp. 125–42.

_____ **and Harris, Laurence.** Industry, the City and the Foreign Exchanges: Theory and Evidence. **In** *Harris, L., et al., eds.*, 1988, pp. 88–115.

Coase, R. H. The Firm, the Market, and the Law. **In** *Coase, R. H.*, 1988, pp. 1–31.

_____. How Should Economists Choose? **In** *[Nutter, G. W.]*, 1988, pp. 63–79.

_____. Industrial Organization: A Proposal for

Research. In *Coase, R. H.*, 1988, *1972*, pp. 57–74.

_____. The Lighthouse in Economics. In *Cowen, T., ed.*, 1988, *1974*, pp. 255–77.

_____. The Lighthouse in Economics. In *Coase, R. H.*, 1988, *1974*, pp. 187–213.

_____. The Marginal Cost Controversy. In *Coase, R. H.*, 1988, *1946*, pp. 75–93.

_____. The Nature of the Firm. In *Coase, R. H.*, 1988, *1937*, pp. 33–55.

_____. The Nature of the Firm: Influence. *J. Law, Econ., Organ.*, Spring 1988, *4*(1), pp. 33–47.

_____. The Nature of the Firm: Meaning. *J. Law, Econ., Organ.*, Spring 1988, *4*(1), pp. 19–32.

_____. The Nature of the Firm: Origin. *J. Law, Econ., Organ.*, Spring 1988, *4*(1), pp. 3–17.

_____. Notes on the Problem of Social Cost. In *Coase, R. H.*, 1988, pp. 157–85.

_____. The Problem of Social Cost. In *Ricketts, M., ed.*, Vol. 2, 1988, *1960*, pp. 14–57.

_____. The Problem of Social Cost. In *Coase, R. H.*, 1988, *1960*, pp. 95–156.

Coate, Douglas and Grossman, Michael. Effects of Alcoholic Beverage Prices and Legal Drinking Ages on Youth Alcohol Use. *J. Law Econ.*, April 1988, *31*(1), pp. 145–71.

Coate, Malcolm B. and Uri, Noel D. A Simultaneous Equations Approach to Modeling Industry Structure and Economic Performance. *Metroecon.*, June 1988, *39*(2), pp. 181–204.

Coates, Daniel E. and Mulligan, James G. Scale Economies and Capacity Utilization: The Importance of Relative Fuel Prices. *Energy Econ.*, April 1988, *10*(2), pp. 140–46.

Coates, Vary T. Office Automation Technology and Home-Based Work. In *Christensen, K. E., ed.*, 1988, pp. 114–25.

Coats, A. W. Economic Rhetoric: The Social and Historical Context. In *Klamer, A.; McCloskey, D. N. and Solow, R. M., eds.*, 1988, pp. 64–84.

_____. Economics and Psychology: A Resurrection Story. In *Earl, P. E., ed.*, 1988, pp. 211–25.

_____. The Educational Revolution and the Professionalization of American Economics. In *Barber, W. J., ed.*, 1988, pp. 340–75.

_____. Enlightenment and Beyond: Political Economy Comes to Japan: From a Western Point of View. In *Sugiyama, C. and Mizuta, H., eds.*, 1988, pp. 273–83.

Coats, Warren L., Jr. Capital Mobility and Monetary Policy: Australia, Japan, and New Zealand. In *Cheng, H.-S., ed.*, 1988, pp. 81–94.

Cobban, Murray A. Tropical Products in the Uruguay Round Negotiations. *World Econ.*, June 1988, *11*(2), pp. 233–48.

Cobble, Dorothy Sue. "Practical Women": Waitress Unionists and the Controversies over Gender Roles in the Food Service Industry, 1900–1980. *Labor Hist.*, Winter 1988, *29*(1), pp. 5–31.

_____. A Self-possessed Woman: A View of FDR's Secretary of Labor, Madame Perkins. *Labor Hist.*, Spring 1988, *29*(2), pp. 225–29.

Cobham, David. A Disequilibrium Monetarist Approach to the Assessment of Monetary Control Regimes. *Brit. Rev. Econ. Issues*, Spring 1988, *10*(22), pp. 1–22.

Cochran, Mark J. and Mjelde, James W. Obtaining Lower and Upper Bounds on the Value of Seasonal Climate Forecasts as a Function of Risk Preferences. *Western J. Agr. Econ.*, December 1988, *13*(2), pp. 285–93.

Cochrane, John H. How Big Is the Random Walk in GNP? *J. Polit. Econ.*, October 1988, *96*(5), pp. 893–920.

_____ **and Sbordone, Argia M.** Multivariate Estimates of the Permanent Components of GNP and Stock Prices. *J. Econ. Dynam. Control*, June–Sept. 1988, *12*(2–3), pp. 255–96.

Cochrane, Steven G. and Vining, Daniel R., Jr. Population Migration in the Developed World: Some Further Comments. *Int. Reg. Sci. Rev.*, 1988, *11*(3), pp. 277–78.

_____ **and Vining, Daniel R., Jr.** Recent Trends in Migration between Core and Peripheral Regions in Developed and Advanced Developing Countries. *Int. Reg. Sci. Rev.*, 1988, *11*(3), pp. 215–43.

Cockburn, Iain and Griliches, Zvi. Industry Effects and Appropriability Measures in the Stock Market's Valuation of R&D and Patents. *Amer. Econ. Rev.*, May 1988, *78*(2), pp. 419–23.

Coddington, Alan. Deficient Foresight: A Troublesome Theme in Keynesian Economics. In *Shaw, G. K., ed.*, Vol. 1, 1988, *1982*, pp. 67–74.

Coderre, Cécile; Denis, Ann and Andrew, Caroline. Women in Management: The Canadian Experience: The Relationship of Professional and Personal Lives. In *Adler, N. J. and Izraeli, D., eds.*, 1988, pp. 250–64.

deCodes, Jose; Baker, Timothy D. and Schumann, Debra. The Hidden Costs of Illness in Developing Countries. In *Sirageldin, I. and Sorkin, A., eds.*, 1988, pp. 127–45.

Codognato, Giulio. Teoria dei giochi ed equilibrio economico generale: Alcuni aspetti. (Game Theory and General Equilibrium: Some Aspects. With English summary.) *Ricerche Econ.*, July–Sept. 1988, *42*(3), pp. 520–35.

Coe, Charles K. The Effects of Cash Management Assistance by States to Local Governments. *Public Budg. Finance*, Summer 1988, *8*(2), pp. 80–90.

Coe, David T. Hysteresis Effects in Aggregate Wage Equations. In *Cross, R., ed.*, 1988, pp. 284–305.

_____; **Durand, Martine and Stiehler, Ulrich.** The Disinflation of the 1980s. *OECD Econ. Stud.*, Autumn 1988, (11), pp. 89–121.

Coe, Jack J. Responses to Some of the Adverse External Effects of Groundwater Withdrawals in California. In *O'Mara, G. T., ed.*, 1988, pp. 51–57.

Coelho, Philip R. P. and Orzechowski, William P. Taxes and Incentives: Horatio Alger vs. the Tax Man. *Atlantic Econ. J.*, September 1988, *16*(3), pp. 31–39.

Coelli, Tim J. and Battese, George E. Prediction

of Firm-Level Technical Efficiencies with a Generalized Frontier Production Function and Panel Data. *J. Econometrics*, July 1988, *38*(3), pp. 387–99.

Coen, Robert M. and Hickman, Bert G. Is European Unemployment Classical or Keynesian? *Amer. Econ. Rev.*, May 1988, *78*(2), pp. 188–93.

Coffee, John C., Jr. After the Crash: Linkages between Stocks and Futures: Trading Systems. In *MacKay, R. J., ed.*, 1988, pp. 65–71.

———. Are Hostile Takeovers Different?: Discussion. In *Browne, L. E. and Rosengren, E. S., eds.*, 1988, pp. 230–42.

———. Shareholders versus Managers: The Strain in the Corporate Web. In *Coffee, J. C., Jr.; Lowenstein, L. and Rose-Ackerman, S., eds.*, 1988, pp. 77–134.

———; **Lowenstein, Louis and Rose-Ackerman, Susan.** Knights, Raiders & Targets: The Impact of the Hostile Takeover: Introduction. In *Coffee, J. C., Jr.; Lowenstein, L. and Rose-Ackerman, S., eds.*, 1988, pp. 1–9.

Coffey, Joseph D. The Design and Impact of Strategic Management Information Systems: Discussion. *Amer. J. Agr. Econ.*, May 1988, *70*(2), pp. 484–85.

Coffin, H. Garth. Agricultural Trade and Policy Reform: Rhetoric and Reality. *Can. J. Agr. Econ.*, November 1988, *36*(3), pp. 383–99.

———. Driving Forces, Instruments, and Institutions in Canadian Agricultural Policies. In *Allen, K. and Macmillan, K., eds.*, 1988, pp. 41–64.

Cogan, John F. The Federal Deficit in the 1990s: A Tale of Two Budgets. In *Anderson, A. and Bark, D. L., eds.*, 1988, pp. 277–87.

Cogger, Kenneth O. Proposals for Research in Time Series Forecasting. *Int. J. Forecasting*, 1988, *4*(3), pp. 403–10.

Cogill, Bruce and Kennedy, Eileen T. The Commercialization of Agriculture and Household-Level Food Security: The Case of Southwestern Kenya. *World Devel.*, September 1988, *16*(9), pp. 1075–81.

Cogoli, A.; Gmünder, F. K. and Nordau, C. G. Cell Biology in Space: From Basic Science to Biotechnology III. In *Egan, J. J., et al.*, 1988, pp. 353–66.

Cohen, Benjamin J. Global Debt: Why is Cooperation so Difficult? In *Guerrieri, P. and Padoan, P. C., eds.*, 1988, pp. 91–111.

Cohen, Bernard P.; Rainwater, Julie and Silver, Steven D. Group Structure and Information Exchange in Innovative Problem Solving. In *Lawler, E. J. and Markovsky, B., eds.*, 1988, pp. 169–94.

Cohen, Cynthia Fryer; Gaines, Jeannie and Jermier, John M. Paying Dues to the Union: A Study of Blue-Collar Workers in a Right-to-Work Environment. *J. Lab. Res.*, Spring 1988, *9*(2), pp. 167–82.

Cohen, Daniel. The Management of the Developing Countries' Debt: Guidelines and Applications to Brazil. *World Bank Econ. Rev.*, January 1988, *2*(1), pp. 77–103.

———. Which LDCs Are Solvent? *Europ. Econ. Rev.*, March 1988, *32*(2–3), pp. 687–93.

———; **Mélitz, Jacques and Oudiz, Gilles.** Le système monéaire européen et l'asymétrie franc–mark. (The EMS and the Frank–Mark Asymetry. With English summary.) *Revue Écon.*, May 1988, *39*(3), pp. 667–77.

——— **and Michel, Philippe.** How Should Control Theory Be Used to Calculate a Time-Consistent Government Policy? *Rev. Econ. Stud.*, April 1988, *55*(2), pp. 263–74.

Cohen, Darrel. Money Demand and the Effects of Fiscal Policies: Comment. *J. Money, Credit, Banking*, November 1988, *20*(4), pp. 698–705.

Cohen, Joel E. Correction [Population Forecasts and Confidence Intervals for Sweden: A Comparison of Model-Based and Empirical Approaches]. *Demography*, May 1988, *25*(2), pp. 315.

Cohen, Joel J. Explaining the Events of October 1987. In *MacKay, R. J., ed.*, 1988, pp. 11–16.

Cohen, John M. and Isaksson, Nils-Ivar. Food Production Strategy Debates in Revolutionary Ethiopia. *World Devel.*, March 1988, *16*(3), pp. 323–48.

Cohen, Kalman J. and Cyert, Richard M. Computer Models in Dynamic Economics. In *Cyert, R. M.*, 1988, *1961*, pp. 163–78.

Cohen, Michael D.; March, James G. and Olsen, Johan P. A Garbage Can Model of Organizational Choice. In *March, J. G.*, 1988, *1972*, pp. 294–334.

Cohen, Michèle and Jaffray, Jean-Yves. Preponderance of the Certainty Effect over Probability Distortion in Decision Making under Risk. In *Munier, B. R., ed.*, 1988, pp. 173–87.

Cohen, Sanford. Does Public Employee Unionism Diminish Democracy? In *Lewin, D., et al., eds.*, 1988, *1979*, pp. 88–98.

Cohen, Stephen and Zysman, John. Muddling Through: American Interests in a Changing International Economy. In *Guerrieri, P. and Padoan, P. C., eds.*, 1988, pp. 162–94.

Cohen, Stephen F. The Stalin Question. In *Cracraft, J., ed.*, 1988, pp. 21–33.

Cohen, Suleiman I. Development Policy in a Multi-provincial Economy: Comments. *Pakistan Devel. Rev.*, Part 1, Winter 1988, *27*(4), pp. 421–24.

———. Manpower Planning Models with Labour Market Adjustment: Applications to Colombia, Republic of Korea and Pakistan. *Econ. Modelling*, January 1988, *5*(1), pp. 19–31.

———. A Social Accounting Matrix Analysis for the Netherlands. *De Economist*, 1988, *136*(2), pp. 253–72.

——— **and Havinga, Ivo C.** Microeconomic Analysis of the Informal Sector—Results of Sample Surveys. *Pakistan Devel. Rev.*, Part 2, Winter 1988, *27*(4), pp. 605–17.

Cohn, Elchanan. History and Prospects of the *Economics of Education Review*. *Econ. Educ. Rev.*, 1988, *7*(2), pp. 165–66.

Cohn, Raymond L. The Determinants of Individual Immigrant Mortality on Sailing Ships,

1836–1853. *Exploration Econ. Hist.*, July 1988, *25*(3), pp. 337–38.

Cohodes, Donald R. PPOs for Medicare? *Inquiry*, Summer 1988, *25*(2), pp. 204–05.

Colaizzo, Raffaele; Leonello, Giuseppe and D'Antonio, Mariano. Mezzogiorno/Centre-North: A Two-Region Model for the Italian Economy. *J. Policy Modeling*, Fall 1988, *10*(3), pp. 437–51.

Colander, David. Economic Methodology, Macroeconomics, and Externalities. In *Pennsylvania Economic Association*, 1988, pp. 1–7.

_____. The Evolution of Keynesian Economics: From Keynesian to New Classical to New Keynesian. In *Hamouda, O. F. and Smithin, J. N., eds., Vol. 1*, 1988, pp. 92–100.

Colby, Bonnie G. Economic Impacts of Water Law—State Law and Water Market Development in the Southwest. *Natural Res. J.*, Fall 1988, *28*(4), pp. 721–49.

_____; **Carpenter, Edwin H. and Cory, Dennis C.** Uncertain Recreation Quality and Wildlife Valuation: Are Conventional Benefit Measures Adequate? *Western J. Agr. Econ.*, December 1988, *13*(2), pp. 153–62.

_____; **Longstreth, Molly and Durham, Catherine A.** The Impact of State Tax Credits and Energy Prices on Adoption of Solar Enegy Systems. *Land Econ.*, November 1988, *64*(4), pp. 347–55.

Colclough, Glenna S. and Beck, E. M. Schooling and Capitalism: The Effect of Urban Economic Structure on the Value of Education. In *Farkas, G. and England, P., eds.*, 1988, pp. 113–39.

Cole, David C. Financial Development in Asia. *Asian-Pacific Econ. Lit.*, September 1988, *2*(2), pp. 26–47.

Cole, David E. and Flynn, Michael S. The U.S. Automotive Industry: Technology and Competitiveness. In *Hicks, D. A., ed.*, 1988, pp. 86–161.

Cole, Harold. Financial Structure and International Trade. *Int. Econ. Rev.*, May 1988, *29*(2), pp. 237–59.

Cole, Ishmail; MacMurray, Robert and Tarullo, Ronald. Regulation, Technological Change, and Productivity Growth in the Coal Industry. In *Pennsylvania Economic Association*, 1988, pp. 682–94.

_____; **MacMurray, Robert and Tarullo, Ronald.** Some Determinants of Official United States Coal Prices. In *Pennsylvania Economic Association*, 1988, pp. 695–706.

Cole, John A. and Chen, Gavin M. The Myths, Facts, and Theories of Ethnic, Small-Scale Enterprise Financing. *Rev. Black Polit. Econ.*, Spring 1988, *16*(4), pp. 111–23.

Cole, William; Sellers, Stephen G. and Bennett, John W. The Importance of Traditional Quality for Foods Containing Vegetable Protein Ingredients. In *Schwarz, F. H., ed.*, 1988, pp. 273–339.

Cole, William E. and Stephens, Mark. The Brazilian Motor Vehicle Industry: A Holistic Approach to Project Evaluation. *J. Econ. Issues*, June 1988, *22*(2), pp. 381–88.

Coleman, David A. British Social Trends since 1900: Population. In *Halsey, A. H., ed.*, 1988, pp. 36–134.

_____ and **McPherson, Klim.** British Social Trends since 1900: Health. In *Halsey, A. H., ed.*, 1988, pp. 398–461.

Coleman, J. R. and Meilke, Karl D. The Influence of Exchange Rates on Red Meat Trade between Canada and the United States. *Can. J. Agr. Econ.*, November 1988, *36*(3), pp. 401–24.

Coleman, James S. The Problems of Order: Where Are Rights to Act Located? *J. Inst. Theoretical Econ.*, April 1988, *144*(2), pp. 367–73.

_____. Social Capital in the Creation of Human Capital. In *Winship, C. and Rosen, S., eds.*, 1988, pp. 95–120.

_____. Social Organization of the Corporation. In *Meyer, J. R. and Gustafson, J. M., eds.*, 1988, pp. 93–111.

Coleman, Jules L. Corrective Justice and Wrongful Gain. In *Coleman, J. L.*, 1988, pp. 184–201.

_____. Crimes, Kickers and Transaction Structures. In *Coleman, J. L.*, 1988, pp. 153–65.

_____. Democracy and Social Choice. In *Coleman, J. L.*, 1988, pp. 290–310.

_____. Efficiency, Auction and Exchange. In *Coleman, J. L.*, 1988, pp. 67–94.

_____. Efficiency, Utility and Wealth Maximization. In *Coleman, J. L.*, 1988, pp. 95–132.

_____. The Foundations of Constitutional Economics. In *Coleman, J. L.*, 1988, pp. 133–50.

_____. Justice in Settlements. In *Coleman, J. L.*, 1988, pp. 202–39.

_____. Market Contractarianism. In *Coleman, J. L.*, 1988, pp. 243–76.

_____. Markets, Morals and the Law: Preface. In *Coleman, J. L.*, 1988, pp. ix–xvii.

_____. Morality and the Theory of Rational Choice. In *Coleman, J. L.*, 1988, pp. 311–42.

_____. The Morality of Strict Tort Liability. In *Coleman, J. L.*, 1988, pp. 166–83.

_____. Negative and Positive Positivism. In *Coleman, J. L.*, 1988, pp. 3–27.

_____. Rethinking the Theory of Legal Rights. In *Coleman, J. L.*, 1988, pp. 28–63.

_____. Unanimity. In *Coleman, J. L.*, 1988, pp. 277–89.

Coleman, Thomas. After the Crash: Linkages between Stocks and Futures: Regulatory Issues. In *MacKay, R. J., ed.*, 1988, pp. 37–40.

Coles, Jeffrey L. and Loewenstein, Uri. Equilibrium Pricing and Portfolio Composition in the Presence of Uncertain Parameters. *J. Finan. Econ.*, December 1988, *22*(2), pp. 279–303.

Colias, John V. An Applied General Equilibrium Model of the United States Economy. In *Motamen, H., ed.*, 1988, pp. 667–82.

Coll, Blanche D. Public Assistance: Reviving the Original Comprehensive Concept of Social Security. In *Nash, G. D.; Pugach, N. H. and Tomasson, R. F., eds.*, 1988, pp. 221–41.

Collard, David A. Catastrophic Risk: Or the Economics of Being Scared. In *[Lecomber, R.]*, 1988, pp. 67–83.

_____. A New Moral Sentiments? A Review [Well-being: Its Meaning, Measurement and Moral Importance]. *Oxford Econ. Pap.*, June 1988, *40*(2), pp. 289–95.

Collet, J. European Programmes in Space-Based Facilities and Transportation. In *Egan, J. J., et al.*, 1988, pp. 201–10.

Collier, Irwin L., Jr. The Simple Analytics (and a Few Pitfalls) of Real Consumption and Purchasing Power Parity Indexes. *Comp. Econ. Stud.*, Winter 1988, *30*(4), pp. 1–16.

_____ **and Gregory, Paul R.** Unemployment in the Soviet Union: Evidence from the Soviet Interview Project. *Amer. Econ. Rev.*, September 1988, *78*(4), pp. 613–32.

_____ **and Papell, David H.** About Two Marks: Refugees and the Exchange Rate before the Berlin Wall. *Amer. Econ. Rev.*, June 1988, *78*(3), pp. 531–42.

Collier, Paul. Oil Shocks and Food Security in Nigeria. *Int. Lab. Rev.*, 1988, *127*(6), pp. 761–82.

Collignon, Frederick C. Benefit–Cost Analyses Conducted by State Agencies. In *Berkowitz, M., ed.*, 1988, pp. 150–60.

Collins, Brenda. Sewing and Social Structure: The Flowerers of Scotland and Ireland. In *Mitchison, R. and Roebuck, P., eds.*, 1988, pp. 242–54.

Collins, D. J. Fringe Benefits Taxation and the Rural Sector. *Rev. Marketing Agr. Econ.*, April 1988, *56*(1), pp. 107–20.

Collins, Daniel W.; Dhaliwal, Dan S. and Doran, B. Michael. The Information of Historical Cost Earnings Relative to Supplemental Reserve-Based Accounting Data in the Extractive Petroleum Industry. *Accounting Rev.*, July 1988, *63*(3), pp. 389–413.

Collins, J. Markham and Bey, Roger P. The Relationship between Before- and After-Tax Yields on Financial Assets. *Financial Rev.*, August 1988, *23*(3), pp. 313–31.

Collins, Julie H. and Wyckoff, James H. Estimates of Tax-Deferred Retirement Savings Behavior. *Nat. Tax J.*, December 1988, *41*(4), pp. 561–72.

Collins, Keith and Vertrees, James. Decoupling and U.S. Farm Policy Reform. *Can. J. Agr. Econ.*, Part 1, December 1988, *36*(4), pp. 733–45.

Collins, Michael. Did Keynes Have the Answer to Unemployment in the 1930s? In *Hillard, J., ed.*, 1988, pp. 64–87.

Collins, Neil and Haslam, R. B. Local Government Finance in the Republic of Ireland—The Aftermath of Rates Abolition. In *Paddison, R. and Bailey, S., eds.*, 1988, pp. 218–29.

Collins, Robert A. The Required Rate of Return for Publicly Held Agricultural Equity: An Arbitrage Pricing Theory Approach. *Western J. Agr. Econ.*, December 1988, *13*(2), pp. 163–68.

_____. Risk Analysis with Single-Index Portfolio Models: An Application to Farm Planning: Re-

ply. *Amer. J. Agr. Econ.*, February 1988, *70*(1), pp. 195–96.

_____ **and Barry, Peter J.** Beta-Adjusted Hurdle Rates for Proprietary Firms. *J. Econ. Bus.*, May 1988, *40*(2), pp. 139–45.

Collins, Ronald K. L. and Skover, David M. The Future of Liberal Legal Scholarship: Commentary. *Mich. Law Rev.*, October 1988, *87*(1), pp. 189–239.

Collins, Susan M. Savings and Growth Experiences of Korea and Japan. *J. Japanese Int. Economies*, September 1988, *2*(3), pp. 328–50.

Collis, David J. The Machine Tool Industry and Industrial Policy, 1955–82. In *Spence, A. M. and Hazard, H. A., eds.*, 1988, pp. 75–114.

Collomp, Catherine. Unions, Civics, and National Identity: Organized Labor's Reaction to Immigration, 1881–1897. *Labor Hist.*, Fall 1988, *29*(4), pp. 450–74.

Colman, David. The CAP in Conflict with Trade and Development. *Europ. Rev. Agr. Econ.*, 1988, *15*(2–3), pp. 123–35.

Coloma, Fernando; Williamson, Carlos and Bustamante, Blanca. El precio social de la mano de obra. (With English summary.) *Cuadernos Econ.*, April 1988, *25*(74), pp. 81–124.

Colomb, Robert M. The Place of Expert Systems in Agricultural Economics: A Comment. *Rev. Marketing Agr. Econ.*, August 1988, *56*(2), pp. 209–10.

Colombard-Prout, Marc. The Global Construction Industry: France. In *Strassmann, W. P. and Wells, J., eds.*, 1988, pp. 104–119.

Colombatto, Enrico and Hamaui, Rony. Domanda di protezionismo e tasso di cambio. (The Demand for Protectionism and the Exchange Rate. With English summary.) *Econ. Polit.*, December 1988, *5*(3), pp. 369–85.

Colombo, J. A. and Anderson, Joan B. Christian Base Communities and Grass-Roots Development. *J. Behav. Econ.*, Summer 1988, *17*(2), pp. 97–112.

Colombo, Massimo G.; Mariotti, Sergio and Cainarca, Gian Carlo. La dinamica diffusiva dell'automazione flessibile. (The Diffusion Pattern of Flexible Automation. With English summary.) *Econ. Lavoro*, Jan.–Mar. 1988, *22*(1), pp. 41–63.

Colombo, Umberto. The Technology Revolution and the Restructuring of the Global Economy. In *Muroyama, J. H. and Stever, H. G., eds.*, 1988, pp. 23–31.

Colton, Timothy J. Gorbachev and the Politics of System Renewal. In *Bialer, S. and Mandelbaum, M., eds.*, 1988, pp. 151–86.

Colwell, Peter F. and Wu, Chunchi. Moral Hazard and Moral Imperative. *J. Risk Ins.*, March 1988, *55*(1), pp. 101–17.

Combe, O. La structure des taux d'interet en France. (The Term Structure of Interest Rates in France. With English summary.) *Écon. Soc.*, January 1988, *22*(1), pp. 249–69.

Comfort, A. M. Alternatives to Infrastructure? Possible Ways Forward for the ERDF: A Perspective from Luxembourg. *Reg. Stud.*, December 1988, *22*(6), pp. 542–51.

Comisso, Ellen. The Politics of Creating Efficient Markets in Socialism: Comments. In *[Holzman, F. D.]*, 1988, pp. 285–99.

Commander, Simon and Killick, Tony. Privatisation in Developing Countries: A Survey of the Issues. In *Cook, P. and Kirkpatrick, C., eds.*, 1988, pp. 91–124.

_____ **and Killick, Tony.** State Divestiture as a Policy Instrument in Developing Countries. *World Devel.*, December 1988, *16*(12), pp. 1465–79.

Commins, Stephen K. and Lofchie, Michael F. Food Deficits and Agricultural Policies in Tropical Africa. In *Wilber, C. K., ed.*, 1988, pp. 303–25.

Common, Michael. 'Poverty and Progress' Revisited. In *[Lecomber, R.]*, 1988, pp. 15–39.

Commons, John R. Institutional Economics. In *Samuels, W. J., ed., Vol. 1*, 1988, *1931*, pp. 18–27.

Comprido, Francisco J. and Trincão, Victor M. Semi-aggregate Consumption in Portugal: 1958–1975. *Economia (Portugal)*, January 1988, *12*(1), pp. 103–14.

Comtois, Claude. L'impact des infrastructures de transport sur la production agricole: le cas des zones économiques spéciales en Chine. (With English summary.) *Can. J. Devel. Stud.*, 1988, *9*(1), pp. 105–16.

Conant, John L. and Wang, Leonard F. S. Corporate Tax Evasion and Output Decisions of the Uncertain Monopolist. *Nat. Tax J.*, December 1988, *41*(4), pp. 579–81.

Condoyanni, L.; O'Hanlon, J. and Ward, C. W. R. Weekend Effects in Stock Market Returns: International Evidence. In *Dimson, E., ed.*, 1988, pp. 52–63.

Conerly, Michael D. and Mansfield, Edward R. An Approximate Test for Comparing Heteroscedastic Regression Models. *J. Amer. Statist. Assoc.*, September 1988, *83*(403), pp. 811–17.

Conforti, D. and Grandinetti, L. An Experience of Advanced Computation Techniques in the Solution of Nonlinearly Constrained Optimization Problems. In *Kurzhanski, A.; Neumann, K. and Pallaschke, D., eds.*, 1988, pp. 69–85.

Confraria, João. A fuga ao imposto sobre o rendimento—um "survey" da literatura. (With English summary.) *Economia (Portugal)*, May 1988, *12*(2), pp. 161–80.

Congdon, Peter Douglas. The Interdependence of Geographical Migration with Job and Housing Mobility in London. *Reg. Stud.*, April 1988, *22*(2), pp. 81–93.

_____. Occupational Mobility and Labour Market Structure: A Multivariate Markov Model. *Scot. J. Polit. Econ.*, August 1988, *35*(3), pp. 208–26.

_____ **and Shepherd, John.** Components of Social Change in Urban Areas. *Urban Stud.*, June 1988, *25*(3), pp. 173–89.

Congleton, Roger D. An Overview of the Contractarian Public Finance of James Buchanan. *Public Finance Quart.*, April 1988, *16*(2), pp. 131–57.

_____. Evaluating Rent-Seeking Losses: Do the Welfare Gains of Lobbyists Count? *Public Choice*, February 1988, *56*(2), pp. 181–84.

Conine, Thomas E., Jr. and Tamarkin, Maurry. Textbook Inconsistencies in Graphing Valuation Equations: A Further Note. *Financial Rev.*, May 1988, *23*(2), pp. 237–41.

Conlan, Timothy J. and Wrightson, Margaret T. Federal Dollars and Congressional Sense: Targeting Aid to Poor People and Poor Places. In *Bell, M. E., ed.*, 1988, pp. 163–90.

Conley, James R.; Wasilewski, Edward J. and Borum, Joan D. The Outlook for Collective Bargaining in 1988. *Mon. Lab. Rev.*, January 1988, *111*(1), pp. 10–23.

Conlisk, John. Optimization Cost. *J. Econ. Behav. Organ.*, April 1988, *9*(3), pp. 213–28.

Connolly, Robert A. and Hirschey, Mark. Market Value and Patents: A Bayesian Approach. *Econ. Letters*, 1988, *27*(1), pp. 83–87.

Connolly, S. J. Albion's Fatal Twigs: Justice and Law in the Eighteenth Century. In *Mitchison, R. and Roebuck, P., eds.*, 1988, pp. 117–25.

Connolly, Thomas J. Nuclear Energy After Chernobyl: Views from Four Countries: United States. *Energy J.*, January 1988, *9*(1), pp. 35–39.

Connor, Gregory and Korajczyk, Robert A. Risk and Return in an Equilibrium APT: Application of a New Test Methodology. *J. Finan. Econ.*, September 1988, *21*(2), pp. 255–89.

Connor, John M. Industrial Organization: Some Applications for Managerial Decisions: Discussion. *Amer. J. Agr. Econ.*, May 1988, *70*(2), pp. 482–83.

Connor-Lajambe, Hélène. Renewable Energy and Long-term Energy Planning. *Energy J.*, July 1988, *9*(3), pp. 143–51.

Connor, Walter D. Changing Times and the Soviet Worker. In *Connor, W. D.*, 1988, pp. 85–113.

_____. From Utopia to Autonomy: Thought and Action in the Eastern European Opposition. In *Connor, W. D.*, 1988, pp. 231–61.

_____. Generations and Politics in the USSR. In *Connor, W. D.*, 1988, *1975*, pp. 50–66.

_____. Social Change and Stability in Eastern Europe. In *Connor, W. D.*, 1988, *1977*, pp. 138–59.

_____. Social Policy in the Gorbachev Era. In *Connor, W. D.*, 1988, pp. 114–37.

_____. Soviet Dissent and Social Complexity. In *Connor, W. D.*, 1988, *1973*, pp. 29–49.

_____. State, Society, and the Soviet Model. In *Connor, W. D.*, 1988, pp. 5–28.

_____. The Successor Generation. In *Connor, W. D.*, 1988, *1983*, pp. 201–30.

_____. Workers and Intellectuals: A Dissident Coalition? In *Connor, W. D.*, 1988, *1980*, pp. 160–81.

_____. Workers and Power. In *Connor, W. D.*, 1988, *1981*, pp. 182–200.

_____. Workers, Politics, and Class Consciousness. In *Connor, W. D.*, 1988, *1979*, pp. 67–84.

Connors, Patrick T. New Deal Labor Policy and

the American Industrial Economy: Review Essay. *Mich. Law Rev.*, May 1988, *86*(6), pp. 1425–29.

Conrad, James and DeBoer, Larry. Do High Interest Rates Encourage Property Tax Delinquency? *Nat. Tax J.*, December 1988, *41*(4), pp. 555–60.

_____ **and DeBoer, Larry.** Rural Property Tax Delinquency and Recession in Agriculture. *Amer. J. Agr. Econ.*, August 1988, *70*(3), pp. 553–59.

Conrad, Jennifer and Kaul, Gautam. Time-Variation in Expected Returns. *J. Bus.*, October 1988, *61*(4), pp. 409–25.

Conrad, Klaus. Theory and Measurement of Productivity and Cost Gaps: A Comparison for the Manufacturing Industry in U.S., Japan and Germany, 1960–1979. In *Eichhorn, W., ed.*, 1988, pp. 725–50.

_____ **and Henseler-Unger, Henseler.** Income Tax Reduction and the Quantification of Welfare Gains—An Applied General Equilibrium Analysis. In *Bös, D.; Rose, M. and Seidl, C., eds.*, 1988, pp. 247–62.

Conradie, Barbara. The Standard Bank and Its Records as an Economic Source. In *Jones, S., ed.*, 1988, pp. 175–79.

Considine, Timothy J. Oil Price Volatility and U.S. Macroeconomic Performance. *Contemp. Policy Issues*, July 1988, *6*(3), pp. 83–96.

Constantinescu, N. N. The System of Economic Sciences at the Academy of High Commercial and Industrial Studies in Bucharest. *Econ. Computat. Cybern. Stud. Res.*, 1988, *23*(3), pp. 33–47.

Constantinides, George M. Comments on Stock Return Seasonality. In *Dimson, E., ed.*, 1988, pp. 123–28.

Constantinides, Marietta A. Optimal Population Growth and the Social Welfare Function. *Eastern Econ. J.*, July–Sept. 1988, *14*(3), pp. 229–38.

Conte, Michael A. and Darrat, Ali F. Economic Growth and the Expanding Public Sector: A Reexamination. *Rev. Econ. Statist.*, May 1988, *70*(2), pp. 322–30.

_____ **and Svejnar, Jan.** Productivity Effects of Worker Participation in Management, Profit-Sharing, Worker Ownership of Assets and Unionization in U.S. Firms. *Int. J. Ind. Organ.*, March 1988, *6*(1), pp. 139–51.

Conti, Vittorio and Silvani, Marco. Il commercio intra-CEE e la posizione relativa dei paesi membri. (Intra-EEC Trade and the Competitive Positions of the Member Countries. With English summary.) *Giorn. Econ.*, Sept.–Oct. 1988, *47*(9–10), pp. 443–74.

Contractor, Farok J. and Lorange, Peter. Cooperative Strategies in International Business: Introduction and a Summary of the Issues. In *Contractor, F. J. and Lorange, P.*, 1988, pp. xxv–xxix.

_____ **and Lorange, Peter.** Why Should Firms Cooperate? The Strategy and Economics Basis for Cooperative Ventures. In *Contractor, F. J. and Lorange, P.*, 1988, pp. 3–30.

Contzen, J. P. The Benefit of Remote Sensing Activities in Europe. In *Egan, J. J., et al.*, 1988, pp. 135–56.

Conway, Delores A. and Reinganum, Marc R. Stable Factors in Security Returns: Identification Using Cross-Validation. *J. Bus. Econ. Statist.*, January 1988, *6*(1), pp. 1–15.

_____ **and Reinganum, Marc R.** Stable Factors in Security Returns: Identification Using Cross-Validation: Reply. *J. Bus. Econ. Statist.*, January 1988, *6*(1), pp. 24–28.

Conway, Elizabeth A. and Levitan, Sar A. Part-Timers: Living on Half-Rations. *Challenge*, May–June 1988, *31*(3), pp. 9–16.

Conway, Patrick. Diminishing Returns to Real Depreciation in Achieving Macroeconomic Goals. *Eastern Econ. J.*, Oct.–Dec. 1988, *14*(4), pp. 371–80.

_____. The Impact of Recent Trade Liberalization Policies in Turkey. In *Nas, T. F. and Odekon, M., eds.*, 1988, pp. 47–67.

_____ **and Bale, Malcolm.** Approximating the Effective Protection Coefficient without Reference to Technological Data. *World Bank Econ. Rev.*, September 1988, *2*(3), pp. 349–63.

_____ **and Gelb, Alan.** Oil Windfalls in a Controlled Economy: A 'Fix-Price' Equilibrium Analysis of Algeria. *J. Devel. Econ.*, February 1988, *28*(1), pp. 63–81.

Conway, Roger K.; Hrubovcak, James and LeBlanc, Michael R. Estimating the Structure of Agricultural Investment: A Stochastic-Coefficients Approach. *J. Bus. Econ. Statist.*, April 1988, *6*(2), pp. 231–40.

_____; **LeBlanc, Michael R. and Swamy, P. A. V. B.** The Stochastic Coefficients Approach to Econometric Modeling: Part I: A Critique of Fixed Coefficients Models. *J. Agr. Econ. Res.*, Spring 1988, *40*(2), pp. 2–10.

_____; **LeBlanc, Michael R. and Swamy, P. A. V. B.** The Stochastic Coefficients Approach to Econometric Modeling, Part II: Description and Motivation. *J. Agr. Econ. Res.*, Summer 1988, *40*(3), pp. 21–30.

_____ **and Mittelhammer, Ron C.** Applying Mixed Estimation in Econometric Research. *Amer. J. Agr. Econ.*, November 1988, *70*(4), pp. 859–66.

Cook, B. A. Discount Effects and Canada's Pacific Halibut Fishery. *Marine Resource Econ.*, 1988, *5*(1), pp. 71–77.

Cook, Christopher J. Commodity Price Distortions and Intraagricultural Income Distribution in Colombia. *J. Devel. Areas*, January 1988, *22*(2), pp. 219–37.

Cook, Earl and Cook, Violetta Burke. Romance and Resources. In *Ehrlich, P. R. and Holdren, J. P., eds.*, 1988, pp. 299–316.

Cook, Edward. Prospects for Polish Agriculture in the 1980s. In *Brada, J. C. and Wadekin, K.-E., eds.*, 1988, pp. 131–45.

Cook, Paul and Hulme, David. The Compatibility of Market Liberalization and Local Economic Development Strategies. *Reg. Stud.*, June 1988, *22*(3), pp. 221–31.

_____ **and Kirkpatrick, Colin.** Privatisation in

Less Developed Countries: An Overview. **In** *Cook, P. and Kirkpatrick, C., eds.*, 1988, pp. 3–44.

_____ **and Kirkpatrick, Colin.** Privatisation in Less Developed Countries: Preface. **In** *Cook, P. and Kirkpatrick, C., eds.*, 1988, pp. xvii–xix.

Cook, Philip J. Increasing the Federal Excise Taxes on Alcoholic Beverages: Editorial. *J. Health Econ.*, March 1988, 7(1), pp. 89–91.

_____. Social Norms and Drunk Driving Countermeasures: Comments. **In** *Graham, J. D., ed.*, 1988, pp. 181–83.

_____ **and Zarkin, Gary A.** Crime and the Business Cycle. **In** *Alper, N. O. and Hellman, D. A., eds.*, 1988, pp. 60–74.

Cook, R. Dennis. Combining Robust and Traditional Least Squares Methods: A Critical Evaluation: Comment. *J. Bus. Econ. Statist.*, October 1988, 6(4), pp. 429–32.

Cook, Richard E. What the Economics Literature Has to Say about Takeovers. **In** *Weidenbaum, M. L. and Chilton, K. W., eds.*, 1988, pp. 1–24.

_____ **and Weidenbaum, Murray L.** Impacts of Takeovers on Financial Markets. **In** *Weidenbaum, M. L. and Chilton, K. W., eds.*, 1988, pp. 63–77.

Cook, Robert J. and Sancar, Fahriye Hazer. Multi-level Modeling for Incorporating Public Perceptions into Comprehensive Planning: Door County Example. *Rev. Reg. Stud.*, Spring 1988, 18(2), pp. 54–69.

Cook, Thomas; Rochfort, William M. and Hodes, Daniel A. The Importance of Regional Economic Analysis and Regional Strategies in an Age of Industrial Restructuring. *Bus. Econ.*, April 1988, 23(2), pp. 46–51.

Cook, Timothy and Hahn, Thomas. The Information Content of Discount Rate Announcements and Their Effect on Market Interest Rates. *J. Money, Credit, Banking*, May 1988, 20(2), pp. 167–80.

Cook, Violetta Burke and Cook, Earl. Romance and Resources. **In** *Ehrlich, P. R. and Holdren, J. P., eds.*, 1988, pp. 299–316.

Cook, Wade D. and Kress, Moshe. Partial and Multiple Match Tournaments. *Math. Soc. Sci.*, June 1988, 15(3), pp. 303–06.

Cooke, Timothy W. Mortgage and Rental Qualification Criteria, Household Location Decisions, and Urban Form. *J. Urban Econ.*, May 1988, 23(3), pp. 354–69.

Cooke, William and Meyer, David. Economic and Political Factors in Formal Grievance Resolution. *Ind. Relat.*, Fall 1988, 27(3), pp. 318–35.

Cookingham, Mary E. Political Economy in the Far West: The University of California and Stanford University. **In** *Barber, W. J., ed.*, 1988, pp. 266–89.

Cool, Karel and Schendel, Dan. Development of the Strategic Management Field: Some Accomplishments and Challenges. **In** *Grant, J. H., ed.*, 1988, pp. 17–31.

Coomans, Géry. Economie productive et écono-

mie financière dans les annees 1920. (Economy of Production and Finance Economy in the Twenties. With English summary.) *Écon. Soc.*, May 1988, 22(5), pp. 13–49.

Coombes, M. G.; Green, A. E. and Owen, D. W. Substantive Issues in the Definition of 'Localities': Evidence from Sub-group Local Labour Market Areas in the West Midlands. *Reg. Stud.*, August 1988, 22(4), pp. 303–18.

Coombs, James and Hall, David O. The Agroenergy Filière: Experiences and Perspectives. **In** *Antonelli, G. and Quadrio-Curzio, A., eds.*, 1988, pp. 257–79.

Coombs, Rod. Technological Opportunities and Industrial Organisation. **In** *Dosi, G., et al., eds.*, 1988, pp. 295–308.

Coomes, Paul A. An Illustration of the Application of Control Methods in Choosing Optimal U.S. Agricultural Policy. *J. Econ. Dynam. Control*, March 1988, 12(1), pp. 161–66.

Cooper, Arnold C.; Dunkelberg, William C. and Woo, Carolyn Y. Entrepreneurial Typologies: Definitions and Implications. **In** *Kirchhoff, B. A., et al., eds.*, 1988, pp. 165–76.

_____; **Dunkelberg, William C. and Woo, Carolyn Y.** Survival and Failure: A Longitudinal Study. **In** *Kirchhoff, B. A., et al., eds.*, 1988, pp. 225–37.

Cooper, Barbara S. and Clauser, Steven B. The Champus Reform Initiative: Tailoring Private-Sector Innovations to Public-Sector Needs. **In** *Scheffler, R. M. and Rossiter, L. F., eds.*, 1988, pp. 247–65.

Cooper, C. Joseph, Jr. White-Collar Pay in Nonservice Industries, March 1988. *Mon. Lab. Rev.*, October 1988, 111(10), pp. 39–41.

Cooper, David J. A Social Analysis of Corporate Pollution Disclosures: A Comment. **In** *Neimark, M., ed.*, 1988, pp. 179–86.

Cooper, Graeme S. Tax Accounting for Deductions. *Australian Tax Forum*, 1988, 5(1), pp. 23–131.

Cooper, Ian and Mello, Antonio S. Default Spreads in the Fixed and in the Floating Interest Rate Markets: A Contingent Claims Approach. **In** *Fabozzi, F. J., ed.*, 1988, pp. 269–89.

Cooper, J. H. The Burden of the Public Debt: A Review. *S. Afr. J. Econ.*, December 1988, 56(4), pp. 278–91.

_____ **and Black, P. A.** Government Financing Requirement: Short and Long-run Consequences. *S. Afr. J. Econ.*, December 1988, 56(4), pp. 292–97.

Cooper, L. G. Market-Share Analysis: Communicating Results through Spreadsheet-Based Simulators. **In** *Gaul, W. and Schader, M., eds.*, 1988, pp. 35–41.

Cooper, M. C. and Milligan, G. W. The Effect of Measurement Error on Determining the Number of Clusters in Cluster Analysis. **In** *Gaul, W. and Schader, M., eds.*, 1988, pp. 319–28.

Cooper, Richard N. An Analysis of the International Energy Agency: Comments by a Some time Practitioner. In *Horwich, G. and Weimer, D. L., eds.*, 1988, pp. 265–84.

———. Industrial Policy and Trade Distortion: A Policy Perspective. In *Spence, A. M. and Hazard, H. A., eds.*, 1988, *1986*, pp. 115–47.

———. To Coordinate or Not to Coordinate? In *Fieleke, N. S., ed.*, 1988, pp. 229–33.

———. Toward an International Commodity Standard? *Cato J.*, Fall 1988, *8*(2), pp. 315–38.

———. U.S. Macroeconomic Policy, 1986–88: Are the Models Useful? In *Bryant, R. C., et al., eds.*, 1988, pp. 255–66.

Cooper, Russel J. Recent Developments in Forecasting with the ORANI Model: Comment. *Australian Econ. Pap.*, Supplement, June 1988, *27*, pp. 105–07.

Cooper, Russell. Labor Contracts and the Role of Monetary Policy in an Overlapping Generations Model. *J. Econ. Theory*, April 1988, *44*(2), pp. 231–50.

———. Will Share Contracts Increase Economic Welfare? *Amer. Econ. Rev.*, March 1988, *78*(1), pp. 138–54.

——— and John, Andrew. Coordinating Coordination Failures in Keynesian Models. *Quart. J. Econ.*, August 1988, *103*(3), pp. 441–63.

——— and Ross, Thomas W. An Intertemporal Model of Warranties. *Can. J. Econ.*, February 1988, *21*(1), pp. 72–86.

——— and Ross, Thomas W. Product Warranties and Moral Hazard. In *Devinney, T. M., ed.*, 1988, pp. 83–98.

Cooper, W. W.; Ahn, T. and Charnes, A. Using Data Envelopment Analysis to Measure the Efficiency of Not-for-Profit Organizations: A Critical Evaluation—A Comment. *Managerial Dec. Econ.*, September 1988, *9*(3), pp. 251–53.

Coox, Alvin D. The Cambridge History of Japan: Volume 6: The Twentieth Century: The Pacific War. In *Duus, P., ed.*, 1988, pp. 315–82.

Copeland, Morris A. Economic Theory and the Natural Science Point of View. In *Samuels, W. J., ed., Vol. 2*, 1988, *1931*, pp. 7–19.

Copeland, Thomas E. and Brennan, Michael J. Beta Changes around Stock Splits: A Note. *J. Finance*, September 1988, *43*(4), pp. 1009–13.

——— and Brennan, Michael J. Stock Splits, Stock Prices, and Transaction Costs. *J. Finan. Econ.*, October 1988, *22*(1), pp. 83–101.

———; Mayers, David and Chen, Nai-Fu. A Comparison of Single and Multifactor Portfolio Performance Methodologies. In *Dimson, E., ed.*, 1988, pp. 254–71.

Coppin, Clayton A. and High, Jack C. Wiley and the Whiskey Industry: Strategic Behavior in the Passage of the Pure Food Act. *Bus. Hist. Rev.*, Summer 1988, *62*(2), pp. 287–309.

Corbae, Dean and Ouliaris, Sam. Cointegration and Tests of Purchasing Power Parity. *Rev. Econ. Statist.*, August 1988, *70*(3), pp. 508–11.

Corbett, Jane. Famine and Household Coping Strategies. *World Devel.*, September 1988, *16*(9), pp. 1099–1112.

Corbo Lioi, Mario. Evolucíon reciente del sistema finnaciero chileno. (With English summary.) *Cuadernos Econ.*, December 1988, *25*(76), pp. 381–89.

Corbo, Vittorio and Nam, Sang-Woo. Korea's Macroeconomic Prospects and Policy Issues for the Next Decade. *World Devel.*, January 1988, *16*(1), pp. 35–45.

Corchón, Luis C. Cost-Prices with Variable Returns. *Metroecon.*, February 1988, *39*(1), pp. 93–99.

——— and Marcos, Félix. Entry, Stackelberg Equilibrium and Reasonable Conjectures. *Int. J. Ind. Organ.*, December 1988, *6*(4), pp. 509–15.

Corcoran, Kris and Nicholas, Stephen. Statistical Appendix: Convicts Transported to New South Wales 1817–40. In *Nicholas, S., ed.*, 1988, pp. 202–24.

Corden, W. Max. The Adjustment Mechanism: Theory and Practice: Discussion. In *Fieleke, N. S., ed.*, 1988, pp. 226–28.

———. An International Debt Facility? *Int. Monet. Fund Staff Pap.*, September 1988, *35*(3), pp. 401–21.

———. Debt Relief and Adjustment Incentives. *Int. Monet. Fund Staff Pap.*, December 1988, *35*(4), pp. 628–43.

———. How Valid Is International Keynesianism? In *Eltis, W. and Sinclair, P. J. N., eds.*, 1988, pp. 391–407.

———. International Trade and Economic Development: Comment. In *Haberler, G.*, 1988, pp. 89–98.

———. Real Exchange-Rate Variability under Pegged and Floating Nominal Exchange-Rate Systems: An Equilibrium Theory: Comment. *Carnegie–Rochester Conf. Ser. Public Policy*, Autumn 1988, *29*, pp. 295–97.

Cordero, Ricardo; Dubacher, René and Zimmermann, Heinz. Zur Entwicklung des neuen Swiss Market Index (SMI) als Grundlage für schweizerische Indexkontrakte: Eine Evaluation potentieller Aktienindices. (On the Development of the Swiss Market Index (SMI) for Index Contracts: An Evaluation of Potential Indices. With English summary.) *Schweiz. Z. Volkswirtsch. Statist.*, December 1988, *124*(4), pp. 575–600.

Cordes, John. Emerging Mineral Trade Issues. In *Richardson, P. R. and Gesing, R., eds.*, 1988, pp. 25–48.

Cordes, Joseph J. The Effect of Tax Policy on the Creation of New Technical Knowledge: An Assessment of the Evidence. In *Cyert, R. M. and Mowery, D. C., eds.*, 1988, pp. 443–80.

Corea, Gamani. Obstacles to South–South Co-operation. In *Sopiee, N.; Hamzah, B. A. and Leong, C. H., eds.*, 1988, pp. 33–37.

Corhay, Albert; Hawawini, Gabriel and Michel, Pierre. The Pricing of Equity on the London Stock Exchange: Seasonality and Size Premium. In *Dimson, E., ed.*, 1988, pp. 197–212.

Coriat, Benjamin. Information Technologies in Small-Scale Footwear Production: Some Lessons from the French Experience. In *Bhalla, A. S. and James, D.*, eds., 1988, pp. 65–74.

Coricelli, Fabrizio and Dosi, Giovanni. Coordination and Order in Economic Change and the Interpretative Power of Economic Theory. In *Dosi, G., et al.*, eds., 1988, pp. 124–47.

Corley, T. A. B. Competition and the Growth of Advertising in the U.S. and Britain, 1800–1914. In *Hausman, W. J.*, ed., 1988, pp. 155–67.

Cormack, R. M. Statistical Challenges in the Environmental Sciences: A Personal View. *J. Roy. Statist. Soc.*, 1988, *151*(1), pp. 201–10.

Cornelius, Peter. Some Arguments against a Global Stabilization Policy by the IMF. *Econ. Int.*, Feb.–March 1988, *41*(1–2), pp. 8–23.

Cornell, Bradford and Engelmann, Kathleen. Measuring the Cost of Corporate Litigation: Five Case Studies. *J. Legal Stud.*, June 1988, *17*(2), pp. 377–99.

Cornes, Richard; Mason, Charles F. and Sandler, Todd. Expectations, the Commons, and Optimal Group Size. *J. Environ. Econ. Manage.*, March 1988, *15*(1), pp. 99–110.

Cornet, Bernard. General Equilibrium Theory and Increasing Returns: Presentation. *J. Math. Econ.*, 1988, *17*(2–3), pp. 103–18.

_____. Topological Properties of the Attainable Set in a Non-convex Production Economy. *J. Math. Econ.*, 1988, *17*(2–3), pp. 275–92.

_____ and Bonnisseau, Jean-Marc. Existence of Equilibria When Firms Follow Bounded Losses Pricing Rules. *J. Math. Econ.*, 1988, *17*(2–3), pp. 119–47.

_____ and Bonnisseau, Jean-Marc. Valuation Equilibrium and Pareto Optimum in Non-convex Economies. *J. Math. Econ.*, 1988, *17*(2–3), pp. 293–308.

Cornett, Marcia Millon. Undetected Theft as a Social Hazard: The Role of Financial Institutions in the Choice of Protection Mechanisms. *J. Risk Ins.*, December 1988, *55*(4), pp. 723–33.

Cornew, Ronald W. Commodity Pool Operators and Their Pools: Expenses and Profitability. *J. Futures Markets*, October 1988, *8*(5), pp. 617–37.

Cornford, Andrew. Suggestions for an Agenda for Institutional International Economics: A Review Article. *J. Econ. Issues*, December 1988, *22*(4), pp. 1225–37.

Cornwell, Christopher and Rupert, Peter. Efficient Estimation with Panel Data: An Empirical Comparison of Instrumental Variables Estimators. *J. Appl. Econometrics*, April 1988, *3*(2), pp. 149–55.

Cornwell, Gretchen T. and Robinson, Warren C. Fertility of U.S. Farm Women during the Electrification Era, 1930–1950. *Population Res. Policy Rev.*, 1988, *7*(3), pp. 277–91.

Correa, Carlos Maria. Computer Software Protection in Developing Countries: A Normative Outlook. *J. World Trade*, February 1988, *22*(1), pp. 23–31.

Correa da Costa, Sergio. Brazil and the Banks. In *Chacel, J. M.; Falk, P. S. and Fleischer, D. V.*, eds., 1988, pp. 17–20.

Correia, Eddie and Budeiri, Priscilla. Antitrust Legislation in the Reagan Era. *Antitrust Bull.*, Summer 1988, *33*(2), pp. 361–93.

Corrigan, E. Gerald. A Balanced Approach to the LDC Debt Problem. *Fed. Res. Bank New York Quart. Rev.*, Spring 1988, *13*(1), pp. 1–6.

_____. Effectiveness of Monetary Policy and the World Financial System. In *Mikdashi, Z.*, ed., 1988, pp. 111–15.

_____. Strengthening International Economic Policy Coordination. *Fed. Res. Bank New York Quart. Rev.*, Autumn 1988, *13*(3), pp. 1–5.

_____. The Worldwide Implications of Financial Innovations. In *Feldstein, M.*, ed. *(II)*, 1988, pp. 257–63.

Corsepius, Uwe and Fischer, Bernhard. Domestic Resource Mobilization in Thailand: A Success Case for Financial Deepening? *Singapore Econ. Rev.*, October 1988, *33*(2), pp. 1–20.

Corsi, Thomas M. and Fanara, Philip, Jr. Driver Management Policies and Motor Carrier Safety. *Logist. Transp. Rev.*, June 1988, *24*(2), pp. 153–63.

_____ and Murphy, Paul R., Jr. Strategic Differentiation among LTL General Freight Carriers: Sales Force Management Policies. *Logist. Transp. Rev.*, September 1988, *24*(3), pp. 217–35.

Cortellese, Claudio and Castillo, Mario. Small and Medium-Scale Industry in the Development of Latin America. *CEPAL Rev.*, April 1988, *(34)*, pp. 127–51.

Cortes, B. S.; Edgmand, M. R. and Rea, J. D. Capital Gains and the Rental Price of Capital. In *Missouri Valley Economic Assoc.*, 1988, pp. 71–75.

Cortes Costa, Mauricio Eduardo. A View from Brazil. In *Walker, C. E. and Bloomfield, M. A.*, eds., 1988, pp. 57–63.

Cory, Dennis C.; Colby, Bonnie G. and Carpenter, Edwin H. Uncertain Recreation Quality and Wildlife Valuation: Are Conventional Benefit Measures Adequate? *Western J. Agr. Econ.*, December 1988, *13*(2), pp. 153–62.

Cory, Floydette C.; Fitzgerald, Michael R. and Lyons, William. From Administration to Oversight: Privatization and Its Aftermath in a Southern City. In *Hula, R. C.*, ed., 1988, pp. 69–83.

Cosimano, Thomas F. The Banking Industry under Uncertain Monetary Policy. *J. Banking Finance*, 1988, *12*(1), pp. 117–39.

_____ and Jansen, Dennis W. Estimates of the Variance of U.S. Inflation Based upon the ARCH Model: A Comment. *J. Money, Credit, Banking*, Part 1, August 1988, *20*(3), pp. 409–21.

_____ and Jansen, Dennis W. Federal Reserve Policy, 1975–1985: An Empirical Analysis. *J. Macroecon.*, Winter 1988, *10*(1), pp. 27–47.

da Costa Garcia, Manuel. Instruction et niveau de vie au Portugal—Analyse critique des résultats. (With English summary.) *Economia (Portugal)*, May 1988, *12*(2), pp. 211–58.

Costa, Julio Castañeda and Vera la Torre, José Carlos. Private Health Care Financing Alternatives. In Zschock, D. K., ed., 1988, pp. 79–97.

Costa, Paolo. Using Input–Output to Forecast Freight Transport Demand. In Bianco, L. and La Bella, A., eds., 1988, pp. 79–120.

_____ and Roson, Roberto. Transport Margins, Transportation Industry and the Multiregional Economy. Some Experiments with a Model for Italy. Ricerche Econ., April–June 1988, 42(2), pp. 273–87.

da Costa Werlang, Sérgio Ribeiro and Dow, James. The Consistency of Welfare Judgments with a Representative Consumer. J. Econ. Theory, April 1988, 44(2), pp. 269–80.

Costanza, Robert and Shrum, Wesley. The Effects of Taxation on Moderating the Conflict Escalation Process: An Experiment Using the Dollar Auction Game. Soc. Sci. Quart., June 1988, 69(2), pp. 416–32.

Costello, Cynthia B. Clerical Home-Based Work: A Case Study of Work and Family. In Christensen, K. E., ed., 1988, pp. 135–45.

Costello, Kenneth W. The Struggle over Electricity Transmission Access. Cato J., Spring–Summer 1988, 8(1), pp. 107–24.

_____. A Welfare Measure of a New Type of Energy Assistance Program. Energy J., July 1988, 9(3), pp. 129–42.

Costrell, Robert M. The Effect of Technical Progress on Productivity, Wages, and the Distribution of Employment: Theory and Postwar Experience in the United States. In Cyert, R. M. and Mowery, D. C., eds., 1988, pp. 73–128.

_____ and Gordon, Myron J. Keynesian Models of the Short Run and the Steady State. J. Econ. (Z. Nationalökon.), 1988, 48(4), pp. 355–73.

Cote, Joseph A. and Buckley, M. Ronald. Measurement Error and Theory Testing in Consumer Research: An Illustration of the Importance of Construct Validation. J. Cons. Res., March 1988, 14(4), pp. 579–82.

Côté, Marcel; Lemelin, Maurice and Toulouse, Jean-Marie. The Management–Industrial Relations Interface: Exploring the Conceptual Linkages. In Hébert, G.; Jain, H. C. and Meltz, N. M., eds.., 1988, pp. 147–86.

Cothren, Richard. Equilibrium Inflation as Determined by a Policy Committee. Quart. J. Econ., May 1988, 103(2), pp. 429–34.

van Cott, T. Norman and Spector, Lee C. Crowding Out, Deficits, and Interest Rates: Comment. Public Choice, July 1988, 58(1), pp. 91–94.

Cottarelli, Carlo. La domanda di carburanti in Italia: stime econometriche ed effetto della armonizzazione delle accise nella CEE. (With English summary.) Polit. Econ., December 1988, 4(3), pp. 433–64.

Cotterill, Ronald W. The Design and Impact of Strategic Management Information Systems. Amer. J. Agr. Econ., May 1988, 70(2), pp. 475–79.

Cotton, Jeremiah. Discrimination and Favoritism in the U.S. Labor Market: The Cost to a Wage Earner of Being Female and Black and the Benefit of Being Male and White. Amer. J. Econ. Soc., January 1988, 47(1), pp. 15–28.

_____. On the Decomposition of Wage Differentials. Rev. Econ. Statist., May 1988, 70(2), pp. 236–43.

Cottrell, Allin F. The Endogeneity of Money: Reply. Scot. J. Polit. Econ., August 1988, 35(3), pp. 295–97.

_____ and Darity, William A., Jr. Marx, Malthus, and Wages. Hist. Polit. Econ., Summer 1988, 20(2), pp. 173–90.

Couch, C. Aspects of Structural Change in Speculative Housing Production: A Case Study in Merseyside. Environ. Planning A, October 1988, 20(10), pp. 1385–96.

Couclelis, H. Of Mice and Men: What Rodent Populations Can Teach Us about Complex Spatial Dynamics. Environ. Planning A, January 1988, 20(1), pp. 99–109.

Coughlin, Cletus C. The Competitive Nature of State Spending on the Promotion of Manufacturing Exports. Fed. Res. Bank St. Louis Rev., May–June 1988, 70(3), pp. 34–42.

_____ and Carraro, Kenneth C. The Dubious Success of Export Subsidies for Wheat. Fed. Res. Bank St. Louis Rev., Nov.–Dec. 1988, 70(6), pp. 38–47.

_____; Chrystal, K. Alec and Wood, Geoffrey E. Protectionist Trade Policies: A Survey of Theory, Evidence and Rationale. Fed. Res. Bank St. Louis Rev., Jan.–Feb. 1988, 70(1), pp. 12–29.

_____ and Fabel, Oliver. State Factor Endowments and Exports: An Alternative to Cross-Industry Studies. Rev. Econ. Statist., November 1988, 70(4), pp. 696–701.

_____ and Mandelbaum, Thomas B. Why Have State Per Capita Incomes Diverged Recently? Fed. Res. Bank St. Louis Rev., Sept.–Oct. 1988, 70(5), pp. 24–36.

Coughlin, Peter. Development Policy and Inappropriate Product Technology: The Kenyan Case. Eastern Afr. Econ. Rev., June 1988, 4(1), pp. 18–35.

_____. Development Policy and Inappropriate Product Technology: The Kenyan Case. In Coughlin, P. and Ikiara, G. K., eds., 1988, pp. 143–68.

_____. Economies of Scale, Capacity Utilization and Import Subsitution: A Focus on Dies, Moulds and Patterns. In Coughlin, P. and Ikiara, G. K., eds., 1988, pp. 112–25.

_____. Investment, Output Growth and Capacity Utilization in an African Economy: A Comment. Eastern Afr. Econ. Rev., June 1988, 4(1), pp. 64–65.

_____. Toward a New Industrialization Strategy in Kenya? In Coughlin, P. and Ikiara, G. K., eds., 1988, pp. 275–303.

_____ and Gachuki, David. Structure and Safeguards for Negotiations with Foreign Investors: Lessons from Kenya. In Coughlin, P. and Ikiara, G. K., eds., 1988, pp. 91–111.

_____ and Ikiara, Gerrishon K. Industrialization

in Kenya: In Search of a Strategy: Introduction. In *Coughlin, P. and Ikiara, G. K., eds.*, 1988, pp. 1–5.

_____; **Mwau, Geoffrey and Begumisa, Gregory.** Tied Aid, Industrial Dependence and New Tactics for Negotiations: Observations from Kenya. In *Coughlin, P. and Ikiara, G. K., eds.*, 1988, pp. 126–42.

Coughlin, Richard M. Social Security: The First Half-Century: General Studies: Comment. In *Nash, G. D.; Pugach, N. H. and Tomasson, R. F., eds.*, 1988, pp. 205–09.

Coulombe, Serge and Parguez, Alain. Le rôle des institutions financières dans le circuit dynamique: L'austérité et le capitalisme rentier public en France. (The Role of Financial Institutions within the Dynamic Circuit: Austerity and State Rentiers Capitalism in France. With English summary.) *Écon. Soc.*, September 1988, 22(9), pp. 85–119.

Coulson, David C. Antitrust Law and Newspapers. In *Picard, R. G., et al., eds.*, 1988, pp. 179–95.

Coulson, N. Edward and Breece, James H. Dynamics of the Transmission of Employment Effects across Metropolitan Areas. *Urban Stud.*, April 1988, 25(2), pp. 145–49.

Courakis, Anthony S. Modelling Portfolio Selection. *Econ. J.*, September 1988, 98(392), pp. 619–42.

Courant, Paul N. and Rubinfeld, Daniel L. Robbing Peter to Pay Peter: The Economics of Local Public Residency Requirements. *J. Urban Econ.*, May 1988, 23(3), pp. 291–306.

Courchane, Marsha J. and Nickerson, David B. Monetary Neutrality and Optimality with Symmetric Partial Information. *Int. Econ. J.*, Winter 1988, 2(4), pp. 57–71.

Courchene, Thomas J. Meech Lake and Socio-Economic Policy. *Can. Public Policy*, Supplement, September 1988, 14, pp. S63–80.

_____ **and Melvin, James R.** A Neoclassical Approach to Regional Economics. In *[Perroux, F.]*, 1988, pp. 169–89.

Courgeau, D. and Lelièvre, E. Estimation of Transition Rates in Dynamic Household Models. In *Keilman, N.; Kuijsten, A. and Vossen, A., eds.*, 1988, pp. 160–76.

Cournot, Augustin. Of the Competition of Producers. In *Daughety, A. F., ed.*, 1988, 1897, pp. 63–72.

Coursey, Don L. Preference Trees, Preference Hierarchies, and Consumer Behavior. *J. Cons. Res.*, December 1988, 15(3), pp. 407–09.

_____ **and Nyquist, Hans.** Applications of Robust Estimation Techniques in Demand Analysis. *Appl. Econ.*, May 1988, 20(5), pp. 595–610.

_____ **and Stanley, Linda R.** Pretrial Bargaining Behavior within the Shadow of the Law: Theory and Experimental Evidence. *Int. Rev. Law Econ.*, December 1988, 8(2), pp. 161–79.

Cousineau, Jean-Michel. Le rapport Forget et l'économie politique de l'assurance-chômage. (With English summary.) *Can. Public Policy*, March 1988, 14(1), pp. 1–6.

Coussy, Jean. Déstabilisation des oligopoles inter-

nationaux? Introduction. (With English summary.) *Écon. Soc.*, Nov.–Dec. 1988, 22(11–12), pp. 5–20.

Cover, James Peery. A Keynesian Macroeconomic Model with New-Classical Econometric Properties. *Southern Econ. J.*, April 1988, 54(4), pp. 831–39.

_____. Optimal Price-Level Flexibility. *J. Macroecon.*, Summer 1988, 10(3), pp. 449–58.

_____ **and Thistle, Paul D.** Time Series, Homicide, and the Deterrent Effect of Capital Punishment. *Southern Econ. J.*, January 1988, 54(3), pp. 615–22.

Covin, Jeffrey G. and Slevin, Dennis P. New Venture Competitive Strategy: An Industry Life Cycle Analysis. In *Kirchhoff, B. A., et al., eds.*, 1988, pp. 446–60.

Coward, E. Walter, Jr. Property, Persistence, and Participation: The State and Traditional Irrigation Systems. In *Bennett, J. W. and Bowen, J. R., eds.*, 1988, pp. 329–42.

Cowell, Frank A. Inequality Decomposition: Three Bad Measures. *Bull. Econ. Res.*, October 1988, 40(4), pp. 309–12.

_____. Poverty Measures, Inequality and Decomposability. In *Bös, D.; Rose, M. and Seidl, C., eds.,*, 1988, pp. 149–66.

_____ **and Gordon, James P. F.** Unwillingness to Pay: Tax Evasion and Public Good Provision. *J. Public Econ.*, August 1988, 36(3), pp. 305–21.

Cowen, Tyler. Public Goods and Externalities: Old and New Perspectives. In *Cowen, T., ed.*, 1988, pp. 1–26.

Cowling, Keith. Oligopoly, Distribution and the Rate of Profit. In *Sawyer, M. C., ed.*, 1988, 1981, pp. 310–39.

_____ **and Mueller, Dennis C.** The Social Costs of Monopoly Power. In *Ricketts, M., ed., Vol. 2*, 1988, 1978, pp. 321–42.

Cox, Anthony D. and Cox, Dena S. What *Does* Familiarity Breed? Complexity as a Moderator of Repetition Effects in Advertisement Evaluation. *J. Cons. Res.*, June 1988, 15(1), pp. 111–16.

Cox, Dena S. and Cox, Anthony D. What *Does* Familiarity Breed? Complexity as a Moderator of Repetition Effects in Advertisement Evaluation. *J. Cons. Res.*, June 1988, 15(1), pp. 111–16.

Cox, James C.; Smith, Vernon L. and Walker, James M. Theory and Individual Behavior of First-Price Auctions. *J. Risk Uncertainty*, March 1988, 1(1), pp. 61–99.

Cox, Larry A. and Griepentrog, Gary L. The Pure-Play Cost of Equity for Insurance Divisions. *J. Risk Ins.*, September 1988, 55(3), pp. 442–52.

_____ **and Griepentrog, Gary L.** Systematic Risk, Unsystematic Risk, and Property-Liability Rate Regulation. *J. Risk Ins.*, December 1988, 55(4), pp. 606–27.

Cox, Stephen and Annis, Sheldon. Community Participation in Rural Water Supply. In *Annis, S. and Hakim, P., eds.*, 1988, pp. 65–72.

Cox, Thomas L. and Chavas, Jean-Paul. A Nonparametric Analysis of Agricultural Technology. *Amer. J. Agr. Econ.*, May 1988, 70(2), pp. 303–10.

Cox, Thomas R. The North American–Japanese Timber Trade: A Survey of Its Social, Economic, and Environmental Impact. In *Richards, J. F. and Tucker, R. P., eds.*, 1988, pp. 164–86.

Cox, W. Michael and Hill, John K. Effects of the Lower Dollar on U.S. Manufacturing: Industry and State Comparisons. *Fed. Res. Bank Dallas Econ. Rev.*, March 1988, pp. 1–9.

_____ **and Parkin, Michael.** Currency Substitution and the International Transmission of Economic Disturbances. *Fed. Res. Bank Dallas Econ. Rev.*, May 1988, pp. 1–12.

Cox, Wendell. Competitive Contracting and the Strategic Prospects of Transit. In *Weicher, J. C., ed.*, 1988, pp. 56–61.

_____. Privatization in the Public Services: Competitive Contracting and the Public Ethic in Urban Public Transport. In *Walker, M. A., ed. (II)*, 1988, pp. 201–32.

Coyne, John and Wright, Mike. Buy-outs and British Industry. In *Johnson, C., ed.*, 1988, 1982, pp. 157–73.

Coyte, Peter C. and Lindsey, C. Robin. Spatial Monopoly and Spatial Monopolistic Competition with Two-Part Pricing. *Economica*, November 1988, 55(220), pp. 461–77.

Cozier, Barry V. and Rahman, Abdul H. Stock Returns, Inflation, and Real Activity in Canada. *Can. J. Econ.*, November 1988, 21(4), pp. 759–74.

Cozzi, Terenzio. Public Finance and Monetary Policy in Italy (1973–83): Trends and Problems. In *Cavanna, H., ed.*, 1988, pp. 120–45.

Cracraft, James. From the Russian Past to the Soviet Present. In *Cracraft, J., ed.*, 1988, pp. 3–12.

Crafts, Nick. The Assessment: British Economic Growth over the Long Run. *Oxford Rev. Econ. Policy*, Spring 1988, 4(1), pp. i–xxi.

Craig, Alton W. J. Mainstream Industrial Relations in Canada. In *Hébert, G.; Jain, H. C. and Meltz, N. M., eds..*, 1988, pp. 9–43.

Craig, James. Privatisation in Malaysia: Present Trends and Future Prospects. In *Cook, P. and Kirkpatrick, C., eds.*, 1988, pp. 248–58.

Craig, Paul; Auburn, Jill Shore and Watt, Kenneth E. F. World Economic Modeling. In *Ehrlich, P. R. and Holdren, J. P., eds.*, 1988, pp. 233–55.

Craig, Steven G. and Sailors, Joel W. State Government Purchases in a Federalist Economy. *Public Choice*, February 1988, 56(2), pp. 121–30.

Craig, Thomas. Air Traffic Congestion: Problems and Prospects. In *Ausubel, J. H. and Herman, R., eds.*, 1988, pp. 222–32.

Craigwell, Roland; Rock, Llewyn and Sealy, Ronald. On the Determination of the External Public Debt: The Case of Barbados. *Soc. Econ. Stud.*, December 1988, 37(4), pp. 137–50.

Crain, Ben W. Is Managed Money the Root of All Evil? *Cato J.*, Fall 1988, 8(2), pp. 279–84.

Crain, W. Mark; Shughart, William F., II and Tollison, Robert D. Legislative Majorities as Nonsalvageable Assets. *Southern Econ. J.*, October 1988, 55(2), pp. 303–14.

_____; **Tollison, Robert D. and Leavens, Donald R.** Laissez-faire in Campaign Finance. *Public Choice*, March 1988, 56(3), pp. 201–12.

Crainic, Teodor Gabriel. Rail Tactical Planning: Issues, Models and Tools. In *Bianco, L. and La Bella, A., eds.*, 1988, pp. 463–509.

von Cramon-Taubadel, Stephan. The EEC's Wheat Trade Policies and International Trade in Differentiated Products: Comment. *Amer. J. Agr. Econ.*, November 1988, 70(4), pp. 941–43.

Crandall, Robert W. The Dardis Paper: Some Suggestions. In *Maynes, E. S. and ACCI Research Committee, eds.*, 1988, pp. 361–63.

_____. The Regional Shift of U.S. Economic Activity. In *Litan, R. E; Lawrence, R. Z. and Schultze, C. L., eds.*, 1988, pp. 154–77.

_____. Should Merger Policy be Changed? An Antitrust Perspective: Discussion. In *Browne, L. E. and Rosengren, E. S., eds.*, 1988, pp. 195–98.

_____. Surprises from Telephone Deregulation and the AT&T Divestiture. *Amer. Econ. Rev.*, May 1988, 78(2), pp. 323–27.

_____. The Use of Cost–Benefit Analysis in Product Safety Regulation. In *Maynes, E. S. and ACCI Research Committee, eds.*, 1988, pp. 61–75.

_____. What Ever Happened to Deregulation? In *Boaz, D., ed.*, 1988, pp. 271–89.

Crane, Donald P. and Miner, John B. Labor Arbitrators' Performance: Views From Union and Management Perspectives. *J. Lab. Res.*, Winter 1988, 9(1), pp. 43–54.

Crane, Edward H. Who Will Lead? In *Boaz, D., ed.*, 1988, pp. 423–28.

Crane-Engel, Melinda and Schanze, Erich. Multilateral Exploration Assistance: The United Nations Programs. In *Tilton, J. E.; Eggert, R. G. and Landsberg, H. H., eds.*, 1988, pp. 227–60.

Crane, Keith. The Economy Five Years after Martial Law. In *Marer, P. and Siwinski, W., eds.*, 1988, pp. 13–24.

_____. Military Spending in Czechoslovakia, Hungary, and Poland. *J. Compar. Econ.*, December 1988, 12(4), pp. 521–45.

Crane, Randall. Second-Best Property Value Capitalization. *Econ. Letters*, 1988, 26(2), pp. 175–78.

Cranford, Brian K. and Stover, Roger D. Interest Yields, Credit Ratings, and Economic Characteristics of State Bonds: Comment. *J. Money, Credit, Banking*, November 1988, 20(4), pp. 691–95.

Cranmer, William H. H. The 'Group-Benefit' Method: A New Methodology for Distributional Analyses of Fiscal Policies in Developing Nations. In *Danziger, S. H. and Portney, K. E., eds.*, 1988, pp. 219–38.

Cranstone, Donald A. The Canadian Mineral Discovery Experience since World War II. In

Tilton, J. E.; Eggert, R. G. and Landsberg, H. H., eds., 1988, pp. 283–329.

Craswell, Richard. Precontractual Investigation as an Optimal Precaution Problem. *J. Legal Stud.*, June 1988, *17*(2), pp. 401–36.

Crawcour, E. Sydney. The Cambridge History of Japan: Volume 6: The Twentieth Century: Industrialization and Technological Change, 1885–1920. In *Duus, P., ed.*, 1988, pp. 385–450.

Crawford, E. Margaret and Clarkson, L. A. Dietary Directions: A Topographical Survey of Irish Diet, 1836. In *Mitchison, R. and Roebuck, P., eds.*, 1988, pp. 171–92.

Crawford, Vincent P. Long-term Relationships Governed by Short-term Contracts. *Amer. Econ. Rev.*, June 1988, *78*(3), pp. 485–99.

Creaco, Salvo. Some Notes on Coproduction. *Econ. Scelte Pubbliche/J. Public Finance Public Choice*, Jan.–April 1988, *6*(1), pp. 33–45.

Cready, William M. Information Value and Investor Wealth: The Case of Earnings Announcements. *J. Acc. Res.*, Spring 1988, *26*(1), pp. 1–27.

Creasey, Pauline. European Defence Firms in Cooperation Agreements. In *Creasey, P. and May, S., eds.*, 1988, pp. 89–164.

_____. The Options and Prospects for Defence Procurement Collaboration. In *Creasey, P. and May, S., eds.*, 1988, pp. 165–92.

_____ **and May, Simon.** The Political and Economic Background. In *Creasey, P. and May, S., eds.*, 1988, pp. 1–30.

Creedy, John. Cohort and Cross-sectional Earnings Profiles: Scientists in Britain and Australia. *J. Econ. Stud.*, 1988, *15*(1), pp. 44–52.

_____. Demographic Effects and Aggregation in a Life Cycle Model. *Metroecon.*, February 1988, *39*(1), pp. 67–81.

_____. Earnings Comparisons between Generations: Some Alternative Approaches. *Manchester Sch. Econ. Soc. Stud.*, September 1988, *56*(3), pp. 268–81.

_____. The Need for Dynamic Analyses: Overview. *Australian Econ. Rev.*, Spring 1988, (83), pp. 76.

_____. Taxation and Compensation to Dependents of Accident Victims. *Int. Rev. Law Econ.*, June 1988, *8*(1), pp. 85–95.

_____. Wicksell on Edgeworth's Tax Paradox. *Scand. J. Econ.*, 1988, *90*(1), pp. 101–12.

_____ **and Disney, Richard F.** The New Pension Scheme in Britain. *Fisc. Stud.*, May 1988, *9*(2), pp. 57–71.

_____ **and Whitfield, Keith.** The Economic Analysis of Internal Labour Markets. *Bull. Econ. Res.*, October 1988, *40*(4), pp. 247–69.

Creigh, Stephen W. Characteristics of the Long-term Unemployed: Evidence from the Labour Force Survey. In *Cross, R., ed.*, 1988, pp. 65–92.

Cremer, Georg. Deployment of Indonesian Migrants in the Middle East: Present Situation and Prospects. *Bull. Indonesian Econ. Stud.*, December 1988, *24*(3), pp. 73–86.

Cremer, Helmuth and Pestieau, Pierre. A Case

for Differential Inheritance Taxation. *Ann. Écon. Statist.*, Jan.–March 1988, (9), pp. 167–82.

_____ **and Pestieau, Pierre.** The Joint Impact of Fertility Differentials and Social Security on the Accumulation and Distribution of Wealth. In *Kessler, D. and Masson, A., eds.*, 1988, pp. 169–85.

Crémer, Jacques and McLean, Richard P. Full Extraction of the Surplus in Bayesian and Dominant Strategy Auctions. *Econometrica*, November 1988, *56*(6), pp. 1247–57.

Crespo, Horacio. The Cartelization of the Mexican Sugar Industry, 1924–1940. In *Albert, B. and Graves, A., eds.*, 1988, pp. 85–96.

Cressie, Noel. A Graphical Procedure for Determining Nonstationarity in Time Series. *J. Amer. Statist. Assoc.*, December 1988, *83*(404), pp. 1108–16.

Crew, Michael A. Equity, Opportunism and the Design of Contractual Relations: Comment. *J. Inst. Theoretical Econ.*, February 1988, *144*(1), pp. 196–99.

_____ **and Rowley, Charles K.** Toward a Public Choice Theory of Monopoly Regulation. *Public Choice*, April 1988, *57*(1), pp. 49–67.

Crichton, Nigel and Farrell, Terrence W. Market Structure and Concentration in the Manufacturing Sector in Trinidad and Tobago. *Soc. Econ. Stud.*, September 1988, *37*(3), pp. 151–92.

Crimmins, Eileen M. and Pramaggiore, Maria T. Changing Health of the Older Working-Age Population and Retirement Patterns over Time. In *Ricardo-Campbell, R. and Lazear, E. P., eds.*, 1988, pp. 132–52.

Criqui, Patrick and Percebois, Jacques. Stratégies énergétiques: Cigales et fourmis. (Energy Strategies: To Avoid or to Manage Energy Dependence?. With English summary.) *Écon. Soc.*, April 1988, *22*(4), pp. 37–57.

_____; **Percebois, Jacques and Bourgeois, Bernard.** Energy Conservation versus Supply Strategies: Implications for Industrial Policy. *Energy J.*, July 1988, *9*(3), pp. 99–111.

Crispo, John. Reconciling Efficiency and Equity in the Employment Relationship. In *Dlugos, G.; Dorow, W. and Weiermair, K., eds.*, 1988, pp. 477–84.

Crissman, Charles C. and Antle, John M. The Market for Innovations and Short-run Technological Change: Evidence from Egypt. *Econ. Develop. Cult. Change*, July 1988, *36*(4), pp. 669–90.

Cristini, Marcela and Chisari, Omar O. El impuesto a la tierra: una discusión de sus efectos económicos para el caso argentino. (Land Tax: A Discussion of Its Economic Effects in the Argentine Case. With English summary.) *Económica (La Plata)*, July–Dec. 1988, *34*(2), pp. 155–84.

Crittenden, R. and Lea, D. A. M. Project Appraisal, Aid and Impact Monitoring: A Comment. *J. Agr. Econ.*, May 1988, *39*(2), pp. 277–79.

Crittenden, Robert and Madden, Carolyn Watts.

Health Insurance for the Uninsured: An Evaluation of Plan Design Preferences. In *Scheffler, R. M. and Rossiter, L. F., eds.*, 1988, pp. 99–112.

Crittenden, Victoria L.; Dolan, Robert J. and Bonoma, Thomas V. Can We Have Rigor and Relevance in Pricing Research? In *Devinney, T. M., ed.*, 1988, pp. 337–59.

Croasdale, Martin. Modelling the Finance of Investment. In *Harris, L., et al., eds.*, 1988, pp. 214–24.

———— **and Harris, Laurence.** Internal Funds and Investment. In *Harris, L., et al., eds.*, 1988, pp. 225–34.

Crocker, Keith J. and Masten, Scott E. Mitigating Contractual Hazards: Unilateral Options and Contract Length. *Rand J. Econ.*, Autumn 1988, 19(3), pp. 327–43.

Crockett, Andrew. Indicators and International Economic Cooperation. *Finance Develop.*, September 1988, 25(3), pp. 20–23.

————. Strengthening International Economic Cooperation: The Role of Indicators in Multilateral Surveillance. In *[Witteveen, H. J.]*, 1988, pp. 1–16.

Crockett, Jean A. and Friend, Irwin. Dividend Policy in Perspective: Can Theory Explain Behavior? *Rev. Econ. Statist.*, November 1988, 70(4), pp. 603–13.

Crockett, Virginia R. Women in Management in Indonesia. In *Adler, N. J. and Izraeli, D., eds.*, 1988, pp. 74–102.

Croll, Elisabeth J. The New Peasant Economy in Chin. In *Feuchtwang, S.; Hussain, A. and Pairault, T., eds., Vol. 1*, 1988, pp. 77–100.

Cromer, Donald L. The Strategic Defense Initiative and Commercial Applications. In *Furino, A., ed.*, 1988, pp. 225–30.

Cron, William L.; Yows, Linda C. and Slocum, John W., Jr. Whose Career Is Likely to Plateau? In *Timpe, A. D., ed.*, 1988, 1987, pp. 266–78.

Cronan, Timothy P.; Wilson, Arlette C. and Glezen, G. William. Forecasting Accounting Information for Auditors' Use in Analytical Reviews. In *Schwartz, B. N., ed.*, 1988, pp. 267–76.

Crone, Theodore. Changing Rates of Return on Rental Property and Condominium Conversions. *Urban Stud.*, February 1988, 25(1), pp. 34–42.

———— **and Voith, Richard.** National Vacancy Rates and the Persistence of Shocks in U.S. Office Markets. *Amer. Real Estate Urban Econ. Assoc. J.*, Winter 1988, 16(4), pp. 437–58.

———— **and Voith, Richard.** Natural Vacancy Rates and the Persistence of Shocks in U.S. Office Markets. In *Pennsylvania Economic Association*, 1988, pp. 470–91.

Crook, J. N. and Schlegelmilch, Bodo B. Firm-Level Determinants of Export Intensity. *Managerial Dec. Econ.*, December 1988, 9(4), pp. 291–300.

Cropper, Maureen L. A Note on the Extinction of Renewable Resources. *J. Environ. Econ. Manage.*, March 1988, 15(1), pp. 64–70.

————; **Deck, Leland B. and McConnell, Kenneth E.** On the Choice of Functional Form for Hedonic Price Functions. *Rev. Econ. Statist.*, November 1988, 70(4), pp. 668–75.

———— **and Sussman, Frances G.** Families and the Economics of Risks to Life. *Amer. Econ. Rev.*, March 1988, 78(1), pp. 255–60.

Cross, Edward M. and Pope, James A. The Optimal Load Size for Ocean Shippers. *Logist. Transp. Rev.*, December 1988, 24(4), pp. 299–315.

Cross, Mark L.; Davidson, Wallace N., III and Thornton, John H. Taxes, Stock Returns and Captive Insurance Subsidiaries. *J. Risk Ins.*, June 1988, 55(2), pp. 331–38.

———— **and Simmons, LeRoy F.** The Underwriting Cycle and the Risk Manager—Authors' Reply. *J. Risk Ins.*, September 1988, 55(3), pp. 561–62.

Cross, Rod. On Psyching Up Economics. In *Earl, P. E., ed.*, 1988, pp. 55–65.

———— **and Allan, Andrew.** On the History of Hysteresis. In *Cross, R., ed.*, 1988, pp. 26–38.

———— **and Hutchinson, Harold.** Hysteresis Effects and Unemployment: An Outline. In *Cross, R., ed.*, 1988, pp. 3–7.

Cross, Sam Y. Treasury and Federal Reserve Foreign Exchange Operations. *Fed. Res. Bull.*, January 1988, 74(1), pp. 14–17.

————. Treasury and Federal Reserve Foreign Exchange Operations. *Fed. Res. Bull.*, April 1988, 74(4), pp. 209–14.

————. Treasury and Federal Reserve Foreign Exchange Operations: May–July 1988. *Fed. Res. Bank New York Quart. Rev.*, Summer 1988, 13(2), pp. 90–95.

————. Treasury and Federal Reserve Foreign Exchange Operations. *Fed. Res. Bull.*, July 1988, 74(7), pp. 430–34.

————. Treasury and Federal Reserve Foreign Exchange Operations. *Fed. Res. Bull.*, October 1988, 74(10), pp. 645–49.

————. Treasury and Federal Reserve Foreign Exchange Operations: February–April 1988. *Fed. Res. Bank New York Quart. Rev.*, Spring 1988, 13(1), pp. 59–65.

————. Treasury and Federal Reserve Foreign Exchange Operations: August–October 1988. *Fed. Res. Bank New York Quart. Rev.*, Autumn 1988, 13(3), pp. 67–72.

Crossley, Rodney. Inflation, Unemployment and the Keynesian Wage Theorem. In *Hillard, J., ed.*, 1988, pp. 88–106.

Crossman, Peter. Balancing the Australian National Accounts. *Econ. Rec.*, March 1988, 64(184), pp. 39–46.

Crosson, Pierre. Improving the Socioeconomic Data Base: A Discussion. In *Hildreth, R. J., et al., eds.*, 1988, pp. 490–95.

Crouzet, Philippe. Instabilité financière et gestion des risques de l'entreprise. (With English summary.) *Revue Écon. Polit.*, Sept.–Oct. 1988, 98(5), pp. 721–30.

Crow, Ben. The Invidious Dilemmas of Capitalist Development: Conclusion. In *Crow, B. and Thorpe, M., et al.*, 1988, pp. 331–48.

―――― **and Bernstein, Henry.** The Expansion of Europe. In *Crow, B. and Thorpe, M., et al.*, 1988, pp. 9–29.

―――― **and Byres, Terry.** New Technology and New Masters for the Indian Countryside. In *Crow, B. and Thorpe, M., et al.*, 1988, pp. 163–81.

―――― **and Johnson, Hazel.** Developing Production on the Land. In *Crow, B. and Thorpe, M., et al.*, 1988, pp. 127–46.

Crowe, B. L. and Hailey, D. M. Recording of Costs in Public Hospitals' MRI Units: Interim Report, July 1986–June 1987. In *Butler, J. R. G. and Doessel, D. P., eds.*, 1988, pp. 154–66.

―――― **and Hailey, D. M.** Work in Progress: Collection and Analysis of Cost Data from Public Hospitals' MRI Units. In *Smith, C. S., ed.*, 1988, pp. 274–89.

Crowe, Marshall. Implications of the Energy Provisions: Comments. In *Schott, J. J. and Smith, M. G., eds.*, 1988, pp. 128–31.

Crowley, Frederick D. and Loviscek, Anthony L. Analyzing Changes in Municipal Bond Ratings: A Different Perspective. *Urban Stud.*, April 1988, *25*(2), pp. 124–32.

Crowson, Philip C. F. A Perspective on Worldwide Exploration for Minerals. In *Tilton, J. E.; Eggert, R. G. and Landsberg, H. H., eds.*, 1988, pp. 21–103.

Crum, Roy L. Meeting Joint Objectives. In *Tavis, L. A., ed.*, 1988, pp. 288–93.

Cruz, Ignacio and Mugica, José M. The Retail Distribution Industry in Spain: Determinants of Its Structuring Process. In *Kaynak, E., ed.*, 1988, pp. 277–98.

Cruz, José Miguel. La fruticultura de exportación: una experiencia de desarrollo empresarial. (Fruit Growing for Export: An Experience in Business Development. With English summary.) *Colección Estud. CIEPLAN*, December 1988, (25), pp. 79–114.

Crysdale, John S. Industrial Classification in the Canadian Census of Manufactures: Towards Less Art and More Science. *Statist. J.*, December 1988, *5*(4), pp. 377–92.

Csaba, László. Coordination of Interests in the CMEA. *Soviet E. Europ. Foreign Trade*, Spring 1988, *24*(1), pp. 37–53.

――――. Restructuring of the Soviet Foreign Trade Mechanism and Possibilities for Interfirm Cooperation in the CMEA. *Acta Oecon.*, 1988, *39*(1–2), pp. 137–54.

Csáki, C., et al. Hungarian Agriculture: Development Potential and Environment. In *Parikh, J. K., ed.*, 1988, pp. 253–95.

Csaplar, Wilfrid W., Jr. and Tower, Edward. Trade and Industrial Policy under Oligopoly: Comment. *Quart. J. Econ.*, August 1988, *103*(3), pp. 599–602.

Csete, László; Harnos, Zsolt and Láng, István. The Enterprisal System of an Adjusting Agriculture in Hungary. *Europ. Rev. Agr. Econ.*, 1988, *15*(2–3), pp. 225–38.

Csige, Eva S. Changing Hungarian Economic Conditions. In *Pennsylvania Economic Association*, 1988, pp. 163–78.

Csikós-Nagy, Béla. A New Approach to East–West Trade. In *Borner, S., ed.*, 1988, pp. 120–31.

Cubbage, Frederick W. and Redmond, Clair H. Portfolio Risk and Returns from Timber Asset Investments. *Land Econ.*, November 1988, *64*(4), pp. 325–37.

Cubbin, John S. and Domberger, Simon. Advertising and Post-entry Oligopoly Behaviour. *J. Ind. Econ.*, December 1988, *37*(2), pp. 123–40.

Cudd, Mike and Morris, Joe. Bias in Journal Ratings. *Financial Rev.*, February 1988, *23*(1), pp. 117–25.

Cuddington, John T. Fiscal Policy, Trade Intervention, and World Interest Rates: Comment. In *Frenkel, J. A., ed.*, 1988, pp. 303–07.

―――― **and Viñals, José M.** Fiscal Policy and the Current Account: What Do Capital Controls Do? *Int. Econ. J.*, Spring 1988, *2*(1), pp. 29–37.

Cude, Brenda J. A Note on the Consumer Benefits of Information: Reply. *J. Cons. Aff.*, Summer 1988, *22*(1), pp. 173.

Cue, Felix M. Income Distribution and Economic Development: A Case Study of the Kuznets' Hypothesis Applied to Puerto Rico. *Rev. Soc. Econ.*, April 1988, *46*(1), pp. 61–80.

Cuevas, Carlos E. Intermediation Costs in an Agricultural Development Bank: A Cost-Function Approach to Measuring Scale Economies. *Amer. J. Agr. Econ.*, May 1988, *70*(2), pp. 273–80.

Cuffaro, Miranda. Una funzione del consumo regionale: un primo tentativo di stima per la sicilia (1951–1985). (A Regional Consumption Function: A Preliminary Estimate for Sicily [1951–1985]. With English summary.) *Econ. Lavoro*, Jan.–Mar. 1988, *22*(1), pp. 99–108.

Cugno, Franco and Ferrero, Mario. Free Access vs. Revenue Sharing as Alternative Systems for Managing Employment Externalities. In *Jones, D. C. and Svejnar, J., eds.*, 1988, pp. 217–33.

Cukierman, Alex. The End of the High Israeli Inflation: An Experiment in Heterodox Stabilization. In *Bruno, M., et al., eds.*, 1988, pp. 48–94.

――――. The End of the High Israeli Inflation: An Experiment in Heterodox Stabilization: Reply. In *Bruno, M., et al., eds.*, 1988, pp. 107–08.

――――. Rapid Inflation—Deliberate Policy or Miscalculation? *Carnegie–Rochester Conf. Ser. Public Policy*, Autumn 1988, *29*, pp. 11–75.

――――. Rapid Inflation—Deliberate Policy or Miscalculation? Reply. *Carnegie–Rochester Conf. Ser. Public Policy*, Autumn 1988, *29*, pp. 81–84.

Culbertson, W. Patton, Jr. and Koraz, Faik. In

terest Rates, the Forward Premium, and Unanticipated Money: Reply. *Southern Econ. J.,* April 1988, *54*(4), pp. 1047–48.

Culem, Claudy G. The Locational Determinants of Direct Investments among Industrialized Countries. *Europ. Econ. Rev.,* April 1988, *32*(4), pp. 885–904.

Culham, Peter and Hartley, Nicholas. Telecommunications Prices under Monopoly and Competition. *Oxford Rev. Econ. Policy,* Summer 1988, *4*(2), pp. 1–19.

Culhane, Dennis and Fried, Marc. Paths in Homelessness: A View from the Street. In *Friedrichs, J., ed.,* 1988, pp. 175–87.

Cullen, L. M.; Smout, T. C. and Gibson, A. Wages and Comparative Development in Ireland and Scotland, 1565–1780. In *Mitchison, R. and Roebuck, P., eds.,* 1988, pp. 105–16.

Cullenberg, Stephen. The Capitalist Enterprise and the Contradictory Movement in the Rate of Profit. *Rev. Radical Polit. Econ.,* Summer–Fall 1988, *20*(2–3), pp. 41–47.

_____. The Politics of Class Analysis versus the Class Analysis of Politics. *Rev. Radical Polit. Econ.,* Summer–Fall 1988, *20*(2–3), pp. 12–17.

Cullingworth, J. Barry and Sparling, William J. Community Energy Planning: Prospects and Potentialities. In *Byrne, J. and Rich, D., eds.,* 1988, pp. 247–82.

Cullis, John G. and Jones, Philip R. Employment of the Disabled: A Rationale for Legislation in the United Kingdom. *Int. Rev. Law Econ.,* June 1988, *8*(1), pp. 37–49.

_____ **and Lewis, Alan.** Preferences, Economics and the Economic Psychology of Public Sector Preference Formation. *J. Behav. Econ.,* Spring 1988, *17*(1), pp. 19–33.

Cullison, William E. On Recognizing Inflation. *Fed. Res. Bank Richmond Econ. Rev.,* July–Aug. 1988, *74*(4), pp. 4–12.

Cullity, John P. and Moore, Geoffrey H. Little-known Facts about Stock Prices and Business Cycles. *Challenge,* March–April 1988, *31*(2), pp. 49–50.

Culpeper, Roy. The Debt Crisis and the World Bank: Adjustment, Workout and Growth. *Can. J. Devel. Stud.,* 1988, *9*(1), pp. 131–36.

Culver, David; Strain, Greg and Ehrensaft, Philip. Cost Structure and Performance of Prairie Grain and Oilseed Farms. *Can. J. Agr. Econ.,* Part 2, December 1988, *36*(4), pp. 845–55.

Culyer, A. J. Medical Care and the Economics of Giving. In *Ricketts, M., ed., Vol. 2,* 1988, *1971,* pp. 310–18.

Cumberland, John H.; Gordon, Patrice L. and McConnell, Virginia D. Regional Marginal Costs and Cost Savings from Economies of Scale in Municipal Waste Treatment: An Application to the Chesapeake Bay Region. *Growth Change,* Fall 1988, *19*(4), pp. 1–13.

Cumby, Robert E. Is It Risk? Explaining Deviations from Uncovered Interest Parity. *J. Monet. Econ.,* September 1988, *22*(2), pp. 279–99.

_____; **Figlewski, Stephen and Cecchetti, Ste-**phen **G.** Estimation of the Optimal Futures Hedge. *Rev. Econ. Statist.,* November 1988, *70*(4), pp. 623–30.

Cumings, Bruce. The Northeast Asian Political Economy under Two Hegemonies. In *Burke, E., III, ed.,* 1988, *1984,* pp. 241–62.

_____. World System and Authoritarian Regimes in Korea, 1948–1984. In *Winckler, E. A. and Greenhalgh, S., eds.,* 1988, pp. 249–69.

Cumming, Christine; Harwood, Alison and Aderhold, Robert. International Linkages among Equities Markets and the October 1987 Market Break. *Fed. Res. Bank New York Quart. Rev.,* Summer 1988, *13*(2), pp. 34–46.

Cummings, L. L. and Gardner, Donald G. Activation Theory and Job Design: Review and Reconceptualization. In *Staw, B. M. and Cummings, L. L., eds.,* 1988, pp. 81–122.

Cummings, Scott, et al. Community Development in a Mexican Squatter Settlement: A Program Evaluation. *Population Res. Policy Rev.,* 1988, *7*(2), pp. 159–88.

Cummins, J. David. Incorporating Risk in Insurance Guaranty Fund Premiums. In *Borba, P. S. and Appel, D., eds.,* 1988, pp. 145–60.

_____. Risk-Based Premiums for Insurance Guaranty Funds. *J. Finance,* September 1988, *43*(4), pp. 823–39.

_____ **and Harrington, Scott E.** The Relationship between Risk and Return: Evidence for Property-Liability Insurance Stocks. *J. Risk Ins.,* March 1988, *55*(1), pp. 15–31.

Cundiff, Edward W. The Evolution of Retailing Institutions across Cultures. In *[Hollander, S. C.],* 1988, pp. 149–62.

Cunningham, Isabella C. M. and Cunningham, William H. Stanley C. Hollander: The Scholar behind Marketing and Retail Theory. In *[Hollander, S. C.],* 1988, pp. 5–7.

Cunningham, Lawrence F., et al. Systematic Risk in the Deregulated Airline Industry. *J. Transp. Econ. Policy,* September 1988, *22*(3), pp. 345–53.

Cunningham, M. T. and White, J. G. The Behaviour of Industrial Buyers in Their Search for Suppliers of Machine Tools. In *Earl, P. E., ed., Vol. 1,* 1988, *1974,* pp. 176–89.

Cunningham, William H. and Cunningham, Isabella C. M. Stanley C. Hollander: The Scholar behind Marketing and Retail Theory. In *[Hollander, S. C.],* 1988, pp. 5–7.

Cunningham, William T. Portuguese Tax Reform. *Bull. Int. Fiscal Doc.,* February 1988, *42*(2), pp. 78–80.

Cuny, Thomas J. Offsetting Collections in the Federal Budget. *Public Budg. Finance,* Autumn 1988, *8*(3), pp. 96–110.

Curbelo Ranero, José Luis. Crecimiento y equidad en una economía regional estancada: El caso de Andalucía (un analisis en el márco de las matrices de contabilidad social). (With English summary.) *Invest. Econ.,* September 1988, *12*(3), pp. 501–18.

Cure, Ken. A British Trade Union View of Organisation and JIT in the UK. In *Holl, U. and Trevor, M., eds.,* 1988, pp. 57–62.

Curiel, Imma J.; Pederzoli, Giorgio and Tijs, Stef H. Reward Allocations in Production Systems. In *Eiselt, H. A. and Pederzoli, G., eds.*, 1988, pp. 186–99.

Curington, William P. Federal versus State Regulation: The Early Years of OSHA. *Soc. Sci. Quart.*, June 1988, 69(2), pp. 341–60.

Curlee, T. Randall; Turhollow, Anthony F. and Das, Sujit. Oil Supply Disruptions and Modelling Methodologies: The Role of LP Models. *Energy Econ.*, April 1988, 10(2), pp. 147–54.

Currid, Michael; Schwab, Arthur J. and Sauer, William J. The Emergence of the High Technology Industry in Southwestern Pennsylvania: A Case Study of Pittsburgh. In *Kirchhoff, B. A., et al., eds.*, 1988, pp. 415–29.

Currie, David. Empirical Macroeconomics for Interdependent Economies: Comparison and Evaluation of Model Simulations: Comment. In *Bryant, R. C., et al., eds.*, 1988, pp. 155–57.

_____. Macroeconomic Policy Design and Control Theory—A Failed Partnership. In *Shaw, G. K., ed., Vol. 2,* 1988, *1985,* pp. 358–79.

_____. Should Fiscal Policy Rule the Roost? The Co-ordination of Monetary and Fiscal Policy. In *Eltis, W. and Sinclair, P. J. N., eds.*, 1988, pp. 295–314.

_____ and Hoffmeyer, Ullrich. Fiscal Policy Co-ordination, Inflation and Reputation in a Natural Rate World. *Greek Econ. Rev.*, 1988, 10(1), pp. 103–32.

_____; Muscatelli, Anton and Vines, David. Macroeconomic Interactions between North and South: Introduction. In *Currie, D. and Vines, D., eds.*, 1988, pp. 1–31.

_____, et al. North–South Interactions: A General-Equilibrium Framework for the Study of Strategic Issues. In *Currie, D. and Vines, D., eds.*, 1988, pp. 65–100.

Currier, Kevin M. An Application of Cremer's Planning Procedure to the Optimal Commodity Taxation Problem. *Econ. Letters*, 1988, 28(2), pp. 123–27.

Curry, David J. The Concept of Quality: New Insights, Unanswered Questions. In *Maynes, E. S. and ACCI Research Committee, eds.*, 1988, pp. 111–42.

Curry, M. and Barnes, T. Time and Narrative in Economic Geography. *Environ. Planning A*, February 1988, 20(2), pp. 141–49.

Curtin, Chris and Shields, Dan. Competition and Control at Work: Rural Miners and the Labour Process. *Econ. Soc. Rev.*, April 1988, 19(3), pp. 159–76.

Curtin, Daniel and Sieling, Mark Scott. Patterns of Productivity Change in Men's and Boys' Suits and Coats. *Mon. Lab. Rev.*, November 1988, 111(11), pp. 25–31.

Curtin, Michael E. The Role of International Institutions in the Debt Crisis. In *Tavis, L. A., ed.*, 1988, pp. 212–22.

Curtis, Donald; Hubbard, Michael and Shepherd, Andrew. Famine and the National and International Economy. In *Curtis, D.; Hubbard, M. and Shepherd, A.*, 1988, pp. 11–27.

Cusack, Thomas R. Public Expenditure Decision-Making: A Comparative Analysis. In *Lybeck, J. A. and Henrekson, M., eds.*, 1988, pp. 59–89.

Cushman, David O. Exchange-Rate Uncertainty and Foreign Direct Investment in the United States. *Weltwirtsch. Arch.*, 1988, 124(2), pp. 322–36.

_____. The Impact of Third-Country Exchange Risk: A Correction. *J. Int. Money Finance*, September 1988, 7(3), pp. 359–60.

_____. U.S. Bilateral Trade Flows and Exchange Risk during the Floating Period. *J. Int. Econ.*, May 1988, 24(3–4), pp. 317–30.

Cuthbertson, Keith. The Demand for M1: A Forward Looking Buffer Stock Model. *Oxford Econ. Pap.*, March 1988, 40(1), pp. 110–31.

_____. Expectations, Learning and the Kalman Filter. *Manchester Sch. Econ. Soc. Stud.*, September 1988, 56(3), pp. 223–46.

_____ and Taylor, Mark P. Monetary Anticipations and the Demand for Money in the U.S.: Further Results. *Southern Econ. J.*, October 1988, 55(2), pp. 326–35.

Cutler, David M. Tax Reform and the Stock Market: An Asset Price Approach. *Amer. Econ. Rev.*, December 1988, 78(5), pp. 1107–17.

_____ and Summers, Lawrence H. The Costs of Conflict Resolution and Financial Distress: Evidence from the Texaco–Pennzoil Litigation. *Rand J. Econ.*, Summer 1988, 19(2), pp. 157–72.

Cutright, Phillips and Smith, Herbert L. Thinking about Change in Illegitimacy Ratios: United States, 1963–1983. *Demography*, May 1988, 25(2), pp. 235–47.

Cuzán, Alfred G.; Moussalli, Stephanie D. and Bundrick, Charles M. Fiscal Expansion and Political Instability in the Iberic–Latin Region. *Public Choice*, December 1988, 59(3), pp. 225–38.

Cwi, David and Strausbaugh, John. The Royalists, the Realists, and the Radicals: A Comparative Analysis of Arts Funding in Canada and the United States. *J. Cult. Econ.*, June 1988, 12(1), pp. 1–26.

Cyert, Richard M. Competition, Growth, and Efficiency. In *Cyert, R. M.*, 1988, *1969,* pp. 36–56.

_____. A Description and Evaluation of Some Firm Simulations. In *Cyert, R. M.*, 1988, *1964,* pp. 179–98.

_____. Oligopoly Price Behaviour and the Business Cycle. In *Cyert, R. M.*, 1988, *1955,* pp. 3–19.

_____. Towards a Control Theory of the Firm. In *Cyert, R. M.*, 1988, pp. 78–91.

_____ and Cohen, Kalman J. Computer Models in Dynamic Economics. In *Cyert, R. M.*, 1988, *1961,* pp. 163–78.

_____; Feigenbaum, Edward A. and March, James G. Models in a Behavioral Theory of the Firm. In *March, J. G.*, 1988, *1959,* pp. 37–60.

_____ and George, Kenneth D. Competition, Growth, and Efficiency. In *Earl, P. E., ed., Vol. 2,* 1988, *1969,* pp. 245–63.

_____ and **Hedrick, Charles L.** Theory of the Firm: Past, Present, and Future; An Interpretation. In *Cyert, R. M.*, 1988, *1972*, pp. 59–77.

_____ and **Kamien, Morton I.** Behavioural Rules and the Theory of the Firm. In *Cyert, R. M.*, 1988, *1967*, pp. 111–21.

_____ and **Lave, Lester B.** Collusion, Conflict, and Economics. In *Cyert, R. M.*, 1988, pp. 92–110.

_____ and **March, James G.** A Behavioural Theory of Organizational Objectives. In *Cyert, R. M.*, 1988, *1959*, pp. 125–38.

_____ and **March, James G.** Organizational Design. In *Cyert, R. M.*, 1988, *1964*, pp. 151–60.

_____ and **March, James G.** Organizational Factors in the Theory of Oligopoly. In *Earl, P. E.*, ed., *Vol. 1*, 1988, *1956*, pp. 332–52.

_____ and **March, James G.** Organizational Structure and Pricing Behavior in an Oligopolistic Market. In *March, J. G.*, 1988, *1955*, pp. 25–36.

_____ and **March, James G.** Organizational Structure and Pricing Behavior in an Oligopolistic Market. In *Earl, P. E.*, ed., *Vol. 1*, 1988, *1955*, pp. 321–31.

_____ and **March, James G.** Research on a Behavioural Theory of the Firm. In *Cyert, R. M.*, 1988, *1960*, pp. 139–50.

_____ and **Mowery, David C.** The Impact of Technological Change on Employment and Economic Growth: Introduction. In *Cyert, R. M. and Mowery, D. C.*, eds., 1988, pp. xxv–xxxiv.

_____ and **Pottinger, Garrel.** Towards a Better Micro-economic Theory. In *Cyert, R. M.*, 1988, *1979*, pp. 201–19.

_____ and **Simon, Herbert A.** The Behavioural Approach: With Emphasis on Economics. In *Earl, P. E.*, ed., *Vol. 1*, 1988, *1983*, pp. 45–58.

_____ and **Simon, Herbert A.** The Behavioural Approach: With Emphasis on Economics. In *Cyert, R. M.*, 1988, *1983*, pp. 220–39.

_____; **Simon, Herbert A. and Trow, Donald B.** Observation of a Business Decision. In *Cyert, R. M.*, 1988, *1956*, pp. 20–35.

Cypher, James M. The Crisis and the Restructuring of Capitalism in the Periphery. In *Zarembka, P.*, ed., 1988, pp. 45–82.

_____. Military Production and Capital Accumulation: A Comment. *J. Post Keynesian Econ.*, Winter 1987–88, *10*(2), pp. 304–09.

Czogala, Ernest and Disney, Peter L. Decision Making in a Probablistic Fuzzy Environment. In *Kacprzyk, J. and Fedrizzi, M.*, eds., 1988, pp. 215–26.

D'Agata, Antonio. Minimum Plant Size and Oligopolistic Markets in a Classical Multisectoral Model. *Australian Econ. Pap.*, December 1988, *27*(51), pp. 298–312.

D'Antonio, Mariano. Sviluppo economico e redistribuzione: il caso del mezzogiorno. (Economic Development and Redistribution: The Case of the "Mezzogiorno." With English summary.)

Econ. Lavoro, Jan.–Mar. 1988, *22*(1), pp. 3–23.

_____; **Colaizzo, Raffaele and Leonello, Giuseppe.** Mezzogiorno/Centre-North: A Two-Region Model for the Italian Economy. *J. Policy Modeling*, Fall 1988, *10*(3), pp. 437–51.

D'Arcy, Stephen P. Use of the CAPM to Discount Property-Liability Loss Reserves. *J. Risk Ins.*, September 1988, *55*(3), pp. 481–91.

_____ and **Chen, K. C.** The Effect of Changes in Pension Plan Interest Rate Assumptions on Security Prices. *J. Econ. Bus.*, August 1988, *40*(3), pp. 243–52.

D'Ascenzo, Michael. Developments in Transfer Pricing Enforcement and Complex Audit Strategy in the Australian Taxation Office. *Australian Tax Forum*, 1988, *5*(4), pp. 471–92.

D'Silva, Brian C. and El Badawi, Ibrahim. Indirect and Direct Taxation of Agriculture in Sudan: The Role of the Government in Agriculture Surplus Extraction. *Amer. J. Agr. Econ.*, May 1988, *70*(2), pp. 431–36.

D'Souza, Dora. Economic Factors and Firms' Financial Structure: An Empirical Study of Cement Companies. *Margin*, Jan.–March 1988, *20*(2), pp. 39–46.

van Daal, J. and Merkies, A. H. Q. M. Nataf's Theorem, Taylor's Expansion and Homogeneity in Consumer Demand. In *Eichhorn, W.*, ed., 1988, pp. 671–89.

_____ and **Merkies, A. H. Q. M.** The Problem of Aggregation of Individual Economic Relations; Consistency and Representativity in a Historical Perspective. In *Eichhorn, W.*, ed., 1988, pp. 607–37.

Dadgostar, Bahram. Integrated Approach to Demand Analysis for Food in Thailand. *Singapore Econ. Rev.*, April 1988, *33*(1), pp. 88–100.

_____. Integrated Approach to Demand Analysis for Meat in Canada. In *Missouri Valley Economic Assoc.*, 1988, pp. 110–15.

Dadkhah, Kamran M. and Mookerjee, Rajen. The Behavior of the Currency Deposit Ratio in India, 1870–1982. *J. Devel. Areas*, April 1988, *22*(3), pp. 359–72.

Dadson, J. A. The Need for Cooperative Reorientation—The Ghanaian Case. In *Hedlund, H.*, ed., 1988, pp. 173–86.

Daduna, Joachim R. A Decision Support System for Vehicle Scheduling in Public Transport. In *Gaul, W. and Schader, M.*, eds., 1988, pp. 93–102.

_____ and **Mojsilovic, Miodrag.** Computer-Aided Vehicle and Duty Scheduling Using the HOT Programme System. In *Daduna, J. R. and Wren, A.*, eds., 1988, pp. 133–46.

Dagenais, Denyse L. and Dagenais, Marcel G. Modèle d'analyse du cheminement des étudiants dans un programme universitaire de premier cycle. (A Model for Analyzing the Schooling Process of Students in an Undergraduate Program. With English summary.) *Ann. Écon. Statist.*, April–June 1988, (10), pp. 75–96.

Dagenais, Marcel G. and Dagenais, Denyse L. Modèle d'analyse du cheminement des étudiants dans un programme universitaire de premier cycle. (A Model for Analyzing the Schooling Process of Students in an Undergraduate Program. With English summary.) *Ann. Écon. Statist.*, April–June 1988, (10), pp. 75–96.

Dagnino-Pastore, José María. Adjustment Processes and the Framework of External Debt Negotiations: Comments. In *Feinberg, R. E. and Ffrench-Davis, R., eds.*, 1988, pp. 108–14.

Dagsvik, John K., et al. Female Labour Supply and the Tax Benefit System in France. *Ann. Écon. Statist.*, July–Sept. 1988, (11), pp. 5–40.

————, **et al.** The Impact on Labor Supply of a Shorter Workday: A Micro-econometric Discrete/Continuous Choice Approach. In *Hart, R. A., ed.*, 1988, pp. 208–24.

Dagum, Camilo. Factor Shares in Canada, the United States, and the United Kingdom. In *Asimakopulos, A., ed.*, 1988, pp. 199–223.

Dahbi, Mohammed B. Considerations on Satellite Liability Insurance. In *Egan, J. J., et al.*, 1988, pp. 421–31.

Dahle, Helge K.; Espedal, Magne S. and Ewing, Richard E. Characteristic Petrov-Galerkin Subdomain Methods for Convection-Diffusion Problems. In *Wheeler, M. F., ed.*, 1988, pp. 77–87.

Dahlgran, Roger A.; Smith, Stephen M. and Barkley, David L. High-Technology Manufacturing in the Nonmetropolitan West: Gold or Just Glitter. *Amer. J. Agr. Econ.*, August 1988, 70(3), pp. 560–71.

Dahlman, Carl J. The Problem of Externality. In *Cowen, T., ed.*, 1988, 1979, pp. 209–34.

Dahmén, Erik. 'Development Blocks' in Industrial Economics. *Scand. Econ. Hist. Rev.*, 1988, 36(1), pp. 3–14.

Dahringer, Lee D. and Johnson, Denise R. Lemon Laws: Intent, Experience, and a Proconsumer Model. *J. Cons. Aff.*, Summer 1988, 22(1), pp. 158–70.

Daicoff, Darwin W. Deregulation and Motor Carrier Safety. *Logist. Transp. Rev.*, June 1988, 24(2), pp. 175–84.

Dakin, Stephen R. and Gimpl, Martin L. Management and Magic. In *Earl, P. E., ed., Vol. 1*, 1988, 1984, pp. 217–28.

Dakkak, Ibrahim. Development from Within: A Strategy for Survival. In *Abed, G. T., ed.*, 1988, pp. 287–310.

Dalal, Ardeshir J. Asset Demands and Slutsky Equations When All Assets Are Risky. *Metroecon.*, June 1988, 39(2), pp. 205–21.

Dalal, Meenakshi Nath and Schachter, Gustav. Transmission of International Inflation to India: A Structural Analysis. *J. Devel. Areas*, October 1988, 23(1), pp. 85–103.

Dalal, S. R. and Klein, R. W. A Flexible Class of Discrete Choice Models. *Marketing Sci.*, Summer 1988, 7(3), pp. 232–51.

Dalamagas, Basil A. The Relative Importance of Monetary and Fiscal Actions: Evidence from the Mediterranean EEC Countries. *Economia (Portugal)*, October 1988, 12(3), pp. 293–321.

Dale, Stephen Frederic. Religious Suicide in Islamic Asia: Anticolonial Terrorism in India, Indonesia, and the Philippines. *J. Conflict Resolution*, March 1988, 32(1), pp. 37–59.

Daley, James M. and Martin, James H. Situational Analysis of Bus Riders and Non-riders for Different Transportation Methods. *Logist. Transp. Rev.*, June 1988, 24(2), pp. 185–99.

Daley, Lane A.; Senkow, David W. and Vigeland, Robert L. Analysts' Forecasts, Earnings Variability, and Option Pricing: Empirical Evidence. *Accounting Rev.*, October 1988, 63(4), pp. 563–85.

Dalgic, Tevfik and Kaynak, Erdener. Irish Consumer Attitudes towards Foreign Products: Retail Policy Implications. In *Kaynak, E., ed.*, 1988, pp. 103–12.

Dallago, Bruno. The Irregular Economy in Italy: Facts, Interpretations, Misunderstandings. *Konjunkturpolitik*, 1988, 34(5–6), pp. 352–80.

Dallin, Alexander. Gorbachev's Foreign Policy and the "New Political Thinking" in the Soviet Union. In *Juviler, P. and Kimura, H., eds.*, 1988, pp. 97–113.

————. The Soviet Union Today: Policy-Making in Foreign Affairs. In *Cracraft, J., ed.*, 1988, pp. 53–63.

Dalpé, Robert. Innovation and Technology Policy in a Small Open Economy: The Canadian Case. In *Freeman, C. and Lundvall, B.-A., eds.*, 1988, pp. 250–61.

Dalto, Guy C. Gender, Risk and Access to Tax-Favored Fringe Benefits: A Split Labor Market Approach. *Population Res. Policy Rev.*, 1988, 7(3), pp. 239–53.

Dalton, Clare. How It Was, How It Is. *Mich. Law Rev.*, May 1988, 86(6), pp. 1346–55.

Dalton, Dan R.; Kesner, Idalene F. and Rechner, Paula L. Corporate Governance and Boards of Directors: An International, Comparative Perspective. In *Farmer, R. N. and McGoun, E. G., eds.*, 1988, pp. 95–105.

Dalton, Linda C. and Dalton, Thomas C. The Politics of Measuring Public Sector Performance: Productivity and the Public Organization. In *Kelly, R. M., ed.*, 1988, pp. 19–65.

Dalton, Margaret M. and Mann, Patrick C. Telephone Cost Allocation: Testing the Variability of Costs. *Land Econ.*, August 1988, 64(3), pp. 296–305.

Dalton, Thomas C. and Dalton, Linda C. The Politics of Measuring Public Sector Performance: Productivity and the Public Organization. In *Kelly, R. M., ed.*, 1988, pp. 19–65.

Dalton, Thomas R. Public Good Provision under Uncertainty. *Public Finance*, 1988, 43(1), pp. 56–66.

Dalum, Bent; Fagerberg, Jan and Jørgensen, Ulrik. Small Open Economies in the World Market for Electronics: The Case of the Nordic Countries. In *Freeman, C. and Lundvall, B.-A., eds.*, 1988, pp. 113–38.

Daly, Herman E. Moving to a Steady-State Economy. In *Ehrlich, P. R. and Holdren, J. P., eds.*, 1988, pp. 271–85.

————. On Sustainable Development and National Accounts. In *[Lecomber, R.]*, 1988, pp. 41–56.

Daly, Mary E. Industrial Policy in Scotland and Ireland in the Inter-war Years. In *Mitchison, R. and Roebuck, P.*, eds., 1988, pp. 288–96.

Daly, Michael J.; Lastman, Gary J. and Naquib, Fadle. The Role of Tax-Deductible Saving in the Transition from a Progressive Income Tax to a Progressive Consumption Tax. *Public Finance*, 1988, *43*(3), pp. 349–72.

———; **Mercier, Pierre and Schweitzer, Thomas.** The Impact of Tax Reform on Investment and Saving Incentives in Canada, the United States, the United Kingdom, and Japan. *Econ. Letters*, 1988, *27*(2), pp. 159–65.

Daly, Rex F. *The Journal of Agricultural Economics Research:* Oris V. Wells' Journal Turns 40. *J. Agr. Econ. Res.*, Winter 1988, *40*(1), pp. 7–8.

Damania, Richard and Mair, Douglas. The Ricardian Tradition and Local Property Taxation. *Cambridge J. Econ.*, December 1988, *12*(4), pp. 435–49.

Damill, Mario, et al. As relações financeiras na economia argentina. (With English summary.) *Pesquisa Planejamento Econ.*, August 1988, *18*(2), pp. 297–339.

Dammon, Robert M. A Security Market and Capital Structure Equilibrium under Uncertainty with Progressive Personal Taxes. In *Chen, A. H.*, ed., 1988, pp. 53–74.

——— **and Senbet, Lemma W.** The Effect of Taxes and Depreciation on Corporate Investment and Financial Leverage. *J. Finance*, June 1988, *43*(2), pp. 357–73.

Damodaran, Aswath. Information Structure in International Markets: Measures and Implications. In *Khoury, S. J. and Ghosh, A.*, eds., 1988, pp. 277–97.

Damon, William W. and Bolch, Ben W. Modeling Divorcement in the Retail Petroleum Industry. *Quart. Rev. Econ. Bus.*, Summer 1988, *28*(2), pp. 46–60.

———; **Hinshaw, C. Elton and Bolch, Ben W.** Visual Artists' Rights Act of 1987: A Case of Misguided Legislation. *Cato J.*, Spring–Summer 1988, *8*(1), pp. 71–78.

Dancet, Geert. From a Workable Social Compromise to Conflict: The Case of Belgium. In *Boyer, R.*, ed., 1988, pp. 96–118.

Dandekar, V. M. Agriculture, Employment and Poverty. In *Lucas, R. E. B. and Papanek, G. F.*, eds., 1988, pp. 93–120.

Daneshyar, Arifeen M. Famines: A Political Economy Perspective. In *Pennsylvania Economic Association*, 1988, pp. 507–21.

Danesy, Frank C.; Dlugos, Günter and Dorow, Wolfgang. The Analysis of the Employer Employee Relationship from the Perspective of the Business Politics Approach. In *Dlugos, G.; Dorow, W. and Weiermair, K.*, eds., 1988, pp. 107–18.

Dangel, Cécile. Théorie monétaire de J. M. Keynes: L'hypothèse de séparabilité de la demande de monnaie. (With English summary.) *Rech. Écon. Louvain*, 1988, *54*(4), pp. 439–58.

Daniel, Clive. The Economic and Social Performance of Small Nations. In *Salvatore, D.*, ed., 1988, pp. 199–210.

Daniel, Coldwell, III. A Critique of the Controversy about the Stability of Consumers' Tastes. *J. Econ. Educ.*, Summer 1988, *19*(3), pp. 245–53.

Daniels, Brian P. and Plott, Charles R. Inflation and Expectations in Experimental Markets. In *Tietz, R.; Albers, W. and Selten, R.*, eds., 1988, pp. 198–218.

Daniels, R. and Dewees, Donald N. Prevention and Compensation of Industrial Disease. *Int. Rev. Law Econ.*, June 1988, *8*(1), pp. 51–72.

Danielsen, Albert L. and Kim, Seungwook. OPEC Stability: An Empirical Assessment. *Energy Econ.*, July 1988, *10*(3), pp. 174–84.

Danielson, Anders. Agricultural Development and Demographic Change: A Comment. *Econ. Develop. Cult. Change*, April 1988, *36*(3), pp. 565–70.

Danilov, V. I. and Sotskov, A. I. Coalition-Stable Social Choice Mechanisms. *Matekon*, Winter 1988–89, *25*(2), pp. 45–61.

——— **and Sotskov, A. I.** Stable Blocking in Social Choice Mechanisms. *Matekon*, Fall 1988, *25*(1), pp. 38–53.

Dann, Larry Y. and DeAngelo, Harry. Corporate Financial Policy and Corporate Control: A Study of Defensive Adjustments in Asset and Ownership Structure. *J. Finan. Econ.*, Jan.–March 1988, *20*(1–2), pp. 87–127.

Danns, Donna E. Guyana's Debt Problem. *Soc. Econ. Stud.*, December 1988, *37*(4), pp. 79–106.

Dans, Peter. Standards of Care in Medicine: Commentary. *Inquiry*, Winter 1988, *25*(4), pp. 451–53.

Dant, Rajiv P. and Barnes, James H., Jr. Methodological Concerns in Cross-Cultural Research: Implications for Economic Development. In *Kumcu, E. and Firat, A. F.*, eds., 1988, pp. 149–71.

Danziger, Leif. Costs of Price Adjustment and the Welfare Economics of Inflation and Disinflation. *Amer. Econ. Rev.*, September 1988, *78*(4), pp. 633–46.

———. Is There Anything Perverse about the Labor-Managed Firm? *J. Compar. Econ.*, June 1988, *12*(2), pp. 240–43.

———. Real Shocks, Efficient Risk Sharing, and the Duration of Labor Contracts. *Quart. J. Econ.*, May 1988, *103*(2), pp. 435–40.

Danziger, Sandra K.; Longres, John F. and Sosin, Michael R. The Status of Youth in Wisconsin: Lessons for Policy. In *Danziger, S. H. and Witte, J. F.*, eds., 1988, pp. 151–71.

Danziger, Sheldon H. The Economy, Public Policy, and the Poor. In *Rodgers, H. R., Jr.*, ed., 1988, pp. 3–13.

———. Recent Trends in Poverty and the Antipoverty Effectiveness of Income Transfers. In *Danziger, S. H. and Portney, K. E.*, eds., 1988, pp. 33–46.

——— **and Feaster, Daniel J.** Wealth Distributional Consequences of Life Cycle Models:

Comments. In *Kessler, D. and Masson, A.,* eds., 1988, pp. 319–21.

_____; **Gottschalk, Peter and Smolensky, Eugene.** The Declining Significance of Age in the United States: Trends in the Well-Being of Children and the Elderly since 1939. In *Palmer, J. L.; Smeeding, T. and Torrey, B. B.,* eds., 1988, pp. 29–54.

_____ **and Nichols-Casebolt, Ann.** Poverty and Income Transfers in Wisconsin. In *Danziger, S. H. and Witte, J. F.,* eds., 1988, pp. 133–50.

_____ **and Portney, Kent E.** The Distributional Impacts of Public Policies. In *Danziger, S. H. and Portney, K. E.,* eds., 1988, pp. 1–10.

_____ **and Witte, John F.** State Policy Choices: The Wisconsin Experience: Introduction. In *Danziger, S. H. and Witte, J. F.,* eds., 1988, pp. 3–10.

Danzon, Patricia M. Medical Malpractice Liability. In *Litan, R. E. and Winston, C.,* eds., 1988, pp. 101–27.

_____. The Political Economy of Workers' Compensation: Lessons for Product Liability. *Amer. Econ. Rev.,* May 1988, 78(2), pp. 305–10.

Darby-Dowman, K., et al. Integrated Decision Support Systems for Urban Transport Scheduling: Discussion of Implementation and Experience. In *Daduna, J. R. and Wren, A.,* eds., 1988, pp. 226–39.

Darby, Michael R. Transmission of Real and Monetary Disturbances under Fixed and Floating Exchange Rates: Real Exchange Rates and Freedom of International Trade and Capital Flows. *Cato J.,* Fall 1988, 8(2), pp. 473–75.

Dardanoni, Valentino. Optimal Choices under Uncertainty: The Case of Two-Argument Utility Functions. *Econ. J.,* June 1988, 98(391), pp. 429–50.

_____ **and Hey, John D.** Optimal Consumption under Uncertainty: An Experimental Investigation. *Econ. J.,* Supplement, 1988, 98(390), pp. 105–16.

_____ **and Hey, John D.** A Preliminary Analysis of a Large-Scale Experimental Investigation into Consumption under Uncertainty. In *Tietz, R.; Albers, W. and Selten, R.,* eds., 1988, pp. 51–65.

_____ **and Jones, Andrew M.** Stochastic Habits and the Consumption/Savings Decision. *Stud. Econ.,* 1988, 43(34), pp. 3–12.

_____ **and Lambert, Peter J.** Welfare Rankings of Income Distributions: A Role for the Variance and Some Insights for Tax Reform. *Soc. Choice Welfare,* 1988, 5(1), pp. 1–17.

_____ **and Martina, Riccardo.** "Il nuovo sistema di incentivi sovietico": Alcuni risultati sul modello de Weitzman. (With English summary.) *Stud. Econ.,* 1988, 43(34), pp. 113–37.

Dardis, Rachel. A Follow-Up to Crandall's Comments. In *Maynes, E. S. and ACCI Research Committee,* eds., 1988, pp. 371–73.

_____. International Trade: The Consumer's Stake. In *Maynes, E. S. and ACCI Research Committee,* eds., 1988, pp. 329–59.

_____. Risk Regulation and Consumer Welfare. *J. Cons. Aff.,* Winter 1988, 22(2), pp. 303–18.

Dargavel, John. Changing Capital Structure, the State, and Tasmanian Forestry. In *Richards, J. F. and Tucker, R. P.,* eds., 1988, pp. 189–210.

Daripa, Prabir, et al. On the Simulation of Heterogeneous Petroleum Reservoirs. In *Wheeler, M. F.,* ed., 1988, pp. 89–103.

Darity, William A., Jr. and Cottrell, Allin F. Marx, Malthus, and Wages. *Hist. Polit. Econ.,* Summer 1988, 20(2), pp. 173–90.

_____ **and Horn, Bobbie L.** Involuntary Unemployment Independent of the Labor Market. *J. Post Keynesian Econ.,* Winter 1987–88, 10(2), pp. 216–24.

Darke, Jane and Darke, Roy. Affordable Housing: Roles for the State and the Community. In *Friedrichs, J.,* ed., 1988, pp. 43–56.

Darke, Roy and Darke, Jane. Affordable Housing: Roles for the State and the Community. In *Friedrichs, J.,* ed., 1988, pp. 43–56.

Darling-Hammond, Linda and Nataraj Kirby, Sheila. Parental Schooling Choice: A Case Study of Minnesota. *J. Policy Anal. Manage.,* Spring 1988, 7(3), pp. 506–17.

Darnell, Adrian C. Data Response Techniques. In *Darnell, A. and Evans, L.,* eds., 1988, pp. 1–28.

_____ **and Evans, J. Lynne.** The Holding Cost of Money. *Appl. Econ.,* March 1988, 20(3), pp. 395–405.

Darrat, Ali F. Are Exports an Engine of Growth? A Reply. *Appl. Econ.,* November 1988, 20(11), pp. 1561.

_____. Does Inflation Inhibit or Promote Growth? Some Time Series Evidence. *Quart. J. Bus. Econ.,* Autumn 1988, 27(4), pp. 113–34.

_____. Have Large Budget Deficits Caused Rising Trade Deficits? *Southern Econ. J.,* April 1988, 54(4), pp. 879–87.

_____. Inflation, Unemployment and Monetary Policy: An Evaluation of the Korean Recent Experience. *J. Econ. Devel.,* December 1988, 13(2), pp. 141–50.

_____. The Islamic Interest-Free Banking System: Some Empirical Evidence. *Appl. Econ.,* March 1988, 20(3), pp. 417–25.

_____. On Fiscal Policy and the Stock Market. *J. Money, Credit, Banking,* Part 1, August 1988, 20(3), pp. 353–63.

_____. Rational Expectations and the Role of Monetary Policy: Some Tests Based on the Fisher Equation. *Eastern Econ. J.,* July–Sept. 1988, 14(3), pp. 211–19.

_____ **and Barnhart, Scott W.** Budget Deficits, Money Growth and Causality: Further OECD Evidence. *J. Int. Money Finance,* June 1988, 7(2), pp. 231–42.

_____ **and Conte, Michael A.** Economic Growth and the Expanding Public Sector: A Reexamination. *Rev. Econ. Statist.,* May 1988, 70(2), pp. 322–30.

_____ **and Lopez, Franklin A.** Price Instability and Inflation: Some Tests Based on Rational Expectations Models. *Econ. Letters,* 1988, 26(2), pp. 111–19.

Darst, Robert G., Jr. Environmentalism in the

USSR: The Opposition to the River Diversion Projects. *Soviet Econ.*, July–Sept. 1988, *4*(3), pp. 223–52.

Darton, David and O'Neill, Gerard J. The Changing Role of the Household Economy in a World of Expanding Technology. In *Tisdell, C. and Maitra, P.*, eds., 1988, pp. 217–38.

Darvish, Tikva and Eckstein, Shlomo. A Model for Simultaneous Sensitivity Analysis of Projects. *Appl. Econ.*, January 1988, *20*(1), pp. 113–23.

_____ **and Rosenberg, Jacob.** The Economic Model of Voter Participation: A Further Test. *Public Choice*, February 1988, *56*(2), pp. 185–92.

Darwin, G. H. The Theory of Exchange Value. In *Wood, J. C.*, ed., *Vol. 2*, 1988, *1875*, pp. 89–99.

Daryanani, Raj; Rones, Arthur and Goodman, Laurie S. The Credit Exposure of Cross-Currency and Nondollar Interest Rate Swaps. In *Khoury, S. J. and Ghosh, A.*, eds., 1988, pp. 193–203.

Das-Gupta, A. A New Measure of Fiscal Privilege. *Public Finance Quart.*, April 1988, *16*(2), pp. 244–52.

Das, Somshankar and Stein, Alfred J. Sustaining and Augmenting Competitive Advantage in Emerging Industries in a Global Environment. In *Furino, A.*, ed., 1988, pp. 157–68.

Das, Sujit; Curlee, T. Randall and Turhollow, Anthony F. Oil Supply Disruptions and Modelling Methodologies: The Role of LP Models. *Energy Econ.*, April 1988, *10*(2), pp. 147–54.

Dasgupta, Partha. Lives and Well-Being. *Soc. Choice Welfare*, 1988, *5*(2/3), pp. 103–26.

_____. Lives and Well-Being. In *Gaertner, W. and Pattanaik, P. K.*, eds., 1988, *1988*, pp. 15–38.

_____. Patents, Priority and Imitation or, the Economics of Races and Waiting Games. *Econ. J.*, March 1988, *98*(389), pp. 66–80.

_____. Trust as a Commodity. In *Gambetta, D.*, ed., 1988, pp. 49–72.

_____. The Welfare Economics of Knowledge Production. *Oxford Rev. Econ. Policy*, Winter 1988, *4*(4), pp. 1–12.

_____ **and Stiglitz, Joseph E.** Learning-by-Doing, Market Structure and Industrial and Trade Policies. *Oxford Econ. Pap.*, June 1988, *40*(2), pp. 246–68.

_____ **and Stiglitz, Joseph E.** Potential Competition, Actual Competition, and Economic Welfare. *Europ. Econ. Rev.*, March 1988, *32*(2–3), pp. 569–77.

Dasgupta, Swapan and Mitra, Tapan. Characterization of Intertemporal Optimality in Terms of Decentralizable Conditions: The Discounted Case. *J. Econ. Theory*, August 1988, *45*(2), pp. 274–87.

_____ **and Mitra, Tapan.** Intertemporal Optimality in a Closed Linear Model of Production. *J. Econ. Theory*, August 1988, *45*(2), pp. 288–315.

Dasvarma, Gouranga Lal and Hull, Terence H.

Fertility Trends in Indonesia 1967–1985. *Bull. Indonesian Econ. Stud.*, April 1988, *24*(1), pp. 115–22.

Datar, Srikant M.; Kekre, Sunder and Banker, Rajiv D. Relevant Costs, Congestion and Stochasticity in Production Environments. *J. Acc. Econ.*, July 1988, *10*(3), pp. 171–97.

Datcher-Loury, Linda. Effects of Mother's Home Time on Children's Schooling. *Rev. Econ. Statist.*, August 1988, *70*(3), pp. 367–73.

Datt, Gaurav. Estimating Engel Elasticities with Bootstrap Standard Errors. *Oxford Bull. Econ. Statist.*, August 1988, *50*(3), pp. 325–33.

Datta, Pranati. An Estimate of the Value of Stocks of Consumer Durables in India in March 1979. *Indian Econ. J.*, Oct.–Dec. 1988, *36*(2), pp. 44–49.

Datta, Samar K., et al. Seasonality, Differential Access Interlinking of Labour and Credit. *J. Devel. Stud.*, April 1988, *24*(3), pp. 379–93.

Daughety, Andrew F. Cournot Oligopoly: Characterization and Applications: Introduction, Purpose, and Overview. In *Daughety, A. F.*, ed., 1988, pp. 3–60.

_____. Reconsidering Cournot: The Cournot Equilibrium Is Consistent. In *Daughety, A. F.*, ed., 1988, *1985*, pp. 161–78.

_____ **and Nelson, Forrest D.** An Econometric Analysis of Changes in the Cost and Production Structure of the Trucking Industry, 1953–1982. *Rev. Econ. Statist.*, February 1988, *70*(1), pp. 67–75.

Dauhajre, Andres. Some Warnings Concerning Possible Financial Reform in the Dominican Republic. In *Jorge, A. and Salazar-Carrillo, J.*, eds., 1988, pp. 180–86.

_____ **and Kiguel, Miguel A.** A Dynamic Model of the Open Economy with Sluggish Output. *Int. Econ. Rev.*, November 1988, *29*(4), pp. 587–606.

Daune-Richard, Anne-Marie. Gender Relations and Female Labor: A Consideration of Sociological Categories. In *Jenson, J.; Hagen, E. and Reddy, C.*, eds., 1988, pp. 260–75.

DaVanzo, Julie. Infant Mortality and Socioeconomic Development: Evidence from Malaysian Household Data. *Demography*, November 1988, *25*(4), pp. 581–95.

Dave, Upendra. Inventory Returns and Special Sales in an Order-Level System for Deteriorating Items. *Econ. Computat. Cybern. Stud. Res.*, 1988, *23*(2), pp. 85–91.

Davelaar, Evert Jan and Nijkamp, Peter. The Incubator Hypothesis: Re-vitalization of Metropolitan Areas? *Ann. Reg. Sci.*, November 1988, *22*(3), pp. 48–65.

Davenport-Hines, R. P. T. Trade Associations and the Modernization Crisis of British Industry, 1910–35: Response. In *Yamazaki, H. and Miyamoto, M.*, eds., 1988, pp. 229–31.

_____. Trade Associations and the Modernization Crisis of British Industry, 1910–35. In *Yamazaki, H. and Miyamoto, M.*, eds., 1988, pp. 205–26.

David, Martin H. and Menchik, Paul L. Changes in Cohort Wealth over a Generation. *Demography*, August 1988, *25*(3), pp. 317–35.

David, Paul A. and Bunn, Julie Ann. The Economics of Gateway Technologies and Network Evolution: Lessons from Electricity Supply History. *Info. Econ. Policy*, 1988, 3(2), pp. 165–202.

_____ and Sundstrom, William A. Old-Age Security Motives, Labor Markets, and Farm Family Fertility in Antebellum America. *Exploration Econ. Hist.*, April 1988, 25(2), pp. 164–97.

_____, et al. Cohort Parity Analysis: Statistical Estimates of the Extent of Fertility Control. *Demography*, May 1988, 25(2), pp. 163–88.

Davidson, B. R. Agriculture and the Recovery from the Depression. In *Gregory, R. G. and Butlin, N. G., eds.*, 1988, pp. 273–88.

Davidson, Carl. Equilibrium in Servicing Industries: An Economic Application of Queuing Theory. *J. Bus.*, July 1988, 61(3), pp. 347–67.

_____. Multiunit Bargaining in Oligopolistic Industries. *J. Lab. Econ.*, July 1988, 6(3), pp. 397–422.

_____; Martin, Lawrence and Matusz, Steven J. The Structure of Simple General Equilibrium Models with Frictional Unemployment. *J. Polit. Econ.*, December 1988, 96(6), pp. 1267–93.

Davidson, Carlos and Reich, Michael. Income Inequality: An Inter-industry Analysis. *Ind. Relat.*, Fall 1988, 27(3), pp. 263–86.

Davidson, Gary E. Don't Reregulate Airlines, Open American Skies to Foreign Competition. *J. Policy Anal. Manage.*, Fall 1988, 7(4), pp. 714–18.

Davidson, Judith R. and Stein, Steve. Economic Crisis, Social Polarization, and Community Participation in Health Care. In *Zschock, D. K., ed.*, 1988, pp. 53–77.

Davidson, Paul. Endogeneous Money, the Production Process, and Inflation Analysis. *Écon. Appl.*, 1988, 41(1), pp. 151–69.

_____. Financial Markets, Investment and Employment. In *Kregel, J. A.; Matzner, E. and Roncaglia, A., eds.*, 1988, pp. 73–92.

_____. A Keynesian View of Patinkin's Theory of Employment. In *Shaw, G. K., ed., Vol. 1*, 1988, 1967, pp. 132–51.

_____. A Modest Set of Proposals for Resolving the International Debt Problem. *J. Post Keynesian Econ.*, Winter 1987–88, 10(2), pp. 323–38.

_____. A Post-Keynesian View of Theories and Causes for High Real Interest Rates. In *Arestis, P., ed.*, 1988, pp. 152–82.

_____. Reviving Keynes's Revolution. In *Shaw, G. K., ed., Vol. 1*, 1988, 1984, pp. 38–52.

_____. A Technical Definition of Uncertainty and the Long-run Non-neutrality of Money. *Cambridge J. Econ.*, September 1988, 12(3), pp. 329–37.

_____. Weitzman's Share Economy and the Aggregate Supply Function. In *Hamouda, O. F. and Smithin, J. N., eds., Vol. 2*, 1988, pp. 81–92.

Davidson, Russell and MacKinnon, James G. Double Length Artificial Regressions. *Oxford Bull. Econ. Statist.*, May 1988, 50(2), pp. 203–17.

Davidson, S. and Senn, S. J. Errors in Assessing the Demand for Inpatient Treatment. *Appl. Econ.*, March 1988, 20(3), pp. 407–15.

Davidson, Wallace N., III; Thornton, John H. and Cross, Mark L. Taxes, Stock Returns and Captive Insurance Subsidiaries. *J. Risk Ins.*, June 1988, 55(2), pp. 331–38.

Davidsson, Per. Type of Man and Type of Company Revisited: A Confirmatory Cluster Analysis Approach. In *Kirchhoff, B. A., et al., eds.*, 1988, pp. 88–105.

Davies, Gavyn. Can Financial Markets form 'Rational' Expectations? *Nat. Inst. Econ. Rev.*, May 1988, (124), pp. 77–80.

Davies, Glenn; Kilpatrick, Andrew and Mayes, David G. Fiscal Policy Simulations—A Comparison of UK Models. *Appl. Econ.*, December 1988, 20(12), pp. 1613–34.

Davies, J. E. and Moussa, H. Natural Monopoly and the Invisible Hand. *Econ. Stud. Quart.*, June 1988, 39(2), pp. 118–31.

Davies, James B. Family Size, Household Production, and Life Cycle Saving. *Ann. Écon. Statist.*, Jan.–March 1988, (9), pp. 141–65.

_____ and Kuhn, Peter. Redistribution, Inheritance, and Inequality: An Analysis of Transitions. In *Kessler, D. and Masson, A., eds.*, 1988, pp. 123–43.

_____; St-Hilaire, France and Whalley, John. Some Calculations of Lifetime Tax Incidence. In *Brown, E., ed.*, 1988, 1984, pp. 115–26.

Davies, John E. and Lee, Frederic S. A Post Keynesian Appraisal of the Contestability Criterion. *J. Post Keynesian Econ.*, Fall 1988, 11(1), pp. 3–24.

Davies, R. S. W. and Pollard, Sidney. Studies in Capital Formation in the United Kingdom, 1750–1920: The Iron Industry, 1750–1850. In *Feinstein, C. H. and Pollard, S., eds.*, 1988, pp. 73–104.

Davies, Richard B.; Martin, A. M. and Penn, R. Linear Modelling with Clustered Observations: An Illustrative Example of Earnings in the Engineering Industry. *Environ. Planning A*, August 1988, 20(8), pp. 1069–84.

Davies, Rob and Sanders, David. Adjustment Policies and the Welfare of Children: Zimbabwe, 1980–1985. In *Cornia, G. A.; Jolly, R. and Stewart, F., eds.*, 1988, pp. 272–99.

Daviet, Jean-Pierre. Trade Associations or Agreements and Controlled Competition in France, 1830–1939. In *Yamazaki, H. and Miyamoto, M., eds.*, 1988, pp. 269–95.

_____. Trade Associations or Agreements and Controlled Competition in France, 1830–1939: Response. In *Yamazaki, H. and Miyamoto, M., eds.*, 1988, pp. 297–98.

Davin, Delia. The Implications of Contract Agriculture for the Employment and Status of Chinese Peasant Women. In *Feuchtwang, S.; Hussain, A. and Pairault, T., eds., Vol. 1*, 1988, pp. 137–46.

Daviron, Benoît and Lerin, François. Le Brésil et la dynamique de l'oligopole caféier (1830–1988). (Brazil and the Dynamics of the World Coffee Oligopoly [1830–1988]. With English summary.) *Écon. Soc.*, Nov.–Dec. 1988, 22(11–12), pp. 123–49.

Davis, Anthony and Thiessen, Victor. Public Policy and Social Control in the Atlantic Fisheries. *Can. Public Policy*, March 1988, 14(1), pp. 66–77.

Davis, Charles J. and Mackey, James T. Coalition Costs through Queueing Theory for Shapley Cost Allocations. In *Schwartz, B. N., ed.*, 1988, pp. 85–110.

Davis, H. Ted. A Theory of Tension at a Miscible Displacement Front. In *Wheeler, M. F., ed.*, 1988, pp. 105–10.

Davis, Herbert J. and Rasool, S. Anvaar. A Reconsideration of England's Values Research in Cross-Cultural Management. In *Farmer, R. N. and McGoun, E. G., eds.*, 1988, pp. 109–25.

Davis, J. B. Sraffa, Wittgenstein and Neoclassical Economics. *Cambridge J. Econ.*, March 1988, 12(1), pp. 29–36.

Davis, James H. and Stasson, Mark F. Small Group Performance: Past and Present Research Trends. In *Lawler, E. J. and Markovsky, B., eds.*, 1988, pp. 245–77.

Davis, John H. Cellular Mobile Telephone Services. In *Guile, B. R. and Quinn, J. B., eds. (I)*, 1988, pp. 144–64.

Davis, Kevin and Lewis, Mervyn K. The New Australian Monetary Policy. In *Cheng, H.-S., ed.*, 1988, pp. 247–78.

Davis, Kingsley. Retirement as a Dubious Paradise—Another Point of View. In *Ricardo-Campbell, R. and Lazear, E. P., eds.*, 1988, pp. 191–203.

——. Social Science Approaches to International Migration. *Population Devel. Rev.*, Supplement, 1988, 14, pp. 245–61.

Davis, Lance E.; Gallman, Robert E. and Hutchins, Teresa D. The Decline of U.S. Whaling: Was the Stock of Whales Running Out? *Bus. Hist. Rev.*, Winter 1988, 62(4), pp. 569–95.

Davis, Michael L. Time and Punishment: An Intertemporal Model of Crime. *J. Polit. Econ.*, April 1988, 96(2), pp. 383–90.

—— **and Largay, James A., III.** Reporting Consolidated Gains and Losses on Subsidiary Stock Issuances. *Accounting Rev.*, April 1988, 63(2), pp. 348–63.

Davis, Novelette. Debt Conversion: The Jamaican Experience. *Soc. Econ. Stud.*, December 1988, 37(4), pp. 151–69.

Davis, Peter N. Protecting Waste Assimilation Streamflows by the Law of Water Allocation, Nuisance, and Public Trust, and by Environmental Statutes. *Natural Res. J.*, Spring 1988, 28(2), pp. 357–91.

Davis, Robert. Explaining the Events of October 1987. In *MacKay, R. J., ed.*, 1988, pp. 27–31.

Dawes, Robyn M.; Orbell, John M. and van de Kragt, Alphons J. C. Are People Who Cooper

ate "Rational Altruists"? *Public Choice*, March 1988, 56(3), pp. 233–47.

—— **and Thaler, Richard H.** Anomalies: Cooperation. *J. Econ. Perspectives*, Summer 1988, 2(3), pp. 187–97.

Dawkins, Peter and Baker, Meredith. The Economic Effects of Shorter Standard Working Hours in the Construction Industry: Some Case Study Evidence. *Australian Bull. Lab.*, June 1988, 14(3), pp. 492–506.

Dawley, Alan. A Preface to Synthesis. *Labor Hist.*, Summer 1988, 29(3), pp. 363–77.

Dawson, Patrick. Information Technology and the Control Function of Supervision. In *Knights, D. and Willmott, H., eds.*, 1988, pp. 118–42.

Day, Charles R., Jr. Do Your Managers Really Manage? In *Timpe, A. D., ed.*, 1988, 1985, pp. 81–86.

Day, Ralph L.; MacKay, David B. and Wu, Tsung Wen. Consumer Benefits versus Product Attributes: An Experimental Test. *Quart. J. Bus. Econ.*, Summer 1988, 27(3), pp. 88–113.

Day, Richard B. Leon Trotsky on the Dialectics of Democratic Control. In *[Nove, A.]*, 1988, pp. 1–36.

Day, Richard H. Profits, Learning and the Convergence of Satisficing to Marginalism. In *Earl, P. E., ed., Vol. 1*, 1988, 1967, pp. 149–58.

Day, T. J. and Ashmore, P. E. Effective Discharge for Suspended Sediment Transport in Streams of the Saskatchewan River Basin. *Water Resources Res.*, June 1988, 24(6), pp. 864–70.

Day, Theodore E. and Lewis, Craig M. The Behavior of the Volatility Implicit in the Prices of Stock Index Options. *J. Finan. Econ.*, October 1988, 22(1), pp. 103–22.

Dayton, C. Mitchell and Macready, George B. Concomitant-Variable Latent-Class Models. *J. Amer. Statist. Assoc.*, March 1988, 83(401), pp. 173–78.

De Aruaíjo, Tarcísio Patrúcio; do Vale Souza, Aldemir and Guimarães Neto, Leonardo. Employment Implications of Informal Sector Policies: A Case Study of Greater Recife. *Int. Lab. Rev.*, 1988, 127(2), pp. 243–58.

De Bondt, Werner F. M. and Makhija, Anil K. Throwing Good Money after Bad? Nuclear Power Plant Investment Decisions and the Relevance of Sunk Costs. *J. Econ. Behav. Organ.*, September 1988, 10(2), pp. 173–99.

De Bruyne, G.; Van De Voorde, C. and Van Rompuy, P. Taxation, Wages and Employment in a Unionized Economy. *Tijdschrift Econ. Manage.*, Sept.–Dec. 1988, 33(3/4), pp. 261–70.

De Cannière, Loïc and Moulaert, Frank. Income Inequality and Consumptive Spending Behavior: Empirical Evidence from the 1987–79 Household Budget Survey in Belgium. *J. Post Keynesian Econ.*, Winter 1987–88, 10(2), pp. 225–49.

De Caprariis, Giulio. Structural Changes in Employment in Italy. *Rev. Econ. Cond. Italy*, May–Aug. 1988, (2), pp. 179–203.

De Caro, Gaspare. Le monde atemporel de Léon Walras. (Leon Walras's Timeless World. With English summary.) *Écon. Soc.*, October 1988, 22(10), pp. 105–32.

De Clementi, Maurizio, et al. Cumulative Inflation and Dynamic Input–Output Modelling. In *Ciaschini, M., ed.*, 1988, pp. 149–65.

De Grauwe, Paul. Exchange Rate Variability and the Slowdown in Growth of International Trade. *Int. Monet. Fund Staff Pap.*, March 1988, 35(1), pp. 63–84.

_____ **and Verfaille, Guy.** Exchange Rate Variability, Misalignment, and the European Monetary System. In *Marston, R. C., ed.*, 1988, pp. 77–100.

De Gregori, Thomas R. Instrumental Criteria for Assessing Technology: An Affirmation by Ways of a Reply. In *Samuels, W. J., ed., Vol. 3,* 1988, *1980*, pp. 58–63.

_____. Resources Are Not; They Become: An Institutional Theory. In *Tool, M. R., ed., Vol. 1,* 1988, *1987*, pp. 291–313.

_____. Technology and Ceremonial Behavior: Aspects of Institutonalism. In *Samuels, W. J., ed., Vol. 3,* 1988, *1977*, pp. 48–57.

De Groot, Hans. Decentralization Decisions in Bureaucracies as a Principal–Agent Problem. *J. Public Econ.*, August 1988, 36(3), pp. 323–37.

de Haan, Jakob and Zelhorst, H. Dick. The Relationship between Real Deficits and Real Growth: A Critique. *J. Post Keynesian Econ.*, Fall 1988, 11(1), pp. 148–60.

De Jong, Eelke and Jagen, Henk. The Contribution of the ECU to Exchange-Rate Stability: A Reply. *Banca Naz. Lavoro Quart. Rev.*, September 1988, (166), pp. 331–35.

De Leeuw, J.; van Praag, Bernard M. S. and Kloek, T. Large-Sample Properties of Method of Moment Estimators under Different Data-Generating Processes. *J. Econometrics*, January 1988, 37(1), pp. 157–69.

De Leone, R. and Mangasarian, O. L. Serial and Parallel Solution of Large Scale Linear Programs by Augmented Lagrangian Successive Overrelaxation. In *Kurzhanski, A.; Neumann, K. and Pallaschke, D., eds.,* 1988, pp. 103–24.

De Long, J. Bradford. Productivity Growth, Convergence, and Welfare: Comment. *Amer. Econ. Rev.*, December 1988, 78(5), pp. 1138–54.

_____ **and Summers, Lawrence H.** How Does Macroeconomic Policy Affect Output? *Brookings Pap. Econ. Act.*, 1988, (2), pp. 433–80.

_____ **and Summers, Lawrence H.** Is Increased Price Flexibility Stabilizing? Reply. *Amer. Econ. Rev.*, March 1988, 78(1), pp. 273–76.

De Marchi, N. B. The Noxious Influence of Authority: A Correction of Jevons' Charge. In *Wood, J. C., ed., Vol. 3,* 1988, *1973*, pp. 135–45.

De Mott, Deborah A. Comparative Dimensions of Takeover Regulation. In *Coffee, J. C., Jr.; Lowenstein, L. and Rose-Ackerman, S., eds.,* 1988, pp. 398–435.

De Pelsmacker, Patrick. Marketing, Expenditure and Quality-Adjusted Price Effects on Market Share Evolution in a Segmented Belgian Car Market (1972–81). *Appl. Econ.*, January 1988, 20(1), pp. 15–30.

De Rosa, Luigi. Urbanization and Industrialization in Italy (1861–1921). *J. Europ. Econ. Hist.*, Winter 1988, 17(3), pp. 467–90.

De Soete, G.; Hubert, L. and Arabie, P. On the Use of Simulated Annealing for Combinatorial Data Analysis. In *Gaul, W. and Schader, M., eds.,* 1988, pp. 329–40.

De Vincenti, Claudio. Comportamento d'impresa ed equilibrio macroeconomico. (Behaviour of Firms and Macroeconomic Equilibrium. With English summary.) *Econ. Polit.*, August 1988, 5(2), pp. 179–203.

De Vos, Susan and Holden, Karen C. Measures Comparing Living Arrangements of the Elderly: An Assessment. *Population Devel. Rev.*, December 1988, 14(4), pp. 688–704.

De Vries, Rimmer. On the Need for Higher U.S. Savings. In *Aho, C. M. and Levinson, M.,* 1988, pp. 206–10.

De Vroey, Michel. Inflation: A Non-monetarist Monetary Interpretation. In *Sawyer, M. C., ed.,* 1988, *1984*, pp. 437–55.

Deacon, Ronald W. and Edington, Bonnie Morel. Innovative Concepts in Public–Private Coordination of Benefits for Retirees. In *Scheffler, R. M. and Rossiter, L. F., eds.,* 1988, pp. 45–67.

Deadman, D. and Turner, R. Kerry. Resource Conservation, Sustainability and Technical Change. In *Turner, R. K., ed.,* 1988, pp. 67–101.

Dean, David H. and Dolan, Robert C. Establishing a Mini-data Link. In *Berkowitz, M., ed.,* 1988, pp. 232–55.

_____ **and Dolan, Robert C.** Imputing Benefits to Persons Closed Not Rehabilitated. In *Berkowitz, M., ed.,* 1988, pp. 139–48.

_____ **and Dolan, Robert C.** Using a Better Measure for Services. In *Berkowitz, M., ed.,* 1988, pp. 186–98.

_____ **and Milberg, William.** Using Better Measures of Disability Status. In *Berkowitz, M., ed.,* 1988, pp. 199–231.

Dean, Edwin and Kunze, Kent. Recent Changes in the Growth of U.S. Multifactor Productivity. *Mon. Lab. Rev.*, May 1988, 111(5), pp. 14–22.

Dean, James W. Does Money Supply Endogeneity Matter? *S. Afr. J. Econ.*, March 1988, 56(1), pp. 39–46.

Dean, Ken G. Interregional Flows of Economically Active Persons in France, 1975–1982. *Demography*, February 1988, 25(1), pp. 81–98.

Dean, Peter N. Government Auditing Standards in Twenty-five Countries. In *Most, K. S., ed.,* 1988, pp. 231–44.

_____. Governmental Financial Management Systems in Developing Nations. In *Chan, J. L. and Jones, R. H., eds.,* 1988, pp. 149–74.

DeAngelo, Harry and Dann, Larry Y. Corporate Financial Policy and Corporate Control: A

Study of Defensive Adjustments in Asset and Ownership Structure. *J. Finan. Econ.*, Jan.–March 1988, *20*(1–2), pp. 87–127.

DeAngelo, Linda Elizabeth. Evidence of Earnings Management from the Provision for Bad Debts: Discussion. *J. Acc. Res.*, Supplement, 1988, *26*, pp. 32–40.

⸻. Managerial Competition, Information Costs, and Corporate Governance: The Use of Accounting Performance Measures in Proxy Contests. *J. Acc. Econ.*, January 1988, *10*(1), pp. 3–36.

Dearden, Lorraine and Ravallion, Martin. Social Security in a "Moral Economy": An Empirical Analysis for Java. *Rev. Econ. Statist.*, February 1988, *70*(1), pp. 36–44.

Deardorff, Alan V. and Staiger, Robert W. An Interpretation of the Factor Content of Trade. *J. Int. Econ.*, February 1988, *24*(1–2), pp. 93–107.

⸻; **Stern, Robert M. and Abraham, Filip.** The Impact of Tariffs on Profits in the United States and Other Major Trading Countries. *Weltwirtsch. Arch.*, 1988, *124*(4), pp. 623–34.

⸻; **Stern, Robert M. and Staiger, Robert W.** The Effects of Protection on the Factor Content of Japanese and American Foreign Trade. *Rev. Econ. Statist.*, August 1988, *70*(3), pp. 475–83.

DeAre, Diana and Long, Larry. U.S. Population Redistribution: A Perspective on the Nonmetropolitan Turnaround. *Population Devel. Rev.*, September 1988, *14*(3), pp. 433–50.

Deaton, Angus. Quality, Quantity, and Spatial Variation of Price. *Amer. Econ. Rev.*, June 1988, *78*(3), pp. 418–30.

Deaton, Anne S. and Deaton, Brady J. Educational Reform and Regional Development. In *Beaulieu, L. J., ed.*, 1988, pp. 304–24.

Deaton, Brady J. and Deaton, Anne S. Educational Reform and Regional Development. In *Beaulieu, L. J., ed.*, 1988, pp. 304–24.

⸻; **Johnson, Thomas G. and Kriesel, Warren P.** Investing in Economic Development Infrastructure: A Decision-Making Framework. In *Johnson, T. G.; Deaton, B. J. and Segarra, E., eds.*, 1988, pp. 155–62.

⸻ **and Konyha, Marvin E.** Local Infrastructure Investment in Rural America: Introduction. In *Johnson, T. G.; Deaton, B. J. and Segarra, E., eds.*, 1988, pp. 1–4.

⸻; **McNamara, Kevin T. and Kriesel, Warren P.** Human Capital Stock and Flow and Economic Growth Analysis: Note. *Growth Change*, Winter 1988, *19*(1), pp. 61–66.

⸻; **McNamara, Kevin T. and Kriesel, Warren P.** Manufacturing Location: The Impact of Human Capital Stocks and Flows. *Rev. Reg. Stud.*, Winter 1988, *18*(1), pp. 42–48.

⸻; **Norton, George W. and Bezuneh, Mesfin.** Food Aid Impacts in Rural Kenya. *Amer. J. Agr. Econ.*, February 1988, *70*(1), pp. 181–91.

⸻; **Segarra, Eduardo and Johnson, Thomas G.** Infrastructure Investment: Alternatives and Priorities. In *Johnson, T. G.; Deaton, B. J. and Segarra, E., eds.*, 1988, pp. 261–64.

⸻ **and Weber, Bruce A.** The Economics of Rural Areas. In *Hildreth, R. J., et al., eds.*, 1988, pp. 403–39.

DeBenedetti, George J. Conflicting Federal Policy in the Development of Atlantic Canada. In *Choudhury, M. A., ed.*, 1988, pp. 94–96.

DeBoer, Larry and Conrad, James. Do High Interest Rates Encourage Property Tax Delinquency? *Nat. Tax J.*, December 1988, *41*(4), pp. 555–60.

⸻ **and Conrad, James.** Rural Property Tax Delinquency and Recession in Agriculture. *Amer. J. Agr. Econ.*, August 1988, *70*(3), pp. 553–59.

Decaluwé, Bernard and Martens, André. CGE Modeling and Developing Economies: A Concise Empirical Survey of 73 Applications to 26 Countries. *J. Policy Modeling*, Winter 1988, *10*(4), pp. 529–68.

Dechert, W. D. and Brock, William A. Theorems on Distinguishing Deterministic from Random Systems. In *Barnett, W. A.; Berndt, E. R. and White, H., eds.*, 1988, pp. 247–65.

Deck, Leland B.; McConnell, Kenneth E. and Cropper, Maureen L. On the Choice of Functional Form for Hedonic Price Functions. *Rev. Econ. Statist.*, November 1988, *70*(4), pp. 668–75.

Decker, Paul T. The Effect of Taxation on Labor Supply When On-the-Job Amenities Are Endogenous. *Econ. Letters*, 1988, *27*(1), pp. 89–94.

Deckop, John R. Determinants of Chief Executive Officer Compensation. *Ind. Lab. Relat. Rev.*, January 1988, *41*(2), pp. 215–26.

Deckro, Richard F. and Spahr, Ronald W. A Non-linear Goal Programming Approach to Modeling Intraregional Economic Development. *Rev. Reg. Stud.*, Winter 1988, *18*(1), pp. 10–18.

Deeble, J. S. Health Insurance Forum. In *Butler, J. R. G. and Doessel, D. P., eds.*, 1988, pp. 230–37.

Deely, John and Berger, James O. A Bayesian Approach to Ranking and Selection of Related Means with Alternatives to Analysis-of-Variance Methodology. *J. Amer. Statist. Assoc.*, June 1988, *83*(402), pp. 364–73.

Deere, Donald R. Bilateral Tradings as an Efficient Auction over Time. *J. Polit. Econ.*, February 1988, *96*(1), pp. 100–115.

DeFreitas, Gregory. Hispanic Immigration and Labor Market Segmentation. *Ind. Relat.*, Spring 1988, *27*(2), pp. 195–214.

⸻. Labor Force Competition and the Black–White Wage Gap. *Rev. Black Polit. Econ.*, Winter 1988, *16*(3), pp. 103–13.

Defusco, Richard A.; Philippatos, George C. and Choi, Dosoung. Risk, Return and International Investment by U.S. Corporations. *Appl. Econ.*, September 1988, *20*(9), pp. 1199–1209.

DeGennaro, Ramon P. Payment Delays: Bias in the Yield Curve: Note. *J. Money, Credit, Banking*, November 1988, *20*(4), pp. 684–90.

Degot, Vincent. La communication interne comme marketing des stratégies d'entreprise.

(Internal Communication as the Marketing of Business Firms' Strategies. With English summary.) *Écon. Soc.*, August 1988, *22*(8), pp. 83–109.

Dehez, Pierre. Rendements d'échelle croissants et équilibre général. (With English summary.) *Revue Écon. Polit.*, Nov.–Dec. 1988, *98*(6), pp. 765–800.

_____ **and Drèze, Jacques H.** Competitive Equilibria with Quantity-Taking Producers and Increasing Returns to Scale. *J. Math. Econ.*, 1988, *17*(2–3), pp. 209–30.

_____ **and Drèze, Jacques H.** Distributive Production Sets and Equilibria with Increasing Returns. *J. Math. Econ.*, 1988, *17*(2–3), pp. 231–48.

Dehoog, Ruth Hoogland and Swanson, Bert E. Tax and Spending Effects of Municipal Enterprises: The Case of Florida Electric Utilities. *Public Budg. Finance*, Spring 1988, *8*(1), pp. 48–57.

Deihl, Richard H. Superregional and National Strategies. In *Federal Home Loan Bank of San Francisco*, 1988, pp. 97–103.

Deily, Mary E. Investment Activity and the Exit Decision. *Rev. Econ. Statist.*, November 1988, *70*(4), pp. 595–602.

Deissenberg, Christophe. Long-Run Macroeconometric Stabilization under Bounded Uncertainty. In *Eiselt, H. A. and Pederzoli, G., eds.*, 1988, pp. 306–25.

Dejax, Pierre J. A Methodology for Warehouse Location and Distribution Systems Planning. In *Bianco, L. and La Bella, A., eds.*, 1988, pp. 289–318.

DeJong, Douglas V.; Forsythe, Robert and Uecker, Wilfred C. A Note on the Use of Businessmen as Subjects in Sealed Offer Markets. *J. Econ. Behav. Organ.*, January 1988, *9*(1), pp. 87–100.

Dekkers, W. A. Development of an Experimental Videotex Information System. In *Schiefer, G., ed.*, 1988, pp. 125–33.

Del Boca, Daniela. Women in a Changing Workplace: The Case of Italy. In *Jenson, J.; Hagen, E. and Reddy, C., eds.*, 1988, pp. 120–36.

Delacroix, Jacques; Goodstein, Jerry and Carroll, Glenn R. The Political Environments of Organizations: An Ecological View. In *Staw, B. M. and Cummings, L. L., eds.*, 1988, pp. 359–92.

Delamotte, Yves. Workers' Participation and Personnel Policies in France. *Int. Lab. Rev.*, 1988, *127*(2), pp. 221–41.

Delaney, John Thomas. Teachers' Collective Bargaining Outcomes and Tradeoffs. *J. Lab. Res.*, Fall 1988, *9*(4), pp. 363–77.

_____ **and Feuille, Peter.** Police Interest Arbitration: Awards and Issues. In *Lewin, D., et al., eds.*, 1988, *1984*, pp. 386–98.

_____; **Masters, Marick F. and Schwochau, Susan.** Unionism and Voter Turnout. *J. Lab. Res.*, Summer 1988, *9*(3), pp. 221–36.

_____; **Sockell, Donna and Brockner, Joel.** Bargaining Effects of the Mandatory–Permissive

Distinction. *Ind. Relat.*, Winter 1988, *27*(1), pp. 21–36.

Delany, John. Social Networks and Efficient Resource Allocation: Computer Models of Job Vacancy Allocation through Contacts. In *Wellman, B. and Berkowitz, S. D., eds.*, 1988, pp. 430–51.

Delapierre, Michel. Technology Bunching and Industrial Strategies. In *Urabe, K.; Child, J. and Kagono, T., eds.*, 1988, pp. 145–63.

_____ **and Mytelka, Lynn Krieger.** The Alliance Strategies of European Firms in the Information Technology Industry and the Role of ESPRIT. In *Dunning, J. and Robson, P., eds.*, 1988, pp. 129–51.

_____ **and Mytelka, Lynn Krieger.** Décomposition, recomposition des oligopoles. (Decomposition, Recomposition of Oligopolies. With English summary.) *Écon. Soc.*, Nov.–Dec. 1988, *22*(11–12), pp. 57–83.

Delbono, Flavio. Welfare Consequences of Declining Costs in Asymmetric Duopolies. *Econ. Notes*, 1988, (1), pp. 69–74.

Delfmann, Werner. Zum Problem der Verfahrenswahl bei Nachfrageungewissheit im Mehrproduktunternehmen. (With English summary.) *Z. Betriebswirtshaft*, January 1988, *58*(1), pp. 127–36.

Delgado, Christopher L.; Ranade, C. G. and Jha, Dayanatha. Technological Change, Production Costs, and Supply Response. In *Mellor, J. W. and Ahmed, R., eds.*, 1988, pp. 190–203.

_____; **Reardon, Thomas and Matlon, Peter.** Coping with Household-Level Food Insecurity in Drought-Affected Areas of Burkina Faso. *World Devel.*, September 1988, *16*(9), pp. 1065–74.

Delis, Constantin. Productivity and Economies of Scale in the Athens–Piraeus Area Electric Buses. *Ann. Pub. Co-op. Econ.*, Oct.–Dec. 1988, *59*(4), pp. 493–508.

Dell, Sidney. The Question of Cross-Conditionality. *World Devel.*, May 1988, *16*(5), pp. 557–68.

_____. Stabilization: The Political Economy of Overkill. In *Wilber, C. K., ed.*, 1988, pp. 222–47.

Della Valle, Anna P. Short-run versus Long-run Marginal Cost Pricing. *Energy Econ.*, October 1988, *10*(4), pp. 283–86.

Dellaportas, George. On the Misuses—and Proper Uses—of Statistics: A Critique. *Amer. J. Econ. Soc.*, October 1988, *47*(4), pp. 459–60.

Dellas, Harris. The Implications of International Asset Trade for Monetary Policy. *J. Int. Econ.*, November 1988, *25*(3–4), pp. 365–72.

_____. Time Consistency and the Feasibility of Alternative Exchange Rate Regimes. *J. Monet. Econ.*, November 1988, *22*(3), pp. 461–72.

Dellenbarger, Ann Z. and Deseran, Forrest A. Local Labor Markets in Agricultural Policy Dependent Areas of the South. In *Beaulieu, L. J., ed.*, 1988, pp. 170–80.

Deller, Steven C. and Chicoine, David L. Representative Versus Direct Democracy: A Tiebout

Test of Relative Performance: Comment. *Public Choice*, January 1988, *56*(1), pp. 69–72.

_____; Chicoine, David L. and Walzer, Norman. Economies of Size and Scope in Rural Low-Volume Roads. *Rev. Econ. Statist.*, August 1988, *70*(3), pp. 459–65.

Dellinger, Mark and Pasqualetti, M. J. Hazardous Waste from Geothermal Energy: A Case Study. *J. Energy Devel.*, Spring 1988, *13*(2), pp. 275–95.

Deloche, Régis. En marge d'un bicentenaire: Galiani et l'apologue. (Galiani and the Apologue: A Bicentennial Report. With English summary.) *Revue Écon.*, November 1988, *39*(6), pp. 1143–57.

DeLorme, Charles D., Jr.; Cartwright, Phillip A. and Kespohl, Elke. The Effect of Temporal Aggregation on the Test of Wagner's Law. *Public Finance*, 1988, *43*(3), pp. 373–87.

Delorme, Louis; Roy, Jacques and Rousseau, Jean-Marc. Motor-Carriers Operations Planning Models: A State of the Art. In *Bianco, L. and La Bella, A.*, eds., 1988, pp. 510–45.

Delorme, Robert. The Welfare State and Jobs. In *Kregel, J. A.; Matzner, E. and Roncaglia, A.*, eds., 1988, pp. 177–203.

Delpérée, F. Constitutional Systems and Sources of Law. In *Pizzorusso, A.*, ed., 1988, pp. 88–102.

Delquie, Philippe and de Neufville, Richard. A Model of the Influence of Certainty and Probability "Effects" on the Measurement of Utility. In *Munier, B. R.*, ed., 1988, pp. 189–205.

Deman, S. Stability of Supply Coefficients and Consistency of Supply-Driven and Demand-Driven Input–Output Models. *Environ. Planning A*, June 1988, *20*(6), pp. 811–16.

Demann, M.; Schader, Martin and Tüshaus, U. Developing a Decision Support System for Personnel Disposition in a Garage—Experiences Using the KEE Shell. In *Gaul, W. and Schader, M.*, eds., 1988, pp. 103–15.

Demaria, Giovanni. Del determinismo economico e dei suoi limiti. (On Economic Determinism and Its Limits. With English summary.) *Rivista Int. Sci. Econ. Com.*, January 1988, *35*(1), pp. 1–6.

DeMarzo, Peter Michael. An Extension of the Modigliani–Miller Theorem to Stochastic Economies with Incomplete Markets and Interdependent Securities. *J. Econ. Theory*, August 1988, *45*(2), pp. 353–69.

Dembinski, Pawel H. Quantity versus Allocation of Money: Monetary Problems of the Centrally Planned Economies Reconsidered. *Kyklos*, 1988, *41*(2), pp. 281–300.

Dembo, David; Dias, Clarence and Morehouse, Ward. Trend and Prospects for Developing Countries. In *Research and Info. System for the Non-aligned and Other Developing Countries*, 1988, pp. 153–92.

Demekas, Dimitrios G., et al. The Effects of the Common Agricultural Policy of the European Community: A Survey of the Literature. *J. Common Market Stud.*, December 1988, *27*(2), pp. 113–45.

Dement'ev, Viktor E. and Sukhotin, Iurii V. Economic Reform and the Forces of Inhibition. *Prob. Econ.*, October 1988, *31*(6), pp. 64–70.

_____ and Sukhotin, Iurii V. Property in the System of Socialist Production Relations. *Prob. Econ.*, August 1988, *31*(4), pp. 57–72.

Demeny, Paul. Demography and the Limits to Growth. *Population Devel. Rev.*, Supplement, 1988, *14*, pp. 213–44.

_____. Re-linking Fertility Behavior and Economic Security in Old Age: Reply. *Population Devel. Rev.*, June 1988, *14*(2), pp. 332–37.

_____. Social Science and Population Policy. *Population Devel. Rev.*, September 1988, *14*(3), pp. 451–79.

Demetriades, Panikos O. Macroeconomic Aspects of the Correlation between the Level and Variability of Inflation. *Econ. Letters*, 1988, *26*(2), pp. 121–24.

Demirdjian, Z. S. A Convergent Validity Test of a Theory of Response Error. In *Brown, R. C.*, ed., 1988, pp. 39–48.

Demko, Stephen and Hill, Theodore P. Equitable Distribution of Indivisible Objects. *Math. Soc. Sci.*, October 1988, *16*(2), pp. 145–58.

DeMott, Deborah A. Adventures in Finance. *Mich. Law Rev.*, May 1988, *86*(6), pp. 1185–95.

Demoussis, Michael and Sarris, Alexander H. Greek Experience under the CAP: Lessons and Outlook. *Europ. Rev. Agr. Econ.*, 1988, *15*(1), pp. 89–107.

Dempster, A. P. Probability, Evidence, and Judgment. In *Bell, D. E.; Raiffa, H. and Tversky, A.*, eds., 1988, 1985, pp. 284–92.

Dempster, M. A. H. and Ireland, A. M. MIDAS: An Expert Debt Management Advisory System. In *Gaul, W. and Schader, M.*, eds., 1988, pp. 116–27.

Demsetz, Harold. The Control Function of Private Wealth. In *Demsetz, H.*, 1988, pp. 229–35.

_____. Corporate Control, Insider Trading, and Rates of Return. In *Demsetz, H.*, 1988, *1986*, pp. 223–28.

_____. The Cost of Transacting. In *Demsetz, H.*, 1988, *1968*, pp. 63–81.

_____. Ethics and Efficiency in Property Rights Systems. In *Demsetz, H.*, 1988, *1979*, pp. 261–80.

_____. The Exchange and Enforcement of Property Rights. In *Demsetz, H.*, 1988, *1964*, pp. 31–46.

_____. The Exchange and Enforcement of Property Rights. In *Cowen, T.*, ed., 1988, *1964*, pp. 127–45.

_____. A Framework for the Study of Ownership. In *Demsetz, H.*, 1988, pp. 12–27.

_____. The Meaning of Freedom. In *Demsetz, H.*, 1988, pp. 281–92.

_____. Minorities in the Market Place. In *Demsetz, H.*, 1988, *1965*, pp. 82–103.

_____. Ownership Control and the Firm: Autobiographical Sketch. In *Demsetz, H.*, 1988, pp. 3–11.

_____. The Private Production of Public Goods. In *Cowen, T.*, ed., 1988, *1970*, pp. 111–26.

————. Profit as a Functional Return: Reconsidering Knight's Views. In *Demsetz, H.*, 1988, pp. 236–47.

————. Social Responsibility in the Enterprise Economy. In *Demsetz, H.*, 1988, pp. 251–60.

————. The Structure of Ownership and the Theory of the Firm. In *Demsetz, H.*, 1988, *1983*, pp. 187–201.

————. The Theory of the Firm Revisited. *J. Law, Econ., Organ.*, Spring 1988, *4*(1), pp. 141–61.

————. The Theory of the Firm Revisited. In *Demsetz, H.*, 1988, *1988*, pp. 144–65.

————. Toward a Theory of Property Rights. In *Demsetz, H.*, 1988, *1967*, pp. 104–16.

————. Vertical Integration: Theories and Evidence. In *Demsetz, H.*, 1988, pp. 166–86.

————. When Does the Rule of Liability Matter? In *Demsetz, H.*, 1988, *1972*, pp. 47–62.

————. Why Regulate Utilities. In *Stigler, G. J.*, ed., 1988, *1968*, pp. 267–78.

———— and Alchian, Armen A. Production, Information Costs, and Economic Organization. In *Ricketts, M.*, ed., *Vol. 1*, 1988, *1972*, pp. 312–30.

———— and Alchian, Armen A. Production, Information Costs, and Economic Organization. In *Demsetz, H.*, 1988, *1972*, pp. 119–43.

———— and Lehn, Kenneth. The Structure of Corporate Ownership: Causes and Consequences. In *Demsetz, H.*, 1988, *1985*, pp. 202–22.

Demski, Joel S. and Antle, Rick. The Controllability Principle in Responsible Accounting. *Accounting Rev.*, October 1988, *63*(4), pp. 700–718.

————; **Sappington, David E. M. and Spiller, Pablo T.** Incentive Schemes with Multiple Agents and Bankruptcy Constraints. *J. Econ. Theory*, February 1988, *44*(1), pp. 156–67.

Demyanov, V. F. Continuous Generalized Gradients for Nonsmooth Functions. In *Kurzhanski, A.; Neumann, K. and Pallaschke, D.*, eds., 1988, pp. 24–27.

Den Uyl, Douglas J. Freedom and Virtue Revisited. In *[Rothbard, M. N.]*, 1988, pp. 195–213.

Dendrinos, Dimitrios S. Straightening Out a Nonlinearity in the Dynamics of Labor and Capital Movements: A Reply. *J. Reg. Sci.*, November 1988, *28*(4), pp. 581–82.

Denicolò, Vincenzo. Some Analytics of the Laffer Curve: A Comment. *J. Public Econ.*, February 1988, *35*(1), pp. 129–30.

Denis, Ann; Andrew, Caroline and Coderre, Cécile. Women in Management: The Canadian Experience: The Relationship of Professional and Personal Lives. In *Adler, N. J. and Izraeli, D.*, eds., 1988, pp. 250–64.

Denis, Henri. Sur une tentative récente de dépassement de l'analyse économique usuelle. (On a Recent Attempt at Passing beyond the Common Economic Analysis. With English summary.) *Écon. Appl.*, 1988, *41*(1), pp. 5–17.

DeNisi, Angelo S. and Williams, Kevin J. Cognitive Approaches to Performance Appraisal. In *Ferris, G. R. and Rowland, K. M.*, eds., 1988, pp. 109–55.

Denison, Daniel R.; Chambers, Brian R. and Hart, Stuart L. Founding Team Experience and New Firm Performance. In *Kirchhoff, B. A., et al.*, eds., 1988, pp. 106–18.

Denison, Edward F. Growth and Embodiment: A Reply [On the Importance of the Embodiment of Technology Effect: A Comment on Denison's Growth Accounting Methodology]. *J. Macroecon.*, Winter 1988, *10*(1), pp. 139–42.

Denisov, Michail N.; Pavlov, Vladimir K. and Astakhov, Alexander S. Prospecting and Exploration in the Soviet Union. In *Tilton, J. E.; Eggert, R. G. and Landsberg, H. H.*, eds., 1988, pp. 199–225.

Denning, Karen C. and Ferris, Stephen P. An Empirical Test of the Information Hypothesis Concerning Stock Splits. *Rivista Int. Sci. Econ. Com.*, Oct.–Nov. 1988, *35*(10–11), pp. 1075–84.

Denninger, E. Constitutional Law between Statutory Law and Higher Law. In *Pizzorusso, A.*, ed., 1988, pp. 103–30.

Dennis, David; Tippett, Mark and Bird, Ron. A Stop Loss Approach to Portfolio Insurance. *J. Portfol. Manage.*, Fall 1988, *15*(1), pp. 35–40.

Dennis, Enid. Stock Market Liquidity and Futures Trading. In *Pennsylvania Economic Association*, 1988, pp. 76–84.

————. Stock Market Liquidity and Futures Trading. In *Pennsylvania Economic Association*, 1988, pp. 140–48.

Dennis, William J., Jr. New World Jobs and Old World Policy: Turbulence, Small Business and Employment Growth. In *Association of Private Education*, 1988, pp. 24–31.

Denny, Michael. Productivity Growth and Changes in the Terms of Trade in Canada: Comment. In *Feenstra, R. C.*, ed., 1988, pp. 295–98.

———— and de Fontenay, Alain. Cost Pressures and Relative Productivity in Canadian Telecommunications Firms. In *Dogramaci, A. and Färe, R.*, eds.,, 1988, pp. 131–48.

Denny, Wanda; Levy, Haim and Barlev, Benzion. Using Accounting Data for Portfolio Management. *J. Portfol. Manage.*, Spring 1988, *14*(3), pp. 70–77.

Deno, Kevin T. The Effect of Public Capital on U.S. Manufacturing Activity: 1970 to 1978. *Southern Econ. J.*, October 1988, *55*(2), pp. 400–411.

———— and Mehay, Stephen L. Municipal Utilities and Local Public Finance: A Simultaneous Model. *Public Choice*, June 1988, *57*(3), pp. 201–12.

Denton, Frank T. The Significance of Significance: Rhetorical Aspects of Statistical Hypothesis Testing in Economics. In *Klamer, A.; McCloskey, D. N. and Solow, R. M.*, eds., 1988, pp. 163–83.

————; **Li, S. Neno and Spencer, Byron G.** Health Care in the Economic–Demographic System: Macro-effects of Market Control, Government Intervention, and Population Change. *Southern Econ. J.*, July 1988, *55*(1), pp. 37–56.

_____ and Spencer, Byron G. Endogenous versus Exogenous Fertility: What Difference for the Macroeconomy? In *Lee, R. D.; Arthur, W. B. and Rodgers, G., eds.*, 1988, pp. 183–215.

Denton, Nancy A. and Massey, Douglas S. Residential Segregation of Blacks, Hispanics, and Asians by Socioeconomic Status and Generation. *Soc. Sci. Quart.*, December 1988, 69(4), pp. 797–817.

Denzau, Arthur T. and Greenberg, Edward. Profit and Expenditure Functions in Basic Public Finance: An Expository Note. *Econ. Inquiry*, January 1988, 26(1), pp. 145–58.

Deolalikar, Anil B. Nutrition and Labor Productivity in Agriculture: Estimates for Rural South India. *Rev. Econ. Statist.*, August 1988, 70(3), pp. 406–13.

_____; Wolfe, Barbara L. and Behrman, Jere R. Nutrients: Impacts and Determinants. *World Bank Econ. Rev.*, September 1988, 2(3), pp. 299–320.

DePass, Rudolph E. and Friedenberg, Howard L. Recent Growth in Nonfarm Personal Income. *Surv. Curr. Bus.*, October 1988, 68(10), pp. 23–26.

_____ and Friedenberg, Howard L. State Personal Income, First Quarter 1988. *Surv. Curr. Bus.*, July 1988, 68(7), pp. 134–36.

Deprez, Johan. Mark-Up Pricing in a Monetary Economy: An Extension of Eichner's Megacorp. *Rev. Radical Polit. Econ.*, Summer–Fall 1988, 20(2–3), pp. 127–32.

van Der Wee, Dominique; Barrett, Brendan and Glasson, John. A Local Income and Employment Multiplier Analysis of a Proposed Nuclear Power Station Development at Hinkley Point in Somerset. *Urban Stud.*, June 1988, 25(3), pp. 248–61.

Deravi, M. Keivan. Forecasting Accuracy of Alternative Techniques: A Comparison of Alabama Forecasts. *Reg. Sci. Persp.*, 1988, 18(2), pp. 94–107.

_____; Gregorowicz, Philip and Hegji, Charles E. Balance of Trade Announcements and Movements in Exchange Rates. *Southern Econ. J.*, October 1988, 55(2), pp. 279–87.

_____ and Metghalchi, Massoud. The European Monetary System: A Note. *J. Banking Finance*, September 1988, 12(3), pp. 505–12.

_____ and Steindl, Frank G. Income Taxation and the Demand for Money. *Quart. J. Bus. Econ.*, Spring 1988, 27(2), pp. 23–34.

Derickson, Alan. Industrial Refugees: The Migration of Silicotics from the Mines of North America and South Africa in the Early 20th Century. *Labor Hist.*, Winter 1988, 29(1), pp. 66–89.

_____. "On the Dump Heap": Employee Medical Screening in the Tri-State Zinc-Lead Industry, 1924–1932. *Bus. Hist. Rev.*, Winter 1988, 62(4), pp. 656–77.

DeRidder, Kim J. The Nature and Effects of Acid Rain: A Comparison of Assessments. In *Schmandt, J.; Clarkson, J. and Roderick, H., eds.*, 1988, pp. 31–63.

Dermody, Jaime Cuevas and Prisman, Eliezer Zeev. Term Structure Multiplicity and Clientele in Markets with Transactions Costs and Taxes. *J. Finance*, September 1988, 43(4), pp. 893–911.

Dernberger, Robert F. Financing China's Development: Needs, Sources, and Prospects. In *Dernberger, R. F. and Eckaus, R. S.*, 1988, pp. 12–68.

_____ and Eckaus, Richard S. China and India: Parallels and Differences. In *Dernberger, R. F. and Eckaus, R. S.*, 1988, pp. 1–11.

DeRosa, Dean A. Agricultural Trade and Protection in Asia. *Finance Develop.*, December 1988, 25(4), pp. 50–52.

_____. Asian Preferences and the Gains from MFN Tariff Reductions. *World Econ.*, September 1988, 11(3), pp. 377–96.

_____ and Campbell, Burnham O. Increasing Protectionism and Its Implications for ASEAN–U.S. Economic Relations. In *Tan, L.-H. and Akrasanee, N., eds.*, 1988, pp. 24–63.

Derrick, Frederick W. and Wolken, John D. Cross-Sectional Aggregation and Demand System Estimation. *Atlantic Econ. J.*, June 1988, 16(2), pp. 82.

Derrick, P. Local Fiscal Crisis: Diagnosis and Remedies. *Reg. Stud.*, June 1988, 22(3), pp. 238–41.

Desai, Anand; Kim, E. Han and Bradley, Michael. Synergistic Gains from Corporate Acquisitions and Their Division between the Stockholders of Target and Acquiring Firms. *J. Finan. Econ.*, May 1988, 21(1), pp. 3–40.

Desai, Ashok V. Technology Acquisition and Application: Interpretations of the Indian Experience. In *Lucas, R. E. B. and Papanek, G. F., eds.*, 1988, pp. 163–84.

Desai, Gunvant M. Policy for Rapid Growth in Use of Modern Agricultural Inputs. In *Mellor, J. W. and Ahmed, R., eds.*, 1988, pp. 204–18.

Desai, Meghnad. The Transformation Problem. *J. Econ. Surveys*, 1988, 2(4), pp. 295–333.

_____ and Anderton, R. Modelling Manufacturing Imports. *Nat. Inst. Econ. Rev.*, February 1988, (123), pp. 80–86.

_____ and Shah, Anup. An Econometric Approach to the Measurement of Poverty. *Oxford Econ. Pap.*, September 1988, 40(3), pp. 505–22.

_____ and Weber, Guglielmo. A Keynesian Macro-econometric Model of the UK: 1955–1984. *J. Appl. Econometrics*, January 1988, 3(1), pp. 1–33.

Desai, Padma. Alternative Measures of Import Shares: Theory and Estimates for the Soviet Union. *J. Int. Econ.*, November 1988, 25(3–4), pp. 319–33.

Desaigues, Brigitte. Les régions françaises et le commerce extérieur en 1860. (With English summary.) *Revue Écon. Polit.*, March–April 1988, 98(2), pp. 273–92.

DeSarbo, Wayne S. and Oliver, Richard L. Response Determinants in Satisfaction Judgments. *J. Cons. Res.*, March 1988, *14*(4), pp. 495–507.

Deschamps, Lucien. Power Galore in Space. In *Egan, J. J., et al.*, 1988, pp. 211–25.

Descy, J.-P. and Micha, J.-C. Use of Biological Indices of Water Quality. *Statist. J.*, November 1988, *5*(3), pp. 249–61.

Deseran, Forrest A. and Dellenbarger, Ann Z. Local Labor Markets in Agricultural Policy Dependent Areas of the South. In *Beaulieu, L. J., ed.*, 1988, pp. 170–80.

DesHarnais, Susan; Chesney, James and Fleming, Steven. Trends and Regional Variations in Hospital Utilization and Quality during the First Two Years of the Prospective Payment System. *Inquiry*, Fall 1988, *25*(3), pp. 374–82.

Deshpande, G. P. A 'Candidate Superpower' among the 'Filthy Swines'? Emergence of China in World Politics. In *Mitra, A., ed.*, 1988, pp. 160–68.

Deshpande, Shreesh D. and Philippatos, George C. Leverage Decisions and the Effect of Corporate Eurobond Offerings. *Appl. Econ.*, July 1988, *20*(7), pp. 901–15.

Desormeaux, Jorge; Díaz, Patricio and Wagner, Gert. La tasa social de descuento. (With English summary.) *Cuadernos Econ.*, April 1988, *25*(74), pp. 125–91.

Despiney, Barbara and Elkoubi, Anne. India, the Soviet Union, and Eastern Europe. In *Lavigne, M., ed.*, 1988, pp. 170–81.

Despotakis, Kostas A. and Fisher, Anthony C. Energy in a Regional Economy: A Computable General Equilibrium Model for California. *J. Environ. Econ. Manage.*, September 1988, *15*(3), pp. 313–30.

Desprairies, Pierre. The Implications of the Oil Price Situation for Consuming Countries. In *Mabro, R., ed.*, 1988, pp. 201–13.

Després, Laure. Third World Arms Trade of the Soviet Union and Eastern Europe. In *Lavigne, M., ed.*, 1988, pp. 51–63.

Despres, Leo A. Dependent Development and the Marginality Thesis: A Case Study from Manaus. In *Bennett, J. W. and Bowen, J. R., eds.*, 1988, pp. 293–310.

Desrochers, Martin and Soumis, François. CREW-OPT: Crew Scheduling by Column Generation. In *Daduna, J. R. and Wren, A., eds.*, 1988, pp. 83–90.

Desrosiers, Jacques and Dumas, Yvan. The Shortest Path Problem for the Construction of Vehicle Routes with Pick-Up, Delivery and Time Constraints. In *Eiselt, H. A. and Pederzoli, G., eds.*, 1988, pp. 144–57.

———; **Dumas, Yvan and Soumis, François.** The Multiple Vehicle DIAL-A-RIDE Problem. In *Daduna, J. R. and Wren, A., eds.*, 1988, pp. 15–27.

Desvousges, William H. and Smith, V. Kerry. The Valuation of Environmental Risks and Hazardous Waste Policy. *Land Econ.*, August 1988, *64*(3), pp. 211–19.

Detemple, Jérôme B. and Adler, Michael. Hedging with Futures in an Intertemporal Portfolio Context. *J. Futures Markets*, June 1988, *8*(3), pp. 249–69.

——— **and Adler, Michael.** On the Optimal Hedge of a Nontraded Cash Position. *J. Finance*, March 1988, *43*(1), pp. 143–53.

Deurloo, M. C.; Dieleman, F. M. and Clark, W. A. V. Generalized Log-linear Models of Housing Choice. *Environ. Planning A*, January 1988, *20*(1), pp. 55–69.

Deutsch, Joseph and Kahana, Nava. A Note on the Output Effect of Price Discrimination on a Sales Maximizer. *Managerial Dec. Econ.*, September 1988, *9*(3), pp. 205–07.

——— **and Kahana, Nava.** On the Responses of the Illyrian and Entrepreneurial Monopolies to a Change in Market Conditions: An Extension. *J. Compar. Econ.*, June 1988, *12*(2), pp. 235–39.

Dev, S. Mahendra. Regional Disparities in Agricultural Labour Productivity and Rural Poverty in India. *Indian Econ. Rev.*, July–Dec. 1988, *23*(2), pp. 167–205.

Devarajan, Shantayanan. Natural Resources and Taxation in Computable General Equilibrium Models of Developing Countries. *J. Policy Modeling*, Winter 1988, *10*(4), pp. 505–28.

Devas, Nick. Local Taxation in Indonesia: Opportunities for Reform. *Bull. Indonesian Econ. Stud.*, August 1988, *24*(2), pp. 58–85.

Devens, Richard M., Jr. Employment and Unemployment in the First Half of 1988. *Mon. Lab. Rev.*, August 1988, *111*(8), pp. 15–19.

———. A Movable Beast: Changing Patterns of Regional Unemployment. *Mon. Lab. Rev.*, April 1988, *111*(4), pp. 60–62.

Devereux, Michael. Corporation Tax: The Effect of the 1984 Reforms on the Incentive to Invest. *Fisc. Stud.*, February 1988, *9*(1), pp. 62–79.

———. Non-traded Goods and the International Transmission of Fiscal Policy. *Can. J. Econ.*, May 1988, *21*(2), pp. 265–78.

———. The Optimal Mix of Wage Indexation and Foreign Exchange Market Intervention. *J. Money, Credit, Banking*, Part 1, August 1988, *20*(3), pp. 381–92.

——— **and Anderson, Simon P.** Trade Unions and the Choice of Capital Stock. *Scand. J. Econ.*, 1988, *90*(1), pp. 27–44.

——— **and Bond, Stephen R.** Financial Volatility, the Stock Market Crash and Corporate Investment. *Fisc. Stud.*, May 1988, *9*(2), pp. 72–80.

———; **Purvis, Douglas and Backus, David.** A Positive Theory of Fiscal Policy in Open Economies. In *Frenkel, J. A., ed.*, 1988, pp. 173–91.

Devezeaux de Lavergne, Jean-Guy. Chocs pétroliers et intensité énergétique: Quelques clefs d'analyse. (Oil Price Increase and Energy Ratio: Some Keys of Analysis. With English summary.) *Écon. Soc.*, April 1988, *22*(4), pp. 89–110.

Devi, S. U. Comment on Prof. Brahmananda's Article on 'Jevons' *Theory of Political Economy*—A Centennial Appraisal. In *Wood, J. C., ed.*, Vol. 2, 1988, *1972*, pp. 134–39.

Deville, J. C.; Grosbras, J. M. and Roth, N.

Efficient sampling Algorithms and Balanced Samples. In *Edwards, D. and Raun, N. E.*, eds., 1988, pp. 255–66.

Devine, Frank J. The Dynamics of Today's Brazil. In *Chacel, J. M.; Falk, P. S. and Fleischer, D. V.*, eds., 1988, pp. 86–88.

Devine, James N. Falling Profit Rates and the Causes of the 1929–33 Collapse: Toward a Synthesis. *Rev. Radical Polit. Econ.*, Summer–Fall 1988, *20*(2–3), pp. 87–93.

Devine, T. M. Unrest and Stability in Rural Ireland and Scotland, 1760–1840. In *Mitchison, R. and Roebuck, P.*, eds., 1988, pp. 126–39.

Devinney, Timothy M. Economic Theory and Pricing Behavior: A General Framework. In *Devinney, T. M.*, ed., 1988, pp. 5–34.

_____. Price, Advertising, and Scale as Information-Revelation Mechanisms in Product Markets. In *Devinney, T. M.*, ed., 1988, pp. 63–81.

Devino, Gary T.; Procter, Michael H. and Kaylen, Michael S. Optimal Use of Qualitative Models: An Application to Country Grain Elevator Bankruptcies. *Southern J. Agr. Econ.*, December 1988, *20*(2), pp. 119–25.

Devlin, Susan J. and Cleveland, William S. Locally Weighted Regression: An Approach to Regression Analysis by Local Fitting. *J. Amer. Statist. Assoc.*, September 1988, *83*(403), pp. 596–610.

_____; **Grosse, Eric and Cleveland, William S.** Regression By Local Fitting: Methods, Properties, and Computational Algorithms. *J. Econometrics*, January 1988, *37*(1), pp. 87–114.

Dewald, William G. The Budgetary Importance of Either Eliminating Inflation or Accounting for It. *Bus. Econ.*, January 1988, *23*(1), pp. 34–38.

_____. Monetarism Is Dead; Long Live the Quantity Theory. *Fed. Res. Bank St. Louis Rev.*, July–Aug. 1988, *70*(4), pp. 3–18.

_____; **Thursby, Jerry G. and Anderson, Richard G.** Replication in Empirical Economics: *The Journal of Money, Credit and Banking Project*: Reply. *Amer. Econ. Rev.*, December 1988, *78*(5), pp. 1162–63.

Dewar, Marvin and Blair, Roger D. How to End the Crisis in Medical Malpractice Insurance. *Challenge*, March–April 1988, *31*(2), pp. 36–41.

Dewatripont, Catherine. Industry Wage Flexibility and Employment in the EEC. *Cah. Écon. Bruxelles*, Fourth Trimester 1988, (120), pp. 457–82.

Dewatripont, Mathias. Commitment through Re-negotiation-Proof Contracts with Third Parties. *Rev. Econ. Stud.*, July 1988, *55*(3), pp. 377–89.

_____. The Impact of Trade Unions on Incentives to Deter Entry. *Rand J. Econ.*, Summer 1988, *19*(2), pp. 191–99.

_____ and **Thys-Clement, F.** Employment and Public Deficits: A Vicious Circle? *Tijdschrift Econ. Manage.*, Sept.–Dec. 1988, *33*(3/4), pp. 287–301.

Dewe, Philip; Dunn, Stephen and Richardson,

Ray. Employee Share Option Schemes, Why Workers Are Attracted to Them. *Brit. J. Ind. Relat.*, March 1988, *26*(1), pp. 1–20.

_____ and **Guest, David E.** Why Do Workers Belong to a Trade Union? A Social Psychological Study in the UK Electronics Industry. *Brit. J. Ind. Relat.*, July 1988, *26*(2), pp. 178–94.

Dewees, Donald N. Paying for Asbestos-Related Diseases under Workers' Compensation. In *Burton, J. F., Jr.*, ed., 1988, pp. 45–70.

_____ and **Daniels, R.** Prevention and Compensation of Industrial Disease. *Int. Rev. Law Econ.*, June 1988, *8*(1), pp. 51–72.

Dex, Shirley and Puttick, Ed. Parental Employment and Family Formation. In *Hunt, A.*, ed., 1988, pp. 123–49.

_____ and **Shaw, Lois B.** Women's Working Lives: A Comparison of Women in the United States and Great Britain. In *Hunt, A.*, ed., 1988, pp. 173–95.

_____ and **Sloane, P. J.** Detecting and Removing Discrimination under Equal Opportunities Policies. *J. Econ. Surveys*, 1988, *2*(1), pp. 1–27.

Dey, Dipak K. and Gelfand, Alan E. Improved Estimation of the Disturbance Variance in a Linear Regression Model. *J. Econometrics*, November 1988, *39*(3), pp. 387–95.

Dezséri, Kálmán and Marcelle, Jillían. Debt–Equity Swaps: Solution to a Crisis? *Écon. Appl.*, 1988, *41*(4), pp. 821–55.

Dhaliwal, Dan S.; Doran, B. Michael and Collins, Daniel W. The Information of Historical Cost Earnings Relative to Supplemental Reserve-Based Accounting Data in the Extractive Petroleum Industry. *Accounting Rev.*, July 1988, *63*(3), pp. 389–413.

_____ and **Johnson, W. Bruce.** LIFO Abandonment. *J. Acc. Res.*, Autumn 1988, *26*(2), pp. 236–72.

_____ and **Sunder, Shyam.** Mergers, Acquisitions, and Takeovers: Wealth Effects on Various Economic Agents. In *Libecap, G.*, ed. *(I)*, 1988, pp. 169–90.

Dhanani, Shafiq. The Development of Rural People: Myths and Approaches: Comments. *Pakistan Devel. Rev.*, Part 1, Winter 1988, *27*(4), pp. 393–95.

_____. International Debt and Foreign Dependency: Policy Options for Pakistan: Comments. *Pakistan Devel. Rev.*, Part 2, Winter 1988, *27*(4), pp. 835–36.

_____. A SAM-Based General Equilibrium Model of the Pakistan Economy 1983–84. *Pakistan Devel. Rev.*, Part 2, Winter 1988, *27*(4), pp. 737–48.

Dhar, P. N. The Indian Economy: Past Performance and Current Issues. In *Lucas, R. E. B. and Papanek, G. F.*, eds., 1988, pp. 3–22.

Dhesi, Autar S. The Evolution of IMF amidst World Economic Crisis (A Review of the Latest Addition to the Fund History). *Rivista Int. Sci. Econ. Com.*, Oct.–Nov. 1988, *35*(10–11), pp. 1085–97.

_____ and **Ghuman, B. S.** Aspects of Financing State Plans (with Special Reference to Punjab).

In *Raikhy, P. S. and Gill, S. S., eds.*, 1988, pp. 9–27.

——— **and Ghuman, B. S.** Resource Mobilisation at State Level—A Case Study of Punjab. In *Raikhy, P. S. and Gill, S. S., eds.*, 1988, pp. 186–211.

——— **and Ghuman, B. S.** The Responsiveness of State Taxes—A Comparative Study of Punjab and Haryana. In *Raikhy, P. S. and Gill, S. S., eds.*, 1988, pp. 77–87.

Dholakia, Nikhilesh. The Marketing of Development: An Exploration of Strategic Forms of Development. In *Kumcu, E. and Firat, A. F., eds.*, 1988, pp. 63–78.

——— **and Firat, A. Fuat.** Development in the Era of Globalizing Markets and Consumption Patterns. In *Kumcu, E. and Firat, A. F., eds.*, 1988, pp. 79–101.

Dholakia, Ruby Roy; Sharif, Mohammed and Bhandari, Labdhi. Consumption in the Third World: Challenges for Marketing and Development. In *Kumcu, E. and Firat, A. F., eds.*, 1988, pp. 129–47.

Dhrymes, Phoebus J. and Peristiani, Stavros C. A Comparison of the Forecasting Performance of WEFA and ARIMA Time Series Methods. *Int. J. Forecasting*, 1988, *4*(1), pp. 81–101.

Di Filippo, Armando. Prebisch's Ideas on the World Economy. *CEPAL Rev.*, April 1988, (34), pp. 153–63.

Di Maio, Amedeo. Conjectures and Voluntary Contributions to Public Goods. *Stud. Econ.*, 1988, *43*(36), pp. 113–24.

Di Pillo, G. and Grippo, L. Recent Results on Nondifferentiable Exact Penalty Functions. In *Iri, M. and Yajima, K., eds.*, 1988, pp. 212–20.

Di Tella, Guido and Canavese, Alfredo J. Inflation Stabilization or Hyperinflation Avoidance? The Case of the Austral Plan in Argentina: 1985–87. In *Bruno, M., et al., eds.*, 1988, pp. 153–90.

Diaconescu, G.; Velicanu, M. and Bodea, Constanţa. A Relational Operator for Sorted Join. *Econ. Computat. Cybern. Stud. Res.*, 1988, *23*(2), pp. 33–36.

Diaconis, Persi and Zabell, Sandy L. Updating Subjective Probability. In *Bell, D. E.; Raiffa, H. and Tversky, A., eds.*, 1988, *1982*, pp. 266–83.

Diakosavvas, Dimitris; Horton, Susan and Kerr, Tom. The Social Costs of Higher Food Prices: Some Cross-country Evidence. *World Devel.*, July 1988, *16*(7), pp. 847–56.

Dialynas, Chris P. Bond Yield Spreads Revisited. *J. Portfol. Manage.*, Winter 1988, *14*(2), pp. 57–62.

Diamond, Arthur M., Jr. The Austrian Economists and the Late Hapsburg Viennese Milieu. In *Rothbard, M. N. and Block, W., eds.*, 1988, pp. 157–72.

———. Bibliography of Unusual Applications of Price Theory, A Note. *Amer. Econ.*, Spring 1988, *32*(1), pp. 78–79.

———. Characteristics of Minority Members of the American Economic Association. *Rev.*

Black Polit. Econ., Winter 1988, *16*(3), pp. 77–96.

———. The Empirical Progressiveness of the General Equilibrium Research Program. *Hist. Polit. Econ.*, Spring 1988, *20*(1), pp. 119–35.

Diamond, Jack and Schiller, Christian. Government Arrears in Fiscal Adjustment Programs. In *Blejer, M. I. and Chu, K.-Y., eds.*, 1988, pp. 32–47.

Diamond, Peter A. Aggregate Demand Management in Search Equilibrium. In *Shaw, G. K., ed., Vol. 1*, 1988, *1982*, pp. 321–34.

———. Credit in Search Equilibrium. In *Kohn, M. and Tsiang, S.-C., eds.*, 1988, pp. 36–53.

Diamond, William D. The Effect of Probability and Consequence Levels on the Focus of Consumer Judgments in Risky Situations. *J. Cons. Res.*, September 1988, *15*(2), pp. 280–83.

Dias, Clarence; Morehouse, Ward and Dembo, David. Trend and Prospects for Developing Countries. In *Research and Info. System for the Non-aligned and Other Developing Countries*, 1988, pp. 153–92.

Diatkine, Daniel. La monnaie dans la philosophie politique de Locke. (Money in Locke's Political Philosophy. With English summary.) *Écon. Soc.*, March 1988, *22*(3), pp. 3–16.

———. Morale et enrichissement monétaire chez J. Locke. Réponse. (Morals and Monetary Enrichment in J. Locke: A Reply. With English summary.) *Écon. Soc.*, October 1988, *22*(10), pp. 21–26.

Díaz-Alejandro, Carlos. Delinking North and South: Unshackled or Unhinged? In *Díaz-Alejandro, C. F.*, 1988, *1978*, pp. 73–121.

———. Direct Foreign Investment in Latin America. In *Díaz-Alejandro, C. F.*, 1988, *1970*, pp. 53–72.

———. Good-Bye Financial Repression, Hello Financial Crash. In *Díaz-Alejandro, C. F.*, 1988, *1985*, pp. 264–86.

———. IMF Conditionality: What Kind? In *Díaz-Alejandro, C. F.*, 1988, *1984*, pp. 359–63.

———. International Financial Intermediation: A Long and Tropical View. In *Díaz-Alejandro, C. F.*, 1988, *1982*, pp. 130–63.

———. International Markets for LDCs—The Old and the New. In *Díaz-Alejandro, C. F.*, 1988, *1978*, pp. 122–29.

———. Latin America in the 1930s. In *Díaz-Alejandro, C. F.*, 1988, *1984*, pp. 185–211.

———. Latin American Debt: I Don't Think We Are in Kansas Anymore. In *Díaz-Alejandro, C. F.*, 1988, *1984*, pp. 310–58.

———. No Less Than One Hundred Years of Argentine Economic History Plus Some Comparisons. In *Díaz-Alejandro, C. F.*, 1988, *1984*, pp. 230–60.

———. A Note on the Impact of Devaluation and the Redistributive Effect. In *Díaz-Alejandro, C. F.*, 1988, *1963*, pp. 5–10.

———. On the Import Intensity of Import Substitution. In *Díaz-Alejandro, C. F.*, 1988, *1965*, pp. 11–22.

———. Open Economy, Closed Polity? In *Díaz-Alejandro, C. F.*, 1988, *1983*, pp. 283–309.

_____. Some Characteristics of Recent Export Expansion in Latin America. In *Díaz-Alejandro, C. F.*, 1988, *1974*, pp. 23–42.

_____. Some Economic Lessons of the Early 1980s. In *Díaz-Alejandro, C. F.*, 1988, *1984*, pp. 164–79.

_____. Southern Cone Stabilization Plans. In *Díaz-Alejandro, C. F.*, 1988, pp. 265–82.

_____. Tariffs, Foreign Capital and Immiserizing Growth. In *Díaz-Alejandro, C. F.*, 1988, *1977*, pp. 43–48.

_____. The 1940s in Latin America. In *Díaz-Alejandro, C. F.*, 1988, *1984*, pp. 212–29.

Díaz-Briquets, Sergio. Regional Differences in Development and Living Standards in Revolutionary Cuba. In *Mesa-Lago, C., ed.*, 1988, pp. 45–63.

Diaz, Francisco Gil and Ramos Tercero, Raul. Lessons from Mexico. In *Bruno, M., et al., eds.*, 1988, pp. 361–90.

Diaz Mier, Miguel Angel. The Spanish Position in the GATT Uruguay Round. In *Dicke, D. C. and Petersmann, E.-U., eds.*, 1988, pp. 3–10.

Díaz, Patricio; Wagner, Gert and Desormeaux, Jorge. La tasa social de descuento. (With English summary.) *Cuadernos Econ.*, April 1988, *25*(74), pp. 125–91.

Diaz, Ramon P. Capitalism and Freedom in Latin America. In *Walker, M. A., ed. (I)*, 1988, pp. 245–69.

Diba, Behzad T. and Grossman, Herschel I. Explosive Rational Bubbles in Stock Prices? *Amer. Econ. Rev.*, June 1988, *78*(3), pp. 520–30.

_____ **and Grossman, Herschel I.** Rational Inflationary Bubbles. *J. Monet. Econ.*, January 1988, *21*(1), pp. 35–46.

_____ **and Grossman, Herschel I.** The Theory of Rational Bubbles in Stock Prices. *Econ. J.*, September 1988, *98*(392), pp. 746–54.

DiBona, Charles J. Long-Term Trends in Oil Markets. In *Fried, E. R. and Blandin, N. M., eds.*, 1988, pp. 21–28.

Dichter, Thomas W. The Changing World of Northern NGOs: Problems, Paradoxes, and Possibilities. In *Lewis, J. P., et al.*, 1988, pp. 177–88.

Dick, Harold. Towards a Strategy for Development: Empowerment and Entrepreneurship. In *Abed, G. T., ed.*, 1988, pp. 311–27.

Dicke, Detlev C. Non-reciprocal Treatment. In *Dicke, D. C. and Petersmann, E.-U., eds.*, 1988, pp. 110–21.

Dicke, Hugo, et al. The Economic Effects of Agricultural Policy in West Germany. *Weltwirtsch. Arch.*, 1988, *124*(2), pp. 301–21.

Dicken, P. The Changing Geography of Japanese Foreign Direct Investment in Manufacturing Industry: A Global Perspective. *Environ. Planning A*, May 1988, *20*(5), pp. 633–53.

Dickens, William T. The Effects of Trade on Employment: Techniques and Evidence. In *Tyson, L. D.; Dickens, W. T. and Zysman, J., eds.*, 1988, pp. 41–85.

_____. Public Sector Bargaining Laws Really Matter: Evidence from Ohio and Illinois: Comment. In *Freeman, R. B. and Ichniowski, C., eds.*, 1988, pp. 78–79.

_____ **and Lang, Kevin.** Labor Market Segmentation and the Union Wage Premium. *Rev. Econ. Statist.*, August 1988, *70*(3), pp. 527–30.

_____ **and Lang, Kevin.** Neoclassical and Sociological Perspectives on Segmented Labor Markets. In *Farkas, G. and England, P., eds.*, 1988, pp. 65–88.

_____ **and Lang, Kevin.** The Reemergence of Segmented Labor Market Theory. *Amer. Econ. Rev.*, May 1988, *78*(2), pp. 129–34.

_____ **and Lang, Kevin.** Why It Matters What We Trade: A Case for Active Policy. In *Tyson, L. D.; Dickens, W. T. and Zysman, J., eds.*, 1988, pp. 87–112.

Dickey, D. A. A Reexamination of Friedman's Consumption Puzzle: Comment. *J. Bus. Econ. Statist.*, October 1988, *6*(4), pp. 410–12.

Dickinson, Gerry; Khajuria, Sajay and Beenstock, Michael. The Relationship between Property-Liability Insurance Premiums and Income: An International Analysis. *J. Risk Ins.*, June 1988, *55*(2), pp. 259–72.

Dickinson, Roger. Lessons from Retailers' Price Experiences of the 1950s. In *[Hollander, S. C.]*, 1988, pp. 177–92.

_____; **Herbst, Anthony F. and O'Shaughnessy, John.** Marketing Concept and Customer Orientation. In *Earl, P. E., ed., Vol. 2*, 1988, *1986*, pp. 311–16.

Dicks, Michael R. and Barbarika, Alexander, Jr. Estimating the Costs of Conservation Compliance. *J. Agr. Econ. Res.*, Summer 1988, *40*(3), pp. 12–20.

_____ **and Ervin, David E.** Cropland Diversion for Conservation and Environmental Improvement: An Economic Welfare Analysis. *Land Econ.*, August 1988, *64*(3), pp. 256–68.

Dickson, David. In Search of the Old Irish Poor Law. In *Mitchison, R. and Roebuck, P., eds.*, 1988, pp. 149–59.

Dickson, Michael G. Security on Movable Property and Receivables in Europe: Ireland. In *Dickson, M. G.; Rosener, W. and Storm, P. M., eds.*, 1988, pp. 75–90.

Dickson, Peter G. M. Wealth and Taxes in Eighteenth Century Austria. In *Guarducci, A., ed.*, 1988, pp. 215–43.

Dickson, Vaughan. Price Leadership and Welfare Losses in U.S. Manufacturing: Comment. *Amer. Econ. Rev.*, March 1988, *78*(1), pp. 285–87.

Diday, E.; Gettler-Summa, M. and Ralambondrainy, H. Data Analysis and Expert Systems: Generating Rules from Data. In *Gaul, W. and Schader, M., eds.*, 1988, pp. 161–73.

Diebold, Francis X. An Application of Operational-Subjective Statistical Methods to Rational Expectations: Comment. *J. Bus. Econ. Statist.*, October 1988, *6*(4), pp. 470–72.

_____. Serial Correlation and the Combination of Forecasts. *J. Bus. Econ. Statist.*, January 1988, *6*(1), pp. 105–11.

_____. Testing for Bubbles, Reflecting Barriers and Other Anomalies. *J. Econ. Dynam. Control*, March 1988, *12*(1), pp. 63–70.

_____ and Pauly, Peter. Endogenous Risk in a Portfolio-Balance Rational-Expectations Model of the Deutschemark–Dollar Rate. *Europ. Econ. Rev.*, January 1988, *32*(1), pp. 27–53.

_____ and Pauly, Peter. Has the EMS Reduced Member-Country Exchange Rate Volatility? *Empirical Econ.*, 1988, *13*(2), pp. 81–102.

Diebold, William, Jr. Bilateralism, Multilateralism and Canada in U.S. Trade Policy: Preface. In *Diebold, W., Jr., ed.*, 1988, pp. xv–xviii.

_____. The History and the Issues. In *Diebold, W., Jr., ed.*, 1988, pp. 1–36.

_____. The New Bilateralism? In *Diebold, W., Jr., ed.*, 1988, pp. 128–88.

Diehl, Paul F. and Goertz, Gary. Territorial Changes and Militarized Conflict. *J. Conflict Resolution*, March 1988, *32*(1), pp. 103–22.

Diejomaoh, V. P.; Adeniyi, E. O. and Ayodele, A. I. The Development Planning Experience in Nigeria: Effectiveness, Problems, and Prospects. In *Urrutia, M. and Yukawa, S., eds. (I)*, 1988, pp. 227–62.

Diekmann, A.; Ziegler, R. and Brüderl, J. Stellensuchdauer und Anfangseinkommen bei Hochschulabsolventen. Ein empirischer Beitrag zur Job-Search-Theorie. (Duration of Job Search and First Income of University Graduates: An Empirical Contribution to Job Search Theory. With English summary.) *Z. Wirtschaft. Sozialwissen.*, 1988, *108*(2), pp. 247–70.

Dieleman, F. M.; Clark, W. A. V. and Deurloo, M. C. Generalized Log-linear Models of Housing Choice. *Environ. Planning A*, January 1988, *20*(1), pp. 55–69.

Dieperink, H. and Nijkamp, Peter. Innovative Behaviour, Agglomeration Economies and R&D Infrastructure. *Empirical Econ.*, 1988, *13*(1), pp. 35–57.

Dierickx, I.; Matutes, C. and Neven, Damien J. Indirect Taxation and Cournot Equilibrium. *Int. J. Ind. Organ.*, 1988, *6*(3), pp. 385–99.

Dierker, Egbert and Neuefeind, Wilhelm. Quantity Guided Price Setting. *J. Math. Econ.*, 1988, *17*(2–3), pp. 249–59.

Dierkes, Meinolf. Unternehmenskultur und Unternehmensführung—Konzeptionelle Ansätze und gesicherte Erkenntnisse. (With English summary.) *Z. Betriebswirtschaft*, May–June 1988, *58*(5–6), pp. 554–75.

Dierx, Adriaan H. Estimation of a Human Capital Model of Migration. *Ann. Reg. Sci.*, November 1988, *22*(3), pp. 99–110.

_____. A Life-Cycle Model of Repeat Migration. *Reg. Sci. Urban Econ.*, August 1988, *18*(3), pp. 383–97.

_____. Metropolitan Agglomeration and Sectoral Aggregation. *J. Reg. Sci.*, August 1988, *28*(3), pp. 405–13.

Dietrich, J. Richard; Thompson, Robert B., II and Olsen, Chris. The Influence of Estimation Period News Events on Standardized Market Model Prediction Errors. *Accounting Rev.*, July 1988, *63*(3), pp. 448–71.

Dietz, Frank and van der Straaten, Jan. The Problem of Optimal Exploitation of Natural Resources: The Need for Ecological Limiting Conditions. *Int. J. Soc. Econ.*, 1988, *15*(3–4), pp. 71–79.

Dietz, James L. and James, Dilmus. The Veblen-Commons Award. *J. Econ. Issues*, June 1988, *22*(2), pp. 323–26.

Dietz, Jobst-Walter and Roski, Reinhold. Innovationsmanagement und Diskontinuitäten. (With English summary.) *Z. Betriebswirtshaft*, September 1988, *58*(9), pp. 927–51.

Dietzenbacher, Erik. Estimation of the Leontief Inverse from the Practitioner's Point of View. *Math. Soc. Sci.*, October 1988, *16*(2), pp. 181–87.

_____. Perturbations of Matrices: A Theorem on the Perron Vector and Its Applications to Input–Output Models. *J. Econ. (Z. Nationalökon.)*, 1988, *48*(4), pp. 389–412.

Diewert, W. Erwin. On Tax Reform. *Can. J. Econ.*, February 1988, *21*(1), pp. 1–40.

_____. Test Approaches to International Comparisons. In *Eichhorn, W., ed.*, 1988, pp. 67–86.

_____ and Morrison, Catherine J. Export Supply and Import Demand Functions: A Production Theory Approach. In *Feenstra, R. C., ed.*, 1988, pp. 207–22.

_____ and Ostensoe, Lawrence A. Flexible Functional Forms for Profit Functions and Global Curvature Conditions. In *Barnett, W. A.; Berndt, E. R. and White, H., eds.*, 1988, pp. 43–51.

_____; Ostensoe, Lawrence A. and Cas, Alexandra. Productivity Growth and Changes in the Terms of Trade in Canada. In *Feenstra, R. C., ed.*, 1988, pp. 279–94.

_____ and Wales, T. J. A Normalized Quadratic Semiflexible Functional Form. *J. Econometrics*, March 1988, *37*(3), pp. 327–42.

_____ and Wales, T. J. Normalized Quadratic Systems of Consumer Demand Functions. *J. Bus. Econ. Statist.*, July 1988, *6*(3), pp. 303–12.

Diez, Willi. Markteintritt und Innovation in der deutschen Automobilindustrie: Ein Überblick. (Market Entry and Innovation in German Automotive Industry: A Survey. With English summary.) *Jahr. Nationalökon. Statist.*, June 1988, *204*(6), pp. 491–507.

DiFilippo, Anthony. Military Spending and Government High Technology Policy: A Summary Analysis of Three Industrial Nations. *Rev. Radical Polit. Econ.*, Summer–Fall 1988, *20*(2–3), pp. 296–303.

Dignan, Tony and Haynes, Kingsley E. Evaluating Capital Grants for Regional Development. In *[Perroux, F.]*, 1988, pp. 330–74.

van Dijk, Herman K.; Zellner, Arnold and Bauwens, Luc. Bayesian Specification Analysis and Estimation of Simultaneous Equation Models Using Monte Carlo Methods. *J. Econometrics*, May–June 1988, *38*(1–2), pp. 39–72.

van Dijk, Jouke and Folmer, Hendrik. Differences in Unemployment Duration: A Regional or a Personal Problem? *Appl. Econ.*, September 1988, *20*(9), pp. 1233–51.

Dijkstra, Theo K. Lecture Notes in Economics and Mathematical Systems: On Model Uncertainty and Its Statistical Implications: Introduction. In *Dijkstra, T. K., ed.*, 1988, pp. iii–vi.

_____ **and Veldkamp, J. H.** Data-Driven Selection of Regressors and the Bootstrap. In *Dijkstra, T. K., ed.*, 1988, pp. 17–38.

Dikow, Edmund and Hornung, Ulrich. A Random Boundary Value Problem Modeling Spatial Variability in Porous Media Flow. In *Wheeler, M. F., ed.*, 1988, pp. 111–17.

Dillard, Dudley. The Barter Illusion in Classical and Neoclassical Economics. *Eastern Econ. J.*, Oct.–Dec. 1988, *14*(4), pp. 299–318.

_____. Capitalism. In *Wilber, C. K., ed.*, 1988, pp. 87–95.

_____. Effective Demand and the Monetary Theory of Employment. In *Barrère, A., ed.*, 1988, pp. 49–64.

_____. Money as an Institution of Capitalism. In *Tool, M. R., ed., Vol. 2*, 1988, *1987*, pp. 205–29.

Dillman, Don A. The Social Environment of Agriculture and Rural Areas. In *Hildreth, R. J., et al., eds.*, 1988, pp. 61–81.

Dillon, John L. A SWOT Appraisal of the Australian Profession of Agricultural Economics as at 1988. *Rev. Marketing Agr. Econ.*, December 1988, *56*(3), pp. 340–46.

Dillon, Patricia and Willett, Thomas D. Political Business Cycles: The Political Economy of Money, Inflation, and Unemployment: Introduction and Summary. In *Willett, T. D., ed.*, 1988, pp. 1–31.

Dilnot, Andrew. British Trends since 1900: The Economic Environment. In *Halsey, A. H., ed.*, 1988, pp. 135–61.

_____ **and Kell, Michael.** Top-Rate Tax Cuts and Incentives: Some Empirical Evidence. *Fisc. Stud.*, November 1988, *9*(4), pp. 70–92.

_____; **Kell, Michael and Webb, Steven B.** The 1988 Budget and the Structure of Personal Taxation. *Fisc. Stud.*, May 1988, *9*(2), pp. 38–47.

_____ **and Webb, Steven B.** Reforming National Insurance Contributions. *Fisc. Stud.*, November 1988, *9*(4), pp. 1–24.

_____ **and Webb, Steven B.** The 1988 Social Security Reforms. *Fisc. Stud.*, August 1988, *9*(3), pp. 26–53.

DiLorenzo, Thomas J. Competition and Political Entrepreneurship: Austrian Insights into Public-Choice Theory. In *Rothbard, M. N. and Block, W., eds.*, 1988, pp. 59–71.

_____. Property Rights, Information Costs, and the Economics of Rent Seeking. *J. Inst. Theoretical Econ.*, April 1988, *144*(2), pp. 318–32.

_____ **and High, Jack C.** Antitrust and Competition, Historically Considered. *Econ. Inquiry*, July 1988, *26*(3), pp. 423–35.

Dilullo, Anthony J. U.S. International Transactions, Second Quarter 1988. *Surv. Curr. Bus.*, September 1988, *68*(9), pp. 33–56.

_____. U.S. International Transactions, Third Quarter 1988. *Surv. Curr. Bus.*, December 1988, *68*(12), pp. 19–36.

Dilworth, Peter; Iacono, Salvatore and Bodnar, Judith. Cross-sectional Analysis of Residential Telephone Subscription in Canada. *Info. Econ. Policy*, 1988, *3*(4), pp. 359–78.

Dimand, Robert W. An Early Canadian Contribution to Mathematical Economics: J. B. Cherriman's 1857 Review of Cournot. *Can. J. Econ.*, August 1988, *21*(3), pp. 610–16.

_____. The Development of Keynes's Theory of Employment. In *Hamouda, O. F. and Smithin, J. N., eds., Vol. 1*, 1988, pp. 121–30.

DiMasi, Joseph A. Property Tax Classification and Welfare in Urban Areas: A General Equilibrium Computational Approach. *J. Urban Econ.*, March 1988, *23*(2), pp. 131–49.

Dimitri, Alexandre; Gombeaud, Jean-François and Lavigne, Marie. Prices, Settlements, Gains from Trade. In *Lavigne, M., ed.*, 1988, pp. 64–93.

Dimitri, Nicola. A Short Remark on Learning of Rational Expectations. *Econ. Notes*, 1988, (3), pp. 145–52.

Dimsdale, Nicholas H. Keynes on Interwar Economic Policy. In *Eltis, W. and Sinclair, P. J. N., eds.*, 1988, pp. 317–39.

Dimson, Elroy and Bowers, John. Stock Market Anomalies: Introduction. In *Dimson, E., ed.*, 1988, pp. 3–15.

_____ **and Marsh, Paul.** The Impact of the Small Firm Effect on Event Studies. In *Dimson, E., ed.*, 1988, pp. 220–39.

Dinar, Ariel and Knapp, Keith C. Economic Analysis of On-Farm Solutions to Drainage Problems in Irrigated Agriculture. *Australian J. Agr. Econ.*, April 1988, *32*(1), pp. 1–14.

Dini, Lamberto. International Macroeconomic Policy Cooperation: Where Do We Go from Here? Perspective. In *Guerrieri, P. and Padoan, P. C., eds.*, 1988, pp. 250–53.

_____. The Italian Financial System in the Perspective of 1992. *Banca Naz. Lavoro Quart. Rev.*, December 1988, (167), pp. 441–49.

Dinneen, Gerald P. Global Flows and Barriers. In *Muroyama, J. H. and Stever, H. G., eds.*, 1988, pp. 32–34.

_____. U.S.–Japanese Science and Technology: A Comparative Assessment. In *Uyehara, C. H., ed.*, 1988, pp. 1–26.

Dinopoulos, Elias. A Formalization of the 'Biological' Model of Trade in Similar Products. *J. Int. Econ.*, August 1988, *25*(1–2), pp. 95–110.

_____. Price and Quality Level Comparisons for U.S. Footwear Imports: An Application of Multilateral Index Numbers: Comment. In *Feenstra, R. C., ed.*, 1988, pp. 276–78.

_____ **and Kreinin, Mordechai E.** Effects on the U.S.–Japan Auto VER on European Prices and on U.S. Welfare. *Rev. Econ. Statist.*, August 1988, *70*(3), pp. 484–91.

Dintenfass, Michael. Entrepreneurial Failure Reconsidered: The Case of the Interwar British Coal Industry. *Bus. Hist. Rev.*, Spring 1988, *62*(1), pp. 1–34.

Dionne, Georges and Belisle, Sylvain. Accessibilité aux ressources et demande de revascularisation du myocarde. (Accessibility to Resources and Demand of Heart Revascularization. With English summary.) *Can. J. Econ.*, February 1988, *21*(1), pp. 129–45.

_____ **and Gagne, Robert.** Models and Methodologies in the Analysis of Regulation Effects in Airline Markets. *Int. J. Transport Econ.*, October 1988, *15*(3), pp. 291–312.

_____ **and Gagné, Robert.** Qu'en est-il des rendements d'échelle dans les industries québécoises et ontariennes de transport par camion. (With English summary.) *L'Actual. Econ.*, September 1988, *64*(3), pp. 380–95.

de Dios Ortuzar, Juan. Zahavi's Alpha Relation: Myth or Blessing? *Int. J. Transport Econ.*, June 1988, *15*(2), pp. 189–201.

Director, Steven M. and Englander, Frederick J. Requiring Unemployment Insurance Recipients to Register with the Public Employment Service. *J. Risk Ins.*, June 1988, *55*(2), pp. 245–58.

Dirindin, Nerina. Effetti redistributivi fra generazioni in un sistema sanitario finanziato a ripartizione. (Intergenerational Income Redistribution and Pay-as-You-Go Health System. With English summary.) *Ricerche Econ.*, Oct.–Dec. 1988, *42*(4), pp. 582–605.

_____. Trattamento fiscale delle spese mediche, redistribuzione del reddito e utilizzazione delle risorse. (With English summary.) *Polit. Econ.*, December 1988, *4*(3), pp. 465–93.

Dirrheimer, Manfred J. Wettbewerbsdynamik in der Lebensversicherung. (With English summary.) *Z. Betriebswirtshaft*, July 1988, *58*(7), pp. 683–97.

Discenza, Richard and Smith, Howard L. Is Employee Discipline Obsolete? In *Timpe, A. D., ed.*, 1988, *1985*, pp. 351–62.

Disney, Peter L. and Czogala, Ernest. Decision Making in a Probablistic Fuzzy Environment. In *Kacprzyk, J. and Fedrizzi, M., eds.*, 1988, pp. 215–26.

Disney, Richard F. and Carruth, Alan A. Where Have Two Million Trade Union Members Gone? *Economica*, February 1988, *55*(217), pp. 1–19.

_____ **and Creedy, John.** The New Pension Scheme in Britain. *Fisc. Stud.*, May 1988, *9*(2), pp. 57–71.

Disney, W. Terry; Duffy, Patricia A. and Hardy, William E., Jr. A Markov Chain Analysis of Pork Farm Size Distributions in the South. *Southern J. Agr. Econ.*, December 1988, *20*(2), pp. 57–64.

Dissanayake, Mallika and Giles, David E. A. Household Expenditure in Sri Lanka: An Engel Curve Analysis. *J. Quant. Econ.*, January 1988, *4*(1), pp. 133–56.

DiTomaso, Nancy. Income Determination in Three Internal Labor Markets. In *Farkas, G. and England, P., eds.*, 1988, pp. 217–42.

Divisekera, S. and Felmingham, Bruce S. Growth and Equity in Sri Lanka, 1963–1982. *Econ. Letters*, 1988, *28*(3), pp. 291–93.

Dixey, Rachael. A Means to Get Out of the House: Working-Class Women, Leisure and Bingo. In *Little, J.; Peake, L. and Richardson, P., eds.*, 1988, pp. 117–132.

Dixit, Avinash K. Anti-dumping and Countervailing Duties Under Oligopoly. *Europ. Econ. Rev.*, January 1988, *32*(1), pp. 55–68.

_____. A General Model of R&D Competition and Policy. *Rand J. Econ.*, Autumn 1988, *19*(3), pp. 317–26.

_____. International R&D Competition and Policy. In *Spence, A. M. and Hazard, H. A., eds.*, 1988, pp. 149–71.

_____. Issues of Strategic Trade Policy for Small Countries. In *Haaland, J. I. and Norman, V. D., eds.*, 1988, pp. 133–51.

_____. Optimal Trade and Industrial Policies for the U.S. Automobile Industry. In *Feenstra, R. C., ed.*, 1988, pp. 141–65.

_____. Trade Restraints, Intermediate Goods, and World Market Conditions: Comment. In *Baldwin, R. E., ed. (II)*, 1988, pp. 248–50.

Dixon, Bruce L. and Elam, Emmett W. Examining the Validity of a Test of Futures Market Efficiency. *J. Futures Markets*, June 1988, *8*(3), pp. 365–72.

Dixon, Daryl. Increasing Taxation on Australian Property Income Utilising Inflation Adjustment, Base Broadening and/or Potential Income Taxation. *Australian Tax Forum*, 1988, *5*(1), pp. 13–22.

Dixon, Huw David. A Simple Model of Imperfect Competition with Walrasian Features. In *Cross, R., ed.*, 1988, pp. 129–57.

_____. Unions, Oligopoly and the Natural Range of Employment. *Econ. J.*, December 1988, *98*(393), pp. 1127–47.

Dixon, L. C. W. Automatic Differentiation and Parallel Processing in Optimisation. In *Kurzhanski, A.; Neumann, K. and Pallaschke, D., eds.*, 1988, pp. 86–93.

Dixon, Peter B. and Johnson, David T. Pricing of Queensland Sugar Cane: Appraisal of the Present Formula and a Suggestion for Reform. *Rev. Marketing Agr. Econ.*, April 1988, *56*(1), pp. 27–35.

_____ **and McDonald, Daina.** The Australian Economy: 1987–88 and 1988–89. *Australian Econ. Rev.*, Winter 1988, (82), pp. 3–26.

_____ **and McDonald, Daina.** Forecasts for the Australian Economy: 1988–89 and 1989–90. *Australian Econ. Rev.*, Summer 1988, (84), pp. 3–18.

_____ **and McDonald, Daina.** Some Macroeconomic Aspects of the 1988–89 Budget. *Australian Econ. Rev.*, Spring 1988, (83), pp. 3–11.

_____; **Parmenter, Brian R. and Horridge, Mark.** Forecasting versus Policy Analysis with the ORANI Model. In *Motamen, H., ed.*, 1988, pp. 653–66.

_____ **and Parmenter, B. R.** Recent Developments in Forecasting with the ORANI Model. *Australian Econ. Pap.*, Supplement, June 1988, 27, pp. 92–104.

Dixon, Robert K. Forest Biotechnology Opportunities in Developing Countries. *J. Devel. Areas*, January 1988, *22*(2), pp. 207–18.

Djajić, Slobodan. Exchange Rates, Wages, and

the International Allocation of Capital. *Amer. Econ. Rev.*, May 1988, 78(2), pp. 341–45.

_____. A Model of Trade in Exhaustible Resources. *Int. Econ. Rev.*, February 1988, 29(1), pp. 87–103.

_____ and **Milbourne, Ross D.** A General Equilibrium Model of Guest-Worker Migration: The Source-Country Perspective. *J. Int. Econ.*, November 1988, 25(3–4), pp. 335–51.

Dlugos, Günter; Dorow, Wolfgang and Danesy, Frank C. The Analysis of the Employer Employee Relationship from the Perspective of the Business Politics Approach. In *Dlugos, G.; Dorow, W. and Weiermair, K.*, eds., 1988, pp. 107–18.

Dmitrichev, Igor Ivanovich and Belova, Natalya Fedorovna. Statistics of Time Use in the USSR. *Statist. J.*, December 1988, 5(4), pp. 393–402.

Dnes, Antony W. The Efficiency of Central Planning: A Comment. *Scot. J. Polit. Econ.*, November 1988, 35(4), pp. 404–10.

_____. Rent Seeking, Entrepreneurship, Subjectivism and Property Rights: A Comment. *J. Inst. Theoretical Econ.*, December 1988, 144(5), pp. 891–93.

Doak, Ervin John. Islamic Interest-Free Banking and 100 Percent Money: Comment. *Int. Monet. Fund Staff Pap.*, September 1988, 35(3), pp. 534–36.

Doane, Michael J.; Hartman, Raymond S. and Woo, Chi-Keung. Household Preference for Interruptible Rate Options and the Revealed Value of Service Reliability. *Energy J.*, Special Issue, 1988, 9, pp. 121–34.

_____; **Hartman, Raymond S. and Woo, Chi-Keung.** Households' Perceived Value of Service Reliability: An Analysis of Contingent Valuation Data. *Energy J.*, Special Issue, 1988, 9, pp. 135–49.

Dobb, Maurice. The Sraffa System and Critique of the Neo-classical Theory of Distribution. In *Steedman, I.*, ed., *Vol. 1*, 1988, 1970, pp. 114–29.

Dobbs, Ian M. Risk Aversion, Gambling and the Labour–Leisure Choice. *Scot. J. Polit. Econ.*, May 1988, 35(2), pp. 171–75.

Dobell, Rod and Bergsten, C. Fred. The Canada–United States Free Trade Agreement: The Global Impact: Preface. In *Schott, J. J. and Smith, M. G.*, eds., 1988, pp. vii–ix.

Dobozi, István. The Responsiveness of the Hungarian Economy to Changes in Energy Prices. In *Brada, J. C. and Dobozi, I.*, eds., 1988, pp. 237–65.

Dobric, V.; Momirovic, Konstantin and Radakovic, J. An Expert System for the Interpretation of Results of Canonical Covariance Analysis. In *Edwards, D. and Raun, N. E.*, eds., 1988, pp. 135–41.

Dobroczynski, Michal. The Polish Economy and New Credits. In *Marer, P. and Siwinski, W.*, eds., 1988, pp. 177–82.

Dobrovolny, Georg J. Zur Aussagekraft der Angaben über den Schuldendienst. (The Meaningfulness of Debt Service Data. With English

summary.) *Kredit Kapital*, 1988, 21(1), pp. 143–48.

Dobson, Allen and Sangl, Judith. A Broker Model for Joint Public–Private Supplemental Insurance for the Medicare Population: A Transition to Long-term Care Insurance. In *Scheffler, R. M. and Rossiter, L. F.*, eds., 1988, pp. 23–44.

Dobson, Gregory and Kalish, Shlomo. Positioning and Pricing a Product Line. *Marketing Sci.*, Spring 1988, 7(2), pp. 107–25.

Dobson, William D. The Macroeconomics of Agriculture and Rural America: A Discussion. In *Hildreth, R. J., et al.*, eds., 1988, pp. 396–99.

Döckel, J. A. and Calitz, E. Die bestaansreg van buitebegrotingsfondse. (With English summary.) *J. Stud. Econ. Econometrics*, November 1988, 12(3), pp. 31–39.

Dockner, Engelbert J. and Jørgensen, Steffen. Optimal Pricing Strategies for New Products in Dynamic Oligopolies. *Marketing Sci.*, Fall 1988, 7(4), pp. 315–34.

_____ and **Takahashi, Harutaka.** Further Turnpike Properties for General Capital Accumulation Games. *Econ. Letters*, 1988, 28(4), pp. 321–25.

Dodaro, Santo and Pluta, Leonard. The Antigonish Movement as a Model of Regional Economic Development. In *Choudhury, M. A.*, ed., 1988, pp. 48–70.

Dodge, David A. and Sargent, John H. World Tax Reform: A Progress Report: Canada. In *Pechman, J. A.*, ed., 1988, pp. 43–69.

Dodgshon, R. A. West Highland Chiefdoms, 1500–1745: A Study in Redistributive Exchange. In *Mitchison, R. and Roebuck, P.*, eds., 1988, pp. 27–37.

Dodgson, J. S. and Katsoulacos, Yannis. Quality Competition in Bus Services: Some Welfare Implications of Bus Deregulation. *J. Transp. Econ. Policy*, September 1988, 22(3), pp. 263–81.

Doeksen, Gerald A. Budgeting: The Foundation of Community Service Research and Extension Programs. In *Johnson, T. G.; Deaton, B. J. and Segarra, E.*, eds., 1988, pp. 67–86.

Doeleman, Jacobus A. Social Determinism, Technology and Economic Externalities. In *Tisdell, C. and Maitra, P.*, eds., 1988, pp. 298–321.

Doenecke, Justus D. A Funny Thing Happened on the Way to the Forum or the Reviews of "Mr. First Nighter." In *[Rothbard, M. N.]*, 1988, pp. 383–91.

Doering, Otto; Schmitz, Andrew and Sigurdson, Dale. Domestic Farm Policy and the Gains from Trade: Reply. *Amer. J. Agr. Econ.*, August 1988, 70(3), pp. 740.

Doeringer, Peter B. Market Structure, Jobs, and Productivity: Observations from Jamaica. *World Devel.*, April 1988, 16(4), pp. 465–82.

_____; **Moss, Philip I. and Terkla, David G.** Widespread Labor Stickiness in the New England Offshore Fishing Industry: Implications for Adjustment and Regulation. *Land Econ.*, February 1988, 64(1), pp. 73–82.

Doescher, Tabitha A. and Turner, John A. Social Security Benefits and the Baby-Boom Generation. *Amer. Econ. Rev.*, May 1988, 78(2), pp. 76–80.

Doessel, D. P. Information Output of Diagnostic Tests: An Analysis of Radiology and Endoscopy. In *Butler, J. R. G. and Doessel, D. P.,* eds., 1988, pp. 109–32.

———— **and Butler, J. R. G.** Alternative Schemes for Distributing Transfers to Natural Disaster Victims: Analysis and Implementation. *Econ. Rec.*, March 1988, 64(184), pp. 47–54.

———— **and Cheah, C.-W.** Technology and Health Expenditures in Australia: Results from the Residual Approach. In *Smith, C. S., ed.,* 1988, pp. 1–18.

———— **and Cheah, C.-W.** A Theoretical Note on the Measurement of the Welfare Cost of Health Insurance. In *Butler, J. R. G. and Doessel, D. P., eds.,* 1988, pp. 170–88.

Doherty, Neil A. The Pricing of Reinsurance Contracts. In *Borba, P. S. and Appel, D., eds.,* 1988, pp. 161–77.

———— **and Kang, Han Bin.** Interest Rates and Insurance Price Cycles. *J. Banking Finance,* June 1988, 12(2), pp. 199–214.

————; **Park, Hun Y. and Chen, Andrew H.** The Optimal Capital Structure Decision of Depository Financial Intermediaries. In *Chen, A. H., ed.,* 1988, pp. 91–111.

Doi, Noriyuki. Concentration, Subcontract and Exports in Japanese Manufacturing Industries. *Managerial Dec. Econ.,* June 1988, 9(2), pp. 109–17.

Doignon, Jean-Paul. Partial Structures of Preference. In *Kacprzyk, J. and Roubens, M., eds.,* 1988, pp. 22–35.

Doktor, Robert H. and Chandler, Susan M. Limits of Predictability in Forecasting in the Behavioral Sciences. *Int. J. Forecasting,* 1988, 4(1), pp. 5–14.

Dolado, Juan and Banerjee, Anindya. Tests of the Life Cycle-Permanent Income Hypothesis in the Presence of Random Walks: Asymptotic Theory and Small-Sample Interpretations. *Oxford Econ. Pap.,* December 1988, 40(4), pp. 610–33.

Dolan, Edwin G. Observations on the Use of Textbooks in the Teaching of Principles of Economics: A Comment. *J. Econ. Educ.,* Spring 1988, 19(2), pp. 169–70.

Dolan, Robert C. and Dean, David H. Establishing a Mini-data Link. In *Berkowitz, M., ed.,* 1988, pp. 232–55.

———— **and Dean, David H.** Imputing Benefits to Persons Closed Not Rehabilitated. In *Berkowitz, M., ed.,* 1988, pp. 139–48.

———— **and Dean, David H.** Using a Better Measure for Services. In *Berkowitz, M., ed.,* 1988, pp. 186–98.

Dolan, Robert J.; Bonoma, Thomas V. and Crittenden, Victoria L. Can We Have Rigor and Relevance in Pricing Research? In *Devinney, T. M., ed.,* 1988, pp. 337–59.

Dolebear, F. Trenery, Jr. On the Theory of Optimum Externality. In *Ricketts, M., ed., Vol. 2,* 1988, 1967, pp. 63–76.

Dolezal, Jaroslav. Optimal Control Discrete-Time Systems. In *Iri, M. and Yajima, K., eds.,* 1988, pp. 22–28.

Doll, John P. Traditional Economic Models of Fishing Vessels: A Review with Discussion. *Marine Resource Econ.,* 1988, 5(2), pp. 99–123.

Dollar, David and Wolff, Edward N. Convergence of Industry Labor Productivity among Advanced Economies, 1963–1982. *Rev. Econ. Statist.,* November 1988, 70(4), pp. 549–58.

————; **Wolff, Edward N. and Baumol, William J.** The Factor-Price Equalization Model and Industry Labor Productivity: An Empirical Test across Countries. In *Feenstra, R. C., ed.,* 1988, pp. 23–47.

Dolton, Peter J. A New Breed of Software? GAUSS, MATLAB and PC-ISP: A Comparative Review. *J. Econ. Surveys,* 1988, 2(1), pp. 77–95.

Domatob, Jerry Komia and Vivekananda, Franklin. Maldevelopment and Sub-Saharan African Elites. In *Vivekananda, F., ed.,* 1988, pp. 177–95.

Domberger, Simon and Cubbin, John S. Advertising and Post-entry Oligopoly Behaviour. *J. Ind. Econ.,* December 1988, 37(2), pp. 123–40.

————; **Meadowcroft, Shirley and Thompson, David.** Competition and Efficiency in Refuse Collection: A Reply. *Fisc. Stud.,* February 1988, 9(1), pp. 86–90.

Domenech, Roberto and Cavallo, Domingo. Las políticas macroecónomicas y el tipo de cambio real. Argentina, 1913–1984. (With English summary.) *Desarrollo Econ.,* Oct.–Dec. 1988, 28(111), pp. 375–400.

Dometrius, Nelson C. and Sigelman, Lee. Assessing Personnel Practices in Higher Education: A Cautionary Note. *Econ. Educ. Rev.,* 1988, 7(4), pp. 439–43.

———— **and Sigelman, Lee.** The Cost of Quality: Teacher Testing and Racial–Ethnic Representativeness in Public Education. *Soc. Sci. Quart.,* March 1988, 69(1), pp. 70–82.

Domingo, J.; Romero, C. and Rehman, T. U. Compromise–Risk Programming for Agricultural Resource Allocation Problems: An Illustration. *J. Agr. Econ.,* May 1988, 39(2), pp. 271–76.

Dominguez, Kathryn M.; Fair, Ray C. and Shapiro, Matthew D. Forecasting the Depression: Harvard versus Yale. *Amer. Econ. Rev.,* September 1988, 78(4), pp. 595–612.

Dominguez, Roberto. Some Ideas Concerning the Need to Reform Financial Management in the Public Sector of Developing Countries. In *Most, K. S., ed.,* 1988, pp. 275–86.

Dominique, C. Rene. A Note on Increasing Returns to Advertising. *Econ. Letters,* 1988, 28(4), pp. 381–85.

Domowitz, Ian; Hubbard, Robert Glenn and Petersen, Bruce C. Market Structure and Cyclical Fluctuations in U.S. Manufacturing. *Rev.*

Econ. Statist., February 1988, *70*(1), pp. 55–66.

_____ and Muus, Lars. Likelihood Inference in the Nonlinear Regression Model with Explosive Linear Dynamics. In *Barnett, W. A.; Berndt, E. R. and White, H., eds.*, 1988, pp. 53–72.

Don, Dominique. The "Socialist-Orientated Countries": Privileged Partners? In *Lavigne, M., ed.*, 1988, pp. 125–44.

Donabedian, Avedis. Quality and Cost: Choices and Responsibilities. *Inquiry*, Spring 1988, *25*(1), pp. 90–99.

_____. Quality Assessment and Assurance: Unity of Purpose, Diversity of Means. *Inquiry*, Spring 1988, *25*(1), pp. 173–92.

Donaldson, Cam, et al. Should QALYs Be Programme-Specific? *J. Health Econ.*, September 1988, *7*(3), pp. 239–57.

Donaldson, David and Blackorby, Charles. Cash versus Kind, Self-selection, and Efficient Transfers. *Amer. Econ. Rev.*, September 1988, *78*(4), pp. 691–700.

_____ and Blackorby, Charles. Money Metric Utility: Harmless Normalization? *J. Econ. Theory*, October 1988, *46*(1), pp. 120–29.

_____ and Weymark, John A. Social Choice in Economic Environments. *J. Econ. Theory*, December 1988, *46*(2), pp. 291–308.

Donaldson, Peter J. American Catholicism and the International Family Planning Movement. *Population Stud.*, November 1988, *42*(3), pp. 367–73.

Dong, Yongshun. An Estimation of the Prospects for China's Petroleum Trade. In *Dorian, J. P. and Fridley, D. G., eds.*, 1988, pp. 55–58.

Donges, Juergen B. The International Debt Problem: Comment. In *Borner, S., ed.*, 1988, pp. 61–66.

_____. Lessons for Europe. In *Giersch, H., ed.*, 1988, pp. 362–67.

_____. Restrictiveness and International Transmission of the "New" Protectionism: Comment. In *Baldwin, R. E.; Hamilton, C. B. and Sapir, A., eds.*, 1988, pp. 224–27.

_____. Whither International Trade Policies: Worries about Continuing Protectionism. In *Elliott, K. A. and Williamson, J., eds.*, 1988, pp. 57–92.

Dongili, Paola. F. Gailiani: *Della moneta.* (F. Galiani's *Della moneta.* With English summary.) *Rivista Int. Sci. Econ. Com.*, January 1988, *35*(1), pp. 11–28.

Donkers, Harry W. J. Consumer Price Indices Adjusted for Indirect Taxes and Subsidies in the Netherlands. *Statist. J.*, December 1988, *5*(4), pp. 403–19.

Donley, Edward. Business Implications of Space Programs. In *Egan, J. J., et al.*, 1988, pp. 413–20.

Donnelly, William D. and Rushing, Francis W. A Rationale for Entrepreneurship Education in Secondary Schools. In *Association of Private Education*, 1988, pp. 97–102.

Donnenfeld, Shabtai. Commercial Policy and Imperfect Discrimination by a Foreign Monopol-

ist. *Int. Econ. Rev.*, November 1988, *29*(4), pp. 607–20.

_____. Gains from Trade in Differentiated Products: Japanese Compact Trucks: Comment. In *Feenstra, R. C., ed.*, 1988, pp. 137–39.

_____ and Besanko, David. The Impact of Buyers' Expectations on Entry Deterrence. *Econ. Letters*, 1988, *26*(4), pp. 375–80.

_____ and Besanko, David. Rate of Return Regulation and Product Variety. *J. Public Econ.*, August 1988, *36*(3), pp. 293–304.

_____ and White, Lawrence J. Product Variety and the Inefficiency of Monopoly. *Economica*, August 1988, *55*(219), pp. 393–401.

_____; White, Lawrence J. and Besanko, David. The Multiproduct Firm, Quality Choice, and Regulation. *J. Ind. Econ.*, June 1988, *36*(4), pp. 411–29.

Donohue, John J., III. Determinants of Job Turnover of Young Men and Women in the United States: A Hazard Rate Analysis. In *Schultz, T. Paul, ed.*, 1988, pp. 257–301.

Donovan, James W. The Mexican Experience in Accounting for Inflation. In *Perkins, E. J., ed.*, 1988, pp. 177–88.

Dooley, Michael P. An Econometric Investigation of North–South Interdependence: Discussion. In *Currie, D. and Vines, D., eds.*, 1988, pp. 63–64.

_____. Buy-Backs and Market Valuation of External Debt. *Int. Monet. Fund Staff Pap.*, June 1988, *35*(2), pp. 215–29.

_____. Capital Flight: A Response to Differences in Financial Risks. *Int. Monet. Fund Staff Pap.*, September 1988, *35*(3), pp. 422–36.

_____. International Capital Mobility and Exchange Rate Volatility: Discussion. In *Fieleke, N. S., ed.*, 1988, pp. 189–94.

_____. Self-financed Buy-Backs and Asset Exchanges. *Int. Monet. Fund Staff Pap.*, December 1988, *35*(4), pp. 714–22.

_____; Frankel, Jeffrey A. and Mathieson, Donald J. International Capital Mobility: What Do Saving–Investment Correlations Tell Us? Reply. *Int. Monet. Fund Staff Pap.*, June 1988, *35*(2), pp. 397–98.

Dooley, Peter C. Malthus on Long Swings: The General Case. *Can. J. Econ.*, February 1988, *21*(1), pp. 200–205.

_____. Porter's Hint and Alternative Theories of the Giffen Paradox: A Reply. *Australian Econ. Pap.*, June 1988, *27*(50), pp. 142–44.

Doorley, Thomas H.; Gregg, Alison and Gagnon, Christopher. Professional Services Firms and Information Technology: Ongoing Search for Sustained Competitive Advantage. In *Guile, B. R. and Quinn, J. B., eds. (I)*, 1988, pp. 175–94.

Doorley, Thomas L. and Quinn, James Brian. Key Policy Issues Posed by Services. In *Guile, B. R. and Quinn, J. B., eds. (II)*, 1988, pp. 211–34.

Dopfer, Kurt. Classical Mechanics with an Ethical Dimension: Professor Tinbergen's Economics: Reply. *J. Econ. Issues*, September 1988, *22*(3), pp. 854–56.

_____. Classical Mechanics with an Ethical Dimension: Professor Tinbergen's Economics. *J. Econ. Issues*, September 1988, *22*(3), pp. 675–706.

_____. How Historical Is Schmoller's Economic Thought? *J. Inst. Theoretical Econ.*, June 1988, *144*(3), pp. 552–69.

_____. In Memoriam: Gunnar Myrdal's Contribution to Institutional Economics. *J. Econ. Issues*, March 1988, *22*(1), pp. 227–31.

Dopuch, Nicholas and Pincus, Morton. Evidence on the Choice of Inventory Accounting Methods: LIFO versus FIFO. *J. Acc. Res.*, Spring 1988, *26*(1), pp. 28–59.

Doran, B. Michael; Collins, Daniel W. and Dhaliwal, Dan S. The Information of Historical Cost Earnings Relative to Supplemental Reserve-Based Accounting Data in the Extractive Petroleum Industry. *Accounting Rev.*, July 1988, *63*(3), pp. 389–413.

Doran, Christine. Public Control and Ownership in Queensland's Electricity Industry. *Australian Econ. Hist. Rev.*, March 1988, *28*(1), pp. 60–81.

Doran, Howard E. Specification Tests for the Partial Adjustment and Adaptive Expectations Models. *Amer. J. Agr. Econ.*, August 1988, *70*(3), pp. 713–23.

Dore, M. H. I. The Optimal Depletion of a Theory of Exhaustible Resources: A Comment. *J. Post Keynesian Econ.*, Summer 1988, *10*(4), pp. 646–50.

_____. The Use of Mathematics in Social Explanation. *Sci. Soc.*, Winter 1988–89, *52*(4), pp. 456–69.

Dore, Ronald and Sako, Mari. Teaching or Testing: The Role of the State in Japan. *Oxford Rev. Econ. Policy*, Autumn 1988, *4*(3), pp. 72–81.

Dorfman, Gerald A. and Hanna, Paul R. Can Education Be Reformed? In *Anderson, A. and Bark, D. L., eds.*, 1988, pp. 383–90.

Dorfman, Nancy S. Route 128: The Development of a Regional High Technology Economy. In *Lampe, D., ed.*, 1988, *1983*, pp. 240–74.

Dorfman, Peter W. and Howell, Jon P. Dimensions of National Culture and Effective Leadership Patterns: Hofstede Revisited. In *Farmer, R. N. and McGoun, E. G., eds.*, 1988, pp. 127–50.

Dorfman, Robert. The Political Economy of Environmental Protection: A Conversation. *Eastern Econ. J.*, July–Sept. 1988, *14*(3), pp. 205–09.

Dorgan, J. J. The Occidental Coal Agreement in China. In *Dorian, J. P. and Fridley, D. G., eds.*, 1988, pp. 143–53.

Dorman, Peter. Worker Rights and International Trade: A Case for Intervention. *Rev. Radical Polit. Econ.*, Summer–Fall 1988, *20*(2–3), pp. 241–46.

Dorn, James A. Dollars, Deficits, and Trade. *Cato J.*, Fall 1988, *8*(2), pp. 229–51.

_____. Public Choice and the Constitution: A Madisonian Perspective. In *Gwartney, J. D. and Wagner, R. E., eds.*, 1988, pp. 57–102.

Dornbusch, Rudiger. The Adjustment Mecha-

nism: Theory and Problems. In *Fieleke, N. S., ed.*, 1988, pp. 195–225.

_____. An International Gold Standard without Gold: The McKinnon Standard: How Persuasive? *Cato J.*, Fall 1988, *8*(2), pp. 375–83.

_____. The Buyback Boondoggle: Comment. *Brookings Pap. Econ. Act.*, 1988, (2), pp. 699–703.

_____. Capital Mobility, Flexible Exchange Rates, and Macroeconomic Equilibrium. In *Dornbusch, R.*, 1988, *1976*, pp. 107–24.

_____. Devaluation, Money, and Nontraded Goods. In *Dornbusch, R.*, 1988, *1973*, pp. 5–22.

_____. Doubts About the McKinnon Standard. *J. Econ. Perspectives*, Winter 1988, *2*(1), pp. 105–112.

_____. Exchange Rate Economics: 1986. In *Dornbusch, R.*, 1988, pp. 235–60.

_____. Exchange Rate Risk and the Macroeconomics of Exchange Rate Determination. In *Dornbusch, R.*, 1988, *1983*, pp. 125–51.

_____. Exchange Rates and Fiscal Policy in a Popular Model of International Trade. In *Dornbusch, R.*, 1988, *1975*, pp. 23–41.

_____. Exchange Rates and Prices. In *Dornbusch, R.*, 1988, *1987*, pp. 79–102.

_____. Expectations and Exchange Rate Dynamics. In *Melamed, L., ed.*, 1988, *1976*, pp. 471–87.

_____. Expectations and Exchange Rate Dynamics. In *Dornbusch, R.*, 1988, *1976*, pp. 61–78.

_____. Fiscal Policies, Net Saving, and Real Exchange Rates: The United States, the Federal Republic of Germany, and Japan: Comment. In *Frenkel, J. A., ed.*, 1988, pp. 66–71.

_____. Flexible Exchange Rates and Excess Capital Mobility. In *Melamed, L., ed.*, 1988, *1986*, pp. 489–504.

_____. Inflation, Capital, and Deficit Finance. In *Dornbusch, R.*, 1988, *1977*, pp. 379–90.

_____. Inflation Stabilization and Capital Mobility. In *Dornbusch, R.*, 1988, pp. 391–408.

_____. Intergenerational and International Trade. In *Dornbusch, R.*, 1988, *1985*, pp. 347–65.

_____. Is There a Public Debt Problem in Italy: Discussion. In *Giavazzi, F. and Spaventa, L., eds.*, 1988, pp. 25–33.

_____. Les défis macro-économiques mondiaux des dix années à venir. (World Economic Challenges for the Next Ten Years. With English summary.) *Revue Écon.*, May 1988, *39*(3), pp. 591–613.

_____. Lessons from the German Inflation Experience of the 1920s. In *Dornbusch, R.*, 1988, *1987*, pp. 409–38.

_____. New Directions for Research. In *Marston, R. C., ed.*, 1988, pp. 299–307.

_____. Our LDC Debts. In *Feldstein, M., ed. (II)*, 1988, pp. 162–96.

_____. Peru on the Brink. *Challenge*, Nov.–Dec. 1988, *31*(6), pp. 31–37.

_____. PPP Exchange Rate Rules and Macroeconomic Stability. In *Dornbusch, R.*, 1988, *1982*, pp. 227–34.

_____. Purchasing Power Parity. In *Dornbusch, R.*, 1988, pp. 265–92.

_____. Real and Monetary Aspects of the Effects of Exchange Rate Changes. In *Dornbusch, R.*, 1988, *1974*, pp. 42–60.

_____. Real Interest Rates, Home Goods, and Optimal External Borrowing. In *Dornbusch, R.*, 1988, *1983*, pp. 333–46.

_____. Special Exchange Rates for Capital Account Transactions. In *Dornbusch, R.*, 1988, *1986*, pp. 177–210.

_____. Tariffs and Nontraded Goods. In *Dornbusch, R.*, 1988, *1974*, pp. 323–32.

_____. The Theory of Flexible Exchange Rate Regimes and Macroeconomic Policy. In *Dornbusch, R.*, 1988, *1976*, pp. 152–76.

_____. World Economic Issues of Interest to Latin America. In *Feinberg, R. E. and Ffrench-Davis, R.*, *eds.*, 1988, pp. 11–28.

_____ and Cardoso, Eliana A. Dívida brasileira: Réquiem para a política de *Muddling Through.* (With English summary.) *Pesquisa Planejamento Econ.*, August 1988, *18*(2), pp. 211–38.

_____; Fischer, Stanley and Samuelson, Paul A. Comparative Advantage, Trade, and Payments in a Ricardian Model with a Continuum of Goods. In *Dornbusch, R.*, 1988, *1977*, pp. 293–322.

_____ and Frankel, Jeffrey A. The Flexible Exchange Rate System: Experience and Alternatives. In *Borner, S.*, *ed.*, 1988, pp. 151–97.

_____ and Mussa, Michael L. Consumption, Real Balances, and the Hoarding Function. In *Dornbusch, R.*, 1988, *1975*, pp. 371–78.

_____ and Simonsen, Mario Henrique. Inflation Stabilization: The Role of Incomes Policy and of Monetization. In *Dornbusch, R.*, 1988, pp. 439–65.

_____, et al. The Black Market for Dollars in Brazil. In *Dornbusch, R.*, 1988, *1983*, pp. 211–26.

Doroodian, Khosrow. Stabilization Policies in Developing Countries. *Atlantic Econ. J.*, March 1988, *16*(1), pp. 95.

Dorow, Wolfgang; Danesy, Frank C. and Dlugos, Günter. The Analysis of the Employer Employee Relationship from the Perspective of the Business Politics Approach. In *Dlugos, G.; Dorow, W. and Weiermair, K.*, *eds.*, 1988, pp. 107–18.

Dos Santos Ferreira, Rodolphe and Michel, Philippe. Reflections on the Microeconomic Foundations of the Keynesian Aggregate Supply Function. In *Barrère, A.*, *ed.*, 1988, pp. 251–62.

Dosi, Giovanni. Institutions and Markets in a Dynamic World. *Manchester Sch. Econ. Soc. Stud.*, June 1988, *56*(2), pp. 119–46.

_____. The Nature of the Innovative Process. In *Dosi, G.*, *et al.*, *eds.*, 1988, pp. 221–38.

_____. Sources, Procedures, and Microeconomic Effects of Innovation. *J. Econ. Lit.*, September 1988, *26*(3), pp. 1120–71.

_____ and Coricelli, Fabrizio. Coordination and Order in Economic Change and the Interpretative Power of Economic Theory. In *Dosi, G.*, *et al.*, *eds.*, 1988, pp. 124–47.

_____ and Orsenigo, Luigi. Coordination and Transformation: An Overview of Structures, Behaviours and Change in Evolutionary Environments. In *Dosi, G.*, *et al.*, *eds.*, 1988, pp. 13–37.

_____ and Orsenigo, Luigi. Industrial Structure and Technical Change. In *Heertje, A.*, *ed.*, 1988, pp. 14–37.

_____; Orsenigo, Luigi and Silverberg, Gerald. Innovation, Diversity and Diffusion: A Self-organisation Model. *Econ. J.*, December 1988, *98*(393), pp. 1032–54.

_____ and Soete, Luc. Technical Change and International Trade. In *Dosi, G.*, *et al.*, *eds.*, 1988, pp. 401–31.

Doss, R. G.; Dupré, M. T. and Mehran, F. Employment Promotion Schemes and the Statistical Measurement of Unemployment. *Int. Lab. Rev.*, 1988, *127*(1), pp. 35–51.

Dossal, Mariam. Henry Conybeare and the Politics of Centralised Water Supply in Mid-nineteenth Century Bombay. *Indian Econ. Soc. Hist. Rev.*, Jan.–March 1988, *25*(1), pp. 79–96.

Dotsey, Michael. The Demand for Currency in the United States. *J. Money, Credit, Banking*, February 1988, *20*(1), pp. 22–40.

_____ and King, Robert G. Rational Expectations Business Cycle Models: A Survey. *Fed. Res. Bank Richmond Econ. Rev.*, March–April 1988, *74*(2), pp. 3–15.

Doucet, Ed and Outrata, Edvard. Impact of New Processing Techniques on the Mangement and Organization of Statistical Data Processing. *Statist. J.*, August 1988, *5*(2), pp. 201–10.

Dougan, William R. and Kenyon, Daphne A. Pressure Groups and Public Expenditures: The Flypaper Effect Reconsidered. *Econ. Inquiry*, January 1988, *26*(1), pp. 159–70.

Douglas, Jim, Jr.; Santos, Juan E. and Arbogast, Todd. Two-Phase Immiscible Flow in Naturally Fractured Reservoirs. In *Wheeler, M. F.*, *ed.*, 1988, pp. 47–66.

_____ and Yirang, Yuan. Numerical Simulation of Immiscible Flow in Porous Media Based on Combining the Method of Characteristics with Mixed Finite Element Procedures. In *Wheeler, M. F.*, *ed.*, 1988, pp. 119–31.

Douglas, Norman S. Insider Trading: The Case against the "Victimless Crime" Hypothesis. *Financial Rev.*, May 1988, *23*(2), pp. 127–42.

Douglas, R. O. and de Cleene, T. A. Final Report of the Consultative Committee on Full Imputation and International Tax Reform: Statement. *Bull. Int. Fiscal Doc.*, October 1988, *42*(10), pp. 442–47.

Doukas, John and Travlos, Nickolaos G. The Effect of Corporate Multinationalism on Shareholders' Wealth: Evidence from International Acquisitions. *J. Finance*, December 1988, *43*(5), pp. 1161–75.

Doupnik, Timothy and Evans, Thomas G. The Functional Currency Determination: A Strategy to Smooth Income. In *Most, K. S.*, *ed.*, 1988, pp. 171–82.

Douthitt, Robin A. and Fedyk, Joanne M. The

Influence of Children on Family Life Cycle Spending Behavior: Theory and Applications. *J. Cons. Aff.*, Winter 1988, *22*(2), pp. 220–48.

Doutriaux, Jérôme A. Government Procurement and Research Contracts at Start-Up and Success of Canadian High-Tech Entrepreneurial Firms. **In** *Kirchhoff, B. A., et al., eds.*, 1988, pp. 582–94.

Dovidio, John F.; Rockel, Mark L. and Kealy, Mary Jo. Accuracy in Valuation is a Matter of Degree. *Land Econ.*, May 1988, *64*(2), pp. 158–71.

Dow, Alexander C. and Dow, Sheila C. Idle Balances and Keynesian Theory. *Scot. J. Polit. Econ.*, August 1988, *35*(3), pp. 193–207.

Dow, Alistair. Keynes and Public Policy: A Comment. **In** *Hamouda, O. F. and Smithin, J. N., eds., Vol. 1*, 1988, pp. 77–78.

Dow, Gregory K. The Evolution of Organizational Form: Selection, Efficiency, and the New Institutional Economics. *Econ. Anal. Workers' Manage.*, 1988, *22*(3), pp. 139–67.

_____. Information, Production Decisions, and Intra-firm Bargaining. *Int. Econ. Rev.*, February 1988, *29*(1), pp. 57–79.

_____. Non-cooperative Bargaining in the Theory of the Firm: Some Recent Developments. *Rev. Radical Polit. Econ.*, Summer–Fall 1988, *20*(2–3), pp. 171–76.

Dow, J. C. R. Uncertainty and the Financial Process and Its Consequences for the Power of the Central Bank. *Banca Naz. Lavoro Quart. Rev.*, September 1988, (166), pp. 311–25.

Dow, James and da Costa Werlang, Sérgio Ribeiro. The Consistency of Welfare Judgments with a Representative Consumer. *J. Econ. Theory*, April 1988, *44*(2), pp. 269–80.

Dow, Sheila C. Money Supply Endogeneity. *Écon. Appl.*, 1988, *41*(1), pp. 19–39.

_____. Post Keynesian Economics: Conceptual Underpinnings. *Brit. Rev. Econ. Issues*, Autumn 1988, *10*(23), pp. 1–18.

_____. What Happened to Keynes's Economics? **In** *Hamouda, O. F. and Smithin, J. N., eds., Vol. 1*, 1988, pp. 101–10.

_____ **and Chick, Victoria.** A Post-Keynesian Perspective on the Relation between Banking and Regional Development. **In** *Arestis, P., ed.*, 1988, pp. 219–50.

_____ **and Dow, Alexander C.** Idle Balances and Keynesian Theory. *Scot. J. Polit. Econ.*, August 1988, *35*(3), pp. 193–207.

Dowd, Jeffrey and Hosier, Richard H. Household Energy Use in Zimbabwe: An Analysis of Consumption Patterns and Fuel Choice. **In** *Hosier, R. H., ed. (I)*, 1988, pp. 83–109.

Dowd, Kevin. Automatic Stabilizing Mechanisms under Free Banking. *Cato J.*, Winter 1988, *7*(3), pp. 643–59.

_____. Option Clauses and the Stability of a Laisser Faire Monetary System. *J. Finan. Services Res.*, December 1988, *1*(4), pp. 319–33.

Dowen, Richard J. Beta, Non-systematic Risk and Portfolio Selection. *Appl. Econ.*, February 1988, *20*(2), pp. 221–28.

_____ **and Isberg, Steven C.** Reexamination of the Intervalling Effect on the CAPM Using a Residual Return Approach. *Quart. J. Bus. Econ.*, Summer 1988, *27*(3), pp. 114–29.

Dowgun, Kay M.; Northrup, Herbert R. and Greis, Theresa Diss. The Office and Professional Employees International Union: From "Union Company Union" to Independent Representative. *J. Lab. Res.*, Winter 1988, *9*(1), pp. 91–106.

_____; **Northrup, Herbert R. and Greis, Theresa Diss.** The Office of Professional Employees International Union: Part Two—Mission Unclear and Unrealized. *J. Lab. Res.*, Summer 1988, *9*(3), pp. 251–70.

Dowling, J. Malcolm, Jr. and Rana, Pradumna B. The Impact of Foreign Capital on Growth: Evidences from Asian Developing Countries. *Devel. Econ.*, March 1988, *26*(1), pp. 3–11.

Downes, Andrew S. On the Statistical Measurement of Smallness: A Principal Component Measure of Country Size. *Soc. Econ. Stud.*, September 1988, *37*(3), pp. 75–96.

Downey, H. Kirk and Ireland, R. Duane. Strategic Objectives in Policy Research: An Essay on the Dangers of not Acknowledging Purposeful Behavior. **In** *Lamb, R. and Shrivastava, P., eds.*, 1988, pp. 263–75.

Downs, Thomas W. and Tehranian, Hassan. Predicting Stock Price Responses to Tax Policy Changes. *Amer. Econ. Rev.*, December 1988, *78*(5), pp. 1118–30.

Dowrick, Steve and Nguyen, D. T. A Re-assessment of Australian Economic Growth in the Light of the Convergence Hypothesis. *Australian Econ. Pap.*, December 1988, *27*(51), pp. 196–212.

Doyle, Christopher. Different Selling Strategies in Bertrand Oligopoly. *Econ. Letters*, 1988, *28*(4), pp. 387–90.

Doyle, Joanne M. and Baum, Christopher F. Dynamic Adjustment of Firms' Capital Structures in a Varying-Risk Environment. *J. Econ. Dynam. Control*, March 1988, *12*(1), pp. 127–33.

Doz, Catherine and Bourlange, Danielle. Pseudo-maximum de vraisemblance: Expériences de simulations dans le cadre d'un modèle de Poisson. (Pseudo-maximum Likelihood Estimators: Monte-Carlo Experimentation in the Case of a Poisson Model. With English summary.) *Ann. Écon. Statist.*, April–June 1988, (10), pp. 139–76.

Doz, Yves L. Technology Partnerships between Larger and Smaller Firms: Some Critical Issues. **In** *Contractor, F. J. and Lorange, P.*, 1988, pp. 317–38.

_____. Value Creation through Technology Collaboration. *Aussenwirtschaft*, June 1988, *43*(1/2), pp. 175–89.

_____ **and Prahalad, C. K.** Quality of Management: An Emerging Source of Global Competitive Advantage? **In** *Hood, N. and Vahlne, J.-E., eds.*, 1988, pp. 345–69.

Drábek, Zdenek. The East European Response to the Debt Crisis: A Trade Diversion or a Statistical Aberration? *Comp. Econ. Stud.*, Spring 1988, *30*(1), pp. 29–58.

———. The Natural Resource Intensity of Production Technology in Market and Planned Economies: Austria vs Czechoslovakia. *J. Compar. Econ.*, June 1988, *12*(2), pp. 217–27.

Drache, Daniel and Glasbeek, Harry J. The New Fordism in Canada: Capital's Offensive, Labour's Opportunity. *Econ. Lavoro*, July–Sept. 1988, *22*(3), pp. 47–70.

Drago, Robert. Quality Circle Survival: An Exploratory Analysis. *Ind. Relat.*, Fall 1988, 27(3), pp. 336–51.

——— **and Sloan, Judith.** The Australian Labour Market, June 1988. *Australian Bull. Lab.*, June 1988, *14*(3), pp. 455–68.

——— **and Turnbull, Geoffrey K.** The Incentive Effects of Tournaments with Positive Externalities among Workers. *Southern Econ. J.*, July 1988, 55(1), pp. 100–106.

——— **and Turnbull, Geoffrey K.** Individual versus Group Piece Rates under Team Technologies. *J. Japanese Int. Economies*, March 1988, 2(1), pp. 1–10.

Dragun, Andrew K. Externalities, Property Rights, and Power. **In** *Samuels, W. J., ed., Vol. 3*, 1988, *1983*, pp. 324–37.

Dramais, A. Optimization and the Preparation of Economic Policy: Comments. **In** *Driehuis, W.; Fase, M. M. G. and den Hartog, H., eds.*, 1988, pp. 287–89.

Dranove, David. Demand Inducement and the Physician/Patient Relationship. *Econ. Inquiry*, April 1988, *26*(2), pp. 281–98.

———. Pricing by Non-profit Institutions: The Case of Hospital Cost-Shifting. *J. Health Econ.*, March 1988, 7(1), pp. 47–57.

Draper, James A. Canadian Studies in International Adult Education. *Can. J. Devel. Stud.*, 1988, *9*(2), pp. 283–99.

Draper, Norman R. and Sanders, Elizabeth R. Minimum Bias Estimation—Designs and Decisions. **In** *Fedorov, V. and Lauter, H., eds.*, 1988, pp. 13–22.

Drazen, Allan. Self-fulfilling Optimism in a Trade-Friction Model of the Business Cycle. *Amer. Econ. Rev.*, May 1988, 78(2), pp. 369–72.

———. Stabilization Policy in Open Economies: Introductory Remarks. *Europ. Econ. Rev.*, March 1988, *32*(2–3), pp. 663–68.

——— **and Eckstein, Zvi.** On the Organization of Rural Markets and the Process of Economic Development. *Amer. Econ. Rev.*, June 1988, 78(3), pp. 431–43.

——— **and Helpman, Elhanan.** The Effect of Policy Anticipations on Stabilization Programs. *Europ. Econ. Rev.*, March 1988, *32*(2–3), pp. 680–86.

——— **and Helpman, Elhanan.** Future Stabilization Policies and Inflation. **In** *Kohn, M. and Tsiang, S.-C., eds.*, 1988, pp. 166–84.

——— **and Helpman, Elhanan.** Stabilization with Exchange Rate Management under Uncertainty. **In** *Helpman, E.; Razin, A. and Sadka, E., eds.*, 1988, pp. 310–27.

Drechsler, Laszlo. The Regionalization of and other Recent Developments in the United Na-

tions International Comparison Project. **In** *Salazar-Carrillo, J. and Rao, D. S. P., eds.*, 1988, pp. 5–15.

Dreher, William A. Does Portfolio Insurance Ever Make Sense? *J. Portfol. Manage.*, Summer 1988, *14*(4), pp. 25–32.

Drejer, Jens. World Tax Reform: A Progress Report: Denmark. **In** *Pechman, J. A., ed.*, 1988, pp. 79–92.

Drettakis, E. G. and Sargan, John Denis. Missing Data in an Autoregressive Model. **In** *Sargan, J. D., Vol. 2*, 1988, *1974*, pp. 204–25.

· **Drewer, Stephen P.** The Global Construction Industry: Scandinavia. **In** *Strassmann, W. P. and Wells, J., eds.*, 1988, pp. 160–79.

Drexler, K. Eric. The Coming Era of Nanotechnology. **In** *Forester, T., ed.*, 1988, pp. 361–73.

Dreyer, Jacob S. Fiscal Targets, Monetary Goals and Interest Rates. *Bus. Econ.*, January 1988, 23(1), pp. 28–33.

Drèze, Jacques H. and Dehez, Pierre. Competitive Equilibria with Quantity-Taking Producers and Increasing Returns to Scale. *J. Math. Econ.*, 1988, *17*(2–3), pp. 209–30.

——— **and Dehez, Pierre.** Distributive Production Sets and Equilibria with Increasing Returns. *J. Math. Econ.*, 1988, *17*(2–3), pp. 231–48.

——— **and Wyplosz, Charles.** Autonomy through Cooperation. *Europ. Econ. Rev.*, March 1988, *32*(2–3), pp. 353–62.

——— **and Wyplosz, Charles.** Une stratégie de croissance ambidextre pour l'Europe: L'autonomie par la coopération. (A Two-Handed Approach for Europe: Autonomy through Cooperation. With English summary.) *Revue Écon.*, May 1988, *39*(3), pp. 627–40.

———, **et al.** The Two-Handed Growth Strategy for Europe: Autonomy through Flexible Cooperation. *Rech. Écon. Louvain*, 1988, *54*(1), pp. 5–52.

Driehuis, Wim and van den Noord, Paul J. The Effects of Investment Subsidies on Employment. *Econ. Modelling*, January 1988, 5(1), pp. 32–40.

——— **and van den Noord, Paul J.** Modelling the Effects of Investment Subsidies. **In** *Motamen, H., ed.*, 1988, pp. 473–90.

Driessen, Patrick. The Race Factor in Social Security. *Rev. Black Polit. Econ.*, Fall 1988, *17*(2), pp. 89–105.

Driffill, John. Macroeconomic Policy Games with Incomplete Information: A Survey. *Europ. Econ. Rev.*, March 1988, *32*(2–3), pp. 533–41.

Driscoll, Robert E. Technology and Development in the Asia-Pacific Region. **In** *Kozmetsky, G.; Matsumoto, H. and Smilor, R. W., eds.*, 1988, pp. 87–98.

Driskill, Robert and Cantor, Richard M. Open-Economy Macro Policies and the Micro Foundation of Labor Market Arrangements. *J. Int. Econ.*, February 1988, *24*(1–2), pp. 159–72.

———; **Frenkel, Jacob A. and Bhandari, Jagdeep S.** Capital Mobility and Exchange Rate Over shooting: Reply. *Europ. Econ. Rev.*, January 1988, *32*(1), pp. 203–06.

Driver, Ciaran. The Employment Effects of Expanding Service Industries. In *Barker, T. and Dunne, P., eds.*, 1988, pp. 83–100.

_____ **and Arestis, Philip.** The Endogeneity of the UK Money Supply: A Political Economy Perspective. *Écon. Soc.*, September 1988, *22*(9), pp. 121–38.

_____ **and Arestis, Philip.** The Macrodynamics of the U.S. and U.K. Economies through Two Post-Keynesian Models. In *Arestis, P., ed.*, 1988, pp. 11–40.

_____ **; Kilpatrick, Andrew and Naisbitt, Barry.** The Sensitivity of Estimated Employment Effects in Input–Output Studies. *Econ. Modelling*, April 1988, *5*(2), pp. 145–50.

Driver, H. C.; Baker, Timothy G. and Turvey, Calum Greig. Systematic and Nonsystematic Risk in Farm Portfolio Selection. *Amer. J. Agr. Econ.*, November 1988, *70*(4), pp. 831–36.

Drobny, Andres and Gausden, Robert. Granger-Causality, Real Factor Prices and Employment: A Re-appraisal with UK Data. *Europ. Econ. Rev.*, July 1988, *32*(6), pp. 1261–83.

Druckman, Daniel; Broome, Benjamin J. and Korper, Susan H. Value Differences and Conflict Resolution: Facilitation or Delinking? *J. Conflict Resolution*, September 1988, *32*(3), pp. 489–510.

Drudy, P. J. and Thomas, Ian C. Growth Town Employment in Mid-Wales Re-visited: A Reply. *Urban Stud.*, December 1988, *25*(6), pp. 532–37.

Drugge, Sten E. Factor Prices, Non-neutral Technical Change and Regional Variations in Unemployment Rates. *Ann. Reg. Sci.*, July 1988, *22*(2), pp. 26–36.

Drukker, J. W.; Slot, Brigitte and Brinkman, Henk Jan. Height and Income: A New Method for the Estimation of Historical National Income Series. *Exploration Econ. Hist.*, July 1988, *25*(3), pp. 227–64.

Drysdale, Peter. Japan as a Pacific and World Economic Power. *Australian Econ. Pap.*, December 1988, *27*(51), pp. 159–72.

_____. South Pacific Trade and Development Assistance. In *Kozmetsky, G.; Matsumoto, H. and Smilor, R. W., eds.*, 1988, pp. 73–80.

Du Bois, W. E. B. The Negro Criminal. In *Simms, M. C. and Myers, S. L., Jr., eds.*, 1988, pp. 17–31.

Du, Rensheng. Rural Employment in China: The Choices. *Int. Lab. Rev.*, 1988, *127*(3), pp. 371–80.

Dua, Pami. Multiperiod Forecasts of Interest Rates. *J. Bus. Econ. Statist.*, July 1988, *6*(3), pp. 381–84.

_____. A Policy Reaction Function for Nominal Interest Rates in the UK: 1972Q3–1982Q4. *Bull. Econ. Res.*, January 1988, *40*(1), pp. 57–71.

_____ **and Smyth, David J.** Public Perceptions of Macroeconomic Policy: An Econometric Analysis of the Reagan Presidency. *Rev. Econ. Statist.*, May 1988, *70*(2), pp. 357–61.

Dubacher, René; Zimmermann, Heinz and Cordero, Ricardo. Zur Entwicklung des neuen Swiss Market Index (SMI) als Grundlage für schweizerische Indexkontrakte: Eine Evaluation potentieller Aktienindices. (On the Development of the Swiss Market Index (SMI) for Index Contracts: An Evaluation of Potential Indices. With English summary.) *Schweiz. Z. Volkswirtsch. Statist.*, December 1988, *124*(4), pp. 575–600.

Dubarle, P. Emerging Business in Space: Recent Trends. In *Egan, J. J., et al.*, 1988, pp. 85–108.

Dubé-Rioux, Laurette; Schmitt, Bernd H. and Leclerc, France. Sex Typing and Consumer Behavior: A Test of Gender Schema Theory. *J. Cons. Res.*, June 1988, *15*(1), pp. 122–28.

Dubey, Pradeep and Neyman, Abraham. Payoffs in Nonatomic Economies: An Axiomatic Approach. In *[Shapley, L. S.]*, 1988, *1984*, pp. 207–16.

_____ **and Shubik, Martin.** A Note on an Optimal Garnishing Rule. *Econ. Letters*, 1988, *27*(1), pp. 5–6.

Dubin, Jeffrey A. and Henson, Steven E. An Engineering/Econometric Analysis of Seasonal Energy Demand and Conservation in the Pacific Northwest. *J. Bus. Econ. Statist.*, January 1988, *6*(1), pp. 121–34.

_____ **and Henson, Steven E.** The Distributional Effects of the Federal Energy Tax Act. *Resources & Energy*, September 1988, *10*(3), pp. 191–212.

_____ **and Navarro, Peter.** How Markets for Impure Public Goods Organize: The Case of Household Refuse Collection. *J. Law, Econ., Organ.*, Fall 1988, *4*(2), pp. 217–41.

_____ **and Wilde, Louis L.** An Empirical Analysis of Federal Income Tax Auditing and Compliance. *Nat. Tax J.*, March 1988, *41*(1), pp. 61–74.

Dubin, Robin A. Estimation of Regression Coefficients in the Presence of Spatially Autocorrelated Error Terms. *Rev. Econ. Statist.*, August 1988, *70*(3), pp. 466–74.

Dubini, Paola. Motivational and Environmental Influences on Business Start Ups: Some Hints for Public Policies. In *Kirchhoff, B. A., et al., eds.*, 1988, pp. 31–45.

_____ **and MacMillan, Ian C.** Entrepreneurial Prerequisites in Venture Capital Backed Projects. In *Kirchhoff, B. A., et al., eds.*, 1988, pp. 46–58.

Dubinsky, Alan J., et al. Impact of Sales Supervisor Leadership Behavior on Insurance Agent Attitudes and Performance. *J. Risk Ins.*, March 1988, *55*(1), pp. 132–44.

Dubnoff, Steve; van der Sar, Nico L. and van Praag, Bernard M. S. Evaluation Questions and Income Utility. In *Munier, B. R., ed.*, 1988, pp. 77–96.

_____ **; van der Sar, Nico L. and van Praag, Bernard M. S.** On the Measurement and Explanation of Standards with Respect to Income, Age and Education. *J. Econ. Psych.*, December 1988, *9*(4), pp. 481–98.

Dubœuf, Françoise. Le processus de formation économique du taux de la rente et du taux de salaire chez Smith. (The Economic Formation of the Rent and the Wage Rates in A. Smith. With English summary.) *Écon. Soc.*, October 1988, *22*(10), pp. 27–51.

Dubois, Didier. Possibility Theory: Searching for Normative Foundations. In *Munier, B. R., ed.*, 1988, pp. 601–14.

_____ **and Prade, Henri.** Decision Evaluation Methods under Uncertainty and Imprecision. In *Kacprzyk, J. and Fedrizzi, M., eds.*, 1988, pp. 48–65.

Dubois, Jean-Luc and Grootaert, Christiaan. Tenancy Choice and the Demand for Rental Housing in the Cities of the Ivory Coast. *J. Urban Econ.*, July 1988, *24*(1), pp. 44–63.

Dubois, Robert W. and Brook, Robert H. Assessing Clinical Decision Making: Is the Ideal System Feasible? *Inquiry*, Spring 1988, *25*(1), pp. 59–64.

Duchesneau, Donald A. and Gartner, William B. A Profile of New Venture Success and Failure in an Emerging Industry. In *Kirchhoff, B. A., et al., eds.*, 1988, pp. 372–86.

Duchin, Faye. Analysing Structural Change in the Economy. In *Ciaschini, M., ed.*, 1988, pp. 113–28.

_____. Role of Services in the U.S. Economy. In *Guile, B. R. and Quinn, J. B., eds. (II)*, 1988, pp. 76–98.

Duck, Nigel W. Money, Output and Prices: An Empirical Study Using Long-term Cross Country Data. *Europ. Econ. Rev.*, October 1988, *32*(8), pp. 1603–19.

Duckett, Stephen J. Health Insurance Forum. In *Butler, J. R. G. and Doessel, D. P., eds.*, 1988, pp. 238–41.

_____ **and Broadhead, Peter.** Death to the Oxymoron: The Introduction of 'Rational Hospital Budgetting' in Victoria, or Perhaps More Accurately, an Account of Progress towards That Goal. In *Butler, J. R. G. and Doessel, D. P., eds.*, 1988, pp. 22–33.

Duczkowska-Malysz, K. and Duczkowska-Piasecka, M. Information and Communication in Polish Agriculture: The Main Problems and Features. In *Schiefer, G., ed.*, 1988, pp. 231–36.

Duczkowska-Piasecka, M. and Duczkowska-Malysz, K. Information and Communication in Polish Agriculture: The Main Problems and Features. In *Schiefer, G., ed.*, 1988, pp. 231–36.

Dudek, Frantisek. The Crisis of the Beet Sugar Industry in Czechoslovakia. In *Albert, B. and Graves, A., eds.*, 1988, pp. 36–46.

Dudler, Hermann-Josef. Innovations financiéres risques globaux en matière de surveillance des banques et rôle de la banque centrale. (With English summary.) *Revue Econ. Polit.*, Sept.–Oct. 1988, *98*(5), pp. 615–37.

_____. Money Supply versus Exchange-Rate Targeting: An Asymmetry between the United States and Other Industrial Economies: Comments. In *Giersch, H., ed.*, 1988, pp. 265–68.

Dudley, Leonard and Montmarquette, Claude. A Disequilibrium Model of Public Spending. *Econ. Letters*, 1988, *26*(2), pp. 165–68.

Dudley, Norman J. A Single Decision-Maker Approach to Irrigation Reservoir and Farm Mangement Decision Making. *Water Resources Res.*, May 1988, *24*(5), pp. 633–40.

_____. Volume Sharing of Reservoir Water. *Water Resources Res.*, May 1988, *24*(5), pp. 641–48.

_____ **and Musgrave, Warren F.** Capacity Sharing of Water Reservoirs. *Water Resources Res.*, May 1988, *24*(5), pp. 649–58.

Due, John F. and Meyer, Carrie. Value Added Tax: Dominican Republic. *Bull. Int. Fiscal Doc.*, January 1988, *42*(1), pp. 13–16.

Duffey, Joseph D. Back to the Future: Collaboration and Competition in a New World. In *Furino, A., ed.*, 1988, pp. 75–82.

_____. U.S. Competitiveness: Looking Back and Looking Ahead. In *Starr, M. K., ed.*, 1988, pp. 72–94.

Duffie, Darrell. An Extension of the Black–Scholes Model of Security Valuation. *J. Econ. Theory*, October 1988, *46*(1), pp. 194–204.

Duffy, Christopher T. and O'Hagan, John W. The Arts and Section 32 of the 1984 Finance Act [The Performing Arts and the Public Purse: An Economic Analysis]. *Econ. Soc. Rev.*, January 1988, *19*(2), pp. 147–51.

Duffy, Neal E. Returns-to-Scale Behavior and Manufacturing Agglomeration Economies in U.S. Urban Areas. *Rev. Reg. Stud.*, Fall 1988, *18*(3), pp. 47–54.

Duffy, Patricia A.; Hardy, William E., Jr. and Disney, W. Terry. A Markov Chain Analysis of Pork Farm Size Distributions in the South. *Southern J. Agr. Econ.*, December 1988, *20*(2), pp. 57–64.

_____ **and Knutson, Ronald D.** Reflections on Agricultural Policies and Their Consequences for the South. In *Beaulieu, L. J., ed.*, 1988, pp. 233–48.

Duffy, Sharyn and Paul, Karen. Corporate Responses to the Call for South African Withdrawal. In *Preston, L. E., ed.*, 1988, pp. 211–40.

Dufour, Jean-Marie. Estimators of the Disturbance Variance in Econometric Models: Small-sample Bias and the Existence of Moments. *J. Econometrics*, February 1988, *37*(2), pp. 277–92.

_____. Estimators of the Disturbance Variance in Econometric Models: Small Sample Bias and the Movements: Erratum. *J. Econometrics*, November 1988, *39*(3), pp. 397.

Dugger, William M. An Institutional Analysis of Corporate Power. *J. Econ. Issues*, March 1988, *22*(1), pp. 79–111.

_____. An Institutionalist Theory of Economic Planning. In *Tool, M. R., ed., Vol. 2*, 1988, *1987*, pp. 231–57.

_____. Corporate Power and Economic Performance. In *Peterson, W. C., ed.*, 1988, pp. 83–108.

_____. Methodological Differences Between Institutional and Neoclassical Economics. In *Samuels, W. J., ed., Vol. 2*, 1988, 1979, pp. 84–94.

――――. Property Rights, Law, and John R. Commons. In *Samuels, W. J., ed., Vol. 2*, 1988, 1967, pp. 209–21.

――――. Radical Institutionalism: Basic Concepts. *Rev. Radical Polit. Econ.*, Spring 1988, *20*(1), pp. 1–20.

――――. A Research Agenda for Institutional Economics. *J. Econ. Issues*, December 1988, *22*(4), pp. 983–1002.

Duguay, Pierre and Rabeau, Yves. A Simulation Model of Macroeconomic Effects of Deficit. *J. Macroecon.*, Fall 1988, *10*(4), pp. 539–64.

Duguid, Andrew. Self-Regulation at Lloyd's. In *Goodhart, C., et al.*, 1988, pp. 55–63.

Duharcourt, Pierre. "Théories" et "concept" de la régulation. (Regulation as a Theory and as a Concept. With English summary.) *Écon. Soc.*, May 1988, *22*(5), pp. 135–61.

Duignan, Peter and Gann, L. H. Foreign Policy and National Security: Hope for Africa. In *Anderson, A. and Bark, D. L., eds.*, 1988, pp. 139–51.

Duijkers, Thomas J.; van den Berg, G. M. and Duijsens, I. J., et al. PRINCE: An Expert System for Nonlinear Principal Components Analysis. In *Edwards, D. and Raun, N. E., eds.*, 1988, pp. 149–53.

Duijsens, I. J., et al.; Duijkers, Thomas J. and van den Berg, G. M. PRINCE: An Expert System for Nonlinear Principal Components Analysis. In *Edwards, D. and Raun, N. E., eds.*, 1988, pp. 149–53.

Duisenberg, Willem F. Exchange Rate Policy in a European and Global Perspective. In *[Witteveen, H. J.]*, 1988, pp. 17–31.

Dukakis, Michael S. An Economic Development Program for Massachusetts. In *Lampe, D., ed.*, 1988, pp. 115–37.

Dukes, David V. Reflections on the Role of JFMIP. *Public Budg. Finance*, Winter 1988, *8*(4), pp. 35–44.

Dullaart, M. H. J. Wieser's Theory of Money. *J. Econ. Stud.*, 1988, *15*(3–4), pp. 123–35.

Duloy, John H. and O'Mara, Gerald T. Modeling Efficient Conjunctive Use of Water in the Indus Basin. In *O'Mara, G. T., ed.*, 1988, pp. 128–38.

DuMars, Charles T. and del Rio M., Salvador Beltran. A Survey of the Air and Water Quality Laws of Mexico. *Natural Res. J.*, Fall 1988, *28*(4), pp. 787–813.

Dumas, Bernard. Price Rigidity, International Mobility of Financial Capital and Exchange Rate Volatility: Comments. *Europ. Econ. Rev.*, June 1988, *32*(5), pp. 1165.

Dumas, Mark W. and Henneberger, J. Edwin. Productivity Trends in the Cotton and Synthetic Broad Woven Fabrics Industry. *Mon. Lab. Rev.*, April 1988, *111*(4), pp. 34–38.

Dumas, Yvan and Desrosiers, Jacques. The Shortest Path Problem for the Construction of Vehicle Routes with Pick-Up, Delivery and

Time Constraints. In *Eiselt, H. A. and Pederzoli, G., eds.*, 1988, pp. 144–57.

――――; **Soumis, François and Desrosiers, Jacques.** The Multiple Vehicle DIAL-A-RIDE Problem. In *Daduna, J. R. and Wren, A., eds.*, 1988, pp. 15–27.

Duménil, Gérard and Lévy, Dominique. Équilibrages par les prix et par les quantités dans le cadre d'une micro-économie d'inspiration classique. (With English summary.) *Revue Écon. Polit.*, Jan.–Feb. 1988, *98*(1), pp. 127–49.

Dumett, Raymond E. Sources for Mining Company History in Africa: The History and Records of the Ashanti Goldfields Corporation (Ghana), Ltd. *Bus. Hist. Rev.*, Autumn 1988, *62*(3), pp. 502–15.

Dumitru, V. and Luban, Florica. A Note on the Cardinality Mathematical Programming. *Econ. Computat. Cybern. Stud. Res.*, 1988, *23*(4), pp. 67–72.

Dumke, Rolf H. Income Inequality and Industrialization in Germany, 1850–1913: Images, Trends and Causes of Historical Inequality. In *Uselding, P. J., ed.*, 1988, pp. 1–47.

Dumsday, R. G. and Edwards, Geoff W. Supply and Demand in Agricultural Economics Education. *Rev. Marketing Agr. Econ.*, August 1988, *56*(2), pp. 211–12.

Dunaev, A. The Soviet Space Technology: Trends of Development and Opportunities of Using It on a Commercial Basis. In *Egan, J. J., et al.*, 1988, pp. 473–77.

Duncan, A. and Hassan, J. A. Energy Price Convergence in the European Community, 1960–82. *Appl. Econ.*, January 1988, *20*(1), pp. 73–79.

Duncan, Greg J. and Burkhauser, Richard V. Life Events, Public Policy, and the Economic Vulnerability of Children and the Elderly. In *Palmer, J. L.; Smeeding, T. and Torrey, B. B., eds.*, 1988, pp. 55–88.

―――― **and Hoffman, Saul D.** A Comparison of Choice-Based Multinomial and Nested Logit Models: The Family Structure and Welfare Use Decisions of Divorced or Separated Women. *J. Human Res.*, Fall 1988, *23*(4), pp. 550–62.

―――― **and Hoffman, Saul D.** Multinomial and Conditional Logit Discrete-Choice Models in Demography. *Demography*, August 1988, *25*(3), pp. 415–27.

―――― **and Hoffman, Saul D.** What *Are* the Economic Consequences of Divorce? *Demography*, November 1988, *25*(4), pp. 641–45.

―――― **and Mathiowetz, Nancy A.** Out of Work, Out of Mind: Response Errors in Retrospective Reports of Unemployment. *J. Bus. Econ. Statist.*, April 1988, *6*(2), pp. 221–29.

Duncan, Harley T. State Legislators and Tax Administrators: Can We Talk? In *Gold, S. D., ed.*, 1988, pp. 83–99.

Duncan, Joseph W. Statistics Corner. *Bus. Econ.*, April 1988, *23*(2), pp. 52–54.

Duncan, Peter J. S. The Party and Russian Nationalism in the USSR: From Brezhnev to Gorbachev. In *Potichnyj, P. J., ed.*, 1988, pp. 229–44.

Duncombe, William and Bahl, Roy. State and Local Government Finances: Was There a Structural Break in the Reagan Years? *Growth Change*, Fall 1988, *19*(4), pp. 30–48.

Dungan, D. Peter and Wilson, Thomas A. Modelling Anticipated and Temporary Fiscal Policy Shocks in a Macro-econometric Model of Canada. *Can. J. Econ.*, February 1988, *21*(1), pp. 41–60.

Dunkelberg, William C.; Staten, Michael and Umbeck, John. Market Share/Market Power Revisited: A New Test for an Old Theory. *J. Health Econ.*, March 1988, *7*(1), pp. 73–83.

_____; **Woo, Carolyn Y. and Cooper, Arnold C.** Entrepreneurial Typologies: Definitions and Implications. In *Kirchhoff, B. A., et al., eds.*, 1988, pp. 165–76.

_____; **Woo, Carolyn Y. and Cooper, Arnold C.** Survival and Failure: A Longitudinal Study. In *Kirchhoff, B. A., et al., eds.*, 1988, pp. 225–37.

Dunlop, David W. and Over, A. Mead. Determinants of Drug Imports to Poor Countries: Preliminary Findings and Implications for Financing Primary Health Care. In *Sirageldin, I. and Sorkin, A., eds.*, 1988, pp. 99–125.

Dunlop, John B. and Rowen, Henry S. The Soviet Union: The Crisis of the System and Prospects for Change. In *Anderson, A. and Bark, D. L., eds.*, 1988, pp. 45–55.

Dunlop, John T. Global Interdependence and International Migration: Commentary. In *Cassing, J. H. and Husted, S. L., eds.*, 1988, pp. 184–87.

_____. Have the 1980's Changed U.S. Industrial Relations? *Mon. Lab. Rev.*, May 1988, *111*(5), pp. 29–34.

_____. Labor Markets and Wage Determination: Then and Now. In *Kaufman, B. E., ed.*, 1988, pp. 47–87.

Dunlop, S.; Young, Stephen and Hood, Neil. Global Strategies, Multinational Subsidiary Roles and Economic Impact in Scotland. *Reg. Stud.*, December 1988, *22*(6), pp. 487–97.

Dunn, James E.; Fryar, Edward O., Jr. and Arnold, J. T. Bayesian Evaluation of a Specific Hypothesis. *Amer. J. Agr. Econ.*, August 1988, *70*(3), pp. 685–92.

Dunn, James W. and Shortle, James S. Agricultural Nonpoint Source Pollution Control in Theory and Practice. *Marine Resource Econ.*, 1988, *5*(3), pp. 259–70.

Dunn, John. Trust and Political Agency. In *Gambetta, D., ed.*, 1988, pp. 73–93.

Dunn, Richard and Longley, Paul A. Graphical Assessment of Housing Market Models. *Urban Stud.*, February 1988, *25*(1), pp. 21–33.

_____ **and Wrigley, Neil.** Models of Store Choice and Market Analysis. In *Wrigley, N., ed.*, 1988, pp. 251–71.

Dunn, Stephen; Richardson, Ray and Dewe, Philip. Employee Share Option Schemes, Why Workers Are Attracted to Them. *Brit. J. Ind. Relat.*, March 1988, *26*(1), pp. 1–20.

Dunn, W. Marcus and Hall, Thomas W. Graduate Education and CPA Examination Performance: Some Empirical Evidence. In *Schwartz, B. N., ed.*, 1988, pp. 191–204.

Dunne, Paul. The Structure of Service Employment in the UK. In *Barker, T. and Dunne, P., eds.*, 1988, pp. 101–29.

Dunne, Timothy; Roberts, Mark J. and Samuelson, Larry. Patterns of Firm Entry and Exit in U.S. Manufacturing Industries. *Rand J. Econ.*, Winter 1988, *19*(4), pp. 495–515.

Dunning, John H. International Business, the Recession and Economic Restructuring. In *Hood, N. and Vahlne, J.-E., eds.*, 1988, pp. 84–103.

_____. Transnational Corporations in a Changing World Environment: Are New Theoretical Explanations Required? In *Teng, W. and Wang, N. T., eds.*, 1988, pp. 3–26.

_____ **and Robson, Peter.** Multinational Corporate Integration and Regional Economic Integration. In *Dunning, J. and Robson, P., eds.*, 1988, pp. 1–23.

Dunstan, Roger H. and Schmidt, Ronald H. Structural Changes in Residential Energy Demand. *Energy Econ.*, July 1988, *10*(3), pp. 206–12.

Dupin, Catherine. The Video Market in France: Economics of a New Media. *J. Cult. Econ.*, June 1988, *12*(1), pp. 87–96.

DuPlessis, Robert S. Urban History, Urbanization, and Economic History: Review Article. *J. Econ. Hist.*, March 1988, *48*(1), pp. 150–54.

Dupré, M. T.; Mehran, F. and Doss, R. G. Employment Promotion Schemes and the Statistical Measurement of Unemployment. *Int. Lab. Rev.*, 1988, *127*(1), pp. 35–51.

Dupré, Ruth. Un siècle de finances publiques québécoises: 1867–1969. *L'Actual. Econ.*, December 1988, *64*(4), pp. 559–83.

Duraisamy, P. An Econometric Analysis of Fertility, Child Schooling and Labour Force Participation of Women in Rural Indian Households. *J. Quant. Econ.*, July 1988, *4*(2), pp. 293–316.

Durand, Martine; Stiehler, Ulrich and Coe, David T. The Disinflation of the 1980s. *OECD Econ. Stud.*, Autumn 1988, (11), pp. 89–121.

Durasoff, Douglas. Conflicts between Economic Decentralization and Political Control in the Domestic Reform of Soviet and Post-Soviet Systems. *Soc. Sci. Quart.*, June 1988, *69*(2), pp. 381–98.

Durbin, Elizabeth. Keynes, the British Labour Party and the Economics of Democratic Socialism. In *Hamouda, O. F. and Smithin, J. N., eds., Vol. 1*, 1988, pp. 29–42.

Durbin, J. Is a Philosophical Consensus for Statistics Attainable? *J. Econometrics*, January 1988, *37*(1), pp. 51–61.

_____. Reply to Stephen E. Fienberg's Discussion. *J. Econometrics*, January 1988, *37*(1), pp. 65.

Durcan, James W. and Kirkbride, Paul S. Power and the Bargaining Process: A Comment on Leap and Grigsby. *Ind. Lab. Relat. Rev.*, July 1988, *41*(4), pp. 618–21.

Durden, Garey and Shogren, Jason F. Valuing Non-market Recreation Goods: An Evaluative Survey of the Literature on the Travel Cost and Contingent Valuation Methods. *Rev. Reg. Stud.*, Fall 1988, *18*(3), pp. 1–15.

van Duren, Erna and Martin, Larry J. Government Assistance to Beef Producers in Canada: Implications for International and Interprovincial Trade. *Can. J. Agr. Econ.*, Part 1, December 1988, *36*(4), pp. 689–701.

Durgin, Frank A. The Soviet 1969 Standard Methodology for Investment Allocation versus 'Universally Correct' Methods. In *[Nove, A.]*, 1988, pp. 61–81.

Durham, Catherine A.; Colby, Bonnie G. and Longstreth, Molly. The Impact of State Tax Credits and Energy Prices on Adoption of Solar Enegy Systems. *Land Econ.*, November 1988, *64*(4), pp. 347–55.

Durie, Alastair and Solar, Peter. The Scottish and Irish Linen Industries Compared, 1780–1860. In *Mitchison, R. and Roebuck, P., eds.*, 1988, pp. 211–21.

Durkin, Thomas A. Financial Services Regulation (Not Deregulation) Rules. In *Maynes, E. S. and ACCI Research Committee, eds.*, 1988, pp. 446–51.

Durlauf, Steven N. and Phillips, Peter C. B. Trends versus Random Walks in Time Series Analysis. *Econometrica*, November 1988, *56*(6), pp. 1333–54.

Durojaiye, Bamidele O. and Ikpi, Anthony E. The Monetary Value of Recreational Facilities in a Developing Economy: A Case Study of Three Centers in Nigeria. *Natural Res. J.*, Spring 1988, *28*(2), pp. 315–28.

Durston, John. Rural Social Policy in a Strategy of Sustained Development. *CEPAL Rev.*, December 1988, (36), pp. 83–99.

Dussault, Louis and Lorrain, Jean. Relation between Psychological Characteristics, Administrative Behaviors and Success of Founder Entrepreneurs at the Start-Up Stage. In *Kirchhoff, B. A., et al., eds.*, 1988, pp. 150–64.

Dutkowsky, Donald H. and Foote, William G. The Demand for Money: A Rational Expectations Approach. *Rev. Econ. Statist.*, February 1988, *70*(1), pp. 83–92.

_____ and Foote, William G. Forecasting Discount Window Borrowing. *Int. J. Forecasting*, 1988, *4*(4), pp. 593–603.

Dutt, Amitava Krishna. Convergence and Equilibrium in Two Sector Models of Growth, Distribution and Prices. *J. Econ. (Z. Nationalökon.)*, 1988, *48*(2), pp. 135–58.

_____. Inelastic Demand for Southern Goods, International Demonstration Effects, and Uneven Development. *J. Devel. Econ.*, July 1988, *29*(1), pp. 111–22.

_____. Monopoly Power and Uneven Development: Baran Revisited. *J. Devel. Stud.*, January 1988, *24*(2), pp. 161–76.

Dutta, Bhaskar. Covering Sets and a New Condorcet Choice Correspondence. *J. Econ. Theory*, February 1988, *44*(1), pp. 63–80.

Dutta, Jayasri. The Wage–Goods Constraint on a Developing Economy: Theory and Evidence. *J. Devel. Econ.*, May 1988, *28*(3), pp. 341–63.

Dutter, Rudolf. BLINWDR: An APL-Function Library for Interactively Solving the Problem of Robust and Bounded Influence Regression. In *Edwards, D. and Raun, N. E., eds.*, 1988, pp. 219–24.

Dutton, C. Gilmore, et al. Principles of a High-Quality State Revenue System. In *Gold, S. D., ed.*, 1988, pp. 47–56.

Dutton, Jane E. Perspectives on Strategic Issue Processing: Insights from a Case Study. In *Lamb, R. and Shrivastava, P., eds.*, 1988, pp. 223–44.

Dutton, John and Grennes, Thomas. The Role of Exchange Rates in Trade Models. In *Carter, C. A. and Gardiner, W. H., eds.*, 1988, pp. 87–135.

Dutton, Michael. Basic Facts on the Household Registration System: Editor's Introduction. *Chinese Econ. Stud.*, Fall 1988, *22*(1), pp. 3–21.

Duus, Peter. The Cambridge History of Japan: Volume 6: The Twentieth Century: Introduction. In *Duus, P., ed.*, 1988, pp. 1–52.

_____ and Scheiner, Irwin. The Cambridge History of Japan: Volume 6: The Twentieth Century: Socialism, Liberalism, and Marxism, 1901–1931. In *Duus, P., ed.*, 1988, pp. 654–710.

Duval, Robert. TM or Not TM? A Comment on "International Peace Project in the Middle East." *J. Conflict Resolution*, December 1988, *32*(4), pp. 813–17.

Dvořák, Jiří. Acceleration Strategy of Socio-economic Development and Improvement of the Economic Mechanism. *Czech. Econ. Pap.*, 1988, (25), pp. 7–20.

Dworkin, Anthony Gary and LeCompte, Margaret D. Educational Programs: Indirect Linkages and Unfulfilled Expectations. In *Rodgers, H. R., Jr., ed.*, 1988, pp. 135–67.

Dworkin, James B., et al. Workers' Preferences in Concession Bargaining. *Ind. Relat.*, Winter 1988, *27*(1), pp. 7–20.

Dwyer, Gerald P., Jr. and Hafer, R. W. Are National Stock Markets Linked? *Fed. Res. Bank St. Louis Rev.*, Nov.–Dec. 1988, *70*(6), pp. 3–14.

_____ and Hafer, R. W. Is Money Irrelevant? *Fed. Res. Bank St. Louis Rev.*, May–June 1988, *70*(3), pp. 3–17.

Dybvig, Philip H. Distributional Analysis of Portfolio Choice. *J. Bus.*, July 1988, *61*(3), pp. 369–93.

Dye, Kenneth M. International Harmonization of Governmental Accounting and Auditing Standards: Current Developments. In *Chan, J. L. and Jones, R. H., eds.*, 1988, pp. 11–26.

Dye, Richard F. and Baade, Robert A. An Analysis of the Economic Rationale for Public Subsidization of Sports Stadiums. *Ann. Reg. Sci.*, July 1988, *22*(2), pp. 37–47.

Dye, Ronald A. Earnings Management in an

Overlapping Generations Model. *J. Acc. Res.*, Autumn 1988, *26*(2), pp. 195–235.

Dyer, Alan W. Economic Theory as an Art Form. *J. Econ. Issues*, March 1988, *22*(1), pp. 157–66.

_____. Schumpeter as an Economic Radical: An Economic Sociology Assessed. *Hist. Polit. Econ.*, Spring 1988, *20*(1), pp. 27–41.

_____. Technology as Merchandise and as Gift: Lessons from Private American Aid to the Contras. *J. Econ. Issues*, June 1988, *22*(2), pp. 371–79.

Dyer, Dave. Can Dairy Products Compete? *Can. J. Agr. Econ.*, Part 1, December 1988, *36*(4), pp. 601–11.

Dyer, Douglas and Kagel, John H. Learning in Common Value Auctions. In *Tietz, R.; Albers, W. and Selten, R.*, eds., 1988, pp. 184–97.

Dyk, Timothy B. Full First Amendment Freedom for Broadcasters: The Industry as Eliza on the Ice and Congress as the Friendly Overseer. *Yale J. Regul.*, Summer 1988, *5*(2), pp. 299–329.

Dyker, David A. Restructuring and "Radical Reform": The Articulation of Investment Demand. In *Linz, S. J. and Moskoff, W.*, eds., 1988, pp. 88–109.

Dyl, Edward A. Corporate Control and Management Compensation: Evidence on the Agency Problem. *Managerial Dec. Econ.*, March 1988, *9*(1), pp. 21–25.

_____ **and Maberly, Edwin D.** The Anomaly That Isn't There: A Comment on Friday the Thirteenth. *J. Finance*, December 1988, *43*(5), pp. 1285–86.

Dymond, W. R. The Role of Manpower Policy in the Swedish Model: Comment. In *Kregel, J. A.; Matzner, E. and Roncaglia, A.*, eds., 1988, pp. 162–68.

Dymski, Gary A. A Keynesian Theory of Bank Behavior. *J. Post Keynesian Econ.*, Summer 1988, *10*(4), pp. 499–526.

_____ **and Elliott, John E.** Roemer versus Marx: Alternative Perspectives on Exploitation. *Rev. Radical Polit. Econ.*, Summer–Fall 1988, *20*(2–3), pp. 25–33.

Dymsza, William A. Successes and Failures of Joint Ventures in Developing Countries: Lessons from Experience. In *Contractor, F. J. and Lorange, P.*, 1988, pp. 403–24.

Dyster, Barrie. Public Employment and Assignment to Private Masters, 1788–1821. In *Nicholas, S.*, ed., 1988, pp. 127–51.

Eagan, Vince. The Optimal Depletion of a Theory of Exhaustible Resources: Reply. *J. Post Keynesian Econ.*, Summer 1988, *10*(4), pp. 651–52.

Eagar, Thomas W. The Real Challenge in Materials Engineering. In *Forester, T.*, ed., 1988, *1987*, pp. 241–53.

Eagleburger, Lawrence S. High Technology and American Foreign Policy. In *[Nutter, G. W.]*, 1988, pp. 195–208.

Eakin, Brian Kelly and Kniesner, Thomas J. Estimating a Non-minimum Cost Function for

Hospitals. *Southern Econ. J.*, January 1988, *54*(3), pp. 583–97.

Eales, James S. and Unnevehr, Laurian J. Demand for Beef and Chicken Products: Separability and Structural Change. *Amer. J. Agr. Econ.*, August 1988, *70*(3), pp. 521–32.

Eames, Elizabeth A. Why the Women Went to War: Women and Wealth in Ondo Town, Southwestern Nigeria. In *Clark, G.*, ed., 1988, pp. 81–97.

Earl, Peter E. A Behavioural Analysis of Demand Elasticities. In *Earl, P. E.*, ed., Vol. 2, 1988, *1986*, pp. 190–207.

_____. Behavioural Economics: Volume I: Introduction. In *Earl, P. E.*, ed., Vol. 1, 1988, pp. 1–16.

_____. Behavioural Economics: Volume II: Introduction. In *Earl, P. E.*, ed., Vol. 2, 1988, pp. 1–16.

_____. On Being a Psychological Economist and Winning the Games Economists Play. In *Earl, P. E.*, ed., 1988, pp. 227–42.

_____. Psychological Economics: Introduction. In *Earl, P. E.*, ed., 1988, pp. 1–10.

_____ **and Kay, Neil M.** How Economics Can Accept Shackle's Critique of Economic Doctrines without Arguing Themselves Out of Their Jobs. In *Earl, P. E.*, ed., Vol. 1, 1988, *1985*, pp. 59–73.

Easley, David and Kiefer, Nicholas M. Controlling a Stochastic Process with Unknown Parameters. *Econometrica*, September 1988, *56*(5), pp. 1045–64.

_____ **and O'Hara, Maureen.** Contracts and Asymmetric Information in the Theory of the Firm. *J. Econ. Behav. Organ.*, April 1988, *9*(3), pp. 229–46.

Easley, J. E., Jr.; Johnson, Thomas G. and Kellogg, Robert L. Optimal Timing of Harvest for the North Carolina Bay Scallop Fishery. *Amer. J. Agr. Econ.*, February 1988, *70*(1), pp. 50–62.

Easson, A. J. Tax Incentives for Foreign Investors: People's Republic of China. *Bull. Int. Fiscal Doc.*, November 1988, *42*(11), pp. 467–70.

Easton, George S. Combining Robust and Traditional Least Squares Methods: A Critical Evaluation: Comment. *J. Bus. Econ. Statist.*, October 1988, *6*(4), pp. 432–41.

_____; **Roberts, Harry V. and Tiao, George C.** Making Statistics More Effective in Schools of Business. *J. Bus. Econ. Statist.*, April 1988, *6*(2), pp. 247–60.

Easton, Stephen T.; Gibson, William A. and Reed, Clyde G. Tariffs and Growth: The Dales Hypothesis. *Exploration Econ. Hist.*, April 1988, *25*(2), pp. 147–63.

Easton, Todd. Bargaining and the Determinants of Teacher Salaries. *Ind. Lab. Relat. Rev.*, January 1988, *41*(2), pp. 263–78.

Eastwood, David B. Panel: Market Research and the Consumer Interest: Advertising: A Consumer Economics Perspective. In *Maynes, E. S. and ACCI Research Committee*, eds., 1988, pp. 639–46.

_____; **Brooker, John R. and Terry, Danny E.**

Household Demand for Food Attributes. *J. Behav. Econ.*, Fall 1988, *17*(3), pp. 219–27.

Eastwood, Fiona and Barrell, R. J. The World Economy. *Nat. Inst. Econ. Rev.*, February 1988, (123), pp. 20–33.

_____ **and Barrell, R. J.** The World Economy. *Nat. Inst. Econ. Rev.*, August 1988, (125), pp. 23–39.

_____ **and Barrell, R. J.** The World Economy. *Nat. Inst. Econ. Rev.*, May 1988, (124), pp. 21–35.

Eaton, Jonathan. Foreign-Owned Land. *Amer. Econ. Rev.*, March 1988, *78*(1), pp. 76–88.

_____. Optimal Trade and Industrial Policies for the U.S. Automobile Industry: Comment. **In** *Feenstra, R. C., ed.*, 1988, pp. 166–69.

_____ **and Grossman, Gene M.** Trade and Industrial Policy under Oligopoly: Reply. *Quart. J. Econ.*, August 1988, *103*(3), pp. 603–07.

Eaton, Joseph. Global Interdependence and International Migration: Commentary. **In** *Cassing, J. H. and Husted, S. L., eds.*, 1988, pp. 187–91.

Eatwell, John. The New Palgrave: Economics from A to Z. *Challenge*, March–April 1988, *31*(2), pp. 16–22.

Ebenroth, Carsten Thomas and Karl, Joachim. Code of Conduct, International Investment Contracts, the Debt Crisis, and the Development Process. **In** *Teng, W. and Wang, N. T., eds.*, 1988, pp. 171–79.

Eberle, William D. On U.S. Trade Policy. **In** *Aho, C. M. and Levinson, M.*, 1988, pp. 215–18.

Eberstadt, Nicholas. Democracy and the "Debt Crisis" in Latin America: A Comment. **In** *Eberstadt, N.*, 1988, pp. 121–33.

_____. Famine, Development, and Foreign Aid. **In** *Eberstadt, N.*, 1988, pp. 69–91.

_____. Foreign Aid and American Purpose: Introduction. **In** *Eberstadt, N.*, 1988, pp. 1–16.

_____. "Human Capital" and Foreign Aid in Africa. **In** *Eberstadt, N.*, 1988, pp. 93–100.

_____. More Myths about Aid to Africa. **In** *Eberstadt, N.*, 1988, pp. 101–20.

_____. The Perversion of Foreign Aid. **In** *Eberstadt, N.*, 1988, pp. 17–68.

_____. Recommendations for Restoring Purpose to American Foreign Aid in the 1980s. **In** *Eberstadt, N.*, 1988, pp. 135–58.

Ebert, Udo. A Family of Aggregative Compromise Inequality Measures. *Int. Econ. Rev.*, May 1988, *29*(2), pp. 363–76.

_____. Measurement of Inequality: An Attempt at Unification and Generalization. **In** *Gaertner, W. and Pattanaik, P. K., eds.*, 1988, *1988*, pp. 59–81.

_____. Measurement of Inequality: An Attempt at Unification and Generalization. *Soc. Choice Welfare*, 1988, *5*(2/3), pp. 147–69.

_____. On the Decomposition of Inequality: Partitions into Nonoverlapping Sub-Groups. **In** *Eichhorn, W., ed.*, 1988, pp. 399–412.

_____. On the Evaluation of Tax Systems. **In** *Bös, D.; Rose, M. and Seidl, C., eds.*, 1988, pp. 263–80.

Eberts, Randall W. and Stone, Joe A. Student Achievement in Public Schools: Do Principals Make a Difference? *Econ. Educ. Rev.*, 1988, *7*(3), pp. 291–99.

_____ **and Stone, Joe A.** Teacher Unions and the Productivity of Public Schools. **In** *Lewin, D., et al., eds.*, 1988, *1987*, pp. 555–69.

_____ **and Stone, Joe A.** Unionism and Licensing of Public School Teachers: Impact on Wages and Educational Output: Comment. **In** *Freeman, R. B. and Ichniowski, C., eds.*, 1988, pp. 319–21.

Ebling, K. Anerkennung der steuerlichen Rechtsfähigkeit ausländischer Unternehmungen: Deutschland. (Recognition of Foreign Enterprises as Taxable Entities: Germany. With English summary.) **In** *International Fiscal Association, ed. (I)*, 1988, pp. 227–49.

Ebrahimi, Ahmad and Heady, Christopher J. Tax Design and Household Composition. *Econ. J.*, Supplement, 1988, *98*(390), pp. 83–96.

Ecchia, Giulio. Modelling Advertising as a Barrier to Entry: A Game Theoretic Approach. *Rivista Int. Sci. Econ. Com.*, September 1988, *35*(9), pp. 817–37.

Eccles, Robert G. and White, Harrison C. Price and Authority in Inter–Profit Center Transactions. **In** *Winship, C. and Rosen, S., eds.*, 1988, pp. 17–51.

Echeverry, Diego and Ibbs, C. William. New Construction Technologies for Rebuilding the Nation's Infrastructure. **In** *Ausubel, J. H. and Herman, R., eds.*, 1988, pp. 294–311.

van Eck, Robert and Kazemier, Brugt. Features of the Hidden Economy in the Netherlands. *Rev. Income Wealth*, September 1988, *34*(3), pp. 251–73.

Eckalbar, John C. Profit Sharing in a Competitive Environment. *Econ. Modelling*, October 1988, *5*(4), pp. 396–402.

Eckard, E. Woodrow, Jr. Advertising, Concentration Changes, and Consumer Welfare. *Rev. Econ. Statist.*, May 1988, *70*(2), pp. 340–43.

_____. Erratum [Advertising, Concentration Changes, and Consumer Welfare]. *Rev. Econ. Statist.*, August 1988, *70*(3), pp. 547.

Eckaus, Richard S. Prospects for Development Finance in India. **In** *Dernberger, R. F. and Eckaus, R. S.*, 1988, pp. 69–113.

_____ **and Dernberger, Robert F.** China and India: Parallels and Differences. **In** *Dernberger, R. F. and Eckaus, R. S.*, 1988, pp. 1–11.

Eckel, Catherine C. The Causes and Consequences of Mixed Enterprise. **In** *Preston, L. E., ed.*, 1988, pp. 139–56.

Eckl, Corina L. and Gold, Steven D. Appendix Checklist of Characteristics of a Good State Revenue System. **In** *Gold, S. D., ed.*, 1988, pp. 57–63.

Eckmann, J.-P., et al. Lyapunov Exponents for Stock Returns. **In** *Anderson, P. W.; Arrow, K. J. and Pines, D., eds.*, 1988, pp. 301–04.

Eckstein, Shlomo and Darvish, Tikva. A Model for Simultaneous Sensitivity Analysis of Projects. *Appl. Econ.*, January 1988, *20*(1), pp. 113–23.

Eckstein, Susan. Why Cuban Internationalism? In *Zimbalist, A., ed.*, 1988, pp. 154–81.

Eckstein, Zvi and Bental, Benjamin. Inflation, Deficit, and Seignorage with Expected Stabilization. In *Helpman, E.; Razin, A. and Sadka, E., eds.*, 1988, pp. 238–53.

———— **and Drazen, Allan.** On the Organization of Rural Markets and the Process of Economic Development. *Amer. Econ. Rev.*, June 1988, *78*(3), pp. 431–43.

————; **Stern, Steven and Wolpin, Kenneth I.** Fertility Choice, Land, and the Malthusian Hypothesis. *Int. Econ. Rev.*, May 1988, *29*(2), pp. 353–61.

————; **Weiss, Yoram and Fleising, Asher.** University Policies under Varying Market Conditions: The Training of Electrical Engineers. *Econ. Educ. Rev.*, 1988, *7*(4), pp. 393–403.

Eckwert, Bernhard and Schittko, Ulrich K. Disequilibrium Dynamics. *Scand. J. Econ.*, 1988, *90*(2), pp. 189–209.

———— **and Schittko, Ulrich K.** Intertemporal Aspects in an Aggregated Two-Country Monetary Macro Model. *Empirica*, 1988, *15*(1), pp. 77–94.

Economides, Nicholas and Siow, Aloysius. The Division of Markets is Limited by the Extent of Liquidity (Spatial Competition with Externalities). *Amer. Econ. Rev.*, March 1988, *78*(1), pp. 108–21.

Economopoulos, Andrew J. Illinois Free Banking Experience. *J. Money, Credit, Banking*, May 1988, *20*(2), pp. 249–64.

Eddy, Albert and Seifert, Bruce. Firm Size and Dividend Announcements. *J. Finan. Res.*, Winter 1988, *11*(4), pp. 295–302.

Edel, C. K. and Edel, Matthew. Mexico's Economic Crisis: The Impact of the "Pact." *Rev. Radical Polit. Econ.*, Summer–Fall 1988, *20*(2–3), pp. 247–52.

Edel, Matthew and Edel, C. K. Mexico's Economic Crisis: The Impact of the "Pact." *Rev. Radical Polit. Econ.*, Summer–Fall 1988, *20*(2–3), pp. 247–52.

Edelstein, Michael. Professional Engineers in Australia: Institutional Response in a Developing Economy, 1860–1980. *Australian Econ. Hist. Rev.*, September 1988, *28*(2), pp. 8–32.

Edelstein, Ronald. Cost Requirements for Solar Thermal Electric and Industrial Process Heat. In *West, R. E. and Kreith, F., eds.*, 1988, pp. 337–71.

Eder, Robert W. and Buckley, M. Ronald. The Employment Interview: An Interactionist Perspective. In *Ferris, G. R. and Rowland, K. M., eds.*, 1988, pp. 75–107.

Edgeworth, F. Y. On the Determinateness of Economic Equilibrium. In *Ricketts, M., ed., Vol. 1*, 1988, *1891*, pp. 99–105.

Edgmand, M. R.; Rea, J. D. and Cortes, B. S. Capital Gains and the Rental Price of Capital. In *Missouri Valley Economic Assoc.*, 1988, pp. 71–75.

Edington, Bonnie Morel and Deacon, Ronald W.

Innovative Concepts in Public–Private Coordination of Benefits for Retirees. In *Scheffler, R. M. and Rossiter, L. F., eds.*, 1988, pp. 45–67.

Edirisinghe, Neville. Food Subsidy Changes in Sri Lanka: The Short-Run Effect on the Poor. In *Pinstrup-Andersen, P., ed.*, 1988, pp. 253–66.

Edison, Hali J. and Tryon, Ralph W. An Empirical Analysis of Policy Co-Ordination in the United States, Japan and Europe. In *Motamen, H., ed.*, 1988, pp. 53–70.

Edmister, Robert O. and Merriken, Harry E. Pricing Efficiency in the Mortgage Market. *Amer. Real Estate Urban Econ. Assoc. J.*, Spring 1988, *16*(1), pp. 50–62.

Edwards, C. T. Implications for Manufacturers. *Rev. Marketing Agr. Econ.*, April 1988, *56*(1), pp. 99–104.

Edwards, Duncan. Experience of a British Firm Supplying Components to Japanese Companies. In *Holl, U. and Trevor, M., eds.*, 1988, pp. 47–55.

Edwards, Frank L. and Larwood, Laurie. Strategic Competitive Factors in the Acquisition of Technology: The Case of Major Weapon Systems. In *Gattiker, U. E. and Larwood, L., eds.*, 1988, pp. 55–72.

Edwards, Franklin R. Explaining the Events of October 1987. In *MacKay, R. J., ed.*, 1988, pp. 32–34.

————. Fashions, Fads, and Bubbles in Financial Markets: Comment. In *Coffee, J. C., Jr.; Lowenstein, L. and Rose-Ackerman, S., eds.*, 1988, pp. 69–70.

————. The Future Financial Structure: Fears and Policies. In *Haraf, W. S. and Kushmeider, R. M., eds.*, 1988, pp. 113–55.

————. Futures Trading and Cash Market Volatility: Stock Index and Interest Rate Futures. *J. Futures Markets*, August 1988, *8*(4), pp. 421–39.

————. Policies to Curb Stock Market Volatility. In *Federal Reserve Bank of Kansas City*, 1988, pp. 141–66.

————. Studies of the 1987 Stock Market Crash: Review and Appraisal. *J. Finan. Services Res.*, June 1988, *1*(3), pp. 231–51.

———— **and Ma, Cindy.** Commodity Pool Performance: Is the Information Contained in Pool Prospectuses Useful? *J. Futures Markets*, October 1988, *8*(5), pp. 589–616.

———— **and Neftci, Salih N.** Extreme Price Movements and Margin Levels in Futures Markets. *J. Futures Markets*, December 1988, *8*(6), pp. 639–55.

Edwards, Geoff W. and Dumsday, R. G. Supply and Demand in Agricultural Economics Education. *Rev. Marketing Agr. Econ.*, August 1988, *56*(2), pp. 211–12.

————; **Freebairn, John W. and Alston, Julian M.** Market Distortions and Benefits from Research. *Amer. J. Agr. Econ.*, May 1988, *70*(2), pp. 281–88.

Edwards, Kay P. Using a Systems Framework

for Organizing Family Financial Planning. *J. Cons. Aff.*, Winter 1988, *22*(2), pp. 319–32.

Edwards, Linda N. Equal Employment Opportunity in Japan: A View from the West. *Ind. Lab. Relat. Rev.*, January 1988, *41*(2), pp. 240–50.

Edwards, Meredith and Whiteford, Peter. The Development of Government Policies on Poverty and Income Distribution. *Australian Econ. Rev.*, Spring 1988, (83), pp. 54–73.

Edwards, P. K. and Bain, George Sayers. Why Are Trade Unions Becoming More Popular? Unions and Public Opinion in Britain. *Brit. J. Ind. Relat.*, November 1988, *26*(3), pp. 311–26.

_____ **and Marginson, Paul.** Differences in Perception Between Establishment and Higher Level Managers. In *Marginson, P., et al.*, 1988, pp. 227–57.

_____ **and Marginson, Paul.** Trade Unions, Pay Bargaining and Industrial Action. In *Marginson, P., et al.*, 1988, pp. 123–64.

Edwards, Sebastian. Financial Deregulation and Segmented Capital Markets: The Case of Korea. *World Devel.*, January 1988, *16*(1), pp. 185–94.

_____. La crisis de la deuda externa y las políticas de ajuste estructural en América Latina. (The Foreign Debt Crisis and the Policies for Structural Adjustment in Latin America. With English summary.) *Colección Estud. CIEPLAN*, March 1988, (23), pp. 145–93.

_____. Real and Monetary Determinants of Real Exchange Rate Behavior: Theory and Evidence from Developing Countries. *J. Devel. Econ.*, November 1988, *29*(3), pp. 311–41.

_____. Terms of Trade, Tariffs, and Labor Market Adjustment in Developing Countries. *World Bank Econ. Rev.*, May 1988, *2*(2), pp. 165–85.

_____. The United States and Foreign Competition in Latin America. In *Feldstein, M., ed. (II)*, 1988, pp. 9–64.

Edwards, Steven F. Option Prices for Groundwater Protection. *J. Environ. Econ. Manage.*, December 1988, *15*(4), pp. 475–87.

Edwards, Ward; von Winterfeldt, Detlof and Moody, David L. Simplicity in Decision Analysis: An Example and a Discussion. In *Bell, D. E.; Raiffa, H. and Tversky, A., eds.*, 1988, pp. 443–64.

Eeckhoudt, Louis and Loubergé, Henri. Export Credit Insurance: Comment. *J. Risk Ins.*, December 1988, *55*(4), pp. 742–47.

_____, et al. The Impact of a Probationary Period on the Demand for Insurance. *J. Risk Ins.*, June 1988, *55*(2), pp. 217–28.

_____, et al. The Income-Replacement Ratio: An Insurance Theory Approach. In *Munier, B. R., ed.*, 1988, pp. 641–56.

Efron, Bradley. Three Examples of Computer-Intensive Statistical Inference. In *Edwards, D. and Raun, N. E., eds.*, 1988, pp. 423–31.

Egan, John J. An Introduction to Space Business—What Is All the Fuss About? In *Egan, J. J., et al.*, 1988, pp. 3–18.

Egel, Robert. Canada's Acid Rain Policy: Federal

and Provincial Roles. In *Schmandt, J.; Clarkson, J. and Roderick, H., eds.*, 1988, pp. 137–58.

Egge, Karl A. and Simer, Frank J. An Analysis of the Advice Given by Recent Entrepreneurs to Prospective Entrepreneurs. In *Kirchhoff, B. A., et al., eds.*, 1988, pp. 119–33.

Eggerstedt, Harald. Die Lockerung der Projektbindung als Beitrag zu einer wirksameren Entwicklunshilfepolitik. (Increasing Foreign Aid Effectiveness by Shifting from Project to Non-project Finance. With English summary.) *Konjunkturpolitik*, 1988, *34*(3), pp. 162–83.

_____. Über Regulierung und Deregulierung von Versicherungsmärkten. Eine Replik. (With English summary.) *Z. Betriebswirtshaft*, July 1988, *58*(7), pp. 704–07.

Eggert, Roderick G. Base and Precious Metals Exploration by Major Corporations. In *Tilton, J. E.; Eggert, R. G. and Landsberg, H. H., eds.*, 1988, pp. 105–44.

_____; **Landsberg, Hans H. and Tilton, John E.** World Mineral Exploration: Trends and Economic Issues: Introduction. In *Tilton, J. E.; Eggert, R. G. and Landsberg, H. H., eds.*, 1988, pp. 1–19.

_____ **and Rose, Arthur W.** Exploration in the United States. In *Tilton, J. E.; Eggert, R. G. and Landsberg, H. H., eds.*, 1988, pp. 331–62.

Egol, Morton. Sound Financial Reporting by Nation-States: A Prerequisite to Worldwide Fiscal Stability. In *Chan, J. L. and Jones, R. H., eds.*, 1988, pp. 177–85.

Ehrbar, Hans and Glick, Mark. Structural Change in Profit Rate Differentials: The Post World War II U.S. Economy. *Brit. Rev. Econ. Issues*, Spring 1988, *10*(22), pp. 81–102.

Ehrenberg, Andrew S. C. and Keng, Kau Ah. Patterns of Store Choice. In *Wrigley, N., ed.*, 1988, pp. 225–50.

_____ **and Uncles, Mark D.** Patterns of Store Choice: New Evidence from the USA. In *Wrigley, N., ed.*, 1988, pp. 272–99.

Ehrenberg, Randy A.; Ehrenberg, Ronald G. and Chaykowski, Richard P. Determinants of the Compensation and Mobility of School Superintendents. *Ind. Lab. Relat. Rev.*, April 1988, *41*(3), pp. 386–401.

Ehrenberg, Ronald G. Workers' Compensation, Wages, and the Risk of Injury. In *Burton, J. F., Jr., ed.*, 1988, pp. 71–96.

_____ **and Chaykowski, Richard P.** On Estimating the Effects of Increased Aid to Education. In *Freeman, R. B. and Ichniowski, C., eds.*, 1988, pp. 245–62.

_____; **Chaykowski, Richard P. and Ehrenberg, Randy A.** Determinants of the Compensation and Mobility of School Superintendents. *Ind. Lab. Relat. Rev.*, April 1988, *41*(3), pp. 386–401.

_____; **Rosenberg, Pamela and Li, Jeanne C.** Part-time Employment in the United States. In *Hart, R. A., ed.*, 1988, pp. 256–81.

Ehrenberger, Vlastimil. The Czechoslovak Fuels

and Energy Complex. *Czech. Econ. Digest.*, May 1988, (3), pp. 42–49.

Ehrensaft, Philip; Culver, David and Strain, Greg. Cost Structure and Performance of Prairie Grain and Oilseed Farms. *Can. J. Agr. Econ.*, Part 2, December 1988, *36*(4), pp. 845–55.

Ehrlich, Anne H. Development and Agriculture. In *Ehrlich, P. R. and Holdren, J. P., eds.*, 1988, pp. 75–100.

Ehrlich, Paul R. The Ecology of Nuclear War. In *Ehrlich, P. R. and Holdren, J. P., eds.*, 1988, pp. 181–99.

Ehrlicher, Werner. Die Geld-, Finanz- und Einkommenspolitik im volkswirtschaftlichen Systemzusammenhang. (Monetary, Financial and Income Policy in a National Economic Policy Framework. With English summary.) *Kredit Kapital*, 1988, *21*(2), pp. 163–81.

Ehrmann, Thomas. Die Wohnungsgemeinnützigkeit abschaffen? Ja, aber wann? Ein Beitrag zur optimalen Lebensdauer von Institutionen. (On Deregulation in the German Housing Sector—Immediate Abolition of "Wohnungsgemeinnützigkeit"? With English summary.) *Konjunkturpolitik*, 1988, *34*(1), pp. 56–68.

Eichenbaum, Martin S.; Hansen, Lars Peter and Singleton, Kenneth J. A Time Series Analysis of Representative Agent Models of Consumption and Leisure Choice under Uncertainty. *Quart. J. Econ.*, February 1988, *103*(1), pp. 51–78.

Eichengreen, Barry. The Australian Recovery of the 1930s in International Comparative Perspective. In *Gregory, R. G. and Butlin, N. G., eds.*, 1988, pp. 33–60.

_____. Did International Economic Forces Cause the Great Depression? *Contemp. Policy Issues*, April 1988, *6*(2), pp. 90–114.

_____. The End of Large Public Debts: Discussion. In *Giavazzi, F. and Spaventa, L., eds.*, 1988, pp. 80–84.

_____. International Competition in the Products of U.S. Basic Industries. In *Feldstein, M., ed. (II)*, 1988, pp. 279–353.

_____. Real Exchange Rate Behavior under Alternative International Monetary Regimes: Interwar Evidence. *Europ. Econ. Rev.*, March 1988, *32*(2–3), pp. 363–71.

_____ **and Hatton, T. J.** Interwar Unemployment in International Perspective. *J. Europ. Econ. Hist.*, Spring 1988, *17*(1), pp. 189–94.

_____ **and Hatton, T. J.** Interwar Unemployment in International Perspective: An Overview. In *Eichengreen, B. and Hatton, T. J., eds.*, 1988, pp. 1–59.

_____ **and Portes, Richard.** Les prêts internationaux dans l'entre-deux-guerres: Le point de vue des porteurs de titres. (Foreign Lending in the Interwar Years: The Bondholders' Perspective. With English summary.) *Écon. Appl.*, 1988, *41*(4), pp. 741–71.

_____ **and Wyplosz, Charles.** The Economic Consequences of the Franc Poincaré. In *Helpman, E.; Razin, A. and Sadka, E., eds.*, 1988, pp. 257–86.

Eicher, Carl K. Ending African Hunger: Six Challenges for Scientists, Policymakers and Politicians. In *Asefa, S., ed.*, 1988, pp. 123–44.

Eichhorn, Wolfgang. On a Class of Inequality Measures. *Soc. Choice Welfare*, 1988, *5*(2/3), pp. 171–77.

_____. On a Class of Inequality Measures. In *Gaertner, W. and Pattanaik, P. K., eds.*, 1988, *1988*, pp. 83–89.

_____ **and Gleissner, Winfried.** The Equation of Measurement. In *Eichhorn, W., ed.*, 1988, pp. 19–27.

_____ **and Gleissner, Winfried.** The Solutions of Important Special Cases of the Equation of Measurement. In *Eichhorn, W., ed.*, 1988, pp. 29–37.

Eichler, Gabriel. A Banker's Perspective on Poland's Debt Problem. In *Marer, P. and Siwinski, W., eds.*, 1988, pp. 201–14.

Eichner, Alfred S. Full Employment and the Human Element. *Challenge*, May–June 1988, *31*(3), pp. 4–8.

_____. A Post-Keynesian Short-Period Model. In *Sawyer, M. C., ed.*, 1988, *1979*, pp. 479–504.

_____. Prices and Pricing. In *Tool, M. R., ed.*, Vol. 2, 1988, *1987*, pp. 137–66.

_____. The Reagan Record: A Post Keynesian View. *J. Post Keynesian Econ.*, Summer 1988, *10*(4), pp. 541–56.

_____. A Theory of the Determination of the Mark-Up under Oligopoly. In *Sawyer, M. C., ed.*, 1988, *1973*, pp. 249–65.

_____ **and Arestis, Philip.** The Post-Keynesian and Institutionalist Theory of Money and Credit. *J. Econ. Issues*, December 1988, *22*(4), pp. 1003–21.

_____ **and Kregel, J. A.** An Essay on Post-Keynesian Theory: A New Paradigm in Economics. In *Sawyer, M. C., ed.*, 1988, *1975*, pp. 11–32.

_____ **and Ochoa, Eduardo M.** The Structure of Industrial Prices. *Rev. Radical Polit. Econ.*, Summer–Fall 1988, *20*(2–3), pp. 114–26.

Eichner, Maxine N. Getting Women Work That Isn't Women's Work: Challenging Gender Biases in the Workplace under Title VII. *Yale Law J.*, June 1988, *97*(7), pp. 1397–1417.

Eickelman, Dale F. Oman's Next Generation: Challenges and Prospects. In *Sindelar, H. R., III and Peterson, J. E., eds.*, 1988, pp. 157–80.

Eickhoff, M. Kathryn. The Business Economist at Work: So You Want to be an Economic Consultant. *Bus. Econ.*, July 1988, *23*(3), pp. 53–54.

van Eijk, C. J. and Veeneklaas, F. R. Optimization and the Preparation of Economic Policy. In *Driehuis, W.; Fase, M. M. G. and den Hartog, H., eds.*, 1988, pp. 265–81.

Eilers, Paul H. C. Autoregressive Models with Latent Variables. In *Edwards, D. and Raun, N. E., eds.*, 1988, pp. 363–68.

Eilts, Hermann Frederick. Foreign Policy Perspectives of the Gulf States. In *Sindelar, H. R., III and Peterson, J. E., eds.*, 1988, pp. 16–37.

Einhorn, Hillel J. and Hogarth, Robin M. Behavioral Decision Theory: Processes of Judgment and Choice. In *Bell, D. E.; Raiffa, H. and Tversky, A.,* eds., 1988, *1981,* pp. 113–46.

—— and Hogarth, Robin M. Conceptions of Choice: Reply to Commentaries. In *Bell, D. E.; Raiffa, H. and Tversky, A.,* eds., 1988, *1982,* pp. 147–51.

—— and Hogarth, Robin M. Decision Making under Ambiguity: A Note. In *Munier, B. R.,* ed., 1988, pp. 327–36.

Einhorn, Michael A. The Effect of Load Management upon Transmission and Distribution Costs: A Case Study. *Energy J.,* January 1988, *9*(1), pp. 73–87.

Einy, Ezra. The Shapley Value on Some Lattices of Monotonic Games. *Math. Soc. Sci.,* February 1988, *15*(1), pp. 1–10.

Eisenbeis, Robert A. Can Banking and Commerce Mix? Comment. In *England, C. and Huertas, T.,* eds., 1988, pp. 309–15.

——. Commentary [The Future Financial Structure: Fears and Policies] [Bank Holding Companies: Structure, Performance, and Reform]. In *Haraf, W. S. and Kushmeider, R. M.,* eds., 1988, pp. 203–211.

——. Expanding Bank Powers: The Present Debate. *Cato J.,* Winter 1988, *7*(3), pp. 763–69.

——; Harris, Robert S. and Born, Jeffery A. The Benefits of Geographical and Product Expansion in the Financial Service Industries. *J. Finan. Services Res.,* January 1988, *1*(2), pp. 161–82.

Eisenberg, John M. and Kabcenell, Andrea. Organized Practice and the Quality of Medical Care. *Inquiry,* Spring 1988, *25*(1), pp. 78–89.

Eisenberg, Melvin A. Shareholders versus Managers: The Strain in the Corporate Web: Comment: Golden Parachutes and the Myth of the Web. In *Coffee, J. C., Jr.; Lowenstein, L. and Rose-Ackerman, S.,* eds., 1988, pp. 155–58.

Eisenberg, William M. and McDonald, Helen. Evaluating Workplace Injury and Illness Records; Testing a Procedure. *Mon. Lab. Rev.,* April 1988, *111*(4), pp. 58–60.

Eiser, J. Richard; Spears, Russell and Webley, Paul. Inflationary Expectations and Policy Preferences. *Econ. Letters,* 1988, *28*(3), pp. 239–41.

Eisgruber, Ludwig M. Management Problems of Farms and Agricultural Firms: A Discussion. In *Hildreth, R. J., et al.,* eds., 1988, pp. 298–300.

Eisinger, Peter K. Targeting Economic Development in Wisconsin. In *Danziger, S. H. and Witte, J. F.,* eds., 1988, pp. 96–107.

Eisner, Robert. Extended Accounts for National Income and Product. *J. Econ. Lit.,* December 1988, *26*(4), pp. 1611–84.

——. What's Facing the Next President? *Challenge,* July–August 1988, *31*(4), pp. 22–31.

——. Which Budget Deficit? In *Brown, E.,* ed., 1988, *1984,* pp. 208–14.

—— and Pieper, Paul J. Deficits, Monetary Policy, and Real Economic Activity. In *Arrow,*

K. J. and Boskin, M. J., eds., 1988, pp. 3–38.

—— and Pieper, Paul J. The Relationship between Real Deficits and Real Growth: A Critique: Rejoinder. *J. Post Keynesian Econ.,* Fall 1988, *11*(1), pp. 161–68.

Eizenga, Wietze. European Economic Integration and a System of European Central Banks. In *[Witteveen, H. J.],* 1988, pp. 33–42.

Ekeland, Ivar. Some Variational Problems Arising from Mathematical Economics. In *Ambrosetti, A.; Gori, F. and Lucchetti, R.,* eds., 1988, pp. 1–18.

Ekelund, Robert B., Jr. and Ault, Richard W. Habits in Economic Analysis: Veblen and the Neoclassicals. *Hist. Polit. Econ.,* Fall 1988, *20*(3), pp. 431–45.

—— and Ault, Richard W. Rent Seeking in a Static Model of Zoning. *Amer. Real Estate Urban Econ. Assoc. J.,* Spring 1988, *16*(1), pp. 69–76.

—— and Boudreaux, Don. The Semantic Imp and Regulation: Reply. *J. Inst. Theoretical Econ.,* December 1988, *144*(5), pp. 889–90.

Ekern, Steinar. An Option Pricing Approach to Evaluating Petroleum Projects. *Energy Econ.,* April 1988, *10*(2), pp. 91–99.

Ekinci, Nazim K. Properties of Two Sector General Equilibrium Models. *METU,* 1988, *15*(1–2), pp. 105–30.

Ekirch, Arthur A., Jr. A Utopia for Liberty: Individual Freedom in Austin Tappan Wright's *Islandia.* In *[Rothbard, M. N.],* 1988, pp. 335–40.

Ekland-Olson, Sheldon. Structured Discretion, Racial Bias, and the Death Penalty: The First Decade after *Furman* in Texas. *Soc. Sci. Quart.,* December 1988, *69*(4), pp. 853–73.

Ekstedt, Hasse and Westberg, Lars. Interaction between Economic Growth and Financial Flows: Presentation of a Model Analysing the Impact of Short-Term Financial Disturbances on Economic Growth. In *Motamen, H.,* ed., 1988, pp. 219–43.

Ekstrom, Brenda L. and Leistritz, F. Larry. The Financial Characteristics of Production Units and Producers Experiencing Financial Stress. In *Murdock, S. H. and Leistritz, F. L.,* eds., 1988, pp. 73–95.

El-Ansary, Adel I. and Robles, Fernando. Informal Sector and Economic Development: A Marketing Perspective. In *Kumcu, E. and Firat, A. F.,* eds., 1988, pp. 199–228.

El Badawi, Ibrahim and D'Silva, Brian C. Indirect and Direct Taxation of Agriculture in Sudan: The Role of the Government in Agriculture Surplus Extraction. *Amer. J. Agr. Econ.,* May 1988, *70*(2), pp. 431–36.

El-Erian, Mohamed. Currency Substitution in Egypt and the Yemen Arab Republic: A Comparative Quantitative Analysis. *Int. Monet. Fund Staff Pap.,* March 1988, *35*(1), pp. 85–103.

El-Hodiri, Mohamed A. and Nourzad, Farrokh. A Note on Leontief Technology and Input Substitution. *J. Reg. Sci.*, February 1988, *28*(1), pp. 119–20.

El-Jafari, M. K. and Turay, A. M. Trade, Japanese Voluntary Restraint Agreements and Import Elasticity for Cars in the U.S. *Rivista Int. Sci. Econ. Com.*, February 1988, *35*(2), pp. 195–202.

El Naggar, Said. The Baker Plan: Prospects and Problems in a Changing Oil Market. In *Mabro, R., ed.*, 1988, pp. 275–86.

Elam, Emmett W. Estimated Hedging Risk with Cash Settlement Feeder Cattle Futures. *Western J. Agr. Econ.*, July 1988, *13*(1), pp. 45–52.

_____ **and Dixon, Bruce L.** Examining the Validity of a Test of Futures Market Efficiency. *J. Futures Markets*, June 1988, *8*(3), pp. 365–72.

_____ **and Vaught, Daniel.** Risk and Return in Cattle and Hog Futures. *J. Futures Markets*, February 1988, *8*(1), pp. 79–87.

Elbaz, A. and Heraud, J.-A. L'image et le devenir des fuel-oils lourds dans le secteur industriel. (The Status and the Future for Heavy Oil in the Industrial Sector. With English summary.) *Écon. Soc.*, April 1988, *22*(4), pp. 159–218.

Elder, Harold W. and Misiolek, Walter S. Tax Structure and the Size of Government: An Empirical Analysis of the Fiscal Illusion and Fiscal Stress Arguments. *Public Choice*, June 1988, *57*(3), pp. 233–45.

Eldor, Rafael and Marcus, Alan J. Quotas as Options: Valuation and Equilibrium Implications. *J. Int. Econ.*, May 1988, *24*(3–4), pp. 255–74.

_____; **Pines, David and Schwartz, Aba.** The Demand for Domestic Assets and Consumption Risk. In *Khoury, S. J. and Ghosh, A., eds.*, 1988, pp. 349–62.

_____; **Pines, David and Schwartz, Aba.** Home Asset Preference and Productivity Shocks. *J. Int. Econ.*, August 1988, *25*(1–2), pp. 165–76.

Elegido, J. M. The Nigerian Experience with Tax Clearance Certificates. *Bull. Int. Fiscal Doc.*, June 1988, *42*(6), pp. 263–67.

Elffers, Henk and Hessing, Dick J. A Linear Structural Model for Tax Evasion Measurements. In *Maital, S., ed., Vol. 2*, 1988, pp. 562–67.

_____; **Weigel, Russell H. and Hessing, Dick J.** Research in Tax Resistance: An Integrative Theoretical Scheme for Tax Evasion Behavior. In *Maital, S., ed., Vol. 2*, 1988, pp. 568–76.

Elguero, Eric and Holmes-Junca, Susan. Confidence Regions for Projection Pursuit Density Estimates. In *Edwards, D. and Raun, N. E., eds.*, 1988, pp. 59–63.

Elhance, Arun P. and Lakshmanan, T. R. Infrastructure-Production System Dynamics in National and Regional Systems: An Econometric Study of the Indian Economy. *Reg. Sci. Urban Econ.*, November 1988, *18*(4), pp. 511–31.

Elias, D. J. Information Output of Diagnostic Tests: An Analysis of Radiology and Endoscopy: Discussion. In *Butler, J. R. G. and Doessel, D. P., eds.*, 1988, pp. 133–34.

Elias, Peter. Family Formation, Occupational Mobility and Part-Time Work. In *Hunt, A., ed.*, 1988, pp. 83–104.

_____. Women and Paid Work: Issues of Equality: Preface and Introduction. In *Hunt, A., ed.*, 1988, pp. xiv–xviii.

_____ **and Purcell, Kate.** Women and Paid Work: Prospects for Equality. In *Hunt, A., ed.*, 1988, pp. 196–221.

Elias, Víctor J. Productividad en el sector industrial argentino: 1935–1985. (Productivity in the Industrial Sector of Argentina, 1935–1985. With English summary.) *Económica (La Plata)*, July–Dec. 1988, *34*(2), pp. 185–202.

Eliasson, Gunnar. Schumpeterian Innovation, Market Structure, and the Stability of Industrial Development. In *Hanusch, H., ed.*, 1988, pp. 151–99.

Elishakoff, I. Correlation and Spectral Analysis–A Brief Outline. In *Schiehlen, W. and Wedig, W., eds.*, 1988, pp. 2–13.

_____. Measurement of Characteristics of Stationary Random Processes. In *Schiehlen, W. and Wedig, W., eds.*, 1988, pp. 14–21.

_____. Random Vibration of Multi-Degree-of-Freedom Systems with Associated Effect of Cross-Correlations. In *Schiehlen, W. and Wedig, W., eds.*, 1988, pp. 22–31.

_____. Wide-Band Random Vibration of Continuous Structures with Associated Effect of Cross-Correlation. In *Schiehlen, W. and Wedig, W., eds.*, 1988, pp. 32–42.

Elkan, Walter. Alternatives to Fuelwood in African Towns. *World Devel.*, April 1988, *16*(4), pp. 527–33.

_____. Entrepreneurs and Entrepreneurship in Africa. *World Bank Res. Observer*, July 1988, *3*(2), pp. 171–88.

Elkjær, Jørgen Ravn. Entreprenøren og foretageren i økonomisk teori. (The Concept of "Entrepreneur" and "Undertaker" in Economic Theory. With English summary.) *Nationaløkon. Tidsskr.*, 1988, *126*(1), pp. 96–111.

Elkoubi, Anne and Despiney, Barbara. India, the Soviet Union, and Eastern Europe. In *Lavigne, M., ed.*, 1988, pp. 170–81.

Ellerman, David P. The Kantian Person/Thing Principle in Political Economy. *J. Econ. Issues*, December 1988, *22*(4), pp. 1109–22.

Elliehausen, Gregory E.; Kennickell, Arthur B. and Avery, Robert B. Measuring Wealth with Survey Data: An Evaluation of the 1983 Survey of Consumer Finances. *Rev. Income Wealth*, December 1988, *34*(4), pp. 339–69.

_____ **and Kurtz, Robert D.** Scale Economies in Compliance Costs for Federal Consumer Credit Regulations. *J. Finan. Services Res.*, January 1988, *1*(2), pp. 147–59.

Ellig, Jerome and High, Jack C. The Private Supply of Education: Some Historical Evidence. In *Cowen, T., ed.*, 1988, pp. 361–82.

Elliott, John A. and Shaw, Wayne H. Write-Offs as Accounting Procedures to Manage Perceptions. *J. Acc. Res.*, Supplement, 1988, *26*, pp. 91–119.

Elliott, John E. Some Developments in Marxian

Theory since Schumpeter: Commentary. **In** *Thweatt, W. O., ed.,* 1988, pp. 259–66.

_____ **and Dymski, Gary A.** Roemer versus Marx: Alternative Perspectives on Exploitation. *Rev. Radical Polit. Econ.,* Summer–Fall 1988, *20*(2–3), pp. 25–33.

Ellis, Alan L.; Melton, Robert J. and Komorita, Samuel S. The Effects of Justice Norms in a Bargaining Situation. **In** *Tietz, R.; Albers, W. and Selten, R., eds.,* 1988, pp. 251–67.

Ellis, Christopher J. Labor Market Share Contracts When the Firm Has Two Variable Inputs. *Econ. Inquiry,* October 1988, *26*(4), pp. 767–74.

_____ **and Butler, Alison.** Ranking Alternative Share Contracts under Rational Expectations. *Europ. Econ. Rev.,* July 1988, *32*(6), pp. 1243–59.

Ellis, Mark and Odland, John. Household Organization and the Interregional Variation of Out-Migration Rates. *Demography,* November 1988, *25*(4), pp. 567–79.

Ellis, Mark S. Foreign Investment in Yugoslavia—A Review of the Joint Venture Law with Amendments and Proposed Changes. *Econ. Anal. Workers' Manage.,* 1988, *22*(4), pp. 235–70.

Ellis, Michael G. Navajo Economic Behavior. *J. Behav. Econ.,* Summer 1988, *17*(2), pp. 119–31.

Ellis, R. J. Mark Twain and the Ideology of Southern Slavery. **In** *Archer, L. J., ed.,* 1988, pp. 157–75.

Ellis, R. Jeffrey and Taylor, Natalie T. Success and Failure in Internal Venture Strategy: An Exploratory Study. **In** *Kirchhoff, B. A., et al., eds.,* 1988, pp. 518–33.

Ellis, Randall P. and McGuire, Thomas G. Insurance Principles and the Design of Prospective Payment Systems. *J. Health Econ.,* September 1988, *7*(3), pp. 215–37.

_____ **and Ruhm, Christopher J.** Incentives to Transfer Patients under Alternative Reimbursement Mechanisms. *J. Public Econ.,* December 1988, *37*(3), pp. 381–94.

Ellison, Julian and Browne, Robert S. Impact of the 1975 Tax Cut on Income and Employment in the Black Community. *Rev. Black Polit. Econ.,* Fall 1988, *17*(2), pp. 5–9.

Ellman, Michael. China's OTC Markets. *Comp. Econ. Stud.,* Spring 1988, *30*(1), pp. 59–64.

_____. Contract Brigades and Normless Teams in Soviet Agriculture. **In** *Brada, J. C. and Wadekin, K.-E., eds.,* 1988, pp. 23–33.

Ellsberg, Daniel. Risk, Ambiguity, and the Savage Axioms. **In** *Gärdenfors, P. and Sahlin, N.-E., eds.,* 1988, pp. 245–69.

Elms, J. Martin. The Use of Computers in Bus and Crew Scheduling by London Buses and Its Predecessors: A User's View. **In** *Daduna, J. R. and Wren, A., eds.,* 1988, pp. 262–71.

Elmslie, Bruce. Income Distribution: Comments. **In** *Mangum, G. and Philips, P., eds.,* 1988, pp. 90–92.

Elrod, Terry. Choice Map: Inferring a Product-Market Map from Panel Data. *Marketing Sci.,* Winter 1988, *7*(1), pp. 21–40.

_____. Inferring an Ideal-Point Product-Market Map from Consumer Panel Data. **In** *Gaul, W. and Schader, M., eds.,* 1988, pp. 240–49.

Else, Peter K. Further Thoughts on Public Goods, Private Goods and Mixed Goods. *Scot. J. Polit. Econ.,* May 1988, *35*(2), pp. 115–28.

Elson, Diane. Dominance and Dependency in the World Economy. **In** *Crow, B. and Thorpe, M., et al.,* 1988, pp. 264–87.

Elster, Jon. Economic Order and Social Norms. *J. Inst. Theoretical Econ.,* April 1988, *144*(2), pp. 357–66.

Eltis, David. The Economic Impact of the Ending of the African Slave Trade to the Americas. *Soc. Econ. Stud.,* March–June 1988, *37*(1–2), pp. 143–72.

_____ **and Jennings, Lawrence C.** Trade between Western Africa and the Atlantic World in the Pre-Colonial Era. *Amer. Hist. Rev.,* October 1988, *93*(4), pp. 936–59.

Eltis, Walter. Britain's Budget Deficit in 1967–84: Its Consequences, Causes and Policies to Control It. **In** *Cavanna, H., ed.,* 1988, pp. 76–101.

_____. The Continuing Relevance of Keynes to Economic Policy. **In** *Eltis, W. and Sinclair, P. J. N., eds.,* 1988, pp. 451–63.

_____. The Contrasting Theories of Industrialization of François Quesnay and Adam Smith. *Oxford Econ. Pap.,* June 1988, *40*(2), pp. 269–88.

_____. The Role of Industry in Economic Development: The Contrasting Theories of François Quesnay and Adam Smith. **In** *Arrow, K. J., ed.,* 1988, pp. 175–97.

Ely, Bert. The Big Bust: The 1930–33 Banking Collapse—Its Causes, Its Lessons. **In** *England, C. and Huertas, T., eds.,* 1988, pp. 41–67.

_____. The Future Structure of the Housing Finance System: Commentary. **In** *Haraf, W. S. and Kushmeider, R. M., eds.,* 1988, pp. 337–42.

Elyasiani, Elyas and Meinster, David R. The Performance of Foreign Owned, Minority Owned, and Holding Company Owned Banks in the U.S. *J. Banking Finance,* June 1988, *12*(2), pp. 293–313.

Elzas, B. D. On the Austrian Notion of "Cost" in 1889. *J. Econ. Stud.,* 1988, *15*(3–4), pp. 36–54.

Elzinga, Kenneth G. and Wood, William C. The Costs of the Legal System in Private Antitrust Enforcement. **In** *White, L. J., ed.,* 1988, pp. 107–48.

Embry, Olice H. and Baggarly, A. L. The History and Genealogy of Georgia Federal Bank, FSB. **In** *Perkins, E. J., ed.,* 1988, pp. 256–72.

Emel'ianov, A. Development Trends and the Restructuring of the Food Sphere. *Prob. Econ.,* July 1988, *31*(3), pp. 81–99.

Emerson, Craig. Issues in Minerals Policy. **In** *McKern, B. and Koomsup, P., eds.,* 1988, pp. 51–83.

Emerson, Michael. Regulation or Deregulation

of the Labour Market: Policy Regimes for the Recruitment and Dismissal of Employees in the Industrialised Countries. *Europ. Econ. Rev.*, April 1988, 32(4), pp. 775–817.

Emerson, Robert D. Human Capital for Agriculture: A Discussion. In *Hildreth, R. J., et al., eds.*, 1988, pp. 522–25.

Emery, Douglas R.; Lewellen, Wilbur G. and Mauer, David C. Tax-Timing Options, Leverage, and the Choice of Corporate Form. *J. Finan. Res.*, Summer 1988, 11(2), pp. 99–110.

Emery, Gary W. Positive Theories of Trade Credit. In *Kim, Y. H., ed.*, 1988, pp. 115–30.

Emery, Robert F. Monetary Policy in Taiwan, China. In *Cheng, H.-S., ed.*, 1988, pp. 381–99.

Emmanuel, Arghiri. Le surcroît d'endettement des pays à monnaie internationale: Ses limites et ses contradictions. (The Overdraft of the International Currency Makers: Its Bounds and Blind Alleys. With English summary.) *Écon. Soc.*, June–July 1988, 22(6–7), pp. 113–27.

Emmanuel, Clive R.; Garrod, Neil W. and Frost, Ceri. Segment Reports and Consolidated Financial Statements: The Complementary Twins. In *Gray, S. J. and Coenenberg, A. G., eds.*, 1988, pp. 272–99.

Emmerij, L. New Thinking in Industrial Co-operation between North and South: Comment. In *Jepma, C. J., ed.*, 1988, pp. 74–79.

Emminger, Otmar. The Evolution of the Exchange Rate from "Sacrosanct" Parity to Flexible Monetary Policy Instrument. In *Pohl, H. and Rudolph, B., eds.*, 1988, pp. 1–16.

Emons, Winand. Warranties, Moral Hazard, and the Lemons Problem. *J. Econ. Theory*, October 1988, 46(1), pp. 16–33.

Encarnación, José, Jr. Price Decisions and Employment Equilibrium. *Philippine Rev. Econ. Bus.*, Sept.–Dec. 1988, 25(3–4), pp. 243–53.

Enders, Thomas O. The Latin Debt Problem Can Be Downsized, but Growth Will Be Long in Coming Back. In *Feldstein, M., ed. (II)*, 1988, pp. 64–68.

Enders, Walter. ARIMA and Cointegration Tests of PPP under Fixed and Flexible Exchange Rate Regimes. *Rev. Econ. Statist.*, August 1988, 70(3), pp. 504–08.

Enderwick, Peter. Between Markets and Hierarchies: The Multinational Operations of Japanese General Trading Companies. *Managerial Dec. Econ.*, March 1988, 9(1), pp. 35–40.

Endres, A. M. 'Structural' Economic Thought in New Zealand: The Inter-war Contribution of A. G. B. Fisher. *New Zealand Econ. Pap.*, 1988, 22, pp. 35–49.

_____. Subjectivism, Psychology, and the Modern Austrians: A Comment. In *Earl, P. E., ed.*, 1988, pp. 121–24.

Endres, Alfred and Gäfgen, Gérard. Wettbewerb und Regulierung auf dem bundesdeutschen Lebensversicherungsmarkt. (Competition and Regulation in the W. German Life Insurance Market. With English summary.)

Jahr. Nationalökon. Statist., July 1988, 205(1), pp. 11–29.

Endruweit, Günter. Social Boundaries of Labor Markets. In *Dlugos, G.; Dorow, W. and Weiermair, K., eds.*, 1988, pp. 143–51.

Enelow, James M. A Bayesian Analysis of a Class of Multistage Decision Problems. *J. Conflict Resolution*, December 1988, 32(4), pp. 759–72.

Eng, Robert Y. and Smith, Thomas C. Peasant Families and Population Control in Eighteenth-Century Japan. In *Smith, T. C.*, 1988, 1976, pp. 103–32.

Engelbourg, Saul. John Stewart Kennedy and the Scottish American Investment Company. In *Perkins, E. J., ed.*, 1988, pp. 37–54.

_____ and Schachter, Gustav. The Steadfastness of Economic Dualism in Italy. *J. Devel. Areas*, July 1988, 22(4), pp. 515–25.

Engelbrecht, Hans-Jürgen. Analysis of the Primary Information Sectors of Korea and Japan Using Computable General Equilibrium Models. *Info. Econ. Policy*, 1988, 3(3), pp. 219–39.

Engelbrecht-Wiggans, Richard. Revenue Equivalence in Multi-object Auctions. *Econ. Letters*, 1988, 26(1), pp. 15–19.

Engelmann, Kathleen and Cornell, Bradford. Measuring the Cost of Corporate Litigation: Five Case Studies. *J. Legal Stud.*, June 1988, 17(2), pp. 377–99.

Engels, Benno. South–South Trade: Significance and Aspects. In *Sopiee, N.; Hamzah, B. A. and Leong, C. H., eds.*, 1988, 1986, pp. 137–56.

Engen, Eric M. and Benson, Bruce L. The Market for Laws: An Economic Analysis of Legislation. *Southern Econ. J.*, January 1988, 54(3), pp. 732–45.

England, Catherine. Agency Costs and Unregulated Banks: Could Depositors Protect Themselves? In *England, C. and Huertas, T., eds.*, 1988, pp. 317–43.

_____. Agency Costs and Unregulated Banks: Could Depositors Protect Themselves? *Cato J.*, Winter 1988, 7(3), pp. 771–97.

_____. Financial Services Regulation: Driven by Events. In *Boaz, D., ed.*, 1988, pp. 187–98.

_____. Nonbank Banks Are Not the Problem: Outmoded Regulations Are. In *England, C. and Huertas, T., eds.*, 1988, pp. 251–65.

_____ and Huertas, Thomas F. The Financial Services Revolution: Introduction. In *England, C. and Huertas, T., eds.*, 1988, pp. 1–5.

England, David F. and Laffer, Arthur B. The Case for a 400-Basis-Point Plunge in Interest Rates. In *Canto, V. A. and Laffer, A. B., eds.*, 1988, pp. 55–75.

England, Geoffrey. Some Thoughts on Constitutionalizing the Right to Strike. In *Carter, D. D., et al.*, 1988, pp. 168–213.

England, George W. Potential Constraints upon Management Action as a Function of National Work Meanings and Patterns—Germany, Japan, and the USA. In *Dlugos, G.; Dorow, W. and Weiermair, K., eds.*, 1988, pp. 455–68.

England, Paula; Barton, Margaret and Farkas, George. Structural Effects on Wages: Sociological and Economic Views. In *Farkas, G. and England, P., eds.*, 1988, pp. 93–112.

_____ **and Farkas, George.** Economic and Sociological Views of Industries, Firms, and Jobs. In *Farkas, G. and England, P., eds.*, 1988, pp. 331–46.

England, Richard W. Disaster-Prone Technologies, Environmental Risks, and Profit Maximization. *Kyklos*, 1988, *41*(3), pp. 379–95.

Englander, A. Steven; Evenson, Robert E. and Hanazaki, Masaharu. R&D, Innovation and the Total Factor Productivity Slowdown. *OECD Econ. Stud.*, Autumn 1988, (11), pp. 7–42.

_____ **and Mittelstädt, Axel.** Total Factor Productivity: Macroeconomic and Structural Aspects of the Slowdown. *OECD Econ. Stud.*, Spring 1988, (10), pp. 7–56.

Englander, Ernest J. International Competitiveness: The Failure to Regulate the Biotechnology Industry. In *Hausman, W. J., ed.*, 1988, pp. 143–53.

_____. Technology and Oliver Williamson's Transaction Cost Economics. *J. Econ. Behav. Organ.*, October 1988, *10*(3), pp. 339–53.

Englander, Fred and Englander, Valerie. The Impact of Program and Labor Market Incentives on Applications for Welfare Appeals. *Amer. Econ.*, Fall 1988, *32*(2), pp. 20–25.

_____ **and Englander, Valerie.** Workfare in New Jersey: A Five-Year Assessment. In *Kelly, R. M., ed.*, 1988, pp. 99–111.

Englander, Frederick J. and Director, Steven M. Requiring Unemployment Insurance Recipients to Register with the Public Employment Service. *J. Risk Ins.*, June 1988, *55*(2), pp. 245–58.

Englander, Valerie and Englander, Fred. The Impact of Program and Labor Market Incentives on Applications for Welfare Appeals. *Amer. Econ.*, Fall 1988, *32*(2), pp. 20–25.

_____ **and Englander, Fred.** Workfare in New Jersey: A Five-Year Assessment. In *Kelly, R. M., ed.*, 1988, pp. 99–111.

Engle, Robert F. Estimates of the Variance of U.S. Inflation Based upon the ARCH Model: Reply. *J. Money, Credit, Banking*, Part 1, August 1988, *20*(3), pp. 422–23.

_____; **Wooldridge, Jeffrey M. and Bollerslev, Tim.** A Capital Asset Pricing Model with Time-Varying Covariances. *J. Polit. Econ.*, February 1988, *96*(1), pp. 116–31.

English, B. C., et al. Iowa, USA: An Agricultural Policy Analysis. In *Parikh, J. K., ed.*, 1988, pp. 135–66.

Englund, Peter; Persson, Mats and Brownstone, David. A Microsimulation Model of Swedish Housing Demand. *J. Urban Econ.*, March 1988, *23*(2), pp. 179–98.

_____; **Persson, Mats and Brownstone, David.** Tax Reform and Housing Demand: The Distribution of Welfare Gains and Losses. *Europ. Econ. Rev.*, April 1988, *32*(4), pp. 819–40.

_____ **and Svensson, Lars E. O.** Money and Banking in a Cash-in-Advance Economy. *Int. Econ. Rev.*, November 1988, *29*(4), pp. 681–705.

Englund, Steven R. Japan's High Technology Industries: Lessons and Limitations of Industrial Policy: Review Article. *Mich. Law Rev.*, May 1988, *86*(6), pp. 1232–37.

Engwerda, J. C. On the Set of Obtainable Reference Trajectories Using Minimum Variance Control. *J. Econ. (Z. Nationalökon.)*, 1988, *48*(3), pp. 279–301.

Ennew, C. T., et al. British Potato Stabilisation Policy in a European Context. *J. Agr. Econ.*, January 1988, *39*(1), pp. 43–60.

Enthoven, Adolf J. H. The Future of International Standards in Government Accounting. In *Most, K. S., ed.*, 1988, pp. 207–30.

Enthoven, Alain. Managed Competition of Alternative Delivery Systems. In *Greenberg, W., ed.*, 1988, pp. 83–99.

Entorf, Horst. Die endogene Innovation. Eine mikro-empirische Analyse von Produktphasen als Innovationsindikatoren. (Endogenous Innovations. A Micro-Empirical Analysis of Product Cycle Phases as Indicators of Innovative Activity. With English summary.) *Jahr. Nationalökon. Statist.*, February 1988, *204*(2), pp. 175–89.

Enyedi, György and Ránki, György. Experiences of National Planning in Hungary. In *Urrutia, M. and Yukawa, S., eds. (I)*, 1988, pp. 311–58.

Epple, Dennis; Romer, Thomas and Filimon, Radu. Community Development with Endogenous Land Use Controls. *J. Public Econ.*, March 1988, *35*(2), pp. 133–62.

Epstein, Henry and Nimroody, Rosy. We're Stronger without SDI. *Challenge*, Sept.–Oct. 1988, *31*(5), pp. 44–49.

Epstein, Larry G. Risk Aversion and Asset Prices. *J. Monet. Econ.*, September 1988, *22*(2), pp. 179–92.

_____ **and Chew, Soo Hong.** The Law of Large Numbers and the Attractiveness of Compound Gambles. *J. Risk Uncertainty*, March 1988, *1*(1), pp. 125–32.

_____; **Zilcha, Itzhak and Chew, Soo Hong.** A Correspondence Theorem between Expected Utility and Smooth Utility. *J. Econ. Theory*, October 1988, *46*(1), pp. 186–93.

Epstein, Lenore A. Income of the Aged in 1962: First Findings of the 1963 Survey of the Aged. *Soc. Sec. Bull.*, March 1988, *51*(3), pp. 9–31.

Epstein, Richard A. The Political Economy of Product Liability Reform. *Amer. Econ. Rev.*, May 1988, *78*(2), pp. 311–15.

_____. The Public Trust Doctrine. In *Gwartney, J. D. and Wagner, R. E., eds.*, 1988, 1987, pp. 315–33.

_____. Taxation, Regulation, and Confiscation. In *Gwartney, J. D. and Wagner, R. E., eds.*, 1988, pp. 181–205.

Epstein, Steven A. Business Cycles and the Sense of Time in Medieval Genoa. *Bus. Hist. Rev.*, Summer 1988, *62*(2), pp. 238–60.

Eralp, Atila. West European Perspectives on

North–South Relations. *METU*, 1988, *15*(3–4), pp. 19–46.

Erbas, S. Nuri. Stability of Financing Deviations from Expected Deficits by Money Creation as Opposed to Bond Creation. *J. Macroecon.*, Summer 1988, *10*(3), pp. 469–75.

Erbe, Rainer. Foreign Indebtedness and Economic Growth: The Philippines. In *Gutowski, A. and Holthus, M., eds.*, 1988, 1982, pp. 173–96.

_____. The Significance of External Indebtedness for Capital Formation and Growth in Developing Countries. In *Gutowski, A. and Holthus, M., eds.*, 1988, 1983, pp. 115–38.

_____ **and Schattner, Susanne.** Indicator Systems for the Assessment of the External Debt Situation of Developing Countries. In *Gutowski, A. and Holthus, M., eds.*, 1988, 1980, pp. 45–59.

Erdilek, Asim. The Role of Foreign Investment in the Liberalization of the Turkish Economy. In *Nas, T. F. and Odekon, M., eds.*, 1988, pp. 141–59.

Erdmenger, Jürgen and Stasinopoulos, Dinos. The Shipping Policy of the European Community. *J. Transp. Econ. Policy*, September 1988, *22*(3), pp. 355–60.

Erdos, Joseph and Butcher, Paul. International Social Security Agreements: The U.S. Experience. *Soc. Sec. Bull.*, September 1988, *51*(9), pp. 4–12.

Erekson, O. Homer and Mitroff, Robert C. Equity Trends in Ohio School Finance, 1976–1984. *Econ. Educ. Rev.*, 1988, *7*(2), pp. 245–50.

_____ **and Sullivan, Dennis H.** A Cross-Section Analysis of IRS Auditing. *Nat. Tax J.*, June 1988, *41*(2), pp. 175–89.

Ereshko, F.; Lebedev, V. and Parikh, Kirit S. Agricultural Planning Models for Stavropol Region: Mathematical Description and Simulation Strategies. In *Parikh, J. K., ed.*, 1988, pp. 39–58.

Ergas, Henry. Countervailing Duty Laws and Subsidies to Imperfectly Competitive Industries: Comment. In *Baldwin, R. E.; Hamilton, C. B. and Sapir, A., eds.*, 1988, pp. 334–41.

Erickson, Rodney A.; Ottensmeyer, Edward J. and Humphrey, Craig R. Industrial Development Groups, Organizational Resources, and the Prospects for Effecting Growth in Local Economies. *Growth Change*, Summer 1988, *19*(3), pp. 1–21.

Erie, Steven P.; Rein, Martin and Brackman, Harold. Wedded to the Welfare State: Women against Reaganite Retrenchment. In *Jenson, J.; Hagen, E. and Reddy, C., eds.*, 1988, pp. 214–30.

Erikson, Robert and Fritzell, Johan. The Effects of the Social Welfare System in Sweden on the Well-Being of Children and the Elderly. In *Palmer, J. L.; Smeeding, T. and Torrey, B. B., eds.*, 1988, pp. 309–30.

Erisman, H. Michael. Cuban Foreign Policy and the Latin American Debt Crisis. In *Mesa-Lago, C., ed.*, 1988, pp. 3–18.

Erler, Gisela. The German Paradox: Non-feminization of the Labor Force and Post-industrial Social Policies. In *Jenson, J.; Hagen, E. and Reddy, C., eds.*, 1988, pp. 231–42.

Ermi, Luigi. Temporal Aggregation and Hall's Model of Consumption Behaviour. *Appl. Econ.*, October 1988, *20*(10), pp. 1317–20.

Ermisch, John F. An Economic Perspective on Household Modelling. In *Keilman, N.; Kuijsten, A. and Vossen, A., eds.*, 1988, pp. 23–40.

_____. British Labour Market Responses to Age Distribution Changes. In *Lee, R. D.; Arthur, W. B. and Rodgers, G., eds.*, 1988, pp. 76–86.

_____. Changing Demographic Patterns and the Housing Market with Special Reference to Great Britain. In *Lee, R. D.; Arthur, W. B. and Rodgers, G., eds.*, 1988, pp. 155–82.

_____. Econometric Analysis of Birth Rate Dynamics in Britain. *J. Human Res.*, Fall 1988, *23*(4), pp. 563–76.

_____. Economic Influences on Birth Rates. *Nat. Inst. Econ. Rev.*, November 1988, (126), pp. 71–81.

_____. Fortunes of Birth: The Impact of Generation Size on the Relative Earnings of Young Men. *Scot. J. Polit. Econ.*, August 1988, *35*(3), pp. 266–82.

Erol, Ümit and Koray, Faik. Frequency Domain Analysis of the Neutrality Hypothesis. *Southern Econ. J.*, October 1988, *55*(2), pp. 390–99.

Ervin, David E. Cropland Diversion (Set-Aside) in the U.S. and U.K. *J. Agr. Econ.*, May 1988, *39*(2), pp. 183–95.

_____ **and Dicks, Michael R.** Cropland Diversion for Conservation and Environmental Improvement: An Economic Welfare Analysis. *Land Econ.*, August 1988, *64*(3), pp. 256–68.

Ervin, Osbin L. Appropriating vs. Budgeting: A Comparison of Municipal Fiscal Processes. *Public Budg. Finance*, Winter 1988, *8*(4), pp. 45–53.

Erwee, Ronel. South African Women: Changing Career Patterns. In *Adler, N. J. and Izraeli, D., eds.*, 1988, pp. 213–25.

Erzan, Refik; Laird, Samuel and Yeats, Alexander. On the Potential for Expanding South–South Trade through the Extension of Mutual Preferences among Developing Countries. *World Devel.*, December 1988, *16*(12), pp. 1441–54.

Escarmelle, Jean-François and Monnier, Lionel. La spécificité du comportement de l'investissement des entreprises publiques françaises depuis 1973. (Behavioral Investment Specificities in French Public Enterprises since 1973. With English summary.) *Ann. Pub. Co-op. Econ.*, July–Sept. 1988, *59*(3), pp. 283–305.

de Escobar, Janet Kelly. Venezuela: Letting in the Market. In *Vernon, R., ed.*, 1988, pp. 57–90.

Escribano, C. and Bosch-Domènech, C. Escribano. Regional Allocation of Public Funds: An

Evaluation Index. *Environ. Planning A*, October 1988, *20*(10), pp. 1323–33.

Escribano, J. Briz. European Agriculture and World Food Supply: Report. *Europ. Rev. Agr. Econ.*, 1988, *15*(2–3), pp. 157–58.

Escrivá, José Luis and Espasa, Antoni. An Econometric Model for the Determination of Banking System Excess Reserves. In *Motamen, H., ed.*, 1988, pp. 609–51.

Escude, Guillermo. Dinámica de inventarios y dinero bajo competencia monopolística y salarios de eficiencia. (The Dynamics of Inventories and Money under Monopolistic Competition and Efficiency Wages. With English summary.) *Económica (La Plata)*, Jan.–June 1988, *34*(1), pp. 25–87.

_____. Teoría de las carteras y de la intermediación financiera. (Portfolio and Financial Intermediation Theory. With English summary.) *Económica (La Plata)*, July–Dec. 1988, *34*(2), pp. 203–39.

Escudier, Jean-Louis. Crises mondiale de l'énergie et mutations du système productif au XIXe et au XXe siècle. La crise charbonnière de 1873 et la crise pétrolière de 1973. (World Energetic Crisis and Changes of the French Productive System on the Nineteenth and Twentieth Centuries. The 1873 Coal Crisis and the 1973 Oil Crisis. With English summary.) *Revue Écon.*, March 1988, *39*(2), pp. 369–89.

Eskridge, William N., Jr. Interpreting Legislative Inaction. *Mich. Law Rev.*, October 1988, *87*(1), pp. 67–137.

Esogbue, Augustine O.; Fedrizzi, Mario and Kacprzyk, Janusz. Fuzzy Dynamic Programming with Stochastic Systems. In *Kacprzyk, J. and Fedrizzi, M., eds.*, 1988, pp. 266–85.

Esparza, A. and Waldorf, B. S. Labor Migration to Western Europe: A Commentary. *Environ. Planning A*, August 1988, *20*(8), pp. 1121–24.

Espasa, Antoni and Escrivá, José Luis. An Econometric Model for the Determination of Banking System Excess Reserves. In *Motamen, H., ed.*, 1988, pp. 609–51.

_____ and Sargan, John Denis. The Spectral Estimation of Simultaneous Equation Systems with Lagged Endogenous Variables. In *Sargan, J. D., Vol. 2*, 1988, 1977, pp. 246–69.

Espedal, Magne S.; Ewing, Richard E. and Dahle, Helge K. Characteristic Petrov-Galerkin Subdomain Methods for Convection-Diffusion Problems. In *Wheeler, M. F., ed.*, 1988, pp. 77–87.

Espenshade, Thomas J. and Arthur, W. Brian. Immigration Policy and Immigrants' Ages. *Population Devel. Rev.*, June 1988, *14*(2), pp. 315–26.

_____ and Calhoun, Charles A. Childbearing and Wives' Foregone Earnings. *Population Stud.*, March 1988, *42*(1), pp. 5–37.

Esping-Andersen, Gosta; Rainwater, Lee and Rein, Martin. Institutional and Political Factors Affecting the Well-Being of the Elderly. In *Palmer, J. L.; Smeeding, T. and Torrey, B. B., eds.*, 1988, pp. 333–50.

Esposito, F. Incorporating Knowledge in Decision Support Systems. In *Gaul, W. and Schader, M., eds.*, 1988, pp. 128–44.

Essayyad, Musa and Wu, H. K. The Performance of U.S. International Mutual Funds. *Quart. J. Bus. Econ.*, Autumn 1988, *27*(4), pp. 32–46.

Esser, Klaus. Modification of the Industrialization Model in Latin America. In *Wilber, C. K., ed.*, 1988, pp. 411–28.

Establet, Roger. Subversion dans la reproduction scolaire. (Subversion in Scholar Reproduction. With English summary.) *Revue Écon.*, January 1988, *39*(1), pp. 71–91.

Estanislao, Jesus P. Structural Adjustments in ASEAN. In *Tan, L.-H. and Akrasanee, N., eds.*, 1988, pp. 67–88.

Estep, Tony and Kritzman, Mark. TIPP: Insurance without Complexity. *J. Portfol. Manage.*, Summer 1988, *14*(4), pp. 38–42.

Estevez, Margarita; Hervés, Carlos and Besada, Manuel. Equilibria in Economies with Countably Many Commodities. *Econ. Letters*, 1988, *26*(3), pp. 203–07.

_____; Hervés, Carlos and Besada, Manuel. Existencia de equilibrio en una economía con producción e infinitas mercancias. (With English summary.) *Invest. Econ.*, January 1988, *12*(1), pp. 69–81.

_____; Hervés, Carlos and Besada, Manuel. Núcleo de una economía con infinitas mercancias. (With English summary.) *Invest. Econ.*, September 1988, *12*(3), pp. 445–53.

Estrada, Richard. Hispanic Americans: The Debased Coin of Citizenship. In *Simcox, D. E., ed.*, 1988, pp. 104–15.

Estrella, Arturo. Consistent Margin Requirements: Are They Feasible? *Fed. Res. Bank New York Quart. Rev.*, Summer 1988, *13*(2), pp. 61–79.

_____ and Hirtle, Beverly. Estimating the Funding Gap of the Pension Benefit Guaranty Corporation. *Fed. Res. Bank New York Quart. Rev.*, Autumn 1988, *13*(3), pp. 45–59.

Estrin, Alexander. Administrative Costs for Social Security Programs in Selected Countries. *Soc. Sec. Bull.*, November 1988, *51*(11), pp. 29.

Estrin, Saul; Geroski, Paul A. and Stewart, Geoff. Employee Share Ownership, Profit-Sharing and Participation: An Introduction. *Int. J. Ind. Organ.*, March 1988, *6*(1), pp. 1–6.

_____; Moore, Robert E. and Svejnar, Jan. Market Imperfections, Labor Management, and Earnings Differentials in a Developing Country: Theory and Evidence from Yugoslavia. *Quart. J. Econ.*, August 1988, *103*(3), pp. 465–78.

_____ and Shlomowitz, Ralph. Income Sharing, Employee Ownership and Worker Democracy. *Ann. Pub. Co-op. Econ.*, March 1988, *59*(1), pp. 43–65.

Etherington, Dan M. and Yainshet, Alasebu. The Impact of Income Terms of Trade for Coffee on Capital Goods Imports and Investment in Ethiopia. *Eastern Afr. Econ. Rev.*, June 1988, *4*(1), pp. 48–52.

Ettin, Edward C. Payments System Risk and Public Policy: Commentary. In *Haraf, W. S. and Kushmeider, R. M., eds.*, 1988, pp. 288–95.

Ettlie, John E. The First-Line Supervisor and Advanced Manufacturing Technology. In *Gattiker, U. E. and Larwood, L., eds.*, 1988, pp. 187–206.

Ettlinger, Nancy. American Fertility and Industrial Restructuring: A Possible Link. *Growth Change*, Summer 1988, *19*(3), pp. 75–93.

Etzioni, Amitai. Normative-Affective Factors: Toward a New Decision-Making Model. *J. Econ. Psych.*, June 1988, *9*(2), pp. 125–50.

——. Opening the Preferences: A Socio-economic Research Agenda. In *Earl, P. E., ed.*, Vol. 2, 1988, *1985*, pp. 137–59.

——. Toward a New Paradigm. In *Albanese, P. J., ed.*, 1988, pp. 165–72.

Eun, Cheol S.; Janakiramanan, S. and Alexander, Gordon J. International Listings and Stock Returns: Some Empirical Evidence. *J. Finan. Quant. Anal.*, June 1988, *23*(2), pp. 135–51.

—— **and Resnick, Bruce G.** Estimating the Dependence Structure of Share Prices: A Comparative Study of the United States and Japan. *Financial Rev.*, November 1988, *23*(4), pp. 387–401.

—— **and Resnick, Bruce G.** Exchange Rate Uncertainty, Forward Contracts, and International Portfolio Selection. *J. Finance*, March 1988, *43*(1), pp. 197–215.

Eusebio, J. Romão, et al. Development and Implementation of an Automatic System for Bus and Crew Scheduling at RN-Portugal. In *Daduna, J. R. and Wren, A., eds.*, 1988, pp. 147–59.

Euzéby, Alain. Social Security and Part-time Employment. *Int. Lab. Rev.*, 1988, *127*(5), pp. 545–57.

Evanoff, Douglas D. Branch Banking and Service Accessibility. *J. Money, Credit, Banking*, May 1988, *20*(2), pp. 191–202.

—— **and Fortier, Diana L.** Reevaluation of the Structure–Conduct–Performance Paradigm in Banking. *J. Finan. Services Res.*, June 1988, *1*(3), pp. 277–94.

Evans, Andrew. Hereford: A Case-Study of Bus Deregulation. *J. Transp. Econ. Policy*, September 1988, *22*(3), pp. 283–306.

Evans, David B. Aspects of Health Insurance: Moral Hazards, Agency Problems, and a Welfare Loss Estimate for Australia: Commentary. In *Smith, C. S., ed.*, 1988, pp. 272–73.

——. Survey of Recent Developments. *Bull. Indonesian Econ. Stud.*, December 1988, *24*(3), pp. 3–30.

——. A Theoretical Note on the Measurement of the Welfare Cost of Health Insurance: Discussion. In *Butler, J. R. G. and Doessel, D. P., eds.*, 1988, pp. 189–91.

Evans, Edward A. World Tax Reform: A Progress Report: Australia. In *Pechman, J. A., ed.*, 1988, pp. 15–40.

Evans, J. Lynne. Adjustment Modelling and the Stability of the Demand for Money Function.

Brit. Rev. Econ. Issues, Autumn 1988, *10*(23), pp. 49–76.

——. The Medium-Term Financial Strategy and the Fight against Inflation. In *Darnell, A. and Evans, L., eds.*, 1988, pp. 135–49.

——. Supply-Side Economics. In *Darnell, A. and Evans, L., eds.*, 1988, pp. 89–102.

—— **and Darnell, Adrian C.** The Holding Cost of Money. *Appl. Econ.*, March 1988, *20*(3), pp. 395–405.

Evans, Leonard. Mandatory Seat Belt Use Laws and Occupant Crash Protection in the United States: Present Status and Future Prospects: Comments. In *Graham, J. D., ed.*, 1988, pp. 73–83.

Evans, Lewis and Garber, Steven. Public-Utility Regulators Are Only Human: A Positive Theory of Rational Constraints. *Amer. Econ. Rev.*, June 1988, *78*(3), pp. 444–62.

Evans, Marc A.; McDonald, Lyman and Nowell, Clifford. Length-Biased Sampling in Contingent Valuation Studies. *Land Econ.*, November 1988, *64*(4), pp. 367–71.

Evans, Mark O. A Recursive Inflation–Unemployment Model for Principles of Economics Courses. *J. Econ. Educ.*, Fall 1988, *19*(4), pp. 341–52.

Evans, Merran A. and King, Maxwell L. A Further Class of Tests for Heteroscedasticity. *J. Econometrics*, February 1988, *37*(2), pp. 265–76.

Evans, Owen and Kenward, Lloyd. Macroeconomic Effects of Tax Reform in the United States. *Int. Monet. Fund Staff Pap.*, March 1988, *35*(1), pp. 141–65.

Evans, Patricia. Work Incentives and the Single Mother: Dilemmas of Reform. *Can. Public Policy*, June 1988, *14*(2), pp. 125–36.

Evans, Paul. Are Consumers Ricardian? Evidence for the United States. *J. Polit. Econ.*, October 1988, *96*(5), pp. 983–1004.

——. Are Government Bonds Net Wealth? Evidence for the United States. *Econ. Inquiry*, October 1988, *26*(4), pp. 551–66.

——. The Effects of Fiscal Policy in Korea. *Int. Econ. J.*, Summer 1988, *2*(2), pp. 1–14.

Evans, Thomas G. and Doupnik, Timothy. The Functional Currency Determination: A Strategy to Smooth Income. In *Most, K. S., ed.*, 1988, pp. 171–82.

Evans, Trevor. Finance and the International System: Money Makes the World Go Round. In *Harris, L., et al., eds.*, 1988, pp. 41–68.

Evans, William N. and Luger, Michael I. Geographic Differences in Production Technology. *Reg. Sci. Urban Econ.*, August 1988, *18*(3), pp. 399–424.

Even, William E. Testing Exogeneity in a Probit Model. *Econ. Letters*, 1988, *26*(2), pp. 125–28.

Evensky, Jerry. An Expansion of the Neoclassical Horizon in Economics: The Rent-Seeking Research Program Brings in the Nuances of Social and Political Control. *Amer. J. Econ. Soc.*, April 1988, *47*(2), pp. 223–37.

Evenson, Robert E. Population Growth, Infrastructure, and Real Incomes in North India. In *Lee, R. D., et al., eds.,* 1988, pp. 118–39.

_____. Technological Opportunities and International Technology Transfer in Agriculture. In *Antonelli, G. and Quadrio-Curzio, A., eds.,* 1988, pp. 133–65.

_____; Hanazaki, Masaharu and Englander, A. Steven. R&D, Innovation and the Total Factor Productivity Slowdown. *OECD Econ. Stud.,* Autumn 1988, (11), pp. 7–42.

Evsiukov, Evgenii; Kriuchkov, Nikolai and Bober, Wolfgang. Scientific-Technological Cooperation in Chemistry. *Soviet E. Europ. Foreign Trade,* Spring 1988, 24(1), pp. 54–62.

Evstigneev, R. Theoretical Aspects of Coordinating Economic Interests. *Prob. Econ.,* October 1988, 31(6), pp. 47–63.

Evtushenko, Y.; Mazourik, V. and Ratkin, V. Multicriteria Optimization in the DISO System. In *Kurzhanski, A.; Neumann, K. and Pallaschke, D., eds.,* 1988, pp. 94–102.

Ewing, Richard E. Adaptive Grid-Refinement Techniques for Treating Singularities, Heterogeneities, and Dispersion. In *Wheeler, M. F., ed.,* 1988, pp. 133–48.

_____; Dahle, Helge K. and Espedal, Magne S. Characteristic Petrov-Galerkin Subdomain Methods for Convection-Diffusion Problems. In *Wheeler, M. F., ed.,* 1988, pp. 77–87.

Extejt, Marian M. and Chelius, James R. The Narcotic Effect of Impasse Resolution Procedures. In *Lewin, D., et al., eds.,* 1988, *1985,* pp. 399–411.

Eytan, T. Hanan; Harpaz, Giora and Cakici, Nusret. American vs. European Options on the Value Line Index. *J. Futures Markets,* June 1988, 8(3), pp. 373–88.

_____; Harpaz, Giora and Krull, Steven. The Pricing of Dollar Index Futures Contracts. *J. Futures Markets,* April 1988, 8(2), pp. 127–39.

Ezeala-Harrison, Fidelis. An Application of the Efficiency-Wage Hypothesis to the Modelling of LDC Labour Problems. *J. Econ. Devel.,* June 1988, 13(1), pp. 71–94.

Ezejelue, A. C. Nigeria: Recent Amendments to Tax Laws. *Bull. Int. Fiscal Doc.,* July 1988, 42(7), pp. 315–18.

Ezekiel, Hannan. An Approach to a Food Aid Strategy. *World Devel.,* November 1988, 16(11), pp. 1377–87.

Faas, Ronald C. Nuclear Waste Disposal Policy: Socioeconomic Impact Management Issues. In *Johnston, G. M.; Freshwater, D. and Favero, P., eds.,* 1988, pp. 91–110.

Fabel, Oliver and Coughlin, Cletus C. State Factor Endowments and Exports: An Alternative to Cross-Industry Studies. *Rev. Econ. Statist.,* November 1988, 70(4), pp. 696–701.

Fabella, Raul V. Natural Team Sharing and Team Productivity. *Econ. Letters,* 1988, 27(2), pp. 105–10.

Faber, Malte and Bernholz, Peter. Reflections on a Normative Economic Theory of the Unification of Law. In *Gwartney, J. D. and Wagner, R. E., eds.,* 1988, pp. 229–49.

_____ and Manstetten, Reiner. Der Ursprung der Volkswirtschaftslerhe als Bestimmung und Bergrenzung ihrer Erkenntnisperspektive. (The Origin of Economics as Determination and Limitation of its Epistemological Perspective. With English summary.) *Schweiz. Z. Volkswirtsch. Statist.,* June 1988, 124(2), pp. 97–121.

Faber, Ronald J. and O'Guinn, Thomas C. Expanding the View of Consumer Socialization: A Nonutilitarian Mass-Mediated Perspective. In *Hirschman, E. and Sheth, J. N., eds.,* 1988, pp. 49–77.

Fabi, Bruno. The New Zealand "Green Paper" on Higher Education: The Human Resource Management Dimension. *Australian Bull. Lab.,* March 1988, 14(2), pp. 401–13.

Fabozzi, Frank J. and Ma, Christopher K. The Day-of-the-Week Effect for Derivative Assets: The Case of Gold Futures Options. In *Fabozzi, F. J., ed.,* 1988, pp. 379–88.

_____ and Ma, Christopher K. The Over-the-Counter Market and New York Stock Exchange Trading Halts. *Financial Rev.,* November 1988, 23(4), pp. 427–37.

_____; Moran, Eileen and Ma, Christopher K. Market Uncertainty and the Least-Cost Offering Method of Public Utility Debt: A Note. *J. Finance,* September 1988, 43(4), pp. 1025–34.

_____, et al. A Note on Unsuccessful Tender Offers and Stockholder Returns. *J. Finance,* December 1988, 43(5), pp. 1275–83.

Fackler, James S. and Holland, A. Steven. Indexation and the Effect of a Price-Level Shock on Relative Wage Variability. *Rev. Econ. Statist.,* August 1988, 70(3), pp. 524–26.

Fackler, Paul L. An Analysis of Alternative Market and Governmental Risk Transference Mechanisms. In *Sumner, D. A., ed.,* 1988, pp. 57–77.

Fader, Peter S. and Hauser, John R. Implicit Coalitions in a Generalized Prisoner's Dilemma. *J. Conflict Resolution,* September 1988, 32(3), pp. 553–82.

Fagbemi, Olubunmi A. Registration of Technology Transactions in Nigeria: Another View. *J. World Trade,* August 1988, 22(4), pp. 95–100.

Fagerberg, Jan. International Competitiveness. *Econ. J.,* June 1988, 98(391), pp. 355–74.

_____. International Competitiveness: Errata. *Econ. J.,* December 1988, 98(393), pp. 1203.

_____. Why Growth Rates Differ. In *Dosi, G., et al., eds.,* 1988, pp. 432–57.

_____; Jørgensen, Ulrik and Dalum, Bent. Small Open Economies in the World Market for Electronics: The Case of the Nordic Countries. In *Freeman, C. and Lundvall, B.-A., eds.,* 1988, pp. 113–38.

Fägerlind, Ingemar; Tuijnman, Albert and Chinapah, Vinayagum. Adult Education and Earnings: A 45-Year Longitudinal Study of 834 Swedish Men. *Econ. Educ. Rev.,* 1988, 7(4), pp. 423–37.

Fagin, Claire M. Why the Quick Fix Won't Fix

Today's Nurse Shortage. *Inquiry*, Fall 1988, 25(3), pp. 309–14.

Fahey, Liam and Camerer, Colin. The Regression Paradigm: A Critical Appraisal and Suggested Directions. In *Grant, J. H., ed.*, 1988, pp. 443–59.

Fahey, P. and Hall, J. Does Accessibility to Health Services Improve Health? In *Smith, C. S., ed.*, 1988, pp. 232–48.

Faig, Miquel. Characterization of the Optimal Tax on Money When It Functions as a Medium of Exchange. *J. Monet. Econ.*, July 1988, 22(1), pp. 137–48.

Faigal, Gerardo Ma. A. and Nieva, Claro L. Processed Agricultural Products: Issues for Negotiation between ASEAN and the EC. In *Langhammer, R. J. and Rieger, H. C., eds.*, 1988, pp. 116–28.

Faiña Medin, J. Andrés and Puy Fraga, Pedro. A Framework for a Public Choice Analysis of the European Community. *Econ. Scelte Pubbliche/J. Public Finance Public Choice*, May–Aug. 1988, 6(2), pp. 141–58.

Fair, Ray C. Optimal Choice of Monetary Policy Instruments in a Macroeconometric Model. *J. Monet. Econ.*, September 1988, 22(2), pp. 301–15.

———. Sources of Economic Fluctuations in the United States. *Quart. J. Econ.*, May 1988, 103(2), pp. 313–32.

——— **and Andrews, Donald W. K.** Inference in Nonlinear Econometric Models with Structural Change. *Rev. Econ. Stud.*, October 1988, 55(4), pp. 615–39.

———; **Shapiro, Matthew D. and Dominguez, Kathryn M.** Forecasting the Depression: Harvard versus Yale. *Amer. Econ. Rev.*, September 1988, 78(4), pp. 595–612.

Fajnzylber, Fernando. International Competitiveness: Agreed Goal, Hard Task. *CEPAL Rev.*, December 1988, (36), pp. 7–23.

Falaris, Evangelos M. Migration and Wages of Young Men. *J. Human Res.*, Fall 1988, 23(4), pp. 514–34.

Falcone, David J. and George, David. Inflation and Related Misperceptions. In *Pennsylvania Economic Association*, 1988, pp. 85–102.

Faldyna, František. The Political and Legal Principles of the Draft Bill on the State Enterprise. *Czech. Econ. Digest.*, February 1988, (1), pp. 59–80.

Falk, Ita. A Dynamic Model of Interrelated Renewable Resources: A Case Study of Marine Stocks under Alternative Forms of Ownership with Symmetrical Interspecies Competition. *Resources & Energy*, March 1988, 10(1), pp. 55–77.

Falk, Karl. China's Socioeconomic Progress: The Mainland Revisited Shows Evidence of Advance but Its Overpopulation Is a Big Problem. *Amer. J. Econ. Soc.*, July 1988, 47(3), pp. 363–69.

Falk, Richard. Militarisation and Human Rights in the Third World. In *Wilber, C. K., ed.*, 1988, pp. 468–79.

———. Satisfying Human Needs in a World of

Sovereign States: Rhetoric, Reality, and Vision. In *Wilber, C. K., ed.*, 1988, pp. 560–87.

Falkenberg, Loren and Ponak, Allen. Dispute Resolution Procedures under Canadian Collective Bargaining. *Australian Bull. Lab.*, March 1988, 14(2), pp. 426–48.

Falkinger, Josef. Tax Evasion and Equity: A Theoretical Analysis. *Public Finance*, 1988, 43(3), pp. 388–95.

Falkner, J. C. and Ryan, D. M. Aspects of Bus Crew Scheduling Using a Set Partitioning Model. In *Daduna, J. R. and Wren, A., eds.*, 1988, pp. 91–103.

Fallenbuchl, Zbigniew M. An Overview of the Role of Agriculture in the Polish Economic Crisis. In *Brada, J. C. and Wadekin, K.-E., eds.*, 1988, pp. 125–30.

———. Changes in the Polish Foreign Trade System and Adjustment: Comments. In *[Holzman, F. D.]*, 1988, pp. 370–77.

———. Present State of the Economic Reform. In *Marer, P. and Siwinski, W., eds.*, 1988, pp. 115–30.

Fallis, George; Smith, Lawrence B. and Rosen, Kenneth T. Recent Developments in Economic Models of Housing Markets. *J. Econ. Lit.*, March 1988, 26(1), pp. 29–64.

Falls, Gregory A. and Natke, Paul A. The Demand for Liquid Assets: A Firm Level Analysis. *Southern Econ. J.*, January 1988, 54(3), pp. 630–42.

——— **and Worden, Debra Drecnik.** Consumer Valuation of Protection from Creditor Remedies. *J. Cons. Aff.*, Summer 1988, 22(1), pp. 20–37.

Falvey, Rodney E. Tariffs, Quotas and Piecemeal Policy Reform. *J. Int. Econ.*, August 1988, 25(1–2), pp. 177–83.

Fama, Eugene F. and French, Kenneth R. Business Cycles and the Behavior of Metals Prices. *J. Finance*, December 1988, 43(5), pp. 1075–93.

——— **and French, Kenneth R.** Dividend Yields and Expected Stock Returns. *J. Finan. Econ.*, October 1988, 22(1), pp. 3–25.

——— **and French, Kenneth R.** Permanent and Temporary Components of Stock Prices. *J. Polit. Econ.*, April 1988, 96(2), pp. 246–73.

Faminow, M. D. and Benson, Bruce L. The Impact of Experience on Prices and Profits in Experimental Duopoly Markets. *J. Econ. Behav. Organ.*, June 1988, 9(4), pp. 345–65.

——— **and Benson, Bruce L.** Location Choice and Urban Growth in a Rent-Seeking Society. *Public Finance Quart.*, April 1988, 16(2), pp. 158–77.

Fan, C. Cindy. The Temporal and Spatial Dynamics of City-Size Distributions in China. *Population Res. Policy Rev.*, 1988, 7(2), pp. 123–57.

Fan, Chuen-Mei. Income Tax Policies and the Labor Supply of Female Secondary Income Earners. *Public Finance*, 1988, 43(1), pp. 67–78.

Fan, Qi. A Reasonable Way Should Be Found to Enable Individual Businesspeople to Hire

Hands and Take on Apprentices: Report on an Investigation in Chengdu. *Chinese Econ. Stud.*, Winter 1987–88, *21*(2), pp. 41–45.

Fanara, Philip, Jr. and Corsi, Thomas M. Driver Management Policies and Motor Carrier Safety. *Logist. Transp. Rev.*, June 1988, *24*(2), pp. 153–63.

Fand, David I. Monetary Reform: The Alternatives. *Econ. Scelte Pubbliche/J. Public Finance Public Choice*, Jan.–April 1988, *6*(1), pp. 3–13.

_____. On the Endogenous Money Supply. *J. Post Keynesian Econ.*, Spring 1988, *10*(3), pp. 386–89.

Fandel, Günter and Reese, Joachim. Kostenminimale Kraftwerksteuerung in einem Industriebetrieb. (With English summary.) *Z. Betriebswirtshaft*, January 1988, *58*(1), pp. 137–52.

Fanelli, Jose Maria and Machinea, Jose Luis. Stopping Hyperinflation: The Case of the Austral Plan in Argentina, 1985–87. In *Bruno, M., et al., eds.*, 1988, pp. 111–52.

Fapohunda, Eleanor R. and Todaro, Michael P. Family Structure, Implicit Contracts, and the Demand for Children in Southern Nigeria. *Population Devel. Rev.*, December 1988, *14*(4), pp. 571–94.

Farber, A. and Adam, M. C. Le financement de l'innovation technoligique. Deuxième partie: L'apport de la théorie finanacière. (With English summary.) *Cah. Écon. Bruxelles*, First Trimester 1988, (117), pp. 3–36.

Farber, Henry S. The Evolution of Public Sector Bargaining Laws. In *Freeman, R. B. and Ichniowski, C., eds.*, 1988, pp. 129–66.

_____. The Impact of Firm Acquisitions on Labor: Comment. In *Auerbach, A. J., ed. (I)*, 1988, pp. 28–31.

_____ **and Abraham, Katharine G.** Returns to Seniority in Union and Nonunion Jobs: A New Look at the Evidence. *Ind. Lab. Relat. Rev.*, October 1988, *42*(1), pp. 3–19.

Farber, Kit D. and Rutledge, Gary L. Pollution Abatement and Control Expenditures, 1983–86. *Surv. Curr. Bus.*, May 1988, *68*(5), pp. 22–29.

Färe, Rolf. Efficiency Gains from Addition of Technologies: A Nonparametric Approach. In *Eichhorn, W., ed.*, 1988, pp. 171–76.

_____. Returns to Scale and Size in Agricultural Economics: Comment. *Western J. Agr. Econ.*, July 1988, *13*(1), pp. 149–50.

_____ **and Grosskopf, Shawna.** Measuring Shadow Price Efficiency. In *Dogramaci, A. and Färe, R., eds.,*, 1988, pp. 223–34.

_____; **Grosskopf, Shawna and Lovell, C. A. Knox.** An Indirect Approach to the Evaluation of Producer Performance. *J. Public Econ.*, October 1988, *37*(1), pp. 71–89.

_____; **Grosskopf, Shawna and Lovell, C. A. Knox.** Scale Elasticity and Scale Efficiency. *J. Inst. Theoretical Econ.*, September 1988, *144*(4), pp. 721–29.

_____ **and Lovell, C. A. Knox.** Aggregation and Efficiency. In *Eichhorn, W., ed.*, 1988, pp. 639–47.

_____ **and Primont, Daniel.** Efficiency Measures for Multiplant Firms with Limited Data. In *Eichhorn, W., ed.*, 1988, pp. 177–86.

_____ **and Sawyer, Carl.** Expenditure Constraints and Profit Maximization in U.S. Agriculture: Comment. *Amer. J. Agr. Econ.*, November 1988, *70*(4), pp. 953–54.

Farebrother, R. W. A Survey of Some Recent Econometric Work on Tests for Inequality Constraints. *J. Quant. Econ.*, July 1988, *4*(2), pp. 227–38.

Faria, Hugo Presgrave de A. Macroeconomic Policymaking in a Crisis Environment: Brazil's Cruzado Plan and Beyond. In *Chacel, J. M.; Falk, P. S. and Fleischer, D. V., eds.*, 1988, pp. 42–59.

Faria, Vilmar and Martine, George. Impacts of Social Research on Policy Formulation: Lessons from the Brazilian Experience in the Population Field. *J. Devel. Areas*, October 1988, *23*(1), pp. 43–61.

Farimani, Mehrdad; Buongiorno, Joseph and Thompson, Howard E. A Financial Model of Investment, with an Application to the Paper Industry. *Appl. Econ.*, June 1988, *20*(6), pp. 767–83.

Farkas, George and England, Paula. Economic and Sociological Views of Industries, Firms, and Jobs. In *Farkas, G. and England, P., eds.*, 1988, pp. 331–46.

_____; **England, Paula and Barton, Margaret.** Structural Effects on Wages: Sociological and Economic Views. In *Farkas, G. and England, P., eds.*, 1988, pp. 93–112.

Farley, Reynolds. After the Starting Line: Blacks and Women in an Uphill Race. *Demography*, November 1988, *25*(4), pp. 477–95.

Farmer, J. Doyne and Sidorowich, John J. Can New Approaches to Nonlinear Modeling Improve Economic Forecasts? In *Anderson, P. W.; Arrow, K. J. and Pines, D., eds.*, 1988, pp. 99–115.

Farmer, Richard N. and McGoun, Elton G. Nationalism, Cultural Heterogeneity, and Economic Growth. In *Farmer, R. N. and McGoun, E. G., eds.*, 1988, pp. 3–19.

Farmer, Roger E. A. Money and Contracts. *Rev. Econ. Stud.*, July 1988, *55*(3), pp. 431–46.

_____. What Is a Liquidity Crisis? *J. Econ. Theory*, October 1988, *46*(1), pp. 1–15.

Farooq, Mohammad Omar. Basic Needs Approach, Appropriate Technology, and Institutionalism. *J. Econ. Issues*, June 1988, *22*(2), pp. 363–70.

Farooqui, M. Naseem Iqbal. Gains in Life Expectancy by Elimination of Specified Causes of Death in Pakistan: Comments. *Pakistan Devel. Rev.*, Part 2, Winter 1988, *27*(4), pp. 652–53.

Farrant, Alan. Proper Handling of Subordinate Problems. In *Timpe, A. D., ed.*, 1988, *1985*, pp. 341–44.

Farrell, John B. Establishment Survey Incorporates March 1987 Employment Benchmarks. *Mon. Lab. Rev.*, October 1988, *111*(10), pp. 37–38.

Farrell, John P. and Kostecki, Marian J. Poland's

Top 500. *Comp. Econ. Stud.*, Winter 1988, 30(4), pp. 52–57.

Farrell, Joseph. Communication, Coordination and Nash Equilibrium. *Econ. Letters*, 1988, 27(3), pp. 209–14.

_____. Puzzles: Sylvia, Ice Cream and More. *J. Econ. Perspectives*, Summer 1988, 2(3), pp. 175–82.

_____ **and Gallini, Nancy T.** Second-Sourcing as a Commitment: Monopoly Incentives to Attract Competition. *Quart. J. Econ.*, November 1988, 103(4), pp. 673–94.

_____ **and Saloner, Garth.** Coordination through Committees and Markets. *Rand J. Econ.*, Summer 1988, 19(2), pp. 235–52.

_____ **and Scotchmer, Suzanne.** Partnerships. *Quart. J. Econ.*, May 1988, 103(2), pp. 279–97.

_____ **and Shapiro, Carl.** Dynamic Competition with Switching Costs. *Rand J. Econ.*, Spring 1988, 19(1), pp. 123–37.

Farrell, Kenneth R. The Economics of Rural Areas: A Discussion. In *Hildreth, R. J., et al., eds.*, 1988, pp. 440–42.

_____. U.S.–Canadian Agricultural Trade Challenges: Developing Common Approaches: Epilogue. In *Allen, K. and Macmillan, K., eds.*, 1988, pp. 197–202.

Farrell, L. M. Hedged Real Estate Portfolios and the Wealth Redistribution Effect of Real Estate Option. *Urban Stud.*, December 1988, 25(6), pp. 507–19.

Farrell, Terrence W. and Crichton, Nigel. Market Structure and Concentration in the Manufacturing Sector in Trinidad and Tobago. *Soc. Econ. Stud.*, September 1988, 37(3), pp. 151–92.

Farris, Donald E.; Mullen, John D. and Wohlgenant, Michael K. Input Substitution and the Distribution of Surplus Gains from Lower U.S. Beef-Processing Costs. *Amer. J. Agr. Econ.*, May 1988, 70(2), pp. 245–54.

Farris, Paul L. and Oellermann, Charles M. Note on Trader Concentration Effects in Feeder Cattle Futures and Comparison with Live Cattle. *J. Futures Markets*, February 1988, 8(1), pp. 103–13.

Fase, M. M. G. and van den Heuvel, Paul J. Productivity and Growth: Verdoorn's Law Revisited. *Econ. Letters*, 1988, 28(2), pp. 135–39.

Fasenfest, David. Urban Policies, Social Goals and Producer Incentives: Are Market Mechanisms and Policy Objectives Compatible? In *Hula, R. C., ed.*, 1988, pp. 137–57.

Fashoyin, Tayo. Trade Unions, the State and Labour Mobility in ECOWAS. In *Southall, R., ed.*, 1988, pp. 49–79.

Fatemi, Ali M. and Furtado, Eugene P. H. An Empirical Investigation of the Wealth Effects of Foreign Acquisitions. In *Khoury, S. J. and Ghosh, A., eds.*, 1988, pp. 363–79.

Faulhaber, Gerald R. Deregulation and Innovation in Telecommunications. In *Libecap, G., ed. (II)*, 1988, pp. 107–51.

_____ **and Allen, Franklin.** Optimism Invites

Deception. *Quart. J. Econ.*, May 1988, 103(2), pp. 397–407.

_____ **and Baumol, William J.** Economists as Innovators: Practical Products of Theoretical Research. *J. Econ. Lit.*, June 1988, 26(2), pp. 577–600.

Faustini, Gino. Labour Supply in Italy. *Rev. Econ. Cond. Italy*, May–Aug. 1988, (2), pp. 153–78.

Faux, Jeff. A Cheaper Dollar Is Not Enough. *Challenge*, May–June 1988, 31(3), pp. 42–47.

_____. New Institutions for the Post-Reagan Economy. In *Levine, M. V., et al.*, 1988, pp. 147–67.

Favereau, Olivier. Probability and Uncertainty: "After All, Keynes Was Right." *Écon. Soc.*, October 1988, 22(10), pp. 133–67.

Favero, Carlo. An Econometric Analysis of the Inflation–Unemployment Trade-Off. *Giorn. Econ.*, Jan.–Feb. 1988, 47(1–2), pp. 45–64.

Favero, Philip; Pitt, David G. and Tuthill, Dean F. Land Use Policies, Water Quality, and the Chesapeake Bay. In *Johnston, G. M.; Freshwater, D. and Favero, P., eds.*, 1988, pp. 71–90.

Fawson, Chris and Giroux, Gary. An Empirical Extension of the Municipal Monopoly Model to Provision of Community Infrastructure [Bureaucracy and the Divisibility of Local Public Output]. *Public Choice*, April 1988, 57(1), pp. 79–83.

_____ **and Shumway, C. Richard.** A Nonparametric Investigation of Agricultural Production Behavior for U.S. Subregions. *Amer. J. Agr. Econ.*, May 1988, 70(2), pp. 311–17.

Fazal, Mohd. Human Resources Development and the Planning Process in India: Keynote Address. In *Kohli, U. and Gautam, V., eds.*, 1988, pp. 5–11.

Fazzari, Steven M. and Chirinko, Robert S. Tobin's Q, Non-constant Returns to Scale, and Imperfectly Competitive Product Markets. *Rech. Écon. Louvain*, 1988, 54(3), pp. 259–75.

_____; **Hubbard, Robert Glenn and Petersen, Bruce C.** Financing Constraints and Corporate Investment. *Brookings Pap. Econ. Act.*, 1988, (1), pp. 141–95.

_____; **Hubbard, Robert Glenn and Petersen, Bruce C.** Investment, Financing Decisions, and Tax Policy. *Amer. Econ. Rev.*, May 1988, 78(2), pp. 200–205.

Fearnside, Philip M. China's Three Gorges Dam: "Fatal" Project or Step toward Modernization. *World Devel.*, May 1988, 16(5), pp. 615–30.

Feaster, Daniel J. and Danziger, Sheldon H. Wealth Distributional Consequences of Life Cycle Models: Comments. In *Kessler, D. and Masson, A., eds.*, 1988, pp. 319–21.

_____; **Holden, Karen C. and Burkhauser, Richard V.** The Timing of Falls into Poverty after Retirement and Widowhood. *Demography*, August 1988, 25(3), pp. 405–14.

Featherstone, Allen M.; Schroeder, Ted C. and Burton, Robert O., Jr. Allocation of Farm Financial Stress among Income, Leverage, and Interest Rate Components: A Kansas Example.

Southern J. Agr. Econ., December 1988, *20*(2), pp. 15–24.

_____, et al. The Theoretical Effects of Farm Policies on Optimal Leverage and the Probability of Equity Losses. *Amer. J. Agr. Econ.*, August 1988, *70*(3), pp. 572–79.

Feder, Gershon and Chalamwong, Yongyuth. The Impact of Landownership Security: Theory and Evidence from Thailand. *World Bank Econ. Rev.*, May 1988, *2*(2), pp. 187–204.

_____; Onchan, Tongroj and Chalamwong, Yongyuth. Land Policies and Farm Performance in Thailand's Forest Reserve Areas. *Econ. Develop. Cult. Change*, April 1988, *36*(3), pp. 483–501.

Fedrizzi, Mario and Kacprzyk, Janusz. On Measuring Consensus in the Setting of Fuzzy Preference Relations. In *Kacprzyk, J. and Roubens, M., eds.*, 1988, pp. 129–41.

_____; Kacprzyk, Janusz and Esogbue, Augustine O. Fuzzy Dynamic Programming with Stochastic Systems. In *Kacprzyk, J. and Fedrizzi, M., eds.*, 1988, pp. 266–85.

Fedyk, Frank; Zeesman, Allen and Messinger, Hans. The Size and Distribution of the Poverty Gap in Canada: A Micro Analysis of Variations among Demographic Groups. *Rev. Income Wealth*, September 1988, *34*(3), pp. 275–88.

Fedyk, Joanne M. and Douthitt, Robin A. The Influence of Children on Family Life Cycle Spending Behavior: Theory and Applications. *J. Cons. Aff.*, Winter 1988, *22*(2), pp. 220–48.

Feehan, James P. Efficient Tariff Financing of Public Goods. *J. Int. Econ.*, August 1988, *25*(1–2), pp. 155–64.

Feenberg, Daniel R. Federal Deductibility of State and Local Taxes: A Test of Public Choice by Representative Government: Comment. In *Rosen, H. S., ed.*, 1988, pp. 175–76.

_____ and Rosen, Harvey S. Promises, Promises: The States' Experience with Income Tax Indexing. *Nat. Tax J.*, December 1988, *41*(4), pp. 525–42.

Feeney, Paul W. Credit Ratings in the Eurocommercial Paper Market. *Nat. Westminster Bank Quart. Rev.*, May 1988, pp. 49–59.

Feenstra, Robert C. The Effects of Protection on Domestic Output: Comment. In *Baldwin, R. E., ed. (II)*, 1988, pp. 226–28.

_____. Gains from Trade in Differentiated Products: Japanese Compact Trucks. In *Feenstra, R. C., ed.*, 1988, pp. 119–36.

_____. Incentive Compatible Trade Policies. In *Haaland, J. I. and Norman, V. D., eds.*, 1988, pp. 157–71.

_____. Quality Change under Trade Restraints in Japanese Autos. *Quart. J. Econ.*, February 1988, *103*(1), pp. 131–46.

Feeny, David. Agricultural Expansion and Forest Depletion in Thailand, 1900–1975. In *Richards, J. F. and Tucker, R. P., eds.*, 1988, pp. 112–43.

_____. The Development of Property Rights in Land: A Comparative Study. In *Bates, R. H., ed.*, 1988, pp. 272–99.

_____ and Mestelman, Stuart. Does Ideology Matter?: Anecdotal Experimental Evidence on the Voluntary Provision of Public Goods. *Public Choice*, June 1988, *57*(3), pp. 281–86.

_____ and Stoddart, Greg. Toward Improved Health Technology Policy in Canada: A Proposal for the National Health Technology Assessment Council. *Can. Public Policy*, September 1988, *14*(3), pp. 254–65.

Feeser, Henry R. and Willard, Gary E. Incubators and Performance: A Comparison of High and Low Growth High Tech Firms. In *Kirchhoff, B. A., et al., eds.*, 1988, pp. 549–63.

Fehr-Duda, Helga. Die Investitionstätigkeit öffentlicher Unternehmungen in Österreich. (Public Enterprise Investment in Austria. With English summary.) *Ann. Pub. Co-op. Econ.*, Oct.–Dec. 1988, *59*(4), pp. 509–28.

Fehrs, Donald H.; Benesh, Gary A. and Peterson, David R. Evidence of a Relation between Stock Price Reactions around Cash Dividend Changes and Yields. *J. Finan. Res.*, Summer 1988, *11*(2), pp. 111–23.

Fei, John C. H. and Reynolds, Bruce L. A Tentative Plan for the Rational Sequencing of Overall Reform in China's Economic System. In *Reynolds, B. L., ed.*, 1988, *1987*, pp. 200–212.

Feichtinger, Gustav. Production–Pollution Cycles. In *Kurzhanski, A.; Neumann, K. and Pallaschke, D., eds.*, 1988, pp. 263–76.

_____; Kistner, Klaus-Peter and Luhmer, Alfred. Ein dynamisches Modell des Intensitätssplittings. (With English summary.) *Z. Betriebswirtshaft*, November 1988, *58*(11), pp. 1242–58.

_____; Luhmer, Alfred and Sorger, Gerhard. Optimal Price and Advertising Policy for a Convenience Goods Retailer. *Marketing Sci.*, Spring 1988, *7*(2), pp. 187–201.

Feigenbaum, Bernard and Lowenberg, Anton D. South African Disinvestment: Causes and Effects. *Contemp. Policy Issues*, October 1988, *6*(4), pp. 105–17.

Feigenbaum, Edward A.; March, James G. and Cyert, Richard M. Models in a Behavioral Theory of the Firm. In *March, J. G.*, 1988, *1959*, pp. 37–60.

Feigenbaum, Susan; Karoly, Lynn and Levy, David M. When Votes Are Words Not Deeds: Some Evidence from the Nuclear Freeze Referendum. *Public Choice*, September 1988, *58*(3), pp. 201–16.

Feiger, George M. Economies of Scope and Scale in Financial Services. In *Federal Home Loan Bank of San Francisco*, 1988, pp. 107–17.

Feinberg, Richard E. The Changing Relationship between the World Bank and the International Monetary Fund. *Int. Organ.*, Summer 1988, *42*(3), pp. 545–60.

_____. Latin American Debt: Renegotiating the Adjustment Burden. In *Feinberg, R. E. and Ffrench-Davis, R., eds.*, 1988, pp. 52–76.

_____ and Ffrench-Davis, Ricardo. Development and External Debt in Latin America: Bases for a New Consensus: Overview. In *Feinberg, R. E. and Ffrench-Davis, R., eds.*, 1988, pp. 1–7.

Feinberg, Robert M. Intellectual Property, Injury, and International Trade. *J. World Trade,* April 1988, 22(2), pp. 45–56.

⸻ **and Benson, Bruce L.** An Experimental Investigation of Equilibria Impacts of Information. *Southern Econ. J.,* January 1988, 54(3), pp. 546–61.

⸻ **and Sherman, Roger.** Mutual Forbearance under Experimental Conditions. *Southern Econ. J.,* April 1988, 54(4), pp. 985–93.

Feinerman, E. and Siegel, P. B. A Dynamic Farm-Level Planning Model for Beef Feedlot Production and Marketing. *J. Agr. Econ.,* September 1988, 39(3), pp. 413–25.

Feinman, Jay M. Practical Legal Studies and Critical Legal Studies. *Mich. Law Rev.,* December 1988, 87(3), pp. 724–31.

Feinson, Marjorie Chary; Hansell, Stephen and Mechanic, David. Factors Associated with Medicare Beneficiaries' Interest in HMOs. *Inquiry,* Fall 1988, 25(3), pp. 364–73.

Feinstein, Charles D. Analysis of a Drug-Testing Program for Intercollegiate Athletes. *J. Policy Anal. Manage.,* Spring 1988, 7(3), pp. 548–50.

Feinstein, Charles H. Economic Growth since 1870: Britain's Performance in International Perspective. *Oxford Rev. Econ. Policy,* Spring 1988, 4(1), pp. 1–13.

⸻. National Statistics: Annex B: Gross Annual Value of Dwellings, and Industrial and Commercial Buildings, Great Britain, 1850–1920. In *Feinstein, C. H. and Pollard, S., eds.,* 1988, pp. 411–19.

⸻. National Statistics: Annex C: The Relationship between the Gross Stock of Dwellings and the Gross Annual Value Assessed to Tax, Great Britain, 1850–1920. In *Feinstein, C. H. and Pollard, S., eds.,* 1988, pp. 420–23.

⸻. The Rise and Fall of the Williamson Curve: Review Article. *J. Econ. Hist.,* September 1988, 48(3), pp. 699–729.

⸻. Studies in Capital Formation in the United Kingdom, 1750–1920: Gas, Water, and Electricity Supply Undertakings. In *Feinstein, C. H. and Pollard, S., eds.,* 1988, pp. 302–06.

⸻. Studies in Capital Formation in the United Kingdom, 1750–1920: Mining and Quarrying. In *Feinstein, C. H. and Pollard, S., eds.,* 1988, pp. 281–85.

⸻. Studies in Capital Formation in the United Kingdom, 1750–1920: Stocks and Work in Progress, Overseas Assets, and Land. In *Feinstein, C. H. and Pollard, S., eds.,* 1988, pp. 391–401.

⸻. Studies in Capital Formation in the United Kingdom, 1750–1920: Agriculture. In *Feinstein, C. H. and Pollard, S., eds.,* 1988, pp. 267–80.

⸻. Studies in Capital Formation in the United Kingdom, 1750–1920: Public and Social Services. In *Feinstein, C. H. and Pollard, S., eds.,* 1988, pp. 355–78.

⸻. Studies in Capital Formation in the United Kingdom, 1750–1920: National Statistics: Annex A: Indices of Rent. In *Feinstein, C. H. and Pollard, S., eds.,* 1988, pp. 405–10.

⸻. Studies in Capital Formation in the United Kingdom, 1750–1920: Residential Dwellings. In *Feinstein, C. H. and Pollard, S., eds.,* 1988, pp. 379–90.

⸻. Studies in Capital Formation in the United Kingdom, 1750–1920: Transport and Communications. In *Feinstein, C. H. and Pollard, S., eds.,* 1988, pp. 312–54.

⸻. Studies in Capital Formation in the United Kingdom, 1750–1920: Distribution and Other Services. In *Feinstein, C. H. and Pollard, S., eds.,* 1988, pp. 307–11.

⸻. Studies in Capital Formation in the United Kingdom, 1750–1920: Manufacturing. In *Feinstein, C. H. and Pollard, S., eds.,* 1988, pp. 286–301.

Feinstein, Jonathan S. and Stein, Jeremy. Employee Opportunism and Redundancy in Firms. *J. Econ. Behav. Organ.,* December 1988, 10(4), pp. 401–14.

Feinstein, Steven P. and Goetzmann, William N. The Effect of the "Triple Witching Hour" on Stock Market Volatility. *Fed. Res. Bank Atlanta Econ. Rev.,* Sept.–Oct. 1988, 73(5), pp. 2–18.

Feiwel, George R. The Economics of Joan Robinson. *Rivista Int. Sci. Econ. Com.,* December 1988, 35(12), pp. 1105–40.

Fekete, Ferenc. The Performances of Hungarian Agrarian Production Systems and the Income Producing Capacity of the Partner Farms. *Acta Oecon.,* 1988, 39(3–4), pp. 231–45.

Fekete, János. The World Needs a New 'Witteveen-Facility' In *[Witteveen, H. J.],* 1988, pp. 43–48.

Feketekuty, Geza. International Trade in Services. In *Candilis, W. O., ed.,* 1988, pp. 57–89.

Feld, Scott L. and Grofman, Bernard. The Borda Count in *n*-Dimensional Issue Space. *Public Choice,* November 1988, 59(2), pp. 167–76.

⸻ **and Grofman, Bernard.** Majority Rule Outcomes and the Structure of Debate in One-Issue-at-a-Time Decision-Making. *Public Choice,* December 1988, 59(3), pp. 239–52.

⸻; **Grofman, Bernard and Miller, Nicholas.** Centripetal Forces in Spatial Voting: On the Size of the Yolk. *Public Choice,* October 1988, 59(1), pp. 37–50.

Felder, Joseph. The Supply of Wage Labor, a Subsistence Level of Consumption, and Household Production—The Cobb–Douglas Case. *Amer. Econ.,* Spring 1988, 32(1), pp. 10–18.

Felderer, Bernhard. The Existence of a Neoclassical Steady State When Population Growth Is Negative. *J. Econ. (Z. Nationalökon.),* 1988, 48(4), pp. 413–18.

Feldman, Allan M. and Lee, Kyung-Ho. Existence of Electoral Equilibria with Probabilistic Voting. *J. Public Econ.,* March 1988, 35(2), pp. 205–27.

Feldman, David H. Devaluation and Non-traded Goods in a Labor Migration Model. *Econ. Letters,* 1988, 28(3), pp. 277–80.

Feldman, Marcus W. and Thomas, Ewart A. C. Behavior-Dependent Contexts for Repeated

Plays of the Prisoner's Dilemma. *J. Conflict Resolution*, December 1988, *32*(4), pp. 699–726.

Feldman, Mark. Optimal Collection of Information by Partially Informed Agents: Comment. *Econometric Rev.*, 1988–89, *7*(2), pp. 149–54.

Feldman, Martha S. and March, James G. Information in Organizations as Signal and Symbol. In *March, J. G.*, 1988, *1981*, pp. 409–28.

Feldman, Roger D. Health Care: The Tyranny of the Budget. In *Boaz, D., ed.*, 1988, pp. 223–41.

_____ **and Sloan, Frank A.** Competition among Physicians, Revisited. In *Greenberg, W., ed.*, 1988, pp. 17–39.

Feldstein, Martin S. Counterrevolution in Progress. *Challenge*, July–August 1988, *31*(4), pp. 42–46.

_____. Distinguished Lecture on Economics in Government: Thinking about International Economic Coordination. *J. Econ. Perspectives*, Spring 1988, *2*(2), pp. 3–13.

_____. Domestic Saving and International Capital Movements in the Long Run and the Short Run. In *Melamed, L., ed.*, 1988, *1983*, pp. 247–71.

_____. Economic Policy Objectives and Policymaking in the Major Industrial Countries: Comment. In *Guth, W., ed.*, 1988, pp. 33–37.

_____. The Effects of Fiscal Policies when Incomes Are Uncertain: A Contradiction to Ricardian Equivalence. *Amer. Econ. Rev.*, March 1988, *78*(1), pp. 14–23.

_____. Imputing Corporate Tax Liabilities to Individual Taxpayers. *Nat. Tax J.*, March 1988, *41*(1), pp. 37–59.

_____. International Economic Cooperation: Introduction. In *Feldstein, M., ed. (I)*, 1988, pp. 1–10.

_____. Rethinking International Economic Coordination. *Oxford Econ. Pap.*, June 1988, *40*(2), pp. 205–19.

_____. The Social Time Preference Discount Rate in Cost Benefit Analysis. In *Ricketts, M., ed., Vol. 2*, 1988, *1964*, pp. 191–210.

_____. The United States in the World Economy: Introduction. In *Feldstein, M., ed. (II)*, 1988, pp. 1–8.

Felgran, Steven D. Bank Participation in Real Estate: Conduct, Risk, and Regulation. *New Eng. Econ. Rev.*, Nov.–Dec. 1988, pp. 57–73.

Fellingham, John. The LIFO/FIFO Choice: An Asymmetric Information Approach: Discussion. *J. Acc. Res.*, Supplement, 1988, *26*, pp. 59–62.

Fellman, Johan. Nuisance Parameter Effects in Balanced Designs. In *Fedorov, V. and Lauter, H., eds.*, 1988, pp. 31–36.

Fellowes, Frederick A. and Frey, Donald N. Pictures and Parts: Delivering an Automated Automotive Parts Catalog. In *Guile, B. R. and Quinn, J. B., eds. (I)*, 1988, pp. 36–56.

Felmingham, Bruce S. Intra-firm Diffusion and the Wage Bargain. *Econ. Letters*, 1988, *26*(1), pp. 89–93.

_____. Product Innovation, Market Inter-dependence and Commodity Prices. *Indian Econ. J.*, Oct.–Dec. 1988, *36*(2), pp. 62–73.

_____. Where Is the Australian J-Curve? *Bull. Econ. Res.*, January 1988, *40*(1), pp. 43–56.

_____ **and Divisekera, S.** Growth and Equity in Sri Lanka, 1963–1982. *Econ. Letters*, 1988, *28*(3), pp. 291–93.

Felrice, Barry. Choosing Automatic Restraint Designs for the 1990s: Comments. In *Graham, J. D., ed.*, 1988, pp. 101–04.

Fels, Gerhard. Comments [Labor Market Barriers to More Employment: Causes for an Increase of the Natural Rate? The Case of West Germany] [Distortions, Incentives, and Growth]. In *Giersch, H., ed.*, 1988, pp. 237–42.

Fels, Joachim. Trade Effects of Greece's Accession to the European Community. *J. World Trade*, February 1988, *22*(1), pp. 97–108.

Felsenstein, Daniel and Shachar, Arie. Locational and Organizational Determinants of R&D Employment in High Technology Firms. *Reg. Stud.*, December 1988, *22*(6), pp. 477–86.

Felsenstein, Klaus and Pötzelberger, K. Robust Bayesian Regression Analysis with HPD-Regions. In *Edwards, D. and Raun, N. E., eds.*, 1988, pp. 349–54.

Felsenthal, Dan S.; Maoz, Zeev and Rapoport, Amnon. Proportional Representation: An Empirical Evaluation of Single-Stage, Non-ranked Voting Procedures. *Public Choice*, November 1988, *59*(2), pp. 151–65.

Feltenstein, Andrew; Lebow, David and Sibert, Anne. An Analysis of the Welfare Implications of Alternative Exchange Rate Regimes: An Intertemporal Model with an Application. *J. Policy Modeling*, Winter 1988, *10*(4), pp. 611–29.

Feng, Ai; Wang, Yulu and Zhang, Zhensheng. Why Can a Large City Like Qinhuangdao Not Accommodate a Small Individual Venture? *Chinese Econ. Stud.*, Winter 1987–88, *21*(2), pp. 28–33.

Feng, Cheng Min and Anas, Alex. Invariance of Expected Utilities in Logit Models. *Econ. Letters*, 1988, *27*(1), pp. 41–45.

Feng, Yu-shu. China's Membership of GATT: A Practical Proposal. *J. World Trade*, December 1988, *22*(6), pp. 53–70.

Fenn, P. T. and Bartrip, P. W. J. Factory Fatalities and Regulation in Britain, 1878–1913. *Exploration Econ. Hist.*, January 1988, *25*(1), pp. 60–74.

_____ **and Veljanovski, Cento G.** A Positive Economic Theory of Regulatory Enforcement. *Econ. J.*, December 1988, *98*(393), pp. 1055–70.

Fenoaltea, Stefano. The Extractive Industries in Italy, 1861–1913: General Methods and Specific Estimates. *J. Europ. Econ. Hist.*, Spring 1988, *17*(1), pp. 117–25.

_____. The Growth of Italy's Silk Industry, 1861–1913: A Statistical Reconstruction. *Rivista Storia Econ.*, S.S., October 1988, *5*(3), pp. 275–318.

———. International Resource Flows and Construction Movements in the Atlantic Economy: The Kuznets Cycle in Italy, 1861–1913. *J. Econ. Hist.*, September 1988, *48*(3), pp. 605–37.

Fenstermaker, J. Van; Malone, R. Phil and Stansell, Stanley R. An Analysis of Commercial Bank Common Stock Returns: 1802–97. *Appl. Econ.*, June 1988, *20*(6), pp. 813–41.

Fenton, Kathryn M. and Gellhorn, Ernest. Vertical Restraints during the Reagan Administration: A Program in Search of a Policy. *Antitrust Bull.*, Fall 1988, *33*(3), pp. 543–73.

Fenton, R. W. Market Equilibrium at Negative Prices: The Exchange of Discommodities. *Atlantic Econ. J.*, March 1988, *16*(1), pp. 98.

Fenyes, T. I.; van Zyl, J. and Vink, N. Structural Imbalances in South African Agriculture. *S. Afr. J. Econ.*, June–Sept. 1988, *56*(2–3), pp. 181–95.

Ferchiou, Ridha. The Global Construction Industry: Tunisia. In *Strassmann, W. P. and Wells, J., eds.*, 1988, pp. 199–210.

Ferdinand, Theodore N. The Criminal Patterns of Boston since 1849. In *Alper, N. O. and Hellman, D. A., eds.*, 1988, pp. 40–59.

Fergus, James T.; Luckett, Charles A. and Canner, Glenn B. Home Equity Lines of Credit. *Fed. Res. Bull.*, June 1988, *74*(6), pp. 361–73.

Ferguson, D. G. and Jones, J. C. H. Location and Survival in the National Hockey League. *J. Ind. Econ.*, June 1988, *36*(4), pp. 443–57.

Ferguson, Daniel M. and Hill, Ned C. Negotiating Payment Terms in an Electronic Environment. In *Kim, Y. H., ed.*, 1988, pp. 131–46.

Ferguson, E. James. The American Public Debt and the Rise of the National Economy, 1750–1815. In *Guarducci, A., ed.*, 1988, pp. 843–64.

Ferguson, Robert. Reply [The Trouble with Performance Measurement]. *J. Portfol. Manage.*, Winter 1988, *14*(2), pp. 77–78.

———. What to Do, or Not to Do, about the Markets. *J. Portfol. Manage.*, Summer 1988, *14*(4), pp. 14–19.

Ferguson, Ronald F. and Ladd, Helen F. The New Economic Role of American States: Massachusetts. In *Fosler, R. S., ed.*, 1988, pp. 19–87.

Fernald, Lloyd W. and Solomon, George T. Comparisons of Entrepreneur and College Business Student Values: A Preliminary Investigation. In *Association of Private Education*, 1988, pp. 133–44.

Fernandez de Pinedo, Emiliano. From the Bloomery to the Blast-Furnace: Technical Change in Spanish Iron-Making (1650–1822). *J. Europ. Econ. Hist.*, Spring 1988, *17*(1), pp. 7–31.

Fernstrom, Meredith M. Consumer Affairs: A View from Business. In *Maynes, E. S. and ACCI Research Committee, eds.*, 1988, pp. 621–27.

Ferrand-Bechmann, Dan. Homeless in France: Public and Private Policies. In *Friedrichs, J., ed.*, 1988, pp. 147–55.

Ferrandier, R. and Blanchon, D. L'evolution recente du systeme financier francais: Les mots et les choses. (The Recent Evolution of the French Financial System: Words and Things. With English summary.) *Écon. Soc.*, January 1988, *22*(1), pp. 7–30.

Ferrante, Vittorioemanuele. On the Logical Circularity of the Notion of "Rational Equilibrium." A Comment. *Econ. Notes*, 1988, (2), pp. 93–109.

Ferrara, Peter J. Social Security: Look at Your Pay Stub. In *Boaz, D., ed.*, 1988, pp. 201–09.

Ferrero, Mario and Cugno, Franco. Free Access vs. Revenue Sharing as Alternative Systems for Managing Employment Externalities. In *Jones, D. C. and Svejnar, J., eds.*, 1988, pp. 217–33.

Ferri, Michael G.; Moore, Scott B. and Schirm, David C. Investor Expectations about Callable Warrants. *J. Portfol. Manage.*, Spring 1988, *14*(3), pp. 84–86.

Ferris, J. Stephen and Shaw, Daniel J. Measurement Costs, Relative Evaluation and Mandatory Education Requirements. *Australian Econ. Pap.*, December 1988, *27*(51), pp. 233–46.

Ferris, James M. The Public Spending and Employment Effects of Local Service Contracting. *Nat. Tax J.*, June 1988, *41*(2), pp. 209–17.

———. The Use of Volunteers in Public Service Production: Some Demand and Supply Considerations. *Soc. Sci. Quart.*, March 1988, *69*(1), pp. 3–23.

Ferris, John W. and Klarquist, Virginia L. Productivity Gains Lukewarm for Makers of Nonelectric Heating Equipment. *Mon. Lab. Rev.*, March 1988, *111*(3), pp. 27–32.

Ferris, Kenneth R. and Reichenstein, William R. A Note on the Tax-Induced Clientele Effect and Tax Reform. *Nat. Tax J.*, March 1988, *41*(1), pp. 131–37.

Ferris, Mark E.; Chou, Shuh S. and Grandstaff, Peter J. Forecasting Competitive Behavior: An Assessment of AT&T's Incentive to Extend Its U.S. Network. *Int. J. Forecasting*, 1988, *4*(4), pp. 521–33.

Ferris, Richard; Hayashi, Fumio and Ando, Albert. Life Cycle and Bequest Savings: A Study of Japanese and U.S. Households Based on Data from the 1984 NSFIE and the 1983 Survey of Consumer Finances. *J. Japanese Int. Economies*, December 1988, *2*(4), pp. 450–91.

Ferris, Stephen P. and Chance, Don M. Margin Requirements and Stock Market Volatility. *Econ. Letters*, 1988, *28*(3), pp. 251–54.

——— **and Denning, Karen C.** An Empirical Test of the Information Hypothesis Concerning Stock Splits. *Rivista Int. Sci. Econ. Com.*, Oct.–Nov. 1988, *35*(10–11), pp. 1075–84.

———; **Haugen, Robert A. and Makhija, Anil K.** Predicting Contemporary Volume with Historic Volume at Differential Price Levels: Evidence Supporting the Disposition Effect. *J. Finance*, July 1988, *43*(3), pp. 677–97.

Ferro, Luiz César M.; Braga, Helson C. and San-

tiago, **Gilda Maria C.** Estrutura da proteçao efetiva no Brasil: 1985. (With English summary.) *Pesquisa Planejamento Econ.*, December 1988, *18*(3), pp. 663–84.

Fertig, Klaus. South Korea: Successful Large-Scale International Borrower. In *Gutowski, A. and Holthus, M., eds.*, 1988, *1983*, pp. 197–217.

_____. Turkey: A Model of Successful Rescheduling? In *Gutowski, A. and Holthus, M., eds.*, 1988, pp. 219–32.

Feuchtwang, Stephan and Hussain, Athar. The People's Livelihood and the Incidence of Poverty. In *Feuchtwang, S.; Hussain, A. and Pairault, T., eds., Vol. 1*, 1988, pp. 36–76.

_____; **Hussain, Athar and Pairault, Thierry.** Transforming China's Economy in the Eighties. In *Feuchtwang, S.; Hussain, A. and Pairault, T., eds., Vol. 1*, 1988, pp. 1–6.

_____; **Hussain, Athar and Pairault, Thierry.** Transforming China's Economy in the Eighties, Volume II: Management, Industry and the Urban Economy: Preface. In *Feuchtwang, S.; Hussain, A. and Pairault, T., eds., Vol. 2*, 1988, pp. 1–6.

Feuille, Peter. Selected Benefits and Costs of Compulsory Arbitration. In *Lewin, D., et al., eds.*, 1988, *1979*, pp. 412–30.

_____ **and Delaney, John Thomas.** Police Interest Arbitration: Awards and Issues. In *Lewin, D., et al., eds.*, 1988, *1984*, pp. 386–98.

_____ **and Juris, Hervey.** Police Union Impact on the Formulation of Law Enforcement Policy. In *Lewin, D., et al., eds.*, 1988, *1973*, pp. 542–55.

_____ **and Schwochau, Susan.** Interest Arbitrators and Their Decision Behavior. *Ind. Relat.*, Winter 1988, *27*(1), pp. 37–55.

_____, **et al.** Multiemployer Bargaining among Local Governments. In *Lewin, D., et al., eds.*, 1988, *1977*, pp. 162–70.

Fforde, Adam. Specific Aspects of the Collectivization of Wet-Rice Cultivation: Vietnamese Experience. In *Brada, J. C. and Wadekin, K.-E., eds.*, 1988, pp. 298–309.

Ffrench-Davis, Ricardo. An Outline of a Neostructuralist Approach. *CEPAL Rev.*, April 1988, (34), pp. 37–44.

_____. External Debt, Adjustment, and Development in Latin America. In *Feinberg, R. E. and Ffrench-Davis, R., eds.*, 1988, pp. 29–51.

_____. The Foreign Debt Crisis and Adjustment in Chile: 1976–86. In *Griffith-Jones, S., ed.*, 1988, pp. 113–40.

_____. Panel on Strategies for Confronting the Crisis: Panel. In *Feinberg, R. E. and Ffrench-Davis, R., eds.*, 1988, pp. 274–81.

_____ **and Feinberg, Richard E.** Development and External Debt in Latin America: Bases for a New Consensus: Overview. In *Feinberg, R. E. and Ffrench-Davis, R., eds.*, 1988, pp. 1–7.

_____ **and Marfan, Manuel.** Selective Policies under a Structural Foreign Exchange Shortage. *J. Devel. Econ.*, November 1988, *29*(3), pp. 347–69.

_____ **and Muñoz, Oscar.** El desarrollo económico de América Latina y el marco internacional: 1950–86. (Economic Development in Latin America and the International Framework: 1950–1986. With English summary.) *Colección Estud. CIEPLAN*, March 1988, (23), pp. 13–33.

Fichtenbaum, Rudy. 'Business Cycles,' Turnover and the Rate of Profit: An Empirical Test of Marxian Crisis Theory. *Eastern Econ. J.*, July–Sept. 1988, *14*(3), pp. 221–28.

_____ **and Shahidi, Hushang.** Truncation Bias and the Measurement of Income Inequality. *J. Bus. Econ. Statist.*, July 1988, *6*(3), pp. 335–37.

Fiebig, Denzil G. and Bewley, Ronald. Estimation of Price Elasticities for an International Telephone Demand Model. *J. Ind. Econ.*, June 1988, *36*(4), pp. 393–409.

_____ **and Bewley, Ronald.** A Flexible Logistic Growth Model with Applications in Telecommunications. *Int. J. Forecasting*, 1988, *4*(2), pp. 177–92.

_____; **Seale, James, Jr. and Theil, Henri.** Cross-Country Demand Analysis Based on Three Phases of the International Comparison Project. In *Salazar-Carrillo, J. and Rao, D. S. P., eds.*, 1988, pp. 225–35.

Fiedler, Manfred. Investment by Public Enterprise in the Federal Republic of Germany. *Ann. Pub. Co-op. Econ.*, Oct.–Dec. 1988, *59*(4), pp. 455–73.

Field, Elizabeth B. Free and Slave Labor in the Antebellum South: Perfect Substitutes or Different Inputs? *Rev. Econ. Statist.*, November 1988, *70*(4), pp. 654–59.

_____. The Relative Efficiency of Slavery Revisited: A Translog Production Function Approach. *Amer. Econ. Rev.*, June 1988, *78*(3), pp. 543–49.

Fields, Gary S. Employment and Economic Growth in Costa Rica. *World Devel.*, December 1988, *16*(12), pp. 1493–1509.

Fields, Joseph A. Expense Preference Behavior in Mutual Life Insurers. *J. Finan. Services Res.*, January 1988, *1*(2), pp. 113–29.

_____ **and Venezian, Emilio C.** Informational Asymmetries in Retroactive Insurance: Authors' Reply. *J. Risk Ins.*, September 1988, *55*(3), pp. 555–58.

Fields, M. Andrew and Keown, Arthur J. The Merger Profile and Size Effect Anomalies: An Empirical Examination of Their Relationship. *Quart. J. Bus. Econ.*, Winter 1988, *27*(1), pp. 70–82.

Fields, Paige; Schmit, Joan T. and Pritchett, S. Travis. Punitive Damages: Punishment or Further Compensation? *J. Risk Ins.*, September 1988, *55*(3), pp. 453–66.

Fields, T. Windsor and Hall, Thomas E. Income or Wealth in Money Demand: Comment. *Southern Econ. J.*, April 1988, *54*(4), pp. 1039–42.

Fieleke, Norman S. Economic Interdependence between Nations: Reason for Policy Coordination? *New Eng. Econ. Rev.*, May–June 1988, pp. 21–38.

_____. International Payments Imbalances in Heavily Indebted Developing Countries. In *Fieleke, N. S., ed.*, 1988, pp. 58–89.

_____. International Payments Imbalances in the 1980s: An Overview. In *Fieleke, N. S., ed.*, 1988, pp. 1–18.

Fienberg, Stephen E. Is a Philosophical Concensus for Statistics Available?: Discussion. *J. Econometrics*, January 1988, *37*(1), pp. 63–64.

Fiering, Myron B.; Rogers, Peter P. and **Harrington, Joseph J.** New Approaches to Using Mathematical Programming for Resource Allocation. In *O'Mara, G. T., ed.*, 1988, pp. 122–26.

Fierro, Miguel; Poggie, John J., Jr. and **Pollnac, Richard B.** Factors Influencing the Success of Fishermen's Cooperatives in Ecuador. *Marine Resource Econ.*, 1988, *5*(3), pp. 231–42.

Fig, David. The Political Economy of South African Penetration of Brazil: The Case of the Anglo American Corporation. In *Carlsson, J. and Shaw, T. M., eds.*, 1988, pp. 204–31.

Figlewski, Stephen; Cecchetti, Stephen G. and **Cumby, Robert E.** Estimation of the Optimal Futures Hedge. *Rev. Econ. Statist.*, November 1988, *70*(4), pp. 623–30.

Figueroa, Leonel. Economic Adjustment and Development in Peru: Towards an Alternative Policy. In *Cornia, G. A.; Jolly, R. and Stewart, F., eds.*, 1988, pp. 156–83.

Figurnova, N. Strengthening the Role of Consumers in Balancing the Economy. *Prob. Econ.*, July 1988, *31*(3), pp. 46–61.

Fik, Timothy J. Hierarchical Interaction: The Modeling of a Competing Central Place System. *Ann. Reg. Sci.*, July 1988, *22*(2), pp. 48–69.

_____. Spatial Competition and Price Reporting in Retail Food Markets. *Econ. Geogr.*, January 1988, *64*(1), pp. 29–44.

Fildes, Robert and **Makridakis, Spyros.** Forecasting and Loss Functions. *Int. J. Forecasting*, 1988, *4*(4), pp. 545–50.

Filer, John E.; Moak, Donald L. and **Uze, Barry.** Why Some States Adopt Lotteries and Others Don't. *Public Finance Quart.*, July 1988, *16*(3), pp. 259–83.

Filer, Randall K. and **Petri, Peter A.** A Job-Characteristics Theory of Retirement. *Rev. Econ. Statist.*, February 1988, *70*(1), pp. 123–29.

Filimon, Radu; Epple, Dennis and **Romer, Thomas.** Community Development with Endogenous Land Use Controls. *J. Public Econ.*, March 1988, *35*(2), pp. 133–62.

Filios, Vassilios P. Socio-Historical Analysis of Accounting: The Case of Ancient Greece. *Rivista Int. Sci. Econ. Com.*, March 1988, *35*(3), pp. 259–67.

Filippello, A. Nicholas. Wall Street and U.S. Corporations: The Discipline Imposed on Management. *Bus. Econ.*, July 1988, *23*(3), pp. 27–32.

Filippini, Carlo and **Filippini, Luigi.** Two Theorems on Joint Production. In *Steedman, I., ed., Vol. 2*, 1988, *1982*, pp. 11–15.

Filippini, Luigi and **Filippini, Carlo.** Two Theorems on Joint Production. In *Steedman, I., ed., Vol. 2*, 1988, *1982*, pp. 11–15.

Finch, C. David. World Tax Reform: A Progress Report: Australia: Comment. In *Pechman, J. A., ed.*, 1988, pp. 40–42.

Findlay, Ronald. International Trade and Economic Development: Comment. In *Haberler, G.*, 1988, pp. 99–110.

_____ and **Wellisz, Stanislaw.** The State and the Invisible Hand. *World Bank Res. Observer*, January 1988, *3*(1), pp. 59–80.

Fine, Ben. The British Coal Industry's Contribution to the Political Economy of Paul Sweezy. *Hist. Polit. Econ.*, Summer 1988, *20*(2), pp. 235–50.

_____. From Capital in Production to Capital in Exchange. *Sci. Soc.*, Fall 1988, *52*(3), pp. 326–37.

Finegold, David and **Soskice, David.** The Failure of Training in Britain: Analysis and Prescription. *Oxford Rev. Econ. Policy*, Autumn 1988, *4*(3), pp. 21–53.

Fink, Gerhard. Prospects for the World Economy: Comments. In *Saunders, C. T., ed.*, 1988, pp. 59–60.

_____ and **Gabrisch, Hubert.** Hard-Currency Debt Scenarios. In *Marer, P. and Siwinski, W., eds.*, 1988, pp. 195–99.

Fink, Leon. John R. Commons, Herbert Gutman, and the Burden of Labor History. *Labor Hist.*, Summer 1988, *29*(3), pp. 313–22.

Finkler, Steven A.; Brooten, Dorothy and **Brown, Linda.** Utilization of Inpatient Services under Shortened Lengths of Stay: A Neonatal Care Example. *Inquiry*, Summer 1988, *25*(2), pp. 271–80.

Finlayson, Bob; Lattimore, Ralph and **Ward, Bert.** New Zealand's Price Elasticity of Export Demand Revisited. *New Zealand Econ. Pap.*, 1988, *22*, pp. 25–34.

Finley, Murray H. On the Human Concerns. In *Aho, C. M. and Levinson, M.*, 1988, pp. 218–23.

Finn, Frank J. and **Higham, Ron.** The Performance of Unseasoned New Equity Issues-Cum-Stock Exchange Listings in Australia. *J. Banking Finance*, September 1988, *12*(3), pp. 333–51.

Finn, Thomas J. A Note on the Real Federal Deficit. *Eastern Econ. J.*, July–Sept. 1988, *14*(3), pp. 263–70.

Finnegan, John, Jr.; Benham, William and **Parsons, Patrick R.** Editors and Their Roles. In *Picard, R. G., et al., eds.*, 1988, pp. 91–103.

Finnerty, Joseph E. and **Park, Hun Y.** How to Profit from Program Trading. *J. Portfol. Manage.*, Winter 1988, *14*(2), pp. 40–46.

_____ and **Park, Hun Y.** Intraday Return and Volatility Patterns in the Stock Market: Futures versus Spot. In *Fabozzi, F. J., ed.*, 1988, pp. 301–17.

Finnie, Ross E. and **Beach, Charles M.** Family Background in an Extended Earnings-Generation Model: Further Evidence. *Eastern Econ. J.*, Jan.–March 1988, *14*(1), pp. 39–49.

Finsinger, Jörg. Non-competitive and Protectionist Government Purchasing Behavior. *Europ. Econ. Rev.*, January 1988, *32*(1), pp. 69–80.

_____. Zur Deregulierung von Versicherungsmärkten. (With English summary.) *Z. Betriebswirtshaft*, July 1988, *58*(7), pp. 698–703.

_____ **and Kraft, Kornelius.** Optimales Marketing bei Kostenzuschlagskalkulation am Beispiel von Krankenversicherungen. (Optimal Marketing with Markup-Pricing. The Example of Health Insurance. With English summary.) *Ifo-Studien*, 1988, *34*(4), pp. 275–97.

Finucane, Thomas J. Options on U.S. Treasury Coupon Issues. *Financial Rev.*, November 1988, *23*(4), pp. 403–26.

_____. Some Empirical Evidence on the Use of Financial Leases. *J. Finan. Res.*, Winter 1988, *11*(4), pp. 321–33.

Fiocca, Mariateresa. From the Homo Oeconomicus to the Philanthropic Man. *Econ. Scelte Pubbliche/J. Public Finance Public Choice*, Jan.–April 1988, *6*(1), pp. 47–62.

Fiore, Lyle; Zuber, Richard A. and Johnson, R. Stafford. A Note on the Investment Performances of Different Price-Earnings Stock. *Rivista Int. Sci. Econ. Com.*, Oct.–Nov. 1988, *35*(10–11), pp. 1067–74.

Fiorentini, Gianluca. Struttura produttiva e concentrazione industriale: Il settore manifatturiero italiano, 1951–1981. (Industrial Concentration and Productive Structure. The Italian Manufacturing Sector, 1951–1981. With English summary.) *Giorn. Econ.*, March–April 1988, *47*(3–4), pp. 213–38.

_____ **and Prosperetti, Luigi.** Conflittualità e dimensione d'impianto: Sviluppi teorici e risultanze empiriche. (Conflict and Manufacturers' Size: Theoretical Developments and Empirical Outcome. With English summary.) *Econ. Lavoro*, Apr.–June 1988, *22*(2), pp. 37–58.

Fiorentino, Raúl. Apuntes para una estrategia de desarrollo de la agricultura de riego en la Argentina. (With English summary.) *Desarrollo Econ.*, Jan.–March 1988, *27*(108), pp. 539–58.

Fiorito, Jack; Gallagher, Daniel G. and Fukami, Cynthia V. Satisfaction with Union Representation. *Ind. Lab. Relat. Rev.*, January 1988, *41*(2), pp. 294–307.

Firat, A. Fuat and Dholakia, Nikhilesh. Development in the Era of Globalizing Markets and Consumption Patterns. In *Kumcu, E. and Firat, A. F., eds.*, 1988, pp. 79–101.

_____; **Kumcu, Erdoğan and Karafakioğlu, Mehmet.** The Interface between Marketing and Development: Problems and Prospects. In *Kumcu, E. and Firat, A. F., eds.*, 1988, pp. 317–43.

First National Bank of Boston. The Dilemma of a Mature Economy and Excessive Government Spending. In *Lampe, D., ed.*, 1988, *1971*, pp. 19–24.

_____. The Governor's Message on the Economy of Massachusetts. In *Lampe, D., ed.*, 1988, *1972*, pp. 35–43.

_____. The Impending Fiscal Crisis. In *Lampe, D., ed.*, 1988, *1972*, pp. 50–58.

_____. Look Out, Massachusetts!!! In *Lampe, D., ed.*, 1988, *1972*, pp. 59–73.

_____. The Massachusetts Economy in the 1980s. In *Lampe, D., ed.*, 1988, pp. 188–200.

Firstenberg, Paul M.; Ross, Stephen A. and Zisler, Randall C. Real Estate: The Whole Story. *J. Portfol. Manage.*, Spring 1988, *14*(3), pp. 22–34.

Fischel, Daniel R. Organized Exchanges and the Regulation of Dual Class Common Stock. In *Coffee, J. C., Jr.; Lowenstein, L. and Rose-Ackerman, S., eds.*, 1988, pp. 499–520.

Fischel, William A. and Shapiro, Perry. Takings, Insurance, and Michelman: Comments on Economic Interpretations of "Just Compensation" Law. *J. Legal Stud.*, June 1988, *17*(2), pp. 269–93.

Fischer, Andreas. Money Announcements and the Risk Premium. *Econ. Letters*, 1988, *27*(2), pp. 155–58.

Fischer, Bernhard and Corsepius, Uwe. Domestic Resource Mobilization in Thailand: A Success Case for Financial Deepening? *Singapore Econ. Rev.*, October 1988, *33*(2), pp. 1–20.

Fischer, C. C. Using a PC Econometric Model to Teach Macroeconomics. In *Missouri Valley Economic Assoc.*, 1988, pp. 177–81.

Fischer, Günther; Frohberg, Klaus and Parikh, Kirit S. Agricultural Trade Regimes: Impact on Sector Proportions, Real Incomes and Hunger in the World. *Europ. Rev. Agr. Econ.*, 1988, *15*(4), pp. 397–417.

Fischer, Manfred M. The Economics of Technological Change: Some Major Research Issues and Gaps in Knowledge: Commentary. *Environ. Planning A*, March 1988, *20*(3), pp. 281–84.

_____ **and Nijkamp, Peter.** The Role of Small Firms for Regional Revitalization. *Ann. Reg. Sci.*, February 1988, *22*, pp. 28–42.

_____; **Schubert, U. and Baumann, J.** A Choice-Theoretical Labour-Market Model: Empirical Tests at the Mesolevel. *Environ. Planning A*, August 1988, *20*(8), pp. 1085–1102.

Fischer, Mary Ellen. The Soviet Union Today: Women. In *Cracraft, J., ed.*, 1988, pp. 327–38.

Fischer, Stanley. Examining Alternative Macroeconomic Theories: Comment. *Brookings Pap. Econ. Act.*, 1988, (1), pp. 265–67.

_____. International Macroeconomic Policy Coordination. In *Feldstein, M., ed. (I)*, 1988, pp. 11–43.

_____. The International Monetary System: An Analysis of Alternative Regimes: Comments. *Europ. Econ. Rev.*, June 1988, *32*(5), pp. 1048–51.

_____. Monetary and Fiscal Policy Coordination with a High Public Debt: Discussion. In *Giavazzi, F. and Spaventa, L., eds.*, 1988, pp. 127–31.

_____. A Positive Theory of Fiscal Policy in Open Economies: Comment. In *Frenkel, J. A., ed.*, 1988, pp. 192–93.

_____. Real Balances, the Exchange Rate, and Indexation: Real Variables in Disinflation. *Quart. J. Econ.*, February 1988, *103*(1), pp. 27–49.

_____. Recent Developments in Macroeconomics. *Econ. J.*, June 1988, *98*(391), pp. 294–339.

_____. Stabilization in High Inflation Countries: Analytical Foundations and Recent Experience: Comments. *Carnegie–Rochester Conf. Ser. Public Policy*, Spring 1988, *28*, pp. 85–92.

_____. Symposium on the Slowdown in Productivity Growth. *J. Econ. Perspectives*, Fall 1988, *2*(4), pp. 3–7.

_____; **Samuelson, Paul A. and Dornbusch, Rudiger.** Comparative Advantage, Trade, and Payments in a Ricardian Model with a Continuum of Goods. **In** *Dornbusch, R.*, 1988, *1977*, pp. 293–322.

Fischhoff, Baruch. Judgmental Aspects of Forecasting: Needs and Possible Trends. *Int. J. Forecasting*, 1988, *4*(3), pp. 331–39.

_____ **and Furby, Lita.** Measuring Values: A Conceptual Framework for Interpreting Transactions with Special Reference to Contingent Valuation of Visibility. *J. Risk Uncertainty*, June 1988, *1*(2), pp. 147–84.

_____; **Lichtenstein, Sarah and Slovic, Paul.** Response Mode, Framing, and Information-Processing Effects in Risk Assessment. **In** *Bell, D. E.; Raiffa, H. and Tversky, A., eds.*, 1988, *1982*, pp. 152–66.

_____; **Slovic, Paul and Lichtenstein, Sarah.** Knowing What You Want: Measuring Labile Values. **In** *Bell, D. E.; Raiffa, H. and Tversky, A., eds.*, 1988, *1980*, pp. 398–421.

Fischmar, Dan and Peters, Carl. A Stochastic Dominance Approach to Portfolio Selection. **In** *Pennsylvania Economic Association*, 1988, pp. 650–63.

Fišer, Ivan. The International Investment Bank and Czechoslovak Enterprises. *Czech. Econ. Digest.*, May 1988, (3), pp. 50–55.

Fish, Stanley. Economics in the Human Conversation: Comments from Outside Economics. **In** *Klamer, A.; McCloskey, D. N. and Solow, R. M., eds.*, 1988, pp. 21–30.

Fishburn, Peter C. Expected Utility: An Anniversary and a New Era. *J. Risk Uncertainty*, September 1988, *1*(3), pp. 267–83.

_____. Normative Theories of Decision Making under Risk and under Uncertainty. **In** *Bell, D. E.; Raiffa, H. and Tversky, A., eds.*, 1988, pp. 78–98.

_____. Normative Theories of Decision Making under Risk and under Uncertainty. **In** *Kacprzyk, J. and Roubens, M., eds.*, 1988, pp. 1–21.

_____. Uncertainty Aversion and Separated Effects in Decision Making under Certainty. **In** *Kacprzyk, J. and Fedrizzi, M., eds.*, 1988, pp. 10–25.

_____ **and LaValle, Irving H.** Context-Dependent Choice with Nonlinear and Nontransitive Preferences. *Econometrica*, September 1988, *56*(5), pp. 1221–39.

_____ **and LaValle, Irving H.** The Structure of SSB Utilities for Decision under Uncertainty. *Math. Soc. Sci.*, June 1988, *15*(3), pp. 217–30.

_____ **and LaValle, Irving H.** Transitivity is Equivalent to Independence for States-Additive SSB Utilities. *J. Econ. Theory*, February 1988, *44*(1), pp. 202–08.

_____; **Merrill, Samuel, III and Brams, Steven J.** The Problem of Indeterminacy in Approval, Multiple, and Truncated Voting Systems: Rejoinder. *Public Choice*, November 1988, *59*(2), pp. 149.

_____; **Merrill, Samuel, III and Brams, Steven J.** The Responsiveness of Approval Voting: Comments [The Problem of Indeterminacy in Approval, Multiple, and Truncated Voting Systems]. *Public Choice*, November 1988, *59*(2), pp. 121–31.

_____ **and Roberts, Fred S.** Unique Finite Conjoint Measurement. *Math. Soc. Sci.*, October 1988, *16*(2), pp. 107–43.

Fishelson, Gideon. The Black Market for Foreign Exchange: An International Comparison. *Econ. Letters*, 1988, *27*(1), pp. 67–71.

_____ **and Hoehn, John P.** Quality Adjusted Prices and Weak Complementarity: A New Method for Estimating the Demand for Environmental Services. *Resources & Energy*, December 1988, *10*(4), pp. 337–54.

Fisher, Anthony C. and Arrow, Kenneth J. Environmental Preservation, Uncertainty, and Irreversibility. **In** *Ricketts, M., ed., Vol. 2*, 1988, *1974*, pp. 226–33.

_____ **and Despotakis, Kostas A.** Energy in a Regional Economy: A Computable General Equilibrium Model for California. *J. Environ. Econ. Manage.*, September 1988, *15*(3), pp. 313–30.

Fisher, Brian S. Agricultural Economics Training at the University of Sydney. *Rev. Marketing Agr. Econ.*, August 1988, *56*(2), pp. 229.

_____ **and Hinchy, Mike.** Benefits from Price Stabilization to Producers and Processors: The Australian Buffer-Stock Scheme for Wool. *Amer. J. Agr. Econ.*, August 1988, *70*(3), pp. 604–15.

_____ **and Wall, Charles A.** Supply Response and the Theory of Production and Profit Functions. *Rev. Marketing Agr. Econ.*, December 1988, *56*(3), pp. 383–404.

Fisher, Franklin M. Production-Theoretic Input Price Indices and the Measurement of Real Aggregate Input Use. **In** *Eichhorn, W., ed.*, 1988, pp. 87–98.

_____ **and Stahl, Dale O., II.** On Stability Analysis with Disequilibrium Awareness. *J. Econ. Theory*, December 1988, *46*(2), pp. 309–21.

Fisher, Jacob. Postwar Changes in the Income Position of the Aged. *Soc. Sec. Bull.*, December 1988, *51*(12), pp. 19–22.

Fisher, Joseph M. Contingent and Noncontingent Attorney's Fees in Personal Injury Cases. *Contemp. Policy Issues*, July 1988, *6*(3), pp. 108–21.

Fisher, Louis. The Executive Budget—An Idea

Whose Time Has Passed: Comments. *Public Budg. Finance*, Spring 1988, *8*(1), pp. 100–03.

Fisher, Mark E. and Thurman, Walter N. Chickens, Eggs, and Causality, or Which Came First? *Amer. J. Agr. Econ.*, May 1988, *70*(2), pp. 237–38.

Fisher, P. G. and Hughes Hallett, Andrew J. Efficient Solution Techniques for Linear and Non-linear Rational Expectations Models. *J. Econ. Dynam. Control*, November 1988, *12*(4), pp. 635–57.

_____, **et al.** Comparative Properties of Models of the UK Economy. *Nat. Inst. Econ. Rev.*, August 1988, (125), pp. 69–87.

Fisher, Peter S. Absentee Ownership of Farmland and State and Local Tax Policy: Income Tax Promotes Absenteeism, but the Property Tax Can Be Used to Strengthen Family Farms. *Amer. J. Econ. Soc.*, January 1988, *47*(1), pp. 29–40.

Fisher, Ronald C. Tax Deductibility and Municipal Budget Structure: Comment. In *Rosen, H. S.*, ed., 1988, pp. 127–36.

Fisher, Stephen. Lisbon as a Port Town in the Eighteenth Century. In *Cavaciocchi, S.*, ed., 1988, pp. 703–29.

Fishlow, Albert. Alternative Approaches and Solutions to the Debt of Developing Countries. In *Borner, S.*, ed., 1988, pp. 3–20.

Fishman, Arthur. Dynamic Sales Discriminate against Uninformed Consumers in a Competitive Market. *Econ. Letters*, 1988, *27*(1), pp. 23–25.

Fishman, Michael J. A Theory of Preemptive Takeover Bidding. *Rand J. Econ.*, Spring 1988, *19*(1), pp. 88–101.

Fisk, George. Interactive Systems Frameworks for Analyzing Spacetime Changes in Marketing Organization and Processes. In *[Hollander, S. C.]*, 1988, pp. 55–69.

Fissel, Gary S. International Economic Policy Co-ordination: Policy Analysis in a Staggered Wage-Setting Model. *J. Econ. Dynam. Control*, March 1988, *12*(1), pp. 93–100.

Fitch, Lyle C. The Rocky Road to Privatization. *Amer. J. Econ. Soc.*, January 1988, *47*(1), pp. 1–14.

Fitoussi, Jean-Paul and Le Cacheux, Jacques. On Macroeconomic Implications of Price Setting in the Open Economy. *Amer. Econ. Rev.*, May 1988, *78*(2), pp. 335–40.

Fitzgerald, Bruce and Monson, Terry. Export Credit and Insurance for Export Promotion. *Finance Develop.*, December 1988, *25*(4), pp. 53–55.

FitzGerald, E. V. K. Stabilization and Economic Justice: The Case of Nicaragua. In *Wilber, C. K.*, ed., 1988, pp. 248–59.

_____. State Accumulation and Market Equilibria: An Application of Kalecki–Kornai Analysis to Planned Economies in the Third World. *J. Devel. Stud.*, July 1988, *24*(4), pp. 50–74.

_____ **and Wuyts, Marc.** Markets within Planning: Socialist Economic Management in the Third World: Introduction. *J. Devel. Stud.*, July 1988, *24*(4), pp. 1–14.

Fitzgerald, Edward Peter. Did France's Colonial Empire Make Economic Sense? A Perspective from the Postwar Decade, 1946–1956. *J. Econ. Hist.*, June 1988, *48*(2), pp. 373–85.

Fitzgerald, Frank T. Errata [The Sovietization of Cuba Thesis' Revisited]. *Sci. Soc.*, Summer 1988, *52*(2), pp. 132.

_____. The "Sovietization of Cuba Thesis" Revisited. In *Zimbalist, A.*, ed., 1988, pp. 137–53.

Fitzgerald, John and Bradley, John. Industrial Output and Factor Input Determination in an Econometric Model of a Small Open Economy. *Europ. Econ. Rev.*, July 1988, *32*(6), pp. 1227–41.

Fitzgerald, Michael R.; Lyons, William and Cory, Floydette C. From Administration to Oversight: Privatization and Its Aftermath in a Southern City. In *Hula, R. C.*, ed., 1988, pp. 69–83.

Fitzmaurice, John. An Analysis of the European Community's Co-operation Procedure. *J. Common Market Stud.*, June 1988, *26*(4), pp. 389–400.

Fitzpatrick, Dennis B.; Settle, John W. and Petry, Glenn H. An Empirical Examination of Rate of Return Regulation in the Electric Utility Industry: 1971–1982. *J. Econ. Bus.*, February 1988, *40*(1), pp. 27–44.

Fitzpatrick, Sheila. Sources of Change in Soviet History: State, Society, and the Entrepreneurial Tradition. In *Bialer, S. and Mandelbaum, M.*, eds., 1988, pp. 37–62.

FitzRoy, Felix R. Employment and Hours in Equilibrium and Disequilibrium. In *Hart, R. A.*, ed., 1988, pp. 129–39.

_____. The Modern Corporation: Efficiency, Control, and Comparative Organization. *Kyklos*, 1988, *41*(2), pp. 239–62.

_____ **and Buck, Andrew J.** Inflation and Productivity Growth in the Federal Republic of Germany. *J. Post Keynesian Econ.*, Spring 1988, *10*(3), pp. 428–44.

Fixler, Dennis and Bental, Benjamin. Firm Behavior and the Externalities of Technological Leadership. *Europ. Econ. Rev.*, November 1988, *32*(9), pp. 1731–46.

Fizel, John L.; Mentzer, Marc S. and Louie, Kenneth K. T. CEO Tenure and Firm Performance. In *Missouri Valley Economic Assoc.*, 1988, pp. 1–6.

Fjornes, Bjoern; Stern, Helman I. and Ceder, Avishai. OPTIBUS: A Scheduling Package. In *Daduna, J. R. and Wren, A.*, eds., 1988, pp. 212–25.

Flaherty, Patrick. The Socio-economics Dynamics of Stalinism. *Sci. Soc.*, Spring 1988, *52*(1), pp. 35–58.

Flaherty, Sean. Mature Collective Bargaining and Rank and File Militancy: Breaking the Peace of the "Treaty of Detroit." In *Zarembka, P.*, ed., 1988, pp. 241–80.

Flaig, Gebhard and Stadler, Manfred. Beschäftigungseffekte privater F&E-Aufwendungen. Eine Panaldaten-Analyse. (The Effects of Private R and D Expenditures on Employment. An Analysis with Panel Data. With English summary.) *Z. Wirtschaft. Sozialwissen.*, 1988, *108*(1), pp. 43–61.

Flam, Harry. Countervailing Duty Laws and Subsidies to Imperfectly Competitive Industries: Comment. In *Baldwin, R. E.; Hamilton, C. B. and Sapir, A., eds.*, 1988, pp. 341–45.

Flamholtz, Eric G.; Randle, Yvonne and Sackmann, Sonja. Personnel Management: The Tone of Tomorrow. In *Timpe, A. D., ed.*, 1988, *1986*, pp. 33–41.

Flamm, Kenneth. The Changing Pattern of Industrial Robot Use. In *Cyert, R. M. and Mowery, D. C., eds.*, 1988, pp. 267–328.

Flanagan, Robert J. Unemployment as a Hiring Problem. *OECD Econ. Stud.*, Autumn 1988, (11), pp. 123–54.

Flannery, Mark J. Payments System Risk and Public Policy. In *Haraf, W. S. and Kushmeider, R. M., eds.*, 1988, pp. 261–87.

_____ **and Protopapadakis, Aris A.** From T-Bills to Common Stocks: Investigating the Generality of Intra-Week Return Seasonality. *J. Finance*, June 1988, *43*(2), pp. 431–50.

Flaschel, Peter and Semmler, Willi. On the Integration of Dual and Cross-Dual Adjustment Processes in Leontief Systems. *Ricerche Econ.*, July–Sept. 1988, *42*(3), pp. 403–32.

Flassbeck, Heiner. Die Standortqualität der Bundesrepublik Deutschland. (The Attractiveness of the Federal Republic as an Industry Location. With English summary.) *Konjunkturpolitik*, 1988, *34*(5–6), pp. 255–67.

Flegg, A. T. The Demographic Effects of Income Redistribution and Accelerated Economic Growth Revisited. *Oxford Bull. Econ. Statist.*, May 1988, *50*(2), pp. 183–94.

Fleischer, David V. Brazil's Economic and Political Future: Epilogue. In *Chacel, J. M.; Falk, P. S. and Fleischer, D. V., eds.*, 1988, pp. 257–59.

Fleischmann, Bernhard. Operations-Research-Modelle und -Verfahren in der Produktionsplanung. (With English summary.) *Z. Betriebswirtshaft*, March 1988, *58*(3), pp. 347–72.

Fleisher, Arthur A., III, et al. Crime or Punishment? Enforcement of the NCAA Football Cartel. *J. Econ. Behav. Organ.*, December 1988, *10*(4), pp. 433–51.

Fleishman, John A. The Effects of Decision Framing and Others' Behavior on Cooperation in a Social Dilemma. *J. Conflict Resolution*, March 1988, *32*(1), pp. 162–80.

Fleising, Asher; Eckstein, Zvi and Weiss, Yoram. University Policies under Varying Market Conditions: The Training of Electrical Engineers. *Econ. Educ. Rev.*, 1988, *7*(4), pp. 393–403.

Fleming, J. M. Price and Output Policy of State Enterprise: A Symposium: Comment. In *Meade, J., Vol. 2*, 1988, pp. 22–30.

Fleming, Steven; DesHarnais, Susan and Chesney, James. Trends and Regional Variations in Hospital Utilization and Quality during the First Two Years of the Prospective Payment System. *Inquiry*, Fall 1988, *25*(3), pp. 374–82.

Flemings, Merton C. and Clark, Joel P. Ad-

vanced Materials and the Economy. In *Forester, T., ed.*, 1988, *1986*, pp. 163–78.

Flemming, John S. Debt and Taxes. *Scot. J. Polit. Econ.*, November 1988, *35*(4), pp. 305–17.

_____. Debt and Taxes in War and Peace: The Closed Economy Case. In *Arrow, K. J. and Boskin, M. J., eds.*, 1988, pp. 201–23.

_____. Interest Rates and Macroeconomic Policy. In *Eltis, W. and Sinclair, P. J. N., eds.*, 1988, pp. 235–45.

_____. International Coordination of Economic Policies: Scope, Method, and Effects: Comment. In *Guth, W., ed.*, 1988, pp. 197–200.

_____. Macroeconomic Modelling for Economic Policy: Comments. In *Driehuis, W.; Fase, M. M. G. and den Hartog, H., eds.*, 1988, pp. 147–49.

_____. The Management of Public Debt and Financial Markets: Discussion. In *Giavazzi, F. and Spaventa, L., eds.*, 1988, pp. 167–72.

_____. Prospects for the OECD Area Economy. In *Mabro, R., ed.*, 1988, pp. 191–200.

Fleurbaey, Marc. Rational Behaviour and Adaptation. In *Munier, B. R., ed.*, 1988, pp. 459–81.

Flew, Antony. Particular Liberties against the General Will. In *[Rothbard, M. N.]*, 1988, pp. 214–28.

Flinn, J.C. and Hazell, Peter B. R. Production Instability and Modern Rice Technology: A Philippine Case Study. *Devel. Econ.*, March 1988, *26*(1), pp. 34–50.

Flint, David. A True and Fair View in Consolidated Accounts. In *Gray, S. J. and Coenenberg, A. G., eds.*, 1988, pp. 15–38.

Flood, Lennart R. Effects of Taxes on Non-market Work: The Swedish Case. *J. Public Econ.*, July 1988, *36*(2), pp. 259–67.

Flood, Robert P. Coordination of Monetary and Fiscal Policies in the Industrial Economies: Comment. In *Frenkel, J. A., ed.*, 1988, pp. 118–20.

_____. Rapid Inflation—Deliberate Policy or Miscalculation? Comment. *Carnegie–Rochester Conf. Ser. Public Policy*, Autumn 1988, 29, pp. 77–79.

_____ **and Marion, Nancy.** Determinants of the Spread in a Two-Tier Foreign Exchange Market. *Econ. Letters*, 1988, *27*(2), pp. 173–78.

Flora, Cornelia Butler and Flora, Jan L. Community Stores in Rural Colombia: Organizing the Means of Consumption. In *Annis, S. and Hakim, P., eds.*, 1988, pp. 117–31.

Flora, Jan L. and Flora, Cornelia Butler. Community Stores in Rural Colombia: Organizing the Means of Consumption. In *Annis, S. and Hakim, P., eds.*, 1988, pp. 117–31.

Florescu, Mihail. Computer-Assisted Research and Design Performances and Prospects. *Econ. Computat. Cybern. Stud. Res.*, 1988, *23*(1), pp. 17–21.

Florian, Michael and Guélat, Jacques. The Prediction of Multicommodity Freight Flows: A Multiproduct Multimode Model and a Solution Algorithm. In *Bianco, L. and La Bella, A., eds.*, 1988, pp. 150–85.

Florida, Richard; Kenney, Martin and Mair, Andrew. The New Geography of Automobile Production: Japanese Transplants in North America. *Econ. Geogr.*, October 1988, *64*(4), pp. 352–73.

Florkowski, Wojciech J.; Hill, Lowell D. and Zareba, Marian. The Impact of Agricultural Policy Changes on Food Production in Poland. *Comp. Econ. Stud.*, Fall 1988, *30*(3), pp. 16–32.

Flowers, Marilyn R. Shared Tax Sources in a Leviathan Model of Federalism. *Public Finance Quart.*, January 1988, *16*(1), pp. 67–77.

_____. Tuition Tax Credits and the Public Schools. *Nat. Tax J.*, March 1988, *41*(1), pp. 87–96.

Floyd, Steven W. A Micro Level Model of Information Technology Use by Managers. In *Gattiker, U. E. and Larwood, L., eds.*, 1988, pp. 123–42.

Fluckiger, Yves. The Theory of Economic Integration in Presence of Transfers between Members of a Customs Union. *Economia (Portugal)*, October 1988, *12*(3), pp. 277–92.

Flynn, David M. Sponsorship, Infrastructure and New Organizations: Exploration of an Ecological Model into Fourteen Regions. In *Kirchhoff, B. A., et al., eds.*, 1988, pp. 238–53.

Flynn, John J. Legal Reasoning, Antitrust Policy and the Social "Science" of Economics. *Antitrust Bull.*, Winter 1988, *33*(4), pp. 713–43.

_____. The Reagan Administration's Antitrust Policy, "Original Intent" and the Legislative History of the Sherman Act. *Antitrust Bull.*, Summer 1988, *33*(2), pp. 259–307.

Flynn, Joseph E. and Mayo, John W. The Effects of Regulation on Research and Development: Theory and Evidence. *J. Bus.*, July 1988, *61*(3), pp. 321–36.

Flynn, Michael S. and Cole, David E. The U.S. Automotive Industry: Technology and Competitiveness. In *Hicks, D. A., ed.*, 1988, pp. 86–161.

Flynn, Patricia M. Lowell: A High Tech Success Story. In *Lampe, D., ed.*, 1988, *1984*, pp. 275–94.

Fodella, Gianni. Eastasia towards World Economic Supremacy: A European View. *Rivista Int. Sci. Econ. Com.*, February 1988, *35*(2), pp. 99–118.

Fogarty, Michael S. and Garofalo, Gasper A. Urban Spatial Structure and Productivity Growth in the Manufacturing Sector of Cities. *J. Urban Econ.*, January 1988, *23*(1), pp. 60–70.

Fogel, Joshua A. The Debates over the Asiatic Mode of Production in Soviet Russia, China, and Japan. *Amer. Hist. Rev.*, February 1988, *93*(1), pp. 56–79.

Fogel, Walter and Lewin, David. Wage Determination in the Public Sector. In *Lewin, D., et al., eds.*, 1988, *1974*, pp. 447–72.

Folbre, Nancy and Hartmann, Heidi I. The Rhetoric of Self-Interest: Ideology and Gender in Economic Theory. In *Klamer, A.; McCloskey, D. N. and Solow, R. M., eds.*, 1988, pp. 184–203.

_____ **and Wagman, Barnet.** The Feminization of Inequality: Some New Patterns. *Challenge*, Nov.–Dec. 1988, *31*(6), pp. 55–59.

Folk-Williams, John A. The Use of Negotiated Agreements to Resolve Water Disputes Involving Indian Rights. *Natural Res. J.*, Winter 1988, *28*(1), pp. 63–103.

Folkerts-Landau, David F. I. and Mathieson, Donald J. Innovation, Institutional Changes, and Regulatory Response in International Financial Markets. In *Haraf, W. S. and Kushmeider, R. M., eds.*, 1988, pp. 392–423.

Folkes, Valerie S. The Availability Heuristic and Perceived Risk. *J. Cons. Res.*, June 1988, *15*(1), pp. 13–23.

_____. Recent Attribution Research in Consumer Behavior: A Review and New Directions. *J. Cons. Res.*, March 1988, *14*(4), pp. 548–65.

Follain, James R. and Brueckner, Jan K. The Rise and Fall of the ARM: An Econometric Analysis of Mortgage Choice. *Rev. Econ. Statist.*, February 1988, *70*(1), pp. 93–102.

_____ **and Ling, David C.** Another Look at Tenure Choice, Inflation, and Taxes. *Amer. Real Estate Urban Econ. Assoc. J.*, Fall 1988, *16*(3), pp. 207–29.

Folmer, Hendrik. Autocorrelation Pre-testing in Linear Models with AR(1) Errors. In *Dijkstra, T. K., ed.*, 1988, pp. 39–55.

_____ **and van Dijk, Jouke.** Differences in Unemployment Duration: A Regional or a Personal Problem? *Appl. Econ.*, September 1988, *20*(9), pp. 1233–51.

Fomby, Thomas B. and Hill, R. Carter. Small-Sigma Approximations and the Minimaxity of Stein-Rules under Nonnormality. In *Rhodes, G. F., Jr. and Fomby, T. B., eds.*, 1988, pp. 193–209.

_____; **Slottje, Daniel J. and Haslag, Joseph H.** A Study of the Relationship between Economic Growth and Inequality: The Case of Mexico. *Fed. Res. Bank Dallas Econ. Rev.*, May 1988, pp. 13–25.

Fon, Vincy. Free-Riding versus Paying under Uncertainty. *Public Finance Quart.*, October 1988, *16*(4), pp. 464–81.

_____ **and Paringer, Lynn.** Price Discrimination in Medicine: The Case of Medicare. *Quart. Rev. Econ. Bus.*, Spring 1988, *28*(1), pp. 49–68.

Fonda, Nickie and Hayes, Chris. Education, Training and Business Performance. *Oxford Rev. Econ. Policy*, Autumn 1988, *4*(3), pp. 108–19.

Fong, Chan Onn. Energy Cost and Economic Development in Malaysia. *Devel. Econ.*, March 1988, *26*(1), pp. 68–89.

Fong, Geoffrey T.; Krantz, David H. and Nisbett, Richard E. The Effects of Statistical Training on Thinking about Everyday Problems. In *Bell, D. E.; Raiffa, H. and Tversky, A., eds.*, 1988, *1986*, pp. 299–340.

Fong, H. Gifford and Tang, Eric M. P. Immunized Bond Portfolios in Portfolio Protection. *J. Portfol. Manage.*, Winter 1988, *14*(2), pp. 63–68.

Fong, Pang Eng. Development Strategies and Labour Market Changes in Singapore. In *Pang, E. F., ed.*, 1988, pp. 195–242.

_____. Structural Change and Labour Market Developments: The Comparative Experiences of Five ASEAN Countries and Australia. In *Pang, E. F., ed.*, 1988, pp. 1–12.

_____ and Pew, Ong Nai. Labour Absorption in Hong Kong and Singapore since 1970. *Philippine Rev. Econ. Bus.*, March–June 1988, 25(1–2), pp. 71–99.

Fontela, Emilio and Antille, Gabrielle. Origine et distribution de la productivité globale. (The Origin and the Distribution of Total Productivity. With English summary.) *Schweiz. Z. Volkswirtsch. Statist.*, September 1988, 124(3), pp. 277–88.

de Fontenay, Alain and Denny, Michael. Cost Pressures and Relative Productivity in Canadian Telecommunications Firms. In *Dogramaci, A. and Färe, R., eds.,*, 1988, pp. 131–48.

Fontiveros, Domingo and Palma, Pedro A. A Comparative Sensitivity Analysis of the MODVEN VII Macroeconomic Model for Venezuela. *Econ. Modelling*, October 1988, 5(4), pp. 286–346.

Foot, David K. and Li, Jeanne C. Youth Unemployment: A Reply. *Can. Public Policy*, March 1988, 14(1), pp. 109–11.

_____ and Stager, David A. A. Differential Effects of Advanced Degrees on Lawyers' Earnings. *Econ. Educ. Rev.*, 1988, 7(4), pp. 385–92.

Foot, S. P. H. and Webber, Michael. Profitability and Accumulation. *Econ. Geogr.*, October 1988, 64(4), pp. 335–51.

Foote, William G. and Asheghian, Parviz. Exchange Rate Devaluation: A Monetary Model and Empirical Investigation. *Eastern Econ. J.*, April–June 1988, 14(2), pp. 181–87.

_____ and Dutkowsky, Donald H. The Demand for Money: A Rational Expectations Approach. *Rev. Econ. Statist.*, February 1988, 70(1), pp. 83–92.

_____ and Dutkowsky, Donald H. Forecasting Discount Window Borrowing. *Int. J. Forecasting*, 1988, 4(4), pp. 593–603.

Forbes, Kevin F. Pricing of Related Products by a Multiproduct Monopolist. *Rev. Ind. Organ.*, Spring 1988, 3(3), pp. 55–73.

_____. Product Differentiation, Oligopolistic Interdependence, Market Share, and Profits. *Econ. Letters*, 1988, 26(4), pp. 381–86.

Forbes, Malcolm S., Jr. A Record of Success. In *Boaz, D., ed.*, 1988, pp. 405–11.

Forbes, Shawn M. and Beranek, William. The Tax-Clientele CAPM and Firm-Size Effects: The Evidence. *Quart. J. Bus. Econ.*, Autumn 1988, 27(4), pp. 87–112.

Forbes, William. Stock Exchange Reactions to Monopoly and Merger Commission Reports. *Appl. Econ.*, July 1988, 20(7), pp. 929–38.

Ford, Deborah Ann and Gilligan, Michele. The Effect of Lead Paint Abatement Laws on Rental Property Values. *Amer. Real Estate Urban Econ. Assoc. J.*, Spring 1988, 16(1), pp. 84–94.

Ford, Gerald. Challenges to American Policy. In *Anderson, A. and Bark, D. L., eds.*, 1988, pp. 535–44.

Ford, Ina Kay and Sturm, Philip. CPI Revision Provides More Accuracy in the Medical Care Services Component. *Mon. Lab. Rev.*, April 1988, 111(4), pp. 17–26.

Ford, Michael and Holmquist, Frank. The State and Economy in Kenya: Review Essay. *African Econ. Hist.*, 1988, (17), pp. 153–63.

Ford, William F. The Public Policy Roots of Recent Thrift Crises. In *[Nutter, G. W.]*, 1988, pp. 215–25.

Foreman, Joshua N. and Beckman, Steven R. An Experimental Test of the Baumol–Tobin Transactions Demand for Money. *J. Money, Credit, Banking*, Part 1, August 1988, 20(3), pp. 291–305.

Foreman-Peck, James and Manning, Dorothy. How Well Is BT Performing? An International Comparison of Telecommunications Total Factor Productivity. *Fisc. Stud.*, August 1988, 9(3), pp. 54–67.

_____ and Manning, Dorothy. Telecommunications in Italy. In *Foreman-Peck, J. and Müller, J., eds.*, 1988, pp. 181–201.

_____ and Manning, Dorothy. Telecommunications in Norway. In *Foreman-Peck, J. and Müller, J., eds.*, 1988, pp. 221–36.

_____ and Manning, Dorothy. Telecommunications in the United Kingdom. In *Foreman-Peck, J. and Müller, J., eds.,*, 1988, pp. 257–78.

_____ and Müller, Jürgen. The Changing European Telecommunications Systems. In *Foreman-Peck, J. and Müller, J., eds.,*, 1988, pp. 23–51.

Forest, Yvon and Friedmann, John. The Politics of Place: Toward a Political Economy of Territorial Planning. In *[Perroux, F.]*, 1988, pp. 115–30.

Forester, Tom. The Materials Revolution: Superconductors, New Materials, and the Japanese Challenge: Introduction. In *Forester, T., ed.*, 1988, pp. 1–20.

Forges, Françoise. Can Sunspots Replace a Mediator? *J. Math. Econ.*, 1988, 17(4), pp. 347–68.

Forget, Evelyn L. and Manouchehri, Shahram. Keynes's Neglected Heritage: The Classical Microfoundations of *The General Theory*. *J. Post Keynesian Econ.*, Spring 1988, 10(3), pp. 401–13.

Forker, Olan D. and Liu, Donald J. Generic Fluid Milk Advertising, Demand Expansion, and Supply Response: The Case of New York City. *Amer. J. Agr. Econ.*, May 1988, 70(2), pp. 229–36.

Forlai, Luigi and Bianchi, Patrizio. The European Domestic Appliance Industry, 1945–1987. In *de Jong, H. W., ed.*, 1988, pp. 269–96.

Form, William, et al. The Impact of Technology on Work Organization and Work Outcomes: A Conceptual Framework and Research

Agenda. In *Farkas, G. and England, P., eds.*, 1988, pp. 303–28.

Formby, John P.; Keeler, James P. and Thistle, Paul D. X-efficiency, Rent-Seeking and Social Costs. *Public Choice*, May 1988, 57(2), pp. 115–26.

⸺ **and Millner, Edward L.** Opportunity Cost and Economic Rent. *Rivista Int. Sci. Econ. Com.*, September 1988, 35(9), pp. 801–16.

⸺ **and Thistle, Paul D.** On One Parameter Functional Forms for Lorenz Curves. *Eastern Econ. J.*, Jan.–March 1988, 14(1), pp. 81–85.

Formery, Zoé and Bureau, Dominique. Quand peut-on justifier des aides aux exportations? (When Can Export Subsidies Be Justified? With English summary.) *Ann. Écon. Statist.*, Oct.–Dec. 1988, (12), pp. 109–26.

Fornell, Claes. Corporate Consumer Affairs Departments: Retrospect and Prospect. In *Maynes, E. S. and ACCI Research Committee, eds.*, 1988, pp. 595–619.

⸺ **and Wernerfelt, Birger.** A Model for Customer Complaint Management. *Marketing Sci.*, Summer 1988, 7(3), pp. 287–98.

Forni, Floreal H. and Benencia, Roberto. Asalariados y campesinos pobres: El recurso familiar y la produccion de mano de obra. Estudios de casos en la provincia de Santiago del Estero. (With English summary.) *Desarrollo Econ.*, July–Sept. 1988, 28(110), pp. 245–79.

⸺ **and Benencia, Roberto.** Demographic Strategies in an Underdeveloped Region of a Modern Country: The Case of Santiago del Estero, Argentina. In *Vlassoff, C. and Barkat-e-Khuda, eds.*, 1988, pp. 73–82.

Fornoga, Coca and Mihăiță, N. V. Applications of the Information Theory to Multicriterial Analysis of Products Quality. *Econ. Computat. Cybern. Stud. Res.*, 1988, 23(4), pp. 37–44.

Forrest, Anne; Viscusi, W. Kip and Magat, Wesley A. Altruistic and Private Valuations of Risk Reduction. *J. Policy Anal. Manage.*, Winter 1988, 7(2), pp. 227–45.

Forrest, David and Naisbitt, Barry. The Sensitivity of Regional Unemployment Rates to the National Trade Cycle. *Reg. Stud.*, April 1988, 22(2), pp. 149–53.

Forrest, J. and Poulsen, M. F. Correlates of Energy Use: Domestic Electricity Consumption in Sydney. *Environ. Planning A*, March 1988, 20(3), pp. 327–38.

Forrest, Ray and Murie, Alan. The New Homeless in Britain. In *Friedrichs, J., ed.*, 1988, pp. 129–45.

Forssell, Osmo. Growth and Changes in the Structure of the Finnish Economy in the 1960s and 1970s. In *Ciaschini, M., ed.*, 1988, pp. 287–302.

Forster, Bruce A. Spatial Economic Theory of Pollution Control: Reflections on a Paradox. *J. Environ. Econ. Manage.*, December 1988, 15(4), pp. 470–74.

Forster, C. Unemployment and the Australian Economic Recovery of the 1930s. In *Gregory, R. G. and Butlin, N. G., eds.*, 1988, pp. 289–310.

Forster, D. Lynn; Sherrick, Bruce J. and Irwin, Scott H. Returns to Farm Real Estate Revisited. *Amer. J. Agr. Econ.*, August 1988, 70(3), pp. 580–87.

Forsund, Finn R. and Hjalmarsson, Lennart. Choice of Technology and Long-Run Technical Change in Energy-Intensive Industries. *Energy J.*, July 1988, 9(3), pp. 79–97.

Forsyth, D. J. C.; Jebuni, C. D. and Love, J. H. Market Structure and LDCs' Manufactured Export Performance. *World Devel.*, December 1988, 16(12), pp. 1511–20.

Forsythe, Robert; Uecker, Wilfred C. and DeJong, Douglas V. A Note on the Use of Businessmen as Subjects in Sealed Offer Markets. *J. Econ. Behav. Organ.*, January 1988, 9(1), pp. 87–100.

Fort, Rodney D. The Median Voter, Setters, and Non-repeated Construction Bond Issues. *Public Choice*, March 1988, 56(3), pp. 213–31.

⸺ **; Budd, William and Rosenman, Robert.** Perceptions, Fear, and Economic Loss: An Application of Prospect Theory to Environmental Decision Making. *Policy Sci.*, 1988, 21(4), pp. 327–50.

⸺ **and Quirk, James.** Normal Backwardation and the Inventory Effect. *J. Polit. Econ.*, February 1988, 96(1), pp. 81–99.

Fortenberry, Joseph E. A History of the Antitrust Law of Vertical Practices. In *Zerbe, R. O., Jr., ed.*, 1988, pp. 133–259.

Fortescue, Stephen. The Primary Party Organizations of Branch Ministries. In *Potichnyj, P. J., ed.*, 1988, pp. 26–47.

Fortier, Diana L. and Evanoff, Douglas D. Reevaluation of the Structure–Conduct–Performance Paradigm in Banking. *J. Finan. Services Res.*, June 1988, 1(3), pp. 277–94.

Fortin, Bernard and Bernier, André. The Welfare Cost of Unemployment in Quebec: Harberger's Triangle Meets Okun's Gap. *Can. J. Econ.*, February 1988, 21(1), pp. 161–81.

Fortin, Carlos. Power, Bargaining and the Latin American Debt Negotiations: Some Political Perspectives. In *Griffith-Jones, S., ed.*, 1988, pp. 308–35.

Fortin, Michel and Khoury, Nabil T. Effectiveness of Hedging Interest Rate Risks and Stock Market Risks with Financial Futures. *J. Futures Markets*, June 1988, 8(3), pp. 319–34.

Förtsch, Frank and Weck, Manfred. Application of Multicriteria Optimization to Structural Systems. In *Iri, M. and Yajima, K., eds.*, 1988, pp. 471–83.

Fortune, Peter. Municipal Bond Yields: Whose Tax Rates Matter? *Nat. Tax J.*, June 1988, 41(2), pp. 219–33.

Fosberg, Richard H. and Madura, Jeff. Intertemporal Exchange Rate Risk: Implications for Corporate Exposure. *Rivista Int. Sci. Econ. Com.*, Oct.–Nov. 1988, 35(10–11), pp. 1053–60.

Foshee, Andrew W.; Burbee, Clark R. and McNiel, Douglas W. Superfund Taxes and Expenditures: Regional Redistributions. *Rev. Reg. Stud.*, Winter 1988, 18(1), pp. 4–9.

Fosler, R. Scott. The New Economic Role of American States: Conclusion. In *Fosler, R. S., ed.*, 1988, pp. 309–29.

_____. The New Economic Role of American States: Overview. In *Fosler, R. S., ed.*, 1988, pp. 1–18.

Foster, C. D. Accountability in the Development of Policy for Local Taxation of People and Business. *Reg. Stud.*, June 1988, 22(3), pp. 245–50.

Foster, James E. and Shorrocks, Anthony F. Inequality and Poverty Orderings. *Europ. Econ. Rev.*, March 1988, 32(2–3), pp. 654–61.

_____ and Shorrocks, Anthony F. Poverty Orderings. *Econometrica*, January 1988, 56(1), pp. 173–77.

_____ and Shorrocks, Anthony F. Poverty Orderings and Welfare Dominance. In *Gaertner, W. and Pattanaik, P. K., eds.*, 1988, *1988*, pp. 91–110.

_____ and Shorrocks, Anthony F. Poverty Orderings and Welfare Dominance. *Soc. Choice Welfare*, 1988, 5(2/3), pp. 179–98.

Foster, John and Malley, James. The Domestic and Foreign-Owned Sectors of Scottish Manufacturing: A Macroeconomic Approach to Their Relative Performance and Prospects. *Scot. J. Polit. Econ.*, August 1988, 35(3), pp. 250–65.

Fosu, Augustin Kwasi. Trends in Relative Earnings Gains by Black Women: Implications for the Future. *Rev. Black Polit. Econ.*, Summer 1988, 17(1), pp. 31–45.

_____ and Huq, Md. Shamsul. Price Inflation and Wage Inflation: A Cause–Effect Relationship? *Econ. Letters*, 1988, 27(1), pp. 35–40.

Fotheringham, A. Stewart. Consumer Store Choice and Choice Set Definition. *Marketing Sci.*, Summer 1988, 7(3), pp. 299–310.

_____. Market Share Analysis Techniques: A Review and Illustration of Current U.S. Practice. In *Wrigley, N., ed.*, 1988, pp. 120–59.

Foulds, L. R. Forestry Applications of Operations Research. In *Iri, M. and Yajima, K., eds.*, 1988, pp. 594–603.

Fourie, F. C. v. N. Die Aktiwiteite en Benadering van die Raad op Mededinging: 1980–1983. (With English summary). *J. Stud. Econ. Econometrics*, March 1988, 12(1), pp. 17–35.

Fourment, Antoine. Security on Movable Property and Receivables in Europe: France. In *Dickson, M. G.; Rosener, W. and Storm, P. M., eds.*, 1988, pp. 37–57.

Fournier, Gary M.; Rasmussen, David W. and Serow, William J. Elderly Migration as a Response to Economic Incentives. *Soc. Sci. Quart.*, June 1988, 69(2), pp. 245–60.

_____; Rasmussen, David W. and Serow, William J. Elderly Migration: For Sun and Money. *Population Res. Policy Rev.*, 1988, 7(2), pp. 189–99.

Fowkes, Tony and Wardman, Mark. The Design of Stated Preference Travel Choice Experiments. *J. Transp. Econ. Policy*, January 1988, 22(1), pp. 27–44.

Fowlkes, Edward B.; Freeny, Anne E. and Landwehr, James M. Evaluating Logistic Models for Large Contingency Tables. *J. Amer. Statist. Assoc.*, September 1988, 83(403), pp. 611–22.

Fox, Douglas R. and Tapscott, Tracy R. The U.S. National Income and Product Accounts: Revised Estimates. *Surv. Curr. Bus.*, July 1988, 68(7), pp. 8–37.

Fox, Glenn; Brinkman, George L. and Horbasz, Chris N. A Comparison of *Ex Post* and *Ex Ante* Measures of Producers' Surplus in Estimating the Returns to Canadian Federal Sheep Research. *Can. J. Agr. Econ.*, November 1988, 36(3), pp. 489–500.

_____; Brinkman, George L. and Widmer, Lorne. The Rate of Return to Agricultural Research in a Small Country: The Case of Beef Cattle Research in Canada. *Can. J. Agr. Econ.*, March 1988, 36(1), pp. 23–35.

Fox, James Alan and Hellman, Daryl A. Location and Other Correlates of Campus Crime. In *Alper, N. O. and Hellman, D. A., eds.*, 1988, pp. 16–39.

Fox, Karl A. Econometrics Needs a History: Two Cases of Conspicuous Neglect. In *Sengupta, J. K. and Kadekodi, G. K., eds.*, 1988, pp. 23–47.

Fox, M. F. Canada's Agricultural and Forest Lands: Issues and Policy. *Can. Public Policy*, September 1988, 14(3), pp. 266–81.

Fox, Pauline and Brotman, Billie Ann. The Impact of Economic Conditions on the Incidence of Arson: Comment. *J. Risk Ins.*, December 1988, 55(4), pp. 751–54.

Fox, William F. and Murray, Matthew. Economic Aspects of Taxing Services. *Nat. Tax J.*, March 1988, 41(1), pp. 19–36.

Foxall, Gordon R. Consumer Innovativeness: Novelty-Seeking, Creativity and Cognitive Style. In *Hirschman, E. and Sheth, J. N., eds.*, 1988, pp. 79–113.

_____. Marketing New Technology: Markets, Hierarchies, and User-Initiated Innovation. *Managerial Dec. Econ.*, September 1988, 9(3), pp. 237–50.

Foxley, Alejandro. The Foreign Debt Problem from a Latin American Viewpoint. In *Feinberg, R. E. and Ffrench-Davis, R., eds.*, 1988, pp. 77–100.

_____. Latin American Development after the Debt Crisis. In *Tavis, L. A., ed.*, 1988, pp. 69–101.

van Fraassen, Bas C. The Pragmatic Theory of Explanation. In *Pitt, J. C., ed.*, 1988, pp. 136–55.

Fraker, Thomas and Moffitt, Robert. The Effect of Food Stamps on Labor Supply: A Bivariate Selection Model. *J. Public Econ.*, February 1988, 35(1), pp. 25–56.

Francia, Joseph H. An Economic Analysis of Co-operative Labour among Philippine Rice Farmers. In *Attwood, D. W. and Baviskar, B. S., eds.*, 1988, pp. 259–81.

Francis, Jack Clark; Kim, Wi-Saeng and Lee, Jae Won. Investment Performance of Common Stocks in Relation to Insider Ownership. *Financial Rev.*, February 1988, 23(1), pp. 53–64.

Francis, James. The Florida Sales Tax on Services: What Really Went Wrong? In *Gold, S. D., ed.*, 1988, pp. 129–52.

Francis, Jere R. and Simon, Daniel T. The Effects of Auditor Change on Audit Fees: Tests of Price Cutting and Price Recovery. *Accounting Rev.*, April 1988, 63(2), pp. 255–69.

_____ **and Wilson, Earl R.** Auditor Changes: A Joint Test of Theories Relating to Agency Costs and Auditor Differentiation. *Accounting Rev.*, October 1988, 63(4), pp. 663–82.

Francken, Dick and Kuylen, Ton. Level of Own Contribution towards a Public Service as an Indicator for Consumer Appraisal. In *Maital, S., ed., Vol. 1*, 1988, pp. 97–113.

Francks, Penelope. Learning from Japan: Plant Imports and Technology Transfer in the Chinese Iron and Steel Industry. *J. Japanese Int. Economies*, March 1988, 2(1), pp. 42–62.

Franco, Gustavo H. B. O imposto inflacionário durante quatro hiperinflações. (With English summary.) *Pesquisa Planejamento Econ.*, August 1988, 18(2), pp. 341–60.

François, Pierre and Leunis, Joseph. The Impact of Belgian Public Policy upon Retailing: The Case of the Second Padlock Law. In *Kaynak, E., ed.*, 1988, pp. 135–53.

Frank, Andre Gunder. American Roulette in the Globonomic Casino: Retrospect and Prospect on the World Economic Crisis Today. In *Zarembka, P., ed.*, 1988, pp. 3–43.

_____. The Development of Underdevelopment. In *Wilber, C. K., ed.*, 1988, pp. 109–20.

Frank, Murray Z. An Intertemporal Model of Industrial Exit. *Quart. J. Econ.*, May 1988, 103(2), pp. 333–44.

_____; **Gencay, Ramazan and Stengos, Thanasis.** International Chaos? *Europ. Econ. Rev.*, October 1988, 32(8), pp. 1569–84.

_____ **and Stengos, Thanasis.** Chaotic Dynamics in Economic Time-Series. *J. Econ. Surveys*, 1988, 2(2), pp. 103–33.

_____ **and Stengos, Thanasis.** Some Evidence Concerning Macroeconomic Chaos. *J. Monet. Econ.*, November 1988, 22(3), pp. 423–38.

_____ **and Stengos, Thanasis.** The Stability of Canadian Macroeconomic Data as Measured by the Largest Lyapunov Exponent. *Econ. Letters*, 1988, 27(1), pp. 11–14.

Frank, Robert H. The Functional Role of Preferences. *J. Behav. Econ.*, Spring 1988, 17(1), pp. 7–18.

_____. Passions within Reason: The Strategic Role of the Emotions. In *Maital, S., ed., Vol. 2*, 1988, pp. 769–83.

Franke, Günter. Debt-Equity Swaps aus finanzierungstheoretischer Perspektive. (With English summary.) *Z. Betriebswirtshaft*, January 1988, 58(1), pp. 187–97.

Franke, Reiner. Integrating the Financing of Production and a Rate of Interest into Production Price Models. *Cambridge J. Econ.*, June 1988, 12(2), pp. 257–72.

_____. A Note on the Lotka–Volterra Gravitation Process and Its Pleasant Properties. *Manches-*

ter Sch. Econ. Soc. Stud., June 1988, 56(2), pp. 147–57.

_____. Some Problems Concerning the Notion of Cost-Minimizing Systems in the Framework of Joint Production. In *Steedman, I., ed., Vol. 2*, 1988, *1986*, pp. 16–25.

_____ **and Kattermann, Dieter.** Konsumnachfrage und technologische Arbeitslosigkeit in einem Input–Output-Modellrahmen. (Consumption Demand and Technological Unemployment in an Input–Output Framework. With English summary.) *Jahr. Nationalökon. Statist.*, June 1988, 204(6), pp. 518–30.

_____ **and Weghorst, W.** Complex Dynamics in a Simple Input–Output Model without the Full Capacity Utilization Hypothesis. *Metroecon.*, February 1988, 39(1), pp. 1–29.

Franke, Siegfried F. Arbeitsmarkt und Schattenökonomie. (Labour Market and Shadow Economy. With English summary.) *Jahr. Nationalökon. Statist.*, October 1988, 205(4), pp. 300–15.

Frankel, Jeffrey A. Ambiguous Policy Multipliers in Theory and in Empirical Models. In *Bryant, R. C., et al., eds.*, 1988, pp. 17–26.

_____. The Implications of Conflicting Models for Coordination between Monetary and Fiscal Policymakers. In *Bryant, R. C., et al., eds.*, 1988, pp. 238–54.

_____. International Capital Flows and Domestic Economic Policies. In *Feldstein, M., ed. (II)*, 1988, pp. 559–625.

_____. International Capital Mobility and Exchange Rate Volatility. In *Fieleke, N. S., ed.*, 1988, pp. 162–88.

_____. International Nominal Targeting: A Proposal for Policy Coordination. In *Fieleke, N. S., ed.*, 1988, pp. 234–39.

_____. Public Debt and Households' Demand for Monetary Assets in Italy: 1970–86: Discussion. In *Giavazzi, F. and Spaventa, L., eds.*, 1988, pp. 244–49.

_____. Recent Estimates of Time-Variation in the Conditional Variance and in the Exchange Risk Premium. *J. Int. Money Finance*, March 1988, 7(1), pp. 115–25.

_____. Tax Policy and International Competitiveness: Comment. In *Frenkel, J. A., ed.*, 1988, pp. 375–80.

_____ **and Dornbusch, Rudiger.** The Flexible Exchange Rate System: Experience and Alternatives. In *Borner, S., ed.*, 1988, pp. 151–97.

_____ **and Froot, Kenneth A.** Chartists, Fundamentalists and the Demand for Dollars. *Greek Econ. Rev.*, 1988, 10(1), pp. 49–102.

_____ **and MacArthur, Alan T.** Political vs. Currency Premia in International Real Interest Rate Differentials: A Study of Forward Rates for 24 Countries. *Europ. Econ. Rev.*, June 1988, 32(5), pp. 1083–114.

_____; **Mathieson, Donald J. and Dooley, Michael P.** International Capital Mobility: What Do Saving–Investment Correlations Tell Us? Reply. *Int. Monet. Fund Staff Pap.*, June 1988, 35(2), pp. 397–98.

_____ **and Rockett, Katharine E.** International

Macroeconomic Policy Coordination When Policymakers Do Not Agree on the True Model. *Amer. Econ. Rev.*, June 1988, *78*(3), pp. 318–40.

Frankel, Linda D.; Fulman, Diane and Howell, James M. The Massachusetts Experience. In *Lampe, D., ed.*, 1988, pp. 348–57.

_____ **and Howell, James M.** Economic Revitalization and Job Creation in America's Oldest Industrial Region. In *Lampe, D., ed.*, 1988, pp. 295–313.

Frankel, S. Herbert. Adam Smith's "Invisible Hand" in a Velvet Glove. In *[Nutter, G. W.]*, 1988, pp. 7–21.

Franks, Julian R.; Harris, Robert S. and Mayer, Colin. Means of Payment in Takeovers: Results for the United Kingdom and the United States. In *Auerbach, A. J., ed. (I)*, 1988, pp. 221–58.

_____ **; Karki, J. and Selby, M. J. P.** Loan Guarantees, Wealth Transfers and Incentives to Invest. *J. Ind. Econ.*, September 1988, *37*(1), pp. 47–65.

Frantz, Roger and Singh, Harinder. Intrafirm (In) Efficiencies: Neoclassical and X-Efficiency Perspectives. *J. Econ. Issues*, September 1988, *22*(3), pp. 856–63.

_____ **and Singh, Harinder.** Maximization Postulate: Type I and Type II Errors. *J. Post Keynesian Econ.*, Fall 1988, *11*(1), pp. 100–107.

Franz, Wolfgang. Sectoral Uncertainty and Unemployment: Comment. In *Hart, R. A., ed.*, 1988, pp. 364–66.

Frasca, Francesco M. and Paladini, Ruggero. The Distributive Effects of Taxation of the Public Debt in Italy. *Econ. Notes*, 1988, (3), pp. 5–28.

Fraser, Cynthia and Hite, Robert E. Compensation as an Alternative to Ownership in Developing Markets: Beliefs, Attitudes and Uses. *J. World Trade*, December 1988, *22*(6), pp. 95–106.

_____ **; Hite, Robert E. and Sauer, Paul L.** Increasing Contributions in Solicitation Campaigns: The Use of Large and Small Anchorpoints. *J. Cons. Res.*, September 1988, *15*(2), pp. 284–87.

Fraser, Douglas A. and Widick, B. J. The Challenges of Competitiveness: A Labor View. In *Starr, M. K., ed.*, 1988, pp. 159–84.

Fraser, L.; Purtill, A. and Hall, N. Supply Response in Broadacre Agriculture. *Rev. Marketing Agr. Econ.*, December 1988, *56*(3), pp. 361–74.

Fraser, R. W. Impact of Exchange Rate Fluctuations on the Mining Sector. *Rev. Marketing Agr. Econ.*, April 1988, *56*(1), pp. 96–99.

_____. A Method for Evaluating Supply Response to Price Underwriting. *Australian J. Agr. Econ.*, April 1988, *32*(1), pp. 22–36.

Fratianni, Michele. The European Monetary System: How Well Has It Worked? *Cato J.*, Fall 1988, *8*(2), pp. 477–501.

_____. International Macroeconomic Policy Cooperation: Where Do We Go from Here? Per-

spective. In *Guerrieri, P. and Padoan, P. C., eds.*, 1988, pp. 254–62.

Fratoe, Frank A. Social Capital of Black Business Owners. *Rev. Black Polit. Econ.*, Spring 1988, *16*(4), pp. 33–50.

Frauendorfer, K. Solving SLP Recource Problems: The Case of Stochastic Technology Matrix, RHS and Objective. In *Iri, M. and Yajima, K., eds.*, 1988, pp. 90–100.

Frazer, Peter. The Regulation of Takeovers in Great Britain. In *Coffee, J. C., Jr.; Lowenstein, L. and Rose-Ackerman, S., eds.*, 1988, pp. 436–51.

Frazier, Mark. Opening Space: New Roles for International Launch Facilities. In *Egan, J. J., et al.*, 1988, pp. 227–33.

Frech, H. E., III. Health Care in America: The Political Economy of Hospitals and Health Insurance: Introduction. In *Frech, H. E., III, ed.*, 1988, pp. 1–23.

_____. Monopoly in Health Insurance: The Economics of *Kartell v. Blue Shield of Massachusetts*. In *Frech, H. E., III, ed.*, 1988, pp. 293–322.

_____. Preferred Provider Organizations and Health Care Competition. In *Frech, H. E., III, ed.*, 1988, pp. 353–372.

_____ **and Ginsburg, Paul B.** Competition among Health Insurers, Revisited. In *Greenberg, W., ed.*, 1988, pp. 57–69.

Frecka, Thomas J.; Park, Hun Y. and Wei, K. C. John. A Further Investigation of the Risk–Return Relation for Commodity Futures. In *Fabozzi, F. J., ed.*, 1988, pp. 357–77.

Frederick, Kenneth D. Market Failure and the Efficiency of Irrigated Agriculture: Comment. In *O'Mara, G. T., ed.*, 1988, pp. 31–32.

Frederiksen, Harald D.; Perry, Christopher and Barghouti, Shawki. Irrigation: Issues, Policies and Lending Strategies. In *Roberts, C., ed.*, 1988, pp. 71–78.

Fredriksen, Tor and Grønhaug, Kjell. Concentration Ratios, Strategy and Performance: The Case of the Norwegian Telecommunications Industry. *Managerial Dec. Econ.*, December 1988, *9*(4), pp. 257–62.

_____ **and Grønhaug, Kjell.** Exploring the Impact of Governmental Incentives on Regional Growth. *Liiketaloudellinen Aikak.*, 1988, *37*(4), pp. 278–88.

Freear, John and Wetzel, William E. Equity Financing for New Technology-Based Firms. In *Kirchhoff, B. A., et al., eds.*, 1988, pp. 347–67.

Freebairn, John W. An Economic Perspective on Recent Changes in the Taxation of Australian Business Income. *Australian Tax Forum*, 1988, *5*(4), pp. 493–521.

_____. Sectoral Implications of Changes in Exchange Rates and Interest Rates: Comment. *Rev. Marketing Agr. Econ.*, April 1988, *56*(1), pp. 104–06.

_____. The Share Market Crash and Australian Agriculture. *Rev. Marketing Agr. Econ.*, April 1988, *56*(1), pp. 140–42.

_____ and **Alston, Julian M.** Producer Price Equalization. *Rev. Marketing Agr. Econ.*, December 1988, *56*(3), pp. 306–40.

_____; **Alston, Julian M. and Edwards, Geoff W.** Market Distortions and Benefits from Research. *Amer. J. Agr. Econ.*, May 1988, *70*(2), pp. 281–88.

_____; **Porter, Michael and Walsh, Cliff.** Tax Cuts: Desirable and Practical. *Australian Tax Forum*, 1988, *5*(3), pp. 285–99.

_____ and **Sarris, Alexander H.** Endogenous Price Policies and International Wheat Prices: Reply. *Amer. J. Agr. Econ.*, August 1988, *70*(3), pp. 747–49.

Freedman, Audrey. How the 1980's Have Changed Industrial Relations. *Mon. Lab. Rev.*, May 1988, *111*(5), pp. 35–38.

Freedman, D. A.; Navidi, W. and Peters, S. C. On the Impact of Variable Selection in Fitting Regression Equations. In *Dijkstra, T. K., ed.,* 1988, pp. 1–16.

Freedman, David H. and Hollister, Robinson G., Jr. Special Employment Programmes in OECD Countries. *Int. Lab. Rev.*, 1988, *127*(3), pp. 317–34.

Freedman, Martin and Jaggi, Bikki. An Analysis of the Impact of Corporate Pollution Disclosures: A Reply. In *Neimark, M., ed.,* 1988, pp. 193–97.

Freedman, Ronald, et al. Local Area Variations in Reproductive Behaviour in the People's Republic of China, 1973–1982. *Population Stud.*, March 1988, *42*(1), pp. 39–57.

Freeman, A. Myrick, III. Reply [One More Externality Article]. *J. Environ. Econ. Manage.*, September 1988, *15*(3), pp. 386.

Freeman, Christopher. Diffusion: The Spread of New Technology to Firms, Sectors, and Nations. In *Heertje, A., ed.,* 1988, pp. 38–70.

_____. Japan: A New National System of Innovation? In *Dosi, G., et al., eds.,* 1988, pp. 330–48.

_____. Technical Change and Economic Theory: Introduction. In *Dosi, G., et al., eds.,* 1988, pp. 1–8.

_____. Technology Gaps, International Trade and the Problems of Smaller and Less-Developed Economies. In *Freeman, C. and Lundvall, B.-A., eds.,* 1988, pp. 67–84.

_____ and **Perez, Carlota.** Structural Crises of Adjustment, Business Cycles and Investment Behaviour. In *Dosi, G., et al., eds.,* 1988, pp. 38–66.

Freeman, David M. Water Water Everywhere in Irrigated Agriculture, and Not a Drop with Constant Meaning. In *Bennett, J. W. and Bowen, J. R., eds.,* 1988, pp. 311–28.

Freeman, Gary P. Voters, Bureaucrats, and the State: On the Autonomy of Social Security Policymaking. In *Nash, G. D.; Pugach, N. H. and Tomasson, R. F., eds.,* 1988, pp. 145–79.

Freeman, Harry L. Implications of Global Financial Intermediation. In *Mikdashi, Z., ed.,* 1988, pp. 73–84.

_____. Services and Investments: Comments. In *Schott, J. J. and Smith, M. G., eds.,* 1988, pp. 151–53.

Freeman, Katherine B. The Significance of Motivational Variables in International Public Welfare Expenditures: A Reply. *Econ. Develop. Cult. Change,* January 1988, *36*(2), pp. 397–99.

Freeman, Richard B. Contraction and Expansion: The Divergence of Private Sector and Public Sector Unionism in the United States. *J. Econ. Perspectives,* Spring 1988, *2*(2), pp. 63–88.

_____. Does the New Generation of Labor Economists Know More Than the Old Generation? In *Kaufman, B. E., ed.,* 1988, pp. 205–32.

_____. Evaluating the European View that the United States Has No Unemployment Problem. *Amer. Econ. Rev.*, May 1988, *78*(2), pp. 294–99.

_____. The Relation of Criminal Activity to Black Youth Employment. In *Simms, M. C. and Myers, S. L., Jr., eds.,* 1988, pp. 99–107.

_____. Union Density and Economic Performance: An Analysis of U.S. States. *Europ. Econ. Rev.*, March 1988, *32*(2–3), pp. 707–16.

_____ and **Bloom, David E.** Economic Development and the Timing and Components of Population Growth. *J. Policy Modeling,* April 1988, *10*(1), pp. 57–81.

_____ and **Ichniowski, Casey.** The Public Sector Look of American Unionism: Introduction. In *Freeman, R. B. and Ichniowski, C., eds.,* 1988, pp. 1–15.

_____; **Ichniowski, Casey and Zax, Jeffrey S.** Collective Organization of Labor in the Public Sector: Appendix A. In *Freeman, R. B. and Ichniowski, C., eds.,* 1988, pp. 365–98.

_____ and **Valletta, Robert G.** The Effects of Public Sector Labor Laws on Labor Market Institutions and Outcomes. In *Freeman, R. B. and Ichniowski, C., eds.,* 1988, pp. 81–103.

_____ and **Valletta, Robert G.** The NBER Public Sector Collective Bargaining Law Data Set: Appendix B. In *Freeman, R. B. and Ichniowski, C., eds.,* 1988, pp. 399–419.

Freeman, Robert J.; Willits, Stephen D. and Clancy, Donald K. Public Employee Retirement System Reports: A Study of Knowledgeable User Information Processing Ability. In *Chan, J. L. and Rowan, H. J., eds.,* 1988, pp. 3–48.

Freeman, Scott. Banking as the Provision of Liquidity. *J. Bus.*, January 1988, *61*(1), pp. 45–64.

Freeny, Anne E.; Landwehr, James M. and Fowlkes, Edward B. Evaluating Logistic Models for Large Contingency Tables. *J. Amer. Statist. Assoc.*, September 1988, *83*(403), pp. 611–22.

Frees, Edward W. Estimating the Cost of a Warranty. *J. Bus. Econ. Statist.*, January 1988, *6*(1), pp. 79–86.

_____ and **Cho, David Chinhyung.** Estimating the Volatility of Discrete Stock Prices. *J. Finance,* June 1988, *43*(2), pp. 451–66.

Freese, V.; Meulders, D. and Plasman, R. Bilan des recherches sur l'aménagement et la réduction du temps de travail en Belgique (1975–1987). (With English summary.) *Cah. Écon.*

Bruxelles, First Trimester 1988, (117), pp. 67–106.

Freire, Paulo. Pedagogy of the Oppressed. **In** *Wilber, C. K., ed.*, 1988, pp. 541–59.

de Freitas, Arlei and Solnik, Bruno. International Factors of Stock Price Behavior. **In** *Khoury, S. J. and Ghosh, A., eds.*, 1988, pp. 259–76.

Fremling, Gertrud M. and Lott, John R., Jr. Televising Legislatures: Some Thoughts on Whether Politicians are Search Goods. *Public Choice*, July 1988, 58(1), pp. 73–78.

French, Dan W. and Martin, Linda J. The Measurement of Option Mispricing. *J. Banking Finance*, December 1988, 12(4), pp. 537–50.

French, George. Contracts and the Provision of Durability. *Quart. Rev. Econ. Bus.*, Spring 1988, 28(1), pp. 6–20.

French, Kenneth R. and Fama, Eugene F. Business Cycles and the Behavior of Metals Prices. *J. Finance*, December 1988, 43(5), pp. 1075–93.

_____ **and Fama, Eugene F.** Dividend Yields and Expected Stock Returns. *J. Finan. Econ.*, October 1988, 22(1), pp. 3–25.

_____ **and Fama, Eugene F.** Permanent and Temporary Components of Stock Prices. *J. Polit. Econ.*, April 1988, 96(2), pp. 246–73.

French, Michael Thomas. An Efficiency Test for Occupational Safety Regulation. *Southern Econ. J.*, January 1988, 54(3), pp. 675–93.

Frenkel, Jacob A. An Introduction to International Aspects of Fiscal Policies. **In** *Frenkel, J. A., ed.*, 1988, pp. 1–19.

_____. The Coordination of Economic Policies. **In** *Fieleke, N. S., ed.*, 1988, pp. 240–43.

_____. Turbulence in the Foreign Exchange Markets and Macroeconomic Policies. **In** *Melamed, L., ed.*, 1988, 1983, pp. 445–69.

_____ **and Aizenman, Joshua.** Sectoral Wages and the Real Exchange Rate. *J. Int. Econ.*, February 1988, 24(1–2), pp. 69–91.

_____; **Bhandari, Jagdeep S. and Driskill, Robert.** Capital Mobility and Exchange Rate Overshooting: Reply. *Europ. Econ. Rev.*, January 1988, 32(1), pp. 203–06.

_____ **and Goldstein, Morris.** Exchange Rate Volatility and Misalignment: Evaluating Some Proposals for Reform. **In** *Federal Reserve Bank of Kansas City*, 1988, pp. 185–220.

_____ **and Goldstein, Morris.** A Guide to Target Zones. **In** *Melamed, L., ed.*, 1988, 1986, pp. 183–221.

_____ **and Goldstein, Morris.** The International Monetary System: Developments and Prospects. *Cato J.*, Fall 1988, 8(2), pp. 285–306.

_____; **Goldstein, Morris and Masson, Paul R.** International Coordination of Economic Policies: Scope, Methods, and Effects. **In** *Guth, W., ed.*, 1988, pp. 149–92.

_____ **and Razin, Assaf.** Budget Deficits under Alternative Tax Systems: International Effects. *Int. Monet. Fund Staff Pap.*, June 1988, 35(2), pp. 297–315.

_____ **and Razin, Assaf.** International Aspects of Budget Deficits with Distortionary Taxes. **In** *Helpman, E.; Razin, A. and Sadka, E., eds.*, 1988, pp. 145–62.

Frenkel, Stephen J. Australian Employers in the Shadow of the Labor Accords. *Ind. Relat.*, Spring 1988, 27(2), pp. 166–79.

Freshwater, David. Acid Rain: An Issue in Canadian–U.S. Relations. **In** *Johnston, G. M.; Freshwater, D. and Favero, P., eds.*, 1988, pp. 113–34.

Freund, Deborah A. Has Public Sector Contracting with Health Maintenance Organisations in the United States Saved Money? **In** *Smith, C. S., ed.*, 1988, pp. 148–60.

_____ **and Hurley, Robert E.** Determinants of Provider Selection or Assignment in a Mandatory Case Management Program and Their Implications for Utilization. *Inquiry*, Fall 1988, 25(3), pp. 402–10.

Frey, Bruno S. Bargaining Perversities, Institutions, and International Economic Relations: Perspective. **In** *Guerrieri, P. and Padoan, P. C., eds.*, 1988, pp. 51–57.

_____. Explaining the Growth of Government: International Perspectives. **In** *Lybeck, J. A. and Henrekson, M., eds.*, 1988, pp. 21–28.

_____. Ipsative and Objective Limits to Human Behavior. *J. Behav. Econ.*, Winter 1988, 17(4), pp. 229–48.

_____. Regulations by Consensus: The Practice of International Investment Agreements: Comment. *J. Inst. Theoretical Econ.*, February 1988, 144(1), pp. 176–79.

_____ **and Buhofer, Heinz.** Prisoners and Property Rights. *J. Law Econ.*, April 1988, 31(1), pp. 19–46.

_____ **and Gygi, Beat.** Die Fairness von Preisen. (The Fairness of Prices. With English summary.) *Schweiz. Z. Volkswirtsch. Statist.*, December 1988, 124(4), pp. 519–41.

_____ **and Pommerehne, Werner W.** Die Geltung deutschsprachiger ökonomen in der Welt. (The Reputation of German Speaking Economists in the World. With English summary.) *Jahr. Nationalökon. Statist.*, May 1988, 204(5), pp. 406–22.

_____ **and Schneider, Friedrich.** Politico-Economic Models of Macroeconomic Policy: A Review of the Empirical Evidence. **In** *Willett, T. D., ed.*, 1988, pp. 239–75.

Frey, Donald N. and Fellowes, Frederick A. Pictures and Parts: Delivering an Automated Automotive Parts Catalog. **In** *Guile, B. R. and Quinn, J. B., eds. (I)*, 1988, pp. 36–56.

Frey, John B. Marketing Mix Reactions to Entry: Commentary. *Marketing Sci.*, Fall 1988, 7(4), pp. 386–87.

Frey, William H. Migration and Metropolitan Decline in Developed Countries: A Comparative Study. *Population Devel. Rev.*, December 1988, 14(4), pp. 595–628.

_____. The Re-emergence of Core Region Growth: A Return to the Metropolis? *Int. Reg. Sci. Rev.*, 1988, 11(3), pp. 261–67.

Frick, Bernd; Stengelhofen, Theo and Sadowski, Dieter. Wer beschäftigt Schwerbehinderte? Erste Einsichten aus einem laufenden Forschungsprojekt. (With English summary.) *Z. Betriebswirtshaft*, January 1988, 58(1), pp. 37–50.

Fried, Edward R. The Impact of Lower Oil Prices on Importing Countries. In *Mabro, R., ed.*, 1988, pp. 215–23.

_____. Oil Security: An Economic Phenomenon. In *Fried, E. R. and Blandin, N. M., eds.*, 1988, pp. 55–64.

Fried, Joel and Howitt, Peter W. Fiscal Deficits, International Trade and Welfare. *J. Int. Econ.*, February 1988, 24(1–2), pp. 1–22.

Fried, Marc and Culhane, Dennis. Paths in Homelessness: A View from the Street. In *Friedrichs, J., ed.*, 1988, pp. 175–87.

Frieden, Jeff. Sectoral Conflict and Foreign Economic Policy, 1914–1940. *Int. Organ.*, Winter 1988, 42(1), pp. 59–90.

_____. Sectoral Conflict and U.S. Foreign Economic Policy, 1914–1940. In *Ikenberry, G. J.; Lake, D. A. and Mastanduno, M., eds.*, 1988, pp. 59–90.

Friedenberg, Howard L. and DePass, Rudolph E. Recent Growth in Nonfarm Personal Income. *Surv. Curr. Bus.*, October 1988, 68(10), pp. 23–26.

_____ and DePass, Rudolph E. State Personal Income, First Quarter 1988. *Surv. Curr. Bus.*, July 1988, 68(7), pp. 134–36.

_____; Renshaw, Vernon and Johnson, Kenneth P. Tracking the BEA Regional Projections, 1983–86. *Surv. Curr. Bus.*, June 1988, 68(6), pp. 23–27.

_____; Renshaw, Vernon and Trott, Edward A., Jr. Gross State Product by Industry, 1963–86. *Surv. Curr. Bus.*, May 1988, 68(5), pp. 30–46.

Frieder, Larry A. The Interstate Banking Landscape: Legislative Policies and Rationale. *Contemp. Policy Issues*, April 1988, 6(2), pp. 41–66.

Friedland, Robert B. and Chollet, Deborah J. Employer Financing of Long-term Care. In *Scheffler, R. M. and Rossiter, L. F., eds.*, 1988, pp. 3–22.

Friedman, Abraham and Shapira, Zur. Expert and Amateur Inflation Expectations. In *Maital, S., ed., Vol. 1*, 1988, pp. 335–41.

Friedman, Benjamin M. Conducting Monetary Policy by Controlling Currency Plus Noise: Comment. *Carnegie–Rochester Conf. Ser. Public Policy*, Autumn 1988, 29, pp. 205–12.

_____. Evolution Prevails. *Challenge*, July–August 1988, 31(4), pp. 47–52.

_____. Is There a Corporate Debt Crisis? Comment. *Brookings Pap. Econ. Act.*, 1988, (1), pp. 126–30.

_____. Lessons on Monetary Policy from the 1980s. *J. Econ. Perspectives*, Summer 1988, 2(3), pp. 51–72.

_____. Monetary Policy without Quantity Variables. *Amer. Econ. Rev.*, May 1988, 78(2), pp. 440–45.

_____ and Warshawsky, Mark J. Annuity Prices and Saving Behavior in the United States. In *Bodie, Z.; Shoven, J. B. and Wise, D. A., eds.*, 1988, pp. 53–77.

Friedman, Brian L. Productivity Trends in Department Stores, 1967–86. *Mon. Lab. Rev.*, March 1988, 111(3), pp. 17–21.

Friedman, David D. Diamonds are a Government's Best Friend: Burden-free Taxes on Goods Valued for their Values: Comment. *Amer. Econ. Rev.*, March 1988, 78(1), pp. 297.

_____. Does Altruism Produce Efficient Outcomes? Marshall versus Kaldor. *J. Legal Stud.*, January 1988, 17(1), pp. 1–13.

Friedman, Gerald. Strike Success and Union Ideology: The United States and France, 1880–1914. *J. Econ. Hist.*, March 1988, 48(1), pp. 1–25.

Friedman, Irving S. The Development Role of the IMF and the World Bank: The U.S. Stance. In *Yochelson, J., ed.*, 1988, pp. 119–32.

Friedman, James W. A Non-cooperative Equilibrium for Supergames. In *Daughety, A. F., ed.*, 1988, 1971, pp. 142–57.

_____. On the Strategic Importance of Prices versus Quantities. *Rand J. Econ.*, Winter 1988, 19(4), pp. 607–22.

Friedman, Joseph; Jimenez, Emmanuel and Mayo, Stephen K. The Demand for Tenure Security in Developing Countries. *J. Devel. Econ.*, September 1988, 29(2), pp. 185–98.

Friedman, Judith J. Central Business Districts: What Saves Sales? *Soc. Sci. Quart.*, June 1988, 69(2), pp. 325–40.

Friedman, Michael. Explanation and Scientific Understanding. In *Pitt, J. C., ed.*, 1988, 1974, pp. 188–98.

Friedman, Milton. Capitalism and Freedom. In *Walker, M. A., ed. (I)*, 1988, pp. 47–57.

_____. The Case for Flexible Exchange Rates. In *Melamed, L., ed.*, 1988, 1953, pp. 3–42.

_____. Market Mechanisms and Central Economic Planning. In *[Nutter, G. W.]*, 1988, pp. 27–46.

_____. The Merits of Flexible Exchange Rates: Introduction. In *Melamed, L., ed.*, 1988, pp. xix–xxv.

_____. Money and the Stock Market. *J. Polit. Econ.*, April 1988, 96(2), pp. 221–45.

_____. A Proposal for Resolving the U.S. Balance of Payments Problem: *Confidential Memorandum to President-Elect Richard Nixon.* In *Melamed, L., ed.*, 1988, pp. 429–38.

_____. A Statistical Note on the Gastil–Wright Survey of Freedom. In *Walker, M. A., ed. (I)*, 1988, pp. 121–25.

_____ and Friedman, Rose D. The Tide in the Affairs of Men. In *Anderson, A. and Bark, D. L., eds.*, 1988, pp. 455–68.

Friedman, Monroe. Models of Consumer Choice Behavior. In *van Raaij, W. F.; van Veldhoven, G. M. and Wärneryd, K.-E., eds.*, 1988, pp. 333–57.

_____ and Rees, Jennifer. A Behavioral Science Assessment of Selected Principles of Consumer Education. *J. Cons. Aff.*, Winter 1988, 22(2), pp. 284–302.

Friedman, Rose D. and Friedman, Milton. The Tide in the Affairs of Men. In *Anderson, A. and Bark, D. L., eds.*, 1988, pp. 455–68.

Friedman, Susan Krug. Forecasting a Seasonal Population. *Bus. Econ.*, July 1988, 23(3), pp. 48–52.

Friedmann, Harriet. Form and Substance in the

Analysis of the World Economy. In *Wellman, B. and Berkowitz, S. D., eds.*, 1988, pp. 304–25.

Friedmann, John and Forest, Yvon. The Politics of Place: Toward a Political Economy of Territorial Planning. In *[Perroux, F.]*, 1988, pp. 115–30.

Friedrichs, Jürgen. Affordable Housing and Homelessness: A Comparative View. In *Friedrichs, J., ed.*, 1988, pp. 5–10.

_____. Large New Housing Estates: The Crisis of Affordable Housing. In *Friedrichs, J., ed.*, 1988, pp. 89–101.

Friend, Irwin and Crockett, Jean A. Dividend Policy in Perspective: Can Theory Explain Behavior? *Rev. Econ. Statist.*, November 1988, *70*(4), pp. 603–13.

_____ and Hasbrouck, Joel. Determinants of Capital Structure. In *Chen, A. H., ed.*, 1988, pp. 1–19.

_____ and Lang, Larry H. P. An Empirical Test of the Impact of Managerial Self-interest on Corporate Capital Structure. *J. Finance*, June 1988, *43*(2), pp. 271–81.

_____ and Lang, Larry H. P. The Size Effect on Stock Returns: Is It Simply a Risk Effect Not Adequately Reflected by the Usual Measures? *J. Banking Finance*, 1988, *12*(1), pp. 13–30.

Fries, Clarence E. A Proposed Procedure for Incorporating Interindustry Relationships in the Design and Analysis of Empirical Forecasting Studies. In *Schwartz, B. N., ed.*, 1988, pp. 71–84.

Fries, Timothy Leonard. A Note on the Protective Effect of Tariffs and Quotas under Uncertainty. *J. Int. Econ.*, February 1988, *24*(1–2), pp. 173–81.

Friman, H. Richard. Rocks, Hard Places, and the New Protectionism: Textile Trade Policy Choices in the United States and Japan. *Int. Organ.*, Autumn 1988, *42*(4), pp. 689–723.

Frimpong-Ansah, Jonathan H. The Debt Problem of Developing Countries and Proposed Solutions: Comments. In *Elliott, K. A. and Williamson, J., eds.*, 1988, pp. 185–87.

Friscia, A. Blake. The System Is Resilient. In *Tavis, L. A., ed.*, 1988, pp. 208–11.

Friss, Lois. The Nursing Shortage: Do We Dislike It Enough to Cure It? *Inquiry*, Summer 1988, *25*(2), pp. 232–42.

Frisvold, George; Mines, Richard and Perloff, Jeffrey M. The Effects of Job Site Sanitation and Living Conditions on the Health and Welfare of Agricultural Workers. *Amer. J. Agr. Econ.*, November 1988, *70*(4), pp. 875–85.

Fritsch, Winston. Brazil's Growth Prospects: Domestic Savings, External Finance and OECD Performance Interactions. In *Currie, D. and Vines, D., eds.*, 1988, pp. 253–78.

_____ and Modiano, Eduardo Marco. A restrição externa ao crescimento econômico brasileiro: Uma perspectiva de longo prazo. (With English summary.) *Pesquisa Planejamento Econ.*, August 1988, *18*(2), pp. 271–96.

Fritsche, Heiko and Mott, Peter. INTERPLAN—

An Interactive Program System for Crew Scheduling and Rostering of Public Transport. In *Daduna, J. R. and Wren, A., eds.*, 1988, pp. 200–211.

Fritscher, Wolfgang and von der Ohe, Werner D. Certain Theoretical Premises as Alternatives to the Modernization Theory. In *Vivekananda, F., ed.*, 1988, pp. 30–50.

Fritz, Richard G. and McHone, W. Warren. Forecasting Local Business Activity from Aggregate Indicators. *Ann. Reg. Sci.*, March 1988, *22*(1), pp. 63–74.

Fritzell, Johan and Erikson, Robert. The Effects of the Social Welfare System in Sweden on the Well-Being of Children and the Elderly. In *Palmer, J. L.; Smeeding, T. and Torrey, B. B., eds.*, 1988, pp. 309–30.

Froeschl, K. A. and Grossmann, W. Statistical Structures for Analyzing Time-Dependent Observations. In *Gaul, W. and Schader, M., eds.*, 1988, pp. 145–60.

Froeschle, Claude; Torre, Dominique and Arena, Richard. Formation des prix et équilibre classique. Un examen préliminaire. (Price Formation and Classical Equilibrium: A Preliminary Investigation. With English summary.) *Revue Écon.*, November 1988, *39*(6), pp. 1097–1117.

Frohberg, Klaus; Parikh, Kirit S. and Fischer, Günther. Agricultural Trade Regimes: Impact on Sector Proportions, Real Incomes and Hunger in the World. *Europ. Rev. Agr. Econ.*, 1988, *15*(4), pp. 397–417.

Frohloff-Kulke, Heidrun. Spatial Disparities in West Malaysia. In *Schätzl, L. H., ed.*, 1988, pp. 53–95.

Frohn, Joachim. An Econometric Model for the World Market Price of Sugar with Price Expectations. *Z. Wirtschaft. Sozialwissen.*, 1988, *108*(3), pp. 423–38.

_____. Rationale Erwartungen und empirische Erwartungsmodelle. (Rational Expectations and Empirical Expectation Models. With English summary.) *Ifo-Studien*, 1988, *34*(4), pp. 241–54.

Froot, Kenneth A. Credibility, Real Interest Rates, and the Optimal Speed of Trade Liberalization. *J. Int. Econ.*, August 1988, *25*(1–2), pp. 71–93.

_____ and Frankel, Jeffrey A. Chartists, Fundamentalists and the Demand for Dollars. *Greek Econ. Rev.*, 1988, *10*(1), pp. 49–102.

Frost, Ceri; Emmanuel, Clive R. and Garrod, Neil W. Segment Reports and Consolidated Financial Statements: The Complementary Twins. In *Gray, S. J. and Coenenberg, A. G., eds.*, 1988, pp. 272–99.

Frost, Peter A. and Savarino, James E. For Better Performance: Constrain Portfolio Weights. *J. Portfol. Manage.*, Fall 1988, *15*(1), pp. 29–34.

Froyen, Richard T. and Benavie, Arthur. The Impact of Monetary and Fiscal Policy on Aggregate Demand: Fixed versus Flexible Deposit Rates. *Quart. Rev. Econ. Bus.*, Summer 1988, *28*(2), pp. 71–87.

_____ and Benavie, Arthur. Price Level Determinancy and Nominal Interest Rate Pegging. *Oxford Econ. Pap.*, December 1988, *40*(4), pp. 634–45.

_____ **and Waud, Roger N.** Real Business Cycles and the Lucas Paradigm. *Econ. Inquiry*, April 1988, *26*(2), pp. 183–201.

Fry, Maxwell J. Money Supply Responses to Exogenous Shocks in Turkey. In *Nas, T. F. and Odekon, M., eds.*, 1988, pp. 85–114.

_____; **Lilien, David M. and Wadhwa, Wilima.** Monetary Policy in Pacific Basin Developing Countries. In *Cheng, H.-S., ed.*, 1988, pp. 153–70.

Fry, Vanessa; Walker, Ian and Blundell, Richard. Modelling the Take-up of Means-tested Benefits: the Case of Housing Benefits in the United Kingdom. *Econ. J.*, Supplement, 1988, *98*(390), pp. 58–74.

Fryar, Edward O., Jr.; Arnold, J. T. and Dunn, James E. Bayesian Evaluation of a Specific Hypothesis. *Amer. J. Agr. Econ.*, August 1988, *70*(3), pp. 685–92.

Fryde, Edmund B. The Financial Policies of the Royal Governments and Popular Resistance to Them in France and England, c. 1290–c. 1420. In *Guarducci, A., ed.*, 1988, pp. 295–327.

Frydl, Edward J. The Free Cash Flow Theory of Takeovers: A Financial Perspective on Mergers and Acquisitions and the Economy: Discussion. In *Browne, L. E. and Rosengren, E. S., eds.*, 1988, pp. 144–48.

Fu, Tsu-tan, et al. Producer Attitudes toward Peanut Market Alternatives: An Application of Multivariate Probit Joint Estimation. *Amer. J. Agr. Econ.*, November 1988, *70*(4), pp. 910–18.

Fuà, Giorgio. Small-Scale Industry in Rural Areas: The Italian Experience. In *Arrow, K. J., ed.*, 1988, pp. 259–79.

Fuchs, Gérard. Is Error Learning Behaviour Stabilizing? In *Grandmont, J.-M., ed.*, 1988, *1979*, pp. 286–303.

_____ **and Laroque, Guy.** Dynamics of Temporary Equilibria and Expectations. In *Grandmont, J.-M., ed.*, 1988, *1976*, pp. 249–70.

Fuchs, Lawrence. Principles vs. Expediency in U.S. Immigration Policy. In *Simcox, D. E., ed.*, 1988, pp. 245–57.

Fuchs-Seliger, S. On the Role of Income Compensation Functions as Money-Metric Utility Functions. In *Eichhorn, W., ed.*, 1988, pp. 221–37.

Fudenberg, Drew; Kreps, David M. and Levine, David K. On the Robustness of Equilibrium Refinements. *J. Econ. Theory*, April 1988, *44*(2), pp. 354–80.

_____ **and Levine, David K.** Open-Loop and Closed-Loop Equilibria in Dynamic Games with Many Players. *J. Econ. Theory*, February 1988, *44*(1), pp. 1–18.

Fudge, Judy. Labour, the New Constitution and Old Style Liberalism. In *Carter, D. D., et al.*, 1988, pp. 61–111.

Fuglister, Jayne; Meeting, David and Rozen, Etzmun. Teaching the Qualitative Characteristics of Accounting Information in the Standard Setting Process: A Technique Using SFAS No. 96. In *Pennsylvania Economic Association*, 1988, pp. 601–13.

Fuguet, Jean-Luc; Lai Tong, Hew Wah and Nancy, Gilles. Mobilité imparfaite des capitaux et dynamique des cours de change. Le cas du SME. (Imperfect Capital Mobility and Exchange Rates Dynamics: The EMS Case. With English summary.) *Revue Écon.*, September 1988, *39*(5), pp. 921–50.

Fuguitt, Glenn V.; Heaton, Tim B. and Lichter, Daniel T. Monitoring the Metropolitanization Process. *Demography*, February 1988, *25*(1), pp. 115–28.

Fuhr, Joseph P., Jr. Antitrust and Regulation: Forestalling Competition in the Telecommunications Terminal Equipment Market. *Rev. Ind. Organ.*, Spring 1988, *3*(3), pp. 101–26.

Fuhrer, Jeffrey C. Estimation of Time-Varying Weights on Alternative Expectations Models: An Application of Non-linear Time-Varying Parameter Estimation. *J. Econ. Dynam. Control*, March 1988, *12*(1), pp. 55–61.

_____. On the Information Content of Consumer Survey Expectations. *Rev. Econ. Statist.*, February 1988, *70*(1), pp. 140–44.

Fuhrken, Gebhard and Richter, Marcel K. Algebra and Topology in Cardinal Utility Theory. In *Eichhorn, W., ed.*, 1988, pp. 139–52.

Fuhrmann, Wilfried. Die Theorie rationaler Erwartungen: Das Ende der Konjunkturpolitik? (Is the Rational Expectations Theory the End of Trade Cycle Policy? With English summary.) *Kredit Kapital*, 1988, *21*(1), pp. 67–91.

Fujii, Edwin T. and Hawley, Clifford B. On the Accuracy of Tax Perceptions. *Rev. Econ. Statist.*, May 1988, *70*(2), pp. 344–47.

Fujii, Nobuo. Existence of an Optimal Domain in a Domain Optimization Problem. In *Iri, M. and Yajima, K., eds.*, 1988, pp. 251–58.

_____; **Muramatsu, Yasuyuki and Goto, Yoshito.** Second Order Necessary Optimality Conditions for Domain Optimization Problem with a Neumann Problem. In *Iri, M. and Yajima, K., eds.*, 1988, pp. 259–68.

Fujimoto, Akimi. The Economics of Land Tenure and Rice Productions in a Double-Cropping Village in Southern Thailand. *Devel. Econ.*, September 1988, *26*(3), pp. 189–211.

Fujimoto, Takao. The Existence, Uniqueness and Global Stability of Competitive Equilibrium under Gross Substitutability: A Difference Equation Approach. *Econ. Stud. Quart.*, September 1988, *39*(3), pp. 271–76.

_____ **and Krause, Ulrich.** More Theorems on Joint Production. *J. Econ. (Z. Nationalökon.)*, 1988, *48*(2), pp. 189–96.

Fujita, Masahisa. A Monopolistic Competition Model of Spatial Agglomeration. *Reg. Sci. Urban Econ.*, February 1988, *18*(1), pp. 87–124.

_____; **Ogawa, Hideaki and Thisse, Jacques-François.** A Spatial Competition Approach to Central Place Theory: Some Basic Principles. *J. Reg. Sci.*, November 1988, *28*(4), pp. 477–94.

_____ **and Rivera-Batiz, Francisco L.** Agglomeration and Heterogeneity in Space. *Reg. Sci. Urban Econ.*, February 1988, *18*(1), pp. 1–5.

Fujita, Teiichirō. Local Trade Associations (*Dōgyō Kumiai*) in Prewar Japan. In *Yamazaki, H. and Miyamoto, M., eds.*, 1988, pp. 87–113.

_____. Local Trade Associations (*Dōgyō Kumiai*) in Prewar Japan: Response. In *Yamazaki, H. and Miyamoto, M., eds.*, 1988, pp. 118–19.

Fujiwara, Takako. Collective Choice Rules and Bargaining Solutions. *Keio Econ. Stud.*, 1988, *25*(1), pp. 39–49.

Fukami, Cynthia V.; Fiorito, Jack and Gallagher, Daniel G. Satisfaction with Union Representation. *Ind. Lab. Relat. Rev.*, January 1988, *41*(2), pp. 294–307.

Fukiharu, Toshitaka. The Structure of Lucas-Type Neutrality of Money. *Kobe Univ. Econ.*, 1988, (34), pp. 41–77.

Fukuda, Shin-ichi. Time Aggregated Information and Volatility of Exchange Rate. *Econ. Stud. Quart.*, June 1988, *39*(2), pp. 132–48.

_____; **Horiuchi, Akiyoshi and Packer, Frank.** What Role Has the "Main Bank" Played in Japan? *J. Japanese Int. Economies*, June 1988, *2*(2), pp. 159–80.

_____ **and Teruyama, Hiroshi.** Some International Evidence on Inventory Fluctuations. *Econ. Letters*, 1988, *28*(3), pp. 225–30.

Fukui, Haruhiro. The Cambridge History of Japan: Volume 6: The Twentieth Century: Postwar Politics, 1945–1973. In *Duus, P., ed.*, 1988, pp. 154–213.

Fukuoh, Takeshi. Trade Associations in Germany in the Late Nineteenth and Early Twentieth Centuries: Comment. In *Yamazaki, H. and Miyamoto, M., eds.*, 1988, pp. 262–64.

Fukushima, Masatoshi. On Two Classes of Smooth Measures for Symmetric Markov Processes. In *Métivier, M. and Watanabe, S., eds.te*, 1988, pp. 17–27.

Fulcher, James. On the Explanation of Industrial Relations Diversity: Labour Movements, Employers and the State in Britain and Sweden. *Brit. J. Ind. Relat.*, July 1988, *26*(2), pp. 246–74.

Fuller, Stephen W.; Nichols, John P. and Capps, Oral, Jr. Assessing Opportunities in Food and Fiber Processing and Distribution. *Amer. J. Agr. Econ.*, May 1988, *70*(2), pp. 462–68.

_____; **Peterson, E. Wesley F. and Viscencio-Brambila, Hector.** A Welfare Analysis of Port User Fees: The Case of Grain and Soybean Exports. *Southern J. Agr. Econ.*, December 1988, *20*(2), pp. 101–08.

Fuller, Wayne A.; Battese, George E. and Harter, Rachel M. An Error-Components Model for Prediction of County Crop Areas Using Survey and Satellite Data. *J. Amer. Statist. Assoc.*, March 1988, *83*(401), pp. 28–36.

Fullerton, Don. Eliminating State and Local Tax Deductibility: A General Equilibrium Model of Revenue Effects: Comment. In *Rosen, H. S., ed.*, 1988, pp. 210–14.

_____ **and Lyon, Andrew B.** Tax Neutrality and Intangible Capital. In *Summers, L. H., ed.*, 1988, pp. 63–88.

Fullerton, Howard N., Jr. An Evaluation of Labor Force Projections to 1985. *Mon. Lab. Rev.*, November 1988, *111*(11), pp. 7–17.

Fullerton, Ronald A. Modern Western Marketing as a Historical Phenomenon: Theory and Illustration. In *[Hollander, S. C.]*, 1988, pp. 71–89.

_____ **and Nevett, Terence.** Advertising: The Archaeology of Marketing: Introduction. In *[Hollander, S. C.]*, 1988, pp. 193–94.

_____ **and Nevett, Terence.** The Evolution of Marketing Thought: Introduction. In *[Hollander, S. C.]*, 1988, pp. 1–4.

_____ **and Nevett, Terence.** Historical Perspectives on Retailing: Introduction. In *[Hollander, S. C.]*, 1988, pp. 147–48.

_____ **and Nevett, Terence.** The Importance of Marketing History and Stanley Hollander's Contribution to It. In *[Hollander, S. C.]*, 1988, pp. xi–xix.

_____ **and Nevett, Terence.** Marketing and Economic Development over Time: Introduction. In *[Hollander, S. C.]*, 1988, pp. 109–11.

_____ **and Nevett, Terence.** Marketing in Historical Context: Introduction. In *[Hollander, S. C.]*, 1988, pp. 53–54.

Fulman, Diane and Howell, James M. A Four-Point Program for the Northeast. In *Lampe, D., ed.*, 1988, pp. 138–54.

_____; **Howell, James M. and Frankel, Linda D.** The Massachusetts Experience. In *Lampe, D., ed.*, 1988, pp. 348–57.

Fulop, Christina. Public Policy and a Marketing Technique 1969–1985: Comparative Pricing and Bargain Offer Claims. In *Kaynak, E., ed.*, 1988, pp. 197–207.

van Fulpen, Hans. An Analysis of the Housing Market in the Netherlands. *Urban Stud.*, June 1988, *25*(3), pp. 190–203.

Funatsu, Hideki. Export Credit Insurance: Author's Reply. *J. Risk Ins.*, December 1988, *55*(4), pp. 748–50.

_____. A Note on the Stability of the Harris–Todaro Model with Capital Mobility. *Economica*, February 1988, *55*(217), pp. 119–21.

Funck, Rolf; Koblo, Reiner and Kowalski, Jan. Information Technology, the Urban System and Urban Policy Consequences. In *Orishimo, I.; Hewings, G. J. D. and Nijkamp, P., eds.*, 1988, pp. 125–40.

Fung, Hung-Gay; Ricks, Michael and Wilson, William W. Option Price Behavior in Grain Futures Markets. *J. Futures Markets*, February 1988, *8*(1), pp. 47–65.

Fung, K. C. Strategic Trade Policies, Differentiated Duopoly and Intra-industry Trade. *Int. Econ. J.*, Autumn 1988, *2*(3), pp. 19–34.

Fung, K. K. On the Slippery Slope: Conformance vs Defection in a Multi-Party Prisoners' Dilemma. *J. Econ. Behav. Organ.*, June 1988, *9*(4), pp. 325–43.

Funk, Michael; Sveikauskas, Leo and Gowdy, John M. Urban Productivity: City Size or Industry Size. *J. Reg. Sci.*, May 1988, *28*(2), pp. 185–202.

Funk, Sandra G.; Rapoport, Amnon and Zwick,

Rami. Selection of Portfolios with Risky and Riskless Assets: Experimental Tests of Two Expected Utility Models. *J. Econ. Psych.*, June 1988, 9(2), pp. 169–94.

Funke, Helmut. Mean Value Properties of the Weights of Linear Price Indices. In *Eichhorn, W., ed.*, 1988, pp. 99–115.

Fuqua, Don. Commercial Space and the User Community. In *Egan, J. J., et al.*, 1988, pp. 453–55.

Furby, Lita and Fischhoff, Baruch. Measuring Values: A Conceptual Framework for Interpreting Transactions with Special Reference to Contingent Valuation of Visibility. *J. Risk Uncertainty*, June 1988, 1(2), pp. 147–84.

Furino, Antonio. Cooperation and Competition in the Global Economy: Overview. In *Furino, A., ed.*, 1988, pp. 3–18.

_____ **and Kozmetsky, George.** Emerging Policies and Strategies. In *Furino, A., ed.*, 1988, pp. 257–64.

Furlong, Frederick T. Changes in Bank Risk-Taking. *Fed. Res. Bank San Francisco Econ. Rev.*, Spring 1988, (2), pp. 45–56.

Furnham, Adrian F. Unemployment. In *van Raaij, W. F.; van Veldhoven, G. M. and Wärneryd, K.-E., eds.*, 1988, pp. 595–637.

_____ **and Cleare, Anthony.** School Children's Conceptions of Economics: Prices, Wages, Investments and Strikes. *J. Econ. Psych.*, December 1988, 9(4), pp. 467–79.

Furniss, Tim. Satellite Launcher World Market to the End of the Century. In *Egan, J. J., et al.*, 1988, pp. 237–57.

Fürst, Hedegard. Problems in the Statistical Measurement of Unemployment in the Community. *Econ. Lavoro*, Apr.–June 1988, 22(2), pp. 59–87.

Fürstenberg, Friedrich. The Future of the Working Society. In *Dlugos, G.; Dorow, W. and Weiermair, K., eds.*, 1988, pp. 3–10.

von Furstenberg, George M. Life Cycle Saving: A General Paradigm or a Caricature of the Petite-Bourgeoisie? *Ann. Écon. Statist.*, Jan.–March 1988, (9), pp. 183–98.

_____ **and Maasoumi, Esfandiar.** Macroeconomic Implications of the Information Revolution. *Amer. Econ. Rev.*, May 1988, 78(2), pp. 178–81.

Furtado, Eugene P. H. and Fatemi, Ali M. An Empirical Investigation of the Wealth Effects of Foreign Acquisitions. In *Khoury, S. J. and Ghosh, A., eds.*, 1988, pp. 363–79.

Furtan, W. H.; Van Kooten, G. C. and Schmitz, Andrew. The Economics of Storing a Non-storable Commodity. *Can. J. Econ.*, August 1988, 21(3), pp. 579–86.

Furubotn, Eirik G. Codetermination and the Modern Theory of the Firm: A Property-Rights Analysis. *J. Bus.*, April 1988, 61(2), pp. 165–81.

_____. Health Economics and the New Institutionalism: Some Observations on the Nature and Potential of Property-Rights Analysis. In *Furubotn, E. G. and Richter, R., eds.*, 1988, pp. 131–46.

Fusfeld, Daniel R. The Development of Economic Institutions. In *Samuels, W. J., ed., Vol. 3*, 1988, 1977, pp. 221–62.

Fusfeld, Herbert. Technology and Public Policy. *Aussenwirtschaft*, June 1988, 43(1/2), pp. 29–43.

G-Yohannes, Arefaine. The Derivation of Simple Formulas for Comparing Investment Alternatives with and without Load and Account Fees. *J. Cons. Aff.*, Winter 1988, 22(2), pp. 333–41.

_____. Mortgage Refinancing. *J. Cons. Aff.*, Summer 1988, 22(1), pp. 85–95.

van der Gaag, Jacques and Vijverberg, Wim. A Switching Regression Model for Wage Determinants in the Public and Private Sectors of a Developing Country. *Rev. Econ. Statist.*, May 1988, 70(2), pp. 244–52.

Gabel, H. Landis. Privatization: Its Motives and Likely Consequences. In *Preston, L. E., ed.*, 1988, pp. 157–80.

Gabel, Jon R. and Jensen, Gail A. The Erosion of Purchased Health Insurance. *Inquiry*, Fall 1988, 25(3), pp. 328–43.

Gabriel, K. R. Some Thoughts on Comparing Multivariate Data with the Map Locations at Which They Are Observed. In *Gaul, W. and Schader, M., eds.*, 1988, pp. 341–54.

Gabriel, Luciano and Loderer, Claudio. Political Progress and Government Growth—A Theoretical and Empirical Investigation. *J. Inst. Theoretical Econ.*, April 1988, 144(2), pp. 267–95.

Gabriel, Stuart A.; Justman, Moshe and Levy, Amnon. Determinants of Internal Migration in Israel: Expected Returns and Risks. *Appl. Econ.*, May 1988, 20(5), pp. 679–90.

_____ **and Levy, Daniel.** Expectations, Information, and Migration: The Case of the West Bank and Gaza. *Appl. Econ.*, January 1988, 20(1), pp. 1–13.

_____ **and Nothaft, Frank E.** Rental Housing Markets and the Natural Vacancy Rate. *Amer. Real Estate Urban Econ. Assoc. J.*, Winter 1988, 16(4), pp. 419–29.

Gabriele, Salvatore and Arnell, Nigel W. The Performance of the Two-Component Extreme Value Distribution in Regional Flood Frequency Analysis. *Water Resources Res.*, June 1988, 24(6), pp. 879–87.

Gabrielli, Daniel; Plihon, Dominique and Boutillier, Michel. La baisse des taux d'intérêt en France: Quels effets en attendre? (Consequences of the Decrease in the Level of Interest Rates in France. With English summary.) *Revue Écon.*, July 1988, 39(4), pp. 841–76.

Gabrisch, Hubert and Fink, Gerhard. Hard-Currency Debt Scenarios. In *Marer, P. and Siwinski, W., eds.*, 1988, pp. 195–99.

Gachuki, David and Coughlin, Peter. Structure and Safeguards for Negotiations with Foreign Investors: Lessons from Kenya. In *Coughlin, P. and Ikiara, G. K., eds.*, 1988, pp. 91–111.

Gaddie, Robert and Zoller, Maureen. New Stage of Process Price System Developed for the Producer Price Index. *Mon. Lab. Rev.*, April 1988, 111(4), pp. 3–16.

Gadiel, David. Management of Health and Family Welfare Programs in Developing Countries: Discussion. In *Butler, J. R. G. and Doessel, D. P., eds.*, 1988, pp. 217–20.

Gaertner, Wulf. Binary Inversions and Transitive Majorities. In *Eichhorn, W., ed.*, 1988, pp. 153–67.

————— **and Jungeilges, Jochen.** A Non-linear Model of Interdependent Consumer Behaviour. *Econ. Letters*, 1988, 27(2), pp. 145–50.

————— **and Pattanaik, Prasanta K.** An Interview with Amartya Sen. *Soc. Choice Welfare*, 1988, 5(1), pp. 69–79.

Gaeth, Gary J. and Levin, Irwin P. How Consumers Are Affected by the Framing of Attribute Information before and after Consuming the Product. *J. Cons. Res.*, December 1988, 15(3), pp. 374–78.

Gafar, John S. The Determinants of Import Demand in Trinidad and Tobago: 1967–84. *Appl. Econ.*, March 1988, 20(3), pp. 303–13.

—————. Economic Growth and Economic Policy: Employment and Unemployment in Jamaica, 1972–1984. *J. Devel. Areas*, October 1988, 23(1), pp. 63–83.

Gaffard, Jean-Luc. De l'economie de decouverts a l'economie de placements de titres negociables: Enjeux et difficultes d'une transition. (From an Overdraft Economy to an Auto-Economy: The Stakes and the Difficulties of a Transition. With English summary.) *Écon. Soc.*, January 1988, 22(1), pp. 31–47.

————— **and Pollin, Jean-Paul.** Réflexions sur l'instabilité des économies monétaires. (With English summary.) *Revue Écon. Polit.*, Sept.–Oct. 1988, 98(5), pp. 599–614.

Gäfgen, Gérard and Endres, Alfred. Wettbewerb und Regulierung auf dem bundesdeutschen Lebensversicherungsmarkt. (Competition and Regulation in the W. German Life Insurance Market. With English summary.) *Jahr. Nationalökon. Statist.*, July 1988, 205(1), pp. 11–29.

Gafni, Amiram and Westman, Mina. Hypertension Labelling as a Stressful Event Leading to an Increase in Absenteeism: A Possible Explanation for an Empirically Measured Phenomenon. In *Maital, S., ed., Vol. 2*, 1988, pp. 507–27.

Gagey, F.; Laroque, Guy and Lollivier, S. Monetary and Fiscal Policies in a General Equilibrium Model. In *Grandmont, J.-M., ed.*, 1988, 1986, pp. 217–45.

Gagné, Robert. Analysis of Regulation Effects in the Trucking Industry: A Technological Approach. In *Bianco, L. and La Bella, A., eds.*, 1988, pp. 409–42.

————— **and Dionne, Georges.** Models and Methodologies in the Analysis of Regulation Effects in Airline Markets. *Int. J. Transport Econ.*, October 1988, 15(3), pp. 291–312.

————— **and Dionne, Georges.** Qu'en est-il des rendements d'échelle dans les industries québécoises et ontariennes de transport par ca-

mion. (With English summary.) *L'Actual. Econ.*, September 1988, 64(3), pp. 380–95.

Gagnon, Christopher; Doorley, Thomas H. and Gregg, Alison. Professional Services Firms and Information Technology: Ongoing Search for Sustained Competitive Advantage. In *Guile, B. R. and Quinn, J. B., eds. (I)*, 1988, pp. 175–94.

Gagnon, Joseph E. Short-run Models and Long-run Forecasts: A Note on the Permanence of Output Fluctuations. *Quart. J. Econ.*, May 1988, 103(2), pp. 415–24.

Gahan, Eoin. The Impact of Expert Systems. *Industry Devel.*, January 1988, (23), pp. 81–97.

Gahin, Fikry S. The Financial Feasibility of Tax-Sheltered Individual Retirement Plans: A Reply. *J. Risk Ins.*, March 1988, 55(1), pp. 164–67.

Gahlen, Bernhard. Relative Preise und Strukturwandel bei Inflation. (Relative Prices and Structural Change under Inflation. With English summary.) *Ifo-Studien*, 1988, 34(1), pp. 1–42.

Gahvari, Firouz. Does the Laffer Curve Ever Slope Down? *Nat. Tax J.*, June 1988, 41(2), pp. 266–69.

—————. Lump-Sum Taxation and the Superneutrality and Optimum Quantity of Money in Life Cycle Growth Models. *J. Public Econ.*, August 1988, 36(3), pp. 339–67.

Gaidar, Egor T. The Process of Normalization: An Economic Observation. *Prob. Econ.*, September 1988, 31(5), pp. 82–98.

—————. Short-term and Long-term Goals in the Economy. *Prob. Econ.*, January 1988, 30(9), pp. 34–52.

Gaignery, Gilles P. Access to Revenue Canada, Taxation Files. In *Canadian Tax Foundation*, 1988, pp. 7.1–8.

Gaiha, Raghav. Income Mobility in Rural India. *Econ. Develop. Cult. Change*, January 1988, 36(2), pp. 279–302.

—————. On Measuring the Risk of Poverty in Rural India. In *Srinivasan, T. N. and Bardhan, P. K., eds.*, 1988, pp. 219–61.

Gaildraud, Isabelle. La consommation énergétique industrielle du monde occidental sur 1970–1985: Un modèle simple et robuste. (Western Energetic Industrial Consumption: 1970–1985. With English summary.) *Écon. Soc.*, April 1988, 22(4), pp. 29–35.

Gaile, Gary L. Choosing Locations for Small Town Development to Enable Market and Employment Expansion: The Case of Kenya. *Econ. Geogr.*, July 1988, 64(3), pp. 242–54.

Gaines, Jeannie; Jermier, John M. and Cohen, Cynthia Fryer. Paying Dues to the Union: A Study of Blue-Collar Workers in a Right-to-Work Environment. *J. Lab. Res.*, Spring 1988, 9(2), pp. 167–82.

Gal-Or, Esther. The Advantages of Imprecise Information. *Rand J. Econ.*, Summer 1988, 19(2), pp. 266–75.

—————. Exit with Incomplete Information about Cost. *Info. Econ. Policy*, 1988, 3(3), pp. 241–63.

_____. Information Transmission—Cournot and Bertrand Equilibria. In *Daughety, A. F., ed.*, 1988, *1986*, pp. 342–52.

_____. The Informational Advantages or Disadvantages of Horizontal Mergers. *Int. Econ. Rev.*, November 1988, *29*(4), pp. 639–61.

_____. Oligopolistic Nonlinear Tariffs. *Int. J. Ind. Organ.*, June 1988, *6*(2), pp. 199–221.

Gal, Samuel and Landsberger, Michael. On "Small Sample" Properties of Experience Rating Insurance Contracts. *Quart. J. Econ.*, February 1988, *103*(1), pp. 233–43.

Galai, Dan. Corporate Income Taxes and the Valuation of the Claims on the Corporation. In *Chen, A. H., ed.*, 1988, pp. 75–90.

Galal, Esam E. Application of Microcomputers in Primary Health Delivery Services in Egypt. In *Bhalla, A. S. and James, D., eds.*, 1988, pp. 137–48.

Galambos, Louis. The American Trade Association Movement Revisited. In *Yamazaki, H. and Miyamoto, M., eds.*, 1988, pp. 121–35.

_____. The American Trade Association Movement Revisited: Response. In *Yamazaki, H. and Miyamoto, M., eds.*, 1988, p. 138.

_____. Looking for the Boundaries of Technological Determinism: A Brief History of the U.S. Telephone System. In *Mayntz, R. and Hughes, T. P., eds.*, 1988, pp. 135–53.

_____. What Have CEOs Been Doing? *J. Econ. Hist.*, June 1988, *48*(2), pp. 243–58.

Galante, Steven P.; Jackson, Susan E. and Schuler, Randall S. Matching Effective HR Practices with Competitive Strategy. In *Timpe, A. D., ed.*, 1988, *1987*, pp. 113–23.

Galatin, Malcolm. Does the Translog Index of Technical Change Measure Technical Change: United States 1948–76? *Atlantic Econ. J.*, December 1988, *16*(4), pp. 52–61.

_____. Technical Change and the Measurement of Productivity in an Input–Output Model. *J. Macroecon.*, Fall 1988, *10*(4), pp. 613–32.

Galaty, John G. Pastoral and Agro-pastoral Migration in Tanzania: Factors of Economy, Ecology and Demography in Cultural Perspective. In *Bennett, J. W. and Bowen, J. R., eds.*, 1988, pp. 163–83.

_____. Scale, Politics and Co-operation in Organizations for East African Development. In *Attwood, D. W. and Baviskar, B. S., eds.*, 1988, pp. 282–308.

Galbraith, Craig S. and Kay, Neil M. Towards a Theory of Multinational Enterprise. In *Earl, P. E., ed., Vol. 2*, 1988, *1986*, pp. 71–87.

Galbraith, James K. The Grammar of Political Economy. In *Klamer, A.; McCloskey, D. N. and Solow, R. M., eds.*, 1988, pp. 221–39.

_____. Let's Try Export-Led Growth. *Challenge*, May–June 1988, *31*(3), pp. 37–41.

_____. Paradox among the Paradigms: A Comment on Eichner, Meltzer, Bowles and Co-workers, and Miles. *J. Post Keynesian Econ.*, Summer 1988, *10*(4), pp. 567–71.

Galbraith, John Kenneth. Time and the New Industrial State. *Amer. Econ. Rev.*, May 1988, *78*(2), pp. 373–76.

_____. The World Economy in Perspective. *J. Econ. Devel.*, December 1988, *13*(2), pp. 7–16.

Galbriath, John W. Modelling Expectations Formation with Measurement Errors. *Econ. J.*, June 1988, *98*(391), pp. 412–28.

Gale, Douglas. A Note on Conjectural Equilibria. In *Grandmont, J.-M., ed.*, 1988, *1978*, pp. 441–46.

_____. Price Setting and Competition in a Simple Duopoly Model. *Quart. J. Econ.*, November 1988, *103*(4), pp. 729–39.

Galeotti, Marzio. Tobin's Marginal 'q' and Tests of the Firm's Dynamic Equilibrium. *J. Appl. Econometrics*, Oct.–Dec. 1988, *3*(4), pp. 267–77.

Galiègue, X. Désinvestissement et Durée de vie du capital dans la théorie keynésienne: Un essai de clarification. (Disinvestment and Fixed Capital Length of Life within the Keynesian Theory: A Clarification Attempt. With English summary.) *Écon. Appl.*, 1988, *41*(2), pp. 389–412.

Galindo, Osmil and Musgrove, Philip. Do the Poor Pay More? Retail Food Prices in Northeast Brazil. *Econ. Develop. Cult. Change*, October 1988, *37*(1), pp. 91–109.

Galizzi, Giovanni. Constraints on Quantity Adjustments: Increased in Productivity, Fixity of Land and Labour, and Changes in the International Monetary System. In *Antonelli, G. and Quadrio-Curzio, A., eds.*, 1988, pp. 103–22.

Gallagher, Daniel G.; Fukami, Cynthia V. and Fiorito, Jack. Satisfaction with Union Representation. *Ind. Lab. Relat. Rev.*, January 1988, *41*(2), pp. 294–307.

Gallagher, Martin. Exogeneity Testing: A Note [Are Exports an Engine of Growth]. *Appl. Econ.*, November 1988, *20*(11), pp. 1559–60.

Gallagher, Paul. The Grain Sector of the European Community: Policy Formation, Price Determination, and Implications for Trade. *Amer. J. Agr. Econ.*, November 1988, *70*(4), pp. 767–78.

Gallagher, Timothy J. and Block, Stanley B. How Much Do Bank Trust Departments Use Derivatives? *J. Portfol. Manage.*, Fall 1988, *15*(1), pp. 12–15.

Gallaway, Lowell; Sollars, David and Vedder, Richard. The Tullock–Bastiat Hypothesis, Inequality-Transfer Curve and the Natural Distribution of Income. *Public Choice*, March 1988, *56*(3), pp. 285–94.

Galler, H. Microsimulation of Household Formation and Dissolution. In *Keilman, N.; Kuijsten, A. and Vossen, A., eds.*, 1988, pp. 139–59.

Galli, Giampaolo. Public Debt and Households' Demand for Monetary Assets in Italy: 1970–86: Discussion. In *Giavazzi, F. and Spaventa, L., eds.*, 1988, pp. 250–54.

_____ **and Masera, Rainer S.** Government Deficits and Debts. The Necessity and Cost of Adjustment: The Case of Italy. In *Eltis, W. and Sinclair, P. J. N., eds.*, 1988, pp. 175–215.

Gallicchio, Salvatore J. and Bye, Barry V. A Note on Sampling Variance Estimates for Social Security Program Participants: From the Survey of Income and Program Participation. *Soc. Sec. Bull.*, October 1988, *51*(10), pp. 4–21.

Galliker, Franz. The New Banking Environment—A Risky Game. In *Mikdashi, Z., ed.*, 1988, pp. 123–28.

Gallini, Nancy T. and Farrell, Joseph. Second-Sourcing as a Commitment: Monopoly Incentives to Attract Competition. *Quart. J. Econ.*, November 1988, *103*(4), pp. 673–94.

_____; **Schmitz, Andrew and Carter, Colin A.** Producer–Consumer Trade-offs in Export Cartels: The Wheat Cartel Case: Reply. *Amer. J. Agr. Econ.*, November 1988, *70*(4), pp. 946.

Gallivan, W. J. Development Experience in Cape Breton. In *Choudhury, M. A., ed.*, 1988, pp. 154–58.

Gallman, Robert E. Changes in the Level of Literacy in a New Community of Early America. *J. Econ. Hist.*, September 1988, *48*(3), pp. 567–82.

_____; **Hutchins, Teresa D. and Davis, Lance E.** The Decline of U.S. Whaling: Was the Stock of Whales Running Out? *Bus. Hist. Rev.*, Winter 1988, *62*(4), pp. 569–95.

Gallo, Francesca and Baldessari, Bruno. A Robustness Property of the Projection Pursuit Methods in Sampling from Separably Dependent Random Vectors. In *Edwards, D. and Raun, N. E., eds.*, 1988, pp. 65–70.

Galloway, Patrick R. Basic Patterns in Annual Variations in Fertility, Nuptiality, Mortality, and Prices in Pre-industrial Europe. *Population Stud.*, July 1988, *42*(2), pp. 275–302.

Galor, Oded. The Long-run Implications of a Hicks-Neutral Technical Progress. *Int. Econ. Rev.*, February 1988, *29*(1), pp. 177–83.

Galper, Harvey; Lucke, Robert and Toder, Eric. A General Equilibrium Analysis of Tax Reform. In *Aaron, H. J.; Galper, H. and Pechman, J. A., eds.*, 1988, pp. 59–108.

_____; **Pechman, Joseph A. and Aaron, Henry J.** Uneasy Compromise: Problems of a Hybrid Income–Consumption Tax: Introduction. In *Aaron, H. J.; Galper, H. and Pechman, J. A., eds.*, 1988, pp. 1–13.

_____ and **Pollock, Stephen H.** Models of State Income Tax Reform. In *Gold, S. D., ed.*, 1988, pp. 107–28.

Galperin, Efim A. The Beta-Algorithm for Mathematical Programming. In *Eiselt, H. A. and Pederzoli, G., eds.*, 1988, pp. 38–48.

Galster, George C. Residential Segregation in American Cities: A Contrary Review. *Population Res. Policy Rev.*, 1988, *7*(2), pp. 93–112.

_____ and **Hesser, Garry W.** Evaluating and Redesigning Subsidy Policies for Home Rehabilitation. *Policy Sci.*, 1988, *21*(1), pp. 67–95.

Galy, Michel. Le marché des changes est-il efficient? Une comparaison entre les monnaies flottantes et celles du mécanisme de change européen. (Is the Foreign Exchange Market Efficient? With English summary.) *Revue Écon.*, September 1988, *39*(5), pp. 913–20.

Gamber, Edward N. Long-term Risk-Sharing Wage Contracts in an Economy Subject to Per-manent and Temporary Shocks. *J. Lab. Econ.*, January 1988, *6*(1), pp. 83–99.

Gambetta, Diego. Can We Trust Trust? In *Gambetta, D., ed.*, 1988, pp. 213–37.

_____. Mafia: The Price of Distrust. In *Gambetta, D., ed.*, 1988, pp. 158–75.

Gammill, James F., Jr. and Marsh, Terry A. Trading Activity and Price Behavior in the Stock and Stock Index Futures Markets in October 1987. *J. Econ. Perspectives*, Summer 1988, *2*(3), pp. 25–44.

Gamser, Matthew S. Innovation, Technical Assistance, and Development: The Importance of Technology Users. *World Devel.*, June 1988, *16*(6), pp. 711–21.

Gan, Wee Bang. Monetary Policy and Nominal Interest Rate in a Developing Country: The Case of Malaysia. *Singapore Econ. Rev.*, April 1988, *33*(1), pp. 21–39.

Gandar, John M. and Zuber, Richard A. Lifting the Television Blackout on No-Shows at Football Games. *Atlantic Econ. J.*, June 1988, *16*(2), pp. 63–73.

_____, **et al.** Testing Rationality in the Point Spread Betting Market. *J. Finance*, September 1988, *43*(4), pp. 995–1008.

Gandolfo, Giancarlo and Petit, Maria Luisa. The Optimal Degree of Wage-Indexation in the Italian Economy: Rerunning History by Dynamic Optimization. In *[Goodwin, R. M.]*, 1988, pp. 120–26.

Gang, Ira N. and Tower, Edward. The Stahl–Alexeev Paradox: A Note. *J. Econ. Theory*, February 1988, *44*(1), pp. 189–91.

Ganley, Joe and Grahl, John. Competition and Efficiency in Refuse Collection: A Critical Comment. *Fisc. Stud.*, February 1988, *9*(1), pp. 80–85.

Gann, L. H. and Duignan, Peter. Foreign Policy and National Security: Hope for Africa. In *Anderson, A. and Bark, D. L., eds.*, 1988, pp. 139–51.

Gann, Pamela Brooks. What Has Happened to the Tax Legislative Process? *Mich. Law Rev.*, May 1988, *86*(6), pp. 1196–1216.

Gannon, Martin J. Managerial Ignorance. In *Timpe, A. D., ed.*, 1988, *1983*, pp. 103–12.

Ganssmann, Heiner. Abstract Labour as a Metaphor? A Comment [Heterogeneous Labour, Money Wages, and Marx's Theory]. *Hist. Polit. Econ.*, Fall 1988, *20*(3), pp. 461–70.

Gapinski, James H. The Economic Right Triangle of Nonprofit Theater. *Soc. Sci. Quart.*, September 1988, *69*(3), pp. 756–63.

_____. Tourism's Contribution to the Demand for London's Lively Arts. *Appl. Econ.*, July 1988, *20*(7), pp. 957–68.

_____ and **Kumar, T. Krishna.** In Estimating the Elasticity of Factor Substitution by Nonlinear Least Squares. In *Sengupta, J. K. and Kadekodi, G. K., eds.*, 1988, pp. 157–68.

Garber, Harry D. The Role of Consumption Taxes in Tax Reform around the World. *Nat. Tax J.*, September 1988, *41*(3), pp. 357–64.

Garber, Peter M. Inflation Stabilization: Israel:

Comment. In *Bruno, M., et al., eds.*, 1988, pp. 95–98.

Garber, Steven. Minimum Legal Drinking Ages and Highway Safety: A Methodological Critique. In *Graham, J. D., ed.*, 1988, pp. 116–50.

———— **and Evans, Lewis.** Public-Utility Regulators Are Only Human: A Positive Theory of Rational Constraints. *Amer. Econ. Rev.*, June 1988, *78*(3), pp. 444–62.

———— **and Poirier, Dale J.** The Design and Summary of Public Subjective–Predictive Analyses: Comment [An Application of Operational-Subjective Statistical Methods to Rational Expectations]. *J. Bus. Econ. Statist.*, October 1988, *6*(4), pp. 466–69.

Garcia, Gillian. The FSLIC Is "Broke" in More Ways Than One. *Cato J.*, Winter 1988, *7*(3), pp. 727–41.

————. The FSLIC Is "Broke" in More Ways Than One. In *England, C. and Huertas, T., eds.*, 1988, pp. 235–49.

García, Jaime; Polo, Clemente and Raymond, José Luis. Una nota sobre la relación empleo-capital en españa: 1955–1984. (With English summary.) *Invest. Econ.*, January 1988, *12*(1), pp. 177–95.

Garcia, Márcio Gomes Pinto. Um modelo de consistência multissetorial para a economia brasileira. (With English summary.) *Pesquisa Planejamento Econ.*, August 1988, *18*(2), pp. 401–52.

Garcia, Marito. Food Subsidies in the Philippines: Preliminary Results. In *Pinstrup-Andersen, P., ed.*, 1988, pp. 206–18.

————; **Jacinto, Elizabeth and Senauer, Benjamin.** Determinants of the Intrahousehold Allocation of Food in the Rural Philippines. *Amer. J. Agr. Econ.*, February 1988, *70*(1), pp. 170–80.

Garcia-Mata, C. and Shaffner, F. I. Solar and Economic Relationships: A Preliminary Report. In *Wood, J. C., ed., Vol. 3*, 1988, *1934*, pp. 15–54.

Garcia, Philip; Hudson, Michael A. and Waller, Mark L. The Pricing Efficiency of Agricultural Futures Markets: An Analysis of Previous Research Results. *Southern J. Agr. Econ.*, July 1988, *20*(1), pp. 119–30.

————; **Zapata, Hector O. and Hudson, Michael A.** Identifying Causal Relationships between Nonstationary Stochastic Processes: An Examination of Alternative Approaches in Small Sample. *Western J. Agr. Econ.*, December 1988, *13*(2), pp. 202–15.

————, **et al.** Pricing Efficiency in the Live Cattle Futures Market: Further Interpretation and Measurement. *Amer. J. Agr. Econ.*, February 1988, *70*(1), pp. 162–69.

García, Ricardo. El costa social de la divisa. (With English summary.) *Cuadernos Econ.*, April 1988, *25*(74), pp. 39–79.

Garcia Rocha, Adalberto. Inequality and Growth in Mexico. In *Jorge, A. and Salazar-Carrillo, J., eds.*, 1988, pp. 199–202.

Gardener, E. P. M. Innovation and New Struc-

tural Frontiers in Banking. In *[Frowen, S.]*, 1988, pp. 7–29.

Gärdenfors, Peter and Sahlin, Nils-Eric. Bayesian Decision Theory—Foundations and Problems. In *Gärdenfors, P. and Sahlin, N.-E., eds.*, 1988, pp. 1–15.

———— **and Sahlin, Nils-Eric.** Unreliable Probabilities, Risk Taking, and Decision Making. In *Gärdenfors, P. and Sahlin, N.-E., eds.*, 1988, pp. 313–34.

Gardiner, Walter H. and Carter, Colin A. Issues Associated with Elasticities in International Agricultural Trade. In *Carter, C. A. and Gardiner, W. H., eds.*, 1988, pp. 1–16.

Gardner, Bruce L. Efficient Redistribution through Commodity Markets. In *Stigler, G. J., ed.*, 1988, *1983*, pp. 479–97.

————. Export Policy, Deficiency Payments, and a Consumption Tax: Comments. *J. Agr. Econ. Res.*, Winter 1988, *40*(1), pp. 38–41.

————. International Competition in Agriculture and U.S. Farm Policy. In *Feldstein, M., ed. (II)*, 1988, pp. 423–60.

————. Panel Discussion: Summary and Reactions. In *Sumner, D. A., ed.*, 1988, pp. 171–73.

Gardner, Donald G. and Cummings, L. L. Activation Theory and Job Design: Review and Reconceptualization. In *Staw, B. M. and Cummings, L. L., eds.*, 1988, pp. 81–122.

Gardner, Everette S., Jr. and Makridakis, Spyros. The Future of Forecasting. *Int. J. Forecasting*, 1988, *4*(3), pp. 325–30.

Gardner, John C. and Swanson, G. A. Not-for-Profit Accounting and Auditing in the Early Eighteenth Century: Some Archival Evidence. *Accounting Rev.*, July 1988, *63*(3), pp. 436–47.

Gardner, Mark L. and Long, C. Richard. Alternative U.S. Monetary and Deficit Reduction Policies for the 1980s. *J. Money, Credit, Banking*, Part 1, August 1988, *20*(3), pp. 336–52.

Gardner, Michael. Enterprise Allocation System in the Offshore Groundfish Sector in Atlantic Canada. *Marine Resource Econ.*, 1988, *5*(4), pp. 389–414.

Gardner, Mona J.; Mills, Dixie L. and Scott, William L. Expense Preference and Minority Banking: A Note. *Financial Rev.*, February 1988, *23*(1), pp. 105–15.

Gardner, Richard L. and Young, Robert A. Assessing Strategies for Control of Irrigation-Induced Salinity in the Upper Colorado River Basin. *Amer. J. Agr. Econ.*, February 1988, *70*(1), pp. 37–49.

Garegnani, Pierangelo. Capital and Effective Demand. In *Barrère, A., ed.*, 1988, pp. 197–230.

————. Heterogeneous Capital, the Production Function and the Theory of Distribution. In *Steedman, I., ed., Vol. 1*, 1988, *1970*, pp. 144–73.

————. Switching of Techniques. In *Steedman, I., ed., Vol. 1*, 1988, *1966*, pp. 130–43.

Garen, John E. Compensating Wage Differentials and the Endogeneity of Job Riskiness. *Rev. Econ. Statist.*, February 1988, *70*(1), pp. 9–16.

_____. Empirical Studies of the Job Matching Hypothesis. In *Ehrenberg, R. G., ed.*, 1988, pp. 187–24.

_____. Wage Growth and the Black–White Wage Differential. *Quart. Rev. Econ. Bus.*, Autumn 1988, 28(3), pp. 28–42.

_____ and Krislov, Joseph. An Examination of the New American Strike Statistics in Analysing Aggregate Strike Incidence. *Brit. J. Ind. Relat.*, March 1988, 26(1), pp. 75–84.

Garfinkel, Irwin; McLanahan, Sara S. and Wong, Patrick. Child Support and Dependency. In *Rodgers, H. R., Jr., ed.*, 1988, pp. 66–85.

_____ and Oellerich, Donald T. Alternative Child Support Regimes: Distributional Impacts and a Crude Benefit–Cost Analysis. In *Danziger, S. H. and Portney, K. E., eds.*, 1988, pp. 67–86.

_____; Wong, Patrick and Nichols-Casebolt, Ann. Reforming Wisconsin's Child Support System. In *Danziger, S. H. and Witte, J. F., eds.*, 1988, pp. 172–86.

Garg, S. K. and Pritchett, J. W. Pressure Interference Data Analysis for Two-Phase (Water/Steam) Geothermal Reservoirs. *Water Resources Res.*, June 1988, 24(6), pp. 843–52.

Gargiulo, Gerardo R. Gasto militar y polótica de defensa. (With English summary.) *Desarrollo Econ.*, April–June 1988, 28(109), pp. 89–104.

Garkovich, Lorraine E. and Bokemeier, Janet L. Factors Associated with Women's Attitudes toward Farming. In *Beaulieu, L. J., ed.*, 1988, pp. 120–40.

Gärling, E. and Gärling, T. Distance Minimization in Downtown Pedestrian Shopping. *Environ. Planning A*, April 1988, 20(4), pp. 547–54.

Gärling, T. and Gärling, E. Distance Minimization in Downtown Pedestrian Shopping. *Environ. Planning A*, April 1988, 20(4), pp. 547–54.

Garnaut, Ross. Asia's Giant. *Australian Econ. Pap.*, December 1988, 27(51), pp. 173–86.

Garner, Catherine; Main, Brian G. M. and Raffe, David. The Distribution of School-Leaver Unemployment within Scottish Cities. *Urban Stud.*, April 1988, 25(2), pp. 133–44.

Garner, Richard L. Long-term Silver Mining Trends in Spanish America: A Comparative Analysis of Peru and Mexico. *Amer. Hist. Rev.*, October 1988, 93(4), pp. 898–935.

Garnier, Bernard and Gasse, Yvon. Training Entrepreneurs through Newspapers and Creating New Businesses. In *Kirchhoff, B. A., et al., eds.*, 1988, pp. 254–65.

Garofalo, Gasper A. and Fogarty, Michael S. Urban Spatial Structure and Productivity Growth in the Manufacturing Sector of Cities. *J. Urban Econ.*, January 1988, 23(1), pp. 60–70.

_____ and Malhotra, Devinder M. Aggregation of Capital and Its Substitution with Energy. *Eastern Econ. J.*, July–Sept. 1988, 14(3), pp. 251–62.

_____ and Malhotra, Devinder M. Analysis of Regional Productivity with Capital as a Quasi-

fixed Factor. *Reg. Sci. Urban Econ.*, November 1988, 18(4), pp. 533–47.

Garrett, Elizabeth H. and Macey, Jonathan R. Market Discipline by Depositors: A Summary of the Theoretical and Empirical Arguments. *Yale J. Regul.*, Winter 1988, 5(1), pp. 215–39.

Garrett, John R. Monetary Policy Coordination in the European Economic Community. *Rev. Radical Polit. Econ.*, Summer–Fall 1988, 20(2–3), pp. 163–70.

Garrison, Charles B. Labor Supply Response in Keynes's Theory of Involuntary Unemployment. *J. Post Keynesian Econ.*, Winter 1987–88, 10(2), pp. 183–201.

Garrison, Roger W. Professor Rothbard and the Theory of Interest. In *[Rothbard, M. N.]*, 1988, pp. 44–55.

_____ and Bellante, Don. Phillips Curves and Hayekian Triangles: Two Perspectives on Monetary Dynamics. *Hist. Polit. Econ.*, Summer 1988, 20(2), pp. 207–34.

_____; Short, Eugenie D. and O'Driscoll, Gerald P., Jr. Financial Stability and FDIC Insurance. In *England, C. and Huertas, T., eds.*, 1988, pp. 187–207.

Garrod, Neil W.; Frost, Ceri and Emmanuel, Clive R. Segment Reports and Consolidated Financial Statements: The Complementary Twins. In *Gray, S. J. and Coenenberg, A. G., eds.*, 1988, pp. 272–99.

Garten, Helen A. Still Banking on the Market: A Comment on the Failure of Market Discipline. *Yale J. Regul.*, Winter 1988, 5(1), pp. 241–51.

Gartner, William B. and Duchesneau, Donald A. A Profile of New Venture Success and Failure in an Emerging Industry. In *Kirchhoff, B. A., et al., eds.*, 1988, pp. 372–86.

_____ and Thomas, Robert J. An Exploration of the Methods Used by New Firms to Estimate Future Sales. In *Kirchhoff, B. A., et al., eds.*, 1988, pp. 461–76.

Garvey, George E. Policy Implications of the Georgetown Study. In *White, L. J., ed.*, 1988, pp. 389–97.

Gary-Bobo, Robert. Equilibre Général et Concurrence Imparfaite: un tour d'horizon. (With English summary.) *Rech. Écon. Louvain*, 1988, 54(1), pp. 53–84.

Gaskin, Steven P. Marketing Mix Reactions to Entry: Commentary. *Marketing Sci.*, Fall 1988, 7(4), pp. 388–89.

Gasparetto, Marialuisa Manfredini. L'economia della famiglia. (The Economics of the Family. With English summary.) *Rivista Int. Sci. Econ. Com.*, April–May 1988, 35(4–5), pp. 393–408.

Gasparski, Piotr and Tyszka, Tadeusz. Justification of Decisions Made in Adverse Circumstances. In *Maital, S., ed., Vol. 1*, 1988, pp. 176–85.

Gasse, Yvon and Garnier, Bernard. Training Entrepreneurs through Newspapers and Creating New Businesses. In *Kirchhoff, B. A., et al., eds.*, 1988, pp. 254–65.

Gasser, Theo and Jennen-Steinmetz, Christine. A Unifying Approach to Nonparametric Regression Estimation. *J. Amer. Statist. Assoc.*, December 1988, 83(404), pp. 1084–89.

Gasson, R. Farm Diversification and Rural Development. *J. Agr. Econ.*, May 1988, 39(2), pp. 175–82.

_____ **and Potter, C.** Conservation through Land Diversion: A Survey of Farmers' Attitudes. *J. Agr. Econ.*, September 1988, 39(3), pp. 340–51.

_____, **et al.** The Farm as a Family Business: A Review. *J. Agr. Econ.*, January 1988, 39(1), pp. 1–41.

Gastil, Raymond D. and Wright, Lindsay M. The State of the World Political and Economic Freedom. In *Walker, M. A., ed. (I)*, 1988, pp. 85–119.

Gately, Dermot. Taking Off: The U.S. Demand for Air Travel and Jet Fuel. *Energy J.*, October 1988, 9(4), pp. 63–91.

Gates, Marilyn. Institutionalizing Dependency: The Impact of Two Decades of Planned Agricultural Modernization on Peasants in the Mexican State of Campeche. *J. Devel. Areas*, April 1988, 22(3), pp. 293–320.

Gates, Stephen and Shrivastava, Paul. Locating Doctoral Dissertations in Strategic Management. In *Lamb, R. and Shrivastava, P., eds.*, 1988, pp. 277–98.

Gathon, Henry-Jean. La distribution de l'eau en Belgique: Prix, coût et efficacité. (With English summary.) *Cah. Écon. Bruxelles*, Third Trimester 1988, (119), pp. 371–84.

Gatignon, Hubert and Anderson, Erin. The Multinational Corporation's Degree of Control over Foreign Subsidiaries: An Empirical Test of a Transaction Cost Explanation. *J. Law, Econ., Organ.*, Fall 1988, 4(2), pp. 305–36.

Gatto, Joseph P.; Kelejian, Harry H. and Stephan, Scott W. Stochastic Generalizations of Demand Systems with an Application to Telecommunications. *Info. Econ. Policy*, 1988, 3(4), pp. 283–309.

_____, **et al.** Interstate Switched Access Demand Analysis. *Info. Econ. Policy*, 1988, 3(4), pp. 333–58.

Gattuso, James L. Antitrust: An Incomplete Revolution. In *Boaz, D., ed.*, 1988, pp. 261–70.

Gaudet, Gérard; Amigues, Jean-Pierre and Moreaux, Michel. Bertrand and Cournot Equilibrium Price Paths in a Nonrenewable Resource Differentiated Product Duopoly. In *Eiselt, H. A. and Pederzoli, G., eds.*, 1988, pp. 343–57.

_____ **and Lasserre, Pierre.** On Comparing Monopoly and Competition in Exhaustible Resource Exploitation. *J. Environ. Econ. Manage.*, December 1988, 15(4), pp. 412–18.

Gauger, Jean. Disaggregate Level Evidence on Monetary Neutrality. *Rev. Econ. Statist.*, November 1988, 70(4), pp. 676–80.

Gauhar, Altaf. Free Flow of Information: Myths and Shibboleths. In *Sopiee, N.; Hamzah, B. A. and Leong, C. H., eds.*, 1988, 1983, pp. 327–48.

Gaul, W.; Böckenholt, I. and Both, M. PROLOG-Based Decision Support for Data Analysis in Marketing. In *Gaul, W. and Schader, M., eds.*, 1988, pp. 19–34.

_____ **and Schaer, A.** A PROLOG-Based PC-Implementation for New Product Introduction. In *Gaul, W. and Schader, M., eds.*, 1988, pp. 42–53.

Gault, John C. and Aït-Laoussine, Nordine. The 1986 Oil Price War: An Economic Fiasco. In *Mabro, R., ed.*, 1988, pp. 81–103.

Gausden, Robert and Drobny, Andres. Granger-Causality, Real Factor Prices and Employment: A Re-appraisal with UK Data. *Europ. Econ. Rev.*, July 1988, 32(6), pp. 1261–83.

Gautam, Vinayshil and Kohli, Uddesh. Human Resources Development and the Planning Process in India: Preface. In *Kohli, U. and Gautam, V., eds.*, 1988, pp. v–xi.

_____ **and Mohan, S.** Job Stress and Health Dimensions of Managerial Effectiveness—HRD Approach. In *Kohli, U. and Gautam, V., eds.*, 1988, pp. 224–35.

Gautschi, David and Betancourt, Roger. The Economics of Retail Firms. *Managerial Dec. Econ.*, June 1988, 9(2), pp. 133–44.

Gauvin, Annie and Bouillaguet-Bernard, Patricia. Female Labour Reserves and the Restructuring of Employment in Booms and Slumps in France. In *Rubery, J., ed.*, 1988, pp. 48–73.

_____ **and Bouillaguet-Bernard, Patricia.** Women's Employment, the State and the Family in France: Contradiction of State Policy for Women's Employment. In *Rubery, J., ed.*, 1988, pp. 163–90.

Gaver, Kenneth M.; Horsky, Dan and Narasimhan, Chakravarthi. Invariant Estimators for Market Share Systems and Their Finite Sample Behavior. *Marketing Sci.*, Spring 1988, 7(2), pp. 169–86.

Gavrilă, I. and Tigănescu, E. Development and Modernization of the Planning and Statistic Education in the Conditions of Training the Specialists. *Econ. Computat. Cybern. Stud. Res.*, 1988, 23(3), pp. 25–31.

Gay, Antonio and Modica, Salvatore. Complete Irreflexive Preferences: A Definition. *Econ. Letters*, 1988, 28(3), pp. 205–08.

Gay, David M. and Welsch, Roy E. Maximum Likelihood and Quasi-likelihood for Nonlinear Exponential Family Regression Models. *J. Amer. Statist. Assoc.*, December 1988, 83(404), pp. 990–98.

Gayle, Dennis John. Singaporean Market Socialism: Some Implications for Development Theory. *Int. J. Soc. Econ.*, 1988, 15(7), pp. 53–75.

Geary, Frank. Balanced and Unbalanced Growth in XIXth Century Europe. *J. Europ. Econ. Hist.*, Fall 1988, 17(2), pp. 349–57.

Geen, Gerry and Nayar, Mark. Individual Transferable Quotas in the Southern Bluefin Tuna Fishery: An Economic Appraisal. *Marine Resource Econ.*, 1988, 5(4), pp. 365–87.

Gehr, Adam K., Jr. Undated Futures Markets. *J. Futures Markets*, February 1988, 8(1), pp. 89–97.

Gehrels, Franz. On the Coming Senescence of American Manufacturing Competence: Discussion. In *Hanusch, H., ed.*, 1988, pp. 383–85.

Gehrig, Wilhelm. On the Shannon–Theil Concentration Measure and Its Characterizations. In *Eichhorn, W., ed.*, 1988, pp. 413–27.

Gehrlein, William V. Probability Calculations for Transitivity of the Simple Majority Rule. *Econ. Letters*, 1988, 27(4), pp. 311–15.

Geistfeld, Loren V. The Price Quality Relationship: The Evidence We Have, The Evidence We Need. In *Maynes, E. S. and ACCI Research Committee, eds.*, 1988, pp. 143–72.

Gekker, Ruvin. Veto Theorems with Expansion Consistency Conditions and without the Weak Pareto Principle. *Math. Soc. Sci.*, February 1988, 15(1), pp. 73–80.

Gel'bras, V. G. The Issue of Sovereignty of the Socialist Enterprise. *Prob. Econ.*, March 1988, 30(11), pp. 30–33.

Gelb, Alan and Conway, Patrick. Oil Windfalls in a Controlled Economy: A 'Fix-Price' Equilibrium Analysis of Algeria. *J. Devel. Econ.*, February 1988, 28(1), pp. 63–81.

Gelfand, Alan E. and Dey, Dipak K. Improved Estimation of the Disturbance Variance in a Linear Regression Model. *J. Econometrics*, November 1988, 39(3), pp. 387–95.

Gellhorn, Ernest. The Operation of the Litigation System: Comment. In *White, L. J., ed.*, 1988, pp. 240–43.

_____ and Fenton, Kathryn M. Vertical Restraints during the Reagan Administration: A Program in Search of a Policy. *Antitrust Bull.*, Fall 1988, 33(3), pp. 543–73.

Gellner, Ernest. Trust, Cohesion, and the Social Order. In *Gambetta, D., ed.*, 1988, pp. 142–57.

Gelski, Richard A. Tax Treatment of Computer Software: Australia. In *International Fiscal Association, ed. (II)*, 1988, pp. 183–202.

Geman, Donald and Branch, Ben. The Valuation of Stochastic Cash Flows. *Quart. J. Bus. Econ.*, Winter 1988, 27(1), pp. 148–78.

Gemery, Henry A. and Hogendorn, Jan S. Continuity in West African Monetary History? An Outline of Monetary Development. *African Econ. Hist.*, 1988, (17), pp. 127–46.

_____, et al. *Voyagers to the West:* A Review. *Bus. Hist. Rev.*, Winter 1988, 62(4), pp. 678–91.

Gemmell, Norman. Debt and the Developing Countries: A Simple Model of Optimal Borrowing. *J. Devel. Stud.*, January 1988, 24(2), pp. 197–213.

_____. Debt Servicing Costs and the Growth of Public Expenditure. *Public Finance*, 1988, 43(2), pp. 223–35.

Gemmill, Gordon. The Contribution of Futures and Options Markets to a Revised Agricultural Policy. *Europ. Rev. Agr. Econ.*, 1988, 15(4), pp. 457–75.

Gemünden, Hans Georg. "Promotors"—Key Persons for the Development and Marketing of Innovative Industrial Products. In *Grønhaug, K. and Kaufmann, G., eds.*, 1988, pp. 347–74.

Gencay, Ramazan; Stengos, Thanasis and Frank, Murray Z. International Chaos? *Europ. Econ. Rev.*, October 1988, 32(8), pp. 1569–84.

Gendreau, Francoise; Rault, A. and Anglard, Patrick. Model Building for Decision Aid in the Agri-economic Field. In *Motamen, H., ed.*, 1988, pp. 283–311.

Genovese, Frank C. An Examination of Proposals for a U.S. Industrial Policy. *Amer. J. Econ. Soc.*, October 1988, 47(4), pp. 441–53.

Gensemer, Susan H. Intransitive Indifference and Incomparability. *Econ. Letters*, 1988, 26(4), pp. 311–14.

_____. On Numerical Representations of Semiorders. *Math. Soc. Sci.*, June 1988, 15(3), pp. 277–86.

Genser, Bernd. Measuring the Burden of Taxation: An Index Number Approach. In *Eichhorn, W., ed.*, 1988, pp. 499–518.

Gentry, James A. Management of Information, Competitive Advantage and Short-Run Financial Management Systems. In *Kim, Y. H., ed.*, 1988, pp. 177–85.

_____; Whitford, David T. and Newbold, Paul. Predicting Industrial Bond Ratings with a Probit Model and Funds Flow Components. *Financial Rev.*, August 1988, 23(3), pp. 269–86.

Georgakopoulos, Theodore A. The Impact of Accession on Agricultural Incomes in Greece. *Europ. Rev. Agr. Econ.*, 1988, 15(1), pp. 79–88.

George, David and Falcone, David J. Inflation and Related Misperceptions. In *Pennsylvania Economic Association*, 1988, pp. 85–102.

George, Donald A. R. Theory, Policy and Arrow. *J. Econ. Surveys*, 1988, 2(4), pp. 373–75.

George, Kenneth D. and Cyert, Richard M. Competition, Growth, and Efficiency. In *Earl, P. E., ed., Vol. 2*, 1988, 1969, pp. 245–63.

George, P. S. Costs and Benefits of Food Subsidies in India. In *Pinstrup-Andersen, P., ed.*, 1988, pp. 229–41.

George, Peter J. and Sworden, Philip J. John Beverley Robinson and the Commercial Empire of the St. Lawrence. In *Uselding, P. J., ed.*, 1988, pp. 217–42.

George, Shanti. Co-operatives and Indian Dairy Policy: More Anand Than Pattern. In *Attwood, D. W. and Baviskar, B. S., eds.*, 1988, pp. 394–426.

Georgescu-Roegen, Nicholas. An Emigrant from a Developing Country: Autobiographical Notes—I. *Banca Naz. Lavoro Quart. Rev.*, March 1988, (164), pp. 3–31.

_____. Closing Remarks: About Economic Growth—A Variation on a Theme by David Hilbert. *Econ. Develop. Cult. Change*, Supplement, April 1988, 36(3), pp. S291–307.

_____. The Interplay between Institutional and Material Factors: The Problem and Its Status. In *Kregel, J. A.; Matzner, E. and Roncaglia, A., eds.*, 1988, pp. 297–326.

Georgiev, T., et al. Northeast Bulgaria: A Model for Optimizing Agroindustrial Production Structures. In *Parikh, J. K., ed.*, 1988, pp. 297–329.

Gérard, Marcel and Vanden Berghe, Carine. An Endogenously Time-Varying Parameter (TVP) Model of Investment Behaviour: Theory and Application to Belgian Data. In *Motamen, H., ed.*, 1988, pp. 183–201.

Gerardi, D.; Avdoulos, A. and Locker, H. Krijnse. Some Experiments with Phase IV ICP-Data. In *Salazar-Carrillo, J. and Rao, D. S. P., eds.*, 1988, pp. 93–112.

Gerber, Larry G. Corporatism in Comparative Perspective: The Impact of the First World War on American and British Labor Relations. *Bus. Hist. Rev.*, Spring 1988, 62(1), pp. 93–127.

Gereffi, Gary. The Pharmaceuticals Market. In *Zschock, D. K., ed.*, 1988, pp. 165–96.

Gerelli, Emilio and Bernardi, Luigi. World Tax Reform: A Progress Report: Italy: Comment. In *Pechman, J. A., ed.*, 1988, pp. 147–53.

Gerhaeusser, Klaus. Price Dispersion and Inflation: A Test of Causality. *Appl. Econ.*, May 1988, 20(5), pp. 701–09.

_____. Störungen der Signalfunktion relativer Preise. Analyse eines Dekompositionsverfahrens. (Distortions in the Signalling Function of Relative Prices. An Analysis of a Decomposition Approach. With English summary.) *Jahr. Nationalökon. Statist.*, September 1988, 205(3), pp. 245–62.

Gerhart, Barry and Haberfeld, Yitchak. Comment: Re-examining "Employment Discrimination: An Empirical Test of Forward versus Reverse Regression" [Reverse Regression and Salary Discrimination]. *J. Human Res.*, Winter 1988, 23(1), pp. 138–44.

Gerking, Shelby; de Haan, Menno and Schulze, William. The Marginal Value of Job Safety: A Contingent Valuation Study. *J. Risk Uncertainty*, June 1988, 1(2), pp. 185–99.

Gerla, Harry S. A Micro-microeconomic Approach to Antitrust Law: Games Managers Play. *Mich. Law Rev.*, April 1988, 86(5), pp. 892–929.

Gerlach, Stefan. World Business Cycles under Fixed and Flexible Exchange Rates. *J. Money, Credit, Banking*, November 1988, 20(4), pp. 621–32.

_____ and Klock, John. State-Space Estimates of International Business Cycles. *Econ. Letters*, 1988, 28(3), pp. 231–34.

Gerlowski, Daniel A. Spatial Entry Deterrence under Oligopoly. *J. Reg. Sci.*, November 1988, 28(4), pp. 531–40.

Germany, J. David. On the Roles of International Financial Markets and Their Relevance for Economic Policy: Comment. *J. Money, Credit, Banking*, Part 2, August 1988, 20(3), pp. 554–58.

Gerner, Jennifer L. Product Safety: A Review. In *Maynes, E. S. and ACCI Research Committee, eds.*, 1988, pp. 37–59.

_____. Research on Consumer Satisfaction and Dissatisfaction. In *Maynes, E. S. and ACCI Research Committee, eds.*, 1988, pp. 749–52.

Geronimus, Arline T. and Korenman, Sanders D. Comments on Pampel and Pillai's "Patterns

and Determinants of Infant Mortality in Developed Nations, 1950–1975." *Demography*, February 1988, 25(1), pp. 155–58.

Geroski, Paul A. In Pursuit of Monopoly Power: Recent Quantitative Work in Industrial Economics. *J. Appl. Econometrics*, April 1988, 3(2), pp. 107–23.

_____ and Jacquemin, Alexis. The Persistence of Profits: A European Comparison. *Econ. J.*, June 1988, 98(391), pp. 375–89.

_____; Jacquemin, Alexis and de Ghellinck, Elisabeth. Inter-industry Variations in the Effect of Trade on Industry Performance. *J. Ind. Econ.*, September 1988, 37(1), pp. 1–19.

_____; Stewart, Geoff and Estrin, Saul. Employee Share Ownership, Profit-Sharing and Participation: An Introduction. *Int. J. Ind. Organ.*, March 1988, 6(1), pp. 1–6.

Gerrard, Bill. Keynesian Economics: The Road to Nowhere? In *Hillard, J., ed.*, 1988, pp. 125–52.

Gerritsen, Rolf and Abbott, Jacky. Shifting to Certainty? Australian Rural Policy in 1987: Review. *Rev. Marketing Agr. Econ.*, April 1988, 56(1), pp. 9–26.

Gershfield, Edward M. Private Property in Talmudic Legal Tradition. *Int. J. Soc. Econ.*, 1988, 15(8), pp. 45–53.

Gershuny, Jonathan and Robinson, John P. Historical Changes in the Household Division of Labor. *Demography*, November 1988, 25(4), pp. 537–52.

Gerson, J. and Kahn, S. B. Factors Determining Real Exchange Rate Change in South Africa. *S. Afr. J. Econ.*, June–Sept. 1988, 56(2–3), pp. 124–35.

Gerson, Judith M. and Kraut, Robert E. Clerical Work at Home or in the Office: The Difference It Makes. In *Christensen, K. E., ed.*, 1988, pp. 49–64.

Gertler, M. S. Some Problems of Time in Economic Geography. *Environ. Planning A*, February 1988, 20(2), pp. 151–64.

Gertler, Mark. Financial Structure and Aggregate Economic Activity: An Overview. *J. Money, Credit, Banking*, Part 2, August 1988, 20(3), pp. 559–88.

_____ and Hubbard, Robert Glenn. Financial Factors in Business Fluctuations. In *Federal Reserve Bank of Kansas City*, 1988, pp. 33–71.

Gertler, Paul J. A Latent-Variable Model of Quality Determination. *J. Bus. Econ. Statist.*, January 1988, 6(1), pp. 97–104.

_____ and Anton, James J. External Markets and Regulation. *J. Public Econ.*, November 1988, 37(2), pp. 243–60.

Gertner, Robert; Gibbons, Robert and Scharfstein, David. Simultaneous Signalling to the Capital and Product Markets. *Rand J. Econ.*, Summer 1988, 19(2), pp. 173–90.

Gesing, Renka and Wojciechowski, Margot. Prospects for Minerals in the '90s: Digest of Discussions. In *Richardson, P. R. and Gesing, R., eds.*, 1988, pp. 111–28.

Gessaman, Paul H. The WAEA as Heir-Apparent

of a Regional Mandate. *Western J. Agr. Econ.*, July 1988, *13*(1), pp. 134–39.

Getis, Arthur. Economic Heterogeneity within Large Metropolitan Areas. *Growth Change*, Winter 1988, *19*(1), pp. 31–42.

Gettler-Summa, M.; Ralambondrainy, H. and Diday, E. Data Analysis and Expert Systems: Generating Rules from Data. In *Gaul, W. and Schader, M., eds.*, 1988, pp. 161–73.

Getzen, Thomas E. U.S. GNP and Health Expenditures: Lags in a Strong Time Series Relationship. In *Pennsylvania Economic Association*, 1988, pp. 753–76.

Gevers, L. and Hoet-Mulquin, M.-E. Public Expenditures and Welfare Policy: A Study of Local Decisions in the Walloon Region. *Tijdschrift Econ. Manage.*, Sept.–Dec. 1988, *33*(3/4), pp. 355–74.

Geweke, John. An Application of Operational-Subjective Statistical Methods to Rational Expectations: Comment. *J. Bus. Econ. Statist.*, October 1988, *6*(4), pp. 465–66.

——. Antithetic Acceleration of Monte Carlo Integration in Bayesian Inference. *J. Econometrics*, May–June 1988, *38*(1–2), pp. 73–89.

——. Comment on Poirer: Operational Bayesian Methods in Econometrics. *J. Econ. Perspectives*, Winter 1988, *2*(1), pp. 159–66.

——. Exact Inference in Models with Autoregressive Conditional Heteroscedasticity. In *Barnett, W. A.; Berndt, E. R. and White, H., eds.*, 1988, pp. 73–104.

——. The Secular and Cyclical Behavior of Real GDP in 19 OECD Countries, 1957–1983. *J. Bus. Econ. Statist.*, October 1988, *6*(4), pp. 479–86.

——; **Godfrey, Leslie G. and Tremayne, A. R.** Diagnostics for the Diagnostics: Discussion of "Checks of Model Adequacy for Univariate Time Series Models and Their Application to Econometric Relationships." *Econometric Rev.*, 1988, *7*(1), pp. 59–62.

Geyer, H. S. On Urbanization in South Africa. *S. Afr. J. Econ.*, June–Sept. 1988, *56*(2–3), pp. 154–72.

Geyer-Schulz, A.; Taudes, A. and Wagner, U. Exploring the Possibilities of an Improvement of Stochastic Market Models by Rule-Based Systems. In *Gaul, W. and Schader, M., eds.*, 1988, pp. 54–66.

Ghadar, Fariborz. Oil: The Power of an Industry. In *Vernon, R., ed.*, 1988, pp. 231–53.

Ghafoor, A. Education and Technical Efficiency in Pakistan's Agriculture: Comments. *Pakistan Devel. Rev.*, Part 2, Winter 1988, *27*(4), pp. 696–97.

Ghani, Ejaz; Malik, Sohail J. and Mushtaq, Mohammad. Consumption Patterns of Major Food Items in Pakistan: Provincial, Sectoral and Inter-temporal Differences 1979–1984-85. *Pakistan Devel. Rev.*, Part 2, Winter 1988, *27*(4), pp. 751–59.

——; **Mushtaq, Muhammad and Qureshi, Sarfraz Khan.** Taxes and Subsidies on Agricultural Producers as Elements of Intersectoral Transfer of Resources: Magnitude of the Transfer

and Search for Policy Options. *Pakistan Devel. Rev.*, Part 2, Winter 1988, *27*(4), pp. 551–56.

Ghannadian, Farhad and Schneider, Howard. Financial Growth versus Economic Development in Turkey, Portugal and Greece 1968–1983. *J. Econ. Devel.*, June 1988, *13*(1), pp. 39–50.

Ghatak, S. Towards a Second Green Revolution: From Chemicals to New Biological Techniques in Agriculture in the Tropics for Sustainable Development. In *Turner, R. K., ed.*, 1988, pp. 145–69.

Ghauri, Pervez N. and Kaynak, Erdener. Retail Distribution Systems in Sweden. In *Kaynak, E., ed.*, 1988, pp. 181–96.

Ghaus, Aisha and Pasha, Hafiz A. Buoyancy of Provincial Tax Revenues in Pakistan. *Pakistan Econ. Soc. Rev.*, Winter 1988, *26*(2), pp. 127–49.

Ghebremedhin, Tesfa G. Assessing the Impacts of Technology on Southern Agriculture and Rural Communities. *Southern J. Agr. Econ.*, July 1988, *20*(1), pp. 45–52.

de Ghellinck, Elisabeth; Geroski, Paul A. and Jacquemin, Alexis. Inter-industry Variations in the Effect of Trade on Industry Performance. *J. Ind. Econ.*, September 1988, *37*(1), pp. 1–19.

Gherity, James A. Mill's "Friendly Critic"—Thornton or Whewell? *Manchester Sch. Econ. Soc. Stud.*, September 1988, *56*(3), pp. 282–85.

Ghilarducci, Teresa. The Impact of Internal Union Politics on the 1981 UMWA Strike. *Ind. Relat.*, Fall 1988, *27*(3), pp. 371–84.

——. Strategic Use of Pension Funds since 1978. *Rev. Radical Polit. Econ.*, Winter 1988, *20*(4), pp. 23–39.

Ghosh, Alak. Changing Economic Scenario in 2001 A.D.: India and the World. *Indian Econ. J.*, April–June 1988, *35*(4), pp. 1–17.

Ghosh, Alo and Khoury, Sarkis J. Recent Developments in International Banking and Finance, Volume II: Overview. In *Khoury, S. J. and Ghosh, A., eds.*, 1988, pp. 1–43.

Ghosh, Atish R. and Masson, Paul R. International Policy Coordination in a World with Model Uncertainty. *Int. Monet. Fund Staff Pap.*, June 1988, *35*(2), pp. 230–58.

Ghosh, Chinmoy and Wollridge, J. Randall. An Analysis of Shareholder Reaction to Dividend Cuts and Omissions. *J. Finan. Res.*, Winter 1988, *11*(4), pp. 281–94.

Ghosh, Damayanti; Aigner, Dennis J. and Schneider, Friedrich. Me and My Shadow: Estimating the Size of the U.S. Hidden Economy from Time Series Data. In *Barnett, W. A.; Berndt, E. R. and White, H., eds.*, 1988, pp. 297–334.

Ghosh, Sukesh K. Optimum Monetary Growth in a Closed and an Open Economy. *Manchester Sch. Econ. Soc. Stud.*, December 1988, *56*(4), pp. 377–82.

Ghuman, B. S. Estimation of Engel Elasticities through Concentration Curves: An Application at Regional Level. *Margin*, April–June 1988, 20(3), pp. 57–78.

_____ **and Dhesi, Autar S.** Aspects of Financing State Plans (with Special Reference to Punjab). In *Raikhy, P. S. and Gill, S. S., eds.*, 1988, pp. 9–27.

_____ **and Dhesi, Autar S.** Resource Mobilisation at State Level—A Case Study of Punjab. In *Raikhy, P. S. and Gill, S. S., eds.*, 1988, pp. 186–211.

_____ **and Dhesi, Autar S.** The Responsiveness of State Taxes—A Comparative Study of Punjab and Haryana. In *Raikhy, P. S. and Gill, S. S., eds.*, 1988, pp. 77–87.

Ghysels, Eric. A Study toward a Dynamic Theory of Seasonality for Economic Time Series. *J. Amer. Statist. Assoc.*, March 1988, 83(401), pp. 168–72.

_____ **and Nerlove, Marc.** Seasonality in Surveys: A Comparison of Belgian, French and German Business Tests. *Europ. Econ. Rev.*, January 1988, 32(1), pp. 81–99.

Giambiagi, Fabio. Paridades cambiais, dívida externa e ajustamento: Reflexões sobre o caso brasileiro—1983/87. (With English summary.) *Pesquisa Planejamento Econ.*, August 1988, 18(2), pp. 453–68.

Gianessi, Leonard P., et al. Welfare Implications of Restricted Triazine Herbicide Use in the Chesapeake Bay Region. *Marine Resource Econ.*, 1988, 5(3), pp. 243–58.

Gianfrancesco, Frank D. The Choice Among Medical Insurance Plans: Comment. *Amer. Econ. Rev.*, March 1988, 78(1), pp. 277–80.

Giannaros, Demetrios S. Government Transfers, Growth and Unemployment Effects on Poverty: An Empirical Investigation. In *Missouri Valley Economic Assoc.*, 1988, pp. 84–91.

Giavazzi, Francesco. Incentives to Fix the Exchange Rate. *Europ. Econ. Rev.*, March 1988, 32(2–3), pp. 382–87.

_____ **and Giovannini, Alberto.** Modèles du SME: L'Europe n'est-elle qu'une zone deutsche mark? (Models of the EMS: Is Europe a Greater Deutschmark Area? With English summary.) *Revue Écon.*, May 1988, 39(3), pp. 641–66.

_____ **and Pagano, Marco.** The Advantage of Tying One's Hands: EMS Discipline and Central Bank Credibility. *Europ. Econ. Rev.*, June 1988, 32(5), pp. 1055–75.

_____; **Sheen, Jeff R. and Wyplosz, Charles.** The Real Exchange Rate and the Fiscal Aspects of a Natural Resource Discovery. *Oxford Econ. Pap.*, September 1988, 40(3), pp. 427–50.

Gibbons, Robert. Learning in Equilibrium Models of Arbitration. *Amer. Econ. Rev.*, December 1988, 78(5), pp. 896–912.

_____; **Scharfstein, David and Gertner, Robert.** Simultaneous Signalling to the Capital and Product Markets. *Rand J. Econ.*, Summer 1988, 19(2), pp. 173–90.

Gibbons, Sam M. U.S. Trade Legislation and Intellectual Property Rights. In *Walker, C. E. and Bloomfield, M. A., eds.*, 1988, pp. 169–70.

Gibbs, Barrie; Keen, Kevin and Lucas, Rob G. Innovation and Human Resource Productivity in Canada: A Comparison of "High" and "Low" Technology Industries. In *Gattiker, U. E. and Larwood, L., eds.*, 1988, pp. 93–120.

Gibbs, D. C. Restructuring in the Manchester Clothing Industry: Technical Change and Interrelationships between Manufacturers and Retailers. *Environ. Planning A*, September 1988, 20(9), pp. 1219–33.

Gibbs, Ernest. The Vocational Rehabilitation Data Base and the Estimation of Benefit–Cost Ratios. In *Berkowitz, M., ed.*, 1988, pp. 74–118.

_____ **and Hall-Kane, Anita G.** Correcting for Zero Wages at Referral. In *Berkowitz, M., ed.*, 1988, pp. 119–39.

Gibbs, Lawrence B. World Tax Reform: A Progress Report: United States. In *Pechman, J. A., ed.*, 1988, pp. 245–51.

Gibbs, Murray and Mashayekhi, Mina. Services: Cooperation for Development. *J. World Trade*, April 1988, 22(2), pp. 81–107.

Gibson, A.; Cullen, L. M. and Smout, T. C. Wages and Comparative Development in Ireland and Scotland, 1565–1780. In *Mitchison, R. and Roebuck, P., eds.*, 1988, pp. 105–16.

Gibson, Cosette M. and Smith, Stephen M. Industrial Diversification in Nonmetropolitan Counties and Its Effect on Economic Stability. *Western J. Agr. Econ.*, December 1988, 13(2), pp. 193–201.

Gibson, Donald R.; Kurtz, David L. and Boone, Louis E. Rating Logistics and Transportation Faculties on the Basis of Editorial Review Board Memberships. *Logist. Transp. Rev.*, December 1988, 24(4), pp. 684–90.

Gibson, Lay. The Long-term Impacts of the Telecommunication Industry and Information Technology. In *Orishimo, I.; Hewings, G. J. D. and Nijkamp, P., eds.*, 1988, pp. 107–24.

Gibson, William A.; Reed, Clyde G. and Easton, Stephen T. Tariffs and Growth: The Dales Hypothesis. *Exploration Econ. Hist.*, April 1988, 25(2), pp. 147–63.

Gideonse, Sarah K. and Meyers, William R. Why "Workfare" Fails. *Challenge*, Jan.–Feb. 1988, 31(1), pp. 44–49.

Gidlow, R. M. Exchange Rate Policy, Export Base and Gold Mining Taxation. *S. Afr. J. Econ.*, March 1988, 56(1), pp. 24–38.

_____. Workings of a Managed Floating Exchange Rate System for the Rand. *S. Afr. J. Econ.*, June–Sept. 1988, 56(2–3), pp. 136–153.

Giersch, Herbert. Growth through Liberalisation. *Nat. Inst. Econ. Rev.*, May 1988, (124), pp. 72–74.

Giertz, J. Fred and Chicoine, David L. Uniformity in a Dual Assessment System. *Nat. Tax J.*, June 1988, 41(2), pp. 247–55.

Giffen, Janice. The Allocation of Investment in the Soviet Union: Criteria for the Efficiency of Investment. In *[Nove, A.]*, 1988, pp. 44–60.

Gifford, Michael N. A Briefing by the Canadian

Agricultural Negotiator. In *Allen, K. and Mac-millan, K., eds.*, 1988, pp. 9–13.

———. Trade Liberalization: Theory and Reality: Discussion. *Can. J. Agr. Econ.*, Part 1, December 1988, *36*(4), pp. 597–99.

Giga, Soichiro. Development of the Studies of Socialist Enterprise in Japan and "Innovation" of the Socialist Enterprise. In *Urabe, K.; Child, J. and Kagono, T., eds.*, 1988, pp. 361–67.

Gigengack, Richard; Jepma, Catrinus J. and Brakman, Steven. The Speed of Adjustment as a Measure for Competitiveness. *Empirica*, 1988, *15*(1), pp. 161–78.

Gigliotti, Ernesto. L'avenir du secteur des soins de santé en Belgique á la lumière des expériences étrangères. (The Future of the Belgian Health Sector in the Light of Foreign Experience. With English summary.) *Ann. Pub. Co-op. Econ.*, Oct.–Dec. 1988, *59*(4), pp. 475–92.

Gil, María Angeles. Probablistic-Possibilistic Approach to Some Statistical Problems with Fuzzy Experimental Observations. In *Kacprzyk, J. and Fedrizzi, M., eds.*, 1988, pp. 286–306.

Gil Sanz, Agustín. La empresa pública en un mercado oligopolístico: Análisis comparativo de las reglas de precio igual a coste marginal y precio igual a coste medio. (With English summary.) *Invest. Econ.*, September 1988, *12*(3), pp. 401–24.

Gilad, Benjamin; Kaish, Stanley and Loeb, Peter D. From Economic Behavior to Behavoiral Economics: The Behavioral Uprising in Economics. In *Earl, P. E., ed., Vol. 2*, 1988, *1984*, pp. 437–58.

———; **Kaish, Stanley and Ronen, Joshua.** The Entrepreneurial Way with Information. In *Maital, S., ed., Vol. 2*, 1988, pp. 480–503.

Gilbert, Christopher L. Buffer Stocks, Hedging and Risk Reduction. *Bull. Econ. Res.*, October 1988, *40*(4), pp. 271–86.

——— **and Anderson, Ronald W.** Commodity Agreements and Commodity Markets: Lessons from Tin. *Econ. J.*, March 1988, *98*(389), pp. 1–15.

——— **and Powell, Andrew.** The Use of Commodity Contracts for the Management of Developing Country Commodity Risks. In *Currie, D. and Vines, D., eds.*, 1988, pp. 147–79.

Gilbert, David John. Use of a Simple Age-Structured Bioeconomic Model to Estimate Optimal Long-run Surpluses. *Marine Resource Econ.*, 1988, *5*(1), pp. 23–42.

Gilbert, Geoffrey. Toward the Welfare State: Some British Views on the 'Right to Subsistence,' 1768–1834. *Rev. Soc. Econ.*, October 1988, *46*(2), pp. 144–63.

Gilbert, Neil and Moon, Ailee. Analyzing Welfare Effort: An Appraisal of Comparative Methods. *J. Policy Anal. Manage.*, Winter 1988, *7*(2), pp. 326–40.

Gilbert, R. Alton. A Comparison of Proposals to Restructure the U.S. Financial System. *Fed. Res. Bank St. Louis Rev.*, July–Aug. 1988, *70*(4), pp. 58–73.

——— **and Belongia, Michael T.** The Effects of

Affiliation with Large Bank Holding Companies on Commercial Bank Lending to Agriculture. *Amer. J. Agr. Econ.*, February 1988, *70*(1), pp. 69–78.

Gilboa, Itzhak. The Complexity of Computing Best-Response Automata in Repeated Games. *J. Econ. Theory*, August 1988, *45*(2), pp. 342–52.

——— **and Schmeidler, David.** Information Dependent Games: Can Common Sense Be Common Knowledge? *Econ. Letters*, 1988, *27*(3), pp. 215–21.

Gilchrist, Robert and Scallan, Antony. FUNI-GIRLS: A Prototype Functional Programming Language for the Analysis of Generalized Linear Models. In *Edwards, D. and Raun, N. E., eds.*, 1988, pp. 213–18.

Giles, David E. A. The Estimation of Allocation Models with Autocorrelated Disturbances. *Econ. Letters*, 1988, *28*(2), pp. 147–50.

——— **and Dissanayake, Mallika.** Household Expenditure in Sri Lanka: An Engel Curve Analysis. *J. Quant. Econ.*, January 1988, *4*(1), pp. 133–56.

——— **and Ullah, Aman.** The Positive-Part Stein-Rule Estimator and Tests of Linear Hypotheses. *Econ. Letters*, 1988, *26*(1), pp. 49–51.

Gilg, Andrew W. Switzerland: Structural Change within Stability. In *Williams, A. M. and Shaw, G., eds.*, 1988, pp. 123–44.

Giliberto, S. Michael. A Note on the Use of Appraisal Data in Indexes of Performance Measurement. *Amer. Real Estate Urban Econ. Assoc. J.*, Spring 1988, *16*(1), pp. 77–83.

Gill, Andrew M. Choice of Employment Status and the Wages of Employees and the Self-employed: Some Further Evidence. *J. Appl. Econometrics*, July–Sept. 1988, *3*(3), pp. 229–34.

Gill, David and Tropper, Peter. Emerging Stock Markets in Developing Countries. *Finance Develop.*, December 1988, *25*(4), pp. 28–37.

Gill, Rajiv and Bawa, R. S. Tax Effort in India—An Inter-state Analysis. In *Raikhy, P. S. and Gill, S. S., eds.*, 1988, pp. 114–26.

Gill, Sucha Singh. Economic Basis of Emerging Tension in Centre–State Relations: A Case Study of Punjab. In *Raikhy, P. S. and Gill, S. S., eds.*, 1988, pp. 169–85.

———. Resource Mobilisation and Economic Development—A Regional Dimension of Punjab. In *Raikhy, P. S. and Gill, S. S., eds.*, 1988, pp. 1–8.

Gilland, Bernard. Population, Economic Growth, and Energy Demand, 1985–2020. *Population Devel. Rev.*, June 1988, *14*(2), pp. 233–44.

Gillen, David W.; Oum, Tae Hoon and Tretheway, Michael W. Entry Barriers and Anti-competitive Behaviour in a Deregulated Airline Market: The Case of Canada. *Int. J. Transport Econ.*, February 1988, *15*(1), pp. 29–41.

———; **Stanbury, W. T. and Tretheway, Michael W.** Duopoly in Canada's Airline Industry: Consequences and Policy Issues. *Can. Public Policy*, March 1988, *14*(1), pp. 15–31.

Gillen, William J. and Guccione, Antonio. A

Common Error in the Geometry of Macroeconomic Models. *J. Macroecon.*, Winter 1988, *10*(1), pp. 149–51.

_____ **and Guccione, Antonio.** Simon's Model of Rural–Urban Migration: A Proof of Johansen's Conjecture. *Reg. Sci. Urban Econ.*, August 1988, *18*(3), pp. 447–50.

Gillespie, A. and Williams, H. Telecommunications and the Reconstruction of Regional Comparative Advantage. *Environ. Planning A*, October 1988, *20*(10), pp. 1311–21.

Gillespie, Raymond. Landed Society and the Interregnum in Ireland and Scotland. In *Mitchison, R. and Roebuck, P., eds.*, 1988, pp. 38–47.

Gillespie, Thomas S. and Sherman, H. A. Recognition of Foreign Enterprises as Taxable Entities: Canada. In *International Fiscal Association, ed. (I)*, 1988, pp. 331–46.

Gillette, Charles C. and Raiklin, Ernest. The Nature of Contemporary Soviet Commodity Production. *Int. J. Soc. Econ.*, 1988, *15*(5–6), pp. 65–136.

Gillette, Clayton P. Plebiscites, Participation, and Collective Action in Local Government Law. *Mich. Law Rev.*, April 1988, *86*(5), pp. 930–88.

Gillette, Dean. Combining Communications and Computing: Telematics Infrastructures. In *Ausubel, J. H. and Herman, R., eds.*, 1988, pp. 233–48.

Gilley, Otis W.; Shieh, Yeung-Nan and Williams, Nancy A. Transportation Rates and Location of the Firm: A Comparative Static Analysis. *J. Reg. Sci.*, May 1988, *28*(2), pp. 231–38.

Gilliam, K. P. and Allsbrook, O. O., Jr. A Cyclical Interpretation of Money. *Kredit Kapital*, 1988, *21*(2), pp. 243–52.

Gilligan, John J. New Corporate Vision as a Prerequisite to New Directions. In *Tavis, L. A., ed.*, 1988, pp. 317–20.

Gilligan, Michele and Ford, Deborah Ann. The Effect of Lead Paint Abatement Laws on Rental Property Values. *Amer. Real Estate Urban Econ. Assoc. J.*, Spring 1988, *16*(1), pp. 84–94.

Gillin, L. Murray and Hindle, Kevin. Some Key Success Factors in Australian New Venture Management. In *Kirchhoff, B. A., et al., eds.*, 1988, pp. 387–402.

Gillis, William R. and Beierlein, James G. The Pennsylvania Agricultural-Access Program. In *Johnson, T. G.; Deaton, B. J. and Segarra, E., eds.*, 1988, pp. 131–34.

Gilmer, R. H., Jr. Risk and Return: A Question of the Holding Period. *J. Econ. Bus.*, May 1988, *40*(2), pp. 129–37.

_____ **and Stock, Duane R.** Yield Volatility of Discount Coupon Bonds. *J. Finan. Res.*, Fall 1988, *11*(3), pp. 189–200.

Gilpin, Robert G. The Implications of the Changing Trade Regime for U.S.–Japanese Relations. In *Inoguchi, T. and Okimoto, D. I., eds.*, 1988, pp. 138–70.

Gilroy, Bernard Michael. Discussion to Session 3: Industrial Targeting for High-Technology Industries. *Aussenwirtschaft*, June 1988, *43*(1/2), pp. 259–66.

_____ **and Broll, Udo.** Intra-industry Trade and Differences in Technology. *Scot. J. Polit. Econ.*, November 1988, *35*(4), pp. 399–403.

Gilson, J. C.; Chadee, D. and Saint-Louis, R. U.S. CVDs and Canadian Hog Exports: Methodological and Measurement Issues. *Can. J. Agr. Econ.*, Part 1, December 1988, *36*(4), pp. 669–87.

Gilson, Ronald J.; Scholes, Myron S. and Wolfson, Mark A. Taxation and the Dynamics of Corporate Control: The Uncertain Case for Tax-Motivated Acquisitions. In *Coffee, J. C., Jr.; Lowenstein, L. and Rose-Ackerman, S., eds.*, 1988, pp. 271–99.

Gilula, Zvi; Krieger, Abba M. and Ritov, Yaakov. Ordinal Association in Contingency Tables: Some Interpretive Aspects. *J. Amer. Statist. Assoc.*, June 1988, *83*(402), pp. 540–45.

Gimpl, Martin L. and Dakin, Stephen R. Management and Magic. In *Earl, P. E., ed., Vol. 1*, 1988, *1984*, pp. 217–28.

Ginarlis, John and Pollard, Sidney. Studies in Capital Formation in the United Kingdom, 1750–1920: Roads and Waterways, 1750–1850. In *Feinstein, C. H. and Pollard, S., eds.*, 1988, pp. 182–224.

Ginevra, Edoardo. Il problema degli incentivi al rimborso del debito estero in un modello di crescita ottimizzante. (The Issue of the Incentives to Foreign Debt Reimbursement in an Optimizing Growth Model. With English summary.) *Giorn. Econ.*, July–Aug. 1988, *47*(7–8), pp. 363–99.

van Ginneken, W. Employment and Labour Income Trends in China (1978–86). In *van Ginneken, W., ed.*, 1988, pp. 133–62.

_____. Employment and Labour Incomes: A Cross-Country Analysis (1971–86). In *van Ginneken, W., ed.*, 1988, pp. 1–31.

Ginsburg, Douglas H. Legal Rules, Takeover Strategies, and Defensive Tactics: Comment. In *Coffee, J. C., Jr.; Lowenstein, L. and Rose-Ackerman, S., eds.*, 1988, pp. 452–54.

Ginsburg, Martin D. Mergers and Takeovers: Taxes, Capital Structure, and the Incentives of Managers: Comment. In *Coffee, J. C., Jr.; Lowenstein, L. and Rose-Ackerman, S., eds.*, 1988, pp. 366–67.

Ginsburg, Paul B. The Emphasis on Measurement in Quality Assurance: Reasons and Implications: Commentary. *Inquiry*, Winter 1988, *25*(4), pp. 434–36.

_____. Public Insurance Programs: Medicare and Medicaid. In *Frech, H. E., III, ed.*, 1988, pp. 179–218.

_____ **and Frech, H. E., III.** Competition among Health Insurers, Revisited. In *Greenberg, W., ed.*, 1988, pp. 57–69.

_____ **and Hammons, Glenn T.** Competition and the Quality of Care: The Importance of Information. *Inquiry*, Spring 1988, *25*(1), pp. 108–15.

Ginsburgh, Victor A. and Mercenier, Jean. Macroeconomic Models and Microeconomic Theory: The Contribution of General Equilibrium Theory. In *Driehuis, W.; Fase, M. M. G. and den Hartog, H., eds.*, 1988, pp. 291–335.

_____ and **Michel, Philippe**. Adjustment Costs, Concentration and Price Behaviour. *J. Ind. Econ.*, June 1988, *36*(4), pp. 477–81.

_____ and **Van der Heyden, Ludo**. On Extending the Negishi Approach to Computing Equilibria: The Case of Government Price Support Policies. *J. Econ. Theory*, February 1988, *44*(1), pp. 168–78.

Gintis, Herbert and Bowles, Samuel. Contested Exchange: Political Economy and Modern Economic Theory. *Amer. Econ. Rev.*, May 1988, *78*(2), pp. 145–50.

Ginzberg, Eli. My Life Philosophy. *Amer. Econ.*, Spring 1988, *32*(1), pp. 3–9.

Giordano, Lorraine. Beyond Taylorism: Computerisation and QWL Programmes in the Production Process. In *Knights, D. and Willmott, H., eds.*, 1988, pp. 163–96.

Giorgi, Giorgio and Meriggi, Maria Rosa. On the Hierarchy of Some Qualitative Structures in the Von Neumann and Related Models. *Metroecon.*, June 1988, *39*(2), pp. 121–40.

Giovannini, Alberto. Capital Controls and Public Finance: The Experience in Italy. In *Giavazzi, F. and Spaventa, L., eds.*, 1988, pp. 177–211.

_____. Exchange Rates and Traded Goods Prices. *J. Int. Econ.*, February 1988, *24*(1–2), pp. 45–68.

_____. On the Effectiveness of Discrete Devaluation in Balance of Payments Adjustment: Comment. In *Marston, R. C., ed.*, 1988, pp. 210–13.

_____. The Real Exchange Rate, the Capital Stock, and Fiscal Policy. *Europ. Econ. Rev.*, November 1988, *32*(9), pp. 1747–67.

_____ and **Giavazzi, Francesco**. Modèles du SME: L'Europe n'est-elle qu'une zone deutsche mark? (Models of the EMS: Is Europe a Greater Deutschmark Area? With English summary.) *Revue Écon.*, May 1988, *39*(3), pp. 641–66.

_____ and **Jorion, Philippe**. Foreign Exchange Risk Premia Volatility Once Again [Interest Rates and Risk Premia in the Stock Market and in the Foreign Exchange Market]. *J. Int. Money Finance*, March 1988, *7*(1), pp. 111–13.

Giovannini, Enrico. A Methodology for an Early Estimate of Quarterly National Accounts. *Econ. Int.*, Aug.–Nov. 1988, *41*(3–4), pp. 197–215.

Gipouloux, François. Industrial Restructuring and Autonomy of Enterprises in China: Is Reform Possible? In *Feuchtwang, S.; Hussain, A. and Pairault, T., eds., Vol. 2*, 1988, pp. 107–17.

Girardin, Eric. Dépenses publiques anticipées et balance courante. Un test pour les sept principaux pays de l'OCDE. (Expected Public Spending and the Current Account: A Test for the Seven Main OECD Countries. With English summary.) *Revue Écon.*, September 1988, *39*(5), pp. 1061–74.

_____ and **Marois, William**. Fiscal Policy in an Open Economy: An Empirical Study of O.E.C.D. Countries. *Brit. Rev. Econ. Issues*, Autumn 1988, *10*(23), pp. 77–110.

Giroux, Gary and Fawson, Chris. An Empirical Extension of the Municipal Monopoly Model to Provision of Community Infrastructure [Bureaucracy and the Divisibility of Local Public Output]. *Public Choice*, April 1988, *57*(1), pp. 79–83.

Girvan, Norman P. C. Y. Thomas and *The Poor and the Powerless:* The Limitations of Conventional Radicalism. *Soc. Econ. Stud.*, December 1988, *37*(4), pp. 53–74.

_____. Trade: Comments. *Soc. Econ. Stud.*, March–June 1988, *37*(1–2), pp. 173–79.

Gisser, Micha. Price Leadership and Welfare Losses in U.S. Manufacturing: Reply. *Amer. Econ. Rev.*, March 1988, *78*(1), pp. 288–89.

Gitlow, Howard S. and Hertz, Paul T. Chain Reaction: The Impact of Managing Quality on Profits, Wages, and Employment. *Rivista Int. Sci. Econ. Com.*, August 1988, *35*(8), pp. 757–67.

Gitmez, Ali S. Developmental Outcomes of External Migration: The Turkish Experience. *METU*, 1988, *15*(1–2), pp. 1–21.

del Giudice, Michele and Cardarelli, Aldo. World Tax Reform: A Progress Report: Italy. In *Pechman, J. A., ed.*, 1988, pp. 141–46.

Givoly, Dan and Lakonishok, Josef. Divergence of Earnings Expectations: The Effect on Stock Market Response to Earnings Signals. In *Dimson, E., ed.*, 1988, pp. 272–89.

Gjesdal, Frøystein. Piecewise Linear Incentive Schemes. *Scand. J. Econ.*, 1988, *90*(3), pp. 305–28.

Glade, William P. Multinationals and the Third World. In *Tool, M. R., ed., Vol. 2*, 1988, *1987*, pp. 471–502.

_____. Rescheduling as Ritual. In *Tavis, L. A., ed.*, 1988, pp. 244–52.

Gladwin, Christina H. Assessing the Impacts of Technology on Southern Agriculture and Rural Communities: Discussion. *Southern J. Agr. Econ.*, July 1988, *20*(1), pp. 53–55.

Glahe, Fred and Vorhies, Frank. Political Liberty and Social Development: An Empirical Investigation. *Public Choice*, July 1988, *58*(1), pp. 45–71.

Glanz, Milton P. and Kerns, Wilmer L. Private Social Welfare Expenditures, 1972–85. *Soc. Sec. Bull.*, August 1988, *51*(8), pp. 3–10.

Glasbeek, Harry J. and Drache, Daniel. The New Fordism in Canada: Capital's Offensive, Labour's Opportunity. *Econ. Lavoro*, July–Sept. 1988, *22*(3), pp. 47–70.

Glascock, John L. and Meyer, Donald J. Assessing the Regulatory Process in an International Context: Mixed Currency SDRs and U.S. Bank Equity Returns. *Atlantic Econ. J.*, March 1988, *16*(1), pp. 39–46.

Glaser, Paul F. Using Technology for Competitive Advantage: The ATM Experience at Citicorp. In *Guile, B. R. and Quinn, J. B., eds. (I)*, 1988, pp. 108–14.

Glasmeier, Amy. Factors Governing the Development of High Tech Industry Agglomerations: A Tale of Three Cities. *Reg. Stud.*, August 1988, 22(4), pp. 287–301.

Glassman, Debra A. and Redish, Angela. Currency Depreciation in Early Modern England and France. *Exploration Econ. Hist.*, January 1988, 25(1), pp. 75–97.

Glasson, John; van Der Wee, Dominique and Barrett, Brendan. A Local Income and Employment Multiplier Analysis of a Proposed Nuclear Power Station Development at Hinkley Point in Somerset. *Urban Stud.*, June 1988, 25(3), pp. 248–61.

Glaz'ev, S. Iu. and L'vov, D. S. Theoretical and Applied Aspects of the Management of Scientific–Technical Progress. *Matekon*, Spring 1988, 24(3), pp. 80–100.

Glazer, Amihai and Grofman, Bernard. Limitations of the Spatial Model. *Public Choice*, August 1988, 58(2), pp. 161–67.

_____ **and Hassin, Refael.** Optimal Contests. *Econ. Inquiry*, January 1988, 26(1), pp. 133–43.

Gleason, Joyce P. and Walstad, William B. An Empirical Test of an Inventory Model of Student Study Time. *J. Econ. Educ.*, Fall 1988, 19(4), pp. 315–21.

Gleicher, David. Bonus Formulae and Central Planning. *Rev. Radical Polit. Econ.*, Summer–Fall 1988, 20(2–3), pp. 133–37.

_____; **Swanson, Paul A. and Alcorn, John.** Toward a General Model of Price, Choice of Technique and Distribution in a Centrally-Planned, Socialist Economy. *Econ. Planning*, 1988, 22(3), pp. 117–35.

Gleick, Peter H. The Effects of Future Climatic Changes on International Water Resources: The Colorado River, the United States, and Mexico. *Policy Sci.*, 1988, 21(1), pp. 23–39.

Gleissner, Winfried and Eichhorn, Wolfgang. The Equation of Measurement. In *Eichhorn, W., ed.*, 1988, pp. 19–27.

_____ **and Eichhorn, Wolfgang.** The Solutions of Important Special Cases of the Equation of Measurement. In *Eichhorn, W., ed.*, 1988, pp. 29–37.

Glennon, Dennis and Lane, Julia I. The Estimation of Age/Earnings Profiles in Wrongful Death and Injury Cases: Author's Reply. *J. Risk Ins.*, March 1988, 55(1), pp. 174–79.

Glewwe, Paul. Economic Liberalization and Income Inequality: Further Evidence on the Sri Lanka Experience. *J. Devel. Econ.*, March 1988, 28(2), pp. 233–46.

_____. Response to Ravallion and Jayasuriya [The Distribution of Income in Sri Lanka in 1969–70 and 1980–81: A Decomposition Analysis]. *J. Devel. Econ.*, March 1988, 28(2), pp. 257–60.

_____. Self-Employment Incomes in Sri Lanka: 1969–70 to 1981–82. In *van Ginneken, W., ed.*, 1988, pp. 85–132.

Glezen, G. William; Cronan, Timothy P. and Wilson, Arlette C. Forecasting Accounting Information for Auditors' Use in Analytical Re-

views. In *Schwartz, B. N., ed.*, 1988, pp. 267–76.

Glick, Mark and Ehrbar, Hans. Structural Change in Profit Rate Differentials: The Post World War II U.S. Economy. *Brit. Rev. Econ. Issues*, Spring 1988, 10(22), pp. 81–102.

Glick, Reuven. Financial Market Changes and Monetary Policy in Pacific Basin Countries. In *Cheng, H.-S., ed.*, 1988, pp. 17–42.

_____. Saving–Investment Determinants of Japan's External Balance. *Fed. Res. Bank San Francisco Econ. Rev.*, Summer 1988, (3), pp. 3–14.

_____ **and Cheng, Hang-Sheng.** Monetary Policy Changes in Pacific Basin Countries. In *Cheng, H.-S., ed.*, 1988, pp. 3–14.

Glickman, Norman J. and Woodward, Douglas P. The Location of Foreign Direct Investment in the United States: Patterns and Determinants. *Int. Reg. Sci. Rev.*, 1988, 11(2), pp. 137–54.

Glombowski, Jörg and Krüger, Michael. A Short-Period Growth Cycle Model. *Rech. Écon. Louvain*, 1988, 54(4), pp. 423–38.

Glosten, Lawrence R. and Harris, Lawrence E. Estimating the Components of the Bid/Ask Spread. *J. Finan. Econ.*, May 1988, 21(1), pp. 123–42.

Gluch, Erich and Riedel, Jürgen. The Global Construction Industry: The Federal Republic of Germany. In *Strassmann, W. P. and Wells, J., eds.*, 1988, pp. 120–40.

Glugiewicz, Ewa and Gruchman, Bohdan. The Role of Innovations in Regional Economic Restructuring in Eastern Europe. In *Aydalot, P. and Keeble, D., eds.*, 1988, pp. 221–32.

Glymour, Clark and Spirtes, Peter. Latent Variables, Causal Models and Overidentifying Constraints. *J. Econometrics*, Sept.–Oct. 1988, 39(1–2), pp. 175–98.

Glyn, Andrew. Behind the Profitability Trends. *Econ. Rev. (Keizai Kenkyu)*, July 1988, 39(3), pp. 230–41.

_____. Colliery Results and Closures after the 1984–85 Coal Dispute. *Oxford Bull. Econ. Statist.*, May 1988, 50(2), pp. 161–73.

_____ **and Rowthorn, Robert E.** West European Unemployment: Corporatism and Structural Change. *Amer. Econ. Rev.*, May 1988, 78(2), pp. 194–99.

Glynn, Dermot. Economic Regulation of the Privatized Water Industry. In *Johnson, C., ed.*, 1988, pp. 77–92.

Glytsos, Nicholas P. Remittances in Temporary Migration: A Theoretical Model and Its Testing with the Greek–German Experience. *Weltwirtsch. Arch.*, 1988, 124(3), pp. 524–49.

Gmünder, F. K.; Nordau, C. G. and Cogoli, A. Cell Biology in Space: From Basic Science to Biotechnology III. In *Egan, J. J., et al., 1988*, pp. 353–66.

Göbel, Thomas. Becoming American: Ethnic Workers and the Rise of the CIO. *Labor Hist.*, Spring 1988, 29(2), pp. 173–98.

Góczán, László. A New Land Evaluation in Hungary Based on Ecological Potential. *Statist. J.*, November 1988, 5(3), pp. 279–87.

Goddard, Ellen W. Export Demand Elasticities in the World Market for Beef. In *Carter, C. A. and Gardiner, W. H., eds.*, 1988, pp. 225–53.

———— **and Holloway, Garth J.** An Approach to Examining Relative Efficiency in the Canadian Livestock Slaughtering Industry. *Can. J. Agr. Econ.*, July 1988, 36(2), pp. 207–20.

———— **and Tielu, A.** Assessing the Effectiveness of Fluid Milk Advertising in Ontario. *Can. J. Agr. Econ.*, July 1988, 36(2), pp. 261–78.

Goddard, Robert W. The People Focus. In *Timpe, A. D., ed.*, 1988, *1984*, pp. 9–13.

Goddeeris, John H. Compensating Differentials and Self-selection: An Application to Lawyers. *J. Polit. Econ.*, April 1988, 96(2), pp. 411–28.

————, **et al.** Hospital Rate Setting: National Evidence and Issues for Wisconsin. In *Danziger, S. H. and Witte, J. F., eds.*, 1988, pp. 208–28.

Godden, David. Nice Work If You Can Get It! *Rev. Marketing Agr. Econ.*, August 1988, 56(2), pp. 151–52.

Godfrey, A. Blanton and Kolesar, Peter J. Role of Quality in Achieving World Class Competitiveness. In *Starr, M. K., ed.*, 1988, pp. 213–38.

Godfrey, Christine. Licensing and the Demand for Alcohol. *Appl. Econ.*, November 1988, 20(11), pp. 1541–58.

Godfrey, Leslie G.; McAleer, Michael and McKenzie, Colin R. Variable Addition and La-Grange Multiplier Tests for Linear and Logarithmic Regression Models. *Rev. Econ. Statist.*, August 1988, 70(3), pp. 492–503.

———— **and Tremayne, A. R.** Checks of Model Adequacy for Univariate Time Series Models and Their Application to Econometric Relationships: Reply. *Econometric Rev.*, 1988, 7(1), pp. 63–64.

———— **and Tremayne, A. R.** Checks of Model Adequacy for Univariate Time Series Models and Their Application to Econometric Relationships. *Econometric Rev.*, 1988, 7(1), pp. 1–42.

————; **Tremayne, A. R. and Geweke, John.** Diagnostics for the Diagnostics: Discussion of "Checks of Model Adequacy for Univariate Time Series Models and Their Application to Econometric Relationships." *Econometric Rev.*, 1988, 7(1), pp. 59–62.

Godley, Wynne. Manufacturing and the Future of the British Economy. In *Barker, T. and Dunne, P., eds.*, 1988, pp. 5–14.

———— **and Nordhaus, William D.** Pricing in the Trade Cycle. In *Sawyer, M. C., ed.*, 1988, *1972*, pp. 227–48.

Godoy, Ricardo A. Small-scale Mining and Agriculture among the Jukumani Indians, Northern Potosí, Bolivia. *J. Devel. Stud.*, January 1988, 24(2), pp. 177–96.

Goedhuys, D. W. The South African Reserve Bank and the Course of the Economy. In *Jones, S., ed.*, 1988, pp. 105–12.

Goertz, Gary and Diehl, Paul F. Territorial Changes and Militarized Conflict. *J. Conflict Resolution*, March 1988, 32(1), pp. 103–22.

de Góes, Walder. Military and Political Transition. In *Chacel, J. M.; Falk, P. S. and Fleischer, D. V., eds.*, 1988, pp. 120–29.

Goett, Andrew A.; McFadden, Daniel L. and Woo, Chi-Keung. Estimating Household Value of Electrical Service Reliability with Market Research Data. *Energy J.*, Special Issue, 1988, 9, pp. 105–20.

Goetz, Andrew R.; Brown, Lawrence A. and Brea, Jorge A. Policy Aspects of Development and Individual Mobility: Migration and Circulation from Ecuador's Rural Sierra. *Econ. Geogr.*, April 1988, 64(2), pp. 147–70.

Goetze, David. Voluntary Siting of Unwanted Facilities. In *Hula, R. C., ed.*, 1988, pp. 204–22.

———— **and Orbell, John M.** Understanding and Cooperation in Social Dilemmas. *Public Choice*, June 1988, 57(3), pp. 275–79.

Goetzmann, William N. and Feinstein, Steven P. The Effect of the "Triple Witching Hour" on Stock Market Volatility. *Fed. Res. Bank Atlanta Econ. Rev.*, Sept.–Oct. 1988, 73(5), pp. 2–18.

Goff, Brian L.; Shughart, William F., II and Tollison, Robert D. Disqualification by Decree: Amateur Rules as Barriers to Entry. *J. Inst. Theoretical Econ.*, June 1988, 144(3), pp. 515–23.

Gofman, K. G.; Albegov, M. M. and Volkonskii, V. A. Optimizational Realism or Economic Nihilism? *Matekon*, Summer 1988, 24(4), pp. 61–71.

Gofran, K. A. Salient Features of the 1987–88 National Budget: Bangladesh. *Bull. Int. Fiscal Doc.*, February 1988, 42(2), pp. 81–83.

————. Some Highlights of the 1988/89 Budget: Bangladesh. *Bull. Int. Fiscal Doc.*, December 1988, 42(12), pp. 534–36.

Goga, A.; Baron, T. and Ivan, I. Modelling the Cost of the Quality of Programme Systems. *Econ. Computat. Cybern. Stud. Res.*, 1988, 23(2), pp. 21–31.

Goisis, Gianandrea. Dissonanze (Certe) e consonanze (auspicabili) nel sistema sanitario italiano. (Incongruities (Certain) and Congruities (Desirable) in the Italian Health System. With English summary.) *Rivista Int. Sci. Econ. Com.*, March 1988, 35(3), pp. 239–58.

Gokturk, S. S. and Masarani, F. On the Probabilities of the Mutual Agreement Match. *J. Econ. Theory*, February 1988, 44(1), pp. 192–201.

Golbe, Devra L. Risk-Taking by Firms Near Bankruptcy. *Econ. Letters*, 1988, 28(1), pp. 75–79.

———— **and White, Lawrence J.** Mergers and Acquisitions in the U.S. Economy: An Aggregate and Historical Overview. In *Auerbach, A. J., ed. (II)*, 1988, pp. 25–47.

———— **and White, Lawrence J.** A Time-Series Analysis of Mergers and Acquisitions in the U.S. Economy. In *Auerbach, A. J., ed. (I)*, 1988, pp. 265–302.

Gold, Joseph. Mexico and the Development of the Practice of the International Monetary Fund. *World Devel.*, October 1988, *16*(10), pp. 1127–42.

Gold, Marsha. Common Sense on Extending DRG Concepts to Pay for Ambulatory Care. *Inquiry*, Summer 1988, *25*(2), pp. 281–89.

Gold, Steven D. A Review of Recent State Tax Reform Activity. In *Gold, S. D., ed.*, 1988, pp. 11–30.

_____. The Unfinished Agenda for State Tax Reform: Introduction. In *Gold, S. D., ed.*, 1988, pp. 1–9.

_____ and **Eckl, Corina L.** Appendix Checklist of Characteristics of a Good State Revenue System. In *Gold, S. D., ed.*, 1988, pp. 57–63.

Gold, Thomas B. Colonial Origins of Taiwanese Capitalism. In *Winckler, E. A. and Greenhalgh, S., eds.*, 1988, pp. 101–17.

_____. Entrepreneurs, Multinationals, and the State. In *Winckler, E. A. and Greenhalgh, S., eds.*, 1988, pp. 175–205.

Goldberg, Gertrude S. and Cherry, Robert. Fresh Start of False Start? *Challenge*, May–June 1988, *31*(3), pp. 48–51.

Goldberg, Joseph P. The Landmark Provisions of Ratified ILO Conventions. *Mon. Lab. Rev.*, June 1988, *111*(6), pp. 53–55.

Goldberg, Lawrence G. and Greenberg, Warren. Health Insurance without Provider Influence: The Limits of Cost Containment. In *Greenberg, W., ed.*, 1988, pp. 71–81.

_____ and **Hanweck, Gerald A.** What We Can Expect from Interstate Banking. *J. Banking Finance*, 1988, *12*(1), pp. 51–67.

Goldberg, Marvin E.; Brucks, Merrie and Armstrong, Gary M. Children's Use of Cognitive Defenses against Television Advertising: A Cognitive Response Approach. *J. Cons. Res.*, March 1988, *14*(4), pp. 471–82.

Goldberg, Michael A.; Avery, Robert B. and Belton, Terrence M. Market Discipline in Regulating Bank Risk: New Evidence from the Capital Markets. *J. Money, Credit, Banking*, November 1988, *20*(4), pp. 597–610.

_____; **Helsley, Robert W. and Levi, Maurice D.** On the Development of International Financial Centers. *Ann. Reg. Sci.*, February 1988, *22*, pp. 81–94.

Goldberg, Michael J. The Propensity to Sue and the Duty of Fair Representation: A Second Point of View [Tactical Use of the Union's Duty of Fair Representation: An Empirical Analysis]. *Ind. Lab. Relat. Rev.*, April 1988, *41*(3), pp. 456–61.

Goldberg, Moshe; Hirsch, Seev and Sassoon, D. M. An Analysis of the American–Israeli Free Trade Area Agreement. *World Econ.*, June 1988, *11*(2), pp. 281–300.

Goldberg, Paul. Consistency in Soviet Investment Rules. *J. Compar. Econ.*, June 1988, *12*(2), pp. 244–47.

Goldberg, Ray A. Company Strategies in a Reconstructed Global Seed Industry. In *Goldberg, R. A., ed., Vol. 8*, 1988, pp. 265–289.

_____. A Global Agribusiness Market Revolution: The Restructuring of Agribusiness. In *Goldberg, R. A., ed., Vol. 9*, 1988, pp. 145–55.

Goldberg, Samuel and Ianchilovici, Beatriz. El stock de capital en la Argentina. (With English summary.) *Desarrollo Econ.*, July–Sept. 1988, *28*(110), pp. 281–304.

Goldberg, Sanford H. and Langer, Marshall J. Recognition of Foreign Enterprises as Taxable Entities: United States. In *International Fiscal Association, ed. (I)*, 1988, pp. 387–98.

Goldberg, Victor P. Accountable Accountants: Is Third-Party Liability Necessary? *J. Legal Stud.*, June 1988, *17*(2), pp. 295–312.

_____. Clarifying the Record: A Comment. *J. Inst. Theoretical Econ.*, December 1988, *144*(5), pp. 885–88.

_____. Impossibility and Related Excuses. *J. Inst. Theoretical Econ.*, February 1988, *144*(1), pp. 100–116.

Golden, John, et al. Modeling the Ratings Game: Publication Performance, Departmental Characteristics, and Graduate Faculty Ratings in Economics. *Quart. Rev. Econ. Bus.*, Spring 1988, *28*(1), pp. 101–09.

Goldenberg, David H. Trading Frictions and Futures Price Movements. *J. Finan. Quant. Anal.*, December 1988, *23*(4), pp. 465–81.

Goldfarb, Robert S. Choice under Uncertainty: Problems Solved and Unsolved: Correspondence. *J. Econ. Perspectives*, Spring 1988, *2*(2), pp. 179–81.

_____. Income Distribution: Comments. In *Mangum, G. and Philips, P., eds.*, 1988, pp. 88–90.

_____. International Division of Labor: Comments. In *Mangum, G. and Philips, P., eds.*, 1988, pp. 349–53.

Goldfeld, Stephen M. and Quandt, Richard E. Budget Constraints, Bailouts, and the Firm under Central Planning. *J. Compar. Econ.*, December 1988, *12*(4), pp. 502–20.

Goldfrank, Walter. Silk and Steel: Italy and Japan between the Two World Wars. In *Burke, E., III, ed.*, 1988, pp. 218–40.

Goldin, Claudia. Maximum Hours Legislation and Female Employment: A Reassessment. *J. Polit. Econ.*, February 1988, *96*(1), pp. 189–205.

Goldin, Kenneth D. Equal Access vs. Selective Access: A Critique of Public Goods Theory. In *Cowen, T., ed.*, 1988, *1977*, pp. 69–92.

Golding, Edward and Zalokar, Nadja. Unisex Insurance. In *Brown, E., ed.*, 1988, pp. 85–92.

Goldman, Fred and Grossman, Michael. The Impact of Public Health Policy: The Case of Community Health Centers. *Eastern Econ. J.*, Jan.–March 1988, *14*(1), pp. 63–72.

Goldman, Marshall I. Gorbachev and Economic Reform in the Soviet Union. *Eastern Econ. J.*, Oct.–Dec. 1988, *14*(4), pp. 331–35.

_____. The Soviet Union Today: The Consumer. In *Cracraft, J., ed.*, 1988, pp. 191–97.

_____ and **Goldman, Merle.** Soviet and Chinese Economic Reform. *Foreign Aff.*, 1987–88, *66*(3), pp. 551–73.

Goldman, Merle and Goldman, Marshall I. Soviet and Chinese Economic Reform. *Foreign Aff.*, 1987–88, *66*(3), pp. 551–73.

Goldschmid, Harvey J. Comment on the Policy Implications of the Georgetown Study. In *White, L. J., ed.*, 1988, pp. 412–15.

Goldschmidt, Peter. Domestic Appliance Energy Usage in Western Australia. *Energy Econ.*, April 1988, *10*(2), pp. 155–62.

Goldsmith, Arthur A. Policy Dialogue, Conditionality, and Agricultural Development: Implications of India's Green Revolution. *J. Devel. Areas*, January 1988, *22*(2), pp. 179–97.

Goldstein, Daniel J. Building Local Capability in Latin America. In *Research and Info. System for the Non-aligned and Other Developing Countries*, 1988, pp. 385–419.

Goldstein, Judith. Ideas, Institutions, and American Trade Policy. In *Ikenberry, G. J.; Lake, D. A. and Mastanduno, M., eds.*, 1988, pp. 179–217.

_____. Ideas, Institutions, and American Trade Policy. *Int. Organ.*, Winter 1988, *42*(1), pp. 179–217.

Goldstein, Morris and Frenkel, Jacob A. Exchange Rate Volatility and Misalignment: Evaluating Some Proposals for Reform. In *Federal Reserve Bank of Kansas City*, 1988, pp. 185–220.

_____ and Frenkel, Jacob A. A Guide to Target Zones. In *Melamed, L., ed.*, 1988, *1986*, pp. 183–221.

_____ and Frenkel, Jacob A. The International Monetary System: Developments and Prospects. *Cato J.*, Fall 1988, *8*(2), pp. 285–306.

_____; Masson, Paul R. and Frenkel, Jacob A. International Coordination of Economic Policies: Scope, Methods, and Effects. In *Guth, W., ed.*, 1988, pp. 149–92.

Goldstein, Nance. A Preliminary Look at the Impact of Military R&D Spending on the U.S. Software Industry. *Rev. Radical Polit. Econ.*, Summer–Fall 1988, *20*(2–3), pp. 290–95.

Golembe, Carter H. Historic Competitive Barriers in the Financial Services Industry. In *Federal Home Loan Bank of San Francisco*, 1988, pp. 33–42.

Golembiewski, Robert T. Policy Initiatives in Worksite Research: Implications from Research on a Phase Model of Burn-Out. In *Kelly, R. M., ed.*, 1988, pp. 209–27.

Golen, Steven P.; Looney, Stephen W. and White, Richard A. An Empirical Examination of CPA Perceptions of Communication Barriers between Auditor and Client. In *Schwartz, B. N., ed.*, 1988, pp. 233–49.

Golinelli, Roberto; Stagni, Anna and Bosi, Paolo. Effetti macroeconomici e settoriali dell'armonizzazione dell'Iva e delle accise: la valutazione del modello Hermes-Italia. (With English summary.) *Polit. Econ.*, December 1988, *4*(3), pp. 361–84.

Gollas, Manuel. Comments on the Mexican Economy in 1984. In *Jorge, A. and Salazar-Carrillo, J., eds.*, 1988, pp. 195–98.

Golley, Frank B. Human Population from an Eco-

logical Perspective. *Population Devel. Rev.*, Supplement, 1988, *14*, pp. 199–210.

Golob, T. F. and Meurs, H. Modeling the Dynamics of Passenger Travel Demand by Using Structural Equations. *Environ. Planning A*, September 1988, *20*(9), pp. 1197–1218.

Gombeaud, Jean-François; Lavigne, Marie and Dimitri, Alexandre. Prices, Settlements, Gains from Trade. In *Lavigne, M., ed.*, 1988, pp. 64–93.

Gombola, Michael J.; Kahl, Douglas R. and Nunn, Kenneth P., Jr. Valuation of the Preferred Stock Sinking Fund Feature: A Time-Series Approach. *J. Finan. Res.*, Spring 1988, *11*(1), pp. 33–42.

_____ and Ogden, William S. Effects of a Sinking Fund on Preferred Stock Marketability: A Probit Analysis. *Quart. J. Bus. Econ.*, Summer 1988, *27*(3), pp. 41–56.

Gomes-Casseres, Benjamin. Joint Venture Cycles: The Evolution of Ownership Strategies of U.S. MNEs, 1945–75. In *Contractor, F. J. and Lorange, P.*, 1988, pp. 111–28.

Gómez, E. Games with Convex Payoff Function in the First Variable. *Int. J. Game Theory*, 1988, *17*(3), pp. 201–04.

Gómez, Luis Carlos. Health Status of the Peruvian Population. In *Zschock, D. K., ed.*, 1988, pp. 15–52.

de Gómez, Martha Isabel; Ramírez, Clara and Reyes, Alvaro. Employment and Labour Incomes in Colombia, 1976–85. In *van Ginneken, W., ed.*, 1988, pp. 33–59.

Gomez-Samper, Henry and Villalba, Julian. A Venezuelan Paradox: The Prospects for Attracting (or Repatriating) Foreign Investment. In *Jorge, A. and Salazar-Carrillo, J., eds.*, 1988, pp. 189–94.

Gómez Villegas, Joaquín. La industria española según su stock de capital: 1964–1981. (With English summary.) *Invest. Econ.*, May 1988, *12*(2), pp. 337–98.

Gomulka, Stanislaw. The Gerschenkron Phenomenon and Systemic Factors in the Post-1975 Growth Slowdown. *Europ. Econ. Rev.*, March 1988, *32*(2–3), pp. 451–58.

_____. Reforms the IMF and the World Bank Should Promote in Poland. In *Marer, P. and Siwinski, W., eds.*, 1988, pp. 279–301.

_____. Soviet Equilibrium Technological Gap and the Post-1975 Productivity Slowdown. *Econ. Planning*, 1988, *22*(1–2), pp. 1–17.

_____ and Rostowski, Jacek. An International Comparison of Material Intensity. *J. Compar. Econ.*, December 1988, *12*(4), pp. 475–501.

Gonçalves, Esmeralda and Gouriéroux, Christian. Agrégation de processus autorégressifs d'ordre 1. (Aggregating Autoregressive Processes. With English summary.) *Ann. Écon. Statist.*, Oct.–Dec. 1988, (12), pp. 127–49.

Gönenç, Rauf. Changing Economics of International Trade in Services. In *Guile, B. R. and Quinn, J. B., eds. (II)*, 1988, pp. 167–86.

Gontier, Jean-Louis and Mathe, Jean-Charles. Gestion de la dimension technologique de l'entreprise: prolongements. (Technological Aspects in Firm Management. Continuation. With English summary.) *Écon. Soc.*, August 1988, 22(8), pp. 37–59.

Gonzales Arrieta, Gerardo M. Interest Rates, Savings, and Growth in LDCs: An Assessment of Recent Empirical Research. *World Devel.*, May 1988, 16(5), pp. 589–605.

González-Bendiksen, Jaime. Tax Treatment of Computer Software: Colombia. In *International Fiscal Association, ed. (II)*, 1988, pp. 281–304.

Gonzalez, Jorge G. Effects of Direct Foreign Investment in the Presence of Sector-Specific Unemployment. *Int. Econ. J.*, Summer 1988, 2(2), pp. 15–27.

González, Norberto. An Economic Policy for Development. *CEPAL Rev.*, April 1988, (34), pp. 7–17.

Gonzalez-Paramo, José M. and Tang, De-Piao. Optimal Intervention in the Presence of "Categorical Equity" Objectives. *Public Finance*, 1988, 43(1), pp. 79–95.

Gonzalez, Roberto and Rofman, Edmundo. On Stochastic Control Problems: An Algorithm for the Value Function and the Optimal Policy— Some Applications. In *Iri, M. and Yajima, K., eds.*, 1988, pp. 80–89.

Gonzalez, Rodolfo A. and Mehay, Stephen L. Non-clearing Labor Markets and Minority Employment in Municipal Government. *J. Lab. Res.*, Spring 1988, 9(2), pp. 127–37.

Good, David. Individuals, Interpersonal Relations, and Trust. In *Gambetta, D., ed.*, 1988, pp. 31–48.

Good, David H. and Pirog-Good, Maureen A. A Simultaneous Probit Model of Crime and Employment for Black and White Teenage Males. In *Simms, M. C. and Myers, S. L., Jr., eds.*, 1988, pp. 109–27.

Goodall, Brian. Changing Patterns and Structure of European Tourism. In *Goodall, B. and Ashworth, G., eds.*, 1988, pp. 18–38.

_____. How Tourists Choose Their Holidays: An Analytical Framework. In *Goodall, B. and Ashworth, G., eds.*, 1988, pp. 1–17.

_____ **and Ashworth, Gregory.** Tourist Images: Marketing Considerations. In *Goodall, B. and Ashworth, G., eds.*, 1988, pp. 213–38.

Goodchild, M. F.; Klinkenberg, B. and Janelle, D. G. Space–Time Diaries and Travel Characteristics for Different Levels of Respondent Aggregation. *Environ. Planning A*, July 1988, 20(7), pp. 891–906.

Goode, Richard. World Tax Reform: A Progress Report: Overview. In *Pechman, J. A., ed.*, 1988, pp. 269–75.

Goodfriend, Marvin. Bureau Analysis and Central Banking: A Review Essay. *J. Monet. Econ.*, November 1988, 22(3), pp. 517–22.

_____. Central Banking under the Gold Standard. *Carnegie–Rochester Conf. Ser. Public Policy*, Autumn 1988, 29, pp. 85–124.

_____. Federal Reserve Interest Rate Smoothing. In *England, C. and Huertas, T., eds.*, 1988, pp. 227–34.

_____. Federal Reserve Interest Rate Smoothing. *Cato J.*, Winter 1988, 7(3), pp. 719–26.

_____. Financial Structure and Aggregate Economic Activity: An Overview: Comment. *J. Money, Credit, Banking*, Part 2, August 1988, 20(3), pp. 589–93.

_____ **and King, Robert G.** Financial Deregulation, Monetary Policy, and Central Banking. *Fed. Res. Bank Richmond Econ. Rev.*, May–June 1988, 74(3), pp. 3–22.

_____ **and King, Robert G.** Financial Deregulation, Monetary Policy, and Central Banking. In *Haraf, W. S. and Kushmeider, R. M., eds.*, 1988, pp. 216–53.

_____ **and McCallum, Bennett T.** Theoretical Analysis of the Demand for Money. *Fed. Res. Bank Richmond Econ. Rev.*, Jan.–Feb. 1988, 74(1), pp. 16–24.

Goodhart, Charles A. E. Bank Insolvency and Deposit Insurance: A Proposal. In *[Frowen, S.]*, 1988, pp. 49–68.

_____. The Costs of Regulation. In *Goodhart, C., et al.*, 1988, pp. 17–31.

_____. The Flexible Exchange Rate System: Experience and Alternatives: Comment. In *Borner, S., ed.*, 1988, pp. 198–208.

_____. The Foreign Exchange Market: A Random Walk with a Dragging Anchor. *Economica*, November 1988, 55(220), pp. 437–60.

_____. The International Transmission of Asset Price Volatility. In *Federal Reserve Bank of Kansas City*, 1988, pp. 79–119.

_____. The Political Economy of Monetary Policy Decisions. *Kredit Kapital*, 1988, 21(1), pp. 1–7.

Goodland, Robert. Management of Cultural Property in Bank Projects. *Finance Develop.*, March 1988, 25(1), pp. 48–49.

Goodman, Allen C. An Econometric Model of Housing Price, Permanent Income, Tenure Choice, and Housing Demand. *J. Urban Econ.*, May 1988, 23(3), pp. 327–53.

Goodman, John and Berridge, John. The British Universities Industrial Relations Association: The First 35 Years. *Brit. J. Ind. Relat.*, July 1988, 26(2), pp. 155–77.

Goodman, John C. and Porter, Philip K. Theory of Competitive Regulatory Equilibrium. *Public Choice*, October 1988, 59(1), pp. 51–66.

Goodman, Laurie S.; Daryanani, Raj and Rones, Arthur. The Credit Exposure of Cross-Currency and Nondollar Interest Rate Swaps. In *Khoury, S. J. and Ghosh, A., eds.*, 1988, pp. 193–203.

_____ **and Vijayaraghavan, N. R.** Combining Various Futures Contracts to Get Better Hedges. In *Fabozzi, F. J., ed.*, 1988, pp. 257–68.

Goodman, Marshall R. Creating a Private-Sector Orientation through Public–Private Partnerships: The Experience of Employment and Training Programmes. In *Hula, R. C., ed.*, 1988, pp. 223–41.

Goodstein, Jerry; Carroll, Glenn R. and Delacroix, Jacques. The Political Environments of Organizations: An Ecological View. In *Staw,*

B. M. and Cummings, L. L., eds., 1988, pp. 359–92.

Goodwin, Craufurd D. The Heterogeneity of the Economists' Discourse: Philosopher, Priest, and Hired Gun. In *Klamer, A.; McCloskey, D. N. and Solow, R. M.*, eds., 1988, pp. 207–20.

Goodwin, H. L., Jr., et al. Factors Affecting Fresh Potato Price in Selected Terminal Markets. *Western J. Agr. Econ.*, December 1988, *13*(2), pp. 233–43.

Goodwin, Richard M. The Multiplier/Accelerator Discretely Revisited. In *[Goodwin, R. M.]*, 1988, pp. 19–29.

———. My Life and Times in the Shadow of Keynes. In *Hamouda, O. F. and Smithin, J. N.*, eds., Vol. 1, 1988, pp. 141–45.

Goodwin, Stacey. Preemption of Private Remedies in Interstate Water Pollution Disputes: *International Paper Company vs. Oullette. Natural Res. J.*, Fall 1988, *28*(4), pp. 863–71.

van Gool, W.; Kümmel, R. and Groscurth, H.-M. Energy Optimization in Industrial Models. In *Iri, M. and Yajima, K.*, eds., 1988, pp. 518–29.

Goolsby, Jerry and Hunt, Shelby D. The Rise and Fall of the Functional Approach to Marketing: A Paradigm Displacement Perspective. In *[Hollander, S. C.]*, 1988, pp. 35–51.

Goossens, Martine; Peeters, Stefaan and Pepermans, Guido. Interwar Unemployment in Belgium. In *Eichengreen, B. and Hatton, T. J.*, eds., 1988, pp. 289–324.

Gootzeit, Michael J. Nominal and Super Inflation in Modern Monetary Theory. *Econ. Notes*, 1988, (2), pp. 37–49.

———. Wicksell on Credit and Inflation. *Amer. Econ.*, Spring 1988, *32*(1), pp. 24–28.

Gopalakrishnan, Chennat. Culture, Economic Development, and Quality of Life: A Speculative Comment on the Case of Kerala, India. *Amer. J. Econ. Soc.*, October 1988, *47*(4), pp. 455–57.

Góra, Zielona and Kisielewicz, Michał. Existence of Optimal Trajectory of Mayer: Problem for Neutral Functional Differential Inclusions. In *Kurzhanski, A.; Neumann, K. and Pallaschke, D.*, eds., 1988, pp. 227–31.

Gordon, Daniel V. The Effect of Price Deregulation on the Competitive Behaviour of Retail Drug Firms. *Appl. Econ.*, May 1988, *20*(5), pp. 641–52.

———; **Singh, Balbir and Bjørndal, Trond.** Economies of Scale in the Norwegian Fish-Meal Industry: Implications for Policy Decisions. *Appl. Econ.*, October 1988, *20*(10), pp. 1321–32.

Gordon, David. In Defense of Rights. In *[Rothbard, M. N.]*, 1988, pp. 229–35.

Gordon, David M. Global Transformation or Decay?: Alternative Perspectives on Recent Changes in the World Economy. In *Mangum, G. and Philips, P.*, eds., 1988, pp. 309–47.

———. The Un-natural Rate of Unemployment: An Econometric Critique of the NAIRU Hy-

pothesis. *Amer. Econ. Rev.*, May 1988, *78*(2), pp. 117–23.

Gordon, Gil E. Corporate Hiring Practices for Telecommuting Homeworkers. In *Christensen, K. E.*, ed., 1988, pp. 65–78.

Gordon, Ian. Evaluating the Effects of Employment Changes on Local Unemployment. *Reg. Stud.*, April 1988, *22*(2), pp. 135–47.

———. Interdistrict Migration in Great Britain 1980–81: A Multistream Model with a Commuting Option. *Environ. Planning A*, July 1988, *20*(7), pp. 907–24.

Gordon, James P. F. and Cowell, Frank A. Unwillingness to Pay: Tax Evasion and Public Good Provision. *J. Public Econ.*, August 1988, *36*(3), pp. 305–21.

Gordon, Kathryn M. European Review of Agricultural Economics: Introduction. *Europ. Rev. Agr. Econ.*, 1988, *15*(4), pp. 305–08.

——— **and Chauveau, Jean-Marie.** World Price Uncertainty and Agricultural Policy Formulation under Rational Expectations. *Europ. Rev. Agr. Econ.*, 1988, *15*(4), pp. 437–56.

Gordon, Lawrence A. and Hamer, Michelle M. Rates of Return and Cash Flow Profiles: An Extension. *Accounting Rev.*, July 1988, *63*(3), pp. 514–21.

Gordon, Myron J. and Costrell, Robert M. Keynesian Models of the Short Run and the Steady State. *J. Econ. (Z. Nationalökon.)*, 1988, *48*(4), pp. 355–73.

Gordon, Patrice L.; McConnell, Virginia D. and Cumberland, John H. Regional Marginal Costs and Cost Savings from Economies of Scale in Municipal Waste Treatment: An Application to the Chesapeake Bay Region. *Growth Change*, Fall 1988, *19*(4), pp. 1–13.

Gordon, Richard K., Jr. Income Tax Compliance and Sanctions in Developing Countries: An Outline of Issues. *Bull. Int. Fiscal Doc.*, January 1988, *42*(1), pp. 3–12.

Gordon, Richard L. Coal in U.S. Land Policy. In *Byrne, J. and Rich, D.*, eds., 1988, pp. 139–72.

Gordon, Robert Aaron. Rigor and Relevance in a Changing Institutional Setting. In *Samuels, W. J.*, ed., Vol. 2, 1988, *1976*, pp. 124–37.

Gordon, Robert J. Back to the Future: European Unemployment Today Viewed from America in 1939. *Brookings Pap. Econ. Act.*, 1988, (1), pp. 271–304.

———. Comments [The Case for Rules in the Conduct of Monetary Policy: A Concrete Example] [The Rules-versus-Discretion Debate in the Light of Recent Experience]. In *Giersch, H.*, ed., 1988, pp. 64–71.

———. Entwicklungen der Konjunkturtheorie in der Nachkriegszeit: Eine konsequent neukeynesianische Perspektive. (Postwar Developments in Business Cycle Theory: An Unabashedly New-Keynesian Perspective. With English summary.) *Ifo-Studien*, 1988, *34*(2–3), pp. 193–221.

———. The Role of Wages in the Inflation Process. *Amer. Econ. Rev.*, May 1988, *78*(2), pp. 276–83.

_____. Wage Gaps versus Output Gaps: Is There a Common Story for All of Europe? In *Giersch, H., ed.*, 1988, pp. 97–151.

_____ and Baily, Martin Neil. The Productivity Slowdown, Measurement Issues, and the Explosion of Computer Power. *Brookings Pap. Econ. Act.*, 1988, (2), pp. 347–420.

Gordon, Roger H. Tax Policy and International Competitiveness: Comment. In *Frenkel, J. A., ed.*, 1988, pp. 380–86.

_____ and Slemrod, Joel. Do We Collect Any Revenue from Taxing Capital Income? In *Summers, L. H., ed.*, 1988, pp. 89–130.

_____ and Varian, Hal R. Intergenerational Risk Sharing. *J. Public Econ.*, November 1988, 37(2), pp. 185–202.

Gordon, Stewart. Burhanpur: Entrepot and Hinterland, 1650–1750. *Indian Econ. Soc. Hist. Rev.*, Oct.–Dec. 1988, 25(4), pp. 425–42.

Gordon, Wendell. Institutionalized Consumption Patterns in Underdeveloped Countries. In *Samuels, W. J., ed., Vol. 3*, 1988, 1973, pp. 289–309.

_____. Welfare Maxima in Economics. In *Samuels, W. J., ed., Vol. 3*, 1988, 1983, pp. 152–67.

Gorelick, Steven M. A Review of Groundwater Management Models. In *O'Mara, G. T., ed.*, 1988, pp. 103–21.

Gorelyi, V. S. Accounting in Cuba. In *Bailey, D. T., ed.*, 1988, pp. 59–75.

Gorini, Stefano. Debt, Wealth and the Rate of Growth: An Exercise in Equilibrium Dynamics. In *Arrow, K. J. and Boskin, M. J., eds.*, 1988, pp. 292–309.

Gorlin, Jacques J. The Business Community and the Uruguay Round. In *Walker, C. E. and Bloomfield, M. A., eds.*, 1988, pp. 170–79.

Gort, Michael and Wall, Richard A. Financial Markets and the Limits of Regulation. *Managerial Dec. Econ.*, March 1988, 9(1), pp. 65–73.

_____ and Wall, Richard A. Foresight and Public Utility Regulation. *J. Polit. Econ.*, February 1988, 96(1), pp. 177–88.

de Gorter, H. and Meilke, Karl D. Impacts of the Common Agricultural Policy on International Wheat Prices. *J. Agr. Econ.*, May 1988, 39(2), pp. 217–29.

Gorton, Gary. Banking Panics and Business Cycles. *Oxford Econ. Pap.*, December 1988, 40(4), pp. 751–81.

Goryunov, Igor Y.; Hitt, Michael A. and Ireland, R. Duane. The Context of Innovation: Investment in R&D and Firm Performance. In *Gattiker, U. E. and Larwood, L., eds.*, 1988, pp. 73–92.

Goss, Ernst. Prior Geographic Mobility and Job Search Length. *Rev. Reg. Stud.*, Winter 1988, 18(1), pp. 49–54.

Goto, Akira; Peck, Merton J. and Levin, Richard C. Picking Losers: Public Policy toward Declining Industries in Japan. In *Shoven, J. B., ed.*, 1988, pp. 195–239.

Goto, Yoshito; Fujii, Nobuo and Muramatsu, Yasuyuki. Second Order Necessary Optimality Conditions for Domain Optimization Problem

with a Neumann Problem. In *Iri, M. and Yajima, K., eds.*, 1988, pp. 259–68.

Gottfried, Robert R. The Effect of Recreation Communities on Local Land Prices: The Case of Beech Mountain. *Amer. Econ.*, Spring 1988, 32(1), pp. 59–65.

Gottfries, Nils and Persson, Torsten. Empirical Examinations of the Information Sets of Economic Agents. *Quart. J. Econ.*, February 1988, 103(1), pp. 251–59.

Gottheil, Fred M. Military Production, Capital Accumulation, and Economic Crisis: A Reply. *J. Post Keynesian Econ.*, Winter 1987–88, 10(2), pp. 318–22.

Gottlieb, Jonathan E. and Pauker, Stephen G. Whether or Not to Administer Amphotericin to an Immunosuppressed Patient with Hematologic Malignancy and Undiagnosed Fever. In *Bell, D. E.; Raiffa, H. and Tversky, A., eds.*, 1988, 1981, pp. 569–87.

Gottret, Pablo E.; Shumway, C. Richard and Saez, Roberto R. Multiproduct Supply and Input Demand in U.S. Agriculture. *Amer. J. Agr. Econ.*, May 1988, 70(2), pp. 330–37.

Gottschalk, Peter. The Impact of Taxes and Transfers on Job Search. *J. Lab. Econ.*, July 1988, 6(3), pp. 362–75.

_____; Smolensky, Eugene and Danziger, Sheldon H. The Declining Significance of Age in the United States: Trends in the Well-Being of Children and the Elderly since 1939. In *Palmer, J. L.; Smeeding, T. and Torrey, B. B., eds.*, 1988, pp. 29–54.

_____; Wissoker, Doug and Berry, Steven. An Error Components Model of the Impact of Plant Closing on Earnings. *Rev. Econ. Statist.*, November 1988, 70(4), pp. 701–07.

Goucher, Candice L. The Impact of German Colonial Rule on the Forests of Togo. In *Richards, J. F. and Tucker, R. P., eds.*, 1988, pp. 56–69.

Goudie, A. W. and Hansen, S. L. The Effect of Dividend Controls on Company Behavior. *Appl. Econ.*, February 1988, 20(2), pp. 143–64.

Gould, Brian W.; Koroluk, Robert M. and Spriggs, John. Separate Crop Accounts for the Western Grain Stabilization Program. *Can. J. Agr. Econ.*, November 1988, 36(3), pp. 443–57.

Gould, Jewell C. and Nelson, F. Howard. Teachers' Unions and Excellence in Education: Comment. *J. Lab. Res.*, Fall 1988, 9(4), pp. 379–87.

Gould, Stephanie G. and Palmer, John L. Outcomes, Interpretations, and Policy Implications. In *Palmer, J. L.; Smeeding, T. and Torrey, B. B., eds.*, 1988, pp. 413–42.

Gould, Stephen J. Consumer Attitudes toward Health and Health Care: A Differential Perspective. *J. Cons. Aff.*, Summer 1988, 22(1), pp. 96–118.

Goulet, Denis. "Development" . . . or Liberation? In *Wilber, C. K., ed.*, 1988, pp. 480–87.

_____ and Wilber, Charles K. The Human Dilemma of Development. In *Wilber, C. K., ed.*, 1988, pp. 459–67.

Gouni, Lucien and Torrion, Phillippe. Risk and Cost of Failure in the French Electricity System. *Energy J.*, Special Issue, 1988, *9*, pp. 33–37.

Gourevitch, Peter. Fascism and Economic Policy Controversies: National Responses to the Global Crisis of the Division of Labor. In *Burke, E., III, ed.*, 1988, *1984*, pp. 183–217.

Gouriéroux, Christian and Gonçalves, Esmeralda. Agrégation de processus autorégressifs d'ordre 1. (Aggregating Autoregressive Processes. With English summary.) *Ann. Écon. Statist.*, Oct.–Dec. 1988, (12), pp. 127–49.

_____ **and Peaucelle, Irina.** Fonctions de production représentatives de fonctions à complémentarité stricte. (With English summary.) *L'Actual. Écon.*, June 1988, *64*(2), pp. 209–30.

Gourlaouen, Jean-Pierre. Une nouvelle exploration de la structure a terme des taux d'interet. (A New Insight into the Term Structure of Interest Rates. With English summary.) *Écon. Soc.*, January 1988, *22*(1), pp. 271–300.

Govind, Har. Promissory Estoppel in Tax Assessments: International. *Bull. Int. Fiscal Doc.*, November 1988, *42*(11), pp. 473–78.

Govindaraju, R. S.; Jones, S. E. and Kavvas, M. L. On the Diffusion Wave Model for Overland Flow 1. Solution for Steep Slopes. *Water Resources Res.*, May 1988, *24*(5), pp. 734–44.

_____ **; Jones, S. E. and Kavvas, M. L.** On the Diffusion Wave Model for Overland Flow 2. Steady State Analysis. *Water Resources Res.*, May 1988, *24*(5), pp. 745–54.

Gow, David D. The Provision of Technical Assistance: A View from the Trenches. *Can. J. Devel. Stud.*, 1988, *9*(1), pp. 81–103.

_____ **and Morss, Elliott R.** The Notorious Nine: Critical Problems in Project Implementation. *World Devel.*, December 1988, *16*(12), pp. 1399–1418.

Gowa, Joanne. Public Goods and Political Institutions: Trade and Monetary Policy Processes in the United States. In *Ikenberry, G. J.; Lake, D. A. and Mastanduno, M., eds.*, 1988, pp. 15–32.

_____. Public Goods and Political Institutions: Trade and Monetary Policy Processes in the United States. *Int. Organ.*, Winter 1988, *42*(1), pp. 15–32.

Gowdy, John M. Entropy and Bioeconomics— The New Paradigm Nicholas Georgescu-Roegen: Review Article. *Int. J. Soc. Econ.*, 1988, *15*(7), pp. 81–84.

_____. The Entropy Law and Marxian Value Theory. *Rev. Radical Polit. Econ.*, Summer–Fall 1988, *20*(2–3), pp. 34–40.

_____; **Funk, Michael and Sveikauskas, Leo.** Urban Productivity: City Size or Industry Size. *J. Reg. Sci.*, May 1988, *28*(2), pp. 185–202.

_____ **and Yesilada, Atilla.** Decision Making under Conditions of Turbulence and Uncertainty: The Case of the Kinked Demand Curve. *Eastern Econ. J.*, Oct.–Dec. 1988, *14*(4), pp. 399–408.

Gowland, David H. The Process of Financial Deregulation after the Recent World Stock Market Crisis. *Rev. Econ. Cond. Italy*, Sept.–Dec. 1988, (3), pp. 353–69.

Goyder, Catherine and Goyder, Hugh. Case Studies of Famine: Ethiopia. In *Curtis, D.; Hubbard, M. and Shepherd, A.*, 1988, pp. 73–110.

Goyder, Hugh and Goyder, Catherine. Case Studies of Famine: Ethiopia. In *Curtis, D.; Hubbard, M. and Shepherd, A.*, 1988, pp. 73–110.

Graafland, Johann J. Hysteresis in Unemployment in the Netherlands. *De Economist*, 1988, *136*(4), pp. 508–38.

Grabowski, Richard. Early Japanese Development: The Role of Trade, 1885–1940. *Quart. J. Bus. Econ.*, Winter 1988, *27*(1), pp. 104–29.

_____. Economies of Scale in Agriculture and the Ray-Homothetic Production Function: An Empirical Illustration from the Philippines. *Singapore Econ. Rev.*, October 1988, *33*(2), pp. 40–48.

_____. The Theory of Induced Institutional Innovation: A Critique. *World Devel.*, March 1988, *16*(3), pp. 385–94.

_____ **and Aly, Hassan Y.** Technical Change, Technical Efficiency, and Input Usage in Taiwanese Agricultural Growth. *Appl. Econ.*, July 1988, *20*(7), pp. 889–99.

_____ **and Pasurka, Carl.** Farmer Education and Economic Efficiency: Northern Farms in 1860. *Econ. Letters*, 1988, *28*(4), pp. 315–20.

_____ **and Pasurka, Carl.** The Relative Technical Efficiency of Northern and Southern U.S. Farms in 1860. *Southern Econ. J.*, January 1988, *54*(3), pp. 598–614.

_____ **and Pasurka, Carl.** The Technical Efficiency of Japanese Agriculture, 1878–1940. *Devel. Econ.*, June 1988, *26*(2), pp. 172–86.

Grachev, M. The Management of Labor under New Conditions of Economic Growth. *Prob. Econ.*, November 1988, *31*(7), pp. 34–57.

Graddy, Duane B. and Homaifar, Ghassem. Equity Yields in Models Considering Higher Moments of the Return Distribution. *Appl. Econ.*, March 1988, *20*(3), pp. 325–34.

Gradstein, Mark and Nitzan, Shmuel. Participation, Decision Aggregation and Internal Information Gathering in Organizational Decision Making. *J. Econ. Behav. Organ.*, December 1988, *10*(4), pp. 415–31.

_____; **Spiegel, Uriel and Ben Zion, Uri.** Financing of Public Goods and Noncooperative Theory of Bargaining. *J. Public Econ.*, December 1988, *37*(3), pp. 345–57.

Grady, Dennis O. Governors and Markets: Corporate Recruitment from the Gubernatorial Perspective. In *Hula, R. C., ed.*, 1988, pp. 43–55.

Grady, Mark F. Common Law Control of Strategic Behavior: Railroad Sparks and the Farmer. *J. Legal Stud.*, January 1988, *17*(1), pp. 15–42.

Grady, William R.; McLaughlin, Steven D. and

Hayward, Mark D. Changes in the Retirement Process among Older Men in the United States: 1972–1980. *Demography*, August 1988, 25(3), pp. 371–86.

Graeser, Paul. Human Capital in a Centrally Planned Economy: Evidence. *Kyklos*, 1988, 41(1), pp. 75–98.

Graetz, Michael J. and Sunley, Emil M. Minimum Taxes and Comprehensive Tax Reform. In *Aaron, H. J.; Galper, H. and Pechman, J. A., eds.*, 1988, pp. 385–419.

Graf v. d. Schulenburg, J.-Matthias. Hospital Finance in Switzerland: Comment. In *Furubotn, E. G. and Richter, R., eds.*, 1988, pp. 121–30.

_____ **and Schlesinger, Harris.** Mehr Markt im Gesundheitswesen. (With English summary.) *J. Inst. Theoretical Econ.*, April 1988, 144(2), pp. 396–402.

Graff, Gordon. Ceramics Take on Tough Tasks. In *Forester, T., ed.*, 1988, 1983, pp. 179–92.

_____ . High-Performance Plastics. In *Forester, T., ed.*, 1988, 1986, pp. 203–13.

Graham, Avy D. How Has Vesting Changed since Passage of Employee Retirement Income Security Act? *Mon. Lab. Rev.*, August 1988, 111(8), pp. 20–25.

Graham, Fred C. The Fisher Hypothesis: A Critique of Recent Results and Some New Evidence. *Southern Econ. J.*, April 1988, 54(4), pp. 961–68.

Graham, J. D. and Borth, D. An Inventory Evaluation Approach for Common Use Stock Range Units in British Columbia. *Can. J. Agr. Econ.*, July 1988, 36(2), pp. 279–94.

_____ **and MacGregor, R. J.** The Impact of Lower Grains and Oilseeds Prices on Canada's Grains Sector: A Regional Programming Approach. *Can. J. Agr. Econ.*, March 1988, 36(1), pp. 51–67.

_____ ; **Webber, C. A. and MacGregor, R. J.** A Regional Analysis of Direct Government Assistance Programs in Canada and Their Impacts on the Beef and Hog Sectors. *Can. J. Agr. Econ.*, Part 2, December 1988, 36(4), pp. 915–28.

Graham, John D. Injury Control, Traffic Safety, and Evaluation Research. In *Graham, J. D., ed.*, 1988, pp. 1–23.

_____ **and Henrion, Max.** Choosing Automatic Restraint Designs for the 1990s. In *Graham, J. D., ed.*, 1988, pp. 90–100.

_____ **and Latimer, Eric.** Themes and Future Directions. In *Graham, J. D., ed.*, 1988, pp. 263–76.

Graham, John L. Buyer–Seller Negotiations around the Pacific Rim: Differences in Fundamental Exchange Processes. *J. Cons. Res.*, June 1988, 15(1), pp. 48–54.

_____ . Deference Given the Buyer: Variations across Twelve Cultures. In *Contractor, F. J. and Lorange, P.*, 1988, pp. 473–85.

Graham, John W. and Beller, Andrea H. Child Support Payments: Evidence from Repeated Cross Sections. *Amer. Econ. Rev.*, May 1988, 78(2), pp. 81–85.

_____ **and Bradley, Michael G.** Education and Asset Composition. *Econ. Educ. Rev.*, 1988, 7(2), pp. 209–20.

Graham, Loren R. The Soviet Union Today: Science Policy and Organization. In *Cracraft, J., ed.*, 1988, pp. 223–33.

Graham, Margaret B. W. R&D and Competition in England and the United States: The Case of the Aluminum Dirigible. *Bus. Hist. Rev.*, Summer 1988, 62(2), pp. 261–85.

Graham, Otis, Jr. Immigration and the National Interest. In *Simcox, D. E., ed.*, 1988, pp. 124–36.

Graham, Stanley L. and Boyd, John H. The Profitability and Risk Effects of Allowing Bank Holding Companies to Merge with Other Financial Firms: A Simulation Study. *Fed. Res. Bank Minn. Rev.*, Spring 1988, 12(2), pp. 3–20.

Graham-Tomasi, Theodore. A Theoretical and Empirical Approach to the Value of Information in Risky Markets: A Comment. *Rev. Econ. Statist.*, August 1988, 70(3), pp. 543–45.

Grahl, John. Productivity Slowdown and Financial Tensions. In *Arestis, P., ed.*, 1988, pp. 183–218.

_____ **and Ganley, Joe.** Competition and Efficiency in Refuse Collection: A Critical Comment. *Fisc. Stud.*, February 1988, 9(1), pp. 80–85.

Grais, Bernard. A Sample Rotation Plan for the Community Labour Force Survey: Lessons Learned from Experience in France. *Econ. Lavoro*, Oct.–Dec. 1988, 22(4), pp. 3–32.

Gram, Harvey N. Duality and Positive Profits. In *Steedman, I., ed., Vol. 2*, 1988, 1985, pp. 162–78.

_____ . Two-Sector Models in the Theory of Capital and Growth. In *Steedman, I., ed., Vol. 1*, 1988, 1976, pp. 174–86.

Gramatzki, Hans-Erich. Employment Policy in the USSR—Limitations on Enterprises' Personnel and Wage Policies. In *Dlugos, G.; Dorow, W. and Weiermair, K., eds.*, 1988, pp. 247–59.

Gramm, Cynthia L.; Hendricks, Wallace E. and Kahn, Lawrence M. Inflation Uncertainty and Strike Activity. *Ind. Relat.*, Winter 1988, 27(1), pp. 114–29.

Gramm, Warren S. The Movement from Real to Abstract Value Theory, 1817–1959. *Cambridge J. Econ.*, June 1988, 12(2), pp. 225–46.

_____ . Rise and Decline of the Maximization Principle. *J. Behav. Econ.*, Fall 1988, 17(3), pp. 157–72.

Grammatikos, Theoharry; Makhija, Anil K. and Thompson, Howard E. Financing Corporate Takeovers by Individuals Seeking Control. *Managerial Dec. Econ.*, September 1988, 9(3), pp. 227–35.

Granbois, Donald H. and Olshavsky, Richard W. Consumer Decision Making—Fact or Fiction? In *Earl, P. E., ed., Vol. 2*, 1988, 1979, pp. 160–67.

Grandinetti, L. and Conforti, D. An Experience

of Advanced Computation Techniques in the Solution of Nonlinearly Constrained Optimization Problems. In *Kurzhanski, A.; Neumann, K. and Pallaschke, D., eds.*, 1988, pp. 69–85.

Grandmont, Jean Michel. Continuity Properties of a von Neumann-Morgenstern Utility. In *Grandmont, J.-M., ed.*, 1988, *1972*, pp. 87–99.

_____. On the Short-Run Equilibrium in a Monetary Economy. In *Grandmont, J.-M., ed.*, 1988, *1974*, pp. 165–80.

_____. Temporary Equilibrium Theory: An Addendum. In *Grandmont, J.-M., ed.*, 1988, pp. 41–84.

_____. Temporary General Equilibrium Theory. In *Grandmont, J.-M., ed.*, 1988, *1977*, pp. 3–40.

_____ **and Hildenbrand, Werner.** Stochastic Processes of Temporary Equilibria. In *Grandmont, J.-M., ed.*, 1988, *1974*, pp. 307–37.

_____; **Laroque, Guy and Younes, Yves.** Equilibrium with Quantity Rationing and Recontracting. In *Grandmont, J.-M., ed.*, 1988, *1978*, pp. 404–22.

_____ **and Younes, Yves.** On the Efficiency of a Monetary Equilibrium. In *Grandmont, J.-M., ed.*, 1988, *1973*, pp. 199–215.

_____ **and Younes, Yves.** On the Role of Money and the Existence of a Monetary Equilibrium. In *Grandmont, J.-M., ed.*, 1988, *1972*, pp. 181–98.

Grandstaff, Peter J.; Ferris, Mark E. and Chou, Shuh S. Forecasting Competitive Behavior: An Assessment of AT&T's Incentive to Extend Its U.S. Network. *Int. J. Forecasting*, 1988, *4*(4), pp. 521–33.

de la Grandville, Olivier. Strokes of Genius. *J. Macroecon.*, Fall 1988, *10*(4), pp. 493–95.

Granger, C. Fuzzy Reasoning for Classification: An Expert System Approach. In *Gaul, W. and Schader, M., eds.*, 1988, pp. 174–84.

Granger, Clive W. J. Causality, Cointegration, and Control. *J. Econ. Dynam. Control*, June–Sept. 1988, *12*(2–3), pp. 551–59.

_____. Some Comments on Econometric Methodology. *Econ. Rec.*, December 1988, *64*(187), pp. 327–30.

_____. Some Recent Developments in a Concept of Causality. *J. Econometrics*, Sept.–Oct. 1988, *39*(1–2), pp. 199–211.

Granick, David. Property Rights vs. Transaction Costs in Comparative Systems Analysis. *J. Inst. Theoretical Econ.*, December 1988, *144*(5), pp. 871–77.

Granovetter, Mark. The Sociological and Economic Approaches to Labor Market Analysis: A Social Structural View. In *Farkas, G. and England, P., eds.*, 1988, pp. 187–216.

Grant, John H. Strategy in Research and Practice. In *Grant, J. H., ed.*, 1988, pp. 5–15.

Grant, K. Gary. Producer–Consumer Trade-offs in Export Cartels: The Wheat Cartel Case: Comment. *Amer. J. Agr. Econ.*, November 1988, *70*(4), pp. 944–45.

Grant, Lindsey. How Many Americans? In *Simcox, D. E., ed.*, 1988, pp. 269–82.

Grant, Warren R.; Rister, M. Edward and Brorsen, B. Wade. Some Effects of Rice Quality on Rough Rice Prices. *Southern J. Agr. Econ.*, July 1988, *20*(1), pp. 131–40.

Granziol, Markus J. and Holzgang, Anna. The Contribution of Inflation to the Level and the Variability of Nominal Interest Rates: Some Multi-country Evidence. *Schweiz. Z. Volkswirtsch. Statist.*, December 1988, *124*(4), pp. 559–73.

Grasso, Fabio. Su un'applicazione del metodo degli scenari: Un modello previsionale per il numbero delle pensioni afferenti al fondo pensioni dei lavoratori dipendenti del settore privato. (On the Application of the Scenario Method: A Forecasting Model for the Number of Pensions Pertaining to the Private Sector Employers Pensions Fund. With English summary.) *Econ. Lavoro*, Oct.–Dec. 1988, *22*(4), pp. 103–18.

Graumann, U. Concepts for the Identification of Suitable Videotex Information. In *Schiefer, G., ed.*, 1988, pp. 191–94.

_____ **and Christiansen, M.** Current Developments: Closed User Group Plant Production: A New Service of TELE AGRAR. In *Schiefer, G., ed.*, 1988, pp. 173–76.

_____ **and Römer, B.** Videotex Activities in European Agriculture—An Overview. In *Schiefer, G., ed.*, 1988, pp. 33–45.

Gravelle, Jane G. Minimum Taxes and Comprehensive Tax Reform: Comments. In *Aaron, H. J.; Galper, H. and Pechman, J. A., eds.*, 1988, pp. 419–29.

_____. U.S. Taxes and Trade Performance: Discussion. *Nat. Tax J.*, September 1988, *41*(3), pp. 341–42.

Gravelle, Pierre. Tax Treaties: Concepts, Objectives and Types: Canada. *Bull. Int. Fiscal Doc.*, December 1988, *42*(12), pp. 522–26.

Graves, Adrian. Crisis and Change in the Australian Sugar Industry, 1914–1939. In *Albert, B. and Graves, A., eds.*, 1988, pp. 142–56.

_____ **and Albert, Bill.** The World Sugar Economy in War and Depression: 1914–40: Introduction. In *Albert, B. and Graves, A., eds.*, 1988, pp. 1–25.

Graves, Peter E.; Sexton, Robert L. and Lee, Dwight R. On Mandatory Deposits, Fines, and the Control of Litter. *Natural Res. J.*, Fall 1988, *28*(4), pp. 837–47.

Graves, Philip E. and Knapp, Thomas A. Mobility Behavior of the Elderly. *J. Urban Econ.*, July 1988, *24*(1), pp. 1–8.

_____, **et al.** The Robustness of Hedonic Price Estimation: Urban Air Quality. *Land Econ.*, August 1988, *64*(3), pp. 220–33.

Graves, Ronald L. and Brada, Josef C. The Slowdown in Soviet Defense Expenditures. *Southern Econ. J.*, April 1988, *54*(4), pp. 969–84.

Gray, Cheryl W. and Linn, Johannes F. Improving Public Finance for Development. *Finance Develop.*, September 1988, *25*(3), pp. 2–5.

Gray, H. Peter. Intra-industry Trade: An "Untidy" Phenomenon. *Weltwirtsch. Arch.*, 1988, *124*(2), pp. 221–29.

Gray, Jack. The State and the Rural Economy in the Chinese People's Republic. In *White, G., ed.*, 1988, pp. 193–234.

Gray, Jo Anna. Wage Rigidity and Unemployment: A Review Essay. *J. Monet. Econ.*, September 1988, *22*(2), pp. 335–42.

Gray, John. Hayek, the Scottish School, and Contemporary Economics. In *Winston, G. C. and Teichgraeber, R. F., III, eds.*, 1988, pp. 53–70.

Gray, Patricia and Singer, Hans W. Trade Policy and Growth of Developing Countries: Some New Data. *World Devel.*, March 1988, *16*(3), pp. 395–403.

Gray, Ronald H. Fundamentals of the Epidemiologic and Demographic Transitions. In *Siragel-din, I. and Sorkin, A., eds.*, 1988, pp. 25–42.

Graziano, Loretta. Economic Measurement, Public Policy, and Human Cognition: An Analytical Framework. In *Maital, S., ed., Vol. 2*, 1988, pp. 784–811.

Graziosi, Andrea. Economisti sovietici degli anni venti. (With English summary.) *Stud. Econ.*, 1988, *43*(35), pp. 129–45.

Grbich, Yuri and Walker, Marilyn. The Tax Code Needs Rewriting. *Australian Tax Forum*, 1988, *5*(3), pp. 385–94.

Greaney, Thomas L. Competitive Reform in Health Care: The Vulnerable Revolution. *Yale J. Regul.*, Winter 1988, *5*(1), pp. 179–213.

Green, A. E.; Owen, D. W. and Coombes, M. G. Substantive Issues in the Definition of 'Localities': Evidence from Sub-group Local Labour Market Areas in the West Midlands. *Reg. Stud.*, August 1988, *22*(4), pp. 303–18.

Green, Alan G. and MacKinnon, Mary. Unemployment and relief in Canada. In *Eichengreen, B. and Hatton, T. J., eds.*, 1988, pp. 353–96.

_____ **and Sparks, Gordon R.** A Macro Interpretation of Recovery: Australia and Canada. In *Gregory, R. G. and Butlin, N. G., eds.*, 1988, pp. 89–112.

Green, Christopher J. Adjustment Costs and Mean–Variance Efficiency in UK Financial Markets. In *Motamen, H., ed.*, 1988, pp. 119–40.

_____ **and Keating, Giles.** Capital Asset Pricing under Alternative Policy Regimes. *Econ. Modelling*, April 1988, *5*(2), pp. 133–44.

Green, D. Hayden. Panel: The Role of Various Organizations in Consumer Education: The Role of Secondary Schools. In *Maynes, E. S. and ACCI Research Committee, eds.*, 1988, pp. 819–29.

Green, David Jay. A Demand-Determined Model of the Residual Fuel Oil Market. *Energy Econ.*, April 1988, *10*(2), pp. 125–39.

_____. The World Oil Market: An Examination Using Small-Scale Models. *Energy J.*, July 1988, *9*(3), pp. 61–77.

Green, Francis. Neoclassical and Marxian Conceptions of Production. *Cambridge J. Econ.*, September 1988, *12*(3), pp. 299–312.

_____. The Trade Union Wage Gap in Britain: Some New Estimates. *Econ. Letters*, 1988, *27*(2), pp. 183–87.

_____ **and Potepan, Michael J.** Vacation Time and Unionism in the U.S. and Europe. *Ind. Relat.*, Spring 1988, *27*(2), pp. 180–94.

Green, Gary P. and McNamara, Kevin T. Traditional and Non-traditional Opportunities and Alternatives for Local Economic Development. In *Beaulieu, L. J., ed.*, 1988, pp. 288–303.

Green, Janet M. and Hirsch, Werner Z. Anti-strike Laws and Their Effects on Work Stoppages by Public School Teachers. *J. Urban Econ.*, November 1988, *24*(3), pp. 331–51.

Green, Jerry R. Demographics, Market Failure, and Social Security. In *Wachter, S. M., ed.*, 1988, pp. 3–16.

_____. Share Repurchases and Acquisitions: An Analysis of Which Firms Participate: Comment. In *Auerbach, A. J., ed. (I)*, 1988, pp. 217–20.

_____. Temporary General Equilibrium in a Sequential Trading Model with Spot and Futures Transactions. In *Grandmont, J.-M., ed.*, 1988, *1973*, pp. 115–35.

_____ **and Jullien, Bruno.** Ordinal Independence in Nonlinear Utility Theory. *J. Risk Uncertainty*, December 1988, *1*(4), pp. 355–87.

Green, Mick. A Modelling Approach to Multiple Correspondence Analysis. In *Edwards, D. and Raun, N. E., eds.*, 1988, pp. 317–22.

Green, Paul E.; Carmone, F. J., Jr. and Schaffer, C. M. An Individual Importance Weights Model for Conjoint Analysis. In *Gaul, W. and Schader, M., eds.*, 1988, pp. 250–57.

_____; **Helsen, Kristiaan and Shandler, Bruce.** Conjoint Internal Validity under Alternative Profile Presentations. *J. Cons. Res.*, December 1988, *15*(3), pp. 392–97.

_____; **Krieger, Abba M. and Schaffer, C. M.** Dominated Options in Consumer Tradeoff Modeling: Is Their Occurrence Recognized? In *Gaul, W. and Schader, M., eds.*, 1988, pp. 258–67.

Green, Reginald Herbold. Unmanageable—Toward Sub-Saharan African Debt Bargaining? In *Griffith-Jones, S., ed.*, 1988, pp. 245–81.

Green, Richard K. and Baldwin, Robert E. The Effects of Protection on Domestic Output. In *Baldwin, R. E., ed. (II)*, 1988, pp. 205–26.

Green, Sharon L.; Lewis, Barry L. and Patton, James M. The Effects of Information Choice and Information Use on Analysts' Predictions of Municipal Bond Rating Changes. *Accounting Rev.*, April 1988, *63*(2), pp. 270–82.

Greenawalt, Mary Brady and Sinkey, Joseph F., Jr. Bank Loan-Loss Provisions and the Income-Smoothing Hypothesis: An Empirical Analysis, 1976–84. *J. Finan. Services Res.*, December 1988, *1*(4), pp. 301–18.

Greenaway, David. Economic Development and International Trade: An Introduction. In *Greenaway, D., ed.*, 1988, pp. 1–5.

_____. Effective Tariff Protection in the United Kingdom. *Oxford Bull. Econ. Statist.*, August 1988, *50*(3), pp. 313–24.

_____. Evaluating the Structure of Protection in Less Developed Countries. In *Greenaway, D., ed.*, 1988, pp. 77–94.

_____. Intra-industry Trade, Intra-firm Trade and European Integration: Evidence, Gains and Policy Aspects. In *Dunning, J. and Robson, P., eds.*, 1988, pp. 51–70.

_____ and Milner, Chris. Intra Industry Trade and the Shifting of Protection across Sectors. *Europ. Econ. Rev.*, April 1988, *32*(4), pp. 927–45.

_____ and Milner, Chris. Some Features of 'True Protection': A Reply. *J. Devel. Stud.*, October 1988, *25*(1), pp. 122–25.

_____ and Nam, Chong Hyun. Industrialisation and Macroeconomic Performance in Developing Countries under Alternative Trade Strategies. *Kyklos*, 1988, *41*(3), pp. 419–35.

Greenbaum, Stuart I. and Akella, Srinivas R. Savings and Loan Ownership Structure and Expense-Preference. *J. Banking Finance*, September 1988, *12*(3), pp. 419–37.

Greenberg, David I. The Reality of Modern Product Liability Law: Compensating the Injured Consumer. In *Maynes, E. S. and ACCI Research Committee, eds.*, 1988, pp. 797–99.

Greenberg, Edward and Denzau, Arthur T. Profit and Expenditure Functions in Basic Public Finance: An Expository Note. *Econ. Inquiry*, January 1988, *26*(1), pp. 145–58.

Greenberg, Joseph. Payoffs in Generalized Sequential Bargaining Games. *Econ. Letters*, 1988, *28*(1), pp. 33–35.

_____. A Strategic Aspect of the Strong Positive Association Condition. *Econ. Letters*, 1988, *26*(3), pp. 225–26.

_____ and Shitovitz, Benyamin. Consistent Voting Rules for Competitive Local Public Goods Economies. *J. Econ. Theory*, December 1988, *46*(2), pp. 223–36.

Greenberg, Maurice R. The United States and World Services Trade. In *Feldstein, M., ed. (II)*, 1988, pp. 407–13.

Greenberg, Warren. Competition in the Health Care Sector: Ten Years Later: Introduction. In *Greenberg, W., ed.*, 1988, pp. 1–3.

_____ and Goldberg, Lawrence G. Health Insurance without Provider Influence: The Limits of Cost Containment. In *Greenberg, W., ed.*, 1988, pp. 71–81.

Greene, David. Agricultural Performance and Policy in India: A Brief Overview and Some Lessons. In *Roberts, C., ed.*, 1988, pp. 93–99.

Greenfield, Patricia A. The NLRB's Deferral to Arbitration before and after *Olin:* An Empirical Analysis. *Ind. Lab. Relat. Rev.*, October 1988, *42*(1), pp. 34–49.

Greenhalgh, Leonard. Managing Conflict. In *Timpe, A. D., ed.*, 1988, *1986*, pp. 324–33.

_____; Jick, Todd and McKersie, Robert B. Change and Continuity: The Role of a Labor–Management Committee in Facilitating Work Force Change during Retrenchment. In *Lewin, D., et al., eds.*, 1988, *1981*, pp. 569–80.

Greenhalgh, Susan. Families and Networks in Taiwan's Economic Development. In *Winck-*

ler, E. A. and Greenhalgh, S., eds., 1988, pp. 224–45.

_____. Fertility as Mobility: Sinic Transitions. *Population Devel. Rev.*, December 1988, *14*(4), pp. 629–74.

_____. Supranational Processes of Income Distribution. In *Winckler, E. A. and Greenhalgh, S., eds.*, 1988, pp. 67–100.

_____ and Winckler, Edwin A. Analytical Issues and Historical Episodes. In *Winckler, E. A. and Greenhalgh, S., eds.*, 1988, pp. 3–19.

Greenhut, M. L. and Phillips, Owen R. A Path to Efficiently Regulated Transport Rates. *Int. J. Transport Econ.*, October 1988, *15*(3), pp. 243–55.

Greenman, Jonathan V. Asymmetry in Conversation: A Capital Stock Analysis. In *Motamen, H., ed.*, 1988, pp. 245–64.

Greenspan, Alan. Coordination Could Be Washed Out. In *Melamed, L., ed.*, 1988, *1986*, pp. 441–44.

_____. Excerpts from the Council of Economic Advisors *Report to the President*, 1975, 1976, 1977. In *Melamed, L., ed.*, 1988, pp. 297–328.

_____. Innovation and Regulation of Banks in the 1990s. *Fed. Res. Bull.*, December 1988, *74*(12), pp. 783–87.

_____. Prospects for International Economic Cooperation. In *Feldstein, M., ed. (I)*, 1988, pp. 61–65.

_____. Statement to the Joint Economic Committee, March 15, 1988. *Fed. Res. Bull.*, May 1988, *74*(5), pp. 301–04.

_____. Statement to the U.S. House Committee on Banking, Finance and Urban Affairs, February 23, 1988. *Fed. Res. Bull.*, April 1988, *74*(4), pp. 225–31.

_____. Statement to the U.S. House Subcommittee on Financial Institutions Supervision, Regulation and Insurance of the Committee on Banking, Finance and Urban Affairs, November 18, 1987. *Fed. Res. Bull.*, January 1988, *74*(1), pp. 20–27.

_____. Statement to the U.S. House Subcommittee on Telecommunications and Finance of the Committee on Energy and Commerce, May 19, 1988. *Fed. Res. Bull.*, July 1988, *74*(7), pp. 445–50.

_____. Statement to the U.S. House Subcommittees on Domestic Monetary Policy and on International Finance, Trade and Monetary Policy of the Committee on Banking, Finance and Urban Affairs, December 18, 1987. *Fed. Res. Bull.*, February 1988, *74*(2), pp. 103–05.

_____. Statement to the U.S. Senate, Committee on Banking, Housing, and Urban Affairs, December 1, 1987. *Fed. Res. Bull.*, February 1988, *74*(2), pp. 91–103.

_____. Statement to the U.S. Senate Committee on Banking, Housing, and Urban Affairs, March 31, 1988. *Fed. Res. Bull.*, May 1988, *74*(5), pp. 312–16.

_____. Statement to the U.S. Senate Committee on Banking, Housing, and Urban Affairs, February 2, 1988. *Fed. Res. Bull.*, April 1988, *74*(4), pp. 217–25.

———. Statement to the U.S. Senate Committee on Banking, Housing, and Urban Affairs, July 13, 1988. *Fed. Res. Bull.*, September 1988, 74(9), pp. 607–13.

———. Statement to the U.S. Senate Committee on the Budget, March 2, 1988. *Fed. Res. Bull.*, May 1988, 74(5), pp. 293–97.

Greenspan, David. College Football's Biggest Fumble: The Economic Impact of the Supreme Court's Decision in *National Collegiate Athletic Association v. Board of Regents of the University of Oklahoma. Antitrust Bull.*, Spring 1988, 33(1), pp. 1–65.

Greenspan, Edward L. Tax Evasion Is a Crime! In *Canadian Tax Foundation*, 1988, pp. 1.1–9.

Greenstein, Robert and Hutchinson, Frederick. State Tax Relief for Low-Income People. In *Gold, S. D., ed.*, 1988, pp. 153–76.

Greenwald, Bruce C. and Stein, Jeremy. The Task Force Report: The Reasoning behind the Recommendations. *J. Econ. Perspectives*, Summer 1988, 2(3), pp. 3–23.

——— **and Stiglitz, Joseph E.** Examining Alternative Macroeconomic Theories. *Brookings Pap. Econ. Act.*, 1988, (1), pp. 207–60.

——— **and Stiglitz, Joseph E.** Imperfect Information, Finance Constraints, and Business Fluctuations. In *Kohn, M. and Tsiang, S.-C., eds.*, 1988, pp. 103–40.

——— **and Stiglitz, Joseph E.** Money, Imperfect Information, and Economic Fluctuations. In *Kohn, M. and Tsiang, S.-C., eds.*, 1988, pp. 141–65.

——— **and Stiglitz, Joseph E.** Pareto Inefficiency of Market Economies: Search and Efficiency Wage Models. *Amer. Econ. Rev.*, May 1988, 78(2), pp. 351–55.

Greenwood, Daphne T. A Comment on *Evolutionary Economics I: Foundations of Institutionalist Thought. J. Econ. Issues*, March 1988, 22(1), pp. 249–51.

——— **and Wolff, Edward N.** Relative Wealth Holdings of Children and the Elderly in the United States, 1962–83. In *Palmer, J. L.; Smeeding, T. and Torrey, B. B., eds.*, 1988, pp. 123–48.

Greenwood, Jeremy. Indexing, Inflation, and Economic Policy: A Review Essay. *J. Monet. Econ.*, July 1988, 22(1), pp. 165–73.

———; **Hercowitz, Zvi and Huffman, Gregory W.** Investment, Capacity Utilization, and the Real Business Cycle. *Amer. Econ. Rev.*, June 1988, 78(3), pp. 402–17.

——— **and Huffman, Gregory W.** On Modelling the Natural Rate of Unemployment with Indivisible Labour. *Can. J. Econ.*, August 1988, 21(3), pp. 587–609.

Greenwood, John G. Monetary Policy in Thailand. In *Cheng, H.-S., ed.*, 1988, pp. 303–19.

Greenwood, Justin; Williams, Allan M. and Shaw, Gareth. The United Kingdom: Market Responses and Public Policy. In *Williams, A. M. and Shaw, G., eds.*, 1988, pp. 162–79.

Greenwood, Michael J. Changing Patterns of Migration and Regional Economic Growth in the U.S.: A Demographic Perspective. *Growth Change*, Fall 1988, 19(4), pp. 68–87.

Greenwood, Ronald G. and Wrege, Charles. The War against Isolated Plants by Central Stations, 1901–1918. In *Perkins, E. J., ed.*, 1988, pp. 189–99.

Greer, Charles R. and Labig, Chalmer E., Jr. Grievance Initiation: A Literature Survey and Suggestions for Future Research. *J. Lab. Res.*, Winter 1988, 9(1), pp. 1–27.

Greer, Douglas F. The Concentration of Economic Power. In *Peterson, W. C., ed.*, 1988, pp. 53–81.

Greer, R. Clyde and Urick, J. J. An Annual Model of Purebred Breeding Bull Price. *Western J. Agr. Econ.*, July 1988, 13(1), pp. 1–6.

Gregersen, Birgitte. Public-Sector Participation in Innovation Systems. In *Freeman, C. and Lundvall, B.-A., eds.*, 1988, pp. 262–78.

Gregg, Alison; Gagnon, Christopher and Doorley, Thomas H. Professional Services Firms and Information Technology: Ongoing Search for Sustained Competitive Advantage. In *Guile, B. R. and Quinn, J. B., eds. (I)*, 1988, pp. 175–94.

Gregg, Paul A.; Britton, Andrew and Joyce, Michael. The Home Economy. *Nat. Inst. Econ. Rev.*, November 1988, (126), pp. 6–17.

———; **Britton, Andrew and Joyce, Michael.** The Home Economy. *Nat. Inst. Econ. Rev.*, August 1988, (125), pp. 6–22.

——— **and Machin, S. J.** Unions and the Incidence of Performance Linked Pay Schemes in Britain. *Int. J. Ind. Organ.*, March 1988, 6(1), pp. 97–107.

——— **and Worswick, G. D. N.** Recession and Recovery in Britain: The 1930s and the 1980s. *Nat. Inst. Econ. Rev.*, November 1988, (126), pp. 44–50.

Gregg, S. R.; Mulvey, J. M. and Wolpert, J. A Stochastic Planning System for Siting and Closing Public Service Facilities. *Environ. Planning A*, January 1988, 20(1), pp. 83–98.

Gregorowicz, Philip; Hegji, Charles E. and Deravi, M. Keivan. Balance of Trade Announcements and Movements in Exchange Rates. *Southern Econ. J.*, October 1988, 55(2), pp. 279–87.

Gregory, Gene. New Materials Technology in Japan. In *Forester, T., ed.*, 1988, 1987, pp. 119–40.

Gregory, Paul R. and Collier, Irwin L., Jr. Unemployment in the Soviet Union: Evidence from the Soviet Interview Project. *Amer. Econ. Rev.*, September 1988, 78(4), pp. 613–32.

——— **and Kohlhase, Janet E.** The Earnings of Soviet Workers: Evidence from the Soviet Interview Project. *Rev. Econ. Statist.*, February 1988, 70(1), pp. 23–35.

Gregory, Robert G. Recovery from the Depression: An Overview. In *Gregory, R. G. and Butlin, N. G., eds.*, 1988, pp. 1–32.

———. A Sad and Sorry Story: Industry Policy for the Australian Motor Vehicle Industry. In *Spence, A. M. and Hazard, H. A., eds.*, 1988, pp. 173–96.

———. Some Recent Developments in Macro-econometric Modelling in the United Kingdom: Comment. *Australian Econ. Pap.*, Supplement, June 1988, *27*, pp. 26–28.

———; Ho, V. and McDermott, L. Sharing the Burden: The Australian Labour Market during the 1930s. In *Gregory, R. G. and Butlin, N. G., eds.*, 1988, pp. 217–44.

———, et al. The Australian and U.S. Labour Markets in the 1930s. In *Eichengreen, B. and Hatton, T. J., eds.*, 1988, pp. 397–430.

Greifinger, Robert. An Ethical Model for Improving the Patient–Physician Relationship: Commentary. *Inquiry*, Winter 1988, *25*(4), pp. 467–68.

Greis, Theresa Diss; Dowgun, Kay M. and Northrup, Herbert R. The Office and Professional Employees International Union: From "Union Company Union" to Independent Representative. *J. Lab. Res.*, Winter 1988, *9*(1), pp. 91–106.

———; Dowgun, Kay M. and Northrup, Herbert R. The Office of Professional Employees International Union: Part Two—Mission Unclear and Unrealized. *J. Lab. Res.*, Summer 1988, *9*(3), pp. 251–70.

Grenier, Gilles. Participation au marché du travail, revenus et langues au Québec: le cas des femmes mariées. (Labour Force Participation, Earnings and Languages in Quebec: The Case of Married Women. With English summary.) *L'Actual. Econ.*, March 1988, *64*(1), pp. 5–22.

Grennes, Thomas. Farm-support Policies Compatible with Trade Liberalization. *World Econ.*, March 1988, *11*(1), pp. 109–17.

——— and Dutton, John. The Role of Exchange Rates in Trade Models. In *Carter, C. A. and Gardiner, W. H., eds.*, 1988, pp. 87–135.

Greskovits, Béla. Western Technological Policies and the Approach of Hungarian Industrial Policy. *Acta Oecon.*, 1988, *39*(1–2), pp. 95–109.

Gressani, Daniela; Guiso, Luigi and Visco, Ignazio. Disinflation in Italy: An Analysis with the Econometric Model of the Bank of Italy. *J. Policy Modeling*, Summer 1988, *10*(2), pp. 163–203.

Grether, David M.; Schwartz, Alan and Wilde, Louis L. Uncertainty and Shopping Behaviour: An Experimental Analysis. *Rev. Econ. Stud.*, April 1988, *55*(2), pp. 323–42.

Griepentrog, Gary L. and Cox, Larry A. The Pure-Play Cost of Equity for Insurance Divisions. *J. Risk Ins.*, September 1988, *55*(3), pp. 442–52.

——— and Cox, Larry A. Systematic Risk, Unsystematic Risk, and Property-Liability Rate Regulation. *J. Risk Ins.*, December 1988, *55*(4), pp. 606–27.

Grieves, R. and Sheehan, Richard G. Sunspots and Cycles: A Test of Causation. In *Wood, J. C., ed., Vol. 3*, 1988, *1978*, pp. 189–92.

Griffin, Charles C. and Birdsall, Nancy M. Fertility and Poverty in Developing Countries. *J. Policy Modeling*, April 1988, *10*(1), pp. 29–55.

Griffin, James M. A Test of the Free Cash Flow Hypothesis: Results from the Petroleum Indus-

try. *Rev. Econ. Statist.*, February 1988, *70*(1), pp. 76–82.

——— and Baltagi, Badi H. A General Index of Technical Change. *J. Polit. Econ.*, February 1988, *96*(1), pp. 20–41.

——— and Baltagi, Badi H. A Generalized Error Component Model with Heteroscedastic Disturbances. *Int. Econ. Rev.*, November 1988, *29*(4), pp. 745–53.

——— and Jones, Clifton T. Economies of Scale in a Multiplant Technology: Evidence from the Oilpatch. *Econ. Inquiry*, January 1988, *26*(1), pp. 107–22.

Griffin, John C., Jr. and Rouse, William. Counter-Trade as a Third World Strategy of Development. In *Wilber, C. K., ed.*, 1988, pp. 508–32.

Griffin, Joseph P. and Calabrese, Michael R. Coping with Extraterritoriality Disputes. *J. World Trade*, June 1988, *22*(3), pp. 5–25.

Griffin, Keith. Growth and Impoverishment in the Rural Areas of Asia. In *Wilber, C. K., ed.*, 1988, pp. 326–63.

———. Observations on Economic Policy in Post-Revolution Nicaragua. *Rev. Radical Polit. Econ.*, Summer–Fall 1988, *20*(2–3), pp. 260–65.

———. Toward a Cooperative Settlement of the Debt Problem. *Finance Develop.*, June 1988, *25*(2), pp. 12–14.

Griffin, Ronald C., et al. Economic Prospects for Sprinkle Irrigating Rice in Texas. *Southern J. Agr. Econ.*, July 1988, *20*(1), pp. 103–17.

Griffith, G. R. and Vere, D. T. Supply and Demand Interactions in the New South Wales Prime Lamb Market. *Rev. Marketing Agr. Econ.*, December 1988, *56*(3), pp. 287–305.

Griffith-Jones, S. Debt Crisis Management, an Analytical Framework. In *Griffith-Jones, S., ed.*, 1988, pp. 1–39.

———. Managing World Debt: Conclusions and Policy Recommendations. In *Griffith-Jones, S., ed.*, 1988, pp. 336–80.

Griffiths, Adrian. Drug Supply and Use in Developing Countries: Problems and Policies. In *Bell, D. E. and Reich, M. R., eds.*, 1988, pp. 349–77.

Griffiths, William E. Bayesian Econometrics and How to Get Rid of Those Wrong Signs. *Rev. Marketing Agr. Econ.*, April 1988, *56*(1), pp. 36–56.

Grift, Yolanda K. The Excess Burden of the Tax and Social Premium System for Dutch Married Women. *De Economist*, 1988, *136*(2), pp. 185–204.

Grigalunas, Thomas A. and Opaluch, James J. Assessing Liability for Damages under CERCLA: A New Approach for Providing Incentives for Pollution Avoidance? *Natural Res. J.*, Summer 1988, *28*(3), pp. 509–33.

———, et al. Measuring Damages to Marine Natural Resources from Pollution Incidents under CERCLA: Applications of an Integrated Ocean Systems/Economic Model. *Marine Resource Econ.*, 1988, *5*(1), pp. 1–21.

Grignon, Claude. Les enquêtes sur la consommation et la sociologie des goûts. (The Consumption Enquiries and the Sociology of Tastes: The Case of Food Habits. With English summary.) *Revue Écon.*, January 1988, *39*(1), pp. 15–32.

Grignon, Julie and Vaillancourt, François. Revenu, caractéristiques sociodémographiques et dépenses des ménages au Canada en 1978 et 1982. (With English summary.) *L'Actual. Econ.*, June 1988, *64*(2), pp. 231–50.

Grigsby, David W. and Leap, Terry L. Power and the Bargaining Process: Reply. *Ind. Lab. Relat. Rev.*, July 1988, *41*(4), pp. 622–26.

Griliches, Zvi. Capital-Skill Complementarity. In *Griliches, Z.*, 1988, *1969*, pp. 213–19.

_____. Capital Stock in Investment Functions: Some Problems of Concept and Measurement. In *Griliches, Z.*, 1988, *1963*, pp. 123–43.

_____. Congruence versus Profitability: A False Dichotomy. In *Griliches, Z.*, 1988, *1960*, pp. 53–55.

_____. Hedonic Price Indexes for Automobiles: An Econometric Analysis of Quality Change. In *Griliches, Z.*, 1988, *1971*, pp. 76–104.

_____. Hedonic Price Indexes Revisited. In *Griliches, Z.*, 1988, *1971*, pp. 105–18.

_____. Hybrid Corn: An Exploration in the Economics of Technological Change. In *Griliches, Z.*, 1988, *1957*, pp. 27–52.

_____. Measuring Inputs in Agriculture: A Critical Survey. In *Griliches, Z.*, 1988, *1960*, pp. 58–75.

_____. Notes on the Role of Education in Production Functions and Growth Accounting. In *Griliches, Z.*, 1988, *1970*, pp. 147–81.

_____. Postscript on Agricultural and Other Production Functions. In *Griliches, Z.*, 1988, pp. 306–07.

_____. Postscript on Diffusion. In *Griliches, Z.*, 1988, pp. 56–57.

_____. Postscript on Education and Economic Growth. In *Griliches, Z.*, 1988, pp. 220–23.

_____. Postscript on Hedonics. In *Griliches, Z.*, 1988, pp. 119–22.

_____. Productivity Puzzles and R&D: Another Nonexplanation. *J. Econ. Perspectives*, Fall 1988, *2*(4), pp. 9–21.

_____. Research Costs and Social Returns: Hybrid Corn and Related Innovations. In *Griliches, Z.*, 1988, *1958*, pp. 227–43.

_____. Research Expenditures and Growth Accounting. In *Griliches, Z.*, 1988, *1973*, pp. 244–67.

_____. Research Expenditures, Education, and the Aggregate Agricultural Production Function. In *Griliches, Z.*, 1988, *1964*, pp. 292–305.

_____. The Sources of Measured Productivity Growth: United States Agriculture, 1940–1960. In *Griliches, Z.*, 1988, *1963*, pp. 271–91.

_____. Union/Nonunion Wage Gaps in the Public Sector: Comment. In *Freeman, R. B. and Ichniowski, C., eds.*, 1988, pp. 193–94.

_____ and Cockburn, Iain. Industry Effects and Appropriability Measures in the Stock Market's Valuation of R&D and Patents. *Amer. Econ. Rev.*, May 1988, *78*(2), pp. 419–23.

_____ and Jorgenson, Dale W. The Explanation of Productivity Change. In *Griliches, Z.*, 1988, *1967*, pp. 308–50.

_____ and Mason, W. M. Education, Income, and Ability. In *Griliches, Z.*, 1988, *1973*, pp. 182–212.

Grilli, Enzo R. Changes in the Structure of Trade and New Forms of Adjustment Policy: Perspective. In *Guerrieri, P. and Padoan, P. C., eds.*, 1988, pp. 229–35.

_____. Macro-economic Determinants of Trade Protection. *World Econ.*, September 1988, *11*(3), pp. 313–26.

_____ and Yang, Maw Cheng. Primary Commodity Prices, Manufactured Goods Prices, and the Terms of Trade of Developing Countries: What the Long Run Shows. *World Bank Econ. Rev.*, January 1988, *2*(1), pp. 1–47.

Grilli, Vittorio U. The Term Structure in the United States, Japan, and West Germany: A Comment. *Carnegie–Rochester Conf. Ser. Public Policy*, Spring 1988, *28*, pp. 315–17.

Grimes, Paul W. and Ray, Margaret A. Right-to-Work Legislation and Employment Growth in the 1980s: A Shift-Share Analysis. *Reg. Sci. Persp.*, 1988, *18*(2), pp. 78–93.

Grimm, Curtis M. and Harris, Robert G. A Qualitative Choice Analysis of Rail Routings: Implications for Vertical Foreclosure and Competition Policy. *Logist. Transp. Rev.*, March 1988, *24*(1), pp. 49–67.

Grinblatt, Mark and Johnson, Herb. A Put Option Paradox. *J. Finan. Quant. Anal.*, March 1988, *23*(1), pp. 23–26.

Grinols, Earl L. Export Supply and Import Demand Functions: A Production Theory Approach: Comment. In *Feenstra, R. C., ed.*, 1988, pp. 223–29.

_____ and Matusz, Steven J. Some Welfare Implications of Job Mobility in General Equilibrium. *Amer. Econ. Rev.*, March 1988, *78*(1), pp. 261–66.

Grinyer, Peter H.; McKiernan, Peter and Yasai-Ardekani, Masoud. Market, Organizational, and Managerial Correlates of Economic Performance in the U.K. Electrical Engineering Industry. In *Grant, J. H., ed.*, 1988, pp. 147–79.

Grippo, L. and Di Pillo, G. Recent Results on Nondifferentiable Exact Penalty Functions. In *Iri, M. and Yajima, K., eds.*, 1988, pp. 212–20.

_____; Lampariello, F. and Lucidi, S. Newton-Type Algorithms with Nonmonotone Line Search for Large-Scale Unconstrained Optimization. In *Iri, M. and Yajima, K., eds.*, 1988, pp. 187–96.

Grisley, William and Herendeen, James B. A Dynamic "q" Model of Investment, Financing and Asset Pricing: An Empirical Test for the Agricultural Sector. *Southern Econ. J.*, October 1988, *55*(2), pp. 360–73.

Grody, Allan and Keith, Christopher. Electronic Automation at the New York Stock Exchange. In *Guile, B. R. and Quinn, J. B., eds. (I)*, 1988, pp. 82–107.

Groenewald, J. A. and van Zyl, J. Effects of Protection on South African Commercial Agriculture. *J. Agr. Econ.*, September 1988, 39(3), pp. 387–401.

Groenewegen, Peter D. Alfred Marshall and the Establishment of the Cambridge Economic Tripos. *Hist. Polit. Econ.*, Winter 1988, 20(4), pp. 627–67.

_____. Pickering's Collected Malthus: A Review Article. *J. Polit. Econ.*, April 1988, 96(2), pp. 429–46.

Grofman, Bernard and Feld, Scott L. The Borda Count in *n*-Dimensional Issue Space. *Public Choice*, November 1988, 59(2), pp. 167–76.

_____ and Feld, Scott L. Majority Rule Outcomes and the Structure of Debate in One-Issue-at-a-Time Decision-Making. *Public Choice*, December 1988, 59(3), pp. 239–52.

_____ and Glazer, Amihai. Limitations of the Spatial Model. *Public Choice*, August 1988, 58(2), pp. 161–67.

_____ and Migalski, Michael. The Return of the Native: The Supply Elasticity of the American Indian Population 1960–1980. *Public Choice*, April 1988, 57(1), pp. 85–88.

_____; Miller, Nicholas and Feld, Scott L. Centripetal Forces in Spatial Voting: On the Size of the Yolk. *Public Choice*, October 1988, 59(1), pp. 37–50.

_____ and Norrander, Barbara. A Rational Choice Model of Citizen Participation in High and Low Commitment Electoral Activities. *Public Choice*, May 1988, 57(2), pp. 187–92.

Gronau, Reuben. Consumption Technology and the Intrafamily Distribution of Resources: Adult Equivalence Scales Reexamined. *J. Polit. Econ.*, December 1988, 96(6), pp. 1183–1205.

_____. Sex-Related Wage Differentials and Women's Interrupted Labor Careers—The Chicken or the Egg. *J. Lab. Econ.*, July 1988, 6(3), pp. 277–301.

Grønhaug, Kjell and Fredriksen, Tor. Concentration Ratios, Strategy and Performance: The Case of the Norwegian Telecommunications Industry. *Managerial Dec. Econ.*, December 1988, 9(4), pp. 257–62.

_____ and Fredriksen, Tor. Exploring the Impact of Governmental Incentives on Regional Growth. *Liiketaloudellinen Aikak.*, 1988, 37(4), pp. 278–88.

_____ and Haugland, Sven Arne. Quality Perceptions in International Distribution Channels. *Liiketaloudellinen Aikak.*, 1988, 37(2), pp. 107–15.

_____ and Kaufmann, Geir. Innovation: A Cross-Disciplinary Perspective: Introduction. In *Grønhaug, K. and Kaufmann, G., eds.*, 1988, pp. 1–10.

_____ and Reve, Torger. Entrepreneurship and Strategic Management: Synergy or Antagony? In *Grønhaug, K. and Kaufmann, G., eds.*, 1988, pp. 331–45.

Grønhaug, Reidar. Continuity in the Potential for Innovation. In *Grønhaug, K. and Kaufmann, G., eds.*, 1988, pp. 491–514.

Gronicki, Miroslaw; Quandt, Richard E. and

Charemza, Wojciech. Modelling Parallel Markets in Centrally Planned Economies: The Case of the Automobile Market in Poland. *Europ. Econ. Rev.*, April 1988, 32(4), pp. 861–83.

Groot, Loek F. M.; Schippers, Jacques J. and Siegers, Joop J. The Effect of Interruptions and Part-time Work on Women's Wage Rate: A Test of the Variable-Intensity Model. *De Economist*, 1988, 136(2), pp. 220–38.

Grootaert, Christiaan and Dubois, Jean-Luc. Tenancy Choice and the Demand for Rental Housing in the Cities of the Ivory Coast. *J. Urban Econ.*, July 1988, 24(1), pp. 44–63.

Gros, Daniel. Dual Exchange Rates in the Presence of Incomplete Market Separation: Long-run Effectiveness and Policy Implications. *Int. Monet. Fund Staff Pap.*, September 1988, 35(3), pp. 437–60.

Grosbras, J. M.; Roth, N. and Deville, J. C. Efficient sampling Algorithms and Balanced Samples. In *Edwards, D. and Raun, N. E., eds.*, 1988, pp. 255–66.

Groscurth, H.-M.; van Gool, W. and Kümmel, R. Energy Optimization in Industrial Models. In *Iri, M. and Yajima, K., eds.*, 1988, pp. 518–29.

Grosh, Barbara L. Comparing Parastatal and Private Manufacturing Firms: Would Privatization Improve Performance? In *Coughlin, P. and Ikiara, G. K., eds.*, 1988, pp. 251–64.

Gross, Barbara L. and Sheth, Jagdish N. Parallel Development of Marketing and Consumer Behavior: A Historical Perspective. In *[Hollander, S. C.]*, 1988, pp. 9–33.

Gross, David J. Estimating Willingness to Pay for Housing Characteristics: An Application of the Ellickson Bid-Rent Model. *J. Urban Econ.*, July 1988, 24(1), pp. 95–112.

Gross, Dominique M. The Relative Importance of Some Causes of Unemployment: The Case of West Germany. *Weltwirtsch. Arch.*, 1988, 124(3), pp. 501–23.

Gross, E.; Hogan, Warren P. and Sharpe, Ian G. Market Information and Potential Insolvency of Australian Financial Institutions. *Australian Econ. Pap.*, June 1988, 27(50), pp. 44–64.

Gross, Martin. A Semi-strong Test of the Efficiency of the Aluminum and Copper Markets at the LME. *J. Futures Markets*, February 1988, 8(1), pp. 67–77.

Grossbard-Shechtman, Amyra. Virtue, Work and Marriage. In *Maital, S., ed., Vol. 1*, 1988, pp. 199–211.

Grossbard-Shechtman, Shoshana A. and Neuman, Shoshana. Women's Labor Supply and Marital Choice. *J. Polit. Econ.*, December 1988, 96(6), pp. 1294–1302.

Grossbart, Sanford and Carlson, Les. Parental Style and Consumer Socialization of Children. *J. Cons. Res.*, June 1988, 15(1), pp. 77–94.

Grosse, Eric; Cleveland, William S. and Devlin, Susan J. Regression By Local Fitting: Methods, Properties, and Computational Algorithms. *J. Econometrics*, January 1988, 37(1), pp. 87–114.

Grosse

Grosse, Robert. Resolving Latin America's Transfer Problem. *World Econ.*, September 1988, 11(3), pp. 417–36.

Grosser, Günter. Empirical Evidence of Effects of Policy Coordination among Major Industrial Countries since Rambouillet Summit of 1975. In *Guth, W., ed.*, 1988, pp. 110–35.

Grosskopf, Shawna and Färe, Rolf. Measuring Shadow Price Efficiency. In *Dogramaci, A. and Färe, R., eds.*, 1988, pp. 223–34.

_____; Hayes, Kathy J. and Porter-Hudak, Susan. Pension Funding and Local Labor Costs: A Dynamic Analysis of Illinois Police Pension Funds. *Southern Econ. J.*, January 1988, 54(3), pp. 572–82.

_____; Lovell, C. A. Knox and Färe, Rolf. An Indirect Approach to the Evaluation of Producer Performance. *J. Public Econ.*, October 1988, 37(1), pp. 71–89.

_____; Lovell, C. A. Knox and Färe, Rolf. Scale Elasticity and Scale Efficiency. *J. Inst. Theoretical Econ.*, September 1988, 144(4), pp. 721–29.

Grossman, Gene M. Trade Restraints, Intermediate Goods, and World Market Conditions: Comment. In *Baldwin, R. E., ed. (II)*, 1988, pp. 250–55.

_____ and Eaton, Jonathan. Trade and Industrial Policy under Oligopoly: Reply. *Quart. J. Econ.*, August 1988, 103(3), pp. 603–07.

_____ and Horn, Henrik. Infant-Industry Protection Reconsidered: The Case of Informational Barriers to Entry. *Quart. J. Econ.*, November 1988, 103(4), pp. 767–87.

_____ and Shapiro, Carl. Counterfeit-Product Trade. *Amer. Econ. Rev.*, March 1988, 78(1), pp. 59–75.

_____ and Shapiro, Carl. Foreign Counterfeiting of Status Goods. *Quart. J. Econ.*, February 1988, 103(1), pp. 79–100.

Grossman, Gregory. A Tonsorial View of the Soviet Second Economy. In *[Nove, A.]*, 1988, pp. 165–92.

Grossman, Herschel I. and Diba, Behzad T. Explosive Rational Bubbles in Stock Prices? *Amer. Econ. Rev.*, June 1988, 78(3), pp. 520–30.

_____ and Diba, Behzad T. Rational Inflationary Bubbles. *J. Monet. Econ.*, January 1988, 21(1), pp. 35–46.

_____ and Diba, Behzad T. The Theory of Rational Bubbles in Stock Prices. *Econ. J.*, September 1988, 98(392), pp. 746–54.

_____ and Van Huyck, John B. Sovereign Debt as a Contingent Claim: Excusable Default, Repudiation, and Reputation. *Amer. Econ. Rev.*, December 1988, 78(5), pp. 1088–97.

Grossman, Jonathan. The Careers of 18 Labor Secretaries. *Mon. Lab. Rev.*, February 1988, 111(2), pp. 11–18.

Grossman, Michael. Alcohol Taxes and Highway Safety: Comments. In *Graham, J. D., ed.*, 1988, pp. 220–22.

_____ and Coate, Douglas. Effects of Alcoholic Beverage Prices and Legal Drinking Ages on Youth Alcohol Use. *J. Law Econ.*, April 1988, 31(1), pp. 145–71.

Grube

_____ and Goldman, Fred. The Impact of Public Health Policy: The Case of Community Health Centers. *Eastern Econ. J.*, Jan.–March 1988, 14(1), pp. 63–72.

Grossman, Philip J. Government and Economic Growth: A Non-linear Relationship. *Public Choice*, February 1988, 56(2), pp. 193–200.

_____. Growth in Government and Economic Growth: The Australian Experience. *Australian Econ. Pap.*, June 1988, 27(50), pp. 33–43.

Grossman, Sanford J. An Analysis of the Implications for Stock and Futures Price Volatility of Program Trading and Dynamic Hedging Strategies. *J. Bus.*, July 1988, 61(3), pp. 275–98.

_____. Insurance Seen and Unseen: The Impact on Markets. *J. Portfol. Manage.*, Summer 1988, 14(4), pp. 5–8.

_____. Program Trading and Stock and Futures Price Volatility. *J. Futures Markets*, August 1988, 8(4), pp. 413–19.

_____ and Hart, Oliver D. One Share–One Vote and the Market for Corporate Control. *J. Finan. Econ.*, Jan.–March 1988, 20(1–2), pp. 175–202.

_____ and Miller, Merton H. Liquidity and Market Structure. *J. Finance*, July 1988, 43(3), pp. 617–37.

Grossmann, W. and Froeschl, K. A. Statistical Structures for Analyzing Time-Dependent Observations. In *Gaul, W. and Schader, M., eds.*, 1988, pp. 145–60.

Grote, Gerhard and Kühn, Horst. Comparative Advantage and Its Use in the Foreign Trade of the Socialist Countries. *Soviet E. Europ. Foreign Trade*, Fall 1988, 24(3), pp. 31–53.

_____; Luft, Christa and Blessing, Helmut. Foreign Trade, Growth of the Socialist National Economy, and Comprehensive Intensification. *Soviet E. Europ. Foreign Trade*, Fall 1988, 24(3), pp. 71–95.

Ground, Richard Lynn. The Genesis of Import Substitution in Latin America. *CEPAL Rev.*, December 1988, (36), pp. 179–203.

Grout, Paul A. Employee Share Ownership and Privatisation: Some Theoretical Issues. *Econ. J.*, Supplement, 1988, 98(390), pp. 97–104.

_____ and Jewitt, Ian. Employee Buy-Outs: Some Theoretical Issues. *Int. J. Ind. Organ.*, March 1988, 6(1), pp. 33–45.

Grub, Phillip D. and Lin, Jian Hai. Foreign Investment in China: Myths and Realities. *J. Econ. Devel.*, December 1988, 13(2), pp. 17–40.

_____ and Sudweeks, Bryan L. Securities Markets and the People's Republic of China. *J. Econ. Devel.*, June 1988, 13(1), pp. 51–69.

Grubb, Farley. The Auction of Redemptioner Servants, Philadelphia, 1771–1804: An Economic Analysis. *J. Econ. Hist.*, September 1988, 48(3), pp. 583–603.

Grubb, W. Norton. Vocationalizing Higher Education: The Causes of Enrollment and Completion in Public Two-Year Colleges, 1970–1980. *Econ. Educ. Rev.*, 1988, 7(3), pp. 301–19.

Grube, R. Corwin and Joy, O. Maurice. Some Evidence on the Efficacy of Security Credit

Regulation in the OTC Equity Market. *J. Finan. Res.*, Summer 1988, *11*(2), pp. 137–42.

Grubel, Herbert G. Direct and Embodied Trade in Services, or Where Is the Service Trade Problem? In *Lee, C. H. and Naya, S., eds.*, 1988, pp. 53–72.

_____. Drifting Apart: Canadian and U.S. Labor Markets. *Contemp. Policy Issues*, January 1988, *6*(1), pp. 39–55.

Gruben, William C. The New Mexico Economy: Outlook for 1989. *Fed. Res. Bank Dallas Econ. Rev.*, November 1988, pp. 21–36.

_____ **and Long, William T., III.** Forecasting the Texas Economy: Applications and Evaluations of a Systematic Multivariate Time Series Model. *Fed. Res. Bank Dallas Econ. Rev.*, January 1988, pp. 11–28.

_____; **Martens, Joann E. and Schmidt, Ronald H.** Interstate Shifts in Nonresidential Construction. *Fed. Res. Bank Dallas Econ. Rev.*, July 1988, pp. 26–37.

Grubert, Harry and Mutti, John. U.S. Taxes and Trade Performance. *Nat. Tax J.*, September 1988, *41*(3), pp. 317–25.

Gruchman, Bohdan and Glugiewicz, Ewa. The Role of Innovations in Regional Economic Restructuring in Eastern Europe. In *Aydalot, P. and Keeble, D., eds.*, 1988, pp. 221–32.

Gruchy, Allan G. Government Intervention and the Social Control of Business: The Neoinstitutionalist Position. In *Samuels, W. J., ed., Vol. 2*, 1988, *1974*, pp. 269–83.

_____. Neoinstitutionalism and the Economics of Dissent. In *Samuels, W. J., ed., Vol. 1*, 1988, *1969*, pp. 53–67.

_____. A New Look at Institutionalism: Discussion. In *Samuels, W. J., ed., Vol. 1*, 1988, *1957*, pp. 38–40.

Gruen, Fred. The Exchange Rate—Can We, Should We Do Something about It? Comment. *Rev. Marketing Agr. Econ.*, April 1988, *56*(1), pp. 88–90.

Gruenspecht, Howard K. Dumping and Dynamic Competition. *J. Int. Econ.*, November 1988, *25*(3–4), pp. 225–48.

_____. Export Subsidies for Differentiated Products. *J. Int. Econ.*, May 1988, *24*(3–4), pp. 331–44.

von Grumbkow, Jasper and Poiesz, Theo B. C. Economic Well-Being, Job Satisfaction, Income Evaluation and Consumer Satisfaction: An Integrative Attempt. In *van Raaij, W. F.; van Veldhoven, G. M. and Wärneryd, K.-E., eds.*, 1988, pp. 571–93.

_____ **and Schoormans, Jan.** Attitudes towards the Dutch Social Security System. In *Maital, S., ed., Vol. 2*, 1988, pp. 718–28.

Grundfest, Joseph A. Explaining the Events of October 1987. In *MacKay, R. J., ed.*, 1988, pp. 22–26.

_____. Panel Discussion: Corporate Takeovers and Public Policy: Remarks. In *Auerbach, A. J., ed. (I)*, 1988, pp. 311–19.

_____. Why are the Parts Worth More than the Sum? "Chop Shop," A Corporate Valuation Model: Discussion. In *Browne, L. E. and Rosengren, E. S., eds.*, 1988, pp. 96–101.

Grunert, Klaus G. Information Processing from the Consumer's Perspective: Comments. In *Maynes, E. S. and ACCI Research Committee, eds.*, 1988, pp. 219–24.

Grünewald, Werner. Fructbarkeitstafeln. (Fertility Life Tables. With English summary.) *Jahr. Nationalökon. Statist.*, March 1988, *204*(3), pp. 241–54.

Grüske, Karl-Dieter. The Role of Government in Changing Industrial Societies: A Schumpeter Perspective: Discussion. In *Hanusch, H., ed.*, 1988, pp. 315–21.

Guadry, Marc J. I. and Blum, Ulrich C. H. An Example of Correlation among Residuals in Directly Ordered Data. *Econ. Letters*, 1988, *26*(4), pp. 335–40.

Guasch, J. Luis and Bhattacharya, Sudipto. Heterogeneity, Tournaments, and Hierarchies. *J. Polit. Econ.*, August 1988, *96*(4), pp. 867–81.

Gubitz, Andrea. Collapse of the Purchasing Power Parity in the Light of Co-integrated Variables? *Weltwirtsch. Arch.*, 1988, *124*(4), pp. 667–74.

Guccione, Antonio and Gillen, William J. A Common Error in the Geometry of Macroeconomic Models. *J. Macroecon.*, Winter 1988, *10*(1), pp. 149–51.

_____ **and Gillen, William J.** Simon's Model of Rural–Urban Migration: A Proof of Johansen's Conjecture. *Reg. Sci. Urban Econ.*, August 1988, *18*(3), pp. 447–50.

_____, **et al.** Interregional Feedbacks in Input–Output Models: The Least Upper Bound. *J. Reg. Sci.*, August 1988, *28*(3), pp. 397–404.

Gucik, Marek. "Mini-restructuring": Experiences and Conclusions from 1985–1986. *Eastern Europ. Econ.*, Winter 1988–89, 27(2), pp. 91–103.

Gudeman, Stephen. Frontiers as Marginal Economies. In *Bennett, J. W. and Bowen, J. R., eds.*, 1988, pp. 213–16.

Güder, Faruk and Morris, James G. Objective Function Approximation: An Application to Spatial Price Equilibrium Models. *Amer. J. Agr. Econ.*, May 1988, *70*(2), pp. 391–96.

Guélat, Jacques and Florian, Michael. The Prediction of Multicommodity Freight Flows: A Multiproduct Multimode Model and a Solution Algorithm. In *Bianco, L. and La Bella, A., eds.*, 1988, pp. 150–85.

Guerard, John B., Jr. Stationarity and Outliers in Annual Accounting Earnings. *Econ. Letters*, 1988, *26*(4), pp. 369–73.

_____ **and Alpert, William T.** Employment, Unemployment and the Minimum Wage: A Causality Model. *Appl. Econ.*, November 1988, *20*(11), pp. 1453–64.

Guerguil, Martine. Some Thoughts on the Definition of the Informal Sector. *CEPAL Rev.*, August 1988, (35), pp. 57–65.

Guerrero, Isabel and Blejer, Mario I. Stabilization Policies and Income Distribution in the Philippines. *Finance Develop.*, December 1988, *25*(4), pp. 6–8.

Guerrieri, Paolo and Padoan, Pier Carlo. International Cooperation and the Role of Macroeconomic Regimes. In *Guerrieri, P. and Padoan, P. C., eds.*, 1988, pp. 1–27.

Guesnerie, Roger. Regulation as an Adverse Selection Problem: An Introduction to the Literature. *Europ. Econ. Rev.*, March 1988, *32*(2–3), pp. 473–81.

_____ **and Chiappori, Pierre André.** Endogenous Fluctuations under Rational Expectations. *Europ. Econ. Rev.*, March 1988, *32*(2–3), pp. 389–97.

_____ **and Oddou, Claude.** Increasing Returns to Size and Their Limits. *Scand. J. Econ.*, 1988, *90*(3), pp. 259–73.

Guess, George M. Budgetary Cutback and Transit System Performance: The Case of MARTA. *Public Budg. Finance*, Spring 1988, *8*(1), pp. 58–68.

Guest, David E. and Dewe, Philip. Why Do Workers Belong to a Trade Union? A Social Psychological Study in the UK Electronics Industry. *Brit. J. Ind. Relat.*, July 1988, *26*(2), pp. 178–94.

Gueullette, Agota Anna. Hungarian Policy on Imports of Licenses and the Assimilation of Transferred Know-How. *Europ. Econ. Rev.*, March 1988, *32*(2–3), pp. 611–17.

_____, **et al.** La modernisation de l'appareil productif en Hongrie. (The Modernization of the Productive Activities in Hungary. With English summary.) *Écon. Soc.*, February 1988, *22*(2), pp. 107–74.

Guex, Philippe. L'autonomie des filiales des entreprises multinationales suisses: Une analyse contextuelle. (Autonomy of Subsidiaries of Swiss Multinational Corporations: A Contextual Analysis. With English summary.) *Schweiz. Z. Volkswirtsch. Statist.*, September 1988, *124*(3), pp. 317–32.

Guger, Alois and Walterskirchen, Ewald. Fiscal and Monetary Policy in the Keynes–Kalecki Tradition. In *Kregel, J. A.; Matzner, E. and Roncaglia, A., eds.*, 1988, pp. 103–32.

Guha, Amalendu. Development Alternative and Social Alternative: Utopia or Possibility? In *Vivekananda, F., ed.*, 1988, pp. 3–29.

_____ **and Vivekananda, Franklin.** Structural Theory of Overdevelopment and Underdevelopment. In *Vivekananda, F., ed.*, 1988, pp. 165–75.

Guhan, S. Aid for the Poor: Performance and Possibilities in India. In *Lewis, J. P., et al.*, 1988, pp. 189–208.

Gui, Benedetto. Gli effetti occupazionali dei sussidi marginali all'occupazione. Un inquadramento. (A Framework for the Effects on Employment of Marginal Employment Subsidiaries. With English summary.) *Econ. Lavoro*, July–Sept. 1988, *22*(3), pp. 27–46.

_____. On Unemployment in Weitzman's Share Economy. In *Jones, D. C. and Svejnar, J., eds.*, 1988, pp. 209–16.

Guidotti, Pablo E. Insulation Properties under Dual Exchange Rates. *Can. J. Econ.*, November 1988, *21*(4), pp. 799–813.

Guile, Bruce R. Introduction to Services Indus-

tries Policy Issues. In *Guile, B. R. and Quinn, J. B., eds. (II)*, 1988, pp. 1–15.

_____ **and Quinn, James Brian.** Managing Innovation in Services. In *Guile, B. R. and Quinn, J. B., eds. (I)*, 1988, pp. 1–8.

Guilkey, David K.; Popkin, Barry M. and Haines, Pamela S. Modeling Food Consumption Decisions as a Two-Step Process. *Amer. J. Agr. Econ.*, August 1988, *70*(3), pp. 543–52.

_____, **et al.** Child Spacing in the Philippines: The Effect of Current Characteristics and Rural Development. *Population Stud.*, July 1988, *42*(2), pp. 259–73.

Guillaumont, Patrick; Guillaumont, Sylviane and Plane, Patrick. Participating in African Monetary Unions: An Alternative Evaluation. *World Devel.*, May 1988, *16*(5), pp. 569–76.

Guillaumont, Sylviane; Plane, Patrick and Guillaumont, Patrick. Participating in African Monetary Unions: An Alternative Evaluation. *World Devel.*, May 1988, *16*(5), pp. 569–76.

Guille, Howard. Industrial Democracy—The Current Position. *Australian Bull. Lab.*, September 1988, *14*(4), pp. 610–20.

Guimarães Neto, Leonardo; De Aruaíjo, Tarcísio Patrúcio and do Vale Souza, Aldemir. Employment Implications of Informal Sector Policies: A Case Study of Greater Recife. *Int. Lab. Rev.*, 1988, *127*(2), pp. 243–58.

Guiot, Jean M. and Lefoll, Jean. Cardinal Utility: An Empirical Test. In *Munier, B. R., ed.*, 1988, pp. 97–102.

Guiso, Luigi; Visco, Ignazio and Gressani, Daniela. Disinflation in Italy: An Analysis with the Econometric Model of the Bank of Italy. *J. Policy Modeling*, Summer 1988, *10*(2), pp. 163–203.

Guitián, Manuel. Empirical Evidence of Effects of Policy Coordination among Major Industrial Countries since Rambouillet Summit of 1975: Comment. In *Guth, W., ed.*, 1988, pp. 142–48.

_____. Three Views on Restoring Growth: Comment. In *Bruno, M., et al., eds.*, 1988, pp. 399–404.

Guitton, Henri. The Foundations of Keynesian Analysis: Some Remarks. In *Barrère, A., ed.*, 1988, pp. 263–64.

_____. The Imperfections of a Modern Economy or of Modern Economics? *Int. J. Soc. Econ.*, 1988, *15*(2), pp. 14–50.

Gul, Faruk and Sonnenschein, Hugo. On Delay in Bargaining with One-Sided Uncertainty. *Econometrica*, May 1988, *56*(3), pp. 601–11.

Gülalp, Haldun. Capital Accumulation and the State. In *Williams, M., ed.*, 1988, pp. 134–54.

Gulhati, Ravi and Nallari, Raj. Reform of Foreign Aid Policies: The Issue of Inter-country Allocation in Africa. *World Devel.*, October 1988, *16*(10), pp. 1167–84.

Gültekin, N. Bülent and Inselbag, Işik. Financial Markets in Turkey. In *Nas, T. F. and Odekon, M., eds.*, 1988, pp. 129–40.

Gunatilleke, Godfrey. Planning in Uncertainty:

The Case of Sri Lanka. In *Urrutia, M. and Yukawa, S., eds. (I),* 1988, pp. 33–106.

Gunderson, Les C. and Keck, Donald B. Optical Fibers: Where Light Outperforms Electrons. In *Forester, T., ed.,* 1988, *1983,* pp. 214–29.

Gunderson, Morley. Labour Economics and Industrial Relations. In *Hébert, G.; Jain, H. C. and Meltz, N. M., eds..,* 1988, pp. 45–72.

—— **and Pesando, James E.** The Case for Allowing Mandatory Retirement. *Can. Public Policy,* March 1988, *14*(1), pp. 32–39.

—— **and Pesando, James E.** Retirement Incentives Contained in Occupational Pension Plans and Their Implications for the Mandatory Retirement Debate. *Can. J. Econ.,* May 1988, *21*(2), pp. 244–64.

—— **and Weiermair, Klaus.** Labour Market Rigidities: Economic Analysis of Alternative Work Schedules Including Overtime Restrictions. In *Dlugos, G.; Dorow, W. and Weiermair, K., eds.,* 1988, pp. 153–63.

Günlük-Şenesen, Gülay. Hatali Veri Matrislerini Düzeltme Yöntemleri ve Türkiye'nin 1973 Nihai Talep Verileri. (Methods for Adjustment of Unbalanced Data Matrices and Turkey's 1973 Final Demand Data. With English summary.) *METU,* 1988, *15*(1–2), pp. 85–104.

—— **and Bates, J. M.** Some Experiments with Methods of Adjusting Unbalanced Data Matrices. *J. Roy. Statist. Soc.,* 1988, *151*(3), pp. 473–90.

Güntensperger, Heinz and Wasserfallen, Walter. Gasoline Consumption and the Stock of Motor Vehicles: An Empirical Analysis for the Swiss Economy. *Energy Econ.,* October 1988, *10*(4), pp. 276–82.

Gunter, Frank R. In Bed with the Elephant: Canadian–United States Economic Relations. In *Thornton, R. J.; Hyclak, T. and Aronson, J. R., eds.,* 1988, pp. 61–79.

Gunter, Lewell and Vasavada, Utpal. Dynamic Labour Demand Schedules for U.S. Agriculture. *Appl. Econ.,* June 1988, *20*(6), pp. 803–12.

Gunto, Samuel J. and Kravitz, David A. Modeling Coalition Formation in Inessential Probabilistic Games. In *Tietz, R.; Albers, W. and Selten, R., eds.,* 1988, pp. 268–85.

Guo, Yonggang. Survey and Analysis of the Sense of Employment Awareness among Young People in Chaoyang District Schools. *Chinese Econ. Stud.,* Summer 1988, *21*(4), pp. 6–25.

Gupta, Anil K. and Sapienza, Harry J. The Pursuit of Diversity by Venture Capital Firms: Antecedents and Implications. In *Kirchhoff, B. A., et al., eds.,* 1988, pp. 290–302.

Gupta, Atul and Misra, Lalatendu. Illegal Insider Trading: Is It Rampant before Corporate Takeovers? *Financial Rev.,* November 1988, *23*(4), pp. 453–64.

Gupta, J. R. Some Aspects of Fiscal Policy in Punjab with Refernce to the Agricultural Sector. In *Raikhy, P. S. and Gill, S. S., eds.,* 1988, pp. 28–52.

Gupta, Kanhaya L. Interest Rate Determination

in a Small Open Economy: Singapore. *Econ. Letters,* 1988, *27*(3), pp. 283–85.

——. Macroeconomic Determinants of Growth: Some Implications of Disaggregation. *Appl. Econ.,* June 1988, *20*(6), pp. 843–52.

—— **and Moazzami, Bakhtiar.** Dynamic Specification and the Demand for Money Function. *Econ. Letters,* 1988, *27*(3), pp. 229–31.

Gupta, Manash Ranjan. Efficiency of Labour, Industrial Wage, and Investment in Health. *J. Quant. Econ.,* January 1988, *4*(1), pp. 19–31.

——. Migration, Welfare, Inequality and Shadow Wage. *Oxford Econ. Pap.,* September 1988, *40*(3), pp. 477–86.

Gupta, R. D. Human Resources Development in Power Sector. In *Kohli, U. and Gautam, V., eds.,* 1988, pp. 94–103.

Gupta, Satyadev. Profits, Investment, and Causality: An Examination of Alternative Paradigms. *Southern Econ. J.,* July 1988, *55*(1), pp. 9–20.

Gupta, Sunil and Wilton, Peter C. Combination of Economic Forecasts: An Odds-Matrix Approach. *J. Bus. Econ. Statist.,* July 1988, *6*(3), pp. 373–79.

Guralnik, Jack M. and Yanagishita, Machiko. Changing Mortality Patterns that Led Life Expectancy in Japan to Surpass Sweden's: 1972–1982. *Demography,* November 1988, *25*(4), pp. 611–24.

Guran, M.; Văduva, I. and Megheşan, V. Informatics and the Technical and Scientific Evolution. *Econ. Computat. Cybern. Stud. Res.,* 1988, *23*(1), pp. 31–44.

Guria, Jagadish C. Effects of the Recent Road Transport Deregulation on Rail Freight Demands in New Zealand. *Int. J. Transport Econ.,* June 1988, *15*(2), pp. 169–87.

——. Inter-temporal Pricing in an Integrated Passenger Transport System. *Int. J. Transport Econ.,* October 1988, *15*(3), pp. 271–90.

Gurney, Andrew. The Exchange Rate, Interest Rates and the Current Balance in a Forward-Looking Model. *Nat. Inst. Econ. Rev.,* August 1988, (125), pp. 40–55.

—— **and Barrell, R. J.** The World Economy. *Nat. Inst. Econ. Rev.,* November 1988, (126), pp. 18–31.

——; **Joyce, Michael and Britton, Andrew.** The Home Economy. *Nat. Inst. Econ. Rev.,* February 1988, (123), pp. 6–19.

——; **Joyce, Michael and Britton, Andrew.** The Home Economy. *Nat. Inst. Econ. Rev.,* May 1988, (124), pp. 7–20.

Gurrieri, Adolfo. Medina Echavarría and the Future of Latin America. *CEPAL Rev.,* August 1988, (35), pp. 73–78.

Gustafson, Cole R.; Barry, Peter J. and Sonka, Steven T. Machinery Investment Decisions: A Simulated Analysis for Cash Grain Farms. *Western J. Agr. Econ.,* December 1988, *13*(2), pp. 244–53.

Gustafson, James M. and Johnson, Elmer W. Efficiency, Morality, and Managerial Effectiveness. In *Meyer, J. R. and Gustafson, J. M., eds.,* 1988, pp. 193–209.

_____ and Meyer, John R. For Whom Does the Corporation Toil?: Epilogue. In *Meyer, J. R. and Gustafson, J. M., eds.*, 1988, pp. 211–34.

Gustafson, Thane. The Crisis of the Soviet System of Power and Mikhail Gorbachev's Political Strategy. In *Bialer, S. and Mandelbaum, M., eds.*, 1988, pp. 187–229.

Gustafson, Thomas A. Poverty among the Elderly: Where Are the Holes in the Safety Net? Comment. In *Bodie, Z.; Shoven, J. B. and Wise, D. A., eds.*, 1988, pp. 134–38.

Gustavson, Sandra G. and Trieschmann, James S. Universal Life Insurance as an Alternative to the Joint and Survivor Annuity. *J. Risk Ins.*, September 1988, 55(3), pp. 529–38.

Gustman, Alan L. and Steinmeier, Thomas L. A Model for Analyzing Youth Labor Market Policies. *J. Lab. Econ.*, July 1988, 6(3), pp. 376–96.

Guth, Michael A. S. Profitable Destabilizing Speculation. A Survey with Some Modern Uncertainty Theory Insights. *Rivista Int. Sci. Econ. Com.*, June 1988, 35(6), pp. 523–38.

Güth, Werner. On the Behavioral Approach to Distributive Justice—A Theoretical and Experimental Investigation. In *Maital, S., ed.*, Vol. 2, 1988, pp. 703–17.

_____ and Tietz, Reinhard. Ultimatum Bargaining for a Shrinking Cake—An Experimental Analysis. In *Tietz, R.; Albers, W. and Selten, R., eds.*, 1988, pp. 111–28.

Guth, Wilfried. Economic Policy Coordination: Introductory Remarks. In *Guth, W., ed.*, 1988, pp. ix–xi.

_____. Economic Policy Coordination: Summary and Conclusions. In *Guth, W., ed.*, 1988, pp. 201–16.

Gutierrez, Leandro and Korol, Juan Carlos. Historia de empresas y crecimiento industrial en la Argentina. El caso de la Fábrica Argentina de Alpargatas. (With English summary.) *Desarrollo Econ.*, Oct.–Dec. 1988, 28(111), pp. 401–24.

Gutowski, Armin. The Developing Countries' External Debt, Real Capital Transfers and Investment. In *Gutowski, A. and Holthus, M., eds.*, 1988, 1984, pp. 139–70.

_____. A New Round of Rescheduling? In *Gutowski, A. and Holthus, M., eds.*, 1988, 1986, pp. 315–42.

_____ and Holthus, Manfred. Limits to International Indebtedness. In *Gutowski, A. and Holthus, M., eds.*, 1988, 1983, pp. 93–114.

Guttentag, Jack M. Restructuring Depository Institutions. In *Federal Home Loan Bank of San Francisco*, 1988, pp. 45–64.

Guttmann, Robert. Crisis and Reform of the International Monetary System. In *Arestis, P., ed.*, 1988, pp. 251–99.

Guy, Clifford M. Information Technology and Retailing: The Implications for Analysis and Forecasting. In *Wrigley, N., ed.*, 1988, pp. 305–22.

Guy, Donna J. Refinería Argentina, 1888–1930: Límites de la tecnología azucarera en una economía periférica. (With English summary.) *Desarrollo Econ.*, Oct.–Dec. 1988, 28(111), pp. 353–73.

Guyer, Philipp. Discussion to Session 1: Innovation and Competition Policy. *Aussenwirtschaft*, June 1988, 43(1/2), pp. 151–53.

Guyomard, Herve. Quasi-fixed Factors and Production Theory—The Case of Self-employed Labour in French Agriculture. *Irish J. Agr. Econ. Rural Soc.*, 1988, 13, pp. 21–33.

Gwartney, James D. and Wagner, Richard E. Public Choice and Constitutional Order. In *Gwartney, J. D. and Wagner, R. E., eds.*, 1988, pp. 29–56.

_____ and Wagner, Richard E. Public Choice and the Conduct of Representative Government. In *Gwartney, J. D. and Wagner, R. E., eds.*, 1988, pp. 3–28.

Gwynne, Gretchen and Zschock, Dieter K. Health Care in Peru: Inferences and Options. In *Zschock, D. K., ed.*, 1988, pp. 259–71.

Gyapong, Anthony Owusu and Gyimah-Brempong, Kwabena. Demand for Factors of Production: A Study of Michigan's Municipal Police Departments. *Appl. Econ.*, November 1988, 20(11), pp. 1421–33.

_____ and Gyimah-Brempong, Kwabena. Factor Substitution, Price Elasticity of Factor Demand and Returns to Scale in Police Production: Evidence from Michigan. *Southern Econ. J.*, April 1988, 54(4), pp. 863–78.

Gygi, Beat and Frey, Bruno S. Die Fairness von Preisen. (The Fairness of Prices. With English summary.) *Schweiz. Z. Volkswirtsch. Statist.*, December 1988, 124(4), pp. 519–41.

Gyimah-Brempong, Kwabena. Agricultural Development and the Size Distribution of Personal Income: The Tropical African Experience. *World Devel.*, April 1988, 16(4), pp. 483–88.

_____ and Gyapong, Anthony Owusu. Demand for Factors of Production: A Study of Michigan's Municipal Police Departments. *Appl. Econ.*, November 1988, 20(11), pp. 1421–33.

_____ and Gyapong, Anthony Owusu. Factor Substitution, Price Elasticity of Factor Demand and Returns to Scale in Police Production: Evidence from Michigan. *Southern Econ. J.*, April 1988, 54(4), pp. 863–78.

Gyllenhammar, Pehr. Fifteen Years of Major Structural Changes in Manufacturing. In *Muroyama, J. H. and Stever, H. G., eds.*, 1988, pp. 80–85.

Gyllström, Björn. Government versus Agricultural Marketing Cooperatives in Kenya. In *Hedlund, H., ed.*, 1988, pp. 37–69.

Gyohten, Toyoo. Economic Policy Objectives and Policymaking in the Major Industrial Countries: Comment. In *Guth, W., ed.*, 1988, pp. 37–40.

Gyourko, Joseph and Tracy, Joseph. An Analysis of Public- and Private-Sector Wages Allowing for Endogenous Choices of Both Government and Union Status. *J. Lab. Econ.*, April 1988, 6(2), pp. 229–53.

Haag, Günter; Munz, Martin and Reiner, Rolf.

The Estimation of Parameters. In *Weidlich, W. and Haag, G.*, eds., 1988, pp. 33–59.

———; Munz, Martin and Reiner, Rolf. Tests of Significance in the Ranking Regression Analysis. In *Weidlich, W. and Haag, G.*, eds., 1988, pp. 345–54.

——— and Weidlich, Wolfgang. Concepts of the Dynamic Migration Model. In *Weidlich, W. and Haag, G.*, eds., 1988, pp. 9–20.

——— and Weidlich, Wolfgang. The Migratory Equations of Motion. In *Weidlich, W. and Haag, G.*, eds., 1988, pp. 21–32.

———, et al. Comparative Analysis of Interregional Migration. In *Weidlich, W. and Haag, G.*, eds., 1988, pp. 285–311.

———, et al. Federal Republic of Germany. In *Weidlich, W. and Haag, G.*, eds., 1988, pp. 65–100.

Haaga, John G. Reliability of Retrospective Survey Data on Infant Feeding. *Demography*, May 1988, 25(2), pp. 307–14.

Haagsma, Auke. A View from the European Community. In *Walker, C. E. and Bloomfield, M. A.*, eds., 1988, pp. 65–75.

Haaland, Jan I. and Norman, Victor D. Modelling Trade and Trade Policy: Introduction. In *Haaland, J. I. and Norman, V. D.*, eds., 1988, pp. 1–10.

———, et al. VEMOD: A Ricardo–Heckscher–Ohlin–Jones Model of World Trade. In *Haaland, J. I. and Norman, V. D.*, eds., 1988, pp. 35–54.

de Haan, J. and Zelhorst, D. The Empirical Evidence on the Ricardian Equivalence Hypothesis. *Kredit Kapital*, 1988, 21(3), pp. 407–21.

de Haan, Menno; Schulze, William and Gerking, Shelby. The Marginal Value of Job Safety: A Contingent Valuation Study. *J. Risk Uncertainty*, June 1988, 1(2), pp. 185–99.

Haaparanta, Pertti J. Dual Exchange Markets and Intervention. *Can. J. Econ.*, November 1988, 21(4), pp. 814–25.

———. Liberalisation and Capital Flight. *Econ. Soc. Rev.*, July 1988, 19(4), pp. 237–48.

———. Liberalization Policies and Welfare in a Financially Repressed Economy: Comment. *Int. Monet. Fund Staff Pap.*, March 1988, 35(1), pp. 205–08.

———. Structural Impacts of External Price Disturbances with Different Wage Indexation Schemes. *Empirica*, 1988, 15(1), pp. 51–63.

Haas, Michael. Violent Schools—Unsafe Schools: The Case of Hawaii. *J. Conflict Resolution*, December 1988, 32(4), pp. 727–58.

Hába, Zdeněk. Ownership in the Restructuring Process. *Czech. Econ. Digest.*, December 1988, (8), pp. 38–47.

———. Waves of Unequal Height: Economic Reforms in Czechoslovakia. *Czech. Econ. Digest.*, October 1988, (6), pp. 45–61.

Habeck, M.; Brown, Deborah J. and Abbott, Philip C. Sources of Export Earnings Instability: The Role of Agriculture. *J. Agr. Econ.*, January 1988, 39(1), pp. 69–79.

Haber, Lawrence D. Identifying the Disabled: Concepts and Methods in the Measurement of Disability. *Soc. Sec. Bull.*, May 1988, 51(5), pp. 11–28.

Haber, Lawrence J. and Levy, David T. Decision Making in the Multiproduct Firm: Adaptability and Firm Organization. *Managerial Dec. Econ.*, December 1988, 9(4), pp. 331–38.

Haberer, Jean-Yves. The Integration of the Financial Markets—A French Perspective. In *Mikdashi, Z.*, ed., 1988, pp. 85–102.

Haberfeld, Yitchak and Gerhart, Barry. Comment: Re-examining "Employment Discrimination: An Empirical Test of Forward versus Reverse Regression" [Reverse Regression and Salary Discrimination]. *J. Human Res.*, Winter 1988, 23(1), pp. 138–44.

Haberler, Gottfried. The International Monetary System and Proposals for International Policy Coordination. In *Melamed, L.*, ed., 1988, 1987, pp. 125–58.

———. The International Monetary System—Once Again. In *Melamed, L.*, ed., 1988, 1987, pp. 159–66.

———. International Trade and Economic Development: Introduction. In *Haberler, G.*, 1988, pp. 1–15.

———. International Trade and Economic Development. In *Haberler, G.*, 1988, pp. 17–53.

———. Liberal and Illiberal Development Policy. In *Haberler, G.*, 1988, pp. 55–87.

———. Liberal and Illiberal Trade Policy: The Messy World of the Second Best. In [*Witteveen, H. J.*], 1988, pp. 49–59.

———. Should Floating Continue? *Cato J.*, Fall 1988, 8(2), pp. 307–14.

———. Wage and Price Rigidities, Supply Restrictions, and the Problem of Stagflation. In *Willett, T. D.*, ed., 1988, pp. 145–76.

Haberman, Shelby J. A Warning on the Use of Chi-Squared Statistics with Frequency Tables with Small Expected Cell Counts. *J. Amer. Statist. Assoc.*, June 1988, 83(402), pp. 555–60.

Habib, Philip C. Foreign Policy and National Security: Looking at the Middle East. In *Anderson, A. and Bark, D. L.*, eds., 1988, pp. 76–87.

Habibullah, Muzafar Shah. Price Expectation Formation and the Demand for Loans in a Developing Economy: The Case of Malaysian Agriculture. *Singapore Econ. Rev.*, April 1988, 33(1), pp. 68–87.

Habte, Aklilu and Harbison, Ralph W. External Aid for African Education. *Finance Develop.*, March 1988, 25(1), pp. 25–27.

Hackenberg, Robert A. Upending Malthus: The Household Role in Philippine Food Gains and Fertility Losses, 1970–1980. In *Vlassoff, C. and Barkat-e-Khuda*, eds., 1988, pp. 7–20.

Hackenbruch, Michael and Wilkens, Herbert. Direktinvestitionen als Element der weltwirtschaftlichen Verflechtung der Wirtschaft der Bundesrepublik Deutschland. (Direct Foreign Investment as an Element of Worldwide Interdependence of the West German Economy. With English summary.) *Aussenwirtschaft*, December 1988, 43(4), pp. 505–48.

Hackett, Judith C. State Rural Development Policies: An Emerging Government Initiative. In *Beaulieu, L. J., ed.*, 1988, pp. 276–87.

Hacking, Ian. Slightly More Realistic Personal Probability. In *Gärdenfors, P. and Sahlin, N.-E., eds.*, 1988, 1967, pp. 118–35.

Hackl, Jo Watson and Testani, Rosa Anna. Second Generation State Takeover Statutes and Shareholder Wealth: An Empirical Study. *Yale Law J.*, May 1988, 97(6), pp. 1193–1231.

Hackman, Steven T. and Passy, Ury. Projectively-Convex Sets and Functions. *J. Math. Econ.*, 1988, 17(1), pp. 55–68.

Hackney, James R., Jr. A Proposal for State Funding of Municipal Tort Liability. *Yale Law J.*, December 1988, 98(2), pp. 389–407.

Hadar, Josef and Seo, Tae Kun. Asset Proportions in Optimal Portfolios. *Rev. Econ. Stud.*, July 1988, 55(3), pp. 459–68.

Haddad, Kamal and Salehizadeh, Mehdi. An Application of Options to Foreign Exchange Rate Forecasting. *Quart. J. Bus. Econ.*, Winter 1988, 27(1), pp. 42–69.

Hadjimatheou, George. The Effectiveness of Monetary Policy in the Presence of Liquidity Constraints. In *[Frowen, S.]*, 1988, pp. 150–66.

Hadley, Jack. Medicare Spending and Mortality Rates of the Elderly. *Inquiry*, Winter 1988, 25(4), pp. 485–93.

Hady, Thomas F. The Economics of Rural Areas: A Discussion. In *Hildreth, R. J., et al., eds.*, 1988, pp. 447–51.

Hafer, R. W. and Dwyer, Gerald P., Jr. Are National Stock Markets Linked? *Fed. Res. Bank St. Louis Rev.*, Nov.–Dec. 1988, 70(6), pp. 3–14.

_____ and Dwyer, Gerald P., Jr. Is Money Irrelevant? *Fed. Res. Bank St. Louis Rev.*, May–June 1988, 70(3), pp. 3–17.

_____ and Haslag, Joseph H. The FOMC in 1987: The Effects of a Falling Dollar and the Stock Market Collapse. *Fed. Res. Bank St. Louis Rev.*, March–April 1988, 70(2), pp. 3–16.

_____ and Hein, Scott E. Further Evidence on the Relationship between Federal Government Debt and Inflation. *Econ. Inquiry*, April 1988, 26(2), pp. 239–51.

_____; Sheehan, Richard G. and Belongia, Michael T. On the Temporal Stability of the Interest Rate–Weekly Money Relationship. *Rev. Econ. Statist.*, August 1988, 70(3), pp. 516–20.

Hagedorn, Homer J. 'Everybody into the Pool.' In *Timpe, A. D., ed.*, 1988, 1984, pp. 42–52.

Hagemann, Harald and Kurz, Heinz D. The Return of the Same Truncation Period and Reswitching of Techniques in Neo-Austrian and More General Models. In *Steedman, I., ed.*, Vol. 1, 1988, 1976, pp. 187–217.

Hagemann, Robert P.; Jones, Brian R. and Montador, R. Bruce. Tax Reform in OECD Countries: Motives, Constraints and Practice. *OECD Econ. Stud.*, Spring 1988, (10), pp. 185–226.

Hagen, Elisabeth and Jenson, Jane. Paradoxes and Promises: Work and Politics in the Postwar Years. In *Jenson, J.; Hagen, E. and Reddy, C., eds.*, 1988, pp. 3–16.

Hagen, James M. and Ruttan, Vernon W. Development Policy under Eisenhower and Kennedy. *J. Devel. Areas*, October 1988, 23(1), pp. 1–30.

von Hagen, Jürgen. Alternative Operating Regimes for Money Stock Control in West Germany: An Empirical Evaluation. *Weltwirtsch. Arch.*, 1988, 124(1), pp. 89–107.

_____. Geldmengensteuerung mit stochastischem Operationsziel. Zur Interpretation der Politik des Federal Reserve Board seit 1982. (Money Supply Management with a Stochastic Money Supply Target. With English summary.) *Kredit Kapital*, 1988, 21(3), pp. 346–62.

_____ and Neumann, Manfred J. M. An Aggregate Supply Function for the Open Economy with Flexible Exchange Rates. *J. Inst. Theoretical Econ.*, September 1988, 144(4), pp. 658–70.

_____ and Neumann, Manfred J. M. Instability versus Dynamics: A Study in West German Demand for Money. *J. Macroecon.*, Summer 1988, 10(3), pp. 327–49.

Hagen, Kåre P. Incentive Compatible Trade Policies: Comment. In *Haaland, J. I. and Norman, V. D., eds.*, 1988, pp. 173–75.

_____. Optimal Shadow Prices for Public Production. *J. Public Econ.*, February 1988, 35(1), pp. 119–27.

Hagen, Ole. Expected Utility Theory and Ordinalism. A Political Marriage. In *Munier, B. R., ed.*, 1988, pp. 209–20.

Hagenaars, Aldi and de Vos, Klaas. The Definition and Measurement of Poverty. *J. Human Res.*, Spring 1988, 23(2), pp. 211–21.

Hagerty, Kathleen M. and Siegel, Daniel R. On the Observational Equivalence of Managerial Contracts under Conditions of Moral Hazard and Self-selection. *Quart. J. Econ.*, May 1988, 103(2), pp. 425–28.

Haggard, Stephan. The Institutional Foundations of Hegemony: Explaining the Reciprocal Trade Agreements Act of 1934. In *Ikenberry, G. J.; Lake, D. A. and Mastanduno, M., eds.*, 1988, pp. 91–119.

_____. The Institutional Foundations of Hegemony: Explaining the Reciprocal Trade Agreements Act of 1934. *Int. Organ.*, Winter 1988, 42(1), pp. 91–119.

_____. The Philippines: Picking Up after Marcos. In *Vernon, R., ed.*, 1988, pp. 91–121.

_____. The Politics of Industrialization in the Republic of Korea and Taiwan. In *Hughes, H., ed.*, 1988, pp. 260–82.

Hagiwara, Shintaro; Noguchi, Yasuhiko and Masui, Kazuhito. Anti-dumping Laws in Japan. *J. World Trade*, August 1988, 22(4), pp. 35–50.

Hahm, Sangmoon. Information Acquisition in an Incomplete Information Model of Business Cycles: Corrigendum. *J. Monet. Econ.*, July 1988, 22(1), pp. 175.

Hahn, Frank H. On Involuntary Unemployment. In *Shaw, G. K., ed., Vol. 2, 1988, 1987*, pp. 103–18.

———. On Monetary Theory. *Econ. J.*, December 1988, 98(393), pp. 957–73.

———. On Non-Walrasian Equilibria. In *Grandmont, J.-M., ed., 1988, 1978*, pp. 423–39.

Hahn, Jeffrey W. The Evolution of the Local Soviets. In *Potichnyj, P. J., ed.*, 1988, pp. 142–58.

Hahn, Robert W. Innovative Approaches for Revising the Clean Air Act. *Natural Res. J.*, Winter 1988, 28(1), pp. 171–88.

———. Promoting Efficiency and Equity through Institutional Design. *Policy Sci.*, 1988, 21(1), pp. 41–66.

Hahn, Thomas and Cook, Timothy. The Information Content of Discount Rate Announcements and Their Effect on Market Interest Rates. *J. Money, Credit, Banking*, May 1988, 20(2), pp. 167–80.

Hahn, William F. Effects of Income Distribution on Meat Demand. *J. Agr. Econ. Res.*, Spring 1988, 40(2), pp. 19–24.

Haid, Alfred and Müller, Jürgen. Telecommunications in the Federal Republic of Germany. In *Foreman-Peck, J. and Müller, J., eds.,,* 1988, pp. 155–80.

Hailbronner, Kay and Bierwagen, Rainer M. Input, Downstream, Upstream, Secondary, Diversionary and Components or Subassembly Dumping. *J. World Trade*, June 1988, 22(3), pp. 27–59.

Hailey, D. M. and Crowe, B. L. Recording of Costs in Public Hospitals' MRI Units: Interim Report, July 1986–June 1987. In *Butler, J. R. G. and Doessel, D. P., eds.*, 1988, pp. 154–66.

——— **and Crowe, B. L.** Work in Progress: Collection and Analysis of Cost Data from Public Hospitals' MRI Units. In *Smith, C. S., ed.*, 1988, pp. 274–89.

Haines, M.; Pitts, E. and Jenkins, T. N. Dairy Industry Structure and Milk Price Comparisons: A Further Comment. *J. Agr. Econ.*, September 1988, 39(3), pp. 446–49.

Haines, Michael R. and Anderson, Barbara A. Essays in Exploration: New Demographic History of the Late 19th-Century United States. *Exploration Econ. Hist.*, October 1988, 25(4), pp. 341–65.

Haines, Pamela S.; Guilkey, David K. and Popkin, Barry M. Modeling Food Consumption Decisions as a Two-Step Process. *Amer. J. Agr. Econ.*, August 1988, 70(3), pp. 543–52.

Haines, Ted and Walters, Vivienne. Workers' Use and Knowledge of the 'Internal Responsibility System': Limits to Participation in Occupational Health and Safety. *Can. Public Policy*, December 1988, 14(4), pp. 411–23.

Haitjema, Henk M. and Kraemer, Stephen R. A New Analytic Function for Modeling Partially Penetrating Wells. *Water Resources Res.*, May 1988, 24(5), pp. 683–90.

Hajda, Joseph. Changing Perspectives in East–West Agriculture Trade: United States–Soviet Relations, 1972–84. In *Brada, J. C. and Wadekin, K.-E., eds.*, 1988, pp. 397–407.

Hájek, O. and Loparo, K. A. Bilinear Control: Geometric Properties of Reachable Sets. In *Eiselt, H. A. and Pederzoli, G., eds.*, 1988, pp. 262–73.

Hájek, Petr. Towards a Probabilistic Analysis of MYCIN-like Expert Systems. In *Edwards, D. and Raun, N. E., eds.*, 1988, pp. 117–21.

Håkansson, Håkan and Johanson, Jan. Formal and Informal Cooperation Strategies in International Networks. In *Contractor, F. J. and Lorange, P.*, 1988, pp. 369–79.

Hakes, David R. Evidence of a Scitovsky Stagflation Thesis. *Rev. Radical Polit. Econ.*, Winter 1988, 20(4), pp. 74–80.

———. Monetary Policy and Presidential Elections: A Nonpartisan Political Cycle. *Public Choice*, May 1988, 57(2), pp. 175–82.

———. October 1979: Did the Federal Reserve Change Policy Objectives? *J. Econ. Bus.*, May 1988, 40(2), pp. 159–67.

Halal, William E. Political Economy in an Information Age: The Convergence of a "New Capitalism" and a "New Socialism." In *Preston, L. E., ed.*, 1988, pp. 1–27.

Hale, David D. Policies to Curb Stock Market Volatility: Commentary. In *Federal Reserve Bank of Kansas City*, 1988, pp. 173–84.

———. Why No Recession in 1989 nor a Great Depression in 1990. *Bus. Econ.*, July 1988, 23(3), pp. 38–42.

Hale, F. Dennis. Editorial Diversity and Concentration. In *Picard, R. G., et al., eds.*, 1988, pp. 161–76.

Halevi, Joseph. Beyond Temporary Equilibrium: A Comment. *Écon. Appl.*, 1988, 41(3), pp. 609–12.

Halikias, John G. The Determination of Greek Exports: A Disaggregated Model, 1961–1985. *Rivista Int. Sci. Econ. Com.*, April–May 1988, 35(4–5), pp. 473–86.

Hall, A. D. and Pesaran, M. Hashem. Tests of Non-nested Linear Regression Models Subject to Linear Restrictions. *Econ. Letters*, 1988, 27(4), pp. 341–48.

Hall, A. E.; Ndoye, Mbaye and Bingen, R. James. California Cowpeas and Food Policy in Senegal. *World Devel.*, July 1988, 16(7), pp. 857–65.

Hall, Bronwyn H. The Effect of Takeover Activity on Corporate Research and Development. In *Auerbach, A. J., ed. (I)*, 1988, pp. 69–96.

Hall, Chris. Demand for Treatment and Choice of Provider: General Practitioner or Accident and Emergency Unit: Commentary. In *Smith, C. S., ed.*, 1988, pp. 125–26.

Hall, Christopher D. and Busche, Kelly. An Exception to the Risk Preference Anomaly. *J. Bus.*, July 1988, 61(3), pp. 337–46.

Hall, David O. and Coombs, James. The Agroenergy Filière: Experiences and Perspectives. In *Antonelli, G. and Quadrio-Curzio, A., eds.*, 1988, pp. 257–79.

Hall, Graham and Lewis, Pam. Development Agencies and the Supply of Finance to Small Firms. *Appl. Econ.*, December 1988, *20*(12), pp. 1675–87.

Hall, J. and Fahey, P. Does Accessibility to Health Services Improve Health? In *Smith, C. S., ed.*, 1988, pp. 232–48.

Hall-Kane, Anita G. and Gibbs, Ernest. Correcting for Zero Wages at Referral. In *Berkowitz, M., ed.*, 1988, pp. 119–39.

Hall, N.; Fraser, L. and Purtill, A. Supply Response in Broadacre Agriculture. *Rev. Marketing Agr. Econ.*, December 1988, *56*(3), pp. 361–74.

Hall, Peter H. Telecommuting, Work from Home and Economic Change. In *Tisdell, C. and Maitra, P., eds.*, 1988, pp. 239–59.

_____; Marron, J. S. and Härdle, Wolfgang. How Far Are Automatically Chosen Regression Smoothing Parameters from Their Optimum? *J. Amer. Statist. Assoc.*, March 1988, *83*(401), pp. 86–95.

_____; Marron, J. S. and Härdle, Wolfgang. How Far Are Automatically Chosen Regression Smoothing Parameters from Their Optimum?: Rejoinder. *J. Amer. Statist. Assoc.*, March 1988, *83*(401), pp. 100–01.

Hall, R. L. and Hitch, C. J. Price Theory and Business Behaviour. In *Sawyer, M. C., ed.*, 1988, *1939*, pp. 205–26.

Hall, Randolph W. Median, Mean, and Optimum as Facility Locations. *J. Reg. Sci.*, February 1988, *28*(1), pp. 65–81.

Hall, Robert E. Examining Alternative Macroeconomic Theories: Comment. *Brookings Pap. Econ. Act.*, 1988, (1), pp. 261–64.

_____. Financial Factors in Business Fluctuations: Commentary. In *Federal Reserve Bank of Kansas City*, 1988, pp. 73–78.

_____. Fluctuations in Equilibrium Unemployment. *Amer. Econ. Rev.*, May 1988, *78*(2), pp. 269–75.

_____. Intertemporal Substitution in Consumption. *J. Polit. Econ.*, April 1988, *96*(2), pp. 339–57.

_____. Job Switching and Job Satisfaction in the U.S. Labor Market: Comment. *Brookings Pap. Econ. Act.*, 1988, (2), pp. 587–91.

_____. The Relation between Price and Marginal Cost in U.S. Industry. *J. Polit. Econ.*, October 1988, *96*(5), pp. 921–47.

_____ and Rabushka, Alvin. An Efficient, Equitable Tax for the 1990s. In *Anderson, A. and Bark, D. L., eds.*, 1988, pp. 301–10.

Hall, Stephen G. Rationality and Siegel's Paradox, the Importance of Coherency in Expectations. *Appl. Econ.*, November 1988, *20*(11), pp. 1533–40.

_____ and Henry, Brian. The Disequilibrium Approach to Modelling the Labour Market. In *Beenstock, M., ed.*, 1988, pp. 49–69.

_____ and Kennally, G. F. Analysing Unstable Policy Prescriptions in Linear Difference Models with Rational Expectations. *Bull. Econ. Res.*, June 1988, *40*(3), pp. 217–25.

Hall, Thomas E. and Fields, T. Windsor. Income or Wealth in Money Demand: Comment. *Southern Econ. J.*, April 1988, *54*(4), pp. 1039–42.

Hall, Thomas W. and Dunn, W. Marcus. Graduate Education and CPA Examination Performance: Some Empirical Evidence. In *Schwartz, B. N., ed.*, 1988, pp. 191–204.

_____ and Tsay, Jeffrey J. An Evaluation of the Performance of Portfolios Selected from Value Line Rank One Stocks: 1976–1982. *J. Finan. Res.*, Fall 1988, *11*(3), pp. 227–40.

Hall, V. B. Design of the NIF88 Model: Comment. *Australian Econ. Pap.*, Supplement, June 1988, *27*, pp. 171–74.

Hallam, Arne. Measuring Economic Welfare: Is Theory a Cookbook for Empirical Analysis? *Amer. J. Agr. Econ.*, May 1988, *70*(2), pp. 442–47.

_____ and Pope, Rulon D. Aggregation of Inputs under Risk. *Amer. J. Agr. Econ.*, November 1988, *70*(4), pp. 826–30.

_____ and Pope, Rulon D. Separability Testing in Production Economics. *Amer. J. Agr. Econ.*, February 1988, *70*(1), pp. 142–52.

_____ and Pope, Rulon D. Testing Separability of Production Using Flexible Functional Form Profit Functions. *Econ. Letters*, 1988, *26*(3), pp. 265–70.

Haller, Hans. Competition in a Stock Market with Small Firms. *J. Econ. (Z. Nationalökon.)*, 1988, *48*(3), pp. 243–61.

_____. Manipulation of Endowments in Replica Economies: An Example. *Europ. Econ. Rev.*, July 1988, *32*(6), pp. 1375–83.

Hallin, Marc and Mélard, Guy. Rank-Based Tests for Randomness against First-Order Serial Dependence. *J. Amer. Statist. Assoc.*, December 1988, *83*(404), pp. 1117–28.

Hallwirth, Volker. Geld- und Lohnpolitik als Instrumente der Beschäftigungspolitik. Eine Theorie der Koordinierung der Wirtschaftspolitik. (Money, Wages and Employment. With English summary.) *Jahr. Nationalökon. Statist.*, August 1988, *205*(2), pp. 131–49.

Hallwood, C. Paul. Host Regions and the Globalization of the Offshore Oil Supply Industry: The Case of Aberdeen. *Int. Reg. Sci. Rev.*, 1988, *11*(2), pp. 155–66.

Halm, Glenn and Shiells, Clinton R. Damage Control: Yen Appreciation and the Japanese Labor Market. *Mon. Lab. Rev.*, November 1988, *111*(11), pp. 3–6.

Halmai, Péter and Sipos, Aladár. Organization System and Economic Mechanism in Hungarian Agriculture. *Acta Oecon.*, 1988, *39*(3–4), pp. 199–230.

Halperin, Daniel and Steuerle, C. Eugene. Indexing the Tax System for Inflation. In *Aaron, H. J.; Galper, H. and Pechman, J. A., eds.*, 1988, pp. 347–72.

Halsey, A. H. British Social Trends since 1900: Higher Education. In *Halsey, A. H., ed.*, 1988, pp. 268–96.

_____. British Social Trends since 1900: Schools. In *Halsey, A. H., ed.*, 1988, pp. 226–67.

_____. Statistics and Social Trends in Britain. In *Halsey, A. H., ed.*, 1988, pp. 1–35.

Halstead, John M. and Johnson, Thomas G. Using Fiscal Impact Models in Local Infrastructure Investment Decisions. In *Johnson, T. G.; Deaton, B. J. and Segarra, E., eds.*, 1988, pp. 99–107.

Halsted, G. B. Professor Jevons's Criticism of Boole's Logical System. In *Wood, J. C., ed., Vol. 1*, 1988, *1878*, pp. 26–29.

Haltiwanger, John C. and Maccini, Louis J. A Model of Inventory and Layoff Behaviour under Uncertainty. *Econ. J.*, September 1988, *98*(392), pp. 731–45.

Halvadakis, Constantinos P. and Lekakis, Joseph N. Biogas System Planning: A Techno-economic Perspective. *J. Energy Devel.*, Autumn 1988, *14*(1), pp. 115–31.

Hama, Mary Y. and Chern, Wen S. Food Expenditure and Nutrient Availability in Elderly Households. *J. Cons. Aff.*, Summer 1988, *22*(1), pp. 3–19.

Hamada, Fumimasa. A Macroeconomic Model with the Rate of Unemployment as a Risk Probability Under the Government Budget Restraint. In *Uno, K. and Shishido, S., eds.*, 1988, pp. 65–79.

Hamada, Koichi. International Policy Co-ordination within a World of Structural Change: Concluding Remarks. In *Borner, S., ed.*, 1988, pp. 389–91.

_____ **and Patrick, Hugh T.** Japan and the International Monetary Regime. In *Inoguchi, T. and Okimoto, D. I., eds.*, 1988, pp. 108–37.

Hamada, Robert, et al. The Role of Statistics in Accounting, Marketing, Finance, and Production. *J. Bus. Econ. Statist.*, April 1988, *6*(2), pp. 261–72.

Hamaui, Rony and Bissaro, Gianantonio. The Choice of Invoice Currency in an Inter-temporal Model of Price Setting. *Giorn. Econ.*, March–April 1988, *47*(3–4), pp. 139–61.

_____ **and Colombatto, Enrico.** Domanda di protezionismo e tasso di cambio. (The Demand for Protectionism and the Exchange Rate. With English summary.) *Econ. Polit.*, December 1988, *5*(3), pp. 369–85.

Hambrick, Donald C. Strategies for Mature Industrial-Product Businesses: A Taxonomic Approach. In *Grant, J. H., ed.*, 1988, pp. 107–45.

_____ **and MacMillan, Ian C.** Capital Intensity, Market Share Instability, and Profits—The Case for Asset Parsimony. In *Lamb, R. and Shrivastava, P., eds.*, 1988, pp. 207–22.

Hamdallah, Ahmed; Haw, In-Mu and Ruland, William. Investor Evaluation of Overfunded Pension Plan Terminations. *J. Finan. Res.*, Spring 1988, *11*(1), pp. 81–88.

Hamdan, Bassam and Rudolph, Patricia M. An Analysis of Post-deregulation Savings-and-Loan Failures. *Amer. Real Estate Urban Econ. Assoc. J.*, Spring 1988, *16*(1), pp. 17–33.

Hamel, G. and Prahalad, C. K. Creating Global Strategic Capability. In *Hood, N. and Vahlne, J.-E., eds.*, 1988, pp. 5–39.

Hamer, Michelle M. and Gordon, Lawrence A. Rates of Return and Cash Flow Profiles: An Extension. *Accounting Rev.*, July 1988, *63*(3), pp. 514–21.

Hamermesh, Daniel S. The Demand for Workers and Hours and the Effects of Job Security Policies: Theory and Evidence. In *Hart, R. A., ed.*, 1988, pp. 9–32.

_____. Employer Size, Pay, and the Ability to Pay in the Public Sector: Comment. In *Freeman, R. B. and Ichniowski, C., eds.*, 1988, pp. 214–15.

_____. Plant Closings and the Value of the Firm. *Rev. Econ. Statist.*, November 1988, *70*(4), pp. 580–86.

Hames, M. J.; Clements, R. T. and Hansen, C. D. The Reserve Bank Econometric Model of the New Zealand Economy. *Econ. Modelling*, April 1988, *5*(2), pp. 83–132.

Hamid, Shahnaz and Bilquees, Faiz. Employment Situation and Economic Exploitation of Poor Earning Women in Rawalpindi. *Pakistan Devel. Rev.*, Part 2, Winter 1988, *27*(4), pp. 791–98.

Hamill, Jim. British Acquisitions in the United States. *Nat. Westminster Bank Quart. Rev.*, August 1988, pp. 2–17.

Hamilton, Billy C. Comments on the Taxation of Services under State Sales Taxes [Sales Tax on Services: Revenue or Reform?]. *Nat. Tax J.*, September 1988, *41*(3), pp. 411–13.

Hamilton, Bob; Mohammad, Sharif and Whalley, John. Applied General Equilibrium Analysis and Perspective on Growth Performance. *J. Policy Modeling*, Summer 1988, *10*(2), pp. 281–97.

Hamilton, Carl B. Restrictiveness and International Transmission of the "New" Protectionism. In *Baldwin, R. E.; Hamilton, C. B. and Sapir, A., eds.*, 1988, pp. 199–224.

_____. Sampson Proposal—A Reply to Aubrey Silberston. *World Econ.*, June 1988, *11*(2), pp. 302–04.

Hamilton, David B. Institutional Economics and Consumption. In *Tool, M. R., ed., Vol. 2*, 1988, *1987*, pp. 113–36.

_____. Social Security: The First Half-Century: Specific Studies: Comment. In *Nash, G. D.; Pugach, N. H. and Tomasson, R. F., eds.*, 1988, pp. 301–06.

_____. Veblen and Commons: A Case of Theoretical Convergence. In *Samuels, W. J., ed., Vol. 1*, 1988, *1974*, pp. 211–19.

Hamilton, Gary G. and Biggart, Nicole Woolsey. Market, Culture, and Authority: A Comparative Analysis of Management and Organization in the Far East. In *Winship, C. and Rosen, S., eds.*, 1988, pp. 52–94.

Hamilton, James D. Are the Macroeconomic Effects of Oil-Price Changes Symmetric? A Comment. *Carnegie–Rochester Conf. Ser. Public Policy*, Spring 1988, *28*, pp. 369–78.

_____. A Neoclassical Model of Unemployment and the Business Cycle. *J. Polit. Econ.*, June 1988, *96*(3), pp. 593–617.

_____. Rational-Expectations Econometric Analysis of Changes in Regime: An Investigation of the Term Structure of Interest Rates. *J. Econ. Dynam. Control*, June–Sept. 1988, *12*(2–3), pp. 385–423.

_____. Role of the International Gold Standard in Propagating the Great Depression. *Contemp. Policy Issues*, April 1988, *6*(2), pp. 67–89.

Hamilton, L. S. Forestry and Watershed Management. In *Ives, J. and Pitt, D. C., eds.*, 1988, pp. 99–131.

_____ **and Pearce, A. J.** Soil and Water Impacts of Deforestation. In *Ives, J. and Pitt, D. C., eds.*, 1988, pp. 75–98.

Hamlen, Susan S.; Hamlen, William A., Jr. and Kasper, George M. The Distributed Lag Effects of Monetary Policy on Interest Rates Using Harmonic Transformations with a Pretest. *Southern Econ. J.*, April 1988, *54*(4), pp. 1002–11.

Hamlen, William A., Jr.; Kasper, George M. and Hamlen, Susan S. The Distributed Lag Effects of Monetary Policy on Interest Rates Using Harmonic Transformations with a Pretest. *Southern Econ. J.*, April 1988, *54*(4), pp. 1002–11.

Hamman, Robert L. and Boyko, Olga. Effect of Environmental Regulation on the Ability of Business Firms in the United States and Japan to Compete in International Trade. In *Pennsylvania Economic Association*, 1988, pp. 428–38.

Hammer, Jane N. and Quible, Zane. Office Automation's Impact on Personnel. In *Timpe, A. D., ed.*, 1988, *1984*, pp. 238–45.

Hammer, Jeffrey S. and Braverman, Avishay. Computer Models for Agricultural Policy Analysis. *Finance Develop.*, June 1988, *25*(2), pp. 34–37.

Hammer, Jerry A. Hedging and Risk Aversion in the Foreign Currency Market. *J. Futures Markets*, December 1988, *8*(6), pp. 657–86.

Hammer, Peter J. Free Speech and the "Acid Bath": An Evaluation and Critique of Judge Richard Posner's Economic Interpretation of the First Amendment. *Mich. Law Rev.*, November 1988, *87*(2), pp. 499–536.

Hammett, A. Lawton; Chen, Nen-Jing and Ames, Glenn C. W. Implications of a Tariff on Imported Canadian Softwood Lumber. *Can. J. Agr. Econ.*, March 1988, *36*(1), pp. 69–81.

Hammond, J. Daniel. How Different Are Hicks and Friedman on Method? [Predictions and Causes: A Comparison of Friedman and Hicks on Method]. *Oxford Econ. Pap.*, June 1988, *40*(2), pp. 392–94.

Hammond, Peter J. Consequentialism and the Independence Axiom. In *Munier, B. R., ed.*, 1988, pp. 503–15.

_____. Consequentialist Demographic Norms and Parenting Rights. In *Gaertner, W. and Pattanaik, P. K., eds.*, 1988, *1988*, pp. 39–57.

_____. Consequentialist Demographic Norms and Parenting Rights. *Soc. Choice Welfare*, 1988, *5*(2/3), pp. 127–45.

_____. Orderly Decision Theory: A Comment. *Econ. Philos.*, October 1988, *4*(2), pp. 292–97.

_____. Overlapping Expectations and Hart's Conditions for Equilibrium in a Securities Model. In *Grandmont, J.-M., ed.*, 1988, *1983*, pp. 156–61.

_____. Principles for Evaluating Public Sector Projects. In *Hare, P. G., ed.*, 1988, pp. 15–44.

Hammond, Valerie. Women in Management in Great Britain. In *Adler, N. J. and Izraeli, D., eds.*, 1988, pp. 168–85.

Hammons, Glenn T. and Ginsburg, Paul B. Competition and the Quality of Care: The Importance of Information. *Inquiry*, Spring 1988, *25*(1), pp. 108–15.

Hammoudeh, Shawkat. The Oil Market and Its Impact on the Economic Development of the Oil-Exporting Countries. *J. Energy Devel.*, Spring 1988, *13*(2), pp. 297–324.

Hamnett, Chris and Randolph, Bill. Labour and Housing Market Change in London: A Longitudinal Analysis, 1971–1981. *Urban Stud.*, October 1988, *25*(5), pp. 380–98.

Hamouda, Omar F. and Harcourt, G. C. Post Keynesianism: From Criticism to Coherence? *Bull. Econ. Res.*, January 1988, *40*(1), pp. 1–33.

_____ **and Smithin, John N.** Rational Behavior with Deficient Foresight. *Eastern Econ. J.*, July–Sept. 1988, *14*(3), pp. 277–85.

_____ **and Smithin, John N.** Uncertainty and Economic Analysis: Some Remarks. *Econ. J.*, March 1988, *98*(389), pp. 159–64.

_____ **and Tarshis, Lorie.** Stagflation for Our Grandchildren. In *Hamouda, O. F. and Smithin, J. N., eds., Vol. 2*, 1988, pp. 205–08.

Hamrin, Robert D. Sorry Americans—You're Still Not "Better Off." *Challenge*, Sept.–Oct. 1988, *31*(5), pp. 50–52.

Han, Jae-Dong and Casas, Francois R. Achieving Pareto Superiority under Free Trade: An Alternative to the Dixit–Norman Scheme. *Int. Econ. J.*, Winter 1988, *2*(4), pp. 1–7.

Hanami, Tadashi. Unfair Labor Practices: Law and Practice. In *Japan Institute of Labour, ed.*, 1988, *1983*, pp. 127–30.

Hanazaki, Masaharu; Englander, A. Steven and Evenson, Robert E. R&D, Innovation and the Total Factor Productivity Slowdown. *OECD Econ. Stud.*, Autumn 1988, (11), pp. 7–42.

Hancock, John and LeLoup, Lance T. Congress and the Reagan Budgets: An Assessment. *Public Budg. Finance*, Autumn 1988, *8*(3), pp. 30–54.

Hancock, Susan and Blandy, Richard. The Australian Labour Market, September 1988. *Australian Bull. Lab.*, September 1988, *14*(4), pp. 535–63.

_____ **and Sloan, Judith.** The Australian Labour Market, March 1988. *Australian Bull. Lab.*, March 1988, *14*(2), pp. 390–99.

Hand, John and Brooks, Robert. Evaluating the Performance of Stock Portfolios with Index Futures Contracts. *J. Futures Markets*, February 1988, *8*(1), pp. 33–46.

Handa, Jagdish. Substitution among Currencies:

A Preferred Habitat Hypothesis. *Int. Econ. J.*, Summer 1988, *2*(2), pp. 41–61.

Handler, Douglas P. The PC Corner: Confessions of a Forecaster. *Bus. Econ.*, April 1988, *23*(2), pp. 55–57.

Hands, D. Wade. Ad Hocness in Economics and the Popperian Tradition. In *de Marchi, N., ed.*, 1988, pp. 121–37.

Hanel, Peter. L'effet des dépenses en R&D sur la productivité de travail au Québec. (With English summary.) *L'Actual. Econ.*, September 1988, *64*(3), pp. 396–415.

Hanf, Claus-Hennig. Adjustment Necessities in European Agricultural Economics Research. *Europ. Rev. Agr. Econ.*, 1988, *15*(2–3), pp. ix–xvi.

Hanif, Muhammad; Tam, S. M. and Brewer, K. R. W. How Nearly Can Model-Based Prediction and Design-Based Estimation Be Reconciled? *J. Amer. Statist. Assoc.*, March 1988, *83*(401), pp. 129–32.

Hanink, Dean M. An Extended Linder Model of International Trade. *Econ. Geogr.*, October 1988, *64*(4), pp. 322–34.

_____. Nonintegration of Regional Labor Markets: The Case of Large U.S. Cities from February 1980 through December 1983. *Environ. Planning A*, October 1988, *20*(10), pp. 1397–1410.

Haniotis, Tassos and Ames, Glenn C. W. The 'Oilseed Tax' and U.S. Soyabean Exports to the Enlarged European Community. *Europ. Rev. Agr. Econ.*, 1988, *15*(1), pp. 39–54.

_____; **Baffes, John and Ames, Glenn C. W.** The Demand and Supply of U.S. Agricultural Exports: The Case of Wheat, Corn, and Soybeans. *Southern J. Agr. Econ.*, December 1988, *20*(2), pp. 45–55.

Hanley, Nicholas. Using Contingent Valuation to Value Environmental Improvements. *Appl. Econ.*, April 1988, *20*(4), pp. 541–49.

Hanna, John B. Assessing Your People Potential. In *Timpe, A. D., ed.*, 1988, *1984*, pp. 63–67.

Hanna, Paul R. and Dorfman, Gerald A. Can Education Be Reformed? In *Anderson, A. and Bark, D. L., eds.*, 1988, pp. 383–90.

Hannan, E. J. and McDougall, A. J. Regression Procedures for ARMA Estimation. *J. Amer. Statist. Assoc.*, June 1988, *83*(402), pp. 490–98.

Hannan, Timothy H. and Hanweck, Gerald A. Bank Insolvency Risk and the Market for Large Certificates of Deposit. *J. Money, Credit, Banking*, May 1988, *20*(2), pp. 203–11.

Hannesson, Rögnvaldur. Fixed or Variable Catch Quotas? The Importance of Population Dynamics and Stock Dependent Costs. *Marine Resource Econ.*, 1988, *5*(4), pp. 415–32.

Hannum, Robert C. and Longbotham, C. Roger. Measuring Inequality between Income Distributions. In *Brown, R. C., ed.*, 1988, pp. 55–72.

Hanrahan, J. R.; Kushner, J. and Masse, I. The Effect of Changes in Tax Legislation on the Purchase/Lease Decision in the Public Sector. *Nat. Tax J.*, March 1988, *41*(1), pp. 123–30.

Hanrahan, Nancy and Wood, Robert. The Corporate Alternative Minimum Tax as a State Revenue Source. *Nat. Tax J.*, September 1988, *41*(3), pp. 445–50.

Hansell, Stephen; Mechanic, David and Feinson, Marjorie Chary. Factors Associated with Medicare Beneficiaries' Interest in HMOs. *Inquiry*, Fall 1988, *25*(3), pp. 364–73.

Hansen, C. D.; Hames, M. J. and Clements, R. T. The Reserve Bank Econometric Model of the New Zealand Economy. *Econ. Modelling*, April 1988, *5*(2), pp. 83–132.

Hansen, Charles E. and Tennant, Wesley L. Historical Cost Review. In *West, R. E. and Kreith, F., eds.*, 1988, pp. 372–413.

Hansen, Gary D. and Sargent, Thomas J. Straight Time and Overtime in Equilibrium. *J. Monet. Econ.*, March–May 1988, *21*(2–3), pp. 281–308.

Hansen, Gerd. Comments [Wage Gaps versus Output Gaps: Is There a Common Story for All of Europe?] [Compositional Effects and Unemployment in the United States and Europe]. In *Giersch, H., ed.*, 1988, pp. 166–71.

Hansen, Lars Peter. A Central-Limit for Instrumental Variables Estimators of Linear Time Series Models. In *Barnett, W. A.; Berndt, E. R. and White, H., eds.*, 1988, pp. 139–55.

_____; **Heaton, John C. and Ogaki, Masao.** Efficiency Bounds Implied by Multiperiod Conditional Moment Restrictions. *J. Amer. Statist. Assoc.*, September 1988, *83*(403), pp. 863–71.

_____; **Singleton, Kenneth J. and Eichenbaum, Martin S.** A Time Series Analysis of Representative Agent Models of Consumption and Leisure Choice under Uncertainty. *Quart. J. Econ.*, February 1988, *103*(1), pp. 51–78.

Hansen, Niles. Regional Consequences of Structural Changes in the National and International Division of Labor. *Int. Reg. Sci. Rev.*, 1988, *11*(2), pp. 121–36.

_____. Small and Medium-Size Cities in Development. In *[Perroux, F.]*, 1988, pp. 318–29.

Hansen, Nis Graulund. Den nye ADAM—nogle kritikpunkter. (A Critical Survey of Recent Changes in the Danish Macroeconomic Model ADAM. With English summary.) *Nationaløkon. Tidsskr.*, 1988, *126*(2), pp. 254–60.

Hansen, Reginald. Gustav Schmollers Beitrag zur allgemeinen Steurlehre. Rückblick und Besinnung zum 150. Geburtstag von Gustav Schmoller. (The Contribution of Gustav Schmoller to the Theory of Taxation. With English summary.) *Jahr. Nationalökon. Statist.*, November 1988, *205*(5), pp. 443–56.

Hansen, Robert G. Auctions with Endogenous Quantity. *Rand J. Econ.*, Spring 1988, *19*(1), pp. 44–58.

_____ **and Samuelson, William F.** Evolution in Economic Games. *J. Econ. Behav. Organ.*, October 1988, *10*(3), pp. 315–38.

Hansen, Robert S.; Pinkerton, John M. and Ma, Tai. The Allocation Ratio Decision in the Underwritten Rights Offering. In *Chen, A. H., ed.*, 1988, pp. 201–25.

Hansen, S. L. and Goudie, A. W. The Effect of

Dividend Controls on Company Behavior. *Appl. Econ.*, February 1988, *20*(2), pp. 143–64.

Hansen, Tore. Financial Development in Norwegian Local Government. In *Paddison, R. and Bailey, S., eds.*, 1988, pp. 171–89.

Hansen, Ulf. Nuclear Energy After Chernobyl: Views from Four Countries: Germany. *Energy J.*, January 1988, *9*(1), pp. 27–30.

Hansen, W. Lee. "Real" Books and Textbooks. *J. Econ. Educ.*, Summer 1988, *19*(3), pp. 271–74.

_____. A Research and Evaluation Agenda for DEEP and Precollege Economic Education: A Comment. *J. Econ. Educ.*, Winter 1988, *19*(1), pp. 14–16.

_____; Reeves, Roxanne W. and Stampen, Jacob O. Implications of Redefining Independent Student Status. *Econ. Educ. Rev.*, 1988, *7*(1), pp. 85–99.

_____ and Rhodes, Marilyn S. Student Debt Crisis: Are Students Incurring Excessive Debt? *Econ. Educ. Rev.*, 1988, *7*(1), pp. 101–12.

_____; Stampen, Jacob O. and Reeves, Roxanne W. The Impact of Student Earnings in Offsetting "Unmet Needs." *Econ. Educ. Rev.*, 1988, *7*(1), pp. 113–26.

Hansmann, Henry. Ownership of the Firm. *J. Law, Econ., Organ.*, Fall 1988, *4*(2), pp. 267–304.

Hanson, Donald A.; Sterner, Thomas and Boyd, Gale A. Decomposition of Changes in Energy Intensity. *Energy Econ.*, October 1988, *10*(4), pp. 309–12.

Hanson, Gregory D.; Kolajo, Ebenezer F. and Martin, Neil R., Jr. Forecast Errors and Farm Firm Growth. *J. Agr. Econ. Res.*, Fall 1988, *40*(4), pp. 2–11.

Hanson, John R., II. Third World Incomes before World War I: Some Comparisons. *Exploration Econ. Hist.*, July 1988, *25*(3), pp. 323–36.

_____. Why Isn't the Whole World Developed? A Traditional View. *J. Econ. Hist.*, September 1988, *48*(3), pp. 668–72.

Hanson, Mark E. and York, Dan W. The Impact of Oil Price Shocks on Economic Growth in Middle-Income Developing Countries. *J. Energy Devel.*, Autumn 1988, *14*(1), pp. 79–102.

Hanson, Patricia and Kuemmerling, Robert A. Inflation Holds Steady during the First Half. *Mon. Lab. Rev.*, October 1988, *111*(10), pp. 13–17.

Hanson, Philip. The Economics of Research and Development: Some East–West Comparisons. *Europ. Econ. Rev.*, March 1988, *32*(2–3), pp. 604–10.

_____. Navrozov versus the Agency. In *[Nove, A.]*, 1988, pp. 153–64.

Hanson, Royce. Water Supply and Distribution: The Next 50 Years. In *Ausubel, J. H. and Herman, R., eds.*, 1988, pp. 258–77.

Hanson, Susan and Pratt, Geraldine. Reconceptualizing the Links between Home and Work in Urban Geography. *Econ. Geogr.*, October 1988, *64*(4), pp. 299–321.

Hansson, Bengt. Risk Aversion as a Problem of Conjoint Measurement. In *Gärdenfors, P. and Sahlin, N.-E., eds.*, 1988, pp. 136–58.

Hansson, S. O. Rights and the Liberal Paradoxes. *Soc. Choice Welfare*, November 1988, *5*(4), pp. 287–302.

Hanusch, Horst. Evolutionary Economics: Introduction. In *Hanusch, H., ed.*, 1988, pp. 1–7.

Hanweck, Gerald A. and Goldberg, Lawrence G. What We Can Expect from Interstate Banking. *J. Banking Finance*, 1988, *12*(1), pp. 51–67.

_____ and Hannan, Timothy H. Bank Insolvency Risk and the Market for Large Certificates of Deposit. *J. Money, Credit, Banking*, May 1988, *20*(2), pp. 203–11.

Haque, Mohammed Ohidul. Estimation of Engel Elasticities from the Box–Cox Engel Function. *Metroecon.*, October 1988, *39*(3), pp. 317–35.

Haque, Nadeem U. Fiscal Policy and Private Sector Saving Behavior in Developing Economies. *Int. Monet. Fund Staff Pap.*, June 1988, *35*(2), pp. 316–35.

Hara, Terushi. Trade Associations or Agreements and Controlled Competition in France, 1830–1939: Comment. In *Yamazaki, H. and Miyamoto, M., eds.*, 1988, pp. 296–97.

Haraf, William S. Principal Policy Conclusions and Recommendations of the Financial Services Regulation Project. In *Haraf, W. S. and Kushmeider, R. M., eds.*, 1988, pp. 431–39.

_____. Restructuring Banking & Financial Services in America: Preface. In *Haraf, W. S. and Kushmeider, R. M., eds.*, 1988, pp. xiii–xvii.

_____. Toward a Sound Financial System. In *England, C. and Huertas, T., eds.*, 1988, pp. 181–85.

_____. Toward a Sound Financial System. *Cato J.*, Winter 1988, *7*(3), pp. 677–81.

_____ and Kushmeider, Rose Marie. Redefining Financial Markets. In *Haraf, W. S. and Kushmeider, R. M., eds.*, 1988, pp. 1–33.

Haraksingh, Kusha. Sugar, Labour and Livelihood in Trinidad, 1940–1970. *Soc. Econ. Stud.*, March–June 1988, *37*(1–2), pp. 271–91.

_____. The Uneasy Relationship: Peasants, Plantocrats and the Trinidad Sugar Industry, 1919–1938. In *Albert, B. and Graves, A., eds.*, 1988, pp. 109–20.

Harberger, Arnold C. Growth, Industrialization and Economic Structure: Latin America and East Asia Compared. In *Hughes, H., ed.*, 1988, pp. 164–94.

_____. The Incidence of the Corporation Income Tax. In *Ricketts, M., ed., Vol. 1*, 1988, *1962*, pp. 333–58.

_____. Indexing the Tax System for Inflation: Comments. In *Aaron, H. J.; Galper, H. and Pechman, J. A., eds.*, 1988, pp. 380–83.

_____. World Inflation Revisited. In *Helpman, E.; Razin, A. and Sadka, E., eds.*, 1988, pp. 217–37.

Harbison, Ralph W. and Habte, Aklilu. External Aid for African Education. *Finance Develop.*, March 1988, *25*(1), pp. 25–27.

Harcourt, G. C. Nicholas Kaldor, 12 May 1908–30 September 1986. *Economica*, May 1988, *55*(218), pp. 159–70.

_____. Piero Sraffa Memorial Issue: Introduction. *Cambridge J. Econ.*, March 1988, *12*(1), pp. 1–5.

———— and **Hamouda, Omar F.** Post Keynesianism: From Criticism to Coherence? *Bull. Econ. Res.*, January 1988, *40*(1), pp. 1–33.

———— and **Kenyon, Peter.** Pricing and the Investment Decision. In *Sawyer, M. C., ed.*, 1988, *1976*, pp. 266–94.

———— and **Massaro, Vincent G.** Mr. Sraffa's Production of Commodities. In *Steedman, I., ed.*, Vol. 1, 1988, *1964*, pp. 29–41.

———— and **Massaro, Vincent G.** A Note on Mr. Sraffa's Sub-systems. In *Steedman, I., ed.*, Vol. 1, 1988, *1964*, pp. 21–28.

Hardaker, J. Brian. Contribution to Swapmeet Discussion. *Rev. Marketing Agr. Econ.*, August 1988, *56*(2), pp. 223.

————; **Pannell, David J. and Patten, Louise H.** Utility-Efficient Programming for Whole-Farm Planning. *Australian J. Agr. Econ.*, Aug.–Dec. 1988, *32*(2–3), pp. 88–97.

Hardee-Cleaveland, Karen and Banister, Judith. Fertility Policy and Implementation in China, 1986–88. *Population Devel. Rev.*, June 1988, *14*(2), pp. 245–86.

Hardin, Garrett. Cassandra's Role in the Population Wrangle. In *Ehrlich, P. R. and Holdren, J. P., eds.*, 1988, pp. 3–16.

Härdle, Wolfgang. Efficient Nonparametric Smoothing in High Dimensions Using Interactive Graphical Techniques. In *Edwards, D. and Raun, N. E., eds.*, 1988, pp. 17–30.

———— and **Bowman, Adrian W.** Bootstrapping in Nonparametric Regression: Local Adaptive Smoothing and Confidence Bands. *J. Amer. Statist. Assoc.*, March 1988, *83*(401), pp. 102–10.

————; **Hall, Peter H. and Marron, J. S.** How Far Are Automatically Chosen Regression Smoothing Parameters from Their Optimum?: Rejoinder. *J. Amer. Statist. Assoc.*, March 1988, *83*(401), pp. 100–01.

————; **Hall, Peter H. and Marron, J. S.** How Far Are Automatically Chosen Regression Smoothing Parameters from Their Optimum? *J. Amer. Statist. Assoc.*, March 1988, *83*(401), pp. 86–95.

Hardouvelis, Gikas A. Economic News, Exchange Rates and Interest Rates. *J. Int. Money Finance*, March 1988, *7*(1), pp. 23–35.

————. Evidence on Stock Market Speculative Bubbles: Japan, the United States, and Great Britain. *Fed. Res. Bank New York Quart. Rev.*, Summer 1988, *13*(2), pp. 4–16.

————. Margin Requirements and Stock Market Volatility. *Fed. Res. Bank New York Quart. Rev.*, Summer 1988, *13*(2), pp. 80–89.

————. The Predictive Power of the Term Structure during Recent Monetary Regimes. *J. Finance*, June 1988, *43*(2), pp. 339–56.

Hardt, John P. and Boone, Jean F. A New U.S. Economic Policy toward Poland. In *Marer, P. and Siwinski, W., eds.*, 1988, pp. 335–44.

Hardy, Chandra. It Is Time to Rethink Our Development Strategies. In *Tavis, L. A., ed.*, 1988, pp. 155–60.

Hardy, William E., Jr.; Disney, W. Terry and

Duffy, Patricia A. A Markov Chain Analysis of Pork Farm Size Distributions in the South. *Southern J. Agr. Econ.*, December 1988, *20*(2), pp. 57–64.

Hare, Paul G. Economics of Publicly Provided Private Goods and Services. In *Hare, P. G., ed.*, 1988, pp. 68–101.

————. Surveys in Public Sector Economics: An Overview. In *Hare, P. G., ed.*, 1988, pp. 1–11.

————. What Can China Learn from the Hungarian Economic Reforms? In *Feuchtwang, S.; Hussain, A. and Pairault, T., eds.*, Vol. 2, 1988, pp. 51–66.

Harford, Jon D. and Marcus, Richard D. A General Equilibrium Model of the Volunteer Military. *Southern Econ. J.*, October 1988, *55*(2), pp. 472–84.

Haririan, Mehdi. Demonstrable Biases against State-Owned Enterprises. In *Pennsylvania Economic Association*, 1988, pp. 727–44.

Harker, Patrick T. Dispersed Spatial Price Equilibrium. *Environ. Planning A*, March 1988, *20*(3), pp. 353–68.

————. Issues and Models for Planning and Regulating Freight Transport Systems. In *Bianco, L. and La Bella, A., eds.*, 1988, pp. 374–408.

Harkin, Michael. AgriLine—A Videotex Service for Irish Farmers. In *Schiefer, G., ed.*, 1988, pp. 103–21.

————. Videotex, Information and Communication in European Agriculture: Review and Outlook: A Summary of the Seminar. In *Schiefer, G., ed.*, 1988, pp. 249–52.

Harl, Neil E. Technological Innovations with Implications for Agricultural Economics: A Discussion. In *Hildreth, R. J., et al., eds.*, 1988, pp. 109–15.

Harley, C. Knick. Ocean Freight Rates and Productivity, 1740–1913: The Primacy of Mechanical Invention Reaffirmed. *J. Econ. Hist.*, December 1988, *48*(4), pp. 851–76.

Harlow, W. V. and Brown, Keith C. Market Overreaction: Magnitude and Intensity. *J. Portfol. Manage.*, Winter 1988, *14*(2), pp. 6–13.

————; **Tinic, Seha M. and Brown, Keith C.** Risk Aversion, Uncertain Information, and Market Efficiency. *J. Finan. Econ.*, December 1988, *22*(2), pp. 355–85.

Harmon, Oskar Ragnar. The Income Elasticity of Demand for Single-Family Owner-Occupied Housing: An Empirical Reconciliation. *J. Urban Econ.*, September 1988, *24*(2), pp. 173–85.

———— and **Potepan, Michael J.** Housing Adjustment Costs: Their Impact on Mobility and Housing Demand Elasticities. *Amer. Real Estate Urban Econ. Assoc. J.*, Winter 1988, *16*(4), pp. 459–78.

Harmstone, Richard C. Background to Gorbachev's Investment Strategy. *Comp. Econ. Stud.*, Winter 1988, *30*(4), pp. 58–91.

Harnos, Zsolt; Láng, István and Csete, László. The Enterprisal System of an Adjusting Agriculture in Hungary. *Europ. Rev. Agr. Econ.*, 1988, *15*(2–3), pp. 225–38.

Harootunian, H. D. and Najita, Tetsuo. Japanese Revolt against the West: Political and Cultural Criticism in the Twentieth Century. In *Duus, P., ed.,* 1988, pp. 711–74.

Harpaz, Giora. The Non-optimality of the Over-the-Counter Options Dividend Protection. *Econ. Letters,* 1988, 27(1), pp. 55–59.

_____; **Cakici, Nusret and Eytan, T. Hanan.** American vs. European Options on the Value Line Index. *J. Futures Markets,* June 1988, 8(3), pp. 373–88.

_____; **Krull, Steven and Eytan, T. Hanan.** The Pricing of Dollar Index Futures Contracts. *J. Futures Markets,* April 1988, 8(2), pp. 127–39.

Harper-Fender, Ann. Organizational Change in the Hudson's Bay Company after 1831. In *Pennsylvania Economic Association,* 1988, pp. 294–308.

Harper, Ian R. Monetary Policy in a Deregulated Financial System. *Australian Econ. Rev.,* Summer 1988, (84), pp. 58–63.

_____. The SRD Requirement and Monetary Policy. *Econ. Rec.,* September 1988, 64(186), pp. 178–86.

_____ **and Lim, G. C.** Financial Implications of the Commonwealth Budget Surplus. *Australian Econ. Rev.,* Summer 1988, (84), pp. 19–25.

Harr, Michael and Kohli, Rajiv. The Role of Contract Research Organizations in Successful International Space Commercialization. In *Egan, J. J., et al.,* 1988, pp. 317–29.

Harrigan, Frank J. and McGilvray, James. The Measurement of Interindustry Linkages. *Ricerche Econ.,* April–June 1988, 42(2), pp. 325–43.

Harrigan, Kathryn Rudie. Strategic Alliances and Partner Asymmetries. In *Contractor, F. J. and Lorange, P.,* 1988, pp. 205–26.

Harrington, Charlene; Newcomer, Robert J. and Moore, Thomas Gale. Factors That Contribute to Medicare HMO Risk Contract Success. *Inquiry,* Summer 1988, 25(2), pp. 251–62.

Harrington, David H. The Status of Southern Agriculture. In *Beaulieu, L. J., ed.,* 1988, pp. 30–50.

Harrington, James W., Jr. and Amrhein, Carl G. Location, Technical Change and Labour Migration in a Heterogeneous Industry. *Reg. Stud.,* December 1988, 22(6), pp. 515–29.

_____ **and Barnas, D. J.** Foreign-Owned Firms and Regional–Functional Specialization. *Environ. Planning A,* July 1988, 20(7), pp. 937–52.

Harrington, Joseph E., Jr. and Chang, Myong-Hun. The Effects of Irreversible Investment in Durable Capacity on the Incentive for Horizontal Merger. *Southern Econ. J.,* October 1988, 55(2), pp. 443–53.

Harrington, Joseph J.; Fiering, Myron B. and Rogers, Peter P. New Approaches to Using Mathematical Programming for Resource Allocation. In *O'Mara, G. T., ed.,* 1988, pp. 122–26.

Harrington, Scott E. Prices and Profits in the Liability Insurance Market. In *Litan, R. E. and Winston, C., eds.,* 1988, pp. 42–100.

_____. The Relationship between Standard Premium Loss Ratios and Firm Size in Workers' Compensation Insurance. In *Borba, P. S. and Appel, D., eds.,* 1988, pp. 95–107.

_____ **and Cummins, J. David.** The Relationship between Risk and Return: Evidence for Property-Liability Insurance Stocks. *J. Risk Ins.,* March 1988, 55(1), pp. 15–31.

Harrington, Winston. Efficient vs Open-Access Use of Public Facilities in the Long Run. *J. Environ. Econ. Manage.,* December 1988, 15(4), pp. 462–69.

_____. Enforcement Leverage When Penalties Are Restricted. *J. Public Econ.,* October 1988, 37(1), pp. 29–53.

Harris, A. H. and Cairns, J. A. Firm Location and Differential Barriers to Entry in the Offshore Oil Supply Industry. *Reg. Stud.,* December 1988, 22(6), pp. 499–506.

Harris, Bernard. Unemployment, Insurance and Health in Interwar Britain. In *Eichengreen, B. and Hatton, T. J., eds.,* 1988, pp. 149–83.

Harris, Beverly and Cecutti, Albert. Quality of Working Life: The Challenge of Occupational Health and Safety. In *Richardson, P. R. and Gesing, R., eds.,* 1988, pp. 105–09.

Harris, Britton. Speculations on the Future of Energy and Planning. In *Byrne, J. and Rich, D., eds.,* 1988, pp. 283–95.

Harris, Chauncy D. The Soviet Union Today: Basic Geography. In *Cracraft, J., ed.,* 1988, pp. 137–53.

Harris, Daniel and Herzel, Leo. Litigation in the United States. *Nat. Westminster Bank Quart. Rev.,* November 1988, pp. 14–27.

Harris, Donald J. Capital, Distribution, and the Aggregate Production Function. In *Steedman, I., ed., Vol. 1,* 1988, *1973,* pp. 218–31.

_____. The Circuit of Capital and the 'Labour Problem' in Capitalist Development. *Soc. Econ. Stud.,* March–June 1988, 37(1–2), pp. 15–31.

_____. On the Classical Theory of Competition. *Cambridge J. Econ.,* March 1988, 12(1), pp. 139–67.

Harris, Duane G. Management Problems of Farms and Agricultural Firms: A Discussion. In *Hildreth, R. J., et al., eds.,* 1988, pp. 301–06.

Harris, Edwin C. Civil Penalties under the Income Tax Act. In *Canadian Tax Foundation,* 1988, pp. 9.1–24.

Harris, Fred R. Social Security: The First Half-Century: Specific Studies: Comment. In *Nash, G. D.; Pugach, N. H. and Tomasson, R. F., eds.,* 1988, pp. 299–301.

Harris, Frederick H. deB. Capital Intensity and the Firm's Cost of Capital. *Rev. Econ. Statist.,* November 1988, 70(4), pp. 587–94.

_____. Testable Competing Hypotheses from Structure–Performance Theory: Efficient Structure versus Market Power. *J. Ind. Econ.,* March 1988, 36(3), pp. 267–80.

Harris, Geoffrey Thomas. Research Output in

Australian University Economics Departments, 1974–83. *Australian Econ. Pap.*, June 1988, 27(50), pp. 102–10.

Harris, I. W. Hong Kong: Salaries Tax: The Goepfert Case. *Bull. Int. Fiscal Doc.*, June 1988, 42(6), pp. 251–52.

_____. 1988/89 Budget: Hong Kong. *Bull. Int. Fiscal Doc.*, May 1988, 42(5), pp. 223–25.

Harris, Laurence. Alternative Perspectives on the Financial System. In *Harris, L., et al., eds.*, 1988, pp. 7–35.

_____. Financial Reform and Economic Growth: A New Interpretation of South Korea's Experience. In *Harris, L., et al., eds.*, 1988, pp. 368–88.

_____. The IMF and Mechanisms of Integration. In *Crow, B. and Thorpe, M., et al.*, 1988, pp. 310–30.

_____. Money and Finance with Undeveloped Banking in the Occupied Territories. In *Abed, G. T., ed.*, 1988, pp. 191–222.

_____. The UK Economy at a Crossroads. In *Allen, J. and Massey, D., eds.*, 1988, pp. 7–44.

_____ and **Coakley, Jerry.** Evaluating the Role of the Financial System. In *Harris, L., et al., eds.*, 1988, pp. 125–42.

_____ and **Coakley, Jerry.** Industry, the City and the Foreign Exchanges: Theory and Evidence. In *Harris, L., et al., eds.*, 1988, pp. 88–115.

_____ and **Croasdale, Martin.** Internal Funds and Investment. In *Harris, L., et al., eds.*, 1988, pp. 225–34.

Harris, Lawrence E. Intra-day Stock Return Patterns. In *Dimson, E., ed.*, 1988, pp. 91–108.

_____. Predicting Contemporary Volume with Historic Volume at Differential Price Levels: Evidence Supporting the Disposition Effect: Discussion. *J. Finance*, July 1988, 43(3), pp. 698–99.

_____ and **Glosten, Lawrence R.** Estimating the Components of the Bid/Ask Spread. *J. Finan. Econ.*, May 1988, 21(1), pp. 123–42.

Harris, Milton and Raviv, Artur. Some Results on Incentive Contracts with Applications to Education and Employment, Health Insurance, and Law Enforcement. In *Ricketts, M., ed., Vol. 1, 1988, 1978*, pp. 220–30.

_____ and **Raviv, Artur.** Corporate Control Contests and Capital Structure. *J. Finan. Econ.*, Jan.–March 1988, 20(1–2), pp. 55–86.   .

_____ and **Raviv, Artur.** Corporate Governance: Voting Rights and Majority Rules. *J. Finan. Econ.*, Jan.–March 1988, 20(1–2), pp. 203–35.

Harris, Nigel. New Bourgeoisies? *J. Devel. Stud.*, January 1988, 24(2), pp. 237–49.

Harris, R. J. and Nicholls, J. R. Methodology in International Acquisitions: An Exploratory Study. *Managerial Dec. Econ.*, June 1988, 9(2), pp. 101–07.

Harris, Richard I. D. Industrial Policy and International Competition in Wide-Bodied Jet Aircraft: Comment. In *Baldwin, R. E., ed. (II)*, 1988, pp. 72–74.

_____. Market Structure and External Control

in the Regional Economies of Great Britain. *Scot. J. Polit. Econ.*, November 1988, 35(4), pp. 334–60.

_____. Modelling the Demand for Factors of Production in the Mechanical Engineering Industry of Northern Ireland, 1954–79. *Econ. Soc. Rev.*, July 1988, 19(4), pp. 249–63.

_____. Technological Change and Regional Development in the UK: Evidence from the SPRU Database on Innovations. *Reg. Stud.*, October 1988, 22(5), pp. 361–74.

_____ and **Beaumont, P. B.** Sub-systems of Industrial Relations: The Spatial Dimension in Britain. *Brit. J. Ind. Relat.*, November 1988, 26(3), pp. 397–407.

_____ and **Wass, V. J.** The Structure of Collective Bargaining in Northern Ireland, 1973–84. *Econ. Soc. Rev.*, January 1988, 19(2), pp. 99–122.

Harris, Robert G. and Grimm, Curtis M. A Qualitative Choice Analysis of Rail Routings: Implications for Vertical Foreclosure and Competition Policy. *Logist. Transp. Rev.*, March 1988, 24(1), pp. 49–67.

Harris, Robert S.; Born, Jeffery A. and Eisenbeis, Robert A. The Benefits of Geographical and Product Expansion in the Financial Service Industries. *J. Finan. Services Res.*, January 1988, 1(2), pp. 161–82.

_____; **Mayer, Colin and Franks, Julian R.** Means of Payment in Takeovers: Results for the United Kingdom and the United States. In *Auerbach, A. J., ed. (I)*, 1988, pp. 221–58.

Harris, Thomas N. Performance Testing Domestic Cookstoves for Zimbabwe. In *Hosier, R. H., ed. (I)*, 1988, pp. 142–59.

_____. The Prospect for Application of Renewable Energy Technologies in Zimbabwe's Rural Domestic and Agricultural Sectors. In *Hosier, R. H., ed. (I)*, 1988, pp. 199–242.

Harris, Thomas R. Assisting Local Government Needs: The Nevada Experience. In *Johnson, T. G.; Deaton, B. J. and Segarra, E., eds.*, 1988, pp. 127–30.

Harrison, Bennett. The Economic Development of Massachusetts. In *Lampe, D., ed.*, 1988, 1974, pp. 74–88.

_____ and **Bluestone, Barry.** The Growth of Low-Wage Employment: 1963–86. *Amer. Econ. Rev.*, May 1988, 78(2), pp. 124–28.

Harrison, Carolyn M.; Burgess, Jacquelin and Limb, Melanie. Exploring Environmental Values Through the Medium of Small Groups: 2. Illustrations of a Group at Work. *Environ. Planning A*, April 1988, 20(4), pp. 457–76.

_____; **Burgess, Jacquelin and Limb, Melanie.** Exploring Environmental Values through the Medium of Small Groups: 1. Theory and Practice. *Environ. Planning A*, March 1988, 20(3), pp. 309–26.

_____; **Limb, Melanie and Burgess, Jacquelin.** People, Parks and the Urban Green: A Study of Popular Meanings and Values for Open Spaces in the City. *Urban Stud.*, December 1988, 25(6), pp. 455–73.

Harrison, Glenn W. Predatory Pricing in a Multiple Market Experiment: A Note. *J. Econ. Behav. Organ.*, June 1988, 9(4), pp. 405–17.

Harrison, J. Richard and March, James G. Decision-Making and Postdecision Surprises. **In** *March, J. G.*, 1988, *1984*, pp. 228–49.

Harrison, Mark. Soviet Industrial Expansion under Late Stalinism (1945–55): The Short-run Dynamic of Civilian Output from Demobilisation to Rearmament. *J. Europ. Econ. Hist.*, Fall 1988, 17(2), pp. 359–78.

Harrison, Paul D.; West, Stephen G. and Reneau, J. Hal. Initial Attributions and Information-Seeking by Superiors and Subordinates in Production Variance Investigations. *Accounting Rev.*, April 1988, 63(2), pp. 307–20.

Harrison, Richard T. and Mason, Colin M. Risk Finance, the Equity Gap and New Venture Formation in the United Kingdom: The Impact of the Business Expansion Scheme. **In** *Kirchhoff, B. A., et al., eds.*, 1988, pp. 595–609.

Harrison, Robert S. and Wilber, Charles K. The Methodological Basis of Institutional Economics: Pattern Model, Storytelling, and Holism. **In** *Samuels, W. J., ed., Vol. 2*, 1988, *1978*, pp. 95–123.

Harrison, William B. Embattled Institution: Old and New Adversaries of the Federal Reserve System. *Soc. Sci. Quart.*, September 1988, 69(3), pp. 646–59.

Harriss, Barbara. Limitations of the 'Lessons from India.' **In** *Curtis, D.; Hubbard, M. and Shepherd, A.*, 1988, pp. 157–70.

Harsanyi, John C. Assessing Other People's Utilities. **In** *Munier, B. R., ed.*, 1988, pp. 127–38.

Harstad, Ronald M. Dual Ceteris Paribus Comparisons: Some Initial Thoughts on Laboratory Isolation of Equilibrium Forces in Auction Markets. **In** *Tietz, R.; Albers, W. and Selten, R., eds.*, 1988, pp. 173–83.

Hart, Keith. Kinship, Contract, and Trust: The Economic Organization of Migrants in an African City Slum. **In** *Gambetta, D., ed.*, 1988, pp. 176–93.

Hart, Oliver D. Capital Structure as a Control Mechanism in Corporations. *Can. J. Econ.*, August 1988, 21(3), pp. 467–76.

_____. Characteristics of Targets of Hostile and Friendly Takeovers: Comment. **In** *Auerbach, A. J., ed. (I)*, 1988, pp. 129–34.

_____. Incomplete Contracts and the Theory of the Firm. *J. Law, Econ., Organ.*, Spring 1988, 4(1), pp. 119–39.

_____. A Model of Imperfect Competition with Keynesian Features. **In** *Grandmont, J.-M., ed.*, 1988, *1982*, pp. 447–76.

_____. On the Existence of Equilibrium in a Securities Model. **In** *Grandmont, J.-M., ed.*, 1988, *1974*, pp. 137–55.

_____ **and Grossman, Sanford J.** One Share–One Vote and the Market for Corporate Control. *J. Finan. Econ.*, Jan.–March 1988, 20(1–2), pp. 175–202.

_____ **and Moore, John.** Incomplete Contracts and Renegotiation. *Econometrica*, July 1988, 56(4), pp. 755–85.

_____ **and Tirole, Jean.** Contract Renegotiation and Coasian Dynamics. *Rev. Econ. Stud.*, October 1988, 55(4), pp. 509–40.

Hart, R. F. G. Aspects of Health Insurance: Moral Hazard, Agency Problems, and a Welfare Loss Estimate for Australia. **In** *Smith, C. S., ed.*, 1988, pp. 253–71.

Hart, Robert A. The Theory of Demand and Supply of Labour—The Post-Keynesian View: Comment. **In** *Kregel, J. A.; Matzner, E. and Roncaglia, A., eds.*, 1988, pp. 43–47.

_____ **and Kawasaki, Seiichi.** Payroll Taxes and Factor Demand. **In** *Ehrenberg, R. G., ed.*, 1988, pp. 257–85.

_____ **and McGregor, Peter G.** The Returns to Labour Services in West German Manufacturing Industry. *Europ. Econ. Rev.*, April 1988, 32(4), pp. 947–63.

_____ **and Wilson, Nicholas.** The Demand for Workers and Hours: Micro Evidence from the U.K. Metal Working Industry. **In** *Hart, R. A., ed.*, 1988, pp. 162–79.

Hart, Sergiu and Mas-Colell, Andreu. The Potential of the Shapley Value. **In** *[Shapley, L. S.]*, 1988, pp. 127–37.

_____ **and Neyman, Abraham.** Values of Nonatomic Vector Measure Games: Are They Linear Combinations of the Measures? *J. Math. Econ.*, 1988, 17(1), pp. 31–40.

Hart, Stuart L.; Denison, Daniel R. and Chambers, Brian R. Founding Team Experience and New Firm Performance. **In** *Kirchhoff, B. A., et al., eds.*, 1988, pp. 106–18.

Harte, John. Acid Rain. **In** *Ehrlich, P. R. and Holdren, J. P., eds.*, 1988, pp. 125–46.

Harter, Rachel M.; Fuller, Wayne A. and Battese, George E. An Error-Components Model for Prediction of County Crop Areas Using Survey and Satellite Data. *J. Amer. Statist. Assoc.*, March 1988, 83(401), pp. 28–36.

Hartland-Thunberg, Penelope. China and the GATT: Time for Modernization. **In** *Yochelson, J., ed.*, 1988, pp. 175–202.

Hartley, Keith. Aerospace: The Political Economy of an Industry. **In** *de Jong, H. W., ed.*, 1988, pp. 329–54.

_____. The European Defence Market and Industry. **In** *Creasey, P. and May, S., eds.*, 1988, pp. 31–59.

Hartley, Nicholas and Culham, Peter. Telecommunications Prices under Monopoly and Competition. *Oxford Rev. Econ. Policy*, Summer 1988, 4(2), pp. 1–19.

Hartley, Peter R. The Liquidity Services of Money. *Int. Econ. Rev.*, February 1988, 29(1), pp. 1–24.

_____ **and Kyle, Albert S.** Real Interest Rates and Home Goods: A Two-Period Model. *Econ. Rec.*, September 1988, 64(186), pp. 168–77.

_____ **and Walsh, Carl E.** Financial Intermediation, Monetary Policy, and Equilibrium Business Cycles. *Fed. Res. Bank San Francisco Econ. Rev.*, Fall 1988, (4), pp. 19–28.

Hartman, Raymond S. Self-Selection Bias in the

Evaluation of Voluntary Energy Conservation Programs. *Rev. Econ. Statist.*, August 1988, *70*(3), pp. 448–58.

_____; **Woo, Chi-Keung and Doane, Michael J.** Household Preference for Interruptible Rate Options and the Revealed Value of Service Reliability. *Energy J.*, Special Issue, 1988, *9*, pp. 121–34.

_____; **Woo, Chi-Keung and Doane, Michael J.** Households' Perceived Value of Service Reliability: An Analysis of Contingent Valuation Data. *Energy J.*, Special Issue, 1988, *9*, pp. 135–49.

Hartman, Richard. Money, Inflation, and Investment. *J. Monet. Econ.*, November 1988, *22*(3), pp. 473–84.

Hartmann, Heidi I. The Political Economy of Comparable Worth. In *Mangum, G. and Philips, P., eds.*, 1988, pp. 217–34.

_____ **and Folbre, Nancy.** The Rhetoric of Self-Interest: Ideology and Gender in Economic Theory. In *Klamer, A.; McCloskey, D. N. and Solow, R. M., eds.*, 1988, pp. 184–203.

Hartog, Joop. An Ordered Response Model for Allocation and Earnings. *Kyklos*, 1988, *41*(1), pp. 113–41.

_____. Poverty and the Measurement of Individual Welfare: A Review Article. *J. Human Res.*, Spring 1988, *23*(2), pp. 243–66.

_____ **and Bierens, Herman J.** Estimating a Hedonic Earnings Function with a Nonparametric Method. *Empirical Econ.*, 1988, *13*(3–4), pp. 267–94.

_____ **and Bierens, Herman J.** Non-linear Regression with Discrete Explanatory Variables, with an Application to the Earnings Function. *J. Econometrics*, July 1988, *38*(3), pp. 269–99.

_____; **Mekkelholt, Eddie and van Ophem, Hans.** Testing the Relevance of Job Search for Job Mobility. *Econ. Letters*, 1988, *27*(3), pp. 299–303.

_____ **and Odink, J. G.** Equity and Efficiency in Holland: An Overview. In *Brenner, Y. S.; Reijnders, J. P. G. and Spithoven, A. H. G. M., eds.*, 1988, pp. 190–208.

_____ **and Oosterbeek, Hessel.** Education, Allocation and Earnings in the Netherlands: Overschooling? *Econ. Educ. Rev.*, 1988, *7*(2), pp. 185–94.

Hartu, C. Program for Computer-Assisted of Economic Analysis and Forecasting. *Econ. Computat. Cybern. Stud. Res.*, 1988, *23*(2), pp. 15–20.

Hartwick, John M. Robert Wallace and Malthus and the Ratios. *Hist. Polit. Econ.*, Fall 1988, *20*(3), pp. 357–79.

_____ **and Yeung, David.** Interest Rate and Output Price Uncertainty and Industry Equilibrium for Non-renewable Resource Extracting Firms. *Resources & Energy*, March 1988, *10*(1), pp. 1–14.

Hartwick, Jon; Warshaw, Paul R. and Sheppard, Blair H. The Theory of Reasoned Action: A Meta-analysis of Past Research with Recommendations for Modifications and Future Research. *J. Cons. Res.*, December 1988, *15*(3), pp. 325–43.

Hartzell, David J., et al. A Look at Real Estate Duration. *J. Portfol. Manage.*, Fall 1988, *15*(1), pp. 16–24.

Haruna, Shoji. Industry Equilibrium with Uncertainty and Labor-Managed Firms. *Econ. Letters*, 1988, *26*(1), pp. 83–88.

_____. The Production Strategy of a Labor-Managed Firm and Price Uncertainty. *Econ. Anal. Workers' Manage.*, 1988, *22*(1–2), pp. 53–62.

Harvey, A. C. and Stock, James H. Continuous Time Autoregressive Models with Common Stochastic Trends. *J. Econ. Dynam. Control*, June–Sept. 1988, *12*(2–3), pp. 365–84.

Harvey, Campbell R. The Real Term Structure and Consumption Growth. *J. Finan. Econ.*, December 1988, *22*(2), pp. 305–33.

Harvey, D. R. Research Priorities in Agriculture. *J. Agr. Econ.*, January 1988, *39*(1), pp. 81–97.

Harvey, Edward B. and Murthy, K. S. R. Forecasting Manpower Demand and Supply: A Model for the Accounting Profession in Canada. *Int. J. Forecasting*, 1988, *4*(4), pp. 551–62.

Harvey, F. D. Herodotus and the Man-Footed Creature. In *Archer, L. J., ed.*, 1988, pp. 42–52.

Harvey, James W. and McCrohan, Kevin F. Voluntary Compliance and the Effectiveness of Public and Non-profit Institutions: American Philanthropy and Taxation. *J. Econ. Psych.*, September 1988, *9*(3), pp. 369–86.

Harwood, Alison; Aderhold, Robert and Cumming, Christine. International Linkages among Equities Markets and the October 1987 Market Break. *Fed. Res. Bank New York Quart. Rev.*, Summer 1988, *13*(2), pp. 34–46.

Hasan, M. Aynul. Financial Repression, Financial Development and Structure of Savings in Pakistan: Comment. *Pakistan Devel. Rev.*, Part 2, Winter 1988, *27*(4), pp. 712–13.

_____. Is There a Phillips Curve in Pakistan? *Pakistan Devel. Rev.*, Part 2, Winter 1988, *27*(4), pp. 839–49.

_____. What Remains of the Case for Flexible Exchange Rates? Comments. *Pakistan Devel. Rev.*, Part 1, Winter 1988, *27*(4), pp. 449–50.

_____; **Kadir, S. Ghulam and Mahmud, S. Fakhre.** Substitutability of Pakistan's Monetary Assets under Alternative Monetary Aggregates. *Pakistan Devel. Rev.*, Autumn 1988, *27*(3), pp. 317–26.

Hasan, Parvez. Domestic Adjustment Policies and External Economic Shocks. *Int. Econ. J.*, Spring 1988, *2*(1), pp. 53–68.

Hasbrouck, Joel. Trades, Quotes, Inventories, and Information. *J. Finan. Econ.*, December 1988, *22*(2), pp. 229–52.

_____ **and Friend, Irwin.** Determinants of Capital Structure. In *Chen, A. H., ed.*, 1988, pp. 1–19.

_____ **and Schwartz, Robert A.** Liquidity and Execution Costs in Equity Markets. *J. Portfol. Manage.*, Spring 1988, *14*(3), pp. 10–16.

Hasegawa, Tsuyoshi. Gorbachev, the New Thinking of Soviet Foreign-Security Policy and the Military: Recent Trends and Implications. **In**

Juviler, P. and Kimura, H., eds., 1988, pp. 115–47.

Hasenkamp, Georg and Kracht-Müntz, Birgit. Indices of Allocation Inefficiencies for Heterogeneous Labor. In *Eichhorn, W., ed.*, 1988, pp. 751–66.

Hashemzadeh, Nozar and Taylor, Philip. Stock Prices, Money Supply, and Interest Rates: The Question of Causality. *Appl. Econ.*, December 1988, *20*(12), pp. 1603–11.

Hashimoto, Jurō. The Development of Business Associations in Prewar Japan: Comment. In *Yamazaki, H. and Miyamoto, M.*, eds., 1988, pp. 46–49.

Hashimoto, Masanori and Raisian, John. The Structure and Short-Run Adaptability of Labor Markets in Japan and the United States. In *Hart, R. A.*, ed., 1988, pp. 314–40.

Haskel, Jonathan and Jackman, Richard. Long-term Unemployment in Britain and the Effects of the Community Programme. *Oxford Bull. Econ. Statist.*, November 1988, *50*(4), pp. 379–408.

Haslag, Joseph H.; Fomby, Thomas B. and Slottje, Daniel J. A Study of the Relationship between Economic Growth and Inequality: The Case of Mexico. *Fed. Res. Bank Dallas Econ. Rev.*, May 1988, pp. 13–25.

_____ **and Hafer, R. W.** The FOMC in 1987: The Effects of a Falling Dollar and the Stock Market Collapse. *Fed. Res. Bank St. Louis Rev.*, March–April 1988, *70*(2), pp. 3–16.

Haslam, R. B. and Collins, Neil. Local Government Finance in the Republic of Ireland—The Aftermath of Rates Abolition. In *Paddison, R. and Bailey, S.*, eds., 1988, pp. 218–29.

Hassan, J. A. and Duncan, A. Energy Price Convergence in the European Community, 1960–82. *Appl. Econ.*, January 1988, *20*(1), pp. 73–79.

Hassan, M. Kabir. The Immigration of Third World Scientists and Engineers to the United States: Theoretical, Empirical and Policy Evaluations. *Pakistan J. Appl. Econ.*, Summer 1988, *7*(1), pp. 43–58.

Hassan, Rashid M. and Hertzler, Greg. Deforestation from the Overexploitation of Wood Resources as a Cooking Fuel: A Dynamic Approach to Pricing Energy Resources in Sudan. *Energy Econ.*, April 1988, *10*(2), pp. 163–68.

Hasselberg, Frank and Steinmann, Horst. Der strategische Managementprozess—Vorüberlegungen für eine Neuorientierung. (With English summary.) *Z. Betriebswirtschaft*, December 1988, *58*(12), pp. 1308–22.

Hassell, John M.; Jennings, Robert H. and Lasser, Dennis J. Management Earnings Forecasts: Their Usefulness as a Source of Firm-Specific Information to Security Analysts. *J. Finan. Res.*, Winter 1988, *11*(4), pp. 303–19.

Hasselman, B. H.; Kok, J. H. M. and Okker, V. R. FREIA and Employment Policies in the Netherlands. In *Hopkins, M. J. D.*, ed., 1988, pp. 103–31.

Hassin, Refael and Glazer, Amihai. Optimal Con-

tests. *Econ. Inquiry*, January 1988, *26*(1), pp. 133–43.

Hassler, James B.; Shalaby, Seif and Yanagida, John F. United States Market Share of Latin American Wheat Imports: Disaggregated Analysis and Application of the Armington Model. *J. Econ. Stud.*, 1988, *15*(5), pp. 24–33.

Hata, Ikuhiko. The Cambridge History of Japan: Volume 6: The Twentieth Century: Continental Expansion, 1905–1941. In *Duus, P.*, ed., 1988, pp. 271–314.

Hatanaka, Toshiharu and Uosaki, Katsuji. Optimal Input for Autoregressive Model Discrimination Based on the Kullback's Divergence. In *Iri, M. and Yajima, K.*, eds., 1988, pp. 101–08.

Hatcher, Larry and Ross, Timothy L. Gainsharing Plans—How Managers Evaluate Them. In *Timpe, A. D.*, ed., 1988, *1986*, pp. 213–25.

Hathaway, Dale E. Linkages between Bilateral and Multilateral Negotiations in Agriculture: Discussion. In *Allen, K. and Macmillan, K.*, eds., 1988, pp. 179–81.

_____ **and Miner, William M.** World Agriculture in Crisis: Reforming Government Policies. In *Miner, W. M. and Hathaway, D. E.*, eds., 1988, pp. 37–110.

Hättenschwiler, P. Konsumlenkung bei Lebensmittelrationierung. Decision Support System zur Rationenplanung. (Decision Support System for Determining Food Rations during Crisis Time. With English summary.) *Schweiz. Z. Volkswirtsch. Statist.*, September 1988, *124*(3), pp. 431–44.

Hatton, T. J. Institutional Change and Wage Rigidity in the UK, 1880–1985. *Oxford Rev. Econ. Policy*, Spring 1988, *4*(1), pp. 74–86.

_____. Profit Sharing in British Industry, 1865–1913. *Int. J. Ind. Organ.*, March 1988, *6*(1), pp. 69–90.

_____. A Quarterly Model of the Labour Market in Interwar Britain. *Oxford Bull. Econ. Statist.*, February 1988, *50*(1), pp. 1–25.

_____. The Recovery of the 1930s and Economic Policy in Britain. In *Gregory, R. G. and Butlin, N. G.*, eds., 1988, pp. 61–88.

_____ **and Bailey, R. E.** Female Labour Force Participation in Interwar Britain. *Oxford Econ. Pap.*, December 1988, *40*(4), pp. 695–718.

_____ **and Eichengreen, Barry.** Interwar Unemployment in International Perspective: An Overview. In *Eichengreen, B. and Hatton, T. J.*, eds., 1988, pp. 1–59.

_____ **and Eichengreen, Barry.** Interwar Unemployment in International Perspective. *J. Europ. Econ. Hist.*, Spring 1988, *17*(1), pp. 189–94.

Haubrich, Joseph G. Optimal Financial Structure in Exchange Economies. *Int. Econ. Rev.*, May 1988, *29*(2), pp. 217–35.

Hauer, Charles R. Cost Requirements for Passive Solar Heating and Cooling. In *West, R. E. and Kreith, F.*, eds., 1988, pp. 309–36.

Haug, Werner. Ausblick auf die Zukunft der schweizerischen Bevölkerung: Bevölkerungsperspektiven 1986–2025. (Outlook on the Future of the Swiss Population: Population Prospects 1986–2025. With English summary.) *Schweiz. Z. Volkswirtsch. Statist.*, June 1988, *124*(2), pp. 193–210.

Haugen, Robert A.; Makhija, Anil K. and Ferris, Stephen P. Predicting Contemporary Volume with Historic Volume at Differential Price Levels: Evidence Supporting the Disposition Effect. *J. Finance*, July 1988, *43*(3), pp. 677–97.

_____ **and Senbet, Lemma W.** Bankruptcy and Agency Costs: Their Significance to the Theory of Optimal Capital Structure. *J. Finan. Quant. Anal.*, March 1988, *23*(1), pp. 27–38.

Haugen, Steven E. and Horrigan, Michael W. The Declining Middle-Class Thesis: A Sensitivity Analysis. *Mon. Lab. Rev.*, May 1988, *111*(5), pp. 3–13.

Haugland, Sven Arne and Grønhaug, Kjell. Quality Perceptions in International Distribution Channels. *Liiketaloudellinen Aikak.*, 1988, *37*(2), pp. 107–15.

Haulman, Clyde A. and Hausman, William J. Political Economy at the College of William and Mary. **In** *Perkins, E. J., ed.*, 1988, pp. 110–23.

Haurin, Donald R. The Duration of Marketing Time of Residential Housing. *Amer. Real Estate Urban Econ. Assoc. J.*, Winter 1988, *16*(4), pp. 396–410.

_____ **and Haurin, R. Jean.** Net Migration, Unemployment, and the Business Cycle. *J. Reg. Sci.*, May 1988, *28*(2), pp. 239–54.

_____ **and Hendershott, Patric H.** Adjustments in the Real Estate Market. *Amer. Real Estate Urban Econ. Assoc. J.*, Winter 1988, *16*(4), pp. 343–53.

Haurin, R. Jean and Haurin, Donald R. Net Migration, Unemployment, and the Business Cycle. *J. Reg. Sci.*, May 1988, *28*(2), pp. 239–54.

Haus, Ber. Forms of Employment and Payment under Conditions of Manpower Shortage in Poland. **In** *Dlugos, G.; Dorow, W. and Weiermair, K., eds.*, 1988, pp. 419–25.

Hausch, Donald B. A Model of Sequential Auctions. *Econ. Letters*, 1988, *26*(3), pp. 227–33.

Hauser, Heinz. Foreign Trade Policy and the Function of Rules for Trade Policy Making. **In** *Dicke, D. C. and Petersmann, E.-U., eds.*, 1988, pp. 18–38.

_____ **; Hösli, Madeleine and Nydegger, Alfred.** Die Schweiz vor dem EG-Bennenmarkt. (Switzerland and the Completion of the EC Internal Market. With English summary.) *Aussenwirtschaft*, September 1988, *43*(3), pp. 327–65.

Hauser, John R. Competitive Price and Positioning Strategies. *Marketing Sci.*, Winter 1988, *7*(1), pp. 76–91.

_____ **and Fader, Peter S.** Implicit Coalitions in a Generalized Prisoner's Dilemma. *J. Conflict Resolution*, September 1988, *32*(3), pp. 553–82.

_____ **and Wernerfelt, Birger.** Existence and Uniqueness of Price Equilibria in Defender [Defensive Marketing Strategies]. *Marketing Sci.*, Winter 1988, *7*(1), pp. 92–93.

Häuser, Karl. Historical School and "Methodenstreit." *J. Inst. Theoretical Econ.*, June 1988, *144*(3), pp. 532–42.

Hausker, Karl. Oil Import Fees: Measuring the Costs and Benefits. *J. Energy Devel.*, Spring 1988, *13*(2), pp. 171–85.

Hausman, Daniel M. An Appraisal of Popperian Methodology. **In** *de Marchi, N., ed.*, 1988, pp. 65–85.

_____. Economic Methodology and Philosophy of Science. **In** *Winston, G. C. and Teichgraeber, R. F., III, eds.*, 1988, pp. 88–116.

_____ **and McPherson, Michael S.** Standards. *Econ. Philos.*, April 1988, *4*(1), pp. 1–7.

Hausman, Jerry A. and MacKie-Mason, Jeffrey K. Innovation and International Trade Policy: Some Lessons from the U.S. *Oxford Rev. Econ. Policy*, Winter 1988, *4*(4), pp. 56–72.

_____ **and MacKie-Mason, Jeffrey K.** Price Discrimination and Patent Policy. *Rand J. Econ.*, Summer 1988, *19*(2), pp. 253–65.

_____ **and Poterba, James M.** Comportement des ménages et réforme fiscale de 1986. (House Behavior and the Tax Reform Act of 1986. With English summary.) *Ann. Écon. Statist.*, July–Sept. 1988, (11), pp. 159–82.

Hausman, William J. and Haulman, Clyde A. Political Economy at the College of William and Mary. **In** *Perkins, E. J., ed.*, 1988, pp. 110–23.

Haveman, Robert H. Conclusion: Modelling the Accumulation and Distribution of Wealth—An Overview and a Point of View. **In** *Kessler, D. and Masson, A., eds.*, 1988, pp. 323–28.

_____. Facts vs. Fiction in Social Policy. *Challenge*, March–April 1988, *31*(2), pp. 23–28.

_____. New Policy for the New Poverty. *Challenge*, Sept.–Oct. 1988, *31*(5), pp. 27–36.

_____ **; Wolfe, Barbara L. and Warlick, Jennifer.** Labor Market Behavior of Older Men: Estimates from a Trichotomous Choice Model. *J. Public Econ.*, July 1988, *36*(2), pp. 153–75.

_____, **et al.** Disparities in Well-Being among U.S. Children over Two Decades: 1962–83. **In** *Palmer, J. L.; Smeeding, T. and Torrey, B. B., eds.*, 1988, pp. 149–70.

Havenner, Arthur and Aoki, Masanao. An Instrumental Variables Interpretation of Linear Systems Theory Estimation. *J. Econ. Dynam. Control*, March 1988, *12*(1), pp. 49–54.

_____ **and Cerchi, Marlene.** Cointegration and Stock Prices: The Random Walk on Wall Street Revisited. *J. Econ. Dynam. Control*, June–Sept. 1988, *12*(2–3), pp. 333–46.

_____ **and Modjtahedi, Bagher.** Foreign Exchange Rates: A Multiple Currency and Maturity Analysis. *J. Econometrics*, February 1988, *37*(2), pp. 251–64.

Havighurst, Clark C. Applying Antitrust Law to Collaboration in the Production of Information: The Case of Medical Technology Assessment. *Law Contemp. Probl.*, Spring 1988, *51*(2), pp. 341–79.

_____. The Questionable Cost-Containment Record of Commercial Health Insurers. **In** *Frech, H. E., III, ed.*, 1988, pp. 221–58.

Havinga, Ivo C. Environmental Crises and Environmental Policies in Asian Countries: Comments. *Pakistan Devel. Rev.*, Part 2, Winter 1988, *27*(4), pp. 777–78.

_____ **and Cohen, Suleiman I.** Microeconomic Analysis of the Informal Sector—Results of Sample Surveys. *Pakistan Devel. Rev.*, Part 2, Winter 1988, *27*(4), pp. 605–17.

Havrilesky, Thomas. Electoral Cycles in Economic Policy. *Challenge*, July–August 1988, *31*(4), pp. 14–21.

_____. Endogeneity of the Inflationary Impact of an Aggregate Supply Shock. *J. Macroecon.*, Winter 1988, *10*(1), pp. 49–62.

_____. Monetary Policy Signaling from the Administration to the Federal Reserve. *J. Money, Credit, Banking*, February 1988, *20*(1), pp. 83–101.

_____. Two Monetary and Fiscal Policy Myths. In *Willett, T. D., ed.*, 1988, pp. 320–36.

Haw, In-Mu and Lustgarten, Steven. Evidence on Income Measurement Properties of ASR No. 190 and SFAS No. 33 Data. *J. Acc. Res.*, Autumn 1988, *26*(2), pp. 331–52.

_____ **and Ro, Byung T.** An Analysis of the Impact of Corporate Pollution Disclosures: A Comment. In *Neimark, M., ed.*, 1988, pp. 187–91.

_____; **Ruland, William and Hamdallah, Ahmed.** Investor Evaluation of Overfunded Pension Plan Terminations. *J. Finan. Res.*, Spring 1988, *11*(1), pp. 81–88.

Hawawini, Gabriel; Michel, Pierre and Corhay, Albert. The Pricing of Equity on the London Stock Exchange: Seasonality and Size Premium. In *Dimson, E., ed.*, 1988, pp. 197–212.

Hawke, G. R. Depression and Recovery in New Zealand. In *Gregory, R. G. and Butlin, N. G., eds.*, 1988, pp. 113–34.

Hawkins, Murray; Adamowicz, Wiktor L. and Higginson, Nancy. Pricing Relationships in Interdependent North American Hog Markets: The Impact of the Countervailing Duty. *Can. J. Agr. Econ.*, November 1988, *36*(3), pp. 501–18.

Hawley, Clifford B. and Fujii, Edwin T. On the Accuracy of Tax Perceptions. *Rev. Econ. Statist.*, May 1988, *70*(2), pp. 344–47.

Hawthorn, Geoffrey. Three Ironies in Trust. In *Gambetta, D., ed.*, 1988, pp. 111–26.

Hay, A. M. Transport Research in a Free Market Society: Commentary. *Environ. Planning A*, June 1988, *20*(6), pp. 705–06.

Hay, Donald and Vickers, John. The Reform of UK Competition Policy. *Nat. Inst. Econ. Rev.*, August 1988, (125), pp. 56–68.

Hay, Joel W. and Anderson, Gerard. The Hospital Services Market: A Disequilibrium Analysis. *Southern Econ. J.*, January 1988, *54*(3), pp. 656–65.

Hay, Roger W. Famine Incomes and Employment: Has Botswana Anything to Teach Africa? *World Devel.*, September 1988, *16*(9), pp. 1113–25.

_____ **and Rukuni, Mandivamba.** SADCC Food Security Strategies: Evolution and Role. *World Devel.*, September 1988, *16*(9), pp. 1013–24.

Hayakawa, Hiroaki. Price Structure Information, Ex-ante Rational Expectations, and Policy Neutrality: An Optimization Approach. *J. Macroecon.*, Fall 1988, *10*(4), pp. 497–514.

Hayami, Yujiro and Honma, Masayoshi. In Search of Agricultural Policy Reform in Japan. *Europ. Rev. Agr. Econ.*, 1988, *15*(4), pp. 367–95.

_____; **Kawagoe, Toshihiko and Morooka, Yoshinori.** Middlemen and Peasants: The Structure of the Indonesian Soybean Market. *Devel. Econ.*, March 1988, *26*(1), pp. 51–67.

_____ **and Otsuka, Keijiro.** Theories of Share Tenancy: A Critical Survey. *Econ. Develop. Cult. Change*, October 1988, *37*(1), pp. 31–68.

_____; **Ruttan, Vernon W. and Kawagoe, Toshihiko.** The Intercountry Agricultural Production Function and Productivity Differences among Countries: Reply. *J. Devel. Econ.*, February 1988, *28*(1), pp. 125–26.

Hayashi, Fumio; Ando, Albert and Ferris, Richard. Life Cycle and Bequest Savings: A Study of Japanese and U.S. Households Based on Data from the 1984 NSFIE and the 1983 Survey of Consumer Finances. *J. Japanese Int. Economies*, December 1988, *2*(4), pp. 450–91.

_____; **Ito, Takatoshi and Slemrod, Joel.** Housing Finance Imperfections, Taxation, and Private Saving: A Comparative Simulation Analysis of the United States and Japan. *J. Japanese Int. Economies*, September 1988, *2*(3), pp. 215–38.

Hayden, F. Gregory. Evolution of Time Constructs and Their Impact on Socioeconomic Planning. In *Tool, M. R., ed., Vol. 1*, 1988, 1987, pp. 329–60.

_____. Values, Beliefs, and Attitudes in a Sociotechnical Setting. *J. Econ. Issues*, June 1988, *22*(2), pp. 415–26.

Haydu, Frank W., III. Financial Innovation and Corporate Mergers: Discussion. In *Browne, L. E. and Rosengren, E. S., eds.*, 1988, pp. 74–77.

Hayenga, Marvin L. and Schroeder, Ted C. Comparison of Selective Hedging and Options Strategies in Cattle Feedlot Risk Management. *J. Futures Markets*, April 1988, *8*(2), pp. 141–56.

Hayes, Adrian C. and Bhattacharyya, Amit K. Cottage Industry and Fertility in a Village in West Bengal, India. In *Vlassoff, C. and Barkat-e-Khuda, eds.*, 1988, pp. 49–57.

Hayes, Chris and Fonda, Nickie. Education, Training and Business Performance. *Oxford Rev. Econ. Policy*, Autumn 1988, *4*(3), pp. 108–19.

Hayes, Dermot and Schmitz, Andrew. The Price and Welfare Implications of Current Conflicts between the Agricultural Policies of the United States and the European Community. In *Baldwin, R. E.; Hamilton, C. B. and Sapir, A., eds.*, 1988, pp. 67–99.

Hayes, J. P. Divided Opinions on Sanctions

against South Africa. *World Econ.*, June 1988, *11*(2), pp. 267–80.

Hayes, Kathy J.; Molina, David J. and Slottje, Daniel J. Measuring Preference Variation across North America. *Economica*, November 1988, *55*(220), pp. 525–39.

_____; **Porter-Hudak, Susan and Grosskopf, Shawna.** Pension Funding and Local Labor Costs: A Dynamic Analysis of Illinois Police Pension Funds. *Southern Econ. J.*, January 1988, *54*(3), pp. 572–82.

Hayford, Stephen L. and Sinicropi, Anthony V. Bargaining Rights Status of Public Sector Supervisors. In *Lewin, D., et al., eds.*, 1988, *1976*, pp. 129–52.

Hayghe, Howard V. Employers and Child Care: What Roles Do They Play? *Mon. Lab. Rev.*, September 1988, *111*(9), pp. 38–44.

Haynes, Kingsley E. and Dignan, Tony. Evaluating Capital Grants for Regional Development. In *[Perroux, F.]*, 1988, pp. 330–74.

Haynes, Robin. The Urban Distribution of Lung Cancer Mortality in England and Wales 1980–1983. *Urban Stud.*, December 1988, *25*(6), pp. 497–506.

Haynes, Stephen E. Identification of Interest Rates and International Capital Flows. *Rev. Econ. Statist.*, February 1988, *70*(1), pp. 103–11.

_____ **and Stone, Joe A.** Does the Political Business Cycle Dominate U.S. Unemployment and Inflation? Some New Evidence. In *Willett, T. D., ed.*, 1988, pp. 276–93.

_____ **and Stone, Joe A.** Short Communications: Reply [Impact of the Terms of Trade on the U.S. Trade Balance: A Reexamination]. *J. Bus. Econ. Statist.*, January 1988, *6*(1), pp. 138–40.

Hayward, John. World Bank Extension: Policy and Issues. In *Roberts, C., ed.*, 1988, pp. 59–63.

Hayward, Mark D.; Grady, William R. and McLaughlin, Steven D. Changes in the Retirement Process among Older Men in the United States: 1972–1980. *Demography*, August 1988, *25*(3), pp. 371–86.

Hazari, Bharat R. and Athukorala, Premachandra. Market Penetration of Manufactured Imports from Developing Countries: The Australian Experience. *J. World Trade*, October 1988, *22*(5), pp. 49–65.

Hazell, Peter B. R. Changing Patterns of Variability in Cereal Prices and Production. In *Mellor, J. W. and Ahmed, R., eds.*, 1988, pp. 27–52.

_____. Risk and Uncertainty in Domestic Production and Prices. In *Mellor, J. W. and Ahmed, R., eds.*, 1988, pp. 94–102.

_____ **and Flinn, J.C.** Production Instability and Modern Rice Technology: A Philippine Case Study. *Devel. Econ.*, March 1988, *26*(1), pp. 34–50.

Hazewinkel, M. Lectures on Linear and Nonlinear Filtering. In *Schiehlen, W. and Wedig, W., eds.*, 1988, pp. 103–35.

Hazledine, Tim. Review Article and Comment: Canada–U.S. Free Trade? Not So Elementary,

Watson. *Can. Public Policy*, June 1988, *14*(2), pp. 204–13.

Hazlett, Thomas W. Economic Origins of Apartheid. *Contemp. Policy Issues*, October 1988, *6*(4), pp. 85–104.

Heady, Christopher J. Optimal Taxation with Fixed Wages and Induced Migration. *Oxford Econ. Pap.*, September 1988, *40*(3), pp. 560–74.

_____. The Structure of Income and Commodity Taxation. In *Hare, P. G., ed.*, 1988, pp. 186–216.

_____ **and Ebrahimi, Ahmad.** Tax Design and Household Composition. *Econ. J.*, Supplement, 1988, *98*(390), pp. 83–96.

Heald, David. The Relevance of UK Privatisation for LDCs. In *Cook, P. and Kirkpatrick, C., eds.*, 1988, pp. 68–90.

Healey, Derek T. Countertrade: Solution or Problem? In *[Clark, C.]*, 1988, pp. 139–67.

Healy, Kevin. From Field to Factory: Vertical Integration in Bolivia. In *Annis, S. and Hakim, P., eds.*, 1988, pp. 195–208.

_____ **and Zorn, Elayne.** Lake Titicaca's Campesino-Controlled Tourism. In *Annis, S. and Hakim, P., eds.*, 1988, pp. 45–57.

Healy, Paul M. and Palepu, Krishna G. Earnings Information Conveyed by Dividend Initiations and Omissions. *J. Finan. Econ.*, September 1988, *21*(2), pp. 149–75.

Hearn, James C. Attendance at Higher-Cost Colleges: Ascribed, Socioeconomic, and Academic Influences on Student Enrollment Patterns. *Econ. Educ. Rev.*, 1988, *7*(1), pp. 65–76.

Hearn, Jeff and Parkin, P. Wendy. Women, Men, and Leadership: A Critical Review of Assumptions, Practices, and Change in the Industrialized Nations. In *Adler, N. J. and Izraeli, D., eds.*, 1988, pp. 17–40.

Hearne, John. Entrepreneurial Clubs: Some Aspects of Pricing and Welfare. *Bull. Econ. Res.*, June 1988, *40*(3), pp. 197–206.

Hearth, Douglas and Melicher, Ronald W. A Time Series Analysis of Aggregate Business Failure Activity and Credit Conditions. *J. Econ. Bus.*, November 1988, *40*(4), pp. 319–33.

Heath, David C. and Jarrow, Robert A. Ex-dividend Stock Price Behavior and Arbitrage Opportunities. *J. Bus.*, January 1988, *61*(1), pp. 95–108.

Heath, John Richard. Obstacles to Small Farm Development in the Commonwealth Caribbean. *Amer. J. Econ. Soc.*, October 1988, *47*(4), pp. 427–40.

Heath, Julia A. and Ciscel, David H. Patriarchy, Family Structure and the Exploitation of Women's Labor. *J. Econ. Issues*, September 1988, *22*(3), pp. 781–94.

Heath, Will Carrington. Von Neumann/Morgenstern Decision Making and Harsanyi's Theory of Justice: After Rawls and Nozick, If It Risks Personal Freedom and Individual Liberty, Can It Be Really Just? *Amer. J. Econ. Soc.*, July 1988, *47*(3), pp. 355–62.

Heaton, Hal. On the Possible Tax-Driven Arbitrage Opportunities in the New Municipal Bond Futures Contract. *J. Futures Markets,* June 1988, *8*(3), pp. 291–302.

Heaton, John C.; Ogaki, Masao and Hansen, Lars Peter. Efficiency Bounds Implied by Multiperiod Conditional Moment Restrictions. *J. Amer. Statist. Assoc.,* September 1988, *83*(403), pp. 863–71.

Heaton, Tim B.; Lichter, Daniel T. and Fuguitt, Glenn V. Monitoring the Metropolitanization Process. *Demography,* February 1988, *25*(1), pp. 115–28.

Hébert, Claude. Léon Walras et les associations populaires coopératives. (With English summary.) *Revue Écon. Polit.,* March–April 1988, *98*(2), pp. 252–72.

Hébert, G.; Jain, H. C. and Meltz, Noah M. The State of the Art in Industrial Relations: Conclusion. In *Hébert, G.; Jain, H. C. and Meltz, N. M., eds..,* 1988, pp. 281–90.

_____; **Jain, H. C. and Meltz, Noah M.** The State of the Art in IR: Some Questions and Concepts. In *Hébert, G.; Jain, H. C. and Meltz, N. M., eds..,* 1988, pp. 1–8.

Hecht, Jacqueline. French Utopian Socialists and the Population Question: "Seeking the Future City." *Population Devel. Rev.,* Supplement, 1988, *14*, pp. 49–73.

Heckman, James J. Time Constraints and Household Demand Functions. In *Schultz, T. Paul, ed.,* 1988, pp. 3–14.

_____ **and MaCurdy, Thomas E.** Empirical Tests of Labor-Market Equilibrium: An Evaluation. *Carnegie–Rochester Conf. Ser. Public Policy,* Spring 1988, *28*, pp. 231–58.

Heckman, Nancy E. Minimax Estimates in a Semiparametric Model. *J. Amer. Statist. Assoc.,* December 1988, *83*(404), pp. 1090–96.

Heclo, Hugh. Generational Politics. In *Palmer, J. L.; Smeeding, T. and Torrey, B. B., eds.,* 1988, pp. 381–411.

Hecox, Walter E. Structural Adjustment, Donor Conditionality and Industrialization in Kenya. In *Coughlin, P. and Ikiara, G. K., eds.,* 1988, pp. 190–217.

Hedge, Shantaram P. An Empirical Analysis of Implicit Delivery Options in the Treasury Bond Futures Contract. *J. Banking Finance,* September 1988, *12*(3), pp. 469–92.

Hedlund, Hans. A Cooperative Revisited in Kenya. In *Hedlund, H., ed.,* 1988, pp. 15–35.

_____. Cooperatives Revisited: Introduction. In *Hedlund, H., ed.,* 1988, pp. 7–13.

Hedlund, Stefan. Soviet Union: The Anomaly of Private-cum-Socialist Agriculture. *Amer. J. Agr. Econ.,* May 1988, *70*(2), pp. 417–22.

Hedrick, Charles L. and Cyert, Richard M. Theory of the Firm: Past, Present, and Future; An Interpretation. In *Cyert, R. M., 1988, 1972,* pp. 59–77.

Heermann, Stephen and Stephens, Daniel B. Dependence of Anisotropy on Saturation in a Stratified Sand. *Water Resources Res.,* May 1988, *24*(5), pp. 770–78.

Heertje, Arnold. An Important Letter from

W. S. Jevons to L. Walras. In *Wood, J. C., ed., Vol. 3,* 1988, *1982,* pp. 261–65.

_____. Schumpeter and Technical Change. In *Hanusch, H., ed.,* 1988, pp. 71–89.

_____. Technical and Financial Innovation. In *Heertje, A., ed.,* 1988, pp. 1–13.

Heffernan, Kathleen D. Struggle against Dependence: Nontraditional Export Growth in Central America and the Caribbean: Honduras. In *Paus, E., ed.,* 1988, pp. 123–43.

Heffey, Peter G. Civil Liability of Tax Practitioners. *Australian Tax Forum,* 1988, *5*(3), pp. 301–37.

Hefner, James and Barnett, Marguerite R. Implications of Revenue Sharing for Black Political and Economic Goals. *Rev. Black Polit. Econ.,* Fall 1988, *17*(2), pp. 45–63.

Hefzi, Hassan; Ifflander, A. James and Smith, David B. Municipal Bond Market Risk Measures and Bond Ratings. In *Schwartz, B. N., ed.,* 1988, pp. 111–27.

Hegazy, Youseff and Bernstein, Mark Allen. The Economic Costs of Electricity Shortages: A Case Study of Egypt. *Energy J.,* Special Issue, 1988, *9*, pp. 173–89.

Hegde, Shantaram P. and Nunn, Kenneth P., Jr. Non-infinitesimal Rate Changes and Macaulay Duration. *J. Portfol. Manage.,* Winter 1988, *14*(2), pp. 69–73.

Hegji, Charles E. Base Drift and the Behavior of Interest Rates. *Econ. Notes,* 1988, (3), pp. 137–44.

_____. Interest Rates, the Forward Premium, and Unanticipated Money: Comment. *Southern Econ. J.,* April 1988, *54*(4), pp. 1043–46.

_____. Monetary Policy, Capital Aggregation, and the Behavior of Interest Rates. *Quart. J. Bus. Econ.,* Spring 1988, *27*(2), pp. 35–50.

_____; **Deravi, M. Keivan and Gregorowicz, Philip.** Balance of Trade Announcements and Movements in Exchange Rates. *Southern Econ. J.,* October 1988, *55*(2), pp. 279–87.

ter Heide, H. and Scholten, H. Application of Household Models in Regional Planning. In *Keilman, N.; Kuijsten, A. and Vossen, A., eds.,* 1988, pp. 209–24.

Heidel, Waltraut and Marschall, Wolfgang. Some Qualitative Interrelations between Science and Production. *Soviet E. Europ. Foreign Trade,* Spring 1988, *24*(1), pp. 108–24.

Heien, Dale M. and Pompelli, Greg. The Demand for Beef Products: Cross-Section Estimation of Demographic and Economic Effects. *Western J. Agr. Econ.,* July 1988, *13*(1), pp. 37–44.

_____ **and Wessells, Cathy Roheim.** The Demand for Dairy Products: Structure, Prediction, and Decomposition. *Amer. J. Agr. Econ.,* May 1988, *70*(2), pp. 219–28.

_____ **and Wessells, Cathy Roheim.** The Nutritional Impact of the Dairy Price Support Program. *J. Cons. Aff.,* Winter 1988, *22*(2), pp. 201–19.

van der Heijden, R. E. C. M. and Timmermans, H. J. P. The Spatial Transferability of a Decompositional Multi-attribute Preference Model.

Environ. Planning A, August 1988, *20*(8), pp. 1013–25.

Heijdra, Ben J. Neoclassical Economics and the Psychology of Risk and Uncertainty. In *Earl, P. E., ed.*, 1988, pp. 67–84.

_____ and Lowenberg, Anton D. The Neoclassical Economic Research Program: Some Lakatosian and Other Considerations. *Australian Econ. Pap.*, December 1988, *27*(51), pp. 272–84.

_____; **Lowenberg, Anton D. and Mallick, Robert J.** Marxism, Methodological Individualism, and the New Institutional Economics. *J. Inst. Theoretical Econ.*, April 1988, *144*(2), pp. 296–317.

Heijman, Willem J. M. Böhm-Bawerk on Time Preference: Economic Action Based on Future Needs. *J. Econ. Stud.*, 1988, *15*(3–4), pp. 79–91.

_____. The Need for a Steady State Economy. *Int. J. Soc. Econ.*, 1988, *15*(3–4), pp. 80–87.

Heikkila, Eric. Multicollinearity in Regression Models with Multiple Distance Measures. *J. Reg. Sci.*, August 1988, *28*(3), pp. 345–62.

Heilbroner, Robert L. Adam Smith's Capitalism. In *Heilbroner, R. L.*, 1988, pp. 134–64.

_____. Behind the Veil of Economics. In *Heilbroner, R. L.*, 1988, pp. 13–34.

_____. Capitalism as a Regime. In *Heilbroner, R. L.*, 1988, pp. 35–62.

_____. On the Future of Capitalism. In *Heilbroner, R. L.*, 1988, pp. 63–79.

_____. The Problem of Value. In *Heilbroner, R. L.*, 1988, pp. 104–33.

_____. Rhetoric and Ideology. In *Klamer, A.; McCloskey, D. N. and Solow, R. M., eds.*, 1988, pp. 38–43.

_____. Schumpeter's Vision. In *Heilbroner, R. L.*, 1988, pp. 165–84.

_____. Vision and Ideology. In *Heilbroner, R. L.*, 1988, pp. 185–99.

_____. The World of Work. In *Heilbroner, R. L.*, 1988, pp. 80–103.

Heilbrun, James. Nonprofit versus Profit-Making Firms: A Comment. *J. Cult. Econ.*, December 1988, *12*(2), pp. 87–92.

Heilemann, Ullrich. Collective Bargaining and Macroeconomic Performance: The Case of West Germany. In *Motamen, H., ed.*, 1988, pp. 491–506.

Heim, Carol E. Government Research Establishments, State Capacity and Distribution of Industry Policy in Britain. *Reg. Stud.*, October 1988, *22*(5), pp. 375–86.

Hein, Scott E. and Hafer, R. W. Further Evidence on the Relationship between Federal Government Debt and Inflation. *Econ. Inquiry*, April 1988, *26*(2), pp. 239–51.

_____ and Spudeck, Raymond E. Forecasting the Daily Federal Funds Rate. *Int. J. Forecasting*, 1988, *4*(4), pp. 581–91.

Heineke, John M. and Shefrin, Hersh M. Exact Aggregation and the Finite Basis Property. *Int. Econ. Rev.*, August 1988, *29*(3), pp. 525–38.

Heiner, Ronald A. Imperfect Decisions and Routinized Production: Implications for Evolutionary Modeling and Inertial Technical Change. In *Dosi, G., et al., eds.*, 1988, pp. 148–69.

_____. Imperfect Decisions in Organizations: Toward a Theory of Internal Structure. *J. Econ. Behav. Organ.*, January 1988, *9*(1), pp. 25–44.

_____. The Necessity of Delaying Economic Adjustment. *J. Econ. Behav. Organ.*, October 1988, *10*(3), pp. 255–86.

_____. The Necessity of Imperfect Decisions. *J. Econ. Behav. Organ.*, July 1988, *10*(1), pp. 29–55.

Heinesen, Eskil. De seneste ændringer i Danmarks Statistiks økonomiske model ADAM. (The Latest Developments of the Danish Macroeconomic Model ADAM. With English summary.) *Nationaløkon. Tidsskr.*, 1988, *126*(2), pp. 217–28.

Heinkel, Robert and Kraus, Alan. Measuring Event Impacts in Thinly Traded Stocks. *J. Finan. Quant. Anal.*, March 1988, *23*(1), pp. 71–88.

Heinrichs, Wolfgang. Growth and the Foreign Balance: Experience and Problems of the German Democratic Republic. In *Saunders, C. T., ed.*, 1988, pp. 111–22.

_____ and Schulz, Gerhard. Political Economy and Modern Productive Forces. *Eastern Europ. Econ.*, Winter 1988–89, *27*(2), pp. 5–43.

Heinsohn, Gunnar and Steiger, Otto. Monetary Theory and the Historiography of Money, or Debts, Interest and Technical Progress in Economies with and without Private Ownership. *Écon. Soc.*, September 1988, *22*(9), pp. 139–53.

Heintz, H. Theodore, Jr. Advocacy Coalitions and the OCS Leasing Debate: A Case Study in Policy Evolution. *Policy Sci.*, 1988, *21*(2–3), pp. 213–38.

_____ and Jenkins-Smith, Hank C. Advocacy Coalitions and the Practice of Policy Analysis. *Policy Sci.*, 1988, *21*(2–3), pp. 263–77.

Heinze, G. Wolfgang and Kill, Heinrich H. The Development of the German Railroad System. In *Mayntz, R. and Hughes, T. P., eds.*, 1988, pp. 105–34.

Heisbourg, François. Public Policy and the Creation of a European Arms Market. In *Creasey, P. and May, S., eds.*, 1988, pp. 60–88.

Heise, Michael. Lohnpolitik bei Terms-of-Trade Änderungen: Eine angebotstheoretische Analyse. (Wage Policy and the Terms-of-Trade: The Results of a Supply-Side Model. With English summary.) *Jahr. Nationalökon. Statist.*, October 1988, *205*(4), pp. 332–47.

Heiser, W. J. and Meulman, J. J. Second Order Regression and Distance Analysis. In *Gaul, W. and Schader, M., eds.*, 1988, pp. 368–80.

Heiskanen, Ikka and Martikainen, Tuomo. The Finnish Public Sector: Its Growth and Changing Role in 1960–1984. In *Lybeck, J. A. and Henrekson, M., eds.*, 1988, pp. 357–89.

Hekman, John S. and Browne, Lynn E. New England's Economy in the 1980s. In *Lampe, D., ed.*, 1988, *1981*, pp. 169–87.

Helberger, Christof. Die Struktur der Erwerbstätigen im sozio-ökonomischen Panel im Vergleich mit der amtlichen Erwerbsstatistik. (The Structure of the Labour Force in the "Socio-Economic Panel" Compared with Official Statistics. With English summary.) *Z. Wirtschaft. Sozialwissen.*, 1988, *108*(2), pp. 227–45.

―――― **and Knepel, Helmut.** How Big Is the Shadow Economy? A Re-analysis of the Unobserved-Variable Approach of B. S. Frey and H. Weck-Hannemann. *Europ. Econ. Rev.*, April 1988, *32*(4), pp. 965–76.

Helkie, William L. and Hooper, Peter. An Empirical Analysis of the External Deficit, 1980–86. In *Bryant, R. C.; Holtham, G. and Hooper, P., eds.*, 1988, pp. 10–56.

Helleiner, Gerald K. Primary Commodity Markets: Recent Trends and Research Requirements. In *Elliott, K. A. and Williamson, J., eds.*, 1988, pp. 197–215.

Heller, H. Robert. Implementing Monetary Policy. *Fed. Res. Bull.*, July 1988, *74*(7), pp. 419–29.

―――― . Statement to the U.S. House Subcommittee on Commerce, Consumer Protection, and Competitiveness of the Committee on Energy and Commerce, September 9, 1988. *Fed. Res. Bull.*, November 1988, *74*(11), pp. 743–51.

―――― . Statement to the U.S. House Subcommittee on Commerce, Consumer, and Monetary Affairs of the Committee on Government Operations, November 19, 1987. *Fed. Res. Bull.*, January 1988, *74*(1), pp. 31–37.

―――― . Statement to the U.S. Senate Committee on Banking, Housing, and Urban Affairs, May 25, 1988. *Fed. Res. Bull.*, July 1988, *74*(7), pp. 458–65.

Heller, Peter. Fund-Supported Adjustment Programs and the Poor. *Finance Develop.*, December 1988, *25*(4), pp. 2–5.

Hellerstein, Walter. Florida's Sales Tax on Services. *Nat. Tax J.*, March 1988, *41*(1), pp. 1–18.

―――― . Is "Internal Consistency" Foolish? Reflections on an Emerging Commerce Clause Restraint on State Taxation. *Mich. Law Rev.*, October 1988, *87*(1), pp. 138–88.

Hellinger, Fred J. National Forecasts of the Medical Care Costs of AIDS: 1988–1992. *Inquiry*, Winter 1988, *25*(4), pp. 469–84.

Helliwell, John F. Comparative Macroeconomics of Stagflation. *J. Econ. Lit.*, March 1988, *26*(1), pp. 1–28.

―――― . Empirical Macroeconomics for Interdependent Economies: What Next? In *Bryant, R. C., et al., eds.*, 1988, pp. 131–48.

Hellman, Daryl A. and Fox, James Alan. Location and Other Correlates of Campus Crime. In *Alper, N. O. and Hellman, D. A., eds.*, 1988, pp. 16–39.

Hellmann, Donald C. Japanese Politics and Foreign Policy: Elitist Democracy within an American Greenhouse. In *Inoguchi, T. and Okimoto, D. I., eds.*, 1988, pp. 345–78.

Hellsten, Martin. Socially Optimal Forestry. *J. Environ. Econ. Manage.*, December 1988, *15*(4), pp. 387–94.

Hellwig, Martin F. Equity, Opportunism, and

the Design of Contractual Relations: Comment. *J. Inst. Theoretical Econ.*, February 1988, *144*(1), pp. 200–207.

―――― . A Note on the Specification of Interfirm Communication in Insurance Markets with Adverse Selection. *J. Econ. Theory*, October 1988, *46*(1), pp. 154–63.

―――― . Time Consistency and Trigger Mechanisms in Open-Economy Monetary Policy Games: Comment. In *Borner, S., ed.*, 1988, pp. 360–68.

Helm, Dieter. Regulating the Electricity Supply Industry. *Fisc. Stud.*, August 1988, *9*(3), pp. 86–105.

―――― . Reply [Predictions and Causes: A Comparison of Friedman and Hicks on Method]. *Oxford Econ. Pap.*, June 1988, *40*(2), pp. 395–96.

―――― ; **Kay, John and Thompson, David.** Energy Policy and the Role of the State in the Market for Energy. *Fisc. Stud.*, February 1988, *9*(1), pp. 41–61.

―――― **and Yarrow, George.** The Assessment: The Regulation of Utilities. *Oxford Rev. Econ. Policy*, Summer 1988, *4*(2), pp. i–xxxi.

Helman, Amir. Professional Managers in the Kibbutz. In *Maital, S., ed., Vol. 1*, 1988, pp. 345–56.

Helmberger, Peter G. and Miranda, Mario J. The Effects of Commodity Price Stabilization Programs. *Amer. Econ. Rev.*, March 1988, *78*(1), pp. 46–58.

Helmbold, Lois Rita. Downward Occupational Mobility during the Great Depression: Urban Black and White Working Class Women. *Labor Hist.*, Spring 1988, *29*(2), pp. 135–72.

Helme, Marcia P. A Mixed Integer Programming Model for Planning an Integrated Services Network. In *Eiselt, H. A. and Pederzoli, G., eds.*, 1988, pp. 103–23.

Helmers, Glenn A.; Atwood, Joseph A. and Watts, Myles J. Chance-Constrained Financing as a Response to Financial Risk. *Amer. J. Agr. Econ.*, February 1988, *70*(1), pp. 79–89.

Helms, Billy P. and Jean, William H. The Identification of Stochastic Dominance Efficient Sets by Moment Combination Orderings. *J. Banking Finance*, June 1988, *12*(2), pp. 243–53.

Helmstädter, Ernst. The Irrelevance of Keynes to German Economic Policy and to International Economic Co-operation in the 1980s. In *Eltis, W. and Sinclair, P. J. N., eds.*, 1988, pp. 411–27.

Helmuth, John A. Nuclear Power Plant Capital Costs and Turnkey Estimates. *Amer. Econ.*, Fall 1988, *32*(2), pp. 66–70.

―――― **and Vetsuypens, Michael R.** Airline Deregulation: Additional Evidence from the Capital Markets. *Quart. J. Bus. Econ.*, Spring 1988, *27*(2), pp. 117–38.

Helpman, Elhanan. Growth, Technological Progress, and Trade. *Empirica*, 1988, *15*(1), pp. 5–25.

―――― . Imperfect Competition and International Trade: Evidence from Fourteen Industrial

Countries. In *Spence, A. M. and Hazard, H. A.*, eds., 1988, pp. 197–220.

_____. Inflation Stabilization: Israel: Comment. In *Bruno, M., et al.*, eds., 1988, pp. 102–07.

_____. Macroeconomic Effects of Price Controls: The Role of Market Structure. *Econ. J.*, June 1988, *98*(391), pp. 340–54.

_____. Trade Patterns under Uncertainty with Country Specific Shocks. *Econometrica*, May 1988, *56*(3), pp. 645–59.

_____ and **Drazen, Allan.** The Effect of Policy Anticipations on Stabilization Programs. *Europ. Econ. Rev.*, March 1988, *32*(2–3), pp. 680–86.

_____ and **Drazen, Allan.** Future Stabilization Policies and Inflation. In *Kohn, M. and Tsiang, S.-C.*, eds., 1988, pp. 166–84.

_____ and **Drazen, Allan.** Stabilization with Exchange Rate Management under Uncertainty. In *Helpman, E.; Razin, A. and Sadka, E.*, eds., 1988, pp. 310–27.

_____ and **Leiderman, Leonardo.** Stabilization in High Inflation Countries: Analytical Foundations and Recent Experience. *Carnegie–Rochester Conf. Ser. Public Policy*, Spring 1988, *28*, pp. 9–84.

Helsen, Kristiaan; Shandler, Bruce and Green, Paul E. Conjoint Internal Validity under Alternative Profile Presentations. *J. Cons. Res.*, December 1988, *15*(3), pp. 392–97.

Helsley, Robert W.; Levi, Maurice D. and Goldberg, Michael A. On the Development of International Financial Centers. *Ann. Reg. Sci.*, February 1988, *22*, pp. 81–94.

Hemmerdinger, Louis and Holt, Alan. Space Station Payload Accommodations. In *Egan, J. J., et al.*, 1988, pp. 261–81.

Hemming, Richard and Mansoor, Ali M. Is Privatization the Answer? *Finance Develop.*, September 1988, *25*(3), pp. 31–33.

Hempel, Carl G. Studies in the Logic of Explanation: Postscript. In *Pitt, J. C.*, ed., 1988, *1965*, pp. 47–50.

_____ and **Oppenheim, Paul.** Studies in the Logic of Explanation. In *Pitt, J. C.*, ed., 1988, *1948*, pp. 9–46.

Hempel, George H. and Peavy, John W., III. The Penn Square Bank Failure: Effect on Commercial Bank Security Returns—A Note. *J. Banking Finance*, 1988, *12*(1), pp. 141–50.

Hendershott, Patric H. and Haurin, Donald R. Adjustments in the Real Estate Market. *Amer. Real Estate Urban Econ. Assoc. J.*, Winter 1988, *16*(4), pp. 343–53.

_____ and **Smith, Marc T.** Housing Inventory Change and the Role of Existing Structures, 1961–1985. *Amer. Real Estate Urban Econ. Assoc. J.*, Winter 1988, *16*(4), pp. 364–78.

Henderson, Dale W. Roundtable on Exchange Rate Policy: Comment. In *Marston, R. C.*, ed., 1988, pp. 156–62.

_____ and **Canzoneri, Matthew B.** Is Sovereign Policymaking Bad? *Carnegie–Rochester Conf. Ser. Public Policy*, Spring 1988, *28*, pp. 93–140.

_____ and **Canzoneri, Matthew B.** Time Consistency and Trigger Mechanisms in Open-Economy Monetary Policy Games. In *Borner, S.*, ed., 1988, pp. 338–55.

_____; **Symansky, Steven A. and Bryant, Ralph C.** Estimates of the Consequences of Policy Actions Derived from Model Simulations. In *Bryant, R. C., et al.*, eds., 1988, pp. 63–91.

Henderson, David; Tweeten, Luther G. and Schriener, Dean. Intra-regional Development: Agricultural and Nodal Adjustment in Oklahoma's Southern High Plains. *Reg. Sci. Persp.*, 1988, *18*(2), pp. 44–59.

Henderson, J. Stephen W. and Stonehouse, D. Peter. Effects of Soil Tillage and Time of Planting on Corn Yields and Farm Profits in Southern Ontario. *Can. J. Agr. Econ.*, March 1988, *36*(1), pp. 127–41.

Henderson, J. V. Locational Pattern of Heavy Industries: Decentralization Is More Efficient. *J. Policy Modeling*, Winter 1988, *10*(4), pp. 569–80.

Henderson, John P. Political Economy and the Service of the State: The University of Wisconsin. In *Barber, W. J.*, ed., 1988, pp. 318–39.

Henderson, Lenneal J., Jr. Energy Policy and Socioeconomic Growth in Low-Income Communities. *Rev. Black Polit. Econ.*, Fall 1988, *17*(2), pp. 11–27.

Henderson, Margaret. Thesis Titles for Degrees in the United Kingdom 1986/87 and 1987/88. *Econ. J.*, March 1988, *98*(389), pp. 175–83.

Henderson, Mary, et al. Private-Sector Medical Case Management for High-Cost Illness. In *Scheffler, R. M. and Rossiter, L. F.*, eds., 1988, pp. 213–45.

Henderson, Yolanda K. Financial Intermediaries under Value-Added Taxation. *New Eng. Econ. Rev.*, July–Aug. 1988, pp. 37–50.

_____. Further Base Broadening: A Possible Source of Tax Revenues? *New Eng. Econ. Rev.*, March–April 1988, pp. 33–45.

_____, et al. Planning for New England's Electricity Requirements. *New Eng. Econ. Rev.*, Jan.–Feb. 1988, pp. 3–30.

Hendricks, Kenneth and Porter, Robert H. An Empirical Study of an Auction with Asymmetric Information. *Amer. Econ. Rev.*, December 1988, *78*(5), pp. 865–83.

_____; **Weiss, Andrew and Wilson, Charles A.** The War of Attrition in Continuous Time with Complete Information. *Int. Econ. Rev.*, November 1988, *29*(4), pp. 663–80.

Hendricks, Wallace E.; Kahn, Lawrence M. and Gramm, Cynthia L. Inflation Uncertainty and Strike Activity. *Ind. Relat.*, Winter 1988, *27*(1), pp. 114–29.

Hendrickson, Christina. Abandonment of Hazardous Waste Sites in the Course of Bankruptcy Proceedings. *Natural Res. J.*, Winter 1988, *28*(1), pp. 189–98.

Hendrickson, Jene' D.; Sorooshian, Soroosh and Brazil, Larry E. Comparison of Newton-Type and Direct Search Algorithms for Calibration of Conceptual Rainfall–Runoff Models. *Water Resources Res.*, May 1988, *24*(5), pp. 691–700.

Hendry, David F. Encompassing. *Nat. Inst. Econ. Rev.*, August 1988, (125), pp. 88–92.

———. The Encompassing Implications of Feedback versus Feedforward Mechanisms in Econometrics. *Oxford Econ. Pap.*, March 1988, *40*(1), pp. 132–49.

——— **and Neale, Adrian J.** Interpreting Long-run Equilibrium Solutions in Conventional Macro Models: A Comment. *Econ. J.*, September 1988, *98*(392), pp. 808–17.

———; **Neale, Adrian J. and Srba, Frank.** Econometric Analysis of Small Linear Systems Using PC-FIML. *J. Econometrics*, May–June 1988, *38*(1–2), pp. 203–26.

Hénin, Pierre-Yves and Michel, Philippe. An IS–LM Representation of Macroeconomic Equilibria with Rationing. In *Barrère, A., ed.*, 1988, pp. 93–110.

Henley, Andrew. Price Formation and Market Structure: The Case of the Inter-war Coal Industry. *Oxford Bull. Econ. Statist.*, August 1988, *50*(3), pp. 263–78.

Hennart, Jean-François. Upstream Vertical Integration in the Aluminum and Tin Industries: A Comparative Study of the Choice between Market and Intrafirm Coordination. *J. Econ. Behav. Organ.*, April 1988, *9*(3), pp. 281–99.

Henneberger, J. Edwin and Dumas, Mark W. Productivity Trends in the Cotton and Synthetic Broad Woven Fabrics Industry. *Mon. Lab. Rev.*, April 1988, *111*(4), pp. 34–38.

Hennings, K. H. George Darwin, Jevons, and the Rate of Interest. In *Wood, J. C., ed., Vol. 3*, 1988, *1979*, pp. 160–73.

Hennipman, Pieter. Communications: A New Look at the Ordinalist Revolution: Comments on Cooter and Rappoport. *J. Econ. Lit.*, March 1988, *26*(1), pp. 80–85.

Henrekson, Magnus. Swedish Government Growth: A Disequilibrium Analysis. In *Lybeck, J. A. and Henrekson, M., eds.*, 1988, pp. 93–132.

——— **and Lybeck, Johan A.** Explaining the Growth of Government: Editors' Introduction and Summary. In *Lybeck, J. A. and Henrekson, M., eds.*, 1988, pp. 3–19.

——— **and Lybeck, Johan A.** Explaining the Growth of Government in Sweden: A Disequilibrium Approach. *Public Choice*, June 1988, *57*(3), pp. 213–32.

Henrichsmeyer, Wilhelm. A European Community Approach to Decoupling: A Commentary. In *Miner, W. M. and Hathaway, D. E., eds.*, 1988, pp. 159–65.

——— **and Ostermeyer-Schlöder, A.** Productivity Growth and Factor Adjustment in EC Agriculture. *Europ. Rev. Agr. Econ.*, 1988, *15*(2–3), pp. 137–54.

Henrion, Max and Graham, John D. Choosing Automatic Restraint Designs for the 1990s. In *Graham, J. D., ed.*, 1988, pp. 90–100.

Henriot, Peter J. and Jameson, Kenneth P. International Debt, Austerity, and the Poor. In *Tavis, L. A., ed.*, 1988, pp. 13–56.

Henriques, Irene and Vaillancourt, François. The Demand for Child Care Services in Can-

ada. *Appl. Econ.*, March 1988, *20*(3), pp. 385–94.

Henry, Brian and Hall, Stephen G. The Disequilibrium Approach to Modelling the Labour Market. In *Beenstock, M., ed.*, 1988, pp. 49–69.

Henry, D. P. and Mays, W. Exhibition of the Work of W. Stanley Jevons. In *Wood, J. C., ed., Vol. 3*, 1988, *1952*, pp. 55–57.

——— **and Mays, W.** Jevons and Logic. In *Wood, J. C., ed., Vol. 1*, 1988, *1953*, pp. 167–87.

Henry, Guy; Peterson, E. Wesley F. and Paggi, Mechel. Quality Restrictions as Barriers to Trade: The Case of European Community Regulations on the Use of Hormones. *Western J. Agr. Econ.*, July 1988, *13*(1), pp. 82–91.

Henry, Mark S. Infrastructure Needs in South Carolina: Factors to Consider in Allocating State Resources to Local Areas. In *Johnson, T. G.; Deaton, B. J. and Segarra, E., eds.*, 1988, pp. 135–39.

———. Southern Farms and Rural Communities: Developing Directions for Economic Development Research and Policy. *Southern J. Agr. Econ.*, July 1988, *20*(1), pp. 13–28.

——— **and Mulkey, David.** Development Strategies in the Rural South: Issues and Alternatives. In *Beaulieu, L. J., ed.*, 1988, pp. 249–64.

Henseler-Unger, Henseler and Conrad, Klaus. Income Tax Reduction and the Quantification of Welfare Gains—An Applied General Equilibrium Analysis. In *Bös, D.; Rose, M. and Seidl, C., eds.,*, 1988, pp. 247–62.

Hensher, David A.; Barnard, Peter O. and Truong, Truong P. The Role of Stated Preference Methods in Studies of Travel Choice. *J. Transp. Econ. Policy*, January 1988, *22*(1), pp. 45–58.

Hensler, Deborah R. Researching Civil Justice: Problems and Pitfalls. *Law Contemp. Probl.*, Summer 1988, *51*(3), pp. 55–65.

Henson, Steven E. and Dubin, Jeffrey A. An Engineering/Econometric Analysis of Seasonal Energy Demand and Conservation in the Pacific Northwest. *J. Bus. Econ. Statist.*, January 1988, *6*(1), pp. 121–34.

——— **and Dubin, Jeffrey A.** The Distributional Effects of the Federal Energy Tax Act. *Resources & Energy*, September 1988, *10*(3), pp. 191–212.

Henton, Douglas and Waldhorn, Steven A. The New Economic Role of American States: California. In *Fosler, R. S., ed.*, 1988, pp. 201–47.

Henze, A. and Zeddies, J. EC Programmes, Economic Effects and Cost Benefit Considerations on Adjustments in EC Agriculture. *Europ. Rev. Agr. Econ.*, 1988, *15*(2–3), pp. 191–210.

Henzler, Herbert. Von der strategischen Planung zur strategischen Führung: Versuch einer Positionsbestimmung. (With English summary.) *Z. Betriebswirtshaft*, December 1988, *58*(12), pp. 1286–1307.

Hepworth, Mark E. and Waterson, Michael. Information Technology and the Spatial Dynamics of Capital. *Info. Econ. Policy*, 1988, *3*(2), pp. 143–63.

Heraud, J.-A. and Elbaz, A. L'image et le devenir des fuel-oils lourds dans le secteur industriel. (The Status and the Future for Heavy Oil in the Industrial Sector. With English summary.) *Écon. Soc.*, April 1988, *22*(4), pp. 159–218.

Herbener, Jeffrey. Austrian Methodology: The Preferred Tax Type. In *Rothbard, M. N. and Block, W., eds.*, 1988, pp. 97–111.

Herber, Bernard P. The Antarctic Treaty, International Collective Consumption, and United States Policy. *Tijdschrift Econ. Manage.*, Sept.–Dec. 1988, *33*(3/4), pp. 375–92.

_____. Federal Income Tax Reform in the United States: How Did It Happen? What Did It Do? Where Do We Go from Here? *Amer. J. Econ. Soc.*, October 1988, *47*(4), pp. 391–408.

Herberg, Horst and Knies, Dietmar. The Employment of a Rigid Wage Ration in Small Open Economies with Sector-Specific Capital. *J. Inst. Theoretical Econ.*, September 1988, *144*(4), pp. 671–83.

Herbert, John H. Weather, the Estimation of Residential Energy Demand Relationships and the Reporting of Data. *Energy Econ.*, October 1988, *10*(4), pp. 324–25.

_____ and Barber, Linda J. Regional Residential Natural Gas Demand: Comments. *Resources & Energy*, December 1988, *10*(4), pp. 387–91.

Herbst, Anthony F. and Maberly, Edwin D. A Further Investigation of the Day-of-the-Week Effect in the Gold Market: A Comment. *J. Futures Markets*, June 1988, *8*(3), pp. 389–90.

_____; O'Shaughnessy, John and Dickinson, Roger. Marketing Concept and Customer Orientation. In *Earl, P. E., ed., Vol. 2, 1988, 1986*, pp. 311–16.

Hercok, A. V. V. Accounting in Czechoslovakia. In *Bailey, D. T., ed.*, 1988, pp. 76–93.

Hercowitz, Zvi. The Israeli Economy: Maturing through Crises: A Review Essay. *J. Monet. Econ.*, January 1988, *21*(1), pp. 185–90.

_____; Huffman, Gregory W. and Greenwood, Jeremy. Investment, Capacity Utilization, and the Real Business Cycle. *Amer. Econ. Rev.*, June 1988, *78*(3), pp. 402–17.

Herendeen, James B. A Dynamic Model of the Banking Firm: Pricing and Growth of Loans and Deposits. In *Pennsylvania Economic Association*, 1988, pp. 125–39.

_____. A Simple Model of Bank Intermediation: Comment. In *Pennsylvania Economic Association*, 1988, pp. 149–50.

_____ and Grisley, William. A Dynamic "q" Model of Investment, Financing and Asset Pricing: An Empirical Test for the Agricultural Sector. *Southern Econ. J.*, October 1988, *55*(2), pp. 360–73.

Herendeen, Robert A. Net Energy Considerations. In *West, R. E. and Kreith, F., eds.*, 1988, pp. 255–73.

Herer, Wiktor. Planning the Development of Agriculture under the Conditions of Polish Economic Reform. In *Brada, J. C. and Wadekin, K.-E., eds.*, 1988, pp. 170–79.

Hergert, Michael and Morris, Deigan. Trends in International Collaborative Agreements. In *Contractor, F. J. and Lorange, P.*, 1988, pp. 99–109.

Heri, Erwin W. Money Demand Regressions and Monetary Targeting: Theory and Stylized Evidence. *Schweiz. Z. Volkswirtsch. Statist.*, June 1988, *124*(2), pp. 123–49.

Hermalin, Benjamin E. and Weisbach, Michael S. The Determinants of Board Composition. *Rand J. Econ.*, Winter 1988, *19*(4), pp. 589–606.

Herman, Arthur S. Productivity in Selected Industries and Government Services in 1986. *Mon. Lab. Rev.*, April 1988, *111*(4), pp. 51–57.

Herman, Edward S. The U.S. Economic Destabilization of Nicaragua. *Rev. Radical Polit. Econ.*, Summer–Fall 1988, *20*(2–3), pp. 271–76.

_____ and Lowenstein, Louis. The Efficiency Effects of Hostile Takeovers. In *Coffee, J. C., Jr.; Lowenstein, L. and Rose-Ackerman, S., eds.*, 1988, pp. 211–40.

Herman, Robert and Ausubel, Jesse H. Cities and Infrastructure: Synthesis and Perspectives. In *Ausubel, J. H. and Herman, R., eds.*, 1988, pp. 1–21.

_____, et al. The Dynamic Characterization of Cities. In *Ausubel, J. H. and Herman, R., eds.*, 1988, pp. 22–70.

Hernández B., Luis. Recognition of Foreign Enterprises as Taxable Entities: Peru. In *International Fiscal Association, ed. (I)*, 1988, pp. 535–44.

Hernández D., Alejandro and Stockman, Alan C. Exchange Controls, Capital Controls, and International Financial Markets. *Amer. Econ. Rev.*, June 1988, *78*(3), pp. 362–74.

Hernández-Iglesias, Feliciano and Riboud, Michelle. Intergenerational Effects on Fertility Behavior and Earnings Mobility in Spain. *Rev. Econ. Statist.*, May 1988, *70*(2), pp. 253–58.

Hernstein, Richard J. A Behavioural Alternative to Utility Maximisation. In *Maital, S., ed., Vol. 1*, 1988, pp. 3–60.

Héroux, Lise; Laroche, Michel and McGown, K. Lee. Consumer Product Label Information Processing: An Experiment Involving Time Pressure and Distraction. *J. Econ. Psych.*, June 1988, *9*(2), pp. 195–214.

Herr, Ellen M. Capital Expenditures by Majority-Owned Foreign Affiliates of U.S. Companies, 1988. *Surv. Curr. Bus.*, March 1988, *68*(3), pp. 21–26.

_____. U.S. Business Enterprises Acquired or Established by Foreign Direct Investors in 1987. *Surv. Curr. Bus.*, May 1988, *68*(5), pp. 50–58.

Herr, Hansjörg. Der Goldstandard und die währungspolitische Diskussion der Klassik. (The Gold Standard and the Monetary Discussion of the Classical School. With English summary.) *Konjunkturpolitik*, 1988, *34*(1), pp. 36–55.

Herrero, Carmen and Villar, Antonio Netario. A Characterization of Economies with the Non-substitution Property. *Econ. Letters*, 1988, *26*(2), pp. 147–52.

_____ and **Villar, Antonio Netario.** General Equilibrium in a Non-linear Leontief Framework. *Manchester Sch. Econ. Soc. Stud.*, June 1988, *56*(2), pp. 159–66.

Herrero, M. J. and Binmore, Ken G. Matching and Bargaining in Dynamic Markets. *Rev. Econ. Stud.*, January 1988, *55*(1), pp. 17–31.

_____ and **Binmore, Ken G.** Security Equilibrium. *Rev. Econ. Stud.*, January 1988, *55*(1), pp. 33–48.

Herring, Richard J. Innovation, Institutional Changes, and Regulatory Response in International Financial Markets: Commentary. In *Haraf, W. S. and Kushmeider, R. M., eds.*, 1988, pp. 424–30.

Herriot, Roger, et al. Enhanced Demographic–Economic Data Sets. *Surv. Curr. Bus.*, November 1988, *68*(11), pp. 44–48.

Herriott, Scott R.; Levinthal, Daniel and March, James G. Learning from Experience in Organizations. In *March, J. G.*, 1988, *1985*, pp. 219–27.

Herrmann, Mark and Lin, Biing-Hwan. The Demand and Supply of Norwegian Atlantic Salmon in the United States and the European Community. *Can. J. Agr. Econ.*, November 1988, *36*(3), pp. 459–71.

Herrmann, Robert O. Consumer Complaints and Redress—What We Know and What We Don't Know. In *Maynes, E. S. and ACCI Research Committee, eds.*, 1988, pp. 727–30.

_____; **Walsh, Edward J. and Warland, Rex H.** The Organizations of the Consumer Movement: A Comparative Perspective: Panel. In *Maynes, E. S. and ACCI Research Committee, eds.*, 1988, pp. 469–94.

Herrmann, Roland. The International Allocation of Trade-Tied Aid: A Quantitative Analysis for the Export Quota Scheme in Coffee. *Weltwirtsch. Arch.*, 1988, *124*(4), pp. 675–700.

_____ and **Cathie, John.** The Southern African Customs Union, Cereal Price Policy in South Africa, and Food Security in Botswana. *J. Devel. Stud.*, April 1988, *24*(3), pp. 394–414.

Hersch, Philip L. and McDougall, Gerald S. Voting for 'Sin' in Kansas. *Public Choice*, May 1988, *57*(2), pp. 127–39.

_____; **Netter, Jeffry M. and Poulsen, Annette B.** Insider Trading: The Law, the Theory, the Evidence. *Contemp. Policy Issues*, July 1988, *6*(3), pp. 1–13.

Hershbarger, Robert A. and Miller, Ronald K. The Impact of Economic Conditions on the Incidence of Arson: A Reply. *J. Risk Ins.*, December 1988, *55*(4), pp. 755–57.

Hershey, John C.; Kunreuther, Howard C. and Schoemaker, Paul J. H. Sources of Bias in Assessment Procedures for Utility Functions. In *Bell, D. E.; Raiffa, H. and Tversky, A., eds.*, 1988, *1982*, pp. 422–42.

Hertel, Thomas W. General Equilibrium Incidence of Natural Resource Subsidies: The Three Factor Case. *J. Environ. Econ. Manage.*, June 1988, *15*(2), pp. 206–23.

_____ and **Preckel, Paul V.** Approximating Linear Programs with Summary Functions: Pseudodata with an Infinite Sample. *Amer. J. Agr. Econ.*, May 1988, *70*(2), pp. 397–402.

_____ and **Preckel, Paul V.** Commodity-Specific Effects of the Conservation Reserve Program. *J. Agr. Econ. Res.*, Summer 1988, *40*(3), pp. 2–11.

_____ and **Tsigas, Marinos E.** Tax Policy and U.S. Agriculture: A General Equilibrium Analysis. *Amer. J. Agr. Econ.*, May 1988, *70*(2), pp. 289–302.

Hertz, Paul T. and Gitlow, Howard S. Chain Reaction: The Impact of Managing Quality on Profits, Wages, and Employment. *Rivista Int. Sci. Econ. Com.*, August 1988, *35*(8), pp. 757–67.

Hertzler, Greg. Dynamically Optimal and Approximately Optimal Beef Cattle Diets Formulated by Nonlinear Programming. *Western J. Agr. Econ.*, July 1988, *13*(1), pp. 7–17.

_____ and **Hassan, Rashid M.** Deforestation from the Overexploitation of Wood Resources as a Cooking Fuel: A Dynamic Approach to Pricing Energy Resources in Sudan. *Energy Econ.*, April 1988, *10*(2), pp. 163–68.

Hervés, Carlos; Besada, Manuel and Estevez, Margarita. Equilibria in Economies with Countably Many Commodities. *Econ. Letters*, 1988, *26*(3), pp. 203–07.

_____; **Besada, Manuel and Estévez, Margarita.** Existencia de equilibrio en una economía con producción e infinitas mercancías. (With English summary.) *Invest. Econ.*, January 1988, *12*(1), pp. 69–81.

_____; **Besada, Manuel and Estévez, Margarita.** Núcleo de una economía con infinitas mercancías. (With English summary.) *Invest. Econ.*, September 1988, *12*(3), pp. 445–53.

Herz, Diane E. Employment Characteristics of Older Women, 1987. *Mon. Lab. Rev.*, September 1988, *111*(9), pp. 3–12.

Herzel, Leo and Harris, Daniel. Litigation in the United States. *Nat. Westminster Bank Quart. Rev.*, November 1988, pp. 14–27.

Hess, Eric. Steuerliche Behandlung von 'Computer Software': Schweiz. (Tax Treatment of Computer Software: Switzerland. With English summary.) In *International Fiscal Association, ed. (II)*, 1988, pp. 527–48.

Hess, Peter N. Static and Dynamic Cross-Sections: Inferences for the Contemporary Fertility Transition. *J. Econ. Devel.*, June 1988, *13*(1), pp. 95–119.

_____ and **Mullan, Brendan.** The Military Burden and Public Education Expenditures in Contemporary Developing Nations: Is There a Trade-off? *J. Devel. Areas*, July 1988, *22*(4), pp. 497–514.

Hess, T. M. and Morris, J. Agricultural Flood Alleviation Benefit Assessment: A Case Study. *J. Agr. Econ.*, September 1988, *39*(3), pp. 402–12.

Hessel, Marek P.; Mooney, Marta and Zeleny, Milan. Integrated Process Management: A Management Technology for the New Competitive Era. In *Starr, M. K., ed.*, 1988, pp. 121–58.

Hesser, Garry W. and Galster, George C. Evaluating and Redesigning Subsidy Policies for Home Rehabilitation. *Policy Sci.*, 1988, *21*(1), pp. 67–95.

Hessing, Dick J. and Elffers, Henk. A Linear Structural Model for Tax Evasion Measurements. In *Maital, S., ed., Vol. 2*, 1988, pp. 562–67.

_____; Elffers, Henk and Weigel, Russell H. Research in Tax Resistance: An Integrative Theoretical Scheme for Tax Evasion Behavior. In *Maital, S., ed., Vol. 2*, 1988, pp. 568–76.

Hessing, Dick J., et al. Tax Evasion Research: Measurement Strategies and Theoretical Models. In *van Raaij, W. F.; van Veldhoven, G. M. and Wärneryd, K.-E., eds.*, 1988, pp. 517–37.

Heston, Alan and Summers, Robert. Comparing International Comparisons. In *Salazar-Carrillo, J. and Rao, D. S. P., eds.*, 1988, pp. 263–81.

_____ and Summers, Robert. A New Set of International Comparisons of Real Product and Price Levels Estimates for 130 Countries, 1950–1985. *Rev. Income Wealth*, March 1988, *34*(1), pp. 1–25.

_____ and Summers, Robert. What We Have Learned about Prices and Quantities from International Comparisons: 1987. *Amer. Econ. Rev.*, May 1988, *78*(2), pp. 467–73.

Hettich, Walter and Winer, Stanley L. Economic and Political Foundations of Tax Structure. *Amer. Econ. Rev.*, September 1988, *78*(4), pp. 701–12.

Hettne, Björn. Newly Industrializing Countries and the Political Economy of South–South Relations: India. In *Carlsson, J. and Shaw, T. M., eds.*, 1988, pp. 76–100.

_____ and Sterner, Thomas. Mexico as a Regional Power. In *Carlsson, J. and Shaw, T. M., eds.*, 1988, pp. 48–75.

Hetzel, Robert L. The Monetary Responsibilities of a Central Bank. *Fed. Res. Bank Richmond Econ. Rev.*, Sept.–Oct. 1988, *74*(5), pp. 19–31.

Heuman, Gad. Runaway Slaves in Nineteenth-Century Barbados. In *Archer, L. J., ed.*, 1988, pp. 206–24.

Heuson, Andrea J. Managing the Short-term Interest Rate Exposure Inherent in Adjustable Rate Mortgage Loans. *Amer. Real Estate Urban Econ. Assoc. J.*, Summer 1988, *16*(2), pp. 160–72.

_____. Mortgage Terminations and Pool Characteristics: Some Additional Evidence. *J. Finan. Res.*, Summer 1988, *11*(2), pp. 143–52.

_____. The Term Premia Relationship Implicit in the Term Structure of Treasury Bills. *J. Finan. Res.*, Spring 1988, *11*(1), pp. 13–20.

Heuts, R. M. J. and Bronckers, J. H. J. M. Forecasting the Dutch Heavy Truck Market: A Multivariate Approach. *Int. J. Forecasting*, 1988, *4*(1), pp. 57–79.

van den Heuvel, Paul J. Energy Dissipation, Op-

eration Time, and Production Speed. *Resources & Energy*, March 1988, *10*(1), pp. 31–54.

_____ and Fase, M. M. G. Productivity and Growth: Verdoorn's Law Revisited. *Econ. Letters*, 1988, *28*(2), pp. 135–39.

Hewett, Ed A. Soviet Central Planning: Probing the Limits of the Traditional Model. In *[Holzman, F. D.]*, 1988, pp. 305–39.

_____. Soviet Oil. In *Mabro, R., ed.*, 1988, pp. 129–39.

_____; Wolf, Thomas A. and Brada, Josef C. Economic Stabilization, Structural Adjustment, and Economic Reform. In *[Holzman, F. D.]*, 1988, pp. 3–36.

_____, et al. The 19th Conference of the CPSU: A *Soviet Economy* Roundtable. *Soviet Econ.*, April–June 1988, *4*(2), pp. 103–36.

Hewings, Geoffrey J. D. and Jensen, Rodney C. Emerging Challenges in Regional Input–Output Analysis. *Ann. Reg. Sci.*, February 1988, 22, pp. 43–53.

_____; Jensen, Rodney C. and West, G. R. The Study of Regional Economic Structure Using Input–Output Tables. *Reg. Stud.*, June 1988, *22*(3), pp. 209–20.

_____; Sonis, Michael and Jensen, Rodney C. Technical Innovation and Input–Output Analysis. In *Orishimo, I.; Hewings, G. J. D. and Nijkamp, P., eds.*, 1988, pp. 163–94.

Hewlett, James and Cantor, Robin. The Economics of Nuclear Power: Further Evidence on Learning, Economies of Scale, and Regulatory Effects. *Resources & Energy*, December 1988, *10*(4), pp. 315–35.

Hey, Jeanne C.; King, Arthur E. and Brada, Josef C. Inter-regional and Inter-organizational Differences in Agricultural Efficiency in Czechoslovakia. In *Brada, J. C. and Wadekin, K.-E., eds.*, 1988, pp. 334–43.

Hey, John D. Experimental Investigations into Economic Behaviour under Uncertainty. In *Munier, B. R., ed.*, 1988, pp. 147–62.

_____. A Pilot Experimental Investigation into Optimal Consumption under Uncertainty. In *Maital, S., ed., Vol. 2*, 1988, pp. 653–67.

_____. Prospects for Mathematical Psychological Economics. In *Earl, P. E., ed.*, 1988, pp. 85–99.

_____. Satisficing versus Optimizing Behaviour: Search for Rules for Search. In *Earl, P. E., ed., Vol. 1*, 1988, *1982*, pp. 159–75.

_____ and Dardanoni, Valentino. Optimal Consumption under Uncertainty: An Experimental Investigation. *Econ. J.*, Supplement, 1988, *98*(390), pp. 105–16.

_____ and Dardanoni, Valentino. A Preliminary Analysis of a Large-Scale Experimental Investigation into Consumption under Uncertainty. In *Tietz, R.; Albers, W. and Selten, R., eds.*, 1988, pp. 51–65.

_____ and Martina, Riccardo. Reactions to Reactions and Conjectures about Conjectures. *Scot. J. Polit. Econ.*, August 1988, *35*(3), pp. 283–90.

Heymann, Daniel. Inflation Stabilization: Argentina: Comment. **In** *Bruno, M., et al., eds.,* 1988, pp. 191–95.

Heyne, Paul. The Foundations of Law and of Economics: Can the Blind Lead the Blind? **In** *Zerbe, R. O., Jr., ed.,* 1988, pp. 53–71.

Heywood, John S. Industrial Concentration and Fringe Benefits. *Rev. Ind. Organ.,* Fall 1988, *3*(4), pp. 119–38.

_____. Market Structure and the Pattern of Black-Owned Firms. *Rev. Black Polit. Econ.,* Spring 1988, *16*(4), pp. 65–76.

_____. The Structural Determinants of Corporate Campaign Activity. *Quart. Rev. Econ. Bus.,* Spring 1988, *28*(1), pp. 39–48.

_____. The Union Wage Profile of Women: Potential vs. Actual Experience. *Econ. Letters,* 1988, *27*(2), pp. 189–93.

_____ **and Belman, Dale L.** Incentive Schemes and Racial Wage Discrimination. *Rev. Black Polit. Econ.,* Summer 1988, *17*(1), pp. 47–56.

_____ **and Belman, Dale L.** Public Wage Differentials and the Public Administration "Industry." *Ind. Relat.,* Fall 1988, *27*(3), pp. 385–93.

Hickerson, Steven R. Instrumental Valuation: The Normative Compass of Institutional Economics. **In** *Tool, M. R., ed., Vol. 1,* 1988, *1987,* pp. 167–93.

Hickey, Paul B. Administrative Issues Arising from Tax Reform. **In** *Canadian Tax Foundation,* 1988, pp. 3.1–25.

Hickman, Bert G. The U.S. Economy and the International Transmission Mechanism. **In** *Bryant, R. C., et al., eds.,* 1988, pp. 92–130.

_____ **and Coen, Robert M.** Is European Unemployment Classical or Keynesian? *Amer. Econ. Rev.,* May 1988, *78*(2), pp. 188–93.

Hickok, Susan; Bell, Linda A. and Ceglowski, Janet. The Competitiveness of U.S. Manufactured Goods: Recent Changes and Prospects. *Fed. Res. Bank New York Quart. Rev.,* Spring 1988, *13*(1), pp. 7–22.

_____ **and Klitgaard, Thomas.** U.S. Trade with Taiwan and South Korea. *Fed. Res. Bank New York Quart. Rev.,* Autumn 1988, *13*(3), pp. 60–66.

Hicks, Donald A. Is New Technology Enough? Making and Remaking U.S. Basic Industries: Introduction and Overview. **In** *Hicks, D. A., ed.,* 1988, pp. 1–18.

Hicks, John. A Conversation with Sir John Hicks about "Value and Capital." *Eastern Econ. J.,* Jan.–March 1988, *14*(1), pp. 1–6.

_____. Towards a More General Theory. **In** *Kohn, M. and Tsiang, S.-C., eds.,* 1988, pp. 6–14.

_____. IS–LM: An Explanation. **In** *Shaw, G. K., ed., Vol. 1,* 1988, *1980,* pp. 22–37.

Hickson, Warren. Death to the Oxymoron: The Introduction of 'Rational Hospital Budgeting' in Victoria, or Perhaps More Accurately, an Account of Progress towards That Goal: Discussion. **In** *Butler, J. R. G. and Doessel, D. P., eds.,* 1988, pp. 34–37.

Hidalgo, Luís Ortiz. Recognition of Foreign Enterprises as Taxable Entities: Mexico. **In** *Inter-*

national Fiscal Association, ed. (I), 1988, pp. 467–77.

Hiemenz, Ulrich. Expansion of ASEAN–EC Trade in Manufacturers: Pertinent Issues and Recent Developments. *Devel. Econ.,* December 1988, *26*(4), pp. 341–66.

Hieronimus, Anne-Marie. ESA Space Commercialisation Effort. **In** *Egan, J. J., et al.,* 1988, pp. 109–16.

Hietala, Paula. Inside a Statistical Expert System: Statistical Methods Employed in the ESTES System. **In** *Edwards, D. and Raun, N. E., eds.,* 1988, pp. 163–68.

Higano, Y. and Kohno, Hirotada. Optimal Reorganization of Greater Tokyo: An Industrial Complex of Agglomeration and Scale Economies. 2. *Environ. Planning A,* September 1988, *20*(9), pp. 1145–64.

_____ **and Kohno, Hirotada.** Optimal Reorganization of Greater Tokyo: An Industrial Complex of Agglomeration and Scale Economies. l. *Environ. Planning A,* August 1988, *20*(8), pp. 1103–20.

Higgins, B. H. W. S. Jevons—A Centenary Estimate. **In** *Wood, J. C., ed., Vol. 1,* 1988, *1935,* pp. 50–58.

Higgins, Benjamin. Regional Development and Efficiency of the National Economy. **In** *[Perroux, F.],* 1988, pp. 193–224.

_____. Regional Economic Development: François Perroux. **In** *[Perroux, F.],* 1988, pp. 31–47.

_____ **and Savoie, Donald J.** The Economics and Politics of Regional Development: Introduction. **In** *[Perroux, F.],* 1988, pp. 1–27.

_____ **and Savoie, Donald J.** Regional Economic Development: Conclusions. **In** *[Perroux, F.],* 1988, pp. 375–84.

Higgins, Christopher I. Empirical Analysis and Intergovernmental Policy Consultation. **In** *Bryant, R. C., et al., eds.,* 1988, pp. 285–96.

Higgins, M. L. and Bera, Anil K. A Joint Test for Arch and Bilinearity in the Regression Model. *Econometric Rev.,* 1988–89, *7*(2), pp. 171–81.

Higginson, John. Disputing the Machines: Scientific Management and the Transformation of the Work Routine at the Union Miniere du Haut-Katanga, 1918–1930. *African Econ. Hist.,* 1988, (17), pp. 1–21.

Higginson, Nancy; Hawkins, Murray and Adamowicz, Wiktor L. Pricing Relationships in Interdependent North American Hog Markets: The Impact of the Countervailing Duty. *Can. J. Agr. Econ.,* November 1988, *36*(3), pp. 501–18.

Higgs, Peter J. How Domestic Economic Conditions Influence the Real Exchange Rate. *Rev. Marketing Agr. Econ.,* April 1988, *56*(1), pp. 82–88.

_____; **Parmenter, B. R. and Rimmer, Russell J.** A Hybrid Top-Down, Bottom-Up Regional Computable General Equilibrium Model. *Int. Reg. Sci. Rev.,* 1988, *11*(3), pp. 317–28.

_____ **and Stoeckel, Andy.** The Relative Significance of a Range of Economic Policies for Improving Australia's Balance of Trade. *Austra-lian J. Agr. Econ.*, Aug.–Dec. 1988, *32*(2–3), pp. 69–87.

Higgs, Robert. Can the Constitution Protect Private Rights during National Emergencies? In *Gwartney, J. D. and Wagner, R. E., eds.*, 1988, pp. 369–86.

_____. Hard Coals Make Bad Law: Congressional Parochialism versus National Defense. *Cato J.*, Spring–Summer 1988, *8*(1), pp. 79–106.

High, Jack C. and Coppin, Clayton A. Wiley and the Whiskey Industry: Strategic Behavior in the Passage of the Pure Food Act. *Bus. Hist. Rev.*, Summer 1988, *62*(2), pp. 287–309.

_____ and DiLorenzo, Thomas J. Antitrust and Competition, Historically Considered. *Econ. Inquiry*, July 1988, *26*(3), pp. 423–35.

_____ and Ellig, Jerome. The Private Supply of Education: Some Historical Evidence. In *Cowen, T., ed.*, 1988, pp. 361–82.

High, S. Hugh. W. H. Hutt and Apartheid. *Managerial Dec. Econ.*, Special Issue, Winter 1988, pp. 59–63.

Higham, Ron and Finn, Frank J. The Performance of Unseasoned New Equity 'Issues-Cum-Stock Exchange Listings in Australia. *J. Banking Finance*, September 1988, *12*(3), pp. 333–51.

Highfield, Richard A. and Zellner, Arnold. Calculation of Maximum Entropy Distributions and Approximation of Marginal Posterior Distributions. *J. Econometrics*, February 1988, *37*(2), pp. 195–209.

Highfill, Jannett K.; Sattler, Edward L. and Scott, Robert C. Advantage to a Risk Neutral Firm of Flexible Resources under Demand Uncertainty. *Southern Econ. J.*, April 1988, *54*(4), pp. 934–49.

Highsmith, Robert J. Professional Developments and Opportunities. *J. Econ. Educ.*, Winter 1988, *19*(1), pp. 97–100.

_____ and Baumol, William J. Variables Affecting Success in Economic Education: Preliminary Findings from a New Data Base. *Amer. Econ. Rev.*, May 1988, *78*(2), pp. 257–62.

Higuchi, Yoshio and Mincer, Jacob. Wage Structures and Labor Turnover in the United States and Japan. *J. Japanese Int. Economies*, June 1988, *2*(2), pp. 97–133.

Hihn, Jairus M. and Johnson, Charles R. Evaluation Techniques for Paired Ratio-Comparison Matrices in a Hierarchical Decision Model. In *Eichhorn, W., ed.*, 1988, pp. 269–88.

Hildebrandt, Eckart. Work, Participation and Co-determination in Computer-Based Manufacturing. In *Knights, D. and Willmott, H., eds.*, 1988, pp. 50–65.

Hildenbrand, Werner and Grandmont, Jean Michel. Stochastic Processes of Temporary Equilibria. In *Grandmont, J.-M., ed.*, 1988, *1974*, pp. 307–37.

Hildreth, R. J. and Castle, Emery N. Agricultural Economics at a Crossroads: An Overview. In *Hildreth, R. J., et al., eds.*, 1988, pp. 3–13.

Hilke, John C. and Nelson, Philip B. Diversifica-tion and Predation. *J. Ind. Econ.*, September 1988, *37*(1), pp. 107–11.

Hill, Bette S.; Blaser, C. Jean and Balmer, Pamela W. Practical Issues in Developing Competitive Contracting for Home Care Services. In *Hula, R. C., ed.*, 1988, pp. 84–95.

Hill, Charles W. L. Internal Capital Market Controls and Financial Performance in Multidivisional Firms. *J. Ind. Econ.*, September 1988, *37*(1), pp. 67–83.

Hill, Elizabeth T. A Hypothesis about Execution Rates in the United States: Comment. In *Pennsylvania Economic Association*, 1988, pp. 530–31.

Hill, Forest G. A New Look at Institutionalism: Discussion. In *Samuels, W. J., ed., Vol. 1*, 1988, *1957*, pp. 40–43.

Hill, Hal. Some Neglected Issues in Factor Proportions and Ownership: An Indonesian Case Study. *Weltwirtsch. Arch.*, 1988, *124*(2), pp. 341–55.

Hill, I. D. Some Aspects of Elections—To Fill One Seat or Many. *J. Roy. Statist. Soc.*, 1988, *151*(2), pp. 243–75.

Hill, Joanne M.; Jain, Anshuman and Wood, Robert A., Jr. Insurance: Volatility Risk and Futures Mispricing. *J. Portfol. Manage.*, Winter 1988, *14*(2), pp. 23–29.

Hill, John K. and Brown, Stephen P. A. Lower Oil Prices and State Employment. *Contemp. Policy Issues*, July 1988, *6*(3), pp. 60–68.

_____ and Cox, W. Michael. Effects of the Lower Dollar on U.S. Manufacturing: Industry and State Comparisons. *Fed. Res. Bank Dallas Econ. Rev.*, March 1988, pp. 1–9.

Hill, Lowell D.; Zareba, Marian and Florkowski, Wojciech J. The Impact of Agricultural Policy Changes on Food Production in Poland. *Comp. Econ. Stud.*, Fall 1988, *30*(3), pp. 16–32.

Hill, Marianne T. Modelling the Macroeconomic Impact of Aid. *Bangladesh Devel. Stud.*, March 1988, *16*(1), pp. 1–25.

Hill, Ned C. and Ferguson, Daniel M. Negotiating Payment Terms in an Electronic Environment. In *Kim, Y. H., ed.*, 1988, pp. 131–46.

_____ and Sartoris, William L. The Relationship between Credit Policies and Firm Financial Characteristics. In *Kim, Y. H., ed.*, 1988, pp. 99–114.

Hill, P. J.; Jackstadt, Steve and Huskey, Lee. The Making of an Economist: Comment. *J. Econ. Perspectives*, Fall 1988, *2*(4), pp. 209–12.

Hill, Peter. Recent Developments in Index Number Theory and Practice. *OECD Econ. Stud.*, Spring 1988, (10), pp. 123–48.

Hill, Peter J. and Anderson, Terry L. Constitutional Constraints, Entrepreneurship, and the Evolution of Property Rights. In *Gwartney, J. D. and Wagner, R. E., eds.*, 1988, pp. 207–27.

Hill, R. Carter and Fomby, Thomas B. Small-Sigma Approximations and the Minimaxity of Stein-Rules under Nonnormality. In *Rhodes, G. F., Jr. and Fomby, T. B., eds.*, 1988, pp. 193–209.

_____ **and Koray, Faik.** Money, Debt, and Economic Activity. *J. Macroecon.*, Summer 1988, *10*(3), pp. 351–70.

Hill, Raymond. Problems and Policy for Pesticide Exports to Less Developed Countries. *Natural Res. J.*, Fall 1988, *28*(4), pp. 699–720.

Hill, Ronald J. The *Apparatchiki* and Soviet Political Development. In *Potichnyj, P. J., ed.*, 1988, pp. 3–25.

Hill, Theodore P. and Demko, Stephen. Equitable Distribution of Indivisible Objects. *Math. Soc. Sci.*, October 1988, *16*(2), pp. 145–58.

Hillard, John. J. M. Keynes: The Last of the Cambridge Economists. In *Hillard, J., ed.*, 1988, pp. 1–17.

Hillard, Michael and McIntyre, Richard. The "Labor Shortage" and the Crisis in the Reproduction of the United States Working Class. *Rev. Radical Polit. Econ.*, Summer–Fall 1988, *20*(2–3), pp. 196–202.

Hiller, E. A. Sturgis, Jr. Personnel—Every Manager's Responsibility. In *Timpe, A. D., ed.*, 1988, *1983*, pp. 19–23.

Hillinger, Claude and Weser, Thilo. The Aggregation Problem in Business Cycle Theory. *J. Econ. Dynam. Control*, March 1988, *12*(1), pp. 37–40.

_____ **and Weser, Thilo.** Die Aggregationsproblematik in der Konjunkturtheorie. (The Aggregation Problem in Business Cycle Theory. With English summary.) *Jahr. Nationalökon. Statist.*, April 1988, *204*(4), pp. 326–41.

Hillman, Arye L. The Political Economy of Protectionism: Tariffs and Retaliation in the Timber Industry: Comment. In *Baldwin, R. E., ed. (II)*, 1988, pp. 364–68.

_____. Tariff-Revenue Transfers to Protectionist Interests: Compensation for Reduced Protection or Supplementary Reward for Successful Lobbying? *Public Choice*, August 1988, *58*(2), pp. 169–72.

_____ **and Ursprung, Heinrich W.** Domestic Politics, Foreign Interests, and International Trade Policy. *Amer. Econ. Rev.*, September 1988, *78*(4), pp. 719–45.

Hills, John. World Tax Reform: A Progress Report: United Kingdom: Comment. In *Pechman, J. A., ed.*, 1988, pp. 236–43.

Hilton, Ronald W. Risk Attitude under Two Alternative Theories of Choice under Risk. *J. Econ. Behav. Organ.*, March 1988, *9*(2), pp. 119–36.

_____; **Swieringa, Robert J. and Turner, Martha J.** Product Pricing, Accounting Costs and Use of Product-Costing Systems. *Accounting Rev.*, April 1988, *63*(2), pp. 195–218.

Himsworth, Chris. The Legal Limits of Local Autonomy. In *Bailey, S. J. and Paddison, R., eds.*, 1988, pp. 60–74.

Hinchy, Mike and Fisher, Brian S. Benefits from Price Stabilization to Producers and Processors: The Australian Buffer-Stock Scheme for Wool. *Amer. J. Agr. Econ.*, August 1988, *70*(3), pp. 604–15.

Hindelang, Thomas J. and Chiang, Thomas C. Forward Rate, Spot Rate and Risk Premium:

An Empirical Analysis. *Weltwirtsch. Arch.*, 1988, *124*(1), pp. 74–88.

Hindle, Kevin and Gillin, L. Murray. Some Key Success Factors in Australian New Venture Management. In *Kirchhoff, B. A., et al., eds.*, 1988, pp. 387–402.

Hindley, Brian. Dumping and the Far East Trade of the European Community. *World Econ.*, December 1988, *11*(4), pp. 445–63.

_____. Service Sector Protection: Considerations for Developing Countries. *World Bank Econ. Rev.*, May 1988, *2*(2), pp. 205–24.

Hines, James R., Jr. Decentralization in the Public Sector: An Empirical Study of State and Local Government: Comment. In *Rosen, H. S., ed.*, 1988, pp. 29–32.

_____. Taxation and U.S. Multinational Investment. In *Summers, L. H., ed.*, 1988, pp. 33–61.

_____ **and Auerbach, Alan J.** Investment Tax Incentives and Frequent Tax Reforms. *Amer. Econ. Rev.*, May 1988, *78*(2), pp. 211–16.

Hines, Ruth D. Popper's Methodology of Falsificationism and Accounting Research. *Accounting Rev.*, October 1988, *63*(4), pp. 657–62.

Hingson, Ralph. Mandatory Seat Belt Use Laws and Occupant Crash Protection in the United States: Present Status and Future Prospects: Comments. In *Graham, J. D., ed.*, 1988, pp. 84–89.

Hinich, Melvin J.; Patterson, Douglas and Brockett, Patrick L. Bispectral-Based Tests for the Detection of Gaussianity and Linearity in Time Series. *J. Amer. Statist. Assoc.*, September 1988, *83*(403), pp. 657–64.

_____ **and Wolinsky, Murray A.** A Test for Aliasing Using Bispectral Analysis. *J. Amer. Statist. Assoc.*, June 1988, *83*(402), pp. 499–502.

Hinojosa, Rene C. and Pigozzi, Bruce William. Economic Base and Input–Output Multipliers: An Empirical Linkage. *Reg. Sci. Persp.*, 1988, *18*(2), pp. 3–13.

Hinrichsen, Diederich and Motscha, Matthias. Optimization Problems in the Robustness Analysis of Linear State Space Systems. In *Gomez Fernandez, J. A., et al., eds.*, 1988, pp. 54–78.

Hinshaw, C. Elton; Bolch, Ben W. and Damon, William W. Visual Artists' Rights Act of 1987: A Case of Misguided Legislation. *Cato J.*, Spring–Summer 1988, *8*(1), pp. 71–78.

Hinterberger, Friedrich and Müller, Klause. Verteilungswirkungen der Einkommensteuertarifreform 1990. (The Reform of the Income Scale in 1990: Distributive Effects. With English summary.) *Z. Wirtschaft. Sozialwissen.*, 1988, *108*(3), pp. 355–69.

von Hippel, Eric. Lead Users: A Source of Novel Product Concepts. In *Grønhaug, K. and Kaufmann, G., eds.*, 1988, *1986*, pp. 387–406.

_____. Novel Product Concepts from Lead Users. In *Urabe, K.; Child, J. and Kagono, T., eds.*, 1988, pp. 81–101.

Hippo, Yasuyuki and Tamura, Saburo. The Global Construction Industry: Japan. In *Strass-*

mann, W. P. and Wells, J., eds., 1988, pp. 59–85.

Hirata, Akira. Promotion of Manufactured Exports in Developing Countries. *Devel. Econ.*, December 1988, *26*(4), pp. 422–37.

Hirono, Ryokichi. Japan: Model for East Asian Industrialization? In *Hughes, H., ed.*, 1988, pp. 241–59.

Hirota, Kaoru. Probablistic Sets—A Survey. In *Kacprzyk, J. and Fedrizzi, M., eds.*, 1988, pp. 184–96.

_____ **and Pedrycz, Witold.** Probablistic Sets in Classification and Pattern Recognition. In *Kacprzyk, J. and Fedrizzi, M., eds.*, 1988, pp. 342–52.

Hirš, J., et al. Nitra, Czechoslavia: Regional and Technological Development of Agriculture. In *Parikh, J. K., ed.*, 1988, pp. 167–208.

Hirsch, Barry T. Trucking Regulation, Unionization, and Labor Earnings: 1973–85. *J. Human Res.*, Summer 1988, *23*(3), pp. 296–319.

Hirsch, Seev. Anti-dumping Actions in Brussels and East–West Trade. *World Econ.*, December 1988, *11*(4), pp. 465–84.

_____; **Kalish, Shlomo and Katznelson, Shauli.** Effects of Knowledge and Service Intensities on Domestic and Export Performance. *Weltwirtsch. Arch.*, 1988, *124*(2), pp. 230–41.

_____; **Sassoon, D. M. and Goldberg, Moshe.** An Analysis of the American–Israeli Free Trade Area Agreement. *World Econ.*, June 1988, *11*(2), pp. 281–300.

Hirsch, Werner Z. An Inquiry into Effects of Mobile Home Park Rent Control. *J. Urban Econ.*, September 1988, *24*(2), pp. 212–26.

_____ **and Green, Janet M.** Anti-strike Laws and Their Effects on Work Stoppages by Public School Teachers. *J. Urban Econ.*, November 1988, *24*(3), pp. 331–51.

Hirschberg, Joseph G.; Molina, David J. and Slottje, Daniel J. A Selection Criterion for Choosing between Functional Forms of Income Distribution. *Econometric Rev.*, 1988–89, *7*(2), pp. 183–97.

Hirschey, Mark and Connolly, Robert A. Market Value and Patents: A Bayesian Approach. *Econ. Letters*, 1988, *27*(1), pp. 83–87.

Hirschhorn, Larry. Computers and Jobs: Services and the New Mode of Production. In *Cyert, R. M. and Mowery, D. C., eds.*, 1988, pp. 377–415.

Hirschman, Albert O. How Keynes Was Spread from America. *Challenge*, Nov.–Dec. 1988, *31*(6), pp. 4–7.

_____. The Principle of Conservation and Mutation of Social Energy. In *Annis, S. and Hakim, P., eds.*, 1988, pp. 7–14.

_____ **and Lindblom, Charles E.** Economic Development, Research and Development, Policy Making: Some Converging Views. In *Lindblom, C. E.*, 1988, *1962*, pp. 191–211.

Hirschman, Elizabeth C. The Ideology of Consumption: A Structural-Syntactical Analysis of "Dallas" and "Dynasty." *J. Cons. Res.*, December 1988, *15*(3), pp. 344–59.

_____. Upper Class WASPS as Consumers: A

Humanist Inquiry. In *Hirschman, E. and Sheth, J. N., eds.*, 1988, pp. 115–48.

Hirshhorn, Ron and Kaell, Arthur. A Framework for Evaluating Public Corporations. *Ann. Pub. Co-op. Econ.*, April–June 1988, *59*(2), pp. 141–56.

Hirshleifer, David. Risk, Futures Pricing, and the Organization of Production in Commodity Markets. *J. Polit. Econ.*, December 1988, *96*(6), pp. 1206–20.

Hirshleifer, Jack. Investment Decision under Uncertainty: Applications of the State-Preference Approach. In *Ricketts, M., ed., Vol. 1*, 1988, *1966*, pp. 70–95.

_____ **and Martinez Coll, Juan Carlos.** What Strategies Can Support the Evolutionary Emergence of Cooperation? *J. Conflict Resolution*, June 1988, *32*(2), pp. 367–98.

Hirte, Georg and Wiegard, Wolfgang. An Introduction to Applied General Equilibrium Tax Modelling (With a Preliminary Application to the Reform of Factor Taxes in the FRG). In *Bös, D.; Rose, M. and Seidl, C., eds.,*, 1988, pp. 167–203.

Hirtle, Beverly and Estrella, Arturo. Estimating the Funding Gap of the Pension Benefit Guaranty Corporation. *Fed. Res. Bank New York Quart. Rev.*, Autumn 1988, *13*(3), pp. 45–59.

Hirvonen, Martti. Eräiden suurten suomalaisyritysten teknillinen ja taloudellinen tehokkuus. (Technical and Economic Efficiency in Some Large Finnish Firms. With English summary.) *Liiketaloudellinen Aikak.*, 1988, *37*(1), pp. 29–54.

Hisnanick, John J. and Kymn, Kern O. Econometric Techniques Applied to Productivity Growth Estimation. *Atlantic Econ. J.*, September 1988, *16*(3), pp. 88.

Hisrich, Robert D. Developing New Industries through New and Established Small Businesses. In *Furino, A., ed.*, 1988, pp. 197–209.

_____ **and Brush, Candida G.** Women Entrepreneurs: Strategic Origins Impact on Growth. In *Kirchhoff, B. A., et al., eds.*, 1988, pp. 612–25.

Hitch, C. J. and Hall, R. L. Price Theory and Business Behaviour. In *Sawyer, M. C., ed.*, 1988, *1939*, pp. 205–26.

Hitchens, D. M. W. N. and O'Farrell, P. N. Alternative Theories of Small-Firm Growth: A Critical Review. *Environ. Planning A*, October 1988, *20*(10), pp. 1365–83.

_____ **and O'Farrell, P. N.** The Comparative Performance of Small Manufacturing Companies Located in the Mid West and Northern Ireland. *Econ. Soc. Rev.*, April 1988, *19*(3), pp. 177–98.

_____ **and O'Farrell, P. N.** The Relative Competitiveness and Performance of Small Manufacturing Firms in Scotland and the Mid-west of Ireland: An Analysis of Matched Pairs. *Reg. Stud.*, October 1988, *22*(5), pp. 399–415.

Hite, James C. and Ulbrich, Holley H. Subsidizing Water Users or Water Systems? *Land Econ.*, November 1988, *64*(4), pp. 377–80.

Hite, Peggy A. An Examination of the Impact of

Subject Selection on Hypothetical and Self-Reported Taxpayer Noncompliance. *J. Econ. Psych.*, December 1988, 9(4), pp. 445–66.

Hite, Robert E. and Fraser, Cynthia. Compensation as an Alternative to Ownership in Developing Markets: Beliefs, Attitudes and Uses. *J. World Trade*, December 1988, 22(6), pp. 95–106.

_____; **Sauer, Paul L. and Fraser, Cynthia.** Increasing Contributions in Solicitation Campaigns: The Use of Large and Small Anchorpoints. *J. Cons. Res.*, September 1988, 15(2), pp. 284–87.

Hitt, Michael A.; Ireland, R. Duane and Goryunov, Igor Y. The Context of Innovation: Investment in R&D and Firm Performance. In *Gattiker, U. E. and Larwood, L.*, eds., 1988, pp. 73–92.

Hitzhusen, Fred; Hushak, Leroy J. and Oo, Tin Htut. Factors Related to Errors in Ex-ante Evaluation of Agricultural Projects in Developing Countries. *J. Devel. Areas*, January 1988, 22(2), pp. 199–206.

Hixson, William. Seven Misconceptions in Economic Thought. *Écon. Soc.*, September 1988, 22(9), pp. 35–55.

Hjalmarsson, Lennart and Forsund, Finn R. Choice of Technology and Long-Run Technical Change in Energy-Intensive Industries. *Energy J.*, July 1988, 9(3), pp. 79–97.

Hjorth-Andersen, Christian. Evidence on Agglomeration in Quality Space. *J. Ind. Econ.*, December 1988, 37(2), pp. 209–23.

Hladik, Karen J. R&D and International Joint Ventures. In *Contractor, F. J. and Lorange, P.*, 1988, pp. 187–203.

Ho, Lok Sang. Government Deficit Financing and Stabilisation. *J. Econ. Stud.*, 1988, 15(5), pp. 34–44.

Ho, Thomas S. Y. and Lee, Sang Bin. The Pricing of Corporate Bond Provisions under Interest Rate Risks. In *Chen, A. H.*, ed., 1988, pp. 139–62.

_____ **and Michaely, Roni.** Information Quality and Market Efficiency. *J. Finan. Quant. Anal.*, March 1988, 23(1), pp. 53–70.

Ho, V.; McDermott, L. and Gregory, Robert G. Sharing the Burden: The Australian Labour Market during the 1930s. In *Gregory, R. G. and Butlin, N. G.*, eds., 1988, pp. 217–44.

Hoaas, David J. The Forgotten Contribution of a Wage Tip. *Amer. Econ.*, Fall 1988, 32(2), pp. 35–40.

Hoag, John H.; Browne, M. Neil and Wheeler, Mark. Does a Professor's Reputation Affect Course Selection? In *Missouri Valley Economic Assoc.*, 1988, pp. 182–91.

Hoagland, Porter, III. The Conservation and Disposal of Ocean Hard Minerals: A Comparison of Ocean Mining Codes in the United States. *Natural Res. J.*, Summer 1988, 28(3), pp. 451–508.

Hoare, A. G. Geographical Aspects of British Overseas Trade: A Framework and a Review. *Environ. Planning A*, October 1988, 20(10), pp. 1345–64.

Hobbelink, Henk and Vellve, Renee. Role of Public Research and NGOs. In *Research and Info. System for the Non-aligned and Other Developing Countries*, 1988, pp. 349–67.

Hobbes, Garry and Saunders, Peter G. Income Inequality in Australia in an International Comparative Perspective. *Australian Econ. Rev.*, Spring 1988, (83), pp. 25–34.

Hobbs, Daryl. Factors Influencing the Demand for Rural Infrastructure. In *Johnson, T. G.; Deaton, B. J. and Segarra, E.*, eds., 1988, pp. 51–60.

Hobbs, P. N. Recognition of Foreign Enterprises as Taxable Entities: United Kingdom. In *International Fiscal Association*, ed. (I), 1988, pp. 565–85.

Hoch, Stephen J. Who Do We Know: Predicting the Interests and Opinions of the American Consumer. *J. Cons. Res.*, December 1988, 15(3), pp. 315–24.

Hochman, Eithan; Just, Richard E. and Zilberman, David. Estimation of Multicrop Production Functions: Reply. *Amer. J. Agr. Econ.*, August 1988, 70(3), pp. 733–34.

Hochman, Harold M. and Barthold, Thomas A. Addiction as Extreme-Seeking. *Econ. Inquiry*, January 1988, 26(1), pp. 89–106.

Hochman, Oded and Luski, Israel. Advertising and Economic Welfare: Comment. *Amer. Econ. Rev.*, March 1988, 78(1), pp. 290–96.

Hochman, Shalom and Palmon, Oded. A Tax-Induced Clientele for Index-Linked Corporate Bonds. *J. Finance*, December 1988, 43(5), pp. 1257–63.

Hodder, James E. Corporate Capital Structure in the United States and Japan: Financial Intermediation and Implications of Financial Deregulation. In *Shoven, J. B.*, ed., 1988, pp. 241–63.

Hodes, Daniel A.; Cook, Thomas and Rochfort, William M. The Importance of Regional Economic Analysis and Regional Strategies in an Age of Industrial Restructuring. *Bus. Econ.*, April 1988, 23(2), pp. 46–51.

Hodge, I. D. Property Institutions and Environmental Improvement. *J. Agr. Econ.*, September 1988, 39(3), pp. 369–75.

_____. A Reassessment of the Role of County Council Smallholdings. *J. Agr. Econ.*, May 1988, 39(2), pp. 243–53.

Hodgson, Dennis. Orthodoxy and Revisionism in American Demography. *Population Devel. Rev.*, December 1988, 14(4), pp. 541–69.

Hodgson, Geoff. On Informational Reductionism: A Reply to Kay. *J. Econ. Issues*, March 1988, 22(1), pp. 244–49.

_____ **and Steedman, Ian.** Depreciation of Machines of Changing Efficiency: A Note. In *Steedman, I.*, ed., Vol. 2, 1988, 1977, pp. 26–32.

Hodoshima, Jiro. The Effect of Truncation on the Identifiability of Regression Coefficients. *J. Amer. Statist. Assoc.*, December 1988, 83(404), pp. 1055–56.

Hodrick, Robert J. Expansionary Fiscal Policy

and International Interdependence: Comment. In *Frenkel, J. A., ed.*, 1988, pp. 265–69.

Hodson, Randy. Good Jobs and Bad Management: How New Problems Evoke Old Solutions in High-Tech Settings. In *Farkas, G. and England, P., eds.*, 1988, pp. 247–79.

Hoehn, John P.; Blomquist, Glenn C. and Berger, Mark C. New Estimates of Quality of Life in Urban Areas. *Amer. Econ. Rev.*, March 1988, *78*(1), pp. 89–107.

_____ **and Fishelson, Gideon.** Quality Adjusted Prices and Weak Complementarity: A New Method for Estimating the Demand for Environmental Services. *Resources & Energy*, December 1988, *10*(4), pp. 337–54.

van der Hoek, M. Peter. An Incomes Policy for the Professions: The Dutch Experience. *Amer. J. Econ. Soc.*, January 1988, *47*(1), pp. 71–80.

Hoekman, Bernard M. Services as the Quid Pro Quo for a Safeguards Code. *World Econ.*, June 1988, *11*(2), pp. 203–15.

_____ **and Stern, Robert M.** Conceptual Issues Relating to Services in the International Economy. In *Lee, C. H. and Naya, S., eds.*, 1988, pp. 7–25.

Hoekman, Jacob M. and Berg, Sanford V. Entrepreneurship over the Product Life Cycle: Joint Venture Strategies in the Netherlands. In *Contractor, F. J. and Lorange, P.*, 1988, pp. 145–67.

Hoekstra, B. L. Perspectives on Early Use of Low Earth Orbit for Space Manufacturing. In *Egan, J. J., et al.*, 1988, pp. 385–92.

Hoel, Michael and Calmfors, Lars. Work Sharing and Overtime. *Scand. J. Econ.*, 1988, *90*(1), pp. 45–62.

_____ **and Moene, Karl O.** Profit Sharing, Unions and Investments. *Scand. J. Econ.*, 1988, *90*(4), pp. 493–505.

_____ **and Nymoen, Ragnar.** The Supply Side of RIKMOD: Short-run Producer Behaviour in a Model of Monopolistic Competition. *Econ. Modelling*, January 1988, *5*(1), pp. 58–70.

_____ **and Nymoen, Ragnar.** The Supply Side of RIKMOD: Short-Run Producer Behaviour in a Model of Monopolistic Competition. In *Motamen, H., ed.*, 1988, pp. 381–405.

_____ **and Nymoen, Ragnar.** Wage Formation in Norwegian Manufacturing: An Empirical Application of a Theoretical Bargaining Model. *Europ. Econ. Rev.*, April 1988, *32*(4), pp. 977–97.

Hoem, Jan M. and Borgan, Ørnulf. Demographic Reproduction Rates and the Estimation of an Expected Total Count per Person in an Open Population. *J. Amer. Statist. Assoc.*, September 1988, *83*(403), pp. 886–91.

Hoerter, Darrell and Wiseman, Michael. Metropolitan Development in the San Francisco Bay Area. *Ann. Reg. Sci.*, November 1988, *22*(3), pp. 11–33.

Hoet-Mulquin, M.-E. and Gevers, L. Public Expenditures and Welfare Policy: A Study of Local Decisions in the Walloon Region. *Tijdschrift Econ. Manage.*, Sept.–Dec. 1988, *33*(3/4), pp. 355–74.

Hoffer, George E.; Pruitt, Stephen W. and Reilly, Robert J. The Effect of Media Presentation on the Formation of Economic Expectations: Some Initial Evidence. *J. Econ. Psych.*, September 1988, *9*(3), pp. 315–25.

_____ **; Pruitt, Stephen W. and Reilly, Robert J.** The Impact of Product Recalls on the Wealth of Sellers: A Reexamination. *J. Polit. Econ.*, June 1988, *96*(3), pp. 663–70.

Hofferth, Sandra L.; Kahn, Joan R. and Kalsbeek, William D. National Estimates of Teenage Sexual Activity: Evaluating the Comparability of Three National Surveys. *Demography*, May 1988, *25*(2), pp. 189–204.

Hofflander, Alfred E. and Nye, Blaine F. Experience Rating in Medical Professional Liability Insurance. *J. Risk Ins.*, March 1988, *55*(1), pp. 150–57.

Hoffman, Elizabeth and Carlos, Ann M. Game Theory and the North American Fur Trade: A Reply. *J. Econ. Hist.*, September 1988, *48*(3), pp. 681.

Hoffman, George. Improving the Socioeconomic Data Base: A Discussion. In *Hildreth, R. J., et al., eds.*, 1988, pp. 496–98.

_____. World Grain Prospects for the 1990s. *Can. J. Agr. Econ.*, Part 2, December 1988, *36*(4), pp. 789–97.

Hoffman, Lutz. UNCTAD and Trade Liberalization. In *Dicke, D. C. and Petersmann, E.-U., eds.*, 1988, pp. 323–39.

Hoffman, Saul D. and Duncan, Greg J. A Comparison of Choice-Based Multinomial and Nested Logit Models: The Family Structure and Welfare Use Decisions of Divorced or Separated Women. *J. Human Res.*, Fall 1988, *23*(4), pp. 550–62.

_____ **and Duncan, Greg J.** Multinomial and Conditional Logit Discrete-Choice Models in Demography. *Demography*, August 1988, *25*(3), pp. 415–27.

_____ **and Duncan, Greg J.** What *Are* the Economic Consequences of Divorce? *Demography*, November 1988, *25*(4), pp. 641–45.

Hoffmann, Hans E. W. Intospace: Support to European Industrial Users. In *Egan, J. J., et al.*, 1988, pp. 309–15.

Hoffmeister, J. Ronald and Spindt, Paul A. The Micromechanics of the Federal Funds Market: Implications for Day-of-the-Week Effects in Funds Rate Variability. *J. Finan. Quant. Anal.*, December 1988, *23*(4), pp. 401–16.

Hoffmeyer, Erik. Economic Policy Objectives and Policymaking in the Major Industrial Countries: Comment. In *Guth, W., ed.*, 1988, pp. 40–43.

Hoffmeyer, Ullrich and Currie, David. Fiscal Policy Coordination, Inflation and Reputation in a Natural Rate World. *Greek Econ. Rev.*, 1988, *10*(1), pp. 103–32.

Hoffstadt, Josef. Computer-Aided Scheduling in Urban Mass Transit Companies: Past, Present and Future. In *Daduna, J. R. and Wren, A., eds.*, 1988, pp. 1–7.

Hofler, Richard; Thompson, Henry and Clark, Don P. Separability of Capital and Labor in

U.S. Manufacturing. *Econ. Letters*, 1988, *26*(2), pp. 197–201.

Hofmann, Hans. Addendum [Arbeitsproduktivitätsentwicklung, Strukturwandel und Unternehmenskonzentration in der westdeutschen Industrie (Growth of Labour Productivity, Structural Change, and Firm Concentration in West German Industry)]. *Z. Wirtschaft. Sozialwissen.*, 1988, *108*(2), pp. 285–86.

_____. Arbeitsproduktivitätsentwicklung, Strukturwandel und Unternehmenskonzentration in der westdeutschen Industrie. (Growth of Labour Productivity, Structural Change and Firm Concentration in West German Industry. With English summary.) *Z. Wirtschaft. Sozialwissen.*, 1988, *108*(1), pp. 25–41.

Hoftyzer, John and Mixon, J. Wilson, Jr. National Origins of Saudi Arabia's Imports. *J. Energy Devel.*, Autumn 1988, *14*(1), pp. 45–54.

Hogan, Timothy D. The Effects of Growth upon Local Inflation Rates. *Ann. Reg. Sci.*, July 1988, *22*(2), pp. 70–79.

Hogan, Warren P.; Sharpe, Ian G. and Gross, E. Market Information and Potential Insolvency of Australian Financial Institutions. *Australian Econ. Pap.*, June 1988, *27*(50), pp. 44–64.

Hogan, William W. and Broadman, Harry G. Is an Oil Tariff Justified? An American Debate: The Numbers Say Yes. *Energy J.*, July 1988, *9*(3), pp. 7–29.

Hogarth, Jeanne M. Accepting an Early Retirement Bonus: An Empirical Study. *J. Human Res.*, Winter 1988, *23*(1), pp. 21–33.

Hogarth, Robin M. and Einhorn, Hillel J. Behavioral Decision Theory: Processes of Judgment and Choice. In *Bell, D. E.; Raiffa, H. and Tversky, A., eds.*, 1988, *1981*, pp. 113–46.

_____ **and Einhorn, Hillel J.** Conceptions of Choice: Reply to Commentaries. In *Bell, D. E.; Raiffa, H. and Tversky, A., eds.*, 1988, *1982*, pp. 147–51.

_____ **and Einhorn, Hillel J.** Decision Making under Ambiguity: A Note. In *Munier, B. R., ed.*, 1988, pp. 327–36.

_____ **and Makridakis, Spyros.** Forecasting and Planning: An Evolution. In *Earl, P. E., ed., Vol. 1*, 1988, *1981*, pp. 193–216.

Hogendorn, Jan S. A Cautionary Tale. *Challenge*, May–June 1988, *31*(3), pp. 52–55.

_____ **and Gemery, Henry A.** Continuity in West African Monetary History? An Outline of Monetary Development. *African Econ. Hist.*, 1988, (17), pp. 127–46.

Hogg, Robert V. Combining Robust and Traditional Least Squares Methods: A Critical Evaluation: Comment. *J. Bus. Econ. Statist.*, October 1988, *6*(4), pp. 428.

Hoh, Ronald. The Effectiveness of Mediation in Public Sector Arbitration Systems: The Iowa Experience. In *Lewin, D., et al., eds.*, 1988, *1984*, pp. 373–86.

Hohenberg, Paul M. and Lees, Lynn Hollen. How Cities Grew in the Western World: A Systems Approach. In *Ausubel, J. H. and Herman, R., eds.*, 1988, pp. 71–84.

Hohmann, Karl. Energy Consumption in the GDR's Agriculture. In *Brada, J. C. and Wadekin, K.-E., eds.*, 1988, pp. 209–22.

Höhn, Siegfried. JIT in Large Complex Companies. In *Holl, U. and Trevor, M., eds.*, 1988, pp. 85–87.

Hojman, David E. Sex and the Labour Market: Wage Discrimination in Latin American Manufacturing. *J. Econ. Devel.*, December 1988, *13*(2), pp. 123–39.

Holahan, John. The Impact of Alternative Hospital Payment Systems on Medicaid Costs. *Inquiry*, Winter 1988, *25*(4), pp. 517–32.

Holbek, Jonny. The Innovation Design Dilemma: Some Notes on Its Relevance and Solutions. In *Grønhaug, K. and Kaufmann, G., eds.*, 1988, pp. 253–77.

Holbik, Karel. Monetary Aspects of United States–Japan Economic Relations. *Rivista Int. Sci. Econ. Com.*, February 1988, *35*(2), pp. 157–70.

Holbrook, Morris B. The Psychoanalytic Interpretation of Consumer Behavior: I Am an Animal. In *Hirschman, E. and Sheth, J. N., eds.*, 1988, pp. 149–78.

_____ **and O'Shaughnessy, John.** On the Scientific Status of Consumer Research and the Need for an Interpretive Approach to Studying Consumption Behavior. *J. Cons. Res.*, December 1988, *15*(3), pp. 398–402.

_____; **Stephens, Debra and Anand, Punam.** The Formation of Affective Judgments: The Cognitive–Affective Model versus the Independence Hypothesis. *J. Cons. Res.*, December 1988, *15*(3), pp. 386–91.

Holcombe, Randall G. The Role of Government. In *[Rothbard, M. N.]*, 1988, pp. 269–82.

Holden, Karen C. Physically Demanding Occupations, Health, and Work after Retirement: Findings from the New Beneficiary Survey. *Soc. Sec. Bull.*, November 1988, *51*(11), pp. 3–15.

_____; **Burkhauser, Richard V. and Feaster, Daniel J.** The Timing of Falls into Poverty after Retirement and Widowhood. *Demography*, August 1988, *25*(3), pp. 405–14.

_____ **and De Vos, Susan.** Measures Comparing Living Arrangements of the Elderly: An Assessment. *Population Devel. Rev.*, December 1988, *14*(4), pp. 688–704.

Holden, Kenneth and Peel, David A. A Comparison of Some Inflation, Growth and Unemployment Forecasts. *J. Econ. Stud.*, 1988, *15*(5), pp. 45–52.

Holden, Steinar. Local and Central Wage Bargaining. *Scand. J. Econ.*, 1988, *90*(1), pp. 93–99.

Holder, Harold D. Alcohol Taxes and Highway Safety: Comments. In *Graham, J. D., ed.*, 1988, pp. 223–26.

Holderness, B. A. Studies in Capital Formation in the United Kingdom, 1750–1920: Agriculture, 1770–1860. In *Feinstein, C. H. and Pollard, S., eds.*, 1988, pp. 9–34.

Holderness, Clifford G. and Sheehan, Dennis P. The Role of Majority Shareholders in Publicly

Held Corporations: An Exploratory Analysis. *J. Finan. Econ.*, Jan.–March 1988, *20*(1–2), pp. 317–46.

Holdren, Cheryl E. Toxic Substances: A Cause for Concern? In *Ehrlich, P. R. and Holdren, J. P., eds.*, 1988, pp. 147–69.

Holdren, John P. Backing Away from the Brink: What Could and Should Be Done to Reduce the Danger of Nuclear War. In *Ehrlich, P. R. and Holdren, J. P., eds.*, 1988, pp. 201–31.

Holl, P. and Pickering, J. F. The Determinants and Effects of Actual, Abandoned and Contested Mergers. *Managerial Dec. Econ.*, March 1988, *9*(1), pp. 1–19.

Holland, A. Steven. The Changing Responsiveness of Wages to Price-Level Shocks: Explicit and Implicit Indexation. *Econ. Inquiry*, April 1988, *26*(2), pp. 265–79.

———. Indexation and the Effect of Inflation Uncertainty on Real GNP. *J. Bus.*, October 1988, *61*(4), pp. 473–84.

——— **and Fackler, James S.** Indexation and the Effect of a Price-Level Shock on Relative Wage Variability. *Rev. Econ. Statist.*, August 1988, *70*(3), pp. 524–26.

Holland, David C. Workers' Self-Management before and after 1981. In *Marer, P. and Siwinski, W., eds.*, 1988, pp. 133–41.

Holland, John H. The Global Economy as an Adaptive Process. In *Anderson, P. W.; Arrow, K. J. and Pines, D., eds.*, 1988, pp. 117–24.

Holland, Rodger G. and Sutton, Nancy A. The Liability Nature of Unfunded Pension Obligations since ERISA. *J. Risk Ins.*, March 1988, *55*(1), pp. 32–58.

Hollander, Abraham and Lasserre, Pierre. Monopoly and the Preemption of Competitive Recycling. *Int. J. Ind. Organ.*, December 1988, *6*(4), pp. 489–97.

Holländer, Heinz. Increasing Returns and the Foundations of Unemployment Theory: A Note. *Econ. J.*, March 1988, *98*(389), pp. 165–71.

Hollander, Samuel. John Stuart Mill Interpretation since Schumpeter: Commentary. In *Thweatt, W. O., ed.*, 1988, pp. 163–78.

Hollas, Daniel R. and Stansell, Stanley R. An Examination of the Economic Efficiency of Class I Railroads: A Profit Function Analysis. *Rev. Ind. Organ.*, Fall 1988, *3*(4), pp. 93–117.

——— **and Stansell, Stanley R.** An Examination of the Effect of Ownership Form on Price Efficiency: Proprietary, Cooperative and Municipal Electric Utilities. *Southern Econ. J.*, October 1988, *55*(2), pp. 336–50.

——— **and Stansell, Stanley R.** Regulation, Interfirm Rivalry, and the Economic Efficiency of Natural Gas Distribution Facilities. *Quart. Rev. Econ. Bus.*, Winter 1988, *28*(4), pp. 21–37.

Hollenhorst, Jerome J. and Kohn, Robert E. Production Uncertainty and Pollution. *Southern Econ. J.*, October 1988, *55*(2), pp. 454–62.

Holleran, Philip M. and Schwarz, Margaret. Another Look at Comparable Worth's Impact on

Black Women. *Rev. Black Polit. Econ.*, Winter 1988, *16*(3), pp. 97–102.

Hollingsworth, A. T. and Hoyer, Denise Tanguay. How Supervisors Can Shape Behavior. In *Timpe, A. D., ed.*, 1988, *1985*, pp. 77–80.

Hollister, Robinson G., Jr. and Freedman, David H. Special Employment Programmes in OECD Countries. *Int. Lab. Rev.*, 1988, *127*(3), pp. 317–34.

Holloway, David. The Soviet Union Today: Arms Control. In *Cracraft, J., ed.*, 1988, pp. 126–34.

Holloway, Garth J. and Goddard, Ellen W. An Approach to Examining Relative Efficiency in the Canadian Livestock Slaughtering Industry. *Can. J. Agr. Econ.*, July 1988, *36*(2), pp. 207–20.

Holloway, Thomas M. The Relationship between Federal Deficits/Debt and Interest Rates. *Amer. Econ.*, Spring 1988, *32*(1), pp. 29–38.

Holly, Alberto and Magnus, Jan R. A Note on Instrumental Variables and Maximum Likelihood Estimation Procedures. *Ann. Écon. Statist.*, April–June 1988, (10), pp. 121–38.

——— **and Rockinger, Georg Michael.** Exact and Approximate Distribution of the *t* Ratio Test Statistic in an AR(1) Model. In *Barnett, W. A.; Berndt, E. R. and White, H., eds.*, 1988, pp. 157–70.

Holly, Sean and Longbottom, Andrew. Company Acquisitions, Investment and Tobin's *Q*: Evidence for the United Kingdom. *J. Econ. Bus.*, May 1988, *40*(2), pp. 103–15.

——— **and Smith, Peter.** Compositional Effects and Unemployment in the United States and Europe. In *Giersch, H., ed.*, 1988, pp. 152–65.

Holm, Søren and Walukiewicz, Stanislaw. Column/Constraint Generation for Quadratic Assignment Problems. In *Iri, M. and Yajima, K., eds.*, 1988, pp. 287–98.

Holmberg, Ingvar and Sarafoglou, Nicias. Interregional Migration in Individual Countries: Sweden. In *Weidlich, W. and Haag, G., eds.*, 1988, pp. 223–60.

Holmes, D. J.; Wu, C. F. Jeff and Holt, D. The Effect of Two-stage Sampling on the *F* Statistic. *J. Amer. Statist. Assoc.*, March 1988, *83*(401), pp. 150–59.

Holmes, James M. and Hutton, Patricia A. A Functional-Form, Distribution-Free Alternative to Parametric Analysis of Granger Causal Models. In *Rhodes, G. F., Jr. and Fomby, T. B., eds.*, 1988, pp. 211–25.

——— **and Manning, Richard.** Memory and Market Stability: The Case of the Cobweb. *Econ. Letters*, 1988, *28*(1), pp. 1–7.

Holmes-Junca, Susan and Elguero, Eric. Confidence Regions for Projection Pursuit Density Estimates. In *Edwards, D. and Raun, N. E., eds.*, 1988, pp. 59–63.

Holmes, Thomas P. The Offsite Impact of Soil Erosion on the Water Treatment Industry. *Land Econ.*, November 1988, *64*(4), pp. 356–66.

Holmlund, Bertil. Fiscal and Monetary Policy in

the Keynes–Kalecki Tradition: Comment. **In**
Kregel, J. A.; Matzner, E. and Roncaglia, A.,
eds., 1988, pp. 133–34.
_____ **and Lundborg, Per.** Unemployment Insurance and Union Wage Setting. *Scand. J.*
Econ., 1988, *90*(2), pp. 161–72.
_____ **and Pencavel, John.** The Determination
of Wages, Employment, and Work Hours in
an Economy with Centralised Wage-Setting:
Sweden, 1950–83. *Econ. J.*, December 1988,
98(393), pp. 1105–26.
Holmquist, Carin and Sundin, Elisabeth. Women
as Entrepreneurs in Sweden: Conclusions from
a Survey. **In** *Kirchhoff, B. A., et al., eds.*, 1988,
pp. 626–42.
Holmquist, Frank and Ford, Michael. The State
and Economy in Kenya: Review Essay. *African*
Econ. Hist., 1988, (17), pp. 153–63.
Holmstrom, Bengt. Breach of Trust in Hostile
Takeovers: Comment. **In** *Auerbach, A. J., ed.*
(I), 1988, pp. 56–61.
Holt, Alan and Hemmerdinger, Louis. Space Station Payload Accommodations. **In** *Egan, J. J.,*
et al., 1988, pp. 261–81.
Holt, Charles A. An Experimental Test of the
Consistent-Conjectures Hypothesis. **In**
Daughety, A. F., ed., 1988, *1985*, pp. 179–
97.
Holt, D.; Holmes, D. J. and Wu, C. F. Jeff.
The Effect of Two-stage Sampling on the *F*
Statistic. *J. Amer. Statist. Assoc.*, March 1988,
83(401), pp. 150–59.
Holt, Matthew T. and Aradhyula, Satheesh V.
GARCH Time-Series Models: An Application
to Retail Livestock Prices. *Western J. Agr.*
Econ., December 1988, *13*(2), pp. 365–74.
_____ **and Johnson, Stanley R.** Supply Dynamics
in the U.S. Hog Industry. *Can. J. Agr. Econ.*,
July 1988, *36*(2), pp. 313–35.
Holter, Darryl. Sources of CIO Success: The New
Deal Years in Milwaukee. *Labor Hist.*, Spring
1988, *29*(2), pp. 199–224.
Holtfrerich, Carl-Ludwig. Relations between
Monetary Authorities and Governmental Institutions: The Case of Germany from the 19th
Century to the Present. **In** *Toniolo, G., ed.*,
1988, pp. 105–59.
Holtham, Gerald. Foreign Responses to U.S.
Macroeconomic Policies. **In** *Bryant, R. C., et*
al., eds., 1988, pp. 267–84.
_____ **and Bryant, Ralph C.** The U.S. External
Deficit: Diagnosis, Prognosis, and Cure. **In**
Bryant, R. C.; Holtham, G. and Hooper, P.,
eds., 1988, pp. 57–81.
_____**; Hooper, Peter and Bryant, Ralph C.**
Consensus and Diversity in the Model Simulations. **In** *Bryant, R. C., et al., eds.*, 1988, pp.
27–62.
_____**; Hooper, Peter and Bryant, Ralph C.** External Deficits and the Dollar: The Pit and the
Pendulum: Introduction. **In** *Bryant, R. C.;*
Holtham, G. and Hooper, P., eds., 1988, pp.
1–9.
Holthausen, Robert W. and Verrecchia, Robert
E. The Effect of Sequential Information Releases on the Variance of Price Changes in an

Intertemporal Multi-asset Market. *J. Acc.*
Res., Spring 1988, *26*(1), pp. 82–106.
Holthus, Manfred. Developments in External Indebtedness since 1973. **In** *Gutowski, A. and*
Holthus, M., eds., 1988, *1980*, pp. 11–44.
_____. External Indebtedness and Debt-Service
Capacity of Developing Countries. **In** *Gutowski, A. and Holthus, M., eds.*, 1988, *1981*, pp.
61–89.
_____ **and Gutowski, Armin.** Limits to International Indebtedness. **In** *Gutowski, A. and Holthus, M., eds.*, 1988, *1983*, pp. 93–114.
_____ **and Stanzel, Klaus.** The Credit Standing
of Developing Countries: Criteria for Assessing
External Debt. **In** *Gutowski, A. and Holthus,*
M., eds., 1988, *1984*, pp. 277–314.
Holtmann, A. G. Theories of Non-profit Institutions. *J. Econ. Surveys*, 1988, *2*(1), pp. 29–
45.
Holtz-Eakin, Douglas. The Line Item Veto and
Public Sector Budgets: Evidence from the
States. *J. Public Econ.*, August 1988, *36*(3),
pp. 269–92.
_____. Testing for Individual Effects in Autoregressive Models. *J. Econometrics*, November
1988, *39*(3), pp. 297–307.
_____ **and McGuire, Therese J.** State Grants-in-Aid and Municipal Government Budgets: A
Case Study of New Jersey. **In** *Bell, M. E.,*
ed., 1988, pp. 229–65.
_____**; Newey, Whitney K. and Rosen, Harvey**
S. Estimating Vector Autoregressions with
Panel Data. *Econometrica*, November 1988,
56(6), pp. 1371–95.
_____ **and Rosen, Harvey S.** Tax Deductibility
and Municipal Budget Structure. **In** *Rosen,*
H. S., ed., 1988, pp. 107–26.
Holub, Hans Werner and Tappeiner, Gottfried.
Qualitative Evaluation of Techniques of Aggregation. *Jahr. Nationalökon. Statist.*, November
1988, *205*(5), pp. 385–99.
Holzach, Robert. The Changing Face of Banking
Services and Strategies. **In** *Mikdashi, Z., ed.*,
1988, pp. 11–24.
Holzer, Harry J. Can We Solve Black Youth Unemployment? *Challenge*, Nov.–Dec. 1988,
31(6), pp. 43–49.
_____. The Effects of Public Sector Unionism
on Pay, Employment, Department Budgets,
and Municipal Expenditures: Comment. **In**
Freeman, R. B. and Ichniowski, C., eds., 1988,
pp. 361–63.
_____. Search Method Use by Unemployed
Youth. *J. Lab. Econ.*, January 1988, *6*(1), pp.
1–20.
Holzgang, Anna and Granziol, Markus J. The
Contribution of Inflation to the Level and the
Variability of Nominal Interest Rates: Some
Multi-country Evidence. *Schweiz. Z. Volkswirtsch. Statist.*, December 1988, *124*(4), pp.
559–73.
Homaifar, Ghassem and Graddy, Duane B.
Equity Yields in Models Considering Higher
Moments of the Return Distribution. *Appl.*
Econ., March 1988, *20*(3), pp. 325–34.
_____, **et al.** American Presidential Elections and

Returns of Defence Industry Stocks. *Appl. Econ.*, July 1988, *20*(7), pp. 985–93.

Homer, Pierce and Kinscherff, Paul. The International Joint Commission: The Role It Might Play. In *Schmandt, J.; Clarkson, J. and Roderick, H., eds.*, 1988, pp. 190–216.

Homsy, G. M. and Meiburg, E. Vortex Methods for Porous Media Flows. In *Wheeler, M. F., ed.*, 1988, pp. 199–225.

Honadle, Beth Walter. The Federal Government's Role in Community Infrastructure in the 1980s and Beyond. In *Johnson, T. G.; Deaton, B. J. and Segarra, E., eds.*, 1988, pp. 257–59.

Honda, Yuzo. A Size Correction to the Lagrange Multiplier Test for Heteroskedasticity. *J. Econometrics*, July 1988, *38*(3), pp. 375–86.

Hondros, E. D. Materials, Year 2000. In *Forester, T., ed.*, 1988, pp. 61–84.

van den Honert, R. C. and Barr, G. D. I. Diversifying Mergers and Risk: A Comment. *J. Econ. Stud.*, 1988, *15*(5), pp. 53–64.

Honey, Michael and Boris, Eileen. Gender, Race, and the Policies of the Labor Department. *Mon. Lab. Rev.*, February 1988, *111*(2), pp. 26–36.

Hong, Kyttack. Interest Rate, Corporate Saving and Household Saving in Korea and Taiwan. *J. Econ. Devel.*, June 1988, *13*(1), pp. 195–207.

Hong, Lee Fook. A Summary of the 1988 Budget's Tax Proposals: Singapore. *Bull. Int. Fiscal Doc.*, May 1988, *42*(5), pp. 213–16.

Hong, Wontack. A Developing Country's Perspective of the International Trade System. In *Borner, S., ed.*, 1988, pp. 102–19.

————. Time Preference in Dynamic Trade Models: An Empirical Critique. *Econ. Develop. Cult. Change*, July 1988, *36*(4), pp. 741–51.

Hong, Y. and Pagan, Adrian. Some Simulation Studies of Nonparametric Estimators. *Empirical Econ.*, 1988, *13*(3–4), pp. 251–66.

Hong, Zhunyan and Ma, Bin. Enlivening Large State Enterprises: Where Is the Motive Force? In *Reynolds, B. L., ed.*, 1988, *1987*, pp. 213–18.

Honma, Masayoshi and Hayami, Yujiro. In Search of Agricultural Policy Reform in Japan. *Europ. Rev. Agr. Econ.*, 1988, *15*(4), pp. 367–95.

Honohan, Patrick and Browne, F. X. Portfolio Choice in Irish Financial Markets. *Econ. Modelling*, January 1988, *5*(1), pp. 9–18.

Hood, Neil; Dunlop, S. and Young, Stephen. Global Strategies, Multinational Subsidiary Roles and Economic Impact in Scotland. *Reg. Stud.*, December 1988, *22*(6), pp. 487–97.

———— **and Vahlne, Jan-Erik.** Strategies in Global Competition: Concluding Perspectives. In *Hood, N. and Vahlne, J.-E., eds.*, 1988, pp. 390–93.

———— **and Young, Stephen.** Inward Investment and the EC: UK Evidence on Corporate Integration Strategies. In *Dunning, J. and Robson, P., eds.*, 1988, pp. 91–104.

———— **and Young, Stephen.** Note on Exchange

Rate Fluctuations and the Foreign-Owned Sector in Scotland. *Scot. J. Polit. Econ.*, February 1988, *35*(1), pp. 77–83.

Hoogduin, L. H. On the Character of Macroeconomics, Macroeconomic Policy and Econometrics: The Need for Another Macroeconomic Policy Conception. *Banca Naz. Lavoro Quart. Rev.*, March 1988, (164), pp. 105–25.

———— **and Van Der Feltz, W. J.** Rational Formation of Expectations: Keynesian Uncertainty and Davidson's (Non)-Ergodicity-Criterium. *Metroecon.*, June 1988, *39*(2), pp. 105–19.

Hoogervorst, N. Y. P. Economic Systems and Resource Adjustment: Report. *Europ. Rev. Agr. Econ.*, 1988, *15*(2–3), pp. 223–24.

Hook, Sidney and Machan, Tibor R. A Dialogue on Marxism. *Int. J. Soc. Econ.*, 1988, *15*(11–12), pp. 105–30.

Hooke, Gus. Interest Rates, the Exchange Rate and Farmers. *Rev. Marketing Agr. Econ.*, April 1988, *56*(1), pp. 91–96.

Hooks, Donald L. and Zumpano, Leonard V. The Real Estate Brokerage Market: A Critical Reevaluation. *Amer. Real Estate Urban Econ. Assoc. J.*, Spring 1988, *16*(1), pp. 1–16.

Hooper, Peter; Bryant, Ralph C. and Holtham, Gerald. Consensus and Diversity in the Model Simulations. In *Bryant, R. C., et al., eds.*, 1988, pp. 27–62.

————; **Bryant, Ralph C. and Holtham, Gerald.** External Deficits and the Dollar: The Pit and the Pendulum: Introduction. In *Bryant, R. C.; Holtham, G. and Hooper, P., eds.*, 1988, pp. 1–9.

———— **and Helkie, William L.** An Empirical Analysis of the External Deficit, 1980–86. In *Bryant, R. C.; Holtham, G. and Hooper, P., eds.*, 1988, pp. 10–56.

Hoover, Kevin D. Money, Prices and Finance in the New Monetary Economics. *Oxford Econ. Pap.*, March 1988, *40*(1), pp. 150–67.

————. On the Pitfalls of Untested Common-Factor Restrictions: The Case of the Inverted Fisher Hypothesis. *Oxford Bull. Econ. Statist.*, May 1988, *50*(2), pp. 125–38.

Hope, Einar. Market Structure and Innovation. In *Grønhaug, K. and Kaufmann, G., eds.*, 1988, pp. 475–90.

Hope, Julie and Miller, Paul W. Financing Tertiary Education: An Examination of the Issues. *Australian Econ. Rev.*, Summer 1988, (84), pp. 37–57.

Hopenhayn, Benjamin. Prebisch: A Classic and Heterodox Thinker. *CEPAL Rev.*, April 1988, (34), pp. 165–77.

Hopkins, Jack W. The Eradication of Smallpox: Organizational Learning and Innovation in International Health Administration. *J. Devel. Areas*, April 1988, *22*(3), pp. 321–32.

Hopkins, Kevin R. Social Welfare Policy: A Failure of Vision. In *Boaz, D., ed.*, 1988, pp. 211–21.

Hopkins, Michael. Employment Forecasting and the Employment Problem: Conclusion. In *Hopkins, M. J. D., ed.*, 1988, pp. 210–47.

————. Employment Forecasting: The Employment Problem in Industrialised Countries: Introduction. In *Hopkins, M. J. D., ed.,* 1988, pp. 1–9.

Hopkins, Nicholas S. Co-operatives and the Noncooperative Sector in Tunisia and Egypt. In *Attwood, D. W. and Baviskar, B. S., eds.,* 1988, pp. 211–30.

Hopkins, Raymond F. Political Calculations in Subsidizing Food. In *Pinstrup-Andersen, P., ed.,* 1988, pp. 107–26.

Hopkins, Sandra. Official Australian Intervention in Foreign Exchange Markets, 1977 to 1986. *Econ. Letters,* 1988, *26*(1), pp. 73–75.

Hoppe, Hans-Hermann. From the Economics of Laissez Faire to the Ethics of Libertarianism. In *[Rothbard, M. N.],* 1988, pp. 56–76.

Hopper, David. Current Major Issues in India's Economic Policy. In *Lucas, R. E. B. and Papanek, G. F., eds.,* 1988, pp. 23–25.

Hoque, Asraul. Farm Size and Economic-Allocative Efficiency in Bangladesh Agriculture. *Appl. Econ.,* October 1988, *20*(10), pp. 1353–68.

———; **Magnus, Jan R. and Pesaran, Bahram.** The Exact Multi-period Mean-Square Forecast Error for the First-Order Autoregressive Model. *J. Econometrics,* November 1988, *39*(3), pp. 327–46.

Horbasz, Chris N.; Fox, Glenn and Brinkman, George L. A Comparison of *Ex Post* and *Ex Ante* Measures of Producers' Surplus in Estimating the Returns to Canadian Federal Sheep Research. *Can. J. Agr. Econ.,* November 1988, *36*(3), pp. 489–500.

Horgan, Constance M.; Taylor, Amy K. and Shrt, Pamela Farley. Medigap Insurance: Friend or Foe in Reducing Medicare Deficits? In *Frech, H. E., III, ed.,* 1988, pp. 145–77.

Horioka, Charles Yuji. Saving for Housing Purchase in Japan. *J. Japanese Int. Economies,* September 1988, *2*(3), pp. 351–84.

———. Tenure Choice and Housing Demand in Japan. *J. Urban Econ.,* November 1988, *24*(3), pp. 289–309.

Horiuchi, Akiyoshi; Packer, Frank and Fukuda, Shin-ichi. What Role Has the "Main Bank" Played in Japan? *J. Japanese Int. Economies,* June 1988, *2*(2), pp. 159–80.

Horiuchi, Shiro and Preston, Samuel H. Age-Specific Growth Rates: The Legacy of Past Population Dynamics. *Demography,* August 1988, *25*(3), pp. 429–41.

Horlacher, David E. and MacKellar, F. Landis. Population Growth versus Economic Growth (?). In *Salvatore, D., ed.,* 1988, pp. 25–44.

Horlick, Gary N.; Oliver, Geoffrey D. and Steger, Debra P. Dispute Resolution Mechanisms. In *Schott, J. J. and Smith, M. G., eds.,* 1988, pp. 65–86.

Horlick, Max. Earnings Replacement Rate of Old-Age Benefits: An International Comparison: Commentary. *Soc. Sec. Bull.,* August 1988, *51*(8), pp. 12, 48–49.

———. The Earnings Replacement Rate of Old-Age Benefits: An International Comparison.

Soc. Sec. Bull., August 1988, *51*(8), pp. 13–26.

Hormats, Robert D. Exchange Rate Volatility and Misalignment: Evaluating Some Proposals for Reform: Commentary. In *Federal Reserve Bank of Kansas City,* 1988, pp. 225–31.

———. Priorities and Prescriptions for the Next President. In *Aho, C. M. and Levinson, M.,* 1988, pp. 191–201.

Horn, Bobbie L. and Darity, William A., Jr. Involuntary Unemployment Independent of the Labor Market. *J. Post Keynesian Econ.,* Winter 1987–88, *10*(2), pp. 216–24.

Horn, Gustav Adolf. Die Bedeutung der Lohnentwicklung für eine kapitalintensivere Produktion. (Wages and Capital-Intensive Production. With English summary.) *Konjunkturpolitik,* 1988, *34*(3), pp. 150–61.

Horn, Henrik and Grossman, Gene M. Infant-Industry Protection Reconsidered: The Case of Informational Barriers to Entry. *Quart. J. Econ.,* November 1988, *103*(4), pp. 767–87.

——— **and Persson, Torsten.** Exchange Rate Policy, Wage Formation and Credibility. *Europ. Econ. Rev.,* October 1988, *32*(8), pp. 1621–36.

——— **and Wolinsky, Asher.** Bilateral Monopolies and Incentives for Merger. *Rand J. Econ.,* Autumn 1988, *19*(3), pp. 408–19.

——— **and Wolinsky, Asher.** Worker Substitutability and Patterns of Unionisation. *Econ. J.,* June 1988, *98*(391), pp. 484–97.

Horn, Manfred. Zur staatlichen Politik und Regulierung im Energiebereich. (General Considerations Regarding Energy Policy and Energy Regulation. With English summary.) *Konjunkturpolitik,* 1988, *34*(3), pp. 136–49.

Horn, Peter and Simes, Richard M. Design of the NIF88 Model. *Australian Econ. Pap.,* Supplement, June 1988, *27*, pp. 155–70.

Horn, Robert N. An Age-Adjusted Unemployment Rate. *Challenge,* July–August 1988, *31*(4), pp. 56–58.

——— **and Jerome, Robert T., Jr.** GOSGAME: A Simulation of the Planning Process in the Soviet Union. *Comp. Econ. Stud.,* Spring 1988, *30*(1), pp. 104–19.

Hornbaker, Robert H. and Mapp, Harry P. A Dynamic Analysis of Water Savings from Advanced Irrigation Technology. *Western J. Agr. Econ.,* December 1988, *13*(2), pp. 307–15.

Horne, Jocelyn and Masson, Paul R. Scope and Limits of International Economic Cooperation and Policy Coordination. *Int. Monet. Fund Staff Pap.,* June 1988, *35*(2), pp. 259–96.

Horner, Melchior R. The Value of the Corporate Voting Right: Evidence from Switzerland. *J. Banking Finance,* 1988, *12*(1), pp. 69–83.

Horner, Robert D. Superregional and National Strategies. In *Federal Home Loan Bank of San Francisco,* 1988, pp. 91–95.

Horney, Mary Jean and McElroy, Marjorie B. The Household Allocation Problem: Empirical Results from a Bargaining Model. In *Schultz, T. Paul, ed.,* 1988, pp. 15–38.

Hornik, Jacob. Cognitive Thoughts Mediating

Compliance in Multiple Request Situations. *J. Econ. Psych.*, March 1988, *9*(1), pp. 69–79.

_____. Diurnal Variation in Consumer Response. *J. Cons. Res.*, March 1988, *14*(4), pp. 588–91.

Hornung, Ulrich and Dikow, Edmund. A Random Boundary Value Problem Modeling Spatial Variability in Porous Media Flow. In *Wheeler, M. F., ed.*, 1988, pp. 111–17.

Horowitz, Harold. Challenges for Research on the Training of Arts Administrators. *J. Cult. Econ.*, December 1988, *12*(2), pp. 19–38.

Horowitz, Joel L. The Asymptotic Efficiency of Semiparametric Estimators for Censored Linear Regression Models. *Empirical Econ.*, 1988, *13*(3–4), pp. 122–40.

_____. Semiparametric M-Estimation of Censored Linear Regression Models. In *Rhodes, G. F., Jr. and Fomby, T. B., eds.*, 1988, pp. 45–83.

_____. What Should We Expect from Models of the Sale Process and Price Formation in Housing Markets. *Environ. Planning A*, June 1988, *20*(6), pp. 829–31.

Horowitz, Morris A. Arbitrator Behavior in Public Sector Wage Disputes: Comment. In *Freeman, R. B. and Ichniowski, C., eds.*, 1988, pp. 125–27.

Horridge, Mark. Tariffs in Australia: Theory, History and Effects. *Australian Econ. Rev.*, Winter 1988, (82), pp. 61–73.

_____; **Dixon, Peter B. and Paramenter, Brian R.** Forecasting versus Policy Analysis with the ORANI Model. In *Motamen, H., ed.*, 1988, pp. 653–66.

Horrigan, Brian R. Are Reserve Requirements Relevant for Economic Stabilization. *J. Monet. Econ.*, January 1988, *21*(1), pp. 97–105.

Horrigan, Michael W. and Haugen, Steven E. The Declining Middle-Class Thesis: A Sensitivity Analysis. *Mon. Lab. Rev.*, May 1988, *111*(5), pp. 3–13.

Horsky, Dan and Mate, Karl. Dynamic Advertising Strategies of Competing Durable Good Producers. *Marketing Sci.*, Fall 1988, *7*(4), pp. 356–67.

_____; **Narasimhan, Chakravarthi and Gaver, Kenneth M.** Invariant Estimators for Market Share Systems and Their Finite Sample Behavior. *Marketing Sci.*, Spring 1988, *7*(2), pp. 169–86.

Horst, R. Outer Cut Methods in Global Optimization. In *Kurzhanski, A.; Neumann, K. and Pallaschke, D., eds.*, 1988, pp. 28–40.

Horton, Raymond D. Fiscal Stress and Labor Power. In *Lewin, D., et al., eds.*, 1988, *1986*, pp. 473–94.

_____ **and Brecher, Charles.** Community Power and Municipal Budgets. In *Rubin, I. S., ed.*, 1988, pp. 148–64.

Horton, Susan. Birth Order and Child Nutritional Status: Evidence from the Philippines. *Econ. Develop. Cult. Change*, January 1988, *36*(2), pp. 341–54.

_____; **Kerr, Tom and Diakosavvas, Dimitris.** The Social Costs of Higher Food Prices: Some

Cross-country Evidence. *World Devel.*, July 1988, *16*(7), pp. 847–56.

Horvat, Branko. A Model of Many Capital Goods. *Econ. Anal. Workers' Manage.*, 1988, *22*(4), pp. 227–34.

_____. A Model with Many Consumer Goods and One Capital Good. *Econ. Anal. Workers' Manage.*, 1988, *22*(3), pp. 169–76.

_____. The Pure Labour Theory of Prices and Technological Change. *Econ. Anal. Workers' Manage.*, 1988, *22*(1–2), pp. 1–34.

Horvath, Janos. Soviet Economic Reforms are Destined to Fizzle. *Challenge*, March–April 1988, *31*(2), pp. 50–52.

Horváth, László. Marketing and Innovation Strategy in a Major Hungarian Enterprise—Taurus. In *Saunders, C. T., ed.*, 1988, pp. 279–93.

Horvath, Philip A. Disintermediation Revisited. *Financial Rev.*, August 1988, *23*(3), pp. 301–12.

_____. A Measurement of the Errors in Intraperiod Compounding and Bond Valuation: A Short Extension. *Financial Rev.*, August 1988, *23*(3), pp. 359–63.

Horverak, Øyvind. Marx's View of Competition and Price Determination. *Hist. Polit. Econ.*, Summer 1988, *20*(2), pp. 275–97.

Horvitz, Paul M. Commentary [Financial Stability and the Federal Safety Net] [Regulating Bank Safety and Performance]. In *Haraf, W. S. and Kushmeider, R. M., eds.*, 1988, pp. 100–103.

Horwich, George; Jenkins-Smith, Hank C. and Weimer, David Leo. The International Energy Agency's Mandatory Oil-Sharing Agreement: Tests of Efficiency, Equity, and Practicality. In *Horwich, G. and Weimer, D. L., eds.*, 1988, pp. 104–33.

_____ **and Miller, Bradley A.** Oil Import Quotas in the Context of the International Energy Agency Sharing Agreement. In *Horwich, G. and Weimer, D. L., eds.*, 1988, pp. 134–78.

_____ **and Weimer, David Leo.** The Economics of International Oil Sharing. *Energy J.*, October 1988, *9*(4), pp. 17–33.

_____ **and Weimer, David Leo.** International Oil Sharing and Policy Coordination: A Critical Summary. In *Horwich, G. and Weimer, D. L., eds.*, 1988, pp. 285–306.

Horwitch, Mel. The Emergence of Value-Creation Networks in Corporate Strategy. In *Uyehara, C. H., ed.*, 1988, pp. 188–217.

Horwitz, Bertrand and Normolle, Daniel. Federal Agency R&D Contract Awards and the FASB Rule for Privately-Funded R&D. *Accounting Rev.*, July 1988, *63*(3), pp. 414–35.

Hoshino, Yasuo. An Analysis of Mergers among the Credit Associations in Japan. *Rivista Int. Sci. Econ. Com.*, February 1988, *35*(2), pp. 135–56.

Hosier, Richard H. The Economics of Deforestation in Eastern Africa. *Econ. Geogr.*, April 1988, *64*(2), pp. 121–36.

_____ **and Dowd, Jeffrey.** Household Energy Use in Zimbabwe: An Analysis of Consumption

Patterns and Fuel Choice. In *Hosier, R. H.*, *ed. (I)*, 1988, pp. 83–109.

_____ and Mazambani, David. Zimbabwe's Informal Sector: Its Nature and Energy-Use Patterns. In *Hosier, R. H., ed. (II)*, 1988, pp. 74–98.

Hosios, Arthur J. Staggered Employment Contracts under Asymmetric Information. *Int. Econ. Rev.*, May 1988, *29*(2), pp. 271–95.

_____; Stiglitz, Joseph E. and Arnott, Richard J. Implicit Contracts, Labor Mobility, and Unemployment. *Amer. Econ. Rev.*, December 1988, *78*(5), pp. 1046–66.

Hosking, Geoffrey. The Soviet Union Today: The Politics of Literature. In *Cracraft, J., ed.*, 1988, pp. 272–83.

Hösli, Madeleine; Nydegger, Alfred and Hauser, Heinz. Die Schweiz vor dem EG-Bennenmarkt. (Switzerland and the Completion of the EC Internal Market. With English summary.) *Aussenwirtschaft*, September 1988, *43*(3), pp. 327–65.

Hosono, Akio. The Financial System and Development: The Formation of Financial Institutions for Labour-Intensive Sectors. In *Urrutia, M., ed.*, 1988, pp. 268–87.

Hossain, Kamal. Foreign Trade in the Present and a New International Economic Order: Introduction. In *Dicke, D. C. and Petersmann, E.-U., eds.*, 1988, pp. 11–17.

_____. South–South Co-operation: Strategies for the 1980s. In *Sopiee, N.; Hamzah, B. A. and Leong, C. H., eds.*, 1988, *1983*, pp. 101–15.

Hossain, M. M. and Morris, P. Australia's Import Demand for Printing and Writing Paper: A Short Run Estimate. *Australian Econ. Pap.*, June 1988, *27*(50), pp. 128–35.

Hossain, Mahabub and Chowdhury, Omar Haider. Tax Structure of Bangladesh: An Overview. *Bangladesh Devel. Stud.*, December 1988, *16*(4), pp. 65–91.

Hossain, Md. Akhtar. A Quarterly Short Run Money Demand Model for Bangladesh 1974:1–1985:4. *Bangladesh Devel. Stud.*, September 1988, *16*(3), pp. 1–30.

_____. Tax and Non-tax Revenue Elasticities in Bangladesh, 1974–1985. *Singapore Econ. Rev.*, October 1988, *33*(2), pp. 79–99.

_____. Theories of Inflation and Balance of Payments in Developing Countries: A Survey. *Indian Econ. J.*, July–September 1988, *36*(1), pp. 55–75.

Hossain, S. M. and Rahman, Atiur. Demand Constraints and the Future Viability of Grameen Bank Credit Programme—An Econometric Study of the Expenditure Pattern of Rural Households. *Bangladesh Devel. Stud.*, June 1988, *16*(2), pp. 1–20.

Hosseini, Hamid. Notions of Private Property in Islamic Economics in Contemporary Iran: A Review of Literature. *Int. J. Soc. Econ.*, 1988, *15*(9), pp. 51–61.

Hosseinzadeh, Esmail. Global Debt: Causes and Cures. *Rev. Radical Polit. Econ.*, Summer–Fall 1988, *20*(2–3), pp. 223–33.

Hotaka, Ryosuke. The Foundation of Data Mod-

els. In *Uno, K. and Shishido, S., eds.*, 1988, pp. 247–53.

Hotchkiss, Julie and Wright, Randall D. A General Model of Unemployment Insurance with and without Short-Term Compensation. In *Ehrenberg, R. G., ed.*, 1988, pp. 91–131.

Hotelling, Harold. Stability in Competition. In *Ricketts, M., ed., Vol. 1*, 1988, *1929*, pp. 114–30.

Hotes, F. L. Responses to Some of the Adverse External Effects of Grondwater Withdrawals in California: Comment. In *O'Mara, G. T., ed.*, 1988, pp. 57.

Hotz, V. Joseph; Kydland, Finn E. and Sedlacek, Guilherme L. Intertemporal Preferences and Labor Supply. *Econometrica*, March 1988, *56*(2), pp. 335–60.

_____ and Miller, Robert A. An Empirical Analysis of Life Cycle Fertility and Female Labor Supply. *Econometrica*, January 1988, *56*(1), pp. 91–118.

Hough, Jerry F. The Politics of the 19th Party Conference. *Soviet Econ.*, April–June 1988, *4*(2), pp. 137–43.

Houpt, James V. International Banking Trends for U.S. Banks and Banking Markets. *Fed. Res. Bull.*, May 1988, *74*(5), pp. 289–90.

House, Ernest R. and Madura, William. Race, Gender, and Jobs: Losing Ground on Employment. *Policy Sci.*, 1988, *21*(4), pp. 351–82.

House, Lewis L. and Ward, Michael D. A Theory of the Behavioral Power of Nations. *J. Conflict Resolution*, March 1988, *32*(1), pp. 3–36.

House, Robert J. Power and Personality in Complex Organizations. In *Staw, B. M. and Cummings, L. L., eds.*, 1988, pp. 305–57.

Houseman, Susan N. Shorter Working Time and Job Security: Labor Adjustment in the Steel Industry. In *Hart, R. A., ed.*, 1988, pp. 64–85.

Houston, Arthur L., Jr. A Comparison of the Reinvestment Risk of the Price Level Adjusted Mortgage and the Standard Fixed Payment Mortgage. *Amer. Real Estate Urban Econ. Assoc. J.*, Spring 1988, *16*(1), pp. 34–49.

Houthhakker, Hendrik S. Factors Shaping Long-Term Oil Markets. In *Fried, E. R. and Blandin, N. M., eds.*, 1988, pp. 29–34.

Houtman, R. and Bouman, F. J. A. Pawnbroking as an Instrument of Rural Banking in the Third World. *Econ. Develop. Cult. Change*, October 1988, *37*(1), pp. 69–89.

Houweling, Henk and Siccama, Jan G. Power Transitions as a Cause of War. *J. Conflict Resolution*, March 1988, *32*(1), pp. 87–102.

Hovenkamp, Herbert. Regulatory Conflict in the Gilded Age: Federalism and the Railroad Problem. *Yale Law J.*, May 1988, *97*(6), pp. 1017–72.

_____. Treble Damages Reform. *Antitrust Bull.*, Summer 1988, *33*(2), pp. 233–58.

Howard, Bill. Some Views on Management within Universities. *Australian Bull. Lab.*, March 1988, *14*(2), pp. 414–25.

Howard, C. Douglas and Kalotay, Andrew J. Embedded Call Options and Refunding Efficiency. In *Fabozzi, F. J., ed.*, 1988, pp. 97–117.

Howard, Daniel J. and Sawyer, Alan G. Recall, Recognition and the Dimensionality of Memory for Print Advertisements: An Interpretative Reappraisal. *Marketing Sci.*, Winter 1988, 7(1), pp. 94–98.

Howard, Michael C. The General Equilibrium Theory of Distribution. In *Asimakopulos, A., ed.*, 1988, pp. 181–97.

_____ **and King, J. E.** Henryk Grossmann and the Breakdown of Capitalism. *Sci. Soc.*, Fall 1988, 52(3), pp. 290–309.

Howard, Wayne H. and Shumway, C. Richard. Dynamic Adjustment in the U.S. Dairy Industry. *Amer. J. Agr. Econ.*, November 1988, 70(4), pp. 837–47.

Howe, Eric C. and Stabler, Jack C. Service Exports and Regional Growth in the Postindustrial Era. *J. Reg. Sci.*, August 1988, 28(3), pp. 303–15.

Howe, John S. and Shilling, James D. Capital Structure Theory and REIT Security Offerings. *J. Finance*, September 1988, 43(4), pp. 983–93.

Howe, Keith M. Valuation of the Growth Firm under Inflation and Differential Personal Taxes. *Quart. J. Bus. Econ.*, Autumn 1988, 27(4), pp. 20–31.

Howe, Wayne J. Education and Demographics: How Do They Affect Unemployment Rates? *Mon. Lab. Rev.*, January 1988, 111(1), pp. 3–9.

_____ **and Ulmer, Mark G.** Job Gains Strong in 1987; Unemployment Rate Declines. *Mon. Lab. Rev.*, February 1988, 111(2), pp. 57–67.

Howell, Craig; Clem, Andrew and Kuemmerling, Robert A. Domestic Price Rise during 1987 Reflects Swing of Energy Prices. *Mon. Lab. Rev.*, June 1988, 111(6), pp. 20–26.

Howell, James M. Alternatives for the Northeast: Choices and Costs. In *Lampe, D., ed.*, 1988, 1975, pp. 89–114.

_____ **and Frankel, Linda D.** Economic Revitalization and Job Creation in America's Oldest Industrial Region. In *Lampe, D., ed.*, 1988, pp. 295–313.

_____; **Frankel, Linda D. and Fulman, Diane.** The Massachusetts Experience. In *Lampe, D., ed.*, 1988, pp. 348–57.

_____ **and Fulman, Diane.** A Four-Point Program for the Northeast. In *Lampe, D., ed.*, 1988, pp. 138–54.

Howell, Jon P. and Dorfman, Peter W. Dimensions of National Culture and Effective Leadership Patterns: Hofstede Revisited. In *Farmer, R. N. and McGoun, E. G., eds.*, 1988, pp. 127–50.

Howells, Peter and Bain, Keith. The Teaching of Money. *Brit. Rev. Econ. Issues*, Spring 1988, 10(22), pp. 55–79.

Howenstine, Ned G. U.S. Affiliates of Foreign Companies: Operations in 1986. *Surv. Curr. Bus.*, May 1988, 68(5), pp. 59–75.

Howitt, Peter W. Business Cycles with Costly Search and Recruiting. *Quart. J. Econ.*, February 1988, 103(1), pp. 147–65.

_____. Money and the Timing of Transactions in Intermediated Exchange. In *Kohn, M. and Tsiang, S.-C., eds.*, 1988, pp. 54–70.

_____. Wage Flexibility and Employment. In *Hamouda, O. F. and Smithin, J. N., eds., Vol. 2*, 1988, pp. 61–69.

_____ **and Fried, Joel.** Fiscal Deficits, International Trade and Welfare. *J. Int. Econ.*, February 1988, 24(1–2), pp. 1–22.

_____ **and McAfee, R. Preston.** Stability of Equilibria with Externalities. *Quart. J. Econ.*, May 1988, 103(2), pp. 261–77.

Howlader, Ali Ahmed; Kabir, M. and Moslehuddin, M. Husband–Wife Communication and Status of Women as a Determinant of Contraceptive Use in Rural Bangladesh. *Bangladesh Devel. Stud.*, March 1988, 16(1), pp. 85–97.

Howland, Jonathan. Social Norms and Drunk Driving Countermeasures. In *Graham, J. D., ed.*, 1988, pp. 163–80.

Howland, Marie. Plant Closures and Local Economic Conditions. *Reg. Stud.*, June 1988, 22(3), pp. 193–207.

_____ **and Peterson, George E.** Labor Market Conditions and the Reemployment of Displaced Workers. *Ind. Lab. Relat. Rev.*, October 1988, 42(1), pp. 109–22.

_____ **and Peterson, George E.** The Response of City Economies to National Business Cycles. *J. Urban Econ.*, January 1988, 23(1), pp. 71–85.

Howsen, Roy M. and Thompsom, William F. The Impact of Changes in Research and Development and Productivity on Changes in Concentration. In *Missouri Valley Economic Assoc.*, 1988, pp. 12–17.

Howson, Susan K. Economists as Policy-Makers: Editing the Papers of James Meade, Lionel Robbins, and The Economic Advisory Council. In *Moggridge, D. E., ed.*, 1988, pp. 129–52.

_____. Monetary Policy and the Labour Government in the 1940s. In *Hamouda, O. F. and Smithin, J. N., eds., Vol. 1*, 1988, pp. 43–49.

_____. 'Socialist' Monetary Policy: Monetary Thought in the Labour Party in the 1940s. *Hist. Polit. Econ.*, Winter 1988, 20(4), pp. 543–64.

Hoy, Frank; Vaught, Bobby C. and Buchanan, W. Wary. Any Development Program Can Work. In *Timpe, A. D., ed.*, 1988, 1985, pp. 307–15.

Hoy, John C. Higher Skills and the New England Economy. In *Lampe, D., ed.*, 1988, 1986, pp. 331–47.

Hoy, Michael. Insurance Provision under a Solvency Requirement. *Econ. Letters*, 1988, 28(3), pp. 273–76.

_____. Risk Management and the Value of Symmetric Information in Insurance Markets. *Economica*, August 1988, 55(219), pp. 355–64.

Hoyer, Denise Tanguay and Hollingsworth, A. T. How Supervisors Can Shape Behavior. In *Timpe, A. D., ed.*, 1988, 1985, pp. 77–80.

Hrinda, Vasil and Větrovský, Jiří. Direct Relations: Clearing Operations in the National Currencies of Czechoslovakia and the Soviet Union. *Czech. Econ. Digest.*, June 1988, (4), pp. 13–20.

Hrnčíř, Miroslav. Criteria for Allocation of Resources in an Open Planned Economy. *Czech. Econ. Pap.*, 1988, (25), pp. 79–97.

Hrubovcak, James; LeBlanc, Michael R. and Conway, Roger K. Estimating the Structure of Agricultural Investment: A Stochastic-Coefficients Approach. *J. Bus. Econ. Statist.*, April 1988, *6*(2), pp. 231–40.

Hryniewicz, Olgierd. Estimation of Life-Time with Fuzzy Prior Information: Application in Reliability. In *Kacprzyk, J. and Fedrizzi, M., eds.*, 1988, pp. 307–21.

Hsieh, David A. The Statistical Properties of Daily Foreign Exchange Rates: 1974–1983. *J. Int. Econ.*, February 1988, *24*(1–2), pp. 129–45.

_____ **and Manas-Anton, Luis.** Empirical Regularities in the Deutsche Mark Futures Options. In *Fabozzi, F. J., ed.*, 1988, pp. 183–208.

Hsing, Yu and Brar, Jagjit S. Estimation of Flexible Elasticities of Demand for Seafood. In *Missouri Valley Economic Assoc.*, 1988, pp. 122–27.

Hsu, Andy; Talwar, Prem P. and Singh, Saraswati P. Tests of Multiple Causality among Monetary and Fiscal Aggregates and Stock Prices. *J. Quant. Econ.*, January 1988, *4*(1), pp. 89–106.

Hsu, Chen-Min. Quantity Expectations and Unemployment in Non-Walrasian Economics. *Int. Econ. J.*, Autumn 1988, *2*(3), pp. 61–77.

Hsu, George J. Y.; Leung, PingSun and Ching, Chauncey T. K. Energy Planning in Taiwan: An Alternative Approach Using a Multiobjective Programming and Input–Output Model. *Energy J.*, January 1988, *9*(1), pp. 53–72.

Hsu, Shih-Hsun and Stefanou, Spiro E. Temporal Risk Aversion in a Phased Deregulation Game. *J. Econ. Dynam. Control*, March 1988, *12*(1), pp. 181–87.

Hsu, Yu-sheng; Liu, Chwen-chi and Ulveling, Edwin F. Predictive Power of Weekly Money Stock Announcements. *Econ. Letters*, 1988, *26*(2), pp. 159–64.

Hsueh, L. Paul and Kidwell, David S. The Impact of a State Bond Guarantee on State Credit Markets and Individual Municipalities. *Nat. Tax J.*, June 1988, *41*(2), pp. 235–45.

Hu, Michael Y. and Bruning, Edward R. Profitability, Firm Size, Efficiency and Flexibility in the U.S. Domestic Airline Industry. *Int. J. Transport Econ.*, October 1988, *15*(3), pp. 313–27.

Hu, Sheng Cheng. Pensions in Labor Contracts. *Int. Econ. Rev.*, August 1988, *29*(3), pp. 477–92.

_____ **and Huang, Roger D.** On the Determinants of Individual Demand for Pension Annuities. *J. Econ. Bus.*, August 1988, *40*(3), pp. 253–63.

Hu, Teh-wei. Teaching About the American Economy in the People's Republic of China. *J. Econ. Educ.*, Winter 1988, *19*(1), pp. 87–96.

_____ **and Yang, Bong-Min.** The Demand for and Supply of Physician Services in the U.S.: A Disequilibrium Analysis. *Appl. Econ.*, August 1988, *20*(8), pp. 995–1006.

Hua, Chang-ming and Bianco, Lucien. Implementation and Resistance: The Single-Child Family Policy. In *Feuchtwang, S.; Hussain, A. and Pairault, T., eds., Vol. 1*, 1988, pp. 147–68.

Hua, Ying and Cao, Shuzhen. Over Three Hundred People Apply for Jobs with the Hilton Hotel. *Chinese Econ. Stud.*, Summer 1988, *21*(4), pp. 26–28.

Huang, Jichun. Policies for the Development of China's Nonferrous Metals Industry. In *Dorian, J. P. and Fridley, D. G., eds.*, 1988, pp. 117–23.

Huang, Kuo S. An Inverse Demand System for U.S. Composite Foods. *Amer. J. Agr. Econ.*, November 1988, *70*(4), pp. 902–09.

Huang, Roger D. and Hu, Sheng Cheng. On the Determinants of Individual Demand for Pension Annuities. *J. Econ. Bus.*, August 1988, *40*(3), pp. 253–63.

_____ **and Jo, Hoje.** Tests of Market Models: Heteroskedasticity or Misspecification? *J. Banking Finance*, September 1988, *12*(3), pp. 439–55.

Huang, Ronghan. Development of Groundwater for Agriculture in the Lower Yellow River Alluvial Basin. In *O'Mara, G. T., ed.*, 1988, pp. 80–84.

Huang, Wei-Chiao. An Empirical Analysis of Foreign Student Brain Drain to the United States. *Econ. Educ. Rev.*, 1988, *7*(2), pp. 231–43.

Hubbard, Michael. Drought Relief and Drought-Proofing in the State of Gujarat, India. In *Curtis, D.; Hubbard, M. and Shepherd, A.*, 1988, pp. 120–31.

_____ ; **Shepherd, Andrew and Curtis, Donald.** Famine and the National and International Economy. In *Curtis, D.; Hubbard, M. and Shepherd, A.*, 1988, pp. 11–27.

Hubbard, N. J. and Jeffrey, D. Foreign Tourism, the Hotel Industry and Regional Economic Performance. *Reg. Stud.*, August 1988, *22*(4), pp. 319–29.

Hubbard, Robert Glenn. Annuity Prices and Saving Behavior in the United States: Comment. In *Bodie, Z.; Shoven, J. B. and Wise, D. A., eds.*, 1988, pp. 78–84.

_____ **and Gertler, Mark.** Financial Factors in Business Fluctuations. In *Federal Reserve Bank of Kansas City*, 1988, pp. 33–71.

_____ **and Judd, Kenneth L.** Capital Market Imperfections and Tax Policy Analysis in the Life Cycle Model. *Ann. Écon. Statist.*, Jan.–March 1988, (9), pp. 111–39.

_____ ; **Petersen, Bruce C. and Domowitz, Ian.** Market Structure and Cyclical Fluctuations in U.S. Manufacturing. *Rev. Econ. Statist.*, February 1988, *70*(1), pp. 55–66.

_____ ; **Petersen, Bruce C. and Fazzari, Steven M.** Financing Constraints and Corporate Investment. *Brookings Pap. Econ. Act.*, 1988, (1), pp. 141–95.

_____; Petersen, Bruce C. and Fazzari, Steven M. Investment, Financing Decisions, and Tax Policy. *Amer. Econ. Rev.*, May 1988, 78(2), pp. 200–205.

Huber, Joel; Magat, Wesley A. and Viscusi, W. Kip. Consumer Processing of Hazard Warning Information. *J. Risk Uncertainty*, June 1988, 1(2), pp. 201–32.

_____; Magat, Wesley A. and Viscusi, W. Kip. Paired Comparison and Contingent Valuation Approaches to Morbidity Risk Valuation. *J. Environ. Econ. Manage.*, December 1988, 15(4), pp. 395–411.

_____; Payne, John and Simonson, Itamar. The Relationship between Prior Brand Knowledge and Information Acquisition Order. *J. Cons. Res.*, March 1988, 14(4), pp. 566–78.

Huber, Oswald. Mental Representation in Multistage Decision Making. In *Tietz, R.; Albers, W. and Selten, R., eds.*, 1988, pp. 66–81.

Huber, Peter. Environmental Hazards and Liability Law. In *Litan, R. E. and Winston, C., eds.*, 1988, pp. 128–54.

Huber, Vandra L.; Northcraft, Gregory B. and Neale, Margaret A. The Effects of Cognitive Bias and Social Influence on Human Resources Management Decisions. In *Ferris, G. R. and Rowland, K. M., eds.*, 1988, pp. 157–89.

Huberman, Gur. Optimality of Periodicity. *Rev. Econ. Stud.*, January 1988, 55(1), pp. 127–38.

_____ and Kahn, Charles M. Limited Contract Enforcement and Strategic Renegotiation. *Amer. Econ. Rev.*, June 1988, 78(3), pp. 471–84.

_____ and Kahn, Charles M. Strategic Renegotiation. *Econ. Letters*, 1988, 28(2), pp. 117–21.

_____ and Kahn, Charles M. Two-sided Uncertainty and "Up-or-Out" Contracts. *J. Lab. Econ.*, October 1988, 6(4), pp. 423–44.

Hubert, L.; Arabie, P. and De Soete, G. On the Use of Simulated Annealing for Combinatorial Data Analysis. In *Gaul, W. and Schader, M., eds.*, 1988, pp. 329–40.

Hübler, Olaf. Beschäftigungseffekte durch Gewinnbeteiligung? (Employment Effects by Profit Sharing? With English summary.) *Konjunkturpolitik*, 1988, 34(5–6), pp. 291–309.

_____. The Demand for Workers and Hours: Micro Evidence from the U.K. Metal Working Industry: Comment. In *Hart, R. A., ed.*, 1988, pp. 180–84.

Huckins, Larry E. and Carnevale, John T. Federal Grants-in-Aid: Theoretical Concerns, Design Issues, and Implementation Strategy. In *Bell, M. E., ed.*, 1988, pp. 41–62.

Huddleston, Barbara and von Braun, Joachim. Implications of Food Aid for Price Policy in Recipient Countries. In *Mellor, J. W. and Ahmed, R., eds.*, 1988, pp. 253–63.

Hudec, Robert E. Dispute Resolution Mechanisms: Comments. In *Schott, J. J. and Smith, M. G., eds.*, 1988, pp. 87–95.

_____. Dispute Settlement in Agricultural Trade Matters: The Lessons of the GATT Experience.

In *Allen, K. and Macmillan, K., eds.*, 1988, pp. 145–53.

_____. Legal Issues in US–EC Trade Policy: GATT Litigation 1960–1985. In *Baldwin, R. E.; Hamilton, C. B. and Sapir, A., eds.*, 1988, pp. 17–58.

Hudson, Carl D.; Slovin, Myron B. and Sushka, Marie E. Corporate Commercial Paper, Note Issuance Facilities, and Shareholder Wealth. *J. Int. Money Finance*, September 1988, 7(3), pp. 289–302.

Hudson, John. Government Popularity and the State of the Economy. *Manchester Sch. Econ. Soc. Stud.*, December 1988, 56(4), pp. 319–30.

Hudson, Laurel Anderson and Ozanne, Julie L. Alternative Ways of Seeking Knowledge in Consumer Research. *J. Cons. Res.*, March 1988, 14(4), pp. 508–21.

Hudson, Michael A. Keynes, Hayek and the Monetary Economy. In *Hillard, J., ed.*, 1988, pp. 172–84.

_____; Garcia, Philip and Zapata, Hector O. Identifying Causal Relationships between Nonstationary Stochastic Processes: An Examination of Alternative Approaches in Small Sample. *Western J. Agr. Econ.*, December 1988, 13(2), pp. 202–15.

_____; Waller, Mark L. and Garcia, Philip. The Pricing Efficiency of Agricultural Futures Markets: An Analysis of Previous Research Results. *Southern J. Agr. Econ.*, July 1988, 20(1), pp. 119–30.

Huertas, Thomas F. Can Banking and Commerce Mix? *Cato J.*, Winter 1988, 7(3), pp. 743–62.

_____. Can Banking and Commerce Mix? In *England, C. and Huertas, T., eds.*, 1988, pp. 289–307.

_____. Commentary [The Future Financial Structure: Fears and Policies] [Bank Holding Companies: Structure, Performance, and Reform]. In *Haraf, W. S. and Kushmeider, R. M., eds.*, 1988, pp. 211–15.

_____. Redesigning Financial Regulation. *Challenge*, Jan.–Feb. 1988, 31(1), pp. 37–43.

_____ and England, Catherine. The Financial Services Revolution: Introduction. In *England, C. and Huertas, T., eds.*, 1988, pp. 1–5.

Hufbauer, Gary C. and Schott, Jeffrey J. Improving U.S. Trade Performance: The Outlook to 1990. In *Yochelson, J., ed.*, 1988, pp. 225–37.

Huff, David L.; Lutz, James M. and Srivastava, Rajendra. A Geographical Analysis of the Innovativeness of States. *Econ. Geogr.*, April 1988, 64(2), pp. 137–46.

Huff, H. Bruce. A Canadian Perspective on Measuring Trade Effects of Domestic Agricultural Policies. In *Allen, K. and Macmillan, K., eds.*, 1988, pp. 101–10.

_____. The OECD Trade Mandate Study: Implications for Farm Policy. *Can. J. Agr. Econ.*, Part 1, December 1988, 36(4), pp. 643–48.

Huffman, Gregory W. and Greenwood, Jeremy. On Modelling the Natural Rate of Unemployment with Indivisible Labour. *Can. J. Econ.*, August 1988, 21(3), pp. 587–609.

_____; **Greenwood, Jeremy and Hercowitz, Zvi.** Investment, Capacity Utilization, and the Real Business Cycle. *Amer. Econ. Rev.*, June 1988, 78(3), pp. 402–17.

Huffman, Wallace E. Human Capital for Agriculture. In *Hildreth, R. J., et al., eds.*, 1988, pp. 499–517.

_____; **Miranowski, John A. and Tegene, Abebayehu.** Dynamic Corn Supply Functions: A Model with Explicit Optimization. *Amer. J. Agr. Econ.*, February 1988, 70(1), pp. 103–11.

Huffstutler, Clyde and Bingham, Barbara. Productivity Growth Slows in the Organic Chemicals Industry. *Mon. Lab. Rev.*, June 1988, 111(6), pp. 44–51.

Huggins, Nathan I. Herbert Gutman and Afro-American History. *Labor Hist.*, Summer 1988, 29(3), pp. 323–35.

Hughes, Dean W. and Penson, John B., Jr. Financial Conditions in the Farm Sector through 1990: An Update. In *Goldberg, R. A., ed., Vol. 8*, 1988, pp. 1–28.

_____, **et al.** Social Costs and Benefits of Subsidized Credit for the Farm Sector. In *Goldberg, R. A., ed., Vol. 8*, 1988, pp. 29–63.

Hughes, Gordon A. Rates Reform and the Housing Market. In *Bailey, S. J. and Paddison, R., eds.*, 1988, pp. 109–29.

Hughes Hallett, Andrew J. Commodities, Debt and North–South Cooperation: A Cautionary Tale from the Structuralist Camp. In *Currie, D. and Vines, D., eds.*, 1988, pp. 106–40.

_____. How Much Could the International Coordination of Economic Policies Achieve? An Example from US–EEC Policy-Making. In *Motamen, H., ed.*, 1988, pp. 71–101.

_____. Professor Chow's *Econometrics:* A Review. *J. Appl. Econometrics*, April 1988, 3(2), pp. 157–64.

_____ **and Fisher, P. G.** Efficient Solution Techniques for Linear and Non-linear Rational Expectations Models. *J. Econ. Dynam. Control*, November 1988, 12(4), pp. 635–57.

_____ **and Petit, Maria Luisa.** Trade-off Reversals in Macroeconomic Policy. *J. Econ. Dynam. Control*, March 1988, 12(1), pp. 85–91.

Hughes, Helen. Primary Commodity Markets: Recent Trends and Research Requirements: Comments. In *Elliott, K. A. and Williamson, J., eds.*, 1988, pp. 216–19.

_____. Too Little, Too Late: Australia's Future in the Pacific Economy. *Australian Econ. Pap.*, December 1988, 27(51), pp. 187–95.

Hughes, Jesse W. and Motekat, Janne. Tax Expenditures for Local Governments. *Public Budg. Finance*, Winter 1988, 8(4), pp. 68–73.

Hughes, Kirsty. Concentration and Diversification of R&D in a Conglomerate World. *Oxford Bull. Econ. Statist.*, August 1988, 50(3), pp. 243–61.

Hughes, Michael D. A Stochastic Frontier Cost Function for Residential Child Care Provision. *J. Appl. Econometrics*, July–Sept. 1988, 3(3), pp. 203–14.

Hughes, Patricia J. and Schwartz, Eduardo S. The LIFO/FIFO Choice: An Asymmetric Information Approach. *J. Acc. Res.*, Supplement, 1988, 26, pp. 41–58.

Hughes, Peter R. and Hutchinson, Gillian. Is Unemployment Irreversible? *Appl. Econ.*, January 1988, 20(1), pp. 31–42.

_____ **and Hutchinson, Gillian.** Unemployment, Irreversibility and the Long-term Unemployed. In *Cross, R., ed.*, 1988, pp. 93–114.

Huirne, R. B. M., et al. The Economic Optimisation of Sow Replacement Decisions by Stochastic Dynamic Programming. *J. Agr. Econ.*, September 1988, 39(3), pp. 426–38.

Hula, David G. Advertising, New Product Profit Expectations, and the Firm's R and D Investment Decisions. *Appl. Econ.*, January 1988, 20(1), pp. 125–42.

Hula, Richard C. Using Markets to Implement Public Policy. In *Hula, R. C., ed.*, 1988, pp. 3–18.

Hull, Frank, et al. Strategic Partnerships between Technological Entrepreneurs in the United States and Large Corporations in Japan and the United States. In *Contractor, F. J. and Lorange, P.*, 1988, pp. 445–56.

Hull, John and White, Alan. An Analysis of the Bias in Option Pricing Caused by a Stochastic Volatility. In *Fabozzi, F. J., ed.*, 1988, pp. 29–61.

_____ **and White, Alan.** The Use of the Control Variate Technique in Option Pricing. *J. Finan. Quant. Anal.*, September 1988, 23(3), pp. 237–51.

Hull, Terence H. and Dasvarma, Gouranga Lal. Fertility Trends in Indonesia 1967–1985. *Bull. Indonesian Econ. Stud.*, April 1988, 24(1), pp. 115–22.

Hulme, David and Cook, Paul. The Compatibility of Market Liberalization and Local Economic Development Strategies. *Reg. Stud.*, June 1988, 22(3), pp. 221–31.

Hulten, Charles R. and Klayman, Robert A. Investment Incentives in Theory and Practice. In *Aaron, H. J.; Galper, H. and Pechman, J. A., eds.*, 1988, pp. 317–38.

_____ **and Schwab, Robert M.** Income Originating in the State and Local Sector. In *Rosen, H. S., ed.*, 1988, pp. 215–48.

Hultman, Charles W. and McGee, L. Randolph. Factors Influencing Foreign Investment in the U.S., 1970–1986. *Rivista Int. Sci. Econ. Com.*, Oct.–Nov. 1988, 35(10–11), pp. 1061–66.

Humbert, Marc. De l'oligopole à la concurrence systémique. (From Oligopoly to Systemic Competition. With English summary.) *Écon. Soc.*, Nov.–Dec. 1988, 22(11–12), pp. 241–60.

Humby, Clive. Store Choice, Store Location and Market Analysis: Some Final Observations on Future Research Priorities. In *Wrigley, N., ed.*, 1988, pp. 323–27.

Humphrey, Arthur. Biotechnology. In *Uyehara, C. H., ed.*, 1988, pp. 162–77.

Humphrey, Craig R.; Erickson, Rodney A. and Ottensmeyer, Edward J. Industrial Development Groups, Organizational Resources, and the Prospects for Effecting Growth in Local

Economies. *Growth Change*, Summer 1988, *19*(3), pp. 1–21.

Humphrey, David B. and Berger, Allen N. Interstate Banking and the Payments System. *J. Finan. Services Res.*, January 1988, *1*(2), pp. 131–45.

Humphrey, John. Industrialization in Brazil: The Miracle and its Aftermath. In *Crow, B. and Thorpe, M., et al.*, 1988, pp. 216–41.

Humphrey, Thomas M. Rival Notions of Money. *Fed. Res. Bank Richmond Econ. Rev.*, Sept.–Oct. 1988, *74*(5), pp. 3–9.

———. The Trade Theorist's Sacred Diagram: Its Origin and Early Development. *Fed. Res. Bank Richmond Econ. Rev.*, Jan.–Feb. 1988, *74*(1), pp. 3–15.

Humphries, Jane. Women's Employment in Restructuring America: The Changing Experience of Women in Three Recessions. In *Rubery, J., ed.*, 1988, pp. 15–47.

——— **and Rubery, Jill.** Recession and Exploitation: British Women in a Changing Workplace, 1979–85. In *Jenson, J.; Hagen, E. and Reddy, C., eds.*, 1988, pp. 85–105.

Hundley, Greg. Education and Union Membership. *Brit. J. Ind. Relat.*, July 1988, *26*(2), pp. 195–201.

———. Taxation and Strikes: The Post-War Experience in Three Countries. *Brit. J. Ind. Relat.*, March 1988, *26*(1), pp. 57–61.

———. Who Joins Unions in the Public Sector? The Effects of Individual Characteristics and the Law. *J. Lab. Res.*, Fall 1988, *9*(4), pp. 301–23.

Hung, N. M. and Schmitt, Nicolas. Quality Competition and Threat of Entry in Duopoly. *Econ. Letters*, 1988, *27*(3), pp. 287–92.

Hunkin, Faleomavaega Eni F., Jr. Some Observations on the Present and Future Potentials of Economic Development in the Pacific Region. In *Kozmetsky, G.; Matsumoto, H. and Smilor, R. W., eds.*, 1988, pp. 49–56.

Hunt, Audrey. The Effects of Caring for the Elderly and Infirm on Women's Employment. In *Hunt, A., ed.*, 1988, pp. 150–72.

———. Women and Paid Work: Issues of Equality. An Overview. In *Hunt, A., ed.*, 1988, pp. 1–22.

Hunt, H. Allan; Krueger, Alan B. and Burton, John F., Jr. The Impact of Open Competition in Michigan on the Employers' Costs of Workers' Compensation. In *Borba, P. S. and Appel, D., eds.*, 1988, pp. 109–44.

Hunt, H. Keith. Consumer Satisfaction/Dissatisfaction and the Consumer Interest. In *Maynes, E. S. and ACCI Research Committee, eds.*, 1988, pp. 731–47.

Hunt, Kim S. Obstacles to Doing More with Less: Illustrations from the Kansas Experience. In *Kelly, R. M., ed.*, 1988, pp. 127–39.

Hunt, Shelby D. and Goolsby, Jerry. The Rise and Fall of the Functional Approach to Marketing: A Paradigm Displacement Perspective. In *[Hollander, S. C.]*, 1988, pp. 35–51.

Hunt, Simon. World Supply–Demand Pattern for

Metals in the 1990s. In *Richardson, P. R. and Gesing, R., eds.*, 1988, pp. 49–66.

Hunter, Laurie. Unemployment and Industrial Relations. *Brit. J. Ind. Relat.*, July 1988, *26*(2), pp. 202–28.

Hunter, Linda C. and Markusen, James R. Per-Capita Income as a Determinant of Trade. In *Feenstra, R. C., ed.*, 1988, pp. 89–109.

Hunter, William Curt and Walker, Mary Beth. Assessing the Fairness of Investment Bankers' Fees. *Fed. Res. Bank Atlanta Econ. Rev.*, March–April 1988, *73*(2), pp. 2–7.

Hunter, William J. and Rankin, Carol H. The Composition of Public Sector Compensation: The Effects of Unionization and Bureaucratic Size. *J. Lab. Res.*, Winter 1988, *9*(1), pp. 29–42.

Huntington, Samuel P. The U.S.—Decline or Renewal? *Foreign Aff.*, Winter 1988–89, *67*(2), pp. 76–96.

Huppes, Gjalt. New Instruments for Environmental Policy: A Perspective. *Int. J. Soc. Econ.*, 1988, *15*(3–4), pp. 42–50.

Huq, M. M. Indigenous Technological Capability in Developing Countries: A Preliminary Approach to Identification. *Pakistan Devel. Rev.*, Part 2, Winter 1988, *27*(4), pp. 517–25.

Huq, Md. Shamsul and Fosu, Augustin Kwasi. Price Inflation and Wage Inflation: A Cause–Effect Relationship? *Econ. Letters*, 1988, *27*(1), pp. 35–40.

Hurd, Michael D. Forecasting the Consumption and Wealth of the Elderly. In *Wachter, S. M., ed.*, 1988, pp. 47–69.

———. Pensions and Turnover: Comment. In *Bodie, Z.; Shoven, J. B. and Wise, D. A., eds.*, 1988, pp. 188–90.

Hurd, Richard W. and Kriesky, Jill K. Communications: 'The Rise and Demise of PATCO' Reconstructed. In *Lewin, D., et al., eds.*, 1988, 1986, pp. 267–78.

——— **and McElwain, Adrienne.** Organizing Clerical Workers: Determinants of Success. *Ind. Lab. Relat. Rev.*, April 1988, *41*(3), pp. 360–73.

Hurley, Robert E. and Freund, Deborah A. Determinants of Provider Selection or Assignment in a Mandatory Case Management Program and Their Implications for Utilization. *Inquiry*, Fall 1988, *25*(3), pp. 402–10.

Hurwicz, Leonid and Majumdar, Mukul. Optimal Intertemporal Allocation Mechanisms and Decentralization of Decisions. *J. Econ. Theory*, August 1988, *45*(2), pp. 228–61.

Hurwitz, Jon. Determinants of Legislative Cue Selection. *Soc. Sci. Quart.*, March 1988, *69*(1), pp. 212–23.

Hurwitz, Mark A. and Caves, Richard E. Persuasion or Information? Promotion and the Shares of Brand Name and Generic Pharmaceuticals. *J. Law Econ.*, October 1988, *31*(2), pp. 299–320.

Husain, Aasim Mairaj. Forgiveness, Buybacks, and Exit Bonds: An Analysis of Alternate Debt Relief Strategies. *Pakistan Devel. Rev.*, Part 2, Winter 1988, *27*(4), pp. 819–28.

Husain, Fazal; Zahid, G. M. and Sarmad, Khwaja. Investment and Inequality in Pakistan's Education Sector. *Pakistan Devel. Rev.*, Part 2, Winter 1988, 27(4), pp. 677–84.

Huschens, Stefan and Becker, Otwin. Bounded Rational Strategies in Sequential Bargaining: An Experiment and a Learning by Evolution Strategy. In *Tietz, R.; Albers, W. and Selten, R., eds.*, 1988, pp. 129–41.

Hush, Lawrence W. and Peroff, Kathleen. The Variety of State Capital Budgets: A Survey. *Public Budg. Finance*, Summer 1988, 8(2), pp. 67–79.

Hushak, Leroy J.; Miller, Gay Y. and Rosenblatt, Joseph M. The Effects of Supply Shifts on Producers' Surplus. *Amer. J. Agr. Econ.*, November 1988, 70(4), pp. 886–91.

_____; Oo, Tin Htut and Hitzhusen, Fred. Factors Related to Errors in Ex-ante Evaluation of Agricultural Projects in Developing Countries. *J. Devel. Areas*, January 1988, 22(2), pp. 199–206.

Huskey, Lee; Hill, P. J. and Jackstadt, Steve. The Making of an Economist: Comment. *J. Econ. Perspectives*, Fall 1988, 2(4), pp. 209–12.

_____ and Knapp, Gunnar. Effects of Transfers on Remote Regional Economies: The Transfer Economy in Rural Alaska. *Growth Change*, Spring 1988, 19(2), pp. 25–39.

Huss, William R. A Move toward Scenario Analysis. *Int. J. Forecasting*, 1988, 4(3), pp. 377–88.

Hussain, Athar and Feuchtwang, Stephan. The People's Livelihood and the Incidence of Poverty. In *Feuchtwang, S.; Hussain, A. and Pairault, T., eds., Vol. 1*, 1988, pp. 36–76.

_____; Pairault, Thierry and Feuchtwang, Stephan. Transforming China's Economy in the Eighties. In *Feuchtwang, S.; Hussain, A. and Pairault, T., eds., Vol. 1*, 1988, pp. 1–6.

_____; Pairault, Thierry and Feuchtwang, Stephan. Transforming China's Economy in the Eighties, Volume II: Management, Industry and the Urban Economy: Preface. In *Feuchtwang, S.; Hussain, A. and Pairault, T., eds., Vol. 2*, 1988, pp. 1–6.

Husson, Bruno. Les prises de contrôle sur le marché français enrichissent-elles les actionnaires? (Shareholders Wealth and Takeovers on the French Market. With English summary.) *Finance*, December 1988, 9(2), pp. 35–56.

Husted, Steven L. The Ongoing Revolution in American Banking: Commentary. In *Cassing, J. H. and Husted, S. L., eds.*, 1988, pp. 91–93.

_____ and Cassing, James H. Capital, Technology, and Labor in the New Global Economy: Introduction. In *Cassing, J. H. and Husted, S. L., eds.*, 1988, pp. xvii–xxvii.

Hustedde, Ronald J. and Pulver, Glen C. Regional Variables That Influence the Allocation of Venture Capital: The Role of Banks. *Rev. Reg. Stud.*, Spring 1988, 18(2), pp. 1–9.

Huston, John H. and Butler, Richard V. The Ef-

fects of Fortress Hubs on Airline Fares and Service: The Early Returns. *Logist. Transp. Rev.*, September 1988, 24(3), pp. 203–15.

_____; Spencer, Roger W. and Sciortino, John J. Risk and Income Distribution. *J. Econ. Psych.*, September 1988, 9(3), pp. 399–408.

Hutchens, Robert M. Changes in the Legal Mandatory Retirement Age: Labor Force Participation Implications: Discussion. In *Ricardo-Campbell, R. and Lazear, E. P., eds.*, 1988, pp. 406–12.

_____. Do Job Opportunities Decline with Age? *Ind. Lab. Relat. Rev.*, October 1988, 42(1), pp. 89–99.

_____ and Lampman, Robert J. The Future of Workers' Compensation. In *Burton, J. F., Jr., ed.*, 1988, pp. 113–40.

Hutcheson, Thomas L.; Stern, Joseph J. and Mallon, Richard D. Foreign Exchange Regimes and Industrial Growth in Bangladesh. *World Devel.*, December 1988, 16(12), pp. 1419–39.

Hutchins, Teresa D.; Davis, Lance E. and Gallman, Robert E. The Decline of U.S. Whaling: Was the Stock of Whales Running Out? *Bus. Hist. Rev.*, Winter 1988, 62(4), pp. 569–95.

Hutchinson, Dianne and Nicholas, Stephen. Theory and Business History: New Approaches to Institutional Change. *J. Europ. Econ. Hist.*, Fall 1988, 17(2), pp. 411–25.

Hutchinson, Frederick and Greenstein, Robert. State Tax Relief for Low-Income People. In *Gold, S. D., ed.*, 1988, pp. 153–76.

Hutchinson, Gillian and Hughes, Peter R. Is Unemployment Irreversible? *Appl. Econ.*, January 1988, 20(1), pp. 31–42.

_____ and Hughes, Peter R. Unemployment, Irreversibility and the Long-term Unemployed. In *Cross, R., ed.*, 1988, pp. 93–114.

Hutchinson, Harold and Cross, Rod. Hysteresis Effects and Unemployment: An Outline. In *Cross, R., ed.*, 1988, pp. 3–7.

Hutchinson, R. W. and McKillop, D. G. Risk Analysis with Single-Index Portfolio Models: An Application to Farm Planning: Comment. *Amer. J. Agr. Econ.*, February 1988, 70(1), pp. 192–94.

Hutchinson, William K. and Knelman, Suzanne Ward. Bond Rates and Causality. *J. Macroecon.*, Summer 1988, 10(3), pp. 459–67.

Hutchison, Michael M. Monetary Control with an Exchange Rate Objective: The Bank of Japan, 1973–86. *J. Int. Money Finance*, September 1988, 7(3), pp. 261–71.

_____ and Cargill, Thomas F. The Response of the Bank of Japan to Macroeconomic and Financial Change. In *Cheng, H.-S., ed.*, 1988, pp. 227–46.

Hutchison, Terence W. Austrian Economics: Roots and Ramifications Reconsidered: Introduction. *J. Econ. Stud.*, 1988, 15(3–4), pp. 7–12.

_____. The Case for Falsification. In *de Marchi, N., ed.*, 1988, pp. 169–81.

_____. Gustav Schmoller and the Problems of Today. *J. Inst. Theoretical Econ.*, June 1988, 144(3), pp. 527–31.

_____. The Politics and Philosophy in Jevons's Political Economy. In *Wood, J. C., ed., Vol. 1, 1988, 1982*, pp. 383–95.

Hüther, Michael. Die "Sattelzeitgerechte" Entrstehung der Nationalökonomie. Eine Beitrag zur Dogmengeschichte. (The "Sattelzeitgerechte" Development of Economics. A Contribution to the History of Dogmas. With English summary.) *Jahr. Nationalökon. Statist.*, August 1988, *205*(2), pp. 150–62.

Huttenrauch, Roland. Environmental Considerations and the Assessment of Quality. In *Maynes, E. S. and ACCI Research Committee, eds.*, 1988, pp. 173–76.

Huttman, Elizabeth. Homelessness as a Housing Problem in an Inner City in the U.S. In *Friedrichs, J., ed.*, 1988, pp. 157–74.

Huttman, John. The Automobile in the 1920s: The Critical Decade. In *Perkins, E. J., ed.*, 1988, pp. 200–210.

Hutton, Patricia A. and Holmes, James M. A Functional-Form, Distribution-Free Alternative to Parametric Analysis of Granger Causal Models. In *Rhodes, G. F., Jr. and Fomby, T. B., eds.*, 1988, pp. 211–25.

Hwa, Erh-Cheng. The Contribution of Agriculture to Economic Growth: Some Empirical Evidence. *World Devel.*, November 1988, *16*(11), pp. 1329–39.

Hwang, Hong and Mai, Chao-cheng. Advertising and Industrial Location. *Int. J. Ind. Organ.*, June 1988, *6*(2), pp. 223–31.

_____ **and Mai, Chao-cheng.** On the Equivalence of Tariffs and Quotas under Duopoly: A Conjectural Variation Approach. *J. Int. Econ.*, May 1988, *24*(3–4), pp. 373–80.

_____ **and Mai, Chao-cheng.** Optimal Export Subsidies and Marginal Cost Differentials. *Econ. Letters*, 1988, *27*(3), pp. 279–82.

_____ **and Mai, Chao-cheng.** Why Voluntary Export Restraints Are Voluntary: An Extension. *Can. J. Econ.*, November 1988, *21*(4), pp. 877–82.

Hwang, Sean-Shong and Murdock, Steve H. Population Size and Residential Segregation: An Empirical Evaluation of Two Perspectives. *Soc. Sci. Quart.*, December 1988, *69*(4), pp. 818–34.

Hyclak, Thomas. Canada in the 1980s: An Overview of the Issues. In *Thornton, R. J.; Hyclak, T. and Aronson, J. R., eds.*, 1988, pp. xv–xxii.

_____. Real Wages and Unemployment in Local Labor Markets: Pennsylvania MSAs, 1975–86. *Growth Change*, Summer 1988, *19*(3), pp. 45–52.

Hyden, Goran. Approaches to Co-operative Development: Blueprint versus Greenhouse. In *Attwood, D. W. and Baviskar, B. S., eds.*, 1988, pp. 149–71.

Hynes, M. and Jackson, Randall W. Demographics in Demographic–Economic Models: A Note on the Basic Activity–Commodity Framework. *Environ. Planning A*, November 1988, *20*(11), pp. 1531–36.

_____ **and Jackson, Randall W.** Demographics in Demographic–Economic Models: A Reply.

Environ. Planning A, November 1988, *20*(11), pp. 1543–45.

Iacono, Salvatore; Bodnar, Judith and Dilworth, Peter. Cross-sectional Analysis of Residential Telephone Subscription in Canada. *Info. Econ. Policy*, 1988, *3*(4), pp. 359–78.

Iams, Howard M. and Ycas, Martynas A. Women, Marriage, and Social Security Benefits. *Soc. Sec. Bull.*, May 1988, *51*(5), pp. 3–9.

Ianchilovici, Beatriz and Goldberg, Samuel. El stock de capital en la Argentina. (With English summary.) *Desarrollo Econ.*, July–Sept. 1988, *28*(110), pp. 281–304.

Iannaccone, Laurence R. A Formal Model of Church and Sect. In *Winship, C. and Rosen, S., eds.*, 1988, pp. 241–68.

Ibarra, David. Comments on the Mexican Financial System. In *Urrutia, M., ed.*, 1988, pp. 110–21.

_____. Crisis and the External Sector in Latin America. In *Feinberg, R. E. and Ffrench-Davis, R., eds.*, 1988, pp. 117–46.

Ibbs, C. William and Echeverry, Diego. New Construction Technologies for Rebuilding the Nation's Infrastructure. In *Ausubel, J. H. and Herman, R., eds.*, 1988, pp. 294–311.

Ibrahim, A. and Schektman, Y. Evolving Principal Clusters: Theory and Application to Management Monitoring. In *Gaul, W. and Schader, M., eds.*, 1988, pp. 291–98.

Ibrahim, Ibrahim B. The Impact of the Oil Price Decline on Arab Economic Relationships. In *Mabro, R., ed.*, 1988, pp. 237–58.

Ichiishi, Tatsuro. Core-Like Solutions for Games with Probabilistic Choice of Strategies. *Math. Soc. Sci.*, February 1988, *15*(1), pp. 51–60.

Ichikawa, Akira. Stability and Control of Linear Periodic Systems. In *Iri, M. and Yajima, K., eds.*, 1988, pp. 70–79.

Ichikawa, Kaoru. Estimated Optimal Lags for the Optimization of Models: A Method for Estimating the Optimal Lag between Economic Variables: In *Motamen, H., ed.*, 1988, pp. 313–26.

Ichioka, Osamu. The Value-Added Tax in Japan: A Numerical General Equilibrium Evaluation. *J. Japanese Int. Economies*, March 1988, *2*(1), pp. 11–41.

Ichniowski, Casey. Police Recognition Strikes: Illegal and Ill-Fated. *J. Lab. Res.*, Spring 1988, *9*(2), pp. 183–97.

_____. Public Sector Union Growth and Bargaining Laws: A Proportional Hazards Approach with Time-Varying Treatments. In *Freeman, R. B. and Ichniowski, C., eds.*, 1988, pp. 19–38.

_____ **and Freeman, Richard B.** The Public Sector Look of American Unionism: Introduction. In *Freeman, R. B. and Ichniowski, C., eds.*, 1988, pp. 1–15.

_____ **and Zax, Jeffrey S.** The Effects of Public Sector Unionism on Pay, Employment, Department Budgets, and Municipal Expenditures. In *Freeman, R. B. and Ichniowski, C., eds.*, 1988, pp. 323–61.

_____; **Zax, Jeffrey S. and Freeman, Richard**

B. Collective Organization of Labor in the Public Sector: Appendix A. In *Freeman, R. B. and Ichniowski, C., eds.*, 1988, pp. 365–98.

Ide, Toyonari and Takayama, Akira. Marshallian Stability, Long-run Equilibrium and the Pattern of Specialization under Factor-Market Distortions in the Pure Theory of International Trade. *Econ. Letters*, 1988, 27(3), pp. 265–70.

_____ **and Takayama, Akira.** Scale Economies, Perverse Comparative Statics Results, the Marshallian Stability and the Long-run Equilibrium for a Small Open Economy. *Econ. Letters*, 1988, 27(3), pp. 257–63.

Ietto-Gillies, Grazia. Internationalization of Production: An Analysis Based on Labour. *Brit. Rev. Econ. Issues*, Autumn 1988, 10(23), pp. 19–47.

Ievoli, Corrado. L'integrazione monetaria europea: alcune note in merito ad un recente contributo. (With English summary.) *Stud. Econ.*, 1988, 43(35), pp. 147–62.

_____. La crisi dell'economia italiana: incubo del passato o realta' attuale? Alcune considerazioni su un recente volume curato dall'ente Einaudi. (With English summary.) *Stud. Econ.*, 1988, 43(34), pp. 139–66.

Iffland, Charles. International Banking at the Crossroads of World Economic Relations. In *Mikdashi, Z., ed.*, 1988, pp. 1–5.

Ifflander, A. James; Smith, David B. and Hefzi, Hassan. Municipal Bond Market Risk Measures and Bond Ratings. In *Schwartz, B. N., ed.*, 1988, pp. 111–27.

Iglesias García, Fe. Changes in Cane Cultivation in Cuba, 1860–1900. *Soc. Econ. Stud.*, March–June 1988, 37(1–2), pp. 341–63.

Ignatiev, Alex and Chu, C. W. Epitaxial Thin Film Growth in Outer Space. In *Egan, J. J., et al.*, 1988, pp. 283–97.

Ihde, Gösta B. Die relative Betriebstiefe als strategischer Erfolgsfaktor. (With English summary.) *Z. Betriebswirtshaft*, January 1988, 58(1), pp. 13–23.

Ihlanfeldt, Keith R. Intra-metropolitan Variation in Earnings and Labor Market Distribution: An Econometric Analysis of the Atlanta Labor Market. *Southern Econ. J.*, July 1988, 55(1), pp. 123–40.

Ihonvbere, Julius O. and Shaw, Timothy M. Petroleum Proletariat: Nigerian Oil Workers in Contextual and Comparative Perspective. In *Southall, R., ed.*, 1988, pp. 80–108.

Ihori, Toshihiro. Debt and Burden and Intergeneration Equity. In *Arrow, K. J. and Boskin, M. J., eds.*, 1988, pp. 149–91.

_____. Optimal Deficits in a Growing Economy. *J. Japanese Int. Economies*, December 1988, 2(4), pp. 525–42.

Iida, Keisuke. Third World Solidarity: The Group of 77 in the UN General Assembly. *Int. Organ.*, Spring 1988, 42(2), pp. 375–95.

Ikeda, Syunsuke; Parker, Gary and Kimura, Yoshitaka. Stable Width and Depth of Straight Gravel Rivers with Heterogeneous Bed Materials. *Water Resources Res.*, May 1988, 24(5), pp. 713–22.

Ikeda, Takanobu. On Quantity-Constrained Perception Equilibria: The Pure-Exchange Economy Case. *Keio Econ. Stud.*, 1988, 25(2), pp. 19–40.

Ikenberry, G. John. An Institutional Approach to American Foreign Economic Policy: Conclusion. In *Ikenberry, G. J.; Lake, D. A. and Mastanduno, M., eds.*, 1988, pp. 219–43.

_____. Conclusion: An Institutional Approach to American Foreign Economic Policy. *Int. Organ.*, Winter 1988, 42(1), pp. 219–43.

_____. Market Solutions for State Problems: The International and Domestic Politics of American Oil Decontrol. *Int. Organ.*, Winter 1988, 42(1), pp. 151–77.

_____. Market Solutions for State Problems: The International and Domestic Politics of American Oil Decontrol. In *Ikenberry, G. J.; Lake, D. A. and Mastanduno, M., eds.*, 1988, pp. 151–77.

_____; **Lake, David A. and Mastanduno, Michael.** Approaches to Explaining American Foreign Economic Policy: Introduction. In *Ikenberry, G. J.; Lake, D. A. and Mastanduno, M., eds.*, 1988, pp. 1–14.

_____; **Lake, David A. and Mastanduno, Michael.** Introduction: Approaches to Explaining American Foreign Economic Policy. *Int. Organ.*, Winter 1988, 42(1), pp. 1–14.

Ikerd, John E. Agricultural and Rural Areas Approaching the Twenty-first Century: A Synthesis of Extension Issues. In *Hildreth, R. J., et al., eds.*, 1988, pp. 537–44.

Ikiara, Gerrishon K. The Role of Government Institutions in Kenya's Industrialization. In *Coughlin, P. and Ikiara, G. K., eds.*, 1988, pp. 218–50.

_____ **and Coughlin, Peter.** Industrialization in Kenya: In Search of a Strategy: Introduction. In *Coughlin, P. and Ikiara, G. K., eds.*, 1988, pp. 1–5.

Ikpi, Anthony E. and Durojaiye, Bamidele O. The Monetary Value of Recreational Facilities in a Developing Economy: A Case Study of Three Centers in Nigeria. *Natural Res. J.*, Spring 1988, 28(2), pp. 315–28.

Ilardi, Barbara C. and McMahon, Anne M. Organizational Legitimacy and Performance Evaluation. In *Lawler, E. J. and Markovsky, B., eds.*, 1988, pp. 217–44.

Im, Bae-Geun; Kaserman, David L. and Melese, Francois. Rent Seeking and the Allowed Rate of Return: A Recursive Model. *Rev. Ind. Organ.*, Fall 1988, 3(4), pp. 27–51.

Im, Eric Iksoon and Cauley, Jon. Intervention Policy Analysis of Skyjackings and Other Terrorist Incidents. *Amer. Econ. Rev.*, May 1988, 78(2), pp. 27–31.

Imai, Ken'ichi and Itami, Hiroyuki. Allocations of Labor and Capital in Japan and the United States. In *Okimoto, D. I. and Rohlen, T. P., eds.*, 1988, pp. 112–18.

Imai, Mitsuaki. Why Consumer Education in Japan? In *Maynes, E. S. and ACCI Research Committee, eds.*, 1988, pp. 495–98.

Imai, Ryukichi. Nuclear Power after Chernobyl. In *Mabro, R., ed.,* 1988, pp. 177–88.

Imbriani, Cesare and Roberti, Paolo. Tax Harmonies and Disharmonies: Harmonization by Itself Is Not Enough. *Rev. Econ. Cond. Italy,* Sept.–Dec. 1988, (3), pp. 371–97.

Imhoff, Eugene A., Jr. and Thomas, Jacob K. Economic Consequences of Accounting Standards: The Lease Disclosure Rule Change. *J. Acc. Econ.,* December 1988, *10*(4), pp. 277–310.

van Imhoff, Evert and Ritzen, Jozef M. M. Optimal Economic Growth and Non-stable Population. *De Economist,* 1988, *136*(3), pp. 339–57.

Imhoff, Gary and Bikales, Gerda. A Kind of Discordant Harmony: Issues in Assimilation. In *Simcox, D. E., ed.,* 1988, *1985,* pp. 137–50.

Imowitz, Robert. Market Research in the Consumer Interest: The Views of a Practicing Market Researcher. In *Maynes, E. S. and ACCI Research Committee, eds.,* 1988, pp. 647–52.

Inagami, Takeshi. Changing Japanese-Style Employment Practices. In *Japan Institute of Labour, ed.,* 1988, *1986,* pp. 40–43.

_____. The Growth of the Service Economy and Labor Unions. In *Japan Institute of Labour, ed.,* 1988, *1985,* pp. 73–76.

_____. Labor Front Unification and Zenmin Rokyo: The Emergence of Neo-corporatism. In *Japan Institute of Labour, ed.,* 1988, *1986,* pp. 82–85.

_____. The Rapid Rise in the Value of the Yen, Deindustrialization and Employment Adjustment. In *Japan Institute of Labour, ed.,* 1988, *1987,* pp. 26–31.

_____. Technology Transfer and Humanware. In *Japan Institute of Labour, ed.,* 1988, pp. 22–25.

Infante, Ricardo. Brazil's External Debt Outlook, 1986–1990: Comments. In *Feinberg, R. E. and Ffrench-Davis, R., eds.,* 1988, pp. 206–09.

Ingberg, Mikael. Bolagsskattens struktur och neutralitet vid skattereformen. (The Structure and Neutrality of Corporate Income Tax in the Tax Reform. With English summary.) *Ekon. Samfundets Tidskr.,* 1988, *41*(4), pp. 255–65.

Ingberman, Daniel E. and Inman, Robert P. The Political Economy of Fiscal Policy. In *Hare, P. G., ed.,* 1988, pp. 105–60.

Ingersoll, Robert S. East Asia and the U.S. Economy. In *Feldstein, M., ed. (II),* 1988, pp. 141–51.

Ingham, Alan; Ulph, Alistair and Toker, Mehmet. A Vintage Model of Scrapping and Investment. *Rech. Écon. Louvain,* 1988, *54*(2), pp. 169–89.

Ingraham, Patricia W. and Anderson, Stephen H. Assessing the Relationships between Program Design and Productivity: A Framework for Analysis. In *Kelly, R. M., ed.,* 1988, pp. 85–98.

Ingram, Helen M. State Government Officials' Role in U.S./Mexico Transboundary Resource Issues. *Natural Res. J.,* Summer 1988, *28*(3), pp. 431–49.

_____ **and Nunn, Susan Christopher.** Informa-

tion, the Decision Forum, and Third-Party Effects in Water Transfers. *Water Resources Res.,* April 1988, *24*(4), pp. 473–80.

Inkeles, Alex and Usui, Chikako. The Retirement Decision in Cross-National Perspective. In *Ricardo-Campbell, R. and Lazear, E. P., eds.,* 1988, pp. 273–96.

Inkster, Ian. Britain and the Single Factor Thesis Once More—A Comment on Kristine Bruland. *J. Europ. Econ. Hist.,* Spring 1988, *17*(1), pp. 187–88.

_____. The Institutionalist Theory of Economic Development, Technological Progress and Social Change: A Comment on James H. Street. *J. Econ. Issues,* December 1988, *22*(4), pp. 1243–47.

Inman, Robert P. Federal Assistance and Local Services in the United States: The Evolution of a New Federalist Fiscal Order. In *Rosen, H. S., ed.,* 1988, pp. 33–74.

_____. Medicare and the Health Care Costs of Retirees: Problems in Choosing the Future: Comment. In *Wachter, S. M., ed.,* 1988, pp. 175–77.

_____ **and Ingberman, Daniel E.** The Political Economy of Fiscal Policy. In *Hare, P. G., ed.,* 1988, pp. 105–60.

Innes, Jon T. and Thornton, Robert J. The Status of Master's Programs in Economics. *J. Econ. Perspectives,* Winter 1988, *2*(1), pp. 171–78.

Innes, Robert and Carman, Hoy F. Tax Reform and Beef Cow Replacement Strategy. *Western J. Agr. Econ.,* December 1988, *13*(2), pp. 254–66.

Inoguchi, Takashi. The Ideas and Structures of Foreign Policy: Looking Ahead with Caution. In *Inoguchi, T. and Okimoto, D. I., eds.,* 1988, pp. 23–63.

_____ **and Okimoto, Daniel I.** The Political Economy of Japan: Vol. 2: The Changing International Context: Introduction. In *Inoguchi, T. and Okimoto, D. I., eds.,* 1988, pp. 1–20.

Inose, Hiroshi. Information Technology in an International Perspective. In *Orishimo, I.; Hewings, G. J. D. and Nijkamp, P., eds.,* 1988, pp. 66–70.

_____. Technological Advances and Challenges in the Telecommunications Sector. In *Muroyama, J. H. and Stever, H. G., eds.,* 1988, pp. 62–67.

Inotai, András. Competition between the European CMEA and Rapidly Industrializing Countries on the OECD Market for Manufactured Goods: Facts, Trends, and Economic Policy Implications. *Empirica,* 1988, *15*(1), pp. 189–204.

_____. International Competitiveness and Imports. *Acta Oecon.,* 1988, *39*(1–2), pp. 45–60.

Inoue, Tadashi and Kiyono, Kazuharu. Optimal Restriction on Foreign Trade and Investment with a Nontraded Good. *Econ. Stud. Quart.,* September 1988, *39*(3), pp. 246–57.

Inoue, Touru and Osano, Hiroshi. Implicit Contracts in the Japanese Labor Market. *J. Japanese Int. Economies,* June 1988, *2*(2), pp. 181–98.

Inouye, Carolyn J. and Astin, Alexander W. How Public Policy at the State Level Affects Private Higher Education Institutions. *Econ. Educ. Rev.*, 1988, 7(1), pp. 47–63.

Inselbag, Işik and Gültekin, N. Bülent. Financial Markets in Turkey. In *Nas, T. F. and Odekon, M., eds.*, 1988, pp. 129–40.

Intrator, Jacob and Weiss, Joseph. Tree Indexing Methods for Transportation Algorithms for Long Problems. *Econ. Computat. Cybern. Stud. Res.*, 1988, 23(4), pp. 81–87.

Inukai, Ichiro. Industrialization in Resource-Rich Developing Countries: A Comparative Survey. In *Urrutia, M. and Yukawa, S., eds. (II)*, 1988, pp. 41–65.

Ioannides, Yannis M. Life Cycle Consumption, Labor Supply and Housing. *Ann. Écon. Statist.*, Jan.–March 1988, (9), pp. 93–110.

Ionescu, C.; Bulgaru, M. and Stroe, R. Turning to Account the Results of the Scientific Research of Economic Cybernetics and Economic Informatics in the Instructional–Educational Process. *Econ. Computat. Cybern. Stud. Res.*, 1988, 23(4), pp. 25–36.

_____ **and Ionescu, N.** Statistical Training of Economists. *Econ. Computat. Cybern. Stud. Res.*, 1988, 23(3), pp. 49–61.

Ionescu, N. and Ionescu, C. Statistical Training of Economists. *Econ. Computat. Cybern. Stud. Res.*, 1988, 23(3), pp. 49–61.

Ippolito, Pauline M. The Economics of Information in Consumer Markets: What Do We Know? What Do We Need to Know? In *Maynes, E. S. and ACCI Research Committee, eds.*, 1988, pp. 235–63.

Ippolito, Richard A. Future Sources of Retirement Income: Whither the Baby Boom: Comment. In *Wachter, S. M., ed.*, 1988, pp. 97–101.

_____. A Look at Very Early Retirees: Discussion. In *Ricardo-Campbell, R. and Lazear, E. P., eds.*, 1988, pp. 266–72.

_____. A Study of the Regulatory Effect of the Employee Retirement Income Security Act. *J. Law Econ.*, April 1988, 31(1), pp. 85–125.

Ipsen, Dirk. Schumpeterian Innovation, Market Structure, and the Stability of Industrial Development: Discussion. In *Hanusch, H., ed.*, 1988, pp. 199–204.

Iqbal, Farrukh. The Determinants of Moneylender Interest Rates: Evidence from Rural India. *J. Devel. Stud.*, April 1988, 24(3), pp. 364–78.

_____. External Financing for Korea: The Next Phase. *World Devel.*, January 1988, 16(1), pp. 137–55.

Iqbal, M. Qamar. Use of Inequality Measures in Calculating Income Elasticities. *Pakistan J. Appl. Econ.*, Summer 1988, 7(1), pp. 59–67.

Iqbal, Zafar and Chaudhry, M. Ghaffar. Regional Distribution of Agricultural Incomes in Pakistan: An Intertemporal Analysis. *Pakistan Devel. Rev.*, Part 2, Winter 1988, 27(4), pp. 537–46.

_____ **and Sheikh, Khalid Hameed.** Determinants of the Declining Share of Agricultural Labour Force to Total Labour Force in Pakistan. *Pakistan Devel. Rev.*, Part 2, Winter 1988, 27(4), pp. 561–65.

Irelan, Lola M. Retirement History Study: Introduction. *Soc. Sec. Bull.*, March 1988, 51(3), pp. 32–37.

Ireland, A. M. and Dempster, M. A. H. MIDAS: An Expert Debt Management Advisory System. In *Gaul, W. and Schader, M., eds.*, 1988, pp. 116–27.

Ireland, Norman J. An Illustrative Production Function for Labour-Managed Firms. *Bull. Econ. Res.*, June 1988, 40(3), pp. 241–45.

_____. Internal Labour Markets and Democratic Labour-Managed Firms. *Scand. J. Econ.*, 1988, 90(4), pp. 585–602.

_____ **and Law, Peter J.** Management Design under Labor Management. *J. Compar. Econ.*, March 1988, 12(1), pp. 1–23.

_____; **Law, Peter J. and Askildsen, Jan Erik.** Some Consequences of Differential Shareholdings among Members in a Labor-Managed and Labor-Owned Firm. In *Jones, D. C. and Svejnar, J., eds.*, 1988, pp. 65–81.

Ireland, R. Duane and Downey, H. Kirk. Strategic Objectives in Policy Research: An Essay on the Dangers of not Acknowledging Purposeful Behavior. In *Lamb, R. and Shrivastava, P., eds.*, 1988, pp. 263–75.

_____; **Goryunov, Igor Y. and Hitt, Michael A.** The Context of Innovation: Investment in R&D and Firm Performance. In *Gattiker, U. E. and Larwood, L., eds.*, 1988, pp. 73–92.

Irfan, Mohammad and Arif, Ghulam Mohammad. Landlessness in Rural Areas of Pakistan and Policy Options: A Preliminary Investigation. *Pakistan Devel. Rev.*, Part 2, Winter 1988, 27(4), pp. 567–74.

Ironmonger, Duncan. Statistical Perspectives and Economic Stability. In *[Clark, C.]*, 1988, pp. 32–48.

Ironside, R. G. and Christy, Craig V. Performance of High-Technology Firms in a Peripheral Resource-Based Economy: Alberta, Canada. *Growth Change*, Fall 1988, 19(4), pp. 88–100.

Irsch, Norbert. Die Entwicklung der Rentabilität kleiner, mittlerer und grosser Unternehmen in der Bundesrepublik Deutschland in der ersten Hälfte der 80er Jahre. (The Development of the Profitability of Small, Medium-Sized, and Large Companies in the Federal Republic of Germany in the First Half of the 1980s. With English summary.) *Konjunkturpolitik*, 1988, 34(2), pp. 69–84.

_____. Zum Zusammenhang von Unternehmensgrösse und Rentabilität in der Bundesrepublik Deutschland in der Mitte der 80er Jahre. (Contributions to the Dependence of Company Size and Profitability in the Federal Republic of Germany in the Middle of the 80s. With English summary.) *Jahr. Nationalökon. Statist.*, December 1988, 205(6), pp. 519–37.

Irwin, Douglas A. Welfare Effects of British Free Trade: Debate and Evidence from the 1840s.

J. Polit. Econ., December 1988, *96*(6), pp. 1142–64.

———— **and Rausser, Gordon C.** The Political Economy of Agricultural Policy Reform. *Europ. Rev. Agr. Econ.*, 1988, *15*(4), pp. 349–66.

Irwin, James R. Exploring the Affinity of Wheat and Slavery in the Virginia Piedmont. *Exploration Econ. Hist.*, July 1988, *25*(3), pp. 295–322.

Irwin, Scott H.; Forster, D. Lynn and Sherrick, Bruce J. Returns to Farm Real Estate Revisited. *Amer. J. Agr. Econ.*, August 1988, *70*(3), pp. 580–87.

————; **Lukac, Louis P. and Brorsen, B. Wade.** Similarity of Computer Guided Technical Trading Systems. *J. Futures Markets*, February 1988, *8*(1), pp. 1–13.

————; **Lukac, Louis P. and Brorsen, B. Wade.** A Test of Futures Market Disequilibrium Using Twelve Different Technical Trading Systems. *Appl. Econ.*, May 1988, *20*(5), pp. 623–39.

Isaac, R. Mark. Remnants of Regulation. In *Libecap, G., ed. (II)*, 1988, pp. 173–91.

———— **and Reynolds, Stanley S.** Appropriability and Market Structure in a Stochastic Invention Model. *Quart. J. Econ.*, November 1988, *103*(4), pp. 647–71.

———— **and Walker, James M.** Communication and Free-Riding Behavior: The Voluntary Contribution Mechanism. *Econ. Inquiry*, October 1988, *26*(4), pp. 585–608.

———— **and Walker, James M.** Group Size Effects in Public Goods Provision: The Voluntary Contributions Mechanism. *Quart. J. Econ.*, February 1988, *103*(1), pp. 179–99.

Isaacs, Arnold H. South Africa and Botswana, Lesotho and Swaziland: A Galtung Approach to Dependence Relations. In *Carlsson, J. and Shaw, T. M., eds.*, 1988, pp. 232–67.

Isaki, Shoji. Euro–Japanese Industrial Collaboration: Experience and Prospects. In *Holl, U. and Trevor, M., eds.*, 1988, pp. 13–25.

Isakson, Hans R. Valuation Analysis of Commercial Real Estate Using the Nearest Neighbors Appraisal Technique. *Growth Change*, Spring 1988, *19*(2), pp. 11–24.

Isaksson, Nils-Ivar and Cohen, John M. Food Production Strategy Debates in Revolutionary Ethiopia. *World Devel.*, March 1988, *16*(3), pp. 323–48.

Isard, Peter. Exchange Rate Modeling: An Assessment of Alternative Approaches. In *Bryant, R. C., et al., eds.*, 1988, pp. 183–201.

Isberg, Steven C. and Dowen, Richard J. Reexamination of the Intervalling Effect on the CAPM Using a Residual Return Approach. *Quart. J. Bus. Econ.*, Summer 1988, *27*(3), pp. 114–29.

Isenberg, Daniel J. How Senior Managers Think. In *Bell, D. E.; Raiffa, H. and Tversky, A., eds.*, 1988, *1984*, pp. 525–39.

Isenberg, Dorene L. Is There a Case for Minsky's Financial Fragility Hypothesis in the 1920s?

J. Econ. Issues, December 1988, *22*(4), pp. 1045–69.

Ishi, Hiromitsu. Corporate Tax Burden and Tax Incentives in Japan. In *Shoven, J. B., ed.*, 1988, pp. 97–120.

————. Historical Background of the Japanese Tax System. *Hitotsubashi J. Econ.*, June 1988, *29*(1), pp. 1–20.

Ishii, Yasunori. Welfare and Efficiency under Uncertainty. *J. Econ. (Z. Nationalökon.)*, 1988, *48*(2), pp. 175–88.

Ishikawa, Shigeru. Problems of Late Industrialisation: An Asian Perspective. In *Arrow, K. J., ed.*, 1988, pp. 85–104.

———— **and Kiyokawa, Yukihiko.** The Significance of Standardization in the Development of the Machine-Tool Industry: The Cases of Japan and China (Part II). *Hitotsubashi J. Econ.*, June 1988, *29*(1), pp. 73–88.

Ishikawa, Tsuneo. Saving and Labor Supply Behavior of Aged Households in Japan. *J. Japanese Int. Economies*, December 1988, *2*(4), pp. 417–49.

Ishizawa, Suezo. Increasing Returns, Public Inputs, and International Trade. *Amer. Econ. Rev.*, September 1988, *78*(4), pp. 794–95.

Islam, Nurul. Agricultural Growth, Technological Progress, and Rural Poverty. In *Lewis, J. P., et al.*, 1988, pp. 121–31.

————. Agriculture in GATT Negotiations and Developing Countries. In *Miner, W. M. and Hathaway, D. E., eds.*, 1988, pp. 169–89.

————. Economic Interdependence between Rich and Poor Nations. In *Sopiee, N.; Hamzah, B. A. and Leong, C. H., eds.*, 1988, *1983*, pp. 399–420.

————. Primary Commodity Markets: Recent Trends and Research Requirements. In *Elliott, K. A. and Williamson, J., eds.*, 1988, pp. 220–27.

Islam, Rafiqul. Aid to Bangladesh: For Self Reliance or for Maldevelopment? In *Vivekananda, F., ed.*, 1988, pp. 123–33.

Islam, Rizwanul and Rahman, Atiq. Labour Use in Rural Bangladesh—An Empirical Analysis. *Bangladesh Devel. Stud.*, December 1988, *16*(4), pp. 1–40.

Islam, Sadequl. Labor's Share of Income in an Open Economy: The Case of Canada. *Rev. Radical Polit. Econ.*, Summer–Fall 1988, *20*(2–3), pp. 214–22.

Islam, Safiqul. On the Controversies of Development and the Conceptual Evaluation of Maldevelopment. In *Vivekananda, F., ed.*, 1988, pp. 71–103.

Islam, Shafiqul. The International Debt Problem: Comment. In *Borner, S., ed.*, 1988, pp. 52–60.

Islam, Tajul and Sobhan, Rehman. Foreign Aid and Domestic Resource Mobilisation in Bangladesh. *Bangladesh Devel. Stud.*, June 1988, *16*(2), pp. 21–44.

Ismail, Zafar H. and Pasha, Hafiz A. Determinants of Success of Industrial Estates in Pakistan. *Pakistan Econ. Soc. Rev.*, Summer 1988, *26*(1), pp. 1–19.

Isogai, Takafumi. Data Plotting Methods for Checking Multivariate Normality and Related Ideas. In *Edwards, D. and Raun, N. E., eds.*, 1988, pp. 87–92.

Iszkowski, Jan. Annual and Multi-year Statistical Programmes. *Statist. J.*, December 1988, 5(4), pp. 421–28.

Itami, Hiroyuki. The Japanese Corporate System and Technology Accumulation. In *Urabe, K.; Child, J. and Kagono, T., eds.*, 1988, pp. 27–46.

_____ **and Imai, Ken'ichi.** Allocations of Labor and Capital in Japan and the United States. In *Okimoto, D. I. and Rohlen, T. P., eds.*, 1988, pp. 112–18.

Ito, Takatoshi. Labor Contracts with Voluntary Quits. *J. Lab. Econ.*, January 1988, 6(1), pp. 100–131.

_____. Use of (Time–Domain) Vector Autoregressions to Test Uncovered Interest Parity. *Rev. Econ. Statist.*, May 1988, 70(2), pp. 296–305.

_____ **and Park, Jin Hyuk.** Political Business Cycles in the Parliamentary System. *Econ. Letters*, 1988, 27(3), pp. 233–38.

_____; **Slemrod, Joel and Hayashi, Fumio.** Housing Finance Imperfections, Taxation, and Private Saving: A Comparative Simulation Analysis of the United States and Japan. *J. Japanese Int. Economies*, September 1988, 2(3), pp. 215–38.

Itoh, Motoshige. International Co-ordination of Domestic Industrial Policies. In *Borner, S., ed.*, 1988, pp. 324–37.

_____ **and Komiya, Ryutaro.** Japan's International Trade and Trade Policy, 1955–1984. In *Inoguchi, T. and Okimoto, D. I., eds.*, 1988, pp. 173–224.

_____ **and Krishna, Kala.** Content Protection and Oligopolistic Interactions. *Rev. Econ. Stud.*, January 1988, 55(1), pp. 107–25.

Ivan, I.; Goga, A. and Baron, T. Modelling the Cost of the Quality of Programme Systems. *Econ. Computat. Cybern. Stud. Res.*, 1988, 23(2), pp. 21–31.

Ivánek, Jiří and Stejskal, Bretislav. Automatic Acquisition of Knowledge Base from Data without Expert: ESOD (Expert System from Observational Data). In *Edwards, D. and Raun, N. E., eds.*, 1988, pp. 175–80.

Ivanov, E. A. The New Quality of Central Planning. *Prob. Econ.*, June 1988, 31(2), pp. 19–32.

Iverson, Kristine. The Government's Role in Regulating Home Employment. In *Christensen, K. E., ed.*, 1988, pp. 149–56.

Ives, Jack D. Development in the Face of Uncertainty. In *Ives, J. and Pitt, D. C., eds.*, 1988, pp. 54–74.

Iwama, M. and Magee, F. R. Computers and Communications. In *Uyehara, C. H., ed.*, 1988, pp. 143–60.

Iwasaki, Yumi and Simon, Herbert A. Causal Ordering, Comparative Statics, and Near Decomposability. *J. Econometrics*, Sept.–Oct. 1988, 39(1–2), pp. 149–73.

Iyenger, N. Sreenivasa and Raghuprasad, Shailaja. Estimation of Additive Engel Curves in the Presence of Heteroscedasticity. *J. Quant. Econ.*, July 1988, 4(2), pp. 329–39.

Izraeli, Dafna N. Women's Movement into Management in Israel. In *Adler, N. J. and Izraeli, D., eds.*, 1988, pp. 186–212.

_____ **and Adler, Nancy J.** Women in Management Worldwide. In *Adler, N. J. and Izraeli, D., eds.*, 1988, pp. 3–16.

Jablonowski, Mark. The Underwriting Cycle and the Risk Manager: Comment. *J. Risk Ins.*, September 1988, 55(3), pp. 559–60.

Jablonski, Mary; Rosenblum, Larry and Kunze, Kent. Productivity, Age, and Labor Composition Changes in the U.S. *Mon. Lab. Rev.*, September 1988, 111(9), pp. 34–38.

Jacinto, Elizabeth; Senauer, Benjamin and Garcia, Marito. Determinants of the Intrahousehold Allocation of Food in the Rural Philippines. *Amer. J. Agr. Econ.*, February 1988, 70(1), pp. 170–80.

Jacklin, Charles J. and Bhattacharya, Sudipto. Distinguishing Panics and Information-Based Bank Runs: Welfare and Policy Implications. *J. Polit. Econ.*, June 1988, 96(3), pp. 568–92.

Jackman, Richard. Local Government Finance and Macroeconomic Policy. In *Bailey, S. J. and Paddison, R., eds.*, 1988, pp. 172–89.

_____. Profit-Sharing in a Unionised Economy with Imperfect Competition. *Int. J. Ind. Organ.*, March 1988, 6(1), pp. 47–57.

_____ **and Haskel, Jonathan.** Long-term Unemployment in Britain and the Effects of the Community Programme. *Oxford Bull. Econ. Statist.*, November 1988, 50(4), pp. 379–408.

_____ **and Kan, Bertrand.** Structural Unemployment: A Reply. *Oxford Bull. Econ. Statist.*, February 1988, 50(1), pp. 83–87.

_____ **and Layard, Richard.** Trade Unions, The Nairu and a Wage-Inflation Tax. In *Shaw, G. K., ed., Vol. 2*, 1988, pp. 46–53.

Jackson, A. A.; McLeod, Joan C. and Omawale. Household Food Consumption Behaviour in St. James, Jamaica. *Soc. Econ. Stud.*, September 1988, 37(3), pp. 213–35.

Jackson, Bernard S. Biblical Laws of Slavery: A Comparative Approach. In *Archer, L. J., ed.*, 1988, pp. 86–101.

Jackson, Gary L. The Residential Demand for Electricity in the TVA Power Service Area: Applicance Consumption from 1979 to 1986. *Energy J.*, January 1988, 9(1), pp. 89–93.

Jackson, Gregory A. Did College Choice Change during the Seventies? *Econ. Educ. Rev.*, 1988, 7(1), pp. 15–27.

Jackson, Jacquelyne Johnson. Seeking Common Ground for Blacks and Immigrants. In *Simcox, D. E., ed.*, 1988, pp. 92–103.

Jackson, John D. and Boyd, James W. A Statistical Approach to Modeling the Behavior of Bond Raters. *J. Behav. Econ.*, Fall 1988, 17(3), pp. 173–93.

Jackson, John E. The New Economic Role of American States: Michigan. In *Fosler, R. S., ed.*, 1988, pp. 89–137.

Jackson, John H. Consistency of Export-Restraint Arrangements with the GATT. *World Econ.*, December 1988, *11*(4), pp. 485–500.

_____. Constructing a Constitution for Trade in Services. *World Econ.*, June 1988, *11*(2), pp. 187–202.

Jackson, Lauren Hite and Wallach, Arthur E. Getting an Answer to "How Am I Doing?" In *Timpe, A. D., ed.*, 1988, *1985*, pp. 145–51.

Jackson, Margaret A. and Boyd, Neil T. Reducing the Risks of Pleasure: Responding to AIDS in Canada. *Can. Public Policy*, December 1988, *14*(4), pp. 347–60.

Jackson, Matthew O. and Barbarà, Salvador. Maximin, Leximin, and the Protective Criterion: Characterizations and Comparisons. *J. Econ. Theory*, October 1988, *46*(1), pp. 34–44.

Jackson, Peter M. The Role of Government in Changing Industrial Societies: A Schumpeter Perspective. In *Hanusch, H., ed.*, 1988, pp. 285–308.

_____ and Palmer, A. J. The Economics of Internal Organisation: The Efficiency of Parastatals in LDCs. In *Cook, P. and Kirkpatrick, C., eds.*, 1988, pp. 195–213.

Jackson, R. Gordon. Aid and Development. In *Kozmetsky, G.; Matsumoto, H. and Smilor, R. W., eds.*, 1988, pp. 133–36.

Jackson, Ralph W. The Effect of Approved Vendors Lists on Industrial Marketing. In *Woodside, A. G., ed.*, 1988, pp. 79–94.

Jackson, Randall W. and Hynes, M. Demographics in Demographic–Economic Models: A Reply. *Environ. Planning A*, November 1988, *20*(11), pp. 1543–45.

_____ and Hynes, M. Demographics in Demographic–Economic Models: A Note on the Basic Activity–Commodity Framework. *Environ. Planning A*, November 1988, *20*(11), pp. 1531–36.

Jackson, Ray. A Museum Cost Function. *J. Cult. Econ.*, June 1988, *12*(1), pp. 41–50.

Jackson, Susan E.; Schuler, Randall S. and Galante, Steven P. Matching Effective HR Practices with Competitive Strategy. In *Timpe, A. D., ed.*, 1988, *1987*, pp. 113–23.

Jackstadt, Steve; Huskey, Lee and Hill, P. J. The Making of an Economist: Comment. *J. Econ. Perspectives*, Fall 1988, *2*(4), pp. 209–12.

Jacob, Adolf-Friedrich. Preispolitik im internationalen Bankgescháft. (With English summary.) *Z. Betriebswirtshaft*, September 1988, *58*(9), pp. 981–96.

Jacobs, Gordon L. and Lessard, Pierre. Tax Treatment of Computer Software: Canada. In *International Fiscal Association, ed. (II)*, 1988, pp. 253–80.

Jacobs, Jerry A. and Breiger, Ronald L. Careers, Industries, and Occupations: Industrial Segmentation Reconsidered. In *Farkas, G. and England, P., eds.*, 1988, pp. 43–63.

Jacobsson, Staffan. Intra-industry Specialization and Development Models for the Capital Goods Sector. *Weltwirtsch. Arch.*, 1988, *124*(1), pp. 14–37.

Jacoby, Sanford M. Employee Attitude Surveys in Historical Perspective. *Ind. Relat.*, Winter 1988, *27*(1), pp. 74–93.

_____ and Mitchell, Daniel J. B. Measurement of Compensation: Union and Nonunion. *Ind. Relat.*, Spring 1988, *27*(2), pp. 215–31.

_____ and Pearl, Maury Y. Labor Market Contracting and Wage Dispersion. *J. Lab. Res.*, Winter 1988, *9*(1), pp. 65–77.

Jacquemin, Alexis. Cooperative Agreements in R&D and European Antitrust Policy. *Europ. Econ. Rev.*, March 1988, *32*(2–3), pp. 551–60.

_____. Echanges internationaux et stratégies collusives. (With English summary.) *Rech. Écon. Louvain*, 1988, *54*(1), pp. 85–102.

_____ and d'Aspremont, Claude. Cooperative and Noncooperative R&D in Duopoly with Spillovers. *Amer. Econ. Rev.*, December 1988, *78*(5), pp. 1133–37.

_____ and Geroski, Paul A. The Persistence of Profits: A European Comparison. *Econ. J.*, June 1988, *98*(391), pp. 375–89.

_____; de Ghellinck, Elisabeth and Geroski, Paul A. Inter-industry Variations in the Effect of Trade on Industry Performance. *J. Ind. Econ.*, September 1988, *37*(1), pp. 1–19.

_____ and Sapir, André. European Integration or World Integration? *Weltwirtsch. Arch.*, 1988, *124*(1), pp. 127–39.

_____ and Sapir, André. International Trade and Integration of the European Community: An Econometric Analysis. *Europ. Econ. Rev.*, September 1988, *32*(7), pp. 1439–49.

Jacquet, Pierre. Gérer l'interdépendance économique internationale: Coordination discrétionnaire ou règles instiutionnelles? (How to Manage International Economic Interdependence: Discretionary Cooperation or Institutional Rules. With English summary.) *Revue Écon.*, May 1988, *39*(3), pp. 615–25.

Jadlow, Janice W. and Jadlow, Joseph M. Risk, Rent Seeking and the Social Cost of Monopoly Power. *Managerial Dec. Econ.*, March 1988, *9*(1), pp. 59–63.

Jadlow, Joseph M. and Jadlow, Janice W. Risk, Rent Seeking and the Social Cost of Monopoly Power. *Managerial Dec. Econ.*, March 1988, *9*(1), pp. 59–63.

Jaeger, Albert and Keuschnigg, Christian. Adjusting Unsustainable Budget Deficits and Crowding Out. *Jahr. Nationalökon. Statist.*, December 1988, *205*(6), pp. 492–505.

Jaeger, Carlo and Weber, Arnd. Lohndynamik und Arbeitslosigkeit. (With English summary.) *Kyklos*, 1988, *41*(3), pp. 479–506.

Jafarey, Saqib; Nishimura, Kazuo and Benhabib, Jess. The Dynamics of Efficient Intertemporal Allocations with Many Agents, Recursive Preferences, and Production. *J. Econ. Theory*, April 1988, *44*(2), pp. 301–20.

Jaffe, Adam B. Demand and Supply Influences in R&D Intensity and Productivity Growth. *Rev. Econ. Statist.*, August 1988, *70*(3), pp. 431–37.

Jaffe, Austin J. Toward an Evolutionary Theory of Trade Associations: The Case of Real Estate

Appraisers. *Amer. Real Estate Urban Econ. Assoc. J.*, Fall 1988, *16*(3), pp. 230–56.

Jaffé, W. Menger, Jevons and Walras De-homogenized. In *Wood, J. C., ed., Vol. 3*, 1988, *1976*, pp. 146–59.

Jaffray, Jean-Yves. An Axiomatic Model of Choice under Risk Which Is Compatible with the Certainty Effect. In *Munier, B. R., ed.*, 1988, pp. 313–25.

_____ **and Cohen, Michèle.** Preponderence of the Certainty Effect over Probability Distortion in Decision Making under Risk. In *Munier, B. R., ed.*, 1988, pp. 173–87.

Jagannathan, N. Vijay. Corruption, Delivery Systems and Property Rights: Rejoinder. *World Devel.*, November 1988, *16*(11), pp. 1393–94.

Jagannathan, Ravi and Chari, V. V. Banking Panics, Information, and Rational Expectations Equilibrium. *J. Finance*, July 1988, *43*(3), pp. 749–61.

_____; **Ofer, Aharon R. and Chari, V. V.** Seasonalities in Security Returns: The Case of Earnings Announcements. *J. Finan. Econ.*, May 1988, *21*(1), pp. 101–21.

Jagen, Henk and De Jong, Eelke. The Contribution of the ECU to Exchange-Rate Stability: A Reply. *Banca Naz. Lavoro Quart. Rev.*, September 1988, (166), pp. 331–35.

Jager, Henk and de Jong, Eelke. The Private Ecu's Potential Impact on Global and European Exchange Rate Stability. *Banca Naz. Lavoro Quart. Rev.*, March 1988, (164), pp. 33–59.

Jaggi, Bikki. A Comparative Analysis of Worker Participation in the United States and Europe. In *Dlugos, G.; Dorow, W. and Weiermair, K., eds.*, 1988, pp. 443–54.

_____ **and Freedman, Martin.** An Analysis of the Impact of Corporate Pollution Disclosures: A Reply. In *Neimark, M., ed.*, 1988, pp. 193–97.

Jahera, John S., Jr.; Lloyd, William P. and Page, Daniel E. Does Business Diversification Affect Performance?: Some Further Evidence. *Quart. J. Bus. Econ.*, Winter 1988, *27*(1), pp. 130–47.

Jaidah, Ali M. Producers' Policies: Past and Future. In *Mabro, R., ed.*, 1988, pp. 71–80.

Jain, Anshuman; Wood, Robert A., Jr. and Hill, Joanne M. Insurance: Volatility Risk and Futures Mispricing. *J. Portfol. Manage.*, Winter 1988, *14*(2), pp. 23–29.

Jain, Arvind K. An Agency Theoretic Explanation of Capital Flight. *Econ. Letters*, 1988, *28*(1), pp. 41–45.

Jain, H. C.; Meltz, Noah M. and Hébert, G. The State of the Art in Industrial Relations: Conclusion. In *Hébert, G.; Jain, H. C. and Meltz, N. M., eds.*, 1988, pp. 281–90.

_____; **Meltz, Noah M. and Hébert, G.** The State of the Art in IR: Some Questions and Concepts. In *Hébert, G.; Jain, H. C. and Meltz, N. M., eds.*, 1988, pp. 1–8.

Jain, Prem C. Response of Hourly Stock Prices and Trading Volume to Economic News. *J. Bus.*, April 1988, *61*(2), pp. 219–31.

_____ **and Joh, Gun-Ho.** The Dependence between Hourly Prices and Trading Volume. *J. Finan. Quant. Anal.*, September 1988, *23*(3), pp. 269–83.

Jain, Rita S. Employer-Sponsored Dental Insurance Eases the Pain. *Mon. Lab. Rev.*, October 1988, *111*(10), pp. 18–23.

_____. Employer-Sponsored Vision Care Brought into Focus. *Mon. Lab. Rev.*, September 1988, *111*(9), pp. 19–23.

Jain, Satish K. Characterization of Monotonicity and Neutrality for Binary Paretian Social Decision Rules. *Math. Soc. Sci.*, June 1988, *15*(3), pp. 307–12.

Jakobsen, Arvid S. How to Observe a Leontief Paradox—And How Not to. In *Ciaschini, M., ed.*, 1988, pp. 217–30.

Jakubson, George. The Sensitivity of Labor-Supply Parameter Estimates to Unobserved Individual Effects: Fixed- and Random-Effects Estimates in a Nonlinear Model Using Panel Data. *J. Lab. Econ.*, July 1988, *6*(3), pp. 302–29.

Jamal, Haroon and Butt, Mohammed Sabihuddin. A Monetarist Approach to Inflation for Pakistan. *Pakistan Econ. Soc. Rev.*, Winter 1988, *26*(2), pp. 69–88.

_____ **and Malik, Salman.** Shifting Patterns in Developmental Rank Ordering: A Case Study of the Districts of Sind Province. *Pakistan Devel. Rev.*, Summer 1988, *27*(2), pp. 159–82.

Jamal, Vali. Coping under Crisis in Uganda. *Int. Lab. Rev.*, 1988, *127*(6), pp. 679–701.

_____. Getting the Crisis Right: Missing Perspectives on Africa. *Int. Lab. Rev.*, 1988, *127*(6), pp. 655–78.

_____. Somalia: Survival in a "Doomed" Economy. *Int. Lab. Rev.*, 1988, *127*(6), pp. 783–812.

_____ **and Weeks, John.** The Vanishing Rural–Urban Gap in Sub-Saharan Africa. *Int. Lab. Rev.*, 1988, *127*(3), pp. 271–92.

James, Christopher. The Use of Loan Sales and Standby Letters of Credit by Commercial Banks. *J. Monet. Econ.*, November 1988, *22*(3), pp. 395–422.

James, Dilmus. Accumulation and Utilization of Internal Technological Capabilities in the Third World. *J. Econ. Issues*, June 1988, *22*(2), pp. 339–53.

_____. Skill Requirements of New Technology Applications to Traditional Sectors. In *Bhalla, A. S. and James, D., eds.*, 1988, pp. 38–50.

_____ **and Bhalla, Ajit S.** New Technologies and Development: Experiences in "Technology Blending": Introduction. In *Bhalla, A. S. and James, D., eds.*, 1988, pp. 1–9.

_____ **and Bhalla, Ajit S.** New Technologies and Development: Experiences in "Technology Blending": Conclusions and Lessons. In *Bhalla, A. S. and James, D., eds.*, 1988, pp. 287–305.

_____ **and Bhalla, Ajit S.** Some Conceptual and Policy Issues. In *Bhalla, A. S. and James, D., eds.*, 1988, pp. 28–37.

_____ **and Dietz, James L.** The Veblen–Commons Award. *J. Econ. Issues*, June 1988, 22(2), pp. 323–26.

_____; Lalkaka, Rustam and Malik, Khalid. Cloning of Tea in Malawi. In *Bhalla, A. S. and James, D., eds.*, 1988, pp. 258–68.

_____ and Street, James H. Institutionalism, Structuralism, and Dependency in Latin America. In *Samuels, W. J., ed., Vol. 3*, 1988, 1982, pp. 204–20.

James, Estelle. Student Aid and College Attendance: Where Are We Now and Where Do We Go from Here? *Econ. Educ. Rev.*, 1988, 7(1), pp. 1–13.

James, Kenneth. Production Management in Small and Medium Businesses in the ASEAN Region: An Overview. In *James, K. and Akrasanee, N., eds.*, 1988, pp. 1–18.

_____ and Akrasanee, Narongchai. Small and Medium Business Improvement in the ASEAN Region: Production Management: Preface. In *James, K. and Akrasanee, N., eds.*, 1988, pp. ix–x.

James, Patrick and Brecher, Michael. Patterns of Crisis Management. *J. Conflict Resolution*, September 1988, 32(3), pp. 426–56.

James, Walter D., III. Financial Institutions and Hazardous Waste Litigation: Limiting the Exposure to Superfund Liability. *Natural Res. J.*, Spring 1988, 28(2), pp. 329–55.

James, Wendy. Perceptions from an African Slaving Frontier. In *Archer, L. J., ed.*, 1988, pp. 130–41.

Jameson, Kenneth P. Education's Role in Rural Areas of Latin America. *Econ. Educ. Rev.*, 1988, 7(3), pp. 333–43.

_____ and Henriot, Peter J. International Debt, Austerity, and the Poor. In *Tavis, L. A., ed.*, 1988, pp. 13–56.

Jamieson, Barbara and Amirkhalkhali, Saleh. Provincial Public Finance in the Atlantic Region, 1965–1984. *Can. Public Policy*, June 1988, 14(2), pp. 197–203.

Jamison, Dean T. and Moock, Peter R. Educational Development in Sub-Saharan Africa. *Finance Develop.*, March 1988, 25(1), pp. 22–24.

Jammalamadaka, S. Rao; Chib, Siddhartha and Tiwari, Ram C. Bayes Prediction Density and Regression Estimation—A Semiparametric Approach. *Empirical Econ.*, 1988, 13(3–4), pp. 209–22.

_____; Chib, Siddhartha and Tiwari, Ram C. Bayes Prediction in Regressions with Elliptical Errors. *J. Econometrics*, July 1988, 38(3), pp. 349–60.

Jampel, Wilhelm. The Chemical Industry in the East. *Soviet E. Europ. Foreign Trade*, Spring 1988, 24(1), pp. 63–107.

Jamshidian, Farshid and Zhu, Yu. Analysis of Bonds with Imbedded Options. In *Fabozzi, F. J., ed.*, 1988, pp. 63–95.

Janáček, Kamil. Growth and Equilibrium. *Czech. Econ. Digest.*, August 1988, (5), pp. 58–66.

Janakiramanan, S.; Alexander, Gordon J. and Eun, Cheol S. International Listings and Stock

Returns: Some Empirical Evidence. *J. Finan. Quant. Anal.*, June 1988, 23(2), pp. 135–51.

Janeba, Vladimír. Experience Gained from the Comprehensive Experiment. *Czech. Econ. Digest.*, June 1988, (4), pp. 44–50.

Janelle, D. G.; Goodchild, M. F. and Klinkenberg, B. Space–Time Diaries and Travel Characteristics for Different Levels of Respondent Aggregation. *Environ. Planning A*, July 1988, 20(7), pp. 891–906.

Janhunen, O. Information Technology and Statistical Product Development. *Statist. J.*, August 1988, 5(2), pp. 193–200.

Jani, B. M. Centre–State Financial Relations with Special Reference to North-west Region. In *Raikhy, P. S. and Gill, S. S., eds.*, 1988, pp. 212–27.

Janiszewski, Chris. Preconscious Processing Effects: The Independence of Attitude Formation and Conscious Thought. *J. Cons. Res.*, September 1988, 15(2), pp. 199–209.

Janowitz, M. F. Induced Social Welfare Functions. *Math. Soc. Sci.*, June 1988, 15(3), pp. 261–76.

Jansen, Dennis W. and Bradley, Michael D. Informational Implications of Money, Interest Rate, and Price Rules. *Econ. Inquiry*, July 1988, 26(3), pp. 437–48.

_____ and Bradley, Michael D. New Classical Models, Policy Effectiveness and the Money Rule/Interest Rule Debate. In *Missouri Valley Economic Assoc.*, 1988, pp. 39–45.

_____ and Bradley, Michael D. Price Rules, Wage Indexing, and Optimal Monetary Policy. *J. Macroecon.*, Fall 1988, 10(4), pp. 515–37.

_____ and Cosimano, Thomas F. Estimates of the Variance of U.S. Inflation Based upon the ARCH Model: A Comment. *J. Money, Credit, Banking*, Part 1, August 1988, 20(3), pp. 409–21.

_____ and Cosimano, Thomas F. Federal Reserve Policy, 1975–1985: An Empirical Analysis. *J. Macroecon.*, Winter 1988, 10(1), pp. 27–47.

Jansen, H. G. P. and Mueller, R. A. E. Farmer and Farm Concepts in Measuring Adoption Lags. *J. Agr. Econ.*, January 1988, 39(1), pp. 121–24.

Janson, Marius A. Combining Robust and Traditional Least Squares Methods: A Critical Evaluation. *J. Bus. Econ. Statist.*, October 1988, 6(4), pp. 415–27.

_____. Combining Robust and Traditional Least Squares Methods: A Critical Evaluation: Reply. *J. Bus. Econ. Statist.*, October 1988, 6(4), pp. 450–51.

Janssen, J. and van Brussel, P. Classification of Microcomputers and Marketing Interpretation. In *Gaul, W. and Schader, M., eds.*, 1988, pp. 355–67.

Jansson, Arne and Söderberg, Johan. Corn-Price Rises and Equalisation: Real Wages in Stockholm 1650–1719. *Scand. Econ. Hist. Rev.*, 1988, 36(2), pp. 42–67.

de Janvry, Alain. Issues in World Agriculture—A Third World Perspective: A Discussion. In

Hildreth, R. J., et al., eds., 1988, pp. 170–76.

_____ **and Sadoulet, Elisabeth.** The Conditions for Compatibility between Aid and Trade in Agriculture. *Econ. Develop. Cult. Change,* October 1988, 37(1), pp. 1–30.

Jappelli, Tullio. Consumo, indebitamento delle famiglie e razionamento del credito. (Consumption, Households Debt and Credit Rationing. With English summary.) *Giorn. Econ.,* Nov.–Dec. 1988, 47(11–12), pp. 545–73.

_____ **and Modigliani, Franco.** The Determinants of Interest Rates in the Italian Economy. *Rev. Econ. Cond. Italy,* Jan.–April 1988, (1), pp. 9–34.

_____ **and Ripa di Meana, Andrea.** The Behavior of Inflation and Interest Rates: Evidence from Italian National History. *J. Econ. Dynam. Control,* March 1988, 12(1), pp. 27–35.

Jaramillo, Felipe. Subsidies, Countervailing Duties and Developing Countries. In *Dicke, D. C. and Petersmann, E.-U., eds.,* 1988, pp. 263–66.

Jarousse, Jean-Pierre. Mobilité professionnelle et représentations du fonctionnement du marché du travail. (Job Turnover and Alternative Theoretical Conceptions of the Labor Market. With English summary.) *Écon. Appl.,* 1988, 41(3), pp. 503–22.

_____. Working Less to Earn More: An Application to the Analysis of Rigidity in Educational Choices. *Econ. Educ. Rev.,* 1988, 7(2), pp. 195–207.

Jarrell, Gregg A. Financial Innovation and Corporate Mergers. In *Browne, L. E. and Rosengren, E. S., eds.,* 1988, pp. 52–73.

_____. On the Underlying Motivations for Corporate Takeovers and Restructurings. In *Libecap, G., ed. (I),* 1988, pp. 13–41.

_____. Panel Discussion: Corporate Takeovers and Public Policy: Remarks. In *Auerbach, A. J., ed. (I),* 1988, pp. 320–21.

_____ **and Bradley, Michael.** Evidence on the Gains from Mergers and Takeovers: Comment. In *Coffee, J. C., Jr.; Lowenstein, L. and Rose-Ackerman, S., eds.,* 1988, pp. 253–59.

_____; **Brickley, James A. and Netter, Jeffry M.** The Market for Corporate Control: The Empirical Evidence Since 1980. *J. Econ. Perspectives,* Winter 1988, 2(1), pp. 49–68.

_____ **and Peltzman, Sam.** The Impact of Product Recalls on the Wealth of Sellers. In *Stigler, G. J., ed.,* 1988, 1985, pp. 612–33.

_____ **and Poulsen, Annette B.** Dual-Class Recapitalizations as Antitakeover Mechanisms: The Recent Evidence. *J. Finan. Econ.,* Jan.–March 1988, 20(1–2), pp. 129–52.

Jarrett, Jerry V. The New Midamerican Opportunity. In *Association of Private Education,* 1988, pp. 5–13.

Jarrett, Steven; Taylor, Carl E. and Parker, Robert L. The Evolving Chinese Rural Health Care System. In *Sirageldin, I. and Sorkin, A., eds.,* 1988, pp. 219–36.

Jarrow, Robert A. and Heath, David C. Ex-dividend Stock Price Behavior and Arbitrage Opportunities. *J. Bus.,* January 1988, 61(1), pp. 95–108.

_____ **and Oldfield, George S.** Forward Options and Futures Options. In *Fabozzi, F. J., ed.,* 1988, pp. 15–28.

Jarsulic, Marc. Financial Instability and Income Distribution. *J. Econ. Issues,* June 1988, 22(2), pp. 545–53.

Jaruga, Alicja. Accounting in Poland. In *Bailey, D. T., ed.,* 1988, pp. 122–32.

_____. Governmental Accounting, Auditing and Financial Reporting in East European Nations. In *Chan, J. L. and Jones, R. H., eds.,* 1988, pp. 105–21.

_____ **and Brzezin, W.** Accounting Evolution in a Planned Economy. In *Bailey, D. T., ed.,* 1988, pp. 41–58.

Jasentuliyana, Nandasiri and Chipman, Ralph. Satellite Remote Sensing in Developing Countries: The Experience of West Africa. In *Bhalla, A. S. and James, D., eds.,* 1988, pp. 223–40.

Jaspersen, Fred. Panel on Strategies for Confronting the Crisis: Panel. In *Feinberg, R. E. and Ffrench-Davis, R., eds.,* 1988, pp. 263–68.

Jasso, Guillermina and Rosenzweig, Mark R. How Well Do U.S. Immigrants Do?: Vintage Effects, Emigration Selectivity, and Occupational Mobility. In *Schultz, T. Paul, ed.,* 1988, pp. 229–53.

Jauregui, Roman Guillermo. Recognition of Foreign Enterprises as Taxable Entities: Argentina. In *International Fiscal Association, ed. (I),* 1988, pp. 251–68.

Jayaraman, Narayanan and Shastri, Kuldeep. The Valuation Impacts of Specially Designated Dividends. *J. Finan. Quant. Anal.,* September 1988, 23(3), pp. 301–12.

Jayasuriya, D. C. Pharmaceuticals, Patents and the Third World. *J. World Trade,* December 1988, 22(6), pp. 117–21.

Jayasuriya, Sisira K. Testing the Multilateral Version of Purchasing Power Parity: An Application to Burma and Jordan under the SDR Peg, 1981–85: A Comment. *Appl. Econ.,* September 1988, 20(9), pp. 1275–76.

_____ **and Athukorala, Premachandra.** Parentage and Factor Proportions: A Comparative Study of Third-World Multinationals in Sri Lankan Manufacturing. *Oxford Bull. Econ. Statist.,* November 1988, 50(4), pp. 409–23.

_____ **and Manning, Chris.** Survey of Recent Developments. *Bull. Indonesian Econ. Stud.,* August 1988, 24(2), pp. 3–41.

_____ **and Ravallion, Martin.** Liberalization and Inequality in Sri Lanka: A Comment [The Distribution of Income in Sri Lanka in 1969–70 and 1980–81: A Decomposition Analysis]. *J. Devel. Econ.,* March 1988, 28(2), pp. 247–55.

Jayne, Edward Randolph, II. The Economic Impact of Defense. *Bus. Econ.,* October 1988, 23(4), pp. 31–37.

Jean, William H. and Helms, Billy P. The Identification of Stochastic Dominance Efficient Sets by Moment Combination Orderings. *J. Banking Finance*, June 1988, *12*(2), pp. 243–53.

Jeanfils, Philippe. Structure du coût salarial, emploi et nature du chûmage: une analyse de déséquilibre. (With English summary.) *Cah. Écon. Bruxelles*, Third Trimester 1988, (119), pp. 333–70.

Jeannot, Thomas M. Philosophical Presuppositions of Marx's Labour Theory of Value. *Int. J. Soc. Econ.*, 1988, *15*(1), pp. 33–57.

Jebuni, C. D.; Love, J. H. and Forsyth, D. J. C. Market Structure and LDCs' Manufactured Export Performance. *World Devel.*, December 1988, *16*(12), pp. 1511–20.

Jedlicki, Claudio. De l'affectation de l'importation d'épargne étrangère dans le cas des grands débiteurs de l'Amérique Latine. (On Allocation of Foreign Savings in the Most Highly Indebted Countries of Latin America. With English summary.) *Écon. Appl.*, 1988, *41*(4), pp. 875–901.

Jefferson, Gary H. The Aggregate Production Function and Productivity Growth: Verdoorn's Law Revisited. *Oxford Econ. Pap.*, December 1988, *40*(4), pp. 671–91.

Jeffrey, D. and Hubbard, N. J. Foreign Tourism, the Hotel Industry and Regional Economic Performance. *Reg. Stud.*, August 1988, *22*(4), pp. 319–29.

Jeffrey, Richard C. Probable Knowledge. In *Gärdenfors, P. and Sahlin, N.-E., eds.*, 1988, pp. 86–96.

Jeffrey, Scott R. Future Financial Performance and Potential Structural Adjustments in Traditional Dairy Farming. *Can. J. Agr. Econ.*, Part 2, December 1988, *36*(4), pp. 871–79.

Jegers, Marc. The Price Cost Margin–Internal Rate of Return Relation: A Contribution to an Eternal Dispute. *Metroecon.*, October 1988, *39*(3), pp. 337–39.

Jemison, David. Value Creation and Acquisition Integration: The Role of Strategic Capability Transfer. In *Libecap, G., ed. (I)*, 1988, pp. 191–218.

Jen, Frank C. Financial Planning and Control for Commercial and Industrial Enterprises in China. *Financial Rev.*, May 1988, *23*(2), pp. 161–74.

Jen, Lo-Sun and Martin, Henry L. Are Ore Grades Declining? The Canadian Experience, 1939–89. In *Tilton, J. E.; Eggert, R. G. and Landsberg, H. H., eds.*, 1988, pp. 419–44.

Jena, Suruchi and Mitra, A. K. Effects of Outliers in Regression Analysis: A Study with Reference to Groundnut Productivity Data of Orissa. *Indian J. Quant. Econ.*, 1988, *4*(1), pp. 41–48.

Jencks, Christopher; Palmer, John L. and Smeeding, Timothy M. The Uses and Limits of Income Comparisons. In *Palmer, J. L.; Smeeding, T. and Torrey, B. B., eds.*, 1988, pp. 9–27.

_____ **and Torrey, Barbara Boyle.** Beyond Income and Poverty: Trends in Social Welfare among Children and the Elderly since 1960. In *Palmer, J. L.; Smeeding, T. and Torrey, B. B., eds.*, 1988, pp. 229–73.

Jenkins, D. T. Studies in Capital Formation in the United Kingdom, 1750–1920: The Wool Textile Industry, 1780–1850. In *Feinstein, C. H. and Pollard, S., eds.*, 1988, pp. 126–40.

Jenkins, Larry. An Approximate Solution to a Capacitated Plant Location Problem under Uncertain Demand. In *Eiselt, H. A. and Pederzoli, G., eds.*, 1988, pp. 174–85.

Jenkins, Rhys. Transnational Corporations and Third World Consumption: Implications of Competitive Strategies. *World Devel.*, November 1988, *16*(11), pp. 1363–70.

Jenkins-Smith, Hank C. Analytical Debates and Policy Learning: Analysis and Change in the Federal Bureaucracy. *Policy Sci.*, 1988, *21*(2–3), pp. 169–211.

_____ **and Heintz, H. Theodore, Jr.** Advocacy Coalitions and the Practice of Policy Analysis. *Policy Sci.*, 1988, *21*(2–3), pp. 263–77.

_____; **Weimer, David Leo and Horwich, George.** The International Energy Agency's Mandatory Oil-Sharing Agreement: Tests of Efficiency, Equity, and Practicality. In *Horwich, G. and Weimer, D. L., eds.*, 1988, pp. 104–33.

Jenkins, Stephen. Calculating Income Distribution Indices from Micro-data. *Nat. Tax J.*, March 1988, *41*(1), pp. 139–42.

_____. Empirical Measurement of Horizontal Inequity. *J. Public Econ.*, December 1988, *37*(3), pp. 305–29.

_____. The Joint Impact of Fertility Differentials and Social Security on the Accumulation and Distribution of Wealth: Comment. In *Kessler, D. and Masson, A., eds.*, 1988, pp. 186–90.

_____. Reranking and the Analysis of Income Redistribution. *Scot. J. Polit. Econ.*, February 1988, *35*(1), pp. 65–76.

Jenkins, T. N.; Haines, M. and Pitts, E. Dairy Industry Structure and Milk Price Comparisons: A Further Comment. *J. Agr. Econ.*, September 1988, *39*(3), pp. 446–49.

Jenkinson, Tim J. The NAIRU: Statistical Fact or Theoretical Straitjacket? In *Cross, R., ed.*, 1988, pp. 365–77.

_____ **and Beckerman, Wilfred.** What Stopped the Inflation? Unemployment or Commodity Prices? In *Shaw, G. K., ed., Vol. 2*, 1988, *1986*, pp. 250–65.

_____ **and Mayer, Colin.** The Privatisation Process in France and the U.K. *Europ. Econ. Rev.*, March 1988, *32*(2–3), pp. 482–90.

Jenkis, Helmut W. Gorbachev's Economic Reforms: a Structural or a Technical Alteration? *Int. J. Soc. Econ.*, 1988, *15*(1), pp. 3–32.

Jennen-Steinmetz, Christine and Gasser, Theo. A Unifying Approach to Nonparametric Regression Estimation. *J. Amer. Statist. Assoc.*, December 1988, *83*(404), pp. 1084–89.

Jenner, M. G. and Barney, G. O. Development, Security and North–South Relations: A Look into the Future. In *Jepma, C. J., ed.*, 1988, pp. 41–55.

Jennergren, L. Peter and Sørensen, Bjarne G. Price Formation in the Danish Stock Market in the 1890s. *Scand. Econ. Hist. Rev.*, 1988, 36(2), pp. 3–24.

Jennings, Lawrence C. and Eltis, David. Trade between Western Africa and the Atlantic World in the Pre-Colonial Era. *Amer. Hist. Rev.*, October 1988, 93(4), pp. 936–59.

Jennings, Robert H.; Lasser, Dennis J. and Hassell, John M. Management Earnings Forecasts: Their Usefulness as a Source of Firm-Specific Information to Security Analysts. *J. Finan. Res.*, Winter 1988, 11(4), pp. 303–19.

Jensen, Arne. The Telecommunication System in Society. **In** *Orishimo, I.; Hewings, G. J. D. and Nijkamp, P., eds.*, 1988, pp. 29–38.

Jensen, Flemming Dalby and Christoffersen, René M. Pensionsreform og den finansielle sektor. (Pension Savings and the Financial Sector. With English summary.) *Nationaløkon. Tidsskr.*, 1988, 126(2), pp. 205–16.

Jensen, Gail A. and Gabel, Jon R. The Erosion of Purchased Health Insurance. *Inquiry*, Fall 1988, 25(3), pp. 328–43.

Jensen, Hans E. The Theory of Human Nature. **In** *Tool, M. R., ed., Vol. 1,* 1988, 1987, pp. 89–123.

Jensen, James T. Implications of the Energy Provisions: Comment. **In** *Schott, J. J. and Smith, M. G., eds.*, 1988, pp. 131–35.

_____. Oil and Energy Demand: Outlook and Issues. **In** *Mabro, R., ed.*, 1988, pp. 17–40.

Jensen, Michael C. Characteristics of Targets of Hostile and Friendly Takeovers: Comment. **In** *Auerbach, A. J., ed. (I),* 1988, pp. 134–36.

_____. The Free Cash Flow Theory of Takeovers: A Financial Perspective on Mergers and Acquisitions and the Economy. **In** *Browne, L. E. and Rosengren, E. S., eds.*, 1988, pp. 102–43.

_____. The Takeover Controversy: Analysis and Evidence. **In** *Coffee, J. C., Jr.; Lowenstein, L. and Rose-Ackerman, S., eds.*, 1988, pp. 314–54.

_____. Takeovers: Their Causes and Consequences. *J. Econ. Perspectives*, Winter 1988, 2(1), pp. 21–48.

_____; **Murphy, Kevin J. and Baker, George P.** Compensation and Incentives: Practice vs. Theory. *J. Finance*, July 1988, 43(3), pp. 593–616.

_____ **and Warner, Jerold B.** The Distribution of Power among Corporate Managers, Shareholders, and Directors. *J. Finan. Econ.*, Jan.–March 1988, 20(1–2), pp. 3–24.

Jensen, Peter R. and Schap, David. Pathways to Pension Portability. *Challenge*, Jan.–Feb. 1988, 31(1), pp. 53–55.

Jensen, Richard. Information Capacity and Innovation Adoption. *Int. J. Ind. Organ.*, 1988, 6(3), pp. 335–50.

Jensen, Rodney C. and Hewings, Geoffrey J. D. Emerging Challenges in Regional Input–Output Analysis. *Ann. Reg. Sci.*, February 1988, 22, pp. 43–53.

_____; **Hewings, Geoffrey J. D. and Sonis, Michael.** Technical Innovation and Input–Output

Analysis. **In** *Orishimo, I.; Hewings, G. J. D. and Nijkamp, P., eds.*, 1988, pp. 163–94.

_____; **West, G. R. and Hewings, Geoffrey J. D.** The Study of Regional Economic Structure Using Input–Output Tables. *Reg. Stud.*, June 1988, 22(3), pp. 209–20.

Jenson, Jane. The Limits of 'and the' Discourse: French Women as Marginal Workers. **In** *Jenson, J.; Hagen, E. and Reddy, C., eds.*, 1988, pp. 155–72.

_____ **and Hagen, Elisabeth.** Paradoxes and Promises: Work and Politics in the Postwar Years. **In** *Jenson, J.; Hagen, E. and Reddy, C., eds.*, 1988, pp. 3–16.

Jeong, Jin-Ho and Maasoumi, Esfandiar. A Comparison of GRF and Other Reduced-Form Estimators in Simultaneous Equations Models. *J. Econometrics*, January 1988, 37(1), pp. 115–34.

Jepma, Catrinus J. The Impact of Untying Aid of the European Community Countries. *World Devel.*, July 1988, 16(7), pp. 797–805.

_____. North–South: Co-operation in Retrospect and Prospect: Introduction. **In** *Jepma, C. J., ed.*, 1988, pp. 1–24.

_____. Some Broad Development Policy Scenarios. **In** *Jepma, C. J., ed.*, 1988, pp. 207–25.

_____; **Brakman, Steven and Gigengack, Richard.** The Speed of Adjustment as a Measure for Competitiveness. *Empirica*, 1988, 15(1), pp. 161–78.

Jeppesen, Svend Erik; Paulsen, Knud B. and Schneider, Friedrich. Telecommunications in Denmark. **In** *Foreman-Peck, J. and Müller, J., eds.,*, 1988, pp. 109–29.

Jéquier, Nicolas and Bhalla, Ajit S. Telecommunications for Rural Development. **In** *Bhalla, A. S. and James, D., eds.*, 1988, pp. 269–83.

Jerdee, Thomas H. and Rosen, Benson. Managing Older Workers' Careers. **In** *Ferris, G. R. and Rowland, K. M., eds.*, 1988, pp. 37–74.

Jermakowicz, Wladyslaw W. Foundations and Prospects for Soviet Economic Reforms: 1949 to 1987. **In** *Liebowitz, R. D., ed.*, 1988, pp. 111–45.

_____. Reform Cycles in Poland, the USSR, the GDR, and Czechoslovakia. **In** *Marer, P. and Siwinski, W., eds.*, 1988, pp. 81–91.

Jermier, John M.; Cohen, Cynthia Fryer and Gaines, Jeannie. Paying Dues to the Union: A Study of Blue-Collar Workers in a Right-to-Work Environment. *J. Lab. Res.*, Spring 1988, 9(2), pp. 167–82.

Jerome, Robert T., Jr. and Horn, Robert N. GOSGAME: A Simulation of the Planning Process in the Soviet Union. *Comp. Econ. Stud.*, Spring 1988, 30(1), pp. 104–19.

Jerrell, Max E. and Morgan, James M. Modeling Labor Demand in a State Econometric Model. *Rev. Reg. Stud.*, Fall 1988, 18(3), pp. 31–40.

Jesse, Edward V. State Policy Choices: The Wisconsin Experience: Agricultural Policy. **In** *Danziger, S. H. and Witte, J. F., eds.*, 1988, pp. 231–49.

Jessell, Kenneth A.; McDaniel, William R. and McCarty, Daniel E. Discounted Cash Flow with Explicit Reinvestment Rates: Tutorial and Extension. *Financial Rev.*, August 1988, *23*(3), pp. 369–85.

Jeuland, Abel P. and Shugan, Steven M. Channel of Distribution Profits When Channel Members Form Conjectures: Note. *Marketing Sci.*, Spring 1988, *7*(2), pp. 202–10.

———— **and Shugan, Steven M.** Competitive Pricing Behavior in Distribution Systems. In *Devinney, T. M., ed.*, 1988, pp. 219–37.

———— **and Shugan, Steven M.** Reply to: Managing Channel Profits: Comment. *Marketing Sci.*, Winter 1988, *7*(1), pp. 103–06.

Jevons, H. S. William Stanley Jevons: His Scientific Contributions. In *Wood, J. C., ed., Vol. 1,* 1988, *1934,* pp. 44–49.

Jevons, H. W. William Stanley Jevons: His Life. In *Wood, J. C., ed., Vol. 1,* 1988, *1934,* pp. 37–43.

Jevons, T. E. Mr. Wicksteed's Notes upon Jevons. In *Wood, J. C., ed., Vol. 2,* 1988, *1889,* pp. 46–48.

Jewell, Nicholas P.; Wu, C. F. Jeff and Tsui, Kwok-Leung. A Nonparametric Approach to the Truncated Regression Problem. *J. Amer. Statist. Assoc.*, September 1988, *83*(403), pp. 785–92.

Jewitt, Ian. Justifying the First-Order Approach to Principal–Agent Problems. *Econometrica*, September 1988, *56*(5), pp. 1177–90.

———— **and Grout, Paul A.** Employee Buy-Outs: Some Theoretical Issues. *Int. J. Ind. Organ.*, March 1988, *6*(1), pp. 33–45.

Ježek, Jiří. International Economic Organizations. *Czech. Econ. Digest.*, August 1988, (5), pp. 51–57.

Jha, Dayanatha; Delgado, Christopher L. and Ranade, C. G. Technological Change, Production Costs, and Supply Response. In *Mellor, J. W. and Ahmed, R., eds.,* 1988, pp. 190–203.

Jha, Shri L. K. Human Resources Development and the Planning Process in India: Valedictory Address. In *Kohli, U. and Gautam, V., eds.,* 1988, pp. 280–86.

Jia, Yunzhen. The Future Market for China's Coal. In *Dorian, J. P. and Fridley, D. G., eds.,* 1988, pp. 59–63.

Jick, Todd; McKersie, Robert B. and Greenhalgh, Leonard. Change and Continuity: The Role of a Labor–Management Committee in Facilitating Work Force Change during Retrenchment. In *Lewin, D., et al., eds.,* 1988, *1981,* pp. 569–80.

Jiggins, Janice. Beware the Greeks Bearing Gifts: Reflections on Donor Behaviour and Cooperative Performance. In *Hedlund, H., ed.,* 1988, pp. 109–23.

Jimenez, Emmanuel. Urban Services and Rural Infrastructure. *Finance Develop.*, September 1988, *25*(3), pp. 6–8.

————**; Lockheed, Marlaine and Wattanawaha, Nongnuch.** The Relative Efficiency of Private and Public Schools: The Case of Thailand. *World Bank Econ. Rev.*, May 1988, *2*(2), pp. 139–64.

————**; Mayo, Stephen K. and Friedman, Joseph.** The Demand for Tenure Security in Developing Countries. *J. Devel. Econ.*, September 1988, *29*(2), pp. 185–98.

Jinyan, Li. People's Republic of China: Taxation of Private Business and Private Investors. *Bull. Int. Fiscal Doc.*, October 1988, *42*(10), pp. 415–20.

Jirousek, Radim and Kríz, O. An Expert System Accepting Knowledge in a Form of Statistical Data. In *Edwards, D. and Raun, N. E., eds.,* 1988, pp. 123–28.

Jo, Hoje and Huang, Roger D. Tests of Market Models: Heteroskedasticity or Misspecification? *J. Banking Finance*, September 1988, *12*(3), pp. 439–55.

Joachimsthaler, Erich A. and Lastovicka, John L. Improving the Detection of Personality–Behavior Relationships in Consumer Research. *J. Cons. Res.*, March 1988, *14*(4), pp. 583–87.

Joanette, François P. and VanDerhei, Jack L. Economic Determinants for the Choice of Actuarial Cost Methods. *J. Risk Ins.*, March 1988, *55*(1), pp. 59–74.

Joaquin, Domingo Castelo. A Reconsideration of the Focal Outcomes Approach to Portfolio Selection. *J. Post Keynesian Econ.*, Summer 1988, *10*(4), pp. 631–45.

Jobse, Rein B. and Needham, Barrie. The Economic Future of the Randstad, Holland. *Urban Stud.*, August 1988, *25*(4), pp. 282–96.

Jobson, J. D. Stable Factors in Security Returns: Identification Using Cross-Validation: Comment. *J. Bus. Econ. Statist.*, January 1988, *6*(1), pp. 16–20.

———— **and Korkie, Bob M.** The Trouble with Performance Measurement: Comment. *J. Portfol. Manage.*, Winter 1988, *14*(2), pp. 74–76.

Joerding, Wayne. Are Stock Prices Excessively Sensitive to Current Information? *J. Econ. Behav. Organ.*, January 1988, *9*(1), pp. 71–85.

————. Excess Stock Price Volatility as a Misspecified Euler Equation. *J. Finan. Quant. Anal.*, September 1988, *23*(3), pp. 253–67.

Joerges, Bernward. Large Technical Systems: Concepts and Issues. In *Mayntz, R. and Hughes, T. P., eds.,* 1988, pp. 9–36.

Jog, S. D.; Khaled, S. M. and Sethuraman, T. V. Market Saturation in Indian Conditions: Cement Industry: A Case Study. *Indian Econ. J.*, Jan.–March 1988, *35*(3), pp. 39–46.

Jogan, S. Some Specific Elements Concerning the Legislative Process of the S.F.R. of Yugoslavia. In *Pizzorusso, A., ed.,* 1988, pp. 332–41.

Joh, Gun-Ho and Jain, Prem C. The Dependence between Hourly Prices and Trading Volume. *J. Finan. Quant. Anal.*, September 1988, *23*(3), pp. 269–83.

Johansen, Leif. A Calculus Approach to the Theory of the Core of an Exchange Economy. In *Ricketts, M., ed., Vol. 1,* 1988, *1978,* pp. 106–13.

Johansen, Søren. Statistical Analysis of Cointegration Vectors. *J. Econ. Dynam. Control*, June–Sept. 1988, *12*(2–3), pp. 231–54.

Johanson, Jan and Håkansson, Håkan. Formal

and Informal Cooperation Strategies in International Networks. In *Contractor, F. J. and Lorange, P.*, 1988, pp. 369–79.

————— **and Mattsson, Lars-Gunnar.** Internationalisation in Industrial Systems—A Network Approach. In *Hood, N. and Vahlne, J.-E., eds.*, 1988, pp. 287–314.

Johansson, Per-Olov. Option Value: Comment. *Land Econ.*, February 1988, *64*(1), pp. 86–87.

————— **and Kriström, B.** Measuring Values for Improved Air Quality from Discrete Response Data: Two Experiments. *J. Agr. Econ.*, September 1988, *39*(3), pp. 439–45.

Johansson, Ulla-Stina and Montgomery, Henry. Life Values: Their Structure and Relation to Life Situation. In *Maital, S., ed., Vol. 1*, 1988, pp. 420–37.

John, A. Meredith. Plantation Slave Mortality in Trinidad. *Population Stud.*, July 1988, *42*(2), pp. 161–82.

—————; **Menken, Jane A. and Trussell, James.** Estimating the Distribution of Interval Length: Current Status and Retrospective History Data. *Population Stud.*, March 1988, *42*(1), pp. 115–27.

John, Andrew and Cooper, Russell. Coordinating Coordination Failures in Keynesian Models. *Quart. J. Econ.*, August 1988, *103*(3), pp. 441–63.

John, George and Weitz, Barton A. Forward Integration into Distribution: An Empirical Test of Transaction Cost Analysis. *J. Law, Econ., Organ.*, Fall 1988, *4*(2), pp. 337–55.

Johnes, Geraint. Shake-Outs and Shake-Ins of Labour: An Example of the Riemann–Hugoniot Catastrophe? *Indian Econ. J.*, Oct.–Dec. 1988, *36*(2), pp. 24–29.

Johns, M. Vernon. Importance Sampling for Bootstrap Confidence Intervals. *J. Amer. Statist. Assoc.*, September 1988, *83*(403), pp. 709–14.

Johnsen, Arve. The Outlook for Norwegian Oil. In *Mabro, R., ed.*, 1988, pp. 141–45.

Johnson, Björn. An Institutional Approach to the Small-Country Problem. In *Freeman, C. and Lundvall, B.-A., eds.*, 1988, pp. 279–97.

Johnson, Bruce. OMB and the Budget Examiner: Changes in the Reagan Era. *Public Budg. Finance*, Winter 1988, *8*(4), pp. 3–21.

Johnson, Charles J. and Clark, Allen L. Mineral Exploration in Developing Countries: Botswana and Papua New Guinea Case Studies. In *Tilton, J. E.; Eggert, R. G. and Landsberg, H. H., eds.*, 1988, pp. 145–78.

Johnson, Charles R. and Hihn, Jairus M. Evaluation Techniques for Paired Ratio-Comparison Matrices in a Hierarchical Decision Model. In *Eichhorn, W., ed.*, 1988, pp. 269–88.

Johnson, Christopher. The Economics of Britain's Electricity Privatization. In *Johnson, C., ed.*, 1988, pp. 60–76.

—————. Privatization and Ownership: Introduction. In *Johnson, C., ed.*, 1988, pp. 1–8.

Johnson, D. Gale. Constraints on Price Adjustments: Structural, Institutional and Financial Rigidities. In *Antonelli, G. and Quadrio-Curzio, A., eds.*, 1988, pp. 81–102.

—————. Economic Reforms in the People's Republic of China. *Econ. Develop. Cult. Change*, Supplement, April 1988, *36*(3), pp. S225–45.

—————. Paradoxes in World Agriculture. In *Anderson, A. and Bark, D. L., eds.*, 1988, pp. 237–49.

—————. Policy Implications. In *Schwarz, F. H., ed.*, 1988, pp. 1–10.

—————. The Soviet Union Today: Agriculture. In *Cracraft, J., ed.*, 1988, pp. 198–209.

—————. U.S.–Canadian Agricultural Trade Challenges: Developing Common Approaches: Summing Up: The U.S. Perspective. In *Allen, K. and Macmillan, K., eds.*, 1988, pp. 189–92.

Johnson, D. S. and Browne, B. M. Infant Mortality in Inter-war Northern Ireland. In *Mitchison, R. and Roebuck, P., eds.*, 1988, pp. 277–87.

Johnson, Dale A.; Shows, E. Warren and Power, Fred B. Lump-Sum Awards in Workers' Compensation: Comment. *J. Risk Ins.*, December 1988, *55*(4), pp. 734–39.

Johnson, David. The Measurement of Poverty in Australia: 1981–82 and 1985–86. *Australian Econ. Rev.*, Spring 1988, (83), pp. 13–24.

Johnson, David R. The Currency Denomination of Long-term Debt in the Canadian Corporate Sector: An Empirical Analysis. *J. Int. Money Finance*, March 1988, *7*(1), pp. 77–90.

Johnson, David T. and Dixon, Peter B. Pricing of Queensland Sugar Cane: Appraisal of the Present Formula and a Suggestion for Reform. *Rev. Marketing Agr. Econ.*, April 1988, *56*(1), pp. 27–35.

Johnson, Denise R. and Dahringer, Lee D. Lemon Laws: Intent, Experience, and a Proconsumer Model. *J. Cons. Aff.*, Summer 1988, *22*(1), pp. 158–70.

Johnson, Douglas H. Sudanese Military Slavery from the Eighteenth to the Twentieth Century. In *Archer, L. J., ed.*, 1988, pp. 142–56.

Johnson, Elmer W. and Gustafson, James M. Efficiency, Morality, and Managerial Effectiveness. In *Meyer, J. R. and Gustafson, J. M., eds.*, 1988, pp. 193–209.

Johnson, F. Reed and Smith, V. Kerry. How Do Risk Perceptions Respond to Information? The Case of Radon. *Rev. Econ. Statist.*, February 1988, *70*(1), pp. 1–8.

Johnson, G. V.; Miltz, D. and Braden, J. B. Standards versus Prices Revisited: The Case of Agricultural Non-point Source Pollution. *J. Agr. Econ.*, September 1988, *39*(3), pp. 360–68.

Johnson, Glenn L. Technological Innovations with Implications for Agricultural Economics. In *Hildreth, R. J., et al., eds.*, 1988, pp. 82–108.

Johnson, Harry G. The Case for Flexible Exchange Rates, 1969. In *Melamed, L., ed.*, 1988, 1973, pp. 43–70.

Johnson, Hazel. Survival and Change on the Land. In *Crow, B. and Thorpe, M., et al.*, 1988, pp. 147–62.

————— **and Crow, Ben.** Developing Production on the Land. In *Crow, B. and Thorpe, M., et al.*, 1988, pp. 127–46.

Johnson, Herb and Blomeyer, Edward C. An Empirical Examination of the Pricing of American Put Options. *J. Finan. Quant. Anal.*, March 1988, *23*(1), pp. 13–22.

_____; Castanias, Rick and Chung, Ki-Young. Dividend Spreads. *J. Bus.*, July 1988, *61*(3), pp. 299–319.

_____ and Grinblatt, Mark. A Put Option Paradox. *J. Finan. Quant. Anal.*, March 1988, *23*(1), pp. 23–26.

Johnson, Howard. Labour Systems in Postemancipation Bahamas. *Soc. Econ. Stud.*, March–June 1988, *37*(1–2), pp. 181–201.

Johnson, James D. and Baum, Kenneth. Improving the Socioeconomic Data Base: A Discussion. In *Hildreth, R. J., et al., eds.*, 1988, pp. 484–89.

Johnson, Kenneth P.; Friedenberg, Howard L. and Renshaw, Vernon. Tracking the BEA Regional Projections, 1983–86. *Surv. Curr. Bus.*, June 1988, *68*(6), pp. 23–27.

Johnson, Kirsten. Women and the Rural Energy Economy of Zimbabwe: Research Findings and Policy Issues. In *Hosier, R. H., ed. (I)*, 1988, pp. 110–41.

Johnson, L. E. *The Legacy of Ricardo:* A Review Article. *Rivista Int. Sci. Econ. Com.*, August 1988, *35*(8), pp. 781–96.

Johnson, Lester W. Cigarette Advertising and Public Policy. *Int. J. Soc. Econ.*, 1988, *15*(7), pp. 76–80.

Johnson, Manuel H. Current Perspectives on Monetary Policy. *Cato J.*, Fall 1988, *8*(2), pp. 253–60.

_____. Statement to the U.S. House Subcommittee on International Development Institutions and Finance and the Subcommittee on International Finance, Trade and Monetary Policy of the Committee on Banking, Finance and Urban Affairs, March 9, 1988. *Fed. Res. Bull.*, May 1988, *74*(5), pp. 297–300.

_____. Statement to the U.S. Senate Committee on Banking, Housing, and Urban Affairs, September 8, 1988. *Fed. Res. Bull.*, November 1988, *74*(11), pp. 733–43.

Johnson, Merrill L. Labor Environment and the Location of Electrical Machinery Employment in the U.S. South. *Growth Change*, Spring 1988, *19*(2), pp. 56–74.

Johnson, Michael D. Comparability and Hierarchical Processing in Multialternative Choice. *J. Cons. Res.*, December 1988, *15*(3), pp. 303–14.

Johnson, Nan E. The Pace of Births over the Life Course: Implications for the Minority-Group Status Hypothesis. *Soc. Sci. Quart.*, March 1988, *69*(1), pp. 95–107.

Johnson, Neal S. and Adams, Richard M. Benefits of Increased Streamflow: The Case of the John Day River Steelhead Fishery. *Water Resources Res.*, November 1988, *24*(11), pp. 1839–46.

Johnson, Omotunde E. G. Agriculture and Fund-Supported Adjustment Programs. *Finance Develop.*, June 1988, *25*(2), pp. 38–40.

Johnson, Paul Edward. On the Theory of Political Competition: Comparative Statics from a General Allocative Perspective. *Public Choice*, September 1988, *58*(3), pp. 217–35.

Johnson, Paul R. Issues in World Agriculture—A U.S. Perspective: A Discussion. In *Hildreth, R. J., et al., eds.*, 1988, pp. 168–70.

_____ and Alston, Julian M. Factor Price Equalisation among International Farmland Markets. *Australian J. Agr. Econ.*, Aug.–Dec. 1988, *32*(2–3), pp. 142–52.

Johnson, Peter. A Note on the Modelling of the Formation Decision: Two Studies Compared [Firm Formation in Manufacturing] [New Firm Formation—A Labour Market Approach to Industrial Entry]. *Scot. J. Polit. Econ.*, May 1988, *35*(2), pp. 176–80.

_____. Small Business Policy and Entrepreneurship. In *Darnell, A. and Evans, L., eds.*, 1988, pp. 43–56.

Johnson, Philip McBride. After the Crash: Linkages between Stocks and Futures: Trading Systems. In *MacKay, R. J., ed.*, 1988, pp. 72–74.

Johnson, Phyllis and Martin, David. South Africa Imposes Sanctions against Its Neighbours. In *United Nations*, 1988, pp. 56–83.

Johnson, R. Stafford; Fiore, Lyle and Zuber, Richard A. A Note on the Investment Performances of Different Price-Earnings Stock. *Rivista Int. Sci. Econ. Com.*, Oct.–Nov. 1988, *35*(10–11), pp. 1067–74.

Johnson, Richard A. and Weerahandi, Samaradasa. A Bayesian Solution to the Multivariate Behrens–Fisher Problem. *J. Amer. Statist. Assoc.*, March 1988, *83*(401), pp. 145–49.

Johnson, Robert A. and Loopesko, Bonnie. Realignment of the Yen–Dollar Exchange Rate: Aspects of the Adjustment Process in Japan. In *Marston, R. C., ed.*, 1988, pp. 105–44.

Johnson, Sam H., III. Large-Scale Irrigation and Drainage Schemes in Pakistan. In *O'Mara, G. T., ed.*, 1988, pp. 58–77.

Johnson, Stanley R. Quantitative Techniques. In *Hildreth, R. J., et al., eds.*, 1988, pp. 177–98.

_____ and Holt, Matthew T. Supply Dynamics in the U.S. Hog Industry. *Can. J. Agr. Econ.*, July 1988, *36*(2), pp. 313–35.

_____ and Teklu, Tesfaye. Demand Systems from Cross-Section Data: An Application to Indonesia. *Can. J. Agr. Econ.*, March 1988, *36*(1), pp. 83–101.

Johnson, Stephen; Kotlikoff, Laurence J. and Samuelson, William F. Consumption, Computation Mistakes, and Fiscal Policy. *Amer. Econ. Rev.*, May 1988, *78*(2), pp. 408–12.

Johnson, Steven B. and VanDerhei, Jack L. Fiduciary Decision Making and the Nature of Private Pension Fund Investment Behavior. *J. Risk Ins.*, December 1988, *55*(4), pp. 692–700.

Johnson, Thomas G. Economic Theories of Infrastructure Decision-Making. In *Johnson, T. G.; Deaton, B. J. and Segarra, E., eds.*, 1988, pp. 7–20.

_____; Deaton, Brady J. and Segarra, Eduardo. Infrastructure Investment: Alternatives and

Priorities. In *Johnson, T. G.; Deaton, B. J. and Segarra, E.*, eds., 1988, pp. 261–64.

_____ **and Halstead, John M.** Using Fiscal Impact Models in Local Infrastructure Investment Decisions. In *Johnson, T. G.; Deaton, B. J. and Segarra, E.*, eds., 1988, pp. 99–107.

_____; **Kellogg, Robert L. and Easley, J. E., Jr.** Optimal Timing of Harvest for the North Carolina Bay Scallop Fishery. *Amer. J. Agr. Econ.*, February 1988, 70(1), pp. 50–62.

_____; **Kriesel, Warren P. and Deaton, Brady J.** Investing in Economic Development Infrastructure: A Decision-Making Framework. In *Johnson, T. G.; Deaton, B. J. and Segarra, E.*, eds., 1988, pp. 155–62.

Johnson, Thomas S. U.S. External Debt and LDC Debt: Twin Problems. In *Feldstein, M.*, ed. *(II)*, 1988, pp. 196–201.

Johnson, W. Bruce. Debt Refunding and Shareholder Wealth: The Price Effects of Debt-for-Debt Exchange Offer Announcements. *Financial Rev.*, February 1988, 23(1), pp. 1–23.

_____ **and Dhaliwal, Dan S.** LIFO Abandonment. *J. Acc. Res.*, Autumn 1988, 26(2), pp. 236–72.

Johnson, William G. and Lambrinos, James. Disability Related Categories: An Alternative to Wage Loss Benefits for Injured Workers. In *Borba, P. S. and Appel, D.*, eds., 1988, pp. 35–57.

Johnson, William R. Income Redistribution in a Federal System. *Amer. Econ. Rev.*, June 1988, 78(3), pp. 570–73.

_____ **and Skinner, Jonathan.** Accounting for Changes in the Labor Supply of Recently Divorced Women. *J. Human Res.*, Fall 1988, 23(4), pp. 417–36.

Johnston, Bruce F. The Political Economy of Agricultural and Rural Development. In *Asefa, S.*, ed., 1988, pp. 35–45.

Johnston, George M. The Role of Economics in Natural Resource and Environmental Policy Analysis. In *Johnston, G. M.; Freshwater, D. and Favero, P.*, eds., 1988, pp. 1–18.

Johnston, K. and Clark, Gordon L. The Geography of U.S. Union Elections: Addenda. *Environ. Planning A*, July 1988, 20(7), pp. 979–82.

Johnston, Warren E. The WAEA—Which Niche in the Profession? *Western J. Agr. Econ.*, July 1988, 13(1), pp. 140–48.

Johnston, Wesley J. and Benton, W. C. Bargaining, Negotiations, and Personal Selling. In *van Raaij, W. F.; van Veldhoven, G. M. and Wärneryd, K.-E.*, eds., 1988, pp. 449–71.

Johnstone, Iain. How Far Are Automatically Chosen Regression Smoothing Parameters from Their Optimum?: Comment. *J. Amer. Statist. Assoc.*, March 1988, 83(401), pp. 99.

Joines, Douglas H. Deficits and Money Growth in the United States: Reply. *J. Monet. Econ.*, January 1988, 21(1), pp. 155–60.

_____; **Phillips, G. Michael and Clark, Truman A.** Social Security Payments, Money Supply Announcements, and Interest Rates. *J. Monet. Econ.*, September 1988, 22(2), pp. 257–78.

Jolly, Richard. Poverty and Adjustment in the 1990s. In *Lewis, J. P., et al.*, 1988, pp. 163–75.

_____. A UNICEF Perspective on the Effects of Economic Crises and What Can Be Done. In *Bell, D. E. and Reich, M. R.*, eds., 1988, pp. 81–102.

Jones, Andrew M. and Dardanoni, Valentino. Stochastic Habits and the Consumption/Savings Decision. *Stud. Econ.*, 1988, 43(34), pp. 3–12.

_____ **and Posnett, John.** The Revenue and Welfare Effects of Cigarette Taxes. *Appl. Econ.*, September 1988, 20(9), pp. 1223–32.

Jones, Barbara A. P. NEA Presidential Address: Economics Programs at Historically Black Colleges and Universities. *Rev. Black Polit. Econ.*, Winter 1988, 16(3), pp. 5–14.

Jones, Brian R.; Montador, R. Bruce and Hagemann, Robert P. Tax Reform in OECD Countries: Motives, Constraints and Practice. *OECD Econ. Stud.*, Spring 1988, (10), pp. 185–226.

Jones, Byrd L. A Quest for National Leadership: Institutionalization of Economics at Harvard. In *Barber, W. J.*, ed., 1988, pp. 95–131.

Jones, C. Vaughan. The Law of Demand and Commodities Sold at a Rate Schedule. *Amer. Econ.*, Spring 1988, 32(1), pp. 39–43.

Jones, Clifton T. and Griffin, James M. Economies of Scale in a Multiplant Technology: Evidence from the Oilpatch. *Econ. Inquiry*, January 1988, 26(1), pp. 107–22.

Jones, David C. The Use of Accounting for Municipal Management Purposes. In *Most, K. S.*, ed., 1988, pp. 297–308.

Jones, David D. How Do We Pay for the Budget Deficit? *Challenge*, Nov.–Dec. 1988, 31(6), pp. 60–61.

Jones, David R. The Soviet Union Today: The Armed Forces: Organization and Deployment. In *Cracraft, J.*, ed., 1988, pp. 89–104.

Jones, Donald W. Monopsony and Plant Location in a Thünen Land Use Model. *J. Reg. Sci.*, August 1988, 28(3), pp. 317–27.

_____. Some Simple Economics of Improved Cookstove Programs in Developing Countries. *Resources & Energy*, September 1988, 10(3), pp. 247–64.

Jones, Douglas N. Regulatory Concepts, Propositions, and Doctrines: Casualties and Survivors. *J. Econ. Issues*, December 1988, 22(4), pp. 1089–1108.

Jones, E. L. and Anderson, J. L. Natural Disasters and the Historical Response. *Australian Econ. Hist. Rev.*, March 1988, 28(1), pp. 3–20.

Jones, George. On the Necessity of Cardinal Utility: Presidential Address. *J. Agr. Econ.*, September 1988, 39(3), pp. 311–25.

Jones, Ian. An Evaluation of YTS. *Oxford Rev. Econ. Policy*, Autumn 1988, 4(3), pp. 54–71.

Jones, J. C. H. and Ferguson, D. G. Location and Survival in the National Hockey League. *J. Ind. Econ.*, June 1988, 36(4), pp. 443–57.

_____ **and Walsh, William D.** Salary Determination in the National Hockey League: The Effects of Skills, Franchise Characteristics, and Discrimination. *Ind. Lab. Relat. Rev.*, July 1988, *41*(4), pp. 592–604.

Jones, J. Morgan and Landwehr, Jane T. Removing Heterogeneity Bias from Logit Model Estimation. *Marketing Sci.*, Winter 1988, *7*(1), pp. 41–59.

Jones, John B., Jr. and Mattson, Robert N. Tax Treatment of Computer Software: General Report. In *International Fiscal Association, ed. (II)*, 1988, pp. 19–44.

Jones, John, Jr. Matrix Differential Equations and Lyapunov Transformations. In *Eiselt, H. A. and Pederzoli, G., eds.*, 1988, pp. 1–14.

Jones, Jonathan D. Seasonal Variation in Interest Rates. *Atlantic Econ. J.*, June 1988, *16*(2), pp. 47–58.

_____ and Bezdek, Roger H. Federal Categorical Grants-in-Aid and State–Local Government Expenditures. *Public Finance*, 1988, *43*(1), pp. 39–55.

_____ and Khilji, Nasir M. Money Growth, Inflation, and Causality (Empirical Evidence for Pakistan, 1973–85). *Pakistan Devel. Rev.*, Spring 1988, *27*(1), pp. 45–58.

_____ and Sattar, Zaidi. Money, Inflation, Output, and Causality: The Bangladesh Case, 1974–1985. *Bangladesh Devel. Stud.*, March 1988, *16*(1), pp. 73–83.

_____ and Walsh, Michael J. More Evidence on the "Border Tax" Effect: The Case of West Virginia, 1979–84. *Nat. Tax J.*, June 1988, *41*(2), pp. 261–65.

Jones, Kit J. Fifty Years of Economic Research: A Brief History of the National Institute of Economic and Social Research 1938–88. *Nat. Inst. Econ. Rev.*, May 1988, (124), pp. 36–62.

Jones, Larry E. The Characteristics Model, Hedonic Prices, and the Clientele Effect. *J. Polit. Econ.*, June 1988, *96*(3), pp. 551–67.

Jones, Lonnie L.; Murdock, Steve H. and Leistritz, F. Larry. Economic-Demographic Projection Models: An Overview of Recent Developments for Infrastructure Analysis. In *Johnson, T. G.; Deaton, B. J. and Segarra, E., eds.*, 1988, pp. 87–97.

Jones, Peter C. Corporate Debt Restructuring in LDCs. *Finance Develop.*, December 1988, *25*(4), pp. 34–36.

Jones, Peter d'A. Henry George and British Socialism. *Amer. J. Econ. Soc.*, October 1988, *47*(4), pp. 473–91.

Jones, Peter T. and Teece, David J. The Research Agenda on Competitiveness: A Program of Research for the Nation's Business Schools. In *Furino, A., ed.*, 1988, pp. 101–14.

_____ and Teece, David J. What We Know and What We Don't Know about Competitiveness. In *Furino, A., ed.*, 1988, pp. 265–330.

Jones, Philip R. Defense Alliances and International Trade. *J. Conflict Resolution*, March 1988, *32*(1), pp. 123–40.

_____ and Cullis, John G. Employment of the Disabled: A Rationale for Legislation in the United Kingdom. *Int. Rev. Law Econ.*, June 1988, *8*(1), pp. 37–49.

Jones, Rich and Whalley, John. Regional Effects of Taxes in Canada: An Applied General Equilibrium Approach. *J. Public Econ.*, October 1988, *37*(1), pp. 1–28.

Jones, Robert and Black, Fischer. Simplifying Portfolio Insurance for Corporate Pension Plans. *J. Portfol. Manage.*, Summer 1988, *14*(4), pp. 33–37.

Jones, Ronald W. Tax Wedges and Mobile Capital. In *Haaland, J. I. and Norman, V. D., eds.*, 1988, pp. 119–30.

Jones, Rowan H. Converting the Recognized Needs of Municipal Financial Report Users into Responsive Accounting Systems. In *Most, K. S., ed.*, 1988, pp. 287–95.

_____ and Chan, James L. Comparative Governmental Accounting: An Introductory Note. In *Chan, J. L. and Jones, R. H., eds.*, 1988, pp. 3–10.

_____ and Pendlebury, Maurice. Governmental Accounting, Auditing and Financial Reporting in the United Kingdom. In *Chan, J. L. and Jones, R. H., eds.*, 1988, pp. 52–81.

Jones, S. E.; Kavvas, M. L. and Govindaraju, R. S. On the Diffusion Wave Model for Overland Flow 2. Steady State Analysis. *Water Resources Res.*, May 1988, *24*(5), pp. 745–54.

_____; Kavvas, M. L. and Govindaraju, R. S. On the Diffusion Wave Model for Overland Flow 1. Solution for Steep Slopes. *Water Resources Res.*, May 1988, *24*(5), pp. 734–44.

Jones, Stephen R. G. The Relationship between Unemployment Spells and Reservation Wages as a Test of Search Theory. *Quart. J. Econ.*, November 1988, *103*(4), pp. 741–65.

Jones, Stuart. Banking and Business in South Africa: Introduction. In *Jones, S., ed.*, 1988, pp. 1–25.

_____. The Visible Hand and the Top 100 Companies in South Africa, 1964–84. In *Jones, S., ed.*, 1988, pp. 133–53.

de Jong, Eelke. Expectation Formation: Criteria and an Assessment. *De Economist*, 1988, *136*(4), pp. 435–67.

_____ and Jager, Henk. The Private Ecu's Potential Impact on Global and European Exchange Rate Stability. *Banca Naz. Lavoro Quart. Rev.*, March 1988, (164), pp. 33–59.

de Jong, Henk Wouter. Market Structures in the European Economic Community. In *de Jong, H. W., ed.*, 1988, pp. 1–39.

_____. The Structure of European Industry: Introduction. In *de Jong, H. W., ed.*, 1988, pp. xi–xii.

Jongen, Stephane. L'actionnariat des salaries: Ses principales formes. (Employee Ownership: The Principal Types. With English summary.) *Ann. Pub. Co-op. Econ.*, April–June 1988, *59*(2), pp. 229–55.

de Jongh, P. J.; de Wet, T. and Welsh, A. H. Mallows-Type Bounded-Influence–Regression Trimmed Means. *J. Amer. Statist. Assoc.*, September 1988, *83*(403), pp. 805–10.

Jonish, James. Laser Technology for Land Level-

ling in Egypt. In *Bhalla, A. S. and James, D.,
eds.*, 1988, pp. 205–22.

Jonscher, Charles. Information and Productivity:
An Attempted Replication of an Empirical Exercise: Rejoinder. *Info. Econ. Policy*, 1988,
3(1), pp. 69–73.

Jonsson, Ernst. Local Government Finance in
Sweden—Present Status and Recent Trends.
In *Paddison, R. and Bailey, S., eds.*, 1988,
pp. 190–217.

Jonung, Lars. Knut Wicksell's Unpublished
Manuscripts: A First Glance. *Europ. Econ.
Rev.*, March 1988, 32(2–3), pp. 503–11.

_____ **and Bordo, Michael D.** Some Qualms
about the Test of the Institutionalist Hypothesis of the Long-run Behavior of Velocity: Reply.
Econ. Inquiry, July 1988, 26(3), pp. 547–49.

_____ **and Laidler, David E.** Are Perceptions
of Inflation Rational? Some Evidence for Sweden. *Amer. Econ. Rev.*, December 1988, 78(5),
pp. 1080–87.

Jordan, Bradford D. and Pettengill, Glenn N.
A Comprehensive Examination of Volume Effects and Seasonality in Daily Security Returns.
J. Finan. Res., Spring 1988, 11(1), pp. 57–70.

_____; **Verbrugge, James A. and Burns, Richard
M.** Returns to Initial Shareholders in Savings
Institution Conversions: Evidence and Regulatory Implications. *J. Finan. Res.*, Summer
1988, 11(2), pp. 125–36.

Jordan, J. S. The Continuity of Optimal Dynamic
Decision Rules. In *Grandmont, J.-M., ed.*,
1988, 1977, pp. 101–12.

_____. A Stability Problem with Nonstationary
Overlapping Generations Equilibria. *J. Econ.
Theory*, August 1988, 45(2), pp. 425–33.

Jordan, Jerry L. The Economic Role of Government. *Bus. Econ.*, January 1988, 23(1), pp. 14–
20.

_____. Weakening the Dollar: The Tax No One
Has to Vote For. In *Boaz, D., ed.*, 1988, pp.
175–86.

**Jordan, John M.; Meador, Mark and Walters,
Stephen J. K.** Effects of Department Size and
Organization on the Research Productivity of
Academic Economists. *Econ. Educ. Rev.*,
1988, 7(2), pp. 251–55.

Jordan, Peter G. and Polenske, Karen R. Multiplier Impacts of Fishing Activities in New England and Nova Scotia. In *Ciaschini, M., ed.*,
1988, pp. 325–66.

Jordan, William Chester. Women and Credit in
the Middle Ages: Problems and Directions. *J.
Europ. Econ. Hist.*, Spring 1988, 17(1), pp.
33–62.

Jorge, Antonio and Salazar-Carrillo, Jorge. Foreign Investment, Debt and Economic Growth
in Latin America: An Introductory Overview.
In *Jorge, A. and Salazar-Carrillo, J., eds.*,
1988, pp. 3–10.

_____ **and Salazar-Carrillo, Jorge.** The Use of
Prices for Comparisons in Developing Command Economies. In *Salazar-Carrillo, J. and
Rao, D. S. P., eds.*, 1988, pp. 299–304.

Jørgensen, Steffen and Dockner, Engelbert J.
Optimal Pricing Strategies for New Products

in Dynamic Oligopolies. *Marketing Sci.*, Fall
1988, 7(4), pp. 315–34.

**Jørgensen, Ulrik; Dalum, Bent and Fagerberg,
Jan.** Small Open Economies in the World Market for Electronics: The Case of the Nordic
Countries. In *Freeman, C. and Lundvall,
B.-A., eds.*, 1988, pp. 113–38.

Jorgenson, Dale W. Productivity and Economic
Growth in Japan and the United States. *Amer.
Econ. Rev.*, May 1988, 78(2), pp. 217–22.

_____. Productivity and Postwar U.S. Economic
Growth. *J. Econ. Perspectives*, Fall 1988, 2(4),
pp. 23–41.

_____ **and Griliches, Zvi.** The Explanation of
Productivity Change. In *Griliches, Z.*, 1988,
1967, pp. 308–50.

_____; **Slesnick, Daniel T. and Stoker, Thomas
M.** Two-Stage Budgeting and Exact Aggregation. *J. Bus. Econ. Statist.*, July 1988, 6(3),
pp. 313–25.

Jörin, R. The Videotex Program "Research and
Advice" in Switzerland. In *Schiefer, G., ed.*,
1988, pp. 135–44.

Jorion, Philippe and Giovannini, Alberto. Foreign Exchange Risk Premia Volatility Once
Again [Interest Rates and Risk Premia in the
Stock Market and in the Foreign Exchange
Market]. *J. Int. Money Finance*, March 1988,
7(1), pp. 111–13.

Joseph, Rebecca. Labour Conditions in the Indonesian Batik Industry. In *Kathuria, S.; Miralao, V. and Joseph, R.*, 1988, pp. 57–70.

_____. Women's Roles in the Indonesian Batik
Industry: Some Implications of Occupational
Segregation in Crafts. In *Kathuria, S.; Miralao,
V. and Joseph, R.*, 1988, pp. 71–89.

Josephson, R. M. and Zbeetnoff, D. M. The
Value of Probability Distribution Information
for Fertilizer Application Decisions. *Can. J.
Agr. Econ.*, Part 2, December 1988, 36(4), pp.
837–44.

Joshi, Heather and Overton, Elizabeth. Forecasting the Female Labour Force in Britain. *Int.
J. Forecasting*, 1988, 4(2), pp. 269–85.

_____ **and Owen, Susan.** Demographic Predictors of Women's Work in Postwar Britain.
In *Schultz, T. Paul, ed.*, 1988, pp. 401–47.

Joshi, Vijay and Bliss, Christopher. Exchange
Rate Protection and Exchange Rate Conflict.
Oxford Econ. Pap., June 1988, 40(2), pp. 365–
77.

Joskow, Paul L. Asset Specificity and the Structure of Vertical Relationships: Empirical Evidence. *J. Law, Econ., Organ.*, Spring 1988,
4(1), pp. 95–117.

_____. Price Adjustment in Long-term Contracts: The Case of Coal. *J. Law Econ.*, April
1988, 31(1), pp. 47–83.

Jossa, Bruno. Lotta di classe e distribuzione del
reddito in Kalecki. (With English summary.)
Stud. Econ., 1988, 43(35), pp. 3–32.

Jouini, Elyes. A Remark on Clarke's Normal Cone
and the Marginal Cost Pricing Rule. *J. Math.
Econ.*, 1988, 17(2–3), pp. 309–15.

Joutz, Frederick L. Informational Efficiency Tests
of Quarterly Macroeconometric GNP Forecasts

from 1976 to 1985. *Managerial Dec. Econ.*, December 1988, *9*(4), pp. 311–30.

Jovanovic, Boyan and Bull, Clive. Mismatch versus Derived-Demand Shift as Causes of Labour Mobility. *Rev. Econ. Stud.*, January 1988, *55*(1), pp. 169–75.

———— **and Rosenthal, Robert W.** Anonymous Sequential Games. *J. Math. Econ.*, 1988, *17*(1), pp. 77–87.

Joy, O. Maurice and Grube, R. Corwin. Some Evidence on the Efficacy of Security Credit Regulation in the OTC Equity Market. *J. Finan. Res.*, Summer 1988, *11*(2), pp. 137–42.

Joyce, Joseph P. Policy Assignments for Central Bank Activities. *Int. Econ. J.*, Winter 1988, *2*(4), pp. 9–20.

Joyce, Michael; Britton, Andrew and Gurney, Andrew. The Home Economy. *Nat. Inst. Econ. Rev.*, February 1988, (123), pp. 6–19.

————; **Britton, Andrew and Gurney, Andrew.** The Home Economy. *Nat. Inst. Econ. Rev.*, May 1988, (124), pp. 7–20.

————; **Gregg, Paul A. and Britton, Andrew.** The Home Economy. *Nat. Inst. Econ. Rev.*, August 1988, (125), pp. 6–22.

————; **Gregg, Paul A. and Britton, Andrew.** The Home Economy. *Nat. Inst. Econ. Rev.*, November 1988, (126), pp. 6–17.

Judd, E. Maren. The Literature of Agribusiness, 1986. In *Goldberg, R. A., ed., Vol. 8*, 1988, pp. 291–310.

————. The Literature of Agribusiness, 1987. In *Goldberg, R. A., ed., Vol. 9*, 1988, pp. 157–75.

Judd, Kenneth L. and Hubbard, Robert Glenn. Capital Market Imperfections and Tax Policy Analysis in the Life Cycle Model. *Ann. Écon. Statist.*, Jan.–March 1988, (9), pp. 111–39.

Judd, Richard W. Saving the Fisherman as Well as the Fish: Conservation and Commercial Rivalry in Maine's Lobster Industry, 1872–1933. *Bus. Hist. Rev.*, Winter 1988, *62*(4), pp. 596–625.

Judge, George and Yi, Gang. Statistical Model Selection Criteria. *Econ. Letters*, 1988, *28*(1), pp. 47–51.

Judge, Guy. Quattro: The Professional Spreadsheet. *J. Econ. Surveys*, 1988, *2*(2), pp. 169–76.

Jullien, Bruno. Competitive Business Cycles in an Overlapping Generations Economy with Productive Investment. *J. Econ. Theory*, October 1988, *46*(1), pp. 45–65.

———— **and Green, Jerry R.** Ordinal Independence in Nonlinear Utility Theory. *J. Risk Uncertainty*, December 1988, *1*(4), pp. 355–87.

Juma, Calestous and Clark, Norman G. Evolutionary Theories in Economic Thought. In *Dosi, G., et al., eds.*, 1988, pp. 197–218.

Jung, Woon-Oh and Kwon, Young K. Disclosure When the Market Is Unsure of Information Endowment of Managers. *J. Acc. Res.*, Spring 1988, *26*(1), pp. 146–53.

Jungeilges, Jochen and Gaertner, Wulf. A Nonlinear Model of Interdependent Consumer Behaviour. *Econ. Letters*, 1988, *27*(2), pp. 145–50.

Junger, Peter D. Evaluating Uncertain Evidence with Sir Thomas Bayes: A Note for Teachers. *J. Econ. Perspectives*, Spring 1988, *2*(2), pp. 176–78.

Jungermann, Helmut. Time Preferences: The Expectation and Evaluation of Decision Consequences as a Function of Time. In *Maital, S., ed., Vol. 2*, 1988, pp. 579–92.

Junius, Theo. Price Formation in Input–Output Analysis. *Econ. Letters*, 1988, *26*(2), pp. 153–57.

Junk, Paul E. and O'Brien, A. Maureen. Some Social Costs of Unemployment: A Regional Analysis. In *Missouri Valley Economic Assoc.*, 1988, pp. 7–11.

Junne, Gerd. Incidence of Biotechnology Advances on Developing Countries. In *Research and Info. System for the Non-aligned and Other Developing Countries*, 1988, pp. 193–206.

Juravich, Tom and Shergold, Peter R. The Impact of Unions on the Voting Behavior of Their Members. *Ind. Lab. Relat. Rev.*, April 1988, *41*(3), pp. 374–85.

Jurewitz, John L. Deregulation of Electricity: A View from Utility Management. *Contemp. Policy Issues*, July 1988, *6*(3), pp. 25–41.

Juris, Hervey and Feuille, Peter. Police Union Impact on the Formulation of Law Enforcement Policy. In *Lewin, D., et al., eds.*, 1988, *1973*, pp. 542–55.

Jussawalla, Meheroo; Snow, Marcellus S. and Braunstein, Yale M. Major Issues in Information Services Trade. In *Lee, C. H. and Naya, S., eds.*, 1988, pp. 77–95.

Just, Richard E. Making Economic Welfare Analysis Useful in the Policy Process: Implications of the Public Choice Literature. *Amer. J. Agr. Econ.*, May 1988, *70*(2), pp. 448–53.

———— **and Zilberman, David.** The Effects of Agricultural Development Policies on Income Distribution and Technological Change in Agriculture. *J. Devel. Econ.*, March 1988, *28*(2), pp. 193–216.

———— **and Zilberman, David.** A Methodology for Evaluating Equity Implications of Environmental Policy Decisions in Agriculture. *Land Econ.*, February 1988, *64*(1), pp. 37–52.

————; **Zilberman, David and Hochman, Eithan.** Estimation of Multicrop Production Functions: Reply. *Amer. J. Agr. Econ.*, August 1988, *70*(3), pp. 733–34.

Justice, S. Craig. The Financial Linkages between the Development and Acquisition of Technology. *J. Econ. Issues*, June 1988, *22*(2), pp. 355–62.

Justman, Moshe; Levy, Amnon and Gabriel, Stuart A. Determinants of Internal Migration in Israel: Expected Returns and Risks. *Appl. Econ.*, May 1988, *20*(5), pp. 679–90.

———— **and Mehrez, Abraham.** Extremal Configurations for Optimal Prevention and Damage Control. *Europ. Econ. Rev.*, October 1988, *32*(8), pp. 1637–43.

_____ and **Teubal, Morris.** A Framework for an Explicit Industry and Technology Policy for Israel and Some Specific Proposals. In *Freeman, C. and Lundvall, B.-A., eds.*, 1988, pp. 226–49.

Juviler, Peter H. Prospects for *Perestroika:* New Goals, Old Interests. In *Juviler, P. and Kimura, H., eds.*, 1988, pp. 21–47.

_____ and **Kimura, Hiroshi.** Gorbachev's Reforms: U.S. and Japanese Assessments: Introduction. In *Juviler, P. and Kimura, H., eds.*, 1988, pp. xi–xxi.

Ka, Chih-ming and Selden, Mark. Original Accumulation, Equality, and Late Industrialization: The Cases of Socialist China and Capitalist Taiwan. In *Selden, M.*, 1988, *1986*, pp. 101–28.

Kabashima, Ikuo and Matsubara, Nozomu. Voters' Choice in the Tanaka Verdict Election: An Analysis of Aggregate Election Data with MK Ratio. In *Uno, K. and Shishido, S., eds.*, 1988, pp. 175–88.

Kabcenell, Andrea and Eisenberg, John M. Organized Practice and the Quality of Medical Care. *Inquiry*, Spring 1988, *25*(1), pp. 78–89.

Kabir, M. and Mangla, I. Effects of Financial Innovations on the Money Demand Function: Canadian Evidence. *Appl. Econ.*, September 1988, *20*(9), pp. 1263–73.

_____; **Moslehuddin, M. and Howlader, Ali Ahmed.** Husband–Wife Communication and Status of Women as a Determinant of Contraceptive Use in Rural Bangladesh. *Bangladesh Devel. Stud.*, March 1988, *16*(1), pp. 85–97.

_____ and **Ridler, Neil B.** Cultivation of Fish and Shellfish: Implications for Regional Economic Development. In *Choudhury, M. A., ed.*, 1988, pp. 116–25.

Kabir, Rezaul. Estimating Import and Export Demand Function: The Case of Bangladesh. *Bangladesh Devel. Stud.*, December 1988, *16*(4), pp. 115–27.

Kacapyr, Elia and Thomas, Wade L. An Index of Economic Activity in Tompkins County. In *Pennsylvania Economic Association*, 1988, pp. 664–81.

Kacker, Madhav. The Role of Global Retailers in World Development. In *Kaynak, E., ed.*, 1988, pp. 33–42.

Kacprzyk, Janusz; Esogbue, Augustine O. and Fedrizzi, Mario. Fuzzy Dynamic Programming with Stochastic Systems. In *Kacprzyk, J. and Fedrizzi, M., eds.*, 1988, pp. 266–85.

_____ and **Fedrizzi, Mario.** On Measuring Consensus in the Setting of Fuzzy Preference Relations. In *Kacprzyk, J. and Roubens, M., eds.*, 1988, pp. 129–41.

Kadane, Joseph B. and Winkler, Robert L. Separating Probability Elicitation from Utilities. *J. Amer. Statist. Assoc.*, June 1988, *83*(402), pp. 357–63.

Kádár, Béla. World Economic Growth and East–West Economic Cooperation in the 1980s. In *Brada, J. C. and Dobozi, I., eds.*, 1988, pp. 197–217.

Kadekodi, Gopal K. Energy Pricing in a Welfare Framework: Issues in Equity, Efficiency and

Exhaustibility. In *Sengupta, J. K. and Kadekodi, G. K., eds.*, 1988, pp. 51–62.

_____; **Kumar, T. Krishna and Sengupta, Jati K.** The Scientific Work of Gerhard Tintner. In *Sengupta, J. K. and Kadekodi, G. K., eds.*, 1988, pp. 3–22.

Kader, Ahmad A. The Relationship between Exports and Growth and the Identification Problem. *Atlantic Econ. J.*, September 1988, *16*(3), pp. 86.

Kadir, S. Ghulam; Mahmud, S. Fakhre and Hasan, M. Aynul. Substitutability of Pakistan's Monetary Assets under Alternative Monetary Aggregates. *Pakistan Devel. Rev.*, Autumn 1988, *27*(3), pp. 317–26.

Kadiyala, K. Rao and Lockwood, Larry J. Measuring Investment Performance with a Stochastic Parameter Regression Model. *J. Banking Finance*, September 1988, *12*(3), pp. 457–67.

_____ and **Lockwood, Larry J.** Risk Measurement for Event-Dependent Security Returns. *J. Bus. Econ. Statist.*, January 1988, *6*(1), pp. 43–49.

Kadyampakeni, James. Pricing Policies in Africa with Special Reference to Agricultural Development in Malawi. *World Devel.*, November 1988, *16*(11), pp. 1299–1315.

Kaell, Arthur and Hirshhorn, Ron. A Framework for Evaluating Public Corporations. *Ann. Pub. Co-op. Econ.*, April–June 1988, *59*(2), pp. 141–56.

Kaempfer, William H. and Lowenberg, Anton D. Determinants of the Economic and Political Effects of Trade Sanctions. *S. Afr. J. Econ.*, December 1988, *56*(4), pp. 270–77.

_____ and **Lowenberg, Anton D.** South Africa's Vulnerability to Oil Sanctions. *J. Energy Devel.*, Autumn 1988, *14*(1), pp. 19–44.

_____ and **Lowenberg, Anton D.** The Theory of International Economic Sanctions: A Public Choice Approach. *Amer. Econ. Rev.*, September 1988, *78*(4), pp. 786–93.

_____; **Marks, Stephen V. and Willett, Thomas D.** Why Do Large Countries Prefer Quantitative Trade Restrictions? *Kyklos*, 1988, *41*(4), pp. 625–46.

_____ and **Moffett, Michael H.** Impact of Anti-apartheid Sanctions on South Africa: Some Trade and Financial Evidence. *Contemp. Policy Issues*, October 1988, *6*(4), pp. 118–29.

Kaen, Fred R.; Simos, Evangelos O. and Triantis, John E. A Term Structure Monetary Model of Exchange Rate Determination. *Econ. Notes*, 1988, (2), pp. 82–92.

Kafka, A. Conditionality: A Double Paradox: Comment. In *Jepma, C. J., ed.*, 1988, pp. 122–24.

_____. Protection, Trade and Development: Comment. In *Jepma, C. J., ed.*, 1988, pp. 101–03.

Kagel, John H. and Dyer, Douglas. Learning in Common Value Auctions. In *Tietz, R.; Albers, W. and Selten, R., eds.*, 1988, pp. 184–97.

Kahana, Nava and Deutsch, Joseph. A Note on the Output Effect of Price Discrimination on a Sales Maximizer. *Managerial Dec. Econ.*, September 1988, 9(3), pp. 205–07.

_____ **and Deutsch, Joseph.** On the Responses of the Illyrian and Entrepreneurial Monopolies to a Change in Market Conditions: An Extension. *J. Compar. Econ.*, June 1988, 12(2), pp. 235–39.

_____ **and Nitzan, Shmuel.** Production Theory with Profit-Constrained Revenue-Maximization: The Duality Approach. *Managerial Dec. Econ.*, December 1988, 9(4), pp. 269–73.

_____ **and Spiegel, Uriel.** On the Definition of Price Discrimination. *Econ. Inquiry*, October 1988, 26(4), pp. 775–77.

Kahane, Yehuda; Kroll, Yoram and Briys, Eric. Voluntary Insurance Coverage, Compulsory Insurance, and Risky–Riskless Portfolio Opportunities. *J. Risk Ins.*, December 1988, 55(4), pp. 713–22.

Kahl, Douglas R.; Nunn, Kenneth P., Jr. and Gombola, Michael J. Valuation of the Preferred Stock Sinking Fund Feature: A Time-Series Approach. *J. Finan. Res.*, Spring 1988, 11(1), pp. 33–42.

Kahl, Kandice H. An Analysis of Alternative Market and Governmental Risk Transference Mechanisms: Reaction. In *Sumner, D. A., ed.*, 1988, pp. 79–83.

Kahl, Klaus-Dietrich. Über die Verwendung von Finanzierungskennziffern. (With English summary.) *Z. Betriebswirtshaft*, February 1988, 58(2), pp. 252–66.

Kahle, Egbert. Unternehmensführung und Unternehmenskultur. Zur Bedeutung der Unternehmensidentität als Erfolgsfaktor. (With English summary.) *Z. Betriebswirtshaft*, November 1988, 58(11), pp. 1228–41.

Kahley, William J. Florida's Challenge: Managing Growth. *Fed. Res. Bank Atlanta Econ. Rev.*, Jan.–Feb. 1988, 73(1), pp. 14–23.

_____. Long-term Prospects for the Southeastern States. *Fed. Res. Bank Atlanta Econ. Rev.*, Jan.–Feb. 1988, 73(1), pp. 2–5.

Kahn, Alfred E. Surprises of Airline Deregulation. *Amer. Econ. Rev.*, May 1988, 78(2), pp. 316–22.

Kahn, Alfred J. and Kamerman, Sheila B. Social Policy and Children in the United States and Europe. In *Palmer, J. L.; Smeeding, T. and Torrey, B. B., eds.*, 1988, pp. 351–80.

Kahn, Barbara E. and Sarin, Rakesh K. Modeling Ambiguity in Decisions under Uncertainty. *J. Cons. Res.*, September 1988, 15(2), pp. 265–72.

Kahn, Charles M. The Use of Complicated Models as Explanations: A Re-examination of Williamson's Late 19th-Century America. In *Uselding, P. J., ed.*, 1988, pp. 185–216.

_____ **and Huberman, Gur.** Limited Contract Enforcement and Strategic Renegotiation. *Amer. Econ. Rev.*, June 1988, 78(3), pp. 471–84.

_____ **and Huberman, Gur.** Strategic Renegotiation. *Econ. Letters*, 1988, 28(2), pp. 117–21.

_____ **and Huberman, Gur.** Two-sided Uncer-

tainty and "Up-or-Out" Contracts. *J. Lab. Econ.*, October 1988, 6(4), pp. 423–44.

_____ **and Mookherjee, Dilip.** A Competitive Efficiency Wage Model with Keynesian Features. *Quart. J. Econ.*, November 1988, 103(4), pp. 609–45.

Kahn, James A. Social Security, Liquidity, and Early Retirement. *J. Public Econ.*, February 1988, 35(1), pp. 97–117.

Kahn, James R. and Balkan, Erol. The Value of Changes in Deer Hunting Quality: A Travel Cost Approach. *Appl. Econ.*, April 1988, 20(4), pp. 533–39.

_____ **and Clark, David E.** The Social Benefits of Urban Cultural Amenities. *J. Reg. Sci.*, August 1988, 28(3), pp. 363–77.

_____; **Ofek, Haim and Clark, David.** City Size, Quality of Life, and the Urbanization Deflator of the GNP: 1910–1984. *Southern Econ. J.*, January 1988, 54(3), pp. 701–14.

Kahn, Joan R.; Kalsbeek, William D. and Hofferth, Sandra L. National Estimates of Teenage Sexual Activity: Evaluating the Comparability of Three National Surveys. *Demography*, May 1988, 25(2), pp. 189–204.

Kahn, Lawrence M.; Gramm, Cynthia L. and Hendricks, Wallace E. Inflation Uncertainty and Strike Activity. *Ind. Relat.*, Winter 1988, 27(1), pp. 114–29.

_____ **and Low, Stuart A.** Systematic and Random Search: A Synthesis. *J. Human Res.*, Winter 1988, 23(1), pp. 1–20.

_____ **and Sherer, Peter D.** Racial Differences in Professional Basketball Players' Compensation. *J. Lab. Econ.*, January 1988, 6(1), pp. 40–61.

Kahn, Richard. Malinvaud on Keynes. In *Shaw, G. K., ed., Vol. 1*, 1988, 1977, pp. 53–66.

_____. Unemployment as Seen by the Keynesians. In *Shaw, G. K., ed., Vol. 1*, 1988, 1976, pp. 152–67.

Kahn, S. B. and Gerson, J. Factors Determining Real Exchange Rate Change in South Africa. *S. Afr. J. Econ.*, June–Sept. 1988, 56(2–3), pp. 124–35.

Kahneman, Daniel. Experimental Economics: A Psychological Perspective. In *Tietz, R.; Albers, W. and Selten, R., eds.*, 1988, pp. 11–18.

_____ **and Tversky, Amos.** Prospect Theory: An Analysis of Decision under Risk. In *Gärdenfors, P. and Sahlin, N.-E., eds.*, 1988, 1979, pp. 183–214.

_____ **and Tversky, Amos.** Prospect Theory: An Analysis of Decision under Risk. In *Earl, P. E., ed., Vol. 1*, 1988, 1979, pp. 253–81.

Kaila, Martti M. and Kauranen, Ilkka. Regional Activation Projects and Small Firms: Application of the Learning-Based, Adaptive Approach. *Liiketaloudellinen Aikak.*, 1988, 37(3), pp. 179–92.

Kaimowitz, David. Nicaragua's Experience with Agricultural Planning: From State-Centred Accumulation to the Strategic Alliance with the Peasantry. *J. Devel. Stud.*, July 1988, 24(4), pp. 115–35.

Kain, Michael. Recent Trends in World Agricultural Trade. *Nat. Westminster Bank Quart. Rev.*, May 1988, pp. 14–24.

Kaiser, Carl P. Layoffs, Average Hours, and Unemployment Insurance in U.S. Manufacturing Industries: Erratum. *Quart. Rev. Econ. Bus.*, Summer 1988, 28(2), pp. 113.

Kaiser, Frederick M. U.S. Customs Service User Fees: A Variety of Charges and Counter-Charges. *Public Budg. Finance*, Autumn 1988, 8(3), pp. 78–95.

Kaiser, Harry M.; Streeter, Deborah H. and Liu, Donald J. Price versus Stock Effect Policies for Reducing Excess Milk Production. *Western J. Agr. Econ.*, December 1988, 13(2), pp. 277–84.

_____; **Streeter, Deborah H. and Liu, Donald J.** Welfare Comparisons of U.S. Dairy Policies with and without Mandatory Supply Control. *Amer. J. Agr. Econ.*, November 1988, 70(4), pp. 848–58.

Kaiser, Robert G. The U.S.S.R. in Decline. *Foreign Aff.*, Winter 1988–89, 67(2), pp. 97–113.

Kaish, Stanley; Loeb, Peter D. and Gilad, Benjamin. From Economic Behavior to Behavoiral Economics: The Behavioral Uprising in Economics. In *Earl, P. E., ed., Vol. 2*, 1988, *1984*, pp. 437–58.

_____; **Ronen, Joshua and Gilad, Benjamin.** The Entrepreneurial Way with Information. In *Maital, S., ed., Vol. 2*, 1988, pp. 480–503.

Kaiyama, Michihiro. Inter-city Migration and Evaluation of Changes in Urban Transport System: An Extention of the Alonso–Wheaton Model to a Two-City Model. (In Japanese. With English summary.) *Econ. Stud. Quart.*, June 1988, 39(2), pp. 174–85.

Kaizuka, Keimei. World Tax Reform: A Progress Report: Japan: Comment. In *Pechman, J. A., ed.*, 1988, pp. 162–69.

Kajii, Atsushi. Note on Equilibria without Ordered Preferences in Topological Vector Spaces. *Econ. Letters*, 1988, 27(1), pp. 1–4.

Kakwani, N. Income Inequality, Welfare and Poverty in a Developing Economy with Applications to Sri Lanka. In *Gaertner, W. and Pattanaik, P. K., eds.*, 1988, *1988*, pp. 111–34.

_____. Income Inequality, Welfare and Poverty in a Developing Economy with Applications to Sri Lanka. *Soc. Choice Welfare*, 1988, 5(2/3), pp. 199–222.

Kalaba, Robert and Tesfatsion, Leigh. The Flexible Least Squares Approach to Time-Varying Linear Regression. *J. Econ. Dynam. Control*, March 1988, 12(1), pp. 43–48.

Kalai, Ehud and Samet, Dov. Weighted Shapley Values. In *[Shapley, L. S.]*, 1988, pp. 83–99.

_____; **Samet, Dov and Stanford, William.** A Note on Reactive Equilibria in the Discounted Prisoner's Dilemma and Associated Games. *Int. J. Game Theory*, 1988, 17(3), pp. 177–86.

_____ **and Stanford, William.** Finite Rationality and Interpersonal Complexity in Repeated Games. *Econometrica*, March 1988, 56(2), pp. 397–410.

Kaldor, Nicholas. The Irrelevance of Equilibrium

Economics. In *Sawyer, M. C., ed.*, 1988, *1972*, pp. 61–79.

_____. The Role of Effective Demand in the Short Run and the Long Run. In *Barrère, A., ed.*, 1988, pp. 153–60.

_____ **and Trevithick, James.** A Keynesian Perspective on Money. In *Sawyer, M. C., ed.*, 1988, *1981*, pp. 101–19.

Kalecki, Michal. Class Struggle and the Distribution of National Income. In *Sawyer, M. C., ed.*, 1988, *1971*, pp. 354–61.

Kaliel, Dale; Chase, Darren and Ross, Carlyle. Economics of Cow-Calf Production in Alberta. *Can. J. Agr. Econ.*, Part 2, December 1988, 36(4), pp. 821–36.

Kalirajan, K. P. and Shand, R. T. Firm and Product-Specific Technical Efficiencies in a Multi-product Cycle System. *J. Devel. Stud.*, October 1988, 25(1), pp. 83–96.

_____ **and Shand, R. T.** Multi-output Self Dual Profit Function and Factor Demand Equations: Primal with Constraints on Inputs. *J. Quant. Econ.*, July 1988, 4(2), pp. 261–78.

Kalish, Shlomo. Pricing New Products from Birth to Decline: An Expository Review. In *Devinney, T. M., ed.*, 1988, pp. 119–44.

_____ **and Dobson, Gregory.** Positioning and Pricing a Product Line. *Marketing Sci.*, Spring 1988, 7(2), pp. 107–25.

_____; **Katznelson, Shauli and Hirsch, Seev.** Effects of Knowledge and Service Intensities on Domestic and Export Performance. *Weltwirtsch. Arch.*, 1988, 124(2), pp. 230–41.

Kallberg, Jarl G. and Kao, Duen-Li. Statistical Models in Credit Management. In *Kim, Y. H., ed.*, 1988, pp. 147–74.

Kalleberg, Arne L. and Berg, Ivar. Work Structures and Markets: An Analytic Framework. In *Farkas, G. and England, P., eds.*, 1988, pp. 3–17.

_____ **and Lincoln, James R.** The Structure of Earnings Inequality in the United States and Japan. In *Winship, C. and Rosen, S., eds.*, 1988, pp. 121–53.

Kallon, Kelfala M. An Empirical Analysis of Money Demand in Five Sub-Saharan African Countries. In *Pennsylvania Economic Association*, 1988, pp. 46–57.

Kalotay, Andrew J. and Howard, C. Douglas. Embedded Call Options and Refunding Efficiency. In *Fabozzi, F. J., ed.*, 1988, pp. 97–117.

Kalsbeek, William D.; Hofferth, Sandra L. and Kahn, Joan R. National Estimates of Teenage Sexual Activity: Evaluating the Comparability of Three National Surveys. *Demography*, May 1988, 25(2), pp. 189–204.

Kalt, Joseph P. The Impact of Domestic Environmental Regulatory Policies on U.S. International Competitiveness. In *Spence, A. M. and Hazard, H. A., eds.*, 1988, pp. 221–62.

_____. The Political Economy of Protectionism: Tariffs and Retaliation in the Timber Industry. In *Baldwin, R. E., ed. (II)*, 1988, pp. 339–64.

de Kam, Flip. World Tax Reform: A Progress Report: Netherlands: Comment. In *Pechman, J. A., ed.*, 1988, pp. 180–85.

Kamakura, Wagner A.; Ratchford, Brian T. and Agrawal, Jagdish. Measuring Market Efficiency and Welfare Loss. *J. Cons. Res.*, December 1988, *15*(3), pp. 289–302.

Kamarás, F. Some Issues in Modelling Household Behaviour of the Aged in Hungary. In *Keilman, N.; Kuijsten, A. and Vossen, A., eds.*, 1988, pp. 195–208.

Kamarck, Andrew M. The Special Case of Africa. In *Bell, D. E. and Reich, M. R., eds.*, 1988, pp. 199–222.

Kamath, Shyam J. Illegal Arbitrage in Dual Commodity Markets. *Atlantic Econ. J.*, September 1988, *16*(3), pp. 87.

_____. Partially Suppressed Markets: Controls, Rent Seeking and the Cost of Protection in the Indian Sugar Industry. *Weltwirtsch. Arch.*, 1988, *124*(1), pp. 140–60.

Kamba, Walter J. The Role of Universities in South–South Co-operation. In *Sopiee, N.; Hamzah, B. A. and Leong, C. H., eds.*, 1988, *1986*, pp. 375–84.

Kambhu, John. Unilateral Disclosure of Private Information by a Regulated Firm. *J. Econ. Behav. Organ.*, July 1988, *10*(1), pp. 57–82.

Kamecki, Zbigniew. The Current State of the Economy. In *Marer, P. and Siwinski, W., eds.*, 1988, pp. 61–62.

Kamel, Nawal; Mohnen, Pierre and Roy, Paul-Martel. Demande de travail et d'heures supplémentaires: étude empirique pour le Canada et le Québec. (With English summary.) *L'Actual. Econ.*, March 1988, *64*(1), pp. 23–43.

Kamerman, Sheila B. and Kahn, Alfred J. Social Policy and Children in the United States and Europe. In *Palmer, J. L.; Smeeding, T. and Torrey, B. B., eds.*, 1988, pp. 351–80.

Kamerud, Dana B. Benefits and Costs of the 55 mph Speed Limit: New Estimates and Their Implications. *J. Policy Anal. Manage.*, Winter 1988, *7*(2), pp. 341–52.

_____. Evaluating the New 65 MPH Speed Limit. In *Graham, J. D., ed.*, 1988, pp. 231–56.

Kamien, Morton I. and Cyert, Richard M. Behavioural Rules and the Theory of the Firm. In *Cyert, R. M.*, 1988, *1967*, pp. 111–21.

_____; **Tauman, Yair and Zang, Israel.** Optimal License Fees for a New Product. *Math. Soc. Sci.*, August 1988, *16*(1), pp. 77–106.

Kamin, Steven and Yagci, Fahrettin. Macroeconomic Policies and Adjustment in Yugoslavia: Some Counterfactual Simulations. In *Motamen, H., ed.*, 1988 , pp. 713–30.

Kamiya, Kazuya. Existence and Uniqueness of Equilibria with Increasing Returns. *J. Math. Econ.*, 1988, *17*(2–3), pp. 149–78.

_____. On the Survival Assumption in Marginal (Cost) Pricing. *J. Math. Econ.*, 1988, *17*(2–3), pp. 261–73.

Kamma, Sreenivas; Weintrop, Joseph and Wier, Peggy. Investors' Perceptions of the Delaware Supreme Court Decision in Unocal v. Mesa.

J. Finan. Econ., Jan.–March 1988, *20*(1–2), pp. 419–30.

Kan, Bertrand and Jackman, Richard. Structural Unemployment: A Reply. *Oxford Bull. Econ. Statist.*, February 1988, *50*(1), pp. 83–87.

Kanafani, Adib and Lan, Lawrence H. Development of Pricing Strategies for Airport Parking—A Case Study at San Francisco Airport. *Int. J. Transport Econ.*, February 1988, *15*(1), pp. 55–76.

Kanaroglou, Pavlos S. and Boots, Barry N. Incorporating the Effects of Spatial Structure in Discrete Choice Models of Migration. *J. Reg. Sci.*, November 1988, *28*(4), pp. 495–509.

Kanbur, S. M. Ravi and Besley, Timothy J. Food Subsidies and Poverty Alleviation. *Econ. J.*, September 1988, *98*(392), pp. 701–19.

_____ **and McIntosh, James P.** Dual Economy Models: Retrospect and Prospect. *Bull. Econ. Res.*, April 1988, *40*(2), pp. 83–113.

_____ **and Stromberg, Jan-Olov.** Income Transitions and Income Distribution Dominance. *J. Econ. Theory*, August 1988, *45*(2), pp. 408–16.

Kandel, Abraham. Theory and Applications of Fuzzy Statistics. In *Kacprzyk, J. and Fedrizzi, M., eds.*, 1988, pp. 89–112.

Kandori, Michihiro. Equivalent Equilibria. *Int. Econ. Rev.*, August 1988, *29*(3), pp. 401–17.

Kane, Alex and Marcus, Alan J. The Delivery Option on Forward Contracts: A Note. *J. Finan. Quant. Anal.*, September 1988, *23*(3), pp. 337–41.

_____ **and Marks, Stephen Gary.** Performance Evaluation of Market Timers: Theory and Evidence. *J. Finan. Quant. Anal.*, December 1988, *23*(4), pp. 425–35.

Kane, Edward J. Adapting Financial Services Regulation to a Changing Economic Environment. In *Libecap, G., ed. (II)*, 1988, pp. 61–94.

_____. Fedbashing and the Role of Monetary Arrangements in Managing Political Stress. In *Willett, T. D., ed.*, 1988, pp. 479–89.

_____. How Market Forces Influence the Structure of Financial Regulation. In *Haraf, W. S. and Kushmeider, R. M., eds.*, 1988, pp. 343–82.

_____. The Impact of a New Federal Reserve Chairman. *Contemp. Policy Issues*, January 1988, *6*(1), pp. 89–97.

_____. Interaction of Financial and Regulatory Innovation. *Amer. Econ. Rev.*, May 1988, *78*(2), pp. 328–34.

_____ **and Unal, Haluk.** Change in Market Assessments of Deposit-Institution Riskiness. *J. Finan. Services Res.*, June 1988, *1*(3), pp. 207–29.

_____ **and Unal, Haluk.** Two Approaches to Assessing the Interest Rate Sensitivity of Deposit Institution Equity Returns. In *Chen, A. H., ed.*, 1988, pp. 113–37.

Kane, Robert L. and Kane, Rosalie A. Long-term Care: Variations on a Quality Assurance Theme. *Inquiry*, Spring 1988, *25*(1), pp. 132–46.

Kane, Rosalie A. and Kane, Robert L. Long-term Care: Variations on a Quality Assurance Theme. *Inquiry*, Spring 1988, 25(1), pp. 132–46.

Kaneda, Hiromitsu. Agricultural Stagnation in the 1920's, a Macroeconomic Perspective. *Hitotsubashi J. Econ.*, June 1988, 29(1), pp. 37–57.

Kaneda, Tatsuo. Gorbachev's Economic Reforms. In *Juviler, P. and Kimura, H., eds.*, 1988, pp. 81–95.

Kaneko, Mamoru. The Conventionally Stable Sets in Noncooperative Games with Limited Observations: An Application to Monopoly and Oligopoly. *Econ. Stud. Quart.*, December 1988, 39(4), pp. 335–55.

Kaneko, Yukio. An Empirical Study on Non-survey Forecasting of the Input Coefficient Matrix in a Leontief Model. *Econ. Modelling*, January 1988, 5(1), pp. 41–48.

—— **and Nidaira, Koh'ichi.** Towards Basic Human Needs in Relation to Public Health and Nutrition. In *Bell, D. E. and Reich, M. R., eds.*, 1988, pp. 241–63.

Kanel, Don. The Human Predicament: Society, Institutions, and Individuals. *J. Econ. Issues*, June 1988, 22(2), pp. 427–34.

——. Property and Economic Power as Issues in Institutional Economics. In *Samuels, W. J., ed.*, *Vol. 3*, 1988, *1974*, pp. 359–72.

——, **et al.** Theory, Research, and Policy: Perspectives from the Land Tenure Center. In *Bennett, J. W. and Bowen, J. R., eds.*, 1988, pp. 387–410.

Kanemoto, Yoshitsugu. Hedonic Prices and the Benefits of Public Projects. *Econometrica*, July 1988, 56(4), pp. 981–89.

Kang, Cheol-Joon. International Loan to Developing Countries as a Risk Sharing Contract. *Int. Econ. J.*, Summer 1988, 2(2), pp. 75–81.

Kang, Han Bin and Doherty, Neil A. Interest Rates and Insurance Price Cycles. *J. Banking Finance*, June 1988, 12(2), pp. 199–214.

Kang, Hyosuk and Chen, Andrew H. Financial Implications of ERISA: Theory and Evidence. *J. Econ. Bus.*, August 1988, 40(3), pp. 193–208.

Kang, Jung M. and Kwon, Jene K. An Estimation of Import Demand, Export Supply and Technical Change for Korea. *Appl. Econ.*, December 1988, 20(12), pp. 1661–74.

Kang, Suk. Fair Distribution Rule in a Cooperative Enterprise: Note. *J. Compar. Econ.*, March 1988, 12(1), pp. 89–92.

Kangun, Norman and Carlson, Les. Demographic Discontinuity: Another Explanation for Consumerism? *J. Cons. Aff.*, Summer 1988, 22(1), pp. 55–73.

Kannappan, Subbiah. Urban Labor Markets and Development. *World Bank Res. Observer*, July 1988, 3(2), pp. 189–206.

Kanne, Marvin E. John Dewey's Conception of Moral Good. *J. Econ. Issues*, December 1988, 22(4), pp. 1213–23.

Kanoh, Satoru. The Reduction of the Width of Confidence Bands in Linear Regression. *J.*

Amer. Statist. Assoc., March 1988, 83(401), pp. 116–22.

Kant, Chander. Endogenous Transfer Pricing and the Effects of Uncertain Regulation. *J. Int. Econ.*, February 1988, 24(1–2), pp. 147–57.

——. Foreign Subsidiary, Transfer Pricing and Tariffs. *Southern Econ. J.*, July 1988, 55(1), pp. 162–70.

Kantarelis, D. and Veendorp, E. C. H. Live and Let Live Type Behavior in a Multi-market Setting with Demand Fluctuations. *J. Econ. Behav. Organ.*, September 1988, 10(2), pp. 235–44.

Kantawala, B. S. India's Imports on Bilateral Basis: Does It Benefit? *Indian Econ. J.*, April–June 1988, 35(4), pp. 44–56.

Kanter, Rosabeth Moss. When a Thousand Flowers Bloom: Structural, Collective, and Social Conditions for Innovation in Organization. In *Staw, B. M. and Cummings, L. L., eds.*, 1988, pp. 169–211.

Kanth, Rajani. On Ricardo and All That: A Reply. *Rev. Radical Polit. Econ.*, Winter 1988, 20(4), pp. 92–93.

Kanto, Antti J. Covariances between Estimated Autocorrelations of an ARMA Process. *Econ. Letters*, 1988, 26(3), pp. 253–58.

Kantor, Brian. Hutt's Views on Money. *Managerial Dec. Econ.*, Special Issue, Winter 1988, pp. 79–83.

——. The Pricing of Electricity in South Africa: A Critical Assessment of the De Villiers Commission of Inquiry. *Managerial Dec. Econ.*, December 1988, 9(4), pp. 301–09.

Kantor, Laurence and Lombra, Raymond E. Is Interest Rate Volatility Necessarily Harmful? *J. Econ. Bus.*, February 1988, 40(1), pp. 17–25.

Kao, Duen-Li and Kallberg, Jarl G. Statistical Models in Credit Management. In *Kim, Y. H., ed.*, 1988, pp. 147–74.

Kao, Kai and Tremblay, Victor J. Cigarette "Health Scare," Excise Taxes, and Advertising Ban: Comment. *Southern Econ. J.*, January 1988, 54(3), pp. 770–76.

Kaosa-ard, Mingsarn Santikarn and Akrasanee, Narongchai. U.S.–Thai Relations: Selected Case Studies in Agribusiness. In *Tan, L.-H. and Akrasanee, N., eds.*, 1988, pp. 177–99.

Kaplan, Eileen. Women Entrepreneurs: Constructing a Framework to Examine Venture Success and Failure. In *Kirchhoff, B. A., et al., eds.*, 1988, pp. 643–53.

Kaplan, Steven E., et al. An Examination of Tax Reporting Recommendations of Professional Tax Preparers. *J. Econ. Psych.*, December 1988, 9(4), pp. 427–43.

Kaplanis, Evi C. Stability and Forecasting of the Comovement Measures of International Stock Market Returns. *J. Int. Money Finance*, March 1988, 7(1), pp. 63–75.

Kaplinsky, Raphael. Restructuring the Capitalist Labour Process: Some Lessons from the Car Industry. *Cambridge J. Econ.*, December 1988, 12(4), pp. 451–70.

Kaplow, Louis. Savings Incentives in a Hybrid

Income Tax: Comments. In *Aaron, H. J.; Galper, H. and Pechman, J. A., eds.*, 1988, pp. 300–308.

Kapoor, Bhushan L. Analysis of Personal Earnings and Sex Differentials in the Industrial Sector in Punjab. *Indian J. Quant. Econ.*, 1988, *4*(1), pp. 21–40.

_____ **and Mann, Prem S.** Earnings Differentials between Public, Private and Joint Sectors in Punjab (India). *Devel. Stud.*, October 1988, *25*(1), pp. 97–111.

Kapp, K. William. In Defense of Institutional Economics. In *Samuels, W. J., ed., Vol. 1*, 1988, *1968*, pp. 92–107.

_____. The Nature and Significance of Institutional Economics. In *Samuels, W. J., ed., Vol. 1*, 1988, *1976*, pp. 68–91.

Kapplin, Steven D. and Schwartz, Arthur L., Jr. Public Real Estate Limited Partnership Returns: A Preliminary Comparison with Other Investments. *Amer. Real Estate Urban Econ. Assoc. J.*, Spring 1988, *16*(1), pp. 63–68.

Kapstein, Ethan B. Brazil: Continued State Dominance. In *Vernon, R., ed.*, 1988, pp. 122–48.

Kapteyn, Arie and Alessie, Rob J. M. Preference Formation, Incomes, and the Distribution of Welfare. *J. Behav. Econ.*, Spring 1988, *17*(1), pp. 77–96.

_____; **Kooreman, Peter and Willemse, Rob.** Some Methodological Issues in the Implementation of Subjective Poverty Definitions. *J. Human Res.*, Spring 1988, *23*(2), pp. 222–42.

Kapur, Basant K. Capital Mobility and Exchange Rate Overshooting: Comment. *Europ. Econ. Rev.*, January 1988, *32*(1), pp. 199–202.

Kapur, Deep and Ravallion, Martin. Rational Expectations as Long-run Equilibria: Tests for Indian Securities. *Econ. Letters*, 1988, *26*(4), pp. 363–67.

Karacaoglu, Girol and Kohn, Meir. Devaluation, Capital Mobility, and Expectations in an Optimizing Model. *J. Int. Econ.*, February 1988, *24*(1–2), pp. 23–44.

_____ **and Ursprung, Heinrich W.** Exchange Rate Dynamics under Gradual Portfolio Adjustment. *J. Macroecon.*, Fall 1988, *10*(4), pp. 565–89.

Karafakioğlu, Mehmet; Firat, A. Fuat and Kumcu, Erdoğan. The Interface between Marketing and Development: Problems and Prospects. In *Kumcu, E. and Firat, A. F., eds.*, 1988, pp. 317–43.

Karafiath, Imre. Using Dummy Variables in the Event Methodology. *Financial Rev.*, August 1988, *23*(3), pp. 351–57.

Karagedov, R. G. The Economics of Shortage: Pages from the Book by J. Kornai. *Prob. Econ.*, November 1988, *31*(7), pp. 13–33.

Karake, Zeinab A. Effects of Eastern European and Western Technologies on LDCs: A Macroeconometric Analysis. *Appl. Econ.*, August 1988, *20*(8), pp. 1099–114.

Karakitsos, Elias. An Analysis of the Asymmetrical Effects of Fiscal Policy between the United States and Europe. *Oxford Bull. Econ. Statist.*, August 1988, *50*(3), pp. 279–300.

_____. Asymmetrical Effects of Monetary Policy between the U.S. and Europe. *J. Econ. Dynam. Control*, March 1988, *12*(1), pp. 79–84.

_____. The Transmission of Monetary Policy in Interdependent Economies: An Empirical Investigation of the U.S. and Europe. In *[Frowen, S.]*, 1988, pp. 126–49.

Karalasingham, Ponniah. Recognition of Foreign Enterprises as Taxable Entities: Sri Lanka. In *International Fiscal Association, ed. (I)*, 1988, pp. 587–96.

Karamouzis, Nicholas and Lombra, Raymond E. Forecasts and U.S. Monetary Policy, 1974–78: The Role of Openness: A Note. *J. Money, Credit, Banking*, Part 1, August 1988, *20*(3), pp. 402–08.

Karathanassis, G. and Philippas, N. Estimation of Bank Stock Price Parameters and the Variance Components Model. *Appl. Econ.*, April 1988, *20*(4), pp. 497–507.

Karatsu, Hajime. How to Cope with Grey Part of Management in System Modelling and Optimization in Japanese Industry. In *Iri, M. and Yajima, K., eds.*, 1988, pp. 14–21.

_____. Improving the Quality of Life through Technology. In *Muroyama, J. H. and Stever, H. G., eds.*, 1988, pp. 177–80.

Karatzas, George. The Greek Hyperinflation and Stabilization of 1943–46: A Comment. *J. Econ. Hist.*, March 1988, *48*(1), pp. 138–39.

Karayiannis, Anastassios D. Democritus on Ethics and Economics. *Rivista Int. Sci. Econ. Com.*, April–May 1988, *35*(4–5), pp. 369–91.

Kardasz, Stanley W. and Stollery, Kenneth. Price Formation in Canadian Manufacturing Industries. *Appl. Econ.*, April 1988, *20*(4), pp. 473–83.

_____ **and Stollery, Kenneth R.** Market Structure and Price Adjustment in Canadian Manufacturing Industries. *J. Econ. Bus.*, November 1988, *40*(4), pp. 335–42.

Kardes, Frank R. Spontaneous Inference Processes in Advertising: The Effects of Conclusion Omission and Involvement on Persuasion. *J. Cons. Res.*, September 1988, *15*(2), pp. 225–33.

Kareken, John H. Commentary [Financial Stability and the Federal Safety Net] [Regulating Bank Safety and Performance]. In *Haraf, W. S. and Kushmeider, R. M., eds.*, 1988, pp. 104–08.

Karier, Thomas. New Evidence on the Effect of Unions and Imports on Monopoly Power. *J. Post Keynesian Econ.*, Spring 1988, *10*(3), pp. 414–27.

Karikari, John A. International Competitiveness and Industry Pricing in Canadian Manufacturing. *Can. J. Econ.*, May 1988, *21*(2), pp. 410–26.

_____. Tariffs and International Price Leadership. *Quart. Rev. Econ. Bus.*, Autumn 1988, *28*(3), pp. 53–66.

Karim, Mehtab S. Comparative Health Policies: A World of Difference: Comments. *Pakistan Devel. Rev.*, Part 1, Winter 1988, *27*(4), pp. 493–94.

Kariya, Takeaki. The Class of Models for which the Durbin–Watson Test is Locally Optimal. *Int. Econ. Rev.*, February 1988, *29*(1), pp. 167–75.

Karki, J.; Selby, M. J. P. and Franks, Julian R. Loan Guarantees, Wealth Transfers and Incentives to Invest. *J. Ind. Econ.*, September 1988, *37*(1), pp. 47–65.

Karl, Joachim and Ebenroth, Carsten Thomas. Code of Conduct, International Investment Contracts, the Debt Crisis, and the Development Process. In *Teng, W. and Wang, N. T., eds.*, 1988, pp. 171–79.

Karlsson, Christer. Corporate Families to Handle Galloping Technology. In *Hood, N. and Vahlne, J.-E., eds.*, 1988, pp. 158–76.

Karmann, Alexander. Finanzintermediäre und Effektivität der Geldpolitik. (Financial Intermediaries and Effective Monetary Policies. With English summary.) *Kredit Kapital*, 1988, *21*(2), pp. 197–220.

_____ **and Nakhaeizadeh, Gholamreza.** Erwartungsbildung und aggregierter Konsum-Einkommen-Prozess. Eine klassische und Bayessche Analyse für die Bundesrepublik Deutschland. (Expectations Building and the Aggregate Consumption: A Classical. With English summary.) *Jahr. Nationalökon. Statist.*, February 1988, *204*(2), pp. 120–39.

Karmel, T. and Maclachlan, M. Occupational Sex Segregation—Increasing or Decreasing? *Econ. Rec.*, September 1988, *64*(186), pp. 187–95.

Karni, Edi and Safra, Zvi. "Preference Reversals" and the Theory of Decision Making under Risk. In *Munier, B. R., ed.*, 1988, pp. 163–72.

Karnik, Ajit V. Public Expenditure and National Income: An Examination of the Causal Mechanism. *Indian J. Quant. Econ.*, 1988, *4*(1), pp. 61–72.

_____ **; Nachane, Dilip M. and Nadkarni, Ramesh M.** Co-integration and Causality Testing of the Energy–GDP Relationship: A Cross-country Study. *Appl. Econ.*, November 1988, *20*(11), pp. 1511–31.

Karoly, Lynn; Levy, David M. and Feigenbaum, Susan. When Votes Are Words Not Deeds: Some Evidence from the Nuclear Freeze Referendum. *Public Choice*, September 1988, *58*(3), pp. 201–16.

Karp, Larry S. Dynamic Hedging with Uncertain Production. *Int. Econ. Rev.*, November 1988, *29*(4), pp. 621–37.

Karp, Philip E. Struggle against Dependence: Nontraditional Export Growth in Central America and the Caribbean: Guatemala. In *Paus, E., ed.*, 1988, pp. 65–83.

_____. Struggle against Dependence: Nontraditional Export Growth in Central America and the Caribbean: Belize. In *Paus, E., ed.*, 1988, pp. 103–22.

Karpoff, Jonathan M. Costly Short Sales and the Correlation of Returns with Volume. *J. Finan. Res.*, Fall 1988, *11*(3), pp. 173–88.

_____ **and Walkling, Ralph A.** Short-term Trading around Ex-dividend Days. *J. Finan. Econ.*, September 1988, *21*(2), pp. 291–98.

Karran, Terence. Local Taxing and Local Spending: International Comparisons. In *Paddison, R. and Bailey, S., eds.*, 1988, pp. 53–83.

Karsten, Siegfried G. China's Approach to Social Market Economics: The Chinese Variant of Market Socialism Seeks to Escape from the Difficultuies of Central Command Planning. *Amer. J. Econ. Soc.*, April 1988, *47*(2), pp. 129–48.

Karunaratne, Neil Dias. Macro-economic Determinants of Australia's Current Account, 1977–1986. *Weltwirtsch. Arch.*, 1988, *124*(4), pp. 713–28.

_____. Monetarist Perspectives of Papua New Guinea's Hard Currency Strategy. *World Devel.*, July 1988, *16*(7), pp. 807–20.

_____. Symbiotics of Telecommunications, Trade and Development. *Econ. Int.*, Feb.–March 1988, *41*(1–2), pp. 44–61.

Karyd, Arne. Affordable Housing and the Market. In *Friedrichs, J., ed.*, 1988, pp. 59–73.

Kaserman, David L.; Barnett, Andy H. and Ault, Richard W. The Rising Incidence of Co-authorship in Economics: Further Evidence. *Rev. Econ. Statist.*, August 1988, *70*(3), pp. 539–43.

_____ **; Melese, Francois and Im, Bae-Geun.** Rent Seeking and the Allowed Rate of Return: A Recursive Model. *Rev. Ind. Organ.*, Fall 1988, *3*(4), pp. 27–51.

Kashyap, A. K., et al. Further Results on Estimating Linear Regression Models with Partial Prior Information. *Econ. Modelling*, January 1988, *5*(1), pp. 49–57.

Kashyap, S. P. Growth of Small-size Enterprises in India: Its Nature and Content. *World Devel.*, June 1988, *16*(6), pp. 667–81.

Kaske, Karlheinz. Organizing for and Meeting the Global Challenge. In *Rosow, J. M., ed.*, 1988, pp. 81–89.

Kasman, Bruce and Pigott, Charles. Interest Rate Divergences among the Major Industrial Nations. *Fed. Res. Bank New York Quart. Rev.*, Autumn 1988, *13*(3), pp. 28–44.

Kasnakoğlu, Zehra. Estimation of Price Elasticities for Turkish Exports Using Cross Section Data. *METU*, 1988, *15*(3–4), pp. 1–18.

Kasper, Daniel M. Liberalizing Airline Services: How to Get from Here to There. *World Econ.*, March 1988, *11*(1), pp. 91–107.

Kasper, George M.; Hamlen, Susan S. and Hamlen, William A., Jr. The Distributed Lag Effects of Monetary Policy on Interest Rates Using Harmonic Transformations with a Pretest. *Southern Econ. J.*, April 1988, *54*(4), pp. 1002–11.

Kasper, Hans. On Problem Perception, Dissatisfaction and Brand Loyalty. *J. Econ. Psych.*, September 1988, *9*(3), pp. 387–97.

Kassalow, Everett M. Concession Bargaining: Towards New Roles for American Unions and Managers. *Int. Lab. Rev.*, 1988, *127*(5), pp. 573–92.

Kassier, W. E. and Vink, N. The 'Tragedy of the Commons' and Livestock Farming in

Southern Africa: Reply. *S. Afr. J. Econ.*, June–Sept. 1988, *56*(2–3), pp. 218–24.

Kassim-Momodu, Momodu. Transfer of Technology in the Petroleum Industry: The Nigerian Experience. *J. World Trade*, August 1988, *22*(4), pp. 51–66.

Kast, Robert. A Generalisation of Rational Behaviour. In *Munier, B. R., ed.*, 1988, pp. 419–34.

Kasten, Richard A. and Sammartino, Frank J. Distributional Analyses of Three Deficit Reduction Options Affecting Social Security Cash Benefits. In *Danziger, S. H. and Portney, K. E., eds.*, 1988, pp. 116–48.

Katayama, Sei-ichi; Toyoda, Toshihisa and Ohtani, Kazuhiro. Estimation of Structural Change in the Import and Export Equations: An International Comparison. In *Uno, K. and Shishido, S., eds.*, 1988, pp. 52–64.

Katerere, Yemi. Fuelwood Consumption and Supply Patterns, Tree-Planting Practices, and Farm Forestry in Rural Zimbabwe. In *Hosier, R. H., ed. (I)*, 1988, pp. 160–84.

Kathuria, Sanjay. Indian Craft Exports for the Global Market. In *Kathuria, S.; Miralao, V. and Joseph, R.*, 1988, pp. 1–29.

Kato, Hirotaka. Keynes: The Instability of Capitalism: A Review Essay. *J. Monet. Econ.*, January 1988, *21*(1), pp. 161–74.

Kato, Hiroyuki. Transfer of Rural Labor Force in Contemporary China. *Kobe Univ. Econ.*, 1988, (34), pp. 79–99.

Katrak, Homi. Payments for Imported Technologies, Market-Rivalry and Adaptive Activity in the Newly Industrialising Countries. *J. Devel. Stud.*, October 1988, *25*(1), pp. 43–54.

_____. R&D, International Production and Trade: The Technological Gap Theory in a Factor-Endowment Model. *Manchester Sch. Econ. Soc. Stud.*, September 1988, *56*(3), pp. 205–22.

Katsaitis, O. Seasonality and the Estimation of Dynamic Demand Systems: Some Exploratory Results. *Econ. Letters*, 1988, *26*(2), pp. 129–32.

Katseli, Louka T. On the Effectiveness of Discrete Devaluation in Balance of Payments Adjustment. In *Marston, R. C., ed.*, 1988, pp. 195–210.

Katsoulacos, Yannis. On Incentives to Cooperate in R&D When Imitation Is Difficult: A Simple Economic Model. *Aussenwirtschaft*, June 1988, *43*(1/2), pp. 141–50.

_____ **and Dodgson, J. S.** Quality Competition in Bus Services: Some Welfare Implications of Bus Deregulation. *J. Transp. Econ. Policy*, September 1988, *22*(3), pp. 263–81.

_____; **Ulph, David T. and Beath, John A.** R&D Rivalry vs R&D Cooperation under Uncertainty. *Rech. Écon. Louvain*, 1988, *54*(4), pp. 373–84.

Kattermann, Dieter and Franke, Reiner. Konsumnachfrage und technologische Arbeitslosigkeit in einem Input–Output-Modellrahmen. (Consumption Demand and Technological Unemployment in an Input–Output Framework.

With English summary.) *Jahr. Nationalökon. Statist.*, June 1988, *204*(6), pp. 518–30.

Katz, Arnold. The Viability of Labor-Managed Firms with Cournot–Nash Workers in a Mixed Economy with Profit-Maximizing Firms. In *Jones, D. C. and Svejnar, J., eds.*, 1988, pp. 133–48.

Katz, Avery. Judicial Decisionmaking and Litigation Expenditure. *Int. Rev. Law Econ.*, December 1988, *8*(2), pp. 127–43.

Katz, Barbara Goody and Owen, Joel. An Equilibrium Model of a Second Economy Market in a Centrally Planned Economy. *J. Compar. Econ.*, December 1988, *12*(4), pp. 546–69.

Katz, Eliakim and Alperovich, Gershon. The Location Decision and Employment Suburbanization. *Urban Stud.*, June 1988, *25*(3), pp. 243–47.

_____ **and Anam, Mahmudul.** Rent-Seeking and Second Best Economics. *Public Choice*, December 1988, *59*(3), pp. 215–24.

_____ **and Appelbaum, Elie.** Portfolio Diversification and Taxation. *Econ. Letters*, 1988, *26*(2), pp. 189–95.

_____ **and Smith, J. Barry.** Rent-Seeking and Optimal Regulation in Replenishable Resource Industries. *Public Choice*, October 1988, *59*(1), pp. 25–36.

Katz, Jorge and Bercovich, Néstor. Innovación genética, esfuerzos públicos de investigación y desarrollo y la frontera tecnológica internacional: nuevos híbridos en el inta. (With English summary.) *Desarrollo Econ.*, July–Sept. 1988, *28*(110), pp. 209–43.

Katz, Julius L. Implications for the Uruguay Round: Comments. In *Schott, J. J. and Smith, M. G., eds.*, 1988, pp. 177–80.

Katz, Lawrence F. Some Recent Developments in Labor Economics and Their Implications for Macroeconomics. *J. Money, Credit, Banking*, Part 2, August 1988, *20*(3), pp. 507–22.

Katzenstein, Peter J. Japan, Switzerland of the Far East? In *Inoguchi, T. and Okimoto, D. I., eds.*, 1988, pp. 275–304.

Katzman, Martin T. Pollution Liability Insurance and Catastrophic Environmental Risk. *J. Risk Ins.*, March 1988, *55*(1), pp. 75–100.

_____. Societal Risk Management through the Insurance Market. In *Hula, R. C., ed.*, 1988, pp. 21–42.

Katznelson, Shauli; Hirsch, Seev and Kalish, Shlomo. Effects of Knowledge and Service Intensities on Domestic and Export Performance. *Weltwirtsch. Arch.*, 1988, *124*(2), pp. 230–41.

Kauffman, Stuart A. The Evolution of Economic Webs. In *Anderson, P. W.; Arrow, K. J. and Pines, D., eds.*, 1988, pp. 125–46.

Kaufman, Bruce E. The Postwar View of Labor Markets and Wage Determination. In *Kaufman, B. E., ed.*, 1988, pp. 145–203.

_____ **and Martinez-Vazquez, Jorge.** Voting for Wage Concessions: The Case of the 1982 GM–UAW Negotiations. *Ind. Lab. Relat. Rev.*, January 1988, *41*(2), pp. 183–94.

Kaufman, Daniel J., Jr. Factors Affecting the

Magnitude of Premiums Paid to Target-Firm Shareholders in Corporate Acquisitions. *Financial Rev.*, November 1988, *23*(4), pp. 465–82.

Kaufman, George G. Bank Runs: Causes, Benefits, and Costs. *Cato J.*, Winter 1988, *7*(3), pp. 559–87.

―――. Securities Activities of Commercial Banks: Recent Changes in the Economic and Legal Environments. *J. Finan. Services Res.*, January 1988, *1*(2), pp. 183–99.

―――. The Truth about Bank Runs. In *England, C. and Huertas, T., eds.*, 1988, pp. 9–40.

――― **and Benston, George J.** Regulating Bank Safety and Performance. In *Haraf, W. S. and Kushmeider, R. M., eds.*, 1988, pp. 63–99.

―――; **Latta, Cynthia M. and Bierwag, G. O.** Duration Models: A Taxonomy. *J. Portfol. Manage.*, Fall 1988, *15*(1), pp. 50–54.

Kaufman, Herbert M. FNMA's Role in Deregulated Markets: Implications from Past Behavior. *J. Money, Credit, Banking*, November 1988, *20*(4), pp. 673–83.

Kaufman, Michael. Democracy and Social Transformation in Jamaica. *Soc. Econ. Stud.*, September 1988, *37*(3), pp. 45–73.

Kaufman, Richard F. Economic Trends and Defence Burdens in the United States and the Soviet Union. In *Saunders, C. T., ed.*, 1988, pp. 357–61.

Kaufman, Roger T. An International Comparison of Okun's Laws. *J. Compar. Econ.*, June 1988, *12*(2), pp. 182–203.

Kaufmann, Geir and Grønhaug, Kjell. Innovation: A Cross-Disciplinary Perspective: Introduction. In *Grønhaug, K. and Kaufmann, G., eds.*, 1988, pp. 1–10.

Kaufmann, Patrick J. and Stern, Louis W. Relational Exchange Norms, Perceptions of Unfairness, and Retained Hostility in Commercial Litigation. *J. Conflict Resolution*, September 1988, *32*(3), pp. 534–52.

Kaufold, Howard and Brown, Eleanor. Human Capital Accumulation and the Optimal Level of Unemployment Insurance Provision. *J. Lab. Econ.*, October 1988, *6*(4), pp. 493–514.

Kaul, Gautam and Conrad, Jennifer. Time-Variation in Expected Returns. *J. Bus.*, October 1988, *61*(4), pp. 409–25.

Kaul, P. K. Successes and Future Prospects. In *Lucas, R. E. B. and Papanek, G. F., eds.*, 1988, pp. 361–63.

Kaul, Sushila; Pandey, R. K. and Kumar, Ashok. Agricultural Field Wages in Orissa: An Economic Study. *Margin*, Oct.–Dec. 1988, *21*(1), pp. 72–78.

Kauper, Thomas E. The Role of Quality of Health Care Considerations in Antitrust Analysis. *Law Contemp. Probl.*, Spring 1988, *51*(2), pp. 273–340.

――― **and Snyder, Edward A.** Private Antitrust Cases That Follow on Government Cases. In *White, L. J., ed.*, 1988, pp. 329–70.

Kaur, Narinder and Singhal, K. C. India's Export Instabilty. *Margin*, Oct.–Dec. 1988, *21*(1), pp. 54–61.

Kauranen, Ilkka and Kaila, Martti M. Regional

Activation Projects and Small Firms: Application of the Learning-Based, Adaptive Approach. *Liiketaloudellinen Aikak.*, 1988, *37*(3), pp. 179–92.

Kavanaugh, Karen and Chelius, James R. Workers' Compensation and the Level of Occupational Injuries. *J. Risk Ins.*, June 1988, *55*(2), pp. 315–23.

Kavee, Robert C. and Zhu, Yu. Performance of Portfolio Insurance Strategies. *J. Portfol. Manage.*, Spring 1988, *14*(3), pp. 48–54.

Kavoossi, Masoud. The Postrevolutionary Iranian Economy: Opportunities and Constraints. *Bus. Econ.*, April 1988, *23*(2), pp. 34–40.

Kavvas, M. L.; Govindaraju, R. S. and Jones, S. E. On the Diffusion Wave Model for Overland Flow 2. Steady State Analysis. *Water Resources Res.*, May 1988, *24*(5), pp. 745–54.

―――; **Govindaraju, R. S. and Jones, S. E.** On the Diffusion Wave Model for Overland Flow 1. Solution for Steep Slopes. *Water Resources Res.*, May 1988, *24*(5), pp. 734–44.

Kawagoe, Toshihiko; Hayami, Yujiro and Ruttan, Vernon W. The Intercountry Agricultural Production Function and Productivity Differences among Countries: Reply. *J. Devel. Econ.*, February 1988, *28*(1), pp. 125–26.

―――; **Morooka, Yoshinori and Hayami, Yujiro.** Middlemen and Peasants: The Structure of the Indonesian Soybean Market. *Devel. Econ.*, March 1988, *26*(1), pp. 51–67.

Kawaller, Ira G.; Koch, Paul D. and Koch, Timothy W. The Relationship between the S&P 500 Index and S&P 500 Index Futures Prices. *Fed. Res. Bank Atlanta Econ. Rev.*, May–June 1988, *73*(3), pp. 2–10.

――― **and Koch, Timothy W.** Managing Cash Flow Risk in Stock Index Futures: The Tail Hedge. *J. Portfol. Manage.*, Fall 1988, *15*(1), pp. 41–44.

Kawano, Masamichi. The Effect of the Transfer in a Two-Class Model. *Metroecon.*, October 1988, *39*(3), pp. 299–315.

Kawasaki, Seiichi. Labor Demand and Standard Working Time in Dutch Manufacturing, 1954–1982: Comment. In *Hart, R. A., ed.*, 1988, pp. 206–07.

――― **and Hart, Robert A.** Payroll Taxes and Factor Demand. In *Ehrenberg, R. G., ed.*, 1988, pp. 257–85.

Kay, Cristóbal. El desarrollo agrario en Cuba: reformas ecónomicas y colectivización. (With English summary.) *Desarrollo Econ.*, Jan.–March 1988, *27*(108), pp. 559–87.

Kay, Geoffrey. Economic Forms and the Possibility of Crisis. In *Williams, M., ed.*, 1988, pp. 80–95.

―――. Right and Force: A Marxist Critique of Contract and the State. In *Williams, M., ed.*, 1988, pp. 115–33.

Kay, John. The Forms of Regulation. In *Goodhart, C., et al.*, 1988, pp. 33–42.

――― **and Keen, Michael J.** Measuring the Inefficiencies of Tax Systems. *J. Public Econ.*, April 1988, *35*(3), pp. 265–87.

―――; **Thompson, David and Helm, Dieter.** Energy Policy and the Role of the State in the Market for Energy. *Fisc. Stud.*, February 1988, *9*(1), pp. 41–61.

Kay, Neil M. The R&D Function: Corporate Strategy and Structure. **In** *Dosi, G., et al., eds.*, 1988, pp. 282–94.

_____. Three Different Ways to Tie Your Shoelaces: Comment on Hodgson. *J. Econ. Issues*, March 1988, *22*(1), pp. 233–44.

_____ **and Earl, Peter E.** How Economics Can Accept Shackle's Critique of Economic Doctrines without Arguing Themselves Out of Their Jobs. **In** *Earl, P. E., ed., Vol. 1*, 1988, *1985*, pp. 59–73.

_____ **and Galbraith, Craig S.** Towards a Theory of Multinational Enterprise. **In** *Earl, P. E., ed., Vol. 2*, 1988, *1986*, pp. 71–87.

Kayaalp, Orhan. Ugo Mazzola and the Italian Theory of Public Goods. *Hist. Polit. Econ.*, Spring 1988, *20*(1), pp. 15–25.

Kaylen, Michael S. Vector Autoregression Forecasting Models: Recent Developments Applied to the U.S. Hog Market. *Amer. J. Agr. Econ.*, August 1988, *70*(3), pp. 701–12.

_____ **and Brandt, Jon A.** A Note on Qualitative Forecast Evaluation: Comment. *Amer. J. Agr. Econ.*, May 1988, *70*(2), pp. 415–16.

_____; **Devino, Gary T. and Procter, Michael H.** Optimal Use of Qualitative Models: An Application to Country Grain Elevator Bankruptcies. *Southern J. Agr. Econ.*, December 1988, *20*(2), pp. 119–25.

Kaynak, Erdener. Application of Theories of Retailing to Developing Economies. **In** *Kaynak, E., ed.*, 1988, pp. 249–64.

_____. Changes and Developments of Retail Systems in Developing Countries. **In** *Kaynak, E., ed.*, 1988, pp. 299–307.

_____. Global Franchising: European and North American Perspectives. **In** *Kaynak, E., ed.*, 1988, pp. 43–50.

_____. Global Retailing: Integrative Statement. **In** *Kaynak, E., ed.*, 1988, pp. 3–19.

_____ **and Dalgic, Tevfik.** Irish Consumer Attitudes towards Foreign Products: Retail Policy Implications. **In** *Kaynak, E., ed.*, 1988, pp. 103–12.

_____ **and Ghauri, Pervez N.** Retail Distribution Systems in Sweden. **In** *Kaynak, E., ed.*, 1988, pp. 181–96.

_____ **and Rice, Gillian.** Retail Systems in Developing Countries: Some Insights from the Middle East. **In** *Kaynak, E., ed.*, 1988, pp. 265–76.

Kazakevich, D. M. Incentives for Intensification under Full Financial Accountability. *Matekon*, Fall 1988, *25*(1), pp. 18–37.

Kazemi, Hossein B. An Alternative Testable Form of the Consumption CAPM. *J. Finance*, March 1988, *43*(1), pp. 61–70.

_____. A Multiperiod Asset-Pricing Model with Unobservable Market Portfolio: A Note. *J. Finance*, September 1988, *43*(4), pp. 1015–24.

Kazemier, Brugt and van Eck, Robert. Features of the Hidden Economy in the Netherlands. *Rev. Income Wealth*, September 1988, *34*(3), pp. 251–73.

Kazgan, Gülten. Marketing in Economic Development. **In** *Kumcu, E. and Firat, A. F., eds.*, 1988, pp. 39–61.

Kazi, Shahnaz. Microeconomic Analysis of the Informal Sector—Results of Sample Surveys: Comments. *Pakistan Devel. Rev.*, Part 2, Winter 1988, *27*(4), pp. 618–19.

_____ **and Raza, Bilquees.** Households Headed by Women: Income, Employment and Household Organization. *Pakistan Devel. Rev.*, Part 2, Winter 1988, *27*(4), pp. 781–87.

Kealy, Mary Jo; Dovidio, John F. and Rockel, Mark L. Accuracy in Valuation is a Matter of Degree. *Land Econ.*, May 1988, *64*(2), pp. 158–71.

_____ **and Rockel, Mark L.** Merit Scholarships Are No Quick Fix for College Quality. *Econ. Educ. Rev.*, 1988, *7*(3), pp. 345–55.

Kealy, Walter G., Jr. International Travel and Passenger Fares, 1987. *Surv. Curr. Bus.*, May 1988, *68*(5), pp. 47–49.

Keane, Dennis M.; MacDonald, S. Leslie and Woo, Chi-Keung. Estimating Residential Partial Outage Cost with Market Research Data. *Energy J.*, Special Issue, 1988, *9*, pp. 151–59.

Keane, Michael; Moffitt, Robert and Runkle, David. Real Wages over the Business Cycle: Estimating the Impact of Heterogeneity with Micro Data. *J. Polit. Econ.*, December 1988, *96*(6), pp. 1232–66.

Kearl, J. R. The Covariance Structure of Earnings and Income, Compensatory Behavior, and On-the-Job Investments. *Rev. Econ. Statist.*, May 1988, *70*(2), pp. 214–23.

Kearney, Colm. Exchange Rate Dynamics and the Term Structure of Interest Rates. *Econ. Soc. Rev.*, April 1988, *19*(3), pp. 199–213.

_____ **and MacDonald, Ronald.** Assets Markets, the Current Account and Exchange Rate Determination: An Empirical Model of the Sterling/Dollar Rate 1973–1983. *Australian Econ. Pap.*, December 1988, *27*(51), pp. 213–32.

Keating, Barry and Bundt, Thomas. Depository Institution Competition in the Deregulated Environment: The Case of the Large Credit Union. *Appl. Econ.*, October 1988, *20*(10), pp. 1333–42.

Keating, Giles and Green, Christopher J. Capital Asset Pricing under Alternative Policy Regimes. *Econ. Modelling*, April 1988, *5*(2), pp. 133–44.

Keating, Michael. Local Government Reform and Finance in France. **In** *Paddison, R. and Bailey, S., eds.*, 1988, pp. 154–70.

Keck, Donald B. and Gunderson, Les C. Optical Fibers: Where Light Outperforms Electrons. **In** *Forester, T., ed.*, 1988, *1983*, pp. 214–29.

Kedia, Banwari L. and Bigler, William R., Jr. Environment, Strategy, and Performance: An Empirical Analysis in Two Service Industries. **In** *Grant, J. H., ed.*, 1988, pp. 181–217.

Keeble, David. High-Technology Industry and Local Environments in the United Kingdom. **In** *Aydalot, P. and Keeble, D., eds.*, 1988, pp. 65–98.

_____ **and Aydalot, Philippe.** High-Technology

Industry and Innovative Environments in Europe: An Overview. In *Aydalot, P. and Keeble, D., eds.*, 1988, pp. 1–21.

Keech, William R. and Chappell, Henry W., Jr. The Unemployment Rate Consequences of Partisan Monetary Policies. *Southern Econ. J.*, July 1988, 55(1), pp. 107–22.

Keefauver, William L. Communications: An Industry Perspective. In *Walker, C. E. and Bloomfield, M. A., eds.*, 1988, pp. 143–49.

Keehn, Richard H. and Smiley, Gene. Margin Purchases, Brokers' Loans and the Bull Market of the Twenties. In *Hausman, W. J., ed.*, 1988, pp. 129–42.

_____ and Smiley, Gene. U.S. Bank Failures, 1932–1933: A Provisional Analysis. In *Perkins, E. J., ed.*, 1988, pp. 136–56.

Keeler, Emmett B.; Carter, Grace M. and Trude, Sally. Insurance Aspects of DRG Outlier Payments. *J. Health Econ.*, September 1988, 7(3), pp. 193–214.

_____; Manning, Willard G. and Wells, Kenneth B. The Demand for Episodes of Mental Health Services. *J. Health Econ.*, December 1988, 7(4), pp. 369–92.

_____ and Rolph, John E. The Demand for Episodes of Treatment in the Health Insurance Experiment. *J. Health Econ.*, December 1988, 7(4), pp. 337–67.

Keeler, James P.; Thistle, Paul D. and Formby, John P. X-efficiency, Rent-Seeking and Social Costs. *Public Choice*, May 1988, 57(2), pp. 115–26.

Keeler, Theodore E. and Ying, John S. Measuring the Benefits of a Large Public Investment: The Case of the U.S. Federal-Aid Highway System. *J. Public Econ.*, June 1988, 36(1), pp. 69–85.

Keeley, Michael C. Bank Capital Regulation in the 1980s: Effective or Ineffective? *Fed. Res. Bank San Francisco Econ. Rev.*, Winter 1988, (1), pp. 3–20.

Keen, Howard, Jr. Use of Weekly and Other Monthly Data as Predictors of the Industrial Production Index. *Bus. Econ.*, January 1988, 23(1), pp. 44–48.

Keen, Kevin; Lucas, Rob G. and Gibbs, Barrie. Innovation and Human Resource Productivity in Canada: A Comparison of "High" and "Low" Technology Industries. In *Gattiker, U. E. and Larwood, L., eds.*, 1988, pp. 93–120.

Keen, Michael J. and Kay, John. Measuring the Inefficiencies of Tax Systems. *J. Public Econ.*, April 1988, 35(3), pp. 265–87.

Keenan, Donald and Rubin, Paul H. Shadow Interest Groups and Safety Regulation. *Int. Rev. Law Econ.*, June 1988, 8(1), pp. 21–36.

Keeney, Ralph L. Value-Focused Thinking and the Study of Values. In *Bell, D. E.; Raiffa, H. and Tversky, A., eds.*, 1988, pp. 465–94.

Keep, Ewart and Mayhew, Ken. The Assessment: Education, Training and Economic Performance. *Oxford Rev. Econ. Policy*, Autumn 1988, 4(3), pp. i–xv.

Keevil, Norman B., Jr. Future Challenges Facing the Canadian Minerals Industry: A Private Sector View. In *Richardson, P. R. and Gesing, R., eds.*, 1988, pp. 3–9.

Kehoe, Patrick J. Fiscal Policies and International Financial Markets: Comment. In *Frenkel, J. A., ed.*, 1988, pp. 221–27.

_____. On the Roles of International Financial Markets and Their Relevance for Economic Policy: Comment. *J. Money, Credit, Banking*, Part 2, August 1988, 20(3), pp. 550–54.

Kehoe, Timothy J. Computation and Multiplicity of Economic Equilibria. In *Anderson, P. W.; Arrow, K. J. and Pines, D., eds.*, 1988, pp. 147–67.

_____, et al. A General Equilibrium Analysis of the 1986 Tax Reform in Spain. *Europ. Econ. Rev.*, March 1988, 32(2–3), pp. 334–42.

Keiding, Hans. Er den offentlige sektor for stor? (The Size of the Public Sector. With English summary.) *Nationaløkon. Tidsskr.*, 1988, 126(1), pp. 1–12.

Keigher, Sharon M. State Medicaid Budgeting in Hard Times: Implications for Long-term Care. *Public Budg. Finance*, Summer 1988, 8(2), pp. 49–66.

Keil, Manfred W. Is the Political Business Cycle Really Dead? *Southern Econ. J.*, July 1988, 55(1), pp. 86–99.

Keilany, Ziad and Rabin, Alan. Absolute Liquidity Preference and the Pigou Effect: A Reply [A Note on the Incompatibility of the Pigou Effect and a Liquidity Trap]. *J. Post Keynesian Econ.*, Summer 1988, 10(4), pp. 655–57.

Keilman, N. Dynamic Household Models. In *Keilman, N.; Kuijsten, A. and Vossen, A., eds.*, 1988, pp. 123–38.

_____ and Keyfitz, Nathan. Recurrent Issues in Dynamic Household Modelling. In *Keilman, N.; Kuijsten, A. and Vossen, A., eds.*, 1988, pp. 254–85.

Keim, Donald B. Stock Market Regularities: A Synthesis of the Evidence and Explanations. In *Dimson, E., ed.*, 1988, pp. 16–39.

Keim, Gerald D.; Baysinger, Barry D. and Zeithaml, Carl P. Toward an Integrated Strategic Management Process: An Empirical Review of Corporate Political Strategy. In *Grant, J. H., ed.*, 1988, pp. 377–93.

_____ and Zardkoohi, Asghar. Looking for Leverage in PAC Markets: Corporate and Labor Contributions Considered. *Public Choice*, July 1988, 58(1), pp. 21–34.

Keith, Christopher and Grody, Allan. Electronic Automation at the New York Stock Exchange. In *Guile, B. R. and Quinn, J. B., eds. (I)*, 1988, pp. 82–107.

Keith, Verna M. and Smith, David P. The Current Differential in Black and White Life Expectancy. *Demography*, November 1988, 25(4), pp. 625–32.

Keizer, P. K. Wage Formation in the Context of Collective Bargaining: Reply. *De Economist*, 1988, 136(4), pp. 538–40.

Kekre, Sunder; Banker, Rajiv D. and Datar, Srikant M. Relevant Costs, Congestion and Stochasticity in Production Environments. *J. Acc. Econ.*, July 1988, 10(3), pp. 171–97.

Keleher, Robert E. Price Level Changes and the Adjustment Process under Fixed Rates. *Cato J.*, Fall 1988, 8(2), pp. 385–92.

Kelejian, Harry H.; Stephan, Scott W. and Gatto, Joseph P. Stochastic Generalizations of Demand Systems with an Application to Telecommunications. *Info. Econ. Policy*, 1988, 3(4), pp. 283–309.

Kell, Michael and Dilnot, Andrew. Top-Rate Tax Cuts and Incentives: Some Empirical Evidence. *Fisc. Stud.*, November 1988, 9(4), pp. 70–92.

————; **Webb, Steven B. and Dilnot, Andrew.** The 1988 Budget and the Structure of Personal Taxation. *Fisc. Stud.*, May 1988, 9(2), pp. 38–47.

Kellar, Jeffrey H. New Methodology Reduces Importance of Used Cars in the Revised CPI. *Mon. Lab. Rev.*, December 1988, 111(12), pp. 34–36.

Kelleher, Jeanette and Bennett, Paul. The International Transmission of Stock Price Disruption in October 1987. *Fed. Res. Bank New York Quart. Rev.*, Summer 1988, 13(2), pp. 17–33.

Kellenbenz, Hermann. Frederic C. Lane. *J. Europ. Econ. Hist.*, Spring 1988, 17(1), pp. 159–84.

Keller Brown, Linda. Female Managers in the United States and in Europe: Corporate Boards, M.B.A. Credentials, and the Image/Illusion of Progress. In *Adler, N. J. and Izraeli, D., eds.*, 1988, pp. 265–74.

Keller, Wouter J. and Bethlehem, Jelke G. New Perspectives in Computer Assisted Survey Processing. In *Edwards, D. and Raun, N. E., eds.*, 1988, pp. 377–88.

Kelley, Allen C. Australia: The Coming of Age. *Australian Econ. Rev.*, Winter 1988, (82), pp. 27–44.

————. Economic Consequences of Population Change in the Third World. *J. Econ. Lit.*, December 1988, 26(4), pp. 1685–1728.

————. Population Pressures, Saving, and Investment in the Third World: Some Puzzles. *Econ. Develop. Cult. Change*, April 1988, 36(3), pp. 449–64.

———— **and Schmidt, Robert M.** The Demographic Transition and Population Policy in Egypt. In *Schultz, T. Paul, ed.*, 1988, pp. 69–110.

Kelley, Edward W., Jr. and Angell, Wayne D. Statement to the U.S. House Subcommittee on Domestic Monetary Policy of the Committee on Banking, Finance and Urban Affairs, May 3, 1988. *Fed. Res. Bull.*, July 1988, 74(7), pp. 437–45.

Kelley, James F., Jr. Coping With the Career Plateau. In *Timpe, A. D., ed.*, 1988, 1985, pp. 289–99.

Kelley, Patricia C. and Mahon, John F. The Politics of Toxic Wastes: Multinational Corporations as Facilitators of Transnational Public Policy. In *Preston, L. E., ed.*, 1988, pp. 59–86.

Kelley, Paul L. Current Issues in East–West Trade Relations. In *Brada, J. C. and Wadekin, K.-E., eds.*, 1988, pp. 385–96.

Kelley, Rita Mae. Success, Productivity and the Public Sector. In *Kelly, R. M., ed.*, 1988, pp. 1–16.

Kelley, Robin D. G. "Comrades, Praise Gawd for Lenin and Them!": Ideology and Culture among Black Communists in Alabama, 1930–1935. *Sci. Soc.*, Spring 1988, 52(1), pp. 59–82.

Kelley, Thomas P. The Dingell Hearings and Related AICPA Initiatives. In *Neimark, M., ed.*, 1988, pp. 157–65.

Kellman, Mitchell and Chow, Peter C. Y. Anti-LDC Bias in the U.S. Tariff Structure: A Test of Source versus Product Characteristics. *Rev. Econ. Statist.*, November 1988, 70(4), pp. 648–53.

Kellogg, Christopher B. and Wang, Stanley D. H. An Econometric Model for American Lobster. *Marine Resource Econ.*, 1988, 5(1), pp. 61–70.

Kellogg, Robert L. Modeling Soviet Modernization: An Economy in Transition. *Soviet Econ.*, Jan.–March 1988, 4(1), pp. 36–56.

————; **Easley, J. E., Jr. and Johnson, Thomas G.** Optimal Timing of Harvest for the North Carolina Bay Scallop Fishery. *Amer. J. Agr. Econ.*, February 1988, 70(1), pp. 50–62.

———— **and Leggett, Robert E.** The Soviet Union: An Economy in Transition and Its Prospects for Economic Growth. In *Liebowitz, R. D., ed.*, 1988, pp. 23–51.

Kelly, Aidan and Brannick, Teresa. Explaining the Strike-Proneness of British Companies in Ireland. *Brit. J. Ind. Relat.*, March 1988, 26(1), pp. 37–55.

Kelly, Austin and Krumm, Ronald. Multiperiod Migration Patterns: The Timing and Frequency of Household Responses. *J. Reg. Sci.*, May 1988, 28(2), pp. 255–70.

Kelly, Gary Wayne. Some Regulatory Determinants of Bank Risk Behavior: Comment. *J. Money, Credit, Banking*, May 1988, 20(2), pp. 265–69.

Kelly, Jerry S. Computational Complexity. *Soc. Choice Welfare*, November 1988, 5(4), pp. 313–17.

————. A Minimal Manipulability and Local Strategy-Proofness. *Soc. Choice Welfare*, 1988, 5(1), pp. 81–85.

————. Rights and Social Choice: Comment. *Econ. Philos.*, October 1988, 4(2), pp. 316–25.

————. Social Choice and Computational Complexity. *J. Math. Econ.*, 1988, 17(1), pp. 1–8.

Kelly, Kenneth. The Analysis of Causality in Escape Clause Cases. *J. Ind. Econ.*, December 1988, 37(2), pp. 187–207.

Kelly, William. Needed: New Statistics for a New Economics. In *Brown, R. C., ed.*, 1988, pp. 49–53.

Kelly, William A., Jr.; Nardinelli, Clark and Wallace, Myles S. Should' We Sell the Fed? *Cato J.*, Spring–Summer 1988, 8(1), pp. 125–38.

Kelsey, David. The Economics of Chaos or the Chaos of Economics. *Oxford Econ. Pap.*, March 1988, 40(1), pp. 1–31.

————. Policies to Achieve a Better Distribution

of Income: Or Is a Dollar a Dollar? *Oxford Econ. Pap.*, September 1988, *40*(3), pp. 577–83.

_____. What is Responsible for the "Paretian Epidemic"? *Soc. Choice Welfare*, November 1988, *5*(4), pp. 303–06.

Kemal, A. R. Pakistan's Experience with Manufacturing of Components for Consumer Durables. *Pakistan Devel. Rev.*, Part 2, Winter 1988, *27*(4), pp. 863–73.

Kemme, David M. Economic Reform and Foreign Trade in Poland: Comments. In *[Holzman, F. D.]*, 1988, pp. 378–83.

Kemp, John R. "Money Can't Buy Me Love": Paradoxes and Expected Utility Theory: A Clarification. *Scot. J. Polit. Econ.*, May 1988, *35*(2), pp. 149–61.

Kemp, Murray C. and Shimomura, Koji. The Impossibility of Global Absolute Advantage in the Heckscher–Ohlin Model of Trade. *Oxford Econ. Pap.*, September 1988, *40*(3), pp. 575–76.

Kempf, Hubert. Rational Expectations, Imperfect Price Adjustment and the Optimality of Monetary Policy. *J. Econ. (Z. Nationalökon.)*, 1988, *48*(3), pp. 223–41.

Kempton, R. A. and Talbot, M. The Development of New Crop Varieties. *J. Roy. Statist. Soc.*, 1988, *151*(2), pp. 327–41.

Kenderov, P. S. Generic Uniqueness of the Solution of "Max Min" Problems. In *Kurzhanski, A.; Neumann, K. and Pallaschke, D., eds.*, 1988, pp. 41–48.

Kendrick, John W. Productivity in Services. In *Guile, B. R. and Quinn, J. B., eds. (II)*, 1988, pp. 99–117.

Kenen, Peter B. International Money and Macroeconomics. In *Elliott, K. A. and Williamson, J., eds.*, 1988, pp. 5–41.

Kenessey, Zoltan E. The Four Megasectors of the Economy in an International Context. In *Salazar-Carrillo, J. and Rao, D. S. P., eds.*, 1988, pp. 179–94.

_____, et al. Recent Developments in Economic Statistics at the Federal Reserve: Part 1. *Bus. Econ.*, October 1988, *23*(4), pp. 47–52.

Keng, Kau Ah and Ehrenberg, Andrew S. C. Patterns of Store Choice. In *Wrigley, N., ed.*, 1988, pp. 225–50.

Kennally, G. F. and Hall, Stephen G. Analysing Unstable Policy Prescriptions in Linear Difference Models with Rational Expectations. *Bull. Econ. Res.*, June 1988, *40*(3), pp. 217–25.

Kennan, John. An Econometric Analysis of Fluctuations in Aggregate Labor Supply and Demand. *Econometrica*, March 1988, *56*(2), pp. 317–33.

_____ and Riezman, Raymond. Do Big Countries Win Tariff Wars? *Int. Econ. Rev.*, February 1988, *29*(1), pp. 81–85.

Kennedy, Eileen T. Alternatives to Consumer-Oriented Food Subsidies for Achieving Nutritional Objectives. In *Pinstrup-Andersen, P., ed.*, 1988, pp. 147–58.

_____ and Cogill, Bruce. The Commercialization of Agriculture and Household-Level Food Se-

curity: The Case of Southwestern Kenya. *World Devel.*, September 1988, *16*(9), pp. 1075–81.

Kennedy, John and Vanzetti, David. Endogenous Price Policies and International Wheat Prices: Comment. *Amer. J. Agr. Econ.*, August 1988, *70*(3), pp. 743–46.

Kennedy, W. J. D. and Carpenter, Susan L. The Denver Metropolitan Water Roundtable: A Case Study in Researching Agreements. *Natural Res. J.*, Winter 1988, *28*(1), pp. 21–35.

Kennelly, B. Welfarism, IIA and Arrovian Constitutional Rules. *Soc. Choice Welfare*, November 1988, *5*(4), pp. 307–11.

Kennett, Steve and Beatty, David. Striking Back: Fighting Words, Social Protest and Political Participation in Free and Democratic Societies. In *Carter, D. D., et al.*, 1988, pp. 214–66.

Kenney, George B. and Bowen, H. Kent. New Materials. In *Uyehara, C. H., ed.*, 1988, pp. 62–89.

Kenney, Martin and Buttel, Frederick H. Prospects and Strategies for Overcoming Dependence. In *Research and Info. System for the Non-aligned and Other Developing Countries.*, 1988, pp. 315–48.

_____; Mair, Andrew and Florida, Richard. The New Geography of Automobile Production: Japanese Transplants in North America. *Econ. Geogr.*, October 1988, *64*(4), pp. 352–73.

Kennickell, Arthur B.; Avery, Robert B. and Elliehausen, Gregory E. Measuring Wealth with Survey Data: An Evaluation of the 1983 Survey of Consumer Finances. *Rev. Income Wealth*, December 1988, *34*(4), pp. 339–69.

Kent, Calvin A. Subsistence Rights, Economic Liberty and the Constitution. In *Association of Private Education*, 1988, pp. 32–46.

Kenton, R. Hours at Work: Jevons' Labor Theory After 100 Years. In *Wood, J. C., ed., Vol. 2*, 1988, *1971*, pp. 112–15.

Kenward, Lloyd and Evans, Owen. Macroeconomic Effects of Tax Reform in the United States. *Int. Monet. Fund Staff Pap.*, March 1988, *35*(1), pp. 141–65.

Kenwood, George. The Use of Statistics for Policy Advising: Colin Clark in Queensland, 1938–52. In *[Clark, C.]*, 1988, pp. 107–22.

Kenyon, Daphne A. Implicit Aid to State and Local Governments through Federal Tax Deductibility. In *Bell, M. E., ed.*, 1988, pp. 63–99.

_____ and Dougan, William R. Pressure Groups and Public Expenditures: The Flypaper Effect Reconsidered. *Econ. Inquiry*, January 1988, *26*(1), pp. 159–70.

Kenyon, Peter and Harcourt, G. C. Pricing and the Investment Decision. In *Sawyer, M. C., ed.*, 1988, *1976*, pp. 266–94.

Keohane, Robert O. Bargaining Perversities, Institutions, and International Economic Relations. In *Guerrieri, P. and Padoan, P. C., eds.*, 1988, pp. 28–50.

_____. The Rhetoric of Economics as Viewed by a Student of Politics. In *Klamer, A.; McClos-*

key, D. N. and Solow, R. M., eds., 1988, pp. 240–46.

Keown, Arthur J. and Fields, M. Andrew. The Merger Profile and Size Effect Anomalies: An Empirical Examination of Their Relationship. *Quart. J. Bus. Econ.*, Winter 1988, *27*(1), pp. 70–82.

Kephart, George. Heterogeneity and the Implied Dynamics of Regional Growth Rates: Was the Nonmetropolitan Turnaround an Artifact of Aggregation? *Demography*, February 1988, *25*(1), pp. 99–113.

Kephart, Robert and Peterson, Dyanne. Himself, at Sixty with Apologies to Ogden Nash. In *[Rothbard, M. N.]*, 1988, pp. 392–94.

de Kergos, Yann. Traitement fiscal du logiciel dans l'informatique: France. (Tax Treatment of Computer Software: France. With English summary.) In *International Fiscal Association, ed. (II)*, 1988, pp. 359–77.

Kerin, John. Exchange Rates and Interest Rates: Where to Now? Implications for Farmers, Miners and Manufacturers: Opening Speech. *Rev. Marketing Agr. Econ.*, April 1988, *56*(1), pp. 57–59.

Kerin, Paul D. Some Implications of Sunk, Congestion and Seasonal Opening Costs within a Regional Grain Handling and Transport System. *J. Transp. Econ. Policy*, May 1988, *22*(2), pp. 175–96.

Kern, William S. Frank Knight on Preachers and Economic Policy: A 19th Century Liberal Anti-Religionist, He Thought Religion Should Support the Status Quo. *Amer. J. Econ. Soc.*, January 1988, *47*(1), pp. 61–69.

———. The Lemon Principle, Democratic Politics, and Frank Knight's First Law of Talk. *Public Choice*, October 1988, *59*(1), pp. 83–87.

Kerner, Antonín. Affordable Housing in a Socialist Country: The Case of Prague. In *Friedrichs, J., ed.*, 1988, pp. 75–88.

———. Reflections on the Draft Bill on the State Enterprise. *Czech. Econ. Digest.*, April 1988, (2), pp. 47–65.

Kerner, Donna O. "Hard Work" and Informal Sector Trade in Tanzania. In *Clark, G., ed.*, 1988, pp. 41–56.

Kerns, Wilmer L. and Glanz, Milton P. Private Social Welfare Expenditures, 1972–85. *Soc. Sec. Bull.*, August 1988, *51*(8), pp. 3–10.

Kerr, Clark. The Neoclassical Revisionists in Labor Economics (1940–1960)—R.I.P.m. In *Kaufman, B. E., ed.*, 1988, pp. 1–46.

Kerr, Tom; Diakosavvas, Dimitris and Horton, Susan. The Social Costs of Higher Food Prices: Some Cross-country Evidence. *World Devel.*, July 1988, *16*(7), pp. 847–56.

Kerr, William A. The Canada–United States Free Trade Agreement and the Livestock Sector: The Second-Stage Negotiations. *Can. J. Agr. Econ.*, Part 2, December 1988, *36*(4), pp. 895–903.

———. Danish Beef Exports to Canada—A Multinational Dispute. *J. Econ. Stud.*, 1988, *15*(1), pp. 32–43.

———; **McLachlan, D. L. and Apuzzo, A.** The

Canada–U.S. Free Trade Agreement: A Canadian Perspective. *J. World Trade*, August 1988, *22*(4), pp. 9–34.

Kerre, Hassan O. Industrialization and the Low-Level Production Trap: Handtools and Cutlery in Kenya. *Eastern Afr. Econ. Rev.*, December 1988, *4*(2), pp. 40–48.

Kersten, H. M. P. and Balk, B. M. The Precision of Consumer Price Indices Caused by the Sampling Variability of Budget Surveys; An Example. In *Eichhorn, W., ed.*, 1988, pp. 49–58.

Kerton, Robert R. Time for a "Wingspread." In *Maynes, E. S. and ACCI Research Committee, eds.*, 1988, pp. 585–88.

Kervin, John. Sociology, Psychology, and Industrial Relations. In *Hébert, G.; Jain, H. C. and Meltz, N. M., eds..*, 1988, pp. 187–242.

Keskinen, A. Benefits of Using Videotex Services: An Experiment for Farmers—A Nationwide Cooperation Project in Finland. In *Schiefer, G., ed.*, 1988, pp. 55–60.

Keskinok, Çağatay. Comments on the Recent Debates on Privatization of Services and Goods Provided Publicly. *METU*, 1988, *15*(3–4), pp. 75–88.

Kesner, Idalene F.; Rechner, Paula L. and Dalton, Dan R. Corporate Governance and Boards of Directors: An International, Comparative Perspective. In *Farmer, R. N. and McGoun, E. G., eds.*, 1988, pp. 95–105.

Kespohl, Elke; DeLorme, Charles D., Jr. and Cartwright, Phillip A. The Effect of Temporal Aggregation on the Test of Wagner's Law. *Public Finance*, 1988, *43*(3), pp. 373–87.

Kessler, Denis and Masson, André. Equal vs. Unequal Estate Sharing: Comments. In *Kessler, D. and Masson, A., eds.*, 1988, pp. 117–19.

——— **and Masson, André.** Le cycle de vie de la théorie du cycle de vie. (The Life Cycle of the Life Cycle Hypothesis. With English summary.) *Ann. Écon. Statist.*, Jan.–March 1988, (9), pp. 1–27.

——— **and Masson, André.** Modelling the Accumulation and Distribution of Wealth: Introduction. In *Kessler, D. and Masson, A., eds.*, 1988, pp. 1–18.

——— **and Masson, André.** On Five Hot Issues on Wealth Distribution. *Europ. Econ. Rev.*, March 1988, *32*(2–3), pp. 644–53.

——— **and Masson, André.** Wealth Distributional Consequences of Life Cycle Models. In *Kessler, D. and Masson, A., eds.*, 1988, pp. 287–318.

Kessler, Jeffrey L. and Millstein, Ira M. The Antitrust Legacy of the Reagan Administration. *Antitrust Bull.*, Fall 1988, *33*(3), pp. 505–41.

Kester, W. Carl. Capital and Ownership Structure: A Comparison of U.S. and Japanese Manufacturing Corporations. In *Spence, A. M. and Hazard, H. A., eds.*, 1988, pp. 263–87.

Kets de Vries, Manfred F. R. and Miller, Danny. Personality, Culture, and Organization. In *Albanese, P. J., ed.*, 1988, pp. 81–99.

Ketz, J. Edward and Kunitake, Walter K. An Evaluation of the Conceptual Framework: Can

It Resolve the Issues Related to Accounting for Income Taxes? In *Schwartz, B. N., ed.,* 1988, pp. 37–54.

Keudel, Walter. Computer-Aided Line Network Design (DIANA) and Minimization of Transfer Times in Networks (FABIAN) In *Daduna, J. R. and Wren, A., eds.,* 1988, pp. 315–26.

Keuning, Steven J. and de Ruijter, Willem A. Guidelines to the Construction of a Social Accounting Matrix. *Rev. Income Wealth,* March 1988, *34*(1), pp. 71–100.

Keuschnigg, Christian and Jaeger, Albert. Adjusting Unsustainable Budget Deficits and Crowding Out. *Jahr. Nationalökon. Statist.,* December 1988, *205*(6), pp. 492–505.

Keyfitz, Barbara Lee. An Analytic Model for Change of Type in Three-Phase Flow. In *Wheeler, M. F., ed.,* 1988, pp. 149–60.

Keyfitz, Nathan. Some Demographic Properties of Transfer Schemes: How to Achieve Equity Between the Generations. In *Lee, R. D.; Arthur, W. B. and Rodgers, G., eds.,* 1988, pp. 92–105.

_____ **and Keilman, N.** Recurrent Issues in Dynamic Household Modelling. In *Keilman, N.; Kuijsten, A. and Vossen, A., eds.,* 1988, pp. 254–85.

Keynes, John Maynard. The General Theory of Employment. In *Shaw, G. K., ed., Vol. 1,* 1988, *1937,* pp. 7–21.

_____. William Stanley Jevons 1835–1882: A Centenary Allocution on His Life and Work as Economist and Statistician. In *Wood, J. C., ed., Vol. 1,* 1988, *1936,* pp. 59–93.

Khabarova, T. On the Socialist Modification of Value. *Prob. Econ.,* September 1988, *31*(5), pp. 49–55.

Khajuria, Sajay; Beenstock, Michael and Dickinson, Gerry. The Relationship between Property-Liability Insurance Premiums and Income: An International Analysis. *J. Risk Ins.,* June 1988, *55*(2), pp. 259–72.

Khakee, Abdul. The Rationale for Urban Government Action for Arts Funding. *J. Cult. Econ.,* December 1988, *12*(2), pp. 1–18.

Khaled, S. M.; Sethuraman, T. V. and Jog, S. D. Market Saturation in Indian Conditions: Cement Industry: A Case Study. *Indian Econ. J.,* Jan.–March 1988, *35*(3), pp. 39–46.

Khalidi, Raja. The Economy of the Palestinian Arabs in Israel. In *Abed, G. T., ed.,* 1988, pp. 37–70.

Khalil, Mohammad and Mansour, Ali H. Iraqi Prewar Economic Structure. *J. Energy Devel.,* Spring 1988, *13*(2), pp. 187–95.

Khamis, Salem H. Suggested Methods for Consistent Temporal–Spatial Comparisons. In *Salazar-Carrillo, J. and Rao, D. S. P., eds.,* 1988, pp. 67–73.

Khan, Aliya H. Landlessness in Rural Areas of Pakistan and Policy Options: A Preliminary Investigation: Comments. *Pakistan Devel. Rev.,* Part 2, Winter 1988, *27*(4), pp. 575–76.

_____ **and Saqib, Najamus.** On an Empirical Definition of Money for Pakistan. *Pakistan*

Devel. Rev., Part 2, Winter 1988, *27*(4), pp. 853–57.

Khan, Aman R. The Impact of Recent Oil Price Changes on the Natural Gas Industry. In *Mabro, R., ed.,* 1988, pp. 149–63.

Khan, Ashfaque H. Factor Demand in Pakistan's Manufacturing Sector. *Int. Econ. J.,* Autumn 1988, *2*(3), pp. 51–59.

_____. Financial Repression, Financial Development and Structure of Savings in Pakistan. *Pakistan Devel. Rev.,* Part 2, Winter 1988, *27*(4), pp. 701–11.

_____. Fiscal Dependence on Trade Taxes and Economic Development: A Case Study of Pakistan. *Public Finance,* 1988, *43*(1), pp. 96–112.

_____. Is There a Phillips Curve in Pakistan? Comments. *Pakistan Devel. Rev.,* Part 2, Winter 1988, *27*(4), pp. 850–51.

_____. Macroeconomic Policy and Private Investment in Pakistan. *Pakistan Devel. Rev.,* Autumn 1988, *27*(3), pp. 277–91.

_____. Public Spending and Deficits: Evidence from a Developing Economy. *Public Finance,* 1988, *43*(3), pp. 396–402.

Khan, Azizur R. Population Growth and Access to Land: An Asian Perspective. In *Lee, R. D., et al., eds.,* 1988, pp. 143–61.

Khan, Ghulam Ishaq. Fifth Annual General Meeting of the Pakistan Society of Development Economists (PSDE) Islamabad, January 4–6, 1989: Inaugural Address. *Pakistan Devel. Rev.,* Part 1, Winter 1988, *27*(4), pp. 347–53.

Khan, Habibullah and Zerby, John. Relationships between Technological Change and Social Development: A Comparative Study. In *Tisdell, C. and Maitra, P., eds.,* 1988, pp. 166–87.

Khan, Haider Ali. Impact of Trade Sanctions on South Africa: A Social Accounting Matrix Approach. *Contemp. Policy Issues,* October 1988, *6*(4), pp. 130–40.

Khan, Kameel I. Petroleum Taxation and Contracts in the Third World—A Law and Policy Perspective. *J. World Trade,* February 1988, *22*(1), pp. 67–88.

Khan, M. Ali. Development Policy in a Multiprovincial Economy. *Pakistan Devel. Rev.,* Part 1, Winter 1988, *27*(4), pp. 399–418.

_____. Ioffe's Normal Cone and the Foundations of Welfare Economics: An Example. *Econ. Letters,* 1988, *28*(1), pp. 15–19.

_____. What Remains of the Case for Flexible Exchange Rates? Comments. *Pakistan Devel. Rev.,* Part 1, Winter 1988, *27*(4), pp. 446–48.

Khan, Mahmood Hasan. Conditions of Agricultural Growth in Developing Countries: Comments. *Pakistan Devel. Rev.,* Part 1, Winter 1988, *27*(4), pp. 469–70.

_____. The Development of Rural People: Myths and Approaches. *Pakistan Devel. Rev.,* Part 1, Winter 1988, *27*(4), pp. 379–90.

Khan, Mohsin S. Islamic Interest-Free Banking: Reply. *Int. Monet. Fund Staff Pap.,* September 1988, *35*(3), pp. 537.

_____ **and Knight, Malcolm D.** Import Compression and Export Performance in Developing Countries. *Rev. Econ. Statist.,* May 1988, *70*(2), pp. 315–21.

Khan, Shahrukh Rafi. Henry George and an Alternative Islamic Land Tenure System. *Econ. Develop. Cult. Change*, July 1988, 36(4), pp. 721–39.

_____ and Ali, Syed Zahid. Some Findings on Higher Educated Unemployment in Pakistan. *Can. J. Devel. Stud.*, 1988, 9(2), pp. 261–78.

Khan, Shulamit and Lang, Kevin. Efficient Estimation of Structural Hedonic Systems. *Int. Econ. Rev.*, February 1988, 29(1), pp. 157–66.

Khan, Zubeda. Fertility Histories: With and without Restrictions—An Analysis of PLM Data. *Pakistan Devel. Rev.*, Part 2, Winter 1988, 27(4), pp. 671–74.

Khandker, Rezaul K. Offer Heterogeneity in a Two State Model of Sequential Search. *Rev. Econ. Statist.*, May 1988, 70(2), pp. 259–65.

Khandker, Shahidur R. Determinants of Women's Time Allocation in Rural Bangladesh. *Econ. Develop. Cult. Change*, October 1988, 37(1), pp. 111–26.

_____. Input Management Ability, Occupational Patterns, and Farm Productivity in Bangladesh Agriculture. *J. Devel. Stud.*, January 1988, 24(2), pp. 214–31.

Khanna, Kailash C. India: Budget 1988/89: May the Rain Gods Come to Our Rescue. *Bull. Int. Fiscal Doc.*, June 1988, 42(6), pp. 247–50.

Kharadia, V. C. The Behaviour of Income Velocity of Money in India: Implications for Monetary Theory and Policy. *Indian Econ. J.*, July–September 1988, 36(1), pp. 1–17.

Kharas, Homi J. and Kiguel, Miguel A. Monetary Policy and Foreign Debt: The Experiences of the Far East Countries. In *Cheng, H.-S., ed.*, 1988, pp. 95–124.

_____ and Levinsohn, James. LDC Savings Rates and Debt Crises. *World Devel.*, July 1988, 16(7), pp. 779–86.

Khatkhate, Deena R. Assessing the Impact of Interest Rates in Less Developed Countries. *World Devel.*, May 1988, 16(5), pp. 577–88.

Khazzoom, J. Daniel. Gasoline Conservation versus Pollution Control: Unintended Consequences, Continued. *J. Policy Anal. Manage.*, Fall 1988, 7(4), pp. 710–14.

Khemani, R. S. and Shapiro, D. M. On Entry and Mobility Barriers. *Antitrust Bull.*, Spring 1988, 33(1), pp. 115–34.

Khilji, Nasir M. and Jones, Jonathan D. Money Growth, Inflation, and Causality (Empirical Evidence for Pakistan, 1973–85). *Pakistan Devel. Rev.*, Spring 1988, 27(1), pp. 45–58.

Khoury, Nabil T. and Fortin, Michel. Effectiveness of Hedging Interest Rate Risks and Stock Market Risks with Financial Futures. *J. Futures Markets*, June 1988, 8(3), pp. 319–34.

Khoury, Sarkis J. and Ghosh, Alo. Recent Developments in International Banking and Finance, Volume II: Overview. In *Khoury, S. J. and Ghosh, A., eds.*, 1988, pp. 1–43.

Khoylian, Roubina; MacMillan, Ian C. and Kulow, David M. Venture Capitalists' Involvement in Their Investments: Extent and Performance. In *Kirchhoff, B. A., et al., eds.*, 1988, pp. 303–23.

Khundker, Nasreen. The Fuzziness of the Informal Sector: Can We Afford to Throw Out the Baby with the Bath Water? Comment. *World Devel.*, October 1988, 16(10), pp. 1263–65.

Khusro, A. M. The Poverty of Poverty Analysis in India. In *Lucas, R. E. B. and Papanek, G. F., eds.*, 1988, pp. 145–47.

Kiani, M. Framurz Khan and Nazli, Samina. Dynamics of Birth Spacing in Pakistan. *Pakistan Devel. Rev.*, Part 2, Winter 1988, 27(4), pp. 655–57.

Kidane, Amdetsion and Lee, Joe W. Tobacco Consumption Pattern: A Demographic Analysis. *Atlantic Econ. J.*, December 1988, 16(4), pp. 92.

Kidwell, David S. and Blackwell, David W. An Investigation of Cost Differences between Public Sales and Private Placements of Debt. *J. Finan. Econ.*, December 1988, 22(2), pp. 253–78.

_____ and Hsueh, L. Paul. The Impact of a State Bond Guarantee on State Credit Markets and Individual Municipalities. *Nat. Tax J.*, June 1988, 41(2), pp. 235–45.

Kiefer, David M. A History of the U.S. Federal Budget and Fiscal Policy. *Public Finance*, 1988, 43(1), pp. 113–37.

_____ and Philips, Peter. Doubts Regarding the Human Capital Theory of Racial Inequality. *Ind. Relat.*, Spring 1988, 27(2), pp. 251–62.

_____ and Philips, Peter. Race and Human Capital: An Institutionalist Response. In *Mangum, G. and Philips, P., eds.*, 1988, pp. 117–43.

Kiefer, Márta. External Economic Adjustment and Major Industrial Development Concepts. *Eastern Europ. Econ.*, Spring 1988, 26(3), pp. 5–21.

Kiefer, Nicholas M. Economic Duration Data and Hazard Functions. *J. Econ. Lit.*, June 1988, 26(2), pp. 646–79.

_____. Employment Contracts, Job Search Theory, and Labour Turnover: Preliminary Empirical Results. *J. Appl. Econometrics*, July–Sept. 1988, 3(3), pp. 169–86.

_____. Optimal Collection of Information by Partially Informed Agents: Reply. *Econometric Rev.*, 1988–89, 7(2), pp. 161–63.

_____. Optimal Collection of Information by Partially Informed Agents. *Econometric Rev.*, 1988–89, 7(2), pp. 113–48.

_____ and Easley, David. Controlling a Stochastic Process with Unknown Parameters. *Econometrica*, September 1988, 56(5), pp. 1045–64.

_____ and Nyarko, Yaw. Control of a Linear Regression Process with Unknown Parameters. In *Barnett, W. A.; Berndt, E. R. and White, H., eds.*, 1988, pp. 105–20.

de Kieffer, Donald E. Foreign Policy Trade Controls and the GATT. *J. World Trade*, June 1988, 22(3), pp. 73–80.

Kierans, Thomas. Federal Government Policy Issues and Current Privatization Initiatives. In *Walker, M. A., ed. (II)*, 1988, pp. 141–51.

Kierzkowski, Henryk. Issues of Strategic Trade Policy for Small Countries: Comment. In *Haa-*

land, J. I. and Norman, V. D., eds., 1988, pp. 153–55.

———. A New International Trading System: Comment. In *Borner, S., ed.*, 1988, pp. 139–44.

———. Strategic Trade, Embargoes, and Imperfect Competition. In *Baldwin, R. E.; Hamilton, C. B. and Sapir, A., eds.*, 1988, pp. 135–52.

Kieser, Alfred. Adapting Organizations to Micro-Electronics—and Micro-electronics to Organizations: Experiences in the Federal Republic of Germany. In *Urabe, K.; Child, J. and Kagono, T., eds.*, 1988, pp. 319–36.

Kiesling, Herbert J. Symposium on Tax Reform: Correspondence. *J. Econ. Perspectives*, Spring 1988, *2*(2), pp. 175–76.

Kiesner, W. F. Entrepreneurship, Is the Grass Really Greener? In *Association of Private Education*, 1988, pp. 145–55.

Kiguel, Miguel A. and Dauhajre, Andres. A Dynamic Model of the Open Economy with Sluggish Output. *Int. Econ. Rev.*, November 1988, *29*(4), pp. 587–606.

——— **and Kharas, Homi J.** Monetary Policy and Foreign Debt: The Experiences of the Far East Countries. In *Cheng, H.-S., ed.*, 1988, pp. 95–124.

——— **and Liviatan, Nissan.** Inflationary Rigidities and Orthodox Stabilization Policies: Lessons from Latin America. *World Bank Econ. Rev.*, September 1988, *2*(3), pp. 273–98.

Kikkawa, Takeo. Functions of Japanese Trade Associations before World War II: The Case of Cartel Organizations. In *Yamazaki, H. and Miyamoto, M., eds.*, 1988, pp. 53–83.

———. Functions of Japanese Trade Associations before World War II: The Case of Cartel Organizations: Response. In *Yamazaki, H. and Miyamoto, M., eds.*, 1988, pp. 85–86.

Kilcollin, Thomas Eric. After the Crash: Linkages between Stocks and Futures: Trading Systems. In *MacKay, R. J., ed.*, 1988, pp. 75–78.

Kill, Heinrich H. and Heinze, G. Wolfgang. The Development of the German Railroad System. In *Mayntz, R. and Hughes, T. P., eds.*, 1988, pp. 105–34.

Killick, Tony and Commander, Simon. Privatisation in Developing Countries: A Survey of the Issues. In *Cook, P. and Kirkpatrick, C., eds.*, 1988, pp. 91–124.

——— **and Commander, Simon.** State Divestiture as a Policy Instrument in Developing Countries. *World Devel.*, December 1988, *16*(12), pp. 1465–79.

Killing, J. Peter. Understanding Alliances: The Role of Task and Organizational Complexity. In *Contractor, F. J. and Lorange, P.*, 1988, pp. 55–67.

Kilmer, Richard L. and Taylor, Timothy G. An Analysis of Market Structure and Pricing in the Florida Celery Industry. *Southern J. Agr. Econ.*, December 1988, *20*(2), pp. 35–43.

Kilpatrick, Andrew; Mayes, David G. and Davies, Glenn. Fiscal Policy Simulations—A Comparison of UK Models. *Appl. Econ.*, December 1988, *20*(12), pp. 1613–34.

——— **and Moir, Christopher.** Developments in the UK's International Trading Performance. In *Barker, T. and Dunne, P., eds.*, 1988, pp. 141–69.

——— **and Naisbitt, Barry.** Energy Intensity, Industrial Structure and the 1970s' Productivity Slowdown. *Oxford Bull. Econ. Statist.*, August 1988, *50*(3), pp. 229–41.

———; **Naisbitt, Barry and Driver, Ciaran.** The Sensitivity of Estimated Employment Effects in Input–Output Studies. *Econ. Modelling*, April 1988, *5*(2), pp. 145–50.

Kilss, Beth and Scheuren, Frederick J. The 1973 CPS–IRS–SSA Exact Match Study. *Soc. Sec. Bull.*, July 1988, *51*(7), pp. 23–31.

Kim, Benjamin J. C. Real Wage Response to Monetary Shocks: A Disaggregated Analysis. *J. Macroecon.*, Spring 1988, *10*(2), pp. 183–200.

———. A Time-Series Study of the Employment–Real Wage Relationship: An International Comparison. *J. Econ. Bus.*, February 1988, *40*(1), pp. 67–78.

Kim, Bong Chin and Labys, Walter C. Application of the Translog Model of Energy Substitution to Developing Countries: The Case of Korea. *Energy Econ.*, October 1988, *10*(4), pp. 313–23.

Kim, C. S. and Schaible, Glenn. Estimation of Transition Probabilities Using Median Absolute Deviations. *J. Agr. Econ. Res.*, Fall 1988, *40*(4), pp. 12–19.

Kim, Chan-Wung and Chang, Eric C. Day of the Week Effects and Commodity Price Changes. *J. Futures Markets*, April 1988, *8*(2), pp. 229–41.

Kim, Daesik and Santomero, Anthony M. Risk in Banking and Capital Regulation. *J. Finance*, December 1988, *43*(5), pp. 1219–33.

Kim, Do Hoon. Le gain spécifique de l'échange international de biens intermédiaires. (With English summary.) *Revue Écon. Polit.*, July–Aug. 1988, *98*(4), pp. 530–50.

Kim, E. Han; Bradley, Michael and Desai, Anand. Synergistic Gains from Corporate Acquisitions and Their Division between the Stockholders of Target and Acquiring Firms. *J. Finan. Econ.*, May 1988, *21*(1), pp. 3–40.

Kim, H. Youn. Analyzing the Indirect Production Function for U.S. Manufacturing. *Southern Econ. J.*, October 1988, *55*(2), pp. 494–504.

———. The Consumer Demand for Education. *J. Human Res.*, Spring 1988, *23*(2), pp. 173–92.

———. The Econometric Modelling of Aggregate Consumer Behaviour: A Comment. *Europ. Econ. Rev.*, April 1988, *32*(4), pp. 1013–17.

——— **and Clark, Robert M.** Economies of Scale and Scope in Water Supply. *Reg. Sci. Urban Econ.*, November 1988, *18*(4), pp. 479–502.

Kim, Hyung-Ki. Institutional Framework for Decision Making in Korean Public Enterprises: Some Implications for Developing Countries. In *Streeten, P., ed.*, 1988, pp. 212–26.

Kim, Insu; Neiss, Hubert and Aghevli, Bijan B. Growth and Adjustment: Experiences of Selected Subcontinent Countries. In *Streeten, P., ed.*, 1988, pp. 30–53.

Kim, Jae-Cheol. Information and Interrelations between the Dealer and Private Markets. *Metroecon.*, June 1988, *39*(2), pp. 161–79.

Kim, Ji-Hong. The Effects of Tariffs and Export Subsidies on Entry Barriers and Investment. *Int. Econ. J.*, Winter 1988, *2*(4), pp. 73–93.

Kim, Jin-Hyun and Yang, Bong-Min. Voluntary Health Insurance and Providers' Price Discounting Behaviour in Korea. In *Butler, J. R. G. and Doessel, D. P.*, eds., 1988, pp. 192–206.

Kim, Joong-Woong. Economic Development and Financial Liberalization in the Republic of Korea: Policy Reforms and Future Prospects. In *Urrutia, M., ed.*, 1988, pp. 137–71.

Kim, K. H. and Roush, F. W. Strategic Tariff Equilibrium and Optimal Tariffs. *Math. Soc. Sci.*, April 1988, *15*(2), pp. 105–34.

Kim, K. Kyu. Organizational Coordination and Performance in Hospital Accounting Information Systems: An Empirical Investigation. *Accounting Rev.*, July 1988, *63*(3), pp. 472–89.

Kim, Kihwan. Korea in the 1990s: Making the Transition to a Developed Economy. *World Devel.*, January 1988, *16*(1), pp. 7–18.

Kim, Kwan S. Continuing Crisis in Sub-Saharan Africa. In *Tavis, L. A., ed.*, 1988, pp. 102–18.

———. East Asian Coping Strategies: The South Korean Case. In *Tavis, L. A., ed.*, 1988, pp. 119–37.

——— **and Clements, Benedict J.** Comércio exterior e distribuição de renda: O caso brasileiro. (With English summary.) *Pesquisa Planejamento Econ.*, April 1988, *18*(1), pp. 17–36.

Kim, Kyung-Hwan and Mills, Edwin S. Korean Development and Urbanization: Prospects and Problems. *World Devel.*, January 1988, *16*(1), pp. 157–67.

Kim, Linsu. The Transfer of Programmable Automation Technology to a Rapidly Developing Country: An Initial Assessment. *Int. Econ. J.*, Summer 1988, *2*(2), pp. 29–39.

Kim, Moon K. and Wu, Chunchi. Effects of Inflation on Capital Structure. *Financial Rev.*, May 1988, *23*(2), pp. 183–200.

Kim, Moshe. The Structure of Technology with Endogenous Capital Utilization. *Int. Econ. Rev.*, February 1988, *29*(1), pp. 111–30.

——— **and Moore, Giora.** Economic vs. Accounting Depreciation. *J. Acc. Econ.*, April 1988, *10*(2), pp. 111–25.

Kim, Seungwook and Danielsen, Albert L. OPEC Stability: An Empirical Assessment. *Energy Econ.*, July 1988, *10*(3), pp. 174–84.

Kim, Sooyong. The Korean Construction Industry as an Exporter of Services. *World Bank Econ. Rev.*, May 1988, *2*(2), pp. 225–38.

Kim, Sun-Woong. Capitalizing on the Weekend Effect. *J. Portfol. Manage.*, Spring 1988, *14*(3), pp. 59–63.

Kim, T. John and Suh, Sunduck. Toward Developing a National Transportation Planning Model: A Bilevel Programming Approach for

Korea. *Ann. Reg. Sci.*, February 1988, *22*, pp. 65–80.

Kim, Tae-Kyun; Baumel, C. Phillip and Lee, Tenpao. Impact of Deregulation on the Financial Performance of the Class I Railroads: Heuristic Models of Pooled Time-Series and Cross-Sectional Data. *Logist. Transp. Rev.*, September 1988, *24*(3), pp. 281–96.

Kim, Taeho and Miles, James A. On the Valuation of FDIC Deposit Insurance: An Empirical Study Using Contingent Claims Analysis. *Quart. J. Bus. Econ.*, Autumn 1988, *27*(4), pp. 47–68.

Kim, Wan-Soon and Yun, K. Y. Fiscal Policy and Development in Korea. *World Devel.*, January 1988, *16*(1), pp. 65–83.

Kim, Wi-Saeng; Lee, Jae Won and Francis, Jack Clark. Investment Performance of Common Stocks in Relation to Insider Ownership. *Financial Rev.*, February 1988, *23*(1), pp. 53–64.

——— **and Lyn, Esmeralda O.** Excess Market Value, Market Power, and Inside Ownership Structure. *Rev. Ind. Organ.*, Fall 1988, *3*(4), pp. 1–25.

Kim, Won Bae. Population Redistribution Policy in Korea: A Review. *Population Res. Policy Rev.*, 1988, *7*(1), pp. 49–77.

Kim, Woncheol and Ro, Kongkyun. A Causal VARMA Model Analysis with an Application to Canadian Money and Income Data. *Appl. Econ.*, September 1988, *20*(9), pp. 1167–83.

Kim, Woo-choong. The Era of Pacific Coprosperity. In *Feldstein, M., ed. (II)*, 1988, pp. 152–58.

Kim, Yong Cheol and Stulz, Rene M. The Eurobond Market and Corporate Financial Policy: A Test of the Clientele Hypothesis. *J. Finan. Econ.*, December 1988, *22*(2), pp. 189–205.

Kim, Yong H. and Srinivasan, Venkat. Decision Support for Working Capital Management: A Conceptual Framework. In *Kim, Y. H., ed.*, 1988, pp. 187–216.

——— **and Srinivasan, Venkat.** Integrating Corporate Strategy and Multinational Capital Budgeting: An Analytical Framework. In *Khoury, S. J. and Ghosh, A., eds.*, 1988, pp. 381–97.

Kim, Yooman M. A Theory of Internationally Diversified Production under Uncertainty: Effects of Exchange Rate Fluctuations on Return Performance and Risk Associated with Direct Foreign Investment. *J. Econ. Devel.*, June 1988, *13*(1), pp. 155–73.

Kim, Young Sik. Financial Market Behavior and Balance of Payments during the Periods of Partial Financial Reform in Korea, 1976–81. *Devel. Econ.*, September 1988, *26*(3), pp. 247–63.

Kimball, Miles S. Farmers' Cooperatives as Behavior Toward Risk. *Amer. Econ. Rev.*, March 1988, *78*(1), pp. 224–32.

Kimbrough, Kent P. Optimal Tax Policy for Balance of Payments Objectives. In *Frenkel, J. A., ed.*, 1988, pp. 309–37.

Kimenyi, Mwangi S. International Trade, Immiserizing Growth, and the Prisoner's Dilemma:

Evidence from Kenya. *Eastern Afr. Econ. Rev.*, June 1988, *4*(1), pp. 53–63.

Kimura, Hiroshi. Gorbachev's "New Thinking" and the Asian-Pacific Region. In *Juviler, P. and Kimura, H., eds.*, 1988, pp. 149–70.

_____ **and Juviler, Peter H.** Gorbachev's Reforms: U.S. and Japanese Assessments: Introduction. In *Juviler, P. and Kimura, H., eds.*, 1988, pp. xi–xxi.

Kimura, Yoshitaka; Ikeda, Syunsuke and Parker, Gary. Stable Width and Depth of Straight Gravel Rivers with Heterogeneous Bed Materials. *Water Resources Res.*, May 1988, *24*(5), pp. 713–22.

Kinal, Terrence and Lahiri, Kajal. A Model for Ex Ante Real Interest Rates and Derived Inflation Forecasts. *J. Amer. Statist. Assoc.*, September 1988, *83*(403), pp. 665–73.

Kincaid, G. Russell. Policy Implications of Structural Changes in Financial Markets. *Finance Develop.*, March 1988, *25*(1), pp. 2–5.

Kind, Paolo; Poli, Giorgio and Basevi, Giorgio. Economic Cooperation and Confrontation between Europe and the U.S.A.: A Game-Theoretic Approach to the Analysis of International Monetary and Trade Policies. In *Baldwin, R. E.; Hamilton, C. B. and Sapir, A., eds.*, 1988, pp. 369–88.

Kindleberger, Charles P. Bank Failures: The 1930s and the 1980s. In *Kindleberger, C. P.*, 1988, *1986*, pp. 69–93.

_____. Distress in International Financial Markets. In *Kindleberger, C. P.*, 1988, pp. 110–20.

_____. Dominance and Leadership in the International Economy: Exploitation, Public Goods, and Free Rides. In *Kindleberger, C. P.*, 1988, *1978*, pp. 185–95.

_____. Economic Development and International Responsibility. In *Kindleberger, C. P.*, 1988, *1987*, pp. 143–52.

_____. Economic Responsibility. In *Kindleberger, C. P.*, 1988, pp. 196–210.

_____. The European Community: Hierarchy or Federation? In *Kindleberger, C. P.*, 1988, *1986*, pp. 161–66.

_____. The Financial Crises of the 1930s and the 1980s: Similarities and Differences. *Kyklos*, 1988, *41*(2), pp. 171–86.

_____. Government and International Trade. In *Kindleberger, C. P.*, 1988, *1978*, pp. 211–29.

_____. Hierarchy versus Inertial Cooperation. In *Kindleberger, C. P.*, 1988, *1986*, pp. 153–60.

_____. Il "lunedí nero" del 1987: considerazioni in prospettiva storica. (Is There Going to Be a Depression? With English summary.) *Rivista Storia Econ.*, S.S., June 1988, *5*(2), pp. 221–33.

_____. International Capital Movements and Foreign Exchange Markets in Crisis: The 1930s and the 1980s. In *Kindleberger, C. P.*, 1988, *1986*, pp. 49–68.

_____. International Public Goods without International Government. In *Kindleberger, C. P.*, 1988, *1986*, pp. 123–42.

_____. Is There Going to Be a Depression? In *Kindleberger, C. P.*, 1988, pp. 3–15.

_____. New Forms of Internationalisation in Business: Concluding Remarks. In *Borner, S., ed.*, 1988, pp. 385–88.

_____. Overtrading, Sometimes Followed by Revulsion and Discredit. In *Kindleberger, C. P.*, 1988, *1987*, pp. 16–28.

_____. Reflections on Current Changes in National and International Capital Markets. In *Kindleberger, C. P.*, 1988, *1987*, pp. 29–48.

_____. Reversible and Irreversible Processes in Economics. In *Kindleberger, C. P.*, 1988, *1986*, pp. 94–106.

_____. Standards as Public, Collective and Private Goods. In *Kindleberger, C. P.*, 1988, *1983*, pp. 167–84.

_____. W. Arthur Lewis Lecture: The Lewis Model of "Economic Growth with Unlimited Supplies of Labor." *Rev. Black Polit. Econ.*, Winter 1988, *16*(3), pp. 15–24.

_____. The 1930s and the 1980s: Parallels and Differences. *Banca Naz. Lavoro Quart. Rev.*, June 1988, (165), pp. 135–45.

Kindred, Hugh M. Modern Methods of Processing Overseas Trade. *J. World Trade*, December 1988, *22*(6), pp. 5–17.

King, Arthur E.; Brada, Josef C. and Hey, Jeanne C. Inter-regional and Inter-organizational Differences in Agricultural Efficiency in Czechoslovakia. In *Brada, J. C. and Wadekin, K.-E., eds.*, 1988, pp. 334–43.

King, B. Frank and Avery, David. A Tale of Two Georgias. *Fed. Res. Bank Atlanta Econ. Rev.*, Jan.–Feb. 1988, *73*(1), pp. 24–35.

King, David A. and Sinden, J. A. Influence of Soil Conservation on Farm Land Values. *Land Econ.*, August 1988, *64*(3), pp. 242–55.

King, David N. Fiscal Federalism. In *Paddison, R. and Bailey, S., eds.*, 1988, pp. 6–29.

_____. The Future Role of Grants in Local Government Finance. In *Bailey, S. J. and Paddison, R., eds.*, 1988, pp. 130–49.

King, Desmond. Sources of Local Finance in the United States. In *Paddison, R. and Bailey, S., eds.*, 1988, pp. 84–115.

King, J. Charles. Contract, Utility, and the Evaluation of Institutions. *Cato J.*, Spring–Summer 1988, *8*(1), pp. 29–52.

King, J. E. and Howard, Michael C. Henryk Grossmann and the Breakdown of Capitalism. *Sci. Soc.*, Fall 1988, *52*(3), pp. 290–309.

_____ **and Regan, P.** Recent Trends in Labour's Share. In *Brenner, Y. S.; Reijnders, J. P. G. and Spithoven, A. H. G. M., eds.*, 1988, pp. 54–86.

King, Jane and Slesser, Malcolm. Resource Accounting: An Application to Development Planning. *World Devel.*, February 1988, *16*(2), pp. 293–303.

King, Maxwell L. and Evans, Merran A. A Further Class of Tests for Heteroscedasticity. *J. Econometrics*, February 1988, *37*(2), pp. 265–76.

King, Mervyn. A General Equilibrium Analysis of Tax Reform: Comments. In *Aaron, H. J.;*

Galper, H. and Pechman, J. A., eds., 1988, pp. 108–12.

———. Lessons from General Equilibrium Models: Comments. In Aaron, H. J.; Galper, H. and Pechman, J. A., eds., 1988, pp. 50–53.

——— and Roell, Ailsa. The Regulation of Takeovers and the Stock Market. Nat. Westminster Bank Quart. Rev., February 1988, pp. 2–14.

King, Michael J. Viscous Fingering and Probabilistic Simulation. In Wheeler, M. F., ed., 1988, pp. 161–76.

King, Robert G. Money Demand in the United Staes: A Quantitative Review: Comment. Carnegie–Rochester Conf. Ser. Public Policy, Autumn 1988, 29, pp. 169–72.

——— and Dotsey, Michael. Rational Expectations Business Cycle Models: A Survey. Fed. Res. Bank Richmond Econ. Rev., March–April 1988, 74(2), pp. 3–15.

——— and Goodfriend, Marvin. Financial Deregulation, Monetary Policy, and Central Banking. In Haraf, W. S. and Kushmeider, R. M., eds., 1988, pp. 216–53.

——— and Goodfriend, Marvin. Financial Deregulation, Monetary Policy, and Central Banking. Fed. Res. Bank Richmond Econ. Rev., May–June 1988, 74(3), pp. 3–22.

———; Plosser, Charles I. and Rebelo, Sergio T. Production, Growth and Business Cycles: I. The Basic Neoclassical Model. J. Monet. Econ., March–May 1988, 21(2–3), pp. 195–232.

———; Plosser, Charles I. and Rebelo, Sergio T. Production, Growth and Business Cycles: II. New Directions. J. Monet. Econ., March–May 1988, 21(2–3), pp. 309–41.

King, Robert P. and Sonka, Steven T. Management Problems of Farms and Agricultural Firms. In Hildreth, R. J., et al., eds., 1988, pp. 270–97.

———, et al. The Agricultural Risk Management Simulator Microcomputer Program. Southern J. Agr. Econ., December 1988, 20(2), pp. 165–71.

King, Ronald H.; Patton, W. E., III and Puto, Christopher P. Individual and Joint Decision-Making in Industrial Purchasing. In Woodside, A. G., ed., 1988, pp. 95–117.

King, Russell. Italy: Multi-faceted Tourism. In Williams, A. M. and Shaw, G., eds., 1988, pp. 58–79.

King, Stephen R. Is Increased Price Flexibility Stabilizing? Comment. Amer. Econ. Rev., March 1988, 78(1), pp. 0234.

King, Thomas E. and Ortegren, Alan K. Accounting for Hybrid Securities: The Case of Adjustable Rate Convertible Notes. Accounting Rev., July 1988, 63(3), pp. 522–35.

King, Thomas R. and Murnighan, J. Keith. Stability and Outcome Tradeoffs in Asymmetric Dilemmas: Conditions Promoting the Discovery of Alternating Solutions. In Tietz, R.; Albers, W. and Selten, R., eds., 1988, pp. 85–94.

King, William R. Strategic Management Decision

Support Systems. In Grant, J. H., ed., 1988, pp. 237–59.

Kingery, W. David. Looking to the Future in Ceramics. In Forester, T., ed., 1988, pp. 315–28.

Kingsland, Sharon. Evolution and Debates over Human Progress from Darwin to Sociobiology. Population Devel. Rev., Supplement, 1988, 14, pp. 167–98.

Kinnard, William N., et al. The First Twenty Years of AREUEA. Amer. Real Estate Urban Econ. Assoc. J., Summer 1988, 16(2), pp. 189–205.

Kinniry, Fran; Koziara, Edward and Yan, Chiou-Shuang. The Economic Performance of the Presidents 1909–1946: A Preliminary View. In Pennsylvania Economic Association, 1988, pp. 260–69.

Kinnucan, Henry, et al. Processor Demand and Price-Markup Functions for Catfish: A Disaggregated Analysis with Implications for the Off-Flavor Problem. Southern J. Agr. Econ., December 1988, 20(2), pp. 81–91.

Kinnunen, Juha. The Time Series Properties of Accrual versus Cash-Based Income Variables: Empirical Evidence from Listed Finnish Firms. Liiketaloudellinen Aikak., 1988, 37(2), pp. 162–71.

Kinscherff, Paul and Homer, Pierce. The International Joint Commission: The Role It Might Play. In Schmandt, J.; Clarkson, J. and Roderick, H., eds., 1988, pp. 190–216.

Kinsey, Jean. International Trade and Trade-Offs for Third World Consumers: A Matter of Entitlements. In Maynes, E. S. and ACCI Research Committee, eds., 1988, pp. 405–11.

Kintner, Hallie J. Determinants of Temporal and Areal Variation in Infant Mortality in Germany, 1871–1933. Demography, November 1988, 25(4), pp. 597–609.

Kipnis, Baruch A. and Swyngedouw, Erik A. Manufacturing Plant Size—Toward a Regional Strategy. A Case Study in Limburg, Belgium. Urban Stud., February 1988, 25(1), pp. 43–52.

Kirby, Alison J. Trade Associations as Information Exchange Mechanisms. Rand J. Econ., Spring 1988, 19(1), pp. 138–46.

Kirby, Michael G. and Lewis, Philip E. T. A New Approach to Modelling the Effects of Incomes Policies. Econ. Letters, 1988, 28(1), pp. 81–85.

Kirby, Ronald F. The Prospects for Greater Private Sector Involvement in Urban Transportation. In Weicher, J. C., ed., 1988, pp. 23–28.

Kirchgässner, Gebhard and Pommerehne, Werner W. Government Spending in Federal Systems: A Comparison between Switzerland and Germany. In Lybeck, J. A. and Henrekson, M., eds., 1988, pp. 327–56.

Kirchler, Erich. Diary Reports on Daily Economic Decisions of Happy versus Unhappy Couples. J. Econ. Psych., September 1988, 9(3), pp. 327–57.

———. Household Economic Decision Making. In van Raaij, W. F.; van Veldhoven, G. M.

and Wärneryd, K.-E., eds., 1988, pp. 258–92.
———. The Long Arm of Unemployment—
Change of Marital Power after Job Loss. In
Maital, S., ed., Vol. 1, 1988, pp. 212–27.
Kirchner, Christian. The New Institutional Eco-
nomics Applied to Monetary Economics: Com-
ment. J. Inst. Theoretical Econ., February
1988, 144(1), pp. 231–36.
Kirim, Arman. Transnational Corporations, Oli-
gopoly and Industrialisation: An Interpretive
Survey. METU, 1988, 15(1–2), pp. 23–48.
———. Türkiye Imalat Sanayiinde Teknoloji Ihra-
cati. (With English summary.) METU, 1988,
15(3–4), pp. 159–79.
Kirk, Robert. Determinants of Occupational
Shifts in Urban Labor Markets. Reg. Sci.
Persp., 1988, 18(2), pp. 60–77.
Kirkbride, Paul S. and Durcan, James W. Power
and the Bargaining Process: A Comment on
Leap and Grigsby. Ind. Lab. Relat. Rev., July
1988, 41(4), pp. 618–21.
Kirkby, Richard. Urban Housing Policy after
Mao. In Feuchtwang, S.; Hussain, A. and Pai-
rault, T., eds., Vol. 1, 1988, pp. 227–44.
Kirkham, G. E. 'To Pay the Rent and Lay Up
Riches': Economic Opportunity in Eighteenth-
Century North–West Ulster. In Mitchison, R.
and Roebuck, P., eds., 1988, pp. 95–104.
Kirkley, James E. and Strand, Ivar E., Jr. The
Technology and Management of Multi-species
Fisheries. Appl. Econ., October 1988, 20(10),
pp. 1279–92.
Kirkpatrick, Colin and Cook, Paul. Privatisation
in Less Developed Countries: An Overview.
In Cook, P. and Kirkpatrick, C., eds., 1988,
pp. 3–44.
——— and Cook, Paul. Privatisation in Less De-
veloped Countries: Preface. In Cook, P. and
Kirkpatrick, C., eds., 1988, pp. xvii–xix.
Kirschke, Dieter. Agriculture: Trade and Protec-
tion: Comment. In Baldwin, R. E.; Hamilton,
C. B. and Sapir, A., eds., 1988, pp. 124–31.
Kirton, Claremont D. Public Policy and Private
Capital in the Transition to Socialism: Grenada
1979–83. Soc. Econ. Stud., September 1988,
37(3), pp. 125–50.
Kirton, M. J. Adaptors and Innovators: Problem
Solvers in Organizations. In Grønhaug, K. and
Kaufmann, G., eds., 1988, pp. 65–85.
Kirzner, Israel M. The Economic Calculation De-
bate: Lessons for Austrians. In Rothbard,
M. N. and Block, W., eds., 1988, pp. 1–18.
———. Welfare Economics: A Modern Austrian
Perspective. In [Rothbard, M. N.], 1988, pp.
77–88.
Kischka, Peter. On the Effects of Bayesian Learn-
ing for a Risk-Averse Consumer. In Eichhorn,
W., ed., 1988, pp. 289–95.
Kiselev, S. V. and Petrikov, A. V. The Innovative
Potential of Managers of Agro-Industrial Enter-
prises. Prob. Econ., June 1988, 31(2), pp. 44–
59.
Kisielewicz, Michał and Góra, Zielona. Existence
of Optimal Trajectory of Mayer: Problem for
Neutral Functional Differential Inclusions. In

Kurzhanski, A.; Neumann, K. and Pallaschke,
D., eds., 1988, pp. 227–31.
Kistner, Klaus-Peter and Luhmer, Alfred. Ein
dynamisches Modell des Betriebsmitteleinsatzes. (With English summary.) Z. Betriebswirtshaft, January 1988, 58(1), pp. 63–83.
———; Luhmer, Alfred and Feichtinger, Gustav. Ein dynamisches Modell des Intensitätssplittings. (With English summary.) Z. Betriebswirtshaft, November 1988, 58(11), pp.
1242–58.
Kitahara, Yasusada. Telecommunications in an
Advanced Information Society: A Japanese Perspective. In Orishimo, I.; Hewings, G. J. D.
and Nijkamp, P., eds., 1988, pp. 39–46.
Kitamura, T., et al. Japan's Suwa Basin: A Regional Agricultural Model. In Parikh, J. K.,
ed., 1988, pp. 209–51.
Kitcher, Philip. Explanatory Unification. In Pitt,
J. C., ed., 1988, 1981, pp. 167–87.
Kitterer, Wolfgang. Der Einfluss der Alters-
sicherung auf die gesamtwirtschaftliche Kapital-
bildung. (The Influence of Pension Plans on
Overall Capital Formation. With English summary.) Kredit Kapital, 1988, 21(3), pp. 383–
406.
———. Staatsverschuldung und intertemporale
Allokation. (Public Debt and Intertemporal Re-
source Allocation. With English summary.)
Jahr. Nationalökon. Statist., April 1988,
204(4), pp. 346–63.
Kiyokawa, Yukihiko and Ishikawa, Shigeru. The
Significance of Standardization in the Development of the Machine-Tool Industry: The Cases
of Japan and China (Part II). Hitotsubashi J.
Econ., June 1988, 29(1), pp. 73–88.
Kiyono, Kazuharu and Inoue, Tadashi. Optimal
Restriction on Foreign Trade and Investment
with a Nontraded Good. Econ. Stud. Quart.,
September 1988, 39(3), pp. 246–57.
——— and Inoue, Tadashi. Optimal Restriction
on Foreign Trade and Investment with a Nontraded Good. Econ. Stud. Quart., September
1988, 39(3), pp. 246–57.
——— and Okuno-Fujiwara, Masahiro. Second-
Mover Advantage in R&D Innovation and Imitation in Dynamic Oligopoly. Econ. Stud.
Quart., December 1988, 39(4), pp. 356–77.
Kiyotaki, Nobuhiro. Multiple Expectational Equi-
libria under Monopolistic Competition. Quart.
J. Econ., November 1988, 103(4), pp. 695–713.
Kjeldsen-Kragh, S. Størrelsesøkonomi i dansk
landbrug. (The Size Economies in Danish Agri-
culture. With English summary.) Nationalø-
kon. Tidsskr., 1988, 126(1), pp. 43–57.
Klaassen, Jan. The Netherlands and the Seventh
Directive. In Gray, S. J. and Coenenberg,
A. G., eds., 1988, pp. 117–27.
Klacek, Jan. Economic Growth and Efficiency:
A Comparative Efficiency Approach. Europ.
Econ. Rev., March 1988, 32(2–3), pp. 443–50.
Klachko, Wolodymyr. An Analysis of Consumer's
Disposable Money Income and Saving Deposit
in the Soviet Union. J. Econ. Devel., Decem-
ber 1988, 13(2), pp. 41–56.
Klaiss, H. and Nitsch, J. The Economics of En-

ergy and Cooperation with Energy-Producing Countries. In *Winter, C.-J. and Nitsch, J., eds.*, 1988, pp. 368–74.

Klamer, Arjo. Economics as Discourse. In *de Marchi, N., ed.*, 1988, pp. 259–78.

_____. Negotiating a New Conversation about Economics. In *Klamer, A.; McCloskey, D. N. and Solow, R. M., eds.*, 1988, pp. 265–79.

_____ **and McCloskey, Donald N.** Economics in the Human Conversation. In *Klamer, A.; McCloskey, D. N. and Solow, R. M., eds.*, 1988, pp. 3–20.

Klant, J. J. The Natural Order. In *de Marchi, N., ed.*, 1988, pp. 87–117.

Klarquist, Virginia L. and Ferris, John W. Productivity Gains Lukewarm for Makers of Non-electric Heating Equipment. *Mon. Lab. Rev.*, March 1988, *111*(3), pp. 27–32.

_____ **and Wilder, Patricia S.** Retail Hardware Stores Register Productivity Gain. *Mon. Lab. Rev.*, May 1988, *111*(5), pp. 39–43.

Klas, Anton. A System of Models for Macroeconomic Analysis and Its Uses in Simulating Economic Development. *Czech. Econ. Pap.*, 1988, (25), pp. 99–128.

Klatt, Lawrence A. A Study of Small Business/ Entrepreneurial Education in Colleges and Universities. In *Association of Private Education*, 1988, pp. 103–08.

Klayman, Robert A. and Hulten, Charles R. Investment Incentives in Theory and Practice. In *Aaron, H. J.; Galper, H. and Pechman, J. A., eds.*, 1988, pp. 317–38.

Kleber, P. Materials Processing in Space. In *Egan, J. J., et al., eds.*, 1988, pp. 55–72.

Kleidon, Allan W. Bubbles, Fads and Stock Price Volatility Tests: A Partial Evaluation: Discussion. *J. Finance*, July 1988, *43*(3), pp. 656–60.

_____. The Probability of Gross Violations of a Present Value Variance Inequality: Reply. *J. Polit. Econ.*, October 1988, *96*(5), pp. 1093–96.

Kleijweg, Aad; Thurik, A. Roy and Nooteboom, Bart. Normal Costs and Demand Effects in Price Setting: A Study of Retailing. *Europ. Econ. Rev.*, April 1988, *32*(4), pp. 999–1011.

Kleiman, Ephraim. Benefits and Burdens of Indexed Debt: Some Lessons from Israel's Experience. In *Arrow, K. J. and Boskin, M. J., eds.*, 1988, pp. 264–87.

Kleiman, Mark A. R. and Mockler, Richard W. With This Test I Thee Wed: Evaluating Premarital AIDS Testing. *J. Policy Anal. Manage.*, Spring 1988, *7*(3), pp. 557–62.

Klein, April and Rosenfeld, James. The Impact of Targeted Share Repurchases on the Wealth of Non-participating Shareholders. *J. Finan. Res.*, Summer 1988, *11*(2), pp. 89–97.

_____ **and Rosenfeld, James.** Targeted Share Repurchases and Top Management Changes. *J. Finan. Econ.*, Jan.–March 1988, *20*(1–2), pp. 493–506.

Klein, Benjamin. Vertical Integration as Organizational Ownership: The Fisher Body–General Motors Relationship Revisited. *J. Law, Econ., Organ.*, Spring 1988, *4*(1), pp. 199–213.

_____ **and Murphy, Kevin M.** Vertical Restraints as Contract Enforcement Mechanisms. *J. Law Econ.*, October 1988, *31*(2), pp. 265–97.

Klein, Burton H. Luck, Necessity, and Dynamic Flexibility. In *Hanusch, H., ed.*, 1988, pp. 95–127.

Klein, Christoph. Measurement by Public Opinion Polls and Consequences for Modelling Pure Competition. In *Eichhorn, W., ed.*, 1988, pp. 297–309.

Klein, K. K., et al. A Bioeconomic Evaluation of Fababeans in Broiler Chick Diets. *Can. J. Agr. Econ.*, July 1988, *36*(2), pp. 337–47.

Klein, Lawrence R. Carrying Forward the Tinbergen Initiative in Macroeconometrics. *De Economist*, March 1988, *136*(1), pp. 3–21.

_____. Carrying Forward the Tinbergen Initiative in Macroeconometrics. *Rev. Soc. Econ.*, December 1988, *46*(3), pp. 231–51.

_____. Global Monetarism. In *[Clark, C.]*, 1988, pp. 168–76.

_____. The LINK Model and Its Use in International Scenario Analysis. In *Motamen, H., ed.*, 1988, pp. 1–10.

_____. The Statistical Approach to Economics. *J. Econometrics*, January 1988, *37*(1), pp. 7–26.

_____ **and Bond, Daniel L.** The Medium-Term Outlook for the World Economy and the Implications for East–West Economic Relations. In *Saunders, C. T., ed.*, 1988, pp. 33–46.

_____; **Marwah, Kanta and Bodkin, Ronald G.** Keynes and the Origins of Macroeconometric Modelling. In *Hamouda, O. F. and Smithin, J. N., eds., Vol. 2*, 1988, pp. 3–11.

Klein, Linda S. and Peterson, David R. Investor Expectations of Volatility Increases around Large Stock Splits as Implied in Call Option Premia. *J. Finan. Res.*, Spring 1988, *11*(1), pp. 71–80.

Klein, Philip A. An Institutionalist View of Development Economics. In *Samuels, W. J., ed., Vol. 3*, 1988, 1977, pp. 263–85.

_____. Changing Perspectives on the Factors of Production. *J. Econ. Issues*, September 1988, *22*(3), pp. 795–809.

_____. Economics: Allocation or Valuation? In *Samuels, W. J., ed., Vol. 3*, 1988, 1974, pp. 90–116.

_____. Of Paradigms and Politics. *J. Econ. Issues*, June 1988, *22*(2), pp. 435–41.

_____. Power and Economic Performance: The Institutionalist View. In *Tool, M. R., ed., Vol. 1*, 1988, 1987, pp. 389–425.

Klein, R. W. and Dalal, S. R. A Flexible Class of Discrete Choice Models. *Marketing Sci.*, Summer 1988, *7*(3), pp. 232–51.

Klein, Rudolf. Privatization and the Welfare State. In *Johnson, C., ed.*, 1988, 1984, pp. 30–46.

Klein, Thomas. A Specification Separating Family Size and Individual Age Effects on Subjective Equivalence Scales: A Note. *Rev. Income Wealth*, June 1988, *34*(2), pp. 209–19.

Klein, Yehuda L. An Econometric Model of the Joint Production and Consumption of Residential Space Heat. *Southern Econ. J.*, October 1988, *55*(2), pp. 351–59.

Kleiner, Morris M. and Bouillon, Marvin L. Providing Business Information to Production Workers: Correlates of Compensation and Profitability. *Ind. Lab. Relat. Rev.*, July 1988, *41*(4), pp. 605–17.

—— **and Petree, Daniel L.** Unionism and Licensing of Public School Teachers: Impact on Wages and Educational Output. In *Freeman, R. B. and Ichniowski, C.*, *eds.*, 1988, pp. 305–19.

Kleinman, Daniel Lee and Kloppenburg, Jack, Jr. The Genetic Resources Controversy. In *Research and Info. System for the Non-aligned and Other Developing Countries*, 1988, pp. 279–312.

Klemperer, Paul D. Welfare Effects of Entry into Markets with Switching Costs. *J. Ind. Econ.*, December 1988, *37*(2), pp. 159–65.

—— **and Meyer, Margaret A.** Consistent Conjectures Equilibria: A Reformulation Showing Non-uniqueness. *Econ. Letters*, 1988, *27*(2), pp. 111–15.

—— **and Meyer, Margaret A.** Price Competition vs. Quantity Competition: The Role of Uncertainty. In *Daughety, A. F.*, *ed.*, 1988, *1986*, pp. 229–61.

Klemt, Wolf-Dieter and Stemme, Wolfgang. Schedule Synchronization for Public Transit Networks. In *Daduna, J. R. and Wren, A.*, *eds.*, 1988, pp. 327–35.

Klepper, Steven. Bounding the Effects of Measurement Error in Regressions Involving Dichotomous Variables. *J. Econometrics*, March 1988, *37*(3), pp. 343–59.

——. Regressor Diagnostics for the Classical Errors-In-Variables Model. *J. Econometrics*, February 1988, *37*(2), pp. 225–50.

Kliemann, W. Analysis of Nonlinear Stochastic Systems. In *Schiehlen, W. and Wedig, W.*, *eds.*, 1988, pp. 43–102.

Klijzing, F. Household Data from Surveys Containing Information for Individuals. In *Keilman, N.; Kuijsten, A. and Vossen, A.*, *eds.*, 1988, pp. 43–55.

Kliman, Andrew J. The Profit Rate under Continuous Technological Change. *Rev. Radical Polit. Econ.*, Summer–Fall 1988, *20*(2–3), pp. 283–89.

Kling, Arnold. The Rise in Bank Failures from a Macroeconomic Perspective. *J. Finan. Services Res.*, December 1988, *1*(4), pp. 353–64.

Kling, Catherine L. Comparing Welfare Estimates of Environmental Quality Changes from Recreation Demand Models. *J. Environ. Econ. Manage.*, September 1988, *15*(3), pp. 331–40.

——. The Reliability of Estimates of Environmental Benefits from Recreation Demand Models. *Amer. J. Agr. Econ.*, November 1988, *70*(4), pp. 892–901.

—— **and Bockstael, Nancy E.** Valuing Environmental Quality: Weak Complementarity with Sets of Goods. *Amer. J. Agr. Econ.*, August 1988, *70*(3), pp. 654–62.

Kling, Robert W. Building an Institutionalist The-

ory of Regulation. *J. Econ. Issues*, March 1988, *22*(1), pp. 197–209.

——. Trucking Deregulation: Evolution of a New Power Structure. *J. Econ. Issues*, December 1988, *22*(4), pp. 1201–11.

Klinkenberg, B.; Janelle, D. G. and Goodchild, M. F. Space–Time Diaries and Travel Characteristics for Different Levels of Respondent Aggregation. *Environ. Planning A*, July 1988, *20*(7), pp. 891–906.

Klitgaard, Thomas and Hickok, Susan. U.S. Trade with Taiwan and South Korea. *Fed. Res. Bank New York Quart. Rev.*, Autumn 1988, *13*(3), pp. 60–66.

Klock, David R. and Babbel, David F. Insurance Pedagogy: Executive Opinions and Priorities. *J. Risk Ins.*, December 1988, *55*(4), pp. 701–12.

Klock, John and Gerlach, Stefan. State-Space Estimates of International Business Cycles. *Econ. Letters*, 1988, *28*(3), pp. 231–34.

Klodt, Henning. De-industrialization in West Germany. *Jahr. Nationalökon. Statist.*, June 1988, *204*(6), pp. 531–40.

Kloek, T. Macroeconomic Models and Econometrics. In *Driehuis, W.; Fase, M. M. G. and den Hartog, H.*, *eds.*, 1988, pp. 343–88.

——; **De Leeuw, J. and van Praag, Bernard M. S.** Large-Sample Properties of Method of Moment Estimators under Different Data-Generating Processes. *J. Econometrics*, January 1988, *37*(1), pp. 157–69.

Klofsten, Magnus, et al. Internal and External Resources in Technology-Based Spin-offs: A Survey. In *Kirchhoff, B. A., et al.*, *eds.*, 1988, pp. 430–43.

Klok, Pieter-Jan and Bressers, Hans. Fundamentals for a Theory of Policy Instruments. *Int. J. Soc. Econ.*, 1988, *15*(3–4), pp. 22–41.

Klonglan, Gerald. The Economics of Rural Areas: A Discussion. In *Hildreth, R. J., et al.*, *eds.*, 1988, pp. 442–46.

Klonsky, Karen. Pest Management: Factors Influencing Farmer Decisionmaking. In *Johnston, G. M.; Freshwater, D. and Favero, P.*, *eds.*, 1988, pp. 201–25.

Kloock, Josef. Erfolgskontrolle mit der differenziert-kumulativen Abweichungsanalyse. (With English summary.) *Z. Betriebswirtshaft*, March 1988, *58*(3), pp. 423–34.

Kloppenburg, Jack, Jr. and Kleinman, Daniel Lee. The Genetic Resources Controversy. In *Research and Info. System for the Non-aligned and Other Developing Countries*, 1988, pp. 279–312.

Kloten, Norbert. The Impact of Innovations and Globalisation of Financial Markets on Monetary Policy: The German Case. In *[Frowen, S.]*, 1988, pp. 69–84.

——. Recent Experience with Macroeconomic Policy in the Federal Republic of Germany. In *Saunders, C. T.*, *ed.*, 1988, pp. 65–90.

Klotz, Valentin. Staff Suggestion Schemes. *Int. Lab. Rev.*, 1988, *127*(3), pp. 335–53.

Kluger, Brian D. Welfare Effects from Non-linear Taxation of Multiproduct Monopoly. *Manage-*

rial Dec. Econ., December 1988, *9*(4), pp. 283–85.

van de Klundert, Th. A Macroeconomic Two-Country Model with Price-Discriminating Monopolists. *J. Econ. (Z. Nationalökon.)*, 1988, *48*(1), pp. 19–34.

_____ **and Peters, Peter J.** Price Inertia in a Macroeconomic Model of Monopolistic Competition. *Economica*, May 1988, *55*(218), pp. 203–17.

Kluson, Václav. Values, Needs, and Motivation: Elements of the Economic Mechanism Basic to Intensive Development. *Eastern Europ. Econ.*, Fall 1988, *27*(1), pp. 45–64.

Kmenta, J. Macroeconomic Models and Econometrics: Comments. In *Driehuis, W.; Fase, M. M. G. and den Hartog, H., eds.*, 1988, pp. 399–404.

Kmietowicz, Z. W. Estimation Problems in Analysing Tanzanian Manufacturing: A Comment. *Eastern Afr. Econ. Rev.*, June 1988, *4*(1), pp. 66–71.

Knaap, Gerrit J. and Nelson, Arthur C. The Effects of Regional Land Use Control in Oregon: A Theoretical and Empirical Review. *Rev. Reg. Stud.*, Spring 1988, *18*(2), pp. 37–46.

Knapp, Gunnar and Huskey, Lee. Effects of Transfers on Remote Regional Economies: The Transfer Economy in Rural Alaska. *Growth Change*, Spring 1988, *19*(2), pp. 25–39.

Knapp, Keith C. and Dinar, Ariel. Economic Analysis of On-Farm Solutions to Drainage Problems in Irrigated Agriculture. *Australian J. Agr. Econ.*, April 1988, *32*(1), pp. 1–14.

Knapp, Thomas A. and Graves, Philip E. Mobility Behavior of the Elderly. *J. Urban Econ.*, July 1988, *24*(1), pp. 1–8.

Kneen, Peter. Soviet Domestic Economic Policy since Brezhnev. In *Darnell, A. and Evans, L., eds.*, 1988, pp. 29–42.

Kneese, Allen V. The Economics of Natural Resources. *Population Devel. Rev.*, Supplement, 1988, *14*, pp. 281–309.

Kneeshaw, John and Mayer, Helmut. Financial Market Structure and Regulatory Change. In *Heertje, A., ed.*, 1988, pp. 127–57.

Knell, Mark. The Economics of Shortage and the Socialist Enterprise: A Criticism of the Walrasian and Non-Walrasian Approach. *Rev. Radical Polit. Econ.*, Summer–Fall 1988, *20*(2–3), pp. 143–48.

Knelman, Suzanne Ward and Hutchinson, William K. Bond Rates and Causality. *J. Macroecon.*, Summer 1988, *10*(3), pp. 459–67.

Knepel, Helmut and Helberger, Christof. How Big Is the Shadow Economy? A Re-analysis of the Unobserved-Variable Approach of B. S. Frey and H. Weck-Hannemann. *Europ. Econ. Rev.*, April 1988, *32*(4), pp. 965–76.

Knickman, James R. Private Long-term Care Insurance: Alleviating Market Problems with Public–Private Partnerships. In *Scheffler, R. M. and Rossiter, L. F., eds.*, 1988, pp. 135–48.

Knieps, Günter and Sommer, Heini. Kostenaufteilung bei Mehrzweckprojekten. (Fair and Ef-

ficient Cost Allocations of Multipurpose Projects—Theory and Empirical Tests. With English summary.) *Schweiz. Z. Volkswirtsch. Statist.*, June 1988, *124*(2), pp. 151–74.

Knies, Dietmar and Herberg, Horst. The Employment of a Rigid Wage Ration in Small Open Economies with Sector-Specific Capital. *J. Inst. Theoretical Econ.*, September 1988, *144*(4), pp. 671–83.

Kniesner, Thomas J. Some Recent Developments in Labor Economics and Their Implications for Macroeconomics: Comment. *J. Money, Credit, Banking*, Part 2, August 1988, *20*(3), pp. 526–30.

_____ **and Eakin, Brian Kelly.** Estimating a Nonminimum Cost Function for Hospitals. *Southern Econ. J.*, January 1988, *54*(3), pp. 583–97.

_____ **and Leeth, John D.** Simulating Hedonic Labor Market Models: Computational Issues and Policy Applications. *Int. Econ. Rev.*, November 1988, *29*(4), pp. 755–89.

_____; **McElroy, Marjorie B. and Wilcox, Steven P.** Getting into Poverty without a Husband, and Getting Out, With or Without. *Amer. Econ. Rev.*, May 1988, *78*(2), pp. 86–90.

Knif, Johan. Finnish Beta Coefficients Empirical Evidence of Instability. *Liiketaloudellinen Aikak.*, 1988, *37*(1), pp. 3–17.

Knight, Alan. Debt Bondage in Latin America. In *Archer, L. J., ed.*, 1988, pp. 102–17.

Knight, Frank H. A New Look at Institutionalism: Discussion. In *Samuels, W. J., ed., Vol. 1,* 1988, *1957*, pp. 43–46.

Knight, Malcolm D. and Khan, Mohsin S. Import Compression and Export Performance in Developing Countries. *Rev. Econ. Statist.*, May 1988, *70*(2), pp. 315–21.

_____ **and Masson, Paul R.** Economic Interactions and the Fiscal Policies of Major Industrial Countries: 1980–1988. *Greek Econ. Rev.*, 1988, *10*(1), pp. 185–237.

_____ **and Masson, Paul R.** Fiscal Policies, Net Saving, and Real Exchange Rates: The United States, the Federal Republic of Germany, and Japan. In *Frenkel, J. A., ed.*, 1988, pp. 21–66.

Knight, Prentice L., III and Barff, Richard A. Dynamic Shift-Share Analysis. *Growth Change*, Spring 1988, *19*(2), pp. 1–10.

Knight, Russell M. Spinoff Entrepreneurs: How Corporations Really Create Entrepreneurs. In *Kirchhoff, B. A., et al., eds.*, 1988, pp. 134–49.

Knight, Thomas R. The Propensity to Sue and the Duty of Fair Representation: Reply [Tactical Use of the Union's Duty of Fair Representation: An Empirical Analysis]. *Ind. Lab. Relat. Rev.*, April 1988, *41*(3), pp. 461–64.

Knights, David. Risk, Financial Self-discipline, and Commodity Relations: An Analysis of the Growth and Development of Life Insurance in Contemporary Capitalism. In *Neimark, M., ed.*, 1988, pp. 47–69.

_____; **Willmott, Hugh and Burnes, Bernard.** New Technology and the Labour Process: Introduction. **In** *Knights, D. and Willmott, H.,* *eds.,* 1988, pp. 1–19.

Knodell, Jane. Interregional Financial Integration and the Banknote Market: The Old Northwest, 1815–1845. *J. Econ. Hist.,* June 1988, *48(2),* pp. 287–98.

_____. Mainstream Macroeconomics and the "Neutrality" of Finance: A Critical Analysis. *Écon. Soc.,* September 1988, *22(9),* pp. 155–84.

Knoedler, Janet T. and Munkirs, John R. Petroleum Producing and Consuming Countries: A Coalescence of Interests. *J. Econ. Issues,* March 1988, *22(1),* pp. 17–31.

Knoester, Anthonie. Pigou and Buffer Effects in Monetary Economics. *Kredit Kapital,* 1988, *21(1),* pp. 92–117.

_____. Supply-Side Policies in Four OECD Countries. **In** *Motamen, H., ed.,* 1988, pp. 31–51.

Knoll, Michael S. Uncertainty, Efficiency, and the Brokerage Industry. *J. Law Econ.,* April 1988, *31(1),* pp. 249–63.

Knöös, Suzanne. Recognition of Foreign Enterprises as Taxable Entities: Sweden. **In** *International Fiscal Association, ed. (I),* 1988, pp. 597–607.

Knopke, Philip. Measuring Productivity Change under Different Levels of Assistance: The Australian Dairy Industry. *Australian J. Agr. Econ.,* Aug.–Dec. 1988, *32(2–3),* pp. 113–28.

Knowlton, Winthrop and Millstein, Ira M. Can the Board of Directors Help the American Corporation Earn the Immortality It Holds So Dear? **In** *Meyer, J. R. and Gustafson, J. M., eds.,* 1988, pp. 169–91.

Knudsen, D. C. On the Stability of Trade Partnerships. *Environ. Planning A,* October 1988, *20(10),* pp. 1335–43.

Knudsen, Odin. Developing Country Perspective: Southern Agriculture and the World Economy: The Multilateral Trade Negotiations. *Southern J. Agr. Econ.,* July 1988, *20(1),* pp. 59–64.

Knudson, Mary K. and Ruttan, Vernon W. Research and Development of a Biological Innovation: Commercial Hybrid Wheat. *Food Res. Inst. Stud.,* 1988, *21(1),* pp. 45–68.

Knutson, Ronald D. Technological Innovations with Implications for Agricultural Economists: A Discussion. **In** *Hildreth, R. J., et al., eds.,* 1988, pp. 115–20.

_____ **and Duffy, Patricia A.** Reflections on Agricultural Policies and Their Consequences for the South. **In** *Beaulieu, L. J., ed.,* 1988, pp. 233–48.

Ko, Richard K.; Bechter, Dan M. and Chmura, Christine. Fifth District Indexes of Manufacturing Output. *Fed. Res. Bank Richmond Econ. Rev.,* May–June 1988, *74(3),* pp. 23–33.

Kobayashi, Hiroshi. Trade Associations and Public Relations: Comment. **In** *Yamazaki, H. and Miyamoto, M., eds.,* 1988, pp. 168–70.

Kobayashi, Yoshihiro. An Economic Analysis of Japanese Bureaucracy. **In** *Choudhury, M. A., ed.,* 1988, pp. 25–47.

Kobayashi, Yotaro. Changes in International Mar-

keting Techniques. **In** *Cassing, J. H. and Husted, S. L., eds.,* 1988, pp. 127–35.

Kobeš, Josef and Rybnikář, Karel. The Concept of the Plan in the Conditions of the Restructuring of the Economic Mechanism. *Czech. Econ. Digest.,* November 1988, (7), pp. 43–57.

Koblo, Reiner; Kowalski, Jan and Funck, Rolf. Information Technology, the Urban System and Urban Policy Consequences. **In** *Orishimo, I.; Hewings, G. J. D. and Nijkamp, P., eds.,* 1988, pp. 125–40.

Kobrin, Stephen J. Strategic Integration in Fragmented Environments: Social and Political Assessment by Subsidiaries of Multinational Firms. **In** *Hood, N. and Vahlne, J.-E., eds.,* 1988, pp. 104–20.

_____. Trends in Ownership of U.S. Manufacturing Subsidiaries in Developing Countries: An Interindustry Analysis. **In** *Contractor, F. J. and Lorange, P.,* 1988, pp. 129–42.

Koch, Helmut. Strategische Unternehmensplanung und Risiko. (With English summary.) *Z. Betriebswirtshaft,* October 1988, *58(10),* pp. 1033–51.

_____. Zur Konzeption einer pragmatisch orientierten Unternehmensheorie. (The Conception of Pragmatically Oriented Enterprise Theory. With English summary.) *Z. Wirtschaft. Sozialwissen.,* 1988, *108(1),* pp. 99–111.

Koch, James V. and Vander Hill, C. Warren. Is There Discrimination in the "Black Man's Game"? *Soc. Sci. Quart.,* March 1988, *69(1),* pp. 83–94.

Koch-Nielsen, Robert. World Tax Reform: A Progress Report: Denmark: Comment. **In** *Pechman, J. A., ed.,* 1988, pp. 92–94.

Koch, Paul D.; Koch, Timothy W. and Kawaller, Ira G. The Relationship between the S&P 500 Index and S&P 500 Index Futures Prices. *Fed. Res. Bank Atlanta Econ. Rev.,* May–June 1988, *73(3),* pp. 2–10.

_____ **and Rasche, Robert H.** An Examination of the Commerce Department Leading-Indicator Approach. *J. Bus. Econ. Statist.,* April 1988, *6(2),* pp. 167–87.

_____; **Rosensweig, Jeffrey A. and Whitt, Joseph A., Jr.** The Dynamic Relationship between the Dollar and U.S. Prices: An Intensive Empirical Investigation. *J. Int. Money Finance,* June 1988, *7(2),* pp. 181–204.

_____ **and Rosenweig, Jeffrey A.** The U.S. Dollar and the "Delayed J-Curve." *Fed. Res. Bank Atlanta Econ. Rev.,* July–Aug. 1988, *73(4),* pp. 2–15.

Koch, Timothy W. and Kawaller, Ira G. Managing Cash Flow Risk in Stock Index Futures: The Tail Hedge. *J. Portfol. Manage.,* Fall 1988, *15(1),* pp. 41–44.

_____; **Kawaller, Ira G. and Koch, Paul D.** The Relationship between the S&P 500 Index and S&P 500 Index Futures Prices. *Fed. Res. Bank Atlanta Econ. Rev.,* May–June 1988, *73(3),* pp. 2–10.

_____; **MacDonald, S. Scott and Peterson, Richard L.** Using Futures to Improve Treasury Bill

Portfolio Performance. *J. Futures Markets*, April 1988, *8*(2), pp. 167–84.

Kochan, Thomas A. The Politics of Interest Arbitration. In *Lewin, D., et al., eds.*, 1988, *1978*, pp. 76–88.

_____. A Theory of Multilateral Collective Bargaining in City Governments. In *Lewin, D., et al., eds.*, 1988, *1974*, pp. 195–221.

Kochevrin, Iu. The Neoclassical Theory of Production and Distribution. *Prob. Econ.*, March 1988, *30*(11), pp. 6–29.

Kochin, Levis A. and Parks, Richard W. Was the Tax-Exempt Bond Market Inefficient or Were Future Expected Tax Rates Negative? *J. Finance*, September 1988, *43*(4), pp. 913–31.

Kodde, David A. Unemployment Expectations and Human Capital Formation. *Europ. Econ. Rev.*, October 1988, *32*(8), pp. 1645–60.

_____ and Ritzen, Jozef M. M. Direct and Indirect Effects of Parental Education Level on the Demand for Higher Education. *J. Human Res.*, Summer 1988, *23*(3), pp. 356–71.

Koedijk, Kees G. and Belongia, Michael T. Testing the Expectations Model of the Term Structure: Some Conjectures on the Effects of Institutional Changes. *Fed. Res. Bank St. Louis Rev.*, Sept.–Oct. 1988, *70*(5), pp. 37–45.

_____ and Bomhoff, Eduard J. Bilateral Exchange Rates and Risk Premia. *J. Int. Money Finance*, June 1988, *7*(2), pp. 205–20.

Koehler, Anne B. and Murphree, Emily S. A Comparison of Results from State Space Forecasting with Forecasts from the Makridakis Competition. *Int. J. Forecasting*, 1988, *4*(1), pp. 45–55.

Koehler, C. U. Information and Dialog Programs for Agriculture in the German Videotex System. In *Schiefer, G., ed.*, 1988, pp. 155–59.

Koekkoek, K. A. The Integration of Developing Countries in the GATT System. *World Devel.*, August 1988, *16*(8), pp. 947–57.

_____. Trade in Services, the Developing Countries and the Uruguay Round. *World Econ.*, March 1988, *11*(1), pp. 151–55.

Koeller, C. Timothy; Ballantine, John W. and Cleveland, Frederick W. Corporate Profitability and Competitive Circumstance. *Eastern Econ. J.*, Jan.–March 1988, *14*(1), pp. 7–18.

Koenig, Dolores. The Culture and Social Organization of USAID Development Projects in West Africa. In *Bennett, J. W. and Bowen, J. R., eds.*, 1988, pp. 345–64.

Koenker, Roger. Asymptotic Theory and Econometric Practice. *J. Appl. Econometrics*, April 1988, *3*(2), pp. 139–47.

_____. Combining Robust and Traditional Least Squares Methods: A Critical Evaluation: Comment. *J. Bus. Econ. Statist.*, October 1988, *6*(4), pp. 447–49.

Kofler, Eduard and Zweifel, Peter. Exploiting Linear Partial Information for Optimal Use of Forecasts: With an Application to U.S. Economic Policy. *Int. J. Forecasting*, 1988, *4*(1), pp. 15–32.

Kogan, Ninel. The Economics of Evaluating New

Technology: The Soviet Chemical Machine Building Industry. *Comp. Econ. Stud.*, Spring 1988, *30*(1), pp. 1–28.

Kogels, Han A. Tax Treatment of Computer Software: Netherlands. In *International Fiscal Association, ed. (II)*, 1988, pp. 453–70.

Kogelschatz, Hartmut. On the Identification of Key Sectors: Critical Theoretical and Empirical Analysis of Key Sector Indices. In *Eichhorn, W., ed.*, 1988, pp. 767–91.

Kogut, Bruce. County Patterns in International Competition: Appropriability and Oligopolistic Agreement. In *Hood, N. and Vahlne, J.-E., eds.*, 1988, pp. 315–40.

_____. A Study of the Life Cycle of Joint Ventures. In *Contractor, F. J. and Lorange, P.*, 1988, pp. 169–85.

_____ and Singh, Harbir. Entering the United States by Joint Venture: Competitive Rivalry and Industry Structure. In *Contractor, F. J. and Lorange, P.*, 1988, pp. 241–51.

Kohama, Hirohisa. A Note on Outward-Looking Policy and Growth Performance: The Republic of Korea and Selected Latin American Countries. In *Urrutia, M., ed.*, 1988, pp. 122–34.

_____ and Urata, Shujiro. The Impact of the Recent Yen Appreciation on the Japanese Economy. *Devel. Econ.*, December 1988, *26*(4), pp. 323–40.

Kohers, Theodor and Mullis, David. An Update on Economies of Scale in Credit Unions. *Appl. Econ.*, December 1988, *20*(12), pp. 1653–59.

Köhler, Claus. Economic Policy in a Framework of Internationalised Economic Relations. In *[Frowen, S.]*, 1988, pp. 85–101.

Köhler, Richard. Möglichkeiten zur Förderung der Produktinnovation in mittelständischen Unternehmen. (With English summary.) *Z. Betriebswirtshaft*, August 1988, *58*(8), pp. 812–27.

Kohler, Wilhelm K. Modeling Heckscher–Ohlin Comparative Advantage in Regression Equations: A Critical Survey. *Empirica*, 1988, *15*(2), pp. 263–93.

Kohlhase, Janet E. and Gregory, Paul R. The Earnings of Soviet Workers: Evidence from the Soviet Interview Project. *Rev. Econ. Statist.*, February 1988, *70*(1), pp. 23–35.

Kohli, Martin. Wages, Work Effort, and Productivity. *Rev. Radical Polit. Econ.*, Summer–Fall 1988, *20*(2–3), pp. 190–95.

Kohli, Rajiv and Harr, Michael. The Role of Contract Research Organizations in Successful International Space Commercialization. In *Egan, J. J., et al.*, 1988, pp. 317–29.

Kohli, Uddesh and Gautam, Vinayshil. Human Resources Development and the Planning Process in India: Preface. In *Kohli, U. and Gautam, V., eds.*, 1988, pp. v–xi.

Kohli, Ulrich. A Note on Banknote Characteristics and the Demand for Currency by Denomination. *J. Banking Finance*, September 1988, *12*(3), pp. 389–99.

_____ and Morey, Edward R. U.S. Imports by Origin: A Characteristics Approach. *Kyklos*, 1988, *41*(1), pp. 51–74.

Kohn, Meir. Monetary Analysis, the Equilibrium Method, and Keynes's "General Theory." In *Shaw, G. K., ed., Vol. 1*, 1988, *1986*, pp. 75–108.

_____. On the Differing Effects of Different Types of Inflation on the Real Rate of Interest. In *Kohn, M. and Tsiang, S.-C., eds.*, 1988, pp. 85–102.

_____ **and Karacaoglu, Girol.** Devaluation, Capital Mobility, and Expectations in an Optimizing Model. *J. Int. Econ.*, February 1988, *24*(1–2), pp. 23–44.

Kohn, Robert E. Efficient Scale of the Pollution-Abating Firm. *Land Econ.*, February 1988, *64*(1), pp. 53–61.

_____. The HQ Production Function. *Econ. Rec.*, June 1988, *64*(185), pp. 133–35.

_____. Transactions Costs and the Controversial Good or Service [Optimal Quantity of a Controversial Good or Service]. *Public Choice*, April 1988, *57*(1), pp. 89–93.

_____ **and Hollenhorst, Jerome J.** Production Uncertainty and Pollution. *Southern Econ. J.*, October 1988, *55*(2), pp. 454–62.

Kohno, Hirotada and Higano, Y. Optimal Reorganization of Greater Tokyo: An Industrial Complex of Agglomeration and Scale Economies. 1. *Environ. Planning A*, August 1988, *20*(8), pp. 1103–20.

_____ **and Higano, Y.** Optimal Reorganization of Greater Tokyo: An Industrial Complex of Agglomeration and Scale Economies. 2. *Environ. Planning A*, September 1988, *20*(9), pp. 1145–64.

_____ **and Mitomo, Hitoshi.** Optimal Pricing of Telecommunications Service in an Advanced Information-Oriented Society. In *Orishimo, I.; Hewings, G. J. D. and Nijkamp, P., eds.*, 1988, pp. 195–213.

Koide, Hiroyuki. Spatial Provision of Local Public Goods with Spillover Effects. *Reg. Sci. Urban Econ.*, May 1988, *18*(2), pp. 283–305.

Kok, J. H. M.; Okker, V. R. and Hasselman, B. H. FREIA and Employment Policies in the Netherlands. In *Hopkins, M. J. D., ed.*, 1988, pp. 103–31.

Kol, J. and Mennes, L. B. M. Protection, Trade and Development. In *Jepma, C. J., ed.*, 1988, pp. 80–94.

Kolajo, Ebenezer F.; Martin, Neil R., Jr. and Hanson, Gregory D. Forecast Errors and Farm Firm Growth. *J. Agr. Econ. Res.*, Fall 1988, *40*(4), pp. 2–11.

Kolari, James; Mahajan, Arvind and Saunders, Edward M., Jr. The Effect of Changes in Reserve Requirements on Bank Stock Prices. *J. Banking Finance*, June 1988, *12*(2), pp. 183–98.

Kolchin, Michael G. and Smackey, Bruce M. Chrysler Canada: Positioning for the Future. In *Thornton, R. J.; Hyclak, T. and Aronson, J. R., eds.*, 1988, pp. 145–67.

Kolderie, Ted and Blazar, William A. The New Economic Role of American States: Minnesota. In *Fosler, R. S., ed.*, 1988, pp. 291–308.

Kole, Linda S. Expansionary Fiscal Policy and International Interdependence. In *Frenkel, J. A., ed.*, 1988, pp. 229–65.

Kolehmainen, Juhani. Socialpolitikens utvecklingsbanor. (Development Lines in Social Policy. With English summary.) *Ekon. Samfundets Tidskr.*, 1988, *41*(2), pp. 99–116.

Kolesar, Peter J. and Godfrey, A. Blanton. Role of Quality in Achieving World Class Competitiveness. In *Starr, M. K., ed.*, 1988, pp. 213–38.

Kolganov, A. I. and Buzgalin, A. V. Methods of State Management of the Economy. *Prob. Econ.*, April 1988, *30*(12), pp. 6–17.

Koller, Roland H., II. On the Source of Entrepreneurial Ideas. In *Kirchhoff, B. A., et al., eds.*, 1988, pp. 194–207.

Kolluri, Bharat R. Further Evidence on the Shifting of Corporate Income Tax in Privately Owned Electric Utilities, 1948–1984. *Public Finance Quart.*, October 1988, *16*(4), pp. 493–507.

Kolm, Jan E. Regional and National Consequences of Globalizing Industries of the Pacific Rim. In *Muroyama, J. H. and Stever, H. G., eds.*, 1988, pp. 106–40.

Kolm, Serge-Christophe. Economics in Europe and in the U.S. *Europ. Econ. Rev.*, January 1988, *32*(1), pp. 207–12.

_____. Unemployment Resulting from Preferences on Wages or Prices. In *Hamouda, O. F. and Smithin, J. N., eds., Vol. 2*, 1988, pp. 102–18.

Kolodko, Grzegorz W. Economic Change and Shortageflation under Centrally Planned Economies. *Econ. Scelte Pubbliche/J. Public Finance Public Choice*, Jan.–April 1988, *6*(1), pp. 15–32.

Kolodny, Richard and Suhler, Diane Rizzuto. The Effects of New Debt Issues on Existing Security Holders. *Quart. J. Bus. Econ.*, Spring 1988, *27*(2), pp. 51–72.

Kolpin, Van W. A Note on Tight Extensive Game Forms. *Int. J. Game Theory*, 1988, *17*(3), pp. 187–91.

Kolsen, H. M. Cost Recovery in Inter-state Land Transport in Australia. *Int. J. Transport Econ.*, October 1988, *15*(3), pp. 257–70.

Kolstad, Charles D. and Wolak, Frank A. Measuring Relative Market Power in the Western U.S. Coal Market Using Shapley Values. *Resources & Energy*, December 1988, *10*(4), pp. 293–314.

Komárek, Valtr. Conditions and Limits of Economic and Social Advancement in the Czechoslovak Socialist Republic—Part I. *Czech. Econ. Digest.*, December 1988, (8), pp. 3–18.

_____. Conditions and Limits of Economic and Social Advancement in the Czechoslovak Socialist Republic—Part II. *Czech. Econ. Digest.*, December 1988, (8), pp. 19–37.

Kominski, Gerald F. and Price, Kurt F. Using Patient Age in Defining DRGs for Medicare Payment. *Inquiry*, Winter 1988, *25*(4), pp. 494–503.

Komiya, Ryutaro. Japan's Foreign Direct Investment: Facts and Theoretical Considerations. In *Borner, S., ed.*, 1988, pp. 241–89.

———— **and Itoh, Motoshige.** Japan's International Trade and Trade Policy, 1955–1984. In *Inoguchi, T. and Okimoto, D. I., eds.*, 1988, pp. 173–224.

Komlos, John. Agricultural Productivity in America and Eastern Europe: A Comment. *J. Econ. Hist.*, September 1988, *48*(3), pp. 655–64.

————. The Birth-Baptism Interval and the Estimate of English Population in the Eighteenth Century. In *Uselding, P. J., ed.*, 1988, pp. 301–16.

————. The Food Budget of English Workers: A Comment. *J. Econ. Hist.*, March 1988, *48*(1), pp. 149.

————. Is Free Trade Passé? Comment. *J. Econ. Perspectives*, Fall 1988, *2*(4), pp. 207–09.

————. On the Role of Crises in Historical Perspective: Comment. *Population Devel. Rev.*, March 1988, *14*(1), pp. 159–64.

———— **and Steinmann, Gunter.** Population Growth and Economic Development in the Very Long Run: A Simulation Model of Three Revolutions. *Math. Soc. Sci.*, August 1988, *16*(1), pp. 49–63.

Komorita, Samuel S.; Ellis, Alan L. and Melton, Robert J. The Effects of Justice Norms in a Bargaining Situation. In *Tietz, R.; Albers, W. and Selten, R., eds.*, 1988, pp. 251–67.

Komorowska, E.; Stépień, J. and Mażbic-Kulma, B. Location Problem and Its Applications in Distribution of Petrol Products. In *Kurzhanski, A.; Neumann, K. and Pallaschke, D., eds.*, 1988, pp. 277–92.

Kondonassis, A. J.; Malliaris, A. G. and Robinson, N. S. Political Instability and Economic Development: An Economic History Case Study of Greece, 1948–1966: A Reply. *J. Europ. Econ. Hist.*, Spring 1988, *17*(1), pp. 185–86.

Könekamp, R. William Stanley Jevons (1835–1882): Some Biographical Notes. In *Wood, J. C., ed., Vol. 1*, 1988, *1962*, pp. 233–50.

————. The Work of Harriet Ann Jevons (1838–1910) after Her Husband's Death. In *Wood, J. C., ed., Vol. 3*, 1988, *1982*, pp. 230–60.

Kong, Randolph. Cooperative Approaches among Tax Administrations to Prevent and Counteract International Tax Evasion and Avoidance: Trinidad and Tabago. *Bull. Int. Fiscal Doc.*, December 1988, *42*(12), pp. 526–30.

König, Heinz and Pohlmeier, Winfried. A Dynamic Model of Labor Utilization. In *Hart, R. A., ed.*, 1988, pp. 112–25.

———— **and Pohlmeier, Winfried.** Employment, Labour Utilization and Procyclical Labour Productivity. *Kyklos*, 1988, *41*(4), pp. 551–72.

Konijn, N. A Crop Production and Environment Model. In *Parikh, J. K., ed.*, 1988, pp. 15–37.

Konijn, P. A. B. Kalker and Plantenga, J. Characteristics Explaining Business Success of Entrepreneurs versus Managers. *J. Behav. Econ.*, Summer 1988, *17*(2), pp. 133–42.

Koning, Hendrik Elle. Cutting Taxes: The Neth-

erlands Follows the Trend by Introducing Radical New Proposals. *Bull. Int. Fiscal Doc.*, Aug.–Sept. 1988, *42*(8–9), pp. 344–46.

———— **and Witteveen, Dirk.** World Tax Reform: A Progress Report: Netherlands. In *Pechman, J. A., ed.*, 1988, pp. 171–80.

Konjing, Chaiwat. Agricultural Diversification in ASEAN. In *Langhammer, R. J. and Rieger, H. C., eds.*, 1988, pp. 1–59.

Kono, Shigemi and Preston, Samuel H. Trends in Well-Being of Children and the Elderly in Japan. In *Palmer, J. L.; Smeeding, T. and Torrey, B. B., eds.*, 1988, pp. 277–307.

Kono, Toyohiro. Factors Affecting the Creativity of Organizations—An Approach from the Analysis of New Product Development. In *Urabe, K.; Child, J. and Kagono, T., eds.*, 1988, pp. 105–44.

Konrad, Kai A. Intergenerationelle Gerechtigkeit bei bestandsabhängigen Extraktionskosten. Intergenerational Equity in the Case of Stock-Dependent Extraction Costs. With English summary.) *Jahr. Nationalökon. Statist.*, November 1988, *205*(5), pp. 400–409.

Kontorovich, Vladimir. The Process of Organizational Innovation in a Command Economy. *J. Inst. Theoretical Econ.*, December 1988, *144*(5), pp. 878–84.

————. Prototype Statistics as Indicators of Soviet R&D Priorities in Civilian and Military Machinery Production. *Comp. Econ. Stud.*, Fall 1988, *30*(3), pp. 1–15.

Konyha, Marvin E. and Deaton, Brady J. Local Infrastructure Investment in Rural America: Introduction. In *Johnson, T. G.; Deaton, B. J. and Segarra, E., eds.*, 1988, pp. 1–4.

Koo, Anthony Y. C. and Quan, Nguyen T. Concentration of Land Holdings and Income: Reply. *J. Devel. Econ.*, September 1988, *29*(2), pp. 233–34.

Koo, Suk Mo and Lee, Jae Won. Trade-off between Economic Growth and Income Equality: A Re-evaluation. In *Brenner, Y. S.; Reijnders, J. P. G. and Spithoven, A. H. G. M., eds.*, 1988, pp. 155–77.

Koo, Won W.; Thompson, Stanley R. and Larson, Donald W. Effects of Ocean Freight Rate Changes on the U.S. Grain Distribution System. *Logist. Transp. Rev.*, March 1988, *24*(1), pp. 85–100.

————; **Wilson, William W. and Wilson, Wesley W.** Modal Competition and Pricing in Grain Transport. *J. Transp. Econ. Policy*, September 1988, *22*(3), pp. 319–37.

Kooi, J. Netherlands: Pensions: A Survey of Recent Developments. *Bull. Int. Fiscal Doc.*, Aug.–Sept. 1988, *42*(8–9), pp. 360–64.

Kooij, Pim. Peripheral Cities and Their Regions in the Dutch Urban System until 1900. *J. Econ. Hist.*, June 1988, *48*(2), pp. 357–71.

Kooiman, P. Macroeconomic Models and Microeconomic Theory: Comments. In *Driehuis, W.; Fase, M. M. G. and den Hartog, H., eds.*, 1988, pp. 337–42.

Kool, Clemens J. M. and Tatom, John A. International Linkages in the Term Structure of Interest Rates. *Fed. Res. Bank St. Louis Rev.*, July–Aug. 1988, *70*(4), pp. 30–43.

_____; de Vries, Casper G. and Boon, Martin. Simulating Currency Substitution Bias. *Econ. Letters*, 1988, *28*(3), pp. 269–72.

Koomsup, Praipol. The ASEAN–Australian Trade Pattern in Fuels and Minerals. In *McKern, B. and Koomsup, P., eds.*, 1988, pp. 13–50.

_____. Minerals and Energy in Thailand: Production, Consumption and Trade. In *McKern, B. and Koomsup, P., eds.*, 1988, pp. 310–63.

Kooreman, Peter; Willemse, Rob and Kapteyn, Arie. Some Methodological Issues in the Implementation of Subjective Poverty Definitions. *J. Human Res.*, Spring 1988, *23*(2), pp. 222–42.

Koot, Willem T. M. Underlying Dilemmas in the Management of International Joint Ventures. In *Contractor, F. J. and Lorange, P.*, 1988, pp. 347–67.

Kopcke, Richard W. Inflation, Taxes, and Interest Rates. *New Eng. Econ. Rev.*, July–Aug. 1988, pp. 3–14.

_____. Tax Reform and Stock Prices. *New Eng. Econ. Rev.*, March–April 1988, pp. 3–21.

Kopecky, Kenneth J. A Mean–Variance Framework for Analyzing Reserve Requirements and Monetary Control. *J. Banking Finance*, 1988, *12*(1), pp. 151–60.

_____. Rational Bank Behavior, Interest Rates, and the Price Level in a Staggered Reserve Accounting System. *J. Macroecon.*, Summer 1988, *10*(3), pp. 389–405.

Kopp, Pierre and Caro, Jean-Yves. Quelques repères sur les services publics de radio et télévision en Europe. (An International Comparison of the Public Services of Radio and Television in 17 European Countries. With English summary.) *Revue Écon.*, May 1988, *39*(3), pp. 573–86.

Koppel, Bruce. The Future of Official Development Assistance to Rural Asia. *Devel. Econ.*, June 1988, *26*(2), pp. 103–24.

Koppelman, Andrew. The Miscegenation Analogy: Sodomy Law as Sex Discrimination. *Yale Law J.*, November 1988, *98*(1), pp. 145–64.

Koppelman, Stanley A. Progressivity Effects of the Tax Reform Act of 1986. *Nat. Tax J.*, September 1988, *41*(3), pp. 285–90.

_____. Should Interest Deductions Be Limited? Comments. In *Aaron, H. J.; Galper, H. and Pechman, J. A., eds.*, 1988, pp. 230–36.

Korajczyk, Robert A. and Connor, Gregory. Risk and Return in an Equilibrium APT: Application of a New Test Methodology. *J. Finan. Econ.*, September 1988, *21*(2), pp. 255–89.

Koray, Faik and Chan, Pingfai. Fiscal Policy and Stabilization of Exchange Rates under Alternative Criteria. *Can. J. Econ.*, February 1988, *21*(1), pp. 96–114.

_____ and Erol, Ümit. Frequency Domain Analysis of the Neutrality Hypothesis. *Southern Econ. J.*, October 1988, *55*(2), pp. 390–99.

_____ and Hill, R. Carter. Money, Debt, and Economic Activity. *J. Macroecon.*, Summer 1988, *10*(3), pp. 351–70.

Koraz, Faik and Culbertson, W. Patton, Jr. Interest Rates, the Forward Premium, and Unanticipated Money: Reply. *Southern Econ. J.*, April 1988, *54*(4), pp. 1047–48.

Korb, Lawrence J. The Reagan Defense Budget and Program: The Buildup That Collapsed. In *Boaz, D., ed.*, 1988, pp. 83–94.

Korbonski, Andrzej. Polish Agriculture and Martial Law, or What Happened to the Smychka? In *Brada, J. C. and Wadekin, K.-E., eds.*, 1988, pp. 146–58.

Kordes, Frans G. Court of Audit, A European Phenomenon: The Situation in the Netherlands. In *Most, K. S., ed.*, 1988, pp. 245–55.

Kordos, Jan. Time Use Surveys in Poland. *Statist. J.*, August 1988, *5*(2), pp. 159–68.

Korenman, Sanders D. and Geronimus, Arline T. Comments on Pampel and Pillai's "Patterns and Determinants of Infant Mortality in Developed Nations, 1950–1975." *Demography*, February 1988, *25*(1), pp. 155–58.

Korkie, Bob M. and Jobson, J. D. The Trouble with Performance Measurement: Comment. *J. Portfol. Manage.*, Winter 1988, *14*(2), pp. 74–76.

Korkman, Sixten. Beskattningen av förmögenhetsinkomst. (Taxation of Capital Incomes. With English summary.) *Ekon. Samfundets Tidskr.*, 1988, *41*(4), pp. 233–39.

_____. Vägvalet vid beskattningen av kapitalinkomster. (The Choice of Basic Principles in Capital Income Taxation. With English summary.) *Ekon. Samfundets Tidskr.*, 1988, *41*(1), pp. 25–29.

Kornai, János. Individual Freedom and Reform of the Socialist Economy. *Europ. Econ. Rev.*, March 1988, *32*(2–3), pp. 233–67.

Kornreich, Jerome S. Myths. In *Timpe, A. D., ed.*, 1988, *1984*, pp. 226–31.

Korol, Juan Carlos and Gutierrez, Leandro. Historia de empresas y crecimiento industrial en la Argentina. El caso de la Fábrica Argentina de Alpargatas. (With English summary.) *Desarrollo Econ.*, Oct.–Dec. 1988, *28*(111), pp. 401–24.

Koroluk, Robert M.; Spriggs, John and Gould, Brian W. Separate Crop Accounts for the Western Grain Stabilization Program. *Can. J. Agr. Econ.*, November 1988, *36*(3), pp. 443–57.

Korostelev, V. A. The Rebirth of Small-Scale Commodity Production. *Prob. Econ.*, December 1988, *31*(8), pp. 43–57.

Korper, Susan H.; Druckman, Daniel and Broome, Benjamin J. Value Differences and Conflict Resolution: Facilitation or Delinking? *J. Conflict Resolution*, September 1988, *32*(3), pp. 489–510.

Kort, Peter M. Optimal Dynamic Investment Policy under Financial Restrictions and Adjustment Costs. *Europ. Econ. Rev.*, November 1988, *32*(9), pp. 1769–76.

Kortan, Jerzy. The Development of the Labour Market in Poland—Restrictions for Management. In *Dlugos, G.; Dorow, W. and Weiermair, K., eds.*, 1988, pp. 261–71.

Korteweg, Pieter. The International Monetary System and the Strength and Vicissitudes of the American Dollar. In *[Witteveen, H. J.]*, 1988, pp. 61–77.

Korth, Christopher M. The Vulnerability in the International Financial System. In *Tavis, L. A., ed.*, 1988, pp. 169–204.

Korzec, Michel. Contract Labor, the "Right to Work" and New Labor Laws in the People's Republic of China. *Comp. Econ. Stud.*, Summer 1988, *30*(2), pp. 117–49.

Kosacoff, Bernardo and Azpiazú, Daniel. Exports and Industrialization in Argentina, 1973–1986. *CEPAL Reb.*, December 1988, (36), pp. 61–81.

Kōsai, Yutaka. The Cambridge History of Japan: Volume 6: The Twentieth Century: The Postwar Japanese Economy, 1945–1973. In *Duus, P., ed.*, 1988, pp. 494–537.

Koschatzhy, Knut. Development of Industrial Systems in West Malaysia. In *Schätzl, L. H., ed.*, 1988, pp. 96–168.

Koshiba, Tesshu. Intra-industry Trade in the Manufacturing Industries of Japan. In *Ciaschini, M., ed.*, 1988, pp. 179–200.

Koshiro, Kazutoshi. The Employment Effects of Microelectronic Technology. In *Japan Institute of Labour, ed.*, *1988, 1983*, pp. 5–9.

Kosicki, George. A Note about Savings as a "Nonpositional Good." *Eastern Econ. J.*, July–Sept. 1988, *14*(3), pp. 271–76.

Kosmicke, Ralph and Opsal, Scott D. The Effect of Volatility on Investment Returns. *J. Portfol. Manage.*, Winter 1988, *14*(2), pp. 14–19.

Kossoudji, Sherrie A. English Language Ability and the Labor Market Opportunities of Hispanic and East Asian Immigrant Men. *J. Lab. Econ.*, April 1988, *6*(2), pp. 205–28.

Kostakov, Vladimir G. Full Employment: How Do We Understand It? *Prob. Econ.*, February 1988, *30*(10), pp. 85–102.

_____. Labor Problems in Light of *Perestroyka*. *Soviet Econ.*, Jan.–March 1988, *4*(1), pp. 95–101.

Kostecki, Marian J. and Farrell, John P. Poland's Top 500. *Comp. Econ. Stud.*, Winter 1988, *30*(4), pp. 52–57.

Kosters, Martinus J. Changing Tourism Requires a Different Management Approach. In *Goodall, B. and Ashworth, G., eds.*, 1988, pp. 198–212.

Kostiainen, Seppo and Taimio, Heikki. Interest Rate Policy with Expectations of Devaluation. *Scand. J. Econ.*, 1988, *90*(2), pp. 211–24.

Kostin, L. Restructuring the System of Payment of Labor. *Prob. Econ.*, July 1988, *31*(3), pp. 62–80.

Kosuge, Toshio and Tonaka, Masatomo. Project on the Pacific Region: A Proposal for the Formation of Education Relationship Networks. In *Kozmetsky, G.; Matsumoto, H. and Smilor, R. W., eds.*, 1988, pp. 161–79.

Kotler, Philip. The Convenience Store: Past Development, and Future Prospects. In *[Hollander, S. C.]*, 1988, pp. 163–75.

_____. The Potential Contributions of Marketing

Thinking to Economic Development. In *Kumcu, E. and Firat, A. F., eds.*, 1988, pp. 1–10.

Kotlikoff, Laurence J. Defined Benefit versus Defined Contribution Pension Plans: What Are the Real Trade-offs? Comment. In *Bodie, Z.; Shoven, J. B. and Wise, D. A., eds.*, 1988, pp. 161–62.

_____. How Tight Was the Reagan Administration's First-Term Fiscal Policy? In *Boaz, D., ed.*, 1988, pp. 17–27.

_____. Intergenerational Transfers and Savings. *J. Econ. Perspectives*, Spring 1988, *2*(2), pp. 41–58.

_____. The Relationship of Productivity to Age. In *Ricardo-Campbell, R. and Lazear, E. P., eds.*, 1988, pp. 100–125.

_____. What Microeconomics Teaches Us about the Dynamic Macro Effects of Fiscal Policy. *J. Money, Credit, Banking*, Part 2, August 1988, *20*(3), pp. 479–95.

_____ and Pakes, Ariel. Looking for the News in the Noise. Additional Stochastic Implications of Optimal Consumption Choice. *Ann. Écon. Statist.*, Jan.–March 1988, (9), pp. 29–46.

_____; Persson, Torsten and Svensson, Lars E. O. Social Contracts as Assets: A Possible Solution to the Time-Consistency Problem. *Amer. Econ. Rev.*, September 1988, *78*(4), pp. 662–77.

_____; Samuelson, William F. and Johnson, Stephen. Consumption, Computation Mistakes, and Fiscal Policy. *Amer. Econ. Rev.*, May 1988, *78*(2), pp. 408–12.

_____; Shoven, John B. and Boskin, Michael J. Personal Security Accounts: A Proposal for Fundamental Social Security Reform. In *Wachter, S. M., ed.*, 1988, pp. 179–206.

_____ and Summers, Lawrence H. The Contribution of Intergenerational Transfers to Total Wealth: A Reply. In *Kessler, D. and Masson, A., eds.*, 1988, pp. 53–67.

_____ and Wise, David A. Pension Backloading, Wage Taxes, and Work Disincentives. In *Summers, L. H., ed.*, 1988, pp. 161–96.

Kotlove, Barry S. Recent Privatization in Soviet Housing Markets. *METU*, 1988, *15*(3–4), pp. 103–23.

Kotowitz, Yehuda. A Model of Advertising and Learning. In *Maital, S., ed.*, *Vol. 1*, 1988, pp. 144–54.

Kounias, Stratis. Testing for Outliers in Linear Models and Bonferroni Significance Levels. In *Fedorov, V. and Lauter, H., eds.*, 1988, pp. 176–80.

Koustas, Zisimos. Is There a Phillips Curve in Canada? A Rational Expectations Approach. *J. Macroecon.*, Summer 1988, *10*(3), pp. 421–33.

_____ and Stengos, Thanasis. Testing for Short-run Money Neutrality in a Small Open Economy: The Case of Canada. *Empirical Econ.*, 1988, *13*(2), pp. 103–20.

Kovacić, William E. Public Choice and the Public Interest: Federal Trade Commission Antitrust Enforcement during the Reagan Administration. *Antitrust Bull.*, Fall 1988, *33*(3), pp. 467–504.

Kovačic, Zlatko. Makroekonometrijski modeli u Jugoslaviji. (Macroeconometric Models in Yugoslavia. With English summary.) *Econ. Anal. Workers' Manage.*, 1988, *22*(4), pp. 289–319.

Kovács, János and Tarján, Tamás. Cycle and Replacement. *Acta Oecon.*, 1988, *39*(3–4), pp. 325–40.

Kovaleff, Theodore P. Antitrust in Camelot: A Lost Opportunity? In *Perkins, E. J., ed.*, 1988, pp. 100–109.

Köves, András. The External Economic Environment and Programme of Stabilization in Hungary: Thoughts after the Preparation of a Forecast. *Acta Oecon.*, 1988, *39*(1–2), pp. 3–22.

Kowalski, Jan; Funck, Rolf and Koblo, Reiner. Information Technology, the Urban System and Urban Policy Consequences. In *Orishimo, I.; Hewings, G. J. D. and Nijkamp, P., eds.*, 1988, pp. 125–40.

Koziara, Edward; Yan, Chiou-Shuang and Kinniry, Fran. The Economic Performance of the Presidents 1909–1946: A Preliminary View. In *Pennsylvania Economic Association*, 1988, pp. 260–69.

_____; Yan, Chiou-Shuang and Quinn, John. Other Measures of the Economic Performance of Presidents. In *Pennsylvania Economic Association*, 1988, pp. 270–78.

Kozin, F. Structural Parameter Identification Techniques. In *Schiehlen, W. and Wedig, W., eds.*, 1988, pp. 137–200.

Kozmetsky, George. Securing the Future through Technology Venturing. In *Furino, A., ed.*, 1988, pp. 181–96.

_____ and Furino, Antonio. Emerging Policies and Strategies. In *Furino, A., ed.*, 1988, pp. 257–64.

Krabbe, Jacob J. Menger's Valuation of Nature: An Atomistic and "Organistic" Approach. *J. Econ. Stud.*, 1988, *15*(3–4), pp. 55–63.

_____. Pitfalls in Environmental Policy: Introduction. *Int. J. Soc. Econ.*, 1988, *15*(3–4), pp. 5–7.

_____ and Backhaus, Jürgen G. Henry George's Theory and an Application to Industrial Siting. *Int. J. Soc. Econ.*, 1988, *15*(3–4), pp. 103–19.

Kracht-Müntz, Birgit and Hasenkamp, Georg. Indices of Allocation Inefficiencies for Heterogeneous Labor. In *Eichhorn, W., ed.*, 1988, pp. 751–66.

Kračun, Davorin. A Cost-Push Model of Galloping Inflation: The Case of Yugoslavia. In *Motamen, H., ed.*, 1988, pp. 507–38.

Kraemer, Stephen R. and Haitjema, Henk M. A New Analytic Function for Modeling Partially Penetrating Wells. *Water Resources Res.*, May 1988, *24*(5), pp. 683–90.

Kraft, Daryl F. and Arthur, Louise M. The Effects of Technological Change on the Economic Impact of Agricultural Drought in Manitoba. *Can. J. Agr. Econ.*, July 1988, *36*(2), pp. 221–37.

Kraft, Kornelius. The Adjustment of Workers and Hours to Changes in Product Demand. In *Dlu-*

gos, G.; Dorow, W. and Weiermair, K., eds., 1988, pp. 351–62.

_____. Die Effekte einer Arbeitszeitverkürzung bei Berücksichtigung von Fixkosten und Überstunden. (The Effects of a Reduction in Standard Working-Time under Consideration of Fixed Costs and Overtime. With English summary.) *Jahr. Nationalökon. Statist.*, April 1988, *204*(4), pp. 316–25.

_____ and Finsinger, Jörg. Optimales Marketing bei Kostenzuschlagskalkulation am Beispiel von Krankenversicherungen. (Optimal Marketing with Markup-Pricing. The Example of Health Insurance. With English summary.) *Ifo-Studien*, 1988, *34*(4), pp. 275–97.

Kraft, Steven E. Use of Natural Resources in a Market Economy: Ethical and Legal Perspectives. *Int. J. Soc. Econ.*, 1988, *15*(3–4), pp. 8–21.

van de Kragt, Alphons J. C.; Dawes, Robyn M. and Orbell, John M. Are People Who Cooperate "Rational Altruists"? *Public Choice*, March 1988, *56*(3), pp. 233–47.

Kraizberg, Elli. The Option to Deliver Prematurely Associated with Forward Contracts: Analysis of a Timing Option. In *Khoury, S. J. and Ghosh, A., eds.*, 1988, pp. 227–58.

Krakover, Shaul and Casetti, Emilio. Directionally Biased Metropolitan Growth: A Model and a Case Study. *Econ. Geogr.*, January 1988, *64*(1), pp. 17–28.

Krämer, Christoph and Rolfes, Bernd. Erfolgsorientierte Steuerung marktbezogener Organisationseinheiten in Kreditinstituten. (Success-Oriented Management of Organizational Units of Credit Institutions Operating Cost to the Market. With English summary.) *Kredit Kapital*, 1988, *21*(1), pp. 118–42.

Kramer, Gerald H. and Snyder, James M. Fairness, Self-interest, and the Politics of the Progressive Income Tax. *J. Public Econ.*, July 1988, *36*(2), pp. 197–230.

Kramer, John M. The Soviet Union Today: Environmental Problems. In *Cracraft, J., ed.*, 1988, pp. 154–63.

Kramer, Larry. Consent Decrees and the Rights of Third Parties. *Mich. Law Rev.*, November 1988, *87*(2), pp. 321–64.

Kramer, Randall A. Stability and Farm Programs: A Case Study of Feed Grain Markets: Reaction. In *Sumner, D. A., ed.*, 1988, pp. 109–11.

Krämer, Walter; Ploberger, Werner and Alt, Raimund. Testing for Structural Change in Dynamic Models. *Econometrica*, November 1988, *56*(6), pp. 1355–69.

Kranich, Laurence J. Altruism and Efficiency: A Welfare Analysis of the Walrasian Mechanism with Transfers. *J. Public Econ.*, August 1988, *36*(3), pp. 369–86.

Krantz, David H.; Nisbett, Richard E. and Fong, Geoffrey T. The Effects of Statistical Training on Thinking about Everyday Problems. In *Bell, D. E.; Raiffa, H. and Tversky, A., eds.*, 1988, *1986*, pp. 299–340.

Krantz, Olle. New Estimates of Swedish Historical GDP since the Beginning of the Nineteenth

Century. *Rev. Income Wealth*, June 1988, *34*(2), pp. 165–81.

Kranzberg, Melvin and Smith, Cyril Stanley. Materials in History and Society. In *Forester, T., ed.*, 1988, *1979*, pp. 85–118.

Krashevski, Richard S. What Is So Natural about High Unemployment? *Amer. Econ. Rev.*, May 1988, *78*(2), pp. 289–93.

Krashinsky, Michael. The Case for Eliminating Mandatory Retirement: Why Economics and Human Rights Need not Conflict. *Can. Public Policy*, March 1988, *14*(1), pp. 40–51.

Krasner, Stephen D. Is Protection Due to Financial Instability? A Sceptical View: Perspective. In *Guerrieri, P. and Padoan, P. C., eds.*, 1988, pp. 155–61.

———. Japan and the United States: Prospects for Stability. In *Inoguchi, T. and Okimoto, D. I., eds.*, 1988, pp. 381–413.

Krasnička, Jan. Future Scientific-Technological Profile of Czechoslovakia in the International Context. *Czech. Econ. Digest.*, June 1988, (4), pp. 38–43.

Krattenmaker, Thomas G. and Pitofsky, Robert. Antitrust Merger Policy and the Reagan Administration. *Antitrust Bull.*, Summer 1988, *33*(2), pp. 211–32.

Kraus, Alan and Heinkel, Robert. Measuring Event Impacts in Thinly Traded Stocks. *J. Finan. Quant. Anal.*, March 1988, *23*(1), pp. 71–88.

Kraus, Aleksander. Strategic Planning and Innovation in a Yugoslavia Self-management Enterprise—Metalservis. In *Saunders, C. T., ed.*, 1988, pp. 269–77.

Kraus, Jon. The Political Economy of Trade Union–State Relations in Radical and Populist Regimes in Africa. In *Southall, R., ed.*, 1988, pp. 171–210.

Kraus, Michael. Gorbachev's Reforms and East Europe. In *Liebowitz, R. D., ed.*, 1988, pp. 161–73.

Krause-Junk, Gerold. Überlegungen zu einem künftigen europäischen Körperschaftsteuersystem. (Reflections on a Future European Corporation Tax System. With English summary.) *Konjunkturpolitik*, 1988, *34*(5–6), pp. 268–90.

———. World Tax Reform: A Progress Report: Germany: Comment. In *Pechman, J. A., ed.*, 1988, pp. 127–40.

Krause, Lawrence B. Economic Trends in the United States and Their Implications for ASEAN. In *Tan, L.-H. and Akrasanee, N., eds.*, 1988, pp. 3–23.

———. Hong Kong and Singapore: Twins or Kissing Cousins? *Econ. Develop. Cult. Change*, Supplement, April 1988, *36*(3), pp. S45–66.

Krause, Ulrich and Fujimoto, Takao. More Theorems on Joint Production. *J. Econ. (Z. Nationalökon.)*, 1988, *48*(2), pp. 189–96.

Krauss, Ellis S. and Muramatsu, Michio. Japanese Political Economy Today: The Patterned Pluralist Model. In *Okimoto, D. I. and Rohlen, T. P., eds.*, 1988, pp. 208–10.

Krauss, Melvyn. Foreign Aid, Protectionism, and

National Security. In *Anderson, A. and Bark, D. L., eds.*, 1988, pp. 225–35.

Kraut, Robert E. Homework: What Is It and Who Does It? In *Christensen, K. E., ed.*, 1988, pp. 30–48.

——— and **Gerson, Judith M.** Clerical Work at Home or in the Office: The Difference It Makes. In *Christensen, K. E., ed.*, 1988, pp. 49–64.

Krautkraemer, Jeffrey A. The Cut-Off Grade and the Theory of Extraction. *Can. J. Econ.*, February 1988, *21*(1), pp. 146–60.

Krautmann, Anthony C. and Barnard, Jerald R. Population Growth among U.S. Regions and Metropolitan Areas: A Test for Causality. *J. Reg. Sci.*, February 1988, *28*(1), pp. 103–18.

——— and **Solow, John L.** Economies of Scale in Nuclear Power Generation. *Southern Econ. J.*, July 1988, *55*(1), pp. 70–85.

Kravis, Irving B. and Lipsey, Robert E. National Price Levels and the Prices of Tradables and Nontradables. *Amer. Econ. Rev.*, May 1988, *78*(2), pp. 474–78.

Kravitz, David A. and Gunto, Samuel J. Modeling Coalition Formation in Inessential Probabilistic Games. In *Tietz, R.; Albers, W. and Selten, R., eds.*, 1988, pp. 268–85.

Kreager, Philip. New Light on Graunt. *Population Stud.*, March 1988, *42*(1), pp. 129–40.

Krebsbach-Gnath, Camilla and Antal, Araine Berthoin. Women in Management: Unused Resources in the Federal Republic of Germany. In *Adler, N. J. and Izraeli, D., eds.*, 1988, pp. 141–56.

Kregel, J. A. Economic Methodology in the Face of Uncertainty: The Modelling Methods of Keynes and the Post-Keynesians. In *Sawyer, M. C., ed.*, 1988, *1976*, pp. 44–60.

———. Financial Innovation and the Organisation of Stock Market Trading. *Banca Naz. Lavoro Quart. Rev.*, December 1988, (167), pp. 367–86.

———. The Multiplier and Liquidity Preference: Two Sides of the Theory of Effective Demand. In *Barrère, A., ed.*, 1988, pp. 231–50.

———. The Theory of Demand and Supply of Labour—The Post-Keynesian View. In *Kregel, J. A.; Matzner, E. and Roncaglia, A., eds.*, 1988, pp. 27–42.

——— and **Eichner, Alfred S.** An Essay on Post-Keynesian Theory: A New Paradigm in Economics. In *Sawyer, M. C., ed.*, 1988, *1975*, pp. 11–32.

———; **Matzner, Egon and Roncaglia, Alessandro.** Barriers to Full Employment: Introduction. In *Kregel, J. A.; Matzner, E. and Roncaglia, A., eds.*, 1988, pp. 1–5.

Krehbiel, Timothy L. and Yunker, James A. Investment Analysis by the Individual Investor. *Quart. Rev. Econ. Bus.*, Winter 1988, *28*(4), pp. 90–101.

Kreider, Rosalie and Black, Robert A. Critical Legal Studies and Economic Analysis: A Survey. In *Pennsylvania Economic Association*, 1988, pp. 492–506.

Krein, Sheila Fitzgerald and Beller, Andrea H. Educational Attainment of Children from Single-Parent Families: Differences by Exposure, Gender, and Race. *Demography*, May 1988, 25(2), pp. 221–34.

Kreinin, Mordechai E. How Closed is Japan's Market? Additional Evidence. *World Econ.*, December 1988, 11(4), pp. 529–42.

———— and Dinopoulos, Elias. Effects on the U.S.–Japan Auto VER on European Prices and on U.S. Welfare. *Rev. Econ. Statist.*, August 1988, 70(3), pp. 484–91.

Kremers, Jeroen J. M. Long-run Limits on the U.S. Federal Debt. *Econ. Letters*, 1988, 28(3), pp. 259–62.

Kreps, David M. In Honor of Sandy Grossman, Winner of the John Bates Clark Medal. *J. Econ. Perspectives*, Spring 1988, 2(2), pp. 111–35.

————; Levine, David K. and Fudenberg, Drew. On the Robustness of Equilibrium Refinements. *J. Econ. Theory*, April 1988, 44(2), pp. 354–80.

———— and Scheinkman, José A. Quantity Precommitment and Betrand Competition Yield Cournot Outcomes. In *Daughety, A. F., ed.*, 1988, 1983, pp. 201–17.

Kresin, Vladimir Z. Soviet Science in Practice: An Inside View. In *Cracraft, J., ed.*, 1988, pp. 234–44.

Kresl, Peter K. Talking Past Each Other: Frustration of the Trade Talks. In *Thornton, R. J.; Hyclak, T. and Aronson, J. R., eds.*, 1988, pp. 115–29.

Kress, Moshe and Cook, Wade D. Partial and Multiple Match Tournaments. *Math. Soc. Sci.*, June 1988, 15(3), pp. 303–06.

Kressel, Kenneth. Labor Mediation: An Exploratory Survey. In *Lewin, D., et al., eds.*, 1988, pp. 351–73.

Kreuter, Josef. Enterprise Strategies: Comments. In *Saunders, C. T., ed.*, 1988, pp. 330–36.

Kreutzer, David and Lee, Dwight R. Tax Evasion and Monopoly Output Decisions: A Reply. *Nat. Tax J.*, December 1988, 41(4), pp. 583–84.

Kridel, Donald J. A Consumer Surplus Approach to Predicting Extended Area Service (EAS) Development and Stimulation Rates. *Info. Econ. Policy*, 1988, 3(4), pp. 379–90.

Krieger, Abba M.; Ritov, Yaakov and Gilula, Zvi. Ordinal Association in Contingency Tables: Some Interpretive Aspects. *J. Amer. Statist. Assoc.*, June 1988, 83(402), pp. 540–45.

————; Schaffer, C. M. and Green, Paul E. Dominated Options in Consumer Tradeoff Modeling: Is Their Occurrence Recognized? In *Gaul, W. and Schader, M., eds.*, 1988, pp. 258–67.

Krieger, Douglas J. National Forest Management: The Issue of Below-Cost Sales. In *Johnston, G. M.; Freshwater, D. and Favero, P., eds.*, 1988, pp. 135–58.

Krieger, Sandra and Sternlight, Peter D. Monetary Policy and Open Market Operations during 1987. *Fed. Res. Bank New York Quart. Rev.*, Spring 1988, 13(1), pp. 41–58.

Kriesel, Warren P.; Deaton, Brady J. and Johnson, Thomas G. Investing in Economic Development Infrastructure: A Decision-Making Framework. In *Johnson, T. G.; Deaton, B. J. and Segarra, E., eds.*, 1988, pp. 155–62.

————; Deaton, Brady J. and McNamara, Kevin T. Human Capital Stock and Flow and Economic Growth Analysis: Note. *Growth Change*, Winter 1988, 19(1), pp. 61–66.

————; Deaton, Brady J. and McNamara, Kevin T. Manufacturing Location: The Impact of Human Capital Stocks and Flows. *Rev. Reg. Stud.*, Winter 1988, 18(1), pp. 42–48.

Kriesky, Jill K. and Hurd, Richard W. Communications: 'The Rise and Demise of PATCO' Reconstructed. In *Lewin, D., et al., eds.*, 1988, 1986, pp. 267–78.

Kriesler, Peter. Kalecki's Pricing Theory Revisited. *J. Post Keynesian Econ.*, Fall 1988, 11(1), pp. 108–30.

————. On Dobb's Interpretation of Jevons on Ricardo. In *Wood, J. C., ed., Vol. 3*, 1988, 1984, pp. 294–97.

Krilek, Jozef. The New Law on Agricultural Cooperatives. *Czech. Econ. Digest.*, June 1988, (4), pp. 59–70.

Krinsky, Itzhak and Chan, M. W. Luke. Expectation Formation and Portfolio Models for Life Insurers. *J. Risk Ins.*, December 1988, 55(4), pp. 682–91.

Krishna, Kala. High-Tech Trade Policy. In *Baldwin, R. E.; Hamilton, C. B. and Sapir, A., eds.*, 1988, pp. 285–311.

————. Long-Run Effects of the Strong Dollar: Comment. In *Marston, R. C., ed.*, 1988, pp. 294–98.

————. Market Access and International Competition: A Simulation Study of 16K Random Access Memories: Comment. In *Feenstra, R. C., ed.*, 1988, pp. 198–202.

————. Strategic Models, Market Structure, and State Trading: An Application to Agriculture: Comment. In *Baldwin, R. E., ed. (II)*, 1988, pp. 105–07.

———— and Itoh, Motoshige. Content Protection and Oligopolistic Interactions. *Rev. Econ. Stud.*, January 1988, 55(1), pp. 107–25.

Krishna, Raj. Ideology and Economic Policy. *Indian Econ. Rev.*, Jan.–June 1988, 23(1), pp. 1–26.

Krishnaiah, J. and Krishnamoorthy, S. Estimation of Engel Elasticities for Grain in Andhra Pradesh. *Margin*, Jan.–March 1988, 20(2), pp. 31–38.

Krishnamoorthy, S. and Krishnaiah, J. Estimation of Engel Elasticities for Grain in Andhra Pradesh. *Margin*, Jan.–March 1988, 20(2), pp. 31–38.

Krishnamurthi, Lakshman and Raj, S. P. A Model of Brand Choice and Purchase Quantity Price Sensitivities. *Marketing Sci.*, Winter 1988, 7(1), pp. 1–20.

Krishnamurty, J. Unemployment in India: The Broad Magnitudes and Characteristics. In *Sri-*

nivasan, T. N. and Bardhan, P. K., eds., 1988, pp. 294–315.

Krishnan, Vijaya. Occupational Status, Earnings, and Fertility Expectations: Development and Estimation of a Causal Model. *De Economist*, 1988, *136*(3), pp. 358–82.

Krishnaswamy, K. S. Economic Change in China: Some Impressions. In *Mitra, A., ed.*, 1988, pp. 62–86.

Krislov, Joseph and Garen, John E. An Examination of the New American Strike Statistics in Analysing Aggregate Strike Incidence. *Brit. J. Ind. Relat.*, March 1988, *26*(1), pp. 75–84.

Krislov, Marvin. Ensuring Tenant Consultation before Public Housing Is Demolished or Sold. *Yale Law J.*, July 1988, *97*(8), pp. 1745–64.

Kristensen, Kai and Amundsen, Rolf. En vurdering af den danske punktafgiftsstruktur. (Is the Danish Commodity Tax Structure Optimal? With English summary.) *Nationaløkon. Tidsskr.*, 1988, *126*(3), pp. 323–34.

Kriström, B. and Johansson, Per-Olov. Measuring Values for Improved Air Quality from Discrete Response Data: Two Experiments. *J. Agr. Econ.*, September 1988, *39*(3), pp. 439–45.

Kritz, Ernesto. Crisis y cambio: Estructura productiva y mercado de trabajo en America Latina después de los años '80. (With English summary.) *Desarrollo Econ.*, April–June 1988, *28*(109), pp. 43–66.

Kritzman, Mark and Estep, Tony. TIPP: Insurance without Complexity. *J. Portfol. Manage.*, Summer 1988, *14*(4), pp. 38–42.

Kriuchkov, Nikolai; Bober, Wolfgang and Evsiukov, Evgenii. Scientific-Technological Cooperation in Chemistry. *Soviet E. Europ. Foreign Trade*, Spring 1988, *24*(1), pp. 54–62.

Kříž, Karel. New Principles in the International Socialist Division of Labour. *Czech. Econ. Digest.*, November 1988, (7), pp. 58–66.

Kríž, O. and Jiroušek, Radim. An Expert System Accepting Knowledge in a Form of Statistical Data. In *Edwards, D. and Raun, N. E., eds.*, 1988, pp. 123–28.

Kroch, Eugene. Bounds on Specification Error Arising From Data Proxies. *J. Econometrics*, January 1988, *37*(1), pp. 171–92.

Kroes, Eric P. and Sheldon, Robert J. Stated Preference Methods. *J. Transp. Econ. Policy*, January 1988, *22*(1), pp. 11–25.

Kroiher, Jaroslav and Plachý, Jan. The Role of the System of Plan-Base Management in Speeding Up Scientific–Technological Development. *Czech. Econ. Digest.*, April 1988, (2), pp. 13–29.

Kroll, Heidi. Transaction Cost Economics and Planned Failure: Vertical Integration and Steel Utilization in Soviet Machine Building. *J. Inst. Theoretical Econ.*, December 1988, *144*(5), pp. 857–64.

Kröll, W. The Role of a National Research Establishment in Preparing for Industrial Utilization of Space. In *Egan, J. J., et al.*, 1988, pp. 465–71.

Kroll, Yoram; Briys, Eric and Kahane, Yehuda. Voluntary Insurance Coverage, Compulsory Insurance, and Risky–Riskless Portfolio Opportunities. *J. Risk Ins.*, December 1988, *55*(4), pp. 713–22.

_____; **Levy, Haim and Rapoport, Amnon.** Experimental Tests of the Separation Theorem and the Capital Asset Pricing Model. *Amer. Econ. Rev.*, June 1988, *78*(3), pp. 500–519.

Kromphardt, Jürgen. Erklärung der Wachstumsschwäche seit den 70er Jahren aus konjunktureller und langfristiger Perspektive. (Explanations of the Economic Slowdown since the 1970s from a Business Cycle and a Long-term Point of View. With English summary.) *Ifo-Studien*, 1988, *34*(2–3), pp. 117–32.

Krtscha, Manfred. Axiomatic Characterization of Statistical Price Indices. In *Eichhorn, W., ed.*, 1988, pp. 117–33.

Krueger, Alan B. Are Public Sector Workers Paid More Than Their Alternative Wage? Evidence from Longitudinal Data and Job Queues. In *Freeman, R. B. and Ichniowski, C., eds.*, 1988, pp. 217–40.

_____. The Determinants of Queues for Federal Jobs. *Ind. Lab. Relat. Rev.*, July 1988, *41*(4), pp. 567–81.

_____; **Burton, John F., Jr. and Hunt, H. Allan.** The Impact of Open Competition in Michigan on the Employers' Costs of Workers' Compensation. In *Borba, P. S. and Appel, D., eds.*, 1988, pp. 109–44.

_____ **and Summers, Lawrence H.** Efficiency Wages and the Inter-industry Wage Structure. *Econometrica*, March 1988, *56*(2), pp. 259–93.

Krueger, Anne O. The Problems of the LDCs' Debt. In *Feldstein, M., ed. (II)*, 1988, pp. 201–14.

_____. Prospects for Liberalising the International Trading System. In *Borner, S., ed.*, 1988, pp. 79–101.

_____; **Schiff, Maurice and Valdés, Alberto.** Agricultural Incentives in Developing Countries: Measuring the Effect of Sectoral and Economy-wide Policies. *World Bank Econ. Rev.*, September 1988, *2*(3), pp. 255–71.

Krueger, Russell C. U.S. International Transactions, First Quarter 1988. *Surv. Curr. Bus.*, June 1988, *68*(6), pp. 28–69.

Krüger, Michael and Glombowski, Jörg. A Short-Period Growth Cycle Model. *Rech. Écon. Louvain*, 1988, *54*(4), pp. 423–38.

Krugman, Paul R. Desindustrialización, reindustrialización y tipo de cambio real. (Deindustrialization, Reindustrialization, and the Real Exchange Rate. With English summary.) *Estud. Econ.*, July–Dec. 1988, *3*(2), pp. 149–67.

_____. Exchange Rate Volatility and Misalignment: Evaluating Some Proposals for Reform: Commentary. In *Federal Reserve Bank of Kansas City*, 1988, pp. 221–24.

_____. Financing vs. Forgiving a Debt Overhang. *J. Devel. Econ.*, November 1988, *29*(3), pp. 253–68.

_____. International Aspects of U.S. Monetary and Fiscal Policy. In *Melamed, L., ed.*, 1988, *1983*, pp. 273–96.

_____. International Payments Imbalances in Japan, Germany, and the United States: Discussion. In *Fieleke, N. S., ed.*, 1988, pp. 51–53.

_____. Long-Run Effects of the Strong Dollar. In *Marston, R. C., ed.*, 1988, pp. 277–94.

_____. Multistage International Competition. In *Spence, A. M. and Hazard, H. A., eds.*, 1988, pp. 289–300.

_____. The Persistent U.S. Trade Deficit. *Australian Econ. Pap.*, December 1988, 27(51), pp. 149–58.

_____. Rethinking International Trade. *Bus. Econ.*, April 1988, 23(2), pp. 7–12.

_____. Sustainability and the Decline of the Dollar. In *Bryant, R. C.; Holtham, G. and Hooper, P., eds.*, 1988, pp. 82–99.

_____ and Baldwin, Richard E. Industrial Policy and International Competition in Wide-Bodied Jet Aircraft. In *Baldwin, R. E., ed. (II)*, 1988, pp. 45–71.

_____ and Baldwin, Richard E. Market Access and International Competition: A Simulation Study of 16K Random Access Memories. In *Feenstra, R. C., ed.*, 1988, pp. 171–97.

de Kruijk, Hans and van Tongeren, Frank. Growth, Employment and Education: An Application of Multicriteria Analysis to Pakistan. *Pakistan Devel. Rev.*, Part 2, Winter 1988, 27(4), pp. 725–33.

Krull, Steven; Eytan, T. Hanan and Harpaz, Giora. The Pricing of Dollar Index Futures Contracts. *J. Futures Markets*, April 1988, 8(2), pp. 127–39.

Krumm, Ronald and Kelly, Austin. Multiperiod Migration Patterns: The Timing and Frequency of Household Responses. *J. Reg. Sci.*, May 1988, 28(2), pp. 255–70.

Krus, Lech and Bronisz, Piotr. Application of Generalized Raiffa Solution to Multicriteria Bargaining Support. In *Iri, M. and Yajima, K., eds.*, 1988, pp. 207–11.

Kruse, Douglas L. International Trade and the Labor Market Experience of Displaced Workers. *Ind. Lab. Relat. Rev.*, April 1988, 41(3), pp. 402–17.

Kruse, Jörn. Irreversibilität und natürliche Markteintrittsbarrieren. (Sunk Costs and Natural Entry Barriers. With English summary.) *Jahr. Nationalökon. Statist.*, June 1988, 204(6), pp. 508–17.

Kruse, Rudolf and Meyer, Klaus Dieter. Confidence Intervals for the Parameters of a Linguistic Random Variable. In *Kacprzyk, J. and Fedrizzi, M., eds.*, 1988, pp. 113–23.

Kruseman, Jean-Louis and Capron, Henri. Is Political Rivalry an Incentive to Vote? *Public Choice*, January 1988, 56(1), pp. 31–43.

Krutilla, Kerry and Boyd, Roy. The Politics and Consequences of Protectionism: A Case Study in the North American Lumber Market. *J. Policy Modeling*, Winter 1988, 10(4), pp. 601–09.

Kruvant, W. J. and Moody, C. E., Jr. Joint Bidding, Entry, and the Price of OCS Leases. *Rand J. Econ.*, Summer 1988, 19(2), pp. 276–84.

Krzyzaniak, Marian and Bastani, Sharokh. The Incidence of the U.S. Corporation Income Tax: An Old Problem Revisited. *Public Finance*, 1988, 43(2), pp. 165–94.

Krzyzanowski, J. European Agricultural Policies in a Global Context: Report. *Europ. Rev. Agr. Econ.*, 1988, 15(2–3), pp. 190.

Ksiensik, Monika Isis and Wendt, Dirk. Normative and Individual Strategies in Social Dilemmata. In *Tietz, R.; Albers, W. and Selten, R., eds.*, 1988, pp. 21–36.

Kubarych, Roger M. After the Crash: Linkages between Stocks and Futures: Trading Systems. In *MacKay, R. J., ed.*, 1988, pp. 79–83.

Kubin, Konrad W. The United States and the Seventh Directive. In *Gray, S. J. and Coenenberg, A. G., eds.*, 1988, pp. 155–88.

Kuboniwa, Masaaki. Prospects for Restructuring the Soviet Price and Finance System. *Hitotsubashi J. Econ.*, December 1988, 29(2), pp. 143–63.

_____. Stepwise Aggregation for Optimal Planning. *Hitotsubashi J. Econ.*, June 1988, 29(1), pp. 89–99.

Kubursi, Atif A. Jobs, Education and Development: The Case of the West Bank. In *Abed, G. T., ed.*, 1988, pp. 223–43.

_____ and Butterfield, D. W. Banker's Preferences and Monetary Control. *Écon. Appl.*, 1988, 41(1), pp. 109–27.

Kucher, Eckhard and Simon, Hermann. Die Bestimmung empirischer Preisabsatzfunktionen: Methoden, Befunde, Erfahrungen. (With English summary.) *Z. Betriebswirtshaft*, January 1988, 58(1), pp. 171–83.

Kuckshinrichs, Wilhelm and Ströbele, Wolfgang J. On the Optimal Transition to a Backstop Technology with Uncertainty as to the Cost of the Substitute. *J. Inst. Theoretical Econ.*, June 1988, 144(3), pp. 496–514.

Kudla, Ronald J. and McInish, Thomas H. Divergence of Opinion and Corporate Spin-offs. *Quart. Rev. Econ. Bus.*, Summer 1988, 28(2), pp. 20–29.

Kuemmerling, Robert A. and Hanson, Patricia. Inflation Holds Steady during the First Half. *Mon. Lab. Rev.*, October 1988, 111(10), pp. 13–17.

_____; Howell, Craig and Clem, Andrew. Domestic Price Rise during 1987 Reflects Swing of Energy Prices. *Mon. Lab. Rev.*, June 1988, 111(6), pp. 20–26.

Kuenstler, Peter. Local Employment Initiatives: Some Recent Developments. *Int. Lab. Rev.*, 1988, 127(4), pp. 463–78.

Kuenzel, Rainer. The Erosion of Profitability in Postwar West Germany: Hypotheses on the Dialectics of Accumulation and Social Relations. *Econ. Rev. (Keizai Kenkyu)*, July 1988, 39(3), pp. 209–20.

Kugler, Peter. An Empirical Note on the Term Structure and Interest Rate Stabilization Policies. *Quart. J. Econ.*, November 1988, 103(4), pp. 789–92.

_____. Intertemporal Substitution and Random Changes in Preferences: Time Series Evidence for Four Countries. *Empirical Econ.*, 1988, *13*(1), pp. 17–34.

———. Intertemporal Substitution, Taste Shocks and Cointegration. *Econ. Letters*, 1988, *26*(3), pp. 235–39.

———. Lohndiskriminierung in der Schweiz: Evidenz von Mikrodaten. (Wage Discrimination in Switzerland: Evidence of Individual Data. With English summary.) *Schweiz. Z. Volkswirtsch. Statist.*, March 1988, *124*(1), pp. 23–47.

———; Müller, Urs and Sheldon, George. Struktur der Arbeitsnachfrage im technologischen Wandel—Eine empirische Analyse für die Bundesrepublik Deutschland. (With English summary.) *Weltwirtsch. Arch.*, 1988, *124*(3), pp. 490–500.

——— and Schwendener, Peter. Arbeitsangebot, Grenzsteuerbelastung und der permanente Lohnsatz: Empirische Ergebnisse für die Schweiz. (Labour Supply, Marginal Taxes, and Permanent Wages: Empirical Evidence for Switzerland. With English summary.) *Schweiz. Z. Volkswirtsch. Statist.*, September 1988, *124*(3), pp. 243–57.

Kühn, Bernhard; Rose, Manfred and Kungl, Hans. Incidence Effects of Changing the German Income Tax Rate Schedule. In *Bös, D.; Rose, M. and Seidl, C., eds.,*, 1988, pp. 205–46.

Kuhn, Betsey A. A Note: Do Futures Prices Always Reflect the Cheapest Deliverable Grade of the Commodity? *J. Futures Markets*, February 1988, *8*(1), pp. 99–102.

Kühn, Horst and Grote, Gerhard. Comparative Advantage and Its Use in the Foreign Trade of the Socialist Countries. *Soviet E. Europ. Foreign Trade*, Fall 1988, *24*(3), pp. 31–53.

Kuhn, Peter. A Nonuniform Pricing Model of Union Wages and Employment. *J. Polit. Econ.*, June 1988, *96*(3), pp. 473–508.

———. Unions in a General Equilibrium Model of Firm Formation. *J. Lab. Econ.*, January 1988, *6*(1), pp. 62–82.

——— and Davies, James B. Redistribution, Inheritance, and Inequality: An Analysis of Transitions. In *Kessler, D. and Masson, A., eds.*, 1988, pp. 123–43.

Kuhn, Rick. Labour Movement Economic Thought in the 1930s: Underconsumptionism and Keynesian Economics. *Australian Econ. Hist. Rev.*, September 1988, *28*(2), pp. 53–74.

Kuijsten, A. Application of Household Models in Studying the Family Life Cycle. In *Keilman, N.; Kuijsten, A. and Vossen, A., eds.*, 1988, pp. 179–94.

——— and Vossen, A. Modelling Household Formation and Dissolution: Introduction. In *Keilman, N.; Kuijsten, A. and Vossen, A., eds.*, 1988, pp. 3–12.

Kuipers, Simon K. The Trade Cycle under Capital Shortage and Labour Shortage: On Witteveen's Synthesis of the Overinvestment and Underinvestment Theory of the Trade Cycle. In *[Witteveen, H. J.]*, 1988, pp. 79–117.

——— and Boertje, Bert. On the Causes of the

Rise in the Liquidity Ratio in the Netherlands during the Early Eighties. *De Economist*, March 1988, *136*(1), pp. 50–90.

Kula, Erhun. The Case of Land Misallocation in Northern Ireland. *Irish J. Agr. Econ. Rural Soc.*, 1988, *13*, pp. 65–72.

———. The Inadequacy of the Entitlement Approach to Explain and Remedy Famines. *J. Devel. Stud.*, October 1988, *25*(1), pp. 112–16.

——— and McKillop, D. G. A Planting Function for Private Afforestation in Northern Ireland. *J. Agr. Econ.*, January 1988, *39*(1), pp. 133–40.

Kulatilaka, Nalin and Marcus, Alan J. General Formulation of Corporate Options. In *Chen, A. H., ed.*, 1988, pp. 183–99.

——— and Marks, Stephen Gary. The Strategic Value of Flexibility: Reducing the Ability to Compromise. *Amer. Econ. Rev.*, June 1988, *78*(3), pp. 574–80.

Kulchycky, Ksenia; Blomström, Magnus and Lipsey, Robert E. U.S. and Swedish Direct Investment and Exports. In *Baldwin, R. E., ed. (II)*, 1988, pp. 259–97.

Kulikov, V. V. The Structure and Forms of Socialist Property. *Prob. Econ.*, May 1988, *31*(1), pp. 14–29.

Kulis, Stephen. Emotional Distress Following AFDC Cutbacks. *Soc. Sci. Quart.*, June 1988, *69*(2), pp. 399–415.

Kulkarni, Kishore and Chakraborty, Debasish. Effects of Output Growth on Balance of Payments. *Margin*, Oct.–Dec. 1988, *21*(1), pp. 41–53.

Kulke, Elmar. Limiting Factors in Industrialization: A Case Study of Kelantan. In *Schätzl, L. H., ed.*, 1988, pp. 169–241.

Kullberg, Rolf. Bankverksamhetens risker och centralbankens roll. (The Risks of Banking and the Role of the Central Bank. With English summary.) *Ekon. Samfundets Tidskr.*, 1988, *41*(1), pp. 35–48.

Kulow, David M.; Khoylian, Roubina and MacMillan, Ian C. Venture Capitalists' Involvement in Their Investments: Extent and Performance. In *Kirchhoff, B. A., et al., eds.*, 1988, pp. 303–23.

Kulshreshtha, Surendra N. and Russell, K. Dale. An Ex Post Evaluation of the Contributions of Irrigation to Regional Development in Alberta: A Case Study. *Rev. Reg. Stud.*, Spring 1988, *18*(2), pp. 10–22.

——— and Tewari, Devi D. Impacts of Rising Energy Prices on Saskatchewan Agriculture. *Can. J. Agr. Econ.*, July 1988, *36*(2), pp. 239–60.

Kultravut, Sunee; Akrasanee, Narongchai and Sestakupt, Pharadorn. Technical Efficiency and Production Management: The Thai Experience. In *James, K. and Akrasanee, N., eds.*, 1988, pp. 164–207.

Kumar, Ashok; Kaul, Sushila and Pandey, R. K. Agricultural Field Wages in Orissa: An Economic Study. *Margin*, Oct.–Dec. 1988, *21*(1), pp. 72–78.

Kumar, Gopalakrishna. On Prices and Economic Power: Explaining Recent Changes in Intersectoral Relations in the Indian Economy. *J. Devel. Stud.*, October 1988, 25(1), pp. 25–42.

Kumar, K. Ravi and Sudharshan, D. Pre-emptive Product Positioning Strategies under Market Share Restrictions. *Managerial Dec. Econ.*, June 1988, 9(2), pp. 93–99.

Kumar, Nagesh. Biotechnology Revolution and the Third World: An Overview. In *Research and Info. System for the Non-aligned and Other Developing Countries*, 1988, pp. 1–30.

——— and Panchamukhi, V. R. Impact on Commodity Exports. In *Research and Info. System for the Non-aligned and Other Developing Countries*, 1988, pp. 207–24.

Kumar, Remesh C. On Optimal Domestic Processing of Exhaustible Natural Resource Exports. *J. Environ. Econ. Manage.*, September 1988, 15(3), pp. 341–54.

Kumar, Rishi; Mathur, Vijay K. and Stein, Sheldon H. A Dynamic Model of Regional Population Growth and Decline. *J. Reg. Sci.*, August 1988, 28(3), pp. 379–95.

Kumar, Shubh K. Design, Income Distribution, and Consumption Effects of Maize Pricing Policies in Zambia. In *Pinstrup-Andersen, P., ed.*, 1988, pp. 289–300.

———. Effect of Seasonal Food Shortage on Agricultural Production in Zambia. *World Devel.*, September 1988, 16(9), pp. 1051–63.

——— and Alderman, Harold. Food Consumption and Nutritional Effects of Consumer-Oriented Food Subsidies. In *Pinstrup-Andersen, P., ed.*, 1988, pp. 36–48.

Kumar, T. Krishna and Gapinski, James H. In Estimating the Elasticity of Factor Substitution by Nonlinear Least Squares. In *Sengupta, J. K. and Kadekodi, G. K., eds.*, 1988, pp. 157–68.

———; Sengupta, Jati K. and Kadekodi, Gopal K. The Scientific Work of Gerhard Tintner. In *Sengupta, J. K. and Kadekodi, G. K., eds.*, 1988, pp. 3–22.

Kumari, Anchala. Probabilistic Model of Population Projection. In *Brown, R. C., ed.*, 1988, pp. 73–85.

Kumbhakar, Subal C. Estimation of Input-Specific Technical and Allocative Inefficiency in Stochastic Frontier Models. *Oxford Econ. Pap.*, September 1988, 40(3), pp. 535–49.

———. On the Estimation of Technical and Allocative Inefficiency Using Stochastic Frontier Functions: The Case of U.S. Class 1 Railroads. *Int. Econ. Rev.*, November 1988, 29(4), pp. 727–43.

——— and Serletis, Apostolos. A Financial Theory of the Financial Firm. *J. Quant. Econ.*, July 1988, 4(2), pp. 201–12.

Kumcu, Erdoğan; Karafakioğlu, Mehmet and Firat, A. Fuat. The Interface between Marketing and Development: Problems and Prospects. In *Kumcu, E. and Firat, A. F., eds.*, 1988, pp. 317–43.

Kumcu, M. Ercan. Exchange Rate Liberalization and Economic Stability: The Turkish Experi-

ence. In *Nas, T. F. and Odekon, M., eds.*, 1988, pp. 69–83.

Kume, Ikuo. Changing Relations among the Government, Labor, and Business in Japan after the Oil Crisis. *Int. Organ.*, Autumn 1988, 42(4), pp. 659–87.

Kümmel, R.; Groscurth, H.-M. and van Gool, W. Energy Optimization in Industrial Models. In *Iri, M. and Yajima, K., eds.*, 1988, pp. 518–29.

Kumon, Shumpei and Tanaka, Akihiko. From Prestige to Wealth to Knowledge. In *Inoguchi, T. and Okimoto, D. I., eds.*, 1988, pp. 64–82.

Kungl, Hans; Kühn, Bernhard and Rose, Manfred. Incidence Effects of Changing the German Income Tax Rate Schedule. In *Bös, D.; Rose, M. and Seidl, C., eds.*, 1988, pp. 205–46.

Kunihiro, Michihiko. International Trade Policy and Trade Negotiations. In *Feldstein, M., ed. (I)*, 1988, pp. 211–18.

Kunitake, Walter K. and Ketz, J. Edward. An Evaluation of the Conceptual Framework: Can It Resolve the Issues Related to Accounting for Income Taxes? In *Schwartz, B. N., ed.*, 1988, pp. 37–54.

Kunreuther, Howard C.; Schoemaker, Paul J. H. and Hershey, John C. Sources of Bias in Assessment Procedures for Utility Functions. In *Bell, D. E.; Raiffa, H. and Tversky, A., eds.*, 1988, 1982, pp. 422–42.

Kunze, Kent and Dean, Edwin. Recent Changes in the Growth of U.S. Multifactor Productivity. *Mon. Lab. Rev.*, May 1988, 111(5), pp. 14–22.

———; Jablonski, Mary and Rosenblum, Larry. Productivity, Age, and Labor Composition Changes in the U.S. *Mon. Lab. Rev.*, September 1988, 111(9), pp. 34–38.

Kuo, Shyanjaw and Ritchken, Peter H. Option Bounds with Finite Revision Opportunities. *J. Finance*, June 1988, 43(2), pp. 301–08.

Kupchan, Charles A. NATO and the Persian Gulf: Examining Intra-alliance Behavior. *Int. Organ.*, Spring 1988, 42(2), pp. 317–46.

Kupka, Václav and Špak, Michal. Prognostication Work and the Strategy of Czechoslovak Development. *Czech. Econ. Digest.*, May 1988, (3), pp. 13–32.

Küpper, Hans-Ulrich. Investitionstheoretische versus kontrolltheoretische Abschreibung: Alternative oder gleichartige Konzepte einer entscheidungsorientierten Kostenrechnung? (With English summary.) *Z. Betriebswirtshaft*, March 1988, 58(3), pp. 397–415.

Kurabayashi, Y. and Sakuma, I. A Reconsideration of the Concept of International Prices for the International Comparison of Real GDP. In *Salazar-Carrillo, J. and Rao, D. S. P., eds.*, 1988, pp. 39–57.

Kuran, Timur. The Tenacious Past: Theories of Personal and Collective Conservatism. *J. Econ. Behav. Organ.*, September 1988, 10(2), pp. 143–71.

Kurashvili, B. P. Restructuring and the Enterprise. *Prob. Econ.*, September 1988, *31*(5), pp. 23–46.

Kuroda, Masahiro. A Method of Estimation for the Updating Transaction Matrix in the Input–Output Relationships. In *Uno, K. and Shishido, S., eds.*, 1988, pp. 128–48.

Kuroda, Yoshimi. The Output Bias of Technological Change in Postwar Japanese Agriculture. *Amer. J. Agr. Econ.*, August 1988, *70*(3), pp. 663–73.

_____ **and Yotopoulos, Pan A.** A Subjective Equilibrium Approach to the Value of Children in the Agricultural Household. *Pakistan Devel. Rev.*, Autumn 1988, *27*(3), pp. 229–76.

Kurth, Michael M. Teachers' Unions and Excellence in Education: Reply. *J. Lab. Res.*, Fall 1988, *9*(4), pp. 389–94.

_____ **and Reid, Joseph D., Jr.** Public Employees in Political Firms: Part A. The Patronage Era. *Public Choice*, December 1988, *59*(3), pp. 253–62.

Kurtz, David L.; Boone, Louis E. and Gibson, Donald R. Rating Logistics and Transportation Faculties on the Basis of Editorial Review Board Memberships. *Logist. Transp. Rev.*, December 1988, *24*(4), pp. 684–90.

Kurtz, Jerome. Investment Incentives in Theory and Practice: Comments. In *Aaron, H. J.; Galper, H. and Pechman, J. A., eds.*, 1988, pp. 338–42.

Kurtz, Robert D. and Elliehausen, Gregory E. Scale Economies in Compliance Costs for Federal Consumer Credit Regulations. *J. Finan. Services Res.*, January 1988, *1*(2), pp. 147–59.

Kurz, Heinz D. Rent Theory in a Multisectoral Model. In *Steedman, I., ed., Vol. 2*, 1988, *1978*, pp. 179–200.

_____. Sraffa's Contribution to the Debate in Capital Theory. In *Steedman, I., ed., Vol. 1*, 1988, *1985*, pp. 42–63.

_____ **and Hagemann, Harald.** The Return of the Same Truncation Period and Reswitching of Techniques in Neo-Austrian and More General Models. In *Steedman, I., ed., Vol. 1*, 1988, *1976*, pp. 187–217.

Kurz, Mordecai. Coalitional Value. In *[Shapley, L. S.]*, 1988, pp. 155–73.

Kurz, Rudi. How to Harness Technology? *Jahr. Nationalökon. Statist.*, August 1988, *205*(2), pp. 163–74.

Kushma, John J. Participation and the Democratic Agenda: Theory and Praxis. In *Levine, M. V., et al.*, 1988, pp. 14–48.

_____. Realizing the Promise of Democracy in America's Third Century. In *Levine, M. V., et al.*, 1988, pp. 198–205.

Kushman, John E. Increasing Competition through Deregulation: Do Consumers Win or Lose? In *Maynes, E. S. and ACCI Research Committee, eds.*, 1988, pp. 413–39.

Kushmeider, Rose Marie and Haraf, William S. Redefining Financial Markets. In *Haraf, W. S. and Kushmeider, R. M., eds.*, 1988, pp. 1–33.

Kushner, J.; Masse, I. and Hanrahan, J. R. The Effect of Changes in Tax Legislation on the

Purchase/Lease Decision in the Public Sector. *Nat. Tax J.*, March 1988, *41*(1), pp. 123–30.

Kushner, Rose. An Ethical Model for Improving the Patient–Physician Relationship: Commentary. *Inquiry*, Winter 1988, *25*(4), pp. 465–67.

Kushnirsky, F. I. Soviet Economic Reform: An Analysis and a Model. In *Linz, S. J. and Moskoff, W., eds.*, 1988, pp. 44–72.

Kutay, A. Technological Change and Spatial Transformation in an Information Economy: 1. A Structural Model of Transition in the Urban System. *Environ. Planning A*, May 1988, *20*(5), pp. 569–93.

_____. Technological Change and Spatial Transformation in an Information Economy: 2. The Influence of New Information Technology on the Urban System. *Environ. Planning A*, June 1988, *20*(6), pp. 707–18.

Kutner, George W. Black–Scholes Revisited: Some Important Details [The Pricing of Options and Corporate Liabilities]. *Financial Rev.*, February 1988, *23*(1), pp. 95–104.

Kutscher, Ronald E. Growth of Services Employment in the United States. In *Guile, B. R. and Quinn, J. B., eds. (II)*, 1988, pp. 47–75.

_____. Structural Change of Employment in the United States. In *Candilis, W. O., ed.*, 1988, pp. 23–44.

Kuttner, Robert L. A Progressive Labor Agenda after Reagan. *Challenge*, Sept.–Oct. 1988, *31*(5), pp. 4–11.

Kuttner, Thomas S. Constitution as Covenant: Labour Law, Labour Boards, and the Courts from the Old to the New Dispensation. In *Carter, D. D., et al.*, 1988, pp. 32–60.

Kuwahara, Yasuo. The Entrepreneurs in the Japanese Software Industry. In *Japan Institute of Labour, ed.*, 1988, *1986*, pp. 18–21.

_____. From "Adaptation" to "Control": Labor and Management Response to Technological Innovation in Japan. In *Japan Institute of Labour, ed.*, 1988, *1984*, pp. 14–17.

_____. The Industrial Locus of Trade Unionism in Japan: The Vicissitudes of Union Membership by Industry. In *Japan Institute of Labour, ed.*, 1988, *1983*, pp. 68–72.

_____. What Does the Increase of Temporary Workers Bring to the Japanese Employment System? In *Japan Institute of Labour, ed.*, 1988, *1985*, pp. 116–19.

Kuwayama, Mikio. International Primary Commodity Marketing and Latin America. *CEPAL Rev.*, April 1988, (34), pp. 77–108.

Kuylen, Ton and Francken, Dick. Level of Own Contribution towards a Public Service as an Indicator for Consumer Appraisal. In *Maital, S., ed., Vol. 1*, 1988, pp. 97–113.

Kuznets, Paul W. An East Asian Model of Economic Development: Japan, Taiwan, and South Korea. *Econ. Develop. Cult. Change*, Supplement, April 1988, *36*(3), pp. S11–43.

_____. Employment Absorption in South Korea: 1970–1980. *Philippine Rev. Econ. Bus.*, March–June 1988, *25*(1–2), pp. 41–70.

Kverneland, Adne. Japan's Industry Structure—

Barriers to Global Competition. In *Hood, N. and Vahlne, J.-E., eds.*, 1988, pp. 225–55.

Kwack, Sung Y. Exchange Rate Effects on Korea's Economy. *Int. Econ. J.*, Summer 1988, 2(2), pp. 101–09.

_____. Korea's Exchange Rate Policy in a Changing Economic Environment. *World Devel.*, January 1988, 16(1), pp. 169–83.

_____ **and Leipziger, Danny M.** Factors Affecting the Accumulation of External Debt: Hypotheses and Evidence from Korea. *J. Econ. Devel.*, December 1988, 13(2), pp. 111–22.

Kwan, Andy C. C. and Sim, Ah-Boon. Generalised Portmanteau Statistics and Tests of Randomness: A Note on Their Applications to Residuals from a Fitted ARMA Model. *Econ. Letters*, 1988, 26(4), pp. 341–47.

Kwan, Clarence C. Y.; Chamberlain, Trevor W. and Cheung, C. Sherman. Cash versus Futures Prices and the Weekend Effect: The Canadian Evidence. In *Fabozzi, F. J., ed.*, 1988, pp. 329–39.

_____ **and Cheung, C. Sherman.** A Note on Simple Criteria for Optimal Portfolio Selection. *J. Finance*, March 1988, 43(1), pp. 241–45.

Kwan, Raymond S. K. Co-ordination of Joint Headways. In *Daduna, J. R. and Wren, A., eds.*, 1988, pp. 304–14.

Kwok, Ben and Veall, Michael R. The Jackknife and Regression with AR(1) Errors. *Econ. Letters*, 1988, 26(3), pp. 247–52.

Kwon, Ik-Whan and Safranski, Scott R. Religious Groups and Management Value Systems. In *Farmer, R. N. and McGoun, E. G., eds.*, 1988, pp. 171–83.

Kwon, Jene K. and Kang, Jung M. An Estimation of Import Demand, Export Supply and Technical Change for Korea. *Appl. Econ.*, December 1988, 20(12), pp. 1661–74.

Kwon, Tecksung. Is the Observed Intra-industry Trade a Statistical Artifact? *Int. Econ. J.*, Spring 1988, 2(1), pp. 69–84.

Kwon, Young K. and Jung, Woon-Oh. Disclosure When the Market Is Unsure of Information Endowment of Managers. *J. Acc. Res.*, Spring 1988, 26(1), pp. 146–53.

Kyburg, Henry E. Bets and Beliefs. In *Gärdenfors, P. and Sahlin, N.-E., eds.*, 1988, pp. 101–17.

Kydland, Finn E. and Prescott, Edward C. The Workweek of Capital and Its Cyclical Implications. *J. Monet. Econ.*, March–May 1988, 21(2–3), pp. 343–60.

_____; **Sedlacek, Guilherme L. and Hotz, V. Joseph.** Intertemporal Preferences and Labor Supply. *Econometrica*, March 1988, 56(2), pp. 335–60.

Kyer, Ben L.; Mixon, J. Wilson, Jr. and Uri, Noel D. Taxes, Transfer Payments and Automatic Stabilization in the United States. Impact and Trends. *Econ. Notes*, 1988, (2), pp. 50–60.

Kyle, Albert S. and Hartley, Peter R. Real Interest Rates and Home Goods: A Two-Period Model. *Econ. Rec.*, September 1988, 64(186), pp. 168–77.

Kymn, Kern O. and Hisnanick, John J. Econometric Techniques Applied to Productivity Growth Estimation. *Atlantic Econ. J.*, September 1988, 16(3), pp. 88.

L'Ecuyer, Pierre. Computing Optimal Checkpointing Policies: A Dynamic Programming Approach. In *Eiselt, H. A. and Pederzoli, G., eds.*, 1988, pp. 214–29.

_____ **and Breton, Michèle.** On the Existence of Sequential Equilibria in Markov Renewal Games. In *Eiselt, H. A. and Pederzoli, G., eds.*, 1988, pp. 200–213.

L'vov, D. S. and Glaz'ev, S. Iu. Theoretical and Applied Aspects of the Management of Scientific–Technical Progress. *Matekon*, Spring 1988, 24(3), pp. 80–100.

La Bella, Agostino and Campisi, Domenico. Evaluating the Economic Impact of Transportation Investment: An Input–Output Approach. In *Bianco, L. and La Bella, A., eds.*, 1988, pp. 443–62.

_____ **and Campisi, Domenico.** Transportation Investment and Dynamic Equilibrium in a Multiregional Input–Output System. In *Iri, M. and Yajima, K., eds.*, 1988, pp. 416–25.

_____ **and Campisi, Domenico.** Transportation Supply and Economic Growth in a Multiregional System. *Environ. Planning A*, July 1988, 20(7), pp. 925–36.

La Ferney, Preston E. and Lee, John E., Jr. Agricultural and Rural Areas Approaching the Twenty-first Century: A Synthesis of Research Issues. In *Hildreth, R. J., et al., eds.*, 1988, pp. 545–51.

La Nauze, J. A. The Conception of Jevons's Utility Theory. In *Wood, J. C., ed., Vol. 3*, 1988, 1953, pp. 58–60.

_____. Jevons in Sydney. In *Wood, J. C., ed., Vol. 1*, 1988, 1941, pp. 109–24.

La Porte, Todd R. The United States Air Traffic System: Increasing Reliability in the Midst of Rapid Growth. In *Mayntz, R. and Hughes, T. P., eds.*, 1988, pp. 215–44.

Laarman, Jan G. Export of Tropical Hardwoods in the Twentieth Century. In *Richards, J. F. and Tucker, R. P., eds.*, 1988, pp. 147–63.

Labán, Raúl and Meller, Patricio. Estimaçao de elasticidades variáveis no mercado de trabalho do Chile. (With English summary.) *Pesquisa Planejamento Econ.*, December 1988, 18(3), pp. 529–59.

Laband, David N. Transactions Costs and Production in a Legislative Setting. *Public Choice*, May 1988, 57(2), pp. 183–86.

_____ **and Sophocleus, John P.** The Social Cost of Rent-Seeking: First Estimates. *Public Choice*, September 1988, 58(3), pp. 269–75.

LaBarbera, Priscilla A. The Nouveaux Riches: Conspicuous Consumption and the Issue of Self-Fulfillment. In *Hirschman, E. and Sheth, J. N., eds.*, 1988, pp. 179–210.

Laber, Gene. Regulators' Decisions on Rates of Return: Recent Experience in the Telephone Industry. *Quart. J. Bus. Econ.*, Spring 1988, 27(2), pp. 3–22.

Labia, J. F. N. The Rhetoric of Economics (Review Article). *S. Afr. J. Econ.*, March 1988, *56*(1), pp. 47–60.

Labig, Chalmer E., Jr. and Greer, Charles R. Grievance Initiation: A Literature Survey and Suggestions for Future Research. *J. Lab. Res.*, Winter 1988, *9*(1), pp. 1–27.

Labouérie, P. Private and Official Capital Flows to Developing Countries: Comment. In *Jepma, C. J., ed.*, 1988, pp. 141–44.

Labys, Walter C. and Kim, Bong Chin. Application of the Translog Model of Energy Substitution to Developing Countries: The Case of Korea. *Energy Econ.*, October 1988, *10*(4), pp. 313–23.

Lacey, Nelson. The Competitiveness of the Property–Casualty Insurance Industry: A Look at Market Equity Values and Premium Prices. *Yale J. Regul.*, Summer 1988, *5*(2), pp. 501–16.

Lacey, Nelson J. Recent Evidence on the Liability Crisis. *J. Risk Ins.*, September 1988, *55*(3), pp. 499–508.

Lächler, Ulrich. Credibility and the Dynamics of Disinflation in Open Economies: A Note on the Southern Cone Experiments. *J. Devel. Econ.*, May 1988, *28*(3), pp. 285–307.

Lachmann, L. M. The Huttian Philosophy. *Managerial Dec. Econ.*, Special Issue, Winter 1988, pp. 13–15.

Lacivita, Charles J. and Seaks, Terry G. Forecasting Accuracy and the Choice of First Difference or Percentage Change Regression Models. *Int. J. Forecasting*, 1988, *4*(2), pp. 261–68.

Lacker, Jeffrey M. Inside Money and Real Output. *Econ. Letters*, 1988, *28*(1), pp. 9–14.

Lacombe, John J., II and Sleemi, Fehmida R. Wage Adjustments in Contracts Negotiated in Private Industry in 1987. *Mon. Lab. Rev.*, May 1988, *111*(5), pp. 23–28.

Lacy, Stephen. Content of Joint Operation Newspapers. In *Picard, R. G., et al., eds.*, 1988, pp. 147–60.

Lad, Frank and Blattenberger, Gail. An Application of Operational-Subjective Statistical Methods to Rational Expectations. *J. Bus. Econ. Statist.*, October 1988, *6*(4), pp. 453–64.

——— **and Blattenberger, Gail.** An Application of Operational-Subjective Statistical Methods to Rational Expectations: Reply. *J. Bus. Econ. Statist.*, October 1988, *6*(4), pp. 475–77.

Ladd, George W. Costs and Goals of the Multiproduct Firm. *Managerial Dec. Econ.*, December 1988, *9*(4), pp. 279–81.

Ladd, Helen F. Income Originating in the State and Local Sector: Comment. In *Rosen, H. S., ed.*, 1988, pp. 248–54.

———. The Meaning of Balance for State-Local Tax Systems. In *Gold, S. D., ed.*, 1988, pp. 31–46.

——— **and Bradbury, Katharine L.** City Taxes and Property Tax Bases. *Nat. Tax J.*, December 1988, *41*(4), pp. 503–23.

——— **and Ferguson, Ronald F.** The New Eco-

nomic Role of American States: Massachusetts. In *Fosler, R. S., ed.*, 1988, pp. 19–87.

Laffer, Arthur B. and Canto, Victor A. Conclusions on Supply-Side Portfolio Strategies. In *Canto, V. A. and Laffer, A. B., eds.*, 1988, pp. 165–74.

——— **and Canto, Victor A.** The Fat Cats Portfolio Strategy. In *Canto, V. A. and Laffer, A. B., eds.*, 1988, pp. 121–41.

——— **and Canto, Victor A.** The State Competitive Environment: 1986–1987 Update. In *Canto, V. A. and Laffer, A. B., eds.*, 1988, pp. 103–19.

——— **and Clark, Truman A.** Are Small Cap Stocks Still Alive? In *Canto, V. A. and Laffer, A. B., eds.*, 1988, pp. 9–24.

——— **and Clark, Truman A.** The Impact of Tax Reform on Income-Producing Real Estate. In *Canto, V. A. and Laffer, A. B., eds.*, 1988, pp. 25–53.

——— **and England, David F.** The Case for a 400-Basis-Point Plunge in Interest Rates. In *Canto, V. A. and Laffer, A. B., eds.*, 1988, pp. 55–75.

Laffont, Jean-Jacques. Hidden Gaming in Hierarchies: Facts and Models. *Econ. Rec.*, December 1988, *64*(187), pp. 295–306.

———; **Le Pottier, Jacques and Aragon, Yves.** Testing the Democratic Hypothesis in the Provision of Local Public Goods. *J. Public Econ.*, July 1988, *36*(2), pp. 139–51.

———; **Le Pottier, Jacques and Aragon, Yves.** Test de l'hypothèse démocratique dans le décisions budgétaires communales. (Test of the Democratic Hypothesis in French Communities. With English summary.) *Revue Écon.*, March 1988, *39*(2), pp. 405–20.

——— **and Rochet, Jean-Charles.** Stock Market Portfolios and the Segmentation of the Insurance Market. *Scand. J. Econ.*, 1988, *90*(3), pp. 435–46.

——— **and Tirole, Jean.** The Dynamics of Incentive Contracts. *Econometrica*, September 1988, *56*(5), pp. 1153–75.

——— **and Tirole, Jean.** Repeated Auctions of Incentive Contracts, Investment, and Bidding Parity with an Application to Takeovers. *Rand J. Econ.*, Winter 1988, *19*(4), pp. 516–37.

Lafourcade, Olivier. Research and Extension: Lending Strategies. In *Roberts, C., ed.*, 1988, pp. 65–69.

Lafuente Feléz, Alberto and Lecha, Gabriel. Determinantes sectoriales del nacimiento de empresas en la industria española. (With English summary.) *Invest. Econ.*, May 1988, *12*(2), pp. 329–35.

Lager, Christian. The Use of a Social Accounting Matrix for Comparative Static Equilibrium Modelling. In *Ciaschini, M., ed.*, 1988, pp. 75–89.

Lago, John R. and Nathan, Richard P. Intergovernmental Relations in the Reagan Era. *Public Budg. Finance*, Autumn 1988, *8*(3), pp. 15–29.

Lagos M., Luis Felipe. El Efecto de los Shocks Externos sobre el Producto: Un Análisis para la Economiá Chilena. (With English summary.) *Cuadernos Econ.*, August 1988, *25*(75), pp. 215–28.

Lagutkin, V. and Baskin, A. Economic Ties, Plan, and Contract. *Prob. Econ.*, April 1988, *30*(12), pp. 73–87.

Lah, Barbara L. Right to Trial by Jury in an Action for Civil Penalties and Injunctive Relief under the Clean Water Act. *Natural Res. J.*, Summer 1988, *28*(3), pp. 607–22.

Lahera, Eugenio. Technical Change and Productive Restructuring. *CEPAL Rev.*, December 1988, (36), pp. 33–47.

Lahiri, Kajal and Kinal, Terrence. A Model for Ex Ante Real Interest Rates and Derived Inflation Forecasts. *J. Amer. Statist. Assoc.*, September 1988, *83*(403), pp. 665–73.

———; **Teigland, Christie and Zaporowski, Mark.** Interest Rates and the Subjective Probability Distribution of Inflation Forecasts. *J. Money, Credit, Banking*, May 1988, *20*(2), pp. 233–48.

——— **and Zaporowski, Mark.** A Comparison of Alternative Real Rate Estimates. *Oxford Bull. Econ. Statist.*, August 1988, *50*(3), pp. 303–12.

Lahiri, Sajal. Scale-Dependent Input–Output Analysis: A Survey and an Application to Interregional Modelling. *Ricerche Econ.*, April–June 1988, *42*(2), pp. 243–56.

——— **and Batra, Raveendra N.** Labour Turnover Cost and the Curious Properties of the Mobile Capital Harris–Todaro Model. *Europ. Econ. Rev.*, July 1988, *32*(6), pp. 1369–74.

——— **and Ono, Yoshiyasu.** Helping Minor Firms Reduces Welfare. *Econ. J.*, December 1988, *98*(393), pp. 1199–1202.

Lahiri, Supriya. On Certain Aspects of Energy Pricing Issues and Policies in Egypt. *J. Energy Devel.*, Spring 1988, *13*(2), pp. 223–38.

Lahti, Ari and Virén, Matti. Examining the Role of Expectations in a Macromodel. *Econ. Modelling*, October 1988, *5*(4), pp. 347–53.

Lai, Cheng-chung. European Cooperativism in Chinese Perspective. *Ann. Pub. Co-op. Econ.*, July–Sept. 1988, *59*(3), pp. 369–77.

———. The Kuznets Effect Revisited. *S. Afr. J. Econ.*, June–Sept. 1988, *56*(2–3), pp. 173–80.

Lai, Ching-chong and Chang, Wen-Ya. Fixed Exchange Rates and Capital Mobility Regulations. *Indian Econ. J.*, April–June 1988, *35*(4), pp. 18–24.

——— **and Chang, Wen-Ya.** Tax Evasion and Tax Collections: An Aggregate Demand–Aggregate Supply Analysis. *Public Finance*, 1988, *43*(1), pp. 138–46.

——— **and Chen, Chau-nan.** Capital Mobility, Trade-Balance Elasticity, and Exchange Rate Dynamics. *Southern Econ. J.*, July 1988, *55*(1), pp. 211–14.

———; **Tsaur, Tien-wang and Chen, Chau-nan.** The Loanable Funds Theory and the Dynamics of Exchange Rates: The Mundell Model Revisited. *J. Int. Money Finance*, June 1988, *7*(2), pp. 221–29.

Lai, K. C. Project Impact Monitoring—A Rejoin-

der. *J. Agr. Econ.*, May 1988, *39*(2), pp. 281–82.

Lai Tong, Hew Wah; Nancy, Gilles and Fuguet, Jean-Luc. Mobilité imparfaite des capitaux et dynamique des cours de change. Le cas du SME. (Imperfect Capital Mobility and Exchange Rates Dynamics: The EMS Case. With English summary.) *Revue Écon.*, September 1988, *39*(5), pp. 921–50.

Lai, Tsong-Yue and Ang, James S. Functional Forms of the Capital Asset Pricing Model under Different Market Risk Regimes. *Financial Rev.*, August 1988, *23*(3), pp. 345–50.

——— **and Ang, James S.** On Optimal Pension Funding Policy. *J. Econ. Bus.*, August 1988, *40*(3), pp. 229–38.

Laibman, David. Cyclical Growth and Intersectoral Dynamics. *Rev. Radical Polit. Econ.*, Summer–Fall 1988, *20*(2–3), pp. 107–13.

——— **and Nell, Edward J.** Reswitching, Wicksell Effects, and the Neoclassical Production Function. In *Steedman, I., ed., Vol. 1*, 1988, 1977, pp. 232–42.

Laidler, David E. British Monetary Orthodoxy in the 1870s. *Oxford Econ. Pap.*, March 1988, *40*(1), pp. 74–109.

———. Development Policy in a Multi-provincial Economy: Comments. *Pakistan Devel. Rev.*, Part 1, Winter 1988, *27*(4), pp. 419–20.

———. Income Tax Incentives for Owner-Occupied Housing. In *Ricketts, M., ed., Vol. 2*, 1988, 1969, pp. 343–69.

———. Jevons on Money. In *Wood, J. C., ed., Vol. 3*, 1988, 1982, pp. 204–29.

———. Some Macroeconomic Implications of Price Stickiness. *Manchester Sch. Econ. Soc. Stud.*, March 1988, *56*(1), pp. 37–54.

———. Taking Money Seriously. *Can. J. Econ.*, November 1988, *21*(4), pp. 687–713.

———. What Remains of the Case for Flexible Exchange Rates? *Pakistan Devel. Rev.*, Part 1, Winter 1988, *27*(4), pp. 425–45.

——— **and Jonung, Lars.** Are Perceptions of Inflation Rational? Some Evidence for Sweden. *Amer. Econ. Rev.*, December 1988, *78*(5), pp. 1080–87.

Laine, Pekka. Varvsindustrins problem och framtidsutsikter. (Problems and Future Prospects for the Shipbuilding Industry. With English summary.) *Ekon. Samfundets Tidskr.*, 1988, *41*(2), pp. 117–22.

Laing, James D. Sequential Games of Status: A Replication. In *Tietz, R.; Albers, W. and Selten, R., eds.*, 1988, pp. 286–302.

Laird, Betty A. and Laird, Roy D. The Zveno and Collective Contracts: The End of Soviet Collectivization? In *Brada, J. C. and Wadekin, K.-E., eds.*, 1988, pp. 34–44.

Laird, Melvin R. Beyond the Tower Commission. In *[Nutter, G. W.]*, 1988, pp. 293–302.

Laird, Nan M. and Baker, Stuart G. Regression Analysis for Categorical Variables with Outcome Subject to Nonignorable Nonresponse. *J. Amer. Statist. Assoc.*, March 1988, *83*(401), pp. 62–69.

Laird, Roy D. and Laird, Betty A. The Zveno

and Collective Contracts: The End of Soviet Collectivization? In *Brada, J. C. and Wadekin, K.-E., eds.*, 1988, pp. 34–44.

Laird, Samuel and Nogués, Julio J. Manufactured Export Performance of the Highly Indebted Countries. *Devel. Econ.*, December 1988, *26*(4), pp. 403–21.

_____ **and Yeats, Alexander.** A Note on the Aggregation Bias in Current Procedures for the Measurement of Trade Barriers. *Bull. Econ. Res.*, April 1988, *40*(2), pp. 133–43.

_____; **Yeats, Alexander and Erzan, Refik.** On the Potential for Expanding South–South Trade through the Extension of Mutual Preferences among Developing Countries. *World Devel.*, December 1988, *16*(12), pp. 1441–54.

Laisney, François and Baccouche, Rafiq. Évaluation de six propositions de réforme de la TVA sur données microéconomiques. (With English summary.) *L'Actual. Econ.*, June 1988, *64*(2), pp. 178–208.

_____ **and Blundell, Richard.** A Labour Supply Model for Married Women in France: Taxation, Hours Constraints and Job Seekers. *Ann. Écon. Statist.*, July–Sept. 1988, (11), pp. 41–71.

Laitinen, Erkki K. Framework for an Effective Decision Support System: Part I. *Liiketaloudellinen Aikak.*, 1988, *37*(4), pp. 289–307.

Laitner, John. Bequests, Gifts, and Social Security. *Rev. Econ. Stud.*, April 1988, *55*(2), pp. 275–99.

Lakdawala, D. T. The Balance between Industry and Agriculture in Economic Development: The Indian Experience. In *Arrow, K. J., ed.*, 1988, pp. 49–75.

_____. Planning for Minimum Needs. In *Srinivasan, T. N. and Bardhan, P. K., eds.*, 1988, pp. 389–401.

Lake, David A. The State and American Trade Strategy in the Pre-hegemonic Era. In *Ikenberry, G. J.; Lake, D. A. and Mastanduno, M., eds.*, 1988, pp. 33–58.

_____. The State and American Trade Strategy in the Pre-hegemonic Era. *Int. Organ.*, Winter 1988, *42*(1), pp. 33–58.

_____; **Mastanduno, Michael and Ikenberry, G. John.** Approaches to Explaining American Foreign Economic Policy: Introduction. In *Ikenberry, G. J.; Lake, D. A. and Mastanduno, M., eds.*, 1988, pp. 1–14.

_____; **Mastanduno, Michael and Ikenberry, G. John.** Introduction: Approaches to Explaining American Foreign Economic Policy. *Int. Organ.*, Winter 1988, *42*(1), pp. 1–14.

Lake, Larry W. A Marriage of Geology and Reservoir Engineering. In *Wheeler, M. F., ed.*, 1988, pp. 177–98.

Lakhan, V. C.; Rawana, D. and Lall, A. Resource Allocation in Agriculture: The Guyana Experience. *Can. J. Devel. Stud.*, 1988, *9*(2), pp. 235–48.

Lakhani, Hyder. The Effect of Pay and Retention Bonuses on Quit Rates in the U.S. Army. *Ind. Lab. Relat. Rev.*, April 1988, *41*(3), pp. 430–38.

Lakhman, I. L.; Levin, M. I. and Polterovich, V. M. The Mechanism of Negotiated Prices and Problems of Its Improvement. *Matekon*, Summer 1988, *24*(4), pp. 27–60.

Lakonishok, Josef. The Size Effect and Event Studies: A Discussion. In *Dimson, E., ed.*, 1988, pp. 215–219.

_____ **and Givoly, Dan.** Divergence of Earnings Expectations: The Effect on Stock Market Response to Earnings Signals. In *Dimson, E., ed.*, 1988, pp. 272–89.

Lakshmanan, T. R. and Elhance, Arun P. Infrastructure-Production System Dynamics in National and Regional Systems: An Econometric Study of the Indian Economy. *Reg. Sci. Urban Econ.*, November 1988, *18*(4), pp. 511–31.

Laky, Teréz. Half-Hearted Organizational Decentralization: The Small State Enterprise. *Acta Oecon.*, 1988, *39*(3–4), pp. 247–70.

Lal, Deepak. The Determinants of Urban Unemployment in India. *Indian Econ. Rev.*, Jan.–June 1988, *23*(1), pp. 61–81.

_____. Ideology and Industrialization in India and East Asia. In *Hughes, H., ed.*, 1988, pp. 195–240.

_____. The Misconceptions of "Development Economics." In *Wilber, C. K., ed.*, 1988, pp. 28–36.

_____. Trends in Real Wages in Rural India 1880–1980. In *Srinivasan, T. N. and Bardhan, P. K., eds.*, 1988, pp. 265–93.

Lalkaka, Rustam; Malik, Khalid and James, Dilmus. Cloning of Tea in Malawi. In *Bhalla, A. S. and James, D., eds.*, 1988, pp. 258–68.

Lall, A.; Lakhan, V. C. and Rawana, D. Resource Allocation in Agriculture: The Guyana Experience. *Can. J. Devel. Stud.*, 1988, *9*(2), pp. 235–48.

Lall, Sanjaya. Recent Trends in International Business: A New Analysis: Comment. In *Borner, S., ed.*, 1988, pp. 290–93.

Lam, David. Lorenz Curves, Inequality, and Social Welfare under Changing Population Composition. *J. Policy Modeling*, April 1988, *10*(1), pp. 141–62.

_____. Marriage Markets and Assortative Mating with Household Public Goods: Theoretical Results and Empirical Implications. *J. Human Res.*, Fall 1988, *23*(4), pp. 462–87.

Lambert, Peter J. Net Fiscal Incidence Progressivity: Some Approaches to Measurement. In *Eichhorn, W., ed.*, 1988, pp. 519–32.

_____. Okun's Bucket: A Leak and Two Splashes? *J. Econ. Stud.*, 1988, *15*(1), pp. 71–78.

_____ **and Dardanoni, Valentino.** Welfare Rankings of Income Distributions: A Role for the Variance and Some Insights for Tax Reform. *Soc. Choice Welfare*, 1988, *5*(1), pp. 1–17.

_____ **and Pfähler, Wilhelm.** On Aggregate Measures of the Net Redistributive Impact of Taxation and Government Expenditure. *Public Finance Quart.*, April 1988, *16*(2), pp. 178–202.

Lambert, Wendy; Rundall, Thomas G. and Sofaer, Shoshanna. Uncompensated Hospital Care in California: Private and Public Hospital

Responses to Competitive Market Forces. **In** *Scheffler, R. M. and Rossiter, L. F., eds.*, 1988, pp. 113–33.

Lamberte, Mario B. Financial Liberalization and the Internal Structure of Capital Markets: The Philippine Case. **In** *Urrutia, M., ed.*, 1988, pp. 201–67.

Lambrinos, James and Johnson, William G. Disability Related Categories: An Alternative to Wage Loss Benefits for Injured Workers. **In** *Borba, P. S. and Appel, D., eds.*, 1988, pp. 35–57.

Lambson, Val Eugene. Aggregate Efficiency, Market Demand, and the Sustainability of Collusion. *Int. J. Ind. Organ.*, June 1988, 6(2), pp. 263–71.

————. Trade Restraints, Intermediate Goods, and World Market Conditions. **In** *Baldwin, R. E., ed. (II)*, 1988, pp. 233–48.

de Lame, Jean and Autenne, Jacques. Traitement fiscal du logiciel dans l'informatique: Belgique. (Tax Treatment of Computer Software: Belgium. With English summary.) **In** *International Fiscal Association, ed. (II)*, 1988, pp. 221–40.

Lamfalussy, Alexandre. Globalization of Financial Markets: International Supervisory and Regulatory Issues. **In** *Federal Reserve Bank of Kansas City*, 1988, pp. 133–40.

Lamm, Richard D. Crisis: The Uncompetitive Society. **In** *Starr, M. K., ed.*, 1988, pp. 12–42.

Lamont, Jacques. The Transition to Computerized Bus and Crew Scheduling at the Montréal Urban Community Transit Company. **In** *Daduna, J. R. and Wren, A., eds.*, 1988, pp. 272–78.

Lampariello, F.; Lucidi, S. and Grippo, L. Newton-Type Algorithms with Nonmonotone Line Search for Large-Scale Unconstrained Optimization. **In** *Iri, M. and Yajima, K., eds.*, 1988, pp. 187–96.

Lampe, David R. The Massachusetts Miracle: The Making of a Miracle. **In** *Lampe, D., ed.*, 1988, pp. 1–18.

Lampert, Ada. Sex Differences in Mate Selection on the Kibbutz. **In** *Maital, S., ed., Vol. 1*, 1988, pp. 376–86.

Lampman, Robert J. JFK's Four Consumer Rights: A Retrospective View. **In** *Maynes, E. S. and ACCI Research Committee, eds.*, 1988, pp. 19–33.

———— **and Hutchens, Robert M.** The Future of Workers' Compensation. **In** *Burton, J. F., Jr., ed.*, 1988, pp. 113–40.

———— **and McBride, Timothy D.** Changes in the Pattern of State and Local Government Revenues and Expenditures in Wisconsin, 1960–1983. **In** *Danziger, S. H. and Witte, J. F., eds.*, 1988, pp. 35–69.

Lamy, Robert E. and Billingsley, Randall S. The Regulation of International Lending: IMF Support, the Debt Crisis, and Bank Stockholder Wealth. *J. Banking Finance*, June 1988, 12(2), pp. 255–74.

———— **and Thompson, G. Rodney.** Risk Premia and the Pricing of Primary Issue Bonds. *J.*

Banking Finance, December 1988, 12(4), pp. 585–601.

————; **Thompson, G. Rodney and Billingsley, Randall S.** The Choice among Debt, Equity, and Convertible Bonds. *J. Finan. Res.*, Spring 1988, 11(1), pp. 43–55.

Lan, Lawrence H. and Kanafani, Adib. Development of Pricing Strategies for Airport Parking—A Case Study at San Francisco Airport. *Int. J. Transport Econ.*, February 1988, 15(1), pp. 55–76.

Lancaster, Kelvin J. A New Approach to Consumer Theory. **In** *Ricketts, M., ed., Vol. 1*, 1988, 1966, pp. 19–44.

———— **and Lipsey, Richard G.** The General Theory of Second Best. **In** *Ricketts, M., ed., Vol. 2*, 1988, 1956, pp. 121–42.

Lancry, Pierre-Jean and Saldanha, Fernando B. A Psychological Opponent Processes Theory of Consumption. **In** *Maital, S., ed., Vol. 1*, 1988, pp. 114–33.

Landau, Ralph and Rosenberg, Nathan. Strategies for U.S. Economic Growth. **In** *Muroyama, J. H. and Stever, H. G., eds.*, 1988, pp. 159–76.

Lande, Robert H. The Rise and (Coming) Fall of Efficiency as the Ruler of Antitrust. *Antitrust Bull.*, Fall 1988, 33(3), pp. 429–65.

Landefeld, J. Steven. Why Have Returns to Capital Fallen? Long-term Trend or Short-term Problem? *Bus. Econ.*, January 1988, 23(1), pp. 21–27.

———— **and Young, Kan H.** U.S. Trade in Services: 1970–1985. **In** *Candilis, W. O., ed.*, 1988, pp. 91–126.

Landers, A. J. and Robson, T. F. Systems Analysis in Mechanization Management. **In** *Schiefer, G., ed.*, 1988, pp. 205–24.

Landers, John and Mouzas, Anastasia. Burial Seasonality and Causes of Death in London 1670–1819. *Population Stud.*, March 1988, 42(1), pp. 59–83.

Landes, Elisabeth M. Insurance, Liability, and Accidents: A Theoretical and Empirical Investigation of the Effect of No-Fault on Accidents. **In** *Stigler, G. J., ed.*, 1988, 1982, pp. 461–78.

Landes, Thomas and Loistl, Otto. Zur Berechnung des internen Zinssatzes unter Unsicherheit. Kommentar zu den gleichnamigen Anmerkungen von Werner Dinkelbach. (With English summary.) *Z. Betriebswirtshaft*, March 1988, 58(3), pp. 435–39.

Landesmann, Michael A. Demand versus Supply Determinants of Disproportional Growth in Open Economies. **In** *Ciaschini, M., ed.*, 1988, pp. 99–111.

————. Where Do We Go from Here? 1. Technical Change and Dynamics. *Cambridge J. Econ.*, March 1988, 12(1), pp. 169–77.

Landmann, Oliver. Current Issues in the International Macroeconomic Policy Debate. **In** *Borner, S., ed.*, 1988, pp. 307–23.

Landon, Stuart. Production Technique, External Shocks, and Unemployment. *J. Macroecon.*, Summer 1988, 10(3), pp. 371–87.

Landry, Larry. The New Economic Role of American States: Arizona. In *Fosler, R. S., ed.*, 1988, pp. 249–68.

Landsberg, Hans H.; Tilton, John E. and Eggert, Roderick G. World Mineral Exploration: Trends and Economic Issues: Introduction. In *Tilton, J. E.; Eggert, R. G. and Landsberg, H. H., eds.*, 1988, pp. 1–19.

Landsberger, Michael and Gal, Samuel. On "Small Sample" Properties of Experience Rating Insurance Contracts. *Quart. J. Econ.*, February 1988, *103*(1), pp. 233–43.

Landskroner, Yoram. Optimal Production and Portfolio Investment Decisions. *Managerial Dec. Econ.*, September 1988, *9*(3), pp. 221–25.

_____ **and Bar-Yosef, Sasson.** Government Subsidies and the Value of the Firm. *Managerial Dec. Econ.*, March 1988, *9*(1), pp. 41–47.

Landsman, Wayne R. and Magliolo, Joseph. Cross-sectional Capital Market Research and Model Specification. *Accounting Rev.*, October 1988, *63*(4), pp. 586–604.

Landwehr, James M.; Fowlkes, Edward B. and Freeny, Anne E. Evaluating Logistic Models for Large Contingency Tables. *J. Amer. Statist. Assoc.*, September 1988, *83*(403), pp. 611–22.

Landwehr, Jane T. and Jones, J. Morgan. Removing Heterogeneity Bias from Logit Model Estimation. *Marketing Sci.*, Winter 1988, *7*(1), pp. 41–59.

Lane, J. A.; Ceuppens, P. R. and Peel, David A. Critical Bounds for MA(2) and MA(3) Processes. *Econ. Letters*, 1988, *27*(2), pp. 133–40.

Lane, Julia I. and Blewett, Robert A. Development Rights and the Differential Assessment of Agricultural Land: Fractional Valuation of Farmland Is Ineffective for Preserving Open Space and Subsidizes Speculation. *Amer. J. Econ. Soc.*, April 1988, *47*(2), pp. 195–205.

_____ **and Glennon, Dennis.** The Estimation of Age/Earnings Profiles in Wrongful Death and Injury Cases: Author's Reply. *J. Risk Ins.*, March 1988, *55*(1), pp. 174–79.

Lane, Walter F.; Randolph, William C. and Berenson, Stephen A. Adjusting the CPI Shelter Index to Compensate for Effect of Depreciation. *Mon. Lab. Rev.*, October 1988, *111*(10), pp. 34–37.

Lane, Walter J. Compulsory Trademark Licensing. *Southern Econ. J.*, January 1988, *54*(3), pp. 643–55.

Lanen, William N. and Thompson, Rex. Stock Price Reactions as Surrogates for the Net Cash Flow Effects of Corporate Policy Decisions. *J. Acc. Econ.*, December 1988, *10*(4), pp. 311–34.

Laney, James D. The Impact of Perceived Familiarity and Perceived Importance on Economic Reasoning in Time-Allocation Decisions. *J. Econ. Educ.*, Summer 1988, *19*(3), pp. 209–16.

Laney, Leroy O. The Reserve Role of the Dollar and the United States as Net Debtor. *Fed. Res. Bank Dallas Econ. Rev.*, September 1988, pp. 1–13.

_____ **and Burdekin, Richard C. K.** Fiscal Policymaking and the Central Bank Institutional Constraint. *Kyklos*, 1988, *41*(4), pp. 647–62.

Láng, István; Csete, László and Harnos, Zsolt. The Enterprisal System of an Adjusting Agriculture in Hungary. *Europ. Rev. Agr. Econ.*, 1988, *15*(2–3), pp. 225–38.

Lang, Kevin. Job Signalling and Welfare Improving Minimum Wage Laws: Reply. *Econ. Inquiry*, July 1988, *26*(3), pp. 533–36.

_____ **and Dickens, William T.** Labor Market Segmentation and the Union Wage Premium. *Rev. Econ. Statist.*, August 1988, *70*(3), pp. 527–30.

_____ **and Dickens, William T.** Neoclassical and Sociological Perspectives on Segmented Labor Markets. In *Farkas, G. and England, P., eds.*, 1988, pp. 65–88.

_____ **and Dickens, William T.** The Reemergence of Segmented Labor Market Theory. *Amer. Econ. Rev.*, May 1988, *78*(2), pp. 129–34.

_____ **and Dickens, William T.** Why It Matters What We Trade: A Case for Active Policy. In *Tyson, L. D.; Dickens, W. T. and Zysman, J., eds.*, 1988, pp. 87–112.

_____ **and Khan, Shulamit.** Efficient Estimation of Structural Hedonic Systems. *Int. Econ. Rev.*, February 1988, *29*(1), pp. 157–66.

Lang, Larry H. P. and Friend, Irwin. An Empirical Test of the Impact of Managerial Self-interest on Corporate Capital Structure. *J. Finance*, June 1988, *43*(2), pp. 271–81.

_____ **and Friend, Irwin.** The Size Effect on Stock Returns: Is It Simply a Risk Effect Not Adequately Reflected by the Usual Measures? *J. Banking Finance*, 1988, *12*(1), pp. 13–30.

Langbein, John H. The Twentieth-Century Revolution in Family Wealth Transmission. *Mich. Law Rev.*, February 1988, *86*(4), pp. 722–51.

Langenfeld, James and Scheffman, David T. Innovation and U.S. Competition Policy. *Aussenwirtschaft*, June 1988, *43*(1/2), pp. 45–95.

Langer, Gary F. Corn: A Classical Landscape. *Econ. Notes*, 1988, (1), pp. 5–21.

Langer, Marshall J. and Goldberg, Sanford H. Recognition of Foreign Enterprises as Taxable Entities: United States. In *International Fiscal Association, ed. (I)*, 1988, pp. 387–98.

Langfeldt, Enno and Trapp, Peter. Experiences in Macroeconomic Forecasting in the Federal Republic of Germany 1976–1987. *Jahr. Nationalökon. Statist.*, November 1988, *205*(5), pp. 427–42.

Langhammer, Rolf J. Do the ACP Trade Preferences Discriminate against ASEAN Agricultural Products? In *Langhammer, R. J. and Rieger, H. C., eds.*, 1988, pp. 155–84.

_____. Financing of Foreign Direct Investment and Trade Flows: The Case of Indonesia. *Bull. Indonesian Econ. Stud.*, April 1988, *24*(1), pp. 97–114.

_____ **and Rieger, Hans Christoph.** ASEAN and the EC: Trade in Tropical Agricultural Products: Preface. In *Langhammer, R. J. and Rieger, H. C., eds.*, 1988, pp. xiii–xiv.

Langille, Brian. Revolution without Foundation: The Grammar of Scepticism and Law. In *Carter, D. D., et al.*, 1988, pp. 112–67.

Langlois, Richard N. Are Economic Models Applicable to Politics? *Econ. Scelte Pubbliche/J. Public Finance Public Choice*, May–Aug. 1988, 6(2), pp. 83–93.

_____. Economic Change and the Boundaries of the Firm. *J. Inst. Theoretical Econ.*, September 1988, 144(4), pp. 635–57.

Langsam, Joseph A. and Bookstaber, Richard. Portfolio Insurance Trading Rules. *J. Futures Markets*, February 1988, 8(1), pp. 15–31.

Languetin, Pierre. Monetary Policy and Financial Innovations. In *Mikdashi, Z., ed.*, 1988, pp. 103–09.

_____. Transformation of the Banking and Financial Environment. In *Mikdashi, Z., ed.*, 1988, pp. 7–10.

Langwell, Kathryn and Brown, Randall S. Enrollment Patterns in Medicare HMOs: Implications for Access to Care. In *Scheffler, R. M. and Rossiter, L. F., eds.*, 1988, pp. 69–96.

Lankford, R. Hamilton. Measuring Welfare Changes in Settings with Imposed Quantities. *J. Environ. Econ. Manage.*, March 1988, 15(1), pp. 45–63.

Lanyi, A. Private and Official Capital Flows to Developing Countries. In *Jepma, C. J., ed.*, 1988, pp. 125–40.

Lányi, Kamilla. Enterprise Behaviour in the 1980s: Beliefs and Reality: Some Conclusions of Recent Case Studies. *Acta Oecon.*, 1988, 39(1–2), pp. 123–35.

Lanza, Alessandro and Rampa, Giorgio. A Model for Assessing the Growth Opportunities of EEC Countries When Interdependence Is Not Ruled Out. In *Ciaschini, M., ed.*, 1988, pp. 367–90.

Lapan, Harvey E. The Optimal Tariff, Production Lags, and Time Consistency. *Amer. Econ. Rev.*, June 1988, 78(3), pp. 395–401.

_____ and **Brown, Douglas M.** Utility Maximization, Individual Production, and Market Equilibrium. *Southern Econ. J.*, October 1988, 55(2), pp. 374–89.

_____ and **Choi, E. Kwan.** Tariffs versus Quotas under Uncertainty: Restricting Imports and the Role of Preference. *Int. Econ. J.*, Winter 1988, 2(4), pp. 35–55.

_____ and **Sandler, Todd.** To Bargain or Not to Bargain: That Is the Question. *Amer. Econ. Rev.*, May 1988, 78(2), pp. 16–21.

Lapidoth, Arye. Israel: "Administrative Offences" in Aid of Tax Enforcement. *Bull. Int. Fiscal Doc.*, October 1988, 42(10), pp. 421–23.

_____. The "New Approach" towards Construction of Tax Statutes Adopted by the Israeli Courts. *Bull. Int. Fiscal Doc.*, April 1988, 42(4), pp. 170–79.

Lapidus, Gail Warshofsky. Gorbachev's Agenda: Domestic Reforms and Foreign Policy Reassessments. In *Juviler, P. and Kimura, H., eds.*, 1988, pp. 1–20.

Lapkoff, Shelley and Lee, Ronald D. Intergenerational Flows of Time and Goods: Conse-

quences of Slowing Population Growth. *J. Polit. Econ.*, June 1988, 96(3), pp. 618–51.

LaPlante, Mitchell P. and Rice, Dorothy P. Chronic Illness, Disability, and Increasing Longevity. In *Sullivan, S. and Lewin, M. E., eds.*, 1988, pp. 9–55.

Lapointe, Alain and Le Goff, Jean-Pierre. Canadian Television: An Alternative to Caplan–Sauvageau. *Can. Public Policy*, September 1988, 14(3), pp. 245–53.

Laporte, Gilbert and Nobert, Yves. A Vehicle Flow Model for the Optimal Design of a Two-Echelon Distribution System. In *Eiselt, H. A. and Pederzoli, G., eds.*, 1988, pp. 158–73.

Lappe, Lothar. The Use of Technology and the Development of Qualifications: How the Debate about the Labour Process Is Viewed in German Industrial Sociology. In *Knights, D. and Willmott, H., eds.*, 1988, pp. 230–64.

Lara-Resende, André and Arida, Persio. Inflationary Inertia and Monetary Reform: Brazil. In *Chacel, J. M.; Falk, P. S. and Fleischer, D. V., eds.*, 1988, pp. 27–41.

Lardy, Nicholas R. People's Republic of China: Systematic and Structural Change in a North China Township. *Amer. J. Agr. Econ.*, May 1988, 70(2), pp. 439.

Largay, James A., III and Davis, Michael L. Reporting Consolidated Gains and Losses on Subsidiary Stock Issuances. *Accounting Rev.*, April 1988, 63(2), pp. 348–63.

de Largentaye, Jean. L'écueil de l'économie monétaire. (The Scourge of Saving in the Monetary Economy. With English summary.) *Écon. Soc.*, September 1988, 22(9), pp. 11–19.

Larkin, Andrew. Denmark's Agricultural Institutions: An Instrumental Evaluation. *J. Econ. Issues*, December 1988, 22(4), pp. 1123–41.

Laroche, Michel; McGown, K. Lee and Héroux, Lise. Consumer Product Label Information Processing: An Experiment Involving Time Pressure and Distraction. *J. Econ. Psych.*, June 1988, 9(2), pp. 195–214.

Laroque, Guy and Benhabib, Jess. On Competitive Cycles in Productive Economies. *J. Econ. Theory*, June 1988, 45(1), pp. 145–70.

_____ and **Fuchs, Gérard.** Dynamics of Temporary Equilibria and Expectations. In *Grandmont, J.-M., ed.*, 1988, 1976, pp. 249–70.

_____; **Lollivier, S. and Gagey, F.** Monetary and Fiscal Policies in a General Equilibrium Model. In *Grandmont, J.-M., ed.*, 1988, 1986, pp. 217–45.

_____; **Younes, Yves and Grandmont, Jean Michel.** Equilibrium with Quantity Rationing and Recontracting. In *Grandmont, J.-M., ed.*, 1988, 1978, pp. 404–22.

de Larosière, J. Exchange Rates and the Adjustment Process. In *Melamed, L., ed.*, 1988, 1979, pp. 387–93.

Larraín B., Felipe and Larraín C., Aníbal. El Caso del Dinero Desaparecido: Chile, 1984–1986. (With English summary.) *Cuadernos Econ.*, August 1988, 25(75), pp. 247–82.

Larraín C., Aníbal and Larraín B., Felipe. El Caso del Dinero Desaparecido: Chile, 1984–

1986. (With English summary.) *Cuadernos Econ.*, August 1988, *25*(75), pp. 247–82.

Larsen, Arne. Landbrugsprotektionismens omkostninger. (The Costs of Agricultural Protectionism. With English summary.) *Nationaløkon. Tidsskr.*, 1988, *126*(1), pp. 31–42.

Larsen, Niels and Nielsen, Jens Christian. Estimation af en dansk eksport model. (Estimation of a Model of Demand and Supply of Danish Exportables. With English summary.) *Nationaløkon. Tidsskr.*, 1988, *126*(1), pp. 75–82.

Larson, Arthur. Tensions of the Next Decade. In *Burton, J. F., Jr., ed.*, 1988, pp. 21–43.

Larson, Donald W.; Koo, Won W. and Thompson, Stanley R. Effects of Ocean Freight Rate Changes on the U.S. Grain Distribution System. *Logist. Transp. Rev.*, March 1988, *24*(1), pp. 85–100.

Larson, Douglas M. Exact Welfare Measurement for Producers under Uncertainty. *Amer. J. Agr. Econ.*, August 1988, *70*(3), pp. 597–603.

Larson, Eric D.; Ross, Marc H. and Williams, Robert H. Beyond the Era of Materials. In *Forester, T., ed.*, 1988, *1986*, pp. 141–59.

Larson, Richard C. Operations Research and the Services Industries. In *Guile, B. R. and Quinn, J. B., eds. (I)*, 1988, pp. 115–43.

LaRue, L. H. Antitrust and Politics. *Antitrust Bull.*, Winter 1988, *33*(4), pp. 745–77.

Larwood, Laurie and Edwards, Frank L. Strategic Competitive Factors in the Acquisition of Technology: The Case of Major Weapon Systems. In *Gattiker, U. E. and Larwood, L., eds.*, 1988, pp. 55–72.

Lasden, Martin. Prima Donnas: Living with Them When You Can't Live without Them. In *Timpe, A. D., ed.*, 1988, *1984*, pp. 129–35.

Lashgari, Malek K. An Information Theoretic Design for Measuring Accuracy of Forecasts. *Atlantic Econ. J.*, June 1988, *16*(2), pp. 83.

Lasser, Dennis J.; Hassell, John M. and Jennings, Robert H. Management Earnings Forecasts: Their Usefulness as a Source of Firm-Specific Information to Security Analysts. *J. Finan. Res.*, Winter 1988, *11*(4), pp. 303–19.

Lasserre, J. B. Decision Horizon, Overtaking and 1-Optimality Criteria in Optimal Control. In *Eiselt, H. A. and Pederzoli, G., eds.*, 1988, pp. 247–61.

Lasserre, Pierre and Gaudet, Gérard. On Comparing Monopoly and Competition in Exhaustible Resource Exploitation. *J. Environ. Econ. Manage.*, December 1988, *15*(4), pp. 412–18.

_____ **and Hollander, Abraham.** Monopoly and the Preemption of Competitive Recycling. *Int. J. Ind. Organ.*, December 1988, *6*(4), pp. 489–97.

_____ **and Ouellette, Pierre.** On Measuring and Comparing Total Factor Productivities in Extractive and Non-extractive Sectors. *Can. J. Econ.*, November 1988, *21*(4), pp. 826–34.

Lassibille, Gérard. La formación de las rentas del trabajo en Andalucia. (With English summary.) *Invest. Econ.*, September 1988, *12*(3), pp. 483–99.

Lastman, Gary J.; Naquib, Fadle and Daly, Michael J. The Role of Tax-Deductible Saving in the Transition from a Progressive Income Tax to a Progressive Consumption Tax. *Public Finance*, 1988, *43*(3), pp. 349–72.

Lastovicka, John L. and Joachimsthaler, Erich A. Improving the Detection of Personality–Behavior Relationships in Consumer Research. *J. Cons. Res.*, March 1988, *14*(4), pp. 583–87.

Latham, A. J. H. From Competition to Constraint: The International Rice Trade in the Nineteenth and Twentieth Centuries. In *Hausman, W. J., ed.*, 1988, pp. 91–102.

Latham, Judith. The Reviewer's Craft. *J. Agr. Econ. Res.*, Winter 1988, *40*(1), pp. 42–46.

Latham, Roger. Lorenz-Dominating Income Tax Functions. *Int. Econ. Rev.*, February 1988, *29*(1), pp. 185–200.

Latham, William R., III and Wang, Young-Doo. Energy and State Economic Growth: Some New Evidence. *J. Energy Devel.*, Spring 1988, *13*(2), pp. 197–221.

Latimer, Eric and Graham, John D. Themes and Future Directions. In *Graham, J. D., ed.*, 1988, pp. 263–76.

Latimore, James. Indirect Provision of Government Services: Contracts and Productivity. In *Kelly, R. M., ed.*, 1988, pp. 113–24.

Latin, Howard. Good Science, Bad Regulation, and Toxic Risk Assessment. *Yale J. Regul.*, Winter 1988, *5*(1), pp. 89–148.

Latos, Charles J. Nonwhite Migration 1960–1970: The Role of Employment Opportunities. *Rev. Black Polit. Econ.*, Winter 1988, *16*(3), pp. 53–62.

Latsis, Otto. The Problem of Rates of Growth in Socialist Construction: Reflections of an Economist. *Prob. Econ.*, August 1988, *31*(4), pp. 73–95.

_____. Why Are You Pushing?: To L. Popkova, Author of the Letter "Where Are the Pirogi Meatier?" *Prob. Econ.*, February 1988, *30*(10), pp. 56–60.

Latta, Cynthia M.; Bierwag, G. O. and Kaufman, George G. Duration Models: A Taxonomy. *J. Portfol. Manage.*, Fall 1988, *15*(1), pp. 50–54.

Lattimore, Ralph; Ward, Bert and Finlayson, Bob. New Zealand's Price Elasticity of Export Demand Revisited. *New Zealand Econ. Pap.*, 1988, *22*, pp. 25–34.

de Lattre, André. The 'Quest for National and Global Stability' and Developing Countries. In *[Witteveen, H. J.]*, 1988, pp. 119–36.

Latzer, Michael and Bauer, Johannes M. Telecommunications in Austria. In *Foreman-Peck, J. and Müller, J., eds.,*, 1988, pp. 53–85.

Lau, Ho-Fuk and Lee, Kam-Hon. Development of Supermarkets in Hong Kong: Current Status and Future Trends. In *Kaynak, E., ed.*, 1988, pp. 321–29.

Lau, Lawrence J. and Yotopoulos, Pan A. Do Country Idiosyncracies Matter in Estimating a Production Function for World Agriculture? *J. Econ. Devel.*, June 1988, *13*(1), pp. 7–19.

Lau, Teik Soon. Development of Human Resources: A Singaporean View. In *Kozmetsky,*

G.; Matsumoto, H. and Smilor, R. W., eds., 1988, pp. 127–30.

Lauby, Jennifer and Stark, Oded. Individual Migration as a Family Strategy: Young Women in the Philippines. *Population Stud.*, November 1988, 42(3), pp. 473–86.

Lauenroth, H. G. Computer Aided Scenarios for CIM Innovation Strategies. *Econ. Computat. Cybern. Stud. Res.*, 1988, 23(2), pp. 57–63.

von Laufenberg, Jürgen. Produktmengenänderungen und anteilige Beschäftigungsabweichungen bei nicht ausgelasteten Anlagen. (With English summary.) Z. *Betriebswirtshaft,* March 1988, 58(3), pp. 416–22.

Laulajainen, Risto. The Spatial Dimension of an Acquisition. *Econ. Geogr.*, April 1988, 64(2), pp. 171–87.

Laumas, G. S. and McMillin, W. Douglas. The Impact of Anticipated and Unanticipated Policy Actions on the Stock Market. *Appl. Econ.*, March 1988, 20(3), pp. 377–84.

Launois, R. and Sailly, P. Mehr Markt im Gesundheitswesen: Einige Überlegungen aus französischer Sicht. (With English summary.) *J. Inst. Theoretical Econ.*, April 1988, 144(2), pp. 403–06.

Laurent, Jean-Paul and Brillet, Jean-Louis. The Reliability of Control Experiments: Comparison of the Sources of Error. *J. Econ. Dynam. Control*, March 1988, 12(1), pp. 173–79.

Laurent, Thierry and Cahuc, Pierre. Emploi et négociations salariales en concurrence monopolistique: théorie et estimation. (Bargaining under Monopolistic Competition: Theory and Evidence. With English summary.) *Écon. Appl.*, 1988, 41(3), pp. 543–69.

Lauritzen, Finn. Nye ADAM of gamle ADAM. (The Extensions of the Danish Macroeconomic Model ADAM. With English summary.) *Nationaløkon. Tidsskr.*, 1988, 126(2), pp. 244–53.

Laursen, Karsten. Hjælper udviklingsbistanden? (Does Development Aid Aid? With English summary.) *Nationaløkon. Tidsskr.*, 1988, 126(1), pp. 58–62.

Laussel, Didier. Chocs et contrechocs pétroliers, salaires rigides et anticipations rationnelles: Quelques résultats paradoxaux. (With English summary.) *Revue Écon. Polit.*, Nov.–Dec. 1988, 98(6), pp. 850–65.

_____; **Montet, Christian and Peguin-Feissolle, Anne.** Optimal Trade Policy under Oligopoly: A Calibrated Model of the Europe–Japan Rivalry in the EEC Car Market. *Europ. Econ. Rev.*, September 1988, 32(7), pp. 1547–65.

Läuter, Henning. Conditioned Estimators of Nonlinear Parameters. **In** Fedorov, V. and Lauter, H., eds., 1988, pp. 106–13.

Läuter, J. Stable Decisions in Discriminant, Regression and Factor Analysis. **In** Fedorov, V. and Lauter, H., eds., 1988, pp. 181–88.

Laux, Helmut. Grundprobleme der Ermittlung optimaler erfolgsabhängiger Anreizsysteme. (With English summary.) Z. *Betriebswirtshaft,* January 1988, 58(1), pp. 24–36.

_____. Optimale Prämienfunktionen bei Informationsasymmetrie. (With English summary.) Z. *Betriebswirtshaft,* May–June 1988, 58(5–6), pp. 588–612.

Laux-Meiselbach, Wolfgang. Impossibility of Exclusion and Characteristics of Public Goods. *J. Public Econ.*, June 1988, 36(1), pp. 127–37.

LaValle, Irving H. and Fishburn, Peter C. Context-Dependent Choice with Nonlinear and Nontransitive Preferences. *Econometrica*, September 1988, 56(5), pp. 1221–39.

_____ **and Fishburn, Peter C.** The Structure of SSB Utilities for Decision under Uncertainty. *Math. Soc. Sci.*, June 1988, 15(3), pp. 217–30.

_____ **and Fishburn, Peter C.** Transitivity is Equivalent to Independence for States-Additive SSB Utilities. *J. Econ. Theory*, February 1988, 44(1), pp. 202–08.

Lavando, Italo. Analisi del monopolio di un bene durevole quandro effetti di esperienza influiscono sui costi e sulla domanda. (An Analysis of a Monopolist's Behaviour When Experience Effects Affect Both Demand and Costs. With English summary.) *Giorn. Econ.*, Sept.–Oct. 1988, 47(9–10), pp. 495–507.

Lave, Judith R., et al. The Decision to Seek an Exemption from PPS. *J. Health Econ.*, June 1988, 7(2), pp. 165–71.

_____, **et al.** The Early Effects of Medicare's Prospective Payment System on Psychiatry. *Inquiry*, Fall 1988, 25(3), pp. 354–63.

Lave, Lester B. Alcohol Taxes and Highway Safety: Comments. **In** Graham, J. D., ed., 1988, pp. 227–30.

_____. The Greenhouse Effect: What Government Actions Are Needed? *J. Policy Anal. Manage.*, Spring 1988, 7(3), pp. 460–70.

_____ **and Cyert, Richard M.** Collusion, Conflict, and Economics. **In** Cyert, R. M., 1988, pp. 92–110.

Lavigne, Marie. Cooperation and Assistance: How Efficient and How Much? **In** Lavigne, M., ed., 1988, pp. 94–111.

_____. East–South and North–South Relations: A Comparison. **In** Lavigne, M., ed., 1988, pp. 112–21.

_____. East–South Relations in the World Economy: Introduction to Part One. **In** Lavigne, M., ed., 1988, pp. 3–8.

_____. East–South Trade: Trends, Partners, Commodity Composition, Balances. **In** Lavigne, M., ed., 1988, pp. 22–50.

_____. The Evolution of CMEA Institutions and Policies and the Need for Structural Adjustment. **In** [Holzman, F. D.], 1988, pp. 147–69.

_____. La modernisation des activites productives dans les pays Europeens du CAEM et l'integration socialiste: Conflits ou interaction? (The Modernization of the Productive Activities in the European CMEA countries and the Socialist Integration: Conflicts or Interaction? With English summary.) *Écon. Soc.*, February 1988, 22(2), pp. 175–201.

_____; **Dimitri, Alexandre and Gombeaud, Jean-François.** Prices, Settlements, Gains from Trade. **In** Lavigne, M., ed., 1988, pp. 64–93.

———— and Renaudie, Françoise. A General View of the Third World. In *Lavigne, M., ed.*, 1988, pp. 9–21.

Lavoie, Marc and Seccareccia, Mario. Money, Interest and Rentiers: The Twilight of Rentier Capitalism in Keynes's *General Theory.* In *Hamouda, O. F. and Smithin, J. N., eds., Vol. 2*, 1988, pp. 145–58.

Law, Alton D. External Economy Arguments for Commodity Stockpiling: A Comment. *Bull. Econ. Res.*, April 1988, *40*(2), pp. 153–57.

Law, C. M. Public–Private Partnership in Urban Revitalization in Britain. *Reg. Stud.*, October 1988, *22*(5), pp. 446–51.

Law, Peter J.; Askildsen, Jan Erik and Ireland, Norman J. Some Consequences of Differential Shareholdings among Members in a Labor-Managed and Labor-Owned Firm. In *Jones, D. C. and Svejnar, J., eds.*, 1988, pp. 65–81.

———— and Ireland, Norman J. Management Design under Labor Management. *J. Compar. Econ.*, March 1988, *12*(1), pp. 1–23.

Law, Warren A. Evidence on the Gains from Mergers and Takeovers: Comment. In *Coffee, J. C., Jr.; Lowenstein, L. and Rose-Ackerman, S., eds.*, 1988, pp. 260–63.

Lawler, K. A.; Seddighi, H. R. and Clark, C. J. The Structure of the Charity Sector in England and Wales: A Statistical Analysis. *Appl. Econ.*, March 1988, *20*(3), pp. 335–50.

Lawless, P. British Inner Urban Policy: A Review. *Reg. Stud.*, December 1988, *22*(6), pp. 531–42.

Lawrence, Denis. Recent Developments in Applying Duality Theory. *Rev. Marketing Agr. Econ.*, December 1988, *56*(3), pp. 375–82.

Lawrence, Edward C. and Arshadi, Nasser. The Distributional Impact of Foreign Deposits on Federal Deposit Insurance Premia. *J. Banking Finance*, 1988, *12*(1), pp. 105–15.

Lawrence, Robert Z. Exchange Rates and U.S. Auto Competitiveness: Comment. In *Marston, R. C., ed.*, 1988, pp. 237–40.

————. Global Adjustments to a Shrinking U.S. Trade Deficit: Comment. *Brookings Pap. Econ. Act.*, 1988, (2), pp. 668–72.

————. The International Dimension. In *Litan, R. E; Lawrence, R. Z. and Schultze, C. L., eds.*, 1988, pp. 23–65.

————. Whither International Trade Policies: Worries about Continuing Protectionism: Comments. In *Elliott, K. A. and Williamson, J., eds.*, 1988, pp. 93–96.

————; Schultze, Charles L. and Litan, Robert E. American Living Standards: Threats and Challenges: Introduction. In *Litan, R. E; Lawrence, R. Z. and Schultze, C. L., eds.*, 1988, pp. 1–22.

Lawrence, William; Bachmann, Laurie McGavin and von Stumm, Michael. Tracking Recent Trends in the International Market for Art Theft. *J. Cult. Econ.*, June 1988, *12*(1), pp. 51–71.

Lawson, Ann M. and Young, Kan H. Exchange Rates and the Competitive Price Positions of U.S. Exports and Imports. *Bus. Econ.*, April 1988, *23*(2), pp. 13–19.

Lawson, Colin. Exchange Rates, Tax-Subsidy Schemes, and the Revenue from Foreign Trade in a Centrally Planned Economy. *Econ. Planning*, 1988, *22*(1–2), pp. 72–77.

Lawson, Gerlad H. Foreign Currency Translation, Cash Flow Analysis and Consolidated Accounts. In *Gray, S. J. and Coenenberg, A. G., eds.*, 1988, pp. 244–71.

Lawson, Tony. Probability and Uncertainty in Economic Analysis. *J. Post Keynesian Econ.*, Fall 1988, *11*(1), pp. 38–65.

————. Uncertainty and Economic Analysis. In *Sawyer, M. C., ed.*, 1988, 1985, pp. 80–98.

Layard, Richard. Is Incomes Policy the Answer to Unemployment? In *Shaw, G. K., ed., Vol. 2*, 1988, 1982, pp. 33–46.

———— and Jackman, Richard. Trade Unions, The Nairu and a Wage-Inflation Tax. In *Shaw, G. K., ed., Vol. 2*, 1988, pp. 46–53.

———— and Nickell, Stephen J. The Case for Subsidising Extra Jobs. In *Shaw, G. K., ed., Vol. 2*, 1988, 1980, pp. 10–32.

Layman, Thomas A. Monetary Policy and Financial Reform in Korea. In *Cheng, H.-S., ed.*, 1988, pp. 353–79.

Layson, Stephen. Third-Degree Price Discrimination, Welfare and Profits: A Geometrical Analysis. *Amer. Econ. Rev.*, December 1988, *78*(5), pp. 1131–32.

Layton, Roger A. Industrial Development and Traditional Distribution: Are They Compatible? In *Kumcu, E. and Firat, A. F., eds.*, 1988, pp. 173–99.

Lazar, Fred. Structural/Strategic Dumping: A Comment on Richard Boltuck's "An Economic Analysis of Dumping." *J. World Trade*, June 1988, *22*(3), pp. 91–93.

————. Survey of Ontario Manufacturing. *Can. Public Policy*, March 1988, *14*(1), pp. 78–91.

Lazarcik, Gregor. Comparative Performance of Agricultural Output, Inputs, and Productivity in Eastern Europe, 1965–83. In *Brada, J. C. and Wadekin, K.-E., eds.*, 1988, pp. 313–33.

Lazear, Edward P. Employment-at-Will, Job Security, and Work Incentives. In *Hart, R. A., ed.*, 1988, pp. 39–61.

————. The Labor Market and International Competitiveness. In *Anderson, A. and Bark, D. L., eds.*, 1988, pp. 367–81.

————. The Relationship of Productivity to Age: Discussion. In *Ricardo-Campbell, R. and Lazear, E. P., eds.*, 1988, pp. 126–31.

————. Symposium on Public and Private Unionization. *J. Econ. Perspectives*, Spring 1988, *2*(2), pp. 59–62.

———— and Moore, Robert L. Pensions and Turnover. In *Bodie, Z.; Shoven, J. B. and Wise, D. A., eds.*, 1988, pp. 163–88.

Lazonick, William. Financial Commitment and Economic Performance: Ownership and Control in the American Industrial Corporation. In *Hausman, W. J., ed.*, 1988, pp. 115–28.

Le Bas, Christian. Formules de productivité, progrès technique et rendements croissants.

Les propriétés dynamiques d'un schéma kaldorien. (Formulae for Productivity, Technical Progress and Increasing Returns. The Dynamic Properties of a Kaldorian Scheme. With English summary.) *Écon. Appl.*, 1988, *41*(3), pp. 633–48.

Le Cacheux, Jacques and Fitoussi, Jean-Paul. On Macroeconomic Implications of Price Setting in the Open Economy. *Amer. Econ. Rev.*, May 1988, *78*(2), pp. 335–40.

Le Fort V., Guillermo R. The Relative Price of Nontraded Goods, Absorption, and Exchange Rate Policy in Chile, 1974–82. *Int. Monet. Fund Staff Pap.*, June 1988, *35*(2), pp. 336–70.

Le Gall, J. P. and Andrieu, J. N. Reconnaissance de la personnalité fiscale des entreprises entreprises étrangères: France. (Recognition of Foreign Enterprises as Taxable Entities: France. With English summary.) In *International Fiscal Association, ed. (I)*, 1988, pp. 411–29.

Le Goff, Jean-Pierre and Lapointe, Alain. Canadian Television: An Alternative to Caplan–Sauvageau. *Can. Public Policy*, September 1988, *14*(3), pp. 245–53.

Le Héron, Edwin. Préférence pour la liquidité en économie mondiale. (Liquidity Preference in World Economics. With English summary.) *Écon. Appl.*, 1988, *41*(2), pp. 413–37.

_____. Problèmes posés par la notion de capacité de transfert international élargie. (Problems about the Widened Capacity of International Transfer. With English summary.) *Écon. Soc.*, June–July 1988, *22*(6–7), pp. 53–68.

Le Heron, R. The Internationalisation of New Zealand Forestry Companies and the Social Reappraisal of New Zealand's Exotic Forest Resource. *Environ. Planning A*, April 1988, *20*(4), pp. 489–515.

Le Pen, Claude. Réglementation des prix et formes de la concurrence dans l'industrie pharmaceutique. (Price Regulation and Competition Patterns in the Ethical Drug Industry in France. With English summary.) *Revue Écon.*, November 1988, *39*(6), pp. 1159–91.

Le Pottier, Jacques; Aragon, Yves and Laffont, Jean-Jacques. Testing the Democratic Hypothesis in the Provision of Local Public Goods. *J. Public Econ.*, July 1988, *36*(2), pp. 139–51.

_____; **Aragon, Yves and Laffont, Jean-Jacques.** Test de l'hypothèse démocratique dans le décisions budgétaires communales. (Test of the Democratic Hypothesis in French Communities. With English summary.) *Revue Écon.*, March 1988, *39*(2), pp. 405–20.

Lea, D. A. M. and Crittenden, R. Project Appraisal, Aid and Impact Monitoring: A Comment. *J. Agr. Econ.*, May 1988, *39*(2), pp. 277–79.

Lea, J. D. and Shonkwiler, J. S. Misspecification in Simultaneous Systems: An Alternative Test and Its Application to a Model of the Shrimp Market. *Southern J. Agr. Econ.*, December 1988, *20*(2), pp. 65–72.

Leach, John E. The Optimal Indexation of Asym-

metric Information Contracts. *Can. J. Econ.*, February 1988, *21*(1), pp. 61–71.

_____. Underemployment with Liquidity-Constrained Multi-period Firms. *J. Econ. Theory*, February 1988, *44*(1), pp. 81–98.

Leader, Shelah. The Treatment of Women Under Medicare. In *Sullivan, S. and Lewin, M. E., eds.*, 1988, pp. 131–44.

Leahy, Patrick J. U.S. Congressional Approaches to Reconciling Intellectual Property Rights. In *Walker, C. E. and Bloomfield, M. A., eds.*, 1988, pp. 77–81.

Leamer, Edward E. Cross-Section Estimation of the Effects of Trade Barriers. In *Feenstra, R. C., ed.*, 1988, pp. 51–82.

_____. Measures of Openness. In *Baldwin, R. E., ed. (II)*, 1988, pp. 147–200.

_____. The Sensitivity of International Comparisons of Capital Stock Measures to Different "Real" Exchange Rates. *Amer. Econ. Rev.*, May 1988, *78*(2), pp. 479–83.

_____. Things That Bother Me. *Econ. Rec.*, December 1988, *64*(187), pp. 331–35.

Lean, Lim Lin. Labour Markets, Labour Flows and Structural Change in Peninsular Malaysia. In *Pang, E. F., ed.*, 1988, pp. 100–138.

Leap, Terry L. and Grigsby, David W. Power and the Bargaining Process: Reply. *Ind. Lab. Relat. Rev.*, July 1988, *41*(4), pp. 622–26.

Leape, J. I. and Atkinson, Anthony B. The Economic Analysis of Tax Reform: Introduction. *Europ. Econ. Rev.*, March 1988, *32*(2–3), pp. 319–24.

Leary, Thomas B. Private Antitrust Litigation: New Evidence, New Learning: Comment. In *White, L. J., ed.*, 1988, pp. 385–86.

Lease, Ronald C.; Smith, Clifford W., Jr. and Brickley, James A. Ownership Structure and Voting on Antitakeover Amendments. *J. Finan. Econ.*, Jan.–March 1988, *20*(1–2), pp. 267–91.

Leatham, David J. and Baker, Timothy G. Farmers' Choice of Fixed and Adjustable Interest Rate Loans. *Amer. J. Agr. Econ.*, November 1988, *70*(4), pp. 803–12.

Leathers, Howard; Chavas, Jean-Paul and Pope, Rulon D. Competitive Industry Equilibrium under Uncertainty and Free Entry. *Econ. Inquiry*, April 1988, *26*(2), pp. 331–44.

Leavens, Donald R.; Crain, W. Mark and Tollison, Robert D. Laissez-faire in Campaign Finance. *Public Choice*, March 1988, *56*(3), pp. 201–12.

LeBarge, Karin Peterson. Daily Trading Estimates for Treasury Bond Futures Contract Prices. *J. Futures Markets*, October 1988, *8*(5), pp. 533–61.

LeBaron, Dean and Speidell, Lawrence S. Why are the Parts Worth More than the Sum? "Chop Shop," A Corporate Valuation Model. In *Browne, L. E. and Rosengren, E. S., eds.*, 1988, pp. 78–95.

Lebedev, V.; Parikh, Kirit S. and Ereshko, F. Agricultural Planning Models for Stavropol Region: Mathematical Description and Simulation

Strategies. In *Parikh, J. K., ed.*, 1988, pp. 39–58.

LeBlanc, Larry J.; Chon, Kyung S. and Boyce, David E. Network Equilibrium Models of Urban Location and Travel Choices: A Retrospective Survey. *J. Reg. Sci.*, May 1988, *28*(2), pp. 159–83.

LeBlanc, Michael R.; Conway, Roger K. and Hrubovcak, James. Estimating the Structure of Agricultural Investment: A Stochastic-Coefficients Approach. *J. Bus. Econ. Statist.*, April 1988, *6*(2), pp. 231–40.

_____ **and Reilly, John M.** Energy Policy Analysis: Alternative Modeling Approaches. In *Johnston, G. M.; Freshwater, D. and Favero, P., eds.*, 1988, pp. 244–71.

_____; **Swamy, P. A. V. B. and Conway, Roger K.** The Stochastic Coefficients Approach to Econometric Modeling: Part I: A Critique of Fixed Coefficients Models. *J. Agr. Econ. Res.*, Spring 1988, *40*(2), pp. 2–10.

_____; **Swamy, P. A. V. B. and Conway, Roger K.** The Stochastic Coefficients Approach to Econometric Modeling, Part II: Description and Motivation. *J. Agr. Econ. Res.*, Summer 1988, *40*(3), pp. 21–30.

Lebow, David; Sibert, Anne and Feltenstein, Andrew. An Analysis of the Welfare Implications of Alternative Exchange Rate Regimes: An Intertemporal Model with an Application. *J. Policy Modeling*, Winter 1988, *10*(4), pp. 611–29.

Lebowitz, Michael A. Errata [The Political Economy of Wage Labor]. *Sci. Soc.*, Summer 1988, *52*(2), pp. 132.

_____. Is "Analytical Marxism" Marxism? *Sci. Soc.*, Summer 1988, *52*(2), pp. 191–214.

Lecaillon, Jacques. Concentration et collusion. (With English summary.) *Revue Écon. Polit.*, Nov.–Dec. 1988, *98*(6), pp. 801–22.

Lecha, Gabriel and Lafuente Feléz, Alberto. Determinantes sectoriales del nacimiento de empresas en la industria española. (With English summary.) *Invest. Econ.*, May 1988, *12*(2), pp. 329–35.

Leclerc, France; Dubé-Rioux, Laurette and Schmitt, Bernd H. Sex Typing and Consumer Behavior: A Test of Gender Schema Theory. *J. Cons. Res.*, June 1988, *15*(1), pp. 122–28.

Leclercq, Vincent and Tubiana, Laurence. La remise en cause du rôle des États-Unis dans le fonctionnement oligopoliste des marchés du blé et du soja. (The Challenge to the United States' Role in the Oligopolistic Operation of the Wheat and Soya Markets. With English summary.) *Écon. Soc.*, Nov.–Dec. 1988, *22*(11–12), pp. 105–22.

LeCompte, Margaret D. and Dworkin, Anthony Gary. Educational Programs: Indirect Linkages and Unfulfilled Expectations. In *Rodgers, H. R., Jr., ed.*, 1988, pp. 135–67.

Lecraw, Donald J. Countertrade: A Form of Cooperative International Business Arrangement. In *Contractor, F. J. and Lorange, P.*, 1988, pp. 425–42.

Leddin, Anthony. Interest and Price Parity and Foreign Exchange Market Efficiency: The Irish Experience in the European Monetary System. *Econ. Soc. Rev.*, April 1988, *19*(3), pp. 215–31.

Ledent, Jacques. Interregional Migration in Individual Countries: Canada. In *Weidlich, W. and Haag, G., eds.*, 1988, pp. 101–30.

Ledesma, Rodolfo G. Banks' Loan Demand Perceptions and Rationality. *Atlantic Econ. J.*, December 1988, *16*(4), pp. 90.

Lee, Catherine and Saunders, Michael. Personal Equity Plans: Success or Failure? *Fisc. Stud.*, November 1988, *9*(4), pp. 36–50.

Lee, Chan Keun. A Study on the Efficiency of the Eurobond Market. In *Khoury, S. J. and Ghosh, A., eds.*, 1988, pp. 131–91.

Lee, Che-fu and Tien, H. Yuan. New Demographics and Old Designs: The Chinese Family amid Induced Population Transition. *Soc. Sci. Quart.*, September 1988, *69*(3), pp. 605–28.

Lee, Cheng F. and Alderson, Michael J. Corporate Pension Policy and Capital Structure Decisions. *J. Econ. Bus.*, August 1988, *40*(3), pp. 209–28.

_____ **and Chen, Andrew H.** Special Issue on Pensions: Introduction. *J. Econ. Bus.*, August 1988, *40*(3), pp. 191.

_____; **Chen, K. C. and Beatty, Randolph P.** On the Nonstationarity of Convertible Bond Betas: Theory and Evidence. *Quart. Rev. Econ. Bus.*, Autumn 1988, *28*(3), pp. 15–27.

_____ **and Wu, Chunchi.** Expectation Formation and Financial Ratio Adjustment Processes. *Accounting Rev.*, April 1988, *63*(2), pp. 292–306.

Lee, Cheng-Few and McDonald, Bill. An Analysis of Nonlinearities, Heteroscedasticity, and Functional Form in the Market Model. *J. Bus. Econ. Statist.*, October 1988, *6*(4), pp. 505–09.

Lee, Chul Song and Lee, Tai Ro. Recognition of Foreign Enterprises as Taxable Entities: Republic of Korea. In *International Fiscal Association, ed. (I)*, 1988, pp. 559–64.

Lee, Chung H. and Naya, Seiji. Patterns of Trade and Investment in Services in the Asia-Pacific Region. In *Lee, C. H. and Naya, S., eds.*, 1988, pp. 27–52.

_____ **and Naya, Seiji.** Trade in East Asian Development with Comparative Reference to Southeast Asian Experiences. *Econ. Develop. Cult. Change*, Supplement, April 1988, *36*(3), pp. S123–52.

_____ **and Naya, Seiji.** U.S.–ASEAN Trade and Investment in Services: An American Viewpoint. In *Tan, L.-H. and Akrasanee, N., eds.*, 1988, pp. 146–73.

Lee, Daniel Y. An Empirical Analysis of Money Demand in Five Sub-Saharan African Countries: Comments. In *Pennsylvania Economic Association*, 1988, pp. 58–59.

Lee, David R. Labor Market Dynamics in the U.S. Food Sector. *Amer. J. Agr. Econ.*, February 1988, *70*(1), pp. 90–102.

Lee, Dwight R. Free Riding and Paid Riding in the Fight against Terrorism. *Amer. Econ. Rev.*, May 1988, *78*(2), pp. 22–26.

_____; **Graves, Peter E. and Sexton, Robert L.**

On Mandatory Deposits, Fines, and the Control of Litter. *Natural Res. J.*, Fall 1988, *28*(4), pp. 837–47.

_____ **and Kreutzer, David.** Tax Evasion and Monopoly Output Decisions: A Reply. *Nat. Tax J.*, December 1988, *41*(4), pp. 583–84.

_____ **and McKenzie, Richard B.** Helping the Poor through Governmental Poverty Programs: The Triumph of Rhetoric over Reality. In *Gwartney, J. D. and Wagner, R. E., eds.*, 1988, pp. 387–408.

_____ **and Sexton, Robert L.** A Pollution Control Approach to Analysis of the Balanced Budget Amendment. *Amer. J. Econ. Soc.*, October 1988, *47*(4), pp. 423–26.

Lee, Eric Youngkoo and Szenberg, Michael. Analysis of Factors Determining the Compensation of Editors of Economics Journals. *Amer. Econ.*, Fall 1988, *32*(2), pp. 76–78.

_____ **and Szenberg, Michael.** The Price, Quantity and Welfare Effects of U.S. Trade Protection: The Case of Footwear. *Int. Econ. J.*, Winter 1988, *2*(4), pp. 95–110.

Lee, Frederic S. Costs, Increasing Costs, and Technical Progress: Response to the Critics [Post-Keynesian View of Average Direct Cost: A Critical Evaluation of the Theory and the Empirical Evidence]. *J. Post Keynesian Econ.*, Spring 1988, *10*(3), pp. 489–91.

_____. A New Dealer in Agriculture: G. C. Means and the Writing of *Industrial Prices*. *Rev. Soc. Econ.*, October 1988, *46*(2), pp. 180–202.

_____ **and Davies, John E.** A Post Keynesian Appraisal of the Contestability Criterion. *J. Post Keynesian Econ.*, Fall 1988, *11*(1), pp. 3–24.

Lee, Gloria L. Managerial Strategies, Information Technology and Engineers. In *Knights, D. and Willmott, H., eds.*, 1988, pp. 91–117.

Lee, Henry. Electricity and Gas: The U.S. East. *Energy J.*, October 1988, *9*(4), pp. 121–25.

Lee, Hong J. and Pinches, George E. On Optimal Insurance Purchasing. *J. Risk Ins.*, March 1988, *55*(1), pp. 145–49.

Lee, Hyunok and Chambers, Robert G. Expenditure Constraints and Profit Maximization in U.S. Agriculture: Reply. *Amer. J. Agr. Econ.*, November 1988, *70*(4), pp. 955–56.

Lee, Jack C. Nested Rotterdam Model: Applications to Marketing Research with Special References to Telecommunications Demand. *Int. J. Forecasting*, 1988, *4*(2), pp. 193–206.

Lee, Jae Won; Francis, Jack Clark and Kim, Wi-Saeng. Investment Performance of Common Stocks in Relation to Insider Ownership. *Financial Rev.*, February 1988, *23*(1), pp. 53–64.

_____ **and Koo, Suk Mo.** Trade-off between Economic Growth and Income Equality: A Reevaluation. In *Brenner, Y. S.; Reijnders, J. P. G. and Spithoven, A. H. G. M., eds.*, 1988, pp. 155–77.

Lee, Joe W. and Kidane, Amdetsion. Tobacco Consumption Pattern: A Demographic Analy-

sis. *Atlantic Econ. J.*, December 1988, *16*(4), pp. 92.

Lee, John E., Jr. Anniversary Articles. *J. Agr. Econ. Res.*, Winter 1988, *40*(1), pp. 3–4.

_____ **and La Ferney, Preston E.** Agricultural and Rural Areas Approaching the Twenty-first Century: A Synthesis of Research Issues. In *Hildreth, R. J., et al., eds.*, 1988, pp. 545–51.

Lee, John G. and Teague, Paul W. Risk Efficient Perennial Crop Selection: A MOTAD Approach to Citrus Production. *Southern J. Agr. Econ.*, December 1988, *20*(2), pp. 145–52.

Lee, K. C. and Borooah, Vani K. The Effect of Changes in Britain's Industrial Structure on Female Relative Pay and Employment. *Econ. J.*, September 1988, *98*(392), pp. 818–32.

Lee, Kam-Hon and Lau, Ho-Fuk. Development of Supermarkets in Hong Kong: Current Status and Future Trends. In *Kaynak, E., ed.*, 1988, pp. 321–29.

Lee, Katherine L. and Bosch, Darrell J. The Farm Level Effects of Better Access to Information: The Case of Dart. *Southern J. Agr. Econ.*, December 1988, *20*(2), pp. 109–18.

Lee, Kevin. Inflation and Labour Market Adjustment: The UK Experience. *Economica*, August 1988, *55*(219), pp. 409–16.

Lee, Ki-Young and Chang, Chung-Sik. Anomalies in the Stock Returns over Trading and Nontrading Periods: Further Evidence in the Korean Stock Market. *Quart. J. Bus. Econ.*, Spring 1988, *27*(2), pp. 139–61.

Lee, Kiong Hock. Universal Primary Education: An African Dilemma. *World Devel.*, December 1988, *16*(12), pp. 1481–91.

_____ **and Nagaraj, Shyamala.** Earnings and the Principal Components of Job Performance. *Econ. Letters*, 1988, *26*(1), pp. 95–97.

Lee, Kye Sik. Rational and Non-rational Expectations of Inflation in Korea. *World Devel.*, January 1988, *16*(1), pp. 195–205.

Lee, Kyung-Ho and Feldman, Allan M. Existence of Electoral Equilibria with Probabilistic Voting. *J. Public Econ.*, March 1988, *35*(2), pp. 205–27.

Lee, Li Way. The Predator–Prey Theory of Addiction. *J. Behav. Econ.*, Winter 1988, *17*(4), pp. 249–62.

Lee, Margaret. The Coal Industry Tribunal: The Case for Its Retention. *Australian Bull. Lab.*, December 1988, *15*(1), pp. 3–19.

Lee, Maw Lin and Chao, Shu-Wen. Effects of Social Security on Personal Saving. *Econ. Letters*, 1988, *28*(4), pp. 365–68.

_____ **and Liu, Ben-chieh.** Measuring Socioeconomic Effects When Using Income as Quality of Life Indicator. *Amer. J. Econ. Soc.*, April 1988, *47*(2), pp. 167–75.

Lee, Ronald D. Demographic Fluctuations and Labour Markets. In *Lee, R. D.; Arthur, W. B. and Rodgers, G., eds.*, 1988, pp. 9–11.

_____. Population, Food, and Rural Development: Introduction. In *Lee, R. D., et al., eds.*, 1988, pp. 3–8.

_____ **and Lapkoff, Shelley.** Intergenerational Flows of Time and Goods: Consequences of Slowing Population Growth. *J. Polit. Econ.*, June 1988, *96*(3), pp. 618–51.

Lee, Sang Bin and Ho, Thomas S. Y. The Pricing of Corporate Bond Provisions under Interest Rate Risks. In *Chen, A. H., ed.*, 1988, pp. 139–62.

Lee, Tai Ro and Lee, Chul Song. Recognition of Foreign Enterprises as Taxable Entities: Republic of Korea. In *International Fiscal Association, ed. (I)*, 1988, pp. 559–64.

Lee, Tenpao; Kim, Tae-Kyun and Baumel, C. Phillip. Impact of Deregulation on the Financial Performance of the Class I Railroads: Heuristic Models of Pooled Time-Series and Cross-Sectional Data. *Logist. Transp. Rev.*, September 1988, *24*(3), pp. 281–96.

Lee, Thea M. Contradictions in the Teaching of Neoclassical Theory. *Rev. Radical Polit. Econ.*, Summer–Fall 1988, *20*(2–3), pp. 7–11.

Lee, Tom K. Does Conditional Covariance or Conditional Variance Explain Time Varying Risk Premia in Foreign Exchange Returns? *Econ. Letters*, 1988, *27*(4), pp. 371–73.

_____. Settlement System and the Day-of-the-Week Effect. *Econ. Letters*, 1988, *26*(4), pp. 353–56.

Lee (Tsao), Yuan. ASEAN–U.S. Trade in Services: An ASEAN Perspective. In *Tan, L.-H. and Akrasanee, N., eds.*, 1988, pp. 115–45.

Lee, Y. and Schmidt, C. G. Evolution of Urban Spatial Cognition: Patterns of Change in Guangzhou, China. *Environ. Planning A*, March 1988, *20*(3), pp. 339–51.

Leeds, Michael A. Rank-Order Tournaments and Worker Incentives. *Atlantic Econ. J.*, June 1988, *16*(2), pp. 74–77.

Leeds, Roger S. Turkey: Rhetoric and Reality. In *Vernon, R., ed.*, 1988, pp. 149–78.

Lees, Lynn Hollen and Hohenberg, Paul M. How Cities Grew in the Western World: A Systems Approach. In *Ausubel, J. H. and Herman, R., eds.*, 1988, pp. 71–84.

Leeth, John D. and Kniesner, Thomas J. Simulating Hedonic Labor Market Models: Computational Issues and Policy Applications. *Int. Econ. Rev.*, November 1988, *29*(4), pp. 755–89.

de Leeuw, Frank. Gross Product by Industry: Comments on Recent Criticisms. *Surv. Curr. Bus.*, July 1988, *68*(7), pp. 132–33.

de Leeuw, Jan. Model Selection in Multinomial Experiments. In *Dijkstra, T. K., ed.*, 1988, pp. 118–38.

Lefeber, R. and van der Linde, J. G. International Energy Agency Captures the Development of European Community Energy Law. *J. World Trade*, October 1988, *22*(5), pp. 5–25.

Lefebvre, Élisabeth and Lefebvre, Louis A. The Innovative Business Firm in Canada: An Empirical Study of CAD/CAM Firms. *Int. Lab. Rev.*, 1988, *127*(4), pp. 497–513.

_____ **and Lefebvre, Louis A.** Technologie et libre-échange une complicité souhaitable.

(With English summary.) *L'Actual. Econ.*, December 1988, *64*(4), pp. 616–29.

Lefebvre, Louis A. and Lefebvre, Élisabeth. The Innovative Business Firm in Canada: An Empirical Study of CAD/CAM Firms. *Int. Lab. Rev.*, 1988, *127*(4), pp. 497–513.

_____ **and Lefebvre, Élisabeth.** Technologie et libre-échange une complicité souhaitable. (With English summary.) *L'Actual. Econ.*, December 1988, *64*(4), pp. 616–29.

Leff, Mark H. Speculating in Social Security Futures: The Perils of Payroll Tax Financing, 1939–1950. In *Nash, G. D.; Pugach, N. H. and Tomasson, R. F., eds.*, 1988, pp. 243–78.

Leff, Nathaniel H. Policy Research for Improved Organizational Performance: A Case from the World Bank. *J. Econ. Behav. Organ.*, June 1988, *9*(4), pp. 393–403.

_____ **and Sato, Kazuo.** Estimating Investment and Savings Functions for Developing Countries, with an Application to Latin America. *Int. Econ. J.*, Autumn 1988, *2*(3), pp. 1–17.

Leffler, Keith B. and Rucker, Randal R. To Harvest or Not to Harvest? An Analysis of Cutting Behavior on Federal Timber Sales Contracts. *Rev. Econ. Statist.*, May 1988, *70*(2), pp. 207–13.

Lefkin, Peter A. Shattering Some Myths on the Insurance Liability: A Comment. *Yale J. Regul.*, Summer 1988, *5*(2), pp. 417–25.

Lefoll, Jean and Guiot, Jean M. Cardinal Utility: An Empirical Test. In *Munier, B. R., ed.*, 1988, pp. 97–102.

Legendre, François; Morin, Pierre and Chevallier, Jean-Yves. L'investissement dans un contexte de faible croissance et de taux d'intérêt élevés. Une étude sur données individuelles du comportement des entreprises industrielles françaises. (With English summary.) *Rech. Écon. Louvain*, 1988, *54*(2), pp. 221–49.

Leggett, Robert E. Gorbachev's Reform Program: "Radical" or More of the Same? In *Linz, S. J. and Moskoff, W., eds.*, 1988, pp. 23–43.

_____ **and Kellogg, Robert L.** The Soviet Union: An Economy in Transition and Its Prospects for Economic Growth. In *Liebowitz, R. D., ed.*, 1988, pp. 23–51.

Legler, John B.; Sylla, Richard and Wallis, John J. U.S. City Finances and the Growth of Government, 1859–1902. *J. Econ. Hist.*, June 1988, *48*(2), pp. 347–56.

Legvold, Robert. War, Weapons, and Soviet Foreign Policy. In *Bialer, S. and Mandelbaum, M., eds.*, 1988, pp. 97–132.

Lehman, Cheryl R. Accounting Ethics: Surviving Survival of the Fittest. In *Neimark, M., ed.*, 1988, pp. 71–82.

Lehman, Dale E. and Max, Wendy. A Behavioral Model of Timber Supply. *J. Environ. Econ. Manage.*, March 1988, *15*(1), pp. 71–86.

Lehmann, Bruce N. and Modest, David M. The Empirical Foundations of the Arbitrage Pricing Theory. *J. Finan. Econ.*, September 1988, *21*(2), pp. 213–54.

Lehmann-Waffenschmidt, Marco. Technolgie-transfer und Transfer des Wertmassstabes

"Geld" in W. G. Waffenschmidts ganzheitlichen Ordnungsmodellen. (Technology Transfer and Transfer of Money as a Measure of Value in W. G. Waffenschmidt's Integrative Ordering Models. With English summary.) *Jahr. Nationalökon. Statist.*, March 1988, *204*(3), pp. 208–30.

Lehn, Kenneth and Demsetz, Harold. The Structure of Corporate Ownership: Causes and Consequences. In *Demsetz, H.*, 1988, *1985*, pp. 202–22.

———— **and Poulsen, Annette B.** Leveraged Buyouts: Wealth Created or Wealth Redistributed? In *Weidenbaum, M. L. and Chilton, K. W.*, *eds.*, 1988, pp. 46–62.

Lehrer, Ehud. An Axiomatization of the Banzhaf Value. *Int. J. Game Theory*, 1988, *17*(2), pp. 89–99.

————. Repeated Games with Stationary Bounded Recall Strategies. *J. Econ. Theory*, October 1988, *46*(1), pp. 130–44.

Lehrer, Evelyn L. Determinants of Marital Instability: A Cox-regression Model. *Appl. Econ.*, February 1988, *20*(2), pp. 195–210.

Lehtinen, Raimo. Kraven på en skattereform från skattebetalarens synpunkt. (The Need for Tax Reform from the Taxpayer's Point of View. With English summary.) *Ekon. Samfundets Tidskr.*, 1988, *41*(1), pp. 31–33.

Leibenstein, Harvey. A Branch of Economics Is Missing: Micro-Micro Theory. In *Earl, P. E.*, *ed.*, *Vol. 1*, 1988, *1979*, pp. 19–44.

———— **and Weiermair, Klaus.** X-Efficiency, Managerial Discretion, and the Nature of Employment-Relations: A Game-Theoretical Approach. In *Dlugos, G.; Dorow, W. and Weiermair, K.*, *eds.*, 1988, pp. 79–94.

Leibold, Marius. New Approaches in Developing Export-Orientated Business Leaders. *J. Stud. Econ. Econometrics*, November 1988, *12*(3), pp. 49–61.

————. Structural Market Changes and Global Retailing Strategy Approaches. In *Kaynak, E.*, *ed.*, 1988, pp. 51–61.

Leibowitz, Arleen; Waite, Linda J. and Witsberger, Christina. Child Care for Preschoolers: Differences by Child's Age. *Demography*, May 1988, *25*(2), pp. 205–20.

Leibowitz, S. J. and Palmer, J. P. Assessing Assessments of Economics Departments. *Quart. Rev. Econ. Bus.*, Summer 1988, *28*(2), pp. 88–113.

Leiderman, Leonardo. The Term Structure in the United States, Japan, and West Germany: Comment. *Carnegie–Rochester Conf. Ser. Public Policy*, Spring 1988, *28*, pp. 319–23.

———— **and Blejer, Mario I.** Modeling and Testing Ricardian Equivalence: A Survey. *Int. Monet. Fund Staff Pap.*, March 1988, *35*(1), pp. 1–35.

———— **and Helpman, Elhanan.** Stabilization in High Inflation Countries: Analytical Foundations and Recent Experience. *Carnegie–Rochester Conf. Ser. Public Policy*, Spring 1988, *28*, pp. 9–84.

———— **and Razin, Assaf.** Effects of Government Finance: Testing Ricardian Neutrality. In *Helpman, E.; Razin, A. and Sadka, E.*, *eds.*, 1988, pp. 107–21.

———— **and Razin, Assaf.** Foreign Trade Shocks and the Dynamics of High Inflation: Israel, 1978–85. *J. Int. Money Finance*, December 1988, *7*(4), pp. 411–23.

———— **and Razin, Assaf.** Testing Ricardian Neutrality with an Intertemporal Stochastic Model. *J. Money, Credit, Banking*, February 1988, *20*(1), pp. 1–21.

Leigh, David R. Business Planning Is People Planning. In *Timpe, A. D.*, *ed.*, 1988, *1984*, pp. 68–76.

Leigh, J. Paul and Berger, Mark C. The Effect of Alcohol Use on Wages. *Appl. Econ.*, October 1988, *20*(10), pp. 1343–51.

Leigh, Wilhelmina A. The Social Preference for Fair Housing: During the Civil Rights Movement and Since. *Amer. Econ. Rev.*, May 1988, *78*(2), pp. 156–62.

———— **and Mitchell, Mildred O.** Public Housing and the Black Community. *Rev. Black Polit. Econ.*, Fall 1988, *17*(2), pp. 107–29.

Leijonhufvud, Axel. Did Keynes Mean Anything? Rejoinder [The Significance of Monetary Disequilibrium]. *Cato J.*, Spring–Summer 1988, *8*(1), pp. 209–17.

————. Effective Demand Failures. In *Shaw, G. K.*, *ed.*, *Vol. 1*, 1988, *1973*, pp. 210–31.

————. Political Business Cycles: The Political Economy of Money, Inflation, and Unemployment: Introduction. In *Willett, T. D.*, *ed.*, 1988, pp. xv–xxii.

———— **and Aoki, Masanao.** The Stock-Flow Analysis of Investment. In *Kohn, M. and Tsiang, S.-C.*, *eds.*, 1988, pp. 206–29.

Leipert, Christian and Simonis, Udo Ernst. Environmental Damage—Environmental Expenditures: Statistical Evidence on the Federal Republic of Germany. *Int. J. Soc. Econ.*, 1988, *15*(7), pp. 37–52.

Leipziger, Danny M. Editor's Introduction: Korea's Transition to Maturity. *World Devel.*, January 1988, *16*(1), pp. 1–5.

————. Industrial Restructuring in Korea. *World Devel.*, January 1988, *16*(1), pp. 121–35.

———— **and Kwack, Sung Y.** Factors Affecting the Accumulation of External Debt: Hypotheses and Evidence from Korea. *J. Econ. Devel.*, December 1988, *13*(2), pp. 111–22.

Leistritz, F. Larry and Ekstrom, Brenda L. The Financial Characteristics of Production Units and Producers Experiencing Financial Stress. In *Murdock, S. H. and Leistritz, F. L.*, *eds.*, 1988, pp. 73–95.

————; **Jones, Lonnie L. and Murdock, Steve H.** Economic-Demographic Projection Models: An Overview of Recent Developments for Infrastructure Analysis. In *Johnson, T. G.; Deaton, B. J. and Segarra, E.*, *eds.*, 1988, pp. 87–97.

———— **and Murdock, Steve H.** The Farm Financial Crisis: Socioeconomic Dimensions and Implications for Producers and Rural Areas: Introduction. In *Murdock, S. H. and Leistritz, F. L.*, *eds.*, 1988, pp. 1–9.

_____ **and Murdock, Steve H.** Financial Characteristics of Farms and of Farm Financial Markets and Policies in the United States. In *Murdock, S. H. and Leistritz, F. L., eds.*, 1988, pp. 13–28.

_____ **and Murdock, Steve H.** Financing Infrastructure in Rapid Growth Communities: The North Dakota Experience. In *Johnson, T. G.; Deaton, B. J. and Segarra, E., eds.*, 1988, pp. 141–54.

_____ **and Murdock, Steve H.** Policy Alternatives and Research Agenda. In *Murdock, S. H. and Leistritz, F. L., eds.*, 1988, pp. 169–84.

_____, **et al.** Producer Reactions and Adaptations. In *Murdock, S. H. and Leistritz, F. L., eds.*, 1988, pp. 97–111.

Leithäuser, Gerhard. Crisis Despite Flexibility: The Case of West Germany. In *Boyer, R., ed.*, 1988, pp. 171–88.

Lekakis, Joseph N. and Halvadakis, Constantinos P. Biogas System Planning: A Techno-economic Perspective. *J. Energy Devel.*, Autumn 1988, *14*(1), pp. 115–31.

Leland, Hayne and Rubinstein, Mark. Comments on the Market Crash: Six Months After. *J. Econ. Perspectives*, Summer 1988, *2*(3), pp. 45–50.

Lele, Uma. Agricultural Growth, Domestic Policies, the External Environment and Assistance to Africa: Lessons of a Quarter Century. In *Roberts, C., ed.*, 1988, pp. 119–98.

_____. Empowering Africa's Rural Poor: Problems and Prospects in Agricultural Development. In *Lewis, J. P., et al.*, 1988, pp. 73–92.

_____. Foreign Assistance and Agricultural Development: Implications of the Past 25 Years for Policy Conditionality, Capacity Building and Sustainability. In *Asefa, S., ed.*, 1988, pp. 47–66.

Lelièvre, E. and Courgeau, D. Estimation of Transition Rates in Dynamic Household Models. In *Keilman, N.; Kuijsten, A. and Vossen, A., eds.*, 1988, pp. 160–76.

Leloup, Lance T. The Executive Budget—An Idea Whose Time Has Passed: Comments. *Public Budg. Finance*, Spring 1988, *8*(1), pp. 104–07.

_____. From Microbudgeting to Macrobudgeting: Evolution in Theory and Practice. In *Rubin, I. S., ed.*, 1988, pp. 19–42.

_____ **and Hancock, John.** Congress and the Reagan Budgets: An Assessment. *Public Budg. Finance*, Autumn 1988, *8*(3), pp. 30–54.

Lemaire, Jean. A Comparative Analysis of Most European and Japanese Bonus-malus Systems. *J. Risk Ins.*, December 1988, *55*(4), pp. 660–81.

Leman, Christopher K. and Paarlberg, Robert L. The Continued Political Power of Agricultural Interests. In *Hildreth, R. J., et al., eds.*, 1988, pp. 32–60.

Lemelin, Maurice; Toulouse, Jean-Marie and Côté, Marcel. The Management–Industrial Relations Interface: Exploring the Conceptual

Linkages. In *Hébert, G.; Jain, H. C. and Meltz, N. M., eds..*, 1988, pp. 147–86.

Lemettre, Jean-François. Les oligopoles technologiques: Quelques hypotheses sur les oligopoles de ressources. (Technological Oligopolies: Some Assumptions on Oligopolies of Resources. With English summary.) *Écon. Soc.*, Nov.–Dec. 1988, *22*(11–12), pp. 201–20.

Lemola, Tarmo and Lovio, Raimo. Possibilities for a Small Country in High-Technology Production: The Electronics Industry in Finland. In *Freeman, C. and Lundvall, B.-A., eds.*, 1988, pp. 139–55.

Lenel, Hans Otto. Hard-Coal Mining: A Divided and Protected Market. In *de Jong, H. W., ed.*, 1988, pp. 61–79.

Lenhard, R. J., et al. Measurement and Simulation of One-Dimensional Transient Three-Phase Flow for Monotonic Liquid Drainage. *Water Resources Res.*, June 1988, *24*(6), pp. 853–63.

Lenk, Peter J. The Logistic Normal Distribution for Bayesian, Nonparametric, Predictive Densities. *J. Amer. Statist. Assoc.*, June 1988, *83*(402), pp. 509–16.

Lensberg, Terje. Stability and the Nash Solution. *J. Econ. Theory*, August 1988, *45*(2), pp. 330–41.

_____ **and Thomson, William.** Characterizing the Nash Bargaining Solution without Pareto-Optimality. *Soc. Choice Welfare*, 1988, *5*(2/3), pp. 247–59.

_____ **and Thomson, William.** Characterizing the Nash Bargaining Solution without Pareto-Optimality. In *Gaertner, W. and Pattanaik, P. K., eds.*, 1988, *1988*, pp. 159–71.

Lenti, Renata Targetti and Civardi, Marisa Bottiroli. The Distribution of Personal Income at the Sectoral Level in Italy: A SAM Model. *J. Policy Modeling*, Fall 1988, *10*(3), pp. 453–68.

Lentz, George H. and Stern, Jerrold J. The "Cap Rate," 1966–1984: Comment. *Land Econ.*, November 1988, *64*(4), pp. 381–83.

Lenway, Stefanie Ann. Between War and Commerce: Economic Sanctions as a Tool of Statecraft. *Int. Organ.*, Spring 1988, *42*(2), pp. 397–426.

Leon, H. and Molana, H. Testing Some Restrictions in a Time Series Cross-Section Model: A Study of Seven LDCs. *Manchester Sch. Econ. Soc. Stud.*, March 1988, *56*(1), pp. 1–15.

Leon, Hyginus. The Monetary Approach to the Balance of Payments—A Simple Test of Jamaican Data. *Soc. Econ. Stud.*, December 1988, *37*(4), pp. 1–37.

Léonard, Jacques. L'économie d'endettement international: Des déterminants logiques aux solutions d'une crise. (The International Indebtedness Economy: From the Logical Determinants to the Solutions to a Crisis. With English summary.) *Écon. Appl.*, 1988, *41*(4), pp. 709–40.

Leonard, Jonathan S. Technological Change and the Extent of Frictional and Structural Unemployment. **In** *Cyert, R. M. and Mowery, D. C., eds.*, 1988, pp. 43–71.

Leonello, Giuseppe; D'Antonio, Mariano and Colaizzo, Raffaele. Mezzogiorno/Centre-North: A Two-Region Model for the Italian Economy. *J. Policy Modeling*, Fall 1988, *10*(3), pp. 437–51.

Leonesio, Michael V. In-Kind Transfers and Work Incentives. *J. Lab. Econ.*, October 1988, *6*(4), pp. 515–29.

_____. Predicting the Effects of In-kind Transfers on Labor Supply. *Southern Econ. J.*, April 1988, *54*(4), pp. 901–12.

Leontidou, Lila. Greece: Prospects and Contradictions of Tourism in the 1980s. **In** *Williams, A. M. and Shaw, G., eds.*, 1988, pp. 80–100.

Leotsarakos, Christos and McCord, Mark R. Investigating Utility and Value Functions with an "Assessment Cube" **In** *Munier, B. R., ed.*, 1988, pp. 59–75.

Lepani, Charles. Potential Determinants of the Role of the Pacific Islands Region in the International Economy of the Twenty-first Century. **In** *Kozmetsky, G.; Matsumoto, H. and Smilor, R. W., eds.*, 1988, pp. 43–48.

Lepistö, Arto. Nuclear Energy After Chernobyl: Views from Four Countries: Finland. *Energy J.*, January 1988, *9*(1), pp. 41–42.

Leppel, Karen and Clain, Suzanne Heller. The Growth in Involuntary Part-Time Employment of Men and Women. *Appl. Econ.*, September 1988, *20*(9), pp. 1155–66.

Lerin, François and Daviron, Benoît. Le Brésil et la dynamique de l'oligopole caféier (1830–1988). (Brazil and the Dynamics of the World Coffee Oligopoly [1830–1988]. With English summary.) *Écon. Soc.*, Nov.–Dec. 1988, *22*(11–12), pp. 123–49.

Lerman, Donald L. and Mikesell, James J. Impacts of Adding Net Worth to the Poverty Definition. *Eastern Econ. J.*, Oct.–Dec. 1988, *14*(4), pp. 357–70.

Lerman, Zvi and Levy, Haim. Testing the Predictive Power of Ex-Post Efficient Portfolios. *J. Finan. Res.*, Fall 1988, *11*(3), pp. 241–54.

Lerner, Abba P. The Concept of Monopoly and the Measurement of Monopoly Power. **In** *Ricketts, M., ed., Vol. 1*, 1988, *1934*, pp. 131–49.

_____. Functional Finance and the Federal Debt. **In** *Shaw, G. K., ed., Vol. 2*, 1988, *1943*, pp. 269–82.

Lerohl, M. L. Issues in Canadian Agricultural Economic Data: A Selected Review. *Can. J. Agr. Econ.*, July 1988, *36*(2), pp. 175–86.

Leroy, Marcel. Strategies toward Full Employment in Isolated Regions. **In** *Choudhury, M. A., ed.*, 1988, pp. 138–47.

Lesage, Alain. Industrial Structure and International Trade: An Evolutionary Perspective. *Empirica*, 1988, *15*(1), pp. 179–87.

Lesage, James P. and Magura, Michael. A Regional Payroll Forecasting Model That Uses Bayesian Shrinkage Techniques for Data Pooling. *Reg. Sci. Persp.*, 1988, *18*(1), pp. 100–116.

Leslie, Derek. Employment during the Thatcher

Years: Did They Fall or Were They Pushed? *Appl. Econ.*, June 1988, *20*(6), pp. 785–802.

Leslie, Joanne. Women's Work and Child Nutrition in the Third World. *World Devel.*, November 1988, *16*(11), pp. 1341–62.

_____; **Lycette, Margaret A. and Buvinić, Mayra.** Weathering Economic Crises: The Crucial Role of Women in Health. **In** *Bell, D. E. and Reich, M. R., eds.*, 1988, pp. 307–48.

Leslie, T. E. C. Untitled Review of the Second Edition. **In** *Wood, J. C., ed., Vol. 2*, 1988, *1879*, pp. 23–27.

Lesourd, J. B. Risk and Flexibility in Microeconomic Production Theory: Principles, and Application to Energy-Saving Investment. **In** *Munier, B. R., ed.*, 1988, pp. 595–600.

Lessard, Donald R. and Tschoegl, Adrian E. Panama's International Banking Center: The Direct Employment Effects. *J. Banking Finance*, 1988, *12*(1), pp. 43–50.

Lessard, Pierre and Jacobs, Gordon L. Tax Treatment of Computer Software: Canada. **In** *International Fiscal Association, ed. (II)*, 1988, pp. 253–80.

Lesser, W. Canadian Seeds Act: Does it Mimic Plant Breeders' Rights Legislation? *Can. J. Agr. Econ.*, November 1988, *36*(3), pp. 519–29.

Lessinger, Johanna. Trader vs. Developer: The Market Relocation Issue in an Indian City. **In** *Clark, G., ed.*, 1988, pp. 139–64.

Lester, David and Yang, Bijou. A Hypothesis about Execution Rates in the United States. **In** *Pennsylvania Economic Association*, 1988, pp. 522–29.

Lester, Richard A. Wages, Benefits, and Company Employment Systems. **In** *Kaufman, B. E., ed.*, 1988, pp. 89–115.

Lesthaeghe, Ron and Surkyn, Johan. Cultural Dynamics and Economic Theories of Fertility Change. *Population Devel. Rev.*, March 1988, *14*(1), pp. 1–45.

Letwin, Oliver. International Experience in the Politics of Privatization. **In** *Walker, M. A., ed. (II)*, 1988, pp. 49–60.

Leung, PingSun and Bowen, Richard L. Using Input–Output Analysis to Estimate Tax Exporting and Tax Pyramiding in Hawaii. *Ann. Reg. Sci.*, March 1988, *22*(1), pp. 49–62.

_____; **Ching, Chauncey T. K. and Hsu, George J. Y.** Energy Planning in Taiwan: An Alternative Approach Using a Multiobjective Programming and Input–Output Model. *Energy J.*, January 1988, *9*(1), pp. 53–72.

Leung, Y. Interregional Equilibrium and Fuzzy Linear Programming: 1. *Environ. Planning A*, January 1988, *20*(1), pp. 25–40.

_____. Interregional Equilibrium and Fuzzy Linear Programming: 2. *Environ. Planning A*, February 1988, *20*(2), pp. 219–30.

Leunis, Joseph and François, Pierre. The Impact of Belgian Public Policy upon Retailing: The Case of the Second Padlock Law. **In** *Kaynak, E., ed.*, 1988, pp. 135–53.

Leuthold, Jane H. A Forecasting Model for State

Expenditures. *Public Choice*, January 1988, 56(1), pp. 45–55.

Leuthold, Raymond M. and Naik, Gopal. Cash and Futures Price Relationships for Nonstorable Commodities: An Empirical Analysis Using a General Theory. *Western J. Agr. Econ.*, December 1988, 13(2), pp. 327–38.

_____ and Sarassoro, Gboroton F. Offshore Commodity Hedging under Floating Exchange Rates: Comment. *Amer. J. Agr. Econ.*, August 1988, 70(3), pp. 724–26.

Levedahl, J. William. Coupon Redeemers: Are They Better Shoppers? *J. Cons. Aff.*, Winter 1988, 22(2), pp. 264–83.

Levi, Isaac. On Indeterminate Probabilities. In *Gärdenfors, P. and Sahlin, N.-E.*, eds., 1988, pp. 287–312.

Levi, Maurice D. Weekend Effects in Stock Market Returns: An Overview. In *Dimson, E.*, ed., 1988, pp. 43–51.

_____; Goldberg, Michael A. and Helsley, Robert W. On the Development of International Financial Centers. *Ann. Reg. Sci.*, February 1988, 22, pp. 81–94.

Levich, Richard M. Financial Innovations in International Financial Markets. In *Feldstein, M.*, ed. (II), 1988, pp. 215–57.

Levin, Dan. Stackelberg, Cournot and Collusive Monopoly: Performance and Welfare Comparisons. *Econ. Inquiry*, April 1988, 26(2), pp. 317–30.

Levin, David J. Alternative Measure of the State and Local Government Fiscal Position: Revised and Updated Estimates. *Surv. Curr. Bus.*, November 1988, 68(11), pp. 24–25.

_____. State and Local Government Fiscal Position in 1987. *Surv. Curr. Bus.*, February 1988, 68(2), pp. 25–27.

Levin, Irwin P. An Associative Model of the Effects of Information Frame on Consumer Behavior. In *Maital, S.*, ed., Vol. 1, 1988, pp. 137–43.

_____ and Gaeth, Gary J. How Consumers Are Affected by the Framing of Attribute Information before and after Consuming the Product. *J. Cons. Res.*, December 1988, 15(3), pp. 374–78.

Levin, Jay H. The Effects of Government Intervention in a Dynamic Model of the Spot and Forward Exchange Markets. *Int. Econ. J.*, Spring 1988, 2(1), pp. 1–20.

Levin, M. I.; Polterovich, V. M. and Lakhman, I. L. The Mechanism of Negotiated Prices and Problems of Its Improvement. *Matekon*, Summer 1988, 24(4), pp. 27–60.

Levin, Michael D. Accountability and Legitimacy in Traditional Co-operation in Nigeria. In *Attwood, D. W. and Baviskar, B. S.*, eds., 1988, pp. 330–42.

Levin, Richard C. Appropriability, R&D Spending, and Technological Performance. *Amer. Econ. Rev.*, May 1988, 78(2), pp. 424–28.

_____; Goto, Akira and Peck, Merton J. Picking Losers: Public Policy toward Declining Industries in Japan. In *Shoven, J. B.*, ed., 1988, pp. 195–239.

_____ and Reiss, Peter C. Cost-Reducing and Demand-Creating R&D with Spillovers. *Rand J. Econ.*, Winter 1988, 19(4), pp. 538–56.

Levine, A. L. Sraffa, Okun, and the Theory of the Imperfectly Competitive Firm. *J. Econ. Behav. Organ.*, January 1988, 9(1), pp. 101–05.

_____ and Arcelus, F. J. Merit Goods and Public Choice: The Case of Higher Education—Reply. *Public Finance*, 1988, 43(3), pp. 471–72.

Levine, Charles H. and Benda, Peter M. The Assignment and Institutionalization of Functions at OMB: Lessons from Two Cases in Work Force Management. In *Rubin, I. S.*, ed., 1988, pp. 70–99.

Levine, David K. and Fudenberg, Drew. Open-Loop and Closed-Loop Equilibria in Dynamic Games with Many Players. *J. Econ. Theory*, February 1988, 44(1), pp. 1–18.

_____; Fudenberg, Drew and Kreps, David M. On the Robustness of Equilibrium Refinements. *J. Econ. Theory*, April 1988, 44(2), pp. 354–80.

Levine, David P. Marx's Theory of Income Distribution. In *Asimakopulos, A.*, ed., 1988, pp. 49–74.

Levine, Howard J. and Oosterhuis, Paul W. Tax Treatment of Computer Software: United States. In *International Fiscal Association*, ed. (II), 1988, pp. 333–58.

Levine, Joel H. and Spadaro, John. Occupational Mobility: A Structural Model. In *Wellman, B. and Berkowitz, S. D.*, eds., 1988, pp. 452–75.

Levine, Marc V. Economic Development in States and Cities: Toward Democratic and Strategic Planning in State and Local Government. In *Levine, M. V.*, et al., 1988, pp. 111–46.

_____. The State and Democracy in America—Historical Patterns and Current Possibilities: Introduction. In *Levine, M. V.*, et al., 1988, pp. 1–13.

Levine, Paul and Smith, Peter. The Gains from Optimal Control in a Small Econometric Model of the UK. *J. Econ. Dynam. Control*, March 1988, 12(1), pp. 13–18.

_____; Smith, Peter and Budd, Alan. Real Wage Adjustment and Long-term Unemployment. In *Cross, R.*, ed., 1988, pp. 41–64.

_____; Smith, Peter and Budd, Alan. Unemployment, Vacancies and the Long-term Unemployed. *Econ. J.*, December 1988, 98(393), pp. 1071–91.

Levine, Phillip B. and Mitchell, Olivia S. The Baby Boom's Legacy: Relative Wages in the Twenty-First Century. *Amer. Econ. Rev.*, May 1988, 78(2), pp. 66–69.

Levine, Susan. Class and Gender: Herbert Gutman and the Women of "Shoe City." *Labor Hist.*, Summer 1988, 29(3), pp. 344–55.

Levins, Richard A.; Brown, Earl H. and Rosson, C. Parr. Soybean Trader: A Microcomputer Simulation of International Agricultural Trade. *Southern J. Agr. Econ.*, July 1988, 20(1), pp. 153–57.

Levinsohn, James. Empirics of Taxes on Differentiated Products: The Case of Tariffs in the U.S.

Automobile Industry. In *Baldwin, R. E., ed. (II)*, 1988, pp. 11–40.

_____ and **Kharas, Homi J.** LDC Savings Rates and Debt Crises. *World Devel.*, July 1988, *16*(7), pp. 779–86.

Levinson, Alfred. The Service Sector in International Trade. *Amer. Econ.*, Spring 1988, *32*(1), pp. 66–70.

Levinson, Arik M. Reexaming Teacher Preferences and Compensating Wages. *Econ. Educ. Rev.*, 1988, *7*(3), pp. 357–64.

Levinson, Marc. The Shaky Case for Aiding Investment. In *Brown, E., ed.*, 1988, *1986*, pp. 183–86.

_____ and **Aho, C. Michael.** The Economy after Reagan. *Foreign Aff.*, Winter 1988–89, *67*(2), pp. 10–25.

Levinthal, Daniel. A Survey of Agency Models of Organizations. *J. Econ. Behav. Organ.*, March 1988, *9*(2), pp. 153–85.

_____ and **March, James G.** A Model of Adaptive Organizational Search. In *March, J. G.*, 1988, *1981*, pp. 187–218.

_____; **March, James G. and Herriott, Scott R.** Learning from Experience in Organizations. In *March, J. G.*, 1988, *1985*, pp. 219–27.

Levis, Mario. Size Related Anomalies and Trading Activity of UK Institutional Investors. In *Dimson, E., ed.*, 1988, pp. 155–75.

Levitan, Sar A. and Conway, Elizabeth A. Part-Timers: Living on Half-Rations. *Challenge*, May–June 1988, *31*(3), pp. 9–16.

Levitskii, E. M. Statistical Analysis and Forecasting the Effect of Scientific and Technical Progress Factors on the Economy's Growth. *Matekon*, Winter 1988–89, *25*(2), pp. 4–19.

Levitt, Arthur, Jr. and Stewart, Gordon C. Can American Business Compete? A Perspective from Midrange Growth Companies. In *Starr, M. K., ed.*, 1988, pp. 271–98.

Levratto, Nadine. Rationnement ou equilibre du marche du credit: Une approche fondee sur le comportement des banques. (Equilibrium Credit Rationing: A Study Based on the Banking Firm Behaviour. With English summary.) *Écon. Soc.*, January 1988, *22*(1), pp. 81–103.

Levy, Amnon; Gabriel, Stuart A. and Justman, Moshe. Determinants of Internal Migration in Israel: Expected Returns and Risks. *Appl. Econ.*, May 1988, *20*(5), pp. 679–90.

_____ and **Spivak, Avia.** How Does the Public Perceive an Unprecedented Rise in Inflation: The Case of Inflationary Expectations in Israel. *J. Macroecon.*, Spring 1988, *10*(2), pp. 273–82.

Levy, Brian. The Determinants of Manufacturing Ownership in Less Developed Countries: A Comparative Analysis. *J. Devel. Econ.*, March 1988, *28*(2), pp. 217–231.

_____. The State-Owned Enterprise as an Entrepreneurial Substitute in Developing Countries: The Case of Nitrogen Fertilizer. *World Devel.*, October 1988, *16*(10), pp. 1199–1211.

Levy, Daniel and Gabriel, Stuart A. Expectations, Information, and Migration: The Case

of the West Bank and Gaza. *Appl. Econ.*, January 1988, *20*(1), pp. 1–13.

Levy, David M. Increasing the Likelihood Value by Adding Constraints. *Econ. Letters*, 1988, *28*(1), pp. 57–61.

_____. The Market for Fame and Fortune. *Hist. Polit. Econ.*, Winter 1988, *20*(4), pp. 615–25.

_____. Utility-Enhancing Consumption Constraints. *Econ. Philos.*, April 1988, *4*(1), pp. 69–88.

_____; **Feigenbaum, Susan and Karoly, Lynn.** When Votes Are Words Not Deeds: Some Evidence from the Nuclear Freeze Referendum. *Public Choice*, September 1988, *58*(3), pp. 201–16.

Levy, David T. Short-term Leasing and Monopoly Power: The Case of IBM. *J. Inst. Theoretical Econ.*, September 1988, *144*(4), pp. 611–34.

_____ and **Haber, Lawrence J.** Decision Making in the Multiproduct Firm: Adaptability and Firm Organization. *Managerial Dec. Econ.*, December 1988, *9*(4), pp. 331–38.

Levy, Dominique and Duménil, Gérard. Équilibrages par les prix et par les quantités dans le cadre d'une micro-économie d'inspiration classique. (With English summary.) *Revue Écon. Polit.*, Jan.–Feb. 1988, *98*(1), pp. 127–49.

Levy, E. and Nobay, A. R. Using Bivariate Autoregressive Representations in Testing Exact Expectations Relations. *Econ. Letters*, 1988, *28*(4), pp. 343–49.

Lévy, Émile. La demande en économie de la santé. (With English summary.) *Revue Écon. Polit.*, July–Aug. 1988, *98*(4), pp. 445–507.

Levy, Frank S. Incomes, Families, and Living Standards. In *Litan, R. E; Lawrence, R. Z. and Schultze, C. L., eds.*, 1988, pp. 108–53.

_____ and **Michel, Richard C.** Work for Welfare: How Much Good Will It Do? In *Brown, E., ed.*, 1988, *1986*, pp. 54–60.

Lévy-Garboua, Louis. The Intergenerational Transmission of Wealth and the Rise and Fall of Families: Comments. In *Kessler, D. and Masson, A., eds.*, 1988, pp. 166–68.

_____ and **Robin, Jean-Marc.** Les représentations implicites des goûts dans les modèles dynamiques de demande. (The Implicit Representation of Tastes in Dynamic Demand Models. With English summary.) *Revue Écon.*, January 1988, *39*(1), pp. 33–55.

Levy, Haim; Barlev, Benzion and Denny, Wanda. Using Accounting Data for Portfolio Management. *J. Portfol. Manage.*, Spring 1988, *14*(3), pp. 70–77.

_____ and **Lerman, Zvi.** Testing the Predictive Power of Ex-Post Efficient Portfolios. *J. Finan. Res.*, Fall 1988, *11*(3), pp. 241–54.

_____; **Rapoport, Amnon and Kroll, Yoram.** Experimental Tests of the Separation Theorem and the Capital Asset Pricing Model. *Amer. Econ. Rev.*, June 1988, *78*(3), pp. 500–519.

Lévy-Leboyer, Maurice. The French Electrical Power System: An Inter-country Comparison.

In *Mayntz, R. and Hughes, T. P., eds.*, 1988, pp. 245–62.

_____. The Quintessential Alfred Chandler. *Bus. Hist. Rev.*, Autumn 1988, *62*(3), pp. 516–21.

Levy, Mickey D. Origins and Effects of the Deficit. In *Boaz, D., ed.*, 1988, pp. 45–69.

Lévy, Pierre. L'histoire inachevée de la préférence pour la liquidité. (The Liquidity Preference Theory: An Unfinished Story. With English summary.) *Écon. Appl.*, 1988, *41*(2), pp. 289–330.

_____. La préférence pour la liquidité: Une théorie générale de la détention des richesses durables. (The Liquidity Preference as a General Theory of Asset Holding. With English summary.) *Écon. Appl.*, 1988, *41*(2), pp. 333–54.

Levy, Santiago. Efectos macroeconómicos del control de precios: Un análisis de equilibrio general a corto plazo. (The Macroeconomic Effects of Price Controls: A Short-run General Equilibrium Analysis. With English summary.) *Estud. Econ.*, Jan.–June 1988, *3*(1), pp. 27–56.

Levy, Shlomit. The Structure of Social Values in Israel. In *Maital, S., ed., Vol. 1*, 1988, pp. 389–402.

Levy, Sidney J. Marketing Research as a Dialogue. In *Maynes, E. S. and ACCI Research Committee, eds.*, 1988, pp. 653–58.

Levy, Victor. Aid and Growth in Sub-Saharan Africa: The Recent Experience. *Europ. Econ. Rev.*, November 1988, *32*(9), pp. 1777–95.

Lewbel, Arthur. An Exactly Aggregable Trigonometric Engel Curve Demand System. *Econometric Rev.*, 1988, *7*(1), pp. 97–102.

_____. Exact Aggregation, Distribution Parameterizations, and a Nonlinear Representative Consumer. In *Rhodes, G. F., Jr. and Fomby, T. B., eds.*, 1988, pp. 253–90.

Lewellen, Wilbur G. and Mauer, David C. Tax Options and Corporate Capital Structures. *J. Finan. Quant. Anal.*, December 1988, *23*(4), pp. 387–400.

_____; **Mauer, David C. and Emery, Douglas R.** Tax-Timing Options, Leverage, and the Choice of Corporate Form. *J. Finan. Res.*, Summer 1988, *11*(2), pp. 99–110.

Lewin, David. Technological Change in the Public Sector: The Case of Sanitation Service. In *Lewin, D., et al., eds.*, 1988, *1987*, pp. 287–319.

_____ **and Bartel, Ann.** Wages and Unionism in the Public Sector: The Case of Police. In *Lewin, D., et al., eds.*, 1988, *1981*, pp. 494–506.

_____ **and Fogel, Walter.** Wage Determination in the Public Sector. In *Lewin, D., et al., eds.*, 1988, *1974*, pp. 447–72.

_____ **and McCormick, Mary.** Coalition Bargaining in Municipal Government: The New York City Experience. In *Lewin, D., et al., eds.*, 1988, *1981*, pp. 170–92.

_____ **and Strauss, George.** Behavioral Research in Industrial Relations: Introduction. *Ind. Relat.*, Winter 1988, *27*(1), pp. 1–6.

_____, **et al.** Productivity Bargaining in New York—What Went Wrong? 1981 Update: The New York City Sanitation Agreement. In *Lewin, D., et al., eds.*, 1988, pp. 239–40.

_____, **et al.** Public Sector Labor Relations: Analysis and Readings: Conclusions and Future Issues. In *Lewin, D., et al., eds.*, 1988, pp. 581–92.

_____, **et al.** Public Sector Labor Relations: Analysis and Readings: Background and Overview. In *Lewin, D., et al., eds.*, 1988, pp. 1–19.

Lewin, Marion Ein and Sullivan, Sean. The Economics and Ethics of Long-Term Care and Disability: Introduction and Overview. In *Sullivan, S. and Lewin, M. E., eds.*, 1988, pp. 1–8.

Lewin, Peter. Political Business Cycles and the Capital Stock: Variations on an Austrian Theme. In *Willett, T. D., ed.*, 1988, pp. 294–97.

Lewington, Paul and Beenstock, Michael. Macroeconomic Policy and Aggregate Supply in the UK. In *Motamen, H., ed.*, 1988, pp. 327–52.

Lewis, Alain A. An Infinite Version of Arrow's Theorem in the Effective Setting. *Math. Soc. Sci.*, August 1988, *16*(1), pp. 41–48.

_____. Lower Bounds on Degrees of Game-Theoretic Structures. *Math. Soc. Sci.*, August 1988, *16*(1), pp. 1–39.

_____ **and Sundaram, Rangarajan.** An Alternate Approach to Axiomatizations of the von Neumann/Morgenstern Characteristic Function. *Math. Soc. Sci.*, April 1988, *15*(2), pp. 145–56.

Lewis, Alan. Some Methods in Psychological Economics. In *Earl, P. E., ed.*, 1988, pp. 189–210.

_____ **and Cullis, John G.** Preferences, Economics and the Economic Psychology of Public Sector Preference Formation. *J. Behav. Econ.*, Spring 1988, *17*(1), pp. 19–33.

Lewis, Alan L. A Simple Algorithm for the Portfolio Selection Problem. *J. Finance*, March 1988, *43*(1), pp. 71–82.

Lewis, Barry L.; Patton, James M. and Green, Sharon L. The Effects of Information Choice and Information Use on Analysts' Predictions of Municipal Bond Rating Changes. *Accounting Rev.*, April 1988, *63*(2), pp. 270–82.

Lewis, Carol W. and Tenzer, Morton J. Community Collaboration: Public–Private Partnerships in Connecticut. In *Hula, R. C., ed.*, 1988, pp. 99–110.

Lewis, Craig M. and Day, Theodore E. The Behavior of the Volatility Implicit in the Prices of Stock Index Options. *J. Finan. Econ.*, October 1988, *22*(1), pp. 103–22.

Lewis, David. Causal Decision Theory. In *Gärdenfors, P. and Sahlin, N.-E., eds.*, 1988, pp. 377–405.

Lewis, Geoffrey W. and Ulph, David T. Poverty, Inequality and Welfare. *Econ. J.*, Supplement, 1988, *98*(390), pp. 117–31.

_____; **Ulph, David T. and Beath, John A.** Policy Targeting in a New Welfare Framework with Poverty. In *Hare, P. G., ed.*, 1988, pp. 161–85.

Lewis, H. Gregg. Union/Nonunion Wage Gaps

in the Public Sector. In *Freeman, R. B. and Ichniowski, C., eds.*, 1988, pp. 169–93.

Lewis, Jacqueline A. Assessing the Effect of the Polytechnic, Wolverhampton on the Local Community. *Urban Stud.*, February 1988, 25(1), pp. 53–61.

_____ and **Armstrong, Kathleen M.** Technological Innovation and Labour Market Adjustments. *Scot. J. Polit. Econ.*, May 1988, 35(2), pp. 162–70.

Lewis, Jim and Williams, Allan M. Portugal: Market Segmentation and Regional Specialisation. In *Williams, A. M. and Shaw, G., eds.*, 1988, pp. 101–22.

Lewis, John P. Strengthening the Poor: Some Lessons for the International Community. In *Lewis, J. P., et al.*, 1988, pp. 3–26.

Lewis, Karen K. Inflation Risk and Asset Market Disturbances: The Mean–Variance Model Revisited. *J. Int. Money Finance*, September 1988, 7(3), pp. 273–88.

_____. The Persistence of the 'Peso Problem' When Policy Is Noisy. *J. Int. Money Finance*, March 1988, 7(1), pp. 5–21.

_____. Testing the Portfolio Balance Model: A Multi-lateral Approach. *J. Int. Econ.*, February 1988, 24(1–2), pp. 109–27.

Lewis, Kenneth A. Estimating the Cost of Equity Capital for Electric Utilities, Market-to-Book Recovery, and the Theory of Regulation: 1969–1984. *Land Econ.*, May 1988, 64(2), pp. 101–13.

Lewis, Mervyn K. Off-Balance Sheet Activities and Financial Innovation in Banking. *Banca Naz. Lavoro Quart. Rev.*, December 1988, (167), pp. 387–410.

_____ and **Davis, Kevin.** The New Australian Monetary Policy. In *Cheng, H.-S., ed.*, 1988, pp. 247–78.

Lewis, Pam and Hall, Graham. Development Agencies and the Supply of Finance to Small Firms. *Appl. Econ.*, December 1988, 20(12), pp. 1675–87.

Lewis, Philip E. T. and Kirby, Michael G. A New Approach to Modelling the Effects of Incomes Policies. *Econ. Letters*, 1988, 28(1), pp. 81–85.

_____, et al. Taxation, Cost of Capital and Investment in Australian Agriculture. *Australian J. Agr. Econ.*, April 1988, 32(1), pp. 15–21.

Lewis, Tracy R. and Brander, James A. Bankruptcy Costs and the Theory of Oligopoly. *Can. J. Econ.*, May 1988, 21(2), pp. 221–43.

_____ and **Brander, James A.** Oligopoly and Financial Structure: The Limited Liability Effect. In *Daughety, A. F., ed.*, 1988, 1986, pp. 421–43.

_____ and **Sappington, David E. M.** Regulating a Monopolist with Unknown Demand. *Amer. Econ. Rev.*, December 1988, 78(5), pp. 986–98.

_____ and **Sappington, David E. M.** Regulating a Monopolist with Unknown Demand and Cost Functions. *Rand J. Econ.*, Autumn 1988, 19(3), pp. 438–57.

Lewis, Verne B. Reflections on Budget Systems. *Public Budg. Finance*, Spring 1988, 8(1), pp. 4–19.

Lewyn, Marc J. and Ponsoldt, James F. Judicial Activism, Economic Theory and the Role of Summary Judgment in Sherman Act Conspiracy Cases: The Illogic of *Matsushita. Antitrust Bull.*, Fall 1988, 33(3), pp. 575–613.

Leyden, Dennis Patrick. Intergovernmental Grants and Successful Tax Limitation Referenda. *Public Choice*, May 1988, 57(2), pp. 141–54.

Li, Chunwen. Some Questions That Need to Be Solved in Developing Individual Businesses. *Chinese Econ. Stud.*, Winter 1987–88, 21(2), pp. 37–40.

Li, Jeanne C.; Ehrenberg, Ronald G. and Rosenberg, Pamela. Part-time Employment in the United States. In *Hart, R. A., ed.*, 1988, pp. 256–81.

_____ and **Foot, David K.** Youth Unemployment: A Reply. *Can. Public Policy*, March 1988, 14(1), pp. 109–11.

Li, Jinyan. Value Added Tax: People's Republic of China. *Bull. Int. Fiscal Doc.*, January 1988, 42(1), pp. 17–22.

Li, S. Neno; Spencer, Byron G. and Denton, Frank T. Health Care in the Economic–Demographic System: Macro-effects of Market Control, Government Intervention, and Population Change. *Southern Econ. J.*, July 1988, 55(1), pp. 37–56.

Li, Y. and Apedaile, L. P. A Simulation of Economic Effects of Technology Transfer in Cereal Production. *Can. J. Agr. Econ.*, November 1988, 36(3), pp. 473–88.

Li, Zheng and Zhang, Jian. P.R.C.'s Price Reform and the Trend in Energy Prices. *Energy J.*, Special Issue, 1988, 9, pp. 45–69.

Liang, Ching-ing Hou and Liang, Kuo-shu. Development Policy Formation and Future Policy Priorities in the Republic of China. *Econ. Develop. Cult. Change*, Supplement, April 1988, 36(3), pp. S67–101.

Liang, Kuo-shu and Liang, Ching-ing Hou. Development Policy Formation and Future Policy Priorities in the Republic of China. *Econ. Develop. Cult. Change*, Supplement, April 1988, 36(3), pp. S67–101.

Liang, Ming-Yih. A Note on Financial Dualism and Interest Rate Policies: A Loanable Funds Approach. *Int. Econ. Rev.*, August 1988, 29(3), pp. 539–49.

Liang, Nellie and Rhoades, Stephen A. Geographic Diversification and Risk in Banking. *J. Econ. Bus.*, November 1988, 40(4), pp. 271–84.

Lianos, T. P. and Rizopoulos, G. Estimation of Social Welfare Weights in Agricultural Policy: The Case of Greek Cotton. *J. Agr. Econ.*, January 1988, 39(1), pp. 61–68.

Libby, Lawrence W. Southern Farms and Rural Communities: Developing Directions for Economic Development Research and Policy: Discussion. *Southern J. Agr. Econ.*, July 1988, 20(1), pp. 29–32.

Lichtblau, John H. Oil Import Dependency and

Crises. In *Fried, E. R. and Blandin, N. M.*, eds., 1988, pp. 35–39.

Lichtenberg, Erik; Parker, Douglas D. and Zilberman, David. Marginal Analysis of Welfare Costs of Environmental Policies: The Case of Pesticide Regulation. *Amer. J. Agr. Econ.*, November 1988, *70*(4), pp. 867–74.

——— **and Zilberman, David.** Efficient Regulation of Environmental Health Risks. *Quart. J. Econ.*, February 1988, *103*(1), pp. 167–78.

Lichtenberg, Frank R. Estimation of the Internal Adjustment Costs Model Using Longitudinal Establishment Data. *Rev. Econ. Statist.*, August 1988, *70*(3), pp. 421–30.

———. The Private R&D Investment Response to Federal Design and Technical Competitions. *Amer. Econ. Rev.*, June 1988, *78*(3), pp. 550–59.

Lichtenstein, Donald R.; Bloch, Peter H. and Black, William C. Correlates of Price Acceptability. *J. Cons. Res.*, September 1988, *15*(2), pp. 243–52.

Lichtenstein, Peter M. Toward a Classical Reconstruction of the Economic Theory of Self-Management. In *Jones, D. C. and Svejnar, J.*, eds., 1988, pp. 107–32.

Lichtenstein, Sarah; Fischhoff, Baruch and Slovic, Paul. Knowing What You Want: Measuring Labile Values. In *Bell, D. E.; Raiffa, H. and Tversky, A.*, eds., 1988, *1980*, pp. 398–421.

———; **Slovic, Paul and Fischhoff, Baruch.** Response Mode, Framing, and Information-Processing Effects in Risk Assessment. In *Bell, D. E.; Raiffa, H. and Tversky, A.*, eds., 1988, *1982*, pp. 152–66.

Lichtenthal, J. David. Group Decision Making in Organizational Buying: A Role Structure Approach. In *Woodside, A. G.*, ed., 1988, pp. 119–57.

Lichter, Daniel T. Race and Underemployment: Black Employment Hardship in the Rural South. In *Beaulieu, L. J.*, ed., 1988, pp. 181–97.

———; **Fuguitt, Glenn V. and Heaton, Tim B.** Monitoring the Metropolitanization Process. *Demography*, February 1988, *25*(1), pp. 115–28.

Lichty, Richard W.; Lim, Kai H. and O'Brien, A. Maureen. An Analysis of Labor Productivity Effects on Regional Growth. *Reg. Sci. Persp.*, 1988, *18*(1), pp. 43–57.

Liddle, Roger F. and Monahan, John F. A Stationary Stochastic Approximation Method. *J. Econometrics*, May–June 1988, *38*(1–2), pp. 91–102.

Lidström, Per; Lyttkens, Carl Hampus and Vedovato, Claudio. Military Expenditures in Developing Countries: A Comment on Deger and Sen [Military Expenditure, Spin-Off and Economic Development]. *J. Devel. Econ.*, February 1988, *28*(1), pp. 105–10.

Liebhafsky, H. H. An Institutionalist Evaluation of the Recent *Apparently*, but only *Apparently* Fatal Attack on Institutionalism [The Institutionalist and *On the Origin of Species:* A Case

of Mistaken Identity]. *J. Econ. Issues*, September 1988, *22*(3), pp. 837–51.

———. Commons and Clark on Law and Economics. In *Samuels, W. J.*, ed., Vol. 2, 1988, *1976*, pp. 239–52.

———. Law and Economics from Different Perspectives. In *Tool, M. R.*, ed., Vol. 2, 1988, *1987*, pp. 391–418.

Liebowitz, S. J. Price Differentials and Price Discrimination: Reply and Extensions. *Econ. Inquiry*, October 1988, *26*(4), pp. 779–83.

Liefert, William Mark. The Full Cost of Soviet Oil and Natural Gas Production. *Comp. Econ. Stud.*, Summer 1988, *30*(2), pp. 1–20.

Lien, Da-Hsiang Donald. Appropriate Scientific Research and Brain Drain: A Simple Model. *J. Devel. Econ.*, July 1988, *29*(1), pp. 77–87.

———. Coalitions in Competitive Bribery Games. *Math. Soc. Sci.*, April 1988, *15*(2), pp. 189–96.

———. Hedger Response to Multiple Grades of Delivery on Futures Markets. *J. Futures Markets*, December 1988, *8*(6), pp. 687–702.

——— **and Rearden, David.** Missing Measurements in Limited Dependent Variable Models. *Econ. Letters*, 1988, *26*(1), pp. 33–36.

Liepmann, Peter and Biehler, Hermann. Personelle Verbindungen und intersektorale Finanzbeziehungen zwischen den grössten deutschen. (Interlocking Directorates and Intersectoral Financial Relations between Large-scale Enterprises in Germany. With English summary.) *Jahr. Nationalökon. Statist.*, January 1988, *204*(1), pp. 48–68.

Liew, Chong K. and Liew, Chung J. A Comparative Study of Household Interactive Variable Input–Output (HIVIO) Model and the Conventional Input–Output Models. *J. Urban Econ.*, July 1988, *24*(1), pp. 64–84.

——— **and Liew, Chung J.** Measuring the Effect of Cost Variation on Industrial Outputs. *J. Reg. Sci.*, November 1988, *28*(4), pp. 563–78.

Liew, Chung J. and Liew, Chong K. A Comparative Study of Household Interactive Variable Input–Output (HIVIO) Model and the Conventional Input–Output Models. *J. Urban Econ.*, July 1988, *24*(1), pp. 64–84.

——— **and Liew, Chong K.** Measuring the Effect of Cost Variation on Industrial Outputs. *J. Reg. Sci.*, November 1988, *28*(4), pp. 563–78.

Light, Walter. How the Workplace Has Changed in 75 Years. *Mon. Lab. Rev.*, February 1988, *111*(2), pp. 19–25.

Lilien, David M.; Wadhwa, Wilima and Fry, Maxwell J. Monetary Policy in Pacific Basin Developing Countries. In *Cheng, H.-S.*, ed., 1988, pp. 153–70.

Lilien, Gary L. and Yoon, Eunsang. An Exploratory Analysis of the Dynamic Behavior of Price Elasticity over the Product Life Cycle: An Empirical Analysis of Industrial Chemical Products. In *Devinney, T. M.*, ed., 1988, pp. 261–87.

———; **Yoon, Eunsang and Choffray, Jean-Marie.** New Industrial Product Performance:

Models and Empirical Analysis. In *Woodside, A. G., ed.*, 1988, pp. 49–77.

Lilien, Steven; Mellman, Martin and Pastena, Victor. Accounting Changes: Successful versus Unsuccessful Firms. *Accounting Rev.*, October 1988, 63(4), pp. 642–56.

Liljeblom, Eva and Berglund, Tom. Market Serial Correlation on a Small Security Market: A Note. *J. Finance*, December 1988, 43(5), pp. 1265–74.

Lilley, William, III. The Competitiveness Issue. In *Walker, C. E. and Bloomfield, M. A., eds.*, 1988, pp. 179–80.

Lim, David. Export Instability and Economic Growth in Resource-Rich Countries. In *Urrutia, M. and Yukawa, S., eds. (II)*, 1988, pp. 66–89.

———. Tax Effort and Expenditure Policy in Resource-Rich Countries. In *Urrutia, M. and Yukawa, S., eds. (II)*, 1988, pp. 128–53.

Lim, G. C. and Harper, Ian R. Financial Implications of the Commonwealth Budget Surplus. *Australian Econ. Rev.*, Summer 1988, (84), pp. 19–25.

Lim, Hank and Wong, John. The Changing Role of Singapore in the Trading and Processing of Mineral Resources. In *McKern, B. and Koomsup, P., eds.*, 1988, pp. 290–309.

Lim, Jeen-Su and Olshavsky, Richard W. Impacts of Consumers' Familiarity and Product Class on Price–Quality Inference and Product Evaluations. *Quart. J. Bus. Econ.*, Summer 1988, 27(3), pp. 130–46.

Lim, Kai H.; O'Brien, A. Maureen and Lichty, Richard W. An Analysis of Labor Productivity Effects on Regional Growth. *Reg. Sci. Persp.*, 1988, 18(1), pp. 43–57.

Lim, Youngil. An Empirical Study of Disequilibrium in North–South Trade: Discussion. In *Currie, D. and Vines, D., eds.*, 1988, pp. 209–13.

Limam, Mohamed M. T. and Thomas, David R. Simultaneous Tolerance Intervals for the Linear Regression Model. *J. Amer. Statist. Assoc.*, September 1988, 83(403), pp. 801–04.

Limb, Melanie; Burgess, Jacquelin and Harrison, Carolyn M. People, Parks and the Urban Green: A Study of Popular Meanings and Values for Open Spaces in the City. *Urban Stud.*, December 1988, 25(6), pp. 455–73.

———; **Harrison, Carolyn M. and Burgess, Jacquelin.** Exploring Environmental Values Through the Medium of Small Groups: 2. Illustrations of a Group at Work. *Environ. Planning A*, April 1988, 20(4), pp. 457–76.

———; **Harrison, Carolyn M. and Burgess, Jacquelin.** Exploring Environmental Values through the Medium of Small Groups: 1. Theory and Practice. *Environ. Planning A*, March 1988, 20(3), pp. 309–26.

Limerick, Patrick. The Big Bang: Integration of Financial Markets. In *Mikdashi, Z., ed.*, 1988, pp. 61–71.

Lin, Biing-Hwan and Herrmann, Mark. The Demand and Supply of Norwegian Atlantic Salmon in the United States and the European

Community. *Can. J. Agr. Econ.*, November 1988, 36(3), pp. 459–71.

Lin, Ching-yuan. East Asia and Latin America as Contrasting Models. *Econ. Develop. Cult. Change*, Supplement, April 1988, 36(3), pp. S153–97.

Lin, Cyril Zhiren. China's Economic Reforms II: Western Perspectives. *Asian-Pacific Econ. Lit.*, March 1988, 2(1), pp. 1–25.

Lin, Jian Hai and Grub, Phillip D. Foreign Investment in China: Myths and Realities. *J. Econ. Devel.*, December 1988, 13(2), pp. 17–40.

Lin, Justin Yifu. The Household Responsibility System in China's Agricultural Reform: A Theoretical and Empirical Study. *Econ. Develop. Cult. Change*, Supplement, April 1988, 36(3), pp. S199–224.

Lin, Kuan-Pin. Revealed Preference Theory and Logic Programming. *Econ. Computat. Cybern. Stud. Res.*, 1988, 23(2), pp. 65–73.

Lin, Winston T. The Dynamic Behavior of Production in the Extractive Industry. *Resources & Energy*, September 1988, 10(3), pp. 225–46.

———. Regional Residential Natural Gas Demand: Reply. *Resources & Energy*, December 1988, 10(4), pp. 393–94.

Lin, Y. Joseph. Oligopoly and Vertical Integration: Note. *Amer. Econ. Rev.*, March 1988, 78(1), pp. 251–54.

———. Price Matching in a Model of Equilibrium Price Dispersion. *Southern Econ. J.*, July 1988, 55(1), pp. 57–69.

Lince, Guillermo Maldonado. The Challenges Facing Latin America in the World Today. *CEPAL Rev.*, April 1988, (34), pp. 63–76.

Lincoln, David. Employment Practices, Sugar Technology, and Sugar Mill Labour: Crisis and Change in the South African Sugar Industry, 1914–1939. In *Albert, B. and Graves, A., eds.*, 1988, pp. 221–33.

Lincoln, James R. and Kalleberg, Arne L. The Structure of Earnings Inequality in the United States and Japan. In *Winship, C. and Rosen, S., eds.*, 1988, pp. 121–53.

Lind, Robert C. and Arrow, Kenneth J. Uncertainty and the Evaluation of Public Investment Decisions. In *Ricketts, M., ed., Vol. 2*, 1988, 1970, pp. 211–25.

Linda, Remo. The Food and Drinks Industry: Large Firm Strategies. In *de Jong, H. W., ed.*, 1988, pp. 127–56.

Lindauer, David L.; Meesook, Oey Astra and Suebsaeng, Parita. Government Wage Policy in Africa: Some Findings and Policy Issues. *World Bank Res. Observer*, January 1988, 3(1), pp. 1–25.

Lindbeck, Assar. Consequences of the Advanced Welfare State. *World Econ.*, March 1988, 11(1), pp. 19–37.

———. Individual Freedom and Welfare State Policy. *Europ. Econ. Rev.*, March 1988, 32(2–3), pp. 295–318.

——— **and Snower, Dennis J.** Cooperation, Harassment, and Involuntary Unemployment: An

Insider–Outsider Approach. *Amer. Econ. Rev.*, March 1988, 78(1), pp. 167–88.

_____ and Snower, Dennis J. Job Security, Work Incentives and Unemployment. *Scand. J. Econ.*, 1988, 90(4), pp. 453–74.

_____ and Snower, Dennis J. Long-term Unemployment and Macroeconomic Policy. *Amer. Econ. Rev.*, May 1988, 78(2), pp. 38–43.

_____ and Snower, Dennis J. Union Activity, Unemployment Persistence and Wage-Employment Ratchets. In *Cross, R., ed.*, 1988, pp. 117–28.

_____ and Weibull, Jörgen W. Altruism and Time Consistency: The Economics of Fait Accompli. *J. Polit. Econ.*, December 1988, 96(6), pp. 1165–82.

_____ and Weibull, Jörgen W. Welfare Effects of Alternative Forms of Public Spending. *Europ. Econ. Rev.*, January 1988, 32(1), pp. 101–27.

Lindblom, Charles E. American Politics since 1970. In *Lindblom, C. E.*, 1988, 1982, pp. 101–13.

_____. Another State of Mind. In *Lindblom, C. E.*, 1988, 1982, pp. 279–304.

_____. Bargaining: The Hidden Hand in Government. In *Lindblom, C. E.*, 1988, 1955, pp. 139–70.

_____. Changing Views on Conflict between Freedom and Equality. In *Lindblom, C. E.*, 1988, 1980, pp. 95–99.

_____. Democracy and Economic Structure. In *Lindblom, C. E.*, 1988, 1962, pp. 25–66.

_____. Democracy and Market System: Introduction. In *Lindblom, C. E.*, 1988, pp. 9–21.

_____. Democracy and the Economy. In *Lindblom, C. E.*, 1988, 1983, pp. 115–35.

_____. Democratization in the U. S. and Its Problems. In *Lindblom, C. E.*, 1988, 1980, pp. 83–94.

_____. Integration of Economics and the Other Social Sciences through Policy Analysis. In *Lindblom, C. E.*, 1988, 1972, pp. 263–77.

_____. New Decision-Making Procedures Governing Research on and Treatment of Catastrophic Diseases. In *Lindblom, C. E.*, 1988, 1970, pp. 213–36.

_____. The Rediscovery of the Market. In *Lindblom, C. E.*, 1988, 1966, pp. 67–82.

_____. The Science of "Muddling Through" In *Lindblom, C. E.*, 1988, 1959, pp. 171–90.

_____. Still Muddling, Not Yet Through. In *Lindblom, C. E.*, 1988, 1979, pp. 237–59.

_____. Who Needs What Social Research for Policy Making? In *Lindblom, C. E.*, 1988, 1984, pp. 305–35.

_____ and Hirschman, Albert O. Economic Development, Research and Development, Policy Making: Some Converging Views. In *Lindblom, C. E.*, 1988, 1962, pp. 191–211.

van der Linde, J. G. and Lefeber, R. International Energy Agency Captures the Development of European Community Energy Law. *J. World Trade*, October 1988, 22(5), pp. 5–25.

van der Linden, J. T. J. M. Economic Thought

in the Netherlands: The Contribution of Professor Jan Tinbergen. *Rev. Soc. Econ.*, December 1988, 46(3), pp. 270–82.

_____ and de Wolff, P. Jan Tinbergen: A Quantitative Economist. *Rev. Soc. Econ.*, December 1988, 46(3), pp. 312–25.

Lindenberg, Marc. Central America: Crisis and Economic Strategy 1930–1985, Lessons from History. *J. Devel. Areas*, January 1988, 22(2), pp. 155–77.

_____. Central America's Elusive Economic Recovery. *World Devel.*, February 1988, 16(2), pp. 237–54.

Lindenberg, Siegwart. Contractual Relations and Weak Solidarity: The Behavioral Basis of Restraints on Gain-Maximization. *J. Inst. Theoretical Econ.*, February 1988, 144(1), pp. 39–58.

Linder, Jane C. Computers, Corporate Culture and Change. In *Timpe, A. D., ed.*, 1988, 1985, pp. 195–206.

Linder, Stephen H. Managing Support for Social Research and Development: Research Goals, Risk, and Policy Instruments. *J. Policy Anal. Manage.*, Fall 1988, 7(4), pp. 621–42.

Lindgren, Björn. Krankenhausfinanzierung in Selbstverwaltung: Comments from a Swedish Perspective. *J. Inst. Theoretical Econ.*, April 1988, 144(2), pp. 427–31.

Lindley, Robert M. Women and Paid Work: Issues of Equality: Foreword. In *Hunt, A., ed.*, 1988, pp. xii–xiii.

Lindqvist, Lars-Johan; Paltschik, Mikael and Sevón, Guje. Consumers' and Producers' Basic Evaluation—An Investigation of Objects in the Field of Music. *Liiketaloudellinen Aikak.*, 1988, 37(3), pp. 193–211.

Lindsay, Cotton M. and Maloney, Michael T. A Model and Some Evidence Concerning the Influence of Discrimination on Wages. *Econ. Inquiry*, October 1988, 26(4), pp. 645–60.

_____ and Maloney, Michael T. Party Politics and the Price of Payola. *Econ. Inquiry*, April 1988, 26(2), pp. 203–21.

Lindsay, Robert V. Direct Investment into the United States. In *Feldstein, M., ed. (II)*, 1988, pp. 550–57.

Lindsey, C. Robin and Coyte, Peter C. Spatial Monopoly and Spatial Monopolistic Competition with Two-Part Pricing. *Economica*, November 1988, 55(220), pp. 461–77.

Lindsey, Lawrence B. Did ERTA Raise the Share of Taxes Paid by Upper-Income Taxpayers? Will TRA86 Be a Retreat? In *Summers, L. H., ed.*, 1988, pp. 131–60.

_____. Federal Deductibility of State and Local Taxes: A Test of Public Choice by Representative Government. In *Rosen, H. S., ed.*, 1988, pp. 137–75.

_____. Supply Side Lessons for Reducing the Deficit. *Bus. Econ.*, October 1988, 23(4), pp. 13–18.

Lindsey, Phoebe and Newhouse, Joseph P. Do Second Opinion Programs Improve Outcomes? *J. Health Econ.*, September 1988, 7(3), pp. 285–88.

Lindström, Anders. New Directions in Swedish Management. **In** *Rosow, J. M., ed.*, 1988, pp. 177–98.

Lindstrom, Mary J. and Bates, Douglas M. Newton–Raphson and EM Algorithms for Linear Mixed-Effects Models for Repeated-Measures Data. *J. Amer. Statist. Assoc.*, December 1988, *83*(404), pp. 1014–22.

Ling, David C. and Follain, James R. Another Look at Tenure Choice, Inflation, and Taxes. *Amer. Real Estate Urban Econ. Assoc. J.*, Fall 1988, *16*(3), pp. 207–29.

_____ **and Smith, Marc T.** Another Look at Mortgage Revenue Bonds [The Efficiency and Distribution of Mortgage Revenue Bond Subsidies: The Effects of Behavioral Responses]. *J. Policy Anal. Manage.*, Spring 1988, *7*(3), pp. 562–64.

Lingen, Cai. Efficient Conjunctive Use of Surface and Groundwater in the People's Victory Canal. **In** *O'Mara, G. T., ed.*, 1988, pp. 84–86.

Linger, Juyne and Choate, Pat. Meeting the Technology Challenge: Toward a U.S. Agenda. **In** *Yochelson, J., ed.*, 1988, pp. 19–32.

Link, Albert N.; Seaks, Terry G. and Woodbery, Sabrina R. Firm Size and R&D Spending: Testing for Functional Form. *Southern Econ. J.*, April 1988, *54*(4), pp. 1027–32.

Link, Charles R. Returns to Nursing Education: 1970–84. *J. Human Res.*, Summer 1988, *23*(3), pp. 372–87.

Linke, Charles M. and Bryan, William R. Estimating Present Value of Future Earnings: Experience with Dedicated Portfolios. *J. Risk Ins.*, June 1988, *55*(2), pp. 273–86.

_____ **and Bryan, William R.** The Estimation of the Age/Earnings Profiles in Wrongful Death and Injury Cases: Comment. *J. Risk Ins.*, March 1988, *55*(1), pp. 168–73.

Linke, Erich. International Trade and the Consumer: Report on an OECD Symposium. **In** *Maynes, E. S. and ACCI Research Committee, eds.*, 1988, pp. 364–70.

Linke, W. The Headship Rate Approach in Modelling Households: The Case of the Federal Republic of Germany. **In** *Keilman, N.; Kuijsten, A. and Vossen, A., eds.*, 1988, pp. 108–22.

Linn, Johannes F. and Gray, Cheryl W. Improving Public Finance for Development. *Finance Develop.*, September 1988, *25*(3), pp. 2–5.

Linn, Scott C. and Lockwood, Larry J. Short-term Stock Price Patterns: NYSE, AMEX, OTC. *J. Portfol. Manage.*, Winter 1988, *14*(2), pp. 30–34.

_____ **and Pinegar, J. Michael.** The Effect of Issuing Preferred Stock on Common and Preferred Stockholder Wealth. *J. Finan. Econ.*, October 1988, *22*(1), pp. 155–84.

Linnakangas, Esko. Recognition of Foreign Enterprises as Taxable Entities: Finland. **In** *International Fiscal Association, ed. (I)*, 1988, pp. 399–410.

Linneman, Peter. The Effects of Consumer Safety Standards: The 1973 Mattress Flammability

Standard. **In** *Stigler, G. J., ed.*, 1988, *1980*, pp. 441–60.

Linnemann, Hans. Population Growth and Food: Some Comments. **In** *Lee, R. D., et al., eds.*, 1988, pp. 40–47.

_____ **and van Beers, Cees.** Measures of Export–Import Similarity, and the Linder Hypothesis Once Again. *Weltwirtsch. Arch.*, 1988, *124*(3), pp. 445–57.

Linowes, David F. Effective Public Policy and Government Management: The Accountant's Role. **In** *Chan, J. L. and Jones, R. H., eds.*, 1988, pp. 186–97.

Linsenmayer, Tadd. U.S. Ends ILO Moratorium by Ratifying Two Conventions. *Mon. Lab. Rev.*, June 1988, *111*(6), pp. 52–53.

Linz, Susan J. The Impact of Soviet Economic Reform: Evidence from the Soviet Interview Project. **In** *Linz, S. J. and Moskoff, W., eds.*, 1988, pp. 129–46.

_____. Management's Response to Tautness in Soviet Planning: Evidence from the Soviet Interview Project. *Comp. Econ. Stud.*, Spring 1988, *30*(1), pp. 65–103.

_____ **and Moskoff, William.** Reorganization and Reform in the Soviet Economy: Introduction. **In** *Linz, S. J. and Moskoff, W., eds.*, 1988, pp. vii–x.

Liossatos, Panagis. A Note on the Kurabayashi/ Sakuma Concept of International Prices for the International Comparison of Real GDP. **In** *Salazar-Carrillo, J. and Rao, D. S. P., eds.*, 1988, pp. 59–66.

Lipartito, Kenneth. Getting Down to Cases: Baker & Botts and the Texas Railroad Commission. **In** *Perkins, E. J., ed.*, 1988, pp. 27–36.

Lipietz, Alan. The L K.imits of Bank Nationalisation in France. **In** *Harris, L., et al., eds.*, 1988, pp. 389–402.

Lipiński, Jan. Problems of Controlling Markets and Resource Allocation in Conditions of Excess Demand: The Polish Case. **In** *Saunders, C. T., ed.*, 1988, pp. 231–53.

Lippi, Marco. On the Dynamic Shape of Aggrated Error Correction Models. *J. Econ. Dynam. Control*, June–Sept. 1988, *12*(2–3), pp. 561–85.

_____. On the Dynamics of Aggregate Macroequations: From Simple Microbehaviors to Complex Macrorelationships. **In** *Dosi, G., et al., eds.*, 1988, pp. 170–96.

Lippit, Victor D. Class Structure, Modes of Production and Economic Development. *Rev. Radical Polit. Econ.*, Summer–Fall 1988, *20*(2–3), pp. 18–24.

Lippman, Steven A. and McCardle, Kevin F. Preemption in R&D Races. *Europ. Econ. Rev.*, October 1988, *32*(8), pp. 1661–69.

Lipset, Seymour Martin. Vote for the Other Guy: The Counterintuitive Character of Recent U.S. Politics. **In** *Anderson, A. and Bark, D. L., eds.*, 1988, pp. 401–11.

Lipsey, Richard G. Global Imbalances and American Trade Policy. *Atlantic Econ. J.*, June 1988, *16*(2), pp. 1–11.

_____. The Understanding and Control of Inflation: Is There a Crisis in Macro-economics? In *Shaw, G. K., ed., Vol. 2*, 1988, *1981*, pp. 175–206.

———— and Lancaster, Kelvin J. The General Theory of Second Best. In *Ricketts, M., ed., Vol. 2*, 1988, *1956*, pp. 121–42.

Lipsey, Robert E. Changing Patterns of International Investment in and by the United States. In *Feldstein, M., ed. (II)*, 1988, pp. 475–545.

———— and Kravis, Irving B. National Price Levels and the Prices of Tradables and Nontradables. *Amer. Econ. Rev.*, May 1988, *78*(2), pp. 474–78.

————; Kulchycky, Ksenia and Blomström, Magnus. U.S. and Swedish Direct Investment and Exports. In *Baldwin, R. E., ed. (II)*, 1988, pp. 259–97.

Lipson, Charles. The International Organization of Third World Debt. In *Bates, R. H., ed.*, 1988, *1981*, pp. 12–46.

Lipton, Michael. The Place of Agricultural Research in the Development of Sub-Saharan Africa. *World Devel.*, October 1988, *16*(10), pp. 1231–57.

Lipumba, Nguyuru, et al. A Supply Constrained Macroeconometric Model of Tanzania. *Econ. Modelling*, October 1988, *5*(4), pp. 354–76.

Liroff, Richard A. EPA's Bubble Policy: The Theory of Marketable Pollution Permits Confronts Reality. In *Hula, R. C., ed.*, 1988, pp. 242–61.

Liski, Erkki P. and Nummi, Tapio. Comparing Sensitivity of Models to Missing Data in the GMANOVA. In *Edwards, D. and Raun, N. E., eds.*, 1988, pp. 311–16.

Litan, Robert E. Reuniting Investment and Commercial Banking. In *England, C. and Huertas, T., eds.*, 1988, pp. 269–87.

————. Reuniting Investment and Commercial Banking. *Cato J.*, Winter 1988, *7*(3), pp. 803–21.

————. The Risks of Recession. In *Litan, R. E; Lawrence, R. Z. and Schultze, C. L., eds.*, 1988, pp. 66–107.

————; Lawrence, Robert Z. and Schultze, Charles L. American Living Standards: Threats and Challenges: Introduction. In *Litan, R. E; Lawrence, R. Z. and Schultze, C. L., eds.*, 1988, pp. 1–22.

————; Swire, Peter and Winston, Clifford. The U.S. Liability System: Background and Trends. In *Litan, R. E. and Winston, C., eds.*, 1988, pp. 1–15.

———— and Winston, Clifford. Policy Options. In *Litan, R. E. and Winston, C., eds.*, 1988, pp. 223–41.

Litaor, M. Iggy. Review of Soil Solution Samplers. *Water Resources Res.*, May 1988, *24*(5), pp. 727–33.

Litman, Barry. Microeconomic Foundations. In *Picard, R. G., et al., eds.*, 1988, pp. 3–34.

Little, I. M. D. The Macro-economic Effects of Foreign Aid: Issues and Evidence: Comment. In *Jepma, C. J., ed.*, 1988, pp. 204–06.

Little, Jane Sneddon. At Stake in the U.S.–Canada Free Trade Agreement: Modest Gains or a Significant Setback. *New Eng. Econ. Rev.*, May–June 1988, pp. 3–20.

————. Foreign Investment in the United States: A Cause for Concern? *New Eng. Econ. Rev.*, July–Aug. 1988, pp. 51–58.

Little, Jo; Peake, Linda and Richardson, Pat. Geography and Gender in the Urban Environment: Introduction. In *Little, J.; Peake, L. and Richardson, P., eds.*, 1988, pp. 1–20.

Little, Peter D. Irrigation Associations among Pastoralists: Some Organizational and Theoretical Considerations from Northern Kenya. In *Attwood, D. W. and Baviskar, B. S., eds.*, 1988, pp. 309–29.

Little, Roderick J. A. Missing-Data Adjustments in Large Surveys. *J. Bus. Econ. Statist.*, July 1988, *6*(3), pp. 287–96.

————. Missing-Data Adjustments in Large Surveys: Reply. *J. Bus. Econ. Statist.*, July 1988, *6*(3), pp. 300–301.

Littlechild, Stephen C. Controls on Advertising: An Examination of Some Economic Arguments. In *Earl, P. E., ed., Vol. 2*, 1988, *1982*, pp. 298–310.

————. Economic Regulation of Privatised Water Authorities and Some Further Reflections. *Oxford Rev. Econ. Policy*, Summer 1988, *4*(2), pp. 40–68.

———— and Beesley, Michael. Privatization: Principles, Problems and Priorities. In *Johnson, C., ed.*, 1988, *1983*, pp. 11–29.

Littlejohn, Gary. Central Planning and Market Relations in Socialist Societies. *J. Devel. Stud.*, July 1988, *24*(4), pp. 75–101.

Littler, Craig R. Technology, Innovation and Labour–Management Strategies. In *Urabe, K.; Child, J. and Kagono, T., eds.*, 1988, pp. 337–58.

Litvak, Isaiah A. Small Business, Competition and Freer Trade: The Canadian–U.S. Case. *J. World Trade*, February 1988, *22*(1), pp. 33–46.

Litzenberger, Robert H. and Barclay, Michael J. Announcement Effects of New Equity Issues and the Use of Intraday Price Data. *J. Finan. Econ.*, May 1988, *21*(1), pp. 71–99.

Liu, Ben-chieh and Lee, Maw Lin. Measuring Socioeconomic Effects When Using Income as Quality of Life Indicator. *Amer. J. Econ. Soc.*, April 1988, *47*(2), pp. 167–75.

Liu, Chwen-chi; Ulveling, Edwin F. and Hsu, Yu-sheng. Predictive Power of Weekly Money Stock Announcements. *Econ. Letters*, 1988, *26*(2), pp. 159–64.

Liu, Dawei and Wang, Qiang. Survey Report on the "Difficulty in Recruiting Labor" in Beijing Municipality. *Chinese Econ. Stud.*, Summer 1988, *21*(4), pp. 45–64.

Liu, Donald J. and Forker, Olan D. Generic Fluid Milk Advertising, Demand Expansion, and Supply Response: The Case of New York City. *Amer. J. Agr. Econ.*, May 1988, *70*(2), pp. 229–36.

————; Kaiser, Harry M. and Streeter, Deborah H. Price versus Stock Effect Policies for Reducing Excess Milk Production. *Western J. Agr. Econ.*, December 1988, *13*(2), pp. 277–84.

_____; **Kaiser, Harry M.** and **Streeter, Deborah H.** Welfare Comparisons of U.S. Dairy Policies with and without Mandatory Supply Control. *Amer. J. Agr. Econ.*, November 1988, *70*(4), pp. 848–58.

Liu, H.-L. Two-Sector Nonmonocentric Urban Land-Use Model with Variable Density. *Environ. Planning A*, April 1988, *20*(4), pp. 477–88.

Liu, Jin-Tan; Butler, J. S. and **Quddus, Munir.** Variability of Inflation and the Dispersion of Relative Prices: Evidence from the Chinese Hyperinflation of 1946–1949. *Econ. Letters*, 1988, *27*(3), pp. 239–44.

Liu, Jung-chao; Shih, Jun-ji and **Mai, Chao-cheng.** A General Analysis of the Output Effect under Third-Degree Price Discrimination. *Econ. J.*, March 1988, *98*(389), pp. 149–58.

Liu, Pak-Wai and **Wong, Yue-Chim.** The Distribution of Benefits among Public Housing Tenants in Hong Kong and Related Policy Issues. *J. Urban Econ.*, January 1988, *23*(1), pp. 1–20.

Liu, Pu. The Relationships between Absolute and Relative Risk Aversion—A Note. *Atlantic Econ. J.*, December 1988, *16*(4), pp. 77–78.

_____ and **Thakor, Anjan V.** Interest Yields, Credit Ratings, and Economic Characteristics of State Bonds: Reply. *J. Money, Credit, Banking*, November 1988, *20*(4), pp. 696–97.

Livernois, John R. Estimates of Marginal Discovery Costs for Oil and Gas. *Can. J. Econ.*, May 1988, *21*(2), pp. 379–93.

Liviatan, Nissan. Inflation Stabilization: Israel: Comment. In *Bruno, M., et al., eds.*, 1988, pp. 98–102.

_____. On the Interaction between Monetary and Fiscal Policies under Perfect Foresight. *Oxford Econ. Pap.*, March 1988, *40*(1), pp. 193–203.

_____ and **Kiguel, Miguel A.** Inflationary Rigidities and Orthodox Stabilization Policies: Lessons from Latin America. *World Bank Econ. Rev.*, September 1988, *2*(3), pp. 273–98.

Livingston, Felix R. Constitutional Jurisprudence and Economic Efficiency. In *Association of Private Education*, 1988, pp. 14–23.

Livne, Zvi A. The Bargaining Problem with an Uncertain Conflict Outcome. *Math. Soc. Sci.*, June 1988, *15*(3), pp. 287–302.

Ljung, Per and **Basu, D. N.** Irrigation Management and Scheduling: Study of an Irrigation System in India. In *O'Mara, G. T., ed.*, 1988, pp. 178–94.

Ljungh, Claes. World Tax Reform: A Progress Report: Sweden. In *Pechman, J. A., ed.*, 1988, pp. 187–211.

Ljungqvist, Lars and **Christiano, Lawrence J.** Money Does Granger-Cause Output in the Bivariate Money–Output Relation. *J. Monet. Econ.*, September 1988, *22*(2), pp. 217–35.

_____, **et al.** The Convergence of Multivariate 'Unit Root' Distributions to Their Asymptotic Limits: The Case of Money–Income Causality.

J. Econ. Dynam. Control, June–Sept. 1988, *12*(2–3), pp. 489–502.

Llewellyn, David T. Integration of European Financial Markets: Implications for Banking. *Rev. Econ. Cond. Italy*, Sept.–Dec. 1988, (3), pp. 303–31.

_____ and **Tew, Brian.** The Sterling Money Market and the Determination of Interest Rates. *Nat. Westminster Bank Quart. Rev.*, May 1988, pp. 25–37.

Lloyd, A. G. The Importance of Agriculture: What Hope for Agriculture, and What Needs Doing? *Rev. Marketing Agr. Econ.*, April 1988, *56*(1), pp. 129–34.

Lloyd, Peter J. An Economic Approach to the Design of AIDS Policies. In *Smith, C. S., ed.*, 1988, pp. 206–25.

_____ and **Schweinberger, Albert G.** Trade Expenditure Functions and the Gains from Trade. *J. Int. Econ.*, May 1988, *24*(3–4), pp. 275–97.

Lloyd, William P.; Page, Daniel E. and **Jahera, John S., Jr.** Does Business Diversification Affect Performance?: Some Further Evidence. *Quart. J. Bus. Econ.*, Winter 1988, *27*(1), pp. 130–47.

Loasby, Brian J. Making Location Policy Work. In *Earl, P. E., ed., Vol. 2*, 1988, *1967*, pp. 264–77.

_____. Management Economics and the Theory of the Firm. In *Earl, P. E., ed., Vol. 1*, 1988, *1967*, pp. 461–72.

_____. Managerial Decision Processes. In *Earl, P. E., ed., Vol. 1*, 1988, *1967*, pp. 353–65.

Lobdell, Richard A. Women in the Jamaican Labour Force, 1881–1921. *Soc. Econ. Stud.*, March–June 1988, *37*(1–2), pp. 203–40.

Lobez, Frédéric. Le rationnement du crédit: une synthèse. (Credit Rationing: A Survey. With English summary.) *Finance*, December 1988, *9*(2), pp. 57–89.

Locay, Luis. Medical Doctors: Determinants of Location. In *Zschock, D. K., ed.*, 1988, pp. 133–63.

Locker, H. Krijnse; Gerardi, D. and **Avdoulos, A.** Some Experiments with Phase IV ICP-Data. In *Salazar-Carrillo, J.* and *Rao, D. S. P., eds.*, 1988, pp. 93–112.

Lockett, Martin. The Urban Collective Economy. In *Feuchtwang, S.; Hussain, A.* and *Pairault, T., eds., Vol. 2*, 1988, pp. 118–37.

Lockheed, Marlaine; Wattanawaha, Nongnuch and **Jimenez, Emmanuel.** The Relative Efficiency of Private and Public Schools: The Case of Thailand. *World Bank Econ. Rev.*, May 1988, *2*(2), pp. 139–64.

Lockwood, Ben and **Manning, Alan.** Inequality and Inefficiency in a Model of Occupational Choice with Asymmetric Information. *J. Public Econ.*, November 1988, *37*(2), pp. 147–69.

Lockwood, Larry J. and **Kadiyala, K. Rao.** Measuring Investment Performance with a Stochastic Parameter Regression Model. *J. Banking Finance*, September 1988, *12*(3), pp. 457–67.

_____ and **Kadiyala, K. Rao.** Risk Measurement for Event-Dependent Security Returns. *J. Bus. Econ. Statist.*, January 1988, *6*(1), pp. 43–49.

_____ and **Linn, Scott C.** Short-term Stock Price Patterns: NYSE, AMEX, OTC. *J. Portfol. Manage.*, Winter 1988, *14*(2), pp. 30–34.

Loderer, Claudio and Gabriel, Luciano. Political Progress and Government Growth—A Theoretical and Empirical Investigation. *J. Inst. Theoretical Econ.*, April 1988, *144*(2), pp. 267–95.

_____ and **Zimmermann, Heinz.** Stock Offerings in a Different Institutional Setting: The Swiss Case, 1973–1983. *J. Banking Finance*, September 1988, *12*(3), pp. 353–78.

Lodewijks, John. Arthur M. Okun: Economics for Policymaking. *J. Econ. Surveys*, 1988, *2*(3), pp. 245–64.

_____. Arthur Okun and the Lucasian Critique. *Australian Econ. Pap.*, December 1988, *27*(51), pp. 253–71.

Loeb, Peter D. The Determinants of Motor Vehicle Accidents—A Specification Error Analysis. *Logist. Transp. Rev.*, March 1988, *24*(1), pp. 33–48.

_____; **Gilad, Benjamin and Kaish, Stanley.** From Economic Behavior to Behavoiral Economics: The Behavioral Uprising in Economics. **In** *Earl, P. E., ed., Vol. 2, 1988, 1984,* pp. 437–58.

von Loesch, Achim. Privatisierungen und Privatisierungsdiskussion in der Bundesrepublik Deutschland. (Privatization in the Federal Republic of Germany. Discussion and Implementation. With English summary.) *Ann. Pub. Coop. Econ.*, March 1988, *59*(1), pp. 67–83.

Loesch, Jacques. Security on Movable Property and Receivables in Europe: Luxembourg. **In** *Dickson, M. G.; Rosener, W. and Storm, P. M., eds., 1988,* pp. 108–22.

Loewenstein, Mark A. and McClure, James E. Taxes and Financial Leasing. *Quart. Rev. Econ. Bus.*, Spring 1988, *28*(1), pp. 21–38.

Loewenstein, Uri and Coles, Jeffrey L. Equilibrium Pricing and Portfolio Composition in the Presence of Uncertain Parameters. *J. Finan. Econ.*, December 1988, *22*(2), pp. 279–303.

Loewy, Michael B. Equilibrium Policy in an Overlapping Generations Economy. *J. Monet. Econ.*, November 1988, *22*(3), pp. 485–99.

_____. The Incompatibility of Valued Money and Equilibrium Policy. *Econ. Letters*, 1988, *28*(2), pp. 157–61.

_____. Reaganomics and Reputation Revisited. *Econ. Inquiry*, April 1988, *26*(2), pp. 253–63.

Loeys, Jan and Berlin, Mitchell. Bond Covenants and Delegated Monitoring. *J. Finance*, June 1988, *43*(2), pp. 397–412.

Lofchie, Michael F. and Commins, Stephen K. Food Deficits and Agricultural Policies in Tropical Africa. **In** *Wilber, C. K., ed., 1988,* pp. 303–25.

Logan, J. and Trengove, C. D. Health Insurance Forum. **In** *Butler, J. R. G. and Doessel, D. P., eds., 1988,* pp. 242–45.

Logue, Dennis E.; Noser, Eugene A., Jr. and Berkowitz, Stephen A. The Total Cost of Transactions on the NYSE. *J. Finance*, March 1988, *43*(1), pp. 97–112.

Lohr, Kathleen N. Outcome Measurement: Concepts and Questions. *Inquiry*, Spring 1988, *25*(1), pp. 37–50.

Loinger, Guy and Peyrache, Veronique. Technological Clusters and Regional Economic Restructuring. **In** *Aydalot, P. and Keeble, D., eds., 1988,* pp. 121–38.

Loistl, Otto and Landes, Thomas. Zur Berechnung des internen Zinssatzes unter Unsicherheit. Kommentar zu den gleichnamigen Anmerkungen von Werner Dinkelbach. (With English summary.) *Z. Betriebswirtshaft*, March 1988, *58*(3), pp. 435–39.

Loizides, Ioannis. The Decomposition of Progressivity Indices with Applications to the Greek Taxation System. *Public Finance*, 1988, *43*(2), pp. 236–47.

Lok, Sang Ho. Towards an Optimal Public Housing Policy. *Urban Stud.*, June 1988, *25*(3), pp. 204–11.

Lollivier, S.; Gagey, F. and Laroque, Guy. Monetary and Fiscal Policies in a General Equilibrium Model. **In** *Grandmont, J.-M., ed., 1988, 1986,* pp. 217–45.

Lomakin S., Alexandra and Valdés Prieto, Salvador. Percepción sobre la Garantía Estatal a los Depósitos Durante 1987 en Chile. (With English summary.) *Cuadernos Econ.*, August 1988, *25*(75), pp. 229–45.

Lomax, David F. The Big Bang—18 Months After. *Nat. Westminster Bank Quart. Rev.*, August 1988, pp. 18–30.

de Lombaerde, P. Kompensatietechnieken in de Oost–Westhandel. (Compensation Techniques in East–West Trade. With English summary.) *S. Afr. J. Econ.*, December 1988, *56*(4), pp. 329–39.

Lombra, Raymond E. Monetary Policy: The Rhetoric versus the Record. **In** *Willett, T. D., ed., 1988,* pp. 337–65.

_____ and **Kantor, Laurence.** Is Interest Rate Volatility Necessarily Harmful? *J. Econ. Bus.*, February 1988, *40*(1), pp. 17–25.

_____ and **Karamouzis, Nicholas.** Forecasts and U.S. Monetary Policy, 1974–78: The Role of Openness: A Note. *J. Money, Credit, Banking*, Part 1, August 1988, *20*(3), pp. 402–08.

Lonaeus, Hakan. How the Bank Finances Its Operations. *Finance Develop.*, September 1988, *25*(3), pp. 40–42.

Loncarevic, Ivan. Price Policy and Price Formation in the Yugoslav Agro-Food Sector. **In** *Brada, J. C. and Wadekin, K.-E., eds., 1988,* pp. 246–68.

Long, Burl F. and Babb, Emerson M. Alternative Enterprises for Strengthening Southern Agriculture. **In** *Beaulieu, L. J., ed., 1988,* pp. 344–57.

Long, C. Richard and Gardner, Mark L. Alternative U.S. Monetary and Deficit Reduction Policies for the 1980s. *J. Money, Credit, Banking*, Part 1, August 1988, *20*(3), pp. 336–52.

Long, David A. The Budgetary Implications of Welfare Reform: Lessons from Four State Initiatives. *J. Policy Anal. Manage.*, Winter 1988, *7*(2), pp. 289–99.

Long, David E. Saudi Arabia and Its Neighbors: Preoccupied Paternalism. In *Sindelar, H. R., III and Peterson, J. E., eds.*, 1988, pp. 181–97.

Long, James E. Taxation and IRA Participation: Re-examination and Confirmation. *Nat. Tax J.*, December 1988, *41*(4), pp. 585–89.

_____ **and Toma, Eugenia Froedge.** The Determinants of Private School Attendance, 1970–1980. *Rev. Econ. Statist.*, May 1988, *70*(2), pp. 351–57.

Long, John F. and Pryor, Edward T. Comparative Demographic Effects of Canadian–U.S. Immigration Flows. *Statist. J.*, August 1988, *5*(2), pp. 135–57.

Long, Larry and DeAre, Diana. U.S. Population Redistribution: A Perspective on the Nonmetropolitan Turnaround. *Population Devel. Rev.*, September 1988, *14*(3), pp. 433–50.

_____; **Tucker, C. Jack and Urton, William L.** Measuring Migration Distances: Self-reporting and Indirect Methods. *J. Amer. Statist. Assoc.*, September 1988, *83*(403), pp. 674–78.

_____; **Tucker, C. Jack and Urton, William L.** Migration Distances: An International Comparison. *Demography*, November 1988, *25*(4), pp. 633–40.

Long, William T., III and Gruben, William C. Forecasting the Texas Economy: Applications and Evaluations of a Systematic Multivariate Time Series Model. *Fed. Res. Bank Dallas Econ. Rev.*, January 1988, pp. 11–28.

Longbotham, C. Roger and Hannum, Robert C. Measuring Inequality between Income Distributions. In *Brown, R. C., ed.*, 1988, pp. 55–72.

Longbottom, Andrew and Holly, Sean. Company Acquisitions, Investment and Tobin's Q: Evidence for the United Kingdom. *J. Econ. Bus.*, May 1988, *40*(2), pp. 103–15.

Longley, Paul A. and Dunn, Richard. Graphical Assessment of Housing Market Models. *Urban Stud.*, February 1988, *25*(1), pp. 21–33.

Longres, John F.; Sosin, Michael R. and Danziger, Sandra K. The Status of Youth in Wisconsin: Lessons for Policy. In *Danziger, S. H. and Witte, J. F., eds.*, 1988, pp. 151–71.

Longstreth, Molly; Durham, Catherine A. and Colby, Bonnie G. The Impact of State Tax Credits and Energy Prices on Adoption of Solar Enegy Systems. *Land Econ.*, November 1988, *64*(4), pp. 347–55.

Longva, Svein; Olsen, Øystein and Strøm, Steinar. Total Elasticities of Energy Demand Analysed within a General Equilibrium Model. *Energy Econ.*, October 1988, *10*(4), pp. 298–308.

Lonmo, O. Victor. The Auto Sector: Comments. In *Schott, J. J. and Smith, M. G., eds.*, 1988, pp. 113–16.

Lonzi, Marco. Unicité du TIR et Intérêts cumulés: Un commentaire. (TIR Unicity and Cumulated Interest: Remarks. With English summary.) *Écon. Soc.*, August 1988, *22*(8), pp. 25–36.

Loo, Jean C. H. Common Stock Returns, Expected Inflation, and the Rational Expectations Hypothesis. *J. Finan. Res.*, Summer 1988, *11*(2), pp. 165–71.

Loomes, Graham. Different Experimental Procedures for Obtaining Valuations of Risky Actions: Implications for Utility Theory. In *Munier, B. R., ed.*, 1988, pp. 37–57.

_____. Further Evidence of the Impact of Regret and Disappointment in Choice under Uncertainty. *Economica*, February 1988, *55*(217), pp. 47–62.

_____. When Actions Speak Louder Than Prospects. *Amer. Econ. Rev.*, June 1988, *78*(3), pp. 463–70.

Loomis, John B. The Bioeconomic Effects of Timber Harvesting on Recreational and Commercial Salmon and Steelhead Fishing: A Case Study of the Siuslaw National Forest. *Marine Resource Econ.*, 1988, *5*(1), pp. 43–60.

_____ **and Revier, Charles F.** Measuring Regressivity of Excise Taxes: A Buyers Index. *Public Finance Quart.*, July 1988, *16*(3), pp. 301–14.

Looney, Robert E. Economic Environments Conducive to Indigenous Third World Arms Production. *Singapore Econ. Rev.*, October 1988, *33*(2), pp. 66–78.

_____. The Impact of Technology Transfer on the Structure of the Saudi Arabian Labor Force. *J. Econ. Issues*, June 1988, *22*(2), pp. 485–92.

_____. Infrastructure Investment and Inflation in Saudi Arabia. *J. Energy Devel.*, Autumn 1988, *14*(1), pp. 103–13.

Looney, Stephen W.; White, Richard A. and Golen, Steven P. An Empirical Examination of CPA Perceptions of Communication Barriers between Auditor and Client. In *Schwartz, B. N., ed.*, 1988, pp. 233–49.

Loopesko, Bonnie and Johnson, Robert A. Realignment of the Yen–Dollar Exchange Rate: Aspects of the Adjustment Process in Japan. In *Marston, R. C., ed.*, 1988, pp. 105–44.

Loos, Marleen and Vuchelen, Jef. Het gezinsvermogen (1970–1987). (With English summary.) *Cah. Écon. Bruxelles*, 2nd Trimester 1988, (118), pp. 219–36.

Loparo, K. A. and Hájek, O. Bilinear Control: Geometric Properties of Reachable Sets. In *Eiselt, H. A. and Pederzoli, G., eds.*, 1988, pp. 262–73.

Lopes, Lola L. Economics as Psychology: A Cognitive Assay of the French and American Schools of Risk Theory. In *Munier, B. R., ed.*, 1988, pp. 405–17.

Lopez, Adolfo. The Paradox of International Comparisons. In *Salazar-Carrillo, J. and Rao, D. S. P., eds.*, 1988, pp. 295–98.

Lopez Casasnovas, Guillem and Wagstaff, Adam. La combinacion de los factores productivos en el hospital: Una aproximación a la función de producción. (With English summary.) *Invest. Ecón.*, May 1988, *12*(2), pp. 305–27.

Lopez, Elena and Chung, Ching-Fan. A Regional Analysis of Food Consumption in Spain. *Econ. Letters*, 1988, *26*(3), pp. 209–13.

_____; Chung, Ching-Fan and Theil, Henri. Tracing the Composition Changes of Japan's Consumer Budget, 1920–1980. *Empirical Econ.*, 1988, *13*(1), pp. 59–64.

Lopez, Franklin A. and Darrat, Ali F. Price Instability and Inflation: Some Tests Based on Rational Expectations Models. *Econ. Letters*, 1988, *26*(2), pp. 111–19.

López García, Miguel Angel. Seguridad Social y crecimiento demográfico en un modelo de ciclo vital. (With English summary.) *Invest. Ecón.*, September 1988, *12*(3), pp. 455–71.

Lopez, Rigoberto A.; Adelaja, Adesoji O. and Andrews, Margaret S. The Effects of Suburbanization on Agriculture. *Amer. J. Agr. Econ.*, May 1988, *70*(2), pp. 346–58.

Lorange, Peter. Co-operative Strategies: Planning and Control Considerations. In *Hood, N. and Vahlne, J.-E., eds.*, 1988, pp. 370–89.

_____. Monitoring Strategic Progress and Ad Hoc Strategy Modification. In *Grant, J. H., ed.*, 1988, pp. 261–85.

_____. Stimulating Strategic Direction Setting in Professional Groups: The Case of an Academic Department. In *Lamb, R. and Shrivastava, P., eds.*, 1988, pp. 299–320.

_____ and Contractor, Farok J. Cooperative Strategies in International Business: Introduction and a Summary of the Issues. In *Contractor, F. J. and Lorange, P.*, 1988, pp. xxv–xxix.

_____ and Contractor, Farok J. Why Should Firms Cooperate? The Strategy and Economics Basis for Cooperative Ventures. In *Contractor, F. J. and Lorange, P.*, 1988, pp. 3–30.

Loranger, Thomas J. and Brakke, David F. The Extent of Snowpack Influence on Water Chemistry in a North Cascades Lake. *Water Resources Res.*, May 1988, *24*(5), pp. 723–26.

Lorenz, Edward H. Neither Friends nor Strangers: Informal Networks of Subcontracting in French Industry. In *Gambetta, D., ed.*, 1988, pp. 194–210.

Lorenz, Hans-Walter. Neuere Entwicklungen in der Theorie dynamischer ökonomischer Systeme. (Recent Developments in the Theory of Dynamical Economic Systems. With English summary.) *Jahr. Nationalökon. Statist.*, April 1988, *204*(4), pp. 295–315.

Lorenz, Wilhelm and Wagner, Joachim. The Earnings Function under Test. *Econ. Letters*, 1988, *27*(1), pp. 95–99.

_____ and Wagner, Joachim. Gibt es kompensierende Lohndifferentiale in der Bundesrepublik Deutschland? (A Test of the Theory of Compensating Wage Differentials for the Federal Republic of Germany. With English summary.) *Z. Wirtschaft. Sozialwissen.*, 1988, *108*(3), pp. 371–81.

Lorenzo, María José. Sistemas completos de demanda para la economía española. (With English summary.) *Invest. Ecón.*, January 1988, *12*(1), pp. 83–131.

Lórincze, Péter. Economic Relations between Hungary and the United States. In *Brada, J. C. and Dobozi, I., eds.*, 1988, pp. 219–35.

Lorrain, Jean and Dussault, Louis. Relation be-
tween Psychological Characteristics, Administrative Behaviors and Success of Founder Entrepreneurs at the Start-Up Stage. In *Kirchhoff, B. A., et al., eds.*, 1988, pp. 150–64.

Lorsch, Jay W. Managing Culture: The Invisible Barrier to Strategic Change. In *Earl, P. E., ed., Vol. 1*, 1988, *1986*, pp. 419–33.

Loschky, David. Mid-XIX Century Military Spending Patterns. *J. Europ. Econ. Hist.*, Spring 1988, *17*(1), pp. 127–30.

Lotspeich, Richard. The Economics of Research and Development: Comment. *Resources & Energy*, June 1988, *10*(2), pp. 185–89.

Lott, John R., Jr. Brand Names, Ignorance, and Quality Guaranteeing Premiums. *Appl. Econ.*, February 1988, *20*(2), pp. 165–76.

_____. Some Thoughts on Tullock's New Definition of Rent Seeking. *Contemp. Policy Issues*, October 1988, *6*(4), pp. 48–49.

_____ and Fremling, Gertrud M. Televising Legislatures: Some Thoughts on Whether Politicians are Search Goods. *Public Choice*, July 1988, *58*(1), pp. 73–78.

Lotz, Peter. Den økonomiske væksts: Komponenter. (The Growth Accounting Method of Explaining Changes in Productivity. With English summary.) *Nationaløkon. Tidsskr.*, 1988, *126*(3), pp. 351–66.

Loubergé, Henri and Chesney, Marc. Les options sur devises: une revue des modèles théoriques et des travaux empiriques. (Currency Options: A Survey of Theoretical and Empirical Work. With English summary.) *Finance*, December 1988, *9*(2), pp. 7–33.

_____ and Eeckhoudt, Louis. Export Credit Insurance: Comment. *J. Risk Ins.*, December 1988, *55*(4), pp. 742–47.

_____ and Schlesinger, Harris. Cutting the Cake with a Stranger: Egoism and Altruism with Imperfect Information. *J. Econ. Behav. Organ.*, December 1988, *10*(4), pp. 377–88.

_____ and Van Tiel, Pieter. Contrôle des changes et risque politique: Une étude économétrique des cas français et suisse. (Capital Flows Controls and Political Risk: An Econometric Study of the Swiss and French Cases. With English summary.) *Revue Écon.*, September 1988, *39*(5), pp. 951–72.

Louie, Kenneth K. T.; Fizel, John L. and Mentzer, Marc S. CEO Tenure and Firm Performance. In *Missouri Valley Economic Assoc.*, 1988, pp. 1–6.

Louri, Helen. Urban Growth and Productivity: The Case of Greece. *Urban Stud.*, October 1988, *25*(5), pp. 433–38.

Louviere, Jordan J. Conjoint Analysis Modelling of Stated Preferences. *J. Transp. Econ. Policy*, January 1988, *22*(1), pp. 93–119.

Love, J. H. and Ashcroft, Brian K. The Regional Interest in UK Mergers Policy. *Reg. Stud.*, August 1988, *22*(4), pp. 341–44.

_____; Forsyth, D. J. C. and Jebuni, C. D. Market Structure and LDCs' Manufactured Export Performance. *World Devel.*, December 1988, *16*(12), pp. 1511–20.

Love, James P. and Branson, William H. U.S. Manufacturing and the Real Exchange Rate. In *Marston, R. C., ed.*, 1988, pp. 241–70.

Lovejoy, Lora Mills. The Comparative Value of Pensions in the Public and Private Sectors. *Mon. Lab. Rev.*, December 1988, *111*(12), pp. 18–26.

———; Blostin, Allan P. and Burke, Thomas P. Disability and Insurance Plans in the Public and Private Sector. *Mon. Lab. Rev.*, December 1988, *111*(12), pp. 9–17.

Lovejoy, P. Management Buy-Outs and Policy Responses in the West Midlands. *Reg. Stud.*, August 1988, *22*(4), pp. 344–47.

Lovell, C. A. Knox and Färe, Rolf. Aggregation and Efficiency. In *Eichhorn, W., ed.*, 1988, pp. 639–47.

———; Färe, Rolf and Grosskopf, Shawna. An Indirect Approach to the Evaluation of Producer Performance. *J. Public Econ.*, October 1988, *37*(1), pp. 71–89.

———; Färe, Rolf and Grosskopf, Shawna. Scale Elasticity and Scale Efficiency. *J. Inst. Theoretical Econ.*, September 1988, *144*(4), pp. 721–29.

———; Sarkar, Asani and Sickles, Robin C. Testing for Aggregation Bias in Efficiency Measurement. In *Eichhorn, W., ed.*, 1988, pp. 187–206.

——— and Schmidt, Peter. A Comparison of Alternative Approaches to the Measurement of Productive Efficiency. In *Dogramaci, A. and Färe, R., eds.,*, 1988, pp. 3–32.

———; Sickles, Robin C. and Warren, Ronald S., Jr. The Effect of Unionization On Labor Productivity: Some Additional Evidence. *J. Lab. Res.*, Winter 1988, *9*(1), pp. 55–63.

Lovell, Malcolm R., Jr. Europe's Lessons for America. In *Simcox, D. E., ed.*, 1988, pp. 229–44.

Loveman, Gary W. and Tilly, Chris. Good Jobs or Bad Jobs? Evaluating the American Job Creation Experience. *Int. Lab. Rev.*, 1988, *127*(5), pp. 593–611.

——— and Tilly, Chris. Good Jobs or Bad Jobs: What Does the Evidence Say? *New Eng. Econ. Rev.*, Jan.–Feb. 1988, pp. 46–65.

Lovett, William A. Solving the U.S. Trade Deficit and Competitiveness Problem. *J. Econ. Issues*, June 1988, *22*(2), pp. 459–67.

Lovio, Raimo and Lemola, Tarmo. Possibilities for a Small Country in High-Technology Production: The Electronics Industry in Finland. In *Freeman, C. and Lundvall, B.-A., eds.*, 1988, pp. 139–55.

Loviscek, Anthony L. and Crowley, Frederick D. Analyzing Changes in Municipal Bond Ratings: A Different Perspective. *Urban Stud.*, April 1988, *25*(2), pp. 124–32.

Low, Linda. Privatisation in Singapore. In *Cook, P. and Kirkpatrick, C., eds.*, 1988, pp. 259–80.

Low, Stuart A. and Kahn, Lawrence M. Systematic and Random Search: A Synthesis. *J. Human Res.*, Winter 1988, *23*(1), pp. 1–20.

Lowdermilk, Max K. Large-Scale Irrigation and

Drainage Schemes in Pakistan: Comment. In *O'Mara, G. T., ed.*, 1988, pp. 77–79.

Lowe, E. A. and Shaw, R. W. An Analysis of Managerial Biasing: Evidence from a Company's Budgeting Process. In *Earl, P. E., ed.*, *Vol. 1*, 1988, *1968*, pp. 366–77.

Lowell, B. Lindsay; Taylor, Lowell J. and Bean, Frank D. Undocumented Mexican Immigrants and the Earnings of Other Workers in the United States. *Demography*, February 1988, *25*(1), pp. 35–52.

Lowenberg, Anton D. and Feigenbaum, Bernard. South African Disinvestment: Causes and Effects. *Contemp. Policy Issues*, October 1988, *6*(4), pp. 105–17.

——— and Heijdra, Ben J. The Neoclassical Economic Research Program: Some Lakatosian and Other Considerations. *Australian Econ. Pap.*, December 1988, *27*(51), pp. 272–84.

——— and Kaempfer, William H. Determinants of the Economic and Political Effects of Trade Sanctions. *S. Afr. J. Econ.*, December 1988, *56*(4), pp. 270–77.

——— and Kaempfer, William H. South Africa's Vulnerability to Oil Sanctions. *J. Energy Devel.*, Autumn 1988, *14*(1), pp. 19–44.

——— and Kaempfer, William H. The Theory of International Economic Sanctions: A Public Choice Approach. *Amer. Econ. Rev.*, September 1988, *78*(4), pp. 786–93.

———; Mallick, Robert J. and Heijdra, Ben J. Marxism, Methodological Individualism, and the New Institutional Economics. *J. Inst. Theoretical Econ.*, April 1988, *144*(2), pp. 296–317.

Lowenberg-DeBoer, J. and Turvey, Calum Greig. Farm-to-Farm Productivity Differences and Whole-Farm Production Functions. *Can. J. Agr. Econ.*, July 1988, *36*(2), pp. 295–312.

Lowenfeld, Andreas F. What the GATT Says (or Does Not Say). In *Diebold, W., Jr., ed.*, 1988, pp. 55–68.

Lowenstein, Louis and Herman, Edward S. The Efficiency Effects of Hostile Takeovers. In *Coffee, J. C., Jr.; Lowenstein, L. and Rose-Ackerman, S., eds.*, 1988, pp. 211–40.

———; Rose-Ackerman, Susan and Coffee, John C., Jr. Knights, Raiders & Targets: The Impact of the Hostile Takeover: Introduction. In *Coffee, J. C., Jr.; Lowenstein, L. and Rose-Ackerman, S., eds.*, 1988, pp. 1–9.

Lower, Ann K. Pipeline Engineering and Microelectronics Applications in the Iron Ore Industry in Northern Mexico. In *Bhalla, A. S. and James, D., eds.*, 1988, pp. 97–111.

Lower, Milton D. The Concept of Technology within the Institutionalist Perspective. In *Tool, M. R., ed., Vol. 1*, 1988, *1987*, pp. 197–226.

Lowery, David; Brunn, Stanley D. and Webster, Gerald R. The Spatial Impact of Reaganomics: A Test of Six Models. *Growth Change*, Fall 1988, *19*(4), pp. 49–67.

Lown, Cara S. The Credit–Output Link vs. the Money–Output Link: New Evidence. *Fed. Res. Bank Dallas Econ. Rev.*, November 1988, pp. 1–10.

Lowry, Mark Newton. Petroleum Product Storage by Competitive Crude Oil Processors. *Resources & Energy*, June 1988, *10*(2), pp. 95–110.

_____. Precautionary Storage of Refinery Products: The Case of Distillate Fuel Oil. *Energy Econ.*, October 1988, *10*(4), pp. 254–60.

_____. Working Stocks and Speculative Stocks. *Econ. Letters*, 1988, *28*(4), pp. 311–14.

Lowry, S. Todd. Insights from Ancient Views on Distribution. In *Brenner, Y. S.; Reijnders, J. P. G. and Spithoven, A. H. G. M., eds.*, 1988, pp. 226–38.

Loyd, Max I. Stability and the Tobacco Program: Reaction. In *Sumner, D. A., ed.*, 1988, pp. 139–42.

Lu, Aiguo and Selden, Mark. The Reform of Landownership and the Political Economy of Contemporary China. In *Selden, M.*, 1988, pp. 181–99.

Lu, Allen H.; Schmittroth, F. and Yeh, William W.-G. Sequential Estimation of Aquifer Parameters. *Water Resources Res.*, May 1988, *24*(5), pp. 670–82.

Lu, Ting Gang. Governmental Accounting and Auditing in China: Evolution and Current Reforms. In *Chan, J. L. and Jones, R. H., eds.*, 1988, pp. 122–48.

Luban, Florica and Dumitru, V. A Note on the Cardinality Mathematical Programming. *Econ. Computat. Cybern. Stud. Res.*, 1988, *23*(4), pp. 67–72.

Lubian, Diego. Are Exchange Rates Too Volatile? *Ricerche Econ.*, Oct.–Dec. 1988, *42*(4), pp. 630–51.

Lubinsky, David and Pregibon, Daryl. Data Analysis as Search. *J. Econometrics*, May–June 1988, *38*(1–2), pp. 247–68.

Lucas, Rob G.; Gibbs, Barrie and Keen, Kevin. Innovation and Human Resource Productivity in Canada: A Comparison of "High" and "Low" Technology Industries. In *Gattiker, U. E. and Larwood, L., eds.*, 1988, pp. 93–120.

Lucas, Robert E. B. Demand for India's Manufactured Exports. *J. Devel. Econ.*, July 1988, *29*(1), pp. 63–75.

_____. Guest Worker Emigration and Remittances. In *Salvatore, D., ed.*, 1988, pp. 125–38.

_____. India's Industrial Policy. In *Lucas, R. E. B. and Papanek, G. F., eds.*, 1988, pp. 185–202.

_____ and Stark, Oded. Migration, Remittances, and the Family. *Econ. Develop. Cult. Change*, April 1988, *36*(3), pp. 465–81.

Lucas, Robert E., Jr. Money Demand in the United States: A Quantitative Review. *Carnegie–Rochester Conf. Ser. Public Policy*, Autumn 1988, *29*, pp. 137–67.

_____. On the Mechanics of Economic Development. *J. Monet. Econ.*, July 1988, *22*(1), pp. 3–42.

Luce, R. Duncan. Rank-Dependent, Subjective Expected-Utility Representations. *J. Risk Uncertainty*, September 1988, *1*(3), pp. 305–32.

Lucey, Brian M. Efficiency in the Forward Exchange Market: An Application of Cointegra-

tion. *Econ. Soc. Rev.*, October 1988, *20*(1), pp. 25–36.

Lucey, Paul A. The Soviet Union Today: Religion. In *Cracraft, J., ed.*, 1988, pp. 315–26.

Lucidi, S.; Grippo, L. and Lampariello, F. Newton-Type Algorithms with Nonmonotone Line Search for Large-Scale Unconstrained Optimization. In *Iri, M. and Yajima, K., eds.*, 1988, pp. 187–96.

Lücke, Matthias. Economies of Scale in Protected Manufacturing Industries in Developing Countries—The Case of the Brazilian Passenger Car Industry. *Industry Devel.*, October 1988, (24), pp. 35–55.

Lucke, Robert; Toder, Eric and Galper, Harvey. A General Equilibrium Analysis of Tax Reform. In *Aaron, H. J.; Galper, H. and Pechman, J. A., eds.*, 1988, pp. 59–108.

Luckett, Charles A. Personal Bankruptcies. *Fed. Res. Bull.*, September 1988, *74*(9), pp. 591–603.

_____; Canner, Glenn B. and Fergus, James T. Home Equity Lines of Credit. *Fed. Res. Bull.*, June 1988, *74*(6), pp. 361–73.

Luckett, Dudley G. A Pedagogical Note on the Use of Margin Credit. *J. Econ. Educ.*, Fall 1988, *19*(4), pp. 337–40.

Luckett, James P. Housing the Poor: Shelter by Tax Shelter. In *Brown, E., ed.*, 1988, pp. 160–66.

Ludden, David. Agrarian Commercialism in Eighteenth Century South India: Evidence from the 1823 Tirunelveli Census. *Indian Econ. Soc. Hist. Rev.*, Oct.–Dec. 1988, *25*(4), pp. 493–519.

Luder, Klaus G. Governmental Accounting in West European Countries: With Special Reference to the Federal Republic of Germany. In *Chan, J. L. and Jones, R. H., eds.*, 1988, pp. 82–104.

Lüders Sch., Rolf. Veinticinco años de ingeniería social en Chile: Un breve ensayo sobre la historia económica del período 1963–1988. (With English summary.) *Cuadernos Econ.*, December 1988, *25*(76), pp. 331–80.

Ludlow, Stephen; Stern, Nicholas and Ahmad, Ehtisham. Demand Response in Pakistan: A Modification of the Linear Expenditure System for 1976. *Pakistan Devel. Rev.*, Autumn 1988, *27*(3), pp. 293–308.

Luedde-Neurath, Richard. State Intervention and Export-Oriented Development in South Korea. In *White, G., ed.*, 1988, pp. 68–112.

Luft, Christa; Blessing, Helmut and Grote, Gerhard. Foreign Trade, Growth of the Socialist National Economy, and Comprehensive Intensification. *Soviet E. Europ. Foreign Trade*, Fall 1988, *24*(3), pp. 71–95.

Luft, Harold S. HMOs and the Quality of Care. *Inquiry*, Spring 1988, *25*(1), pp. 147–56.

Luger, Michael I. Federal Tax Reform and the Interjurisdictional Mobility Impulse. *J. Urban Econ.*, March 1988, *23*(2), pp. 235–50.

_____ and Evans, William N. Geographic Differences in Production Technology. *Reg. Sci. Urban Econ.*, August 1988, *18*(3), pp. 399–424.

Luhmann, Niklas. Familiarity, Confidence, Trust: Problems and Alternatives. In *Gambetta, D., ed.*, 1988, pp. 94–107.

Luhmer, Alfred; Feichtinger, Gustav and Kistner, Klaus-Peter. Ein dynamisches Modell des Intensitätssplittings. (With English summary.) *Z. Betriebswirtshaft*, November 1988, *58*(11), pp. 1242–58.

———— **and Kistner, Klaus-Peter.** Ein dynamisches Modell des Betriebsmitteleinsatzes. (With English summary.) *Z. Betriebswirtshaft*, January 1988, *58*(1), pp. 63–83.

————; **Sorger, Gerhard and Feichtinger, Gustav.** Optimal Price and Advertising Policy for a Convenience Goods Retailer. *Marketing Sci.*, Spring 1988, *7*(2), pp. 187–201.

Luijben, Thom; Boomsma, Anne and Molenaar, Ivo W. Modification of Factor Analysis Models in Covariance Structure Analysis: A Monte Carlo Study. In *Dijkstra, T. K., ed.*, 1988, pp. 70–101.

Lukac, Louis P.; Brorsen, B. Wade and Irwin, Scott H. Similarity of Computer Guided Technical Trading Systems. *J. Futures Markets*, February 1988, *8*(1), pp. 1–13.

————; **Brorsen, B. Wade and Irwin, Scott H.** A Test of Futures Market Disequilibrium Using Twelve Different Technical Trading Systems. *Appl. Econ.*, May 1988, *20*(5), pp. 623–39.

Lukács, O. Hungarian Trade in Consumer Goods—Some Questions Related to Changes in Enterprise Structure. *Acta Oecon.*, 1988, *39*(3–4), pp. 369–83.

Lukaschin, Y. P. Analysis of Data When Constructing an Adaptive Regression Model. In *Fedorov, V. and Lauter, H., eds.*, 1988, pp. 189–94.

Lukaszewicz, Aleksander. Domestic and External Macro-policies: Comments. In *Saunders, C. T., ed.*, 1988, pp. 228–29.

Luksus, Edmund J. A Use of Inductive Logic in Corporate Economic Analysis. In *Brown, R. C., ed.*, 1988, pp. 87–104.

Lumijärvi, Olli-Pekka. Suboptimization in a Profit Center Organization: A Field Study. *Liiketaloudellinen Aikak.*, 1988, *37*(2), pp. 116–31.

Lumsden, Keith and Scott, Alex. A Characteristics Approach to the Evaluation of Economics Software Packages. *J. Econ. Educ.*, Fall 1988, *19*(4), pp. 353–62.

Lund, Adrian K. and Williams, Allan F. Mandatory Seat Belt Use Laws and Occupant Crash Protection in the Untied States: Present Status and Future Prospects. In *Graham, J. D., ed.*, 1988, pp. 51–72.

Lundahl, Mats. Self-defeating and Welfare-Improving DUP Redistribution of Capital Assets. *Econ. Letters*, 1988, *26*(2), pp. 179–82.

Lundberg, Lars. The Role of Comparative Costs for Determining Inter- and Intra-industry Trade with Developing Countries. *Europ. Econ. Rev.*, November 1988, *32*(9), pp. 1699–1710.

————. Technology, Factor Proportions and Competitiveness. *Scand. J. Econ.*, 1988, *90*(2), pp. 173–88.

Lundberg, Shelly J. Labor Supply of Husbands and Wives: A Simultaneous Equations Approach. *Rev. Econ. Statist.*, May 1988, *70*(2), pp. 224–35.

Lundborg, Per and Holmlund, Bertil. Unemployment Insurance and Union Wage Setting. *Scand. J. Econ.*, 1988, *90*(2), pp. 161–72.

Lundholm, Russell J. Price-Signal Relations in the Presence of Correlated Public and Private Information. *J. Acc. Res.*, Spring 1988, *26*(1), pp. 107–18.

Lundvall, Bengt-Åke. Innovation as an Interactive Process: From User–Producer Interaction to the National System of Innovation. In *Dosi, G., et al., eds.*, 1988, pp. 349–69.

———— **and Andersen, Esben Sloth.** Small National Systems of Innovation Facing Technological Revolutions: An Analytical Framework. In *Freeman, C. and Lundvall, B.-A., eds.*, 1988, pp. 9–36.

Lundy, Loretta. The GATT Safeguards Debacle and the Canadian Textiles and Clothing Policy: A Proposal for an Equitable Approch to North–South Relations. *J. World Trade*, December 1988, *22*(6), pp. 71–94.

Lung, Yannick. Complexity and Spatial Dynamics Modelling. From Catastrophe Theory to Self-organizing Process: A Review of the Literature. *Ann. Reg. Sci.*, July 1988, *22*(2), pp. 81–111.

Lusetti, Dino; Brox, James and Carvalho, Emanuel. Input Substitution in Canadian Manufacturing: An Application of the CES-Translog Production Function. *Atlantic Econ. J.*, June 1988, *16*(2), pp. 22–46.

Lusht, Kenneth M. The Real Estate Pricing Puzzle. *Amer. Real Estate Urban Econ. Assoc. J.*, Summer 1988, *16*(2), pp. 95–104.

Luski, Israel and Hochman, Oded. Advertising and Economic Welfare: Comment. *Amer. Econ. Rev.*, March 1988, *78*(1), pp. 290–96.

Lüst, Reimar. Europe's Future in Space. In *Egan, J. J., et al., eds.*, 1988, pp. 457–63.

Lustgarten, Steven and Haw, In-Mu. Evidence on Income Measurement Properties of ASR No. 190 and SFAS No. 33 Data. *J. Acc. Res.*, Autumn 1988, *26*(2), pp. 331–52.

Lustig, Nora. Del estructuralismo al neoestructuralismo: La búsqueda de un paradigma heterodoxo. (From Structuralism to Neo-Structuralism: Searching for an Unorthodox Paradigm. With English summary.) *Colección Estud. CIEPLAN*, March 1988, (23), pp. 35–50.

————. Fiscal Cost and Welfare Effects of the Maize Subsidy in Mexico. In *Pinstrup-Andersen, P., ed.*, 1988, pp. 277–88.

Luten, Daniel B. Energy and Material Resources. In *Ehrlich, P. R. and Holdren, J. P., eds.*, 1988, pp. 101–10.

Luther, Norman Y. and Cho, Lee-Jay. Reconstruction of Birth Histories from Census and Household Survey Data. *Population Stud.*, November 1988, *42*(3), pp. 451–72.

Lütkepohl, Helmut. Prediction Tests for Structural Stability. *J. Econometrics*, November 1988, *39*(3), pp. 267–96.

Lütolf, Franz. The Debt Problem: From Crisis Management towards Sustainable Solutions. **In** *Borner, S., ed.*, 1988, pp. 21–37.

Lutz, James M.; Srivastava, Rajendra and Huff, David L. A Geographical Analysis of the Innovativeness of States. *Econ. Geogr.*, April 1988, *64*(2), pp. 137–46.

Luzadis, Rebecca A. and Mitchell, Olivia S. Changes in Pension Incentives through Time. *Ind. Lab. Relat. Rev.*, October 1988, *42*(1), pp. 100–108.

Luzar, E. Jane. Natural Resource Management in Agriculture: An Institutional Analysis of the 1985 Farm Bill. *J. Econ. Issues*, June 1988, *22*(2), pp. 563–70.

Luzón, José L. Housing in Socialist Cuba: An Analysis Using Cuban Censuses of Population and Housing. **In** *Mesa-Lago, C., ed.*, 1988, pp. 65–83.

Lybeck, Johan A. Comparing Government Growth Rates: the Non-Institutional vs. the Institutional Approach. **In** *Lybeck, J. A. and Henrekson, M., eds.*, 1988, pp. 29–47.

_____ **and Henrekson, Magnus.** Explaining the Growth of Government: Editors' Introduction and Summary. **In** *Lybeck, J. A. and Henrekson, M., eds.*, 1988, pp. 3–19.

_____ **and Henrekson, Magnus.** Explaining the Growth of Government in Sweden: A Disequilibrium Approach. *Public Choice*, June 1988, *57*(3), pp. 213–32.

Lyberg, Lars and Sundgren, Bo. The Impact of the Development of EDP on Statistical Methodology and Survey Techniques. *Statist. J.*, August 1988, *5*(2), pp. 169–91.

Lycette, Margaret A. and Buvinić, Mayra. Women, Poverty, and Development in the Third World. **In** *Lewis, J. P., et al.*, 1988, pp. 149–62.

_____ **; Buvinić, Mayra and Leslie, Joanne.** Weathering Economic Crises: The Crucial Role of Women in Health. **In** *Bell, D. E. and Reich, M. R., eds.*, 1988, pp. 307–48.

Lyles, Majorie A. Learning among Joint Venture-Sophisticated Firms. **In** *Contractor, F. J. and Lorange, P.*, 1988, pp. 301–16.

Lyn, Esmeralda O. and Kim, Wi-Saeng. Excess Market Value, Market Power, and Inside Ownership Structure. *Rev. Ind. Organ.*, Fall 1988, *3*(4), pp. 1–25.

Lynch, John G., Jr.; Marmorstein, Howard and Weigold, Michael F. Choices from Sets Including Remembered Brands: Use of Recalled Attributes and Prior Overall Evaluations. *J. Cons. Res.*, September 1988, *15*(2), pp. 169–84.

Lynch, Lisa M. Are Public Sector Workers Paid More Than Their Alternative Wage? Evidence from Longitudinal Data and Job Queues: Comment. **In** *Freeman, R. B. and Ichniowski, C., eds.*, 1988, pp. 240–42.

Lynch, P. Review of 'Papers and Correspondence of William Stanley Jevons, Volumes I and II.' **In** *Wood, J. C., ed.*, *Vol. 3*, 1988, *1973*, pp. 130–34.

Lynk, Edward L. The Depletion of U.K. North Sea Oil. *Scot. J. Polit. Econ.*, November 1988, *35*(4), pp. 318–33.

Lynk, William J. Physician Price Fixing under the Sherman Act: An Indirect Test of the *Maricopa* Issues. *J. Health Econ.*, June 1988, *7*(2), pp. 95–109.

Lynn, Susan A. Profiling Benefit Segments in a Business Market for a Professional Service. **In** *Woodside, A. G., ed.*, 1988, pp. 159–99.

Lynne, Gary D. Allocatable Fixed Inputs and Jointness in Agricultural Production: Implications for Economic Modeling: Comment. *Amer. J. Agr. Econ.*, November 1988, *70*(4), pp. 947–49.

_____. Machinery Replacement, Multiple Optima, and the 1986 Tax Reform Act. *Southern J. Agr. Econ.*, July 1988, *20*(1), pp. 179–87.

_____ **; Shonkwiler, J. S. and Rola, Leandro R.** Attitudes and Farmer Conservation Behavior. *Amer. J. Agr. Econ.*, February 1988, *70*(1), pp. 12–19.

Lyon, Andrew B. and Fullerton, Don. Tax Neutrality and Intangible Capital. **In** *Summers, L. H., ed.*, 1988, pp. 63–88.

Lyon, Thomas P. and Schlesinger, Benjamin. Gas Utility Supply Planning: Risk Management and Regulatory Oversight. *Energy J.*, July 1988, *9*(3), pp. 153–60.

Lyons, Richard K. Tests of the Foreign Exchange Risk Premium Using the Expected Second Moments Implied by Option Pricing. *J. Int. Money Finance*, March 1988, *7*(1), pp. 91–108.

Lyons, Susan M. C. and van Waardenburg, Dirk A. Some Aspects of the International Tax Treaty Strategy of the Netherlands: Unilateral Relief and Tax Treaties. *Bull. Int. Fiscal Doc.*, Aug.–Sept. 1988, *42*(8–9), pp. 374–400.

Lyons, Thomas P. Concentration and Specialization in Chinese Agriculture, 1979–1985. *J. Devel. Areas*, July 1988, *22*(4), pp. 437–55.

Lyons, William; Cory, Floydette C. and Fitzgerald, Michael R. From Administration to Oversight: Privatization and Its Aftermath in a Southern City. **In** *Hula, R. C., ed.*, 1988, pp. 69–83.

Lypny, Gregory J. Hedging Foreign Exchange Risk with Currency Futures: Portfolio Effects. *J. Futures Markets*, December 1988, *8*(6), pp. 703–15.

Lys, Thomas and Sivaramakrishnan, Konduru. Earnings Expectations and Capital Restructuring: The Case of Equity-for-Debt Swaps. *J. Acc. Res.*, Autumn 1988, *26*(2), pp. 273–99.

Lyson, Thomas A. Economic Development in the Rural South—An Uneven Past—An Uncertain Future. **In** *Beaulieu, L. J., ed.*, 1988, pp. 265–75.

Lyttkens, Carl Hampus. Workers' Compensation and Employees' Safety Incentives in Sweden. *Int. Rev. Law Econ.*, December 1988, *8*(2), pp. 181–85.

_____ **; Vedovato, Claudio and Lidström, Per.** Military Expenditures in Developing Countries: A Comment on Deger and Sen [Military Expenditure, Spin-Off and Economic Development]. *J. Devel. Econ.*, February 1988, *28*(1), pp. 105–10.

Ma, Barry K. Convergence in Inner Probability Measure and the Nonlinear Least Squares Estimator. *J. Quant. Econ.*, July 1988, *4*(2), pp. 213–25.

Ma, Bin and Hong, Zhunyan. Enlivening Large State Enterprises: Where Is the Motive Force? **In** *Reynolds, B. L., ed.*, 1988, *1987*, pp. 213–18.

Ma, Ching-to Albert. Implementation in Dynamic Job Transfers. *Econ. Letters*, 1988, *28*(4), pp. 391–95.

_____. Unique Implementation of Incentive Contracts with Many Agents. *Rev. Econ. Stud.*, October 1988, *55*(4), pp. 555–72.

_____; **Moore, John and Turnbull, Stephen.** Stopping Agents from "Cheating." *J. Econ. Theory*, December 1988, *46*(2), pp. 355–72.

Ma, Christopher K. and Fabozzi, Frank J. The Day-of-the-Week Effect for Derivative Assets: The Case of Gold Futures Options. **In** *Fabozzi, F. J., ed.*, 1988, pp. 379–88.

_____ **and Fabozzi, Frank J.** The Over-the-Counter Market and New York Stock Exchange Trading Halts. *Financial Rev.*, November 1988, *23*(4), pp. 427–37.

_____; **Fabozzi, Frank J. and Moran, Eileen.** Market Uncertainty and the Least-Cost Offering Method of Public Utility Debt: A Note. *J. Finance*, September 1988, *43*(4), pp. 1025–34.

_____ **and Rao, Ramesh P.** Information Asymmetry and Options Trading. *Financial Rev.*, February 1988, *23*(1), pp. 39–51.

_____; **Rao, Ramesh P. and Weinraub, Herbert J.** The Seasonality in Convertible Bond Markets: A Stock Effect or Bond Effect? *J. Finan. Res.*, Winter 1988, *11*(4), pp. 335–47.

_____ **and Soenen, Luc A.** Arbitrage Opportunities in Metal Futures Markets. *J. Futures Markets*, April 1988, *8*(2), pp. 199–209.

Ma, Cindy and Edwards, Franklin R. Commodity Pool Performance: Is the Information Contained in Pool Prospectuses Useful? *J. Futures Markets*, October 1988, *8*(5), pp. 589–616.

Ma, Tai; Hansen, Robert S. and Pinkerton, John M. The Allocation Ratio Decision in the Underwritten Rights Offering. **In** *Chen, A. H., ed.*, 1988, pp. 201–25.

Maasoumi, Esfandiar. Contributions of Denis Sargan to the Theory of Finite Sample Distributions and Dynamic Econometric Models. **In** *Sargan, J. D., Vol. 2*, 1988, pp. 1–17.

_____. Denis Sargan and His Seminal Contributions to Economic and Econometric Theory. **In** *Sargan, J. D., Vol. 1*, 1988, pp. 1–18.

_____. On Econometric Methodology. *Econ. Rec.*, December 1988, *64*(187), pp. 340–43.

_____ **and von Furstenberg, George M.** Macroeconomic Implications of the Information Revolution. *Amer. Econ. Rev.*, May 1988, *78*(2), pp. 178–81.

_____ **and Jeong, Jin-Ho.** A Comparison of GRF and Other Reduced-Form Estimators in Simultaneous Equations Models. *J. Econometrics*, January 1988, *37*(1), pp. 115–34.

_____ **and Nickelsburg, Gerald.** Multivariate Measures of Well-Being and an Analysis of Inequality in the Michigan Data. *J. Bus. Econ. Statist.*, July 1988, *6*(3), pp. 326–34.

Maberly, Edwin D. The Other Friday "Bull" Effect: A Chance Occurrence or the Harbinger of Yet Another Puzzling Anomaly? A Note! *J. Futures Markets*, December 1988, *8*(6), pp. 723–24.

_____ **and Dyl, Edward A.** The Anomaly That Isn't There: A Comment on Friday the Thirteenth. *J. Finance*, December 1988, *43*(5), pp. 1285–86.

_____ **and Herbst, Anthony F.** A Further Investigation of the Day-of-the-Week Effect in the Gold Market: A Comment. *J. Futures Markets*, June 1988, *8*(3), pp. 389–90.

Mabro, Robert. The 1986 Oil Price Crisis: Economic Effects and Policy Responses: Introduction. **In** *Mabro, R., ed.*, 1988, pp. 1–14.

MacArthur, Alan T. and Frankel, Jeffrey A. Political vs. Currency Premia in International Real Interest Rate Differentials: A Study of Forward Rates for 24 Countries. *Europ. Econ. Rev.*, June 1988, *32*(5), pp. 1083–114.

MacAulay, T. G. Co-operative Research in Agricultural Economics. *Rev. Marketing Agr. Econ.*, December 1988, *56*(3), pp. 347–51.

_____ **and Piggott, R. R.** Agricultural Economics at the University of New England. *Rev. Marketing Agr. Econ.*, August 1988, *56*(2), pp. 226–28.

MacBean, Alasdair I. Global Savings, Investment and Adjustment: On Micro- and Macroeconomic Foundations of North–South Financial Interdependence: Discussion. **In** *Currie, D. and Vines, D., eds.*, 1988, pp. 249–52.

_____ **and Nguyen, D. T.** Export Instability and Growth Performance. **In** *Greenaway, D., ed.*, 1988, pp. 95–116.

Maccini, Louis J. and Haltiwanger, John C. A Model of Inventory and Layoff Behaviour under Uncertainty. *Econ. J.*, September 1988, *98*(392), pp. 731–45.

Maccoby, Michael and Brooks, Harvey. Corporations and the Work Force. **In** *Meyer, J. R. and Gustafson, J. M., eds.*, 1988, pp. 113–31.

MacCrimmon, Kenneth R. Essence of Strategy: Ends, Means and Conditions. **In** *Grant, J. H., ed.*, 1988, pp. 49–72.

MacDonald, Gary Alan. Labor Law's Alter Ego Doctrine: The Role of Employer Motive in Corporate Transformations. *Mich. Law Rev.*, April 1988, *86*(5), pp. 1024–60.

MacDonald, Glenn M. The Economics of Rising Stars. *Amer. Econ. Rev.*, March 1988, *78*(1), pp. 155–66.

_____. Job Mobility in Market Equilibrium. *Rev. Econ. Stud.*, January 1988, *55*(1), pp. 153–68.

_____. Symposium on New Directions in the Economic Analysis of Organizations: Foreword. *Can. J. Econ.*, August 1988, *21*(3), pp. 441–43.

MacDonald, Gordon J. Scientific Basis for the Greenhouse Effect. *J. Policy Anal. Manage.*, Spring 1988, *7*(3), pp. 425–44.

MacDonald, J. A. The Concept of a National Comptroller (Accountant). In *Most, K. S., ed.*, 1988, pp. 265–74.

Macdonald, James E. and Valentin, E. K. The Brave New World of Organ Transplantation: Issues and Challenges from a Consumer Affairs Perspective. *J. Cons. Aff.*, Summer 1988, 22(1), pp. 119–35.

Macdonald, Kenneth and Ridge, John. British Social Trends since 1900: Social Mobility. In *Halsey, A. H., ed.*, 1988, pp. 202–25.

MacDonald, Ronald. Purchasing Power Parity: Some 'Long Run' Evidence from the Recent Float. *De Economist*, 1988, 136(2), pp. 238–52.

_____ and Kearney, Colm. Assets Markets, the Current Account and Exchange Rate Determination: An Empirical Model of the Sterling/Dollar Rate 1973–1983. *Australian Econ. Pap.*, December 1988, 27(51), pp. 213–32.

_____ and Speight, Alan E. H. The Term Structure of Interest Rates in the UK. *Bull. Econ. Res.*, October 1988, 40(4), pp. 287–99.

_____ and Taylor, Mark P. Metals Prices, Efficiency and Cointegration: Some Evidence from the London Metal Exchange. *Bull. Econ. Res.*, June 1988, 40(3), pp. 235–39.

_____ and Taylor, Mark P. Testing Rational Expectations and Efficiency in the London Metal Exchange. *Oxford Bull. Econ. Statist.*, February 1988, 50(1), pp. 41–52.

_____ and Torrance, Thomas S. Covered Interest Parity and UK Monetary 'News.' *Econ. Letters*, 1988, 26(1), pp. 53–56.

_____ and Torrance, Thomas S. Exchange Rates and the "News": Some Evidence Using U.K. Survey Data. *Manchester Sch. Econ. Soc. Stud.*, March 1988, 56(1), pp. 69–76.

_____ and Torrance, Thomas S. Monetary Policy and the Real Interest Rate: Some U.K. Evidence. *Scot. J. Polit. Econ.*, November 1988, 35(4), pp. 361–71.

_____ and Torrance, Thomas S. On Risk, Rationality and Excessive Speculation in the Deutschmark–U.S. Dollar Exchange Market: Some Evidence Using Survey Data. *Oxford Bull. Econ. Statist.*, May 1988, 50(2), pp. 107–23.

MacDonald, S. Leslie; Woo, Chi-Keung and Keane, Dennis M. Estimating Residential Partial Outage Cost with Market Research Data. *Energy J.*, Special Issue, 1988, 9, pp. 151–59.

MacDonald, S. Scott; Peterson, Richard L. and Koch, Timothy W. Using Futures to Improve Treasury Bill Portfolio Performance. *J. Futures Markets*, April 1988, 8(2), pp. 167–84.

MacDonnell, Lawrence J. Natural Resources Dispute Resolution: An Overview. *Natural Res. J.*, Winter 1988, 28(1), pp. 5–19.

de Macedo, Jorge Braga. The Use of Commodity Contracts for the Management of Developing Country Commodity Risks: Discussion. In *Currie, D. and Vines, D., eds.*, 1988, pp. 180–84.

Macedo, Roberto. Brazilian Children and the Economic Crisis: The Evidence from the State of São Paulo. In *Cornia, G. A.; Jolly, R. and Stewart, F., eds.*, 1988, pp. 28–56.

_____. Inflation Stabilization: Brazil: Comment. In *Bruno, M., et al., eds.*, 1988, pp. 294–98.

Macey, Jonathan R. and Garrett, Elizabeth H. Market Discipline by Depositors: A Summary of the Theoretical and Empirical Arguments. *Yale J. Regul.*, Winter 1988, 5(1), pp. 215–39.

_____ and Miller, Geoffrey P. *Trans Union* Reconsidered. *Yale Law J.*, November 1988, 98(1), pp. 127–43.

Macfarlane, Alison and McPherson, C. K. The Quality of Official Health Statistics. *J. Roy. Statist. Soc.*, 1988, 151(2), pp. 342–48.

MacGregor, B. D.; Adams, C. D. and Baum, A. E. The Availability of Land for Inner City Development: A Case Study of Inner Manchester. *Urban Stud.*, February 1988, 25(1), pp. 62–76.

MacGregor, R. J. and Graham, J. D. The Impact of Lower Grains and Oilseeds Prices on Canada's Grains Sector: A Regional Programming Approach. *Can. J. Agr. Econ.*, March 1988, 36(1), pp. 51–67.

_____; Graham, J. D. and Webber, C. A. A Regional Analysis of Direct Government Assistance Programs in Canada and Their Impacts on the Beef and Hog Sectors. *Can. J. Agr. Econ.*, Part 2, December 1988, 36(4), pp. 915–28.

Machak, Joseph A.; Spivey, W. Allen and Rose, Elizabeth L. A Survey of the Teaching of Statistics in M.B.A. Programs. *J. Bus. Econ. Statist.*, April 1988, 6(2), pp. 273–82.

Machan, Tibor R. Economic Analysis and the Pursuit of Liberty. In *Walker, M. A., ed. (I)*, 1988, pp. 355–62.

_____. Ethics vs. Coercion: Morality or Just Values? In *[Rothbard, M. N.]*, 1988, pp. 236–46.

_____. Marxism: A Bourgeois Critique. *Int. J. Soc. Econ.*, 1988, 15(11–12), pp. 1–104.

_____ and Hook, Sidney. A Dialogue on Marxism. *Int. J. Soc. Econ.*, 1988, 15(11–12), pp. 105–30.

Macharzina, Klaus. Recent Advances in European Accounting: An Assessment by Use of the Accounting Culture Concept. In *Most, K. S., ed.*, 1988, pp. 131–47.

Machin, S. J. and Gregg, Paul A. Unions and the Incidence of Performance Linked Pay Schemes in Britain. *Int. J. Ind. Organ.*, March 1988, 6(1), pp. 97–107.

Machina, Mark J. Cardinal Properties of "Local Utility Functions" In *Munier, B. R., ed.*, 1988, pp. 339–44.

_____. Choice under Uncertainty: Problems Solved and Unsolved: Response. *J. Econ. Perspectives*, Spring 1988, 2(2), pp. 181–83.

_____. Generalized Expected Utility Analysis and the Nature of Observed Violations of the Independence Axiom. In *Gärdenfors, P. and Sahlin, N.-E., eds.*, 1988, 1983, pp. 215–39.

Machinea, Jose Luis and Fanelli, Jose Maria. Stopping Hyperinflation: The Case of the Austral Plan in Argentina, 1985–87. In *Bruno, M.*, *et al., eds.*, 1988, pp. 111–52.

Machlup, Fritz. Growth Rates, Trade Balances, and Exchange Rates. In *Melamed, L., ed.*, 1988, *1982*, pp. 167–82.

Maciejewicz, Jan and Monkiewicz, Jan. Trade and Foreign Investment in Services. The East European Dimension. *Konjunkturpolitik*, 1988, *34*(4), pp. 239–54.

MacInnes, Allan I. The Impact of the Civil Wars and Interregnum: Political Disruption and Social Change within Scottish Gaeldom. In *Mitchison, R. and Roebuck, P., eds.*, 1988, pp. 58–69.

MacKay, David B.; Wu, Tsung Wen and Day, Ralph L. Consumer Benefits versus Product Attributes: An Experimental Test. *Quart. J. Bus. Econ.*, Summer 1988, *27*(3), pp. 88–113.

Mackay, Robert J. After the Crash: Linkages between Stocks & Futures: Introduction. In *MacKay, R. J., ed.*, 1988, pp. 1–8.

MacKellar, F. Landis and Horlacher, David E. Population Growth versus Economic Growth (?). In *Salvatore, D., ed.*, 1988, pp. 25–44.

_____ **and Vining, Daniel R., Jr.** Research Policy and Review 26: Where Does the United States Stand in the Global Resource Scarcity Debate? *Environ. Planning A*, December 1988, *20*(12), pp. 1567–73.

Mackenzie, Brian and Woodall, Roy. Economic Productivity of Base Metal Exploration in Australia and Canada. In *Tilton, J. E.; Eggert, R. G. and Landsberg, H. H., eds.*, 1988, pp. 363–417.

Mackenzie, G. A. Social Security Issues in Developing Countries: The Latin America Experience. *Int. Monet. Fund Staff Pap.*, September 1988, *35*(3), pp. 496–522.

Mackenzie, Suzanne. Balancing Our Space and Time: The Impact of Women's Organisation on the British City, 1920–1980. In *Little, J.; Peake, L. and Richardson, P., eds.*, 1988, pp. 41–60.

Mackey, James T. and Davis, Charles J. Coalition Costs through Queueing Theory for Shapley Cost Allocations. In *Schwartz, B. N., ed.*, 1988, pp. 85–110.

Mackey, Timothy C. Is Bilateralism Possible? Discussion. In *Allen, K. and Macmillan, K., eds.*, 1988, pp. 183–88.

Mackie, J. A. C. Economic Growth in the ASEAN Region: The Political Underpinnings. In *Hughes, H., ed.*, 1988, pp. 283–326.

MacKie-Mason, Jeffrey K. and Hausman, Jerry A. Innovation and International Trade Policy: Some Lessons from the U.S. *Oxford Rev. Econ. Policy*, Winter 1988, *4*(4), pp. 56–72.

_____ **and Hausman, Jerry A.** Price Discrimination and Patent Policy. *Rand J. Econ.*, Summer 1988, *19*(2), pp. 253–65.

MacKinnon, James G. and Davidson, Russell. Double Length Artificial Regressions. *Oxford Bull. Econ. Statist.*, May 1988, *50*(2), pp. 203–17.

_____ **and Milbourne, Ross D.** Are Price Equa-

tions Really Money Demand Equations on Their Heads? *J. Appl. Econometrics*, Oct.–Dec. 1988, *3*(4), pp. 295–305.

MacKinnon, Mary and Green, Alan G. Unemployment and relief in Canada. In *Eichengreen, B. and Hatton, T. J., eds.*, 1988, pp. 353–96.

Mackintosh, Maureen and Wuyts, Marc. Accumulation, Social Services and Socialist Transition in the Third World: Reflections on Decentralised Planning Based on the Mozambican Experience. *J. Devel. Stud.*, July 1988, *24*(4), pp. 136–79.

MacKlem, Tiff. A Note on Models with Generated Covariances. *Oxford Bull. Econ. Statist.*, May 1988, *50*(2), pp. 219–23.

Maclachlan, M. and Karmel, T. Occupational Sex Segregation—Increasing or Decreasing? *Econ. Rec.*, September 1988, *64*(186), pp. 187–95.

MacLean, L. C. and Sutherland, W. R. S. Sensitivity Analysis of Optimal Growth Plans with Exogenous Capital Stocks. *J. Econ. (Z. Nationalökon.)*, 1988, *48*(3), pp. 263–78.

MacLennan, B. Jevons's Philosophy of Science. In *Wood, J. C., ed., Vol. 1*, 1988, *1972*, pp. 251–67.

MacLennan, Carol. The Democratic Administration of Government. In *Levine, M. V., et al.*, 1988, pp. 49–78.

Macleod, John. Emerging Trends in World Mineral Competition: A View from Down Under. In *Richardson, P. R. and Gesing, R., eds.*, 1988, pp. 11–23.

MacLeod, W. Bentley. Equity, Efficiency, and Incentives in Cooperative Teams. In *Jones, D. C. and Svejnar, J., eds.*, 1988, pp. 5–23.

_____ **and Malcomson, James M.** Reputation and Hierarchy in Dynamic Models of Employment. *J. Polit. Econ.*, August 1988, *96*(4), pp. 832–54.

_____ **; Norman, G. and Thisse, Jacques-François.** Price Discrimination and Equilibrium in Monopolistic Competition. *Int. J. Ind. Organ.*, December 1988, *6*(4), pp. 429–46.

MacMillan, Ian C. and Dubini, Paola. Entrepreneurial Prerequisites in Venture Capital Backed Projects. In *Kirchhoff, B. A., et al., eds.*, 1988, pp. 46–58.

_____ **and Hambrick, Donald C.** Capital Intensity, Market Share Instability, and Profits—The Case for Asset Parsimony. In *Lamb, R. and Shrivastava, P., eds.*, 1988, pp. 207–22.

_____ **; Kulow, David M. and Khoylian, Roubina.** Venture Capitalists' Involvement in Their Investments: Extent and Performance. In *Kirchhoff, B. A., et al., eds.*, 1988, pp. 303–23.

_____ **and Scheinberg, Sari.** An 11 Country Study of Motivations to Start a Business. In *Kirchhoff, B. A., et al., eds.*, 1988, pp. 669–87.

MacMillan, J. A.; Arthur, Louise M. and Smith, M. Economic Evaluation Methodology for an Alberta Agro-energy Project. *Can. J. Agr. Econ.*, Part 2, December 1988, *36*(4), pp. 905–13.

MacMinn, Richard D. and Martin, John D. Uncertainty, the Fisher Model, and Corporate Financial Theory. In *Chen, A. H., ed.*, 1988, pp. 227–64.

MacMurray, Robert; Tarullo, Ronald and Cole, Ishmail. Regulation, Technological Change, and Productivity Growth in the Coal Industry. In *Pennsylvania Economic Association*, 1988, pp. 682–94.

———; **Tarullo, Ronald and Cole, Ishmail.** Some Determinants of Official United States Coal Prices. In *Pennsylvania Economic Association*, 1988, pp. 695–706.

Macneil, Ian R. Contract Remedies: A Need for Better Efficiency Analysis. *J. Inst. Theoretical Econ.*, February 1988, *144*(1), pp. 6–30.

MacNeil, Teresa. Notes on Cape Breton Development. In *Choudhury, M. A., ed.*, 1988, pp. 148–53.

MacPherson, Alan. Industrial Innovation in the Small Business Sector: Empirical Evidence from Metropolitan Toronto. *Environ. Planning A*, July 1988, *20*(7), pp. 953–71.

———. New Product Development among Small Toronto Manufacturers: Empirical Evidence on the Role of Technical Service Linkages. *Econ. Geogr.*, January 1988, *64*(1), pp. 62–75.

Macpherson, David A. Self-employment and Married Women. *Econ. Letters*, 1988, *28*(3), pp. 281–84.

MacRae, Duncan, Jr. and Whittington, Dale. Assessing Preferences in Cost–Benefit Analysis: Reflections on Rural Water Supply Evaluation in Haiti. *J. Policy Anal. Manage.*, Winter 1988, *7*(2), pp. 246–63.

Macready, George B. and Dayton, C. Mitchell. Concomitant-Variable Latent-Class Models. *J. Amer. Statist. Assoc.*, March 1988, *83*(401), pp. 173–78.

MaCurdy, Thomas E. and Heckman, James J. Empirical Tests of Labor-Market Equilibrium: An Evaluation. *Carnegie–Rochester Conf. Ser. Public Policy*, Spring 1988, *28*, pp. 231–58.

Maczak, Antoni. State Revenues and National Income: Poland and the Crisis of the Seventeenth Century. In *Guarducci, A., ed.*, 1988, pp. 677–702.

Madan, Dilip B. Risk Measurement in Semimartingale Models with Multiple Consumption Goods [Consumption Correlatedness and Risk Measurement in Economies with Nontraded Assets and Heterogeneos Information]. *J. Econ. Theory*, April 1988, *44*(2), pp. 398–412.

Madden, Carolyn Watts and Crittenden, Robert. Health Insurance for the Uninsured: An Evaluation of Plan Design Preferences. In *Scheffler, R. M. and Rossiter, L. F., eds.*, 1988, pp. 99–112.

Madden, Gary G. Aggregate Studies of Automobile Demand: A Review. *Int. J. Transport Econ.*, June 1988, *15*(2), pp. 129–58.

Madden, J. P. and Stefanou, Spiro E. Economies of Size Revisited. *J. Agr. Econ.*, January 1988, *39*(1), pp. 125–32.

Madden, Janice Fanning. Communications: The Distribution of Economic Losses among Displaced Workers: Measurement Methods Matter. *J. Human Res.*, Winter 1988, *23*(1), pp. 93–107.

Madden, Moss. Demographics in Demographic–Economic Models: Notes on Two Activity–Commodity Frameworks. *Environ. Planning A*, November 1988, *20*(11), pp. 1537–42.

——— **and Batey, Peter W. J.** The Treatment of Migration in an Extended Input–Output Modelling Framework. *Ricerche Econ.*, April–June 1988, *42*(2), pp. 344–66.

Maddison, Angus. Ultimate and Proximate Growth Causality: A Critique of Mancur Olson on the Rise and Decline of Nations. *Scand. Econ. Hist. Rev.*, 1988, *36*(2), pp. 25–29.

——— **and van Ark, Bart.** Comparison of Real Output and Purchasing Power—Brazil/USA and Mexico/USA. In *Salazar-Carrillo, J. and Rao, D. S. P., eds.*, 1988, pp. 153–77.

Madison, Bernice. The Soviet Social Security System: Its Legal Structure and Fair Hearings Process. In *Potichnyj, P. J., ed.*, 1988, pp. 179–200.

Madura, Jeff and Fosberg, Richard H. Intertemporal Exchange Rate Risk: Implications for Corporate Exposure. *Rivista Int. Sci. Econ. Com.*, Oct.–Nov. 1988, *35*(10–11), pp. 1053–60.

Madura, William and House, Ernest R. Race, Gender, and Jobs: Losing Ground on Employment. *Policy Sci.*, 1988, *21*(4), pp. 351–82.

Maekawa, Koichi. Comparing the Wald, *LR* and *LM* Tests for Heteroscedasticity in a Linear Regression Model. *Econ. Letters*, 1988, *26*(1), pp. 37–41.

Maeshiro, Asatoshi and Vali, Shapoor. Pitfalls in the Estimation of a Differenced Model. *J. Bus. Econ. Statist.*, October 1988, *6*(4), pp. 511–15.

Mafune, Yonosuke. Corporate Social Performance and Policy in Japan. In *Preston, L. E., ed.*, 1988, pp. 291–303.

Magas, Istvan. Changing Positions of U.S. Exporters of Manufactures: High-Technology Trade. In *Missouri Valley Economic Assoc.*, 1988, pp. 97–109.

Magat, Wesley A.; Forrest, Anne and Viscusi, W. Kip. Altruistic and Private Valuations of Risk Reduction. *J. Policy Anal. Manage.*, Winter 1988, *7*(2), pp. 227–45.

———; **Viscusi, W. Kip and Huber, Joel.** Consumer Processing of Hazard Warning Information. *J. Risk Uncertainty*, June 1988, *1*(2), pp. 201–32.

———; **Viscusi, W. Kip and Huber, Joel.** Paired Comparison and Contingent Valuation Approaches to Morbidity Risk Valuation. *J. Environ. Econ. Manage.*, December 1988, *15*(4), pp. 395–411.

Magdalinos, Michael A. The Local Power of the Tests of Overidentifying Restrictions. *Int. Econ. Rev.*, August 1988, *29*(3), pp. 509–24.

Magee, F. R. and Iwama, M. Computers and Communications. In *Uyehara, C. H., ed.*, 1988, pp. 143–60.

Magee, Lonnie. The Behaviour of a Modified Box–Cox Regression Model When Some Values of the Dependent Variable are Close to Zero. *Rev. Econ. Statist.*, May 1988, *70*(2), pp. 362–66.

———; **Robb, A. Leslie and Burbidge, John B.** Alternative Transformations to Handle Extreme Values of the Dependent Variable. *J. Amer. Statist. Assoc.*, March 1988, *83*(401), pp. 123–27.

Magenheim, Ellen B. and Mueller, Dennis C. Are Acquiring-Firm Shareholders Better Off after an Acquisition? In *Coffee, J. C., Jr.; Lowenstein, L. and Rose-Ackerman, S., eds.*, 1988, pp. 171–93.

——— **and Murrell, Peter.** How to Haggle and to Stay Firm: Barter as Hidden Price Discrimination. *Econ. Inquiry*, July 1988, *26*(3), pp. 449–59.

Maggs, Peter B. The Soviet Union Today: Law. In *Cracraft, J., ed.*, 1988, pp. 339–48.

Magilligan, Robert J. and Rothschild, Leonard W., Jr. United States: The Definition of Residency for Federal Income Tax Purposes. *Bull. Int. Fiscal Doc.*, July 1988, *42*(7), pp. 324–28.

Magliolo, Joseph and Landsman, Wayne R. Cross-sectional Capital Market Research and Model Specification. *Accounting Rev.*, October 1988, *63*(4), pp. 586–604.

Magnus, Anne; Stoelwinder, Johannes U. and Abernethy, Margaret A. An Assessment of Alternative Models for Costing Nursing Services: A Measurement Theory Perspective. In *Smith, C. S., ed.*, 1988, pp. 127–44.

Magnus, Jan R. and Holly, Alberto. A Note on Instrumental Variables and Maximum Likelihood Estimation Procedures. *Ann. Écon. Statist.*, April–June 1988, (10), pp. 121–38.

———; **Pesaran, Bahram and Hoque, Asraul.** The Exact Multi-period Mean-Square Forecast Error for the First-Order Autoregressive Model. *J. Econometrics*, November 1988, *39*(3), pp. 327–46.

——— **and Woodland, Alan D.** On the Maximum Likelihood Estimation of Multivariate Regression Models Containing Serially Correlated Error Components. *Int. Econ. Rev.*, November 1988, *29*(4), pp. 707–25.

Magura, Michael and Lesage, James P. A Regional Payroll Forecasting Model That Uses Bayesian Shrinkage Techniques for Data Pooling. *Reg. Sci. Persp.*, 1988, *18*(1), pp. 100–116.

Mahabir, Dhanayshar and Cairns, Robert D. Contestability: A Revisionist View. *Economica*, May 1988, *55*(218), pp. 269–76.

Mahajan, Arvind and Saunders, Edward M., Jr. An Empirical Examination of Composite Stock Index Futures Pricing. *J. Futures Markets*, April 1988, *8*(2), pp. 211–28.

———; **Saunders, Edward M., Jr. and Kolari, James.** The Effect of Changes in Reserve Requirements on Bank Stock Prices. *J. Banking Finance*, June 1988, *12*(2), pp. 183–98.

Mahajan, V. S. Role of Remittances in Resource Mobilisation in North West Region. In *Raikhy, P. S. and Gill, S. S., eds.*, 1988, pp. 65–76.

Mahajan, Vijay and Wind, Yoram. New Product Forecasting Models: Directions for Research

and Implementation. *Int. J. Forecasting*, 1988, *4*(3), pp. 341–58.

Mahar, Dennis J. Population Growth and Human Carrying Capacity in Sub-Saharan Africa. In *Salvatore, D., ed.*, 1988, pp. 59–76.

Mahé, L. P. and Tavéra, C. Bilateral Harmonization of EC and U.S. Agricultural Policies. *Europ. Rev. Agr. Econ.*, 1988, *15*(4), pp. 327–48.

Mahmood, Mir Annice. Is Foreign Aid an Obstruction to Democracy and Development in the Third World? Comments. *Pakistan Devel. Rev.*, Part 2, Winter 1988, *27*(4), pp. 532–34.

——— **and Sahibzada, Shamim A.** The Economic Rate of Return in Small and Household Manufacturing Industries. *Pakistan Devel. Rev.*, Part 2, Winter 1988, *27*(4), pp. 875–83.

Mahmood, Moazam. Agricultural Prices in Pakistan: A Multimarket Analysis: Comments. *Pakistan Devel. Rev.*, Part 2, Winter 1988, *27*(4), pp. 593–94.

———. A General Theoretical Framework for Analyzing Capital Accumulation in Agriculture. *Pakistan Devel. Rev.*, Part 2, Winter 1988, *27*(4), pp. 621–30.

Mahmood, Riaz and Sarmad, Khwaja. Prospects for Expanding Trade between SAARC and ASEAN Countries. *Pakistan Devel. Rev.*, Summer 1988, *27*(2), pp. 129–36.

Mahmud, S. Fakhre and Chishti, Salim. Energy Substitution in Pakistan's Manufacturing. *Pakistan Econ. Soc. Rev.*, Summer 1988, *26*(1), pp. 57–64.

———; **Hasan, M. Aynul and Kadir, S. Ghulam.** Substitutability of Pakistan's Monetary Assets under Alternative Monetary Aggregates. *Pakistan Devel. Rev.*, Autumn 1988, *27*(3), pp. 317–26.

Mahmud, Simeen. Exploring the Relationship between Women's Work and Fertility: The Bangladesh Context. *Bangladesh Devel. Stud.*, December 1988, *16*(4), pp. 99–113.

Mahon, John F. and Kelley, Patricia C. The Politics of Toxic Wastes: Multinational Corporations as Facilitators of Transnational Public Policy. In *Preston, L. E., ed.*, 1988, pp. 59–86.

Mahoney, Patrick I. The Recent Behavior of Demand Deposits. *Fed. Res. Bull.*, April 1988, *74*(4), pp. 195–208.

Mai, Chao-cheng and Hwang, Hong. Advertising and Industrial Location. *Int. J. Ind. Organ.*, June 1988, *6*(2), pp. 223–31.

——— **and Hwang, Hong.** On the Equivalence of Tariffs and Quotas under Duopoly: A Conjectural Variation Approach. *J. Int. Econ.*, May 1988, *24*(3–4), pp. 373–80.

——— **and Hwang, Hong.** Optimal Export Subsidies and Marginal Cost Differentials. *Econ. Letters*, 1988, *27*(3), pp. 279–82.

——— **and Hwang, Hong.** Why Voluntary Export Restraints Are Voluntary: An Extension. *Can. J. Econ.*, November 1988, *21*(4), pp. 877–82.

———; **Liu, Jung-chao and Shih, Jun-ji.** A General Analysis of the Output Effect under Third-Degree Price Discrimination. *Econ. J.*, March 1988, *98*(389), pp. 149–58.

Maiden, C. J. Appropriate Technology and Economic Growth. In *Kozmetsky, G.; Matsumoto, H. and Smilor, R. W., eds.*, 1988, pp. 83–86.

Maidique, Modesto A. and Zirger, Billie Jo. The New Product Learning Cycle. In *Grønhaug, K. and Kaufmann, G., eds.*, 1988, *1985*, pp. 407–31.

Maier, Steven F. Float Management: The Impact of Regulatory and Technological Changes, Electronic Funds Transfer and National Banking. In *Kim, Y. H., ed.*, 1988, pp. 67–78.

Mailath, George J. An Abstract Two-Period Game with Simultaneous Signaling—Existence of Separating Equilibria. *J. Econ. Theory*, December 1988, *46*(2), pp. 373–94.

———. On the Behavior of Separating Equilibria of Signaling Games with a Finite Set of Types as the Set of Types Becomes Dense in an Interval. *J. Econ. Theory*, April 1988, *44*(2), pp. 413–24.

Maillard, Bénédicte and Sneessens, Henri. Investment, Sales Constraints and Profitability in France, 1957–1985. *Rech. Écon. Louvain*, 1988, *54*(2), pp. 151–67.

Maillard, Didier and Milleron, Jean-Claude. World Tax Reform: A Progress Report: France. In *Pechman, J. A., ed.*, 1988, pp. 95–112.

Maillat, Denis and Vasserot, Jean-Yves. Economic and Territorial Conditions for Indigenous Revival in Europe's Industrial Regions. In *Aydalot, P. and Keeble, D., eds.*, 1988, pp. 163–83.

Maillet, Peirre. Summary of the Conference. *Empirica*, 1988, *15*(1), pp. 227–34.

Main, Brian G. M. Hourly Earnings of Female Part-time versus Full-time Employees. *Manchester Sch. Econ. Soc. Stud.*, December 1988, *56*(4), pp. 331–44.

———. The Lifetime Attachment of Women to the Labour Market. In *Hunt, A., ed.*, 1988, pp. 23–51.

———. Women's Hourly Earnings: The Influence of Work Histories on Rates of Pay. In *Hunt, A., ed.*, 1988, pp. 105–22.

———; **Raffe, David and Garner, Catherine.** The Distribution of School-Leaver Unemployment within Scottish Cities. *Urban Stud.*, April 1988, *25*(2), pp. 133–44.

——— **and Shelly, Michael A.** School Leavers and the Search for Employment. *Oxford Econ. Pap.*, September 1988, *40*(3), pp. 487–504.

Main, Gloria L. and Main, Jackson T. Economic Growth and the Standard of Living in Southern New England, 1640–1774. *J. Econ. Hist.*, March 1988, *48*(1), pp. 27–46.

Main, Jackson T. and Main, Gloria L. Economic Growth and the Standard of Living in Southern New England, 1640–1774. *J. Econ. Hist.*, March 1988, *48*(1), pp. 27–46.

Main, Ombretta. Lifting Trade Barriers in Nonhomogeneous Industries. *Ricerche Econ.*, Oct.–Dec. 1988, *42*(4), pp. 678–94.

Maindiratta, Ajay and Banker, Rajiv D. Nonparametric Analysis of Technical and Allocative Efficiencies in Production. *Econometrica*, November 1988, *56*(6), pp. 1315–32.

Mainwaring, L. A Neo-Ricardian Analysis of International Trade. In *Steedman, I:, ed., Vol. 2*, 1988, pp. 201–17.

Maiolo, John R.; Blomo, Vito J. and Orbach, Michael. Competition and Conflict in the U.S. Atlantic Coast Menhaden Industry. *Amer. J. Econ. Soc.*, January 1988, *47*(1), pp. 41–60.

Mair, Andrew; Florida, Richard and Kenney, Martin. The New Geography of Automobile Production: Japanese Transplants in North America. *Econ. Geogr.*, October 1988, *64*(4), pp. 352–73.

Mair, Douglas. Raw Material Prices and Kalecki's Wage Share Theory: A Comment. *J. Post Keynesian Econ.*, Spring 1988, *10*(3), pp. 482–86.

——— **and Damania, Richard.** The Ricardian Tradition and Local Property Taxation. *Cambridge J. Econ.*, December 1988, *12*(4), pp. 435–49.

Mairesse, Jacques. Les lois de la production ne sont plus ce qu'elles étaient: Une introduction à l'économétrie des panels. (The Laws of Production Are Not What They Used to Be: An Introduction to the Econometrics of Panel Data. With English summary.) *Revue Écon.*, January 1988, *39*(1), pp. 225–71.

Maisto, Guglielmo. Tax Treatment of Computer Software: Italy. In *International Fiscal Association, ed. (II)*, 1988, pp. 389–97.

Maital, Shlomo. Applied Behavioural Economics, Volume I: Introduction. In *Maital, S., ed., Vol. 1*, 1988, pp. xi–xiv.

———. Novelty, Comfort, and Pleasure: Inside the Utility-Function Black Box. In *Albanese, P. J., ed.*, 1988, pp. 1–29.

Maitra, Priyatosh. Population Growth, Technological Change and Economic Development—The Indian Case, with a Critique of Marxist Interpretation. In *Tisdell, C. and Maitra, P., eds.*, 1988, pp. 9–34.

Maitra, Tares. Rural Poverty in West Bengal. In *Srinivasan, T. N. and Bardhan, P. K., eds.*, 1988, pp. 402–49.

Majerus, David W. Price vs. Quantity Competition in Oligopoly Supergames. *Econ. Letters*, 1988, *27*(3), pp. 293–97.

Majmudar, Madhavi. The Multi-Fibre Arrangement (MFA IV) 1986–1991: A Move towards a Liberalized System? *J. World Trade*, April 1988, *22*(2), pp. 109–25.

Major, Philip J.; Mollett, Nina and Clark, Ian N. Development and Implementation of New Zealand's ITQ Management System. *Marine Resource Econ.*, 1988, *5*(4), pp. 325–49.

Majumdar, Mukul. Decentralization in Infinite Horizon Economies: An Introduction. *J. Econ. Theory*, August 1988, *45*(2), pp. 217–27.

——— **and Brock, William A.** On Characterizing Optimal Competitive Programs in Terms of Decentralizable Conditions. *J. Econ. Theory*, August 1988, *45*(2), pp. 262–73.

——— **and Hurwicz, Leonid.** Optimal Intertemporal Allocation Mechanisms and Decentralization of Decisions. *J. Econ. Theory*, August 1988, *45*(2), pp. 228–61.

Majumder, Amita. A Note on Optimal Commodity Taxation in India. *Econ. Letters*, 1988, 27(2), pp. 167–71.

Mak, James and White Kenneth. Tourism in Asia and the Pacific. In *Lee, C. H. and Naya, S.*, eds., 1988, pp. 121–49.

Mak, King-Tim. Approximate Separability and Aggregation. *J. Econ. Theory*, June 1988, 45(1), pp. 200–206.

———. General Homothetic Production Correspondences. In *Dogramaci, A. and Färe, R.*, eds., 1988, pp. 235–49.

———. Separability and the Existence of Aggregates. In *Eichhorn, W.*, ed., 1988, pp. 649–70.

Makar, Scott D. and Blair, Roger D. The Structure of Florida's Medical Malpractice Insurance Market: If It Ain't Broke, Don't Fix It. *Yale J. Regul.*, Summer 1988, 5(2), pp. 427–53.

Makarim, Wajdi; Verzilli, Andrew G. and Awerbuch, Patricia. Frustration Equilibrium and Disequilibrium Positions: Has Anything Changed in Eight Years? In *Pennsylvania Economic Association*, 1988, pp. 32–43.

Makarov, Valery L. On Long-term Directions of Research by TsEMI AN SSSR. *Matekon*, Summer 1988, 24(4), pp. 5–26.

———. On the Strategy for Implementing Economic Reform in the USSR. *Amer. Econ. Rev.*, May 1988, 78(2), pp. 457–60.

Makela, Carole J. Content Is Not Enough. In *Maynes, E. S. and ACCI Research Committee*, eds., 1988, pp. 885–89.

Makhija, Anil K. and De Bondt, Werner F. M. Throwing Good Money after Bad? Nuclear Power Plant Investment Decisions and the Relevance of Sunk Costs. *J. Econ. Behav. Organ.*, September 1988, 10(2), pp. 173–99.

———; **Ferris, Stephen P. and Haugen, Robert A.** Predicting Contemporary Volume with Historic Volume at Differential Price Levels: Evidence Supporting the Disposition Effect. *J. Finance*, July 1988, 43(3), pp. 677–97.

———; **Thompson, Howard E. and Grammatikos, Theoharry.** Financing Corporate Takeovers by Individuals Seeking Control. *Managerial Dec. Econ.*, September 1988, 9(3), pp. 227–35.

Maki, Atsushi. The Estimation of a Complete Demand System Using the Marginal Rates of Substitution: An Indifference Map Interpretation of the Houthakker–Taylor Model. *Econ. Stud. Quart.*, March 1988, 39(1), pp. 64–76.

Maki, Dennis R. and Ng, Ignace. Strike Activity of U.S. Institutions in Canada. *Brit. J. Ind. Relat.*, March 1988, 26(1), pp. 63–73.

Mäki, Uskali. How to Combine Rhetoric and Realism in the Methodology of Economics. *Econ. Philos.*, April 1988, 4(1), pp. 89–109.

———. Realism, Economics, and Rhetoric: A Rejoinder. *Econ. Philos.*, April 1988, 4(1), pp. 167–69.

Makin, John H. Japan's Investment in America: Is It a Threat? *Challenge*, Nov.–Dec. 1988, 31(6), pp. 8–16.

Makinen, Gail E. The German Inflation 1914–1923: Review Article. *Atlantic Econ. J.*, September 1988, 16(3), pp. 46–54.

———. The Greek Hyperinflation and Stabilization of 1943–1946: A Reply. *J. Econ. Hist.*, March 1988, 48(1), pp. 140–42.

———. Inflation Stabilization in Bolivia: Comment. In *Bruno, M., et al.*, eds., 1988, pp. 347–53.

———; **Anderson, Robert B. and Bomberger, William A.** The Demand for Money, the "Reform Effect," and the Money Supply Process in Hyperinflations: The Evidence from Greece and Hungary II Reexamined. *J. Money, Credit, Banking*, November 1988, 20(4), pp. 653–72.

——— **and Woodward, G. Thomas.** The Transition from Hyperinflation to Stability: Some Evidence. *Eastern Econ. J.*, Jan.–March 1988, 14(1), pp. 19–26.

Makridakis, Spyros. Metaforecasting: Ways of Improving Forecasting Accuracy and Usefulness. *Int. J. Forecasting*, 1988, 4(3), pp. 467–91.

——— **and Fildes, Robert.** Forecasting and Loss Functions. *Int. J. Forecasting*, 1988, 4(4), pp. 545–50.

——— **and Gardner, Everette S., Jr.** The Future of Forecasting. *Int. J. Forecasting*, 1988, 4(3), pp. 325–30.

——— **and Hogarth, Robin M.** Forecasting and Planning: An Evolution. In *Earl, P. E.*, ed., Vol. 1, 1988, 1981, pp. 193–216.

Maks, J. A. H. and van Witteloostuijn, A. Walras: A Hicksian *avant la lettre*. *Écon. Appl.*, 1988, 41(3), pp. 595–608.

Maksimovic, Vojislav. Capital Structure in Repeated Oligopolies. *Rand J. Econ.*, Autumn 1988, 19(3), pp. 389–407.

———; **Zechner, Josef and Brennan, Michael J.** Vendor Financing. *J. Finance*, December 1988, 43(5), pp. 1127–41.

Maksy, Mostafa M. Articulation Problems between the Balance Sheet and the Funds Statement. *Accounting Rev.*, October 1988, 63(4), pp. 683–99.

Malanowski, Kazimierz. Higher Order Sensitivity of Solutions to Convex Programming Problems without Strict Complementarity. In *Iri, M. and Yajima, K.*, eds., 1988, pp. 148–64.

Malatesta, Paul H. and Walkling, Ralph A. Poison Pill Securities: Stockholder Wealth, Profitability, and Ownership Structure. *J. Finan. Econ.*, Jan.–March 1988, 20(1–2), pp. 347–76.

Malcomson, James M. Some Analytics of the Laffer Curve: Reply. *J. Public Econ.*, February 1988, 35(1), pp. 131–32.

——— **and MacLeod, W. Bentley.** Reputation and Hierarchy in Dynamic Models of Employment. *J. Polit. Econ.*, August 1988, 96(4), pp. 832–54.

——— **and Spinnewyn, Frans.** The Multiperiod Principal–Agent Problem. *Rev. Econ. Stud.*, July 1988, 55(3), pp. 391–407.

Malczewski, J. and Ogryczak, W. A Multiobjective Approach to the Reorganization of Health-Service Areas: A Case Study. *Environ. Planning A*, November 1988, 20(11), pp. 1461–70.

Male, Sarah. Non-price Barriers to Home Ownership. *Econ. Rec.*, March 1988, *64*(184), pp. 26–38.

Malecki, E. J. The Challenge of Rural Development: Commentary. *Environ. Planning A*, May 1988, *20*(5), pp. 567–68.

Malenbaum, Wilfred. Amartya Sen on Future Development Policy and Program: Review Article. *Econ. Develop. Cult. Change*, January 1988, *36*(2), pp. 401–09.

Malfi, Lucio. Government Production in ESA and SNA Tables. In *Ciaschini, M., ed.*, 1988, pp. 61–74.

Malhotra, Devinder M. and Garofalo, Gasper A. Aggregation of Capital and Its Substitution with Energy. *Eastern Econ. J.*, July–Sept. 1988, *14*(3), pp. 251–62.

———— **and Garofalo, Gasper A.** Analysis of Regional Productivity with Capital as a Quasi-fixed Factor. *Reg. Sci. Urban Econ.*, November 1988, *18*(4), pp. 533–47.

Malhotra, Naresh K. Self Concept and Product Choice: An Integrated Perspective. *J. Econ. Psych.*, March 1988, *9*(1), pp. 1–28.

Malhotra, R. N. Beyond Adjustment: The Asian Experience: Opening Remarks. In *Streeten, P., ed.*, 1988, pp. 18–29.

Malik, Khalid; James, Dilmus and Lalkaka, Rustam. Cloning of Tea in Malawi. In *Bhalla, A. S. and James, D., eds.*, 1988, pp. 258–68.

Malik, Muhammad Hussain. On an Empirical Definition of Money for Pakistan: Comments. *Pakistan Devel. Rev.*, Part 2, Winter 1988, *27*(4), pp. 858–59.

————. Some New Evidence on the Incidence of Poverty in Pakistan. *Pakistan Devel. Rev.*, Part 2, Winter 1988, *27*(4), pp. 509–15.

Malik, Salman and Jamal, Haroon. Shifting Patterns in Developmental Rank Ordering: A Case Study of the Districts of Sind Province. *Pakistan Devel. Rev.*, Summer 1988, *27*(2), pp. 159–82.

Malik, Sohail J. and Battese, George E. Estimation of Elasticities of Substitution for CES and VES Production Functions using Firm-Level Data for Food-Processing Industries in Pakistan. *Pakistan Devel. Rev.*, Spring 1988, *27*(1), pp. 59–71.

————; **Mushtaq, Mohammad and Ghani, Ejaz.** Consumption Patterns of Major Food Items in Pakistan: Provincial, Sectoral and Inter-temporal Differences 1979–1984-85. *Pakistan Devel. Rev.*, Part 2, Winter 1988, *27*(4), pp. 751–59.

Malinvaud, Edmond. Distributional Aspects of the Life Cycle Theory of Saving: Comments. In *Kessler, D. and Masson, A., eds.*, 1988, pp. 236–39.

————. I macroeconomisti di fronte alle indagini sulla popolazione attiva. (Macroeconomists Confronted with the Working Population Surveys. With English summary.) *Econ. Lavoro*, Apr.–June 1988, *22*(2), pp. 3–11.

Maliţa, M. Scientific Concepts in the System Theory. *Econ. Computat. Cybern. Stud. Res.*, 1988, *23*(1), pp. 23–29.

Malixi, Margaret and Bahmani-Oskooee, Mohsen. Exchange Rate Flexibility and the LDCs Demand for International Reserves. *J. Quant. Econ.*, July 1988, *4*(2), pp. 317–28.

Maljutov, M. B. Design and Analysis in Generalized Regression Model F. In *Fedorov, V. and Lauter, H., eds.*, 1988, pp. 72–76.

Malkiel, Burton G. The Brady Commission Report: A Critique. *J. Portfol. Manage.*, Summer 1988, *14*(4), pp. 9–13.

Mallela, Parthasaradhi and Yoo, Sang-Hee. On the Inadequacy of Sufficient Conditions under 'Limited Information' Identification. *Econ. Letters*, 1988, *27*(4), pp. 337–39.

Malley, James and Foster, John. The Domestic and Foreign-Owned Sectors of Scottish Manufacturing: A Macroeconomic Approach to Their Relative Performance and Prospects. *Scot. J. Polit. Econ.*, August 1988, *35*(3), pp. 250–65.

Malliaris, A. G.; Robinson, N. S. and Kondonassis, A. J. Political Instability and Economic Development: An Economic History Case Study of Greece, 1948–1966: A Reply. *J. Europ. Econ. Hist.*, Spring 1988, *17*(1), pp. 185–86.

Mallick, Robert J.; Heijdra, Ben J. and Lowenberg, Anton D. Marxism, Methodological Individualism, and the New Institutional Economics. *J. Inst. Theoretical Econ.*, April 1988, *144*(2), pp. 296–317.

Mallon, Richard D.; Hutcheson, Thomas L. and Stern, Joseph J. Foreign Exchange Regimes and Industrial Growth in Bangladesh. *World Devel.*, December 1988, *16*(12), pp. 1419–39.

Mallory, Charles D. La pollution est non convexe. (With English summary.) *L'Actual. Econ.*, June 1988, *64*(2), pp. 251–61.

Mallows, C. L. Bayesian Variable Selection in Linear Regression: Comment. *J. Amer. Statist. Assoc.*, December 1988, *83*(404), pp. 1034–35.

Malmgren, Harald B. Information, Expectations and the Theory of the Firm. In *Earl, P. E., ed.*, Vol. 2, 1988, *1961*, pp. 34–56.

————. Innovation and the Global Economic Environment. In *Yochelson, J., ed.*, 1988, pp. 3–18.

Malone, R. Phil; Stansell, Stanley R. and Fenstermaker, J. Van. An Analysis of Commercial Bank Common Stock Returns: 1802–97. *Appl. Econ.*, June 1988, *20*(6), pp. 813–41.

Maloney, Michael T. and Brady, Gordon L. Capital Turnover and Marketable Pollution Rights. *J. Law Econ.*, April 1988, *31*(1), pp. 203–26.

———— **and Lindsay, Cotton M.** A Model and Some Evidence Concerning the Influence of Discrimination on Wages. *Econ. Inquiry*, October 1988, *26*(4), pp. 645–60.

———— **and Lindsay, Cotton M.** Party Politics and the Price of Payola. *Econ. Inquiry*, April 1988, *26*(2), pp. 203–21.

———— **and McCormick, Robert E.** Excess Capacity, Cyclical Production, and Merger Motives: Some Evidence from the Capital Markets. *J. Law Econ.*, October 1988, *31*(2), pp. 321–50.

———— **and McGregor, Rob Roy, III.** Financing the Unemployment Insurance System and the

Interest Group Theory of Government. *Public Choice*, March 1988, 56(3), pp. 249–58.

Maloney, Tim and Ratti, Ronald A. Divergent Trends in the Discouragement of Adult Men, Adult Women, and Teenagers: 1970–1986. *Econ. Letters*, 1988, 28(1), pp. 93–96.

Malueg, David A. Repeated Insurance Contracts with Differential Learning. *Rev. Econ. Stud.*, January 1988, 55(1), pp. 177–81.

Maluwa, Tiyanjana. Legal Aspects of the Niger River under the Niamey Treaties. *Natural Res. J.*, Fall 1988, 28(4), pp. 671–97.

Mama, E. Touna. Dette extérieure et seuil d'endettement supportable. (External Debt and Sustainable Debt. With English summary.) *Écon. Soc.*, June–July 1988, 22(6–7), pp. 37–51.

Mamalakis, Markos. Foreign Investment and Unilateral Transfers. In *Jorge, A. and Salazar-Carrillo, J., eds.*, 1988, pp. 29–40.

Manage, Neela and Marlow, Michael L. Expenditures and Receipts in State and Local Government Finances: Reply. *Public Choice*, December 1988, 59(3), pp. 287–90.

Manas-Anton, Luis and Hsieh, David A. Empirical Regularities in the Deutsche Mark Futures Options. In *Fabozzi, F. J., ed.*, 1988, pp. 183–208.

Manchester, Joyce. The Baby Boom, Housing, and Financial Flows. *Amer. Econ. Rev.*, May 1988, 78(2), pp. 70–75.

Mandel, R. and Bank, B. Quantitative Stability of (Mixed-) Integer Linear Optimization Problems. In *Kurzhanski, A.; Neumann, K. and Pallaschke, D., eds.*, 1988, pp. 3–15.

Mandelbaum, Thomas B. The District Business Economy in 1987: The Expansion Continues. *Fed. Res. Bank St. Louis Rev.*, March–April 1988, 70(2), pp. 17–28.

———— **and Coughlin, Cletus C.** Why Have State Per Capita Incomes Diverged Recently? *Fed. Res. Bank St. Louis Rev.*, Sept.–Oct. 1988, 70(5), pp. 24–36.

Manders, A. Production Technology and Distribution Theory. In *Brenner, Y. S.; Reijnders, J. P. G. and Spithoven, A. H. G. M., eds.*, 1988, pp. 211–25.

Manegold, D. Recent Changes in EC Agricultural Policy: A 1987–88 Policy Review. *Rev. Marketing Agr. Econ.*, August 1988, 56(2), pp. 153–78.

Maneschi, Andrea. The Place of Lord Kahn's *The Economics of the Short Period* in the Theory of Imperfect Competition. *Hist. Polit. Econ.*, Summer 1988, 20(2), pp. 155–71.

Mănescu, Manea. Alma Mater Scientiae Oeconomicae Romaniae. *Econ. Computat. Cybern. Stud. Res.*, 1988, 23(3), pp. 5–12.

————. The Importance of the Setting Up of the Romanian Unitary National State for Romania's Socio-Economic Development. *Econ. Computat. Cybern. Stud. Res.*, 1988, 23(4), pp. 5–13.

————. The System-Model-Information-Cybernetics Dialectics in the Conditions of the Contemporary Technical–Scientific Revolution, of

Economic and Social Development. *Econ. Computat. Cybern. Stud. Res.*, 1988, 23(1), pp. 11–16.

Mangan, John and Shorten, Brett. Micro-economic Employment Initiatives in Regional New South Wales. *Reg. Stud.*, April 1988, 22(2), pp. 162–66.

Mangasarian, O. L. and De Leone, R. Serial and Parallel Solution of Large Scale Linear Programs by Augmented Lagrangian Successive Overrelaxation. In *Kurzhanski, A.; Neumann, K. and Pallaschke, D., eds.*, 1988, pp. 103–24.

Mangla, I. and Kabir, M. Effects of Financial Innovations on the Money Demand Function: Canadian Evidence. *Appl. Econ.*, September 1988, 20(9), pp. 1263–73.

Mangum, Garth. International Division of Labor: Comments. In *Mangum, G. and Philips, P., eds.*, 1988, pp. 353–55.

———— **and Philips, Peter.** Three Worlds of Labor Economics: Introduction. In *Mangum, G. and Philips, P., eds.*, 1988, pp. 3–18.

Mangum, Stephen L. Comparable Worth: The Institutional Economist's Approach. In *Mangum, G. and Philips, P., eds.*, 1988, pp. 201–16.

————. The Male–Female Comparable Worth Debate: Alterntive Economic Perspectives on an Issue That Cuts across the Social Sciences. *Amer. J. Econ. Soc.*, April 1988, 47(2), pp. 149–65.

Mankiw, N. Gregory. How Does Macroeconomic Policy Affect Output? Comment. *Brookings Pap. Econ. Act.*, 1988, (2), pp. 481–85.

————. Imperfect Competition and the Keynesian Cross. *Econ. Letters*, 1988, 26(1), pp. 7–13.

————. New Issues in Corporate Finance: Comments. *Europ. Econ. Rev.*, June 1988, 32(5), pp. 1183–86.

————. Recent Developments in Macroeconomics: A Very Quick Refresher Course. *J. Money, Credit, Banking*, Part 2, August 1988, 20(3), pp. 436–49.

———— **and Blanchard, Olivier Jean.** Consumption: Beyond Certainty Equivalence. *Amer. Econ. Rev.*, May 1988, 78(2), pp. 173–77.

————; **Romer, David and Ball, Laurence.** The New Keynesian Economics and the Output–Inflation Trade-off. *Brookings Pap. Econ. Act.*, 1988, (1), pp. 1–65.

———— **and Summers, Lawrence H.** Money Demand and the Effects of Fiscal Policies: Reply. *J. Money, Credit, Banking*, November 1988, 20(4), pp. 715–17.

Manley, Michael. South–South Co-operation: Challenge to Political Process. In *Sopiee, N.; Hamzah, B. A. and Leong, C. H., eds.*, 1988, pp. 29–32.

Mann, Arthur J. and Smith, Robert. Tax Attitudes and Tax Evasion in Puerto Rico: A Survey of Upper Income Professionals. *J. Econ. Devel.*, June 1988, 13(1), pp. 121–41.

Mann, Catherine L. Industrial Policy and International Competition in Wide-Bodied Jet Air craft: Comment. In *Baldwin, R. E., ed. (II)*, 1988, pp. 74–77.

Mann, Cindy and Albelda, Randy. Jobs, Fathers and the States: Welfare Policy and the New Federalism. *Rev. Radical Polit. Econ.*, Summer–Fall 1988, *20*(2–3), pp. 61–67.

Mann, Duncan P. A Model Based on Individual Behavior. In *Berkowitz, M., ed.*, 1988, pp. 62–69.

_____ **and Wissink, Jennifer P.** Money-Back Contracts with Double Moral Hazard. *Rand J. Econ.*, Summer 1988, *19*(2), pp. 285–92.

Mann, Patrick C. and Dalton, Margaret M. Telephone Cost Allocation: Testing the Variability of Costs. *Land Econ.*, August 1988, *64*(3), pp. 296–305.

Mann, Prem S. and Kapoor, Bhushan L. Earnings Differentials between Public, Private and Joint Sectors in Punjab (India). *J. Devel. Stud.*, October 1988, *25*(1), pp. 97–111.

Mannan, M. A. Preference for Son, Desire for Additional Children and Contraceptive Use in Bangladesh. *Bangladesh Devel. Stud.*, September 1988, *16*(3), pp. 31–57.

Mannari, Hiroshi and Marsh, Robert M. The Changing Industrial Relations Scene in Japan and Its Impact on Managerial Behavior. In *Dlugos, G.; Dorow, W. and Weiermair, K., eds.*, 1988, pp. 273–87.

Manne, Henry G. Some Perspectives on Contractual Relations: Concluding Remarks. *J. Inst. Theoretical Econ.*, February 1988, *144*(1), pp. 237–41.

Männel, Wolfgang. Besonderheiten der internen Rechnungslegung öffentlicher Unternehmungen und Verwaltungen. (With English summary.) *Z. Betriebswirtshaft*, August 1988, *58*(8), pp. 839–57.

Manning, Alan. A Model of the Labour Market with Some Marxian and Keynesian Features. *Europ. Econ. Rev.*, November 1988, *32*(9), pp. 1797–1816.

_____ **and Alogoskoufis, George.** Wage Setting and Unemployment Persistence in Europe, Japan and the USA. *Europ. Econ. Rev.*, March 1988, *32*(2–3), pp. 698–706.

_____ **and Lockwood, Ben.** Inequality and Inefficiency in a Model of Occupational Choice with Asymmetric Information. *J. Public Econ.*, November 1988, *37*(2), pp. 147–69.

Manning, Chris. Rural Employment Creation in Java: Lessons from the Green Revolution and Oil Boom. *Population Devel. Rev.*, March 1988, *14*(1), pp. 47–80.

_____ **and Jayasuriya, Sisira K.** Survey of Recent Developments. *Bull. Indonesian Econ. Stud.*, August 1988, *24*(2), pp. 3–41.

Manning, Christopher A. The Determinants of Intercity Home Building Site Price Differences. *Land Econ.*, February 1988, *64*(1), pp. 1–14.

Manning, D. N. Household Demand for Energy in the UK. *Energy Econ.*, January 1988, *10*(1), pp. 59–78.

Manning, Dorothy and Foreman-Peck, James. How Well Is BT Performing? An International Comparison of Telecommunications Total Factor Productivity. *Fisc. Stud.*, August 1988, *9*(3), pp. 54–67.

_____ **and Foreman-Peck, James.** Telecommunications in Italy. In *Foreman-Peck, J. and Müller, J., eds.*, 1988, pp. 181–201.

_____ **and Foreman-Peck, James.** Telecommunications in Norway. In *Foreman-Peck, J. and Müller, J., eds.*, 1988, pp. 221–36.

_____ **and Foreman-Peck, James.** Telecommunications in the United Kingdom. In *Foreman-Peck, J. and Müller, J., eds.*, 1988, pp. 257–78.

_____, **et al.** Telecommunications in Spain. In *Foreman-Peck, J. and Müller, J., eds.*, 1988, pp. 237–55.

Manning, Ian. Are Tax Cuts Practicable? *Australian Tax Forum*, 1988, *5*(3), pp. 265–83.

Manning, Kingsley; Norburn, David and Birley, Sue. Implementing Corporate Venturing. In *Lamb, R. and Shrivastava, P., eds.*, 1988, pp. 165–79.

Manning, Patrick. The Anthropology of Slavery: Review Essay. *African Econ. Hist.*, 1988, (17), pp. 147–52.

Manning, Richard and Holmes, James M. Memory and Market Stability: The Case of the Cobweb. *Econ. Letters*, 1988, *28*(1), pp. 1–7.

Manning, Travis W. Methods in Economics. *Can. J. Agr. Econ.*, Part 2, December 1988, *36*(4), pp. 775–87.

Manning, Willard G.; Wells, Kenneth B. and Keeler, Emmett B. The Demand for Episodes of Mental Health Services. *J. Health Econ.*, December 1988, *7*(4), pp. 369–92.

Mannion, R.; Tillack, R. and Vincent, D. Effects of Petroleum Product Excises on Agriculture. *Rev. Marketing Agr. Econ.*, April 1988, *56*(1), pp. 121–28.

Mannix, Elizabeth A.; Thompson, Leigh L. and Bazerman, Max H. Groups as Mixed-Motive Negotiations. In *Lawler, E. J. and Markovsky, B., eds.*, 1988, pp. 195–216.

Manns, Curtis L. and March, James G. Financial Adversity, Internal Competition, and Curriculum Change in a University. In *March, J. G.*, 1988, *1978*, pp. 61–75.

Manouchehi, S. More on the Monetary Approach to the Balance of Payments. In *Missouri Valley Economic Assoc.*, 1988, pp. 30–33.

Manouchehri, Shahram and Forget, Evelyn L. Keynes's Neglected Heritage: The Classical Microfoundations of *The General Theory. J. Post Keynesian Econ.*, Spring 1988, *10*(3), pp. 401–13.

Manser, Marilyn E. and McDonald, Richard J. An Analysis of Substitution Bias in Measuring Inflation, 1959–85. *Econometrica*, July 1988, *56*(4), pp. 909–30.

Mansfield, Charles Y. Tax Administration in Developing Countries: An Economic Perspective. *Int. Monet. Fund Staff Pap.*, March 1988, *35*(1), pp. 181–97.

Mansfield, Edward R. and Conerly, Michael D. An Approximate Test for Comparing Heteroscedastic Regression Models. *J. Amer. Statist.*

Assoc., September 1988, *83*(403), pp. 811–17.

Mansfield, Edwin. Industrial R&D in Japan and the United States: A Comparative Study. *Amer. Econ. Rev.*, May 1988, *78*(2), pp. 223–28.

_____. Intellectual Property Rights, Technological Change, and Economic Growth. In *Walker, C. E. and Bloomfield, M. A., eds.*, 1988, pp. 3–26.

Manski, Charles F. Identification of Binary Response Models. *J. Amer. Statist. Assoc.*, September 1988, *83*(403), pp. 729–38.

Mansoor, Ali M. The Budgetary Impact of Privatization. In *Blejer, M. I. and Chu, K.-Y., eds.*, 1988, pp. 48–56.

_____. The Fiscal Impact of Privatisation. In *Cook, P. and Kirkpatrick, C., eds.*, 1988, pp. 180–94.

_____ and Hemming, Richard. Is Privatization the Answer? *Finance Develop.*, September 1988, *25*(3), pp. 31–33.

Mansour, Ali H. and Khalil, Mohammad. Iraqui Prewar Economic Structure. *J. Energy Devel.*, Spring 1988, *13*(2), pp. 187–95.

Mansour, Antoine. The West Bank Economy: 1948–1984. In *Abed, G. T., ed.*, 1988, pp. 71–99.

Manstetten, Reiner and Faber, Malte. Der Ursprung der Volkswirtschaftslerhe als Bestimmung und Bergrenzung ihrer Erkenntnisperspektive. (The Origin of Economics as Determination and Limitation of its Epistemological Perspective. With English summary.) *Schweiz. Z. Volkswirtsch. Statist.*, June 1988, *124*(2), pp. 97–121.

Mansury, R. Taxation of Income from Capital: Two Issues: Indonesia. *Bull. Int. Fiscal Doc.*, May 1988, *42*(5), pp. 226–31.

Manuelli, Rodolfo and Sargent, Thomas J. Models of Business Cycles: A Review Essay. *J. Monet. Econ.*, November 1988, *22*(3), pp. 523–42.

Maoz, Zeev; Rapoport, Amnon and Felsenthal, Dan S. Proportional Representation: An Empirical Evaluation of Single-Stage, Non-ranked Voting Procedures. *Public Choice*, November 1988, *59*(2), pp. 151–65.

Mapp, Harry P. Irrigated Agriculture on the High Plains: An Uncertain Future. *Western J. Agr. Econ.*, December 1988, *13*(2), pp. 339–47.

_____ and Hornbaker, Robert H. A Dynamic Analysis of Water Savings from Advanced Irrigation Technology. *Western J. Agr. Econ.*, December 1988, *13*(2), pp. 307–15.

Maracchi, G., et al. An Information System for Agricultural Productivity. In *Parikh, J. K., ed.*, 1988, pp. 59–97.

Marando, Vincent L. and Reeves, Mavis Mann. State Responsiveness and Local Government Reorganization. *Soc. Sci. Quart.*, December 1988, *69*(4), pp. 996–1004.

Maranto, Cheryl L. Corporate Characteristics and Union Organizing. *Ind. Relat.*, Fall 1988, *27*(3), pp. 352–70.

Marasini, Donata. Aree di integrazione economica nell'america centromeridionale. (Hierar-chical Areas of Economic Integration in Central South America. With English summary.) *Rivista Int. Sci. Econ. Com.*, July 1988, *35*(7), pp. 663–74.

_____. Una nota sul test di J. S. Maritz. (On J. S. Maritz's Test. With English summary.) *Rivista Int. Sci. Econ. Com.*, September 1988, *35*(9), pp. 847–52.

Maravall, Agustín. A Note on Minimum Mean Squared Error Estimation of Signals with Unit Roots. *J. Econ. Dynam. Control*, June–Sept. 1988, *12*(2–3), pp. 589–93.

_____. The Use of ARIMA Models in Unobserved-Components Estimation: An Application to Spanish Monetary Control. In *Barnett, W. A.; Berndt, E. R. and White, H., eds.*, 1988, pp. 171–96.

Marcel, Mario and Palma, J. Gabriel. Third World Debt and Its Effects on the British Economy: A Southern View of Economic Mismanagement in the North. *Cambridge J. Econ.*, September 1988, *12*(3), pp. 361–400.

Marcelle, Jillían and Dezséri, Kálmán. Debt–Equity Swaps: Solution to a Crisis? *Écon. Appl.*, 1988, *41*(4), pp. 821–55.

Marcet, Albert and Sargent, Thomas J. The Fate of Systems with "Adaptive" Expectations. *Amer. Econ. Rev.*, May 1988, *78*(2), pp. 168–72.

March, James C. and March, James G. Performance Sampling in Social Matches. In *March, J. G.*, 1988, *1978*, pp. 359–83.

March, James G. Ambiguity and Accounting: The Elusive Link between Information and Decision-Making. In *March, J. G.*, 1988, *1987*, pp. 384–408.

_____. Bounded Rationality, Ambiguity, and the Engineering of Choice. In *Bell, D. E.; Raiffa, H. and Tversky, A., eds.*, 1988, *1978*, pp. 33–57.

_____. Bounded Rationality, Ambiguity, and the Engineering of Choice. In *March, J. G.*, 1988, *1978*, pp. 266–93.

_____. The Business Firm as a Political Coalition. In *March, J. G.*, 1988, *1962*, pp. 101–15.

_____. A Chronicle of Speculations about Decision-Making in Organizations. In *March, J. G.*, 1988, pp. 1–21.

_____. Footnotes to Organizational Change. In *March, J. G.*, 1988, *1981*, pp. 167–86.

_____. The Power of Power. In *March, J. G.*, 1988, *1966*, pp. 116–49.

_____. The Technology of Foolishness. In *March, J. G.*, 1988, pp. 253–65.

_____. Variable Risk Preferences and Adaptive Aspirations. *J. Econ. Behav. Organ.*, January 1988, *9*(1), pp. 5–24.

_____ and Cyert, Richard M. A Behavioural Theory of Organizational Objectives. In *Cyert, R. M.*, 1988, *1959*, pp. 125–38.

_____ and Cyert, Richard M. Organizational Design. In *Cyert, R. M.*, 1988, *1964*, pp. 151–60.

_____ and Cyert, Richard M. Organizational Factors in the Theory of Oligopoly. In *Earl, P. E., ed., Vol. 1*, 1988, *1956*, pp. 332–52.

_____ and Cyert, Richard M. Organizational Structure and Pricing Behavior in an Oligopolistic Market. In *March, J. G.*, 1988, *1955*, pp. 25–36.

_____ and Cyert, Richard M. Organizational Structure and Pricing Behavior in an Oligopolistic Market. In *Earl, P. E.*, ed., *Vol. 1*, 1988, *1955*, pp. 321–31.

_____ and Cyert, Richard M. Research on a Behavioural Theory of the Firm. In *Cyert, R. M.*, 1988, *1960*, pp. 139–50.

_____; Cyert, Richard M. and Feigenbaum, Edward A. Models in a Behavioral Theory of the Firm. In *March, J. G.*, 1988, *1959*, pp. 37–60.

_____ and Feldman, Martha S. Information in Organizations as Signal and Symbol. In *March, J. G.*, 1988, *1981*, pp. 409–28.

_____ and Harrison, J. Richard. Decision-Making and Postdecision Surprises. In *March, J. G.*, 1988, *1984*, pp. 228–49.

_____; Herriott, Scott R. and Levinthal, Daniel. Learning from Experience in Organizations. In *March, J. G.*, 1988, *1985*, pp. 219–27.

_____ and Levinthal, Daniel. A Model of Adaptive Organizational Search. In *March, J. G.*, 1988, *1981*, pp. 187–218.

_____ and Manns, Curtis L. Financial Adversity, Internal Competition, and Curriculum Change in a University. In *March, J. G.*, 1988, *1978*, pp. 61–75.

_____ and March, James C. Performance Sampling in Social Matches. In *March, J. G.*, 1988, *1978*, pp. 359–83.

_____ and Olsen, Johan P. The Uncertainty of the Past: Organizational Learning under Ambiguity. In *March, J. G.*, 1988, *1975*, pp. 335–58.

_____; Olsen, Johan P. and Cohen, Michael D. A Garbage Can Model of Organizational Choice. In *March, J. G.*, 1988, *1972*, pp. 294–334.

_____; Sætren, Harald and Baier, Vicki Eaton. Implementation and Ambiguity. In *March, J. G.*, 1988, *1986*, pp. 150–64.

_____ and Sevón, Guje. Behavioral Perspectives on Theories of the Firm. In *van Raaij, W. F.; van Veldhoven, G. M. and Wärneryd, K.-E.*, eds., 1988, pp. 369–402.

_____ and Sevón, Guje. Gossip, Information and Decision-Making. In *March, J. G.*, 1988, *1984*, pp. 429–42.

_____ and Shapira, Zur. Managerial Perspectives on Risk and Risk-Taking. In *March, J. G.*, 1988, *1987*, pp. 76–97.

Marchand, Claude. Structural and Cyclical Factors in the Transmission Patterns of Unemployment in OECD Countries. *Reg. Stud.*, April 1988, *22*(2), pp. 121–34.

Marchese, Carla and Brosio, Giorgio. The Growth of Government under Different Redistributive Rules: A Long Term Study of the Italian Case. *Public Finance Quart.*, October 1988, *16*(4), pp. 439–63.

_____ and Brosio, Giorgio. The Growth of Public Expenditure in Italy since the Second World War. In *Lybeck, J. A. and Henrekson, M.*, eds., 1988, pp. 187–200.

Marchese, Grazia and Branson, William H. International Payments Imbalances in Japan, Germany, and the United States. In *Fieleke, N. S.*, ed., 1988, pp. 19–50.

Marchetti, Cesare. Infrastructures for Movement: Past and Future. In *Ausubel, J. H. and Herman, R.*, eds., 1988, pp. 146–74.

de Marchi, Neil. The History of Dutch Macroeconomic Modelling (1936–1986): Comments. In *Driehuis, W.; Fase, M. M. G. and den Hartog, H.*, eds., 1988, pp. 89–92.

_____. John Stuart Mill Interpretation since Schumpeter. In *Thweatt, W. O.*, ed., 1988, pp. 137–62.

_____. Popper and the LSE Economists. In *de Marchi, N.*, ed., 1988, pp. 139–66.

_____. The Popperian Legacy in Economics: Introduction. In *de Marchi, N.*, ed., 1988, pp. 1–15.

Marchington, Mick. The Changing Nature of Industrial Relations in the UK and Its Impact on Management Behaviour. In *Dlugos, G.; Dorow, W. and Weiermair, K.*, eds., 1988, pp. 207–20.

Marco, Luc. La démographie des entreprises: theories et statistiques. (The Demography of Enterprises: Theories and Statistics. With English summary.) *Écon. Soc.*, August 1988, *22*(8), pp. 111–42.

Marcos, Félix and Corchón, Luis C. Entry, Stackelberg Equilibrium and Reasonable Conjectures. *Int. J. Ind. Organ.*, December 1988, *6*(4), pp. 509–15.

Marcus, Alan J. and Eldor, Rafael. Quotas as Options: Valuation and Equilibrium Implications. *J. Int. Econ.*, May 1988, *24*(3–4), pp. 255–74.

_____ and Kane, Alex. The Delivery Option on Forward Contracts: A Note. *J. Finan. Quant. Anal.*, September 1988, *23*(3), pp. 337–41.

_____ and Kulatilaka, Nalin. General Formulation of Corporate Options. In *Chen, A. H.*, ed., 1988, pp. 183–99.

_____; Merton, Robert C. and Bodie, Zvi. Defined Benefit versus Defined Contribution Pension Plans: What Are the Real Trade-offs? In *Bodie, Z.; Shoven, J. B. and Wise, D. A.*, eds., 1988, pp. 139–60.

Marcus, Alfred and Bromiley, Philip. The Rationale for Regulation: Shareholder Losses under Various Assumptions about Managerial Cognition. *J. Law, Econ., Organ.*, Fall 1988, *4*(2), pp. 357–72.

Marcus, Richard D. and Harford, Jon D. A General Equilibrium Model of the Volunteer Military. *Southern Econ. J.*, October 1988, *55*(2), pp. 472–84.

Marczewski, Jean. Economic Fluctuations in France 1815–1938. *J. Europ. Econ. Hist.*, Fall 1988, *17*(2), pp. 259–66.

Marer, Paul. Centrally Planned Economies in the IMF, the World Bank, and the GATT. In *[Holzman, F. D.]*, 1988, pp. 223–55.

_____. Comparing the Foreign Economic Strategies of Market and Centrally Planned Economies. In *Saunders, C. T., ed.*, 1988, pp. 183–216.

_____. How to Create Markets in Eastern Europe: The Hungarian Case: Comments. In *[Holzman, F. D.]*, 1988, pp. 300–304.

_____. Poland's Debt Situation in Global Perspective. In *Marer, P. and Siwinski, W., eds.*, 1988, pp. 241–49.

_____. What Roles for the IMF and the World Bank in Poland? In *Marer, P. and Siwinski, W., eds.*, 1988, pp. 273–77.

_____ and Siwinski, Wlodzimierz. Creditworthiness and Reform in Poland: Western and Polish Perspectives: Introduction. In *Marer, P. and Siwinski, W., eds.*, 1988, pp. xv–xxiii.

Marfan, Manuel and Ffrench-Davis, Ricardo. Selective Policies under a Structural Foreign Exchange Shortage. *J. Devel. Econ.*, November 1988, *29*(3), pp. 347–69.

Marginson, Paul. Centralized Control or Establishment Autonomy? In *Marginson, P., et al.*, 1988, pp. 183–226.

_____ and Edwards, P. K. Differences in Perception Between Establishment and Higher Level Managers. In *Marginson, P., et al.*, 1988, pp. 227–57.

_____ and Edwards, P. K. Trade Unions, Pay Bargaining and Industrial Action. In *Marginson, P., et al.*, 1988, pp. 123–64.

_____ and Sisson, Keith. The Enterprises in Profile. In *Marginson, P., et al.*, 1988, pp. 21–50.

_____ and Sisson, Keith. The Management of Employees. In *Marginson, P., et al.*, 1988, pp. 80–122.

_____, et al. Beyond the Workplace: Managing Industrial Relations in the Multi-Establishment Enterprise: Conclusions. In *Marginson, P., et al.*, 1988, pp. 258–69.

_____, et al. Structure, Strategy and Choice. In *Marginson, P., et al.*, 1988, pp. 1–20.

_____, et al. What Do Corporate Offices Really Do? *Brit. J. Ind. Relat.*, July 1988, *26*(2), pp. 229–45.

Margo, Robert. Interwar Unemployment in the United States: Evidence from the 1940 Census Sample. In *Eichengreen, B. and Hatton, T. J., eds.*, 1988, pp. 325–52.

Margolis, Louis I. Financial Market Volatility: Overview. In *Federal Reserve Bank of Kansas City*, 1988, pp. 233–41.

Margolis, Marvin S. An Index of Industrial Production for Lancaster County. In *Pennsylvania Economic Association*, 1988, pp. 707–24.

Marien, Patrick and Vuchelen, Jef. The Exchange Market Announcement Effects of Belgian Discount Rate Changes. *Europ. Econ. Rev.*, July 1988, *32*(6), pp. 1335–47.

Marin, Carlos M. and Smith, Mark Griffin. Water Resources Assessment: A Spatial Equilibrium Approach. *Water Resources Res.*, June 1988, *24*(6), pp. 793–801.

_____ and Swallow, Stephen K. Long Run Price Inflexibility and Efficiency Loss for Municipal Water Supply. *J. Environ. Econ. Manage.*, June 1988, *15*(2), pp. 233–47.

Marin, Dalia. Import-Led Innovation: The Case of the Austrian Textile Industry. *Weltwirtsch. Arch.*, 1988, *124*(3), pp. 550–65.

Marina Borghesani, Maria Erminia. Sulle leggi finanziarie subadditive e scomponibili. (On the Subadditive and Decomposable Financial Laws. With English summary.) *Giorn. Econ.*, May–June 1988, *47*(5–6), pp. 309–18.

Marini, Giancarlo. Flexible Exchange Rates and Stabilizing Speculation. *J. Int. Money Finance*, June 1988, *7*(2), pp. 251–57.

_____. Policy Effectiveness and Design in New Classical Models. *Oxford Econ. Pap.*, December 1988, *40*(4), pp. 646–54.

_____ and Attanasio, Orazio P. Countercyclical Policy and the Phillips Curve. Some Evidence for OECD Countries. *Econ. Notes*, 1988, (3), pp. 51–68.

_____ and van der Ploeg, Frederick. Finite Horizons and the Non-neutrality of Money. *Econ. Letters*, 1988, *26*(1), pp. 57–61.

_____ and van der Ploeg, Frederick. Monetary and Fiscal Policy in an Optimising Model with Capital Accumulation and Finite Lives. *Econ. J.*, September 1988, *98*(392), pp. 772–86.

Marino, Anthony M. Monopoly, Liability and Regulation. *Southern Econ. J.*, April 1988, *54*(4), pp. 913–27.

_____. Products Liability and Scale Effects in a Long-run Competitive Equilibrium. *Int. Rev. Law Econ.*, June 1988, *8*(1), pp. 97–107.

_____ and Sicilian, Joseph. The Incentive for Conservation Investment in Regulated Utilities. *J. Environ. Econ. Manage.*, June 1988, *15*(2), pp. 173–88.

Marion, Nancy and Flood, Robert P. Determinants of the Spread in a Two-Tier Foreign Exchange Market. *Econ. Letters*, 1988, *27*(2), pp. 173–78.

Mariotti, Sergio. Italian Inward and Outward Direct Investment: A Comparison. In *Onida, F. and Viesti, G., eds.*, 1988, pp. 133–49.

_____; Cainarca, Gian Carlo and Colombo, Massimo G. La dinamica diffusiva dell'automazione flessibile. (The Diffusion Pattern of Flexible Automation. With English summary.) *Econ. Lavoro*, Jan.–Mar. 1988, *22*(1), pp. 41–63.

Maritim, H. K. Instability of Marketed Output of Maize in Kenya. *Eastern Afr. Econ. Rev.*, December 1988, *4*(2), pp. 9–12.

Marjit, Sugata. A Simple Model of Technology Transfer. *Econ. Letters*, 1988, *26*(1), pp. 63–67.

_____. Tariff, Technical Progress and Trade with Vertical Specialization. *Keio Econ. Stud.*, 1988, *25*(1), pp. 51–57.

Mark, Jerome A. Measuring Productivity in Services Industries. In *Guile, B. R. and Quinn, J. B., eds. (II)*, 1988, pp. 139–59.

_____. Productivity in Service Industries. In *Candilis, W. O., ed.*, 1988, pp. 45–55.

Mark, Nelson C. Time-Varying Betas and Risk Premia in the Pricing of Forward Foreign Exchange Contracts. *J. Finan. Econ.*, December 1988, *22*(2), pp. 335–54.

_____ and **Cantor, Richard M.** The International Transmission of Real Business Cycles. *Int. Econ. Rev.*, August 1988, *29*(3), pp. 493–507.

van der Mark, Ronald; Alsters, Theo and Nijkamp, Peter. Evaluation of Regional Incubator Profiles for Small and Medium Sized Enterprises. *Reg. Stud.*, April 1988, *22*(2), pp. 95–105.

Markey, James P. The Labor Market Problems of Today's High School Dropouts. *Mon. Lab. Rev.*, June 1988, *111*(6), pp. 36–43.

Markey, Ray. The Aristocracy of Labour and Productivity Re-organization in NSW, c. 1880–1900. *Australian Econ. Hist. Rev.*, March 1988, *28*(1), pp. 43–59.

Markley, Deborah M. Changing Financial markets and the Impact on Rural Communities: An Alternative Research Approach. In *Beaulieu, L. J., ed.*, 1988, pp. 158–69.

Marks, Barry R.; Raman, K. K. and Benson, Earl D. Tax Effort as an Indicator of Fiscal Stress. *Public Finance Quart.*, April 1988, *16*(2), pp. 203–18.

Marks, Denton. More on Rent Control: A Response to Yang and Dennis [Public Choice and Rent Control]. *Atlantic Econ. J.*, June 1988, *16*(2), pp. 78–79.

Marks, Leonard, Jr. The Retrenchment of Multinational Banks. In *Tavis, L. A., ed.*, 1988, pp. 240–43.

Marks, Russell E., Jr. Brazil's Economic and Political Future: Foreword: Brazil's Place in the 1980s. In *Chacel, J. M.; Falk, P. S. and Fleischer, D. V., eds.*, 1988, pp. xi–xiv.

Marks, Stephen Gary and Kane, Alex. Performance Evaluation of Market Timers: Theory and Evidence. *J. Finan. Quant. Anal.*, December 1988, *23*(4), pp. 425–35.

_____ and **Kulatilaka, Nalin.** The Strategic Value of Flexibility: Reducing the Ability to Compromise. *Amer. Econ. Rev.*, June 1988, *78*(3), pp. 574–80.

Marks, Stephen V. Influences on Legislator Voting: Theory and an Example. In *Brown, E., ed.*, 1988, pp. 24–33.

_____. Teaching Guide: Abortion Economics. *Econ. Inquiry*, January 1988, *26*(1), pp. 175–79.

_____ and **McArthur, John.** Constituent Interest vs. Legislator Ideology: The Role of Political Opportunity Cost. *Econ. Inquiry*, July 1988, *26*(3), pp. 461–70.

_____; **Willett, Thomas D. and Kaempfer, William H.** Why Do Large Countries Prefer Quantitative Trade Restrictions? *Kyklos*, 1988, *41*(4), pp. 625–46.

Markusen, James R. Production, Trade, and Migration with Differentiated, Skilled Workers. *Can. J. Econ.*, August 1988, *21*(3), pp. 492–506.

_____ and **Hunter, Linda C.** Per-Capita Income as a Determinant of Trade. In *Feenstra, R. C., ed.*, 1988, pp. 89–109.

_____ and **Venables, Anthony J.** Trade Policy with Increasing Returns and Imperfect Competition: Contradictory Results from Competing

Assumptions. *J. Int. Econ.*, May 1988, *24*(3–4), pp. 299–316.

Marland, Gregg and Weinberg, Alvin M. Longevity of Infrastructure. In *Ausubel, J. H. and Herman, R., eds.*, 1988, pp. 312–32.

Marlow, Michael L. Fiscal Decentralization and Government Size. *Public Choice*, March 1988, *56*(3), pp. 259–69.

_____. Private Sector Shrinkage and the Growth of Industrialized Economies: Reply. *Public Choice*, September 1988, *58*(3), pp. 285–94.

_____ and **Manage, Neela.** Expenditures and Receipts in State and Local Government Finances: Reply. *Public Choice*, December 1988, *59*(3), pp. 287–90.

_____ and **Orzechowski, William P.** Controlling Leviathan through Tax Reduction. *Public Choice*, September 1988, *58*(3), pp. 237–45.

Marme, Christopher and Wells, Paul. Hick's Wage-Theorem and Keynes's *General Theory*. In *Hamouda, O. F. and Smithin, J. N., eds.*, Vol. 2, 1988, pp. 93–101.

Marmorstein, Howard; Weigold, Michael F. and Lynch, John G., Jr. Choices from Sets Including Remembered Brands: Use of Recalled Attributes and Prior Overall Evaluations. *J. Cons. Res.*, September 1988, *15*(2), pp. 169–84.

Marois, William and Girardin, Eric. Fiscal Policy in an Open Economy: An Empirical Study of O.E.C.D. Countries. *Brit. Rev. Econ. Issues*, Autumn 1988, *10*(23), pp. 77–110.

Marquette, R. Penny and Wilson, Earl R. Evaluating the Effects of Multicollinearity: A Note on the Use of Ridge Regression. In *Schwartz, B. N., ed.*, 1988, pp. 143–56.

Marquez, Jaime. Cyclical and Secular Trade Elasticities: An Application to LDC Exports. *J. Econ. Dynam. Control*, March 1988, *12*(1), pp. 71–76.

_____. International Policy Coordination and the Reduction of the U.S. Trade Deficit. *J. Econ. Dynam. Control*, March 1988, *12*(1), pp. 19–25.

_____ and **McNeilly, Caryl.** Income and Price Elasticities for Exports of Developing Countries. *Rev. Econ. Statist.*, May 1988, *70*(2), pp. 306–14.

_____ and **Schinasi, Garry J.** Measures of Money and the Monetary Model of the Canadian–U.S. Dollar Exchange Rate. *Econ. Letters*, 1988, *26*(2), pp. 183–88.

Marr, M. Wayne and Spivey, Michael F. The Cost Relationship between Competitive and Negotiated Preferred Stock Sales under Different Credit Market Conditions. *Quart. J. Bus. Econ.*, Summer 1988, *27*(3), pp. 23–40.

Marrelli, Massimo and Martina, Riccardo. Tax Evasion and Strategic Behaviour of the Firms. *J. Public Econ.*, October 1988, *37*(1), pp. 55–69.

Marrese, Michael and Vaňous, Jan. The Content and Controversy of Soviet Trade Relations with Eastern Europe, 1970–1984. In *[Holzman, F. D.]*, 1988, pp. 185–220.

Marris, Stephen. International Macroeconomic Policy Cooperation: Where Do We Go from

Here? **In** *Guerrieri, P. and Padoan, P. C.,* *eds.*, 1988, pp. 236–49.

Marron, Donald B. The Globalization of Capital. **In** *Rosow, J. M., ed.*, 1988, pp. 53–78.

Marron, J. S. Automatic Smoothing Parameter Selection: A Survey. *Empirical Econ.*, 1988, *13*(3–4), pp. 187–208.

_____; **Härdle, Wolfgang and Hall, Peter H.** How Far Are Automatically Chosen Regression Smoothing Parameters from Their Optimum?: Rejoinder. *J. Amer. Statist. Assoc.*, March 1988, *83*(401), pp. 100–01.

_____; **Härdle, Wolfgang and Hall, Peter H.** How Far Are Automatically Chosen Regression Smoothing Parameters from Their Optimum? *J. Amer. Statist. Assoc.*, March 1988, *83*(401), pp. 86–95.

Marschall, Wolfgang and Heidel, Waltraut. Some Qualitative Interrelations between Science and Production. *Soviet E. Europ. Foreign Trade*, Spring 1988, *24*(1), pp. 108–24.

Marselli, Riccardo and Vannini, Marco E. C. The Holmes–Smyth Effect: Some Preliminary Exercises with the UK Demand for Narrow Money. *Appl. Econ.*, June 1988, *20*(6), pp. 711–20.

Marsh, C., et al. The View of Academic Social Scientists on the 1991 UK Census of Population: A Report of the Economic and Social Research Council Working Group. *Environ. Planning A*, July 1988, *20*(7), pp. 851–89.

Marsh, James Barney. Data Problems in Marine Resource Economics. **In** *Brown, R. C., ed.*, 1988, pp. 105–27.

Marsh, John M. The Effects of the Dairy Termination Program on Live Cattle and Wholesale Beef Prices. *Amer. J. Agr. Econ.*, November 1988, *70*(4), pp. 919–28.

Marsh, John S. An EC Approach to Decoupling. **In** *Miner, W. M. and Hathaway, D. E., eds.*, 1988, pp. 141–57.

Marsh, Paul and Dimson, Elroy. The Impact of the Small Firm Effect on Event Studies. **In** *Dimson, E., ed.*, 1988, pp. 220–39.

Marsh, Robert M. and Mannari, Hiroshi. The Changing Industrial Relations Scene in Japan and Its Impact on Managerial Behavior. **In** *Dlugos, G.; Dorow, W. and Weiermair, K., eds.*, 1988, pp. 273–87.

Marsh, Terry A. and Gammill, James F., Jr. Trading Activity and Price Behavior in the Stock and Stock Index Futures Markets in October 1987. *J. Econ. Perspectives*, Summer 1988, *2*(3), pp. 25–44.

Marshall, A. Mr. Jevons' 'Theory of Political Economy.' **In** *Wood, J. C., ed., Vol. 2*, 1988, *1872*, pp. 17–22.

Marshall, Albert W. and Olkin, Ingram. Families of Multivariate Distributions. *J. Amer. Statist. Assoc.*, September 1988, *83*(403), pp. 834–41.

Marshall, J. V. Recording of Costs in Public Hospitals' MRI Units: Interim Report, July 1986–June 1987: Discussion. **In** *Butler, J. R. G. and Doessel, D. P., eds.*, 1988, pp. 167–69.

Marshall, Jorge and Montt, Felipe. Privatisation

in Chile. **In** *Cook, P. and Kirkpatrick, C., eds.*, 1988, pp. 281–307.

Marshall, Paul and Tomkins, Cyril. Incorporating Discounted Cash Flow Contours onto a BCG Portfolio Matrix Using Limit Pricing. *Managerial Dec. Econ.*, June 1988, *9*(2), pp. 119–26.

Marshall, Ray. Immigration in the Golden State: The Tarnished Dream. **In** *Simcox, D. E., ed.*, 1988, pp. 181–98.

_____. The International Division of Labor. **In** *Mangum, G. and Philips, P., eds.*, 1988, pp. 274–308.

_____. Jobs: The Shifting Structure of Global Employment. **In** *Sewell, J. W. and Tucker, S. K., eds.*, 1988, pp. 167–94.

Marshall, William J. and Weingast, Barry R. The Industrial Organization of Congress; or, Why Legislatures, Like Firms, Are Not Organized as Markets. *J. Polit. Econ.*, February 1988, *96*(1), pp. 132–63.

Marsteller, William and Blanchfield, Robert. Rising Export and Import Prices in 1987 Reversed the Trend of Recent Years. *Mon. Lab. Rev.*, June 1988, *111*(6), pp. 3–19.

Marston, Richard C. Exchange Rate Policy Reconsidered. **In** *Feldstein, M., ed. (I)*, 1988, pp. 79–136.

_____. International Payments Imbalances of the East Asian Developing Economies: Discussion. **In** *Fieleke, N. S., ed.*, 1988, pp. 152–56.

_____. Realignment of the Yen–Dollar Exchange Rate: Aspects of the Adjustment Process in Japan: Comment. **In** *Marston, R. C., ed.*, 1988, pp. 144–48.

Martan, Leslaw. Measures for the Activation of Employees in Poland and the Limitations of These Measures. **In** *Dlugos, G.; Dorow, W. and Weiermair, K., eds.*, 1988, pp. 411–18.

Martellaro, Joseph A. Some Aspects of Economic Reform in the USSR, Post-1965. *Rivista Int. Sci. Econ. Com.*, December 1988, *35*(12), pp. 1155–72.

Martellato, Dino and Batten, David F. Modelling Interregional Trade within Input–Output Systems. *Ricerche Econ.*, April–June 1988, *42*(2), pp. 204–21.

Martens, André and Decaluwé, Bernard. CGE Modeling and Developing Economies: A Concise Empirical Survey of 73 Applications to 26 Countries. *J. Policy Modeling*, Winter 1988, *10*(4), pp. 529–68.

Martens, Joann E.; Schmidt, Ronald H. and Gruben, William C. Interstate Shifts in Nonresidential Construction. *Fed. Res. Bank Dallas Econ. Rev.*, July 1988, pp. 26–37.

Mårtenson, Rita. Cross-Cultural Similarities and Differences in Multinational Retailing. **In** *Kaynak, E., ed.*, 1988, pp. 21–32.

Marti-Recober, M.; Muñoz-Gracia, M. Pilar and Pages-Fita, J. Estimation of ARMA Process Parameters and Noise Variance by Means of a Non Linear Filtering Algorithm. **In** *Edwards, D. and Raun, N. E., eds.*, 1988, pp. 357–62.

Martikainen, Tuomo and Heiskanen, Ikka. The Finnish Public Sector: Its Growth and Changing Role in 1960–1984. In *Lybeck, J. A. and Henrekson, M., eds.*, 1988, pp. 357–89.

Martin, A. M.; Penn, R. and Davies, Richard B. Linear Modelling with Clustered Observations: An Illustrative Example of Earnings in the Engineering Industry. *Environ. Planning A*, August 1988, *20*(8), pp. 1069–84.

Martin, David and Johnson, Phyllis. South Africa Imposes Sanctions against Its Neighbours. In *United Nations*, 1988, pp. 56–83.

Martin, David Dale. Beyond Capitalism: A Role for Markets? In *Samuels, W. J., ed., Vol. 3*, 1988, *1974*, pp. 310–23.

Martín Del Campo, Enrique. Technology and the World Economy: The Case of the American Hemisphere. In *Muroyama, J. H. and Stever, H. G., eds.*, 1988, pp. 141–58.

Martin, Fernand. The Influence of Unemployment Insurance Benefits upon the Social Cost of Labor in Lagging Regions. In *[Perroux, F.]*, 1988, pp. 244–68.

Martin, Henry L. and Jen, Lo-Sun. Are Ore Grades Declining? The Canadian Experience, 1939–89. In *Tilton, J. E.; Eggert, R. G. and Landsberg, H. H., eds.*, 1988, pp. 419–44.

Martin, James H. and Daley, James M. Situational Analysis of Bus Riders and Non-riders for Different Transportation Methods. *Logist. Transp. Rev.*, June 1988, *24*(2), pp. 185–99.

Martin, Jean-Marie. L'intensité énergétique de l'activité économique dans les pays industrialisés: Les évolutions de très longue période livrent-elles des enseignements utiles? (The Energy Intensity of the Industrial Countries: Will the Very Long Term Developments Be Instructive? With English summary.) *Écon. Soc.*, April 1988, *22*(4), pp. 9–27.

Martin, John D. and MacMinn, Richard D. Uncertainty, the Fisher Model, and Corporate Financial Theory. In *Chen, A. H., ed.*, 1988, pp. 227–64.

Martin, John P. The Structure and Short-Run Adaptability of Labor Markets in Japan and the United States: Comment. In *Hart, R. A., ed.*, 1988, pp. 341–43.

Martin, Juan Antonio de Vicente. Tax Treatment of Computer Software: Spain. In *International Fiscal Association, ed. (II)*, 1988, pp. 319–32.

Martin, Juan M. F. Interaction between the Public and Private Sectors and the Overall Efficiency of the Economy. *CEPAL Rev.*, December 1988, (36), pp. 101–16.

Martin, Larry J. and van Duren, Erna. Government Assistance to Beef Producers in Canada: Implications for International and Interprovincial Trade. *Can. J. Agr. Econ.*, Part 1, December 1988, *36*(4), pp. 689–701.

Martin, Lawrence; Matusz, Steven J. and Davidson, Carl. The Structure of Simple General Equilibrium Models with Frictional Unemployment. *J. Polit. Econ.*, December 1988, *96*(6), pp. 1267–93.

Martin, Linda G. and Ogawa, Naohiro. The Effects of Cohort Size on Relative Wages in Japan. In *Lee, R. D.; Arthur, W. B. and Rodgers, G., eds.*, 1988, pp. 59–75.

Martin, Linda J. and French, Dan W. The Measurement of Option Mispricing. *J. Banking Finance*, December 1988, *12*(4), pp. 537–50.

Martin, Marshall A. Stability and Farm Programs: A Case Study of Feed Grain Markets. In *Sumner, D. A., ed.*, 1988, pp. 85–107.

Martin, Michael V. The Spanish Accession to the EC and Its Likely Impacts on Agricultural Trade and Development in Morocco. *J. Agr. Econ.*, January 1988, *39*(1), pp. 141–45.

———, **et al.** The Impacts of the Conservation Reserve Program on Rural Communities: The Case of Three Oregon Counties. *Western J. Agr. Econ.*, December 1988, *13*(2), pp. 225–32.

Martin, Neil R., Jr.; Hanson, Gregory D. and Kolajo, Ebenezer F. Forecast Errors and Farm Firm Growth. *J. Agr. Econ. Res.*, Fall 1988, *40*(4), pp. 2–11.

Martin, Philip. Network Recruitment and Labor Displacement. In *Simcox, D. E., ed.*, 1988, pp. 67–91.

Martin, Ray. State and Regional Strategies. In *Federal Home Loan Bank of San Francisco*, 1988, pp. 85–89.

Martin, Ricardo and Selowsky, Marcelo. External Shocks and the Demand for Adjustment Finance. *World Bank Econ. Rev.*, January 1988, *2*(1), pp. 105–21.

——— **and van Wijnbergen, S.** Efficient Pricing of Natural Gas: A Case Study of Egypt. *J. Public Econ.*, July 1988, *36*(2), pp. 177–96.

Martin, Robert E. Franchising and Risk Management. *Amer. Econ. Rev.*, December 1988, *78*(5), pp. 954–68.

Martin, Roderick. The Management of Industrial Relations and New Technology. In *Marginson, P., et al.*, 1988, pp. 165–82.

Martin, Stephen. Market Power and/or Efficiency? *Rev. Econ. Statist.*, May 1988, *70*(2), pp. 331–35.

———. The Measurement of Profitability and the Diagnosis of Market Power. *Int. J. Ind. Organ.*, 1988, *6*(3), pp. 301–21.

Martin, William E. Back to the Future: A Willingness to Play Reexamined. *Western J. Agr. Econ.*, July 1988, *13*(1), pp. 112–20.

Martin, William F. Energy Policy and U.S. National Priorities. In *Fried, E. R. and Blandin, N. M., eds.*, 1988, pp. 71–76.

Martina, Riccardo and Dardanoni, Valentino. "Il nuovo sistema di incentivi sovietico": Alcuni risultati sul modello de Weitzman. (With English summary.) *Stud. Econ.*, 1988, *43*(34), pp. 113–37.

——— **and Hey, John D.** Reactions to Reactions and Conjectures about Conjectures. *Scot. J. Polit. Econ.*, August 1988, *35*(3), pp. 283–90.

——— **and Marrelli, Massimo.** Tax Evasion and Strategic Behaviour of the Firms. *J. Public Econ.*, October 1988, *37*(1), pp. 55–69.

Martine, George. Frontier Expansion, Agricultural Modernization, and Population Trends in Brazil. In *Lee, R. D., et al., eds.*, 1988, pp. 187–203.

——— **and Faria, Vilmar.** Impacts of Social Research on Policy Formulation: Lessons from the Brazilian Experience in the Population Field. *J. Devel. Areas*, October 1988, *23*(1), pp. 43–61.

Martinello, Felice. Insurance in a Unionized Labour Market: An Empirical Test. *Can. J. Econ.*, May 1988, *21*(2), pp. 394–409.

_____ **and West, Edwin G.** The Optimal Size of the Tuition Tax Credit. *Public Finance Quart.*, October 1988, *16*(4), pp. 425–38.

Martínez-Alier, Joan and Roca Jusmet, Jordi. Economía política del corporativismo en el Estado español: Del franquismo al posfranquismo. (With English summary.) *Desarrollo Econ.*, April–June 1988, *28*(109), pp. 3–38.

Martinez Coll, Juan Carlos and Hirshleifer, Jack. What Strategies Can Support the Evolutionary Emergence of Cooperation? *J. Conflict Resolution*, June 1988, *32*(2), pp. 367–98.

Martinez-Giralt, Xavier and Neven, Damien J. Can Price Competition Dominate Market Segmentation? *J. Ind. Econ.*, June 1988, *36*(4), pp. 431–42.

Martínez Mongay, Carlos and Pascual Lapeña, Nuria. Productividad multifactor y efecto capacidad de la industria española 1971–1981. (With English summary.) *Invest. Ecón.*, September 1988, *12*(3), pp. 425–44.

_____ **and Pascual Lapeña, Nuria.** Sobre el análisis de la eslasticidad de sustitución en condiciones de equilibrio temporal. (With English summary.) *Invest. Ecón.*, May 1988, *12*(2), pp. 279–303.

Martinez Oliva, Juan Carlos. Policy-Makers' "Revealed Preferences" and Macroeconomic Policy Coordination: An Appraisal. *Econ. Notes*, 1988, (1), pp. 22–40.

_____. Reddito e Disoccupazione negli Stati Uniti e in Europa: 1979–1985. (With English summary.) *Econ. Int.*, Feb.–March 1988, *41*(1–2), pp. 62–87.

_____ **and Sinn, Stefan.** The Game-Theoretic Approach to International Policy Coordination: Assessing the Role of Targets. *Weltwirtsch. Arch.*, 1988, *124*(2), pp. 252–68.

Martinez-Piedra, Alberto. The Economy of Guatemala: Recent Developments. In *Jorge, A. and Salazar-Carrillo, J., eds.*, 1988, pp. 140–61.

Martinez-Vazquez, Jorge and Kaufman, Bruce E. Voting for Wage Concessions: The Case of the 1982 GM–UAW Negotiations. *Ind. Lab. Relat. Rev.*, January 1988, *41*(2), pp. 183–94.

_____ **and Sjoquist, David L.** Property Tax Financing, Renting, and the Level of Local Expenditures. *Southern Econ. J.*, October 1988, *55*(2), pp. 424–31.

Martino, A. A. Software for the Legislator. In *Pizzorusso, A., ed.*, 1988, pp. 342–71.

Martirena-Mantel, Ana María. Distorsiones domésticas y ordenamiento óptimo de políticas comerciales en la economía abierta. (With English summary.) *Desarrollo Econ.*, Jan.–March 1988, *27*(108), pp. 505–38.

Martires, Concepcion R. Management and Its Impact on Productivity in the Philippine Work Setting of Food and Garments Industries. *Philippine Rev. Econ. Bus.*, Sept.–Dec. 1988, *25*(3–4), pp. 271–93.

Martlew, Clive and Bailey, Stephen J. A Poll Tax for Britain? In *Bailey, S. J. and Paddison, R., eds.*, 1988, pp. 75–91.

Marty, Alvin L. and Chaloupka, Frank J. Optimal Inflation Rates: A Generalization. *J. Money, Credit, Banking*, February 1988, *20*(1), pp. 141–44.

Maruani, Margaret and Borzeix, Anni. When a Strike Comes Marching Home. In *Jenson, J.; Hagen, E. and Reddy, C., eds.*, 1988, pp. 245–59.

Marvasti, A. Alternative Regimes for the Exploitation of Manganese Nodules and Their Impacts. *J. Policy Modeling*, Summer 1988, *10*(2), pp. 317–19.

Marvel, Mary K. The Impact of Sunset Review: A Study of Real Estate Licensing. *Public Choice*, July 1988, *58*(1), pp. 79–84.

Marwah, Kanta and Bodkin, Ronald G. Trends in Macroeconomic Modeling: The Past Quarter Century. *J. Policy Modeling*, Summer 1988, *10*(2), pp. 299–315.

_____; **Bodkin, Ronald G. and Klein, Lawrence R.** Keynes and the Origins of Macroeconometric Modelling. In *Hamouda, O. F. and Smithin, J. N., eds., Vol. 2*, 1988, pp. 3–11.

_____ **and Palsson, Halldor P.** Direct Interventions, Interest Rate Shocks and Monetary Disturbances in the Canadian Foreign Exchange Market: A Simulation Study. In *Motamen, H., ed.*, 1988, pp. 407–55.

März, Eduard. Anti-Say's Law versus Say's Law: A Change in Paradigm: Comments. In *Hanusch, H., ed.*, 1988, pp. 53–64.

Mas-Colell, Andreu. Four Lectures on the Differentiable Approach to General Equilibrium Theory. In *Ambrosetti, A.; Gori, F. and Lucchetti, R., eds.*, 1988, pp. 19–43.

_____ **and Hart, Sergiu.** The Potential of the Shapley Value. In *[Shapley, L. S.]*, 1988, pp. 127–37.

Masarani, F. and Gokturk, S. S. On the Probabilities of the Mutual Agreement Match. *J. Econ. Theory*, February 1988, *44*(1), pp. 192–201.

Maschler, Michael; Owen, Guillermo and Peleg, Bezalel. Paths Leading to the Nash Set. In *[Shapley, L. S.]*, 1988, pp. 321–30.

Masciandaro, Donato. Teoria dell'assetto istituzionale della Banca Centrale: Riflessi sul controllo monetario e sulla politica fiscale. (On a Theory of the Central Bank's Institutional Setting: Some Reflexions on Monetary Control and Fiscal Policy. With English summary.) *Giorn. Econ.*, Jan.–Feb. 1988, *47*(1–2), pp. 65–97.

_____ **and Tabellini, Guido.** Monetary Regimes and Fiscal Deficits: A Comparative Analysis. In *Cheng, H.-S., ed.*, 1988, pp. 125–52.

Mascolo, João Luiz and Pereira, Pedro L. Valls. Testes de exogeneidade da moeda para a economia brasileira. (With English summary.) *Pesquisa Planejamento Econ.*, December 1988, *18*(3), pp. 595–613.

Masera, Rainer S. and Galli, Giampaolo. Government Deficits and Debts. The Necessity and Cost of Adjustment: The Case of Italy. In *Eltis, W. and Sinclair, P. J. N., eds.*, 1988, pp. 175–215.

Mashaw, Jerry L. Lessons for the Administration of Workers' Compensation from the Social Security Disability Insurance Program. In *Burton, J. F., Jr., ed.*, 1988, pp. 97–111.

———. Mendeloff's *The Dilemma of Toxic Substance Regulation: How Overregulation Causes Underregulation. Rand J. Econ.*, Autumn 1988, *19*(3), pp. 489–94.

Mashayekhi, Mina and Gibbs, Murray. Services: Cooperation for Development. *J. World Trade*, April 1988, *22*(2), pp. 81–107.

Maskin, Eric and Tirole, Jean. A Theory of Dynamic Oligopoly, I: Overview and Quantity Competition with Large Fixed Costs. *Econometrica*, May 1988, *56*(3), pp. 549–69.

——— **and Tirole, Jean.** A Theory of Dynamic Oligopoly, II: Price Competition, Kinked Demand Curves, and Edgeworth Cycles. *Econometrica*, May 1988, *56*(3), pp. 571–99.

——— **and Tirole, Jean.** A Theory of Dynamic Oligopoly, III, Cournot Competition: Corrigendum. *Europ. Econ. Rev.*, September 1988, *32*(7), pp. 1567–68.

Maskus, Keith E. The Factor Content of Consumption in Canada and the United States: A Two-Country Test of the Heckscher–Ohlin–Vanek Model: Comment. In *Feenstra, R. C., ed.*, 1988, pp. 18–21.

Mason, Andrew. Population Growth, Aggregate Saving, and Economic Development. In *Salvatore, D., ed.*, 1988, pp. 45–57.

———. The Replacement Effect and Comparisons of Per Capita Income across Countries: A Short Note. *Demography*, February 1988, *25*(1), pp. 141–44.

———. Saving, Economic Growth, and Demographic Change. *Population Devel. Rev.*, March 1988, *14*(1), pp. 113–44.

Mason, Charles F.; Sandler, Todd and Cornes, Richard. Expectations, the Commons, and Optimal Group Size. *J. Environ. Econ. Manage.*, March 1988, *15*(1), pp. 99–110.

Mason, Colin M. and Harrison, Richard T. Risk Finance, the Equity Gap and New Venture Formation in the United Kingdom: The Impact of the Business Expansion Scheme. In *Kirchhoff, B. A., et al., eds.*, 1988, pp. 595–609.

Mason, Janet; Pilla, Lou and McKendrick, Joseph. The Challenge to Middle Managers. In *Timpe, A. D., ed.*, 1988, *1984*, pp. 14–18.

Mason, Paul M. and Borg, Mary O. The Budgetary Incidence of a Lottery to Support Education. *Nat. Tax J.*, March 1988, *41*(1), pp. 75–85.

Mason, Roger S. The Psychological Economics of Conspicuous Consumption. In *Earl, P. E., ed.*, 1988, pp. 147–62.

Mason, Scott P. and Baldwin, Carliss Y. Evaluation of Government Subsidies to Large-Scale Energy Projects: A Contingent Claims Approach. In *Fabozzi, F. J., ed.*, 1988, pp. 169–81.

Mason, W. M. and Griliches, Zvi. Education, Income, and Ability. In *Griliches, Z.*, 1988, *1973*, pp. 182–212.

Massachusetts High Technology Council. A New Social Contract for Massachusetts. In *Lampe, D., ed.*, 1988, pp. 155–68.

Massad, Carlos. International Money and Macroeconomics: Comments. In *Elliott, K. A. and Williamson, J., eds.*, 1988, pp. 42–45.

Massaro, Vincent G. and Harcourt, G. C. Mr. Sraffa's Production of Commodities. In *Steedman, I., ed., Vol. 1*, 1988, *1964*, pp. 29–41.

——— **and Harcourt, G. C.** A Note on Mr. Sraffa's Sub-systems. In *Steedman, I., ed., Vol. 1*, 1988, *1964*, pp. 21–28.

Masse, I.; Hanrahan, J. R. and Kushner, J. The Effect of Changes in Tax Legislation on the Purchase/Lease Decision in the Public Sector. *Nat. Tax J.*, March 1988, *41*(1), pp. 123–30.

Massey, Doreen. What Is an Economy Anyway? In *Allen, J. and Massey, D., eds.*, 1988, pp. 229–59.

———. What's Happening to UK Manufacturing? In *Allen, J. and Massey, D., eds.*, 1988, pp. 45–90.

——— **and Allen, John.** Restructuring Britain: The Economy in Question: Introduction. In *Allen, J. and Massey, D., eds.*, 1988, pp. 1–6.

Massey, Douglas S. Economic Development and International Migration in Comparative Perspective. *Population Devel. Rev.*, September 1988, *14*(3), pp. 383–413.

——— **and Denton, Nancy A.** Residential Segregation of Blacks, Hispanics, and Asians by Socioeconomic Status and Generation. *Soc. Sci. Quart.*, December 1988, *69*(4), pp. 797–817.

Masson, André. Permanent Income, Age and the Distribution of Wealth. *Ann. Écon. Statist.*, Jan.–March 1988, (9), pp. 227–56.

——— **and Kessler, Denis.** Equal vs. Unequal Estate Sharing: Comments. In *Kessler, D. and Masson, A., eds.*, 1988, pp. 117–19.

——— **and Kessler, Denis.** Le cycle de vie de la théorie du cycle de vie. (The Life Cycle of the Life Cycle Hypothesis. With English summary.) *Ann. Écon. Statist.*, Jan.–March 1988, (9), pp. 1–27.

——— **and Kessler, Denis.** Modelling the Accumulation and Distribution of Wealth: Introduction. In *Kessler, D. and Masson, A., eds.*, 1988, pp. 1–18.

——— **and Kessler, Denis.** On Five Hot Issues on Wealth Distribution. *Europ. Econ. Rev.*, March 1988, *32*(2–3), pp. 644–53.

——— **and Kessler, Denis.** Wealth Distributional Consequences of Life Cycle Models. In *Kessler, D. and Masson, A., eds.*, 1988, pp. 287–318.

Masson, Paul R. Deriving Small Models from Large Models. In *Bryant, R. C., et al., eds.*, 1988, pp. 322–27.

———. Empirical Macroeconomics for Interdependent Economies: Comparison and Evaluation of Model Simulations: Comment. In *Bryant, R. C., et al., eds.*, 1988, pp. 151–52.

———. Strategies for Modeling Exchange Rates

and Capital Flows in Multicountry Models. *J. Policy Modeling*, Summer 1988, *10*(2), pp. 205–28.

_____; Frenkel, Jacob A. and Goldstein, Morris. International Coordination of Economic Policies: Scope, Methods, and Effects. In *Guth, W., ed.*, 1988, pp. 149–92.

_____ and Ghosh, Atish R. International Policy Coordination in a World with Model Uncertainty. *Int. Monet. Fund Staff Pap.*, June 1988, *35*(2), pp. 230–58.

_____ and Horne, Jocelyn. Scope and Limits of International Economic Cooperation and Policy Coordination. *Int. Monet. Fund Staff Pap.*, June 1988, *35*(2), pp. 259–96.

_____ and Knight, Malcolm D. Economic Interactions and the Fiscal Policies of Major Industrial Countries: 1980–1988. *Greek Econ. Rev.*, 1988, *10*(1), pp. 185–237.

_____ and Knight, Malcolm D. Fiscal Policies, Net Saving, and Real Exchange Rates: The United States, the Federal Republic of Germany, and Japan. In *Frenkel, J. A., ed.*, 1988, pp. 21–66.

_____, et al. MULTIMOD: A Multi-regional Econometric Model. In *International Monetary Fund Research Department*, 1988, pp. 50–104.

Masson, Robert T. and Chiang, Shih-Chen. Domestic Industrial Structure and Export Quality. *Int. Econ. Rev.*, May 1988, *29*(2), pp. 261–70.

Massone, Pedro. Taxation of Income Derived by Non-Residents in Latin America. *Bull. Int. Fiscal Doc.*, April 1988, *42*(4), pp. 147–69.

Mastanduno, Michael. Trade as a Strategic Weapon: American and Alliance Export Control Policy in the Early Postwar Period. *Int. Organ.*, Winter 1988, *42*(1), pp. 121–50.

_____. Trade as a Strategic Weapon: American and Alliance Export Control Policy in the Early Postwar Period. In *Ikenberry, G. J.; Lake, D. A. and Mastanduno, M., eds.*, 1988, pp. 121–150.

_____; Ikenberry, G. John and Lake, David A. Approaches to Explaining American Foreign Economic Policy: Introduction. In *Ikenberry, G. J.; Lake, D. A. and Mastanduno, M., eds.*, 1988, pp. 1–14.

_____; Ikenberry, G. John and Lake, David A. Introduction: Approaches to Explaining American Foreign Economic Policy. *Int. Organ.*, Winter 1988, *42*(1), pp. 1–14.

Masten, Scott E. Equity, Opportunism, and the Design of Contractual Relations. *J. Inst. Theoretical Econ.*, February 1988, *144*(1), pp. 180–95.

_____. A Legal Basis for the Firm. *J. Law, Econ., Organ.*, Spring 1988, *4*(1), pp. 181–98.

_____. Minimum Bill Contracts: Theory and Policy. *J. Ind. Econ.*, September 1988, *37*(1), pp. 85–97.

_____ and Crocker, Keith J. Mitigating Contractual Hazards: Unilateral Options and Contract Length. *Rand J. Econ.*, Autumn 1988, *19*(3), pp. 327–43.

Masters, Marick F. Federal Employee Unions and Political Action. In *Lewin, D., et al., eds.*, 1988, *1985*, pp. 98–122.

_____ and Robertson, John D. The Impact of Organized Labor on Public Employment: A Comparative Analysis. *J. Lab. Res.*, Fall 1988, *9*(4), pp. 347–62.

_____; Schwochau, Susan and Delaney, John Thomas. Unionism and Voter Turnout. *J. Lab. Res.*, Summer 1988, *9*(3), pp. 221–36.

_____ and Zaardkoohi, Asghar. Congressional Support for Unions' Positions across Diverse Legislation. *J. Lab. Res.*, Spring 1988, *9*(2), pp. 149–65.

Masui, Kazuhito; Hagiwara, Shintaro and Noguchi, Yasuhiko. Anti-dumping Laws in Japan. *J. World Trade*, August 1988, *22*(4), pp. 35–50.

Masulis, Ronald W. and Trueman, Brett. Corporate Investment and Dividend Decisions under Differential Personal Taxation. *J. Finan. Quant. Anal.*, December 1988, *23*(4), pp. 369–85.

Mata, Leonardo. A Public Health Approach to the "Food–Malnutrition–Economic Recession" Complex. In *Bell, D. E. and Reich, M. R., eds.*, 1988, pp. 265–75.

Mate, Karl and Horsky, Dan. Dynamic Advertising Strategies of Competing Durable Good Producers. *Marketing Sci.*, Fall 1988, *7*(4), pp. 356–67.

Mathe, Jean-Charles and Gontier, Jean-Louis. Gestion de la dimension technologique de l'entreprise: prolongements. (Technological Aspects in Firm Management. Continuation. With English summary.) *Écon. Soc.*, August 1988, *22*(8), pp. 37–59.

Mathers, Constance Jones. Family Partnerships and International Trade in Early Modern Europe: Merchants from Burgos in England and France, 1470–1570. *Bus. Hist. Rev.*, Autumn 1988, *62*(3), pp. 367–97.

Mathews, Russell. Specific Purpose Payments and the Commonwealth Grants Commission: Commentary. In *Smith, C. S., ed.*, 1988, pp. 39–44.

Mathewson, G. Frank and Carr, Jack L. Unlimited Liability as a Barrier to Entry. *J. Polit. Econ.*, August 1988, *96*(4), pp. 766–84.

_____ and Winter, Ralph A. On Vertical Restraints and the Law: A Reply. *Rand J. Econ.*, Summer 1988, *19*(2), pp. 298–301.

Mathias, Peter and O'Brien, Patrick. The Social and Economic Burden of Tax Revenue Collected for Central Government in Britain and France, 1715–85. In *Guarducci, A., ed.*, 1988, pp. 805–42.

Mathiasen, David G. The Evolution of the Office of Management and Budget under President Reagan. *Public Budg. Finance*, Autumn 1988, *8*(3), pp. 3–14.

Mathiesen, Lars. International Trade in Gains: Domestic Policies and Trade Impacts: Comment. In *Haaland, J. I. and Norman, V. D., eds.*, 1988, pp. 69–70.

Mathieson, Donald J. Exchange Rate Arrangements and Monetary Policy. In *Cheng, H.-S.,* ed., 1988, pp. 43–80.

———; **Dooley, Michael P.** and **Frankel, Jeffrey A.** International Capital Mobility: What Do Saving–Investment Correlations Tell Us? Reply. *Int. Monet. Fund Staff Pap.,* June 1988, *35*(2), pp. 397–98.

——— and **Folkerts-Landau, David F. I.** Innovation, Institutional Changes, and Regulatory Response in International Financial Markets. In *Haraf, W. S. and Kushmeider, R. M., eds.,* 1988, pp. 392–423.

Mathieson, John A. Struggle against Dependence: Nontraditional Export Growth in Central America and the Caribbean: Dominican Republic. In *Paus, E., ed.,* 1988, pp. 41–63.

———. Struggle against Dependence: Nontraditional Export Growth in Central America and the Caribbean: Jamaica. In *Paus, E., ed.,* 1988, pp. 145–68.

Mathiowetz, Nancy A. and **Duncan, Greg J.** Out of Work, Out of Mind: Response Errors in Retrospective Reports of Unemployment. *J. Bus. Econ. Statist.,* April 1988, *6*(2), pp. 221–29.

Mathis, Edward J.; Zech, Charles E. and **Webster, Elaine.** The Impact of Foreign Exports on State Economies: An Economic Base Multiplier Analysis. In *Missouri Valley Economic Assoc.,* 1988, pp. 25–29.

Mathis, John E. and **Mayo, John W.** The Effectiveness of Mandatory Fuel Efficiency Standards in Reducing the Demand for Gasoline. *Appl. Econ.,* February 1988, *20*(2), pp. 211–19.

Mathur, Rajul. The Delay in the Formation of the Reserve Bank of India: The India Office Perspective. *Indian Econ. Soc. Hist. Rev.,* April–June 1988, *25*(2), pp. 133–69.

Mathur, Vijay K. and **Park, Keehwan.** Production Technology Uncertainty and the Optimal Location of the Firm. *J. Reg. Sci.,* February 1988, *28*(1), pp. 51–64.

———; **Stein, Sheldon H.** and **Kumar, Rishi.** A Dynamic Model of Regional Population Growth and Decline. *J. Reg. Sci.,* August 1988, *28*(3), pp. 379–95.

Matin, K. M. Growth and Adjustment: Experiences of Selected Subcontinent Countries: Comments. In *Streeten, P., ed.,* 1988, pp. 54–67.

Matioukhine, G. The International Debt Problem: Comment. In *Borner, S., ed.,* 1988, pp. 67–71.

Matlon, Peter; Delgado, Christopher L. and **Reardon, Thomas.** Coping with Household-Level Food Insecurity in Drought-Affected Areas of Burkina Faso. *World Devel.,* September 1988, *16*(9), pp. 1065–74.

Mato, Gonzalo. Investment Demand at the Firm Level: The Case of Spain. *Rech. Écon. Louvain,* 1988, *54*(3), pp. 325–36.

Matosich, Andrew J. and **Matosich, Bonnie K.** Machine Building: *Perestroyka's* Sputtering Engine. *Soviet Econ.,* April–June 1988, *4*(2), pp. 144–76.

Matosich, Bonnie K. and **Matosich, Andrew J.**

Machine Building: *Perestroyka's* Sputtering Engine. *Soviet Econ.,* April–June 1988, *4*(2), pp. 144–76.

Matoušek, Jiří. Draft Law on Cooperative Farming. *Czech. Econ. Digest.,* February 1988, (1), pp. 47–58.

Matsebula, M. S. Entrepreneurial Success in Swaziland's Urban Informal Sector: A Profit-Function Framework. *Eastern Afr. Econ. Rev.,* June 1988, *4*(1), pp. 36–41.

Matsubara, Nozomu and **Kabashima, Ikuo.** Voters' Choice in the Tanaka Verdict Election: An Analysis of Aggregate Election Data with MK Ratio. In *Uno, K. and Shishido, S., eds.,* 1988, pp. 175–88.

Matsuda, Takako. Intelligent User Interface of Different Statistical Packages with a Knowledge-Based System. In *Uno, K. and Shishido, S., eds.,* 1988, pp. 280–303.

Matsuda, Yoshiro. Manufacturing and Corporation Firm System in Meiji Japan. In *Uno, K. and Shishido, S., eds.,* 1988, pp. 202–37.

Matsushima, Hitoshi. A New Approach to the Implementation Problem. *J. Econ. Theory,* June 1988, *45*(1), pp. 128–44.

Matsuyama, Kiminori. Life-Cycle Saving and Comparative Advantage in the Long Run. *Econ. Letters,* 1988, *28*(4), pp. 375–79.

———. Terms-of-Trade, Factor Intensities and the Current Account in a Life-Cycle Model. *Rev. Econ. Stud.,* April 1988, *55*(2), pp. 247–62.

Mattei, Andrés Ramos. The Plantations of the Southern Coast of Puerto Rico: 1880–1910. *Soc. Econ. Stud.,* March–June 1988, *37*(1–2), pp. 365–404.

di Matteo, Massimo. Goodwin and the Evolution of a Capitalistic Economy: An Afterthought. In *[Goodwin, R. M.],* 1988, pp. 93–101.

Mattesini, Fabrizio. Screening in the Credit Market with Loans of Variable Size. *Rivista Int. Sci. Econ. Com.,* Oct.–Nov. 1988, *35*(10–11), pp. 967–91.

Matteuzzi, Massimo. Nota sulla tassazione dei titoli pubblici e incentivi alla speculazione per le imprese. (With English summary.) *Polit. Econ.,* December 1988, *4*(3), pp. 495–505.

Matthews, H. Lee and **Overdahl, James A.** The Use of NYMEX Options to Forecast Crude Oil Prices. *Energy J.,* October 1988, *9*(4), pp. 135–47.

Matthews, Jacqueline. Multinational Corporations in SADCC (Southern African Development Coordination Conference). In *Jones, S., ed.,* 1988, pp. 155–74.

Matthews, M. H., et al. The Influence of the Neighbourhood on Teacher Characteristics: A Case Study of Coventry. *Environ. Planning A,* May 1988, *20*(5), pp. 681–88.

Matthews, Robin C. O. Research on Productivity and the Productivity Gap. *Nat. Inst. Econ. Rev.,* May 1988, (124), pp. 66–72.

———. The Work of Robert M. Solow. *Scand. J. Econ.,* 1988, *90*(1), pp. 13–16.

——— and **Bowen, Alex.** Keynesian and Other Explanations of Post-war Macroeconomic

Trends. In *Eltis, W. and Sinclair, P. J. N.*, eds., 1988, pp. 354–88.

Matthiessen, Poul Christian. De demografiske perspektiver i pensionsdebatten. (The Development of the Danish Population by Age from 1985 to 2025. With English summary.) *Nationaløkon. Tidsskr.*, 1988, *126*(2), pp. 124–31.

Mattson, Robert N. and Jones, John B., Jr. Tax Treatment of Computer Software: General Report. In *International Fiscal Association, ed. (II)*, 1988, pp. 19–44.

Mattsson, Lars-Gunnar and Johanson, Jan. Internationalisation in Industrial Systems—A Network Approach. In *Hood, N. and Vahlne, J.-E.*, eds., 1988, pp. 287–314.

Matusz, Steven J. U.S. and Swedish Direct Investment and Exports: Comment. In *Baldwin, R. E.*, ed. (II), 1988, pp. 297–99.

———; **Davidson, Carl and Martin, Lawrence.** The Structure of Simple General Equilibrium Models with Frictional Unemployment. *J. Polit. Econ.*, December 1988, *96*(6), pp. 1267–93.

——— **and Grinols, Earl L.** Some Welfare Implications of Job Mobility in General Equilibrium. *Amer. Econ. Rev.*, March 1988, *78*(1), pp. 261–66.

Matuszewski, Pierre. Partial Public Privatization in Quebec Soquem/Cambior. In *Walker, M. A.*, ed. (II), 1988, pp. 185–99.

Matutes, C.; Neven, Damien J. and Dierickx, I. Indirect Taxation and Cournot Equilibrium. *Int. J. Ind. Organ.*, 1988, *6*(3), pp. 385–99.

Matutes, Carmen and Regibeau, Pierre. "Mix and Match": Product Compatibility without Network Externalities. *Rand J. Econ.*, Summer 1988, *19*(2), pp. 221–34.

Matzner, Egon; Roncaglia, Alessandro and Kregel, J. A. Barriers to Full Employment: Introduction. In *Kregel, J. A.; Matzner, E. and Roncaglia, A.*, eds., 1988, pp. 1–5.

Mauer, David C.; Emery, Douglas R. and Lewellen, Wilbur G. Tax-Timing Options, Leverage, and the Choice of Corporate Form. *J. Finan. Res.*, Summer 1988, *11*(2), pp. 99–110.

——— **and Lewellen, Wilbur G.** Tax Options and Corporate Capital Structures. *J. Finan. Quant. Anal.*, December 1988, *23*(4), pp. 387–400.

Mauleón, Ignacio. A Quarterly Econometric Model for the Spanish Economy. In *Motamen, H.*, ed., 1988, pp. 683–712.

Maurenen, Tapani. Review of Research in Economic and Social History in Finland in the 1970s and 1980s. *Scand. Econ. Hist. Rev.*, 1988, *36*(3), pp. 23–41.

Maurer, O. The Use of Videotex in Austrian Agriculture—Present Stage of Development and Tendencies for the Future. In *Schiefer, G.*, ed., 1988, pp. 145–51.

Maussner, Alfred. Luck, Necessity, and Dynamic Flexibility: Discussion. In *Hanusch, H.*, ed., 1988, pp. 129–36.

———. Strom- und Bestandsrestriktionen in makroökonomischen Modellen. (Flow and Stock Constraints in Macroeconomic Models. With

English summary.) *Jahr. Nationalökon. Statist.*, October 1988, *205*(4), pp. 316–31.

Max, Wendy and Lehman, Dale E. A Behavioral Model of Timber Supply. *J. Environ. Econ. Manage.*, March 1988, *15*(1), pp. 71–86.

Maxfield, Linda Drazga. The 1982 New Beneficiary Survey: An Introduction. *Soc. Sec. Bull.*, March 1988, *51*(3), pp. 38–46.

Maxwell, Ken. Health Insurance Forum. In *Butler, J. R. G. and Doessel, D. P.*, eds., 1988, pp. 246–49.

Maxwell, Nan L. Economic Returns to Migration: Marital Status and Gender Differences. *Soc. Sci. Quart.*, March 1988, *69*(1), pp. 108–21.

Maxwell, Philip and Peter, Matthew. Income Inequality in Small Regions: A Study of Australian Statistical Divisions. *Rev. Reg. Stud.*, Winter 1988, *18*(1), pp. 19–27.

May, Ann Mari and Sellers, John R. Contemporary Philosophy of Science and Neoinstitutional Thought. *J. Econ. Issues*, June 1988, *22*(2), pp. 397–405.

May, Eleanor G.; Ress, C. William and Salmon, Walter J. Future Trends in Retailing: Merchandise Line Trends and Store Trends 1980–1990. In *Kaynak, E.*, ed., 1988, pp. 333–48.

May, J. Douglas. The Political Economy of Development in Atlantic Canada. In *Choudhury, M. A.*, ed., 1988, pp. 71–83.

May, Simon and Creasey, Pauline. The Political and Economic Background. In *Creasey, P. and May, S.*, eds., 1988, pp. 1–30.

Mayer, Charles. North American Agriculture in an Interdependent World: Challenges and Opportunities. In *Allen, K. and Macmillan, K.*, eds., 1988, pp. 119–22.

Mayer, Colin. New Issues in Corporate Finance. *Europ. Econ. Rev.*, June 1988, *32*(5), pp. 1167–83.

———. The Real Value of Company Accounts. *Fisc. Stud.*, February 1988, *9*(1), pp. 1–17.

———; **Franks, Julian R. and Harris, Robert S.** Means of Payment in Takeovers: Results for the United Kingdom and the United States. In *Auerbach, A. J.*, ed. (I), 1988, pp. 221–58.

——— **and Jenkinson, Tim J.** The Privatisation Process in France and the U.K. *Europ. Econ. Rev.*, March 1988, *32*(2–3), pp. 482–90.

Mayer, Helmut and Kneeshaw, John. Financial Market Structure and Regulatory Change. In *Heertje, A.*, ed., 1988, pp. 127–57.

Mayer-Kress, Gottfried and Saperstein, Alvin M. A Nonlinear Dynamical Model of the Impact of SDI on the Arms Race. *J. Conflict Resolution*, December 1988, *32*(4), pp. 636–70.

Mayer, Leo V. A Briefing by the U.S. Agricultural Negotiator. In *Allen, K. and Macmillan, K.*, eds., 1988, pp. 15–20.

Mayer, Martin. Remarks on the Financial Services Industry. In *Federal Home Loan Bank of San Francisco*, 1988, pp. 69–73.

Mayer, Peter C. The Theory of Political Patronage. In *Zerbe, R. O., Jr.*, ed., 1988, pp. 91–111.

Mayer, Robert N. Consumer Safety and the Issue

Emergence Process. In *Maynes, E. S. and ACCI Research Committee, eds.*, 1988, pp. 82–96.

Mayer, Thomas. Absolute Liquidity Preference and the Pigou Effect: A Comment [A Note on the Incompatibility of the Pigou Effect and a Liquidity Trap]. *J. Post Keynesian Econ.*, Summer 1988, *10*(4), pp. 653–54.

_____. The Empirical Significance of the Real Balance Effect. In *Shaw, G. K., ed., Vol. 1*, 1988, *1959*, pp. 115–31.

_____. Interpreting Federal Reserve Behavior. *J. Behav. Econ.*, Winter 1988, *17*(4), pp. 263–77.

_____. The Keynesian Legacy: Does Countercyclical Policy Pay Its Way? In *Willett, T. D., ed.*, 1988, pp. 129–44.

_____. Modigliani on Monetarism: A Response [The Monetarist Controversy Revisited]. *Contemp. Policy Issues*, October 1988, *6*(4), pp. 19–24.

_____. United States Monetary Policy. In *Cheng, H.-S., ed.*, 1988, pp. 201–25.

_____ and **Willett, Thomas D.** Evaluating Proposals for Fundamental Monetary Reform. In *Willett, T. D., ed.*, 1988, pp. 398–423.

Mayers, David; Chen, Nai-Fu and Copeland, Thomas E. A Comparison of Single and Multifactor Portfolio Performance Methodologies. In *Dimson, E., ed.*, 1988, pp. 254–71.

_____ and **Smith, Clifford W., Jr.** Ownership Structure across Lines of Property-Casualty Insurance. *J. Law Econ.*, October 1988, *31*(2), pp. 351–78.

Mayes, David G.; Davies, Glenn and Kilpatrick, Andrew. Fiscal Policy Simulations—A Comparison of UK Models. *Appl. Econ.*, December 1988, *20*(12), pp. 1613–34.

Mayhew, Anne. The Beginnings of Institutionalism. In *Tool, M. R., ed., Vol. 1*, 1988, *1987*, pp. 21–48.

_____ and **Campen, James T.** The National Banking System and Southern Economic Growth: Evidence from One Southern City, 1870–1900. *J. Econ. Hist.*, March 1988, *48*(1), pp. 127–37.

Mayhew, Ken and Keep, Ewart. The Assessment: Education, Training and Economic Performance. *Oxford Rev. Econ. Policy*, Autumn 1988, *4*(3), pp. i–xv.

Mayland, Kenneth T. Quantitative Measures of Pent-Up Demand and Consumer Satiation. *Bus. Econ.*, January 1988, *23*(1), pp. 39–43.

Maynard, Alan. Privatizing the National Health Service. In *Johnson, C., ed.*, 1988, *1983*, pp. 47–59.

Maynes, E. Scott. The First Word, the Last Word. In *Maynes, E. S. and ACCI Research Committee, eds.*, 1988, pp. 3–16.

_____. Weights, Cardinality, and Scaling in Assessing Quality. In *Maynes, E. S. and ACCI Research Committee, eds.*, 1988, pp. 177–84.

Mayntz, Renate and Scheider, Volker. The Dynamics of System Development in a Comparative Perspective: Interactive Videotex in Germany, France, and Britain. In *Mayntz, R. and Hughes, T. P., eds.*, 1988, pp. 263–98.

Mayo, John W. and Flynn, Joseph E. The Effects of Regulation on Research and Development: Theory and Evidence. *J. Bus.*, July 1988, *61*(3), pp. 321–36.

_____ and **Mathis, John E.** The Effectiveness of Mandatory Fuel Efficiency Standards in Reducing the Demand for Gasoline. *Appl. Econ.*, February 1988, *20*(2), pp. 211–19.

Mayo, Stephen K.; Friedman, Joseph and Jimenez, Emmanuel. The Demand for Tenure Security in Developing Countries. *J. Devel. Econ.*, September 1988, *29*(2), pp. 185–98.

Mayper, Alan G.; Welker, Robert B. and Wiggins, Casper E. Accounting and Review Services: Perceptions of the Message within the CPA's Report. In *Schwartz, B. N., ed.*, 1988, pp. 219–32.

Mays, W. Jevons's Conception of Scientific Method. In *Wood, J. C., ed., Vol. 1*, 1988, *1962*, pp. 212–32.

_____ and **Henry, D. P.** Exhibition of the Work of W. Stanley Jevons. In *Wood, J. C., ed., Vol. 3*, 1988, *1952*, pp. 55–57.

_____ and **Henry, D. P.** Jevons and Logic. In *Wood, J. C., ed., Vol. 1*, 1988, *1953*, pp. 167–87.

Mazambani, David and Hosier, Richard H. Zimbabwe's Informal Sector: Its Nature and Energy-Use Patterns. In *Hosier, R. H., ed. (II)*, 1988, pp. 74–98.

Mażbic-Kulma, B.; Komorowska, E. and Stępień, J. Location Problem and Its Applications in Distribution of Petrol Products. In *Kurzhanski, A.; Neumann, K. and Pallaschke, D., eds.*, 1988, pp. 277–92.

Mazerolle, Fabrice. Marchés du travail et théories du commerce international. (With English summary.) *Revue Écon. Polit.*, Jan.–Feb. 1988, *98*(1), pp. 90–110.

_____ and **Mucchielli, Jean-Louis.** Commerce intra-branche et intra-produit dans la spécialisation internationale de la France: 1960–1985. (Intra-industry, Intra-product Trade and International Specialization: The French Experience between 1960–1985. With English summary.) *Revue Écon.*, November 1988, *39*(6), pp. 1193–1217.

Mazey, Sonia. European Community Action on Behalf of Women: The Limits of Legislation. *J. Common Market Stud.*, September 1988, *27*(1), pp. 63–84.

Mazis, Michael B. Overlooked Mechanisms for Conveying Information to Consumers. In *Maynes, E. S. and ACCI Research Committee, eds.*, 1988, pp. 225–30.

Mazlish, B. Jevons' Science and His 'Second Nature.' In *Wood, J. C., ed., Vol. 1*, 1988, *1986*, pp. 419–31.

Mazourik, V.; Ratkin, V. and Evtushenko, Y. Multicriteria Optimization in the DISO System. In *Kurzhanski, A.; Neumann, K. and Pallaschke, D., eds.*, 1988, pp. 94–102.

Mazower, Mark. Economic Diplomacy between Great Britain and Greece in the 1930s. *J. Europ. Econ. Hist.*, Winter 1988, *17*(3), pp. 603–19.

Mazumdar, Tridib and Monroe, Kent B. Pricing-Decision Models: Recent Developments and Research Opportunities. In *Devinney, T. M., ed.*, 1988, pp. 361–88.

Mazursky, David and Schul, Yaacov. The Effects of Advertisement Encoding on the Failure to Discount Information: Implications for the Sleeper Effect. *J. Cons. Res.*, June 1988, *15*(1), pp. 24–36.

Mazzoleni, Piera and Castagnoli, Erio. From an Oriental Market to the European Monetary System: Some Fuzzy-Sets-Related Ideas. In *Kacprzyk, J. and Fedrizzi, M., eds.*, 1988, pp. 389–99.

Mazzonis, Danielle. The Use of High Technology in the Cottage Silk Industry in Como, Italy. In *Bhalla, A. S. and James, D., eds.*, 1988, pp. 75–84.

Mbaku, John M. Political Instability and Economic Development in Sub-Saharan Africa: Some Recent Evidence. *Rev. Black Polit. Econ.*, Summer 1988, *17*(1), pp. 89–112.

Mbat, David Okon. Public Debt Policy and Management in Nigeria 1965–1983: A Critical Appraisal. *Public Finance*, 1988, *43*(3), pp. 403–13.

McAdam, M. Bruce. Equipment Leasing: An Integral Part of Financial Services. *Bus. Econ.*, July 1988, *23*(3), pp. 43–47.

McAfee, R. Preston and Howitt, Peter W. Stability of Equilibria with Externalities. *Quart. J. Econ.*, May 1988, *103*(2), pp. 261–77.

_____ **and McMillan, John.** Multidimensional Incentive Compatibility and Mechanism Design. *J. Econ. Theory*, December 1988, *46*(2), pp. 335–54.

_____ **and McMillan, John.** Search Mechanisms. *J. Econ. Theory*, February 1988, *44*(1), pp. 99–123.

_____ **and Williams, Michael A.** Can Event Studies Detect Anticompetitive Mergers? *Econ. Letters*, 1988, *28*(2), pp. 199–203.

McAleer, Michael. Some Comments on Testing Time Series Models. *Econometric Rev.*, 1988, *7*(1), pp. 49–57.

_____ **; McKenzie, Colin R. and Godfrey, Leslie G.** Variable Addition and LaGrange Multiplier Tests for Linear and Logarithmic Regression Models. *Rev. Econ. Statist.*, August 1988, *70*(3), pp. 492–503.

_____ **and Tse, Y. K.** A Sequential Testing Procedure for Outliers and Structural Change. *Econometric Rev.*, 1988, *7*(1), pp. 103–11.

McAllister, Richard and Brewin, Christopher. Annual Review of the Activities of the European Communities in 1987. *J. Common Market Stud.*, June 1988, *26*(4), pp. 431–67.

McArthur, John and Marks, Stephen V. Constituent Interest vs. Legislator Ideology: The Role of Political Opportunity Cost. *Econ. Inquiry*, July 1988, *26*(3), pp. 461–70.

McAvinchey, Ian D. A Comparison of Unemployment, Income and Mortality Interaction for Five European Countries. *Appl. Econ.*, April 1988, *20*(4), pp. 453–71.

McBride, Richard D. and Zufryden, Fred S. An Integer Programming Approach to the Optimal Product Line Selection Problem. *Marketing Sci.*, Spring 1988, *7*(2), pp. 126–40.

McBride, Timothy D. and Lampman, Robert J. Changes in the Pattern of State and Local Government Revenues and Expenditures in Wisconsin, 1960–1983. In *Danziger, S. H. and Witte, J. F., eds.*, 1988, pp. 35–69.

McCaffrey, Neil. Rothbard as Cultural Conservative. In *[Rothbard, M. N.]*, 1988, pp. 395–97.

McCain, Roger A. Increasing "Alienation": The Work Environment and the Direction of Technical Progress under Alternative Forms of Enterprise Organization. In *Jones, D. C. and Svejnar, J., eds.*, 1988, pp. 83–105.

_____. Learning by Doing in Capitalist and Illyrian Firms: A Control Theoretic Exploration. *Econ. Anal. Workers' Manage.*, 1988, *22*(1–2), pp. 35–52.

McCall, Charles W. Rule of Reason versus Mechanical Tests in the Adjudication of Price Predation. *Rev. Ind. Organ.*, Spring 1988, *3*(3), pp. 15–44.

McCallum, Bennett T. The Case for Rules in the Conduct of Monetary Policy: A Concrete Example. In *Giersch, H., ed.*, 1988, pp. 26–44.

_____. Entwicklungen der Konjunkturtheorie in der Nachkriegszeit: Eine gemässigt klassische Perspektive. (Postwar Developments in Business Cycle Theory: A Moderately Classical Perspective. With English summary.) *Ifo-Studien*, 1988, *34*(2–3), pp. 175–91.

_____. Postwar Developments in Business Cycle Theory: A Moderately Classical Perspective. *J. Money, Credit, Banking*, Part 2, August 1988, *20*(3), pp. 459–71.

_____. Robustness Properties of a Rule for Monetary Policy: Reply. *Carnegie–Rochester Conf. Ser. Public Policy*, Autumn 1988, *29*, pp. 213–14.

_____. Robustness Properties of a Rule for Monetary Policy. *Carnegie–Rochester Conf. Ser. Public Policy*, Autumn 1988, *29*, pp. 173–203.

_____. The Role of Demand Management in the Maintenance of Full Employment. In *Eltis, W. and Sinclair, P. J. N., eds.*, 1988, pp. 25–41.

_____. The Treatment of Expectations in Large Multicountry Econometric Models: Comment. In *Bryant, R. C., et al., eds.*, 1988, pp. 179–81.

_____ **and Goodfriend, Marvin.** Theoretical Analysis of the Demand for Money. *Fed. Res. Bank Richmond Econ. Rev.*, Jan.–Feb. 1988, *74*(1), pp. 16–24.

McCallum, John. Is Increased Credibility Stabilizing? *J. Money, Credit, Banking*, May 1988, *20*(2), pp. 155–66.

_____. Les taux de chômage canadien et américain dans les années 1980: un test de trois hypothèses. (With English summary.) *L'Actual. Econ.*, December 1988, *64*(4), pp. 494–508.

McCann, Ewen. Budget Deficits and Asset Sales. *New Zealand Econ. Pap.*, 1988, *22*, pp. 51–60.

McCann, H. Gilman and White, Douglas R. Cites

and Fights: Material Entailment Analysis of the Eighteenth-Century Chemical Revolution. In *Wellman, B. and Berkowitz, S. D., eds.*, 1988, pp. 380–400.

McCardle, Kevin F. and Lippman, Steven A. Preemption in R&D Races. *Europ. Econ. Rev.*, October 1988, 32(8), pp. 1661–69.

McCarl, Bruce A. Preference among Risky Prospects under Constant Risk Aversion. *Southern J. Agr. Econ.*, December 1988, 20(2), pp. 25–33.

_____ **and Parandvash, Gholam Hossein.** Irrigation Development versus Hydroelectric Generation: Can Interruptible Irrigation Play a Role? *Western J. Agr. Econ.*, December 1988, 13(2), pp. 267–76.

McCarthy, C. L. Structural Development of South African Manufacturing Industry—A Policy Perspective. *S. Afr. J. Econ.*, March 1988, 56(1), pp. 1–23.

McCarthy, Dennis M. P. Bureaucracy, Business, and Africa during the Colonial Period: Who Did What to Whom and with What Consequences? In *Uselding, P. J., ed.*, 1988, pp. 81–152.

McCarthy, E. Jerome. Marketing Orientedness and Economic Development. In *[Hollander, S. C.]*, 1988, pp. 133–46.

McCarthy, Joseph E. and Melicher, Ronald W. Analysis of Bond Rating Changes in a Portfolio Context. *Quart. J. Bus. Econ.*, Autumn 1988, 27(4), pp. 69–86.

_____ **and Zaima, Janis K.** The Impact of Bond Rating Changes on Common Stocks and Bonds: Tests of the Wealth Redistribution Hypothesis. *Financial Rev.*, November 1988, 23(4), pp. 483–98.

McCarthy, Paul I. Poland's Long Road Back to Creditworthiness. In *Marer, P. and Siwinski, W., eds.*, 1988, pp. 227–39.

McCarty, Daniel E.; Jessell, Kenneth A. and McDaniel, William R. Discounted Cash Flow with Explicit Reinvestment Rates: Tutorial and Extension. *Financial Rev.*, August 1988, 23(3), pp. 369–85.

McChesney, Fred S. The Cinderella School of Tax Reform: A Comment. *Contemp. Policy Issues*, October 1988, 6(4), pp. 65–69.

McClain, John O. Dominant Tracking Signals. *Int. J. Forecasting*, 1988, 4(4), pp. 563–72.

McCleery, Robert K. and Reynolds, Clark W. The Political Economy of Immigration Law: Impact of Simpson–Rodino on the United States and Mexico. *J. Econ. Perspectives*, Summer 1988, 2(3), pp. 117–31.

McClelland, Charles E. Social Security: The First Half-Century: General Studies: Comment. In *Nash, G. D.; Pugach, N. H. and Tomasson, R. F., eds.*, 1988, pp. 209–13.

McClelland, John W. and Vroomen, Harry. Stationarity Assumptions and Technical Change in Supply Response Analysis. *J. Agr. Econ. Res.*, Fall 1988, 40(4), pp. 20–24.

_____ **and Wetzstein, Michael E.** Investment and Disinvestment Principles with Nonconstant Prices and Varying Firm Size Applied

to Beef-Breeding Herds: Comment. *Amer. J. Agr. Econ.*, November 1988, 70(4), pp. 936–37.

_____; **Wetzstein, Michael E. and Musser, Wesley N.** Returns to Scale and Size in Agricultural Economics: Reply. *Western J. Agr. Econ.*, July 1988, 13(1), pp. 151–52.

McClements, L. D. The Bardsley and McRae Test for a Method of Estimating Equivalence Scales: Comment. *J. Public Econ.*, November 1988, 37(2), pp. 261–63.

McClennen, Edward F. Dynamic Choice and Rationality. In *Munier, B. R., ed.*, 1988, pp. 517–36.

_____. Ordering and Independence: A Comment. *Econ. Philos.*, October 1988, 4(2), pp. 298–308.

_____. Sure-Thing Doubts. In *Gärdenfors, P. and Sahlin, N.-E., eds..,*, 1988, *1983*, pp. 166–82.

McClintock, Brent. Recent Theories of Direct Foreign Investment: An Institutionalist Perspective. *J. Econ. Issues*, June 1988, 22(2), pp. 477–84.

McCloskey, Donald N. The Consequences of Rhetoric. In *Klamer, A.; McCloskey, D. N. and Solow, R. M., eds.*, 1988, pp. 280–93.

_____. The Rhetoric of Law and Economics. *Mich. Law Rev.*, February 1988, 86(4), pp. 752–67.

_____. Thick and Thin Methodologies in the History of Economic Thought. In *de Marchi, N., ed.*, 1988, pp. 245–57.

_____. Towards a Rhetoric of Economics. In *Winston, G. C. and Teichgraeber, R. F., III, eds.*, 1988, pp. 13–29.

_____. Two Replies and a Dialogue on the Rhetoric of Economics: Mäki, Rappaport, and Rosenberg. *Econ. Philos.*, April 1988, 4(1), pp. 150–66.

_____ **and Klamer, Arjo.** Economics in the Human Conversation. In *Klamer, A.; McCloskey, D. N. and Solow, R. M., eds.*, 1988, pp. 3–20.

McClure, Charles E., Jr. A General Equilibrium Analysis of Tax Reform: Comments. In *Aaron, H. J.; Galper, H. and Pechman, J. A., eds.*, 1988, pp. 112–14.

McClure, J. Harold, Jr. PPP, Interest Rate Parities, and the Modified Fisher Effect in the Presence of Tax Agreements: A Comment. *J. Int. Money Finance*, September 1988, 7(3), pp. 347–50.

_____ **and Willett, Thomas D.** The Inflation Tax. In *Willett, T. D., ed.*, 1988, pp. 177–85.

McClure, James A. Preparing for Emergencies. In *Fried, E. R. and Blandin, N. M., eds.*, 1988, pp. 83–86.

McClure, James E. and Loewenstein, Mark A. Taxes and Financial Leasing. *Quart. Rev. Econ. Bus.*, Spring 1988, 28(1), pp. 21–38.

McCluskey, Martha T. Rethinking Equality and Difference: Disability Discrimination in Public Transportation. *Yale Law J.*, April 1988, 97(5), pp. 863–80.

McCombie, J. S. L. A Synoptic View of Regional

Growth and Unemployment: II—The Post-Keynesian Theory. *Urban Stud.*, October 1988, *25*(5), pp. 399–417.

_____. A Synoptic View of Regional Growth and Unemployment: I—The Neoclassical Theory. *Urban Stud.*, August 1988, *25*(4), pp. 267–81.

_____. Keynes and the Nature of Involuntary Unemployment. *J. Post Keynesian Econ.*, Winter 1987–88, *10*(2), pp. 202–15.

McCombs, Maxwell E. Concentration, Monopoly, and Content. In *Picard, R. G., et al., eds.*, 1988, pp. 129–37.

McConnell, Campbell R. The Principles of Economics from Now until Then: A Response. *J. Econ. Educ.*, Spring 1988, *19*(2), pp. 148–51.

McConnell, Kenneth E. Heterogeneous Preferences for Congestion. *J. Environ. Econ. Manage.*, September 1988, *15*(3), pp. 251–58.

_____; **Cropper, Maureen L. and Deck, Leland B.** On the Choice of Functional Form for Hedonic Price Functions. *Rev. Econ. Statist.*, November 1988, *70*(4), pp. 668–75.

McConnell, Virginia D.; Cumberland, John H. and Gordon, Patrice L. Regional Marginal Costs and Cost Savings from Economies of Scale in Municipal Waste Treatment: An Application to the Chesapeake Bay Region. *Growth Change*, Fall 1988, *19*(4), pp. 1–13.

McCord, Mark R. and Leotsarakos, Christos. Investigating Utility and Value Functions with an "Assessment Cube" In *Munier, B. R., ed.*, 1988, pp. 59–75.

McCorkle, Constance M. "You Can't Eat Cotton": Cash Crops and the Cereal Code of Honor in Burkina Faso. In *Bennett, J. W. and Bowen, J. R., eds.*, 1988, pp. 105–23.

McCormick, Barry. Quit Rates over Time in a Job-Rationed Labour Market: The British Manufacturing Sector, 1971–1983. *Economica*, February 1988, *55*(217), pp. 81–94.

_____. Unstable Job Attachments and the Changing Structure of British Unemployment 1973–83. *Econ. J.*, Supplement, 1988, *98*(390), pp. 132–47.

McCormick, Douglas. Biotechnology: Promise Redeemed. In *Furino, A., ed.*, 1988, pp. 141–56.

McCormick, Ken. Important Parallels between Veblen and Keynes. In *Missouri Valley Economic Assoc.*, 1988, pp. 116–21.

_____ **and Raiklin, Ernest.** Soviet Men on the Road to Utopia: A Moral–Psychological Sketch. *Int. J. Soc. Econ.*, 1988, *15*(10), pp. 3–62.

_____ **and Raiklin, Ernest.** Three Views of Productive Labor. In *Missouri Valley Economic Assoc.*, 1988, pp. 141–44.

McCormick, Mary and Lewin, David. Coalition Bargaining in Municipal Government: The New York City Experience. In *Lewin, D., et al., eds.*, 1988, *1981*, pp. 170–92.

McCormick, Robert E. and Maloney, Michael T. Excess Capacity, Cyclical Production, and Merger Motives: Some Evidence from the Capital Markets. *J. Law Econ.*, October 1988, *31*(2), pp. 321–50.

_____ **and Meiners, Roger E.** University Governance: A Property Rights Perspective. *J. Law Econ.*, October 1988, *31*(2), pp. 423–42.

_____; **Shughart, William F., II and Tollison, Robert D.** The Disinterest in Deregulation: Reply. *Amer. Econ. Rev.*, March 1988, *78*(1), pp. 284.

McCormick, William O. Selected Military Transactions in the U.S. International Accounts, 1983–87. *Surv. Curr. Bus.*, June 1988, *68*(6), pp. 70–75.

McCracken, Gerald H. Preventing Tax Evasion through Enforcement: The Government Perspective. In *Canadian Tax Foundation*, 1988, pp. 2.1–14.

McCracken, Michael C. America's International Problems: As Seen by Her Largest Trading Partner. *Bus. Econ.*, April 1988, *23*(2), pp. 29–33.

McCrate, Elaine. The Effect of Schooling and Labor Market Expectations on Teenage Childbearing. *Rev. Radical Polit. Econ.*, Summer–Fall 1988, *20*(2–3), pp. 203–07.

_____. Gender Differences: The Role of Endogenous Preferences and Collective Action. *Amer. Econ. Rev.*, May 1988, *78*(2), pp. 235–39.

McCraw, Thomas K. The Evolution of the Corporation in the United States. In *Meyer, J. R. and Gustafson, J. M., eds.*, 1988, pp. 1–20.

_____. Thinking about Competition. In *Hausman, W. J., ed.*, 1988, pp. 9–29.

McCready, Douglas J. Ramsey Pricing: A Method for Setting Fees in Social Service Organizations. *Amer. J. Econ. Soc.*, January 1988, *47*(1), pp. 97–110.

McCreary, Edward A. Technology Marketing: The Three-Level Sell and Other Market Developments. In *Furino, A., ed.*, 1988, pp. 169–78.

McCrickard, Donald L. and Allen, Stuart D. Deficits and Monetary Growth in the United States: A Comment. *J. Monet. Econ.*, January 1988, *21*(1), pp. 143–53.

McCrohan, Kevin F. and Harvey, James W. Voluntary Compliance and the Effectiveness of Public and Non-profit Institutions: American Philanthropy and Taxation. *J. Econ. Psych.*, September 1988, *9*(3), pp. 369–86.

McCue, Michael J.; McCue, Tom and Wheeler, John R. C. An Assessment of Hospital Acquisition Prices. *Inquiry*, Summer 1988, *25*(2), pp. 290–96.

McCue, Tom; Wheeler, John R. C. and McCue, Michael J. An Assessment of Hospital Acquisition Prices. *Inquiry*, Summer 1988, *25*(2), pp. 290–96.

McCulloch, Rachel. International Competition in Services. In *Feldstein, M., ed. (II)*, 1988, pp. 367–406.

_____. Macroeconomic Policy and Trade Performance: International Implications of U.S. Budget Deficits. In *Baldwin, R. E.; Hamilton, C. B. and Sapir, A., eds.*, 1988, pp. 349–68.

_____. Unexpected Real Consequences of Floating Exchange Rates. In *Melamed, L., ed.*, 1988, *1983*, pp. 223–44.

_____. United States–Japan Economic Relations.

In *Baldwin, R. E., ed. (II)*, 1988, pp. 305–30.

McCullough, Laurence B. An Ethical Model for Improving the Patient–Physician Relationship. *Inquiry*, Winter 1988, 25(4), pp. 454–65.

McCurdy, Thomas H. An Efficiency Frontier Model: An Analysis of the Macroeconomic Implications of Structural Shocks. *Econ. Notes*, 1988, (3), pp. 69–95.

_____ **and Morgan, Ieuan G.** Testing the Martingale Hypothesis in Deutsche Mark Futures with Models Specifying the Form of Heteroscedasticity. *J. Appl. Econometrics*, July–Sept. 1988, 3(3), pp. 187–202.

McCusker, Jane; Stoddard, Anne M. and Sorensen, Andrew A. Do HMOs Reduce Hospitalization of Terminal Cancer Patients? *Inquiry*, Summer 1988, 25(2), pp. 263–70.

McCusker, John J. The View from British North America. *Bus. Hist. Rev.*, Winter 1988, 62(4), pp. 691–96.

McDaniel, William R.; McCarty, Daniel E. and Jessell, Kenneth A. Discounted Cash Flow with Explicit Reinvestment Rates: Tutorial and Extension. *Financial Rev.*, August 1988, 23(3), pp. 369–85.

McDavid, James. Privatizing Local Government Services in Canada. In *Walker, M. A., ed. (II)*, 1988, pp. 101–16.

McDermott, John. Corporate Form: A Unitary Theory of Technology, Property and Social Class. *Rev. Radical Polit. Econ.*, Spring 1988, 20(1), pp. 21–45.

McDermott, L.; Gregory, Robert G. and Ho, V. Sharing the Burden: The Australian Labour Market during the 1930s. In *Gregory, R. G. and Butlin, N. G., eds.*, 1988, pp. 217–44.

McDonald, Bill and Lee, Cheng-Few. An Analysis of Nonlinearities, Heteroscedasticity, and Functional Form in the Market Model. *J. Bus. Econ. Statist.*, October 1988, 6(4), pp. 505–09.

_____ **; Miller, Robert E. and Balvers, Ronald J.** Underpricing of New Issues and the Choice of Auditor as a Signal of Investment Banker Reputation. *Accounting Rev.*, October 1988, 63(4), pp. 605–22.

McDonald, Brian and Boldt, David. Review: Aremos Data Management and Econometric Software, Version 1.0. *Econ. Inquiry*, April 1988, 26(2), pp. 365–67.

McDonald, Daina. A Description of Recent Developments in the Australian Economy: An Update to 1987–88. *Australian Econ. Rev.*, Spring 1988, (83), pp. 77–80.

_____. A Description of Recent Developments in the Australian Economy in an Historical Context. *Australian Econ. Rev.*, 1st Quarter 1988, (81), pp. 42–57.

_____ **and Dixon, Peter B.** The Australian Economy: 1987–88 and 1988–89. *Australian Econ. Rev.*, Winter 1988, (82), pp. 3–26.

_____ **and Dixon, Peter B.** Forecasts for the Australian Economy: 1988–89 and 1989–90. *Australian Econ. Rev.*, Summer 1988, (84), pp. 3–18.

_____ **and Dixon, Peter B.** Some Macroeconomic Aspects of the 1988–89 Budget. *Australian Econ. Rev.*, Spring 1988, (83), pp. 3–11.

McDonald, Forrest. Economic Freedom and the Constitution: The Design of the Framers. In *Gwartney, J. D. and Wagner, R. E., eds.*, 1988, pp. 335–50.

McDonald, Helen and Eisenberg, William M. Evaluating Workplace Injury and Illness Records; Testing a Procedure. *Mon. Lab. Rev.*, April 1988, 111(4), pp. 58–60.

McDonald, Ian and Robinson, Peter B. A Multisectoral Dynamic Optimization Model for Energy/Petrochemical Decision Making in Zimbabwe and the SADCC. In *Hosier, R. H., ed. (II)*, 1988, pp. 126–37.

McDonald, John and Spindler, Zane A. Benefit-Induced Female Sole Parenthood in Australia, 1973–85. *Australian Econ. Pap.*, June 1988, 27(50), pp. 1–19.

McDonald, John F. and d'Ouville, Edmond L. Constraints on Land Consumption and Urban Rent Gradients. *J. Urban Econ.*, November 1988, 24(3), pp. 279–88.

_____ **and d'Ouville, Edmond L.** Highway Traffic Flow and the 'Uneconomic' Region of Production. *Reg. Sci. Urban Econ.*, November 1988, 18(4), pp. 503–09.

McDonald, Lyman; Nowell, Clifford and Evans, Marc A. Length-Biased Sampling in Contingent Valuation Studies. *Land Econ.*, November 1988, 64(4), pp. 367–71.

McDonald, Richard J. and Manser, Marilyn E. An Analysis of Substitution Bias in Measuring Inflation, 1959–85. *Econometrica*, July 1988, 56(4), pp. 909–30.

McDonald, Trish and Rimmer, Malcolm. Award Structure and the Second Tier. *Australian Bull. Lab.*, June 1988, 14(3), pp. 469–91.

McDougall, A. J. and Hannan, E. J. Regression Procedures for ARMA Estimation. *J. Amer. Statist. Assoc.*, June 1988, 83(402), pp. 490–98.

McDougall, Barbara. Political Perspectives. In *Schott, J. J. and Smith, M. G., eds.*, 1988, pp. 181–86.

McDougall, Gerald S. and Cho, Dong W. Demand Estimates for New General Aviation Aircraft: A User-Cost Approach. *Appl. Econ.*, March 1988, 20(3), pp. 315–24.

_____ **and Cho, Dong W.** Explaining General Aviation Turbine Utilization. *Logist. Transp. Rev.*, March 1988, 24(1), pp. 68–83.

_____ **and Hersch, Philip L.** Voting for 'Sin' in Kansas. *Public Choice*, May 1988, 57(2), pp. 127–39.

McDougall, Patricia P. and Robinson, Richard B., Jr. New Venture Performance: Patterns of Strategic Behavior in Different Industries. In *Kirchhoff, B. A., et al., eds.*, 1988, pp. 477–91.

McDowell, George R. Limitations of Theoretical Foundations of Infrastructure Investment Decision-Making. In *Johnson, T. G.; Deaton, B. J. and Segarra, E., eds.*, 1988, pp. 61–63.

McElroy, Marjorie B. and Burmeister, Edwin.

Arbitrage Pricing Theory as a Restricted Non-linear Multivariate Regression Model: Iterated Nonlinear Seemingly Unrelated Regression Estimates. *J. Bus. Econ. Statist.*, January 1988, 6(1), pp. 29–42.

_____ and Burmeister, Edwin. Joint Estimation of Factor Sensitivities and Risk Premia for the Arbitrage Pricing Theory. *J. Finance*, July 1988, 43(3), pp. 721–33.

_____ and Horney, Mary Jean. The Household Allocation Problem: Empirical Results from a Bargaining Model. In *Schultz, T. Paul, ed.*, 1988, pp. 15–38.

_____; Wilcox, Steven P. and Kniesner, Thomas J. Getting into Poverty without a Husband, and Getting Out, With or Without. *Amer. Econ. Rev.*, May 1988, 78(2), pp. 86–90.

McElwain, Adrienne and Hurd, Richard W. Organizing Clerical Workers: Determinants of Success. *Ind. Lab. Relat. Rev.*, April 1988, 41(3), pp. 360–73.

McEnally, Richard W.; Chambers, Donald R. and Carleton, Willard T. Immunizing Default-free Bond Portfolios with a Duration Vector. *J. Finan. Quant. Anal.*, March 1988, 23(1), pp. 89–104.

McEwin, R. Ian. Workplace Accident Compensation Reform—A Reappraisal. *Australian Econ. Rev.*, Winter 1988, (82), pp. 45–60.

McFadden, Daniel L.; Woo, Chi-Keung and Goett, Andrew A. Estimating Household Value of Electrical Service Reliability with Market Research Data. *Energy J.*, Special Issue, 1988, 9, pp. 105–20.

McFarland, Henry B. Evaluating q as an Alternative to the Rate of Return in Measuring Profitability. *Rev. Econ. Statist.*, November 1988, 70(4), pp. 614–22.

McGahagan, Thomas A. First Glimpses of the Invisible Hand: Seventeenth Century Arguments for Capitalism? In *Pennsylvania Economic Association*, 1988, pp. 225–44.

McGahey, Richard. Crime and Employment Research: A Continuing Deadlock? In *Simms, M. C. and Myers, S. L., Jr., eds.*, 1988, pp. 223–30.

McGartland, Albert. A Comparison of Two Marketable Discharge Permits Systems. *J. Environ. Econ. Manage.*, March 1988, 15(1), pp. 35–44.

McGee, John and Thomas, Howard. Making Sense of Complex Industries. In *Hood, N. and Vahlne, J.-E., eds.*, 1988, pp. 40–78.

McGee, L. Randolph and Hultman, Charles W. Factors Influencing Foreign Investment in the U.S., 1970–1986. *Rivista Int. Sci. Econ. Com.*, Oct.–Nov. 1988, 35(10–11), pp. 1061–66.

McGee, M. Kevin. Invariant Resource Supply and Tax Incidence in a Lifecycle Growth Model. *Public Finance Quart.*, October 1988, 16(4), pp. 482–92.

McGeer, Peter. The Challenge of New Materials. In *Richardson, P. R. and Gesing, R., eds.*, 1988, pp. 87–103.

McGibany, James M. and Nourzad, Farrokh. Money Demand and the Effects of Fiscal Poli-

cies: Comment. *J. Money, Credit, Banking*, November 1988, 20(4), pp. 706–14.

_____ and Nourzad, Farrokh. The Substitutability of Real Capital and Financial Assets. *Appl. Econ.*, November 1988, 20(11), pp. 1445–51.

McGillicuddy, John F. The Internationalization of Financial Markets. In *Rosow, J. M., ed.*, 1988, pp. 201–17.

McGillicuddy, Neil B.; Welton, Gary L. and Pruitt, Dean G. The Role of Caucusing in Community Mediation. *J. Conflict Resolution*, March 1988, 32(1), pp. 181–202.

McGilvray, James and Harrigan, Frank J. The Measurement of Interindustry Linkages. *Ricerche Econ.*, April–June 1988, 42(2), pp. 325–43.

McGlynn, Elizabeth A., et al. Quality-of-Care Research in Mental Health: Responding to the Challenge. *Inquiry*, Spring 1988, 25(1), pp. 157–70.

McGoldrick, Peter J. Spatial Price Differentiation by Chain Store Retailers. In *Kaynak, E., ed.*, 1988, pp. 167–80.

McGoun, Elton G. and Farmer, Richard N. Nationalism, Cultural Heterogeneity, and Economic Growth. In *Farmer, R. N. and McGoun, E. G., eds.*, 1988, pp. 3–19.

McGovern, George. The 1988 Election: U.S. Foreign Policy at a Watershed. *Foreign Aff.*, 1987–88, 66(3), pp. 614–29.

McGown, K. Lee; Héroux, Lise and Laroche, Michel. Consumer Product Label Information Processing: An Experiment Involving Time Pressure and Distraction. *J. Econ. Psych.*, June 1988, 9(2), pp. 195–214.

McGrath, Paul; Arshanapalli, Gangadha and Skeels, Jack W. The Importance of Strike Size in Strike Research. *Ind. Lab. Relat. Rev.*, July 1988, 41(4), pp. 582–91.

McGregor, Peter G. The Demand for Money in a Period Analysis Context, the Irrelevance of the "Choice of Market" and the Loanable Funds-Liquidity Preference Debate. *Australian Econ. Pap.*, June 1988, 27(50), pp. 136–41.

_____. Hysteresis and Unemployment Policy: The Case for Activism. In *Cross, R., ed.*, 1988, pp. 402–06.

_____. Keynes on Ex-ante Saving and the Rate of Interest. *Hist. Polit. Econ.*, Spring 1988, 20(1), pp. 107–18.

_____ and Hart, Robert A. The Returns to Labour Services in West German Manufacturing Industry. *Europ. Econ. Rev.*, April 1988, 32(4), pp. 947–63.

McGregor, Rob Roy, III and Maloney, Michael T. Financing the Unemployment Insurance System and the Interest Group Theory of Government. *Public Choice*, March 1988, 56(3), pp. 249–58.

McGuckin, Robert H. and Pascoe, George A., Jr. The Longitudinal Research Database: Status and Research Possibilities. *Surv. Curr. Bus.*, November 1988, 68(11), pp. 30–37.

McGuire, Therese J. and Holtz-Eakin, Douglas. State Grants-in-Aid and Municipal Government Budgets: A Case Study of New Jersey. **In** *Bell, M. E., ed.*, 1988, pp. 229–65.

McGuire, Thomas G. and Ellis, Randall P. Insurance Principles and the Design of Prospective Payment Systems. *J. Health Econ.*, September 1988, 7(3), pp. 215–37.

McHone, W. Warren and Fritz, Richard G. Forecasting Local Business Activity from Aggregate Indicators. *Ann. Reg. Sci.*, March 1988, 22(1), pp. 63–74.

McHugh, Kevin E. Determinants of Black Interstate Migration, 1965–70 and 1975–80. *Ann. Reg. Sci.*, March 1988, 22(1), pp. 36–48.

McHugh, Richard J. and Wilkinson, James T. A Random Effects Approach to Substate Growth Models: A Comment on "The Determinants of Country Growth." *J. Reg. Sci.*, May 1988, 28(2), pp. 271–73.

McInish, Thomas H. and Kudla, Ronald J. Divergence of Opinion and Corporate Spin-offs. *Quart. Rev. Econ. Bus.*, Summer 1988, 28(2), pp. 20–29.

McIntire, John; Rosenzweig, Mark R. and Binswanger, Hans P. From Land Abundance to Land Scarcity: The Effects of Population Growth on Production Relations in Agrarian Economies. **In** *Lee, R. D., et al., eds.*, 1988, pp. 77–100.

McIntosh, Christopher S. and Bessler, David A. Forecasting Agricultural Prices Using a Bayesian Composite Approach. *Southern J. Agr. Econ.*, December 1988, 20(2), pp. 73–80.

McIntosh, James P. and Kanbur, S. M. Ravi. Dual Economy Models: Retrospect and Prospect. *Bull. Econ. Res.*, April 1988, 40(2), pp. 83–113.

McIntyre, Alister. Marketing of Commodities: Approaches and Arrangements for Developing Countries. **In** *Sopiee, N.; Hamzah, B. A. and Leong, C. H., eds.*, 1988, 1986, pp. 197–211.

———. South–South Trade and Economic Cooperation: Some Notes on Future Strategy. **In** *Sopiee, N.; Hamzah, B. A. and Leong, C. H., eds.*, 1988, pp. 157–64.

McIntyre, Michael J. Australian Measures to Curb Tax Haven Abuses: A United States Perspective. *Australian Tax Forum*, 1988, 5(4), pp. 419–49.

———. Implications of U.S. Tax Reform for Distributive Justice. *Australian Tax Forum*, 1988, 5(2), pp. 219–44.

———. Rosen's Marriage Tax Computations: What Do They Mean? [The Marriage Tax is Down but Not Out]. *Nat. Tax J.*, June 1988, 41(2), pp. 257–58.

McIntyre, Richard and Hillard, Michael. The "Labor Shortage" and the Crisis in the Reproduction of the United States Working Class. *Rev. Radical Polit. Econ.*, Summer–Fall 1988, 20(2–3), pp. 196–202.

——— and Medley, Joseph. Democratic Reform of the Fed: The Impact of Class Relations on Policy Formation. *Rev. Radical Polit. Econ.*, Summer–Fall 1988, 20(2–3), pp. 156–62.

McIntyre, Robert S. Are States Overtaxing or Un-

dertaxing Corporations? **In** *Gold, S. D., ed.*, 1988, pp. 197–217.

McKaig, Dianne. Consumer Affairs Professionals and the Consumer Interest. **In** *Maynes, E. S. and ACCI Research Committee, eds.*, 1988, pp. 633–37.

McKay, Niccie L. An Econometric Analysis of Costs and Scale Economies in the Nursing Home Industry. *J. Human Res.*, Winter 1988, 23(1), pp. 57–75.

McKay, Roberta V. International Competition: Its Impact on Employment. **In** *Christensen, K. E., ed.*, 1988, pp. 95–113.

McKee, Arnold. Not by Logic Alone. *Rev. Soc. Econ.*, October 1988, 46(2), pp. 212–15.

McKee, David L. Some Reflections on Cruise Ships and the Economic Development of Small Island Nations. *Can. J. Devel. Stud.*, 1988, 9(2), pp. 249–59.

McKee, Michael. Political Competition and the Roman Catholic Schools: Ontario, Canada. *Public Choice*, January 1988, 56(1), pp. 57–67.

McKee, Michael J. and Quick, Perry D. Sales Tax on Services: Revenue or Reform? *Nat. Tax J.*, September 1988, 41(3), pp. 395–409.

McKendrick, Joseph; Mason, Janet and Pilla, Lou. The Challenge to Middle Managers. **In** *Timpe, A. D., ed.*, 1988, 1984, pp. 14–18.

McKenna, C. J. Bargaining and Strategic Search. *Econ. Letters*, 1988, 28(2), pp. 129–34.

McKenna, Edward; Wade, Maurice and Zannoni, Diane. Keynes, Rawls, Uncertainty, and the Liberal Theory of the State. *Econ. Philos.*, October 1988, 4(2), pp. 221–41.

McKenzie, Colin R. Rational Expectations in Financial Markets and the Murphy Model: Comment. *Australian Econ. Pap.*, Supplement, June 1988, 27, pp. 89–91.

———; Godfrey, Leslie G. and McAleer, Michael. Variable Addition and LaGrange Multiplier Tests for Linear and Logarithmic Regression Models. *Rev. Econ. Statist.*, August 1988, 70(3), pp. 492–503.

McKenzie, Ed. A Note on Using the Integrated Form of ARIMA Forecasts. *Int. J. Forecasting*, 1988, 4(1), pp. 117–24.

McKenzie, George. Applied Welfare Economics and Frisch's Conjecture. **In** *Bös, D.; Rose, M. and Seidl, C., eds.,*, 1988, pp. 1–20.

McKenzie, Lionel W. A Limit Theorem on the Core. *Econ. Letters*, 1988, 27(1), pp. 7–9.

McKenzie, Richard B. The Relative Restrictiveness of Tariffs and Quotas: A Reinterpretation from a Rent-Seeking Perspective. *Public Choice*, July 1988, 58(1), pp. 85–90.

——— and Lee, Dwight R. Helping the Poor through Governmental Poverty Programs: The Triumph of Rhetoric over Reality. **In** *Gwartney, J. D. and Wagner, R. E., eds.*, 1988, pp. 387–408.

McKern, Bruce. Minerals in the Economies of the ASEAN Countries and Australia. **In** *McKern, B. and Koomsup, P., eds.*, 1988, pp. 1–12.

———. The Minerals Industries of ASEAN and Australia: Problems and Prospects: Conclusions and Prospects. In *McKern, B. and Koomsup, P., eds.,* 1988, pp. 364–73.

McKersie, Robert B. Productivity Bargaining in New York—What Went Wrong? Afterword. In *Lewin, D., et al., eds.,* 1988, *1980,* pp. 236–38.

_____; **Greenhalgh, Leonard and Jick, Todd.** Change and Continuity: The Role of a Labor–Management Committee in Facilitating Work Force Change during Retrenchment. In *Lewin, D., et al., eds.,* 1988, *1981,* pp. 569–80.

McKibbin, Warwick J. The Economics of International Policy Coordination. *Econ. Rec.,* December 1988, *64*(187), pp. 241–53.

_____. Policy Analysis with the MSG2 Model. *Australian Econ. Pap.,* Supplement, June 1988, *27,* pp. 126–50.

_____ **and Sachs, Jeffrey D.** Comparing the Global Performance of Alternative Exchange Arrangements. *J. Int. Money Finance,* December 1988, *7*(4), pp. 387–410.

_____ **and Sachs, Jeffrey D.** Coordination of Monetary and Fiscal Policies in the Industrial Economies. In *Frenkel, J. A., ed.,* 1988, pp. 73–113.

_____ **and Siegloff, Eric S.** A Note on Aggregate Investment in Australia. *Econ. Rec.,* September 1988, *64*(186), pp. 209–15.

McKiernan, Peter; Yasai-Ardekani, Masoud and Grinyer, Peter H. Market, Organizational, and Managerial Correlates of Economic Performance in the U.K. Electrical Engineering Industry. In *Grant, J. H., ed.,* 1988, pp. 147–79.

McKillop, D. G. and Hutchinson, R. W. Risk Analysis with Single-Index Portfolio Models: An Application to Farm Planning: Comment. *Amer. J. Agr. Econ.,* February 1988, *70*(1), pp. 192–94.

_____ **and Kula, Erhun.** A Planting Function for Private Afforestation in Northern Ireland. *J. Agr. Econ.,* January 1988, *39*(1), pp. 133–40.

McKinnon, Ronald I. An International Gold Standard without Gold. *Cato J.,* Fall 1988, *8*(2), pp. 351–73.

_____. Monetary and Exchange Rate Policies for International Financial Stability: A Proposal. *J. Econ. Perspectives,* Winter 1988, *2*(1), pp. 83–103.

_____. Money Supply versus Exchange-Rate Targeting: An Asymmetry between the United States and Other Industrial Economies. In *Giersch, H., ed.,* 1988, pp. 245–64.

McLachlan, D. L.; Apuzzo, A. and Kerr, William A. The Canada–U.S. Free Trade Agreement: A Canadian Perspective. *J. World Trade,* August 1988, *22*(4), pp. 9–34.

McLanahan, Sara S. Family Structure and Dependency: Early Transitions to Female Household Headship. *Demography,* February 1988, *25*(1), pp. 1–16.

_____; **Wong, Patrick and Garfinkel, Irwin.** Child Support and Dependency. In *Rodgers, H. R., Jr., ed.,* 1988, pp. 66–85.

McLaughlin, Catherine G. Market Responses to HMOs: Price Competition or Rivalry? *Inquiry,* Summer 1988, *25*(2), pp. 207–18.

_____ **and Brown, Lawrence D.** 'May the Third Force Be With You': Community Programs for Affordable Health Care. In *Scheffler, R. M. and Rossiter, L. F., eds.,* 1988, pp. 187–211.

McLaughlin, Josetta S. and Wokutch, Richard E. The Sociopolitical Context of Occupational Injuries. In *Preston, L. E., ed.,* 1988, pp. 113–37.

McLaughlin, Kenneth J. Aspects of Tournament Models: A Survey. In *Ehrenberg, R. G., ed.,* 1988, pp. 225–56.

McLaughlin, Mary M. and Wolfson, Martin H. The Profitability of Insured Commercial Banks in 1987. *Fed. Res. Bull.,* July 1988, *74*(7), pp. 403–18.

McLaughlin, Steven D.; Hayward, Mark D. and Grady, William R. Changes in the Retirement Process among Older Men in the United States: 1972–1980. *Demography,* August 1988, *25*(3), pp. 371–86.

McLean, Ian W. Unequal Sacrifice: Distributional Aspects of Depression and Recovery in Australia. In *Gregory, R. G. and Butlin, N. G., eds.,* 1988, pp. 335–56.

McLean, Kenneth A. How Market Forces Influence the Structure of Financial Regulation: Commentary. In *Haraf, W. S. and Kushmeider, R. M., eds.,* 1988, pp. 383–86.

McLean-Meyinsse, Patricia E. and Okunade, Albert Ade. Factor Demands of Louisiana Rice Producers: An Econometric Investigation. *Southern J. Agr. Econ.,* December 1988, *20*(2), pp. 127–35.

McLean, Richard P. and Crémer, Jacques. Full Extraction of the Surplus in Bayesian and Dominant Strategy Auctions. *Econometrica,* November 1988, *56*(6), pp. 1247–57.

McLennan, Kenneth. Global Competition and the Special Challenges of Developing Countries: A U.S. Perspective. In *Furino, A., ed.,* 1988, pp. 233–43.

McLeod, Joan C.; Omawale and Jackson, A. A. Household Food Consumption Behaviour in St. James, Jamaica. *Soc. Econ. Stud.,* September 1988, *37*(3), pp. 213–35.

McLin, Jon. The Petroleum Price Rollercoaster: Some Social and Economic Effects in Producing Countries. *Int. Lab. Rev.,* 1988, *127*(4), pp. 409–28.

McLure, Charles E., Jr. Lessons from General Equilibrium Models: Comments. In *Aaron, H. J.; Galper, H. and Pechman, J. A., eds.,* 1988, pp. 53–57.

_____. Tax Competition: Is What's Good for the Private Goose Also Good for the Public Gander? In *Brown, E., ed.,* 1988, *1986,* pp. 222–32.

_____. Tax Policy for the 1990s: Tending to Unfinished Business. In *Anderson, A. and Bark, D. L., eds.,* 1988, pp. 289–300.

_____. The VAT and Other Revenue Sources. *Bus. Econ.,* October 1988, *23*(4), pp. 19–24.

_____. The 1986 Act: Tax Reform's Finest Hour

or Death Throes of the Income Tax? *Nat. Tax J.*, September 1988, *41*(3), pp. 303–15.

McMahon, Anne M. and Ilardi, Barbara C. Organizational Legitimacy and Performance Evaluation. In *Lawler, E. J. and Markovsky, B., eds.*, 1988, pp. 217–44.

McMahon, Gary. Dual Factor Price Equalization: Elements of a Theory. *World Devel.*, August 1988, *16*(8), pp. 903–12.

McMahon, Patrick C. and Taylor, Mark P. Longrun Purchasing Power Parity in the 1920s. *Europ. Econ. Rev.*, January 1988, *32*(1), pp. 179–97.

McMahon, Walter W. Potential Resource Recovery in Higher Education in the Developing Countries and the Parents' Expected Contribution. *Econ. Educ. Rev.*, 1988, *7*(1), pp. 135–52.

McManus, Walter S. Aggregation and "the" Elasticity of Substitution. *Amer. Econ.*, Fall 1988, *32*(2), pp. 41–44.

McMillan, Henry and Baesel, Jerome B. The Role of Demographic Factors in Interest Rate Forecasting. *Managerial Dec. Econ.*, September 1988, *9*(3), pp. 187–95.

McMillan, John and McAfee, R. Preston. Multidimensional Incentive Compatibility and Mechanism Design. *J. Econ. Theory*, December 1988, *46*(2), pp. 335–54.

—— **and McAfee, R. Preston.** Search Mechanisms. *J. Econ. Theory*, February 1988, *44*(1), pp. 99–123.

—— **and Morgan, Peter B.** Price Dispersion, Price Flexibility, and Repeated Purchasing. *Can. J. Econ.*, November 1988, *21*(4), pp. 883–902.

McMillan, Melville L. and Amoako-Tuffour, Joe. An Examination of Preferences for Local Public Sector Outputs. *Rev. Econ. Statist.*, February 1988, *70*(1), pp. 45–54.

McMillin, W. Douglas. Money Growth Volatility and the Macroeconomy. *J. Money, Credit, Banking*, Part 1, August 1988, *20*(3), pp. 319–35.

—— **and Beard, Thomas R.** Do Budget Deficits Matter? Some Pre–World War II Evidence. *J. Econ. Bus.*, November 1988, *40*(4), pp. 295–308.

—— **and Laumas, G. S.** The Impact of Anticipated and Unanticipated Policy Actions on the Stock Market. *Appl. Econ.*, March 1988, *20*(3), pp. 377–84.

McMullen, B. Starr and Bible, Thomas D. Sources of Profit Risk for Small Wood Product Manufacturing Firms in the Pacific Northwest. *Land Econ.*, May 1988, *64*(2), pp. 184–95.

—— **and Stanley, Linda R.** The Impact of Deregulation on the Production Structure of the Motor Carrier Industry. *Econ. Inquiry*, April 1988, *26*(2), pp. 299–316.

McNamar, R. T. Evolution of the International Debt Challenge. In *Feldstein, M., ed. (1)*, 1988, pp. 305–20.

McNamara, Kevin T. and Green, Gary P. Traditional and Non-traditional Opportunities and Alternatives for Local Economic Development. In *Beaulieu, L. J., ed.*, 1988, pp. 288–303.

——**; Kriesel, Warren P. and Deaton, Brady J.** Human Capital Stock and Flow and Economic Growth Analysis: Note. *Growth Change*, Winter 1988, *19*(1), pp. 61–66.

——**; Kriesel, Warren P. and Deaton, Brady J.** Manufacturing Location: The Impact of Human Capital Stocks and Flows. *Rev. Reg. Stud.*, Winter 1988, *18*(1), pp. 42–48.

McNees, Stephen K. How Accurate Are Macroeconomic Forecasts? *New Eng. Econ. Rev.*, July–Aug. 1988, pp. 15–36.

——. On the Future of Macroeconomic Forecasting. *Int. J. Forecasting*, 1988, *4*(3), pp. 359–62.

McNeil, Barbara J. The Emphasis on Measurement in Quality Assurance: Reasons and Implications: Commentary. *Inquiry*, Winter 1988, *25*(4), pp. 433–34.

—— **and Cleary, Paul D.** Patient Satisfaction as an Indicator of Quality Care. *Inquiry*, Spring 1988, *25*(1), pp. 25–36.

——**; Pauker, Stephen G. and Pauker, Susan P.** The Effects of Private Attitudes on Public Policy: Prenatal Screening for Neural Tube Defects as a Prototype. In *Bell, D. E.; Raiffa, H. and Tversky, A., eds.*, 1988, *1981*, pp. 588–98.

——**; Pauker, Stephen G. and Tversky, Amos.** On the Framing of Medical Decisions. In *Bell, D. E.; Raiffa, H. and Tversky, A., eds.*, 1988, pp. 562–68.

McNeill, John R. Deforestation in the Araucaria Zone of Southern Brazil, 1900–1983. In *Richards, J. F. and Tucker, R. P., eds.*, 1988, pp. 15–32.

McNeilly, Caryl and Marquez, Jaime. Income and Price Elasticities for Exports of Developing Countries. *Rev. Econ. Statist.*, May 1988, *70*(2), pp. 306–14.

McNelis, Paul D. Indexation and Stabilization: Theory and Experience. *World Bank Res. Observer*, July 1988, *3*(2), pp. 157–69.

—— **and Bigman, David.** Inventory Mangement and Economic Instability in High Inflation Economies: A Macrodynamic Simulation. *J. Policy Modeling*, Summer 1988, *10*(2), pp. 229–47.

McNichols, Maureen. A Comparison of the Skewness of Stock Return Distributions at Earnings and Non-earnings Announcement Dates. *J. Acc. Econ.*, July 1988, *10*(3), pp. 239–73.

—— **and Wilson, G. Peter.** Evidence of Earnings Management from the Provision for Bad Debts. *J. Acc. Res.*, Supplement, 1988, *26*, pp. 1–31.

McNicoll, Geoffrey and Cain, Mead. Population Growth and Agrarian Outcomes. In *Lee, R. D., et al., eds.*, 1988, pp. 101–17.

McNiel, Douglas W.; Foshee, Andrew W. and Burbee, Clark R. Superfund Taxes and Expenditures: Regional Redistributions. *Rev. Reg. Stud.*, Winter 1988, *18*(1), pp. 4–9.

McNutt, Patrick A. A Note on Altruism. *Int. J. Soc. Econ.*, 1988, *15*(9), pp. 62–64.

McPherson, C. K. and Macfarlane, Alison. The Quality of Official Health Statistics. *J. Roy. Statist. Soc.*, 1988, *151*(2), pp. 342–48.

McPherson, Klim and Coleman, David A. British Social Trends since 1900: Health. In *Halsey, A. H., ed.*, 1988, pp. 398–461.

McPherson, M. Peter. Political Perspectives: Comments. In *Schott, J. J. and Smith, M. G., eds.*, 1988, pp. 187–95.

McPherson, Michael S. On Assessing the Impact of Federal Student Aid. *Econ. Educ. Rev.*, 1988, *7*(1), pp. 77–84.

_____. Reuniting Economics and Philosophy. In *Winston, G. C. and Teichgraeber, R. F., III, eds.*, 1988, pp. 71–87.

_____ and Hausman, Daniel M. Standards. *Econ. Philos.*, April 1988, *4*(1), pp. 1–7.

McQueen, David. The Hidden Microeconomics of John Maynard Keynes. In *Hamouda, O. F. and Smithin, J. N., eds., Vol. 1*, 1988, pp. 111–20.

McReady, Douglas J. Municipal Finances in Canada: Issues of Local Finance and the Case for User Charges. In *Paddison, R. and Bailey, S., eds.*, 1988, pp. 116–31.

McTaggart, Douglas. Agricultural Price Variability in a Neoclassical Framework. *Can. J. Agr. Econ.*, November 1988, *36*(3), pp. 539–48.

Meacci, Ferdinando. The Principles of Capital in Luigi Einaudi's Work. *Giorn. Econ.*, Sept.–Oct. 1988, *47*(9–10), pp. 475–93.

Meacher, Michael. The Future of Finance. In *Harris, L., et al., eds.*, 1988, pp. 3–6.

Mead, Lawrence M. The Potential for Work Enforcement: A Study of WIN. *J. Policy Anal. Manage.*, Winter 1988, *7*(2), pp. 264–88.

Mead, Margaret. Australian On-line Information Sources for Business and Economics. *Australian Econ. Rev.*, 1st Quarter 1988, (81), pp. 28–41.

Meade, Ellen E. Exchange Rates, Adjustment, and the J-Curve. *Fed. Res. Bull.*, October 1988, *74*(10), pp. 633–44.

Meade, James. The Adjustment of Savings to Investment in a Growing Economy. In *Meade, J., Vol. 2*, 1988, *1963*, pp. 398–415.

_____. The Adjustment Processes of Labour Cooperatives with Constant Returns to Scale and Perfect Competition. In *Meade, J., Vol. 2*, 1988, *1979*, pp. 201–10.

_____. The Amount of Money and the Banking System. In *Meade, J., Vol. 1*, 1988, *1934*, pp. 26–32.

_____. The Balance-of-Payments Problems of a European Free-Trade Area. In *Meade, J., Vol. 3*, 1988, *1957*, pp. 212–28.

_____. Benelux: The Formation of the Common Customs. In *Meade, J., Vol. 3*, 1988, *1956*, pp. 177–89.

_____. Bretton Woods, GATT, and the Balance of Payments: A Second Round? In *Meade, J., Vol. 3*, 1988, *1952*, pp. 148–60.

_____. Bretton Woods, Havana and the United Kingdom Balance of Payments. In *Meade, J., Vol. 3*, 1988, *1948*, pp. 81–94.

_____. The Case for Variable Exchange Rates.

In *Meade, J., Vol. 3*, 1988, *1955*, pp. 161–76.

_____. Comment [Monetarism: An Interpretation and an Assessment] [The Monetarist Counter Revolution Today—An Appraisal]. In *Meade, J., Vol. 1*, 1988, *1981*, pp. 376–82.

_____. The Common Market: Is There an Alternative. In *Meade, J., Vol. 3*, 1988, *1962*, pp. 274–84.

_____. Control of Inflation. In *Meade, J., Vol. 1*, 1988, *1946*, pp. 275–96.

_____. The Control of Inflation. In *Meade, J., Vol. 1*, 1988, *1958*, pp. 297–320.

_____. Degrees of Competitive Speculation. In *Meade, J., Vol. 2*, 1988, *1949*, pp. 78–89.

_____. Different Forms of Share Economy. In *Meade, J., Vol. 2*, 1988, *1986*, pp. 211–48.

_____. Economic Planning. In *Meade, J., Vol. 1*, 1988, *1945*, pp. 265–74.

_____. The Effect on Employment of a Change in the Employer's Social Security Contribution. In *Meade, J., Vol. 1*, 1988, *1942*, pp. 193–98.

_____. The Effects of Savings on Consumption in a State of Steady Growth. In *Meade, J., Vol. 2*, 1988, *1962*, pp. 389–97.

_____. The Exchange Policy of a Socialist Government. In *Meade, J., Vol. 3*, 1988, pp. 11–26.

_____. Exchange-Rate Flexibility. In *Meade, J., Vol. 3*, 1988, *1966*, pp. 297–312.

_____. External Economies and Diseconomies in a Competitive Situation. In *Meade, J., Vol. 2*, 1988, *1952*, pp. 90–102.

_____. Financial Aspects of War Economy. In *Meade, J., Vol. 1*, 1988, *1940*, pp. 106–17.

_____. Financial Policy and the Balance of Payments. In *Meade, J., Vol. 3*, 1988, *1948*, pp. 67–80.

_____. The Future of International Trade and Payments. In *Meade, J., Vol. 3*, 1988, *1961*, pp. 229–43.

_____. A Geometrical Representation of Balance-of-Payments Policy. In *Meade, J., Vol. 3*, 1988, *1949*, pp. 133–47.

_____. Government Intervention in the Post-War Economy. In *Meade, J., Vol. 2*, 1988, *1942*, pp. 9–15.

_____. The Inheritance of Inequalities: Some Biological, Demographic, Social, and Economic Factors. In *Meade, J., Vol. 2*, 1988, *1973*, pp. 352–72.

_____. Internal Measures for the Prevention of General Unemployment. In *Meade, J., Vol. 1*, 1988, pp. 171–83.

_____. International Commodity Agreements. In *Meade, J., Vol. 3*, 1988, *1964*, pp. 285–96.

_____. International Economic Co-operation. In *Meade, J., Vol. 3*, 1988, *1933*, pp. 1–10.

_____. Is the National Debt a Burden? In *Meade, J., Vol. 2*, 1988, *1958*, pp. 296–314.

_____. Is the National Debt a Burden? A Correction. In *Meade, J., Vol. 2*, 1988, *1959*, pp. 315–16.

_____. James Meade. In *Meade, J., Vol. 1*, 1988, pp. 1–5.

_____. The Keynesian Revolution. In *Meade, J., Vol. 1*, 1988, *1975*, pp. 343–48.

_____. Labour-Managed Firms in Conditions of Imperfect Competition. In *Meade, J.*, *Vol. 2*, 1988, *1974*, pp. 192–200.

_____. Life-Cycle Savings, Inheritance and Economic Growth. In *Meade, J.*, *Vol. 2*, 1988, *1966*, pp. 429–50.

_____. Little's *Critique of Welfare Economics*. In *Meade, J.*, *Vol. 2*, 1988, *1959*, pp. 103–08.

_____. Maintenance of Full Employment. In *Meade, J.*, *Vol. 1*, 1988, *1943*, pp. 199–232.

_____. Mauritius: A Case Study in Malthusian Economics. In *Meade, J.*, *Vol. 2*, 1988, *1961*, pp. 375–88.

_____. The Meaning of "Internal Balance." In *Meade, J.*, *Vol. 1*, 1988, *1978*, pp. 349–62.

_____. Monetary Policy and Fiscal Policy: Impact Effects with a New Keynesian 'Assignment' of Weapons to Targets. In *Meade, J.*, *Vol. 3*, 1988, pp. 354–87.

_____. Mr Lerner on *The Economics of Control*. In *Meade, J.*, *Vol. 2*, 1988, *1945*, pp. 32–50.

_____. National Income, National Expenditure and the Balance of Payments. In *Meade, J.*, *Vol. 3*, 1988, *1948*, pp. 95–132.

_____. A New Keynesian Approach to Full Employment. In *Meade, J.*, *Vol. 1*, 1988, *1983*, pp. 383–97.

_____. A New Keynesian Bretton Woods. In *Meade, J.*, *Vol. 3*, 1988, *1984*, pp. 338–53.

_____. Next Steps in Domestic Economic Policy. In *Meade, J.*, *Vol. 2*, 1988, *1949*, pp. 285–95.

_____. Notes on the Elasticity of Substitution. In *Meade, J.*, *Vol. 2*, 1988, *1933*, pp. 3–8.

_____. On Stagflation. In *Meade, J.*, *Vol. 1*, 1988, *1978*, pp. 363–75.

_____. The Optimal Balance between Economies of Scale and Variety of Products: An Illustrative Model. In *Meade, J.*, *Vol. 2*, 1988, *1974*, pp. 183–91.

_____. Outline of Economic Policy for a Labour Government. In *Meade, J.*, *Vol. 1*, 1988, *1935*, pp. 33–78.

_____. Population Explosion, the Standard of Living and Social Conflict. In *Meade, J.*, *Vol. 2*, 1988, *1967*, pp. 451–72.

_____. The Post-War International Settlement and the United Kingdom Balance of Payments. In *Meade, J.*, *Vol. 3*, 1988, pp. 36–66.

_____. The Post-War Treatment of the National Debt. In *Meade, J.*, *Vol. 2*, 1988, *1945*, pp. 251–84.

_____. Poverty in the Welfare State. In *Meade, J.*, *Vol. 2*, 1988, *1972*, pp. 317–51.

_____. Price and Output Policy of State Enterprise: A Symposium: Rejoinder. In *Meade, J.*, *Vol. 2*, 1988, pp. 30–31.

_____. Price and Output Policy of State Enterprise: A Symposium. In *Meade, J.*, *Vol. 2*, 1988, *1944*, pp. 16–22.

_____. The Price Mechanism and the Australian Balance of Payments. In *Meade, J.*, *Vol. 3*, 1988, *1956*, pp. 190–205.

_____. A Proposal for an International Commercial Union. In *Meade, J.*, *Vol. 3*, 1988, pp. 27–35.

_____. Public Works in Their International As-

pect. In *Meade, J.*, *Vol. 1*, 1988, *1933*, pp. 6–25.

_____. The Rate of Profit in a Growing Economy. In *Meade, J.*, *Vol. 2*, 1988, *1963*, pp. 416–24.

_____. The Rate of Profit in a Growing Economy. In *Meade, J.*, *Vol. 2*, 1988, *1965*, pp. 425–28.

_____. A Simplified Model of Mr. Keynes' System. In *Meade, J.*, *Vol. 1*, 1988, *1937*, pp. 79–90.

_____. Sir William Beveridge's *Full Employment in a Free Society* and the White Paper on Employment Policy (Command 6527). In *Meade, J.*, *Vol. 1*, 1988, *1944*, pp. 233–64.

_____. The Socialisation of Industries. Memorandum by the Economic Section of the Cabinet Secretariat. In *Meade, J.*, *Vol. 2*, 1988, pp. 51–77.

_____. A Strategy for Commodity Policy. In *Meade, J.*, *Vol. 3*, 1988, *1978*, pp. 313–23.

_____. Structural Changes in the Rate of Interest and the Rate of Foreign Exchange to Preserve Equilibrium in the Balance of Payments and the Budget Balance. In *Meade, J.*, *Vol. 3*, 1988, *1984*, pp. 224–37.

_____. The Theory of Indicative Planning. In *Meade, J.*, *Vol. 2*, 1988, *1970*, pp. 109–57.

_____. The Theory of Labour-Managed Firms and of Profit Sharing. In *Ricketts, M., ed.*, *Vol. 1*, 1988, *1972*, pp. 262–88.

_____. The Theory of Labour-Managed Firms and of Profit Sharing. In *Meade, J.*, *Vol. 2*, 1988, *1972*, pp. 158–82.

_____. UK, Commonwealth and Common Market. In *Meade, J.*, *Vol. 3*, 1988, *1962*, pp. 244–73.

_____. Variations in the Rate of Social Security Contributions as a Means of Stabilising the Demand for Labour. In *Meade, J.*, *Vol. 1*, 1988, *1944*, pp. 184–92.

_____. Wage-Fixing Revisited. In *Meade, J.*, *Vol. 1*, 1988, *1985*, pp. 398–422.

_____. Wage-Rates, the Cost of Living, and the Balance of Payments. In *Meade, J.*, *Vol. 3*, 1988, *1957*, pp. 206–11.

_____. Wages and Prices in a Mixed Economy. In *Meade, J.*, *Vol. 1*, 1988, *1971*, pp. 321–42.

_____ **and Andrews, P. W. S.** Summary of Replies to Questions on Effects of Interest Rates. In *Meade, J.*, *Vol. 1*, 1988, *1938*, pp. 91–105.

_____ **and Stone, Richard.** The Construction of Tables of National Income, Expenditure, Savings and Investment. In *Meade, J.*, *Vol. 1*, 1988, *1941*, pp. 118–35.

_____ **and Stone, Richard.** National Income and Expenditure. In *Meade, J.*, *Vol. 1*, 1988, *1944*, pp. 152–70.

_____; **Stone, Richard and Champernowne, D. G.** The Precision of National Income Estimates. In *Meade, J.*, *Vol. 1*, 1988, *1942*, pp. 136–51.

Meade, Nigel. A Modified Logistic Model Applied to Human Populations. *J. Roy. Statist. Soc.*, 1988, *151*(3), pp. 491–98.

Meador, Mark; Walters, Stephen J. K. and Jordan, John M. Effects of Department Size and Organization on the Research Productivity of

Academic Economists. *Econ. Educ. Rev.*, 1988, 7(2), pp. 251–55.

Meadowcroft, Shirley; Thompson, David and Domberger, Simon. Competition and Efficiency in Refuse Collection: A Reply. *Fisc. Stud.*, February 1988, 9(1), pp. 86–90.

Meadows, Donella H. How Can We Improve Our Chances? In *Ehrlich, P. R. and Holdren, J. P., eds.*, 1988, pp. 287–98.

_____. -T3The Limits to Growth-U3 Revisited. In *Ehrlich, P. R. and Holdren, J. P., eds.*, 1988, pp. 257–70.

Meagher, G. A. and Agrawal, Nisha. Structural Reform, Macro Policies and Income Distribution. *Australian Econ. Rev.*, Spring 1988, (83), pp. 42–52.

Mechanic, David; Feinson, Marjorie Chary and Hansell, Stephen. Factors Associated with Medicare Beneficiaries' Interest in HMOs. *Inquiry*, Fall 1988, 25(3), pp. 364–73.

Mechlin, George F. and Berg, Daniel. Evaluating Research—ROI is Not Enough. In *Grønhaug, K. and Kaufmann, G., eds.*, 1988, 1980, pp. 433–42.

Medick, Hans. Industrialisation before Industrialisation? Rural Industries in Europe and the Genesis of Capitalism. *Indian Econ. Soc. Hist. Rev.*, July–Sept. 1988, 25(3), pp. 371–84.

Medley, Joseph and McIntyre, Richard. Democratic Reform of the Fed: The Impact of Class Relations on Policy Formation. *Rev. Radical Polit. Econ.*, Summer–Fall 1988, 20(2–3), pp. 156–62.

Medoff, James L. and Brown, Charles C. Employer Size, Pay, and the Ability to Pay in the Public Sector. In *Freeman, R. B. and Ichniowski, C., eds.*, 1988, pp. 195–213.

_____ **and Brown, Charles C.** The Impact of Firm Acquisitions on Labor. In *Auerbach, A. J., ed. (I)*, 1988, pp. 9–25.

Medoff, Marshall H. An Economic Analysis of the Demand for Abortions. *Econ. Inquiry*, April 1988, 26(2), pp. 353–59.

Meegan, Richard. A Crisis of Mass Production? In *Allen, J. and Massey, D., eds.*, 1988, pp. 136–83.

Meek, Ronald L. Mr. Sraffa's Rehabilitation of Classical Economics. In *Steedman, I., ed., Vol. 2*, 1988, 1961, pp. 377–94.

Meen, Geoffrey. International Comparisons of the UK's Long-run Economic Performance. *Oxford Rev. Econ. Policy*, Spring 1988, 4(1), pp. xxii–xli.

van der Meer, J. and van den Berg, L. Dynamics of Urban Systems: General Trends and Dutch Experiences. *Environ. Planning A*, November 1988, 20(11), pp. 1471–86.

van der Meer, T. and Merkies, A. H. Q. M. A Theoretical Foundation for Constant Market Share Analysis. *Empirical Econ.*, 1988, 13(2), pp. 65–80.

Meeropol, Michael. Reaganomics Has Failed on Its Own Terms. *Challenge*, Jan.–Feb. 1988, 31(1), pp. 50–53.

Meese, Edwin, III. Criminal Justice: A Public

Policy Imperative. In *Anderson, A. and Bark, D. L., eds.*, 1988, pp. 427–37.

Meese, Richard A. and Rogoff, Kenneth. Was It Real? The Exchange Rate-Interest Differential Relation over the Modern Floating-Rate Period. *J. Finance*, September 1988, 43(4), pp. 933–48.

Meesook, Oey Astra and Chernichovsky, Dov. Urban-Rural Food and Nutrition Consumption Patterns in Indonesia. In *Sirageldin, I. and Sorkin, A., eds.*, 1988, pp. 193–205.

_____; **Suebsaeng, Parita and Lindauer, David L.** Government Wage Policy in Africa: Some Findings and Policy Issues. *World Bank Res. Observer*, January 1988, 3(1), pp. 1–25.

Meeting, David; Rozen, Etzmun and Fuglister, Jayne. Teaching the Qualitative Characteristics of Accounting Information in the Standard Setting Process: A Technique Using SFAS No. 96. In *Pennsylvania Economic Association*, 1988, pp. 601–13.

Megheşan, V.; Guran, M. and Văduva, I. Informatics and the Technical and Scientific Evolution. *Econ. Computat. Cybern. Stud. Res.*, 1988, 23(1), pp. 31–44.

Mehay, Stephen L. and Deno, Kevin T. Municipal Utilities and Local Public Finance: A Simultaneous Model. *Public Choice*, June 1988, 57(3), pp. 201–12.

_____ **and Gonzalez, Rodolfo A.** Non-clearing Labor Markets and Minority Employment in Municipal Government. *J. Lab. Res.*, Spring 1988, 9(2), pp. 127–37.

Mehdian, S., et al. Toward an Appraisal of the FMHA Farm Credit Program: A Case Study of the Efficiency of Borrowers in Southern Illinois. *Southern J. Agr. Econ.*, December 1988, 20(2), pp. 93–99.

Mehmet, Ozay. The NIC Challenge and the Changing Structure of World Trade: Some Implications for Regional Development. In *Choudhury, M. A., ed.*, 1988, pp. 13–24.

Mehr, Barry D. Canada–U.S. Agricultural Trade: Market Realities and Opportunities. In *Allen, K. and Macmillan, K., eds.*, 1988, pp. 75–79.

_____. Opportunities for Canadian Producers: Industry Development and New Markets. *Can. J. Agr. Econ.*, Part 1, December 1988, 36(4), pp. 703–10.

Mehra, Rajnish. On the Existence and Representation of Equilibrium in an Economy with Growth and Nonstationary Consumption. *Int. Econ. Rev.*, February 1988, 29(1), pp. 131–35.

_____ **and Prescott, Edward C.** The Equity Risk Premium: A Solution? *J. Monet. Econ.*, July 1988, 22(1), pp. 133–36.

Mehra, Yash P. The Forecast Performance of Alternative Models of Inflation. *Fed. Res. Bank Richmond Econ. Rev.*, Sept.–Oct. 1988, 74(5), pp. 10–18.

Mehran, F.; Doss, R. G. and Dupré, M. T. Employment Promotion Schemes and the Statistical Measurement of Unemployment. *Int. Lab. Rev.*, 1988, 127(1), pp. 35–51.

Mehrez, Abraham. Two Managerial Economics Approaches to the R&D Decision Process.

Managerial Dec. Econ., June 1988, 9(2), pp. 163–72.

_____ and Justman, Moshe. Extremal Configurations for Optimal Prevention and Damage Control. *Europ. Econ. Rev.*, October 1988, 32(8), pp. 1637–43.

Mehrotra, Sunil. Marketing Mix Reactions to Entry: Commentary. *Marketing Sci.*, Fall 1988, 7(4), pp. 390.

Mehta, Ashok. Myth of the Optimal Capital Structure. *Indian Econ. J.*, Oct.–Dec. 1988, 36(2), pp. 74–81.

Mehta, Cyrus R.; Patel, Nitin R. and Senchaudhuri, P. Exact Non-parametric Significance Tests. In *Edwards, D. and Raun, N. E., eds.*, 1988, pp. 227–32.

Mehta, Dileep R. and Tai, Lawrence S. T. Trade and Investment Behavior in U.S. and Japanese Manufacturing Industries: 1962–1981. *Hitotsubashi J. Econ.*, June 1988, 29(1), pp. 59–71.

Mehta, Fredie A. Growth, Controls and the Private Sector. In *Lucas, R. E. B. and Papanek, G. F., eds.*, 1988, pp. 203–13.

Mehta, Ghanshyam. Some General Theorems on the Existence of Order-Preserving Functions. *Math. Soc. Sci.*, April 1988, 15(2), pp. 135–43.

Meiburg, E. and Homsy, G. M. Vortex Methods for Porous Media Flows. In *Wheeler, M. F., ed.*, 1988, pp. 199–225.

Meidner, Rudolf. The Role of Manpower Policy in the Swedish Model. In *Kregel, J. A.; Matzner, E. and Roncaglia, A., eds.*, 1988, pp. 143–61.

Meier, Peter M. and Cassedy, Edward S. Planning for Electric Power in Developing Countries in the Face of Change. In *Byrne, J. and Rich, D., eds.*, 1988, pp. 53–100.

Meier, Walter. Security on Movable Property and Receivables in Europe: Switzerland. In *Dickson, M. G.; Rosener, W. and Storm, P. M., eds.*, 1988, pp. 172–86.

Meigs, A. James. Dollars and Deficits: Substituting False for Real Problems. *Cato J.*, Fall 1988, 8(2), pp. 533–53.

_____. Evolution in Banking. In *England, C. and Huertas, T., eds.*, 1988, pp. 345–48.

_____. Evolution in Banking. *Cato J.*, Winter 1988, 7(3), pp. 799–802.

Meilke, Karl D. and Coleman, J. R. The Influence of Exchange Rates on Red Meat Trade between Canada and the United States. *Can. J. Agr. Econ.*, November 1988, 36(3), pp. 401–24.

_____ and de Gorter, H. Impacts of the Common Agricultural Policy on International Wheat Prices. *J. Agr. Econ.*, May 1988, 39(2), pp. 217–29.

_____ and Moschini, Giancarlo. Sustainable Rates of Return for Milk Quotas in Ontario. *Can. J. Agr. Econ.*, March 1988, 36(1), pp. 119–26.

Meiners, Hubert and Binswanger, Hans Christoph. Von der Wirtschafgemeinschaft (EWG) zur Wirtschafts- und Umweltgemeinschaft (EWUG). (The Expansion of the European Economic Community into a European Economic and Environmental Community. With English summary.) *Aussenwirtschaft*, September 1988, 43(3), pp. 399–421.

Meiners, Roger E. and McCormick, Robert E. University Governance: A Property Rights Perspective. *J. Law Econ.*, October 1988, 31(2), pp. 423–42.

_____ and Nardinelli, Clark. Schmoller, the Methodenstreit, and the Development of Economic History. *J. Inst. Theoretical Econ.*, June 1988, 144(3), pp. 543–51.

Meinster, David R. and Elyasiani, Elyas. The Performance of Foreign Owned, Minority Owned, and Holding Company Owned Banks in the U.S. *J. Banking Finance*, June 1988, 12(2), pp. 293–313.

Meissner, Frank; Berman, Brian W. and Ben David, Moshe. Export Marketing for Off-Season Fresh Produce: The Case of Agrexco, Israel. In *Kumcu, E. and Firat, A. F., eds.*, 1988, pp. 253–83.

Meixner, Wilda F. and Welker, Robert B. Judgment Consensus and Auditor Experience: An Examination of Organizational Relations. *Accounting Rev.*, July 1988, 63(3), pp. 505–13.

Mekkelholt, Eddie; van Ophem, Hans and Hartog, Joop. Testing the Relevance of Job Search for Job Mobility. *Econ. Letters*, 1988, 27(3), pp. 299–303.

Meklin, Pentti. Julkisen liikelaitoksen liiketaloudellinen ja yhteiskunnallinen päämäärä. Esimerkkinä Suomen Valtionrautatiet. (Commercial and Social Objectives in a State Enterprise: The Case of the Finnish State Railways. With English summary.) *Liiketaloudellinen Aikak.*, 1988, 37(4), pp. 346–54.

Melamed, Leo. Evolution of the International Monetary Market. *Cato J.*, Fall 1988, 8(2), pp. 393–404.

_____. The International Monetary Market. In *Melamed, L., ed.*, 1988, pp. 417–27.

Meland, Creighton R., Jr. Modern Investment Management and the Prudent Man Rule: Review Article. *Mich. Law Rev.*, May 1988, 86(6), pp. 1237–43.

Mélard, Guy and Hallin, Marc. Rank-Based Tests for Randomness against First-Order Serial Dependence. *J. Amer. Statist. Assoc.*, December 1988, 83(404), pp. 1117–28.

Melenberg, Bertrand; Weber, Guglielmo and Alessie, Rob J. M. Consumption, Leisure and Earnings-Related Liquidity Constraints: A Note. *Econ. Letters*, 1988, 27(1), pp. 101–04.

Melese, Francois; Im, Bae-Geun and Kaserman, David L. Rent Seeking and the Allowed Rate of Return: A Recursive Model. *Rev. Ind. Organ.*, Fall 1988, 3(4), pp. 27–51.

_____ and Michel, Philippe. The Hazard Rate and the Hotelling Rule. *Atlantic Econ. J.*, December 1988, 16(4), pp. 43–51.

Melfi, C. A. and Rogers, Alan J. A Test for the Existence of Allocative Inefficiency in Firms. *J. Appl. Econometrics*, January 1988, 3(1), pp. 69–80.

Melichar, Emmanuel. Agricultural Finance:

Turning the Corner on Problem Farm Debt. In *Goldberg, R. A., ed., Vol. 8*, 1988, pp. 65–94.

Melicher, Ronald W. and Cherin, Antony C. Impact of Branch Banking on Bank Firm Risk via Geographic Market Diversification. *Quart. J. Bus. Econ.*, Spring 1988, 27(2), pp. 73–95.

_____ **and Hearth, Douglas.** A Time Series Analysis of Aggregate Business Failure Activity and Credit Conditions. *J. Econ. Bus.*, November 1988, 40(4), pp. 319–33.

_____ **and McCarthy, Joseph E.** Analysis of Bond Rating Changes in a Portfolio Context. *Quart. J. Bus. Econ.*, Autumn 1988, 27(4), pp. 69–86.

Melick, William R. U.S. International Transactions in 1987. *Fed. Res. Bull.*, May 1988, 74(5), pp. 279–88.

Melino, Angelo. The Term Structure of Interest Rates: Evidence and Theory. *J. Econ. Surveys*, 1988, 2(4), pp. 335–66.

Mélitz, Jacques. Exchange Rate Variability, Misalignment, and the European Monetary System: Comment. In *Marston, R. C., ed.*, 1988, pp. 100–103.

_____. Monetary Discipline, Germany, and the European Monetary System. *Kredit Kapital*, 1988, 21(4), pp. 481–512.

_____. The Prospect of a Depreciating Dollar and Possible Tension Inside the EMS. *Schweiz. Z. Volkswirtsch. Statist.*, March 1988, 124(1), pp. 1–21.

_____; **Oudiz, Gilles and Cohen, Daniel.** Le système monéaire européen et l'asymétrie franc-mark. (The EMS and the Frank–Mark Asymetry. With English summary.) *Revue Écon.*, May 1988, 39(3), pp. 667–77.

Melka, Richard F. and Mukerjee, Gautam. Criteria Ranking for Low-Level Waste Sites: A Guide for Policymakers. In *Pennsylvania Economic Association*, 1988, pp. 453–69.

Melkote, Srinivas R. Agricultural Extension and the Small Farmer: Revealing the Communication Gap in an Extension Project in Kenya. *J. Devel. Areas*, January 1988, 22(2), pp. 239–51.

Meller, Patricio. América Latina y la condicionalidad del fondo monetario internacional y del banco mundial. (Latin America and the International Monetary Fund and the World Bank Conditionalities. With English summary.) *Colección Estud. CIEPLAN*, March 1988, (23), pp. 195–237.

_____. El cobre y la generación de recursos externos durante el régimen militar. (Copper and the Generation of Foreign Resources during the Military Regime. With English summary.) *Colección Estud. CIEPLAN*, June 1988, (24), pp. 85–111.

_____ **and Labán, Raúl.** Estimaçao de elasticidades variáveis no mercado de trabalho do Chile. (With English summary.) *Pesquisa Planejamento Econ.*, December 1988, 18(3), pp. 529–59.

Mellman, Martin; Pastena, Victor and Lilien, Steven. Accounting Changes: Successful versus Unsuccessful Firms. *Accounting Rev.*, October 1988, 63(4), pp. 642–56.

Mello, Antonio S. and Cooper, Ian. Default Spreads in the Fixed and in the Floating Interest Rate Markets: A Contingent Claims Approach. In *Fabozzi, F. J., ed.*, 1988, pp. 269–89.

Mellor, Earl F. and Parks, William, II. A Year's Work: Labor Force Activity from a Different Perspective. *Mon. Lab. Rev.*, September 1988, 111(9), pp. 13–18.

Mellor, John W. Food and Development: The Critical Nexus between Developing and Developed Countries. In *Antonelli, G. and Quadrio-Curzio, A., eds.*, 1988, pp. 175–83.

_____. Food Demand in Developing Countries and the Transition of World Agriculture. *Europ. Rev. Agr. Econ.*, 1988, 15(4), pp. 419–36.

_____. Food Production, Consumption and Development Strategy. In *Lucas, R. E. B. and Papanek, G. F., eds.*, 1988, pp. 53–76.

_____. Global Food Balances and Food Security. *World Devel.*, September 1988, 16(9), pp. 997–1011.

_____. Issues in World Agriculture—A U.S. Perspective. In *Hildreth, R. J., et al., eds.*, 1988, pp. 158–67.

_____. Research Needs for an Agricultural and Employment Growth Strategy. In *Mellor, J. W.*, 1988, pp. 55–75.

_____. United States Agriculture in the Global Context. In *Asefa, S., ed.*, 1988, pp. 67–86.

_____ **and Ahmed, Raisuddin.** Agricultural Price Policy for Accelerating Growth: Conclusions. In *Mellor, J. W. and Ahmed, R., eds.*, 1988, pp. 265–91.

_____ **and Ahmed, Raisuddin.** Agricultural Price Policy—The Context and the Approach. In *Mellor, J. W. and Ahmed, R., eds.*, 1988, pp. 1–10.

Melman, Seymour. Economic Consequences of the Arms Race: The Second-Rate Economy. *Amer. Econ. Rev.*, May 1988, 78(2), pp. 55–59.

_____. The Impact of Economics on Technology. In *Samuels, W. J., ed., Vol. 3*, 1988, 1975, pp. 168–81.

Melnick, Glenn A. and Zwanziger, Jack. The Effects of Hospital Competition and the Medicare PPS Program on Hospital Cost Behavior in California. *J. Health Econ.*, December 1988, 7(4), pp. 301–20.

Melnick, Rafi. Prices, Wages, and Import Prices in Israel: 1970–1983. *J. Appl. Econometrics*, January 1988, 3(1), pp. 53–67.

Melnik, Arie and Plaut, Steven E. International Lending, Private-Sector "Country Risk," and Stabilization Policy. In *Khoury, S. J. and Ghosh, A., eds.*, 1988, pp. 121–29.

de Melo, Jaime. Computable General Equilibrium Models for Trade Policy Analysis in Developing Countries: A Survey. *J. Policy Modeling*, Winter 1988, 10(4), pp. 469–503.

_____. The Macro-economic Effects of Foreign Aid: Issues and Evidence. In *Jepma, C. J., ed.*, 1988, pp. 187–203.

_____. SAM-Based Models: An Introduction. *J. Policy Modeling*, Fall 1988, *10*(3), pp. 321–25.

_____. Some Broad Development Policy Scenerios: Comment. In *Jepma, C. J., ed.*, 1988, pp. 226–27.

_____ **and Bark, Taeho.** Export Quota Allocations, Export Earnings, and Market Diversification. *World Bank Econ. Rev.*, September 1988, *2*(3), pp. 341–48.

_____ **and Messerlin, Patrick A.** Price, Quality and Welfare Effects of European VERs on Japanese Autos. *Europ. Econ. Rev.*, September 1988, *32*(7), pp. 1527–46.

Melody, William H. Information: An Emerging Dimension of Institutional Analysis. In *Tool, M. R., ed., Vol. 1*, 1988, *1987*, pp. 361–87.

Melossi, Dario. Political Business Cycles and Imprisonment Rates in Italy: Report on a Work in Progress. In *Simms, M. C. and Myers, S. L., Jr., eds.*, 1988, pp. 211–18.

Melton, Robert J.; Komorita, Samuel S. and Ellis, Alan L. The Effects of Justice Norms in a Bargaining Situation. In *Tietz, R.; Albers, W. and Selten, R., eds.*, 1988, pp. 251–67.

Meltz, Noah M. The Industrial Relations Systems Model as an Analytical Tool. In *Maital, S., ed., Vol. 2*, 1988, pp. 613–19.

_____; **Hébert, G. and Jain, H. C.** The State of the Art in Industrial Relations: Conclusion. In *Hébert, G.; Jain, H. C. and Meltz, N. M., eds..*, 1988, pp. 281–90.

_____; **Hébert, G. and Jain, H. C.** The State of the Art in IR: Some Questions and Concepts. In *Hébert, G.; Jain, H. C. and Meltz, N. M., eds..*, 1988, pp. 1–8.

Meltzer, Allan H. Economic Policies and Actions in the Reagan Administration. *J. Post Keynesian Econ.*, Summer 1988, *10*(4), pp. 528–40.

_____. Restructuring Banking & Financial Services in America: The Policy Proposals in the AEI Studies. In *Haraf, W. S. and Kushmeider, R. M., eds.*, 1988, pp. 440–47.

_____ **and Brunner, Karl.** Money and Credit in the Monetary Transmission Process. *Amer. Econ. Rev.*, May 1988, *78*(2), pp. 446–51.

_____ **and Brunner, Karl.** Stabilization Policies and Labor Markets. *Carnegie–Rochester Conf. Ser. Public Policy*, Spring 1988, *28*, pp. 1–8.

_____ **and Richard, Scott F.** A Rational Theory of the Size of Government. In *Ricketts, M., ed., Vol. 1*, 1988, *1981*, pp. 375–88.

Meltzer, Judith W. Financing Long-Term Care: A Major Obstacle to Reform. In *Sullivan, S. and Lewin, M. E., eds.*, 1988, pp. 56–72.

Melvin, James R. and Courchene, Thomas J. A Neoclassical Approach to Regional Economics. In *[Perroux, F.]*, 1988, pp. 169–89.

_____ **and Scheffman, David T.** The Effects of Oil Price Changes on Urban Structure: Some Theoretical and Simulation Results. In *Byrne, J. and Rich, D., eds.*, 1988, pp. 215–46.

Melvin, Michael. The Dollarization of Latin America as a Market-Enforced Monetary Reform: Evidence and Implications. *Econ. Develop. Cult. Change*, April 1988, *36*(3), pp. 543–58.

_____. Monetary Confidence, Privately Produced Monies, and Domestic and International Monetary Reform. In *Willett, T. D., ed.*, 1988, pp. 435–59.

Memon, Ali. Voluntary Organizations and Ethnic Minority Business Development in Inner Cities: A Comment. *Reg. Stud.*, April 1988, *22*(2), pp. 155–60.

Mencher, Joan P. Peasants and Agricultural Laborers: An Analytical Assessment of Issues Involved in Their Organizing. In *Srinivasan, T. N. and Bardhan, P. K., eds.*, 1988, pp. 526–48.

Menchik, Paul L. Unequal Estate Division: Is It Altruism, Reverse Bequests, or Simply Noise? In *Kessler, D. and Masson, A., eds.*, 1988, pp. 105–16.

_____ **and David, Martin H.** Changes in Cohort Wealth over a Generation. *Demography*, August 1988, *25*(3), pp. 317–35.

Menck, Thomas and Uelner, Adalbert. World Tax Reform: A Progress Report: Germany. In *Pechman, J. A., ed.*, 1988, pp. 119–27.

Mendenhall, Richard R. and Nichols, William D. Bad News and Differential Market Reactions to Announcements of Earlier-Quarters versus Fourth-Quarter Earnings. *J. Acc. Res.*, Supplement, 1988, *26*, pp. 63–86.

Mendes, Antonio. Brazil: The Debt–Equity Conversion Programme: A Follow Up. *Bull. Int. Fiscal Doc.*, July 1988, *42*(7), pp. 300–303.

_____. The Debt–Equity Conversion Programme: Brazil. *Bull. Int. Fiscal Doc.*, February 1988, *42*(2), pp. 75–77.

Méndez, José A. and Brada, Josef C. An Estimate of the Dynamic Effects of Economic Integration. *Rev. Econ. Statist.*, February 1988, *70*(1), pp. 163–68.

_____ **and Brada, Josef C.** Exchange Rate Risk, Exchange Rate Regime and the Volume of International Trade. *Kyklos*, 1988, *41*(2), pp. 263–80.

_____ **and Brada, Josef C.** How Effective Is the CMEA? An International Comparison. In *Brada, J. C. and Dobozi, I., eds.*, 1988, pp. 171–95.

Menezes, C. F. and Tressler, J. H. The Comparative Statics of a Competitive Industry Facing Demand Uncertainty. *Econ. Letters*, 1988, *26*(4), pp. 315–19.

Meng, Werner. International Regulation of Subsidies and Economic Development. In *Dicke, D. C. and Petersmann, E.-U., eds.*, 1988, pp. 235–62.

Mengle, David L. and Vital, Christian. SIC: Switzerland's New Electronic Interbank Payment System. *Fed. Res. Bank Richmond Econ. Rev.*, Nov.–Dec. 1988, *74*(6), pp. 12–27.

_____ **and Walter, John R.** A Review of Bank Performance in the Fifth District, 1987. *Fed. Res. Bank Richmond Econ. Rev.*, July–Aug. 1988, *74*(4), pp. 13–18.

Menken, Jane A.; Trussell, James and John, A. Meredith. Estimating the Distribution of Interval Length: Current Status and Retrospective History Data. *Population Stud.*, March 1988, *42*(1), pp. 115–27.

_____ **and Watkins, Susan Cotts.** On the Role of Crises in Historical Perspective: Reply. *Population Devel. Rev.*, March 1988, *14*(1), pp. 165–70.

Menkhoff, Lukas. Inflationsgefahr durch Überschreiten von Geldmengenzielen? (Inflationary Risks as a Result of Overshooting Money Supply Targets? With English summary.) *Kredit Kapital*, 1988, *21*(4), pp. 513–31.

Mennerick, Lewis A. and Najafizadeh, Mehrangiz. Worldwide Educational Expansion from 1950 to 1980: The Failure of the Expansion of Schooling in Developing Countries. *J. Devel. Areas*, April 1988, *22*(3), pp. 333–57.

Mennes, L. B. M. Optimization and the Preparation of Economic Policy: Comments. **In** *Driehuis, W.; Fase, M. M. G. and den Hartog, H., eds.,* 1988, pp. 283–85.

_____ **and Kol, J.** Protection, Trade and Development. **In** *Jepma, C. J., ed.,* 1988, pp. 80–94.

Mentzer, John T. and Pisharodi, R. Mohan. Transportation as an Industrial Marketing Service. **In** *Woodside, A. G., ed.,* 1988, pp. 201–21.

Mentzer, Marc S.; Louie, Kenneth K. T. and Fizel, John L. CEO Tenure and Firm Performance. **In** *Missouri Valley Economic Assoc.,* 1988, pp. 1–6.

Menzie, Elmer L. Harmonization of Farm Policy for Free Interprovincial Trade. *Can. J. Agr. Econ.*, Part 1, December 1988, *36*(4), pp. 649–63.

_____ **and Prentice, Barry E.** Formal and Informal Nontariff Barriers to Agricultural Trade between the United States and Canada. **In** *Allen, K. and Macmillan, K., eds.,* 1988, pp. 123–38.

Menzler-Hokkanen, Ingeborg. EC Trade Policies in Tropical Agricultural Products. **In** *Langhammer, R. J. and Rieger, H. C., eds.,* 1988, pp. 60–115.

_____. Time Series Properties of Comparative Advantage Indices. *Weltwirtsch. Arch.*, 1988, *124*(2), pp. 242–51.

de Meo, Giuseppe. Effetti economici delle migrazioni e divario Sud–Nord. (Migration and South–North Economic Gap. With English summary.) *Rivista Storia Econ.*, S.S., June 1988, *5*(2), pp. 151–72.

Mera, Koichi. The Emergence of Migration Cycles? *Int. Reg. Sci. Rev.*, 1988, *11*(3), pp. 269–75.

Meran, Georg. Employment and Hours in Equilibrium and Disequilibrium: Comment. **In** *Hart, R. A., ed.,* 1988, pp. 140–41.

_____. Zur Kontroverse über die Wettbewerbswirkungen eines Umweltlizenzmarktes. (With English summary.) *Z. Wirtschaft. Sozialwissen.*, 1988, *108*(3), pp. 439–50.

Mercenier, Jean and Ginsburgh, Victor A. Macroeconomic Models and Microeconomic Theory: The Contribution of General Equilibrium

Theory. **In** *Driehuis, W.; Fase, M. M. G. and den Hartog, H., eds.,* 1988, pp. 291–335.

_____ **and Sekkat, Khalid.** Money Stock Targeting and Money Supply: An Intertemporal Optimization Approach (with an Application to Canada). *J. Appl. Econometrics*, July–Sept. 1988, *3*(3), pp. 215–28.

Mercier, Pierre; Schweitzer, Thomas and Daly, Michael J. The Impact of Tax Reform on Investment and Saving Incentives in Canada, the United States, the United Kingdom, and Japan. *Econ. Letters*, 1988, *27*(2), pp. 159–65.

Meredith, David. Full Circle?: Contemporary Views on Transportation. **In** *Nicholas, S., ed.,* 1988, pp. 14–27.

Mergen, François, et al. Forestry Research: A Provisional Global Inventory. *Econ. Develop. Cult. Change*, October 1988, *37*(1), pp. 149–71.

Mergos, George J. and Yotopoulos, Pan A. Demand for Feed Inputs in the Greek Livestock Sector. *Europ. Rev. Agr. Econ.*, 1988, *15*(1), pp. 1–17.

Meriggi, Maria Rosa and Giorgi, Giorgio. On the Hierarchy of Some Qualitative Structures in the Von Neumann and Related Models. *Metroecon.*, June 1988, *39*(2), pp. 121–40.

Merino, Catherine L. Compromising Immigration Reform: The Creation of a Vulnerable Subclass. *Yale Law J.*, December 1988, *98*(2), pp. 409–26.

Merkies, A. H. Q. M. and van Daal, J. Nataf's Theorem, Taylor's Expansion and Homogeneity in Consumer Demand. **In** *Eichhorn, W., ed.,* 1988, pp. 671–89.

_____ **and van Daal, J.** The Problem of Aggregation of Individual Economic Relations; Consistency and Representativity in a Historical Perspective. **In** *Eichhorn, W., ed.,* 1988, pp. 607–37.

_____ **and van der Meer, T.** A Theoretical Foundation for Constant Market Share Analysis. *Empirical Econ.*, 1988, *13*(2), pp. 65–80.

Merkin, Victor. Intra-COMECON Bargaining and World Energy Prices: A Backdoor Connection? *Comp. Econ. Stud.*, Winter 1988, *30*(4), pp. 24–51.

Merl, Stephan. Did the Kolkhoz System Really Fulfill the Initial Aims of the Party in the 1930s? **In** *Brada, J. C. and Wadekin, K.-E., eds.,* 1988, pp. 77–97.

Merriam, Ida C. Economic Status of the Aged: Commentary. *Soc. Sec. Bull.*, December 1988, *51*(12), pp. 17–18, 45.

_____. Social Welfare in the United States, 1934–54. *Soc. Sec. Bull.*, June 1988, *51*(6), pp. 21–33.

Merrick, John J., Jr. Hedging with Mispriced Futures. *J. Finan. Quant. Anal.*, December 1988, *23*(4), pp. 451–64.

_____. Portfolio Insurance with Stock Index Futures. *J. Futures Markets*, August 1988, *8*(4), pp. 441–55.

_____. Replication in Empirical Economics: *The Journal of Money, Credit and Banking Project:*

Comment. *Amer. Econ. Rev.*, December 1988, 78(5), pp. 1160–61.

Merrifield, John D. The Impact of Selected Abatement Strategies on Transnational Pollution, the Terms of Trade, and Factor Rewards: A General Equilibrium Approach. *J. Environ. Econ. Manage.*, September 1988, 15(3), pp. 259–84.

Merriken, Harry E. and Edmister, Robert O. Pricing Efficiency in the Mortgage Market. *Amer. Real Estate Urban Econ. Assoc. J.*, Spring 1988, 16(1), pp. 50–62.

Merrill, Richard A. FDA's Implementation of the Delaney Clause: Repudiation of Congressional Choice or Reasoned Adaptation to Scientific Progress? *Yale J. Regul.*, Winter 1988, 5(1), pp. 1–88.

Merrill, Samuel, III; Brams, Steven J. and Fishburn, Peter C. The Problem of Indeterminacy in Approval, Multiple, and Truncated Voting Systems: Rejoinder. *Public Choice*, November 1988, 59(2), pp. 149.

_____; **Brams, Steven J. and Fishburn, Peter C.** The Responsiveness of Approval Voting: Comments [The Problem of Indeterminacy in Approval, Multiple, and Truncated Voting Systems]. *Public Choice*, November 1988, 59(2), pp. 121–31.

Merrill, Stephen A. The Internationalization of Technology: Balancing U.S. Interests. In *Yochelson, J., ed.*, 1988, pp. 33–49.

Mertens, Jean-François. Nondifferentiable TU Markets: The Value. In *[Shapley, L. S.]*, 1988, pp. 235–64.

_____. The Shapley Value in the Non Differentiable Case. *Int. J. Game Theory*, 1988, 17(1), pp. 1–65.

Merton, Robert C.; Bodie, Zvi and Marcus, Alan J. Defined Benefit versus Defined Contribution Pension Plans: What Are the Real Trade-offs? In *Bodie, Z.; Shoven, J. B. and Wise, D. A., eds.*, 1988, pp. 139–60.

van der Merwe, C. A. and Roux, J. J. J. Frequency Models for the Distribution of Personal Income in the RSA. In *Brown, R. C., ed.*, 1988, pp. 165–95.

Mesa-Lago, Carmelo. Cuban Statistics: One More Time. In *Mesa-Lago, C., ed.*, 1988, pp. 133–45.

_____. Medical Care Under Social Security: Coverage, Costs, and Financing. In *Zschock, D. K., ed.*, 1988, pp. 229–58.

_____. Social Insurance: The Experience of Three Countries in the English-Speaking Caribbean. *Int. Lab. Rev.*, 1988, 127(4), pp. 479–96.

Meško, Ivan. Nonsmooth and Nonconvex Models of the Business Process. *Econ. Anal. Workers' Manage.*, 1988, 22(1–2), pp. 63–80.

Messéan, A. Nonlinear Regression: Methodological and Software Aspects. In *Edwards, D. and Raun, N. E., eds.*, 1988, pp. 299–310.

Messenberg, Roberto P.; Bier, Amaury G. and Paulani, Leda Maria. A crise do saneamento no Brasil: Reforma tributária, uma falsa resposta. (With English summary.) *Pesquisa Pla-*

nejamento Econ., April 1988, 18(1), pp. 161–96.

Messere, Kenneth C. World Tax Reform: A Progress Report: Overview. In *Pechman, J. A., ed.*, 1988, pp. 277–89.

Messerlin, Patrick A. The Developing Countries and the Uruguay Round Negotiations on the Antidumping Code. In *Dicke, D. C. and Petersmann, E.-U., eds.*, 1988, pp. 163–86.

_____ **and de Melo, Jaime.** Price, Quality and Welfare Effects of European VERs on Japanese Autos. *Europ. Econ. Rev.*, September 1988, 32(7), pp. 1527–46.

Messerschmidt, Donald A. Success in Small Farmer Development: Paper Making at Pang and Nanglibang, Nepal. *World Devel.*, June 1988, 16(6), pp. 733–50.

Messick, David M.; Allison, Scott T. and Samuelson, Charles D. Framing and Communication Effects on Group Members' Responses to Environmental and Social Uncertainty. In *Maital, S., ed., Vol. 2*, 1988, pp. 677–700.

Messinger, Hans; Fedyk, Frank and Zeesman, Allen. The Size and Distribution of the Poverty Gap in Canada: A Micro Analysis of Variations among Demographic Groups. *Rev. Income Wealth*, September 1988, 34(3), pp. 275–88.

Mestelman, Stuart and Chan, Kenneth S. Institutions, Efficiency and the Strategic Behaviour of Sponsors and Bureaus. *J. Public Econ.*, October 1988, 37(1), pp. 91–102.

_____ **and Feeny, David.** Does Ideology Matter?: Anecdotal Experimental Evidence on the Voluntary Provision of Public Goods. *Public Choice*, June 1988, 57(3), pp. 281–86.

_____ **and Welland, Douglas.** Advance Production in Experimental Markets. *Rev. Econ. Stud.*, October 1988, 55(4), pp. 641–54.

Metcalfe, J. S. The Diffusion of Innovation: An Interpretative Survey. In *Dosi, G., et al., eds.*, 1988, pp. 560–89.

_____ **and Steedman, Ian.** Reswitching and Primary Input Use. In *Steedman, I., ed., Vol. 1*, 1988, 1972, pp. 243–60.

Metghalchi, Massoud and Deravi, M. Keivan. The European Monetary System: A Note. *J. Banking Finance*, September 1988, 12(3), pp. 505–12.

Metzen, Edward J. A College Course in Consumer Education: A Critique. In *Maynes, E. S. and ACCI Research Committee, eds.*, 1988, pp. 879–84.

Meulders, D.; Plasman, R. and Freese, V. Bilan des recherches sur l'aménagement et la réduction du temps de travail en Belgique (1975–1987). (With English summary.) *Cah. Écon. Bruxelles*, First Trimester 1988, (117), pp. 67–106.

Meulendyke, Ann-Marie. Can the Federal Reserve Influence whether the Money Supply Is Endogenous? A Comment. *J. Post Keynesian Econ.*, Spring 1988, 10(3), pp. 390–97.

_____. A Review of Federal Reserve Policy Targets and Operating Guides in Recent Decades. *Fed. Res. Bank New York Quart. Rev.*, Autumn 1988, 13(3), pp. 6–17.

Meulman, J. J. and Heiser, W. J. Second Order Regression and Distance Analysis. In *Gaul, W. and Schader, M., eds.*, 1988, pp. 368–80.

Meurs, H. and Golob, T. F. Modeling the Dynamics of Passenger Travel Demand by Using Structural Equations. *Environ. Planning A*, September 1988, *20*(9), pp. 1197–1218.

Mey, Abram. Replacement Value Accounting Theory: The "Circular Flow" and the Calculation of Value. In *Most, K. S., ed.*, 1988, pp. 3–21.

Meyanathan, Sahathavan. ASEAN–Australia Interests in Mineral Commodity Associations and Agreements. In *McKern, B. and Koomsup, P., eds.*, 1988, pp. 85–115.

_____. Minerals Trade and Economic Development in Malaysia. In *McKern, B. and Koomsup, P., eds.*, 1988, pp. 209–54.

Meyer, Bruce D. Classification-Error Models and Labor-Market Dynamics. *J. Bus. Econ. Statist.*, July 1988, *6*(3), pp. 385–90.

Meyer, Carrie and Due, John F. Value Added Tax: Dominican Republic. *Bull. Int. Fiscal Doc.*, January 1988, *42*(1), pp. 13–16.

Meyer, D. Does Drought Really Depress Beef Prices in South Africa? *J. Stud. Econ. Econometrics*, July 1988, *12*(2), pp. 7–14.

Meyer, David and Cooke, William. Economic and Political Factors in Formal Grievance Resolution. *Ind. Relat.*, Fall 1988, *27*(3), pp. 318–35.

Meyer, David L. and Rule, Charles F. An Antitrust Enforcement Policy to Maximize the Economic Wealth of All Consumers. *Antitrust Bull.*, Winter 1988, *33*(4), pp. 677–712.

Meyer, David R. The Industrial Retardation of Southern Cities, 1860–1880. *Exploration Econ. Hist.*, October 1988, *25*(4), pp. 366–86.

Meyer, Donald J. Competition and Bidding Behavior: Some Evidence from the Rice Market. *Econ. Inquiry*, January 1988, *26*(1), pp. 123–32.

_____ **and Glascock, John L.** Assessing the Regulatory Process in an International Context: Mixed Currency SDRs and U.S. Bank Equity Returns. *Atlantic Econ. J.*, March 1988, *16*(1), pp. 39–46.

Meyer, Fred A., Jr. and Baker, Ralph E. Neighbourhood Co-production of Protection: A Private Sector Response to Crime. In *Hula, R. C., ed.*, 1988, pp. 111–20.

Meyer, Jack and Robison, Lindon J. Hedging under Output Price Randomness. *Amer. J. Agr. Econ.*, May 1988, *70*(2), pp. 268–72.

Meyer, Jack A. and Moon, Marilyn. Health Care Spending on Children and the Elderly. In *Palmer, J. L.; Smeeding, T. and Torrey, B. B., eds.*, 1988, pp. 171–200.

Meyer, John R. and Gustafson, James M. For Whom Does the Corporation Toil?: Epilogue. In *Meyer, J. R. and Gustafson, J. M., eds.*, 1988, pp. 211–34.

_____ **and Tye, William B.** Toward Achieving Workable Competition in Industries Undergoing a Transition to Deregulation: A Contractual

Equilibrium Approach. *Yale J. Regul.*, Summer 1988, *5*(2), pp. 273–97.

Meyer, Klaus Dieter and Kruse, Rudolf. Confidence Intervals for the Parameters of a Linguistic Random Variable. In *Kacprzyk, J. and Fedrizzi, M., eds.*, 1988, pp. 113–23.

Meyer, Margaret A. and Klemperer, Paul D. Consistent Conjectures Equilibria: A Reformulation Showing Non-uniqueness. *Econ. Letters*, 1988, *27*(2), pp. 111–15.

_____ **and Klemperer, Paul D.** Price Competition vs. Quantity Competition: The Role of Uncertainty. In *Daughety, A. F., ed.*, 1988, *1986*, pp. 229–61.

Meyer, Neil and Sparks, Gordon R. Policy Decisions Affecting Rationalization of the Prairie Grain Transportation System: Implications for the St. Lawrence Seaway System. *Can. J. Agr. Econ.*, Part 2, December 1988, *36*(4), pp. 941–50.

_____; **Stabler, Jack C. and Van Kooten, G. C.** Methodological Issues in the Evaluation of Regional Resource Development Projects. *Ann. Reg. Sci.*, July 1988, *22*(2), pp. 13–25.

Meyer, Peter B. Combining New Job Creation with Advanced Technology Adoptions: British Innovative Local Economic Efforts. *J. Econ. Issues*, June 1988, *22*(2), pp. 443–49.

Meyer, Willi. Schmoller's Research Programme, His Psychology, and the Autonomy of Social Sciences. *J. Inst. Theoretical Econ.*, June 1988, *144*(3), pp. 570–80.

Meyer zu Selhausen, Hermann. Erfassung und Steuerung des Zinsänderungsrisikos einer Bank mit Hilfe eines Modells der Aktiv-Passiv-Koordination. (Recording and Managing a Bank's Interest Variation Risk on the Basis of an Assets/Liabilities Coordination Model. With English summary.) *Kredit Kapital*, 1988, *21*(4), pp. 556–91.

Meyers, Gary G. West European Perspectives on Greater East–West Economic Interaction. In *Liebowitz, R. D., ed.*, 1988, pp. 97–110.

Meyers, K. and Thomas, V. Development Lending and Conditionality. In *Jepma, C. J., ed.*, 1988, pp. 145–60.

Meyers, Robert J. and Oehmke, James F. Instability and Risk as Rationales for Farm Programs. In *Sumner, D. A., ed.*, 1988, pp. 1–22.

Meyers, Roy T. Biennial Budgeting by the U.S. Congress. *Public Budg. Finance*, Summer 1988, *8*(2), pp. 21–32.

Meyers, William R. and Gideonse, Sarah K. Why "Workfare" Fails. *Challenge*, Jan.–Feb. 1988, *31*(1), pp. 44–49.

de Meza, David. The Efficacy of Effluent Charges. *Can. J. Econ.*, February 1988, *21*(1), pp. 182–86.

_____. Package Size and the Suppression of Variety. *Int. J. Ind. Organ.*, 1988, *6*(3), pp. 363–71.

_____ **and Webb, David C.** Credit Market Efficiency and Tax Policy in the Presence of Screening Costs. *J. Public Econ.*, June 1988, *36*(1), pp. 1–22.

Mezias, Stephen J. Aspiration Level Effects: An Empirical Investigation. *J. Econ. Behav. Organ.*, December 1988, *10*(4), pp. 389–400.

Mézière, Dominique. Economie d'énergie et diversification des approvisionnements dans l'industrie: Un bilan. (Energy Conservation and Diversification of Energy Supplies in Industry: The Results. With English summary.) *Écon. Soc.*, April 1988, *22*(4), pp. 133–58.

Miceli, Thomas J. Information Costs and the Organization of the Real Estate Brokerage Industry in the U.S. and Great Britain. *Amer. Real Estate Urban Econ. Assoc. J.*, Summer 1988, *16*(2), pp. 173–88.

Micha, J.-C. and Descy, J.-P. Use of Biological Indices of Water Quality. *Statist. J.*, November 1988, *5*(3), pp. 249–61.

Michael, Michael S. and Chang, Winston W. Optimum Tariff and Its Optimum Revenue Distribution. *Econ. Letters*, 1988, *28*(4), pp. 369–74.

Michael, Robert T. Why Did the U.S. Divorce Rate Double within a Decade? In *Schultz, T. Paul, ed.*, 1988, pp. 367–99.

Michaels, Robert J. Addiction, Compulsion, and the Technology of Consumption. *Econ. Inquiry*, January 1988, *26*(1), pp. 75–88.

_____. The Design of Rent-Seeking Competitions. *Public Choice*, January 1988, *56*(1), pp. 17–29.

Michaely, Roni and Ho, Thomas S. Y. Information Quality and Market Efficiency. *J. Finan. Quant. Anal.*, March 1988, *23*(1), pp. 53–70.

Michel, Kay and Specht, Günter. Integrierte Technologie- und Marktplanung mit Innovationsportfolios. (With English summary.) *Z. Betriebswirtshaft*, April 1988, *58*(4), pp. 502–20.

Michel, Philippe and Cohen, Daniel. How Should Control Theory Be Used to Calculate a Time-Consistent Government Policy? *Rev. Econ. Stud.*, April 1988, *55*(2), pp. 263–74.

_____ **and Dos Santos Ferreira, Rodolphe.** Reflections on the Microeconomic Foundations of the Keynesian Aggregate Supply Function. In *Barrère, A., ed.*, 1988, pp. 251–62.

_____ **and Ginsburgh, Victor A.** Adjustment Costs, Concentration and Price Behaviour. *J. Ind. Econ.*, June 1988, *36*(4), pp. 477–81.

_____ **and Hénin, Pierre-Yves.** An *IS–LM* Representation of Macroeconomic Equilibria with Rationing. In *Barrère, A., ed.*, 1988, pp. 93–110.

_____ **and Melese, Francois.** The Hazard Rate and the Hotelling Rule. *Atlantic Econ. J.*, December 1988, *16*(4), pp. 43–51.

Michel, Pierre; Corhay, Albert and Hawawini, Gabriel. The Pricing of Equity on the London Stock Exchange: Seasonality and Size Premium. In *Dimson, E., ed.*, 1988, pp. 197–212.

Michel, Richard C. and Levy, Frank S. Work for Welfare: How Much Good Will It Do? In *Brown, E., ed.*, 1988, 1986, pp. 54–60.

Michelet, Christian Fr. Recognition of Foreign Enterprises as Taxable Entities: Norway. In *International Fiscal Association, ed. (I)*, 1988, pp. 479–92.

Michener, Ron. Backing Theories and the Currencies of Eighteenth-Century America: A Comment. *J. Econ. Hist.*, September 1988, *48*(3), pp. 682–92.

Michie, Ranald C. The Canadian Securities Market, 1850–1914. *Bus. Hist. Rev.*, Spring 1988, *62*(1), pp. 35–73.

_____. The Finance of Innovation in Late Victorian and Edwardian Britain: Possibilities and Constraints. *J. Europ. Econ. Hist.*, Winter 1988, *17*(3), pp. 491–530.

Michl, Thomas R. The Two-Stage Decline in U.S. Nonfinancial Corporate Profitability, 1948–1986. *Rev. Radical Polit. Econ.*, Winter 1988, *20*(4), pp. 1–22.

_____. The Wage–Profit Frontier and Declining Profitability in U.S. Manufacturing. *Rev. Radical Polit. Econ.*, Summer–Fall 1988, *20*(2–3), pp. 80–86.

Mickiewicz, Ellen. The Soviet Union Today: The Mass Media. In *Cracraft, J., ed.*, 1988, pp. 293–300.

Micklin, Philip P. and Bond, Andrew R. Reflections on Environmentalism and the River Diversion Projects. *Soviet Econ.*, July–Sept. 1988, *4*(3), pp. 253–74.

Micossi, Stefano. The Single European Market: Finance. *Banca Naz. Lavoro Quart. Rev.*, June 1988, (165), pp. 217–35.

Micwitz, Gösta. Skattereformen—i vilket syfe? En paneldebatt. (Three Contributions to the Debate on the Proposed Tax Reform in Finland. With English summary.) *Ekon. Samfundets Tidskr.*, 1988, *41*(1), pp. 21–22.

Middleton, Elliott. An Alternative to the Random Utility Approach in Modeling the Preference for Variety. In *Maital, S., ed., Vol. 1*, 1988, pp. 155–60.

Middleton, Roger. The Size of the Public Sector. In *Darnell, A. and Evans, L., eds.*, 1988, pp. 103–17.

Miegel, Meinhard. The Welfare State and Jobs: Comment. In *Kregel, J. A.; Matzner, E. and Roncaglia, A., eds.*, 1988, pp. 204–08.

Migalski, Michael and Grofman, Bernard. The Return of the Native: The Supply Elasticity of the American Indian Population 1960–1980. *Public Choice*, April 1988, *57*(1), pp. 85–88.

Mihăiţă, N. V. and Fornoga, Coca. Applications of the Information Theory to Multicriterial Analysis of Products Quality. *Econ. Computat. Cybern. Stud. Res.*, 1988, *23*(4), pp. 37–44.

Mihaljek, Dubravko. Errata [Sequencing of Economic Liberalization Policies in Developing Countries: A Review of Principal Issues and Results]. *Econ. Anal. Workers' Manage.*, 1988, *22*(4), pp. 325.

_____. Sequencing of Economic Liberalization Policies in Developing Countries: A Survey of Principal Issues and Results. *Econ. Anal. Workers' Manage.*, 1988, *22*(1–2), pp. 81–132.

Mihályi, Peter. Cycles or Shocks: East European Investments, 1950–1985. *Econ. Planning*, 1988, *22*(1–2), pp. 41–56.

Mikdashi, Zuhayr. Whither the 'New Finance'? A Synthesis of Issues and an Essay of Reflection. In *Mikdashi, Z., ed.,* 1988, pp. 129–45.

Mikesell, James J. and Lerman, Donald L. Impacts of Adding Net Worth to the Poverty Definition. *Eastern Econ. J.,* Oct.–Dec. 1988, *14*(4), pp. 357–70.

Mikesell, John L. and Bowman, John H. Uniform Assessment of Agricultural Property for Taxation: Improvements from System Reform. *Land Econ.,* February 1988, *64*(1), pp. 28–36.

_____ **and Zorn, Kurt.** State Lotteries for Public Revenue. *Public Budg. Finance,* Spring 1988, *8*(1), pp. 38–47.

Mikesell, Raymond F. The Changing Demand for Industrial Raw Materials. In *Sewell, J. W. and Tucker, S. K., eds.,* 1988, pp. 139–66.

Mikhail, W. M. and Sargan, John Denis. A General Approximation to the Distribution of Instrumental Variables Estimates. In *Sargan, J. D., Vol. 2,* 1988, *1971,* pp. 18–56.

Mikkelson, Wayne H. and Partch, M. Megan. Withdrawn Security Offerings. *J. Finan. Quant. Anal.,* June 1988, *23*(2), pp. 119–33.

Miklius, Walter. Issues in Ocean Shipping and the Asia-Pacific Region. In *Lee, C. H. and Naya, S., eds.,* 1988, pp. 97–120.

Milan, Edwin and Reyes, Edna A. Employment Strategies for Accelerated Economic Growth: The Philippine Experience. *Philippine Rev. Econ. Bus.,* March–June 1988, *25*(1–2), pp. 151–84.

Milberg, William. A Product Line Life Cycle Model of Intra-industry Trade. *Eastern Econ. J.,* Oct.–Dec. 1988, *14*(4), pp. 389–97.

_____. Welfare Measurement for Cost–Benefit Analysis. In *Berkowitz, M., ed.,* 1988, pp. 28–45.

_____ **and Dean, David H.** Using Better Measures of Disability Status. In *Berkowitz, M., ed.,* 1988, pp. 199–231.

Milbourne, Ross D. Disequilibrium Buffer Stock Models: A Survey. *J. Econ. Surveys,* 1988, *2*(3), pp. 187–208.

_____. A Theorem Regarding Elasticities of the Transactions Demand for Money. *Econ. Letters,* 1988, *27*(2), pp. 151–54.

_____ **and Djajic, Slobodan.** A General Equilibrium Model of Guest-Worker Migration: The Source-Country Perspective. *J. Int. Econ.,* November 1988, *25*(3–4), pp. 335–51.

_____ **and Mackinnon, James G.** Are Price Equations Really Money Demand Equations on Their Heads? *J. Appl. Econometrics,* Oct.–Dec. 1988, *3*(4), pp. 295–305.

Milbrath, Robert S. New Directions for Research on Cooperative Type Work Organizations. *Rev. Soc. Econ.,* April 1988, *46*(1), pp. 24–45.

Milde, Hellmuth. Wage and Quantity Setting with Asymmetric Quality Information: A Note. *Z. Wirtschaft. Sozialwissen.,* 1988, *108*(1), pp. 63–70.

_____ **and Riley, John G.** Signaling in Credit Markets. *Quart. J. Econ.,* February 1988, *103*(1), pp. 101–29.

Miles, James A. and Beranek, William. The Ex-

cess Return Argument and Double Leverage. *Financial Rev.,* May 1988, *23*(2), pp. 143–50.

_____ **and Kim, Taeho.** On the Valuation of FDIC Deposit Insurance: An Empirical Study Using Contingent Claims Analysis. *Quart. J. Bus. Econ.,* Autumn 1988, *27*(4), pp. 47–68.

Miles, Marc A. An Evaluation of Reagan's Economic Policies from an Incentivist (Supply-Side) Perspective. *J. Post Keynesian Econ.,* Summer 1988, *10*(4), pp. 557–66.

Milgate, Murray. Money, Capital and Forced Saving. *Cambridge J. Econ.,* March 1988, *12*(1), pp. 43–54.

Milgrom, Paul. Employment Contracts, Influence Activities, and Efficient Organization Design. *J. Polit. Econ.,* February 1988, *96*(1), pp. 42–60.

_____ **and Roberts, John.** An Economic Approach to Influence Activities in Organizations. In *Winship, C. and Rosen, S., eds.,* 1988, pp. 154–79.

_____ **and Roberts, John.** Communication and Inventory as Substitutes in Organizing Production. *Scand. J. Econ.,* 1988, *90*(3), pp. 275–89.

_____ **and Roberts, John.** Economic Theories of the Firm: Past, Present, and Future. *Can. J. Econ.,* August 1988, *21*(3), pp. 444–58.

Milkovich, George T. A Strategic Perspective on Compensation Management. In *Ferris, G. R. and Rowland, K. M., eds.,* 1988, pp. 263–88.

Millar, Annie. Selecting Capital Investment Projects for Local Governments. *Public Budg. Finance,* Autumn 1988, *8*(3), pp. 63–77.

Millar, Campbell and Roseveare, Debbie. Testing the Rationality of Manufacturers' Inflationary Expectations. *New Zealand Econ. Pap.,* 1988, *22,* pp. 3–13.

Millar, James R. The Soviet Union Today: The Economy: An Overview. In *Cracraft, J., ed.,* 1988, pp. 177–90.

Miller, Bradley A. and Horwich, George. Oil Import Quotas in the Context of the International Energy Agency Sharing Agreement. In *Horwich, G. and Weimer, D. L., eds.,* 1988, pp. 134–78.

Miller, C. A.; Wheeler, Mary F. and Moissis, D. E. A Parametric Study of Viscous Fingering in Miscible Displacement by Numerical Simulation. In *Wheeler, M. F., ed.,* 1988, pp. 227–47.

Miller, Danny and Kets de Vries, Manfred F. R. Personality, Culture, and Organization. In *Albanese, P. J., ed.,* 1988, pp. 81–99.

Miller, Edward M. Growth and Embodiment: A Reply [On the Importance of the Embodiment of Technology Effect: A Comment on Denison's Growth Accounting Methodology]. *J. Macroecon.,* Winter 1988, *10*(1), pp. 143–48.

_____. On the Systematic Risk of Expansion Investment. *Quart. Rev. Econ. Bus.,* Autumn 1988, *28*(3), pp. 67–77.

_____. Profit Margins and Concentration. *Atlantic Econ. J.,* March 1988, *16*(1), pp. 96.

_____. Used Capital: Implications for Isoquants, Production Functions, and Shepard's Lemma.

Eastern Econ. J., April–June 1988, *14*(2), pp. 141–52.

_____. Why a Weekend Effect? *J. Portfol. Manage.*, Summer 1988, *14*(4), pp. 43–48.

Miller, Edythe S. Institutional Economics: Philosophy, Methodology and Theory. In *Samuels, W. J., ed., Vol. 2*, 1988, *1978*, pp. 50–62.

Miller, Frances H. Vertical Restraints and Powerful Health Insurers: Exclusionary Conduct Masquerading as Managed Care? *Law Contemp. Probl.*, Spring 1988, *51*(2), pp. 195–236.

Miller, Gay Y.; Rosenblatt, Joseph M. and Hushak, Leroy J. The Effects of Supply Shifts on Producers' Surplus. *Amer. J. Agr. Econ.*, November 1988, *70*(4), pp. 886–91.

Miller, Geoffrey P. and Macey, Jonathan R. *Trans Union* Reconsidered. *Yale Law J.*, November 1988, *98*(1), pp. 127–43.

Miller, Gerald H. Virtues of a State Value-Added Tax. In *Gold, S. D., ed.*, 1988, pp. 227–33.

Miller, Green R. Educational Quality: The Impact of the Teachers' Union. In *Missouri Valley Economic Assoc.*, 1988, pp. 92–96.

Miller, J. R. and Robison, M. H. Cross-Hauling and Nonsurvey Input–Output Models: Some Lessons from Small-Area Timber Economies. *Environ. Planning A*, November 1988, *20*(11), pp. 1523–30.

Miller, James C., III. It's Time to Free the Mails. *Cato J.*, Spring–Summer 1988, *8*(1), pp. 199–204.

_____. Spending and Deficits. In *[Nutter, G. W.]*, 1988, pp. 273–88.

Miller, James P. and Bluestone, Herman. Prospects for Service Sector Employment Growth in Non-metropolitan America. *Rev. Reg. Stud.*, Winter 1988, *18*(1), pp. 28–41.

Miller, John A. Military Spending and Economic Crises: A Comment. *J. Post Keynesian Econ.*, Winter 1987–88, *10*(2), pp. 310–17.

Miller, Marcus H. Hysteresis in Ouput and Employment: A Comment. In *Cross, R., ed.*, 1988, pp. 397–401.

_____. Price Rigidity, International Mobility of Financial Capital and Exchange Rate Volatility: Comments. *Europ. Econ. Rev.*, June 1988, *32*(5), pp. 1162–64.

_____ **and Sutherland, Alan.** Measures of Fiscal Stance and Rules for Stabilising the Economy: The Case for Separating Measurement from Policy. In *Eltis, W. and Sinclair, P. J. N., eds.*, 1988, pp. 216–32.

_____ **and Williamson, John.** The International Monetary System: An Analysis of Alternative Regimes. *Europ. Econ. Rev.*, June 1988, *32*(5), pp. 1031–48.

Miller, Mark. Employer Sanctions in Europe: Deterrence without Discrimination. In *Simcox, D. E., ed.*, 1988, pp. 217–28.

Miller, Merton H. Explaining the Events of October 1987. In *MacKay, R. J., ed.*, 1988, pp. 17–21.

_____. The Modigliani–Miller Propositions after Thirty Years. *J. Econ. Perspectives*, Fall 1988, *2*(4), pp. 99–120.

_____ **and Grossman, Sanford J.** Liquidity and

Market Structure. *J. Finance*, July 1988, *43*(3), pp. 617–37.

_____ **and Musgrave, Richard A.** Built-In Flexibility. In *Shaw, G. K., ed., Vol. 2*, 1988, *1948*, pp. 283–89.

Miller, Michael K.; Mulkey, David and Beaulieu, Lionel J. Community Forces and Their Influence on Farm Structure. In *Beaulieu, L. J., ed.*, 1988, pp. 211–32.

_____; **Stokes, C. Shannon and Warland, Rex H.** The Effect of Legalization and Public Funding of Abortion on Neonatal Mortality: An Intervention Analysis. *Population Res. Policy Rev.*, 1988, *7*(1), pp. 79–92.

Miller, Nicholas; Feld, Scott L. and Grofman, Bernard. Centripetal Forces in Spatial Voting: On the Size of the Yolk. *Public Choice*, October 1988, *59*(1), pp. 37–50.

Miller, Norman C. and Chakraborty, Debasish. Economic Growth and the Balance of Payments. *J. Econ. Devel.*, December 1988, *13*(2), pp. 57–79.

Miller, Paul W. Economic Models of Fertility Behaviour in Australia. *Australian Econ. Pap.*, June 1988, *27*(50), pp. 65–82.

_____ **and Chiswick, Barry R.** Earnings in Canada: The Roles of Immigrant Generation, French Ethnicity, and Language. In *Schultz, T. Paul, ed.*, 1988, pp. 183–228.

_____ **and Hope, Julie.** Financing Tertiary Education: An Examination of the Issues. *Australian Econ. Rev.*, Summer 1988, (84), pp. 37–57.

Miller, Preston J. What Microeconomics Teaches Us about the Dynamic Macro Effects of Fiscal Policy: Comment. *J. Money, Credit, Banking*, Part 2, August 1988, *20*(3), pp. 500–506.

Miller, Robert A. Innovation and Reputation. *J. Polit. Econ.*, August 1988, *96*(4), pp. 741–65.

_____ **and Hotz, V. Joseph.** An Empirical Analysis of Life Cycle Fertility and Female Labor Supply. *Econometrica*, January 1988, *56*(1), pp. 91–118.

Miller, Robert E.; Balvers, Ronald J. and McDonald, Bill. Underpricing of New Issues and the Choice of Auditor as a Signal of Investment Banker Reputation. *Accounting Rev.*, October 1988, *63*(4), pp. 605–22.

Miller, Robert F. Recent Agricultural Policy in Yugoslavia: A Return to the Private Sector? In *Brada, J. C. and Wadekin, K.-E., eds.*, 1988, pp. 225–45.

Miller, Ronald E. and Blair, Peter D. Measuring Spatial Linkages. *Ricerche Econ.*, April–June 1988, *42*(2), pp. 288–310.

Miller, Ronald K. and Hershbarger, Robert A. The Impact of Economic Conditions on the Incidence of Arson: A Reply. *J. Risk Ins.*, December 1988, *55*(4), pp. 755–57.

Miller, Stephen M. Are Saving and Investment Co-integrated? *Econ. Letters*, 1988, *27*(1), pp. 31–34.

_____. The Beveridge–Nelson Decomposition of Economic Time Series: Another Economical Computational Method. *J. Monet. Econ.*, January 1988, *21*(1), pp. 141–42.

_____. Counterfactual Experiments of Deregulation on Banking Structure. *Quart. Rev. Econ. Bus.*, Winter 1988, *28*(4), pp. 38–49.

_____. International Capital Mobility: What Do Saving–Investment Correlations Tell Us? Comment. *Int. Monet. Fund Staff Pap.*, June 1988, *35*(2), pp. 391–96.

_____ and Ahking, Francis W. Models of Business Cycles: A Review Essay. *Eastern Econ. J.*, April–June 1988, *14*(2), pp. 197–202.

_____ and Chiang, Alpha C. Inflation Expectations, Wealth Perception, and Consumption Expenditure. *Eastern Econ. J.*, Jan.–March 1988, *14*(1), pp. 27–38.

Miller, Steven L. Student Test Scores and Textbook Deficienciies: Is There a Relationship? In *Association of Private Education*, 1988, pp. 78–84.

Miller, Ted R. Willingness to Pay: Pandora's Box or Palliative for Liability Problems. *J. Policy Anal. Manage.*, Winter 1988, *7*(2), pp. 363–67.

Miller, Timothy I. and Bartlett, Robin L. Executive Earnings by Gender: A Case Study. *Soc. Sci. Quart.*, December 1988, *69*(4), pp. 892–909.

Miller, Tom W. A Systems View of Short-term Investment Management. In *Kim, Y. H., ed.*, 1988, pp. 39–66.

Miller, Van V. and Smeltz, Wayne J. An Empirical and Historical Examination of How Organizations Manage and Manipulate Their Environments: The FASB Example. In *Grant, J. H., ed.*, 1988, pp. 361–75.

Milleron, Jean-Claude and Maillard, Didier. World Tax Reform: A Progress Report: France. In *Pechman, J. A., ed.*, 1988, pp. 95–112.

Millett, Peter [Sir]. Artificial Tax Avoidance—The English and American Approach. *Australian Tax Forum*, 1988, *5*(1), pp. 1–12.

Milligan, G. W. and Cooper, M. C. The Effect of Measurement Error on Determining the Number of Clusters in Cluster Analysis. In *Gaul, W. and Schader, M., eds.*, 1988, pp. 319–28.

Millner, Edward L. and Formby, John P. Opportunity Cost and Economic Rent. *Rivista Int. Sci. Econ. Com.*, September 1988, *35*(9), pp. 801–16.

_____; Pratt, Michael D. and Reilly, Robert J. A Re-examination of Harrison's Experimental Test for Risk Aversion. *Econ. Letters*, 1988, *27*(4), pp. 317–19.

Mills, David E. Preemptive Investment Timing. *Rand J. Econ.*, Spring 1988, *19*(1), pp. 114–22.

Mills, Dixie L.; Scott, William L. and Gardner, Mona J. Expense Preference and Minority Banking: A Note. *Financial Rev.*, February 1988, *23*(1), pp. 105–15.

Mills, Edwin S. and Kim, Kyung-Hwan. Korean Development and Urbanization: Prospects and Problems. *World Devel.*, January 1988, *16*(1), pp. 157–67.

Mills, Leonard O. and Boschen, John F. Tests of the Relation between Money and Output

in the Real Business Cycle Model. *J. Monet. Econ.*, November 1988, *22*(3), pp. 355–74.

Mills, P. D. Latest Developments in UK Agricultural Videotex Services. In *Schiefer, G., ed.*, 1988, pp. 63–72.

Mills, Terence C. and Wood, Geoffrey E. Interest Rates and the Conduct of Monetary Policy. In *Eltis, W. and Sinclair, P. J. N., eds.*, 1988, pp. 246–67.

Millstein, Ira M. The Georgetown Study of Private Antitrust Litigation: Some Policy Implications. In *White, L. J., ed.*, 1988, pp. 399–405.

_____ and Kessler, Jeffrey L. The Antitrust Legacy of the Reagan Administration. *Antitrust Bull.*, Fall 1988, *33*(3), pp. 505–41.

_____ and Knowlton, Winthrop. Can the Board of Directors Help the American Corporation Earn the Immortality It Holds So Dear? In *Meyer, J. R. and Gustafson, J. M., eds.*, 1988, pp. 169–91.

Millward, Neil and Blanchflower, David G. Trade Unions and Employment Change: An Analysis of British Establishment Data. *Europ. Econ. Rev.*, March 1988, *32*(2–3), pp. 717–26.

Millward, Robert. Measured Sources of Inefficiency in the Performance of Private and Public Enterprises in LDCs. In *Cook, P. and Kirkpatrick, C., eds.*, 1988, pp. 143–61.

Milne, Frank. Arbitrage and Diversification in a General Equilibrium Asset Economy. *Econometrica*, July 1988, *56*(4), pp. 815–40.

_____ and Shefrin, Hersh M. *Ex Post* Efficiency and *Ex Post* Welfare: Some Fundamental Considerations. *Economica*, February 1988, *55*(217), pp. 63–79.

Milne, W. J. and Barber, G. M. Modelling Internal Migration in Kenya: An Econometric Analysis with Limited Data. *Environ. Planning A*, September 1988, *20*(9), pp. 1185–96.

Milner, Chris. Trade Strategies and Economic Development: Theory and Evidence. In *Greenaway, D., ed.*, 1988, pp. 55–76.

_____. Weighting Considerations in the Measurement and Modelling of Intra-industry Trade. *Appl. Econ.*, March 1988, *20*(3), pp. 295–301.

_____ and Greenaway, David. Intra Industry Trade and the Shifting of Protection across Sectors. *Europ. Econ. Rev.*, April 1988, *32*(4), pp. 927–45.

_____ and Greenaway, David. Some Features of 'True Protection': A Reply. *J. Devel. Stud.*, October 1988, *25*(1), pp. 122–25.

Milner, Helen and Snyder, Jack. Lost Hegemony? *Int. Organ.*, Autumn 1988, *42*(4), pp. 749–50.

Milon, J. Walter. A Nested Demand Shares Model of Artificial Marine Habitat Choice by Sport Anglers. *Marine Resource Econ.*, 1988, *5*(3), pp. 191–213.

_____. Travel Cost Methods for Estimating the Recreational Use Benefits of Artificial Marine Habitat. *Southern J. Agr. Econ.*, July 1988, *20*(1), pp. 87–101.

Milovidov, A. and Rimashevskaia, N. M. On Improving State Assistance to Families with Children. *Prob. Econ.*, November 1988, *31*(7), pp. 72–81.

Miltz, D.; Braden, J. B. and Johnson, G. V. Standards versus Prices Revisited: The Case of Agricultural Non-point Source Pollution. *J. Agr. Econ.*, September 1988, *39*(3), pp. 360–68.

Minarik, Joseph J. Fiscal Reality and Exploding Myths. *Challenge*, July–August 1988, *31*(4), pp. 4–13.

———. Individual Income Tax Issues as Revised by Tax Reform. *Nat. Tax J.*, September 1988, *41*(3), pp. 291–301.

Mincer, Jacob and Higuchi, Yoshio. Wage Structures and Labor Turnover in the United States and Japan. *J. Japanese Int. Economies*, June 1988, *2*(2), pp. 97–133.

Miner, John B. and Crane, Donald P. Labor Arbitrators' Performance: Views From Union and Management Perspectives. *J. Lab. Res.*, Winter 1988, *9*(1), pp. 43–54.

Miner, William M. Resolving Subsidy, Countervail, and Import Disruption Issues in Canadian–U.S. Agricultural Trade. In *Allen, K. and Macmillan, K., eds.,* 1988, pp. 139–43.

——— **and Hathaway, Dale E.** World Agriculture in Crisis: Reforming Government Policies. In *Miner, W. M. and Hathaway, D. E., eds.,* 1988, pp. 37–110.

Mines, Richard; Perloff, Jeffrey M. and Frisvold, George. The Effects of Job Site Sanitation and Living Conditions on the Health and Welfare of Agricultural Workers. *Amer. J. Agr. Econ.*, November 1988, *70*(4), pp. 875–85.

Minford, Patrick. Comments [Wage Gaps versus Output Gaps: Is There a Common Story for All of Europe?] [Compositional Effects and Unemployment in the United States and Europe]. In *Giersch, H., ed.,* 1988, pp. 172–78.

———. Interest Rates and Bond Financed Deficits in a Ricardian Two-Party Democracy. *Weltwirtsch. Arch.*, 1988, *124*(3), pp. 387–402.

———. Monetary and Fiscal Policy Coordination with a High Public Debt: Discussion. In *Giavazzi, F. and Spaventa, L., eds.,* 1988, pp. 132–34.

———. A New Classical Model of the Labour Market. In *Beenstock, M., ed.,* 1988, pp. 105–44.

———. Outlook after the Budget. *Fisc. Stud.*, May 1988, *9*(2), pp. 30–37.

———. Wages and Unemployment Half a Century On. In *Eltis, W. and Sinclair, P. J. N., eds.,* 1988, pp. 45–64.

———; **Ashton, Paul and Peel, Michael.** The Effects of Housing Distortions on Unemployment. *Oxford Econ. Pap.*, June 1988, *40*(2), pp. 322–45.

——— **and Canzoneri, Matthew B.** When International Policy Coordination Matters: An Empirical Analysis. *Appl. Econ.*, September 1988, *20*(9), pp. 1137–54.

Mingat, Alain. Mesure et analyse de l'égalité et de l'équité en éducation. (Analysing and Measuring Equality and Equity in the Education System. With English summary.) *Revue Écon.*, January 1988, *39*(1), pp. 93–112.

——— **and Salmon, Pierre.** Alterable Electorates in the Context of Residential Mobility. *Public Choice*, October 1988, *59*(1), pp. 67–82.

Mini, Piero V. John Maynard Keynes on the Method of Economics. *Economia (Portugal)*, May 1988, *12*(2), pp. 181–95.

Minne, Bert. Two Types of Pattern of Specialization of the Economic Environment of a Highly Industrialized Country in Western Europe. *Empirica*, 1988, *15*(1), pp. 127–38.

Minnis, Peter. Taxation, Inflation and the Measurement of Real Interest. *Australian Tax Forum*, 1988, *5*(3), pp. 339–57.

Minns, Richard. The Management of Shareholdings in Large Manufacturing Companies. In *Harris, L., et al., eds.,* 1988, pp. 143–69.

———. Pension Funds: An Alternative View. In *Harris, L., et al., eds.,* 1988, pp. 325–39.

Mino, Kazuo. The Long-run Effects of Income Taxation under Endogenous Technical Progress. *Econ. Letters*, 1988, *27*(4), pp. 367–70.

———. Stabilization Effect of Endogenous Money Supply in a Descriptive Neoclassical Growth Model. *J. Macroecon.*, Winter 1988, *10*(1), pp. 125–37.

Minsky, Hyman P. Back from the Brink. *Challenge*, Jan.–Feb. 1988, *31*(1), pp. 22–28.

———. Global Debt: Why Is Cooperation So Difficult? Perspective. In *Guerrieri, P. and Padoan, P. C., eds.,* 1988, pp. 117–22.

Mintert, James and Schroeder, Ted C. Hedging Feeder Steers and Heifers in the Cash-Settled Feeder Cattle Futures Market. *Western J. Agr. Econ.*, December 1988, *13*(2), pp. 316–26.

Mintz, Jack M. An Empirical Estimate of Corporate Tax Refundability and Effective Tax Rates. *Quart. J. Econ.*, February 1988, *103*(1), pp. 225–31.

Mintzberg, Henry. Generic Strategies: Toward a Comprehensive Framework. In *Lamb, R. and Shrivastava, P., eds.,* 1988, pp. 1–67.

——— **and Mintzberg, Yvette.** Strategy Making as Craft. In *Urabe, K.; Child, J. and Kagono, T., eds.,* 1988, pp. 167–96.

———, **et al.** Strategy of Design: A Study of "Architects in Co-Partnership." In *Grant, J. H., ed.,* 1988, pp. 311–59.

Mintzberg, Yvette and Mintzberg, Henry. Strategy Making as Craft. In *Urabe, K.; Child, J. and Kagono, T., eds.,* 1988, pp. 167–96.

Mintzer, Irving. Living in a Warmer World: Challenges for Policy Analysis and Management. *J. Policy Anal. Manage.*, Spring 1988, *7*(3), pp. 445–59.

Miralao, Virginia. Labour Conditions in the Philippine Craft Industries. In *Kathuria, S.; Miralao, V. and Joseph, R.,* 1988, pp. 30–56.

Miranda, Casimiro V., Jr. Criteria for the Regional Allocation of Public Resources. *Philippine Rev. Econ. Bus.*, Sept.–Dec. 1988, *25*(3–4), pp. 295–305.

Miranda, Mario J. and Helmberger, Peter G. The Effects of Commodity Price Stabilization Programs. *Amer. Econ. Rev.*, March 1988, *78*(1), pp. 46–58.

Miranda Serrano, Rafael. Los teoremas de

Stiemke y Tucker: una demostración original y su interpretación económica. (With English summary.) *Invest. Ecón.*, January 1988, *12*(1), pp. 159–67.

Miranowski, John A.; Tegene, Abebayehu and Huffman, Wallace E. Dynamic Corn Supply Functions: A Model with Explicit Optimization. *Amer. J. Agr. Econ.*, February 1988, *70*(1), pp. 103–11.

Miranti, Paul J. Professionalism and Nativism: The Competition in Securing Public Accountancy Legislation in New York during the 1890s. *Soc. Sci. Quart.*, June 1988, *69*(2), pp. 361–80.

Mirman, Leonard J. and Reisman, Haim. Price Fluctuations When Only Prices Reveal Information. *Econ. Letters*, 1988, *27*(4), pp. 305–10.

Miron, Jeffrey A. and Zeldes, Stephen P. Seasonality, Cost Shocks, and the Production Smoothing Models of Inventories. *Econometrica*, July 1988, *56*(4), pp. 877–908.

Mirowski, Philip. Adam Smith, Empiricism, and the Rate of Profit in Eighteenth-Century England. In *Mirowski, P.*, 1988, *1982*, pp. 191–209.

_____. Energy and Energetics in Economic Theory: A Review Essay. *J. Econ. Issues*, September 1988, *22*(3), pp. 811–30.

_____. How to Protect Economics from Science. In *Mirowski, P.*, 1988, pp. 1–8.

_____. Institutions as a Solution Concept in a Game Theory Context. In *Mirowski, P.*, 1988, pp. 75–93.

_____. Is There a Mathematical Neoinstitutional Economics? In *Mirowski, P.*, 1988, pp. 57–74.

_____. Is There a Mathematical Neoinstitutional Economics? In *Samuels, W. J., ed., Vol. 2*, 1988, *1981*, pp. 63–83.

_____. Macroeconomic Instability and the "Natural" Processes in Early Neoclassical Economics. In *Mirowski, P.*, 1988, *1984*, pp. 45–54.

_____. Macroeconomic Instability and the 'Natural' Processes in Early Neoclassical Economics. In *Wood, J. C., ed., Vol. 3*, 1988, *1984*, pp. 283–93.

_____. Morishima on Marx. In *Mirowski, P.*, 1988, pp. 171–88.

_____. Nelson and Winter's *Evolutionary Theory of Economic Change*. In *Mirowski, P.*, 1988, pp. 161–70.

_____. The Philosophical Bases of Institutionalist Economics. In *Tool, M. R., ed., Vol. 1*, 1988, *1987*, pp. 51–88.

_____. The Philosophical Foundations of Institutionalist Economics. In *Mirowski, P.*, 1988, *1987*, pp. 106–33.

_____. Physics and the "Marginalist Revolution." In *Mirowski, P.*, 1988, *1984*, pp. 11–30.

_____. Rhetoric, Mathematics, and the Nature of Neoclassical Economic Theory. In *Mirowski, P.*, 1988, pp. 137–60.

_____. The Role of Conservation Principles in Twentieth-Century Economic Theory. In *Mirowski, P.*, 1988, pp. 94–105.

_____. The Sciences Were Never at War? Some

Early Skirmishes between Physicists and Economists. In *Mirowski, P.*, 1988, pp. 31–44.

_____. Shall I Compare Thee to a Minkowski–Ricardo–Leontief–Metzler Matrix of the Mosak–Hicks Type? In *Klamer, A.; McCloskey, D. N. and Solow, R. M., eds.*, 1988, *1987*, pp. 117–45.

_____. What Do Markets Do? Market Efficacy and the Economic Historian. In *Mirowski, P.*, 1988, *1987*, pp. 210–32.

Mirrlees, Catriona and Parker, Julia. British Social Trends since 1900: Housing. In *Halsey, A. H., ed.*, 1988, pp. 357–97.

_____ **and Parker, Julia.** British Social Trends since 1900: Welfare. In *Halsey, A. H., ed.*, 1988, pp. 462–517.

Mishel, Lawrence R. Advance Notice of Plant Closings: Benefits Outweigh the Costs. *Challenge*, July–August 1988, *31*(4), pp. 58–61.

_____ **and Simon, Jacqueline.** The State of Working America. *Challenge*, Nov.–Dec. 1988, *31*(6), pp. 50–51.

Mishkin, Frederic S. Causes of Changing Financial Market Volatility: Commentary. In *Federal Reserve Bank of Kansas City*, 1988, pp. 23–32.

_____. The Information in the Term Structure: Some Further Results. *J. Appl. Econometrics*, Oct.–Dec. 1988, *3*(4), pp. 307–14.

Misiolek, Walter S. Pollution Control Through Price Incentives: The Role of Rent Seeking Costs in Monopoly Markets. *J. Environ. Econ. Manage.*, March 1988, *15*(1), pp. 1–8.

_____ **and Elder, Harold W.** Tax Structure and the Size of Government: An Empirical Analysis of the Fiscal Illusion and Fiscal Stress Arguments. *Public Choice*, June 1988, *57*(3), pp. 233–45.

Misra, Lalatendu and Gupta, Atul. Illegal Insider Trading: Is It Rampant before Corporate Takeovers? *Financial Rev.*, November 1988, *23*(4), pp. 453–64.

Missaggia, Maria Giovanna. Nota sulle statistiche ufficiali per l'industria in Italia: 1885–1903. (Note on Official Statistics for Industry in Italy: 1885–1903. With English summary.) *Rivista Storia Econ.*, S.S., June 1988, *5*(2), pp. 234–54.

Mistral, Jacques. International Policy Co-ordination within a World of Structural Change: Comment. In *Borner, S., ed.*, 1988, pp. 356–59.

Mitani, Taichirō. The Cambridge History of Japan: Volume 6: The Twentieth Century: The Establishment of Party Cabinets, 1898–1932. In *Duus, P., ed.*, 1988, pp. 55–96.

Mitchell, A. A. The Development of a Knowledge Based Media Planning System. In *Gaul, W. and Schader, M., eds.*, 1988, pp. 67–79.

Mitchell, Daniel J. B. and Jacoby, Sanford M. Measurement of Compensation: Union and Nonunion. *Ind. Relat.*, Spring 1988, *27*(2), pp. 215–31.

Mitchell, Douglas W. Explicit Interest and Demand Deposit Service Charges: Comment. *J. Money, Credit, Banking*, May 1988, *20*(2), pp. 270–74.

_____. The Feasibility of Perpetual Deficits. *J. Macroecon.*, Summer 1988, *10*(3), pp. 407–19.

_____. Velocity Variance Comparisons under Alternative Policy Regimes. *Atlantic Econ. J.*, December 1988, *16*(4), pp. 37–42.

Mitchell, J. Brooks and Ponthieu, Louis D. Deals: A Comparison of Entrepreneur and Executive Perceptions. In *Association of Private Education*, 1988, pp. 125–32.

Mitchell, Janet. Financial Constraints and the Trade-off between Salaries and Savings in Labor-Managed Firms. *J. Compar. Econ.*, September 1988, *12*(3), pp. 362–79.

Mitchell, Jean M. and Benson, Bruce L. Rent Seekers Who Demand Government Production: Bureaucratic Output and the Price of Complements. *Public Choice*, January 1988, *56*(1), pp. 3–16.

Mitchell, Jeremy. An Electronic Future? In *Maynes, E. S. and ACCI Research Committee, eds.*, 1988, pp. 307–11.

_____. Privatization, Competition and Airline Deregulation: A View from Abroad. In *Maynes, E. S. and ACCI Research Committee, eds.*, 1988, pp. 452–56.

Mitchell, Mark L. and Mulherin, J. Harold. Finessing the Political System: The Cigarette Advertising Ban. *Southern Econ. J.*, April 1988, *54*(4), pp. 855–62.

Mitchell, Mildred O. and Leigh, Wilhelmina A. Public Housing and the Black Community. *Rev. Black Polit. Econ.*, Fall 1988, *17*(2), pp. 107–29.

Mitchell, Olivia S. The Relation of Age to Workplace Injuries. *Mon. Lab. Rev.*, July 1988, *111*(7), pp. 8–13.

_____. Trends in the Labor Force Activity of the Elderly in the United States, 1940–1980: Discussion. In *Ricardo-Campbell, R. and Lazear, E. P., eds.*, 1988, pp. 76–83.

_____. Worker Knowledge of Pension Provisions. *J. Lab. Econ.*, January 1988, *6*(1), pp. 21–39.

_____ and Levine, Phillip B. The Baby Boom's Legacy: Relative Wages in the Twenty-First Century. *Amer. Econ. Rev.*, May 1988, *78*(2), pp. 66–69.

_____ and Luzadis, Rebecca A. Changes in Pension Incentives through Time. *Ind. Lab. Relat. Rev.*, October 1988, *42*(1), pp. 100–108.

Mitchell, T. J. and Beauchamp, J. J. Bayesian Variable Selection in Linear Regression: Rejoinder. *J. Amer. Statist. Assoc.*, December 1988, *83*(404), pp. 1035–36.

_____ and Beauchamp, J. J. Bayesian Variable Selection in Linear Regression. *J. Amer. Statist. Assoc.*, December 1988, *83*(404), pp. 1023–32.

Mitchell, Wesley C. Commons on Institutional Economics. In *Samuels, W. J., ed., Vol. 1*, 1988, *1935*, pp. 135–52.

_____. Commons on Legal Foundations of Capitalism. In *Samuels, W. J., ed., Vol. 2*, 1988, *1924*, pp. 195–208.

Mitchell, William C. Inflation and Politics: Six

Theories in Search of Reality. In *Willett, T. D., ed.*, 1988, pp. 63–99.

_____. Virginia, Rochester, and Bloomington: Twenty-five Years of Public Choice and Political Science. *Public Choice*, February 1988, *56*(2), pp. 101–19.

Mitchison, Rosalind. Who Were the Poor in Scotland, 1690–1830? In *Mitchison, R. and Roebuck, P., eds.*, 1988, pp. 140–48.

_____ and Roebuck, Peter. Economy and Society in Scotland and Ireland: 1500–1939: Introduction. In *Mitchison, R. and Roebuck, P., eds.*, 1988, pp. 1–13.

Mitomo, Hitoshi and Kohno, Hirotada. Optimal Pricing of Telecommunications Service in an Advanced Information-Oriented Society. In *Orishimo, I.; Hewings, G. J. D. and Nijkamp, P., eds.*, 1988, pp. 195–213.

Mitra, A. K. and Jena, Suruchi. Effects of Outliers in Regression Analysis: A Study with Reference to Groundnut Productivity Data of Orissa. *Indian J. Quant. Econ.*, 1988, *4*(1), pp. 41–48.

Mitra, Ashok. China: Issues in Development: Introduction. In *Mitra, A., ed.*, 1988, pp. i–vii.

Mitra, Tapan and Dasgupta, Swapan. Characterization of Intertemporal Optimality in Terms of Decentralizable Conditions: The Discounted Case. *J. Econ. Theory*, August 1988, *45*(2), pp. 274–87.

_____ and Dasgupta, Swapan. Intertemporal Optimality in a Closed Linear Model of Production. *J. Econ. Theory*, August 1988, *45*(2), pp. 288–315.

Mitroff, Ian I. Marrying Two Schools of Policy Research: What is an Adequate Method for Complex Problems? In *Grant, J. H., ed.*, 1988, pp. 33–42.

Mitroff, Robert C. and Erekson, O. Homer. Equity Trends in Ohio School Finance, 1976–1984. *Econ. Educ. Rev.*, 1988, *7*(2), pp. 245–50.

Mitsuo, Kishi, et al. Modelling Support System for System Dynamics. In *Iri, M. and Yajima, K., eds.*, 1988, pp. 60–69.

Mittal, Banwari. The Role of Affective Choice Mode in the Consumer Purchase of Expressive Products. *J. Econ. Psych.*, December 1988, *9*(4), pp. 499–524.

Mittal, Dutt Kumar. Declining Share of Labour in Revenues of Public Enterprises (1974–75 to 1985–86). *Indian Econ. J.*, Oct.–Dec. 1988, *36*(2), pp. 82–87.

Mittelhammer, Ron C. and Conway, Roger K. Applying Mixed Estimation in Econometric Research. *Amer. J. Agr. Econ.*, November 1988, *70*(4), pp. 859–66.

Mittelstädt, Axel. Hours Reductions within Large-scale Macroeconomic Models: Conflict between Theory and Empirical Application: Comment. In *Hart, R. A., ed.*, 1988, pp. 253–55.

_____ and Englander, A. Steven. Total Factor Productivity: Macroeconomic and Structural Aspects of the Slowdown. *OECD Econ. Stud.*, Spring 1988, (10), pp. 7–56.

Mixon, J. Wilson, Jr. and Hoftyzer, John. National Origins of Saudi Arabia's Imports. *J. Energy Devel.*, Autumn 1988, *14*(1), pp. 45–54.

_____; **Uri, Noel D. and Kyer, Ben L.** Taxes, Transfer Payments and Automatic Stabilization in the United States. Impact and Trends. *Econ. Notes*, 1988, (2), pp. 50–60.

Miyagiwa, Kaz. Corporate Income Tax Incidence in the Presence of Sector-Specific Unemployment. *J. Public Econ.*, October 1988, *37*(1), pp. 103–12.

_____. International Transfer of Localized Technology and Factor Income in the Ricardo–Viner Trade Model. *Can. J. Econ.*, November 1988, *21*(4), pp. 736–46.

Miyajima, Hideaki. Local Trade Associations (*Dōgyō Kumiai*) in Prewar Japan: Comment. In *Yamazaki, H. and Miyamoto, M., eds.*, 1988, pp. 114–18.

Miyake, Mitsunobu. On the Nash Social Welfare Function and the Continuity Axioms. *Econ. Stud. Quart.*, December 1988, *39*(4), pp. 291–302.

Miyamoto, Matao. The Development of Business Associations in Prewar Japan: Response. In *Yamazaki, H. and Miyamoto, M., eds.*, 1988, pp. 50–52.

_____. The Development of Business Associations in Prewar Japan. In *Yamazaki, H. and Miyamoto, M., eds.*, 1988, pp. 1–45.

_____. Trade Associations in Business History: Concluding Remarks. In *Yamazaki, H. and Miyamoto, M., eds.*, 1988, pp. 299–318.

Miyazaaki, Isamu. International Money and Macroeconomics: Comments. In *Elliott, K. A. and Williamson, J., eds.*, 1988, pp. 46–47.

Miyazaki, Hajime. Contract Curves and Slutsky Equations in a Theory of the Labor-Managed Firm. In *Jones, D. C. and Svejnar, J., eds.*, 1988, pp. 25–63.

Mizoguchi, Toshiyuki. Analysis of Household Economic Data on the HOMEDAS Data-Base. In *Uno, K. and Shishido, S., eds.*, 1988, pp. 149–55.

_____ **and Nojima, Noriyuki.** Economic Time-Series Database of Japan's Former Colonies (COTEDAS): 1885–1945: An Example of Historical Statistics Database. In *Uno, K. and Shishido, S., eds.*, 1988, pp. 238–44.

Mizsei, Kálmán. Is the Hungarian Economic Mechanism a Model to Be Emulated? *Eastern Europ. Econ.*, Summer 1988, *26*(4), pp. 58–71.

Mizukami, Koichi and Wu, Hansheng. Incentive Stackelberg Strategies in Linear Quadratic Differential Games with Two Noncooperative Followers. In *Iri, M. and Yajima, K., eds.*, 1988, pp. 436–45.

Mizuta, Hiroshi. Enlightenment and Beyond: Political Economy Comes to Japan: Historical Introduction. In *Sugiyama, C. and Mizuta, H., eds.*, 1988, pp. 3–33.

_____. For Domestic Colonization: Political Economy in Sapporo Agricultural College. In *Sugiyama, C. and Mizuta, H., eds.*, 1988, pp. 121–26.

_____ **and Suzuki, Mikihisa.** His Majesty's University: Tokyo Imperial University. In *Sugiyama, C. and Mizuta, H., eds.*, 1988, pp. 97–120.

Mjelde, James W. and Cochran, Mark J. Obtaining Lower and Upper Bounds on the Value of Seasonal Climate Forecasts as a Function of Risk Preferences. *Western J. Agr. Econ.*, December 1988, *13*(2), pp. 285–93.

_____ **and Talpaz, Hovav.** Crop Irrigation Scheduling via Simulation-Based Experimentation. *Western J. Agr. Econ.*, December 1988, *13*(2), pp. 184–92.

_____, **et al.** Valuing Forecast Characteristics in a Dynamic Agricultural Production System. *Amer. J. Agr. Econ.*, August 1988, *70*(3), pp. 674–84.

Mo, Jie-ping. Entry and Structures of Interest Groups in Assignment Games. *J. Econ. Theory*, October 1988, *46*(1), pp. 66–96.

Mo, Zhen. Tighten Control over Big Labor-Hiring Households in Rural Areas. *Chinese Econ. Stud.*, Winter 1987–88, *21*(2), pp. 90–99.

Moak, Donald L.; Uze, Barry and Filer, John E. Why Some States Adopt Lotteries and Others Don't. *Public Finance Quart.*, July 1988, *16*(3), pp. 259–83.

Moatti, Marie. Discretization and Markov Modelling of a State Variable in Dynamic Programming. In *Iri, M. and Yajima, K., eds.*, 1988, pp. 530–38.

Moazzami, Bakhtiar and Gupta, Kanhaya L. Dynamic Specification and the Demand for Money Function. *Econ. Letters*, 1988, *27*(3), pp. 229–31.

Mobley, Mary F.; Bearden, William O. and Teel, Jesse E. An Investigation of Individual Responses to Tensile Price Claims. *J. Cons. Res.*, September 1988, *15*(2), pp. 273–79.

Mockler, Richard W. and Kleiman, Mark A. R. With This Test I Thee Wed: Evaluating Premarital AIDS Testing. *J. Policy Anal. Manage.*, Spring 1988, *7*(3), pp. 557–62.

Modest, David M. and Lehmann, Bruce N. The Empirical Foundations of the Arbitrage Pricing Theory. *J. Finan. Econ.*, September 1988, *21*(2), pp. 213–54.

Modiano, Eduardo Marco. The Cruzado First Attempt: The Brazilian Stabilization Program of February 1986. In *Bruno, M., et al., eds.*, 1988, pp. 215–58.

_____. Repasses mensais x reajustes trimestrais. (With English summary.) *Pesquisa Planejamento Econ.*, April 1988, *18*(1), pp. 83–99.

_____ **and Fritsch, Winston.** A restrição externa ao crescimento econômico brasileiro: Uma perspectiva de longo prazo. (With English summary.) *Pesquisa Planejamento Econ.*, August 1988, *18*(2), pp. 271–96.

Modica, Salvatore and Gay, Antonio. Complete Irreflexive Preferences: A Definition. *Econ. Letters*, 1988, *28*(3), pp. 205–08.

Modigliani, Franco. Measuring the Contribution of Intergenerational Transfers to Total Wealth:

Conceptual Issues and Empirical Findings. **In** *Kessler, D. and Masson, A., eds.*, 1988, pp. 21–52.

_____. MM—Past, Present, Future. *J. Econ. Perspectives*, Fall 1988, 2(4), pp. 149–58.

_____. The Monetarist Controversy or, Should We Forsake Stabilization Policies? **In** *Shaw, G. K., ed., Vol. 1*, 1988, 1977, pp. 191–209.

_____. The Monetarist Controversy Revisited. *Contemp. Policy Issues*, October 1988, 6(4), pp. 3–18.

_____. Reagan's Economic Policies: A Critique. *Oxford Econ. Pap.*, September 1988, 40(3), pp. 397–426.

_____. The Role of Intergenerational Transfers and Life Cycle Saving in the Accumulation of Wealth. *J. Econ. Perspectives*, Spring 1988, 2(2), pp. 15–40.

_____ **and Jappelli, Tullio.** The Determinants of Interest Rates in the Italian Economy. *Rev. Econ. Cond. Italy*, Jan.–April 1988, (1), pp. 9–34.

Modjtahedi, Bagher. Dynamics of Real Interest Differentials: An Empirical Investigation. *Europ. Econ. Rev.*, July 1988, 32(6), pp. 1191–1211.

_____ **and Havenner, Arthur.** Foreign Exchange Rates: A Multiple Currency and Maturity Analysis. *J. Econometrics*, February 1988, 37(2), pp. 251–64.

Moehring, H. B. Symbol versus Substance in Legislative Activity: The Case of Illegal Immigration. *Public Choice*, June 1988, 57(3), pp. 287–94.

Moen, Jon R. Diversity and Balanced Growth: Tennessee Stays on Track. *Fed. Res. Bank Atlanta Econ. Rev.*, Jan.–Feb. 1988, 73(1), pp. 58–66.

_____. Past and Current Trends in Retirement: American Men from 1860 to 1980. *Fed. Res. Bank Atlanta Econ. Rev.*, July–Aug. 1988, 73(4), pp. 16–27.

Moene, Karl O. A Reformulation of the Harris–Todaro Mechanism with Endogenous Wages. *Econ. Letters*, 1988, 27(4), pp. 387–90.

_____. Unions' Threats and Wage Determination. *Econ. J.*, June 1988, 98(391), pp. 471–83.

_____ **and Hoel, Michael.** Profit Sharing, Unions and Investments. *Scand. J. Econ.*, 1988, 90(4), pp. 493–505.

Moffett, Michael H. and Kaempfer, William H. Impact of Anti-apartheid Sanctions on South Africa: Some Trade and Financial Evidence. *Contemp. Policy Issues*, October 1988, 6(4), pp. 118–29.

Moffitt, L. Joe. Incorporating Environmental Considerations in Pest Control Advice for Farmers. *Amer. J. Agr. Econ.*, August 1988, 70(3), pp. 628–34.

Moffitt, Robert and Fraker, Thomas. The Effect of Food Stamps on Labor Supply: A Bivariate Selection Model. *J. Public Econ.*, February 1988, 35(1), pp. 25–56.

_____; **Runkle, David and Keane, Michael.** Real Wages over the Business Cycle: Estimating the Impact of Heterogeneity with Micro Data. *J. Polit. Econ.*, December 1988, 96(6), pp. 1232–66.

Mogensen, Gunnar Viby. Recent Danish Research in Economic History—A Survey. *Scand. Econ. Hist. Rev.*, 1988, 36(3), pp. 5–22.

Moggridge, D. E. Editing Modern Economists: Introduction. **In** *Moggridge, D. E., ed.*, 1988, pp. 11–17.

_____. The Keynesian Revolution in Historical Perspective. **In** *Hamouda, O. F. and Smithin, J. N., eds., Vol. 1*, 1988, pp. 50–60.

_____. On Editing Keynes. **In** *Moggridge, D. E., ed.*, 1988, pp. 67–90.

Moghadam, Fatemeh E. An Historical Interpretation of the Iranian Revolution. *Cambridge J. Econ.*, December 1988, 12(4), pp. 401–18.

_____. Nomadic Invasions and the Development of Productive Forces: An Historical Study of Iran (1000–1800). *Sci. Soc.*, Winter 1988–89, 52(4), pp. 389–412.

Moghadam, K. and Ballard, K. P. Small Area Modeling of the Industrial Sector (SAMIS): An Integrated Econometric–Interindustry Approach. *Environ. Planning A*, May 1988, 20(5), pp. 655–68.

Mohabbat, Khan A. The Productivity of Money: Some Empirical Evidence from Italy. *Rivista Int. Sci. Econ. Com.*, Oct.–Nov. 1988, 35(10–11), pp. 1021–30.

Mohamad, Mahathir. A Keynote Address to the South. **In** *Sopiee, N.; Hamzah, B. A. and Leong, C. H., eds.*, 1988, pp. 3–10.

Mohammad, Ali; Afzal, Mohammad and Raja, Tariq Aslam. Some Differentials in Infant and Child Mortality Risks in Pakistan 1962–1986. *Pakistan Devel. Rev.*, Part 2, Winter 1988, 27(4), pp. 635–42.

Mohammad, Faiz and Tahir, Sayyid. Agricultural Prices in Pakistan: A Multimarket Analysis. *Pakistan Devel. Rev.*, Part 2, Winter 1988, 27(4), pp. 577–92.

Mohammad, Sharif; Whalley, John and Hamilton, Bob. Applied General Equilibrium Analysis and Perspective on Growth Performance. *J. Policy Modeling*, Summer 1988, 10(2), pp. 281–97.

Mohammed, Azizali F. Contrasting External Debt Experience: Asia and Latin America. **In** *Streeten, P., ed.*, 1988, pp. 106–12.

Mohan, J. Spatial Aspects of Health-care Employment in Britain, 2: Current Policy Initiatives. *Environ. Planning A*, February 1988, 20(2), pp. 203–17.

_____. Spatial Aspects of Health-Care Employment in Britain: 1. Aggregate Trends. *Environ. Planning A*, January 1988, 20(1), pp. 7–23.

Mohan, Rakesh and Sabot, Richard. Educational Expansion and the Inequality of Pay: Colombia 1973–78. *Oxford Bull. Econ. Statist.*, May 1988, 50(2), pp. 175–82.

Mohan, S. and Gautam, Vinayshil. Job Stress and Health Dimensions of Managerial Effectiveness—HRD Approach. **In** *Kohli, U. and Gautam, V., eds.*, 1988, pp. 224–35.

Mohatarem, Mustafa. The Auto Sector: Comments. In *Schott, J. J. and Smith, M. G., eds.*, 1988, pp. 110–13.

Mohnen, Pierre; Roy, Paul-Martel and Kamel, Nawal. Demande de travail et d'heures supplémentaires: étude empirique pour le Canada et le Québec. (With English summary.) *L'Actual. Econ.*, March 1988, *64*(1), pp. 23–43.

Mohod, Sudham B. Political Maldevelopment: The Genesis of the Current Political and Social Unrest in India. In *Vivekananda, F., ed.*, 1988, pp. 104–22.

Mohr, Ernst U. Appropriation of Common Access Natural Resources through Exploration: The Relevance of the Open-Loop Concept. *Int. Econ. Rev.*, May 1988, *29*(2), pp. 307–19.

_____. International Borrowing and Exhaustible Resources: Note on a Liquidity Creditworthiness Conflict. *Europ. Econ. Rev.*, July 1988, *32*(6), pp. 1385–92.

_____. On the Incredibility of Perfect Threats in Repeated Games: Note. *Int. Econ. Rev.*, August 1988, *29*(3), pp. 551–55.

Mohr, Lillian H. The Role of the Federal Government. In *Maynes, E. S. and ACCI Research Committee, eds.*, 1988, pp. 830–35.

Möhring, R. H.; Radermacher, F. J. and Bartusch, M. M-Machine Unit Time Scheduling: A Report on Ongoing Research. In *Kurzhanski, A.; Neumann, K. and Pallaschke, D., eds.*, 1988, pp. 165–212.

Mohtadi, Hamid. Growth-Distribution Trade-offs: The Role of Capacity Utilisation. *Cambridge J. Econ.*, December 1988, *12*(4), pp. 419–33.

_____ **and Arora, Harjit.** Stagflation and Monetary Stabilization Policies in a Disequilibrium Framework: The Case of South Korea. *J. Post Keynesian Econ.*, Summer 1988, *10*(4), pp. 602–17.

Mohtadi, Shahruz. The Stabilization of the Effective Exchange Rates of the Less Developed Countries under Alternative Exchange Rate Arrangements. *J. Econ. Devel.*, June 1988, *13*(1), pp. 143–54.

Moinuddin, Hasan. Grey Area Trade Policies. In *Dicke, D. C. and Petersmann, E.-U., eds.*, 1988, pp. 197–202.

Moir, Christopher and Kilpatrick, Andrew. Developments in the UK's International Trading Performance. In *Barker, T. and Dunne, P., eds.*, 1988, pp. 141–69.

Moiseev, N. N., et al. The Development of Mathematical Economic Methods: Results, Problems, Prospects. *Matekon*, Fall 1988, *25*(1), pp. 54–88.

Moissis, D. E.; Miller, C. A. and Wheeler, Mary F. A Parametric Study of Viscous Fingering in Miscible Displacement by Numerical Simulation. In *Wheeler, M. F., ed.*, 1988, pp. 227–47.

Mojsilovic, Miodrag and Daduna, Joachim R. Computer-Aided Vehicle and Duty Scheduling Using the HOT Programme System. In *Daduna, J. R. and Wren, A., eds.*, 1988, pp. 133–46.

Mokyr, Joel. Economics, History, and Human Biology: Review Article. *Econ. Develop. Cult. Change*, April 1988, *36*(3), pp. 559–64.

_____. Is There Still Life in the Pessimist Case? Consumption during the Industrial Revolution, 1790–1850. *J. Econ. Hist.*, March 1988, *48*(1), pp. 69–92.

Molana, H. and Leon, H. Testing Some Restrictions in a Time Series Cross-Section Model: A Study of Seven LDCs. *Manchester Sch. Econ. Soc. Stud.*, March 1988, *56*(1), pp. 1–15.

Moledo, Leonardo; Sauber, Beatriz and Szyld, Daniel B. Positive Solutions for the Leontief Dynamic Input–Output Model. In *Ciaschini, M., ed.*, 1988, pp. 91–97.

Molenaar, Ivo W. Statistical Consultants and Statistical Expert Systems. In *Edwards, D. and Raun, N. E., eds.*, 1988, pp. 187–92.

_____; **Luijben, Thom and Boomsma, Anne.** Modification of Factor Analysis Models in Covariance Structure Analysis: A Monte Carlo Study. In *Dijkstra, T. K., ed.*, 1988, pp. 70–101.

Molenda, Danuta. Technological Innovation in Central Europe between the XIVth and the XVIIth Centuries. *J. Europ. Econ. Hist.*, Spring 1988, *17*(1), pp. 63–84.

Molho, Lazaros and Sundararajan, V. Financial Reform and Monetary Control in Indonesia. In *Cheng, H.-S., ed.*, 1988, pp. 321–51.

_____ **and Sundararajan, V.** Financial Reform in Indonesia. *Finance Develop.*, December 1988, *25*(4), pp. 43–45.

Molina, David J. and Nieswiadomy, Michael L. Urban Water Demand Estimates under Increasing Block Rates. *Growth Change*, Winter 1988, *19*(1), pp. 1–12.

_____; **Slottje, Daniel J. and Basmann, Robert L.** A Note on Measuring Veblen's Theory of Conspicuous Consumption. *Rev. Econ. Statist.*, August 1988, *70*(3), pp. 531–35.

_____; **Slottje, Daniel J. and Hayes, Kathy J.** Measuring Preference Variation across North America. *Economica*, November 1988, *55*(220), pp. 525–39.

_____; **Slottje, Daniel J. and Hirschberg, Joseph G.** A Selection Criterion for Choosing between Functional Forms of Income Distribution. *Econometric Rev.*, 1988–89, *7*(2), pp. 183–97.

Moll, Peter G. The Intercountry Agricultural Production Function and Productivity Differences Among Countries: Comment. *J. Devel. Econ.*, February 1988, *28*(1), pp. 121–24.

_____. Transition to Freehold in the South African Reserves. *World Devel.*, March 1988, *16*(3), pp. 349–60.

Molle, Willem. Oil Refineries and Petrochemical Industries: Moving into Maturity. In *de Jong, H. W., ed.*, 1988, pp. 41–60.

_____ **and van Mourik, Aad.** International Movements of Labour under Conditions of Economic Integration: The Case of Western Europe. *J. Common Market Stud.*, March 1988, *26*(3), pp. 317–42.

Møller, Michael and Nielsen, Niels Chr. Pension

i OD-sammenhæng. (Pension Reform and Profit Sharing. With English summary.) *Nationaløkon. Tidsskr.*, 1988, *126*(2), pp. 171–82.

Mollett, Nina; Clark, Ian N. and Major, Philip J. Development and Implementation of New Zealand's ITQ Management System. *Marine Resource Econ.*, 1988, *5*(4), pp. 325–49.

Molta, David J. and Ammons, David N. Productivity Emphasis in Local Government: An Assessment of the Impact of Selected Policy Environment Factors. In *Kelly, R. M., ed.*, 1988, pp. 69–83.

Molyneux, Philip G. Real Tax Rates versus Nominal Tax Rates—The Impact of Tax Preferences. *Australian Tax Forum*, 1988, *5*(3), pp. 373–83.

Momirovic, Konstantin; Radakovic, J. and Dobric, V. An Expert System for the Interpretation of Results of Canonical Covariance Analysis. In *Edwards, D. and Raun, N. E., eds.*, 1988, pp. 135–41.

Monahan, George E. and Nti, Kofi O. Optimal Pricing and Advertising for New Products with Repeat Purchases. In *Devinney, T. M., ed.*, 1988, pp. 145–65.

Monahan, John F. and Liddle, Roger F. A Stationary Stochastic Approximation Method. *J. Econometrics*, May–June 1988, *38*(1–2), pp. 91–102.

Moncarz, Raul. Financial and Capital Flows in Central America in the 1980s. In *Jorge, A. and Salazar-Carrillo, J., eds.*, 1988, pp. 123–39.

Moncur, James E. T. and Pollock, Richard L. Scarcity Rents for Water: A Valuation and Pricing Model. *Land Econ.*, February 1988, *64*(1), pp. 62–72.

Monderer, Dov. A Probabilistic Problem Arising in Economics. *J. Math. Econ.*, 1988, *17*(4), pp. 321–38.

_____. Values and Semivalues on Subspaces of Finite Games. *Int. J. Game Theory*, 1988, *17*(4), pp. 301–10.

_____ and **Neyman, Abraham.** Values of Smooth Nonatomic Games: The Method of Multilinear Approximation. In *[Shapley, L. S.]*, 1988, pp. 217–34.

Mongar, Tom. Political Economy of the Conservative Swing. In *Zarembka, P., ed.*, 1988, pp. 205–40.

Mongin, Philippe. Assessing Other People's Utilities: Comment. In *Munier, B. R., ed.*, 1988, pp. 139–44.

_____ and **Walliser, Bernard.** Infinite Regressions in the Optimizing Theory of Decision. In *Munier, B. R., ed.*, 1988, pp. 435–57.

Monheit, Alan C. and Mueller, Curt D. Insurance Coverage and the Demand for Dental Care: Results for Non-aged White Adults. *J. Health Econ.*, March 1988, *7*(1), pp. 59–72.

_____ and **Schur, Claudia L.** The Dynamics of Health Insurance Loss: A Tale of Two Cohorts. *Inquiry*, Fall 1988, *25*(3), pp. 315–27.

_____; **Short, Pamela Farley and Cantor, Joel C.** The Dynamics of Medicaid Enrollment. *Inquiry*, Winter 1988, *25*(4), pp. 504–16.

Monjardet, Bernard. A Generalisation of Probabilistic Consistency: Linearity Conditions for

Valued Preference Relations. In *Kacprzyk, J. and Roubens, M., eds.*, 1988, pp. 36–53.

Monkiewicz, Grazyna and Monkiewicz, Jan. East–South Capital Cooperation: An Unexploited Possibility. *J. World Trade*, June 1988, *22*(3), pp. 61–72.

Monkiewicz, Jan. East–West–South Cooperation and Worldwide Technology Flows: A Hope or a Myth? *Rivista Int. Sci. Econ. Com.*, April–May 1988, *35*(4–5), pp. 437–56.

_____ and **Maciejewicz, Jan.** Trade and Foreign Investment in Services. The East European Dimension. *Konjunkturpolitik*, 1988, *34*(4), pp. 239–54.

_____ and **Monkiewicz, Grazyna.** East–South Capital Cooperation: An Unexploited Possibility. *J. World Trade*, June 1988, *22*(3), pp. 61–72.

Monnier, Lionel and Escarmelle, Jean-François. La spécificité du comportement de l'investissement des entreprises publiques françaises depuis 1973. (Behavioral Investment Specificities in French Public Enterprises since 1973. With English summary.) *Ann. Pub. Co-op. Econ.*, July–Sept. 1988, *59*(3), pp. 283–305.

Monroe, Kent B. and Mazumdar, Tridib. Pricing-Decision Models: Recent Developments and Research Opportunities. In *Devinney, T. M., ed.*, 1988, pp. 361–88.

_____ and **Rao, Akshay R.** The Moderating Effect of Prior Knowledge on Cue Utilization in Product Evaluations. *J. Cons. Res.*, September 1988, *15*(2), pp. 253–64.

Monroe, Margaret A. Indeterminacy of Price and Quantity in Futures Markets. *J. Futures Markets*, October 1988, *8*(5), pp. 575–88.

Monson, Terry and Fitzgerald, Bruce. Export Credit and Insurance for Export Promotion. *Finance Develop.*, December 1988, *25*(4), pp. 53–55.

Montador, R. Bruce; Hagemann, Robert P. and Jones, Brian R. Tax Reform in OECD Countries: Motives, Constraints and Practice. *OECD Econ. Stud.*, Spring 1988, (10), pp. 185–226.

Montani, Guido. Scarce Natural Resources and Income Distribution. In *Steedman, I., ed., Vol. 2*, 1988, *1975*, pp. 218–51.

Montesano, Aldo. A Generalized Measure of Risk Aversion, without the Independence Axiom. In *Munier, B. R., ed.*, 1988, pp. 629–37.

Montet, C. Reswitching and Primary Input Use: A Comment. In *Steedman, I., ed., Vol. 1*, 1988, *1979*, pp. 261–66.

Montet, Christian; Peguin-Feissolle, Anne and Laussel, Didier. Optimal Trade Policy under Oligopoly: A Calibrated Model of the Europe–Japan Rivalry in the EEC Car Market. *Europ. Econ. Rev.*, September 1988, *32*(7), pp. 1547–65.

Montgomery, Cynthia A. and Wernerfelt, Birger. Diversification, Ricardian Rents, and Tobin's q. *Rand J. Econ.*, Winter 1988, *19*(4), pp. 623–32.

_____ and **Wernerfelt, Birger.** Tobin's q and the Importance of Focus in Firm Performance.

Amer. Econ. Rev., March 1988, 78(1), pp. 246–50.

Montgomery, David. Gutman's Agenda for Future Historical Research. *Labor Hist.*, Summer 1988, 29(3), pp. 299–312.

Montgomery, David B. On Negative Binomial Distribution: Comment. *J. Bus. Econ. Statist.*, April 1988, 6(2), pp. 163–64.

Montgomery, Edward and Shaw, Kathryn. The Real Wage–Employment Relationship: An Industry Analysis. *Econ. Letters*, 1988, 26(3), pp. 241–46.

_____ **and Wascher, William.** Creative Destruction and the Behavior of Productivity over the Business Cycle. *Rev. Econ. Statist.*, February 1988, 70(1), pp. 168–72.

Montgomery, Henry and Johansson, Ulla-Stina. Life Values: Their Structure and Relation to Life Situation. In *Maital, S., ed., Vol. 1,* 1988, pp. 420–37.

Montgomery, Mark. Hours of Part-time and Full-time Workers at the Same Firm. *Ind. Relat.*, Fall 1988, 27(3), pp. 394–406.

_____. On the Determinants of Employer Demand for Part-Time Workers. *Rev. Econ. Statist.*, February 1988, 70(1), pp. 112–17.

Montgomery, Mark R. How Large Is Too Large? Implications of the City Size Literature for Population Policy and Research. *Econ. Develop. Cult. Change,* July 1988, 36(4), pp. 691–720.

_____; **Cheung, Paul P. L. and Sulak, Donna B.** Rates of Courtship and First Marriage in Thailand. *Population Stud.*, November 1988, 42(3), pp. 375–88.

Monti, Mario. Monetary and Financial Integration: Short Term and Long Term Prospects. *Rev. Econ. Cond. Italy,* Sept.–Dec. 1988, (3), pp. 425–33.

Montias, John M. On Hierarchies and Economic Reforms. *J. Inst. Theoretical Econ.*, December 1988, 144(5), pp. 832–38.

Montilla, Armando. Consolidation of Net Income and Losses: Venezuela. *Bull. Int. Fiscal Doc.*, May 1988, 42(5), pp. 232–34.

Montmarquette, Claude and Dudley, Leonard. A Disequilibrium Model of Public Spending. *Econ. Letters*, 1988, 26(2), pp. 165–68.

Montrucchio, Luigi. The Occurrence of Erratic Fluctuations in Models of Optimization over Infinite Horizon. In *[Goodwin, R. M.],* 1988, pp. 83–92.

_____ **and Boldrin, Michele.** Acyclicity and Stability for Intertemporal Optimization Models. *Int. Econ. Rev.*, February 1988, 29(1), pp. 137–46.

Montt, Felipe and Marshall, Jorge. Privatisation in Chile. In *Cook, P. and Kirkpatrick, C., eds.,* 1988, pp. 281–307.

Montuschi, Luisa. La inversión en el proceso del crecimiento económico argentino 1950–1980. (Investment in the Process of the Argentine Economic Growth 1950–1980. With English summary.) *Económica (La Plata),* Jan.–June 1988, 34(1), pp. 89–112.

Moock, Peter R. and Jamison, Dean T. Educa-

tional Development in Sub-Saharan Africa. *Finance Develop.*, March 1988, 25(1), pp. 22–24.

Moody, C. E., Jr. and Kruvant, W. J. Joint Bidding, Entry, and the Price of OCS Leases. *Rand J. Econ.*, Summer 1988, 19(2), pp. 276–84.

Moody, David L.; Edwards, Ward and von Winterfeldt, Detlof. Simplicity in Decision Analysis: An Example and a Discussion. In *Bell, D. E.; Raiffa, H. and Tversky, A., eds.,* 1988, pp. 443–64.

Mooers, Stephanie L. A Reevaluation of Royal Justice under Henry I of England. *Amer. Hist. Rev.*, April 1988, 93(2), pp. 340–58.

Mookerjee, Rajen. The Stock Market and the Economy: The Indian Experience 1949–1981. *Indian Econ. J.*, Oct.–Dec. 1988, 36(2), pp. 30–43.

_____ **and Dadkhah, Kamran M.** The Behavior of the Currency Deposit Ratio in India, 1870–1982. *J. Devel. Areas*, April 1988, 22(3), pp. 359–72.

Mookherjee, Dilip. Involuntary Unemployment and Worker Self-selection. *J. Econ. Theory,* June 1988, 45(1), pp. 171–88.

_____ **and Kahn, Charles M.** A Competitive Efficiency Wage Model with Keynesian Features. *Quart. J. Econ.*, November 1988, 103(4), pp. 609–45.

Moomaw, Ronald L. Agglomeration Economies: Localization or Urbanization? *Urban Stud.*, April 1988, 25(2), pp. 150–61.

_____; **Thompson, Richard P. and Olson, Kent W.** Redwood National Park Expansion: Impact on Old-Growth Redwood Stumpage Prices. *Land Econ.*, August 1988, 64(3), pp. 269–75.

Moon, Ailee and Gilbert, Neil. Analyzing Welfare Effort: An Appraisal of Comparative Methods. *J. Policy Anal. Manage.*, Winter 1988, 7(2), pp. 326–40.

Moon, Hiwhoa. Whither International Trade Policies: Worries about Continuing Protectionism: Comments. In *Elliott, K. A. and Williamson, J., eds.,* 1988, pp. 96–100.

Moon, Marilyn and Meyer, Jack A. Health Care Spending on Children and the Elderly. In *Palmer, J. L.; Smeeding, T. and Torrey, B. B., eds.,* 1988, pp. 171–200.

Moon, Soo-Young and Post, Gerald V. A Pooled Cross-section Time-Series Approach to Business Failures in 18 U.S. Cities. *J. Econ. Bus.*, February 1988, 40(1), pp. 45–56.

Mooney, Marta; Zeleny, Milan and Hessel, Marek P. Integrated Process Management: A Management Technology for the New Competitive Era. In *Starr, M. K., ed.,* 1988, pp. 121–58.

Mooney, Pat Roy. Biotechnology and the North–South Conflict. In *Research and Info. System for the Non-aligned and Other Developing Countries,* 1988, pp. 243–78.

Moore, B. C.; Rhodes, J. and Tyler, P. Geographical Variations in Industrial Costs. *Scot. J. Polit. Econ.*, February 1988, 35(1), pp. 22–50.

_____; **Rhodes, J. and Tyler, P.** The Rate Burden: An Accounting Framework for Assessing the Effect of Local Taxes on Business. *Reg. Stud.*, October 1988, *22*(5), pp. 387–97.

Moore, Basil J. The Endogeneity of Money: A Comment. *Scot. J. Polit. Econ.*, August 1988, *35*(3), pp. 291–94.

———. The Endogenous Money Supply. *J. Post Keynesian Econ.*, Spring 1988, *10*(3), pp. 372–85.

———. The Endogenous Money Supply: Concluding Comments. *J. Post Keynesian Econ.*, Spring 1988, *10*(3), pp. 398–400.

———. Keynes's Treatment of Interest. In *Hamouda, O. F. and Smithin, J. N., eds., Vol. 2*, 1988, pp. 121–29.

———. Unpacking the Post Keynesian Black Box: Bank Lending and the Money Supply. In *Sawyer, M. C., ed.*, 1988, *1983*, pp. 120–39.

———. Unpacking the Post-Keynesian Black Box: Wages, Bank Lending and the Money Supply. In *Arestis, P., ed.*, 1988, pp. 122–51.

Moore, Christopher and Richardson, Jeremy J. The Politics and Practice of Corporate Responsibility in Great Britain. In *Preston, L. E., ed.*, 1988, pp. 267–90.

Moore, F. C. T. Do Higher Order Desires Resolve Conflict? In *Liu, S. and Allinson, R. E., eds.*, 1988, pp. 59–67.

Moore, Geoffrey H. and Cullity, John P. Little-known Facts about Stock Prices and Business Cycles. *Challenge*, March–April 1988, *31*(2), pp. 49–50.

Moore, Giora and Kim, Moshe. Economic vs. Accounting Depreciation. *J. Acc. Econ.*, April 1988, *10*(2), pp. 111–25.

Moore, J. E., II and Wiggins, L. L. Linearized, Optimally Configured Urban System Models: A Profit-Maximizing Formulation. *Environ. Planning A*, March 1988, *20*(3), pp. 369–90.

Moore, Joe. Production Control: Workers' Control in Early Postwar Japan. In *Tsurumi, E. P., ed.*, 1988, pp. 14–35.

Moore, John. Contracting between Two Parties with Private Information. *Rev. Econ. Stud.*, January 1988, *55*(1), pp. 49–69.

——— **and Hart, Oliver D.** Incomplete Contracts and Renegotiation. *Econometrica*, July 1988, *56*(4), pp. 755–85.

——— **and Repullo, Rafael.** Subgame Perfect Implementation. *Econometrica*, September 1988, *56*(5), pp. 1191–1220.

———; **Turnbull, Stephen and Ma, Ching-to Albert.** Stopping Agents from "Cheating." *J. Econ. Theory*, December 1988, *46*(2), pp. 355–72.

Moore, John H. Knowledge Transfers in the United States. *Europ. Econ. Rev.*, March 1988, *32*(2–3), pp. 591–603.

———. Science and Public Policy. In *[Nutter, G. W.]*, 1988, pp. 255–30.

Moore, Jonathan S. Enforcing Foreign Ownership Claims in the Antiquities Market. *Yale Law J.*, February 1988, *97*(3), pp. 466–87.

Moore, Laurence. Stated Preference Analysis and New Store Location. In *Wrigley, N., ed.*, 1988, pp. 203–20.

Moore, Lynden. Agricultural Protection in Britain and Its Economy-Wide Effects. *World Econ.*, June 1988, *11*(2), pp. 249–65.

Moore, Mark H. Policies to Achieve Discrimination on the Effective Price of Heroin. In *Alper, N. O. and Hellman, D. A., eds.*, 1988, pp. 225–37.

Moore, Michael J. and Viscusi, W. Kip. Doubling the Estimated Value of Life: Results Using New Occupational Fatality Data. *J. Policy Anal. Manage.*, Spring 1988, *7*(3), pp. 476–90.

——— **and Viscusi, W. Kip.** The Quantity-Adjusted Value of Life. *Econ. Inquiry*, July 1988, *26*(3), pp. 369–88.

Moore, Mick. Economic Growth and the Rise of Civil Society: Agriculture in Taiwan and South Korea. In *White, G., ed.*, 1988, pp. 113–52.

Moore, Raymond E. Recognition of Foreign Enterprises as Taxable Entities: Hong Kong. In *International Fiscal Association, ed. (I)*, 1988, pp. 431–37.

Moore, Robert E.; Svejnar, Jan and Estrin, Saul. Market Imperfections, Labor Management, and Earnings Differentials in a Developing Country: Theory and Evidence from Yugoslavia. *Quart. J. Econ.*, August 1988, *103*(3), pp. 465–78.

Moore, Robert L. and Lazear, Edward P. Pensions and Turnover. In *Bodie, Z.; Shoven, J. B. and Wise, D. A., eds.*, 1988, pp. 163–88.

Moore, Scott B.; Schirm, David C. and Ferri, Michael G. Investor Expectations about Callable Warrants. *J. Portfol. Manage.*, Spring 1988, *14*(3), pp. 84–86.

Moore, Thomas Gale. Regulation, Reregulation, or Deregulation: The Issue for the 1990s. In *Anderson, A. and Bark, D. L., eds.*, 1988, pp. 323–34.

———; **Harrington, Charlene and Newcomer, Robert J.** Factors That Contribute to Medicare HMO Risk Contract Success. *Inquiry*, Summer 1988, *25*(2), pp. 251–62.

Moore, William J. and Newman, Robert J. A Cross-section Analysis of the Postwar Decline in American Trade Union Membership. *J. Lab. Res.*, Spring 1988, *9*(2), pp. 111–25.

Moore, William T. and Sartoris, William L. On the Existence of a Dividend Clientele in the Market for Electric Utility Stocks. *Quart. Rev. Econ. Bus.*, Spring 1988, *28*(1), pp. 88–100.

Moorer, Thomas H. Global Evolution since World War II. In *[Nutter, G. W.]*, 1988, pp. 105–11.

Moorthy, K. Sridhar. Consumer Expectations and the Pricing of Durables. In *Devinney, T. M., ed.*, 1988, pp. 99–114.

———. Product and Price Competition in a Duopoly. *Marketing Sci.*, Spring 1988, *7*(2), pp. 141–68.

———. Strategic Decentralization in Channels. *Marketing Sci.*, Fall 1988, *7*(4), pp. 335–55.

Morais, Nina. Sex Discrimination and the Fourteenth Amendment: Lost History. *Yale Law J.*, May 1988, *97*(6), pp. 1153–72.

Morales, Juan-Antonio. Inflation Stabilization in

Bolivia. In *Bruno, M., et al., eds.*, 1988, pp. 307–46.

Moran, Cristian. A Structural Model for Developing Countries' Manufactured Exports. *World Bank Econ. Rev.*, September 1988, *2*(3), pp. 321–40.

Moran, Eileen; Ma, Christopher K. and Fabozzi, Frank J. Market Uncertainty and the Least-Cost Offering Method of Public Utility Debt: A Note. *J. Finance*, September 1988, *43*(4), pp. 1025–34.

Moran, Emilio F. Social Reproduction in Agricultural Frontiers. In *Bennett, J. W. and Bowen, J. R., eds.*, 1988, pp. 199–212.

Moran, Larry R. Motor Vehicles, Model Year 1988. *Surv. Curr. Bus.*, November 1988, *68*(11), pp. 20–21.

Moran, Theodore H. Multinational Corporations and North-South Relations: Old Threats and New Opportunities in the Coming Decade. In *Tavis, L. A., ed.*, 1988, pp. 267–83.

_____ **and Pearson, Charles S.** Tread Carefully in the Field of TRIP Measures. *World Econ.*, March 1988, *11*(1), pp. 119–34.

Morandé, Felipe G. Domestic Currency Appreciation and Foreign Capital Inflows: What Comes First? (Chile, 1977–82). *J. Int. Money Finance*, December 1988, *7*(4), pp. 447–66.

Morawski, Witold. A Sociologist Looks at Public Opinion, Politics, and Reform. In *Marer, P. and Siwinski, W., eds.*, 1988, pp. 93–102.

Mørch, Niels. Recognition of Foreign Enterprises as Taxable Entities: Denmark. In *International Fiscal Association, ed. (I)*, 1988, pp. 363–71.

Mørck, Randall; Shleifer, Andrei and Vishny, Robert W. Characteristics of Targets of Hostile and Friendly Takeovers. In *Auerbach, A. J., ed. (I)*, 1988, pp. 101–29.

_____; **Shleifer, Andrei and Vishny, Robert W.** Management Ownership and Market Valuation: An Empirical Analysis. *J. Finan. Econ.*, Jan.–March 1988, *20*(1–2), pp. 293–315.

Mordacq, Patrick. Les nouveaux instruments financiers et l'information des actionnaires. (With English summary.) *Revue Écon. Polit.*, Sept.–Oct. 1988, *98*(5), pp. 713–20.

Moré, Jorge J. Trust Regions and Projected Gradients. In *Iri, M. and Yajima, K., eds.*, 1988, pp. 1–13.

Moreaux, Michel and Boyer, Marcel. Rational Rationing in Stackelberg Equilibria. *Quart. J. Econ.*, May 1988, *103*(2), pp. 409–14.

_____; **Gaudet, Gérard and Amigues, Jean-Pierre.** Bertrand and Cournot Equilibrium Price Paths in a Nonrenewable Resource Differentiated Product Duopoly. In *Eiselt, H. A. and Pederzoli, G., eds.*, 1988, pp. 343–57.

Morehouse, Ward; Dembo, David and Dias, Clarence. Trend and Prospects for Developing Countries. In *Research and Info. System for the Non-aligned and Other Developing Countries*, 1988, pp. 153–92.

Moreno, Ramon. Exchange Rates and Monetary Policy in Singapore and Hong Kong. In *Cheng, H.-S., ed.*, 1988, pp. 173–200.

_____. Saving, Investment, and the U.S. Exter-nal Balance. *Fed. Res. Bank San Francisco Econ. Rev.*, Fall 1988, (4), pp. 3–17.

Moretto, Michele. Ciclo economico e decisioni di occupazione dell'impresa: Una analisi in condizioni di incertezza. (Business Cycle and Employment Decisions of the Firm: An Analysis under Uncertainty. With English summary.) *Econ. Polit.*, August 1988, *5*(2), pp. 205–35.

Morey, Edward R. and Kohli, Ulrich. U.S. Imports by Origin: A Characteristics Approach. *Kyklos*, 1988, *41*(1), pp. 51–74.

Morgan, David R. and Brudney, Jeffrey L. Local Government Productivity: Efficiency and Equity. In *Kelly, R. M., ed.*, 1988, pp. 163–75.

Morgan, George Emir; Shome, Dilip K. and Smith, Stephen D. Optimal Futures Positions for Large Banking Firms. *J. Finance*, March 1988, *43*(1), pp. 175–95.

Morgan, Ieuan G. and McCurdy, Thomas H. Testing the Martingale Hypothesis in Deutsche Mark Futures with Models Specifying the Form of Heteroscedasticity. *J. Appl. Econometrics*, July–Sept. 1988, *3*(3), pp. 187–202.

Morgan, James M. and Jerrell, Max E. Modeling Labor Demand in a State Econometric Model. *Rev. Reg. Stud.*, Fall 1988, *18*(3), pp. 31–40.

Morgan, James N. Consumer Choice Is More Than Search. In *Maynes, E. S. and ACCI Research Committee, eds.*, 1988, pp. 277–305.

_____. A Note on the Consumer Benefits of Information. *J. Cons. Aff.*, Summer 1988, *22*(1), pp. 171–72.

Morgan, Mary. Finding a Satisfactory Empirical Model. In *de Marchi, N., ed.*, 1988, pp. 199–211.

Morgan, Peter B. and McMillan, John. Price Dispersion, Price Flexibility, and Repeated Purchasing. *Can. J. Econ.*, November 1988, *21*(4), pp. 883–902.

Morgan, Richard. Drought Relief Programmes in Botswana. In *Curtis, D.; Hubbard, M. and Shepherd, A.*, 1988, pp. 112–20.

Morgan, Theodore. Theory versus Empiricism in Academic Economics: Update and Comparisons. *J. Econ. Perspectives*, Fall 1988, *2*(4), pp. 159–64.

Morgan, Theresa A. Medicare Reform. In *Pennsylvania Economic Association*, 1988, pp. 560–73.

Mori, Kei. Developing User-Participated Database in Econometric Models. In *Uno, K. and Shishido, S., eds.*, 1988, pp. 304–14.

_____. A Marine Ranch Concept Using a Sunflower ("Himawari"). In *Kozmetsky, G.; Matsumoto, H. and Smilor, R. W., eds.*, 1988, pp. 109–18.

Moriguchi, Chikashi. Japan's Energy Policy during the 1970s. In *Shoven, J. B., ed.*, 1988, pp. 301–17.

Morin, Pierre; Chevallier, Jean-Yves and Legendre, François. L'investissement dans un contexte de faible croissance et de taux d'intérêt élevés. Une étude sur données individuelles du comportement des entreprises industrielles françaises. (With English summary.) *Rech. Écon. Louvain*, 1988, *54*(2), pp. 221–49.

Morini, Annalisa. Goods Transport in Urban Areas: A Comparison between the United States and Italy. In *Bianco, L. and La Bella, A., eds.,* 1988, pp. 352–73.

Morishima, Michio and Catephores, George. Anti-Say's Law versus Say's Law: A Change in Paradigm. In *Hanusch, H., ed.,* 1988, pp. 23–53.

_____ **and Catephores, George.** Anti-Say's Law versus Say's Law: A Change in Paradigm: Reply. In *Hanusch, H., ed.,* 1988, pp. 68–70.

Morita, Tsuneo. The Structure of Capital Financing: A Hungarian Case Study. *Econ. Planning*, 1988, *22*(1–2), pp. 78–87.

Morley, Richard. The Dutch Disease. In *Darnell, A. and Evans, L., eds.,* 1988, pp. 163–77.

Morley, Samuel A. Relative Wages, Labor Force Structure, and the Distribution of Income in the Short and Long Run. *Econ. Develop. Cult. Change*, July 1988, *36*(4), pp. 651–68.

Morlok, Edward K. Current Trends and Perspectives on Freight Transport in North America. In *Bianco, L. and La Bella, A., eds.,* 1988, pp. 1–49.

Morooka, Yoshinori; Hayami, Yujiro and Kawagoe, Toshihiko. Middlemen and Peasants: The Structure of the Indonesian Soybean Market. *Devel. Econ.*, March 1988, *26*(1), pp. 51–67.

Morrill, Richard L. Intra Metropolitan Demographic Structure: A Seattle Example. *Ann. Reg. Sci.*, March 1988, *22*(1), pp. 1–16.

_____ . Migration Regions and Population Redistribution. *Growth Change*, Winter 1988, *19*(1), pp. 43–60.

Morris, Cynthia and Adelman, Irma. Interactions between Agriculture and Industry during the Nineteenth Century. In *Antonelli, G. and Quadrio-Curzio, A., eds.,* 1988, pp. 23–31.

Morris, Deigan and Hergert, Michael. Trends in International Collaborative Agreements. In *Contractor, F. J. and Lorange, P.,* 1988, pp. 99–109.

Morris, Ira; Webley, Paul and Robben, Henry. Social Comparison and Tax Evasion in a Shop Simulation. In *Maital, S., ed., Vol. 2,* 1988, pp. 553–61.

Morris, J. and Hess, T. M. Agricultural Flood Alleviation Benefit Assessment: A Case Study. *J. Agr. Econ.*, September 1988, *39*(3), pp. 402–12.

Morris, J. L. Producer Services and the Regions: The Case of Large Accountancy Firms. *Environ. Planning A*, June 1988, *20*(6), pp. 741–59.

Morris, James G. and Güder, Faruk. Objective Function Approximation: An Application to Spatial Price Equilibrium Models. *Amer. J. Agr. Econ.*, May 1988, *70*(2), pp. 391–96.

Morris, Joe and Cudd, Mike. Bias in Journal Ratings. *Financial Rev.*, February 1988, *23*(1), pp. 117–25.

Morris, John Richard. Enforcement of Property Rights and the Provision of Public Good Attributes. *Info. Econ. Policy*, 1988, *3*(2), pp. 91–108.

Morris, Michael H. and Nichols, William D. Consistency Exceptions: Materiality Judgments and Audit Firm Structure. *Accounting Rev.*, April 1988, *63*(2), pp. 237–54.

Morris, P. and Hossain, M. M. Australia's Import Demand for Printing and Writing Paper: A Short Run Estimate. *Australian Econ. Pap.*, June 1988, *27*(50), pp. 128–35.

Morrisey, Michael A. and Alexander, Jeffrey A. Hospital–Physician Integration and Hospital Costs. *Inquiry*, Fall 1988, *25*(3), pp. 388–401.

_____ ; **Sloan, Frank A. and Valvona, Joseph.** Defining Geographic Markets for Hospital Care. *Law Contemp. Probl.*, Spring 1988, *51*(2), pp. 165–94.

Morrison, Andrew R. and Becker, Charles M. The Determinants of Urban Population Growth in Sub-Saharan Africa. *Econ. Develop. Cult. Change*, January 1988, *36*(2), pp. 259–78.

Morrison, Catherine J. Capacity Utilization and Productivity Measurement: An Application to the U.S. Automobile Industry. In *Dogramaci, A. and Färe, R., eds.,,* 1988, pp. 163–93.

_____ . Quasi-Fixed Inputs in U.S. and Japanese Manufacturing: A Generalized Leontief Restricted Cost Function Approach. *Rev. Econ. Statist.*, May 1988, *70*(2), pp. 275–87.

_____ . Subequilibrium in the North American Steel Industries: A Study of Short Run Biases from Regulation and Utilisation Fluctuations. *Econ. J.*, June 1988, *98*(391), pp. 390–411.

_____ **and Diewert, W. Erwin.** Export Supply and Import Demand Functions: A Production Theory Approach. In *Feenstra, R. C., ed.,* 1988, pp. 207–22.

Morrison, Charles E. Japan and the ASEAN Countries: The Evolution of Japan's Regional Role. In *Inoguchi, T. and Okimoto, D. I., eds.,* 1988, pp. 414–45.

Morrison, Donald G. and Schmittlein, David C. Generalizing the NBD Model for Customer Purchases: What Are the Implications and Is It Worth the Effort? *J. Bus. Econ. Statist.*, April 1988, *6*(2), pp. 145–59.

_____ **and Schmittlein, David C.** Generalizing the NBD Model for Customer Purchases: What Are the Implications and Is It Worth the Effort? Reply. *J. Bus. Econ. Statist.*, April 1988, *6*(2), pp. 165–66.

Morrison, Malcolm H. Changes in the Legal Mandatory Retirement Age: Labor Force Participation Implications. In *Ricardo-Campbell, R. and Lazear, E. P., eds.,* 1988, pp. 378–405.

Morrison, Randall Clark. Regulatory Problems in the Securitization of Bank Assets. In *Kemper, R. L., ed.,* 1988, pp. 147–212.

Morrison, Thomas K. and Chu, Ke-young. World Non-oil Primary Commodity Markets: Reply [A Medium-term Framework of Analysis]. *Int. Monet. Fund Staff Pap.*, March 1988, *35*(1), pp. 204.

_____ **and Wattleworth, Michael.** Causes of the 1984–86 Commodity Price Decline. *Finance Develop.*, June 1988, *25*(2), pp. 31–33.

_____ and Wattleworth, Michael. The 1984–86 Commodity Recession: Analysis of Underlying Causes. *Int. Monet. Fund Staff Pap.*, June 1988, 35(2), pp. 371–81.

Morrison, W. S. G. Technology Upgradation and Human Resources Development in the Maritime Industry. In *Kohli, U. and Gautam, V.,* eds., 1988, pp. 104–12.

Morriss, Andrew. Supporting Structures for Resolving Environmental Disputes among Friendly Neighbors. In *Schmandt, J.; Clarkson, J. and Roderick, H.,* eds., 1988, pp. 217–52.

_____; Schmandt, Jurgen and Roderick, Hilliard. Acid Rain Is Different. In *Schmandt, J.; Clarkson, J. and Roderick, H.,* eds., 1988, pp. 7–30.

Morrisson, Christian. Jean Lhomme, de l'économie à l'histoire (1901–1987). (Jean Lhomme, from Economy to History (1901–1987). With English summary.) *Revue Écon.*, May 1988, 39(3), pp. 497–510.

_____; Atkinson, Anthony B. and Bourguignon, François. Earnings Mobility. *Europ. Econ. Rev.*, March 1988, 32(2–3), pp. 619–32.

Morrow-Jones, H. A. The Housing Life-Cycle and the Transition from Renting to Owning a Home in the United States: A Multistate Analysis. *Environ. Planning A*, September 1988, 20(9), pp. 1165–84.

Morse, Dale and Shaw, Wayne H. Investing in Bankrupt Firms. *J. Finance*, December 1988, 43(5), pp. 1193–1206.

Morse, Jeremy. The Great Inflation and Its Aftermath. In *[Witteveen, H. J.],* 1988, pp. 137–41.

Morss, Elliott R. and Gow, David D. The Notorious Nine: Critical Problems in Project Implementation. *World Devel.*, December 1988, 16(12), pp. 1399–1418.

Mortensen, Dale T. Matching: Finding a Partner for Life or Otherwise. In *Winship, C. and Rosen, S.,* eds., 1988, pp. 215–40.

_____. Wages, Separations, and Job Tenure: On-the-Job Specific Training or Matching? *J. Lab. Econ.*, October 1988, 6(4), pp. 445–71.

_____ and Neumann, George R. Estimating Structural Models of Unemployment and Job Duration. In *Barnett, W. A.; Berndt, E. R. and White, H.,* eds., 1988, pp. 335–55.

Mortensen, Michael. Mikroøkonomisk pristeori og makroøkonomiske modeller. (Microeconomic Explanations of Price Behavior and Macroeconomic Models. With English summary.) *Nationaløkon. Tidsskr.*, 1988, 126(1), pp. 83–95.

Mortimer, Kate. The Securities and Investments Board. In *Goodhart, C., et al.,* 1988, pp. 45–54.

Morton, Desmond. Labour and Industrial Relations History in English-Speaking Canada. In *Hébert, G.; Jain, H. C. and Meltz, N. M.,* eds.., 1988, pp. 243–60.

Morton, John S. and Buckles, Stephen. The Effects of Advanced Placement on College Introductory Economics Courses. *Amer. Econ. Rev.*, May 1988, 78(2), pp. 263–68.

Morton, S. Strategic Voting in Repeated Referenda. *Soc. Choice Welfare*, 1988, 5(1), pp. 45–68.

Morus, Steven A. and Cargill, Thomas F. A Vector Autoregression Model of the Nevada Economy. *Fed. Res. Bank San Francisco Econ. Rev.*, Winter 1988, (1), pp. 21–32.

Moschini, Giancarlo. The Cost Structure of Ontario Dairy Farms: A Microeconometric Analysis. *Can. J. Agr. Econ.*, July 1988, 36(2), pp. 187–206.

_____. A Model of Production with Supply Management for the Canadian Agricultural Sector. *Amer. J. Agr. Econ.*, May 1988, 70(2), pp. 318–29.

_____ and Meilke, Karl D. Sustainable Rates of Return for Milk Quotas in Ontario. *Can. J. Agr. Econ.*, March 1988, 36(1), pp. 119–26.

_____; Prescott, David M. and Stengos, Thanasis. Nonparametric Kernel Estimation Applied to Forecasting: An Evaluation Based on the Bootstrap. *Empirical Econ.*, 1988, 13(3–4), pp. 141–54.

Moschos, Demetrios and Bedrossian, Arakel. Industrial Structure, Concentration and the Speed of Price Adjustment. *J. Ind. Econ.*, June 1988, 36(4), pp. 459–76.

Moseley, Fred. The Increase of Unproductive Labor in the Postwar U.S. Economy. *Rev. Radical Polit. Econ.*, Summer–Fall 1988, 20(2–3), pp. 100–106.

_____. The Rate of Surplus Value, the Organic Composition, and the General Rate of Profit in the U.S. Economy, 1947–67: A Critique and Update of Wolff's Estimates. *Amer. Econ. Rev.*, March 1988, 78(1), pp. 298–303.

Moser, James T. and Born, Jeffery A. An Investigation into the Role of the Market Portfolio in the Arbitrage Pricing Theory. *Financial Rev.*, August 1988, 23(3), pp. 287–99.

_____; Officer, Dennis T. and Born, Jeffery A. Changes in Dividend Policy and Subsequent Earnings. *J. Portfol. Manage.*, Summer 1988, 14(4), pp. 56–62.

Moses, Resio. Accessibility, Population, and Human Resources. In *Kozmetsky, G.; Matsumoto, H. and Smilor, R. W.,* eds., 1988, pp. 121–26.

Moskoff, William and Linz, Susan J. Reorganization and Reform in the Soviet Economy: Introduction. In *Linz, S. J. and Moskoff, W.,* eds., 1988, pp. vii–x.

Moslehuddin, M.; Howlader, Ali Ahmed and Kabir, M. Husband–Wife Communication and Status of Women as a Determinant of Contraceptive Use in Rural Bangladesh. *Bangladesh Devel. Stud.*, March 1988, 16(1), pp. 85–97.

Mosley, Paul. On Persuading a Leopard to Change His Spots: Optimal Strategies for Donors and Recipients of Conditional Development Aid. In *Bates, R. H.,* ed., 1988, pp. 47–79.

_____. Privatisation, Policy-Based Lending and

World Bank Behaviour. In *Cook, P. and Kirkpatrick, C., eds.*, 1988, pp. 125–40.

──────. Towards a "Satisficing" Theory of Economic Policy. In *Earl, P. E., ed., Vol. 2*, 1988, *1976*, pp. 319–32.

──────. Trade and Aid. In *Greenaway, D., ed.*, 1988, pp. 166–73.

Mosley, W. Henry and Sirageldin, Ismail. Health Services and Population Planning Programs: A Review of Interrelations. In *Sirageldin, I. and Sorkin, A., eds.*, 1988, pp. 3–23.

Moss, Philip I. Employment Gains by Minorities, Women in Large City Government, 1976–83. *Mon. Lab. Rev.*, November 1988, *111*(11), pp. 18–24.

──────; **Terkla, David G. and Doeringer, Peter B.** Widespread Labor Stickiness in the New England Offshore Fishing Industry: Implications for Adjustment and Regulation. *Land Econ.*, February 1988, *64*(1), pp. 73–82.

Mote, Victor L. The BAM and Pacific Development. In *Liebowitz, R. D., ed.*, 1988, pp. 175–87.

Motekat, Janne and Hughes, Jesse W. Tax Expenditures for Local Governments. *Public Budg. Finance*, Winter 1988, *8*(4), pp. 68–73.

Motley, Brian. Should M2 Be Redefined? *Fed. Res. Bank San Francisco Econ. Rev.*, Winter 1988, (1), pp. 33–51.

Motscha, Matthias and Hinrichsen, Diederich. Optimization Problems in the Robustness Analysis of Linear State Space Systems. In *Gomez Fernandez, J. A., et al., eds.*, 1988, pp. 54–78.

Mott, Peter and Fritsche, Heiko. INTERPLAN— An Interactive Program System for Crew Scheduling and Rostering of Public Transport. In *Daduna, J. R. and Wren, A., eds.*, 1988, pp. 200–211.

Mott, Tracy and Baghestani, Hamid. The Money Supply Process under Alternative Federal Reserve Operating Procedures: An Empirical Examination. *Southern Econ. J.*, October 1988, *55*(2), pp. 485–93.

da Motta, Ronaldo Serôa and da Rocha Ferreira, Léo. The Brazilian National Alcohol Programme: An Economic Reappraisal and Adjustments. *Energy Econ.*, July 1988, *10*(3), pp. 229–34.

Mougeot, Michel and Naegelen, Florence. Analyse micro-économique du Code des marchés publics. (The French Public Procurement Code: A Theoretical Analysis. With English summary.) *Revue Écon.*, July 1988, *39*(4), pp. 725–52.

Mouhammed, Adil H. The Irrelevance of Rational Expectations to Developing Countries. In *Missouri Valley Economic Assoc.*, 1988, pp. 145–54.

Moulaert, Frank and De Cannière, Loïc. Income Inequality and Consumptive Spending Behavior: Empirical Evidence from the 1987–79 Household Budget Survey in Belgium. *J. Post Keynesian Econ.*, Winter 1987–88, *10*(2), pp. 225–49.

Moulen, Joël and Andjiga, Nicolas G. Binary Games in Constitutional Form and Collective Choice. *Math. Soc. Sci.*, October 1988, *16*(2), pp. 189–201.

Moulik, T. K. Energy and Development Options: The Case of India. *J. Energy Devel.*, Spring 1988, *13*(2), pp. 239–73.

Moulin, Hervé. Condorcet's Principle Implies the No Show Paradox. *J. Econ. Theory*, June 1988, *45*(1), pp. 53–64.

────── **and Thomson, William.** Can Everyone Benefit from Growth? Two Difficulties. *J. Math. Econ.*, 1988, *17*(4), pp. 339–45.

Mountain, Dean C. The Rotterdam Model: An Approximation in Variable Space. *Econometrica*, March 1988, *56*(2), pp. 477–84.

────── **and Chan, M. W. Luke.** The Interactive and Causal Relationships Involving Precious Metal Price Movements: An Analysis of the Gold and Silver Markets. *J. Bus. Econ. Statist.*, January 1988, *6*(1), pp. 69–77.

Mounts, William Stewart; Sowell, Clifford and Boyes, William J. The Federal Reserve as a Bureaucracy: An Examination of Expense-Preference Behavior. *J. Money, Credit, Banking*, May 1988, *20*(2), pp. 181–90.

Mourdoukoutas, Panos. Seasonal Employment, Seasonal Unemployment and Unemployment Compensation: The Case of the Tourist Industry of the Greek Islands. *Amer. J. Econ. Soc.*, July 1988, *47*(3), pp. 315–29.

van Mourik, Aad and Molle, Willem. International Movements of Labour under Conditions of Economic Integration: The Case of Western Europe. *J. Common Market Stud.*, March 1988, *26*(3), pp. 317–42.

Moussa, H. and Davies, J. E. Natural Monopoly and the Invisible Hand. *Econ. Stud. Quart.*, June 1988, *39*(2), pp. 118–31.

Moussalli, Stephanie D.; Bundrick, Charles M. and Cuzán, Alfred G. Fiscal Expansion and Political Instability in the Iberic–Latin Region. *Public Choice*, December 1988, *59*(3), pp. 225–38.

Moutos, Thomas and Scarth, William M. Stabilization Policy within a Currency Area. *Scot. J. Polit. Econ.*, November 1988, *35*(4), pp. 387–97.

────── **and Vines, David.** A Prototype Macroeconomic Model with Integrated Financial and Commodity Markets. *Econ. Notes*, 1988, (1), pp. 51–68.

Mouzas, Anastasia and Landers, John. Burial Seasonality and Causes of Death in London 1670–1819. *Population Stud.*, March 1988, *42*(1), pp. 59–83.

Movit, Charles H. and Roberts, Bryan W. Modeling Soviet Modernization: An Economy in Transition: A Comment. *Soviet Econ.*, Jan.–March 1988, *4*(1), pp. 57–64.

Mowery, David C. The Diffusion of New Manufacturing Technologies. In *Cyert, R. M. and Mowery, D. C., eds.*, 1988, pp. 481–509.

────── **and Cyert, Richard M.** The Impact of Technological Change on Employment and Economic Growth: Introduction. In *Cyert,*

R. M. and Mowery, D. C., eds., 1988, pp. xxv–xxxiv.

Moxon, Richard W.; Roehl, Thomas W. and Truitt, J. Frederick. International Cooperative Ventures in the Commercial Aircraft Industry: Gains, Sure, But What's My Share? In Contractor, F. J. and Lorange, P., 1988, pp. 255–77.

Moy, Joyanna. An Analysis of Unemployment and Other Labor Market Indicators in 10 Countries. Mon. Lab. Rev., April 1988, 111(4), pp. 39–50.

Moyes, P. A Note on Minimally Progressive Taxation and Absolute Income Inequality. In Gaertner, W. and Pattanaik, P. K., eds., 1988, 1988, pp. 139–46.

_____. A Note on Minimally Progressive Taxation and Absolute Income Inequality. Soc. Choice Welfare, 1988, 5(2/3), pp. 227–34.

Moyo, Nelson P. The State, Planning and Labour: Towards Transforming the Colonial Labour Process in Zimbabwe. J. Devel. Stud., July 1988, 24(4), pp. 203–17.

Moyo, Sam; Chidiya, Charles and Weiner, Dan. Energy Use in Zimbabwe's Agricultural Sector. In Hosier, R. H., ed. (I), 1988, pp. 20–59.

Mporogomyi, Kilonsi. Cooperatives and Development in Tanzania: Theory and Evidence of Lost Opportunities. In Hedlund, H., ed., 1988, pp. 71–91.

Mrak, Mojmir. Developing Countries' External Debt and South–South Economic Co-operation. In Sopiee, N.; Hamzah, B. A. and Leong, C. H., eds., 1988, 1985, pp. 291–305.

Mroczkowski, Piotr. History of Poland's Relations with the IMF and the World Bank. In Marer, P. and Siwinski, W., eds., 1988, pp. 253–57.

Mroz, John Edwin. Perestroika and Economic Security. In Aganbegyan, A. and Timofeyev, T., 1988, pp. 9–23.

Mtoi, M. T. T. and Phillips, T. P. Farming System Analysis of an Alternative Production System for Peasant Farming in Morogoro, Tanzania. Can. J. Agr. Econ., March 1988, 36(1), pp. 143–53.

Mucchielli, Jean-Louis and Mazerolle, Fabrice. Commerce intra-branche et intra-produit dans la spécialisation internationale de la France: 1960–1985. (Intra-industry, Intra-product Trade and International Specialization: The French Experience between 1960–1985. With English summary.) Revue Écon., November 1988, 39(6), pp. 1193–1217.

Muczyk, Jan P. and Reimann, Bernard C. Has Participative Management Been Oversold? In Timpe, A. D., ed., 1988, 1987, pp. 157–63.

Mudd, Shannon B. Disaggregating the Dollar Index: Trade in Textiles and Apparel. Fed. Res. Bank Atlanta Econ. Rev., March–April 1988, 73(2), pp. 28–33.

von zur Muehlen, Peter and Swamy, P. A. V. B. Further Thoughts on Testing for Causality with Econometric Models. J. Econometrics, Sept.–Oct. 1988, 39(1–2), pp. 105–47.

Muellbauer, John. Habits, Rationality and Myopia in the Life Cycle Consumption Function.

Ann. Écon. Statist., Jan.–March 1988, (9), pp. 47–70.

Mueller, Charles C. Conflitos intragovernamentais e a formaÂao de políticas de preços agrícolas no Brasil. (With English summary.) Pesquisa Planejamento Econ., December 1988, 18(3), pp. 685–708.

Mueller, Curt D. and Monheit, Alan C. Insurance Coverage and the Demand for Dental Care: Results for Non-aged White Adults. J. Health Econ., March 1988, 7(1), pp. 59–72.

Mueller, Dennis C. Anarchy, the Market, and the State. Southern Econ. J., April 1988, 54(4), pp. 821–30.

_____ and Cowling, Keith. The Social Costs of Monopoly Power. In Ricketts, M., ed., Vol. 2, 1988, 1978, pp. 321–42.

_____ and Magenheim, Ellen B. Are Acquiring-Firm Shareholders Better Off after an Acquisition? In Coffee, J. C., Jr.; Lowenstein, L. and Rose-Ackerman, S., eds., 1988, pp. 171–93.

Mueller, Franz H. Economic History and History of Economics. Rev. Soc. Econ., October 1988, 46(2), pp. 164–79.

Mueller, Hans. Protection and Market Power in the Steel Industry. Challenge, Sept.–Oct. 1988, 31(5), pp. 52–55.

Mueller, Milan and Clark, W. A. V. Hispanic Relocation and Spatial Assimilation: A Case Study. Soc. Sci. Quart., June 1988, 69(2), pp. 468–75.

Mueller, R. A. E. and Jansen, H. G. P. Farmer and Farm Concepts in Measuring Adoption Lags. J. Agr. Econ., January 1988, 39(1), pp. 121–24.

Muench, Thomas J. Quantum Agglomeration Formation during Growth in a Combined Economic/Gravity Model. J. Urban Econ., March 1988, 23(2), pp. 199–214.

Mueser, Peter R. and White, Michael J. Implications of Boundary Choice for the Measurement of Residential Mobility. Demography, August 1988, 25(3), pp. 443–59.

Muet, P.-A. A Comparative Analysis of Actual Dutch Macroeconomic Models: Comments. In Driehuis, W.; Fase, M. M. G. and den Hartog, H., eds., 1988, pp. 207–14.

Mugica, José M. and Cruz, Ignacio. The Retail Distribution Industry in Spain: Determinants of Its Structuring Process. In Kaynak, E., ed., 1988, pp. 277–98.

Mühl, Richard. The Wage Policy and the Restructuring Process. Czech. Econ. Digest., November 1988, (7), pp. 67–78.

Muir, Allan. Fuzzy Evaluation of Communicators. In Kacprzyk, J. and Fedrizzi, M., eds., 1988, pp. 145–51.

Mujahid-Mukhtar, Eshya and Mukhtar, Hanid. Agricultural Performance in the Punjabs: A Statistical Evaluation. Pakistan Econ. Soc. Rev., Winter 1988, 26(2), pp. 89–108.

Mujica R., Patricio. Políticas de Tipo de Cambio: Un Modelo de Tres Países. (With English summary.) Cuadernos Econ., August 1988, 25(75), pp. 197–214.

Mujżel, Jan. Democracy or Technocracy: Discussion: The Second Stage of the Reform. *Eastern Europ. Econ.*, Spring 1988, *26*(3), pp. 72–87.

Mukerjee, Gautam and Melka, Richard F. Criteria Ranking for Low-Level Waste Sites: A Guide for Policymakers. In *Pennsylvania Economic Association*, 1988, pp. 453–69.

Mukherjee, Smriti. Fluctuations in World Economy and India's Export Sector. *Margin*, Jan.–March 1988, *20*(2), pp. 65–73.

Mukherji, Anjan and Sanyal, Amal. Uncertainty, Liquidity and the Demand for Money. *Keio Econ. Stud.*, 1988, *25*(1), pp. 1–19.

Mukhtar, Eshya Mujahid. Growth, Employment and Education: An Application of Multicriteria Analysis to Pakistan: Comments. *Pakistan Devel. Rev.*, Part 2, Winter 1988, *27*(4), pp. 734–35.

———— **and Mukhtar, Hanid.** Input Use and Productivity across Farm Sizes: A Comparison of the Two Punjabs. *Pakistan Devel. Rev.*, Part 2, Winter 1988, *27*(4), pp. 595–604.

Mukhtar, Hanid. Consumption Patterns of Major Food Items in Pakistan: Provincial, Sectoral and Inter-temporal Differences 1979–1984-85: Comments. *Pakistan Devel. Rev.*, Part 2, Winter 1988, *27*(4), pp. 760–61.

————. Regional Distribution of Agricultural Incomes in Pakistan: An Intertemporal Analysis: Comments. *Pakistan Devel. Rev.*, Part 2, Winter 1988, *27*(4), pp. 547–49.

———— **and Mujahid-Mukhtar, Eshya.** Agricultural Performance in the Punjabs: A Statistical Evaluation. *Pakistan Econ. Soc. Rev.*, Winter 1988, *26*(2), pp. 89–108.

———— **and Mukhtar, Eshya Mujahid.** Input Use and Productivity across Farm Sizes: A Comparison of the Two Punjabs. *Pakistan Devel. Rev.*, Part 2, Winter 1988, *27*(4), pp. 595–604.

Mulat, Teshome. Education Policy and the Regional Distribution of Schools in Ethiopia. *Eastern Afr. Econ. Rev.*, December 1988, *4*(2), pp. 13–20.

Mulberg, Ruthellen; Oberheu, Howard and Scott, Charles G. SSA's Outreach Efforts to Contact Beneficiaries Eligible for SSI Payments. *Soc. Sec. Bull.*, January 1988, *51*(1), pp. 12–17.

Mulder, Christian. Testing Korteweg's Rational Expectations Model for a Small Open Economy. *De Economist*, March 1988, *136*(1), pp. 22–49.

Mulford, Charles W. and Schneider, Arnold. An Empirical Study of Structural and Controllable Factors Affecting Faculty Evaluations. In *Schwartz, B. N., ed.*, 1988, pp. 205–15.

Mulherin, J. Harold and Mitchell, Mark L. Finessing the Political System: The Cigarette Advertising Ban. *Southern Econ. J.*, April 1988, *54*(4), pp. 855–62.

Mulkey, David; Beaulieu, Lionel J. and Miller, Michael K. Community Forces and Their Influence on Farm Structure. In *Beaulieu, L. J., ed.*, 1988, pp. 211–32.

———— **and Henry, Mark S.** Development Strategies in the Rural South: Issues and Alternatives. In *Beaulieu, L. J., ed.*, 1988, pp. 249–64.

Mullan, Brendan and Hess, Peter N. The Military Burden and Public Education Expenditures in Contemporary Developing Nations: Is There a Trade-off? *J. Devel. Areas*, July 1988, *22*(4), pp. 497–514.

Mullen, John D.; Wohlgenant, Michael K. and Farris, Donald E. Input Substitution and the Distribution of Surplus Gains from Lower U.S. Beef-Processing Costs. *Amer. J. Agr. Econ.*, May 1988, *70*(2), pp. 245–54.

————, **et al.** The Consumption Behaviour of Farmers: A Review of the Evidence. *Rev. Marketing Agr. Econ.*, August 1988, *56*(2), pp. 179–93.

Müller, A. L. Gedagtes oor die aard, inhoud en betekenis van ekonomiese geskiedenis. (With English summary.) *J. Stud. Econ. Econometrics*, November 1988, *12*(3), pp. 41–48.

————. Soviet Technology and the West, 1945–1985. *S. Afr. J. Econ.*, December 1988, *56*(4), pp. 317–28.

Müller, Anton P. Internationale Determinanten der Geldpolitik. (International Monetary Policy Determinants. With English summary.) *Kredit Kapital*, 1988, *21*(1), pp. 34–44.

Muller, Charlotte. Retirement and Health Coverage: Problems Affecting Homework. In *Christensen, K. E., ed.*, 1988, pp. 177–88.

Muller, Eitan and Peles, Yoram C. The Dynamic Adjustment of Optimal Durability and Quality. *Int. J. Ind. Organ.*, December 1988, *6*(4), pp. 499–507.

Muller, Frederik. Flexible Coefficients for Interregional Input–Output Models. *Ricerche Econ.*, April–June 1988, *42*(2), pp. 257–72.

Müller-Graff, Peter-Christian. Franchising: A Case of Long-term Contracts. *J. Inst. Theoretical Econ.*, February 1988, *144*(1), pp. 122–44.

Müller, Heinz H. and Blanco, José Antonio. Put-Optionen als Instrumente der Portfolioinsurance: Investitionsstrategien für institutionelle Anleger? (Puts as Instruments of Portfolio Insurance: Investment Strategies for Institutional Investors? With English summary.) *Schweiz. Z. Volkswirtsch. Statist.*, September 1988, *124*(3), pp. 391–404.

Müller, Jürgen. Telecommunications in Belgium. In *Foreman-Peck, J. and Müller, J., eds.*, 1988, pp. 87–107.

———— **and Foreman-Peck, James.** The Changing European Telecommunications Systems. In *Foreman-Peck, J. and Müller, J., eds.*, 1988, pp. 23–51.

———— **and Haid, Alfred.** Telecommunications in the Federal Republic of Germany. In *Foreman-Peck, J. and Müller, J., eds.*, 1988, pp. 155–80.

Müller, Klause and Hinterberger, Friedrich. Verteilungswirkungen der Einkommensteuertarifreform 1990. (The Reform of the Income Scale in 1990: Distributive Effects. With English summary.) *Z. Wirtschaft. Sozialwissen.*, 1988, *108*(3), pp. 355–69.

Müller, Paul and Rothengatter, Werner. Measuring the Relevance of Natural Resources for

Production. *Jahr. Nationalökon. Statist.*, February 1988, *204*(2), pp. 99–119.

Muller, R. Andrew. Some Economics of the GRAND Canal. *Can. Public Policy*, June 1988, *14*(2), pp. 162–74.

Müller, Urs. Der Einfluss von Kreditrationierung auf das Investitionsvolumen. (The Impact of Credit Rationing on Investment Activities. With English summary.) *Schweiz. Z. Volkswirtsch. Statist.*, September 1988, *124*(3), pp. 421–30.

_____; **Sheldon, George and Kugler, Peter.** Struktur der Arbeitsnachfrage im technologischen Wandel—Eine empirische Analyse für die Bundesrepublik Deutschland. (With English summary.) *Weltwirtsch. Arch.*, 1988, *124*(3), pp. 490–500.

Muller, Walter J., III and Woodford, Michael. Determinacy of Equilibrium in Stationary Economies with Both Finite and Infinite Lived Consumers. *J. Econ. Theory*, December 1988, *46*(2), pp. 255–90.

Mullick, M. A. Hussein. Is Foreign Aid an Obstruction to Democracy and Development in the Third World? *Pakistan Devel. Rev.*, Part 2, Winter 1988, *27*(4), pp. 529–32.

Mulligan, James G. and Coates, Daniel E. Scale Economies and Capacity Utilization: The Importance of Relative Fuel Prices. *Energy Econ.*, April 1988, *10*(2), pp. 140–46.

Mullineaux, Donald J. Competitive Monies and the Suffolk Bank System: Reply. *Southern Econ. J.*, July 1988, *55*(1), pp. 220–23.

Mullins, D. and Wang, T.-F. A Model of Income Distribution, Employment, and Growth for South Africa: A Semi-closed Input–Output Approach. *J. Stud. Econ. Econometrics*, November 1988, *12*(3), pp. 11–30.

Mullins, Daniel; Bretschneider, Stuart and Straussman, Jeffrey D. Do Revenue Forecasts Influence Budget Setting? A Small Group Experiment. *Policy Sci.*, 1988, *21*(4), pp. 305–25.

Mullis, David and Kohers, Theodor. An Update on Economies of Scale in Credit Unions. *Appl. Econ.*, December 1988, *20*(12), pp. 1653–59.

Mullner, Ross M.; Young, Gaylen W. and Andersen, Ronald M. Health Care Coalitions: Continuity and Change. In *Scheffler, R. M. and Rossiter, L. F., eds.*, 1988, pp. 165–85.

Mullor-Sebastian, Alicia. A New Approach to the Relationship between Export Instability and Economic Development. *Econ. Develop. Cult. Change*, January 1988, *36*(2), pp. 217–36.

Mulvey, J. M.; Wolpert, J. and Gregg, S. R. A Stochastic Planning System for Siting and Closing Public Service Facilities. *Environ. Planning A*, January 1988, *20*(1), pp. 83–98.

Mumbengegwi, Clever. The Political Economy of Agricultural Producer Cooperative Development in Post-independence Zimbabwe. In *Hedlund, H., ed.*, 1988, pp. 153–72.

Mumtaz, Soofia. Economic Development and Traditional Social Structures: Some Theoretical Considerations. *Pakistan Devel. Rev.*, Part 2, Winter 1988, *27*(4), pp. 501–07.

Mun, Kin-chok. Chinese Retailing in a Changing Environment. In *Kaynak, E., ed.*, 1988, pp. 211–26.

Munarriz, Mayu T. Socioeconomic Changes in Tondo Foreshore: An Evaluation of a Slum Upgrading Project. *Philippine Rev. Econ. Bus.*, Sept.–Dec. 1988, *25*(3–4), pp. 255–70.

Munasinghe, Mohan. The Economics of Rural Electrification Projects. *Energy Econ.*, January 1988, *10*(1), pp. 3–17.

_____. Energy Economics in Developing Countries: Analytical Framework and Problems of Application. *Energy J.*, January 1988, *9*(1), pp. 1–17.

_____. Optimal Planning, Supply Quality and Shortage Costs in Power Systems: Case of Costa Rica. *Energy J.*, Special Issue, 1988, *9*, pp. 43–75.

_____. Rural Electrification: International Experience and Policy in Indonesia. *Bull. Indonesian Econ. Stud.*, August 1988, *24*(2), pp. 87–106.

_____ **and Sanghvi, A.** Reliability of Electricity Supply, Outage Costs and Value of Service: An Overview. *Energy J.*, Special Issue, 1988, *9*, pp. 1–18.

Munasirei, David K. Methodology for the Assessment of Land-Use in Zimbabwe. In *Hosier, R. H., ed. (I)*, 1988, pp. 60–82.

_____. Woodfuel Harvesting and Soil Erosion in Zimbabwe. In *Hosier, R. H., ed. (I)*, 1988, pp. 185–98.

Munch, James M. and Swasy, John L. Rhetorical Question, Summarization Frequency, and Argument Strength Effects on Recall. *J. Cons. Res.*, June 1988, *15*(1), pp. 69–76.

Munden, Ted. Nuclear Fuel. *Energy J.*, October 1988, *9*(4), pp. 131–34.

Mundheim, Robert H. One Share, One Vote: Comment. In *Coffee, J. C., Jr.; Lowenstein, L. and Rose-Ackerman, S., eds.*, 1988, pp. 521–23.

Mundlak, Yair. Capital Accumulation, the Choice of Techniques, and Agricultural Output. In *Mellor, J. W. and Ahmed, R., eds.*, 1988, pp. 171–89.

Munera, Hector A. A Large Scale Empirical Test for the Linearizied Moments Model (LMM): Compatibility between Theory and Observation. In *Munier, B. R., ed.*, 1988, pp. 291–311.

Mung, Malcolm. A System Wide Approach to Forecast the Demand for Business Toll Services. *Int. J. Forecasting*, 1988, *4*(4), pp. 535–44.

Munger, Michael C. On the Political Participation of the Firm in the Electoral Process: An Update. *Public Choice*, March 1988, *56*(3), pp. 295–98.

Munier, Bertrand R. A Guide to Decision-Making under Uncertainty. In *Munier, B. R., ed.*, 1988, pp. 1–34.

Münich, Hans. Consequences of Self-Help Promotion for Cooperative Development Policy in Africa. In *Hedlund, H., ed.*, 1988, pp. 187–205.

Munkirs, John R. The Dichotomy: Views of a

Fifth Generation Institutionalist. *J. Econ. Issues,* December 1988, 22(4), pp. 1035–44.

_____. Economic Power: History and Institutions. In *Peterson, W. C., ed.,* 1988, pp. 27–52.

_____. The Existence and Exercise of Corporate Power: An Opaque Fact. In *Tool, M. R., ed., Vol. 2,* 1988, *1987,* pp. 261–88.

_____. Technological Change: Disaggregation and Overseas Production. *J. Econ. Issues,* June 1988, 22(2), pp. 469–75.

_____ and Knoedler, Janet T. Petroleum Producing and Consuming Countries: A Coalescence of Interests. *J. Econ. Issues,* March 1988, 22(1), pp. 17–31.

Munn, Charles W. Aspects of Bank Finance for Industry: Scotland 1845–1914. In *Mitchison, R. and Roebuck, P., eds.,* 1988, pp. 233–41.

Munnell, Alicia H. Personal Security Accounts: A Proposal for Fundamental Social Security Reform: Comment. In *Wachter, S. M., ed.,* 1988, pp. 207–08.

_____. Public versus Private Provision of Retirement Income. *New Eng. Econ. Rev.,* May–June 1988, pp. 51–58.

_____. Savings Incentives in a Hybrid Income Tax: Comments. In *Aaron, H. J.; Galper, H. and Pechman, J. A., eds.,* 1988, pp. 309–15.

_____. Wealth Transfer Taxation: The Relative Role for Estate and Income Taxes. *New Eng. Econ. Rev.,* Nov.–Dec. 1988, pp. 3–28.

Münnich, Frank E. Reforming Hospital Finance in West Germany: Propositions and Obstacles. In *Furubotn, E. G. and Richter, R., eds.,* 1988, pp. 51–69.

Muñoz-Gracia, M. Pilar; Pages-Fita, J. and Marti-Recober, M. Estimation of ARMA Process Parameters and Noise Variance by Means of a Non Linear Filtering Algorithm. In *Edwards, D. and Raun, N. E., eds.,* 1988, pp. 357–62.

Muñoz, Oscar. El Estado y los empresarios: experiencias comparadas y sus implicancias para Chile. (The State and Private Enterprise: A Comparison of Different Experiences and Their Implications for Chile. With English summary.) *Colección Estud. CIEPLAN,* December 1988, (25), pp. 5–53.

_____ and Ffrench-Davis, Ricardo. El desarrollo económico de América Latina y el marco internacional: 1950–86. (Economic Development in Latin America and the International Framework: 1950–1986. With English summary.) *Colección Estud. CIEPLAN,* March 1988, (23), pp. 13–33.

Munro, John H. Deflation and the Petty Coinage Problem in the Late-Medieval Economy: The Case of Flanders, 1334–1484. *Exploration Econ. Hist.,* October 1988, 25(4), pp. 387–423.

Munro, Katherine. Monetary Policy, Commercial Banking and the Political Imperative, 1965–85. In *Jones, S., ed.,* 1988, pp. 113–32.

Munz, Martin and Rabino, Giovanni. Interregional Migration in Individual Countries: Italy. In *Weidlich, W. and Haag, G., eds.,* 1988, pp. 185–221.

_____ and Reiner, Rolf. A Computer Program for the Estimation of Utilities and Mobilities. In *Weidlich, W. and Haag, G., eds.,* 1988, pp. 365–81.

_____ and Reiner, Rolf. Ranking Regression Analysis of the Global Mobility. In *Weidlich, W. and Haag, G., eds.,* 1988, pp. 355–64.

_____; Reiner, Rolf and Haag, Günter. The Estimation of Parameters. In *Weidlich, W. and Haag, G., eds.,* 1988, pp. 33–59.

_____; Reiner, Rolf and Haag, Günter. Tests of Significance in the Ranking Regression Analysis. In *Weidlich, W. and Haag, G., eds.,* 1988, pp. 345–54.

Muramatsu, Michio and Krauss, Ellis S. Japanese Political Economy Today: The Patterned Pluralist Model. In *Okimoto, D. I. and Rohlen, T. P., eds.,* 1988, pp. 208–10.

Muramatsu, Yasuyuki; Goto, Yoshito and Fujii, Nobuo. Second Order Necessary Optimality Conditions for Domain Optimization Problem with a Neumann Problem. In *Iri, M. and Yajima, K., eds.,* 1988, pp. 259–68.

Muraro, Gilberto. Les objectifs dans l'evaluation des investissements publics. (Objectives in the Evaluation of Public Investment. With English summary.) *Ann. Pub. Coop. Econ.,* March 1988, 59(1), pp. 23–42.

Murata, Minoru. The Flexibility of Labor Market in Japan. In *Dlugos, G.; Dorow, W. and Weiermair, K., eds.,* 1988, pp. 289–97.

Murdoch, James C. and Thayer, Mark A. Hedonic Price Estimation of Variable Urban Air Quality. *J. Environ. Econ. Manage.,* June 1988, 15(2), pp. 143–46.

Murdock, Diane and Steinwald, Bruce. Payments for Outliers under Medicare's Prospective Payment System: Editorial. *J. Health Econ.,* September 1988, 7(3), pp. 291–96.

Murdock, Steve H. and Albrecht, Don E. The Effects of the Farm Crisis on Rural Communities and Community Residents. In *Beaulieu, L. J., ed.,* 1988, pp. 198–210.

_____ and Albrecht, Don E. The Structural Characteristics of U.S. Agriculture: Historical Patterns and Precursors of Producers' Adaptations to the Crisis. In *Murdock, S. H. and Leistritz, F. L., eds.,* 1988, pp. 29–44.

_____ and Hwang, Sean-Shong. Population Size and Residential Segregation: An Empirical Evaluation of Two Perspectives. *Soc. Sci. Quart.,* December 1988, 69(4), pp. 818–34.

_____ and Leistritz, F. Larry. The Farm Financial Crisis: Socioeconomic Dimensions and Implications for Producers and Rural Areas: Introduction. In *Murdock, S. H. and Leistritz, F. L., eds.,* 1988, pp. 1–9.

_____ and Leistritz, F. Larry. Financial Characteristics of Farms and of Farm Financial Markets and Policies in the United States. In *Murdock, S. H. and Leistritz, F. L., eds.,* 1988, pp. 13–28.

_____ and Leistritz, F. Larry. Financing Infrastructure in Rapid Growth Communities: The North Dakota Experience. In *Johnson, T. G.;*

Deaton, B. J. and Segarra, E., eds., 1988, pp. 141–54.

_____ **and Leistritz, F. Larry.** Policy Alternatives and Research Agenda. In *Murdock, S. H. and Leistritz, F. L., eds.*, 1988, pp. 169–84.

_____; **Leistritz, F. Larry and Jones, Lonnie L.** Economic-Demographic Projection Models: An Overview of Recent Developments for Infrastructure Analysis. In *Johnson, T. G.; Deaton, B. J. and Segarra, E., eds.*, 1988, pp. 87–97.

_____, **et al.** Demographic Characteristics of Rural Residents in Financial Distress and Social and Community Impacts of the Farm Crisis. In *Murdock, S. H. and Leistritz, F. L., eds.*, 1988, pp. 113–40.

_____, **et al.** Demographic, Socioeconomic and Service Characteristics of Rural Areas in the United States: The Human Resources Base for the Response to the Crisis. In *Murdock, S. H. and Leistritz, F. L., eds.*, 1988, pp. 45–69.

_____, **et al.** The Implications of the Current Farm Crisis for Rural America. In *Murdock, S. H. and Leistritz, F. L., eds.*, 1988, pp. 141–68.

Mureithi, Leopold P. Development Planning in Kenya. In *Urrutia, M. and Yukawa, S., eds. (I)*, 1988, pp. 198–226.

Murie, Alan and Forrest, Ray. The New Homeless in Britain. In *Friedrichs, J., ed.*, 1988, pp. 129–45.

Murillo, Gabriel and Cartier, William. Urbanization, the Informal Sector and Migration: Issues for Research and Cooperation. *Can. J. Devel. Stud.*, 1988, 9(1), pp. 7–17.

Murillo, Juan A. Modern Bridge Construction and Engineering Services. In *Guile, B. R. and Quinn, J. B., eds. (I)*, 1988, pp. 165–74.

Murnane, Richard J. Education and the Productivity of the Work Force: Looking Ahead. In *Litan, R. E; Lawrence, R. Z. and Schultze, C. L., eds.*, 1988, pp. 215–45.

_____. On Estimating the Effects of Increased Aid to Education: Comment. In *Freeman, R. B. and Ichniowski, C., eds.*, 1988, pp. 263–69.

Murnighan, J. Keith and King, Thomas R. Stability and Outcome Tradeoffs in Asymmetric Dilemmas: Conditions Promoting the Discovery of Alternating Solutions. In *Tietz, R.; Albers, W. and Selten, R., eds.*, 1988, pp. 85–94.

_____; **Roth, Alvin E. and Schoumaker, Francoise.** Risk Aversion in Bargaining: An Experimental Study. *J. Risk Uncertainty*, March 1988, 1(1), pp. 101–24.

_____; **Schoumaker, Francoise and Roth, Alvin E.** The Deadline Effect in Bargaining: Some Experimental Evidence. *Amer. Econ. Rev.*, September 1988, 78(4), pp. 806–23.

Murota, Takeshi. Demand and Supply Values of Information. *Info. Econ. Policy*, 1988, 3(1), pp. 25–34.

Muroyama, Janet H. and Stever, H. Guyford. Globalization of Technology: International Perspectives: Overview. In *Muroyama, J. H. and Stever, H. G., eds.*, 1988, pp. 1–11.

Murphree, Emily S. and Koehler, Anne B. A Comparison of Results from State Space Forecasting with Forecasts from the Makridakis Competition. *Int. J. Forecasting*, 1988, 4(1), pp. 45–55.

Murphy, C. W. An Overview of the Murphy Model. *Australian Econ. Pap.*, Supplement, June 1988, 27, pp. 175–99.

_____. Rational Expectations in Financial Markets and the Murphy Model. *Australian Econ. Pap.*, Supplement, June 1988, 27, pp. 61–88.

Murphy, D. G. Zimbabwe: Foreign Shareholders' Liquidation Dividends. *Bull. Int. Fiscal Doc.*, June 1988, 42(6), pp. 255–58.

Murphy, Edward E. International Comparisons of Real Product and Public Policy. In *Salazar-Carrillo, J. and Rao, D. S. P., eds.*, 1988, pp. 289–93.

Murphy, Eithne. Comparative Advantage in Dairying: An Intra-national Study for Ireland. *Irish J. Agr. Econ. Rural Soc.*, 1988, 13, pp. 47–63.

Murphy, J. Carter. Reflections on the Exchange Rate System. In *Melamed, L., ed.*, 1988, 1985, pp. 71–80.

Murphy, John Austin. A Discounted Cash-Flow Model of Fixed-Income Securities Subject to Multiple Calls. *Southern Econ. J.*, July 1988, 55(1), pp. 21–36.

Murphy, Kevin J.; Baker, George P. and Jensen, Michael C. Compensation and Incentives: Practice vs. Theory. *J. Finance*, July 1988, 43(3), pp. 593–616.

Murphy, Kevin M. and Becker, Gary S. The Family and the State. *J. Law Econ.*, April 1988, 31(1), pp. 1–18.

_____ **and Becker, Gary S.** A Theory of Rational Addiction. *J. Polit. Econ.*, August 1988, 96(4), pp. 675–700.

_____ **and Klein, Benjamin.** Vertical Restraints as Contract Enforcement Mechanisms. *J. Law Econ.*, October 1988, 31(2), pp. 265–97.

_____; **Plant, Mark and Welch, Finis R.** Cohort Size and Earnings in the USA. In *Lee, R. D.; Arthur, W. B. and Rodgers, G., eds.*, 1988, pp. 39–58.

Murphy, M.; Sullivan, O. and Brown, A. Sources of Data for Modelling Household Change with Special Reference to the OPCS 1% Longitudinal Study. In *Keilman, N.; Kuijsten, A. and Vossen, A., eds.*, 1988, pp. 56–66.

Murphy, Patrick E. How Can Marketing Research Contribute to the Consumer Interest? In *Maynes, E. S. and ACCI Research Committee, eds.*, 1988, pp. 659–64.

Murphy, Paul R., Jr. and Corsi, Thomas M. Strategic Differentiation among LTL General Freight Carriers: Sales Force Management Policies. *Logist. Transp. Rev.*, September 1988, 24(3), pp. 217–35.

Murphy, Robert G. Optimal Tax Policy for Balance of Payments Objectives: Comment. In *Frenkel, J. A., ed.*, 1988, pp. 344–47.

_____. Sector-Specific Capital and Real Exchange Rate Dynamics. *J. Econ. Dynam. Control*, March 1988, *12*(1), pp. 7–12.

Murray, Alan I. and Reshef, Yonatan. Toward a Neoinstitutionalist Approach in Industrial Relations. *Brit. J. Ind. Relat.*, March 1988, *26*(1), pp. 85–97.

Murray, Alan P. The Business Economist at Work: The Credit Division of Fuji Bank, Ltd. *Bus. Econ.*, January 1988, *23*(1), pp. 49–50.

Murray, Hugh. Management Education and the MBA: It's Time for a Rethink. *Managerial Dec. Econ.*, Special Issue, Winter 1988, pp. 71–78.

Murray, Jane; Weiss, Andrew A. and Bartels, Robert. The Role of Consumer and Business Sentiment in Forecasting Telecommunications Traffic. *J. Econ. Psych.*, June 1988, *9*(2), pp. 215–32.

Murray, Kenneth J. Complying with the R&D Rules. In *Canadian Tax Foundation*, 1988, pp. 6.1–17.

Murray, Matthew and Fox, William F. Economic Aspects of Taxing Services. *Nat. Tax J.*, March 1988, *41*(1), pp. 19–36.

Murray, Patrick. Karl Marx as a Historical Materialist Historian of Political Economy. *Hist. Polit. Econ.*, Spring 1988, *20*(1), pp. 95–105.

Murray, Robin. Pension Funds and Local Authority Investments. In *Harris, L., et al., eds.*, 1988, pp. 306–24.

Murrell, David and Rector, Andrew. Dualism in the Maritime Provinces: 1961–1981 A Social Indicator Approach. In *Choudhury, M. A., ed.*, 1988, pp. 97–115.

Murrell, Peter and Magenheim, Ellen B. How to Haggle and to Stay Firm: Barter as Hidden Price Discrimination. *Econ. Inquiry*, July 1988, *26*(3), pp. 449–59.

Murtagh, F. and Adorf, H.-M. Clustering Based on Neural Network Processing. In *Edwards, D. and Raun, N. E., eds.*, 1988, pp. 239–44.

Murthy, K. S. R. and Harvey, Edward B. Forecasting Manpower Demand and Supply: A Model for the Accounting Profession in Canada. *Int. J. Forecasting*, 1988, *4*(4), pp. 551–62.

Murthy, Radha. Determination of the Spot Exchange Rate: Japanese Yen per US Dollar: Comments. In *Pennsylvania Economic Association*, 1988, pp. 387.

_____. Oil Price Shocks and the Exchange Rate. In *Pennsylvania Economic Association*, 1988, pp. 362–71.

Muscarella, Chris J. Price Performance of Initial Public Offerings of Master Limited Partnership Units. *Financial Rev.*, November 1988, *23*(4), pp. 513–21.

Muscatelli, Anton; Vines, David and Currie, David. Macroeconomic Interactions between North and South: Introduction. In *Currie, D. and Vines, D., eds.*, 1988, pp. 1–31.

Muscatelli, Vito Antonio. Alternative Models of Buffer Stock Money: An Empirical Investigation. *Scot. J. Polit. Econ.*, February 1988, *35*(1), pp. 1–21.

_____. Policy Rules, Feedback Effects and Ex-

change Rate Dynamics. *Econ. Notes*, 1988, (3), pp. 96–111.

_____. The Specification of Asset Demands in Portfolio Models of the Exchange Rate. *Econ. Notes*, 1988, (1), pp. 135–42.

Musella, Marco. La curva di Phillips derivata da un modello kaleckiano. (With English summary.) *Stud. Econ.*, 1988, *43*(35), pp. 105–28.

Musgrave, John C. Fixed Reproducible Tangible Wealth in the United States, 1984–87. *Surv. Curr. Bus.*, August 1988, *68*(8), pp. 84–87.

Musgrave, Peggy B. Foreign Reactions to U.S. Tax Reform: Comments in Session [International Tax Competition: The Foreign Government Response in Canada and Other Countries]. *Nat. Tax J.*, September 1988, *41*(3), pp. 365–66.

Musgrave, Richard A. Fiscal Pressure on the "Tax State": Discussion. In *Hanusch, H., ed.*, 1988, pp. 273–78.

_____. Indexing the Tax System for Inflation: Comments. In *Aaron, H. J.; Galper, H. and Pechman, J. A., eds.*, 1988, pp. 376–80.

_____. Public Debt and Intergeneration Equity. In *Arrow, K. J. and Boskin, M. J., eds.*, 1988, pp. 133–46.

_____. U.S. Fiscal Policy, Keynes, and Keynesian Economics. *J. Post Keynesian Econ.*, Winter 1987–88, *10*(2), pp. 171–82.

_____ **and Miller, Merton H.** Built-In Flexibility. In *Shaw, G. K., ed., Vol. 2*, 1988, *1948*, pp. 283–89.

Musgrave, Simon and Stern, Nicholas. Alcohol: Demand and Taxation under Monopoly and Oligopoly in South India in the 1970s. *J. Devel. Econ.*, February 1988, *28*(1), pp. 1–41.

Musgrave, Warren F. Structural Change and Adjustment in the Australian Rural Sector: The Socio-economic Consequences of Being a Low-Cost Residual Supplier. In *Tisdell, C. and Maitra, P., eds.*, 1988, pp. 135–65.

_____ **and Dudley, Norman J.** Capacity Sharing of Water Reservoirs. *Water Resources Res.*, May 1988, *24*(5), pp. 649–58.

Musgrove, Philip and Galindo, Osmil. Do the Poor Pay More? Retail Food Prices in Northeast Brazil. *Econ. Develop. Cult. Change*, October 1988, *37*(1), pp. 91–109.

Mushkatel, Alvin H. and Weschler, Louis. Privatism in Local Land Use Development: The Use of Exactions, Impact Fees and Impact Taxes by Municipalities. In *Hula, R. C., ed.*, 1988, pp. 121–33.

Mushtaq, Mohammad; Ghani, Ejaz and Malik, Sohail J. Consumption Patterns of Major Food Items in Pakistan: Provincial, Sectoral and Inter-temporal Differences 1979–1984-85. *Pakistan Devel. Rev.*, Part 2, Winter 1988, *27*(4), pp. 751–59.

Mushtaq, Muhammad; Qureshi, Sarfraz Khan and Ghani, Ejaz. Taxes and Subsidies on Agricultural Producers as Elements of Intersectoral Transfer of Resources: Magnitude of the Transfer and Search for Policy Options. *Pakistan Devel. Rev.*, Part 2, Winter 1988, *27*(4), pp. 551–56.

Musquar, Philippe; Bellis, Jean-François and Vermulst, Edwin. The New EEC Regulation on Unfair Pricing Practices in Maritime Transport: A Forerunner of the Extension of Unfair Trade Concepts to Services? *J. World Trade*, February 1988, *22*(1), pp. 47–65.

Mussa, Michael L. The International Transmission of Asset Price Volatility: Commentary. In *Federal Reserve Bank of Kansas City*, 1988, pp. 127–32.

——. The Role of Official Intervention. In *Melamed, L., ed.*, 1988, *1981*, pp. 331–59.

—— **and Dornbusch, Rudiger.** Consumption, Real Balances, and the Hoarding Function. In *Dornbusch, R.*, 1988, *1975*, pp. 371–78.

Musser, Wesley N.; McClelland, John W. and Wetzstein, Michael E. Returns to Scale and Size in Agricultural Economics: Reply. *Western J. Agr. Econ.*, July 1988, *13*(1), pp. 151–52.

Mutén, Leif. A New International Tax Order? *Bull. Int. Fiscal Doc.*, November 1988, *42*(11), pp. 471–72.

——. World Tax Reform: A Progress Report: Sweden: Comment. In *Pechman, J. A., ed.*, 1988, pp. 211–17.

Muth, John F. Rational Expectations and the Theory of Price Movements. In *Ricketts, M., ed.*, Vol. 1, 1988, *1961*, pp. 186–206.

Muth, Richard F. Housing Market Dynamics. *Reg. Sci. Urban Econ.*, August 1988, *18*(3), pp. 345–56.

Mutlu, Servet. The Spatial Urban Hierarchy in Turkey: Its Structure and Some of Its Determinants. *Growth Change*, Summer 1988, *19*(3), pp. 53–74.

Muto, Shigeo, et al. On Big Boss Games. *Econ. Stud. Quart.*, December 1988, *39*(4), pp. 303–21.

Mutti, John. U.S. and Swedish Direct Investment and Exports: Comment. In *Baldwin, R. E., ed. (II)*, 1988, pp. 300–302.

—— **and Grubert, Harry.** U.S. Taxes and Trade Performance. *Nat. Tax J.*, September 1988, *41*(3), pp. 317–25.

Muus, Lars and Domowitz, Ian. Likelihood Inference in the Nonlinear Regression Model with Explosive Linear Dynamics. In *Barnett, W. A.; Berndt, E. R. and White, H., eds.*, 1988, pp. 53–72.

Muzyka, Daniel F. The Management of Failure: A Key to Organizational Entrepreneurship. In *Kirchhoff, B. A., et al., eds.*, 1988, pp. 501–17.

Mwanyimi-Mbomba, Mandjumba. L'agriculture africaine dans la zone de Kalemie (territoire d'Albertville) de 1933 à 1952. (With English summary.) *Can. J. Devel. Stud.*, 1988, *9*(2), pp. 219–33.

Mwase, Ngila R. L. Road Haulage Pricing in Developing Countries: The Tanzanian Experience. *Eastern Afr. Econ. Rev.*, December 1988, *4*(2), pp. 32–39.

——. Road Transport Pricing in Developing Countries: The Tanzanian Case. *Int. J. Transport Econ.*, October 1988, *15*(3), pp. 329–43.

Mwau, Geoffrey; Begumisa, Gregory and Coughlin, Peter. Tied Aid, Industrial Dependence and New Tactics for Negotiations: Observations from Kenya. In *Coughlin, P. and Ikiara, G. K., eds.*, 1988, pp. 126–42.

Mwega, F. M. Short-run Shifting of Manufacturers' Sales Taxes in Kenya: Revisited. *Eastern Afr. Econ. Rev.*, June 1988, *4*(1), pp. 42–47.

Myers, Lester H. Quantitative Techniques: A Discussion. In *Hildreth, R. J., et al., eds.*, 1988, pp. 204–07.

Myers, Ramon H. Mainland China's March toward a New Socialism. In *Anderson, A. and Bark, D. L., eds.*, 1988, pp. 63–75.

——. Review Article: Land and Labor in China. *Econ. Develop. Cult. Change*, July 1988, *36*(4), pp. 797–806.

Myers, Robert J. Actuarial Aspects of Financing Old-Age and Survivors Insurance. *Soc. Sec. Bull.*, November 1988, *51*(11), pp. 18–26.

——. Actuarial Research and Analysis: Commentary. *Soc. Sec. Bull.*, November 1988, *51*(11), pp. 16–17.

——. The Value of Ideal Contingency Markets in Agriculture. *Amer. J. Agr. Econ.*, May 1988, *70*(2), pp. 255–67.

Myers, Samuel L., Jr. The Economics of Race and Crime: Introduction. In *Simms, M. C. and Myers, S. L., Jr., eds.*, 1988, pp. 5–15.

—— **and Sabol, William J.** Unemployment and Racial Differences in Imprisonment. In *Simms, M. C. and Myers, S. L., Jr., eds.*, 1988, pp. 189–209.

Myerson, Roger B. and Aumann, Robert J. Endogenous Formation of Links between Players and of Coalitions: An Application of the Shapley Value. In *[Shapley, L. S.]*, 1988, pp. 175–91.

Myles, Gareth D. Some Implications of Quality Differentials for Optimal Taxation. *Econ. J.*, Supplement, 1988, *98*(390), pp. 148–60.

Myrdal, Gunnar. Inequality of Justice. In *Simms, M. C. and Myers, S. L., Jr., eds.*, 1988, pp. 81–98.

Mytelka, Lynn Krieger and Delapierre, Michel. The Alliance Strategies of European Firms in the Information Technology Industry and the Role of ESPRIT. In *Dunning, J. and Robson, P., eds.*, 1988, pp. 129–51.

—— **and Delapierre, Michel.** Décomposition, recomposition des oligopoles. (Decomposition, Recomposition of Oligopolies. With English summary.) *Écon. Soc.*, Nov.–Dec. 1988, *22*(11–12), pp. 57–83.

Nachane, Dilip M.; Nadkarni, Ramesh M. and Karnik, Ajit V. Co-integration and Causality Testing of the Energy–GDP Relationship: A Cross-country Study. *Appl. Econ.*, November 1988, *20*(11), pp. 1511–31.

—— **and Rao, M. J. Manohar.** Varying Parameter Models: An Optimal Control Formulation. *J. Quant. Econ.*, January 1988, *4*(1), pp. 59–79.

Nachman, David C. Stochastic Equilibria. *J. Math. Econ.*, 1988, *17*(1), pp. 69–75.

Naciri, M. Ahmed and Bloom, Robert. An Analysis of the Accounting Standard-Setting Framework in Two European Countries: France and the Netherlands. In *Most, K. S., ed.*, 1988, pp. 69–85.

Nadeau, Serge. A Model to Measure the Effects of Taxes on the Real and Financial Decisions of the Firm. *Nat. Tax J.*, December 1988, 41(4), pp. 467–81.

Nadiri, M. Ishaq and Bernstein, Jeffrey I. Interindustry R&D Spillovers, Rates of Return, and Production in High-Tech Industries. *Amer. Econ. Rev.*, May 1988, 78(2), pp. 429–34.

_____ **and Prucha, Ingmar R.** On the Computation of Estimators in Systems with Implicitly Defined Variables. *Econ. Letters*, 1988, 26(2), pp. 141–45.

Nadkarni, Ramesh M.; Karnik, Ajit V. and Nachane, Dilip M. Co-integration and Causality Testing of the Energy–GDP Relationship: A Cross-country Study. *Appl. Econ.*, November 1988, 20(11), pp. 1511–31.

Naegelen, Florence. L'enchère optimale dans l'hypothèse de dépendance des évaluations: Une caractérisation. (Optimal Auction with Dependent Values: A Characterization. With English summary.) *Ann. Écon. Statist.*, April–June 1988, (10), pp. 23–43.

_____ **and Mougeot, Michel.** Analyse micro-économique du Code des marchés publics. (The French Public Procurement Code: A Theoretical Analysis. With English summary.) *Revue Écon.*, July 1988, 39(4), pp. 725–52.

Naert, Philippe and Bultez, Alain. SH.A.R.P.: SHelf Allocation for Retailers' Profit. *Marketing Sci.*, Summer 1988, 7(3), pp. 211–31.

Naeve, Peter and Westerhoff, Thomas. On Inference Process. In *Edwards, D. and Raun, N. E., eds.*, 1988, pp. 193–98.

Nagano, Atsushi. World Tax Reform: A Progress Report: Japan. In *Pechman, J. A., ed.*, 1988, pp. 155–62.

Nagano, Yoshiko. The Oligopolistic Structure of the Philippine Sugar Industry during the Great Depression. In *Albert, B. and Graves, A., eds.*, 1988, pp. 170–81.

Nagaraj, Shyamala and Lee, Kiong-Hock. Earnings and the Principal Components of Job Performance. *Econ. Letters*, 1988, 26(1), pp. 95–97.

Nagarajan, P. Kenya's Fiscal Stance in the Course of Development, 1965–83. *Bull. Int. Fiscal Doc.*, January 1988, 42(1), pp. 23–30.

Nagel, Julie Jaffee. Identity and Career Choice in Music. *J. Cult. Econ.*, December 1988, 12(2), pp. 67–76.

Nagel, Stuart S. The New Productivity. In *Kelly, R. M., ed.*, 1988, pp. 231–46.

Naggar, Tahany. The Role of International Trade. In *Pennsylvania Economic Association*, 1988, pp. 331–45.

Naggl, Walter. Use of Anticipations Data in the Anticipations Model. In *Motamen, H., ed.*, 1988, pp. 165–82.

Nagle, Thomas T. and Novak, Kenneth. The Roles of Segmentation and Awareness in Explaining Variations in Price Markups. In *Devinney, T. M., ed.*, 1988, pp. 313–32.

Nagurney, Anna. Algorithms for Oligopolistic Market Equilibrium Problems. *Reg. Sci. Urban Econ.*, August 1988, 18(3), pp. 425–45.

Nagy, András. Why Does It Not Work? *Acta Oecon.*, 1988, 39(1–2), pp. 23–44.

Nahmijas, Alberto and Pera, Alberto. Capital Market Efficiency and Newly Issued Common Stocks: An Analytical Study of Italian Data (1983–1986). *Rev. Econ. Cond. Italy*, Jan.–April 1988, (1), pp. 49–74.

Naik, Gopal and Leuthold, Raymond M. Cash and Futures Price Relationships for Nonstorable Commodities: An Empirical Analysis Using a General Theory. *Western J. Agr. Econ.*, December 1988, 13(2), pp. 327–38.

Nair, D. P. Operational Efficiency of Public Utilities—Need for Professionalism and Accountability: A Case Study of Public Sector Road Transport in Kerala. *Indian Econ. J.*, Jan.–March 1988, 35(3), pp. 86–94.

Nairn, Alasdair G. M. and O'Neill, Gerard J. Population Density Functions: A Differential Equation Approach. *J. Reg. Sci.*, February 1988, 28(1), pp. 89–102.

_____ **; Parr, John B. and O'Neill, Gerard J.** Metropolitan Density Functions: A Further Exploration. *Reg. Sci. Urban Econ.*, November 1988, 18(4), pp. 463–78.

Naisbitt, Barry; Driver, Ciaran and Kilpatrick, Andrew. The Sensitivity of Estimated Employment Effects in Input–Output Studies. *Econ. Modelling*, April 1988, 5(2), pp. 145–50.

_____ **and Forrest, David.** The Sensitivity of Regional Unemployment Rates to the National Trade Cycle. *Reg. Stud.*, April 1988, 22(2), pp. 149–53.

_____ **and Kilpatrick, Andrew.** Energy Intensity, Industrial Structure and the 1970s' Productivity Slowdown. *Oxford Bull. Econ. Statist.*, August 1988, 50(3), pp. 229–41.

Naish, Howard F. Imperfect Competition, Price Adjustment Costs, and the Long-run Phillips Curve. *J. Macroecon.*, Winter 1988, 10(1), pp. 103–24.

_____. Optimal Union Wage Setting Behaviour and the Non-neutrality of Anticipated Monetary Changes. *Oxford Econ. Pap.*, June 1988, 40(2), pp. 346–64.

_____. The Optimality of Partial Price Adjustment Policies. *Econ. Inquiry*, October 1988, 26(4), pp. 741–66.

Naito, Masahisa. Japanese Petroleum Policy. In *Mabro, R., ed.*, 1988, pp. 225–34.

Najafizadeh, Mehrangiz and Mennerick, Lewis A. Worldwide Educational Expansion from 1950 to 1980: The Failure of the Expansion of Schooling in Developing Countries. *J. Devel. Areas*, April 1988, 22(3), pp. 333–57.

Najita, Tetsuo and Harootunian, H. D. Japanese Revolt against the West: Political and Cultural Criticism in the Twentieth Century. In *Duus, P., ed.*, 1988, pp. 711–74.

Nakakita, Tōru. The Globalization of Japanese Firms and Its Influence on Japan's Trade with Developing Countries. *Devel. Econ.*, December 1988, 26(4), pp. 306–22.

Nakamori, Seiichi and Tokumaru, Hidekatsu. Identification of Linear Discrete-Time Stochastic System Using Covariance Information. In *Iri, M. and Yajima, K., eds.*, 1988, pp. 109–18.

Nakamori, Y. Development of a Computer System for Model Selection. In *Fedorov, V. and Lauter, H., eds.*, 1988, pp. 195–204.

Nakamura, Shinichiro. Testing Integrability Conditions in a Dynamic Framework. In *Eichhorn, W., ed.*, 1988, pp. 793–807.

Nakamura, Takafusa. The Cambridge History of Japan: Volume 6: The Twentieth Century: Depression, Recovery, and War, 1920–1945. In *Duus, P., ed.*, 1988, pp. 451–93.

Nakatani, Iwao. Curing Trade Imbalance by International Tax Coordination. In *Shoven, J. B., ed.*, 1988, pp. 173–94.

Nakatani, Takeshi. Aggregate Demand Policy in the Open Macro Economy. *Kobe Univ. Econ.*, 1988, (34), pp. 25–40.

Nakhaeizadeh, Gholamreza and Karmann, Alexander. Erwartungsbildung und aggregierter Konsum-Einkommen-Prozess. Eine klassische und Bayessche Analyse für die Bundesrepublik Deutschland. (Expectations Building and the Aggregate Consumption: A Classical. With English summary.) *Jahr. Nationalökon. Statist.*, February 1988, 204(2), pp. 120–39.

Nakicenovic, Nebojsa. Dynamics and Replacement of U.S. Transport Infrastructures. In *Ausubel, J. H. and Herman, R., eds.*, 1988, pp. 175–221.

Nakosteen, Robert A. and Zimmer, Michael A. Mobility of Labor between Employers and Industries. In *Missouri Valley Economic Assoc.*, 1988, pp. 155–67.

Nalebuff, Barry J. Blockades, Carrier Missions, Secret Intelligence, and More. *J. Econ. Perspectives*, Fall 1988, 2(4), pp. 181–89.

_____. Minimal Nuclear Deterrence. *J. Conflict Resolution*, September 1988, 32(3), pp. 411–25.

_____. Puzzles: Penny Stocks, Discount Brokers, Better Bidding, and More. *J. Econ. Perspectives*, Winter 1988, 2(1), pp. 179–85.

_____ and Caplin, Andrew S. On 64%–Majority Rule. *Econometrica*, July 1988, 56(4), pp. 787–814.

Nallari, Raj. Bifurcations and Chaos with Applications in Economics. *J. Quant. Econ.*, July 1988, 4(2), pp. 185–200.

_____ and Gulhati, Ravi. Reform of Foreign Aid Policies: The Issue of Inter-country Allocation in Africa. *World Devel.*, October 1988, 16(10), pp. 1167–84.

Nam, Chong Hyun and Greenaway, David. Industrialisation and Macroeconomic Performance in Developing Countries under Alternative Trade Strategies. *Kyklos*, 1988, 41(3), pp. 419–35.

Nam, Sang-Woo. Alternative Growth and Adjustment Strategies of Newly Industrializing Countries in Southeast Asia. In *Streeten, P., ed.*, 1988, pp. 68–94.

_____ and Corbo, Vittorio. Korea's Macroeconomic Prospects and Policy Issues for the Next Decade. *World Devel.*, January 1988, 16(1), pp. 35–45.

Namboodiri, K. S. and Ray, D. Granger's Causality—An Indian Experience. *J. Quant. Econ.*, July 1988, 4(2), pp. 279–91.

Nancy, Gilles; Fuguet, Jean-Luc and Lai Tong, Hew Wah. Mobilité imparfaite des capitaux et dynamique des cours de change. Le cas du SME. (Imperfect Capital Mobility and Exchange Rates Dynamics: The EMS Case. With English summary.) *Revue Écon.*, September 1988, 39(5), pp. 921–50.

Nandakumar, Parameswar. Oil Price Increases and the Structure of Small Open Economies. *Weltwirtsch. Arch.*, 1988, 124(4), pp. 653–66.

_____. Public Sector Expansion in a Mixed Open Economy with a Real Wage Restriction. *Econ. Letters*, 1988, 28(2), pp. 189–92.

Nankervis, J. C. and Savin, N. E. The Exact Moments of the Least-Squares Estimator for the Autoregressive Model. *J. Econometrics*, March 1988, 37(3), pp. 381–88.

_____ and Savin, N. E. The Student's t Approximation in a Stationary First Order Autoregressive Model. *Econometrica*, January 1988, 56(1), pp. 119–45.

Naor, Jacob. Innovative Retailing in Hungary—A Case Study in Innovation. In *Kaynak, E., ed.*, 1988, pp. 227–48.

Napier, Nancy K. and Peterson, Richard B. Putting Human Resource Management at the Line Manager Level. In *Timpe, A. D., ed.*, 1988, 1984, pp. 87–102.

Naples, Michele I. Industrial Conflict, the Quality of Worklife, and the Productivity Slowdown in U.S. Manufacturing. *Eastern Econ. J.*, April–June 1988, 14(2), pp. 157–66.

_____. Is a Uniform Profit Rate Possible? A Logical–Historical Analysis [Abstract Labor and Its Value Form]. *Sci. Soc.*, Spring 1988, 52(1), pp. 89–93.

Naquib, Fadle; Daly, Michael J. and Lastman, Gary J. The Role of Tax-Deductible Saving in the Transition from a Progressive Income Tax to a Progressive Consumption Tax. *Public Finance*, 1988, 43(3), pp. 349–72.

Naqvi, K. A. and Robinson, Joan. The Badly Behaved Production Function. In *Steedman, I., ed., Vol. 1*, 1988, 1967, pp. 328–40.

Naqvi, Nadeem and Beladi, Hamid. Urban Unemployment and Non-immiserizing Growth. *J. Devel. Econ.*, May 1988, 28(3), pp. 365–76.

Naranjo, Edgar L. Ecuador: Foreign Debt Swaps. *Bull. Int. Fiscal Doc.*, October 1988, 42(10), pp. 440.

Narasimham, Gorti V. L.; Swamy, P. A. V. B. and Reed, R. C. Productivity Analysis of U.S. Manufacturing Using a Stochastic-Coefficients Production Function. *J. Bus. Econ. Statist.*, July 1988, 6(3), pp. 339–49.

Narasimhan, Chakravarthi. Competitive Promotional Strategies. *J. Bus.*, October 1988, 61(4), pp. 427–49.

_____. A Model of Discounting for Repeat Sales. In *Devinney, T. M., ed.*, 1988, pp. 171–92.

_____; Gaver, Kenneth M. and Horsky, Dan. Invariant Estimators for Market Share Systems and Their Finite Sample Behavior. *Marketing Sci.*, Spring 1988, 7(2), pp. 169–86.

Narayan, S. Human Resource Development in Mining: The Coal Industry. In *Kohli, U. and Gautam, V., eds.*, 1988, pp. 140–54.

Narayana, A. V. L. and Panagariya, Arvind. Excise Tax Evasion: A Welfare cum Crime Theoretic Analysis. *Public Finance*, 1988, 43(2), pp. 248–60.

Narayana, N. S. S.; Parikh, Kirit S. and Srinivasan, T. N. Rural Works Programs in India: Costs and Benefits. *J. Devel. Econ.*, September 1988, 29(2), pp. 131–56.

Narayanan, M. P. Debt versus Equity under Asymmetric Information. *J. Finan. Quant. Anal.*, March 1988, 23(1), pp. 39–51.

Narayanaswamy, C. R. A Mean–Variance Synthesis of Corporate Financial Theory: A Note. *J. Finance*, June 1988, 43(2), pp. 529–30.

Nardinelli, Clark. Productivity in Nineteenth Century France and Britain: A Note on the Comparisons. *J. Europ. Econ. Hist.*, Fall 1988, 17(2), pp. 427–34.

_____. Were Children Exploited during the Industrial Revolution? In *Uselding, P. J., ed.*, 1988, pp. 243–76.

_____ and Meiners, Roger E. Schmoller, the Methodenstreit, and the Development of Economic History. *J. Inst. Theoretical Econ.*, June 1988, 144(3), pp. 543–51.

_____; Wallace, Myles S. and Kelly, William A., Jr. Should We Sell the Fed? *Cato J.*, Spring–Summer 1988, 8(1), pp. 125–38.

_____; Wallace, Myles S. and Warner, John T. State Business Cycles and Their Relationship to the National Cycle: Structural and Institutional Determinants. *Southern Econ. J.*, April 1988, 54(4), pp. 950–60.

Nardone, Thomas. Finance, Insurance, and Real Estate: Employment Growth during 1982–87. *Mon. Lab. Rev.*, July 1988, 111(7), pp. 24–27.

Nardozzi, Giangiacomo. A Central Bank between the Government and the Credit System: The Bank of Italy after World War II. In *Toniolo, G., ed.*, 1988, pp. 161–96.

_____. La questione economica nella società italiana. Note su un libro postumo di Fausto Vicarelli. (Economic Questions in the Italian Society: The Crisis of the 70s and Its Aftermath. With English summary.) *Econ. Polit.*, December 1988, 5(3), pp. 409–15.

Narjes, Karl-Heinz. "Space Commerce '88'" Conference: Thursday, February 25th, in Montreux: Introductory Remarks. In *Egan, J. J., et al.*, 1988, pp. 445–52.

Nas, Tevfik F. Problems and Prospects: A Commentary. In *Nas, T. F. and Odekon, M., eds.*, 1988, pp. 185–200.

Nash, Christopher A. and Bowers, John. Alternative Approaches to the Valuation of Environmental Resources. In *Turner, R. K., ed.*, 1988, pp. 118–42.

_____ and Whiteing, A. E. Mode Choice: A Total

Distribution Cost Approach. In *Bianco, L. and La Bella, A., eds.*, 1988, pp. 121–49.

Nash, Elizabeth K.; Shumway, C. Richard and Pope, Rulon D. Allocatable Fixed Inputs and Jointness in Agricultural Production: Implications for Economic Modeling: Reply. *Amer. J. Agr. Econ.*, November 1988, 70(4), pp. 950–52.

Nash, Gerald D.; Pugach, Noel H. and Tomasson, Richard F. An Overview of American Social Security, 1935–1985. In *Nash, G. D.; Pugach, N. H. and Tomasson, R. F., eds.*, 1988, pp. 3–28.

Nash, John. Non-cooperative Games. In *Daughety, A. F., ed.*, 1988, 1951, pp. 82–93.

Nasir, Zafar Mueen and Ali, Syed Mubashir. Gains in Life Expectancy by Elimination of Specified Causes of Death in Pakistan. *Pakistan Devel. Rev.*, Part 2, Winter 1988, 27(4), pp. 645–51.

Näslund, Bertil. Dynamic Behavior of a Labor-Managed Team. *Scand. J. Econ.*, 1988, 90(4), pp. 575–84.

_____. Nya Finansiella Instrument och Deras Användning i Företagens Kapitalförvaltning. (New Financial Instruments and Their Application in Financial Management. With English summary.) *Liiketaloudellinen Aikak.*, 1988, 37(4), pp. 306–19.

Nataraj Kirby, Sheila and Darling-Hammond, Linda. Parental Schooling Choice: A Case Study of Minnesota. *J. Policy Anal. Manage.*, Spring 1988, 7(3), pp. 506–17.

Nath, Raghu. Comparative Management Research and International Strategic Planning. In *Farmer, R. N. and McGoun, E. G., eds.*, 1988, pp. 187–201.

Nathan, Richard P. and Lago, John R. Intergovernmental Relations in the Reagan Era. *Public Budg. Finance*, Autumn 1988, 8(3), pp. 15–29.

National Endowment for the Arts. Artist Employment in 1986. *J. Cult. Econ.*, June 1988, 12(1), pp. 81–86.

Natke, Paul A. and Falls, Gregory A. The Demand for Liquid Assets: A Firm Level Analysis. *Southern Econ. J.*, January 1988, 54(3), pp. 630–42.

von Natzmer, Wulfheinrich. Budget Consolidation, Effective Demand and Employment. In *Motamen, H., ed.*, 1988, pp. 203–18.

Nau, Henry R. The United States and the NICs in the Uruguay Round: Bargaining Barriers. In *Yochelson, J., ed.*, 1988, pp. 203–23.

Naudts, B. and Schokkaert, E. Government Debt and Interest Rates in Belgium 1974–1986. *Tijdschrift Econ. Manage.*, Sept.–Dec. 1988, 33(3/4), pp. 339–54.

Naughton, Barry. Macroeconomic Policy and Response in the Chinese Economy: The Impact of the Reform Process. In *Reynolds, B. L., ed.*, 1988, 1987, pp. 44–63.

Naughton, Michael C. The Determinants of Regulators' Preferences: Discrimination in Electricity Pricing. *J. Behav. Econ.*, Winter 1988, 17(4), pp. 279–94.

Navajas, Fernando and Porto, Alberto. Características distributivas, presupuestos familiares y el impacto distributivo de las tarifas públicas. (Distributional Characteristics of Goods, Household Budgets, and Distributional Effects of Public Prices. With English summary.) *Económica (La Plata)*, Jan.–June 1988, *34*(1), pp. 113–25.

Navalkar, M. P. and Subramanian, T. A. Human Resource Development in Scientific Institutions with Special Reference to Department of Atomic Energy. In *Kohli, U. and Gautam, V.*, eds., 1988, pp. 264–69.

Navarro, Peter. Comparative Energy Policy: The Economics of Nuclear Power in Japan and the United States. *Energy J.*, October 1988, *9*(4), pp. 1–15.

_____. The Income Elasticity of Corporate Contributions. *Quart. Rev. Econ. Bus.*, Winter 1988, *28*(4), pp. 66–75.

_____. Why Do Corporations Give to Charity? *J. Bus.*, January 1988, *61*(1), pp. 65–93.

_____ **and Carson, Richard T.** A Seller's (and Buyer's) Guide to the Job Market for Beginning Academic Economists. *J. Econ. Perspectives*, Spring 1988, *2*(2), pp. 137–48.

_____ **and Carson, Richard T.** Fundamental Issues in Natural Resource Damage Assessment. *Natural Res. J.*, Fall 1988, *28*(4), pp. 815–36.

_____ **and Dubin, Jeffrey A.** How Markets for Impure Public Goods Organize: The Case of Household Refuse Collection. *J. Law, Econ., Organ.*, Fall 1988, *4*(2), pp. 217–41.

Navidi, W.; Peters, S. C. and Freedman, D. A. On the Impact of Variable Selection in Fitting Regression Equations. In *Dijkstra, T. K.*, ed., 1988, pp. 1–16.

Navrozov, Lev. Assessing the CIA's 'Soviet Economic Indices.' In *[Nove, A.]*, 1988, pp. 112–52.

Nawe, Julita. The Health and Working Conditions of Tanzania's Workforce: A Research Note. *Eastern Afr. Econ. Rev.*, December 1988, *4*(2), pp. 65–67.

Naya, Seiji. The Role of Trade Policies in the Industrialization of Rapidly Growing Asian Developing Countries. In *Hughes, H.*, ed., 1988, pp. 64–94.

_____ **and Lee, Chung H.** Patterns of Trade and Investment in Services in the Asia-Pacific Region. In *Lee, C. H. and Naya, S.*, eds., 1988, pp. 27–52.

_____ **and Lee, Chung H.** Trade in East Asian Development with Comparative Reference to Southeast Asian Experiences. *Econ. Develop. Cult. Change*, Supplement, April 1988, *36*(3), pp. S123–52.

_____ **and Lee, Chung H.** U.S.–ASEAN Trade and Investment in Services: An American Viewpoint. In *Tan, L.-H. and Akrasanee, N.*, eds., 1988, pp. 146–73.

_____ **and Ramstetter, Eric D.** Policy Interactions and Direct Foreign Investment in East and Southeast Asia. *J. World Trade*, April 1988, *22*(2), pp. 57–71.

Nayar, Mark and Geen, Gerry. Individual Transferable Quotas in the Southern Bluefin Tuna Fishery: An Economic Appraisal. *Marine Resource Econ.*, 1988, *5*(4), pp. 365–87.

de Nayer, Marie-Christine and Brac de La Perrière, Gilles. Le matif et la gestion du risque. (With English summary.) *Revue Écon. Polit.*, Sept.–Oct. 1988, *98*(5), pp. 701–12.

Naylor, J. C. and Smith, A. F. M. Econometric Illustrations of Novel Numerical Integration Strategies for Bayesian Inference. *J. Econometrics*, May–June 1988, *38*(1–2), pp. 103–25.

Nayyar, Deepak. The External Sector in Chinese Economic Development. In *Mitra, A.*, ed., 1988, pp. 87–114.

_____. India's Export Performance, 1970–85: Underlying Factors and Constraints. In *Lucas, R. E. B. and Papanek, G. F.*, eds., 1988, pp. 217–52.

_____. The Political Economy of International Trade in Services. *Cambridge J. Econ.*, June 1988, *12*(2), pp. 279–98.

_____. Some Reflections on the Uruguay Round and Trade in Services. *J. World Trade*, October 1988, *22*(5), pp. 35–47.

Nazarenko, Victor I. The Development of the Agro-industrial Complex of the USSR. In *Goldberg, R. A.*, ed., *Vol. 9*, 1988, pp. 9–41.

_____. Major Principles of Future Activities of Joint Ventures in the USSR Involving Soviet Organizations and Foreign Companies. In *Goldberg, R. A.*, ed., *Vol. 9*, 1988, pp. 1–7.

Nazli, Samina and Kiani, M. Framurz Khan. Dynamics of Birth Spacing in Pakistan. *Pakistan Devel. Rev.*, Part 2, Winter 1988, *27*(4), pp. 655–57.

Nazmi, Nader. Jean-Paul Sartre on Economics. *Rev. Radical Polit. Econ.*, Winter 1988, *20*(4), pp. 85–91.

Ndoye, Mbaye; Bingen, R. James and Hall, A. E. California Cowpeas and Food Policy in Senegal. *World Devel.*, July 1988, *16*(7), pp. 857–65.

Ndubizu, Gordian A. Analysis of the Economic Consequences of Foreign Currency Standards: A Classification Issue. In *Most, K. S.*, ed., 1988, pp. 183–200.

Neal, Anne deHayden. A Perspective from the Recording Industry. In *Walker, C. E. and Bloomfield, M. A.*, eds., 1988, pp. 135–41.

Neale, Adrian J. and Hendry, David F. Interpreting Long-run Equilibrium Solutions in Conventional Macro Models: A Comment. *Econ. J.*, September 1988, *98*(392), pp. 808–17.

_____; **Srba, Frank and Hendry, David F.** Econometric Analysis of Small Linear Systems Using PC-FIML. *J. Econometrics*, May–June 1988, *38*(1–2), pp. 203–26.

Neale, Margaret A.; Huber, Vandra L. and Northcraft, Gregory B. The Effects of Cognitive Bias and Social Influence on Human Resources Management Decisions. In *Ferris, G. R. and Rowland, K. M.*, eds., 1988, pp. 157–89.

Neale, Walter C. Evolutionary Economics: Volume 1: Foundations of Institutional Thought:

Institutions. In *Tool, M. R., ed., Vol. 1,* 1988, *1987,* pp. 227–56.

_____. Language and Economics. In *Samuels, W. J., ed., Vol. 2,* 1988, *1982,* pp. 177–91.

Near, Janet P. Reactions to the Career Plateau. In *Timpe, A. D., ed.,* 1988, *1984,* pp. 256–63.

Neary, Hugh M. The Comparative Statics of the Ward–Domar Labor-Managed Firm: A Profit-Function Approach. *J. Compar. Econ.,* June 1988, *12*(2), pp. 159–81.

Neary, Peter. ARMOD: A Small Numerical Macroeconomic World Model with Non-clearing Markets: Comment. In *Haaland, J. I. and Norman, V. D., eds.,* 1988, pp. 31–34.

_____. Determinants of the Equilibrium Real Exchange Rate. *Amer. Econ. Rev.,* March 1988, *78*(1), pp. 210–15.

_____. Export Subsidies and National Welfare. *Empirica,* 1988, *15*(2), pp. 243–61.

_____. Stability of the Mobile-Capital Harris–Todaro Model: Some Further Results. *Economica,* February 1988, *55*(217), pp. 123–27.

_____. Tariffs, Quotas, and Voluntary Export Restraints with and without Internationally Mobile Capital. *Can. J. Econ.,* November 1988, *21*(4), pp. 714–35.

_____ and **Ruane, Frances P.** International Capital Mobility, Shadow Prices, and the Cost of Protection. *Int. Econ. Rev.,* November 1988, *29*(4), pp. 571–85.

_____ and **Stiglitz, Joseph E.** Toward a Reconstruction of Keynesian Economics: Expectations and Constrained Equilibria. In *Shaw, G. K., ed., Vol. 1,* 1988, *1983,* pp. 283–312.

Neck, Reinhard and Schneider, Friedrich. The Growth of the Public Sector in Austria: An Exploratory Analysis. In *Lybeck, J. A. and Henrekson, M., eds.,* 1988, pp. 231–63.

Neckar, David H. and de la Torre, José. Forecasting Political Risks for International Operations. *Int. J. Forecasting,* 1988, *4*(2), pp. 221–41.

Needham, Barrie and Jobse, Rein B. The Economic Future of the Randstad, Holland. *Urban Stud.,* August 1988, *25*(4), pp. 282–96.

Neef, Arthur and Thomas, James. International Comparisons of Productivity and Unit Labor Cost Trends in Manufacturing. *Mon. Lab. Rev.,* December 1988, *111*(12), pp. 27–33.

Neelin, Janet; Sonnenschein, Hugo and Spiegel, Matthew. A Further Test of Noncooperative Bargaining Theory: Comment. *Amer. Econ. Rev.,* September 1988, *78*(4), pp. 824–36.

Neftci, Salih N. and Edwards, Franklin R. Extreme Price Movements and Margin Levels in Futures Markets. *J. Futures Markets,* December 1988, *8*(6), pp. 639–55.

Negandhi, Anant R. Indian Foreign Investment Policie. In *Teng, W. and Wang, N. T., eds.,* 1988, pp. 121–35.

Negishi, T. A Note on Jevons's Law of Indifference and Competitive Equilibrium. In *Wood, J. C., ed., Vol. 3,* 1988, *1982,* pp. 193–203.

Nehls, Carl. Custodial Package Tracking at Fed-

eral Express. In *Guile, B. R. and Quinn, J. B., eds. (I),* 1988, pp. 57–81.

Neill, Jon R. Another Theorem on Using Market Demands to Determine Willingness to Pay for Non-traded Goods. *J. Environ. Econ. Manage.,* June 1988, *15*(2), pp. 224–32.

Neiss, Hubert; Aghevli, Bijan B. and Kim, Insu. Growth and Adjustment: Experiences of Selected Subcontinent Countries. In *Streeten, P., ed.,* 1988, pp. 30–53.

Nelder, John A. How Should the Statistical Expert System and Its User See Each Other. In *Edwards, D. and Raun, N. E., eds.,* 1988, pp. 107–16.

Nelissen, Jan H. M. and van den Akker, Piet A. M. Are Demographic Developments Influenced by Social Security. *J. Econ. Psych.,* March 1988, *9*(1), pp. 81–114.

Nell, Edward J. On Monetary Circulation and the Rate of Exploitation. In *Arestis, P., ed.,* 1988, pp. 72–121.

_____ and **Laibman, David.** Reswitching, Wicksell Effects, and the Neoclassical Production Function. In *Steedman, I., ed., Vol. 1,* 1988, *1977,* pp. 232–42.

Nelles, H. V. Commerce in a Cold Climate: Bliss on Canadian Business History. *Bus. Hist. Rev.,* Summer 1988, *62*(2), pp. 310–16.

Nelson, Arthur C. and Knaap, Gerrit J. The Effects of Regional Land Use Control in Oregon: A Theoretical and Empirical Review. *Rev. Reg. Stud.,* Spring 1988, *18*(2), pp. 37–46.

Nelson, Charles R. Spurious Trend and Cycle in the State Space Decomposition of a Time Series with a Unit Root. *J. Econ. Dynam. Control,* June–Sept. 1988, *12*(2–3), pp. 475–88.

_____ and **Siegel, Andrew F.** Long-term Behavior of Yield Curves. *J. Finan. Quant. Anal.,* March 1988, *23*(1), pp. 105–10.

Nelson, Clarence W. Modeling the Impact of an Energy Price Shock on Interregional Income Transfer. *Fed. Res. Bank Minn. Rev.,* Summer 1988, *12*(3), pp. 2–17.

Nelson, F. Howard and Gould, Jewell C. Teachers' Unions and Excellence in Education: Comment. *J. Lab. Res.,* Fall 1988, *9*(4), pp. 379–87.

Nelson, Forrest D. and Daughety, Andrew F. An Econometric Analysis of Changes in the Cost and Production Structure of the Trucking Industry, 1953–1982. *Rev. Econ. Statist.,* February 1988, *70*(1), pp. 67–75.

Nelson, Hans and Bos, Marko. Indirect Taxation and the Completion of the Internal Market of the EC. *J. Common Market Stud.,* September 1988, *27*(1), pp. 27–44.

Nelson, Helen Ewing. The Issues in Regulation and Deregulation. In *Maynes, E. S. and ACCI Research Committee, eds.,* 1988, pp. 457–61.

_____. Reflections on Research in the Consumer Interest. In *Maynes, E. S. and ACCI Research Committee, eds.,* 1988, pp. 97–101.

Nelson, Joan. The Political Economy of Stabilization: Commitment, Capacity, and Public Response. In *Bates, R. H., ed.,* 1988, *1984,* pp. 80–130.

Nelson, Julie A. Household Economies of Scale in Consumption: Theory and Evidence. *Econometrica*, November 1988, 56(6), pp. 1301–14.

Nelson, Mack C. and Beauford, E. Yvonne. Social and Economic Conditions of Black Farm Households: Status and Prospects. In *Beaulieu, L. J., ed.*, 1988, pp. 99–119.

Nelson, Paul S. Rational Expectations in Experimental Duopoly Markets. *J. Behav. Econ.*, Fall 1988, 17(3), pp. 195–206.

Nelson, Philip B. and Hilke, John C. Diversification and Predation. *J. Ind. Econ.*, September 1988, 37(1), pp. 107–11.

Nelson, Randy A. and Primeaux, Walter J., Jr. The Effects of Competition on Transmission and Distribution Costs in the Municipal Electric Industry. *Land Econ.*, November 1988, 64(4), pp. 338–46.

Nelson, Ray D. and Antonovitz, Frances. Forward and Futures Markets and the Competitive Firm under Price Uncertainty. *Southern Econ. J.*, July 1988, 55(1), pp. 182–95.

Nelson, Reed E. and Thakur, Manab. The Organization of the Mexican Maquiladora: A Contextual Analysis. In *Farmer, R. N. and McGoun, E. G., eds.*, 1988, pp. 75–94.

Nelson, Richard R. Assessing Private Enterprise: An Exegesis of Tangled Doctrine. In *Earl, P. E., ed., Vol. 2*, 1988, *1981*, pp. 278–97.

_____. Institutions Supporting Technical Change in the United States. In *Dosi, G., et al., eds.*, 1988, pp. 312–29.

_____. Modelling the Connections in the Cross Section between Technical Progress and R&D Intensity. *Rand J. Econ.*, Autumn 1988, 19(3), pp. 478–85.

_____. State Labor Laws: Changes during 1987. *Mon. Lab. Rev.*, January 1988, 111(1), pp. 38–61.

_____ and Winter, Sidney G. Firm and Industry Response to Changed Market Conditions: An Evolutionary Approach. In *Earl, P. E., ed., Vol. 1*, 1988, *1980*, pp. 434–57.

Nelson, Richard W. Optimal Banking Structure: Implications for Interstate Banking. *Contemp. Policy Issues*, April 1988, 6(2), pp. 13–23.

Nelson, Theron R. and Rabianski, Joseph. Consumer Preferences in Housing Market Analysis: An Application of Multidimensional Scaling Techniques. *Amer. Real Estate Urban Econ. Assoc. J.*, Summer 1988, 16(2), pp. 138–59.

Nelson, William J., Jr. Workers' Compensation: Coverage, Benefits, and Costs, 1985. *Soc. Sec. Bull.*, January 1988, 51(1), pp. 4–9.

_____. Workers' Compensation: 1980–84 Benchmark Revisions. *Soc. Sec. Bull.*, July 1988, 51(7), pp. 4–21.

Nentjes, Andries. Hayek and Keynes: A Comparative Analysis of Their Monetary Views. *J. Econ. Stud.*, 1988, 15(3–4), pp. 136–51.

_____ and Wiersma, Doede. Innovation and Pollution Control. *Int. J. Soc. Econ.*, 1988, 15(3–4), pp. 51–70.

Neri, Fabio. Immigration and the Italian Labour Market: A Contradiction? *Rev. Econ. Cond. Italy*, May–Aug. 1988, (2), pp. 141–52.

Nerlove, Marc and Beggs, John J. Biases in Dynamic Models with Fixed Effects. *Econ. Letters*, 1988, 26(1), pp. 29–31.

_____ and Ghysels, Eric. Seasonality in Surveys: A Comparison of Belgian, French and German Business Tests. *Europ. Econ. Rev.*, January 1988, 32(1), pp. 81–99.

_____; Razin, Assaf and Sadka, Efraim. A Bequest-Constrained Economy: Welfare Analysis. *J. Public Econ.*, November 1988, 37(2), pp. 203–20.

Nesbitt, Dale M. and Choi, Thomas Y. Is an Oil Tariff Justified? An American Debate: The Numbers Say No. *Energy J.*, July 1988, 9(3), pp. 31–59.

Ness, Gayl D. and Brechin, Steven R. Bridging the Gap: International Organizations as Organizations. *Int. Organ.*, Spring 1988, 42(2), pp. 245–73.

Nesslein, Thomas S. Housing: The Market versus the Welfare State Model Revisited. *Urban Stud.*, April 1988, 25(2), pp. 95–108.

Netter, Jeffry M.; Jarrell, Gregg A. and Brickley, James A. The Market for Corporate Control: The Empirical Evidence Since 1980. *J. Econ. Perspectives*, Winter 1988, 2(1), pp. 49–68.

_____; Poulsen, Annette B. and Hersch, Philip L. Insider Trading: The Law, the Theory, the Evidence. *Contemp. Policy Issues*, July 1988, 6(3), pp. 1–13.

_____ and Ryngaert, Michael. Shareholder Wealth Effects of the Ohio Antitakeover Law. *J. Law, Econ., Organ.*, Fall 1988, 4(2), pp. 373–83.

Neu, C. R. International Trade in Banking Services. In *Baldwin, R. E.; Hamilton, C. B. and Sapir, A., eds.*, 1988, pp. 245–69.

Neubauer, Günter. Reforming Hospital Finance in West Germany: Propositions and Obstacles: Comment. In *Furubotn, E. G. and Richter, R., eds.*, 1988, pp. 71–77.

Neuberger, Egon and Ben-Ner, Avner. Towards an Economic Theory of the Firm in the Centrally Planned Economy: Transaction Costs: Internalization and Externalization. *J. Inst. Theoretical Econ.*, December 1988, 144(5), pp. 839–48.

Neuefeind, Wilhelm and Dierker, Egbert. Quantity Guided Price Setting. *J. Math. Econ.*, 1988, 17(2–3), pp. 249–59.

de Neufville, Richard and Delquie, Philippe. A Model of the Influence of Certainty and Probability "Effects" on the Measurement of Utility. In *Munier, B. R., ed.*, 1988, pp. 189–205.

Neuman, Shoshana and Grossbard-Shechtman, Shoshana A. Women's Labor Supply and Marital Choice. *J. Polit. Econ.*, December 1988, 96(6), pp. 1294–1302.

Neuman, Stephanie G. Arms, Aid and the Superpowers. *Foreign Aff.*, Summer 1988, 66(5), pp. 1044–66.

Neumann, Dean, et al. Policy Functions for Capital Accumulation Paths. *J. Econ. Theory*, October 1988, 46(1), pp. 205–14.

Neumann, George R. and Mortensen, Dale T. Estimating Structural Models of Unemployment and Job Duration. In *Barnett, W. A.; Berndt, E. R. and White, H., eds.*, 1988, pp. 335–55.

Neumann, Helmut. Effiziente Entlassungen durch Sozialpläne? (Efficient Lay-Offs and Severance Payments. With English summary.) *Jahr. Nationalökon. Statist.*, December 1988, 205(6), pp. 506–18.

Neumann, Manfred J. M. Beschleunigte steuerliche Abschreibung und Kapitalertrag nach Steuern in einem lagfristigen Wachstumsgleichgewicht. (Accelerated Depreciation and the Rate of Return after Taxation in a Steady State Equilibrium of Economic Growth. With English summary.) *Jahr. Nationalökon. Statist.*, April 1988, 204(4), pp. 342–45.

———. Industrial Organization and Public Policy. *Int. J. Ind. Organ.*, June 1988, 6(2), pp. 155–66.

———. Money Supply versus Exchange-Rate Targeting: An Asymmetry between the United States and Other Industrial Economies: Comments. In *Giersch, H., ed.*, 1988, pp. 269–75.

——— **and von Hagen, Jürgen.** An Aggregate Supply Function for the Open Economy with Flexible Exchange Rates. *J. Inst. Theoretical Econ.*, September 1988, 144(4), pp. 658–70.

——— **and von Hagen, Jürgen.** Instability versus Dynamics: A Study in West German Demand for Money. *J. Macroecon.*, Summer 1988, 10(3), pp. 327–49.

Neumark, David. Employers' Discriminatory Behavior and the Estimation of Wage Discrimination. *J. Human Res.*, Summer 1988, 23(3), pp. 279–95.

———. Gender Differences in Family Effects on Human Capital and Earnings: An Empirical Study of Siblings. In *Maital, S., ed., Vol. 1*, 1988, pp. 228–51.

Neuthinger, Egon. Anatomie eines Wachstumspfades—Zur wirtschaftlichen Entwicklung in der Bundesrepublik Deutschland seit 1983—Rückschauende Analyse, Ausblick und wirtschaftspolitische Bewertung. (Anatomy of a Growth Path—Economic Development in the Federal Republic of Germany—Analysis in Retrospect, Outlook and Economic Policy Assessment. With English summary.) *Konjunkturpolitik*, 1988, 34(4), pp. 185–238.

Nevalainen, Kari and Shanmugam, Ramalingam. Analyzing Environmental Time Series: A Review and Finnish Case Study. *Statist. J.*, November 1988, 5(3), pp. 315–38.

Neven, Damien J.; Dierickx, I. and Matutes, C. Indirect Taxation and Cournot Equilibrium. *Int. J. Ind. Organ.*, 1988, 6(3), pp. 385–99.

——— **and Martinez-Giralt, Xavier.** Can Price Competition Dominate Market Segmentation? *J. Ind. Econ.*, June 1988, 36(4), pp. 431–42.

das Neves, João Luís César. Equilíbrio de pobreza: Esboço de formulação e estudo empírico. (With English summary.) *Economia (Portugal)*, January 1988, 12(1), pp. 1–52.

Nevett, Terence. Advertising Control through Self-Regulation: Some Policy Implications for Developing Countries. In *Kumcu, E. and Firat, A. F., eds.*, 1988, pp. 229–51.

———. American Influences on British Advertising before 1920. In *[Hollander, S. C.]*, 1988, pp. 223–40.

——— **and Fullerton, Ronald A.** Advertising: The Archaeology of Marketing: Introduction. In *[Hollander, S. C.]*, 1988, pp. 193–94.

——— **and Fullerton, Ronald A.** The Evolution of Marketing Thought: Introduction. In *[Hollander, S. C.]*, 1988, pp. 1–4.

——— **and Fullerton, Ronald A.** Historical Perspectives on Retailing: Introduction. In *[Hollander, S. C.]*, 1988, pp. 147–48.

——— **and Fullerton, Ronald A.** The Importance of Marketing History and Stanley Hollander's Contribution to It. In *[Hollander, S. C.]*, 1988, pp. xi–xix.

——— **and Fullerton, Ronald A.** Marketing and Economic Development over Time: Introduction. In *[Hollander, S. C.]*, 1988, pp. 109–11.

——— **and Fullerton, Ronald A.** Marketing in Historical Context: Introduction. In *[Hollander, S. C.]*, 1988, pp. 53–54.

Nevile, John W. and Tran-Nam, Binh. The Effects of Birthplace on Male Earnings in Australia. *Australian Econ. Pap.*, June 1988, 27(50), pp. 83–101.

Nevins, James L. Mechatronics. In *Uyehara, C. H., ed.*, 1988, pp. 92–140.

Newbery, David M. The Analysis of Agricultural Price Reform. *J. Public Econ.*, February 1988, 35(1), pp. 1–24.

———. Charging for Roads. *World Bank Res. Observer*, July 1988, 3(2), pp. 119–38.

———. Market Failure and the Efficiency of Irrigated Agriculture: Comment. In *O'Mara, G. T., ed.*, 1988, pp. 32–33.

———. On the Accuracy of the Mean–Variance Approximation for Futures Markets. *Econ. Letters*, 1988, 28(1), pp. 63–68.

———. Road Damage Externalities and Road User Charges. *Econometrica*, March 1988, 56(2), pp. 295–316.

———. Road User Charges in Britain. *Econ. J.*, Supplement, 1988, 98(390), pp. 161–76.

———; **Zilberman, David and Bigman, David.** New Approaches in Agricultural Policy Research: Discussion. *Amer. J. Agr. Econ.*, May 1988, 70(2), pp. 460–61.

Newbold, Paul and Bera, Anil K. Checks of Model Adequacy for Univariate Time Series Models and Their Applications to Econometric Relationships: Comment. *Econometric Rev.*, 1988, 7(1), pp. 43–48.

———; **Gentry, James A. and Whitford, David T.** Predicting Industrial Bond Ratings with a Probit Model and Funds Flow Components. *Financial Rev.*, August 1988, 23(3), pp. 269–86.

Newcomer, Robert J.; Moore, Thomas Gale and Harrington, Charlene. Factors That Contribute to Medicare HMO Risk Contract Success. *Inquiry*, Summer 1988, 25(2), pp. 251–62.

Newell, Andrew and Symons, J. S. V. The Macroeconomics of the Interwar Years: International

Comparisons. In *Eichengreen, B. and Hatton, T. J., eds.*, 1988, pp. 61–96.

Newell, Dianne. The Rationality of Mechanization in the Pacific Salmon-Canning Industry before the Second World War. *Bus. Hist. Rev.*, Winter 1988, *62*(4), pp. 626–55.

van Newenhizen, Jill and Saari, Donald G. Is Approval Voting an 'Unmitigated Evil'? A Response [The Problem of Indeterminacy in Approval, Multiple, and Truncated Voting Systems]. *Public Choice*, November 1988, *59*(2), pp. 133–47.

_____ **and Saari, Donald G.** The Problem of Indeterminacy in Approval, Multiple, and Truncated Voting Systems. *Public Choice*, November 1988, *59*(2), pp. 101–20.

Newey, Whitney K. Adaptive Estimation of Regression Models via Moment Restrictions. *J. Econometrics*, July 1988, *38*(3), pp. 301–39.

_____; **Rosen, Harvey S. and Holtz-Eakin, Douglas.** Estimating Vector Autoregressions with Panel Data. *Econometrica*, November 1988, *56*(6), pp. 1371–95.

Newhouse, Joseph P. Has the Erosion of the Medical Marketplace Ended? In *Greenberg, W., ed.*, 1988, pp. 41–56.

_____ **and Byrne, Daniel J.** Did Medicare's Prospective Payment System Cause Length of Stay to Fall? *J. Health Econ.*, December 1988, *7*(4), pp. 413–16.

_____ **and Lindsey, Phoebe.** Do Second Opinion Programs Improve Outcomes? *J. Health Econ.*, September 1988, *7*(3), pp. 285–88.

Newman, John L. A Stochastic Dynamic Model of Fertility. In *Schultz, T. Paul, ed.*, 1988, pp. 41–68.

Newman, Mark D. Southern Agriculture and the World Economy: The Multilateral Trade Negotiations: Introduction. *Southern J. Agr. Econ.*, July 1988, *20*(1), pp. 57–58.

Newman, Paul. An Explanation for Accounting Income Smoothing: Discussion. *J. Acc. Res.*, Supplement, 1988, *26*, pp. 140–43.

Newman, Peter. Production of Commodities by Means of Commodities. In *Steedman, I., ed., Vol. 1*, 1988, pp. 64–81.

_____ **and Vassilakis, Spyros.** Sraffa and Imperfect Competition. *Cambridge J. Econ.*, March 1988, *12*(1), pp. 37–42.

Newman, Robert J. and Moore, William J. A Cross-section Analysis of the Postwar Decline in American Trade Union Membership. *J. Lab. Res.*, Spring 1988, *9*(2), pp. 111–25.

_____ **and Sullivan, Dennis H.** Econometric Analysis of Business Tax Impacts on Industrial Location: What Do We Know, and How Do We Know It? *J. Urban Econ.*, March 1988, *23*(2), pp. 215–34.

Newmark, Craig M. Does Horizontal Price Fixing Raise Price? A Look at the Bakers of Washington Case. *J. Law Econ.*, October 1988, *31*(2), pp. 469–84.

_____. Is Antitrust Enforcement Effective? Comment. *J. Polit. Econ.*, December 1988, *96*(6), pp. 1315–28.

Neyman, Abraham and Dubey, Pradeep. Payoffs

in Nonatomic Economies: An Axiomatic Approach. In *[Shapley, L. S.]*, 1988, *1984*, pp. 207–16.

_____ **and Hart, Sergiu.** Values of Non-atomic Vector Measure Games: Are They Linear Combinations of the Measures? *J. Math. Econ.*, 1988, *17*(1), pp. 31–40.

_____ **and Monderer, Dov.** Values of Smooth Nonatomic Games: The Method of Multilinear Approximation. In *[Shapley, L. S.]*, 1988, pp. 217–34.

Ng, Ignace and Maki, Dennis R. Strike Activity of U.S. Institutions in Canada. *Brit. J. Ind. Relat.*, March 1988, *26*(1), pp. 63–73.

Ng, Kenneth. Free Banking Laws and Barriers to Entry in Banking, 1838–1860. *J. Econ. Hist.*, December 1988, *48*(4), pp. 877–89.

Ng, Yew-Kwang. Economic Efficiency versus Egalitarian Rights. *Kyklos*, 1988, *41*(2), pp. 215–37.

_____. Is a Dollar a Dollar? A Response. *Oxford Econ. Pap.*, September 1988, *40*(3), pp. 584–86.

Nguyen, D. T. and Dowrick, Steve. A Re-assessment of Australian Economic Growth in the Light of the Convergence Hypothesis. *Australian Econ. Pap.*, December 1988, *27*(51), pp. 196–212.

_____ **and MacBean, Alasdair I.** Export Instability and Growth Performance. In *Greenaway, D., ed.*, 1988, pp. 95–116.

_____ **and Siriwardana, A. Mahinda.** The Relationship between Output Growth and Unemployment: A Re-examination of Okun's Law in Australia. *Australian Econ. Rev.*, 1st Quarter 1988, (81), pp. 16–27.

Nguyen, Godefroy Dang. Telecommunications in France. In *Foreman-Peck, J. and Müller, J., eds.,*, 1988, pp. 131–54.

Nguyen, Hung T. On Combining Uncertainty Measures. In *Kacprzyk, J. and Fedrizzi, M., eds.*, 1988, pp. 124–34.

Nguyen, Sang and Picard, Guy. Estimation of Interregional Freight Flows Using Input/Output Analysis. In *Bianco, L. and La Bella, A., eds.*, 1988, pp. 186–209.

Nguyen, The-Hiep and Bernier, Gilles. Beta and q in a Simultaneous Framework with Pooled Data. *Rev. Econ. Statist.*, August 1988, *70*(3), pp. 520–24.

Nhova, Charles. Zimbabwe: Energy Imperatives in the Transportation Sector. In *Hosier, R. H., ed. (II)*, 1988, pp. 50–73.

Ní Bhrolcháin, Máire. The Contraceptive Confidence Idea: An Empirical Investigation. *Population Stud.*, July 1988, *42*(2), pp. 205–25.

Nicholas, Stephen. The Care and Feeding of Convicts. In *Nicholas, S., ed.*, 1988, pp. 180–98.

_____. The Convict Labour Market. In *Nicholas, S., ed.*, 1988, pp. 111–26.

_____. A New Past. In *Nicholas, S., ed.*, 1988, pp. 199–201.

_____. The Organisation of Public Work. In *Nicholas, S., ed.*, 1988, pp. 152–66.

_____ **and Carlos, Ann M.** "Giants of an Earlier Capitalism": The Chartered Trading Companies as Modern Multinationals. *Bus. Hist. Rev.*, Autumn 1988, *62*(3), pp. 398–419.

_____ and Corcoran, Kris. Statistical Appendix: Convicts Transported to New South Wales 1817–40. In *Nicholas, S., ed.*, 1988, pp. 202–24.

_____ and Hutchinson, Dianne. Theory and Business History: New Approaches to Institutional Change. *J. Europ. Econ. Hist.*, Fall 1988, *17*(2), pp. 411–25.

_____ and Shergold, Peter R. Convicts as Migrants. In *Nicholas, S., ed.*, 1988, pp. 43–61.

_____ and Shergold, Peter R. Convicts as Workers. In *Nicholas, S., ed.*, 1988, pp. 62–84.

_____ and Shergold, Peter R. A Labour Aristocracy in Chains. In *Nicholas, S., ed.*, 1988, pp. 98–108.

_____ and Shergold, Peter R. Transportation as Global Migration. In *Nicholas, S., ed.*, 1988, pp. 28–39.

_____ and Shergold, Peter R. Unshackling the Past. In *Nicholas, S., ed.*, 1988, pp. 3–13.

Nicholls, David. Haiti: Race, Slavery and Independence (1804–1825). In *Archer, L. J., ed.*, 1988, pp. 225–38.

Nicholls, J. R. and Harris, R. J. Methodology in International Acquisitions: An Exploratory Study. *Managerial Dec. Econ.*, June 1988, *9*(2), pp. 101–07.

Nichols-Casebolt, Ann and Danziger, Sheldon H. Poverty and Income Transfers in Wisconsin. In *Danziger, S. H. and Witte, J. F., eds.*, 1988, pp. 133–50.

_____; Garfinkel, Irwin and Wong, Patrick. Reforming Wisconsin's Child Support System. In *Danziger, S. H. and Witte, J. F., eds.*, 1988, pp. 172–86.

Nichols, John P.; Capps, Oral, Jr. and Fuller, Stephen W. Assessing Opportunities in Food and Fiber Processing and Distribution. *Amer. J. Agr. Econ.*, May 1988, *70*(2), pp. 462–68.

Nichols, William D. and Mendenhall, Richard R. Bad News and Differential Market Reactions to Announcements of Earlier-Quarters versus Fourth-Quarter Earnings. *J. Acc. Res.*, Supplement, 1988, *26*, pp. 63–86.

_____ and Morris, Michael H. Consistency Exceptions: Materiality Judgments and Audit Firm Structure. *Accounting Rev.*, April 1988, *63*(2), pp. 237–54.

Nicholson, C. Local Budgetary Development, Relative Efficiency and Local Fiscal Crisis. *Reg. Stud.*, June 1988, *22*(3), pp. 241–45.

Nickell, Stephen J. Imperfect Competition and the Labour Market. In *Beenstock, M., ed.*, 1988, pp. 145–67.

_____. The NAIRU: Some Theory and Statistical Facts. In *Cross, R., ed.*, 1988, pp. 378–85.

_____. The Supply Side and Macroeconomic Modeling. In *Bryant, R. C., et al., eds.*, 1988, pp. 202–18.

_____. Wages and Economic Activity. In *Eltis, W. and Sinclair, P. J. N., eds.*, 1988, pp. 65–75.

_____. Why Is Wage Inflation in Britain So High? In *Cross, R., ed.*, 1988, pp. 256–83.

_____ and Layard, Richard. The Case for Subsidising Extra Jobs. In *Shaw, G. K., ed.*, Vol. 2, 1988, *1980*, pp. 10–32.

_____ and Wadhwani, Sushil. Unions, Wages and Employment: Tests Based on U.K. Firm-Level Data. *Europ. Econ. Rev.*, March 1988, *32*(2–3), pp. 727–33.

Nickelsburg, Gerald and Maasoumi, Esfandiar. Multivariate Measures of Well-Being and an Analysis of Inequality in the Michigan Data. *J. Bus. Econ. Statist.*, July 1988, *6*(3), pp. 326–34.

Nickerson, David B. and Courchane, Marsha J. Monetary Neutrality and Optimality with Symmetric Partial Information. *Int. Econ. J.*, Winter 1988, *2*(4), pp. 57–71.

Nickum, James E. All Is Not Wells in North China: Irrigation in Yucheng County. In *O'Mara, G. T., ed.*, 1988, pp. 87–94.

Nicolaides, Phedon. A General Equilibrium Method for Evaluating Customs Unions. *Econ. Int.*, Aug.–Nov. 1988, *41*(3–4), pp. 216–24.

_____. Limits to the Expansion of Neoclassical Economics. *Cambridge J. Econ.*, September 1988, *12*(3), pp. 313–28.

Nicoletti, Giuseppe. A Cross-Country Analysis of Private Consumption, Inflation and the "Debt Neutrality Hypothesis." *OECD Econ. Stud.*, Autumn 1988, (11), pp. 41–87.

Nicoll, William. The Long March of the EC's 1988 Budget. *J. Common Market Stud.*, December 1988, *27*(2), pp. 161–69.

de Nicolò, Vinsenzo. Learning by Doing and Cyclical Growth. In *[Goodwin, R. M.]*, 1988, 62–82.

Niculsecu-Mizil, E. Some Theoretical and Applied Considerations Regarding the Living Systems Social–Economic Cybernetic Systems Analogy. *Econ. Computat. Cybern. Stud. Res.*, 1988, *23*(1), pp. 45–53.

Nidaira, Koh'ichi and Kaneko, Yukio. Towards Basic Human Needs in Relation to Public Health and Nutrition. In *Bell, D. E. and Reich, M. R., eds.*, 1988, pp. 241–63.

Niehans, Jürg. International Coordination of Economic Policies: Scope, Method, and Effects: Comment. In *Guth, W., ed.*, 1988, pp. 192–97.

Nielsen, Jens Christian and Larsen, Niels. Estimation af en dansk eksport model. (Estimation of a Model of Demand and Supply of Danish Exportables. With English summary.) *Nationaløkon. Tidsskr.*, 1988, *126*(1), pp. 75–82.

Nielsen, Lars Tyge. Comparative Risk Aversion. *Econ. Letters*, 1988, *27*(4), pp. 321–25.

_____. Uniqueness of Equilibrium in the Classical Capital Asset Pricing Model. *J. Finan. Quant. Anal.*, September 1988, *23*(3), pp. 329–36.

Nielsen, Michael Teit. The Pareto Domination of Irrational Expectations over Rational Expectations. *J. Econ. Theory*, December 1988, *46*(2), pp. 322–34.

Nielsen, Niels Chr. and Møller, Michael. Pension i OD-sammenhæng. (Pension Reform and Profit Sharing. With English summary.) *Na-*

tionaløkon. Tidsskr., 1988, *126*(2), pp. 171–82.

Niemann, Hans-Werner. Russian Business in the Brüning Era. In *Pohl, H. and Rudolph, B.*, *eds.*, 1988, pp. 77–94.

Nier, Keith A. and Butrica, Andrew J. Telegraphy Becomes a World System: Paradox and Progress in Technology and Management. In *Perkins, E. J., ed.*, 1988, pp. 211–26.

Niessen, Hermann. The Seventh Directive on Consolidated Accounts within the Framework of Company Law Harmonisation in the European Community. In *Gray, S. J. and Coenenberg, A. G., eds.*, 1988, pp. 3–12.

Nieswiadomy, Michael L. Input Substitution in Irrigated Agriculture in the High Plains of Texas, 1970–80. *Western J. Agr. Econ.*, July 1988, *13*(1), pp. 63–70.

———— **and Molina, David J.** Urban Water Demand Estimates under Increasing Block Rates. *Growth Change*, Winter 1988, *19*(1), pp. 1–12.

———— **and Silberberg, Eugene.** Calculating Changes in Worklife Expectancies and Lost Earnings in Personal Injury Cases. *J. Risk Ins.*, September 1988, *55*(3), pp. 492–98.

———— **and Slottje, D. J.** Estimating Lost Future Earnings Using the New Worklife Tables: A Comment. *J. Risk Ins.*, September 1988, *55*(3), pp. 539–44.

Nieuwenhuis, J. W. Stability Analysis by Means of Modern Linear Systems Theory. *Econ. Letters*, 1988, *28*(1), pp. 53–56.

Nieva, Claro L. and Faigal, Gerardo Ma. A. Processed Agricultural Products: Issues for Negotiation between ASEAN and the EC. In *Langhammer, R. J. and Rieger, H. C., eds.*, 1988, pp. 116–28.

Nigg, Dudley M. State and Regional Strategies. In *Federal Home Loan Bank of San Francisco*, 1988, pp. 77–82.

Niggle, Christopher J. The Increasing Importance of Financial Capital in the U.S. Economy. *J. Econ. Issues*, June 1988, *22*(2), pp. 581–88.

Nightingale, John. Information and Productivity: An Attempted Replication of an Empirical Exercise. *Info. Econ. Policy*, 1988, *3*(1), pp. 55–67.

Nijkamp, Peter. Environmental Problems and Employment Opportunities: Comment. In *Kregel, J. A.; Matzner, E. and Roncaglia, A., eds.*, 1988, pp. 288–90.

————. Information Center Policy in a Spatial Development Perspective. *Econ. Develop. Cult. Change*, October 1988, *37*(1), pp. 173–93.

———— **and Brouwer, Floor.** Design and Structure Analysis of Integrated Environmental Planning Models. *Europ. Rev. Agr. Econ.*, 1988, *15*(1), pp. 19–38.

———— **and Davelaar, Evert Jan.** The Incubator Hypothesis: Re-vitalization of Metropolitan Areas? *Ann. Reg. Sci.*, November 1988, *22*(3), pp. 48–65.

———— **and Dieperink, H.** Innovative Behaviour, Agglomeration Economies and R&D Infra-

structure. *Empirical Econ.*, 1988, *13*(1), pp. 35–57.

———— **and Fischer, Manfred M.** The Role of Small Firms for Regional Revitalization. *Ann. Reg. Sci.*, February 1988, *22*, pp. 28–42.

————; **van der Mark, Ronald and Alsters, Theo.** Evaluation of Regional Incubator Profiles for Small and Medium Sized Enterprises. *Reg. Stud.*, April 1988, *22*(2), pp. 95–105.

———— **and Perrels, Adriaan.** Impacts of Electricity Rates on Industrial Location. *Energy Econ.*, April 1988, *10*(2), pp. 107–16.

———— **and Reggiani, A.** Dynamic Spatial Interaction Models: New Directions. *Environ. Planning A*, November 1988, *20*(11), pp. 1449–60.

———— **and Rouwendal, Jan.** Intergenerational Discount Rates in Long-term Plan Evaluation. *Public Finance*, 1988, *43*(2), pp. 195–211.

———— **and Salomon, Ilan.** Telecommunication and the Tyranny of Space. In *Orishimo, I.; Hewings, G. J. D. and Nijkamp, P., eds.*, 1988, pp. 91–106.

————; **Scholten, H. and Brouwer, Floor.** Hybrid Log-Linear Models for Spatial Interaction and Stability Analysis. *Metroecon.*, February 1988, *39*(1), pp. 43–65.

———— **and Soeteman, Frits.** Ecologically Sustainable Economic Development: Key Issues for Strategic Environmental Management. *Int. J. Soc. Econ.*, 1988, *15*(3–4), pp. 88–102.

———— **and Sonis, Michael.** Qualitative Impact Analysis for Dynamic Spatial Systems. *Econ. Geogr.*, July 1988, *64*(3), pp. 226–41.

Nijman, Theodore E. and Palm, Franz C. Consistent Estimation of Regression Models with Incompletely Observed Exogenous Variables. *Ann. Écon. Statist.*, Oct.–Dec. 1988, (12), pp. 151–75.

Nikolopoulos, Andreas. Trends in the Development of Industrial Democracy in Greece and Their Impact on Management Discretion. In *Dlugos, G.; Dorow, W. and Weiermair, K., eds.*, 1988, pp. 221–31.

Nikonov, Aleksandr A. The Development of Cooperation and the Resolution of the Food Problem. *Prob. Econ.*, October 1988, *31*(6), pp. 84–100.

————. "The Responsibility of Science and for Science": An Inteview with the President of VASKhNIL. *Prob. Econ.*, September 1988, *31*(5), pp. 67–81.

————, **et al.** Stavropol, USSR: An Agricultural Management Model. In *Parikh, J. K., ed.*, 1988, pp. 101–134.

Nimroody, Rosy and Epstein, Henry. We're Stronger without SDI. *Challenge*, Sept.–Oct. 1988, *31*(5), pp. 44–49.

Nirmala, V. and Subramaniyan, G. The Economic Efficiency of High-Yielding, Irrigated Cotton in India. *Margin*, July–Sept. 1988, *20*(4), pp. 80–88.

Niroomand, Farhang. Inter- versus Intra-industry Trade: A Note on U.S. Trends, 1963–1980. *Weltwirtsch. Arch.*, 1988, *124*(2), pp. 337–40.

———— **and Bahmani-Oskooee, Mohsen.** On the Exchange-Rate Elasticity of the Demand for

International Reserves: Some Evidence from Industrial Countries. *Weltwirtsch. Arch.*, 1988, *124*(1), pp. 161–68.

Nisbett, Richard E.; Fong, Geoffrey T. and Krantz, David H. The Effects of Statistical Training on Thinking about Everyday Problems. In *Bell, D. E.; Raiffa, H. and Tversky, A., eds.*, 1988, *1986*, pp. 299–340.

Nishikawa, Jun. The World Crisis and Transnational Corporations. In *Teng, W. and Wang, N. T., eds.*, 1988, pp. 93–106.

Nishimizu, Mieko; Page, John M., Jr. and Bateman, Deborah A. Regional Productivity Differentials and Development Policy in Yugoslavia, 1965–1978. *J. Compar. Econ.*, March 1988, *12*(1), pp. 24–42.

Nishimura, Kazuo; Benhabib, Jess and Jafarey, Saqib. The Dynamics of Efficient Intertemporal Allocations with Many Agents, Recursive Preferences, and Production. *J. Econ. Theory*, April 1988, *44*(2), pp. 301–20.

Nishimura, Kiyohiko G. Expectational Coordination Failure. *Econ. Stud. Quart.*, December 1988, *39*(4), pp. 322–34.

_____. A Note on Price Rigidity: Pledging Stable Prices under Sluggish Information Diffusion and Costly Search. *J. Econ. Behav. Organ.*, July 1988, *10*(1), pp. 121–31.

Nishino, Terutaro. To Promote Economic Self-Reliance: A Proposal for Pacific Island Countries. In *Kozmetsky, G.; Matsumoto, H. and Smilor, R. W., eds.*, 1988, pp. 153–60.

Nishisato, S. Market Segmentation by Dual Scaling through Generalized Forced Classification. In *Gaul, W. and Schader, M., eds.*, 1988, pp. 268–78.

Nishizawa, Tamotsu and Sugihara, Shirō. In the 'Commercial Metropolis' Osaka: Schools of Commerce and Law. In *Sugiyama, C. and Mizuta, H., eds.*, 1988, pp. 189–207.

_____ **and Sugiyama, Chūhei.** 'Captain of Industry': Tokyo Commercial School at Hitotsubashi. In *Sugiyama, C. and Mizuta, H., eds.*, 1988, pp. 151–69.

Niskanen, William A. Evaluating Government Policy. In *Association of Private Education*, 1988, pp. 1–4.

_____. Macroeconomic Issues for Europe in the 1980s: Can the NAIRU Be Tamed? Comment. In *Giersch, H., ed.*, 1988, pp. 23–25.

_____. Nonmarket Decision Making: The Peculiar Economics of Bureaucracy. In *Ricketts, M., ed., Vol. 1*, 1988, *1968*, pp. 249–61.

_____. A Primer on Energy Security Policy. In *Fried, E. R. and Blandin, N. M., eds.*, 1988, pp. 98–102.

_____. Public Choice and Constitutional Economics: Foreword: The Erosion of the Economic Constitution. In *Gwartney, J. D. and Wagner, R. E., eds.*, 1988, pp. xi–xiii.

_____. Reflections on Reaganomics. In *Boaz, D., ed.*, 1988, pp. 9–15.

_____. The Uneasy Relation between the Budget and Trade Deficits. *Cato J.*, Fall 1988, *8*(2), pp. 507–19.

_____. What Microeconomics Teaches Us about

the Dynamic Macro Effects of Fiscal Policy: Comment. *J. Money, Credit, Banking*, Part 2, August 1988, *20*(3), pp. 496–99.

Nissan, Edward and Caveny, Regina. Regional Population Growth Rate Differences: Note. *Growth Change*, Winter 1988, *19*(1), pp. 67–74.

_____ **and Caveny, Regina.** Relative Concentration of Sales and Assets in American Business. *Southern Econ. J.*, April 1988, *54*(4), pp. 928–33.

_____ **and Caveny, Regina.** Relative Welfare Improvements of Low Income versus High Income Countries. *World Devel.*, May 1988, *16*(5), pp. 607–14.

Nisticò, Sergio. Prezzi naturali e conflitto distributivo in Smith e Ricardo. (With English summary.) *Stud. Econ.*, 1988, *43*(36), pp. 125–54.

Nitsch, J. Energy Supply Structures and the Role of Gaseous Energy Carriers. In *Winter, C.-J. and Nitsch, J., eds.*, 1988, pp. 13–29.

_____ **and Klaiss, H.** The Economics of Energy and Cooperation with Energy-Producing Countries. In *Winter, C.-J. and Nitsch, J., eds.*, 1988, pp. 368–74.

_____ **and Voigt, C.** Hydrogen in a Future Energy Supply System. In *Winter, C.-J. and Nitsch, J., eds.*, 1988, pp. 314–57.

_____ **and Voigt, C.** Hydrogen's Potential. In *Winter, C.-J. and Nitsch, J., eds.*, 1988, pp. 293–313.

_____ **and Voigt, C.** Launch Concepts for Nonfossil Hydrogen. In *Winter, C.-J. and Nitsch, J., eds.*, 1988, pp. 358–67.

Nitsch, Thomas O. Social Catholicism: Birth and Tradition of Solidarism. *Int. J. Soc. Econ.*, 1988, *15*(9), pp. 3–38.

Nitta, Michio. Birth of Rengo and Reformation of Union Organization. In *Japan Institute of Labour, ed.*, 1988, *1988*, pp. 86–89.

_____. Trends in Wage Profile: Reestablishment of Length-of-Service-Based Wages? In *Japan Institute of Labour, ed.*, 1988, *1985*, pp. 36–39.

_____. Will Employment Practices and Industrial Relations Change? Union Leaders' View. In *Japan Institute of Labour, ed.*, 1988, *1987*, pp. 44–47.

Nitzan, Shmuel and Gradstein, Mark. Participation, Decision Aggregation and Internal Information Gathering in Organizational Decision Making. *J. Econ. Behav. Organ.*, December 1988, *10*(4), pp. 415–31.

_____ **and Kahana, Nava.** Production Theory with Profit-Constrained Revenue-Maximization: The Duality Approach. *Managerial Dec. Econ.*, December 1988, *9*(4), pp. 269–73.

Niv, Amittai and Bar-On, Dan. The Transition from a "Simple" Industry to a "Sophisticated" One in the Future Kibbutz. In *Maital, S., ed., Vol. 1*, 1988, pp. 357–75.

Nkomo, Jabavu C.; Robinson, Peter B. and Ram, Bonnie. Industrial Energy Consumption, Conservation Strategies and Policy Options in Zimbabwe. In *Hosier, R. H., ed. (II)*, 1988, pp. 26–49.

Nobay, A. R. and Levy, E. Using Bivariate Autoregressive Representations in Testing Exact Expectations Relations. *Econ. Letters*, 1988, *28*(4), pp. 343–49.

Nobel, Nico. Netherlands: Mandatory Publication of Resolutions and Rulings is Necessary for Fair and Just Taxation. *Bull. Int. Fiscal Doc.*, Aug.–Sept. 1988, *42*(8–9), pp. 352–54.

Nobel, Peter. Das EG-Binnenmarktprogramm und die Weiterentwicklung des schweizerischen Gesellschaftsrechts. (The EEC Integration and the Further Development of the Swiss Company Law. With English summary.) *Aussenwirtschaft*, September 1988, *43*(3), pp. 423–48.

Nobert, Yves and Laporte, Gilbert. A Vehicle Flow Model for the Optimal Design of a Two-Echelon Distribution System. In *Eiselt, H. A. and Pederzoli, G., eds.*, 1988, pp. 158–73.

Nobes, Christopher. An Historical-Comparative Perspective of Governmental Accounting. In *Chan, J. L. and Jones, R. H., eds.*, 1988, pp. 198–206.

_____. The United Kingdom and the Seventh Directive. In *Gray, S. J. and Coenenberg, A. G., eds.*, 1988, pp. 128–42.

Noble, Charles. Rebuilding the Regulatory State: Prospects for Environmental and Worker Protection. In *Levine, M. V., et al.*, 1988, pp. 79–110.

Nocera, Simon and Blackwell, Michael. The Impact of Debt to Equity Conversion. *Finance Develop.*, June 1988, *25*(2), pp. 15–17.

Nochteff, Hugo J. Industrial Revolution, Technological Paradigm and Regional Alternatives. *CEPAL Rev.*, December 1988, (36), pp. 25–32.

Noether, Monica. Competition among Hospitals. *J. Health Econ.*, September 1988, *7*(3), pp. 259–84.

Noguchi, Tasuku. High Technology and Its Impact on Business Management. In *Urabe, K.; Child, J. and Kagono, T., eds.*, 1988, pp. 303–18.

Noguchi, Yasuhiko; Masui, Kazuhito and Hagiwara, Shintaro. Anti-dumping Laws in Japan. *J. World Trade*, August 1988, *22*(4), pp. 35–50.

Nogueira Ramos, Pedro. Uma curva de oferta de crédito com vários regimes. (With English summary.) *Economia (Portugal)*, October 1988, *12*(3), pp. 371–85.

Nogués, Julio J. La economía política del proteccionismo y la liberalización en la Argentina. (With English summary.) *Desarrollo Econ.*, July–Sept. 1988, *28*(110), pp. 159–82.

_____ and Laird, Samuel. Manufactured Export Performance of the Highly Indebted Countries. *Devel. Econ.*, December 1988, *26*(4), pp. 403–21.

Noh, Inchul. Test of Rationality of Adaptive Expectations in the German Hyperinflation. *Int. Econ. J.*, Spring 1988, *2*(1), pp. 39–52.

Nojima, Noriyuki and Mizoguchi, Toshiyuki. Economic Time-Series Database of Japan's Former Colonies (COTEDAS): 1885–1945: An Example of Historical Statistics Database. In *Uno, K. and Shishido, S., eds.*, 1988, pp. 238–44.

Nolan, Peter and Brown, William. Wages and Labour Productivity: The Contribution of Industrial Relations Research to the Understanding of Pay Determination. *Brit. J. Ind. Relat.*, November 1988, *26*(3), pp. 339–61.

Noland, Marcus. The Determinants of International Specialization in Manufactured Goods, 1965–1980. *Econ. Stud. Quart.*, September 1988, *39*(3), pp. 216–32.

_____. Japanese Household Portfolio Allocation Behavior. *Rev. Econ. Statist.*, February 1988, *70*(1), pp. 135–39.

Noll, Roger G. Private Antitrust Litigation: Comment: Settlement Incentives and Follow-on Litigation. In *White, L. J., ed.*, 1988, pp. 371–78.

Noller, C. W. Jevons on Cost. In *Wood, J. C., ed., Vol. 2*, 1988, *1972*, pp. 129–33.

Nomura, Masuo. On Exact Small Sample Properties of Ordinary Ridge Estimators. *Econ. Letters*, 1988, *27*(3), pp. 251–55.

van den Noord, Paul J. The SEO Econometric Model of the Netherlands Economy (SECMON) In *Driehuis, W.; Fase, M. M. G. and den Hartog, H., eds.*, 1988, pp. 433–55.

_____ and Driehuis, Wim. The Effects of Investment Subsidies on Employment. *Econ. Modelling*, January 1988, *5*(1), pp. 32–40.

_____ and Driehuis, Wim. Modelling the Effects of Investment Subsidies. In *Motamen, H., ed.*, 1988, pp. 473–90.

Noori, Esmail and Baghestani, Hamid. On the Rationality of the Michigan Monthly Survey of Inflationary Expectations. *Econ. Letters*, 1988, *27*(4), pp. 333–35.

Nooteboom, Bart. The Facts about Small Business and the Real Values of Its 'Life World': A Social Philosophical Interpretation of This Sector of the Modern Economy. *Amer. J. Econ. Soc.*, July 1988, *47*(3), pp. 299–314.

_____; Kleijweg, Aad and Thurik, A. Roy. Normal Costs and Demand Effects in Price Setting: A Study of Retailing. *Europ. Econ. Rev.*, April 1988, *32*(4), pp. 999–1011.

_____; Thurik, A. Roy and Vollebregt, J. A. C. Do Retail Margins Differ between European Countries? A Comparative Study. In *Kaynak, E., ed.*, 1988, pp. 155–66.

Norburn, David; Birley, Sue and Manning, Kingsley. Implementing Corporate Venturing. In *Lamb, R. and Shrivastava, P., eds.*, 1988, pp. 165–79.

Nord, Stephen; Phelps, John J. and Sheets, Robert G. An Analysis of the Economic Impact of the Service Sector on Underemployment in Major Metropolitan Areas in the United States. *Urban Stud.*, October 1988, *25*(5), pp. 418–32.

Nord, Walter R., et al. Work Values and the Conduct of Organizational Behavior. In *Staw, B. M. and Cummings, L. L., eds.*, 1988, pp. 1–42.

Nordau, C. G.; Cogoli, A. and Gmünder, F. K.

Cell Biology in Space: From Basic Science to Biotechnology III. In *Egan, J. J., et al.*, 1988, pp. 353–66.

Nordbotten, Svein. Experiments with Probabilistic Consultation Systems. In *Edwards, D. and Raun, N. E., eds.*, 1988, pp. 181–86.

Nordhaus, William D. Can the Share Economy Conquer Stagflation? *Quart. J. Econ.*, February 1988, *103*(1), pp. 201–17.

———. The Productivity Slowdown, Measurement Issues, and the Explosion of Computer Power: Comment. *Brookings Pap. Econ. Act.*, 1988, (2), pp. 421–24.

——— **and Godley, Wynne.** Pricing in the Trade Cycle. In *Sawyer, M. C., ed.*, 1988, *1972*, pp. 227–48.

Nordstrom, Kjell and Vahlne, Jan-Erik. Choice of Market Channel in a Strategic Perspective. In *Hood, N. and Vahlne, J.-E., eds.*, 1988, pp. 256–81.

Noreen, Eric. An Empirical Comparison of Probit and OLS Regression Hypothesis Tests. *J. Acc. Res.*, Spring 1988, *26*(1), pp. 119–33.

Norel, P.; Quenan, C. and Sarry, M.-C. Stratégies bancaires et risque-pays. (International Banking Strategies and Country-Risk. With English summary.) *Écon. Appl.*, 1988, *41*(4), pp. 857–72.

Norgaard, Richard B. The Biological Control of Cassava Mealybug in Africa. *Amer. J. Agr. Econ.*, May 1988, *70*(2), pp. 366–71.

———. The Oyster Beds of Ao Ban Don. *Land Econ.*, February 1988, *64*(1), pp. 83–85.

Noriega del Valle, Enrique. Tax Treatment of Computer Software: Peru. In *International Fiscal Association, ed. (II)*, 1988, pp. 471–83.

Norman, G.; Thisse, Jacques-François and MacLeod, W. Bentley. Price Discrimination and Equilibrium in Monopolistic Competition. *Int. J. Ind. Organ.*, December 1988, *6*(4), pp. 429–46.

Norman, Victor D. and Haaland, Jan I. Modelling Trade and Trade Policy: Introduction. In *Haaland, J. I. and Norman, V. D., eds.*, 1988, pp. 1–10.

Normolle, Daniel and Horwitz, Bertrand. Federal Agency R&D Contract Awards and the FASB Rule for Privately-Funded R&D. *Accounting Rev.*, July 1988, *63*(3), pp. 414–35.

Norrander, Barbara and Grofman, Bernard. A Rational Choice Model of Citizen Participation in High and Low Commitment Electoral Activities. *Public Choice*, May 1988, *57*(2), pp. 187–92.

Norrbin, Stefan C. Determinants of Differences in Regional Cyclical Variability. *Rev. Reg. Stud.*, Fall 1988, *18*(3), pp. 16–22.

——— **and Schlagenhauf, Don E.** An Inquiry into the Sources of Macroeconomic Fluctuations. *J. Monet. Econ.*, July 1988, *22*(1), pp. 43–70.

Norris, Donald F. Microcomputers in Financial Mangement: Case Studies of Eight American Cities. *Public Budg. Finance*, Spring 1988, *8*(1), pp. 69–82.

Norsa, Aldo. The Global Construction Industry:

Italy. In *Strassmann, W. P. and Wells, J., eds.*, 1988, pp. 86–103.

North-Coombes, M. D. Struggles in the Canefields: Small Growers in Mauritius 1921–1937. In *Albert, B. and Graves, A., eds.*, 1988, pp. 194–208.

North, Douglass C. Ideology and Political/Economic Institutions. *Cato J.*, Spring–Summer 1988, *8*(1), pp. 15–28.

———. Institutions, Economic Growth and Freedom: An Historical Introduction. In *Walker, M. A., ed. (I)*, 1988, pp. 3–25.

——— **and Wallis, John Joseph.** Should Transaction Costs Be Subtracted from Gross National Product? *J. Econ. Hist.*, September 1988, *48*(3), pp. 651–54.

North, Gary. Why Murray Rothbard Will Never Win the Nobel Prize! In *[Rothbard, M. N.]*, 1988, pp. 89–109.

North, Michael. The Lighterman Business in the Baltic Ports: Danzig, Elbing and Königsberg (Sixteenth–Eighteenth Centuries). In *Cavaciocchi, S., ed.*, 1988, pp. 541–49.

Northcraft, Gregory B.; Neale, Margaret A. and Huber, Vandra L. The Effects of Cognitive Bias and Social Influence on Human Resources Management Decisions. In *Ferris, G. R. and Rowland, K. M., eds.*, 1988, pp. 157–89.

Northrop, Emily M. Economic Growth and Poverty Reductions: Important Mitigating Factors. *Eastern Econ. J.*, Oct.–Dec. 1988, *14*(4), pp. 349–56.

Northrup, Herbert R. The Rise and Demise of PATCO. In *Lewin, D., et al., eds.*, 1988, *1984*, pp. 240–67.

———. The Rise and Demise of PATCO: Reply. In *Lewin, D., et al., eds.*, 1988, pp. 279–87.

———**; Campbell, Duncan C. and Slowinski, Betty J.** Multinational Union–Management Consultation in Europe: Resurgence in the 1980s? *Int. Lab. Rev.*, 1988, *127*(5), pp. 525–43.

———**; Greis, Theresa Diss and Dowgun, Kay M.** The Office and Professional Employees International Union: From "Union Company Union" to Independent Representative. *J. Lab. Res.*, Winter 1988, *9*(1), pp. 91–106.

———**; Greis, Theresa Diss and Dowgun, Kay M.** The Office of Professional Employees International Union: Part Two—Mission Unclear and Unrealized. *J. Lab. Res.*, Summer 1988, *9*(3), pp. 251–70.

Norton, Bruce. Epochs and Essences: A Review of Marxist Long-Wave and Stagnation Theories. *Cambridge J. Econ.*, June 1988, *12*(2), pp. 203–24.

Norton, Desmond A. G. Employment Relationships in Irish Counties 1881–1971. *Econ. Soc. Rev.*, July 1988, *19*(4), pp. 265–81.

———. On the Economic Theory of Smuggling. *Economica*, February 1988, *55*(217), pp. 107–18.

Norton, Edgar and Pittman, Russell. M-Form Organization and Firm Profitability. *Rev. Ind. Organ.*, Spring 1988, *3*(3), pp. 1–14.

Norton, Gale Ann. The Limitless Federal Taxing

Power. In *Gwartney, J. D. and Wagner, R. E., eds.*, 1988, *1983*, pp. 253–84.

Norton, George W.; Bezuneh, Mesfin and Deaton, Brady J. Food Aid Impacts in Rural Kenya. *Amer. J. Agr. Econ.*, February 1988, *70*(1), pp. 181–91.

Norton, Seth W. An Empirical Look at Franchising as an Organizational Form. *J. Bus.*, April 1988, *61*(2), pp. 197–218.

———. Regulation, the OPEC Oil Supply Shock, and Wealth Effects for Electric Utilities. *Econ. Inquiry*, April 1988, *26*(2), pp. 223–38.

Norwood, Janet L. The Measurement of Unemployment. *Amer. Econ. Rev.*, May 1988, *78*(2), pp. 284–88.

———. Measuring the Cost and Incidence of Employee Benefits. *Mon. Lab. Rev.*, August 1988, *111*(8), pp. 3–8.

Noser, Eugene A., Jr.; Berkowitz, Stephen A. and Logue, Dennis E. The Total Cost of Transactions on the NYSE. *J. Finance*, March 1988, *43*(1), pp. 97–112.

Nothaft, Frank E. and Gabriel, Stuart A. Rental Housing Markets and the Natural Vacancy Rate. *Amer. Real Estate Urban Econ. Assoc. J.*, Winter 1988, *16*(4), pp. 419–29.

Notin, Bernard. La théorie du circuit et le débat libre-echange/protectionnisme. (Circuit Theory: Free Trade vs. Protectionism. With English summary.) *Écon. Soc.*, June–July 1988, *22*(6–7), pp. 147–63.

Noto, Nonna A. Revenue and Expenditure Turnbacks. In *Bell, M. E., ed.*, 1988, pp. 125–62.

Nournoff, S. J. Transnational Corporation Investment in China: A View from the Outside. In *Teng, W. and Wang, N. T., eds.*, 1988, pp. 199–222.

Nourse, Hugh O. The "Cap Rate," 1966–1984: Reply. *Land Econ.*, November 1988, *64*(4), pp. 384–85.

——— **and Ahn, Jeong Keun.** Spatial Economic Interdependence in an Urban Hierarchy System. *J. Reg. Sci.*, August 1988, *28*(3), pp. 421–32.

———; **Okoruwa, A. Ason and Terza, Joseph V.** Estimating Patronization Shares for Urban Retail Centers: An Extension of the Poisson Gravity Model. *J. Urban Econ.*, November 1988, *24*(3), pp. 241–59.

Nourzad, Farrokh and El-Hodiri, Mohamed A. A Note on Leontief Technology and Input Substitution. *J. Reg. Sci.*, February 1988, *28*(1), pp. 119–20.

——— **and McGibany, James M.** Money Demand and the Effects of Fiscal Policies: Comment. *J. Money, Credit, Banking*, November 1988, *20*(4), pp. 706–14.

——— **and McGibany, James M.** The Substitutability of Real Capital and Financial Assets. *Appl. Econ.*, November 1988, *20*(11), pp. 1445–51.

Novak, Kenneth and Nagle, Thomas T. The Roles of Segmentation and Awareness in Explaining Variations in Price Markups. In *Devinney, T. M., ed.*, 1988, pp. 313–32.

Nove, Alec. Labor Incentives in Soviet Kolkhozy.

In *Brada, J. C. and Wadekin, K.-E., eds.*, 1988, pp. 13–22.

———. Ortona on Stalinism: A Comment. *Écon. Appl.*, 1988, *41*(3), pp. 649–51.

Novos, Ian E. and Waldman, Michael. Complementarity and Partial Nonexcludability: An Analysis of the Software/Computer Market. *J. Inst. Theoretical Econ.*, June 1988, *144*(3), pp. 443–61.

Novshek, William. On the Existence of Cournot Equilibrium. In *Daughety, A. F., ed.*, 1988, *1985*, pp. 103–21.

——— **and Sonnenschein, Hugo.** Cournot and Walras Equilibrium. In *Daughety, A. F., ed.*, 1988, *1978*, pp. 271–316.

Nowakowski, Marek and Chanas, Stefan. From Fuzzy Data to a Single Action—A Simulation Approach. In *Kacprzyk, J. and Fedrizzi, M., eds.*, 1988, pp. 331–41.

Nowell, Clifford; Evans, Marc A. and McDonald, Lyman. Length-Biased Sampling in Contingent Valuation Studies. *Land Econ.*, November 1988, *64*(4), pp. 367–71.

Nowotny, Kenneth. Transmission Technology and Electric Utility Regulation. *J. Econ. Issues*, June 1988, *22*(2), pp. 555–62.

Nti, Kofi O. Capital Asset Prices in an Oligopolistic Market. *J. Econ. (Z. Nationalökon.)*, 1988, *48*(1), pp. 35–57.

——— **and Monahan, George E.** Optimal Pricing and Advertising for New Products with Repeat Purchases. In *Devinney, T. M., ed.*, 1988, pp. 145–65.

Nugent, Jeffrey B. Foreign Aid, Economic Development and Income Distribution: Some Inferences from a CGE Model for Egypt. In *Sengupta, J. K. and Kadekodi, G. K., eds.*, 1988, pp. 63–90.

——— **and Azabou, Mongi.** Contractual Choice in Tax Collection Activities: Some Implications of the Experience with Tax Farming. *J. Inst. Theoretical Econ.*, September 1988, *144*(4), pp. 684–705.

Nummi, Tapio and Liski, Erkki P. Comparing Sensitivity of Models to Missing Data in the GMANOVA. In *Edwards, D. and Raun, N. E., eds.*, 1988, pp. 311–16.

———; **Nurhonen, Markku and Puntanen, S.** Computer-Aided Illustration of Regression Diagnostics. In *Edwards, D. and Raun, N. E., eds.*, 1988, pp. 93–98.

Nunamaker, Thomas R. Using Data Envelopment Analysis to Measure the Efficiency of Non-Profit Organizations: A Critical Evaluation—Reply. *Managerial Dec. Econ.*, September 1988, *9*(3), pp. 255–56.

Núñez del Prado, Arturo. Economies of Difficult Viability: An Option to Be Examined. *CEPAL Rev.*, December 1988, (36), pp. 161–77.

Nunn, Kenneth P., Jr.; Gombola, Michael J. and Kahl, Douglas R. Valuation of the Preferred Stock Sinking Fund Feature: A Time-Series Approach. *J. Finan. Res.*, Spring 1988, *11*(1), pp. 33–42.

——— **and Hegde, Shantaram P.** Non-infinitesimal Rate Changes and Macaulay Duration. *J.*

Portfol. Manage., Winter 1988, *14*(2), pp. 69–73.

Nunn, Susan Christopher and Ingram, Helen M. Information, the Decision Forum, and Third-Party Effects in Water Transfers. *Water Resources Res.*, April 1988, *24*(4), pp. 473–80.

Nunziante, Gianni. Security on Movable Property and Receivables in Europe: Italy. In *Dickson, M. G.; Rosener, W. and Storm, P. M., eds.*, 1988, pp. 91–107.

Nurhonen, Markku; Puntanen, S. and Nummi, Tapio. Computer-Aided Illustration of Regression Diagnostics. In *Edwards, D. and Raun, N. E., eds.*, 1988, pp. 93–98.

Nurmi, Hannu. Assumptions of Individual Preferences in the Theory of Voting Procedures. In *Kacprzyk, J. and Roubens, M., eds.*, 1988, pp. 142–55.

_____ **and Berg, Sven.** Making Choices in the Old-Fashioned Way. *Econ. Scelte Pubbliche/J. Public Finance Public Choice*, May–Aug. 1988, *6*(2), pp. 95–113.

Nuti, Domenico Mario. Capitalism, Socialism and Steady Growth. In *Steedman, I., ed., Vol. 2*, 1988, *1973*, pp. 252–77.

_____. Codetermination, Profit Sharing, and Full Employment. In *Jones, D. C. and Svejnar, J., eds.*, 1988, pp. 169–83.

_____. Competitive Valuation and Efficiency of Capital Investment in the Socialist Economy. *Europ. Econ. Rev.*, March 1988, *32*(2–3), pp. 459–64.

_____. Domestic and External Macro-policies: Comments. In *Saunders, C. T., ed.*, 1988, pp. 219–22.

_____. 'Vulgar Economy' in the Theory of Income Distribution. In *Steedman, I., ed., Vol. 1*, 1988, *1970*, pp. 267–73.

Nutzinger, Hans G. Employee Participation by Codetermination, Labor Law, and Collective Bargaining. In *Dlugos, G.; Dorow, W. and Weiermair, K., eds.*, 1988, pp. 301–12.

Nyarko, Yaw. On Characterizing Optimality of Stochastic Competitive Processes. *J. Econ. Theory*, August 1988, *45*(2), pp. 316–29.

_____ **and Kiefer, Nicholas M.** Control of a Linear Regression Process with Unknown Parameters. In *Barnett, W. A.; Berndt, E. R. and White, H., eds.*, 1988, pp. 105–20.

Nydegger, Alfred; Hauser, Heinz and Hösli, Madeleine. Die Schweiz vor dem EG-Bennenmarkt. (Switzerland and the Completion of the EC Internal Market. With English summary.) *Aussenwirtschaft*, September 1988, *43*(3), pp. 327–65.

Nye, Blaine F. and Hofflander, Alfred E. Experience Rating in Medical Professional Liability Insurance. *J. Risk Ins.*, March 1988, *55*(1), pp. 150–57.

Nye, John Vincent. Game Theory and the North American Fur Trade: A Comment. *J. Econ. Hist.*, September 1988, *48*(3), pp. 677–80.

Nyers, Rezsö. National Economic Objectives and the Hungarian Reform Process in the 1980s. In *Brada, J. C. and Dobozi, I., eds.*, 1988, pp. 33–51.

Nyhus, Douglas. The INFORUM-ERI International System of Macroeconomic Input–Output Models. In *Ciaschini, M., ed.*, 1988, pp. 391–410.

Nyman, John A. Excess Demand, the Percentage of Medicaid Patients, and the Quality of Nursing Home Care. *J. Human Res.*, Winter 1988, *23*(1), pp. 76–92.

_____. The Marginal Cost of Nursing Home Care: New York, 1983. *J. Health Econ.*, December 1988, *7*(4), pp. 393–412.

Nymoen, Ragnar and Hoel, Michael. The Supply Side of RIKMOD: Short-Run Producer Behaviour in a Model of Monopolistic Competition. In *Motamen, H., ed.*, 1988, pp. 381–405.

_____ **and Hoel, Michael.** The Supply Side of RIKMOD: Short-run Producer Behaviour in a Model of Monopolistic Competition. *Econ. Modelling*, January 1988, *5*(1), pp. 58–70.

_____ **and Hoel, Michael.** Wage Formation in Norwegian Manufacturing: An Empirical Application of a Theoretical Bargaining Model. *Europ. Econ. Rev.*, April 1988, *32*(4), pp. 977–97.

Nyong'o, P. Anyang'. The Possibilities and Historical Limitations of Import-Substitution Industrialization in Kenya. In *Coughlin, P. and Ikiara, G. K., eds.*, 1988, pp. 6–50.

Nyquist, Hans and Coursey, Don L. Applications of Robust Estimation Techniques in Demand Analysis. *Appl. Econ.*, May 1988, *20*(5), pp. 595–610.

Nystad, Arild N. On the Economics of Improved Oil Recovery: The Optimal Recovery Factor from Oil and Gas Reservoirs. *Energy J.*, October 1988, *9*(4), pp. 49–61.

O'Brien, A. Maureen and Junk, Paul E. Some Social Costs of Unemployment: A Regional Analysis. In *Missouri Valley Economic Assoc.*, 1988, pp. 7–11.

_____; **Lichty, Richard W. and Lim, Kai H.** An Analysis of Labor Productivity Effects on Regional Growth. *Reg. Sci. Persp.*, 1988, *18*(1), pp. 43–57.

O'Brien, Anthony Patrick. Factory Size, Economies of Scale, and the Great Merger Wave of 1898–1902. *J. Econ. Hist.*, September 1988, *48*(3), pp. 639–49.

O'Brien, Denis P. Classical Reassessments. In *Thweatt, W. O., ed.*, 1988, pp. 179–220.

_____. Lionel Charles Robbins, 1898–1984. *Econ. J.*, March 1988, *98*(389), pp. 104–25.

O'Brien, Gerard. A Question of Attitude: Responses to the New Poor Law in Ireland and Scotland. In *Mitchison, R. and Roebuck, P., eds.*, 1988, pp. 160–70.

O'Brien, Gordon E. Work and Leisure. In *van Raaij, W. F.; van Veldhoven, G. M. and Wärneryd, K.-E., eds.*, 1988, pp. 539–68.

O'Brien, Leslie. Between Capital and Labour: Trade Unionism in Malaysia. In *Southall, R., ed.*, 1988, pp. 136–70.

O'Brien, Patricia C. Analysts' Forecasts as Earnings Expectations. *J. Acc. Econ.*, January 1988, *10*(1), pp. 53–83.

O'Brien, Patrick and Mathias, Peter. The Social

and Economic Burden of Tax Revenue Collected for Central Government in Britain and France, 1715–85. In *Guarducci, A., ed.*, 1988, pp. 805–42.

O'Brien, Thomas J. The Mechanics of Portfolio Insurance. *J. Portfol. Manage.*, Spring 1988, *14*(3), pp. 40–47.

O'Brien, Thomas S. and Taylor, Stuart R. The Problem of Sparsity in Education Provision. *Urban Stud.*, December 1988, *25*(6), pp. 520–26.

O'Bryen, David. Financial Taxes in Australia. *Australian Tax Forum*, 1988, *5*(3), pp. 359–72.

O'Connell, Joan. Sterilization and Interest Rates. *J. Int. Money Finance*, December 1988, *7*(4), pp. 425–28.

O'Connell, Stephen A. and Zeldes, Stephen P. Rational Ponzi Games. *Int. Econ. Rev.*, August 1988, *29*(3), pp. 431–50.

O'Donnell, Guillermo. State and Alliances in Argentina, 1956–1976. In *Bates, R. H., ed.*, 1988, *1978*, pp. 176–205.

O'Donnell, Margaret G. Charlotte Perkins Gilman's Economic Interpretation of the Role of Women at the Turn of the Century. *Soc. Sci. Quart.*, March 1988, *69*(1), pp. 177–92.

O'Dowd, Mary. Land and Lordship in Sixteenth- and Early Seventeenth-Century Ireland. In *Mitchison, R. and Roebuck, P., eds.*, 1988, pp. 17–26.

O'Driscoll, Gerald P., Jr. Bank Failures: The Deposit Insurance Connection. *Contemp. Policy Issues*, April 1988, *6*(2), pp. 1–12.

————. Deposit Insurance in Theory and Practice. *Cato J.*, Winter 1988, *7*(3), pp. 661–75.

————. Deposit Insurance in Theory and Practice. In *England, C. and Huertas, T., eds.*, 1988, pp. 165–79.

————; Garrison, Roger W. and Short, Eugenie D. Financial Stability and FDIC Insurance. In *England, C. and Huertas, T., eds.*, 1988, pp. 187–207.

O'Farrell, P. N. and Hitchens, D. M. W. N. Alternative Theories of Small-Firm Growth: A Critical Review. *Environ. Planning A*, October 1988, *20*(10), pp. 1365–83.

———— and Hitchens, D. M. W. N. The Comparative Performance of Small Manufacturing Companies Located in the Mid West and Northern Ireland. *Econ. Soc. Rev.*, April 1988, *19*(3), pp. 177–98.

———— and Hitchens, D. M. W. N. The Relative Competitiveness and Performance of Small Manufacturing Firms in Scotland and the Mid-west of Ireland: An Analysis of Matched Pairs. *Reg. Stud.*, October 1988, *22*(5), pp. 399–415.

O'Guinn, Thomas C. and Faber, Ronald J. Expanding the View of Consumer Socialization: A Nonutilitarian Mass-Mediated Perspective. In *Hirschman, E. and Sheth, J. N., eds.*, 1988, pp. 49–77.

O'Hagan, John W. and Duffy, Christopher T. The Arts and Section 32 of the 1984 Finance Act [The Performing Arts and the Public Purse: An Economic Analysis]. *Econ. Soc. Rev.*, January 1988, *19*(2), pp. 147–51.

O'Hagan, L. Richard. The Politics of Canada. In *Thornton, R. J.; Hyclak, T. and Aronson, J. R., eds.*, 1988, pp. 15–31.

O'Hanlon, J.; Ward, C. W. R. and Condoyanni, L. Weekend Effects in Stock Market Returns: International Evidence. In *Dimson, E., ed.*, 1988, pp. 52–63.

O'Hara, Maureen and Easley, David. Contracts and Asymmetric Information in the Theory of the Firm. *J. Econ. Behav. Organ.*, April 1988, *9*(3), pp. 229–46.

O'Haver, Robert. The Business Economist at Work: Litigation Consulting. *Bus. Econ.*, October 1988, *23*(4), pp. 53–55.

O'Higgins, Eleanor R. E. Innovation, Entrepreneurship, Efficiency and Strategy-Manager Fit in Irish Agricultural Co-operatives. In *Maital, S., ed., Vol. 2*, 1988, pp. 458–79.

O'Higgins, Michael. The Allocation of Public Resources to Children and the Elderly in OECD Countries. In *Palmer, J. L.; Smeeding, T. and Torrey, B. B., eds.*, 1988, pp. 201–28.

O'Higgins, Niall. The Progressivity of Government Taxation and Expenditure: A Comparison of Two Measures of Redistributive Impact with an Application to Ireland. *Stud. Econ.*, 1988, *43*(35), pp. 65–91.

O'Keefe, Hsu. Applicability of Economic Evaluation to China's Urban Transportation Projects in a Changing Society. In *Tisdell, C. and Maitra, P., eds.*, 1988, pp. 116–34.

O'Leary, James J. The Changing Pattern of Foreign Investment in the United States. *Bus. Econ.*, July 1988, *23*(3), pp. 21–26.

————. Trends in Ownership of the Exploding Federal Debt: Problems and Consequences for Government Policy and Our Financial Markets. *Bus. Econ.*, October 1988, *23*(4), pp. 25–30.

O'Loughlin, J. Immigration to Western Europe, 1952–1982: A Time-Series Analysis of Movement to Sweden, France, and Essen: Reply. *Environ. Planning A*, August 1988, *20*(8), pp. 1125–27.

O'Malley, William J. Culture and Industrialization. In *Hughes, H., ed.*, 1988, pp. 327–43.

O'Mara, Gerald T. The Efficient Use of Surface Water and Groundwater in Irrigation: An Overview of the Issues. In *O'Mara, G. T., ed.*, 1988, pp. 1–17.

————. Groundwater as a Constraint to Irrigation: Comment. In *O'Mara, G. T., ed.*, 1988, pp. 176–77.

———— and Duloy, John H. Modeling Efficient Conjunctive Use of Water in the Indus Basin. In *O'Mara, G. T., ed.*, 1988, pp. 128–38.

O'Mara, L. P. The Medium Term Outlook for the Real Exchange Rate and Real Interest Rates. *Rev. Marketing Agr. Econ.*, April 1988, *56*(1), pp. 60–67.

O'Neil, Brian F. and Bommer, Michael R. W. Analysis of Alternative Distribution Strategies. *Logist. Transp. Rev.*, September 1988, *24*(3), pp. 237–47.

O'Neil, Cherie J. and Thompson, G. Rodney.

Taxation and IRA Participation: Response. *Nat. Tax J.*, December 1988, *41*(4), pp. 591–93.

O'Neill, Brian. Choosing Automatic Restraint Designs for the 1990s: Comment. In *Graham, J. D., ed.*, 1988, pp. 105–10.

O'Neill, Gerard J. and Darton, David. The Changing Role of the Household Economy in a World of Expanding Technology. In *Tisdell, C. and Maitra, P., eds.*, 1988, pp. 217–38.

_____ **and Nairn, Alasdair G. M.** Population Density Functions: A Differential Equation Approach. *J. Reg. Sci.*, February 1988, *28*(1), pp. 89–102.

_____; **Nairn, Alasdair G. M. and Parr, John B.** Metropolitan Density Functions: A Further Exploration. *Reg. Sci. Urban Econ.*, November 1988, *18*(4), pp. 463–78.

O'Neill, June. Poverty: Programs and Policies. In *Anderson, A. and Bark, D. L., eds.*, 1988, pp. 349–66.

O'Neill, Paul H. Quality and Efficiency—The Keys to the Global Market. In *Rosow, J. M., ed.*, 1988, pp. 111–20.

O'Riordan, Timothy. The Politics of Sustainability. In *Turner, R. K., ed.*, 1988, pp. 29–50.

O'Shaughnessy, John; Dickinson, Roger and Herbst, Anthony F. Marketing Concept and Customer Orientation. In *Earl, P. E., ed., Vol. 2*, 1988, *1986*, pp. 311–16.

_____ **and Holbrook, Morris B.** On the Scientific Status of Consumer Research and the Need for an Interpretive Approach to Studying Consumption Behavior. *J. Cons. Res.*, December 1988, *15*(3), pp. 398–402.

Oakeshott, Robert. The Beginnings of an Employee-Owned Sector. In *Johnson, C., ed.*, 1988, *1985*, pp. 174–86.

Oates, Wallace E. And One More Reply [One More Externality Article]. *J. Environ. Econ. Manage.*, September 1988, *15*(3), pp. 384–85.

_____. On the Measurement of Congestion in the Provision of Local Public Goods. *J. Urban Econ.*, July 1988, *24*(1), pp. 85–94.

_____ **and Schwab, Robert M.** Economic Competition among Jurisdictions: Efficiency Enhancing or Distortion Inducing? *J. Public Econ.*, April 1988, *35*(3), pp. 333–54.

_____ **and Wallis, John Joseph.** Decentralization in the Public Sector: An Empirical Study of State and Local Government. In *Rosen, H. S., ed.*, 1988, pp. 5–28.

_____ **and Wallis, John Joseph.** Does Economic Sclerosis Set in with Age? An Empirical Study of the Olson Hypothesis. *Kyklos*, 1988, *41*(3), pp. 397–417.

Oaxaca, Ronald L. and Ransom, Michael R. Searching for the Effect of Unionism on the Wages of Union and Nonunion Workers. *J. Lab. Res.*, Spring 1988, *9*(2), pp. 139–48.

Obel, Børge and Burton, Richard M. Opportunism, Incentives, and the M-Form Hypothesis: A Laboratory Study. *J. Econ. Behav. Organ.*, July 1988, *10*(1), pp. 99–119.

Oberender, Peter and Rüter, Georg. The Steel Industry: A Crisis of Adaptation. In *de Jong, H. W., ed.*, 1988, pp. 81–104.

Oberheu, Howard; Scott, Charles G. and Mulberg, Ruthellen. SSA's Outreach Efforts to Contact Beneficiaries Eligible for SSI Payments. *Soc. Sec. Bull.*, January 1988, *51*(1), pp. 12–17.

Oberoi, R. C.; Singh, Kamlesh and Sharma, H. R. Rural Farm Size and Inequality: A Case Study. *Margin*, Jan.–March 1988, *20*(2), pp. 47–53.

Obeysekera, J. T. B.; Bartolini, Paolo and Salas, Jose D. Multivariate Periodic ARMA (1, 1) Processes. *Water Resources Res.*, August 1988, *24*(8), pp. 1237–46.

Oblath, Gábor. Exchange Rate Policy in the Reform Package. *Acta Oecon.*, 1988, *39*(1–2), pp. 81–93.

Obstfeld, Maurice. The Advantage of Tying One's Hands: EMS Discipline and Central Bank Credibility: Comments. *Europ. Econ. Rev.*, June 1988, *32*(5), pp. 1077–82.

_____. Capital Controls and Public Finance: The Experience in Italy: Discussion. In *Giavazzi, F. and Spaventa, L., eds.*, 1988, pp. 212–16.

_____. Macroeconomic Policy Design in an Interdependent World Economy: An Analysis of Three Contingencies: Comment. In *Frenkel, J. A., ed.*, 1988, pp. 155–64.

_____. Reforming the Exchange Rate System. *Cato J.*, Fall 1988, *8*(2), pp. 443–49.

_____. Sources of Misalignment in the 1980s: Comment. In *Marston, R. C., ed.*, 1988, pp. 31–38.

_____ **and Calvo, Guillermo A.** Optimal Time-Consistent Fiscal Policy with Finite Lifetimes. *Econometrica*, March 1988, *56*(2), pp. 411–32.

_____ **and Calvo, Guillermo A.** Optimal Time-Consistent Fiscal Policy with Finite Lifetimes: Analysis and Extensions. In *Helpman, E.; Razin, A. and Sadka, E., eds.*, 1988, pp. 163–98.

Ochoa, Eduardo M. and Eichner, Alfred S. The Structure of Industrial Prices. *Rev. Radical Polit. Econ.*, Summer–Fall 1988, *20*(2–3), pp. 114–26.

Oczkowski, Edward. A Theory of Market Quantity Controls: The Use of Disequilibrium and Bargaining Theories. *Australian Econ. Pap.*, December 1988, *27*(51), pp. 285–97.

Oddou, Claude and Guesnerie, Roger. Increasing Returns to Size and Their Limits. *Scand. J. Econ.*, 1988, *90*(3), pp. 259–73.

Odedokun, M. O. Effectiveness of Selective Credit Policies: Alternative Framework of Evaluation. *World Devel.*, August 1988, *16*(8), pp. 913–19.

Odekon, Mehmet. Liberalization and the Turkish Economy: A Comparative Analysis. In *Nas, T. F. and Odekon, M., eds.*, 1988, pp. 29–46.

Odink, J. G. and Hartog, Joop. Equity and Efficiency in Holland: An Overview. In *Brenner, Y. S.; Reijnders, J. P. G. and Spithoven, A. H. G. M., eds.*, 1988, pp. 190–208.

Odland, John. Sources of Change in the Process of Population Redistribution in the United

States, 1955–1980. *Environ. Planning A*, June 1988, *20*(6), pp. 789–809.

―――― **and Ellis, Mark.** Household Organization and the Interregional Variation of Out-Migration Rates. *Demography*, November 1988, *25*(4), pp. 567–79.

Odom, William E. How Far Can Economic and Social Reform Go in the Soviet Union? In *Liebowitz, R. D., ed.*, 1988, pp. 69–95.

Oechsler, Walter A. Employee Severance—Regulations and Procedures. In *Dlugos, G.; Dorow, W. and Weiermair, K., eds.*, 1988, pp. 397–410.

Oehmke, James F. and Meyers, Robert J. Instability and Risk as Rationales for Farm Programs. In *Sumner, D. A., ed.*, 1988, pp. 1–22.

Oellerich, Donald T. and Garfinkel, Irwin. Alternative Child Support Regimes: Distributional Impacts and a Crude Benefit–Cost Analysis. In *Danziger, S. H. and Portney, K. E., eds.*, 1988, pp. 67–86.

Oellermann, Charles M. and Farris, Paul L. Note on Trader Concentration Effects in Feeder Cattle Futures and Comparison with Live Cattle. *J. Futures Markets*, February 1988, *8*(1), pp. 103–13.

Oesch, Richard. Anerkennung der steuerlichen Rechtsfähigkeit ausländischer Unternehmungen: Schweiz. (Recognition of Foreign Enterprises as Taxable Entities: Switzerland. With English summary.) In *International Fiscal Association, ed. (I)*, 1988, pp. 609–34.

Ofek, Haim; Clark, David and Kahn, James R. City Size, Quality of Life, and the Urbanization Deflator of the GNP: 1910–1984. *Southern Econ. J.*, January 1988, *54*(3), pp. 701–14.

Ofer, Aharon R.; Chari, V. V. and Jagannathan, Ravi. Seasonalities in Security Returns: The Case of Earnings Announcements. *J. Finan. Econ.*, May 1988, *21*(1), pp. 101–21.

Officer, Dennis T.; Born, Jeffery A. and Moser, James T. Changes in Dividend Policy and Subsequent Earnings. *J. Portfol. Manage.*, Summer 1988, *14*(4), pp. 56–62.

Offutt, Susan. Aggregating Crop Production Data: A Random Coefficient Approach. *J. Agr. Econ. Res.*, Spring 1988, *40*(2), pp. 11–18.

Ofori-Amoah, Benjamin. Improving Existing Indigenous Technologies as a Strategy for the Appropriate Technology Concept in Ghana. *Industry Devel.*, January 1988, (23), pp. 57–79.

Ogaki, Masao; Hansen, Lars Peter and Heaton, John C. Efficiency Bounds Implied by Multiperiod Conditional Moment Restrictions. *J. Amer. Statist. Assoc.*, September 1988, *83*(403), pp. 863–71.

Ogata, Shijuro. Japan and the Integration of Financial Markets. In *Mikdashi, Z., ed.*, 1988, pp. 55–59.

―――― . Japan at a Turning Point. *Aussenwirtschaft*, June 1988, *43*(1/2), pp. 5–11.

Ogawa, Hideaki; Thisse, Jacques-François and Fujita, Masahisa. A Spatial Competition Approach to Central Place Theory: Some Basic Principles. *J. Reg. Sci.*, November 1988, *28*(4), pp. 477–94.

Ogawa, Naohiro and Martin, Linda G. The Effects of Cohort Size on Relative Wages in Japan. In *Lee, R. D.; Arthur, W. B. and Rodgers, G., eds.*, 1988, pp. 59–75.

Ogden, Joseph P. and Tucker, Alan L. The Relative Valuation of American Currency Spot and Futures Options: Theory and Empirical Tests. *J. Finan. Quant. Anal.*, December 1988, *23*(4), pp. 351–68.

Ogden, William S. The Need for Change in Managing LDC Debt. In *Feldstein, M., ed. (I)*, 1988, pp. 283–90.

―――― **and Gombola, Michael J.** Effects of a Sinking Fund on Preferred Stock Marketability: A Probit Analysis. *Quart. J. Bus. Econ.*, Summer 1988, *27*(3), pp. 41–56.

Ogino, Katsuya. Stackelberg Game Model Incorporating Public Participation for Electric Generating System Development. In *Iri, M. and Yajima, K., eds.*, 1988, pp. 446–54.

ÓGráda, Cormac and Allen, Robert C. On the Road Again with Arthur Young: English, Irish, and French Agriculture during the Industrial Revolution. *J. Econ. Hist.*, March 1988, *48*(1), pp. 93–116.

Ogryczak, W. and Malczewski, J. A Multiobjective Approach to the Reorganization of Health-Service Areas: A Case Study. *Environ. Planning A*, November 1988, *20*(11), pp. 1461–70.

Ohanian, Lee E. The Spurious Effects of Unit Roots on Vector Autoregressions: A Monte Carlo Study. *J. Econometrics*, November 1988, *39*(3), pp. 251–66.

Ohashi, Isao. Specific Human Capital, Wages and Quits in Japanese Manufacturing Industries. *Econ. Stud. Quart.*, June 1988, *39*(2), pp. 97–117.

von der Ohe, Werner D. and Fritscher, Wolfgang. Certain Theoretical Premises as Alternatives to the Modernization Theory. In *Vivekananda, F., ed.*, 1988, pp. 30–50.

Ohkawa, Kazushi. On the Methodology of Comparative Studies. In *Urrutia, M., ed.*, 1988, pp. 7–14.

Ohlin, Göran P. Determinants and Consequences of Population Theories. In *Salvatore, D., ed.*, 1988, pp. 13–23.

Ohno, Koichi. Changes in Trade Structure and Factor Intensity: A Case Study of the Republic of Korea. *Devel. Econ.*, December 1988, *26*(4), pp. 367–85.

Ohse, Takateru. Epidemiology of Hunger in Africa. In *Bell, D. E. and Reich, M. R., eds.*, 1988, pp. 223–40.

Ohsfeldt, Robert L. The Effect of AMA Membership on Physicians' Earnings. *Ind. Lab. Relat. Rev.*, October 1988, *42*(1), pp. 20–33.

―――― . Implicit Markets and the Demand for Housing Characteristics. *Reg. Sci. Urban Econ.*, August 1988, *18*(3), pp. 321–43.

―――― **and Smith, Barton A.** Assessing the Accuracy of Structural Parameter Estimates in Analyses of Implicit Markets. *Land Econ.*, May 1988, *64*(2), pp. 135–46.

Ohta, H. and Wako, T. The Output Effects of Spatial Price Discrimination Revisited. *J. Reg. Sci.*, February 1988, 28(1), pp. 83–87.

Ohta, Makoto. Did the Gasoline Price Increases Change Consumer Evaluations of Cars in Japan during 1970–83? A Note. *Econ. Stud. Quart.*, March 1988, 39(1), pp. 87–92.

Ohta, Toshiaki. Work Rules in Japan. *Int. Lab. Rev.*, 1988, 127(5), pp. 627–39.

Ohtani, Kazuhiro. Optimal Levels of Significance of a Pre-test in Estimating the Disturbance Variance after the Pre-test for a Linear Hypothesis on Coefficients in a Linear Regression. *Econ. Letters*, 1988, 28(2), pp. 151–56.

_____; **Katayama, Sei-ichi and Toyoda, Toshihisa.** Estimation of Structural Change in the Import and Export Equations: An International Comparison. In *Uno, K. and Shishido, S., eds.*, 1988, pp. 52–64.

Ohyama, Michihiro. Predictive and Imitative Expectations in Macro-dynamic Theories. *Keio Econ. Stud.*, 1988, 25(2), pp. 1–17.

Oi, Walter Y. How Valuable Are Matched Data Files? (A Comment on "Enhanced Demographic-Economic Data Sets.") *Surv. Curr. Bus.*, November 1988, 68(11), pp. 49–50.

_____. The Indirect Effect of Technology on Retail Trade. In *Cyert, R. M. and Mowery, D. C., eds.*, 1988, pp. 329–75.

_____ **and Burstein, Meyer Louis.** Monopoly, Competition and Variability of Market Prices. In *Burstein, M. L.*, 1988, pp. 249–55.

Ojo, Olatunde J. B. Nigeria: The Political Economy of Dependent Industrialization and Foreign Policy. In *Carlsson, J. and Shaw, T. M., eds.*, 1988, pp. 121–50.

Okabe, A., et al. The Statistical Analysis of a Distribution of Activity Points in Relation to Surface-Like Elements. *Environ. Planning A*, May 1988, 20(5), pp. 609–20.

Okada, A. Asymmetric Multidimensional Scaling of Car Switching Data. In *Gaul, W. and Schader, M., eds.*, 1988, pp. 279–90.

_____. Perfect Equilibrium Points and Lexicographic Domination. *Int. J. Game Theory*, 1988, 17(3), pp. 225–39.

Okafor, F. O. E. The PAIGC and the Economic Development of Guinea-Bissau: Ideology and Reality. *Devel. Econ.*, June 1988, 26(2), pp. 125–40.

Okamoto, Masanori B. A Notion of Granger-Causality in Multivariate Systems of Economic Time Series. In *Brown, R. C., ed.*, 1988, pp. 129–38.

Okayama, Reiko. Trade Associations and the Modernization Crisis of British Industry, 1910–35: Comment. In *Yamazaki, H. and Miyamoto, M., eds.*, 1988, pp. 227–29.

Okidi, C. O. The State and the Management of International Drainage Basins in Africa. *Natural Res. J.*, Fall 1988, 28(4), pp. 645–69.

Okimoto, Daniel I. Political Inclusivity: The Domestic Structure of Trade. In *Inoguchi, T. and Okimoto, D. I., eds.*, 1988, pp. 305–44.

_____ **and Inoguchi, Takashi.** The Political Economy of Japan: Vol. 2: The Changing International Context: Introduction. In *Inoguchi, T. and Okimoto, D. I., eds.*, 1988, pp. 1–20.

Okisho, Nobuo. On Marx's Reproduction Scheme. *Kobe Univ. Econ.*, 1988, (34), pp. 1–24.

Okita, Saburo. Domestic Economic Policy and International Capital Flows. In *Feldstein, M., ed. (II)*, 1988, pp. 627–33.

Okker, V. R. The CPB Econometric Model of the Netherlands Economy (FREIA-KOMPAS) In *Driehuis, W.; Fase, M. M. G. and den Hartog, H., eds.*, 1988, pp. 457–81.

_____; **Hasselman, B. H. and Kok, J. H. M.** FREIA and Employment Policies in the Netherlands. In *Hopkins, M. J. D., ed.*, 1988, pp. 103–31.

Okoruwa, A. Ason; Terza, Joseph V. and Nourse, Hugh O. Estimating Patronization Shares for Urban Retail Centers: An Extension of the Poisson Gravity Model. *J. Urban Econ.*, November 1988, 24(3), pp. 241–59.

Okrasa, W. Redistribution and the Two Dimensions of Inequality: An East–West Comparison. *Europ. Econ. Rev.*, March 1988, 32(2–3), pp. 633–43.

Okuguchi, Koji and Szidarovszky, Ferenc. Dynamics of the Cournot Oligopoly with Multiproduct Firms. *Math. Soc. Sci.*, October 1988, 16(2), pp. 159–69.

_____ **and Szidarovszky, Ferenc.** A Linear Oligopoly Model with Adaptive Expectations: Stability Reconsidered. *J. Econ. (Z. Nationalökon.)*, 1988, 48(1), pp. 79–82.

_____ **and Szidarovszky, Ferenc.** A Note on Global Asymptotic Stability of Non-linear Difference Equations. *Econ. Letters*, 1988, 26(4), pp. 349–52.

Okunade, Albert Ade. and McLean-Meyinsse, Patricia E. Factor Demands of Louisiana Rice Producers: An Econometric Investigation. *Southern J. Agr. Econ.*, December 1988, 20(2), pp. 127–35.

Okuno-Fujiwara, Masahiro. Interdependence of Industries, Coordination Failure and Strategic Promotion of an Industry. *J. Int. Econ.*, August 1988, 25(1–2), pp. 25–43.

_____ **and Kiyono, Kazuharu.** Second-Mover Advantage in R&D Innovation and Imitation in Dynamic Oligopoly. *Econ. Stud. Quart.*, December 1988, 39(4), pp. 356–77.

Ölander, Folke. Consumer Information in the Electronic Data Media. In *Maital, S., ed., Vol. 1*, 1988, pp. 63–72.

_____. Consumer Satisfaction/Dissatisfaction and the Consumer Interest. In *Maynes, E. S. and ACCI Research Committee, eds.*, 1988, pp. 753–59.

_____. Salient Issues in Current European Consumer Policy Research. In *Maynes, E. S. and ACCI Research Committee, eds.*, 1988, pp. 547–83.

Oldak, P. G. Economic Theory and the Practice of Restructuring: Responses and Opinions. *Prob. Econ.*, October 1988, 31(6), pp. 71–83.

_____. A Qualitatively New Stage in the Development of Soviet Society. *Prob. Econ.*, June 1988, 31(2), pp. 60–74.

Oldfield, George S. and Jarrow, Robert A. Forward Options and Futures Options. In *Fabozzi, F. J., ed.*, 1988, pp. 15–28.

Oldford, R. Wayne. Object-Oriented Software Representations for Statistical Data. *J. Econometrics*, May–June 1988, 38(1–2), pp. 227–46.

Ølgaard, Anders. Den forkalkede boligpolitik. (Danish Housing Policy. With English summary.) *Nationaløkon. Tidsskr.*, 1988, 126(3), pp. 267–85.

_____. Pensionsdebatten. (The Danish Debate on Pension Schemes. With English summary.) *Nationaløkon. Tidsskr.*, 1988, 126(2), pp. 119–23.

Olien, Diana Davids and Olien, Roger M. Competition for Capital in Two Oil Ventures. In *Hausman, W. J., ed.*, 1988, pp. 169–78.

Olien, Roger M. and Olien, Diana Davids. Competition for Capital in Two Oil Ventures. In *Hausman, W. J., ed.*, 1988, pp. 169–78.

Oliveira, G. C., et al. A Representation of Spatial Cross Correlations in Large Stochastic Seasonal Streamflow Models. *Water Resources Res.*, May 1988, 24(5), pp. 781–85.

Oliver, Geoffrey D.; Steger, Debra P. and Horlick, Gary N. Dispute Resolution Mechanisms. In *Schott, J. J. and Smith, M. G., eds.*, 1988, pp. 65–86.

Oliver, Richard L. and DeSarbo, Wayne S. Response Determinants in Satisfaction Judgments. *J. Cons. Res.*, March 1988, 14(4), pp. 495–507.

Olivera, Julio H. G. Inflexibilidad descendente de las tasas de interés. (With English summary.) *Desarrollo Econ.*, April–June 1988, 28(109), pp. 39–42.

Olkin, Ingram and Marshall, Albert W. Families of Multivariate Distributions. *J. Amer. Statist. Assoc.*, September 1988, 83(403), pp. 834–41.

Ollerenshaw, Philip. Aspects of Bank Lending in Post-Famine Ireland. In *Mitchison, R. and Roebuck, P., eds.*, 1988, pp. 222–32.

Olmer, Lionel H. The Role of Services. In *Feldstein, M., ed. (II)*, 1988, pp. 413–20.

Olsen, Chris; Dietrich, J. Richard and Thompson, Robert B., II. The Influence of Estimation Period News Events on Standardized Market Model Prediction Errors. *Accounting Rev.*, July 1988, 63(3), pp. 448–71.

Olsen, Johan P.; Cohen, Michael D. and March, James G. A Garbage Can Model of Organizational Choice. In *March, J. G.*, 1988, 1972, pp. 294–334.

_____ and March, James G. The Uncertainty of the Past: Organizational Learning under Ambiguity. In *March, J. G.*, 1988, 1975, pp. 335–58.

Olsen, John G. and Carnes, Richard B. Productivity Shows a Decline in Automotive Repair Shops. *Mon. Lab. Rev.*, March 1988, 111(3), pp. 22–26.

Olsen, Øystein; Strøm, Steinar and Longva, Svein. Total Elasticities of Energy Demand Analysed within a General Equilibrium Model. *Energy Econ.*, October 1988, 10(4), pp. 298–308.

Olsen, Randall J. Cross-Sectional Methods for Estimating the Replacement of Infant Deaths. In *Schultz, T. Paul, ed.*, 1988, pp. 111–36.

Olsen, Trond E. Strategic Considerations in Invention and Innovation; The Case of Natural Resources Revisited. *Econometrica*, July 1988, 56(4), pp. 841–49.

_____ and Stensland, Gunnar. Optimal Shutdown Decisions in Resource Extraction. *Econ. Letters*, 1988, 26(3), pp. 215–18.

Olshavsky, Richard W. Determinants of Information Use: Beyond the Simple Cost–Benefit Model. In *Maynes, E. S. and ACCI Research Committee, eds.*, 1988, pp. 231–34.

_____ and Granbois, Donald H. Consumer Decision Making—Fact or Fiction? In *Earl, P. E., ed., Vol. 2*, 1988, 1979, pp. 160–67.

_____ and Lim, Jeen-Su. Impacts of Consumers' Familiarity and Product Class on Price–Quality Inference and Product Evaluations. *Quart. J. Bus. Econ.*, Summer 1988, 27(3), pp. 130–46.

Olson, Dennis O. and Weddleton, John. Estimating Undisclosed Earnings Data. *Ann. Reg. Sci.*, March 1988, 22(1), pp. 84–90.

Olson, James E. Toward a Global Information Age. In *Rosow, J. M., ed.*, 1988, pp. 93–108.

Olson, Jerry C. and Celsi, Richard L. The Role of Involvement in Attention and Comprehension Processes. *J. Cons. Res.*, September 1988, 15(2), pp. 210–24.

Olson, Jon; Osborn, Richard N. and Strickstein, Aubrey. Cooperative Multinational R&D Ventures: Interpretation and Negotiation in Emerging Systems. In *Gattiker, U. E. and Larwood, L., eds.*, 1988, pp. 33–54.

Olson, Kent W.; Moomaw, Ronald L. and Thompson, Richard P. Redwood National Park Expansion: Impact on Old-Growth Redwood Stumpage Prices. *Land Econ.*, August 1988, 64(3), pp. 269–75.

Olson, Mancur. The Productivity Slowdown, the Oil Shocks, and the Real Cycle. *J. Econ. Perspectives*, Fall 1988, 2(4), pp. 43–69.

Olson, Margrethe H. Corporate Culture and the Homeworker. In *Christensen, K. E., ed.*, 1988, pp. 126–34.

Olsson, P. AgroVision: The Agricultural Videotex System in Sweden. In *Schiefer, G., ed.*, 1988, pp. 51–54.

Olsson, Rolf. Management for Success in Modern Agriculture. *Europ. Rev. Agr. Econ.*, 1988, 15(2–3), pp. 239–59.

Olsson, Sven-Olof. Swedish–Polish Trade Negotiations at the End of the Second World War and Their Results. *Scand. Econ. Hist. Rev.*, 1988, 36(2), pp. 30–41.

Olteanu, I. The Growth-Development-Progress Model and the Openings to New Paradigms: Some Preliminary Remarks. *Econ. Computat. Cybern. Stud. Res.*, 1988, 23(1), pp. 67–82.

Oman, Charles P. Cooperative Strategies in Developing Countries: The New Forms of Investment. In *Contractor, F. J. and Lorange, P.*, 1988, pp. 383–402.

Omawale; Jackson, A. A. and McLeod, Joan C. Household Food Consumption Behaviour in

St. James, Jamaica. *Soc. Econ. Stud.*, September 1988, *37*(3), pp. 213–35.

Omberg, Edward. Efficient Discrete Time Jump Process Models in Option Pricing. *J. Finan. Quant. Anal.*, June 1988, *23*(2), pp. 161–74.

Ominami, Carlos. Desindustrialización y reestructuracion industrial en América Latina: Los ejemplos de Argentina, Brasil y Chile. (Deindustrialization and Industrial Restructuring in Latin America: The Cases of Argentina, Brazil and Chile. With English summary.) *Colección Estud. CIEPLAN*, March 1988, (23), pp. 87–115.

Omori, Ikuo. For Diffusing Economic Knowledge: Tokyo Senmon Gakko (Waseda). In *Sugiyama, C. and Mizuta, H., eds.*, 1988, pp. 171–87.

Onchan, Tongroj; Chalamwong, Yongyuth and Feder, Gershon. Land Policies and Farm Performance in Thailand's Forest Reserve Areas. *Econ. Develop. Cult. Change*, April 1988, *36*(3), pp. 483–501.

Öncü, Ahmet. The Extent of Financial Repression in the Turkish Economy during 1971–1985. *METU*, 1988, *15*(1–2), pp. 73–84.

Ondrack, Daniel. The Impact of Environmental Trends on the Legitimacy of Trade Unions in Canada. In *Dlugos, G.; Dorow, W. and Weiermair, K., eds.*, 1988, pp. 165–76.

Ondrich, Jan and Blackley, Paul R. A Limited Joint-Choice Model for Discrete and Continuous Housing Characteristics. *Rev. Econ. Statist.*, May 1988, *70*(2), pp. 266–74.

Oneal, Frances H. and Oneal, John R. Hegemony, Imperialism, and the Profitability of For-eign Investments. *Int. Organ.*, Spring 1988, *42*(2), pp. 347–73.

Oneal, John R. and Oneal, Frances H. Hegemony, Imperialism, and the Profitability of Foreign Investments. *Int. Organ.*, Spring 1988, *42*(2), pp. 347–73.

Ong, Aihwa. Industrial Development and Rural Malay Households: Changing Strategies of Reproduction. In *Vlassoff, C. and Barkat-e-Khuda, eds.*, 1988, pp. 21–35.

Onida, Fabrizio. Patterns of International Specialisation and Technological Competitiveness in Italian Manufacturing Industry. In *Onida, F. and Viesti, G., eds.*, 1988, pp. 6–29.

—————— **and Viesti, Gianfranco.** Italy as an International Investor: Summary and Conclusions. In *Onida, F. and Viesti, G., eds.*, 1988, pp. 150–57.

Onishi, Akira. Projections of the OECD Economies in the Global Perspective, 1986–2000: Policy Simulations by the FUGI Global Macroeconomic Model. In *Motamen, H., ed.*, 1988, pp. 11–30.

Onishi, Haruo. On a Variable Selection Procedure for a Modified Limited Information Maximum Likelihood Method. In *Uno, K. and Shishido, S., eds.*, 1988, pp. 269–79.

Ono, Yoshiyasu and Lahiri, Sajal. Helping Minor Firms Reduces Welfare. *Econ. J.*, December 1988, *98*(393), pp. 1199–1202.

Onuma, Ayumi. Conditioned Preferences and the Maximin Justice between Generations. *Econ.*

Stud. Quart., September 1988, *39*(3), pp. 258–70.

Oo, Tin Htut; Hitzhusen, Fred and Hushak, Leroy J. Factors Related to Errors in Ex-ante Evaluation of Agricultural Projects in Developing Countries. *J. Devel. Areas*, January 1988, *22*(2), pp. 199–206.

Oort, Conrad J. Freedom of Capital Movements in the European Community. In *[Witteveen, H. J.]*, 1988, pp. 143–57.

Oosterbeek, Hessel and Hartog, Joop. Education, Allocation and Earnings in the Netherlands: Overschooling? *Econ. Educ. Rev.*, 1988, *7*(2), pp. 185–94.

Oosterhaven, Jan. On the Plausibility of the Supply-Driven Input–Output Model. *J. Reg. Sci.*, May 1988, *28*(2), pp. 203–17.

Oosterhuis, Paul W. and Levine, Howard J. Tax Treatment of Computer Software: United States. In *International Fiscal Association, ed. (II)*, 1988, pp. 333–58.

Opaluch, James J. and Grigalunas, Thomas A. Assessing Liability for Damages under CERCLA: A New Approach for Providing Incentives for Pollution Avoidance? *Natural Res. J.*, Summer 1988, *28*(3), pp. 509–33.

van Ophem, Hans; Hartog, Joop and Mekkelholt, Eddie. Testing the Relevance of Job Search for Job Mobility. *Econ. Letters*, 1988, *27*(3), pp. 299–303.

Opler, Tim C. The Effect of Inflationary Pressure on Government Expenditure. *Econ. Letters*, 1988, *28*(4), pp. 331–34.

Opp, Karl-Dieter. Contractual Relations and Weak Solidarity: The Behavioral Basis of Restraints on Gain-Maximization: Comment. *J. Inst. Theoretical Econ.*, February 1988, *144*(1), pp. 67–72.

——————. Spontaneous Order and Tit for Tat: Some Hypotheses and an Empirical Test. *J. Inst. Theoretical Econ.*, April 1988, *144*(2), pp. 374–85.

Oppenheim, Paul and Hempel, Carl G. Studies in the Logic of Explanation. In *Pitt, J. C., ed.*, 1988, *1948*, pp. 9–46.

Oprescu, G. and Andrei, Anca. Optimizing the Physical Production Plan at the Level of Economic Units. *Econ. Computat. Cybern. Stud. Res.*, 1988, *23*(3), pp. 75–85.

Opromolla, Paolo and Checchi, Daniele. The Role of Financial Sectors in Business Cycle Analysis. *Rivista Int. Sci. Econ. Com.*, March 1988, *35*(3), pp. 269–94.

Opsal, Scott D. and Kosmicke, Ralph. The Effect of Volatility on Investment Returns. *J. Portfol. Manage.*, Winter 1988, *14*(2), pp. 14–19.

Orbach, Michael; Maiolo, John R. and Blomo, Vito J. Competition and Conflict in the U.S. Atlantic Coast Menhaden Industry. *Amer. J. Econ. Soc.*, January 1988, *47*(1), pp. 41–60.

Orbell, John. Studies in Capital Formation in the United Kingdom, 1750–1920: The Corn Milling Industry, 1750–1820. In *Feinstein, C. H. and Pollard, S., eds.*, 1988, pp. 141–63.

Orbell, John M. and Goetze, David. Understand

ing and Cooperation in Social Dilemmas. *Public Choice*, June 1988, 57(3), pp. 275–79.

_____; van de Kragt, Alphons J. C. and Dawes, Robyn M. Are People Who Cooperate "Rational Altruists"? *Public Choice*, March 1988, 56(3), pp. 233–47.

Ord, J. Keith. Future Developments in Forecasting: The Time Series Connexion. *Int. J. Forecasting*, 1988, 4(3), pp. 389–401.

Orden, David and Schuh, G. Edward. The Macroeconomics of Agriculture and Rural America. In *Hildreth, R. J., et al., eds.*, 1988, pp. 347–83.

Ordover, Janusz A. and Baumol, William J. Antitrust Policy and High-Technology Industries. *Oxford Rev. Econ. Policy*, Winter 1988, 4(4), pp. 13–34.

d'Orey, Vasco; Turnovsky, Stephen J. and Basar, Tamer. Dynamic Strategic Monetary Policies and Coordination in Interdependent Economies. *Amer. Econ. Rev.*, June 1988, 78(3), pp. 341–61.

Orishimo, Isao. Development of Informatics and Possible Changes in Urbanisation Processes. In *Orishimo, I.; Hewings, G. J. D. and Nijkamp, P., eds.*, 1988, pp. 250–64.

Orlando, Frank S. Comparing the Incomes of Countries. In *Salazar-Carrillo, J. and Rao, D. S. P., eds.*, 1988, pp. 283–87.

Orlikowski, Wanda J. Computer Technology in Organisations: Some Critical Notes. In *Knights, D. and Willmott, H., eds.*, 1988, pp. 20–49.

Orme, Christopher. The Calculation of the Information Matrix Test for Binary Data Models. *Manchester Sch. Econ. Soc. Stud.*, December 1988, 56(4), pp. 370–76.

Orme-Johnson, David W., et al. International Peace Project in the Middle East: The Effects of the Maharishi Technology of the Unified Field. *J. Conflict Resolution*, December 1988, 32(4), pp. 776–812.

Ormiston, Michael B. and Phillips, Owen R. Nonlinear Price Schedules and Tied Products. *Economica*, May 1988, 55(218), pp. 219–33.

Ormond, Barbara A. and Berman, Peter. Changes in Health Care Demand and Supply Accompanying Economic Development. In *Sirageldin, I. and Sorkin, A., eds.*, 1988, pp. 147–72.

Orosel, Gerhard O. Price Rigidity, International Mobility of Financial Capital and Exchange Rate Volatility. *Europ. Econ. Rev.*, June 1988, 32(5), pp. 1155–62.

Orr, Adrian B. and Batchelor, Roy A. Inflation Expectations Revisited. *Economica*, August 1988, 55(219), pp. 317–31.

Orsenigo, Luigi and Dosi, Giovanni. Coordination and Transformation: An Overview of Structures, Behaviours and Change in Evolutionary Environments. In *Dosi, G., et al., eds.*, 1988, pp. 13–37.

_____ and Dosi, Giovanni. Industrial Structure and Technical Change. In *Heertje, A., ed.*, 1988, pp. 14–37.

_____; Silverberg, Gerald and Dosi, Giovanni.

Innovation, Diversity and Diffusion: A Self-organisation Model. *Econ. J.*, December 1988, 98(393), pp. 1032–54.

Orshansky, Mollie. Counting the Poor: Another Look at the Poverty Profile. *Soc. Sec. Bull.*, October 1988, 51(10), pp. 25–51.

_____. The Poverty Measure: Commentary. *Soc. Sec. Bull.*, October 1988, 51(10), pp. 22–24.

Orsini, Marie Antoinette. Consumer Policy and the European Economic Community (EEC) In *Maynes, E. S. and ACCI Research Committee, eds.*, 1988, pp. 510–21.

Orski, C. Kenneth. New Solutions to Old Problems in Public Transportation. In *Weicher, J. C., ed.*, 1988, pp. 3–7.

Ortaliz, Wilhelm G. Trade Regimes and Export Strategies with Reference to South Asia: Comments. In *Streeten, P., ed.*, 1988, pp. 160–65.

Ortega, Emiliano. Agriculture as Viewed by ECLAC. *CEPAL Rev.*, August 1988, (35), pp. 13–39.

Ortegren, Alan K. and King, Thomas E. Accounting for Hybrid Securities: The Case of Adjustable Rate Convertible Notes. *Accounting Rev.*, July 1988, 63(3), pp. 522–35.

Ortiz, Guillermo. Inflation Stabilization: Brazil: Comment. In *Bruno, M., et al., eds.*, 1988, pp. 298–302.

Ortoleva, P. and Chadam, J. Reaction-Infiltration Instabilities. In *Wheeler, M. F., ed.*, 1988, pp. 67–76.

Ortona, Guido. Further Comments on the Relationship between Inflation Rate and Development Level in OECD Countries. *Econ. Lavoro*, Jan.–Mar. 1988, 22(1), pp. 109–15.

_____. How a Convention Is Adopted: The Choice May Be Casual. *Econ. Scelte Pubbliche/ J. Public Finance Public Choice*, Sept.–Dec. 1988, 6(3), pp. 227–35.

_____. A Theory of Transition to Stalinism. *Écon. Appl.*, 1988, 41(1), pp. 73–107.

_____. A Theory of Transition to Stalinism: A Reply. *Écon. Appl.*, 1988, 41(3), pp. 653–56.

Orzechowski, William P. and Coelho, Philip R. P. Taxes and Incentives: Horatio Alger vs. the Tax Man. *Atlantic Econ. J.*, September 1988, 16(3), pp. 31–39.

_____ and Marlow, Michael L. Controlling Leviathan through Tax Reduction. *Public Choice*, September 1988, 58(3), pp. 237–45.

Osano, Hiroshi and Inoue, Touru. Implicit Contracts in the Japanese Labor Market. *J. Japanese Int. Economies*, June 1988, 2(2), pp. 181–98.

Osawa, Machiko. Working Mothers: Changing Patterns of Employment and Fertility in Japan. *Econ. Develop. Cult. Change*, July 1988, 36(4), pp. 623–50.

Osberg, Lars. The "Disappearance" of Involuntary Unemployment. *J. Econ. Issues*, September 1988, 22(3), pp. 707–27.

_____ and Siddiq, Fazley. The Inequality of Wealth in Britain's North American Colonies: The Importance of the Relatively Poor. *Rev. Income Wealth*, June 1988, 34(2), pp. 143–63.

Osborn, Denise R. Seasonality and Habit Persistence in a Life Cycle Model of Consumption. *J. Appl. Econometrics*, Oct.–Dec. 1988, *3*(4), pp. 255–66.

_____, et al. Seasonality and the Order of Integration for Consumption. *Oxford Bull. Econ. Statist.*, November 1988, *50*(4), pp. 361–77.

Osborn, Richard N.; Strickstein, Aubrey and Olson, Jon. Cooperative Multinational R&D Ventures: Interpretation and Negotiation in Emerging Systems. In *Gattiker, U. E. and Larwood, L., eds.*, 1988, pp. 33–54.

Osborne, Dale K. Cartel Problems. In *Ricketts, M., ed., Vol. 1*, 1988, *1976*, pp. 150–59.

_____. Competition and Geographical Integration in Commercial Bank Lending. *J. Banking Finance*, 1988, *12*(1), pp. 85–103.

Osborne, R. D., et al. Trends in Higher Education Participation in Northern Ireland. *Econ. Soc. Rev.*, July 1988, *19*(4), pp. 283–301.

Osgood, Eugenia V. The Soviet Union Today: Military Strategy in the Nuclear Age. In *Cracraft, J., ed.*, 1988, pp. 114–25.

Oshima, Harry T. Full Employment Growth in Japan and Taiwan. *Philippine Rev. Econ. Bus.*, March–June 1988, *25*(1–2), pp. 1–39.

_____. Human Resources in East Asia's Secular Growth. *Econ. Develop. Cult. Change*, Supplement, April 1988, *36*(3), pp. S103–22.

Osipov, Yu. S. Control Problems under Insufficient Information. In *Iri, M. and Yajima, K., eds.*, 1988, pp. 29–51.

Ossa, Cristián. Adjustment Processes and the Framework of External Debt Negotiations: Comments. In *Feinberg, R. E. and Ffrench-Davis, R., eds.*, 1988, pp. 101–07.

Ossa, Fernando. El sistema monetario internacional en los últimos veinticinco años (1963–1988). (With English summary.) *Cuadernos Econ.*, December 1988, *25*(76), pp. 405–30.

Ostensoe, Lawrence A.; Cas, Alexandra and Diewert, W. Erwin. Productivity Growth and Changes in the Terms of Trade in Canada. In *Feenstra, R. C., ed.*, 1988, pp. 279–94.

_____ and Diewert, W. Erwin. Flexible Functional Forms for Profit Functions and Global Curvature Conditions. In *Barnett, W. A.; Berndt, E. R. and White, H., eds.*, 1988, pp. 43–51.

Osterfeld, David. Caste and Class: The Rothbardian View of Governments and Markets. In *[Rothbard, M. N.]*, 1988, pp. 283–328.

_____. "Social Utility" and Government Transfers of Wealth: An Austrian Perspective. In *Rothbard, M. N. and Block, W., eds.*, 1988, pp. 79–95.

Osterloh, Margit. Management between "Old" and "New" Production Concepts and Its Dependence on Factors in the System of Vocational Training and Employment. In *Dlugos, G.; Dorow, W. and Weiermair, K., eds.*, 1988, pp. 193–206.

Osterman, Melvin H., Jr. Productivity Bargaining in New York—What Went Wrong? In *Lewin, D., et al., eds.*, 1988, *1980*, pp. 221–36.

Ostermeyer-Schlöder, A. and Henrichsmeyer,

Wilhelm. Productivity Growth and Factor Adjustment in EC Agriculture. *Europ. Rev. Agr. Econ.*, 1988, *15*(2–3), pp. 137–54.

Ostmann, Axel. Limits of Rational Behaviour in Cooperatively Played Normal Form Games. In *Tietz, R.; Albers, W. and Selten, R., eds.*, 1988, pp. 317–32.

Østrup, Finn. Pensionsordninger i EF-landene. (Pension Schemes in EC Countries. With English summary.) *Nationaløkon. Tidsskr.*, 1988, *126*(2), pp. 132–43.

Ostry, Jonathan D. The Balance of Trade, Terms of Trade, and Real Exchange Rate: An Intertemporal Optimizing Framework. *Int. Monet. Fund Staff Pap.*, December 1988, *35*(4), pp. 541–73.

Oswald, Andrew J. Unions and Employment: Tests Using Aggregate and Microeconomic Data: Introduction. *Europ. Econ. Rev.*, March 1988, *32*(2–3), pp. 695–97.

_____ and Blanchflower, David G. Internal and External Influences upon Pay Settlements. *Brit. J. Ind. Relat.*, November 1988, *26*(3), pp. 363–70.

_____ and Blanchflower, David G. Profit-Related Pay: Prose Discovered. *Econ. J.*, September 1988, *98*(392), pp. 720–30.

_____ and Carruth, Alan A. Testing for Multiple Natural Rates of Unemployment in the British Economy: A Preliminary Investigation. In *Cross, R., ed.*, 1988, pp. 232–55.

Otani, Ichiro and Sassanpour, Cyrus. Financial, Exchange Rate, and Wage Policies in Singapore, 1979–86. *Int. Monet. Fund Staff Pap.*, September 1988, *35*(3), pp. 474–95.

Otsuka, Keijiro and Hayami, Yujiro. Theories of Share Tenancy: A Critical Survey. *Econ. Develop. Cult. Change*, October 1988, *37*(1), pp. 31–68.

Ott, Alfred E. Der erste Sachverständigenrat zur Begutachtung der gesamtwirtschaftlichen Entwicklung—Eineige Reminiszenzen. (The First German Economic Council—Some Reminiscences. With English summary.) *Jahr. Nationalökon. Statist.*, July 1988, *205*(1), pp. 1–10.

_____. Laffer-Kurve und Verbrauchsbesteuerung. (Laffer-Curve and Expenditures Taxation. With English summary.) *Ifo-Studien*, 1988, *34*(4), pp. 299–305.

Ott, Mack. Have U.S. Exports Been Larger Than Reported? *Fed. Res. Bank St. Louis Rev.*, Sept.–Oct. 1988, *70*(5), pp. 3–23.

Ottensmeyer, Edward J.; Humphrey, Craig R. and Erickson, Rodney A. Industrial Development Groups, Organizational Resources, and the Prospects for Effecting Growth in Local Economies. *Growth Change*, Summer 1988, *19*(3), pp. 1–21.

Otto, Daniel M. Graphical Presentation of a Two-Person, Two-Good (One Public and One Private) World. In *Johnson, T. G.; Deaton, B. J. and Segarra, E., eds.*, 1988, pp. 21–25.

_____. Issues in the Supply of Public Infrastructure. In *Johnson, T. G.; Deaton, B. J. and Segarra, E., eds.*, 1988, pp. 27–36.

Oudiz, Gilles. The International Monetary System: An Analysis of Alternative Regimes: Comments. *Europ. Econ. Rev.*, June 1988, *32*(5), pp. 1051–54.

_____. Macroeconomic Policy Coordination: Where Should We Stand? In *Giersch, H., ed.*, 1988, pp. 278–91.

_____; Cohen, Daniel and Mélitz, Jacques. Le système monéaire européen et l'asymétrie franc–mark. (The EMS and the Frank–Mark Asymetry. With English summary.) *Revue Écon.*, May 1988, *39*(3), pp. 667–77.

Ouellette, Pierre and Lasserre, Pierre. On Measuring and Comparing Total Factor Productivities in Extractive and Non-extractive Sectors. *Can. J. Econ.*, November 1988, *21*(4), pp. 826–34.

Ouliaris, Sam and Corbae, Dean. Cointegration and Tests of Purchasing Power Parity. *Rev. Econ. Statist.*, August 1988, *70*(3), pp. 508–11.

_____ and Phillips, Peter C. B. Testing for Cointegration Using Principal Components Methods. *J. Econ. Dynam. Control*, June–Sept. 1988, *12*(2–3), pp. 205–30.

Oum, Tae Hoon and Tretheway, Michael W. Ramsey Pricing in the Presence of Externality Costs. *J. Transp. Econ. Policy*, September 1988, *22*(3), pp. 307–17.

_____; Tretheway, Michael W. and Gillen, David W. Entry Barriers and Anti-competitive Behaviour in a Deregulated Airline Market: The Case of Canada. *Int. J. Transport Econ.*, February 1988, *15*(1), pp. 29–41.

Oustapassidis, K. Structural Characteristics of Agricultural Co-operatives in Britain. *J. Agr. Econ.*, May 1988, *39*(2), pp. 231–42.

Outrata, Edvard and Doucet, Ed. Impact of New Processing Techniques on the Mangement and Organization of Statistical Data Processing. *Statist. J.*, August 1988, *5*(2), pp. 201–10.

Outrequin, Philippe. La consommation spécifique d'énergie. (The Specific Energy Consumption in Industry. With English summary.) *Écon. Soc.*, April 1988, *22*(4), pp. 111–32.

Outreville, J. Francois. The Long-run and Short-run Demand for Cash Balances: The Case of Insurance Companies. *Quart. Rev. Econ. Bus.*, Winter 1988, *28*(4), pp. 76–89.

d'Ouville, Edmond L. and McDonald, John F. Constraints on Land Consumption and Urban Rent Gradients. *J. Urban Econ.*, November 1988, *24*(3), pp. 279–88.

_____ and McDonald, John F. Highway Traffic Flow and the 'Uneconomic' Region of Production. *Reg. Sci. Urban Econ.*, November 1988, *18*(4), pp. 503–09.

Ouyang, Ling-Nan. Joint Ventures in China: Problems and Solutions. *Financial Rev.*, May 1988, *23*(2), pp. 175–81.

Ovchinnikov, Sergei V. and Ozernoy, Vladimir M. Identifying Noninferior Decision Alternatives Based on Fuzzy Binary Relations. In *Kacprzyk, J. and Roubens, M., eds.*, 1988, pp. 82–95.

Over, A. Mead and Dunlop, David W. Determinants of Drug Imports to Poor Countries: Pre-liminary Findings and Implications for Financing Primary Health Care. In *Sirageldin, I. and Sorkin, A., eds.*, 1988, pp. 99–125.

Overdahl, James A. The Early Exercise of Options on Treasury Bond Futures. *J. Finan. Quant. Anal.*, December 1988, *23*(4), pp. 437–49.

_____ and Matthews, H. Lee. The Use of NYMEX Options to Forecast Crude Oil Prices. *Energy J.*, October 1988, *9*(4), pp. 135–47.

Overgaard, Erik. Tax Treatment of Computer Software: Denmark. In *International Fiscal Association, ed. (II)*, 1988, pp. 305–17.

Overman, E. Samuel. Methodology and Epistemology for Social Science: Selected Papers: Introduction: Social Science and Donald T. Campbell. In *Campbell, D. T.*, 1988, pp. vii–xix.

Overton, Elizabeth and Joshi, Heather. Forecasting the Female Labour Force in Britain. *Int. J. Forecasting*, 1988, *4*(2), pp. 269–85.

Owen, D. W.; Coombes, M. G. and Green, A. E. Substantive Issues in the Definition of 'Localities': Evidence from Sub-group Local Labour Market Areas in the West Midlands. *Reg. Stud.*, August 1988, *22*(4), pp. 303–18.

Owen, Guillermo. Multilinear Extensions of Games. In *[Shapley, L. S.]*, 1988, pp. 139–51.

_____ and Carreras, Francesc. Evaluation of the Catalonian Parliament, 1980–1984. *Math. Soc. Sci.*, February 1988, *15*(1), pp. 87–92.

_____; Peleg, Bezalel and Maschler, Michael. Paths Leading to the Nash Set. In *[Shapley, L. S.]*, 1988, pp. 321–30.

Owen, Joel and Katz, Barbara Goody. An Equilibrium Model of a Second Economy Market in a Centrally Planned Economy. *J. Compar. Econ.*, December 1988, *12*(4), pp. 546–69.

Owen, John D. A Dynamic Model of Labor Utilization: Comment. In *Hart, R. A., ed.*, 1988, pp. 126–28.

_____. Work-Time Reduction in the U.S. and Western Europe. *Mon. Lab. Rev.*, December 1988, *111*(12), pp. 41–45.

Owen, P. Dorian. Invariance Results for FIML Estimation of an Integrated Model of Expenditure and Portfolio Behaviour. *J. Quant. Econ.*, July 1988, *4*(2), pp. 239–46.

Owen, Robert F. and Perrakis, Stylianos. An International Duopoly Model under Exchange Rate Uncertainty. *Revue Écon.*, September 1988, *39*(5), pp. 1035–60.

Owen, Roger. Economic Development in Mandatory Palestine: 1918–1948. In *Abed, G. T., ed.*, 1988, pp. 13–35.

Owen, Susan and Joshi, Heather. Demographic Predictors of Women's Work in Postwar Britain. In *Schultz, T. Paul, ed.*, 1988, pp. 401–47.

Owen, Thomas C. Four Episodes of Corporate Law Reform in the Russian Empire, 1836–1914. In *Uselding, P. J., ed.*, 1988, pp. 277–99.

Owens, Raymond E. Agricultural Summary and

Outlook. *Fed. Res. Bank Richmond Econ. Rev.*, Jan.–Feb. 1988, *74*(1), pp. 25–28.

Owers, James E. and Sufrin, Sidney C. The Ethics of Anti Trust. *Rivista Int. Sci. Econ. Com.*, April–May 1988, *35*(4–5), pp. 359–68.

Owsinski, Jan W. and Romanowicz, Tomasz M. A Population-Type Model of Car Market Dynamics. In *Iri, M. and Yajima, K., eds.*, 1988, pp. 385–94.

Oxelheim, Lars and Wihlborg, Clas G. Hedging and Managing Exchange Rate and Related Macroeconomic Exposure. In *Khoury, S. J. and Ghosh, A., eds.*, 1988, pp. 321–47.

Oxford, Thomas P.; Taylor, Carol A. and Charney, Alberta H. A Recursive Conjoint Modeling Approach to State Severance Tax Analysis: Mining Florida Phosphates. *Resources & Energy*, December 1988, *10*(4), pp. 355–86.

Oxley, Deborah. Female Convicts. In *Nicholas, S., ed.*, 1988, pp. 85–97.

Ozanne, Julie L. and Hudson, Laurel Anderson. Alternative Ways of Seeking Knowledge in Consumer Research. *J. Cons. Res.*, March 1988, *14*(4), pp. 508–21.

Ozawa, Terutomo. Nascent General Trading Companies (GTCs) in Asia: Progress and Prospects. *Rivista Int. Sci. Econ. Com.*, February 1988, *35*(2), pp. 119–34.

Özcan, Yusuf Ziya. Occupational Structure and Social Mobility in Turkey, 1968. *METU*, 1988, *15*(1–2), pp. 151–82.

Ozernoy, Vladimir M. and Ovchinnikov, Sergei V. Identifying Noninferior Decision Alternatives Based on Fuzzy Binary Relations. In *Kacprzyk, J. and Roubens, M., eds.*, 1988, pp. 82–95.

Paarlberg, Don. Domestic Food and Agricultural Policy Research Directions: A Discussion. In *Hildreth, R. J., et al., eds.*, 1988, pp. 155–57.

_____. Forty Years in Retrospect. *J. Agr. Econ. Res.*, Winter 1988, *40*(1), pp. 5–6.

Paarlberg, Philip L.; Patterson, Paul M. and Abbott, Philip C. Supplier Substitutability by Importers: Implications for Assessing the 1980 U.S. Grain Embargo. *Southern J. Agr. Econ.*, December 1988, *20*(2), pp. 1–14.

Paarlberg, Robert L. U.S. Agriculture and the Developing World: Opportunities for Joint Gains. In *Sewell, J. W. and Tucker, S. K., eds.*, 1988, pp. 119–38.

_____. U.S. Interests in International Agricultural Policy. In *Yochelson, J., ed.*, 1988, pp. 239–60.

_____ and **Leman, Christopher K.** The Continued Political Power of Agricultural Interests. In *Hildreth, R. J., et al., eds.*, 1988, pp. 32–60.

Paass, Gerhard. Disclosure Risk and Disclosure Avoidance for Microdata. *J. Bus. Econ. Statist.*, October 1988, *6*(4), pp. 487–500.

de Pablo, Juan Carlos. Inflation Stabilization: Argentina: Comment. In *Bruno, M., et al., eds.*, 1988, pp. 195–201.

Pace, D. Gene. Modernization in Brazil: The De-

cline of the *Caudilhos*, 1822–1889. In *Perkins, E. J., ed.*, 1988, pp. 166–76.

Pace, Kelley and Shieh, Yeung-Nan. The Moses–Predohl Pull and the Location Decision of the Firm [On Sufficient Conditions for Interior Location in the Triangle Space: A Comment]. *J. Reg. Sci.*, February 1988, *28*(1), pp. 121–26.

Pachauri, R. K. and Srivastava, Leena. Integrated Energy Planning in India: A Modeling Approach. *Energy J.*, October 1988, *9*(4), pp. 35–48.

Paci, Pierella. Tax-Based Incomes Policies: Will They Work? Have They Worked? *Fisc. Stud.*, May 1988, *9*(2), pp. 81–94.

Pack, Janet Rothenberg. The Congress and Fiscal Policy. *Public Choice*, August 1988, *58*(2), pp. 101–22.

Packard, Michael D. and Reno, Virginia P. A Look at Very Early Retirees. In *Ricardo-Campbell, R. and Lazear, E. P., eds.*, 1988, pp. 243–65.

Packard, Norman H. Dynamics of Development: A Simple Model for Dynamics Away from Attractors. In *Anderson, P. W.; Arrow, K. J. and Pines, D., eds.*, 1988, pp. 169–76.

Packer, Frank; Fukuda, Shin-ichi and Horiuchi, Akiyoshi. What Role Has the "Main Bank" Played in Japan? *J. Japanese Int. Economies*, June 1988, *2*(2), pp. 159–80.

Paddison, Ronan. The British Reform in Its International Context. In *Bailey, S. J. and Paddison, R., eds.*, 1988, pp. 190–204.

_____. Federalism and the Bolstering of Australian Local Government Finance. In *Paddison, R. and Bailey, S., eds.*, 1988, pp. 132–53.

_____ and **Bailey, Stephen J.** Local Government Finance: International Perspectives: Introduction. In *Paddison, R. and Bailey, S., eds.*, 1988, pp. 1–5.

_____ and **Bailey, Stephen J.** Local Government Finance: International Perspectives: Conclusions. In *Paddison, R. and Bailey, S., eds.*, 1988, pp. 254–64.

_____ and **Bailey, Stephen J.** The Reform of Local Government Finance in Britain: Introduction. In *Bailey, S. J. and Paddison, R., eds.*, 1988, pp. 1–5.

_____ and **Bailey, Stephen J.** The Reform of Local Government Finance in Britain: Conclusion. In *Bailey, S. J. and Paddison, R., eds.*, 1988, pp. 205–18.

Paddock, James L.; Siegel, Daniel R. and Smith, James L. Option Valuation of Claims on Real Assets: The Case of Offshore Petroleum Leases. *Quart. J. Econ.*, August 1988, *103*(3), pp. 479–508.

Padgett, Carol. Investment and Financial Decision Making in the UK Company Sector. *Rech. Écon. Louvain*, 1988, *54*(2), pp. 191–220.

Padilla Gimeno, Rafael. La demanda de servicios turísticos en España. (With English summary.) *Invest. Econ.*, January 1988, *12*(1), pp. 133–57.

Padoa-Schioppa, Tommaso. The ECUs Coming of Age. In *[Witteveen, H. J.]*, 1988, pp. 159–73.

———. "Milan, Hannover, 1992." *Rev. Econ. Cond. Italy*, Sept.–Dec. 1988, (3), pp. 435–44.

Padoan, Pier Carlo. Global Debt: Why Is Cooperation So Difficult? Perspective. In *Guerrieri, P. and Padoan, P. C., eds.*, 1988, pp. 112–16.

——— **and Guerrieri, Paolo.** International Cooperation and the Role of Macroeconomic Regimes. In *Guerrieri, P. and Padoan, P. C., eds.*, 1988, pp. 1–27.

Pagan, Adrian. Comment on Poirier: Dogma or Doubt? *J. Econ. Perspectives*, Winter 1988, 2(1), pp. 153–58.

———. A Note on the Magnitude of Risk Premia [The Implications of Mean–Variance Optimization for Four Questions in International Macroeconomics]. *J. Int. Money Finance*, March 1988, 7(1), pp. 109–10.

——— **and Hong, Y.** Some Simulation Studies of Nonparametric Estimators. *Empirical Econ.*, 1988, 13(3–4), pp. 251–66.

——— **and Ullah, Aman.** The Econometric Analysis of Models with Risk Terms. *J. Appl. Econometrics*, April 1988, 3(2), pp. 87–105.

Pagano, Marco. The Management of Public Debt and Financial Markets. In *Giavazzi, F. and Spaventa, L., eds.*, 1988, pp. 135–66.

——— **and Giavazzi, Francesco.** The Advantage of Tying One's Hands: EMS Discipline and Central Bank Credibility. *Europ. Econ. Rev.*, June 1988, 32(5), pp. 1055–75.

Paganoni, Luigi. On a Functional Equation with Applications to Measurement in Economics. In *Eichhorn, W., ed.*, 1988, pp. 39–45.

Pagden, Anthony. The Destruction of Trust and Its Economic Consequences in the Case of Eighteenth-Century Naples. In *Gambetta, D., ed.*, 1988, pp. 127–41.

Page, Daniel E.; Jahera, John S., Jr. and Lloyd, William P. Does Business Diversification Affect Performance?: Some Further Evidence. *Quart. J. Bus. Econ.*, Winter 1988, 27(1), pp. 130–47.

Page, John M., Jr.; Bateman, Deborah A. and Nishimizu, Mieko. Regional Productivity Differentials and Development Policy in Yugoslavia, 1965–1978. *J. Compar. Econ.*, March 1988, 12(1), pp. 24–42.

Page, Talbot. Pivot Mechanisms as a Link between Probability and Preference Revelation. *J. Econ. Theory*, February 1988, 44(1), pp. 43–62.

Pages-Fita, J.; Marti-Recober, M. and Muñoz-Gracia, M. Pilar. Estimation of ARMA Process Parameters and Noise Variance by Means of a Non Linear Filtering Algorithm. In *Edwards, D. and Raun, N. E., eds.*, 1988, pp. 357–62.

Paggi, Mechel; Henry, Guy and Peterson, E. Wesley F. Quality Restrictions as Barriers to Trade: The Case of European Community Regulations on the Use of Hormones. *Western J. Agr. Econ.*, July 1988, 13(1), pp. 82–91.

Paige, Jeffery. One, Two, or Many Vietnams? Social Theory and Peasant Revolution in Vietnam and Guatemala. In *Burke, E., III, ed.*, 1988, 1983, pp. 145–79.

Paine, Frank T. and Schilit, Warren Keith. An Empirical Examination of the Strategic Decision Making Process. In *Grant, J. H., ed.*, 1988, pp. 293–309.

Painter, An. The Future of Environmental Dispute Resolution. *Natural Res. J.*, Winter 1988, 28(1), pp. 145–70.

Painter, Nell Irvin. Remembering Herbert Gutman. *Labor Hist.*, Summer 1988, 29(3), pp. 336–43.

Pairault, Thierry. Ideology and Industrialization in China 1949–83. In *Feuchtwang, S.; Hussain, A. and Pairault, T., eds.*, Vol. 2, 1988, pp. 26–50.

———; **Feuchtwang, Stephan and Hussain, Athar.** Transforming China's Economy in the Eighties. In *Feuchtwang, S.; Hussain, A. and Pairault, T., eds.*, Vol. 1, 1988, pp. 1–6.

———; **Feuchtwang, Stephan and Hussain, Athar.** Transforming China's Economy in the Eighties, Volume II: Management, Industry and the Urban Economy: Preface. In *Feuchtwang, S.; Hussain, A. and Pairault, T., eds.*, Vol. 2, 1988, pp. 1–6.

Paixão, J. and Branco, I. M. Bus Scheduling with a Fixed Number of Vehicles. In *Daduna, J. R. and Wren, A., eds.*, 1988, pp. 28–40.

Pajak, Roger F. Soviet Designs and Dilemmas in the Gulf Region. In *Sindelar, H. R., III and Peterson, J. E., eds.*, 1988, pp. 61–85.

Pajestka, Józef. Global Shifts and Their Impact on National Policies. In *Saunders, C. T., ed.*, 1988, pp. 47–58.

Pake, George E. Driving Technologies. In *Muroyama, J. H. and Stever, H. G., eds.*, 1988, pp. 37–40.

Pakes, Ariel. The Effect of Takeover Activity on Corporate Research and Development: Comment. In *Auerbach, A. J., ed. (I)*, 1988, pp. 97–100.

——— **and Kotlikoff, Laurence J.** Looking for the News in the Noise. Additional Stochastic Implications of Optimal Consumption Choice. *Ann. Écon. Statist.*, Jan.–March 1988, (9), pp. 29–46.

Pal, Leslie A. Sense and Sensibility: Comments. *Can. Public Policy*, March 1988, 14(1), pp. 7–14.

Pal, Padmaja; Bhattacharya, N. and Chatterjee, G. S. Variations in Level of Living across Regions and Social Groups in Rural India, 1963/1964 and 1973/1974. In *Srinivasan, T. N. and Bardhan, P. K., eds.*, 1988, pp. 154–218.

Pal, Surendra and Waldauer, Charles. Imbalanced Faculty: A Persistent Problem in Higher Education. *J. Policy Anal. Manage.*, Fall 1988, 7(4), pp. 718–21.

Paladini, Ruggero and Frasca, Francesco M. The Distributive Effects of Taxation of the Public Debt in Italy. *Econ. Notes*, 1988, (3), pp. 5–28.

Paldam, Martin and Zeuthen, Hans E. The Expansion of the Public Sector in Denmark—A

Post Festum? In *Lybeck, J. A. and Henrekson, M., eds.*, 1988, pp. 157–86.

Palepu, Krishna G. Bad News and Differential Market Reactions to Announcements of Earlier-Quarters versus Fourth-Quarter Earnings: Discussion. *J. Acc. Res.*, Supplement, 1988, *26*, pp. 87–90.

_____ **and Healy, Paul M.** Earnings Information Conveyed by Dividend Initiations and Omissions. *J. Finan. Econ.*, September 1988, *21*(2), pp. 149–75.

Palerm, Angel. Selective Policies under a Structural Foreign Exchange Shortage: Comments. *J. Devel. Econ.*, November 1988, *29*(3), pp. 371–74.

Palfrey, Thomas R. Uncertainty Resolution, Private Information Aggregation, and the Cournot Competitive Limit. In *Daughety, A. F., ed.*, 1988, *1985*, pp. 353–72.

_____ **and Rosenthal, Howard.** Private Incentives in Social Dilemmas: The Effects of Incomplete Information and Altruism. *J. Public Econ.*, April 1988, *35*(3), pp. 309–32.

Palia, Aspy P. and Williams, Harold R. The U.S. Trigger Price Mechanism: Econometric Analysis of Its Impact on Steel Imports. *Rivista Int. Sci. Econ. Com.*, April–May 1988, *35*(4–5), pp. 457–71.

Palley, Thomas I. Bank Lending, Discount Window Borrowing, and the Endogenous Money Supply: A Theoretical Framework. *J. Post Keynesian Econ.*, Winter 1987–88, *10*(2), pp. 282–303.

_____. The Effect of Unemployment Among Union Members on Union Wage Contracts. *Atlantic Econ. J.*, September 1988, *16*(3), pp. 19–30.

Palloni, Alberto. On the Role of Crises in Historical Perspective: An Exchange. *Population Devel. Rev.*, March 1988, *14*(1), pp. 145–58.

Palm, Franz C. Macroeconomic Models and Econometrics: Comment. In *Driehuis, W.; Fase, M. M. G. and den Hartog, H., eds.*, 1988, pp. 389–98.

_____ **and Nijman, Theodore E.** Consistent Estimation of Regression Models with Incompletely Observed Exogenous Variables. *Ann. Écon. Statist.*, Oct.–Dec. 1988, (12), pp. 151–75.

de Palma, André. Modélisation de la demande temporelle pour le téléphone. (Forecast of the Temporal Demand for Telephones. With English summary.) *Ann. Écon. Statist.*, Oct.–Dec. 1988, (12), pp. 63–87.

_____ **and Anderson, Simon P.** Spatial Price Discrimination with Heterogeneous Products. *Rev. Econ. Stud.*, October 1988, *55*(4), pp. 573–92.

_____ **and Papageorgiou, Yorgos Y.** Heterogeneity in Tastes and Urban Structure. *Reg. Sci. Urban Econ.*, February 1988, *18*(1), pp. 37–56.

_____; **Thisse, Jacques-François and Anderson, Simon P.** The CES and the Logit: Two Related Models of Heterogeneity. *Reg. Sci. Urban Econ.*, February 1988, *18*(1), pp. 155–64.

_____; **Thisse, Jacques-François and Anderson, Simon P.** A Representative Consumer Theory of the Logit Model. *Int. Econ. Rev.*, August 1988, *29*(3), pp. 461–66.

Palma, J. Gabriel and Marcel, Mario. Third World Debt and Its Effects on the British Economy: A Southern View of Economic Mismanagement in the North. *Cambridge J. Econ.*, September 1988, *12*(3), pp. 361–400.

Palma, Pedro A. and Fontiveros, Domingo. A Comparative Sensitivity Analysis of the MODVEN VII Macroeconomic Model for Venezuela. *Econ. Modelling*, October 1988, *5*(4), pp. 286–346.

Palmer, A. J. and Jackson, Peter M. The Economics of Internal Organisation: The Efficiency of Parastatals in LDCs. In *Cook, P. and Kirkpatrick, C., eds.*, 1988, pp. 195–213.

Palmer, C. M. and Sloyan, M. J. The Experience of the UK Meat and Livestock Commission in Providing Videotex Services in Great Britain. In *Schiefer, G., ed.*, 1988, pp. 73–86.

Palmer, J. P. and Leibowitz, S. J. Assessing Assessments of Economics Departments. *Quart. Rev. Econ. Bus.*, Summer 1988, *28*(2), pp. 88–113.

Palmer, John L. and Gould, Stephanie G. Outcomes, Interpretations, and Policy Implications. In *Palmer, J. L.; Smeeding, T. and Torrey, B. B., eds.*, 1988, pp. 413–42.

_____; **Smeeding, Timothy M. and Jencks, Christopher.** The Uses and Limits of Income Comparisons. In *Palmer, J. L.; Smeeding, T. and Torrey, B. B., eds.*, 1988, pp. 9–27.

_____; **Smeeding, Timothy M. and Torrey, Barbara Boyle.** The Vulnerable: Introduction. In *Palmer, J. L.; Smeeding, T. and Torrey, B. B., eds.*, 1988, pp. 1–6.

Palmer, Michael. China's New Inheritance Law: Some Preliminary Observations. In *Feuchtwang, S.; Hussain, A. and Pairault, T., eds.*, Vol. 1, 1988, pp. 169–97.

Palmer, R. Heather. The Challenges and Prospects for Quality Assessment and Assurance in Ambulatory Care. *Inquiry*, Spring 1988, *25*(1), pp. 119–31.

Palmer, Richard. Statistical Mechanics Approaches to Complex Optimization Problems. In *Anderson, P. W.; Arrow, K. J. and Pines, D., eds.*, 1988, pp. 177–93.

Palmer, Sarah. The Eighteenth Century Ports of London and Liverpool: Private v. Corporate Promotion. In *Cavaciocchi, S., ed.*, 1988, pp. 381–97.

Palmeter, N. David. The Antidumping Emperor: Editorial. *J. World Trade*, August 1988, *22*(4), pp. 5–7.

_____. Exchange Rates and Antidumping Determinations. *J. World Trade*, April 1988, *22*(2), pp. 73–80.

_____. Gray Market Imports: No Black and White Answer. *J. World Trade*, October 1988, *22*(5), pp. 89–92.

Palmon, Oded and Hochman, Shalom. A Tax-Induced Clientele for Index-Linked Corporate

Bonds. *J. Finance*, December 1988, *43*(5), pp. 1257–63.

Palmquist, Raymond B. Welfare Measurement for Environmental Improvements Using the Hedonic Model: The Case of Nonparametric Marginal Prices. *J. Environ. Econ. Manage.*, September 1988, *15*(3), pp. 297–312.

Palócz, Éva. Services in the World Economy. *Acta Oecon.*, 1988, *39*(1–2), pp. 171–83.

Pálovics, Irén and Ujhelyi, Tamás. European Agricultural Policy in a Global Context: The European CMEA Countries. *Europ. Rev. Agr. Econ.*, 1988, *15*(2–3), pp. 173–86.

Pålsson, Anne-Marie. Hushållens sparande i portföljvalsperspektiv. Analys med svenska data. (Household Savings in the Light of Portfolio Management. An Analysis Using Swedish Data. With English summary.) *Ekon. Samfundets Tidskr.*, 1988, *41*(3), pp. 147–65.

Palsson, Halldor P. and Marwah, Kanta. Direct Interventions, Interest Rate Shocks and Monetary Disturbances in the Canadian Foreign Exchange Market: A Simulation Study. In *Motamen, H., ed.*, 1988, pp. 407–55.

_____ **and West, Edwin G.** Parental Choice of School Characteristics: Estimation Using State-Wide Data. *Econ. Inquiry*, October 1988, *26*(4), pp. 725–40.

Paltschik, Mikael; Sevón, Guje and Lindqvist, Lars-Johan. Consumers' and Producers' Basic Evaluation—An Investigation of Objects in the Field of Music. *Liiketaloudellinen Aikak.*, 1988, *37*(3), pp. 193–211.

Pampel, Fred C. and Pillai, Vijayan. Teenage Fertility and Infant Mortality: Reply. *Demography*, February 1988, *25*(1), pp. 159–61.

Panagariya, Arvind. A Theoretical Explanation of Some Stylized Facts of Economic Growth. *Quart. J. Econ.*, August 1988, *103*(3), pp. 509–26.

_____ **and Narayana, A. V. L.** Excise Tax Evasion: A Welfare cum Crime Theoretic Analysis. *Public Finance*, 1988, *43*(2), pp. 248–60.

Panas, Epaminondas E. and Bitros, George C. Measuring Product Prices under Conditions of Quality Change: The Case of Passenger Cars in Greece. *J. Ind. Econ.*, December 1988, *37*(2), pp. 167–86.

Panattoni, Lorenzo. Interactive Preference Elicitation in Macroeconomic Decision Models. *J. Econ. Dynam. Control*, March 1988, *12*(1), pp. 109–16.

_____ **and Calzolari, Giorgio.** Alternative Estimators of FIML Covariance Matrix: A Monte Carlo Study. *Econometrica*, May 1988, *56*(3), pp. 701–14.

_____ **and Calzolari, Giorgio.** Finite Sample Performance of the Robust Wald Test in Simultaneous Equation Systems. In *Rhodes, G. F., Jr. and Fomby, T. B., eds.*, 1988, pp. 163–91.

Panchamukhi, V. R. and Kumar, Nagesh. Impact on Commodity Exports. In *Research and Info. System for the Non-aligned and Other Developing Countries*, 1988, pp. 207–24.

Pandey, R. K.; Kumar, Ashok and Kaul, Sushila.

Agricultural Field Wages in Orissa: An Economic Study. *Margin*, Oct.–Dec. 1988, *21*(1), pp. 72–78.

Panek, Emil. Consumption Turnpike in a Nonlinear Model of the Input–Output Type. In *Ciaschini, M., ed.*, 1988, pp. 253–59.

Panico, Carlo. Marx on the Banking Sector and the Interest Rate: Some Notes for a Discussion. *Sci. Soc.*, Fall 1988, *52*(3), pp. 310–25.

_____. Sraffa on Money and Banking. *Cambridge J. Econ.*, March 1988, *12*(1), pp. 7–28.

Pankow, Max. Steuerliche Behandlung von 'Computer Software': Deutschland. (Tax Treatment of Computer Software: Germany. With English summary.) In *International Fiscal Association, ed. (II)*, 1988, pp. 139–59.

Pannell, David J. An Integrated Package for Linear Programming. *Rev. Marketing Agr. Econ.*, August 1988, *56*(2), pp. 234–35.

_____. The Place of Expert Systems in Agricultural Economics. *Rev. Marketing Agr. Econ.*, August 1988, *56*(2), pp. 206–09.

_____. Weed Management: A Review of Applied Economics Research in Australia. *Rev. Marketing Agr. Econ.*, December 1988, *56*(3), pp. 255–69.

_____; **Patten, Louise H. and Hardaker, J. Brian.** Utility-Efficient Programming for Whole-Farm Planning. *Australian J. Agr. Econ.*, Aug.–Dec. 1988, *32*(2–3), pp. 88–97.

Panova, Galina. Recent Developments in Soviet Banking. *Nat. Westminster Bank Quart. Rev.*, August 1988, pp. 31–38.

Papageorgiou, Yorgos Y. and de Palma, André. Heterogeneity in Tastes and Urban Structure. *Reg. Sci. Urban Econ.*, February 1988, *18*(1), pp. 37–56.

_____ **and Pines, David.** The Impact of Transportation Cost Uncertainty on Urban Structure. *Reg. Sci. Urban Econ.*, May 1988, *18*(2), pp. 247–60.

Papanek, Gustav F. Poverty in India. In *Lucas, R. E. B. and Papanek, G. F., eds.*, 1988, pp. 121–44.

Papathanasis, A. and Vasillopulos, Christopher. The Remedies of Antitrust under Functional Integration. In *Pennsylvania Economic Association*, 1988, pp. 626–38.

Papell, David H. Expectations and Exchange Rate Dynamics after a Decade of Floating. *J. Int. Econ.*, November 1988, *25*(3–4), pp. 303–17.

_____ **and Collier, Irwin L., Jr.** About Two Marks: Refugees and the Exchange Rate before the Berlin Wall. *Amer. Econ. Rev.*, June 1988, *78*(3), pp. 531–42.

Papi, Luca. Domanda di moneta e struttura dinamica: Uno studio applicato all'Italia. (Monetary Demand and Dynamical Structure: The Case of Italy. With English summary.) *Giorn. Econ.*, March–April 1988, *47*(3–4), pp. 163–85.

Papps, Ivy. Deregulation and Privatisation. In *Darnell, A. and Evans, L., eds.*, 1988, pp. 57–69.

Paqueo, Vicente B. and Boulier, Bryan L. On the Theory and Measurement of the Determinants of Mortality. *Demography*, May 1988, *25*(2), pp. 249–63.

Parai, Amar K. The Incidence of Corporate Income Tax under Variable Returns to Scale. *Public Finance*, 1988, *43*(3), pp. 414–24.

———. Trade Creation, Trade Diversion and Elastic Labor Supply. *Math. Soc. Sci.*, October 1988, *16*(2), pp. 171–79.

Paramenter, Brian R.; Horridge, Mark and Dixon, Peter B. Forecasting versus Policy Analysis with the ORANI Model. In *Motamen, H., ed.*, 1988, pp. 653–66.

Parandvash, Gholam Hossein and McCarl, Bruce A. Irrigation Development versus Hydroelectric Generation: Can Interruptible Irrigation Play a Role? *Western J. Agr. Econ.*, December 1988, *13*(2), pp. 267–76.

Parguez, Alain. Croissance et accumulation au-delà du seuil critique d'endettement. (Growth and Accumulation beyond the Critical Level of Borrowing. With English summary.) *Écon. Soc.*, June–July 1988, *22*(6–7), pp. 89–99.

——— **and Coulombe, Serge.** Le rôle des institutions financières dans le circuit dynamique: L'austérité et le capitalisme rentier public en France. (The Role of Financial Institutions within the Dynamic Circuit: Austerity and State Rentiers Capitalism in France. With English summary.) *Écon. Soc.*, September 1988, *22*(9), pp. 85–119.

Pari, Robert and Caks, John. A Note on Bond Defeasance. *Financial Rev.*, May 1988, *23*(2), pp. 233–36.

Parigi, Bruno M. A Model of Borrowing and Lending with Reputation and Incomplete Information. *Rivista Int. Sci. Econ. Com.*, Oct.–Nov. 1988, *35*(10–11), pp. 951–66.

Parikh, Ashok. An Econometric Analysis of Fertilizer Demand in Bangladesh Using Cross-Section and Time-Series Data. *J. Quant. Econ.*, January 1988, *4*(1), pp. 157–71.

———. An Econometric Study on Estimation of Trade Shares Using the Almost Ideal Demand System in the World Link. *Appl. Econ.*, August 1988, *20*(8), pp. 1017–39.

———. A Review of the Macro Model for the Third Five Year Plan. *Bangladesh Devel. Stud.*, June 1988, *16*(2), pp. 45–56.

———. Some Views on the Construction of Monetary Sector within the Technical Framework of Macro Model. *Bangladesh Devel. Stud.*, December 1988, *16*(4), pp. 93–97.

——— **and Starmer, C.** The Relationship between the Money Supply and Prices in Bangladesh. *Bangladesh Devel. Stud.*, September 1988, *16*(3), pp. 59–70.

Parikh, J. K. Bangladesh: Agricultural, Biomass, and Environment. In *Parikh, J. K., ed.*, 1988, pp. 331–64.

———. Sustainable Development in Agriculture: Introduction. In *Parikh, J. K., ed.*, 1988, pp. 1–11.

———. Sustainable Development of Agricultural Systems: Concerns, Approaches, and Policy Insights. In *Parikh, J. K., ed.*, 1988, pp. 367–85.

Parikh, Kirit S.; Ereshko, F. and Lebedev, V. Agricultural Planning Models for Stavropol Region: Mathematical Description and Simulation Strategies. In *Parikh, J. K., ed.*, 1988, pp. 39–58.

———**; Fischer, Günther and Frohberg, Klaus.** Agricultural Trade Regimes: Impact on Sector Proportions, Real Incomes and Hunger in the World. *Europ. Rev. Agr. Econ.*, 1988, *15*(4), pp. 397–417.

———**; Srinivasan, T. N. and Narayana, N. S. S.** Rural Works Programs in India: Costs and Benefits. *J. Devel. Econ.*, September 1988, *29*(2), pp. 131–56.

Paringer, Lynn and Fon, Vincy. Price Discrimination in Medicine: The Case of Medicare. *Quart. Rev. Econ. Bus.*, Spring 1988, *28*(1), pp. 49–68.

Paris, Quirino. Long-run Comparative Statics under Output and Land Price Uncertainty. *Amer. J. Agr. Econ.*, February 1988, *70*(1), pp. 133–41.

Pařízek, Pavel and Špaček, Petr. Foreign-Exchange Financial Relations. *Czech. Econ. Digest.*, June 1988, (4), pp. 21–37.

Park, C. Whan. Changes in International Marketing Techniques: Commentary. In *Cassing, J. H. and Husted, S. L., eds.*, 1988, pp. 136–38.

Park, Hun Y.; Bera, Anil K. and Bubnys, Edward. Conditional Heteroscedasticity in the Market Model and Efficient Estimates of Betas. *Financial Rev.*, May 1988, *23*(2), pp. 201–14.

———**; Chen, Andrew H. and Doherty, Neil A.** The Optimal Capital Structure Decision of Depository Financial Intermediaries. In *Chen, A. H., ed.*, 1988, pp. 91–111.

——— **and Finnerty, Joseph E.** How to Profit from Program Trading. *J. Portfol. Manage.*, Winter 1988, *14*(2), pp. 40–46.

——— **and Finnerty, Joseph E.** Intraday Return and Volatility Patterns in the Stock Market: Futures versus Spot. In *Fabozzi, F. J., ed.*, 1988, pp. 301–17.

———**; Wei, K. C. John and Frecka, Thomas J.** A Further Investigation of the Risk–Return Relation for Commodity Futures. In *Fabozzi, F. J., ed.*, 1988, pp. 357–77.

Park, Jin Hyuk and Ito, Takatoshi. Political Business Cycles in the Parliamentary System. *Econ. Letters*, 1988, *27*(3), pp. 233–38.

Park, Joon Y. and Phillips, Peter C. B. Asymptotic Equivalence of Ordinary Least Squares and Generalized Least Squares in Regressions with Integrated Regressors. *J. Amer. Statist. Assoc.*, March 1988, *83*(401), pp. 111–15.

——— **and Phillips, Peter C. B.** On the Formulation of Wald Tests of Nonlinear Restrictions. *Econometrica*, September 1988, *56*(5), pp. 1065–83.

Park, Keehwan and Mathur, Vijay K. Production Technology Uncertainty and the Optimal Location of the Firm. *J. Reg. Sci.*, February 1988, *28*(1), pp. 51–64.

Park, Se-Hark. A Decomposition Analysis of Manufacturing Value Added and Structural

Change by Industry and Region, 1963–80. *Devel. Econ.*, September 1988, 26(3), pp. 264–91.

Park, Se-Il. Labor Issues in Korea's Future. *World Devel.*, January 1988, 16(1), pp. 99–119.

Park, Thae S. Federal Personal Income Tax Liabilities and Payments: Revised and Updated Estimates, 1984–86. *Surv. Curr. Bus.*, September 1988, 68(9), pp. 21–22.

———— **and Reeb, Jane S.** Relationship between Personal Income and Adjusted Gross Income, 1984–86. *Surv. Curr. Bus.*, August 1988, 68(8), pp. 23–27.

Park, Tong Whan. South Korea and the Ambiguities of South–South Cooperation in the Pacific Rim. In *Carlsson, J. and Shaw, T. M., eds.*, 1988, pp. 268–94.

Park, Ungsuh K. A Bird's Eye View of Korean Economic Development. In *Park, U. K.*, 1988, pp. 35–47.

————. Commodity Trade and Technological Cooperation between Korea and France. In *Park, U. K.*, 1988, pp. 209–22.

————. Economic Development Model of Japan: Transferability to Korea and Taiwan. In *Park, U. K.*, 1988, *1985*, pp. 153–86.

————. Economic Developments Strategy of the PRC: A Comparative Study to Korea. In *Park, U. K.*, 1988, *1983*, pp. 88–120.

————. Export Competition between and Comparative Advantages of Newly Industrializing Countries. In *Park, U. K.*, 1988, *1980*, pp. 267–87.

————. Importance of Mutual Trade between South Korea and East Europe. In *Park, U. K.*, 1988, *1984*, pp. 136–50.

————. Inter-industry Effect of Cumulative Wage Indexation. In *Park, U. K.*, 1988, *1979*, pp. 249–64.

————. Intra-ASEAN Relationship: Cooperation and Conflict. In *Park, U. K.*, 1988, *1986*, pp. 187–208.

————. Korea's Economy at a Turning Point. In *Park, U. K.*, 1988, *1980*, pp. 27–34.

————. Korean Domestic Trade Policy Process and Role of the Private Sector in the Uruguay Round. In *Park, U. K.*, 1988, pp. 325–43.

————. Modernization of the Industrial Sector: The Second Round of Reform in the PRC. In *Park, U. K.*, 1988, *1986*, pp. 121–35.

————. The Modernization Program of the PRC and Its Impacts on Korea. In *Park, U. K.*, 1988, *1979*, pp. 51–87.

————. Patterns and Problems of Korean Economic Development. In *Park, U. K.*, 1988, pp. 3–26.

————. Structural Inter-dependence of Economies of Korea and Japan: An Analysis of Combined Input–Output Table. In *Park, U. K.*, 1988, pp. 309–24.

————. Structure and Specialization in Korea–U.S. Trade. In *Park, U. K.*, 1988, pp. 288–308.

————. Studies of the Disaggregated Australian Export Functions. In *Park, U. K.*, 1988, *1980*, pp. 223–48.

Parkash, Om. Growth of Sales Tax Revenue in Punjab. In *Raikhy, P. S. and Gill, S. S., eds.*, 1988, pp. 88–113.

Parker, Dennis J. and Sewell, W. R. Derrick. Evolving Water Institutions in England and Wales: An Assessment of Two Decades of Experience. *Natural Res. J.*, Fall 1988, 28(4), pp. 751–85.

Parker, Douglas D.; Zilberman, David and Lichtenberg, Erik. Marginal Analysis of Welfare Costs of Environmental Policies: The Case of Pesticide Regulation. *Amer. J. Agr. Econ.*, November 1988, 70(4), pp. 867–74.

Parker, Gary; Kimura, Yoshitaka and Ikeda, Syunsuke. Stable Width and Depth of Straight Gravel Rivers with Heterogeneous Bed Materials. *Water Resources Res.*, May 1988, 24(5), pp. 713–22.

Parker, Jeffrey A. Private Financing of Mass Transit. In *Weicher, J. C., ed.*, 1988, pp. 29–37.

Parker, John. The Effective Patent Life of Pharmaceuticals in New Zealand—A Simulation. In *Butler, J. R. G. and Doessel, D. P., eds.*, 1988, pp. 135–53.

Parker, Julia and Mirrlees, Catriona. British Social Trends since 1900: Housing. In *Halsey, A. H., ed.*, 1988, pp. 357–97.

———— **and Mirrlees, Catriona.** British Social Trends since 1900: Welfare. In *Halsey, A. H., ed.*, 1988, pp. 462–517.

Parker, Richard. Conversational Interaction: Directions for Qualitative Marketing and Consumer Research. In *Hirschman, E. and Sheth, J. N., eds.*, 1988, pp. 211–45.

Parker, Robert L.; Jarrett, Steven and Taylor, Carl E. The Evolving Chinese Rural Health Care System. In *Sirageldin, I. and Sorkin, A., eds.*, 1988, pp. 219–36.

Parkin, David and Yule, Brian. Patient Charges and the Demand for Dental Care in Scotland, 1962–81. *Appl. Econ.*, February 1988, 20(2), pp. 229–42.

Parkin, Michael. A Method for Determining Whether Parameters in Aggregative Models are Structural. *Carnegie–Rochester Conf. Ser. Public Policy*, Autumn 1988, 29, pp. 215–52.

———— **and Cox, W. Michael.** Currency Substitution and the International Transmission of Economic Disturbances. *Fed. Res. Bank Dallas Econ. Rev.*, May 1988, pp. 1–12.

Parkin, P. Wendy and Hearn, Jeff. Women, Men, and Leadership: A Critical Review of Assumptions, Practices, and Change in the Industrialized Nations. In *Adler, N. J. and Izraeli, D., eds.*, 1988, pp. 17–40.

Parkoła, Andrzej and Rapacki, Ryszard. The Second Phase of the Reform: Proposals in the Area of Foreign Trade. *Eastern Europ. Econ.*, Summer 1988, 26(4), pp. 72–90.

Parks, Richard W. and Kochin, Levis A. Was the Tax-Exempt Bond Market Inefficient or Were Future Expected Tax Rates Negative? *J. Finance*, September 1988, 43(4), pp. 913–31.

Parks, William, II and Mellor, Earl F. A Year's

Work: Labor Force Activity from a Different Perspective. *Mon. Lab. Rev.*, September 1988, *111*(9), pp. 13–18.

Parlange, J.-Y., et al. Extension and Practical Limitations of the One-Dimension Intercept. *Water Resources Res.*, May 1988, *24*(5), pp. 779–80.

Parmenter, B. R. and Dixon, Peter B. Recent Developments in Forecasting with the ORANI Model. *Australian Econ. Pap.*, Supplement, June 1988, *27*, pp. 92–104.

———; **Rimmer, Russell J. and Higgs, Peter J.** A Hybrid Top-Down, Bottom-Up Regional Computable General Equilibrium Model. *Int. Reg. Sci. Rev.*, 1988, *11*(3), pp. 317–28.

Paroush, Jacob. The Domino Effect and the Supervision of the Banking System. *J. Finance*, December 1988, *43*(5), pp. 1207–18.

Parpart, Jane L. Women, Work and Collective Labour Action in Africa. **In** *Southall, R., ed.*, 1988, pp. 238–55.

Parr, John B. Incomes, Trade, and the Balance of Payments within an Urban System. *J. Reg. Sci.*, February 1988, *28*(1), pp. 1–14.

———; **O'Neill, Gerard J. and Nairn, Alasdair G. M.** Metropolitan Density Functions: A Further Exploration. *Reg. Sci. Urban Econ.*, November 1988, *18*(4), pp. 463–78.

Parrinello, Sergio. Il ruolo di una scuola estiva di economia. (The Role of a Summer School in Economics. With English summary.) *Econ. Polit.*, December 1988, *5*(3), pp. 335–41.

———. "On Foreign Trade" and the Ricardian Model of Trade. *J. Post Keynesian Econ.*, Summer 1988, *10*(4), pp. 585–601.

Parrish, Rudolph and Carsel, Robert F. Developing Joint Probability Distributions of Soil Water Retention Characteristics. *Water Resources Res.*, May 1988, *24*(5), pp. 755–69.

Parry, Charles W. Basic Materials in a Global Economy. **In** *Feldstein, M., ed. (II)*, 1988, pp. 354–58.

Parry, Thomas G. Foreign Investment and Industry in the Pacific Islands. *J. Devel. Areas*, April 1988, *22*(3), pp. 381–99.

———. The Multinational Enterprise and Restrictive Conditions in International Technology Transfer: Some New Australian Evidence. *J. Ind. Econ.*, March 1988, *36*(3), pp. 359–65.

———. The Role of Foreign Capital in East Asian Industrialization, Growth and Development. **In** *Hughes, H., ed.*, 1988, pp. 95–128.

Parsons, Carol A. The Changing Shape of Domestic Employment in High-Tech Industry: The Case of International Trade in Semiconductors. **In** *Tyson, L. D.; Dickens, W. T. and Zysman, J., eds.*, 1988, pp. 237–67.

———. The Domestic Employment Consequences of Managed International Competition in Apparel. **In** *Tyson, L. D.; Dickens, W. T. and Zysman, J., eds.*, 1988, pp. 113–55.

Parsons, Charles K. Computer Technology: Implications for Human Resources Management. **In** *Ferris, G. R. and Rowland, K. M., eds.*, 1988, pp. 1–36.

Parsons, Donald O. Changing Health of the Older

Working-Age Population and Retirement Patterns over Time: Discussion. **In** *Ricardo-Campbell, R. and Lazear, E. P., eds.*, 1988, pp. 153–61.

Parsons, John E. Bubble, Bubble, How Much Trouble? Financial Markets, Capitalist Development and Capitalist Crises. *Sci. Soc.*, Fall 1988, *52*(3), pp. 260–89.

———. Contractual Forms for Industrial Cooperation: New Thinking in the East . . . and in the West? **In** *Liebowitz, R. D., ed.*, 1988, pp. 147–59.

Parsons, Kenneth H. A New Look at Institutionalism: Discussion. **In** *Samuels, W. J., ed., Vol. 1*, 1988, *1957*, pp. 46–51.

Parsons, Patrick R.; Finnegan, John, Jr. and Benham, William. Editors and Their Roles. **In** *Picard, R. G., et al., eds.*, 1988, pp. 91–103.

Partch, M. Megan and Mikkelson, Wayne H. Withdrawn Security Offerings. *J. Finan. Quant. Anal.*, June 1988, *23*(2), pp. 119–33.

Parthemos, James. The Federal Reserve Act of 1913 in the Stream of U.S. Monetary History. *Fed. Res. Bank Richmond Econ. Rev.*, July–Aug. 1988, *74*(4), pp. 19–28.

Pascale, Richard and Rohlen, Thomas P. The Mazda Turnaround. **In** *Okimoto, D. I. and Rohlen, T. P., eds.*, 1988, pp. 149–69.

Pascarella, Perry. Plugging in the 'People Factors.' **In** *Timpe, A. D., ed.*, 1988, *1985*, pp. 3–8.

Pascoe, George A., Jr. and McGuckin, Robert H. The Longitudinal Research Database: Status and Research Possibilities. *Surv. Curr. Bus.*, November 1988, *68*(11), pp. 30–37.

Pascual Lapeña, Nuria and Martínez Mongay, Carlos. Productividad multifactor y efecto capacidad de la industria española 1971–1981. (With English summary.) *Invest. Econ.*, September 1988, *12*(3), pp. 425–44.

——— **and Martinez Mongay, Carlos.** Sobre el análisis de la eslasticidad de sustitución en condiciones de equilibrio temporal. (With English summary.) *Invest. Econ.*, May 1988, *12*(2), pp. 279–303.

Pasetta, Vesna. Model of Organizational Structure of the Selfmanaged Firm. *Econ. Anal. Workers' Manage.*, 1988, *22*(3), pp. 197–220.

Pasha, Hafiz A. and Ghaus, Aisha. Buoyancy of Provincial Tax Revenues in Pakistan. *Pakistan Econ. Soc. Rev.*, Winter 1988, *26*(2), pp. 127–49.

——— **and Ismail, Zafar H.** Determinants of Success of Industrial Estates in Pakistan. *Pakistan Econ. Soc. Rev.*, Summer 1988, *26*(1), pp. 1–19.

Pashigian, B. Peter. Consequences and Causes of Public Ownership of Urban Transit Facilities. **In** *Stigler, G. J., ed.*, 1988, *1976*, pp. 404–25.

———. Demand Uncertainty and Sales: A Study of Fashion and Markdown Pricing. *Amer. Econ. Rev.*, December 1988, *78*(5), pp. 936–53.

———. Environmental Regulation: Whose Self-

Interests Are Being Protected. **In** *Stigler, G. J., ed.*, 1988, *1985*, pp. 498–534.

_____. Why Have Some Farmers Opposed Futures Markets? *J. Polit. Econ.*, April 1988, *96*(2), pp. 371–82.

Pasinetti, Luigi L. Growing Subsystems, Vertically Hyper-integrated Sectors and the Labour Theory of Value. *Cambridge J. Econ.*, March 1988, *12*(1), pp. 125–34.

_____. The Notion of Vertical Integration in Economic Analysis. **In** *Steedman, I., ed., Vol. 2*, 1988, *1973*, pp. 278–306.

_____. On 'Non-substitution' in Production Models. **In** *Steedman, I., ed., Vol. 1*, 1988, *1977*, pp. 313–18.

_____. Paradoxes in Capital Theory: A Symposium: Changes in the Rate of Profit and Switches of Techniques. **In** *Steedman, I., ed., Vol. 1*, 1988, *1966*, pp. 274–88.

_____. Rate of Profit and Income Distribution in Relation to the Rate of Economic Growth. **In** *Sawyer, M. C., ed.*, 1988, *1962*, pp. 297–309.

_____. Sraffa on Income Distribution. *Cambridge J. Econ.*, March 1988, *12*(1), pp. 135–38.

_____. Switches of Technique and the "Rate of Return" in Capital Theory. **In** *Steedman, I., ed., Vol. 1*, 1988, *1969*, pp. 289–312.

_____. Technical Progress and International Trade. *Empirica*, 1988, *15*(1), pp. 139–47.

Pasour, E. C., Jr. Economic Efficiency and Public Policy. **In** *[Rothbard, M. N.]*, 1988, pp. 110–24.

Pasqualetti, M. J. and Dellinger, Mark. Hazardous Waste from Geothermal Energy: A Case Study. *J. Energy Devel.*, Spring 1988, *13*(2), pp. 275–95.

Pasquarello, Thomas E. Human Rights and U.S. Bilateral Aid Allocations to Africa. **In** *Cingranelli, D. L., ed.*, 1988, pp. 236–54.

Pasquero, Jean. Comparative Research: The Case for Middle-Range Methodologies. **In** *Preston, L. E., ed.*, 1988, pp. 181–209.

Passicot, Andres. Foreign Investment and Development: The Experience of Chile: 1974–84. **In** *Jorge, A. and Salazar-Carrillo, J., eds.*, 1988, pp. 233–44.

Passos, Adelaide B. Recognition of Foreign Enterprises as Taxable Entities: South Africa. **In** *International Fiscal Association, ed. (I)*, 1988, pp. 211–26.

Passy, Ury and Hackman, Steven T. Projectively-Convex Sets and Functions. *J. Math. Econ.*, 1988, *17*(1), pp. 55–68.

Pastena, Victor; Lilien, Steven and Mellman, Martin. Accounting Changes: Successful versus Unsuccessful Firms. *Accounting Rev.*, October 1988, *63*(4), pp. 642–56.

Pastore, Mario H. Mean–Variance Analysis of Portfolios of Dependent Investments: An Extension. *J. Econ. Bus.*, May 1988, *40*(2), pp. 147–57.

Pasurka, Carl and Grabowski, Richard. Farmer Education and Economic Efficiency: Northern

Farms in 1860. *Econ. Letters*, 1988, *28*(4), pp. 315–20.

_____ **and Grabowski, Richard.** The Relative Technical Efficiency of Northern and Southern U.S. Farms in 1860. *Southern Econ. J.*, January 1988, *54*(3), pp. 598–614.

_____ **and Grabowski, Richard.** The Technical Efficiency of Japanese Agriculture, 1878–1940. *Devel. Econ.*, June 1988, *26*(2), pp. 172–86.

Patat, Jean-Pierre. Les autorités monétaires face à l'instabilité et aux nouveaux risques du système financier. (With English summary.) *Revue Écon. Polit.*, Sept.–Oct. 1988, *98*(5), pp. 747–63.

Patel, A. S. Co-operative Dairying and Rural Development: A Case Study of AMUL. **In** *Attwood, D. W. and Baviskar, B. S., eds.*, 1988, pp. 362–77.

Patel, Nitin R.; Senchaudhuri, P. and Mehta, Cyrus R. Exact Non-parametric Significance Tests. **In** *Edwards, D. and Raun, N. E., eds.*, 1988, pp. 227–32.

Patel, Pari and Pavitt, Keith. The International Distribution and Determinants of Technological Activities. *Oxford Rev. Econ. Policy*, Winter 1988, *4*(4), pp. 35–55.

Pathy, Jaganath. The Structure of the Indian Working Class and Conventional Unionism. **In** *Southall, R., ed.*, 1988, pp. 109–35.

Patnaik, Utsa. Three Communes and a Production Brigade: The Contract Responsibility System in China. **In** *Mitra, A., ed.*, 1988, pp. 34–61.

Patrick, George F. Mallee Wheat Farmers' Demand for Crop and Rainfall Insurance. *Australian J. Agr. Econ.*, April 1988, *32*(1), pp. 37–49.

Patrick, Hugh T. Japan's Foreign Direct Investment: Facts and Theoretical Considerations: Comment. **In** *Borner, S., ed.*, 1988, pp. 294–99.

_____ **and Hamada, Koichi.** Japan and the International Monetary Regime. **In** *Inoguchi, T. and Okimoto, D. I., eds.*, 1988, pp. 108–37.

Patrick, Robert J., Jr. Comments on U.S. Tax Structures and Competitiveness. *Nat. Tax J.*, September 1988, *41*(3), pp. 343–45.

Patrizi, Vincenzo and Rossi, Nicola. Gli effetti redistributivi del progetto europeo di armonizzazione delle imposte indirette. (With English summary.) *Polit. Econ.*, December 1988, *4*(3), pp. 409–32.

Pattanaik, Prasanta K. On the Consistency of Libertarian Values. *Economica*, November 1988, *55*(220), pp. 517–24.

_____ **and Gaertner, Wulf.** An Interview with Amartya Sen. *Soc. Choice Welfare*, 1988, *5*(1), pp. 69–79.

Patten, Louise H.; Hardaker, J. Brian and Pannell, David J. Utility-Efficient Programming for Whole-Farm Planning. *Australian J. Agr. Econ.*, Aug.–Dec. 1988, *32*(2–3), pp. 88–97.

Patterson, Douglas; Brockett, Patrick L. and Hinich, Melvin J. Bispectral-Based Tests for the Detection of Gaussianity and Linearity in

Time Series. *J. Amer. Statist. Assoc.*, September 1988, *83*(403), pp. 657–64.

Patterson, K. D. and Stephenson, M. J. Stock–Flow Consistent Accounting: A Macroeconomic Perspective. *Econ. J.*, September 1988, *98*(392), pp. 787–800.

Patterson, Paul M.; Abbott, Philip C. and Paarlberg, Philip L. Supplier Substitutability by Importers: Implications for Assessing the 1980 U.S. Grain Embargo. *Southern J. Agr. Econ.*, December 1988, *20*(2), pp. 1–14.

Patterson, Perry L. The Soviet Union Today: Foreign Trade. In *Cracraft, J., ed.*, 1988, pp. 210–19.

Patterson, William P. Managing the Maverick—Or . . . How to Get a "Wild Duck" to Fly in Formation. In *Timpe, A. D., ed.*, 1988, *1987*, pp. 136–42.

Patton, James M.; Green, Sharon L. and Lewis, Barry L. The Effects of Information Choice and Information Use on Analysts' Predictions of Municipal Bond Rating Changes. *Accounting Rev.*, April 1988, *63*(2), pp. 270–82.

Patton, Judd W. Austrian Theory of the Business Cycle. In *Association of Private Education*, 1988, pp. 47–53.

Patton, W. E., III; Puto, Christopher P. and King, Ronald H. Individual and Joint Decision-Making in Industrial Purchasing. In *Woodside, A. G., ed.*, 1988, pp. 95–117.

Pätzold, Jürgen. Stabilisierungspolitik im Konflikt zwischen sozialpolitischer Verantwortung und Sicherung der dynamischen Effizienz. (Stabilization Policy: The Conflict between Social Responsibility and Dynamic Efficiency. With English summary.) *Jahr. Nationalökon. Statist.*, September 1988, *205*(3), pp. 229–44.

Pauker, Stephen G. and Gottlieb, Jonathan E. Whether or Not to Administer Amphotericin to an Immunosuppressed Patient with Hematologic Malignancy and Undiagnosed Fever. In *Bell, D. E.; Raiffa, H. and Tversky, A., eds.*, 1988, *1981*, pp. 569–87.

_____; **Pauker, Susan P. and McNeil, Barbara J.** The Effects of Private Attitudes on Public Policy: Prenatal Screening for Neural Tube Defects as a Prototype. In *Bell, D. E.; Raiffa, H. and Tversky, A., eds.*, 1988, *1981*, pp. 588–98.

_____; **Tversky, Amos and McNeil, Barbara J.** On the Framing of Medical Decisions. In *Bell, D. E.; Raiffa, H. and Tversky, A., eds.*, 1988, pp. 562–68.

Pauker, Susan P.; McNeil, Barbara J. and Pauker, Stephen G. The Effects of Private Attitudes on Public Policy: Prenatal Screening for Neural Tube Defects as a Prototype. In *Bell, D. E.; Raiffa, H. and Tversky, A., eds.*, *1981*, 1988, pp. 588–98.

Paukert, Felix. Price Policies as a Form of Incomes Policy in Developing Countries: 2. Instruments and Effects. *Int. Lab. Rev.*, 1988, *127*(3), pp. 293–316.

_____. Price Policies as a Form of Incomes Policy in Developing Countries: 1. Objectives and In-

struments. *Int. Lab. Rev.*, 1988, *127*(2), pp. 135–51.

Paul, Ellen Frankel. Comparable Worth: Theoretical Foundations. In *[Rothbard, M. N.]*, 1988, pp. 125–38.

_____. W. Stanley Jevons: Economic Revolutionary, Political Utilitarian. In *Wood, J. C., ed.*, Vol. 1, 1988, *1979*, pp. 311–28.

Paul, Jeffrey. Historical Entitlement and the Right to Natural Resources. In *[Rothbard, M. N.]*, 1988, pp. 247–65.

Paul, Karen and Duffy, Sharyn. Corporate Responses to the Call for South African Withdrawal. In *Preston, L. E., ed.*, 1988, pp. 211–40.

Paul, Patrick B. Tax Treatment of Computer Software: Hong Kong. In *International Fiscal Association, ed. (II)*, 1988, pp. 378–87.

Paul, Robert D. Why Is the Government in the Pension Business? Comment. In *Wachter, S. M., ed.*, 1988, pp. 40–43.

Paul, Ron. The Political Importance of Murray N. Rothbard. In *[Rothbard, M. N.]*, 1988, pp. 329–32.

Paul, Samuel. Governments and Grassroots Organizations: From Co-existence to Collaboration. In *Lewis, J. P., et al.*, 1988, pp. 61–71.

Paul, Satya. Household Composition and the Measurement of Disparity in Levels of Living. *Indian Econ. Rev.*, Jan.–June 1988, *23*(1), pp. 83–106.

Paulani, Leda Maria; Messenberg, Roberto P. and Bier, Amaury G. A crise do saneamento no Brasil: Reforma tributária, uma falsa resposta. (With English summary.) *Pesquisa Planejamento Econ.*, April 1988, *18*(1), pp. 161–96.

Pauli, Gunter A. and Wright, Richard W. International Trade in Financial Services: The Japanese Challenge. In *Guile, B. R. and Quinn, J. B., eds. (II)*, 1988, pp. 187–210.

Paulino, Leonardo A. Trends in Cereal Supply, Demand, Trade, and Stocks. In *Mellor, J. W. and Ahmed, R., eds.*, 1988, pp. 13–26.

Paulsen, Knud B.; Schneider, Friedrich and Jeppesen, Svend Erik. Telecommunications in Denmark. In *Foreman-Peck, J. and Müller, J., eds.,*, 1988, pp. 109–29.

Paulsen, Michael B. and Pogue, Thomas F. Higher Education Enrollment: The Interaction of Labor Market Conditions, Curriculum, and Selectivity. *Econ. Educ. Rev.*, 1988, *7*(3), pp. 275–90.

Paulson, Steve and Albin, Tom. Environmental and Economic Interests in Canada and the United States. In *Schmandt, J.; Clarkson, J. and Roderick, H., eds.*, 1988, pp. 107–36.

_____; **Britton, Barbara and Albin, Tom.** The U.S. Policy Response to Acid Rain. In *Schmandt, J.; Clarkson, J. and Roderick, H., eds.*, 1988, pp. 159–84.

Paulus, John D. After the Dollar Crash: The World Turned Upside Down. *Challenge*, Jan.–Feb. 1988, *31*(1), pp. 4–10.

_____ **and Waite, Stephen R.** The 1980s Merger Wave: An Industrial Organization Perspective:

Discussion. In *Browne, L. E. and Rosengren, E. S.*, eds., 1988, pp. 38–51.

Pauly, Mark V. Competition in Health Insurance Markets. *Law Contemp. Probl.*, Spring 1988, *51*(2), pp. 237–71.

_____. Hospital Finance and the Behavior of American For-Profit and Not-for-Profit Hospitals. In *Furubotn, E. G. and Richter, R.*, eds., 1988, pp. 1–43.

_____. Insurance, Information, Quality, and Medical Markets. In *Smith, C. S.*, ed., 1988, pp. 45–55.

_____. Is Medical Care Different? Old Questions, New Answers. In *Greenberg, W.*, ed., 1988, pp. 5–15.

_____. Market Power, Monopsony, and Health Insurance Markets. *J. Health Econ.*, June 1988, *7*(2), pp. 111–28.

_____. Market Share and the Illusion of Power: Can Blue Cross Force Hospitals to Discount? Reply. *J. Health Econ.*, March 1988, *7*(1), pp. 85–87.

_____. Medicare and the Health Care Costs of Retirees: Problems in Choosing the Future. In *Wachter, S. M.*, ed., 1988, pp. 149–73.

_____. More Market in the West German Health Care System: Comments from a U.S. Perspective. *J. Inst. Theoretical Econ.*, April 1988, *144*(2), pp. 407–11.

_____. A Primer on Competition in Medical Markets. In *Frech, H. E., III*, ed., 1988, pp. 27–71.

Pauly, Peter. Unemployment Prospects for the OECD Area: Alternative Scenarios with the Project LINK System. In *Hopkins, M. J. D.*, ed., 1988, pp. 157–83.

_____ **and Diebold, Francis X.** Endogenous Risk in a Portfolio-Balance Rational-Expectations Model of the Deutschemark–Dollar Rate. *Europ. Econ. Rev.*, January 1988, *32*(1), pp. 27–53.

_____ **and Diebold, Francis X.** Has the EMS Reduced Member-Country Exchange Rate Volatility? *Empirical Econ.*, 1988, *13*(2), pp. 81–102.

Paus, Eva. A Critical Look at Nontraditional Export Demand: The Caribbean Basin Initiative. In *Paus, E.*, ed., 1988, pp. 193–213.

_____. Economic Development in Central America and the Caribbean: The Role of Nontraditional Exports. In *Paus, E.*, ed., 1988, pp. 1–17.

Pauwels, Wilfried. Measuring Welfare Changes in Quantity Constrained Regimes. In *Bös, D.; Rose, M. and Seidl, C.*, eds.,, 1988, pp. 49–70.

Pavelka, František. Changeover to a Single-Element Exchange Rate. *Czech. Econ. Digest.*, February 1988, (1), pp. 37–46.

Pavitt, Keith. International Patterns of Technological Accumulation. In *Hood, N. and Vahlne, J.-E.*, eds., 1988, pp. 126–57.

_____ **and Patel, Pari.** The International Distribution and Determinants of Technological Activities. *Oxford Rev. Econ. Policy*, Winter 1988, *4*(4), pp. 35–55.

Pavlov, Valentin S. An Important Component of

Restructuring. *Prob. Econ.*, March 1988, *30*(11), pp. 78–98.

Pavlov, Vladimir K.; Astakhov, Alexander S. and Denisov, Michail N. Prospecting and Exploration in the Soviet Union. In *Tilton, J. E.; Eggert, R. G. and Landsberg, H. H.*, eds., 1988, pp. 199–225.

Pavlova, N. and Rimashevskaia, N. M. The System of Pension Security. *Prob. Econ.*, May 1988, *31*(1), pp. 74–88.

Pawitra, Ted. The 10th Congress of the Indonesian Economics Association. *Bull. Indonesian Econ. Stud.*, April 1988, *24*(1), pp. 123–25.

Paxson, Christina H. and Altonji, Joseph G. Labor Supply Preferences, Hours Constraints, and Hours–Wage Trade-Offs. *J. Lab. Econ.*, April 1988, *6*(2), pp. 254–76.

Payne, Clive; Cleave, Nancy and Brown, Philip. Adding New Statistical Techniques to Standard Software Systems: A Review. In *Edwards, D. and Raun, N. E.*, eds., 1988, pp. 207–11.

Payne, John; Simonson, Itamar and Huber, Joel. The Relationship between Prior Brand Knowledge and Information Acquisition Order. *J. Cons. Res.*, March 1988, *14*(4), pp. 566–78.

Paz, Miguel and Tecson, David J. Argentina's Debt to the Equity Conversion Program. *J. World Trade*, October 1988, *22*(5), pp. 81–87.

Pázman, Andrej. Flat Gaussian Nonlinear Regression Models. In *Fedorov, V. and Lauter, H.*, eds., 1988, pp. 120–24.

Pazos, Felipe. Foreign Investment Revisited. In *Jorge, A. and Salazar-Carrillo, J.*, eds., 1988, pp. 17–28.

_____. Raúl Prebisch, Central Banker. *CEPAL Rev.*, April 1988, (34), pp. 179–95.

Peach, Ceri, et al. British Social Trends since 1900: Immigration and Ethnicity. In *Halsey, A. H.*, ed., 1988, pp. 561–615.

Peach, James T. Distribution and Economic Progress. In *Tool, M. R.*, ed., *Vol. 2*, 1988, *1987*, pp. 77–111.

Peach, Terry. David Ricardo: A Review of Some Interpretative Issues. In *Thweatt, W. O.*, ed., 1988, pp. 103–31.

_____. Samuel Hollander's *Classical Economics:* A Review Article. *Manchester Sch. Econ. Soc. Stud.*, June 1988, *56*(2), pp. 167–76.

Peacock, Alan T. An Economic Analysis of Economic Advice Giving. *Atlantic Econ. J.*, September 1988, *16*(3), pp. 1–10.

Peake, Linda and Bondi, Liz. Gender and the City: Urban Politics Revisited. In *Little, J.; Peake, L. and Richardson, P.*, eds., 1988, pp. 21–40.

_____; **Richardson, Pat and Little, Jo.** Geography and Gender in the Urban Environment: Introduction. In *Little, J.; Peake, L. and Richardson, P.*, eds., 1988, pp. 1–20.

Pearce, A. J. and Hamilton, L. S. Soil and Water Impacts of Deforestation. In *Ives, J. and Pitt, D. C.*, eds., 1988, pp. 75–98.

Pearce, David. Optimal Prices for Sustainable Development. In *[Lecomber, R.]*, 1988, pp. 57–66.

_____. The Sustainable Use of Natural Resources

in Developing Countries. In *Turner, R. K., ed.*, 1988, pp. 102–17.

Pearce, Douglas K. and Roley, V. Vance. Firm Characteristics, Unanticipated Inflation, and Stock Returns. *J. Finance*, September 1988, 43(4), pp. 965–81.

Pearce, Robert D. and Casson, Mark. Intra-firm Trade and the Developing Countries. In *Greenaway, D., ed.*, 1988, pp. 132–56.

Pearl, Maury Y. and Jacoby, Sanford M. Labor Market Contracting and Wage Dispersion. *J. Lab. Res.*, Winter 1988, 9(1), pp. 65–77.

Pearse, Peter H. Property Rights and the Development of Natural Resource Policies in Canada. *Can. Public Policy*, September 1988, 14(3), pp. 307–20.

Pearson, Charles S. and Moran, Theodore H. Tread Carefully in the Field of TRIP Measures. *World Econ.*, March 1988, 11(1), pp. 119–34.

Pearson, K. R. Automating the Computation of Solutions of Large Economic Models. *Econ. Modelling*, October 1988, 5(4), pp. 385–95.

Pearson, Mark and Smith, Stephen. 1992: Issues in Indirect Taxation. *Fisc. Stud.*, November 1988, 9(4), pp. 25–35.

Peattie, Mark R. The Japanese Colonial Empire, 1895–1945. In *Duus, P., ed.*, 1988, pp. 217–70.

Peaucelle, Irina and Gouriéroux, Christian. Fonctions de production représentatives de fonctions à complémentarité stricte. (With English summary.) *L'Actual. Econ.*, June 1988, 64(2), pp. 209–30.

_____ and Petit, Pascal. Profit et formes de motivations salariales. A propos de quelques études comparatives de l'école radicale américaine. (Profit and Work Incentives. With English summary.) *Écon. Appl.*, 1988, 41(1), pp. 41–71.

Peavy, John W., III and Hempel, George H. The Penn Square Bank Failure: Effect on Commercial Bank Security Returns—A Note. *J. Banking Finance*, 1988, 12(1), pp. 141–50.

Pecchenino, Rowena A. The Loan Contract: Mechanism of Financial Control. *Econ. J.*, March 1988, 98(389), pp. 126–37.

Pechman, Joseph A. Tax Reform: Theory and Practice. In *Brown, E., ed.*, 1988, 1987, pp. 170–82.

_____. World Tax Reform: A Progress Report: Introduction. In *Pechman, J. A., ed.*, 1988, pp. 1–14.

_____; Aaron, Henry J. and Galper, Harvey. Uneasy Compromise: Problems of a Hybrid Income–Consumption Tax: Introduction. In *Aaron, H. J.; Galper, H. and Pechman, J. A., eds.*, 1988, pp. 1–13.

Peck, James. On the Existence of Sunspot Equilibria in an Overlapping Generations Model. *J. Econ. Theory*, February 1988, 44(1), pp. 19–42.

Peck, Merton J. The Large Japanese Corporation. In *Meyer, J. R. and Gustafson, J. M., eds.*, 1988, pp. 21–42.

_____; Levin, Richard C. and Goto, Akira. Picking Losers: Public Policy toward Declining In-

dustries in Japan. In *Shoven, J. B., ed.*, 1988, pp. 195–239.

Peck, Richard M. Power, Majority Voting, and Linear Income Tax Schedules. *J. Public Econ.*, June 1988, 36(1), pp. 53–67.

Peck, Stephen C.; Bosch, Deborah K. and Weyant, John P. Industrial Energy Demand: A Simple Structural Approach. *Resources & Energy*, June 1988, 10(2), pp. 111–33.

Pécsi, Kálmán. Reform and Commodity Production: Views of a Hungarian Economist. *Prob. Econ.*, December 1988, 31(8), pp. 58–79.

Peddle, Michael T. An Empirical Investigation of the Relationship between Community Characteristics and the Presence of Industrial Parks. *Reg. Sci. Persp.*, 1988, 18(2), pp. 14–28.

Pederzoli, Giorgio; Tijs, Stef H. and Curiel, Imma J. Reward Allocations in Production Systems. In *Eiselt, H. A. and Pederzoli, G., eds.*, 1988, pp. 186–99.

Pedrycz, Witold and Hirota, Kaoru. Probablistic Sets in Classification and Pattern Recognition. In *Kacprzyk, J. and Fedrizzi, M., eds.*, 1988, pp. 342–52.

Peek, Joe. Inflation and the Excess Taxation of Personal Interest Income. *New Eng. Econ. Rev.*, March–April 1988, pp. 46–52.

_____ and Rosengren, Eric S. The Stock Market and Economic Activity. *New Eng. Econ. Rev.*, May–June 1988, pp. 39–50.

Peek, Peter. How Equitable Are Rural Development Projects? *Int. Lab. Rev.*, 1988, 127(1), pp. 73–89.

Peel, David A. and Holden, Kenneth. A Comparison of Some Inflation, Growth and Unemployment Forecasts. *J. Econ. Stud.*, 1988, 15(5), pp. 45–52.

_____; Lane, J. A. and Ceuppens, P. R. Critical Bounds for MA(2) and MA(3) Processes. *Econ. Letters*, 1988, 27(2), pp. 133–40.

_____ and Pope, Peter F. Economic Surprises and the Behaviour of Asset Prices: Some Analyses and Further Empirical Results. *Econ. Letters*, 1988, 27(4), pp. 375–79.

_____ and Thomas, Dennis A. Outcome Uncertainty and the Demand for Football: An Analysis of Match Attendances in the English Football League. *Scot. J. Polit. Econ.*, August 1988, 35(3), pp. 242–49.

Peel, Michael; Minford, Patrick and Ashton, Paul. The Effects of Housing Distortions on Unemployment. *Oxford Econ. Pap.*, June 1988, 40(2), pp. 322–45.

Peeters, Stefaan; Pepermans, Guido and Goossens, Martine. Interwar Unemployment in Belgium. In *Eichengreen, B. and Hatton, T. J., eds.*, 1988, pp. 289–324.

Peguin-Feissolle, Anne; Laussel, Didier and Montet, Christian. Optimal Trade Policy under Oligopoly: A Calibrated Model of the Europe–Japan Rivalry in the EEC Car Market. *Europ. Econ. Rev.*, September 1988, 32(7), pp. 1547–65.

Peirce, Jon. Aquaculture and Changing Regional Development Strategy. In *Choudhury, M. A., ed.*, 1988, pp. 126–37.

Peirson, John. The Importance of Being Unimportant: Marshall's Third Rule of Derived Demand. *Scot. J. Polit. Econ.*, May 1988, *35*(2), pp. 105–14.

Pejovich, Svetozar. Freedom, Property Rights and Innovation in Socialism. In *Walker, M. A., ed. (I)*, 1988, pp. 323–39.

Peleg, Bezalel and d'Aspremont, Claude. Ordinal Bayesian Incentive Compatible Representations of Committees. *Soc. Choice Welfare*, November 1988, *5*(4), pp. 261–79.

_____; **Maschler, Michael and Owen, Guillermo.** Paths Leading to the Nash Set. In *[Shapley, L. S.]*, 1988, pp. 321–30.

Peles, Yoram C. On the Depreciation of Automobiles. *Int. J. Transport Econ.*, February 1988, *15*(1), pp. 43–54.

_____ **and Muller, Eitan.** The Dynamic Adjustment of Optimal Durability and Quality. *Int. J. Ind. Organ.*, December 1988, *6*(4), pp. 499–507.

Pelikan, Pavel. Can the Imperfect Innovation Systems of Capitalism be Outperformed? In *Dosi, G., et al., eds.*, 1988, pp. 370–98.

Pelkmans, Jacques. Is Protection Due to Financial Instability? A Sceptical View. In *Guerrieri, P. and Padoan, P. C., eds.*, 1988, pp. 123–54.

Pellanda, Anna. Power or Economic Law? *Rivista Int. Sci. Econ. Com.*, April–May 1988, *35*(4–5), pp. 345–58.

_____. Quando si scrive di storia delle dottrine economiche "a peso" mentre se ne vorrebbe favorire il decollo istituzionale. (Writing on History of Economic Doctrines "by Weight" Instead of Encouraging Its Institutional Advancement. With English summary.) *Rivista Int. Sci. Econ. Com.*, August 1988, *35*(8), pp. 769–80.

Pellechio, Anthony J. Taxation, Rental Income, and Optimal Holding Periods for Real Property. *Nat. Tax J.*, March 1988, *41*(1), pp. 97–107.

Pelosi, Guido. Taylor e la rivoluzione industriale. (With English summary.) *Stud. Econ.*, 1988, *43*(35), pp. 163–74.

Peltonen, Matti. Agrarian World Market and Finnish Farm Economy: The Agrarian Transition in Finland in Late Nineteenth and Early Twentieth Centuries. *Scand. Econ. Hist. Rev.*, 1988, *36*(1), pp. 26–45.

Peltzman, Sam. An Economic Interpretation of the History of Congressional Voting in the Twentieth Century. In *Stigler, G. J., ed.*, 1988, *1985*, pp. 116–48.

_____. An Evaluation of Consumer Protection Legislation: The 1962 Drug Amendments. In *Stigler, G. J., ed.*, 1988, *1973*, pp. 303–48.

_____. The Effects of Automobile Safety Regulation. In *Stigler, G. J., ed.*, 1988, *1975*, pp. 349–403.

_____. The Growth of Government. In *Stigler, G. J., ed.*, 1988, *1980*, pp. 3–84.

_____. Toward a More General Theory of Regulation. In *Stigler, G. J., ed.*, 1988, *1976*, pp. 234–66.

_____ **and Jarrell, Gregg A.** The Impact of Product Recalls on the Wealth of Sellers. In *Stigler, G. J., ed.*, 1988, *1985*, pp. 612–33.

Pelzman, Joseph and Schoepfle, Gregory K. The Impact of the Caribbean Basin Economic Recovery Act on Caribbean Nations' Exports and Development. *Econ. Develop. Cult. Change*, July 1988, *36*(4), pp. 753–96.

Pemberton, James. Expectations and Adjustment: An Alternative Approach with an Application to Overlapping Wage Contracts. *Economica*, August 1988, *55*(219), pp. 379–91.

_____. A 'Managerial' Model of the Trade Union. *Econ. J.*, September 1988, *98*(392), pp. 755–71.

Penati, Alessandro. Expansionary Fiscal Policy and International Interdependence: Comment. In *Frenkel, J. A., ed.*, 1988, pp. 269–71.

_____ **and Protopapadakis, Aris A.** The Effect of Implicit Deposit Insurance on Banks' Portfolio Choices with an Application to International "Overexposure." *J. Monet. Econ.*, January 1988, *21*(1), pp. 107–26.

Pencak, William. Alexander Hamilton's Economic Program as a Possible Model for Third World Development. In *Pennsylvania Economic Association*, 1988, pp. 247–59.

_____. First Glimpses of the Invisible Hand: Seventeenth Century Arguments for Capitalism? Comment. In *Pennsylvania Economic Association*, 1988, p. 245.

_____. The Missing Branch in the Family Tree of Economics: The Place of Gustav Schmoller: Comment. In *Pennsylvania Economic Association*, 1988, p. 246.

_____. Mortgage Lending and Manufacturing Decentralization: 1890–1900: Comment. In *Pennsylvania Economic Association*, 1988, pp. 319–20.

_____. Organizational Change in the Hudson's Bay Company, 1821–1841: Comment. In *Pennsylvania Economic Association*, 1988, p. 309.

Pencavel, John and Holmlund, Bertil. The Determination of Wages, Employment, and Work Hours in an Economy with Centralised Wage-Setting: Sweden, 1950–83. *Econ. J.*, December 1988, *98*(393), pp. 1105–26.

Pendlebury, Maurice and Jones, Rowan H. Governmental Accounting, Auditing and Financial Reporting in the United Kingdom. In *Chan, J. L. and Jones, R. H., eds.*, 1988, pp. 52–81.

Penm, Jammie H. An Econometric Study of the Demand for Bottled, Canned and Bulk Beer. *Econ. Rec.*, December 1988, *64*(187), pp. 268–74.

Penn, R.; Davies, Richard B. and Martin, A. M. Linear Modelling with Clustered Observations: An Illustrative Example of Earnings in the Engineering Industry. *Environ. Planning A*, August 1988, *20*(8), pp. 1069–84.

Pennacchi, George G. Loan Sales and the Cost of Bank Capital. *J. Finance*, June 1988, *43*(2), pp. 375–96.

Penner, Rudolph G. The Consequences of Persistent Large Budget Deficits. In *Cavanna, H.,* ed., 1988, pp. 41–75.

———. The Economics and the Morality of the Budget Deficit. *Bus. Econ.,* October 1988, *23*(4), pp. 6–12.

———. On the Budget Process. *Contemp. Policy Issues,* October 1988, *6*(4), pp. 32–36.

Penney, M. O. Tax Treatment of Computer Software: United Kingdom. In *International Fiscal Association,* ed. *(II),* 1988, pp. 493–507.

Pennington, Robert L. International Trade/Commercial Policy Myths and Reality: High School Texts versus Teacher Perceptions. In *Association of Private Education,* 1988, pp. 54–63.

Pennisi, Giuseppe. Cost–Benefit Analysis: Credibility and Feasibility—A Comment. *Econ. Scelte Pubbliche/J. Public Finance Public Choice,* May–Aug. 1988, *6*(2), pp. 135–39.

Penny, Nicholas J. and Broom, David. The Tesco Approach to Store Location. In *Wrigley, N.,* ed., 1988, pp. 106–19.

Penouil, Marc. La Zone Franc élargit-elle la capacité d'endettement des pays membres? (Does the Franc Area Enlarge the Debt Capacity of Its Members? With English summary.) *Écon. Soc.,* June–July 1988, *22*(6–7), pp. 129–46.

Penrose, Edith. Defending the Price of Oil. *Energy J.,* January 1988, *9*(1), pp. 19–25.

Penson, John B., Jr. and Babula, Ronald A. Japanese Monetary Policies and U.S. Agricultural Exports. *J. Agr. Econ. Res.,* Winter 1988, *40*(1), pp. 11–18.

——— and **Hughes, Dean W.** Financial Conditions in the Farm Sector through 1990: An Update. In *Goldberg, R. A.,* ed., Vol. 8, 1988, pp. 1–28.

——— and **Talpaz, Hovav.** Endogenization of Final Demand and Primary Input Supply in Input–Output Analysis. *Appl. Econ.,* June 1988, *20*(6), pp. 739–52.

Penugonda, Shrinivas. The Debt Crisis of Third World Countries: A Case Study of Mexico. In *Pennsylvania Economic Association,* 1988, pp. 777–99.

Pepall, Lynne. A Clustering Analysis of the Effects of Import Penetration on Product Variety. *Oxford Econ. Pap.,* December 1988, *40*(4), pp. 655–70.

Pepermans, Guido; Goossens, Martine and Peeters, Stefaan. Interwar Unemployment in Belgium. In *Eichengreen, B. and Hatton, T. J.,* eds., 1988, pp. 289–324.

Pequin-Feissolle, A. An Attempt to Provide Supplementary Information in Modelling: Bayesian Inference and Organisational Weight. *J. Stud. Econ. Econometrics,* July 1988, *12*(2), pp. 37–54.

Pera, Alberto and Nahmijas, Alberto. Capital Market Efficiency and Newly Issued Common Stocks: An Analytical Study of Italian Data (1983–1986). *Rev. Econ. Cond. Italy,* Jan.–April 1988, (1), pp. 49–74.

Peracchi, Franco. Semi-parametric and Robust Estimators in Econometrics: An Overview. *Ricerche Econ.,* July–Sept. 1988, *42*(3), pp. 489–506.

Percebois, Jacques; Bourgeois, Bernard and Criqui, Patrick. Energy Conservation versus Supply Strategies: Implications for Industrial Policy. *Energy J.,* July 1988, *9*(3), pp. 99–111.

——— and **Criqui, Patrick.** Stratégies énergétiques: Cigales et fourmis. (Energy Strategies: To Avoid or to Manage Energy Dependence?. With English summary.) *Écon. Soc.,* April 1988, *22*(4), pp. 37–57.

Pereira, Alfredo M. On the Existence and Uniqueness of Optimal Output Path for CRTS Firms in Adjustment Costs Technologies. *Economia (Portugal),* January 1988, *12*(1), pp. 97–102.

——— and **Shoven, John B.** Survey of Dynamic Computational General Equilibrium Models for Tax Policy Evaluation. *J. Policy Modeling,* Fall 1988, *10*(3), pp. 401–36.

Pereira, Dennyson Francis. Usage of Survey Instruments in Assessing Organisation Excellence: A Research Based Case Presentation. In *Kohli, U. and Gautam, V.,* eds., 1988, pp. 155–71.

Pereira, Pedro L. Valls and Mascolo, João Luiz. Testes de exogeneidade da moeda para a economia brasileira. (With English summary.) *Pesquisa Planejamento Econ.,* December 1988, *18*(3), pp. 595–613.

Perelman, Michael. High Technology, Intellectual Property, and Public Goods: The Rationality of Socialism. *Rev. Radical Polit. Econ.,* Summer–Fall 1988, *20*(2–3), pp. 277–82.

———. The q-Ratio and Replacement Investment: An Extension of Keynesian Theory. In *Hamouda, O. F. and Smithin, J. N.,* eds., Vol. 2, 1988, pp. 41–48.

Perelman, Sergio and Pestieau, Pierre. Technical Performance in Public Enterprises: A Comparative Study of Railways and Postal Services. *Europ. Econ. Rev.,* March 1988, *32*(2–3), pp. 432–41.

Perera, Nelson. Demand for Money in Sri Lanka 1960–1984. *Indian Econ. J.,* July–September 1988, *36*(1), pp. 18–32.

Peretz, Paul. Modelling the Provision of Industrial Development Incentives. In *Hula, R. C.,* ed., 1988, pp. 158–78.

Perevedentsev, Viktor I. Changes in the Structure of Employment and Entry into the Work Force. *Prob. Econ.,* October 1988, *31*(6), pp. 6–28.

——— and **Belkin, V. D.** The Food Problem and the Lessons of Akchi. *Prob. Econ.,* April 1988, *30*(12), pp. 18–42.

Pérez-Amaral, Teodosio and Todó-Rovira, Adolfo. Social Security and Private Saving: A Reconsideration of the Assumptions. *Appl. Econ.,* August 1988, *20*(8), pp. 1057–69.

Perez, Carlota. New Technologies and Development. In *Freeman, C. and Lundvall, B.-A.,* eds., 1988, pp. 85–97.

——— and **Freeman, Christopher.** Structural Crises of Adjustment, Business Cycles and Investment Behaviour. In *Dosi, G., et al.,* eds., 1988, pp. 38–66.

——— and **Soete, Luc.** Catching Up in Technology: Entry Barriers and Windows of Opportunity. In *Dosi, G., et al., eds.*, 1988, pp. 458–79.

Pérez de Ayala, J. L. Reconnaissance de la personnalité fiscale des entreprises étrangères: Espagne. (Recognition of Foreign Enterprises as Taxable Entities: Spain. With English summary.) In *International Fiscal Association, ed. (I)*, 1988, pp. 373–85.

Pérez, Juan A. Pérez. Tax Treatment of Computer Software: Uruguay. In *International Fiscal Association, ed. (II)*, 1988, pp. 549–66.

Pérez, Lisandro. Cuban Women in the U.S. Labor Force: A Comment. In *Mesa-Lago, C., ed.*, 1988, pp. 159–64.

Peristiani, Stavros C. and Dhrymes, Phoebus J. A Comparison of the Forecasting Performance of WEFA and ARIMA Time Series Methods. *Int. J. Forecasting*, 1988, *4*(1), pp. 81–101.

Perkins, Dwight Heald. Reforming China's Economic System. *J. Econ. Lit.*, June 1988, *26*(2), pp. 601–45.

Perkins, H. C. Bulldozers in the Southern Part of Heaven: Defending Place against Rapid Growth. Part 2: The Alliance Strikes Back. *Environ. Planning A*, April 1988, *20*(4), pp. 435–56.

_____. Bulldozers in the Southern Part of Heaven: Defending Place against Rapid Growth. Part 1: Local Residents' Interpretations of Rapid Urban Growth in a Free-Standing Service-Class Town. *Environ. Planning A*, March 1988, *20*(3), pp. 285–308.

Perkins, James O. N. and Van Hoa, Tran. Twenty-five per Cent Forty Years On. In *[Clark, C.]*, 1988, pp. 123–38.

Perkins, John. Convict Labour and the Australian Agricultural Company. In *Nicholas, S., ed.*, 1988, pp. 167–79.

_____. The German Beet-Sugar Industry and the Nazi Machtergreifung of 1933. In *Albert, B. and Graves, A., eds.*, 1988, pp. 26–35.

Perlis, Mark. Indexing the Tax System for Inflation: Comments. In *Aaron, H. J.; Galper, H. and Pechman, J. A., eds.*, 1988, pp. 373–76.

Perlman, Jacob. The Continuous Work-History Sample: The First 12 Years. *Soc. Sec. Bull.*, April 1988, *51*(4), pp. 13–20.

Perlman, Mark. On the Coming Senescence of American Manufacturing Competence. In *Hanusch, H., ed.*, 1988, pp. 343–83.

Perlman, Richard. Education and Training: An American Perspective. *Oxford Rev. Econ. Policy*, Autumn 1988, *4*(3), pp. 82–93.

Perlo, Victor. Deterioration of Black Economic Conditions in the 1980s. *Rev. Radical Polit. Econ.*, Summer–Fall 1988, *20*(2–3), pp. 55–60.

Perloff, Jeffrey M. and Berck, Peter. The Dynamic Annihilation of a Rational Competitive Fringe by a Low-Cost Dominant Firm. *J. Econ. Dynam. Control*, November 1988, *12*(4), pp. 659–78.

_____; Frisvold, George and Mines, Richard. The Effects of Job Site Sanitation and Living Conditions on the Health and Welfare of Agri-

cultural Workers. *Amer. J. Agr. Econ.*, November 1988, *70*(4), pp. 875–85.

_____ and Rubinfeld, Daniel L. Settlements in Private Antitrust Litigation. In *White, L. J., ed.*, 1988, pp. 149–84.

Perng, Fai-nan. The Balance of Payments Adjustment Process in Taiwan, Republic of China. In *Fieleke, N. S., ed.*, 1988, pp. 157–61.

Peroff, Kathleen and Hush, Lawrence W. The Variety of State Capital Budgets: A Survey. *Public Budg. Finance*, Summer 1988, *8*(2), pp. 67–79.

Perold, André F. The Implementation Shortfall: Paper versus Reality. *J. Portfol. Manage.*, Spring 1988, *14*(3), pp. 4–9.

Perrakis, Stylianos. Preference-Free Option Prices When the Stock Returns Can Go Up, Go Down, or Stay the Same. In *Fabozzi, F. J., ed.*, 1988, pp. 209–35.

_____ and Owen, Robert F. An International Duopoly Model under Exchange Rate Uncertainty. *Revue Écon.*, September 1988, *39*(5), pp. 1035–60.

Perrault, Jean-Louis. Régulation et déploiement historique d'une industrie: Une analyse retrospective des industries électriques et électroniques. (Regulation and Historical Spread of an Industry: An Electrical and Electronics Industries Retrospect. With English summary.) *Écon. Soc.*, Nov.–Dec. 1988, *22*(11–12), pp. 173–98.

Perrels, Adriaan and Nijkamp, Peter. Impacts of Electricity Rates on Industrial Location. *Energy Econ.*, April 1988, *10*(2), pp. 107–16.

Perri, Stefano. The Substitution of Machinery for Labour and "The Two Ricardo Effects." *Rivista Int. Sci. Econ. Com.*, June 1988, *35*(6), pp. 507–22.

Perri, Timothy J. Salary Prospects, Unemployment, and Work Effort. *J. Econ. Bus.*, February 1988, *40*(1), pp. 57–66.

Perrin, Jean-Claude. New Technologies, Local Synergies and Regional Policies in Europe. In *Aydalot, P. and Keeble, D., eds.*, 1988, pp. 139–62.

Perron, Pierre. Challenges to Canada's Mining Industry: A Personal Prospective. In *Richardson, P. R. and Gesing, R., eds.*, 1988, pp. 77–86.

_____. Trends and Random Walks in Macroeconomic Time Series: Further Evidence from a New Approach. *J. Econ. Dynam. Control*, June–Sept. 1988, *12*(2–3), pp. 297–332.

Perrot, Jean. L'influence de l'utilisation du temps sur la réussite des étudiants en France. (With English summary.) *L'Actual. Écon.*, March 1988, *64*(1), pp. 44–67.

Perroux, François. Peregrinations of an Economist and the Choice of His Route. In *[Perroux, F.]*, 1988, *1980*, pp. 77–90.

_____. The Pole of Development's New Place in a General Theory of Economic Activity. In *[Perroux, F.]*, 1988, pp. 48–76.

Perry, Christopher; Barghouti, Shawki and Frederiksen, Harald D. Irrigation: Issues, Policies and Lending Strategies. In *Roberts, C.,* *ed.*, 1988, pp. 71–78.

Perry, James L. and Angle, Harold L. Union Member Attitudes and Bargaining Unit Stability in Urban Transit. In *Lewin, D., et al., eds.,* 1988, *1984*, pp. 152–62.

Perry, Lee Tom and Sandholtz, Kurt W. A "Liberating Form" for Radical Product Innovation. In *Gattiker, U. E. and Larwood, L., eds.,* 1988, pp. 9–31.

Perry, Seymour and Chu, Flora. Selecting Medical Technologies in Developing Countries. In *Bell, D. E. and Reich, M. R., eds.,* 1988, pp. 379–99.

Perry, Stephen. Downward Occupational Mobility and Part-Time Women Workers. *Appl. Econ.,* April 1988, *20*(4), pp. 485–95.

_____. The Supply of Female Part-time Labour over the Life Cycle. *Appl. Econ.,* December 1988, *20*(12), pp. 1579–87.

Persico, Pasquale. R&D Expenditure and Localized Technological Progress: A Theoretical Approach to Explain Some Recent R&D Performances in Manufacturing Industry. *Stud. Econ.,* 1988, *43*(34), pp. 13–23.

Persky, Allan. Abatement of Pollution in Models with Stochastic Penalties. *Southern Econ. J.,* October 1988, *55*(2), pp. 463–71.

Persky, Joseph J. and Camacho, Antonio. The Internal Organization of Complex Teams: Bounded Rationality and the Logic of Hierarchies. *J. Econ. Behav. Organ.,* June 1988, *9*(4), pp. 367–80.

_____ **and White, William D.** A Rather Neoclassical Contribution to Marxian Rent Theory. *Land Econ.,* May 1988, *64*(2), pp. 196–98.

Persson, Mats; Brownstone, David and Englund, Peter. A Microsimulation Model of Swedish Housing Demand. *J. Urban Econ.,* March 1988, *23*(2), pp. 179–98.

_____**; Brownstone, David and Englund, Peter.** Tax Reform and Housing Demand: The Distribution of Welfare Gains and Losses. *Europ. Econ. Rev.,* April 1988, *32*(4), pp. 819–40.

Persson, Torsten. Credibility of Macroeconomic Policy: An Introduction and a Broad Survey. *Europ. Econ. Rev.,* March 1988, *32*(2–3), pp. 519–32.

_____ **and Gottfries, Nils.** Empirical Examinations of the Information Sets of Economic Agents. *Quart. J. Econ.,* February 1988, *103*(1), pp. 251–59.

_____ **and Horn, Henrik.** Exchange Rate Policy, Wage Formation and Credibility. *Europ. Econ. Rev.,* October 1988, *32*(8), pp. 1621–36.

_____ **and Svensson, Lars E. O.** Checks and Balances on the Government Budget. In *Helpman, E.; Razin, A. and Sadka, E., eds.,* 1988, pp. 199–214.

_____**; Svensson, Lars E. O. and Kotlikoff, Laurence J.** Social Contracts as Assets: A Possible Solution to the Time-Consistency Problem. *Amer. Econ. Rev.,* September 1988, *78*(4), pp. 662–77.

Pertl, Mars A. and Sprecher, C. Ronald. Intraindustry Effects of the MGM Grand Fire.

Quart. J. Bus. Econ., Spring 1988, *27*(2), pp. 96–116.

Pervushin, S. P. Full Cost Accounting: Organizational and Methodological Foundations. *Prob. Econ.,* January 1988, *30*(9), pp. 53–69.

Perz, S. and Rolewicz, S. On Inverse-Image of Non-oriented Graphs. In *Kurzhanski, A.; Neumann, K. and Pallaschke, D., eds.,* 1988, pp. 213–24.

Pesando, James E. and Gunderson, Morley. The Case for Allowing Mandatory Retirement. *Can. Public Policy,* March 1988, *14*(1), pp. 32–39.

_____ **and Gunderson, Morley.** Retirement Incentives Contained in Occupational Pension Plans and Their Implications for the Mandatory Retirement Debate. *Can. J. Econ.,* May 1988, *21*(2), pp. 244–64.

_____ **and Plourde, André.** The October 1979 Change in the U.S. Monetary Regime: Its Impact on the Forecastability of Canadian Interest Rates. *J. Finance,* March 1988, *43*(1), pp. 217–39.

Pesaran, Bahram; Hoque, Asraul and Magnus, Jan R. The Exact Multi-period Mean-Square Forecast Error for the First-Order Autoregressive Model. *J. Econometrics,* November 1988, *39*(3), pp. 327–46.

Pesaran, M. Hashem. On the Policy Ineffectiveness Proposition and a Keynesian Alternative: A Rejoinder. *Econ. J.,* June 1988, *98*(391), pp. 504–08.

_____. The Role of Theory in Applied Econometrics. *Econ. Rec.,* December 1988, *64*(187), pp. 336–39.

_____ **and Hall, A. D.** Tests of Non-nested Linear Regression Models Subject to Linear Restrictions. *Econ. Letters,* 1988, *27*(4), pp. 341–48.

Pesek, Boris P. Banks' Supply Function and the Equilibrium Quantity of Money. In *Pesek, B. P.,* 1988, *1970,* pp. 124–57.

_____. Equilibrium Level of Transaction Services of Money. In *Pesek, B. P.,* 1988, *1973,* pp. 108–23.

_____. In Defence of Neoclasssical Monetary Theory. In *Pesek, B. P.,* 1988, *1982,* pp. 199–207.

_____. Microeconomics of Banking. In *Pesek, B. P.,* 1988, pp. 39–60.

_____. Microeconomics of Money. In *Pesek, B. P.,* 1988, *1986,* pp. 15–38.

_____. Microeconomics of Money and Banking and Other Essays: Introduction. In *Pesek, B. P.,* 1988, pp. 1–12.

_____. Modern Bank Deposits and the Theory of Optimum Undefined Money. In *Pesek, B. P.,* 1988, *1979,* pp. 85–107.

_____. Monetary Theory in the Post-Robertson "Alice in Wonderland" Era. In *Pesek, B. P.,* 1988, *1976,* pp. 161–98.

_____. A Note on Permanent Income Theory. In *Pesek, B. P.,* 1988, *1979,* pp. 230–35.

_____. A Note on Permanent Income Theory: Reply. In *Pesek, B. P.,* 1988, *1981,* pp. 240–41.

_____. There Is Another Bank Reform in the Wings. In *Pesek, B. P.*, 1988, *1982*, pp. 262–67.

_____ and Saving, Thomas R. Monetary Policy, Taxes, and the Rate of Interest. In *Pesek, B. P.*, 1988, *1963*, pp. 208–29.

Peshekhonov, Iu. Social Justice and Public Consumption Funds. *Prob. Econ.*, May 1988, *31*(1), pp. 60–73.

Peskin, Henry M. One More Externality Article. *J. Environ. Econ. Manage.*, September 1988, *15*(3), pp. 380–81.

Pesola, Jarmo. Lagerteoretiska modeller och dekomponering av kassa. (Inventory-Theoretical Models and the Decomposition of Cash. Optimization of Cash Management. With English summary.) *Ekon. Samfundets Tidskr.*, 1988, *41*(3), pp. 167–79.

Pestano, Armando. Petroleum Product Pricing in the Philippines. *Energy J.*, Special Issue, 1988, 9, pp. 1–14.

Pestieau, Pierre and Cremer, Helmuth. A Case for Differential Inheritance Taxation. *Ann. Écon. Statist.*, Jan.–March 1988, (9), pp. 167–82.

_____ and Cremer, Helmuth. The Joint Impact of Fertility Differentials and Social Security on the Accumulation and Distribution of Wealth. In *Kessler, D. and Masson, A.*, eds., 1988, pp. 169–85.

_____ and Perelman, Sergio. Technical Performance in Public Enterprises: A Comparative Study of Railways and Postal Services. *Europ. Econ. Rev.*, March 1988, *32*(2–3), pp. 432–41.

Peston, Maurice H. Aspects of the Theory of Fiscal Policy. In *Eltis, W. and Sinclair, P. J. N.*, eds., 1988, pp. 102–23.

_____. The Tax Mix and Effective Demand. In *Shaw, G. K.*, ed., *Vol. 2*, 1988, *1971*, pp. 313–16.

Peter, Matthew and Maxwell, Philip. Income Inequality in Small Regions: A Study of Australian Statistical Divisions. *Rev. Reg. Stud.*, Winter 1988, *18*(1), pp. 19–27.

Peteri, Z. Problems of the Legislative Process in the Socialist Countries of Europe. In *Pizzorusso, A.*, ed., 1988, pp. 306–31.

Peters, Carl and Fischmar, Dan. A Stochastic Dominance Approach to Portfolio Selection. In *Pennsylvania Economic Association*, 1988, pp. 650–63.

Peters, Donald L. Receipts and Expenditures of State Governments and of Local Governments: Revised and Updated Estimates, 1984–87. *Surv. Curr. Bus.*, September 1988, *68*(9), pp. 23–25.

Peters, H. Elizabeth. Retrospective versus Panel Data in Analyzing Lifecycle Events. *J. Human Res.*, Fall 1988, *23*(4), pp. 488–513.

Peters, Lawrence H. and Sheridan, John E. Turnover Research Methodology: A Critique of Traditional Designs and a Suggested Survival Model Alternative. In *Ferris, G. R. and Rowland, K. M.*, eds., 1988, pp. 231–62.

Peters, Pauline E. The Ideology and Practice of Tswana Borehole Syndicates: Co-operative or

Corporation? In *Attwood, D. W. and Baviskar, B. S.*, eds., 1988, pp. 23–45.

Peters, Peter J. and van de Klundert, Th. Price Inertia in a Macroeconomic Model of Monopolistic Competition. *Economica*, May 1988, *55*(218), pp. 203–17.

Peters, S. C.; Freedman, D. A. and Navidi, W. On the Impact of Variable Selection in Fitting Regression Equations. In *Dijkstra, T. K.*, ed., 1988, pp. 1–16.

Peters, Wolfgang. A Pension Insurance System in an Overlapping Generations Model. *J. Inst. Theoretical Econ.*, December 1988, *144*(5), pp. 813–30.

_____ and Bös, Dieter. Privatization, Internal Control, and Internal Regulation. *J. Public Econ.*, July 1988, *36*(2), pp. 231–58.

Petersen, Bruce C.; Domowitz, Ian and Hubbard, Robert Glenn. Market Structure and Cyclical Fluctuations in U.S. Manufacturing. *Rev. Econ. Statist.*, February 1988, *70*(1), pp. 55–66.

_____; Fazzari, Steven M. and Hubbard, Robert Glenn. Financing Constraints and Corporate Investment. *Brookings Pap. Econ. Act.*, 1988, (1), pp. 141–95.

_____; Fazzari, Steven M. and Hubbard, Robert Glenn. Investment, Financing Decisions, and Tax Policy. *Amer. Econ. Rev.*, May 1988, *78*(2), pp. 200–205.

Petersen, John E. The Municipal Bond Market in a Changing Economy. *Public Budg. Finance*, Winter 1988, *8*(4), pp. 22–34.

Petersen, Jørn Henrik. Danish Economists on the Issue of Funding versus Pay-as-You-Go. *Scand. Econ. Hist. Rev.*, 1988, *36*(1), pp. 15–25.

_____. A Note on Old-Age Pensions, Demography and the Distribution between Generations. *J. Inst. Theoretical Econ.*, April 1988, *144*(2), pp. 333–42.

Petersen, William. Marxism and the Population Question: Theory and Practice. *Population Devel. Rev.*, Supplement, 1988, *14*, pp. 77–101.

Petersmann, Ernst-Ulrich. Grey Area Trade Policy and the Rule of Law. *J. World Trade*, April 1988, *22*(2), pp. 23–44.

_____. Grey Area Trade Restrictions and International Law. In *Dicke, D. C. and Petersmann, E.-U.*, eds., 1988, pp. 203–207.

_____. Proposals for Improvements in the GATT Dispute Settlement System. In *Dicke, D. C. and Petersmann, E.-U.*, eds., 1988, pp. 340–93.

_____. Strengthening GATT Procedures for Settling Trade Disputes. *World Econ.*, March 1988, *11*(1), pp. 55–89.

Peterson, David R.; Fehrs, Donald H. and Benesh, Gary A. Evidence of a Relation between Stock Price Reactions around Cash Dividend Changes and Yields. *J. Finan. Res.*, Summer 1988, *11*(2), pp. 111–23.

_____ and Klein, Linda S. Investor Expectations of Volatility Increases around Large Stock

Splits as·Implied in Call Option Premia. *J. Finan. Res.*, Spring 1988, *11*(1), pp. 71–80.

_____; **Scott, Elton and Tucker, Alan L.** Tests of the Black–Scholes and Constant Elasticity of Variance Currency Call Option Valuation Models. *J. Finan. Res.*, Fall 1988, *11*(3), pp. 201–13.

_____ **and Tucker, Alan L.** Implied Spot Rates as Predictors of Currency Returns: A Note [Option Prices as Predictors of Equilibrium Stock Prices]. *J. Finance*, March 1988, *43*(1), pp. 247–58.

_____ **and Wall, Larry D.** Capital Changes at Large Affiliated Banks. *J. Finan. Services Res.*, June 1988, *1*(3), pp. 253–75.

Peterson, Dyanne and Kephart, Robert. Himself, at Sixty with Apologies to Ogden Nash. In *[Rothbard, M. N.]*, 1988, pp. 392–94.

Peterson, E. Wesley F.; Paggi, Mechel and Henry, Guy. Quality Restrictions as Barriers to Trade: The Case of European Community Regulations on the Use of Hormones. *Western J. Agr. Econ.*, July 1988, *13*(1), pp. 82–91.

_____; **Viscencio-Brambila, Hector and Fuller, Stephen W.** A Welfare Analysis of Port User Fees: The Case of Grain and Soybean Exports. *Southern J. Agr. Econ.*, December 1988, *20*(2), pp. 101–08.

Peterson, George E. and Howland, Marie. Labor Market Conditions and the Reemployment of Displaced Workers. *Ind. Lab. Relat. Rev.*, October 1988, *42*(1), pp. 109–22.

_____ **and Howland, Marie.** The Response of City Economies to National Business Cycles. *J. Urban Econ.*, January 1988, *23*(1), pp. 71–85.

Peterson, J. E. The Future of Federalism in the United Arab Emirates. In *Sindelar, H. R., III and Peterson, J. E.*, eds., 1988, pp. 198–230.

_____ **and Sindelar, H. Richard, III.** Crosscurrents in the Gulf: Preface. In *Sindelar, H. R., III and Peterson, J. E.*, eds., 1988, pp. xiii–xviii.

Peterson, John. Export Shares and Revealed Comparative Advantage. A Study of International Travel. *Appl. Econ.*, March 1988, *20*(3), pp. 351–65.

Peterson, Milo O. Gross Product by Industry, 1987. *Surv. Curr. Bus.*, April 1988, *68*(4), pp. 25.

Peterson, Pamela P. Reincorporation: Motives and Shareholder Wealth. *Financial Rev.*, May 1988, *23*(2), pp. 151–60.

Peterson, Peter G. Deficit, Debt, and Demographics: Some International Aspects. In *Feldstein, M., ed. (II)*, 1988, pp. 633–44.

Peterson, Richard B. and Napier, Nancy K. Putting Human Resource Management at the Line Manager Level. In *Timpe, A. D., ed.*, 1988, *1984*, pp. 87–102.

Peterson, Richard L.; Koch, Timothy W. and MacDonald, S. Scott. Using Futures to Improve Treasury Bill Portfolio Performance. *J. Futures Markets*, April 1988, *8*(2), pp. 167–84.

Peterson, Rodney. Industrial Power: Meaning and Measurement. In *Peterson, W. C., ed.*, 1988, pp. 1–25.

Peterson, Wallace C. Economic Policy Imperatives of the American Bishops' *Pastoral Letter*. *J. Econ. Issues*, December 1988, *22*(4), pp. 1023–33.

_____. The Macroeconomic Legacy of Reaganomics. *J. Econ. Issues*, March 1988, *22*(1), pp. 1–16.

_____. Macroeconomic Theory and Policy in an Institutionalist Perspective. In *Tool, M. R., ed.*, Vol. 2, 1988, *1987*, pp. 169–203.

_____. Market Power and the Economy: Concluding Observations. In *Peterson, W. C., ed.*, 1988, pp. 157–69.

Pethe, Abhay. Robust Policy Analysis: A Tentative Approach. *Indian J. Quant. Econ.*, 1988, *4*(1), pp. 49–60.

Pethig, Rüdiger. Copyrights and Copying Costs: A New Price-Theoretic Approach. *J. Inst. Theoretical Econ.*, June 1988, *144*(3), pp. 462–95.

Petit, Maria Luisa and Gandolfo, Giancarlo. The Optimal Degree of Wage-Indexation in the Italian Economy: Rerunning History by Dynamic Optimization. In *[Goodwin, R. M.]*, 1988, pp. 120–26.

_____ **and Hughes Hallett, Andrew J.** Trade-off Reversals in Macroeconomic Policy. *J. Econ. Dynam. Control*, March 1988, *12*(1), pp. 85–91.

Petit, Pascal. Problems of the State in Dealing with the System of Wage/Labour Relations: The Case of France. In *Boyer, R., ed.*, 1988, pp. 26–57.

_____ **and Peaucelle, Irina.** Profit et formes de motivations salariales. A propos de quelques études comparatives de l'école radicale américaine. (Profit and Work Incentives. With English summary.) *Écon. Appl.*, 1988, *41*(1), pp. 41–71.

Petith, Howard C. Purposely Induced Asymmetric Information. *Bull. Econ. Res.*, October 1988, *40*(4), pp. 301–08.

Petr, Jerry L. Economic Power and the Political Process. In *Peterson, W. C., ed.*, 1988, pp. 127–55.

_____. The Nature and Necessity of the Mixed Economy. In *Tool, M. R., ed.*, Vol. 2, 1988, *1987*, pp. 27–50.

Petree, Daniel L. and Kleiner, Morris M. Unionism and Licensing of Public School Teachers: Impact on Wages and Educational Output. In *Freeman, R. B. and Ichniowski, C., eds.*, 1988, pp. 305–19.

Petrella, Frank. Henry George and the Classical Scientific Research Program: The Economics of Republican Millenialism. *Amer. J. Econ. Soc.*, April 1988, *47*(2), pp. 239–56.

_____. Henry George and the Classical Scientific Research Program: George's Modification of It and His Real Significance for Future Generations. *Amer. J. Econ. Soc.*, July 1988, *47*(3), pp. 371–84.

Petri, Peter A. Korea's Export Niche: Origins and Prospects. *World Devel.*, January 1988, *16*(1), pp. 47–63.

_____. United States–Japan Economic Relations: Comment. In *Baldwin, R. E., ed. (II)*, 1988, pp. 334–37.

_____ and Filer, Randall K. A Job-Characteristics Theory of Retirement. *Rev. Econ. Statist.*, February 1988, *70*(1), pp. 123–29.

Petrikov, A. V. and Kiselev, S. V. The Innovative Potential of Managers of Agro-Industrial Enterprises. *Prob. Econ.*, June 1988, *31*(2), pp. 44–59.

Petrochilos, George A. Foreign Direct Investment and Concentration in Greek Manufacturing. *Brit. Rev. Econ. Issues*, Spring 1988, *10*(22), pp. 23–53.

Petrović, Pavle. Price Distortion and Income Dispersion in a Labor-Managed Economy: Evidence from Yugoslavia. *J. Compar. Econ.*, December 1988, *12*(4), pp. 592–603.

Petry, Francois. The Policy Impact of Canadian Party Programs: Public Expenditure Growth and Contagion from the Left. *Can. Public Policy*, December 1988, *14*(4), pp. 376–89.

Petry, Glenn H. A Statistical Analysis of Worldwide Coauthorship Relationships in Scholarly Journals of Business. *J. Econ. Bus.*, May 1988, *40*(2), pp. 169–76.

_____; Fitzpatrick, Dennis B. and Settle, John W. An Empirical Examination of Rate of Return Regulation in the Electric Utility Industry: 1971–1982. *J. Econ. Bus.*, February 1988, *40*(1), pp. 27–44.

_____ and Settle, John W. A Comprehensive Analysis of Worldwide Scholarly Productivity in Selected U.S. Business Journals. *Quart. Rev. Econ. Bus.*, Autumn 1988, *28*(3), pp. 88–104.

Pettengill, Glenn N. and Jordan, Bradford D. A Comprehensive Examination of Volume Effects and Seasonality in Daily Security Returns. *J. Finan. Res.*, Spring 1988, *11*(1), pp. 57–70.

Pettway, Richard H.; Tapley, T. Craig and Yamada, Takeshi. The Impacts of Financial Deregulation upon Trading Efficiency and the Levels of Risk and Return of Japanese Banks. *Financial Rev.*, August 1988, *23*(3), pp. 243–68.

Petty, John R. National Interests and Global Obligations: A Call for Meaningful Dialogue. In *Feldstein, M., ed. (I)*, 1988, pp. 151–56.

_____. On U.S. Development Assistance. In *Aho, C. M. and Levinson, M.*, 1988, pp. 223–26.

Pevzner, Iakov A. Radical Economic Reform and Problems of Political Economy. *Prob. Econ.*, January 1988, *30*(9), pp. 19–33.

Pew, Ong Nai and Fong, Pang Eng. Labour Absorption in Hong Kong and Singapore since 1970. *Philippine Rev. Econ. Bus.*, March–June 1988, *25*(1–2), pp. 71–99.

Peyrache, Veronique and Loinger, Guy. Technological Clusters and Regional Economic Restructuring. In *Aydalot, P. and Keeble, D., eds.*, 1988, pp. 121–38.

Pezzey, John. Market Mechanisms of Pollution Control: 'Polluter Pays', Economic and Practical Aspects. In *Turner, R. K., ed.*, 1988, pp. 190–242.

Pfähler, Wilhelm. Distributional Equity and Measurement of Tax Progressivity. In *Eichhorn, W., ed.*, 1988, pp. 533–48.

_____. On Measuring the Welfare Cost of Public Expenditure: A Simple General Equilibrium Approach. In *Bös, D.; Rose, M. and Seidl, C., eds.*, 1988, pp. 317–37.

_____ and Lambert, Peter J. On Aggregate Measures of the Net Redistributive Impact of Taxation and Government Expenditure. *Public Finance Quart.*, April 1988, *16*(2), pp. 178–202.

Pfeffer, Jeffrey and Baron, James N. Taking the Workers Back Out: Recent Trends in the Structuring of Employment. In *Staw, B. M. and Cummings, L. L., eds.*, 1988, pp. 257–303.

Pfeffermann, Guy and Weigel, Dale R. The Private Sector and the Policy Environment. *Finance Develop.*, December 1988, *25*(4), pp. 25–27.

Pfingsten, Andreas. Measures of Tax Progression—An Axiomatic Approach. In *Eichhorn, W., ed.*, 1988, pp. 549–62.

_____. Progressive Taxation and Redistributive Taxation: Different Labels for the Same Product? In *Gaertner, W. and Pattanaik, P. K., eds.*, 1988, *1988*, pp. 147–58.

_____. Progressive Taxation and Redistributive Taxation: Different Labels for the Same Product? *Soc. Choice Welfare*, 1988, *5*(2/3), pp. 235–46.

Pflaumer, Peter. Confidence Intervals for Population Projections Based on Monte Carlo Methods. *Int. J. Forecasting*, 1988, *4*(1), pp. 135–42.

Pfleiderer, Paul and Admati, Anat R. Selling and Trading on Information in Financial Markets. *Amer. Econ. Rev.*, May 1988, *78*(2), pp. 96–103.

Pfouts, Ralph W. The Gorbachev Economic Proposals and the U.S. Economy. *Atlantic Econ. J.*, March 1988, *16*(1), pp. 1–6.

_____ and Rosefielde, Steven. Economic Optimization and Technical Efficiency in Soviet Enterprises Jointly Regulated by Plans and Incentives. *Europ. Econ. Rev.*, July 1988, *32*(6), pp. 1285–99.

Pham, Dang. France and the Seventh Directive. In *Gray, S. J. and Coenenberg, A. G., eds.*, 1988, pp. 76–94.

Phan, Duc-Loi. The CAP and Comparative Advantage Changes: The Case of Processed Food and Agricultural Products. *Empirica*, 1988, *15*(1), pp. 149–60.

Phaneuf, Louis. Hystérésis du chômage: faits, théories et politiques. (With English summary.) *L'Actual. Econ.*, December 1988, *64*(4), pp. 509–31.

_____ and Ambler, Steve. Interest Rate Innovations and the Business Cycle. *Econ. Letters*, 1988, *26*(4), pp. 305–09.

Phelps, Charles E. Alcohol Taxes and Highway Safety. In *Graham, J. D., ed.*, 1988, pp. 197–219.

_____. Death and Taxes: An Opportunity for

Substitution. *J. Health Econ.*, March 1988, 7(1), pp. 1–24.

Phelps, Charlotte DeMonte. Caring and Family Income. *J. Econ. Behav. Organ.*, July 1988, 10(1), pp. 83–98.

————. Explaining Choice of Hypothetical Marriage Partner by a Motive Measure of Preferences: Evidence on May's Theory of Aggregation of Preference Patterns. *J. Behav. Econ.*, Spring 1988, 17(1), pp. 57–76.

————. Is Altruism the Dominant Motivation in the Family? In *Maital, S., ed.*, Vol. 1, 1988, pp. 189–98.

Phelps, Edmund S. Recent Developments in Macroeconomics: A Very Quick Refresher Course: Comment. *J. Money, Credit, Banking,* Part 2, August 1988, 20(3), pp. 456–58.

————. A Working Model of Slump and Recovery from Disturbances to Capital-Goods Demand in an Open Nonmonetary Economy. *Amer. Econ. Rev.*, May 1988, 78(2), pp. 346–50.

———— and Velupillai, Kumaraswamy. Optimum Fiscal Policy When Monetary Policy Is Bound by a Rule: Ramsey Redux. In *Arrow, K. J. and Boskin, M. J., eds.*, 1988, pp. 116–30.

Phelps, John J.; Sheets, Robert G. and Nord, Stephen. An Analysis of the Economic Impact of the Service Sector on Underemployment in Major Metropolitan Areas in the United States. *Urban Stud.*, October 1988, 25(5), pp. 418–32.

Phelps, Michael. Price and Output Effects of Monetary and Fiscal Policy under Flexible Exchange Rates. *Int. Monet. Fund Staff Pap.*, March 1988, 35(1), pp. 209–12.

———— and Bennett, John S. The Supply Multiplier with a Self-Employed Private Sector. *Econ. Planning*, 1988, 22(3), pp. 101–08.

Philippas, N. and Karathanassis, G. Estimation of Bank Stock Price Parameters and the Variance Components Model. *Appl. Econ.*, April 1988, 20(4), pp. 497–507.

Philippatos, George C.; Choi, Dosoung and Defusco, Richard A. Risk, Return and International Investment by U.S. Corporations. *Appl. Econ.*, September 1988, 20(9), pp. 1199–1209.

———— and Deshpande, Shreesh D. Leverage Decisions and the Effect of Corporate Eurobond Offerings. *Appl. Econ.*, July 1988, 20(7), pp. 901–15.

Philips, Peter and Kiefer, David M. Doubts Regarding the Human Capital Theory of Racial Inequality. *Ind. Relat.*, Spring 1988, 27(2), pp. 251–62.

———— and Kiefer, David M. Race and Human Capital: An Institutionalist Response. In *Mangum, G. and Philips, P., eds.*, 1988, pp. 117–43.

———— and Mangum, Garth. Three Worlds of Labor Economics: Introduction. In *Mangum, G. and Philips, P., eds.*, 1988, pp. 3–18.

———— and Segal, William. Production Process, Work Organization, and Labor Relations in the Postwar California Food Processing Industry. *Rev. Radical Polit. Econ.*, Summer–Fall 1988, 20(2–3), pp. 208–13.

Phillips, A. W. Stabilisation Policy and the Time-Forms of Lagged Responses. In *Shaw, G. K., ed.*, Vol. 2, 1988, 1957, pp. 300–312.

Phillips, G. Michael; Clark, Truman A. and Joines, Douglas H. Social Security Payments, Money Supply Announcements, and Interest Rates. *J. Monet. Econ.*, September 1988, 22(2), pp. 257–78.

Phillips, Garry D. A. Erratum [Recursions for the Two Stage Least Squares Estimators]. *J. Econometrics*, March 1988, 37(3), pp. 395.

————. Testing for Serial Correlation after Three Stage Least Squares Estimation. *Bull. Econ. Res.*, April 1988, 40(2), pp. 145–51.

Phillips, Keith R. New Tools for Analyzing the Texas Economy: Indexes of Coincident and Leading Economic Indicators. *Fed. Res. Bank Dallas Econ. Rev.*, July 1988, pp. 1–13.

Phillips, Llad. The Economics of Race and Crime: Comments. In *Simms, M. C. and Myers, S. L., Jr., eds.*, 1988, pp. 219–21.

———— and Votey, Harold L., Jr. Rational Choice Models of Crimes by Youth. In *Simms, M. C. and Myers, S. L., Jr., eds.*, 1988, pp. 129–87.

Phillips, Owen R. and Greenhut, M. L. A Path to Efficiently Regulated Transport Rates. *Int. J. Transport Econ.*, October 1988, 15(3), pp. 243–55.

———— and Ormiston, Michael B. Nonlinear Price Schedules and Tied Products. *Economica*, May 1988, 55(218), pp. 219–33.

———— and Schutte, David P. Identifying Profitable Self-service Markets: A Test in Gasoline Retailing. *Appl. Econ.*, February 1988, 20(2), pp. 263–72.

Phillips-Patrick, Frederick J. and Schneeweis, Thomas. The "Weekend Effect" for Stock Indexes and Stock Index Futures: Dividend and Interest Rate Effects. *J. Futures Markets*, February 1988, 8(1), pp. 115–21.

Phillips, Peter C. B. Conditional and Unconditional Statistical Independence. *J. Econometrics*, July 1988, 38(3), pp. 341–48.

————. Reflections on Econometric Methodology. *Econ. Rec.*, December 1988, 64(187), pp. 344–59.

————. Regression Theory for Near-Integrated Time Series. *Econometrica*, September 1988, 56(5), pp. 1021–43.

———— and Durlauf, Steven N. Trends versus Random Walks in Time Series Analysis. *Econometrica*, November 1988, 56(6), pp. 1333–54.

———— and Ouliaris, Sam. Testing for Cointegration Using Principal Components Methods. *J. Econ. Dynam. Control*, June–Sept. 1988, 12(2–3), pp. 205–30.

———— and Park, Joon Y. Asymptotic Equivalence of Ordinary Least Squares and Generalized Least Squares in Regressions with Integrated Regressors. *J. Amer. Statist. Assoc.*, March 1988, 83(401), pp. 111–15.

———— and Park, Joon Y. On the Formulation of Wald Tests of Nonlinear Restrictions. *Econometrica*, September 1988, 56(5), pp. 1065–83.

Phillips, Robyn S. Residential Capitalization

Rates: Explaining Intermetropolitan Variation, 1974–1979. *J. Urban Econ.*, May 1988, *23*(3), pp. 278–90.

———. Unravelling the Residential Rent-Value Puzzle: An Empirical Investigation. *Urban Stud.*, December 1988, *25*(6), pp. 487–96.

Phillips, Ronnie J. Veblen and Simons on Credit and Monetary Reform. *Southern Econ. J.*, July 1988, *55*(1), pp. 171–81.

———. 'War News' and Black Market Exchange Rate Deviations from Purchasing Power Parity: Wartime South Vietnam. *J. Int. Econ.*, November 1988, *25*(3–4), pp. 373–78.

Phillips, T. P. and Mtoi, M. T. T. Farming System Analysis of an Alternative Production System for Peasant Farming in Morogoro, Tanzania. *Can. J. Agr. Econ.*, March 1988, *36*(1), pp. 143–53.

Phillips, William D., Jr. Spain's Northern Shipping Industry in the Sixteenth Century. *J. Europ. Econ. Hist.*, Fall 1988, *17*(2), pp. 267–301.

Phillips, William H. and Bordo, Michael D. Faithful Index to the Ambitions and Fortunes of the State: The Development of Political Economy at South Carolina College. In *Barber, W. J., ed.*, 1988, pp. 42–71.

Phipps, Tim T. and Chambers, Robert G. Accumulation and Rental Behavior in the Market for Farmland. *Western J. Agr. Econ.*, December 1988, *13*(2), pp. 294–306.

Phlips, Louis. Price Discrimination: A Survey of the Theory. *J. Econ. Surveys*, 1988, *2*(2), pp. 135–67.

Phylaktis, Kate. Capital Controls: The Case of Argentina. *J. Int. Money Finance*, September 1988, *7*(3), pp. 303–20.

Piasecki, K. Fuzzy P-Measures and Their Application in Decision Making. In *Kacprzyk, J. and Fedrizzi, M., eds.*, 1988, pp. 75–88.

Picard, Guy and Nguyen, Sang. Estimation of Interregional Freight Flows Using Input/Output Analysis. In *Bianco, L. and La Bella, A., eds.*, 1988, pp. 186–209.

Picard, Pierre. La tarification optimale des télécommunications: Une présentation synthétique. (Optimal Pricing for Telecommunications: An Overview. With English summary.) *Ann. Écon. Statist.*, Oct.–Dec. 1988, (12), pp. 27–62.

Picard, Robert G. Pricing Behavior of Newspapers. In *Picard, R. G., et al., eds.*, 1988, pp. 55–69.

———, et al. Press Concentration and Monopoly: New Perspectives on Newspaper Ownership and Operation: Policy Implications. In *Picard, R. G., et al., eds.*, 1988, pp. 197–208.

Picciotto, Robert. Modeling Efficient Conjunctive Use of Water in the Indus Basin: Comment. In *O'Mara, G. T., ed.*, 1988, pp. 138–40.

———. Pricing and Trade: Issues, Policies and Lending Strategies. In *Roberts, C., ed.*, 1988, pp. 79–80.

Picht, Hartmut. Government Size and Public Choices. *Kyklos*, 1988, *41*(3), pp. 437–58.

Pickens, T. Boone. The Stockholder Revolution.

In *Weidenbaum, M. L. and Chilton, K. W., eds.*, 1988, pp. 25–33.

Pickering, J. F. A Behavioural Model of the Demand for Consumer Durables. In *Earl, P. E., ed., Vol. 2*, 1988, *1981*, pp. 217–35.

———, and Holl, P. The Determinants and Effects of Actual, Abandoned and Contested Mergers. *Managerial Dec. Econ.*, March 1988, *9*(1), pp. 1–19.

Pickett, E. E. and Whiting, R. G. On the Estimation of Probabilistic Functions of Markov Chains. In *Fedorov, V. and Lauter, H., eds.*, 1988, pp. 205–13.

Pickford, M. On the Welfare Function of the Commerce Commission. *New Zealand Econ. Pap.*, 1988, *22*, pp. 15–24.

Pickup, Laurie. Hard to get around: A Study of Women's Travel Mobility. In *Little, J.; Peake, L. and Richardson, P., eds.*, 1988, pp. 98–116.

Picot, Arnold and Wenger, Ekkehard. The Employment Relation from the Transactions Cost Perspective. In *Dlugos, G.; Dorow, W. and Weiermair, K., eds.*, 1988, pp. 29–43.

Piderit, John J. Values, Population, and International Responsibility. In *Salvatore, D., ed.*, 1988, pp. 211–24.

Pieper, Paul J. and Eisner, Robert. Deficits, Monetary Policy, and Real Economic Activity. In *Arrow, K. J. and Boskin, M. J., eds.*, 1988, pp. 3–38.

———, and Eisner, Robert. The Relationship between Real Deficits and Real Growth: A Critique: Rejoinder. *J. Post Keynesian Econ.*, Fall 1988, *11*(1), pp. 161–68.

Pieptea, Dan R. and Prisman, Eliezer Zeev. The Monday Effect and Speculative Opportunities in the Stock-Index Futures Market. In *Fabozzi, F. J., ed.*, 1988, pp. 319–28.

Pierce, Glenn L. and Bowers, William J. Arbitrariness and Discrimination under Post-*Furman* Capital Statutes. In *Alper, N. O. and Hellman, D. A., eds.*, 1988, pp. 150–71.

———, and Bowers, William J. The Bartley–Fox Gun Law's Short-term Impact on Crime in Boston. In *Alper, N. O. and Hellman, D. A., eds.*, 1988, pp. 201–24.

——— and Bowers, William J. Deterrence or Brutalization: What Is the Effect of Executions? In *Alper, N. O. and Hellman, D. A., eds.*, 1988, pp. 172–200.

Pierce, John C., et al. Public Information on Acid Rain in Canada and the United States. *Soc. Sci. Quart.*, March 1988, *69*(1), pp. 193–202.

Pierenkemper, Toni. Trade Associations in Germany in the Late Nineteenth and Early Twentieth Centuries: Response. In *Yamazaki, H. and Miyamoto, M., eds.*, 1988, pp. 264–67.

———. Trade Associations in Germany in the Late Nineteenth and Early Twentieth Centuries. In *Yamazaki, H. and Miyamoto, M., eds.*, 1988, pp. 223–61.

Pierre, Guy. The Frustrated Development of the Haitian Sugar Industry between 1915/18 and 1938/39: International Financial and Commercial Rivalries. In *Albert, B. and Graves, A., eds.*, 1988, pp. 121–30.

Piesse, Jennie and Wood, Douglas. The Information Value of Failure Predictions in Credit Assessment. *J. Banking Finance*, June 1988, *12*(2), pp. 275–92.

Pieters, Rik G. M. Attitude-Behavior Relationships. In *van Raaij, W. F.; van Veldhoven, G. M. and Wärneryd, K.-E., eds.*, 1988, pp. 147–204.

———— and van Raaij, W. Fred. Functions and Management of Affect: Applications to Economic Behavior. *J. Econ. Psych.*, June 1988, *9*(2), pp. 251–82.

———— and van Raaij, W. Fred. The Role of Affect in Economic Behavior. In *van Raaij, W. F.; van Veldhoven, G. M. and Wärneryd, K.-E., eds.*, 1988, pp. 108–42.

———— and Verplanken, Bas. The Joy of Thinking about Nuclear Energy. In *Maital, S., ed., Vol. 2*, 1988, pp. 537–49.

Piggott, John. The Distribution of Wealth: What Is It, What Does It Mean, and Is It Important? *Australian Econ. Rev.*, Spring 1988, (83), pp. 35–41.

————. General Equilibrium Computation Applied to Public Sector Issues. In *Hare, P. G., ed.*, 1988, pp. 248–98.

Piggott, R. R. and MacAulay, T. G. Agricultural Economics at the University of New England. *Rev. Marketing Agr. Econ.*, August 1988, *56*(2), pp. 226–28.

Pigott, Charles and Kasman, Bruce. Interest Rate Divergences among the Major Industrial Nations. *Fed. Res. Bank New York Quart. Rev.*, Autumn 1988, *13*(3), pp. 28–44.

Pigozzi, Bruce William and Hinojosa, Rene C. Economic Base and Input–Output Multipliers: An Empirical Linkage. *Reg. Sci. Persp.*, 1988, *18*(2), pp. 3–13.

Piha, Kalevi. Business Ethics and Business Philosophy. *Liiketaloudellinen Aikak.*, 1988, *37*(3), pp. 212–24.

Pihlanto, Pekka. Onko laskentatoimi (kirjanpito) vain rahaprosessin kuvausta? (Is Accounting Merely a Description of the Monetary Process of the Enterprise? The Social Copnstructionist View of Accounting. With English summary.) *Liiketaloudellinen Aikak.*, 1988, *37*(4), pp. 320–45.

Piiasheva, L. I. and Pinsker, B. S. Prices and Cost Accounting. *Prob. Econ.*, March 1988, *30*(11), pp. 34–40.

Pikkarainen, Pentti. Can We Measure the Pressure on the Finnish Markka? *Liiketaloudellinen Aikak.*, 1988, *37*(2), pp. 132–41.

Pilati, Massimo and Salvemini, Severino. Il contributo della teoria dell'agenzia allo sviluppo del capitalismo manageriale. (A Contribution of the Agency Theory to the Development of Managerial Capitalism. With English summary.) *Giorn. Econ.*, March–April 1988, *47*(3–4), pp. 187–211.

Pilla, Lou; McKendrick, Joseph and Mason, Janet. The Challenge to Middle Managers. In *Timpe, A. D., ed.*, 1988, *1984*, pp. 14–18.

Pillai, Vijayan and Pampel, Fred C. Teenage Fertility and Infant Mortality: Reply. *Demography*, February 1988, *25*(1), pp. 159–61.

Pillet, Gonzague. Water, Wind and Soil: Hidden Keys to the Water Planet Earth and to Economic Macroprocesses. *Energy J.*, January 1988, *9*(1), pp. 43–52.

———— and Baranzini, Andrea. Procédure d'évaluation de la part de l'environnement dans un produit économique. (Evaluation Procedure of the Role of Environment at the Interface with Economic Systems. With English summary.) *Écon. Appl.*, 1988, *41*(1), pp. 129–50.

Pilon, Roger. Property Rights, Takings, and a Free Society. In *Gwartney, J. D. and Wagner, R. E., eds.*, 1988, *1982*, pp. 151–79.

Pimental, David. Industrialized Agriculture and Natural Resources. In *Ehrlich, P. R. and Holdren, J. P., eds.*, 1988, pp. 53–74.

Pinches, George E. and Lee, Hong J. On Optimal Insurance Purchasing. *J. Risk Ins.*, March 1988, *55*(1), pp. 145–49.

Pinckney, Thomas C. and Valdés, Alberto. Short-run Supply Management and Food Security: Results from Pakistan and Kenya. *World Devel.*, September 1988, *16*(9), pp. 1025–34.

Pincus, J. J. Australian Budgetary Policies in the 1930s. In *Gregory, R. G. and Butlin, N. G., eds.*, 1988, pp. 173–92.

Pincus, Morton and Dopuch, Nicholas. Evidence on the Choice of Inventory Accounting Methods: LIFO versus FIFO. *J. Acc. Res.*, Spring 1988, *26*(1), pp. 28–59.

Pinder, David. The Netherlands: Tourist Development in a Crowded Society. In *Williams, A. M. and Shaw, G., eds.*, 1988, pp. 214–29.

Pindyck, Robert S. Capital Risk and Models of Investment Behaviour. In *Motamen, H., ed.*, 1988, pp. 103–17.

————. Irreversible Investment, Capacity Choice, and the Value of the Firm. *Amer. Econ. Rev.*, December 1988, *78*(5), pp. 969–85.

————. Risk Aversion and Determinants of Stock Market Behavior. *Rev. Econ. Statist.*, May 1988, *70*(2), pp. 183–90.

Pinegar, J. Michael and Chang, Eric C. Does the Market Reward Risk in Non-January Months? *J. Portfol. Manage.*, Fall 1988, *15*(1), pp. 55–57.

———— and Chang, Eric C. A Fundamental Study of the Seasonal Risk–Return Relationship: A Note. *J. Finance*, September 1988, *43*(4), pp. 1035–39.

———— and Linn, Scott C. The Effect of Issuing Preferred Stock on Common and Preferred Stockholder Wealth. *J. Finan. Econ.*, October 1988, *22*(1), pp. 155–84.

Pines, David and Papageorgiou, Yorgos Y. The Impact of Transportation Cost Uncertainty on Urban Structure. *Reg. Sci. Urban Econ.*, May 1988, *18*(2), pp. 247–60.

————; Schwartz, Aba and Eldor, Rafael. The Demand for Domestic Assets and Consumption Risk. In *Khoury, S. J. and Ghosh, A., eds.*, 1988, pp. 349–62.

————; Schwartz, Aba and Eldor, Rafael. Home

Asset Preference and Productivity Shocks. *J. Int. Econ.*, August 1988, *25*(1–2), pp. 165–76.

Pingali, Prabhu L. and Binswanger, Hans P. Population Density and Farming Systems: The Changing Locus of Innovations and Technical Change. **In** *Salvatore, D., ed.*, 1988, pp. 165–86.

——— **and Binswanger, Hans P.** Population Density and Farming Systems: The Changing Locus of Innovations and Technical Change. **In** *Lee, R. D., et al., eds.*, 1988, pp. 51–76.

——— **and Binswanger, Hans P.** Technological Priorities for Farming in Sub-Saharan Africa. *World Bank Res. Observer*, January 1988, *3*(1), pp. 81–98.

Pini, Paolo and Segnana, Luisa. "Economia Politica": Alcune valutazioni dopo quattro anni. (*Economia Politica:* An Assessment after Four Years. With English summary.) *Econ. Polit.*, August 1988, *5*(2), pp. 237–64.

Pinkerton, Evelyn W. Cooperative Management of Local Fisheries: A Route to Development. **In** *Bennett, J. W. and Bowen, J. R., eds.*, 1988, pp. 257–73.

Pinkerton, John M.; Ma, Tai and Hansen, Robert S. The Allocation Ratio Decision in the Underwritten Rights Offering. **In** *Chen, A. H., ed.*, 1988, pp. 201–25.

———; **Shome, Dilip K. and Smith, Stephen D.** The Purchasing Power of Money and Nominal Interest Rates: A Re-examination. *J. Finance*, December 1988, *43*(5), pp. 1113–25.

Pinsker, B. S. and Piiasheva, L. I. Prices and Cost Accounting. *Prob. Econ.*, March 1988, *30*(11), pp. 34–40.

Pinson, Christian R. A. and Roberto, Eduardo L. Consumer Behavior and the Marketing Activities of Firms. **In** *van Raaij, W. F.; van Veldhoven, G. M. and Wärneryd, K.-E., eds.*, 1988, pp. 295–330.

Pinstrup-Andersen, Per. Assuring Food Security and Adequate Nutrition for the Poor. **In** *Bell, D. E. and Reich, M. R., eds.*, 1988, pp. 147–75.

———. Food Security and Structural Adjustment. **In** *Roberts, C., ed.*, 1988, pp. 205–23.

———. Food Subsidies: Consumer Welfare and Producer Incentives. **In** *Mellor, J. W. and Ahmed, R., eds.*, 1988, pp. 241–52.

———. The Social and Economic Effects of Consumer-Oriented Food Subsidies: A Summary of Current Evidence. **In** *Pinstrup-Andersen, P., ed.*, 1988, pp. 3–18.

———. Some Microeconomic Policy Implications of Consumer-Oriented Food Subsidies. **In** *Pinstrup-Andersen, P., ed.*, 1988, pp. 331–40.

——— **and Alderman, Harold.** The Effectiveness of Consumer-Oriented Food Subsidies in Reaching Rationing and Income Transfer Goals. **In** *Pinstrup-Andersen, P., ed.*, 1988, pp. 21–35.

Pintz, Peter. Environmental Crises and Environmental Policies in Asian Countries. *Pakistan Devel. Rev.*, Part 2, Winter 1988, *27*(4), pp. 765–76.

Pirani, A. and Serbolisca, A. Information and Advisory Systems for the Farming Industry. **In** *Schiefer, G., ed.*, 1988, pp. 237–46.

Pirie, Madsen. Principles of Privatization. **In** *Walker, M. A., ed. (II)*, 1988, pp. 3–14.

Pirog-Good, Maureen A. and Good, David H. A Simultaneous Probit Model of Crime and Employment for Black and White Teenage Males. **In** *Simms, M. C. and Myers, S. L., Jr., eds.*, 1988, pp. 109–27.

Pisharodi, R. Mohan and Mentzer, John T. Transportation as an Industrial Marketing Service. **In** *Woodside, A. G., ed.*, 1988, pp. 201–21.

Pissarides, Christopher A. The Search Equilibrium Approach to Fluctuations in Employment. *Amer. Econ. Rev.*, May 1988, *78*(2), pp. 363–68.

Pissulla, Petra. Romania and Hungary in the IMF and Implications for Poland. **In** *Marer, P. and Siwinski, W., eds.*, 1988, pp. 259–72.

Pitayanon, Sumalee. Labour Market Changes and Economic Development in Thailand. **In** *Pang, E. F., ed.*, 1988, pp. 243–77.

Pitchik, Carolyn and Schotter, Andrew. Honesty in a Model of Strategic Information Transmission: Correction. *Amer. Econ. Rev.*, December 1988, *78*(5), pp. 1164.

——— **and Schotter, Andrew.** Perfect Equilibria in Budget-Constrained Sequential Auctions: An Experimental Study. *Rand J. Econ.*, Autumn 1988, *19*(3), pp. 363–88.

Piterman, Sylvia. Inflation Stabilization: Argentina: Comment. **In** *Bruno, M., et al., eds.*, 1988, pp. 209–12.

——— **and Bruno, Michael.** Israel's Stabilization: A Two-Year Review. **In** *Bruno, M., et al., eds.*, 1988, pp. 3–47.

Pitkin, John and Börsch-Supan, Axel. On Discrete Choice Models of Housing Demand. *J. Urban Econ.*, September 1988, *24*(2), pp. 153–72.

Pitofsky, Robert and Krattenmaker, Thomas G. Antitrust Merger Policy and the Reagan Administration. *Antitrust Bull.*, Summer 1988, *33*(2), pp. 211–32.

Pitsvada, Bernard T. The Executive Budget—An Idea Whose Time Has Passed. *Public Budg. Finance*, Spring 1988, *8*(1), pp. 85–94.

Pitt, D. C. Deforestation: Social Dynamics in Watersheds and Mountain Ecosystems: Introduction. **In** *Ives, J. and Pitt, D. C., eds.*, 1988, pp. xi–xiii.

———. Poverty, Women and Young People. **In** *Ives, J. and Pitt, D. C., eds.*, 1988, pp. 191–223.

Pitt, David G.; Tuthill, Dean F. and Favero, Philip. Land Use Policies, Water Quality, and the Chesapeake Bay. **In** *Johnston, G. M.; Freshwater, D. and Favero, P., eds.*, 1988, pp. 71–90.

Pittle, R. David. Product Safety: The Views of a Former Regulator. **In** *Maynes, E. S. and ACCI Research Committee, eds.*, 1988, pp. 102–07.

Pittman, Russell. Rent-Seeking and Market Structure: Comment. *Public Choice*, August 1988, *58*(2), pp. 173–85.

_____ and Norton, Edgar. M-Form Organization and Firm Profitability. *Rev. Ind. Organ.*, Spring 1988, 3(3), pp. 1–14.

Pitts, E.; Jenkins, T. N. and Haines, M. Dairy Industry Structure and Milk Price Comparisons: A Further Comment. *J. Agr. Econ.*, September 1988, 39(3), pp. 446–49.

Pitts, Robert A. and Radosh, Jerome. Beyond Wage Differentials as a Criterion in Selecting an Offshore Manufacturing Site: The Case of Tuna Processing in Thailand. In *Pennsylvania Economic Association*, 1988, pp. 404–16.

Piva, Francesco and Toniolo, Gianni. Unemployment in the 1930s: The Case of Italy. In *Eichengreen, B. and Hatton, T. J.*, eds., 1988, pp. 221–45.

Pizzorusso, A. The Law-Making Process as a Juridical and Political Activity. In *Pizzorusso, A.*, ed., 1988, pp. 1–87.

Pla, Josep M. Ensemble des possibilités de production, fonction de production et fonction de coût: une présentation de la dualité. (With English summary.) *L'Actual. Econ.*, September 1988, 64(3), pp. 416–41.

Plachý, Jan and Kroiher, Jaroslav. The Role of the System of Plan-Base Management in Speeding Up Scientific–Technological Development. *Czech. Econ. Digest.*, April 1988, (2), pp. 13–29.

Placone, Dennis L. and Blair, Dudley W. Expense-Preference Behavior, Agency Costs, and Firm Organization: The Savings and Loan Industry. *J. Econ. Bus.*, February 1988, 40(1), pp. 1–15.

Planche, Alain. L'incertitude monétaire comme fondement du surendettement. (Monetary Uncertainty as a Basis of Over-Endebtment. With English summary.) *Écon. Soc.*, June–July 1988, 22(6–7), pp. 101–12.

Plane, Patrick. Les facteurs de déséquilibre des paiements courants en union monétaire ouest africaine (1970–1983). (With English summary.) *Revue Écon. Polit.*, Jan.–Feb. 1988, 98(1), pp. 111–26.

_____; Guillaumont, Patrick and Guillaumont, Sylviane. Participating in African Monetary Unions: An Alternative Evaluation. *World Devel.*, May 1988, 16(5), pp. 569–76.

Plant, Mark; Welch, Finis R. and Murphy, Kevin M. Cohort Size and Earnings in the USA. In *Lee, R. D.; Arthur, W. B. and Rodgers, G.*, eds., 1988, pp. 39–58.

Plante-Failé, Marianne and Zwemmer, J. W. Netherlands: Interest: Withholding Tax or No Withholding Tax? *Bull. Int. Fiscal Doc.*, Aug.–Sept. 1988, 42(8–9), pp. 365–67.

Plantenga, J. and Konijn, P. A. B. Kalker. Characteristics Explaining Business Success of Entrepreneurs versus Managers. *J. Behav. Econ.*, Summer 1988, 17(2), pp. 133–42.

Plasman, R.; Freese, V. and Meulders, D. Bilan des recherches sur l'aménagement et la réduction du temps de travail en Belgique (1975–1987). (With English summary.) *Cah. Écon. Bruxelles*, First Trimester 1988, (117), pp. 67–106.

Plasmans, Joseph and Vanroelen, Annemie. Reducing Working Time for Reducing Unemployment? A Macroeconomic Simulation Study for the Belgian Economy. In *Motamen, H.*, ed., 1988, pp. 561–608.

Plaut, Steven E. and Melnik, Arie. International Lending, Private-Sector "Country Risk," and Stabilization Policy. In *Khoury, S. J. and Ghosh, A.*, eds., 1988, pp. 121–29.

Plesko, George A. The Accuracy of Government Forecasts and Budget Projections. *Nat. Tax J.*, December 1988, 41(4), pp. 483–501.

Pletnev, E. P. Clearly Defining the Basic Link. *Prob. Econ.*, March 1988, 30(11), pp. 41–46.

Plewis, Ian. Assessing and Understanding the Educational Progress of Children from Different Ethnic Groups. *J. Roy. Statist. Soc.*, 1988, 151(2), pp. 316–26.

Plihon, Dominique; Boutillier, Michel and Gabrielli, Daniel. La baisse des taux d'intérêt en France: Quels effets en attendre? (Consequences of the Decrease in the Level of Interest Rates in France. With English summary.) *Revue Écon.*, July 1988, 39(4), pp. 841–76.

Pliskin, Jeffrey. A Further Theoretical Result for Generalized Ridge Regression Estimators. *Econ. Letters*, 1988, 26(2), pp. 133–35.

Ploberger, Werner; Alt, Raimund and Krämer, Walter. Testing for Structural Change in Dynamic Models. *Econometrica*, November 1988, 56(6), pp. 1355–69.

van der Ploeg, Frederick. International Interdependence and Policy Coordination in Economies with Real and Nominal Wage Rigidity. *Greek Econ. Rev.*, 1988, 10(1), pp. 1–48.

_____. International Policy Coordination in Interdependent Monetary Economies. *J. Int. Econ.*, August 1988, 25(1–2), pp. 1–23.

_____ and Attanasio, Orazio P. Real Effects of Demand- and Supply-Side Policies in Interdependent Economies. *Econ. Modelling*, April 1988, 5(2), pp. 151–64.

_____ and Marini, Giancarlo. Finite Horizons and the Non-neutrality of Money. *Econ. Letters*, 1988, 26(1), pp. 57–61.

_____ and Marini, Giancarlo. Monetary and Fiscal Policy in an Optimising Model with Capital Accumulation and Finite Lives. *Econ. J.*, September 1988, 98(392), pp. 772–86.

du Plooy, R. M. Productivity in South African Industry. *S. Afr. J. Econ.*, March 1988, 56(1), pp. 82–93.

Plosser, Charles I.; Rebelo, Sergio T. and King, Robert G. Production, Growth and Business Cycles: I. The Basic Neoclassical Model. *J. Monet. Econ.*, March–May 1988, 21(2–3), pp. 195–232.

_____; Rebelo, Sergio T. and King, Robert G. Production, Growth and Business Cycles: II. New Directions. *J. Monet. Econ.*, March–May 1988, 21(2–3), pp. 309–41.

Plott, Charles R. and Daniels, Brian P. Inflation and Expectations in Experimental Markets. In *Tietz, R.; Albers, W. and Selten, R.*, eds., 1988, pp. 198–218.

_____; Porter, David P. and Banks, Jeffrey S.

An Experimental Analysis of Unanimity in Public Goods Provision Mechanisms. *Rev. Econ. Stud.*, April 1988, *55*(2), pp. 301–22.

_____ **and Sunder, Shyam.** Rational Expectations and the Aggregation of Diverse Information in Laboratory Security Markets. *Econometrica*, September 1988, *56*(5), pp. 1085–1118.

Plourde, André. On Aspects of Oil and Gas Trade. *Energy J.*, October 1988, *9*(4), pp. 107–10.

_____ **and Pesando, James E.** The October 1979 Change in the U.S. Monetary Regime: Its Impact on the Forecastability of Canadian Interest Rates. *J. Finance*, March 1988, *43*(1), pp. 217–39.

Plourde, Charles and Yeung, David. A Note on Hayashi's Neoclassical Interpretation of Tobin's *q*. *Atlantic Econ. J.*, June 1988, *16*(2), pp. 81.

Plowiec, Urszula. Economic Reform and Foreign Trade in Poland. In *[Holzman, F. D.]*, 1988, pp. 340–69.

Plowman, David H. Employer Associations and Bargaining Structures: An Australian Perspective. *Brit. J. Ind. Relat.*, November 1988, *26*(3), pp. 371–96.

Pluta, Leonard and Dodaro, Santo. The Antigonish Movement as a Model of Regional Economic Development. In *Choudhury, M. A., ed.*, 1988, pp. 48–70.

Poddar, Satya. Issues in Integration of Federal and Provincial Sales Taxes: A Canadian Perspective. *Nat. Tax J.*, September 1988, *41*(3), pp. 369–80.

Podder, Nripesh. Technology and Its Transfer to Less Developed Economies. In *Tisdell, C. and Maitra, P., eds.*, 1988, pp. 63–91.

Podesta, Bruno and Scurrah, Martin J. The Experience of Worker Self-management in Peru and Chile. In *Annis, S. and Hakim, P., eds.*, 1988, pp. 132–53.

Podgursky, Michael. Job Displacement and Labor Market Adjustment: Evidence from the Displaced Worker Surveys. In *Cyert, R. M. and Mowery, D. C., eds.*, 1988, pp. 3–41.

Podkaminer, Leon. Disequilibrium in Poland's Consumer Markets: Further Evidence on Intermarket Spillovers. *J. Compar. Econ.*, March 1988, *12*(1), pp. 43–60.

Podolski, T. M. The Cross Report: A Critical Appraisal of the Study Group's Evaluation of Issues of Monetary and Prudential Policy. *Brit. Rev. Econ. Issues*, Spring 1988, *10*(22), pp. 103–14.

Poggie, John J., Jr.; Pollnac, Richard B. and Fierro, Miguel. Factors Influencing the Success of Fishermen's Cooperatives in Ecuador. *Marine Resource Econ.*, 1988, *5*(3), pp. 231–42.

Pogodzinski, J. M. Amenities in an Urban General Equilibrium Model. *J. Urban Econ.*, November 1988, *24*(3), pp. 260–78.

Pogue, Thomas F. and Bentick, Brian L. The Impact on Development Timing of Property and Profit Taxation. *Land Econ.*, November 1988, *64*(4), pp. 317–24.

_____ **and Paulsen, Michael B.** Higher Education Enrollment: The Interaction of Labor Market Conditions, Curriculum, and Selectivity. *Econ. Educ. Rev.*, 1988, *7*(3), pp. 275–90.

Pohjola, Matti. Concentration of Shareholder Voting Power in Finnish Industrial Companies. *Scand. J. Econ.*, 1988, *90*(2), pp. 245–53.

Pohl, Hans. The Society for Business History: A Decade of Work. In *Pohl, H. and Rudolph, B., eds.*, 1988, pp. 17–39.

Pohle, Monika. A Review of the New Literature on Banking History. In *Pohl, H. and Rudolph, B., eds.*, 1988, pp. 121–30.

Pohlmeier, Winfried and König, Heinz. A Dynamic Model of Labor Utilization. In *Hart, R. A., ed.*, 1988, pp. 112–25.

_____ **and König, Heinz.** Employment, Labour Utilization and Procyclical Labour Productivity. *Kyklos*, 1988, *41*(4), pp. 551–72.

Poiesz, Theo B. C. and von Grumbkow, Jasper. Economic Well-Being, Job Satisfaction, Income Evaluation and Consumer Satisfaction: An Integrative Attempt. In *van Raaij, W. F.; van Veldhoven, G. M. and Wärneryd, K.-E., eds.*, 1988, pp. 571–93.

_____ **and Sol, Jopy.** The Individual Evaluation of the Dutch Social Security System: Results of an Initial Investigation. In *Maital, S., ed., Vol. 2*, 1988, pp. 752–65.

Poirier, Dale J. Causal Relationships and Replicability. *J. Econometrics*, Sept.–Oct. 1988, *39*(1–2), pp. 213–34.

_____. Frequentist and Subjectivist Perspectives on the Problems of Model Building in Economics. *J. Econ. Perspectives*, Winter 1988, *2*(1), pp. 121–44.

_____. The Subjectivist Response. *J. Econ. Perspectives*, Winter 1988, *2*(1), pp. 167–70.

_____ **and Garber, Steven.** The Design and Summary of Public Subjective–Predictive Analyses: Comment [An Application of Operational-Subjective Statistical Methods to Rational Expectations]. *J. Bus. Econ. Statist.*, October 1988, *6*(4), pp. 466–69.

_____ **and Ruud, Paul A.** Probit with Dependent Observations. *Rev. Econ. Stud.*, October 1988, *55*(4), pp. 593–614.

Poisson, Véronique. The Renegotiation of the 1982 Gas Contract between France and the USSR. *Soviet E. Europ. Foreign Trade*, Summer 1988, *24*(2), pp. 26–37.

Poitras, Geoffrey. Arbitrage Boundaries, Treasury Bills, and Covered Interest Parity. *J. Int. Money Finance*, December 1988, *7*(4), pp. 429–45.

Polak, Jacques J. Conditionality: A Double Paradox: Comment. In *Jepma, C. J., ed.*, 1988, pp. 120–21.

_____. Development, Security and North–South Relations: A Look into the Future: Comment. In *Jepma, C. J., ed.*, 1988, pp. 56–58.

_____. Economic Policy Objectives and Policy-making in the Major Industrial Countries. In *Guth, W., ed.*, 1988, pp. 1–25.

_____. The History of Dutch Macroeconomic Modelling (1936–1986): Comments. In *Driehuis, W.; Fase, M. M. G. and den Hartog, H., eds.*, 1988, pp. 93–98.

──────. The Impasse Concerning the Role of the SDR. In *[Witteveen, H. J.]*, 1988, pp. 175–89.

Poland, William B. The Importance of Including Uncertainties in Economic Generation Reliability Planning. *Energy J.*, Special Issue, 1988, 9, pp. 19–32.

Polaschewski, Edwin. On the Inter-Relation Between Large and Small Enterprises in a Socialist Economy: The Case of the GDR. In *Urabe, K.; Child, J. and Kagono, T., eds.*, 1988, pp. 243–52.

Polemarchakis, H. M. Portfolio Choice, Exchange Rates, and Indeterminacy. *J. Econ. Theory*, December 1988, 46(2), pp. 414–21.

Polenske, Karen R. Growth Pole Theory and Strategy Reconsidered: Domination, Linkages, and Distribution. In *[Perroux, F.]*, 1988, pp. 91–111.

──────. **and Jordan, Peter G.** Multiplier Impacts of Fishing Activities in New England and Nova Scotia. In *Ciaschini, M., ed.*, 1988, pp. 325–66.

Poli, Giorgio; Basevi, Giorgio and Kind, Paolo. Economic Cooperation and Confrontation between Europe and the U.S.A.: A Game-Theoretic Approach to the Analysis of International Monetary and Trade Policies. In *Baldwin, R. E.; Hamilton, C. B. and Sapir, A., eds.*, 1988, pp. 369–88.

Policinski, Mark R. The Japanese Technical Literature Act of 1986. In *Uyehara, C. H., ed.*, 1988, pp. 57–61.

Polinsky, A. Mitchell. Detrebling versus Decoupling Antitrust Damages: Lessons from the Theory of Enforcement. In *White, L. J., ed.*, 1988, pp. 87–94.

──────. **and Rubinfeld, Daniel L.** The Deterrent Effects of Settlements and Trials. *Int. Rev. Law Econ.*, June 1988, 8(1), pp. 109–16.

──────. **and Rubinfeld, Daniel L.** The Welfare Implications of Costly Litigation for the Level of Liability. *J. Legal Stud.*, January 1988, 17(1), pp. 151–64.

Polishuk, Paul and Blustain, Harvey. Fiber Optics: Technology Diffusion and Industrial Competitiveness. In *Hicks, D. A., ed.*, 1988, pp. 308–42.

Pollak, Robert A. Tied Transfers and Paternalistic Preferences. *Amer. Econ. Rev.*, May 1988, 78(2), pp. 240–44.

Pollard, J. H. On the Decomposition of Changes in Expectation of Life and Differentials in Life Expectancy. *Demography*, May 1988, 25(2), pp. 265–76.

Pollard, Sidney. Studies in Capital Formation in the United Kingdom, 1750–1920: Coal Mining. In *Feinstein, C. H. and Pollard, S., eds.*, 1988, pp. 35–72.

──────. Studies in Capital Formation in the United Kingdom, 1750–1920: The Insurance Policies. In *Feinstein, C. H. and Pollard, S., eds.*, 1988, pp. 225–56.

──────. **and Davies, R. S. W.** Studies in Capital Formation in the United Kingdom, 1750–1920: The Iron Industry, 1750–1850. In *Feinstein,*

C. H. and Pollard, S., eds., 1988, pp. 73–104.

──────. **and Ginarlis, John.** Studies in Capital Formation in the United Kingdom, 1750–1920: Roads and Waterways, 1750–1850. In *Feinstein, C. H. and Pollard, S., eds.*, 1988, pp. 182–224.

Pollard, Stephen K. and Canarella, Giorgio. Efficiency in Foreign Exchange Markets: A Vector Autoregression Approach. *J. Int. Money Finance*, September 1988, 7(3), pp. 331–46.

Pollay, Richard W. Current Events That Are Making Advertising History. In *[Hollander, S. C.]*, 1988, pp. 195–221.

Pollin, Jean-Paul and Gaffard, Jean-Luc. Réflexions sur l'instabilité des économies monétaires. (With English summary.) *Revue Écon. Polit.*, Sept.–Oct. 1988, 98(5), pp. 599–614.

Pollin, Robert. The Growth of U.S. Household Debt: Demand-Side Influences. *J. Macroecon.*, Spring 1988, 10(2), pp. 231–48.

Pollitt, Brian H. The Collaboration of Maurice Dobb in Sraffa's Edition of Ricardo. *Cambridge J. Econ.*, March 1988, 12(1), pp. 55–65.

──────. The Cuban Sugar Economy in the 1930s. In *Albert, B. and Graves, A., eds.*, 1988, pp. 97–108.

Pollnac, Richard B.; Fierro, Miguel and Poggie, John J., Jr. Factors Influencing the Success of Fishermen's Cooperatives in Ecuador. *Marine Resource Econ.*, 1988, 5(3), pp. 231–42.

Pollock, Alex. Society and Change in the Northern Jordan Valley. In *Abed, G. T., ed.*, 1988, pp. 245–58.

Pollock, David H. Raúl Prebisch versus the U.S. Government: Changing Perceptions over Time. *Can. J. Devel. Stud.*, 1988, 9(1), pp. 121–29.

Pollock, Richard L. and Moncur, James E. T. Scarcity Rents for Water: A Valuation and Pricing Model. *Land Econ.*, February 1988, 64(1), pp. 62–72.

Pollock, Stephen H. and Galper, Harvey. Models of State Income Tax Reform. In *Gold, S. D., ed.*, 1988, pp. 107–28.

Pollock, Vivienne. The Seafishing Industry in County Down and Its Scottish Connections, 1860–1939. In *Mitchison, R. and Roebuck, P., eds.*, 1988, pp. 255–66.

Polo, Clemente; Raymond, José Luis and García, Jaime. Una nota sobre la relación empleo-capital en españa: 1955–1984. (With English summary.) *Invest. Econ.*, January 1988, 12(1), pp. 177–95.

Polonsky, M. J.; Scott, D. R. and Suchard, Hazel T. Motivations of South African Emigrants. *Appl. Econ.*, October 1988, 20(10), pp. 1293–1315.

Polopolus, Leo and Beilock, Richard. Ranking of Agricultural Economics Departments: Influence of Regional Journals, Joint Authorship, and Self-Citations. *Amer. J. Agr. Econ.*, May 1988, 70(2), pp. 403–09.

Poloz, Stephen S. and Boothe, Paul M. Unstable Money Demand and the Monetary Model of the Exchange Rate. *Can. J. Econ.*, November 1988, 21(4), pp. 785–98.

Polt, Wolfgang and Braun, Ernest. High Technology and Competitiveness: An Austrian Perspective. In *Freeman, C. and Lundvall, B.-A., eds.*, 1988, pp. 203–25.

Polterovich, V. M.; Lakhman, I. L. and Levin, M. I. The Mechanism of Negotiated Prices and Problems of Its Improvement. *Matekon*, Summer 1988, *24*(4), pp. 27–60.

Poluha, Eva. The Producers' Cooperative as an Option for Women—A Case Study from Ethiopia. In *Hedlund, H., ed.*, 1988, pp. 139–52.

Polzin, Paul E., et al. Forecasting Accuracy and Structural Stability of the Economic Base Model. *Rev. Reg. Stud.*, Spring 1988, *18*(2), pp. 23–36.

Pombo, Fernando. Security on Movable Property and Receivables in Europe: Spain. In *Dickson, M. G.; Rosener, W. and Storm, P. M., eds.*, 1988, pp. 153–71.

Pomfret, Richard. World Steel Trade at a Crossroads. *J. World Trade*, June 1988, *22*(3), pp. 81–89.

Pommerehne, Werner W. Measuring Environmental Benefits: A Comparison of Hedonic Technique and Contingent Valuation. In *Bös, D.; Rose, M. and Seidl, C., eds.,*, 1988, pp. 363–400.

_____ and Frey, Bruno S. Die Geltung deutschsprachiger ökonomen in der Welt. (The Reputation of German Speaking Economists in the World. With English summary.) *Jahr. Nationalökon. Statist.*, May 1988, *204*(5), pp. 406–22.

_____ and Kirchgässner, Gebhard. Government Spending in Federal Systems: A Comparison between Switzerland and Germany. In *Lybeck, J. A. and Henrekson, M., eds.*, 1988, pp. 327–56.

Pommerenke, Pamela Lynne. Comparable Worth: A Panacea for Discrimination against Women in the Labor Market? *Amer. Econ.*, Spring 1988, ·*32*(1), pp. 44–48.

Pomp, Richard D. State Tax Expenditure Budgets—And Beyond. In *Gold, S. D., ed.*, 1988, pp. 65–81.

Pompelli, Greg and Heien, Dale M. The Demand for Beef Products: Cross-Section Estimation of Demographic and Economic Effects. *Western J. Agr. Econ.*, July 1988, *13*(1), pp. 37–44.

Ponak, Allen and Falkenberg, Loren. Dispute Resolution Procedures under Canadian Collective Bargaining. *Australian Bull. Lab.*, March 1988, *14*(2), pp. 426–48.

Pond, Lallon and Tucker, Alan L. The Probability Distribution of Foreign Exchange Price Changes: Tests of Candidate Processes. *Rev. Econ. Statist.*, November 1988, *70*(4), pp. 638–47.

Ponnambalam, Kumaraswamy and Adams, Barry J. Comment on "Error Analysis of Conventional Discrete and Gradient Dynamic Programming." *Water Resources Res.*, June 1988, *24*(6), pp. 888–89.

Ponsoldt, James F. Antitrust Legislation: Introduction. *Antitrust Bull.*, Summer 1988, *33*(2), pp. 201–09.

_____ and Lewyn, Marc J. Judicial Activism, Economic Theory and the Role of Summary Judgment in Sherman Act Conspiracy Cases: The Illogic of *Matsushita. Antitrust Bull.*, Fall 1988, *33*(3), pp. 575–613.

Pontecorvo, Giulio. The State Worldwide Fishery Statistics: A Modest Proposal. *Marine Resource Econ.*, 1988, *5*(2), pp. 79–81.

Ponthieu, Louis D. and Mitchell, J. Brooks. Deals: A Comparison of Entrepreneur and Executive Perceptions. In *Association of Private Education*, 1988, pp. 125–32.

Poole, Michael. Factors Affecting the Development of Employee Financial Participation in Contemporary Britain: Evidence from a National Survey. *Brit. J. Ind. Relat.*, March 1988, *26*(1), pp. 21–36.

Poole, Robert W., Jr. Fire Protection. In *Cowen, T., ed.*, 1988, *1980*, pp. 305–25.

_____. Leisure and Recreational Services. In *Cowen, T., ed.*, 1988, *1980*, pp. 327–39.

_____. The Limits of Privatization. In *Walker, M. A., ed. (II)*, 1988, pp. 79–91.

Poole, William. Monetary Policy Lessons of Recent Inflation and Disinflation. *J. Econ. Perspectives*, Summer 1988, *2*(3), pp. 73–100.

_____. Monetary Policy: Monetarism to Fine-Tuning. In *Boaz, D., ed.*, 1988, pp. 157–73.

Poore, M. E. D. Deforestation: Social Dynamics in Watersheds and Mountain Ecosystems: Conclusion. In *Ives, J. and Pitt, D. C., eds.*, 1988, pp. 242–44.

Pope, Clayne. Income Distribution: Comments. In *Mangum, G. and Philips, P., eds.*, 1988, pp. 83–88.

Pope, James A. and Cross, Edward M. The Optimal Load Size for Ocean Shippers. *Logist. Transp. Rev.*, December 1988, *24*(4), pp. 299–315.

_____ and Talley, Wayne K. Inventory Costs and Optimal Ship Size. *Logist. Transp. Rev.*, June 1988, *24*(2), pp. 107–20.

Pope, Peter F. and Peel, David A. Economic Surprises and the Behaviour of Asset Prices: Some Analyses and Further Empirical Results. *Econ. Letters*, 1988, *27*(4), pp. 375–79.

Pope, Robin Elizabeth. Additional Perspectives on Modelling Health Insurance Decisions: Discussion. In *Smith, C. S., ed.*, 1988, pp. 189–205.

_____. The Bayesian Approach: Irreconcilable with Expected Utility Theory? In *Munier, B. R., ed.*, 1988, pp. 221–30.

Pope, Rulon D. Developments in Economics of Importance to Agricultural Economics. In *Hildreth, R. J., et al., eds.*, 1988, pp. 238–56.

_____. A New Parametric Test for the Structure of Risk Preferences. *Econ. Letters*, 1988, *27*(2), pp. 117–21.

_____ and Hallam, Arne. Aggregation of Inputs under Risk. *Amer. J. Agr. Econ.*, November 1988, *70*(4), pp. 826–30.

_____ and Hallam, Arne. Separability Testing in Production Economics. *Amer. J. Agr. Econ.*, February 1988, *70*(1), pp. 142–52.

_____ and Hallam, Arne. Testing Separability

of Production Using Flexible Functional Form Profit Functions. *Econ. Letters*, 1988, *26*(3), pp. 265–70.

_____; **Leathers, Howard and Chavas, Jean-Paul.** Competitive Industry Equilibrium under Uncertainty and Free Entry. *Econ. Inquiry*, April 1988, *26*(2), pp. 331–44.

_____; **Nash, Elizabeth K. and Shumway, C. Richard.** Allocatable Fixed Inputs and Jointness in Agricultural Production: Implications for Economic Modeling: Reply. *Amer. J. Agr. Econ.*, November 1988, *70*(4), pp. 950–52.

_____ **and Tolley, H. Dennis.** Testing for Stochastic Dominance. *Amer. J. Agr. Econ.*, August 1988, *70*(3), pp. 693–700.

Popkin, Barry M.; Haines, Pamela S. and Guilkey, David K. Modeling Food Consumption Decisions as a Two-Step Process. *Amer. J. Agr. Econ.*, August 1988, *70*(3), pp. 543–52.

_____; **Schwartz, J. Brad and Akin, John S.** Price and Income Elasticities of Demand for Modern Health Care: The Case of Infant Delivery in the Philippines. *World Bank Econ. Rev.*, January 1988, *2*(1), pp. 49–76.

Popkin, Samuel L. Public Choice and Peasant Organization. In *Bates, R. H., ed.*, 1988, pp. 245–71.

Popkova, L. Where Are the *Pirogi* Meatier? *Prob. Econ.*, February 1988, *30*(10), pp. 44–48.

Popper, Steven W. The Diffusion of Numerically Controlled Machine Tools in Hungary. In *Brada, J. C. and Dobozi, I., eds.*, 1988, pp. 111–51.

_____ **and Tyson, Laura D'Andrea.** The New Hungarian Economic Reforms and Their Effects on Enterprise Behavior. In *Jones, D. C. and Svejnar, J., eds.*, 1988, pp. 327–65.

Porcano, Thomas M. Correlates of Tax Evasion. *J. Econ. Psych.*, March 1988, *9*(1), pp. 47–67.

Poret, Pierre. Un modèle estimé de demande de capital en déséquilibre dans l'industrie française. (With English summary.) *Rech. Écon. Louvain*, 1988, *54*(4), pp. 409–21.

Porket, J. L. Social Deprivation under Soviet Full Employment. In *Potichnyj, P. J., ed.*, 1988, pp. 161–78.

Porta, Pier Luigi. The Classical Theory of Price: A Note on the Sraffian Interpretation. *Écon. Soc.*, October 1988, *22*(10), pp. 53–74.

_____. La nuova edizione del "Palgrave's Dictionary." (The New Edition of the Palgrave's Dictionary. With English summary.) *Giorn. Econ.*, Nov.–Dec. 1988, *47*(11–12), pp. 601–06.

Porter, David P.; Banks, Jeffrey S. and Plott, Charles R. An Experimental Analysis of Unanimity in Public Goods Provision Mechanisms. *Rev. Econ. Stud.*, April 1988, *55*(2), pp. 301–22.

Porter-Hudak, Susan; Grosskopf, Shawna and Hayes, Kathy J. Pension Funding and Local Labor Costs: A Dynamic Analysis of Illinois Police Pension Funds. *Southern Econ. J.*, January 1988, *54*(3), pp. 572–82.

Porter, Michael; Walsh, Cliff and Freebairn, John W. Tax Cuts: Desirable and Practical.

Australian Tax Forum, 1988, *5*(3), pp. 285–99.

Porter, Philip K. and Goodman, John C. Theory of Competitive Regulatory Equilibrium. *Public Choice*, October 1988, *59*(1), pp. 51–66.

Porter, Richard C. Environmental Negotiation: Its Potential and Its Economic Efficiency. *J. Environ. Econ. Manage.*, June 1988, *15*(2), pp. 129–42.

_____. Supply and Demand Variations and Export Earnings Instability: Further Comment. *Econ. Develop. Cult. Change*, April 1988, *36*(3), pp. 573–75.

Porter, Robert H. A Study of Cartel Stability: The Joint Executive Committee, 1880–1886. In *Daughety, A. F., ed.*, 1988, *1983*, pp. 402–20.

_____ **and Hendricks, Kenneth.** An Empirical Study of an Auction with Asymmetric Information. *Amer. Econ. Rev.*, December 1988, *78*(5), pp. 865–83.

Portes, Richard and Eichengreen, Barry. Les prêts internationaux dans l'entre-deux-guerres: Le point de vue des porteurs de titres. (Foreign Lending in the Interwar Years: The Bondholders' Perspective. With English summary.) *Écon. Appl.*, 1988, *41*(4), pp. 741–71.

_____; **Quandt, Richard E. and Yeo, Stephen.** Tests of the Chronic Shortage Hypothesis: The Case of Poland. *Rev. Econ. Statist.*, May 1988, *70*(2), pp. 288–95.

_____ **and Santorum, Anita.** Money and the Consumption Goods Market in China. In *Reynolds, B. L., ed.*, 1988, *1987*, pp. 64–81.

Portney, Kent E. Politics and Distributional Impact Studies: The Dilemma of Economic Analysis in the Policy-Making Process. In *Danziger, S. H. and Portney, K. E., eds.*, 1988, pp. 239–48.

_____ **and Danziger, Sheldon H.** The Distributional Impacts of Public Policies. In *Danziger, S. H. and Portney, K. E., eds.*, 1988, pp. 1–10.

Portny, Stanley E. Collection of Data by State Agencies. In *Berkowitz, M., ed.*, 1988, pp. 160–82.

Porto, Alberto and Navajas, Fernando. Características distributivas, presupuestos familiares y el impacto distributivo de las tarifas públicas. (Distributional Characteristics of Goods, Household Budgets, and Distributional Effects of Public Prices. With English summary.) *Económica (La Plata)*, Jan.–June 1988, *34*(1), pp. 113–25.

Pöschke, J. and Rogge, V. Experiments for Manufacturing Metallic Compounds during the D1-Mission. In *Egan, J. J., et al.*, 1988, pp. 369–83.

Posner, Richard A. The Social Costs of Monopoly and Regulation. In *Stigler, G. J., ed.*, 1988, *1975*, pp. 279–300.

_____. A Theory of Primitive Society, With Special Reference to Law. In *Stigler, G. J., ed.*, 1988, *1980*, pp. 149–206.

Posnett, John and Jones, Andrew M. The Revenue and Welfare Effects of Cigarette Taxes.

Appl. Econ., September 1988, *20*(9), pp. 1223–32.

_____ **and Sandler, Todd.** Transfers, Transaction Costs and Charitable Intermediaries. *Int. Rev. Law Econ.*, December 1988, *8*(2), pp. 145–60.

Possen, Uri M. and Benninga, Simon. Fiscal Policy and the Term Structure of Interest Rates. *J. Public Econ.*, December 1988, *37*(3), pp. 331–44.

Post, Gerald V. and Moon, Soo-Young. A Pooled Cross-section Time-Series Approach to Business Failures in 18 U.S. Cities. *J. Econ. Bus.*, February 1988, *40*(1), pp. 45–56.

Postlep, Rolf-Dieter. An Evolutionary Approach to Inflation: Prices, Productivity, and Innovation: Discussion. In *Hanusch, H., ed.*, 1988, pp. 249–53.

Postma, H.; Soderstrom, E. J. and Carpenter, W. W. "Profiting" from Technology Transfer: A Novel Approach. In *Furino, A., ed.*, 1988, pp. 211–24.

Postner, Harry H. Linkages between Macro and Micro Business Accounts: Implications for Economic Measurement. *Rev. Income Wealth*, September 1988, *34*(3), pp. 313–35.

Potepan, Michael J. and Green, Francis. Vacation Time and Unionism in the U.S. and Europe. *Ind. Relat.*, Spring 1988, *27*(2), pp. 180–94.

_____ **and Harmon, Oskar Ragnar.** Housing Adjustment Costs: Their Impact on Mobility and Housing Demand Elasticities. *Amer. Real Estate Urban Econ. Assoc. J.*, Winter 1988, *16*(4), pp. 459–78.

Poterba, James M. Are Consumers Forward Looking? Evidence from Fiscal Experiments. *Amer. Econ. Rev.*, May 1988, *78*(2), pp. 413–18.

_____. Capital Gains Taxation in the United States: Realization, Revenue, and Rhetoric: Comment. *Brookings Pap. Econ. Act.*, 1988, (2), pp. 632–35.

_____. The Effects of Taxation on the Merger Decision: Comment. In *Auerbach, A. J., ed. (I)*, 1988, pp. 183–87.

_____. Financing Constraints and Corporate Investment: Comment. *Brookings Pap. Econ. Act.*, 1988, (1), pp. 200–204.

_____ **and Auerbach, Alan J.** Why Have Corporate Tax Revenues Declined? In *Helpman, E.; Razin, A. and Sadka, E., eds.*, 1988, pp. 33–49.

_____ **and Hausman, Jerry A.** Comportement des ménages et réforme fiscale de 1986. (House Behavior and the Tax Reform Act of 1986. With English summary.) *Ann. Écon. Statist.*, July–Sept. 1988, (11), pp. 159–82.

_____ **and Summers, Lawrence H.** Mean Reversion in Stock Prices. *J. Finan. Econ.*, October 1988, *22*(1), pp. 27–59.

Potier, Jean-Pierre. Léon Walras, critique de l'enseignement de l'économie politique en France au XIXe siècle. (With English summary.) *Revue Écon. Polit.*, March–April 1988, *98*(2), pp. 232–51.

Potiowsky, Thomas P.; Smith, W. James and

Vaughan, Michael B. Inferring Collusion from Pricing Behavior: The American Tobacco Case Reexamined. *Atlantic Econ. J.*, September 1988, *16*(3), pp. 40–45.

Potter, C. and Gasson, R. Conservation through Land Diversion: A Survey of Farmers' Attitudes. *J. Agr. Econ.*, September 1988, *39*(3), pp. 340–51.

Potter, Harley D. Some Conceptual Aspects of Measuring Homogeneity of Industrial Data from Manufacturing Censuses and Surveys. *Statist. J.*, December 1988, *5*(4), pp. 359–75.

Potter, Joseph E. Does Family Planning Reduce Infant Mortality? Comment. *Population Devel. Rev.*, March 1988, *14*(1), pp. 179–87.

Pottier, Claude. Local Innovation and Large Firm Strategies in Europe. In *Aydalot, P. and Keeble, D., eds.*, 1988, pp. 99–120.

Pottinger, Garrel and Cyert, Richard M. Towards a Better Micro-economic Theory. In *Cyert, R. M.*, 1988, *1979*, pp. 201–19.

Pötzelberger, K. and Felsenstein, Klaus. Robust Bayesian Regression Analysis with HPD-Regions. In *Edwards, D. and Raun, N. E., eds.*, 1988, pp. 349–54.

Pouliquen, Alain. The Contract Brigades: Towards a Neo-collectivism in Soviet Agriculture? In *Brada, J. C. and Wadekin, K.-E., eds.*, 1988, pp. 45–54.

Poulon, Frédéric. Le circuit en économie ouverte et la capacité d'endettement international. (The Circuit–Flux Theory in an Open Economy and the International Debt Capacity. With English summary.) *Écon. Soc.*, June–July 1988, *22*(6–7), pp. 7–20.

_____. The Short Period of Keynesian Analysis and the Time-Period of the Circuit. In *Barrère, A., ed.*, 1988, pp. 161–68.

Poulon-Lafaye, Nicole. Comptabilité nationale et circuit keynésien en économie ouverte. (National Accounts and Keynesian Circuit in an Open Economy. With English summary.) *Écon. Soc.*, June–July 1988, *22*(6–7), pp. 21–36.

_____. La controverse de 1929 entre Keynes, Ohlin et Rueff sur le problème des transferts internationaux est-elle anachronique? (Is It True That the 1929 Keynes, Ohlin, Rueff Controversy Addressing International Transfers Is Obsolete? With English summary.) *Écon. Soc.*, September 1988, *22*(9), pp. 73–84.

Poulsen, Annette B.; Hersch, Philip L. and Netter, Jeffry M. Insider Trading: The Law, the Theory, the Evidence. *Contemp. Policy Issues*, July 1988, *6*(3), pp. 1–13.

_____ **and Jarrell, Gregg A.** Dual-Class Recapitalizations as Antitakeover Mechanisms: The Recent Evidence. *J. Finan. Econ.*, Jan.–March 1988, *20*(1–2), pp. 129–52.

_____ **and Lehn, Kenneth.** Leveraged Buyouts: Wealth Created or Wealth Redistributed? In *Weidenbaum, M. L. and Chilton, K. W., eds.*, 1988, pp. 46–62.

Poulsen, M. F. and Forrest, J. Correlates of Energy Use: Domestic Electricity Consumption in Sydney. *Environ. Planning A*, March 1988, 20(3), pp. 327–38.

Pound, John. The Information Effects of Takeover Bids and Resistance. *J. Finan. Econ.*, December 1988, 22(2), pp. 207–27.

_____. Proxy Contests and the Efficiency of Shareholder Oversight. *J. Finan. Econ.*, Jan.–March 1988, 20(1–2), pp. 237–65.

Pourciau, Susan and Smith, David B. A Comparison of the Financial Characteristics of December and Non-December Year-End Companies. *J. Acc. Econ.*, December 1988, 10(4), pp. 335–44.

Pourgerami, Abbas. The Political Economy of Development: A Cross-national Causality Test of Development–Democracy–Growth Hypothesis. *Public Choice*, August 1988, 58(2), pp. 123–41.

_____. Socioeconomic Determinants of Political Democracy. *Atlantic Econ. J.*, March 1988, 16(1), pp. 94.

Pourian, Heydar. International Securities Markets: Integration, Regulation, and Methods for Extraterritorial Conflict Resolution. In *Khoury, S. J. and Ghosh, A., eds.*, 1988, pp. 105–19.

Powell, Andrew and Gilbert, Christopher L. The Use of Commodity Contracts for the Management of Developing Country Commodity Risks. In *Currie, D. and Vines, D., eds.*, 1988, pp. 147–79.

Powell, David E. The Soviet Union Today: A Troubled Society. In *Cracraft, J., ed.*, 1988, pp. 349–64.

Powell-Griner, Eve. Differences in Infant Mortality among Texas Anglos, Hispanics, and Blacks. *Soc. Sci. Quart.*, June 1988, 69(2), pp. 452–67.

Power, Fred B.; Johnson, Dale A. and Shows, E. Warren. Lump-Sum Awards in Workers' Compensation: Comment. *J. Risk Ins.*, December 1988, 55(4), pp. 734–39.

Power, Marilyn. Women, the State and the Family in the U.S.: Reaganomics and the Experience of Women. In *Rubery, J., ed.*, 1988, pp. 140–62.

Powers, Brian and Browne, M. Neil. Henry George and Comparable Worth: Hypothetical Markets as a Stimulus for Reforming the Labor Market. *Amer. J. Econ. Soc.*, October 1988, 47(4), pp. 461–71.

Powers, David R. Higher Education–Industry Partnerships: Procedural Rules and Guidelines. In *Powers, D. R., et al.*, 1988, pp. 328–46.

_____ and Powers, Mary F. Benefits of Cooperation between Higher Education and Industry. In *Powers, D. R., et al.*, 1988, pp. 3–30.

_____ and Powers, Mary F. Cooperative Approaches to Education and Research. In *Powers, D. R., et al.*, 1988, pp. 31–75.

_____ and Powers, Mary F. Creating Successful Partnerships. In *Powers, D. R., et al.*, 1988, pp. 119–68.

_____ and Powers, Mary F. Establishing Sound

Contracts and Oversight Procedures. In *Powers, D. R., et al.*, 1988, pp. 197–228.

_____ and Powers, Mary F. Examples of Innovative Alliances. In *Powers, D. R., et al.*, 1988, pp. 76–118.

_____ and Powers, Mary F. Future Challenges and Opportunities for Educational Alliances. In *Powers, D. R., et al.*, 1988, pp. 229–40.

_____ and Powers, Mary F. Reconciling Differing Needs of Academe and Industry. In *Powers, D. R., et al.*, 1988, pp. 169–96.

Powers, Mary F. and Powers, David R. Benefits of Cooperation between Higher Education and Industry. In *Powers, D. R., et al.*, 1988, pp. 3–30.

_____ and Powers, David R. Cooperative Approaches to Education and Research. In *Powers, D. R., et al.*, 1988, pp. 31–75.

_____ and Powers, David R. Creating Successful Partnerships. In *Powers, D. R., et al.*, 1988, pp. 119–68.

_____ and Powers, David R. Establishing Sound Contracts and Oversight Procedures. In *Powers, D. R., et al.*, 1988, pp. 197–228.

_____ and Powers, David R. Examples of Innovative Alliances. In *Powers, D. R., et al.*, 1988, pp. 76–118.

_____ and Powers, David R. Future Challenges and Opportunities for Educational Alliances. In *Powers, D. R., et al.*, 1988, pp. 229–40.

_____ and Powers, David R. Reconciling Differing Needs of Academe and Industry. In *Powers, D. R., et al.*, 1988, pp. 169–96.

Powers, Mary G. Development and the Status of Women: Indicators and Measures. In *Salvatore, D., ed.*, 1988, pp. 187–98.

Powers, Ronald C. Institutions and Agricultural Economics in the Twenty-first Century: A Discussion. In *Hildreth, R. J., et al., eds.*, 1988, pp. 340–42.

Powers, Susan G. The Role of Capital Discards in Multifactor Productivity Measurement. *Mon. Lab. Rev.*, June 1988, 111(6), pp. 27–35.

Pownall, Roger and Stuart, Brian. The IMF's Compensatory and Contingency Financing Facility. *Finance Develop.*, December 1988, 25(4), pp. 9–11.

Pozdena, Randall Johnston. Banks Affiliated with Bank Holding Companies: A New Look at Their Performance. *Fed. Res. Bank San Francisco Econ. Rev.*, Fall 1988, (4), pp. 29–40.

Pozdniakov, E. Is It Possible to Be "A Little Pregnant?" A Dilettante's Opinion. *Prob. Econ.*, February 1988, 30(10), pp. 49–55.

Poznanski, Kazimierz Z. The Competitiveness of Polish Industry and Indebtedness. In *Marer, P. and Siwinski, W., eds.*, 1988, pp. 45–60.

_____. The CPE Aversion to Innovations: Alternative Theoretical Explanations. *Econ. Planning*, 1988, 22(3), pp. 136–45.

Pozo, Susan. Monetary Operating Procedures and Exchange Rate Volatility. *Quart. J. Bus. Econ.*, Summer 1988, 27(3), pp. 3–22.

Pozzana, Roberto and Zaninotto, Enrico. Technical Efficiency and Market Structure for Retail

Firms: A Nonparametric Approach. *Ricerche Econ.*, Oct.–Dec. 1988, *42*(4), pp. 606–29.

van Praag, Bernard M. S. Climate Equivalence Scales: An Application of a General Method. *Europ. Econ. Rev.*, April 1988, *32*(4), pp. 1019–24.

_____; Dubnoff, S. and van der Sar, N. L. Evaluation Questions and Income Utility. In *Munier, B. R., ed.*, 1988, pp. 77–96.

_____; Dubnoff, Steve and van der Sar, Nico L. On the Measurement and Explanation of Standards with Respect to Income, Age and Education. *J. Econ. Psych.*, December 1988, *9*(4), pp. 481–98.

_____; Kloek, T. and De Leeuw, J. Large-Sample Properties of Method of Moment Estimators under Different Data-Generating Processes. *J. Econometrics*, January 1988, *37*(1), pp. 157–69.

_____ and Van der Sar, Nico L. Household Cost Functions and Equivalence Scales. *J. Human Res.*, Spring 1988, *23*(2), pp. 193–210.

_____ and van Weeren, J. Memory and Anticipation Processes and Their Significance for Social Security and Income Inequality. In *Maital, S., ed., Vol. 2*, 1988, pp. 731–51.

Prachowny, Martin F. J. Who Are the Volunteers in the Battle against Budget Deficits? *Public Choice*, August 1988, *58*(2), pp. 143–59.

Prade, Henri and Dubois, Didier. Decision Evaluation Methods under Uncertainty and Imprecision. In *Kacprzyk, J. and Fedrizzi, M., eds.*, 1988, pp. 48–65.

Pradhan, Hemanta K. Exchange Rate Variability of the Rupee and India's Exports. *Margin*, July–Sept. 1988, *20*(4), pp. 28–47.

Praet, Jean-Claude. Modélisation dynamique de l'investissement: analyse en termes de schémas d'anticipations. (With English summary.) *Cah. Écon. Bruxelles*, Fourth Trimester 1988, (120), pp. 433–56.

Praet, Peter and Vuchelen, Jef. Exogenous Shocks and Consumer Confidence in Four Major European Countries. *Appl. Econ.*, April 1988, *20*(4), pp. 561–67.

Prag, Jules B. Thinking about Government Deficits I: Domestic Ramifications. In *Brown, E., ed.*, 1988, pp. 202–07.

_____. Thinking about Government Deficits II: International Ramifications. In *Brown, E., ed.*, 1988, pp. 235–37.

Prager, Carol A. L. Poverty in North America: Losing Ground? *Can. Public Policy*, March 1988, *14*(1), pp. 52–65.

Práger, László. On Openness: An Approach to a Set of Problems. *Soviet E. Europ. Foreign Trade*, Summer 1988, *24*(2), pp. 93–107.

Prahalad, C. K. and Doz, Yves L. Quality of Management: An Emerging Source of Global Competitive Advantage? In *Hood, N. and Vahlne, J.-E., eds.*, 1988, pp. 345–69.

_____ and Hamel, G. Creating Global Strategic Capability. In *Hood, N. and Vahlne, J.-E., eds.*, 1988, pp. 5–39.

Prais, S. J. Two Approaches to the Economics

of Education: A Methodological Note. *Econ. Educ. Rev.*, 1988, *7*(2), pp. 257–60.

_____ and Wagner, Karin. Productivity and Management: The Training of Foremen in Britain and Germany. *Nat. Inst. Econ. Rev.*, February 1988, (123), pp. 34–47.

Prakash, B. A. Changing Structure of Employment in Kerala. *Margin*, Oct.–Dec. 1988, *21*(1), pp. 62–71.

Prakash, Om. On Coinage in Mughal India. *Indian Econ. Soc. Hist. Rev.*, Oct.–Dec. 1988, *25*(4), pp. 475–91.

Prakke, Frits. The Financing of Technical Innovation. In *Heertje, A., ed.*, 1988, pp. 71–100.

Pramaggiore, Maria T. and Crimmins, Eileen M. Changing Health of the Older Working-Age Population and Retirement Patterns over Time. In *Ricardo-Campbell, R. and Lazear, E. P., eds.*, 1988, pp. 132–52.

Prasad, S. S. R.; Unni, N. V. M. and Bowonder, B. Dynamics of Fuelwood Prices in India: Policy Implications. *World Devel.*, October 1988, *16*(10), pp. 1213–29.

Prasad, Y. Eswara. An Econometric Analysis of Cotton Production in Guntur District of Andhra Pradesh. *Margin*, Oct.–Dec. 1988, *21*(1), pp. 79–86.

Prasartset, Suthy. Technological Domination by the Transnational Corporation in Thailand. In *Teng, W. and Wang, N. T., eds.*, 1988, pp. 145–63.

Prasnikar, Janez and Svejnar, Jan. Economic Behavior of Yugoslav Enterprises. In *Jones, D. C. and Svejnar, J., eds.*, 1988, pp. 237–311.

Prat, Georges and Bethenod, Jean-Marie. Reformulation de la demande de monnaie et dynamique monetaire: France, 1964–1983. (A New Formulation of the "Standard" Model of Demand for Money. With English summary.) *Écon. Soc.*, January 1988, *22*(1), pp. 205–47.

Pratt, Edmund T., Jr. Changing Realities: The Need for Business–Government Cooperation. In *Feldstein, M., ed. (I)*, 1988, pp. 218–24.

_____. Growing to Serve the Global Marketplace. In *Rosow, J. M., ed.*, 1988, pp. 123–44.

Pratt, Geraldine and Hanson, Susan. Reconceptualizing the Links between Home and Work in Urban Geography. *Econ. Geogr.*, October 1988, *64*(4), pp. 299–321.

Pratt, John W. Aversion to One Risk in the Presence of Others. *J. Risk Uncertainty*, December 1988, *1*(4), pp. 395–413.

_____ and Schlaifer, Robert. On the Interpretation and Observation of Laws. *J. Econometrics*, Sept.–Oct. 1988, *39*(1–2), pp. 23–52.

Pratt, Michael D.; Reilly, Robert J. and Millner, Edward L. A Re-examination of Harrison's Experimental Test for Risk Aversion. *Econ. Letters*, 1988, *27*(4), pp. 317–19.

Pratt, Richard T. Functional Competition from Wall Street. In *Federal Home Loan Bank of San Francisco*, 1988, pp. 143–49.

Prebble, John. Recognition of Foreign Enterprises as Taxable Entities: New Zealand. In

International Fiscal Association, ed. (I), 1988, pp. 493–509.

Prebisch, Raúl. Dependence, Interdependence and Development. *CEPAL Rev.*, April 1988, (34), pp. 197–205.

Preckel, Paul V. and Hertel, Thomas W. Approximating Linear Programs with Summary Functions: Pseudodata with an Infinite Sample. *Amer. J. Agr. Econ.*, May 1988, 70(2), pp. 397–402.

_____ **and Hertel, Thomas W.** Commodity-Specific Effects of the Conservation Reserve Program. *J. Agr. Econ. Res.*, Summer 1988, 40(3), pp. 2–11.

Preeg, Ernest H. The Decline of the North–South Dichotomy: Policy Implications for a Changing International Economic Order. In *Yochelson, J., ed.*, 1988, pp. 77–95.

Pregibon, Daryl and Lubinsky, David. Data Analysis as Search. *J. Econometrics*, May–June 1988, 38(1–2), pp. 247–68.

Premo, Jerome C. Privatization in Practice: The Case of New Jersey Transit. In *Weicher, J. C., ed.*, 1988, pp. 16–20.

Prentice, Barry E. Harmonization of Farm Policy for Freer Interprovincial Trade: Discussion. *Can. J. Agr. Econ.*, Part 1, December 1988, 36(4), pp. 665–67.

_____ **and Menzie, Elmer L.** Formal and Informal Nontariff Barriers to Agricultural Trade between the United States and Canada. In *Allen, K. and Macmillan, K., eds.*, 1988, pp. 123–38.

Prentis, Roger A., et al. Pharmaceutical Innovation and R&D Investment in the UK. *Managerial Dec. Econ.*, September 1988, 9(3), pp. 197–203.

Prescott, David M.; Stengos, Thanasis and Moschini, Giancarlo. Nonparametric Kernel Estimation Applied to Forecasting: An Evaluation Based on the Bootstrap. *Empirical Econ.*, 1988, 13(3–4), pp. 141–54.

Prescott, Edward C. Robert M. Solow's Neoclassical Growth Model: An Influential Contribution to Economics. *Scand. J. Econ.*, 1988, 90(1), pp. 7–12.

_____ **and Kydland, Finn E.** The Workweek of Capital and Its Cyclical Implications. *J. Monet. Econ.*, March–May 1988, 21(2–3), pp. 343–60.

_____ **and Mehra, Rajnish.** The Equity Risk Premium: A Solution? *J. Monet. Econ.*, July 1988, 22(1), pp. 133–36.

_____; **Smith, Bruce D. and Boyd, John H.** Organizations in Economic Analysis. *Can. J. Econ.*, August 1988, 21(3), pp. 477–91.

Pressler, Jonathan. How to Avoid the Paretian–Libertarian Paradox: A Reply. *Econ. Philos.*, October 1988, 4(2), pp. 326–32.

Pressman, Steven. The Feminization of Poverty: Causes and Remedies. *Challenge*, March–April 1988, 31(2), pp. 57–61.

Preston, Anne E. The Effects of Property Rights on Labor Costs of Nonprofit Firms: An Application to the Day Care Industry. *J. Ind. Econ.*, March 1988, 36(3), pp. 337–50.

_____. The Nonprofit Firm: A Potential Solution to Inherent Market Failures. *Econ. Inquiry*, July 1988, 26(3), pp. 493–506.

Preston, I. P. and Besley, Timothy J. Invariance and the Axiomatics of Income Tax Progression: A Comment. *Bull. Econ. Res.*, April 1988, 40(2), pp. 159–63.

Preston, Lee E. and Windsor, Duane. Corporate Governance, Social Policy, and Social Performance in the Multinational Corporation. In *Preston, L. E., ed.*, 1988, pp. 45–58.

Preston, Samuel H. The Relation between Actual and Intrinsic Growth Rates: Reply. *Population Stud.*, November 1988, 42(3), pp. 495–501.

_____ **and Horiuchi, Shiro.** Age-Specific Growth Rates: The Legacy of Past Population Dynamics. *Demography*, August 1988, 25(3), pp. 429–41.

_____ **and Kono, Shigemi.** Trends in Well-Being of Children and the Elderly in Japan. In *Palmer, J. L.; Smeeding, T. and Torrey, B. B., eds.*, 1988, pp. 277–307.

Preusse, Heinz Gert. The Indirect Approach to Trade Liberalization: Dynamic Consideration on Liberalization-cum-Stabilization Policies in Latin America. *World Devel.*, August 1988, 16(8), pp. 883–97.

Prezas, Alexandros P. Interactions of the Firm's Real and Financial Decisions. *Appl. Econ.*, April 1988, 20(4), pp. 551–60.

Price, Catherine and Bradley, Ian. The Economic Regulation of Private Industries by Price Constraints. *J. Ind. Econ.*, September 1988, 37(1), pp. 99–106.

Price, Colin. Does Social Cost–Benefit Analysis Measure Overall Utility Change? *Econ. Letters*, 1988, 26(4), pp. 357–61.

Price, Kurt F. and Kominski, Gerald F. Using Patient Age in Defining DRGs for Medicare Payment. *Inquiry*, Winter 1988, 25(4), pp. 494–503.

Price, Richard Tudor. Dairy-Substitute Products: Impact on the Canadian Industry. *Can. J. Agr. Econ.*, Part 1, December 1988, 36(4), pp. 613–19.

Price, Robert and Bain, George Sayers. British Social Trends since 1900: The Labour Force. In *Halsey, A. H., ed.*, 1988, pp. 162–201.

Price, Simon. Unemployment and Worker Quality. In *Cross, R., ed.*, 1988, pp. 158–79.

_____ **and Chatterji, Monojit.** Unions, Dutch Disease and Unemployment. *Oxford Econ. Pap.*, June 1988, 40(2), pp. 302–21.

Prichard, J. Robert S. A Systematic Approach to Comparative Law: The Effect of Cost, Fee, and Financing Rules on the Development of the Substantive Law. *J. Legal Stud.*, June 1988, 17(2), pp. 451–75.

Priest, George L. The Disappearance of the Consumer from Modern Products Liability Law. In *Maynes, E. S. and ACCI Research Committee, eds.*, 1988, pp. 771–91.

_____. Products Liability Law and the Accident Rate. In *Litan, R. E. and Winston, C., eds.*, 1988, pp. 184–222.

Priestley, M. B. Current Developments in Time

Series Modelling. *J. Econometrics*, January 1988, *37*(1), pp. 67–86.

Primeaux, Walter J., Jr. What Can Regulators Regulate? The Case of Electric Utility Rates of Return. *Managerial Dec. Econ.*, June 1988, *9*(2), pp. 145–52.

_____ **and Nelson, Randy A.** The Effects of Competition on Transmission and Distribution Costs in the Municipal Electric Industry. *Land Econ.*, November 1988, *64*(4), pp. 338–46.

Primont, Daniel and Färe, Rolf. Efficiency Measures for Multiplant Firms with Limited Data. In *Eichhorn, W., ed.*, 1988, pp. 177–86.

Prindle, David F. Labor Union Ideology in the Screen Actors Guild. *Soc. Sci. Quart.*, September 1988, *69*(3), pp. 675–86.

Pringle, John J. and Wall, Larry D. Interest Rate Swaps: A Review of the Issues. *Fed. Res. Bank Atlanta Econ. Rev.*, Nov.–Dec. 1988, *73*(6), pp. 22–40.

Prisman, Eliezer Zeev and Dermody, Jaime Cuevas. Term Structure Multiplicity and Clientele in Markets with Transactions Costs and Taxes. *J. Finance*, September 1988, *43*(4), pp. 893–911.

_____ **and Pieptea, Dan R.** The Monday Effect and Speculative Opportunities in the Stock-Index Futures Market. In *Fabozzi, F. J., ed.*, 1988, pp. 319–28.

_____ **and Shores, Marilyn R.** Duration Measures for Specific Term Structure Estimations and Applications to Bond Portfolio Immunization. *J. Banking Finance*, September 1988, *12*(3), pp. 493–504.

Pristavko, G. V. and Sonin, I. M. Stochastic Models of Management of Parallel Multistage Programs. *Matekon*, Summer 1988, *24*(4), pp. 72–90.

Pritchett, J. W. and Garg, S. K. Pressure Interference Data Analysis for Two-Phase (Water/Steam) Geothermal Reservoirs. *Water Resources Res.*, June 1988, *24*(6), pp. 843–52.

Pritchett, S. Travis; Fields, Paige and Schmit, Joan T. Punitive Damages: Punishment or Further Compensation? *J. Risk Ins.*, September 1988, *55*(3), pp. 453–66.

Procter, Michael H.; Kaylen, Michael S. and Devino, Gary T. Optimal Use of Qualitative Models: An Application to Country Grain Elevator Bankruptcies. *Southern J. Agr. Econ.*, December 1988, *20*(2), pp. 119–25.

Pronzato, Luc and Walter, Eric. Robust Experiment Designs for Nonlinear Regression Models. In *Fedorov, V. and Lauter, H., eds.*, 1988, pp. 77–86.

Proops, John L. R. Energy Intensities, Input–Output Analysis and Economic Development. In *Ciaschini, M., ed.*, 1988, pp. 201–15.

Prosperetti, Luigi and Fiorentini, Gianluca. Conflittualità e dimensione d'impianto: Sviluppi teorici e risultanze empiriche. (Conflict and Manufacturers' Size: Theoretical Developments and Empirical Outcome. With English summary.) *Econ. Lavoro*, Apr.–June 1988, *22*(2), pp. 37–58.

Prosser, Richard and Baldwin, Nick. World Oil Market Simulation. *Energy Econ.*, July 1988, *10*(3), pp. 185–98.

Prost, Antoine. Catholic Conservatives, Population, and the Family in Twentieth Century France. *Population Devel. Rev.*, Supplement, 1988, *14*, pp. 147–64.

Protopapadakis, Aris A. and Benninga, Simon. The Equilibrium Pricing of Exchange Rates and Assets when Trade Takes Time. *J. Int. Money Finance*, June 1988, *7*(2), pp. 129–49.

_____ **and Flannery, Mark J.** From T-Bills to Common Stocks: Investigating the Generality of Intra-Week Return Seasonality. *J. Finance*, June 1988, *43*(2), pp. 431–50.

_____ **and Penati, Alessandro.** The Effect of Implicit Deposit Insurance on Banks' Portfolio Choices with an Application to International "Overexposure." *J. Monet. Econ.*, January 1988, *21*(1), pp. 107–26.

Prucha, Ingmar R. and Nadiri, M. Ishaq. On the Computation of Estimators in Systems with Implicitly Defined Variables. *Econ. Letters*, 1988, *26*(2), pp. 141–45.

Pruitt, Dean G.; McGillicuddy, Neil B. and Welton, Gary L. The Role of Caucusing in Community Mediation. *J. Conflict Resolution*, March 1988, *32*(1), pp. 181–202.

Pruitt, Stephen W.; Reilly, Robert J. and Hoffer, George E. The Effect of Media Presentation on the Formation of Economic Expectations: Some Initial Evidence. *J. Econ. Psych.*, September 1988, *9*(3), pp. 315–25.

_____**; Reilly, Robert J. and Hoffer, George E.** The Impact of Product Recalls on the Wealth of Sellers: A Reexamination. *J. Polit. Econ.*, June 1988, *96*(3), pp. 663–70.

_____**; Wei, K. C. John and White, Richard E.** The Impact of Union-Sponsored Boycotts on the Stock Prices of Target Firms. *J. Lab. Res.*, Summer 1988, *9*(3), pp. 285–89.

_____ **and White, Richard E.** The CRISMA Trading System: Who Says Technical Analysis Can't Beat the Market? *J. Portfol. Manage.*, Spring 1988, *14*(3), pp. 55–58.

Prust, Jim. Partial Recovery from the Economic Crisis. In *Marer, P. and Siwinski, W., eds.*, 1988, pp. 3–11.

Pryke, Richard. Richard Lecomber: A Memoir and Tribute. In *[Lecomber, R.]*, 1988, pp. 5–13.

Pryor, Edward T. and Long, John F. Comparative Demographic Effects of Canadian–U.S. Immigration Flows. *Statist. J.*, August 1988, *5*(2), pp. 135–57.

Pryor, Frederic L. Corporatism as an Economic System: A Review Essay. *J. Compar. Econ.*, September 1988, *12*(3), pp. 317–44.

_____. Marxist Regime Series III: Review Article. *J. Compar. Econ.*, June 1988, *12*(2), pp. 248–55.

Przeworska-Rolewicz, D. Smooth Solutions of Linear Equations with Scalar Coefficients in a Right Invertible Operator. In *Kurzhanski, A.; Neumann, K. and Pallaschke, D., eds.*, 1988, pp. 232–60.

Psacharopoulos, George. Education and Development: A Review. *World Bank Res. Observer*, January 1988, *3*(1), pp. 99–116.

——— and Steier, Francis. Education and the Labor Market in Venezuela, 1975–1984. *Econ. Educ. Rev.*, 1988, *7*(3), pp. 321–32.

Pucik, Vladimir. Strategic Alliances with the Japanese: Implications for Human Resource Management. In *Contractor, F. J. and Lorange, P.*, 1988, pp. 487–98.

Puffert, Douglas J. and Boskin, Michael J. The Financial Impact of Social Security by Cohort under Alternative Financing Assumptions. In *Ricardo-Campbell, R. and Lazear, E. P., eds.*, 1988, pp. 207–32.

Pugach, Noel H.; Tomasson, Richard F. and Nash, Gerald D. An Overview of American Social Security, 1935–1985. In *Nash, G. D.; Pugach, N. H. and Tomasson, R. F., eds.*, 1988, pp. 3–28.

Pugel, Thomas A. and White, Lawrence J. An Empirical Analysis of the Underwriting Spreads on Initial Public Offerings. *Quart. Rev. Econ. Bus.*, Winter 1988, *28*(4), pp. 6–20.

Pugliaresi, Lucian. Policy Tests for Energy Security. In *Fried, E. R. and Blandin, N. M., eds.*, 1988, pp. 111–15.

Puhakka, Mikko and Böhm, Volker. Rationing and Optimality in Overlapping Generations Models. *Scand. J. Econ.*, 1988, *90*(2), pp. 225–32.

Puig, Jean-Pierre. The Forecasting of Employment and Unemployment Using the French Model DMS. In *Hopkins, M. J. D., ed.*, 1988, pp. 43–77.

Puig Junoy, Jaume. Gasto farmacéutico en España: efectos de la participación del usuario en el coste. (With English summary.) *Invest. Econ.*, January 1988, *12*(1), pp. 45–68.

Puiu, Al. Traditions and Prospects in the Economic Higher Education. *Econ. Computat. Cybern. Stud. Res.*, 1988, *23*(3), pp. 13–24.

Pullen, John M. Recent Literature on Malthus: Commentary. In *Thweatt, W. O., ed.*, 1988, pp. 85–102.

Pulley, Lawrence B. and Rapping, Leonard A. Speculation, Deregulation, and the Interest Rate. In *Rapping, L. A.*, 1988, *1985*, pp. 126–35.

Pulver, Glen C. Needed Institutional Change to Provide Local Infrastructure. In *Johnson, T. G.; Deaton, B. J. and Segarra, E., eds.*, 1988, pp. 215–27.

——— and Hustedde, Ronald J. Regional Variables That Influence the Allocation of Venture Capital: The Role of Banks. *Rev. Reg. Stud.*, Spring 1988, *18*(2), pp. 1–9.

———; Rogers, Glenn and Shaffer, Ron E. Identification of Local Capital Markets for Policy Research. *Rev. Reg. Stud.*, Winter 1988, *18*(1), pp. 55–66.

Pumain, Denise. Interregional Migration in Individual Countries: France. In *Weidlich, W. and Haag, G., eds.*, 1988, pp. 131–53.

Puntanen, S.; Nummi, Tapio and Nurhonen, Markku. Computer-Aided Illustration of Re-

gression Diagnostics. In *Edwards, D. and Raun, N. E., eds.*, 1988, pp. 93–98.

Punzo, Lionello F. Harrodian Macrodynamics in Generalized Coordinates. In *[Goodwin, R. M.]*, 1988, pp. 30–52.

Purcaru, I. On a Generalization of the Measure of Information. *Econ. Computat. Cybern. Stud. Res.*, 1988, *23*(2), pp. 43–45.

Purcell, John. The Structure and Function of Personnel Management. In *Marginson, P., et al.*, 1988, pp. 51–79.

Purcell, Kate and Elias, Peter. Women and Paid Work: Prospects for Equality. In *Hunt, A., ed.*, 1988, pp. 196–221.

Purcell, Randall B. Help the NICs. *Challenge*, May–June 1988, *31*(3), pp. 55–57.

Puri, Anil K. and Van Lierop, Johannes. Forecasting Housing Starts. *Int. J. Forecasting*, 1988, *4*(1), pp. 125–34.

Purohit, B. C. Firm Size and Saving Behaviour: A Study of Selected Indian Engineering Firms. *Indian Econ. Rev.*, Jan.–June 1988, *23*(1), pp. 107–20.

Purohit, Mahesh C. Taxation of Contracts for Work: Policy Imperatives for a Sales Tax System in a Developing Country: India. *Bull. Int. Fiscal Doc.*, January 1988, *42*(1), pp. 31–33.

Purtill, A.; Hall, N. and Fraser, L. Supply Response in Broadacre Agriculture. *Rev. Marketing Agr. Econ.*, December 1988, *56*(3), pp. 361–74.

Purtschert, Robert. Möglichkeiten und Grenzen der Gemeinschaftswerbung. (With English summary.) *Z. Betriebswirtshaft*, April 1988, *58*(4), pp. 521–34.

Purvis, Douglas; Backus, David and Devereux, Michael. A Positive Theory of Fiscal Policy in Open Economies. In *Frenkel, J. A., ed.*, 1988, pp. 173–91.

Pusateri, C. Joseph. Westinghouse Broadcasting and the Development of Integrated Group Operations in the Broadcasting Industry. In *Perkins, E. J., ed.*, 1988, pp. 1–12.

Putler, Daniel S. and Zilberman, David. Computer Use in Agriculture: Evidence from Tulare County, California. *Amer. J. Agr. Econ.*, November 1988, *70*(4), pp. 790–802.

Putnam, Robert D. Diplomacy and Domestic Politics: The Logic of Two-Level Games. *Int. Organ.*, Summer 1988, *42*(3), pp. 427–60.

Puto, Christopher P.; King, Ronald H. and Patton, W. E., III. Individual and Joint Decision-Making in Industrial Purchasing. In *Woodside, A. G., ed.*, 1988, pp. 95–117.

Putterman, Louis. Asset Specificity, Governance, and the Employment Relation. In *Dlugos, G.; Dorow, W. and Weiermair, K., eds.*, 1988, pp. 45–62.

———. The Firm as Association versus the Firm as Commodity: Efficiency, Rights, and Ownership. *Econ. Philos.*, October 1988, *4*(2), pp. 243–66.

———. Marx and Disequilibrium: Comment. *Econ. Philos.*, October 1988, *4*(2), pp. 333–36.

———. People's Republic of China: Systemic and Structural Change in a North China Township.

Amer. J. Agr. Econ., May 1988, *70*(2), pp. 423–30.

_____. Ration Subsidies and Incentives in the Pre-reform Chinese Commune. *Economica*, May 1988, *55*(218), pp. 235–47.

_____. Regulation by Consensus: The Practice of International Investment Agreements: Comment. *J. Inst. Theoretical Econ.*, February 1988, *144*(1), pp. 172–75.

_____ and Skillman, Gil, Jr. The Incentive Effects of Monitoring under Alternative Compensation Schemes. *Int. J. Ind. Organ.*, March 1988, *6*(1), pp. 109–19.

Puttick, Ed and Dex, Shirley. Parental Employment and Family Formation. In *Hunt, A., ed.*, 1988, pp. 123–49.

Puy Fraga, Pedro and Faiña Medin, J. Andrés. A Framework for a Public Choice Analysis of the European Community. *Econ. Scelte Pubbliche/J. Public Finance Public Choice*, May–Aug. 1988, *6*(2), pp. 141–58.

Pyatt, Graham. A SAM Approach to Modeling. *J. Policy Modeling*, Fall 1988, *10*(3), pp. 327–52.

Pyke, Thomas N., Jr. Satellite Remote Sensing for Resources Development. In *Egan, J. J., et al.*, 1988, pp. 157–66.

Pyle, Kenneth B. Japan, the World, and the Twenty-first Century. In *Inoguchi, T. and Okimoto, D. I., eds.*, 1988, pp. 446–86.

Pyo, Hak K. Estimates of Capital Stock and Capital/Output Coefficients by Industries: Korea (1953–86). *Int. Econ. J.*, Autumn 1988, *2*(3), pp. 79–121.

Qian, GuiRu. A View from a Commercial Official of the People's Republic of China. In *Walker, C. E. and Bloomfield, M. A., eds.*, 1988, pp. 83–91.

Qian, Yingyi. Urban and Rural Household Saving in China. *Int. Monet. Fund Staff Pap.*, December 1988, *35*(4), pp. 592–627.

Quadrio-Curzio, Alberto and Antonelli, Gilberto. The Development of an Agro-technological System between Market Pulls and Structural Pushes. In *Antonelli, G. and Quadrio-Curzio, A., eds.*, 1988, pp. 1–16.

Quaglieri, Philip L. The New People of Power: The Backgrounds and Careers of Top Labor Leaders. *J. Lab. Res.*, Summer 1988, *9*(3), pp. 271–84.

Quan, Nguyen T. The Prediction Sum of Squares as a General Measure for Regression Diagnostics. *J. Bus. Econ. Statist.*, October 1988, *6*(4), pp. 501–04.

_____ and Koo, Anthony Y. C. Concentration of Land Holdings and Income: Reply. *J. Devel. Econ.*, September 1988, *29*(2), pp. 233–34.

Quandt, Richard E. and Asch, Peter. Betting Bias in 'Exotic' Bets. *Econ. Letters*, 1988, *28*(3), pp. 215–19.

_____; Charemza, Wojciech and Gronicki, Miroslaw. Modelling Parallel Markets in Centrally Planned Economies: The Case of the Automobile Market in Poland. *Europ. Econ. Rev.*, April 1988, *32*(4), pp. 861–83.

_____ and Goldfeld, Stephen M. Budget Constraints, Bailouts, and the Firm under Central Planning. *J. Compar. Econ.*, December 1988, *12*(4), pp. 502–20.

_____; Yeo, Stephen and Portes, Richard. Tests of the Chronic Shortage Hypothesis: The Case of Poland. *Rev. Econ. Statist.*, May 1988, *70*(2), pp. 288–95.

Quandt, William B. The Middle East Factor. In *Fried, E. R. and Blandin, N. M., eds.*, 1988, pp. 45–48.

Quddus, Munir; Liu, Jin-Tan and Butler, J. S. Variability of Inflation and the Dispersion of Relative Prices: Evidence from the Chinese Hyperinflation of 1946–1949. *Econ. Letters*, 1988, *27*(3), pp. 239–44.

Quenan, C.; Sarry, M.-C. and Norel, P. Stratégies bancaires et risque-pays. (International Banking Strategies and Country-Risk. With English summary.) *Écon. Appl.*, 1988, *41*(4), pp. 857–72.

Quesem, Md. Abul. Farmers' Participation in the Paddy Markets, Their Marketed Surplus and Factors Affecting It in Bangladesh: A Reply. *Bangladesh Devel. Stud.*, March 1988, *16*(1), pp. 109–11.

Quible, Zane and Hammer, Jane N. Office Automation's Impact on Personnel. In *Timpe, A. D., ed.*, 1988, *1984*, pp. 238–45.

Quibria, M. G. Migration, Trade Unions, and the Informal Sector: A Note on Calvo. *Int. Econ. Rev.*, August 1988, *29*(3), pp. 557–63.

_____. A Note on International Migration, Nontraded Goods and Economic Welfare in the Source Country. *J. Devel. Econ.*, May 1988, *28*(3), pp. 377–87.

_____. On Generalizing the Economic Analysis of International Migration: A Note. *Can. J. Econ.*, November 1988, *21*(4), pp. 874–76.

Quick, Perry D. and McKee, Michael J. Sales Tax on Services: Revenue or Reform? *Nat. Tax J.*, September 1988, *41*(3), pp. 395–409.

Quigg, Donald J. Intellectual Property Rights, Technological Change, and Economic Growth: Discussion: Safeguarding Intellectual Property—Stimulus to Economic Expansion. In *Walker, C. E. and Bloomfield, M. A., eds.*, 1988, pp. 33–46.

Quiggin, John. Murray River Salinity—An Illustrative Model. *Amer. J. Agr. Econ.*, August 1988, *70*(3), pp. 635–45.

_____. Private and Common Property Rights in the Economics of the Environment. *J. Econ. Issues*, December 1988, *22*(4), pp. 1071–87.

_____. Scattered Landholdings in Common Property Systems. *J. Econ. Behav. Organ.*, March 1988, *9*(2), pp. 187–201.

Quijano, Alicia M. Capital Expenditures by Majority-Owned Foreign Affiliates of U.S. Companies, 1988 and 1989. *Surv. Curr. Bus.*, September 1988, *68*(9), pp. 26–32.

Quilkey, John. Teaching Marketing. *Rev. Marketing Agr. Econ.*, August 1988, *56*(2), pp. 224–25.

Quinlivan, Gary M. Oil Price Shocks and the Exchange Rate: A Reply. In *Pennsylvania Economic Association*, 1988, pp. 372–76.

Quinn, Brian. The International Transmission of Asset Price Volatility: Commentary. In *Federal Reserve Bank of Kansas City*, 1988, pp. 121–26.

Quinn, Dennis P. Investment Incentives: A Five Country Test of the Lindblom Hypothesis. In *Preston, L. E., ed.*, 1988, pp. 87–111.

Quinn, James Brian. Services Technology and Manufacturing: Cornerstones of the U.S. Economy. In *Guile, B. R. and Quinn, J. B., eds. (I)*, 1988, pp. 9–35.

———. Technology in Services: Past Myths and Future Challenges. In *Guile, B. R. and Quinn, J. B., eds. (II)*, 1988, pp. 16–46.

——— **and Doorley, Thomas L.** Key Policy Issues Posed by Services. In *Guile, B. R. and Quinn, J. B., eds. (II)*, 1988, pp. 211–34.

——— **and Guile, Bruce R.** Managing Innovation in Services. In *Guile, B. R. and Quinn, J. B., eds. (I)*, 1988, pp. 1–8.

Quinn, John; Koziara, Edward and Yan, Chiou-Shuang. Other Measures of the Economic Performance of Presidents. In *Pennsylvania Economic Association*, 1988, pp. 270–78.

Quinn, Victoria, et al. Crisis-Proofing the Economy: The Response of Botswana to Economic Recession and Drought. In *Cornia, G. A.; Jolly, R. and Stewart, F., eds.*, 1988, pp. 3–27.

Quintas, Luis G. Constructing Bimatrix Games with Unique Equilibrium Points. *Math. Soc. Sci.*, February 1988, *15*(1), pp. 61–72.

———. Uniqueness of Nash Equilibrium Points in Bimatrix Games. *Econ. Letters*, 1988, *27*(2), pp. 123–27.

Quintieri, Beniamino and Rosati, Furio Camillo. Fiscal Policy and Labor Supply. *Public Finance*, 1988, *43*(3), pp. 425–39.

Quintyn, Marc. Money Demand in Belgium—One Step Ahead in Search of Its Stability. *Cah. Écon. Bruxelles*, First Trimester 1988, (117), pp. 37–65.

Quirk, James and Fort, Rodney D. Normal Backwardation and the Inventory Effect. *J. Polit. Econ.*, February 1988, *96*(1), pp. 81–99.

Quirk, Peter J. and Schoofs, Viktor. Forward Foreign Exchange Markets in LDCs. *Finance Develop.*, September 1988, *25*(3), pp. 36–39.

Quirmbach, Herman C. Comparative Statics for Oligopoly: Demand Shift Effects. *Int. Econ. Rev.*, August 1988, *29*(3), pp. 451–59.

Quiroz, Jorge; Barahona, Pablo and Valdés, Alberto. Reformas económicas en la agricultura y respuesta de la producción agregada: Chile 1960–1987. (With English summary.) *Cuadernos Econ.*, December 1988, *25*(76), pp. 389–403.

Quizon, Jaime B. and Binswanger, Hans P. Distributional Consequences of Alternative Food Policies in India. In *Pinstrup-Andersen, P., ed.*, 1988, pp. 301–19.

Qureshi, Moeen A. Lending Strategies for Agricultural Development. In *Roberts, C., ed.*, 1988, pp. 51–58.

Qureshi, Sarfraz Khan. Conditions of Agricultural Growth in Developing Countries: Comments.

Pakistan Devel. Rev., Part 1, Winter 1988, *27*(4), pp. 471–72.

———; **Ghani, Ejaz and Mushtaq, Muhammad.** Taxes and Subsidies on Agricultural Producers as Elements of Intersectoral Transfer of Resources: Magnitude of the Transfer and Search for Policy Options. *Pakistan Devel. Rev.*, Part 2, Winter 1988, *27*(4), pp. 551–56.

Quyen, N. V. The Optimal Depletion and Exploration of a Nonrenewable Resource. *Econometrica*, November 1988, *56*(6), pp. 1467–71.

ten Raa, Thijs. An Alternative Treatment of Secondary Products in Input–Output Analysis: Frustration. *Rev. Econ. Statist.*, August 1988, *70*(3), pp. 535–38.

——— **and Berliant, Marcus.** A Foundation of Location Theory: Consumer Preferences and Demand. *J. Econ. Theory*, April 1988, *44*(2), pp. 336–53.

Raab, Michael S. The Transparency Theory: An Alternative Approach to Glass–Steagall Issues. *Yale Law J.*, March 1988, *97*(4), pp. 603–22.

Raab, Raymond L. and Wong, Shee Q. A Note on Causality and the Structure–Performance Controversy. *Rev. Ind. Organ.*, Spring 1988, *3*(3), pp. 45–53.

van Raad, Kees. Netherlands: Issues in the Application of Tax Treaty Non-discrimination Clauses. *Bull. Int. Fiscal Doc.*, Aug.–Sept. 1988, *42*(8–9), pp. 347–51.

———. Recognition of Foreign Enterprises as Taxable Entities: General Report. In *International Fiscal Association, ed. (I)*, 1988, pp. 19–66.

van Raaij, W. Fred. Information Processing and Decision Making: Cognitive Aspects of Economic Behaviour. In *van Raaij, W. F.; van Veldhoven, G. M. and Wärneryd, K.-E., eds.*, 1988, pp. 74–106.

———. The Use of Natural Resources. In *van Raaij, W. F.; van Veldhoven, G. M. and Wärneryd, K.-E., eds.*, 1988, pp. 639–55.

——— **and Pieters, Rik G. M.** Functions and Management of Affect: Applications to Economic Behavior. *J. Econ. Psych.*, June 1988, *9*(2), pp. 251–82.

——— **and Pieters, Rik G. M.** The Role of Affect in Economic Behavior. In *van Raaij, W. F.; van Veldhoven, G. M. and Wärneryd, K.-E., eds.*, 1988, pp. 108–42.

Rabeau, Yves and Duguay, Pierre. A Simulation Model of Macroeconomic Effects of Deficit. *J. Macroecon.*, Fall 1988, *10*(4), pp. 539–64.

Rabianski, Joseph and Nelson, Theron R. Consumer Preferences in Housing Market Analysis: An Application of Multidimensional Scaling Techniques. *Amer. Real Estate Urban Econ. Assoc. J.*, Summer 1988, *16*(2), pp. 138–59.

Rabin, Alan and Keilany, Ziad. Absolute Liquidity Preference and the Pigou Effect: A Reply [A Note on the Incompatibility of the Pigou Effect and a Liquidity Trap]. *J. Post Keynesian Econ.*, Summer 1988, *10*(4), pp. 655–57.

Rabino, Giovanni and Munz, Martin. Interregional Migration in Individual Countries: Italy.

In *Weidlich, W. and Haag, G., eds.,* 1988, pp. 185–221.

Rabinowicz, Wlodzimierz. Ratifiability and Stability. In *Gärdenfors, P. and Sahlin, N.-E., eds.,* 1988, pp. 406–25.

Rabinowitz, Gad and Ritchken, Peter H. Capital Budgeting Using Contingent Claims Analysis: A Tutorial. In *Fabozzi, F. J., ed.,* 1988, pp. 119–43.

Rabushka, Alvin. Economic, Civil, and Political Freedoms: The Cases of Singapore and Hong Kong. In *Walker, M. A., ed. (I),* 1988, pp. 151–83.

_____. The Tax Reform Act of 1986: Concentrated Costs, Diffuse Benefits—An Inversion of Public Choice. *Contemp. Policy Issues,* October 1988, *6*(4), pp. 50–64.

_____ and Hall, Robert E. An Efficient, Equitable Tax for the 1990s. In *Anderson, A. and Bark, D. L., eds.,* 1988, pp. 301–10.

Raczkowski, Stanislaw. Factors Influencing Creditworthiness. In *Marer, P. and Siwinski, W., eds.,* 1988, pp. 165–73.

Raczynski, Dagmar. Social Policy, Poverty, and Vulnerable Groups: Children in Chile. In *Cornia, G. A.; Jolly, R. and Stewart, F., eds.,* 1988, pp. 57–92.

_____ and Serrano, Claudia. Planificación para el desarrollo local? La experiencia en algunos municipios de Santiago. (Planning for Local Development? The Experience of Some Municipalities in Santiago. With English summary.) *Colección Estud. CIEPLAN,* June 1988, (24), pp. 37–62.

Radaelli, Giorgio. EMS Stability, Capital Controls, and Foreign Exchange Market Intervention. *Greek Econ. Rev.,* 1988, *10*(1), pp. 133–61.

Radakovic, J.; Dobric, V. and Momirovic, Konstantin. An Expert System for the Interpretation of Results of Canonical Covariance Analysis. In *Edwards, D. and Raun, N. E., eds.,* 1988, pp. 135–41.

Radecki, Lawrence J. and Reinhart, Vincent. The Globalization of Financial Markets and the Effectiveness of Monetary Policy Instruments. *Fed. Res. Bank New York Quart. Rev.,* Autumn 1988, *13*(3), pp. 18–27.

Radermacher, F. J.; Bartusch, M. and Möhring, R. H. M-Machine Unit Time Scheduling: A Report on Ongoing Research. In *Kurzhanski, A.; Neumann, K. and Pallaschke, D., eds.,* 1988, pp. 165–212.

Radice, Hugo. Keynes and the Policy of Practical Protectionism. In *Hillard, J., ed.,* 1988, pp. 153–71.

Radner, Daniel B. Interagency Data Matching Projects for Research Purposes: Commentary. *Soc. Sec. Bull.,* July 1988, *51*(7), pp. 22, 56–57.

Radner, Roy. A Behavioral Model of Cost Reduction. In *Earl, P. E., ed.,* Vol. 1, 1988, *1975,* pp. 381–402.

_____. Collusive Behavior in Noncooperative Epsilon-Equilibria of Oligopolies with Long but Finite Lives. In *Daughety, A. F., ed.,* 1988, *1980,* pp. 122–41.

Radonja, Pero J. Optimum State Estimation Using a New Class of Robust Doubly Optimized Recursive Estimators. In *Iri, M. and Yajima, K., eds.,* 1988, pp. 119–28.

Radosevich, George. Legal Considerations for Coping with Externalities in Irrigated Agriculture. In *O'Mara, G. T., ed.,* 1988, pp. 34–46.

Radosh, Jerome and Pitts, Robert A. Beyond Wage Differentials as a Criterion in Selecting an Offshore Manufacturing Site: The Case of Tuna Processing in Thailand. In *Pennsylvania Economic Association,* 1988, pp. 404–16.

Radovanac, Mirko and Willumsen, L. G. Testing the Practical Value of the UMOT Model. *Int. J. Transport Econ.,* June 1988, *15*(2), pp. 203–23.

Rădulescu, M. and Rădulescu, S. Optimizations in Distributed Database Systems. *Econ. Computat. Cybern. Stud. Res.,* 1988, *23*(4), pp. 51–65.

Rădulescu, S. and Rădulescu, M. Optimizations in Distributed Database Systems. *Econ. Computat. Cybern. Stud. Res.,* 1988, *23*(4), pp. 51–65.

Radvanyi, Jean. The Experiments in Georgia, 1974–1984: Quest for a New Organization in the Soviet Agricultural System. In *Brada, J. C. and Wadekin, K.-E., eds.,* 1988, pp. 110–22.

Radzicki, Michael J. Institutional Dynamics: An Extension of the Institutionalist Approach to Socioeconomic Analysis. *J. Econ. Issues,* September 1988, *22*(3), pp. 633–65.

_____. A Note on Kelsey's "The Economics of Chaos or the Chaos of Economics." *Oxford Econ. Pap.,* December 1988, *40*(4), pp. 692–93.

Raeside, R. The Use of Sigmoids in Modelling and Forecasting Human Populations. *J. Roy. Statist. Soc.,* 1988, *151*(3), pp. 499–513.

Rafalko, Robert J. Henry George and the Contemporary Debate over Industrial Protectionism. *Amer. J. Econ. Soc.,* January 1988, *47*(1), pp. 111–25.

Raff, Daniel M. G. Wage Determination Theory and the Five-Dollar Day at Ford. *J. Econ. Hist.,* June 1988, *48*(2), pp. 387–99.

Raffe, David; Garner, Catherine and Main, Brian G. M. The Distribution of School-Leaver Unemployment within Scottish Cities. *Urban Stud.,* April 1988, *25*(2), pp. 133–44.

Raffiee, Kambiz and Wendel, Jeanne. The Effects of Alternative Regulatory Policies on Utility Investment Strategies. *Southern Econ. J.,* April 1988, *54*(4), pp. 840–54.

Rafiquzzaman, M. Invention, Market Structure, Cost Reduction Uncertainty and the Optimal Patent Term. *J. Econ. (Z. Nationalökon.),* 1988, *48*(3), pp. 303–12.

Rafuse, Robert W., Jr. A Strategy for Intergovernmental Fiscal Reform in the Remainder of the Eighties. In *Bell, M. E., ed.,* 1988, pp. 267–96.

Ragan, James F., Jr. and Tremblay, Carol Horton. Testing for Employee Discrimination by Race and Sex. *J. Human Res.*, Winter 1988, *23*(1), pp. 123–37.

Raghuprasad, Shailaja and Iyenger, N. Sreenivasa. Estimation of Additive Engel Curves in the Presence of Heteroscedasticity. *J. Quant. Econ.*, July 1988, *4*(2), pp. 329–39.

Rahardjo, M. Dawam. Efficiency and Production Management in Small and Medium Businesses: The Indonesian Case. In *James, K. and Akrasanee, N., eds.*, 1988, pp. 19–54.

Rahiala, Markku and Teräsvirta, Timo. Formation of Firms' Production Decisions in Finnish Manufacturing Industries. *J. Appl. Econometrics*, April 1988, *3*(2), pp. 125–37.

Rahman, Abdul H. and Cozier, Barry V. Stock Returns, Inflation, and Real Activity in Canada. *Can. J. Econ.*, November 1988, *21*(4), pp. 759–74.

Rahman, Atiq and Islam, Rizwanul. Labour Use in Rural Bangladesh—An Empirical Analysis. *Bangladesh Devel. Stud.*, December 1988, *16*(4), pp. 1–40.

Rahman, Atiur and Hossain, S. M. Demand Constraints and the Future Viability of Grameen Bank Credit Programme—An Econometric Study of the Expenditure Pattern of Rural Households. *Bangladesh Devel. Stud.*, June 1988, *16*(2), pp. 1–20.

Rahman, Pk. Md. Motiur. Some Aspects of Income Distribution in Rural Bangladesh. *Appl. Econ.*, August 1988, *20*(8), pp. 1007–15.

Rahmeyer, Fritz. An Evolutionary Approach to Inflation: Prices, Productivity, and Innovation. In *Hanusch, H., ed.*, 1988, pp. 205–38.

Rahn, Richard. Supply-Side Success. In *Boaz, D., ed.*, 1988, pp. 71–79.

Rahuma, Ali A. and Veeman, Terrence S. Productivity Growth in the Prairie Grain Sector and Its Major Soil Zones, 1960s to 1980s. *Can. J. Agr. Econ.*, Part 2, December 1988, *36*(4), pp. 857–70.

Raiatskas, R. L., et al. The Development of Mathematical Economic Methods: Results, Problems, Prospects (Continued). *Matekon*, Winter 1988–89, *25*(2), pp. 62–87.

Raico, Ralph. John Prince Smith and the German Free-Trade Movement. In *[Rothbard, M. N.]*, 1988, pp. 341–51.

Raiffa, Howard and Bell, David E. Marginal Value and Intrinsic Risk Aversion. In *Bell, D. E.; Raiffa, H. and Tversky, A., eds.*, 1988, pp. 384–97.

_____ and Bell, David E. Risky Choice Revisited. In *Bell, D. E.; Raiffa, H. and Tversky, A., eds.*, 1988, pp. 99–112.

_____; Tversky, Amos and Bell, David E. Descriptive, Normative, and Prescriptive Interactions in Decision Making. In *Bell, D. E.; Raiffa, H. and Tversky, A., eds.*, 1988, pp. 9–30.

Raikhy, P. S. Public Sector and Resource Mobilisation in Punjab. In *Raikhy, P. S. and Gill, S. S., eds.*, 1988, pp. 53–64.

_____ and Bhushan, Bharat. Role of Financial Institutions—An Inter State Analysis. In *Raikhy, P. S. and Gill, S. S., eds.*, 1988, pp. 152–68.

Raiklin, Ernest. On the Nature and Origin of Soviet Turnover Taxes. *Int. J. Soc. Econ.*, 1988, *15*(5–6), pp. 3–64.

_____. The Soviet Union in Transition (The Question is Open to Discussion). *Int. J. Soc. Econ.*, 1988, *15*(7), pp. 5–36.

_____ and Gillette, Charles C. The Nature of Contemporary Soviet Commodity Production. *Int. J. Soc. Econ.*, 1988, *15*(5–6), pp. 65–136.

_____ and McCormick, Ken. Soviet Men on the Road to Utopia: A Moral–Psychological Sketch. *Int. J. Soc. Econ.*, 1988, *15*(10), pp. 3–62.

_____ and McCormick, Ken. Three Views of Productive Labor. In *Missouri Valley Economic Assoc.*, 1988, pp. 141–44.

Railton, Peter. A Deductive–Nomological Model of Probabilistic Explanation. In *Pitt, J. C., ed.*, 1988, *1978*, pp. 119–35.

Rainelli, P. and Bonnieux, F. Agricultural Policy and Environment in Developed Countries. *Europ. Rev. Agr. Econ.*, 1988, *15*(2–3), pp. 263–81.

Rainwater, Julie; Silver, Steven D. and Cohen, Bernard P. Group Structure and Information Exchange in Innovative Problem Solving. In *Lawler, E. J. and Markovsky, B., eds.*, 1988, pp. 169–94.

Rainwater, Lee; Rein, Martin and Esping-Andersen, Gosta. Institutional and Political Factors Affecting the Well-Being of the Elderly. In *Palmer, J. L.; Smeeding, T. and Torrey, B. B., eds.*, 1988, pp. 333–50.

Raisian, John and Hashimoto, Masanori. The Structure and Short-Run Adaptability of Labor Markets in Japan and the United States. In *Hart, R. A., ed.*, 1988, pp. 314–40.

_____; Ward, Michael P. and Welch, Finis R. Implementing Comparable Worth: Conceptual Issues and Impacts. In *Mangum, G. and Philips, P., eds.*, 1988, pp. 183–200.

Raitz, Karl. Advantages of Place as Perceived by Sunbelt Promoters. *Growth Change*, Fall 1988, *19*(4), pp. 14–29.

Raj, Baldev and Siklos, Pierre L. The Role of Fiscal Policy in the St. Louis Model: Nonparametric Estimates for a Small Open Economy. *Empirical Econ.*, 1988, *13*(3–4), pp. 169–86.

_____ and Siklos, Pierre L. Some Qualms about the Test of the Institutional Hypothesis of the Long-run Behavior of Velocity. *Econ. Inquiry*, July 1988, *26*(3), pp. 537–45.

Raj, S. P. and Krishnamurthi, Lakshman. A Model of Brand Choice and Purchase Quantity Price Sensitivities. *Marketing Sci.*, Winter 1988, *7*(1), pp. 1–20.

Raja, Tariq Aslam; Mohammad, Ali and Afzal, Mohammad. Some Differentials in Infant and Child Mortality Risks in Pakistan 1962–1986. *Pakistan Devel. Rev.*, Part 2, Winter 1988, *27*(4), pp. 635–42.

Rajan, Roby. Entrepreneurship and Rent Seeking

in India. *Cato J.*, Spring–Summer 1988, *8*(1), pp. 165–84.

Rajapatirana, Sarath. Foreign Trade and Economic Development: Sri Lanka's Experience. *World Devel.*, October 1988, *16*(10), pp. 1143–57.

Rajdl, Lubomír. Stocks—Impediment and Reserve. *Czech. Econ. Digest.*, August 1988, (5), pp. 26–43.

Rakitskii, B. Problems of Restructuring the Political Economy of Socialism. *Prob. Econ.*, August 1988, *31*(4), pp. 24–41.

Rakodi, Carole. Upgrading in Chawama, Lusaka: Displacement or Differentiation? *Urban Stud.*, August 1988, *25*(4), pp. 297–318.

Rakshit, Mihir. Uses and Abuses of Instruments for Resource Mobilization: The Indian Experience. In *Lucas, R. E. B. and Papanek, G. F., eds.*, 1988, pp. 319–42.

Ralambondrainy, H.; Diday, E. and Gettler-Summa, M. Data Analysis and Expert Systems: Generating Rules from Data. In *Gaul, W. and Schader, M., eds.*, 1988, pp. 161–73.

Rall, Wilhelm. Strategic Planning in a Changing Competitive Environment. In *Saunders, C. T., ed.*, 1988, pp. 315–29.

Ram, Bonnie; Nkomo, Jabavu C. and Robinson, Peter B. Industrial Energy Consumption, Conservation Strategies and Policy Options in Zimbabwe. In *Hosier, R. H., ed. (II)*, 1988, pp. 26–49.

Ram, Rati. Additional Evidence on Causality between Government Revenue and Government Expenditure. *Southern Econ. J.*, January 1988, *54*(3), pp. 763–69.

———. Economic Development and Income Inequality: Further Evidence on the U-Curve Hypothesis. *World Devel.*, November 1988, *16*(11), pp. 1371–76.

———. Inflation and Relative-Price Variability: Effect of Temporal Aggregation. *Econ. Letters*, 1988, *28*(2), pp. 141–46.

———. A Multicountry Perspective on Causality between Government Revenue and Government Expenditure. *Public Finance*, 1988, *43*(2), pp. 261–70.

———. Relation between Inflation and Relative-Price Variability in the United States: Evidence from Data for the 1980s. *Econ. Letters*, 1988, *27*(2), pp. 129–32.

——— and **Singh, Ram D.** Farm Households in Rural Burkina Faso: Some Evidence on Allocative and Direct Return to Schooling, and Male–Female Labor Productivity Differentials. *World Devel.*, March 1988, *16*(3), pp. 419–24.

Ramachandran, Padma. HRD for Training Institutions. In *Kohli, U. and Gautam, V., eds.*, 1988, pp. 257–63.

Ramachandran, S. and Biswas, D. K. Infrastructure Development: The Indian Perspective. In *Research and Info. System for the Non-aligned and Other Developing Countries*, 1988, pp. 443–51.

Raman, K. K.; Benson, Earl D. and Marks, Barry R. Tax Effort as an Indicator of Fiscal

Stress. *Public Finance Quart.*, April 1988, *16*(2), pp. 203–18.

Ramanujam, Vasudevan and Venkatraman, N. Modeling the Effectiveness of a Strategic Planning System. In *Lamb, R. and Shrivastava, P., eds.*, 1988, pp. 113–38.

Ramaprasad, Arkalgud and Stubbart, Charles I. Probing Two Chief Executives' Schematic Knowledge of the U.S. Steel Industry Using Cognitive Maps. In *Lamb, R. and Shrivastava, P., eds.*, 1988, pp. 139–64.

Ramazani, Rouhollah K. Socio-political Change in the Gulf: A Climate for Terrorism? In *Sindelar, H. R., III and Peterson, J. E., eds.*, 1988, pp. 127–51.

Ramb, Bernd-Thomas. Elementare Gleichgewichtsbedingungen des staatlichen Rentensystems. (Elemental Equilibrium Conditions of the Social Retirement System. With English summary.) *Jahr. Nationalökon. Statist.*, February 1988, *204*(2), pp. 140–54.

Ramcharran, Harridutt. Residential Demand for Energy in Jamaica. *Energy Econ.*, July 1988, *10*(3), pp. 223–28.

Ramey, Garey and Bagwell, Kyle. Advertising and Limit Pricing. *Rand J. Econ.*, Spring 1988, *19*(1), pp. 59–71.

Ramin, Taghi. A Regression Analysis of Migration to Urban Areas of a Less-Developed Country: The Case of Iran. *Amer. Econ.*, Fall 1988, *32*(2), pp. 26–34.

Ramírez, Clara; Reyes, Alvaro and de Gómez, Martha Isabel. Employment and Labour Incomes in Colombia, 1976–85. In *van Ginneken, W., ed.*, 1988, pp. 33–59.

Ramirez, Jorge, et al. Ex Post Analysis of Flood Control: Benefit–Cost Analysis and the Value of Information. *Water Resources Res.*, August 1988, *24*(8), pp. 1397–1405.

Ramirez, Miguel D. The Composition of Government Spending and the Assignments of Instruments to Targets in a Small Open Economy. *Southern Econ. J.*, October 1988, *55*(2), pp. 432–42.

Ramo, Simon. Globalization of Industry and Implications for the Future. In *Muroyama, J. H. and Stever, H. G., eds.*, 1988, pp. 12–22.

Ramos, Joseph. Inflation Stabilization in Bolivia: Comment. In *Bruno, M., et al., eds.*, 1988, pp. 353–57.

———. Panel on Strategies for Confronting the Crisis: Panel. In *Feinberg, R. E. and Ffrench-Davis, R., eds.*, 1988, pp. 257–62.

———. The Rise and Fall of Capital Markets in the Southern Cone. In *Urrutia, M., ed.*, 1988, pp. 43–81.

Ramos Tercero, Raul. Monopolistic Competition, Credibility and the Output Costs of Disinflation Programs: An Analysis of Price Controls: Comments. *J. Devel. Econ.*, November 1988, *29*(3), pp. 399–401.

——— and **Diaz, Francisco Gil.** Lessons from Mexico. In *Bruno, M., et al., eds.*, 1988, pp. 361–90.

Rampa, Giorgio. Dynamic Determination of the General Level of Activity in a Multisectoral

Model. *Ricerche Econ.*, Oct.–Dec. 1988, *42*(4), pp. 559–81.

_____ and Lanza, Alessandro. A Model for Assessing the Growth Opportunities of EEC Countries When Interdependence Is Not Ruled Out. In *Ciaschini, M., ed.*, 1988, pp. 367–90.

_____ and Rampa, Lorenzo. Fluctuating Growth with Induced Innovations. *Metroecon.*, February 1988, *39*(1), pp. 31–42.

Rampa, Lorenzo and Bianchi, Carluccio. Financial Assets and the Short-run Dynamics of a Capitalist Economy. *Econ. Notes*, 1988, (3), pp. 29–50.

_____ and Rampa, Giorgio. Fluctuating Growth with Induced Innovations. *Metroecon.*, February 1988, *39*(1), pp. 31–42.

Ramphal, Shridath S. For the South, a Time to Think. In *Sopiee, N.; Hamzah, B. A. and Leong, C. H., eds.*, 1988, pp. 11–28.

_____. North–South Co-operation: Why and How the South Must Persist. In *Sopiee, N.; Hamzah, B. A. and Leong, C. H., eds.*, 1988, *1983*, pp. 421–41.

Ramqvist, Lars. Information Technologies in Industry and Society. In *Muroyama, J. H. and Stever, H. G., eds.*, 1988, pp. 45–61.

Ramsay, Harvie and Beirne, Martin. Computer Redesign and 'Labour Process' Theory: Towards a Critical Appraisal. In *Knights, D. and Willmott, H., eds.*, 1988, pp. 197–229.

Ramser, Hans Jürgen. Neuere Beiträge zur Konjunkturtheorie: ein Überblick. (Recent Developments in Business Cycle Theory: A Review. With English summary.) *Ifo-Studien*, 1988, *34*(2–3), pp. 95–115.

Ramsey, Frank P. Truth and Probability. In *Gärdenfors, P. and Sahlin, N.-E., eds.*, 1988, pp. 19–47.

Ramstad, Yngve. A Pragmatist's Quest for Holistic Knowledge: The Scientific Methodology of John R. Commons. In *Samuels, W. J., ed.*, Vol. 2, 1988, *1986*, pp. 138–76.

Ramstetter, Eric D. and Naya, Seiji. Policy Interactions and Direct Foreign Investment in East and Southeast Asia. *J. World Trade*, April 1988, *22*(2), pp. 57–71.

Rana, Pradumna B. Exports, Policy Changes, and Economic Growth in Developing Countries after the 1973 Oil Shock: Comments [1985, Exports, Policy Choices, and Economic Growth in Developing Countries after the 1973 Oil Shock]. *J. Devel. Econ.*, March 1988, *28*(2), pp. 261–64.

_____ and Dowling, J. Malcolm, Jr. The Impact of Foreign Capital on Growth: Evidences from Asian Developing Countries. *Devel. Econ.*, March 1988, *26*(1), pp. 3–11.

Ranade, C. G.; Jha, Dayanatha and Delgado, Christopher L. Technological Change, Production Costs, and Supply Response. In *Mellor, J. W. and Ahmed, R., eds.*, 1988, pp. 190–203.

Rand, James F. Negotiating: Master the Possibilities. In *Timpe, A. D., ed.*, 1988, *1987*, pp. 345–50.

Randall, Alan. Market Failure and the Efficiency of Irrigated Agriculture. In *O'Mara, G. T., ed.*, 1988, pp. 21–30.

_____. Property Institutions and Economic Behavior. In *Samuels, W. J., ed.*, Vol. 3, 1988, *1978*, pp. 338–58.

_____. Resource and Enviromental Economics: A Discussion. In *Hildreth, R. J., et al., eds.*, 1988, pp. 230–33.

Randle, Yvonne; Sackmann, Sonja and Flamholtz, Eric G. Personnel Management: The Tone of Tomorrow. In *Timpe, A. D., ed.*, 1988, *1986*, pp. 33–41.

Randolph, Bill and Hamnett, Chris. Labour and Housing Market Change in London: A Longitudinal Analysis, 1971–1981. *Urban Stud.*, October 1988, *25*(5), pp. 380–98.

Randolph, R. Sean. U.S. Energy Policy toward the Asia-Pacific Region. In *Dorian, J. P. and Fridley, D. G., eds.*, 1988, pp. 37–42.

Randolph, William C. Estimation of Housing Depreciation: Short-term Quality Change and Long-term Vintage Effects. *J. Urban Econ.*, March 1988, *23*(2), pp. 162–78.

_____. Housing Depreciation and Aging Bias in the Consumer Price Index. *J. Bus. Econ. Statist.*, July 1988, *6*(3), pp. 359–71.

_____. A Transformation for Heteroscedastic Error Components Regression Models. *Econ. Letters*, 1988, *27*(4), pp. 349–54.

_____; Berenson, Stephen A. and Lane, Walter F. Adjusting the CPI Shelter Index to Compensate for Effect of Depreciation. *Mon. Lab. Rev.*, October 1988, *111*(10), pp. 34–37.

Rangan, Nanda, et al. The Technical Efficiency of U.S. Banks. *Econ. Letters*, 1988, *28*(2), pp. 169–75.

Rangarajan, C. The Asian Experience and the Role of Multilateral Institutions, Foreign Aid, and Other Financial Sources. In *Streeten, P., ed.*, 1988, pp. 227–48.

_____. India's Foreign Borrowing. In *Lucas, R. E. B. and Papanek, G. F., eds.*, 1988, pp. 253–70.

Rangazas, Peter C. and Abdullah, Dewan A. Money and the Business Cycle: Another Look. *Rev. Econ. Statist.*, November 1988, *70*(4), pp. 680–85.

_____ and Abdullah, Dewan A. Testing Some Monetarist Propositions. *Rev. Econ. Statist.*, February 1988, *70*(1), pp. 173–77.

Ranki, György. Economy and the Second World War: A Few Comparative Issues. *J. Europe. Econ. Hist.*, Fall 1988, *17*(2), pp. 303–47.

_____ and Enyedi, György. Experiences of National Planning in Hungary. In *Urrutia, M. and Yukawa, S., eds. (I)*, 1988, pp. 311–58.

Rankin, Carol H. and Hunter, William J. The Composition of Public Sector Compensation: The Effects of Unionization and Bureaucratic Size. *J. Lab. Res.*, Winter 1988, *9*(1), pp. 29–42.

Rankin, Neil. Macroeconomic Interdependence, Floating Exchange Rates, and Product Substitutability. *Greek Econ. Rev.*, 1988, *10*(1), pp. 162–84.

Ransom, Michael R. and Oaxaca, Ronald L. Searching for the Effect of Unionism on the Wages of Union and Nonunion Workers. *J. Lab. Res.*, Spring 1988, 9(2), pp. 139–48.

Ransom, Roger L. and Sutch, Richard. The Decline of Retirement in the Years before Social Security: U.S. Retirement Patterns, 1870–1940. In *Ricardo-Campbell, R. and Lazear, E. P., eds.*, 1988, pp. 3–26.

Ranson, Baldwin. The Institutionalist Theory of Capital Formation. In *Tool, M. R., ed., Vol. 1*, 1988, *1987*, pp. 315–28.

Ranson, Thomas Baldwin. Education for Modernization: Meritocratic Myths in China, Mexico, the United States, and Japan. *J. Econ. Issues*, September 1988, 22(3), pp. 747–62.

Rantala, Olavi. Tasapainokorko, Korkopolitiikka ja korkojen aikarekenne. (The Equilibrium Rate of Interest, Interest Rate Policy, and the Term Structure of Interest Rates. With English summary.) *Liiketaloudellinen Aikak.*, 1988, 37(2), pp. 147–61.

Rao, Akshay R. and Monroe, Kent B. The Moderating Effect of Prior Knowledge on Cue Utilization in Product Evaluations. *J. Cons. Res.*, September 1988, 15(2), pp. 253–64.

Rao, D. S. Prasada and Salazar-Carrillo, Jorge. A General Equilibrium Approach to the Construction of Multilateral Index Numbers. In *Salazar-Carrillo, J. and Rao, D. S. P., eds.*, 1988, pp. 19–37.

—— **and Salazar-Carrillo, Jorge.** Real Product and Price Comparisons among Latin American Countries. In *Salazar-Carrillo, J. and Rao, D. S. P., eds.*, 1988, pp. 195–205.

Rao, G. N. Canal Irrigation and Agrarian Change in Colonial Andhra: A Study of Godavari District, c. 1850–1890. *Indian Econ. Soc. Hist. Rev.*, Jan.–March 1988, 25(1), pp. 25–60.

Rao, M. J. Manohar and Nachane, Dilip M. Varying Parameter Models: An Optimal Control Formulation. *J. Quant. Econ.*, January 1988, 4(1), pp. 59–79.

Rao, P. K. Planning and Financing Water Resource Development in the United States: A Review and Policy Perspective. *Amer. J. Econ. Soc.*, January 1988, 47(1), pp. 81–96.

Rao, Ram C. Strategic Pricing of Durables under Competition. In *Devinney, T. M., ed.*, 1988, pp. 197–217.

Rao, Ramesh K. S. and Boyle, Glenn W. The Mean-Generalized Coefficient of Variation Selection Rule and Expected Utility Maximization. *Southern Econ. J.*, July 1988, 55(1), pp. 1–18.

Rao, Ramesh P. and Ma, Christopher K. Information Asymmetry and Options Trading. *Financial Rev.*, February 1988, 23(1), pp. 39–51.

——; **Weinraub, Herbert J. and Ma, Christopher K.** The Seasonality in Convertible Bond Markets: A Stock Effect or Bond Effect? *J. Finan. Res.*, Winter 1988, 11(4), pp. 335–47.

Rao, T. V. S. Ramamohan. Demand Uncertainty, Decision Models of the Firm, and Parameter Estimation. *J. Quant. Econ.*, January 1988, 4(1), pp. 45–58.

——. Econometric Estimation of Decision Models under Uncertainty. In *Sengupta, J. K. and Kadekodi, G. K., eds.*, 1988, pp. 135–56.

—— **and Saxena, Rakesh K.** Economic Efficiency of the Organizational Decisions of the Firm. *Rivista Int. Sci. Econ. Com.*, July 1988, 35(7), pp. 675–88.

—— **and Saxena, Rakesh K.** Transaction Costs, Vertical Integration, and X-Efficiency. *Rivista Int. Sci. Econ. Com.*, December 1988, 35(12), pp. 1173–90.

Rao, V. K. R. V. The Balance between Industry and Agriculture in Economic Development: Inaugural Address. In *Arrow, K. J., ed.*, 1988, pp. 3–21.

Rao, V. V. Bhanoji. Income Distribution in East Asian Developing Countries. *Asian-Pacific Econ. Lit.*, March 1988, 2(1), pp. 26–45.

Rapacki, Ryszard and Parkoła, Andrzej. The Second Phase of the Reform: Proposals in the Area of Foreign Trade. *Eastern Europ. Econ.*, Summer 1988, 26(4), pp. 72–90.

Rapoport, Amnon; Felsenthal, Dan S. and Maoz, Zeev. Proportional Representation: An Empirical Evaluation of Single-Stage, Non-ranked Voting Procedures. *Public Choice*, November 1988, 59(2), pp. 151–65.

——; **Kroll, Yoram and Levy, Haim.** Experimental Tests of the Separation Theorem and the Capital Asset Pricing Model. *Amer. Econ. Rev.*, June 1988, 78(3), pp. 500–519.

——; **Zwick, Rami and Funk, Sandra G.** Selection of Portfolios with Risky and Riskless Assets: Experimental Tests of Two Expected Utility Models. *J. Econ. Psych.*, June 1988, 9(2), pp. 169–94.

Rapoport, Anatol. Experiments with N-Person Social Traps II: Tragedy of the Commons. *J. Conflict Resolution*, September 1988, 32(3), pp. 473–88.

——. Experiments with N-Person Social Traps I: Prisoner's Dilemma, Weak Prisoner's Dilemma, Volunteer's Dilemma, and Largest Number. *J. Conflict Resolution*, September 1988, 32(3), pp. 457–72.

——. What Strategies Can Support the Evolutionary Emergence of Cooperation? Comments. *J. Conflict Resolution*, June 1988, 32(2), pp. 399–401.

Rappaport, Steven. Arguments, Truth, and Economic Methodology: A Rejoinder. *Econ. Philos.*, April 1988, 4(1), pp. 170–72.

——. Economic Methodology: Rhetoric or Epistemology? *Econ. Philos.*, April 1988, 4(1), pp. 110–28.

Rapping, Leonard A. America's Budget and Trade Deficits. In *Rapping, L. A.*, 1988, pp. 5–36.

——. Bureaucracy, the Corporation and Economic Policy. In *Rapping, L. A.*, 1988, *1984*, pp. 70–87.

——. The Domestic and International Aspects of Structural Inflation. In *Rapping, L. A.*, 1988, *1979*, pp. 93–112.

——. Economic Policy and the International

Market: The Interest Rate and Third World Debt. In *Rapping, L. A.*, 1988, *1984*, pp. 136–52.

_____. In Search of the Economic Future. In *Rapping, L. A.*, 1988, pp. 155–71.

_____. International Reorganization and American Economic Policy: Preface. In *Rapping, L. A.*, 1988, pp. ix–xix.

_____. Productivity and Workplace Organization. In *Rapping, L. A.*, 1988, pp. 54–69.

_____. Real Wages, Productivity and Technology. In *Rapping, L. A.*, 1988, pp. 37–53.

_____ and **Bennett, Stephen J.** The Causes of High Real Interest Rates in the 1980s. In *Rapping, L. A.*, 1988, pp. 113–25.

_____ and **Pulley, Lawrence B.** Speculation, Deregulation, and the Interest Rate. In *Rapping, L. A.*, 1988, *1985*, pp. 126–35.

Rappoport, Peter. Reply to Professor Hennipman: Communications. *J. Econ. Lit.*, March 1988, *26*(1), pp. 86–91.

Rasche, Robert H. Monetary Policy and Financial Deregulation in the United States. *Kredit Kapital*, 1988, *21*(3), pp. 451–68.

_____ and **Koch, Paul D.** An Examination of the Commerce Department Leading-Indicator Approach. *J. Bus. Econ. Statist.*, April 1988, *6*(2), pp. 167–87.

Rashid, Salim. Economics and the Study of Its Past. *World Devel.*, February 1988, *16*(2), pp. 207–18.

_____. The Irish School of Economic Development: 1720–1750. *Manchester Sch. Econ. Soc. Stud.*, December 1988, *56*(4), pp. 345–69.

_____. Quality in Contestable Markets: A Historical Problem? *Quart. J. Econ.*, February 1988, *103*(1), pp. 245–49.

_____. Recent Literature on Malthus. In *Thweatt, W. O.*, ed., 1988, pp. 53–84.

Raskin, Marcus G. Democracy versus the National Security State. In *Levine, M. V., et al.*, 1988, pp. 168–97.

Rasler, Karen A. and Thompson, William R. Defense Burdens, Capital Formation, and Economic Growth: The Systemic Leader Case. *J. Conflict Resolution*, March 1988, *32*(1), pp. 61–86.

_____ and **Thompson, William R.** War and Systemic Capability Reconcentration. *J. Conflict Resolution*, June 1988, *32*(2), pp. 335–66.

Rasminsky, Louis. Planning the Postwar International System. In *Hamouda, O. F. and Smithin, J. N.*, eds., Vol. 1, 1988, pp. 151–56.

Rasmusen, Eric. Entry for Buyout. *J. Ind. Econ.*, March 1988, *36*(3), pp. 281–99.

_____. Mutual Banks and Stock Banks. *J. Law Econ.*, October 1988, *31*(2), pp. 395–421.

Rasmussen, Bo Sandemann. Stabilization Policies in Open Economies with Imperfect Current Information. *J. Int. Money Finance*, June 1988, *7*(2), pp. 151–66.

Rasmussen, David W.; Serow, William J. and Fournier, Gary M. Elderly Migration as a Response to Economic Incentives. *Soc. Sci. Quart.*, June 1988, *69*(2), pp. 245–60.

_____; **Serow, William J. and Fournier, Gary M.** Elderly Migration: For Sun and Money. *Population Res. Policy Rev.*, 1988, *7*(2), pp. 189–99.

_____ and **Zuehlke, Thomas W.** The Evaluation of Residential Living Space. *Rev. Reg. Stud.*, Spring 1988, *18*(2), pp. 47–53.

_____ and **Zuehlke, Thomas W.** A Search Model of Housing Market Transactions. *Southern Econ. J.*, January 1988, *54*(3), pp. 623–29.

Rasmussen, Wayne D. Approaching the Twenty-first Century: Lessons from History. In *Hildreth, R. J., et al.*, eds., 1988, pp. 21–31.

Rasool, S. Anvaar and Davis, Herbert J. A Reconsideration of England's Values Research in Cross-Cultural Management. In *Farmer, R. N. and McGoun, E. G.*, eds., 1988, pp. 109–25.

Rassuli, Ali and Rassuli, Kathleen M. The Realism of Post Keynesian Economics: A Marketing Perspective. *J. Post Keynesian Econ.*, Spring 1988, *10*(3), pp. 455–73.

Rassuli, Kathleen M. Evidence of Marketing Strategy in the Early Printed Book Trade: An Application of Hollander's Historical Approach. In *[Hollander, S. C.]*, 1988, pp. 91–107.

_____ and **Rassuli, Ali.** The Realism of Post Keynesian Economics: A Marketing Perspective. *J. Post Keynesian Econ.*, Spring 1988, *10*(3), pp. 455–73.

Ratchford, Brian T. The Economics of Information: The Views of a Marketing Economist. In *Maynes, E. S. and ACCI Research Committee*, eds., 1988, pp. 265–69.

_____; **Agrawal, Jagdish and Kamakura, Wagner A.** Measuring Market Efficiency and Welfare Loss. *J. Cons. Res.*, December 1988, *15*(3), pp. 289–302.

Ratick, Samuel J. and Reinert, Kenneth A. A Note on Estimating a Long-run Average Cost Curve for Flue Gas Desulfurization. *J. Environ. Econ. Manage.*, March 1988, *15*(1), pp. 30–34.

Ratkin, V.; Evtushenko, Y. and Mazourik, V. Multicriteria Optimization in the DISO System. In *Kurzhanski, A.; Neumann, K. and Pallaschke, D.*, eds., 1988, pp. 94–102.

Ratnayake, Ravindra. Trade Policy and the Performance of the Manufacturing Sector: Sri Lanka. *Devel. Econ.*, March 1988, *26*(1), pp. 12–33.

Ratti, Remigio. Development Theory, Technological Change and Europe's Frontier Regions. In *Aydalot, P. and Keeble, D.*, eds., 1988, pp. 197–220.

Ratti, Ronald A. and Maloney, Tim. Divergent Trends in the Discouragement of Adult Men, Adult Women, and Teenagers: 1970–1986. *Econ. Letters*, 1988, *28*(1), pp. 93–96.

Rattso, Jorn. Macrodynamic Adjustment Mechanisms in India. *World Devel.*, August 1988, *16*(8), pp. 959–73.

_____. Macroeconomic Adjustments in a Dual Economy under Policy Controlled Domestic Terms of Trade. *Indian Econ. Rev.*, Jan.–June 1988, *23*(1), pp. 45–59.

Räty, Päivi and Suominen, Risto. Breddningen av skattebasen vid beskattning av industriföretag. (The Broadening of the Tax Base in the Taxation of Manufacturing Companies. With English summary.) *Ekon. Samfundets Tidskr.*, 1988, *41*(4), pp. 267–72.

Raubitschek, Ruth S. Hitting the Jackpot: Product Proliferation by Multiproduct Firms under Uncertainty. *Int. J. Ind. Organ.*, December 1988, *6*(4), pp. 469–88.

_____. Multiple Scenario Analysis and Business Planning. In *Lamb, R. and Shrivastava, P., eds.*, 1988, pp. 181–205.

Rault, A.; Anglard, Patrick and Gendreau, Francoise. Model Building for Decision Aid in the Agri-economic Field. In *Motamen, H., ed.*, 1988, pp. 283–311.

Raup, Philip M. Assessing the Significance of the Soviet Market for United States Agricultural Exports. In *Brada, J. C. and Wadekin, K.-E., eds.*, 1988, pp. 408–21.

_____. Institutions and Agricultural Economics in the Twenty-first Century: A Discussion. In *Hildreth, R. J., et al., eds.*, 1988, pp. 342–46.

Rauscher, Michael. OPEC Behavior and the Price of Petroleum. *J. Econ. (Z. Nationalökon.)*, 1988, *48*(1), pp. 59–78.

Rausser, Gordon C. Developments in Economics of Importance to Agricultural Economics: A Discussion. In *Hildreth, R. J., et al., eds.*, 1988, pp. 257–64.

_____. The Macroeconomics of Agriculture and Rural America: A Discussion. In *Hildreth, R. J., et al., eds.*, 1988, pp. 384–95.

_____. Stability Issues and Policy Analysis. In *Sumner, D. A., ed.*, 1988, pp. 143–70.

_____ and Irwin, Douglas A. The Political Economy of Agricultural Policy Reform. *Europ. Rev. Agr. Econ.*, 1988, *15*(4), pp. 349–66.

Raut, L. K. R&D Behaviour of Indian Firms: A Stochastic Control Model. *Indian Econ. Rev.*, July–Dec. 1988, *23*(2), pp. 207–29.

Ravallion, Martin. Expected Poverty under Risk-Induced Welfare Variability. *Econ. J.*, December 1988, *98*(393), pp. 1171–82.

_____. INPRES and Inequality: A Distributional Perspective on the Centre's Regional Disbursements. *Bull. Indonesian Econ. Stud.*, December 1988, *24*(3), pp. 53–71.

_____ and Dearden, Lorraine. Social Security in a "Moral Economy": An Empirical Analysis for Java. *Rev. Econ. Statist.*, February 1988, *70*(1), pp. 36–44.

_____ and Jayasuriya, Sisira K. Liberalization and Inequality in Sri Lanka: A Comment [The Distribution of Income in Sri Lanka in 1969–70 and 1980–81: A Decomposition Analysis]. *J. Devel. Econ.*, March 1988, *28*(2), pp. 247–55.

_____ and Kapur, Deep. Rational Expectations as Long-run Equilibria: Tests for Indian Securities. *Econ. Letters*, 1988, *26*(4), pp. 363–67.

Raven, John. Choice in a Modern Economy: New Concepts of Democracy and Bureaucracy. In *Maital, S., ed., Vol. 2*, 1988, pp. 812–24.

Raven, Peter H. What the Fate of the Rain Forests Means to Us. In *Ehrlich, P. R. and Holdren, J. P., eds.*, 1988, pp. 111–23.

Ravenscraft, David J. The 1980s Merger Wave: An Industrial Organization Perspective. In *Browne, L. E. and Rosengren, E. S., eds.*, 1988, pp. 17–37.

_____ and Scherer, Frederic M. The Long-Run Performance of Mergers and Takeovers. In *Weidenbaum, M. L. and Chilton, K. W., eds.*, 1988, pp. 34–45.

_____ and Scherer, Frederic M. Mergers and Managerial Performance. In *Coffee, J. C., Jr.; Lowenstein, L. and Rose-Ackerman, S., eds.*, 1988, pp. 194–210.

van Ravenstein, Ad and Vijlbrief, Hans. Welfare Cost of Higher Tax Rates: An Empirical Laffer Curve for the Netherlands. *De Economist*, 1988, *136*(2), pp. 205–19.

van Ravenswaay, Eileen O.; Thompson, Stanley R. and Smith, Mark E. Sales Loss Determination in Food Contamination Incidents: An Application to Milk Bans in Hawaii. *Amer. J. Agr. Econ.*, August 1988, *70*(3), pp. 513–20.

Ravichandran, R. and Sa-Aadu, J. Resource Combination and Security Price Reactions: The Case of Real Estate Joint Ventures. *Amer. Real Estate Urban Econ. Assoc. J.*, Summer 1988, *16*(2), pp. 105–22.

Ravid, S. Abraham and Talmor, Eli. Government Financing, Taxation, and Capital Markets. In *Chen, A. H., ed.*, 1988, pp. 21–52.

Raviv, Artur. Means of Payment in Takeovers: Results for the United Kingdom and the United States: Comment. In *Auerbach, A. J., ed. (I)*, 1988, pp. 259–60.

_____ and Harris, Milton. Corporate Control Contests and Capital Structure. *J. Finan. Econ.*, Jan.–March 1988, *20*(1–2), pp. 55–86.

_____ and Harris, Milton. Corporate Governance: Voting Rights and Majority Rules. *J. Finan. Econ.*, Jan.–March 1988, *20*(1–2), pp. 203–35.

_____, and Harris, Milton. Some Results on Incentive Contracts with Applications to Education and Employment, Health Insurance, and Law Enforcement. In *Ricketts, M., ed., Vol. 1*, 1988, *1978*, pp. 220–30.

Rawana, D.; Lall, A. and Lakhan, V. C. Resource Allocation in Agriculture: The Guyana Experience. *Can. J. Devel. Stud.*, 1988, *9*(2), pp. 235–48.

Ray, Anandarup. Agricultural Policies in Developing Countries: National and International Aspects. In *Antonelli, G. and Quadrio-Curzio, A., eds.*, 1988, pp. 33–51.

Ray, D. and Namboodiri, K. S. Granger's Causality—An Indian Experience. *J. Quant. Econ.*, July 1988, *4*(2), pp. 279–91.

Ray, Edward John and Baack, Ben. Federal Transfer Payments in America: Veterans' Pensions and the Rise of Social Security. *Econ. Inquiry*, October 1988, *26*(4), pp. 687–702.

_____ and Baack, Ben. Special Interests and the Nineteenth-Century Roots of the U.S. Military–Industrial Complex. In *Uselding, P. J.,* ed., 1988, pp. 153–69.

Ray, George F. The Diffusion of Innovations: An Update. *Nat. Inst. Econ. Rev.,* November 1988, (126), pp. 51–56.

_____. Innovation in Materials. In *Forester, T.,* ed., 1988, *1986,* pp. 254–72.

Ray, Margaret A. and Grimes, Paul W. Right-to-Work Legislation and Employment Growth in the 1980s: A Shift-Share Analysis. *Reg. Sci. Persp.,* 1988, *18*(2), pp. 78–93.

Ray, Rajat Kanta. The Bazaar: Changing Structural Characteristics of the Indigenous Section of the Indian Economy before and after the Great Depression. *Indian Econ. Soc. Hist. Rev.,* July–Sept. 1988, *25*(3), pp. 263–318.

Ray, Ranjan. Optimal Commodity Taxes in the Presence of Children. *Scand. J. Econ.,* 1988, *90*(1), pp. 75–92.

_____. Optimally Uniform Commodity Taxes in a Non Linear Demographic Demand Model. *Bull. Econ. Res.,* June 1988, *40*(3), pp. 227–33.

Rayack, Wendy. False Fears of Wage-Led Inflation. *Challenge,* Sept.–Oct. 1988, *31*(5), pp. 12–20.

_____. The Impact of Recessions on Two-Parent Families: An Analysis of Earnings-Sensitivity by Family Income Class. *Public Finance Quart.,* January 1988, *16*(1), pp. 101–28.

Raymond, José Luis; García, Jaime and Polo, Clemente. Una nota sobre la relación empleo-capital en españa: 1955–1984. (With English summary.) *Invest. Econ.,* January 1988, *12*(1), pp. 177–95.

Raymond, Richard D. and Sesnowitz, Michael L. The Impact of Sex and Attitudes upon the Earnings of College Graduates. *Eastern Econ. J.,* April–June 1988, *14*(2), pp. 167–79.

_____; **Sesnowitz, Michael L. and Williams, Donald R.** Does Sex Still Matter? New Evidence from the 1980s. *Econ. Inquiry,* January 1988, *26*(1), pp. 43–58.

Raynauld, André. Regional Development in a Federal State. In *[Perroux, F.],* 1988, pp. 225–43.

Raynauld, Jacques. Canadian Regional Cycles: The Québec–Ontario Case Revisited. *Can. J. Econ.,* February 1988, *21*(1), pp. 115–28.

Rayner, Robert K. Some Asymptotic Theory for the Bootstrap in Econometric Models. *Econ. Letters,* 1988, *26*(1), pp. 43–47.

Raza, Bilquees and Kazi, Shahnaz. Households Headed by Women: Income, Employment and Household Organization. *Pakistan Devel. Rev.,* Part 2, Winter 1988, *27*(4), pp. 781–87.

Razin, Assaf and Frenkel, Jacob A. Budget Deficits under Alternative Tax Systems: International Effects. *Int. Monet. Fund Staff Pap.,* June 1988, *35*(2), pp. 297–315.

_____ **and Frenkel, Jacob A.** International Aspects of Budget Deficits with Distortionary Taxes. In *Helpman, E.; Razin, A. and Sadka, E., eds.,* 1988, pp. 145–62.

_____ **and Leiderman, Leonardo.** Effects of Government Finance: Testing Ricardian Neu-

trality. In *Helpman, E.; Razin, A. and Sadka, E., eds.,* 1988, pp. 107–21.

_____ **and Leiderman, Leonardo.** Foreign Trade Shocks and the Dynamics of High Inflation: Israel, 1978–85. *J. Int. Money Finance,* December 1988, *7*(4), pp. 411–23.

_____ **and Leiderman, Leonardo.** Testing Ricardian Neutrality with an Intertemporal Stochastic Model. *J. Money, Credit, Banking,* February 1988, *20*(1), pp. 1–21.

_____; **Sadka, Efraim and Nerlove, Marc.** A Bequest-Constrained Economy: Welfare Analysis. *J. Public Econ.,* November 1988, *37*(2), pp. 203–20.

Razin, E. The Role of Ownership Characteristics in the Industrial Development of Israel's Peripheral Towns. *Environ. Planning A,* September 1988, *20*(9), pp. 1235–52.

Rea, J. D.; Cortes, B. S. and Edgmand, M. R. Capital Gains and the Rental Price of Capital. In *Missouri Valley Economic Assoc.,* 1988, pp. 71–75.

Read, Colin. Advertising and Natural Vacancies in Rental Housing Markets. *Amer. Real Estate Urban Econ. Assoc. J.,* Winter 1988, *16*(4), pp. 354–63.

_____. Price Strategies for Idiosyncratic Goods—The Case of Housing. *Amer. Real Estate Urban Econ. Assoc. J.,* Winter 1988, *16*(4), pp. 379–95.

Read, William J. An Analysis of Auditor Judgment in Nonstatistical Sampling. In *Schwartz, B. N.,* ed., 1988, pp. 251–66.

Reading, Steven L. and Rosenbaum, David I. Market Structure and Import Share: A Regional Market Analysis. *Southern Econ. J.,* January 1988, *54*(3), pp. 694–700.

Reagan, Ronald. The United States and the World in the 1990s. In *Anderson, A. and Bark, D. L., eds.,* 1988, pp. 555–64.

Reams, Margaret A. and Regens, James L. State Strategies for Regulating Groundwater Quality. *Soc. Sci. Quart.,* March 1988, *69*(1), pp. 53–69.

Rearden, David and Lien, Da-Hsiang Donald. Missing Measurements in Limited Dependent Variable Models. *Econ. Letters,* 1988, *26*(1), pp. 33–36.

Reardon, Thomas; Matlon, Peter and Delgado, Christopher L. Coping with Household-Level Food Insecurity in Drought-Affected Areas of Burkina Faso. *World Devel.,* September 1988, *16*(9), pp. 1065–74.

Reati, Angelo and Roland, Gérard. Ondes longues et régulation: le cas allemand. (With English summary.) *Cah. Écon. Bruxelles,* First Trimester 1988, (117), pp. 107–50.

Rebelo, Sergio T.; King, Robert G. and Plosser, Charles I. Production, Growth and Business Cycles: I. The Basic Neoclassical Model. *J. Monet. Econ.,* March–May 1988, *21*(2–3), pp. 195–232.

_____; **King, Robert G. and Plosser, Charles I.** Production, Growth and Business Cycles: II. New Directions. *J. Monet. Econ.,* March–May 1988, *21*(2–3), pp. 309–41.

Rebeyrol, Antoine. A propos des théories prékeynesiennes du cycle: Wicksell, Fisher et Hayek. (On Pre-Keynesian Theories of Business Cycle: Wicksell, Fisher and Hayek. With English summary.) *Écon. Soc.*, March 1988, *22*(3), pp. 95–133.

Rebitzer, James B. Unemployment, Labor Relations, and Unit Labor Costs. *Amer. Econ. Rev.*, May 1988, *78*(2), pp. 389–94.

Rechner, Paula L.; Dalton, Dan R. and Kesner, Idalene F. Corporate Governance and Boards of Directors: An International, Comparative Perspective. In *Farmer, R. N. and McGoun, E. G., eds.*, 1988, pp. 95–105.

Recknagel, Frieder. A Deep Expert System for Water Quality Control of Lake Ecosystems. *Statist. J.*, November 1988, *5*(3), pp. 271–77.

Rector, Andrew and Murrell, David. Dualism in the Maritime Provinces: 1961–1981 A Social Indicator Approach. In *Choudhury, M. A., ed.*, 1988, pp. 97–115.

Redburn, F. Stevens. Never Lost a Penny: An Assessment of Federal Deposit Insurance. *J. Policy Anal. Manage.*, Fall 1988, *7*(4), pp. 687–702.

Redclift, Michael. Economic Models and Environmental Values: A Discourse on Theory. In *Turner, R. K., ed.*, 1988, pp. 51–66.

Reddy, D. Narasimha. Maldevelopment and Marxist Approach. In *Vivekananda, F., ed.*, 1988, pp. 51–60.

Reder, Melvin W. The Rise and Fall of Unions: The Public Sector and the Private. *J. Econ. Perspectives*, Spring 1988, *2*(2), pp. 89–110.

Redish, Angela and Bordo, Michael D. Costs and Benefits of Exchange Rate Stability: Canada's Interwar Experience. *Contemp. Policy Issues*, April 1988, *6*(2), pp. 115–30.

_____ **and Bordo, Michael D.** Was the Establishment of a Canadian Central Bank in 1935 Necessary? In *England, C. and Huertas, T., eds.*, 1988, pp. 69–86.

_____ **and Glassman, Debra A.** Currency Depreciation in Early Modern England and France. *Exploration Econ. Hist.*, January 1988, *25*(1), pp. 75–97.

Redmond, Clair H. and Cubbage, Frederick W. Portfolio Risk and Returns from Timber Asset Investments. *Land Econ.*, November 1988, *64*(4), pp. 325–37.

Redmond, J. Effective Exchange Rates in the Nineteen-Thirties: The European Gold Bloc and North America. *J. Europ. Econ. Hist.*, Fall 1988, *17*(2), pp. 379–410.

Reeb, Jane S. and Park, Thae S. Relationship between Personal Income and Adjusted Gross Income, 1984–86. *Surv. Curr. Bus.*, August 1988, *68*(8), pp. 23–27.

Reece, B. F. The Price-Adjustment Process for Rental Housing: Some Further Evidence. *Amer. Real Estate Urban Econ. Assoc. J.*, Winter 1988, *16*(4), pp. 411–18.

Reed, Clyde G.; Easton, Stephen T. and Gibson, William A. Tariffs and Growth: The Dales Hypothesis. *Exploration Econ. Hist.*, April 1988, *25*(2), pp. 147–63.

Reed, Michael R. and Skees, Jerry R. The Restructuring of Southern Agriculture: Data Needs for Economic and Policy Research. *Southern J. Agr. Econ.*, July 1988, *20*(1), pp. 33–40.

Reed, R. C.; Narasimham, Gorti V. L. and Swamy, P. A. V. B. Productivity Analysis of U.S. Manufacturing Using a Stochastic-Coefficients Production Function. *J. Bus. Econ. Statist.*, July 1988, *6*(3), pp. 339–49.

Reed, William J. and Clarke, Harry R. A Stochastic Analysis of Land Development Timing and Property Valuation. *Reg. Sci. Urban Econ.*, August 1988, *18*(3), pp. 357–81.

Reekie, W. Duncan. A Collection of Essays Compiled as a Memorial to Professor W. H. Hutt: Editorial. *Managerial Dec. Econ.*, Special Issue, Winter 1988, pp. 1–4.

_____. Consumers' Sovereignty Revisited. *Managerial Dec. Econ.*, Special Issue, Winter 1988, pp. 17–25.

Rees, Hedley J. B.; Sahay, Surottam N. and Sinha, Ramesh P. An Econometric Analysis of Workers Participation in Unions. *Indian Econ. J.*, Jan.–March 1988, *35*(3), pp. 61–71.

Rees, J. Pollution Control Objectives and the Regulatory Framework. In *Turner, R. K., ed.*, 1988, pp. 170–89.

Rees, Jennifer and Friedman, Monroe. A Behavioral Science Assessment of Selected Principles of Consumer Education. *J. Cons. Aff.*, Winter 1988, *22*(2), pp. 284–302.

Rees, Joan C. M. and Bromley, Rosemary D. F. The First Five Years of the Swansea Enterprise Zone: An Assessment of Change. *Reg. Stud.*, August 1988, *22*(4), pp. 263–75.

Rees, John and Bradley, R. State Science Policy and Economic Development in the United States: A Critical Perspective. *Environ. Planning A*, August 1988, *20*(8), pp. 999–1012.

Rees, Ray. Inefficiency, Public Enterprise and Privatisation. *Europ. Econ. Rev.*, March 1988, *32*(2–3), pp. 422–31.

_____ **and Apps, Patricia F.** Taxation and the Household. *J. Public Econ.*, April 1988, *35*(3), pp. 355–69.

Reese, Joachim and Fandel, Günter. Kostenminimale Kraftwerksteuerung in einem Industriebetrieb. (With English summary.) *Z. Betriebswirtschaft*, January 1988, *58*(1), pp. 137–52.

Reese, Julie A. Smart Cards: Foreign Technology Points to the Future Development of U.S. Bank Cards. In *Kemper, R. L., ed.*, 1988, pp. 1–34.

Reeves, Mavis Mann and Marando, Vincent L. State Responsiveness and Local Government Reorganization. *Soc. Sci. Quart.*, December 1988, *69*(4), pp. 996–1004.

Reeves, Roxanne W.; Hansen, W. Lee and Stampen, Jacob O. The Impact of Student Earnings in Offsetting "Unmet Needs." *Econ. Educ. Rev.*, 1988, *7*(1), pp. 113–26.

_____; **Stampen, Jacob O. and Hansen, W. Lee.** Implications of Redefining Independent Student Status. *Econ. Educ. Rev.*, 1988, *7*(1), pp. 85–99.

Regalia, Martin A. and Barth, James R. The Evolving Role of Regulation in the Savings and Loan Industry. In *England, C. and Huertas, T., eds.*, 1988, pp. 113–61.

Regan, P. and King, J. E. Recent Trends in Labour's Share. In *Brenner, Y. S.; Reijnders, J. P. G. and Spithoven, A. H. G. M., eds.*, 1988, pp. 54–86.

Regens, James L. and Reams, Margaret A. State Strategies for Regulating Groundwater Quality. *Soc. Sci. Quart.*, March 1988, 69(1), pp. 53–69.

Reggiani, A. and Nijkamp, Peter. Dynamic Spatial Interaction Models: New Directions. *Environ. Planning A*, November 1988, 20(11), pp. 1449–60.

Regibeau, Pierre and Matutes, Carmen. "Mix and Match": Product Compatibility without Network Externalities. *Rand J. Econ.*, Summer 1988, 19(2), pp. 221–34.

Register, Charles A. Hospital Performance under the Medicare Prospective Reimbursement System. *Atlantic Econ. J.*, December 1988, 16(4), pp. 62–76.

_____. Technical Efficiency with the U.S. Postal Service and the Postal Reorganization Act of 1970. *Appl. Econ.*, September 1988, 20(9), pp. 1185–97.

_____. Wages, Productivity, and Costs in Union and Nonunion Hospitals. *J. Lab. Res.*, Fall 1988, 9(4), pp. 325–45.

_____; Sharp, Ansel M. and Stevans, Lonnie K. Profit Incentives and the Hospital Industry: New Evidence. *Atlantic Econ. J.*, March 1988, 16(1), pp. 25–38.

Regling, Klaus P. New Financing Approaches in the Debt Strategy. *Finance Develop.*, March 1988, 25(1), pp. 6–9.

de Regt, Erik R. Labor Demand and Standard Working Time in Dutch Manufacturing, 1954–1982. In *Hart, R. A., ed.*, 1988, pp. 185–205.

Rehbinder, Maria. Reformen av beskattningen av aktiebolag och personbolag. (The Reform of the Taxation of Limited Companies, Sole Traders, and Partnerships. With English summary.) *Ekon. Samfundets Tidskr.*, 1988, 41(4), pp. 241–53.

Rehman, T. U.; Domingo, J. and Romero, C. Compromise–Risk Programming for Agricultural Resource Allocation Problems: An Illustration. *J. Agr. Econ.*, May 1988, 39(2), pp. 271–76.

_____ and Speedy, A. W. UK Farm Planning and Management on AGVISER. In *Schiefer, G., ed.*, 1988, pp. 87–101.

Rehnfeldt, Maria; Barbieri, William M. and Smith, Robert J. Indian Colonization in Paraguay: What Is Success? In *Annis, S. and Hakim, P., eds.*, 1988, pp. 58–64.

Reibstein, David; Bateson, John E. G. and Boulding, William. Conjoint Analysis Reliability: Empirical Findings. *Marketing Sci.*, Summer 1988, 7(3), pp. 271–86.

Reich, Michael. Postwar Racial Income Differences: Trends and Theories. In *Mangum, G. and Philips, P., eds.*, 1988, pp. 144–67.

_____ and Davidson, Carlos. Income Inequality: An Inter-industry Analysis. *Ind. Relat.*, Fall 1988, 27(3), pp. 263–86.

Reich, Michael R. International Trade and Trade-Offs for Third World Consumers. In *Maynes, E. S. and ACCI Research Committee, eds.*, 1988, pp. 375–96.

_____ and Bell, David E. Health, Nutrition, and Economic Crises: Approaches to Policy in the Third World: Introduction and Overview. In *Bell, D. E. and Reich, M. R., eds.*, 1988, pp. 1–13.

Reich, Robert B. Bailout: A Comparative Study in Law and Industrial Structure. In *Spence, A. M. and Hazard, H. A., eds.*, 1988, pp. 301–72.

_____. The Economics of Illusion and the Illusion of Economics. *Foreign Aff.*, 1987–88, 66(3), pp. 516–28.

Reichelderfer, Katherine and Boggess, William G. Government Decision Making and Program Performance: The Case of the Conservation Reserve Program. *Amer. J. Agr. Econ.*, February 1988, 70(1), pp. 1–11.

Reichelstein, Stefan and Reiter, Stanley. Game Forms with Minimal Message Spaces. *Econometrica*, May 1988, 56(3), pp. 661–92.

Reichenstein, William R. and Ferris, Kenneth R. A Note on the Tax-Induced Clientele Effect and Tax Reform. *Nat. Tax J.*, March 1988, 41(1), pp. 131–37.

Reid, G. C. Jevons's Treatment of Dimensionality in 'The Theory of Political Economy': An Essay in the History of Mathematical Economics. In *Wood, J. C., ed., Vol. 2*, 1988, *1972*, pp. 70–83.

Reid, Gary J. How Cities in California Have Responded to Fiscal Pressures since Proposition 13. *Public Budg. Finance*, Spring 1988, 8(1), pp. 20–37.

Reid, J. Norman. Entrepreneurship as a Community Development Strategy for the Rural South. In *Beaulieu, L. J., ed.*, 1988, pp. 325–43.

Reid, Joseph D., Jr. and Kurth, Michael M. Public Employees in Political Firms: Part A. The Patronage Era. *Public Choice*, December 1988, 59(3), pp. 253–62.

Reidy, K. Risk Analysis in Agricultural Development Projects: The Use of the Monte-Carlo Simulation Technique. *Irish J. Agr. Econ. Rural Soc.*, 1988, 13, pp. 35–46.

Reijnders, Jan P. G. Economic Stability and Political Expediency. In *Brenner, Y. S.; Reijnders, J. P. G. and Spithoven, A. H. G. M., eds.*, 1988, pp. 132–52.

Reilly, Frank K. and Wright, David J. A Comparison of Published Betas. *J. Portfol. Manage.*, Spring 1988, 14(3), pp. 64–69.

Reilly, John M. and LeBlanc, Michael R. Energy Policy Analysis: Alternative Modeling Approaches. In *Johnston, G. M.; Freshwater, D. and Favero, P., eds.*, 1988, pp. 244–71.

_____ and Shankle, S. A. Auxiliary Heating in the Residential Sector. *Energy Econ.*, January 1988, 10(1), pp. 29–41.

Reilly, Robert J.; Hoffer, George E. and Pruitt, Stephen W. The Effect of Media Presentation on the Formation of Economic Expectations: Some Initial Evidence. *J. Econ. Psych.*, September 1988, *9*(3), pp. 315–25.

_____; **Hoffer, George E. and Pruitt, Stephen W.** The Impact of Product Recalls on the Wealth of Sellers: A Reexamination. *J. Polit. Econ.*, June 1988, *96*(3), pp. 663–70.

_____; **Millner, Edward L. and Pratt, Michael D.** A Re-examination of Harrison's Experimental Test for Risk Aversion. *Econ. Letters*, 1988, *27*(4), pp. 317–19.

Reimann, Bernard C. and Muczyk, Jan P. Has Participative Management Been Oversold? In *Timpe, A. D., ed.*, 1988, *1987*, pp. 157–63.

Rein, Martin; Brackman, Harold and Erie, Steven P. Wedded to the Welfare State: Women against Reaganite Retrenchment. In *Jenson, J.; Hagen, E. and Reddy, C., eds.*, 1988, pp. 214–30.

_____; **Esping-Andersen, Gosta and Rainwater, Lee.** Institutional and Political Factors Affecting the Well-Being of the Elderly. In *Palmer, J. L.; Smeeding, T. and Torrey, B. B., eds.*, 1988, pp. 333–50.

_____; **Smeeding, Timothy M. and Torrey, Barbara Boyle.** Patterns of Income and Poverty: The Economic Status of Children and the Elderly in Eight Countries. In *Palmer, J. L.; Smeeding, T. and Torrey, B. B., eds.*, 1988, pp. 89–119.

Reinecke, Gerhard. Accounting in the GDR. In *Bailey, D. T., ed.*, 1988, pp. 94–106.

Reiner, Rolf; Haag, Günter and Munz, Martin. The Estimation of Parameters. In *Weidlich, W. and Haag, G., eds.*, 1988, pp. 33–59.

_____; **Haag, Günter and Munz, Martin.** Tests of Significance in the Ranking Regression Analysis. In *Weidlich, W. and Haag, G., eds.*, 1988, pp. 345–54.

_____ **and Munz, Martin.** A Computer Program for the Estimation of Utilities and Mobilities. In *Weidlich, W. and Haag, G., eds.*, 1988, pp. 365–81.

_____ **and Munz, Martin.** Ranking Regression Analysis of the Global Mobility. In *Weidlich, W. and Haag, G., eds.*, 1988, pp. 355–64.

Reinert, Kenneth A. and Ratick, Samuel J. A Note on Estimating a Long-run Average Cost Curve for Flue Gas Desulfurization. *J. Environ. Econ. Manage.*, March 1988, *15*(1), pp. 30–34.

Reinganum, Jennifer F. Plea Bargaining and Prosecutorial Discretion. *Amer. Econ. Rev.*, September 1988, *78*(4), pp. 713–28.

_____ **and Wilde, Louis L.** A Note on Enforcement Uncertainty and Taxpayer Compliance. *Quart. J. Econ.*, November 1988, *103*(4), pp. 793–98.

Reinganum, Marc R. and Conway, Delores A. Stable Factors in Security Returns: Identification Using Cross-Validation: Reply. *J. Bus. Econ. Statist.*, January 1988, *6*(1), pp. 24–28.

_____ **and Conway, Delores A.** Stable Factors in Security Returns: Identification Using Cross-Validation. *J. Bus. Econ. Statist.*, January 1988, *6*(1), pp. 1–15.

Reinhart, Vincent and Radecki, Lawrence J. The Globalization of Financial Markets and the Effectiveness of Monetary Policy Instruments. *Fed. Res. Bank New York Quart. Rev.*, Autumn 1988, *13*(3), pp. 18–27.

Reinke, William A. Health Care in Indonesia: Dealing with Diversity. In *Sirageldin, I. and Sorkin, A., eds.*, 1988, pp. 175–91.

Reinsel, Gregory C. and Ahn, Sung K. Nested Reduced-Rank Autoregressive Models for Multiple Time Series. *J. Amer. Statist. Assoc.*, September 1988, *83*(403), pp. 849–56.

Reinstein, R. A. U.S.–Canadian Trade Agreement: Background and Summary of Energy Provisions. *Energy J.*, October 1988, *9*(4), pp. 95–97.

Reis, Eustáquio José; Bonelli, Regis and Rios, Sandra Maria Polónia. Dívidas e déficits: Projeções para o médio prazo. (With English summary.) *Pesquisa Planejamento Econ.*, August 1988, *18*(2), pp. 239–70.

Reishus, David and Auerbach, Alan J. The Effects of Taxation on the Merger Decision. In *Auerbach, A. J., ed. (I)*, 1988, pp. 157–83.

_____ **and Auerbach, Alan J.** The Impact of Taxation on Mergers and Acquisitions. In *Auerbach, A. J., ed. (II)*, 1988, pp. 69–85.

_____ **and Auerbach, Alan J.** Taxes and the Merger Decision. In *Coffee, J. C., Jr.; Lowenstein, L. and Rose-Ackerman, S., eds.*, 1988, pp. 300–313.

Reisman, Haim. A General Approach to the Arbitrage Pricing Theory (APT). *Econometrica*, March 1988, *56*(2), pp. 473–76.

_____ **and Mirman, Leonard J.** Price Fluctuations When Only Prices Reveal Information. *Econ. Letters*, 1988, *27*(4), pp. 305–10.

Reiss, Peter C.; Bernanke, Ben S. and Bohn, Henning. Alternative Non-nested Specification Tests of Time-Series Investment Models. *J. Econometrics*, March 1988, *37*(3), pp. 293–326.

_____ **and Levin, Richard C.** Cost-Reducing and Demand-Creating R&D with Spillovers. *Rand J. Econ.*, Winter 1988, *19*(4), pp. 538–56.

Reister, David B. A Compact Model of Oil Supply Disruptions. *Resources & Energy*, June 1988, *10*(2), pp. 161–83.

Reiter, Stanley and Reichelstein, Stefan. Game Forms with Minimal Message Spaces. *Econometrica*, May 1988, *56*(3), pp. 661–92.

Reitsma, René F. and Vergoossen, Dick. A Causal Typology of Migration: The Role of Commuting. *Reg. Stud.*, August 1988, *22*(4), pp. 331–40.

Reitz, Jeffrey G. Less Racial Discrimination in Canada, or Simply Less Racial Conflict?: Implications of Comparisons with Britain. *Can. Public Policy*, December 1988, *14*(4), pp. 424–41.

Reitzes, James D. and Rousslang, Donald J. Domestic versus International Capital Mobility: Some Empirical Evidence. *Can. J. Econ.*, May 1988, *21*(2), pp. 312–23.

Remenyi, Joseph V. Partnership in Research: A New Model for Development Assistance. In

Tisdell, C. and Maitra, P., eds., 1988, pp. 92–115.

Remington, Michael. Comments on *K Mart v. Cartier:* Gray Market Trade and EEC Law. *J. World Trade*, October 1988, *22*(5), pp. 93–102.

Renaghan, Thomas M. A New Look at Fiscal Policy in the 1930s. In *Uselding, P. J., ed.*, 1988, pp. 171–83.

Renaud, Paul S. A. and van Winden, Frans A. A. M. Fiscal Behaviour and the Growth of Government in the Netherlands. In *Lybeck, J. A. and Henrekson, M., eds.*, 1988, pp. 133–56.

Renaudie, Françoise and Lavigne, Marie. A General View of the Third World. In *Lavigne, M., ed.*, 1988, pp. 9–21.

Rendeiro, João O. Technical Change and Vertical Disintegration in Global Competition: Lessons from Machine Tools. In *Hood, N. and Vahlne, J.-E., eds.*, 1988, pp. 209–24.

Rendon, Teresa and Salas, Carlos. Wages and Employment in Mexico: Recent Tendencies and Perspectives. *Rev. Radical Polit. Econ.*, Summer–Fall 1988, *20*(2–3), pp. 253–59.

Reneau, J. Hal; Harrison, Paul D. and West, Stephen G. Initial Attributions and Information-Seeking by Superiors and Subordinates in Production Variance Investigations. *Accounting Rev.*, April 1988, *63*(2), pp. 307–20.

Renfrew, Charles B. Special Issues in Antitrust Litigation: Comment. In *White, L. J., ed.*, 1988, pp. 379–80.

Reno, Virginia P. and Packard, Michael D. A Look at Very Early Retirees. In *Ricardo-Campbell, R. and Lazear, E. P., eds.*, 1988, pp. 243–65.

Renshaw, Edward F. The Rationality Model Revisited. *J. Futures Markets*, April 1988, *8*(2), pp. 157–66.

Renshaw, Jean R. Women in Management in the Pacific Islands: Exploring Pacific Stereotypes. In *Adler, N. J. and Izraeli, D., eds.*, 1988, pp. 122–40.

Renshaw, Vernon. Organizing Work in an Information Age. *J. Post Keynesian Econ.*, Summer 1988, *10*(4), pp. 618–30.

_____; **Johnson, Kenneth P. and Friedenberg, Howard L.** Tracking the BEA Regional Projections, 1983–86. *Surv. Curr. Bus.*, June 1988, *68*(6), pp. 23–27.

_____; **Trott, Edward A., Jr. and Friedenberg, Howard L.** Gross State Product by Industry, 1963–86. *Surv. Curr. Bus.*, May 1988, *68*(5), pp. 30–46.

Renversez, Françoise. Innovations financieres, desintermediation et economie d'endettement. (Financial Innovations, Disintermediation, and the French Overdraft Economy. With English summary.) *Écon. Soc.*, January 1988, *22*(1), pp. 49–79.

Renzetti, Steven. An Econometric Study of Industrial Water Demands in British Columbia, Canada. *Water Resources Res.*, October 1988, *24*(10), pp. 1569–73.

Repin, E. N. Do We Properly Calculate the Economic Efficiency of Health Care Activities. *Prob. Econ.*, November 1988, *31*(7), pp. 58–71.

Repullo, Rafael. The Core of an Economy with Transaction Costs. *Rev. Econ. Stud.*, July 1988, *55*(3), pp. 447–58.

_____. A New Characterization of the Efficiency of Equilibrium with Incomplete Markets. *J. Econ. Theory*, April 1988, *44*(2), pp. 217–30.

_____ **and Moore, John.** Subgame Perfect Implementation. *Econometrica*, September 1988, *56*(5), pp. 1191–1220.

Reschovsky, Andrew. Microsimulation Models and State Tax Reform: The Case of Massachusetts. In *Danziger, S. H. and Portney, K. E., eds.*, 1988, pp. 202–16.

Reshef, Yonatan and Murray, Alan I. Toward a Neoinstitutionalist Approach in Industrial Relations. *Brit. J. Ind. Relat.*, March 1988, *26*(1), pp. 85–97.

Resnick, Bruce G. and Eun, Cheol S. Estimating the Dependence Structure of Share Prices: A Comparative Study of the United States and Japan. *Financial Rev.*, November 1988, *23*(4), pp. 387–401.

_____ **and Eun, Cheol S.** Exchange Rate Uncertainty, Forward Contracts, and International Portfolio Selection. *J. Finance*, March 1988, *43*(1), pp. 197–215.

Resnick, Stephen and Wolff, Richard. Marxian Theory and the Rhetorics of Economics. In *Klamer, A.; McCloskey, D. N. and Solow, R. M., eds.*, 1988, pp. 47–63.

_____ **and Wolff, Richard.** Radical Differences among Radical Theories. *Rev. Radical Polit. Econ.*, Summer–Fall 1988, *20*(2–3), pp. 1–6.

Ress, C. William; Salmon, Walter J. and May, Eleanor G. Future Trends in Retailing: Merchandise Line Trends and Store Trends 1980–1990. In *Kaynak, E., ed.*, 1988, pp. 333–48.

Reti, Pál. Technological Change by Central Control: The Case of the Hungarian Electronics Industry. In *Freeman, C. and Lundvall, B.-A., eds.*, 1988, pp. 156–68.

Rettore, Enrico; Torelli, Nicola and Trivellato, Ugo. Disoccupazione e ricerca di lavoro: Convenzioni definitorie e analisi esplorative sull' "attachment" al mercato del lavoro. (Unemployment and Job Search: Defining Conventions and Exploratory Analyses for Labour Market "Attachment." With English summary.) *Econ. Lavoro*, July–Sept. 1988, *22*(3), pp. 71–94.

Reuten, Geert. Value as Social Form. In *Williams, M., ed.*, 1988, pp. 42–61.

Reuter, Edzard. Analyse von Weltabschlüssen nach Bilanzrichtlinien-Gesetz. (With English summary.) *Z. Betriebswirtshaft*, February 1988, *58*(2), pp. 285–303.

Reuter, Peter. Quantity Illusions and Paradoxes of Drug Interdiction: Federal Intervention into Vice Policy. *Law Contemp. Probl.*, Winter 1988, *51*(1), pp. 233–52.

_____. Testing and Deterrence. *J. Policy Anal. Manage.*, Spring 1988, *7*(3), pp. 554–57.

Reutlinger, Shlomo. Income-Augmenting Interventions and Food Self-Sufficiency for Enhancing Food Consumption among the Poor. In *Pinstrup-Andersen, P., ed.*, 1988, pp. 159–67.

Reve, Torger and Grønhaug, Kjell. Entrepreneurship and Strategic Management: Synergy or Antagony? In *Grønhaug, K. and Kaufmann, G., eds.*, 1988, pp. 331–45.

Revier, Charles F. and Loomis, John B. Measuring Regressivity of Excise Taxes: A Buyers Index. *Public Finance Quart.*, July 1988, *16*(3), pp. 301–14.

Rey, Patrick and Stiglitz, Joseph E. Vertical Restraints and Producers' Competition. *Europ. Econ. Rev.*, March 1988, *32*(2–3), pp. 561–68.

Reyes, Alvaro; de Gómez, Martha Isabel and Ramírez, Clara. Employment and Labour Incomes in Colombia, 1976–85. In *van Ginneken, W., ed.*, 1988, pp. 33–59.

Reyes, Edna A. and Milan, Edwin. Employment Strategies for Accelerated Economic Growth: The Philippine Experience. *Philippine Rev. Econ. Bus.*, March–June 1988, *25*(1–2), pp. 151–84.

Reynolds, Bruce L. Trade, Employment, and Inequality in Postreform China. In *Reynolds, B. L., ed.*, 1988, 1987, pp. 189–99.

_____ **and Fei, John C. H.** A Tentative Plan for the Rational Sequencing of Overall Reform in China's Economic System. In *Reynolds, B. L., ed.*, 1988, 1987, pp. 200–212.

_____ **and Wu, Jinglian.** Choosing a Strategy for China's Economic Reform. *Amer. Econ. Rev.*, May 1988, *78*(2), pp. 461–66.

Reynolds, Clark W. Fissures in the Volcano? Central American Economic Prospects. In *Bates, R. H., ed.*, 1988, 1978, pp. 206–36.

_____ **and McCleery, Robert K.** The Political Economy of Immigration Law: Impact of Simpson–Rodino on the United States and Mexico. *J. Econ. Perspectives*, Summer 1988, *2*(3), pp. 117–31.

Reynolds, Lloyd G. Labor Economics Then and Now. In *Kaufman, B. E., ed.*, 1988, pp. 117–43.

Reynolds, Morgan O. Labor Reform: A Blip on the Radarscope. In *Boaz, D., ed.*, 1988, pp. 321–32.

Reynolds, Peter C. Corporate Culture on the Rocks. In *Timpe, A. D., ed.*, 1988, 1986, pp. 53–60.

Reynolds, R. Larry and Barney, L. Dwayne. Economics of Organ Procurement and Allocation. *J. Econ. Issues*, June 1988, *22*(2), pp. 571–79.

Reynolds, Robert J.; Salant, Stephen W. and Switzer, Sheldon. Losses from Horizontal Merger: The Effects of an Exogenous Change in Industry Structure on Cournot–Nash Equilibrium. In *Daughety, A. F., ed.*, 1988, 1983, pp. 373–87.

Reynolds, Stanley S. Plant Closings and Exit Behaviour in Declining Industries. *Economica*, November 1988, *55*(220), pp. 493–503.

_____ **and Isaac, R. Mark.** Appropriability and Market Structure in a Stochastic Invention

Model. *Quart. J. Econ.*, November 1988, *103*(4), pp. 647–71.

Reynolds, Stephen E. and Seninger, Stephen F. Long-Run Determinants of the International Division of Labor. In *Mangum, G. and Philips, P., eds.*, 1988, pp. 249–73.

Rezende, Condorcet Pereira. Recognition of Foreign Enterprises as Taxable Entities: Brazil. In *International Fiscal Association, ed. (I)*, 1988, pp. 321–29.

Rhee, Wookwan. Interest Rates and Wage Indexation. *Int. Econ. J.*, Summer 1988, *2*(2), pp. 63–73.

Rhoades, Stephen A. and Amel, Dean F. Strategic Groups in Banking. *Rev. Econ. Statist.*, November 1988, *70*(4), pp. 685–89.

_____ **and Liang, Nellie.** Geographic Diversification and Risk in Banking. *J. Econ. Bus.*, November 1988, *40*(4), pp. 271–84.

Rhodes, Ed and Wield, David. Divisions of Labour or Labour Divided? International Relocation of Industry. In *Crow, B. and Thorpe, M., et al.*, 1988, pp. 288–309.

Rhodes, George F., Jr. and Sampath, Rajan K. Efficiency, Equity and Cost Recovery Implications of Water Pricing and Allocation Schemes in Developing Countries. *Can. J. Agr. Econ.*, March 1988, *36*(1), pp. 103–17.

Rhodes, J.; Tyler, P. and Moore, B. C. Geographical Variations in Industrial Costs. *Scot. J. Polit. Econ.*, February 1988, *35*(1), pp. 22–50.

_____; **Tyler, P. and Moore, B. C.** The Rate Burden: An Accounting Framework for Assessing the Effect of Local Taxes on Business. *Reg. Stud.*, October 1988, *22*(5), pp. 387–97.

Rhodes, Marilyn S. and Hansen, W. Lee. Student Debt Crisis: Are Students Incurring Excessive Debt? *Econ. Educ. Rev.*, 1988, *7*(1), pp. 101–12.

Riboud, Michelle. Altruisme au sein de la famille, croissance économique et démographie. (Altruism in the Family, Economic Growth and Demography. With English summary.) *Revue Écon.*, January 1988, *39*(1), pp. 127–54.

_____ **and Hernández-Iglesias, Feliciano.** Intergenerational Effects on Fertility Behavior and Earnings Mobility in Spain. *Rev. Econ. Statist.*, May 1988, *70*(2), pp. 253–58.

Ricardo-Campbell, Rita. Aging: Social Security and Medicare. In *Anderson, A. and Bark, D. L., eds.*, 1988, pp. 335–48.

_____. Women: Retirees and Widows. In *Ricardo-Campbell, R. and Lazear, E. P., eds.*, 1988, pp. 84–95.

Ricart i Costa, Joan E. Managerial Task Assignment and Promotions. *Econometrica*, March 1988, *56*(2), pp. 449–66.

Ricca, Sergio. The Changing Role of Public Employment Services. *Int. Lab. Rev.*, 1988, *127*(1), pp. 19–34.

Ricci, Gianni. Applications of Mathematics of the Goodwin Model. In *[Goodwin, R. M.]*, 1988, pp. 53–61.

_____ **and Velupillai, Kumaraswamy.** Lecture Notes in Economics and Mathematical Systems: Growth Cycles and Multisectoral Economics: The Goodwin Tradition: Introduction. In *[Goodwin, R. M.]*, 1988, pp. 1–18.

Rice, Dorothy P. and LaPlante, Mitchell P. Chronic Illness, Disability, and Increasing Longevity. In *Sullivan, S. and Lewin, M. E., eds.*, 1988, pp. 9–55.

Rice, Gillian and Kaynak, Erdener. Retail Systems in Developing Countries: Some Insights from the Middle East. In *Kaynak, E., ed.*, 1988, pp. 265–76.

Rich, Daniel and Byrne, John. Planning for Changing Energy Conditions: Introduction. In *Byrne, J. and Rich, D., eds.*, 1988, pp. 1–8.

Rich, Daniel P. and Wyzan, Michael L. Microeconomic Analysis of Parallel Markets: Comment. *J. Compar. Econ.*, December 1988, *12*(4), pp. 604–09.

Rich, Georg. A New International Trading System: Concluding Remarks. In *Borner, S., ed.*, 1988, pp. 377–80.

Richard, J. F. and Steel, M. F. J. Bayesian Analysis of Systems of Seemingly Unrelated Regression Equations under a Recursive Extended Natural Conjugate Prior Density. *J. Econometrics*, May–June 1988, *38*(1–2), pp. 7–37.

Richard, Scott F. and Meltzer, Allan H. A Rational Theory of the Size of Government. In *Ricketts, M., ed., Vol. 1*, 1988, *1981*, pp. 375–88.

_____ **and Srivastava, Sanjay.** Equilibrium in Economies with Infinitely Many Consumers and Infinitely Many Commodities. *J. Math. Econ.*, 1988, *17*(1), pp. 9–21.

Richards, Daniel J. Some Evidence on the Inflationary Bias of Macroeconomic Policy. *J. Macroecon.*, Summer 1988, *10*(3), pp. 435–47.

Richards, Eric. Regional Imbalance and Poverty in Early Nineteenth-Century Britain. In *Mitchison, R. and Roebuck, P., eds.*, 1988, pp. 193–207.

Richards, Hamish. The Changing Nature of Population Education for Workers. *Int. Lab. Rev.*, 1988, *127*(5), pp. 559–71.

Richards, John F. and Tucker, Richard P. World Deforestation in the Twentieth Century: Introduction. In *Richards, J. F. and Tucker, R. P., eds.*, 1988, pp. 1–12.

Richards, Peter G. The Recent History of Local Fiscal Reform. In *Bailey, S. J. and Paddison, R., eds.*, 1988, pp. 25–41.

Richards, Timothy J. Intellectual Property Rights: Reconciling Divergent Views. In *Walker, C. E. and Bloomfield, M. A., eds.*, 1988, pp. 93–98.

Richardson, B. An Economic Approach to the Design of AIDS Policies: Commentary. In *Smith, C. S., ed.*, 1988, pp. 226–29.

Richardson, D. H. and Wu, M. T. C. A Short-run Monetary Model of Exchange Rate Determination: Stability Tests and Forecasting. *Empirical Econ.*, 1988, *13*(1), pp. 1–15.

Richardson, G. B. Equilibrium, Expectations and Information. In *Earl, P. E., ed., Vol. 2*, 1988, *1959*, pp. 19–33.

_____. The Organisation of Industry. In *Earl, P. E., ed., Vol. 2*, 1988, *1972*, pp. 57–70.

Richardson, Grace E. The Role of Business. In *Maynes, E. S. and ACCI Research Committee, eds.*, 1988, pp. 836–42.

Richardson, Harry W. Monocentric vs. Policentric Models: The Future of Urban Economics in Regional Science. *Ann. Reg. Sci.*, July 1988, *22*(2), pp. 1–12.

_____. National Urban Policies and the Costs and Benefits of Urbanization. In *Salvatore, D., ed.*, 1988, pp. 95–106.

_____. A Review of Techniques for Regional Policy Analysis. In *[Perroux, F.]*, 1988, pp. 142–68.

_____ **and Schwartz, Gerd.** Economic Development, Population and Primacy. *Reg. Stud.*, December 1988, *22*(6), pp. 467–75.

Richardson, J. The Diffusion of Eleven Medical Technologies in Australia. In *Butler, J. R. G. and Doessel, D. P., eds.*, 1988, pp. 78–108.

_____. The Geographic Distribution of Doctors: Does the Market Fail? In *Smith, C. S., ed.*, 1988, pp. 61–95.

_____. Insurance, Information, Quality, and Medical Markets: Commentary. In *Smith, C. S., ed.*, 1988, pp. 56–60.

Richardson, J. David. Exchange Rates and U.S. Auto Competitiveness. In *Marston, R. C., ed.*, 1988, pp. 215–37.

_____. The Factor-Price Equalization Model and Industry Labor Productivity: An Empirical Test across Countries: Comment. In *Feenstra, R. C., ed.*, 1988, pp. 48–49.

_____. International Coordination of Trade Policy. In *Feldstein, M., ed. (I)*, 1988, pp. 167–204.

_____. International Payments Imbalances in Heavily Indebted Developing Countries: Discussion. In *Fieleke, N. S., ed.*, 1988, pp. 98–102.

Richardson, Jeremy J. and Moore, Christopher. The Politics and Practice of Corporate Responsibility in Great Britain. In *Preston, L. E., ed.*, 1988, pp. 267–90.

Richardson, Pat; Little, Jo and Peake, Linda. Geography and Gender in the Urban Environment: Introduction. In *Little, J.; Peake, L. and Richardson, P., eds.*, 1988, pp. 1–20.

Richardson, Pete. Empirical Macroeconomics for Interdependent Economies: Comparison and Evaluation of Model Simulations: Comment. In *Bryant, R. C., et al., eds.*, 1988, pp. 154–55.

_____. The Structure and Simulation Properties of OECD's Interlink Model. *OECD Econ. Stud.*, Spring 1988, (10), pp. 57–122.

_____. A Survey of Non-Dutch European Macroeconometric Models: Some International Perspective: Comments. In *Driehuis, W.; Fase, M. M. G. and den Hartog, H., eds.*, 1988, pp. 259–64.

Richardson, Ray; Dewe, Philip and Dunn, Stephen. Employee Share Option Schemes, Why Workers Are Attracted to Them. *Brit. J. Ind. Relat.*, March 1988, *26*(1), pp. 1–20.

Richardson, Sue. The Development of Government Policies on Poverty and Income Distribution: Comment. *Australian Econ. Rev.*, Spring 1988, (83), pp. 74–75.

Richman, Sheldon L. Commentator on Our Times: A Quest for the Historical Rothbard. In *[Rothbard, M. N.]*, 1988, pp. 352–79.

Richmond, James and Carrera, Cármen. Investment Decisions under Majority Rule. *Economica*, August 1988, 55(219), pp. 365–78.

Richter, C. and Burdakov, O. Parallel Hybrid Optimization Methods. In *Kurzhanski, A.; Neumann, K. and Pallaschke, D.*, eds., 1988, pp. 16–23.

Richter, Kerry. Union Patterns and Children's Living Arrangements in Latin America. *Demography*, November 1988, 25(4), pp. 553–66.

Richter, Marcel K. and Fuhrken, Gebhard. Algebra and Topology in Cardinal Utility Theory. In *Eichhorn, W.*, ed., 1988, pp. 139–52.

Richter, Rudolf. The New Institutional Economics Applied to Monetary Economics. *J. Inst. Theoretical Econ.*, February 1988, 144(1), pp. 208–24.

_____. Views and Comments on Gustav Schmoller and the Methodenstreit. *J. Inst. Theoretical Econ.*, June 1988, 144(3), pp. 524–26.

_____. Views and Comments on the Problem of Order in Economics. *J. Inst. Theoretical Econ.*, April 1988, 144(2), pp. 343.

_____ and Szeifel, Peter. Three Reports on the West German Health Care System: A Collection of Reviews. *J. Inst. Theoretical Econ.*, April 1988, 144(2), pp. 386–87.

Richter, Wolfram F. Comprehensive versus Neutral Income Taxation. In *Bös, D.; Rose, M. and Seidl, C.*, eds.,, 1988, pp. 281–95.

_____ and Bamberg, Günter. Risk-Taking under Progressive Taxation: Three Partial Effects. In *Eichhorn, W.*, ed., 1988, pp. 479–97.

_____; Schwaiger, J. and Buchholz, Wolfgang. Distributional Implications of Equal Sacrifice Rules. *Soc. Choice Welfare*, 1988, 5(2/3), pp. 223–26.

_____; Schwaiger, J. and Buchholz, Wolfgang. Distributional Implications of Equal Sacrifice Rules. In *Gaertner, W. and Pattanaik, P. K.*, eds., 1988, 1988, pp. 135–38.

Rickard, Julie M. Factors Influencing Long-Distance Rail Passenger Trip Rates in Great Britain. *J. Transp. Econ. Policy*, May 1988, 22(2), pp. 209–33.

Ricketts, Erol R. and Sawhill, Isabel V. Defining and Measuring the Underclass. *J. Policy Anal. Manage.*, Winter 1988, 7(2), pp. 316–25.

Ricketts, Martin. Rent-Seeking, Entrepreneurship, Subjectivism, and Property Rights: A Reply. *J. Inst. Theoretical Econ.*, December 1988, 144(5), pp. 894–95.

Ricks, Michael; Wilson, William W. and Fung, Hung-Gay. Option Price Behavior in Grain Futures Markets. *J. Futures Markets*, February 1988, 8(1), pp. 47–65.

Ricks, William E. and Biddle, Gary C. Analyst Forecast Errors and Stock Price Behavior Near the Earnings Announcement Dates of LIFO Adopters. *J. Acc. Res.*, Autumn 1988, 26(2), pp. 169–94.

Ricottilli, Massimo. Le decisioni di investimento per la sostituzione di impianti superati dal progresso tecnico: Il problema della scelta del tempo. (Investment Decisions Concerning Plant Scrapping and Substitution: The Optimum Date Problem. With English summary.) *Econ. Polit.*, December 1988, 5(3), pp. 387–408.

Riddell, Tom. U.S. Military Power, the Terms of Trade, and the Profit Rate. *Amer. Econ. Rev.*, May 1988, 78(2), pp. 60–65.

Riddle, Dorothy I. Public Sector Productivity and Role Conflicts. In *Kelly, R. M.*, ed., 1988, pp. 191–208.

_____ and Brown, Kristopher J. From Complacency to Strategy: Retaining World Class Competitiveness in Services. In *Starr, M. K.*, ed., 1988, pp. 239–70.

Rider, Christine. Interpretations of Capitalism: Four Alternative Texts: A Review Article. *Rev. Radical Polit. Econ.*, Winter 1988, 20(4), pp. 95–103.

_____. Market Reforms in a Shortage Economy. *Rev. Radical Polit. Econ.*, Summer–Fall 1988, 20(2–3), pp. 138–42.

Ridge, John and Macdonald, Kenneth. British Social Trends since 1900: Social Mobility. In *Halsey, A. H.*, ed., 1988, pp. 202–25.

Ridler, Neil B. The *Caisse de Stabilisation* in the Coffee Sector of the Ivory Coast. *World Devel.*, December 1988, 16(12), pp. 1521–26.

_____ and Kabir, M. Cultivation of Fish and Shellfish: Implications for Regional Economic Development. In *Choudhury, M. A.*, ed., 1988, pp. 116–25.

Riebe, K.-E. The Principles of Education in the Use of Computer-Assisted Decision Models by the General Farm Management Adviser. In *Schiefer, G.*, ed., 1988, pp. 227–30.

Riedel, James. The Demand for LDC Exports of Manufactures: Estimates from Hong Kong. *Econ. J.*, March 1988, 98(389), pp. 138–48.

_____. Economic Development in East Asia: Doing What Comes Naturally? In *Hughes, H.*, ed., 1988, pp. 1–38.

_____. Trade as an Engine of Growth: Theory and Evidence. In *Greenaway, D.*, ed., 1988, pp. 25–54.

Riedel, Jürgen and Gluch, Erich. The Global Construction Industry: The Federal Republic of Germany. In *Strassmann, W. P. and Wells, J.*, eds., 1988, pp. 120–40.

Riege, Astrid. The Development of a Small Village to an Important Naval Town in England: Chatham 1550–1697. In *Cavaciocchi, S.*, ed., 1988, pp. 909–35.

Rieger, Hans Christoph and Langhammer, Rolf J. ASEAN and the EC: Trade in Tropical Agricultural Products: Preface. In *Langhammer, R. J. and Rieger, H. C.*, eds., 1988, pp. xiii–xiv.

Rieke, Wolfgang. Jahresversammlung des Internationalen Währungsfonds und der Weltbank 1988 in West-Berlin. (1988 Combined Annual Meeting of the International Monetary Fund and the World Bank Group in West Berlin. With English summary.) *Kredit Kapital*, 1988, *21*(4), pp. 633–40.

Riepe, James S. Functional Competition from Mutual Funds. In *Federal Home Loan Bank of San Francisco*, 1988, pp. 151–61.

Riese, Martin. Raw Material Prices and Kalecki's Wage Share Theory: Reply. *J. Post Keynesian Econ.*, Spring 1988, *10*(3), pp. 487–88.

Riester, Walter. A Trade Union View on JIT in Germany. In *Holl, U. and Trevor, M., eds.*, 1988, pp. 89–91.

Rietveld, Piet. Urban Development Patterns in Indonesia. *Bull. Indonesian Econ. Stud.*, April 1988, *24*(1), pp. 73–95.

_____ **and Rouwendal, Jan.** Search and Mobility in a Housing Market with Limited Supply. *Ann. Reg. Sci.*, November 1988, *22*(3), pp. 80–98.

Rietz, Thomas A. The Equity Risk Premium: A Solution. *J. Monet. Econ.*, July 1988, *22*(1), pp. 117–31.

Riezman, Raymond. Empirics of Taxes on Differentiated Products: The Case of Tariffs in the U.S. Automobile Industry: Comment. In *Baldwin, R. E., ed. (II)*, 1988, pp. 40–41.

_____ **and Kennan, John.** Do Big Countries Win Tariff Wars? *Int. Econ. Rev.*, February 1988, *29*(1), pp. 81–85.

Riggs, Henry E. Innovations: A United States–Japan Perspective. In *Okimoto, D. I. and Rohlen, T. P., eds.*, 1988, pp. 246–52.

Riker, William H. The Place of Political Science in Public Choice. *Public Choice*, June 1988, *57*(3), pp. 247–57.

Riley, Barry and Brittan, Samuel. A People's Stake in North Sea Oil. In *Johnson, C., ed.*, 1988, *1978*, pp. 141–56.

Riley, John G. Ex Post Information in Auctions. *Rev. Econ. Stud.*, July 1988, *55*(3), pp. 409–29.

_____ **and Milde, Hellmuth.** Signaling in Credit Markets. *Quart. J. Econ.*, February 1988, *103*(1), pp. 101–29.

Rima, Ingrid H. Keynes's Vision and Econometric Analysis. In *Hamouda, O. F. and Smithin, J. N., eds., Vol. 2*, 1988, pp. 12–22.

Rimashevskaia, N. M. The Need for New Approaches. *Prob. Econ.*, April 1988, *30*(12), pp. 59–72.

_____ **and Milovidov, A.** On Improving State Assistance to Families with Children. *Prob. Econ.*, November 1988, *31*(7), pp. 72–81.

_____ **and Pavlova, N.** The System of Pension Security. *Prob. Econ.*, May 1988, *31*(1), pp. 74–88.

Rimlinger, Gaston V. Social Security in Trouble. In *Nash, G. D.; Pugach, N. H. and Tomasson, R. F., eds.*, 1988, pp. 181–204.

Rimmer, Lesley. The Intra-family Distribution of Paid Work, 1968–81. In *Hunt, A., ed.*, 1988, pp. 52–82.

Rimmer, Malcolm and McDonald, Trish. Award Structure and the Second Tier. *Australian Bull. Lab.*, June 1988, *14*(3), pp. 469–91.

_____ **and Zappala, Jon.** Labour Market Flexi-

bility and the Second Tier. *Australian Bull. Lab.*, September 1988, *14*(4), pp. 564–91.

Rimmer, P. J. The Internationalization of Engineering Consultancies: Problems of Breaking into the Club. *Environ. Planning A*, June 1988, *20*(6), pp. 761–88.

Rimmer, Russell J. and Bonnell, Sheila Mary. Trends and Cyclical Changes in Real Wages, Productivity and Distribution of Income during the 1930s. In *Brenner, Y. S.; Reijnders, J. P. G. and Spithoven, A. H. G. M., eds.*, 1988, pp. 89–116.

_____; **Higgs, Peter J. and Parmenter, B. R.** A Hybrid Top-Down, Bottom-Up Regional Computable General Equilibrium Model. *Int. Reg. Sci. Rev.*, 1988, *11*(3), pp. 317–28.

Rindfuss, Ronald R.; Bean, Frank D. and Stephen, Elizabeth Hervey. Racial Differences in Contraceptive Choice: Complexity and Implications. *Demography*, February 1988, *25*(1), pp. 53–70.

Rindi, Barbara. The Effects of Financial Futures Trading on Cash Market Prices: A Survey. *Giorn. Econ.*, July–Aug. 1988, *47*(7–8), pp. 333–61.

Ringo, Philip J. Privatization in the Transit Industry. In *Weicher, J. C., ed.*, 1988, pp. 62–67.

del Rio M., Salvador Beltran and DuMars, Charles T. A Survey of the Air and Water Quality Laws of Mexico. *Natural Res. J.*, Fall 1988, *28*(4), pp. 787–813.

Riordan, Michael H. and Sappington, David E. M. Commitment in Procurement Contracting. *Scand. J. Econ.*, 1988, *90*(3), pp. 357–72.

_____ **and Sappington, David E. M.** Optimal Contracts with Public ex post Information. *J. Econ. Theory*, June 1988, *45*(1), pp. 189–99.

Rios, Sandra Maria Polónia; Reis, Eustáquio José and Bonelli, Regis. Dívidas e déficits: Projeções para o médio prazo. (With English summary.) *Pesquisa Planejamento Econ.*, August 1988, *18*(2), pp. 239–70.

Ripa di Meana, Andrea and Jappelli, Tullio. The Behavior of Inflation and Interest Rates: Evidence from Italian National History. *J. Econ. Dynam. Control*, March 1988, *12*(1), pp. 27–35.

Rippe, Wolfgang. Educational Expansion, Change in Organizational Structures, and Managerial Discretion. In *Dlugos, G.; Dorow, W. and Weiermair, K., eds.*, 1988, pp. 363–81.

Risager, Ole. Devaluation, Profitability and Investment. *Scand. J. Econ.*, 1988, *90*(2), pp. 125–40.

_____ **and Andersen, Torben M.** Indkomstpolitikken under firkløverregeringen. (Danish Incomes Policy 1982–87. With English summary.) *Nationaløkon. Tidsskr.*, 1988, *126*(3), pp. 286–302.

_____ **and Andersen, Torben M.** Stabilization Policies, Credibility, and Interest Rate Determination in a Small Open Economy. *Europ. Econ. Rev.*, March 1988, *32*(2–3), pp. 669–79.

Riskær, Sven. Hjælper ulandshjælpen—nok? (Does Development Aid Aid—Enough? With

English summary.) *Nationaløkon. Tidsskr.*, 1988, *126*(1), pp. 63–74.

Riso, Gerald. Role of the Federal Chief Financial Officer. *Public Budg. Finance*, Autumn 1988, *8*(3), pp. 55–62.

Rister, M. Edward. Management Problems of Farms and Agricultural Firms: A Discussion. In *Hildreth, R. J., et al., eds.*, 1988, pp. 307–12.

————; **Brorsen, B. Wade and Grant, Warren R.** Some Effects of Rice Quality on Rough Rice Prices. *Southern J. Agr. Econ.*, July 1988, *20*(1), pp. 131–40.

Ritchken, Peter H. and Chen, Wen-Kuei. Downside Risk Option Pricing Models. In *Khoury, S. J. and Ghosh, A., eds.*, 1988, pp. 205–25.

———— **and Kuo, Shyanjaw.** Option Bounds with Finite Revision Opportunities. *J. Finance*, June 1988, *43*(2), pp. 301–08.

———— **and Rabinowitz, Gad.** Capital Budgeting Using Contingent Claims Analysis: A Tutorial. In *Fabozzi, F. J., ed.*, 1988, pp. 119–43.

Ritov, Yaakov; Gilula, Zvi and Krieger, Abba M. Ordinal Association in Contingency Tables: Some Interpretive Aspects. *J. Amer. Statist. Assoc.*, June 1988, *83*(402), pp. 540–45.

Ritson, Christopher. Economic Systems and Resource Adjustment: Some Comments. *Europ. Rev. Agr. Econ.*, 1988, *15*(2–3), pp. 221–23.

———— **and Swinbank, Alan.** The Common Agricultural Policy, Customs Unions and the Mediterranean Basin. *J. Common Market Stud.*, December 1988, *27*(2), pp. 97–112.

Rittenberg, Libby. Financial Liberalization and Savings in Turkey. In *Nas, T. F. and Odekon, M., eds.*, 1988, pp. 115–27.

Ritter, A. R. M. Cuba's Convertible Currency Debt Problem. *CEPAL Rev.*, December 1988, (36), pp. 117–40.

Ritter, Jay R. The Buying and Selling Behavior of Individual Investors at the Turn of the Year. *J. Finance*, July 1988, *43*(3), pp. 701–17.

Ritz, Zvi and Sudharshan, D. An Evolutionary Analysis of Product-Preference Structure: Toward Managerial Control. In *Eiselt, H. A. and Pederzoli, G., eds.*, 1988, pp. 326–42.

Ritzen, Jozef M. M. and van Imhoff, Evert. Optimal Economic Growth and Non-stable Population. *De Economist*, 1988, *136*(3), pp. 339–57.

———— **and Kodde, David A.** Direct and Indirect Effects of Parental Education Level on the Demand for Higher Education. *J. Human Res.*, Summer 1988, *23*(3), pp. 356–71.

Rivera-Batiz, Francisco L. Increasing Returns, Monopolistic Competition, and Agglomeration Economies in Consumption and Production. *Reg. Sci. Urban Econ.*, February 1988, *18*(1), pp. 125–53.

———— **and Fujita, Masahisa.** Agglomeration and Heterogeneity in Space. *Reg. Sci. Urban Econ.*, February 1988, *18*(1), pp. 1–5.

Rivers, Douglas and Vuong, Quang H. Limited Information Estimators and Exogeneity Tests for Simultaneous Probit Models. *J. Econometrics*, November 1988, *39*(3), pp. 347–66.

Rivlin, Alice M. Economics and the Political Process. In *Brown, E., ed.*, 1988, *1987*, pp. 13–23.

Rizopoulos, G. and Lianos, T. P. Estimation of Social Welfare Weights in Agricultural Policy: The Case of Greek Cotton. *J. Agr. Econ.*, January 1988, *39*(1), pp. 61–68.

Rizzo, Ilde. Fiscal Perception and Public Debt: Some Notes on the Equivalence Issue. *Econ. Scelte Pubbliche/J. Public Finance Public Choice*, Sept.–Dec. 1988, *6*(3), pp. 213–26.

Ro, Byung T. and Haw, In-Mu. An Analysis of the Impact of Corporate Pollution Disclosures: A Comment. In *Neimark, M., ed.*, 1988, pp. 187–91.

Ro, Kongkyun and Kim, Woncheol. A Causal VARMA Model Analysis with an Application to Canadian Money and Income Data. *Appl. Econ.*, September 1988, *20*(9), pp. 1167–83.

Roach, Stephen S. Technology and Services Sector: America's Hidden Competitive Challenge. In *Guile, B. R. and Quinn, J. B., eds. (II)*, 1988, pp. 118–38.

Roback, Jennifer. W. H. Hutt's *The Economics of the Colour Bar. Managerial Dec. Econ.*, Special Issue, Winter 1988, pp. 65–70.

————. Wages, Rents, and Amenities: Differences among Workers and Regions. *Econ. Inquiry*, January 1988, *26*(1), pp. 23–41.

Robb, A. Leslie; Burbidge, John B. and Magee, Lonnie. Alternative Transformations to Handle Extreme Values of the Dependent Variable. *J. Amer. Statist. Assoc.*, March 1988, *83*(401), pp. 123–27.

Robb, Peter. Bihar, the Colonial State and Agricultural Development in India, 1880–1920. *Indian Econ. Soc. Hist. Rev.*, April–June 1988, *25*(2), pp. 205–35.

Robben, Henry; Morris, Ira and Webley, Paul. Social Comparison and Tax Evasion in a Shop Simulation. In *Maital, S., ed., Vol. 2*, 1988, pp. 553–61.

Robbins, Edward Henry and Schatzberg, John D. Callable Bonds: A Risk-Reducing Signalling Mechanism—A Reply. *J. Finance*, September 1988, *43*(4), pp. 1067–73.

Robbins, Lionel. The Place of Jevons in the History of Economic Thought. In *Wood, J. C., ed., Vol. 1*, 1988, *1936*, pp. 94–108.

Robbins, Lynn W. A Positive Role for Graduate Agribusiness Programs in Agricultural Economics. *Western J. Agr. Econ.*, July 1988, *13*(1), pp. 121–27.

Robbins, Walter A. The Importance of Selected Information Items to Municipal Bond Analysts and Their Disclosure in Municipal Annual Reports: An Empirical Assessment. In *Chan, J. L. and Rowan, H. J., eds.*, 1988, pp. 103–27.

Roberds, William. Forecast Accuracy and the Performance of Economic Policy: Is There a Connection? *Fed. Res. Bank Atlanta Econ. Rev.*, Sept.–Oct. 1988, *73*(5), pp. 20–32.

———— **and Stutzer, Michael J.** Variable Rate Loans and Financed Activities: The Case of Adjustable Rate Mortgages. *J. Urban Econ.*, July 1988, *24*(1), pp. 27–37.

Robert, Christian. Performances d'estimateurs à

rétrécisseur en situation de multicolinéarité. (Shrinkage Estimators and Multicollinearity Problems. With English summary.) *Ann. Écon. Statist.*, April–June 1988, (10), pp. 97–119.

Roberti, Paolo. Riflessioni critiche sui principi e sugli strumenti dello "stato del benessere." (Some Critical Reflections on the Principles and Instruments of the Welfare State. With English summary.) *Econ. Lavoro*, July–Sept. 1988, 22(3), pp. 3–25.

_____ **and Imbriani, Cesare.** Tax Harmonies and Disharmonies: Harmonization by Itself Is Not Enough. *Rev. Econ. Cond. Italy*, Sept.–Dec. 1988, (3), pp. 371–97.

Roberto, Eduardo L. and Pinson, Christian R. A. Consumer Behavior and the Marketing Activities of Firms. In *van Raaij, W. F.; van Veldhoven, G. M. and Wärneryd, K.-E., eds.*, 1988, pp. 295–330.

Roberts, Bryan W. and Movit, Charles H. Modeling Soviet Modernization: An Economy in Transition: A Comment. *Soviet Econ.*, Jan.–March 1988, 4(1), pp. 57–64.

Roberts, David J. and Sullivan, Mark J. Marriage and the Income Tax Law: Living Together Compatibly. *Challenge*, Nov.–Dec. 1988, 31(6), pp. 52–53.

Roberts, Fred S. and Fishburn, Peter C. Unique Finite Conjoint Measurement. *Math. Soc. Sci.*, October 1988, 16(2), pp. 107–43.

Roberts, Harry V. and Alwan, Layth C. Time-Series Modeling for Statistical Process Control. *J. Bus. Econ. Statist.*, January 1988, 6(1), pp. 87–95.

_____; **Tiao, George C. and Easton, George S.** Making Statistics More Effective in Schools of Business. *J. Bus. Econ. Statist.*, April 1988, 6(2), pp. 247–60.

Roberts, John and Boskin, Michael J. A Closer Look at Saving Rates in the United States and Japan. In *Shoven, J. B., ed.*, 1988, pp. 121–43.

_____ **and Milgrom, Paul.** An Economic Approach to Influence Activities in Organizations. In *Winship, C. and Rosen, S., eds.*, 1988, pp. 154–79.

_____ **and Milgrom, Paul.** Communication and Inventory as Substitutes in Organizing Production. *Scand. J. Econ.*, 1988, 90(3), pp. 275–89.

_____ **and Milgrom, Paul.** Economic Theories of the Firm: Past, Present, and Future. *Can. J. Econ.*, August 1988, 21(3), pp. 444–58.

Roberts, Mark J. and Aw, Bee Yan. Price and Quality Level Comparisons for U.S. Footwear Imports: An Application of Multilateral Index Numbers. In *Feenstra, R. C., ed.*, 1988, pp. 257–75.

_____ **and Samuelson, Larry.** An Empirical Analysis of Dynamic, Nonprice Competition in an Oligopolistic Industry. *Rand J. Econ.*, Summer 1988, 19(2), pp. 200–220.

_____; **Samuelson, Larry and Dunne, Timothy.** Patterns of Firm Entry and Exit in U.S. Manu-

facturing Industries. *Rand J. Econ.*, Winter 1988, 19(4), pp. 495–515.

Roberts, Paul Craig. How Economists Wrought a Nonsystem. *Cato J.*, Fall 1988, 8(2), pp. 347–49.

_____. Warren Nutter: An Economist for all Time. In *[Nutter, G. W.]*, 1988, pp. 157–68.

Roberts, Peter W. Energy Policy and Planning in the U.K.: The Case of Coal and Regional Development. In *Byrne, J. and Rich, D., eds.*, 1988, pp. 173–214.

Robertson, Frances and Sloan, Judith. A Labour Market Profile of Nurses in Australia. *Australian Bull. Lab.*, June 1988, 14(3), pp. 507–28.

Robertson, G. Mr. Jevons's Formal Logic. In *Wood, J. C., ed., Vol. 1*, 1988, 1876, pp. 11–25.

Robertson, John D. and Masters, Marick F. The Impact of Organized Labor on Public Employment: A Comparative Analysis. *J. Lab. Res.*, Fall 1988, 9(4), pp. 347–62.

Robertson, R. M. Jevons and His Precursors. In *Wood, J. C., ed., Vol. 1*, 1988, 1951, pp. 146–66.

Robin, Jean-Marc and Lévy-Garboua, Louis. Les représentations implicites des goûts dans les modèles dynamiques de demande. (The Implicit Representation of Tastes in Dynamic Demand Models. With English summary.) *Revue Écon.*, January 1988, 39(1), pp. 33–55.

Robins, Philip K. Child Care and Convenience: The Effects of Labor Market Entry Costs on Economic Self-sufficiency among Public Housing Residents. *Soc. Sci. Quart.*, March 1988, 69(1), pp. 122–36.

_____ **and Blau, David M.** Child-Care Costs and Family Labor Supply. *Rev. Econ. Statist.*, August 1988, 70(3), pp. 374–81.

Robinson, Austin. The National Institute: The Early Years. *Nat. Inst. Econ. Rev.*, May 1988, (124), pp. 63–66.

Robinson, Bill and Stark, Graham. The Tax Treatment of Marriage: What Has the Chancellor Really Achieved? *Fisc. Stud.*, May 1988, 9(2), pp. 48–56.

Robinson, Bob H., et al. U.S.–Canadian Trade Liberalization: Key Issues. In *Allen, K. and Macmillan, K., eds.*, 1988, pp. 65–74.

Robinson, Chris. Language Choice: The Distribution of Language Skills and Earnings in a Dual-Language Economy. In *Ehrenberg, R. G., ed.*, 1988, pp. 53–90.

Robinson, Colin. A Liberalized Coal Market? In *Johnson, C., ed.*, 1988, 1987, pp. 93–110.

Robinson, David E. Feed Cost Problems and Feed Freight Assistance in Nova Scotia. *Can. J. Agr. Econ.*, Part 2, December 1988, 36(4), pp. 881–93.

Robinson, David J. and Stella, Peter. Amalgamating Central Bank and Fiscal Deficits. In *Blejer, M. I. and Chu, K.-Y., eds.*, 1988, pp. 20–31.

Robinson, Glen O. The Titanic Remembered: AT&T and the Changing World of Telecommunications: Book Review Essay. *Yale J. Regul.*, Summer 1988, 5(2), pp. 517–45.

Robinson, James C. Hazardous Occupations

within the Job Hierarchy. *Ind. Relat.*, Spring 1988, *27*(2), pp. 241–50.

_____. Market Structure, Employment, and Skill Mix in the Hospital Industry. *Southern Econ. J.*, October 1988, *55*(2), pp. 315–25.

_____. Workplace Hazards and Workers' Desires for Union Representation. *J. Lab. Res.*, Summer 1988, *9*(3), pp. 237–49.

Robinson, Jean R. The Content of a College-University Course in Consumer Education. In *Maynes, E. S. and ACCI Research Committee, eds.*, 1988, pp. 857–73.

Robinson, Joan. Capital Theory Up to Date. In *Steedman, I., ed., Vol. 1*, 1988, *1970*, pp. 319–27.

_____. Prelude to a Critique of Economic Theory. In *Steedman, I., ed., Vol. 1*, 1988, *1961*, pp. 82–87.

_____. The Theory of Distribution. In *Sawyer, M. C., ed.*, 1988, *1960*, pp. 340–53.

_____. Time in Economic Theory. In *Sawyer, M. C., ed.*, 1988, *1980*, pp. 33–43.

_____ and Naqvi, K. A. The Badly Behaved Production Function. In *Steedman, I., ed., Vol. 1*, 1988, *1967*, pp. 328–40.

Robinson, John P. and Gershuny, Jonathan. Historical Changes in the Household Division of Labor. *Demography*, November 1988, *25*(4), pp. 537–52.

Robinson, Kenneth J. The Effect of Monetary Policy on Long-Term Interest Rates: Further Evidence from an Efficient-Markets Approach. *Fed. Res. Bank Dallas Econ. Rev.*, March 1988, pp. 10–16.

Robinson, N. S.; Kondonassis, A. J. and Malliaris, A. G. Political Instability and Economic Development: An Economic History Case Study of Greece, 1948–1966: A Reply. *J. Europ. Econ. Hist.*, Spring 1988, *17*(1), pp. 185–86.

Robinson, Peter B. and McDonald, Ian. A Multisectoral Dynamic Optimization Model for Energy/Petrochemical Decision Making in Zimbabwe and the SADCC. In *Hosier, R. H., ed. (II)*, 1988, pp. 126–37.

_____; Ram, Bonnie and Nkomo, Jabavu C. Industrial Energy Consumption, Conservation Strategies and Policy Options in Zimbabwe. In *Hosier, R. H., ed. (II)*, 1988, pp. 26–49.

_____ and Stoneman, Colin. Economic Modeling for LEAP: Background and Methodology. In *Hosier, R. H., ed. (II)*, 1988, pp. 99–125.

_____, et al. Energy Consumption in Zimbabwe's Manufacturing, Mining, Transport and Commerce Sectors: Concepts, Issues and Problems. In *Hosier, R. H., ed. (II)*, 1988, pp. 1–25.

Robinson, Peter M. Root-*N*-Consistent Semiparametric Regression. *Econometrica*, July 1988, *56*(4), pp. 931–54.

_____. Semiparametric Econometrics: A Survey. *J. Appl. Econometrics*, January 1988, *3*(1), pp. 35–51.

_____. The Stochastic Difference between Econometric Statistics. *Econometrica*, May 1988, *56*(3), pp. 531–48.

_____. Using Gaussian Estimators Robustly. *Oxford Bull. Econ. Statist.*, February 1988, *50*(1), pp. 97–106.

Robinson, Richard B., Jr. and McDougall, Patricia P. New Venture Performance: Patterns of Strategic Behavior in Different Industries. In *Kirchhoff, B. A., et al., eds.*, 1988, pp. 477–91.

Robinson, Roger W., Jr. Financing the East Bloc. In *Anderson, A. and Bark, D. L., eds.*, 1988, pp. 203–14.

Robinson, S. J. and Voss, C. A. Application of Just-in-Time Manufacturing Techniques in the United Kingdom. In *Holl, U. and Trevor, M., eds.*, 1988, pp. 101–04.

_____ and Voss, C. A. Application of Just-in-Time Manufacturing Techniques in the United Kingdom. In *Holl, U. and Trevor, M., eds.*, 1988, pp. 63–70.

Robinson, Sherman and Adelman, Irma. Macroeconomic Adjustment and Income Distribution: Alternative Models Applied to Two Economies. *J. Devel. Econ.*, July 1988, *29*(1), pp. 23–44.

_____ and Adelman, Irma. Macroeconomic Shocks, Foreign Trade, and Structural Adjustment: A General Equilibrium Analysis of the U.S. Economy, 1982–1986. In *Carter, C. A. and Gardiner, W. H., eds.*, 1988, pp. 137–62.

_____ and Roland-Holst, David W. Macroeconomic Structure and Computable General Equilibrium Models. *J. Policy Modeling*, Fall 1988, *10*(3), pp. 353–75.

_____; Woods, Leyla and Tyson, Laura D'Andrea. Conditionality and Adjustment in Hungary and Yugoslavia. In *[Holzman, F. D.]*, 1988, pp. 72–105.

Robinson, Silvan. On Prices and Price Formation. In *Mabro, R., ed.*, 1988, pp. 41–47.

Robinson, Warren C. and Cornwell, Gretchen T. Fertility of U.S. Farm Women during the Electrification Era, 1930–1950. *Population Res. Policy Rev.*, 1988, *7*(3), pp. 277–91.

_____ and Schutjer, Wayne. Agricultural Development and Demographic Change: Reply. *Econ. Develop. Cult. Change*, April 1988, *36*(3), pp. 571–72.

Robinson, William T. Marketing Mix Reactions to Entry. *Marketing Sci.*, Fall 1988, *7*(4), pp. 368–85.

_____. Marketing Mix Reactions to Entry: Reply. *Marketing Sci.*, Fall 1988, *7*(4), pp. 391–92.

Robison, H. David. Industrial Pollution Abatement: The Impact on Balance of Trade. *Can. J. Econ.*, February 1988, *21*(1), pp. 187–99.

Robison, Lindon J. and Meyer, Jack. Hedging under Output Price Randomness. *Amer. J. Agr. Econ.*, May 1988, *70*(2), pp. 268–72.

Robison, M. H. and Miller, J. R. Cross-Hauling and Nonsurvey Input–Output Models: Some Lessons from Small-Area Timber Economies. *Environ. Planning A*, November 1988, *20*(11), pp. 1523–30.

Robison, Richard. Resisting Structural Adjustment: Conflict over Industrial Policy in Indonesia. In *Carlsson, J. and Shaw, T. M., eds.*, 1988, pp. 23–47.

Robles, Fernando and El-Ansary, Adel I. Informal Sector and Economic Development: A Marketing Perspective. In *Kumcu, E. and Firat, A. F., eds.*, 1988, pp. 199–228.

_____ **and Sarathy, Ravi.** Segmenting the Market for Commuter Aircraft. In *Woodside, A. G., ed.*, 1988, pp. 223–47.

Robock, Stefan H. U.S. Policies toward Transnationals. In *Teng, W. and Wang, N. T., eds.*, 1988, pp. 109–20.

Robson, Peter and Dunning, John H. Multinational Corporate Integration and Regional Economic Integration. In *Dunning, J. and Robson, P., eds.*, 1988, pp. 1–23.

Robson, T. F. and Landers, A. J. Systems Analysis in Mechanization Management. In *Schiefer, G., ed.*, 1988, pp. 205–24.

Roca Jusmet, Jordi and Martínez-Alier, Joan. Economía política del corporativismo en el Estado español: Del franquismo al posfranquismo. (With English summary.) *Desarrollo Econ.*, April–June 1988, *28*(109), pp. 3–38.

da Rocha Ferreira, Léo and da Motta, Ronaldo Serôa. The Brazilian National Alcohol Programme: An Economic Reappraisal and Adjustments. *Energy Econ.*, July 1988, *10*(3), pp. 229–34.

Roche, Edward M. Knowledge-Processing Technologies and the Global Strategies of Transnational Corporations: Issues for Developing Countries. In *Teng, W. and Wang, N. T., eds.*, 1988, pp. 75–92.

Roche, Frederick C. Java's Critical Uplands: Is Sustainable Development Possible? *Food Res. Inst. Stud.*, 1988, *21*(1), pp. 1–43.

Rochet, Jean-Charles. Théorie de la négociation: Une sélection de quelques résultats récents. (Bargaining Theory: A Selection of Some Recent Results. With English summary.) *Ann. Écon. Statist.*, Oct.–Dec. 1988, (12), pp. 1–25.

_____ **and Laffont, Jean-Jacques.** Stock Market Portfolios and the Segmentation of the Insurance Market. *Scand. J. Econ.*, 1988, *90*(3), pp. 435–46.

Rochfort, William M.; Hodes, Daniel A. and Cook, Thomas. The Importance of Regional Economic Analysis and Regional Strategies in an Age of Industrial Restructuring. *Bus. Econ.*, April 1988, *23*(2), pp. 46–51.

Rock, Llewyn; Sealy, Ronald and Craigwell, Roland. On the Determination of the External Public Debt: The Case of Barbados. *Soc. Econ. Stud.*, December 1988, *37*(4), pp. 137–50.

Rock, Steven M. The Tax Reform Act of 1986 and State Income Taxes: The Illinois Expectation. *Public Budg. Finance*, Spring 1988, *8*(1), pp. 108–16.

Rockefeller, John D., IV. The United States and the Asia-Pacific Region. In *Kozmetsky, G.; Matsumoto, H. and Smilor, R. W., eds.*, 1988, pp. 139–42.

Rockel, Mark L. and Kealy, Mary Jo. Merit Scholarships Are No Quick Fix for College Quality. *Econ. Educ. Rev.*, 1988, *7*(3), pp. 345–55.

_____ **; Kealy, Mary Jo and Dovidio, John F.** Accuracy in Valuation is a Matter of Degree. *Land Econ.*, May 1988, *64*(2), pp. 158–71.

_____ **and Turner, Robert W.** Estimating Covariances of Parameter Estimates from Different Models. *Econ. Letters*, 1988, *26*(2), pp. 137–40.

Rockett, Katharine E. and Frankel, Jeffrey A. International Macroeconomic Policy Coordination When Policymakers Do Not Agree on the True Model. *Amer. Econ. Rev.*, June 1988, *78*(3), pp. 318–40.

Rockinger, Georg Michael and Holly, Alberto. Exact and Approximate Distribution of the *t* Ratio Test Statistic in an AR(1) Model. In *Barnett, W. A.; Berndt, E. R. and White, H., eds.*, 1988, pp. 157–70.

Rockness, Joanne W. and Schlachter, Paul. Directions for Social Accounting Research: A Survey of Potential Data Sources. In *Neimark, M., ed.*, 1988, pp. 83–94.

Rockwell, Llewellyn H., Jr. Three National Treasures: Hazlitt, Hutt, and Rothbard. In *[Rothbard, M. N.]*, 1988, pp. 139–50.

_____ **and Block, Walter.** Man, Economy, and Liberty: Essays in Honor of Murray N. Rothbard: Introduction. In *[Rothbard, M. N.]*, 1988, pp. ix–xviii.

Rodano, Giorgio and Saltari, Enrico. Futures Markets, Average Opinion and Rational Learning. *Ricerche Econ.*, July–Sept. 1988, *42*(3), pp. 452–69.

Roderick, Hilliard; Morriss, Andrew and Schmandt, Jurgen. Acid Rain Is Different. In *Schmandt, J.; Clarkson, J. and Roderick, H., eds.*, 1988, pp. 7–30.

_____ **; Schmandt, Jurgen and Clarkson, Judith.** Acid Rain and Friendly Neighbors: The Policy Dispute between Canada and the United States: Preface. In *Schmandt, J.; Clarkson, J. and Roderick, H., eds.*, 1988, pp. xiii–xv.

Rodger, Richard. Alternatives to Mass Production: Industrial Dualism and Business Structure in Victorian Scotland. In *Perkins, E. J., ed.*, 1988, pp. 227–41.

Rodgers, Harrell R., Jr. Beyond Welfare: New Approaches to the Problem of Poverty in America: Introduction: The Role of Nonwelfare Social Policies in Reducing Poverty. In *Rodgers, H. R., Jr., ed.*, 1988, pp. vii–xiv.

_____ . Reducing Poverty through Family Support. In *Rodgers, H. R., Jr., ed.*, 1988, pp. 39–65.

Rodgers, Joan R. Intra-industry Trade, Aggregation and the HOS Model. *J. Econ. Stud.*, 1988, *15*(5), pp. 5–23.

Rodino, Peter W., Jr. Let's Fix Only What's Broken: Some Thoughts on Proposed Reform of Private Antitrust Litigation. In *White, L. J., ed.*, 1988, pp. 419–24.

Rodrigues, Mónica Reyes. Recognition of Foreign Enterprises as Taxable Entities: Colombia. In *International Fiscal Association, ed. (I)*, 1988, pp. 347–61.

Rodriguez, Abelardo and Taylor, R. G. Stochastic Modeling of Short-term Cattle Operations. *Amer. J. Agr. Econ.*, February 1988, 70(1), pp. 121–32.

Rodriguez, Carlos Alfredo. Inflation Stabilization: Argentina: Comment. In *Bruno, M., et al., eds.*, 1988, pp. 202–09.

Rodriguez Castellanos, Arturo. Premio por riesgo en el mercado de cambios a plazo. Modelos de valoración de activos financieros: una exploración empírica. (With English summary.) *Invest. Econ.*, May 1988, 12(2), pp. 259–77.

Rodríguez, Ennio. Costa Rica: A Quest for Survival. In *Griffith-Jones, S., ed.*, 1988, pp. 193–210.

_____. The Costa Rican Experience with the International Debt Crisis: Comments. In *Feinberg, R. E. and Ffrench-Davis, R., eds.*, 1988, pp. 232–36.

Rodríguez Fernández, José Miguel. La decisión de distribuir dividendos: Investigación empírica en la gran empresa española. (With English summary.) *Invest. Econ.*, May 1988, 12(2), pp. 243–58.

Rodriguez, Flavia. Foreign Debt, Exchange Rates and Prices. *Soc. Econ. Stud.*, December 1988, 37(4), pp. 227–52.

_____. Recession and Adjustment: The Dominican Case 1983–1985. *Soc. Econ. Stud.*, December 1988, 37(4), pp. 193–226.

Rodríguez, Germán and Cleland, John. The Effect of Parental Education on Marital Fertility in Developing Countries. *Population Stud.*, November 1988, 42(3), pp. 419–42.

_____ and Cleland, John. Modelling Marital Fertility by Age and Duration: An Empirical Appraisal of the Page Model. *Population Stud.*, July 1988, 42(2), pp. 241–57.

Rodríguez, José Luis. The Antecedents and Theoretical Characteristics of Cubanology. In *Zimbalist, A., ed.*, 1988, pp. 22–38.

_____. Cubanology and the Provision of Basic Needs in the Cuban Revolution. In *Zimbalist, A., ed.*, 1988, pp. 83–106.

Rodríguez, Manuel Martín. The Spanish Sugar Industry, 1914–1936. In *Albert, B. and Graves, A., eds.*, 1988, pp. 47–58.

Rodriguez, Ricardo J. Default Risk, Yield Spreads, and Time to Maturity. *J. Finan. Quant. Anal.*, March 1988, 23(1), pp. 111–17.

_____. The Wealth Maximizing Ordering Quantity: An Extension. *Financial Rev.*, May 1988, 23(2), pp. 227–32.

Rodrik, Dani. External Debt and Economic Performance in Turkey. In *Nas, T. F. and Odekon, M., eds.*, 1988, pp. 161–83.

_____. Imperfect Competition, Scale Economies, and Trade Policy in Developing Countries. In *Baldwin, R. E., ed. (II)*, 1988, pp. 109–37.

_____ and Zeckhauser, Richard. The Dilemma of Government Responsiveness. *J. Policy Anal. Manage.*, Fall 1988, 7(4), pp. 601–20.

Rodwin, Lloyd. Some Lessons and Implications of the World Bank's Experience in Urban Development. In *[Perroux, F.]*, 1988, pp. 299–317.

Rodwin, Marc A. and Altman, Stuart H. Halfway Competitive Markets and Ineffective Regulation: The American Health Care System. In *Greenberg, W., ed.*, 1988, pp. 101–17.

Roe, Terry L. Ippolito Extended. In *Maynes, E. S. and ACCI Research Committee, eds.*, 1988, pp. 270–75.

_____ and Antonovitz, Frances. A Theoretical and Empirical Approach to the Value of Information in Risky Markets: A Reply. *Rev. Econ. Statist.*, August 1988, 70(3), pp. 545–47.

Roebuck, Peter. The Economic Situation and Functions of Substantial Landowners 1600–1815: Ulster and Lowland Scotland Compared. In *Mitchison, R. and Roebuck, P., eds.*, 1988, pp. 81–92.

_____ and Mitchison, Rosalind. Economy and Society in Scotland and Ireland: 1500–1939: Introduction. In *Mitchison, R. and Roebuck, P., eds.*, 1988, pp. 1–13.

Roediger, David. Americanism and Fordism—American Style: Kate Richards O'Hare's "Has Henry Ford Made Good?" *Labor Hist.*, Spring 1988, 29(2), pp. 241–52.

Roehl, Thomas W.; Truitt, J. Frederick and Moxon, Richard W. International Cooperative Ventures in the Commercial Aircraft Industry: Gains, Sure, But What's My Share? In *Contractor, F. J. and Lorange, P.*, 1988, pp. 255–77.

Roehrig, Charles S. Conditions for Identification in Nonparametric and Parametric Models. *Econometrica*, March 1988, 56(2), pp. 433–47.

Roell, Ailsa and King, Mervyn. The Regulation of Take-overs and the Stock Market. *Nat. Westminster Bank Quart. Rev.*, February 1988, pp. 2–14.

Roemer, John E. Axiomatic Bargaining Theory on Economic Environments. *J. Econ. Theory*, June 1988, 45(1), pp. 1–31.

Roett, Riordan. Brazil: Economic Crisis and Policy Options. In *Chacel, J. M.; Falk, P. S. and Fleischer, D. V., eds.*, 1988, pp. 110–19.

Rofman, Edmundo and Gonzalez, Roberto. On Stochastic Control Problems: An Algorithm for the Value Function and the Optimal Policy—Some Applications. In *Iri, M. and Yajima, K., eds.*, 1988, pp. 80–89.

Rogers, Alan J. The Bahadur Efficiency of Tests of Some Joint Hypotheses. *J. Amer. Statist. Assoc.*, March 1988, 83(401), pp. 257–64.

_____ and Melfi, C. A. A Test for the Existence of Allocative Inefficiency in Firms. *J. Appl. Econometrics*, January 1988, 3(1), pp. 69–80.

Rogers, Andrei. Age Patterns of Elderly Migration: An International Comparison. *Demography*, August 1988, 25(3), pp. 335–70.

Rogers, Beatrice Lorge. Design and Implementation Considerations for Consumer-Oriented Food Subsidies. In *Pinstrup-Andersen, P., ed.*, 1988, pp. 127–46.

_____. Pakistan's Ration System: Distribution of Costs and Benefits. In *Pinstrup-Andersen, P., ed.*, 1988, pp. 242–52.

Rogers, Carol Ann. A Simple Rule for Managing the Maturity Structure of Government Debt. *Econ. Letters*, 1988, *28*(2), pp. 163–68.

Rogers, David. Environmental Change in the Financial Services Industry. In *Lamb, R. and Shrivastava, P., eds.*, 1988, pp. 89–111.

Rogers, Everett M. The Role of the Research University in the Spin-off of High-Technology Companies. In *Grønhaug, K. and Kaufmann, G., eds.*, 1988, *1986*, pp. 443–55.

Rogers, Glenn; Shaffer, Ron E. and Pulver, Glen C. Identification of Local Capital Markets for Policy Research. *Rev. Reg. Stud.*, Winter 1988, *18*(1), pp. 55–66.

Rogers, Jay. Trends in Transit Financing. In *Weicher, J. C., ed.*, 1988, pp. 38–44.

Rogers, John M. Expenditures of Urban and Rural Consumers, 1972–73 to 1985. *Mon. Lab. Rev.*, March 1988, *111*(3), pp. 41–45.

Rogers, Peter P.; Harrington, Joseph J. and Fiering, Myron B. New Approaches to Using Mathematical Programming for Resource Allocation. In *O'Mara, G. T., ed.*, 1988, pp. 122–26.

Rogers, R. Mark. Improving Monthly Models for Economic Indicators: The Example of an Improved CPI Model. *Fed. Res. Bank Atlanta Econ. Rev.*, Sept.–Oct. 1988, *73*(5), pp. 34–50.

Rogers, Ronald C. The Relationship between Earnings Yield and Market Value: Evidence from the American Stock Exchange. *Financial Rev.*, February 1988, *23*(1), pp. 65–80.

Rogerson, P. A. Alternative Strategies for Selling Land to the Highest Bidder. *Environ. Planning A*, June 1988, *20*(6), pp. 817–28.

_____. What Should We Expect from Models of the Sale Process and Price Formation in Housing Markets: Rebuttal. *Environ. Planning A*, June 1988, *20*(6), pp. 832.

Rogerson, Richard. Indivisible Labor, Lotteries and Equilibrium. *J. Monet. Econ.*, January 1988, *21*(1), pp. 3–16.

_____. Recursive Competitive Equilibrium in Multi-sector Economies. *Int. Econ. Rev.*, August 1988, *29*(3), pp. 419–30.

_____ and Cho, Jang-Ok. Family Labor Supply and Aggregate Fluctuations. *J. Monet. Econ.*, March–May 1988, *21*(2–3), pp. 233–45.

_____ and Wright, Randall D. Involuntary Unemployment in Economies with Efficient Risk Sharing. *J. Monet. Econ.*, November 1988, *22*(3), pp. 501–15.

Rogerson, William P. Price Advertising and the Deterioration of Product Quality. *Rev. Econ. Stud.*, April 1988, *55*(2), pp. 215–29.

Rogge, V. and Pöschke, J. Experiments for Manufacturing Metallic Compounds during the D1-Mission. In *Egan, J. J., et al.*, 1988, pp. 369–83.

Rogoff, Kenneth. A Positive Theory of Fiscal Policy in Open Economies: Comment. In *Frenkel, J. A., ed.*, 1988, pp. 193–95.

_____ and Bulow, Jeremy. The Buyback Boondoggle. *Brookings Pap. Econ. Act.*, 1988, (2), pp. 645–98.

_____ and Bulow, Jeremy. Comprehensive Debt Retirement: The Bolivian Example: Comment. *Brookings Pap. Econ. Act.*, 1988, (2), pp. 714–15.

_____ and Bulow, Jeremy. Multilateral Negotiations for Rescheduling Developing Country Debt: A Bargaining-Theoretic Framework. *Int. Monet. Fund Staff Pap.*, December 1988, *35*(4), pp. 644–57.

_____ and Meese, Richard A. Was It Real? The Exchange Rate-Interest Differential Relation over the Modern Floating-Rate Period. *J. Finance*, September 1988, *43*(4), pp. 933–48.

_____ and Sibert, Anne. Elections and Macroeconomic Policy Cycles. *Rev. Econ. Stud.*, January 1988, *55*(1), pp. 1–16.

Rogowski, Ronald. Structure, Growth, and Power: Three Rationalist Accounts. In *Bates, R. H., ed.*, 1988, *1983*, pp. 300–330.

Rogus, John. Potential Impact of AIDS on African Economic Development. In *Pennsylvania Economic Association*, 1988, pp. 532–47.

Rohlen, Thomas P. Education in Japanese Society. In *Okimoto, D. I. and Rohlen, T. P., eds.*, 1988, pp. 25–31.

_____ and Pascale, Richard. The Mazda Turnaround. In *Okimoto, D. I. and Rohlen, T. P., eds.*, 1988, pp. 149–69.

Rojas, Mauricio. Reflexiones acerca del debate sobre los orígenes de la industrialización Latinoamericana y de su entorno ideológico. (Review of the Debate in the Origins of Industrialization and Its Ideological Context in Latin America. With English summary.) *Colección Estud. CIEPLAN*, March 1988, (23), pp. 67–86.

Rola, Leandro R.; Lynne, Gary D. and Shonkwiler, J. S. Attitudes and Farmer Conservation Behavior. *Amer. J. Agr. Econ.*, February 1988, *70*(1), pp. 12–19.

Roland, Gérard. Product Quality in a Soviet-Type Economy. *Europ. Econ. Rev.*, January 1988, *32*(1), pp. 129–39.

_____ and Reati, Angelo. Ondes longues et régulation: le cas allemand. (With English summary.) *Cah. Écon. Bruxelles*, First Trimester 1988, (117), pp. 107–50.

Roland-Holst, David W. and Robinson, Sherman. Macroeconomic Structure and Computable General Equilibrium Models. *J. Policy Modeling*, Fall 1988, *10*(3), pp. 353–75.

Rolewicz, S. and Perz, S. On Inverse-Image of Non-oriented Graphs. In *Kurzhanski, A.; Neumann, K. and Pallaschke, D., eds.*, 1988, pp. 213–24.

Roley, V. Vance and Pearce, Douglas K. Firm Characteristics, Unanticipated Inflation, and Stock Returns. *J. Finance*, September 1988, *43*(4), pp. 965–81.

Rolfes, Bernd and Krämer, Christoph. Erfolgsorientierte Steuerung marktbezogener Organisationseinheiten in Kreditinstituten. (Success-Oriented Management of Organizational Units of Credit Institutions Operating Cost to the Market. With English summary.) *Kredit Kapital*, 1988, *21*(1), pp. 118–42.

Roll, Richard. Empirical Evidence on Takeover Activity and Shareholder Wealth. In *Coffee,*

J. C., Jr.; Lowenstein, L. and Rose-Ackerman, S., eds., 1988, pp. 241–52.

_____. R^2. *J. Finance*, July 1988, *43*(3), pp. 541–66.

Rollet, Philippe. The Evolution of the Specialization of Industrial Activities in Europe. *Empirica*, 1988, *15*(1), pp. 117–26.

Rolnick, Arthur J. and Weber, Warren E. Explaining the Demand for Free Bank Notes. *J. Monet. Econ.*, January 1988, *21*(1), pp. 47–71.

_____ **and Weber, Warren E.** Explaining the Demand for Free Bank Notes. *Fed. Res. Bank Minn. Rev.*, Spring 1988, *12*(2), pp. 21–35.

Rolph, John E. and Keeler, Emmett B. The Demand for Episodes of Treatment in the Health Insurance Experiment. *J. Health Econ.*, December 1988, *7*(4), pp. 337–67.

Rom, Mark C. and Witte, John F. Power versus Participation: The Wisconsin State Budget Process. In *Danziger, S. H. and Witte, J. F., eds.*, 1988, pp. 13–34.

Romani, Franco. Anti-trust Legislation in a Free Society. *Rev. Econ. Cond. Italy*, Jan.–April 1988, (1), pp. 35–47.

Romano, Joseph P. A Bootstrap Revival of Some Nonparametric Distance Tests. *J. Amer. Statist. Assoc.*, September 1988, *83*(403), pp. 698–708.

Romano, Richard E. A Monopolist Should Always Be Subsidized No Matter How High the Excess Burden. *Can. J. Econ.*, November 1988, *21*(4), pp. 871–73.

_____. A Note on Vertical Integration: Price Discrimination and Successive Monopoly. *Economica*, May 1988, *55*(218), pp. 261–68.

_____. Oligopolistic Competition for Market Share via Voluntary Excess Supply. *Int. J. Ind. Organ.*, December 1988, *6*(4), pp. 447–68.

_____ **and Blair, Roger D.** The Influence of Attitudes toward Risk on the Value of Forecasting. *Quart. J. Econ.*, May 1988, *103*(2), pp. 387–96.

Romanowicz, Tomasz M. and Owsinski, Jan W. A Population-Type Model of Car Market Dynamics. In *Iri, M. and Yajima, K., eds.*, 1988, pp. 385–94.

Römer, B. and Graumann, U. Videotex Activities in European Agriculture—An Overview. In *Schiefer, G., ed.*, 1988, pp. 33–45.

Romer, Christina D. How Does Macroeconomic Policy Affect Output? Comment. *Brookings Pap. Econ. Act.*, 1988, (2), pp. 485–90.

_____. World War I and the Postwar Depression: A Reinterpretation Based on Alternative Estimates of GNP. *J. Monet. Econ.*, July 1988, *22*(1), pp. 91–115.

Romer, David. The Productivity Slowdown, Measurement Issues, and the Explosion of Computer Power: Comment. *Brookings Pap. Econ. Act.*, 1988, (2), pp. 425–28.

_____; **Ball, Laurence and Mankiw, N. Gregory.** The New Keynesian Economics and the Output–Inflation Trade-off. *Brookings Pap. Econ. Act.*, 1988, (1), pp. 1–65.

Römer, Elisabeth M. Konkurrenzforschung. Informationsgrundlage der Wettbewerbsstrate-

gie. (With English summary.) *Z. Betriebswirtshaft*, April 1988, *58*(4), pp. 481–501.

Romer, Thomas. Federal Assistance and Local Services in the United States: The Evolution of a New Federalist Fiscal Order: Comment. In *Rosen, H. S., ed.*, 1988, pp. 74–77.

_____. On James Buchanan's Contributions to Public Economics. *J. Econ. Perspectives*, Fall 1988, *2*(4), pp. 165–79.

_____; **Filimon, Radu and Epple, Dennis.** Community Development with Endogenous Land Use Controls. *J. Public Econ.*, March 1988, *35*(2), pp. 133–62.

Romero, C.; Rehman, T. U. and Domingo, J. Compromise–Risk Programming for Agricultural Resource Allocation Problems: An Illustration. *J. Agr. Econ.*, May 1988, *39*(2), pp. 271–76.

Romero, José. Pérdidas de ingreso por acumulación de factores inducida por aranceles: Un modelo neoaustriaco. (Income Losses Due to Tariff-Induced Factor Accumulation in a Neo-Austrian Model. With English summary.) *Estud. Econ.*, Jan.–June 1988, *3*(1), pp. 57–75.

Roncaglia, Alessandro. The Neo-Ricardian Approach and the Distribution of Income. In *Asimakopulos, A., ed.*, 1988, pp. 159–80.

_____. Wage Costs and Employment: The Sraffian View. In *Kregel, J. A.; Matzner, E. and Roncaglia, A., eds.*, 1988, pp. 9–23.

_____. William Petty and the Conceptual Framework for the Analysis of Economic Development. In *Arrow, K. J., ed.*, 1988, pp. 157–74.

_____; **Kregel, J. A. and Matzner, Egon.** Barriers to Full Employment: Introduction. In *Kregel, J. A.; Matzner, E. and Roncaglia, A., eds.*, 1988, pp. 1–5.

Ronen, Joshua. The Entrepreneur and Society. In *Albanese, P. J., ed.*, 1988, pp. 143–63.

_____. Individual Entrepreneurship and Corporate Entrepreneurship: A Tentative Synthesis. In *Libecap, G., ed. (II)*, 1988, pp. 243–67.

_____ **and Balachandran, Kashi R.** An Approach to Transfer Pricing under Uncertainty. *J. Acc. Res.*, Autumn 1988, *26*(2), pp. 300–314.

_____; **Gilad, Benjamin and Kaish, Stanley.** The Entrepreneurial Way with Information. In *Maital, S., ed., Vol. 2*, 1988, pp. 480–503.

Rones, Arthur; Goodman, Laurie S. and Daryanani, Raj. The Credit Exposure of Cross-Currency and Nondollar Interest Rate Swaps. In *Khoury, S. J. and Ghosh, A., eds.*, 1988, pp. 193–203.

Ronn, Ehud I. Nonadditive Preferences and the Marginal Propensity to Consume. *Amer. Econ. Rev.*, March 1988, *78*(1), pp. 216–23.

Ronning, Gerd. Probleme bei der Schätzung fehlerbehafteter Anteilsgleichungen. (Problems in the Estimation of Share Equations Affected by Errors. With English summary.) *Jahr. Nationalökon. Statist.*, January 1988, *204*(1), pp. 69–82.

Roobeek, Annemieke J. M. Telecommunications: An Industry in Transition. In *de Jong, H. W., ed.*, 1988, pp. 297–328.

Rook, Dennis W. Researching Consumer Fantasy. In *Hirschman, E. and Sheth, J. N.*, eds., 1988, pp. 247–70.

Rooney, Patrick Michael. Worker Participation in Employee-Owned Firms. *J. Econ. Issues*, June 1988, *22*(2), pp. 451–58.

Roosa, Robert V. Financial Market Volatility: Overview. In *Federal Reserve Bank of Kansas City*, 1988, pp. 243–48.

_____. Restoring Stability Within a System of Floating Exchange Rates. In *[Witteveen, H. J.]*, 1988, pp. 191–97.

Root, Franklin R. Some Taxonomies of International Cooperative Arrangements. In *Contractor, F. J. and Lorange, P.*, 1988, pp. 69–80.

van Rooyen, M. and Snyman, J. A. A Multiplex Algorithm for Linear Programming Problems. In *Iri, M. and Yajima, K.*, eds., 1988, pp. 177–86.

Roper, Stephen. Recruitment Methods and Vacancy Duration. *Scot. J. Polit. Econ.*, February 1988, *35*(1), pp. 51–64.

Rorijs, Gertjan and Steerneman, Ton. Pitfalls for Forecasters. In *Dijkstra, T. K.*, ed., 1988, pp. 102–17.

Rosa, Jean-Jacques. Théorie économique de la nationalisation et de la privatisation. (An Economic Theory of Nationalization and Privatization. With English summary.) *Finance*, December 1988, *9*(2), pp. 91–109.

Rosales, Osvaldo. An Assessment of the Structuralist Paradigm for Latin American Development and the Prospects for Its Renovation. *CEPAL Rev.*, April 1988, (34), pp. 19–36.

Rosati, Furio Camillo and Quintieri, Beniamino. Fiscal Policy and Labor Supply. *Public Finance*, 1988, *43*(3), pp. 425–39.

Rose-Ackerman, Susan. Progressive Law and Economics—And the New Administrative Law. *Yale Law J.*, December 1988, *98*(2), pp. 341–68.

_____; Coffee, John C., Jr. and Lowenstein, Louis. Knights, Raiders & Targets: The Impact of the Hostile Takeover: Introduction. In *Coffee, J. C., Jr.; Lowenstein, L. and Rose-Ackerman, S.*, eds., 1988, pp. 1–9.

Rose, Adam and Beaumont, Paul. Interrelational Income-Distribution Multipliers for the West Virginia Economy. *J. Reg. Sci.*, November 1988, *28*(4), pp. 461–75.

_____ and Stevens, Brandt K. Distributional Impacts of Oil and Gas Tax Reforms. *Energy Econ.*, July 1988, *10*(3), pp. 235–41.

Rose, Andrew Kenan. Is the Real Interest Rate Stable? *J. Finance*, December 1988, *43*(5), pp. 1095–1112.

_____; Yellen, Janet L. and Akerlof, George A. Job Switching and Job Satisfaction in the U.S. Labor Market. *Brookings Pap. Econ. Act.*, 1988, (2), pp. 495–582.

_____; Yellen, Janet L. and Akerlof, George A. The New Keynesian Economics and the Output–Inflation Trade-off: Comment. *Brookings Pap. Econ. Act.*, 1988, (1), pp. 66–75.

Rose, Arthur W. and Eggert, Roderick G. Exploration in the United States. In *Tilton, J. E.;*

Eggert, R. G. and Landsberg, H. H., eds., 1988, pp. 331–62.

Rose, Elizabeth L.; Machak, Joseph A. and Spivey, W. Allen. A Survey of the Teaching of Statistics in M.B.A. Programs. *J. Bus. Econ. Statist.*, April 1988, *6*(2), pp. 273–82.

Rose, John T. and Wolken, John D. Thrift Competition and the "Commercial Banking" Line of Commerce. *Atlantic Econ. J.*, December 1988, *16*(4), pp. 24–36.

Rose, Manfred; Kungl, Hans and Kühn, Bernhard. Incidence Effects of Changing the German Income Tax Rate Schedule. In *Bös, D.; Rose, M. and Seidl, C.*, eds., 1988, pp. 205–46.

Rose, Marshall B.; Slaski, Lawrence J. and Rosenthal, Donald H. Economic Value of the Oil and Gas Resources on the Outer Continental Shelf. *Marine Resource Econ.*, 1988, *5*(3), pp. 171–89.

Rose, Mary B. and Snowden, P. N. Bond Issues as a Replacement for Bank Lending to LDCs: A Reconsideration of the Lessons of the 19th Century for the Present Day. *World Devel.*, July 1988, *16*(7), pp. 771–78.

Rose, Nancy E. Production-for-Use or Production-for-Profit?: The Contradictions of Consumer Goods Production in 1930s Work Relief. *Rev. Radical Polit. Econ.*, Spring 1988, *20*(1), pp. 46–61.

Rosefielde, Steven and Pfouts, Ralph W. Economic Optimization and Technical Efficiency in Soviet Enterprises Jointly Regulated by Plans and Incentives. *Europ. Econ. Rev.*, July 1988, *32*(6), pp. 1285–99.

Rosegger, Gerhard. From Hammer to Electric Generator: Technological Advance in Schmoller's Grundriss. *J. Inst. Theoretical Econ.*, June 1988, *144*(3), pp. 591–600.

Rosegrant, Mark W. Legal Considerations for Coping with Externalities in Irrigated Agriculture: Comment. In *O'Mara, G. T.*, ed., 1988, pp. 47–48.

_____ and Siamwalla, Ammar. Government Credit Programs: Justification, Benefits, and Costs. In *Mellor, J. W. and Ahmed, R.*, eds., 1988, pp. 219–38.

Roseman, Daniel. Towards a GATT Code on Trade in Telecommunication Equipment. *World Econ.*, March 1988, *11*(1), pp. 135–49.

Rosen, Benson and Jerdee, Thomas H. Managing Older Workers' Careers. In *Ferris, G. R. and Rowland, K. M.*, eds., 1988, pp. 37–74.

Rosen, Christine. Pollution Control in Late 19th-Century America. In *Perkins, E. J.*, ed., 1988, pp. 13–26.

Rosen, Harvey S. The Effects of Public Sector Labor Laws on Labor Market Institutions and Outcomes: Comment. In *Freeman, R. B. and Ichniowski, C.*, eds., 1988, pp. 103–06.

_____. Fiscal Federalism: Quantitative Studies: Introduction. In *Rosen, H. S.*, ed., 1988, pp. 1–4.

_____. The Marriage Tax Is Down But Not Out. In *Brown, E.*, ed., 1988, *1987*, pp. 145–53.

_____. Thinking about the Tax Consequences of

Marriage [The Marriage Tax is Down but Not Out]. *Nat. Tax J.*, June 1988, *41*(2), pp. 259–60.

_____ and Feenberg, Daniel R. Promises, Promises: The States' Experience with Income Tax Indexing. *Nat. Tax J.*, December 1988, *41*(4), pp. 525–42.

_____ and Holtz-Eakin, Douglas. Tax Deductibility and Municipal Budget Structure. In *Rosen, H. S., ed.*, 1988, pp. 107–26.

_____; Holtz-Eakin, Douglas and Newey, Whitney K. Estimating Vector Autoregressions with Panel Data. *Econometrica*, November 1988, *56*(6), pp. 1371–95.

Rosen, Kenneth T.; Fallis, George and Smith, Lawrence B. Recent Developments in Economic Models of Housing Markets. *J. Econ. Lit.*, March 1988, *26*(1), pp. 29–64.

Rosen, Sherwin. Implicit Contracts: A Survey. In *Shaw, G. K., ed., Vol. 2*, 1988, *1985*, pp. 65–96.

_____. Population Aging and the Timing of Old-Age Benefits: Discussion. In *Ricardo-Campbell, R. and Lazear, E. P., eds.*, 1988, pp. 372–77.

_____. Promotions, Elections and Other Contests. *J. Inst. Theoretical Econ.*, February 1988, *144*(1), pp. 73–90.

_____. Transactions Costs and Internal Labor Markets. *J. Law, Econ., Organ.*, Spring 1988, *4*(1), pp. 49–64.

_____. The Value of Changes in Life Expectancy. *J. Risk Uncertainty*, September 1988, *1*(3), pp. 285–304.

_____ and Topel, Robert H. Housing Investment in the United States. *J. Polit. Econ.*, August 1988, *96*(4), pp. 718–40.

_____ and Winship, Christopher. Introduction: Sociological and Economic Approaches to the Analysis of Social Structure. In *Winship, C. and Rosen, S., eds.*, 1988, pp. 1–16.

Rosen, Stanley. The Private Economy (II): Editor's Introduction. *Chinese Econ. Stud.*, Winter 1987–88, *21*(2), pp. 3–7.

Rosenbaum, David I. and Reading, Steven L. Market Structure and Import Share: A Regional Market Analysis. *Southern Econ. J.*, January 1988, *54*(3), pp. 694–700.

Rosenbaum, S. 100 Years of Heights and Weights. *J. Roy. Statist. Soc.*, 1988, *151*(2), pp. 276–309.

Rosenberg, Alexander. Economics Is Too Important to Be Left to the Rhetoricians. *Econ. Philos.*, April 1988, *4*(1), pp. 129–49.

_____. Rhetoric Is Not Important Enough for Economists to Bother About. *Econ. Philos.*, April 1988, *4*(1), pp. 173–75.

Rosenberg, Christoph B. and Sloan, Frank A. Krankenhausfinanzierung in Selbstverwaltung: Comments from a U.S. Perspective. *J. Inst. Theoretical Econ.*, April 1988, *144*(2), pp. 388–95.

Rosenberg, D. Statistical Science Is User Friendly but Teaching Materials Undermine the Message: $F = t^2$ and Orthogonal Coding. In *Brown, R. C., ed.*, 1988, pp. 139–42.

Rosenberg, Jacob and Darvish, Tikva. The Economic Model of Voter Participation: A Further Test. *Public Choice*, February 1988, *56*(2), pp. 185–92.

Rosenberg, Joshua D. Tax Avoidance and Income Measurement. *Mich. Law Rev.*, November 1988, *87*(2), pp. 365–497.

Rosenberg, L. Joseph. Dillard Department Stores, Inc.: A Look at Several Current Strategies. In *Perkins, E. J., ed.*, 1988, pp. 273–88.

Rosenberg, Maurice. The Impact of Procedure-Impact Studies in the Administration of Justice. *Law Contemp. Probl.*, Summer 1988, *51*(3), pp. 13–30.

Rosenberg, Nathan. New Technologies and Old Debates. In *Bhalla, A. S. and James, D., eds.*, 1988, pp. 13–27.

_____. Technological Change under Capitalism and Socialism. In *Anderson, A. and Bark, D. L., eds.*, 1988, pp. 191–202.

_____ and Landau, Ralph. Strategies for U.S. Economic Growth. In *Muroyama, J. H. and Stever, H. G., eds.*, 1988, pp. 159–76.

_____ and Steinmueller, W. Edward. Why Are Americans Such Poor Imitators? *Amer. Econ. Rev.*, May 1988, *78*(2), pp. 229–34.

Rosenberg, Pamela; Li, Jeanne C. and Ehrenberg, Ronald G. Part-time Employment in the United States. In *Hart, R. A., ed.*, 1988, pp. 256–81.

Rosenberg, Samuel. Racial Wage Gap: Comments. In *Mangum, G. and Philips, P., eds.*, 1988, pp. 169–75.

Rosenberg, Sheila. The Power of Team Play. In *Timpe, A. D., ed.*, 1988, *1983*, pp. 152–56.

Rosenblatt, Joseph M.; Hushak, Leroy J. and Miller, Gay Y. The Effects of Supply Shifts on Producers' Surplus. *Amer. J. Agr. Econ.*, November 1988, *70*(4), pp. 886–91.

Rosenbloom, Joshua L. Straightening Out a Non-linearity in the Dynamics of Labor and Capital Movements: A Comment on Dendrinos's Model [On the Dynamic Stability of Interurban/Regional Labor and Capital Movements]. *J. Reg. Sci.*, November 1988, *28*(4), pp. 579–80.

Rosenblum, Larry; Kunze, Kent and Jablonski, Mary. Productivity, Age, and Labor Composition Changes in the U.S. *Mon. Lab. Rev.*, September 1988, *111*(9), pp. 34–38.

Rosener, Wolfgang. Federal Republic of Germany (Including West Berlin). In *Dickson, M. G.; Rosener, W. and Storm, P. M., eds.*, 1988, pp. 58–74.

Rosenfeld, James and Klein, April. The Impact of Targeted Share Repurchases on the Wealth of Non-participating Shareholders. *J. Finan. Res.*, Summer 1988, *11*(2), pp. 89–97.

_____ and Klein, April. Targeted Share Repurchases and Top Management Changes. *J. Finan. Econ.*, Jan.–March 1988, *20*(1–2), pp. 493–506.

Rosenfeld, Stuart A. The Tale of Two Souths. In *Beaulieu, L. J., ed.*, 1988, pp. 51–71.

Rosengren, Eric S. Is the United States for Sale? Foreign Acquisitions of U.S. Companies. *New*

Eng. Econ. Rev., Nov.–Dec. 1988, pp. 47–56.

_____ and **Browne, Lynn E.** Are Hostile Takeovers Different? In *Browne, L. E. and Rosengren, E. S.*, eds., 1988, pp. 199–229.

_____ and **Browne, Lynn E.** The Merger Boom: An Overview. *New Eng. Econ. Rev.*, March–April 1988, pp. 22–31.

_____ and **Browne, Lynn E.** The Merger Boom: An Overview. In *Browne, L. E. and Rosengren, E. S.*, eds., 1988, pp. 1–16.

_____ and **Peek, Joe.** The Stock Market and Economic Activity. *New Eng. Econ. Rev.*, May–June 1988, pp. 39–50.

Rosenman, Robert; Fort, Rodney D. and Budd, William. Perceptions, Fear, and Economic Loss: An Application of Prospect Theory to Environmental Decision Making. *Policy Sci.*, 1988, *21*(4), pp. 327–50.

Rosensweig, Jeffrey A. Elasticities of Substitution in Caribbean Tourism. *J. Devel. Econ.*, July 1988, *29*(1), pp. 89–100.

_____; **Whitt, Joseph A., Jr. and Koch, Paul D.** The Dynamic Relationship between the Dollar and U.S. Prices: An Intensive Empirical Investigation. *J. Int. Money Finance*, June 1988, *7*(2), pp. 181–204.

Rosenthal, Donald H.; Rose, Marshall B. and Slaski, Lawrence J. Economic Value of the Oil and Gas Resources on the Outer Continental Shelf. *Marine Resource Econ.*, 1988, *5*(3), pp. 171–89.

Rosenthal, Gert. The Costa Rican Experience with the International Debt Crisis: Comments. In *Feinberg, R. E. and Ffrench-Davis, R.*, eds., 1988, pp. 237–40.

_____. ECLAC: Forty Years of Continuity with Change. *CEPAL Rev.*, August 1988, (35), pp. 7–12.

Rosenthal, Howard and Palfrey, Thomas R. Private Incentives in Social Dilemmas: The Effects of Incomplete Information and Altruism. *J. Public Econ.*, April 1988, *35*(3), pp. 309–32.

Rosenthal, Robert W. and Jovanovic, Boyan. Anonymous Sequential Games. *J. Math. Econ.*, 1988, *17*(1), pp. 77–87.

Rosenthal, Stuart S. A Residence Time Model of Housing Markets. *J. Public Econ.*, June 1988, *36*(1), pp. 87–109.

Rosenwaike, Ira and Bradshaw, Benjamin S. The Status of Death Statistics for the Hispanic Population of the Southwest. *Soc. Sci. Quart.*, September 1988, *69*(3), pp. 722–36.

Rosenweig, Jeffrey A. and Koch, Paul D. The U.S. Dollar and the "Delayed J-Curve." *Fed. Res. Bank Atlanta Econ. Rev.*, July–Aug. 1988, *73*(4), pp. 2–15.

Rosenzweig, Mark R. Human Capital, Population Growth, and Economic Development: Beyond Correlations. *J. Policy Modeling*, April 1988, *10*(1), pp. 83–111.

_____. Risk, Implicit Contracts and the Family in Rural Areas of Low-income Countries. *Econ. J.*, December 1988, *98*(393), pp. 1148–70.

_____. Risk, Private Information, and the Family. *Amer. Econ. Rev.*, May 1988, *78*(2), pp. 245–50.

_____; **Binswanger, Hans P. and McIntire, John.** From Land Abundance to Land Scarcity: The Effects of Population Growth on Production Relations in Agrarian Economies. In *Lee, R. D., et al.*, eds., 1988, pp. 77–100.

_____ and **Jasso, Guillermina.** How Well Do U.S. Immigrants Do?: Vintage Effects, Emigration Selectivity, and Occupational Mobility. In *Schultz, T. Paul*, ed., 1988, pp. 229–53.

_____ and **Schultz, T. Paul.** The Stability of Household Production Technology: A Replication. *J. Human Res.*, Fall 1988, *23*(4), pp. 535–49.

_____ and **Wolpin, Kenneth I.** Heterogeneity, Intrafamily Distribution, and Child Health. *J. Human Res.*, Fall 1988, *23*(4), pp. 437–61.

_____ and **Wolpin, Kenneth I.** Migration Selectivity and the Effects of Public Programs. *J. Public Econ.*, December 1988, *37*(3), pp. 265–89.

Roseveare, Debbie and Millar, Campbell. Testing the Rationality of Manufacturers' Inflationary Expectations. *New Zealand Econ. Pap.*, 1988, *22*, pp. 3–13.

Roseveare, Henry. Government Financial Policy and the Money Market in Late Seventeenth Century England. In *Guarducci, A.*, ed., 1988, pp. 703–35.

Rosh, Robert M. Militarization, Human Rights and Basic Needs in the Third World. In *Cingranelli, D. L.*, ed., 1988, pp. 190–204.

_____. Third World Militarization: Security Webs and the States They Ensnare. *J. Conflict Resolution*, December 1988, *32*(4), pp. 671–98.

Rosier, Michel. Chronique de la méthode en histoire de la pensée économieque: Cinq etudes de cas. (With English summary.) *Écon. Soc.*, March 1988, *22*(3), pp. 155–66.

Roskamp, Karl W. Optimal Lifetime Consumption Paths under Equal Yield Income and Consumption Taxes: Correction and Extension. *Public Finance*, 1988, *43*(2), pp. 326–27.

Roski, Reinhold and Dietz, Jobst-Walter. Innovationsmanagement und Diskontinuitäten. (With English summary.) *Z. Betriebswirtshaft*, September 1988, *58*(9), pp. 927–51.

Rosner, Peter. A Note on the Theories of Business Cycle by Hilferding and by Hayek. *Hist. Polit. Econ.*, Summer 1988, *20*(2), pp. 309–19.

Roson, Roberto and Costa, Paolo. Transport Margins, Transportation Industry and the Multiregional Economy. Some Experiments with a Model for Italy. *Ricerche Econ.*, April–June 1988, *42*(2), pp. 273–87.

Rosow, Jerome M. The Global Marketplace—An Overview. In *Rosow, J. M.*, ed., 1988, pp. 1–29.

Ross, Anthony Clunies. Stabilisation Targets and Instruments in Developing Countries. *J. Econ. Stud.*, 1988, *15*(2), pp. 1–74.

Ross, Benjamin. What Is Competition For? *Challenge*, March–April 1988, *31*(2), pp. 42–48.

Ross, Carlyle; Kaliel, Dale and Chase, Darren.

Economics of Cow-Calf Production in Alberta. *Can. J. Agr. Econ.*, Part 2, December 1988, *36*(4), pp. 821–36.

Ross, David R. and Bradburd, Ralph M. A General Measure of Multidimensional Inequality. *Oxford Bull. Econ. Statist.*, November 1988, *50*(4), pp. 429–33.

Ross, G. J. S. Expert Systems for Non-linear Modelling: Progress and Prospects. In *Edwards, D. and Raun, N. E., eds.,* 1988, pp. 155–61.

Ross, H. Laurence. Social Norms and Drunk Driving Countermeasures: Comments. In *Graham, J. D., ed.,* 1988, pp. 184–87.

———— **and Campbell, Donald T.** The Connecticut Crackdown on Speeding: Time-Series Data in Quasi-experimental Analysis. In *Campbell, D. T.,* 1988, *1968*, pp. 222–37.

Ross, Howard N. Price and Margin Rigidity in Deflation: The Great Depression. *Rev. Ind. Organ.*, Fall 1988, *3*(4), pp. 53–91.

Ross, Lee Ann. Collaborative Research for More Effective Foreign Assistance. *World Devel.*, February 1988, *16*(2), pp. 231–36.

Ross, Marc H.; Williams, Robert H. and Larson, Eric D. Beyond the Era of Materials. In *Forester, T., ed.,* 1988, *1986*, pp. 141–59.

Ross, Mary. The Financial Impact of Social Security by Cohort under Alternative Financing Assumptions: Discussion. In *Ricardo-Campbell, R. and Lazear, E. P., eds.,* 1988, pp. 233–42.

Ross, Miceal. Standard European-Type Institutions in a Developing Economy: The Case of Ireland. In *Boyer, R., ed.,* 1988, pp. 81–95.

Ross, Russell T. The Labour Market Position of Aboriginal People in Non-metropolitan New South Wales. *Australian Bull. Lab.*, December 1988, *15*(1), pp. 29–56.

Ross, Stanford G. Developing Countries and the New International Aspects of U.S. Taxation. *Bull. Int. Fiscal Doc.*, March 1988, *42*(3), pp. 104–09.

Ross, Stephen A. Comment on the Modigliani–Miller Propositions. *J. Econ. Perspectives*, Fall 1988, *2*(4), pp. 127–33.

————**; Zisler, Randall C. and Firstenberg, Paul M.** Real Estate: The Whole Story. *J. Portfol. Manage.*, Spring 1988, *14*(3), pp. 22–34.

Ross, Thomas W. Brand Information and Price. *J. Ind. Econ.*, March 1988, *36*(3), pp. 301–13.

————. Movements towards Free Trade and Domestic Market Performance with Imperfect Competition. *Can. J. Econ.*, August 1988, *21*(3), pp. 507–24.

————. On the Price Effects of Mergers with Freer Trade. *Int. J. Ind. Organ.*, June 1988, *6*(2), pp. 233–46.

———— **and Cooper, Russell.** An Intertemporal Model of Warranties. *Can. J. Econ.*, February 1988, *21*(1), pp. 72–86.

———— **and Cooper, Russell.** Product Warranties and Moral Hazard. In *Devinney, T. M., ed.,* 1988, pp. 83–98.

Ross, Timothy L. and Hatcher, Larry. Gainsharing Plans—How Managers Evaluate Them. In *Timpe, A. D., ed.,* 1988, *1986*, pp. 213–25.

Rosser, J. Barkley, Jr.; Sheehan, Richard G. and Ahmed, Ehsan. A Global Model of OECD Aggregate Supply and Demand Using Vector Autoregressive Techniques. *Europ. Econ. Rev.*, November 1988, *32*(9), pp. 1711–29.

Rossi, José W. A demanda por moeda no Brasil: O que ocorreu a partir de 1980? (With English summary.) *Pesquisa Planejamento Econ.*, April 1988, *18*(1), pp. 37–53.

Rossi, Nicola. Budget Share Demographic Translation and the Aggregate Almost Ideal Demand System. *Europ. Econ. Rev.*, July 1988, *32*(6), pp. 1301–18.

————. Government Spending, the Real Interest Rate, and the Behavior of Liquidity-Constrained Consumers in Developing Countries. *Int. Monet. Fund Staff Pap.*, March 1988, *35*(1), pp. 104–40.

———— **and Bollino, C. Andrea.** Public Debt and Households' Demand for Monetary Assets in Italy: 1970–86. In *Giavazzi, F. and Spaventa, L., eds.,* 1988, pp. 222–43.

———— **and Patrizi, Vincenzo.** Gli effetti redistributivi del progetto europeo di armonizzazione delle imposte indirette. (With English summary.) *Polit. Econ.*, December 1988, *4*(3), pp. 409–32.

———— **and Schiantarelli, Fabio.** Error-Correction, "Surprise" Models and the Differential Approach to the Consumption Function. *Metroecon.*, February 1988, *39*(1), pp. 83–91.

Rossi, Peter E. Comparison of Dynamic Factor Demand Models. In *Barnett, W. A.; Berndt, E. R. and White, H., eds.,* 1988, pp. 357–76.

Rossiter, Louis F. and Scheffler, Richard M. Advances in Health Economics and Health Services Research: Preface. In *Scheffler, R. M. and Rossiter, L. F., eds.,* 1988, pp. xiii–xv.

Rosson, C. Parr; Levins, Richard A. and Brown, Earl H. Soybean Trader: A Microcomputer Simulation of International Agricultural Trade. *Southern J. Agr. Econ.*, July 1988, *20*(1), pp. 153–57.

Rostow, Walt W. A Challenge for the Pacific Basin. In *Kozmetsky, G.; Matsumoto, H. and Smilor, R. W., eds.,* 1988, pp. 17–23.

————. The Fourth Industrial Revolution and American Society: Some Reflections on the Past for the Future. In *Furino, A., ed.,* 1988, pp. 63–73.

Rostowski, Jacek and Auerbach, P. Intra-year Fluctuations in Production and Sales: East and West. In *[Nove, A.],* 1988, pp. 82–111.

———— **and Gomulka, Stanislaw.** An International Comparison of Material Intensity. *J. Compar. Econ.*, December 1988, *12*(4), pp. 475–501.

Rotberg, Robert I. Haiti's Past Mortgages Its Future. *Foreign Aff.*, Fall 1988, *67*(1), pp. 93–109.

Rotenberg, Wendy D. and Chan, M. W. Luke. Financial Distress in the Canadian Agricultural Sector: A Macro Analysis. *Can. J. Agr. Econ.*, November 1988, *36*(3), pp. 531–38.

Roth, Alvin E. The Expected Utility of Playing a Game. In *[Shapley, L. S.],* 1988, pp. 51–70.

_____. Laboratory Experimentation in Economics: A Methodological Overview. *Econ. J.*, December 1988, *98*(393), pp. 974–1031.

_____. The Shapley Value: Essays in Honor of Lloyd S. Shapley: Introduction to the Shapley Value. In *[Shapley, L. S.]*, 1988, pp. 1–27.

_____; Murnighan, J. Keith and Schoumaker, Francoise. The Deadline Effect in Bargaining: Some Experimental Evidence. *Amer. Econ. Rev.*, September 1988, *78*(4), pp. 806–23.

_____; Schoumaker, Francoise and Murnighan, J. Keith. Risk Aversion in Bargaining: An Experimental Study. *J. Risk Uncertainty*, March 1988, *1*(1), pp. 101–24.

_____ and Sotomayor, Marilda. Interior Points in the Core of Two-Sided Matching Markets. *J. Econ. Theory*, June 1988, *45*(1), pp. 85–101.

Roth, Gabriel. Private Sector Roles in Urban Public Transport. In *Weicher, J. C.*, ed., 1988, pp. 109–21.

Roth, N.; Deville, J. C. and Grosbras, J. M. Efficient sampling Algorithms and Balanced Samples. In *Edwards, D. and Raun, N. E.*, eds., 1988, pp. 255–66.

Rothbard, Murray N. Timberlake on the Austrian Theory of Money: A Comment [A Critique of Monetarist and Austrian Doctrines on the Utility and Value of Money]. In *Rothbard, M. N. and Block, W.*, eds., 1988, pp. 179–87.

Rothblum, Uriel G. Combinatorial Representations of the Shapley Value Based on Average Relative Payoffs. In *[Shapley, L. S.]*, 1988, pp. 121–26.

Rotheim, Roy J. Keynes and the Language of Probability and Uncertainty. *J. Post Keynesian Econ.*, Fall 1988, *11*(1), pp. 82–99.

Rötheli, Tobias F. Money Demand and Inflation in Switzerland: An Application of the Pascal Lag Technique. *Fed. Res. Bank St. Louis Rev.*, May–June 1988, *70*(3), pp. 43–52.

Rothenberg, Thomas J. Approximate Power Functions for Some Robust Tests of Regression Coefficients. *Econometrica*, September 1988, *56*(5), pp. 997–1019.

Rothenberg, Winifred B. The Emergence of Farm Labor Markets and the Transformation of the Rural Economy: Massachusetts, 1750–1855. *J. Econ. Hist.*, September 1988, *48*(3), pp. 537–66.

Rothengatter, Werner and Müller, Paul. Measuring the Relevance of Natural Resources for Production. *Jahr. Nationalökon. Statist.*, February 1988, *204*(2), pp. 99–119.

Röthlin, N. Die Affäre Tillier & Co. Zum Gegensatz zwischen merkantilistischem Monopol und Handelsfreiheit im 18. Jahrhundert. (The Tiller & Co. Business: An Example of the Difference between Mercantilist Monopoly and Free Trade in the 18th Century. With English summary.) *Schweiz. Z. Volkswirtsch. Statist.*, March 1988, *124*(1), pp. 65–77.

Rothschild, Kurt W. Micro-foundations, Ad Hocery, and Keynesian Theory. *Atlantic Econ. J.*, June 1988, *16*(2), pp. 12–21.

_____. New Information Theoretic Approaches to Labour Market Theory: Comment. In *Kre-*

gel, J. A.; Matzner, E. and Roncaglia, A., eds., 1988, pp. 66–69.

_____. Schumpeter and Technical Change: Discussion. In *Hanusch, H.*, ed., 1988, pp. 90–94.

Rothschild, Leonard W., Jr. and Magilligan, Robert J. United States: The Definition of Residency for Federal Income Tax Purposes. *Bull. Int. Fiscal Doc.*, July 1988, *42*(7), pp. 324–28.

Rothschild, Michael L., et al. Hemispherically Lateralized EEG as a Response to Television Commercials. *J. Cons. Res.*, September 1988, *15*(2), pp. 185–98.

Rothschild, R. The Impact of Market Share, Tariffs and Quotas on the Performance of International Cartels. *Econ. Letters*, 1988, *27*(1), pp. 79–82.

Rothstein, Morton. Centralizing Firms and Spreading Markets: The World of International Grain Traders, 1846–1914. In *Hausman, W. J.*, ed., 1988, pp. 103–13.

Rothstein, Robert L. Epitaph for a Monument to a Failed Protest? A North–South Retrospective. *Int. Organ.*, Autumn 1988, *42*(4), pp. 725–48.

Roubens, Marc and Teghem, Jacques, Jr. Comparison of Methodologies for Multicriteria Feasibility—Constrained Fuzzy and Multiple-Objective Stochastic Linear Programming. In *Kacprzyk, J. and Fedrizzi, M.*, eds., 1988, pp. 240–65.

_____ and Vinke, Philippe. Fuzzy Possibility Graphs and Their Application to Ranking Fuzzy Numbers. In *Kacprzyk, J. and Roubens, M.*, eds., 1988, pp. 119–28.

Roulac, Stephen E. How to Value Real Estate Securities. *J. Portfol. Manage.*, Spring 1988, *14*(3), pp. 35–39.

Roumasset, James and Setboonsarng, Suthad. Second-Best Agricultural Policy: Getting the Price of Thai Rice Right. *J. Devel. Econ.*, May 1988, *28*(3), pp. 323–40.

Round, Jeffery I. Multipliers and Feedback Effects in Interregional Input–Output Models. *Ricerche Econ.*, April–June 1988, *42*(2), pp. 311–24.

Rous, P. and Archer, R. Peut-on desagreger la vitesse de circulation de la monnaie? (How to Disaggregate the Velocity of Money? With English summary.) *Écon. Soc.*, January 1988, *22*(1), pp. 179–203.

Rouse, John W. The Transformation of Manufacturing as a National Priority. In *Furino, A.*, ed., 1988, pp. 117–27.

Rouse, William and Griffin, John C., Jr. Counter-Trade as a Third World Strategy of Development. In *Wilber, C. K.*, ed., 1988, pp. 508–32.

Roush, F. W. and Kim, K. H. Strategic Tariff Equilibrium and Optimal Tariffs. *Math. Soc. Sci.*, April 1988, *15*(2), pp. 105–34.

Rousseau, Jean-Marc. ALIAGES: A System for the Assignment of Bus Routes to Garages. In *Daduna, J. R. and Wren, A.*, eds., 1988, pp. 8–14.

——— **and Blais, J. Y.** Overview of HASTUS Current and Future Versions. In *Daduna, J. R. and Wren, A., eds.*, 1988, pp. 175–87.

———; **Delorme, Louis and Roy, Jacques.** Motor-Carriers Operations Planning Models: A State of the Art. In *Bianco, L. and La Bella, A., eds.*, 1988, pp. 510–45.

Rousslang, Donald J. Import Injury in U.S. Trade Law: An Economic View. *Int. Rev. Law Econ.*, June 1988, 8(1), pp. 117–22.

——— **and Reitzes, James D.** Domestic versus International Capital Mobility: Some Empirical Evidence. *Can. J. Econ.*, May 1988, 21(2), pp. 312–23.

——— **and Suomela, John W.** Calculating the Welfare Costs of Import Restrictions in the Imperfect Substitutes Model. *Appl. Econ.*, May 1988, 20(5), pp. 691–700.

Rouwendal, Jan and Nijkamp, Peter. Intergenerational Discount Rates in Long-term Plan Evaluation. *Public Finance*, 1988, 43(2), pp. 195–211.

——— **and Rietveld, Piet.** Search and Mobility in a Housing Market with Limited Supply. *Ann. Reg. Sci.*, November 1988, 22(3), pp. 80–98.

Roux, J. J. J. and van der Merwe, C. A. Frequency Models for the Distribution of Personal Income in the RSA. In *Brown, R. C., ed.*, 1988, pp. 165–95.

Rowe, Edward R. The Federal Government Reporting Study (Canada and the United States). In *Most, K. S., ed.*, 1988, pp. 257–63.

Rowen, Henry S. U.S. Vulnerability to an Interruption in Gulf Oil Supplies. In *Fried, E. R. and Blandin, N. M., eds.*, 1988, pp. 49–54.

——— **and Dunlop, John B.** The Soviet Union: The Crisis of the System and Prospects for Change. In *Anderson, A. and Bark, D. L., eds.*, 1988, pp. 45–55.

Rowlatt, Penelope A. Analysis of the Recent Path of UK Inflation. *Oxford Bull. Econ. Statist.*, November 1988, 50(4), pp. 335–60.

Rowley, Charles K. and Crew, Michael A. Toward a Public Choice Theory of Monopoly Regulation. *Public Choice*, April 1988, 57(1), pp. 49–67.

———; **Tollison, Robert D. and Anderson, Gary Michael.** Rent Seeking and the Restriction of Human Exchange. *J. Legal Stud.*, January 1988, 17(1), pp. 83–100.

Rowley, Robin. Economic Development and Income Distribution. In *Asimakopulos, A., ed.*, 1988, pp. 225–47.

———. The Keynes–Tinbergen Exchange in Retrospect. In *Hamouda, O. F. and Smithin, J. N., eds., Vol. 2*, 1988, pp. 23–31.

Rowse, John. Constructing a Supply Function for a Depletable Resource. *Resources & Energy*, March 1988, 10(1), pp. 15–29.

———. Does an Exhaustible Resource Usually Have Many Near-Optimal Depletion Paths? *Amer. J. Agr. Econ.*, August 1988, 70(3), pp. 646–53.

Rowthorn, Robert E. Conflict, Inflation and Money. In *Sawyer, M. C., ed.*, 1988, *1977*, pp. 412–36.

———. Demand, Real Wages and Economic Growth. In *Sawyer, M. C., ed.*, 1988, *1981*, pp. 163–201.

——— **and Glyn, Andrew.** West European Unemployment: Corporatism and Structural Change. *Amer. Econ. Rev.*, May 1988, 78(2), pp. 194–99.

Roy, Dilip Kumar. Employment and Growth: Empirical Results from Bangladesh Industries. *Bangladesh Devel. Stud.*, March 1988, 16(1), pp. 55–72.

———. Industrial Policy and Development of Rural Industries in Bangladesh: A Review of Some Issues. *Industry Devel.*, October 1988, (24), pp. 89–111.

———. Some Determinants of Industrial Performance in Bangladesh: A Preliminary Analysis. *Bangladesh Devel. Stud.*, June 1988, 16(2), pp. 81–90.

Roy, Jacques; Rousseau, Jean-Marc and Delorme, Louis. Motor-Carriers Operations Planning Models: A State of the Art. In *Bianco, L. and La Bella, A., eds.*, 1988, pp. 510–45.

Roy, Paul-Martel; Kamel, Nawal and Mohnen, Pierre. Demande de travail et d'heures supplémentaires: étude empirique pour le Canada et le Québec. (With English summary.) *L'Actual. Econ.*, March 1988, 64(1), pp. 23–43.

Roy, Prannoy L. and Bhalla, Surjit S. Mis-specification in Farm Productivity Analysis: The Role of Land Quality. *Oxford Econ. Pap.*, March 1988, 40(1), pp. 55–73.

Roy, Probir. A Mixed Integer 0-1 Programming Heuristic for Resource Allocation in a Decentralized System. In *Iri, M. and Yajima, K., eds.*, 1988, pp. 338–47.

Roy, Tirthankar. Size and Structure of Handloom Weaving in the Mid-Thirties. *Indian Econ. Soc. Hist. Rev.*, Jan.–March 1988, 25(1), pp. 1–24.

Rozeff, Michael S. and Zaman, Mir A. Market Efficiency and Insider Trading: New Evidence. *J. Bus.*, January 1988, 61(1), pp. 25–44.

Rozek, Richard P. A Nonparametric Test for Economies of Scope. *Appl. Econ.*, May 1988, 20(5), pp. 653–63.

———. Protection of Intellectual Property through Licensing: Efficiency Considerations. *J. World Trade*, October 1988, 22(5), pp. 27–34.

Rozen, Etzmun; Fuglister, Jayne and Meeting, David. Teaching the Qualitative Characteristics of Accounting Information in the Standard Setting Process: A Technique Using SFAS No. 96. In *Pennsylvania Economic Association*, 1988, pp. 601–13.

Rozwadowski, Franek. From Recitation Room to Research Seminar: Political Economy at Columbia University. In *Barber, W. J., ed.*, 1988, pp. 169–202.

Ruane, Frances P. International Trade in Banking Services: Comment. In *Baldwin, R. E.; Hamilton, C. B. and Sapir, A., eds.*, 1988, pp. 269–76.

_____ and Neary, Peter. International Capital Mobility, Shadow Prices, and the Cost of Protection. *Int. Econ. Rev.*, November 1988, 29(4), pp. 571–85.

Ruback, Richard S. An Overview of Takeover Defenses. In *Auerbach, A. J., ed. (II)*, 1988, pp. 49–67.

_____. Coercive Dual-Class Exchange Offers. *J. Finan. Econ.*, Jan.–March 1988, 20(1–2), pp. 153–73.

_____. Do Target Shareholders Lose in Unsuccessful Control Contests? In *Auerbach, A. J., ed. (I)*, 1988, pp. 137–52.

_____. Means of Payment in Takeovers: Results for the United Kingdom and the United States: Comment. In *Auerbach, A. J., ed. (I)*, 1988, pp. 260–63.

_____. Mergers and Takeovers: Taxes, Capital Structure, and the Incentives of Managers: Comment. In *Coffee, J. C., Jr.; Lowenstein, L. and Rose-Ackerman, S., eds.*, 1988, pp. 355–57.

Rübel, Markus and Bieg, Hartmut. Ausweis und Bewertung von Devisen- und Zinstermingeschäften in Bankbilanzen—Teil II. (Showing and Valuating Forward Exchange and Interest Rate Futures Deals in Bank Balance Sheets—Part II. With English summary.) *Kredit Kapital*, 1988, 21(3), pp. 422–50.

_____ and Bieg, Hartmut. Ausweis und Bewertung von Devisen- und Zinstermingeschäften in Bankbilanzen—Teil III. (Showing and Valuation of Forward Exchange and Interest Rate Futures Deals in Bank Balance Sheets—Part III. With English summary.) *Kredit Kapital*, 1988, 21(4), pp. 592–624.

_____ and Bieg, Hartmut. Ausweis und Bewertung von Devisen- und Zinstermingeschäften in Bankbilanzen—Teil I. (Showing and Valuating Forward Exchange and Interest Rate Futures Deals on Bank Balance Sheets—Part I. With English summary.) *Kredit Kapital*, 1988, 21(2), pp. 253–77.

Ruben, George. A Review of Collective Bargaining in 1987. *Mon. Lab. Rev.*, January 1988, 111(1), pp. 24–37.

Rubens, Jack H. and Webb, James R. The Effect of Alternative Return Measures on Restricted Mixed-Asset Portfolios. *Amer. Real Estate Urban Econ. Assoc. J.*, Summer 1988, 16(2), pp. 123–37.

Rubenstein, Joshua. The Soviet Union Today: Dissent. In *Cracraft, J., ed.*, 1988, pp. 64–76.

Rubery, Jill. Women and Recession: A Comparative Perspective. In *Rubery, J., ed.*, 1988, pp. 253–86.

_____. Women and Recession: Preface. In *Rubery, J., ed.*, 1988, pp. ix–xii.

_____ and Humphries, Jane. Recession and Exploitation: British Women in a Changing Workplace, 1979–85. In *Jenson, J.; Hagen, E. and Reddy, C., eds.*, 1988, pp. 85–105.

_____ and Tarling, Roger. Women's Employment in Declining Britain. In *Rubery, J., ed.*, 1988, pp. 100–132.

Rubin, Beth A. Inequality in the Working Class: The Unanticipated Consequences of Union Organization and Strikes. *Ind. Lab. Relat. Rev.*, July 1988, 41(4), pp. 553–66.

Rubin, Donald B. Multiple Imputation for Data-Base Construction. In *Edwards, D. and Raun, N. E., eds.*, 1988, pp. 389–400.

Rubin, Irene S. The Authorization Process: Implications for Budget Theory. In *Rubin, I. S., ed.*, 1988, pp. 124–47.

_____. New Directions in Budget Theory: Introduction. In *Rubin, I. S., ed.*, 1988, pp. 1–18.

Rubin, Laura S. State and Local Government Finance in the Current Expansion. *Fed. Res. Bull.*, February 1988, 74(2), pp. 79–88.

Rubin, Marc A. Municipal Audit Fee Determinants. *Accounting Rev.*, April 1988, 63(2), pp. 219–36.

Rubin, Margot S. Advertising and Title VIII: The Discriminatory Use of Models in Real Estate Advertisements. *Yale Law J.*, November 1988, 98(1), pp. 165–85.

Rubin, Paul H. The Economics of Crime. In *Alper, N. O. and Hellman, D. A., eds.*, 1988, pp. 1–15.

_____ and Keenan, Donald. Shadow Interest Groups and Safety Regulation. *Int. Rev. Law Econ.*, June 1988, 8(1), pp. 21–36.

Rubin, Philip A. Satellite Communications. In *Egan, J. J., et al.*, 1988, pp. 37–46.

Rubinfeld, Daniel L. and Courant, Paul N. Robbing Peter to Pay Peter: The Economics of Local Public Residency Requirements. *J. Urban Econ.*, May 1988, 23(3), pp. 291–306.

_____ and Perloff, Jeffrey M. Settlements in Private Antitrust Litigation. In *White, L. J., ed.*, 1988, pp. 149–84.

_____ and Polinsky, A. Mitchell. The Deterrent Effects of Settlements and Trials. *Int. Rev. Law Econ.*, June 1988, 8(1), pp. 109–16.

_____ and Polinsky, A. Mitchell. The Welfare Implications of Costly Litigation for the Level of Liability. *J. Legal Stud.*, January 1988, 17(1), pp. 151–64.

Rubinshtein, A. G. A Model of Interregional Economic Interactions with Two Systems of Prices. *Matekon*, Winter 1988–89, 25(2), pp. 20–32.

Rubinstein, Ariel. Similarity and Decision-Making under Risk (Is There a Utility Theory Resolution to the Allais Paradox?) *J. Econ. Theory*, October 1988, 46(1), pp. 145–53.

_____ and Abreu, Dilip. The Structure of Nash Equilibrium in Repeated Games with Finite Automata. *Econometrica*, November 1988, 56(6), pp. 1259–81.

Rubinstein, Mark and Leland, Hayne. Comments on the Market Crash: Six Months After. *J. Econ. Perspectives*, Summer 1988, 2(3), pp. 45–50.

Rubinstein, W. D. Social Class, Social Attitudes, and British Business Life. *Oxford Rev. Econ. Policy*, Spring 1988, 4(1), pp. 51–58.

Rubio, Gonzalo. Further International Evidence on Asset Pricing: The Case of the Spanish Capital Market. *J. Banking Finance*, June 1988, 12(2), pp. 221–42.

Rubio Llorente, F. Constitutional Jurisdiction as Law-Making. **In** *Pizzorusso, A., ed.*, 1988, pp. 156–85.

Ruccio, David F. and Simon, Lawrence H. Radical Theories of Development: Frank, the Modes of Production School, and Amin. **In** *Wilber, C. K., ed.*, 1988, pp. 121–73.

Rucker, Randal R. and Leffler, Keith B. To Harvest or Not to Harvest? An Analysis of Cutting Behavior on Federal Timber Sales Contracts. *Rev. Econ. Statist.*, May 1988, 70(2), pp. 207–13.

Ruckle, W. H. The Linearizing Projection, Global Theories. *Int. J. Game Theory*, 1988, 17(1), pp. 67–87.

Ruddle, Kenneth. Social Principles Underlying Traditional Inshore Fishery Management Systems in the Pacific Basin. *Marine Resource Econ.*, 1988, 5(4), pp. 351–63.

Rudebusch, Glenn D. Are Productivity Fluctuations Due to Real Supply Shocks? *Econ. Letters*, 1988, 27(4), pp. 327–31.

Rudin, Jeremy R. Central Bank Secrecy, 'Fed Watching,' and the Predictability of Interest Rates. *J. Monet. Econ.*, September 1988, 22(2), pp. 317–34.

Ruding, H. Onno. External Imbalances: Causes, Consequences and Cures. **In** *[Witteveen, H. J.]*, 1988, pp. 199–215.

Rudolph, Franz. Trends in the Process of Socialization. *Eastern Europ. Econ.*, Spring 1988, 26(3), pp. 22–48.

Rudolph, Patricia M. and Hamdan, Bassam. An Analysis of Post-deregulation Savings-and-Loan Failures. *Amer. Real Estate Urban Econ. Assoc. J.*, Spring 1988, 16(1), pp. 17–33.

Rudra, Ashok. Emerging Class Structure in Indian Agriculture. **In** *Srinivasan, T. N. and Bardhan, P. K., eds.*, 1988, pp. 483–500.

Ruegg, Rosalie T. and Short, Walter. Economic Methods. **In** *West, R. E. and Kreith, F., eds.*, 1988, pp. 18–83.

Ruehl, Sonja. Interest Rate Policy and Credit Rationing in Japan: The Evidence. **In** *Harris, L., et al., eds.*, 1988, pp. 346–67.

Ruelle, David. Can Nonlinear Dynamics Help Economists? **In** *Anderson, P. W.; Arrow, K. J. and Pines, D., eds.*, 1988, pp. 195–204.

Ruffin, Roy J. The Missing Link: The Ricardian Approach to the Factor Endowments Theory of Trade. *Amer. Econ. Rev.*, September 1988, 78(4), pp. 759–72.

Ruggie, Mary. Gender, Work, and Social Progress: Some Consequences of Interest Aggregation in Sweden. **In** *Jenson, J.; Hagen, E. and Reddy, C., eds.*, 1988, pp. 173–88.

Ruggles, Steven. The Demography of the Unrelated Individual: 1900–1950. *Demography*, November 1988, 25(4), pp. 521–36.

Rugina, Anghel N. The Theory of the Cheating of the Masses in Modern Times: The Institutional Roots of Social Immorality under Capitalism and Socialism. *Int. J. Soc. Econ.*, 1988, 15(8), pp. 3–44.

_____. The Unending Search for Universal and Lasting Peace: From Leon Walras to Jan Tin-bergen and Beyond. *Rev. Soc. Econ.*, December 1988, 46(3), pp. 283–306.

Rugman, Alan M. Multinational Enterprises and Strategies for International Competitiveness. **In** *Farmer, R. N. and McGoun, E. G., eds.*, 1988, pp. 47–58.

_____ **and Warner, Mark.** Foreign Ownership, Free Trade, and the Canadian Energy Sector. *J. Energy Devel.*, Autumn 1988, 14(1), pp. 1–18.

Ruhl, J. B. Interstate Pollution Control and Resource Development Planning: Outmoded Approaches or Outmoded Politics? *Natural Res. J.*, Spring 1988, 28(2), pp. 293–314.

Ruhm, Christopher J. When 'Equal Opportunity' Is Not Enough: Training Costs and Intergenerational Inequality. *J. Human Res.*, Spring 1988, 23(2), pp. 155–72.

_____ **and Ellis, Randall P.** Incentives to Transfer Patients under Alternative Reimbursement Mechanisms. *J. Public Econ.*, December 1988, 37(3), pp. 381–94.

de Ruijter, Willem A. and Keuning, Steven J. Guidelines to the Construction of a Social Accounting Matrix. *Rev. Income Wealth*, March 1988, 34(1), pp. 71–100.

Ruivenkamp, Guido. Emerging Patterns in the Global Food Chain. **In** *Research and Info. System for the Non-aligned and Other Developing Countries*, 1988, pp. 225–42.

Ruiz, Maria Laura. Oil Price and Competitive Behaviour: A Note on the Target Revenue Model. *Econ. Notes*, 1988, (1), pp. 41–50.

Ruiz Ramirez, Ricardo. Tax Treatment of Computer Software: Mexico. **In** *International Fiscal Association, ed. (II)*, 1988, pp. 425–38.

Rukuni, Mandivamba and Hay, Roger W. SADCC Food Security Strategies: Evolution and Role. *World Devel.*, September 1988, 16(9), pp. 1013–24.

Ruland, William; Hamdallah, Ahmed and Haw, In-Mu. Investor Evaluation of Overfunded Pension Plan Terminations. *J. Finan. Res.*, Spring 1988, 11(1), pp. 81–88.

Rule, Charles F. and Meyer, David L. An Antitrust Enforcement Policy to Maximize the Economic Wealth of All Consumers. *Antitrust Bull.*, Winter 1988, 33(4), pp. 677–712.

Rumler, Miroslav. Neoconservatism versus Keynesism—Most Recent Development Trends in Bourgeois Concepts of State Monopoly Regulation. *Czech. Econ. Pap.*, 1988, (25), pp. 129–40.

Rundall, Thomas G.; Sofaer, Shoshanna and Lambert, Wendy. Uncompensated Hospital Care in California: Private and Public Hospital Responses to Competitive Market Forces. **In** *Scheffler, R. M. and Rossiter, L. F., eds.*, 1988, pp. 113–33.

Runde, Jochen H. Subjectivism, Psychology, and the Modern Austrians. **In** *Earl, P. E., ed.*, 1988, pp. 101–20.

Runge, Carlisle Ford. The Assault on Agricultural Protectionism. *Foreign Aff.*, Fall 1988, 67(1), pp. 133–50.

Runkle, David E. Why No Crunch from the

Crash? *Fed. Res. Bank Minn. Rev.*, Winter 1988, *12*(1), pp. 2–7.

———; **Keane, Michael and Moffitt, Robert.** Real Wages over the Business Cycle: Estimating the Impact of Heterogeneity with Micro Data. *J. Polit. Econ.*, December 1988, *96*(6), pp. 1232–66.

Runner, Diana. Changes in Unemployment Insurance Legislation during 1987. *Mon. Lab. Rev.*, March 1988, *111*(3), pp. 9–16.

Runtze, Julius. Zielsystem und dynamisches Preisgleichgewicht im Oligopol. (Goal System and Dynamic Price Equilibrium in Oligopoly. With English summary.) *Jahr. Nationalökon. Statist.*, May 1988, *204*(5), pp. 456–77.

Ruotolo, A. Carlos. Monopoly and Socialization. In *Picard, R. G., et al., eds.*, 1988, pp. 117–25.

Rupert, Peter and Cornwell, Christopher. Efficient Estimation with Panel Data: An Empirical Comparison of Instrumental Variables Estimators. *J. Appl. Econometrics*, April 1988, *3*(2), pp. 149–55.

Ruppel, Fred J. and Ayuk, Elias T. Cotton Exports: Analysis of the Relationships between Sales and Shipments. *Southern J. Agr. Econ.*, July 1988, *20*(1), pp. 159–69.

Ruppert, David; Carroll, Raymond J. and Wu, C. F. Jeff. The Effect of Estimating Weights in Weighted Least Squares. *J. Amer. Statist. Assoc.*, December 1988, *83*(404), pp. 1045–54.

Rusek, Antonin and Altinkemer, Melike. Determination of the Spot Exchange Rate: Japanese Yen per U.S. Dollar. In *Pennsylvania Economic Association*, 1988, pp. 377–86.

——— **and Sellekaerts, Willy.** Occupation Experience and Performance Determine Labor Income. *Rev. Soc. Econ.*, December 1988, *46*(3), pp. 307–11.

Ruser, John W. and Smith, Robert S. The Effect of OSHA Records-Check Inspections on Reported Occupational Injuries in Manufacturing Establishments. *J. Risk Uncertainty*, December 1988, *1*(4), pp. 415–35.

Rush, Mark and Waldo, Douglas. On the Policy Ineffectiveness Proposition and a Keynesian Alternative. *Econ. J.*, June 1988, *98*(391), pp. 498–503.

Rushdi, A. A. Weather, the Estimation of Residential Energy Demand Relationships and the Reporting of Data: Reply. *Energy Econ.*, October 1988, *10*(4), pp. 325.

Rushing, Francis W. and Donnelly, William D. A Rationale for Entrepreneurship Education in Secondary Schools. In *Association of Private Education*, 1988, pp. 97–102.

Rushton, Gerard. The Roepke Lecture in Economic Geography: Location Theory, Location-Allocation Models, and Service Development Planning in the Third World. *Econ. Geogr.*, April 1988, *64*(2), pp. 97–120.

Rusmich, Ladislav. The Restructuring of the Mechanism of Cooperation among the Socialist States. *Czech. Econ. Digest.*, August 1988, (5), pp. 67–75.

Russell, Gary J. Recovering Measures of Adver-

tising Carryover from Aggregate Data: The Role of the Firm's Decision Behavior. *Marketing Sci.*, Summer 1988, *7*(3), pp. 252–70.

Russell, James S. and Wexley, Kenneth N. Improving Managerial Performance in Assessing Needs and Transferring Training. In *Ferris, G. R. and Rowland, K. M., eds.*, 1988, pp. 289–323.

Russell, K. Dale and Kulshreshtha, Surendra N. An Ex Post Evaluation of the Contributions of Irrigation to Regional Development in Alberta: A Case Study. *Rev. Reg. Stud.*, Spring 1988, *18*(2), pp. 10–22.

Russell, R. Robert. Life-Cycle Savings and the Individual Distribution of Wealth by Class: Comments. In *Kessler, D. and Masson, A., eds.*, 1988, pp. 281–85.

———. On the Axiomatic Approach to the Measurement of Technical Efficiency. In *Eichhorn, W., ed.*, 1988, pp. 207–17.

Russell, Susan D. Cheap Food: Politicization and Provisioning Patterns among the Urban Poor in Manila. In *Bennett, J. W. and Bowen, J. R., eds.*, 1988, pp. 275–92.

Russell, Thomas and Thaler, Richard H. The Relevance of Quasi Rationality in Competitive Markets. In *Bell, D. E.; Raiffa, H. and Tversky, A., eds.*, 1988, pp. 508–24.

Russett, Bruce. U.S. Hegemony: Gone or Merely Diminished, and How Does It Matter? In *Inoguchi, T. and Okimoto, D. I., eds.*, 1988, pp. 83–107.

Russo, J. Edward. Information Processing from the Consumer's Perspective. In *Maynes, E. S. and ACCI Research Committee, eds.*, 1988, pp. 185–217.

Rust, John. Comment on Poirer: The Subjective Perspective of a "Spiritual Bayesian." *J. Econ. Perspectives*, Winter 1988, *2*(1), pp. 145–51.

———. Optimal Collection of Information by Partially Informed Agents: Comments. *Econometric Rev.*, 1988–89, *7*(2), pp. 155–60.

Rustem, Berc. A Constrained Min–Max Algorithm for Rival Models. *J. Econ. Dynam. Control*, March 1988, *12*(1), pp. 101–07.

Rutenberg, David P. Multinational Corporate Planning and National Economic Policies. In *Grant, J. H., ed.*, 1988, pp. 87–105.

Rüter, Georg and Oberender, Peter. The Steel Industry: A Crisis of Adaptation. In *de Jong, H. W., ed.*, 1988, pp. 81–104.

Rutgaizer, V. M., et al. On the Question of Reforming Consumer Prices and the Money Incomes of the Population. *Prob. Econ.*, June 1988, *31*(2), pp. 75–90.

Rutherford, Malcolm. Clarence Ayres and the Instrumental Theory of Value. In *Samuels, W. J., ed., Vol. 3*, 1988, *1981*, pp. 7–23.

———. J. R. Commons's Institutional Economics. In *Samuels, W. J., ed., Vol. 1*, 1988, *1983*, pp. 265–88.

———. Learning and Decision-Making in Economics and Psychology: A Methodological Perspective. In *Earl, P. E., ed.*, 1988, pp. 35–54.

Rutledge, Gary L. and Farber, Kit D. Pollution

Abatement and Control Expenditures, 1983–86. *Surv. Curr. Bus.*, May 1988, 68(5), pp. 22–29.

_____ and Stergioulas, Nikolaos A. Plant and Equipment Expenditures by Business for Pollution Abatement, 1987 and Planned 1988. *Surv. Curr. Bus.*, November 1988, 68(11), pp. 26–29.

Rutman, G. L. and Ault, D. E. The 'Tragedy of the Commons' and Livestock Farming in Southern Africa: A Comment. *S. Afr. J. Econ.*, June–Sept. 1988, 56(2–3), pp. 212–17.

Ruttan, Vernon W. Cultural Endowments and Economic Development: What Can We Learn from Anthropology? *Econ. Develop. Cult. Change*, Supplement, April 1988, 36(3), pp. S247–71.

_____. Technical Change and Agricultural Development. In *Asefa, S., ed.*, 1988, pp. 9–33.

_____ and Hagen, James M. Development Policy under Eisenhower and Kennedy. *J. Devel. Areas*, October 1988, 23(1), pp. 1–30.

_____; Kawagoe, Toshihiko and Hayami, Yujiro. The Intercountry Agricultural Production Function and Productivity Differences among Countries: Reply. *J. Devel. Econ.*, February 1988, 28(1), pp. 125–26.

_____ and Knudson, Mary K. Research and Development of a Biological Innovation: Commercial Hybrid Wheat. *Food Res. Inst. Stud.*, 1988, 21(1), pp. 45–68.

_____ and Wong, Lung-Fai. Sources of Differences in Agricultural Productivity Growth among Socialist Countries. In *Dogramaci, A. and Färe, R., eds.*, 1988, pp. 103–30.

Ruud, Paul A. and Poirier, Dale J. Probit with Dependent Observations. *Rev. Econ. Stud.*, October 1988, 55(4), pp. 593–614.

Ruys, Pieter H. M. Industries with Private and Public Enterprises. *Europ. Econ. Rev.*, March 1988, 32(2–3), pp. 415–21.

Ryan, Cillian. Trade in Services: An Introductory Survey. *Econ. Soc. Rev.*, October 1988, 20(1), pp. 37–48.

Ryan, D. M. and Falkner, J. C. Aspects of Bus Crew Scheduling Using a Set Partitioning Model. In *Daduna, J. R. and Wren, A., eds.*, 1988, pp. 91–103.

Ryan, David L.; Von Hohenbalken, Balder and West, Douglas S. New Competition in Shopping-Center Hierarchies: An Empirical Comparison of Alternative Specifications. *J. Reg. Sci.*, August 1988, 28(3), pp. 329–44.

Ryan, Timothy J. The "Deflouring" of an Industry: Australian Wheat. *Can. J. Agr. Econ.*, Part 1, December 1988, 36(4), pp. 621–32.

Rybczynski, Tad M. Financial Systems and Industrial Re-structuring. *Nat. Westminster Bank Quart. Rev.*, November 1988, pp. 3–13.

_____. The Internationalization of Finance and Business. *Bus. Econ.*, July 1988, 23(3), pp. 14–20.

Rybnikář, Karel and Kobeš, Josef. The Concept of the Plan in the Conditions of the Restructuring of the Economic Mechanism. *Czech. Econ. Digest.*, November 1988, (7), pp. 43–57.

Rychetnik, Luděk. Efficiency and Ownership under Socialism: Social and Group Appropriation. *Econ. Planning*, 1988, 22(1–2), pp. 18–40.

van Ryckeghem, Willy. Panel on Strategies for Confronting the Crisis: Panel. In *Feinberg, R. E. and Ffrench-Davis, R., eds.*, 1988, pp. 269–73.

Rymes, T. K. Keynes and Stable Money. In *Hamouda, O. F. and Smithin, J. N., eds., Vol. 2*, 1988, pp. 130–44.

_____. Keynes's Lectures, 1932–35: Notes of a Representative Student. Problems in Construction of a Synthesis. In *Moggridge, D. E., ed.*, 1988, pp. 91–127.

Ryngaert, Michael. The Effect of Poison Pill Securities on Shareholder Wealth. *J. Finan. Econ.*, Jan.–March 1988, 20(1–2), pp. 377–417.

_____ and Netter, Jeffry M. Shareholder Wealth Effects of the Ohio Antitakeover Law. *J. Law, Econ., Organ.*, Fall 1988, 4(2), pp. 373–83.

Ryrie, William. IFC: Growth and Diversification. *Finance Develop.*, December 1988, 25(4), pp. 22–24.

Ryscavage, Paul. Using the Current Population Survey for Longitudinal Analysis. *Econ. Lavoro*, July–Sept. 1988, 22(3), pp. 119–33.

Rystrom, David and Brastow, Raymond. Wealth Effects of the Drug Price Competition and Patent Term Restoration Act of 1984. *Amer. Econ.*, Fall 1988, 32(2), pp. 59–65.

Sýkora, Slavomír. The Establishment of Joint Enterprises with Partners from Non-Socialist Countries. *Czech. Econ. Digest.*, April 1988, (2), pp. 66–72.

Sa-Aadu, J. and Ravichandran, R. Resource Combination and Security Price Reactions: The Case of Real Estate Joint Ventures. *Amer. Real Estate Urban Econ. Assoc. J.*, Summer 1988, 16(2), pp. 105–22.

_____ and Shilling, James D. Rankings of Contributing Authors to the *AREUEA Journal* by Doctoral Origin and Employer: 1973–1987. *Amer. Real Estate Urban Econ. Assoc. J.*, Fall 1988, 16(3), pp. 257–70.

de Sa, Paulo. La restructuration de l'industrie miniére et métallurgique et ses effets sur les mécanismes de la formation des prix. (Market Structure and Price Formation in the Minerals and Metals Industry. With English summary.) *Écon. Soc.*, Nov.–Dec. 1988, 22(11–12), pp. 151–71.

Saari, Donald G. and van Newenhizen, Jill. Is Approval Voting an 'Unmitigated Evil'? A Response [The Problem of Indeterminacy in Approval, Multiple, and Truncated Voting Systems]. *Public Choice*, November 1988, 59(2), pp. 133–47.

_____ and van Newenhizen, Jill. The Problem of Indeterminacy in Approval, Multiple, and Truncated Voting Systems. *Public Choice*, November 1988, 59(2), pp. 101–20.

Saba, Richard P. and Ault, Richard W. Portfolio Choice with Investor Specific Transaction Costs. *Southern Econ. J.*, April 1988, 54(4), pp. 1012–19.

Sabatier, Paul A. An Advocacy Coalition Framework of Policy Change and the Role of Policy-Oriented Learning Therein. *Policy Sci.*, 1988, 21(2–3), pp. 129–68.

Sabavala, Darius J. Generalizing the NBD Model for Customer Purchases: What Are the Implications and Is It Worth the Effort? Comment. *J. Bus. Econ. Statist.*, April 1988, 6(2), pp. 161–62.

Sabol, William J. and Myers, Samuel L., Jr. Unemployment and Racial Differences in Imprisonment. In *Simms, M. C. and Myers, S. L., Jr., eds.*, 1988, pp. 189–209.

Sabot, Richard and Mohan, Rakesh. Educational Expansion and the Inequality of Pay: Colombia 1973–78. *Oxford Bull. Econ. Statist.*, May 1988, 50(2), pp. 175–82.

Sabourian, Hamid. Wage Norms and Involuntary Unemployment. *Econ. J.*, Supplement, 1988, 98(390), pp. 177–88.

Sacchetto, Claudio. Recognition of Foreign Enterprises as Taxable Entities: Italy. In *International Fiscal Association, ed. (I)*, 1988, pp. 439–58.

Sacco, Pier Luigi. Rational Expectations in Dynamic General Equilibrium Models: A Taxonomic View. *Giorn. Econ.*, May–June 1988, 47(5–6), pp. 253–75.

Saccomanni, Fabrizio. On Multilateral Surveillance. In *Guerrieri, P. and Padoan, P. C., eds.*, 1988, pp. 58–86.

Sachs, Ignacy. Bio-energy and Agro-industries for Decentralised Development. In *Research and Info. System for the Non-aligned and Other Developing Countries*, 1988, pp. 89–101.

———. Market, Non-market, Quasi-market and the 'Real' Economy. In *Arrow, K. J., ed.*, 1988, pp. 218–31.

Sachs, Jeffrey D. Comprehensive Debt Retirement: The Bolivian Example. *Brookings Pap. Econ. Act.*, 1988, (2), pp. 705–13.

———. The Debt Crisis at a Turning Point. *Challenge*, May–June 1988, 31(3), pp. 17–26.

———. Global Adjustments to a Shrinking U.S. Trade Deficit. *Brookings Pap. Econ. Act.*, 1988, (2), pp. 639–67.

———. International Policy Coordination: The Case of the Developing Country Debt Crisis. In *Feldstein, M., ed. (I)*, 1988, pp. 233–78.

———. Políticas comerciales y de tipo de cambio en programas de ajuste orientados al crecimiento. (Trade and Exchange Rate Policies in Growth-Oriented Adjustment Programs. With English summary.) *Estud. Econ.*, Jan.–June 1988, 3(1), pp. 77–108.

——— and Alesina, Alberto. Political Parties and the Business Cycle in the United States, 1948–1984. *J. Money, Credit, Banking*, February 1988, 20(1), pp. 63–82.

——— and Berg, Andrew. The Debt Crisis: Structural Explanations of Country Performance. *J. Devel. Econ.*, November 1988, 29(3), pp. 271–306.

——— and Boone, Peter. Japanese Structural Adjustment and the Balance of Payments. *J. Japanese Int. Economies*, September 1988, 2(3), pp. 286–327.

——— and Burda, Michael C. Assessing High Unemployment in West Germany. *World Econ.*, December 1988, 11(4), pp. 543–63.

——— and McKibbin, Warwick J. Comparing the Global Performance of Alternative Exchange Arrangements. *J. Int. Money Finance*, December 1988, 7(4), pp. 387–410.

——— and McKibbin, Warwick J. Coordination of Monetary and Fiscal Policies in the Industrial Economies. In *Frenkel, J. A., ed.*, 1988, pp. 73–113.

——— and Sundberg, Mark W. International Payments Imbalances of the East Asian Developing Economies. In *Fieleke, N. S., ed.*, 1988, pp. 103–51.

Sackmann, Sonja; Flamholtz, Eric G. and Randle, Yvonne. Personnel Management: The Tone of Tomorrow. In *Timpe, A. D., ed.*, 1988, 1986, pp. 33–41.

Sacks, Stephen R. Transaction Costs in Non-Market Economies. *J. Inst. Theoretical Econ.*, December 1988, 144(5), pp. 865–70.

Sacksteder, Elizabeth M. Securities Regulation for a Changing Market: Option Trader Standing under Rule 10b-5. *Yale Law J.*, March 1988, 97(4), pp. 623–43.

Sadanand, V. Endogenously Determined Price-Setting Monopoly in an Exchange Economy. *J. Econ. Theory*, October 1988, 46(1), pp. 172–78.

Sadka, Efraim; Nerlove, Marc and Razin, Assaf. A Bequest-Constrained Economy: Welfare Analysis. *J. Public Econ.*, November 1988, 37(2), pp. 203–20.

Sadoulet, Elisabeth and de Janvry, Alain. The Conditions for Compatibility between Aid and Trade in Agriculture. *Econ. Develop. Cult. Change*, October 1988, 37(1), pp. 1–30.

Sadowski, Dieter; Frick, Bernd and Stengelhofen, Theo. Wer beschäftigt Schwerbehinderte? Erste Einsichten aus einem laufenden Forschungsprojekt. (With English summary.) *Z. Betriebswirtshaft*, January 1988, 58(1), pp. 37–50.

Sætren, Harald; Baier, Vicki Eaton and March, James G. Implementation and Ambiguity. In *March, J. G.*, 1988, 1986, pp. 150–64.

Sáez, Raúl Eduardo. La selectividad en la política industrial: las experiencias de Japón y Francia. (Selectivity in Industrial Policy: The Experience in Japan and France. With English summary.) *Colección Estud. CIEPLAN*, December 1988, (25), pp. 55–77.

Saez, Roberto R.; Gottret, Pablo E. and Shumway, C. Richard. Multiproduct Supply and Input Demand in U.S. Agriculture. *Amer. J. Agr. Econ.*, May 1988, 70(2), pp. 330–37.

Saffran, Bernard. Recommendations for Further Reading. *J. Econ. Perspectives*, Spring 1988, 2(2), pp. 157–60.

———. Recommendations for Further Reading. *J. Econ. Perspectives*, Summer 1988, 2(3), pp. 183–86.

———. Recommendations for Further Reading. *J. Econ. Perspectives*, Winter 1988, 2(1), pp. 187–89.

Safra, Zvi. On the Structure of Non-manipulable Equilibria. *J. Math. Econ.*, 1988, *17*(1), pp. 23–29.

_____ **and Karni, Edi.** "Preference Reversals" and the Theory of Decision Making under Risk. In *Munier, B. R., ed.*, 1988, pp. 163–72.

_____ **and Zilcha, Itzhak.** Efficient Sets with and without the Expected Utility Hypothesis. *J. Math. Econ.*, 1988, *17*(4), pp. 369–84.

Safranski, Scott R. and Kwon, Ik-Whan. Religious Groups and Management Value Systems. In *Farmer, R. N. and McGoun, E. G., eds.*, 1988, pp. 171–83.

Sagar, Deep. Integrated Rural Development Programme in Uttar Pradesh and Bihar. *Margin*, Oct.–Dec. 1988, *21*(1), pp. 31–40.

Sagari, Silvia B. and Blejer, Mario I. Sequencing the Liberalization of Financial Markets. *Finance Develop.*, March 1988, *25*(1), pp. 18–20.

Sagasti, Francisco R. National Development Planning in Turbulent Times: New Approaches and Criteria for Institutional Design. *World Devel.*, April 1988, *16*(4), pp. 431–48.

Saghafi, Massoud M. Optimal Pricing to Maximize Profits and Achieve Market-Share Targets for Single-Product and Multiproduct Companies. In *Devinney, T. M., ed.*, 1988, pp. 239–55.

_____ **and Attaran, Mohsen.** Concentration Trends and Profitability in the U.S. Manufacturing Sector: 1970–84. *Appl. Econ.*, November 1988, *20*(11), pp. 1497–1510.

Sah, Raaj Kumar and Srinivasan, T. N. Distributional Consequences of Rural Food Levy and Subsidized Urban Rations. *Europ. Econ. Rev.*, January 1988, *32*(1), pp. 141–59.

_____ **and Stiglitz, Joseph E.** Committees, Hierarchies and Polyarchies. *Econ. J.*, June 1988, *98*(391), pp. 451–70.

Sahay, Surottam N.; Sinha, Ramesh P. and Rees, Hedley J. B. An Econometric Analysis of Workers Participation in Unions. *Indian Econ. J.*, Jan.–March 1988, *35*(3), pp. 61–71.

Sahi, S. and Shubik, Martin. A Model of a Sudden-Death Field-Goal Football Game as a Sequential Duel. *Math. Soc. Sci.*, June 1988, *15*(3), pp. 205–15.

Sahibzada, Shamim A. Investment and Inequality in Pakistan's Education Sector: Comments. *Pakistan Devel. Rev.*, Part 2, Winter 1988, *27*(4), pp. 685–86.

_____ **and Mahmood, Mir Annice.** The Economic Rate of Return in Small and Household Manufacturing Industries. *Pakistan Devel. Rev.*, Part 2, Winter 1988, *27*(4), pp. 875–83.

Sahlin, Nils-Eric and Gärdenfors, Peter. Bayesian Decision Theory—Foundations and Problems. In *Gärdenfors, P. and Sahlin, N.-E., eds.*, 1988, pp. 1–15.

_____ **and Gärdenfors, Peter.** Unreliable Probabilities, Risk Taking, and Decision Making. In *Gärdenfors, P. and Sahlin, N.-E., eds.*, 1988, pp. 313–34.

Sahn, David E. The Effect of Price and Income Changes on Food-Energy Intake in Sri Lanka. *Econ. Develop. Cult. Change*, January 1988, *36*(2), pp. 315–40.

_____ **and Alderman, Harold.** The Effects of Human Capital on Wages, and the Determinants of Labor Supply in a Developing Country. *J. Devel. Econ.*, September 1988, *29*(2), pp. 157–83.

Sahu, Bhabatosh. Participative Management for Effective Human Resources Management: Experience of Two Steel Plants. In *Kohli, U. and Gautam, V., eds.*, 1988, pp. 177–95.

Sai, Frederick T. and Birdsall, Nancy M. Family Planning Services in Sub-Saharan Africa. *Finance Develop.*, March 1988, *25*(1), pp. 28–31.

Saijo, Tatsuyoshi. Strategy Space Reduction in Maskin's Theorem: Sufficient Conditions for Nash Implementation. *Econometrica*, May 1988, *56*(3), pp. 693–700.

Sailly, P. and Launois, R. Mehr Markt im Gesundheitswesen: Einige Überlegungen aus französischer Sicht. (With English summary.) *J. Inst. Theoretical Econ.*, April 1988, *144*(2), pp. 403–06.

Sailors, Joel W. and Craig, Steven G. State Government Purchases in a Federalist Economy. *Public Choice*, February 1988, *56*(2), pp. 121–30.

Sainsaulieu, Renaud. Stratégies d'entreprise et communautés sociales de production. (Company Strategies and Social Communities of Production. With English summary.) *Revue Écon.*, January 1988, *39*(1), pp. 155–74.

Saint-Louis, R.; Gilson, J. C. and Chadee, D. U.S. CVDs and Canadian Hog Exports: Methodological and Measurement Issues. *Can. J. Agr. Econ.*, Part 1, December 1988, *36*(4), pp. 669–87.

Saint-Ouen, François. Facing European Integration: The Case of Switzerland. *J. Common Market Stud.*, March 1988, *26*(3), pp. 273–85.

Saito, Osamu. The Other Faces of the Industrial Revolution—A Review Essay. *Econ. Rev. (Keizai Kenkyu)*, April 1988, *39*(2), pp. 180–84.

Sakai, Marcia Y. A Micro-analysis of Business Travel Demand. *Appl. Econ.*, November 1988, *20*(11), pp. 1481–95.

Sakai, Yoshikiyo. Conditional Pareto Optimality of Stationary Equilibrium in a Stochastic Overlapping Generations Model. *J. Econ. Theory*, February 1988, *44*(1), pp. 209–13.

Sakamoto, Arthur and Sandefur, Gary D. American Indian Household Structure and Income. *Demography*, February 1988, *25*(1), pp. 71–80.

_____ **and Sandefur, Gary D.** Improving the Economic Well-Being of Indians in Wisconsin. In *Danziger, S. H. and Witte, J. F., eds.*, 1988, pp. 187–207.

Sakamoto, Masahiro. Whither International Trade Policies: Worries about Continuing Protectionism: Comments. In *Elliott, K. A. and Williamson, J., eds.*, 1988, pp. 100–103.

Sakamoto, Tomohiko. The Japan–U.S. Bilateral Trade. *Fed. Res. Bank San Francisco Econ. Rev.*, Spring 1988, (2), pp. 3–13.

Sakawa, Masatoshi and Seo, Fumiko. Evaluation of Telecommunication Systems with Multiple Criteria Decision Analysis: A Game Theoretic Approach. In *Orishimo, I.; Hewings, G. J. D. and Nijkamp, P.*, eds., 1988, pp. 214–36.

Sako, Mari and Dore, Ronald. Teaching or Testing: The Role of the State in Japan. *Oxford Rev. Econ. Policy*, Autumn 1988, *4*(3), pp. 72–81.

Sakuma, I. and Kurabayashi, Y. A Reconsideration of the Concept of International Prices for the International Comparison of Real GDP. In *Salazar-Carrillo, J. and Rao, D. S. P.*, eds., 1988, pp. 39–57.

Salais, Robert. Why Was Unemployment So Low in France during the 1930s? In *Eichengreen, B. and Hatton, T. J.*, eds., 1988, pp. 247–88.

Salam, Abdul. Taxes and Subsidies on Agricultural Producers as Elements of Intersectoral Transfer of Resources: Magnitude of the Transfer and Search for Policy Options: Comments. *Pakistan Devel. Rev.*, Part 2, Winter 1988, *27*(4), pp. 557–60.

Salama, Elías. Sobre el ingreso nominal como meta intermedia de la política monetaria. (On Nominal Income as an Intermediate Target on Monetary Policy. With English summary.) *Económica (La Plata)*, July–Dec. 1988, *34*(2), pp. 241–74.

Salami, K. A. Impact of Formal Agricultural Credit on Small Farm Development in the Ashanti Region of Ghana. *Eastern Afr. Econ. Rev.*, December 1988, *4*(2), pp. 1–8.

Salandro, Dan; Shastri, Kuldeep and Choi, J. Y. On the Estimation of Bid–Ask Spreads: Theory and Evidence. *J. Finan. Quant. Anal.*, June 1988, *23*(2), pp. 219–30.

Salant, Stephen W.; Switzer, Sheldon and Reynolds, Robert J. Losses from Horizontal Merger: The Effects of an Exogenous Change in Industry Structure on Cournot–Nash Equilibrium. In *Daughety, A. F.*, ed., 1988, *1983*, pp. 373–87.

Salant, Walter S. The Spread of Keynesian Doctrines and Practices in the United States. In *Hamouda, O. F. and Smithin, J. N.*, eds., Vol. *1*, 1988, pp. 61–76.

Salant, William A. Taxes, Income Determination, and the Balanced Budget Theorem. In *Shaw, G. K.*, ed., Vol. 2, 1988, *1957*, pp. 290–99.

Salas, Carlos and Rendon, Teresa. Wages and Employment in Mexico: Recent Tendencies and Perspectives. *Rev. Radical Polit. Econ.*, Summer–Fall 1988, *20*(2–3), pp. 253–59.

Salas, Jose D.; Obeysekera, J. T. B. and Bartolini, Paolo. Multivariate Periodic ARMA (1, 1) Processes. *Water Resources Res.*, August 1988, *24*(8), pp. 1237–46.

Salathe, Larry. Export Responsiveness and U.S. Farm Policy Options for Wheat. *J. Agr. Econ. Res.*, Winter 1988, *40*(1), pp. 19–29.

Salazar-Carrillo, Jorge and de Alonso, Irma Tirado. Real Product and Price Comparisons between Latin America and the Rest of the World. *Rev. Income Wealth*, March 1988, *34*(1), pp. 27–43.

_____ and Jorge, Antonio. Foreign Investment, Debt and Economic Growth in Latin America: An Introductory Overview. In *Jorge, A. and Salazar-Carrillo, J.*, eds., 1988, pp. 3–10.

_____ and Jorge, Antonio. The Use of Prices for Comparisons in Developing Command Economies. In *Salazar-Carrillo, J. and Rao, D. S. P.*, eds., 1988, pp. 299–304.

_____ and Rao, D. S. Prasada. A General Equilibrium Approach to the Construction of Multilateral Index Numbers. In *Salazar-Carrillo, J. and Rao, D. S. P.*, eds., 1988, pp. 19–37.

_____ and Rao, D. S. Prasada. Real Product and Price Comparisons among Latin American Countries. In *Salazar-Carrillo, J. and Rao, D. S. P.*, eds., 1988, pp. 195–205.

Salazar, Melito S., Jr., et al. Problems of Production Management for Small and Medium Enterprises in the Philippines. In *James, K. and Akrasanee, N.*, eds., 1988, pp. 93–125.

Saldanha, Fernando B. and Lancry, Pierre-Jean. A Psychological Opponent Processes Theory of Consumption. In *Maital, S.*, ed., Vol. 1, 1988, pp. 114–33.

Saleem, Samir Taha. Relative Efficiency of Cotton Farms in Sudanese Irrigated Agriculture. *World Devel.*, August 1988, *16*(8), pp. 975–84.

Salehi-Esfahani, Haideh. Informationally Imperfect Labour Markets and the 'Dutch Disease' Problem. *Can. J. Econ.*, August 1988, *21*(3), pp. 617–24.

Salehi-Isfahani, Djavad. Technology and Preferences in the Boserup Model of Agricultural Growth. *J. Devel. Econ.*, March 1988, *28*(2), pp. 175–91.

Salehizadeh, Mehdi and Haddad, Kamal. An Application of Options to Foreign Exchange Rate Forecasting. *Quart. J. Bus. Econ.*, Winter 1988, *27*(1), pp. 42–69.

Salemi, Michael K. and Black, Stanley W. FIML Estimation of the Dollar–Deutschemark Risk Premium in a Portfolio Model. *J. Int. Econ.*, November 1988, *25*(3–4), pp. 205–24.

Salerno, Joseph T. The Neglect of the French Liberal School in Anglo-American Economics: A Critique of Received Explanations. In *Rothbard, M. N. and Block, W.*, eds., 1988, pp. 113–56.

Salin, Pascal. Comments [The Case for Rules in the Conduct of Monetary Policy: A Concrete Example] [The Rules-versus-Discretion Debate in the Light of Recent Experience]. In *Giersch, H.*, ed., 1988, pp. 71–85.

_____. Macroeconomic Policy Coordination: Where Should We Stand? Comments. In *Giersch, H.*, ed., 1988, pp. 292–95.

Salinger, Michael A. Capital Markets, Efficiency, and Corporate Control: Comment. In *Coffee, J. C., Jr.; Lowenstein, L. and Rose-Ackerman, S.*, eds., 1988, pp. 71–73.

_____. Vertical Mergers and Market Foreclosure. *Quart. J. Econ.*, May 1988, *103*(2), pp. 345–56.

Salisbury, Lance; Bascom, Jonathan and Samatar, Abdi. The Political Economy of Livestock

Marketing in Northern Somalia. *African Econ. Hist.*, 1988, (17), pp. 81–97.

Salisbury, Richard F. The Economics of Development through Services: Findings of the McGill Programme among the Cree. In *Bennett, J. W. and Bowen, J. R., eds.*, 1988, pp. 239–56.

Salkever, David S. Morbidity Costs: National Estimates and Economic Determinants. In *Sirageldin, I. and Sorkin, A., eds.*, 1988, pp. 237–88.

Sallai, R. and Schweitzer, Iván. World Economic Environment and the Hungarian Economy: A Conference. *Acta Oecon.*, 1988, 39(1–2), pp. 185–87.

Salmi, Timo, et al. Financial Ratios as Predictors of Firms' Industry Branch. *Liiketaloudellinen Aikak.*, 1988, 37(4), pp. 263–77.

Salmon, Mark. Error Correction Models, Cointegration and the Internal Model Principle. *J. Econ. Dynam. Control*, June–Sept. 1988, 12(2–3), pp. 523–49.

Salmon, Pierre and Mingat, Alain. Alterable Electorates in the Context of Residential Mobility. *Public Choice*, October 1988, 59(1), pp. 67–82.

Salmon, Walter J.; May, Eleanor G. and Ress, C. William. Future Trends in Retailing: Merchandise Line Trends and Store Trends 1980–1990. In *Kaynak, E., ed.*, 1988, pp. 333–48.

Salmon, Wesley C. Statistical Explanation and Causality. In *Pitt, J. C., ed.*, 1988, pp. 75–118.

Salomon, Ilan and Nijkamp, Peter. Telecommunication and the Tyranny of Space. In *Orishimo, I.; Hewings, G. J. D. and Nijkamp, P., eds.*, 1988, pp. 91–106.

Saloner, Garth and Farrell, Joseph. Coordination through Committees and Markets. *Rand J. Econ.*, Summer 1988, 19(2), pp. 235–52.

Salop, Steven C. Evaluating Uncertain Evidence with Sir Thomas Bayes: A Note for Teachers: Response. *J. Econ. Perspectives*, Spring 1988, 2(2), pp. 178–79.

_____. Panel Discussion: Corporate Takeovers and Public Policy: Remarks. In *Auerbach, A. J., ed. (I)*, 1988, pp. 321–25.

_____. A Time-Series Analysis of Mergers and Acquisitions in the U.S. Economy: Comment. In *Auerbach, A. J., ed. (I)*, 1988, pp. 303–07.

_____ and White, Lawrence J. Private Antitrust Litigation: An Introduction and Framework. In *White, L. J., ed.*, 1988, pp. 3–60.

Salorio, Eugene M. The Causes and Consequences of Inconsistent Leadership in Postwar U.S. International Agricultural Policy. In *Goldberg, R. A., ed., Vol. 9*, 1988, pp. 43–102.

Salsbury, Stephen. The Emergence of an Early Large-Scale Technical System: The American Railroad Network. In *Mayntz, R. and Hughes, T. P., eds.*, 1988, pp. 37–68.

Salsecci, Gianluca. Dualistic Economic Structure and Money Non-neutrality. *Econ. Letters*, 1988, 28(4), pp. 295–99.

Saltari, Enrico and Rodano, Giorgio. Futures Markets, Average Opinion and Rational Learning. *Ricerche Econ.*, July–Sept. 1988, 42(3), pp. 452–69.

Salter, Malcolm S. and Weinhold, Wolf A. Corporate Takeovers: Financial Boom or Organizational Bust? In *Coffee, J. C., Jr.; Lowenstein, L. and Rose-Ackerman, S., eds.*, 1988, pp. 135–49.

Saltzman, Gregory M. Bargaining Laws as a Cause and Consequence of the Growth of Teacher Unionism. In *Lewin, D., et al., eds.*, 1988, 1985, pp. 53–75.

_____. Public Sector Bargaining Laws Really Matter: Evidence from Ohio and Illinois. In *Freeman, R. B. and Ichniowski, C., eds.*, 1988, pp. 41–78.

Salvadori, Neri. The Existence of a Two-Class Economy in a General Cambridge Model of Growth and Distribution: An Addendum. *Cambridge J. Econ.*, June 1988, 12(2), pp. 273–78.

_____. Existence of Cost-Minimizing Systems within the Sraffa Framework. In *Steedman, I., ed., Vol. 2*, 1988, 1982, pp. 33–50.

_____. Fixed Capital within a von Neumann–Morishima Model of Growth and Distribution. *Int. Econ. Rev.*, May 1988, 29(2), pp. 341–51.

_____. Fixed Capital within the Sraffa Framework. *J. Econ. (Z. Nationalökon.)*, 1988, 48(1), pp. 1–17.

_____. Switching in Methods of Production and Joint Production. In *Steedman, I., ed., Vol. 2*, 1988, 1985, pp. 51–73.

_____ and Steedman, Ian. Cost Functions and Produced Means of Production: Duality and Capital Theory. In *Steedman, I., ed., Vol. 2*, 1988, 1985, pp. 307–18.

_____ and Steedman, Ian. Joint Production Analysis in a Sraffian Framework. *Bull. Econ. Res.*, June 1988, 40(3), pp. 165–95.

_____ and Steedman, Ian. No Reswitching? No Switching! *Cambridge J. Econ.*, December 1988, 12(4), pp. 481–86.

_____ and Steedman, Ian. A Note about the Interest Rate and the Revenue Function. *Eastern Econ. J.*, April–June 1988, 14(2), pp. 153–56.

Salvas-Bronsard, Lise and Bronsard, Camille. Anticipations rationnelles, fonctions d'anticipations et structure locale de Slutsky. (Rational Expectations, Expectation Functions, and Slutsky Local Structure. With English summary.) *Can. J. Econ.*, November 1988, 21(4), pp. 846–56.

_____ and Bronsard, Camille. Sur trois contributions d'Allais. (With English summary.) *L'Actual. Econ.*, December 1988, 64(4), pp. 481–92.

Salvati, Michele. The Interplay between Institutional and Material Factors: The Problem and Its Status: Comment. In *Kregel, J. A.; Matzner, E. and Roncaglia, A., eds.*, 1988, pp. 336–39.

Salvatore, Dominick. Internal Migration, Urbanization, and Economic Development. In *Salvatore, D., ed.*, 1988, pp. 79–94.

———. The New Protectionism with Nontariff Instruments. In *Saunders, C. T., ed.,* 1988, pp. 155–81.

———. Population Trends and Economic Development: Introduction. In *Salvatore, D., ed.,* 1988, pp. 1–9.

——— and Campano, Fred. Economic Development, Income Inequality and Kuznets' U-shaped Hypothesis. *J. Policy Modeling,* Summer 1988, *10*(2), pp. 265–80.

Salvemini, Severino and Pilati, Massimo. Il contributo della teoria dell'agenzia allo sviluppo del capitalismo manageriale. (A Contribution of the Agency Theory to the Development of Managerial Capitalism. With English summary.) *Giorn. Econ.,* March–April 1988, *47*(3–4), pp. 187–211.

Salyer, Kevin D. The Characterization of Savings under Uncertainty: The Case of Serially Correlated Returns. *Econ. Letters,* 1988, *26*(1), pp. 21–27.

———. Comparative Dynamics and Risk Premia in an Overlapping Generations Model: A Note. *Rev. Econ. Stud.,* October 1988, *55*(4), pp. 667–68.

———. Overlapping Generations and Representative Agent Models of the Equity Premia: Implications from a Growing Economy. *Can. J. Econ.,* August 1988, *21*(3), pp. 565–78.

———. Risk Aversion and Stock Price Volatility When Dividends Are Difference Stationary. *Econ. Letters,* 1988, *28*(3), pp. 255–58.

Salzman, Philip Carl. Labour Formations in a Nomadic Tribe. In *Attwood, D. W. and Baviskar, B. S., eds.,* 1988, pp. 233–58.

Samanta, Subarna K. and Beladi, Hamid. Factor Market Distortions and Backward Incidence of Pollution Control. *Ann. Reg. Sci.,* March 1988, *22*(1), pp. 75–83.

——— and Beladi, Hamid. Unanticipated Monetary Policy and Real Output—Some Evidence from the UK Economy. *Appl. Econ.,* June 1988, *20*(6), pp. 721–29.

——— and Beladi, Hamid. Unanticipated Monetary Policy: Another Look for a Developing Country. *J. Macroecon.,* Spring 1988, *10*(2), pp. 297–307.

Samarasinghe, S. W. R. de A. Sri Lanka: A Case Study from the Third World. In *Bell, D. E. and Reich, M. R., eds.,* 1988, pp. 39–80.

Samatar, Abdi; Salisbury, Lance and Bascom, Jonathan. The Political Economy of Livestock Marketing in Northern Somalia. *African Econ. Hist.,* 1988, (17), pp. 81–97.

Samet, Dov and Kalai, Ehud. Weighted Shapley Values. In *[Shapley, L. S.],* 1988, pp. 83–99.

———; Stanford, William and Kalai, Ehud. A Note on Reactive Equilibria in the Discounted Prisoner's Dilemma and Associated Games. *Int. J. Game Theory,* 1988, *17*(3), pp. 177–86.

Samiei, S. Hossein. An Empirical Study of Disequilibrium in North–South Trade. In *Currie, D. and Vines, D., eds.,* 1988, pp. 185–208.

Sammartino, Frank J. and Kasten, Richard A. Distributional Analyses of Three Deficit Reduction Options Affecting Social Security Cash

Benefits. In *Danziger, S. H. and Portney, K. E., eds.,* 1988, pp. 116–48.

Sampath, Rajan K. and Rhodes, George F., Jr. Efficiency, Equity and Cost Recovery Implications of Water Pricing and Allocation Schemes in Developing Countries. *Can. J. Agr. Econ.,* March 1988, *36*(1), pp. 103–17.

Samper, Diego Giraldo. Agricultural and Sociodemographic Interrelationships: A Study of Three Areas at Different Levels of Development in Tolima, Colombia. In *Vlassoff, C. and Barkat-e-Khuda, eds.,* 1988, pp. 58–72.

Sampson, Anthony A. Efficient Union Bargains with a Random Arbitrator. *Econ. Letters,* 1988, *26*(1), pp. 99–102.

———. Unionized Contracts with Fixed Wage Rates and State-Contingent Employment Levels. *Economica,* February 1988, *55*(217), pp. 95–105.

Sampson, Gary P. International Trade in Banking Services: Comment. In *Baldwin, R. E.; Hamilton, C. B. and Sapir, A., eds.,* 1988, pp. 276–81.

———. Uruguay Round Negotiations on Services Issues and Recent Developments. In *Dicke, D. C. and Petersmann, E.-U., eds.,* 1988, pp. 274–87.

Samson, Ivan. La modernisation des activites productives en RDA. (The Modernization of the Productive Activities in GDR. With English summary.) *Écon. Soc.,* February 1988, *22*(2), pp. 47–77.

Samson, Lucie. Chocs sectoriels et chômage. (With English summary.) *L'Actual. Econ.,* December 1988, *64*(4), pp. 532–44.

Samuel, Wendell A. Tax Reform in Grenada. *Bull. Int. Fiscal Doc.,* March 1988, *42*(3), pp. 123–30.

Samuels, Warren J. An Essay on the Nature and Significance of the Normative Nature of Economics. *J. Post Keynesian Econ.,* Spring 1988, *10*(3), pp. 347–54.

———. Edwin E. Witte's Concept of the Role of Government in the Economy. In *Samuels, W. J., ed., Vol. 2,* 1988, *1967,* pp. 222–38.

———. Institutional Economics, Volume I: Introduction. In *Samuels, W. J., ed., Vol. 1,* 1988, pp. 1–5.

———. Institutional Economics, Volume II: Introduction. In *Samuels, W. J., ed., Vol. 2,* 1988, pp. 1–4.

———. Interrelations Between Legal and Economic Processes. In *Samuels, W. J., ed., Vol. 2,* 1988, *1971,* pp. 253–68.

———. Of Lookout Cows and the Methodology of Economics. *J. Econ. Issues,* September 1988, *22*(3), pp. 864–67.

———. Technology vis-á-vis Institutions in the *JEI:* A Suggested Interpretation. In *Samuels, W. J., ed., Vol. 3,* 1988, *1977,* pp. 65–89.

Samuelson, Charles D.; Messick, David M. and Allison, Scott T. Framing and Communication Effects on Group Members' Responses to Environmental and Social Uncertainty. In *Maital, S., ed., Vol. 2,* 1988, pp. 677–700.

Samuelson, Larry. On the Effects of Indexed

Bonds in Developing Countries. *Oxford Econ. Pap.*, March 1988, *40*(1), pp. 168–92.

_____; **Dunne, Timothy and Roberts, Mark J.** Patterns of Firm Entry and Exit in U.S. Manufacturing Industries. *Rand J. Econ.*, Winter 1988, *19*(4), pp. 495–515.

_____ **and Roberts, Mark J.** An Empirical Analysis of Dynamic, Nonprice Competition in an Oligopolistic Industry. *Rand J. Econ.*, Summer 1988, *19*(2), pp. 200–220.

Samuelson, Paul A. The Critique of Marginal Theory: A Summing Up. In *Steedman, I., ed., Vol. 1*, 1988, *1966*, pp. 341–56.

_____. Diagrammatic Exposition of a Theory of Public Expenditure. In *Ricketts, M., ed., Vol. 2*, 1988, *1955*, pp. 7–13.

_____. How a Certain Internal Consistency Entails the Expected Utility Dogma. *J. Risk Uncertainty*, December 1988, *1*(4), pp. 389–93.

_____. In the Beginning. *Challenge*, July–August 1988, *31*(4), pp. 32–34.

_____. Interactions between the Multiplier Analysis and the Principle of Acceleration. In *Shaw, G. K., ed., Vol. 1*, 1988, *1939*, pp. 111–14.

_____. Mathematical Vindication of Ricardo on Machinery. *J. Polit. Econ.*, April 1988, *96*(2), pp. 274–82.

_____. The Passing of the Guard in Economics. *Eastern Econ. J.*, Oct.–Dec. 1988, *14*(4), pp. 319–29.

_____. The Pure Theory of Public Expenditure. In *Cowen, T., ed.*, 1988, *1954*, pp. 29–33.

_____; **Dornbusch, Rudiger and Fischer, Stanley.** Comparative Advantage, Trade, and Payments in a Ricardian Model with a Continuum of Goods. In *Dornbusch, R.*, 1988, *1977*, pp. 293–322.

_____ **and Solow, Robert M.** Problem of Achieving and Maintaining a Stable Price Level: Analytical Aspects of Anti-inflation Policy. In *Shaw, G. K., ed., Vol. 2*, 1988, *1960*, pp. 138–55.

Samuelson, William F. and Hansen, Robert G. Evolution in Economic Games. *J. Econ. Behav. Organ.*, October 1988, *10*(3), pp. 315–38.

_____; **Johnson, Stephen and Kotlikoff, Laurence J.** Consumption, Computation Mistakes, and Fiscal Policy. *Amer. Econ. Rev.*, May 1988, *78*(2), pp. 408–12.

_____ **and Zeckhauser, Richard.** Status Quo Bias in Decision Making. *J. Risk Uncertainty*, March 1988, *1*(1), pp. 7–59.

Sancar, Fahriye Hazer and Cook, Robert J. Multi-level Modeling for Incorporating Public Perceptions into Comprehensive Planning: Door County Example. *Rev. Reg. Stud.*, Spring 1988, *18*(2), pp. 54–69.

Sand, Paal. The Use of Impact Tables for Policy Applications of Input–Output Models. In *Ciaschini, M., ed.*, 1988, pp. 263–86.

Sand, Peter. Consumer Organizations and Representation in the Developed World. In *Maynes, E. S. and ACCI Research Committee, eds.*, 1988, pp. 499–505.

Sandbach, Jonathan. The Sensitivity of Consump-

tion of Oil Products to Price Changes: An Econometric Investigation. *Energy Econ.*, October 1988, *10*(4), pp. 261–70.

Sandberg, Lars G. and Steckel, Richard H. Overpopulation and Malnutrition Rediscovered: Hard Times in 19th-Century Sweden. *Exploration Econ. Hist.*, January 1988, *25*(1), pp. 1–19.

Sandbrook, Richard. Patrimonialism and the Failing of Parastatals: Africa in Comparative Perspective. In *Cook, P. and Kirkpatrick, C., eds.*, 1988, pp. 162–79.

Sande, I. G. Missing-Data Adjustments in Large Surveys: Comment. *J. Bus. Econ. Statist.*, July 1988, *6*(3), pp. 296–97.

Sandefur, Gary D. and Sakamoto, Arthur. American Indian Household Structure and Income. *Demography*, February 1988, *25*(1), pp. 71–80.

_____ **and Sakamoto, Arthur.** Improving the Economic Well-Being of Indians in Wisconsin. In *Danziger, S. H. and Witte, J. F., eds.*, 1988, pp. 187–207.

_____ **and Tuma, Nancy Brandon.** Trends in the Labor Force Activity of the Elderly in the United States, 1940–1980. In *Ricardo-Campbell, R. and Lazear, E. P., eds.*, 1988, pp. 38–75.

Sandelin, Bo and Aguilar, Renato. Qualitative Response Estimations of the Selling Behaviour in the Swedish Market for Owner-Occupied Houses. *Urban Stud.*, February 1988, *25*(1), pp. 77–84.

Sanderatne, Nimal. The Asian Experience and the Role of Multilateral Institutions, Foreign Aid, and Other Financial Sources: Comments. In *Streeten, P., ed.*, 1988, pp. 249–55.

Sanders, Anthony B. and Unal, Haluk. On the Intertemporal Behavior of the Short-term Rate of Interest. *J. Finan. Quant. Anal.*, December 1988, *23*(4), pp. 417–23.

Sanders, Arthur. Rationality, Self-interest, and Public Attitudes on Public Spending. *Soc. Sci. Quart.*, June 1988, *69*(2), pp. 311–24.

Sanders, David and Davies, Rob. Adjustment Policies and the Welfare of Children: Zimbabwe, 1980–1985. In *Cornia, G. A.; Jolly, R. and Stewart, F., eds.*, 1988, pp. 272–99.

Sanders, Elizabeth R. and Draper, Norman R. Minimum Bias Estimation—Designs and Decisions. In *Fedorov, V. and Lauter, H., eds.*, 1988, pp. 13–22.

Sanders, Larry D. The Restructuring of Southern Agriculture: Data Needs for Economic and Policy Research: Discussion. *Southern J. Agr. Econ.*, July 1988, *20*(1), pp. 41–43.

Sanders, Larry W. Help Your Subordinates Grow. In *Timpe, A. D., ed.*, 1988, *1984*, pp. 285–88.

Sanders, William V. Gender-Based Determinants of Household Production Time. In *Pennsylvania Economic Association*, 1988, pp. 439–52.

Sanderson, Fred H. The Agro-food Filière: A Macroeconomic Study on the Evolution of the Demand Structure and Induced Changes in the Destination of Agricultural Outputs. In *An-*

tonelli, G. and Quadrio-Curzio, A., eds., 1988, pp. 185–208.

Sanderson, Michael. Education and Economic Decline, 1890–1980s. *Oxford Rev. Econ. Policy,* Spring 1988, *4*(1), pp. 38–50.

Sandholtz, Kurt W. and Perry, Lee Tom. A "Liberating Form" for Radical Product Innovation. In *Gattiker, U. E. and Larwood, L.,* eds., 1988, pp. 9–31.

Sandler, Ralph D. Market Share Instability in Commercial Airline Markets and the Impact of Deregulation. *J. Ind. Econ.,* March 1988, *36*(3), pp. 327–35.

Sandler, Todd. Sharing Burdens in NATO. *Challenge,* March–April 1988, *31*(2), pp. 29–35.

_____; **Cornes, Richard and Mason, Charles F.** Expectations, the Commons, and Optimal Group Size. *J. Environ. Econ. Manage.,* March 1988, *15*(1), pp. 99–110.

_____ **and Lapan, Harvey E.** To Bargain or Not to Bargain: That Is the Question. *Amer. Econ. Rev.,* May 1988, *78*(2), pp. 16–21.

_____ **and Posnett, John.** Transfers, Transaction Costs and Charitable Intermediaries. *Int. Rev. Law Econ.,* December 1988, *8*(2), pp. 145–60.

_____ **and Sterbenz, Frederic P.** Externalities, Pigouvian Corrections, and Risk Attitudes. *J. Environ. Econ. Manage.,* December 1988, *15*(4), pp. 488–504.

Sandmo, Agnar. History of Economic Thought: The Scandinavian Contribution: Introductory Remarks. *Europ. Econ. Rev.,* March 1988, *32*(2–3), pp. 491–94.

_____. Optimal Taxation. In *Ricketts, M.,* ed., Vol. 2, 1988, *1976,* pp. 171–88.

_____. Tax Wedges and Mobile Capital: Comment. In *Haaland, J. I. and Norman, V. D.,* eds., 1988, pp. 131–32.

_____ **and Allingham, Michael G.** Income Tax Evasion: A Theoretical Analysis. In *Ricketts, M., ed., Vol. 1,* 1988, *1972,* pp. 359–74.

Sandström, Arne; Wretman, Jan H. and Waldén, Bertil. Variance Estimators of the Gini Coefficient—Probability Sampling. *J. Bus. Econ. Statist.,* January 1988, *6*(1), pp. 113–19.

Sanford, Charles S., Jr. and Votja, George J. Deregulation, Technology, and the "Safety and Soundness" of the Financial System. In *Feldstein, M., ed. (II),* 1988, pp. 264–77.

Sanford, Jonathan E. Feasibility of a World Bank Interest Subsidy Account to Supplement the Existing IDA Program. *World Devel.,* July 1988, *16*(7), pp. 787–96.

_____. The World Bank and Poverty: The Plight of the World's Impoverished Is Still a Major Concern of the International Agency. *Amer. J. Econ. Soc.,* July 1988, *47*(3), pp. 257–75.

Sanford, Scott and Tweeten, Luther G. Farm Income Enhancement Potential for Small, Part-Time Farming Operations in East Central Oklahoma. *Southern J. Agr. Econ.,* December 1988, *20*(2), pp. 153–64.

Sanghvi, A. and Munasinghe, Mohan. Reliability of Electricity Supply, Outage Costs and Value of Service: An Overview. *Energy J.,* Special Issue, 1988, *9,* pp. 1–18.

Sangl, Judith and Dobson, Allen. A Broker Model for Joint Public–Private Supplemental Insurance for the Medicare Population: A Transition to Long-term Care Insurance. In *Scheffler, R. M. and Rossiter, L. F.,* eds., 1988, pp. 23–44.

Sankar, T. L. Structural Adaptation and Public Enterprise Performance: Comments. In *Streeten, P.,* ed., 1988, pp. 208–11.

Santamäki, Tuire. Implications of the Non-homogeneity of Standard and Overtime Hours on the Structure and Cyclical Adjustment of Labor Input. In *Hart, R. A.,* ed., 1988, pp. 90–106.

Santana, Sarah. Some Thoughts on Vital Statistics and Health Status in Cuba. In *Zimbalist, A.,* ed., 1988, pp. 107–18.

Santerre, Rexford E. Representative Versus Direct Democracy: A Tiebout Test of Relative Performance: Reply. *Public Choice,* January 1988, *56*(1), pp. 73–76.

Santi, Lawrence L. The Demographic Context of Recent Changes in the Structure of American Households. *Demography,* November 1988, *25*(4), pp. 509–19.

Santiago, Carlos E. and Thorbecke, Erik. A Multisectoral Framework for the Analysis of Labor Mobility and Development in LDCs: An Application to Postwar Puerto Rico. *Econ. Develop. Cult. Change,* October 1988, *37*(1), pp. 127–48.

Santiago, Gilda Maria C.; Ferro, Luiz César M. and Braga, Helson C. Estrutura da proteçao efetiva no Brasil: 1985. (With English summary.) *Pesquisa Planejamento Econ.,* December 1988, *18*(3), pp. 663–84.

Santiago-Valiente, Wilfredo. Historical Background of the Classical Monetary Theory and the 'Real-Bills' Banking Tradition. *Hist. Polit. Econ.,* Spring 1988, *20*(1), pp. 43–63.

Santini, Danilo J. A Model of Economic Fluctuations and Growth Arising from the Reshaping of Transportation Technology. *Logist. Transp. Rev.,* June 1988, *24*(2), pp. 121–51.

Santomero, Anthony M. The Intermediation Process and the Future of Thrifts. In *Federal Home Loan Bank of San Francisco,* 1988, pp. 187–99.

_____ **and Kim, Daesik.** Risk in Banking and Capital Regulation. *J. Finance,* December 1988, *43*(5), pp. 1219–33.

Santoni, G. J. The October Crash: Some Evidence on the Cascade Theory. *Fed. Res. Bank St. Louis Rev.,* May–June 1988, *70*(3), pp. 18–33.

Santorum, Anita and Portes, Richard. Money and the Consumption Goods Market in China. In *Reynolds, B. L.,* ed., 1988, *1987,* pp. 64–81.

Santos, Juan E.; Arbogast, Todd and Douglas, Jim, Jr. Two-Phase Immiscible Flow in Naturally Fractured Reservoirs. In *Wheeler, M. F.,* ed., 1988, pp. 47–66.

Santos, Teodoro M. The Philippine Minerals Industry, Development and Trade. In *McKern, B. and Koomsup, P.,* eds., 1988, pp. 255–88.

Santucci, Giuseppe and Catarci, Tiziana. GRASP: A Complete Graphical Conceptual Language for Definition and Manipulation of

Statistical Databases. In *Edwards, D. and Raun, N. E., eds.*, 1988, pp. 401–06.

Sanyal, Amal and Mukherji, Anjan. Uncertainty, Liquidity and the Demand for Money. *Keio Econ. Stud.*, 1988, 25(1), pp. 1–19.

Sanyal, S. K. Trends in Landholdings and Poverty in Rural India. In *Srinivasan, T. N. and Bardhan, P. K., eds.*, 1988, pp. 121–53.

Saperstein, Alvin M. and Mayer-Kress, Gottried. A Nonlinear Dynamical Model of the Impact of SDI on the Arms Race. *J. Conflict Resolution*, December 1988, 32(4), pp. 636–70.

Sapienza, Harry J. and Gupta, Anil K. The Pursuit of Diversity by Venture Capital Firms: Antecedents and Implications. In *Kirchhoff, B. A., et al., eds.*, 1988, pp. 290–302.

Sapir, André. International Trade in Telecommunications Services. In *Baldwin, R. E.; Hamilton, C. B. and Sapir, A., eds.*, 1988, pp. 231–43.

_____ and Jacquemin, Alexis. European Integration or World Integration? *Weltwirtsch. Arch.*, 1988, 124(1), pp. 127–39.

_____ and Jacquemin, Alexis. International Trade and Integration of the European Community: An Econometric Analysis. *Europ. Econ. Rev.*, September 1988, 32(7), pp. 1439–49.

Saposnik, Rubin. The Distribution of Income, Incomplete Information and the Rank and Pareto Criteria. *Public Choice*, November 1988, 59(2), pp. 195–202.

Sappington, David E. M. and Adams, William James. Profiting from 'Countervailing' Power: An Effect of Government Control. *Int. J. Ind. Organ.*, 1988, 6(3), pp. 323–33.

_____ and Lewis, Tracy R. Regulating a Monopolist with Unknown Demand. *Amer. Econ. Rev.*, December 1988, 78(5), pp. 986–98.

_____ and Lewis, Tracy R. Regulating a Monopolist with Unknown Demand and Cost Functions. *Rand J. Econ.*, Autumn 1988, 19(3), pp. 438–57.

_____ and Riordan, Michael H. Commitment in Procurement Contracting. *Scand. J. Econ.*, 1988, 90(3), pp. 357–72.

_____ and Riordan, Michael H. Optimal Contracts with Public ex post Information. *J. Econ. Theory*, June 1988, 45(1), pp. 189–99.

_____ and Sibley, David S. Regulating without Cost Information: The Incremental Surplus Subsidy Scheme. *Int. Econ. Rev.*, May 1988, 29(2), pp. 297–306.

_____; Spiller, Pablo T. and Demski, Joel S. Incentive Schemes with Multiple Agents and Bankruptcy Constraints. *J. Econ. Theory*, February 1988, 44(1), pp. 156–67.

Sapsford, David. The Debate over Trends in the Terms of Trade. In *Greenaway, D., ed.*, 1988, pp. 117–31.

_____. Internationally Traded Primary Commodities: A Model of Price Determination. *Appl. Econ.*, April 1988, 20(4), pp. 439–52.

_____. A Reduced Form Real Price Equation for Primary Commodities. *Rivista Int. Sci. Econ. Com.*, March 1988, 35(3), pp. 295–305.

Saqib, Najamus and Khan, Aliya H. On an Empirical Definition of Money for Pakistan. *Pakistan Devel. Rev.*, Part 2, Winter 1988, 27(4), pp. 853–57.

van der Sar, Nico L.; van Praag, Bernard M. S. and Dubnoff, S. Evaluation Questions and Income Utility. In *Munier, B. R., ed.*, 1988, pp. 77–96.

_____; van Praag, Bernard M. S. and Dubnoff, Steve. On the Measurement and Explanation of Standards with Respect to Income, Age and Education. *J. Econ. Psych.*, December 1988, 9(4), pp. 481–98.

Sarafoglou, Nicias and Holmberg, Ingvar. Interregional Migration in Individual Countries: Sweden. In *Weidlich, W. and Haag, G., eds.*, 1988, pp. 223–60.

Saraiva Guerreiro, Ramiro. Brazilian–U.S. Relations. In *Chacel, J. M.; Falk, P. S. and Fleischer, D. V., eds.*, 1988, pp. 252–56.

Sarassoro, Gboroton F. and Leuthold, Raymond M. Offshore Commodity Hedging under Floating Exchange Rates: Comment. *Amer. J. Agr. Econ.*, August 1988, 70(3), pp. 724–26.

Sarathy, Ravi and Robles, Fernando. Segmenting the Market for Commuter Aircraft. In *Woodside, A. G., ed.*, 1988, pp. 223–47.

Sarcinelli, Mario. The Contribution of the ECU to Exchange-Rate Stability: A Comment. *Banca Naz. Lavoro Quart. Rev.*, September 1988, (166), pp. 327–30.

_____. Liberalization and Integration of Financial Markets. *Rev. Econ. Cond. Italy*, Sept.–Dec. 1988, (3), pp. 283–301.

Sargan, John Denis. The Distribution of Wealth. In *Sargan, J. D., Vol. 1*, 1988, *1957*, pp. 39–62.

_____. Econometric Estimators and the Edgeworth Approximation. In *Sargan, J. D., Vol. 2*, 1988, *1976*, pp. 98–132.

_____. The Estimation of Economic Relationships Using Instrumental Variables. In *Sargan, J. D., Vol. 1*, 1988, *1958*, pp. 63–86.

_____. The Estimation of Relationships with Autocorrelated Residuals by the Use of Instrumental Variables. In *Sargan, J. D., Vol. 1*, 1988, *1959*, pp. 87–104.

_____. The Existence of the Moments of Estimated Reduced Form Coefficients. In *Sargan, J. D., Vol. 2*, 1988, pp. 133–57.

_____. The Finite Sample Distribution of FIML Estimators. In *Sargan, J. D., Vol. 2*, 1988, pp. 57–75.

_____. Gram–Charlier Approximations Applied to *t* Ratios of *k*-Class Estimators. In *Sargan, J. D., Vol. 2*, 1988, *1975*, pp. 76–97.

_____. The Identification and Estimation of Sets of Simultaneous Stochastic Equations. In *Sargan, J. D., Vol. 1*, 1988, pp. 236–49.

_____. Identification and Lack of Identification. In *Sargan, J. D., Vol. 1*, 1988, *1983*, pp. 250–80.

_____. Identification in Models with Autoregressive Errors. In *Sargan, J. D., Vol. 1*, 1988, *1983*, pp. 281–304.

_____. The Maximum Likelihood Estimation of Economic Relationships with Autoregressive

Residuals. In *Sargan, J. D., Vol. 1*, 1988, *1961*, pp. 105–17.

_____. A Model of Wage–Price Inflation. In *Sargan, J. D., Vol. 1*, 1988, *1980*, pp. 170–90.

_____. A Note on Mr Blyth's Article. In *Sargan, J. D., Vol. 1*, 1988, *1956*, pp. 36–38.

_____. The Period of Production. In *Sargan, J. D., Vol. 1*, 1988, *1955*, pp. 19–35.

_____. Some Discrete Approximations to Continuous Time Stochastic Models. In *Sargan, J. D., Vol. 2*, 1988, *1974*, pp. 226–45.

_____. Some Experience of Numerical Computation of Edgeworth Approximations. In *Sargan, J. D., Vol. 2*, 1988, pp. 158–71.

_____. Some Tests of Dynamic Specification for a Single Equation. In *Sargan, J. D., Vol. 1*, 1988, *1980*, pp. 191–212.

_____. Testing for Misspecification after Estimating Using Instrumental Variables. In *Sargan, J. D., Vol. 1*, 1988, pp. 213–35.

_____. Three-Stage Least-Squares and Full Maximum Likelihood Estimates. In *Sargan, J. D., Vol. 1*, 1988, *1964*, pp. 118–23.

_____. Wages and Prices in the United Kingdom: A Study in Econometric Methodology. In *Sargan, J. D., Vol. 1*, 1988, pp. 124–58.

_____ and Bhargava, Alok. Estimating Dynamic Random Effects Models from Panel Data Covering Short Time Periods. In *Sargan, J. D., Vol. 2*, 1988, *1983*, pp. 270–96.

_____ and Bhargava, Alok. Maximum Likelihood Estimation of Regression Models with First Order Moving Average Errors When the Root Lies on the Unit Circles. In *Sargan, J. D., Vol. 2*, 1988, *1983*, pp. 182–203.

_____ and Drettakis, E. G. Missing Data in an Autoregressive Model. In *Sargan, J. D., Vol. 2*, 1988, *1974*, pp. 204–25.

_____ and Espasa, Antoni. The Spectral Estimation of Simultaneous Equation Systems with Lagged Endogenous Variables. In *Sargan, J. D., Vol. 2*, 1988, *1977*, pp. 246–69.

_____ and Mikhail, W. M. A General Approximation to the Distribution of Instrumental Variables Estimates. In *Sargan, J. D., Vol. 2*, 1988, *1971*, pp. 18–56.

_____ and Tse, Y. K. Edgeworth Approximations for 2SLS Estimates of a Dynamic Models. In *Sargan, J. D., Vol. 2*, 1988, pp. 172–81.

Sargent, Francis W. The Economic Development of Massachusetts. In *Lampe, D., ed.*, 1988, *1976*, pp. 25–34.

_____. The State's Fiscal Crisis. In *Lampe, D., ed.*, 1988, *1976*, pp. 44–49.

Sargent, John H. and Dodge, David A. World Tax Reform: A Progress Report: Canada. In *Pechman, J. A., ed.*, 1988, pp. 43–69.

Sargent, Thomas J. The Role of Monetary Policy under U.S. Institutions. In *Anderson, A. and Bark, D. L., eds.*, 1988, pp. 311–22.

_____ and Hansen, Gary D. Straight Time and Overtime in Equilibrium. *J. Monet. Econ.*, March–May 1988, *21*(2–3), pp. 281–308.

_____ and Manuelli, Rodolfo. Models of Business Cycles: A Review Essay. *J. Monet. Econ.*, November 1988, *22*(3), pp. 523–42.

_____ and Marcet, Albert. The Fate of Systems with "Adaptive" Expectations. *Amer. Econ. Rev.*, May 1988, *78*(2), pp. 168–72.

_____ and Smith, Bruce D. The Irrelevance of Government Foreign Exchange Operations. In *Helpman, E.; Razin, A. and Sadka, E., eds.*, 1988, pp. 328–45.

Sarin, Rakesh K. and Kahn, Barbara E. Modeling Ambiguity in Decisions under Uncertainty. *J. Cons. Res.*, September 1988, *15*(2), pp. 265–72.

Sarkar, Abhirup. Supply Constraints, Government Subsidies and Industrial Employment. *J. Devel. Econ.*, February 1988, *28*(1), pp. 111–19.

Sarkar, Asani; Sickles, Robin C. and Lovell, C. A. Knox. Testing for Aggregation Bias in Efficiency Measurement. In *Eichhorn, W., ed.*, 1988, pp. 187–206.

Sarma, J. S. Determination of Administered Prices of Foodgrains in India. In *Mellor, J. W. and Ahmed, R., eds.*, 1988, pp. 155–68.

_____. Meat Supply and Demand in Developing Countries: Past Trends and Projections to 2000. In *Schwarz, F. H., ed.*, 1988, pp. 11–69.

Sarmad, Khwaja. The Functional Form of the Aggregate Import Demand Equation: Evidence from Developing Countries. *Pakistan Devel. Rev.*, Autumn 1988, *27*(3), pp. 309–15.

_____. A SAM-Based General Equilibrium Model of the Pakistan Economy 1983–84: Comments. *Pakistan Devel. Rev.*, Part 2, Winter 1988, *27*(4), pp. 749–50.

_____; Husain, Fazal and Zahid, G. M. Investment and Inequality in Pakistan's Education Sector. *Pakistan Devel. Rev.*, Part 2, Winter 1988, *27*(4), pp. 677–84.

_____ and Mahmood, Riaz. Prospects for Expanding Trade between SAARC and ASEAN Countries. *Pakistan Devel. Rev.*, Summer 1988, *27*(2), pp. 129–36.

Sarmiento, Eduardo. Development of Industrial versus Primary Exports. In *Urrutia, M. and Yukawa, S., eds. (II)*, 1988, pp. 90–111.

_____. The Failures of the Capital Market: A Latin American View. In *Urrutia, M., ed.*, 1988, pp. 82–109.

Sarney, José. Brazil: A President's Story. In *Chacel, J. M.; Falk, P. S. and Fleischer, D. V., eds.*, 1988, pp. 97–106.

Sarno, Domenico. "Constant Market Shares Analysis": Un modello alternativo. (With English summary.) *Stud. Econ.*, 1988, *43*(34), pp. 25–52.

Sarris, Alexander H. EC–US Agricultural Trade Confrontation. In *Baldwin, R. E.; Hamilton, C. B. and Sapir, A., eds.*, 1988, pp. 101–24.

_____ and Demoussis, Michael. Greek Experience under the CAP: Lessons and Outlook. *Europ. Rev. Agr. Econ.*, 1988, *15*(1), pp. 89–107.

_____ and Freebairn, John W. Endogenous Price Policies and International Wheat Prices: Reply. *Amer. J. Agr. Econ.*, August 1988, *70*(3), pp. 747–49.

Sarry, M.-C.; Norel, P. and Quenan, C. Stratégies bancaires et risque-pays. (International Banking Strategies and Country-Risk. With English summary.) *Écon. Appl.*, 1988, *41*(4), pp. 857–72.

Sartore, Domenico and Calliari, Sergio. La validità empirica della teoria neoclassica della domanda: Una verifica con i dati italiani 1960–1983. (An Empirical Assessment of the Neoclassical Theory of Demand: The Italian Case 1960–1983. With English summary.) *Rivista Int. Sci. Econ. Com.*, April–May 1988, *35*(4–5), pp. 313–44.

Sartoris, William L. and Hill, Ned C. The Relationship between Credit Policies and Firm Financial Characteristics. In *Kim, Y. H., ed.*, 1988, pp. 99–114.

_____ **and Moore, William T.** On the Existence of a Dividend Clientele in the Market for Electric Utility Stocks. *Quart. Rev. Econ. Bus.*, Spring 1988, *28*(1), pp. 88–100.

Sass, Steven A. An Uneasy Relationship: The Business Community and Academic Economists at the University of Pennsylvania. In *Barber, W. J., ed.*, 1988, pp. 225–40.

Sass, Tim R. A Note on Optimal Price Cutting Behavior under Demand Uncertainty. *Rev. Econ. Statist.*, May 1988, *70*(2), pp. 336–39.

_____. T³ Scientific Word Processing System, Version 2.2: Review. *Econ. Inquiry*, January 1988, *26*(1), pp. 181–82.

Sassano, A. Minimizing Costs in Crude Oil Transportation. In *Bianco, L. and La Bella, A., eds.*, 1988, pp. 319–33.

Sassanpour, Cyrus and Otani, Ichiro. Financial, Exchange Rate, and Wage Policies in Singapore, 1979–86. *Int. Monet. Fund Staff Pap.*, September 1988, *35*(3), pp. 474–95.

Sasseville, Jacques. Implementation of the General Anti-avoidance Rule. In *Canadian Tax Foundation*, 1988, pp. 4.1–16.

Sasson, Albert. Promise in Agriculture, Food and Energy. In *Research and Info. System for the Non-aligned and Other Developing Countries*, 1988, pp. 55–88.

Sassoon, D. M.; Goldberg, Moshe and Hirsch, Seev. An Analysis of the American–Israeli Free Trade Area Agreement. *World Econ.*, June 1988, *11*(2), pp. 281–300.

Sassower, Raphael. Ideology Masked as Science: Shielding Economics from Criticism. *J. Econ. Issues*, March 1988, *22*(1), pp. 167–79.

Sathar, Zeba A. and Akhtar, Afifa. Evidence of Fertility Decline in Karachi. *Pakistan Devel. Rev.*, Part 2, Winter 1988, *27*(4), pp. 659–68.

_____, **et al.** Women's Status and Fertility Change in Pakistan. *Population Devel. Rev.*, September 1988, *14*(3), pp. 415–32.

Sato, Hideto, et al. Conceptual Schema for a Wide-Scope Statistical Database and Its Applications. In *Uno, K. and Shishido, S., eds.*, 1988, pp. 254–68.

Sato, Kazuo. The Role of the IS Balance and Its Macroeconomic Implications: The Case of Japan. *J. Japanese Int. Economies*, September 1988, *2*(3), pp. 239–58.

_____ **and Leff, Nathaniel H.** Estimating Invest-

ment and Savings Functions for Developing Countries, with an Application to Latin America. *Int. Econ. J.*, Autumn 1988, *2*(3), pp. 1–17.

Sato, Ryuzo. The Technology Game and Dynamic Comparative Advantage: An Application to U.S.–Japan Competition. In *Spence, A. M. and Hazard, H. A., eds.*, 1988, pp. 373–98.

Sattar, Zaidi and Jones, Jonathan D. Money, Inflation, Output, and Causality: The Bangladesh Case, 1974–1985. *Bangladesh Devel. Stud.*, March 1988, *16*(1), pp. 73–83.

Sattler, Edward L.; Scott, Robert C. and Highfill, Jannett K. Advantage to a Risk Neutral Firm of Flexible Resources under Demand Uncertainty. *Southern Econ. J.*, April 1988, *54*(4), pp. 934–49.

Sau, Ranjit. Resolving the Triangle of International Debt: A Proposal. *Econ. Int.*, Aug.–Nov. 1988, *41*(3–4), pp. 225–44.

Sauber, Beatriz; Szyld, Daniel B. and Moledo, Leonardo. Positive Solutions for the Leontief Dynamic Input–Output Model. In *Ciaschini, M., ed.*, 1988, pp. 91–97.

Sauer, Paul L.; Fraser, Cynthia and Hite, Robert E. Increasing Contributions in Solicitation Campaigns: The Use of Large and Small Anchorpoints. *J. Cons. Res.*, September 1988, *15*(2), pp. 284–87.

Sauer, Raymond D. Estimates of the Returns to Quality and Coauthorship in Economic Academia. *J. Polit. Econ.*, August 1988, *96*(4), pp. 855–66.

_____, **et al.** Hold Your Bets: Another Look at the Efficiency of the Gambling Market for National Football League Games: Comment. *J. Polit. Econ.*, February 1988, *96*(1), pp. 206–13.

Sauer, William J.; Currid, Michael and Schwab, Arthur J. The Emergence of the High Technology Industry in Southwestern Pennsylvania: A Case Study of Pittsburgh. In *Kirchhoff, B. A., et al., eds.*, 1988, pp. 415–29.

Saul, Mahir. The Efficiency of Private Channels in the Distribution of Cereals in Burkina Faso. In *Bennett, J. W. and Bowen, J. R., eds.*, 1988, pp. 87–104.

Saulnier, Raymond J. The President's Economic Report: A Critique. *J. Portfol. Manage.*, Summer 1988, *14*(4), pp. 66–67.

Saunders, Anthony. Bank Holding Companies: Structure, Performance, and Reform. In *Haraf, W. S. and Kushmeider, R. M., eds.*, 1988, pp. 156–202.

_____ **and Sienkiewicz, Stanley.** The Hedging Performance of ECU Futures Contracts. *J. Futures Markets*, June 1988, *8*(3), pp. 335–52.

_____; **Swary, Itzhak and Aharony, Joseph.** The Effects of DIDMCA on Bank Stockholders' Returns and Risk. *J. Banking Finance*, September 1988, *12*(3), pp. 317–31.

_____ **and Urich, Thomas.** The Effects of Shifts in Monetary Policy and Reserve Accounting Regimes on Bank Reserve Management Behavior in the Federal Funds Market. *J. Banking Finance*, December 1988, *12*(4), pp. 523–35.

_____ and Urich, Thomas. Weekly Variation in the Federal Funds Market: The Weekend Game and Other Effects. In *Dimson, E., ed.*, 1988, pp. 64–73.

Saunders, Caroline M. and Willis, K. G. The Impact of a Development Agency on Employment: Resurrection Discounted? *Appl. Econ.*, January 1988, *20*(1), pp. 81–96.

_____; Willis, K. G. and Benson, J. F. The Impact of Agricultural Policy on the Costs of Nature Conservation. *Land Econ.*, May 1988, *64*(2), pp. 147–57.

Saunders, Edward M., Jr.; Kolari, James and Mahajan, Arvind. The Effect of Changes in Reserve Requirements on Bank Stock Prices. *J. Banking Finance*, June 1988, *12*(2), pp. 183–98.

_____ and Mahajan, Arvind. An Empirical Examination of Composite Stock Index Futures Pricing. *J. Futures Markets*, April 1988, *8*(2), pp. 211–28.

Saunders, Michael and Lee, Catherine. Personal Equity Plans: Success or Failure? *Fisc. Stud.*, November 1988, *9*(4), pp. 36–50.

_____ and Webb, Steven B. Fiscal Privilege and Financial Assets: Some Distributional Effects. *Fisc. Stud.*, November 1988, *9*(4), pp. 51–69.

Saunders, Peter G. Explaining International Differences in Public Expenditure: An Empirical Study. *Public Finance*, 1988, *43*(2), pp. 271–94.

_____. Private Sector Shrinkage and the Growth of Industrialized Economies: Comment. *Public Choice*, September 1988, *58*(3), pp. 277–84.

_____ and Hobbes, Garry. Income Inequality in Australia in an International Comparative Perspective. *Australian Econ. Rev.*, Spring 1988, (83), pp. 25–34.

Saunders, Peter J. An Empirical Investigation of the Effects of Monetary Changes on the U.K. Economy. *Scot. J. Polit. Econ.*, November 1988, *35*(4), pp. 372–86.

_____. Causality of U.S. Agricultural Prices and the Money Supply: Further Empirical Evidence. *Amer. J. Agr. Econ.*, August 1988, *70*(3), pp. 588–96.

Saunders, Phillip. A Research and Evaluation Agenda for DEEP and Precollege Economic Education: A Comment. *J. Econ. Educ.*, Winter 1988, *19*(1), pp. 17–19.

Sav, G. Thomas. Economic Models. In *West, R. E. and Kreith, F., eds.*, 1988, pp. 84–124.

Savarino, James E. and Frost, Peter A. For Better Performance: Constrain Portfolio Weights. *J. Portfol. Manage.*, Fall 1988, *15*(1), pp. 29–34.

Savin, N. E. and Nankervis, J. C. The Exact Moments of the Least-Squares Estimator for the Autoregressive Model. *J. Econometrics*, March 1988, *37*(3), pp. 381–88.

_____ and Nankervis, J. C. The Student's *t* Approximation in a Stationary First Order Autoregressive Model. *Econometrica*, January 1988, *56*(1), pp. 119–45.

Saving, Thomas R. and Pesek, Boris P. Monetary Policy, Taxes, and the Rate of Interest. In *Pesek, B. P., 1988, 1963*, pp. 208–29.

Savit, Robert. When Random Is Not Random: An Introduction to Chaos in Market Prices. *J. Futures Markets*, June 1988, *8*(3), pp. 271–90.

Savitt, Ronald. A Personal View of Historical Explanation in Marketing and Economic Development. In *[Hollander, S. C.]*, 1988, pp. 113–32.

_____. The State of the Art in Marketing and Economic Development. In *Kumcu, E. and Firat, A. F., eds.*, 1988, pp. 11–37.

Savoie, Donald J. and Higgins, Benjamin. The Economics and Politics of Regional Development: Introduction. In *[Perroux, F.]*, 1988, pp. 1–27.

_____ and Higgins, Benjamin. Regional Economic Development: Conclusions. In *[Perroux, F.]*, 1988, pp. 375–84.

Săvulescu, B. and Vasiliu, D. P. Aspects of Queueing Spaces Dimensioning. *Econ. Computat. Cybern. Stud. Res.*, 1988, *23*(4), pp. 45–49.

Sawers, Larry. Poverty Weighted Measures of Social Welfare Change. *World Devel.*, August 1988, *16*(8), pp. 899–901.

Sawhill, Isabel V. Poverty in the U.S.: Why Is It So Persistent? *J. Econ. Lit.*, September 1988, *26*(3), pp. 1073–119.

_____. What about America's Underclass? *Challenge*, May–June 1988, *31*(3), pp. 27–36.

_____ and Ricketts, Erol R. Defining and Measuring the Underclass. *J. Policy Anal. Manage.*, Winter 1988, *7*(2), pp. 316–25.

Sawhney, Bansi L. and Tran, Dang T. Government Deficits, Capital Flows, and Interest Rates. *Appl. Econ.*, June 1988, *20*(6), pp. 753–65.

Sawhney, Shiv and Vasillopulos, Christopher. The Triple Tension of Entrepreneurial Management. In *Pennsylvania Economic Association*, 1988, pp. 614–25.

Sawyer, Alan G. and Howard, Daniel J. Recall, Recognition and the Dimensionality of Memory for Print Advertisements: An Interpretative Reappraisal. *Marketing Sci.*, Winter 1988, *7*(1), pp. 94–98.

Sawyer, Carl and Färe, Rolf. Expenditure Constraints and Profit Maximization in U.S. Agriculture: Comment. *Amer. J. Agr. Econ.*, November 1988, *70*(4), pp. 953–54.

Sawyer, Malcolm C. Financial Markets, Investment and Employment: Comment. In *Kregel, J. A.; Matzner, E. and Roncaglia, A., eds.*, 1988, pp. 99–102.

_____. Post-Keynesian Economics: Introduction. In *Sawyer, M. C., ed.*, 1988, pp. 1–7.

_____. Theories of Monopoly Capitalism. *J. Econ. Surveys*, 1988, *2*(1), pp. 47–76.

Sawyer, W. Charles and Sprinkle, Richard L. EC Enlargement and U.S. Exports: An Analysis of the Trade Effects. *J. World Trade*, February 1988, *22*(1), pp. 89–96.

Sax, Sidney. Health Insurance Forum. In *Butler,*

J. R. G. and Doessel, D. P., eds., 1988, pp. 252–54.

Saxena, R. B. and Bakshi, Heena R. IMF Conditionality—A Third World Perspective. *J. World Trade*, October 1988, 22(5), pp. 67–79.

Saxena, Rakesh K. and Rao, T. V. S. Ramamohan. Economic Efficiency of the Organizational Decisions of the Firm. *Rivista Int. Sci. Econ. Com.*, July 1988, 35(7), pp. 675–88.

_____ **and Rao, T. V. S. Ramamohan.** Transaction Costs, Vertical Integration, and X-Efficiency. *Rivista Int. Sci. Econ. Com.*, December 1988, 35(12), pp. 1173–90.

Saxena, Swati and Stefanou, Spiro E. Education, Experience, and Allocative Efficiency: A Dual Approach. *Amer. J. Agr. Econ.*, May 1988, 70(2), pp. 338–45.

Saxonhouse, Arlene W. and Saxonhouse, Gary R. An Inquiry into the Philosophic Roots of Concepts of Economic Order. *J. Inst. Theoretical Econ.*, April 1988, 144(2), pp. 344–56.

Saxonhouse, Gary R. Comparative Advantage, Structural Adaptation, and Japanese Performance. In *Inoguchi, T. and Okimoto, D. I.*, eds., 1988, pp. 225–48.

_____. Technological Progress and R&D Systems in Japan and the United States. In *Uyehara, C. H.*, ed., 1988, pp. 29–54.

_____ **and Saxonhouse, Arlene W.** An Inquiry into the Philosophic Roots of Concepts of Economic Order. *J. Inst. Theoretical Econ.*, April 1988, 144(2), pp. 344–56.

Sayad, João. Brazil's Economic Stabilization Plan: An Analysis. In *Chacel, J. M.; Falk, P. S. and Fleischer, D. V.*, eds., 1988, pp. 9–16.

Sayan, Serdar. "Iktisat Kurami ve Iktisat Öğretimi": Kara'ya Cevap. (Economics Theory and Economics Education: A Reply. With English summary.) *METU*, 1988, 15(1–2), pp. 191–97.

Sayers, Chera L. and Brock, William A. Is the Business Cycle Characterized by Deterministic Chaos? *J. Monet. Econ.*, July 1988, 22(1), pp. 71–90.

Sayigh, Yusif A. Dispossession and Pauperisation: The Palestinian Economy under Occupation. In *Abed, G. T.*, ed., 1988, pp. 259–85.

Saylor, Thomas Reese. Resolving Agricultural Trade Disputes. In *Allen, K. and Macmillan, K.*, eds., 1988, pp. 155–60.

Sazanami, Yoko. Japan's Trade and Investment in Finance, Information, Communications, and Business Services. In *Lee, C. H. and Naya, S.*, eds., 1988, pp. 153–79.

_____. Recent Trends in Japanese Trade and Capital Flow—Japan vs Western Europe and Asia. *Keio Econ. Stud.*, 1988, 25(1), pp. 21–38.

Sbordone, Argia M. and Cochrane, John H. Multivariate Estimates of the Permanent Components of GNP and Stock Prices. *J. Econ. Dynam. Control*, June–Sept. 1988, 12(2–3), pp. 255–96.

Sbriglia, Patrizia. Recent Developments in the Theory of Innovation and Technical Change. *Stud. Econ.*, 1988, 43(34), pp. 53–90.

Scafuri, Allen J. On Consistency of Conjectures in the Private Provision of Public Goods. *J. Public Econ.*, December 1988, 37(3), pp. 395–98.

Scalera, Domenico. Aspettative inflazionistiche, tassi di interesse, effetto Fisher: l'esperienza italiana tra il 1970 ed il 1987. (With English summary.) *Stud. Econ.*, 1988, 43(36), pp. 69–112.

Scallan, Antony and Gilchrist, Robert. FUNIGIRLS: A Prototype Functional Programming Language for the Analysis of Generalized Linear Models. In *Edwards, D. and Raun, N. E.*, eds., 1988, pp. 213–18.

Scanlan, James P. Ideology and Reform. In *Juviler, P. and Kimura, H.*, eds., 1988, pp. 49–62.

Scarborough, Grace Iusi. Polarity, Power, and Risk in International Disputes. *J. Conflict Resolution*, September 1988, 32(3), pp. 511–33.

Scarth, William M. Built-in Stabilizers. *Can. J. Econ.*, November 1988, 21(4), pp. 747–58.

_____. Deficits and Debt in an Open Economy. *J. Int. Money Finance*, September 1988, 7(3), pp. 351–58.

_____ **and Moutos, Thomas.** Stabilization Policy within a Currency Area. *Scot. J. Polit. Econ.*, November 1988, 35(4), pp. 387–97.

Scazzieri, Roberto. The Legacy of Ricardo. *Atlantic Econ. J.*, December 1988, 16(4), pp. 79–87.

Scerri, M. Research and Development in South African Manufacturing Industries. *S. Afr. J. Econ.*, June–Sept. 1988, 56(2–3), pp. 111–23.

Schaan, Jean-Louis and Beamish, Paul W. Joint Venture General Managers in LDCs. In *Contractor, F. J. and Lorange, P.*, 1988, pp. 279–99.

Schabas, M. Some Reactions to Jevons' Mathematical Program: The Case of Cairnes and Mill. In *Wood, J. C.*, ed., *Vol. 3*, 1988, 1985, pp. 298–315.

_____. The 'Worldly Philosophy' of William Stanley Jevons. In *Wood, J. C.*, ed., *Vol. 1*, 1988, 1984, pp. 401–18.

Schachter, Barry. Open Interest in Stock Options around Quarterly Earnings Announcements. *J. Acc. Res.*, Autumn 1988, 26(2), pp. 353–72.

Schachter, Gustav and Dalal, Meenakshi Nath. Transmission of International Inflation to India: A Structural Analysis. *J. Devel. Areas*, October 1988, 23(1), pp. 85–103.

_____ **and Engelbourg, Saul.** The Steadfastness of Economic Dualism in Italy. *J. Devel. Areas*, July 1988, 22(4), pp. 515–25.

Schader, Martin and Büring, O. KREDIT: KEE-Based Support for Credit Decisions in a Mail-Order Firm. In *Gaul, W. and Schader, M.*, eds., 1988, pp. 83–92.

_____ **and Schmid, Friedrich.** Zur Messung der relativen Konzentration aus gruppierten Daten. Ein Vergleich parametrischer und nichtparametrischer Ansätze. (Measurement of Relative Concentration from Grouped Data. A Comparison of Parametric and Nonparametric Approaches. With English summary.) *Jahr.*

nique in Fixed Capital Systems. In *Steedman, I., ed., Vol. 2*, 1988, *1976*, pp. 74–88.

_____. Relative Prices as a Function of the Rate of Profit: A Mathematical Note. In *Steedman, I., ed., Vol. 2*, 1988, *1976*, pp. 319–46.

_____. Sraffa and Applied Economics: Joint Production. In *Steedman, I., ed., Vol. 2*, 1988, *1985*, pp. 89–112.

Scheiber, Harry N. Original Intent, History, and Doctrine: The Constitution and Economic Liberty. *Amer. Econ. Rev.*, May 1988, *78*(2), pp. 140–44.

Scheide, Joachim. Comments [The Case for Rules in the Conduct of Monetary Policy: A Concrete Example] [The Rules-versus-Discretion Debate in the Light of Recent Experience]. In *Giersch, H., ed.*, 1988, pp. 85–90.

Scheider, Benjamin and Bowen, David E. Services Marketing and Management: Implications for Organizational Behavior. In *Staw, B. M. and Cummings, L. L., eds.*, 1988, pp. 43–80.

Scheider, Volker and Mayntz, Renate. The Dynamics of System Development in a Comparative Perspective: Interactive Videotex in Germany, France, and Britain. In *Mayntz, R. and Hughes, T. P., eds.*, 1988, pp. 263–98.

Scheinberg, Sari and Alänge, Sverker. Swedish Entrepreneurship in a Cross-Cultural Perspective. In *Kirchhoff, B. A., et al., eds.*, 1988, pp. 1–15.

_____ and MacMillan, Ian C. An 11 Country Study of Motivations to Start a Business. In *Kirchhoff, B. A., et al., eds.*, 1988, pp. 669–87.

Scheiner, Irwin and Duus, Peter. The Cambridge History of Japan: Volume 6: The Twentieth Century: Socialism, Liberalism, and Marxism, 1901–1931. In *Duus, P., ed.*, 1988, pp. 654–710.

Scheinkman, José A. Dynamic General Equilibrium Models—Two Examples. In *Ambrosetti, A.; Gori, F. and Lucchetti, R., eds.*, 1988, pp. 44–71.

_____ and Boldrin, Michele. Learning-by-Doing, International Trade and Growth: A Note. In *Anderson, P. W.; Arrow, K. J. and Pines, D., eds.*, 1988, pp. 285–300.

_____ and Kreps, David M. Quantity Precommitment and Betrand Competition Yield Cournot Outcomes. In *Daughety, A. F., ed.*, 1988, *1983*, pp. 201–17.

Schejtman, Alexander. Food Security: Trends and Impact of the Crisis. *CEPAL Rev.*, December 1988, (36), pp. 141–60.

_____. The Peasant Economy: Internal Logic, Articulation, and Persistence. In *Wilber, C. K., ed.*, 1988, pp. 364–92.

Schektman, Y. and Ibrahim, A. Evolving Principal Clusters: Theory and Application to Management Monitoring. In *Gaul, W. and Schader, M., eds.*, 1988, pp. 291–98.

Schelbert-Syfrig, Heidi. Methoden und Probleme der Konjunkturprognose heute. (Methods and Problems to Forecast Business Cycles Today.

With English summary.) *Ifo-Studien*, 1988, *34*(2–3), pp. 147–60.

_____ and Zimmermann, Andreas J. Konkurrenz und Umweltschutz. Wald- und Holzwirtschaft zwischen Ökonomie und Ökologie. (Competition and Environment Protection. With English summary.) *Schweiz. Z. Volkswirtsch. Statist.*, September 1988, *124*(3), pp. 289–302.

Schellhaass, Horst-Manfred. The Disinterest in Efficient Subsidization. *Kyklos*, 1988, *41*(1), pp. 99–111.

_____. Übergangsbedingungen für eine Liberalisierung des Wohnungsmarktes. (The Transition a Deregulated Housing Market. With English summary.) *Z. Wirtschaft. Sozialwissen.*, 1988, *108*(3), pp. 405–21.

Schelling, Thomas C. Economics and Criminal Enterprise. In *Alper, N. O. and Hellman, D. A., eds.*, 1988, pp. 238–57.

_____. The Mind as a Consuming Organ. In *Bell, D. E.; Raiffa, H. and Tversky, A., eds.*, 1988, pp. 343–57.

Schembri, Lawrence L. Macro-economic Stability and Policy Rules in a Two-Sector Model of an Open Economy. *Can. J. Econ.*, February 1988, *21*(1), pp. 87–96.

_____. Per-Capita Income as a Determinant of Trade: Comment. In *Feenstra, R. C., ed.*, 1988, pp. 110–13.

Schendel, Dan and Cool, Karel. Development of the Strategic Management Field: Some Accomplishments and Challenges. In *Grant, J. H., ed.*, 1988, pp. 17–31.

Schenk, Karl-Ernst. Comment on the Theory of Hierarchies and Why It is "Relatively Underdeveloped" for Comparative Purposes. *J. Inst. Theoretical Econ.*, December 1988, *144*(5), pp. 849–56.

Schenker-Wicki, Andrea and Bui, Tung. Co-oP: Un système d'aide à la décision de groupe pour les décisions stratégiques de l'entreprise. (Co-oP: A Group Decision Support System for Multiple Criteria Group Decision Making. With English summary.) *Schweiz. Z. Volkswirtsch. Statist.*, September 1988, *124*(3), pp. 445–54.

Scherer, Frederic M. Corporate Ownership and Control. In *Meyer, J. R. and Gustafson, J. M., eds.*, 1988, pp. 43–66.

_____. Corporate Takeovers: The Efficiency Arguments. *J. Econ. Perspectives*, Winter 1988, *2*(1), pp. 69–82.

_____. Enterprise Ownership and Managerial Behavior. In *Hanusch, H., ed.*, 1988, pp. 137–45.

_____. Mergers and Antitrust. In *Libecap, G., ed. (I)*, 1988, pp. 91–111.

_____. Private Antitrust Litigation: An Introduction and Framework: Comment. In *White, L. J., ed.*, 1988, pp. 95–98.

_____. Time and the New Industrial State: Discussion. *Amer. Econ. Rev.*, May 1988, *78*(2), pp. 380–82.

_____ and Ravenscraft, David J. The Long-Run Performance of Mergers and Takeovers. In *Weidenbaum, M. L. and Chilton, K. W., eds.*, 1988, pp. 34–45.

_____ and **Ravenscraft, David J.** Mergers and Managerial Performance. In *Coffee, J. C., Jr.; Lowenstein, L. and Rose-Ackerman, S., eds.*, 1988, pp. 194–210.

Scherhorn, Gerhard. Self-Fulfillment, Consumer Policy and Consumer Research. In *Maynes, E. S. and ACCI Research Committee, eds.*, 1988, pp. 589–94.

Scherr, Frederick C. The Bankruptcy Cost Puzzle. *Quart. J. Bus. Econ.*, Summer 1988, 27(3), pp. 147–79.

Scherr, Sara J. Incorporating Macroeconomic Variables in Anthropological Research: Examples from a Developing Petroleum Region. In *Bennett, J. W. and Bowen, J. R., eds.*, 1988, pp. 125–42.

Scherrer, Christoph. Mini-Mills: A New Growth Path for the U.S. Steel Industry? *J. Econ. Issues*, December 1988, 22(4), pp. 1179–1200.

Schertz, Lyle P. Improvements in the Rural South: They Won't Come Easy. In *Beaulieu, L. J., ed.*, 1988, pp. 365–74.

Scheuermann, Scott L. Interest on Underpaid and Overpaid Amounts. In *Canadian Tax Foundation*, 1988, pp. 10.1–40.

Scheuren, Frederick J. and Kilss, Beth. The 1973 CPS–IRS–SSA Exact Match Study. *Soc. Sec. Bull.*, July 1988, 51(7), pp. 23–31.

Scheuren, Fritz. Missing-Data Adjustments in Large Surveys: Comment. *J. Bus. Econ. Statist.*, July 1988, 6(3), pp. 298–99.

Schiantarelli, Fabio and Booth, Alison. Reductions in Hours and Employment: What Do Union Models Tell Us? In *Hart, R. A., ed.*, 1988, pp. 142–57.

_____ and **Rossi, Nicola.** Error-Correction, "Surprise" Models and the Differential Approach to the Consumption Function. *Metroecon.*, February 1988, 39(1), pp. 83–91.

Schick, Allen. An Inquiry into the Possibility of a Budgetary Theory. In *Rubin, I. S., ed.*, 1988, pp. 59–69.

Schick, Frederic. Self-knowledge, Uncertainty, and Choice. In *Gärdenfors, P. and Sahlin, N.-E., eds.*, 1988, pp. 270–86.

Schieber, Sylvester J. First Year Impact of SSI on Economic Status of 1973 Adult Assistance Populations. *Soc. Sec. Bull.*, September 1988, 51(9), pp. 19–47.

Schiefer, Gerhard W. Communication Systems for Marketing Support and Production Control in Farm Management. In *Schiefer, G., ed.*, 1988, pp. 195–204.

_____. Videotex in European Agriculture: A Principal View on Development Directions. In *Schiefer, G., ed.*, 1988, pp. 13–25.

_____. Videotex in Use: Experiences from a National Videotex Trial with Farms. In *Schiefer, G., ed.*, 1988, pp. 161–64.

Schiehlen, W. Modeling, Analysis and Estimation of Vehicle Systems. In *Schiehlen, W. and Wedig, W., eds.*, 1988, pp. 243–67.

Schieppati, Cesare. Geographical and Sectoral Pattern of Italian Direct Investment Abroad. In *Onida, F. and Viesti, G., eds.*, 1988, pp. 49–74.

_____ and **Viesti, Gianfranco.** Profiles of Major Italian Multinationals. In *Onida, F. and Viesti, G., eds.*, 1988, pp. 158–79.

Schiff, Maurice; Valdés, Alberto and Krueger, Anne O. Agricultural Incentives in Developing Countries: Measuring the Effect of Sectoral and Economywide Policies. *World Bank Econ. Rev.*, September 1988, 2(3), pp. 255–71.

Schilit, Warren Keith and Paine, Frank T. An Empirical Examination of the Strategic Decision Making Process. In *Grant, J. H., ed.*, 1988, pp. 293–309.

Schiller, Bradley. On the Market for Principles of Economics Textbooks: Innovation and Product Differentiation—A Response. *J. Econ. Educ.*, Spring 1988, 19(2), pp. 183–84.

Schiller, Christian and Diamond, Jack. Government Arrears in Fiscal Adjustment Programs. In *Blejer, M. I. and Chu, K.-Y., eds.*, 1988, pp. 32–47.

Schimberni, Mario. Investing to and from the United States. In *Feldstein, M., ed. (II)*, 1988, pp. 545–50.

Schimek, M. G. A Roughness Penalty Regression Approach for Statistical Graphics. In *Edwards, D. and Raun, N. E., eds.*, 1988, pp. 37–43.

Schinasi, Garry J. Taxation of Capital Gains on Foreign Exchange Transactions and the Non-neutrality of Changes in Anticipated Inflation. *Econ. Letters*, 1988, 26(3), pp. 277–80.

_____ and **Marquez, Jaime.** Measures of Money and the Monetary Model of the Canadian–U.S. Dollar Exchange Rate. *Econ. Letters*, 1988, 26(2), pp. 183–88.

Schinke, Eberhard. The Reform of Agricultural Prices in the German Democratic Republic. In *Brada, J. C. and Wadekin, K.-E., eds.*, 1988, pp. 199–208.

Schintke, Joachim and Stäglin, Reiner. Important Input Coefficients in Market Transaction Tables and Production Flow Tables. In *Ciaschini, M., ed.*, 1988, pp. 43–60.

Schipper, Katherine and Smith, Abbie. Restructuring in the Food Industry. In *Libecap, G., ed. (I)*, 1988, pp. 131–68.

Schippers, Jacques J.; Siegers, Joop J. and Groot, Loek F. M. The Effect of Interruptions and Part-time Work on Women's Wage Rate: A Test of the Variable-Intensity Model. *De Economist*, 1988, 136(2), pp. 220–38.

Schirm, David C.; Ferri, Michael G. and Moore, Scott B. Investor Expectations about Callable Warrants. *J. Portfol. Manage.*, Spring 1988, 14(3), pp. 84–86.

Schittko, Ulrich K. and Eckwert, Bernhard. Disequilibrium Dynamics. *Scand. J. Econ.*, 1988, 90(2), pp. 189–209.

_____ and **Eckwert, Bernhard.** Intertemporal Aspects in an Aggregated Two-Country Monetary Macro Model. *Empirica*, 1988, 15(1), pp. 77–94.

Schittkowski, Klaus. EMP: An Expert System for Mathematical Programming. In *Kurzhanski, A.; Neumann, K. and Pallaschke, D., eds.*, 1988, pp. 125–57.

Schlachter, Paul and Rockness, Joanne W. Directions for Social Accounting Research: A Survey of Potential Data Sources. In *Neimark, M., ed.*, 1988, pp. 83–94.

Schlagenhauf, Don E. and Norrbin, Stefan C. An Inquiry into the Sources of Macroeconomic Fluctuations. *J. Monet. Econ.*, July 1988, 22(1), pp. 43–70.

Schlaifer, Robert and Pratt, John W. On the Interpretation and Observation of Laws. *J. Econometrics*, Sept.–Oct. 1988, 39(1–2), pp. 23–52.

Schlegelmilch, Bodo B. and Crook, J. N. Firm-Level Determinants of Export Intensity. *Managerial Dec. Econ.*, December 1988, 9(4), pp. 291–300.

_____ **and Therivel, Silvia.** The Use of Marketing Research in Engineering Companies: Empirical Evidence from the U.S. and the U.K. In *Woodside, A. G., ed.*, 1988, pp. 249–91.

Schleicher, Heinz. Equité fiscale: une simple expérience. (Fiscal Equity: A Simple Experiment. With English summary.) *Écon. Appl.*, 1988, 41(3), pp. 613–31.

Schlesinger, Benjamin and Lyon, Thomas P. Gas Utility Supply Planning: Risk Management and Regulatory Oversight. *Energy J.*, July 1988, 9(3), pp. 153–60.

Schlesinger, Harris and Graf v. d. Schulenburg, J.-Matthias. Mehr Markt im Gesundheitswesen. (With English summary.) *J. Inst. Theoretical Econ.*, April 1988, 144(2), pp. 396–402.

_____ **and Loubergé, Henri.** Cutting the Cake with a Stranger: Egoism and Altruism with Imperfect Information. *J. Econ. Behav. Organ.*, December 1988, 10(4), pp. 377–88.

_____ **and Venezian, Emilio C.** Compensating Victims of Occupational Diseases: Can We Structure an Effective Policy? In *Borba, P. S. and Appel, D., eds.*, 1988, pp. 59–79.

Schlesinger, Helmut. Economic Policy Objectives and Policymaking in the Major Industrial Countries: Comment. In *Guth, W., ed.*, 1988, pp. 26–33.

_____. Monetary Authorities and the New Banking Environment. In *Mikdashi, Z., ed.*, 1988, pp. 117–22.

_____. The Requirements for Successful International Macroeconomic Cooperation. In *Fieleke, N. S., ed.*, 1988, pp. 244–50.

Schlesinger, James R. Domestic Policies and International Capital Flows. In *Feldstein, M., ed. (II)*, 1988, pp. 644–54.

_____. Oil and National Security: An American Dilemma. In *Fried, E. R. and Blandin, N. M., eds.*, 1988, pp. 8–13.

Schliephake, Dietrich. The Agro-Chemical-Pharmaceutical Filière: A Study on Experiences and Perspectives of Evolution under the Impact of Innovations Affecting Industrial Processing. In *Antonelli, G. and Quadrio-Curzio, A., eds.*, 1988, pp. 231–55.

Schlomann, Heinrich. Zur Spezifikation einer Geldnachfragefunktion für die Bundesrepublik Deutschland von 1974 bis 1986. (On the Specification of a Demand for Money Function for the Federal Republic of Germany from 1974

to 1986. With English summary.) *Ifo-Studien*, 1988, 34(1), pp. 43–68.

Schlotterbeck, Walter A. The Operation of the Litigation System: Comment. In *White, L. J., ed.*, 1988, pp. 244–45.

Schmalensee, Richard. Industrial Economics: An Overview. *Econ. J.*, September 1988, 98(392), pp. 643–81.

Schmandt, Jurgen and Clarkson, Judith. Acid Rain and Friendly Neighbors: The Policy Dispute between Canada and the United States: Conclusions. In *Schmandt, J.; Clarkson, J. and Roderick, H., eds.*, 1988, pp. 253–302.

_____; **Clarkson, Judith and Roderick, Hilliard.** Acid Rain and Friendly Neighbors: The Policy Dispute between Canada and the United States: Preface. In *Schmandt, J.; Clarkson, J. and Roderick, H., eds.*, 1988, pp. xiii–xv.

_____; **Roderick, Hilliard and Morriss, Andrew.** Acid Rain Is Different. In *Schmandt, J.; Clarkson, J. and Roderick, H., eds.*, 1988, pp. 7–30.

Schmeidler, David and Gilboa, Itzhak. Information Dependent Games: Can Common Sense Be Common Knowledge? *Econ. Letters*, 1988, 27(3), pp. 215–21.

Schmid, A. Allan. Resource and Environmental Economics: A Discussion. In *Hildreth, R. J., et al., eds.*, 1988, pp. 234–37.

Schmid, Friedrich and Schader, Martin. Zur Messung der relativen Konzentration aus gruppierten Daten. Ein Vergleich parametrischer und nichtparametrischer Ansätze. (Measurement of Relative Concentration from Grouped Data. A Comparison of Parametric and Nonparametric Approaches. With English summary.) *Jahr. Nationalökon. Statist.*, May 1988, 204(5), pp. 437–55.

Schmid, Gregory. Manufacturing: The Key to Future Jobs. *Challenge*, Nov.–Dec. 1988, 31(6), pp. 54–56.

Schmid, Günther. The Role of Manpower Policy in the Swedish Model: Comment. In *Kregel, J. A.; Matzner, E. and Roncaglia, A., eds.*, 1988, pp. 168–74.

Schmid, J. Principles Emerging from Sociology for Definitions and Typologies of Household Structures. In *Keilman, N.; Kuijsten, A. and Vossen, A., eds.*, 1988, pp. 13–22.

Schmid, Michael. Fiscal Strategies, Foreign Indebtedness, and Overlapping Generations. *Empirica*, 1988, 15(1), pp. 95–115.

Schmidt, C. G. and Lee, Y. Evolution of Urban Spatial Cognition: Patterns of Change in Guangzhou, China. *Environ. Planning A*, March 1988, 20(3), pp. 339–51.

Schmidt, Christian. Programme de recherche benthamien et économie politique britannique: Deux rendez-vou manqués. (Bentham in Research Program and British Political Economy: Two Misunderstandings. With English summary.) *Revue Écon.*, July 1988, 39(4), pp. 809–39.

Schmidt, Elizabeth S. Farmers, Hunters, and Gold-Washers: A Reevaluation of Women's

Roles in Precolonial and Colonial Zimbabwe. *African Econ. Hist.*, 1988, (17), pp. 45–80.

_____. United Nations Sanctions and South Africa: Lessons from the Case of Southern Rhodesia. In *United Nations*, 1988, pp. 21–55.

Schmidt-Hebbel, Klaus. El impacto de escenarios externos alternativos sobre la economía chilena en 1988–1989. (The Impact of Alternative Foreign Scenarios on the Chilean Economy in 1988–1989. With English summary.) *Colección Estud. CIEPLAN*, June 1988, (24), pp. 113–43.

Schmidt, Helmut. Prospects for International Cooperation. In *Feldstein, M., ed. (I)*, 1988, pp. 65–74.

Schmidt, Ingo L. O. The Suitability of Chicago's Approach to Antitrust for EEC and German Competition Policy. *Jahr. Nationalökon. Statist.*, July 1988, *205*(1), pp. 30–42.

Schmidt, Kurt. Mehr zur Meritorik. Kritisches und Alternatives zu der Lehre von den öffentlichen Götern. (More on Meritorics. Some Criticism on and Alternatives to the Theory of Public Goods. With English summary.) *Z. Wirtschaft. Sozialwissen.*, 1988, *108*(3), pp. 383–403.

Schmidt, Peter. Estimation of a Fixed-Effect Cobb–Douglas System Using Panel Data. *J. Econometrics*, March 1988, *37*(3), pp. 361–80.

_____ **and Lovell, C. A. Knox.** A Comparison of Alternative Approaches to the Measurement of Productive Efficiency. In *Dogramaci, A. and Färe, R., eds.,* 1988, pp. 3–32.

Schmidt, Reinhard H., et al. Underpricing bei deutschen Erstemissionen 1984/85. (With English summary.) *Z. Betriebswirtshaft*, November 1988, *58*(11), pp. 1193–1203.

Schmidt, Robert M. and Kelley, Allen C. The Demographic Transition and Population Policy in Egypt. In *Schultz, T. Paul, ed.,* 1988, pp. 69–110.

Schmidt, Roland. Konstanzer Seminar on Monetary Theory and Monetary Policy. *Kredit Kapital,* 1988, *21*(4), pp. 625–32.

Schmidt, Ronald H. Hotelling's Rule Repealed? An Examination of Exhaustible Resource Pricing. *Fed. Res. Bank San Francisco Econ. Rev.*, Fall 1988, (4), pp. 41–54.

_____ **and Dunstan, Roger H.** Structural Changes in Residential Energy Demand. *Energy Econ.*, July 1988, *10*(3), pp. 206–12.

_____; **Gruben, William C. and Martens, Joann E.** Interstate Shifts in Nonresidential Construction. *Fed. Res. Bank Dallas Econ. Rev.*, July 1988, pp. 26–37.

Schmidt-Trenz, H.-J.; Utzig, S. and Schmidtchen, D. Zwang oder nicht Zwang—das ist hier die Frage. Der Verein für Sozialpolitik und seine obligatorische Mitgliederzeitschrift. (To Coerce or Not to Coerce—That Is the Question. The New Requirement by the German Economic Association That Its Members Subscribe to Its Journal. With English summary.) *Jahr. Nationalökon. Statist.*, May 1988, *204*(5), pp. 423–36.

Schmidt, Wolfgang H. Asymptotics for Inade-

quate Nonlinear Models with Heteroscedastic Variances. In *Fedorov, V. and Lauter, H., eds.,* 1988, pp. 125–33.

Schmidtchen, D.; Schmidt-Trenz, H.-J. and Utzig, S. Zwang oder nicht Zwang—das ist hier die Frage. Der Verein für Socialpolitik und seine obligatorische Mitgliederzeitschrift. (To Coerce or Not to Coerce—That Is the Question. The New Requirement by the German Economic Association That Its Members Subscribe to Its Journal. With English summary.) *Jahr. Nationalökon. Statist.*, May 1988, *204*(5), pp. 423–36.

Schmieding, Holger. What about a Liberalization Club for an Open World Economy? *World Econ.*, December 1988, *11*(4), pp. 515–27.

Schmit, Joan T. Lump-Sum Awards in Workers' Compensation: Reply. *J. Risk Ins.*, December 1988, *55*(4), pp. 740–41.

_____; **Pritchett, S. Travis and Fields, Paige.** Punitive Damages: Punishment or Further Compensation? *J. Risk Ins.*, September 1988, *55*(3), pp. 453–66.

Schmitt, Bernard. The Identity of Aggregate Supply and Demand in Time. In *Barrère, A., ed.,* 1988, pp. 169–93.

_____. The International Debt Problem and the 'Clearing Union.' In *Hamouda, O. F. and Smithin, J. N., eds., Vol. 2,* 1988, pp. 194–201.

Schmitt, Bernd H.; Leclerc, France and Dubé-Rioux, Laurette. Sex Typing and Consumer Behavior: A Test of Gender Schema Theory. *J. Cons. Res.*, June 1988, *15*(1), pp. 122–28.

Schmitt, Günther. Was basagen eigentlich agrarsektorale Einkommens- und Produktivitätsmassstäbe? (What Do Agricultural Productivity Measurements Really Mean? With English summary.) *Z. Wirtschaft. Sozialwissen.*, 1988, *108*(1), pp. 710–97.

Schmitt, Nicolas and Hung, N. M. Quality Competition and Threat of Entry in Duopoly. *Econ. Letters*, 1988, *27*(3), pp. 287–92.

Schmitt, Richard. The Materialistic Dialectic. *Sci. Soc.*, Winter 1988–89, *52*(4), pp. 441–56.

Schmittlein, David C. and Morrison, Donald G. Generalizing the NBD Model for Customer Purchases: What Are the Implications and Is It Worth the Effort? *J. Bus. Econ. Statist.*, April 1988, *6*(2), pp. 145–59.

_____ **and Morrison, Donald G.** Generalizing the NBD Model for Customer Purchases: What Are the Implications and Is It Worth the Effort? Reply. *J. Bus. Econ. Statist.*, April 1988, *6*(2), pp. 165–66.

Schmittroth, F.; Yeh, William W.-G. and Lu, Allen H. Sequential Estimation of Aquifer Parameters. *Water Resources Res.*, May 1988, *24*(5), pp. 670–82.

Schmitz, Andrew. U.S.–Canadian Agricultural Trade Challenges: Developing Common Approaches: Summing Up: The Canadian Perspective. In *Allen, K. and Macmillan, K., eds.,* 1988, pp. 193–95.

_____. United States Agricultural Trade: Where

Are the Gains? *Western J. Agr. Econ.*, December 1988, *13*(2), pp. 357–64.

———; **Carter, Colin A. and Gallini, Nancy T.** Producer–Consumer Trade-offs in Export Cartels: The Wheat Cartel Case: Reply. *Amer. J. Agr. Econ.*, November 1988, *70*(4), pp. 946.

———; **Furtan, W. H. and Van Kooten, G. C.** The Economics of Storing a Non-storable Commodity. *Can. J. Econ.*, August 1988, *21*(3), pp. 579–86.

——— **and Hayes, Dermot.** The Price and Welfare Implications of Current Conflicts between the Agricultural Policies of the United States and the European Community. **In** *Baldwin, R. E.; Hamilton, C. B. and Sapir, A., eds.*, 1988, pp. 67–99.

———; **Sigurdson, Dale and Doering, Otto.** Domestic Farm Policy and the Gains from Trade: Reply. *Amer. J. Agr. Econ.*, August 1988, *70*(3), pp. 740.

Schmitz, Heinz-Peter and Scott, David W. Calibrating Histograms with Application to Economic Data. *Empirical Econ.*, 1988, *13*(3–4), pp. 155–68.

Schmulowitz, Jack. SSI and the Low-Income Population: Commentary. *Soc. Sec. Bull.*, September 1988, *51*(9), pp. 18, 68–69.

Schnabel, Jacques A. Restructuring the Black–Scholes Isomorphism. *Atlantic Econ. J.*, June 1988, *16*(2), pp. 85.

Schneeberger, Hans. The Distribution of the Ratio of Two Normal Variables. *Jahr. Nationalökon. Statist.*, June 1988, *204*(6), pp. 541–48.

Schneeweis, Thomas and Phillips-Patrick, Frederick J. The "Weekend Effect" for Stock Indexes and Stock Index Futures: Dividend and Interest Rate Effects. *J. Futures Markets*, February 1988, *8*(1), pp. 115–21.

Schneider, Arnold and Mulford, Charles W. An Empirical Study of Structural and Controllable Factors Affecting Faculty Evaluations. **In** *Schwartz, B. N., ed.*, 1988, pp. 205–15.

Schneider, Dieter. Grundsätze anreizverträglicher innerbetrieblicher Erfolgsrechnung zur Steuerung und Kontrolle von Fertigungs- und Vertriebsentscheidungen. (With English summary.) *Z. Betriebswirtshaft*, November 1988, *58*(11), pp. 1181–92.

———. Reformvorschläge zu einer anreizverträglichen Wirtschaftsrechnung bei mehrperiodiger Lieferung und Leistung. (With English summary.) *Z. Betriebswirtshaft*, December 1988, *58*(12), pp. 1371–86.

Schneider, Elihu and Simmons, James C. Spatial Price Aggregation, Item Weight and Constant Utility. *Rev. Reg. Stud.*, Spring 1988, *18*(2), pp. 70–74.

Schneider, Friedrich. Institutional Economics and Hospital Finance: Some Remarks from the Public Choice Perspective. **In** *Furubotn, E. G. and Richter, R., eds.*, 1988, pp. 147–54.

———. The Role of Government in Changing Industrial Societies: A Schumpeter Perspective: Discussion. **In** *Hanusch, H., ed.*, 1988, pp. 308–15.

——— **and Frey, Bruno S.** Politico-Economic Models of Macroeconomic Policy: A Review of the Empirical Evidence. **In** *Willett, T. D., ed.*, 1988, pp. 239–75.

———; **Ghosh, Damayanti and Aigner, Dennis J.** Me and My Shadow: Estimating the Size of the U.S. Hidden Economy from Time Series Data. **In** *Barnett, W. A.; Berndt, E. R. and White, H., eds.*, 1988, pp. 297–334.

———; **Jeppesen, Svend Erik and Paulsen, Knud B.** Telecommunications in Denmark. **In** *Foreman-Peck, J. and Müller, J., eds.,*, 1988, pp. 109–29.

——— **and Neck, Reinhard.** The Growth of the Public Sector in Austria: An Exploratory Analysis. **In** *Lybeck, J. A. and Henrekson, M., eds.*, 1988, pp. 231–63.

Schneider, Harold K. Principles of Development: A View from Anthropology. **In** *Bennett, J. W. and Bowen, J. R., eds.*, 1988, pp. 61–79.

Schneider, Howard and Ghannadian, Farhad. Financial Growth versus Economic Development in Turkey, Portugal and Greece 1968–1983. *J. Econ. Devel.*, June 1988, *13*(1), pp. 39–50.

Schneider, Johannes. Wage Costs and Employment: The Sraffian View: Comment. **In** *Kregel, J. A.; Matzner, E. and Roncaglia, A., eds.*, 1988, pp. 24–26.

Schneider, Robert R. A Framework for Analyzing Food Subsidies. *World Devel.*, July 1988, *16*(7), pp. 835–45.

Schneider, Stephen H. Climate and Food: Signs of Hope, Despair, and Opportunity. **In** *Ehrlich, P. R. and Holdren, J. P., eds.*, 1988, pp. 17–51.

Schnell, Peter. The Federal Republic of Germany: A Growing International Deficit? **In** *Williams, A. M. and Shaw, G., eds.*, 1988, pp. 196–213.

Schnurnberger, W. Hydrogen as Raw Material. **In** *Winter, C.-J. and Nitsch, J., eds.*, 1988, pp. 56–78.

Schoemaker, Paul J. H.; Hershey, John C. and Kunreuther, Howard C. Sources of Bias in Assessment Procedures for Utility Functions. **In** *Bell, D. E.; Raiffa, H. and Tversky, A., eds.*, 1988, 1982, pp. 422–42.

Schoenberger, Erica. Multinational Corporations and the New International Division of Labor: A Critical Appraisal. *Int. Reg. Sci. Rev.*, 1988, *11*(2), pp. 105–19.

Schoepfle, Gregory K. and Pelzman, Joseph. The Impact of the Caribbean Basin Economic Recovery Act on Caribbean Nations' Exports and Development. *Econ. Develop. Cult. Change*, July 1988, *36*(4), pp. 753–96.

Schofield, J. A. Production Functions in the Sports Industry: An Empirical Analysis of Professional Cricket. *Appl. Econ.*, February 1988, *20*(2), pp. 177–93.

Schokkaert, Erik. Fiscal Preferences and Fiscal Knowledge at the Local Level. *J. Econ. Psych.*, March 1988, *9*(1), pp. 29–46.

——— **and Naudts, B.** Government Debt and Interest Rates in Belgium 1974–1986. *Tijd-*

schrift Econ. Manage., Sept.–Dec. 1988, *33* (3/4), pp. 339–54.

_____ **and Van der Wee, H.** A Quantitative Study of Food Consumption in the Low Countries during the Sixteenth Century. *J. Europ. Econ. Hist.*, Spring 1988, *17*(1), pp. 131–58.

Scholcz, R. L. Accounting in Hungary. In *Bailey, D. T., ed.*, 1988, pp. 107–21.

Schöler, Klaus. Ist Geld wirklich ein Produktionsfaktor? (Money: Is It a Real Production Factor? With English summary.) *Kredit Kapital*, 1988, *21*(2), pp. 182–96.

_____. Zur Effizienz des räumlichen Wettbewerbs. (On the Efficiency of Spatial Competition. With English summary.) *Jahr. Nationalökon. Statist.*, July 1988, *205*(1), pp. 43–49.

Scholes, Myron S. and Wolfson, Mark A. The Cost of Capital and Changes in Tax Regimes. In *Aaron, H. J.; Galper, H. and Pechman, J. A., eds.*, 1988, pp. 157–90.

_____; **Wolfson, Mark A. and Gilson, Ronald J.** Taxation and the Dynamics of Corporate Control: The Uncertain Case for Tax-Motivated Acquisitions. In *Coffee, J. C., Jr.; Lowenstein, L. and Rose-Ackerman, S., eds.*, 1988, pp. 271–99.

Scholing, Eberhard and Timmermann, Vincenz. Why LDC Growth Rates Differ: Measuring "Unmeasurable" Influences. *World Devel.*, November 1988, *16*(11), pp. 1271–94.

Scholl, Russell B. The International Investment Position of the United States in 1987. *Surv. Curr. Bus.*, June 1988, *68*(6), pp. 76–84.

Scholten, H.; Brouwer, Floor and Nijkamp, Peter. Hybrid Log-Linear Models for Spatial Interaction and Stability Analysis. *Metroecon.*, February 1988, *39*(1), pp. 43–65.

_____ **and ter Heide, H.** Application of Household Models in Regional Planning. In *Keilman, N.; Kuijsten, A. and Vossen, A., eds.*, 1988, pp. 209–24.

Scholz, Joachim. Postmaterialist Values and Socialisation. In *Maital, S., ed., Vol. 1*, 1988, pp. 403–11.

Schoney, Richard A.; Van Kooten, G. C. and Weisensel, Ward P. Where Are Saskatchewan Farmland Prices Headed? *Can. J. Agr. Econ.*, March 1988, *36*(1), pp. 37–50.

Schönfelder, Bruno. Relevance and Irrelevance of the Barro Irrelevance Theorem. *J. Econ. (Z. Nationalökon.)*, 1988, *48*(4), pp. 333–54.

Schoofs, Viktor and Quirk, Peter J. Forward Foreign Exchange Markets in LDCs. *Finance Develop.*, September 1988, *25*(3), pp. 36–39.

Schoormans, Jan and von Grumbkow, Jasper. Attitudes towards the Dutch Social Security System. In *Maital, S., ed., Vol. 2*, 1988, pp. 718–28.

Schotman, Peter C. and Bomhoff, Eduard J. The Term Structure in the United States, Japan, and West Germany. *Carnegie–Rochester Conf. Ser. Public Policy*, Spring 1988, *28*, pp. 269–313.

Schott, Jeffrey J. The Free Trade Agreement: A U.S. Assessment. In *Schott, J. J. and Smith, M. G., eds.*, 1988, pp. 1–35.

_____. Implications for the Uruguay Round. In *Schott, J. J. and Smith, M. G., eds.*, 1988, pp. 159–72.

_____ **and Hufbauer, Gary C.** Improving U.S. Trade Performance: The Outlook to 1990. In *Yochelson, J., ed.*, 1988, pp. 225–37.

_____ **and Smith, Murray G.** Services and Investment. In *Schott, J. J. and Smith, M. G., eds.*, 1988, pp. 137–50.

Schotter, Andrew. State-of-Nature Theory and the Rise of Social Institutions. In *Cowen, T., ed.*, 1988, *1981*, pp. 147–77.

_____ **and Pitchik, Carolyn.** Honesty in a Model of Strategic Information Transmission: Correction. *Amer. Econ. Rev.*, December 1988, *78*(5), pp. 1164.

_____ **and Pitchik, Carolyn.** Perfect Equilibria in Budget-Constrained Sequential Auctions: An Experimental Study. *Rand J. Econ.*, Autumn 1988, *19*(3), pp. 363–88.

Schoumaker, Francoise; Murnighan, J. Keith and Roth, Alvin E. Risk Aversion in Bargaining: An Experimental Study. *J. Risk Uncertainty*, March 1988, *1*(1), pp. 101–24.

_____; **Roth, Alvin E. and Murnighan, J. Keith.** The Deadline Effect in Bargaining: Some Experimental Evidence. *Amer. Econ. Rev.*, September 1988, *78*(4), pp. 806–23.

Schram, Sanford F.; Turbett, J. Patrick and Wilken, Paul H. Child Poverty and Welfare Benefits: A Reassessment with State Data of the Claim that American Welfare Breeds Dependence. *Amer. J. Econ. Soc.*, October 1988, *47*(4), pp. 409–22.

Schramm, Gunter. Regional Development and the Value of Migratory Labor—Some Perverse Economic/Technological Interactions. *Ann. Reg. Sci.*, February 1988, *22*, pp. 8–27.

Schriener, Dean; Henderson, David and Tweeten, Luther G. Intra-regional Development: Agricultural and Nodal Adjustment in Oklahoma's Southern High Plains. *Reg. Sci. Persp.*, 1988, *18*(2), pp. 44–59.

Schröder, Jürgen. Negative Net Foreign Position and Exchange Rate. *Jahr. Nationalökon. Statist.*, September 1988, *205*(3), pp. 197–208.

Schroder, W. R. Experiences in Developing an Agricultural Business Curriculum. *Rev. Marketing Agr. Econ.*, August 1988, *56*(2), pp. 217–22.

Schroeder, Edward A., IV. Careers in Economics: A Sample Study of AEA Members. *J. Econ. Educ.*, Fall 1988, *19*(4), pp. 390–92.

Schroeder, Gertrude E. Gorbachev's Economic Reforms. In *Liebowitz, R. D., ed.*, 1988, pp. 53–68.

_____. Organizations and Hierarchies: The Perennial Search for Solutions. In *Linz, S. J. and Moskoff, W., eds.*, 1988, pp. 3–22.

Schroeder, Larry and Bretschneider, Stuart. Evaluation of Commercial Economic Forecasts for Use in Local Government Budgeting. *Int. J. Forecasting*, 1988, *4*(1), pp. 33–43.

Schroeder, Ted C.; Burton, Robert O., Jr. and Featherstone, Allen M. Allocation of Farm Financial Stress among Income, Leverage, and

Interest Rate Components: A Kansas Example. *Southern J. Agr. Econ.*, December 1988, *20*(2), pp. 15–24.

———— and Hayenga, Marvin L. Comparison of Selective Hedging and Options Strategies in Cattle Feedlot Risk Management. *J. Futures Markets*, April 1988, *8*(2), pp. 141–56.

———— and Mintert, James. Hedging Feeder Steers and Heifers in the Cash-Settled Feeder Cattle Futures Market. *Western J. Agr. Econ.*, December 1988, *13*(2), pp. 316–26.

————, et al. Factors Affecting Feeder Cattle Price Differentials. *Western J. Agr. Econ.*, July 1988, *13*(1), pp. 71–81.

Schroeter, John R. Estimating the Degree of Market Power in the Beef Packing Industry. *Rev. Econ. Statist.*, February 1988, *70*(1), pp. 158–62.

Schröter, Harm. Risk and Control in Multinational Enterprise: German Businesses in Scandinavia, 1918–1939. *Bus. Hist. Rev.*, Autumn 1988, *62*(3), pp. 420–43.

Schubert, Eric S. Innovations, Debts, and Bubbles: International Integration of Financial Markets in Western Europe, 1688–1720. *J. Econ. Hist.*, June 1988, *48*(2), pp. 299–306.

Schubert, U.; Baumann, J. and Fischer, Manfred M. A Choice-Theoretical Labour-Market Model: Empirical Tests at the Mesolevel. *Environ. Planning A*, August 1988, *20*(8), pp. 1085–1102.

Schuh, G. Edward. Exchange Rates and Their Role in Agricultural Trade Issues. In *Miner, W. M. and Hathaway, D. E.*, eds., 1988, pp. 193–210.

————. Some Neglected Agricultural Policy Issues in the Uruguay Round of Multilateral Trade Negotiations. In *Roberts, C.*, ed., 1988, pp. 5–12.

————. Trade Liberalization: Theory and Reality. *Can. J. Agr. Econ.*, Part 1, December 1988, *36*(4), pp. 589–96.

———— and Barghouti, Shawki. Agricultural Diversification in Asia. *Finance Develop.*, June 1988, *25*(2), pp. 41–44.

———— and Calegar, Geraldo M. Effects of Brazilian Wheat Subsidies on Income Distribution and Trade. In *Pinstrup-Andersen, P.*, ed., 1988, pp. 267–76.

———— and Orden, David. The Macroeconomics of Agriculture and Rural America. In *Hildreth, R. J., et al.*, eds., 1988, pp. 347–83.

————; Smith, Matthew G. and Schuh, Maria Ignez. The Potential Role of Isolated Soy Protein Food Ingredients in Mexico. In *Schwarz, F. H.*, ed., 1988, pp. 159–87.

Schuh, Maria Ignez; Schuh, G. Edward and Smith, Matthew G. The Potential Role of Isolated Soy Protein Food Ingredients in Mexico. In *Schwarz, F. H.*, ed., 1988, pp. 159–87.

Schul, Yaacov and Mazursky, David. The Effects of Advertisement Encoding on the Failure to Discount Information: Implications for the Sleeper Effect. *J. Cons. Res.*, June 1988, *15*(1), pp. 24–36.

Schuler, Randall S.; Galante, Steven P. and Jack-

son, Susan E. Matching Effective HR Practices with Competitive Strategy. In *Timpe, A. D.*, ed., 1988, *1987*, pp. 113–23.

Schüler, Wolfgang. Der Erfolg in der Lebensversicherung: Entstehung, Darstellung und Beurteilung. (With English summary.) *Z. Betriebswirtschaft*, January 1988, *58*(1), pp. 201–11.

Schulhofer, Stephen J. Criminal Justice Discretion as a Regulatory System. *J. Legal Stud.*, January 1988, *17*(1), pp. 43–82.

Schuller, Bernd-Joachim. Kriminalitet, inkomster och rättsväsendet. En empirisk studie med svenska data. (Criminality, Incomes and the Judicial System. With English summary.) *Ekon. Samfundets Tidskr.*, 1988, *41*(2), pp. 79–97.

Schulmeister, Stephan. Currency Speculation and Dollar Fluctuations. *Banca Naz. Lavoro Quart. Rev.*, December 1988, (167), pp. 343–65.

Schultz, T. Paul. Expansion of Public School Expenditures and Enrollments: Intercountry Evidence on the Effects of Income, Prices, and Population Growth. *Econ. Educ. Rev.*, 1988, *7*(2), pp. 167–83.

————. Heterogeneous Preferences and Migration: Self-Selection, Regional Prices and Programs, and the Behavior of Migrants in Colombia. In *Schultz, T. Paul*, ed., 1988, pp. 163–81.

————. Population Programs: Measuring Their Impact on Fertility and the Personal Distribution of Their Effects. *J. Policy Modeling*, April 1988, *10*(1), pp. 113–39.

———— and Rosenzweig, Mark R. The Stability of Household Production Technology: A Replication. *J. Human Res.*, Fall 1988, *23*(4), pp. 535–49.

Schultz, Theodore W. Dealing with Economic Imbalances between Industry and Agriculture. In *Arrow, K. J.*, ed., 1988, pp. 33–48.

Schultze, Charles L. Back to the Future: European Unemployment Today Viewed from America in 1939: Comment. *Brookings Pap. Econ. Act.*, 1988, (1), pp. 305–10.

————. International Macroeconomics Coordination—Marrying the Economic Models with Political Reality. In *Feldstein, M.*, ed. (I), 1988, pp. 49–60.

————; Litan, Robert E. and Lawrence, Robert Z. American Living Standards: Threats and Challenges: Introduction. In *Litan, R. E; Lawrence, R. Z. and Schultze, C. L.*, eds., 1988, pp. 1–22.

Schulz, Gerhard and Heinrichs, Wolfgang. Political Economy and Modern Productive Forces. *Eastern Europ. Econ.*, Winter 1988–89, *27*(2), pp. 5–43.

Schulz, Ulrich. The Influence of Social Orientation and Generalized Expectancies on Decision Making in Iterated Experimental Games. In *Tietz, R.; Albers, W. and Selten, R.*, eds., 1988, pp. 95–110.

Schulze, William; Gerking, Shelby and de Haan, Menno. The Marginal Value of Job Safety: A

Contingent Valuation Study. *J. Risk Uncertainty*, June 1988, *1*(2), pp. 185–99.

Schulze, William D. The Optimal Use of Nonrenewable Resources: The Theory of Extraction. In *Ricketts, M., ed., Vol. 2*, 1988, *1974*, pp. 253–73.

Schumacher, Dieter. Determinants of the Major Industrialized Countries' Exports to Developing Countries. *World Devel.*, November 1988, *16*(11), pp. 1317–28.

Schumann, Debra; deCodes, Jose and Baker, Timothy D. The Hidden Costs of Illness in Developing Countries. In *Sirageldin, I. and Sorkin, A., eds.*, 1988, pp. 127–45.

Schumann, Laurence. State Regulation of Takeovers and Shareholder Wealth: The Case of New York's 1985 Takeover Statutes. *Rand J. Econ.*, Winter 1988, *19*(4), pp. 557–67.

Schur, Claudia L. and Monheit, Alan C. The Dynamics of Health Insurance Loss: A Tale of Two Cohorts. *Inquiry*, Fall 1988, *25*(3), pp. 315–27.

Schuster, Camille P. Interact Matrix System: A Method for Analyzing Sales Interactions. In *Hirschman, E. and Sheth, J. N., eds.*, 1988, pp. 271–323.

Schutjer, Wayne and Robinson, Warren C. Agricultural Development and Demographic Change: Reply. *Econ. Develop. Cult. Change*, April 1988, *36*(3), pp. 571–72.

Schutte, David P. and Phillips, Owen R. Identifying Profitable Self-service Markets: A Test in Gasoline Retailing. *Appl. Econ.*, February 1988, *20*(2), pp. 263–72.

van Schuur, W. H. The Importance of Unidimensional Unfolding for Marketing Research. In *Gaul, W. and Schader, M., eds.*, 1988, pp. 299–15.

Schwab, Arthur J.; Sauer, William J. and Currid, Michael. The Emergence of the High Technology Industry in Southwestern Pennsylvania: A Case Study of Pittsburgh. In *Kirchhoff, B. A., et al., eds.*, 1988, pp. 415–29.

Schwab, Robert M. and Hulten, Charles R. Income Originating in the State and Local Sector. In *Rosen, H. S., ed.*, 1988, pp. 215–48.

_____ **and Oates, Wallace E.** Economic Competition among Jurisdictions: Efficiency Enhancing or Distortion Inducing? *J. Public Econ.*, April 1988, *35*(3), pp. 333–54.

Schwab, Stewart. A Coasean Experiment on Contract Presumptions. *J. Legal Stud.*, June 1988, *17*(2), pp. 237–68.

Schwaiger, J.; Buchholz, Wolfgang and Richter, Wolfram F. Distributional Implications of Equal Sacrifice Rules. In *Gaertner, W. and Pattanaik, P. K., eds.*, 1988, *1988*, pp. 135–38.

_____ **; Buchholz, Wolfgang and Richter, Wolfram F.** Distributional Implications of Equal Sacrifice Rules. *Soc. Choice Welfare*, 1988, *5*(2/3), pp. 223–26.

Schwalbach, Joachim. Marktanteil und Unternehmensgewinn. (With English summary.) *Z. Betriebswirtshaft*, April 1988, *58*(4), pp. 535–49.

Schwartz, Aba; Eldor, Rafael and Pines, David.

The Demand for Domestic Assets and Consumption Risk. In *Khoury, S. J. and Ghosh, A., eds.*, 1988, pp. 349–62.

_____ **; Eldor, Rafael and Pines, David.** Home Asset Preference and Productivity Shocks. *J. Int. Econ.*, August 1988, *25*(1–2), pp. 165–76.

Schwartz, Alan. The Fairness of Tender Offer Prices in Utilitarian Theory. *J. Legal Stud.*, January 1988, *17*(1), pp. 165–96.

_____. Proposals for Products Liability Reform: A Theoretical Synthesis. *Yale Law J.*, February 1988, *97*(3), pp. 353–419.

_____. The Sole Owner Standard Reviewed. *J. Legal Stud.*, January 1988, *17*(1), pp. 231–35.

_____ **; Wilde, Louis L. and Grether, David M.** Uncertainty and Shopping Behaviour: An Experimental Analysis. *Rev. Econ. Stud.*, April 1988, *55*(2), pp. 323–42.

Schwartz, Anna J. Bank Runs and Deposit Insurance Reform. *Cato J.*, Winter 1988, *7*(3), pp. 589–94.

_____. Financial Stability and the Federal Safety Net. In *Haraf, W. S. and Kushmeider, R. M., eds.*, 1988, pp. 34–62.

_____ **and Bordo, Michael D.** Transmission of Real and Monetary Disturbances under Fixed and Floating Exchange Rates. *Cato J.*, Fall 1988, *8*(2), pp. 451–72.

Schwartz, Arthur L., Jr. and Kapplin, Steven D. Public Real Estate Limited Partnership Returns: A Preliminary Comparison with Other Investments. *Amer. Real Estate Urban Econ. Assoc. J.*, Spring 1988, *16*(1), pp. 63–68.

Schwartz, Davis R. Privatization of State and Local Government Services in the United States. In *Walker, M. A., ed. (II)*, 1988, pp. 239–50.

Schwartz, Eduardo S. and Brennan, Michael J. Time-Invariant Portfolio Insurance Strategies. *J. Finance*, June 1988, *43*(2), pp. 283–99.

_____ **and Hughes, Patricia J.** The LIFO/FIFO Choice: An Asymmetric Information Approach. *J. Acc. Res.*, Supplement, 1988, *26*, pp. 41–58.

Schwartz, Eli. A Quick Step through the Canadian Economy. In *Thornton, R. J.; Hyclak, T. and Aronson, J. R., eds.*, 1988, pp. 33–47.

Schwartz, Gerd and Richardson, Harry W. Economic Development, Population and Primacy. *Reg. Stud.*, December 1988, *22*(6), pp. 467–75.

Schwartz, Hugh H. Economic Perception and Judgment in Small and Medium Size Manufacturing Enterprises: Findings and Preliminary Hypotheses from In-Depth Interviews in Argentina, Mexico and the United States. In *Maital, S., ed., Vol. 2*, 1988, pp. 441–57.

Schwartz, J. Brad and Akin, John S. The Effect of Economic Factors on Contraceptive Choice in Jamaica and Thailand: A Comparison of Mixed Multinomial Logit Results. *Econ. Develop. Cult. Change*, April 1988, *36*(3), pp. 503–27.

_____ **; Akin, John S. and Popkin, Barry M.** Price and Income Elasticities of Demand for Modern Health Care: The Case of Infant Delivery in the Philippines. *World Bank Econ. Rev.*, January 1988, *2*(1), pp. 49–76.

Schwartz, Leonard W. Recent Developments in Hele-Shaw Flow Modeling. In *Wheeler, M. F., ed.*, 1988, pp. 249–61.

Schwartz, Marius and Baumann, Michael G. Entry-Deterrence Externalities and Relative Firm Size. *Int. J. Ind. Organ.*, June 1988, *6*(2), pp. 181–97.

Schwartz, Robert A. A Proposal to Stabilize Stock Prices. *J. Portfol. Manage.*, Fall 1988, *15*(1), pp. 4–11.

_____ **and Hasbrouck, Joel.** Liquidity and Execution Costs in Equity Markets. *J. Portfol. Manage.*, Spring 1988, *14*(3), pp. 10–16.

Schwartz, Saul and Baum, Sandra R. Merit Aid to College Students. *Econ. Educ. Rev.*, 1988, *7*(1), pp. 127–34.

Schwartz, Seymour I. and Zorn, Peter M. A Critique of Quasiexperimental and Statistical Controls for Measuring Program Effects: Application to Urban Growth Control. *J. Policy Anal. Manage.*, Spring 1988, *7*(3), pp. 491–505.

Schwartz, Warren F. Private Antitrust Litigation: An Introduction and Framework: Comment: The Counterfactual and Legal Reform. In *White, L. J., ed.*, 1988, pp. 99–101.

Schwartz, William and Aaron, Henry J. The Painful Prescription: Rationing Hospital Care. In *Brown, E., ed.*, 1988, pp. 97–104.

Schwartzman, Simon. High Technology versus Self-reliance: Brazil Enters the Computer Age. In *Chacel, J. M.; Falk, P. S. and Fleischer, D. V., eds.*, 1988, pp. 67–82.

Schwarz, F. H. Quantifying the Profitability of New Technology. In *Schwarz, F. H., ed.*, 1988, pp. 189–235.

Schwarz, K. Household Trends in Europe after World War II. In *Keilman, N.; Kuijsten, A. and Vossen, A., eds.*, 1988, pp. 67–83.

Schwarz, Margaret and Holleran, Philip M. Another Look at Comparable Worth's Impact on Black Women. *Rev. Black Polit. Econ.*, Winter 1988, *16*(3), pp. 97–102.

Schwarz-Miller, Ann and Talley, Wayne K. The Demand for Air Services Provided by Air Passenger–Cargo Carriers in a Deregulated Environment. *Int. J. Transport Econ.*, June 1988, *15*(2), pp. 159–68.

Schweikhardt, David B. The Role of Values in Economic Theory and Policy: A Comparison of Frank Knight and John R. Commons. *J. Econ. Issues*, June 1988, *22*(2), pp. 407–14.

Schweinberger, Albert G. and Lloyd, Peter J. Trade Expenditure Functions and the Gains from Trade. *J. Int. Econ.*, May 1988, *24*(3–4), pp. 275–97.

de Schweinitz, Karl, Jr. Technology, Ideology, and the State in Economic Development. In *Samuels, W. J., ed., Vol. 3*, 1988, *1974*, pp. 134–51.

Schweitzer, Iván. Will the Industrial Pyramid Be Set Afoot? The Development of Enterprise Size Structure in Hungarian Industry in the 1980s. *Acta Oecon.*, 1988, *39*(1–2), pp. 111–22.

_____ **and Sallai, R.** World Economic Environment and the Hungarian Economy: A Conference. *Acta Oecon.*, 1988, *39*(1–2), pp. 185–87.

Schweitzer, Thomas; Daly, Michael J. and Mercier, Pierre. The Impact of Tax Reform on Investment and Saving Incentives in Canada, the United States, the United Kingdom, and Japan. *Econ. Letters*, 1988, *27*(2), pp. 159–65.

Schweizer, Urs. Externalities and the Coase Theorem: Hypothesis or Result? *J. Inst. Theoretical Econ.*, April 1988, *144*(2), pp. 245–66.

Schwendener, Peter and Kugler, Peter. Arbeitsangebot, Grenzsteuerbelastung und der permanente Lohnsatz: Empirische Ergebnisse für die Schweiz. (Labour Supply, Marginal Taxes, and Permanent Wages: Empirical Evidence for Switzerland. With English summary.) *Schweiz. Z. Volkswirtsch. Statist.*, September 1988, *124*(3), pp. 243–57.

Schwenk, Charles R. and Thomas, Howard. Effects of Strategic Decision Aids on Problem Solving: A Laboratory Experiment. In *Grant, J. H., ed.*, 1988, pp. 399–414.

Schwieterman, Joseph P. Efficiency in Mass Transit: An Inquiry into the Effects of Regulation. In *Weicher, J. C., ed.*, 1988, pp. 82–88.

Schwindt, Richard and Vining, Aidan R. Have a Heart: Increasing the Supply of Transplant Organs for Infants and Children. *J. Policy Anal. Manage.*, Fall 1988, *7*(4), pp. 706–10.

Schwob, Claude. Dirigisme ou libéralisme? La conception hegelienne. (State Interventionism or Liberalism? The Hegelian Conception. With English summary.) *Écon. Soc.*, October 1988, *22*(10), pp. 75–104.

Schwochau, Susan; Delaney, John Thomas and Masters, Marick F. Unionism and Voter Turnout. *J. Lab. Res.*, Summer 1988, *9*(3), pp. 221–36.

_____ **and Feuille, Peter.** Interest Arbitrators and Their Decision Behavior. *Ind. Relat.*, Winter 1988, *27*(1), pp. 37–55.

Schworm, William and Blackorby, Charles. The Existence of Input and Output Aggregates in Aggregate Production Functions. *Econometrica*, May 1988, *56*(3), pp. 613–43.

Sciarra, S. and Wedderburn, Lord. Collective Bargaining as Agreement and as Law: Neo-contractualist and Neo-corporative Tendencies of Our Age. In *Pizzorusso, A., ed.*, 1988, pp. 186–235.

Sciarrone, G. Delivery Problems in Metropolitan Areas Optimizing the Distribution of a Daily Newspaper: An Application to the Turin Daily "La Stampa." In *Bianco, L. and La Bella, A., eds.*, 1988, pp. 334–51.

Sciortino, John J.; Huston, John H. and Spencer, Roger W. Risk and Income Distribution. *J. Econ. Psych.*, September 1988, *9*(3), pp. 399–408.

Scobie, Grant M. Food Subsidies in Egypt: Macroeconomic and Trade Implications. In *Pinstrup-Andersen, P., ed.*, 1988, pp. 196–205.

_____. Macroeconomic and Trade Implications of Consumer-Oriented Food Subsidies. In *Pinstrup-Andersen, P., ed.*, 1988, pp. 49–76.

Scotchmer, Suzanne and Farrell, Joseph. Partnerships. *Quart. J. Econ.*, May 1988, *103*(2), pp. 279–97.

Scott, Alex. Economics in Action. *J. Econ. Surveys*, 1988, *2*(4), pp. 367–71.

_____ and Lumsden, Keith. A Characteristics Approach to the Evaluation of Economics Software Packages. *J. Econ. Educ.*, Fall 1988, *19*(4), pp. 353–62.

Scott, Allen J. and Angel, D. P. The Global Assembly-Operations of U.S. Semiconductor Firms: A Geographical Analysis. *Environ. Planning A*, August 1988, *20*(8), pp. 1047–67.

Scott, Anthony. Development of Property in the Fishery. *Marine Resource Econ.*, 1988, *5*(4), pp. 289–311.

Scott, Charles G.; Mulberg, Ruthellen and Oberheu, Howard. SSA's Outreach Efforts to Contact Beneficiaries Eligible for SSI Payments. *Soc. Sec. Bull.*, January 1988, *51*(1), pp. 12–17.

Scott, D. R.; Suchard, Hazel T. and Polonsky, M. J. Motivations of South African Emigrants. *Appl. Econ.*, October 1988, *20*(10), pp. 1293–1315.

Scott, David W. How Far Are Automatically Chosen Regression Smoothing Parameters from Their Optimum?: Comment. *J. Amer. Statist. Assoc.*, March 1988, *83*(401), pp. 96–98.

_____ and Schmitz, Heinz-Peter. Calibrating Histograms with Application to Economic Data. *Empirical Econ.*, 1988, *13*(3–4), pp. 155–68.

Scott, Elton; Tucker, Alan L. and Peterson, David R. Tests of the Black–Scholes and Constant Elasticity of Variance Currency Call Option Valuation Models. *J. Finan. Res.*, Fall 1988, *11*(3), pp. 201–13.

Scott, Frank A., Jr.; Berger, Mark C. and Blomquist, Glenn C. Impacts of Air Pollution Control Strategies in Kentucky. *Growth Change*, Spring 1988, *19*(2), pp. 40–55.

Scott, John T. Diversification versus Co-operation in R&D Investment. *Managerial Dec. Econ.*, September 1988, *9*(3), pp. 173–86.

Scott, Kenneth E. Contract Remedies: A Need for Better Efficiency Analysis: Comment. *J. Inst. Theoretical Econ.*, February 1988, *144*(1), pp. 31–34.

_____. How Market Forces Influence the Structure of Financial Regulation: Commentary. In *Haraf, W. S. and Kushmeider, R. M., eds.*, 1988, pp. 386–91.

Scott, Robert C. Grade Inflation: A Way Out: A Comment. *J. Econ. Educ.*, Summer 1988, *19*(3), pp. 227–29.

_____; Highfill, Jannett K. and Sattler, Edward L. Advantage to a Risk Neutral Firm of Flexible Resources under Demand Uncertainty. *Southern Econ. J.*, April 1988, *54*(4), pp. 934–49.

Scott, Robert E. Trade and Employment in Automobiles: The Short-Run Success and Long-Run Failure of Protectionist Measures. In *Tyson, L. D.; Dickens, W. T. and Zysman, J., eds.*, 1988, pp. 157–203.

Scott, William L.; Gardner, Mona J. and Mills,

Dixie L. Expense Preference and Minority Banking: A Note. *Financial Rev.*, February 1988, *23*(1), pp. 105–15.

Scotton, R. B. Has Public Sector Contracting with Health Maintenance Organisations in the United States Saved Money? Commentary. In *Smith, C. S., ed.*, 1988, pp. 161–63.

_____. Health Insurance Forum. In *Butler, J. R. G. and Doessel, D. P., eds.*, 1988, pp. 225–29.

Scoville, James G. Hewers of Wood and Drawers of Water: Incomes and Employment in the Traditional Unskilled Sector. *World Devel.*, February 1988, *16*(2), pp. 305–16.

Scriven, Michael. Explanations, Predictions, and Laws. In *Pitt, J. C., ed.*, 1988, *1962*, pp. 51–74.

Scudder, Thayer. The Institute for Development Anthropology: The Case for Anthropological Participation in the Development Process. In *Bennett, J. W. and Bowen, J. R., eds.*, 1988, pp. 365–85.

Scully, Gerald W. The Institutional Framework and Economic Development. *J. Polit. Econ.*, June 1988, *96*(3), pp. 652–62.

Scurrah, Martin J. and Podesta, Bruno. The Experience of Worker Self-management in Peru and Chile. In *Annis, S. and Hakim, P., eds.*, 1988, pp. 132–53.

Seaks, Terry G. and Lacivita, Charles J. Forecasting Accuracy and the Choice of First Difference or Percentage Change Regression Models. *Int. J. Forecasting*, 1988, *4*(2), pp. 261–68.

_____; Woodbery, Sabrina R. and Link, Albert N. Firm Size and R&D Spending: Testing for Functional Form. *Southern Econ. J.*, April 1988, *54*(4), pp. 1027–32.

Seale, James, Jr.; Theil, Henri and Fiebig, Denzil G. Cross-Country Demand Analysis Based on Three Phases of the International Comparison Project. In *Salazar-Carrillo, J. and Rao, D. S. P., eds.*, 1988, pp. 225–35.

Seale, William E. and Barnhill, Theodore M. Optimal Exercise of the Switching Option in Treasury Bond Arbitrages. *J. Futures Markets*, October 1988, *8*(5), pp. 517–32.

Sealy, Ronald; Craigwell, Roland and Rock, Llewyn. On the Determination of the External Public Debt: The Case of Barbados. *Soc. Econ. Stud.*, December 1988, *37*(4), pp. 137–50.

Sears, David L. What Do Employees Want? In *Timpe, A. D., ed.*, 1988, *1984*, pp. 24–28.

Sears, R. Stephen and Wei, K. C. John. The Structure of Skewness Preferences in Asset Pricing Models with Higher Moments: An Empirical Test. *Financial Rev.*, February 1988, *23*(1), pp. 25–38.

Seastrand, Frans. The Effect of Federal, State and Local Tax Rates on Capital Gains: New York State's Experience. *Nat. Tax J.*, September 1988, *41*(3), pp. 415–38.

Sebald, Anthony V. and Bullard, Clark W. Monte Carlo Sensitivity Analysis of Input–Output Models. *Rev. Econ. Statist.*, November 1988, *70*(4), pp. 708–12.

Seccareccia, Mario. Système monétaire et loi d'entropie: La notion geselienne de préférence pour la liquidité. (The Monetary System and Entropy: The Gesellian notion of Liquidity Preference. With English summary.) *Écon. Soc.*, September 1988, 22(9), pp. 57–71.

_____. Systemic Viability and Credit Crunches: An Examination of Recent Canadian Cyclical Fluctuations. *J. Econ. Issues*, March 1988, 22(1), pp. 49–77.

_____ and Lavoie, Marc. Money, Interest and Rentiers: The Twilight of Rentier Capitalism in Keynes's *General Theory*. In *Hamouda, O. F. and Smithin, J. N.*, eds., Vol. 2, 1988, pp. 145–58.

Sechzer, Selig L. The Welfare Effects of Foreign Investment in Tariff Distorted Economies. *J. Int. Econ.*, November 1988, 25(3–4), pp. 379–83.

Seddighi, H. R.; Clark, C. J. and Lawler, K. A. The Structure of the Charity Sector in England and Wales: A Statistical Analysis. *Appl. Econ.*, March 1988, 20(3), pp. 335–50.

Sedlacek, Guilherme L.; Hotz, V. Joseph and Kydland, Finn E. Intertemporal Preferences and Labor Supply. *Econometrica*, March 1988, 56(2), pp. 335–60.

Seel, Barbara. Hausarbeit und Wertschöpfung. (Estimating Value Added by Household Production. With English summary.) *Jahr. Nationalökon. Statist.*, August 1988, 205(2), pp. 97–115.

Seeley, Robert D. and Sellekaerts, Willy. On the Relative Performance of Inflation Models. In *Pennsylvania Economic Association*, 1988, pp. 105–15.

Seeto, Dewey Q. and Woo, Chi-Keung. Optimal Off-Peak Incremental Sales Rate Design in Electricity Pricing. *Energy J.*, January 1988, 9(1), pp. 95–102.

Segal, Uzi. Does the Preference Reversal Phenomenon Necessarily Contradict the Independence Axiom? *Amer. Econ. Rev.*, March 1988, 78(1), pp. 233–36.

_____. Probabilistic Insurance and Anticipated Utility. *J. Risk Ins.*, June 1988, 55(2), pp. 287–97.

_____ and Spivak, Avia. Non-expected Utility Risk Premiums: The Cases of Probability Ambiguity and Outcome Uncertainty. *J. Risk Uncertainty*, September 1988, 1(3), pp. 333–47.

_____; Spivak, Avia and Zeira, Joseph. Precautionary Saving and Risk Aversion: An Anticipated Utility Approach. *Econ. Letters*, 1988, 27(3), pp. 223–27.

Segal, William and Philips, Peter. Production Process, Work Organization, and Labor Relations in the Postwar California Food Processing Industry. *Rev. Radical Polit. Econ.*, Summer–Fall 1988, 20(2–3), pp. 208–13.

Segarra, Eduardo; Johnson, Thomas G. and Deaton, Brady J. Infrastructure Investment: Alternatives and Priorities. In *Johnson, T. G.; Deaton, B. J. and Segarra, E.*, eds., 1988, pp. 261–64.

Seger, Martha R. Financial Markets and Reform.

In *Federal Home Loan Bank of San Francisco,* 1988, pp. 19–27.

_____. Statement to the U.S. Senate Committee on Banking, Housing, and Urban Affairs, March 23, 1988. *Fed. Res. Bull.*, May 1988, 74(5), pp. 307–12.

_____. Statement to the U.S. Senate Subcommittee on Consumer Affairs of the Committee on Banking, Housing, and Urban Affairs, November 18, 1987. *Fed. Res. Bull.*, January 1988, 74(1), pp. 27–31.

Segerson, Kathleen. Uncertainty and Incentives for Nonpoint Pollution Control. *J. Environ. Econ. Manage.*, March 1988, 15(1), pp. 87–98.

_____ and Bromley, Daniel W. State Policy Choices: The Wisconsin Experience: Natural Resource Policy. In *Danziger, S. H. and Witte, J. F.*, eds., 1988, pp. 250–76.

Segerstahl, Boris and Vasko, Tibor. Communication and Regional Planning: Some Systemic Remarks. In *Orishimo, I.; Hewings, G. J. D. and Nijkamp, P.*, eds., 1988, pp. 21–28.

Segerstrom, Paul S. Demons and Repentance. *J. Econ. Theory*, June 1988, 45(1), pp. 32–52.

Segnana, Luisa and Pini, Paolo. "Economia Politica": Alcune valutazioni dopo quattro anni. (*Economia Politica:* An Assessment after Four Years. With English summary.) *Econ. Polit.*, August 1988, 5(2), pp. 237–64.

Seguiti, Maria Laura. An Italian Perspective on U.S. Federal Credit Reform. *Public Budg. Finance*, Winter 1988, 8(4), pp. 54–67.

Seidel, Hans. Austria's Macro-economic Policies in the Last Decade. In *Saunders, C. T.*, ed., 1988, pp. 91–99.

Seidenfeld, Teddy. Decision Theory without "Independence" or without "Ordering": Rejoinder. *Econ. Philos.*, October 1988, 4(2), pp. 309–15.

_____. Decision Theory without "Independence" or without "Ordering": What Is the Difference? *Econ. Philos.*, October 1988, 4(2), pp. 267–90.

Seidl, Christian. Poverty Measurement: A Survey. In *Bös, D.; Rose, M. and Seidl, C.*, eds., 1988, pp. 71–147.

_____. Public Finance in a Democratic Society. *Weltwirtsch. Arch.*, 1988, 124(4), pp. 775–84.

Seifert, Bruce; Akgiray, Vedat and Booth, G. Geoffrey. Distribution Properties of Latin American Black Market Exchange Rates. *J. Int. Money Finance*, March 1988, 7(1), pp. 37–48.

_____ and Eddy, Albert. Firm Size and Dividend Announcements. *J. Finan. Res.*, Winter 1988, 11(4), pp. 295–302.

Seiglie, Carlos. International Conflict and Military Expenditures: An Externality Approach. *J. Conflict Resolution*, March 1988, 32(1), pp. 141–61.

Seike, Atsushi. Analysis of the 1986 Spring Labor Wage Offensive. In *Japan Institute of Labour,* ed., 1988, 1986, pp. 52–55.

Seiling, Mark Scott. Semiconductor Productivity Gains Linked to Multiple Innovations. *Mon. Lab. Rev.*, April 1988, 111(4), pp. 27–33.

Seitz, Helmut. The Estimation of Inflation Forecasts from Business Survey Data. *Appl. Econ.*, April 1988, *20*(4), pp. 427–38.

Seitz, Tycho. Aktuelle Entwicklungstendenzen der Konjunkturforschung. (Recent Tendencies in Business Cycle Research. With English summary.) *Ifo-Studien*, 1988, *34*(2–3), pp. 161–73.

Seják, Josef. An Interpretation of Socially Necessary Costs. *Czech. Econ. Pap.*, 1988, (25), pp. 35–52.

Sejersted, Francis. The Development of Economic History in Norway. *Scand. Econ. Hist. Rev.*, 1988, *36*(3), pp. 42–50.

Sekimoto, Tadahiro. Meeting the Challenge of the 21st Century. In *Rosow, J. M., ed.*, 1988, pp. 147–61.

Sekkat, Khalid. Filières de production et stratégies d'entreprises. (With English summary.) *Cah. Écon. Bruxelles*, 2nd Trimester 1988, (118), pp. 181–98.

———— **and Mercenier, Jean.** Money Stock Targeting and Money Supply: An Intertemporal Optimization Approach (with an Application to Canada). *J. Appl. Econometrics*, July–Sept. 1988, *3*(3), pp. 215–28.

Selby, M. J. P.; Franks, Julian R. and Karki, J. Loan Guarantees, Wealth Transfers and Incentives to Invest. *J. Ind. Econ.*, September 1988, *37*(1), pp. 47–65.

Selden, Mark. City versus Countryside? The Social Consequences of Development Choices in China. In *Selden, M.*, 1988, pp. 153–80.

————. Cooperation and Conflict: Cooperative and Collective Formation in China's Countryside. In *Selden, M.*, 1988, *1982*, pp. 54–100.

————. Income Inequality and the State in Rural China. In *Selden, M.*, 1988, *1985*, pp. 129–52.

————. Marxism and the Peasantry: Collectivization and Strategies of Socialist Agrarian Development. In *Selden, M.*, 1988, *1983*, pp. 31–53.

————. Rethinking China's Socialist Economic Development. In *Selden, M.*, 1988, pp. 3–30.

———— **and Ka, Chih-ming.** Original Accumulation, Equality, and Late Industrialization: The Cases of Socialist China and Capitalist Taiwan. In *Selden, M.*, 1988, *1986*, pp. 101–28.

———— **and Lu, Aiguo.** The Reform of Landownership and the Political Economy of Contemporary China. In *Selden, M.*, 1988, pp. 181–99.

Seldon, Arthur. Economists and the Politician. *Managerial Dec. Econ.*, Special Issue, Winter 1988, pp. 89–94.

Selgin, George A. Accommodating Changes in the Relative Demand for Currency: Free Banking vs. Central Banking. *Cato J.*, Winter 1988, *7*(3), pp. 621–41.

————. Praxeology and Understanding: An Analysis of the Controversy in Austrian Economics. In *Rothbard, M. N. and Block, W., eds.*, 1988, pp. 19–58.

———— **and White, Lawrence H.** Competitive Monies and the Suffolk Bank System: Comment. *Southern Econ. J.*, July 1988, *55*(1), pp. 215–19.

Seligman, Joel. Stock Exchange Rules Affecting Takeovers and Control Transactions. In *Coffee, J. C., Jr.; Lowenstein, L. and Rose-Ackerman, S., eds.*, 1988, pp. 465–98.

Sell, Friedrich L. IS–LM auch in den Tropen: Zu den gesamtwirtschaftlichen Wirkungen von Zinsreformen in Entwicklungsländern. (IS–LM in the Tropics: Assessing the Overall Economic Impact of Interest Rate Reforms in Developing Countries. With English summary.) *Konjunkturpolitik*, 1988, *34*(2), pp. 104–21.

————. "True Exposure": The Analysis of Trade Liberalization in a General Equilibrium Framework. *Weltwirtsch. Arch.*, 1988, *124*(4), pp. 635–52.

Sell, Jane. Types of Public Goods and Free-Riding. In *Lawler, E. J. and Markovsky, B., eds.*, 1988, pp. 119–40.

Sellars, Wilfrid. Theoretical Explanation. In *Pitt, J. C., ed.*, 1988, pp. 156–66.

Sellekaerts, Willy and Rusek, Antonin. Occupation Experience and Performance Determine Labor Income. *Rev. Soc. Econ.*, December 1988, *46*(3), pp. 307–11.

———— **and Seeley, Robert D.** On the Relative Performance of Inflation Models. In *Pennsylvania Economic Association*, 1988, pp. 105–15.

Sellers, John R. and May, Ann Mari. Contemporary Philosophy of Science and Neoinstitutional Thought. *J. Econ. Issues*, June 1988, *22*(2), pp. 397–405.

Sellers, Stephen G.; Bennett, John W. and Cole, William. The Importance of Traditional Quality for Foods Containing Vegetable Protein Ingredients. In *Schwarz, F. H., ed.*, 1988, pp. 273–339.

Sellin, Thorsten. The Negro and the Problem of Law Observance and Administration in the Light of Social Research. In *Simms, M. C. and Myers, S. L., Jr., eds.*, 1988, pp. 71–80.

Selowsky, Marcelo. The Debt Crisis: Structural Explanations of Country Performance: Comments. *J. Devel. Econ.*, November 1988, *29*(3), pp. 307–09.

———— **and Martin, Ricardo.** External Shocks and the Demand for Adjustment Finance. *World Bank Econ. Rev.*, January 1988, *2*(1), pp. 105–21.

Selten, Reinhard. Evolutionary Stability in Extensive Two-Person Games—Correction and Further Development. *Math. Soc. Sci.*, December 1988, *16*(3), pp. 223–66.

———— **and Uhlich, Gerald R.** Order of Strength and Exhaustivity as Additional Hypotheses in Theories for 3-Person Characteristic Function Games. In *Tietz, R.; Albers, W. and Selten, R., eds.*, 1988, pp. 235–50.

Selvanathan, E. Antony. Alcohol Consumption in the UK, 1955–85: A System-Wide Analysis. *Appl. Econ.*, August 1988, *20*(8), pp. 1071–86.

———— **and Clements, Kenneth W.** The Rotterdam Demand Model and Its Application in Marketing. *Marketing Sci.*, Winter 1988, *7*(1), pp. 60–75.

Semmler, Willi and Flaschel, Peter. On the Integration of Dual and Cross-Dual Adjustment

Processes in Leontief Systems. *Ricerche Econ.*, July–Sept. 1988, *42*(3), pp. 403–32.

Semudram, M. and Chye, Tan Eu. The Monetarist versus Neo-Keynesian Controversy over Inflation: The Malaysian Evidence. *Indian Econ. J.*, July–September 1988, *36*(1), pp. 48–54.

Semyonov, Moshe and Shenhav, Yehouda. Investment Dependence, Economic Development, and Female Employment Opportunities in Less Developed Countries. *Soc. Sci. Quart.*, December 1988, *69*(4), pp. 961–78.

Sen, Amartya K. Africa and India: What Do We Have to Learn from Each Other? In *Arrow, K. J.*, ed., 1988, pp. 105–37.

_____. Development: Which Way Now? In *Wilber, C. K.*, ed., 1988, pp. 37–58.

_____. Family and Food: Sex Bias in Poverty. In *Srinivasan, T. N. and Bardhan, P. K.*, eds., 1988, pp. 453–72.

_____. Freedom of Choice: Concept and Content. *Europ. Econ. Rev.*, March 1988, *32*(2–3), pp. 269–94.

_____. Property and Hunger. *Econ. Philos.*, April 1988, *4*(1), pp. 57–68.

_____. Sri Lanka's Achievements: How and When. In *Srinivasan, T. N. and Bardhan, P. K.*, eds., 1988, pp. 549–56.

Sen, Pranab Kumar. The Harmonic Gini Coefficient and Affluence Indexes. *Math. Soc. Sci.*, August 1988, *16*(1), pp. 65–76.

Sen, Sunanda. Contrasting External Debt Experience: Asia and Latin America: Comments. In *Streeten, P.*, ed., 1988, pp. 113–16.

Senauer, Benjamin; Garcia, Marito and Jacinto, Elizabeth. Determinants of the Intrahousehold Allocation of Food in the Rural Philippines. *Amer. J. Agr. Econ.*, February 1988, *70*(1), pp. 170–80.

Senbet, Lemma W. and Dammon, Robert M. The Effect of Taxes and Depreciation on Corporate Investment and Financial Leverage. *J. Finance*, June 1988, *43*(2), pp. 357–73.

_____ and **Haugen, Robert A.** Bankruptcy and Agency Costs: Their Significance to the Theory of Optimal Capital Structure. *J. Finan. Quant. Anal.*, March 1988, *23*(1), pp. 27–38.

Senchack, A. J., Jr. and Woodruff, Catherine S. Intradaily Price–Volume Adjustments of NYSE Stocks to Unexpected Earnings. *J. Finance*, June 1988, *43*(2), pp. 467–91.

Senchaudhuri, P.; Mehta, Cyrus R. and Patel, Nitin R. Exact Non-parametric Significance Tests. In *Edwards, D. and Raun, N. E.*, eds., 1988, pp. 227–32.

Senf, David R. Shift-Share Analysis of Rural Retail Trade Patterns. *Reg. Sci. Persp.*, 1988, *18*(2), pp. 29–43.

Sengupta, Abhijit. On a Criterion of Infinite-Horizon Efficiency. *J. Econ. Theory*, December 1988, *46*(2), pp. 409–13.

Sengupta, Arjun. A Proposal for a Debt-Adjustment Facility in the IMF. *World Econ.*, June 1988, *11*(2), pp. 165–85.

_____. What Is to Be Done with the Japanese Surplus? *Finance Develop.*, September 1988, *25*(3), pp. 24–27.

Sengupta, Jati K. The Active Approach of Stochastic Optimization with New Applications. In *Sengupta, J. K. and Kadekodi, G. K.*, eds., 1988, pp. 93–108.

_____. The Measurement of Productive Efficiency: A Robust Minimax Approach. *Managerial Dec. Econ.*, June 1988, *9*(2), pp. 153–61.

_____. Recent Nonparametric Measures of Productive Efficiency. In *Sengupta, J. K. and Kadekodi, G. K.*, eds., 1988, pp. 169–93.

_____. A Robust Approach to the Measurement of Farrell Efficiency. *Appl. Econ.*, February 1988, *20*(2), pp. 273–83.

_____; **Kadekodi, Gopal K. and Kumar, T. Krishna.** The Scientific Work of Gerhard Tintner. In *Sengupta, J. K. and Kadekodi, G. K.*, eds., 1988, pp. 3–22.

_____ and **Sfeir, Raymond E.** Efficiency Measurement by Data Envelopment Analysis with Econometric Applications. *Appl. Econ.*, March 1988, *20*(3), pp. 285–93.

Seninger, Stephen F. Labor Turnover and Employment Impacts in Regional Labor Markets. *Environ. Planning A*, January 1988, *20*(1), pp. 41–53.

_____ and **Reynolds, Stephen E.** Long-Run Determinants of the International Division of Labor. In *Mangum, G. and Philips, P.*, eds., 1988, pp. 249–73.

Senkow, David W.; Vigeland, Robert L. and Daley, Lane A. Analysts' Forecasts, Earnings Variability, and Option Pricing: Empirical Evidence. *Accounting Rev.*, October 1988, *63*(4), pp. 563–85.

Senn, S. J. and Davidson, S. Errors in Assessing the Demand for Inpatient Treatment. *Appl. Econ.*, March 1988, *20*(3), pp. 407–15.

Sensat, Julius. Methodological Individualism and Marxism. *Econ. Philos.*, October 1988, *4*(2), pp. 189–219.

Senses, Fikret. An Overview of Recent Turkish Experience with Economic Stabilization and Liberalization. In *Nas, T. F. and Odekon, M.*, eds., 1988, pp. 9–28.

Sentana Ivañez, Enrique. Nota sobre la inclusión en el sistema de precios en un modelo de Leontief de dos regimenes de imposición indirecta sobre el consumo. (With English summary.) *Invest. Ecón.*, January 1988, *12*(1), pp. 169–76.

Senti, R. Ein EFTA-EG-Freihandelsvertrag für Dienstleistungen Vorschlag eines Konzeptes. (A Trade Agreement of Services between EFTA- and EC-Countries. With English summary.) *Aussenwirtschaft*, September 1988, *43*(3), pp. 367–84.

Seo, Fumiko and Sakawa, Masatoshi. Evaluation of Telecommunication Systems with Multiple Criteria Decision Analysis: A Game Theoretic Approach. In *Orishimo, I.; Hewings, G. J. D. and Nijkamp, P.*, eds., 1988, pp. 214–36.

Seo, Tae Kun and Hadar, Josef. Asset Proportions in Optimal Portfolios. *Rev. Econ. Stud.*, July 1988, *55*(3), pp. 459–68.

Sephton, Peter S. The Impossible Dream: The IMF and Trend-Stationary Exchange Rates.

Atlantic Econ. J., December 1988, *16*(4), pp. 89.

_____. Money in the Production Function Revisited. *Appl. Econ.*, July 1988, *20*(7), pp. 853–60.

_____. On Interest Rate Innovations and Anticipated Monetary Policy. *Econ. Letters*, 1988, *28*(2), pp. 177–80.

_____. World Non-oil Primary Commodity Markets: Comment [A Medium-term Framework of Analysis]. *Int. Monet. Fund Staff Pap.*, March 1988, *35*(1), pp. 198–203.

Serbolisca, A. and Pirani, A. Information and Advisory Systems for the Farming Industry. In *Schiefer, G., ed.*, 1988, pp. 237–46.

Sergeev, Yaroslav D. and Strongin, Roman G. Effective Algorithm for Global Optimization with Parallel Computations. In *Kurzhanski, A.; Neumann, K. and Pallaschke, D., eds.*, 1988, pp. 158–62.

Serletis, Apostolos. The Empirical Relationship between Money, Prices, and Income Revisited. *J. Bus. Econ. Statist.*, July 1988, *6*(3), pp. 351–58.

_____. New Tests of the Theory of Optimal Seigniorage. *Econ. Letters*, 1988, *27*(4), pp. 361–65.

_____. Translog Flexible Functional Forms and Substitutability of Monetary Assets. *J. Bus. Econ. Statist.*, January 1988, *6*(1), pp. 59–67.

_____ and Atkins, Frank. The Low-Frequency Relationship between Money, Prices and Income. *Appl. Econ.*, July 1988, *20*(7), pp. 877–87.

_____ and Kumbhakar, Subal C. A Financial Theory of the Financial Firm. *J. Quant. Econ.*, July 1988, *4*(2), pp. 201–12.

Serow, William J.; Fournier, Gary M. and Rasmussen, David W. Elderly Migration as a Response to Economic Incentives. *Soc. Sci. Quart.*, June 1988, *69*(2), pp. 245–60.

_____; Fournier, Gary M. and Rasmussen, David W. Elderly Migration: For Sun and Money. *Population Res. Policy Rev.*, 1988, *7*(2), pp. 189–99.

Serra, Pablo. The Excess Utility Functions and the Welfare Adjustment Process. *Econ. Letters*, 1988, *26*(1), pp. 1–5.

Serra, Sérgio B. Brazil's Trade: A View from the South. In *Chacel, J. M.; Falk, P. S. and Fleischer, D. V., eds.*, 1988, pp. 89–94.

Serrano, Claudia and Raczynski, Dagmar. Planificación para el desarrollo local? La experiencia en algunos municipios de Santiago. (Planning for Local Development? The Experience of Some Municipalities in Santiago. With English summary.) *Colección Estud. CIEPLAN*, June 1988, (24), pp. 37–62.

Sertel, Murat R. Characterizing Approval Voting [Axioms for Approval Voting: Direct Proof]. *J. Econ. Theory*, June 1988, *45*(1), pp. 207–11.

_____. Characterizing Fidelity for Reflexive Choices. *Math. Soc. Sci.*, February 1988, *15*(1), pp. 93–95.

_____. Choice, Hull, Continuity and Fidelity:

Note. *Math. Soc. Sci.*, October 1988, *16*(2), pp. 203–06.

_____. A Non-Dictatorial Compromise. *Soc. Choice Welfare*, 1988, *5*(1), pp. 19–29.

_____. Regulation by Participation. *J. Econ. (Z. Nationalökon.)*, 1988, *48*(2), pp. 111–34.

Seshamani, V. Industrial Development in Zambia: Retrospect and Prospect. In *Coughlin, P. and Ikiara, G. K., eds.*, 1988, pp. 51–70.

Seskin, Eugene P. and Sullivan, David F. Plant and Equipment Expenditures, First and Second Quarters and Second Half of 1988. *Surv. Curr. Bus.*, April 1988, *68*(4), pp. 26–30.

_____ and Sullivan, David F. Plant and Equipment Expenditures, the Four Quarters of 1988. *Surv. Curr. Bus.*, September 1988, *68*(9), pp. 18–20.

_____ and Sullivan, David F. Plant and Equipment Expenditures, the Four Quarters of 1988. *Surv. Curr. Bus.*, June 1988, *68*(6), pp. 19–22.

Sesnowitz, Michael L. The Returns to Burglary. In *Alper, N. O. and Hellman, D. A., eds.*, 1988, pp. 143–49.

_____ and Raymond, Richard D. The Impact of Sex and Attitudes upon the Earnings of College Graduates. *Eastern Econ. J.*, April–June 1988, *14*(2), pp. 167–79.

_____; Williams, Donald R. and Raymond, Richard D. Does Sex Still Matter? New Evidence from the 1980s. *Econ. Inquiry*, January 1988, *26*(1), pp. 43–58.

Sessions, David N. and Stevans, Lonnie K. The Derivation of an Implicit Weighting Scheme for Economic Goals and Policies: 1953–1981. *J. Post Keynesian Econ.*, Fall 1988, *11*(1), pp. 26–37.

Sestakupt, Pharadorn; Kultravut, Sunee and Akrasanee, Narongchai. Technical Efficiency and Production Management: The Thai Experience. In *James, K. and Akrasanee, N., eds.*, 1988, pp. 164–207.

Setboonsarng, Suthad and Roumasset, James. Second-Best Agricultural Policy: Getting the Price of Thai Rice Right. *J. Devel. Econ.*, May 1988, *28*(3), pp. 323–40.

Sethi, S. Prakash and Bes, C. Dynamic Stochastic Optimization Problems in the Framework of Forecast and Decision Horizons. In *Eiselt, H. A. and Pederzoli, G., eds.*, 1988, pp. 230–46.

_____ and Steidlmeier, Paul. A New Paradigm of the Business/Society Relationship in the Third World: The Challenge of Liberation Theology. In *Preston, L. E., ed.*, 1988, pp. 29–43.

Sethi, Suresh P. and Taksar, Michael. A Note on Merton's "Optimum Consumption and Portfolio Rules in a Continuous-Time Model." *J. Econ. Theory*, December 1988, *46*(2), pp. 395–401.

Sethness, Charles O. Capital Market Development. *Finance Develop.*, December 1988, *25*(4), pp. 32–33.

Sethuraman, T. V.; Jog, S. D. and Khaled, S. M. Market Saturation in Indian Conditions:

Cement Industry: A Case Study. *Indian Econ. J.*, Jan.–March 1988, *35*(3), pp. 39–46.

Settle, John W. and Petry, Glenn H. A Comprehensive Analysis of Worldwide Scholarly Productivity in Selected U.S. Business Journals. *Quart. Rev. Econ. Bus.*, Autumn 1988, *28*(3), pp. 88–104.

_____; **Petry, Glenn H. and Fitzpatrick, Dennis B.** An Empirical Examination of Rate of Return Regulation in the Electric Utility Industry: 1971–1982. *J. Econ. Bus.*, February 1988, *40*(1), pp. 27–44.

Setubal Filho, Laerte. Private Sector Connection to Development. In *Chacel, J. M.; Falk, P. S. and Fleischer, D. V., eds.*, 1988, pp. 83–85.

Setubal, Olavo Egydio. Brazil's Foreign Policy in the New Republic. In *Chacel, J. M.; Falk, P. S. and Fleischer, D. V., eds.*, 1988, pp. 240–46.

Sevareid, Eric. Ellis Island: The Building of a Heritage. In *Simcox, D. E., ed.*, 1988, *1986*, pp. 119–23.

Severin, Barbara. The USSR: The Livestock Feed Issue. In *Brada, J. C. and Wadekin, K.-E., eds.*, 1988, pp. 344–60.

Sevón, Guje. Det mänskliga kapitalet. (Human Capital. With English summary.) *Ekon. Samfundets Tidskr.*, 1988, *41*(1), pp. 49–54.

_____. Rationalization of Action through Value Development. In *Maital, S., ed., Vol. 1*, 1988, pp. 412–19.

_____; **Lindqvist, Lars-Johan and Paltschik, Mikael.** Consumers' and Producers' Basic Evaluation—An Investigation of Objects in the Field of Music. *Liiketaloudellinen Aikak.*, 1988, *37*(3), pp. 193–211.

_____ **and March, James G.** Behavioral Perspectives on Theories of the Firm. In *van Raaij, W. F.; van Veldhoven, G. M. and Wärneryd, K.-E., eds.*, 1988, pp. 369–402.

_____ **and March, James G.** Gossip, Information and Decision-Making. In *March, J. G.*, 1988, *1984*, pp. 429–42.

Seward, J. Allen and Ambrose, Jan Mills. Best's Ratings, Financial Ratios and Prior Probabilities in Insolvency Prediction. *J. Risk Ins.*, June 1988, *55*(2), pp. 229–44.

Sewell, John W. The Dual Challenge: Managing the Economic Crisis and Technological Change. In *Sewell, J. W. and Tucker, S. K., eds.*, 1988, pp. 3–43.

_____. Strengthening the Poor: What Have We Learned? Foreword. In *Lewis, J. P., et al.*, 1988, pp. ix–xiii.

Sewell, W. R. Derrick and Parker, Dennis J. Evolving Water Institutions in England and Wales: An Assessment of Two Decades of Experience. *Natural Res. J.*, Fall 1988, *28*(4), pp. 751–85.

Sewell, William H., Jr. Uneven Development, the Autonomy of Politics, and the Dockworkers of Nineteenth-Century Marseille. *Amer. Hist. Rev.*, June 1988, *93*(3), pp. 604–37.

Sexton, Robert L. and Lee, Dwight R. A Pollution Control Approach to Analysis of the Bal-

anced Budget Amendment. *Amer. J. Econ. Soc.*, October 1988, *47*(4), pp. 423–26.

_____; **Lee, Dwight R. and Graves, Peter E.** On Mandatory Deposits, Fines, and the Control of Litter. *Natural Res. J.*, Fall 1988, *28*(4), pp. 837–47.

Sexton, Thomas R. and Zilz, Ulrike. On the Wisdom of Mandatory Drug Testing. *J. Policy Anal. Manage.*, Spring 1988, *7*(3), pp. 542–47.

Seyfried, Manfred. Productivity Growth and Technical Change. In *Ciaschini, M., ed.*, 1988, pp. 167–78.

Seyhun, H. Nejat. The Information Content of Aggregate Insider Trading. *J. Bus.*, January 1988, *61*(1), pp. 1–24.

_____. The January Effect and Aggregate Insider Trading. *J. Finance*, March 1988, *43*(1), pp. 129–41.

Seymour, Ian. OPEC at the Crossroads. In *Mabro, R., ed.*, 1988, pp. 119–25.

Sfeir, Raymond E. and Sengupta, Jati K. Efficiency Measurement by Data Envelopment Analysis with Econometric Applications. *Appl. Econ.*, March 1988, *20*(3), pp. 285–93.

Shaaeldin, Elfatih. Sources of Industrial Growth in Kenya, Tanzania, Zambia and Zimbabwe. *Eastern Afr. Econ. Rev.*, December 1988, *4*(2), pp. 21–31.

Shaanan, Joseph. Welfare and Barriers to Entry: An Empirical Study. *Southern Econ. J.*, January 1988, *54*(3), pp. 746–62.

Shachar, Arie and Felsenstein, Daniel. Locational and Organizational Determinants of R&D Employment in High Technology Firms. *Reg. Stud.*, December 1988, *22*(6), pp. 477–86.

Shackle, G. L. S. Elasticities of Surprise in the Concept of Policy. In *[Frowen, S.]*, 1988, pp. 1–6.

Shadid, Mohammed K. Israeli Policy towards Economic Development in the West Bank and Gaza. In *Abed, G. T., ed.*, 1988, pp. 121–37.

Shafer, Glenn. Conceptions of Choice: Savage Revisited. In *Bell, D. E.; Raiffa, H. and Tversky, A., eds.*, 1988, *1986*, pp. 193–234.

_____ **and Tversky, Amos.** Languages and Designs for Probability Judgment. In *Bell, D. E.; Raiffa, H. and Tversky, A., eds.*, 1988, *1985*, pp. 237–65.

Shafer, Jeffrey R. What the U.S. Current-Account Deficit of the 1980s Has Meant for Other OECD Countries. *OECD Econ. Stud.*, Spring 1988, (10), pp. 149–84.

Shaffer, Ron E. Reflections and Directions. In *Johnson, T. G.; Deaton, B. J. and Segarra, E., eds.*, 1988, pp. 229–32.

_____; **Pulver, Glen C. and Rogers, Glenn.** Identification of Local Capital Markets for Policy Research. *Rev. Reg. Stud.*, Winter 1988, *18*(1), pp. 55–66.

Shaffer, Sherrill. Competitive Rationing. *Atlantic Econ. J.*, March 1988, *16*(1), pp. 97.

_____. Regulatory Control over Quantity Risk. *Australian Econ. Pap.*, December 1988, *27*(51), pp. 247–52.

Shaffner, F. I. and Garcia-Mata, C. Solar and

Economic Relationships: A Preliminary Report. In *Wood, J. C., ed., Vol. 3*, 1988, *1934*, pp. 15–54.

Shah, Anup and Desai, Meghnad. An Econometric Approach to the Measurement of Poverty. *Oxford Econ. Pap.*, September 1988, *40*(3), pp. 505–22.

Shah, Anwar Chaudry. An Empirical Analysis of Public Transit Subsidies in Canada. In *Brown, R. C., ed.*, 1988, pp. 15–25.

_____. Optimal Pricing of Externalities for Environmental Protection. In *Brown, R. C., ed.*, 1988, pp. 27–37.

Shah, Salman and Thakor, Anjan V. Private versus Public Ownership: Investment, Ownership Distribution, and Optimality. *J. Finance*, March 1988, *43*(1), pp. 41–59.

Shahidi, Hushang and Fichtenbaum, Rudy. Truncation Bias and the Measurement of Income Inequality. *J. Bus. Econ. Statist.*, July 1988, *6*(3), pp. 335–37.

Shaked, Avner; Sutton, John and Binmore, Ken G. A Further Test of Noncooperative Bargaining Theory: Reply. *Amer. Econ. Rev.*, September 1988, *78*(4), pp. 837–39.

Shalaby, Seif; Yanagida, John F. and Hassler, James B. United States Market Share of Latin American Wheat Imports: Disaggregated Analysis and Application of the Armington Model. *J. Econ. Stud.*, 1988, *15*(5), pp. 24–33.

Shaman, Paul and Stine, Robert A. The Bias of Autoregressive Coefficient Estimators. *J. Amer. Statist. Assoc.*, September 1988, *83*(403), pp. 842–48.

Shamanna, K. Developing People in Small Industry. In *Kohli, U. and Gautam, V., eds.*, 1988, pp. 196–200.

Shammas, Carole. The Food Budget of English Workers: A Reply [Food Expenditures and Economic Well-Being on Early Modern England]. *J. Econ. Hist.*, September 1988, *48*(3), pp. 673–76.

Shan, Pu. The Debt Problem of Developing Countries and Proposed Solutions: Comments. In *Elliott, K. A. and Williamson, J., eds.*, 1988, pp. 187–90.

Shand, R. T. and Kalirajan, K. P. Firm and Product-Specific Technical Efficiencies in a Multiproduct Cycle System. *J. Devel. Stud.*, October 1988, *25*(1), pp. 83–96.

_____ and Kalirajan, K. P. Multi-output Self Dual Profit Function and Factor Demand Equations: Primal with Constraints on Inputs. *J. Quant. Econ.*, July 1988, *4*(2), pp. 261–78.

Shandler, Bruce; Green, Paul E. and Helsen, Kristiaan. Conjoint Internal Validity under Alternative Profile Presentations. *J. Cons. Res.*, December 1988, *15*(3), pp. 392–97.

Shank, Susan E. Women and the Labor Market: The Link Grows Stronger. *Mon. Lab. Rev.*, March 1988, *111*(3), pp. 3–8.

Shankle, S. A. and Reilly, John M. Auxiliary Heating in the Residential Sector. *Energy Econ.*, January 1988, *10*(1), pp. 29–41.

Shanmugam, Ramalingam and Nevalainen, Kari. Analyzing Environmental Time Series: A Review and Finnish Case Study. *Statist. J.*, November 1988, *5*(3), pp. 315–38.

Shapira, Zur and Friedman, Abraham. Expert and Amateur Inflation Expectations. In *Maital, S., ed., Vol. 1*, 1988, pp. 335–41.

_____ and March, James G. Managerial Perspectives on Risk and Risk-Taking. In *March, J. G.*, 1988, *1987*, pp. 76–97.

Shapiro, Aharon H. Moses—Henry George's Inspiration. *Amer. J. Econ. Soc.*, October 1988, *47*(4), pp. 493–501.

Shapiro, Carl and Farrell, Joseph. Dynamic Competition with Switching Costs. *Rand J. Econ.*, Spring 1988, *19*(1), pp. 123–37.

_____ and Grossman, Gene M. Counterfeit-Product Trade. *Amer. Econ. Rev.*, March 1988, *78*(1), pp. 59–75.

_____ and Grossman, Gene M. Foreign Counterfeiting of Status Goods. *Quart. J. Econ.*, February 1988, *103*(1), pp. 79–100.

Shapiro, D. M. and Khemani, R. S. On Entry and Mobility Barriers. *Antitrust Bull.*, Spring 1988, *33*(1), pp. 115–34.

Shapiro, Edward. The Textbook Consumption Function: A Recent Empirical Irregularity, A Note. *Amer. Econ.*, Spring 1988, *32*(1), pp. 74–77.

Shapiro, Matthew D. Political vs. Currency Premia in International Real Interest Rate Differentials: Comments. *Europ. Econ. Rev.*, June 1988, *32*(5), pp. 1114–18.

_____. The Stabilization of the U. S. Economy: Evidence from the Stock Market. *Amer. Econ. Rev.*, December 1988, *78*(5), pp. 1067–79.

_____; Dominguez, Kathryn M. and Fair, Ray C. Forecasting the Depression: Harvard versus Yale. *Amer. Econ. Rev.*, September 1988, *78*(4), pp. 595–612.

Shapiro, Perry and Fischel, William A. Takings, Insurance, and Michelman: Comments on Economic Interpretations of "Just Compensation" Law. *J. Legal Stud.*, June 1988, *17*(2), pp. 269–93.

Shapley, Lloyd S. Utility Comparison and the Theory of Games. In *[Shapley, L. S.]*, 1988, *1969*, pp. 307–19.

_____. A Value for *n*-Person Games. In *[Shapley, L. S.]*, 1988, *1953*, pp. 31–40.

_____ and Shubik, Martin. A Method for Evaluating the Distribution of Power in a Committee System. In *[Shapley, L. S.]*, 1988, *1954*, pp. 41–48.

Sharda, Ramesh and Willett, Keith D. Competing Demands for Water Resources: A Dynamic Joint Maximization Model. *Resources & Energy*, June 1988, *10*(2), pp. 135–59.

_____ and Willett, Keith D. A Dynamic Multimarket Equilibrium Model for the Economic Analysis of Pollution Control Policies. *Environ. Planning A*, March 1988, *20*(3), pp. 391–405.

Sharif, Mohammed; Bhandari, Labdhi and Dholakia, Ruby Roy. Consumption in the Third World: Challenges for Marketing and Development. In *Kumcu, E. and Firat, A. F., eds.*, 1988, pp. 129–47.

Sharir, Shmuel. Does Evidence on Wage Elasticities Contradict the Two Interpretations of Labor-Force Participation Rates? In *Missouri Valley Economic Assoc.*, 1988, pp. 64–70.

Sharma, B. M. and Aradhyula, Satheesh V. Farming Systems: Income Potential and Credit Requirements of Non-viable Farmers in Pithapuram Block, India. *J. Econ. Devel.*, June 1988, *13*(1), pp. 21–37.

Sharma, H. R.; Oberoi, R. C. and Singh, Kamlesh. Rural Farm Size and Inequality: A Case Study. *Margin*, Jan.–March 1988, *20*(2), pp. 47–53.

Sharma, K. L. Economic Interactions between Agriculture and the Non-farm Sectors in Kenya. *Eastern Afr. Econ. Rev.*, June 1988, *4*(1), pp. 12–17.

Sharp, Ansel M.; Stevans, Lonnie K. and Register, Charles A. Profit Incentives and the Hospital Industry: New Evidence. *Atlantic Econ. J.*, March 1988, *16*(1), pp. 25–38.

Sharp, C. Developments in Transport Policy: United Kingdom. *J. Transp. Econ. Policy*, May 1988, *22*(2), pp. 235–38.

Sharp, Keith P. Tests of U.S. Short and Long Interest Rate Seasonality. *Rev. Econ. Statist.*, February 1988, *70*(1), pp. 177–82.

Sharp, Philip R. A Practical Energy Policy for the 1990s. In *Fried, E. R. and Blandin, N. M., eds.*, 1988, pp. 87–97.

Sharpe, Ian G.; Gross, E. and Hogan, Warren P. Market Information and Potential Insolvency of Australian Financial Institutions. *Australian Econ. Pap.*, June 1988, *27*(50), pp. 44–64.

Shastri, Kuldeep; Choi, J. Y. and Salandro, Dan. On the Estimation of Bid–Ask Spreads: Theory and Evidence. *J. Finan. Quant. Anal.*, June 1988, *23*(2), pp. 219–30.

_____ **and Jayaraman, Narayanan.** The Valuation Impacts of Specially Designated Dividends. *J. Finan. Quant. Anal.*, September 1988, *23*(3), pp. 301–12.

Shavell, Steven. Legal Advice about Contemplated Acts: The Decision to Obtain Advice, Its Social Desirability, and Protection of Confidentiality. *J. Legal Stud.*, January 1988, *17*(1), pp. 123–50.

Shaw, Annapurna. The Income Security Function of the Rural Sector: The Case of Calcutta, India. *Econ. Develop. Cult. Change*, January 1988, *36*(2), pp. 303–14.

Shaw, Daigee. On-Site Samples' Regression: Problems of Non-negative Integers, Truncation, and Endogenous Stratification. *J. Econometrics*, February 1988, *37*(2), pp. 211–23.

Shaw, Daniel J. and Ferris, J. Stephen. Measurement Costs, Relative Evaluation and Mandatory Education Requirements. *Australian Econ. Pap.*, December 1988, *27*(51), pp. 233–46.

Shaw, Dayna S. Turnovers and the Male–Female Differential in Secondary School Teachers. In *Pennsylvania Economic Association*, 1988, pp. 548–59.

Shaw, G. B. The Jevonian Criticism of Marx (A Comment on the Rev. P. H. Wicksteed's Article). In *Wood, J. C., ed., Vol. 2*, 1988, *1885*, pp. 100–105.

Shaw, G. K. Revenue Implications of Trade Taxes. In *Greenaway, D., ed.*, 1988, pp. 174–87.

Shaw, Gareth; Greenwood, Justin and Williams, Allan M. The United Kingdom: Market Responses and Public Policy. In *Williams, A. M. and Shaw, G., eds.*, 1988, pp. 162–79.

_____ **and Williams, Allan M.** Tourism and Development: Introduction. In *Williams, A. M. and Shaw, G., eds.*, 1988, pp. 1–11.

_____ **and Williams, Allan M.** Tourism Policies in a Changing Economic Environment. In *Williams, A. M. and Shaw, G., eds.*, 1988, pp. 230–39.

_____ **and Williams, Allan M.** Western European Tourism in Perspective. In *Williams, A. M. and Shaw, G., eds.*, 1988, pp. 12–38.

Shaw, Kathryn and Montgomery, Edward. The Real Wage–Employment Relationship: An Industry Analysis. *Econ. Letters*, 1988, *26*(3), pp. 241–46.

Shaw, Lois B. and Dex, Shirley. Women's Working Lives: A Comparison of Women in the United States and Great Britain. In *Hunt, A., ed.*, 1988, pp. 173–95.

Shaw, R. W. and Lowe, E. A. An Analysis of Managerial Biasing: Evidence from a Company's Budgeting Process. In *Earl, P. E., ed., Vol. 1*, 1988, *1968*, pp. 366–77.

Shaw, Timothy M. and Carlsson, Jerker. Newly Industrializing Countries and South–South: Concepts, Correlates, Controversies and Cases. In *Carlsson, J. and Shaw, T. M., eds.*, 1988, pp. 1–22.

_____ **and Ihonvbere, Julius O.** Petroleum Proletariat: Nigerian Oil Workers in Contextual and Comparative Perspective. In *Southall, R., ed.*, 1988, pp. 80–108.

Shaw, Wayne H. Measuring the Impact of the Safe Harbor Lease Law on Security Prices. *J. Acc. Res.*, Spring 1988, *26*(1), pp. 60–81.

_____ **and Elliott, John A.** Write-Offs as Accounting Procedures to Manage Perceptions. *J. Acc. Res.*, Supplement, 1988, *26*, pp. 91–119.

_____ **and Morse, Dale.** Investing in Bankrupt Firms. *J. Finance*, December 1988, *43*(5), pp. 1193–1206.

Shearer, Michael. Loss of Strict Hyperbolicity of the Buckley-Leverett Equations for Three Phase Flow in a Porous Medium. In *Wheeler, M. F., ed.*, 1988, pp. 263–83.

Shechter, Mordechai. Incorporating Anxiety Induced by Environmental Episodes in Life Valuation. In *Maital, S., ed., Vol. 2*, 1988, pp. 529–36.

Sheehan, Dennis P. and Holderness, Clifford G. The Role of Majority Shareholders in Publicly Held Corporations: An Exploratory Analysis. *J. Finan. Econ.*, Jan.–March 1988, *20*(1–2), pp. 317–46.

Sheehan, Michael F. Corporate Control and the Decapitalization of Subsidiary Corporations: The Looting of the Bangor and Aroostook Railroad. *J. Econ. Issues*, September 1988, 22(3), pp. 729–45.

_____. Institutionalists before Regulatory Commissions: The Value of Doing in Thinking, Teaching, and Writing. *J. Econ. Issues*, December 1988, 22(4), pp. 1169–78.

Sheehan, Richard G.; Ahmed, Ehsan and Rosser, J. Barkley, Jr. A Global Model of OECD Aggregate Supply and Demand Using Vector Autoregressive Techniques. *Europ. Econ. Rev.*, November 1988, 32(9), pp. 1711–29.

_____; **Belongia, Michael T. and Hafer, R. W.** On the Temporal Stability of the Interest Rate–Weekly Money Relationship. *Rev. Econ. Statist.*, August 1988, 70(3), pp. 516–20.

_____ **and Grieves, R.** Sunspots and Cycles: A Test of Causation. In *Wood, J. C., ed., Vol. 3, 1988, 1978*, pp. 189–92.

Sheen, Jeff R.; Wyplosz, Charles and Giavazzi, Francesco. The Real Exchange Rate and the Fiscal Aspects of a Natural Resource Discovery. *Oxford Econ. Pap.*, September 1988, 40(3), pp. 427–50.

Sheets, Robert G.; Nord, Stephen and Phelps, John J. An Analysis of the Economic Impact of the Service Sector on Underemployment in Major Metropolitan Areas in the United States. *Urban Stud.*, October 1988, 25(5), pp. 418–32.

Sheffrin, Steven M. Have Economic Fluctuations Been Dampened? A Look at Evidence Outside the United States. *J. Monet. Econ.*, January 1988, 21(1), pp. 73–83.

Shefrin, Hersh M. and Heineke, John M. Exact Aggregation and the Finite Basis Property. *Int. Econ. Rev.*, August 1988, 29(3), pp. 525–38.

_____ **and Milne, Frank.** *Ex Post* Efficiency and *Ex Post* Welfare: Some Fundamental Considerations. *Economica*, February 1988, 55(217), pp. 63–79.

_____ **and Thaler, Richard H.** The Behavioral Life-Cycle Hypothesis. *Econ. Inquiry*, October 1988, 26(4), pp. 609–43.

Sheikh, Khalid Hameed and Iqbal, Zafar. Determinants of the Declining Share of Agricultural Labour Force to Total Labour Force in Pakistan. *Pakistan Devel. Rev.*, Part 2, Winter 1988, 27(4), pp. 561–65.

Sheikh, Mohammad Amjad and Butt, Abdul Rauf. An Analysis of Gap between Demand for and Supply of Higher Education in Pakistan. *Pakistan Econ. Soc. Rev.*, Summer 1988, 26(1), pp. 41–55.

Sheldon, George. Qualitative Ungleichgewichte auf dem Schweizer Arbeitsmarkt. (Qualitative Imbalances in the Swiss Labor Market. With English summary.) *Schweiz. Z. Volkswirtsch. Statist.*, September 1988, 124(3), pp. 259–75.

_____. Reductions in Hours and Employment: What Do Union Models Tell Us?: Comment. In *Hart, R. A., ed., 1988*, pp. 158–61.

_____; **Kugler, Peter and Müller, Urs.** Struktur der Arbeitsnachfrage im technologischen Wandel—Eine empirische Analyse für die Bundesrepublik Deutschland. (With English sum-

mary.) *Weltwirtsch. Arch.*, 1988, 124(3), pp. 490–500.

Sheldon, Robert J. and Kroes, Eric P. Stated Preference Methods. *J. Transp. Econ. Policy*, January 1988, 22(1), pp. 11–25.

Shelly, Michael A. and Main, Brian G. M. School Leavers and the Search for Employment. *Oxford Econ. Pap.*, September 1988, 40(3), pp. 487–504.

Shen, Longhai. External Cooperation in the Development of China's Energy Technology. In *Dorian, J. P. and Fridley, D. G., eds., 1988*, pp. 137–41.

Shen, T. Y. New Institutionalism and the Erosion of Capitalism. *J. Behav. Econ.*, Fall 1988, 17(3), pp. 207–18.

Sheng, Andrew. Financial Opening in Malaysia. In *Urrutia, M., ed., 1988*, pp. 172–79.

_____. South–South Monetary Arrangements in the Balance. In *Sopiee, N.; Hamzah, B. A. and Leong, C. H., eds., 1988, 1986*, pp. 233–42.

Shenhav, Yehouda and Semyonov, Moshe. Investment Dependence, Economic Development, and Female Employment Opportunities in Less Developed Countries. *Soc. Sci. Quart.*, December 1988, 69(4), pp. 961–78.

Shepard, Donald S. and Benjamin, Elisabeth R. User Fees and Health Financing in Developing Countries: Mobilizing Financial Resources for Health. In *Bell, D. E. and Reich, M. R., eds., 1988*, pp. 401–24.

Shepherd, Andrew. Case Studies of Famine: Sudan. In *Curtis, D.; Hubbard, M. and Shepherd, A., 1988*, pp. 28–72.

_____; **Curtis, Donald and Hubbard, Michael.** Famine and the National and International Economy. In *Curtis, D.; Hubbard, M. and Shepherd, A., 1988*, pp. 11–27.

Shepherd, John and Congdon, Peter Douglas. Components of Social Change in Urban Areas. *Urban Stud.*, June 1988, 25(3), pp. 173–89.

Shepherd, William G. Competition, Contestability, and Transport Mergers. *Int. J. Transport Econ.*, June 1988, 15(2), pp. 113–28.

_____. Public Enterprise: Criteria and Cases. In *de Jong, H. W., ed., 1988*, pp. 355–88.

_____. Self-interest and National Security. *Amer. Econ. Rev.*, May 1988, 78(2), pp. 50–54.

_____. Three "Efficiency School" Hypotheses about Market Power. *Antitrust Bull.*, Summer 1988, 33(2), pp. 395–415.

Sheppard, Blair H.; Hartwick, Jon and Warshaw, Paul R. The Theory of Reasoned Action: A Meta-analysis of Past Research with Recommendations for Modifications and Future Research. *J. Cons. Res.*, December 1988, 15(3), pp. 325–43.

Sheppard, Stephen. The Qualitative Economics of Development Control. *J. Urban Econ.*, November 1988, 24(3), pp. 310–30.

Sherer, Peter D. and Cappelli, Peter. Satisfaction, Market Wages, and Labor Relations: An Airline Study. *Ind. Relat.*, Winter 1988, 27(1), pp. 57–73.

_____ **and Kahn, Lawrence M.** Racial Differences in Professional Basketball Players' Compensation. *J. Lab. Econ.*, January 1988, 6(1), pp. 40–61.

Shergold, Peter R. and Juravich, Tom. The Impact of Unions on the Voting Behavior of Their Members. *Ind. Lab. Relat. Rev.*, April 1988, 41(3), pp. 374–85.

_____ **and Nicholas, Stephen.** Convicts as Migrants. In *Nicholas, S., ed.*, 1988, pp. 43–61.

_____ **and Nicholas, Stephen.** Convicts as Workers. In *Nicholas, S., ed.*, 1988, pp. 62–84.

_____ **and Nicholas, Stephen.** A Labour Aristocracy in Chains. In *Nicholas, S., ed.*, 1988, pp. 98–108.

_____ **and Nicholas, Stephen.** Transportation as Global Migration. In *Nicholas, S., ed.*, 1988, pp. 28–39.

_____ **and Nicholas, Stephen.** Unshackling the Past. In *Nicholas, S., ed.*, 1988, pp. 3–13.

Sheridan, John E. and Peters, Lawrence H. Turnover Research Methodology: A Critique of Traditional Designs and a Suggested Survival Model Alternative. In *Ferris, G. R. and Rowland, K. M., eds.*, 1988, pp. 231–62.

Sherman, Ethel C. Your Attitude Is Your Altitude. In *Timpe, A. D., ed.*, 1988, 1985, pp. 319–23.

Sherman, H. A. and Gillespie, Thomas S. Recognition of Foreign Enterprises as Taxable Entities: Canada. In *International Fiscal Association, ed. (I)*, 1988, pp. 331–46.

Sherman, Howard J. Profit Squeeze in Marx, Keynes, Mitchell, and Kalecki. *Rev. Radical Polit. Econ.*, Summer–Fall 1988, 20(2–3), pp. 94–99.

Sherman, Roger and Feinberg, Robert M. Mutual Forbearance under Experimental Conditions. *Southern Econ. J.*, April 1988, 54(4), pp. 985–93.

Sherman, Sally R. Commentary: Survey Research in Social Security. *Soc. Sec. Bull.*, March 1988, 51(3), pp. 8.

Sherrick, Bruce J.; Irwin, Scott H. and Forster, D. Lynn. Returns to Farm Real Estate Revisited. *Amer. J. Agr. Econ.*, August 1988, 70(3), pp. 580–87.

Sherry, John F., Jr.; Wallendorf, Melanie and Belk, Russell W. A Naturalistic Inquiry into Buyer and Seller Behavior at a Swap Meet. *J. Cons. Res.*, March 1988, 14(4), pp. 449–70.

Sherwood-Call, Carolyn. Exploring the Relationships between National and Regional Economic Fluctuations. *Fed. Res. Bank San Cisco Econ. Rev.*, Summer 1988, (3), pp. 15–25.

Sheshinski, Eytan. Earnings Uncertainty and Intergenerational Transfers. In *Helpman, E.; Razin, A. and Sadka, E., eds.*, 1988, pp. 77–90.

_____. The Optimal Linear Income-Tax. In *Ricketts, M., ed., Vol. 2*, 1988, 1972, pp. 165–70.

Sheth, Jagdish N. and Gross, Barbara L. Parallel Development of Marketing and Consumer Behavior: A Historical Perspective. In *[Hollander, S. C.]*, 1988, pp. 9–33.

Shetty, Sudhir. Limited Liability, Wealth Differences and Tenancy Contracts in Agrarian Econ-

omies. *J. Devel. Econ.*, July 1988, 29(1), pp. 1–22.

Shi, Shou Yong. Rational Expectation Equilibrium under Quasilinear Preferences: A Diagrammatic Approach. *Econ. Letters*, 1988, 26(2), pp. 107–10.

_____. Rothschild–Stiglitz Competitive Insurance Market under Quasilinear Preferences. *Econ. Letters*, 1988, 27(1), pp. 27–30.

Shiba, Tsunemasa and Tsurumi, Hiroki. Bayesian and Non-Bayesian Tests of Independence in Seemingly Unrelated Regressions. *Int. Econ. Rev.*, May 1988, 29(2), pp. 377–95.

Shibata, Hirofumi. Merit Goods and Public Choice: The Case of Higher Education—Comment. *Public Finance*, 1988, 43(3), pp. 466–70.

Shieh, Yeung-Nan. A General Equilibrium Model of Multinational Corporations in Developing Economies: A Further Analysis. *Oxford Econ. Pap.*, June 1988, 40(2), pp. 390–91.

_____. Variable Transportation Rates and the Profit-Maximization Location Theory of the Firm. *Urban Stud.*, August 1988, 25(4), pp. 341–47.

_____ **and Bostaph, S.** W. S. Jevons and Lardner's 'Railway Economy' In *Wood, J. C., ed., Vol. 3*, 1988, 1986, pp. 316–32.

_____ **and Pace, Kelley.** The Moses–Predohl Pull and the Location Decision of the Firm [On Sufficient Conditions for Interior Location in the Triangle Space: A Comment]. *J. Reg. Sci.*, February 1988, 28(1), pp. 121–26.

_____; **Williams, Nancy A. and Gilley, Otis W.** Transportation Rates and Location of the Firm: A Comparative Static Analysis. *J. Reg. Sci.*, May 1988, 28(2), pp. 231–38.

Shields, Dan and Curtin, Chris. Competition and Control at Work: Rural Miners and the Labour Process. *Econ. Soc. Rev.*, April 1988, 19(3), pp. 159–76.

Shields, Gail M. and Shields, Michael P. Families, Migration and Adjusting to Disequilibrium. *Econ. Letters*, 1988, 26(4), pp. 387–92.

Shields, Michael P. and Shields, Gail M. Families, Migration and Adjusting to Disequilibrium. *Econ. Letters*, 1988, 26(4), pp. 387–92.

Shields, Roger E. Aspects of Current International Debt Problems: Is the Problem Insolvency or Illiquidity? In *[Nutter, G. W.]*, 1988, pp. 175–88.

Shiells, Clinton R. and Halm, Glenn. Damage Control: Yen Appreciation and the Japanese Labor Market. *Mon. Lab. Rev.*, November 1988, 111(11), pp. 3–6.

Shih, Jun-ji; Mai, Chao-cheng and Liu, Jung-chao. A General Analysis of the Output Effect under Third-Degree Price Discrimination. *Econ. J.*, March 1988, 98(389), pp. 149–58.

Shih, Y.C. and Chou, W. L. Trade, Determinants, and Causality: A Case of Hong Kong's Exports to the United States. *Int. Econ. J.*, Winter 1988, 2(4), pp. 21–33.

Shih, Yuan-kang. Conflict, Contract, and the

Principles of Justice. In *Liu, S. and Allinson, R. E., eds.*, 1988, pp. 69–88.

Shiller, Robert J. Causes of Changing Financial Market Volatility. In *Federal Reserve Bank of Kansas City*, 1988, pp. 1–22.

_____. Fashions, Fads, and Bubbles in Financial Markets. In *Coffee, J. C., Jr.; Lowenstein, L. and Rose-Ackerman, S., eds.*, 1988, pp. 56–68.

_____. The Probability of Gross Violations of a Present Value Variance Inequality. *J. Polit. Econ.*, October 1988, 96(5), pp. 1089–92.

_____ **and Campbell, John Y.** Interpreting Cointegrated Models. *J. Econ. Dynam. Control*, June–Sept. 1988, 12(2–3), pp. 505–22.

_____ **and Campbell, John Y.** Stock Prices, Earnings, and Expected Dividends. *J. Finance*, July 1988, 43(3), pp. 661–76.

_____ **and Case, Karl E.** The Behavior of Home Buyers in Boom and Post-boom Markets. *New Eng. Econ. Rev.*, Nov.–Dec. 1988, pp. 29–46.

Shilling, A. Gary. A Depression is More Likely than Most Believe. *Bus. Econ.*, July 1988, 23(3), pp. 33–37.

Shilling, James D. and Howe, John S. Capital Structure Theory and REIT Security Offerings. *J. Finance*, September 1988, 43(4), pp. 983–93.

_____ **and Sa-Aadu, J.** Rankings of Contributing Authors to the *AREUEA Journal* by Doctoral Origin and Employer: 1973–1987. *Amer. Real Estate Urban Econ. Assoc. J.*, Fall 1988, 16(3), pp. 257–70.

Shimada, Haruo. Contemporary Challenges for Japanese Trade Unionism. In *Japan Institute of Labour, ed.*, 1988, *1988*, pp. 63–67.

_____. Trade Frictions and Industrial Relations. In *Japan Institute of Labour, ed.*, 1988, *1984*, pp. 59–62.

Shimomura, Koji and Kemp, Murray C. The Impossibility of Global Absolute Advantage in the Heckscher–Ohlin Model of Trade. *Oxford Econ. Pap.*, September 1988, 40(3), pp. 575–76.

Shimotomai, Nobuo. The Reform Movement: Power, Ideology, and Intellectuals. In *Juviler, P. and Kimura, H., eds.*, 1988, pp. 63–79.

Shinkai, Yoichi. The Internationalization of Finance in Japan. In *Inoguchi, T. and Okimoto, D. I., eds.*, 1988, pp. 249–71.

Shionoya, Yuichi. Anti-Say's Law versus Say's Law: A Change in Paradigm: Comments. In *Hanusch, H., ed.*, 1988, pp. 64–67.

Shires, David. Australian/Cairns Group Perspective: Southern Agriculture and the World Economy: The Multilateral Trade Negotiations. *Southern J. Agr. Econ.*, July 1988, 20(1), pp. 69–71.

Shirley, Mary. The Experience with Privatization. *Finance Develop.*, September 1988, 25(3), pp. 34–35.

_____. Promoting the Private Sector. *Finance Develop.*, March 1988, 25(1), pp. 40–43.

Shironin, V. M. and Aven, Petr O. The Reform of the Economic Mechanism. *Prob. Econ.*, June 1988, 31(2), pp. 33–48.

Shishido, Shuntaro. The Japanese Growth Alternatives and the World Economy: Simulations with Tsukuba-FAIS World Econometric Model. In *Uno, K. and Shishido, S., eds.*, 1988, pp. 17–30.

Shitovitz, Benyamin. On Stationary 3-Period Overlapping Generations Models. *J. Econ. Theory*, December 1988, 46(2), pp. 402–08.

_____ **and Greenberg, Joseph.** Consistent Voting Rules for Competitive Local Public Goods Economies. *J. Econ. Theory*, Décember 1988, 46(2), pp. 223–36.

Shiva, V. and Bandyopadhyay, J. The Chipko Movement. In *Ives, J. and Pitt, D. C., eds.*, 1988, pp. 224–41.

Shively, Thomas S. An Analysis of Tests for Regression Coefficient Stability. *J. Econometrics*, November 1988, 39(3), pp. 367–86.

Shleifer, Andrei. Do Target Shareholders Lose in Unsuccessful Control Contests? Comment. In *Auerbach, A. J., ed. (I)*, 1988, pp. 152–53.

_____ **and Summers, Lawrence H.** Breach of Trust in Hostile Takeovers. In *Auerbach, A. J., ed. (I)*, 1988, pp. 33–56.

_____ **and Vishny, Robert W.** The Efficiency of Investment in the Presence of Aggregate Demand Spillovers. *J. Polit. Econ.*, December 1988, 96(6), pp. 1221–31.

_____ **and Vishny, Robert W.** Management Buyouts as a Response to Market Pressure. In *Auerbach, A. J., ed. (II)*, 1988, pp. 87–102.

_____ **and Vishny, Robert W.** Value Maximization and the Acquisition Process. *J. Econ. Perspectives*, Winter 1988, 2(1), pp. 7–20.

_____; **Vishny, Robert W. and Mørck, Randall.** Characteristics of Targets of Hostile and Friendly Takeovers. In *Auerbach, A. J., ed. (I)*, 1988, pp. 101–29.

_____; **Vishny, Robert W. and Morck, Randall.** Management Ownership and Market Valuation: An Empirical Analysis. *J. Finan. Econ.*, Jan.–March 1988, 20(1–2), pp. 293–315.

Shlicht, Ekkehart. Promotions, Elections, and Other Contests: Comment. *J. Inst. Theoretical Econ.*, February 1988, 144(1), pp. 94–99.

Shlomowitz, Ralph and Estrin, Saul. Income Sharing, Employee Ownership and Worker Democracy. *Ann. Pub. Co-op. Econ.*, March 1988, 59(1), pp. 43–65.

Shmanske, Stephen. On the Measurement of Teacher Effectiveness. *J. Econ. Educ.*, Fall 1988, 19(4), pp. 307–14.

Shmelev, Nikolai P. Advances and Debts. *Prob. Econ.*, February 1988, 30(10), pp. 7–43.

_____. Rethinking Price Reform in the USSR. *Soviet Econ.*, Oct.–Dec. 1988, 4(4), pp. 319–27.

Shoemaker, Robbin. The Relative Demand for Inputs: A Decomposition Analysis of U.S. Agricultural Production. *Appl. Econ.*, May 1988, 20(5), pp. 665–78.

Shoenhair, John D. and Winn, Daryl N. Compensation-Based (Dis)incentives for Revenue-Maximizing Behavior: A Test of the "Revised"

Baumol Hypothesis. *Rev. Econ. Statist.*, February 1988, *70*(1), pp. 154–58.

Shoesmith, Gary L. Economies of Scale and Scope in Petroleum Refining. *Appl. Econ.*, December 1988, *20*(12), pp. 1643–52.

Shogren, Jason F. Reducing Moral Hazard Associated with Implied Warranties of Animal Health: Comment. *Amer. J. Agr. Econ.*, May 1988, *70*(2), pp. 410–12.

_____ **and Durden, Garey.** Valuing Non-market Recreation Goods: An Evaluative Survey of the Literature on the Travel Cost and Contingent Valuation Methods. *Rev. Reg. Stud.*, Fall 1988, *18*(3), pp. 1–15.

Shome, Dilip K. and Smith, Stephen D. An Econometric Analysis of Equity Costs and Risk Premiums in the Electric Utility Industry: 1971–1985. *Financial Rev.*, November 1988, *23*(4), pp. 439–52.

_____; **Smith, Stephen D. and Morgan, George Emir.** Optimal Futures Positions for Large Banking Firms. *J. Finance*, March 1988, *43*(1), pp. 175–95.

_____; **Smith, Stephen D. and Pinkerton, John M.** The Purchasing Power of Money and Nominal Interest Rates: A Re-examination. *J. Finance*, December 1988, *43*(5), pp. 1113–25.

Shome, Parthasarathi and Aguirre, Carlos A. The Mexican Value-Added Tax (VAT): Methodology for Calculating the Base. *Nat. Tax J.*, December 1988, *41*(4), pp. 543–54.

Shonkwiler, J. S. and Lea, J. D. Misspecification in Simultaneous Systems: An Alternative Test and Its Application to a Model of the Shrimp Market. *Southern J. Agr. Econ.*, December 1988, *20*(2), pp. 65–72.

_____; **Rola, Leandro R. and Lynne, Gary D.** Attitudes and Farmer Conservation Behavior. *Amer. J. Agr. Econ.*, February 1988, *70*(1), pp. 12–19.

_____ **and Taylor, Timothy G.** Food Processor Price Behavior: Firm-Level Evidence of Sticky Prices. *Amer. J. Agr. Econ.*, May 1988, *70*(2), pp. 239–44.

Shores, Marilyn R. and Prisman, Eliezer Zeev. Duration Measures for Specific Term Structure Estimations and Applications to Bond Portfolio Immunization. *J. Banking Finance*, September 1988, *12*(3), pp. 493–504.

Shorrocks, Anthony F. Aggregation Issues in Inequality Measurement. In *Eichhorn, W., ed.*, 1988, pp. 429–51.

_____. Wealth Holdings and Entrepreneurial Activity. In *Kessler, D. and Masson, A., eds.*, 1988, pp. 241–56.

_____ **and Foster, James E.** Inequality and Poverty Orderings. *Europ. Econ. Rev.*, March 1988, *32*(2–3), pp. 654–61.

_____ **and Foster, James E.** Poverty Orderings. *Econometrica*, January 1988, *56*(1), pp. 173–77.

_____ **and Foster, James E.** Poverty Orderings and Welfare Dominance. In *Gaertner, W. and Pattanaik, P. K., eds.*, 1988, 1988, pp. 91–110.

_____ **and Foster, James E.** Poverty Orderings and Welfare Dominance. *Soc. Choice Welfare*, 1988, *5*(2/3), pp. 179–98.

Short, Eugenie D.; O'Driscoll, Gerald P., Jr. and Garrison, Roger W. Financial Stability and FDIC Insurance. In *England, C. and Huertas, T., eds.*, 1988, pp. 187–207.

Short, J. R. Construction Workers and the City: 1. Analysis. *Environ. Planning A*, June 1988, *20*(6), pp. 719–32.

_____. Construction Workers and the City: 2. An Interview with Jack Mundey. *Environ. Planning A*, June 1988, *20*(6), pp. 733–40.

Short, Pamela Farley; Cantor, Joel C. and Monheit, Alan C. The Dynamics of Medicaid Enrollment. *Inquiry*, Winter 1988, *25*(4), pp. 504–16.

Short, Walter and Ruegg, Rosalie T. Economic Methods. In *West, R. E. and Kreith, F., eds.*, 1988, pp. 18–83.

Shorten, Brett and Mangan, John. Micro-economic Employment Initiatives in Regional New South Wales. *Reg. Stud.*, April 1988, *22*(2), pp. 162–66.

Shortle, James S. and Dunn, James W. Agricultural Nonpoint Source Pollution Control in Theory and Practice. *Marine Resource Econ.*, 1988, *5*(3), pp. 259–70.

Shoup, Carl S. Distribution of Benefits from Government Services: Horizontal Equity. *Public Finance*, 1988, *43*(1), pp. 1–18.

_____. Standards for Distributing a Free Government Service: Crime Protection. In *Alper, N. O. and Hellman, D. A., eds.*, 1988, pp. 104–13.

_____. The Value Added Tax and Developing Countries. *World Bank Res. Observer*, July 1988, *3*(2), pp. 139–56.

Shoven, John B. The Effects of Taxation on the Merger Decision: Comment. In *Auerbach, A. J., ed. (I)*, 1988, pp. 188–89.

_____. Future Social Security Financing Alternatives and National Saving: Comment. In *Wachter, S. M., ed.*, 1988, pp. 144–47.

_____. Intellectual Property Rights and Economic Growth. In *Walker, C. E. and Bloomfield, M. A., eds.*, 1988, pp. 46–52.

_____. Investment Incentives in Theory and Practice: Comments. In *Aaron, H. J.; Galper, H. and Pechman, J. A., eds.*, 1988, pp. 342–46.

_____. Women: Retirees and Widows: Discussion. In *Ricardo-Campbell, R. and Lazear, E. P., eds.*, 1988, pp. 96–99.

_____ **and Bagwell, Laurie Simon.** Share Repurchases and Acquisitions: An Analysis of Which Firms Participate. In *Auerbach, A. J., ed. (I)*, 1988, pp. 191–213.

_____ **and Bernheim, B. Douglas.** Fiscalité et coût du capital: Une comparaison internationale. (Tax Systems and the Cost of Capital: An International Comparison. With English summary.) *Ann. Écon. Statist.*, July–Sept. 1988, (11), pp. 93–116.

_____ **and Bernheim, B. Douglas.** Pension Funding and Saving. In *Bodie, Z.; Shoven, J. B. and Wise, D. A., eds.*, 1988, pp. 85–111.

_____ **and Boskin, Michael J.** Poverty among the Elderly: Where Are the Holes in the Safety

Net? In *Bodie, Z.; Shoven, J. B. and Wise, D. A., eds.*, 1988, pp. 115–34.

_____; **Boskin, Michael J. and Kotlikoff, Laurence J.** Personal Security Accounts: A Proposal for Fundamental Social Security Reform. In *Wachter, S. M., ed.*, 1988, pp. 179–206.

_____ **and Pereira, Alfredo M.** Survey of Dynamic Computational General Equilibrium Models for Tax Policy Evaluation. *J. Policy Modeling*, Fall 1988, *10*(3), pp. 401–36.

_____ **and Tachibanaki, Toshiaki.** The Taxation of Income from Capital in Japan. In *Shoven, J. B., ed.*, 1988, pp. 51–96.

_____; **Wise, David A. and Bodie, Zvi.** Pensions in the U.S. Economy: Introduction. In *Bodie, Z.; Shoven, J. B. and Wise, D. A., eds.*, 1988, pp. 1–8.

Shows, E. Warren; Power, Fred B. and Johnson, Dale A. Lump-Sum Awards in Workers' Compensation: Comment. *J. Risk Ins.*, December 1988, *55*(4), pp. 734–39.

Shrader-Frechette, K. S. Values and Hydrogeological Method: How Not to Site the World's Largest Nuclear Dump. In *Byrne, J. and Rich, D., eds.*, 1988, pp. 101–37.

Shrestha, Keshab. Estimation of a General Linear Model with an Unobservable Stochastic Variable. *Econ. Letters*, 1988, *26*(3), pp. 259–64.

Shrivastava, Paul and Gates, Stephen. Locating Doctoral Dissertations in Strategic Management. In *Lamb, R. and Shrivastava, P., eds.*, 1988, pp. 277–98.

Shriver, Keith A. A Note on the Estimation of Current Cost Depreciation. In *Schwartz, B. N., ed.*, 1988, pp. 129–41.

Shroff, Manu. Observations on the State of the Economy. In *Lucas, R. E. B. and Papanek, G. F., eds.*, 1988, pp. 364–65.

Shrt, Pamela Farley; Horgan, Constance M. and Taylor, Amy K. Medigap Insurance: Friend or Foe in Reducing Medicare Deficits? In *Frech, H. E., III, ed.*, 1988, pp. 145–77.

Shrum, Wesley and Costanza, Robert. The Effects of Taxation on Moderating the Conflict Escalation Process: An Experiment Using the Dollar Auction Game. *Soc. Sci. Quart.*, June 1988, *69*(2), pp. 416–32.

Shubik, Martin. Corporate Control, Efficient Markets, and the Public Good. In *Coffee, J. C., Jr.; Lowenstein, L. and Rose-Ackerman, S., eds.*, 1988, pp. 31–55.

_____ **and Dubey, Pradeep.** A Note on an Optimal Garnishing Rule. *Econ. Letters*, 1988, *27*(1), pp. 5–6.

_____ **and Sahi, S.** A Model of a Sudden-Death Field-Goal Football Game as a Sequential Duel. *Math. Soc. Sci.*, June 1988, *15*(3), pp. 205–15.

_____ **and Shapley, Lloyd S.** A Method for Evaluating the Distribution of Power in a Committee System. In *[Shapley, L. S.]*, 1988, *1954*, pp. 41–48.

Shugan, Steven M. Pricing When Different Outlets Offer Different Assortments of Brands. In *Devinney, T. M., ed.*, 1988, pp. 289–311.

_____ **and Jeuland, Abel P.** Channel of Distribu-

tion Profits When Channel Members Form Conjectures: Note. *Marketing Sci.*, Spring 1988, *7*(2), pp. 202–10.

_____ **and Jeuland, Abel P.** Competitive Pricing Behavior in Distribution Systems. In *Devinney, T. M., ed.*, 1988, pp. 219–37.

_____ **and Jeuland, Abel P.** Reply to: Managing Channel Profits: Comment. *Marketing Sci.*, Winter 1988, *7*(1), pp. 103–06.

Shughart, William F., II. A Public Choice Perspective of the Banking Act of 1933. In *England, C. and Huertas, T., eds.*, 1988, pp. 87–105.

_____. A Public Choice Perspective of the Banking Act of 1933. *Cato J.*, Winter 1988, *7*(3), pp. 595–613.

_____; **Tollison, Robert D. and Anderson, Gary Michael.** A Public Choice Theory of the Great Contraction. *Public Choice*, October 1988, *59*(1), pp. 3–23.

_____; **Tollison, Robert D. and Crain, W. Mark.** Legislative Majorities as Nonsalvageable Assets. *Southern Econ. J.*, October 1988, *55*(2), pp. 303–14.

_____; **Tollison, Robert D. and Goff, Brian L.** Disqualification by Decree: Amateur Rules as Barriers to Entry. *J. Inst. Theoretical Econ.*, June 1988, *144*(3), pp. 515–23.

_____; **Tollison, Robert D. and McCormick, Robert E.** The Disinterest in Deregulation: Reply. *Amer. Econ. Rev.*, March 1988, *78*(1), p. 284.

Shukov, N. S. Mathematical Economics in Russia (1867–1917). *Matekon*, Spring 1988, *24*(3), pp. 3–31.

Shull, Bernard. Interstate Banking and Antitrust Laws: History of Public Policies to Promote Banking Competition. *Contemp. Policy Issues*, April 1988, *6*(2), pp. 24–40.

Shulman, Joel M. and Bygrave, William D. Capital Gains Tax: Bane or Boon for Venture Capital? In *Kirchhoff, B. A., et al., eds.*, 1988, pp. 324–38.

Shultz, George. National Success and International Stability in a Time of Change. In *Anderson, A. and Bark, D. L., eds.*, 1988, pp. 515–26.

Shumavon, Douglas H. Productivity and Social Goals: A Case Study from Cincinnati, Ohio. In *Kelly, R. M., ed.*, 1988, pp. 177–88.

Shumway, C. Richard. Estimation of Multicrop Production Functions: Comment. *Amer. J. Agr. Econ.*, August 1988, *70*(3), pp. 729–32.

_____ **and Alexander, William P.** Agricultural Product Supplies and Input Demands: Regional Comparisons. *Amer. J. Agr. Econ.*, February 1988, *70*(1), pp. 153–61.

_____ **and Fawson, Chris.** A Nonparametric Investigation of Agricultural Production Behavior for U.S. Subregions. *Amer. J. Agr. Econ.*, May 1988, *70*(2), pp. 311–17.

_____ **and Howard, Wayne H.** Dynamic Adjustment in the U.S. Dairy Industry. *Amer. J. Agr. Econ.*, November 1988, *70*(4), pp. 837–47.

_____; **Pope, Rulon D. and Nash, Elizabeth K.** Allocatable Fixed Inputs and Jointness in Agricultural Production: Implications for Economic Modeling: Reply. *Amer. J. Agr. Econ.*, November 1988, *70*(4), pp. 950–52.

_____; **Saez, Roberto R. and Gottret, Pablo E.** Multiproduct Supply and Input Demand in U.S. Agriculture. *Amer. J. Agr. Econ.*, May 1988, *70*(2), pp. 330–37.

Shupp, Franklin R. Uncertainty, Habit Persistence, and Cyclical Price Behavior. *J. Econ. Dynam. Control*, March 1988, *12*(1), pp. 119–25.

Shvyrkov, Vladislav V. The Secret Cause and Known Effects: The New Quality Philosophy in Statistics. In *Brown, R. C., ed.*, 1988, pp. 143–64.

Shy, Oz. A General Equilibrium Model of Pareto Inferior Trade. *J. Int. Econ.*, August 1988, *25*(1–2), pp. 143–54.

Siamwalla, Ammar. Public Stock Management. In *Mellor, J. W. and Ahmed, R., eds.*, 1988, pp. 81–93.

_____. Some Macroeconomic Policy Implications of Consumer-Oriented Food Subsidies. In *Pinstrup-Andersen, P., ed.*, 1988, pp. 323–30.

_____ **and Rosegrant, Mark W.** Government Credit Programs: Justification, Benefits, and Costs. In *Mellor, J. W. and Ahmed, R., eds.*, 1988, pp. 219–38.

_____ **and Valdés, Alberto.** Foreign Trade Regime, Exchange Rate Policy, and the Structure of Incentives. In *Mellor, J. W. and Ahmed, R., eds.*, 1988, pp. 103–23.

Sibal, V. K. Human Resources Development and the Railways. In *Kohli, U. and Gautam, V., eds.*, 1988, pp. 113–39.

Sibert, Anne; Feltenstein, Andrew and Lebow, David. An Analysis of the Welfare Implications of Alternative Exchange Rate Regimes: An Intertemporal Model with an Application. *J. Policy Modeling*, Winter 1988, *10*(4), pp. 611–29.

_____ **and Rogoff, Kenneth.** Elections and Macroeconomic Policy Cycles. *Rev. Econ. Stud.*, January 1988, *55*(1), pp. 1–16.

Sibley, David S. and Sappington, David E. M. Regulating without Cost Information: The Incremental Surplus Subsidy Scheme. *Int. Econ. Rev.*, May 1988, *29*(2), pp. 297–306.

Sicat, Gerardo P. and Virmani, Arvind. Personal Income Taxes in Developing Countries. *World Bank Econ. Rev.*, January 1988, *2*(1), pp. 123–38.

Siccama, Jan G. and Houweling, Henk. Power Transitions as a Cause of War. *J. Conflict Resolution*, March 1988, *32*(1), pp. 87–102.

Sichel, Werner. Principles of Economics Textbooks: Innovation and Product Differentiation—A Response. *J. Econ. Educ.*, Spring 1988, *19*(2), pp. 178–82.

Sichtermann, Barbara. The Conflict between Housework and Employment: Some Notes on Women's Identity. In *Jenson, J.; Hagen, E. and Reddy, C., eds.*, 1988, pp. 276–87.

Sicilian, Joseph and Marino, Anthony M. The Incentive for Conservation Investment in Regulated Utilities. *J. Environ. Econ. Manage.*, June 1988, *15*(2), pp. 173–88.

Sickles, Robin C. Allocative Inefficiency in the Airline Industry: A Case for Deregulation. In *Dogramaci, A. and Färe, R., eds.,*, 1988, pp. 149–62.

_____; **Lovell, C. A. Knox and Sarkar, Asani.** Testing for Aggregation Bias in Efficiency Measurement. In *Eichhorn, W., ed.*, 1988, pp. 187–206.

_____; **Taubman, Paul and Behrman, Jere R.** Age-Specific Death Rates. In *Ricardo-Campbell, R. and Lazear, E. P., eds.*, 1988, pp. 162–83.

_____; **Warren, Ronald S., Jr. and Lovell, C. A. Knox.** The Effect of Unionization On Labor Productivity: Some Additional Evidence. *J. Lab. Res.*, Winter 1988, *9*(1), pp. 55–63.

Sicular, Terry. Plan and Market in China's Agricultural Commerce. *J. Polit. Econ.*, April 1988, *96*(2), pp. 283–307.

_____ **and Weiss, Vanessa.** Grain and Meat in China: Trends in Consumption, Production, and Imports with Special Reference to Isolated Soy Protein Meat Ingredients. In *Schwarz, F. H., ed.*, 1988, pp. 107–57.

Siddayao, Corazon M. Asian Petroleum Pricing Policies Revisited. *Energy J.*, Special Issue, 1988, *9*, pp. 107–25.

Siddharthan, N. S. In-House R&D, Imported Technology, and Firm Size: Lessons from Indian Experience. *Devel. Econ.*, September 1988, *26*(3), pp. 212–21.

_____. International Economic Turmoil: The Process of Creative Destruction. *Indian Econ. J.*, April–June 1988, *35*(4), pp. 57–67.

Siddiq, Fazley and Osberg, Lars. The Inequality of Wealth in Britain's North American Colonies: The Importance of the Relatively Poor. *Rev. Income Wealth*, June 1988, *34*(2), pp. 143–63.

Sidorowich, John J. and Farmer, J. Doyne. Can New Approaches to Nonlinear Modeling Improve Economic Forecasts? In *Anderson, P. W.; Arrow, K. J. and Pines, D., eds.*, 1988, pp. 99–115.

Siebeck, Wolfgang E. Agriculture in the Uruguay Round. In *Roberts, C., ed.*, 1988, pp. 25–32.

Siebert, Horst. Langfristige Lieferverträge im internationalen Ressourcenhandel. (Long-run Contracts in International Resources Trade. With English summary.) *Z. Wirtschaft. Sozialwissen.*, 1988, *108*(2), pp. 195–225.

_____. Strategische Handelspolitik. Theoretische Ansätze und wirtschaftspolitische Empfehlungen. (Strategic Trade Policy. Theoretical Approaches and Policy Applications. With English summary.) *Aussenwirtschaft*, December 1988, *43*(4), pp. 549–84.

Siebrand, Jan C. Macroeconomic Modelling for Economic Policy. In *Driehuis, W.; Fase, M. M. G. and den Hartog, H., eds.*, 1988, pp. 99–135.

_____ **and Swank, Job.** Adjustment Options for the U.S. Economy. In *Motamen, H., ed.*, 1988, pp. 265–82.

Siedl, Christian. The Right Combination of Demand and Supply Policies: The Case for a Two-

Handed Approach: Comments. In *Giersch, H.*, *ed.*, 1988, pp. 353–59.

Siegel, Andrew F. and Nelson, Charles R. Long-term Behavior of Yield Curves. *J. Finan. Quant. Anal.*, March 1988, 23(1), pp. 105–10.

Siegel, Daniel R.; Cheng, C. S. Agnes and Smith, James L. Failure of the Net Profit Share Leasing Experiment for Offshore Petroleum Resources. *Rev. Econ. Statist.*, May 1988, 70(2), pp. 199–206.

_____ **and Hagerty, Kathleen M.** On the Observational Equivalence of Managerial Contracts under Conditions of Moral Hazard and Self-selection. *Quart. J. Econ.*, May 1988, 103(2), pp. 425–28.

_____; **Smith, James L. and Paddock, James L.** Option Valuation of Claims on Real Assets: The Case of Offshore Petroleum Leases. *Quart. J. Econ.*, August 1988, 103(3), pp. 479–508.

Siegel, Harvey. Relativism for Consumer Research? [On Method in Consumer Research: A Critical Relativist Perspective]. *J. Cons. Res.*, June 1988, 15(1), pp. 129–32.

Siegel, Lee M. Educational Malpractice: A Comment. In *Pennsylvania Economic Association*, 1988, pp. 599–600.

_____. Frustration Equilibrium and Disequilibrium Positions: Has Anything Changed in Eight Years? A Comment. In *Pennsylvania Economic Association*, 1988, pp. 44–45.

Siegel, P. B. and Feinerman, E. A Dynamic Farm-Level Planning Model for Beef Feedlot Production and Marketing. *J. Agr. Econ.*, September 1988, 39(3), pp. 413–25.

Siegers, Joop J.; Groot, Loek F. M. and Schippers, Jacques J. The Effect of Interruptions and Part-time Work on Women's Wage Rate: A Test of the Variable-Intensity Model. *De Economist*, 1988, 136(2), pp. 220–38.

Siegfried, John J. Could a Score of Industrial Organization Economists Agree on Competition? *Rev. Ind. Organ.*, Fall 1988, 3(4), pp. 139–48.

Siegloff, Eric S. and McKibbin, Warwick J. A Note on Aggregate Investment in Australia. *Econ. Rec.*, September 1988, 64(186), pp. 209–15.

Sieh, Lee Mei Ling. Malaysian Workers in Singapore. *Singapore Econ. Rev.*, April 1988, 33(1), pp. 101–11.

_____. Production Management in Small and Medium Businesses in Malaysia. In *James, K. and Akrasanee, N., eds.*, 1988, pp. 55–92.

Sieling, Mark Scott and Curtin, Daniel. Patterns of Productivity Change in Men's and Boys' Suits and Coats. *Mon. Lab. Rev.*, November 1988, 111(11), pp. 25–31.

Sienkiewicz, Stanley and Saunders, Anthony. The Hedging Performance of ECU Futures Contracts. *J. Futures Markets*, June 1988, 8(3), pp. 335–52.

Sievers, Mark. A Taxonomy of Economic Regulation. In *Missouri Valley Economic Assoc.*, 1988, pp. 18–24.

Sigelman, Lee and Dometrius, Nelson C. Assessing Personnel Practices in Higher Education:

A Cautionary Note. *Econ. Educ. Rev.*, 1988, 7(4), pp. 439–43.

_____ **and Dometrius, Nelson C.** The Cost of Quality: Teacher Testing and Racial–Ethnic Representativeness in Public Education. *Soc. Sci. Quart.*, March 1988, 69(1), pp. 70–82.

Sigmond, J. P. Development of Dutch Harbours 1500–1800. A Survey. In *Cavaciocchi, S., ed.*, 1988, pp. 881–907.

Sigurdson, Dale; Doering, Otto and Schmitz, Andrew. Domestic Farm Policy and the Gains from Trade: Reply. *Amer. J. Agr. Econ.*, August 1988, 70(3), pp. 740.

Sijben, Jac. J. Financial Innovations, Monetary Policy and Financial Stability. *Kredit Kapital*, 1988, 21(1), pp. 45–66.

Siklos, Pierre L. The Deficit–Interest Rate Link: Empirical Evidence for Canada. *Appl. Econ.*, December 1988, 20(12), pp. 1563–77.

_____. Output–Inflation Trade-offs: Some New Evidence from Postwar U.S. Quarterly Data. *J. Macroecon.*, Spring 1988, 10(2), pp. 249–60.

_____ **and Raj, Baldev.** The Role of Fiscal Policy in the St. Louis Model: Nonparametric Estimates for a Small Open Economy. *Empirical Econ.*, 1988, 13(3–4), pp. 169–86.

_____ **and Raj, Baldev.** Some Qualms about the Test of the Institutional Hypothesis of the Long-run Behavior of Velocity. *Econ. Inquiry*, July 1988, 26(3), pp. 537–45.

Silber, Jacques G. and Berrebi, Z. M. Distance Functions and the Comparison of Development Levels. *Econ. Letters*, 1988, 27(2), pp. 195–200.

Silberberg, Eugene and Nieswiadomy, Michael L. Calculating Changes in Worklife Expectancies and Lost Earnings in Personal Injury Cases. *J. Risk Ins.*, September 1988, 55(3), pp. 492–98.

Silberston, Aubrey. Impracticalities of the Sampson Proposal for Phasing Out the MFA. *World Econ.*, June 1988, 11(2), pp. 301–02.

Siliciano, John A. Negligent Accounting and the Limits of Instrumental Tort Reform. *Mich. Law Rev.*, August 1988, 86(8), pp. 1929–80.

Silipo, Damiano Bruno. Il processo cumulativo wickselliano. (With English summary.) *Stud. Econ.*, 1988, 43(34), pp. 91–111.

Silk, Alvin J. and Bagozzi, Richard P. Reply [Recall, Recognition and the Measurement of Memory for Print Advertisements]. *Marketing Sci.*, Winter 1988, 7(1), pp. 99–102.

Silk, Leonard. On the Twin Deficits and National Security. In *Aho, C. M. and Levinson, M.*, 1988, pp. 201–06.

_____; **Calleo, David P. and Cleveland, Harold van B.** The Dollar and the Defense of the West. *Foreign Aff.*, Spring 1988, 66(4), pp. 846–62.

Silva-Herzog, Jesus. A Latin American Perspective. In *Feldstein, M., ed. (II)*, 1988, pp. 69–77.

de Silva, R. G. L. Imputation System for Corporate Taxation: Sri Lanka. *Bull. Int. Fiscal Doc.*, December 1988, 42(12), pp. 537–40.

Silvani, Marco and Conti, Vittorio. Il commercio

intra-CEE e la posizione relativa dei paesi membri. (Intra-EEC Trade and the Competitive Positions of the Member Countries. With English summary.) *Giorn. Econ.*, Sept.–Oct. 1988, *47*(9–10), pp. 443–74.

da Silveira Lobo, Carlos Augusto. Tax Treatment of Computer Software: Brazil. In *International Fiscal Association, ed. (II)*, 1988, pp. 241–51.

Silver, Brian D. and Anderson, Barbara A. The Effects of the Registration System on the Seasonality of Births: The Case of the Soviet Union. *Population Stud.*, July 1988, *42*(2), pp. 303–20.

Silver, Mick. Average Prices, Unanticipated Prices and Price Variability in the UK for Individual Products. *Appl. Econ.*, May 1988, *20*(5), pp. 569–94.

Silver, Steven D. Interdependencies in Social and Economic Decision Making: A Conditional Logit Model of the Joint Homeownership–Mobility Decision. *J. Cons. Res.*, September 1988, *15*(2), pp. 234–42.

_____; **Cohen, Bernard P. and Rainwater, Julie.** Group Structure and Information Exchange in Innovative Problem Solving. In *Lawler, E. J. and Markovsky, B., eds.*, 1988, pp. 169–94.

Silverberg, Gerald. Modelling Economic Dynamics and Technical Change: Mathematical Approaches to Self-Organisation and Evolution. In *Dosi, G., et al., eds.*, 1988, pp. 531–59.

_____; **Dosi, Giovanni and Orsenigo, Luigi.** Innovation, Diversity and Diffusion: A Self-organisation Model. *Econ. J.*, December 1988, *98*(393), pp. 1032–54.

Silverberg, Stanley C. Regulating Bank Safety and Performance: Commentary. In *Haraf, W. S. and Kushmeider, R. M., eds.*, 1988, pp. 108–12.

Silverman, Dan P. National Socialist Economics: The *Wirtschaftswunder* Reconsidered. In *Eichengreen, B. and Hatton, T. J., eds.*, 1988, pp. 185–220.

Silvestre, Joaquim. Undominated Prices in the Three Good Model. *Europ. Econ. Rev.*, January 1988, *32*(1), pp. 161–178.

Silvestrelli, Maria and Bartolucci, Antonio. The Matching of Transport Demand with Supply in Italy. In *Bianco, L. and La Bella, A., eds.*, 1988, pp. 50–78.

Silvia, John E. and Whall, Barry. Rising Consumer Debt: For Better...or for Worse. *Challenge*, Jan.–Feb. 1988, *31*(1), pp. 55–60.

Sim, Ah-Boon and Kwan, Andy C. C. Generalised Portmanteau Statistics and Tests of Randomness: A Note on Their Applications to Residuals from a Fitted ARMA Model. *Econ. Letters*, 1988, *26*(4), pp. 341–47.

Simai, Mihály. Hungary and the Transnational Corporations. In *Teng, W. and Wang, N. T., eds.*, 1988, pp. 165–70.

_____. Research, Development, Innovation and Technology Flows in Small Countries: The Experience of Hungary. In *Brada, J. C. and Dobozi, I., eds.*, 1988, pp. 153–67.

Simcox, David E. Illegal Immigration: Counting

the Shadow Population. In *Simcox, D. E., ed.*, 1988, pp. 23–30.

_____. Immigration and Social Welfare: The Notion of the Non-revenue Consuming Taxpayer. In *Simcox, D. E., ed.*, 1988, pp. 37–42.

_____. Immigration and the Labor Market: The Repeal of Supply and Demand. In *Simcox, D. E., ed.*, 1988, pp. 31–36.

_____. Immigration Enforcement: A Finger in the Sluice Gates. In *Simcox, D. E., ed.*, 1988, pp. 43–51.

_____. Legal Immigration: The Ceiling That Does Not Seal. In *Simcox, D. E., ed.*, 1988, pp. 13–22.

_____. The Maturing of U.S. Immigration Reform. In *Simcox, D. E., ed.*, 1988, pp. 3–12.

_____. Mexico's Dilemma: Finding a Million Jobs a Year. In *Simcox, D. E., ed.*, 1988, pp. 201–13.

_____. Refugees, Asylum and Sanctuary: National Passion vs. National Interest. In *Simcox, D. E., ed.*, 1988, pp. 52–58.

_____. Unfinished Business in American Immigration Policy. In *Simcox, D. E., ed.*, 1988, pp. 59–63.

Simer, Frank J. and Egge, Karl A. An Analysis of the Advice Given by Recent Entrepreneurs to Prospective Entrepreneurs. In *Kirchhoff, B. A., et al., eds.*, 1988, pp. 119–33.

Simes, Richard M. Macroeconometric Model Evaluation, with Special Reference to the NIF88 Model. *Australian Econ. Pap.*, Supplement, June 1988, *27*, pp. 29–56.

_____ **and Horn, Peter.** Design of the NIF88 Model. *Australian Econ. Pap.*, Supplement, June 1988, *27*, pp. 155–70.

Simmons, James C. The Development of Spatial Price Comparison in the State of Florida. In *Salazar-Carrillo, J. and Rao, D. S. P., eds.*, 1988, pp. 207–22.

_____ **and Schneider, Elihu.** Spatial Price Aggregation, Item Weight and Constant Utility. *Rev. Reg. Stud.*, Spring 1988, *18*(2), pp. 70–74.

Simmons, LeRoy F. and Cross, Mark L. The Underwriting Cycle and the Risk Manager—Authors' Reply. *J. Risk Ins.*, September 1988, *55*(3), pp. 561–62.

Simmons, Phil. Teaching Marketing: Comment. *Rev. Marketing Agr. Econ.*, August 1988, *56*(2), pp. 225–26.

_____. A Theoretical Discussion of the Economic Effects of Buffer Stocks and Buffer Funds. *Australian J. Agr. Econ.*, Aug.–Dec. 1988, *32*(2–3), pp. 129–41.

Simmons, Rex and Adair, John J. From Voucher Auditing to Junkyard Dogs: The Evolution of Federal Inspectors General. *Public Budg. Finance*, Summer 1988, *8*(2), pp. 91–110.

Simms, Margaret C. Transformation in the Educational System: Catalysts for Black Change. *Rev. Black Polit. Econ.*, Summer 1988, *17*(1), pp. 57–65.

_____ **and Swinton, David H.** A Report on the Supply of Black Economists. *Rev. Black Polit. Econ.*, Summer 1988, *17*(1), pp. 67–88.

Simon, Curtis J. Frictional Unemployment and

the Role of Industrial Diversity. *Quart. J. Econ.*, November 1988, *103*(4), pp. 715–28.

Simon, Daniel T. and Francis, Jere R. The Effects of Auditor Change on Audit Fees: Tests of Price Cutting and Price Recovery. *Accounting Rev.*, April 1988, *63*(2), pp. 255–69.

Simon, David. Coping with Low Oil Prices. In *Mabro, R., ed.*, 1988, pp. 49–60.

Simon, Denis Fred. External Incorporation and Internal Reform. In *Winckler, E. A. and Greenhalgh, S., eds.*, 1988, pp. 138–50.

———. Technology Transfer and National Autonomy. In *Winckler, E. A. and Greenhalgh, S., eds.*, 1988, pp. 206–23.

Simon, Herbert A. Rationality as Process and as Product of Thought. In *Bell, D. E.; Raiffa, H. and Tversky, A., eds.*, 1988, *1978*, pp. 58–77.

———. Theories of Decision-Making in Economics and Behavioral Science. In *Earl, P. E., ed.*, Vol. 1, 1988, *1959*, pp. 77–107.

——— **and Cyert, Richard M.** The Behavioural Approach: With Emphasis on Economics. In *Cyert, R. M.*, 1988, *1983*, pp. 220–39.

——— **and Cyert, Richard M.** The Behavioural Approach: With Emphasis on Economics. In *Earl, P. E., ed.*, Vol. 1, 1988, *1983*, pp. 45–58.

——— **and Iwasaki, Yumi.** Causal Ordering, Comparative Statics, and Near Decomposability. *J. Econometrics*, Sept.–Oct. 1988, *39*(1–2), pp. 149–73.

———; **Trow, Donald B. and Cyert, Richard M.** Observation of a Business Decision. In *Cyert, R. M.*, 1988, *1956*, pp. 20–35.

Simon, Hermann. Management strategischer Wettbewerbsvorteile. (With English summary.) *Z. Betriebswirtshaft*, April 1988, *58*(4), pp. 461–80.

——— **and Kucher, Eckhard.** Die Bestimmung empirischer Preisabsatzfunktionen: Methoden, Befunde, Erfahrungen. (With English summary.) *Z. Betriebswirtshaft*, January 1988, *58*(1), pp. 171–83.

Simon, Jacqueline and Mishel, Lawrence R. The State of Working America. *Challenge*, Nov.–Dec. 1988, *31*(6), pp. 50–51.

Simon, Julian L. Re-linking Fertility Behavior and Economic Security in Old Age: Comment. *Population Devel. Rev.*, June 1988, *14*(2), pp. 327–31.

——— **and Ben-Ur, Joseph.** Demand, Cost and Prices in Duopoly. *Energy Econ.*, April 1988, *10*(2), pp. 117–24.

Simon, Lawrence H. and Ruccio, David F. Radical Theories of Development: Frank, the Modes of Production School, and Amin. In *Wilber, C. K., ed.*, 1988, pp. 121–73.

Simon, Roger D. Canada: An Introduction. In *Thornton, R. J.; Hyclak, T. and Aronson, J. R., eds.*, 1988, pp. 1–14.

Simonin, Jean-Pascal. À propos de deux ouvrages de Boisguillebert: L'effet Giffen phénomène de crise ou transformation structurelle. (With English summary.) *Revue Écon. Polit.*, March–April 1988, *98*(2), pp. 209–31.

———. Sur une conséquence paradoxale du paradoxe de Giffen. Application à la crise de la pomme de terre en Irlande au XIXᵉ siècle. (On a Paradoxical Consequence of the Giffen's Paradox. An Application to the Irish Potato. With English summary.) *Revue Écon.*, March 1988, *39*(2), pp. 391–403.

Simonis, Udo Ernst and Leipert, Christian. Environmental Damage—Environmental Expenditures: Statistical Evidence on the Federal Republic of Germany. *Int. J. Soc. Econ.*, 1988, *15*(7), pp. 37–52.

Simons, Thomas W., Jr. Strategy and Tactics in U.S. Foreign Policy toward Eastern Europe. In *Marer, P. and Siwinski, W., eds.*, 1988, pp. 305–14.

Simonsen, Mario Henrique. Price Stabilization and Incomes Policies: Theory and the Brazilian Case Study. In *Bruno, M., et al., eds.*, 1988, pp. 259–86.

———. Rational Expectations, Game Theory and Inflationary Inertia. In *Anderson, P. W.; Arrow, K. J. and Pines, D., eds.*, 1988, pp. 205–41.

——— **and Dornbusch, Rudiger.** Inflation Stabilization: The Role of Incomes Policy and of Monetization. In *Dornbusch, R.*, 1988, pp. 439–65.

Simonson, Donald G. and Stock, Duane R. Tax-Adjusted Duration for Amortizing Debt Instruments. *J. Finan. Quant. Anal.*, September 1988, *23*(3), pp. 313–27.

Simonson, Itamar; Huber, Joel and Payne, John. The Relationship between Prior Brand Knowledge and Information Acquisition Order. *J. Cons. Res.*, March 1988, *14*(4), pp. 566–78.

Simonson, Joy R. Protection of Clerical Homeworkers: From What, by Whom? In *Christensen, K. E., ed.*, 1988, pp. 157–67.

Simos, Evangelos O. and Charos, Evangelos N. The Effects of Human Capital and R&D upon International Trade Flows: Evidence from a Multi-input, Multi-output Model for the United States. *Weltwirtsch. Arch.*, 1988, *124*(4), pp. 701–12.

——— **and Triantis, John E.** A Note on Productivity, Inflation and Causality. *Rivista Int. Sci. Econ. Com.*, September 1988, *35*(9), pp. 839–46.

——— **and Triantis, John E.** The Theory of Permanent Income. In *Pesek, B. P.*, 1988, *1981*, pp. 236–39.

———; **Triantis, John E. and Kaen, Fred R.** A Term Structure Monetary Model of Exchange Rate Determination. *Econ. Notes*, 1988, (2), pp. 82–92.

Simpson, Herb M. Minimum Legal Drinking Ages and Highway Safety: A Methodological Critique: Comments. In *Graham, J. D., ed.*, 1988, pp. 158–62.

Simpson, R. J. Chemical Analysis in Space. In *Egan, J. J., et al.*, 1988, pp. 349–52.

Simpson, Thomas D. Developments in the U.S. Financial System since the Mid-1970s. *Fed. Res. Bull.*, January 1988, *74*(1), pp. 1–13.

Sims, Brian G., et al. Animal-Drawn Implements

for Small Farms in Mexico. *Food Res. Inst. Stud.*, 1988, *21*(1), pp. 69–95.

Sims, Christopher A. Bayesian Skepticism on Unit Root Econometrics. *J. Econ. Dynam. Control*, June–Sept. 1988, *12*(2–3), pp. 463–74.

———. Identifying Policy Effects. In *Bryant, R. C., et al., eds.*, 1988, pp. 305–21.

———. The New Keynesian Economics and the Output–Inflation Trade-off: Comment. *Brookings Pap. Econ. Act.*, 1988, (1), pp. 75–79.

———. Uncertainty across Models. *Amer. Econ. Rev.*, May 1988, *78*(2), pp. 163–67.

Sims, Joe. Private Antitrust Litigation: New Evidence, New Learning: Overview and Data: Comment. In *White, L. J., ed.*, 1988, pp. 102–03.

Sinai, Allen. The Crash of '87 and the Economy of '88. *Challenge*, Jan.–Feb. 1988, *31*(1), pp. 11–21.

Sincich, Terry and Smith, Stanley K. Stability over Time in the Distribution of Population Forecast Errors. *Demography*, August 1988, *25*(3), pp. 461–74.

Sinclair, M. Thea and Sutcliffe, Charles. The Economic Effects on Destination Areas of Foreign Involvement in the Tourism Industry: A Spanish Application. In *Goodall, B. and Ashworth, G., eds.*, 1988, pp. 111–32.

——— and Sutcliffe, Charles. The Estimation of Keynesian Income Multipliers at the Sub-national Level. *Appl. Econ.*, November 1988, *20*(11), pp. 1435–44.

Sinclair, Peter. Is Fiscal Expansion Inflationary? In *Eltis, W. and Sinclair, P. J. N., eds.*, 1988, pp. 139–71.

Sindelar, H. Richard, III and Peterson, J. E. Crosscurrents in the Gulf: Preface. In *Sindelar, H. R., III and Peterson, J. E., eds.*, 1988, pp. xiii–xviii.

Sindelar, Jody L. The Declining Price of Health Insurance. In *Frech, H. E., III, ed.*, 1988, pp. 259–91.

Sinden, J. A. Empirical Tests of Hypothetical Bias in Consumers' Surplus Surveys. *Australian J. Agr. Econ.*, Aug.–Dec. 1988, *32*(2–3), pp. 98–112.

——— and King, David A. Influence of Soil Conservation on Farm Land Values. *Land Econ.*, August 1988, *64*(3), pp. 242–55.

Singer, Alan J. Class-Conscious Coal Miners: Nanty-glo versus the Open Shop in the Post-World War I Era. *Labor Hist.*, Winter 1988, *29*(1), pp. 56–65.

Singer, Hans W. The World Development Report 1987 on the Blessings of 'Outward Orientation': A Necessary Correction. *J. Devel. Stud.*, January 1988, *24*(2), pp. 233–36.

——— and Gray, Patricia. Trade Policy and Growth of Developing Countries: Some New Data. *World Devel.*, March 1988, *16*(3), pp. 395–403.

Singer, Leslie P. Phenomenology and Economics of Art Markets: An Art Historical Perspective. *J. Cult. Econ.*, June 1988, *12*(1), pp. 27–40.

Singh, Ajit. Employment and Output in a Semi-industrial Economy: Modelling Alternative Policy Options in Mexico. In *Hopkins, M. J. D., ed.*, 1988, pp. 184–209.

———. Industrial Policy in Developing Countries: The Foreign Exchange Cost of Exports. *Industry Devel.*, January 1988, (23), pp. 1–43.

Singh, B. R. Human Resources Development in Industrial Sector. In *Kohli, U. and Gautam, V., eds.*, 1988, pp. 172–76.

Singh, Balbir; Bjørndal, Trond and Gordon, Daniel V. Economies of Scale in the Norwegian Fish-Meal Industry: Implications for Policy Decisions. *Appl. Econ.*, October 1988, *20*(10), pp. 1321–32.

Singh, Chetan. Conformity and Conflict: Tribes and the 'Agrarian System' of Mughal India. *Indian Econ. Soc. Hist. Rev.*, July–Sept. 1988, *25*(3), pp. 319–40.

Singh, Duleep. Productivity Scenerio in India—Seventh Five-Year Plan and Human Resource Development. In *Kohli, U. and Gautam, V., eds.*, 1988, pp. 12–25.

Singh, Gurjeet and Chadha, V. An Analysis of Tax Evasion in Punjab. In *Raikhy, P. S. and Gill, S. S., eds.*, 1988, pp. 140–51.

Singh, Harbir and Kogut, Bruce. Entering the United States by Joint Venture: Competitive Rivalry and Industry Structure. In *Contractor, F. J. and Lorange, P.*, 1988, pp. 241–51.

Singh, Harinder. Investigating the Compatibility of Econometric Forecasts and Subjective Expectations: A Suggested Framework. *J. Econ. Psych.*, June 1988, *9*(2), pp. 233–49.

——— and Frantz, Roger. Intrafirm (In) Efficiencies: Neoclassical and X-Efficiency Perspectives. *J. Econ. Issues*, September 1988, *22*(3), pp. 856–63.

——— and Frantz, Roger. Maximization Postulate: Type I and Type II Errors. *J. Post Keynesian Econ.*, Fall 1988, *11*(1), pp. 100–107.

Singh, Harsha V. An Extension of the Simple Analytics of Segmented Grain Markets and the Case for Liberalization. *World Devel.*, June 1988, *16*(6), pp. 759–63.

———. A Comment on Some Features of 'True Protection.' *J. Devel. Stud.*, October 1988, *25*(1), pp. 117–21.

Singh, Kamlesh; Sharma, H. R. and Oberoi, R. C. Rural Farm Size and Inequality: A Case Study. *Margin*, Jan.–March 1988, *20*(2), pp. 47–53.

Singh, Kullar Harbinder. Galtung and Wallerstein on Structural Theory of Imperialism: Roots of Social and Economic Disequilibrium. In *Vivekananda, F., ed.*, 1988, pp. 61–70.

Singh, Lakhwinder and Bhangoo, K. S. Changes in the Structure of Industrial Work Force in Punjab. *Margin*, Jan.–March 1988, *20*(2), pp. 54–64.

Singh, Manmohan. The Balance between Industry and Agriculture in Economic Development: Valedictory Address. In *Arrow, K. J., ed.*, 1988, pp. 138–50.

Singh, Parminder. Automotive Taxation in Punjab. In *Raikhy, P. S. and Gill, S. S.*, eds., 1988, pp. 127–39.

Singh, R. Oumade and Bourne, Compton. External Debt and Adjustment in Caribbean Countries. *Soc. Econ. Stud.*, December 1988, *37*(4), pp. 107–36.

Singh, Radhey S. Estimation of Error Variance in Linear Regression Models with Errors Having Multivariate Student-*t* Distribution with Unknown Degrees of Freedom. *Econ. Letters*, 1988, *27*(1), pp. 47–53.

Singh, Ram D. The Multinationals' Economic Penetration, Growth, Industrial Output, and Domestic Savings in Developing Countries: Another Look. *J. Devel. Stud.*, October 1988, *25*(1), pp. 55–82.

_____ **and Ram, Rati.** Farm Households in Rural Burkina Faso: Some Evidence on Allocative and Direct Return to Schooling, and Male–Female Labor Productivity Differentials. *World Devel.*, March 1988, *16*(3), pp. 419–24.

Singh, S. P. Human Resources Development for Infrastructure and Industry. In *Kohli, U. and Gautam, V.*, eds., 1988, pp. 82–88.

Singh, Saraswati P.; Hsu, Andy and Talwar, Prem P. Tests of Multiple Causality among Monetary and Fiscal Aggregates and Stock Prices. *J. Quant. Econ.*, January 1988, *4*(1), pp. 89–106.

Singh, Vijai P. and Borzutzky, Silvia. The State of the Mature Industrial Region in Western Europe and North America. *Urban Stud.*, June 1988, *25*(3), pp. 212–27.

Singhal, K. C. and Kaur, Narinder. India's Export Instabilty. *Margin*, Oct.–Dec. 1988, *21*(1), pp. 54–61.

Singleton, Kenneth J. Econometric Issues in the Analysis of Equilibrium Business Cycle Models. *J. Monet. Econ.*, March–May 1988, *21*(2–3), pp. 361–86.

_____; **Eichenbaum, Martin S. and Hansen, Lars Peter.** A Time Series Analysis of Representative Agent Models of Consumption and Leisure Choice under Uncertainty. *Quart. J. Econ.*, February 1988, *103*(1), pp. 51–78.

Singson, R. L. Privatization—The U.K. Experience. In *Association of Private Education*, 1988, pp. 73–77.

Sinha, B. N. SICO's Experience with HRD Approaches as Core of OD Effort: An Enviable Success Story. In *Kohli, U. and Gautam, V.*, eds., 1988, pp. 248–56.

Sinha, Dipendra. Irrational Expectations, Unclearing Markets and a Business Cycle That Won't Go Away: The Recent School of New Classical Economists Comes a Cropper on Basic Economic Facts. *Amer. J. Econ. Soc.*, July 1988, *47*(3), pp. 345–54.

Sinha, Ramesh P.; Rees, Hedley J. B. and Sahay, Surottam N. An Econometric Analysis of Workers Participation in Unions. *Indian Econ. J.*, Jan.–March 1988, *35*(3), pp. 61–71.

Sinha, Tapen. Life Cycle Model of Accumulation on Trial: An Eclectic Survey. *Quart. J. Bus. Econ.*, Winter 1988, *27*(1), pp. 83–103.

Sinicropi, Anthony V. and Hayford, Stephen L.

Bargaining Rights Status of Public Sector Supervisors. In *Lewin, D., et al.*, eds., 1988, *1976*, pp. 129–52.

Sinkey, Joseph F., Jr. and Greenawalt, Mary Brady. Bank Loan-Loss Provisions and the Income-Smoothing Hypothesis: An Empirical Analysis, 1976–84. *J. Finan. Services Res.*, December 1988, *1*(4), pp. 301–18.

Sinn, Hans-Werner. The Sahel Problem. *Kyklos*, 1988, *41*(2), pp. 187–213.

_____. U.S. Tax Reform 1981 and 1986: Impact on International Capital Markets and Capital Flows. *Nat. Tax J.*, September 1988, *41*(3), pp. 327–40.

_____. Welfare and Efficiency in Public Economics: Introduction. In *Bös, D.; Rose, M. and Seidl, C.*, eds.,, 1988, pp. vii–xvi.

_____. The 1986 U.S. Tax Reform and the World Capital Market. *Europ. Econ. Rev.*, March 1988, *32*(2–3), pp. 325–33.

Sinn, Stefan and Martinez Oliva, Juan Carlos. The Game-Theoretic Approach to International Policy Coordination: Assessing the Role of Targets. *Weltwirtsch. Arch.*, 1988, *124*(2), pp. 252–68.

Siow, Aloysius and Economides, Nicholas. The Division of Markets is Limited by the Extent of Liquidity (Spatial Competition with Externalities). *Amer. Econ. Rev.*, March 1988, *78*(1), pp. 108–21.

Sipos, Aladár and Halmai, Péter. Organization System and Economic Mechanism in Hungarian Agriculture. *Acta Oecon.*, 1988, *39*(3–4), pp. 199–230.

Sirageldin, Ismail and Mosley, W. Henry. Health Services and Population Planning Programs: A Review of Interrelations. In *Sirageldin, I. and Sorkin, A.*, eds., 1988, pp. 3–23.

Sirc, Ljubo. The End of Central Planning and Self-management? *Managerial Dec. Econ.*, Special Issue, Winter 1988, pp. 85–88.

Sirisena, N. L. and Stoeckel, John. Gender-Specific Socioeconomic Impacts of Development Programs in Sri Lanka. *J. Devel. Areas*, October 1988, *23*(1), pp. 31–42.

Siriwardana, A. Mahinda and Nguyen, D. T. The Relationship between Output Growth and Unemployment: A Re-examination of Okun's Law in Australia. *Australian Econ. Rev.*, 1st Quarter 1988, (81), pp. 16–27.

Siroën, Jean-Marc. La théorie de l'échange international en concurrence monopolistique. Une comparaison des modèles. (International Trade Theory in Monopolistic Competition. A Comparative Analysis of Basic Models. With English summary.) *Revue Écon.*, May 1988, *39*(3), pp. 511–44.

_____. Les aides à l'exportation en concurrence imparfaite avec discrimination des prix et économies d'échelle. (With English summary.) *Revue Écon. Polit.*, May–June 1988, *98*(3), pp. 401–13.

Sisson, Keith and Marginson, Paul. The Enterprises in Profile. In *Marginson, P., et al.*, 1988, pp. 21–50.

_____ **and Marginson, Paul.** The Management

of Employees. **In** *Marginson, P., et al.*, 1988, pp. 80–122.

Sitzer, Scott and Bopp, Anthony E. On the 'Efficiency' of Futures Markets: Another View. *Energy Econ.*, July 1988, *10*(3), pp. 199–205.

Sivakumar, Narayanaswamy and Ben-Horim, Moshe. Evaluating Capital Investment Projects. *Managerial Dec. Econ.*, December 1988, *9*(4), pp. 263–68.

Sivaramakrishnan, Konduru and Lys, Thomas. Earnings Expectations and Capital Restructuring: The Case of Equity-for-Debt Swaps. *J. Acc. Res.*, Autumn 1988, *26*(2), pp. 273–99.

Sivitz, Tracy Ellen. Eliminating the Continuing Effects of the Violation: Compensatory Education as a Remedy for Unlawful School Segregation. *Yale Law J.*, May 1988, *97*(6), pp. 1173–92.

Siwinski, Wlodzimierz. Why Poland Lost Its Creditworthiness. **In** *Marer, P. and Siwinski, W., eds.*, 1988, pp. 25–31.

_____ **and Marer, Paul.** Creditworthiness and Reform in Poland: Western and Polish Perspectives: Introduction. **In** *Marer, P. and Siwinski, W., eds.*, 1988, pp. xv–xxiii.

Siyal, Hussain B. Some Differentials in Infant and Child Mortality Risks in Pakistan 1962–1986: Comments. *Pakistan Devel. Rev.*, Part 2, Winter 1988, *27*(4), pp. 643.

Sjaastad, Larry A. Latin America and the World Economy. **In** *Jorge, A. and Salazar-Carrillo, J., eds.*, 1988, pp. 205–09.

Sjogren, Jane and Baum, Sandra R. Cost-of-Living Adjustments for Social Security Benefits: Their Impact on the Incomes of the Elderly. **In** *Danziger, S. H. and Portney, K. E., eds.*, 1988, pp. 87–115.

Sjoquist, David L. and Biegeleisen, J. Alan. Rational Voting Applied to Choice of Taxes. *Public Choice*, April 1988, *57*(1), pp. 39–47.

_____ **and Martinez-Vazquez, Jorge.** Property Tax Financing, Renting, and the Level of Local Expenditures. *Southern Econ. J.*, October 1988, *55*(2), pp. 424–31.

Sjostrom, William. Monopoly Exclusion of Lower Cost Entry: Loyalty Contracts in Ocean Shipping Conferences. *J. Transp. Econ. Policy*, September 1988, *22*(3), pp. 339–44.

Skaburskis, Andrejs. Criteria for Compensating for the Impacts of Large Projects: The Impact of British Columbia's Revelstoke Dam on Local Government Services. *J. Policy Anal. Manage.*, Fall 1988, *7*(4), pp. 668–86.

_____. The Nature of Canadian Condominium Submarkets and Their Effect on the Evolving Urban Spatial Structure. *Urban Stud.*, April 1988, *25*(2), pp. 109–23.

Skala, Heinz J. Essay on the History of the Development of Many-Valued Logics and Some Related Topics. **In** *Kacprzyk, J. and Fedrizzi, M., eds.*, 1988, pp. 1–9.

_____. On σ-Additive, σ-Coherence, and the Existence of Posteriors. **In** *Munier, B. R., ed.*, 1988, pp. 563–74.

Skeegan, Sam. Six Steps to Hiring Success. **In** *Timpe, A. D., ed.*, 1988, *1985*, pp. 279–84.

Skeels, Jack W.; McGrath, Paul and Arshanapalli, Gangadha. The Importance of Strike Size in Strike Research. *Ind. Lab. Relat. Rev.*, July 1988, *41*(4), pp. 582–91.

Skees, Jerry R. and Reed, Michael R. The Restructuring of Southern Agriculture: Data Needs for Economic and Policy Research. *Southern J. Agr. Econ.*, July 1988, *20*(1), pp. 33–40.

_____ **and Swanson, Louis E.** Farm Structure and Local Society Well-being in the South. **In** *Beaulieu, L. J., ed.*, 1988, pp. 141–57.

Skidelsky, Robert. Keynes's Political Legacy. **In** *Hamouda, O. F. and Smithin, J. N., eds.*, Vol. 1, 1988, pp. 3–28.

_____. Some Aspects of Keynes the Man. **In** *Hamouda, O. F. and Smithin, J. N., eds.*, Vol. 1, 1988, pp. 157–61.

Skillman, Gil, Jr. Bargaining and Replacement in Capitalist Firms. *Rev. Radical Polit. Econ.*, Summer–Fall 1988, *20*(2–3), pp. 177–83.

_____ **and Putterman, Louis.** The Incentive Effects of Monitoring under Alternative Compensation Schemes. *Int. J. Ind. Organ.*, March 1988, *6*(1), pp. 109–19.

Skinner, Jonathan. Risky Income, Life Cycle Consumption, and Precautionary Savings. *J. Monet. Econ.*, September 1988, *22*(2), pp. 237–55.

_____. The Welfare Cost of Uncertain Tax Policy. *J. Public Econ.*, November 1988, *37*(2), pp. 129–45.

_____ **and Johnson, William R.** Accounting for Changes in the Labor Supply of Recently Divorced Women. *J. Human Res.*, Fall 1988, *23*(4), pp. 417–36.

Sklair, Leslie. Transcending the Impasse: Metatheory, Theory, and Empirical Research in the Sociology of Development and Underdevelopment. *World Devel.*, June 1988, *16*(6), pp. 697–709.

Sknolnick, Jerome H. The Social Transformation of Vice. *Law Contemp. Probl.*, Winter 1988, *51*(1), pp. 9–29.

Skolka, Jiri V. Homogeneity of Price Development within Commodity Groups and by Demand Components: Analysis of Input–Output Data for Austria, 1964–76. **In** *Ciaschini, M., ed.*, 1988, pp. 19–41.

Skott, Peter. Finance, Saving and Accumulation. *Cambridge J. Econ.*, September 1988, *12*(3), pp. 339–54.

Skountzos, Theodoros. Social Accounting Matrix Multipliers in a Developing Economy: The Case of Greece. *Econ. Planning*, 1988, *22*(1–2), pp. 57–71.

Skousen, Mark. Murray Rothbard as Investment Advisor. **In** *[Rothbard, M. N.]*, 1988, pp. 151–74.

_____. Saving the Depression: A New Look at World War II. **In** *Rothbard, M. N. and Block, W., eds.*, 1988, pp. 211–26.

Skover, David M. and Collins, Ronald K. L. The Future of Liberal Legal Scholarship: Commentary. *Mich. Law Rev.*, October 1988, *87*(1), pp. 189–239.

Skyrms, Brian. Probability and Causation. *J. Econometrics*, Sept.–Oct. 1988, *39*(1–2), pp. 53–68.

Slade, Margaret E. Grade Selection under Uncertainty: Least Cost Last and Other Anomalies. *J. Environ. Econ. Manage.*, June 1988, *15*(2), pp. 189–205.

_____. Value-Added Total-Factor-Productivity Measurement: A Monte-Carlo Assessment. In *Eichhorn, W.*, ed., 1988, pp. 809–30.

Slaski, Lawrence J.; Rosenthal, Donald H. and Rose, Marshall B. Economic Value of the Oil and Gas Resources on the Outer Continental Shelf. *Marine Resource Econ.*, 1988, *5*(3), pp. 171–89.

Slavinskaia, Larisa. Planning Activity of the CMEA Member Countries: Bourgeois Conceptions and Reality. *Soviet E. Europ. Foreign Trade*, Spring 1988, *24*(1), pp. 6–17.

Slay, Benjamin. Foreign Trade Reforms since 1981. In *Marer, P. and Siwinski, W.*, eds., 1988, pp. 143–50.

Sleemi, Fehmida R. and Lacombe, John J., II. Wage Adjustments in Contracts Negotiated in Private Industry in 1987. *Mon. Lab. Rev.*, May 1988, *111*(5), pp. 23–28.

Slemrod, Joel. Effect of Taxation with International Capital Mobility. In *Aaron, H. J.; Galper, H. and Pechman, J. A.*, eds., 1988, pp. 115–48.

_____ **and Gordon, Roger H.** Do We Collect Any Revenue from Taxing Capital Income? In *Summers, L. H.*, ed., 1988, pp. 89–130.

_____**; Hayashi, Fumio and Ito, Takatoshi.** Housing Finance Imperfections, Taxation, and Private Saving: A Comparative Simulation Analysis of the United States and Japan. *J. Japanese Int. Economies*, September 1988, *2*(3), pp. 215–38.

Slesnick, Daniel T.; Stoker, Thomas M. and Jorgenson, Dale W. Two-Stage Budgeting and Exact Aggregation. *J. Bus. Econ. Statist.*, July 1988, *6*(3), pp. 313–25.

Slesser, Malcolm and King, Jane. Resource Accounting: An Application to Development Planning. *World Devel.*, February 1988, *16*(2), pp. 293–303.

Sleuwaegen, Leo. Multinationals, the European Community and Belgium: Recent Developments. In *Dunning, J. and Robson, P.*, eds., 1988, pp. 153–70.

_____**; Veugelers, Reinhilde and de Bondt, Raymond.** Innovative Strategic Groups in Multinational Industries. *Europ. Econ. Rev.*, April 1988, *32*(4), pp. 905–25.

_____ **and Yamawaki, Hideki.** The Formation of the European Common Market and Changes in Market Structure and Performance. *Europ. Econ. Rev.*, September 1988, *32*(7), pp. 1451–75.

Slevin, Dennis P. and Covin, Jeffrey G. New Venture Competitive Strategy: An Industry Life Cycle Analysis. In *Kirchhoff, B. A., et al.*, eds., 1988, pp. 446–60.

Sloan, Frank A. Property Rights in the Hospital

Industry. In *Frech, H. E., III*, ed., 1988, pp. 103–41.

_____ **and Blumstein, James F.** Antitrust and Hospital Peer Review. *Law Contemp. Probl.*, Spring 1988, *51*(2), pp. 7–92.

_____ **and Feldman, Roger D.** Competition among Physicians, Revisited. In *Greenberg, W.*, ed., 1988, pp. 17–39.

_____ **and Rosenberg, Christoph B.** Krankenhausfinanzierung in Selbstverwaltung: Comments from a U.S. Perspective. *J. Inst. Theoretical Econ.*, April 1988, *144*(2), pp. 388–95.

_____**; Valvona, Joseph and Morrisey, Michael A.** Defining Geographic Markets for Hospital Care. *Law Contemp. Probl.*, Spring 1988, *51*(2), pp. 165–94.

_____, et al. Cost of Capital to the Hospital Sector. *J. Health Econ.*, March 1988, *7*(1), pp. 25–45.

Sloan, Judith and Drago, Robert. The Australian Labour Market, June 1988. *Australian Bull. Lab.*, June 1988, *14*(3), pp. 455–68.

_____ **and Hancock, Susan.** The Australian Labour Market, March 1988. *Australian Bull. Lab.*, March 1988, *14*(2), pp. 390–99.

_____ **and Robertson, Frances.** A Labour Market Profile of Nurses in Australia. *Australian Bull. Lab.*, June 1988, *14*(3), pp. 507–28.

Sloane, P. J. Gender, Pay Equity and Equal Value: A Solution in Search of a Rationale? *Managerial Dec. Econ.*, Special Issue, Winter 1988, pp. 45–50.

_____ **and Chiplin, B.** The Effect of Britain's Anti-discrimination Legislation on Relative Pay and Employment: A Comment. *Econ. J.*, September 1988, *98*(392), pp. 833–38.

_____ **and Dex, Shirley.** Detecting and Removing Discrimination under Equal Opportunities Policies. *J. Econ. Surveys*, 1988, *2*(1), pp. 1–27.

Slocum, John W., Jr.; Cron, William L. and Yows, Linda C. Whose Career Is Likely to Plateau? In *Timpe, A. D.*, ed., 1988, *1987*, pp. 266–78.

Slot, Brigitte; Brinkman, Henk Jan and Drukker, J. W. Height and Income: A New Method for the Estimation of Historical National Income Series. *Exploration Econ. Hist.*, July 1988, *25*(3), pp. 227–64.

Slottje, Daniel J. and Basmann, Robert L. Errata [A New Index of Income Inequality: The *B* Measure]. *Econ. Letters*, 1988, *26*(3), pp. 295–97.

_____**; Basmann, Robert L. and Molina, David J.** A Note on Measuring Veblen's Theory of Conspicuous Consumption. *Rev. Econ. Statist.*, August 1988, *70*(3), pp. 531–35.

_____**; Haslag, Joseph H. and Fomby, Thomas B.** A Study of the Relationship between Economic Growth and Inequality: The Case of Mexico. *Fed. Res. Bank Dallas Econ. Rev.*, May 1988, pp. 13–25.

_____**; Hayes, Kathy J. and Molina, David J.** Measuring Preference Variation across North America. *Economica*, November 1988, *55*(220), pp. 525–39.

_____; Hirschberg, Joseph G. and Molina, David J. A Selection Criterion for Choosing between Functional Forms of Income Distribution. *Econometric Rev.*, 1988–89, 7(2), pp. 183–97.

_____ and Nieswiadomy, Michael L. Estimating Lost Future Earnings Using the New Worklife Tables: A Comment. *J. Risk Ins.*, September 1988, 55(3), pp. 539–44.

Slovic, Paul; Fischhoff, Baruch and Lichtenstein, Sarah. Response Mode, Framing, and Information-Processing Effects in Risk Assessment. In *Bell, D. E.; Raiffa, H. and Tversky, A., eds.*, 1988, 1982, pp. 152–66.

_____; Lichtenstein, Sarah and Fischhoff, Baruch. Knowing What You Want: Measuring Labile Values. In *Bell, D. E.; Raiffa, H. and Tversky, A., eds.*, 1988, 1980, pp. 398–421.

Slovin, Myron B. and Barrett, W. Brian. Economic Volatility and the Demand for Consumer Durables. *Appl. Econ.*, June 1988, 20(6), pp. 731–38.

_____; Sushka, Marie E. and Barrett, W. Brian. Reserve Regulation and Recourse as a Source of Risk Premia in the Federal Funds Market. *J. Banking Finance*, December 1988, 12(4), pp. 575–84.

_____; Sushka, Marie E. and Hudson, Carl D. Corporate Commercial Paper, Note Issuance Facilities, and Shareholder Wealth. *J. Int. Money Finance*, September 1988, 7(3), pp. 289–302.

Slowinski, Betty J.; Northrup, Herbert R. and Campbell, Duncan C. Multinational Union–Management Consultation in Europe: Resurgence in the 1980s? *Int. Lab. Rev.*, 1988, 127(5), pp. 525–43.

Sloyan, M. J. and Palmer, C. M. The Experience of the UK Meat and Livestock Commission in Providing Videotex Services in Great Britain. In *Schiefer, G., ed.*, 1988, pp. 73–86.

Slyadz, N. N. and Borisov, A. N. Decision Making Based on Fuzzy Stochastic and Statistical Dominance. In *Kacprzyk, J. and Fedrizzi, M., eds.*, 1988, pp. 197–214.

Smackey, Bruce M. and Kolchin, Michael G. Chrysler Canada: Positioning for the Future. In *Thornton, R. J.; Hyclak, T. and Aronson, J. R., eds.*, 1988, pp. 145–67.

Small, Annette M. Interstate Trade in Market Milk. *Rev. Marketing Agr. Econ.*, April 1988, 56(1), pp. 135–39.

Small, Kenneth A. and Berechman, J. Research Policy and Review 25. Modeling Land Use and Transportation: An Interpretive Review for Growth Areas. *Environ. Planning A*, October 1988, 20(10), pp. 1285–1309.

_____ and Winston, Clifford. Optimal Highway Durability. *Amer. Econ. Rev.*, June 1988, 78(3), pp. 560–69.

Small, Marshall L. Legal Rules, Takeover Strategies, and Defensive Tactics: Comment. In *Coffee, J. C., Jr.; Lowenstein, L. and Rose-Ackerman, S., eds.*, 1988, pp. 455–58.

Smart, Alan. Resistance to Relocation by Shop-

keepers in a Hong Kong Squatter Area. In *Clark, G., ed.*, 1988, pp. 119–38.

Smart, Bruce. A U.S. Perspective. In *Lucas, R. E. B. and Papanek, G. F., eds.*, 1988, pp. 366–68.

Smart, Josephine. How to Survive in Illegal Street Hawking in Hong Kong. In *Clark, G., ed.*, 1988, pp. 99–117.

Smeeding, Timothy M. Reagan, the Recession, and Poverty: What the Official Estimates Fail to Show. In *Danziger, S. H. and Portney, K. E., eds.*, 1988, pp. 47–64.

_____; Betson, David M. and Warlick, Jennifer L. The Effects of Taxing Unemployment Insurance Benefits Accounting For Induced Labor Supply Responses. In *Danziger, S. H. and Portney, K. E., eds.*, 1988, pp. 149–67.

_____; Jencks, Christopher and Palmer, John L. The Uses and Limits of Income Comparisons. In *Palmer, J. L.; Smeeding, T. and Torrey, B. B., eds.*, 1988, pp. 9–27.

_____; Torrey, Barbara Boyle and Palmer, John L. The Vulnerable: Introduction. In *Palmer, J. L.; Smeeding, T. and Torrey, B. B., eds.*, 1988, pp. 1–6.

_____; Torrey, Barbara Boyle and Rein, Martin. Patterns of Income and Poverty: The Economic Status of Children and the Elderly in Eight Countries. In *Palmer, J. L.; Smeeding, T. and Torrey, B. B., eds.*, 1988, pp. 89–119.

Smeets, Heinz-Dieter. Zur Wahl eines geldpolitischen Indikators für die Bundesrepublik Deutschland. (Selecting a Monetary Indicator for Germany. With English summary.) *Jahr. Nationalökon. Statist.*, November 1988, 205(5), pp. 410–26.

Smeltz, Wayne J. and Miller, Van V. An Empirical and Historical Examination of How Organizations Manage and Manipulate Their Environments: The FASB Example. In *Grant, J. H., ed.*, 1988, pp. 361–75.

Smiley, Gene and Keehn, Richard H. Margin Purchases, Brokers' Loans and the Bull Market of the Twenties. In *Hausman, W. J., ed.*, 1988, pp. 129–42.

_____ and Keehn, Richard H. U.S. Bank Failures, 1932–1933: A Provisional Analysis. In *Perkins, E. J., ed.*, 1988, pp. 136–56.

Smiley, Robert. Empirical Evidence on Strategic Entry Deterrence. *Int. J. Ind. Organ.*, June 1988, 6(2), pp. 167–80.

Smirlock, Michael and Starks, Laura. An Empirical Analysis of the Stock Price–Volume Relationship. *J. Banking Finance*, 1988, 12(1), pp. 31–41.

Smit, E. van der M. and Wesso, G. R. Structural Stability in South African Econometric Models—Some Empirical Results. *J. Stud. Econ. Econometrics*, March 1988, 12(1), pp. 51–71.

Smith, A. F. M. and Naylor, J. C. Econometric Illustrations of Novel Numerical Integration Strategies for Bayesian Inference. *J. Econometrics*, May–June 1988, 38(1–2), pp. 103–25.

Smith, Abbie and Schipper, Katherine. Restructuring in the Food Industry. In *Libecap, G., ed. (I)*, 1988, pp. 131–68.

Smith, Alasdair. East–West Trade, Embargoes, and Expectations. In *Baldwin, R. E.; Hamilton, C. B. and Sapir, A., eds.*, 1988, pp. 153–70.

———. Shadow Price Calculations in Distorted Economies. In *Haaland, J. I. and Norman, V. D., eds.*, 1988, pp. 71–86.

——— and Venables, Anthony J. Completing the Internal Market in the European Community: Some Industry Simulations. *Europ. Econ. Rev.*, September 1988, *32*(7), pp. 1501–25.

Smith, Barbara M. and Wren, Anthony. Experiences with a Crew Scheduling System Based on Set Covering. In *Daduna, J. R. and Wren, A., eds.*, 1988, pp. 104–18.

Smith, Barton A. and Ohsfeldt, Robert L. Assessing the Accuracy of Structural Parameter Estimates in Analyses of Implicit Markets. *Land Econ.*, May 1988, *64*(2), pp. 135–46.

Smith, Brian and White, Robert W. The Deposit Insurance System in Canada: Problems and Proposals for Change. *Can. Public Policy*, December 1988, *14*(4), pp. 331–46.

Smith, Bruce D. Legal Restrictions, "Sunspots," and Peel's Bank Act: The Real Bills Doctrine versus the Quantity Theory Reconsidered. *J. Polit. Econ.*, February 1988, *96*(1), pp. 3–19.

———. The Relationship between Money and Prices: Some Historical Evidence Reconsidered. *Fed. Res. Bank Minn. Rev.*, Summer 1988, *12*(3), pp. 18–32.

———; Boyd, John H. and Prescott, Edward C. Organizations in Economic Analysis. *Can. J. Econ.*, August 1988, *21*(3), pp. 477–91.

——— and Sargent, Thomas J. The Irrelevance of Government Foreign Exchange Operations. In *Helpman, E.; Razin, A. and Sadka, E., eds.*, 1988, pp. 328–45.

Smith, C. E. Output Effects of a Tariff under Flexible Exchange Rates. *J. Int. Econ.*, May 1988, *24*(3–4), pp. 359–71.

Smith, C. Selby. Technology and Health Expenditures in Australia: Results from the Residual Approach: Commentary. In *Smith, C. S., ed.*, 1988, pp. 19–23.

Smith, Chris; Whipp, Richard and Willmott, Hugh. Case-Study Research in Accounting: Methodological Breakthrough or Ideological Weapon? In *Neimark, M., ed.*, 1988, pp. 95–120.

Smith, Clifford W., Jr. and Barclay, Michael J. Corporate Payout Policy: Cash Dividends versus Open-Market Repurchases. *J. Finan. Econ.*, October 1988, *22*(1), pp. 61–82.

———; Brickley, James A. and Lease, Ronald C. Ownership Structure and Voting on Antitakeover Amendments. *J. Finan. Econ.*, Jan.–March 1988, *20*(1–2), pp. 267–91.

——— and Mayers, David. Ownership Structure across Lines of Property-Casualty Insurance. *J. Law Econ.*, October 1988, *31*(2), pp. 351–78.

Smith, Cyril Stanley and Kranzberg, Melvin. Materials in History and Society. In *Forester, T., ed.*, 1988, *1979*, pp. 85–118.

Smith, Dale L. Reagan's National Security Leg-

acy: Model-Based Analyses of Recent Changes in American Policy. *J. Conflict Resolution*, December 1988, *32*(4), pp. 595–625.

Smith, David B. An Investigation of Securities and Exchange Commission Regulation of Auditor Change Disclosures: The Case of Accounting Series Release No. 165. *J. Acc. Res.*, Spring 1988, *26*(1), pp. 134–45.

———; Hefzi, Hassan and Ifflander, A. James. Municipal Bond Market Risk Measures and Bond Ratings. In *Schwartz, B. N., ed.*, 1988, pp. 111–27.

——— and Pourciau, Susan. A Comparison of the Financial Characteristics of December and Non-December Year-End Companies. *J. Acc. Econ.*, December 1988, *10*(4), pp. 335–44.

Smith, David P. and Keith, Verna M. The Current Differential in Black and White Life Expectancy. *Demography*, November 1988, *25*(4), pp. 625–32.

Smith, David W. Reassessments, Waivers, Amended Returns, and Refunds. In *Canadian Tax Foundation*, 1988, pp. 8.1–49.

Smith, Donald J. An Apartment Story: To Introduce the Study of Spot, Forward, and Futures Markets, the Term Structure, and Arbitrage. *J. Econ. Educ.*, Summer 1988, *19*(3), pp. 275–86.

———. Credit Union Rate and Earnings Retention Decisions Under Uncertainty and Taxation. *J. Money, Credit, Banking*, February 1988, *20*(1), pp. 119–31.

Smith, Douglas A. Recent Proposals for Copyright Revision: An Evaluation. *Can. Public Policy*, June 1988, *14*(2), pp. 175–85.

Smith, Fred L., Jr. What Environmental Policy? In *Boaz, D., ed.*, 1988, pp. 333–49.

Smith, Frederick W. Air Cargo Transportation in the Next Economy. In *Guile, B. R. and Quinn, J. B., eds. (II)*, 1988, pp. 160–66.

Smith, Herbert L. and Cutright, Phillips. Thinking about Change in Illegitimacy Ratios: United States, 1963–1983. *Demography*, May 1988, *25*(2), pp. 235–47.

Smith, Hilary H. Drought 1988: Farmers and the Macroeconomy. *Fed. Res. Bank Dallas Econ. Rev.*, September 1988, pp. 15–22.

———. U.S. Agricultural Export Competitiveness: Export Levels, Trade Shares, and the Law of One Price. *Fed. Res. Bank Dallas Econ. Rev.*, July 1988, pp. 14–25.

Smith, Howard L. and Discenza, Richard. Is Employee Discipline Obsolete? In *Timpe, A. D., ed.*, 1988, *1985*, pp. 351–62.

Smith, J. Barry and Katz, Eliakim. Rent-Seeking and Optimal Regulation in Replenishable Resource Industries. *Public Choice*, October 1988, *59*(1), pp. 25–36.

——— and Stelcner, Morton. Labour Supply of Married Women in Canada, 1980. *Can. J. Econ.*, November 1988, *21*(4), pp. 857–70.

Smith, James A. A Model of Daily Municipal Water Use for Short-term Forecasting. *Water Resources Res.*, February 1988, *24*(2), pp. 201–206.

Smith, James L.; Paddock, James L. and Siegel,

Daniel R. Option Valuation of Claims on Real Assets: The Case of Offshore Petroleum Leases. *Quart. J. Econ.*, August 1988, *103*(3), pp. 479–508.

_____; **Siegel, Daniel R. and Cheng, C. S. Agnes.** Failure of the Net Profit Share Leasing Experiment for Offshore Petroleum Resources. *Rev. Econ. Statist.*, May 1988, *70*(2), pp. 199–206.

Smith, James P. and Welch, Finis R. Racial Discrimination: A Human Capital Perspective. In *Mangum, G. and Philips, P., eds.*, 1988, pp. 95–116.

Smith, Keith V. Postwar Working Capital Investments in the United States. In *Kim, Y. H., ed.*, 1988, pp. 17–35.

Smith, L. C., Jr. and Smith, L. Murphy. Teaching Microeconomics with Microcomputer Spreadsheets. *J. Econ. Educ.*, Fall 1988, *19*(4), pp. 363–82.

Smith, L. D. Africa's Crisis. *J. Devel. Stud.*, January 1988, *24*(2), pp. 250–57.

Smith, L. Murphy and Smith, L. C., Jr. Teaching Microeconomics with Microcomputer Spreadsheets. *J. Econ. Educ.*, Fall 1988, *19*(4), pp. 363–82.

Smith, Lawrence B. Economic Implications of Ontario's New Housing Legislation, Bills 11 and 51. *Can. Public Policy*, December 1988, *14*(4), pp. 390–98.

_____; **Rosen, Kenneth T. and Fallis, George.** Recent Developments in Economic Models of Housing Markets. *J. Econ. Lit.*, March 1988, *26*(1), pp. 29–64.

Smith, Lee O. The Cuomo Commission's "New Realism." *Challenge*, Sept.–Oct. 1988, *31*(5), pp. 37–43.

Smith, M.; MacMillan, J. A. and Arthur, Louise M. Economic Evaluation Methodology for an Alberta Agro-energy Project. *Can. J. Agr. Econ.*, Part 2, December 1988, *36*(4), pp. 905–13.

Smith, M. Estellie. The Informal Economy and the State. In *Clark, G., ed.*, 1988, pp. 189–99.

Smith, Marc T. and Hendershott, Patric H. Housing Inventory Change and the Role of Existing Structures, 1961–1985. *Amer. Real Estate Urban Econ. Assoc. J.*, Winter 1988, *16*(4), pp. 364–78.

_____ **and Ling, David C.** Another Look at Mortgage Revenue Bonds [The Efficiency and Distribution of Mortgage Revenue Bond Subsidies: The Effects of Behavioral Responses]. *J. Policy Anal. Manage.*, Spring 1988, *7*(3), pp. 562–64.

Smith, Mark E.; van Ravenswaay, Eileen O. and Thompson, Stanley R. Sales Loss Determination in Food Contamination Incidents: An Application to Milk Bans in Hawaii. *Amer. J. Agr. Econ.*, August 1988, *70*(3), pp. 513–20.

Smith, Mark Griffin and Marin, Carlos M. Water Resources Assessment: A Spatial Equilibrium Approach. *Water Resources Res.*, June 1988, *24*(6), pp. 793–801.

Smith, Marlene A. Income or Wealth in Money

Demand: Comment. *Southern Econ. J.*, April 1988, *54*(4), pp. 1033–38.

Smith, Matthew G. The Introduction of Isolated Soy Protein Food Ingredients in Sweden: Prospective Impacts on Trade, Food Policy, and Agricultural Resource Use. In *Schwarz, F. H., ed.*, 1988, pp. 71–106.

_____; **Schuh, Maria Ignez and Schuh, G. Edward.** The Potential Role of Isolated Soy Protein Food Ingredients in Mexico. In *Schwarz, F. H., ed.*, 1988, pp. 159–87.

Smith, Michael B. The Uruguay Round and the Intellectual Property Agenda. In *Walker, C. E. and Bloomfield, M. A., eds.*, 1988, pp. 163–68.

Smith, Michael L. and Witt, Robert C. Informational Asymmetries in Retroactive Insurance: A Response. *J. Risk Ins.*, September 1988, *55*(3), pp. 548–54.

Smith, Murray G. Exchange Rates and Their Role in Agricultural Trade Issues: A Commentary. In *Miner, W. M. and Hathaway, D. E., eds.*, 1988, pp. 211–14.

_____. The Free Trade Agreement in Context: A Canadian Perspective. In *Schott, J. J. and Smith, M. G., eds.*, 1988, pp. 37–64.

_____. What Is at Stake? In *Diebold, W., Jr., ed.*, 1988, pp. 69–104.

_____ **and Allen, Kristen.** An Overview of Agricultural Issues in the U.S.–Canadian Free Trade Agreement. In *Allen, K. and Macmillan, K., eds.*, 1988, pp. 1–8.

_____ **and Schott, Jeffrey J.** Services and Investment. In *Schott, J. J. and Smith, M. G., eds.*, 1988, pp. 137–50.

Smith, Neil R. Present Trends and Outlook for Metals Markets and Trade in the Asia-Pacific Region. In *Dorian, J. P. and Fridley, D. G., eds.*, 1988, pp. 67–91.

Smith, Nina and Westergård-Nielsen, Niels. Udviklingen i lønforskelle mellem den offentlige og private sektor. (Wage Differentials between the Public and the Private Sector in Denmark. With English summary.) *Nationaløkon. Tidsskr.*, 1988, *126*(1), pp. 13–30.

Smith, Peter; Budd, Alan and Levine, Paul. Real Wage Adjustment and Long-term Unemployment. In *Cross, R., ed.*, 1988, pp. 41–64.

_____; **Budd, Alan and Levine, Paul.** Unemployment, Vacancies and the Long-term Unemployed. *Econ. J.*, December 1988, *98*(393), pp. 1071–91.

_____ **and Holly, Sean.** Compositional Effects and Unemployment in the United States and Europe. In *Giersch, H., ed.*, 1988, pp. 152–65.

_____ **and Levine, Paul.** The Gains from Optimal Control in a Small Econometric Model of the UK. *J. Econ. Dynam. Control*, March 1988, *12*(1), pp. 13–18.

Smith, Richard L. Forecasting Records by Maximum Likelihood. *J. Amer. Statist. Assoc.*, June 1988, *83*(402), pp. 331–38.

Smith, Robert and Mann, Arthur J. Tax Attitudes and Tax Evasion in Puerto Rico: A Survey of

Upper Income Professionals. *J. Econ. Devel.*, June 1988, *13*(1), pp. 121–41.

Smith, Robert C. Financing Black Politics: A Study of Congressional Elections. *Rev. Black Polit. Econ.*, Summer 1988, *17*(1), pp. 5–30.

Smith, Robert J. Private Solutions to Conservation Problems. In *Cowen, T.*, ed., 1988, pp. 341–60.

_____; **Rehnfeldt, Maria and Barbieri, William M.** Indian Colonization in Paraguay: What Is Success? In *Annis, S. and Hakim, P.*, eds., 1988, pp. 58–64.

Smith, Robert S. Comparable Worth: Limited Coverage and the Exacerbation of Inequality. *Ind. Lab. Relat. Rev.*, January 1988, *41*(2), pp. 227–39.

_____ and **Ruser, John W.** The Effect of OSHA Records-Check Inspections on Reported Occupational Injuries in Manufacturing Establishments. *J. Risk Uncertainty*, December 1988, *1*(4), pp. 415–35.

Smith, Rodney T. International Energy Cooperation: The Mismatch between IEA Policy Actions and Policy Goals. In *Horwich, G. and Weimer, D. L.*, eds., 1988, pp. 17–103.

Smith, Roger B. Global Competition—A Strategy for Success. In *Rosow, J. M.*, ed., 1988, pp. 33–50.

Smith, Russell E. Wage Indexation, Turnover, and Nominal-Wage Changes in Brazilian Manufacturing,1966–1976. *J. Devel. Econ.*, March 1988, *28*(2), pp. 159–73.

Smith, Scott D. and Cartwright, David W. Deflators for Purchases of Computers in GNP: Revised and Extended Estimates, 1983–88. *Surv. Curr. Bus.*, November 1988, *68*(11), pp. 22–23.

Smith, Stanley K. and Sincich, Terry. Stability over Time in the Distribution of Population Forecast Errors. *Demography*, August 1988, *25*(3), pp. 461–74.

Smith, Stephen. Excise Duties and the Internal Market. *J. Common Market Stud.*, December 1988, *27*(2), pp. 147–60.

_____. Should UK Local Government Be Financed by a Poll Tax? *Fisc. Stud.*, February 1988, *9*(1), pp. 18–28.

_____ and **Pearson, Mark.** 1992: Issues in Indirect Taxation. *Fisc. Stud.*, November 1988, *9*(4), pp. 25–35.

_____ and **Watson, Sheila.** Consequences of the Abolition of the Inner London Education Authority. *Fisc. Stud.*, August 1988, *9*(3), pp. 68–85.

Smith, Stephen C. On the Incidence of Profit and Equity Sharing: Theory and an Application to the High Tech Sector. *J. Econ. Behav. Organ.*, January 1988, *9*(1), pp. 45–58.

_____ and **Bradley, Michael D.** Employment, Prices, and Money in the Share Economy: An Alternative View. In *Jones, D. C. and Svejnar, J.*, eds., 1988, pp. 201–08.

_____ and **Bradley, Michael D.** On Illyrian Macroeconomics. *Economica*, May 1988, *55*(218), pp. 249–59.

_____ and **Ye, Meng-Hua.** Dynamic Allocation in a Labor-Managed Firm. *J. Compar. Econ.*, June 1988, *12*(2), pp. 204–16.

Smith, Stephen D.; Morgan, George Emir and Shome, Dilip K. Optimal Futures Positions for Large Banking Firms. *J. Finance*, March 1988, *43*(1), pp. 175–95.

_____; **Pinkerton, John M. and Shome, Dilip K.** The Purchasing Power of Money and Nominal Interest Rates: A Re-examination. *J. Finance*, December 1988, *43*(5), pp. 1113–25.

_____ and **Shome, Dilip K.** An Econometric Analysis of Equity Costs and Risk Premiums in the Electric Utility Industry: 1971–1985. *Financial Rev.*, November 1988, *23*(4), pp. 439–52.

Smith, Stephen L. How Much Change at the Store? The Impact of New Technologies and Labour Processes on Managers and Staffs in Retail Distribution. In *Knights, D. and Willmott, H.*, eds., 1988, pp. 143–62.

_____ and **Wield, David.** Banking on the New Technology: Cooperation, Competition and the Clearers. In *Harris, L., et al.*, eds., 1988, pp. 240–73.

_____ and **Wield, David.** New Technology and Bank Work: Banking on It as an 'Organisational Technology.' In *Harris, L., et al.*, eds., 1988, pp. 274–300.

Smith, Stephen M.; Barkley, David L. and Dahlgran, Roger A. High-Technology Manufacturing in the Nonmetropolitan West: Gold or Just Glitter. *Amer. J. Agr. Econ.*, August 1988, *70*(3), pp. 560–71.

_____ and **Gibson, Cosette M.** Industrial Diversification in Nonmetropolitan Counties and Its Effect on Economic Stability. *Western J. Agr. Econ.*, December 1988, *13*(2), pp. 193–201.

Smith, Thomas C. The Discontented. In *Smith, T. C.*, 1988, *1962*, pp. 148–55.

_____. Farm Family By-Employments in Preindustrial Japan. In *Smith, T. C.*, 1988, *1969*, pp. 71–102.

_____. Japan's Aristocratic Revolution. In *Smith, T. C.*, 1988, *1961*, pp. 133–47.

_____. The Land Tax in the Tokugawa Period. In *Smith, T. C.*, 1988, *1958*, pp. 50–70.

_____. "Merit" as Ideology in the Tokugawa Period. In *Smith, T. C.*, 1988, *1967*, pp. 156–72.

_____. Peasant Time and Factory Time in Japan. In *Smith, T. C.*, 1988, *1986*, pp. 199–235.

_____. Premodern Economic Growth: Japan and the West. In *Smith, T. C.*, 1988, *1973*, pp. 15–49.

_____. The Right to Benevolence: Dignity and Japanese Workers, 1890–1920. In *Smith, T. C.*, 1988, *1984*, pp. 236–70.

_____. Ōkuranagatsune and the Technologists. In *Smith, T. C.*, 1988, *1970*, pp. 173–98.

_____ and **Eng, Robert Y.** Peasant Families and Population Control in Eighteenth-Century Japan. In *Smith, T. C.*, 1988, *1976*, pp. 103–32.

Smith, Tony E. A Cost-efficiency Theory of Dispersed Network Equilibria. *Environ. Planning A*, February 1988, *20*(2), pp. 231–66.

_____. Price Equilibria for Markets with Supply Rigidities and Demand Heterogeneity. *Reg. Sci. Urban Econ.*, February 1988, *18*(1), pp. 165–97.

Smith, V. Kerry. Legislating Open Access to a Scarce Resource: A Shortcoming of Policy on Nuclear Waste. *J. Policy Anal. Manage.*, Winter 1988, *7*(2), pp. 367–72.

_____. Selection and Recreation Demand. *Amer. J. Agr. Econ.*, February 1988, *70*(1), pp. 29–36.

_____ **and Desvousges, William H.** The Valuation of Environmental Risks and Hazardous Waste Policy. *Land Econ.*, August 1988, *64*(3), pp. 211–19.

_____ **and Johnson, F. Reed.** How Do Risk Perceptions Respond to Information? The Case of Radon. *Rev. Econ. Statist.*, February 1988, *70*(1), pp. 1–8.

_____, **et al.** Learning about Radon's Risk. *J. Risk Uncertainty*, June 1988, *1*(2), pp. 233–58.

Smith, Vernon L. Electric Power Deregulation: Background and Prospects. *Contemp. Policy Issues*, July 1988, *6*(3), pp. 14–24.

_____; **Suchanek, Gerry L. and Williams, Arlington W.** Bubbles, Crashes, and Endogenous Expectations in Experimental Spot Asset Markets. *Econometrica*, September 1988, *56*(5), pp. 1119–51.

_____; **Walker, James M. and Cox, James C.** Theory and Individual Behavior of First-Price Auctions. *J. Risk Uncertainty*, March 1988, *1*(1), pp. 61–99.

Smith, W. James; Vaughan, Michael B. and Potiowsky, Thomas P. Inferring Collusion from Pricing Behavior: The American Tobacco Case Reexamined. *Atlantic Econ. J.*, September 1988, *16*(3), pp. 40–45.

Smithin, John N. On Flexible Wage Policy. *Écon. Soc.*, March 1988, *22*(3), pp. 135–53.

_____ **and Hamouda, Omar F.** Rational Behavior with Deficient Foresight. *Eastern Econ. J.*, July–Sept. 1988, *14*(3), pp. 277–85.

_____ **and Hamouda, Omar F.** Uncertainty and Economic Analysis: Some Remarks. *Econ. J.*, March 1988, *98*(389), pp. 159–64.

Smithson, Charles W. and Thomas, Christopher R. Measuring the Cost to Consumers of Product Defects: The Value of "Lemon Insurance." *J. Law Econ.*, October 1988, *31*(2), pp. 485–502.

Smits, Willem J. B. Foreign Direct Investment and Export and Import Value: A Cross-Section Study for Thirty Less Developed Countries. *De Economist*, March 1988, *136*(1), pp. 91–117.

Smolensky, Eugene; Danziger, Sheldon H. and Gottschalk, Peter. The Declining Significance of Age in the United States: Trends in the Well-Being of Children and the Elderly since 1939. In *Palmer, J. L.; Smeeding, T. and Torrey, B. B., eds.*, 1988, pp. 29–54.

Smook, Nicholas P. and Wolf, Bernard M. Keynes and the Question of Tariffs. In *Hamouda, O. F. and Smithin, J. N., eds., Vol. 2*, 1988, pp. 169–82.

Smout, T. C.; Gibson, A. and Cullen, L. M. Wages and Comparative Development in Ireland and Scotland, 1565–1780. In *Mitchison, R. and Roebuck, P., eds.*, 1988, pp. 105–16.

Smulovitz, Catalina. Crónica de un final anunciado: Las elecciones de marzo de 1962. (With English summary.) *Desarrollo Econ.*, April–June 1988, *28*(109), pp. 105–19.

Smyth, David J. and Dua, Pami. Public Perceptions of Macroeconomic Policy: An Econometric Analysis of the Reagan Presidency. *Rev. Econ. Statist.*, May 1988, *70*(2), pp. 357–61.

Snape, Richard H. Is Non-discrimination Really Dead? *World Econ.*, March 1988, *11*(1), pp. 1–17.

Sneeden, Emory M. Private Antitrust Litigation: New Evidence, New Learning: Comment: Proposed Changes in Private Antitrust Enforcement, Policy Implications. In *White, L. J., ed.*, 1988, pp. 416–18.

Sneessens, Henri and Maillard, Bénédicte. Investment, Sales Constraints and Profitability in France, 1957–1985. *Rech. Écon. Louvain*, 1988, *54*(2), pp. 151–67.

Snell, Andy and Tonks, Ian. The Sweet Taste of Information: A Study of the Demand for New Brands in the UK Confectionery Industry. *Appl. Econ.*, August 1988, *20*(8), pp. 1041–55.

Snijders, Tom A. B. On Cross-Validation for Predictor Evaluation in Time Series. In *Dijkstra, T. K., ed.*, 1988, pp. 56–69.

Snooks, G. D. Government Unemployment Relief in the 1930s: Aid or Hindrance to Recovery? In *Gregory, R. G. and Butlin, N. G., eds.*, 1988, pp. 311–34.

Snow, Marcellus S. The State as Stopgap: Social Economy and Sustainability of Monopoly in the Telecommunications Sector. *Rev. Soc. Econ.*, April 1988, *46*(1), pp. 1–23.

_____; **Braunstein, Yale M. and Jussawalla, Meheroo.** Major Issues in Information Services Trade. In *Lee, C. H. and Naya, S., eds.*, 1988, pp. 77–95.

Snowball, Doug and Bamber, E. Michael. An Experimental Study of the Effects of Audit Structure in Uncertain Task Environments. *Accounting Rev.*, July 1988, *63*(3), pp. 490–504.

Snowberger, Vinson. Firm Behavior in the Rate Design Phase of the Regulatory Process. *Econ. Letters*, 1988, *27*(4), pp. 381–85.

Snowden, Kenneth A. Mortgage Lending and American Urbanization, 1880–1890. *J. Econ. Hist.*, June 1988, *48*(2), pp. 273–85.

Snowden, P. N. and Rose, Mary B. Bond Issues as a Replacement for Bank Lending to LDCs: A Reconsideration of the Lessons of the 19th Century for the Present Day. *World Devel.*, July 1988, *16*(7), pp. 771–78.

Snower, Dennis J. and Alpern, Steve. "High–Low Search" in Product and Labor Markets. *Amer. Econ. Rev.*, May 1988, *78*(2), pp. 356–62.

_____ **and Lindbeck, Assar.** Cooperation, Harassment, and Involuntary Unemployment: An Insider–Outsider Approach. *Amer. Econ. Rev.*, March 1988, *78*(1), pp. 167–88.

_____ and Lindbeck, Assar. Job Security, Work Incentives and Unemployment. *Scand. J. Econ.*, 1988, *90*(4), pp. 453–74.

_____ and Lindbeck, Assar. Long-term Unemployment and Macroeconomic Policy. *Amer. Econ. Rev.*, May 1988, *78*(2), pp. 38–43.

_____ and Lindbeck, Assar. Union Activity, Unemployment Persistence and Wage-Employment Ratchets. In *Cross, R., ed.*, 1988, pp. 117–28.

Snyder, Donald L. and Andersen, Jay C. Competition for Water: The Issue of Native American Water Rights. *Ann. Reg. Sci.*, February 1988, *22*, pp. 54–64.

Snyder, Edward A. and Kauper, Thomas E. Private Antitrust Cases That Follow on Government Cases. In *White, L. J., ed.*, 1988, pp. 329–70.

Snyder, Jack and Milner, Helen. Lost Hegemony? *Int. Organ.*, Autumn 1988, *42*(4), pp. 749–50.

Snyder, James M. and Kramer, Gerald H. Fairness, Self-interest, and the Politics of the Progressive Income Tax. *J. Public Econ.*, July 1988, *36*(2), pp. 197–230.

Snyman, J. A. and van Rooyen, M. A Multiplex Algorithm for Linear Programming Problems. In *Iri, M. and Yajima, K., eds.*, 1988, pp. 177–86.

So, Alvin Y. Shenzhen Special Economic Zone: China's Struggle for Independent Development. *Can. J. Devel. Stud.*, 1988, *9*(2), pp. 313–23.

Soares, Fernando Brito. Some Reflections on the Reform of CAP. *Europ. Rev. Agr. Econ.*, 1988, *15*(1), pp. 109–12.

Sobel, Irvin. Fifty Years after the *General Theory*: The Lernerian Version. *Rivista Int. Sci. Econ. Com.*, December 1988, *35*(12), pp. 1141–54.

Sobel, Jordan Howard. Metatickles, Ratificationism, and Newcomb-Like Problems without Dominance. In *Munier, B. R., ed.*, 1988, pp. 483–501.

_____. World Bayesianism: Comments on the Hammond/McClennen Debate. In *Munier, B. R., ed.*, 1988, pp. 537–42.

Sobhan, Farooq. Opportunities for South–South Co-operation. In *Sopiee, N.; Hamzah, B. A. and Leong, C. H., eds.*, 1988, *1987*, pp. 59–99.

Sobhan, Rehman and Islam, Tajul. Foreign Aid and Domestic Resource Mobilisation in Bangladesh. *Bangladesh Devel. Stud.*, June 1988, *16*(2), pp. 21–44.

Sobti, Rajiv. Increasing Social Variability and Insurance Equilibrium. *J. Risk Ins.*, September 1988, *55*(3), pp. 509–17.

Sockell, Donna; Brockner, Joel and Delaney, John Thomas. Bargaining Effects of the Mandatory–Permissive Distinction. *Ind. Relat.*, Winter 1988, *27*(1), pp. 21–36.

Söderbaum, Peter. Agriculture—Economics and Ecology: Some Comments. *Europ. Rev. Agr. Econ.*, 1988, *15*(2–3), pp. 297–99.

Söderberg, Johan and Jansson, Arne. Corn-Price Rises and Equalisation: Real Wages in Stock-

holm 1650–1719. *Scand. Econ. Hist. Rev.*, 1988, *36*(2), pp. 42–67.

Soderstrom, E. J.; Carpenter, W. W. and Postma, H. "Profiting" from Technology Transfer: A Novel Approach. In *Furino, A., ed.*, 1988, pp. 211–24.

Soehoed, A. R. Reflections on Industrialisation and Industrial Policy in Indonesia. *Bull. Indonesian Econ. Stud.*, August 1988, *24*(2), pp. 43–57.

Soenen, Luc A. Risk Diversification Characteristics of Currency Cocktails. *J. Econ. Bus.*, May 1988, *40*(2), pp. 177–89.

_____ and Aggarwal, Raj. The Nature and Efficiency of the Gold Market. *J. Portfol. Manage.*, Spring 1988, *14*(3), pp. 18–21.

_____ and Aggarwal, Raj. Private Use of Official Currency Cocktails: The Relative Success of the ECU and the SDR. *Banca Naz. Lavoro Quart. Rev.*, December 1988, (167), pp. 425–40.

_____ and Ma, Christopher K. Arbitrage Opportunities in Metal Futures Markets. *J. Futures Markets*, April 1988, *8*(2), pp. 199–209.

_____ and van Winkel, E. G. F. Predicting Future Spot Rates on the Basis of Forward Rates—A Time Series Approach. *Quart. J. Bus. Econ.*, Summer 1988, *27*(3), pp. 57–87.

Soesastro, Hadi and Sudarsono, Budi. Mineral and Energy Development in Indonesia. In *McKern, B. and Koomsup, P., eds.*, 1988, pp. 161–207.

Soete, Luc. Technical Change and International Implications for Small Countries. In *Freeman, C. and Lundvall, B.-A., eds.*, 1988, pp. 98–110.

_____ and Dosi, Giovanni. Technical Change and International Trade. In *Dosi, G., et al., eds.*, 1988, pp. 401–31.

_____ and Perez, Carlota. Catching Up in Technology: Entry Barriers and Windows of Opportunity. In *Dosi, G., et al., eds.*, 1988, pp. 458–79.

Soeteman, Frits and Nijkamp, Peter. Ecologically Sustainable Economic Development: Key Issues for Strategic Environmental Management. *Int. J. Soc. Econ.*, 1988, *15*(3–4), pp. 88–102.

Sofaer, Shoshanna; Lambert, Wendy and Rundall, Thomas G. Uncompensated Hospital Care in California: Private and Public Hospital Responses to Competitive Market Forces. In *Scheffler, R. M. and Rossiter, L. F., eds.*, 1988, pp. 113–33.

Sofianos, George. Margin Requirements on Equity Instruments. *Fed. Res. Bank New York Quart. Rev.*, Summer 1988, *13*(2), pp. 47–60.

Soh, Byung Hee. Political Instability and Economic Fluctuations in the Republic of Korea. *Public Choice*, June 1988, *57*(3), pp. 259–74.

Söhngen, Ludwig. Planning Shift Work and Duty Roster for Personnel with Variable Workload. In *Daduna, J. R. and Wren, A., eds.*, 1988, pp. 119–32.

Sokoloff, Kenneth L. Inventive Activity in Early Industrial America: Evidence from Patent

Records, 1790–1846. *J. Econ. Hist.*, December 1988, *48*(4), pp. 813–50.

Sokolowska, Joanna. Managing Directors' Motivation to Undertake Risky Economic Actions in the Context of Economy Management in Poland. In *Maital, S., ed., Vol. 1*, 1988, pp. 163–75.

Sol, Jopy and Poiesz, Theo B. C. The Individual Evaluation of the Dutch Social Security System: Results of an Initial Investigation. In *Maital, S., ed., Vol. 2*, 1988, pp. 752–65.

Solar, Peter and Durie, Alastair. The Scottish and Irish Linen Industries Compared, 1780–1860. In *Mitchison, R. and Roebuck, P., eds.*, 1988, pp. 211–21.

Soldaczuk, Józef. Economic Performance, Reform, and Debt-Servicing Capability through 1995. In *Marer, P. and Siwinski, W., eds.*, 1988, pp. 183–91.

Soldo, Beth J. and Wolf, Douglas A. Household Composition Choices of Older Unmarried Women. *Demography*, August 1988, *25*(3), pp. 387–403.

Solimano, Andrés. Mercado de trabalho: Quatro enfoques em busca de um paradigma. (With English summary.) *Pesquisa Planejamento Econ.*, December 1988, *18*(3), pp. 561–94.

_____. Política de remuneraciones en Chile: experiencia pasada, instrumentos y opciones a futuro. (Wage Policies in Chile: Past Experience, Mechanisms and Options for the Future. With English summary.) *Colección Estud. CIEPLAN*, December 1988, (25), pp. 159–90.

Sollars, David; Vedder, Richard and Gallaway, Lowell. The Tullock–Bastiat Hypothesis, Inequality-Transfer Curve and the Natural Distribution of Income. *Public Choice*, March 1988, *56*(3), pp. 285–94.

Sollogoub, Michel. L'inégalité des revenus primaires en France de 1962 à 1979. (The Inequality in the Distribution of Household Primary Incomes in France from 1962 to 1979. With English summary.) *Revue Écon.*, May 1988, *39*(3), pp. 545–72.

Solnick, Loren M. Promotions, Pay, Performance Ratings and Quits. *Eastern Econ. J.*, Jan.–March 1988, *14*(1), pp. 51–62.

Solnik, Bruno and de Freitas, Arlei. International Factors of Stock Price Behavior. In *Khoury, S. J. and Ghosh, A., eds.*, 1988, pp. 259–76.

Solocha, Andrew and Bundt, Thomas. Debt, Deficits and the Dollar. *J. Policy Modeling*, Winter 1988, *10*(4), pp. 581–600.

Solomn, Robert. Exchange Rates, Macroeconomic Policies, and the Debt Problem. In *Feldstein, M., ed. (I)*, 1988, pp. 156–61.

Solomon, Anthony M. After Reagan: Confronting the Changed World Economy: Foreword. In *Aho, C. M. and Levinson, M.*, 1988, pp. vii–xiv.

_____. International Economic Policy Coordination: Present Shortcomings, Future Opportunities. In *[Witteveen, H. J.]*, 1988, pp. 217–29.

_____. Prospects for the LDC Debt Problem. In *Feldstein, M., ed. (I)*, 1988, pp. 278–83.

Solomon, George T. Small Business Management and Entrepreneurial Education in America: A National Survey Overview. In *Association of Private Education*, 1988, pp. 109–18.

_____ **and Fernald, Lloyd W.** Comparisons of Entrepreneur and College Business Student Values: A Preliminary Investigation. In *Association of Private Education*, 1988, pp. 133–44.

Solomon, Michael R. Building Up and Breaking Down: The Impact of Cultural Sorting on Symbolic Consumption. In *Hirschman, E. and Sheth, J. N., eds.*, 1988, pp. 325–51.

Solomon, Richard L. How the Opponent-Process Theory of Acquired Motivation Came into Economics. In *Albanese, P. J., ed.*, 1988, pp. 31–34.

Solon, Gary. Self-selection Bias in Longitudinal Estimation of Wage Gaps. *Econ. Letters*, 1988, *28*(3), pp. 285–90.

_____, **et al.** Sibling and Intergenerational Correlations in Welfare Program Participation. *J. Human Res.*, Summer 1988, *23*(3), pp. 388–96.

Solow, John L. and Krautmann, Anthony C. Economies of Scale in Nuclear Power Generation. *Southern Econ. J.*, July 1988, *55*(1), pp. 70–85.

Solow, Robert M. Bibliography of Robert M. Solow's Publications, 1950–1987. *Scand. J. Econ.*, 1988, *90*(1), pp. 17–26.

_____. Economics in the Human Conversation: Comments from Inside Economics. In *Klamer, A.; McCloskey, D. N. and Solow, R. M., eds.*, 1988, pp. 31–37.

_____. Growth Theory and After. *Amer. Econ. Rev.*, June 1988, *78*(3), pp. 307–17.

_____. Macroeconomic Issues Confronting the Next President. *J. Econ. Educ.*, Summer 1988, *19*(3), pp. 231–36.

_____. On Theories of Unemployment. In *Shaw, G. K., ed., Vol. 2*, 1988, *1980*, pp. 54–64.

_____. Time and the New Industrial State: Discussion. *Amer. Econ. Rev.*, May 1988, *78*(2), pp. 378–80.

_____ **and Blinder, Alan S.** Does Fiscal Policy Matter? In *Shaw, G. K., ed., Vol. 2*, 1988, *1973*, pp. 317–37.

_____ **and Samuelson, Paul A.** Problem of Achieving and Maintaining a Stable Price Level: Analytical Aspects of Anti-inflation Policy. In *Shaw, G. K., ed., Vol. 2*, 1988, *1960*, pp. 138–55.

Soltan, Karol Edward. Democracy, Dictatorship and Decision Costs. *Public Choice*, May 1988, *57*(2), pp. 155–73.

Soltwedel, Rüdiger. Employment Problems in West Germany—The Role of Institutions, Labor Law, and Government Intervention. *Carnegie–Rochester Conf. Ser. Public Policy*, Spring 1988, *28*, pp. 153–219.

_____ **and Trapp, Peter.** Labor Market Barriers to More Employment: Causes for an Increase of the Natural Rate? The Case of West Germany. In *Giersch, H., ed.*, 1988, pp. 181–225.

Solvell, Orjan. Is the Global Automobile Industry Really Global? In *Hood, N. and Vahlne, J.-E., eds.*, 1988, pp. 181–208.

Solzhenitsyn, Aleksandr. Difficulties in the West with the Study of Russian History: A Speech at the Hoover Institution in 1976. In *Anderson, A. and Bark, D. L., eds.*, 1988, pp. 57–61.

Somel, Cem. Stabilization in Underdeveloped Economies: A Fix-Price Approach. *METU*, 1988, *15*(3–4), pp. 47–73.

Sommariva, Andrea and Tullio, Giuseppe. Notes, Comments, Replies: International Gold Flows in Gold Standard Germany: A Test of the Monetary Approach to the Balance of Payments, 1880–1911. *J. Money, Credit, Banking*, February 1988, *20*(1), pp. 132–40.

Sommer, A. A., Jr. One Share, One Vote: Comment. In *Coffee, J. C., Jr.; Lowenstein, L. and Rose-Ackerman, S., eds.*, 1988, pp. 524–29.

Sommer, Heini and Knieps, Günter. Kostenaufteilung bei Mehrzweckprojekten. (Fair and Efficient Cost Allocations of Multipurpose Projects—Theory and Empirical Tests. With English summary.) *Schweiz. Z. Volkswirtsch. Statist.*, June 1988, *124*(2), pp. 151–74.

Sommer, Joseph H. Transformative Torts. *Yale Law J.*, March 1988, *97*(4), pp. 645–64.

van Son, P. and Bonte, J. Health Statistics in the Netherlands for Health Policy and Evaluation: Experience and Developments. *Statist. J.*, August 1988, *5*(2), pp. 123–33.

Søndergaard, Jørgen. Arbejdsløshed, betalingsbalance og velfærdsøkonomi. (Optimal Shadow Prices for an Economy Facing a Foreign Debt Constraint. With English summary.) *Nationaløkon. Tidsskr.*, 1988, *126*(3), pp. 335–50.

Sonin, I. M. and Pristavko, G. V. Stochastic Models of Management of Parallel Multistage Programs. *Matekon*, Summer 1988, *24*(4), pp. 72–90.

Sonis, Michael. Interregional Migration in Individual Countries: Israel. In *Weidlich, W. and Haag, G., eds.*, 1988, pp. 155–84.

_____; **Jensen, Rodney C. and Hewings, Geoffrey J. D.** Technical Innovation and Input–Output Analysis. In *Orishimo, I.; Hewings, G. J. D. and Nijkamp, P., eds.*, 1988, pp. 163–94.

_____ **and Nijkamp, Peter.** Qualitative Impact Analysis for Dynamic Spatial Systems. *Econ. Geogr.*, July 1988, *64*(3), pp. 226–41.

Sonka, Steven T.; Gustafson, Cole R. and Barry, Peter J. Machinery Investment Decisions: A Simulated Analysis for Cash Grain Farms. *Western J. Agr. Econ.*, December 1988, *13*(2), pp. 244–53.

_____ **and King, R. P.** Management Problems of Farms and Agricultural Firms. In *Hildreth, R. J., et al., eds.*, 1988, pp. 270–97.

Sonnenschein, Hugo and Gul, Faruk. On Delay in Bargaining with One-Sided Uncertainty. *Econometrica*, May 1988, *56*(3), pp. 601–11.

_____ **and Novshek, William.** Cournot and Walras Equilibrium. In *Daughety, A. F., ed.*, 1988, *1978*, pp. 271–316.

_____; **Spiegel, Matthew and Neelin, Janet.** A Further Test of Noncooperative Bargaining Theory: Comment. *Amer. Econ. Rev.*, September 1988, *78*(4), pp. 824–36.

Sontheimer, Kevin C. Markets, Morals, Property, and Other Rights: A Rejoinder to the Pastoral Letter. *Contemp. Policy Issues*, January 1988, *6*(1), pp. 69–83.

Sontz, Ann H. L. and Young, Philip K. Y. Is Hard Work the Key to Success? A Socioeconomic Analysis of Immigrant Enterprise. *Rev. Black Polit. Econ.*, Spring 1988, *16*(4), pp. 11–31.

Soper, John C. and Walstad, William B. The Reality of High School Economics: The Teachers' Perspective. In *Association of Private Education*, 1988, pp. 85–96.

_____ **and Walstad, William B.** A Report Card on the Economic Literacy of U.S. High School Students. *Amer. Econ. Rev.*, May 1988, *78*(2), pp. 251–56.

_____ **and Walstad, William B.** What is High School Economics? Posttest Knowledge, Attitudes, and Course Content. *J. Econ. Educ.*, Winter 1988, *19*(1), pp. 37–51.

_____ **and Walstad, William B.** What Is High School Economics? TEL Revision and Pretest Findings. *J. Econ. Educ.*, Winter 1988, *19*(1), pp. 24–36.

Sophocleus, John P. and Laband, David N. The Social Cost of Rent-Seeking: First Estimates. *Public Choice*, September 1988, *58*(3), pp. 269–75.

Sopiee, Noordin. Crisis and Response: The Challenge to South–South Economic Co-operation: The Global Economic Crisis—The Challenge to the South: Introduction. In *Sopiee, N.; Hamzah, B. A. and Leong, C. H., eds.*, 1988, pp. xi–xxvii.

Sorensen, Andrew A.; McCusker, Jane and Stoddard, Anne M. Do HMOs Reduce Hospitalization of Terminal Cancer Patients? *Inquiry*, Summer 1988, *25*(2), pp. 263–70.

Sørensen, Bjarne G. and Jennergren, L. Peter. Price Formation in the Danish Stock Market in the 1890s. *Scand. Econ. Hist. Rev.*, 1988, *36*(2), pp. 3–24.

Sørensen, Christen. Opsparing og beskatning. (Savings Policy and Taxation Policy. With English summary.) *Nationaløkon. Tidsskr.*, 1988, *126*(2), pp. 196–204.

Sorensen, Elaine. There Is Worth to Comparable Worth: A Critique of Raisian, Welch, and Ward. In *Mangum, G. and Philips, P., eds.*, 1988, pp. 235–240.

Sorensen, Eric H. and Arnott, Robert D. The Risk Premium and Stock Market Performance. *J. Portfol. Manage.*, Summer 1988, *14*(4), pp. 50–55.

Sørensen, Georg. Newly Industrializing Countries and the Political Economy of South–South Relations: Brazil. In *Carlsson, J. and Shaw, T. M., eds.*, 1988, pp. 101–20.

Sørensen, Jan Rose and Andersen, Torben M. Exchange Rate Variability and Wage Formation in Open Economies. *Econ. Letters*, 1988, *28*(3), pp. 263–68.

Sørensen, Olav Jull. Development of Marketing Channels for Agricultural Supplies. In *Kumcu, E. and Firat, A. F., eds.*, 1988, pp. 285–316.

Sørensen, Peter Birch. Skatteincitamenter til opsparing og investering: En vurdering af firsernes skattereformer. (Incentive Effects of the Recent Reforms of Danish Capital Income Taxation. With English summary.) *Nationaløkon. Tidsskr.*, 1988, *126*(3), pp. 303–22.

Sørensen, Rune J. The Growth of Public Spending in Norway 1865–1985. In *Lybeck, J. A. and Henrekson, M., eds.*, 1988, pp. 265–98.

Sorge, Arndt. New Technologies and Employment in the 1980s: From Science and Technology to Macroeconomic Modelling: Comment. In *Kregel, J. A.; Matzner, E. and Roncaglia, A., eds.*, 1988, pp. 269–72.

Sorger, Gerhard; Feichtinger, Gustav and Luhmer, Alfred. Optimal Price and Advertising Policy for a Convenience Goods Retailer. *Marketing Sci.*, Spring 1988, *7*(2), pp. 187–201.

Sorkin, Alan L. The Impact of Water and Sanitation on Health and Development. In *Sirageldin, I. and Sorkin, A., eds.*, 1988, pp. 77–98.

Sorooshian, Soroosh; Brazil, Larry E. and Hendrickson, Jene' D. Comparison of Newton-Type and Direct Search Algorithms for Calibration of Conceptual Rainfall–Runoff Models. *Water Resources Res.*, May 1988, *24*(5), pp. 691–700.

Sosin, Michael R.; Danziger, Sandra K. and Longres, John F. The Status of Youth in Wisconsin: Lessons for Policy. In *Danziger, S. H. and Witte, J. F., eds.*, 1988, pp. 151–71.

Soskice, David. Industrial Relations and Unemployment: The Case for Flexible Corporatism. In *Kregel, J. A.; Matzner, E. and Roncaglia, A., eds.*, 1988, pp. 212–26.

——— **and Finegold, David.** The Failure of Training in Britain: Analysis and Prescription. *Oxford Rev. Econ. Policy*, Autumn 1988, *4*(3), pp. 21–53.

Sotomayor, Marilda and Roth, Alvin E. Interior Points in the Core of Two-Sided Matching Markets. *J. Econ. Theory*, June 1988, *45*(1), pp. 85–101.

Sotskov, A. I. and Danilov, V. I. Coalition-Stable Social Choice Mechanisms. *Matekon*, Winter 1988–89, *25*(2), pp. 45–61.

——— **and Danilov, V. I.** Stable Blocking in Social Choice Mechanisms. *Matekon*, Fall 1988, *25*(1), pp. 38–53.

Souder, William E. Technological Change and Its International Diffusion: Commentary. In *Cassing, J. H. and Husted, S. L., eds.*, 1988, pp. 117–19.

Soumis, François and Desrochers, Martin. CREW-OPT: Crew Scheduling by Column Generation. In *Daduna, J. R. and Wren, A., eds.*, 1988, pp. 83–90.

———; **Desrosiers, Jacques and Dumas, Yvan.** The Multiple Vehicle DIAL-A-RIDE Problem. In *Daduna, J. R. and Wren, A., eds.*, 1988, pp. 15–27.

de Sousa, Maria de Conceição Sampaio and Barrantes Hidalgo, Álvaro. Um modelo de equilíbrio geral computável para o estudo de políticas de comércio exterior no Brasil. (With English summary.) *Pesquisa Planejamento Econ.*, August 1988, *18*(2), pp. 379–400.

Southall, Roger. Labour and Unions in Asia and Africa: Introduction. In *Southall, R., ed.*, 1988, pp. 1–31.

de Souza Silva, Jose. Biotechnology in Brazil and Prospects for South–South Cooperation. In *Research and Info. System for the Non-aligned and Other Developing Countries*, 1988, pp. 420–42.

Sowell, Clifford; Boyes, William J. and Mounts, William Stewart. The Federal Reserve as a Bureaucracy: An Examination of Expense-Preference Behavior. *J. Money, Credit, Banking*, May 1988, *20*(2), pp. 181–90.

Sowell, Thomas. Preferential Policies: An International Perspective. In *Anderson, A. and Bark, D. L., eds.*, 1988, pp. 469–76.

Sowey, Eric R. Macroeconometric Model Evaluation with Special Reference to the NIF88 Model: Comment. *Australian Econ. Pap.*, Supplement, June 1988, *27*, pp. 57–60.

Špaček, Petr and Pařízek, Pavel. Foreign-Exchange Financial Relations. *Czech. Econ. Digest.*, June 1988, (4), pp. 21–37.

Spadaro, John and Levine, Joel H. Occupational Mobility: A Structural Model. In *Wellman, B. and Berkowitz, S. D., eds.*, 1988, pp. 452–75.

Spaetling, Dieter. Subjektive Qualitätseinschätzung bei unvollständiger Information über die Güterqualität und individuelles Nachfrageverhalten. (Subjective Quality Appreciation, Incomplete Quality Information, and Individual Consumer Behavior. With English summary.) *Jahr. Nationalökon. Statist.*, September 1988, *205*(3), pp. 263–74.

Spahn, H.-Peter. Fiscal and Monetary Policy in the Keynes–Kalecki Tradition: Comment. In *Kregel, J. A.; Matzner, E. and Roncaglia, A., eds.*, 1988, pp. 134–40.

Spahn, P. Bernd. Turbulenzen auf den Finanzmärkten vor dem Hintergrund der Entwicklungen in der Weltwirtschaft. (Turbulences in Financial Markets on the Background of World Economic Trends. With English summary.) *Konjunkturpolitik*, 1988, *34*(1), pp. 1–35.

Spahr, Ronald W. and Deckro, Richard F. A Non-linear Goal Programming Approach to Modeling Intraregional Economic Development. *Rev. Reg. Stud.*, Winter 1988, *18*(1), pp. 10–18.

Špak, Michal and Kupka, Václav. Prognostication Work and the Strategy of Czechoslovak Development. *Czech. Econ. Digest.*, May 1988, (3), pp. 13–32.

Spalding, Nancy. Democracy and Economic Human Rights in the Third World. In *Cingranelli, D. L., ed.*, 1988, pp. 173–89.

Spalding, Rose J. The Political Implications of Austerity. In *Tavis, L. A., ed.*, 1988, pp. 57–60.

Spalter-Roth, Roberta M. The Sexual Political Economy of Street Vending in Washington, D.C. In *Clark, G., ed.*, 1988, pp. 165–87.

Španěl, Jiři. The Role of Investment in the Modernization of the Machine-Building Industry:

Conditions, Productivity, and Problems. *Eastern Europ. Econ.*, Winter 1988–89, 27(2), pp. 75–90.

Spanos, Aris. Towards a Unifying Methodological Framework for Econometric Modelling. *Econ. Notes*, 1988, (1), pp. 107–34.

Sparks, Gordon R. and Green, Alan G. A Macro Interpretation of Recovery: Australia and Canada. In *Gregory, R. G. and Butlin, N. G., eds.*, 1988, pp. 89–112.

_____ **and Meyer, Neil.** Policy Decisions Affecting Rationalization of the Prairie Grain Transportation System: Implications for the St. Lawrence Seaway System. *Can. J. Agr. Econ.*, Part 2, December 1988, 36(4), pp. 941–50.

Sparling, William J. and Cullingworth, J. Barry. Community Energy Planning: Prospects and Potentialities. In *Byrne, J. and Rich, D., eds.*, 1988, pp. 247–82.

Spatt, Chester S. and Sterbenz, Frederic P. Warrant Exercise, Dividends, and Reinvestment Policy. *J. Finance*, June 1988, 43(2), pp. 493–506.

Spaulding, Jay. The Business of Slavery in the Central Anglo–Egyptian Sudan, 1910–1930. *African Econ. Hist.*, 1988, (17), pp. 23–44.

Spaventa, Luigi. Is There a Public Debt Problem in Italy? In *Giavazzi, F. and Spaventa, L., eds.*, 1988, pp. 1–24.

_____. The Management of Public Debt and Financial Markets: Discussion. In *Giavazzi, F. and Spaventa, L., eds.*, 1988, pp. 173–76.

_____. Rate of Profit, Rate of Growth, and Capital Intensity in a Simple Production Model. In *Steedman, I., ed., Vol. 1*, 1988, *1970*, pp. 357–75.

Spear, Stephen E. Existence and Local Uniqueness of Functional Rational Expectations Equilibria in Dynamic Economic Models. *J. Econ. Theory*, February 1988, 44(1), pp. 124–55.

_____ **and Alesina, Alberto.** An Overlapping Generations Model of Electoral Competition. *J. Public Econ.*, December 1988, 37(3), pp. 359–79.

_____ **and Srivastava, Sanjay.** Markov Rational Expectations Equilibria in an Overlapping Generations Model. In *Grandmont, J.-M., ed.*, 1988, *1986*, pp. 349–79.

Spears, John. Sustainable Natural Resource Management: Implications for World Bank Agriculture Operations. In *Roberts, C., ed.*, 1988, pp. 101–16.

Spears, Russell; Webley, Paul and Eiser, J. Richard. Inflationary Expectations and Policy Preferences. *Econ. Letters*, 1988, 28(3), pp. 239–41.

Specht, Günter and Michel, Kay. Integrierte Technologie- und Marktplanung mit Innovationsportfolios. (With English summary.) *Z. Betriebswirtshaft*, April 1988, 58(4), pp. 502–20.

Spector, Bert A. and Beer, Michael. Managing Human Assets—It's Time for New Thinking. In *Timpe, A. D., ed.*, 1988, *1985*, pp. 232–37.

Spector, Lee C. Female Participation and the Nat-

ural Rate of Unemployment: A Reexamination. *J. Macroecon.*, Spring 1988, 10(2), pp. 309–18.

_____ **and van Cott, T. Norman.** Crowding Out, Deficits, and Interest Rates: Comment. *Public Choice*, July 1988, 58(1), pp. 91–94.

Speedy, A. W. and Rehman, T. U. UK Farm Planning and Management on AGVISER. In *Schiefer, G., ed.*, 1988, pp. 87–101.

Speidell, Lawrence S. and LeBaron, Dean. Why are the Parts Worth More than the Sum? "Chop Shop," A Corporate Valuation Model. In *Browne, L. E. and Rosengren, E. S., eds.*, 1988, pp. 78–95.

Speight, Alan E. H. and MacDonald, Ronald. The Term Structure of Interest Rates in the UK. *Bull. Econ. Res.*, October 1988, 40(4), pp. 287–99.

Spence, A. Michael. International Competitiveness: Introduction. In *Spence, A. M. and Hazard, H. A., eds.*, 1988, pp. xvii–xxiii.

_____. Contestable Markets and the Theory of Industry Structure: A Review Article. In *Ricketts, M., ed., Vol. 1*, 1988, *1983*, pp. 160–69.

Spencer, A. H. Modernisation and Incorporation: The Development of Singapore's Bus Services 1945–1974. *Environ. Planning A*, August 1988, 20(8), pp. 1027–46.

Spencer, Barbara J. Capital Subsidies and Countervailing Duties in Oligopolistic Industries. *J. Int. Econ.*, August 1988, 25(1–2), pp. 45–69.

_____. Countervailing Duty Laws and Subsidies to Imperfectly Competitive Industries. In *Baldwin, R. E.; Hamilton, C. B. and Sapir, A., eds.*, 1988, pp. 313–34.

_____ **and Brander, James A.** Unionized Oligopoly and International Trade Policy. *J. Int. Econ.*, May 1988, 24(3–4), pp. 217–34.

Spencer, Byron G. and Denton, Frank T. Endogenous versus Exogenous Fertility: What Difference for the Macroeconomy? In *Lee, R. D.; Arthur, W. B. and Rodgers, G., eds.*, 1988, pp. 183–215.

_____; **Denton, Frank T. and Li, S. Neno.** Health Care in the Economic–Demographic System: Macro-effects of Market Control, Government Intervention, and Population Change. *Southern Econ. J.*, July 1988, 55(1), pp. 37–56.

Spencer, Roger W.; Sciortino, John J. and Huston, John H. Risk and Income Distribution. *J. Econ. Psych.*, September 1988, 9(3), pp. 399–408.

_____ **and Walz, Daniel T.** Bias in Systems of Survey and Econometric Forecasts. *J. Macroecon.*, Spring 1988, 10(2), pp. 261–71.

Spenner, Kenneth I. Technological Change, Skill Requirements, and Education: The Case for Uncertainty. In *Cyert, R. M. and Mowery, D. C., eds.*, 1988, pp. 131–84.

Spewak, Peter C. Analyzing the Effect of Economic Policy on Solar Markets. In *West, R. E. and Kreith, F., eds.*, 1988, pp. 167–204.

Speyrer, Janet Furman; Carlson, George N. and Brashares, Edith. Distributional Aspects of a

Federal Value-Added Tax. *Nat. Tax J.*, June 1988, *41*(2), pp. 155–74.

Spiegel, Matthew; Neelin, Janet and Sonnenschein, Hugo. A Further Test of Noncooperative Bargaining Theory: Comment. *Amer. Econ. Rev.*, September 1988, *78*(4), pp. 824–36.

Spiegel, Uriel; Ben Zion, Uri and Gradstein, Mark. Financing of Public Goods and Noncooperative Theory of Bargaining. *J. Public Econ.*, December 1988, *37*(3), pp. 345–57.

_____ **and Kahana, Nava.** On the Definition of Price Discrimination. *Econ. Inquiry*, October 1988, *26*(4), pp. 775–77.

Spiller, Cristina Nardi. Lines of Thought on the Evolution of Monetary Economics from Marshall to Keynes: A Review Article. *Rivista Int. Sci. Econ. Com.*, December 1988, *35*(12), pp. 1191–98.

Spiller, Pablo T.; Demski, Joel S. and Sappington, David E. M. Incentive Schemes with Multiple Agents and Bankruptcy Constraints. *J. Econ. Theory*, February 1988, *44*(1), pp. 156–67.

_____ **and Wood, Robert O.** Arbitrage during the Dollar–Sterling Gold Standard, 1899–1908: An Economic Approach. *J. Polit. Econ.*, August 1988, *96*(4), pp. 882–92.

_____ **and Wood, Robert O.** The Estimation of Transaction Costs in Arbitrage Models. *J. Econometrics*, November 1988, *39*(3), pp. 309–26.

Spindler, Hans-Joachim. Risiko- und Renditeeffekte der Diversifikation in Konjunkturkrisen. (With English summary.) *Z. Betriebswirtshaft*, August 1988, *58*(8), pp. 858–75.

Spindler, Zane A. and McDonald, John. Benefit-Induced Female Sole Parenthood in Australia, 1973–85. *Australian Econ. Pap.*, June 1988, *27*(50), pp. 1–19.

_____ **and Walker, Michael A.** Canadian Tax Reform as Public Choice. *Contemp. Policy Issues*, October 1988, *6*(4), pp. 70–84.

Spindt, Paul A. and Hoffmeister, J. Ronald. The Micromechanics of the Federal Funds Market: Implications for Day-of-the-Week Effects in Funds Rate Variability. *J. Finan. Quant. Anal.*, December 1988, *23*(4), pp. 401–16.

Spinelli, Franco. Pasquale Jannaccone: A Neglected Originator of the Monetary Approach to Balance of Payments and Exchanges Rates. *J. Europ. Econ. Hist.*, Winter 1988, *17*(3), pp. 665–97.

Spinnewyn, Frans and Malcomson, James M. The Multiperiod Principal–Agent Problem. *Rev. Econ. Stud.*, July 1988, *55*(3), pp. 391–407.

Spiro, Erwin. The Margo Report: Republic of South Africa. *Bull. Int. Fiscal Doc.*, January 1988, *42*(1), pp. 37–38.

_____. South Africa: The 1988 Budget. *Bull. Int. Fiscal Doc.*, June 1988, *42*(6), pp. 259–62.

Spiro, Peter S. The Effects of Government Debt and Deficits on Interest Rates. *Bus. Econ.*, October 1988, *23*(4), pp. 39–46.

Spirtes, Peter and Glymour, Clark. Latent Variables, Causal Models and Overidentifying Constraints. *J. Econometrics*, Sept.–Oct. 1988, *39*(1–2), pp. 175–98.

Spithoven, A. H. G. M. A Case Study on Functional Income Shares and the Distribution of Income between Investment and Consumption in 1965–85. In *Brenner, Y. S.; Reijnders, J. P. G. and Spithoven, A. H. G. M., eds.*, 1988, pp. 117–31.

Spivak, Avia and Levy, Amnon. How Does the Public Perceive an Unprecedented Rise in Inflation: The Case of Inflationary Expectations in Israel. *J. Macroecon.*, Spring 1988, *10*(2), pp. 273–82.

_____ **and Segal, Uzi.** Non-expected Utility Risk Premiums: The Cases of Probability Ambiguity and Outcome Uncertainty. *J. Risk Uncertainty*, September 1988, *1*(3), pp. 333–47.

_____; **Zeira, Joseph and Segal, Uzi.** Precautionary Saving and Risk Aversion: An Anticipated Utility Approach. *Econ. Letters*, 1988, *27*(3), pp. 223–27.

Spivey, Michael F. and Marr, M. Wayne. The Cost Relationship between Competitive and Negotiated Preferred Stock Sales under Different Credit Market Conditions. *Quart. J. Bus. Econ.*, Summer 1988, *27*(3), pp. 23–40.

Spivey, W. Allen; Rose, Elizabeth L. and Machak, Joseph A. A Survey of the Teaching of Statistics in M.B.A. Programs. *J. Bus. Econ. Statist.*, April 1988, *6*(2), pp. 273–82.

Spooner, Gillian M.; Sunley, Emil M. and Amerkhail, Valerie L. The Fall and Rise of the U.S. Corporate Tax Burden. *Nat. Tax J.*, September 1988, *41*(3), pp. 273–84.

Spoor, Max. Reforming State Finance in Post-1975 Vietnam. *J. Devel. Stud.*, July 1988, *24*(4), pp. 102–14.

Sporkin, Stanley. Legal Rules, Takeover Strategies, and Defensive Tactics: Comment. In *Coffee, J. C., Jr.; Lowenstein, L. and Rose-Ackerman, S., eds.*, 1988, pp. 459–61.

Sprague, Alison. Post-war Fertility and Female Labour Force Participation Rates. *Econ. J.*, September 1988, *98*(392), pp. 682–700.

Sprecher, C. Ronald and Pertl, Mars A. Intra-industry Effects of the MGM Grand Fire. *Quart. J. Bus. Econ.*, Spring 1988, *27*(2), pp. 96–116.

Spremann, Klaus. Reputation, Garantie, Information. (With English summary.) *Z. Betriebswirtshaft*, May–June 1988, *58*(5–6), pp. 613–29.

Spriggs, John; Gould, Brian W. and Koroluk, Robert M. Separate Crop Accounts for the Western Grain Stabilization Program. *Can. J. Agr. Econ.*, November 1988, *36*(3), pp. 443–57.

_____ **and Van Kooten, G. C.** Rationale for Government Intervention in Canadian Agriculture: A Review of Stabilization Programs. *Can. J. Agr. Econ.*, March 1988, *36*(1), pp. 1–21.

Sprinkel, Beryl W. Improving International Performance. In *Melamed, L., ed.*, 1988, pp. 405–13.

_____. Strategies for Effective Fiscal Policy. *Con-*

temp. Policy Issues, October 1988, *6*(4), pp. 25–31.

Sprinkle, Richard L. and Sawyer, W. Charles. EC Enlargement and U.S. Exports: An Analysis of the Trade Effects. *J. World Trade*, February 1988, *22*(1), pp. 89–96.

Spudeck, Raymond E. and Hein, Scott E. Forecasting the Daily Federal Funds Rate. *Int. J. Forecasting*, 1988, *4*(4), pp. 581–91.

Spulber, Daniel F. Bargaining and Regulation with Asymmetric Information about Demand and Supply. *J. Econ. Theory*, April 1988, *44*(2), pp. 251–68.

_____. Optimal Environmental Regulation under Asymmetric Information. *J. Public Econ.*, March 1988, *35*(2), pp. 163–81.

_____. Products Liability and Monopoly in a Contestable Market. *Economica*, August 1988, *55*(219), pp. 333–41.

Squires, Dale. Production Technology, Costs, and Multiproduct Industry Structure: An Application of the Long-run Profit Function to the New England Fishing Industry. *Can. J. Econ.*, May 1988, *21*(2), pp. 359–78.

Squires, Gregory D. and Velez, William. Insurance Redlining and the Process of Discrimination. *Rev. Black Polit. Econ.*, Winter 1988, *16*(3), pp. 63–75.

Srba, Frank; Hendry, David F. and Neale, Adrian J. Econometric Analysis of Small Linear Systems Using PC-FIML. *J. Econometrics*, May–June 1988, *38*(1–2), pp. 203–26.

Sreenivasamurthy, D. and Bisaliah, S. Technological Innovations and Productivity Change in Agriculture. *Margin*, April–June 1988, *20*(3), pp. 51–56.

Srinivasan, Aruna. Mississippi: A Dual Economy. *Fed. Res. Bank Atlanta Econ. Rev.*, Jan.–Feb. 1988, *73*(1), pp. 50–57.

Srinivasan, T. N. Economic Liberalization in China and India: Issues and an Analytical Framework. In *Reynolds, B. L., ed.*, 1988, *1987*, pp. 137–53.

_____. Fertility and Old Age Security in an Overlapping Generations Model. *J. Quant. Econ.*, January 1988, *4*(1), pp. 11–17.

_____. Population Growth and Economic Development. *J. Policy Modeling*, April 1988, *10*(1), pp. 7–28.

_____. Population Growth and Food: An Assessment of Issues, Models, and Projections. In *Lee, R. D., et al., eds.*, 1988, pp. 11–39.

_____ and Bardhan, Pranab K. Rural Poverty in South Asia: Introduction. In *Srinivasan, T. N. and Bardhan, P. K., eds.*, 1988, pp. 1–8.

_____; Narayana, N. S. S. and Parikh, Kirit S. Rural Works Programs in India: Costs and Benefits. *J. Devel. Econ.*, September 1988, *29*(2), pp. 131–56.

_____ and Sah, Raaj Kumar. Distributional Consequences of Rural Food Levy and Subsidized Urban Rations. *Europ. Econ. Rev.*, January 1988, *32*(1), pp. 141–59.

Srinivasan, Venkat and Kim, Yong H. Decision Support for Working Capital Management: A Conceptual Framework. In *Kim, Y. H., ed.*, 1988, pp. 187–216.

_____ and Kim, Yong H. Integrating Corporate Strategy and Multinational Capital Budgeting: An Analytical Framework. In *Khoury, S. J. and Ghosh, A., eds.*, 1988, pp. 381–97.

Srivastava, Leena and Pachauri, R. K. Integrated Energy Planning in India: A Modeling Approach. *Energy J.*, October 1988, *9*(4), pp. 35–48.

Srivastava, P. K. Management of Health and Family Welfare Programs in Developing Countries. In *Butler, J. R. G. and Doessel, D. P., eds.*, 1988, pp. 210–16.

Srivastava, Rajendra; Huff, David L. and Lutz, James M. A Geographical Analysis of the Innovativeness of States. *Econ. Geogr.*, April 1988, *64*(2), pp. 137–46.

Srivastava, Sanjay and Richard, Scott F. Equilibrium in Economies with Infinitely Many Consumers and Infinitely Many Commodities. *J. Math. Econ.*, 1988, *17*(1), pp. 9–21.

_____ and Spear, Stephen E. Markov Rational Expectations Equilibria in an Overlapping Generations Model. In *Grandmont, J.-M., ed.*, 1988, *1986*, pp. 349–79.

Srull, Thomas K. and Burke, Raymond R. Competitive Interference and Consumer Memory for Advertising. *J. Cons. Res.*, June 1988, *15*(1), pp. 55–68.

St-Hilaire, France; Whalley, John and Davies, James B. Some Calculations of Lifetime Tax Incidence. In *Brown, E., ed.*, 1988, *1984*, pp. 115–26.

Staar, Richard F. The Soviet Union Abroad. In *Anderson, A. and Bark, D. L., eds.*, 1988, pp. 153–63.

Staber, Udo and Aldrich, Howard. An Evolutionary View on Changes in Employment Relationships: The Evolution of Organizational Control in the United States. In *Dlugos, G.; Dorow, W. and Weiermair, K., eds.*, 1988, pp. 63–78.

Stabile, Donald R. Veblen's Analysis of Social Movements: Bellamyites, Workers, and Engineers. *J. Econ. Issues*, March 1988, *22*(1), pp. 211–26.

Stabler, Jack C. and Howe, Eric C. Service Exports and Regional Growth in the Postindustrial Era. *J. Reg. Sci.*, August 1988, *28*(3), pp. 303–15.

_____; Van Kooten, G. C. and Meyer, Neil. Methodological Issues in the Evaluation of Regional Resource Development Projects. *Ann. Reg. Sci.*, July 1988, *22*(2), pp. 13–25.

Stabler, Michael J. The Image of Destination Regions: Theoretical and Empirical Aspects. In *Goodall, B. and Ashworth, G., eds.*, 1988, pp. 133–61.

_____ and Ashworth, Gregory. Tourism Development Planning in Languedoc: Le Mission Impossible? In *Goodall, B. and Ashworth, G., eds.*, 1988, pp. 187–97.

Stadler, Manfred and Flaig, Gebhard. Beschäftigungseffekte privater F&E-Aufwendungen. Eine Panaldaten-Analyse. (The Effects of Private R and D Expenditures on Employment.

An Analysis with Panel Data. With English summary.) Z. Wirtschaft. Sozialwissen., 1988, 108(1), pp. 43–61.

Staehle, Wolfgang H. The Changing Face of Personnel Management. In Dlugos, G.; Dorow, W. and Weiermair, K., eds., 1988, pp. 323–33.

_____. Human Resource Managment (HRM)—Eine neue Managementrichtung in den USA? (With English summary.) Z. Betriebswirtshaft, May–June 1988, 58(5–6), pp. 576–87.

Stafford, Frank P. Employment Problems in West Germany: A Comment. Carnegie–Rochester Conf. Ser. Public Policy, Spring 1988, 28, pp. 221–30.

Stageberg, Stephen P. Technological Change and Its Impact on Productivity: The U.S. Steel Industry. Rivista Int. Sci. Econ. Com., June 1988, 35(6), pp. 563–78.

Stager, David A. A. and Foot, David K. Differential Effects of Advanced Degrees on Lawyers' Earnings. Econ. Educ. Rev., 1988, 7(4), pp. 385–92.

Stäglin, Reiner and Schintke, Joachim. Important Input Coefficients in Market Transaction Tables and Production Flow Tables. In Ciaschini, M., ed., 1988, pp. 43–60.

Stagni, Anna; Bosi, Paolo and Golinelli, Roberto. Effetti macroeconomici e settoriali dell'armonizzazione dell'Iva e delle accise: la valutazione del modello Hermes-Italia. (With English summary.) Polit. Econ., December 1988, 4(3), pp. 361–84.

Stahl, Dale O., II. Bertrand Competition for Inputs and Walrasian Outcomes. Amer. Econ. Rev., March 1988, 78(1), pp. 189–201.

_____. On the Instability of Mixed-Strategy Nash Equilibria. J. Econ. Behav. Organ., January 1988, 9(1), pp. 59–69.

_____. Price-Setting Merchants in a Simple Trade Model. J. Int. Econ., May 1988, 24(3–4), pp. 197–216.

_____ and Fisher, Franklin M. On Stability Analysis with Disequilibrium Awareness. J. Econ. Theory, December 1988, 46(2), pp. 309–21.

Stahl, Ingemar. Political and Economic Freedom in the Welfare State: Some Basic Concepts Applied to the Case of Sweden. In Walker, M. A., ed. (I), 1988, pp. 295–305.

Staiger, Robert W. Organized Labor and the Scope of International Specialization. J. Polit. Econ., October 1988, 96(5), pp. 1022–47.

_____. A Specification Test of the Heckscher–Ohlin Theory. J. Int. Econ., August 1988, 25(1–2), pp. 129–41.

_____. United States–Japan Economic Relations: Comment. In Baldwin, R. E., ed. (II), 1988, pp. 330–34.

_____ and Deardorff, Alan V. An Interpretation of the Factor Content of Trade. J. Int. Econ., February 1988, 24(1–2), pp. 93–107.

_____; Deardorff, Alan V. and Stern, Robert M. The Effects of Protection on the Factor Content of Japanese and American Foreign Trade. Rev. Econ. Statist., August 1988, 70(3), pp. 475–83.

Stålhammar, Nils-Olov. Price and Demand Expectations in the Swedish Manufacturing Industry. Scand. J. Econ., 1988, 90(2), pp. 233–43.

Stambaugh, Robert F. The Information in Forward Rates: Implications for Models of the Term Structure. J. Finan. Econ., May 1988, 21(1), pp. 41–70.

_____. Stable Factors in Security Returns: Identification Using Cross-Validation: Comment. J. Bus. Econ. Statist., January 1988, 6(1), pp. 20–21.

Stampen, Jacob O. and Cabrera, Alberto F. The Targeting and Packaging of Student Aid and Its Effect on Attrition. Econ. Educ. Rev., 1988, 7(1), pp. 29–46.

_____; Hansen, W. Lee and Reeves, Roxanne W. Implications of Redefining Independent Student Status. Econ. Educ. Rev., 1988, 7(1), pp. 85–99.

_____; Reeves, Roxanne W. and Hansen, W. Lee. The Impact of Student Earnings in Offsetting "Unmet Needs." Econ. Educ. Rev., 1988, 7(1), pp. 113–26.

Stanbury, W. T.; Tretheway, Michael W. and Gillen, David W. Duopoly in Canada's Airline Industry: Consequences and Policy Issues. Can. Public Policy, March 1988, 14(1), pp. 15–31.

Stancanelli, Néstor E. Developing Countries and Liberalization of Agricultural Trade. In Dicke, D. C. and Petersmann, E.-U., eds., 1988, pp. 208–34.

Standing, Guy. Training, Flexibility and Swedish Full Employment. Oxford Rev. Econ. Policy, Autumn 1988, 4(3), pp. 94–107.

_____. Would Revenue-Sharing Pay Cure Unemployment? Int. Lab. Rev., 1988, 127(1), pp. 1–18.

Standop, Dirk. Intensitätsmässige Anpassungen in Absatzkalkülen bei unsicherer Nachfrage. (With English summary.) Z. Betriebswirtshaft, January 1988, 58(1), pp. 116–26.

Stanfield, J. Ron. The Institutional Economics of Karl Polanyi. In Samuels, W. J., ed., Vol. 1, 1988, 1980, pp. 243–64.

Stanford, William and Kalai, Ehud. Finite Rationality and Interpersonal Complexity in Repeated Games. Econometrica, March 1988, 56(2), pp. 397–410.

_____; Kalai, Ehud and Samet, Dov. A Note on Reactive Equilibria in the Discounted Prisoner's Dilemma and Associated Games. Int. J. Game Theory, 1988, 17(3), pp. 177–86.

Staniford, Andrew J. The Influence of the Supply and Demand Characteristics of Fisheries on the Benefits from Economic Improvement Programs. Australian J. Agr. Econ., April 1988, 32(1), pp. 50–59.

Stanley, Linda R. and Coursey, Don L. Pretrial Bargaining Behavior within the Shadow of the Law: Theory and Experimental Evidence. Int. Rev. Law Econ., December 1988, 8(2), pp. 161–79.

_____ and McMullen, B. Starr. The Impact of Deregulation on the Production Structure of the Motor Carrier Industry. *Econ. Inquiry*, April 1988, *26*(2), pp. 299–316.

_____; Tschirhart, John and Atkinson, Scott E. Revenue Sharing as an Incentive in an Agency Problem: An Example from the National Football League. *Rand J. Econ.*, Spring 1988, *19*(1), pp. 27–43.

Stanley, Ralph L. Privatization and the Challenge of Urban Mobility. In *Weicher, J. C., ed.*, 1988, pp. 11–15.

Stansell, Christine and Wilentz, Sean. Gutman's Legacy. *Labor Hist.*, Summer 1988, *29*(3), pp. 378–90.

Stansell, Stanley R.; Fenstermaker, J. Van and Malone, R. Phil. An Analysis of Commercial Bank Common Stock Returns: 1802–97. *Appl. Econ.*, June 1988, *20*(6), pp. 813–41.

_____ and Hollas, Daniel R. An Examination of the Economic Efficiency of Class I Railroads: A Profit Function Analysis. *Rev. Ind. Organ.*, Fall 1988, *3*(4), pp. 93–117.

_____ and Hollas, Daniel R. An Examination of the Effect of Ownership Form on Price Efficiency: Proprietary, Cooperative and Municipal Electric Utilities. *Southern Econ. J.*, October 1988, *55*(2), pp. 336–50.

_____ and Hollas, Daniel R. Regulation, Interfirm Rivalry, and the Economic Efficiency of Natural Gas Distribution Facilities. *Quart. Rev. Econ. Bus.*, Winter 1988, *28*(4), pp. 21–37.

Stanton, David. Hysteresis: Some Policy Implications. In *Cross, R., ed.*, 1988, pp. 389–91.

Stanworth, John and Stern, Peter. The Development of Franchising in Britain. *Nat. Westminster Bank Quart. Rev.*, May 1988, pp. 38–48.

Stanzel, Klaus and Holthus, Manfred. The Credit Standing of Developing Countries: Criteria for Assessing External Debt. In *Gutowski, A. and Holthus, M., eds.*, 1988, *1984*, pp. 277–314.

_____ and Schattner, Susanne. The Role of the State in Foreign Borrowing by Developing Countries. In *Gutowski, A. and Holthus, M., eds.*, 1988, pp. 253–74.

Stapleton, David C. and Young, Douglas J. Educational Attainment and Cohort Size. *J. Lab. Econ.*, July 1988, *6*(3), pp. 330–61.

Stark, Graham. Partially Transferable Allowances. *Fisc. Stud.*, February 1988, *9*(1), pp. 29–40.

_____ and Robinson, Bill. The Tax Treatment of Marriage: What Has the Chancellor Really Achieved? *Fisc. Stud.*, May 1988, *9*(2), pp. 48–56.

Stark, Oded and Bernheim, B. Douglas. Altruism within the Family Reconsidered: Do Nice Guys Finish Last? *Amer. Econ. Rev.*, December 1988, *78*(5), pp. 1034–45.

_____ and Lauby, Jennifer. Individual Migration as a Family Strategy: Young Women in the Philippines. *Population Stud.*, November 1988, *42*(3), pp. 473–86.

_____ and Lucas, Robert E. B. Migration, Re-

mittances, and the Family. *Econ. Develop. Cult. Change*, April 1988, *36*(3), pp. 465–81.

_____; Taylor, J. Edward and Yitzhaki, Shlomo. Migration, Remittances and Inequality: A Sensitivity Analysis Using the Extended Gini Index. *J. Devel. Econ.*, May 1988, *28*(3), pp. 309–22.

_____ and Yitzhaki, Shlomo. Relative Deprivation and Migration. In *Maital, S., ed.*, Vol. 1, 1988, pp. 269–302.

Starkermann, R. The Apartheid Malady. *Math. Soc. Sci.*, April 1988, *15*(2), pp. 157–77.

Starkie, David. The New Zealand Road Charging System. *J. Transp. Econ. Policy*, May 1988, *22*(2), pp. 239–45.

Starks, Laura and Smirlock, Michael. An Empirical Analysis of the Stock Price–Volume Relationship. *J. Banking Finance*, 1988, *12*(1), pp. 31–41.

Starmer, C. and Parikh, Ashok. The Relationship between the Money Supply and Prices in Bangladesh. *Bangladesh Devel. Stud.*, September 1988, *16*(3), pp. 59–70.

Starodubrovskaia, I. What is the Plan? *Prob. Econ.*, March 1988, *30*(11), pp. 47–59.

Starr, Edward. The Growth of Small Manufacturers: 1976–84. *Bus. Econ.*, April 1988, *23*(2), pp. 41–45.

Starr, Martin K. Global Competitiveness: Getting the U.S. Back on Track: Introduction. In *Starr, M. K., ed.*, 1988, pp. 6–11.

_____ and Ullmann, John E. The Myth of U.S. Industrial Supremacy. In *Starr, M. K., ed.*, 1988, pp. 43–71.

Starr, S. Frederick. The Changing Nature of Change in the USSR. In *Bialer, S. and Mandelbaum, M., eds.*, 1988, pp. 3–35.

Starrett, David A. Effects of Taxes on Saving. In *Aaron, H. J.; Galper, H. and Pechman, J. A., eds.*, 1988, pp. 237–59.

Stasinopoulos, Dinos and Erdmenger, Jürgen. The Shipping Policy of the European Community. *J. Transp. Econ. Policy*, September 1988, *22*(3), pp. 355–60.

Stasny, Elizabeth A. Modeling Nonignorable Nonresponse in Categorical Panel Data with an Example in Estimating Gross Labor-Force Flows. *J. Bus. Econ. Statist.*, April 1988, *6*(2), pp. 207–19.

Stasson, Mark F. and Davis, James H. Small Group Performance: Past and Present Research Trends. In *Lawler, E. J. and Markovsky, B., eds.*, 1988, pp. 245–77.

Staten, Michael; Umbeck, John and Dunkelberg, William C. Market Share/Market Power Revisited: A New Test for an Old Theory. *J. Health Econ.*, March 1988, *7*(1), pp. 73–83.

Stathopoulos, Athanasios N. Future Trends in the Greek Labour Market. In *Dlugos, G.; Dorow, W. and Weiermair, K., eds.*, 1988, pp. 233–46.

Stauber, Steve and Weersink, Alfons. Optimal Replacement Interval and Depreciation Method for a Grain Combine. *Western J. Agr. Econ.*, July 1988, *13*(1), pp. 18–28.

Staudohar, Paul D. The Football Strike of 1987:

The Question of Free Agency. *Mon. Lab. Rev.*, August 1988, *111*(8), pp. 26–31.

Stavins, Robert. A Model of English Demographic Change: 1573–1873. *Exploration Econ. Hist.*, January 1988, *25*(1), pp. 98–116.

Stayman, Douglas M. and Aaker, David A. Are All the Effects of Ad-Induced Feelings Mediated by A_{Ad}? *J. Cons. Res.*, December 1988, *15*(3), pp. 368–733.

de Ste. Croix, G. E. M. Slavery and Other Forms of Unfree Labour. In *Archer, L. J., ed.*, 1988, pp. 19–32.

Stebelsky, Ihor. Food Consumption Patterns in the Soviet Union. In *Brada, J. C. and Wadekin, K.-E., eds.*, 1988, pp. 98–109.

Steckel, Joel H. and Vanhonacker, Wilfried R. A Heterogeneous Conditional Logit Model of Choice. *J. Bus. Econ. Statist.*, July 1988, *6*(3), pp. 391–98.

Steckel, Richard H. The Health and Mortality of Women and Children, 1850–1860. *J. Econ. Hist.*, June 1988, *48*(2), pp. 333–45.

_____ **and Sandberg, Lars G.** Overpopulation and Malnutrition Rediscovered: Hard Times in 19th-Century Sweden. *Exploration Econ. Hist.*, January 1988, *25*(1), pp. 1–19.

Stedman Jones, Gareth. The Mid-century Crisis and the 1848 Revolutions: The Case of England. In *Burke, E., III, ed.*, 1988, *1983*, pp. 72–85.

Steedman, Hilary. Vocational Training in France and Britain: Mechanical and Electrical Craftsman. *Nat. Inst. Econ. Rev.*, November 1988, (126), pp. 57–70.

Steedman, Ian. Basics, Non-Basics and Joint Production. In *Steedman, I., ed., Vol. 2*, 1988, *1977*, pp. 113–17.

_____. Jevon's Theory of Capital and Interest. In *Steedman, I., ed., Vol. 2*, 1988, *1972*, pp. 395–416.

_____. Jevons's Theory of Capital and Interest. In *Wood, J. C., ed., Vol. 3*, 1988, *1972*, pp. 105–26.

_____. Joint Production and Technical Progress. In *Steedman, I., ed., Vol. 2*, 1988, pp. 127–38.

_____. Joint Production and the Wage-Rent Frontier. In *Steedman, I., ed., Vol. 2*, 1988, *1982*, pp. 118–26.

_____. On Input 'Demand Curves.' In *Steedman, I., ed., Vol. 1*, 1988, *1985*, pp. 376–83.

_____. Positive Profits with Negative Surplus Value. In *Steedman, I., ed., Vol. 2*, 1988, *1975*, pp. 417–26.

_____. Returns to Scale and the Switch in Methods of Production. In *Steedman, I., ed., Vol. 2*, 1988, *1980*, pp. 347–55.

_____. Sraffian Economics, Volume I: Introduction. In *Steedman, I., ed., Vol. 1*, 1988, pp. 1–8.

_____. Sraffian Interdependence and Partial Equilibrium Analysis. *Cambridge J. Econ.*, March 1988, *12*(1), pp. 85–95.

_____ **and Hodgson, Geoff.** Depreciation of Machines of Changing Efficiency: A Note. In *Steedman, I., ed., Vol. 2*, 1988, *1977*, pp. 26–32.

_____ **and Metcalfe, J. S.** Reswitching and Primary Input Use. In *Steedman, I., ed., Vol. 1*, 1988, *1972*, pp. 243–60.

_____ **and Salvadori, Neri.** Cost Functions and Produced Means of Production: Duality and Capital Theory. In *Steedman, I., ed., Vol. 2*, 1988, *1985*, pp. 307–18.

_____ **and Salvadori, Neri.** Joint Production Analysis in a Sraffian Framework. *Bull. Econ. Res.*, June 1988, *40*(3), pp. 165–95.

_____ **and Salvadori, Neri.** No Reswitching? No Switching! *Cambridge J. Econ.*, December 1988, *12*(4), pp. 481–86.

_____ **and Salvadori, Neri.** A Note about the Interest Rate and the Revenue Function. *Eastern Econ. J.*, April–June 1988, *14*(2), pp. 153–56.

Steel, M. F. J. and Richard, J. F. Bayesian Analysis of Systems of Seemingly Unrelated Regression Equations under a Recursive Extended Natural Conjugate Prior Density. *J. Econometrics*, May–June 1988, *38*(1–2), pp. 7–37.

Steel, William F. Adjusting Industrial Policy in Sub-Saharan Africa. *Finance Develop.*, March 1988, *25*(1), pp. 36–39.

Steele, G. R. Hayek's Ricardo Effect. *Hist. Polit. Econ.*, Winter 1988, *20*(4), pp. 669–72.

Steele, Richard. Textiles and Apparel: A Basic Industry for a Basic Need. In *Hicks, D. A., ed.*, 1988, pp. 209–54.

Steenkamp, Jan-Benedict E. M. The Relationship between Price and Quality in the Marketplace. *De Economist*, 1988, *136*(4), pp. 491–507.

Steerneman, Ton and Rorijs, Gertjan. Pitfalls for Forecasters. In *Dijkstra, T. K., ed.*, 1988, pp. 102–17.

Stefani, Giorgio. Privatizing Italian State Holdings. *Rivista Int. Sci. Econ. Com.*, Oct.–Nov. 1988, *35*(10–11), pp. 935–50.

_____. Public Enterprise Investments in Italy: Local Transport and Electricity. *Ann. Pub. Coop. Econ.*, July–Sept. 1988, *59*(3), pp. 307–29.

Stefanou, Spiro E. Stochastic Learning by Experience and Returns to Scale. *J. Econ. Dynam. Control*, March 1988, *12*(1), pp. 137–43.

_____ **and Chang, Ching-Cheng.** Specification and Estimation of Asymmetric Adjustment Rates for Quasi-Fixed Factors of Production. *J. Econ. Dynam. Control*, March 1988, *12*(1), pp. 145–51.

_____ **and Hsu, Shih-Hsun.** Temporal Risk Aversion in a Phased Deregulation Game. *J. Econ. Dynam. Control*, March 1988, *12*(1), pp. 181–87.

_____ **and Madden, J. P.** Economies of Size Revisited. *J. Agr. Econ.*, January 1988, *39*(1), pp. 125–32.

_____ **and Saxena, Swati.** Education, Experience, and Allocative Efficiency: A Dual Approach. *Amer. J. Agr. Econ.*, May 1988, *70*(2), pp. 338–45.

Steffen, James R. The Bigness Complex: Industry, Labor, and Government in the American Economy: Review Article. *Mich. Law Rev.*, May 1988, *86*(6), pp. 1247–53.

Steger, Debra P. Canadian–U.S. Agricultural

Trade: A Proposal for Resolving Disputes. **In** *Allen, K. and Macmillan, K., eds.*, 1988, pp. 161–67.

_____; **Horlick, Gary N. and Oliver, Geoffrey D.** Dispute Resolution Mechanisms. **In** *Schott, J. J. and Smith, M. G., eds.*, 1988, pp. 65–86.

Stehling, Frank. Environmental Quality Indices: Problems, Concepts, Examples. **In** *Eichhorn, W., ed.*, 1988, pp. 349–69.

Steidlmeier, Paul and Sethi, S. Prakash. A New Paradigm of the Business/Society Relationship in the Third World: The Challenge of Liberation Theology. **In** *Preston, L. E., ed.*, 1988, pp. 29–43.

Steier, Francis and Psacharopoulos, George. Education and the Labor Market in Venezuela, 1975–1984. *Econ. Educ. Rev.*, 1988, 7(3), pp. 321–32.

Steiger, Otto and Heinsohn, Gunnar. Monetary Theory and the Historiography of Money, or Debts, Interest and Technical Progress in Economies with and without Private Ownership. *Écon. Soc.*, September 1988, 22(9), pp. 139–53.

Steigum, Erling, Jr. ARMOD: A Small Numerical Macroeconomic World Model with Non-clearing Markets. **In** *Haaland, J. I. and Norman, V. D., eds.*, 1988, pp. 11–30.

Stein, Alfred J. and Das, Somshankar. Sustaining and Augmenting Competitive Advantage in Emerging Industries in a Global Environment. **In** *Furino, A., ed.*, 1988, pp. 157–68.

Stein, Herbert. Recent Developments in Macroeconomics: A Very Quick Refresher Course: Comment. *J. Money, Credit, Banking*, Part 2, August 1988, 20(3), pp. 450–56.

Stein, Howard. The State and Crisis in Tanzania: Towards a Systemic Evaluation. **In** *Zarembka, P., ed.*, 1988, pp. 83–121.

Stein, Jeremy C. Takeover Threats and Managerial Myopia. *J. Polit. Econ.*, February 1988, 96(1), pp. 61–80.

_____ **and Feinstein, Jonathan S.** Employee Opportunism and Redundancy in Firms. *J. Econ. Behav. Organ.*, December 1988, 10(4), pp. 401–14.

_____ **and Greenwald, Bruce C.** The Task Force Report: The Reasoning behind the Recommendations. *J. Econ. Perspectives*, Summer 1988, 2(3), pp. 3–23.

Stein, Kenneth. Privatization—A Canadian Perspective. **In** *Walker, M. A., ed. (II)*, 1988, pp. 69–76.

Stein, Morris I. Organizational Effects on Creativity: The Use of Roles in a Technical Audit of Organizations. **In** *Grønhaug, K. and Kaufmann, G., eds.*, 1988, pp. 311–29.

Stein, Sheldon H.; Kumar, Rishi and Mathur, Vijay K. A Dynamic Model of Regional Population Growth and Decline. *J. Reg. Sci.*, August 1988, 28(3), pp. 379–95.

Stein, Steve and Davidson, Judith R. Economic Crisis, Social Polarization, and Community Participation in Health Care. **In** *Zschock, D. K., ed.*, 1988, pp. 53–77.

Stein, William E. and Zwick, Rami. Fuzzy Random Variables. **In** *Kacprzyk, J. and Fedrizzi, M., eds.*, 1988, pp. 66–74.

Steinberg, David I. Sociopolitical Factors and Korea's Future Economic Policies. *World Devel.*, January 1988, 16(1), pp. 19–34.

Steinberg, Ronnie. The Unsubtle Revolution: Women, the State and Equal Employment. **In** *Jenson, J.; Hagen, E. and Reddy, C., eds.*, 1988, pp. 189–213.

Steindl, Frank G. Anticipations of "The Great Contraction"? *Hist. Polit. Econ.*, Spring 1988, 20(1), pp. 65–83.

_____ **and Deravi, M. Keivan.** Income Taxation and the Demand for Money. *Quart. J. Bus. Econ.*, Spring 1988, 27(2), pp. 23–34.

Steindl, Josef. New Lines of Research on the Question of Full Employment. **In** *Kregel, J. A.; Matzner, E. and Roncaglia, A., eds.*, 1988, pp. 343–50.

_____. Stagnation Theory and Stagnation Policy. **In** *Sawyer, M. C., ed.*, 1988, 1979, pp. 149–62.

Steiner, Peter. Wertgrenzen bei geschützten Kaufoptionen. (With English summary.) *Z. Betriebswirtshaft*, March 1988, 58(3), pp. 373–80.

Steinhoff, Patricia G. and Tanaka, Kazuko. Women Managers in Japan. **In** *Adler, N. J. and Izraeli, D., eds.*, 1988, pp. 103–21.

Steinisch, Irmgard. Studies of American Labor History in West Germany. *Labor Hist.*, Fall 1988, 29(4), pp. 531–41.

Steinitz, Klaus. Economic Growth and Economic Strategy. *Eastern Europ. Econ.*, Fall 1988, 27(1), pp. 65–90.

Steinmann, Gunter and Komlos, John. Population Growth and Economic Development in the Very Long Run: A Simulation Model of Three Revolutions. *Math. Soc. Sci.*, August 1988, 16(1), pp. 49–63.

Steinmann, Horst and Hasselberg, Frank. Der strategische Managementprozess—Vorüberlegungen für eine Neuorientierung. (With English summary.) *Z. Betriebswirtshaft*, December 1988, 58(12), pp. 1308–22.

Steinmeier, Thomas L. and Gustman, Alan L. A Model for Analyzing Youth Labor Market Policies. *J. Lab. Econ.*, July 1988, 6(3), pp. 376–96.

Steinmueller, W. Edward. Industry Structure and Government Policies in the U.S. and Japanese Integrated-Circuit Industries. **In** *Shoven, J. B., ed.*, 1988, pp. 319–54.

_____ **and Rosenberg, Nathan.** Why Are Americans Such Poor Imitators? *Amer. Econ. Rev.*, May 1988, 78(2), pp. 229–34.

Steinwald, Bruce and Murdock, Diane. Payments for Outliers under Medicare's Prospective Payment System: Editorial. *J. Health Econ.*, September 1988, 7(3), pp. 291–96.

Stejskal, Bretislav and Ivánek, Jiří. Automatic Acquisition of Knowledge Base from Data without Expert: ESOD (Expert System from Observational Data). **In** *Edwards, D. and Raun, N. E., eds.*, 1988, pp. 175–80.

Stelcner, Morton and Smith, J. Barry. Labour Supply of Married Women in Canada, 1980. *Can. J. Econ.*, November 1988, *21*(4), pp. 857–70.

Stella, Peter and Robinson, David J. Amalgamating Central Bank and Fiscal Deficits. In *Blejer, M. I. and Chu, K.-Y.*, eds., 1988, pp. 20–31.

Stelzer, Irwin. Britain's Newest Import: America's Regulatory Experience. *Oxford Rev. Econ. Policy*, Summer 1988, *4*(2), pp. 69–79.

Stemme, Wolfgang and Klemt, Wolf-Dieter. Schedule Synchronization for Public Transit Networks. In *Daduna, J. R. and Wren, A.*, eds., 1988, pp. 327–35.

Stengelhofen, Theo; Sadowski, Dieter and Frick, Bernd. Wer beschäftigt Schwerbehinderte? Erste Einsichten aus einem laufenden Forschungsprojekt. (With English summary.) *Z. Betriebswirtschaft*, January 1988, *58*(1), pp. 37–50.

Stengos, Thanasis and Frank, Murray Z. Chaotic Dynamics in Economic Time-Series. *J. Econ. Surveys*, 1988, *2*(2), pp. 103–33.

_____ **and Frank, Murray Z.** Some Evidence Concerning Macroeconomic Chaos. *J. Monet. Econ.*, November 1988, *22*(3), pp. 423–38.

_____ **and Frank, Murray Z.** The Stability of Canadian Macroeconomic Data as Measured by the Largest Lyapunov Exponent. *Econ. Letters*, 1988, *27*(1), pp. 11–14.

_____; **Frank, Murray Z. and Gencay, Ramazan.** International Chaos? *Europ. Econ. Rev.*, October 1988, *32*(8), pp. 1569–84.

_____ **and Koustas, Zisimos.** Testing for Short-run Money Neutrality in a Small Open Economy: The Case of Canada. *Empirical Econ.*, 1988, *13*(2), pp. 103–20.

_____; **Moschini, Giancarlo and Prescott, David M.** Nonparametric Kernel Estimation Applied to Forecasting: An Evaluation Based on the Bootstrap. *Empirical Econ.*, 1988, *13*(3–4), pp. 141–54.

Stensland, Gunnar and Olsen, Trond E. Optimal Shutdown Decisions in Resource Extraction. *Econ. Letters*, 1988, *26*(3), pp. 215–18.

Stephan, G. Edward. The Distribution of Service Establishments. *J. Reg. Sci.*, February 1988, *28*(1), pp. 29–40.

Stephan, Gunter. Economic Impact of Emission Standards: A Computational Approach to Waste Water Treatment in Western Europe. In *Bös, D.; Rose, M. and Seidl, C.*, eds., 1988, pp. 401–22.

_____. Minderschätzung künftiger Bedürfnisse. Zur Formalisierung eines psychologischen Phänomens. (Impatience to Consume: The Formalization of a Psychological Phenomenon. With English summary.) *Jahr. Nationalökon. Statist.*, October 1988, *205*(4), pp. 348–62.

_____. A Neo-Austrian Approach to Computable Equilibrium Models: Time to Build Technologies and Imperfect Markets. *Schweiz. Z. Volkswirtsch. Statist.*, March 1988, *124*(1), pp. 49–64.

Stephan, Scott W.; Gatto, Joseph P. and Kelejian, Harry H. Stochastic Generalizations of Demand Systems with an Application to Telecommunications. *Info. Econ. Policy*, 1988, *3*(4), pp. 283–309.

Stephen, Elizabeth Hervey; Rindfuss, Ronald R. and Bean, Frank D. Racial Differences in Contraceptive Choice: Complexity and Implications. *Demography*, February 1988, *25*(1), pp. 53–70.

Stephens, Daniel B. and Heermann, Stephen. Dependence of Anisotropy on Saturation in a Stratified Sand. *Water Resources Res.*, May 1988, *24*(5), pp. 770–78.

Stephens, Debra; Anand, Punam and Holbrook, Morris B. The Formation of Affective Judgments: The Cognitive–Affective Model versus the Independence Hypothesis. *J. Cons. Res.*, December 1988, *15*(3), pp. 386–91.

Stephens, J. Kirker. The Average-Productivity Wage Adjustment Rule: A Further Reconsideration. *J. Post Keynesian Econ.*, Spring 1988, *10*(3), pp. 452–54.

Stephens, Mark and Cole, William E. The Brazilian Motor Vehicle Industry: A Holistic Approach to Project Evaluation. *J. Econ. Issues*, June 1988, *22*(2), pp. 381–88.

Stephenson, M. J. and Patterson, K. D. Stock–Flow Consistent Accounting: A Macroeconomic Perspective. *Econ. J.*, September 1988, *98*(392), pp. 787–800.

Stępień, J.; Mażbic-Kulma, B. and Komorowska, E. Location Problem and Its Applications in Distribution of Petrol Products. In *Kurzhanski, A.; Neumann, K. and Pallaschke, D.*, eds., 1988, pp. 277–92.

Štěrba, Jan. Interview with the Czechoslovak Minister of Foreign Trade, on Amendments of the Law on External Economic Relations. *Czech. Econ. Digest.*, October 1988, (6), pp. 62–70.

Sterbenz, Frederic P. and Sandler, Todd. Externalities, Pigouvian Corrections, and Risk Attitudes. *J. Environ. Econ. Manage.*, December 1988, *15*(4), pp. 488–504.

_____ **and Spatt, Chester S.** Warrant Exercise, Dividends, and Reinvestment Policy. *J. Finance*, June 1988, *43*(2), pp. 493–506.

Sterdyniak, Henri and Bleuze, Eric. L'interdépendance des économies en change flexible: Les apports d'une maquette dynamique. (Interdependence of Economies under Flexible Exchange Rates: The Contributions of Dynamic Model. With English summary.) *Revue Écon.*, September 1988, *39*(5), pp. 999–1033.

Stergioulas, Nikolaos A. and Rutledge, Gary L. Plant and Equipment Expenditures by Business for Pollution Abatement, 1987 and Planned 1988. *Surv. Curr. Bus.*, November 1988, *68*(11), pp. 26–29.

Sterken, Elmer. A Model of Real and Financial Household Behaviour. *De Economist*, 1988, *136*(3), pp. 317–38.

Sterks, C. G. M. and Bakker, B. B. Optimal Legal Standards in Negligence-Based Liability Rules. *De Economist*, 1988, *136*(3), pp. 383–400.

Sterling, Robert R. Confessions of a Failed Empiricist. In *Schwartz, B. N., ed.*, 1988, pp. 3–35.

Sterling, W. P. and Cappelli, Peter. Union Bargaining Decisions and Contract Ratifications: The 1982 and 1984 Auto Agreements. *Ind. Lab. Relat. Rev.*, January 1988, *41*(2), pp. 195–209.

Sterman, John D. Modeling the Formation of Expectations: The History of Energy Demand Forecasts. *Int. J. Forecasting*, 1988, *4*(2), pp. 243–59.

Stern, Ernest. World Bank General Capital Increase. *Finance Develop.*, June 1988, *25*(2), pp. 20–23.

Stern, Gary H. Budget Policy and the Economy. *Cato J.*, Fall 1988, *8*(2), pp. 521–27.

Stern, Helman I.; Ceder, Avishai and Fjornes, Bjoern. OPTIBUS: A Scheduling Package. In *Daduna, J. R. and Wren, A., eds.*, 1988, pp. 212–25.

Stern, Jerrold J. and Lentz, George H. The "Cap Rate," 1966–1984: Comment. *Land Econ.*, November 1988, *64*(4), pp. 381–83.

Stern, Joseph J.; Mallon, Richard D. and Hutcheson, Thomas L. Foreign Exchange Regimes and Industrial Growth in Bangladesh. *World Devel.*, December 1988, *16*(12), pp. 1419–39.

Stern, Louis W. and Kaufmann, Patrick J. Relational Exchange Norms, Perceptions of Unfairness, and Retained Hostility in Commercial Litigation. *J. Conflict Resolution*, September 1988, *32*(3), pp. 534–52.

Stern, Nicholas; Ahmad, Ehtisham and Coady, David. A Complete Set of Shadow Prices for Pakistan: Illustrations for 1975–76. *Pakistan Devel. Rev.*, Spring 1988, *27*(1), pp. 7–43.

_____; Ahmad, Ehtisham and Ludlow, Stephen. Demand Response in Pakistan: A Modification of the Linear Expenditure System for 1976. *Pakistan Devel. Rev.*, Autumn 1988, *27*(3), pp. 293–308.

_____ and Musgrave, Simon. Alcohol: Demand and Taxation under Monopoly and Oligopoly in South India in the 1970s. *J. Devel. Econ.*, February 1988, *28*(1), pp. 1–41.

Stern, Peter and Stanworth, John. The Development of Franchising in Britain. *Nat. Westminster Bank Quart. Rev.*, May 1988, pp. 38–48.

Stern, Robert M. The Effects of Protection on Domestic Output: Comment. In *Baldwin, R. E., ed. (II)*, 1988, pp. 229–31.

_____. U.S. Manufacturing and the Real Exchange Rate: Comment. In *Marston, R. C., ed.*, 1988, pp. 270–75.

_____; Abraham, Filip and Deardorff, Alan V. The Impact of Tariffs on Profits in the United States and Other Major Trading Countries. *Weltwirtsch. Arch.*, 1988, *124*(4), pp. 623–34.

_____ and Hoekman, Bernard M. Conceptual Issues Relating to Services in the International Economy. In *Lee, C. H. and Naya, S., eds.*, 1988, pp. 7–25.

_____; Staiger, Robert W. and Deardorff, Alan V. The Effects of Protection on the Factor Content of Japanese and American Foreign Trade.

Rev. Econ. Statist., August 1988, *70*(3), pp. 475–83.

Stern, Steven; Wolpin, Kenneth I. and Eckstein, Zvi. Fertility Choice, Land, and the Malthusian Hypothesis. *Int. Econ. Rev.*, May 1988, *29*(2), pp. 353–61.

Stern, Steven J. Feudalism, Capitalism, and the World-System in the Perspective of Latin America and the Caribbean. *Amer. Hist. Rev.*, October 1988, *93*(4), pp. 829–72.

_____. Feudalism, Capitalism, and the World-System in the Perspective of Latin America and the Caribbean: Ever More Solitary: Reply. *Amer. Hist. Rev.*, October 1988, *93*(4), pp. 886–97.

Sternberg, Menachem and Arnon, Arie. Forward Credit Commitments and Bank Behavior under Uncertainty: Implications for Monetary Control. *J. Macroecon.*, Fall 1988, *10*(4), pp. 591–612.

Sterner, Thomas; Boyd, Gale A. and Hanson, Donald A. Decomposition of Changes in Energy Intensity. *Energy Econ.*, October 1988, *10*(4), pp. 309–12.

_____ and Hettne, Björn. Mexico as a Regional Power. In *Carlsson, J. and Shaw, T. M., eds.*, 1988, pp. 48–75.

Sternlight, Peter D. and Krieger, Sandra. Monetary Policy and Open Market Operations during 1987. *Fed. Res. Bank New York Quart. Rev.*, Spring 1988, *13*(1), pp. 41–58.

Steuerle, C. Eugene. Pension Funding and Saving: Comment. In *Bodie, Z.; Shoven, J. B. and Wise, D. A., eds.*, 1988, pp. 111–13.

_____. World Tax Reform: A Progress Report: United States. In *Pechman, J. A., ed.*, 1988, pp. 251–60.

_____ and Halperin, Daniel. Indexing the Tax System for Inflation. In *Aaron, H. J.; Galper, H. and Pechman, J. A., eds.*, 1988, pp. 347–72.

Stevans, Lonnie K. An Empirical Model of Property Crime: Deterrence versus Redistribution. *J. Post Keynesian Econ.*, Summer 1988, *10*(4), pp. 572–84.

_____; Register, Charles A. and Sharp, Ansel M. Profit Incentives and the Hospital Industry: New Evidence. *Atlantic Econ. J.*, March 1988, *16*(1), pp. 25–38.

_____ and Sessions, David N. The Derivation of an Implicit Weighting Scheme for Economic Goals and Policies: 1953–1981. *J. Post Keynesian Econ.*, Fall 1988, *11*(1), pp. 26–37.

Steven, Rob. The Japanese Working Class. In *Tsurumi, E. P., ed.*, 1988, pp. 91–111.

Stevens, Anastasia S. Pueblo Water Rights in New Mexico. *Natural Res. J.*, Summer 1988, *28*(3), pp. 535–83.

Stevens, Brandt K. Fiscal Implications of Effluent Charges and Input Taxes. *J. Environ. Econ. Manage.*, September 1988, *15*(3), pp. 285–96.

_____ and Rose, Adam. Distributional Impacts of Oil and Gas Tax Reforms. *Energy Econ.*, July 1988, *10*(3), pp. 235–41.

Stevens, Candice. Advanced Ceramics: Restoring U.S. Competitiveness through Technology

Diffusion. **In** *Hicks, D. A., ed.*, 1988, pp. 255–307.

Stevens, Yvette. Photovoltaic Applications in Rural Areas of Developing Countries: A Survey of Evidence. **In** *Bhalla, A. S. and James, D., eds.*, 1988, pp. 151–70.

Stevenson, David. The Effects of Revolution and Conquest on Scotland. **In** *Mitchison, R. and Roebuck, P., eds.*, 1988, pp. 48–57.

Stevenson, Rodney E. Institutional Economics and the Theory of Production. **In** *Tool, M. R., ed., Vol. 2*, 1988, *1987*, pp. 53–75.

Stever, H. Guyford and Muroyama, Janet H. Globalization of Technology: International Perspectives: Overview. **In** *Muroyama, J. H. and Stever, H. G., eds.*, 1988, pp. 1–11.

Stewart, Doug. Skylines of Fabric. **In** *Forester, T., ed.*, 1988, *1987*, pp. 230–37.

Stewart, Douglas B. and Venieris, Yiannis P. Long-run Social and Economic Responses of Fertility in the United States. *Pakistan Devel. Rev.*, Summer 1988, *27*(2), pp. 137–57.

Stewart, Frances. The International Debt Situation and North–South Relations. **In** *Wilber, C. K., ed.*, 1988, pp. 260–81.

_____. Money and South–South Co-operation. **In** *Sopiee, N.; Hamzah, B. A. and Leong, C. H., eds.*, 1988, *1987*, pp. 243–59.

_____. A Note on Social Cost–Benefit Analysis and Class Conflict in LDCs. **In** *Wilber, C. K., ed.*, 1988, pp. 443–55.

Stewart, G. W. Parallel Linear Algebra in Statistical Computations. **In** *Edwards, D. and Raun, N. E., eds.*, 1988, pp. 3–14.

Stewart, Geoff; Estrin, Saul and Geroski, Paul A. Employee Share Ownership, Profit-Sharing and Participation: An Introduction. *Int. J. Ind. Organ.*, March 1988, *6*(1), pp. 1–6.

Stewart, Gordon C. and Levitt, Arthur, Jr. Can American Business Compete? A Perspective from Midrange Growth Companies. **In** *Starr, M. K., ed.*, 1988, pp. 271–98.

Stewart, Kenneth G. A Direction of Bias Result for the Standard Errors of a Sequential Least Squares Single Equation Rational Expectations Estimator. *Econ. Letters*, 1988, *28*(4), pp. 357–60.

Stewart, Robert B. Negotiations on Acid Rain. **In** *Schmandt, J.; Clarkson, J. and Roderick, H., eds.*, 1988, pp. 64–82.

Stiehler, Ulrich; Coe, David T. and Durand, Martine. The Disinflation of the 1980s. *OECD Econ. Stud.*, Autumn 1988, (11), pp. 89–121.

Stigler, George J. Chicago Studies in Political Economy: Preface. **In** *Stigler, G. J., ed.*, 1988, pp. ix–xviii.

_____. Director's Law of Public Income Redistribution. **In** *Stigler, G. J., ed.*, 1988, *1970*, pp. 106–15.

_____. The Economics of Information. **In** *Ricketts, M., ed., Vol. 1*, 1988, *1961*, pp. 173–85.

_____. Economists and Public Policy. **In** *[Nutter, G. W.]*, 1988, pp. 85–97.

_____. The Effect of Government on Economic Efficiency. *Bus. Econ.*, January 1988, *23*(1), pp. 7–13.

_____. Palgrave's Dictionary of Economics. *J. Econ. Lit.*, December 1988, *26*(4), pp. 1729–36.

_____. Review of 'Papers and Correspondence of William Stanley Jevons, Volume VII: Papers on Political Economy.' **In** *Wood, J. C., ed., Vol. 3*, 1988, *1983*, pp. 277–79.

_____. The Theory of Economic Regulation. **In** *Stigler, G. J., ed.*, 1988, *1971*, pp. 209–33.

_____ **and Becker, Gary S.** Law Enforcement, Malfeasance, and Compensation of Enforcers. **In** *Stigler, G. J., ed.*, 1988, *1974*, pp. 593–611.

Stigler, S. M. Jevons as Statistician. **In** *Wood, J. C., ed., Vol. 1*, 1988, *1982*, pp. 369–82.

Stiglitz, Joseph E. The Cost of Capital and Changes in Tax Regimes: Comments. **In** *Aaron, H. J.; Galper, H. and Pechman, J. A., eds.*, 1988, pp. 190–94.

_____. Money, Credit, and Business Fluctuations. *Econ. Rec.*, December 1988, *64*(187), pp. 307–22.

_____. The New Development Economics. **In** *Wilber, C. K., ed.*, 1988, pp. 393–407.

_____. On the Market for Principles of Economics Textbooks: Innovation and Product Differentiation. *J. Econ. Educ.*, Spring 1988, *19*(2), pp. 171–77.

_____. On the Relevance or Irrelevance of Public Financial Policy. **In** *Arrow, K. J. and Boskin, M. J., eds.*, 1988, pp. 41–75.

_____. Why Financial Structure Matters. *J. Econ. Perspectives*, Fall 1988, *2*(4), pp. 121–26.

_____ **and Arnott, Richard J.** The Basic Analytics of Moral Hazard. *Scand. J. Econ.*, 1988, *90*(3), pp. 383–413.

_____ **and Arnott, Richard J.** Randomization with Asymmetric Information. *Rand J. Econ.*, Autumn 1988, *19*(3), pp. 344–62.

_____; **Arnott, Richard J. and Hosios, Arthur J.** Implicit Contracts, Labor Mobility, and Unemployment. *Amer. Econ. Rev.*, December 1988, *78*(5), pp. 1046–66.

_____ **and Dasgupta, Partha.** Learning-by-Doing, Market Structure and Industrial and Trade Policies. *Oxford Econ. Pap.*, June 1988, *40*(2), pp. 246–68.

_____ **and Dasgupta, Partha.** Potential Competition, Actual Competition, and Economic Welfare. *Europ. Econ. Rev.*, March 1988, *32*(2–3), pp. 569–77.

_____ **and Greenwald, Bruce C.** Examining Alternative Macroeconomic Theories. *Brookings Pap. Econ. Act.*, 1988, (1), pp. 207–60.

_____ **and Greenwald, Bruce C.** Imperfect Information, Finance Constraints, and Business Fluctuations. **In** *Kohn, M. and Tsiang, S.-C., eds.*, 1988, pp. 103–40.

_____ **and Greenwald, Bruce C.** Money, Imperfect Information, and Economic Fluctuations. **In** *Kohn, M. and Tsiang, S.-C., eds.*, 1988, pp. 141–65.

_____ **and Greenwald, Bruce C.** Pareto Inefficiency of Market Economies: Search and Efficiency Wage Models. *Amer. Econ. Rev.*, May 1988, *78*(2), pp. 351–55.

_____ and Neary, Peter. Toward a Reconstruction of Keynesian Economics: Expectations and Constrained Equilibria. In *Shaw, G. K., ed.*, *Vol. 1*, 1988, *1983*, pp. 283–312.

_____ and Rey, Patrick. Vertical Restraints and Producers' Competition. *Europ. Econ. Rev.*, March 1988, *32*(2–3), pp. 561–68.

_____ and Sah, Raaj Kumar. Committees, Hierarchies and Polyarchies. *Econ. J.*, June 1988, *98*(391), pp. 451–70.

Stihl, Hans Peter. Integrating JIT into a Total Production and Marketing System. In *Holl, U. and Trevor, M., eds.*, 1988, pp. 71–83.

Stilwell, Frank. Contemporary Political Economy: Common and Contested Terrain. *Econ. Rec.*, March 1988, *64*(184), pp. 14–25.

Stinchcombe, Arthur L. On Social Factors in Administrative Innovation. In *Grønhaug, K. and Kaufmann, G., eds.*, 1988, *1986*, pp. 375–83.

Stine, Robert A. and Shaman, Paul. The Bias of Autoregressive Coefficient Estimators. *J. Amer. Statist. Assoc.*, September 1988, *83*(403), pp. 842–48.

Stine, William F. The Effect of Local Administrative Stringency on the Provision of AFDC. *Public Finance Quart.*, July 1988, *16*(3), pp. 284–300.

_____. Estimating Property Tax Base Elasticity over Time: Evidence on the Revenue Maximizing Politician. *Public Choice*, July 1988, *58*(1), pp. 35–44.

Stinson, Thomas F. Life Cycle Behavior, Uncertainty, and the Demand for Infrastructure. In *Johnson, T. G.; Deaton, B. J. and Segarra, E., eds.*, 1988, pp. 37–49.

Stith, Kate. Congress' Power of the Purse. *Yale Law J.*, June 1988, *97*(7), pp. 1343–96.

Stober, Thomas L. Incentives for Accruing Costs and Efficiency in Regulated Monopolies Subject to ROE Constraint: Discussion. *J. Acc. Res.*, Supplement, 1988, *26*, pp. 175–81.

Stock, Duane R. and Gilmer, R. H., Jr. Yield Volatility of Discount Coupon Bonds. *J. Finan. Res.*, Fall 1988, *11*(3), pp. 189–200.

_____ and Simonson, Donald G. Tax-Adjusted Duration for Amortizing Debt Instruments. *J. Finan. Quant. Anal.*, September 1988, *23*(3), pp. 313–27.

Stock, James H. Estimating Continuous-Time Processes Subject to Time Deformation: An Application to Postwar U.S. GNP. *J. Amer. Statist. Assoc.*, March 1988, *83*(401), pp. 77–85.

_____. A Reexamination of Friedman's Consumption Puzzle: Reply. *J. Bus. Econ. Statist.*, October 1988, *6*(4), pp. 413–14.

_____. A Reexamination of Friedman's Consumption Puzzle. *J. Bus. Econ. Statist.*, October 1988, *6*(4), pp. 401–07.

_____ and Harvey, A. C. Continuous Time Autoregressive Models with Common Stochastic Trends. *J. Econ. Dynam. Control*, June–Sept. 1988, *12*(2–3), pp. 365–84.

_____ and Watson, Mark W. Testing for Common Trends. *J. Amer. Statist. Assoc.*, December 1988, *83*(404), pp. 1097–1107.

_____ and Watson, Mark W. Variable Trends in Economic Time Series. *J. Econ. Perspectives*, Summer 1988, *2*(3), pp. 147–74.

_____ and West, Kenneth D. Integrated Regressors and Tests of the Permanent-Income Hypothesis. *J. Monet. Econ.*, January 1988, *21*(1), pp. 85–95.

Stockhausen, Gerard L. The Effects of a Quota Threat on a Country with a Monopoly Export Industry. In *Missouri Valley Economic Assoc.*, 1988, pp. 54–63.

Stockman, Alan C. Fiscal Policies and International Financial Markets. In *Frenkel, J. A., ed.*, 1988, pp. 197–217.

_____. On the Roles of International Financial Markets and Their Relevance for Economic Policy. *J. Money, Credit, Banking*, Part 2, August 1988, *20*(3), pp. 531–49.

_____. Price Contracts, Output, and Monetary Disturbances. In *Kohn, M. and Tsiang, S.-C., eds.*, 1988, pp. 71–84.

_____. Real Exchange-Rate Variability under Pegged and Floating Nominal Exchange-Rate Systems: An Equilibrium Theory. *Carnegie–Rochester Conf. Ser. Public Policy*, Autumn 1988, *29*, pp. 259–94.

_____. Sectoral and National Aggregate Disturbances to Industrial Output in Seven European Countries. *J. Monet. Econ.*, March–May 1988, *21*(2–3), pp. 387–409.

_____. The Worldwide Change in the Behavior of Interest Rates and Prices in 1914: Comments. *Europ. Econ. Rev.*, June 1988, *32*(5), pp. 1150–54.

_____ and Hernández D., Alejandro. Exchange Controls, Capital Controls, and International Financial Markets. *Amer. Econ. Rev.*, June 1988, *78*(3), pp. 362–74.

Stockton, David J. Relative Price Dispersion, Aggregate Price Movement, and the Natural Rate of Unemployment. *Econ. Inquiry*, January 1988, *26*(1), pp. 1–22.

Stoddard, Anne M.; Sorensen, Andrew A. and McCusker, Jane. Do HMOs Reduce Hospitalization of Terminal Cancer Patients? *Inquiry*, Summer 1988, *25*(2), pp. 263–70.

Stoddart, Greg and Feeny, David. Toward Improved Health Technology Policy in Canada: A Proposal for the National Health Technology Assessment Council. *Can. Public Policy*, September 1988, *14*(3), pp. 254–65.

Stoeckel, Andy. Should the Exchange Rate Be a Target Variable for Government Policy? *Rev. Marketing Agr. Econ.*, April 1988, *56*(1), pp. 75–77.

_____ and Higgs, Peter J. The Relative Significance of a Range of Economic Policies for Improving Australia's Balance of Trade. *Australian J. Agr. Econ.*, Aug.–Dec. 1988, *32*(2–3), pp. 69–87.

Stoeckel, John and Sirisena, N. L. Gender-Specific Socioeconomic Impacts of Development Programs in Sri Lanka. *J. Devel. Areas*, October 1988, *23*(1), pp. 31–42.

Stoelwinder, Johannes U. and Abernethy, Margaret A. Management Information Systems in

Public Hospitals: The Queen Victoria Medical Centre Experience. In *Butler, J. R. G. and Doessel, D. P.*, eds., 1988, pp. 3–19.

_____; **Abernethy, Margaret A.** and **Magnus, Anne.** An Assessment of Alternative Models for Costing Nursing Services: A Measurement Theory Perspective. In *Smith, C. S.*, ed., 1988, pp. 127–44.

Stoga, Alan J. The United States and the Developing World: Pitfalls, Pratfalls, and Possibilities. In *Yochelson, J.*, ed., 1988, pp. 97–118.

Stoker, Thomas M.; Jorgenson, Dale W. and **Slesnick, Daniel T.** Two-Stage Budgeting and Exact Aggregation. *J. Bus. Econ. Statist.*, July 1988, *6*(3), pp. 313–25.

Stokes, Bruce. On Technology and Economic Policymaking. In *Aho, C. M. and Levinson, M.*, 1988, pp. 226–31.

Stokes, C. Shannon; Warland, Rex H. and **Miller, Michael K.** The Effect of Legalization and Public Funding of Abortion on Neonatal Mortality: An Intervention Analysis. *Population Res. Policy Rev.*, 1988, *7*(1), pp. 79–92.

Stokes, Raymond G. German Energy in the U.S. Post-war Economic Order, 1945–51. *J. Europ. Econ. Hist.*, Winter 1988, *17*(3), pp. 621–39.

Stokey, Nancy L. Learning by Doing and the Introduction of New Goods. *J. Polit. Econ.*, August 1988, *96*(4), pp. 701–17.

Stoll, Hans R. After the Crash: Linkages between Stocks and Futures: Regulatory Issues. In *MacKay, R. J.*, ed., 1988, pp. 41–44.

_____. Index Futures, Program Trading, and Stock Market Procedures. *J. Futures Markets*, August 1988, *8*(4), pp. 391–412.

_____. Portfolio Trading. *J. Portfol. Manage.*, Summer 1988, *14*(4), pp. 20–24.

_____ and **Whaley, Robert E.** Volatility and Futures: Message versus Messenger. *J. Portfol. Manage.*, Winter 1988, *14*(2), pp. 20–22.

Stoll, John R. New Approaches in Agricultural Policy Research: Discussion. *Amer. J. Agr. Econ.*, May 1988, *70*(2), pp. 459.

_____ and **Bowker, J. M.** Use of Dichotomous Choice Nonmarket Methods to Value the Whooping Crane Resource. *Amer. J. Agr. Econ.*, May 1988, *70*(2), pp. 372–81.

Stollery, Kenneth R. and **Kardasz, Stanley W.** Market Structure and Price Adjustment in Canadian Manufacturing Industries. *J. Econ. Bus.*, November 1988, *40*(4), pp. 335–42.

_____ and **Kardasz, Stanley W.** Price Formation in Canadian Manufacturing Industries. *Appl. Econ.*, April 1988, *20*(4), pp. 473–83.

Stolper, Wolfgang F. Development: Theory and Empirical Evidence. In *Hanusch, H.*, ed., 1988, pp. 9–22.

_____. On the Coming Senescence of American Manufacturing Competence: Discussion. In *Hanusch, H.*, ed., 1988, pp. 385–92.

Stone, Bruce. The North China Plain: Comment. In *O'Mara, G. T.*, ed., 1988, pp. 96–99.

_____. Relative Prices in the People's Republic of China: Rural Taxation through Public Monopsony. In *Mellor, J. W. and Ahmed, R.*, eds., 1988, pp. 124–54.

Stone, Eugene F. Moderator Variables in Research: A Review and Analysis of Conceptual and Methodological Issues. In *Ferris, G. R. and Rowland, K. M.*, eds., 1988, pp. 191–229.

Stone, Frank. Dispute Resolution Mechanisms: Comments. In *Schott, J. J. and Smith, M. G.*, eds., 1988, pp. 95–100.

Stone, Jack H. and **Allen, Ralph C.** Managerial Productivity and Firm Size: A Comment on Oi's Managerial Time Allocation Model. *Econ. Inquiry*, January 1988, *26*(1), pp. 171–73.

Stone, Joe A. and **Eberts, Randall W.** Student Achievement in Public Schools: Do Principals Make a Difference? *Econ. Educ. Rev.*, 1988, *7*(3), pp. 291–99.

_____ and **Eberts, Randall W.** Teacher Unions and the Productivity of Public Schools. In *Lewin, D., et al.*, eds., 1988, *1987*, pp. 555–69.

_____ and **Eberts, Randall W.** Unionism and Licensing of Public School Teachers: Impact on Wages and Educational Output: Comment. In *Freeman, R. B. and Ichniowski, C.*, eds., 1988, pp. 319–21.

_____ and **Haynes, Stephen E.** Does the Political Business Cycle Dominate U.S. Unemployment and Inflation? Some New Evidence. In *Willett, T. D.*, ed., 1988, pp. 276–93.

_____ and **Haynes, Stephen E.** Short Communications: Reply [Impact of the Terms of Trade on the U.S. Trade Balance: A Reexamination]. *J. Bus. Econ. Statist.*, January 1988, *6*(1), pp. 138–40.

Stone, Judith Lee. Evaluating the New 65 MPH Speed Limit: Comments. In *Graham, J. D.*, ed., 1988, pp. 259–62.

Stone, Richard. Progress in Balancing the National Accounts. In *[Clark, C.]*, 1988, pp. 21–31.

_____. When Will the War End? *Cambridge J. Econ.*, June 1988, *12*(2), pp. 193–201.

_____; **Champernowne, D. G.** and **Meade, James.** The Precision of National Income Estimates. In *Meade, J.*, Vol. 1, 1988, *1942*, pp. 136–51.

_____ and **Meade, James.** The Construction of Tables of National Income, Expenditure, Savings and Investment. In *Meade, J.*, Vol. 1, 1988, *1941*, pp. 118–35.

_____ and **Meade, James.** National Income and Expenditure. In *Meade, J.*, Vol. 1, 1988, *1944*, pp. 152–70.

Stonecash, Jeffrey M. Fiscal Centralization in the American States: Findings from Another Perspective. *Public Budg. Finance*, Winter 1988, *8*(4), pp. 81–89.

Stonehouse, D. Peter and **Henderson, J. Stephen W.** Effects of Soil Tillage and Time of Planting on Corn Yields and Farm Profits in Southern Ontario. *Can. J. Agr. Econ.*, March 1988, *36*(1), pp. 127–41.

Stoneman, Colin and **Robinson, Peter B.** Economic Modeling for LEAP: Background and Methodology. In *Hosier, R. H.*, ed. *(II)*, 1988, pp. 99–125.

Stoneman, Paul and **Vickers, John.** The Assessment: The Economics of Technology Policy. *Oxford Rev. Econ. Policy*, Winter 1988, *4*(4), pp. i–xvi.

Stoner, James A. F.; Taylor, Arthur R. and Wankel, Charles B. On Waiting for Neither Godot nor the Apocalypse: Practical First Steps to Move U.S. Managers Toward World Class Managing. **In** *Starr, M. K., ed.*, 1988, pp. 185–212.

Stopford, John M. and Baden-Fuller, Charles. Regional-Level Competition in a Mature Industry: The Case of European Domestic Appliances. **In** *Dunning, J. and Robson, P., eds.*, 1988, pp. 71–90.

_____ **and Baden-Fuller, Charles.** Restructuring Mature Industries: The Challenge for Europe. **In** *Urabe, K.; Child, J. and Kagono, T., eds.*, 1988, pp. 225–41.

Storm, Paul M. Security on Movable Property and Receivables in Europe: The Netherlands. **In** *Dickson, M. G.; Rosener, W. and Storm, P. M., eds.*, 1988, pp. 123–41.

Storper, M. Big Structures, Small Events, and Large Processes in Economic Geography. *Environ. Planning A*, February 1988, *20*(2), pp. 165–85.

Story, Joseph C. Gulf Oil Policies in the 1980s. **In** *Sindelar, H. R., III and Peterson, J. E., eds.*, 1988, pp. 110–26.

Stoto, Michael A. Estimating Age-Specific Transition Rates for Population Sub-groups from Successive Surveys: Changes in Adult Rates of Cigarette Smoking. *Population Stud.*, July 1988, *42*(2), pp. 227–39.

Stoughton, Neal M. The Information Content of Corporate Merger and Acquisition Offers. *J. Finan. Quant. Anal.*, June 1988, *23*(2), pp. 175–97.

Stout, D. K. The National Institute and Understanding Technical Change. *Nat. Inst. Econ. Rev.*, May 1988, (124), pp. 80–82.

Stout, David E.; Wygal, Donald E. and Volpi, James. A Comparative Income Statement Approach to Integrating International Topics in the Financial Accounting Curriculum. **In** *Most, K. S., ed.*, 1988, pp. 149–68.

Stout, Lynn A. The Unimportance of Being Efficient: An Economic Analysis of Stock Market Pricing and Securities Regulation. *Mich. Law Rev.*, December 1988, *87*(3), pp. 613–709.

Stover, Roger D. and Cranford, Brian K. Interest Yields, Credit Ratings, and Economic Characteristics of State Bonds: Comment. *J. Money, Credit, Banking*, November 1988, *20*(4), pp. 691–95.

Stowsky, Jay S. The Domestic Employment Consequences of International Trade in Telecommunications Equipment. **In** *Tyson, L. D.; Dickens, W. T. and Zysman, J., eds.*, 1988, pp. 205–36.

van der Straaten, Jan and Dietz, Frank. The Problem of Optimal Exploitation of Natural Resources: The Need for Ecological Limiting Conditions. *Int. J. Soc. Econ.*, 1988, *15*(3–4), pp. 71–79.

Stračár, Ján. New Conditions Must Not Take Us by Surprise. *Czech. Econ. Digest.*, April 1988, (2), pp. 3–12.

Strachey, A. J. S. Mill's Philosophy Tested by Prof. Jevons. **In** *Wood, J. C., ed.*, *Vol. 3*, 1988, pp. 9–10.

Straffin, Philip D., Jr. The Shapley–Shubik and Banzhaf Power Indices as Probabilities. **In** *[Shapley, L. S.]*, 1988, pp. 71–81.

Strain, Greg; Ehrensaft, Philip and Culver, David. Cost Structure and Performance of Prairie Grain and Oilseed Farms. *Can. J. Agr. Econ.*, Part 2, December 1988, *36*(4), pp. 845–55.

Strand, Ivar E., Jr. Economic Rationale in the Development of Fisheries Management: Atlantic Striped Bass. **In** *Johnston, G. M.; Freshwater, D. and Favero, P., eds.*, 1988, pp. 159–77.

_____ **and Kirkley, James E.** The Technology and Management of Multi-species Fisheries. *Appl. Econ.*, October 1988, *20*(10), pp. 1279–92.

Strand, Jon. The Short-run Phillips Curve with Monopoly Unions. *Scand. J. Econ.*, 1988, *90*(1), pp. 63–74.

Strange, Susan. The Persistent Myth of Lost Hegemony: Reply. *Int. Organ.*, Autumn 1988, *42*(4), pp. 751–52.

Strassmann, W. Paul. The Global Construction Industry: The United States. **In** *Strassmann, W. P. and Wells, J., eds.*, 1988, pp. 22–58.

_____. Technology: A Culture Trait, a Logical Category, or Virtue Itself? **In** *Samuels, W. J., ed.*, *Vol. 3*, 1988, *1974*, pp. 117–33.

_____ **and Wells, Jill.** The Global Construction Industry: Conclusion: Comparison and Analysis. **In** *Strassmann, W. P. and Wells, J., eds.*, 1988, pp. 211–58.

_____ **and Wells, Jill.** The Global Construction Industry: Strategies for Entry Growth and Survival: Introduction. **In** *Strassmann, W. P. and Wells, J., eds.*, 1988, pp. 1–21.

Straub, Martin and Wenig, Alois. On the Construction of an Index of Bequest Behavior. **In** *Eichhorn, W., ed.*, 1988, pp. 453–76.

Straubhaar, Thomas. International Labor Migration and Development. **In** *Salvatore, D., ed.*, 1988, pp. 139–61.

_____. International Labour Migration within a Common Market: Some Aspects of EC Experience. *J. Common Market Stud.*, September 1988, *27*(1), pp. 45–62.

Strausbaugh, John and Cwi, David. The Royalists, the Realists, and the Radicals: A Comparative Analysis of Arts Funding in Canada and the United States. *J. Cult. Econ.*, June 1988, *12*(1), pp. 1–26.

Strauss, George. Australian Labor Relations through American Eyes. *Ind. Relat.*, Spring 1988, *27*(2), pp. 131–48.

_____ **and Lewin, David.** Behavioral Research in Industrial Relations: Introduction. *Ind. Relat.*, Winter 1988, *27*(1), pp. 1–6.

Strauss, John. Indirect and Direct Taxation of Agriculture in Sudan: The Role of Government in Agriculture Surplus Extraction: Discussion.

Amer. J. Agr. Econ., May 1988, 70(2), pp. 440–41.

Strauss-Kahn, Dominique. Public Sector Deficits and the Growth of the National Debt. In *Cavanna, H., ed.*, 1988, pp. 146–65.

Strauss-Kahn, M.-O. and Bordes, C. Dispositif de controle monetaire en France et chocs sur la vitesse dans un environnement en mutation. (The French Experience with Targeting and Velocity Shocks in a Changing Environment. With English summary.) *Écon. Soc.*, January 1988, 22(1), pp. 105–53.

Strauss, Robert S. Current Issues in U.S. Trade Policy. In *Feldstein, M., ed. (I)*, 1988, pp. 204–11.

Straussman, Jeffrey D. Rights-Based Budgeting. In *Rubin, I. S., ed.*, 1988, pp. 100–123.

———; **Mullins, Daniel and Bretschneider, Stuart.** Do Revenue Forecasts Influence Budget Setting? A Small Group Experiment. *Policy Sci.*, 1988, 21(4), pp. 305–25.

Streeck, Wolfgang. Industrial Relations and Unemployment: The Case for Flexible Corporatism: Comment. In *Kregel, J. A.; Matzner, E. and Roncaglia, A., eds.*, 1988, pp. 227–32.

Street, Donald R. Jovellanos, an Antecedent to Modern Human Capital Theory. *Hist. Polit. Econ.*, Summer 1988, 20(2), pp. 191–206.

Street, James H. The Contribution of Simon S. Kuznets to Institutionalist Development Theory. *J. Econ. Issues*, June 1988, 22(2), pp. 499–509.

———. The Institutionalist Theory of Economic Development. In *Tool, M. R., ed., Vol. 2*, 1988, 1987, pp. 443–69.

———. The Latin American "Structuralists" and the Institutionalists: Convergence in Development Theory. In *Samuels, W. J., ed., Vol. 3*, 1988, 1967, pp. 185–203.

———. The Making of an Applied Institutionalist. *J. Econ. Issues*, June 1988, 22(2), pp. 327–37.

———; **Arestis, Philip and Tool, Marc R.** In Memoriam: Alfred S. Eichner 1937–1988. *J. Econ. Issues*, December 1988, 22(4), pp. 1239–42.

——— **and James, Dilmus.** Institutionalism, Structuralism, and Dependency in Latin America. In *Samuels, W. J., ed., Vol. 3*, 1988, 1982, pp. 204–20.

Streeten, Paul P. Beyond Adjustment: The Asian Experience: Introduction and Discussion Summary. In *Streeten, P., ed.*, 1988, pp. 1–17.

———. Conditionality: A Double Paradox. In *Jepma, C. J., ed.*, 1988, pp. 107–19.

———. The Double Paradox of Conditionality. In *Tavis, L. A., ed.*, 1988, pp. 138–41.

———. "New" Directions for Private Resource Transfers. In *Tavis, L. A., ed.*, 1988, pp. 294–311.

———. Reflections on the Role of the University and the Developing Countries. *World Devel.*, May 1988, 16(5), pp. 639–40.

———. Surpluses for a Capital-Hungry World. In *Streeten, P., ed.*, 1988, pp. 256–61.

Streeter, Deborah H.; Liu, Donald J. and Kaiser, Harry M. Price versus Stock Effect Policies for Reducing Excess Milk Production. *Western*

J. Agr. Econ., December 1988, 13(2), pp. 277–84.

———; **Liu, Donald J. and Kaiser, Harry M.** Welfare Comparisons of U.S. Dairy Policies with and without Mandatory Supply Control. *Amer. J. Agr. Econ.*, November 1988, 70(4), pp. 848–58.

Streib, Gordon F. The Decline of Retirement in the Years before Social Security: U.S. Retirement Patterns, 1870–1940: Discussion. In *Ricardo-Campbell, R. and Lazear, E. P., eds.*, 1988, pp. 27–37.

Streissler, Erich. New Information Theoretic Approaches to Labour Market Theory. In *Kregel, J. A.; Matzner, E. and Roncaglia, A., eds.*, 1988, pp. 48–65.

Streit, Manfred E. The Mirage of Neo-corporatism. *Kyklos*, 1988, 41(4), pp. 603–24.

Stren, Richard E. Urban Services in Africa: Public Management or Privatisation? In *Cook, P. and Kirkpatrick, C., eds.*, 1988, pp. 217–47.

Strickstein, Aubrey; Olson, Jon and Osborn, Richard N. Cooperative Multinational R&D Ventures: Interpretation and Negotiation in Emerging Systems. In *Gattiker, U. E. and Larwood, L., eds.*, 1988, pp. 33–54.

Strier, Leonid and Chapman, John N. Five-Year Plans for Soviet Agricultural Industries: Are They Relevant as Production Indicators? *Comp. Econ. Stud.*, Fall 1988, 30(3), pp. 71–93.

Ströbele, Wolfgang J. The Optimal Intertemporal Decision on Industrial Production and Harvesting a Renewable Natural Resource. *J. Econ. (Z. Nationalökon.)*, 1988, 48(4), pp. 375–88.

——— **and Kuckshinrichs, Wilhelm.** On the Optimal Transition to a Backstop Technology with Uncertainty as to the Cost of the Substitute. *J. Inst. Theoretical Econ.*, June 1988, 144(3), pp. 496–514.

Stroe, R.; Ionescu, C. and Bulgaru, M. Turning to Account the Results of the Scientific Research of Economic Cybernetics and Economic Informatics in the Instructional–Educational Process. *Econ. Computat. Cybern. Stud. Res.*, 1988, 23(4), pp. 25–36.

Strøm, Steinar; Longva, Svein and Olsen, Øystein. Total Elasticities of Energy Demand Analysed within a General Equilibrium Model. *Energy Econ.*, October 1988, 10(4), pp. 298–308.

Stromberg, Jan-Olov and Kanbur, S. M. Ravi. Income Transitions and Income Distribution Dominance. *J. Econ. Theory*, August 1988, 45(2), pp. 408–16.

Strongin, Roman G. and Sergeev, Yaroslav D. Effective Algorithm for Global Optimization with Parallel Computations. In *Kurzhanski, A.; Neumann, K. and Pallaschke, D., eds.*, 1988, pp. 158–62.

Stroope, John C. An Empirical Analysis of the Impact of ERTA and TEFRA on Tax Compliance. In *Pennsylvania Economic Association*, 1988, pp. 321–30.

Štrougal, Lubomír. From the Program Statement

of the Czechoslovak Federal Government. *Czech. Econ. Digest.*, August 1988, (5), pp. 5–25.

Stroup, Richard L. Buying Misery with Federal Land. *Public Choice*, April 1988, 57(1), pp. 69–77.

Strum, Peter H. Labour Market Simulations for Six OECD Countries Using INTERLINK with a Three-Factor Putty-Clay Supply Block: Results and Their Limitations. In *Hopkins, M. J. D., ed.*, 1988, pp. 132–56.

Strümpel, Burkhard. Work Ethics in Transition. In *Dlugos, G.; Dorow, W. and Weiermair, K., eds.*, 1988, pp. 121–32.

Struyk, Raymond J. The Distribution of Tenant Benefits from Rent Control in Urban Jordan. *Land Econ.*, May 1988, 64(2), pp. 125–34.

_____. Understanding High Housing Vacancy Rates in a Developing Country: Jordan. *J. Devel. Areas*, April 1988, 22(3), pp. 373–80.

Stuart, Brian and Pownall, Roger. The IMF's Compensatory and Contingency Financing Facility. *Finance Develop.*, December 1988, 25(4), pp. 9–11.

Stuart, Robert W. and Abetti, Pier A. Field Study of Technical Ventures—Part III: The Impact of Entrepreneurial and Management Experience on Early Performance. In *Kirchhoff, B. A., et al., eds.*, 1988, pp. 177–93.

Stubbart, Charles I. and Ramaprasad, Arkalgud. Probing Two Chief Executives' Schematic Knowledge of the U.S. Steel Industry Using Cognitive Maps. In *Lamb, R. and Shrivastava, P., eds.*, 1988, pp. 139–64.

Stubbs, Jeans. Gender Constructs of Labour in Prerevolutionary Cuban Tobacco. *Soc. Econ. Stud.*, March–June 1988, 37(1–2), pp. 241–69.

Stukel, Thérèse A. Generalized Logistic Models. *J. Amer. Statist. Assoc.*, June 1988, 83(402), pp. 426–31.

Stulz, Rene M. Capital Mobility and the Current Accounts. *J. Int. Money Finance*, June 1988, 7(2), pp. 167–80.

_____. Managerial Control of Voting Rights: Financing Policies and the Market for Corporate Control. *J. Finan. Econ.*, Jan.–March 1988, 20(1–2), pp. 25–54.

_____ and Kim, Yong Cheol. The Eurobond Market and Corporate Financial Policy: A Test of the Clientele Hypothesis. *J. Finan. Econ.*, December 1988, 22(2), pp. 189–205.

von Stumm, Michael; Lawrence, William and Bachmann, Laurie McGavin. Tracking Recent Trends in the International Market for Art Theft. *J. Cult. Econ.*, June 1988, 12(1), pp. 51–71.

Stumpf, Stephen A. Leadership and Beyond: The Need for Strategic Management Skills. In *Lamb, R. and Shrivastava, P., eds.*, 1988, pp. 245–61.

Sturm, Philip and Ford, Ina Kay. CPI Revision Provides More Accuracy in the Medical Care Services Component. *Mon. Lab. Rev.*, April 1988, 111(4), pp. 17–26.

Sturrock, Thomas and Thies, Clifford F. The

Pension-Augmented Balance Sheet. *J. Risk Ins.*, September 1988, 55(3), pp. 467–80.

Stutsman, Douglas. Wage Competition in the Labor Queue. *J. Post Keynesian Econ.*, Spring 1988, 10(3), pp. 355–69.

Stutzer, Michael J. and Roberds, William. Variable Rate Loans and Financed Activities: The Case of Adjustable Rate Mortgages. *J. Urban Econ.*, July 1988, 24(1), pp. 27–37.

Suarez-Villa, Luis. Metropolitan Evolution, Sectoral Economic Change, and the City Size Distribution. *Urban Stud.*, February 1988, 25(1), pp. 1–20.

Subrahmanyam, Sanjay. On the Significance of Gadflies: The Genoese East India Company of the 1640s. *J. Europ. Econ. Hist.*, Winter 1988, 17(3), pp. 559–81.

_____ and Bayly, C. A. Portfolio Capitalists and the Political Economy of Early Modern India. *Indian Econ. Soc. Hist. Rev.*, Oct.–Dec. 1988, 25(4), pp. 401–24.

Subrahmanyam, Sudha. Finance Commission Transfers in India: A Critical Note. *Indian Econ. Rev.*, Jan.–June 1988, 23(1), pp. 121–38.

Subramanian, Shankar and Carson, Richard T. Robust Regression in the Presence of Heteroscedasticity. In *Rhodes, G. F., Jr. and Fomby, T. B., eds.*, 1988, pp. 85–138.

Subramanian, T. A. and Navalkar, M. P. Human Resource Development in Scientific Institutions with Special Reference to Department of Atomic Energy. In *Kohli, U. and Gautam, V., eds.*, 1988, pp. 264–69.

Subramaniyan, G. and Nirmala, V. The Economic Efficiency of High-Yielding, Irrigated Cotton in India. *Margin*, July–Sept. 1988, 20(4), pp. 80–88.

Suchanek, Gerry L.; Williams, Arlington W. and Smith, Vernon L. Bubbles, Crashes, and Endogenous Expectations in Experimental Spot Asset Markets. *Econometrica*, September 1988, 56(5), pp. 1119–51.

Suchard, Hazel T. Attitudes of Bank Employees to Technological Change: A Survey of the South African Banking Industry. In *Tisdell, C. and Maitra, P., eds.*, 1988, pp. 260–80.

_____; Polonsky, M. J. and Scott, D. R. Motivations of South African Emigrants. *Appl. Econ.*, October 1988, 20(10), pp. 1293–1315.

Sudarsono, Budi and Soesastro, Hadi. Mineral and Energy Development in Indonesia. In *McKern, B. and Koomsup, P., eds.*, 1988, pp. 161–207.

Sudharshan, D. and Kumar, K. Ravi. Pre-emptive Product Positioning Strategies under Market Share Restrictions. *Managerial Dec. Econ.*, June 1988, 9(2), pp. 93–99.

_____ and Ritz, Zvi. An Evolutionary Analysis of Product-Preference Structure: Toward Managerial Control. In *Eiselt, H. A. and Pederzoli, G., eds.*, 1988, pp. 326–42.

Sudweeks, Bryan L. and Grub, Phillip D. Securities Markets and the People's Republic of China. *J. Econ. Devel.*, June 1988, 13(1), pp. 51–69.

Suebsaeng, Parita; Lindauer, David L. and Mee-sook, Oey Astra. Government Wage Policy in Africa: Some Findings and Policy Issues. *World Bank Res. Observer,* January 1988, 3(1), pp. 1–25.

Suedfeld, Peter and Bluck, Susan. Changes in Integrative Complexity Prior to Surprise Attacks. *J. Conflict Resolution,* December 1988, 32(4), pp. 626–35.

Sufrin, Sidney C. Folly as 20/20 Hindsight. *Rivista Int. Sci. Econ. Com.,* March 1988, 35(3), pp. 227–38.

_____. **and Owers, James E.** The Ethics of Anti Trust. *Rivista Int. Sci. Econ. Com.,* April–May 1988, 35(4–5), pp. 359–68.

Sugeno, Kazuo. The Coexistence of Rival Unions at Undertakings and Unfair Labor Practices. In *Japan Institute of Labour, ed.,* 1988, *1984,* pp. 131–35.

_____. Collective Bargaining with Rival Unions: The Supreme Court's More Significant Second Ruling. In *Japan Institute of Labour, ed.,* 1988, *1985,* pp. 136–40.

_____. Final Step toward Revision of the Law Regulating Hours of Work. In *Japan Institute of Labour, ed.,* 1988, pp. 97–102.

_____. The Impact of the Equal Employment Opportunity Law at Its First Stage of Enforcement. In *Japan Institute of Labour, ed.,* 1988, *1987,* pp. 111–15.

Sugihara, Shirō. Economists in Government: Ōkubo Toshimichi, the 'Bismark of Japan', and His Times. In *Sugiyama, C. and Mizuta, H., eds.,* 1988, pp. 211–21.

_____. Economists in Journalism: Liberalism, Nationalism and Their Variants. In *Sugiyama, C. and Mizuta, H., eds.,* 1988, pp. 237–53.

_____. In the Schools of Law: Hōsei, Meiji and Chūō In *Sugiyama, C. and Mizuta, H., eds.,* 1988, pp. 139–49.

_____. **and Nishizawa, Tamotsu.** In the 'Commercial Metropolis' Osaka: Schools of Commerce and Law. In *Sugiyama, C. and Mizuta, H., eds.,* 1988, pp. 189–207.

Sugiura, Ippei. Distributed Control of Econometric Data Bases and Models. In *[Clark, C.],* 1988, pp. 70–103.

Sugiyama, Chūhei. Fukuzawa Yukichi. In *Sugiyama, C. and Mizuta, H., eds.,* 1988, pp. 37–57.

_____. Nishi Amane and Tsuda Mamichi. In *Sugiyama, C. and Mizuta, H., eds.,* 1988, pp. 59–72.

_____. Pioneer Economics Department: Senshū School. In *Sugiyama, C. and Mizuta, H., eds.,* 1988, pp. 127–37.

_____. **and Nishizawa, Tamotsu.** 'Captain of Industry': Tokyo Commercial School at Hitotsubashi. In *Sugiyama, C. and Mizuta, H., eds.,* 1988, pp. 151–69.

Suh, Nam Pyo. Technological Change and Its International Diffusion: Commentary. In *Cassing, J. H. and Husted, S. L., eds.,* 1988, pp. 114–17.

Suh, Sang-Mok and Williamson, David. The Impact of Adjustment and Stabilization Policies on Social Welfare: The South Korean Experiences during 1978–1985. In *Cornia, G. A.; Jolly, R. and Stewart, F., eds.,* 1988, pp. 218–37.

Suh, Seoung Hwan. The Possibility and Impossibility of Intercity Commuting. *J. Urban Econ.,* January 1988, 23(1), pp. 86–100.

Suh, Sunduck and Kim, T. John. Toward Developing a National Transportation Planning Model: A Bilevel Programming Approach for Korea. *Ann. Reg. Sci.,* February 1988, 22, pp. 65–80.

Suh, Yoon S. Noncontrollable Costs and Optimal Performance Measurement. *J. Acc. Res.,* Spring 1988, 26(1), pp. 154–68.

Suhler, Diane Rizzuto and Kolodny, Richard. The Effects of New Debt Issues on Existing Security Holders. *Quart. J. Bus. Econ.,* Spring 1988, 27(2), pp. 51–72.

Sukatme, P. V. Energy Intake and Nutrition: On the Autoregulatory Homeostatic Nature of the Energy Requirement. In *Srinivasan, T. N. and Bardhan, P. K., eds.,* 1988, pp. 365–88.

Sukharev, A. Y. The Legal Education of Workers and Managers in the USSR. *Int. Lab. Rev.,* 1988, 127(5), pp. 613–26.

Sukhotin, Iurii V. and Dement'ev, Viktor E. Economic Reform and the Forces of Inhibition. *Prob. Econ.,* October 1988, 31(6), pp. 64–70.

_____ **and Dement'ev, Viktor E.** Property in the System of Socialist Production Relations. *Prob. Econ.,* August 1988, 31(4), pp. 57–72.

Sukume, Chrispen and Buccola, Steven T. Optimal Grain Pricing and Storage Policy in Controlled Agricultural Economies: Application to Zimbabwe. *World Devel.,* March 1988, 16(3), pp. 361–71.

Sulak, Donna B.; Montgomery, Mark R. and Cheung, Paul P. L. Rates of Courtship and First Marriage in Thailand. *Population Stud.,* November 1988, 42(3), pp. 375–88.

Suliman, Ali Ahmed. Africa: Management of Government Finance in Africa. *Bull. Int. Fiscal Doc.,* June 1988, 42(6), pp. 253–54, 283.

_____. Experience with *Zakat:* The Relation between *Zakat* and Income Tax: The Sudan. *Bull. Int. Fiscal Doc.,* January 1988, 42(1), pp. 34–36.

Sullivan, Daniel G. and Card, David. Measuring the Effect of Subsidized Training Programs on Movements in and out of Employment. *Econometrica,* May 1988, 56(3), pp. 497–530.

Sullivan, David F. and Seskin, Eugene P. Plant and Equipment Expenditures, First and Second Quarters and Second Half of 1988. *Surv. Curr. Bus.,* April 1988, 68(4), pp. 26–30.

_____ **and Seskin, Eugene P.** Plant and Equipment Expenditures, the Four Quarters of 1988. *Surv. Curr. Bus.,* September 1988, 68(9), pp. 18–20.

_____ **and Seskin, Eugene P.** Plant and Equipment Expenditures, the Four Quarters of 1988. *Surv. Curr. Bus.,* June 1988, 68(6), pp. 19–22.

Sullivan, Dennis H. and Erekson, O. Homer. A

Cross-Section Analysis of IRS Auditing. *Nat. Tax J.*, June 1988, *41*(2), pp. 175–89.

_____ **and Newman, Robert J.** Econometric Analysis of Business Tax Impacts on Industrial Location: What Do We Know, and How Do We Know It? *J. Urban Econ.*, March 1988, *23*(2), pp. 215–34.

Sullivan, E. Thomas. The Antitrust Division as a Regulatory Agency: An Enforcement Policy in Transition. **In** *Weidenbaum, M. L. and Chilton, K. W., eds.*, 1988, pp. 106–40.

Sullivan, Gene D. Louisiana: Prospects for a Diversified Economy. *Fed. Res. Bank Atlanta Econ. Rev.*, Jan.–Feb. 1988, *73*(1), pp. 36–48.

_____ **and Wilson, W. Gene.** Crop Costs and Farm Survival. *Fed. Res. Bank Atlanta Econ. Rev.*, March–April 1988, *73*(2), pp. 8–26.

Sullivan, Lawrence A. Special Issues in Antitrust Litigation: Comment. **In** *White, L. J., ed.*, 1988, pp. 381–84.

Sullivan, Mark A. Ireland's Unemployment Problem and Irish Industrial Policy: 1975–1985: A Survey and Evaluation. **In** *Pennsylvania Economic Association*, 1988, pp. 179–95.

Sullivan, Mark J. and Roberts, David J. Marriage and the Income Tax Law: Living Together Compatibly. *Challenge*, Nov.–Dec. 1988, *31*(6), pp. 52–53.

Sullivan, O.; Brown, A. and Murphy, M. Sources of Data for Modelling Household Change with Special Reference to the OPCS 1% Longitudinal Study. **In** *Keilman, N.; Kuijsten, A. and Vossen, A., eds.*, 1988, pp. 56–66.

Sullivan, Patrick J. Financial Sources for Local Infrastructure Investment. **In** *Johnson, T. G.; Deaton, B. J. and Segarra, E., eds.*, 1988, pp. 165–200.

Sullivan, Sean and Lewin, Marion Ein. The Economics and Ethics of Long-Term Care and Disability: Introduction and Overview. **In** *Sullivan, S. and Lewin, M. E., eds.*, 1988, pp. 1–8.

Sullivan, Timothy E. Industrial Transformation and Market Integration along the American Manufacturing Frontier: The Midwest from 1850–1880. **In** *Hausman, W. J., ed.*, 1988, pp. 201–06.

Sumiya, Mikio. Impact of Micro-electronics. **In** *Japan Institute of Labour, ed.*, 1988, *1983*, pp. 10–13.

Summers, Bruce J. Electronic Payments in Retrospect. *Fed. Res. Bank Richmond Econ. Rev.*, March–April 1988, *74*(2), pp. 16–19.

Summers, Lawrence H. Economic Priorities for the Next President. *Challenge*, Sept.–Oct. 1988, *31*(5), pp. 21–26.

_____. Effect of Taxation with International Capital Mobility: Comments. **In** *Aaron, H. J.; Galper, H. and Pechman, J. A., eds.*, 1988, pp. 148–55.

_____. Effects of Taxes on Saving: Comments. **In** *Aaron, H. J.; Galper, H. and Pechman, J. A., eds.*, 1988, pp. 259–65.

_____. A Fair Tax Act That's Bad for Business. **In** *Brown, E., ed.*, 1988, *1987*, pp. 187–95.

_____. Is There a Corporate Debt Crisis? Comment. *Brookings Pap. Econ. Act.*, 1988, (1), pp. 130–36.

_____. Policies to Curb Stock Market Volatility: Commentary. **In** *Federal Reserve Bank of Kansas City*, 1988, pp. 167–71.

_____. Postwar Developments in Business Cycle Theory: A Moderately Classical Perspective: Comment. *J. Money, Credit, Banking*, Part 2, August 1988, *20*(3), pp. 472–76.

_____. Relative Wages, Efficiency Wages, and Keynesian Unemployment. *Amer. Econ. Rev.*, May 1988, *78*(2), pp. 383–88.

_____. Should Keynesian Economics Dispense with the Phillips Curve? **In** *Cross, R., ed.*, 1988, pp. 11–25.

_____. Tax Policy and International Competitiveness. **In** *Spence, A. M. and Hazard, H. A., eds.*, 1988, pp. 399–430.

_____. Tax Policy and International Competitiveness. **In** *Frenkel, J. A., ed.*, 1988, pp. 349–75.

_____. Tax Policy and the Economy: Introduction. **In** *Summers, L. H., ed.*, 1988, pp. vii–x.

_____ **and Barsky, Robert B.** Gibson's Paradox and the Gold Standard. *J. Polit. Econ.*, June 1988, *96*(3), pp. 528–50.

_____ **and Blanchard, Olivier Jean.** Beyond the Natural Rate Hypothesis. *Amer. Econ. Rev.*, May 1988, *78*(2), pp. 182–87.

_____ **and Blanchard, Olivier Jean.** Hysteresis and the European Unemployment Problem. **In** *Cross, R., ed.*, 1988, pp. 306–64.

_____ **and Blanchard, Olivier Jean.** Hysteresis in Unemployment. **In** *Shaw, G. K., ed., Vol. 1*, 1988, *1987*, pp. 313–20.

_____ **and Clark, Kim B.** Labour Force Participation: Timing and Persistence. **In** *Cross, R., ed.*, 1988, pp. 203–31.

_____ **and Cutler, David M.** The Costs of Conflict Resolution and Financial Distress: Evidence from the Texaco–Pennzoil Litigation. *Rand J. Econ.*, Summer 1988, *19*(2), pp. 157–72.

_____ **and De Long, J. Bradford.** How Does Macroeconomic Policy Affect Output? *Brookings Pap. Econ. Act.*, 1988, (2), pp. 433–80.

_____ **and De Long, J. Bradford.** Is Increased Price Flexibility Stabilizing? Reply. *Amer. Econ. Rev.*, March 1988, *78*(1), pp. 273–76.

_____ **and Kotlikoff, Laurence J.** The Contribution of Intergenerational Transfers to Total Wealth: A Reply. **In** *Kessler, D. and Masson, A., eds.*, 1988, pp. 53–67.

_____ **and Krueger, Alan B.** Efficiency Wages and the Inter-industry Wage Structure. *Econometrica*, March 1988, *56*(2), pp. 259–93.

_____ **and Mankiw, N. Gregory.** Money Demand and the Effects of Fiscal Policies: Reply. *J. Money, Credit, Banking*, November 1988, *20*(4), pp. 715–17.

_____ **and Poterba, James M.** Mean Reversion in Stock Prices. *J. Finan. Econ.*, October 1988, *22*(1), pp. 27–59.

_____ **and Shleifer, Andrei.** Breach of Trust in Hostile Takeovers. **In** *Auerbach, A. J., ed. (I)*, 1988, pp. 33–56.

Summers, Robert and Heston, Alan. Comparing International Comparisons. In *Salazar-Carrillo, J. and Rao, D. S. P., eds.*, 1988, pp. 263–81.

—— **and Heston, Alan.** A New Set of International Comparisons of Real Product and Price Levels Estimates for 130 Countries, 1950–1985. *Rev. Income Wealth*, March 1988, 34(1), pp. 1–25.

—— **and Heston, Alan.** What We Have Learned about Prices and Quantities from International Comparisons: 1987. *Amer. Econ. Rev.*, May 1988, 78(2), pp. 467–73.

Sumner, Daniel A. Developments in Economics of Importance to Agricultural Economics: A Discussion. In *Hildreth, R. J., et al., eds.*, 1988, pp. 266–69.

——. Stability and the Tobacco Program. In *Sumner, D. A., ed.*, 1988, pp. 113–37.

Sumner, Michael. Note on Improving the Effectiveness of Effective Tax Rates on Business Investment. *J. Public Econ.*, April 1988, 35(3), pp. 393–96.

Sun, Shu and Sun, Yiyin. The Study and Development of Mineral and Energy Resources in China. In *Dorian, J. P. and Fridley, D. G., eds.*, 1988, pp. 94–104.

Sun, Yiyin and Sun, Shu. The Study and Development of Mineral and Energy Resources in China. In *Dorian, J. P. and Fridley, D. G., eds.*, 1988, pp. 94–104.

Sundaram, K. and Tendulkar, Suresh D. Toward an Explanation of Interregional Variations in Poverty and Unemployment in Rural India. In *Srinivasan, T. N. and Bardhan, P. K., eds.*, 1988, pp. 316–62.

Sundaram, Rangarajan and Lewis, Alain A. An Alternate Approach to Axiomatizations of the von Neumann/Morgenstern Characteristic Function. *Math. Soc. Sci.*, April 1988, 15(2), pp. 145–56.

Sundararajan, S. and Bhole, L. M. Impacts of Devaluation on the Trade Balance. *Margin*, July–Sept. 1988, 20(4), pp. 48–59.

Sundararajan, V. and Molho, Lazaros. Financial Reform and Monetary Control in Indonesia. In *Cheng, H.-S., ed.*, 1988, pp. 321–51.

—— **and Molho, Lazaros.** Financial Reform in Indonesia. *Finance Develop.*, December 1988, 25(4), pp. 43–45.

Sundberg, Mark W. and Sachs, Jeffrey D. International Payments Imbalances of the East Asian Developing Economies. In *Fieleke, N. S., ed.*, 1988, pp. 103–51.

Sundeen, Richard A. Explaining Participation in Coproduction: A Study of Volunteers. *Soc. Sci. Quart.*, September 1988, 69(3), pp. 547–68.

Sunder, Shyam and Dhaliwal, Dan S. Mergers, Acquisitions, and Takeovers: Wealth Effects on Various Economic Agents. In *Libecap, G., ed. (I)*, 1988, pp. 169–90.

—— **and Plott, Charles R.** Rational Expectations and the Aggregation of Diverse Information in Laboratory Security Markets. *Econometrica*, September 1988, 56(5), pp. 1085–1118.

Sundgren, Bo and Lyberg, Lars. The Impact of the Development of EDP on Statistical Methodology and Survey Techniques. *Statist. J.*, August 1988, 5(2), pp. 169–91.

Sundin, Elisabeth and Holmquist, Carin. Women as Entrepreneurs in Sweden: Conclusions from a Survey. In *Kirchhoff, B. A., et al., eds.*, 1988, pp. 626–42.

Sunding, David and Adelman, Irma. Economic Policy and Income Distribution in China. In *Reynolds, B. L., ed.*, 1988, 1987, pp. 154–71.

Sundrum, R. M. Indonesia's Slow Economic Growth 1981–86. *Bull. Indonesian Econ. Stud.*, April 1988, 24(1), pp. 37–72.

Sundstrom, William A. Internal Labor Markets before World War I: On-the-Job Training and Employee Promotion. *Exploration Econ. Hist.*, October 1988, 25(4), pp. 424–45.

——. Organizational Failures and Wage Determination: A Historical Case Study. *J. Econ. Behav. Organ.*, September 1988, 10(2), pp. 201–24.

—— **and David, Paul A.** Old-Age Security Motives, Labor Markets, and Farm Family Fertility in Antebellum America. *Exploration Econ. Hist.*, April 1988, 25(2), pp. 164–97.

Sunga, Preetom S. Conceptual Incongruity in the National Accounts. *Rev. Income Wealth*, December 1988, 34(4), pp. 393–409.

Sungsup, Rhee. Recent Industrial Adjustments of Korean Economy and Underlying Policy Reforms. *Devel. Econ.*, September 1988, 26(3), pp. 222–46.

Sunley, Emil M.; Amerkhail, Valerie L. and Spooner, Gillian M. The Fall and Rise of the U.S. Corporate Tax Burden. *Nat. Tax J.*, September 1988, 41(3), pp. 273–84.

—— **and Graetz, Michael J.** Minimum Taxes and Comprehensive Tax Reform. In *Aaron, H. J.; Galper, H. and Pechman, J. A., eds.*, 1988, pp. 385–419.

van Suntum, Ulrich. Capital and Growth: A Simple Neo-Austrian Approach. *Jahr. Nationalökon. Statist.*, January 1988, 204(1), pp. 1–16.

——. Vindicating Thünen's Tombstone Formula √ap. *Jahr. Nationalökon. Statist.*, May 1988, 204(5), pp. 393–405.

Suomela, John W. and Rousslang, Donald J. Calculating the Welfare Costs of Import Restrictions in the Imperfect Substitutes Model. *Appl. Econ.*, May 1988, 20(5), pp. 691–700.

Suomi, Reima. Applying the Transaction Cost Approach to Building of Inter-organizational Informed Systems. *Liiketaloudellinen Aikak.*, 1988, 37(3), pp. 225–41.

Suominen, Risto and Räty, Päivi. Breddningen av skattebasen vid beskattning av industriföretag. (The Broadening of the Tax Base in the Taxation of Manufacturing Companies. With English summary.) *Ekon. Samfundets Tidskr.*, 1988, 41(4), pp. 267–72.

Suppes, P. Lorenz Curves for Various Processes: A Pluralistic Approach to Equity. In *Gaertner, W. and Pattanaik, P. K., eds.*, 1988, 1988, pp. 1–13.

——. Lorenz Curves for Various Processes: A

Pluralistic Approach to Equity. *Soc. Choice Welfare*, 1988, *5*(2/3), pp. 89–101.

Surkyn, Johan and Lesthaeghe, Ron. Cultural Dynamics and Economic Theories of Fertility Change. *Population Devel. Rev.*, March 1988, *14*(1), pp. 1–45.

Surrey, Michael. The Great Recession 1974–84: Is a 'Keynesist' Approach Plausible? In *Hillard, J., ed.*, 1988, pp. 107–24.

Suruga, Terukazu; Tachibanaki, Toshiaki and Atoda, Naosumi. Statistical Inference of Functional Forms for Income Distribution. *Econ. Stud. Quart.*, March 1988, *39*(1), pp. 14–40.

Sury, M. M. India: Structure and Reform of Indirect Taxes. *Bull. Int. Fiscal Doc.*, October 1988, *42*(10), pp. 424–33.

Sushka, Marie E.; Barrett, W. Brian and Slovin, Myron B. Reserve Regulation and Recourse as a Source of Risk Premia in the Federal Funds Market. *J. Banking Finance*, December 1988, *12*(4), pp. 575–84.

_____ **and Bendeck, Yvette.** Bank Acquisitions and Stockholders' Wealth. *J. Banking Finance*, December 1988, *12*(4), pp. 551–62.

_____; **Hudson, Carl D. and Slovin, Myron B.** Corporate Commercial Paper, Note Issuance Facilities, and Shareholder Wealth. *J. Int. Money Finance*, September 1988, *7*(3), pp. 289–302.

Sussangkarn, Chalongphob and Bell, Clive. Rationing and Adjustment in the Market for Tenancies: The Behavior of Landowning Households in Thanjavur District. *Amer. J. Agr. Econ.*, November 1988, *70*(4), pp. 779–89.

Sussman, Frances G. and Cropper, Maureen L. Families and the Economics of Risks to Life. *Amer. Econ. Rev.*, March 1988, *78*(1), pp. 255–60.

Sustal, J. On the Combination of Vague Evidence of the Probabilistic Origin. In *Kacprzyk, J. and Fedrizzi, M., eds.*, 1988, pp. 135–44.

Sutch, Richard and Ransom, Roger L. The Decline of Retirement in the Years before Social Security: U.S. Retirement Patterns, 1870–1940. In *Ricardo-Campbell, R. and Lazear, E. P., eds.*, 1988, pp. 3–26.

Sutcliffe, Charles and Board, John. Forced Diversification. *Quart. Rev. Econ. Bus.*, Autumn 1988, *28*(3), pp. 43–52.

_____ **and Sinclair, M. Thea.** The Economic Effects on Destination Areas of Foreign Involvement in the Tourism Industry: A Spanish Application. In *Goodall, B. and Ashworth, G., eds.*, 1988, pp. 111–32.

_____ **and Sinclair, M. Thea.** The Estimation of Keynesian Income Multipliers at the Subnational Level. *Appl. Econ.*, November 1988, *20*(11), pp. 1435–44.

Sutcliffe, R. B. Industry and Underdevelopment Re-examined. In *Wilber, C. K., ed.*, 1988, pp. 429–42.

Sutherland, Alan and Miller, Marcus H. Measures of Fiscal Stance and Rules for Stabilising the Economy: The Case for Separating Measurement from Policy. In *Eltis, W. and Sinclair, P. J. N., eds.*, 1988, pp. 216–32.

Sutherland, W. R. S. and MacLean, L. C. Sensitivity Analysis of Optimal Growth Plans with Exogenous Capital Stocks. *J. Econ. (Z. Nationalökon.)*, 1988, *48*(3), pp. 263–78.

Sutton, C. J. Management Behaviour and a Theory of Diversification. In *Earl, P. E., ed., Vol. 1*, 1988, *1973*, pp. 403–18.

Sutton, John; Binmore, Ken G. and Shaked, Avner. A Further Test of Noncooperative Bargaining Theory: Reply. *Amer. Econ. Rev.*, September 1988, *78*(4), pp. 837–39.

Sutton, Nancy A. and Holland, Rodger G. The Liability Nature of Unfunded Pension Obligations since ERISA. *J. Risk Ins.*, March 1988, *55*(1), pp. 32–58.

Sutton, Timothy G. Constitutional Changes in the FASB: A Note. *Public Choice*, October 1988, *59*(1), pp. 89–94.

_____. The Proposed Introduction of Current Cost Accounting in the U.K. *J. Acc. Econ.*, April 1988, *10*(2), pp. 127–49.

Suwa, Yasuo. The Equal Employment Opportunity Law. In *Japan Institute of Labour, ed.*, 1988, *1985*, pp. 103–06.

_____. JNR Reform and Labor Union Trends. In *Japan Institute of Labour, ed.*, 1988, *1987*, pp. 90–93.

_____. Policy for Part-time Workers: A Recent Study Group Report. In *Japan Institute of Labour, ed.*, 1988, *1987*, pp. 48–51.

_____. Transfer and Relocation under Labor Law. In *Japan Institute of Labour, ed.*, 1988, *1986*, pp. 32–35.

Suzuki, Mikihisa and Mizuta, Hiroshi. His Majesty's University: Tokyo Imperial University. In *Sugiyama, C. and Mizuta, H., eds.*, 1988, pp. 97–120.

Suzuki, T. Inter-sector Comparison of Some Manufacturing Industries in India. *Indian Econ. J.*, Jan.–March 1988, *35*(3), pp. 1–29.

Suzuki, Yoshio. International Payments Imbalances in Japan, Germany, and the United States: Discussion. In *Fieleke, N. S., ed.*, 1988, pp. 54–57.

Suzumura, Kotaro. Reduction of Social Choice Problems: A Simple Proof of Arrow's General Possibility Theorem. *Hitotsubashi J. Econ.*, December 1988, *29*(2), pp. 219–31.

Sveikauskas, Leo; Gowdy, John and Funk, Michael. Urban Productivity: City Size or Industry Size. *J. Reg. Sci.*, May 1988, *28*(2), pp. 185–202.

Svejnar, Jan and Conte, Michael A. Productivity Effects of Worker Participation in Management, Profit-Sharing, Worker Ownership of Assets and Unionization in U.S. Firms. *Int. J. Ind. Organ.*, March 1988, *6*(1), pp. 139–51.

_____; **Estrin, Saul and Moore, Robert E.** Market Imperfections, Labor Management, and Earnings Differentials in a Developing Country: Theory and Evidence from Yugoslavia. *Quart. J. Econ.*, August 1988, *103*(3), pp. 465–78.

_____ **and Prasnikar, Janez.** Economic Behavior of Yugoslav Enterprises. In *Jones, D. C. and Svejnar, J., eds.*, 1988, pp. 237–311.

Svensson, Lars E. O. Fiscal Policy, Sticky Goods Prices, and Resource Utilization. In *Kohn, M. and Tsiang, S.-C., eds.*, 1988, pp. 185–205.

———. International Fiscal Policy Transmission. In *Haaland, J. I. and Norman, V. D., eds.*, 1988, pp. 89–118.

———. Trade in Risky Assets. *Amer. Econ. Rev.*, June 1988, 78(3), pp. 375–94.

——— **and Englund, Peter.** Money and Banking in a Cash-in-Advance Economy. *Int. Econ. Rev.*, November 1988, 29(4), pp. 681–705.

———; **Kotlikoff, Laurence J. and Persson, Torsten.** Social Contracts as Assets: A Possible Solution to the Time-Consistency Problem. *Amer. Econ. Rev.*, September 1988, 78(4), pp. 662–77.

——— **and Persson, Torsten.** Checks and Balances on the Government Budget. In *Helpman, E.; Razin, A. and Sadka, E., eds.*, 1988, pp. 199–214.

Svensson, Lars-Gunnar. Fair Wages When Individual Choice Sets Are Incomplete—An Application of a Model with Indivisibilities. *Scand. J. Econ.*, 1988, 90(4), pp. 563–73.

Sverdrup, Harald and Warfvinge, Per. Soil Liming as a Measure to Mitigate Acid Runoff. *Water Resources Res.*, May 1988, 24(5), pp. 701–12.

Svoboda, Pavel. Improved Coordination of National Economic Plans. *Czech. Econ. Digest.*, May 1988, (3), pp. 3–12.

Swallow, Stephen K. and Marin, Carlos M. Long Run Price Inflexibility and Efficiency Loss for Municipal Water Supply. *J. Environ. Econ. Manage.*, June 1988, 15(2), pp. 233–47.

Swaminathan, M. S. Biotechnology and Sustainable Agriculture. In *Research and Info. System for the Non-aligned and Other Developing Countries*, 1988, pp. 33–54.

Swamy, Gurushri. Population Growth and International Migration. In *Salvatore, D., ed.*, 1988, pp. 107–24.

Swamy, P. A. V. B. and Barth, James R. An Application of Operational-Subjective Statistical Methods to Rational Expectations: Comment. *J. Bus. Econ. Statist.*, October 1988, 6(4), pp. 473–74.

———; **Conway, Roger K. and LeBlanc, Michael R.** The Stochastic Coefficients Approach to Econometric Modeling, Part II: Description and Motivation. *J. Agr. Econ. Res.*, Summer 1988, 40(3), pp. 21–30.

———; **Conway, Roger K. and LeBlanc, Michael R.** The Stochastic Coefficients Approach to Econometric Modeling: Part I: A Critique of Fixed Coefficients Models. *J. Agr. Econ. Res.*, Spring 1988, 40(2), pp. 2–10.

——— **and von zur Muehlen, Peter.** Further Thoughts on Testing for Causality with Econometric Models. *J. Econometrics*, Sept.–Oct. 1988, 39(1–2), pp. 105–47.

———; **Reed, R. C. and Narasimham, Gorti V. L.** Productivity Analysis of U.S. Manufacturing Using a Stochastic-Coefficients Production Function. *J. Bus. Econ. Statist.*, July 1988, 6(3), pp. 339–49.

Swaney, James A. Elements of a Neoinstitutional Environmental Economics. In *Tool, M. R., ed., Vol. 2*, 1988, 1987, pp. 321–61.

———. Trading Water: Market Extension, Social Improvement, or What? *J. Econ. Issues*, March 1988, 22(1), pp. 33–47.

Swank, Job and Siebrand, Jan C. Adjustment Options for the U.S. Economy. In *Motamen, H., ed.*, 1988, pp. 265–82.

Swanson, Bert E. Community Power Trends in San Antonio, Texas. In *Perkins, E. J., ed.*, 1988, pp. 87–99.

——— **and Dehoog, Ruth Hoogland.** Tax and Spending Effects of Municipal Enterprises: The Case of Florida Electric Utilities. *Public Budg. Finance*, Spring 1988, 8(1), pp. 48–57.

Swanson, G. A. and Gardner, John C. Not-for-Profit Accounting and Auditing in the Early Eighteenth Century: Some Archival Evidence. *Accounting Rev.*, July 1988, 63(3), pp. 436–47.

Swanson, Louis E. The Human Dimension of the Rural South in Crisis. In *Beaulieu, L. J., ed.*, 1988, pp. 87–98.

——— **and Skees, Jerry R.** Farm Structure and Local Society Well-being in the South. In *Beaulieu, L. J., ed.*, 1988, pp. 141–57.

Swanson, Paul A.; Alcorn, John and Gleicher, David. Toward a General Model of Price, Choice of Technique and Distribution in a Centrally-Planned, Socialist Economy. *Econ. Planning*, 1988, 22(3), pp. 117–35.

Swanson, Peggy E. The International Transmission of Interest Rates: A Note on Causal Relationships between Short-term External and Domestic U.S. Dollar Returns. *J. Banking Finance*, December 1988, 12(4), pp. 563–73.

———. Interrelationships among Domestic and Eurocurrency Deposit Yields: A Focus on the U.S. Dollar. *Financial Rev.*, February 1988, 23(1), pp. 81–94.

Swartz, Caroline and Carlson, Leonard A. The Earnings of Women and Ethnic Minorities, 1959–1979. *Ind. Lab. Relat. Rev.*, July 1988, 41(4), pp. 530–46.

Swary, Itzhak; Aharony, Joseph and Saunders, Anthony. The Effects of DIDMCA on Bank Stockholders' Returns and Risk. *J. Banking Finance*, September 1988, 12(3), pp. 317–31.

Swasy, John L. and Munch, James M. Rhetorical Question, Summarization Frequency, and Argument Strength Effects on Recall. *J. Cons. Res.*, June 1988, 15(1), pp. 69–76.

Swee-Hock, Saw. Population and Labour Force Growth and Patterns in ASEAN Countries. *Philippine Rev. Econ. Bus.*, Sept.–Dec. 1988, 25(3–4), pp. 187–203.

Sweeney, Richard J. Inflation Risk and the Speed of Adjustment in Short-run Money Demand Functions. *Econ. Letters*, 1988, 26(3), pp. 271–76.

———. Some New Filter Rule Tests: Methods and Results. *J. Finan. Quant. Anal.*, September 1988, 23(3), pp. 285–300.

———. Uncertainty, Capital Formation, and Exchange Rates. In *Khoury, S. J. and Ghosh, A., eds.*, 1988, pp. 299–319.

Sweet, Arnold L. and Wilson, James R. Pitfalls in Simulation-Based Evaluation of Forecast Monitoring Schemes. *Int. J. Forecasting*, 1988, 4(4), pp. 573–79.

Swenson, Charles W. Some Preliminary Evidence on Tax-Exempt Municipal Leasing. *Nat. Tax J.*, December 1988, 41(4), pp. 573–77.

Swicegood, Gray, et. al. Language Usage and Fertility in the Mexican-Origin Population of the United States. *Demography*, February 1988, 25(1), pp. 17–33.

Swiderski, Karen A. Economic Reform in a Planned Economy: The Case of Poland. *Finance Develop.*, June 1988, 25(2), pp. 24–27.

Swidler, Steve. An Empirical Investigation of Heterogeneous Expectations, Analysts' Earnings Forecasts, and the Capital Asset Pricing Model. *Quart. J. Bus. Econ.*, Winter 1988, 27(1), pp. 20–41.

Swieringa, Robert J.; Turner, Martha J. and Hilton, Ronald W. Product Pricing, Accounting Costs and Use of Product-Costing Systems. *Accounting Rev.*, April 1988, 63(2), pp. 195–218.

Swinbank, Alan and Ritson, Christopher. The Common Agricultural Policy, Customs Unions and the Mediterranean Basin. *J. Common Market Stud.*, December 1988, 27(2), pp. 97–112.

Swinton, David H. and Simms, Margaret C. A Report on the Supply of Black Economists. *Rev. Black Polit. Econ.*, Summer 1988, 17(1), pp. 67–88.

Swire, Peter; Winston, Clifford and Litan, Robert E. The U.S. Liability System: Background and Trends. In *Litan, R. E. and Winston, C., eds.*, 1988, pp. 1–15.

Switalski, Marion. Hierarchische Produktionsplanung und Aggregation. (With English summary.) *Z. Betriebswirtshaft*, March 1988, 58(3), pp. 381–96.

Switalski, Zbigniew. Choice Functions Associated with Fuzzy Preference Relations. In *Kacprzyk, J. and Roubens, M., eds.*, 1988, pp. 106–18.

Switzer, Sheldon; Reynolds, Robert J. and Salant, Stephen W. Losses from Horizontal Merger: The Effects of an Exogenous Change in Industry Structure on Cournot–Nash Equilibrium. In *Daughety, A. F., ed.*, 1988, *1983*, pp. 373–87.

Swoboda, Alexander K. International Adjustment and the Dollar: Policy Illusions and Economic Constraints: Comment. In *Guth, W., ed.*, 1988, pp. 93–104.

_____. A New Monetary Framework: Concluding Remarks. In *Borner, S., ed.*, 1988, pp. 381–84.

Swofford, James L. and Whitney, Gerald A. Comparison of Nonparametric Tests of Weak Separability for Annual and Quarterly Data on Consumption, Leisure, and Money. *J. Bus. Econ. Statist.*, April 1988, 6(2), pp. 241–46.

Sworden, Philip J. and George, Peter J. John Beverley Robinson and the Commercial Empire of the St. Lawrence. In *Uselding, P. J., ed.*, 1988, pp. 217–42.

Swyngedouw, Erik A. and Kipnis, Baruch A. Manufacturing Plant Size—Toward a Regional Strategy. A Case Study in Limburg, Belgium. *Urban Stud.*, February 1988, 25(1), pp. 43–52.

Sydow, Peter. Intensive Development as an Instrument for Export-Led Growth in the German Democratic Republic. In *Saunders, C. T., ed.*, 1988, pp. 123–31.

Sylla, Richard. The Autonomy of Monetary Authorities: The Case of the U.S. Federal Reserve System. In *Toniolo, G., ed.*, 1988, pp. 17–38.

_____; **Wallis, John J. and Legler, John B.** U.S. City Finances and the Growth of Government, 1859–1902. *J. Econ. Hist.*, June 1988, 48(2), pp. 347–56.

Sylos-Labini, Paolo. The Great Debates on the Laws of Returns and the Value of Capital: When Will Economists Finally Accept Their Own Logic? *Banca Naz. Lavoro Quart. Rev.*, September 1988, (166), pp. 263–91.

_____. Industrial Pricing in the United Kingdom. In *Sawyer, M. C., ed.*, 1988, *1979*, pp. 401–11.

Symansky, Steven A.; Bryant, Ralph C. and Henderson, Dale W. Estimates of the Consequences of Policy Actions Derived from Model Simulations. In *Bryant, R. C., et al., eds.*, 1988, pp. 63–91.

Syme, Geoffrey J. and Thomas, John F. Estimating Residential Price Elasticity of Demand for Water: A Contingent Valuation Approach. *Water Resources Res.*, November 1988, 24(11), pp. 1847–57.

Symons, Gladys L. Women's Occupational Careers in Business: Managers and Entrepreneurs in France and in Canada. In *Adler, N. J. and Izraeli, D., eds.*, 1988, pp. 41–53.

Symons, J. S. V. and Newell, Andrew. The Macroeconomics of the Interwar Years: International Comparisons. In *Eichengreen, B. and Hatton, T. J., eds.*, 1988, pp. 61–96.

Szabó, Judit. Preliminary and Incremental Softness of the Budget Constraint: A Comment on the Gomulka–Kornai Debate. *Econ. Planning*, 1988, 22(3), pp. 109–16.

Szafran, Robert F. The Short-term Instability of Occupational Change. *Soc. Sci. Quart.*, September 1988, 69(3), pp. 748–55.

Szal, Richard. Is There an Agrarian Crisis in Madagascar? *Int. Lab. Rev.*, 1988, 127(6), pp. 735–60.

Szamuely, László. The After-Life of NEP. *Acta Oecon.*, 1988, 39(3–4), pp. 341–55.

Szeifel, Peter and Richter, Rudolf. Three Reports on the West German Health Care System: A Collection of Reviews. *J. Inst. Theoretical Econ.*, April 1988, 144(2), pp. 386–87.

Szenberg, Michael and Lee, Eric Youngkoo. Analysis of Factors Determining the Compensation of Editors of Economics Journals. *Amer. Econ.*, Fall 1988, 32(2), pp. 76–78.

_____ **and Lee, Eric Youngkoo.** The Price, Quantity and Welfare Effects of U.S. Trade Protection: The Case of Footwear. *Int. Econ. J.*, Winter 1988, 2(4), pp. 95–110.

Szidarovszky, Ferenc and Okuguchi, Koji. Dynamics of the Cournot Oligopoly with Multiproduct Firms. *Math. Soc. Sci.*, October 1988, *16*(2), pp. 159–69.

_____ and Okuguchi, Koji. A Linear Oligopoly Model with Adaptive Expectations: Stability Reconsidered. *J. Econ. (Z. Nationalökon.)*, 1988, *48*(1), pp. 79–82.

_____ and Okuguchi, Koji. A Note on Global Asymptotic Stability of Non-linear Difference Equations. *Econ. Letters*, 1988, *26*(4), pp. 349–52.

Szmrecsányi, Tamás. Growth and Crisis of the Brazilian Sugar Industry, 1914–39. *Rivista Storia Econ.*, S.S., June 1988, *5*(2), pp. 193–219.

_____. Growth and Crisis of the Brazilian Sugar Industry, 1914–39. In *Albert, B. and Graves, A., eds.*, 1988, pp. 59–70.

Sznajder, Andrzej. Bedingungen der Gründung von Joint Ventures und ihre Entwicklung in den osteuropäischen Ländern. (With English summary.) *Z. Betriebswirtshaft*, February 1988, *58*(2), pp. 304–23.

Szöke, Gy. A Chapter of Recent Economic History—Mergers of Agricultural Cooperatives over Two Decades in Hungary. *Acta Oecon.*, 1988, *39*(3–4), pp. 357–67.

Szychowski, Mario L. La protección efectiva (Tratamiento de los insumos de bienes domésticos) Argentina 1988. (The Effective Protection [Treatment for Domestic Goods Inputs] Argentina 1988. With English summary.) *Económica (La Plata)*, July–Dec. 1988, *34*(2), pp. 275–97.

Szyld, Daniel B.; Moledo, Leonardo and Sauber, Beatriz. Positive Solutions for the Leontief Dynamic Input–Output Model. In *Ciaschini, M., ed.*, 1988, pp. 91–97.

Tabatabai, Hamid. Agricultural Decline and Access to Food in Ghana. *Int. Lab. Rev.*, 1988, *127*(6), pp. 703–34.

Tabb, William K. What Happened to Black Economic Development? *Rev. Black Polit. Econ.*, Fall 1988, *17*(2), pp. 65–88.

Tabellini, Guido. Centralized Wage Setting and Monetary Policy in a Reputational Equilibrium. *J. Money, Credit, Banking*, February 1988, *20*(1), pp. 102–18.

_____. Learning and the Volatility of Exchange Rates. *J. Int. Money Finance*, June 1988, *7*(2), pp. 243–50.

_____. Monetary and Fiscal Policy Coordination with a High Public Debt. In *Giavazzi, F. and Spaventa, L., eds.*, 1988, pp. 90–126.

_____ and Alesina, Alberto. Credibility and Politics. *Europ. Econ. Rev.*, March 1988, *32*(2–3), pp. 542–50.

_____ and Masciandaro, Donato. Monetary Regimes and Fiscal Deficits: A Comparative Analysis. In *Cheng, H.-S., ed.*, 1988, pp. 125–52.

Tachibanaki, Toshiaki. Education, Occupation, Hierarchy and Earnings. *Econ. Educ. Rev.*, 1988, *7*(2), pp. 221–29.

_____. Flexible Staffing Arrangements and Employers' Short-term Adjustment Strategies: Comment. In *Hart, R. A., ed.*, 1988, pp. 312–13.

_____; Atoda, Naosumi and Suruga, Terukazu. Statistical Inference of Functional Forms for Income Distribution. *Econ. Stud. Quart.*, March 1988, *39*(1), pp. 14–40.

_____ and Shoven, John B. The Taxation of Income from Capital in Japan. In *Shoven, J. B., ed.*, 1988, pp. 51–96.

Taddei, Dominque and Cette, Gilbert. Chômage mixte et politiques économiques. Un modèle de déséquilbre. (Mixed Unemployment and Economic Policies: A Disequilibrium Model. With English summary.) *Revue Écon.*, November 1988, *39*(6), pp. 1119–41.

Tadman, Michael. Slave Trading and the Mentalities of Masters and Slaves in Ante-Bellum America. In *Archer, L. J., ed.*, 1988, pp. 188–205.

Taggart, Robert A., Jr. The Growth of the "Junk" Bond Market and Its Role in Financing Takeovers. In *Auerbach, A. J., ed. (II)*, 1988, pp. 5–24.

_____. A Time-Series Analysis of Mergers and Acquisitions in the U.S. Economy: Comment. In *Auerbach, A. J., ed. (I)*, 1988, pp. 307–09.

Tahir, Sayyid and Mohammad, Faiz. Agricultural Prices in Pakistan: A Multimarket Analysis. *Pakistan Devel. Rev.*, Part 2, Winter 1988, *27*(4), pp. 577–92.

Tai, Lawrence S. T. and Mehta, Dileep R. Trade and Investment Behavior in U.S. and Japanese Manufacturing Industries: 1962–1981. *Hitotsubashi J. Econ.*, June 1988, *29*(1), pp. 59–71.

Taimio, Heikki and Kostiainen, Seppo. Interest Rate Policy with Expectations of Devaluation. *Scand. J. Econ.*, 1988, *90*(2), pp. 211–24.

Tainer, Evelina. English Language Proficiency and the Determination of Earnings among Foreign-Born Men. *J. Human Res.*, Winter 1988, *23*(1), pp. 108–22.

Taira, Koji. Economic Development, Labor Markets, and Industrial Relations in Japan, 1905–1955. In *Duus, P., ed.*, 1988, pp. 606–53.

Tajika, Eiji and Yui, Yuji. Cost of Capital and Effective Tax Rate: A Comparison of U.S. and Japanese Manufacturing Industries. *Hitotsubashi J. Econ.*, December 1988, *29*(2), pp. 181–200.

Takacs, Wendy E. Economic Aspects of Quota License Auctions. *J. World Trade*, December 1988, *22*(6), pp. 39–51.

Takagi, Shinji. A Basket Peg Policy: Operational Issues for Developing Countries. *World Devel.*, February 1988, *16*(2), pp. 271–79.

_____. The Changing Japanese Financial System. *Finance Develop.*, March 1988, *25*(1), pp. 10–13.

_____. Financial Liberalization and the "Bills-Only" Doctrine: A Causality Test of Daily Japanese Data, 1978–85. *Econ. Stud. Quart.*, June 1988, *39*(2), pp. 149–59.

_____. Recent Developments in Japan's Bond and Money Markets. *J. Japanese Int. Economies*, March 1988, *2*(1), pp. 63–91.

_____. Testing the Multilateral Version of Purchasing Power Parity: An Application to Burma and Jordan under the SDR Peg, 1981–85: A Reply. *Appl. Econ.*, September 1988, *20*(9), pp. 1277–78.

Takahashi, Harutaka and Dockner, Engelbert J. Further Turnpike Properties for General Capital Accumulation Games. *Econ. Letters*, 1988, *28*(4), pp. 321–25.

Takahashi, Yoshiaki. The Impact of Increased Utilisation of Microelectronics on Employment, Production Process, and Job Organisation— The Japanese Viewpoint. In *Dlugos, G.; Dorow, W. and Weiermair, K., eds.*, 1988, pp. 427–39.

Takao, Hiroji. Tax Accounting in Japan and Its International Aspects. In *Most, K. S., ed.*, 1988, pp. 111–30.

Takase, Tamotsu. Different Tariff Treatments and the Uruguay Round. *World Econ.*, September 1988, *11*(3), pp. 355–76.

Takayama, Akira and Chao, Chi-chur. Product Differentiation, Heterogeneous Labor, and Non-homotheticity: Statics and Dynamics. *Southern Econ. J.*, October 1988, *55*(2), pp. 263–78.

_____ **and Ide, Toyonari.** Marshallian Stability, Long-run Equilibrium and the Pattern of Specialization under Factor-Market Distortions in the Pure Theory of International Trade. *Econ. Letters*, 1988, *27*(3), pp. 265–70.

_____ **and Ide, Toyonari.** Scale Economies, Perverse Comparative Statics Results, the Marshallian Stability and the Long-run Equilibrium for a Small Open Economy. *Econ. Letters*, 1988, *27*(3), pp. 257–63.

Takekuma, Shin-Ichi. On the Existence of Optimal Stationary States in Capital Accumulation under Uncertainty: A Case of Linear Direct Utility. *Hitotsubashi J. Econ.*, December 1988, *29*(2), pp. 223–34.

Takeshima, Masao. A Model of Bargaining over Wages and Employment. *Keio Econ. Stud.*, 1988, *25*(2), pp. 67–76.

Takeuchi, Sawako. Les dettes extérieures des pays asiatiques et le rôle du Japon. (External Debts of Asian Countries and the Role of Japan. With English summary.) *Écon. Appl.*, 1988, *41*(4), pp. 903–11.

Takeyasu, Yoshimitsu. Science and Technology Policy in Japan. In *Uyehara, C. H., ed.*, 1988, pp. 178–87.

Taksar, Michael and Sethi, Suresh P. A Note on Merton's "Optimum Consumption and Portfolio Rules in a Continuous-Time Model." *J. Econ. Theory*, December 1988, *46*(2), pp. 395–401.

Talarzyk, W. Wayne. New Technologies in Consumer Information. In *Maynes, E. S. and ACCI Research Committee, eds.*, 1988, pp. 312–16.

Talbot, Jonathan. Have Enterprise Zones Encouraged Enterprise? Some Empirical Evidence from Tyneside. *Reg. Stud.*, December 1988, *22*(6), pp. 507–14.

Talbot, M. and Kempton, R. A. The Development of New Crop Varieties. *J. Roy. Statist. Soc.*, 1988, *151*(2), pp. 327–41.

Talbott, W. J. Cost Spreading and Benefit Spreading in Tort Law. In *Zerbe, R. O., Jr., ed.*, 1988, pp. 25–51.

Talele, Chaitram J. Schumpeterian Financing of Economic Development. *Indian Econ. J.*, Jan.–March 1988, *35*(3), pp. 72–85.

Talley, Wayne K. and Pope, James A. Inventory Costs and Optimal Ship Size. *Logist. Transp. Rev.*, June 1988, *24*(2), pp. 107–20.

_____ **and Schwarz-Miller, Ann.** The Demand for Air Services Provided by Air Passenger– Cargo Carriers in a Deregulated Environment. *Int. J. Transport Econ.*, June 1988, *15*(2), pp. 159–68.

Tallman, Ellis. Some Unanswered Questions about Bank Panics. *Fed. Res. Bank Atlanta Econ. Rev.*, Nov.–Dec. 1988, *73*(6), pp. 2–21.

Talmor, Eli and Benninga, Simon. The Interaction of Corporate and Government Financing in General Equilibrium. *J. Bus.*, April 1988, *61*(2), pp. 233–58.

_____ **and Benninga, Simon.** Revenue-Neutral Changes in Corporate and Personal Income Taxes and Government Debt. In *Helpman, E.; Razin, A. and Sadka, E., eds.*, 1988, pp. 50–64.

_____ **and Ravid, S. Abraham.** Government Financing, Taxation, and Capital Markets. In *Chen, A. H., ed.*, 1988, pp. 21–52.

Talpaz, Hovav and Mjelde, James W. Crop Irrigation Scheduling via Simulation-Based Experimentation. *Western J. Agr. Econ.*, December 1988, *13*(2), pp. 184–92.

_____ **and Penson, John B., Jr.** Endogenization of Final Demand and Primary Input Supply in Input–Output Analysis. *Appl. Econ.*, June 1988, *20*(6), pp. 739–52.

_____, **et al.** Economic Optimization of a Growth Trajectory for Broilers. *Amer. J. Agr. Econ.*, May 1988, *70*(2), pp. 382–90.

Talwar, Prem P.; Singh, Saraswati P. and Hsu, Andy. Tests of Multiple Causality among Monetary and Fiscal Aggregates and Stock Prices. *J. Quant. Econ.*, January 1988, *4*(1), pp. 89–106.

Tam, Mo-Yin S. A Mechanism to Induce Ramsey Pricing for Natural Monopoly Firms. *Int. J. Ind. Organ.*, June 1988, *6*(2), pp. 247–61.

Tam, S. M.; Brewer, K. R. W. and Hanif, Muhammad. How Nearly Can Model-Based Prediction and Design-Based Estimation Be Reconciled? *J. Amer. Statist. Assoc.*, March 1988, *83*(401), pp. 129–32.

Tamaki, Mitsushi. A Bayesian Approach to the Best-Choice Problem. *J. Amer. Statist. Assoc.*, December 1988, *83*(404), pp. 1129–33.

Tamaki, Norio. The American Professor's Regime: Political Economy at Keio University, 1890–1912. In *Sugiyama, C. and Mizuta, H., eds.*, 1988, pp. 75–95.

_____. Economists in Parliament: The Fall of Bimetallism in Japan. In *Sugiyama, C. and Mizuta, H., eds.*, 1988, pp. 223–36.

Tamarkin, Maurry and Conine, Thomas E., Jr. Textbook Inconsistencies in Graphing Valuation Equations: A Further Note. *Financial Rev.*, May 1988, *23*(2), pp. 237–41.

Tamaş, I. and Băcescu, M. An Efficient Method of Carrying Out Data Bases. *Econ. Computat. Cybern. Stud. Res.*, 1988, *23*(3), pp. 63–74.

Tamborini, Roberto. The Collapse of Exchange-Rate Theory in the Eighties: The Role of Flaws in Fundamentals. *Econ. Notes*, 1988, (1), pp. 75–106.

Tamura, Hiroyuki. Computer-Aided Multiobjective Decision Making under Risk. In *Orishimo, I.; Hewings, G. J. D. and Nijkamp, P., eds.*, 1988, pp. 237–49.

Tamura, Saburo and Hippo, Yasuyuki. The Global Construction Industry: Japan. In *Strassmann, W. P. and Wells, J., eds.*, 1988, pp. 59–85.

Tan, Chin Tiong and Teoh, Jeannie. Retailing System in Singapore. In *Kaynak, E., ed.*, 1988, pp. 309–19.

Tan, Loong-Hoe and Akrasanee, Narongchai. Changes in the ASEAN–U.S. Economic Environment and Opportunities: An Introductory Overview. In *Tan, L.-H. and Akrasanee, N., eds.*, 1988, pp. xv–xxii.

Tan, S. J. and Vertinsky, Ilan. Strategic Management of International Financial Centers: A Tale of Two Cities. In *Khoury, S. J. and Ghosh, A., eds.*, 1988, pp. 87–104.

Tan, Siew Ee and Wah, Lai Yew. Towards Effective Planning in Malaysia: Some Strategic Issues. In *Urrutia, M. and Yukawa, S., eds. (I)*, 1988, pp. 107–55.

Tan, Tommy Chin-Chiu and Werlang, Sérgio Ribeiro da Costa. The Bayesian Foundations of Solution Concepts of Games. *J. Econ. Theory*, August 1988, *45*(2), pp. 370–91.

Tanabe, Kunio. Centered Newton Method for Mathematical Programming. In *Iri, M. and Yajima, K., eds.*, 1988, pp. 197–206.

Tanaka, Akihiko and Kumon, Shumpei. From Prestige to Wealth to Knowledge. In *Inoguchi, T. and Okimoto, D. I., eds.*, 1988, pp. 64–82.

Tanaka, Kazuko and Steinhoff, Patricia G. Women Managers in Japan. In *Adler, N. J. and Izraeli, D., eds.*, 1988, pp. 103–21.

Tanaka, Yasuhito. On Multiplicity of Consistent Conjectures in Free Entry Oligopoly. *Econ. Letters*, 1988, *28*(2), pp. 109–15.

Tanaka, Yuki. Nuclear Power Plant Gypsies in High-Tech Society. In *Tsurumi, E. P., ed.*, 1988, pp. 149–62.

Tang, Anthony M. Agricultural Poverty in Panama for Asian Perspective. *Philippine Rev. Econ. Bus.*, Sept.–Dec. 1988, *25*(3–4), pp. 205–42.

————. Why Does Overcrowded, Resource-Poor East Asia Succeed—Lessons for the LDCs? Introduction. *Econ. Develop. Cult. Change*, Supplement, April 1988, *36*(3), pp. S5–10.

Tang, De-Piao and Gonzalez-Paramo, José M. Optimal Intervention in the Presence of "Categorical Equity" Objectives. *Public Finance*, 1988, *43*(1), pp. 79–95.

————— and **Yang, David C. H.** Testing for Causal-

ity in the Richardson Arms Race Model. *Math. Soc. Sci.*, April 1988, *15*(2), pp. 197–203.

Tang, Eric M. P. and Fong, H. Gifford. Immunized Bond Portfolios in Portfolio Protection. *J. Portfol. Manage.*, Winter 1988, *14*(2), pp. 63–68.

Tang, Joseph S. H. The Draft Basic Law of Hong Kong and the Constitutional Constraints on Budgetary Expenditure and Revenue. *Bull. Int. Fiscal Doc.*, November 1988, *42*(11), pp. 479–88.

Tang, Yi and Aral, Mustafa M. A New Boundary Element Formulation for Time-Dependent Confined and Unconfined Aquifer Problems. *Water Resources Res.*, June 1988, *24*(6), pp. 831–42.

Tangermann, Stefan. The EC Perspective on Agriculture in the Uruguay Round. In *Roberts, C., ed.*, 1988, pp. 33–43.

————. International Coordination of Agricultural Policy Adjustments. *Europ. Rev. Agr. Econ.*, 1988, *15*(4), pp. 309–25.

Tani, Kouichi. Economic Planning and the Market Economy: Experience in Post-War Japan. In *Urrutia, M. and Yukawa, S., eds. (I)*, 1988, pp. 263–310.

Tanigaki, Kazunori. A Note on Nontraded Goods and the Welfare Effect of Foreign Investment. *J. Int. Econ.*, August 1988, *25*(1–2), pp. 185–87.

Tanino, Tetsuzo. Fuzzy Preference Relations in Group Decision Making. In *Kacprzyk, J. and Roubens, M., eds.*, 1988, pp. 54–71.

Tankut, Gönül. 20. Yüzyilin Planli Başkentleri: Canberra, Ankara, Bresilia, Islamabad. (The Planned Capital Cities of the 20th Century. With English summary.) *METU*, 1988, *15*(1–2), pp. 129–50.

Tann, Jennifer. Fixed Capital Formation in Steam Power, 1775–1825: A Case Study of the Boulton and Watt Engine. In *Feinstein, C. H. and Pollard, S., eds.*, 1988, pp. 164–81.

Tannenwald, Robert. Should Massachusetts Reform Its Bank Tax? *New Eng. Econ. Rev.*, Sept.–Oct. 1988, pp. 23–35.

Tanzi, Vito. Issues in Coordination of Fiscal Policies. *Finance Develop.*, December 1988, *25*(4), pp. 16–19.

————. Tax Reform in Industrial Countries and the Impact of the U.S. Tax Reform Act of 1986. *Bull. Int. Fiscal Doc.*, February 1988, *42*(2), pp. 51–64.

————. Trends in Tax Policy as Revealed by Recent Developments and Research. *Bull. Int. Fiscal Doc.*, March 1988, *42*(3), pp. 97–103.

————— and **Blejer, Mario I.** Public Debt and Fiscal Policy in Developing Countries. In *Arrow, K. J. and Boskin, M. J., eds.*, 1988, pp. 230–63.

————; **Blejer, Mario I. and Teijeiro, Mario O.** The Effects of Inflation on the Measurement of Fiscal Deficits. In *Blejer, M. I. and Chu, K.-Y., eds.*, 1988, pp. 4–19.

Tapley, T. Craig; Yamada, Takeshi and Pettway, Richard H. The Impacts of Financial Deregulation upon Trading Efficiency and the Levels of Risk and Return of Japanese Banks. *Financial Rev.*, August 1988, *23*(3), pp. 243–68.

Taplin, Ian M. What Future for U.S. Trade Unions? *Challenge*, Nov.–Dec. 1988, *31*(6), pp. 38–42.

Tappeiner, Gottfried and Holub, Hans Werner. Qualitative Evaluation of Techniques of Aggregation. *Jahr. Nationalökon. Statist.*, November 1988, *205*(5), pp. 385–99.

Tapscott, Tracy R. and Fox, Douglas R. The U.S. National Income and Product Accounts: Revised Estimates. *Surv. Curr. Bus.*, July 1988, *68*(7), pp. 8–37.

Tarascio, Vincent J. Kondratieff's Theory of Long Cycles. *Atlantic Econ. J.*, December 1988, *16*(4), pp. 1–10.

Tarasov, L. A. The Economy of the Socialist Community: Emergence, Development, Problems. *Prob. Econ.*, November 1988, *31*(7), pp. 82–99.

Tardos, Márton. Can Hungary's Monetary Policy Succeed? *Acta Oecon.*, 1988, *39*(1–2), pp. 61–79.

_____. Domestic and External Macro-policies: Comments. In *Saunders, C. T.*, ed., 1988, pp. 217–19.

_____. How to Create Markets in Eastern Europe: The Hungarian Case. In *[Holzman, F. D.]*, 1988, pp. 259–84.

Tarján, Tamás and Kovács, János. Cycle and Replacement. *Acta Oecon.*, 1988, *39*(3–4), pp. 325–40.

Tarling, Roger and Rubery, Jill. Women's Employment in Declining Britain. In *Rubery, J.*, ed., 1988, pp. 100–132.

Tarr, David G. The Steel Crisis in the United States and the European Community: Causes and Adjustments. In *Baldwin, R. E.; Hamilton, C. B. and Sapir, A.*, eds., 1988, pp. 173–98.

Tarshis, Lorie. Changes in Real and Money Wages. In *Shaw, G. K.*, ed., Vol. 2, 1988, *1939*, pp. 5–9.

_____. The International Debt of the LDCs. In *Hamouda, O. F. and Smithin, J. N.*, eds., Vol. 2, 1988, pp. 183–93.

_____ and Hamouda, Omar F. Stagflation for Our Grandchildren. In *Hamouda, O. F. and Smithin, J. N.*, eds., Vol. 2, 1988, pp. 205–08.

Tarsitano, Agostino. Measuring the Asymmetry of the Lorenz Curve. *Ricerche Econ.*, July–Sept. 1988, *42*(3), pp. 507–19.

Tarsitano, Alberto. Tax Treatment of Computer Software: Argentina. In *International Fiscal Association*, ed. (*II*), 1988, pp. 161–82.

Tarullo, Ronald; Cole, Ishmail and MacMurray, Robert. Regulation, Technological Change, and Productivity Growth in the Coal Industry. In *Pennsylvania Economic Association*, 1988, pp. 682–94.

_____; Cole, Ishmail and MacMurray, Robert. Some Determinants of Official United States Coal Prices. In *Pennsylvania Economic Association*, 1988, pp. 695–706.

Tasgian, Astrig and Cassone, Alberto. Growth and Decline of a Metropolitan Area: The Case

of Torino. *Ann. Reg. Sci.*, November 1988, *22*(3), pp. 34–47.

Taslim, M. A. Tenancy and Interlocking Markets: Issues and Some Evidence. *World Devel.*, June 1988, *16*(6), pp. 655–66.

Tatchell, Michael. The Effect of Teaching on Public Hospital Costs: Evidence from Queensland: Discussion. In *Butler, J. R. G. and Doessel, D. P.*, eds., 1988, pp. 76–77.

Tate, Uday S. and Andrews, Donald R. An Application of the Stock Adjustment Model in Estimating Employment Multipliers for the South Central Louisiana Petroleum Economy, 1964–84: Note. *Growth Change*, Summer 1988, *19*(3), pp. 94–105.

Tatemoto, Masahiro. "A Stabilization Model" after Twenty Years. *Econ. Stud. Quart.*, March 1988, *39*(1), pp. 1–13.

Tatom, John A. Are the Macroeconomic Effects of Oil-Price Changes Symmetric? *Carnegie–Rochester Conf. Ser. Public Policy*, Spring 1988, *28*, pp. 325–68.

_____. The Link between the Value of the Dollar, U.S. Trade and Manufacturing Output: Some Recent Evidence. *Fed. Res. Bank St. Louis Rev.*, Nov.–Dec. 1988, *70*(6), pp. 24–37.

_____. Macroeconomic Effects of the 1986 Oil Price Decline. *Contemp. Policy Issues*, July 1988, *6*(3), pp. 69–82.

_____ and Kool, Clemens J. M. International Linkages in the Term Structure of Interest Rates. *Fed. Res. Bank St. Louis Rev.*, July–Aug. 1988, *70*(4), pp. 30–43.

Tattam, C. Sören R. Security on Movable Property and Receivables in Europe: United Kingdom: England. In *Dickson, M. G.; Rosener, W. and Storm, P. M.*, eds., 1988, pp. 187–205.

Tattara, Giuseppe. External Trade in Italy, 1922–38. Some Evidence from Trade Index Numbers. *Rivista Storia Econ.*, S.S., February 1988, *5*(1), pp. 102–20.

Tau'ili'ili, Uili Meredith. The Role of Technology: A South Pacific Islander's Perspective. In *Kozmetsky, G.; Matsumoto, H. and Smilor, R. W.*, eds., 1988, pp. 99–107.

Taub, B. Efficiency in a Pure Currency Economy with Inflation. *Econ. Inquiry*, October 1988, *26*(4), pp. 567–83.

Taubman, Paul; Behrman, Jere R. and Sickles, Robin C. Age-Specific Death Rates. In *Ricardo-Campbell, R. and Lazear, E. P.*, eds., 1988, pp. 162–83.

Taudes, A.; Wagner, U. and Geyer-Schulz, A. Exploring the Possibilities of an Improvement of Stochastic Market Models by Rule-Based Systems. In *Gaul, W. and Schader, M.*, eds., 1988, pp. 54–66.

Tauile, José Ricardo. Notes on Microelectronic Automation in Brazil. *CEPAL Rev.*, December 1988, (36), pp. 49–59.

Tauman, Yair. The Aumann–Shapley Prices: A Survey. In *[Shapley, L. S.]*, 1988, pp. 279–304.

_____; Zang, Israel and Kamien, Morton I. Optimal License Fees for a New Product. *Math. Soc. Sci.*, August 1988, *16*(1), pp. 77–106.

Tavéra, C. and Mahé, L. P. Bilateral Harmonization of EC and U.S. Agricultural Policies. *Europ. Rev. Agr. Econ.*, 1988, *15*(4), pp. 327–48.

Tavis, Lee A. A Strategic Time for Change. In *Tavis, L. A., ed.*, 1988, pp. 335–63.

Tavlas, George S. The Price Equation, Excess Demand, and Normal Cost Pricing: A Reply. *Appl. Econ.*, December 1988, *20*(12), pp. 1693–97.

——— **and Aschheim, Joseph.** Econometric Modelling of Partial Adjustment: The Cochrane–Orcutt Procedure, Flaws and Remedies. *Econ. Modelling*, January 1988, *5*(1), pp. 2–8.

——— **and Bailey, Martin J.** Trade and Investment under Floating Rates: The U.S. Experience. *Cato J.*, Fall 1988, *8*(2), pp. 421–42.

Tawada, Makoto and Abe, Kenzo. Public Production and the Incidence of a Corporate Income Tax. *Econ. Stud. Quart.*, September 1988, *39*(3), pp. 233–45.

Taylor, Amy K.; Shrt, Pamela Farley and Horgan, Constance M. Medigap Insurance: Friend or Foe in Reducing Medicare Deficits? In *Frech, H. E., III, ed.*, 1988, pp. 145–77.

Taylor, Arthur R.; Wankel, Charles B. and Stoner, James A. F. On Waiting for Neither Godot nor the Apocalypse: Practical First Steps to Move U.S. Managers Toward World Class Managing. In *Starr, M. K., ed.*, 1988, pp. 185–212.

Taylor, Calvin. The Contradictions of Positivist Marxism. In *Williams, M., ed.*, 1988, pp. 62–79.

Taylor, Carl E.; Parker, Robert L. and Jarrett, Steven. The Evolving Chinese Rural Health Care System. In *Sirageldin, I. and Sorkin, A., eds.*, 1988, pp. 219–36.

Taylor, Carol A.; Charney, Alberta H. and Oxford, Thomas P. A Recursive Conjoint Modeling Approach to State Severance Tax Analysis: Mining Florida Phosphates. *Resources & Energy*, December 1988, *10*(4), pp. 355–86.

——— **and Theil, Henri.** Measuring the Size of Revisions of Regional Data. *Econ. Letters*, 1988, *27*(2), pp. 201–04.

——— **and Theil, Henri.** Modeling the Accuracy of Certain Regional Predictions. *Reg. Sci. Urban Econ.*, November 1988, *18*(4), pp. 453–62.

Taylor, Christopher. Inflation and Fiscal Expansion. In *Eltis, W. and Sinclair, P. J. N., eds.*, 1988, pp. 127–38.

Taylor, Frank F. Revolution, Race, and Some Aspects of Foreign Relations in Cuba Since 1959. In *Mesa-Lago, C., ed.*, 1988, pp. 19–41.

Taylor, J. Edward; Vogel, Stephen and Adelman, Irma. Life in a Mexican Village: A SAM Perspective. *J. Devel. Stud.*, October 1988, *25*(1), pp. 7–24.

———; **Yitzhaki, Shlomo and Stark, Oded.** Migration, Remittances and Inequality: A Sensi-

tivity Analysis Using the Extended Gini Index. *J. Devel. Econ.*, May 1988, *28*(3), pp. 309–22.

Taylor, James W. The Role of Risk in Consumer Behavior. In *Earl, P. E., ed., Vol. 2*, 1988, *1974*, pp. 236–42.

Taylor, Jeremy M. G. The Cost of Generalizing Logistic Regression. *J. Amer. Statist. Assoc.*, December 1988, *83*(404), pp. 1078–83.

Taylor, Jim and Twomey, Jim. The Movement of Manufacturing Industry in Great Britain: An Inter-country Analysis, 1972–1981. *Urban Stud.*, June 1988, *25*(3), pp. 228–42.

Taylor, John B. A Method for Determining Whether Parameters in Aggregative Models are Structural: Comment. *Carnegie–Rochester Conf. Ser. Public Policy*, Autumn 1988, *29*, pp. 253–57.

———. The Treatment of Expectations in Large Multicountry Econometric Models. In *Bryant, R. C., et al., eds.*, 1988, pp. 161–79.

Taylor, Lance. Back to Basics: Theory for the Rhetoric in North–South Negotiations. In *Wilber, C. K., ed.*, 1988, pp. 207–21.

———. Macro Constraints on India's Economic Growth. *Indian Econ. Rev.*, July–Dec. 1988, *23*(2), pp. 145–65.

———. Macro Effects of Myriad Shocks: Developing Countries in the World Economy. In *Bell, D. E. and Reich, M. R., eds.*, 1988, pp. 17–37.

Taylor, Leroy. Absorption, Growth and the Balance-of-Payments in a Centre–Periphery Model of World Economy. *Soc. Econ. Stud.*, September 1988, *37*(3), pp. 9–43.

———. The Caribbean and the World Economy: Comments. *Soc. Econ. Stud.*, March–June 1988, *37*(1–2), pp. 65–66.

Taylor, Lester D. A Model of Consumption and Demand Based on Psychological Opponent Processes. In *Albanese, P. J., ed.*, 1988, pp. 35–57.

———. Telecommunications Demand Modeling: The Current State-of-the-Art. *Info. Econ. Policy*, 1988, *3*(4), pp. 277–81.

Taylor, Lowell J.; Bean, Frank D. and Lowell, B. Lindsay. Undocumented Mexican Immigrants and the Earnings of Other Workers in the United States. *Demography*, February 1988, *25*(1), pp. 35–52.

Taylor, Mark P. An Empirical Examination of Long-run Purchasing Power Parity Using Cointegration Techniques. *Appl. Econ.*, October 1988, *20*(10), pp. 1369–81.

———. A DYMIMIC Model of Forward Foreign Exchange Risk, with Estimates for Three Major Exchange Rates. *Manchester Sch. Econ. Soc. Stud.*, March 1988, *56*(1), pp. 55–68.

———. What Do Investment Managers Know? An Empirical Study of Practitioners' Predictions. *Economica*, May 1988, *55*(218), pp. 185–202.

——— **and Cuthbertson, Keith.** Monetary Anticipations and the Demand for Money in the U.S.: Further Results. *Southern Econ. J.*, October 1988, *55*(2), pp. 326–35.

——— **and MacDonald, Ronald.** Metals Prices,

Efficiency and Cointegration: Some Evidence from the London Metal Exchange. *Bull. Econ. Res.*, June 1988, 40(3), pp. 235–39.

_____ and MacDonald, Ronald. Testing Rational Expectations and Efficiency in the London Metal Exchange. *Oxford Bull. Econ. Statist.*, February 1988, 50(1), pp. 41–52.

_____ and McMahon, Patrick C. Long-run Purchasing Power Parity in the 1920s. *Europ. Econ. Rev.*, January 1988, 32(1), pp. 179–97.

Taylor, Natalie T. and Ellis, R. Jeffrey. Success and Failure in Internal Venture Strategy: An Exploratory Study. In *Kirchhoff, B. A., et al., eds.*, 1988, pp. 518–33.

Taylor, Philip and Hashemzadeh, Nozar. Stock Prices, Money Supply, and Interest Rates: The Question of Causality. *Appl. Econ.*, December 1988, 20(12), pp. 1603–11.

Taylor, R. G. and Rodriguez, Abelardo. Stochastic Modeling of Short-term Cattle Operations. *Amer. J. Agr. Econ.*, February 1988, 70(1), pp. 121–32.

Taylor, Richard W. The Valuation of Semiannual Bonds between Interest Payment Dates. *Financial Rev.*, August 1988, 23(3), pp. 365–68.

Taylor, Stephen J. Forecasting Market Prices. *Int. J. Forecasting*, 1988, 4(3), pp. 421–26.

Taylor, Stuart R. and O'Brien, Thomas S. The Problem of Sparsity in Education Provision. *Urban Stud.*, December 1988, 25(6), pp. 520–26.

Taylor, Timothy G. and Kilmer, Richard L. An Analysis of Market Structure and Pricing in the Florida Celery Industry. *Southern J. Agr. Econ.*, December 1988, 20(2), pp. 35–43.

_____ and Shonkwiler, J. S. Food Processor Price Behavior: Firm-Level Evidence of Sticky Prices. *Amer. J. Agr. Econ.*, May 1988, 70(2), pp. 239–44.

Taylor, Wagiha. Alexander Hamilton's Economic Program as a Possible Model for Third World Development: Discussion. In *Pennsylvania Economic Association*, 1988, pp. 800–803.

Taylor, William. Statement to the U.S. House Subcommittee on Commerce, Consumer, and Monetary Affairs of the Committee on Government Operations, March 15, 1988. *Fed. Res. Bull.*, May 1988, 74(5), pp. 304–07.

_____. Statement to the U.S. House Subcommittee on General Oversight and Investigations of the Committee on Banking, Finance and Urban Affairs, April 21, 1988. *Fed. Res. Bull.*, June 1988, 74(6), pp. 376–80.

Teague, Paul W. and Lee, John G. Risk Efficient Perennial Crop Selection: A MOTAD Approach to Citrus Production. *Southern J. Agr. Econ.*, December 1988, 20(2), pp. 145–52.

Teal, Roger F. Contracting for Transit Service. In *Weicher, J. C., ed.*, 1988, pp. 47–55.

Tease, Warren J. The Expectations Theory of the Term Structure of Interest Rates in Australia. *Econ. Rec.*, June 1988, 64(185), pp. 120–27.

_____. Speculative Efficiency and the Exchange Rate: Some Evidence since the Float. *Econ. Rec.*, March 1988, 64(184), pp. 2–13.

Teck, Hoon Hian. Value Added per Worker, Cap-

ital Accumulation, and Technical Progress. *Pakistan Devel. Rev.*, Summer 1988, 27(2), pp. 211–15.

Tecson, David J. and Paz, Miguel. Argentina's Debt to the Equity Conversion Program. *J. World Trade*, October 1988, 22(5), pp. 81–87.

Tedeschi, Piero. Modelli di agenzia e mercato del lavoro: Una rassegna. (Agency Models and the Labour Market: A Survey. With English summary.) *Econ. Polit.*, August 1988, 5(2), pp. 265–319.

Tedlow, Richard S. The Struggle for Dominance in the Automobile Market: The Early Years of Ford and General Motors. In *Hausman, W. J., ed.*, 1988, pp. 49–62.

_____. Trade Associations and Public Relations. In *Yamazaki, H. and Miyamoto, M., eds.*, 1988, pp. 139–67.

_____. Trade Associations and Public Relations: Response. In *Yamazaki, H. and Miyamoto, M., eds.*, 1988, pp. 170–72.

Teece, David J. Technological Change and the Nature of the Firm. In *Dosi, G., et al., eds.*, 1988, pp. 256–81.

_____ and Jones, Peter T. The Research Agenda on Competitiveness: A Program of Research for the Nation's Business Schools. In *Furino, A., ed.*, 1988, pp. 101–14.

_____ and Jones, Peter T. What We Know and What We Don't Know about Competitiveness. In *Furino, A., ed.*, 1988, pp. 265–330.

Teel, Jesse E.; Mobley, Mary F. and Bearden, William O. An Investigation of Individual Responses to Tensile Price Claims. *J. Cons. Res.*, September 1988, 15(2), pp. 273–79.

Tegene, Abebayehu; Huffman, Wallace E. and Miranowski, John A. Dynamic Corn Supply Functions: A Model with Explicit Optimization. *Amer. J. Agr. Econ.*, February 1988, 70(1), pp. 103–11.

Teghem, Jacques, Jr. and Roubens, Marc. Comparison of Methodologies for Multicriteria Feasibility—Constrained Fuzzy and Multiple-Objective Stochastic Linear Programming. In *Kacprzyk, J. and Fedrizzi, M., eds.*, 1988, pp. 240–65.

Tehranian, Hassan and Bruning, Edward R. Stock Market Reactions to Motor Carrier Regulatory Reform. *Int. J. Transport Econ.*, February 1988, 15(1), pp. 7–27.

_____ and Downs, Thomas W. Predicting Stock Price Responses to Tax Policy Changes. *Amer. Econ. Rev.*, December 1988, 78(5), pp. 1118–30.

_____; Trennepohl, Gary L. and Booth, James R. An Empirical Analysis of Insured Portfolio Strategies Using Listing Options. *J. Finan. Res.*, Spring 1988, 11(1), pp. 1–12.

Teigland, Christie; Zaporowski, Mark and Lahiri, Kajal. Interest Rates and the Subjective Probability Distribution of Inflation Forecasts. *J. Money, Credit, Banking*, May 1988, 20(2), pp. 233–48.

Teijeiro, Mario O.; Tanzi, Vito and Blejer, Mario I. The Effects of Inflation on the Measurement of Fiscal Deficits. In *Blejer, M. I. and Chu, K.-Y., eds.*, 1988, pp. 4–19.

Teillet, Pierre. A Concept of Satellite Account in the Revised SNA. *Rev. Income Wealth*, December 1988, *34*(4), pp. 411–39.

Teitelbaum, Michael S. and Winter, Jay M. Population and Resources in Western Intellectual Traditions: Introduction. *Population Devel. Rev.*, Supplement, 1988, *14*, pp. 1–4.

Teixeira Pinto, Luiz Fernando. Recent Changes in Brazil. *Bull. Int. Fiscal Doc.*, December 1988, *42*(12), pp. 531–32.

Teja, Ranjit S. The Case for Earmarked Taxes. *Int. Monet. Fund Staff Pap.*, September 1988, *35*(3), pp. 523–33.

Teka, Tegegne. The State and Rural Cooperatives in Ethiopia. In *Hedlund, H., ed.*, 1988, pp. 125–37.

Teklu, Tesfaye and Johnson, Stanley R. Demand Systems from Cross-Section Data: An Application to Indonesia. *Can. J. Agr. Econ.*, March 1988, *36*(1), pp. 83–101.

Teller, Edward. Deterrence? Defense? Disarmament? The Many Roads toward Stability. In *Anderson, A. and Bark, D. L., eds.*, 1988, pp. 21–32.

Tellez, Luis. Monopolistic Competition, Credibility and the Output Costs of Disinflation Programs: An Analysis of Price Controls: Comments. *J. Devel. Econ.*, November 1988, *29*(3), pp. 403–04.

Tello, Mario D. Exportaciones de manufacturas desde países en desarrollo y política tributaria en un contexto de mercados internacionales imperfectos. (Manufactured Exports from Developing Countries and Government Policy under Imperfect International Markets: Corporate Income Taxes and Exchange Rate. With English summary.) *Estud. Econ.*, July–Dec. 1988, *3*(2), pp. 131–47.

Temin, Peter. An Economic History of American Hospitals. In *Frech, H. E., III, ed.*, 1988, pp. 75–102.

_____. Product Quality and Vertical Integration in the Early Cotton Textile Industry. *J. Econ. Hist.*, December 1988, *48*(4), pp. 891–907.

Tempelmeier, Horst. Kapazitätsplanung für flexible Fertigungssysteme. (With English summary.) *Z. Betriebswirtshaft*, September 1988, *58*(9), pp. 963–80.

Tendler, Judith. What to Think about Cooperatives: A Guide from Bolivia. In *Annis, S. and Hakim, P., eds.*, 1988, pp. 85–116.

Tendulkar, Suresh D. and Sundaram, K. Toward an Explanation of Interregional Variations in Poverty and Unemployment in Rural India. In *Srinivasan, T. N. and Bardhan, P. K., eds.*, 1988, pp. 316–62.

Tennant, Wesley L. and Hansen, Charles E. Historical Cost Review. In *West, R. E. and Kreith, F., eds.*, 1988, pp. 372–413.

Tenzer, Morton J. and Lewis, Carol W. Community Collaboration: Public–Private Partnerships in Connecticut. In *Hula, R. C., ed.*, 1988, pp. 99–110.

Teodorović, Ivan and Bendeković, Jadranko. In-

vestment Decision-Making in Yugoslavia. In *Saunders, C. T., ed.*, 1988, pp. 255–67.

Teoh, Jeannie and Tan, Chin Tiong. Retailing System in Singapore. In *Kaynak, E., ed.*, 1988, pp. 309–19.

Teplitz, Paul V. The Georgetown Project: An Overview of the Data Set and Its Collection. In *White, L. J., ed.*, 1988, pp. 61–81.

Teranishi, Juro. Economic Growth and Regulation of Financial Markets: The Japanese Experience during the Post-War High-Growth Period. In *Urrutia, M., ed.*, 1988, pp. 180–200.

Teräsvirta, Timo and Rahiala, Markku. Formation of Firms' Production Decisions in Finnish Manufacturing Industries. *J. Appl. Econometrics*, April 1988, *3*(2), pp. 125–37.

Terhal, P. Tinbergen on World Peace: A Comparative Historical Perspective. *Rev. Soc. Econ.*, December 1988, *46*(3), pp. 255–69.

Terkla, David G.; Doeringer, Peter B. and Moss, Philip I. Widespread Labor Stickiness in the New England Offshore Fishing Industry: Implications for Adjustment and Regulation. *Land Econ.*, February 1988, *64*(1), pp. 73–82.

Terreblanche, S. J. Strukturele Wanbalanse in die Suid-Afrikaanse Ekonomie. (Structural Imbalances in the South African Economy. With English summary.) *S. Afr. J. Econ.*, March 1988, *56*(1), pp. 61–81.

Terrell, Deane. VAR Forecasting of the Australian Economy: A Preliminary Analysis: Comment. *Australian Econ. Pap.*, Supplement, June 1988, *27*, pp. 121–25.

Terrell, Henry S. The Vulnerability of Multinational Banks to an International Shock. In *Tavis, L. A., ed.*, 1988, pp. 223–39.

Terry, Danny E.; Eastwood, David B. and Brooker, John R. Household Demand for Food Attributes. *J. Behav. Econ.*, Fall 1988, *17*(3), pp. 219–27.

Terry, N. G. The Changing UK Pension System. *Nat. Westminster Bank Quart. Rev.*, May 1988, pp. 2–13.

Terry, Sarah M. External Debt and the Polish Leadership. In *Marer, P. and Siwinski, W., eds.*, 1988, pp. 215–25.

Teruyama, Hiroshi and Fukuda, Shin-ichi. Some International Evidence on Inventory Fluctuations. *Econ. Letters*, 1988, *28*(3), pp. 225–30.

Terweduwe, Dirk and Berlage, Lodewijk. The Classification of Countries by Cluster and by Factor Analysis. *World Devel.*, December 1988, *16*(12), pp. 1527–45.

Terza, Joseph V.; Nourse, Hugh O. and Okoruwa, A. Ason. Estimating Patronization Shares for Urban Retail Centers: An Extension of the Poisson Gravity Model. *J. Urban Econ.*, November 1988, *24*(3), pp. 241–59.

Teschner, Manfred. Arbeitszeitverkürzungen oder ungebrochenes Wirtschaftswachstum im Zuge des technischen Fortschritts? (Shorter Working Hours or Uninterrupted Economic Growth in the Course of Technical Progress? With English summary.) *Konjunkturpolitik*, 1988, *34*(3), pp. 123–35.

Tesfagiorgis, Gebre Hiwet. Comparative Income

Distribution and the Impact of Taxation. *Bull. Int. Fiscal Doc.*, June 1988, *42*(6), pp. 274–83.

Tesfatsion, Leigh and Kalaba, Robert. The Flexible Least Squares Approach to Time-Varying Linear Regression. *J. Econ. Dynam. Control,* March 1988, *12*(1), pp. 43–48.

Testani, Rosa Anna and Hackl, Jo Watson. Second Generation State Takeover Statutes and Shareholder Wealth: An Empirical Study. *Yale Law J.,* May 1988, *97*(6), pp. 1193–1231.

Teubal, Morris and Justman, Moshe. A Framework for an Explicit Industry and Technology Policy for Israel and Some Specific Proposals. In *Freeman, C. and Lundvall, B.-A., eds.,* 1988, pp. 226–49.

Tew, Brian and Llewellyn, David T. The Sterling Money Market and the Determination of Interest Rates. *Nat. Westminster Bank Quart. Rev.,* May 1988, pp. 25–37.

Tewari, Devi D. and Kulshreshtha, Surendra N. Impacts of Rising Energy Prices on Saskatchewan Agriculture. *Can. J. Agr. Econ.,* July 1988, *36*(2), pp. 239–60.

Tewari, R. T. Inter-regional Pattern of Industrialisation in India: 1971–1981. *Indian Econ. J.,* Oct.–Dec. 1988, *36*(2), pp. 1–23.

Tezel, Ahmet. The Value Line Stock Rankings and the Option Model Implied Standard Deviations. *J. Finan. Res.,* Fall 1988, *11*(3), pp. 215–25.

Thakkar, Rasesh B. and Beare, John B. Optimal Government Bond Finance. *J. Macroecon.,* Spring 1988, *10*(2), pp. 217–29.

Thakor, Anjan V. and Liu, Pu. Interest Yields, Credit Ratings, and Economic Characteristics of State Bonds: Reply. *J. Money, Credit, Banking,* November 1988, *20*(4), pp. 696–97.

_____ **and Shah, Salman.** Private versus Public Ownership: Investment, Ownership Distribution, and Optimality. *J. Finance,* March 1988, *43*(1), pp. 41–59.

Thakur, Manab and Nelson, Reed E. The Organization of the Mexican Maquiladora: A Contextual Analysis. In *Farmer, R. N. and McGoun, E. G., eds.,* 1988, pp. 75–94.

Thaler, Richard H. Anomalies: The Winner's Curse. *J. Econ. Perspectives,* Winter 1988, *2*(1), pp. 191–202.

_____ . Toward a Positive Theory of Consumer Choice. In *Earl, P. E., ed., Vol. 2,* 1988, *1980,* pp. 168–89.

_____ . The Ultimatum Game. *J. Econ. Perspectives,* Fall 1988, *2*(4), pp. 195–206.

_____ **and Dawes, Robyn M.** Anomalies: Cooperation. *J. Econ. Perspectives,* Summer 1988, *2*(3), pp. 187–97.

_____ **and Russell, Thomas.** The Relevance of Quasi Rationality in Competitive Markets. In *Bell, D. E.; Raiffa, H. and Tversky, A., eds.,* 1988, pp. 508–24.

_____ **and Shefrin, Hersh M.** The Behavioral Life-Cycle Hypothesis. *Econ. Inquiry,* October 1988, *26*(4), pp. 609–43.

_____ **and Ziemba, William T.** Parimutuel Betting Markets: Racetracks and Lotteries. *J.*

Econ. Perspectives, Spring 1988, *2*(2), pp. 161–74.

Tharakan, P. K. M. and Waelbroeck, Jean. Has Human Capital Become a Scarce Factor in Belgium? *Cah. Écon. Bruxelles,* 2nd Trimester 1988, (118), pp. 159–79.

Thayer, Frederick C., Jr. The Other Side: A Brief Sermon on the History and Necessity of Economic Regulation. In *Maynes, E. S. and ACCI Research Committee, eds.,* 1988, pp. 462–66.

Thayer, Mark A. and Murdoch, James C. Hedonic Price Estimation of Variable Urban Air Quality. *J. Environ. Econ. Manage.,* June 1988, *15*(2), pp. 143–46.

Theen, Rolf H. W. Hierarchical Reform in the Soviet Economy: The Case of Agriculture. In *Linz, S. J. and Moskoff, W., eds.,* 1988, pp. 73–87.

Theil, Henri. Income Inequality and the Progressivity of an Income Tax. *Rev. Soc. Econ.,* December 1988, *46*(3), pp. 252–54.

_____ ; **Fiebig, Denzil G. and Seale, James, Jr.** Cross-Country Demand Analysis Based on Three Phases of the International Comparison Project. In *Salazar-Carrillo, J. and Rao, D. S. P., eds.,* 1988, pp. 225–35.

_____ ; **Lopez, Elena and Chung, Ching-Fan.** Tracing the Composition Changes of Japan's Consumer Budget, 1920–1980. *Empirical Econ.,* 1988, *13*(1), pp. 59–64.

_____ **and Taylor, Carol A.** Measuring the Size of Revisions of Regional Data. *Econ. Letters,* 1988, *27*(2), pp. 201–04.

_____ **and Taylor, Carol A.** Modeling the Accuracy of Certain Regional Predictions. *Reg. Sci. Urban Econ.,* November 1988, *18*(4), pp. 453–62.

Theocharis, Reghinos D. C. Courtois: An Early Contributor to Cost–Benefit Analysis. *Hist. Polit. Econ.,* Summer 1988, *20*(2), pp. 265–73.

Theofanides, Stavros. The Metamorphosis of Development Economics. *World Devel.,* December 1988, *16*(12), pp. 1455–63.

Théret, Bruno and Uri, Didier. La courbe de Laffer dix ans après: Un essai de bilan critique. (The Laffer Curve Ten Years After: A Tentative Critical Survey. With English summary.) *Revue Écon.,* July 1988, *39*(4), pp. 753–808.

Therivel, Silvia and Schlegelmilch, Bodo B. The Use of Marketing Research in Engineering Companies: Empirical Evidence from the U.S. and the U.K. In *Woodside, A. G., ed.,* 1988, pp. 249–91.

Theunisse, Hilda and Aerts, Walter. Belgium and the Seventh Directive. In *Gray, S. J. and Coenenberg, A. G., eds.,* 1988, pp. 41–75.

Thibodeau, Thomas G. and Weicher, John C. Filtering and Housing Markets: An Empirical Analysis. *J. Urban Econ.,* January 1988, *23*(1), pp. 21–40.

Thiel, Carol Tomme. Training Starts With Top-Down Acceptance. In *Timpe, A. D., ed.,* 1988, *1984,* pp. 252–55.

Thiel, Stuart E. Multidimensional Auctions. *Econ. Letters,* 1988, *28*(1), pp. 37–40.

_____ . Some Evidence of the Winner's Curse.

Amer. Econ. Rev., December 1988, 78(5), pp. 884–95.

Thies, Clifford F. and Sturrock, Thomas. The Pension-Augmented Balance Sheet. *J. Risk Ins.*, September 1988, 55(3), pp. 467–80.

Thiessen, Victor and Davis, Anthony. Public Policy and Social Control in the Atlantic Fisheries. *Can. Public Policy*, March 1988, 14(1), pp. 66–77.

Thijssen, Geert. Estimating a Labour Supply Function of Farm Households. *Europ. Rev. Agr. Econ.*, 1988, 15(1), pp. 67–78.

Thirlwall, A. P. Keynesian Employment Theory Is Not Defunct. **In** *Shaw, G. K., ed., Vol. 1, 1988, 1981*, pp. 168–82.

———. Population Growth and economic Development. **In** *[Clark, C.]*, 1988, pp. 177–98.

Thirtle, C. Is Publicly Funded Agricultural Research Excessive? A Reply. *J. Agr. Econ.*, September 1988, 39(3), pp. 456–58.

——— **and Bottomley, P.** Is Publicly Funded Agricultural Research Excessive? *J. Agr. Econ.*, January 1988, 39(1), pp. 99–111.

Thiry, Beranrd. Distributive Effects of the Reform of Value-Added Tax: The Case of Belgium. *Ann. Pub. Co-op. Econ.*, July–Sept. 1988, 59(3), pp. 341–68.

Thisse, Jacques-François and Anderson, Simon P. Price Discrimination in Spatial Competitive Markets. *Europ. Econ. Rev.*, March 1988, 32(2–3), pp. 578–90.

———; **Anderson, Simon P. and de Palma, André.** The CES and the Logit: Two Related Models of Heterogeneity. *Reg. Sci. Urban Econ.*, February 1988, 18(1), pp. 155–64.

———; **Anderson, Simon P. and de Palma, André.** A Representative Consumer Theory of the Logit Model. *Int. Econ. Rev.*, August 1988, 29(3), pp. 461–66.

———; **Fujita, Masahisa and Ogawa, Hideaki.** A Spatial Competition Approach to Central Place Theory: Some Basic Principles. *J. Reg. Sci.*, November 1988, 28(4), pp. 477–94.

———; **MacLeod, W. Bentley and Norman, G.** Price Discrimination and Equilibrium in Monopolistic Competition. *Int. J. Ind. Organ.*, December 1988, 6(4), pp. 429–46.

——— **and Vives, Xavier.** On the Strategic Choice of Spatial Price Policy. *Amer. Econ. Rev.*, March 1988, 78(1), pp. 122–37.

Thistle, Paul D. Uniform Progressivity, Residual Progression, and Single-Crossing. *J. Public Econ.*, October 1988, 37(1), pp. 121–26.

———; **Bishop, John A. and Chakraborti, S.** Large Sample Tests for Absolute Lorenz Dominance. *Econ. Letters*, 1988, 26(3), pp. 291–94.

——— **and Cover, James Peery.** Time Series, Homicide, and the Deterrent Effect of Capital Punishment. *Southern Econ. J.*, January 1988, 54(3), pp. 615–22.

——— **and Formby, John P.** On One Parameter Functional Forms for Lorenz Curves. *Eastern Econ. J.*, Jan.–March 1988, 14(1), pp. 81–85.

———; **Formby, John P. and Keeler, James P.** X-efficiency, Rent-Seeking and Social Costs. *Public Choice*, May 1988, 57(2), pp. 115–26.

Thivierge, Simon and Bernard, Jean-Thomas. Les politiques fiscales et financiéres des services d'électricité: Le cas d'Hydro-Québec. (With English summary.) *Can. Public Policy*, September 1988, 14(3), pp. 239–44.

Thomas, A. M. Human Resources Development for Rural Industries and Artisans Activities. **In** *Kohli, U. and Gautam, V., eds.*, 1988, pp. 63–70.

Thomas, Barry. Employment Policy and the Measurement of (Un)employment. **In** *Darnell, A. and Evans, L., eds.*, 1988, pp. 70–88.

Thomas, Christopher R. and Smithson, Charles W. Measuring the Cost to Consumers of Product Defects: The Value of "Lemon Insurance." *J. Law Econ.*, October 1988, 31(2), pp. 485–502.

Thomas, David R. and Limam, Mohamed M. T. Simultaneous Tolerance Intervals for the Linear Regression Model. *J. Amer. Statist. Assoc.*, September 1988, 83(403), pp. 801–04.

Thomas, Dennis A. and Peel, David A. Outcome Uncertainty and the Demand for Football: An Analysis of Match Attendances in the English Football League. *Scot. J. Polit. Econ.*, August 1988, 35(3), pp. 242–49.

Thomas, Ewart A. C. and Feldman, Marcus W. Behavior-Dependent Contexts for Repeated Plays of the Prisoner's Dilemma. *J. Conflict Resolution*, December 1988, 32(4), pp. 699–726.

Thomas, Frank. The Politics of Growth: The German Telephone System. **In** *Mayntz, R. and Hughes, T. P., eds.*, 1988, pp. 179–213.

Thomas, Gary M. Tax Treatment of Computer Software: Japan. **In** *International Fiscal Association, ed. (II)*, 1988, pp. 399–424.

Thomas, Howard and McGee, John. Making Sense of Complex Industries. **In** *Hood, N. and Vahlne, J.-E., eds.*, 1988, pp. 40–78.

——— **and Schwenk, Charles R.** Effects of Strategic Decision Aids on Problem Solving: A Laboratory Experiment. **In** *Grant, J. H., ed.*, 1988, pp. 399–414.

Thomas, Ian C. and Drudy, P. J. Growth Town Employment in Mid-Wales Re-visited: A Reply. *Urban Stud.*, December 1988, 25(6), pp. 532–37.

Thomas, Jacob K. Corporate Taxes and Defined Benefit Pension Plans. *J. Acc. Econ.*, July 1988, 10(3), pp. 199–237.

——— **and Imhoff, Eugene A., Jr.** Economic Consequences of Accounting Standards: The Lease Disclosure Rule Change. *J. Acc. Econ.*, December 1988, 10(4), pp. 277–310.

Thomas, James and Neef, Arthur. International Comparisons of Productivity and Unit Labor Cost Trends in Manufacturing. *Mon. Lab. Rev.*, December 1988, 111(12), pp. 27–33.

Thomas, John F. and Syme, Geoffrey J. Estimating Residential Price Elasticity of Demand for Water: A Contingent Valuation Approach. *Water Resources Res.*, November 1988, 24(11), pp. 1847–57.

Thomas, Jonathan and Worrall, Tim. Self-enforcing Wage Contracts. *Rev. Econ. Stud.*, October 1988, *55*(4), pp. 541–54.

Thomas, Lacy Glenn. Revealed Bureaucratic Preference: Priorities of the Consumer Product Safety Commission. *Rand J. Econ.*, Spring 1988, *19*(1), pp. 102–13.

Thomas, Lloyd B., Jr. and Abderrezak, Ali. Anticipated Future Budget Deficits and the Term Structure of Interest Rates. *Southern Econ. J.*, July 1988, *55*(1), pp. 150–61.

_____ **and Abderrezak, Ali.** Long-term Interest Rates: The Role of Expected Budget Deficits. *Public Finance Quart.*, July 1988, *16*(3), pp. 341–56.

Thomas, Mark. Labour Market Structure and the Nature of Unemployment in Interwar Britain. In *Eichengreen, B. and Hatton, T. J., eds.*, 1988, pp. 97–148.

_____. Manufacturing and Economic Recovery in Australia, 1932–1937. In *Gregory, R. G. and Butlin, N. G., eds.*, 1988, pp. 245–71.

_____. Slowdown in the Pre-World War One Economy. *Oxford Rev. Econ. Policy*, Spring 1988, *4*(1), pp. 14–24.

Thomas, R. W. Stochastic Carrier Models for the Simulation of Hodgkin's Disease in a System of Regions. *Environ. Planning A*, December 1988, *20*(12), pp. 1575–1601.

Thomas, Robert G. Groundwater as a Constraint to Irrigation. In *O'Mara, G. T., ed.*, 1988, pp. 168–76.

Thomas, Robert J. and Gartner, William B. An Exploration of the Methods Used by New Firms to Estimate Future Sales. In *Kirchhoff, B. A., et al., eds.*, 1988, pp. 461–76.

Thomas, V. and Meyers, K. Development Lending and Conditionality. In *Jepma, C. J., ed.*, 1988, pp. 145–60.

Thomas, Wade L. and Kacapyr, Elia. An Index of Economic Activity in Tompkins County. In *Pennsylvania Economic Association*, 1988, pp. 664–81.

Thomassin, Paul J. and Baker, Laurie. Farm Ownership and Financial Stress. *Can. J. Agr. Econ.*, Part 2, December 1988, *36*(4), pp. 799–811.

Thommessen, Gunnar and Bing, Jon. Tax Treatment of Computer Software: Norway. In *International Fiscal Association, ed. (II)*, 1988, pp. 439–52.

Thompsom, William F. and Howsen, Roy M. The Impact of Changes in Research and Development and Productivity on Changes in Concentration. In *Missouri Valley Economic Assoc.*, 1988, pp. 12–17.

Thompson, David; Domberger, Simon and Meadowcroft, Shirley. Competition and Efficiency in Refuse Collection: A Reply. *Fisc. Stud.*, February 1988, *9*(1), pp. 86–90.

_____; **Helm, Dieter and Kay, John.** Energy Policy and the Role of the State in the Market for Energy. *Fisc. Stud.*, February 1988, *9*(1), pp. 41–61.

Thompson, Dennis. The International Tin Council Litigation. *J. World Trade*, October 1988, *22*(5), pp. 103–11.

Thompson, Frank W. and Anderson, W. H. Locke. Neoclassical Marxism. *Sci. Soc.*, Summer 1988, *52*(2), pp. 215–28.

Thompson, Fred. Taking Full Advantage of State Investment Pools. *J. Policy Anal. Manage.*, Winter 1988, *7*(2), pp. 353–56.

_____ **and Choate, G. Marc.** Budget Makers as Agents: A Preliminary Investigation of Discretionary Behavior under State-Contingent Rewards. *Public Choice*, July 1988, *58*(1), pp. 3–20.

Thompson, G. Rodney; Billingsley, Randall S. and Lamy, Robert E. The Choice among Debt, Equity, and Convertible Bonds. *J. Finan. Res.*, Spring 1988, *11*(1), pp. 43–55.

_____ **and Lamy, Robert E.** Risk Premia and the Pricing of Primary Issue Bonds. *J. Banking Finance*, December 1988, *12*(4), pp. 585–601.

_____ **and O'Neil, Cherie J.** Taxation and IRA Participation: Response. *Nat. Tax J.*, December 1988, *41*(4), pp. 591–93.

Thompson, Gary D. Choice of Flexible Functional Forms: Review and Appraisal. *Western J. Agr. Econ.*, December 1988, *13*(2), pp. 169–83.

Thompson, Gregory L. The Passenger Train in the Motor Age: The California Experience, 1910–1941. In *Hausman, W. J., ed.*, 1988, pp. 219–26.

Thompson, Henry; Clark, Don P. and Hofler, Richard. Separability of Capital and Labor in U.S. Manufacturing. *Econ. Letters*, 1988, *26*(2), pp. 197–201.

Thompson, Howard E. and Ahn, Chang Mo. Jump-Diffusion Processes and the Term Structure of Interest Rates. *J. Finance*, March 1988, *43*(1), pp. 155–74.

_____; **Farimani, Mehrdad and Buongiorno, Joseph.** A Financial Model of Investment, with an Application to the Paper Industry. *Appl. Econ.*, June 1988, *20*(6), pp. 767–83.

_____; **Grammatikos, Theoharry and Makhija, Anil K.** Financing Corporate Takeovers by Individuals Seeking Control. *Managerial Dec. Econ.*, September 1988, *9*(3), pp. 227–35.

Thompson, Lawrence H. Altering the Public/Private Mix of Retirement Incomes. In *Wachter, S. M., ed.*, 1988, pp. 209–26.

Thompson, Leigh L.; Bazerman, Max H. and Mannix, Elizabeth A. Groups as Mixed-Motive Negotiations. In *Lawler, E. J. and Markovsky, B., eds.*, 1988, pp. 195–216.

Thompson, M. and Warburton, M. Uncertainty on a Himalayan Scale. In *Ives, J. and Pitt, D. C., eds.*, 1988, pp. 1–53.

Thompson, Patricia. Public Housing and Displacement: A Response to the Leigh–Mitchell Paper. *Rev. Black Polit. Econ.*, Fall 1988, *17*(2), pp. 131–32.

Thompson, R. S. Price Adjustment and Market Structure: A Single-Industry Study. *Managerial Dec. Econ.*, June 1988, *9*(2), pp. 87–92.

_____. Product Differentiation in the Newspaper Industry: An Hedonic Price Approach. *Appl. Econ.*, March 1988, *20*(3), pp. 367–76.

Thompson, Rex and Lanen, William N. Stock-

Price Reactions as Surrogates for the Net Cash Flow Effects of Corporate Policy Decisions. *J. Acc. Econ.*, December 1988, *10*(4), pp. 311–34.

Thompson, Richard P.; Olson, Kent W. and Moomaw, Ronald L. Redwood National Park Expansion: Impact on Old-Growth Redwood Stumpage Prices. *Land Econ.*, August 1988, *64*(3), pp. 269–75.

Thompson, Robert B. Tender Offer Regulation and the Federalization of State Corporate Law. In *Weidenbaum, M. L. and Chilton, K. W., eds.*, 1988, pp. 78–105.

Thompson, Robert B., II; Olsen, Chris and Dietrich, J. Richard. The Influence of Estimation Period News Events on Standardized Market Model Prediction Errors. *Accounting Rev.*, July 1988, *63*(3), pp. 448–71.

Thompson, Robert L. Agriculture: Growing Government Control. In *Boaz, D., ed.*, 1988, pp. 243–49.

Thompson, Stanley R. and Bond, Gary E. Offshore Commodity Hedging under Floating Exchange Rates: Reply. *Amer. J. Agr. Econ.*, August 1988, *70*(3), pp. 727–28.

_____; Larson, Donald W. and Koo, Won W. Effects of Ocean Freight Rate Changes on the U.S. Grain Distribution System. *Logist. Transp. Rev.*, March 1988, *24*(1), pp. 85–100.

_____; Smith, Mark E. and van Ravenswaay, Eileen O. Sales Loss Determination in Food Contamination Incidents: An Application to Milk Bans in Hawaii. *Amer. J. Agr. Econ.*, August 1988, *70*(3), pp. 513–20.

Thompson, William R. and Rasler, Karen A. Defense Burdens, Capital Formation, and Economic Growth: The Systemic Leader Case. *J. Conflict Resolution*, March 1988, *32*(1), pp. 61–86.

_____ and Rasler, Karen A. War and Systemic Capability Reconcentration. *J. Conflict Resolution*, June 1988, *32*(2), pp. 335–66.

Thomson, James T. Deforestation and Desertification in Twentieth-Century Arid Sahelien Africa. In *Richards, J. F. and Tucker, R. P., eds.*, 1988, pp. 70–90.

Thomson, William. The Manipulability of the Shapley-Value. *Int. J. Game Theory*, 1988, *17*(2), pp. 101–27.

_____. A Study of Choice Correspondences in Economies with a Variable Number of Agents. *J. Econ. Theory*, December 1988, *46*(2), pp. 237–54.

_____ and Chun, Youngsub. Monotonicity Properties of Bargaining Solutions when Applied to Economics. *Math. Soc. Sci.*, February 1988, *15*(1), pp. 11–27.

_____ and Lensberg, Terje. Characterizing the Nash Bargaining Solution without Pareto-Optimality. *Soc. Choice Welfare*, 1988, *5*(2/3), pp. 247–59.

_____ and Lensberg, Terje. Characterizing the Nash Bargaining Solution without Pareto-Optimality. In *Gaertner, W. and Pattanaik, P. K., eds.*, 1988, *1988*, pp. 159–71.

_____ and Moulin, Hervé. Can Everyone Bene-

fit from Growth? Two Difficulties. *J. Math. Econ.*, 1988, *17*(4), pp. 339–45.

Thon, Dominique and Thorlund-Petersen, Lars. Stochastic Dominance and Friedman–Savage Utility Functions. *Math. Soc. Sci.*, December 1988, *16*(3), pp. 305–17.

Thorbecke, Erik and Santiago, Carlos E. A Multisectoral Framework for the Analysis of Labor Mobility and Development in LDCs: An Application to Postwar Puerto Rico. *Econ. Develop. Cult. Change*, October 1988, *37*(1), pp. 127–48.

Thorelli, Hans B. Consumer Problems: Developed and Less Developed Countries. In *Maynes, E. S. and ACCI Research Committee, eds.*, 1988, pp. 523–46.

Thorlund-Petersen, Lars and Thon, Dominique. Stochastic Dominance and Friedman–Savage Utility Functions. *Math. Soc. Sci.*, December 1988, *16*(3), pp. 305–17.

Thorn, Richard S. The Cross Listing of Stocks on the Malaysian and Singapore Stock Exchanges: A Study of Policy Alternatives. *Singapore Econ. Rev.*, April 1988, *33*(1), pp. 1–20.

Thorns, David C. New Solutions to Old Problems: Housing Affordability and Access within Australia and New Zealand. *Environ. Planning A*, January 1988, *20*(1), pp. 71–82.

_____. Who Gets Housed: The Changing Nature of Housing Affordability and Access in Advanced Capitalist Societies. In *Friedrichs, J., ed.*, 1988, pp. 27–41.

Thornton, Arland. Cohabitation and Marriage in the 1980s. *Demography*, November 1988, *25*(4), pp. 497–508.

Thornton, Daniel L. The Borrowed-Reserves Operating Procedure: Theory and Evidence. *Fed. Res. Bank St. Louis Rev.*, Jan.–Feb. 1988, *70*(1), pp. 30–54.

_____. The Effect of Monetary Policy on Short-term Interest Rates. *Fed. Res. Bank St. Louis Rev.*, May–June 1988, *70*(3), pp. 53–72.

_____ and Chrystal, K. Alec. The Macroeconomic Effects of Deficit Spending: A Review. *Fed. Res. Bank St. Louis Rev.*, Nov.–Dec. 1988, *70*(6), pp. 48–60.

_____ and Chrystal, K. Alec. On the Informational Content of Spot and Forward Exchange Rates. *J. Int. Money Finance*, September 1988, *7*(3), pp. 321–30.

Thornton, John. Inflation and Output Growth: Some Time Series Evidence, a Note. *Amer. Econ.*, Fall 1988, *32*(2), pp. 55–58.

Thornton, John H.; Cross, Mark L. and Davidson, Wallace N., III. Taxes, Stock Returns and Captive Insurance Subsidiaries. *J. Risk Ins.*, June 1988, *55*(2), pp. 331–38.

Thornton, Robert J. and Innes, Jon T. The Status of Master's Programs in Economics. *J. Econ. Perspectives*, Winter 1988, *2*(1), pp. 171–78.

Thorp, Rosemary. Three Views on Restoring Growth: Comment. In *Bruno, M., et al., eds.*, 1988, pp. 404–07.

Thorp, S. J. and Trevor, R. G. VAR Forecasting Models of the Australian Economy: A Preliminary Analysis. *Australian Econ. Pap.*, Supplement, June 1988, *27*, pp. 108–20.

Thorpe, Kenneth E. Uncompensated Care Pools and Care to the Uninsured: Lessons from the New York Prospective Hospital Reimbursement Methodology. *Inquiry*, Fall 1988, *25(3)*, pp. 344–53.

_____. The Use of Regression Analysis to Determine Hospital Payment: The Case of Medicare's Indirect Teaching Adjustment. *Inquiry*, Summer 1988, *25(2)*, pp. 219–31.

Thorpe, Mary. Survival and Change in the Third World: Introduction. **In** *Crow, B. and Thorpe, M., et al.*, 1988, pp. 1–6.

Thorsson, Inga. The Arms Race and Development: A Competitive Relationship. **In** *Wilber, C. K., ed.*, 1988, pp. 533–40.

Thottathil, Pelis. The Internal Transfer of Income from Exporters to Importers within a Foreign Exchange Control Regime: An Indian Case. *Appl. Econ.*, September 1988, *20(9)*, pp. 1211–22.

Thoumi, Francisco and Ballestero, Florencio. The Instability of Intra-Latin American and Caribbean Exports and Exchange Rates. **In** *Jorge, A. and Salazar-Carrillo, J., eds.*, 1988, pp. 59–81.

Throop, Adrian W. An Evaluation of Alternative Measures of Expected Inflation. *Fed. Res. Bank San Francisco Econ. Rev.*, Summer 1988, *(3)*, pp. 27–43.

Thürbach, Ralf-Peter. Overview of the Commercial Space Market. **In** *Egan, J. J., et al.*, 1988, pp. 21–36.

Thurik, A. Roy; Nooteboom, Bart and Kleijweg, Aad. Normal Costs and Demand Effects in Price Setting: A Study of Retailing. *Europ. Econ. Rev.*, April 1988, *32(4)*, pp. 999–1011.

_____; **Vollebregt, J. A. C. and Nooteboom, Bart.** Do Retail Margins Differ between European Countries? A Comparative Study. **In** *Kaynak, E., ed.*, 1988, pp. 155–66.

Thurman, Quint. Taxpayer Noncompliance and Attribution Theory: An Experimental Vignette Approach. *Public Finance*, 1988, *43(1)*, pp. 147–56.

Thurman, Walter N. Speculative Carryover: An Empirical Examination of the U.S. Refined Copper Market. *Rand J. Econ.*, Autumn 1988, *19(3)*, pp. 420–37.

_____. Storage, Stability, and Farm Programs: Reaction. **In** *Sumner, D. A., ed.*, 1988, pp. 51–55.

_____ **and Fisher, Mark E.** Chickens, Eggs, and Causality, or Which Came First? *Amer. J. Agr. Econ.*, May 1988, *70(2)*, pp. 237–38.

Thurow, Lester C. A Surge in Inequality. **In** *Brown, E., ed.*, 1988, *1987*, pp. 36–46.

Thursby, Jerry G. Evaluation of Coefficients in Misspecified Regressions with Application to Import Demand. *Rev. Econ. Statist.*, November 1988, *70(4)*, pp. 690–95.

_____; **Anderson, Richard G. and Dewald, William G.** Replication in Empirical Economics: *The Journal of Money, Credit and Banking*

Project: Reply. *Amer. Econ. Rev.*, December 1988, *78(5)*, pp. 1162–63.

_____ **and Thursby, Marie C.** Elasticities in International Trade: Theoretical and Methodological Issues. **In** *Carter, C. A. and Gardiner, W. H., eds.*, 1988, pp. 17–52.

Thursby, Marie C. Strategic Models, Market Structure, and State Trading: An Application to Agriculture. **In** *Baldwin, R. E., ed. (II)*, 1988, pp. 79–105.

_____ **and Thursby, Jerry G.** Elasticities in International Trade: Theoretical and Methodological Issues. **In** *Carter, C. A. and Gardiner, W. H., eds.*, 1988, pp. 17–52.

Thurston, Thom and Allen, Linda. Cash-Futures Arbitrage and Forward-Futures Spreads in the Treasury Bill Market. *J. Futures Markets*, October 1988, *8(5)*, pp. 563–73.

Thury, Gerhard. Intervention Analysis of Consumer Expenditure in Austria. *Empirica*, 1988, *15(2)*, pp. 295–325.

Thwaites, James. History and Industrial Relations in Canada. **In** *Hébert, G.; Jain, H. C. and Meltz, N. M., eds..*, 1988, pp. 261–79.

Thygesen, Niels. International Adjustment and the Dollar: Policy Illusions and Economic Constraints: Comment. **In** *Guth, W., ed.*, 1988, pp. 84–93.

Thys-Clement, F. and Dewatripont, Mathias. Employment and Public Deficits: A Vicious Circle? *Tijdschrift Econ. Manage.*, Sept.–Dec. 1988, *33(3/4)*, pp. 287–301.

Tian, Guoqiang. On the Constrained Walrasian and Lindahl Correspondences. *Econ. Letters*, 1988, *26(4)*, pp. 299–303.

Tiao, George C.; Easton, George S. and Roberts, Harry V. Making Statistics More Effective in Schools of Business. *J. Bus. Econ. Statist.*, April 1988, *6(2)*, pp. 247–60.

Tibshirani, Robert. Estimating Transformations for Regression via Additivity and Variance Stabilization. *J. Amer. Statist. Assoc.*, June 1988, *83(402)*, pp. 394–405.

Tichy, G. E. Anerkennung der steuerlichen Rechtsfähigkeit ausländischer Unternehmungen: Österreich. (Recognition of Foreign Enterprises as Taxable Entities: Austria. With English summary.) **In** *International Fiscal Association, ed. (I)*, 1988, pp. 287–301.

Tickamyer, Ann R. and Tickamyer, Cecil H. Gender and Poverty in Central Appalachia. *Soc. Sci. Quart.*, December 1988, *69(4)*, pp. 874–91.

Tickamyer, Cecil H. and Tickamyer, Ann R. Gender and Poverty in Central Appalachia. *Soc. Sci. Quart.*, December 1988, *69(4)*, pp. 874–91.

Tidalgo, Rosa Linda P. Labour Markets, Labour Flows and Structural Change in the Philippines. **In** *Pang, E. F., ed.*, 1988, pp. 139–94.

Tideman, T. Nicolaus and Tullock, Gordon. A New and Superior Process for Making Social Choices. **In** *Ricketts, M., ed., Vol. 2*, 1988, *1976*, pp. 103–17.

Tiebout, Charles M. A Pure Theory of Local Expenditures. In *Cowen, T., ed.*, 1988, *1956*, pp. 179–91.

――――. A Pure Theory of Local Expenditures. In *Ricketts, M., ed., Vol. 2*, 1988, *1956*, pp. 77–85.

Tielu, A. and Goddard, Ellen W. Assessing the Effectiveness of Fluid Milk Advertising in Ontario. *Can. J. Agr. Econ.*, July 1988, *36*(2), pp. 261–78.

Tiemann, Jonathan. Exact Arbitrage Pricing and the Minimum-Variance Frontier. *J. Finance*, June 1988, *43*(2), pp. 327–38.

Tien, H. Yuan and Lee, Che-fu. New Demographics and Old Designs: The Chinese Family amid Induced Population Transition. *Soc. Sci. Quart.*, September 1988, *69*(3), pp. 605–28.

Tienda, Marta. Human Capital for Agriculture: A Discussion. In *Hildreth, R. J., et al., eds.*, 1988, pp. 517–22.

Tietmeyer, Hans. Empirical Evidence of Effects of Policy Coordination among Major Industrial Countries since Rambouillet Summit of 1975: Comment. In *Guth, W., ed.*, 1988, pp. 135–41.

Tietz, Reinhard. Experimental Economics: Ways to Model Bounded Rational Bargaining Behavior. In *Tietz, R.; Albers, W. and Selten, R., eds.*, 1988, pp. 3–10.

――――― **and Güth, Werner.** Ultimatum Bargaining for a Shrinking Cake—An Experimental Analysis. In *Tietz, R.; Albers, W. and Selten, R., eds.*, 1988, pp. 111–28.

――――― **and Vossebein, Ulrich.** Modeling Investment Behavior in an Experimental Market. In *Tietz, R.; Albers, W. and Selten, R., eds.*, 1988, pp. 219–31.

―――――, **et al.** Semi-normative Properties of Bounded Rational Bargaining Theories. In *Tietz, R.; Albers, W. and Selten, R., eds.*, 1988, pp. 142–59.

Tietzel, Manfred. Zur ökonomischen Theorie des Betrügens und des Fälschens. (On the Economic Theory of Cheating and Falsifying. (With English summary.) *Jahr. Nationalökon. Statist.*, January 1988, *204*(1), pp. 17–35.

Tiganescu, E. and Gavrilă, I. Development and Modernization of the Planning and Statistic Education in the Conditions of Training the Specialists. *Econ. Computat. Cybern. Stud. Res.*, 1988, *23*(3), pp. 25–31.

Tigges, Leann. Dueling Sectors: The Role of Service Industries in the Earnings Process of the Dual Economy. In *Farkas, G. and England, P., eds.*, 1988, pp. 281–301.

Tijs, Stef H.; Curiel, Imma J. and Pederzoli, Giorgio. Reward Allocations in Production Systems. In *Eiselt, H. A. and Pederzoli, G., eds.*, 1988, pp. 186–99.

van Til, Reinold and Chand, Sheetal K. Ghana: Toward Successful Stabilization and Recovery. *Finance Develop.*, March 1988, *25*(1), pp. 32–35.

Tillack, R.; Vincent, D. and Mannion, R. Effects of Petroleum Product Excises on Agriculture. *Rev. Marketing Agr. Econ.*, April 1988, *56*(1), pp. 121–28.

Tilley, Daniel S. and Campbell, Steven K. Performance of the Weekly Gulf –Kansas City Hard-Red Winter Wheat Basis. *Amer. J. Agr. Econ.*, November 1988, *70*(4), pp. 929–35.

Tillinghast, Diana Stover. Limits of Competition. In *Picard, R. G., et al., eds.*, 1988, pp. 71–87.

Tillmann, Georg. Stability in a Simple Pure Consumption Loan Model. In *Grandmont, J.-M., ed.*, 1988, *1983*, pp. 271–85.

Tilly, Charles. Misreading, then Rereading, Nineteenth-Century Social Change. In *Wellman, B. and Berkowitz, S. D., eds.*, 1988, pp. 332–58.

Tilly, Chris and Loveman, Gary W. Good Jobs or Bad Jobs? Evaluating the American Job Creation Experience. *Int. Lab. Rev.*, 1988, *127*(5), pp. 593–611.

――――― **and Loveman, Gary W.** Good Jobs or Bad Jobs: What Does the Evidence Say? *New Eng. Econ. Rev.*, Jan.–Feb. 1988, pp. 46–65.

Tilman, Rick. A Comment on Stabile's Interpretation of Veblen and the Engineers. *J. Econ. Issues*, December 1988, *22*(4), pp. 1247–49.

――――. The Neoinstrumental Theory of Democracy. In *Tool, M. R., ed., Vol. 1*, 1988, *1987*, pp. 427–49.

――――― **and Clarke, Michael.** C. B. Macpherson's Contributions to Democratic Theory. *J. Econ. Issues*, March 1988, *22*(1), pp. 181–96.

Tilton, John E. Material Substitution: Lessons from the Tin-Using Industries. In *Forester, T., ed.*, 1988, *1983*, pp. 287–313.

―――――; **Eggert, Roderick G. and Landsberg, Hans H.** World Mineral Exploration: Trends and Economic Issues: Introduction. In *Tilton, J. E.; Eggert, R. G. and Landsberg, H. H., eds.*, 1988, pp. 1–19.

Timberlake, Richard H., Jr. A Critique of Monetarist and Austrian Doctrines on the Utility and Value of Money: Reply. In *Rothbard, M. N. and Block, W., eds.*, 1988, pp. 189–97.

――――. New Deal Monetary Legislation for the Welfare of the Government. *Cato J.*, Winter 1988, *7*(3), pp. 615–19.

――――. New Deal Monetary Legislation for the Welfare of the Government. In *England, C. and Huertas, T., eds.*, 1988, pp. 107–11.

――――. A Reassessment of C. A. Phillip's Theory of Bank Credit. *Hist. Polit. Econ.*, Summer 1988, *20*(2), pp. 299–308.

Timmer, C. Peter. Crop Diversification in Rice-Based Agricultural Economies: Conceptual and Policy Issues. In *Goldberg, R. A., ed., Vol. 8*, 1988, pp. 95–163.

――――. Food Policy and Economic Adjustment. In *Bell, D. E. and Reich, M. R., eds.*, 1988, pp. 177–97.

――――. Foreign Assistance and American Agriculture. In *Asefa, S., ed.*, 1988, pp. 87–121.

Timmermann, Vincenz and Scholing, Eberhard. Why LDC Growth Rates Differ: Measuring "Unmeasurable" Influences. *World Devel.*, November 1988, *16*(11), pp. 1271–94.

Timmermans, H. J. P. and van der Heijden, R. E. C. M. The Spatial Transferability of a

Decompositional Multi-attribute Preference Model. *Environ. Planning A*, August 1988, *20*(8), pp. 1013–25.

Timofeyev, Timor. Social Aspects of Perestroika. In *Aganbegyan, A. and Timofeyev, T.*, 1988, pp. 45–60.

Timoney, Nicola. Maurice Allais. *Econ. Soc. Rev.*, October 1988, *20*(1), pp. 1–3.

Tims, David and Waterhouse, John. The GAAP in Bank Regulation. *Can. Public Policy*, June 1988, *14*(2), pp. 151–61.

Tinbergen, Jan. Classical Mechanics with an Ethical Dimension: Professor Tinbergen's Economics: A Comment. *J. Econ. Issues*, September 1988, *22*(3), pp. 851–54.

_____. The Role of Errors in Scientific Development. *Rev. Soc. Econ.*, December 1988, *46*(3), pp. 225–30.

_____. The Theory of Income and Wealth Distribution: Introductory Remarks. In *Brenner, Y. S.; Reijnders, J. P. G. and Spithoven, A. H. G. M.*, eds., 1988, pp. 1–7.

_____. The Worst Destabilizer. In *[Witteveen, H. J.]*, 1988, pp. 231–42.

Tinic, Seha M. Anatomy of Initial Public Offerings of Common Stock. *J. Finance*, September 1988, *43*(4), pp. 789–822.

_____ **and Barone-Adesi, Giovanni.** Stock Return Seasonality and the Tests of Asset Pricing Models: Canadian Evidence. In *Dimson, E.*, ed., 1988, pp. 129–46.

_____; **Brown, Keith C. and Harlow, W. V.** Risk Aversion, Uncertain Information, and Market Efficiency. *J. Finan. Econ.*, December 1988, *22*(2), pp. 355–85.

Tinker, Tony. Waiving Goodbye to the TWA Bus: "Paper Prophets" and the Sraffian Critique of Marginalism. In *Neimark, M.*, ed., 1988, pp. 121–41.

Tinsley, La Verne C. State Workers' Compensation: Legislation Enacted in 1987. *Mon. Lab. Rev.*, January 1988, *111*(1), pp. 62–68.

Tippett, Mark; Bird, Ron and Dennis, David. A Stop Loss Approach to Portfolio Insurance. *J. Portfol. Manage.*, Fall 1988, *15*(1), pp. 35–40.

Tirole, Jean. The Multicontract Organization. *Can. J. Econ.*, August 1988, *21*(3), pp. 459–66.

_____ **and Hart, Oliver D.** Contract Renegotiation and Coasian Dynamics. *Rev. Econ. Stud.*, October 1988, *55*(4), pp. 509–40.

_____ **and Laffont, Jean-Jacques.** The Dynamics of Incentive Contracts. *Econometrica*, September 1988, *56*(5), pp. 1153–75.

_____ **and Laffont, Jean-Jacques.** Repeated Auctions of Incentive Contracts, Investment, and Bidding Parity with an Application to Takeovers. *Rand J. Econ.*, Winter 1988, *19*(4), pp. 516–37.

_____ **and Maskin, Eric.** A Theory of Dynamic Oligopoly, I: Overview and Quantity Competition with Large Fixed Costs. *Econometrica*, May 1988, *56*(3), pp. 549–69.

_____ **and Maskin, Eric.** A Theory of Dynamic Oligopoly, II: Price Competition, Kinked De-

mand Curves, and Edgeworth Cycles. *Econometrica*, May 1988, *56*(3), pp. 571–99.

_____ **and Maskin, Eric.** A Theory of Dynamic Oligopoly, III, Cournot Competition: Corrigendum. *Europ. Econ. Rev.*, September 1988, *32*(7), pp. 1567–68.

Tisdell, Clem A. Sustainable Development: Differing Perspectives of Ecologists and Economists, and Relevance to LDCs. *World Devel.*, March 1988, *16*(3), pp. 373–84.

_____. Sustainable Economic Growth, Production and Development: An Overview of Concepts and Changing Views. *Indian J. Quant. Econ.*, 1988, *4*(1), pp. 73–86.

_____ **and Aislabie, Colin J.** Profit Maximization and Marketing Strategies: Demand Rotation and Social Influences [A Note on Price-Advertising Reaction Function]. *Managerial Dec. Econ.*, March 1988, *9*(1), pp. 77–82.

_____ **and Alauddin, Mohammad.** Has the Green Revolution Destabilized Food Production?: Some Evidence from Bangladesh. *Devel. Econ.*, June 1988, *26*(2), pp. 141–60.

_____ **and Alauddin, Mohammad.** Impact of New Agricultural Technology on the Instability of Foodgrain Production and Yield: Data Analysis for Bangladesh and Its Districts. *J. Devel. Econ.*, September 1988, *29*(2), pp. 199–227.

_____ **and Alauddin, Mohammad.** New Agricultural Technology and Sustainable Food Production: Bangladesh's Achievements, Predicament and Prospects. In *Tisdell, C. and Maitra, P.*, eds., 1988, pp. 35–62.

_____ **and Alauddin, Mohammad.** Patterns and Determinants of Adoption of High Yielding Varieties: Farm-Level Evidence from Bangladesh. *Pakistan Devel. Rev.*, Summer 1988, *27*(2), pp. 183–210.

_____ **and Alauddin, Mohammad.** The Use of Input–Output Analysis to Determine the Appropriateness of Technology and Industries: Evidence from Bangladesh. *Econ. Develop. Cult. Change*, January 1988, *36*(2), pp. 369–91.

Tison, Elisabeth; Zumaran Paz, Jorge and Akaishi, Giselda. Latin and Central America: The Challenge to the United States. In *Lavigne, M.*, ed., 1988, pp. 182–211.

Titman, Sheridan D. and Trueman, Brett. An Explanation for Accounting Income Smoothing. *J. Acc. Res.*, Supplement, 1988, *26*, pp. 127–39.

_____ **and Wessels, Roberto E.** The Determinants of Capital Structure Choice. *J. Finance*, March 1988, *43*(1), pp. 1–19.

Titterington, D. M. Optimal Design for Nonlinear Problems. In *Fedorov, V. and Lauter, H.*, eds., 1988, pp. 87–93.

Tivers, Jacqueline. Women with Young Children: Constraints on Activities in the Urban Environment. In *Little, J.; Peake, L. and Richardson, P.*, eds., 1988, pp. 84–97.

Tiwari, K. M. Human Resources Development for Rural Industries. In *Kohli, U. and Gautam, V.*, eds., 1988, pp. 71–81.

Tiwari, Ram C.; Jammalamadaka, S. Rao and

Chib, Siddhartha. Bayes Prediction Density and Regression Estimation—A Semiparametric Approach. *Empirical Econ.*, 1988, *13*(3–4), pp. 209–22.

———; Jammalamadaka, S. Rao and Chib, Siddhartha. Bayes Prediction in Regressions with Elliptical Errors. *J. Econometrics*, July 1988, *38*(3), pp. 349–60.

Tjiptoherijanto, Prijono; Ananta, Aris and Alatas, Secha. Labour Market Developments and Structural Change in Indonesia. In *Pang, E. F., ed.*, 1988, pp. 66–99.

To, Theodore. More Realism in the Prisoner's Dilemma. *J. Conflict Resolution*, June 1988, *32*(2), pp. 402–08.

Tobias, Lester L. Hiring for Excellence. In *Timpe, A. D., ed.*, 1988, *1987*, pp. 264–65.

Tobin, James. Financial Market Volatility: Overview. In *Federal Reserve Bank of Kansas City*, 1988, pp. 249–54.

———. Keynesian Models of Recession and Depression. In *Shaw, G. K., ed., Vol. 1*, 1988, *1975*, pp. 183–90.

———. The Monetarist Counter-Revolution Today—An Appraisal. In *Shaw, G. K., ed., Vol. 2*, 1988, *1981*, pp. 207–20.

———. Money and Income: Post Hoc Ergo Propter Hoc? In *Shaw, G. K., ed., Vol. 2*, 1988, *1970*, pp. 121–37.

———. A Revolution Remembered. *Challenge*, July–August 1988, *31*(4), pp. 35–41.

Tocker, Edwin. A Chemical Industry Perspective. In *Walker, C. E. and Bloomfield, M. A., eds.*, 1988, pp. 151–59.

Todaro, Michael P. and Fapohunda, Eleanor R. Family Structure, Implicit Contracts, and the Demand for Children in Southern Nigeria. *Population Devel. Rev.*, December 1988, *14*(4), pp. 571–94.

Todd, Douglas. Total Factor Productivity Growth and the Productivity Slowdown in the West German Industrial Sector, 1970–1981. *Weltwirtsch. Arch.*, 1988, *124*(1), pp. 108–26.

Todd, Michael J. Polynomial Algorithms for Linear Programming. In *Eiselt, H. A. and Pederzoli, G., eds.*, 1988, pp. 49–66.

Toder, Eric; Galper, Harvey and Lucke, Robert. A General Equilibrium Analysis of Tax Reform. In *Aaron, H. J.; Galper, H. and Pechman, J. A., eds.*, 1988, pp. 59–108.

Todó-Rovira, Adolfo and Pérez-Amaral, Teodosio. Social Security and Private Saving: A Reconsideration of the Assumptions. *Appl. Econ.*, August 1988, *20*(8), pp. 1057–69.

Toedter, Karl-Heinz. Effects of Shorter Hours on Employment in Disequilibrium Models. *Europ. Econ. Rev.*, July 1988, *32*(6), pp. 1319–33.

Toharia, Luis. Partial Fordism: Spain between Political Transition and Economic Crisis. In *Boyer, R., ed.*, 1988, pp. 119–39.

Toker, Mehmet; Ingham, Alan and Ulph, Alistair. A Vintage Model of Scrapping and Investment. *Rech. Écon. Louvain*, 1988, *54*(2), pp. 169–89.

Tokman, Victor E. Urban Employment: Research and Policy in Latin America. *CEPAL Rev.*, April 1988, (34), pp. 109–26.

Tokumaru, Hidekatsu and Nakamori, Seiichi. Identification of Linear Discrete-Time Stochastic System Using Covariance Information. In *Iri, M. and Yajima, K., eds.*, 1988, pp. 109–18.

Tolley, George S. What If Transit Markets Were Freed? In *Weicher, J. C., ed.*, 1988, pp. 89–97.

Tolley, H. Dennis and Pope, Rulon D. Testing for Stochastic Dominance. *Amer. J. Agr. Econ.*, August 1988, *70*(3), pp. 693–700.

Tolliday, Steven. Competition and the Workplace in the British Automobile Industry, 1945–1988. In *Hausman, W. J., ed.*, 1988, pp. 63–77.

Tollison, Robert D. and Anderson, Gary Michael. Democracy, Interest Groups, and the Price of Votes. *Cato J.*, Spring–Summer 1988, *8*(1), pp. 53–70.

——— and Anderson, Gary Michael. Legislative Monopoly and the Size of Government. *Southern Econ. J.*, January 1988, *54*(3), pp. 529–45.

———; Anderson, Gary Michael and Rowley, Charles K. Rent Seeking and the Restriction of Human Exchange. *J. Legal Stud.*, January 1988, *17*(1), pp. 83–100.

———; Anderson, Gary Michael and Shughart, William F., II. A Public Choice Theory of the Great Contraction. *Public Choice*, October 1988, *59*(1), pp. 3–23.

———; Crain, W. Mark and Shughart, William F., II. Legislative Majorities as Nonsalvageable Assets. *Southern Econ. J.*, October 1988, *55*(2), pp. 303–14.

———; Goff, Brian L. and Shughart, William F., II. Disqualification by Decree: Amateur Rules as Barriers to Entry. *J. Inst. Theoretical Econ.*, June 1988, *144*(3), pp. 515–23.

———; Leavens, Donald R. and Crain, W. Mark. Laissez-faire in Campaign Finance. *Public Choice*, March 1988, *56*(3), pp. 201–12.

———; McCormick, Robert E. and Shughart, William F., II. The Disinterest in Deregulation: Reply. *Amer. Econ. Rev.*, March 1988, *78*(1), pp. 284.

——— and Wagner, Richard E. Social Cost, Rent Seeking, and Smoking: A Public Choice Perspective. *Econ. Scelte Pubbliche/J. Public Finance Public Choice*, Sept.–Dec. 1988, *6*(3), pp. 171–86.

Tolonen, Yrjänä. Some Macroeconomic Consequences of Trade with Centrally Planned Economies. *J. Compar. Econ.*, September 1988, *12*(3), pp. 345–61.

Tolwinski, B. A Renegotiation-Proof Solution for a Price Setting Duopoly. In *Eiselt, H. A. and Pederzoli, G., eds.*, 1988, pp. 358–71.

Toma, Eugenia Froedge. State Liquor Licensing, Implicit Contracting, and Dry/Wet Counties. *Econ. Inquiry*, July 1988, *26*(3), pp. 507–24.

——— and Long, James E. The Determinants of Private School Attendance, 1970–1980. *Rev. Econ. Statist.*, May 1988, *70*(2), pp. 351–57.

Toma, Mark. The Role of the Federal Reserve in Reserve Requirement Regulation. *Cato J.*, Winter 1988, *7*(3), pp. 701–18.

———. The Role of the Federal Reserve in Reserve Requirement Regulation. In *England, C. and Huertas, T., eds.*, 1988, pp. 209–26.

Toman, Michael A. and Bohi, Douglas R. Restructuring the IEA Crisis Management Program to Serve Members' Interests Better. In *Horwich, G. and Weimer, D. L., eds.*, 1988, pp. 200–217.

Tomaselli, Sylvana. Moral Philosophy and Population Questions in Eighteenth Century Europe. *Population Devel. Rev.*, Supplement, 1988, *14*, pp. 7–29.

Tomashkevich, V. The Ministry and the Democratism of Management: How to Overcome the "Silent" Power of the Apparatus. *Prob. Econ.*, November 1988, *31*(7), pp. 6–12.

Tomaskovic-Devey, Donald. Market Concentration and Structural Power as Sources of Industrial Productivity. In *Farkas, G. and England, P., eds.*, 1988, pp. 141–54.

Tomasson, Richard F.; Nash, Gerald D. and Pugach, Noel H. An Overview of American Social Security, 1935–1985. In *Nash, G. D.; Pugach, N. H. and Tomasson, R. F., eds.*, 1988, pp. 3–28.

Tombak, Mihkel. The Effect of Technological Uncertainty on the Optimal Location of a Competitive Firm. *J. Urban Econ.*, July 1988, *24*(1), pp. 38–43.

Tomczak, Franciszek. The Development Strategy of Agriculture in Poland. In *Brada, J. C. and Wadekin, K.-E., eds.*, 1988, pp. 159–69.

Tomer, John F. Worker Participation: Paths to Higher Productivity and Well-Being. In *Maital, S., ed., Vol. 2*, 1988, pp. 637–49.

Tomes, Nigel. Inheritance and Inequality within the Family: Equal Division among Unequals, or do the Poor Get More? In *Kessler, D. and Masson, A., eds.*, 1988, pp. 79–104.

———. The Intergenerational Transmission of Wealth and the Rise and Fall of Families. In *Kessler, D. and Masson, A., eds.*, 1988, pp. 147–65.

Tomiak, Monica and Bollman, Ray D. Decoupled Agricultural Policy and the Lack of Production Alternatives. *Can. J. Agr. Econ.*, July 1988, *36*(2), pp. 349–52.

Tomkins, Cyril and Marshall, Paul. Incorporating Discounted Cash Flow Contours onto a BCG Portfolio Matrix Using Limit Pricing. *Managerial Dec. Econ.*, June 1988, *9*(2), pp. 119–26.

Toms, Miroslav. Quantity and Price Parameters in Economic Mechanism: Towards a Synthesis. *Czech. Econ. Pap.*, 1988, (25), pp. 53–77.

Tonaka, Masatomo and Kosuge, Toshio. Project on the Pacific Region: A Proposal for the Formation of Education Relationship Networks. In *Kozmetsky, G.; Matsumoto, H. and Smilor, R. W., eds.*, 1988, pp. 161–79.

van Tongeren, Frank and de Kruijk, Hans. Growth, Employment and Education: An Application of Multicriteria Analysis to Pakistan. *Pakistan Devel. Rev.*, Part 2, Winter 1988, *27*(4), pp. 725–33.

Tongren, Hale N. Determinant Behavior Characteristics of Older Consumers. *J. Cons. Aff.*, Summer 1988, *22*(1), pp. 136–57.

Toniolo, Gianni. Alexander Gerschenkron e l'Italia. Alcune considerazioni nel decimo anniversario della morte. (Alexander Gerschenkron and Italy. Some Considerations on the Tenth Anniversary of His Death. With English summary.) *Rivista Storia Econ.*, S.S., October 1988, *5*(3), pp. 397–404.

——— and Piva, Francesco. Unemployment in the 1930s: The Case of Italy. In *Eichengreen, B. and Hatton, T. J., eds.*, 1988, pp. 221–45.

Tonkin, S. and Webber, Michael. Technical Changes and the Rate of Profit in the Canadian Textile, Knitting, and Clothing Industries. *Environ. Planning A*, November 1988, *20*(11), pp. 1487–1505.

——— and Webber, Michael. Technical Changes and the Rate of Profit in the Canadian Wood, Furniture, and Paper Industries. *Environ. Planning A*, December 1988, *20*(12), pp. 1623–43.

Tonks, Ian and Snell, Andy. The Sweet Taste of Information: A Study of the Demand for New Brands in the UK Confectionery Industry. *Appl. Econ.*, August 1988, *20*(8), pp. 1041–55.

Tonn, B. E. A Method for the Nonstatistical Assessment of Behaviorally-Based Policy Models. *Environ. Planning A*, May 1988, *20*(5), pp. 669–79.

———. Philosophical Aspects of 500-Year Planning. *Environ. Planning A*, November 1988, *20*(11), pp. 1507–22.

Tool, Marc R. The Compulsive Shift to Institutional Analysis. In *Samuels, W. J., ed., Vol. 1*, 1988, *1981*, pp. 108–31.

———. Evolutionary Economics: Volume 1: Foundations of Institutional Thought: Introduction. In *Tool, M. R., ed., Vol. 1*, 1988, pp. 1–17.

———. A Social Value Theory in Neoinstitutional Economics. In *Samuels, W. J., ed., Vol. 3*, 1988, *1977*, pp. 24–47.

———; Street, James H. and Arestis, Philip. In Memoriam: Alfred S. Eichner 1937–1988. *J. Econ. Issues*, December 1988, *22*(4), pp. 1239–42.

Topalov, Christian. Régulation publique du capitalisme et propriété de masse du logement: La "révolution hypothécaire" des années 1930 aux Etats-Unis. (State-Regulated Capitalism and Mass Home Property: The "Mortgage" Revolution of the Thirties in the USA. With English summary.) *Écon. Soc.*, May 1988, *22*(5), pp. 51–99.

Topel, Robert H. Some Recent Developments in Labor Economics and Their Implications for Macroeconomics: Comment. *J. Money, Credit, Banking*, Part 2, August 1988, *20*(3), pp. 523–26.

——— and Rosen, Sherwin. Housing Investment in the United States. *J. Polit. Econ.*, August 1988, *96*(4), pp. 718–40.

——— and Weiss, Laurence. Sectoral Uncertainty and Unemployment. In *Hart, R. A., ed.*, 1988, pp. 344–63.

Topp, Niels-Henrik. Fiscal Policy in Denmark 1930–1945. *Europ. Econ. Rev.*, March 1988, *32*(2–3), pp. 512–18.

Torbert, Preston M. Selected U.S. Law Aspects of Technology-Transfer Contracts between U.S. and Chinese Parties. In *Teng, W. and Wang, N. T., eds.*, 1988, pp. 223–32.

Torelli, Nicola; Trivellato, Ugo and Rettore, Enrico. Disoccupazione e ricerca di lavoro: Convenzioni definitorie e analisi esplorative sull' "attachment" al mercato del lavoro. (Unemployment and Job Search: Defining Conventions and Exploratory Analyses for Labour Market "Attachment." With English summary.) *Econ. Lavoro*, July–Sept. 1988, *22*(3), pp. 71–94.

Torkanovskii, E. Socialist Self-management of Production. *Prob. Econ.*, February 1988, *30*(10), pp. 69–84.

Törnblom, Kjell Y. Positive and Negative Allocations: A Typology and a Model for Conflicting Justice Principles. In *Lawler, E. J. and Markovsky, B., eds.*, 1988, pp. 141–68.

Torous, Walter N. and Ball, Clifford A. Investigating Security-Price Performance in the Presence of Event-Date Uncertainty. *J. Finan. Econ.*, October 1988, *22*(1), pp. 123–53.

Torrance, Thomas S. and MacDonald, Ronald. Covered Interest Parity and UK Monetary 'News.' *Econ. Letters*, 1988, *26*(1), pp. 53–56.

_____ **and MacDonald, Ronald.** Exchange Rates and the "News": Some Evidence Using U.K. Survey Data. *Manchester Sch. Econ. Soc. Stud.*, March 1988, *56*(1), pp. 69–76.

_____ **and MacDonald, Ronald.** Monetary Policy and the Real Interest Rate: Some U.K. Evidence. *Scot. J. Polit. Econ.*, November 1988, *35*(4), pp. 361–71.

_____ **and MacDonald, Ronald.** On Risk, Rationality and Excessive Speculation in the Deutschmark–U.S. Dollar Exchange Market: Some Evidence Using Survey Data. *Oxford Bull. Econ. Statist.*, May 1988, *50*(2), pp. 107–23.

Torre, André. Chocs exogènes et répercussions sur la circulation monétaire nationale. (External Monetary Shocks upon the National Circuit. With English summary.) *Écon. Soc.*, June–July 1988, *22*(6–7), pp. 165–80.

_____. Une approche structurelle de la relation secteur énergétique–système productif. (Structural Analysis of the Relations between Energy Sector and Productive System. With English summary.) *Écon. Soc.*, April 1988, *22*(4), pp. 59–87.

Torre, Dominique; Arena, Richard and Froeschle, Claude. Formation des prix et équilibre classique. Un examen préliminaire. (Price Formation and Classical Equilibrium: A Preliminary Investigation. With English summary.) *Revue Écon.*, November 1988, *39*(6), pp. 1097–1117.

de la Torre, José and Neckar, David H. Forecasting Political Risks for International Operations. *Int. J. Forecasting*, 1988, *4*(2), pp. 221–41.

Torrey, Barbara Boyle. Assets of the Aged: Clues

and Issues. *Population Devel. Rev.*, September 1988, *14*(3), pp. 489–97.

_____ **and Jencks, Christopher.** Beyond Income and Poverty: Trends in Social Welfare among Children and the Elderly since 1960. In *Palmer, J. L.; Smeeding, T. and Torrey, B. B., eds.*, 1988, pp. 229–73.

_____; **Palmer, John L. and Smeeding, Timothy M.** The Vulnerable: Introduction. In *Palmer, J. L.; Smeeding, T. and Torrey, B. B., eds.*, 1988, pp. 1–6.

_____; **Rein, Martin and Smeeding, Timothy M.** Patterns of Income and Poverty: The Economic Status of Children and the Elderly in Eight Countries. In *Palmer, J. L.; Smeeding, T. and Torrey, B. B., eds.*, 1988, pp. 89–119.

Torrion, Phillippe and Gouni, Lucien. Risk and Cost of Failure in the French Electricity System. *Energy J.*, Special Issue, 1988, *9*, pp. 33–37.

Torrisi, Alfio. The International Equities Market: Recent Developments and Prospects. *Rev. Econ. Cond. Italy*, Sept.–Dec. 1988, (3), pp. 333–52.

Torto, Raymond G. and Wheaton, William C. Vacancy Rates and the Future of Office Rents. *Amer. Real Estate Urban Econ. Assoc. J.*, Winter 1988, *16*(4), pp. 430–36.

Toruño, Mayo C. Appraisals and Rational Reconstructions of General Competitive Equilibrium Theory. *J. Econ. Issues*, March 1988, *22*(1), pp. 127–55.

Toshimitzu, Tsuyoshi. Intra-industry Trade and Effective Demand: Product Differentiation, International Price Competition, and Vintage Model. *Kobe Univ. Econ.*, 1988, (34), pp. 117–33.

Tosi, Gilbert. Equilibre d'anticipation rationnelle sur le marché du crédit: Un exemple. (Rational Expectation Equilibrium in Loan Market. With English summary.) *Écon. Appl.*, 1988, *41*(3), pp. 523–42.

Tosini, Elisabetta and Vercellis, Carlo. An Interactive System for Extra-Urban Vehicle and Crew Scheduling Problems. In *Daduna, J. R. and Wren, A., eds.*, 1988, pp. 41–53.

Tosini, Paula. After the Crash: Linkages between Stocks and Futures: Regulatory Issues. In *MacKay, R. J., ed.*, 1988, pp. 45–47.

Tötsch, Inge. Screening in Labour Markets with Heterogeneous Workers. In *Cross, R., ed.*, 1988, pp. 180–200.

Tottle, Graham P. and Bakar, Kamuruddin Abu. Microcomputer Use by the Malaysian Rubber Industry Smallholders Development Authority. In *Bhalla, A. S. and James, D., eds.*, 1988, pp. 85–96.

Toufique, Kazi Ali. Sharecropping: Efficiency and Risk—A Note. *Bangladesh Devel. Stud.*, June 1988, *16*(2), pp. 91–94.

Toulmin, Camilla. Livestock Policy in the Sahel: Why It Must Become More Drought Oriented. In *Curtis, D.; Hubbard, M. and Shepherd, A.*, 1988, pp. 171–77.

Toulouse, Jean-Marie; Côté, Marcel and Lemelin, Maurice. The Management–Industrial Relations Interface: Exploring the Conceptual Linkages. In *Hébert, G.; Jain, H. C. and Meltz, N. M., eds..*, 1988, pp. 147–86.

Toumanoff, Peter. Economic Reform and Industrial Performance in the Soviet Union 1950–1984. In *Linz, S. J. and Moskoff, W., eds.*, 1988, pp. 110–28.

Tovias, Alfred. Discrimination in International Trade—A Review. *Weltwirtsch. Arch.*, 1988, *124*(2), pp. 356–60.

———. Trade Discrimination in the Thirties and Eighties. *World Econ.*, December 1988, *11*(4), pp. 501–14.

Tower, Edward. Explaining the Yeh Paradox: A Comment [The Maximum Revenue Tariff vs. Transfer Payments]. *Eastern Econ. J.*, April–June 1988, *14*(2), pp. 189–92.

——— **and Christiansen, Robert E.** Effect of a Fertilizer Subsidy on Income Distribution and Efficiency in Malawi. *Eastern Afr. Econ. Rev.*, December 1988, *4*(2), pp. 49–58.

——— **and Csaplar, Wilfrid W., Jr.** Trade and Industrial Policy under Oligopoly: Comment. *Quart. J. Econ.*, August 1988, *103*(3), pp. 599–602.

——— **and Gang, Ira N.** The Stahl–Alexeev Paradox: A Note. *J. Econ. Theory*, February 1988, *44*(1), pp. 189–91.

Townley, Peter G. C. and Boadway, Robin W. Social Security and the Failure of Annuity Markets. *J. Public Econ.*, February 1988, *35*(1), pp. 75–96.

Townsend, Robert M. Information Constrained Insurance: The Revelation Principle Extended. *J. Monet. Econ.*, March–May 1988, *21*(2–3), pp. 411–50.

———. Models as Economies. *Econ. J.*, Supplement, 1988, *98*(390), pp. 1–24.

Toyoda, Toshihisa; Ohtani, Kazuhiro and Katayama, Sei-ichi. Estimation of Structural Change in the Import and Export Equations: An International Comparison. In *Uno, K. and Shishido, S., eds.*, 1988, pp. 52–64.

Tracy, Joseph and Gyourko, Joseph. An Analysis of Public- and Private-Sector Wages Allowing for Endogenous Choices of Both Government and Union Status. *J. Lab. Econ.*, April 1988, *6*(2), pp. 229–53.

Train, Kenneth E. Incentives for Energy Conservation in the Commercial and Industrial Sectors. *Energy J.*, July 1988, *9*(3), pp. 113–28.

——— **and Woo, Chi-Keung.** The Cost of Electric Power Interruptions to Commercial Firms. *Energy J.*, Special Issue, 1988, 9, pp. 161–72.

Tran, Dang T. and Sawhney, Bansi L. Government Deficits, Capital Flows, and Interest Rates. *Appl. Econ.*, June 1988, *20*(6), pp. 753–65.

Tran-Nam, Binh and Nevile, John W. The Effects of Birthplace on Male Earnings in Australia. *Australian Econ. Pap.*, June 1988, *27*(50), pp. 83–101.

Tran, Van Tho. Foreign Capital and Technology in the Process of Catching Up by the Developing Countries: The Experience of the Synthetic

Fiber Industry in the Republic of Korea. *Devel. Econ.*, December 1988, *26*(4), pp. 386–402.

Trapp, James N. Investment and Disinvestment Principles with Nonconstant Prices and Varying Firm Size Applied to Beef-Breeding Herds: Reply. *Amer. J. Agr. Econ.*, November 1988, *70*(4), pp. 938–40.

Trapp, Peter and Langfeldt, Enno. Experiences in Macroeconomic Forecasting in the Federal Republic of Germany 1976–1987. *Jahr. Nationalökon. Statist.*, November 1988, *205*(5), pp. 427–42.

——— **and Soltwedel, Rüdiger.** Labor Market Barriers to More Employment: Causes for an Increase of the Natural Rate? The Case of West Germany. In *Giersch, H., ed.*, 1988, pp. 181–225.

Traugott, Mark. The Crowd in the French Revolution of February, 1848. *Amer. Hist. Rev.*, June 1988, *93*(3), pp. 638–52.

———. Interdependencies in Global Crisis: France and England in the Mid-nineteenth Century. In *Burke, E., III, ed.*, 1988, *1983*, pp. 13–24.

Trautmann, S. OPTRAD: A Decision Support System for Portfolio Management in Stock and Options Markets. In *Gaul, W. and Schader, M., eds.*, 1988, pp. 185–203.

Trautwein, Hans-Michael. Zur Entschärfung tarifpolitischer Verteilungskonflikte durch kollektive Kapitalbeteiligung: Das Beispiel der schwedischen Arbeitnehmerfonds. (Wage Policy Conflicts and Collective Stock-Sharing: The Case of the Swedish Wage-Earner Funds. With English summary.) *Jahr. Nationalökon. Statist.*, February 1988, *204*(2), pp. 155–74.

Travers, T. Local Taxation and Services: Present and Future. *Reg. Stud.*, June 1988, *22*(3), pp. 235–38.

Travlos, Nickolaos G. and Doukas, John. The Effect of Corporate Multinationalism on Shareholders' Wealth: Evidence from International Acquisitions. *J. Finance*, December 1988, *43*(5), pp. 1161–75.

de Tray, Dennis. Government Policy, Household Behavior, and the Distribution of Schooling: A Case Study of Malaysia. In *Schultz, T. Paul, ed.*, 1988, pp. 303–36.

Treadgold, M. L. Intercensal Change in Aboriginal Incomes, 1976–1986. *Australian Bull. Lab.*, September 1988, *14*(4), pp. 592–609.

Trebilcock, Michael J. The Role of Insurance Considerations in the Choice of Efficient Civil Liability Rules. *J. Law, Econ., Organ.*, Fall 1988, *4*(2), pp. 243–65.

Trebing, Harry M. Regulation of Industry: An Institutionalist Approach. In *Tool, M. R., ed., Vol. 2*, 1988, *1987*, pp. 289–319.

Trehan, Bharat. The Practice of Monetary Targeting: A Case Study of the West German Experience. *Fed. Res. Bank San Francisco Econ. Rev.*, Spring 1988, (2), pp. 30–44.

——— **and Walsh, Carl E.** Common Trends, the Government's Budget Constraint, and Revenue Smoothing. *J. Econ. Dynam. Control*, June–Sept. 1988, *12*(2–3), pp. 425–44.

Treisman, Michel. The St. Petersburg Paradox and the Expectation Heuristic. In *Maital, S., ed., Vol. 2,* 1988, pp. 668–76.

Trejo Reyes, Saul. Financing vs. Forgiving a Debt Overhang: Comments. *J. Devel. Econ.,* November 1988, *29*(3), pp. 269–70.

Trela, Irene; Whalley, John and Wigle, Randall. International Trade in Grains: Domestic Policies and Trade Impacts. In *Haaland, J. I. and Norman, V. D., eds.,* 1988, pp. 55–67.

Tremayne, A. R.; Geweke, John and Godfrey, Leslie G. Diagnostics for the Diagnostics: Discussion of "Checks of Model Adequacy for Univariate Time Series Models and Their Application to Econometric Relationships." *Econometric Rev.,* 1988, *7*(1), pp. 59–62.

_____ **and Godfrey, Leslie G.** Checks of Model Adequacy for Univariate Time Series Models and Their Application to Econometric Relationships: Reply. *Econometric Rev.,* 1988, *7*(1), pp. 63–64.

_____ **and Godfrey, Leslie G.** Checks of Model Adequacy for Univariate Time Series Models and Their Application to Econometric Relationships. *Econometric Rev.,* 1988, *7*(1), pp. 1–42.

Tremblay, Carol Horton and Ragan, James F., Jr. Testing for Employee Discrimination by Race and Sex. *J. Human Res.,* Winter 1988, *23*(1), pp. 123–37.

_____ **and Tremblay, Victor J.** The Determinants of Horizontal Acquisitions: Evidence from the U.S. Brewing Industry. *J. Ind. Econ.,* September 1988, *37*(1), pp. 21–45.

Tremblay, Victor J. and Kao, Kai. Cigarette "Health Scare," Excise Taxes, and Advertising Ban: Comment. *Southern Econ. J.,* January 1988, *54*(3), pp. 770–76.

_____ **and Tremblay, Carol Horton.** The Determinants of Horizontal Acquisitions: Evidence from the U.S. Brewing Industry. *J. Ind. Econ.,* September 1988, *37*(1), pp. 21–45.

_____ **and Wohl, Lawrence A.** The Thick Point Theorem. *J. Econ. Educ.,* Summer 1988, *19*(3), pp. 269–70.

Treml, Vladimir G. *Perestroyka* and Soviet Statistics. *Soviet Econ.,* Jan.–March 1988, *4*(1), pp. 65–94.

Trengove, C. D. and Logan, J. Health Insurance Forum. In *Butler, J. R. G. and Doessel, D. P., eds.,* 1988, pp. 242–45.

Trennepohl, Gary L.; Booth, James R. and Tehranian, Hassan. An Empirical Analysis of Insured Portfolio Strategies Using Listing Options. *J. Finan. Res.,* Spring 1988, *11*(1), pp. 1–12.

de Trenqualye, Pierre. Stability of the Groves and Ledyard Mechanism. *J. Econ. Theory,* October 1988, *46*(1), pp. 164–71.

Trescott, Paul B. Bank Failures, Interest Rates, and the Great Currency Outflow in the United States, 1929–1933. In *Uselding, P. J., ed.,* 1988, pp. 49–80.

Tresnowski, Bernard R. The Current Interest in Quality Is Nothing New. *Inquiry,* Spring 1988, *25*(1), pp. 3–5.

Tressler, J. H. and Menezes, C. F. The Comparative Statics of a Competitive Industry Facing Demand Uncertainty. *Econ. Letters,* 1988, *26*(4), pp. 315–19.

Tretheway, Michael W.; Gillen, David W. and Oum, Tae Hoon. Entry Barriers and Anti-competitive Behaviour in a Deregulated Airline Market: The Case of Canada. *Int. J. Transport Econ.,* February 1988, *15*(1), pp. 29–41.

_____ **; Gillen, David W. and Stanbury, W. T.** Duopoly in Canada's Airline Industry: Consequences and Policy Issues. *Can. Public Policy,* March 1988, *14*(1), pp. 15–31.

_____ **and Oum, Tae Hoon.** Ramsey Pricing in the Presence of Externality Costs. *J. Transp. Econ. Policy,* September 1988, *22*(3), pp. 307–17.

Treue, Wilhelm. The Bankers Simon and Abraham Oppenheim 1812–1880: The Private Background to Their Professional Activity, Their Role in Politics and Ennoblement. In *Pohl, H. and Rudolph, B., eds.,* 1988, pp. 41–76.

Trevino, Angel Gurria. Debt Restructuring: Mexico as a Case Study. In *Griffith-Jones, S., ed.,* 1988, pp. 64–112.

Trevithick, James and Kaldor, Nicholas. A Keynesian Perspective on Money. In *Sawyer, M. C., ed.,* 1988, *1981,* pp. 101–19.

Trevor, R. G. and Thorp, S. J. VAR Forecasting Models of the Australian Economy: A Preliminary Analysis. *Australian Econ. Pap.,* Supplement, June 1988, *27,* pp. 108–20.

Triantis, John E.; Kaen, Fred R. and Simos, Evangelos O. A Term Structure Monetary Model of Exchange Rate Determination. *Econ. Notes,* 1988, (2), pp. 82–92.

_____ **and Simos, Evangelos O.** A Note on Productivity, Inflation and Causality. *Rivista Int. Sci. Econ. Com.,* September 1988, *35*(9), pp. 839–46.

_____ **and Simos, Evangelos O.** The Theory of Permanent Income. In *Pesek, B. P.,* 1988, *1981,* pp. 236–39.

Tribe, Keith. Friedrich List and the Critique of "Cosmopolitical Economy." *Manchester Sch. Econ. Soc. Stud.,* March 1988, *56*(1), pp. 17–36.

Tribedy, Gopal; Beladi, Hamid and Biswas, Basudeb. A Two Sector Analysis of Protection and Negative Value-Added. *Indian Econ. J.,* April–June 1988, *35*(4), pp. 25–32.

Trieschmann, James S. and Gustavson, Sandra G. Universal Life Insurance as an Alternative to the Joint and Survivor Annuity. *J. Risk Ins.,* September 1988, *55*(3), pp. 529–38.

Trigeorgis, Lenos. A Conceptual Options Framework for Capital Budgeting. In *Fabozzi, F. J., ed.,* 1988, pp. 145–67.

Trigueros, Ignacio. Real and Monetary Determinants of Real Exchange Rate Behavior: Theory and Evidence from Developing Countries: Comment. *J. Devel. Econ.,* November 1988, *29*(3), pp. 343–45.

Trincão, Victor M. and Comprido, Francisco J. Semi-aggregate Consumption in Portugal:

1958–1975. *Economia (Portugal)*, January 1988, *12*(1), pp. 103–14.

Trivedi, Pravin K. Statistical Software Tools (SST) Version 1.1: A Review. *J. Appl. Econometrics*, July–Sept. 1988, *3*(3), pp. 235–39.

———— **and Alexander, J. N.** Incorporating International Competitiveness into the Demand for Labour Function: Some Issues of Specification and Interpretation. *Econ. Rec.*, September 1988, *64*(186), pp. 196–208.

Trivedi, Vishwapati. Corruption, Delivery Systems and Property Rights: A Comment. *World Devel.*, November 1988, *16*(11), pp. 1389–91.

Trivellato, Ugo; Rettore, Enrico and Torelli, Nicola. Disoccupazione e ricerca di lavoro: Convenzioni definitorie e analisi esplorative sull' "attachment" al mercato del lavoro. (Unemployment and Job Search: Defining Conventions and Exploratory Analyses for Labour Market "Attachment." With English summary.) *Econ. Lavoro*, July–Sept. 1988, *22*(3), pp. 71–94.

Trolle, Eskil. Security on Movable Property and Receivables in Europe: Denmark. In *Dickson, M. G.; Rosener, W. and Storm, P. M., eds.*, 1988, pp. 24–36.

Tronti, Leonello. La remunerazione dell'anzianità di lavoro nel settore pubblico. Un'analisi con un modello meccanico. (Rewarding Job Seniority in the Public Sector. With English summary.) *Econ. Lavoro*, Oct.–Dec. 1988, *22*(4), pp. 33–53.

Tronzano, Marco. Exchange-Rate Volatility and Uncovered Interest Parity: An Empirical Note. *Econ. Int.*, Feb.–March 1988, *41*(1–2), pp. 88–100.

————. Is the Foreign-Exchange Market Efficient? Some Evidence from the Recent Floating Period. *Rivista Int. Sci. Econ. Com.*, Oct.–Nov. 1988, *35*(10–11), pp. 1031–51.

Tropper, Peter and Gill, David. Emerging Stock Markets in Developing Countries. *Finance Develop.*, December 1988, *25*(4), pp. 28–37.

Trott, Edward A., Jr.; Friedenberg, Howard L. and Renshaw, Vernon. Gross State Product by Industry, 1963–86. *Surv. Curr. Bus.*, May 1988, *68*(5), pp. 30–46.

Troutt, Marvin D. A Purchase Timing Model for Life Insurance Decision Support Systems. *J. Risk Ins.*, December 1988, *55*(4), pp. 628–43.

Trow, Donald B.; Cyert, Richard M. and Simon, Herbert A. Observation of a Business Decision. In *Cyert, R. M.*, 1988, *1956*, pp. 20–35.

Truchon, Michel and Campbell, Donald E. Boundary Optima and the Theory of Public Goods Supply. *J. Public Econ.*, March 1988, *35*(2), pp. 241–49.

Trude, Sally; Keeler, Emmett B. and Carter, Grace M. Insurance Aspects of DRG Outlier Payments. *J. Health Econ.*, September 1988, *7*(3), pp. 193–214.

Trueman, Brett. A Theory of Noise Trading in Securities Markets. *J. Finance*, March 1988, *43*(1), pp. 83–95.

———— **and Masulis, Ronald W.** Corporate Investment and Dividend Decisions under Differen-

tial Personal Taxation. *J. Finan. Quant. Anal.*, December 1988, *23*(4), pp. 369–85.

———— **and Titman, Sheridan D.** An Explanation for Accounting Income Smoothing. *J. Acc. Res.*, Supplement, 1988, *26*, pp. 127–39.

Truex, Gregory F. Crime in the Development Process. In *Bennett, J. W. and Bowen, J. R., eds.*, 1988, pp. 185–98.

Truitt, J. Frederick; Moxon, Richard W. and Roehl, Thomas W. International Cooperative Ventures in the Commercial Aircraft Industry: Gains, Sure, But What's My Share? In *Contractor, F. J. and Lorange, P.*, 1988, pp. 255–77.

Truong, Truong P.; Hensher, David A. and Barnard, Peter O. The Role of Stated Preference Methods in Studies of Travel Choice. *J. Transp. Econ. Policy*, January 1988, *22*(1), pp. 45–58.

Trussell, James. Does Family Planning Reduce Infant Mortality? An Exchange. *Population Devel. Rev.*, March 1988, *14*(1), pp. 171–78.

————; **John, A. Meredith and Menken, Jane A.** Estimating the Distribution of Interval Length: Current Status and Retrospective History Data. *Population Stud.*, March 1988, *42*(1), pp. 115–27.

Truu, M. L. Approaches to the South African Economy. *J. Stud. Econ. Econometrics*, March 1988, *12*(1), pp. 1–16.

————. Economics of Privatization. *S. Afr. J. Econ.*, December 1988, *56*(4), pp. 251–69.

Tryon, Ralph W. Empirical Macroeconomics for Interdependent Economies: Comparison and Evaluation of Model Simulations: Comment. In *Bryant, R. C., et al., eds.*, 1988, pp. 152–54.

———— **and Edison, Hali J.** An Empirical Analysis of Policy Co-Ordination in the United States, Japan and Europe. In *Motamen, H., ed.*, 1988, pp. 53–70.

Tsakloglou, Panos. Development and Inequality Revisited. *Appl. Econ.*, April 1988, *20*(4), pp. 509–31.

Tsaur, Tien-wang; Chen, Chau-nan and Lai, Ching-chong. The Loanable Funds Theory and the Dynamics of Exchange Rates: The Mundell Model Revisited. *J. Int. Money Finance*, June 1988, *7*(2), pp. 221–29.

Tsay, Jeffrey J. and Hall, Thomas W. An Evaluation of the Performance of Portfolios Selected from Value Line Rank One Stocks: 1976–1982. *J. Finan. Res.*, Fall 1988, *11*(3), pp. 227–40.

Tschetter, John. An Evaluation of BLS Projections of the 1985 Economy. *Mon. Lab. Rev.*, September 1988, *111*(9), pp. 24–33.

Tschirhart, John; Atkinson, Scott E. and Stanley, Linda R. Revenue Sharing as an Incentive in an Agency Problem: An Example from the National Football League. *Rand J. Econ.*, Spring 1988, *19*(1), pp. 27–43.

Tschoegl, Adrian E. The Source and Consequences of Stop Orders: A Conjecture. *Managerial Dec. Econ.*, March 1988, *9*(1), pp. 83–85.

———— **and Lessard, Donald R.** Panama's International Banking Center: The Direct Employment Effects. *J. Banking Finance*, 1988, *12*(1), pp. 43–50.

Tse, Y. K. and McAleer, Michael. A Sequential Testing Procedure for Outliers and Structural Change. *Econometric Rev.*, 1988, 7(1), pp. 103–11.

―――― **and Sargan, John Denis.** Edgeworth Approximations for 2SLS Estimates of a Dynamic Models. In *Sargan, J. D., Vol. 2*, 1988, pp. 172–81.

Tseng, Kuo C. Low Price, Price–Earnings Ratio, Market Value, and Abnormal Stock Returns. *Financial Rev.*, August 1988, *23*(3), pp. 333–43.

Tsiang, Sho-Chieh. The Flow Formulation of a Monetary Model for an Open Economy and the Determination of the Exchange Rate. In *Kohn, M. and Tsiang, S.-C., eds.*, 1988, pp. 15–35.

Tsigas, Marinos E. and Hertel, Thomas W. Tax Policy and U.S. Agriculture: A General Equilibrium Analysis. *Amer. J. Agr. Econ.*, May 1988, *70*(2), pp. 289–302.

Tsipko, A. S. Reflections on the Historical Stability of the Cooperative System. *Prob. Econ.*, May 1988, *31*(1), pp. 30–59.

Tso, Y. Allen. Monetary Expansion, International Trade and Capital Accumulation. *Econ. Rec.*, June 1988, *64*(185), pp. 113–19.

Tsoukalis, Loukas. On Multilateral Surveillance: Perspective. In *Guerrieri, P. and Padoan, P. C., eds.*, 1988, pp. 87–90.

Tsui, Kai Yuen. The Measurement of Export Instability: A Methodological Note. *Econ. Letters*, 1988, *27*(1), pp. 61–65.

Tsui, Kwok-Leung; Jewell, Nicholas P. and Wu, C. F. Jeff. A Nonparametric Approach to the Truncated Regression Problem. *J. Amer. Statist. Assoc.*, September 1988, *83*(403), pp. 785–92.

Tsukahara, Yasuhiro. A Simple Theoretical Model of the Fungibility Hypothesis. *Public Finance*, 1988, *43*(3), pp. 440–44.

Tsukui, Jinkichi, et al. Public Consumption Turnpike Model and the Long Term National Planning of Japan. In *Uno, K. and Shishido, S., eds.*, 1988, pp. 111–27.

Tsuru, Tsuyoshi. Change in the Wage–Unemployment Relation: The Reserve Army Effect in the Postwar Japanese Economy. *Econ. Rev. (Keizai Kenkyu)*, July 1988, *39*(3), pp. 242–52.

Tsurumi, Hiroki and Shiba, Tsunemasa. Bayesian and Non-Bayesian Tests of Independence in Seemingly Unrelated Regressions. *Int. Econ. Rev.*, May 1988, *29*(2), pp. 377–95.

Tsutakawa, Robert K. Mixed Model for Analyzing Geographic Variability in Mortality Rates. *J. Amer. Statist. Assoc.*, March 1988, *83*(401), pp. 37–42.

Tsypkin, Mikhail. The Soviet Union Today: The Armed Forces: The Conscripts. In *Cracraft, J., ed.*, 1988, pp. 105–13.

Tubiana, Laurence and Leclercq, Vincent. La remise en cause du rôle des États-Unis dans le fonctionnement oligopoliste des marchés du blé et du soja. (The Challenge to the United States' Role in the Oligopolistic Operation of the Wheat and Soya Markets. With English summary.) *Écon. Soc.*, Nov.–Dec. 1988, *22*(11–12), pp. 105–22.

Tucci, Marco P. The Stochastic Parameter Problem: A Survey of the Literature. *Econ. Notes*, 1988, (3), pp. 112–36.

Tucker, Alan L. and Ang, James S. The Shareholder Wealth Effects of Corporate Greenmail. *J. Finan. Res.*, Winter 1988, *11*(4), pp. 265–80.

―――― **and Ogden, Joseph P.** The Relative Valuation of American Currency Spot and Futures Options: Theory and Empirical Tests. *J. Finan. Quant. Anal.*, December 1988, *23*(4), pp. 351–68.

―――― **and Peterson, David R.** Implied Spot Rates as Predictors of Currency Returns: A Note [Option Prices as Predictors of Equilibrium Stock Prices]. *J. Finance*, March 1988, *43*(1), pp. 247–58.

――――; **Peterson, David R. and Scott, Elton.** Tests of the Black–Scholes and Constant Elasticity of Variance Currency Call Option Valuation Models. *J. Finan. Res.*, Fall 1988, *11*(3), pp. 201–13.

―――― **and Pond, Lallon.** The Probability Distribution of Foreign Exchange Price Changes: Tests of Candidate Processes. *Rev. Econ. Statist.*, November 1988, *70*(4), pp. 638–47.

Tucker, C. Jack; Urton, William L. and Long, Larry. Measuring Migration Distances: Self-reporting and Indirect Methods. *J. Amer. Statist. Assoc.*, September 1988, *83*(403), pp. 674–78.

――――; **Urton, William L. and Long, Larry.** Migration Distances: An International Comparison. *Demography*, November 1988, *25*(4), pp. 633–40.

Tucker, Irvin B., III. Entrepreneurs and Public-Sector Employees: The Role of Achievement Motivation and Risk in Occupational Choice. *J. Econ. Educ.*, Summer 1988, *19*(3), pp. 259–68.

Tucker, Richard P. The British Empire and India's Forest Resources: The Timberlands of Assam and Kumaon, 1914–1950. In *Richards, J. F. and Tucker, R. P., eds.*, 1988, pp. 91–111.

―――― **and Richards, John F.** World Deforestation in the Twentieth Century: Introduction. In *Richards, J. F. and Tucker, R. P., eds.*, 1988, pp. 1–12.

Tuckman, Howard P. Supply, Human Capital, and the Average Quality Level of the Science and Engineering Labor Force. *Econ. Educ. Rev.*, 1988, 7(4), pp. 405–21.

―――― **and Chang, Cyril F.** Cost Convergence between For-Profit and Not-for-Profit Nursing Homes: Does Competition Matter? *Quart. Rev. Econ. Bus.*, Winter 1988, *28*(4), pp. 50–65.

Tuijnman, Albert; Chinapah, Vinayagum and Fägerlind, Ingemar. Adult Education and Earnings: A 45-Year Longitudinal Study of 834

Swedish Men. *Econ. Educ. Rev.*, 1988, 7(4), pp. 423–37.

van Tulder, Rob. Small European Countries in the International Telecommunications Struggle. In *Freeman, C. and Lundvall, B.-A., eds.*, 1988, pp. 169–83.

Tull, M. T. The Financial Performance of the Fremantle Harbour Trust, 1903 to 1939. *Australian Econ. Hist. Rev.*, March 1988, 28(1), pp. 21–42.

Tullio, Giuseppe and Sommariva, Andrea. Notes, Comments, Replies: International Gold Flows in Gold Standard Germany: A Test of the Monetary Approach to the Balance of Payments, 1880–1911. *J. Money, Credit, Banking*, February 1988, 20(1), pp. 132–40.

Tullock, Gordon. An Economic Analysis of Political Choice. In *Tullock, G.*, 1988, pp. 36–43.

_____. An Economic Approach to Crime. In *Alper, N. O. and Hellman, D. A., eds.*, 1988, pp. 87–103.

_____. The Costs of Rent Seeking: A Metaphysical Problem. *Public Choice*, April 1988, 57(1), pp. 15–24.

_____. Does Punishment Deter Crime? In *Alper, N. O. and Hellman, D. A., eds.*, 1988, pp. 75–86.

_____. Entry Barriers in Politics. In *Tullock, G.*, 1988, pp. 44–54.

_____. The General Irrelevance of the General Impossibility Theorem. In *Tullock, G.*, 1988, pp. 55–68.

_____. How to Do Well While Doing Good! In *Tullock, G.*, 1988, pp. 171–84.

_____. Income Testing and Politics: A Theoretical Model. In *Tullock, G.*, 1988, pp. 136–57.

_____. Majority Voting. In *Tullock, G.*, 1988, pp. 8–35.

_____. A (Partial) Rehabilitation of the Public Interest Theory. In *Tullock, G.*, 1988, pp. 158–70.

_____. Rent Seeking and Tax Reform. *Contemp. Policy Issues*, October 1988, 6(4), pp. 37–47.

_____. The Short Way with Dissenters. In *Tullock, G.*, 1988, pp. 122–35.

_____. A Simple Algebraic Logrolling Model. In *Tullock, G.*, 1988, pp. 81–92.

_____. Social Cost and Government Action. In *Tullock, G.*, 1988, pp. 69–80.

_____. The Social Costs of Reducing Social Cost. In *Tullock, G.*, 1988, pp. 93–103.

_____. The *Calculus*: Postscript after 25 Years. In *Gwartney, J. D. and Wagner, R. E., eds.*, 1988, *1987*, pp. 139–47.

_____. Why So Much Stability? In *Tullock, G.*, 1988, pp. 104–21.

_____. Why the Austrians Are Wrong about Depressions. In *Rothbard, M. N. and Block, W., eds.*, 1988, pp. 73–78.

_____ and **Tideman, T. Nicolaus.** A New and Superior Process for Making Social Choices. In *Ricketts, M., ed., Vol. 2*, 1988, *1976*, pp. 103–17.

Tuma, Elias H. Institutionalized Obstacles to Development: The Case of Egypt. *World Devel.*, October 1988, 16(10), pp. 1185–98.

Tuma, Nancy Brandon and Sandefur, Gary D. Trends in the Labor Force Activity of the Elderly in the United States, 1940–1980. In *Ricardo-Campbell, R. and Lazear, E. P., eds.*, 1988, pp. 38–75.

Tumarkin, Nina. Lenin and His Cult. In *Cracraft, J., ed.*, 1988, pp. 13–20.

Tung, Rosalie L. Toward a Conceptual Paradigm of International Business Negotiations. In *Farmer, R. N. and McGoun, E. G., eds.*, 1988, pp. 203–19.

Tunstall, Allan W. Agricultural Education at RMIHE: Some Personal Views. *Rev. Marketing Agr. Econ.*, August 1988, 56(2), pp. 232–33.

Tuppen, John. France: The Changing Character of a Key Industry. In *Williams, A. M. and Shaw, G., eds.*, 1988, pp. 180–95.

Turatto, Renzo and Brunetta, Renato. Dall'equilibrio marginalista al paradigma generazionale. Comportamenti microeconomici in un modello dinamico di equilibrio sociale. (From the Classical Equilibrium to the Generational Paradigm. Microeconomic Behavior in a Dynamic Model of Social Equilibrium. With English summary.) *Econ. Lavoro*, Apr.–June 1988, 22(2), pp. 13–36.

Turay, A. M. and El-Jafari, M. K. Trade, Japanese Voluntary Restraint Agreements and Import Elasticity for Cars in the U.S. *Rivista Int. Sci. Econ. Com.*, February 1988, 35(2), pp. 195–202.

Turbett, J. Patrick; Wilken, Paul H. and Schram, Sanford F. Child Poverty and Welfare Benefits: A Reassessment with State Data of the Claim that American Welfare Breeds Dependence. *Amer. J. Econ. Soc.*, October 1988, 47(4), pp. 409–22.

Ture, Norman B. The Tax Reform Act of 1986: Revolution or Conterrevolution? In *Boaz, D., ed.*, 1988, pp. 29–43.

Turgeon, Lynn. Where Is the Soviet Union Going? A Review Article. *Rev. Radical Polit. Econ.*, Winter 1988, 20(4), pp. 103–11.

Turhollow, Anthony F.; Das, Sujit and Curlee, T. Randall. Oil Supply Disruptions and Modelling Methodologies: The Role of LP Models. *Energy Econ.*, April 1988, 10(2), pp. 147–54.

Turk, Ivan. Accounting in Yugoslavia. In *Bailey, D. T., ed.*, 1988, pp. 157–72.

Turkington, D. A. and Bowden, R. J. Identification Information and Instruments in Linear Econometric Models with Rational Expectations. *J. Econometrics*, July 1988, 38(3), pp. 361–73.

Turksen, I. B. Stochastic Fuzzy Sets: A Survey. In *Kacprzyk, J. and Fedrizzi, M., eds.*, 1988, pp. 168–83.

Turnau, Irena. The Organization of the European Textile Industry from the Thirteenth to the Eighteenth Century. *J. Europ. Econ. Hist.*, Winter 1988, 17(3), pp. 583–602.

Turnbull, Geoffrey K. The Effects of Local Taxes and Public Services on Residential Development Patterns. *J. Reg. Sci.*, November 1988, 28(4), pp. 541–62.

_____. Market Structure, Location Rents, and the Land Development Process. *J. Urban Econ.*, May 1988, 23(3), pp. 261–77.

_____. Residential Development in an Open City. *Reg. Sci. Urban Econ.*, May 1988, 18(2), pp. 307–20.

_____ **and Drago, Robert.** The Incentive Effects of Tournaments with Positive Externalities among Workers. *Southern Econ. J.*, July 1988, 55(1), pp. 100–106.

_____ **and Drago, Robert.** Individual versus Group Piece Rates under Team Technologies. *J. Japanese Int. Economies*, March 1988, 2(1), pp. 1–10.

Turnbull, Peter J. The Economic Theory of Trade Union Behaviour: A Critique. *Brit. J. Ind. Relat.*, March 1988, 26(1), pp. 99–118.

_____. Industrial Relations and the Seniority Model of Union Behaviour. *Oxford Bull. Econ. Statist.*, February 1988, 50(1), pp. 53–70.

_____ **and Bean, Charles R.** Employment in the British Coal Industry: A Test of the Labour Demand Model. *Econ. J.*, December 1988, 98(393), pp. 1092–1104.

Turnbull, Stephen; Ma, Ching-to Albert and Moore, John. Stopping Agents from "Cheating." *J. Econ. Theory*, December 1988, 46(2), pp. 355–72.

Turner, Donald F. Private Antitrust Enforcement: Policy Recommendations. In *White, L. J., ed.*, 1988, pp. 407–09.

Turner, John. Servants of Two Masters: British Trade Associations in the First Half of the Twentieth Century: Response. In *Yamazaki, H. and Miyamoto, M., eds.*, 1988, pp. 202–03.

_____. Servants of Two Masters: British Trade Associations in the First Half of the Twentieth Century. In *Yamazaki, H. and Miyamoto, M., eds.*, 1988, pp. 173–98.

Turner, John A. Pension Survivors Insurance for Widows. *Econ. Inquiry*, July 1988, 26(3), pp. 403–22.

_____ **and Doescher, Tabitha A.** Social Security Benefits and the Baby-Boom Generation. *Amer. Econ. Rev.*, May 1988, 78(2), pp. 76–80.

Turner, Josephine. The Role of Cooperative Extension. In *Maynes, E. S. and ACCI Research Committee, eds.*, 1988, pp. 849–55.

Turner, Martha J.; Hilton, Ronald W. and Swieringa, Robert J. Product Pricing, Accounting Costs and Use of Product-Costing Systems. *Accounting Rev.*, April 1988, 63(2), pp. 195–218.

Turner, Mary. Labour: Comments. *Soc. Econ. Stud.*, March–June 1988, 37(1–2), pp. 293–99.

Turner, Philip. Savings and Investment, Exchange Rates, and International Imbalances: A Comparison of the United States, Japan, and Germany. *J. Japanese Int. Economies*, September 1988, 2(3), pp. 259–85.

Turner, R. Kerry. Pluralism in Environmental Economics: A Survey of the Sustainable Eco-

nomic Development Debate. *J. Agr. Econ.*, September 1988, 39(3), pp. 352–59.

_____. Sustainability, Resource Conservation and Pollution Control: An Overview. In *Turner, R. K., ed.*, 1988, pp. 1–25.

_____. Wetland Conservation: Economics and Ethics. In *[Lecomber, R.]*, 1988, pp. 121–59.

_____ **and Deadman, D.** Resource Conservation, Sustainability and Technical Change. In *Turner, R. K., ed.*, 1988, pp. 67–101.

Turner, Robert W. and Rockel, Mark L. Estimating Covariances of Parameter Estimates from Different Models. *Econ. Letters*, 1988, 26(2), pp. 137–40.

Turnovsky, Stephen J. The Gains from Fiscal Cooperation in the Two-Commodity Real Trade Model. *J. Int. Econ.*, August 1988, 25(1–2), pp. 111–27.

_____. Macroeconomic Policy Design in an Interdependent World Economy: An Analysis of Three Contingencies: Comment. In *Frenkel, J. A., ed.*, 1988, pp. 164–72.

_____. Monopolistic Competition and Labor Market Adjustment in the Open Economy: Comment. In *Marston, R. C., ed.*, 1988, pp. 189–94.

_____; **Basar, Tamer and d'Orey, Vasco.** Dynamic Strategic Monetary Policies and Coordination in Interdependent Economies. *Amer. Econ. Rev.*, June 1988, 78(3), pp. 341–61.

Turnquist, Mark A. Analyzing Production–Logistics Interactions. In *Bianco, L. and La Bella, A., eds.*, 1988, pp. 258–88.

Turpijn, Wouter. Shadow-Housing: Self-Help of Dwellers in the Netherlands. In *Friedrichs, J., ed.*, 1988, pp. 103–13.

Turunen-Red, Arja H. and Woodland, Alan D. On the Multilateral Transfer Problem: Existence of Pareto Improving International Transfers. *J. Int. Econ.*, November 1988, 25(3–4), pp. 249–69.

Turvey, Calum Greig; Driver, H. C. and Baker, Timothy G. Systematic and Nonsystematic Risk in Farm Portfolio Selection. *Amer. J. Agr. Econ.*, November 1988, 70(4), pp. 831–36.

_____ **and Lowenberg-DeBoer, J.** Farm-to-Farm Productivity Differences and Whole-Farm Production Functions. *Can. J. Agr. Econ.*, July 1988, 36(2), pp. 295–312.

Turvey, Ralph. On Divergences between Social Cost and Private Cost. In *Ricketts, M., ed., Vol. 2*, 1988, 1963, pp. 58–62.

Tüshaus, U. Decision Support for Qualitative Data Analysis: KEE Shell Linked to FORTRAN Programs. In *Gaul, W. and Schader, M., eds.*, 1988, pp. 204–12.

_____; **Demann, M. and Schader, Martin.** Developing a Decision Support System for Personnel Disposition in a Garage—Experiences Using the KEE Shell. In *Gaul, W. and Schader, M., eds.*, 1988, pp. 103–15.

Tussie, Diana. The Coordination of the Latin American Debtors: Is There a Logic behind the Story. In *Griffith-Jones, S., ed.*, 1988, pp. 282–307.

_____. La coordinación de los deudores latinoamericos: Cual es la lógica de su accionar? (With English summary.) *Desarrollo Econ.*, April–June 1988, *28*(109), pp. 67–88.

Tussing, Arlon R. Electricity and Gas: The U.S. West. *Energy J.*, October 1988, *9*(4), pp. 111–19.

_____ **and Van Vactor, Samuel A.** Is an Oil Tariff Justified? An American Debate: Reality Says No. *Energy J.*, July 1988, *9*(3), pp. 1–5.

Tuthill, Dean F.; Favero, Philip and Pitt, David G. Land Use Policies, Water Quality, and the Chesapeake Bay. In *Johnston, G. M.; Freshwater, D. and Favero, P.*, eds., 1988, pp. 71–90.

Tutin, Christian. Intérêt et ajustement: le débat Hayek/Keynes (1931–1932). (Interest and Adjustment: The Hayek/Keynes Debate of 1931–1932. With English summary.) *Écon. Appl.*, 1988, *41*(2), pp. 247–87.

Tversky, Amos; Bell, David E. and Raiffa, Howard. Descriptive, Normative, and Prescriptive Interactions in Decision Making. In *Bell, D. E.; Raiffa, H. and Tversky, A.*, eds., 1988, pp. 9–30.

_____ **and Kahneman, Daniel.** Prospect Theory: An Analysis of Decision under Risk. In *Earl, P. E.*, ed., Vol. 1, 1988, 1979, pp. 253–81.

_____ **and Kahneman, Daniel.** Prospect Theory: An Analysis of Decision under Risk. In *Gärdenfors, P. and Sahlin, N.-E.*, eds., 1988, 1979, pp. 183–214.

_____ **; McNeil, Barbara J. and Pauker, Stephen G.** On the Framing of Medical Decisions. In *Bell, D. E.; Raiffa, H. and Tversky, A.*, eds., 1988, pp. 562–68.

_____ **and Shafer, Glenn.** Languages and Designs for Probability Judgment. In *Bell, D. E.; Raiffa, H. and Tversky, A.*, eds., 1988, 1985, pp. 237–65.

Twaddle, Michael. Slaves and Peasants in Buganda. In *Archer, L. J.*, ed., 1988, pp. 118–29.

Tweeten, Luther G. Agricultural Technology—The Potential Socio-economic Impact. In *Goldberg, R. A.*, ed., Vol. 8, 1988, pp. 183–212.

_____. Are Farmers Predestined to Earn Chronically Low Rates of Return on Resources in the Absence of Government Support Programs? In *Goldberg, R. A.*, ed., Vol. 9, 1988, pp. 113–26.

_____. Domestic Food and Agricultural Policy Research Directions. In *Hildreth, R. J., et al.*, eds., 1988, pp. 121–44.

_____. Elements of a Sound Rural Development Policy. In *Goldberg, R. A.*, ed., Vol. 9, 1988, pp. 103–11.

_____. Farm Activism: A Study in Conflicting Goals, Values, and Beliefs. In *Goldberg, R. A.*, ed., Vol. 8, 1988, pp. 165–82.

_____. A Holistic Macroeconomics of Agriculture. In *Goldberg, R. A.*, ed., Vol. 9, 1988, pp. 127–44.

_____. Is the Family Farm Being Squeezed Out of Business by Monopolies? In *Goldberg, R. A.*, ed., Vol. 8, 1988, pp. 213–43.

_____. Mandatory Supply Control: A Viable Alternative? In *Goldberg, R. A.*, ed., Vol. 8, 1988, pp. 245–263.

_____ **and Sanford, Scott.** Farm Income Enhancement Potential for Small, Part-Time Farming Operations in East Central Oklahoma. *Southern J. Agr. Econ.*, December 1988, *20*(2), pp. 153–64.

_____**; Schriener, Dean and Henderson, David.** Intra-regional Development: Agricultural and Nodal Adjustment in Oklahoma's Southern High Plains. *Reg. Sci. Persp.*, 1988, *18*(2), pp. 44–59.

Twigg, David and Appleby, Colin. Computer Aided Design in the United Kingdom Car Industry. *Nat. Westminster Bank Quart. Rev.*, August 1988, pp. 39–52.

Twight, Charlotte. Government Manipulation of Constitutional-Level Transaction Costs: A General Theory of Transaction-Cost Augmentation and the Growth of Government. *Public Choice*, February 1988, *56*(2), pp. 131–52.

Twomey, Jim and Taylor, Jim. The Movement of Manufacturing Industry in Great Britain: An Inter-country Analysis, 1972–1981. *Urban Stud.*, June 1988, *25*(3), pp. 228–42.

Tybout, James R. The Algebra of Inflation Accounting. *Int. Econ. J.*, Summer 1988, *2*(2), pp. 83–100.

_____ **and Bark, Taeho.** Macro Shocks and Industrial Portfolio Responses: An Econometric Model for LDCs. *Rev. Econ. Statist.*, November 1988, *70*(4), pp. 559–68.

Tye, William B. Pricing Trackage Rights to Preserve Post-merger Rail Competition on Equal Terms. *Logist. Transp. Rev.*, December 1988, *24*(4), pp. 317–48.

_____ **and Meyer, John R.** Toward Achieving Workable Competition in Industries Undergoing a Transition to Deregulation: A Contractual Equilibrium Approach. *Yale J. Regul.*, Summer 1988, *5*(2), pp. 273–97.

Tyebjee, Tyzoon T. Japan's Joint Ventures in the United States. In *Contractor, F. J. and Lorange, P.*, 1988, pp. 457–72.

Tyers, Rod and Anderson, Kym. Imperfect Price Transmission and Implied Trade Elasticities in a Multi-commodity World. In *Carter, C. A. and Gardiner, W. H.*, eds., 1988, pp. 255–95.

_____ **and Anderson, Kym.** Liberalising OECD Agricultural Policies in the Uruguay Round: Effects on Trade and Welfare. *J. Agr. Econ.*, May 1988, *39*(2), pp. 197–216.

Tyler, P.; Moore, B. C. and Rhodes, J. Geographical Variations in Industrial Costs. *Scot. J. Polit. Econ.*, February 1988, *35*(1), pp. 22–50.

_____**; Moore, B. C. and Rhodes, J.** The Rate Burden: An Accounting Framework for Assessing the Effect of Local Taxes on Business. *Reg. Stud.*, October 1988, *22*(5), pp. 387–97.

Tyson, Laura D'Andrea. Competitiveness: An Analysis of the Problem and a Perspective on Future Policy. In *Starr, M. K.*, ed., 1988, pp. 95–120.

_____. Making Policy for National Competitiveness in a Changing World. In *Furino, A., ed.*, 1988, pp. 19–47.

_____ and Castells, Manuel. High-Technology Choices Ahead: Restructuring Interdependence. In *Sewell, J. W. and Tucker, S. K., eds.*, 1988, pp. 55–95.

_____ and Popper, Steven W. The New Hungarian Economic Reforms and Their Effects on Enterprise Behavior. In *Jones, D. C. and Svejnar, J., eds.*, 1988, pp. 327–65.

_____; Robinson, Sherman and Woods, Leyla. Conditionality and Adjustment in Hungary and Yugoslavia. In *[Holzman, F. D.]*, 1988, pp. 72–105.

_____ and Zysman, John. Trade and Employment: An Overview of the Issues and Evidence. In *Tyson, L. D.; Dickens, W. T. and Zysman, J., eds.*, 1988, pp. 1–40.

Tyszka, Tadeusz and Gasparski, Piotr. Justification of Decisions Made in Adverse Circumstances. In *Maital, S., ed., Vol. 1*, 1988, pp. 176–85.

Tzannatos, Zafiris. The Long-run Effects of the Sex Integration of the British Labour Market. *J. Econ. Stud.*, 1988, *15*(1), pp. 5–18.

_____ and Zabalza, Antonio. The Effect of Britain's Anti-discrimination Legislation on Relative Pay and Employment: Reply. *Econ. J.*, September 1988, *98*(392), pp. 839–43.

U.N., F.A.O., Statistics Office. International Comparison of Agricultural Output. In *Salazar-Carrillo, J. and Rao, D. S. P., eds.*, 1988, pp. 115–52.

Ubogu, Roland E. Impacts of External Economic and Trade Policies on Nigeria's Trade Performance 1960–1986. *Econ. Int.*, Feb.–March 1988, *41*(1–2), pp. 101–22.

Uddin, Mohammed Sohrab. Monetary Policy under Alternative Exchange Rates: A Reconsideration: Some Comments. *Indian Econ. J.*, July–September 1988, *36*(1), pp. 95–98.

Udell, Jon G. An Entrepreneurial Approach to Entrepreneurial Research. In *Association of Private Education*, 1988, pp. 119–24.

Uebe, Götz. Joseph Lang aus Freiburg Eine Kreislauftheorie von 1807 zwischen Quesnay und Marx. (Joseph Lang from Freiburg: A Theory of the Circular Flow of Income—An Intermediation between Quesnay and Marx in the Year 1807. With English summary.) *Jahr. Nationalökon. Statist.*, January 1988, *204*(1), pp. 36–47.

Uecker, Wilfred C.; DeJong, Douglas V. and Forsythe, Robert. A Note on the Use of Businessmen as Subjects in Sealed Offer Markets. *J. Econ. Behav. Organ.*, January 1988, *9*(1), pp. 87–100.

Ueda, Kazuo. The Japanese Current-Account Surplus and Fiscal Policy in Japan and the United States. In *Shoven, J. B., ed.*, 1988, pp. 145–72.

Uelner, Adalbert and Menck, Thomas. World Tax Reform: A Progress Report: Germany. In *Pechman, J. A., ed.*, 1988, pp. 119–27.

Uemiya, S. Jevons and Fleeming Jenkin. In

Wood, J. C., ed., Vol. 3, 1988, *1981*, pp. 174–88.

Ugarteche, Oscar. Peru: The Foreign Debt and Heterodox Adjustment Policy under Alan Garcia. In *Griffith-Jones, S., ed.*, 1988, pp. 170–92.

Uhlenberg, Peter. Population Aging and the Timing of Old-Age Benefits. In *Ricardo-Campbell, R. and Lazear, E. P., eds.*, 1988, pp. 353–71.

Uhlich, Gerald R. and Selten, Reinhard. Order of Strength and Exhaustivity as Additional Hypotheses in Theories for 3-Person Characteristic Function Games. In *Tietz, R.; Albers, W. and Selten, R., eds.*, 1988, pp. 235–50.

Ujhelyi, Tamás. Hungary as a Trade Partner for Socialist and Market Economies. In *Brada, J. C. and Wadekin, K.-E., eds.*, 1988, pp. 373–84.

_____ and Pálovics, Irén. European Agricultural Policy in a Global Context: The European CMEA Countries. *Europ. Rev. Agr. Econ.*, 1988, *15*(2–3), pp. 173–86.

Ulbrich, Holley H. and Hite, James C. Subsidizing Water Users or Water Systems? *Land Econ.*, November 1988, *64*(4), pp. 377–80.

_____; Wallace, Myles S. and Bowles, David C. Default Risk and the Effects of Fiscal Policy on Interest Rates: 1929–1945. *Public Finance Quart.*, July 1988, *16*(3), pp. 357–73.

Ulengin, Fusun and Bookbinder, James H. Models for Improving Grain Transportation in Western Canada. *Logist. Transp. Rev.*, December 1988, *24*(4), pp. 349–67.

Ullah, Aman. Non-parametric Estimation of Econometric Functionals. *Can. J. Econ.*, August 1988, *21*(3), pp. 625–58.

_____. Nonparametric Estimation and Hypothesis Testing in Econometric Models. *Empirical Econ.*, 1988, *13*(3–4), pp. 223–49.

_____ and Giles, David E. A. The Positive-Part Stein-Rule Estimator and Tests of Linear Hypotheses. *Econ. Letters*, 1988, *26*(1), pp. 49–51.

_____ and Pagan, Adrian. The Econometric Analysis of Models with Risk Terms. *J. Appl. Econometrics*, April 1988, *3*(2), pp. 87–105.

_____ and Vinod, H. D. Flexible Production Function Estimation by Nonparametric Kernel Estimators. In *Rhodes, G. F., Jr. and Fomby, T. B., eds.*, 1988, pp. 139–60.

_____ and Vinod, H. D. Nonparametric Kernel Estimation of Econometric Parameters. *J. Quant. Econ.*, January 1988, *4*(1), pp. 81–87.

Ullenhag, Kersti. Firms under Expansion: A Theoretical Model and Its Application. *Scand. Econ. Hist. Rev.*, 1988, *36*(2), pp. 68–81.

Ullmann, Arieh A. "Lohnt" sich soziale Verantwortung? Zum Zusammenhang zwischen wirtschaftlichem Unternehmenserfolg und gesellschaftlicher Verantwortung. (With English summary.) *Z. Betriebswirtshaft*, September 1988, *58*(9), pp. 908–26.

Ullmann, John E. The Reagan Administration: A New Issue, with Warmer-Over Ingredients. In *Neimark, M., ed.*, 1988, pp. 167–78.

_____ and Starr, Martin K. The Myth of U.S.

Industrial Supremacy. In *Starr, M. K., ed.*, 1988, pp. 43–71.

Ullmo, Yves. Intermédiation intermédiaires financiers et marché. (With English summary.) *Revue Écon. Polit.*, Sept.–Oct. 1988, *98*(5), pp. 639–54.

Ulmer, Mark G. and Howe, Wayne J. Job Gains Strong in 1987; Unemployment Rate Declines. *Mon. Lab. Rev.*, February 1988, *111*(2), pp. 57–67.

Ulph, Alistair; Toker, Mehmet and Ingham, Alan. A Vintage Model of Scrapping and Investment. *Rech. Écon. Louvain*, 1988, *54*(2), pp. 169–89.

_____ **and Ulph, David T.** Bargaining Structures and Delay in Innovation. *Scand. J. Econ.*, 1988, *90*(4), pp. 475–91.

_____ **and Ulph, David T.** Policies towards Natural Resources and Investment in International Trade. In *[Lecomber, R.]*, 1988, pp. 173–99.

Ulph, David T.; Beath, John A. and Katsoulacos, Yannis. R&D Rivalry vs R&D Cooperation under Uncertainty. *Rech. Écon. Louvain*, 1988, *54*(4), pp. 373–84.

_____; **Beath, John A. and Lewis, Geoffrey W.** Policy Targeting in a New Welfare Framework with Poverty. In *Hare, P. G., ed.*, 1988, pp. 161–85.

_____ **and Lewis, Geoffrey W.** Poverty, Inequality and Welfare. *Econ. J.*, Supplement, 1988, *98*(390), pp. 117–31.

_____ **and Ulph, Alistair.** Bargaining Structures and Delay in Innovation. *Scand. J. Econ.*, 1988, *90*(4), pp. 475–91.

_____ **and Ulph, Alistair.** Policies towards Natural Resources and Investment in International Trade. In *[Lecomber, R.]*, 1988, pp. 173–99.

Ulveling, Edwin F.; Hsu, Yu-sheng and Liu, Chwen-chi. Predictive Power of Weekly Money Stock Announcements. *Econ. Letters*, 1988, *26*(2), pp. 159–64.

Umbeck, John; Dunkelberg, William C. and Staten, Michael. Market Share/Market Power Revisited: A New Test for an Old Theory. *J. Health Econ.*, March 1988, *7*(1), pp. 73–83.

Unal, Haluk and Kane, Edward J. Change in Market Assessments of Deposit-Institution Riskiness. *J. Finan. Services Res.*, June 1988, *1*(3), pp. 207–29.

_____ **and Kane, Edward J.** Two Approaches to Assessing the Interest Rate Sensitivity of Deposit Institution Equity Returns. In *Chen, A. H., ed.*, 1988, pp. 113–37.

_____ **and Sanders, Anthony B.** On the Intertemporal Behavior of the Short-term Rate of Interest. *J. Finan. Quant. Anal.*, December 1988, *23*(4), pp. 417–23.

Uncles, Mark D. and Ehrenberg, Andrew S. C. Patterns of Store Choice: New Evidence from the USA. In *Wrigley, N., ed.*, 1988, pp. 272–99.

Unger, Kurt. Industrial Structure, Technical Change and Microeconomic Behaviour in LDCs. In *Dosi, G., et al., eds.*, 1988, pp. 480–95.

von Ungern-Sternberg, Thomas. Cartel Stability

in Sealed Bid Second Price Auctions. *J. Ind. Econ.*, March 1988, *36*(3), pp. 351–58.

_____. Excess Capacity as a Commitment to Promote Entry. *J. Ind. Econ.*, December 1988, *37*(2), pp. 113–22.

_____. Monopolistic Competition and General Purpose Products. *Rev. Econ. Stud.*, April 1988, *55*(2), pp. 231–46.

_____. Zur Förderung der VANS in der Schweiz. (Value Added Network Services in Switzerland. With English summary.) *Schweiz. Z. Volkswirtsch. Statist.*, September 1988, *124*(3), pp. 365–76.

UNICEF. Adjustment Policies and Programmes to Protect Children and Other Vulnerable Groups in Ghana. In *Cornia, G. A.; Jolly, R. and Stewart, F., eds.*, 1988, pp. 93–125.

_____. Redirecting Adjustment Programmes towards Growth and the Protection of the Poor: The Philippine Case. In *Cornia, G. A.; Jolly, R. and Stewart, F., eds.*, 1988, pp. 184–217.

_____. Sri Lanka: The Social Impact of Economic Policies during the Last Decade. In *Cornia, G. A.; Jolly, R. and Stewart, F., eds.*, 1988, pp. 238–71.

United Nations Secretary-General. External Debt Crisis and Development: The International Debt Situation in Mid-1987. In *Sopiee, N.; Hamzah, B. A. and Leong, C. H., eds.*, 1988, pp. 261–89.

Unnevehr, Laurian J. and Eales, James S. Demand for Beef and Chicken Products: Separability and Structural Change. *Amer. J. Agr. Econ.*, August 1988, *70*(3), pp. 521–32.

Unni, N. V. M.; Bowonder, B. and Prasad, S. S. R. Dynamics of Fuelwood Prices in India: Policy Implications. *World Devel.*, October 1988, *16*(10), pp. 1213–29.

Uno, Kimio. Appreciation of the Yen and the Structural Adjustment—A Multisectoral Industry Analysis of the Japanese Economy. In *Uno, K. and Shishido, S., eds.*, 1988, pp. 80–110.

_____. Quality of Life and Voting Behavior in Japan. In *Uno, K. and Shishido, S., eds.*, 1988, pp. 189–201.

_____. A Survey on Econometric Models and Statistical Databases. In *Uno, K. and Shishido, S., eds.*, 1988, pp. 317–47.

Uosaki, Katsuji and Hatanaka, Toshiharu. Optimal Input for Autoregressive Model Discrimination Based on the Kullback's Divergence. In *Iri, M. and Yajima, K., eds.*, 1988, pp. 101–08.

Uphoff, Norman. Assisted Self-Reliance: Working with, Rather Than for, the Poor. In *Lewis, J. P., et al.*, 1988, pp. 47–59.

Uppal, J. S. Domestic Capital Formation in Indonesia. *J. Econ. Devel.*, December 1988, *13*(2), pp. 151–61.

_____. Indonesia: Central Transfers and Local Finances. *Bull. Int. Fiscal Doc.*, October 1988, *42*(10), pp. 448–53.

Upton, M.; Wise, W. S. and Beck, H. S. Is Publicly Funded Agricultural Research Excessive?

A Comment. *J. Agr. Econ.*, September 1988, 39(3), pp. 453–55.

Urabe, Kuniyoshi. Innovation and the Japanese Management System. In *Urabe, K.; Child, J. and Kagono, T., eds.*, 1988, pp. 3–25.

Urata, Shujiro. The Development of the Motor Vehicle Industry in Post–Second-World-War Japan. *Industry Devel.*, October 1988, (24), pp. 1–33.

———. Economic Growth and Structural Change in the Soviet Economy, 1959–72. In *Ciaschini, M., ed.*, 1988, pp. 303–23.

——— **and Kohama, Hirohisa.** The Impact of the Recent Yen Appreciation on the Japanese Economy. *Devel. Econ.*, December 1988, 26(4), pp. 323–40.

Urban Institute. Mexicans: California's Newest Immigrants. In *Simcox, D. E., ed.*, 1988, pp. 176–80.

Urban, Jan. Prognostic Concept of Czechoslovakia's Participation in International Division of Labour. *Czech. Econ. Digest.*, May 1988, (3), pp. 33–41.

Urban, Michael E. Political Language and Political Change in the USSR: Notes on the Gorbachev Leadership. In *Potichnyj, P. J., ed.*, 1988, pp. 87–106.

Urban, Nicole and Zerbe, Richard O., Jr. Including the Public Interest in Theories of Regulation. In *Zerbe, R. O., Jr., ed.*, 1988, pp. 1–23.

Urbany, Joel E.; Bearden, William O. and Weilbaker, Dan C. The Effect of Plausible and Exaggerated Reference Prices on Consumer Perceptions and Price Search. *J. Cons. Res.*, June 1988, 15(1), pp. 95–110.

Uri, Didier and Théret, Bruno. La courbe de Laffer dix ans après: Un essai de bilan critique. (The Laffer Curve Ten Years After: A Tentative Critical Survey. With English summary.) *Revue Écon.*, July 1988, 39(4), pp. 753–808.

Uri, Noel D. A Note on Determining the Spatial and Product Extent of a Market. *Rev. Reg. Stud.*, Fall 1988, 18(3), pp. 55–64.

———. A Re-examination of the Relationship between Industry Structure and Economic Performance. *Appl. Econ.*, October 1988, 20(10), pp. 1383–1400.

——— **and Coate, Malcolm B.** A Simultaneous Equations Approach to Modeling Industry Structure and Economic Performance. *Metroecon.*, June 1988, 39(2), pp. 181–204.

———; **Kyer, Ben L. and Mixon, J. Wilson, Jr.** Taxes, Transfer Payments and Automatic Stabilization in the United States. Impact and Trends. *Econ. Notes*, 1988, (2), pp. 50–60.

Urich, Thomas and Saunders, Anthony. The Effects of Shifts in Monetary Policy and Reserve Accounting Regimes on Bank Reserve Management Behavior in the Federal Funds Market. *J. Banking Finance*, December 1988, 12(4), pp. 523–33.

——— **and Saunders, Anthony.** Weekly Variation in the Federal Funds Market: The Weekend Game and Other Effects. In *Dimson, E., ed.*, 1988, pp. 64–73.

Urick, J. J. and Greer, R. Clyde. An Annual Model of Purebred Breeding Bull Price. *Western J. Agr. Econ.*, July 1988, 13(1), pp. 1–6.

Urrutia, Miguel. The Changing Nature of Economic Planning in Colombia. In *Urrutia, M. and Yukawa, S., eds. (I)*, 1988, pp. 156–97.

———. Inflation Stabilization: Brazil: Comment. In *Bruno, M., et al., eds.*, 1988, pp. 302–03.

———. New Approaches to Development Planning. In *Urrutia, M. and Yukawa, S., eds. (I)*, 1988, pp. 1–15.

———. The Politics of Economic Development Policies in Resource-Rich Countries. In *Urrutia, M. and Yukawa, S., eds. (II)*, 1988, pp. 154–65.

Ursprung, Heinrich W. and Hillman, Arye L. Domestic Politics, Foreign Interests, and International Trade Policy. *Amer. Econ. Rev.*, September 1988, 78(4), pp. 719–45.

——— **and Karacaoglu, Girol.** Exchange Rate Dynamics under Gradual Portfolio Adjustment. *J. Macroecon.*, Fall 1988, 10(4), pp. 565–89.

Urton, William L.; Long, Larry and Tucker, C. Jack. Measuring Migration Distances: Self-reporting and Indirect Methods. *J. Amer. Statist. Assoc.*, September 1988, 83(403), pp. 674–78.

———; **Long, Larry and Tucker, C. Jack.** Migration Distances: An International Comparison. *Demography*, November 1988, 25(4), pp. 633–40.

Urvoy, Jean-Charles. CHIC Graphic and CHIC Services: RATP-Developed Software Packages for Time-Scheduled Design. In *Daduna, J. R. and Wren, A., eds.*, 1988, pp. 240–49.

Uspenski, Georgi. Major Space Application to the "MIR" Space Station. In *Egan, J. J., et al.*, 1988, pp. 175–80.

Usselman, Steven W. Running the Machine: The Management of Technological Change on American Railroads, 1850–1910. In *Hausman, W. J., ed.*, 1988, pp. 213–18.

Usui, Chikako and Inkeles, Alex. The Retirement Decision in Cross-National Perspective. In *Ricardo-Campbell, R. and Lazear, E. P., eds.*, 1988, pp. 273–96.

Usui, Mikoto. Organizational Problems of a Data Bank For Policy Research. In *Uno, K. and Shishido, S., eds.*, 1988, pp. 3–14.

Utterström, Peter. Tax Treatment of Computer Software: Sweden. In *International Fiscal Association, ed. (II)*, 1988, pp. 509–26.

Utzig, S.; Schmidtchen, D. and Schmidt-Trenz, H.-J. Zwang oder nicht Zwang—das ist hier die Frage. Der Verein für Socialpolitik und seine obligatorische Mitgliederzeitschrift. (To Coerce or Not to Coerce—That Is the Question. The New Requirement by the German Economic Association That Its Members Subscribe to Its Journal. With English summary.) *Jahr. Nationalökon. Statist.*, May 1988, 204(5), pp. 423–36.

Uyehara, Cecil H. U.S.–Japan Science and Technology Exchange: Patterns of Interdependence: Concluding Remarks. In *Uyehara, C. H., ed.*, 1988, pp. 257–63.

Uzawa, Hirofumi. Duality Principles in the Theory of Cost and Production. In *Uzawa, H.*, 1988, *1964*, pp. 87–91.

_____. Iterative Methods for Concave Programming. In *Uzawa, H.*, 1988, *1958*, pp. 135–48.

_____. The Kuhn–Tucker Theorem in Concave Programming. In *Uzawa, H.*, 1988, *1958*, pp. 129–34.

_____. Neutral Inventions and the Stability of Growth Equilibrium. In *Uzawa, H.*, 1988, *1961*, pp. 102–11.

_____. On a Two-Sector Model of Economic Growth, I. In *Uzawa, H.*, 1988, *1962*, pp. 197–205.

_____. On a Two-Sector Model of Economic Growth, II. In *Uzawa, H.*, 1988, *1963*, pp. 206–22.

_____. On the Dynamic Stability of Economic Growth: The Neoclassical versus Keynesian Approaches. In *Uzawa, H.*, 1988, *1974*, pp. 249–80.

_____. On the Economics of Social Overhead Capital. In *Uzawa, H.*, 1988, *1974*, pp. 340–62.

_____. On the Integrability of Demand Functions. In *Uzawa, H.*, 1988, *1971*, pp. 27–64.

_____. On the Stability of Edgeworth's Barter Process. In *Uzawa, H.*, 1988, *1962*, pp. 179–93.

_____. Optimal Growth in a Two-Sector Model of Capital Accumulation. In *Uzawa, H.*, 1988, *1964*, pp. 283–312.

_____. Optimum Fiscal Policy in an Aggregative Model of Economic Growth. In *Uzawa, H.*, 1988, *1969*, pp. 313–39.

_____. Optimum Technical Change in an Aggregative Model of Economic Growth. In *Uzawa, H.*, 1988, *1965*, pp. 112–26.

_____. Preference and Rational Choice in the Theory of Consumption. In *Uzawa, H.*, 1988, *1960*, pp. 3–26.

_____. Prices of the Factors of Production in International Trade. In *Uzawa, H.*, 1988, *1959*, pp. 149–71.

_____. Production Functions with Constant Elasticities of Substitution. In *Uzawa, H.*, 1988, *1963*, pp. 92–101.

_____. Time Preference and the Penrose Effect in a Two-Class Model of Economic Growth. In *Uzawa, H.*, 1988, *1969*, pp. 223–48.

_____. Time Preference, the Consumption Function, and Optimum Asset Holdings. In *Uzawa, H.*, 1988, *1968*, pp. 65–84.

_____. Walras's Existence Theorem and Brouwer's Fixed-Point Theorem. In *Uzawa, H.*, 1988, *1962*, pp. 175–78.

Uzdemir, Alexander P. Solution Methods of Plants Location Dynamic Problems in Continuous-Time. In *Iri, M. and Yajima, K., eds.*, 1988, pp. 701–14.

Uze, Barry; Filer, John E. and Moak, Donald L. Why Some States Adopt Lotteries and Others Don't. *Public Finance Quart.*, July 1988, *16*(3), pp. 259–83.

Văduva, I.; Megheşan, V. and Guran, M. Informatics and the Technical and Scientific Evolution. *Econ. Computat. Cybern. Stud. Res.*, 1988, *23*(1), pp. 31–44.

Vagliasindi, Pietro A. The von Neumann Version of De Viti De Marco's Model: The Case of Public Intermediate Commodities. *Metroecon.*, October 1988, *39*(3), pp. 223–44.

Vaglio, Alessandro. Static and Dynamic Economies of Scale in Export-Led Growth. *Econ. Notes*, 1988, (2), pp. 61–81.

Vahlne, Jan-Erik and Hood, Neil. Strategies in Global Competition: Concluding Perspectives. In *Hood, N. and Vahlne, J.-E., eds.*, 1988, pp. 390–93.

_____ **and Nordstrom, Kjell.** Choice of Market Channel in a Strategic Perspective. In *Hood, N. and Vahlne, J.-E., eds.*, 1988, pp. 256–81.

Vaidyanathan, A. Agricultural Development and Rural Poverty. In *Lucas, R. E. B. and Papanek, G. F., eds.*, 1988, pp. 77–90.

_____. Economic Reform in China: Some Observations. In *Mitra, A., ed.*, 1988, pp. 28–33.

Vaillancourt, François and Blais, André. The Political Economy of Taxation: Some Evidence for Canada. *Public Finance Quart.*, July 1988, *16*(3), pp. 315–29.

_____ **and Grignon, Julie.** Revenu, caractéristiques sociodémographiques et dépenses des ménages au Canada en 1978 et 1982. (With English summary.) *L'Actual. Econ.*, June 1988, *64*(2), pp. 231–50.

_____ **and Henriques, Irene.** The Demand for Child Care Services in Canada. *Appl. Econ.*, March 1988, *20*(3), pp. 385–94.

Valdés, Alberto. Constraints on Adjustments through International Trade: An Analysis of the Relationship between Industrial and Developing Countries. In *Antonelli, G. and Quadrio-Curzio, A., eds.*, 1988, pp. 123–31.

_____. Explicit versus Implicit Food Subsidies: Distribution of Costs. In *Pinstrup-Andersen, P., ed.*, 1988, pp. 77–91.

_____; **Krueger, Anne O. and Schiff, Maurice.** Agricultural Incentives in Developing Countries: Measuring the Effect of Sectoral and Economywide Policies. *World Bank Econ. Rev.*, September 1988, *2*(3), pp. 255–71.

_____ **and Pinckney, Thomas C.** Short-run Supply Management and Food Security: Results from Pakistan and Kenya. *World Devel.*, September 1988, *16*(9), pp. 1025–34.

_____; **Quiroz, Jorge and Barahona, Pablo.** Reformas económicas en la agricultura y respuesta de la producción agregada: Chile 1960–1987. (With English summary.) *Cuadernos Econ.*, December 1988, *25*(76), pp. 389–403.

_____ **and Siamwalla, Ammar.** Foreign Trade Regime, Exchange Rate Policy, and the Structure of Incentives. In *Mellor, J. W. and Ahmed, R., eds.*, 1988, pp. 103–23.

Valdés, Nelson P. Revolution and Paradigms: A Critical Assessment of Cuban Studies. In *Zimbalist, A., ed.*, 1988, pp. 182–211.

Valdés Prieto, Salvador and Lomakin S., Alexandra. Percepción sobre la Garantía Estatal a los Depósitos Durante 1987 en Chile. (With English summary.) *Cuadernos Econ.*, August 1988, *25*(75), pp. 229–45.

Valdez, Marla. Constitutionality of Educational Land Grants and Mississippi State Property Interests under Review in *Papasan v. Allain. Natural Res. J.*, Winter 1988, *28*(1), pp. 199–216.

do Vale Souza, Aldemir; Guimarães Neto, Leonardo and De Aruaíjo, Tarcísio Patrúcio. Employment Implications of Informal Sector Policies: A Case Study of Greater Recife. *Int. Lab. Rev.*, 1988, *127*(2), pp. 243–58.

Valenta, František. Theoretical Aspects of the Intensive Type of Reproduction. *Czech. Econ. Pap.*, 1988, (25), pp. 21–33.

Valentin, E. K. and Macdonald, James E. The Brave New World of Organ Transplantation: Issues and Challenges from a Consumer Affairs Perspective. *J. Cons. Aff.*, Summer 1988, *22*(1), pp. 119–35.

Valentine, T. J. Can Monetary Policy Be Used to Influence the Real Value of the $A in the Short or Long Run? *Rev. Marketing Agr. Econ.*, April 1988, *56*(1), pp. 78–81.

Valentino, Raphael. An Evolutionary Approach to Inflation: Prices, Productivity, and Innovation: Discussion. In *Hanusch, H., ed.*, 1988, pp. 238–49.

Valenzuela, Manuel. Spain: The Phenomenon of Mass Tourism. In *Williams, A. M. and Shaw, G., eds.*, 1988, pp. 39–57.

Vali, Shapoor. Economic Structure and Errors in Multiregional Input–Output Model. *Ricerche Econ.*, April–June 1988, *42*(2), pp. 367–90.

———— **and Maeshiro, Asatoshi.** Pitfalls in the Estimation of a Differenced Model. *J. Bus. Econ. Statist.*, October 1988, *6*(4), pp. 511–15.

Vallageas, Bernard. Intérêt, répartition et théorie des circuits. (Interest, Distribution of Income and "Circuits Theory." With English summary.) *Écon. Appl.*, 1988, *41*(2), pp. 355–88.

Valletta, Robert G. and Freeman, Richard B. The Effects of Public Sector Labor Laws on Labor Market Institutions and Outcomes. In *Freeman, R. B. and Ichniowski, C., eds.*, 1988, pp. 81–103.

———— **and Freeman, Richard B.** The NBER Public Sector Collective Bargaining Law Data Set: Appendix B. In *Freeman, R. B. and Ichniowski, C., eds.*, 1988, pp. 399–419.

Valliant, Richard. Estimation of Laspeyres Price Indexes Using the Prediction Approach for Finite Population Sampling. *J. Bus. Econ. Statist.*, April 1988, *6*(2), pp. 189–96.

Valnet, Frederique and Bodurtha, James N., Jr. Innovation in the International Money and Bond Markets: A Source of Lower Borrowing Costs? In *Khoury, S. J. and Ghosh, A., eds.*, 1988, pp. 45–86.

Valovaia, T. The Difficult Road of Cognition: Reflections on a Timely Book and a Sensational Article. *Prob. Econ.*, February 1988, *30*(10), pp. 61–68.

Valsecchi, Irene. L'ipotesi del buono scuola tra equità ed efficienza. (The Voucher System Hypothesis between Equity and Efficiency. With English summary.) *Rivista Int. Sci. Econ. Com.*, January 1988, *35*(1), pp. 77–90.

Valvona, Joseph; Morrisey, Michael A. and Sloan, Frank A. Defining Geographic Markets for Hospital Care. *Law Contemp. Probl.*, Spring 1988, *51*(2), pp. 165–94.

Van Bael, Ivo. The GATT Dispute Settlement Procedure. *J. World Trade*, August 1988, *22*(4), pp. 67–77.

Van Cleave, William R. Strategic Deterrence, Defense, and Arms Control. In *Anderson, A. and Bark, D. L., eds.*, 1988, pp. 33–43.

Van Damme, Eric. The Impossibility of Stable Renegotiation. *Econ. Letters*, 1988, *26*(4), pp. 321–24.

Van De Voorde, C.; Van Rompuy, P. and De Bruyne, G. Taxation, Wages and Employment in a Unionized Economy. *Tijdschrift Econ. Manage.*, Sept.–Dec. 1988, *33*(3/4), pp. 261–70.

Van de Voorde, E. and Blauwens, G. The Valuation of Time Savings in Commodity Transport. *Int. J. Transport Econ.*, February 1988, *15*(1), pp. 77–87.

Van Der Feltz, W. J. and Hoogduin, L. H. Rational Formation of Expectations: Keynesian Uncertainty and Davidson's (Non)-Ergodicity-Criterium. *Metroecon.*, June 1988, *39*(2), pp. 105–19.

Van der Heyden, Ludo and Ginsburgh, Victor A. On Extending the Negishi Approach to Computing Equilibria: The Case of Government Price Support Policies. *J. Econ. Theory*, February 1988, *44*(1), pp. 168–78.

Van der Sar, Nico L. and van Praag, Bernard M. S. Household Cost Functions and Equivalence Scales. *J. Human Res.*, Spring 1988, *23*(2), pp. 193–210.

Van der Wee, H. and Schokkaert, E. A Quantitative Study of Food Consumption in the Low Countries during the Sixteenth Century. *J. Europ. Econ. Hist.*, Spring 1988, *17*(1), pp. 131–58.

Van Doorslaer, E. K. A. and Van Vliet, R. C. J. A. Disaggregation of the Demand for Hospital Care. *Appl. Econ.*, July 1988, *20*(7), pp. 969–84.

Van Hoa, Tran. Econometric Modelling of Private Consumption Using OECD National Accounts. In *[Clark, C.]*, 1988, pp. 49–69.

———— **and Chaturvedi, A.** The Necessary and Sufficient Conditions for the Uniform Dominance of the Two-Stage Stein Estimators. *Econ. Letters*, 1988, *28*(4), pp. 351–55.

———— **and Perkins, James O. N.** Twenty-five per Cent Forty Years On. In *[Clark, C.]*, 1988, pp. 123–38.

Van Hoomissen, Theresa. Price Dispersion and Inflation: Evidence from Israel. *J. Polit. Econ.*, December 1988, *96*(6), pp. 1303–14.

Van Huyck, John B. and Grossman, Herschel I. Sovereign Debt as a Contingent Claim: Excusable Default, Repudiation, and Reputation. *Amer. Econ. Rev.*, December 1988, *78*(5), pp. 1088–97.

Van Kooten, G. C. Economic Impacts of Supply

Management: Review and Comparison of Alternative Measures of Consumer Welfare Loss. *Can. J. Agr. Econ.*, November 1988, *36*(3), pp. 425–41.

_____; Meyer, Neil and Stabler, Jack C. Methodological Issues in the Evaluation of Regional Resource Development Projects. *Ann. Reg. Sci.*, July 1988, *22*(2), pp. 13–25.

_____; Schmitz, Andrew and Furtan, W. H. The Economics of Storing a Non-storable Commodity. *Can. J. Econ.*, August 1988, *21*(3), pp. 579–86.

_____ and Spriggs, John. Rationale for Government Intervention in Canadian Agriculture: A Review of Stabilization Programs. *Can. J. Agr. Econ.*, March 1988, *36*(1), pp. 1–21.

_____; Weisensel, Ward P. and Schoney, Richard A. Where Are Saskatchewan Farmland Prices Headed? *Can. J. Agr. Econ.*, March 1988, *36*(1), pp. 37–50.

Van Lear, William M. An Oil Price Model. In *Pennsylvania Economic Association*, 1988, pp. 310–18.

Van Lierop, Johannes and Puri, Anil K. Forecasting Housing Starts. *Int. J. Forecasting*, 1988, *4*(1), pp. 125–34.

Van Moeseke, Paul. Efficient Portfolios: Risk Shares and Monetary Policy. In *Sengupta, J. K. and Kadekodi, G. K., eds.*, 1988, pp. 109–22.

Van Offeren, Dick H. Replacement Value Accounting: Theory and Practice. In *Most, K. S., ed.*, 1988, pp. 23–50.

Van Parijs, Philippe. De l'efficience à la liberté. L'économie du bien-être face au défi libertarien. (From Efficiency to Freedom. Welfare Economics and the Libertarian Challenge. With English summary.) *Écon. Appl.*, 1988, *41*(3), pp. 451–78.

Van Rompuy, P.; De Bruyne, G. and Van De Voorde, C. Taxation, Wages and Employment in a Unionized Economy. *Tijdschrift Econ. Manage.*, Sept.–Dec. 1988, *33*(3/4), pp. 261–70.

Van Tiel, Pieter and Loubergé, Henri. Contrôle des changes et risque politique: Une étude économétrique des cas français et suisse. (Capital Flows Controls and Political Risk: An Econometric Study of the Swiss and French Cases. With English summary.) *Revue Écon.*, September 1988, *39*(5), pp. 951–72.

Van Vactor, Samuel A. and Tussing, Arlon R. Is an Oil Tariff Justified? An American Debate: Reality Says No. *Energy J.*, July 1988, *9*(3), pp. 1–5.

Van Vliet, R. C. J. A. and Van Doorslaer, E. K. A. Disaggregation of the Demand for Hospital Care. *Appl. Econ.*, July 1988, *20*(7), pp. 969–84.

Vanackere, Martine. Conditions of Agricultural Day-Labourers in Mexico. *Int. Lab. Rev.*, 1988, *127*(1), pp. 91–110.

Vanberg, Viktor J. and Buchanan, James M. The Politicization of Market Failure. *Public Choice*, May 1988, *57*(2), pp. 101–13.

Vanden Berghe, Carine and Gérard, Marcel. An

Endogenously Time-Varying Parameter (TVP) Model of Investment Behaviour: Theory and Application to Belgian Data. In *Motamen, H., ed.*, 1988, pp. 183–201.

Vander Hill, C. Warren and Koch, James V. Is There Discrimination in the "Black Man's Game"? *Soc. Sci. Quart.*, March 1988, *69*(1), pp. 83–94.

Vander Weide, James H. and Carleton, Willard T. Investor Growth Expectations: Analysts vs. History. *J. Portfol. Manage.*, Spring 1988, *14*(3), pp. 78–82.

Vandergeest, Peter and Buttel, Frederick H. Marx, Weber, and Development Sociology: Beyond the Impasse. *World Devel.*, June 1988, *16*(6), pp. 683–95.

VanDerhei, Jack L. and Joanette, François P. Economic Determinants for the Choice of Actuarial Cost Methods. *J. Risk Ins.*, March 1988, *55*(1), pp. 59–74.

_____ and Johnson, Steven B. Fiduciary Decision Making and the Nature of Private Pension Fund Investment Behavior. *J. Risk Ins.*, December 1988, *55*(4), pp. 692–700.

VanderHoff, James. Direct Evidence on Endogenous Expectation Formation Methods. *Quart. Rev. Econ. Bus.*, Autumn 1988, *28*(3), pp. 6–14.

_____. Relative Price Variability and Monetary Policy Regimes. *J. Macroecon.*, Spring 1988, *10*(2), pp. 283–96.

Vanderkamp, John. Regional Disparities: A Model with Some Econometric Results for Canada. In *[Perroux, F.]*, 1988, pp. 269–96.

Vanheerswynghels, Adinda and Alaluf, Mateo. Local Employment, Training Structures and New Technologies in Traditional Industrial Regions: European Comparisons. In *Aydalot, P. and Keeble, D., eds.*, 1988, pp. 184–96.

Vanhonacker, Wilfried R. and Steckel, Joel H. A Heterogeneous Conditional Logit Model of Choice. *J. Bus. Econ. Statist.*, July 1988, *6*(3), pp. 391–98.

VanHoose, David D. Deposit Market Deregulation, Implicit Deposit Rates, and Monetary Policy. *Atlantic Econ. J.*, December 1988, *16*(4), pp. 11–23.

_____. Deregulation and Oligopolistic Rivalry in Bank Deposit Markets. *J. Banking Finance*, September 1988, *12*(3), pp. 379–88.

_____. Discount Rate Policy and Alternative Federal Reserve Operating Procedures in a Rational Expectations Setting. *J. Econ. Bus.*, November 1988, *40*(4), pp. 285–94.

Vanistendael, Frans. Trends of Tax Reform in Europe. *Australian Tax Forum*, 1988, *5*(2), pp. 133–79.

Vann, Richard J. Recognition of Foreign Enterprises as Taxable Entities: Australia. In *International Fiscal Association, ed. (I)*, 1988, pp. 269–85.

Vannini, Marco E. C. Rational Expectations in Second Moments, the *J*-Curve, and the Harrod Effect. *Econ. Letters*, 1988, *28*(1), pp. 69–73.

_____ and Marselli, Riccardo. The Holmes–Smyth Effect: Some Preliminary Exercises with the UK Demand for Narrow Money. *Appl. Econ.*, June 1988, *20*(6), pp. 711–20.

Vaňous, Jan and Marrese, Michael. The Content and Controversy of Soviet Trade Relations with Eastern Europe, 1970–1984. In *[Holzman, F. D.]*, 1988, pp. 185–220.

Vanroelen, Annemie and Plasmans, Joseph. Reducing Working Time for Reducing Unemployment? A Macroeconomic Simulation Study for the Belgian Economy. In *Motamen, H., ed.*, 1988, pp. 561–608.

Vansnick, Jean-Claude and Bouyssou, Denis. A Note on the Relationships Between Utility and Value Functions. In *Munier, B. R., ed.*, 1988, pp. 103–14.

VanTassell, Larry W. and Bessler, David A. Dynamic Price and Adjustments between Commercial and Purebred Cattle Markets. *Southern J. Agr. Econ.*, December 1988, *20*(2), pp. 137–43.

Vanzetti, David and Kennedy, John. Endogenous Price Policies and International Wheat Prices: Comment. *Amer. J. Agr. Econ.*, August 1988, *70*(3), pp. 743–46.

Varaiya, Nikhil P. The 'Winner's Curse' Hypothesis and Corporate Takeovers. *Managerial Dec. Econ.*, September 1988, *9*(3), pp. 209–19.

Varamini, Hossein and Akkina, Krishna. Rational Expectations and the Term Structure of Interest Rates: An Empirical Study of Group Ten Countries. In *Missouri Valley Economic Assoc.*, 1988, pp. 128–34.

Varga, György. The Role of Small Ventures in the Hungarian Economy. In *Brada, J. C. and Dobozi, I., eds.*, 1988, pp. 69–95.

Varga-Subá, Judit. The "Foreign Trade Limitation" and Cyclical Growth. *Soviet E. Europ. Foreign Trade*, Fall 1988, *24*(3), pp. 6–30.

Varian, Hal R. Estimating Risk Aversion from Arrow–Debreu Portfolio Choice. *Econometrica*, July 1988, *56*(4), pp. 973–79.

_____. Le principe d'arbitrage en économie financiére. (The Arbitrage Principle in Financial Economics. With English summary.) *Ann. Écon. Statist.*, April–June 1988, (10), pp. 1–22.

_____. Revealed Preference with a Subset of Goods. *J. Econ. Theory*, October 1988, *46*(1), pp. 179–85.

_____. Symposium on Takeovers. *J. Econ. Perspectives*, Winter 1988, *2*(1), pp. 3–5.

_____ and Gordon, Roger H. Intergenerational Risk Sharing. *J. Public Econ.*, November 1988, *37*(2), pp. 185–202.

Vartiainen, Henri J. Luck, Necessity, and Dynamic Flexibility: Discussion. In *Hanusch, H., ed.*, 1988, pp. 128–29.

Vasavada, Utpal and Gunter, Lewell. Dynamic Labour Demand Schedules for U.S. Agriculture. *Appl. Econ.*, June 1988, *20*(6), pp. 803–12.

Vasconcellos, Geraldo M. On the Application of Optimal Control Theory to Financial Planning and Forecasting. *J. Econ. Bus.*, November 1988, *40*(4), pp. 309–18.

Vasgerau, Hans-Jürgen. Contract Remedies: A Need for Better Efficiency Analysis: Comment. *J. Inst. Theoretical Econ.*, February 1988, *144*(1), pp. 35–38.

Vashistha, Prem and Bhalla, Surjit S. Income Distribution in India—A Re-examination. In *Srinivasan, T. N. and Bardhan, P. K., eds.*, 1988, pp. 39–68.

Vasiliu, D. P. and Săvulescu, B. Aspects of Queueing Spaces Dimensioning. *Econ. Computat. Cybern. Stud. Res.*, 1988, *23*(4), pp. 45–49.

Vasillopulos, Christopher and Papathanasis, A. The Remedies of Antitrust under Functional Integration. In *Pennsylvania Economic Association*, 1988, pp. 626–38.

_____ and Sawhney, Shiv. The Triple Tension of Entrepreneurial Management. In *Pennsylvania Economic Association*, 1988, pp. 614–25.

Vasko, Tibor and Segerstahl, Boris. Communication and Regional Planning: Some Systemic Remarks. In *Orishimo, I.; Hewings, G. J. D. and Nijkamp, P., eds.*, 1988, pp. 21–28.

Vásquez-Barquero, Antonio. Small-Scale Industry in Rural Areas: The Spanish Experience since the Beginning of This Century. In *Arrow, K. J., ed.*, 1988, pp. 232–58.

Vasserot, Jean-Yves and Maillat, Denis. Economic and Territorial Conditions for Indigenous Revival in Europe's Industrial Regions. In *Aydalot, P. and Keeble, D., eds.*, 1988, pp. 163–83.

Vassilakis, Spyros and Newman, Peter. Sraffa and Imperfect Competition. *Cambridge J. Econ.*, March 1988, *12*(1), pp. 37–42.

Vastrup, Claus. Pensionsreform og stabiliseringspolitik. (Stabilization Aspects of a Compulsory Pension for the Labor Market. With English summary.) *Nationaløkon. Tidsskr.*, 1988, *126*(2), pp. 159–70.

Vaubel, Roland. Macroeconomic Policy Coordination: Where Should We Stand? Comments. In *Giersch, H., ed.*, 1988, pp. 296–300.

Vaughan, Michael B. The Arc Elasticity of Demand: A Note and Comment. *J. Econ. Educ.*, Summer 1988, *19*(3), pp. 254–58.

_____ and Baxter, Scott. Tuition, Unemployment and the Demand for Education: A Case Study for Classroom Use. In *Missouri Valley Economic Assoc.*, 1988, pp. 135–40.

_____; Potiowsky, Thomas P. and Smith, W. James. Inferring Collusion from Pricing Behavior: The American Tobacco Case Reexamined. *Atlantic Econ. J.*, September 1988, *16*(3), pp. 40–45.

Vaughan, Richard. Distributional Aspects of the Life Cycle Theory of Saving. In *Kessler, D. and Masson, A., eds.*, 1988, pp. 193–235.

Vaughan, Therese M. The Financial Feasibility of Tax-Sheltered Individual Retirement Plans: Comment. *J. Risk Ins.*, March 1988, *55*(1), pp. 159–63.

Vaught, Bobby C.; Buchanan, W. Wary and Hoy, Frank. Any Development Program Can Work. In *Timpe, A. D., ed.*, 1988, *1985*, pp. 307–15.

Vaught, Daniel and Elam, Emmett W. Risk and

Return in Cattle and Hog Futures. *J. Futures Markets*, February 1988, *8*(1), pp. 79–87.

Vaupel, James W. Inherited Frailty and Longevity. *Demography*, May 1988, *25*(2), pp. 277–87.

Vavouras, Ioannis S. The Theory of Public Enterprise Restated. *Ann. Pub. Co-op. Econ.*, July–Sept. 1988, *59*(3), pp. 331–40.

Vawter, Irene M. Consumer Affairs: A View from Government. In *Maynes, E. S. and ACCI Research Committee, eds.*, 1988, pp. 628–32.

Veall, Michael R. and Kwok, Ben. The Jackknife and Regression with AR(1) Errors. *Econ. Letters*, 1988, *26*(3), pp. 247–52.

Vedder, Richard; Gallaway, Lowell and Sollars, David. The Tullock–Bastiat Hypothesis, Inequality-Transfer Curve and the Natural Distribution of Income. *Public Choice*, March 1988, *56*(3), pp. 285–94.

Vedovato, Claudio; Lidström, Per and Lyttkens, Carl Hampus. Military Expenditures in Developing Countries: A Comment on Deger and Sen [Military Expenditure, Spin-Off and Economic Development]. *J. Devel. Econ.*, February 1988, *28*(1), pp. 105–10.

Veeman, Michele M. Supply Management Systems: Impact on Interprovincial Trade. *Can. J. Agr. Econ.*, Part 1, December 1988, *36*(4), pp. 711–23.

Veeman, Terrence S. and Rahuma, Ali A. Productivity Growth in the Prairie Grain Sector and Its Major Soil Zones, 1960s to 1980s. *Can. J. Agr. Econ.*, Part 2, December 1988, *36*(4), pp. 857–70.

Veendorp, E. C. H. and Kantarelis, D. Live and Let Live Type Behavior in a Multi-market Setting with Demand Fluctuations. *J. Econ. Behav. Organ.*, September 1988, *10*(2), pp. 235–44.

Veeneklaas, F. R. and van Eijk, C. J. Optimization and the Preparation of Economic Policy. In *Driehuis, W.; Fase, M. M. G. and den Hartog, H., eds.*, 1988, pp. 265–81.

de Veer, J. Conflicts of Interest in the Field of Agricultural Policy. *Europ. Rev. Agr. Econ.*, 1988, *15*(2–3), pp. 155–57.

Vegari, Sheila. A Test for Household Behavior in Response to Government Activities. *Southern Econ. J.*, April 1988, *54*(4), pp. 994–1001.

Végh, Carlos A. Effects of Currency Substitution on the Response of the Current Account to Supply Shocks. *Int. Monet. Fund Staff Pap.*, December 1988, *35*(4), pp. 574–91.

Vehmanen, Lasse. Vähemmistöosuudet konsernissa. (External Interests in the Group of Companies. With English summary.) *Liiketaloudellinen Aikak.*, 1988, *37*(1), pp. 55–68.

Veit, Lawrence A. Foreign Exchange Rates: The U.S. Interest. In *Yochelson, J., ed.*, 1988, pp. 157–73.

──────. On the Case against Excessive Pessimism. In *Aho, C. M. and Levinson, M.*, 1988, pp. 210–15.

Velasco, Andres. Monetarismo y neoestructuralismo: Lecciones macroeconómicas. (Monetarism and Neo-Structuralism: Macroeconomic

Lessons. With English summary.) *Colección Estud. CIEPLAN*, March 1988, (23), pp. 51–65.

van Veldhoven, Gery M. Dynamic Aspects of Economic Behavior: Some Determinants. In *van Raaij, W. F.; van Veldhoven, G. M. and Wärneryd, K.-E., eds.*, 1988, pp. 52–73.

Veldkamp, J. H. and Dijkstra, Theo K. Data-Driven Selection of Regressors and the Bootstrap. In *Dijkstra, T. K., ed.*, 1988, pp. 17–38.

Velez, William and Squires, Gregory D. Insurance Redlining and the Process of Discrimination. *Rev. Black Polit. Econ.*, Winter 1988, *16*(3), pp. 63–75.

Velicanu, M.; Bodea, Constanţa and Diaconescu, G. A Relational Operator for Sorted Join. *Econ. Computat. Cybern. Stud. Res.*, 1988, *23*(2), pp. 33–36.

Veljanovski, Cento G. Financial Regulation—Or Over-regulation? Introduction. In *Goodhart, C., et al.*, 1988, pp. 1–13.

──────. Impossibility and Related Excuses: Comment. *J. Inst. Theoretical Econ.*, February 1988, *144*(1), pp. 117–21.

──────. **and Fenn, P. T.** A Positive Economic Theory of Regulatory Enforcement. *Econ. J.*, December 1988, *98*(393), pp. 1055–70.

Vella, Frank. Generating Conditional Expectations from Models with Selectivity Bias. *Econ. Letters*, 1988, *28*(1), pp. 97–103.

Vellmann, Karlheinz. Herstellkosten-Controlling—Eine Praxisorientierte Darstellung. (With English summary.) *Z. Betriebswirtshaft*, December 1988, *58*(12), pp. 1340–70.

Vellve, Renee and Hobbelink, Henk. Role of Public Research and NGOs. In *Research and Info. System for the Non-aligned and Other Developing Countries*, 1988, pp. 349–67.

Velupillai, Kumaraswamy. Some Swedish Stepping Stones to Modern Macroeconomics. *Eastern Econ. J.*, Jan.–March 1988, *14*(1), pp. 87–98.

──────. **and Phelps, Edmund S.** Optimum Fiscal Policy When Monetary Policy Is Bound by a Rule: Ramsey Redux. In *Arrow, K. J. and Boskin, M. J., eds.*, 1988, pp. 116–30.

──────. **and Ricci, Gianni.** Lecture Notes in Economics and Mathematical Systems: Growth Cycles and Multisectoral Economics: The Goodwin Tradition: Introduction. In *[Goodwin, R. M.]*, 1988, pp. 1–18.

Venables, Anthony J. and Markusen, James R. Trade Policy with Increasing Returns and Imperfect Competition: Contradictory Results from Competing Assumptions. *J. Int. Econ.*, May 1988, *24*(3–4), pp. 299–316.

──────. **and Smith, Alasdair.** Completing the Internal Market in the European Community: Some Industry Simulations. *Europ. Econ. Rev.*, September 1988, *32*(7), pp. 1501–25.

Vencovský, František. Which Way to the Convertible Crown? *Czech. Econ. Digest.*, June 1988, (4), pp. 3–12.

Venetoulias, Aachilles; Welsch, Roy E. and Belsley, David A. Computer Guided Diagnostics.

In *Edwards, D. and Raun, N. E., eds.*, 1988, pp. 99–104.

Venezia, Itzhak. On the Economic Advantages of the Coinsurance Clause. *J. Risk Ins.*, June 1988, 55(2), pp. 307–14.

Venezian, Emilio C. and Fields, Joseph A. Informational Asymmetries in Retroactive Insurance: Authors' Reply. *J. Risk Ins.*, September 1988, 55(3), pp. 555–58.

_____ **and Schlesinger, Harris.** Compensating Victims of Occupational Diseases: Can We Structure an Effective Policy? In *Borba, P. S. and Appel, D., eds.*, 1988, pp. 59–79.

Veneziani, Bruno. La contrattazione collettiva in agricoltura. (Collective Bargaining in Agriculture. With English summary.) *Econ. Lavoro*, Jan.–Mar. 1988, 22(1), pp. 89–97.

Venieris, Yiannis P. and Stewart, Douglas B. Long-run Social and Economic Responses of Fertility in the United States. *Pakistan Devel. Rev.*, Summer 1988, 27(2), pp. 137–57.

Venkataraman, K. The Role of UNIDO. In *Research and Info. System for the Non-aligned and Other Developing Countries.*, 1988, pp. 368–84.

Venkataraman, R. Human Resources Development and the Planning Process in India: Inaugural Address. In *Kohli, U. and Gautam, V., eds.*, 1988, pp. 1–4.

Venkatesh, B. and Verghese, Thomas. Institutional Paper, the Association of the Physically Handicapped: Human Resources Development for the Disabled (Problems and Solution). In *Kohli, U. and Gautam, V., eds.*, 1988, pp. 236–47.

Venkatesh, P. C. and Chiang, Raymond. Insider Holdings and Perceptions of Information Asymmetry: A Note. *J. Finance*, September 1988, 43(4), pp. 1041–48.

Venkateswarlu, Tadiboyina. Econometrics: Survey of Course Reading Materials in Universities in Canada and the United States. *Amer. Econ.*, Spring 1988, 32(1), pp. 80–84.

_____. Mathematical Economics: Survey of Reading Materials in Universities in Canada and the United States. *Amer. Econ.*, Fall 1988, 32(2), pp. 79–83.

Venkatraman, N. and Ramanujam, Vasudevan. Modeling the Effectiveness of a Strategic Planning System. In *Lamb, R. and Shrivastava, P., eds.*, 1988, pp. 113–38.

Venti, Steven F. and Wise, David A. The Determinants of IRA Contributions and the Effect of Limit Changes. In *Bodie, Z.; Shoven, J. B. and Wise, D. A., eds.*, 1988, pp. 9–47.

Vera la Torre, José Carlos and Costa, Julio Castañeda. Private Health Care Financing Alternatives. In *Zschock, D. K., ed.*, 1988, pp. 79–97.

Veranen, Jyrki. Do the Owners Have an Impact on Firm Performance? *Liiketaloudellinen Aikak.*, 1988, 37(2), pp. 142–46.

Verbeke, Alain. Assessing the Effectiveness of Belgian Seaport Policy: A Comparative Institutional Approach. *Ann. Pub. Co-op. Econ.*, April–June 1988, 59(2), pp. 157–74.

Verbeke, Louis H. Security on Movable Property and Receivables in Europe: Belgium. In *Dickson, M. G.; Rosener, W. and Storm, P. M., eds.*, 1988, pp. 7–23.

Verbon, H. A. A. Explaining Pay-as-You-Go Financed Public Pension Systems. *Econ. Letters*, 1988, 28(2), pp. 181–87.

Verbrugge, James A.; Burns, Richard M. and Jordan, Bradford D. Returns to Initial Shareholders in Savings Institution Conversions: Evidence and Regulatory Implications. *J. Finan. Res.*, Summer 1988, 11(2), pp. 125–36.

Verbruggen, Johan P. Two Recent Trends Combined in an Econometric Model for the Netherlands: The Supply-Side and Sectoral Approach. In *Motamen, H., ed.*, 1988, pp. 353–80.

Vercelli, Alessandro. Goodwin and the M-K-S System. In *[Goodwin, R. M.]*, 1988, pp. 102–11.

_____. "Homo oeconomicus" oppure "homo sapiens"? Comportamentismo e razionalismo in economia politica. (Homo Oeconomicus versus Homo Sapiens? Rationalism and Behaviourism in Economics. With English summary.) *Econ. Polit.*, August 1988, 5(2), pp. 169–75.

_____. Technological Flexibility, Financial Fragility and the Recent Revival of Schumpeterian Entrepreneurship. *Rech. Écon. Louvain*, 1988, 54(1), pp. 103–32.

Vercellis, Carlo and Tosini, Elisabetta. An Interactive System for Extra-Urban Vehicle and Crew Scheduling Problems. In *Daduna, J. R. and Wren, A., eds.*, 1988, pp. 41–53.

Verdin, Jo Ann. The Impact of Computer Technology on Human Resource Information System Users. In *Gattiker, U. E. and Larwood, L., eds.*, 1988, pp. 143–59.

Verdoorn, P. J. Factors That Determine the Growth of Labour Productivity: Appendix. In *[Clark, C.]*, 1988, pp. 199–207.

Vere, D. T. and Griffith, G. R. Supply and Demand Interactions in the New South Wales Prime Lamb Market. *Rev. Marketing Agr. Econ.*, December 1988, 56(3), pp. 287–305.

Verfaille, Guy and De Grauwe, Paul. Exchange Rate Variability, Misalignment, and the European Monetary System. In *Marston, R. C., ed.*, 1988, pp. 77–100.

Verge, Pierre. Law and Industrial Relations in Quebec: Object and Context. In *Hébert, G.; Jain, H. C. and Meltz, N. M., eds..*, 1988, pp. 73–105.

Verges, Joaquim. The Determination of Justified Deficits and Rules of Behavior for Public Enterprises, When "External Factors" Are Present. *Ann. Pub. Co-op. Econ.*, March 1988, 59(1), pp. 3–22.

Verghese, Thomas and Venkatesh, B. Institutional Paper, the Association of the Physically Handicapped: Human Resources Development for the Disabled (Problems and Solution). In *Kohli, U. and Gautam, V., eds.*, 1988, pp. 236–47.

Vergoossen, Dick and Reitsma, René F. A Causal Typology of Migration: The Role of Commuting. *Reg. Stud.*, August 1988, 22(4), pp. 331–40.

Verhoef, Grietjie. Aspects of Nedbank's International Activities 1945–73. In *Jones, S., ed.,* 1988, pp. 81–103.

Verillo, Josmar. The Global Construction Industry: Brazil. In *Strassmann, W. P. and Wells, J., eds.,* 1988, pp. 180–98.

Verkooijen, J. K. IMF Policies: The Dilemma of Their Effect on Growth and Income Distribution in Developing Countries, 1980–5. In *Brenner, Y. S.; Reijnders, J. P. G. and Spithoven, A. H. G. M., eds.,* 1988, pp. 178–89.

Verleger, Philip K., Jr. Implications of the Energy Provisions. In *Schott, J. J. and Smith, M. G., eds.,* 1988, pp. 117–27.

———. U.S.–Canadian Trade Agreement: An American Perspective. *Energy J.,* October 1988, 9(4), pp. 99–101.

VerLoren van Themaat, Pieter. The Possibilities for National Measures of Implementation to Strengthen the Legal Quality of International Rules on Foreign Trade. In *Dicke, D. C. and Petersmann, E.-U., eds.,* 1988, pp. 42–57.

Verma, P. C. Exports of Jute Goods from India. *Margin,* July–Sept. 1988, 20(4), pp. 72–79.

Vermaelen, Theo. Size Related Anomalies and Trading Activity of UK Institutional Investors: Discussion. In *Dimson, E., ed.,* 1988, pp. 176–78.

Vermulst, Edwin; Musquar, Philippe and Bellis, Jean-François. The New EEC Regulation on Unfair Pricing Practices in Maritime Transport: A Forerunner of the Extension of Unfair Trade Concepts to Services? *J. World Trade,* February 1988, 22(1), pp. 47–65.

Vernon, Raymond. The Promise and the Challenge. In *Vernon, R., ed.,* 1988, pp. 1–22.

Verny, Sophie. The EEC and CMEA: The Problem of Mutual Recognition. *Soviet E. Europ. Foreign Trade,* Summer 1988, 24(2), pp. 6–25.

Verplanken, Bas and Pieters, Rik G. M. The Joy of Thinking about Nuclear Energy. In *Maital, S., ed., Vol. 2,* 1988, pp. 537–49.

Verrecchia, Robert E. and Holthausen, Robert W. The Effect of Sequential Information Releases on the Variance of Price Changes in an Intertemporal Multi-asset Market. *J. Acc. Res.,* Spring 1988, 26(1), pp. 82–106.

Versace, John. Choosing Automatic Restraint Designs for the 1990s: Comments. In *Graham, J. D., ed.,* 1988, pp. 111–15.

Vertinsky, Ilan and Tan, S. J. Strategic Management of International Financial Centers: A Tale of Two Cities. In *Khoury, S. J. and Ghosh, A., eds.,* 1988, pp. 87–104.

Vertonghen, R. Socio-economic Evaluation of Investments in the Public Sector. *Tijdschrift Econ. Manage.,* Sept.–Dec. 1988, 33(3/4), pp. 245–59.

Vertrees, James and Collins, Keith. Decoupling and U.S. Farm Policy Reform. *Can. J. Agr. Econ.,* Part 1, December 1988, 36(4), pp. 733–45.

Verzilli, Andrew G.; Awerbuch, Patricia and Makarim, Wajdi. Frustration Equilibrium and Disequilibrium Positions: Has Anything Changed in Eight Years? In *Pennsylvania Economic Association,* 1988, pp. 32–43.

——— **and Wieckowski, Tom.** The Economics—If Any—Of Malpractice in Education? In *Pennsylvania Economic Association,* 1988, pp. 591–98.

Větrovský, Jiří and Hrinda, Vasil. Direct Relations: Clearing Operations in the National Currencies of Czechoslovakia and the Soviet Union. *Czech. Econ. Digest.,* June 1988, (4), pp. 13–20.

Vetsuypens, Michael R. and Helmuth, John A. Airline Deregulation: Additional Evidence from the Capital Markets. *Quart. J. Bus. Econ.,* Spring 1988, 27(2), pp. 117–38.

Veugelers, Reinhilde; de Bondt, Raymond and Sleuwaegen, Leo. Innovative Strategic Groups in Multinational Industries. *Europ. Econ. Rev.,* April 1988, 32(4), pp. 905–25.

Veyrat, Bernadette. Sub-Saharan African Countries: Minor Partners, Major Strategic Interests. In *Lavigne, M., ed.,* 1988, pp. 212–24.

Vial, Joaquin. Comparación de modelos macroeconométricos latinoamericanos. (Comparison between Latin American Macroeconometric Models. With English summary.) *Colección Estud. CIEPLAN,* June 1988, (24), pp. 145–81.

Vianello, Fernando. A Critique of Professor Goodwin's "Critique of Sraffa" In *[Goodwin, R. M.],* 1988, pp. 112–19.

Vibe-Pedersen, Jon. Samspilsfænomenet og fordelingen af pensionisternes forbrugsmuligheder. (Tax Rates, Benefit Reduction Rates and Pension Reform. With English summary.) *Nationaløkon. Tidsskr.,* 1988, 126(2), pp. 183–95.

Vicarelli, Fausto. Central Bank Autonomy: A Historical Perspective. In *Toniolo, G., ed.,* 1988, pp. 1–16.

———. Equilibrium and Probability: A Reinterpretation of the Methodological Foundations of the *General Theory.* In *Barrère, A., ed.,* 1988, pp. 112–27.

Vickers, John. Delegation and the Theory of the Firm. In *Daughety, A. F., ed.,* 1988, pp. 391–401.

——— **and Bonanno, Giacomo.** Vertical Separation. *J. Ind. Econ.,* March 1988, 36(3), pp. 257–65.

——— **and Hay, Donald.** The Reform of UK Competition Policy. *Nat. Inst. Econ. Rev.,* August 1988, (125), pp. 56–68.

——— **and Stoneman, Paul.** The Assessment: The Economics of Technology Policy. *Oxford Rev. Econ. Policy,* Winter 1988, 4(4), pp. i–xvi.

——— **and Yarrow, George.** Regulation of Privatised Firms in Britain. *Europ. Econ. Rev.,* March 1988, 32(2–3), pp. 465–72.

Vidali, Carlos. Developing Country Perspectives on the Multilateral Trade Negotiations. In *Roberts, C., ed.,* 1988, pp. 45–48.

Viesti, Gianfranco. International Strategies of Italian Multinationals. In *Onida, F. and Viesti, G., eds.,* 1988, pp. 75–95.

———. Size and Trends of Italian Direct Investment Abroad: A Quantitative Assessment. In *Onida, F. and Viesti, G., eds.*, 1988, pp. 30–48.

———. Technological Interdependence, Market Structure and the Pattern of International Growth of Italian Firms. In *Onida, F. and Viesti, G., eds.*, 1988, pp. 110–32.

——— and Onida, Fabrizio. Italy as an International Investor: Summary and Conclusions. In *Onida, F. and Viesti, G., eds.*, 1988, pp. 150–57.

——— and Schieppati, Cesare. Profiles of Major Italian Multinationals. In *Onida, F. and Viesti, G., eds.*, 1988, pp. 158–79.

Viganó, Jorge A. National Treatment in Trade in Services and Developing Countries. In *Dicke, D. C. and Petersmann, E.-U., eds.*, 1988, pp. 288–91.

Vigeland, Robert L.; Daley, Lane A. and Senkow, David W. Analysts' Forecasts, Earnings Variability, and Option Pricing: Empirical Evidence. *Accounting Rev.*, October 1988, *63*(4), pp. 563–85.

Vijayaraghavan, N. R. and Goodman, Laurie S. Combining Various Futures Contracts to Get Better Hedges. In *Fabozzi, F. J., ed.*, 1988, pp. 257–68.

Vijh, Anand M. Potential Biases from Using Only Trade Prices of Related Securities on Different Exchanges: A Comment. *J. Finance*, September 1988, *43*(4), pp. 1049–55.

Vijlbrief, Hans and van Ravenstein, Ad. Welfare Cost of Higher Tax Rates: An Empirical Laffer Curve for the Netherlands. *De Economist*, 1988, *136*(2), pp. 205–19.

Vijverberg, Wim and van der Gaag, Jacques. A Switching Regression Model for Wage Determinants in the Public and Private Sectors of a Developing Country. *Rev. Econ. Statist.*, May 1988, *70*(2), pp. 244–52.

Vila, Jean-Pierre. New Algorithmic and Software Tools for D-Optimal Design Computation in Nonlinear Regression. In *Edwards, D. and Raun, N. E., eds.*, 1988, pp. 409–14.

Vilas, Carlos M. El populismo latinoamericano: un enfoque estructural. (With English summary.) *Desarrollo Econ.*, Oct.–Dec. 1988, *28*(111), pp. 323–52.

Vilks, Arnis. Approximate Aggregation of Excess Demand Functions. *J. Econ. Theory*, August 1988, *45*(2), pp. 417–24.

———. Consistent Aggregation of a General Equilibrium Model. In *Eichhorn, W., ed.*, 1988, pp. 691–703.

Villalba, Julian and Gomez-Samper, Henry. A Venezuelan Paradox: The Prospects for Attracting (or Repatriating) Foreign Investment. In *Jorge, A. and Salazar-Carrillo, J., eds.*, 1988, pp. 189–94.

Villamil, Anne P. Price Discriminating Monetary Policy: A Nonuniform Pricing Approach. *J. Public Econ.*, April 1988, *35*(3), pp. 385–92.

Villanueva, Delano. Issues in Financial Sector Reform. *Finance Develop.*, March 1988, *25*(1), pp. 14–17.

Villar, Antonio Netario. La lógica de la elección social: Una revisión de los resultados bósicos. (With English summary.) *Invest. Ecón.*, January 1988, *12*(1), pp. 3–44.

———. On the Existence of Pareto Optimal Allocations When Individual Welfare Depends on Relative Consumption. *J. Public Econ.*, August 1988, *36*(3), pp. 387–97.

——— and Herrero, Carmen. A Characterization of Economies with the Non-substitution Property. *Econ. Letters*, 1988, *26*(2), pp. 147–52.

——— and Herrero, Carmen. General Equilibrium in a Non-linear Leontief Framework. *Manchester Sch. Econ. Soc. Stud.*, June 1988, *56*(2), pp. 159–66.

Villarmarzo, Ricardo. Uruguay: Evolution of Taxation and Promotional Regimes. *Bull. Int. Fiscal Doc.*, March 1988, *42*(3), pp. 116–22.

Villarreal, René. External Debt and Adjustment Policies: The Case of Mexico 1982–6. In *Griffith-Jones, S., ed.*, 1988, pp. 40–63.

———. Industrial Restructuring of the Public Steel Industry: The Mexican Case. *Industry Devel.*, October 1988, (24), pp. 57–88.

Viñals, José M. and Berges, Angel. Financial Innovation and Capital Formation. In *Heertje, A., ed.*, 1988, pp. 158–202.

——— and Cuddington, John T. Fiscal Policy and the Current Account: What Do Capital Controls Do? *Int. Econ. J.*, Spring 1988, *2*(1), pp. 29–37.

Vincent, D.; Mannion, R. and Tillack, R. Effects of Petroleum Product Excises on Agriculture. *Rev. Marketing Agr. Econ.*, April 1988, *56*(1), pp. 121–28.

Vincent, Joan. Equality and Enterprise: The Cooperative Movement in the Development Economy of Uganda. In *Attwood, D. W. and Baviskar, B. S., eds.*, 1988, pp. 188–210.

Vincent, Richard. Taxation of Foreign-Source Income: Australia. *Bull. Int. Fiscal Doc.*, November 1988, *42*(11), pp. 493–95.

Vincke, Philippe. {P, Q, I}-Preference Structures. In *Kacprzyk, J. and Roubens, M., eds.*, 1988, pp. 72–81.

Vines, David; Currie, David and Muscatelli, Anton. Macroeconomic Interactions between North and South: Introduction. In *Currie, D. and Vines, D., eds.*, 1988, pp. 1–31.

——— and Moutos, Thomas. A Prototype Macroeconomic Model with Integrated Financial and Commodity Markets. *Econ. Notes*, 1988, (1), pp. 51–68.

Vining, Aidan R. and Schwindt, Richard. Have a Heart: Increasing the Supply of Transplant Organs for Infants and Children. *J. Policy Anal. Manage.*, Fall 1988, *7*(4), pp. 706–10.

——— and Weimer, David Leo. Information Asymmetry Favoring Sellers: A Policy Framework. *Policy Sci.*, 1988, *21*(4), pp. 281–303.

Vining, Daniel R., Jr. and Cochrane, Steven G. Population Migration in the Developed World: Some Further Comments. *Int. Reg. Sci. Rev.*, 1988, *11*(3), pp. 277–78.

——— and Cochrane, Steven G. Recent Trends in Migration between Core and Peripheral Regions in Developed and Advanced Developing Countries. *Int. Reg. Sci. Rev.*, 1988, *11*(3), pp. 215–43.

———— and MacKellar, F. L. Research Policy and Review 26: Where Does the United States Stand in the Global Resource Scarcity Debate? *Environ. Planning A*, December 1988, *20*(12), pp. 1567–73.

Vining, Rutledge. Seeing to It That the Subject of the Science Is the Subject of Its Practice: Towards a Theory of the Outcome of an Economic System's Working. *Rev. Reg. Stud.*, Winter 1988, *18*(1), pp. 1–3.

Vink, N.; Fenyes, T. I. and van Zyl, J. Structural Imbalances in South African Agriculture. *S. Afr. J. Econ.*, June–Sept. 1988, *56*(2–3), pp. 181–95.

———— and Kassier, W. E. The 'Tragedy of the Commons' and Livestock Farming in Southern Africa: Reply. *S. Afr. J. Econ.*, June–Sept. 1988, *56*(2–3), pp. 218–24.

Vinke, Philippe and Roubens, Marc. Fuzzy Possibility Graphs and Their Application to Ranking Fuzzy Numbers. In *Kacprzyk, J. and Roubens, M., eds.*, 1988, pp. 119–28.

Vinning, G. S. and Wegener, M. K. Agricultural Economics Training at the University of Queensland. *Rev. Marketing Agr. Econ.*, August 1988, *56*(2), pp. 230–32.

Vinod, H. D. Dynamic Benefit Cost Ratio Criterion for Practical Sequential Ranking to Encourage Cost Control and Self Help. *Indian Econ. Rev.*, July–Dec. 1988, *23*(2), pp. 263–74.

————. Random Walk in Consumption: Maximum Likelihood and Nonparametrics. In *Rhodes, G. F., Jr. and Fomby, T. B., eds.*, 1988, pp. 291–309.

———— and Ullah, Aman. Flexible Production Function Estimation by Nonparametric Kernel Estimators. In *Rhodes, G. F., Jr. and Fomby, T. B., eds.*, 1988, pp. 139–60.

———— and Ullah, Aman. Nonparametric Kernel Estimation of Econometric Parameters. *J. Quant. Econ.*, January 1988, *4*(1), pp. 81–87.

Violi, Roberto; Bollino, Carlo and Ceriani, Vieri. Il mercato unico europeo e l'armonizzazione dell'iva e delle accise. (With English summary.) *Polit. Econ.*, December 1988, *4*(3), pp. 315–59.

Vipraio, Patrizia Tiberi. International Co-operation among Firms. Problems and Perspectives for Theoretical Analysis. *Econ. Lavoro*, Oct.–Dec. 1988, *22*(4), pp. 55–70.

Virén, Matti. Interest Rates and Budget Deficits: Cross-Country Evidence from the Period 1924–1938. *Econ. Letters*, 1988, *28*(3), pp. 235–38.

———— and Lahti, Ari. Examining the Role of Expectations in a Macromodel. *Econ. Modelling*, October 1988, *5*(4), pp. 347–53.

Virmani, Arvind. Tax Reform in Developing Countries: Issues, Policies, and Information Gaps. *Public Finance*, 1988, *43*(1), pp. 19–38.

———— and Sicat, Gerardo P. Personal Income

Taxes in Developing Countries. *World Bank Econ. Rev.*, January 1988, *2*(1), pp. 123–38.

Visaria, Pravin. Demographic Trends and Population Policy in China. In *Mitra, A., ed.*, 1988, pp. 1–27.

Viscencio-Brambila, Hector; Fuller, Stephen W. and Peterson, E. Wesley F. A Welfare Analysis of Port User Fees: The Case of Grain and Soybean Exports. *Southern J. Agr. Econ.*, December 1988, *20*(2), pp. 101–08.

Visco, Ignazio. Again on Sign Changes upon Deletion of a Variable from a Linear Regression. *Oxford Bull. Econ. Statist.*, May 1988, *50*(2), pp. 225–27.

————; Gressani, Daniela and Guiso, Luigi. Disinflation in Italy: An Analysis with the Econometric Model of the Bank of Italy. *J. Policy Modeling*, Summer 1988, *10*(2), pp. 163–203.

Viscusi, W. Kip. Editor's Introduction. *J. Risk Uncertainty*, June 1988, *1*(2), pp. 139–45.

————. Irreversible Environmental Investments with Uncertain Benefit Levels. *J. Environ. Econ. Manage.*, June 1988, *15*(2), pp. 147–57.

————. Liability for Occupational Accidents and Illnesses. In *Litan, R. E. and Winston, C., eds.*, 1988, pp. 155–83.

————. Pain and Suffering in Product Liability Cases: Systematic Compensation or Capricious Awards? *Int. Rev. Law Econ.*, December 1988, *8*(2), pp. 203–20.

————. Product Liability and Regulation: Establishing the Appropriate Institutional Division of Labor. *Amer. Econ. Rev.*, May 1988, *78*(2), pp. 300–304.

————. Product Liability Litigation with Risk Aversion. *J. Legal Stud.*, January 1988, *17*(1), pp. 101–21.

————; Huber, Joel and Magat, Wesley A. Consumer Processing of Hazard Warning Information. *J. Risk Uncertainty*, June 1988, *1*(2), pp. 201–32.

————; Huber, Joel and Magat, Wesley A. Paired Comparison and Contingent Valuation Approaches to Morbidity Risk Valuation. *J. Environ. Econ. Manage.*, December 1988, *15*(4), pp. 395–411.

————; Magat, Wesley A. and Forrest, Anne. Altruistic and Private Valuations of Risk Reduction. *J. Policy Anal. Manage.*, Winter 1988, *7*(2), pp. 227–45.

———— and Moore, Michael J. Doubling the Estimated Value of Life: Results Using New Occupational Fatality Data. *J. Policy Anal. Manage.*, Spring 1988, *7*(3), pp. 476–90.

———— and Moore, Michael J. The Quantity-Adjusted Value of Life. *Econ. Inquiry*, July 1988, *26*(3), pp. 369–88.

Vishnevskii, Anatolii G. Are Things Moving? On Demographic Processes and Social Policy. *Prob. Econ.*, December 1988, *31*(8), pp. 6–24.

Vishny, Robert W. Do Target Shareholders Lose in Unsuccessful Control Contests? Comment. In *Auerbach, A. J., ed. (1)*, 1988, pp. 153–55.

————; Mørck, Randall and Shleifer, Andrei. Characteristics of Targets of Hostile and

Friendly Takeovers. In *Auerbach, A. J., ed. (I)*, 1988, pp. 101–29.

———; **Morck, Randall and Shleifer, Andrei.** Management Ownership and Market Valuation: An Empirical Analysis. *J. Finan. Econ.*, Jan.–March 1988, 20(1–2), pp. 293–315.

——— **and Shleifer, Andrei.** The Efficiency of Investment in the Presence of Aggregate Demand Spillovers. *J. Polit. Econ.*, December 1988, 96(6), pp. 1221–31.

——— **and Shleifer, Andrei.** Management Buyouts as a Response to Market Pressure. In *Auerbach, A. J., ed. (II)*, 1988, pp. 87–102.

——— **and Shleifer, Andrei.** Value Maximization and the Acquisition Process. *J. Econ. Perspectives*, Winter 1988, 2(1), pp. 7–20.

Vishwanath, Tara. Parallel Search and Information Gathering. *Amer. Econ. Rev.*, May 1988, 78(2), pp. 110–16.

——— **and Burdett, Kenneth.** Balanced Matching and Labor Market Equilibrium. *J. Polit. Econ.*, October 1988, 96(5), pp. 1048–65.

——— **and Burdett, Kenneth.** Declining Reservation Wages and Learning. *Rev. Econ. Stud.*, October 1988, 55(4), pp. 655–65.

Vislie, Jon. Equilibrium in a Market with Sequential Bargaining and Random Outside Options. *Econ. Letters*, 1988, 26(4), pp. 325–28.

Visser, H. Austrian Thinking on International Economics. *J. Econ. Stud.*, 1988, 15(3–4), pp. 106–22.

Vital, Christian and Mengle, David L. SIC: Switzerland's New Electronic Interbank Payment System. *Fed. Res. Bank Richmond Econ. Rev.*, Nov.–Dec. 1988, 74(6), pp. 12–27.

Vitaliano, Donald F. Assessing the Locational Efficiency of a System of Hospitals. *Appl. Econ.*, August 1988, 20(8), pp. 1087–98.

———. Evidence about Debt Equivalence from the Local Public Sector. *Public Finance*, 1988, 43(2), pp. 295–309.

Vitello, Vincenzo. Economia monetaria e valori "naturali" della produzione e dell'occupazione: dall'approccio classico alla "nuova macroeconomia classica." (With English summary.) *Stud. Econ.*, 1988, 43(36), pp. 39–67.

Vito, Giuseppe. Seaport Systems Strategic Planning. In *Bianco, L. and La Bella, A., eds.*, 1988, pp. 546–68.

Vivekananda, Franklin and Domatob, Jerry Komia. Maldevelopment and Sub-Saharan African Elites. In *Vivekananda, F., ed.*, 1988, pp. 177–95.

——— **and Guha, Amalendu.** Structural Theory of Overdevelopment and Underdevelopment. In *Vivekananda, F., ed.*, 1988, pp. 165–75.

Vives, Xavier. Aggregation of Information in Large Cournot Markets. *Econometrica*, July 1988, 56(4), pp. 851–76.

———. Duopoly Information Equilibrium: Cournot and Betrand. In *Daughety, A. F., ed.*, 1988, *1984*, pp. 317–41.

———. On the Efficiency of Bertrand and Cournot Equilibria with Product Differentiation. In *Daughety, A. F., ed.*, 1988, *1985*, pp. 218–28.

———. Sequential Entry, Industry Structure and Welfare. *Europ. Econ. Rev.*, October 1988, 32(8), pp. 1671–87.

——— **and Thisse, Jacques-François.** On the Strategic Choice of Spatial Price Policy. *Amer. Econ. Rev.*, March 1988, 78(1), pp. 122–37.

Vladeck, Bruce C. Quality Assurance through External Controls. *Inquiry*, Spring 1988, 25(1), pp. 100–107.

Vlaisavljevich, Michael. State Business Taxes: The Policy and Research Agendas. In *Gold, S. D., ed.*, 1988, pp. 177–95.

Vlassoff, Carol. Impact of Development on Household Demographic Behaviour. In *Vlassoff, C. and Barkat-e-Khuda, eds.*, 1988, pp. 109–118.

——— **and Barkat-e-Khuda.** Impact of Modernization on Development and Demographic Behaviour: Introduction. In *Vlassoff, C. and Barkat-e-Khuda, eds.*, 1988, pp. 1–4.

van Vliet, Willem. Growth Restrictions and Affordable Housing: Dwellings versus People. In *Friedrichs, J., ed.*, 1988, pp. 13–26.

Voas, Robert B. Social Norms and Drunk Driving Countermeasures: Comments. In *Graham, J. D., ed.*, 1988, pp. 188–96.

Vobruba, Georg and Büchtemann, Christoph F. The Welfare State and Jobs: Comment. In *Kregel, J. A.; Matzner, E. and Roncaglia, A., eds.*, 1988, pp. 208–11.

Vogel, Ezra F. Competition and Cooperation: Learning From Japan. In *Furino, A., ed.*, 1988, pp. 51–61.

Vogel, Stephen; Adelman, Irma and Taylor, J. Edward. Life in a Mexican Village: A SAM Perspective. *J. Devel. Stud.*, October 1988, 25(1), pp. 7–24.

Vogelheim, Elisabeth. Women in a Changing Workplace: The Case of the Federal Republic of Germany. In *Jenson, J.; Hagen, E. and Reddy, C., eds.*, 1988, pp. 106–19.

Vogelsang, Ingo. A Little Paradox in the Design of Regulatory Mechanisms. *Int. Econ. Rev.*, August 1988, 29(3), pp. 467–76.

———. Regulation of Public Utilities and Nationalized Industries. In *Hare, P. G., ed.*, 1988, pp. 45–67.

Vogelstein, John L. Mergers and Takeovers: Taxes, Capital Structure, and the Incentives of Managers: Comment. In *Coffee, J. C., Jr.; Lowenstein, L. and Rose-Ackerman, S., eds.*, 1988, pp. 358–59.

Vohra, Rajiv. On the Existence of Equilibria in Economies with Increasing Returns. *J. Math. Econ.*, 1988, 17(2–3), pp. 179–92.

———. Optimal Regulation under Fixed Rules for Income Distribution. *J. Econ. Theory*, June 1988, 45(1), pp. 65–84.

Voigt, C. and Nitsch, J. Hydrogen in a Future Energy Supply System. In *Winter, C.-J. and Nitsch, J., eds.*, 1988, pp. 314–57.

——— **and Nitsch, J.** Hydrogen's Potential. In *Winter, C.-J. and Nitsch, J., eds.*, 1988, pp. 293–313.

——— **and Nitsch, J.** Launch Concepts for Nonfossil Hydrogen. In *Winter, C.-J. and Nitsch, J., eds.*, 1988, pp. 358–67.

Voith, Richard and Crone, Theodore. National Vacancy Rates and the Persistence of Shocks in U.S. Office Markets. *Amer. Real Estate Urban Econ. Assoc. J.*, Winter 1988, *16*(4), pp. 437–58.

_____ **and Crone, Theodore.** Natural Vacancy Rates and the Persistence of Shocks in U.S. Office Markets. In *Pennsylvania Economic Association*, 1988, pp. 470–91.

Volkmann, Peter. A System of Functional Equations Considered by Krtscha. In *Eichhorn, W., ed.*, 1988, pp. 135–36.

Volkonskii, V. A.; Gofman, K. G. and Albegov, M. M. Optimizational Realism or Economic Nihilism? *Matekon*, Summer 1988, *24*(4), pp. 61–71.

Vollebregt, J. A. C.; Nooteboom, Bart and Thurik, A. Roy. Do Retail Margins Differ between European Countries? A Comparative Study. In *Kaynak, E., ed.*, 1988, pp. 155–66.

Vollmers, A. Clyde. Industrial Concentration in Australian Agribusiness. *Rev. Marketing Agr. Econ.*, August 1988, *56*(2), pp. 194–205.

Volpi, James; Stout, David E. and Wygal, Donald E. A Comparative Income Statement Approach to Integrating International Topics in the Financial Accounting Curriculum. In *Most, K. S., ed.*, 1988, pp. 149–68.

Von Eschen, Donald and Bandyopadhyay, Suraj. Villager Failure to Co-operate: Some Evidence from West Bengal, India. In *Attwood, D. W. and Baviskar, B. S., eds.*, 1988, pp. 112–45.

Von Hohenbalken, Balder; West, Douglas S. and Ryan, David L. New Competition in Shopping-Center Hierarchies: An Empirical Comparison of Alternative Specifications. *J. Reg. Sci.*, August 1988, *28*(3), pp. 329–44.

Vona, S. and Bini Smaghi, L. La coesione dello SME e il ruolo dei fattori esterni: Un'analisi in termini di commercio estero. (Economic Growth and Exchange Rates in the European Monetary System: Their Trade Effects in a Changing External Environment. With English summary.) *Giorn. Econ.*, Jan.–Feb. 1988, *47*(1–2), pp. 3–43.

Vonthron, Jacques. European Community Perspective: Southern Agriculture and the World Economy: The Multilateral Trade Negotiations. *Southern J. Agr. Econ.*, July 1988, *20*(1), pp. 65–67.

Voogd, Henk. Recreational Developments in Gravel Workings: The Limburg Experience. In *Goodall, B. and Ashworth, G., eds.*, 1988, pp. 101–10.

Vorhies, Frank and Glahe, Fred. Political Liberty and Social Development: An Empirical Investigation. *Public Choice*, July 1988, *58*(1), pp. 45–71.

Voronovitskii, M. M. A Simple Model of a Self-intensifying Shortage Due to the Holding of Reserves. *Matekon*, Fall 1988, *25*(1), pp. 3–17.

Vos de Wael, Mariane. La diversification internationale et l'investisseur belge. (With English summary.) *Cah. Écon. Bruxelles*, Third Trimester 1988, (119), pp. 385–424.

de Vos, Klaas and Hagenaars, Aldi. The Definition and Measurement of Poverty. *J. Human Res.*, Spring 1988, *23*(2), pp. 211–21.

Vos, Rob. Global Savings, Investment and Adjustment: On Micro- and Macroeconomic Foundations of North–South Financial Interdependence. In *Currie, D. and Vines, D., eds.*, 1988, pp. 214–48.

_____. Savings, Investment and Foreign Capital Flows: Have Capital Markets Become More Integrated? *J. Devel. Stud.*, April 1988, *24*(3), pp. 310–34.

Vosgerau, Hans-Jürgen. Probleme internationaler Konjunkturtransmission. (Problems of the International Transmission of Business Cycles. With English summary.) *Ifo-Studien*, 1988, *34*(2–3), pp. 133–45.

Vošický, Emilián. Trade Policy: Czechoslovakia—EEC, ECSC, EFTA, OECD. *Czech. Econ. Digest.*, May 1988, (3), pp. 61–65.

Voss, C. A. and Robinson, S. J. Application of Just-in-Time Manufacturing Techniques in the United Kingdom. In *Holl, U. and Trevor, M., eds.*, 1988, pp. 101–04.

_____ **and Robinson, S. J.** Application of Just-in-Time Manufacturing Techniques in the United Kingdom. In *Holl, U. and Trevor, M., eds.*, 1988, pp. 63–70.

Voss, Paul R. A Demographic Portrait of Wisconsin's People. In *Danziger, S. H. and Witte, J. F., eds.*, 1988, pp. 70–95.

Vossebein, Ulrich and Tietz, Reinhard. Modeling Investment Behavior in an Experimental Market. In *Tietz, R.; Albers, W. and Selten, R., eds.*, 1988, pp. 219–31.

Vossen, A. and Bartlema, J. Reflections on Household Modelling. In *Keilman, N.; Kuijsten, A. and Vossen, A., eds.*, 1988, pp. 243–53.

_____ **and Kuijsten, A.** Modelling Household Formation and Dissolution: Introduction. In *Keilman, N.; Kuijsten, A. and Vossen, A., eds.*, 1988, pp. 3–12.

Votey, Harold L., Jr. and Phillips, Llad. Rational Choice Models of Crimes by Youth. In *Simms, M. C. and Myers, S. L., Jr., eds.*, 1988, pp. 129–87.

Votja, George J. and Sanford, Charles S., Jr. Deregulation, Technology, and the "Safety and Soundness" of the Financial System. In *Feldstein, M., ed. (II)*, 1988, pp. 264–77.

de Vries, Casper G. Theory and Relevance of Currency Substitution with Case Studies for Canada and the Netherlands Antilles. *Rev. Econ. Statist.*, August 1988, *70*(3), pp. 512–15.

_____; **Boon, Martin and Kool, Clemens J. M.** Simulating Currency Substitution Bias. *Econ. Letters*, 1988, *28*(3), pp. 269–72.

Vroman, Wayne and Abowd, John M. Disaggregated Wage Developments. *Brookings Pap. Econ. Act.*, 1988, (1), pp. 313–38.

Vrooman, David M. The Ancient Samurai Secret of Daniel Willard: Quality Circles and the Baltimore & Ohio Railroad Cooperative Plan of

1923. In *Perkins, E. J., ed.*, 1988, pp. 55–71.

Vroomen, Harry and McClelland, John W. Stationarity Assumptions and Technical Change in Supply Response Analysis. *J. Agr. Econ. Res.*, Fall 1988, *40*(4), pp. 20–24.

Vu, Joseph D. An Empirical Analysis of Ben Graham's Net Current Asset Value Rule. *Financial Rev.*, May 1988, *23*(2), pp. 215–25.

_____ **and Cinar, E. Mine.** The Effect of Individual Stock Option Expirations on Stock Returns before and after the Introduction of SP 100 Index Options. In *Fabozzi, F. J., ed.*, 1988, pp. 341–56.

Vuchelen, Jef. Het Sneeuwbaleffect en de Sanering van de Belgische Openbare Financiën. (With English summary.) *Cah. Écon. Bruxelles*, Third Trimester 1988, (119), pp. 293–318.

_____ **and Loos, Marleen.** Het gezinsvermogen (1970–1987). (With English summary.) *Cah. Écon. Bruxelles*, 2nd Trimester 1988, (118), pp. 219–36.

_____ **and Marien, Patrick.** The Exchange Market Announcement Effects of Belgian Discount Rate Changes. *Europ. Econ. Rev.*, July 1988, *32*(6), pp. 1335–47.

_____ **and Praet, Peter.** Exogenous Shocks and Consumer Confidence in Four Major European Countries. *Appl. Econ.*, April 1988, *20*(4), pp. 561–67.

Vuchkov, I. N. and Boyadjieva, L. N. Errors in the Factor Level: Parameter Estimation of Heteroscedastic Model and Robustness of the Experimental Designs. In *Fedorov, V. and Lauter, H., eds.*, 1988, pp. 134–43.

Vujačić, Ivan. Marx and Engels on Development and Underdevelopment: The Restoration of a Certain Coherence. *Hist. Polit. Econ.*, Fall 1988, *20*(3), pp. 471–98.

Vuong, Quang H. and Rivers, Douglas. Limited Information Estimators and Exogeneity Tests for Simultaneous Probit Models. *J. Econometrics*, November 1988, *39*(3), pp. 347–66.

van Waardenburg, Dirk A. and Lyons, Susan M. C. Some Aspects of the International Tax Treaty Strategy of the Netherlands: Unilateral Relief and Tax Treaties. *Bull. Int. Fiscal Doc.*, Aug.–Sept. 1988, *42*(8–9), pp. 374–400.

Wachter, Kenneth W. Age Group Growth Rates and Population Momentum. *Population Stud.*, November 1988, *42*(3), pp. 487–94.

Wachter, Michael L. and Williamson, Oliver E. Obligational Markets and the Mechanics of Inflation. In *Earl, P. E., ed., Vol. 2*, 1988, *1978*, pp. 372–95.

Wachter, Susan M. Private and Public Provision of Retirement Insurance. In *Wachter, S. M., ed.*, 1988, pp. ix–xiv.

Waddington, Jeremy. Trade Union Mergers: A Study of Trade Union Structural Dynamics. *Brit. J. Ind. Relat.*, November 1988, *26*(3), pp. 408–30.

Wade, Alice H. Social Security Area Population Projections: 1987. *Soc. Sec. Bull.*, February 1988, *51*(2), pp. 3–30.

Wade, Maurice; Zannoni, Diane and McKenna, Edward. Keynes, Rawls, Uncertainty, and the Liberal Theory of the State. *Econ. Philos.*, October 1988, *4*(2), pp. 221–41.

Wade, Robert. The Management of Irrigation Systems: How to Evoke Trust and Avoid Prisoners' Dilemma. *World Devel.*, April 1988, *16*(4), pp. 489–500.

_____. The Role of Government in Overcoming Market Failure: Taiwan, Republic of Korea and Japan. In *Hughes, H., ed.*, 1988, pp. 129–63.

_____. State Intervention in 'Outward-Looking' Development: Neoclassical Theory and Taiwanese Practice. In *White, G., ed.*, 1988, pp. 30–67.

_____ **and White, Gordon.** Developmental States and Markets in East Asia: An Introduction. In *White, G., ed.*, 1988, pp. 1–29.

Wädekin, Karl-Eugen. Agrarian Structures and Policies in the USSR, China, and Hungary: A Comparative View. In *Brada, J. C. and Wadekin, K.-E., eds.*, 1988, pp. 55–74.

_____. Socialist Agriculture in Transition: Organizational Response to Failing Performance: Introduction. In *Brada, J. C. and Wadekin, K.-E., eds.*, 1988, pp. 1–10.

_____. Soviet Agriculture: A Brighter Prospect? In *[Nove, A.]*, 1988, pp. 193–216.

Wadhva, Charan D. Some Aspects of India's Export Policy and Performance. In *Lucas, R. E. B. and Papanek, G. F., eds.*, 1988, pp. 271–84.

_____. Trade Regimes and Export Strategies with Reference to South Asia: Comments. In *Streeten, P., ed.*, 1988, pp. 165–73.

Wadhwa, Wilima; Fry, Maxwell J. and Lilien, David M. Monetary Policy in Pacific Basin Developing Countries. In *Cheng, H.-S., ed.*, 1988, pp. 153–70.

Wadhwani, Sushil. Profit-Sharing as a Cure for Unemployment: Some Doubts. *Int. J. Ind. Organ.*, March 1988, *6*(1), pp. 59–68.

_____ **and Nickell, Stephen J.** Unions, Wages and Employment: Tests Based on U.K. Firm-Level Data. *Europ. Econ. Rev.*, March 1988, *32*(2–3), pp. 727–33.

Waelbroeck, Jean. Macroeconomic Issues for Europe in the 1980s: Can the NAIRU Be Tamed? In *Giersch, H., ed.*, 1988, pp. 1–22.

_____ **and Burniaux, Jean-Marc.** Agricultural Protection in Europe: Its Impact on Developing Countries. In *Langhammer, R. J. and Rieger, H. C., eds.*, 1988, pp. 129–54.

_____ **and Tharakan, P. K. M.** Has Human Capital Become a Scarce Factor in Belgium? *Cah. Écon. Bruxelles*, 2nd Trimester 1988, (118), pp. 159–79.

Wagenaar, Alexander C. Minimum Legal Drinking Ages and Highway Safety: A Methodological Critique: Comments. In *Graham, J. D., ed.*, 1988, pp. 151–58.

Wagener, Hans-Jürgen. Enterprise Strategies: Comments. In *Saunders, C. T., ed.*, 1988, pp. 337–51.

Wagenhals, Gerhard. Ein Prognosemodell für den Nickelmarkt. (A Forecasting Model for the Nickel Market. With English summary.) *Ifo-Studien*, 1988, *34*(4), pp. 255–74.

_____ and **Ahlheim, Michael.** Exakte Wohlfahrtsmasse in der Nutzen-Kosten-Analyse. (Exact Welfare Measurement in Cost Benefit Analysis. With English summary.) *Z. Wirtschaft. Sozialwissen.*, 1988, *108*(2), pp. 169–93.

Wagman, Barnet and Folbre, Nancy. The Feminization of Inequality: Some New Patterns. *Challenge*, Nov.–Dec. 1988, *31*(6), pp. 55–59.

Wagner, Gert; Desormeaux, Jorge and Díaz, Patricio. La tasa social de descuento. (With English summary.) *Cuadernos Econ.*, April 1988, *25*(74), pp. 125–91.

Wagner, Helmut. Reducing the 'Nairu' by Building New Socio-economic Institutions? *Indian Econ. J.*, Jan.–March 1988, *35*(3), pp. 95–111.

_____. Soll die Bundesbank eine nominelle BSP-Regelpolitik bertrieben? (Should West Germany's Bundesbank Pursue a GNP Regulating Policy? With English summary.) *Kredit Kapital*, 1988, *21*(1), pp. 8–33.

Wagner, Joachim. Innovationen und Entwicklung der Internationalen Wettbewerbsfähigkeit. Eine ökonometrische Untersuchung für Industrien des Verarbeitenden Gewerbes in der Bundesrepublik Deutschland (1979–1984). (Innovations and Changes in International Competitiveness. An Econometric Study for Industries in the FRG, 1979 to 1984. With English summary.) *Jahr. Nationalökon. Statist.*, July 1988, *205*(1), pp. 50–64.

_____ and **Lorenz, Wilhelm.** The Earnings Function under Test. *Econ. Letters*, 1988, *27*(1), pp. 95–99.

_____ and **Lorenz, Wilhelm.** Gibt es kompensierende Lohndifferentiale in der Bundesrepublik Deutschland? (A Test of the Theory of Compensating Wage Differentials for the Federal Republic of Germany. With English summary.) *Z. Wirtschaft. Sozialwissen.*, 1988, *108*(3), pp. 371–81.

Wagner, Karin and Prais, S. J. Productivity and Management: The Training of Foremen in Britain and Germany. *Nat. Inst. Econ. Rev.*, February 1988, (123), pp. 34–47.

Wagner, R. Harrison. Economic Interdependence, Bargaining Power, and Political Influence. *Int. Organ.*, Summer 1988, *42*(3), pp. 461–83.

Wagner, Richard E. The *Calculus of Consent:* A Wicksellian Retrospective. *Public Choice*, February 1988, *56*(2), pp. 153–66.

_____ and **Gwartney, James D.** Public Choice and Constitutional Order. In *Gwartney, J. D. and Wagner, R. E., eds.*, 1988, pp. 29–56.

_____ and **Gwartney, James D.** Public Choice and the Conduct of Representative Government. In *Gwartney, J. D. and Wagner, R. E., eds.*, 1988, pp. 3–28.

_____ and **Tollison, Robert D.** Social Cost, Rent Seeking, and Smoking: A Public Choice Perspective. *Econ. Scelte Pubbliche/J. Public Finance Public Choice*, Sept.–Dec. 1988, *6*(3), pp. 171–86.

Wagner, U.; Geyer-Schulz, A. and Taudes, A. Exploring the Possibilities of an Improvement of Stochastic Market Models by Rule-Based Systems. In *Gaul, W. and Schader, M., eds.*, 1988, pp. 54–66.

Wagner, Wayne H. The Many Dimensions of Risk. *J. Portfol. Manage.*, Winter 1988, *14*(2), pp. 35–39.

Wagstaff, Adam and Lopez Casasnovas, Guillem. La combinacion de los factores productivos en el hospital: Una aproximación a la función de producción. (With English summary.) *Invest. Econ.*, May 1988, *12*(2), pp. 305–27.

Wah, Lai Yew and Tan, Siew Ee. Towards Effective Planning in Malaysia: Some Strategic Issues. In *Urrutia, M. and Yukawa, S., eds. (I)*, 1988, pp. 107–55.

Wahlström, Staffan. Simulating the Distribution of Economic Welfare. The Case of Sweden. *Statist. J.*, August 1988, *5*(2), pp. 101–11.

Wahlund, Richard and Wärneryd, Karl-Erik. Aggregate Saving and the Saving Behavior of Saver Groups in Sweden Accompanying a Tax Reform. In *Maital, S., ed., Vol. 1*, 1988, pp. 73–96.

Wai, Tan Tat. Management of Resource-Based Growth in Different Factor Endowment Conditions. In *Urrutia, M. and Yukawa, S., eds. (II)*, 1988, pp. 112–27.

Waite, Charles A. Service Sector: Its Importance and Prospects for the Future. In *Candilis, W. O., ed.*, 1988, pp. 1–22.

Waite, Linda J.; Witsberger, Christina and Leibowitz, Arleen. Child Care for Preschoolers: Differences by Child's Age. *Demography*, May 1988, *25*(2), pp. 205–20.

Waite, Stephen R. and Paulus, John D. The 1980s Merger Wave: An Industrial Organization Perspective: Discussion. In *Browne, L. E. and Rosengren, E. S., eds.*, 1988, pp. 38–51.

Wakefield, Joseph C. Federal Fiscal Programs. *Surv. Curr. Bus.*, February 1988, *68*(2), pp. 19–24.

Wakker, Peter P. Characterizations of Quasilinear Representations and Specified Forms of These. In *Eichhorn, W., ed.*, 1988, pp. 311–26.

_____. Continuity of Preference Relations for Separable Topologies. *Int. Econ. Rev.*, February 1988, *29*(1), pp. 105–10.

_____. Derived Strengths of Preference Relations on Coordinates. *Econ. Letters*, 1988, *28*(4), pp. 301–06.

Wako, T. and Ohta, H. The Output Effects of Spatial Price Discrimination Revisited. *J. Reg. Sci.*, February 1988, *28*(1), pp. 83–87.

Walbert, Mark S. and Bierma, Thomas J. The Permits Game: Conveying the Logic of Marketable Pollution Permits. *J. Econ. Educ.*, Fall 1988, *19*(4), pp. 383–89.

Waldauer, Charles and Pal, Surendra. Imbalanced Faculty: A Persistent Problem in Higher Education. *J. Policy Anal. Manage.*, Fall 1988, *7*(4), pp. 718–21.

Waldén, Bertil; Sandström, Arne and Wretman, Jan H. Variance Estimators of the Gini Coefficient—Probability Sampling. *J. Bus. Econ. Statist.*, January 1988, *6*(1), pp. 113–19.

Walden, Michael L. Why Unit Prices of Supermarket Products Vary. *J. Cons. Aff.*, Summer 1988, *22*(1), pp. 74–84.

Waldhorn, Steven A. and Henton, Douglas. The New Economic Role of American States: California. In *Fosler, R. S., ed.*, 1988, pp. 201–47.

Waldman, Don E. The Inefficiencies of "Unsuccessful" Price Fixing Agreements. *Antitrust Bull.*, Spring 1988, *33*(1), pp. 67–93.

Waldman, Michael and Novos, Ian E. Complementarity and Partial Nonexcludability: An Analysis of the Software/Computer Market. *J. Inst. Theoretical Econ.*, June 1988, *144*(3), pp. 443–61.

Waldo, Douglas and Rush, Mark. On the Policy Ineffectiveness Proposition and a Keynesian Alternative. *Econ. J.*, June 1988, *98*(391), pp. 498–503.

Wales, T. J. and Diewert, W. Erwin. A Normalized Quadratic Semiflexible Functional Form. *J. Econometrics*, March 1988, *37*(3), pp. 327–42.

———— **and Diewert, W. Erwin.** Normalized Quadratic Systems of Consumer Demand Functions. *J. Bus. Econ. Statist.*, July 1988, *6*(3), pp. 303–12.

Walker, David A. and Chant, Elizabeth M. Small Business Demand for Trade Credit. *Appl. Econ.*, July 1988, *20*(7), pp. 861–76.

Walker, Donald A. The Institutionalist Economic Theories of Clarence Ayres. In *Samuels, W. J., ed., Vol. 1, 1988, 1979*, pp. 192–211.

————. Iteration in Walras's Theory of Tatonnement. *De Economist*, 1988, *136*(3), pp. 299–316.

————. Thorstein Veblen's Economic System. In *Samuels, W. J., ed., Vol. 1, 1988, 1977*, pp. 153–77.

Walker, Gordon. Network Analysis for Cooperative Interfirm Relationships. In *Contractor, F. J. and Lorange, P.*, 1988, pp. 227–40.

Walker, Graham. Canadian Success in Privatization. In *Walker, M. A., ed. (II)*, 1988, pp. 157–66.

————. Labour in Scotland and Northern Ireland: The Inter-war Experience. In *Mitchison, R. and Roebuck, P., eds.*, 1988, pp. 267–76.

Walker, Ian; Blundell, Richard and Fry, Vanessa. Modelling the Take-up of Means-tested Benefits: the Case of Housing Benefits in the United Kingdom. *Econ. J.*, Supplement, 1988, *98*(390), pp. 58–74.

Walker, James M.; Cox, James C. and Smith, Vernon L. Theory and Individual Behavior of First-Price Auctions. *J. Risk Uncertainty*, March 1988, *1*(1), pp. 61–99.

———— **and Isaac, R. Mark.** Communication and Free-Riding Behavior: The Voluntary Contribution Mechanism. *Econ. Inquiry*, October 1988, *26*(4), pp. 585–608.

———— **and Isaac, R. Mark.** Group Size Effects in Public Goods Provision: The Voluntary Contributions Mechanism. *Quart. J. Econ.*, February 1988, *103*(1), pp. 179–99.

———— **and Williams, Arlington W.** Market Behavior in Bid, Offer, and Double Auctions: A Reexamination. *J. Econ. Behav. Organ.*, April 1988, *9*(3), pp. 301–14.

Walker, Jill. Women, the State and the Family in Britain: Thatcher Economics and the Experience of Women. In *Rubery, J., ed.*, 1988, pp. 218–50.

Walker, Marilyn and Grbich, Yuri. The Tax Code Needs Rewriting. *Australian Tax Forum*, 1988, *5*(3), pp. 385–94.

Walker, Mary Beth and Hunter, William Curt. Assessing the Fairness of Investment Bankers' Fees. *Fed. Res. Bank Atlanta Econ. Rev.*, March–April 1988, *73*(2), pp. 2–7.

Walker, Michael A. Freedom, Democracy and Economic Welfare: Preface. In *Walker, M. A., ed. (I)*, 1988, pp. ix–xvi.

———— **and Block, Walter.** Entropy in the Canadian Economics Profession: Sampling Consensus on the Major Issues. *Can. Public Policy*, June 1988, *14*(2), pp. 137–50.

———— **and Spindler, Zane A.** Canadian Tax Reform as Public Choice. *Contemp. Policy Issues*, October 1988, *6*(4), pp. 70–84.

————, **et al.** Canadian–U.S. Trade. *Contemp. Policy Issues*, January 1988, *6*(1), pp. 1–27.

Walker, Nigel. British Social Trends since 1900: Crime and Penal Measures. In *Halsey, A. H., ed.*, 1988, pp. 616–44.

Walker, Patricia C. U.S. Direct Investment Abroad: Detail for Position and Balance of Payments Flow, 1987. *Surv. Curr. Bus.*, August 1988, *68*(8), pp. 42–68.

Walklet, Donn C. From Imagery to Information: Adding Value to Satellite Imagery with Advanced Computer Mapping Systems. In *Egan, J. J., et al.*, 1988, pp. 167–72.

Walkling, Ralph A. and Karpoff, Jonathan M. Short-term Trading around Ex-dividend Days. *J. Finan. Econ.*, September 1988, *21*(2), pp. 291–98.

———— **and Malatesta, Paul H.** Poison Pill Securities: Stockholder Wealth, Profitability, and Ownership Structure. *J. Finan. Econ.*, Jan.–March 1988, *20*(1–2), pp. 347–76.

Wall, Charles A. and Fisher, Brian S. Supply Response and the Theory of Production and Profit Functions. *Rev. Marketing Agr. Econ.*, December 1988, *56*(3), pp. 383–404.

Wall, Larry D. Callable Bonds: A Risk-Reducing Signalling Mechanism—A Comment. *J. Finance*, September 1988, *43*(4), pp. 1057–65.

————. Commercial Bank Profitability: Still Weak in 1987. *Fed. Res. Bank Atlanta Econ. Rev.*, July–Aug. 1988, *73*(4), pp. 28–42.

————. Leverage Ratios of U.S. Nonfinancial Corporations. *Fed. Res. Bank Atlanta Econ. Rev.*, May–June 1988, *73*(3), pp. 12–29.

———— **and Peterson, David R.** Capital Changes at Large Affiliated Banks. *J. Finan. Services Res.*, June 1988, *1*(3), pp. 253–75.

———— **and Pringle, John J.** Interest Rate Swaps: A Review of the Issues. *Fed. Res. Bank Atlanta Econ. Rev.*, Nov.–Dec. 1988, *73*(6), pp. 22–40.

Wall, M. Danny. Toward a Healthy, Competitive

Thrift Industry. **In** *Federal Home Loan Bank of San Francisco*, 1988, pp. 5–14.

Wall, Richard A. and Gort, Michael. Financial Markets and the Limits of Regulation. *Managerial Dec. Econ.*, March 1988, *9*(1), pp. 65–73.

―――― **and Gort, Michael.** Foresight and Public Utility Regulation. *J. Polit. Econ.*, February 1988, *96*(1), pp. 177–88.

Wallace, Cynthia Day. Foreign Direct Investment: A New Climate for Negotiations with the Third World. **In** *Yochelson, J., ed.*, 1988, pp. 113–54.

Wallace, Mack. A Perilous Choice: Minesweepers or Drilling Rigs. **In** *Fried, E. R. and Blandin, N. M., eds.*, 1988, pp. 103–10.

Wallace, Myles S.; Bowles, David C. and Ulbrich, Holley H. Default Risk and the Effects of Fiscal Policy on Interest Rates: 1929–1945. *Public Finance Quart.*, July 1988, *16*(3), pp. 357–73.

――――**; Kelly, William A., Jr. and Nardinelli, Clark.** Should We Sell the Fed? *Cato J.*, Spring–Summer 1988, *8*(1), pp. 125–38.

――――**; Warner, John T. and Nardinelli, Clark.** State Business Cycles and Their Relationship to the National Cycle: Structural and Institutional Determinants. *Southern Econ. J.*, April 1988, *54*(4), pp. 950–60.

――――**; Watson, Sharon B. and Yandle, Bruce.** Environment Regulation: A Financial Markets Test. *Quart. Rev. Econ. Bus.*, Spring 1988, *28*(1), pp. 69–87.

Wallace, Nancy E. The Market Effects of Zoning Undeveloped Land: Does Zoning Follow the Market? *J. Urban Econ.*, May 1988, *23*(3), pp. 307–26.

Wallace, Neil. Another Attempt to Explain an Illiquid Banking System: The Diamond and Dybvig Model with Sequential Service Taken Seriously. *Fed. Res. Bank Minn. Rev.*, Fall 1988, *12*(4), pp. 3–16.

――――. A Suggestion for Oversimplifying the Theory of Money. *Econ. J.*, Supplement, 1988, *98*(390), pp. 25–36.

Wallach, Arthur E. and Jackson, Lauren Hite. Getting an Answer to "How Am I Doing?" **In** *Timpe, A. D., ed.*, 1988, *1985*, pp. 145–51.

Wallach, Michael A. Creativity and Talent. **In** *Grønhaug, K. and Kaufmann, G., eds.*, 1988, *1983*, pp. 13–27.

van de Walle, Dominique. On the Use of the Susenas for Modelling Consumer Behaviour. *Bull. Indonesian Econ. Stud.*, August 1988, *24*(2), pp. 107–22.

Wallendorf, Melanie; Belk, Russell W. and Sherry, John F., Jr. A Naturalistic Inquiry into Buyer and Seller Behavior at a Swap Meet. *J. Cons. Res.*, March 1988, *14*(4), pp. 449–70.

Waller, Christopher J. Alternative Monetary Regimes: Review Article. *Atlantic Econ. J.*, March 1988, *16*(1), pp. 47–52.

Waller, Mark L.; Garcia, Philip and Hudson, Michael A. The Pricing Efficiency of Agricultural Futures Markets: An Analysis of Previous Research Results. *Southern J. Agr. Econ.*, July 1988, *20*(1), pp. 119–30.

Waller, William T., Jr. The Concept of Habit in Economic Analysis. *J. Econ. Issues*, March 1988, *22*(1), pp. 113–26.

――――. Creating Legitimacy, Reciprocity, and Transfer Programs. *J. Econ. Issues*, December 1988, *22*(4), pp. 1143–51.

――――. Radical Institutionalism: Methodological Aspects of the Radical Tradition. *J. Econ. Issues*, September 1988, *22*(3), pp. 667–74.

Wallerstein, Immanuel. Feudalism, Capitalism, and the World-System in the Perspective of Latin America and the Caribbean: Comments on Stern's Critical Tests. *Amer. Hist. Rev.*, October 1988, *93*(4), pp. 873–85.

Wallich, Henry C. Floating as Seen from the Central Bank. **In** *Melamed, L., ed.*, 1988, *1980*, pp. 395–403.

Wallis, John Joseph; Legler, John B. and Sylla, Richard. U.S. City Finances and the Growth of Government, 1859–1902. *J. Econ. Hist.*, June 1988, *48*(2), pp. 347–56.

―――― **and North, Douglass C.** Should Transaction Costs Be Subtracted from Gross National Product? *J. Econ. Hist.*, September 1988, *48*(3), pp. 651–54.

―――― **and Oates, Wallace E.** Decentralization in the Public Sector: An Empirical Study of State and Local Government. **In** *Rosen, H. S., ed.*, 1988, pp. 5–28.

―――― **and Oates, Wallace E.** Does Economic Sclerosis Set in with Age? An Empirical Study of the Olson Hypothesis. *Kyklos*, 1988, *41*(3), pp. 397–417.

Wallis, Kenneth F. Empirical Models and Macroeconomic Policy Analysis. **In** *Bryant, R. C., et al., eds.*, 1988, pp. 225–37.

――――. Some Recent Developments in Macroeconometric Modelling in the United Kingdom. *Australian Econ. Pap.*, Supplement, June 1988, *27*, pp. 7–25.

――――. A Survey of Non-Dutch European Macroeconomic Models: Some International Perspective: Comments. **In** *Driehuis, W.; Fase, M. M. G. and den Hartog, H., eds.*, 1988, pp. 251–57.

―――― **and Burridge, Peter.** Prediction Theory for Autoregressive–Moving Average Processes. *Econometric Rev.*, 1988, *7*(1), pp. 65–95.

Walliser, Bernard and Mongin, Philippe. Infinite Regressions in the Optimizing Theory of Decision. **In** *Munier, B. R., ed.*, 1988, pp. 435–57.

Wallmeier, Hans-Martin. Games with Informants: An Information-Theoretical Approach towards a Game-Theoretical Problem. *Int. J. Game Theory*, 1988, *17*(4), pp. 245–78.

Wallop, Malcolm. A Congressional View. **In** *Walker, C. E. and Bloomfield, M. A., eds.*, 1988, pp. 52–54.

Walsh, Brendan M. Ricardian Equivalence and the Irish Consumption Function: A Comment. *Econ. Soc. Rev.*, October 1988, *20*(1), pp. 49–52.

Walsh, Carl E. Financial Deregulation and Monetary Policy in New Zealand. **In** *Cheng, H.-S., ed.*, 1988, pp. 279–301.

_____. Testing for Real Effects of Monetary Policy Regime Shifts: A Note. *J. Money, Credit, Banking*, Part 1, August 1988, *20*(3), pp. 393–401.

_____ and Hartley, Peter R. Financial Intermediation, Monetary Policy, and Equilibrium Business Cycles. *Fed. Res. Bank San Francisco Econ. Rev.*, Fall 1988, (4), pp. 19–28.

_____ and Trehan, Bharat. Common Trends, the Government's Budget Constraint, and Revenue Smoothing. *J. Econ. Dynam. Control*, June–Sept. 1988, *12*(2–3), pp. 425–44.

Walsh, Cliff; Freebairn, John W. and Porter, Michael. Tax Cuts: Desirable and Practical. *Australian Tax Forum*, 1988, *5*(3), pp. 285–99.

Walsh, David J. Accounting for the Proliferation of Two-Tier Wage Settlements in the U.S. Airline Industry, 1983–1986. *Ind. Lab. Relat. Rev.*, October 1988, *42*(1), pp. 50–62.

Walsh, Edward J.; Warland, Rex H. and Herrmann, Robert O. The Organizations of the Consumer Movement: A Comparative Perspective: Panel. In *Maynes, E. S. and ACCI Research Committee, eds.*, 1988, pp. 469–94.

Walsh, Geoff. Trade Unions and the Media. *Int. Lab. Rev.*, 1988, *127*(2), pp. 205–20.

Walsh, Kieron. Fiscal Crisis and Stress: Origins and Implications. In *Paddison, R. and Bailey, S., eds.*, 1988, pp. 30–52.

Walsh, Michael J. and Jones, Jonathan D. More Evidence on the "Border Tax" Effect: The Case of West Virginia, 1979–84. *Nat. Tax J.*, June 1988, *41*(2), pp. 261–65.

Walsh, Vivien. Technology and the Competitiveness of Small Countries: Review. In *Freeman, C. and Lundvall, B.-A., eds.*, 1988, pp. 37–66.

Walsh, William D. and Jones, J. C. H. Salary Determination in the National Hockey League: The Effects of Skills, Franchise Characteristics, and Discrimination. *Ind. Lab. Relat. Rev.*, July 1988, *41*(4), pp. 592–604.

Walstad, William B. and Gleason, Joyce P. An Empirical Test of an Inventory Model of Student Study Time. *J. Econ. Educ.*, Fall 1988, *19*(4), pp. 315–21.

_____ and Soper, John C. The Reality of High School Economics: The Teachers' Perspective. In *Association of Private Education*, 1988, pp. 85–96.

_____ and Soper, John C. A Report Card on the Economic Literacy of U.S. High School Students. *Amer. Econ. Rev.*, May 1988, *78*(2), pp. 251–56.

_____ and Soper, John C. What is High School Economics? Posttest Knowledge, Attitudes, and Course Content. *J. Econ. Educ.*, Winter 1988, *19*(1), pp. 37–51.

_____ and Soper, John C. What Is High School Economics? TEL Revision and Pretest Findings. *J. Econ. Educ.*, Winter 1988, *19*(1), pp. 24–36.

Walt, Stephen M. Testing Theories of Alliance Formation: The Case of Southwest Asia. *Int. Organ.*, Spring 1988, *42*(2), pp. 275–316.

Walter, Eric and Pronzato, Luc. Robust Experiment Designs for Nonlinear Regression Models. In *Fedorov, V. and Lauter, H., eds.*, 1988, pp. 77–86.

Walter, Ingo. Competitive Performance and Strategic Positioning in International Financial Services. In *Lamb, R. and Shrivastava, P., eds.*, 1988, pp. 69–87.

Walter, John R. and Mengle, David L. A Review of Bank Performance in the Fifth District, 1987. *Fed. Res. Bank Richmond Econ. Rev.*, July–Aug. 1988, *74*(4), pp. 13–18.

Walter, Norbert. The Inflexibility of Labour-Market Related Institutions—Some Observations for Germany. In *Dlugos, G.; Dorow, W. and Weiermair, K., eds.*, 1988, pp. 133–42.

Walters, Alan A. [Sir]. A Critical View of the EMS. *Cato J.*, Fall 1988, *8*(2), pp. 503–06.

_____. Monetary and Fiscal Policy in the UK. In *Eltis, W. and Sinclair, P. J. N., eds.*, 1988, pp. 271–94.

_____. Privatization in British Transport Policy. In *Weicher, J. C., ed.*, 1988, pp. 101–08.

Walters, Forrest E. A General Theoretical Framework for Analyzing Capital Accumulation in Agriculture: Comments. *Pakistan Devel. Rev.*, Part 2, Winter 1988, *27*(4), pp. 631–32.

Walters, Stephen J. K.; Jordan, John M. and Meador, Mark. Effects of Department Size and Organization on the Research Productivity of Academic Economists. *Econ. Educ. Rev.*, 1988, *7*(2), pp. 251–55.

Walters, Vivienne and Haines, Ted. Workers' Use and Knowledge of the 'Internal Responsibility System': Limits to Participation in Occupational Health and Safety. *Can. Public Policy*, December 1988, *14*(4), pp. 411–23.

Walterskirchen, Ewald and Guger, Alois. Fiscal and Monetary Policy in the Keynes–Kalecki Tradition. In *Kregel, J. A.; Matzner, E. and Roncaglia, A., eds.*, 1988, pp. 103–32.

Walton, David R. Does GNP Have a Unit Root? Evidence for the UK. *Econ. Letters*, 1988, *26*(3), pp. 219–24.

Walton, David Ryan. Acquisition of Troubled Thrifts across State Lines: Minimizing the Impact on Interstate Banking Prohibitions. In *Kemper, R. L., ed.*, 1988, pp. 107–46.

Walukiewicz, Stanislaw and Holm, Søren. Column/Constraint Generation for Quadratic Assignment Problems. In *Iri, M. and Yajima, K., eds.*, 1988, pp. 287–98.

Walz, Daniel T. and Spencer, Roger W. Bias in Systems of Survey and Econometric Forecasts. *J. Macroecon.*, Spring 1988, *10*(2), pp. 261–71.

Walzer, Norman; Deller, Steven C. and Chicoine, David L. Economies of Size and Scope in Rural Low-Volume Roads. *Rev. Econ. Statist.*, August 1988, *70*(3), pp. 459–65.

Wan, Henry Y., Jr. Nipponized Confucian Ethos or Incentive-Compatible Institutional Design: Notes on Morishima, "Why Has Japan Succeeded?" *Int. Econ. J.*, Spring 1988, *2*(1), pp. 101–08.

_____ and Clemhout, Simone. A General Dynamic Model of Bargaining—The Perfect Information Case. In *Eiselt, H. A. and Pederzoli, G., eds.*, 1988, pp. 293–305.

Wandschneider, Philip. Dividing the Waters: Designing Management Institutions for the Columbia River. In *Johnston, G. M.; Freshwater, D. and Favero, P., eds.*, 1988, pp. 178–98.

Wang, Feng. The Roles of Individuals' Socioeconomic Characteristics and the Government Family Planning Program in China's Fertility Decline. *Population Res. Policy Rev.*, 1988, 7(3), pp. 255–76.

Wang, Jichuan. Determinants of Fertility Increase in Sichuan, 1981–86. *Population Devel. Rev.*, September 1988, 14(3), pp. 481–88.

Wang, Leonard F. S. and Bowles, David C. Risk Aversion, Forward Markets and the Competitive Labor-Managed Firm under Price Uncertainty. *Managerial Dec. Econ.*, December 1988, 9(4), pp. 275–78.

_____ **and Conant, John L.** Corporate Tax Evasion and Output Decisions of the Uncertain Monopolist. *Nat. Tax J.*, December 1988, 41(4), pp. 579–81.

Wang, Liandong. Enthusiastically Foster Individual Transport Operations; Actively Exercise Management. *Chinese Econ. Stud.*, Winter 1987–88, 21(2), pp. 55–58.

Wang, N. T. China's Learning Curve in Its Relations with Transnational Corporations. In *Teng, W. and Wang, N. T., eds.*, 1988, pp. 251–66.

Wang, Qiang and Liu, Dawei. Survey Report on the "Difficulty in Recruiting Labor" in Beijing Municipality. *Chinese Econ. Stud.*, Summer 1988, 21(4), pp. 45–64.

Wang, Stanley D. H. and Kellogg, Christopher B. An Econometric Model for American Lobster. *Marine Resource Econ.*, 1988, 5(1), pp. 61–74.

Wang, T.-F. and Mullins, D. A Model of Income Distribution, Employment, and Growth for South Africa: A Semi-closed Input–Output Approach. *J. Stud. Econ. Econometrics*, November 1988, 12(3), pp. 11–30.

Wang, Xiaoqiang and Chen, Yizi. Reform: Results and Lessons from the 1985 CESRRI Survey. In *Reynolds, B. L., ed.*, 1988, 1987, pp. 172–88.

Wang, Xionglin. Mineral Resources in China: Geological Exploration and Exploitation. In *Dorian, J. P. and Fridley, D. G., eds.*, 1988, pp. 105–16.

Wang, Young-Doo and Latham, William R., III. Energy and State Economic Growth: Some New Evidence. *J. Energy Devel.*, Spring 1988, 13(2), pp. 197–221.

Wang, Yulu; Zhang, Zhensheng and Feng, Ai. Why Can a Large City Like Qinhuangdao Not Accommodate a Small Individual Venture? *Chinese Econ. Stud.*, Winter 1987–88, 21(2), pp. 28–33.

Wang, Zheng Xian. Transnational Corporations and China's Economic Development. In *Teng, W. and Wang, N. T., eds.*, 1988, pp. 191–97.

Wangwe, Samuel M. Industrialization Experiences from Tanzania 1961–1985. In *Coughlin, P. and Ikiara, G. K., eds.*, 1988, pp. 71–90.

Wankel, Charles B.; Stoner, James A. F. and Taylor, Arthur R. On Waiting for Neither Godot nor the Apocalypse: Practical First Steps to Move U.S. Managers Toward World Class Managing. In *Starr, M. K., ed.*, 1988, pp. 185–212.

Wanna, John. Industrialisation in South Australia: A Reply. *Australian Econ. Hist. Rev.*, September 1988, 28(2), pp. 75–84.

Wannop, U. Do We Need Regional Local Government and Is the Scottish Model Relevant? *Reg. Stud.*, October 1988, 22(5), pp. 439–46.

Warburton, M. and Thompson, M. Uncertainty on a Himalayan Scale. In *Ives, J. and Pitt, D. C., eds.*, 1988, pp. 1–53.

Warburton, Peter and Beenstock, Michael. A Neoclassical Model of the UK Labour Market. In *Beenstock, M., ed.*, 1988, pp. 71–104.

Ward, Benjamin. LEP: An Alternative Criterion for Socio-economic Valuation. *J. Econ. Issues*, September 1988, 22(3), pp. 763–80.

Ward, Bert; Finlayson, Bob and Lattimore, Ralph. New Zealand's Price Elasticity of Export Demand Revisited. *New Zealand Econ. Pap.*, 1988, 22, pp. 25–34.

Ward, C. W. R.; Condoyanni, L. and O'Hanlon, J. Weekend Effects in Stock Market Returns: International Evidence. In *Dimson, E., ed.*, 1988, pp. 52–63.

Ward, John O. Origins of the Tort Reform Movement. *Contemp. Policy Issues*, July 1988, 6(3), pp. 97–107.

Ward, Lorne H. Origins of the Class Structure in Pre-Etruscan Rome, c. 750 B.C.–c. 550 B.C. *Sci. Soc.*, Winter 1988–89, 52(4), pp. 413–40.

Ward, Michael D. and House, Lewis L. A Theory of the Behavioral Power of Nations. *J. Conflict Resolution*, March 1988, 32(1), pp. 3–36.

Ward, Michael P.; Welch, Finis R. and Raisian, John. Implementing Comparable Worth: Conceptual Issues and Impacts. In *Mangum, G. and Philips, P., eds.*, 1988, pp. 183–200.

Ward, Terry. From Mounting Tension to Open Confrontation: The Case of the UK. In *Boyer, R., ed.*, 1988, pp. 58–80.

Wardman, Mark. A Comparison of Revealed Preference and Stated Preference Models of Travel Behaviour. *J. Transp. Econ. Policy*, January 1988, 22(1), pp. 71–91.

_____ **and Fowkes, Tony.** The Design of Stated Preference Travel Choice Experiments. *J. Transp. Econ. Policy*, January 1988, 22(1), pp. 27–44.

Wardrop, A. W. Scheduling Railway Motive Power. In *Daduna, J. R. and Wren, A., eds.*, 1988, pp. 250–61.

Ware, Richard A. The Pentagon's Office of International Security Affairs, 1969–1973 or Two Citizens Go to Washington. In *[Nutter, G. W.]*, 1988, pp. 233–47.

Ware, Roger and Winter, Ralph A. Forward Markets, Currency Options and the Hedging of Foreign Exchange Risk. *J. Int. Econ.*, November 1988, 25(3–4), pp. 291–302.

Warfvinge, Per and Sverdrup, Harald. Soil Liming as a Measure to Mitigate Acid Runoff. *Water Resources Res.*, May 1988, *24*(5), pp. 701–12.

Warland, Rex H.; Herrmann, Robert O. and Walsh, Edward J. The Organizations of the Consumer Movement: A Comparative Perspective: Panel. In *Maynes, E. S. and ACCI Research Committee, eds.*, 1988, pp. 469–94.

_____; **Miller, Michael K. and Stokes, C. Shannon.** The Effect of Legalization and Public Funding of Abortion on Neonatal Mortality: An Intervention Analysis. *Population Res. Policy Rev.*, 1988, *7*(1), pp. 79–92.

Warley, T. K. Linkages between Bilateral and Multilateral Negotiations in Agriculture. In *Allen, K. and Macmillan, K., eds.*, 1988, pp. 169–78.

Warlick, Jennifer; Haveman, Robert and Wolfe, Barbara L. Labor Market Behavior of Older Men: Estimates from a Trichotomous Choice Model. *J. Public Econ.*, July 1988, *36*(2), pp. 153–75.

_____; **Smeeding, Timothy M. and Betson, David M.** The Effects of Taxing Unemployment Insurance Benefits Accounting For Induced Labor Supply Responses. In *Danziger, S. H. and Portney, K. E., eds.*, 1988, pp. 149–67.

Warner, Jerold B. and Jensen, Michael C. The Distribution of Power among Corporate Managers, Shareholders, and Directors. *J. Finan. Econ.*, Jan.–March 1988, *20*(1–2), pp. 3–24.

_____; **Watts, Ross L. and Wruck, Karen H.** Stock Prices and Top Management Changes. *J. Finan. Econ.*, Jan.–March 1988, *20*(1–2), pp. 461–92.

Warner, John T.; Nardinelli, Clark and Wallace, Myles S. State Business Cycles and Their Relationship to the National Cycle: Structural and Institutional Determinants. *Southern Econ. J.*, April 1988, *54*(4), pp. 950–60.

Warner, Mark and Rugman, Alan M. Foreign Ownership, Free Trade, and the Canadian Energy Sector. *J. Energy Devel.*, Autumn 1988, *14*(1), pp. 1–18.

Wärneryd, Karl-Erik. Economic Psychology as a Field of Study. In *van Raaij, W. F.; van Veldhoven, G. M. and Wärneryd, K.-E., eds.*, 1988, pp. 2–41.

_____. The Life and Work of George Katona. In *Earl, P. E., ed., Vol. 2*, 1988, *1982*, pp. 403–33.

_____. The Psychology of Innovative Entrepreneurship. In *van Raaij, W. F.; van Veldhoven, G. M. and Wärneryd, K.-E., eds.*, 1988, pp. 404–47.

_____. Social Influence on Economic Behavior. In *van Raaij, W. F.; van Veldhoven, G. M. and Wärneryd, K.-E., eds.*, 1988, pp. 207–48.

_____ and **Wahlund, Richard.** Aggregate Saving and the Saving Behavior of Saver Groups in Sweden Accompanying a Tax Reform. In *Maital, S., ed., Vol. 1*, 1988, pp. 73–96.

Warr, Peter. Work, Jobs and Unemployment. In *Earl, P. E., ed., Vol. 2*, 1988, *1983*, pp. 396–402.

Warren-Boulton, Frederick R. *Maricopa* and Maximum-Price Agreements: Time for a New Legal Standard? Editorial. *J. Health Econ.*, June 1988, *7*(2), pp. 185–90.

Warren, Charles R. The New Economic Role of American States: Indiana. In *Fosler, R. S., ed.*, 1988, pp. 269–90.

Warren, J. H. Services and Investments: Comments. In *Schott, J. J. and Smith, M. G., eds.*, 1988, pp. 153–58.

Warren, Mashuri L. Cost Requirements for Active Solar Heating and Cooling. In *West, R. E. and Kreith, F., eds.*, 1988, pp. 274–308.

Warren, Michael. Survey Research on Behalf of the Consumer: A View from the United Kingdom. In *Maynes, E. S. and ACCI Research Committee, eds.*, 1988, pp. 665–71.

Warren, Neil A. Flattening the Income Tax Rate Scale through Changes in the Tax Mix. *Australian Tax Forum*, 1988, *5*(2), pp. 181–217.

Warren, Ronald S., Jr.; Lovell, C. A. Knox and Sickles, Robin C. The Effect of Unionization On Labor Productivity: Some Additional Evidence. *J. Lab. Res.*, Winter 1988, *9*(1), pp. 55–63.

Warren, Stephen H. A Creditors' Bargain Perspective of FDIC Policy for Handling Bank Failures (or, the Bargain That's No Bargain at All). In *Kemper, R. L., ed.*, 1988, pp. 77–105.

Warsh, David L. War Stories: Defense Spending and the Growth of the Massachusetts Economy. In *Lampe, D., ed.*, 1988, *1986*, pp. 314–30.

_____. "Yellow Rain" and "Supply-Side Economics": Some Rhetoric That Failed. In *Klamer, A.; McCloskey, D. N. and Solow, R. M., eds.*, 1988, pp. 247–62.

Warshaw, Paul R.; Sheppard, Blair H. and Hartwick, Jon. The Theory of Reasoned Action: A Meta-analysis of Past Research with Recommendations for Modifications and Future Research. *J. Cons. Res.*, December 1988, *15*(3), pp. 325–43.

Warshawsky, Mark J. Pension Plans: Funding, Assets, and Regulatory Environment. *Fed. Res. Bull.*, November 1988, *74*(11), pp. 717–30.

_____. Private Annuity Markets in the United States: 1919–1984. *J. Risk Ins.*, September 1988, *55*(3), pp. 518–28.

_____ and **Abel, Andrew B.** Specification of the Joy of Giving: Insights from Altruism. *Rev. Econ. Statist.*, February 1988, *70*(1), pp. 145–49.

_____ and **Friedman, Benjamin M.** Annuity Prices and Saving Behavior in the United States. In *Bodie, Z.; Shoven, J. B. and Wise, D. A., eds.*, 1988, pp. 53–77.

Wartenberg, Daniel. Groundwater Contamination by Temik Aldicarb Pesticide: The First 8 Months. *Water Resources Res.*, February 1988, *24*(2), pp. 185–94.

Wascher, William and Montgomery, Edward. Creative Destruction and the Behavior of Productivity over the Business Cycle. *Rev. Econ. Statist.*, February 1988, *70*(1), pp. 168–72.

Washida, Toyoaki. Growth Potential in a Non-capitalist Economy. *Econ. Stud. Quart.*, March 1988, *39*(1), pp. 77–86.

_____. Reconstruction of the Generalized Fundamental Marxian Theorem. *Econ. Stud. Quart.*, September 1988, *39*(3), pp. 277–83.

_____. Turnpike Stability of Decomposable Systems and the Efficiency of Growth Planning. In *Ciaschini, M., ed.*, 1988, pp. 129–45.

Wasilewski, Edward J.; Borum, Joan D. and Conley, James R. The Outlook for Collective Bargaining in 1988. *Mon. Lab. Rev.*, January 1988, *111*(1), pp. 10–23.

Wass, V. J. and Harris, Richard I. D. The Structure of Collective Bargaining in Northern Ireland, 1973–84. *Econ. Soc. Rev.*, January 1988, *19*(2), pp. 99–122.

Wasserfallen, Walter. Trends, Random Walks, and the Expectations-Augmented Phillips Curve: Evidence from Six Countries. *J. Money, Credit, Banking*, Part 1, August 1988, *20*(3), pp. 306–18.

_____ and **Güntensperger, Heinz.** Gasoline Consumption and the Stock of Motor Vehicles: An Empirical Analysis for the Swiss Economy. *Energy Econ.*, October 1988, *10*(4), pp. 276–82.

_____ and **Wydler, Daniel.** Underpricing of Newly Issued Bonds: Evidence from the Swiss Capital Market. *J. Finance*, December 1988, *43*(5), pp. 1177–91.

Wassink, Darwin and Carbaugh, Robert. International Economic Sanctions and Economic Theory. *Rivista Int. Sci. Econ. Com.*, March 1988, *35*(3), pp. 217–25.

Waswo, Ann. The Cambridge History of Japan: Volume 6: The Twentieth Century: The Transformation of Rural Society, 1900–1950. In *Duus, P., ed.*, 1988, pp. 541–605.

Watanabe, Akira. Employee Dispatching Business Law. In *Japan Institute of Labour, ed.*, 1988, *1985*, pp. 120–23.

_____. Ordinance and Guidelines for Implementing the Equal Employment Opportunity Law. In *Japan Institute of Labour, ed.*, 1988, *1986*, pp. 107–10.

_____. Outline of Government and Ministerial Ordinances for Implementing the Employee Dispatching Business Law. In *Japan Institute of Labour, ed.*, 1988, *1986*, pp. 124–26.

Watanabe, Kishichi. The Business Ideology of Benjamin Franklin and Japanese Values of the 18th Century. In *Hausman, W. J., ed.*, 1988, pp. 79–90.

Waterhouse, John and Tims, David. The GAAP in Bank Regulation. *Can. Public Policy*, June 1988, *14*(2), pp. 151–61.

Waterman, Anthony M. C. Can 'Economic Policy' be 'Christian'? *Rev. Soc. Econ.*, October 1988, *46*(2), pp. 203–11.

_____. Hume, Malthus, and the Stability of Equilibrium. *Hist. Polit. Econ.*, Spring 1988, *20*(1), pp. 85–94.

_____. Malthus on Long Swings: A Reply. *Can. J. Econ.*, February 1988, *21*(1), pp. 206–07.

Waters, William R. Social Economics: A Solidar-ist Perspective. *Rev. Soc. Econ.*, October 1988, *46*(2), pp. 113–43.

Waterson, Michael. On Vertical Restraints and the Law: A Note. *Rand J. Econ.*, Summer 1988, *19*(2), pp. 293–97.

_____ and **Hepworth, Mark E.** Information Technology and the Spatial Dynamics of Capital. *Info. Econ. Policy*, 1988, *3*(2), pp. 143–63.

Watkins, Susan Cotts and Menken, Jane A. On the Role of Crises in Historical Perspective: Reply. *Population Devel. Rev.*, March 1988, *14*(1), pp. 165–70.

Watson, Harry S. The Effects of Taxation on Partnership Investment. *J. Public Econ.*, June 1988, *36*(1), pp. 111–26.

Watson, Mark W. A Reexamination of Friedman's Consumption Puzzle: Comment. *J. Bus. Econ. Statist.*, October 1988, *6*(4), pp. 408–09.

_____ and **Stock, James H.** Testing for Common Trends. *J. Amer. Statist. Assoc.*, December 1988, *83*(404), pp. 1097–1107.

_____ and **Stock, James H.** Variable Trends in Economic Time Series. *J. Econ. Perspectives*, Summer 1988, *2*(3), pp. 147–74.

Watson, Patrick Kent. The Balance of Payments of Trinidad and Tobago 1973–1983: A Monetary Phenomenon? *J. Econ. Stud.*, 1988, *15*(1), pp. 19–31.

Watson, Sharon B.; Yandle, Bruce and Wallace, Myles S. Environment Regulation: A Financial Markets Test. *Quart. Rev. Econ. Bus.*, Spring 1988, *28*(1), pp. 69–87.

Watson, Sheila and Smith, Stephen. Consequences of the Abolition of the Inner London Education Authority. *Fisc. Stud.*, August 1988, *9*(3), pp. 68–85.

Watson, William G. The Case of the Disputed Benefit: A Reply to Tim Hazledine. *Can. Public Policy*, June 1988, *14*(2), pp. 214–21.

Watt, Kenneth E. F.; Craig, Paul and Auburn, Jill Shore. World Economic Modeling. In *Ehrlich, P. R. and Holdren, J. P., eds.*, 1988, pp. 233–55.

Wattanawaha, Nongnuch; Jimenez, Emmanuel and Lockheed, Marlaine. The Relative Efficiency of Private and Public Schools: The Case of Thailand. *World Bank Econ. Rev.*, May 1988, *2*(2), pp. 139–64.

Watterson, Patricia A. Infant Mortality by Father's Occupation from the 1911 Census of England and Wales. *Demography*, May 1988, *25*(2), pp. 289–306.

_____; **Woodward, J. H. and Woods, R. I.** The Causes of Rapid Infant Mortality Decline in England and Wales, 1861–1921: Part I. *Population Stud.*, November 1988, *42*(3), pp. 343–66.

Wattleworth, Michael. Credit Subsidies in Budgetary Lending: Computation, Effects, and Fiscal Implications. In *Blejer, M. 1. and Chu, K.-Y., eds.*, 1988, pp. 57–70.

_____. The Effects of Collective Devaluation on Commodity Prices and Exports. *Int. Monet. Fund Staff Pap.*, March 1988, *35*(1), pp. 166–80.

_____ and Morrison, Thomas K. Causes of the 1984–86 Commodity Price Decline. *Finance Develop.*, June 1988, *25*(2), pp. 31–33.

_____ and Morrison, Thomas K. The 1984–86 Commodity Recession: Analysis of Underlying Causes. *Int. Monet. Fund Staff Pap.*, June 1988, *35*(2), pp. 371–81.

Watts, Martin. The Average-Productivity Wage Adjustment Rule: A Reconsideration. *J. Post Keynesian Econ.*, Spring 1988, *10*(3), pp. 445–51.

Watts, Michael. On Peasant Diffidence: Non-revolt, Resistance, and Hidden Forms of Political Consciousness in Northern Nigeria, 1900–1945. In *Burke, E., III, ed.*, 1988, pp. 117–44.

Watts, Myles J.; Helmers, Glenn A. and Atwood, Joseph A. Chance-Constrained Financing as a Response to Financial Risk. *Amer. J. Agr. Econ.*, February 1988, *70*(1), pp. 79–89.

Watts, Peter and Bell, Edwina. Building a Statistical Knowledge Base: A Discussion of the Approach Used in the Development of THESEUS, a Statistical Expert System. In *Edwards, D. and Raun, N. E., eds.*, 1988, pp. 143–48.

Watts, Ross L.; Wruck, Karen H. and Warner, Jerold B. Stock Prices and Top Management Changes. *J. Finan. Econ.*, Jan.–March 1988, *20*(1–2), pp. 461–92.

Waud, Roger N. Tax Aversion, Optimal Tax Rates, and Indexation. *Public Finance*, 1988, *43*(2), pp. 310–25.

_____ and Froyen, Richard T. Real Business Cycles and the Lucas Paradigm. *Econ. Inquiry*, April 1988, *26*(2), pp. 183–201.

Waugh, Geoffrey and Byron, Neil. Forestry and Fisheries in the Asian–Pacific Region: Issues in Natural Resource Management. *Asian-Pacific Econ. Lit.*, March 1988, *2*(1), pp. 46–80.

Waverman, Leonard. U.S.–Canadian Trade Agreement: Two Canadian Perspectives. *Energy J.*, October 1988, *9*(4), pp. 103–06.

Wavre, Pierre-Alain. Swiss Investments in Italy from the XVIIIth to the XXth Century. *J. Europ. Econ. Hist.*, Spring 1988, *17*(1), pp. 85–102.

Waymire, Gregory. Write-Offs as Accounting Procedures to Manage Perceptions: Discussion. *J. Acc. Res.*, Supplement, 1988, *26*, pp. 120–26.

Waldorf, B. S. and Esparza, A. Labor Migration to Western Europe: A Commentary. *Environ. Planning A*, August 1988, *20*(8), pp. 1121–24.

Weagley, Robert O. Consumer Default of Delinquent Adjustable-Rate Mortgage Loans. *J. Cons. Aff.*, Summer 1988, *22*(1), pp. 38–54.

Weale, Martin. The Reconciliation of Values, Volumes and Prices in the National Accounts. *J. Roy. Statist. Soc.*, 1988, *151*(1), pp. 211–21.

_____ and Blake, Andrew. Exchange-Rate Targets and Wage Formation. *Nat. Inst. Econ. Rev.*, February 1988, (123), pp. 48–64.

Weatherford, M. Stephen. The International Economy as a Constraint on U.S. Macroeco-

nomic Policymaking. *Int. Organ.*, Autumn 1988, *42*(4), pp. 605–37.

Weatherley, Richard A. Teenage Parenthood and Poverty. In *Rodgers, H. R., Jr., ed.*, 1988, pp. 114–34.

Weaver, Jerry L. Searching for Survival: Urban Ethiopian Refugees in Sudan. *J. Devel. Areas*, July 1988, *22*(4), pp. 457–75.

Weaver, Paul H. After Social Responsibility. In *Meyer, J. R. and Gustafson, J. M., eds.*, 1988, pp. 133–48.

_____. The Intellectual Debate. In *Boaz, D., ed.*, 1988, pp. 413–21.

Webb, Arthur. Early Capitalism in the Cape: The Eastern Province Bank, 1839–73. In *Jones, S., ed.*, 1988, pp. 47–68.

Webb, Cary. A Probabilistic Model for Price Levels in Discontinuous Markets. In *Eichhorn, W., ed.*, 1988, pp. 137–56.

Webb, David C. and de Meza, David. Credit Market Efficiency and Tax Policy in the Presence of Screening Costs. *J. Public Econ.*, June 1988, *36*(1), pp. 1–22.

Webb, James R. and Rubens, Jack H. The Effect of Alternative Return Measures on Restricted Mixed-Asset Portfolios. *Amer. Real Estate Urban Econ. Assoc. J.*, Summer 1988, *16*(2), pp. 123–37.

Webb, Nick C. New Zealand: Final Report of the Consultative Committee on Full Imputation and International Tax Reform. *Bull. Int. Fiscal Doc.*, October 1988, *42*(10), pp. 441–42.

Webb, Richard C. Comprehensive Solutions: Needed But Not Likely. In *Tavis, L. A., ed.*, 1988, pp. 205–07.

_____. Domestic Crisis and Foreign Debt in Peru. In *Feinberg, R. E. and Ffrench-Davis, R., eds.*, 1988, pp. 241–53.

_____. The Problem Is Adjustment, Not Debt. In *Tavis, L. A., ed.*, 1988, pp. 150–54.

Webb, Roy H. Commodity Prices as Predictors of Aggregate Price Change. *Fed. Res. Bank Richmond Econ. Rev.*, Nov.–Dec. 1988, *74*(6), pp. 3–11.

Webb, Steven B. Latin American Debt Today and German Reparations after World War I—A Comparison. *Weltwirtsch. Arch.*, 1988, *124*(4), pp. 745–74.

_____ and Dilnot, Andrew. Reforming National Insurance Contributions. *Fisc. Stud.*, November 1988, *9*(4), pp. 1–24.

_____ and Dilnot, Andrew. The 1988 Social Security Reforms. *Fisc. Stud.*, August 1988, *9*(3), pp. 26–53.

_____; Dilnot, Andrew and Kell, Michael. The 1988 Budget and the Structure of Personal Taxation. *Fisc. Stud.*, May 1988, *9*(2), pp. 38–47.

_____ and Saunders, Michael. Fiscal Privilege and Financial Assets: Some Distributional Effects. *Fisc. Stud.*, November 1988, *9*(4), pp. 51–69.

Webber, C. A.; MacGregor, R. J. and Graham, J. D. A Regional Analysis of Direct Government Assistance Programs in Canada and Their Impacts on the Beef and Hog Sectors. *Can.*

J. Agr. Econ., Part 2, December 1988, *36*(4), pp. 915–28.

Webber, Michael and Foot, S. P. H. Profitability and Accumulation. *Econ. Geogr.*, October 1988, *64*(4), pp. 335–51.

_____ **and Tonkin, S.** Technical Changes and the Rate of Profit in the Canadian Wood, Furniture, and Paper Industries. *Environ. Planning A*, December 1988, *20*(12), pp. 1623–43.

_____ **and Tonkin, S.** Technical Changes and the Rate of Profit in the Canadian Textile, Knitting, and Clothing Industries. *Environ. Planning A*, November 1988, *20*(11), pp. 1487–1505.

Weber, A. European Agricultural Policies in a Global Context: Some Comments. *Europ. Rev. Agr. Econ.*, 1988, *15*(2–3), pp. 187–90.

Weber, Arnd and Jaeger, Carlo. Lohndynamik und Arbeitslosigkeit. (With English summary.) *Kyklos*, 1988, *41*(3), pp. 479–506.

Weber, Bruce A. and Deaton, Brady J. The Economics of Rural Areas. In *Hildreth, R. J., et al., eds.*, 1988, pp. 403–39.

Weber, Ernst Juerg. Currency Competition in Switzerland, 1826–1850. *Kyklos*, 1988, *41*(3), pp. 459–78.

Weber, Guglielmo; Alessie, Rob J. M. and Melenberg, Bertrand. Consumption, Leisure and Earnings-Related Liquidity Constraints: A Note. *Econ. Letters*, 1988, *27*(1), pp. 101–04.

_____ **and Brugiavini, Agar.** L'armonizzazione delle imposte indirette: Effetti sul benessere dei consumatori italiani. (With English summary.) *Polit. Econ.*, December 1988, *4*(3), pp. 385–408.

_____ **and Desai, Meghnad.** A Keynesian Macroeconometric Model of the UK: 1955–1984. *J. Appl. Econometrics*, January 1988, *3*(1), pp. 1–33.

Weber, Robert James. Probabilistic Value for Games. In *[Shapley, L. S.]*, 1988, pp. 101–19.

Weber, Warren E. and Rolnick, Arthur J. Explaining the Demand for Free Bank Notes. *Fed. Res. Bank Minn. Rev.*, Spring 1988, *12*(2), pp. 21–35.

_____ **and Rolnick, Arthur J.** Explaining the Demand for Free Bank Notes. *J. Monet. Econ.*, January 1988, *21*(1), pp. 47–71.

Weber, William P. Manufacturing as a Competitive Strategy. In *Furino, A., ed.*, 1988, pp. 129–39.

Webley, Paul; Eiser, J. Richard and Spears, Russell. Inflationary Expectations and Policy Preferences. *Econ. Letters*, 1988, *28*(3), pp. 239–41.

_____; **Robben, Henry and Morris, Ira.** Social Comparison and Tax Evasion in a Shop Simulation. In *Maital, S., ed., Vol. 2*, 1988, pp. 553–61.

Webster, Elaine; Mathis, Edward J. and Zech, Charles E. The Impact of Foreign Exports on State Economies: An Economic Base Multiplier Analysis. In *Missouri Valley Economic Assoc.*, 1988, pp. 25–29.

Webster, Gerald R.; Lowery, David and Brunn, Stanley D. The Spatial Impact of Reaganomics: A Test of Six Models. *Growth Change*, Fall 1988, *19*(4), pp. 49–67.

Webster, J. P. G. and Williams, N. T. Changes in Cereal Production and Yield Variability on Farms in South East England. *J. Agr. Econ.*, May 1988, *39*(2), pp. 255–62.

Weck, Manfred and Förtsch, Frank. Application of Multicriteria Optimization to Structural Systems. In *Iri, M. and Yajima, K., eds.*, 1988, pp. 471–83.

Weddepohl, H. N. A Comparative Analysis of Actual Dutch Macroeconomic Models: Comments. In *Driehuis, W.; Fase, M. M. G. and den Hartog, H., eds.*, 1988, pp. 215–20.

Wedderburn, Lord and Sciarra, S. Collective Bargaining as Agreement and as Law: Neo-contractualist and Neo-corporative Tendencies of Our Age. In *Pizzorusso, A., ed.*, 1988, pp. 186–235.

Weddleton, John and Olson, Dennis O. Estimating Undisclosed Earnings Data. *Ann. Reg. Sci.*, March 1988, *22*(1), pp. 84–90.

Wedig, Gerard J. Health Status and the Demand for Health: Results on Price Elasticities. *J. Health Econ.*, June 1988, *7*(2), pp. 151–63.

_____, **et al.** Capital Structure, Ownership, and Capital Payment Policy: The Case of Hospitals. *J. Finance*, March 1988, *43*(1), pp. 21–40.

Wedig, W. Parameteric Instability and Process Identification. In *Schiehlen, W. and Wedig, W., eds.*, 1988, pp. 201–42.

Weeks, John. Economic Crisis in Nicaragua: Blaming the Victim. *Rev. Radical Polit. Econ.*, Summer–Fall 1988, *20*(2–3), pp. 266–70.

_____. Value and Protection in the *General Theory*. In *Hillard, J., ed.*, 1988, pp. 185–210.

_____ **and Jamal, Vali.** The Vanishing Rural–Urban Gap in Sub-Saharan Africa. *Int. Lab. Rev.*, 1988, *127*(3), pp. 271–92.

Weerahandi, Samaradasa and Johnson, Richard A. A Bayesian Solution to the Multivariate Behrens–Fisher Problem. *J. Amer. Statist. Assoc.*, March 1988, *83*(401), pp. 145–49.

van Weeren, J. and van Praag, Bernard M. S. Memory and Anticipation Processes and Their Significance for Social Security and Income Inequality. In *Maital, S., ed., Vol. 2*, 1988, pp. 731–51.

Weersink, Alfons and Stauber, Steve. Optimal Replacement Interval and Depreciation Method for a Grain Combine. *Western J. Agr. Econ.*, July 1988, *13*(1), pp. 18–28.

Wegener, M. K. and Vining, G. S. Agricultural Economics Training at the University of Queensland. *Rev. Marketing Agr. Econ.*, August 1988, *56*(2), pp. 230–32.

Weghorst, W. and Franke, Reiner. Complex Dynamics in a Simple Input–Output Model without the Full Capacity Utilization Hypothesis. *Metroecon.*, February 1988, *39*(1), pp. 1–29.

Wei, K. C. John. An Asset-Pricing Theory Unifying the CAPM and APT. *J. Finance*, September 1988, *43*(4), pp. 881–92.

_____ **and Carroll, Carolyn.** Risk, Return, and

Equilibrium: An Extension. *J. Bus.*, October 1988, *61*(4), pp. 485–99.

_____; Frecka, Thomas J. and Park, Hun Y. A Further Investigation of the Risk–Return Relation for Commodity Futures. In *Fabozzi, F. J.*, *ed.*, 1988, pp. 357–77.

_____ and Sears, R. Stephen. The Structure of Skewness Preferences in Asset Pricing Models with Higher Moments: An Empirical Test. *Financial Rev.*, February 1988, *23*(1), pp. 25–38.

_____; White, Richard E. and Pruitt, Stephen W. The Impact of Union-Sponsored Boycotts on the Stock Prices of Target Firms. *J. Lab. Res.*, Summer 1988, *9*(3), pp. 285–89.

Weibull, Jörgen W. and Lindbeck, Assar. Altruism and Time Consistency: The Economics of Fait Accompli. *J. Polit. Econ.*, December 1988, *96*(6), pp. 1165–82.

_____ and Lindbeck, Assar. Welfare Effects of Alternative Forms of Public Spending. *Europ. Econ. Rev.*, January 1988, *32*(1), pp. 101–27.

Weicher, John C. The Future Structure of the Housing Finance System. In *Haraf, W. S. and Kushmeider, R. M.*, *eds.*, 1988, pp. 296–336.

_____ and Thibodeau, Thomas G. Filtering and Housing Markets: An Empirical Analysis. *J. Urban Econ.*, January 1988, *23*(1), pp. 21–40.

Weichert, Ronald and Zietz, Joachim. A Dynamic Singular Equation System of Asset Demand. *Europ. Econ. Rev.*, July 1988, *32*(6), pp. 1349–57.

Weidenaar, Dennis J. and Bartlett, Robin L. An Introduction to the Proceedings of the 1987 Invitational Conference on the Principles of Economics Textbook. *J. Econ. Educ.*, Spring 1988, *19*(2), pp. 109–12.

Weidenbaum, Murray L. International Trade: Better Than Congress. In *Boaz, D.*, *ed.*, 1988, pp. 253–60.

_____. The Role of the Council of Economic Advisers. *J. Econ. Educ.*, Summer 1988, *19*(3), pp. 237–43.

_____. Strategies for Responding to Corporate Takeovers. In *Weidenbaum, M. L. and Chilton, K. W.*, *eds.*, 1988, pp. 141–69.

_____ and Chilton, Kenneth W. Public Policy toward Corporate Takeovers: Introduction. In *Weidenbaum, M. L. and Chilton, K. W.*, *eds.*, 1988, pp. vii–xvi.

_____ and Cook, Richard E. Impacts of Takeovers on Financial Markets. In *Weidenbaum, M. L. and Chilton, K. W.*, *eds.*, 1988, pp. 63–77.

Weidlich, Wolfgang. Derivation of the Master Equation. In *Weidlich, W. and Haag, G.*, *eds.*, 1988, pp. 317–25.

_____. Solutions of the Master Equation. In *Weidlich, W. and Haag, G.*, *eds.*, 1988, pp. 327–44.

_____ and Haag, Günter. Concepts of the Dynamic Migration Model. In *Weidlich, W. and Haag, G.*, *eds.*, 1988, pp. 9–20.

_____ and Haag, Günter. The Migratory Equations of Motion. In *Weidlich, W. and Haag, G.*, *eds.*, 1988, pp. 21–32.

Weiermair, Klaus. Part-Time Labor: Causes and Consequences for Managerial Discretion. In *Dlugos, G.; Dorow, W. and Weiermair, K.*, *eds.*, 1988, pp. 335–49.

_____ and Gunderson, Morley. Labour Market Rigidities: Economic Analysis of Alternative Work Schedules Including Overtime Restrictions. In *Dlugos, G.; Dorow, W. and Weiermair, K.*, *eds.*, 1988, pp. 153–63.

_____ and Leibenstein, Harvey. X-Efficiency, Managerial Discretion, and the Nature of Employment-Relations: A Game-Theoretical Approach. In *Dlugos, G.; Dorow, W. and Weiermair, K.*, *eds.*, 1988, pp. 79–94.

Weigel, Dale R. and Pfeffermann, Guy. The Private Sector and the Policy Environment. *Finance Develop.*, December 1988, *25*(4), pp. 25–27.

Weigel, Russell H.; Hessing, Dick J. and Elffers, Henk. Research in Tax Resistance: An Integrative Theoretical Scheme for Tax Evasion Behavior. In *Maital, S.*, *ed.*, *Vol. 2*, 1988, pp. 568–76.

Weigelt, Keith and Camerer, Colin. Experimental Tests of a Sequential Equilibrium Reputation Model. *Econometrica*, January 1988, *56*(1), pp. 1–36.

Weigold, Michael F.; Lynch, John G., Jr. and Marmorstein, Howard. Choices from Sets Including Remembered Brands: Use of Recalled Attributes and Prior Overall Evaluations. *J. Cons. Res.*, September 1988, *15*(2), pp. 169–84.

Weil, Irwin. The Soviet Union Today: A Survey of the Cultural Scene. In *Cracraft, J.*, *ed.*, 1988, pp. 261–71.

Weilbaker, Dan C.; Urbany, Joel E. and Bearden, William O. The Effect of Plausible and Exaggerated Reference Prices on Consumer Perceptions and Price Search. *J. Cons. Res.*, June 1988, *15*(1), pp. 95–110.

Weiman, David F. Urban Growth on the Periphery of the Antebellum Cotton Belt: Atlanta, 1847–1860. *J. Econ. Hist.*, June 1988, *48*(2), pp. 259–72.

Weimer, David Leo and Horwich, George. The Economics of International Oil Sharing. *Energy J.*, October 1988, *9*(4), pp. 17–33.

_____ and Horwich, George. International Oil Sharing and Policy Coordination: A Critical Summary. In *Horwich, G. and Weimer, D. L.*, *eds.*, 1988, pp. 285–306.

_____; Horwich, George and Jenkins-Smith, Hank C. The International Energy Agency's Mandatory Oil-Sharing Agreement: Tests of Efficiency, Equity, and Practicality. In *Horwich, G. and Weimer, D. L.*, *eds.*, 1988, pp. 104–33.

_____ and Vining, Aidan R. Information Asymmetry Favoring Sellers: A Policy Framework. *Policy Sci.*, 1988, *21*(4), pp. 281–303.

Weinberg, Alvin M. and Marland, Gregg. Longevity of Infrastructure. In *Ausubel, J. H. and Herman, R.*, *eds.*, 1988, pp. 312–32.

Weinberger, Caspar W. National Defense in the

Next Decade. In *Anderson, A. and Bark, D. L., eds.*, 1988, pp. 165–74.

Weindling, Paul. Fascism and Population in Comparative European Perspective. *Population Devel. Rev.*, Supplement, 1988, *14*, pp. 102–21.

Weiner, Dan; Moyo, Sam and Chidiya, Charles. Energy Use in Zimbabwe's Agricultural Sector. In *Hosier, R. H., ed. (I)*, 1988, pp. 20–59.

Weiner, Stuart E. Financial Market Volatility: Introduction. In *Federal Reserve Bank of Kansas City*, 1988, pp. xv–xxix.

Weingast, Barry R. and Marshall, William J. The Industrial Organization of Congress; or, Why Legislatures, Like Firms, Are Not Organized as Markets. *J. Polit. Econ.*, February 1988, *96*(1), pp. 132–63.

Weinhold, Wolf A. and Salter, Malcolm S. Corporate Takeovers: Financial Boom or Organizational Bust? In *Coffee, J. C., Jr.; Lowenstein, L. and Rose-Ackerman, S., eds.*, 1988, pp. 135–49.

Weinraub, Herbert J.; Ma, Christopher K. and Rao, Ramesh P. The Seasonality in Convertible Bond Markets: A Stock Effect or Bond Effect? *J. Finan. Res.*, Winter 1988, *11*(4), pp. 335–47.

Weinrib, Ernest J. Legal Formalism: On the Immanent Rationality of Law. *Yale Law J.*, May 1988, *97*(6), pp. 949–1016.

Weinrobe, Maurice. An Insurance Plan to Guarantee Reverse Mortgages. *J. Risk Ins.*, December 1988, *55*(4), pp. 644–59.

Weins, Thomas B. Issues in the Structural Reform of Chinese Agriculture. In *Reynolds, B. L., ed.*, 1988, *1987*, pp. 82–94.

Weinstein, Maxine and Wood, James W. A Model of Age-Specific Fecundability. *Population Stud.*, March 1988, *42*(1), pp. 85–113.

Weinstein, Milton C. A QALY Is a QALY Is a QALY—Or Is It? Editorial. *J. Health Econ.*, September 1988, *7*(3), pp. 289–90.

Weintraub, E. Roy. Economic Rhetoric among Economists: On the Brittleness of the Orange Equilibrium. In *Klamer, A.; McCloskey, D. N. and Solow, R. M., eds.*, 1988, pp. 146–62.

_____. The Neo-Walrasian Program Is Empirically Progressive. In *de Marchi, N., ed.*, 1988, pp. 213–27.

Weintraub, Sidney. An Eclectic Theory of Income Shares. In *Sawyer, M. C., ed.*, 1988, *1981*, pp. 362–76.

_____. Generalizing Kalecki and Simplifying Macroeconomics. In *Sawyer, M. C., ed.*, 1988, *1979*, pp. 143–48.

_____. Keynesian Demand Serendipity in Supply-Side Economics. In *Shaw, G. K., ed., Vol. 2*, 1988, *1981*, pp. 239–49.

Weintrop, Joseph; Wier, Peggy and Kamma, Sreenivas. Investors' Perceptions of the Delaware Supreme Court Decision in Unocal v. Mesa. *J. Finan. Econ.*, Jan.–March 1988, *20*(1–2), pp. 419–30.

Weir, R. B. Structural Change and Diversification

in Ireland and Scotland. In *Mitchison, R. and Roebuck, P., eds.*, 1988, pp. 297–307.

Weisbach, Michael S. Outside Directors and CEO Turnover. *J. Finan. Econ.*, Jan.–March 1988, *20*(1–2), pp. 431–60.

_____ and Hermalin, Benjamin E. The Determinants of Board Composition. *Rand J. Econ.*, Winter 1988, *19*(4), pp. 589–606.

Weisbrod, Steven R. Regulation of International Banking: A Review Essay. *J. Monet. Econ.*, September 1988, *22*(2), pp. 347–52.

Weisensel, Ward P.; Schoney, Richard A. and Van Kooten, G. C. Where Are Saskatchewan Farmland Prices Headed? *Can. J. Agr. Econ.*, March 1988, *36*(1), pp. 37–50.

Weisman, Dennis L. Default Capacity Tariffs: Smoothing the Transitional Regulatory Asymmetries in the Telecommunications Market. *Yale J. Regul.*, Winter 1988, *5*(1), pp. 149–78.

Weiss, Andrew. High School Graduation, Performance, and Wages. *J. Polit. Econ.*, August 1988, *96*(4), pp. 785–820.

_____; Wilson, Charles A. and Hendricks, Kenneth. The War of Attrition in Continuous Time with Complete Information. *Int. Econ. Rev.*, November 1988, *29*(4), pp. 663–80.

Weiss, Andrew A.; Bartels, Robert and Murray, Jane. The Role of Consumer and Business Sentiment in Forecasting Telecommunications Traffic. *J. Econ. Psych.*, June 1988, *9*(2), pp. 215–32.

Weiss, Charles F. Federal Agency Treatment of Uncertainty in Environmental Impact Statements under the CEQ's Amended NEPA Regulation § 1502.22: Worst Case Analysis or Risk Threshold? *Mich. Law Rev.*, February 1988, *86*(4), pp. 777–821.

Weiss, Elliott J. Mergers and Takeovers: Taxes, Capital Structure, and the Incentives of Managers: Comment. In *Coffee, J. C., Jr.; Lowenstein, L. and Rose-Ackerman, S., eds.*, 1988, pp. 360–65.

Weiss, Jeffrey H. Is Vote-Selling Desirable? *Public Choice*, November 1988, *59*(2), pp. 177–94.

Weiss, Joseph and Intrator, Jacob. Tree Indexing Methods for Transportation Algorithms for Long Problems. *Econ. Computat. Cybern. Stud. Res.*, 1988, *23*(4), pp. 81–87.

Weiss, Laurence. Financial Structure and Aggregate Economic Activity: An Overview: Comment. *J. Money, Credit, Banking*, Part 2, August 1988, *20*(3), pp. 594–96.

_____ and Topel, Robert H. Sectoral Uncertainty and Unemployment. In *Hart, R. A., ed.*, 1988, pp. 344–63.

Weiss, Marc A. The Rise of the Community Builders: The American Real Estate Industry and Urban Land Planning. In *Perkins, E. J., ed.*, 1988, pp. 72–86.

Weiss, Michael D. Expected Utility Theory without Continuous Preferences. In *Munier, B. R., ed.*, 1988, pp. 115–26.

Weiss, U. OPPA—Market Information on Videotex in France. In *Schiefer, G., ed.*, 1988, pp. 177–88.

Weiss, Vanessa and Sicular, Terry. Grain and Meat in China: Trends in Consumption, Production, and Imports with Special Reference to Isolated Soy Protein Meat Ingredients. In *Schwarz, F. H., ed.*, 1988, pp. 107–57.

Weiss, Yoram; Fleising, Asher and Eckstein, Zvi. University Policies under Varying Market Conditions: The Training of Electrical Engineers. *Econ. Educ. Rev.*, 1988, 7(4), pp. 393–403.

Weisskopf, Thomas E. An Analysis of Profitability Changes in Eight Capitalist Economies. *Rev. Radical Polit. Econ.*, Summer–Fall 1988, 20(2–3), pp. 68–79.

――――. The Analytics of Neo-Marxian Crisis Theory: An Illustrative Model. *Econ. Rev. (Keizai Kenkyu)*, July 1988, 39(3), pp. 193–208.

Weisz, Morris. A View of Labor Ministries in Other Nations. *Mon. Lab. Rev.*, July 1988, 111(7), pp. 19–23.

Weitz, Barton A. and John, George. Forward Integration into Distribution: An Empirical Test of Transaction Cost Analysis. *J. Law, Econ., Organ.*, Fall 1988, 4(2), pp. 337–55.

Weitzman, Martin L. Comment on "Can the Share Economy Conquer Stagflation?" *Quart. J. Econ.*, February 1988, 103(1), pp. 219–23.

――――. Consumer's Surplus as an Exact Approximation When Prices Are Appropriately Deflated. *Quart. J. Econ.*, August 1988, 103(3), pp. 543–53.

――――. Increasing Returns and the Foundations of Unemployment Theory: Rejoinder. *Econ. J.*, March 1988, 98(389), pp. 172–74.

von Weizsäcker, C. Christian and Wieland, Bernhard. Current Telecommunications Policy in West Germany. *Oxford Rev. Econ. Policy*, Summer 1988, 4(2), pp. 20–39.

Welch, Finis R.; Murphy, Kevin M. and Plant, Mark. Cohort Size and Earnings in the USA. In *Lee, R. D.; Arthur, W. B. and Rodgers, G., eds.*, 1988, pp. 39–58.

――――; Raisian, John and Ward, Michael P. Implementing Comparable Worth: Conceptual Issues and Impacts. In *Mangum, G. and Philips, P., eds.*, 1988, pp. 183–200.

――――. and Smith, James P. Racial Discrimination: A Human Capital Perspective. In *Mangum, G. and Philips, P., eds.*, 1988, pp. 95–116.

Welch, Robert L. and Chen, David M. On the Properties of the Valuation Formula for an Unprotected American Call Option with Known Dividends and the Computation of Its Implied Standard Deviation. In *Fabozzi, F. J., ed.*, 1988, pp. 237–56.

von Welck, Stephan Frhr. Restrictions on the Export of Space Technology. In *Egan, J. J., et al.*, 1988, pp. 433–42.

Weldon, J. C. The Classical Theory of Distribution. In *Asimakopulos, A., ed.*, 1988, pp. 15–47.

Welford, Richard. Objectives and Growth Aspirations of UK Worker Cooperatives. *Ann. Pub. Co-op. Econ.*, April–June 1988, 59(2), pp. 215–27.

Welker, Robert B. and Meixner, Wilda F. Judg-

ment Consensus and Auditor Experience: An Examination of Organizational Relations. *Accounting Rev.*, July 1988, 63(3), pp. 505–13.

――――; Wiggins, Casper E. and Mayper, Alan G. Accounting and Review Services: Perceptions of the Message within the CPA's Report. In *Schwartz, B. N., ed.*, 1988, pp. 219–32.

Welland, Douglas and Mestelman, Stuart. Advance Production in Experimental Markets. *Rev. Econ. Stud.*, October 1988, 55(4), pp. 641–54.

Wellings, Paul. International Competition and Industrial Decentralization in South Africa: A Comment. *World Devel.*, December 1988, 16(12), pp. 1547–49.

Wellington, Donald C. Empires: Ancient and Modern. *Rivista Int. Sci. Econ. Com.*, March 1988, 35(3), pp. 209–15.

Wellington, Harry H. and Winter, Ralph K., Jr. The Limits of Collective Bargaining in Public Employment. In *Lewin, D., et al., eds.*, 1988, pp. 37–52.

Wellisz, Stanislaw and Findlay, Ronald. The State and the Invisible Hand. *World Bank Res. Observer*, January 1988, 3(1), pp. 59–80.

Wellman, Barry and Berkowitz, S. D. Introduction: Studying Social Structures. In *Wellman, B. and Berkowitz, S. D., eds.*, 1988, pp. 1–14.

Wells, Donald R. Security Reserve Requirements—A Possible Substitute for Deposit Insurance? In *Missouri Valley Economic Assoc.*, 1988, pp. 76–83.

Wells, Jill and Strassmann, W. Paul. The Global Construction Industry: Conclusion: Comparison and Analysis. In *Strassmann, W. P. and Wells, J., eds.*, 1988, pp. 211–58.

――――. and Strassmann, W. Paul. The Global Construction Industry: Strategies for Entry Growth and Survival: Introduction. In *Strassmann, W. P. and Wells, J., eds.*, 1988, pp. 1–21.

Wells, Kenneth B.; Keeler, Emmett B. and Manning, Willard G. The Demand for Episodes of Mental Health Services. *J. Health Econ.*, December 1988, 7(4), pp. 369–92.

Wells, O. V. Agricultural Economics Research: Some Notes on the New Journal. *J. Agr. Econ. Res.*, Winter 1988, 40(1), pp. 9–10.

Wells, Paul and Marme, Christopher. Hick's Wage-Theorem and Keynes's *General Theory*. In *Hamouda, O. F. and Smithin, J. N., eds.*, Vol. 2, 1988, pp. 93–101.

Welsch, Heinz. A Cost Comparison of Alternative Policies for Sulphur Dioxide Control: The Case of the British Power Plant Sector. *Energy Econ.*, October 1988, 10(4), pp. 287–97.

Welsch, Roy E. and Belsley, David A. Modeling Energy Consumption—Using and Abusing Regression Diagnostics: Comment [Combining Robust and Traditional Least Squares Methods: A Critical Evaluation]. *J. Bus. Econ. Statist.*, October 1988, 6(4), pp. 442–47.

――――; Belsley, David A. and Venetoulias, Aachilles. Computer Guided Diagnostics. In

Edwards, D. and Raun, N. E., eds., 1988, pp. 99–104.

_____ **and Gay, David M.** Maximum Likelihood and Quasi-likelihood for Nonlinear Exponential Family Regression Models. *J. Amer. Statist. Assoc.*, December 1988, *83*(404), pp. 990–98.

Welsh, A. H.; de Jongh, P. J. and de Wet, T. Mallows-Type Bounded-Influence–Regression Trimmed Means. *J. Amer. Statist. Assoc.*, September 1988, *83*(403), pp. 805–10.

Welsh, Michael P.; Bishop, Richard C. and Boyle, Kevin J. Validation of Empirical Measures of Welfare Change: Comment. *Land Econ.*, February 1988, *64*(1), pp. 94–98.

Welton, Gary L.; Pruitt, Dean G. and McGillicuddy, Neil B. The Role of Caucusing in Community Mediation. *J. Conflict Resolution*, March 1988, *32*(1), pp. 181–202.

Wendel, Jeanne and Raffiee, Kambiz. The Effects of Alternative Regulatory Policies on Utility Investment Strategies. *Southern Econ. J.*, April 1988, *54*(4), pp. 840–54.

Wendt, Dirk and Ksiensik, Monika Isis. Normative and Individual Strategies in Social Dilemmata. In *Tietz, R.; Albers, W. and Selten, R., eds.*, 1988, pp. 21–36.

Wendt, H. and Bauer, G. H. Water-Splitting Methods. In *Winter, C.-J. and Nitsch, J., eds.*, 1988, pp. 166–208.

Wenger, Ekkehard and Picot, Arnold. The Employment Relation from the Transactions Cost Perspective. In *Dlugos, G.; Dorow, W. and Weiermair, K., eds.*, 1988, pp. 29–43.

Wenger, Morton G. Marxism and Social Research: The Mythology of Epistemology. *Sci. Soc.*, Summer 1988, *52*(2), pp. 133–62.

Wenig, Alois and Straub, Martin. On the Construction of an Index of Bequest Behavior. In *Eichhorn, W., ed.*, 1988, pp. 453–76.

Wenninger, John. Money Demand—Some Long-run Properties. *Fed. Res. Bank New York Quart. Rev.*, Spring 1988, *13*(1), pp. 23–40.

Wenzel, Heinz-Dieter. Fiscal Pressure on the "Tax State": Discussion. In *Hanusch, H., ed.*, 1988, pp. 278–83.

_____. Zur Lösung statischer Zielkonflikte in dynamischen Makrosystemen: Ein Fallbeispiel. (Some Remarks to the Solution of Static Target Realization Problems—An Example. With English summary.) *Jahr. Nationalökon. Statist.*, March 1988, *204*(3), pp. 231–40.

Werczberger, E. and Berechman, J. Incorporating Neighborhood Effects into Spatial Allocation Models. *Environ. Planning A*, May 1988, *20*(5), pp. 595–607.

Werden, Gregory J. The Divergence of SIC Industries from Antitrust Markets: Some Evidence from Price Fixing Cases. *Econ. Letters*, 1988, *28*(2), pp. 193–97.

v. Werder, Axel. Produkthaftungs-Management U.S.-amerikanischer Grossunternehmungen. (With English summary.) *Z. Betriebswirtshaft*, October 1988, *58*(10), pp. 1010–32.

Wergeland, Tor. Shadow Price Calculations in Distorted Economies: Comment. In *Haaland,*

J. I. and Norman, V. D., eds., 1988, pp. 87–88.

Werlang, Sérgio Ribeiro da Costa and Tan, Tommy Chin-Chiu. The Bayesian Foundations of Solution Concepts of Games. *J. Econ. Theory*, August 1988, *45*(2), pp. 370–91.

Werneck, Rogério L. Furquim. Um modelo de simulaçao para análise do financiamento do setor público. (With English summary.) *Pesquisa Planejamento Econ.*, December 1988, *18*(3), pp. 479–528.

Werner, Josua. Die Arbeitslosigkeit in der Bundesrepublik Deutschland Natur, Ursachen und beschäftigungspolitische Optionen. (The Unemployment in the Federal Republic of Germany. With English summary.) *Aussenwirtschaft*, December 1988, *43*(4), pp. 473–504.

Wernerfelt, Birger. General Equilibrium with Real Time Search in Labor and Product Markets. *J. Polit. Econ.*, August 1988, *96*(4), pp. 821–31.

_____. Reputation, Monitoring, and Effort. *Info. Econ. Policy*, 1988, *3*(3), pp. 207–18.

_____. Umbrella Branding as a Signal of New Product Quality: An Example of Signalling by Posting a Bond. *Rand J. Econ.*, Autumn 1988, *19*(3), pp. 458–66.

_____ **and Fornell, Claes.** A Model for Customer Complaint Management. *Marketing Sci.*, Summer 1988, *7*(3), pp. 287–98.

_____ **and Hauser, John R.** Existence and Uniqueness of Price Equilibria in Defender [Defensive Marketing Strategies]. *Marketing Sci.*, Winter 1988, *7*(1), pp. 92–93.

_____ **and Montgomery, Cynthia A.** Diversification, Ricardian Rents, and Tobin's q. *Rand J. Econ.*, Winter 1988, *19*(4), pp. 623–32.

_____ **and Montgomery, Cynthia A.** Tobin's q and the Importance of Focus in Firm Performance. *Amer. Econ. Rev.*, March 1988, *78*(1), pp. 246–50.

Weschler, Louis and Mushkatel, Alvin H. Privatism in Local Land Use Development: The Use of Exactions, Impact Fees and Impact Taxes by Municipalities. In *Hula, R. C., ed.*, 1988, pp. 121–33.

Wescott, Shari H. An Assessment of the Ability of Accounting Numbers to Predict Municipal General Obligation Bond Ratings. In *Chan, J. L. and Rowan, H. J., eds.*, 1988, pp. 79–102.

Weser, Thilo and Hillinger, Claude. The Aggregation Problem in Business Cycle Theory. *J. Econ. Dynam. Control*, March 1988, *12*(1), pp. 37–50.

_____ **and Hillinger, Claude.** Die Aggregationsproblematik in der Konjunkturtheorie. (The Aggregation Problem in Business Cycle Theory. With English summary.) *Jahr. Nationalökon. Statist.*, April 1988, *204*(4), pp. 326–41.

Wessel, Robert H. Significant Third-World Debt Reductions Soon: A Real Possibility. *Rivista Int. Sci. Econ. Com.*, Oct.–Nov. 1988, *35*(10–11), pp. 925–34.

_____. Women in the Labor Forces of the World: Participation, Compensation and Discrimination. *Rivista Int. Sci. Econ. Com.*, January 1988, 35(1), pp. 59–76.

Wessells, Cathy Roheim and Heien, Dale M. The Demand for Dairy Products: Structure, Prediction, and Decomposition. *Amer. J. Agr. Econ.*, May 1988, 70(2), pp. 219–28.

———— **and Heien, Dale M.** The Nutritional Impact of the Dairy Price Support Program. *J. Cons. Aff.*, Winter 1988, 22(2), pp. 201–19.

Wessels, G. M. Die Opkoms en Agteruitgang van die Dollar as Internasionale Sleutelvaluta sedert die Eerste Wêreldoorlog. (With English summary). *J. Stud. Econ. Econometrics*, March 1988, 12(1), pp. 37–50.

Wessels, Roberto E. and Titman, Sheridan D. The Determinants of Capital Structure Choice. *J. Finance*, March 1988, 43(1), pp. 1–19.

————; **Wijmenga, Roel T. and van den Bergh, Willem Max.** Two Tests of the Tax-Loss Selling Hypothesis. In *Dimson, E., ed.*, 1988, pp. 147–54.

Wesso, G. R. and Smit, E. van der M. Structural Stability in South African Econometric Models—Some Empirical Results. *J. Stud. Econ. Econometrics*, March 1988, 12(1), pp. 51–71.

Wesson, Robert. Latin America and the Caribbean: Neighbors and Friends? In *Anderson, A. and Bark, D. L., eds.*, 1988, pp. 103–14.

West, Douglas. Multinational Competition in the British Advertising Agency Business, 1936–1987. *Bus. Hist. Rev.*, Autumn 1988, 62(3), pp. 467–501.

West, Douglas S.; Ryan, David L. and Von Hohenbalken, Balder. New Competition in Shopping-Center Hierarchies: An Empirical Comparison of Alternative Specifications. *J. Reg. Sci.*, August 1988, 28(3), pp. 329–44.

West, Edwin G. Developments in the Literature on Adam Smith: An Evaluative Survey. In *Thweatt, W. O., ed.*, 1988, pp. 13–44.

————. Government Grants to Nonprofit Firms: Still Searching for the Rationale. *J. Cult. Econ.*, December 1988, 12(2), pp. 93–96.

————. Job Signalling and Welfare Improving Minimum Wage Laws. *Econ. Inquiry*, July 1988, 26(3), pp. 525–32.

———— **and Martinello, Felice.** The Optimal Size of the Tuition Tax Credit. *Public Finance Quart.*, October 1988, 16(4), pp. 425–38.

———— **and Palsson, Halldor P.** Parental Choice of School Characteristics: Estimation Using State-Wide Data. *Econ. Inquiry*, October 1988, 26(4), pp. 725–40.

West, G. R.; Hewings, Geoffrey J. D. and Jensen, Rodney C. The Study of Regional Economic Structure Using Input–Output Tables. *Reg. Stud.*, June 1988, 22(3), pp. 209–20.

West, Kenneth D. Asymptotic Normality, When Regressors Have a Unit Root. *Econometrica*, November 1988, 56(6), pp. 1397–1417.

————. Bubbles, Fads and Stock Price Volatility Tests: A Partial Evaluation. *J. Finance*, July 1988, 43(3), pp. 639–56.

————. Dividend Innovations and Stock Price Volatility. *Econometrica*, January 1988, 56(1), pp. 37–61.

————. The Insensitivity of Consumption to News about Income. *J. Monet. Econ.*, January 1988, 21(1), pp. 17–33.

————. On the Interpretation of Near Random-walk Behavior in GNP. *Amer. Econ. Rev.*, March 1988, 78(1), pp. 202–09.

———— **and Stock, James H.** Integrated Regressors and Tests of the Permanent-Income Hypothesis. *J. Monet. Econ.*, January 1988, 21(1), pp. 85–95.

West, Ronald E. Economic Analysis of Solar Thermal Energy Systems: Introduction. In *West, R. E. and Kreith, F., eds.*, 1988, pp. 1–17.

West, Stephen G.; Reneau, J. Hal and Harrison, Paul D. Initial Attributions and Information-Seeking by Superiors and Subordinates in Production Variance Investigations. *Accounting Rev.*, April 1988, 63(2), pp. 307–20.

Westberg, Lars and Ekstedt, Hasse. Interaction between Economic Growth and Financial Flows: Presentation of a Model Analysing the Impact of Short-Term Financial Disturbances on Economic Growth. In *Motamen, H., ed.*, 1988, pp. 219–43.

Westbrook, Robert A. Consumer Satisfaction: An Affirmation of Possibilities. In *Maynes, E. S. and ACCI Research Committee, eds.*, 1988, pp. 760–70.

Westergård-Nielsen, Niels and Smith, Nina. Udviklingen i lønforskelle mellem den offentlige og private sektor. (Wage Differentials between the Public and the Private Sector in Denmark. With English summary.) *Nationaløkon. Tidsskr.*, 1988, 126(1), pp. 13–30.

Westerhoff, Thomas and Naeve, Peter. On Inference Process. In *Edwards, D. and Raun, N. E., eds.*, 1988, pp. 193–98.

Westman, Mina and Gafni, Amiram. Hypertension Labelling as a Stressful Event Leading to an Increase in Absenteeism: A Possible Explanation for an Empirically Measured Phenomenon. In *Maital, S., ed.*, Vol. 2, 1988, pp. 507–27.

Westney, D. Eleanor. Domestic and Foreign Learning Curves in Managing International Cooperative Strategies. In *Contractor, F. J. and Lorange, P.*, 1988, pp. 339–46.

Westoff, Charles F. Is the KAP-Gap Real? *Population Devel. Rev.*, June 1988, 14(2), pp. 225–32.

Weston, Rae and Williams, Alan. Socioeconomic Implications of New Technology in Banking: Some Australian and New Zealand Evidence. In *Tisdell, C. and Maitra, P., eds.*, 1988, pp. 281–97.

de Wet, T.; Welsh, A. H. and de Jongh, P. J. Mallows-Type Bounded-Influence–Regression Trimmed Means. *J. Amer. Statist. Assoc.*, September 1988, 83(403), pp. 805–10.

Wetzel, William E. and Freear, John. Equity Financing for New Technology-Based Firms. In *Kirchhoff, B. A., et al., eds.*, 1988, pp. 347–67.

Wetzstein, Michael E. An Organonic and Modern Problems Approach for Teaching Agricultural

Economics Principles. *Amer. J. Agr. Econ.*, February 1988, *70*(1), pp. 63–68.

_____ and Centner, Terence J. Reducing Moral Hazard Associated with Implied Warranties of Animal Health: Reply. *Amer. J. Agr. Econ.*, May 1988, *70*(2), pp. 413–14.

_____ and McClelland, John W. Investment and Disinvestment Principles with Nonconstant Prices and Varying Firm Size Applied to Beef-Breeding Herds: Comment. *Amer. J. Agr. Econ.*, November 1988, *70*(4), pp. 936–37.

_____; Musser, Wesley N. and McClelland, John W. Returns to Scale and Size in Agricultural Economics: Reply. *Western J. Agr. Econ.*, July 1988, *13*(1), pp. 151–52.

_____, et al. Efficiency Criteria and Risk Aversion: An Empirical Evaluation. *Southern J. Agr. Econ.*, July 1988, *20*(1), pp. 171–78.

Wexley, Kenneth N. and Russell, James S. Improving Managerial Performance in Assessing Needs and Transferring Training. In *Ferris, G. R. and Rowland, K. M., eds.*, 1988, pp. 289–323.

Weyant, John P. Coordinated Stock Drawdowns: Pros and Cons. In *Horwich, G. and Weimer, D. L., eds.*, 1988, pp. 179–99.

_____. Is There Policy-Oriented Learning in the Analysis of Natural Gas Policy Issues? *Policy Sci.*, 1988, *21*(2–3), pp. 239–61.

_____; Peck, Stephen C. and Bosch, Deborah K. Industrial Energy Demand: A Simple Structural Approach. *Resources & Energy*, June 1988, *10*(2), pp. 111–33.

Weymark, John A. and Chakravarty, Satya R. Axiomatizations of the Entropy Numbers Equivalent Index of Industrial Concentration. In *Eichhorn, W., ed.*, 1988, pp. 383–97.

_____ and Donaldson, David. Social Choice in Economic Environments. *J. Econ. Theory*, December 1988, *46*(2), pp. 291–308.

Whalen, Charles J. The Minsky–Simons Connection: A Neglected Thread in the History of Economic Thought. *J. Econ. Issues*, June 1988, *22*(2), pp. 533–44.

Whalen, Thomas and Brønn, Carl. Essentials of Decision Making under Generalized Uncertainty. In *Kacprzyk, J. and Fedrizzi, M., eds.*, 1988, pp. 26–47.

Whaley, Robert E. and Barone-Adesi, Giovanni. On the Valuation of American Put Options on Dividend-Paying Stocks. In *Fabozzi, F. J., ed.*, 1988, pp. 1–13.

_____ and Stoll, Hans R. Volatility and Futures: Message versus Messenger. *J. Portfol. Manage.*, Winter 1988, *14*(2), pp. 20–22.

Whall, Barry and Silvia, John E. Rising Consumer Debt: For Better...or for Worse. *Challenge*, Jan.–Feb. 1988, *31*(1), pp. 55–60.

Whalley, Diane. Neighborhood Variations in Moderate Housing Rehabilitation Program Impacts: An Accounting Model of Housing Quality Change. *Econ. Geogr.*, January 1988, *64*(1), pp. 45–61.

Whalley, John. Implications for the Uruguay Round: Comments. In *Schott, J. J. and Smith, M. G., eds.*, 1988, pp. 173–77.

_____. Lessons from General Equilibrium Models. In *Aaron, H. J.; Galper, H. and Pechman, J. A., eds.*, 1988, pp. 15–50.

_____ and Clarete, Ramon L. Interactions between Trade Policies and Domestic Distortions in a Small Open Developing Country. *J. Int. Econ.*, May 1988, *24*(3–4), pp. 345–58.

_____; Davies, James B. and St-Hilaire, France. Some Calculations of Lifetime Tax Incidence. In *Brown, E., ed.*, 1988, *1984*, pp. 115–26.

_____; Hamilton, Bob and Mohammad, Sharif. Applied General Equilibrium Analysis and Perspective on Growth Performance. *J. Policy Modeling*, Summer 1988, *10*(2), pp. 281–97.

_____ and Jones, Rich. Regional Effects of Taxes in Canada: An Applied General Equilibrium Approach. *J. Public Econ.*, October 1988, *37*(1), pp. 1–28.

_____; Wigle, Randall and Trela, Irene. International Trade in Grains: Domestic Policies and Trade Impacts. In *Haaland, J. I. and Norman, V. D., eds.*, 1988, pp. 55–67.

Wheatley, Simon. Some Tests of International Equity Integration. *J. Finan. Econ.*, September 1988, *21*(2), pp. 177–212.

_____. Some Tests of the Consumption-Based Asset Pricing Model. *J. Monet. Econ.*, September 1988, *22*(2), pp. 193–215.

Wheaton, William C. and Torto, Raymond G. Vacancy Rates and the Future of Office Rents. *Amer. Real Estate Urban Econ. Assoc. J.*, Winter 1988, *16*(4), pp. 430–36.

Wheeler, Hoyt N. Management from an Institutional/Biological Perspective. In *Dlugos, G.; Dorow, W. and Weiermair, K., eds.*, 1988, pp. 95–105.

Wheeler, James O. The Corporate Role of Large Metropolitan Areas in the United States. *Growth Change*, Spring 1988, *19*(2), pp. 75–86.

_____. Spatial Ownership Links of Major Corporations: The Dallas and Pittsburgh Examples. *Econ. Geogr.*, January 1988, *64*(1), pp. 1–16.

Wheeler, Joanna. International: Problems and Paradoxes—The Elusive Tax Incentive. *Bull. Int. Fiscal Doc.*, July 1988, *42*(7), pp. 319–23.

Wheeler, John R. C.; McCue, Michael J. and McCue, Tom. An Assessment of Hospital Acquisition Prices. *Inquiry*, Summer 1988, *25*(2), pp. 290–96.

Wheeler, Joseph C. Sub-sector Planning and Poverty Reduction: A Donor View. In *Lewis, J. P., et al.*, 1988, pp. 209–19.

Wheeler, Mark; Hoag, John H. and Browne, M. Neil. Does a Professor's Reputation Affect Course Selection? In *Missouri Valley Economic Assoc.*, 1988, pp. 182–91.

Wheeler, Mary F.; Moissis, D. E. and Miller, C. A. A Parametric Study of Viscous Fingering in Miscible Displacement by Numerical Simulation. In *Wheeler, M. F., ed.*, 1988, pp. 227–47.

Wheeler, Russell. Empirical Research and the Politics of Judicial Administration: Creating the Federal Judicial Center. *Law Contemp. Probl.*, Summer 1988, *51*(3), pp. 31–53.

Whichard, Obie G. International Services: New Information on U.S. Transactions with Unaffiliated Foreigners. *Surv. Curr. Bus.*, October 1988, *68*(10), pp. 27–34.

_____. International Services Operations of U.S. Multinational Companies. In *Candilis, W. O., ed.*, 1988, pp. 127–54.

_____. U.S. Multinational Companies: Operations in 1986. *Surv. Curr. Bus.*, June 1988, *68*(6), pp. 85–96.

Whinston, Michael D. Exit with Muliplant Firms. *Rand J. Econ.*, Winter 1988, *19*(4), pp. 568–88.

Whipp, Richard; Willmott, Hugh and Smith, Chris. Case-Study Research in Accounting: Methodological Breakthrough or Ideological Weapon? In *Neimark, M., ed.*, 1988, pp. 95–120.

Whitaker, John K. The Distribution Theory of Marshall's *Principles*. In *Asimakopulos, A., ed.*, 1988, pp. 105–32.

_____. Early Flowering in the Old Dominion: Political Economy at the College of William and Mary and the University of Virginia. In *Barber, W. J., ed.*, 1988, pp. 15–41.

_____. Editing Alfred Marshall. In *Moggridge, D. E., ed.*, 1988, pp. 43–66.

_____. Review of 'Papers and Correspondence of William Stanley Jevons, Volumes I–VII.' In *Wood, J. C., ed., Vol. 3*, 1988, *1984*, pp. 280–82.

Whitbread, Chris and Beenstock, Michael. Explaining Changes in the Union Mark-Up for Male Manual Workers in Great Britain, 1953–1983. *Brit. J. Ind. Relat.*, November 1988, *26*(3), pp. 327–38.

White, Alan and Hull, John. An Analysis of the Bias in Option Pricing Caused by a Stochastic Volatility. In *Fabozzi, F. J., ed.*, 1988, pp. 29–61.

_____ and Hull, John. The Use of the Control Variate Technique in Option Pricing. *J. Finan. Quant. Anal.*, September 1988, *23*(3), pp. 237–51.

White, D. L. and Brown, M. A. Stimulating Energy Conservation by Sharing the Savings: A Community-Based Approach. *Environ. Planning A*, April 1988, *20*(4), pp. 517–34.

White, Douglas R. and McCann, H. Gilman. Cites and Fights: Material Entailment Analysis of the Eighteenth-Century Chemical Revolution. In *Wellman, B. and Berkowitz, S. D., eds.*, 1988, pp. 380–400.

White, Eduardo. The Question of Foreign Investments and the Economic Crisis in Latin America. In *Feinberg, R. E. and Ffrench-Davis, R., eds.*, 1988, pp. 147–74.

White, Gordon. Evolving Relations between State and Markets in the Reform of China's Urban-Industrial Economy. In *Feuchtwang, S.; Hussain, A. and Pairault, T., eds., Vol. 2*, 1988, pp. 7–25.

_____. State and Market in China's Labour Reforms. *J. Devel. Stud.*, July 1988, *24*(4), pp. 180–202.

_____. State and Market in China's Socialist In-

dustrialization. In *White, G., ed.*, 1988, pp. 153–92.

_____ and Bowles, Paul. China's Banking Reforms: Aims, Methods and Problems. *Nat. Westminster Bank Quart. Rev.*, November 1988, pp. 28–37.

_____ and Wade, Robert. Developmental States and Markets in East Asia: An Introduction. In *White, G., ed.*, 1988, pp. 1–29.

White, Halbert and Bates, Charles. Efficient Instrumental Variables Estimation of Systems of Implicit Heterogeneous Nonlinear Dynamic Equations with Nonspherical Errors. In *Barnett, W. A.; Berndt, E. R. and White, H., eds.*, 1988, pp. 3–25.

White, Harrison C. Contractual Relations and Weak Solidarity: The Behavioral Basis of Restraints on Gain-Maximization: Comment. *J. Inst. Theoretical Econ.*, February 1988, *144*(1), pp. 59–66.

_____. Varieties of Markets. In *Wellman, B. and Berkowitz, S. D., eds.*, 1988, pp. 226–60.

_____ and Eccles, Robert G. Price and Authority in Inter–Profit Center Transactions. In *Winship, C. and Rosen, S., eds.*, 1988, pp. 17–51.

White, J. G. and Cunningham, M. T. The Behaviour of Industrial Buyers in Their Search for Suppliers of Machine Tools. In *Earl, P. E., ed., Vol. 1*, 1988, *1974*, pp. 176–89.

White, James R. Large Lot Zoning and Subdivision Costs: A Test. *J. Urban Econ.*, May 1988, *23*(3), pp. 370–84.

White, Joseph. What Budgeting Cannot Do: Lessons of Reagan's and Other Years. In *Rubin, I. S., ed.*, 1988, pp. 165–202.

White, K. J. SHAZAM: A Response. *J. Appl. Econometrics*, July–Sept. 1988, *3*(3), pp. 245–47.

White Kennethand Mak, James. Tourism in Asia and the Pacific. In *Lee, C. H. and Naya, S., eds.*, 1988, pp. 121–49.

White, Lawrence H. Depoliticizing the Supply of Money. In *Willett, T. D., ed.*, 1988, pp. 460–78.

_____. Problems Inherent in Political Money Supply Schemes: Some Historical and Theoretical Lessons. In *Willett, T. D., ed.*, 1988, pp. 301–19.

_____. Toward an International Fiat Standard? *Cato J.*, Fall 1988, *8*(2), pp. 339–46.

_____ and Selgin, George A. Competitive Monies and the Suffolk Bank System: Comment. *Southern Econ. J.*, July 1988, *55*(1), pp. 215–19.

White, Lawrence J. Litan's *What Should Banks Do?* A Review Essay. *Rand J. Econ.*, Summer 1988, *19*(2), pp. 305–15.

_____. Litigation and Economic Incentives. In *Zerbe, R. O., Jr., ed.*, 1988, pp. 73–90.

_____. Panel Discussion: Corporate Takeovers and Public Policy: Remarks. In *Auerbach, A. J., ed. (I)*, 1988, pp. 325–32.

_____. Private Antitrust Litigation: New Evidence, New Learning: Foreword. In *White, L. J., ed.*, 1988, pp. xi–xiv.

_____; Besanko, David and Donnenfeld, Shabtai. The Multiproduct Firm, Quality Choice, and Regulation. *J. Ind. Econ.*, June 1988, 36(4), pp. 411–29.

_____ and Donnenfeld, Shabtai. Product Variety and the Inefficiency of Monopoly. *Economica*, August 1988, 55(219), pp. 393–401.

_____ and Golbe, Devra L. Mergers and Acquisitions in the U.S. Economy: An Aggregate and Historical Overview. In *Auerbach, A. J., ed. (II)*, 1988, pp. 25–47.

_____ and Golbe, Devra L. A Time-Series Analysis of Mergers and Acquisitions in the U.S. Economy. In *Auerbach, A. J., ed. (I)*, 1988, pp. 265–302.

_____ and Pugel, Thomas A. An Empirical Analysis of the Underwriting Spreads on Initial Public Offerings. *Quart. Rev. Econ. Bus.*, Winter 1988, 28(4), pp. 6–20.

_____ and Salop, Steven C. Private Antitrust Litigation: An Introduction and Framework. In *White, L. J., ed.*, 1988, pp. 3–60.

White-Means, Shelley I. The Purchase of Medicare Supplements: A Cost Saving Mechanism in the Purchase of Physician Services. *J. Cons. Aff.*, Winter 1988, 22(2), pp. 249–63.

White, Michael. Educational Policy and Economic Goals. *Oxford Rev. Econ. Policy*, Autumn 1988, 4(3), pp. 1–20.

_____. Organization and Content of Work in Relation to Training and Information. *Econ. Lavoro*, Apr.–June 1988, 22(2), pp. 127–37.

White, Michael D. Prices, Unit Labor Costs, Wages, and Causality in the United States, 1947–1982. *Quart. Rev. Econ. Bus.*, Autumn 1988, 28(3), pp. 78–87.

White, Michael J. and Mueser, Peter R. Implications of Boundary Choice for the Measurement of Residential Mobility. *Demography*, August 1988, 25(3), pp. 443–59.

White, Michael V. Jevons in Australia: A Reassessment. In *Wood, J. C., ed., Vol. 1*, 1988, *1982*, pp. 329–50.

_____. Jevons in Australia: Response. In *Wood, J. C., ed., Vol. 1*, 1988, *1984*, pp. 396–98.

_____. Porter's Hint and Alternative Theories of the Giffen Paradox: A Rejoinder. *Australian Econ. Pap.*, June 1988, 27(50), pp. 145–46.

White, Michelle J. Contract Breach and Contract Discharge Due to Impossibility: A Unified Theory. *J. Legal Stud.*, June 1988, 17(2), pp. 353–76.

_____. The Economics of Accidents. *Mich. Law Rev.*, May 1988, 86(6), pp. 1217–31.

_____. Location Choice and Commuting Behavior in Cities with Decentralized Employment. *J. Urban Econ.*, September 1988, 24(2), pp. 129–52.

_____. Urban Commuting Journeys Are Not "Wasteful." *J. Polit. Econ.*, October 1988, 96(5), pp. 1097–110.

White, Richard A.; Golen, Steven P. and Looney, Stephen W. An Empirical Examination of CPA Perceptions of Communication Barriers between Auditor and Client. In *Schwartz, B. N., ed.*, 1988, pp. 233–49.

White, Richard E. and Pruitt, Stephen W. The CRISMA Trading System: Who Says Technical Analysis Can't Beat the Market? *J. Portfol. Manage.*, Spring 1988, 14(3), pp. 55–58.

_____; Pruitt, Stephen W. and Wei, K. C. John. The Impact of Union-Sponsored Boycotts on the Stock Prices of Target Firms. *J. Lab. Res.*, Summer 1988, 9(3), pp. 285–89.

White, Robert W. and Smith, Brian. The Deposit Insurance System in Canada: Problems and Proposals for Change. *Can. Public Policy*, December 1988, 14(4), pp. 331–46.

White, Stephen. Political Socialization in the USSR: April 1979 and After. In *Potichnyj, P. J., ed.*, 1988, pp. 67–86.

White, Wayne E. The Iran–Iraq War: A Challenge to the Arab Gulf States. In *Sindelar, H. R., III and Peterson, J. E., eds.*, 1988, pp. 91–109.

White, William D. and Persky, Joseph J. A Rather Neoclassical Contribution to Marxian Rent Theory. *Land Econ.*, May 1988, 64(2), pp. 196–98.

Whiteford, Peter. Corrigendum [Unemployment and Families]. *Australian Bull. Lab.*, March 1988, 14(2), pp. 400.

_____ and Edwards, Meredith. The Development of Government Policies on Poverty and Income Distribution. *Australian Econ. Rev.*, Spring 1988, (83), pp. 54–73.

Whitehead, David D. Moving toward 1992: A Common Financial Market for Europe? *Fed. Res. Bank Atlanta Econ. Rev.*, Nov.–Dec. 1988, 73(6), pp. 42–51.

Whiteing, A. E. and Nash, Christopher A. Mode Choice: A Total Distribution Cost Approach. In *Bianco, L. and La Bella, A., eds.*, 1988, pp. 121–49.

Whiteman, John L. The Efficiency of Labour and Capital in Australian Manufacturing. *Appl. Econ.*, February 1988, 20(2), pp. 243–61.

Whitfield, Keith. The Australian Wage System and Its Labor Market Effects. *Ind. Relat.*, Spring 1988, 27(2), pp. 149–65.

_____ and Creedy, John. The Economic Analysis of Internal Labour Markets. *Bull. Econ. Res.*, October 1988, 40(4), pp. 247–69.

Whitford, David T.; Newbold, Paul and Gentry, James A. Predicting Industrial Bond Ratings with a Probit Model and Funds Flow Components. *Financial Rev.*, August 1988, 23(3), pp. 269–86.

Whiting, R. G. and Pickett, E. E. On the Estimation of Probabilistic Functions of Markov Chains. In *Fedorov, V. and Lauter, H., eds.*, 1988, pp. 205–13.

Whitley, John D. Manufacturing and Services in UK Macro-models. In *Barker, T. and Dunne, P., eds.*, 1988, pp. 39–62.

_____ and Wilson, R. A. Hours Reductions within Large-scale Macroeconomic Models: Conflict between Theory and Empirical Application. In *Hart, R. A., ed.*, 1988, pp. 228–52.

Whitmer, J. M. Data Needs and Limitations for Public Services Modeling. In *Johnson, T. G.;*

Deaton, B. J. and Segarra, E., eds., 1988, pp. 109–16.

Whitney, Gerald A. and Barnhart, Scott W. Nonparametric Analysis in Parametric Estimation: An Application to Translog Demand Systems. *Rev. Econ. Statist.*, February 1988, *70*(1), pp. 149–53.

———— **and Swofford, James L.** Comparison of Nonparametric Tests of Weak Separability for Annual and Quarterly Data on Consumption, Leisure, and Money. *J. Bus. Econ. Statist.*, April 1988, *6*(2), pp. 241–46.

Whitney, James D. Imperfect Competition and Import Penetration. *Atlantic Econ. J.*, March 1988, *16*(1), pp. 7–18.

————. Winning Games versus Winning Championships: The Economics of Fan Interest and Team Performance. *Econ. Inquiry*, October 1988, *26*(4), pp. 703–24.

Whitt, Joseph A., Jr.; Koch, Paul D. and Rosensweig, Jeffrey A. The Dynamic Relationship between the Dollar and U.S. Prices: An Intensive Empirical Investigation. *J. Int. Money Finance*, June 1988, *7*(2), pp. 181–204.

Whittaker, Joe, et al. Graphical Modelling with Large Numbers of Variables: An Application of Principal Components. In *Edwards, D. and Raun, N. E., eds.*, 1988, pp. 73–79.

Whitten, David O. From Wayland to Ekelund: Political Economy at Auburn University, 1856–1986. In *Perkins, E. J., ed.*, 1988, pp. 124–35.

Whittington, Dale and MacRae, Duncan, Jr. Assessing Preferences in Cost–Benefit Analysis: Reflections on Rural Water Supply Evaluation in Haiti. *J. Policy Anal. Manage.*, Winter 1988, *7*(2), pp. 246–63.

Whyte, A. G. D. A Resource Planning and Management System for Pine Plantations in Fiji. In *Iri, M. and Yajima, K., eds.*, 1988, pp. 565–73.

Whyte, I. D. and Whyte, K. A. Debt and Credit, Poverty and Prosperity in a Seventeenth-Century Scottish Rural Community. In *Mitchison, R. and Roebuck, P., eds.*, 1988, pp. 70–80.

Whyte, K. A. and Whyte, I. D. Debt and Credit, Poverty and Prosperity in a Seventeenth-Century Scottish Rural Community. In *Mitchison, R. and Roebuck, P., eds.*, 1988, pp. 70–80.

Wiarda, Howard J. Toward a Nonethnocentric Theory of Development: Alternative Conceptions from the Third World. In *Wilber, C. K., ed.*, 1988, pp. 59–82.

Wiatrowski, William J. Comparing Employee Benefits in the Public and Private Sectors. *Mon. Lab. Rev.*, December 1988, *111*(12), pp. 3–8.

Wibaut, Serge. Fiscal Reform and Disequilibrium. *Ann. Écon. Statist.*, July–Sept. 1988, (11), pp. 141–57.

Wichmann, Ralph B. Zinsswaps als Spezialfall der Ricardianischen Tauschtheorie. (Interest Swaps as a Special Case of Ricardo's Value in Exchange Theory. With English summary.) *Kredit Kapital*, 1988, *21*(2), pp. 278–87.

Wickens, M. R. and Breusch, T. S. Dynamic Specification, the Long-run and the Estimation of Transformed Regression Models. *Econ. J.*, Supplement, 1988, *98*(390), pp. 189–205.

Wicksell, Knut. A New Principle of Just Taxation. In *Gwartney, J. D. and Wagner, R. E., eds.*, 1988, pp. 117–30.

Wicksteed, P. H. The Jevonian Criticism of Marx: A Rejoinder. In *Wood, J. C., ed., Vol. 2*, 1988, *1885*, pp. 106–08.

————. Jevons's Economic Work. In *Wood, J. C., ed., Vol. 3*, 1988, *1905*, pp. 11–14.

————. On Certain Passages in Jevon's 'Theory of Political Economy.' In *Wood, J. C., ed., Vol. 2*, 1988, *1889*, pp. 28–45.

Wickström, Bo. Analysis of the Effects of Special Retail Promotions in a Consumer Perspective. In *Kaynak, E., ed.*, 1988, pp. 113–31.

————. Retail Innovators—A Study of Attitudes, Behavior, and Sales Success. In *Kaynak, E., ed.*, 1988, pp. 63–85.

Widick, B. J. and Fraser, Douglas A. The Challenges of Competitiveness: A Labor View. In *Starr, M. K., ed.*, 1988, pp. 159–84.

Widmer, Lorne; Fox, Glenn and Brinkman, George L. The Rate of Return to Agricultural Research in a Small Country: The Case of Beef Cattle Research in Canada. *Can. J. Agr. Econ.*, March 1988, *36*(1), pp. 23–35.

Wiebke, Harald. Programmhandel: Fluch oder Segen? (Program Trading: Evil or Blessing? With English summary.) *Konjunkturpolitik*, 1988, *34*(5–6), pp. 310–26.

Wieckowski, Tom and Verzilli, Andrew G. The Economics—If Any—Of Malpractice in Education? In *Pennsylvania Economic Association*, 1988, pp. 591–98.

Wiegard, Wolfgang and Hirte, Georg. An Introduction to Applied General Equilibrium Tax Modelling (With a Preliminary Application to the Reform of Factor Taxes in the FRG). In *Bös, D.; Rose, M. and Seidl, C., eds.*, 1988, pp. 167–203.

Wieland, Bernhard. Telecommunications in the Netherlands. In *Foreman-Peck, J. and Müller, J., eds.*, 1988, pp. 203–19.

———— **and von Weizsäcker, C. Christian.** Current Telecommunications Policy in West Germany. *Oxford Rev. Econ. Policy*, Summer 1988, *4*(2), pp. 20–39.

Wield, David. Industry and Industrialization. In *Crow, B. and Thorpe, M., et al.*, 1988, pp. 187–215.

————. Making a Living. In *Crow, B. and Thorpe, M., et al.*, 1988, pp. 242–60.

———— **and Rhodes, Ed.** Divisions of Labour or Labour Divided? International Relocation of Industry. In *Crow, B. and Thorpe, M., et al.*, 1988, pp. 288–309.

———— **and Smith, Stephen L.** Banking on the New Technology: Cooperation, Competition and the Clearers. In *Harris, L., et al., eds.*, 1988, pp. 240–73.

———— **and Smith, Stephen L.** New Technology and Bank Work: Banking on It as an 'Organisational Technology.' In *Harris, L., et al., eds.*, 1988, pp. 274–300.

Wiemer, Calla. A Framework for Assessing Productivity Loss from Schistosomiasis. *J. Human Res.*, Summer 1988, *23*(3), pp. 320–41.

Wiendahl, Hans-Peter. Erwiderung: Probleme der belastungsorientierten Auftragsfreigabe. (With English summary.) *Z. Betriebswirtshaft,* November 1988, *58*(11), pp. 1224–27.

Wiendieck, Gerd. Quality Circles and Corporate Identity—Towards Overcoming the Crisis of Taylorism. In *Maital, S., ed., Vol. 2,* 1988, pp. 620–36.

Wiener, Hans B. Just-in-Time Systems and Euro–Japanese Industrial Collaboration: Introduction. In *Holl, U. and Trevor, M., eds.,* 1988, pp. 11–12.

Wier, Peggy; Kamma, Sreenivas and Weintrop, Joseph. Investors' Perceptions of the Delaware Supreme Court Decision in Unocal v. Mesa. *J. Finan. Econ.,* Jan.–March 1988, *20*(1–2), pp. 419–30.

Wiersma, Doede and Nentjes, Andries. Innovation and Pollution Control. *Int. J. Soc. Econ.,* 1988, *15*(3–4), pp. 51–70.

Wierzchoń, S. T. Randomness and Fuzziness in a Linear Programming Problem. In *Kacprzyk, J. and Fedrizzi, M., eds.,* 1988, pp. 227–39.

Wiesebach, H. P. F. New Thinking in Industrial Co-operation between North and South. In *Jepma, C. J., ed.,* 1988, pp. 59–73.

Wiesner, Eduardo. Latin America's Policy Response to the Debt Crisis: Learning from Adversity. In *Feldstein, M., ed. (I),* 1988, pp. 290–305.

Wiggins, Casper E.; Mayper, Alan G. and Welker, Robert B. Accounting and Review Services: Perceptions of the Message within the CPA's Report. In *Schwartz, B. N., ed.,* 1988, pp. 219–32.

Wiggins, L. L. and Moore, J. E., II. Linearized, Optimally Configured Urban System Models: A Profit-Maximizing Formulation. *Environ. Planning A,* March 1988, *20*(3), pp. 369–90.

Wiggins, Steven N. Franchising—A Case of Long-term Contracts: Comment. *J. Inst. Theoretical Econ.,* February 1988, *144*(1), pp. 149–51.

Wightman, David. Money and Security: Financing American Troops in Germany and the Trilateral Negotiations of 1966–67. *Rivista Storia Econ.,* S.S., February 1988, *5*(1), pp. 26–77.

Wigle, Randall. Between a Rock and a Hard Place: The Economics of Canada–U.S. Freer Trade. *Can. Public Policy,* March 1988, *14*(1), pp. 104–08.

_____. General Equilibrium Evaluation of Canada–U.S. Trade Liberalization in a Global Context. *Can. J. Econ.,* August 1988, *21*(3), pp. 539–64.

_____; **Trela, Irene and Whalley, John.** International Trade in Grains: Domestic Policies and Trade Impacts. In *Haaland, J. I. and Norman, V. D., eds.,* 1988, pp. 55–67.

Wignaraja, Ganeshan. Concentration of Land Holdings and Income: Comment. *J. Devel. Econ.,* September 1988, *29*(2), pp. 229–32.

Wihlborg, Clas G. and Oxelheim, Lars. Hedging and Managing Exchange Rate and Related Macroeconomic Exposure. In *Khoury, S. J. and Ghosh, A., eds.,* 1988, pp. 321–47.

Wijkander, Hans. Equity and Efficiency in Public Sector Pricing: A Case for Stochastic Rationing. *Econometrica,* November 1988, *56*(6), pp. 1455–65.

Wijkman, Per Magnus. Legal Issues in US–EC Trade Policy: GATT Litigation 1960–1985: Comment. In *Baldwin, R. E.; Hamilton, C. B. and Sapir, A., eds.,* 1988, pp. 58–64.

Wijmenga, Roel T.; van den Bergh, Willem Max and Wessels, Roberto E. Two Tests of the Tax-Loss Selling Hypothesis. In *Dimson, E., ed.,* 1988, pp. 147–54.

Wijnberg, N. N. Depression-Triggered Innovation: A Further Comment on the Kleinknecht–Coombs Discussion. *De Economist,* 1988, *136*(3), pp. 401–02.

van Wijnbergen, Sweder. Fiscal Policy, Trade Intervention, and World Interest Rates: An Empirical Analysis. In *Frenkel, J. A., ed.,* 1988, pp. 273–300.

_____. Inflation, Balance of Payments Crises, and Public Sector Deficits. In *Helpman, E.; Razin, A. and Sadka, E., eds.,* 1988, pp. 287–309.

_____. Monopolistic Competition, Credibility and the Output Costs of Disinflation Programs: An Analysis of Price Controls. *J. Devel. Econ.,* November 1988, *29*(3), pp. 375–98.

_____ **and Martin, Ricardo.** Efficient Pricing of Natural Gas: A Case Study of Egypt. *J. Public Econ.,* July 1988, *36*(2), pp. 177–96.

Wilber, Charles K. and Goulet, Denis. The Human Dilemma of Development. In *Wilber, C. K., ed.,* 1988, pp. 459–67.

_____ **and Harrison, Robert S.** The Methodological Basis of Institutional Economics: Pattern Model, Storytelling, and Holism. In *Samuels, W. J., ed., Vol. 2,* 1988, 1978, pp. 95–123.

Wilcox, Steven J.; Kniesner, Thomas J. and McElroy, Marjorie B. Getting into Poverty without a Husband, and Getting Out, With or Without. *Amer. Econ. Rev.,* May 1988, *78*(2), pp. 86–90.

Wildasin, David E. The (Apparent) Demise of Sales Tax Deductibility: Issues for Analysis and Policy. *Nat. Tax J.,* September 1988, *41*(3), pp. 381–89.

_____. Indirect Distributional Effects in Benefit–Cost Analysis of Small Projects. *Econ. J.,* September 1988, *98*(392), pp. 801–07.

_____. Nash Equilibria in Models of Fiscal Competition. *J. Public Econ.,* March 1988, *35*(2), pp. 229–40.

Wildavsky, Aaron. If You Can't Budget, How Can You Govern? In *Anderson, A. and Bark, D. L., eds.,* 1988, pp. 265–75.

Wilde, Louis L. and Dubin, Jeffrey A. An Empirical Analysis of Federal Income Tax Auditing and Compliance. *Nat. Tax J.,* March 1988, *41*(1), pp. 61–74.

_____; **Grether, David M. and Schwartz, Alan.** Uncertainty and Shopping Behaviour: An Experimental Analysis. *Rev. Econ. Stud.,* April 1988, *55*(2), pp. 323–42.

_____ and **Reinganum, Jennifer F.** A Note on Enforcement Uncertainty and Taxpayer Compliance. *Quart. J. Econ.*, November 1988, *103*(4), pp. 793–98.

Wildemann, Horst. Just-in-Time Systems and Euro–Japanese Industrial Collaboration: Conclusions. In *Holl, U. and Trevor, M., eds.*, 1988, pp. 95–100.

Wilder, Patricia S. and Klarquist, Virginia L. Retail Hardware Stores Register Productivity Gain. *Mon. Lab. Rev.*, May 1988, *111*(5), pp. 39–43.

Wilder, Ronald P. and Amato, Louis. Market Concentration, Efficiency, and Antitrust Policy: Demsetz Revisited. *Quart. J. Bus. Econ.*, Autumn 1988, *27*(4), pp. 3–19.

Wildt, Albert R. and Bruno, Albert V. Toward Understanding Attitude Structure: A Study of the Complimentarity of Multi-attribute Models. In *Earl, P. E., ed., Vol. 2*, 1988, *1975*, pp. 208–16.

Wilen, James E. Limited Entry Licensing: A Retrospective Assessment. *Marine Resource Econ.*, 1988, *5*(4), pp. 313–24.

_____ and **Andrews, Elizabeth J.** Angler Response to Success in the California Salmon Sportfishery: Evidence and Management Implications. *Marine Resource Econ.*, 1988, *5*(2), pp. 125–38.

Wilentz, Sean and Stansell, Christine. Gutman's Legacy. *Labor Hist.*, Summer 1988, *29*(3), pp. 378–90.

Wiles, David. Greek Theatre and the Legitimation of Slavery. In *Archer, L. J., ed.*, 1988, pp. 53–67.

Wiles, Peter. Economic Policies under Andropov and Chernenko (November 1982–February 1984–March 1985). In *[Nove, A.]*, 1988, pp. 217–50.

_____. Soviet Investment Criteria: A Prefatory Note. In *[Nove, A.]*, 1988, pp. 37–43.

Wiley, John Shepard, Jr. Reciprocal Altruism as a Felony: Antitrust and the Prisoner's Dilemma. *Mich. Law Rev.*, August 1988, *86*(8), pp. 1906–28.

Wilhelm, William J. and Allen, Paul R. The Impact of the 1980 Depository Institutions Deregulation and Monetary Control Act on Market Value and Risk: Evidence from the Capital Markets. *J. Money, Credit, Banking*, Part 1, August 1988, *20*(3), pp. 364–80.

Wilhite, Al. Political Parties, Campaign Contributions and Discrimination. *Public Choice*, September 1988, *58*(3), pp. 259–68.

_____. Union PAC Contributions and Legislative Voting. *J. Lab. Res.*, Winter 1988, *9*(1), pp. 79–90.

Wilke, Henk and Wit, Arjaan. Subordinates' Endorsement of an Allocating Leader in a Commons Dilemma: An Equity Theoretical Approach. *J. Econ. Psych.*, June 1988, *9*(2), pp. 151–68.

Wilken, Paul H.; Schram, Sanford F. and Turbett, J. Patrick. Child Poverty and Welfare Benefits: A Reassessment with State Data of the Claim that American Welfare Breeds Dependence. *Amer. J. Econ. Soc.*, October 1988, *47*(4), pp. 409–22.

Wilkens, Herbert and Hackenbruch, Michael. Direktinvestitionen als Element der weltwirtschaftlichen Verflechtung der Wirtschaft der Bundesrepublik Deutschland. (Direct Foreign Investment as an Element of Worldwide Interdependence of the West German Economy. With English summary.) *Aussenwirtschaft*, December 1988, *43*(4), pp. 505–48.

Wilkie, William L. The Marketing Context of Consumer Choice. In *Maynes, E. S. and ACCI Research Committee, eds.*, 1988, pp. 317–26.

Wilkin, Jerzy. The Induced Innovation Model of Agricultural Development and the Socialist Economic System. *Europ. Rev. Agr. Econ.*, 1988, *15*(2–3), pp. 211–20.

Wilking, Louis H. Technology: A Corporation's Major Asset. In *Tavis, L. A., ed.*, 1988, pp. 312–16.

Wilkins, Mira. Business History as a Discipline. In *Hausman, W. J., ed.*, 1988, pp. 1–7.

Wilkinson, Frank. Where Do We Go from Here? 2. Real Wages, Effective Demand and Economic Development. *Cambridge J. Econ.*, March 1988, *12*(1), pp. 179–91.

Wilkinson, James T. and McHugh, Richard J. A Random Effects Approach to Substate Growth Models: A Comment on "The Determinants of Country Growth." *J. Reg. Sci.*, May 1988, *28*(2), pp. 271–73.

Wilkinson, Kenneth P. The Community Crisis in the Rural South. In *Beaulieu, L. J., ed.*, 1988, pp. 72–86.

Wilkinson, Roderick. Who Gets the Promotion? In *Timpe, A. D., ed.*, 1988, *1985*, pp. 249–51.

Willard, Gary E. and Feeser, Henry R. Incubators and Performance: A Comparison of High and Low Growth High Tech Firms. In *Kirchhoff, B. A., et al., eds.*, 1988, pp. 549–63.

Willcox, Walter F. Negro Criminality. In *Simms, M. C. and Myers, S. L., Jr., eds.*, 1988, *1899*, pp. 33–45.

Willekens, F. A Life Course Perspective on Household Dynamics. In *Keilman, N.; Kuijsten, A. and Vossen, A., eds.*, 1988, pp. 87–107.

Willemse, Rob; Kapteyn, Arie and Kooreman, Peter. Some Methodological Issues in the Implementation of Subjective Poverty Definitions. *J. Human Res.*, Spring 1988, *23*(2), pp. 222–42.

Willett, Keith D. and Sharda, Ramesh. Competing Demands for Water Resources: A Dynamic Joint Maximization Model. *Resources & Energy*, June 1988, *10*(2), pp. 135–59.

_____ and **Sharda, Ramesh.** A Dynamic Multimarket Equilibrium Model for the Economic Analysis of Pollution Control Policies. *Environ. Planning A*, March 1988, *20*(3), pp. 391–405.

Willett, Thomas D. Functioning of the Current International Financial System: Strengths, Weaknesses, and Criteria for Evaluation. In *Melamed, L., ed.*, 1988, *1983*, pp. 81–122.

_____. Key Exchange Rate Regimes: A Constitutional Perspective. *Cato J.*, Fall 1988, *8*(2), pp. 405–20.

_____ and Banaian, King. Explaining the Great Stagflation: Toward a Political Economy Framework. In *Willett, T. D., ed.*, 1988, pp. 35–62.

_____ and Banaian, King. Legislation and Political Business Cycles: Comment. *Kyklos*, 1988, *41*(3), pp. 507–11.

_____ and Banaian, King. Models of the Political Process and Their Implications for Stagflation: A Public Choice Perspective. In *Willett, T. D., ed.*, 1988, pp. 100–116.

_____ and Dillon, Patricia. Political Business Cycles: The Political Economy of Money, Inflation, and Unemployment: Introduction and Summary. In *Willett, T. D., ed.*, 1988, pp. 1–31.

_____; Kaempfer, William H. and Marks, Stephen V. Why Do Large Countries Prefer Quantitative Trade Restrictions? *Kyklos*, 1988, *41*(4), pp. 625–46.

_____ and Mayer, Thomas. Evaluating Proposals for Fundamental Monetary Reform. In *Willett, T. D., ed.*, 1988, pp. 398–423.

_____ and McClure, J. Harold, Jr. The Inflation Tax. In *Willett, T. D., ed.*, 1988, pp. 177–85.

_____, et al. Inflation Hypotheses and Monetary Accommodation: Postwar Evidence from the Industrial Countries. In *Willett, T. D., ed.*, 1988, pp. 200–236.

Williams, Alan and Weston, Rae. Socioeconomic Implications of New Technology in Banking: Some Australian and New Zealand Evidence. In *Tisdell, C. and Maitra, P., eds.*, 1988, pp. 281–97.

Williams, Alan H. Priority Setting in Public and Private Health Care: A Guide through the Ideological Jungle. *J. Health Econ.*, June 1988, *7*(2), pp. 173–83.

Williams, Allan F. and Lund, Adrian K. Mandatory Seat Belt Use Laws and Occupant Crash Protection in the Untied States: Present Status and Future Prospects. In *Graham, J. D., ed.*, 1988, pp. 51–72.

Williams, Allan M. and Lewis, Jim. Portugal: Market Segmentation and Regional Specialisation. In *Williams, A. M. and Shaw, G., eds.*, 1988, pp. 101–22.

_____ and Shaw, Gareth. Tourism and Development: Introduction. In *Williams, A. M. and Shaw, G., eds.*, 1988, pp. 1–11.

_____ and Shaw, Gareth. Tourism Policies in a Changing Economic Environment. In *Williams, A. M. and Shaw, G., eds.*, 1988, pp. 230–39.

_____ and Shaw, Gareth. Western European Tourism in Perspective. In *Williams, A. M. and Shaw, G., eds.*, 1988, pp. 12–38.

_____; Shaw, Gareth and Greenwood, Justin. The United Kingdom: Market Responses and Public Policy. In *Williams, A. M. and Shaw, G., eds.*, 1988, pp. 162–79.

Williams, Arlington W.; Smith, Vernon L. and Suchanek, Gerry L. Bubbles, Crashes, and Endogenous Expectations in Experimental Spot Asset Markets. *Econometrica*, September 1988, *56*(5), pp. 1119–51.

_____ and Walker, James M. Market Behavior in Bid, Offer, and Double Auctions: A Reexamination. *J. Econ. Behav. Organ.*, April 1988, *9*(3), pp. 301–14.

Williams, Bernard. Formal Structures and Social Reality. In *Gambetta, D., ed.*, 1988, pp. 3–13.

Williams, C. P. New Directions in Remote Sensing. In *Egan, J. J., et al.*, 1988, pp. 125–31.

Williams, David. Banking and Changes in Industry Structure. In *Barker, T. and Dunne, P., eds.*, 1988, pp. 131–39.

Williams, Donald R.; Raymond, Richard D. and Sesnowitz, Michael L. Does Sex Still Matter? New Evidence from the 1980s. *Econ. Inquiry*, January 1988, *26*(1), pp. 43–58.

Williams, Gerald O. Share Croppers at Sea: The Whaler's "Lay," and Events in the Arctic, 1905–1907. *Labor Hist.*, Winter 1988, *29*(1), pp. 32–55.

Williams, H. and Gillespie, A. Telecommunications and the Reconstruction of Regional Comparative Advantage. *Environ. Planning A*, October 1988, *20*(10), pp. 1311–21.

Williams, Harold R. and Palia, Aspy P. The U.S. Trigger Price Mechanism: Econometric Analysis of Its Impact on Steel Imports. *Rivista Int. Sci. Econ. Com.*, April–May 1988, *35*(4–5), pp. 457–71.

Williams, Jeffrey C. and Wright, Brian D. The Incidence of Market-Stabilising Price Support Schemes. *Econ. J.*, December 1988, *98*(393), pp. 1183–98.

_____ and Wright, Brian D. Measurement of Consumer Gains from Market Stabilization. *Amer. J. Agr. Econ.*, August 1988, *70*(3), pp. 616–27.

Williams, Jeffrey R. A Stochastic Dominance Analysis of Tillage and Crop Insurance Practices in a Semiarid Region. *Amer. J. Agr. Econ.*, February 1988, *70*(1), pp. 112–20.

_____. A Stochastic Dominance Comparison of Reduced Tillage Systems in Corn and Soybean Production under Risk: Comment. *Amer. J. Agr. Econ.*, August 1988, *70*(3), pp. 741–42.

_____ and Bailey, Elizabeth E. Sources of Economic Rent in the Deregulated Airline Industry. *J. Law Econ.*, April 1988, *31*(1), pp. 173–202.

_____, et al. A Microcomputer Model for Irrigation System Evaluation. *Southern J. Agr. Econ.*, July 1988, *20*(1), pp. 145–51.

Williams, John. A Case Study in Privatizing a Major Public Corporation. In *Walker, M. A., ed. (II)*, 1988, pp. 23–38.

Williams, Joseph. Banking Panics, Information, and Rational Expectations Equilibrium: Discussion. *J. Finance*, July 1988, *43*(3), pp. 761–63.

_____. Efficient Signalling with Dividends, Investment, and Stock Repurchases. *J. Finance*, July 1988, *43*(3), pp. 737–47.

Williams, Kevin J. and DeNisi, Angelo S. Cognitive Approaches to Performance Appraisal. In

Ferris, G. R. and Rowland, K. M., eds., 1988, pp. 109–55.

Williams, Michael. Competition Subjects, State and Civil Society. In *Williams, M., ed.,* 1988, pp. 96–114.

_____. The Death and Rebirth of the American Forest: Clearing and Reversion in the United States, 1900–1980. In *Richards, J. F. and Tucker, R. P., eds.,* 1988, pp. 211–29.

_____. Value, Social Form and the State: Introduction. In *Williams, M., ed.,* 1988, pp. 1–20.

Williams, Michael A. and Baumann, Michael G. Output–Inflation Tradeoffs in 34 Countries: Comment. *J. Econ. Bus.,* February 1988, *40*(1), pp. 97–101.

_____ **and McAfee, R. Preston.** Can Event Studies Detect Anticompetitive Mergers? *Econ. Letters,* 1988, *28*(2), pp. 199–203.

Williams, N. T. and Webster, J. P. G. Changes in Cereal Production and Yield Variability on Farms in South East England. *J. Agr. Econ.,* May 1988, *39*(2), pp. 255–62.

Williams, Nancy A.; Gilley, Otis W. and Shieh, Yeung-Nan. Transportation Rates and Location of the Firm: A Comparative Static Analysis. *J. Reg. Sci.,* May 1988, *28*(2), pp. 231–38.

Williams, P. A. A Recursive Model of Intraurban Trip-Making. *Environ. Planning A,* April 1988, *20*(4), pp. 535–46.

Williams, R. E. Dairy Industry Structure and Milk Price Comparisons: A Further Rejoinder. *J. Agr. Econ.,* September 1988, *39*(3), pp. 450–52.

Williams, Robert H.; Larson, Eric D. and Ross, Marc H. Beyond the Era of Materials. In *Forester, T., ed.,* 1988, *1986,* pp. 141–59.

Williams, Ross A. Comment [Income Inequality in Australia in an International Comparative Perspective] [The Distribution of Wealth: What Is It, What Does It Mean, and Is It Important?] [Structural Reform, Macro Policies and Income Distribution]. *Australian Econ. Rev.,* Spring 1988, (83), pp. 53.

Williamson, Carlos; Bustamante, Blanca and Coloma, Fernando. El precio social de la mano de obra. (With English summary.) *Cuadernos Econ.,* April 1988, *25*(74), pp. 81–124.

Williamson, David and Suh, Sang-Mok. The Impact of Adjustment and Stabilization Policies on Social Welfare: The South Korean Experiences during 1978–1985. In *Cornia, G. A.; Jolly, R. and Stewart, F., eds.,* 1988, pp. 218–37.

Williamson, Jeffrey G. Migrant Selectivity, Urbanization, and Industrial Revolutions. *Population Devel. Rev.,* June 1988, *14*(2), pp. 287–314.

Williamson, John. Comment on McKinnons's Monetary Rule. *J. Econ. Perspectives,* Winter 1988, *2*(1), pp. 113–19.

_____. Conflicting Views of the Twin Deficits. *Cato J.,* Fall 1988, *8*(2), pp. 529–32.

_____. International Money and Macroeconomics: Comments. In *Elliott, K. A. and Williamson, J., eds.,* 1988, pp. 48–52.

_____. Profit, Growth and Sales Maximization. In *Ricketts, M., ed., Vol. 1,* 1988, *1966,* pp. 233–48.

_____. Roundtable on Exchange Rate Policy: Comment. In *Marston, R. C., ed.,* 1988, pp. 162–67.

_____ **and Miller, Marcus H.** The International Monetary System: An Analysis of Alternative Regimes. *Europ. Econ. Rev.,* June 1988, *32*(5), pp. 1031–48.

Williamson, John B. and Branco, Kenneth J. Economic Development and Income Distribution: A Cross-National Analysis. *Amer. J. Econ. Soc.,* July 1988, *47*(3), pp. 277–97.

Williamson, John W. Future Policy Directions for Quality Assurance: Lessons from the Health Accounting Experience. *Inquiry,* Spring 1988, *25*(1), pp. 67–77.

Williamson, Oliver E. Breach of Trust in Hostile Takeovers: Comment. In *Auerbach, A. J., ed. (I),* 1988, pp. 61–67.

_____. Corporate Finance and Corporate Governance. *J. Finance,* July 1988, *43*(3), pp. 567–91.

_____. The Economics and Sociology of Organization: Promoting a Dialogue. In *Farkas, G. and England, P., eds.,* 1988, pp. 159–85.

_____. The Logic of Economic Organization. *J. Law, Econ., Organ.,* Spring 1988, *4*(1), pp. 65–93.

_____. Mergers, Acquisitions, and Leveraged Buyouts: An Efficiency Assessment. In *Libecap, G., ed. (I),* 1988, pp. 55–79.

_____. Shareholders versus Managers: The Strain in the Corporate Web: Comment: Shareholders *and* Managers—A Risk-Neutral Perspective. In *Coffee, J. C., Jr.; Lowenstein, L. and Rose-Ackerman, S., eds.,* 1988, pp. 159–67.

_____. Technology and Transaction Cost Economics: A Reply. *J. Econ. Behav. Organ.,* October 1988, *10*(3), pp. 355–63.

_____ **and Wachter, Michael L.** Obligational Markets and the Mechanics of Inflation. In *Earl, P. E., ed., Vol. 2,* 1988, *1978,* pp. 372–95.

Williamson, Stephen D. Liquidity, Banking, and Bank Failures. *Int. Econ. Rev.,* February 1988, *29*(1), pp. 25–43.

Willinger, Marc and Zuscovitch, Ehud. Towards the Economics of Information-Intensive Production Systems: The Case of Advanced Materials. In *Dosi, G., et al., eds.,* 1988, pp. 239–55.

Willis, K. G. The Impact of Factory Development on 'Growth Town' Employment in Mid-Wales: A Comment. *Urban Stud.,* December 1988, *25*(6), pp. 527–31.

_____ **and Benson, J. F.** A Comparison of User Benefits and Costs of Nature Conservation at Three Nature Reserves. *Reg. Stud.,* October 1988, *22*(5), pp. 417–28.

_____ **and Benson, J. F.** Valuation of Wildlife: A Case Study on the Upper Teesdale Site of Special Scientific Interest and Comparison of Methods in Environmental Economics. In *Turner, R. K., ed.,* 1988, pp. 243–64.

———; **Benson, J. F. and Saunders, Caroline M.** The Impact of Agricultural Policy on the Costs of Nature Conservation. *Land Econ.*, May 1988, *64*(2), pp. 147–57.

——— **and Saunders, Caroline M.** The Impact of a Development Agency on Employment: Resurrection Discounted? *Appl. Econ.*, January 1988, *20*(1), pp. 81–96.

Willis, Robert J. Life Cycles, Institutions, and Population Growth: A Theory of the Equilibrium Interest Rate in an Overlapping Generations Model. **In** *Lee, R. D.; Arthur, W. B. and Rodgers, G., eds.,* 1988, pp. 106–38.

Willits, Stephen D.; Clancy, Donald K. and Freeman, Robert J. Public Employee Retirement System Reports: A Study of Knowledgeable User Information Processing Ability. **In** *Chan, J. L. and Rowan, H. J., eds.,* 1988, pp. 3–48.

Willman, Alpo. Balance-of-Payments Crises and Monetary Policy Reactions in a Model with Imperfect Substitutability between Domestic and Foreign Bonds. *Econ. Letters*, 1988, *26*(1), pp. 77–81.

———. The Collapse of the Fixed Exchange Rate Regime with Sticky Wages and Imperfect Substitutability between Domestic and Foreign Bonds. *Europ. Econ. Rev.*, November 1988, *32*(9), pp. 1817–38.

Willman, Paul. Opportunism in Labour Contracting: An Application of the 'Organisational Failures' Framework. **In** *Earl, P. E., ed., Vol. 2,* 1988, *1982*, pp. 119–34.

Willmott, Hugh; Burnes, Bernard and Knights, David. New Technology and the Labour Process: Introduction. **In** *Knights, D. and Willmott, H., eds.,* 1988, pp. 1–19.

———; **Smith, Chris and Whipp, Richard.** Case-Study Research in Accounting: Methodological Breakthrough or Ideological Weapon? **In** *Neimark, M., ed.,* 1988, pp. 95–120.

Willms, Manfred. Macroeconomic Policy Coordination: Where Should We Stand? Comments. **In** *Giersch, H., ed.,* 1988, pp. 301–03.

———. Public Debt and Public Debt Policy in Germany. **In** *Cavanna, H., ed.,* 1988, pp. 102–19.

Willoughby, John. National Economic Management and the Supranational Economy. **In** *Peterson, W. C., ed.,* 1988, pp. 109–25.

Willumsen, L. G. and Radovanac, Mirko. Testing the Practical Value of the UMOT Model. *Int. J. Transport Econ.*, June 1988, *15*(2), pp. 203–23.

Wilman, Elizabeth A. Pricing Policies for Outdoor Recreation. *Land Econ.*, August 1988, *64*(3), pp. 234–41.

Wilshusen, Katherine. U.S.–Canadian Research Groups. **In** *Schmandt, J.; Clarkson, J. and Roderick, H., eds.,* 1988, pp. 83–102.

Wilson, Alan G. Store and Shopping-Centre Location and Size: A Review of British Research and Practice. **In** *Wrigley, N., ed.,* 1988, pp. 160–86.

Wilson, Arlette C.; Glezen, G. William and Cronan, Timothy P. Forecasting Accounting Information for Auditors' Use in Analytical Reviews. **In** *Schwartz, B. N., ed.,* 1988, pp. 267–76.

Wilson, Charles A. On the Optimal Pricing Policy of a Monopolist. *J. Polit. Econ.*, February 1988, *96*(1), pp. 164–76.

———; **Hendricks, Kenneth and Weiss, Andrew.** The War of Attrition in Continuous Time with Complete Information. *Int. Econ. Rev.*, November 1988, *29*(4), pp. 663–80.

Wilson, Earl R. and Francis, Jere R. Auditor Changes: A Joint Test of Theories Relating to Agency Costs and Auditor Differentiation. *Accounting Rev.*, October 1988, *63*(4), pp. 663–82.

——— **and Marquette, R. Penny.** Evaluating the Effects of Multicollinearity: A Note on the Use of Ridge Regression. **In** *Schwartz, B. N., ed.,* 1988, pp. 143–56.

Wilson, Ernest J., III and Callaghy, Thomas M. Africa: Policy, Reality or Ritual? **In** *Vernon, R., ed.,* 1988, pp. 179–230.

Wilson, Fiona. Computer Numerical Control and Constraint. **In** *Knights, D. and Willmott, H., eds.,* 1988, pp. 66–90.

Wilson, Franklin D. Components of Change in Migration and Destination–Propensity Rates for Metropolitan and Nonmetropolitan Areas: 1935–1980. *Demography*, February 1988, *25*(1), pp. 129–39.

Wilson, G. Peter and McNichols, Maureen. Evidence of Earnings Management from the Provision for Bad Debts. *J. Acc. Res.*, Supplement, 1988, *26*, pp. 1–31.

Wilson, H. T. Anti-discrimination Legislation and Its Impact on the Employment Relationship: The Case of Affirmative Action and Equal Pay. **In** *Dlugos, G.; Dorow, W. and Weiermair, K., eds.,* 1988, pp. 383–95.

Wilson, James R. and Sweet, Arnold L. Pitfalls in Simulation-Based Evaluation of Forecast Monitoring Schemes. *Int. J. Forecasting*, 1988, *4*(4), pp. 573–79.

Wilson, L. A., II. Rescuing Politics from the Economists: Privatizing the Public Sector. **In** *Hula, R. C., ed.,* 1988, pp. 59–68.

Wilson, Nicholas and Hart, Robert A. The Demand for Workers and Hours: Micro Evidence from the U.K. Metal Working Industry. **In** *Hart, R. A., ed.,* 1988, pp. 162–79.

Wilson, Paul W. Wage Variation Resulting from Staggered Work Hours. *J. Urban Econ.*, July 1988, *24*(1), pp. 9–26.

Wilson, Robert A. and Whitley, John D. Hours Reductions within Large-scale Macroeconomic Models: Conflict between Theory and Empirical Application. **In** *Hart, R. A., ed.,* 1988, pp. 228–52.

Wilson, Robert B. Credentials and Wage Discrimination. *Scand. J. Econ.*, 1988, *90*(4), pp. 549–62.

Wilson, Rodney. The European Monetary System. **In** *Darnell, A. and Evans, L., eds.,* 1988, pp. 150–62.

———. Third World Debt. **In** *Darnell, A. and Evans, L., eds.,* 1988, pp. 178–91.

Wilson, Stephanie Y. Poverty and Protectionism.

Rev. Black Polit. Econ., Winter 1988, *16*(3), pp. 25–51.

Wilson, Thomas A. and Dungan, D. Peter. Modelling Anticipated and Temporary Fiscal Policy Shocks in a Macro-econometric Model of Canada. *Can. J. Econ.*, February 1988, *21*(1), pp. 41–60.

Wilson, Tom. Local Freedom and Central Control—A Question of Balance. In *Bailey, S. J. and Paddison, R.*, eds., 1988, pp. 92–108.

Wilson, W. Gene. The Lasting Role of Natural Resources in Alabama's Economy. *Fed. Res. Bank Atlanta Econ. Rev.*, Jan.–Feb. 1988, *73*(1), pp. 6–13.

_____. The Southeastern Forest Industry after the Tax Reform Act of 1986. *Fed. Res. Bank Atlanta Econ. Rev.*, May–June 1988, 73(3), pp. 30–35.

_____ and Sullivan, Gene D. Crop Costs and Farm Survival. *Fed. Res. Bank Atlanta Econ. Rev.*, March–April 1988, *73*(2), pp. 8–26.

Wilson, Wesley W.; Koo, Won W. and Wilson, William W. Modal Competition and Pricing in Grain Transport. *J. Transp. Econ. Policy*, September 1988, *22*(3), pp. 319–37.

Wilson, William W.; Fung, Hung-Gay and Ricks, Michael. Option Price Behavior in Grain Futures Markets. *J. Futures Markets*, February 1988, *8*(1), pp. 47–65.

_____; Wilson, Wesley W. and Koo, Won W. Modal Competition and Pricing in Grain Transport. *J. Transp. Econ. Policy*, September 1988, *22*(3), pp. 319–37.

Wilton, David A. and Auld, Douglas A. L. The Impact of Progressive Income Tax Rates on Canadian Negotiated Wage Rates. *Can. J. Econ.*, May 1988, *21*(2), pp. 279–84.

Wilton, Peter C. and Gupta, Sunil. Combination of Economic Forecasts: An Odds-Matrix Approach. *J. Bus. Econ. Statist.*, July 1988, *6*(3), pp. 373–79.

Wiltshaw, D. G. Pedagogic Comment and the Supply of Land for a Particular Use. *Urban Stud.*, October 1988, *25*(5), pp. 439–47.

Winch, Donald. Developments in the Literature on Adam Smith: An Evaluative Survey: Commentary. In *Thweatt, W. O.*, ed., 1988, pp. 45–52.

Winckler, Edwin A. Contending Approaches to East Asian Development. In *Winckler, E. A. and Greenhalgh, S.*, eds., 1988, pp. 20–37.

_____. Elite Political Struggle 1945–1985. In *Winckler, E. A. and Greenhalgh, S.*, eds., 1988, pp. 151–73.

_____. Globalist, Statist, and Network Paradigms in East Asia. In *Winckler, E. A. and Greenhalgh, S.*, eds., 1988, pp. 270–81.

_____. Mass Political Incorporation 1500–2000. In *Winckler, E. A. and Greenhalgh, S.*, eds., 1988, pp. 41–66.

_____ and Greenhalgh, Susan. Analytical Issues and Historical Episodes. In *Winckler, E. A. and Greenhalgh, S.*, eds., 1988, pp. 3–19.

Winckler, Joachim and Bertram, Hans-Henning. Scheduling on Microcomputers Using MI-

CROBUS. In *Daduna, J. R. and Wren, A.*, eds., 1988, pp. 188–99.

Wind, Yoram and Mahajan, Vijay. New Product Forecasting Models: Directions for Research and Implementation. *Int. J. Forecasting*, 1988, *4*(3), pp. 341–58.

van Winden, Frans A. A. M. and Renaud, Paul S. A. Fiscal Behaviour and the Growth of Government in the Netherlands. In *Lybeck, J. A. and Henrekson, M.*, eds., 1988, pp. 133–56.

Windsor, Duane and Preston, Lee E. Corporate Governance, Social Policy, and Social Performance in the Multinational Corporation. In *Preston, L. E.*, ed., 1988, pp. 45–58.

Wineberg, Arthur. The Japanese Patent System: A Non-tariff Barrier to Foreign Business? *J. World Trade*, February 1988, *22*(1), pp. 11–22.

Winegarden, C. R. AFDC and Illegitimacy Ratios: A Vector-Autoregressive Model. *Appl. Econ.*, December 1988, *20*(12), pp. 1589–1601.

_____. The Demographic Effects of Income Redistribution and Accelerated Economic Growth Revisited: A Reply. *Oxford Bull. Econ. Statist.*, May 1988, *50*(2), pp. 195–201.

Winer, Russell S. Behavioral Perspective on Pricing: Buyers' Subjective Perceptions of Price Revisited. In *Devinney, T. M.*, ed., 1988, pp. 35–57.

Winer, Stanley L. and Hettich, Walter. Economic and Political Foundations of Tax Structure. *Amer. Econ. Rev.*, September 1988, *78*(4), pp. 701–12.

Winham, Gilbert R. Why Canada Acted. In *Diebold, W., Jr.*, ed., 1988, pp. 37–54.

Winiecki, Jan. Four Kinds of Fallacies in Comparing Market-Type and Soviet-Type Economies: Issues and Outcomes. *Banca Naz. Lavoro Quart. Rev.*, March 1988, (164), pp. 79–103.

van Winkel, E. G. F. and Soenen, Luc A. Predicting Future Spot Rates on the Basis of Forward Rates—A Time Series Approach. *Quart. J. Bus. Econ.*, Summer 1988, *27*(3), pp. 57–87.

Winkler, Robert L. and Kadane, Joseph B. Separating Probability Elicitation from Utilities. *J. Amer. Statist. Assoc.*, June 1988, *83*(402), pp. 357–63.

Winn, Daryl N. and Shoenhair, John D. Compensation-Based (Dis)incentives for Revenue-Maximizing Behavior: A Test of the "Revised" Baumol Hypothesis. *Rev. Econ. Statist.*, February 1988, *70*(1), pp. 154–58.

Winpenny, Thomas R. From East Liverpool to Gotham: The Mixed Fate of the 19th Century Artisan. In *Perkins, E. J.*, ed., 1988, pp. 242–55.

Winship, Christopher and Rosen, Sherwin. Introduction: Sociological and Economic Approaches to the Analysis of Social Structure. In *Winship, C. and Rosen, S.*, eds., 1988, pp. 1–16.

Winston, Clifford and Calfee, John E. Economic Aspects of Liability Rules and Liability Insurance. In *Litan, R. E. and Winston, C.*, eds., 1988, pp. 16–41.

_____ and Litan, Robert E. Policy Options. In

Litan, R. E. and Winston, C., eds., 1988, pp. 223–41.

_____; **Litan, Robert E. and Swire, Peter.** The U.S. Liability System: Background and Trends. In *Litan, R. E. and Winston, C., eds.*, 1988, pp. 1–15.

_____ **and Small, Kenneth A.** Optimal Highway Durability. *Amer. Econ. Rev.*, June 1988, 78(3), pp. 560–69.

Winston, Gordon C. The Boundaries of Economics: Introduction. In *Winston, G. C. and Teichgraeber, R. F., III, eds.*, 1988, pp. 1–12.

_____. Three Problems with the Treatment of Time in Economics: Perspectives, Repetitiveness, and Time Units. In *Winston, G. C. and Teichgraeber, R. F., III, eds.*, 1988, pp. 30–52.

_____. The Time-Shape of Transactions: Relational Exchange, Repetition and Honesty. In *Maital, S., ed., Vol. 2*, 1988, pp. 593–609.

Winter, C. J. Hydrogen as an Energy Carrier—A Guide. In *Winter, C.-J. and Nitsch, J., eds.*, 1988, pp. 1–10.

Winter, Harvey J. A View from the U.S. State Department. In *Walker, C. E. and Bloomfield, M. A., eds.*, 1988, pp. 99–106.

Winter, James P. Interlocking Directorships and Economic Power. In *Picard, R. G., et al., eds.*, 1988, pp. 105–15.

_____ **and Candussi, Dores A.** Monopoly and Content in Winnipeg. In *Picard, R. G., et al., eds.*, 1988, pp. 139–45.

Winter, Jay M. Socialism, Social Democracy, and Population Questions in Western Europe: 1870–1950. *Population Devel. Rev.*, Supplement, 1988, 14, pp. 122–46.

_____ **and Teitelbaum, Michael S.** Population and Resources in Western Intellectual Traditions: Introduction. *Population Devel. Rev.*, Supplement, 1988, 14, pp. 1–4.

Winter, Ralph A. The Liability Crisis and the Dynamics of Competitive Insurance Markets. *Yale J. Regul.*, Summer 1988, 5(2), pp. 455–99.

_____ **and Mathewson, G. Frank.** On Vertical Restraints and the Law: A Reply. *Rand J. Econ.*, Summer 1988, 19(2), pp. 298–301.

_____ **and Ware, Roger.** Forward Markets, Currency Options and the Hedging of Foreign Exchange Risk. *J. Int. Econ.*, November 1988, 25(3–4), pp. 291–302.

Winter, Ralph K., Jr. and Wellington, Harry H. The Limits of Collective Bargaining in Public Employment. In *Lewin, D., et al., eds.*, 1988, pp. 37–52.

Winter, Sidney G. Economic "Natural Selection" and the Theory of the Firm. In *Earl, P. E., ed., Vol. 1*, 1988, 1964, pp. 108–148.

_____. On Coase, Competence, and the Corporation. *J. Law, Econ., Organ.*, Spring 1988, 4(1), pp. 163–80.

_____ **and Nelson, Richard R.** Firm and Industry Response to Changed Market Conditions: An Evolutionary Approach. In *Earl, P. E., ed., Vol. 1*, 1988, 1980, pp. 434–57.

Winter, William F. Charting a Course for the

Rural South. In *Beaulieu, L. J., ed.*, 1988, pp. 358–64.

von Winterfeldt, Detlof; Moody, David L. and Edwards, Ward. Simplicity in Decision Analysis: An Example and a Discussion. In *Bell, D. E.; Raiffa, H. and Tversky, A., eds.*, 1988, pp. 443–64.

Winters, L. Alan. Completing the European Internal Market: Some Notes on Trade Policy. *Europ. Econ. Rev.*, September 1988, 32(7), pp. 1477–99.

_____. East–West Trade, Embargoes, and Expectations: Comment. In *Baldwin, R. E.; Hamilton, C. B. and Sapir, A., eds.*, 1988, pp. 170–71.

Wirl, Franz. Resource Extraction of Imperfect Substitutes. *Energy Econ.*, July 1988, 10(3), pp. 242–48.

Wise, David A. Saving for Retirement: The U.S. Case. *J. Japanese Int. Economies*, December 1988, 2(4), pp. 385–416.

_____. Social Security Benefits: An Empirical Study of Expectations and Realizations: Discussion. In *Ricardo-Campbell, R. and Lazear, E. P., eds.*, 1988, pp. 346–50.

_____; **Bodie, Zvi and Shoven, John B.** Pensions in the U.S. Economy: Introduction. In *Bodie, Z.; Shoven, J. B. and Wise, D. A., eds.*, 1988, pp. 1–8.

_____ **and Kotlikoff, Laurence J.** Pension Backloading, Wage Taxes, and Work Disincentives. In *Summers, L. H., ed.*, 1988, pp. 161–96.

_____ **and Venti, Steven F.** The Determinants of IRA Contributions and the Effect of Limit Changes. In *Bodie, Z.; Shoven, J. B. and Wise, D. A., eds.*, 1988, pp. 9–47.

Wise, W. S.; Beck, H. S. and Upton, M. Is Publicly Funded Agricultural Research Excessive? A Comment. *J. Agr. Econ.*, September 1988, 39(3), pp. 453–55.

Wiseman, Michael. Obligation and Welfare Policy. *Policy Sci.*, 1988, 21(1), pp. 97–107.

_____. Workfare and Welfare Reform. In *Rodgers, H. R., Jr., ed.*, 1988, pp. 14–38.

_____ **and Hoerter, Darrell.** Metropolitan Development in the San Francisco Bay Area. *Ann. Reg. Sci.*, November 1988, 22(3), pp. 11–33.

Wish, Eric D. Urine Testing of Criminals: What Are We Waiting For? *J. Policy Anal. Manage.*, Spring 1988, 7(3), pp. 551–54.

Wisley, Thomas O. Sequential Signaling and the Leading Indicator Subgroup Indexes. In *Missouri Valley Economic Assoc.*, 1988, pp. 46–53.

Wisman, Jon D. The Dominance of Consensual over Technical Rationality in Confucius' Socioeconomic Thought. *Int. J. Soc. Econ.*, 1988, 15(1), pp. 58–67.

Wissink, Jennifer P. and Mann, Duncan P. Money-Back Contracts with Double Moral Hazard. *Rand J. Econ.*, Summer 1988, 19(2), pp. 285–92.

Wissoker, Doug; Berry, Steven and Gottschalk, Peter. An Error Components Model of the Impact of Plant Closing on Earnings. *Rev. Econ. Statist.*, November 1988, 70(4), pp. 701–07.

Wiswede, Günter. Ökonomische Psychologie–Psychologische Ökonomie Probleme und Befunde wirtschaftspsychologischer Forschung. (Economic Psychology–Psychological Economics. Problems and Results of Economic Psychological Research. With English summary.) *Z. Wirtschaft. Sozialwissen.*, 1988, *108*(4), pp. 503–92.

Wit, Arjaan and Wilke, Henk. Subordinates' Endorsement of an Allocating Leader in a Commons Dilemma: An Equity Theoretical Approach. *J. Econ. Psych.*, June 1988, *9*(2), pp. 151–68.

de Wit, C. T. Environmental Impact of the CAP. *Europ. Rev. Agr. Econ.*, 1988, *15*(2–3), pp. 283–96.

Withers, Glenn. Australian Labour Markets, Labour Flows and Structural Change. In *Pang, E. F., ed.*, 1988, pp. 13–65.

Witsberger, Christina; Leibowitz, Arleen and Waite, Linda J. Child Care for Preschoolers: Differences by Child's Age. *Demography*, May 1988, *25*(2), pp. 205–20.

Witt, Robert C. and Smith, Michael L. Informational Asymmetries in Retroactive Insurance: A Response. *J. Risk Ins.*, September 1988, *55*(3), pp. 548–54.

Witte, Ann Dryden. Earnings and Jobs of Ex-offenders: A Case Study. In *Alper, N. O. and Hellman, D. A., eds.*, 1988, pp. 114–35.

Witte, Edwin E. Institutional Economics as Seen by an Institutional Economist. In *Samuels, W. J., ed., Vol. 1*, 1988, *1954*, pp. 28–37.

Witte, John F. The Growth and Distribution of Tax Expenditures. In *Danziger, S. H. and Portney, K. E., eds.*, 1988, pp. 171–201.

_____. Wisconsin Income Tax Reform. In *Danziger, S. H. and Witte, J. F., eds.*, 1988, pp. 108–29.

_____ **and Danziger, Sheldon H.** State Policy Choices: The Wisconsin Experience: Introduction. In *Danziger, S. H. and Witte, J. F., eds.*, 1988, pp. 3–10.

_____ **and Rom, Mark C.** Power versus Participation: The Wisconsin State Budget Process. In *Danziger, S. H. and Witte, J. F., eds.*, 1988, pp. 13–34.

van Witteloostuijn, Arjen. Maximising and Satisficing Opposite or Equivalent Concepts? *J. Econ. Psych.*, September 1988, *9*(3), pp. 289–313.

_____ **and Maks, J. A. H.** Walras: A Hicksian *avant la lettre*. *Econ. Appl.*, 1988, *41*(3), pp. 595–608.

Witteveen, Dirk and Koning, Hendrik Elle. World Tax Reform: A Progress Report: Netherlands. In *Pechman, J. A., ed.*, 1988, pp. 171–80.

Wittkowski, Knut M. Building a Statistical Expert System with Knowledge Bases of Different Levels of Abstraction. In *Edwards, D. and Raun, N. E., eds.*, 1988, pp. 129–34.

Wittman, Donald. Dispute Resolution, Bargaining, and the Selection of Cases for Trial: A Study of the Generation of Biased and Unbiased Data. *J. Legal Stud.*, June 1988, *17*(2), pp. 313–52.

Witzel, Robert C. Suggestions for Improving the Administration of State Taxes. In *Gold, S. D., ed.*, 1988, pp. 101–06.

Wizarat, Shahida. Inter-industry Productivity Differentials in Pakistan's Large-Scale Manufacturing Sector. *Singapore Econ. Rev.*, October 1988, *33*(2), pp. 49–65.

_____. Simultaneous Estimation of Production Function and Beneficiaries of Growth for a Developing Economy. *Pakistan J. Appl. Econ.*, Summer 1988, *7*(1), pp. 1–17.

Wodopoia, Franz-Josef and Breyer, Friedrich. The Concept of "Scale" and Related Topics in the Specification of Econometric Cost Functions: Theory and Application to Hospitals. In *Eichhorn, W., ed.*, 1988, pp. 707–23.

Wohar, Mark E. Alternative Versions of the Coase Theorem and the Definition of Transaction Costs. *Quart. J. Bus. Econ.*, Winter 1988, *27*(1), pp. 3–19.

_____. How Effective Is Fiscal Policy? The U.S. Experience. *Weltwirtsch. Arch.*, 1988, *124*(3), pp. 458–79.

Wohl, Lawrence A. and Tremblay, Victor J. The Thick Point Theorem. *J. Econ. Educ.*, Summer 1988, *19*(3), pp. 269–70.

Wohlgemuth, Melody J. The Relation between Firm Size and the Informational Content of Earnings. *Quart. J. Bus. Econ.*, Autumn 1988, *27*(4), pp. 135–48.

Wohlgenant, Michael K. Instability and Risk as Rationales for Farm Programs: Reaction. In *Sumner, D. A., ed.*, 1988, pp. 23–25.

_____; **Farris, Donald E. and Mullen, John D.** Input Substitution and the Distribution of Surplus Gains from Lower U.S. Beef-Processing Costs. *Amer. J. Agr. Econ.*, May 1988, *70*(2), pp. 245–54.

Wojciechowska, Urszula. An Important Lesson: Five Years of Studying the Polish Reform. *Eastern Europ. Econ.*, Spring 1988, *26*(3), pp. 49–60.

Wojciechowski, Margot and Gesing, Renka. Prospects for Minerals in the '90s: Digest of Discussions. In *Richardson, P. R. and Gesing, R., eds.*, 1988, pp. 111–28.

Wojciechowski, Waldemar and Cichocki, Krzysztof. Investment Coefficient Matrix in Dynamic Input–Output Models: An Analysis and Prognosis. In *Ciaschini, M., ed.*, 1988, pp. 231–52.

Wokutch, Richard E. and McLaughlin, Josetta S. The Sociopolitical Context of Occupational Injuries. In *Preston, L. E., ed.*, 1988, pp. 113–37.

Wolak, Frank A. and Kolstad, Charles D. Measuring Relative Market Power in the Western U.S. Coal Market Using Shapley Values. *Resources & Energy*, December 1988, *10*(4), pp. 293–314.

Wolf, Bernard M. and Smook, Nicholas P. Keynes and the Question of Tariffs. In *Hamouda, O. F. and Smithin, J. N., eds., Vol. 2*, 1988, pp. 169–82.

Wolf, Charles, Jr. The Rise of Market Forces. In *Anderson, A. and Bark, D. L., eds.*, 1988, pp. 177–89.

Wolf, Douglas A. and Soldo, Beth J. Household Composition Choices of Older Unmarried Women. *Demography*, August 1988, 25(3), pp. 387–403.

Wolf, Frederick D. Federal Government Credit Program: Privatization through Loan Sales. *Public Budg. Finance*, Winter 1988, 8(4), pp. 74–80.

Wolf, Jochen. Zur Integration vager Grössen in LP-Ansätze: Das ō-niveaubegrenzte Fuzzy-Modell. (With English summary.) *Z. Betriebswirtshaft*, September 1988, 58(9), pp. 952–62.

de Wolf, Peter. The Pharmaceutical Industry: Structure, Intervention and Competitive Strength. In *de Jong, H. W., ed.*, 1988, pp. 211–44.

Wolf, Thomas A. Devaluation in Modified Planned Economies: A Preliminary Model for Hungary. In *[Holzman, F. D.]*, 1988, pp. 39–71.

_____. The Simultaneity of the Effects of Devaluation: Implications for Modified Planned Economies. *Acta Oecon.*, 1988, 39(3–4), pp. 303–24.

_____; **Brada, Josef C. and Hewett, Ed A.** Economic Stabilization, Structural Adjustment, and Economic Reform. In *[Holzman, F. D.]*, 1988, pp. 3–36.

Wolf, Walter J. The Relative Merits of Various Protein Food Ingredients. In *Schwarz, F. H., ed.*, 1988, pp. 237–72.

Wolfe, Barbara L.; Behrman, Jere R. and Deolalikar, Anil B. Nutrients: Impacts and Determinants. *World Bank Econ. Rev.*, September 1988, 2(3), pp. 299–320.

_____; **Blau, David M. and Behrman, Jere R.** Schooling and Earnings Distributions with Endogenous Labour Force Participation, Marital Status and Family Size. *Economica*, August 1988, 55(219), pp. 297–316.

_____; **Warlick, Jennifer and Haveman, Robert.** Labor Market Behavior of Older Men: Estimates from a Trichotomous Choice Model. *J. Public Econ.*, July 1988, 36(2), pp. 153–75.

Wolff, Christian C. P. Autoregressive Conditional Heteroscedasticity: A Comparison of ARCH and Random Coefficient Models. *Econ. Letters*, 1988, 27(2), pp. 141–43.

_____. Exchange Rates, Innovations and Forecasting. *J. Int. Money Finance*, March 1988, 7(1), pp. 49–61.

_____. Models of Exchange Rates: A Comparison of Forecasting Results. *Int. J. Forecasting*, 1988, 4(4), pp. 605–07.

Wolff, Edward N. Life-Cycle Savings and the Individual Distribution of Wealth by Class. In *Kessler, D. and Masson, A., eds.*, 1988, pp. 261–80.

_____. The Rate of Surplus Value, the Organic Composition, and the General Rate of Profit in the U.S. Economy, 1947–67: Reply. *Amer. Econ. Rev.*, March 1988, 78(1), pp. 304–06.

_____. Social Security, Pensions and the Life

Cycle Accumulation of Wealth: Some Empirical Tests. *Ann. Écon. Statist.*, Jan.–March 1988, (9), pp. 199–226.

_____ and **Baumol, William J.** Productivity Growth, Convergence, and Welfare: Reply. *Amer. Econ. Rev.*, December 1988, 78(5), pp. 1155–59.

_____; **Baumol, William J. and Dollar, David.** The Factor-Price Equalization Model and Industry Labor Productivity: An Empirical Test across Countries. In *Feenstra, R. C., ed.*, 1988, pp. 23–47.

_____ and **Dollar, David.** Convergence of Industry Labor Productivity among Advanced Economies, 1963–1982. *Rev. Econ. Statist.*, November 1988, 70(4), pp. 549–58.

_____ and **Greenwood, Daphne T.** Relative Wealth Holdings of Children and the Elderly in the United States, 1962–83. In *Palmer, J. L.; Smeeding, T. and Torrey, B. B., eds.*, 1988, pp. 123–48.

de Wolff, P. and van der Linden, J. T. J. M. Jan Tinbergen: A Quantitative Economist. *Rev. Soc. Econ.*, December 1988, 46(3), pp. 312–25.

Wolff, Richard and Resnick, Stephen. Marxian Theory and the Rhetorics of Economics. In *Klamer, A.; McCloskey, D. N. and Solow, R. M., eds.*, 1988, pp. 47–63.

_____ and **Resnick, Stephen.** Radical Differences among Radical Theories. *Rev. Radical Polit. Econ.*, Summer–Fall 1988, 20(2–3), pp. 1–6.

Wolfson, Mark A.; Gilson, Ronald J. and Scholes, Myron S. Taxation and the Dynamics of Corporate Control: The Uncertain Case for Tax-Motivated Acquisitions. In *Coffee, J. C., Jr.; Lowenstein, L. and Rose-Ackerman, S., eds.*, 1988, pp. 271–99.

_____ and **Scholes, Myron S.** The Cost of Capital and Changes in Tax Regimes. In *Aaron, H. J.; Galper, H. and Pechman, J. A., eds.*, 1988, pp. 157–90.

Wolfson, Martin H. and McLaughlin, Mary M. The Profitability of Insured Commercial Banks in 1987. *Fed. Res. Bull.*, July 1988, 74(7), pp. 403–18.

Wolfson, Michael C. Homemaker Pensions and Lifetime Redistribution. *Rev. Income Wealth*, September 1988, 34(3), pp. 221–50.

_____ and **Adler, Hans J.** A Prototype Micro–Macro Link for the Canadian Household Sector. *Rev. Income Wealth*, December 1988, 34(4), pp. 371–92.

Wolfson, Murray. Marx, the Quantity Theory, and the Theory of Value: Comment. *Hist. Polit. Econ.*, Spring 1988, 20(1), pp. 137–40.

Wolfstetter, Elmar and Adolph, Brigitte. Lohnindexierung und Geldpolitik bei informativen Preisen. (Wage Indexation and Monetary Policy if Prices Are Informative. With English summary.) *Z. Wirtschaft. Sozialwissen.*, 1988, 108(3), pp. 335–53.

_____ and **Brown, Murray.** Optimal Unemployment Insurance and Experience Rating. *Scand. J. Econ.*, 1988, 90(4), pp. 529–47.

Wolinsky, Asher. Dynamic Markets with Competitive Bidding. *Rev. Econ. Stud.*, January 1988, 55(1), pp. 71–84.

_____ and Horn, Henrik. Bilateral Monopolies and Incentives for Merger. *Rand J. Econ.*, Autumn 1988, 19(3), pp. 408–19.

_____ and Horn, Henrik. Worker Substitutability and Patterns of Unionisation. *Econ. J.*, June 1988, 98(391), pp. 484–97.

Wolinsky, Murray A. and Hinich, Melvin J. A Test for Aliasing Using Bispectral Analysis. *J. Amer. Statist. Assoc.*, June 1988, 83(402), pp. 499–502.

Wolken, John D. and Derrick, Frederick W. Cross-Sectional Aggregation and Demand System Estimation. *Atlantic Econ. J.*, June 1988, 16(2), pp. 82.

_____ and Rose, John T. Thrift Competition and the "Commercial Banking" Line of Commerce. *Atlantic Econ. J.*, December 1988, 16(4), pp. 24–36.

Wolleb, Enrico. Belated Industrialization: The Case of Italy. In *Boyer, R., ed.*, 1988, pp. 140–70.

Wollridge, J. Randall and Ghosh, Chinmoy. An Analysis of Shareholder Reaction to Dividend Cuts and Omissions. *J. Finan. Res.*, Winter 1988, 11(4), pp. 281–94.

Wolpert, J.; Gregg, S. R. and Mulvey, J. M. A Stochastic Planning System for Siting and Closing Public Service Facilities. *Environ. Planning A*, January 1988, 20(1), pp. 83–98.

Wolpin, Kenneth I.; Eckstein, Zvi and Stern, Steven. Fertility Choice, Land, and the Malthusian Hypothesis. *Int. Econ. Rev.*, May 1988, 29(2), pp. 353–61.

_____ and Rosenzweig, Mark R. Heterogeneity, Intrafamily Distribution, and Child Health. *J. Human Res.*, Fall 1988, 23(4), pp. 437–61.

_____ and Rosenzweig, Mark R. Migration Selectivity and the Effects of Public Programs. *J. Public Econ.*, December 1988, 37(3), pp. 265–89.

Wolter, Frank. A New International Trading System: Comment. In *Borner, S., ed.*, 1988, pp. 132–38.

_____. Protection, Trade and Development: Comment. In *Jepma, C. J., ed.*, 1988, pp. 95–100.

Wong, Christine P. W. Between Plan and Market: The Role of the Local Sector in Post-Mao China. In *Reynolds, B. L., ed.*, 1988, 1987, pp. 95–108.

Wong, David Y. Inflation, Taxation, and Investment in the Open Economy. In *Pennsylvania Economic Association*, 1988, pp. 417–27.

Wong, Jilnaught. Economic Incentives for the Voluntary Disclosure of Current Cost Financial Statements. *J. Acc. Econ.*, April 1988, 10(2), pp. 151–67.

_____. Political Costs and an Intraperiod Accounting Choice for Export Tax Credits. *J. Acc. Econ.*, January 1988, 10(1), pp. 37–51.

Wong, John. Integration of China into the Asian-Pacific Region. *World Econ.*, September 1988, 11(3), pp. 327–54.

_____ and Lim, Hank. The Changing Role of

Singapore in the Trading and Processing of Mineral Resources. In *McKern, B. and Koomsup, P., eds.*, 1988, pp. 290–309.

Wong, Kar-yiu. International Factor Mobility and the Volume of Trade: An Empirical Study. In *Feenstra, R. C., ed.*, 1988, pp. 231–50.

Wong, Kum Poh. Money Multipliers for Singapore. *Singapore Econ. Rev.*, April 1988, 33(1), pp. 40–67.

Wong, Lung-Fai and Ruttan, Vernon W. Sources of Differences in Agricultural Productivity Growth among Socialist Countries. In *Dogramaci, A. and Färe, R., eds.,*, 1988, pp. 103–30.

Wong, Patrick; Garfinkel, Irwin and McLanahan, Sara S. Child Support and Dependency. In *Rodgers, H. R., Jr., ed.*, 1988, pp. 66–85.

_____; Nichols-Casebolt, Ann and Garfinkel, Irwin. Reforming Wisconsin's Child Support System. In *Danziger, S. H. and Witte, J. F., eds.*, 1988, pp. 172–86.

Wong, Shee Q. and Raab, Raymond L. A Note on Causality and the Structure–Performance Controversy. *Rev. Ind. Organ.*, Spring 1988, 3(3), pp. 45–53.

Wong, Yue-Chim and Liu, Pak-Wai. The Distribution of Benefits among Public Housing Tenants in Hong Kong and Related Policy Issues. *J. Urban Econ.*, January 1988, 23(1), pp. 1–20.

Wonnacott, Paul. The Auto Sector. In *Schott, J. J. and Smith, M. G., eds.*, 1988, pp. 101–09.

Woo, Carolyn Y.; Cooper, Arnold C. and Dunkelberg, William C. Entrepreneurial Typologies: Definitions and Implications. In *Kirchhoff, B. A., et al., eds.*, 1988, pp. 165–76.

_____; Cooper, Arnold C. and Dunkelberg, William C. Survival and Failure: A Longitudinal Study. In *Kirchhoff, B. A., et al., eds.*, 1988, pp. 225–37.

Woo, Chi-Keung. Inefficiency of Avoided Cost Pricing of Cogenerated Power. *Energy J.*, January 1988, 9(1), pp. 103–13.

_____. Optimal Electricity Rates and Consumption Externality. *Resources & Energy*, December 1988, 10(4), pp. 277–92.

_____; Doane, Michael J. and Hartman, Raymond S. Household Preference for Interruptible Rate Options and the Revealed Value of Service Reliability. *Energy J.*, Special Issue, 1988, 9, pp. 121–34.

_____; Doane, Michael J. and Hartman, Raymond S. Households' Perceived Value of Service Reliability: An Analysis of Contingent Valuation Data. *Energy J.*, Special Issue, 1988, 9, pp. 135–49.

_____; Goett, Andrew A. and McFadden, Daniel L. Estimating Household Value of Electrical Service Reliability with Market Research Data. *Energy J.*, Special Issue, 1988, 9, pp. 105–20.

_____; Keane, Dennis M. and MacDonald, S. Leslie. Estimating Residential Partial Outage Cost with Market Research Data. *Energy J.*, Special Issue, 1988, 9, pp. 151–59.

_____ and Seeto, Dewey Q. Optimal Off-Peak Incremental Sales Rate Design in Electricity

Pricing. *Energy J.*, January 1988, 9(1), pp. 95–102.

_____ and Train, Kenneth E. The Cost of Electric Power Interruptions to Commercial Firms. *Energy J.*, Special Issue, 1988, 9, pp. 161–72.

Woo, Wing Thye. What Kind of Structural Adjustment Policies for U.S. Trade Difficulties? In *Tan, L.-H. and Akrasanee, N., eds.*, 1988, pp. 89–111.

Wood, Adrian. Brazil's Growth Prospects: Domestic Savings, External Finance and OECD Performance: Discussion. In *Currie, D. and Vines, D., eds.*, 1988, pp. 279–83.

_____. How Much Unemployment Is Structural? *Oxford Bull. Econ. Statist.*, February 1988, 50(1), pp. 71–81.

Wood, Arnold S. Manager vs. Client: What's the Difference? *J. Portfol. Manage.*, Summer 1988, 14(4), pp. 63–65.

Wood, Bruce. British Social Trends since 1900: Urbanisation and Local Government. In *Halsey, A. H., ed.*, 1988, pp. 322–56.

Wood, Douglas and Piesse, Jennie. The Information Value of Failure Predictions in Credit Assessment. *J. Banking Finance*, June 1988, 12(2), pp. 275–92.

Wood, G. Donald. Employment Cost Index Series to Replace Hourly Earnings Index. *Mon. Lab. Rev.*, July 1988, 111(7), pp. 32–35.

_____. A New Measure of the Cost of Compensation Components. *Surv. Curr. Bus.*, November 1988, 68(11), pp. 38–43.

Wood, Geoffrey E. and Chrystal, K. Alec. Are Trade Deficits a Problem? *Fed. Res. Bank St. Louis Rev.*, Jan.–Feb. 1988, 70(1), pp. 3–12.

_____; Coughlin, Cletus C. and Chrystal, K. Alec. Protectionist Trade Policies: A Survey of Theory, Evidence and Rationale. *Fed. Res. Bank St. Louis Rev.*, Jan.–Feb. 1988, 70(1), pp. 12–29.

_____ and Mills, Terence C. Interest Rates and the Conduct of Monetary Policy. In *Eltis, W. and Sinclair, P. J. N., eds.*, 1988, pp. 246–67.

Wood, James W. and Weinstein, Maxine. A Model of Age-Specific Fecundability. *Population Stud.*, March 1988, 42(1), pp. 85–113.

Wood, John Cunningham. William Stanley Jevons: Critical Assessments, Volume III: Commentary. In *Wood, J. C., ed., Vol. 3*, 1988, pp. 3–8.

_____. William Stanley Jevons: Critical Assessments: Volume I: General Commentary. In *Wood, J. C., ed., Vol. 1*, 1988, pp. i–vi.

Wood, Peter W. The Economics of Space Business. In *Egan, J. J., et al.*, 1988, pp. 395–412.

Wood, Richard H., Jr. Literacy and Basic Needs Satisfaction in Mexico. *World Devel.*, March 1988, 16(3), pp. 405–17.

Wood, Robert and Hanrahan, Nancy. The Corporate Alternative Minimum Tax as a State Revenue Source. *Nat. Tax J.*, September 1988, 41(3), pp. 445–50.

Wood, Robert A., Jr.; Hill, Joanne M. and Jain, Anshuman. Insurance: Volatility Risk and Futures Mispricing. *J. Portfol. Manage.*, Winter 1988, 14(2), pp. 23–29.

Wood, Robert O. and Spiller, Pablo T. Arbitrage during the Dollar–Sterling Gold Standard, 1899–1908: An Economic Approach. *J. Polit. Econ.*, August 1988, 96(4), pp. 882–92.

_____ and Spiller, Pablo T. The Estimation of Transaction Costs in Arbitrage Models. *J. Econometrics*, November 1988, 39(3), pp. 309–26.

Wood, Van R. and Burnett, John J. A Proposed Model of the Donation Decision Process. In *Hirschman, E. and Sheth, J. N., eds.*, 1988, pp. 1–47.

Wood, William C. and Elzinga, Kenneth G. The Costs of the Legal System in Private Antitrust Enforcement. In *White, L. J., ed.*, 1988, pp. 107–48.

Woodall, Roy and Mackenzie, Brian. Economic Productivity of Base Metal Exploration in Australia and Canada. In *Tilton, J. E.; Eggert, R. G. and Landsberg, H. H., eds.*, 1988, pp. 363–417.

Woodbery, Sabrina R.; Link, Albert N. and Seaks, Terry G. Firm Size and R&D Spending: Testing for Functional Form. *Southern Econ. J.*, April 1988, 54(4), pp. 1027–32.

Woodbury, Stephen A. Power in the Labor Market: Institutionalist Approaches to Labor Problems. In *Tool, M. R., ed., Vol. 2*, 1988, *1987*, pp. 363–89.

Wooders, Myrna Holtz. Stability of Jurisdiction Structures in Economies with Local Public Goods. *Math. Soc. Sci.*, February 1988, 15(1), pp. 29–49.

_____ and Zame, William R. Values of Large Finite Games. In *[Shapley, L. S.]*, 1988, pp. 195–206.

Woodford, Michael. Expectations, Finance, and Aggregate Instability. In *Kohn, M. and Tsiang, S.-C., eds.*, 1988, pp. 230–61.

_____ and Muller, Walter J., III. Determinacy of Equilibrium in Stationary Economies with Both Finite and Infinite Lived Consumers. *J. Econ. Theory*, December 1988, 46(2), pp. 255–90.

Woodhall, Maureen. Designing a Student Loan Programme for a Developing Country: The Relevance of International Experience. *Econ. Educ. Rev.*, 1988, 7(1), pp. 153–61.

Woodland, Alan D. International Factor Mobility and the Volume of Trade: An Empirical Study: Comment. In *Feenstra, R. C., ed.*, 1988, pp. 251–56.

_____ and Magnus, Jan R. On the Maximum Likelihood Estimation of Multivariate Regression Models Containing Serially Correlated Error Components. *Int. Econ. Rev.*, November 1988, 29(4), pp. 707–25.

_____ and Turunen-Red, Arja H. On the Multilateral Transfer Problem: Existence of Pareto Improving International Transfers. *J. Int. Econ.*, November 1988, 25(3–4), pp. 249–69.

Woodruff, Catherine S. and Senchack, A. J., Jr. Intradaily Price–Volume Adjustments of NYSE

Stocks to Unexpected Earnings. *J. Finance*, June 1988, *43*(2), pp. 467–91.

Woods, J. E. On Switching of Techniques in Two-Sector Models. *Scot. J. Polit. Econ.*, February 1988, *35*(1), pp. 84–91.

Woods, John Cunningham. William Stanley Jevons: Critical Assessments: Volume I: Commentary. In *Wood, J. C., ed., Vol. 1*, 1988, pp. 3–9.

Woods, John R. Retirement-Age Women and Pensions: Findings from the New Beneficiary Survey. *Soc. Sec. Bull.*, December 1988, *51*(12), pp. 5–16.

Woods, Leyla. Enterprise Size, Behavior and Performance in the Reformed Hungarian Economy. In *Brada, J. C. and Dobozi, I., eds.*, 1988, pp. 97–110.

_____; **Tyson, Laura D'Andrea and Robinson, Sherman.** Conditionality and Adjustment in Hungary and Yugoslavia. In *[Holzman, F. D.]*, 1988, pp. 72–105.

Woods, Michael D. Local Government Needs for Infrastructure Planning: The Texas Example. In *Johnson, T. G.; Deaton, B. J. and Segarra, E., eds.*, 1988, pp. 123–26.

Woods, R. I.; Watterson, Patricia A. and Woodward, J. H. The Causes of Rapid Infant Mortality Decline in England and Wales, 1861–1921: Part I. *Population Stud.*, November 1988, *42*(3), pp. 343–66.

Woodward, Douglas P. and Glickman, Norman J. The Location of Foreign Direct Investment in the United States: Patterns and Determinants. *Int. Reg. Sci. Rev.*, 1988, *11*(2), pp. 137–54.

Woodward, G. Thomas. The Real Rate of Interest: Inferences from the New U.K. Indexed Gilts: Comment. *Int. Econ. Rev.*, August 1988, *29*(3), pp. 565–68.

_____ **and Makinen, Gail E.** The Transition from Hyperinflation to Stability: Some Evidence. *Eastern Econ. J.*, Jan.–March 1988, *14*(1), pp. 19–26.

Woodward, J. H.; Woods, R. I. and Watterson, Patricia A. The Causes of Rapid Infant Mortality Decline in England and Wales, 1861–1921: Part I. *Population Stud.*, November 1988, *42*(3), pp. 343–66.

Woodward, R. S. The Effect of Relative Monetary Surprises on Spot Exchange Rates. *Appl. Econ.*, August 1988, *20*(8), pp. 1129–36.

_____. Some New Evidence on the Profitability of One-Way versus Round-Trip Arbitrage. *J. Money, Credit, Banking*, November 1988, *20*(4), pp. 645–52.

Woodward, Susan E. Policy Issues in the Privatization of FNMA and FHLMC. In *Federal Home Loan Bank of San Francisco*, 1988, pp. 169–84.

_____. A Transaction Cost Analysis of Banking Activity and Deposit Insurance. *Cato J.*, Winter 1988, *7*(3), pp. 683–99.

Woodward, Susan L. and Alchian, Armen A. The Firm is Dead; Long Live the Firm: A Review of Oliver E. Williamson's *The Economic Insti-*

tutions of Capitalism. *J. Econ. Lit.*, March 1988, *26*(1), pp. 65–79.

Woodwell, George M. Biotic Services and the Human Estate: A Scheme to Avoid Hidden Taxes. In *Ehrlich, P. R. and Holdren, J. P., eds.*, 1988, pp. 171–79.

Wooldridge, Jeffrey M.; Bollerslev, Tim and Engle, Robert F. A Capital Asset Pricing Model with Time-Varying Covariances. *J. Polit. Econ.*, February 1988, *96*(1), pp. 116–31.

Wooton, Ian. Towards a Common Market: Factor Mobility in a Customs Union. *Can. J. Econ.*, August 1988, *21*(3), pp. 525–38.

Worden, Debra Drecnik and Falls, Gregory A. Consumer Valuation of Protection from Creditor Remedies. *J. Cons. Aff.*, Summer 1988, *22*(1), pp. 20–37.

Wörgötter, Andreas. The Structure of Wage–Price Determination and Unemployment in a Small Open Economy. *Empirica*, 1988, *15*(1), pp. 65–75.

Work, Monroe N. Negro Criminality in the South. In *Simms, M. C. and Myers, S. L., Jr., eds.*, 1988, *1913*, pp. 63–69.

Woroch, Glenn A. Regulatory Risk, Investment, and Welfare. *Rev. Ind. Organ.*, Spring 1988, *3*(3), pp. 75–99.

Worrall, John D. Benefit and Cost Models. In *Berkowitz, M., ed.*, 1988, pp. 45–62.

_____ **and Butler, Richard J.** Experience Rating Matters. In *Borba, P. S. and Appel, D., eds.*, 1988, pp. 81–94.

_____ **and Butler, Richard J.** Labor Market Theory and the Distribution of Workers' Compensation Losses. In *Borba, P. S. and Appel, D., eds.*, 1988, pp. 19–34.

Worrall, Tim and Thomas, Jonathan. Self-enforcing Wage Contracts. *Rev. Econ. Stud.*, October 1988, *55*(4), pp. 541–54.

Worre, Torben. Denmark at the Crossroads: The Danish Referendum of 28 February 1986 on the EC Reform Package. *J. Common Market Stud.*, June 1988, *26*(4), pp. 361–88.

Worswick, G. D. N. and Gregg, Paul A. Recession and Recovery in Britain: The 1930s and the 1980s. *Nat. Inst. Econ. Rev.*, November 1988, (126), pp. 44–50.

Worthington, Virginia E. and Burt, Oscar R. Wheat Acreage Supply Response in the United States. *Western J. Agr. Econ.*, July 1988, *13*(1), pp. 100–111.

Wortman, Max S., Jr. Strategic Management in Nonprofit Organizations: A Research Typology and Research Prospectus. In *Grant, J. H., ed.*, 1988, pp. 415–42.

Wos, Augustyn. Resource Adjustment and Farming Structures: Some Comments. *Europ. Rev. Agr. Econ.*, 1988, *15*(2–3), pp. 260–62.

Woychik, Eric. Regulatory View of Capacity Valuation in California. *Energy J.*, Special Issue, 1988, *9*, pp. 39–42.

Wray, Larry Randall. Profit Expectations and the Investment–Saving Relation. *J. Post Keynesian Econ.*, Fall 1988, *11*(1), pp. 131–47.

Wrege, Charles and Greenwood, Ronald G. The War against Isolated Plants by Central Stations,

1901–1918. In *Perkins, E. J., ed.*, 1988, pp. 189–99.

Wren, Anthony and Chamberlain, Mark. The Development of Micro-BUSMAN: Scheduling on Micro-computers. In *Daduna, J. R. and Wren, A., eds.*, 1988, pp. 160–74.

—— **and Smith, Barbara M.** Experiences with a Crew Scheduling System Based on Set Covering. In *Daduna, J. R. and Wren, A., eds.*, 1988, pp. 104–18.

Wren, Colin. Closure Rates among Assisted and Non-assisted Establishments. *Reg. Stud.*, April 1988, 22(2), pp. 107–19.

Wren-Lewis, Simon. Supply, Liquidity and Credit: A New Version of the Institute's Domestic Econometric Macromodel. *Nat. Inst. Econ. Rev.*, November 1988, (126), pp. 32–43.

Wretman, Jan H.; Waldén, Bertil and Sandström, Arne. Variance Estimators of the Gini Coefficient—Probability Sampling. *J. Bus. Econ. Statist.*, January 1988, 6(1), pp. 113–19.

Wright, Brian D. Storage, Stability, and Farm Programs. In *Sumner, D. A., ed.*, 1988, pp. 27–49.

—— **and Williams, Jeffrey C.** The Incidence of Market-Stabilising Price Support Schemes. *Econ. J.*, December 1988, 98(393), pp. 1183–98.

—— **and Williams, Jeffrey C.** Measurement of Consumer Gains from Market Stabilization. *Amer. J. Agr. Econ.*, August 1988, 70(3), pp. 616–27.

Wright, David J. and Reilly, Frank K. A Comparison of Published Betas. *J. Portfol. Manage.*, Spring 1988, 14(3), pp. 64–69.

Wright, Kevin N. and Cingranelli, David Louis. Correlates of Due Process. In *Cingranelli, D. L., ed.*, 1988, pp. 154–72.

Wright, Lindsay M. and Gastil, Raymond D. The State of the World Political and Economic Freedom. In *Walker, M. A., ed. (I)*, 1988, pp. 85–119.

Wright, Mike and Coyne, John. Buy-outs and British Industry. In *Johnson, C., ed.*, 1988, 1982, pp. 157–73.

Wright, Randall D. The Observational Implications of Labor Contracts in a Dynamic General Equilibrium Model. *J. Lab. Econ.*, October 1988, 6(4), pp. 530–51.

—— **and Hotchkiss, Julie.** A General Model of Unemployment Insurance with and without Short-Term Compensation. In *Ehrenberg, R. G., ed.*, 1988, pp. 91–131.

—— **and Rogerson, Richard.** Involuntary Unemployment in Economies with Efficient Risk Sharing. *J. Monet. Econ.*, November 1988, 22(3), pp. 501–15.

Wright, Richard W. and Pauli, Gunter A. International Trade in Financial Services: The Japanese Challenge. In *Guile, B. R. and Quinn, J. B., eds. (II)*, 1988, pp. 187–210.

Wrightson, Margaret T. and Conlan, Timothy J. Federal Dollars and Congressional Sense: Targeting Aid to Poor People and Poor Places. In *Bell, M. E., ed.*, 1988, pp. 163–90.

Wrigley, E. A. The Limits to Growth: Malthus and the Classical Economists. *Population Devel. Rev.*, Supplement, 1988, 14, pp. 30–48.

Wrigley, Neil. Retail Restructuring and Retail Analysis. In *Wrigley, N., ed.*, 1988, pp. 3–38.

—— **and Dunn, Richard.** Models of Store Choice and Market Analysis. In *Wrigley, N., ed.*, 1988, pp. 251–71.

Wriston, Walter B. Technology and Sovereignty. *Foreign Aff.*, Winter 1988–89, 67(2), pp. 63–75.

Wruck, Karen H.; Warner, Jerold B. and Watts, Ross L. Stock Prices and Top Management Changes. *J. Finan. Econ.*, Jan.–March 1988, 20(1–2), pp. 461–92.

Wu, C. F. Jeff; Holt, D. and Holmes, D. J. The Effect of Two-stage Sampling on the F Statistic. *J. Amer. Statist. Assoc.*, March 1988, 83(401), pp. 150–59.

—— **; Ruppert, David and Carroll, Raymond J.** The Effect of Estimating Weights in Weighted Least Squares. *J. Amer. Statist. Assoc.*, December 1988, 83(404), pp. 1045–54.

—— **; Tsui, Kwok-Leung and Jewell, Nicholas P.** A Nonparametric Approach to the Truncated Regression Problem. *J. Amer. Statist. Assoc.*, September 1988, 83(403), pp. 785–92.

Wu, Chunchi and Colwell, Peter F. Moral Hazard and Moral Imperative. *J. Risk Ins.*, March 1988, 55(1), pp. 101–17.

—— **and Kim, Moon K.** Effects of Inflation on Capital Structure. *Financial Rev.*, May 1988, 23(2), pp. 183–200.

—— **and Lee, Cheng F.** Expectation Formation and Financial Ratio Adjustment Processes. *Accounting Rev.*, April 1988, 63(2), pp. 292–306.

Wu, H. K. and Essayyad, Musa. The Performance of U.S. International Mutual Funds. *Quart. J. Bus. Econ.*, Autumn 1988, 27(4), pp. 32–46.

Wu, Hansheng and Mizukami, Koichi. Incentive Stackelberg Strategies in Linear Quadratic Differential Games with Two Noncooperative Followers. In *Iri, M. and Yajima, K., eds.*, 1988, pp. 436–45.

Wu, Ho-Mou. Unemployment Equilibrium in a Random Economy. *J. Math. Econ.*, 1988, 17(4), pp. 385–400.

Wu, Jinglian and Reynolds, Bruce L. Choosing a Strategy for China's Economic Reform. *Amer. Econ. Rev.*, May 1988, 78(2), pp. 461–66.

—— **and Zhao, Renwei.** The Dual Pricing System in China's Industry. In *Reynolds, B. L., ed.*, 1988, 1987, pp. 19–28.

Wu, Lan. Contracting Cost and Vertical Integration: Discussion of Dr. Lee's Paper. In *Pennsylvania Economic Association*, 1988, pp. 639–41.

Wu, M. T. C. and Richardson, D. H. A Short-run Monetary Model of Exchange Rate Determination: Stability Tests and Forecasting. *Empirical Econ.*, 1988, 13(1), pp. 1–15.

Wu, Tsung Wen; Day, Ralph L. and MacKay, David B. Consumer Benefits versus Product Attributes: An Experimental Test. *Quart. J. Bus. Econ.*, Summer 1988, 27(3), pp. 88–113.

Wu, Yuan-li. Adversaries, Allies, and Foreign Economic Policy. In *[Nutter, G. W.]*, 1988, pp. 137–50.

Wulff, Manfred. Kreditmarkttheoretische Erklärung der Zins- und Zahlungsbilanzentwicklung in einer offenen Volkswirtschaft mit festen Wechselkursen. Konsequenzen für die Geldpolitik. (The Development of Interest Rates and the Balance of Payments in an Open Economy with Fixed Exchange Raates in the Framework of Credit Market Theory. With English summary.) *Jahr. Nationalökon. Statist.*, September 1988, *205*(3), pp. 209–28.

Wulwick, Nancy J. Money and Interest Rates: A Comment. In *Hamouda, O. F. and Smithin, J. N.*, eds., Vol. 2, 1988, pp. 159–61.

Wunnava, Phanindra Venkata. Life Cycle Union Effects Based on a Pooled Regression Technique: Evidence from PSID. *Southern Econ. J.*, April 1988, *54*(4), pp. 1020–26.

Wuyts, Marc and FitzGerald, E. V. K. Markets within Planning: Socialist Economic Management in the Third World: Introduction. *J. Devel. Stud.*, July 1988, *24*(4), pp. 1–14.

_____ **and Mackintosh, Maureen.** Accumulation, Social Services and Socialist Transition in the Third World: Reflections on Decentralised Planning Based on the Mozambican Experience. *J. Devel. Stud.*, July 1988, *24*(4), pp. 136–79.

Wyckoff, James H. To What Extent Is Education a Public Good? In *Brown, E.*, ed., 1988, pp. 2–7.

_____ **and Collins, Julie H.** Estimates of Tax-Deferred Retirement Savings Behavior. *Nat. Tax J.*, December 1988, *41*(4), pp. 561–72.

Wyckoff, Paul Gary. Bureaucracy and the "Publicness" of Local Public Goods. *Public Choice*, March 1988, *56*(3), pp. 271–84.

_____ . A Bureaucratic Theory of Flypaper Effects. *J. Urban Econ.*, January 1988, *23*(1), pp. 115–29.

Wydler, Daniel and Wasserfallen, Walter. Underpricing of Newly Issued Bonds: Evidence from the Swiss Capital Market. *J. Finance*, December 1988, *43*(5), pp. 1177–91.

Wygal, Donald E.; Volpi, James and Stout, David E. A Comparative Income Statement Approach to Integrating International Topics in the Financial Accounting Curriculum. In *Most, K. S.*, ed., 1988, pp. 149–68.

van Wyk, R. J. Technological Advance: Unravelling the Strands. In *Tisdell, C. and Maitra, P.*, eds., 1988, pp. 322–40.

Wylie, Peter J. and Wylie, Raymond F. The Free-Trade Issue in Canada's Relations with the United States. In *Thornton, R. J.; Hyclak, T. and Aronson, J. R.*, eds., 1988, pp. 81–114.

Wylie, Raymond F. and Wylie, Peter J. The Free-Trade Issue in Canada's Relations with the United States. In *Thornton, R. J.; Hyclak, T. and Aronson, J. R.*, eds., 1988, pp. 81–114.

Wyplosz, Charles. Capital Controls and Public Finance: The Experience in Italy: Discussion. In *Giavazzi, F. and Spaventa, L.*, eds., 1988, pp. 217–21.

_____ **and Drèze, Jacques H.** Autonomy through Cooperation. *Europ. Econ. Rev.*, March 1988, *32*(2–3), pp. 353–62.

_____ **and Drèze, Jacques H.** Une stratégie de croissance ambidextre pour l'Europe: L'autonomie par la coopération. (A Two-Handed Approach for Europe: Autonomy through Cooperation. With English summary.) *Revue Écon.*, May 1988, *39*(3), pp. 627–40.

_____ **and Eichengreen, Barry.** The Economic Consequences of the Franc Poincaré. In *Helpman, E.; Razin, A. and Sadka, E.*, eds., 1988, pp. 257–86.

_____ ; **Giavazzi, Francesco and Sheen, Jeff R.** The Real Exchange Rate and the Fiscal Aspects of a Natural Resource Discovery. *Oxford Econ. Pap.*, September 1988, *40*(3), pp. 427–50.

von Wysocki, Klaus. Germany and the Seventh Directive. In *Gray, S. J. and Coenenberg, A. G.*, eds., 1988, pp. 95–104.

Wyszewianski, Leon. The Emphasis on Measurement in Quality Assurance: Reasons and Implications. *Inquiry*, Winter 1988, *25*(4), pp. 424–33.

_____ . Quality of Care: Past Achievements and Future Challenges. *Inquiry*, Spring 1988, *25*(1), pp. 13–22.

Wyzan, Michael L. and Rich, Daniel P. Microeconomic Analysis of Parallel Markets: Comment. *J. Compar. Econ.*, December 1988, *12*(4), pp. 604–09.

Xia, Xianmin. The Energy and Minerals Development Planning Process in the People's Republic of China: An Overview. In *Dorian, J. P. and Fridley, D. G.*, eds., 1988, pp. 93–97.

Xian, Guoming. The Theory of Internalization and the Contemporary International Division of Labor. In *Teng, W. and Wang, N. T.*, eds., 1988, pp. 47–60.

Xiang, Yuanwang and Yuji, Wang. Dynamic Simulation and Optimal Control of Urban Socioeconomic and Eco-environment System. In *Iri, M. and Yajima, K.*, eds., 1988, pp. 462–70.

Xie, Wen Zhi. A Simple Way of Computing the Inverse Moments of a Non-central Chi-Square Random Variable. *J. Econometrics*, March 1988, *37*(3), pp. 389–93.

Xin, Dingguo. The Present and Long-term Energy Strategy of China. In *Dorian, J. P. and Fridley, D. G.*, eds., 1988, pp. 43–54.

Xingwu, Liu and Alatan. China's Policy Towards Her Minority Nationalities. In *Mitra, A.*, ed., 1988, pp. 136–59.

Xiong, Guilin and Zhang, Qiren. Modelling and Optimization of Public Traffic Large Scale Systems. In *Iri, M. and Yajima, K.*, eds., 1988, pp. 426–35.

Xu, Dianqing. Background to a Mathematical Model of Price Reform in China. *Chinese Econ. Stud.*, Spring 1988, *21*(3), pp. 78–91.

Xu, Jing'an. The Stock-Share System: A New Avenue for China's Economic Reform. In *Reynolds, B. L.*, ed., 1988, 1987, pp. 219–24.

Yaari, Menahem E. A Controversial Proposal Concerning Inequality Measurement. *J. Econ. Theory*, April 1988, *44*(2), pp. 381–97.

Yaari, Uzi and Cherkes, Martin. Unions, Default Risk, and Pension Underfunding. *J. Econ. Bus.*, August 1988, *40*(3), pp. 239–42.

Yabuuchi, Shigemi. Partial Revenue Seeking and Welfare. *Econ. Letters*, 1988, *27*(3), pp. 271–78.

Yagci, Fahrettin and Kamin, Steven. Macroeconomic Policies and Adjustment in Yugoslavia: Some Counterfactual Simulations. In *Motamen, H., ed.*, 1988 , pp. 713–30.

Yager, Ronald R. Uncertain Associational Relations: Compatibility and Transition Relations in Reasoning. In *Kacprzyk, J. and Fedrizzi, M., eds.*, 1988, pp. 152–67.

Yaghmaian, Behzad. Internationalization of Capital and the Crisis of the Iranian Economy. *Rev. Radical Polit. Econ.*, Winter 1988, *20*(4), pp. 40–56.

_____ and Bina, Cyrus. Import Substitution and Export Promotion within the Context of the Internationalization of Capital. *Rev. Radical Polit. Econ.*, Summer–Fall 1988, *20*(2–3), pp. 234–40.

Yagüe Guillén, María Jesús. Competencia dinámica en precios: Evidencias en el Sector de Fertilizantes Agrícolas. (With English summary.) *Invest. Econ.*, May 1988, *12*(2), pp. 199–224.

Yahav, Joseph A. and Bickel, Peter J. Richardson Extrapolation and the Bootstrap. *J. Amer. Statist. Assoc.*, June 1988, *83*(402), pp. 387–93.

Yahaya, Jahara. Fishery Management and Regulation in Peninsular Malaysia: Issues and Constraints. *Marine Resource Econ.*, 1988, *5*(2), pp. 83–98.

Yainshet, Alasebu and Etherington, Dan M. The Impact of Income Terms of Trade for Coffee on Capital Goods Imports and Investment in Ethiopia. *Eastern Afr. Econ. Rev.*, June 1988, *4*(1), pp. 48–52.

Yakita, Akira. The Flow Equilibrium and the Neutrality of Money in a Neoclassical Monetary Growth Model. *J. Macroecon.*, Spring 1988, *10*(2), pp. 201–16.

Yalawar, Yalaguresh B. Bombay Stock Exchange: Rates of Return and Efficiency. *Indian Econ. J.*, April–June 1988, *35*(4), pp. 68–121.

Yamada, Atsushi. Cooperative Fuzzy Game with Side-Payments. In *Iri, M. and Yajima, K., eds.*, 1988, pp. 455–61.

Yamada, Takeshi; Pettway, Richard H. and Tapley, T. Craig. The Impacts of Financial Deregulation upon Trading Efficiency and the Levels of Risk and Return of Japanese Banks. *Financial Rev.*, August 1988, *23*(3), pp. 243–68.

Yamaguchi, Kazuomi. The American Trade Association Movement Revisited: Comment. In *Yamazaki, H. and Miyamoto, M., eds.*, 1988, pp. 136–38.

Yamawaki, Hideki and Audretsch, David B. Import Share under International Oligopoly with Differentiated Products: Japanese Imports in U.S. Manufacturing. *Rev. Econ. Statist.*, November 1988, *70*(4), pp. 569–79.

_____ and Audretsch, David B. R&D Rivalry,

Industrial Policy, and U.S.–Japanese Trade. *Rev. Econ. Statist.*, August 1988, *70*(3), pp. 438–47.

_____ and Sleuwaegen, Leo. The Formation of the European Common Market and Changes in Market Structure and Performance. *Europ. Econ. Rev.*, September 1988, *32*(7), pp. 1451–75.

Yamazaki, Hiroaki. Trade Associations in Business History: Introduction. In *Yamazaki, H. and Miyamoto, M., eds.*, 1988, pp. ix–xxiii.

Yamazawa, Ippei. The Generalized System of Preferences and Japan's Imports from Developing Countries. *Hitotsubashi J. Econ.*, December 1988, *29*(2), pp. 117–42.

Yamey, Basil S. Professor Hutt on Monopoly Policy (1934–43). *Managerial Dec. Econ.*, Special Issue, Winter 1988, pp. 27–31.

Yan, Chiou-Shuang; Kinniry, Fran and Koziara, Edward. The Economic Performance of the Presidents 1909–1946: A Preliminary View. In *Pennsylvania Economic Association*, 1988, pp. 260–69.

_____; Quinn, John and Koziara, Edward. Other Measures of the Economic Performance of Presidents. In *Pennsylvania Economic Association*, 1988, pp. 270–78.

Yanagida, John F.; Hassler, James B. and Shalaby, Seif. United States Market Share of Latin American Wheat Imports: Disaggregated Analysis and Application of the Armington Model. *J. Econ. Stud.*, 1988, *15*(5), pp. 24–33.

Yanagishita, Machiko and Guralnik, Jack M. Changing Mortality Patterns that Led Life Expectancy in Japan to Surpass Sweden's: 1972–1982. *Demography*, November 1988, *25*(4), pp. 611–24.

Yandell, Dirk. Audit Information and Incentives for Efficiency. *Amer. Econ.*, Spring 1988, *32*(1), pp. 49–58.

Yandle, Bruce. Antitrust Actions and the Budgeting Process. *Public Choice*, December 1988, *59*(3), pp. 263–75.

_____. Regulators, Legislators and Budget Manipulation. *Public Choice*, February 1988, *56*(2), pp. 167–80.

_____; Wallace, Myles S. and Watson, Sharon B. Environment Regulation: A Financial Markets Test. *Quart. Rev. Econ. Bus.*, Spring 1988, *28*(1), pp. 69–87.

Yang, Bijou and Lester, David. A Hypothesis about Execution Rates in the United States. In *Pennsylvania Economic Association*, 1988, pp. 522–29.

Yang, Bong-Min and Hu, Teh-wei. The Demand for and Supply of Physician Services in the U.S.: A Disequilibrium Analysis. *Appl. Econ.*, August 1988, *20*(8), pp. 995–1006.

_____ and Kim, Jin-Hyun. Voluntary Health Insurance and Providers' Price Discounting Behaviour in Korea. In *Butler, J. R. G. and Doessel, D. P., eds.*, 1988, pp. 192–206.

Yang, Chin W. An Estimation of the Inflation in the Chin and Early Han Dynasties: A Statistical Approach. In *Pennsylvania Economic Association*, 1988, pp. 279–93.

Yang, David C. H. and Tang, De-Piao. Testing for Causality in the Richardson Arms Race Model. *Math. Soc. Sci.*, April 1988, *15*(2), pp. 197–203.

Yang, Guohua. Accomplishments in Employing Workers in Townships and Cities and the New Situation We Face. *Chinese Econ. Stud.*, Summer 1988, *21*(4), pp. 69–91.

Yang, Jeong-Ae and Chae, Suchan. The Unique Perfect Equilibrium of an *N*-Person Bargaining Game. *Econ. Letters*, 1988, *28*(3), pp. 221–23.

Yang, Jianxin. Is "Life Is Difficult, without a Source of Income" the Primary Cause for Rising Crime and Delinquency among Young People Awaiting Job Assignment? *Chinese Econ. Stud.*, Summer 1988, *21*(4), pp. 65–68.

Yang, Maw Cheng and Grilli, Enzo R. Primary Commodity Prices, Manufactured Goods Prices, and the Terms of Trade of Developing Countries: What the Long Run Shows. *World Bank Econ. Rev.*, January 1988, *2*(1), pp. 1–47.

Yaniv, Gideon. Crime and Punishment: A Note on Instrumental Violence. *J. Behav. Econ.*, Summer 1988, *17*(2), pp. 143–48.

_____. Enforcement and Monopsonistic Compliance with the Minimum Wage Law. *Southern Econ. J.*, October 1988, *55*(2), pp. 505–09.

_____. Withholding and Non-withheld Tax Evasion. *J. Public Econ.*, March 1988, *35*(2), pp. 183–204.

Yannopoulos, G. N. Customs Unions and Trade Conflicts: The Enlargement of the European Community: Introduction. In *Yannopoulos, G. N.*, 1988, pp. 1–13.

_____. The Economics of "Flagging Out." *J. Transp. Econ. Policy*, May 1988, *22*(2), pp. 197–207.

_____. The European Community's Common External Commercial Policy. In *Yannopoulos, G. N.*, 1988, *1985*, pp. 14–27.

_____. European Community Trade Options in the New Round of Trade Negotiations. In *Yannopoulos, G. N.*, 1988, pp. 159–70.

_____. The External Trade Effects of the EC's Integrated Mediterranean Programmes. In *Yannopoulos, G. N.*, 1988, pp. 130–58.

_____. The Impact of the Common Agricultural Policy (CAP) on Developing Countries Following the Enlargement of the European Community. In *Yannopoulos, G. N.*, 1988, pp. 57–80.

_____. The Impact of Western European Integration on East–West Trade. In *Yannopoulos, G. N.*, 1988, pp. 28–39.

_____. Prospects for the Manufacturing Exports of the Non-candidate Mediterranean Countries in a Community of Twelve. In *Yannopoulos, G. N.*, 1988, *1984*, pp. 81–94.

_____. The Second Enlargement of the EC and the Trade Interests of the Developing Countries. In *Yannopoulos, G. N.*, 1988, pp. 40–56.

_____. Trade Effects on Third Countries from Spain's Accession to the EC. In *Yannopoulos, G. N.*, 1988, pp. 95–110.

_____. The Trade Interests of the United States and the Enlargement of the EC. In *Yannopoulos, G. N.*, 1988, *1987*, pp. 111–29.

Yano, Toru. Japan as a Civilization. In *Kozmetsky, G.; Matsumoto, H. and Smilor, R. W., eds.*, 1988, pp. 25–41.

Yao, Dennis A. Strategic Responses to Automobile Emissions Control: A Game-Theoretic Analysis. *J. Environ. Econ. Manage.*, December 1988, *15*(4), pp. 419–38.

Yarbrough, Beth V. Imperfect Competition, Scale Economies, and Trade Policy in Developing Countries: Comment. In *Baldwin, R. E., ed. (II)*, 1988, pp. 141–43.

_____ **and Yarbrough, Robert M.** The Transactional Structure of the Firm: A Comparative Survey. *J. Econ. Behav. Organ.*, July 1988, *10*(1), pp. 1–28.

Yarbrough, Robert M. and Yarbrough, Beth V. The Transactional Structure of the Firm: A Comparative Survey. *J. Econ. Behav. Organ.*, July 1988, *10*(1), pp. 1–28.

Yarrow, George and Helm, Dieter. The Assessment: The Regulation of Utilities. *Oxford Rev. Econ. Policy*, Summer 1988, *4*(2), pp. i–xxxi.

_____ **and Vickers, John.** Regulation of Privatised Firms in Britain. *Europ. Econ. Rev.*, March 1988, *32*(2–3), pp. 465–72.

Yasai-Ardekani, Masoud; Grinyer, Peter H. and McKiernan, Peter. Market, Organizational, and Managerial Correlates of Economic Performance in the U.K. Electrical Engineering Industry. In *Grant, J. H., ed.*, 1988, pp. 147–79.

Yasuba, Yasukichi. The Commodity Problem with Special Reference to the South Pacific. In *Kozmetsky, G.; Matsumoto, H. and Smilor, R. W., eds.*, 1988, pp. 67–72.

_____. The Japanese Economy and Economic Policy in the 1930s. In *Gregory, R. G. and Butlin, N. G., eds.*, 1988, pp. 135–71.

Yatchew, Adonis John. Some Tests of Nonparametric Regression Models. In *Barnett, W. A.; Berndt, E. R. and White, H., eds.*, 1988, pp. 121–35.

Yates, Alden P. Technological Advances in the Construction Sector. In *Muroyama, J. H. and Stever, H. G., eds.*, 1988, pp. 68–79.

Yates, Judith. Housing Finance and Deregulation: Predictions and Outcomes. *Australian Econ. Rev.*, 1st Quarter 1988, (81), pp. 3–15.

Ycas, Martynas A. and Iams, Howard M. Women, Marriage, and Social Security Benefits. *Soc. Sec. Bull.*, May 1988, *51*(5), pp. 3–9.

Ye, Meng-Hua and Smith, Stephen C. Dynamic Allocation in a Labor-Managed Firm. *J. Compar. Econ.*, June 1988, *12*(2), pp. 204–16.

Yeager, Leland B. The Austrian School on Money and Gold. *J. Econ. Stud.*, 1988, *15*(3–4), pp. 92–105.

_____. Comments [Labor Market Barriers to More Employment: Causes for an Increase of the Natural Rate? The Case of West Germany] [Distortions, Incentives, and Growth]. In *Giersch, H., ed.*, 1988, pp. 242–43.

_____. Comments [The Case for Rules in the Conduct of Monetary Policy: A Concrete Example] [The Rules-versus-Discretion Debate in the Light of Recent Experience]. In *Giersch, H., ed.*, 1988, pp. 90–94.

_____. Domestic Stability versus Exchange Rate Stability. *Cato J.*, Fall 1988, *8*(2), pp. 261–77.

_____. On Interpreting Keynes: Reply [The Significance of Monetary Disequilibrium]. *Cato J.*, Spring–Summer 1988, *8*(1), pp. 205–08.

_____. Utility and the Social Welfare Function. In *[Rothbard, M. N.]*, 1988, pp. 175–91.

_____. Why Subjectivism? Reply. In *Rothbard, M. N. and Block, W., eds.*, 1988, pp. 209–10.

Yeats, Alexander; Erzan, Refik and Laird, Samuel. On the Potential for Expanding South–South Trade through the Extension of Mutual Preferences among Developing Countries. *World Devel.*, December 1988, *16*(12), pp. 1441–54.

_____ **and Laird, Samuel.** A Note on the Aggregation Bias in Current Procedures for the Measurement of Trade Barriers. *Bull. Econ. Res.*, April 1988, *40*(2), pp. 133–43.

Yeh, William W.-G.; Lu, Allen H. and Schmittroth, F. Sequential Estimation of Aquifer Parameters. *Water Resources Res.*, May 1988, *24*(5), pp. 670–82.

Yeh, Yeong-Her. Consumption Taxes vs. Export Subsidies. *Amer. Econ.*, Spring 1988, *32*(1), pp. 71–73.

_____. The Effects of Changes in Consumers' Preferences and Factor Endowments. *Atlantic Econ. J.*, December 1988, *16*(4), pp. 91.

_____. Factor Intensities, Trade, and Income Distribution. *Atlantic Econ. J.*, June 1988, *16*(2), pp. 84.

Yellen, Janet L. Efficiency Wage Models of Unemployment. In *Shaw, G. K., ed., Vol. 2*, 1988, *1984*, pp. 97–102.

_____ **and Akerlof, George A.** Fairness and Unemployment. *Amer. Econ. Rev.*, May 1988, *78*(2), pp. 44–49.

_____; **Akerlof, George A. and Rose, Andrew Kenan.** Job Switching and Job Satisfaction in the U.S. Labor Market. *Brookings Pap. Econ. Act.*, 1988, (2), pp. 495–582.

_____; **Akerlof, George A. and Rose, Andrew Kenan.** The New Keynesian Economics and the Output–Inflation Trade-off: Comment. *Brookings Pap. Econ. Act.*, 1988, (1), pp. 66–75.

Yeo, Stephen; Portes, Richard and Quandt, Richard E. Tests of the Chronic Shortage Hypothesis: The Case of Poland. *Rev. Econ. Statist.*, May 1988, *70*(2), pp. 288–95.

Yeong, Wee Yong; Ch'ng, Hak Kee and Chang, Zeph-Yun. Production Management Practices of Small and Medium Businesses in Singapore. In *James, K. and Akrasanee, N., eds.*, 1988, pp. 126–63.

Yergin, Daniel. Energy Security in the 1990s. *Foreign Aff.*, Fall 1988, *67*(1), pp. 110–32.

Yesilada, Atilla and Gowdy, John M. Decision Making under Conditions of Turbulence and

Uncertainty: The Case of the Kinked Demand Curve. *Eastern Econ. J.*, Oct.–Dec. 1988, *14*(4), pp. 399–408.

Yeung, David and Hartwick, John M. Interest Rate and Output Price Uncertainty and Industry Equilibrium for Non-renewable Resource Extracting Firms. *Resources & Energy*, March 1988, *10*(1), pp. 1–14.

_____ **and Plourde, Charles.** A Note on Hayashi's Neoclassical Interpretation of Tobin's q. *Atlantic Econ. J.*, June 1988, *16*(2), pp. 81.

Yeutter, Clayton. Negotiating Intellectual Property Rights Protection. In *Walker, C. E. and Bloomfield, M. A., eds.*, 1988, pp. 109–15.

Yi, Gang and Judge, George. Statistical Model Selection Criteria. *Econ. Letters*, 1988, *28*(1), pp. 47–51.

Yi, P. and Chan, Y. Bifurcation and Disaggregation in Lowry–Garin Derivative Models: Theory, Calibration, and Case Study. *Environ. Planning A*, September 1988, *20*(9), pp. 1253–67.

Ying, John S. and Keeler, Theodore E. Measuring the Benefits of a Large Public Investment: The Case of the U.S. Federal-Aid Highway System. *J. Public Econ.*, June 1988, *36*(1), pp. 69–85.

Yip, Chong K. The Employment Effects of Tariffs in an Efficient Bargain Model. *J. Macroecon.*, Summer 1988, *10*(3), pp. 477–85.

Yirang, Yuan and Douglas, Jim, Jr. Numerical Simulation of Immiscible Flow in Porous Media Based on Combining the Method of Characteristics with Mixed Finite Element Procedures. In *Wheeler, M. F., ed.*, 1988, pp. 119–31.

Yitzhaki, Shlomo and Stark, Oded. Relative Deprivation and Migration. In *Maital, S., ed., Vol. 1*, 1988, pp. 269–302.

_____; **Stark, Oded and Taylor, J. Edward.** Migration, Remittances and Inequality: A Sensitivity Analysis Using the Extended Gini Index. *J. Devel. Econ.*, May 1988, *28*(3), pp. 309–22.

Ylä-Liedenpohja, Jouko. Laskelmia korkojen verotuskohtelun muuttamisesta. (Calculations on Changing the Tax Treatment of Interest. With English summary.) *Liiketaloudellinen Aikak.*, 1988, *37*(1), pp. 68–95.

_____. Project Specific Discount Rates: Depreciation, Inflation and Tax Effects. *Liiketaloudellinen Aikak.*, 1988, *37*(1), pp. 18–28.

Yochelson, John. Keeping Pace: U.S. Policies and Global Economic Change: Introduction. In *Yochelson, J., ed.*, 1988, pp. xiii–xxi.

Yoguel, Gabriel and Beccaria, Luis. Apuntes sobre la evolución del empleo industrial en el período 1973–1984. (With English summary.) *Desarrollo Econ.*, Jan.–March 1988, *27*(108), pp. 589–605.

Yohai, Victor J. and Zamar, Ruben H. High Breakdown-Point Estimates of Regression by Means of the Minimization of an Efficient Scale. *J. Amer. Statist. Assoc.*, June 1988, *83*(402), pp. 406–13.

Yoo, Jang H. and Bishop, John A. Cigarette "Health Scare," Excise Taxes and Advertising

Ban: Reply. *Southern Econ. J.*, January 1988, 54(3), pp. 777–79.

Yoo, Sang-Hee and Mallela, Parthasaradhi. On the Inadequacy of Sufficient Conditions under 'Limited Information' Identification. *Econ. Letters*, 1988, 27(4), pp. 337–39.

Yoon, Eunsang; Choffray, Jean-Marie and Lilien, Gary L. New Industrial Product Performance: Models and Empirical Analysis. In *Woodside, A. G., ed.*, 1988, pp. 49–77.

———— **and Lilien, Gary L.** An Exploratory Analysis of the Dynamic Behavior of Price Elasticity over the Product Life Cycle: An Empirical Analysis of Industrial Chemical Products. In *Devinney, T. M., ed.*, 1988, pp. 261–87.

Yoon, Suk-Won. Effects of Tariffs and Nontariff Trade Barriers (NTBs) on the International Rice Trade: A Reactive Programming Model. *J. Econ. Devel.*, June 1988, 13(1), pp. 175–94.

Yordon, Wesley J. Evidence against Diminishing Returns in Manufacturing and Comments on Short-run Models of Price–Output Behavior: Rejoinder. *J. Post Keynesian Econ.*, Spring 1988, 10(3), pp. 492–94.

York, Dan W. and Hanson, Mark E. The Impact of Oil Price Shocks on Economic Growth in Middle-Income Developing Countries. *J. Energy Devel.*, Autumn 1988, 14(1), pp. 79–102.

York, James D. Variety Stores Experience Shifting Trend in Productivity. *Mon. Lab. Rev.*, October 1988, 111(10), pp. 30–33.

Yoshida, Hiroshi. Conceptual Systems of Accounting Theory Formation. In *Most, K. S., ed.*, 1988, pp. 51–66.

Yoshihara, Hideki. Dynamic Synergy and Top Management Leadership: Strategic Innovation in Japanese Companies. In *Urabe, K.; Child, J. and Kagono, T., eds.*, 1988, pp. 47–62.

Yoshii, Masahiko. Development of the Soviet Computer Industry: Can the USSR Be a High-Tech Economy? *Kobe Univ. Econ.*, 1988, (34), pp. 101–15.

Yoshimura, Isao. Leading Actors Promoting Labor Front Unification. In *Japan Institute of Labour, ed.*, 1988, 1983, pp. 77–81.

Yoshinaga, Kohei. Notes on the Foreign Trade Structure of Japan and the Federal Republic of Germany: A Comparative Analysis by Input-Output–Tables. *Hitotsubashi J. Econ.*, June 1988, 29(1), pp. 101–15.

Yoshitomi, Masaru. Empirical Analysis and Intergovernmental Policy Consultation: Comment. In *Bryant, R. C., et al., eds.*, 1988, pp. 297–301.

Yotopoulos, Pan A. and Kuroda, Yoshimi. A Subjective Equilibrium Approach to the Value of Children in the Agricultural Household. *Pakistan Devel. Rev.*, Autumn 1988, 27(3), pp. 229–76.

———— **and Lau, Lawrence J.** Do Country Idiosyncracies Matter in Estimating a Production Function for World Agriculture? *J. Econ. Devel.*, June 1988, 13(1), pp. 7–19.

———— **and Mergos, George J.** Demand for Feed

Inputs in the Greek Livestock Sector. *Europ. Rev. Agr. Econ.*, 1988, 15(1), pp. 1–17.

Youmans, Russ, et al. The Role of Cooperative Extension, USDA, Land Grant Universities, and Rural Development Centers. In *Johnson, T. G.; Deaton, B. J. and Segarra, E., eds.*, 1988, pp. 245–53.

Younes, Yves. Accès asymétrique des agents économiques à des marchés incomplets. (Asymmetric Participation of Economic Agents to Market Structures. With English summary.) *Ann. Écon. Statist.*, Oct.–Dec. 1988, (12), pp. 89–107.

———— **and Grandmont, Jean Michel.** On the Efficiency of a Monetary Equilibrium. In *Grandmont, J.-M., ed.*, 1988, 1973, pp. 199–215.

———— **and Grandmont, Jean Michel.** On the Role of Money and the Existence of a Monetary Equilibrium. In *Grandmont, J.-M., ed.*, 1988, 1972, pp. 181–98.

————; **Grandmont, Jean Michel and Laroque, Guy.** Equilibrium with Quantity Rationing and Recontracting. In *Grandmont, J.-M., ed.*, 1988, 1978, pp. 404–22.

Young, A. A. Jevons' 'Theory of Political Economy.' In *Wood, J. C., ed., Vol. 2*, 1988, 1912, pp. 51–62.

Young, Alastair. Resampling Tests of Statistical Hypotheses. In *Edwards, D. and Raun, N. E., eds.*, 1988, pp. 233–38.

Young, Andrew. Thinking about Cities in the 1990s. In *Anderson, A. and Bark, D. L., eds.*, 1988, pp. 413–25.

Young, Douglas J. and Stapleton, David C. Educational Attainment and Cohort Size. *J. Lab. Econ.*, July 1988, 6(3), pp. 330–61.

Young, Gaylen W.; Andersen, Ronald M. and Mullner, Ross M. Health Care Coalitions: Continuity and Change. In *Scheffler, R. M. and Rossiter, L. F., eds.*, 1988, pp. 165–85.

Young, H. Peyton. Distributive Justice in Taxation. *J. Econ. Theory*, April 1988, 44(2), pp. 321–35.

————. Equal Sacrifice in Taxation. In *Eichhorn, W., ed.*, 1988, pp. 563–73.

————. Individual Contribution and Just Compensation. In *[Shapley, L. S.]*, 1988, pp. 267–78.

Young, Kan H. The Effects of Taxes and Rates of Return on Foreign Direct Investment in the United States. *Nat. Tax J.*, March 1988, 41(1), pp. 109–21.

————. Short Communications: Comment on "A Neglected Method of Separating Demand and Supply in Time Series Regression," by Stephen E. Haynes and Joe A. Stone. *J. Bus. Econ. Statist.*, January 1988, 6(1), pp. 135–38.

———— **and Landefeld, J. Steven.** U.S. Trade in Services: 1970–1985. In *Candilis, W. O., ed.*, 1988, pp. 91–126.

———— **and Lawson, Ann M.** Exchange Rates and the Competitive Price Positions of U.S. Exports and Imports. *Bus. Econ.*, April 1988, 23(2), pp. 13–19.

Young, Ken. Local Government in Britain: Rationale, Structure and Finance. In *Bailey, S. J. and Paddison, R., eds.*, 1988, pp. 6–24.

Young, Leslie and Boyle, Glenn W. Asset Prices, Commodity Prices, and Money: A General Equilibrium, Rational Expectations Model. *Amer. Econ. Rev.*, March 1988, *78*(1), pp. 24–45.

Young, Linda Wilcox. Economic Development and Employment: Agroindustrialization in Mexico's *El Bajío. J. Econ. Issues*, June 1988, *22*(2), pp. 389–96.

Young, Philip K. Y. and Sontz, Ann H. L. Is Hard Work the Key to Success? A Socioeconomic Analysis of Immigrant Enterprise. *Rev. Black Polit. Econ.*, Spring 1988, *16*(4), pp. 11–31.

Young, Robert A. and Bredehoeft, John D. Risk Aversion in Conjunctive Water Use. In *O'Mara, G. T., ed.*, 1988, pp. 155–67.

_____ and Gardner, Richard L. Assessing Strategies for Control of Irrigation-Induced Salinity in the Upper Colorado River Basin. *Amer. J. Agr. Econ.*, February 1988, *70*(1), pp. 37–49.

Young, S. David. The Economic Theory of Regulation: Evidence from the Uniform CPA Examination. *Accounting Rev.*, April 1988, *63*(2), pp. 283–91.

Young, Stephen and Hood, Neil. Inward Investment and the EC: UK Evidence on Corporate Integration Strategies. In *Dunning, J. and Robson, P., eds.*, 1988, pp. 91–104.

_____ and Hood, Neil. Note on Exchange Rate Fluctuations and the Foreign-Owned Sector in Scotland. *Scot. J. Polit. Econ.*, February 1988, *35*(1), pp. 77–83.

_____; Hood, Neil and Dunlop, S. Global Strategies, Multinational Subsidiary Roles and Economic Impact in Scotland. *Reg. Stud.*, December 1988, *22*(6), pp. 487–97.

Yousefi, Mahmood and Abizadeh, Sohrab. An Empirical Re-examination of Wagner's Law. *Econ. Letters*, 1988, *26*(2), pp. 169–73.

_____ and Abizadeh, Sohrab. Growth of Government Expenditure: The Case of Canada. *Public Finance Quart.*, January 1988, *16*(1), pp. 78–100.

Yows, Linda C.; Slocum, John W., Jr. and Cron, William L. Whose Career Is Likely to Plateau? In *Timpe, A. D., ed.*, 1988, *1987*, pp. 266–78.

Yu, Seung-Hum. Health Systems of Korea. In *Sirageldin, I. and Sorkin, A., eds.*, 1988, pp. 207–17.

Yücel, Mine Kuban. Severance Tax Shifting: A Quantitative Analysis. *Resources & Energy*, September 1988, *10*(3), pp. 265–75.

Yücelt, Ugur. Comparative Study of Shopping Styles and Their Effect on Retail Management. In *Kaynak, E., ed.*, 1988, pp. 89–102.

Yue, Piyu and Barnett, William A. Semiparametric Estimation of the Asymptotically Ideal Model: The Aim Demand System. In *Rhodes, G. F., Jr. and Fomby, T. B., eds.*, 1988, pp. 229–51.

Yue, Xiao Zhi. EEC–China: Ten Years after the First Trade Agreement: The Legal Framework

and Its Practical Application. *J. World Trade*, April 1988, *22*(2), pp. 5–21.

Yui, Tsunehiko. Development, Organization, and International Competitiveness of Industrial Enterprises in Japan, 1880–1915. In *Hausman, W. J., ed.*, 1988, pp. 31–48.

_____. Functions of Japanese Trade Associations before World War II: The Case of Cartel Organizations: Comment. In *Yamazaki, H. and Miyamoto, M., eds.*, 1988, pp. 84–85.

Yui, Yuji and Tajika, Eiji. Cost of Capital and Effective Tax Rate: A Comparison of U.S. and Japanese Manufacturing Industries. *Hitotsubashi J. Econ.*, December 1988, *29*(2), pp. 181–200.

Yuji, Wang and Xiang, Yuanwang. Dynamic Simulation and Optimal Control of Urban Socioeconomic and Eco-environment System. In *Iri, M. and Yajima, K., eds.*, 1988, pp. 462–70.

Yukawa, Setsuko. The Arguments for Planning. In *Urrutia, M. and Yukawa, S., eds. (I)*, 1988, pp. 16–32.

_____. Constraints on the Development of Resource-Rich Countries: A Comparative Analysis. In *Urrutia, M. and Yukawa, S., eds. (II)*, 1988, pp. 1–40.

Yule, Brian and Parkin, David. Patient Charges and the Demand for Dental Care in Scotland, 1962–81. *Appl. Econ.*, February 1988, *20*(2), pp. 229–42.

Yun, K. Y. and Kim, Wan-Soon. Fiscal Policy and Development in Korea. *World Devel.*, January 1988, *16*(1), pp. 65–83.

Yunker, James A. A New Perspective on Market Socialism. *Comp. Econ. Stud.*, Summer 1988, *30*(2), pp. 69–116.

_____. Risk-taking as a Justification for Property Income. *J. Compar. Econ.*, March 1988, *12*(1), pp. 74–88.

_____. A World Economic Equalization Program: Refinements and Sensitivity Analysis. *World Devel.*, August 1988, *16*(8), pp. 921–33.

_____ and Krehbiel, Timothy L. Investment Analysis by the Individual Investor. *Quart. Rev. Econ. Bus.*, Winter 1988, *28*(4), pp. 90–101.

Yusoff, Mohammed Bin. Money, Prices, and Balance of Payments in Malaysia. *Indian Econ. J.*, July–September 1988, *36*(1), pp. 33–47.

Yusuf, Abdulqawi A. The Legal Framework for Stable, Remunerative and Equitible Commodity Prices in International Trade. In *Dicke, D. C. and Petersmann, E.-U., eds.*, 1988, pp. 122–46.

_____. The United Nations Draft Code of Conduct on Transfer of Technology: Problems and Prospects. In *Dicke, D. C. and Petersmann, E.-U., eds.*, 1988, pp. 301–11.

Yuzawa, Takeshi. Servants of Two Masters: British Trade Associations in the First Half of the Twentieth Century: Comment. In *Yamazaki, H. and Miyamoto, M., eds.*, 1988, pp. 199–201.

Yvars, Bernard. Dépréciation monétaire et seuil critique d'endettement. (Monetary Depreciation and Critical Level of Borrowing. With English summary.) *Écon. Soc.*, June–July 1988, 22(6–7), pp. 69–88.

van Yzeren, J. Weighting and Additivity Problems of Multilateral Comparison. In *Eichhorn, W., ed.*, 1988, pp. 157–64.

Zaardkoohi, Asghar and Masters, Marick F. Congressional Support for Unions' Positions across Diverse Legislation. *J. Lab. Res.*, Spring 1988, 9(2), pp. 149–65.

Zabalza, Antonio and Arrufat, José Luis. Efficiency and Equity Effects of Reforming the British System of Direct Taxation: A Utility-Based Simulation Methodology. *Economica*, February 1988, 55(217), pp. 21–45.

_____ **and Tzannatos, Zafiris.** The Effect of Britain's Anti-discrimination Legislation on Relative Pay and Employment: Reply. *Econ. J.*, September 1988, 98(392), pp. 839–43.

Zabell, Sandy L. and Diaconis, Persi. Updating Subjective Probability. In *Bell, D. E.; Raiffa, H. and Tversky, A., eds.*, 1988, 1982, pp. 266–83.

Zadrozny, Peter. Analytic Derivatives for Estimation of Discrete-Time, Linear-Quadratic, Dynamic, Optimization Models. *Econometrica*, March 1988, 56(2), pp. 467–72.

_____. A Consistent, Closed-Loop Solution for Infinite-Horizon, Linear-Quadratic, Dynamic Stackelberg Games. *J. Econ. Dynam. Control*, March 1988, 12(1), pp. 155–59.

Zafanolli, Wojtek. A Brief Outline of China's Second Economy. In *Feuchtwang, S.; Hussain, A. and Pairault, T., eds., Vol. 2*, 1988, pp. 138–55.

Zaghini, Enrico. On Non-basic Commodities. In *Steedman, I., ed., Vol. 2*, 1988, 1967, pp. 356–65.

Zahid, G. M.; Sarmad, Khwaja and Husain, Fazal. Investment and Inequality in Pakistan's Education Sector. *Pakistan Devel. Rev.*, Part 2, Winter 1988, 27(4), pp. 677–84.

Zahid, Khan Hasan. Government Budget Deficits and Interest Rates: The Evidence since 1971, Using Alternative Deficit Measures. *Southern Econ. J.*, January 1988, 54(3), pp. 725–31.

Zahler, Roberto. Estrategias financieras latinoamericanas: La experiencia del Cono Sur. (Latin American Financial Strategies: The Experience of the Southern Cone. With English summary.) *Colección Estud. CIEPLAN*, March 1988, (23), pp. 117–43.

Zaichenko, A. Risk and Independence in Innovative Activity. *Prob. Econ.*, October 1988, 31(6), pp. 29–46.

Zaidi, Arif Ali. Comparative Health Policies: A World of Difference: Comments. *Pakistan Devel. Rev.*, Part 1, Winter 1988, 27(4), pp. 495–97.

_____. Evidence of Fertility Decline in Karachi: Comments. *Pakistan Devel. Rev.*, Part 2, Winter 1988, 27(4), pp. 669–70.

Zaidi, Iqbal Mehdi. A Rationing Model of Imports and the Balance of Payments in Developing Countries: Theoretical Framework and an Ap-

plication to the Philippine Economy. *Appl. Econ.*, January 1988, 20(1), pp. 43–61.

Zaima, Janis K. and McCarthy, Joseph E. The Impact of Bond Rating Changes on Common Stocks and Bonds: Tests of the Wealth Redistribution Hypothesis. *Financial Rev.*, November 1988, 23(4), pp. 483–98.

Zajac, Edward E. Telecommunications: An Example of Policy Gone Awry? In *Libecap, G., ed. (II)*, 1988, pp. 221–42.

Zajdela, Hélène. IS–LM: La controverse Hicks–Keynes. (IS–LM: Mr. Hicks and the Keynesians. With English summary.) *Écon. Appl.*, 1988, 41(2), pp. 225–46.

Zakharov, V. S. Credit and Self-Financing. *Prob. Econ.*, December 1988, 31(8), pp. 95–106.

Zalai, Ernó. Recent Changes in the Planned Central Management System of Hungary and Their Background. In *Brada, J. C. and Dobozi, I., eds.*, 1988, pp. 53–65.

Zaleznik, Abraham. Decisions, Coalitions, and the Economy of the Self. In *Albanese, P. J., ed.*, 1988, pp. 101–41.

Zall, Barnaby. The U.S. Refugee Industry: Doing Well by Doing Good. In *Simcox, D. E., ed.*, 1988, pp. 258–68.

Zalokar, Nadja. Male–Female Differences in Occupational Choice and the Demand for General and Occupation-Specific Human Capital. *Econ. Inquiry*, January 1988, 26(1), pp. 59–74.

_____ **and Golding, Edward.** Unisex Insurance. In *Brown, E., ed.*, 1988, pp. 85–92.

Zaman, Arshad. Alternative Growth and Adjustment Strategies of Newly Industrializing Countries in Southeast Asia: Comments. In *Streeten, P., ed.*, 1988, pp. 95–105.

Zaman, Mir A. and Rozeff, Michael S. Market Efficiency and Insider Trading: New Evidence. *J. Bus.*, January 1988, 61(1), pp. 25–44.

Zamanian, Zaman. On the Impossibility of Factor Accumulation Causing a Real Income Loss in a Small, Underdeveloped Economy. In *Missouri Valley Economic Assoc.*, 1988, pp. 34–38.

Zamar, Ruben H. and Yohai, Victor J. High Breakdown-Point Estimates of Regression by Means of the Minimization of an Efficient Scale. *J. Amer. Statist. Assoc.*, June 1988, 83(402), pp. 406–13.

Zame, William R. and Bennett, Elaine. Bargaining in Cooperative Games. *Int. J. Game Theory*, 1988, 17(4), pp. 279–300.

_____ **and Wooders, Myrna Holtz.** Values of Large Finite Games. In *[Shapley, L. S.]*, 1988, pp. 195–206.

von Zameck, Walburga. Im Schatten der Schattenökonomie: Die Hausarbeit. (Shadow Economy and Housework. With English summary.) *Jahr. Nationalökon. Statist.*, October 1988, 205(4), pp. 289–99.

_____. Konjunkturbedingte Defizite und materieller Haushaltsausgleich. (Cyclical Conditioned Deficits and the Annually Balanced Budget. With English summary.) *Jahr. Natio-*

nalökon. Statist., March 1988, *204*(3), pp. 197–207.

Zamir, Shmuel. Topics in Noncooperative Game Theory. In *Ambrosetti, A.; Gori, F. and Lucchetti, R., eds.*, 1988, pp. 72–128.

Zandamela, Rogério L. The Implications of Wage Indexation on the Magnitude of Macroeconomic Fluctuations in a Simple Closed Economy. *Southern Econ. J.*, October 1988, *55*(2), pp. 288–302.

_____. The Macroeconomic Implications of Wage Indexation in a Two-Sector Open Economy. *Weltwirtsch. Arch.*, 1988, *124*(2), pp. 269–86.

Zander, Ernst. Chances for Flexibility in Cooperation between Company Management and Works Councils. In *Dlugos, G.; Dorow, W. and Weiermair, K., eds.*, 1988, pp. 469–75.

Zang, Israel; Kamien, Morton I. and Tauman, Yair. Optimal License Fees for a New Product. *Math. Soc. Sci.*, August 1988, *16*(1), pp. 77–106.

Zangenehzadeh, Hamid. Grade Inflation: A Way Out. *J. Econ. Educ.*, Summer 1988, *19*(3), pp. 217–26.

_____. Grade Inflation: A Way Out: Reply. *J. Econ. Educ.*, Summer 1988, *19*(3), pp. 230.

Zaninotto, Enrico and Pozzana, Roberto. Technical Efficiency and Market Structure for Retail Firms: A Nonparametric Approach. *Ricerche Econ.*, Oct.–Dec. 1988, *42*(4), pp. 606–29.

Zannoni, Diane; McKenna, Edward and Wade, Maurice. Keynes, Rawls, Uncertainty, and the Liberal Theory of the State. *Econ. Philos.*, October 1988, *4*(2), pp. 221–41.

Zant, Wouter. Social Security Wealth and Aggregate Consumption: An Extended Life-Cycle Model Estimated for the Netherlands. *De Economist*, March 1988, *136*(1), pp. 136–53.

Zapata, Hector O.; Hudson, Michael A. and Garcia, Philip. Identifying Causal Relationships between Nonstationary Stochastic Processes: An Examination of Alternative Approaches in Small Sample. *Western J. Agr. Econ.*, December 1988, *13*(2), pp. 202–15.

Zapata, Juan Antonio. Estimating the Externalities of Groundwater Use in Western Argentina. In *O'Mara, G. T., ed.*, 1988, pp. 141–54.

Zaporowski, Mark and Lahiri, Kajal. A Comparison of Alternative Real Rate Estimates. *Oxford Bull. Econ. Statist.*, August 1988, *50*(3), pp. 303–12.

_____; Lahiri, Kajal and Teigland, Christie. Interest Rates and the Subjective Probability Distribution of Inflation Forecasts. *J. Money, Credit, Banking*, May 1988, *20*(2), pp. 233–48.

Zappala, Jon and Rimmer, Malcolm. Labour Market Flexibility and the Second Tier. *Australian Bull. Lab.*, September 1988, *14*(4), pp. 564–91.

Zardkoohi, Asghar. Market Structure and Campaign Contributions: Does Concentration Matter? A Reply. *Public Choice*, August 1988, *58*(2), pp. 187–91.

_____ and Keim, Gerald D. Looking for Leverage in PAC Markets: Corporate and Labor

Contributions Considered. *Public Choice*, July 1988, *58*(1), pp. 21–34.

Zareba, Marian; Florkowski, Wojciech J. and Hill, Lowell D. The Impact of Agricultural Policy Changes on Food Production in Poland. *Comp. Econ. Stud.*, Fall 1988, *30*(3), pp. 16–32.

Zarkin, Gary A. and Biddle, Jeff E. Worker Preferences and Market Compensation for Job Risk. *Rev. Econ. Statist.*, November 1988, *70*(4), pp. 660–67.

_____ and Cook, Philip J. Crime and the Business Cycle. In *Alper, N. O. and Hellman, D. A., eds.*, 1988, pp. 60–74.

Zarowin, Paul. Non-linearities and Nominal Contracting Effects: The Case of the Depreciation Tax Shield. *J. Acc. Econ.*, April 1988, *10*(2), pp. 89–110.

Zaslavsky, Victor. Ethnic Group Divided: Social Stratification and Nationality Policy in the Soviet Union. In *Potichnyj, P. J., ed.*, 1988, pp. 218–28.

Zavatta, Roberto. The Paper Industry in the European Economic Community. In *de Jong, H. W., ed.*, 1988, pp. 105–25.

Zax, Jeffrey S. The Effects of Jurisdiction Types and Numbers on Local Public Finance. In *Rosen, H. S., ed.*, 1988, pp. 79–103.

_____. Fringe Benefits, Income Tax Exemptions, and Implicit Subsidies. *J. Public Econ.*, November 1988, *37*(2), pp. 171–83.

_____. Wages, Nonwage Compensation, and Municipe Unions. *Ind. Relat.*, Fall 1988, *27*(3), pp. 301–17.

_____; Freeman, Richard B. and Ichniowski, Casey. Collective Organization of Labor in the Public Sector: Appendix A. In *Freeman, R. B. and Ichniowski, C., eds.*, 1988, pp. 365–98.

_____ and Ichniowski, Casey. The Effects of Public Sector Unionism on Pay, Employment, Department Budgets, and Municipal Expenditures. In *Freeman, R. B. and Ichniowski, C., eds.*, 1988, pp. 323–61.

Zbeetnoff, D. M. and Josephson, R. M. The Value of Probability Distribution Information for Fertilizer Application Decisions. *Can. J. Agr. Econ.*, Part 2, December 1988, *36*(4), pp. 837–44.

Zech, Charles E.; Webster, Elaine and Mathis, Edward J. The Impact of Foreign Exports on State Economies: An Economic Base Multiplier Analysis. In *Missouri Valley Economic Assoc.*, 1988, pp. 25–29.

Zecher, Richard. After the Crash: Linkages between Stocks and Futures: Regulatory Issues. In *MacKay, R. J., ed.*, 1988, pp. 49–52.

Zechner, Josef; Brennan, Michael J. and Maksimovic, Vojislav. Vendor Financing. *J. Finance*, December 1988, *43*(5), pp. 1127–41.

Zeckhauser, Richard. Health Care in America: The Political Economy of Hospitals and Health Insurance: Foreword. In *Frech, H. E., III, ed.*, 1988, pp. xvii–xxiii.

_____ and Rodrik, Dani. The Dilemma of Government Responsiveness. *J. Policy Anal. Manage.*, Fall 1988, 7(4), pp. 601–20.

_____ and Samuelson, William. Status Quo Bias in Decision Making. *J. Risk Uncertainty*, March 1988, 1(1), pp. 7–59.

Zeddies, J. and Henze, A. EC Programmes, Economic Effects and Cost Benefit Considerations on Adjustments in EC Agriculture. *Europ. Rev. Agr. Econ.*, 1988, 15(2–3), pp. 191–210.

Zee, Howell H. On the Uncertain Fiscal Policy Effects in a Simple Open-Economy Macro Model. *Public Finance*, 1988, 43(3), pp. 445–65.

_____. The Sustainability and Optimality of Government Debt. *Int. Monet. Fund Staff Pap.*, December 1988, 35(4), pp. 658–85.

Zeesman, Allen; Messinger, Hans and Fedyk, Frank. The Size and Distribution of the Poverty Gap in Canada: A Micro Analysis of Variations among Demographic Groups. *Rev. Income Wealth*, September 1988, 34(3), pp. 275–88.

Zehnwirth, Ben. A Generalization of the Kalman Filter for Models with State-Dependent Observation Variance. *J. Amer. Statist. Assoc.*, March 1988, 83(401), pp. 164–67.

Zeira, Joseph. Risk Reducing Fiscal Policies and Economic Growth. In *Helpman, E.; Razin, A. and Sadka, E., eds.*, 1988, pp. 65–74.

_____; Segal, Uzi and Spivak, Avia. Precautionary Saving and Risk Aversion: An Anticipated Utility Approach. *Econ. Letters*, 1988, 27(3), pp. 223–27.

Zeithaml, Carl P.; Keim, Gerald D. and Baysinger, Barry D. Toward an Integrated Strategic Management Process: An Empirical Review of Corporate Political Strategy. In *Grant, J. H., ed.*, 1988, pp. 377–93.

Zeitzer, Ilene R. Disability Case Management in Israel. *Soc. Sec. Bull.*, June 1988, 51(6), pp. 34–37.

Zel'dner, A. Price Relations and Exchange Between Agriculture and Industry. *Prob. Econ.*, January 1988, 30(9), pp. 87–103.

Zeldes, Stephen P. and Miron, Jeffrey A. Seasonality, Cost Shocks, and the Production Smoothing Models of Inventories. *Econometrica*, July 1988, 56(4), pp. 877–908.

_____ and O'Connell, Stephen A. Rational Ponzi Games. *Int. Econ. Rev.*, August 1988, 29(3), pp. 431–50.

Zeleny, Milan; Hessel, Marek P. and Mooney, Marta. Integrated Process Management: A Management Technology for the New Competitive Era. In *Starr, M. K., ed.*, 1988, pp. 121–58.

Zelhorst, D. and de Haan, J. The Empirical Evidence on the Ricardian Equivalence Hypothesis. *Kredit Kapital*, 1988, 21(3), pp. 407–21.

Zelhorst, H. Dick and de Haan, Jakob. The Relationship between Real Deficits and Real Growth: A Critique. *J. Post Keynesian Econ.*, Fall 1988, 11(1), pp. 148–60.

Zelleke, Girma. Deviation of Exchange Rates from Purchasing Power Parity: An Empirical

Study. In *Pennsylvania Economic Association*, 1988, pp. 388–403.

Zellner, Arnold. Bayesian Analysis in Econometrics. *J. Econometrics*, January 1988, 37(1), pp. 27–50.

_____. Causality and Causal Laws in Economics. *J. Econometrics*, Sept.–Oct. 1988, 39(1–2), pp. 7–21.

_____; Bauwens, Luc and van Dijk, Herman K. Bayesian Specification Analysis and Estimation of Simultaneous Equation Models Using Monte Carlo Methods. *J. Econometrics*, May–June 1988, 38(1–2), pp. 39–72.

_____ and Highfield, Richard A. Calculation of Maximum Entropy Distributions and Approximation of Marginal Posterior Distributions. *J. Econometrics*, February 1988, 37(2), pp. 195–209.

Zellner, James A. Industrial Organization: Some Applications for Managerial Decisions. *Amer. J. Agr. Econ.*, May 1988, 70(2), pp. 469–74.

_____. Trade Effects of U.S. Commodity Programs. *J. Agr. Econ. Res.*, Winter 1988, 40(1), pp. 30–37.

Zeman, Karel. Involving the European CMEA Members in the International Division of Labor: The Long-term Outlook. *Soviet E. Europ. Foreign Trade*, Summer 1988, 24(2), pp. 73–92.

_____ and Chomát, Jiří. The Fuels and Energy Balance. *Czech. Econ. Digest.*, June 1988, (4), pp. 71–86.

Zemlička, Jiří. Foreign Prices in the Restructuring of the Economic Mechanism. *Czech. Econ. Digest.*, December 1988, (8), pp. 48–70.

_____. New Principles of Planning in Foreign Trade. *Czech. Econ. Digest.*, November 1988, (7), pp. 21–42.

Zeng, Yi. Changing Demographic Characteristics and the Family Status of Chinese Women. *Population Stud.*, July 1988, 42(2), pp. 183–203.

Zerbato, Michel. Une économie mondiale d'endettement appelle-t-elle un nouveau système monétaire international? (Does a World Overdraft Economy Need a New International Monetary System? With English summary.) *Écon. Soc.*, June–July 1988, 22(6–7), pp. 181–97.

Zerbe, Richard O., Jr. and Urban, Nicole. Including the Public Interest in Theories of Regulation. In *Zerbe, R. O., Jr., ed.*, 1988, pp. 1–23.

Zerby, John and Khan, Habibullah. Relationships between Technological Change and Social Development: A Comparative Study. In *Tisdell, C. and Maitra, P., eds.*, 1988, pp. 166–87.

Zervoyianni, Athina. Exchange Rate Overshooting, Currency Substitution and Monetary Policy. *Manchester Sch. Econ. Soc. Stud.*, September 1988, 56(3), pp. 247–67.

Zeuthen, Hans E. and Paldam, Martin. The Expansion of the Public Sector in Denmark—A Post Festum? In *Lybeck, J. A. and Henrekson, M., eds.*, 1988, pp. 157–86.

Zey, Michael G. Mentor Programs: Making the Right Moves. In *Timpe, A. D., ed.*, 1988, 1985, pp. 300–306.

Zhang, Fengbo. A Theoretical Study of Several Current Macroeconomic Problems. *Chinese Econ. Stud.*, Spring 1988, *21*(3), pp. 40–58.

Zhang, Hongying. Composite Report on the Symposium on Problems of Contracted Youth Labor in Eight Municipalities. *Chinese Econ. Stud.*, Summer 1988, *21*(4), pp. 92–100.

Zhang, Jian and Li, Zheng. P.R.C.'s Price Reform and the Trend in Energy Prices. *Energy J.*, Special Issue, 1988, *9*, pp. 45–69.

Zhang, Qingwu. Basic Facts on the Household Registration System. *Chinese Econ. Stud.*, Fall 1988, *22*(1), pp. 22–106.

Zhang, Qiren and Xiong, Guilin. Modelling and Optimization of Public Traffic Large Scale Systems. In *Iri, M. and Yajima, K., eds.*, 1988, pp. 426–35.

Zhang, Shaojie and Zhao, Yujiang. Restraining the Payment Capability of China's Grass-Roots Banks. *Chinese Econ. Stud.*, Spring 1988, *21*(3), pp. 24–39.

Zhang, Wei-Bin. HOPF Bifurcations in Multisector Models of Optimal Economic Growth. *Econ. Letters*, 1988, *26*(4), pp. 329–34.

_____. Limit Cycles in van der Ploeg's Model of Economic Growth and Conflict over the Distribution of Income. *J. Econ. (Z. Nationalökon.)*, 1988, *48*(2), pp. 159–73.

_____ **and Andersson, Åke E.** The Two-Dimensional Continuous Spatial Input–Output System. *Ricerche Econ.*, April–June 1988, *42*(2), pp. 222–42.

Zhang, Xin. On the Contradiction between the Economic Growth Rate and Improvement of People's Well-Being. *Chinese Econ. Stud.*, Spring 1988, *21*(3), pp. 59–77.

Zhang, Yangui. The Economic Environment and China's Model for the Utilization of Foreign Capital. In *Teng, W. and Wang, N. T., eds.*, 1988, pp. 183–90.

Zhang, Zhensheng; Feng, Ai and Wang, Yulu. Why Can a Large City Like Qinhuangdao Not Accommodate a Small Individual Venture? *Chinese Econ. Stud.*, Winter 1987–88, *21*(2), pp. 28–33.

Zhao, Renwei and Wu, Jinglian. The Dual Pricing System in China's Industry. In *Reynolds, B. L., ed.*, 1988, *1987*, pp. 19–28.

Zhao, Ruizhang. The Hiring of Laborers in Rural Taishan County, Guangdong: A Survey. *Chinese Econ. Stud.*, Winter 1987–88, *21*(2), pp. 73–89.

Zhao, Yujiang and Zhang, Shaojie. Restraining the Payment Capability of China's Grass-Roots Banks. *Chinese Econ. Stud.*, Spring 1988, *21*(3), pp. 24–39.

Zheng, Quan. Theory and Methods for General Optimization—An Integral Approach. In *Eiselt, H. A. and Pederzoli, G., eds.*, 1988, pp. 15–37.

Zhijun, Lin. A Survey of Current Developments in Chinese Accounting. In *Most, K. S., ed.*, 1988, pp. 99–100.

Zhou, Xiaochuan and Zhu, Li. China's Banking System: Current Status, Perspective on Re-

form. In *Reynolds, B. L., ed.*, 1988, *1987*, pp. 109–19.

Zhu, Ang. China's Investment Environment, Laws, and Regulations. In *Dorian, J. P. and Fridley, D. G., eds.*, 1988, pp. 127–36.

Zhu, Li and Zhou, Xiaochuan. China's Banking System: Current Status, Perspective on Reform. In *Reynolds, B. L., ed.*, 1988, *1987*, pp. 109–19.

Zhu, Qingfang. On the Evolution and Changes of Individual Economy and Countermeasures. *Chinese Econ. Stud.*, Winter 1987–88, *21*(2), pp. 100–114.

Zhu, Yu and Jamshidian, Farshid. Analysis of Bonds with Imbedded Options. In *Fabozzi, F. J., ed.*, 1988, pp. 63–95.

_____ **and Kavee, Robert C.** Performance of Portfolio Insurance Strategies. *J. Portfol. Manage.*, Spring 1988, *14*(3), pp. 48–54.

Zhukovin, V. E. Effective Convolutions of Vector Preference Relations in Decision Making Problems. In *Kacprzyk, J. and Roubens, M., eds.*, 1988, pp. 96–105.

Zhuravlev, S. N. The Renewal Cycle of Fixed Assets. *Matekon*, Spring 1988, *24*(3), pp. 52–79.

Ziabrev, N. B. One Problem of the Optimal Planning of the Production of Complex Items. *Matekon*, Winter 1988–89, *25*(2), pp. 33–44.

Ziegert, A. L. The Demand for Housing Additions: An Empirical Analysis. *Amer. Real Estate Urban Econ. Assoc. J.*, Winter 1988, *16*(4), pp. 479–92.

Ziegler, Joseph A. Spatial Variations in Production Costs. *J. Urban Econ.*, January 1988, *23*(1), pp. 101–14.

Ziegler, R.; Brüderl, J. and Diekmann, A. Stellensuchdauer und Anfangseinkommen bei Hochschulabsolventen. Ein empirischer Beitrag zur Job-Search-Theorie. (Duration of Job Search and First Income of University Graduates: An Empirical Contribution to Job Search Theory. With English summary.) *Z. Wirtschaft. Sozialwissen.*, 1988, *108*(2), pp. 247–70.

Ziemba, William T. The Buying and Selling Behavior of Individual Investors at the Turn of the Year: Discussion. *J. Finance*, July 1988, *43*(3), pp. 717–19.

_____ **and Thaler, Richard H.** Parimutuel Betting Markets: Racetracks and Lotteries. *J. Econ. Perspectives*, Spring 1988, *2*(2), pp. 161–74.

Zieschang, Maatthias. Ein dynamisches Wechselkursmodell unter Berücksichtigung wesentlicher Elemente der Finanzmarktansätze und der traditionllen Wechselkurstheorie. (A Dynamic Exchange Rate Model Taking into Account Essential Elements of the Asset Market and the Traditional Exchange Rate Theory. With English summary.) *Z. Wirtschaft. Sozialwissen.*, 1988, *108*(1), pp. 113–30.

Zietz, Joachim. Adequacy Tests for Linear Regression Models: A Nontechnical Overview with Applications. *Jahr. Nationalökon. Statist.*, March 1988, *204*(3), pp. 255–72.

_____. Strategies for Dealing with Agriculture

in the Uruguay Round. *J. Agr. Econ.*, September 1988, *39*(3), pp. 382–86.

_____. Trade Policy and Structural Change in the Private Enterprise System: The Case of the Apparel Industry. In *Association of Private Education*, 1988, pp. 64–72.

_____ and Weichert, Ronald. A Dynamic Singular Equation System of Asset Demand. *Europ. Econ. Rev.*, July 1988, *32*(6), pp. 1349–57.

Zilberfarb, Ben-Zion. The Effects of Foreign Exchange Risk and Return on the Demand for Domestic Balances. *Europ. Econ. Rev.*, July 1988, *32*(6), pp. 1359–68.

Zilberman, David; Bigman, David and Newbery, David M. New Approaches in Agricultural Policy Research: Discussion. *Amer. J. Agr. Econ.*, May 1988, *70*(2), pp. 460–61.

_____; Hochman, Eithan and Just, Richard E. Estimation of Multicrop Production Functions: Reply. *Amer. J. Agr. Econ.*, August 1988, *70*(3), pp. 733–34.

_____ and Just, Richard E. The Effects of Agricultural Development Policies on Income Distribution and Technological Change in Agriculture. *J. Devel. Econ.*, March 1988, *28*(2), pp. 193–216.

_____ and Just, Richard E. A Methodology for Evaluating Equity Implications of Environmental Policy Decisions in Agriculture. *Land Econ.*, February 1988, *64*(1), pp. 37–52.

_____ and Lichtenberg, Erik. Efficient Regulation of Environmental Health Risks. *Quart. J. Econ.*, February 1988, *103*(1), pp. 167–78.

_____; Lichtenberg, Erik and Parker, Douglas D. Marginal Analysis of Welfare Costs of Environmental Policies: The Case of Pesticide Regulation. *Amer. J. Agr. Econ.*, November 1988, *70*(4), pp. 867–74.

_____ and Putler, Daniel S. Computer Use in Agriculture: Evidence from Tulare County, California. *Amer. J. Agr. Econ.*, November 1988, *70*(4), pp. 790–802.

Zilcha, Itzhak; Chew, Soo Hong and Epstein, Larry G. A Correspondence Theorem between Expected Utility and Smooth Utility. *J. Econ. Theory*, October 1988, *46*(1), pp. 186–93.

_____ and Safra, Zvi. Efficient Sets with and without the Expected Utility Hypothesis. *J. Math. Econ.*, 1988, *17*(4), pp. 369–84.

Zilz, Ulrike and Sexton, Thomas R. On the Wisdom of Mandatory Drug Testing. *J. Policy Anal. Manage.*, Spring 1988, *7*(3), pp. 542–47.

Zimbalist, Andrew. Cuba's External Economy: Reflections on Export Dependence, Soviet Aid and Foreign Debt. *Comp. Econ. Stud.*, Summer 1988, *30*(2), pp. 21–46.

_____. Cuban Political Economy and Cubanology: An Overview. In *Zimbalist, A., ed.*, 1988, pp. 1–21.

_____. Interpreting Cuban Planning: Between a Rock and a Hard Place. In *Zimbalist, A., ed.*, 1988, pp. 66–82.

_____. Quinquennial Growth Rates in the CMEA: A Note on Eurocentrism. *Comp. Econ. Stud.*, Fall 1988, *30*(3), pp. 94–95.

_____. Struggle against Dependence: Nontradi-

tional Export Growth in Central America and the Caribbean: Costa Rica. In *Paus, E., ed.*, 1988, pp. 21–40.

_____. Struggle against Dependence: Nontraditional Export Growth in Central America and the Caribbean: Panama. In *Paus, E., ed.*, 1988, pp. 85–102.

_____. Struggle against Dependence: Nontraditional Export Growth in Central America and the Caribbean: Cuba. In *Paus, E., ed.*, 1988, pp. 169–92.

_____ and Brundenius, Claes. Cubanology and Cuban Economic Performance. In *Zimbalist, A., ed.*, 1988, pp. 39–65.

Zimmer, Michael A. and Nakosteen, Robert A. Mobility of Labor between Employers and Industries. In *Missouri Valley Economic Assoc.*, 1988, pp. 155–67.

Zimmerman, Dennis. The Intergovernmental Struggle over Tax-Exempt Bond Reform. In *Bell, M. E., ed.*, 1988, pp. 101–23.

Zimmerman, Gary C. and Bennett, Barbara A. U.S. Banks' Exposure to Developing Countries: An Examination of Recent Trends. *Fed. Res. Bank San Francisco Econ. Rev.*, Spring 1988, (2), pp. 14–29.

Zimmerman, Martin B. Regulatory Treatment of Abandoned Property: Incentive Effects and Policy Issues. *J. Law Econ.*, April 1988, *31*(1), pp. 127–44.

_____ and Borenstein, Severin. Market Incentives for Safe Commercial Airline Operation. *Amer. Econ. Rev.*, December 1988, *78*(5), pp. 913–35.

Zimmermann, Andreas J. and Schelbert-Syfrig, Heidi. Konkurrenz und Umweltschutz. Wald- und Holzwirtschaft zwischen Ökonomie und Ökologie. (Competition and Environment Protection. With English summary.) *Schweiz. Z. Volkswirtsch. Statist.*, September 1988, *124*(3), pp. 289–302.

Zimmermann, Friedrich. Austria: Contrasting Tourist Seasons and Contrasting Regions. In *Williams, A. M. and Shaw, G., eds.*, 1988, pp. 145–61.

Zimmermann, Heinz. Eine Analyse des Couponabschlages bei schweizerischen Optionsanleihen. (The Coupon Discount of Bonds with Warrants in Switzerland: An Empirical Analysis. With English summary.) *Schweiz. Z. Volkswirtsch. Statist.*, September 1988, *124*(3), pp. 405–19.

_____; Cordero, Ricardo and Dubacher, René. Zur Entwicklung des neuen Swiss Market Index (SMI) als Grundlage für schweizerische Indexkontrakte: Eine Evaluation potentieller Aktienindices. (On the Development of the Swiss Market Index (SMI) for Index Contracts: An Evaluation of Potential Indices. With English summary.) *Schweiz. Z. Volkswirtsch. Statist.*, December 1988, *124*(4), pp. 575–600.

_____ and Loderer, Claudio. Stock Offerings in a Different Institutional Setting: The Swiss Case, 1973–1983. *J. Banking Finance*, September 1988, *12*(3), pp. 353–78.

Zimmermann, Horst. Fiscal Pressure on the "Tax

State." In *Hanusch, H.*, ed., 1988, pp. 255–73.

Zimmermann, Jean-Benoît. L'équilibre oligopolistique face à la transformation des modes d'organisation industrielle et de la concurrence. (Oligopolistic Equilibrium Face with the Transformation of Industrial Organization and Competition. With English summary.) *Écon. Soc.*, Nov.–Dec. 1988, 22(11–12), pp. 221–40.

Zimmermann, Klaus. Environmental Problems and Employment Opportunities: Comment. In *Kregel, J. A.; Matzner, E. and Roncaglia, A.*, eds., 1988, pp. 291–94.

——. Umweltpolitik und integrierte Technologien: Entwicklungen und Determinanten in empirischer Analyse. (Environmental Policy and Integrated Technologies: Patterns and Determinants of Technological Adjustment in German Industry. With English summary.) *Konjunkturpolitik*, 1988, 34(5–6), pp. 327–51.

Zimmermann, Klaus F. The Impact on Labor Supply of a Shorter Workday: A Microeconometric Discrete/Continuous Choice Approach: Comment. In *Hart, R. A.*, ed., 1988, pp. 225–27.

——. Wurzeln der modernen ökonomischen Bevölkerungstheorie in der deutschen Forschung um 1900. (Roots of Modern Population Economics in the German Literature around 1900. With English summary.) *Jahr. Nationalökon. Statist.*, August 1988, 205(2), pp. 116–30.

Zinam, Oleg. On Resolution of Conflicting Preferences, Economists' Black Boxes and Paradigmatic Myopia. *Rivista Int. Sci. Econ. Com.*, June 1988, 35(6), pp. 489–506.

Zingler, Ervin K. Veblen vs. Commons: A Comparative Evaluation. In *Samuels, W. J.*, ed., *Vol. 1*, 1988, *1974*, pp. 220–42.

Zini, Álvaro Antônio, Jr. Funçoes de exportaçao e de importaçao para o Brasil. (With English summary.) *Pesquisa Planejamento Econ.*, December 1988, 18(3), pp. 615–61.

Zinkhan, F. Christian. Is Enhanced Bank Prestige a Possible Motive for Bank Mergers? *J. Behav. Econ.*, Summer 1988, 17(2), pp. 149–56.

Zioganas, Christos M. Defining and Determining a 'Fair' Standard of Living for the Farm Family. *Europ. Rev. Agr. Econ.*, 1988, 15(1), pp. 55–65.

Zirger, Billie Jo and Maidique, Modesto A. The New Product Learning Cycle. In *Grønhaug, K. and Kaufmann, G.*, eds., 1988, *1985*, pp. 407–31.

Zis, George. Flexible Exchange Rates: The Failure of a Cure. In *[Frowen, S.]*, 1988, pp. 102–13.

Zisler, Randall C.; Firstenberg, Paul M. and Ross, Stephen A. Real Estate: The Whole Story. *J. Portfol. Manage.*, Spring 1988, 14(3), pp. 22–34.

Zodrow, George R. Eliminating State and Local Tax Deductibility: A General Equilibrium Model of Revenue Effects. In *Rosen, H. S.*, ed., 1988, pp. 177–210.

——. The Windfall Recapture Tax: Issues of

Theory and Design. *Public Finance Quart.*, October 1988, 16(4), pp. 387–424.

Zola, Irving Kenneth. Policies and Programs Concerning Aging and Disability: Toward a Unifying Agenda. In *Sullivan, S. and Lewin, M. E.*, eds., 1988, pp. 90–130.

Zoller, Maureen and Gaddie, Robert. New Stage of Process Price System Developed for the Producer Price Index. *Mon. Lab. Rev.*, April 1988, 111(4), pp. 3–16.

Zorn, Elayne and Healy, Kevin. Lake Titicaca's Campesino-Controlled Tourism. In *Annis, S. and Hakim, P.*, eds., 1988, pp. 45–57.

Zorn, Kurt and Mikesell, John L. State Lotteries for Public Revenue. *Public Budg. Finance*, Spring 1988, 8(1), pp. 38–47.

Zorn, Peter M. An Analysis of Household Mobility and Tenure Choice: An Empirical Study of Korea. *J. Urban Econ.*, September 1988, 24(2), pp. 113–28.

—— and Schwartz, Seymour I. A Critique of Quasiexperimental and Statistical Controls for Measuring Program Effects: Application to Urban Growth Control. *J. Policy Anal. Manage.*, Spring 1988, 7(3), pp. 491–505.

Zschock, Dieter K. Health Care in Peru: Resources and Policy: Introduction. In *Zschock, D. K.*, ed., 1988, pp. 1–14.

——. The Ministry of Health: Financing and Coverage. In *Zschock, D. K.*, ed., 1988, pp. 197–227.

—— and Gwynne, Gretchen. Health Care in Peru: Inferences and Options. In *Zschock, D. K.*, ed., 1988, pp. 259–71.

Zuber, Richard A. and Gandar, John M. Lifting the Television Blackout on No-Shows at Football Games. *Atlantic Econ. J.*, June 1988, 16(2), pp. 63–73.

——; Johnson, R. Stafford and Fiore, Lyle. A Note on the Investment Performances of Different Price-Earnings Stock. *Rivista Int. Sci. Econ. Com.*, Oct.–Nov. 1988, 35(10–11), pp. 1067–74.

Zuberi, Habib A. and Beladi, Hamid. Environmental Constraints and a Dynamic Model for Energy Development. *Energy Econ.*, January 1988, 10(1), pp. 18–28.

Zuckerman, Dror. Job Search with General Stochastic Offer Arrival Rates. *J. Econ. Dynam. Control*, November 1988, 12(4), pp. 679–84.

Zuckerman, Gilroy J. and Bublitz, Bruce O. Discounting Deferred Taxes: A New Approach. In *Schwartz, B. N.*, ed., 1988, pp. 55–69.

Zuckerman, Stephen. Controlling Medicare Outlays: Will Prepaid Health Plans Work? In *Brown, E.*, ed., 1988, pp. 78–84.

Zuehlke, Thomas W. and Rasmussen, David W. The Evaluation of Residential Living Space. *Rev. Reg. Stud.*, Spring 1988, 18(2), pp. 47–53.

—— and Rasmussen, David W. A Search Model of Housing Market Transactions. *Southern Econ. J.*, January 1988, 54(3), pp. 623–29.

Zufryden, Fred S. and McBride, Richard D. An Integer Programming Approach to the Optimal

Product Line Selection Problem. *Marketing Sci.*, Spring 1988, 7(2), pp. 126–40.

Zuidema, J. R. Carl Menger, Author of a Research Programme. *J. Econ. Stud.*, 1988, 15(3–4), pp. 13–35.

Zuidema, R. P. On the Austrian Contribution to Capital Theory. *J. Econ. Stud.*, 1988, 15(3–4), pp. 64–78.

Zumaran Paz, Jorge; Akaishi, Giselda and Tison, Elisabeth. Latin and Central America: The Challenge to the United States. In *Lavigne, M., ed.*, 1988, pp. 182–211.

Zumpano, Leonard V. and Hooks, Donald L. The Real Estate Brokerage Market: A Critical Re-evaluation. *Amer. Real Estate Urban Econ. Assoc. J.*, Spring 1988, 16(1), pp. 1–16.

Zund, André. Switzerland and the Seventh Directive. In *Gray, S. J. and Coenenberg, A. G., eds.*, 1988, pp. 143–54.

Zupan, Mark A. The Relative Size of Supply/Demand Elasticity and Tax Incidence. *Econ. Inquiry*, April 1988, 26(2), pp. 361–63.

Zurayk, Huda. Health Information for Public Health Policies and Services in Developing Countries. In *Sirageldin, I. and Sorkin, A., eds.*, 1988, pp. 57–73.

Zuscovitch, Ehud. Prix relatifs et relativité des prix. (On Relative Prices and Price Relativity. With English summary.) *Écon. Appl.*, 1988, 41(3), pp. 479–502.

_____ **and Willinger, Marc.** Towards the Economics of Information-Intensive Production Systems: The Case of Advanced Materials. In *Dosi, G., et al., eds.*, 1988, pp. 239–55.

Zuvekas, Clarence. The Economic Crisis in Central America. In *Jorge, A. and Salazar-Carrillo, J., eds.*, 1988, pp. 101–22.

Zwanziger, Jack and Melnick, Glenn A. The Effects of Hospital Competition and the Medicare PPS Program on Hospital Cost Behavior in California. *J. Health Econ.*, December 1988, 7(4), pp. 301–20.

Zwartendyk, Jan. Prospects for the Canadian Mineral Endowment. In *Richardson, P. R. and Gesing, R., eds.*, 1988, pp. 67–76.

von Zwehl, Wolfgang. Die Kalkulation kommunaler Benutzungsgebren in betriebswirtschaftlicher Sicht. (With English summary.) *Z. Betriebswirtshaft*, January 1988, 58(1), pp. 155–70.

Zweifel, Peter. Das Jahresgutachten 1987 des Sachverständigenrats für die Konzertierte Aktion im Gesundheitswesen: Ein Kommentar aus schweizerischer Sicht. (With English summary.) *J. Inst. Theoretical Econ.*, April 1988, 144(2), pp. 418–26.

_____. Hospital Finance in Switzerland. In *Furubotn, E. G. and Richter, R., eds.*, 1988, pp. 79–120.

_____. Premium Rebates for No Claims: The West German Experience. In *Frech, H. E., III, ed.*, 1988, pp. 323–52.

_____ **and Beck, K.** Warum eine Grenzkostentarifierung für Elektrizität? (Why Marginal Cost Pricing of Electricity? With English summary.) *Schweiz. Z. Volkswirtsch. Statist.*, December 1988, 124(4), pp. 543–58.

_____ **and Kofler, Eduard.** Exploiting Linear Partial Information for Optimal Use of Forecasts: With an Application to U.S. Economic Policy. *Int. J. Forecasting*, 1988, 4(1), pp. 15–32.

Zwemmer, J. W. and Plante-Failé, Marianne. Netherlands: Interest: Withholding Tax or No Withholding Tax? *Bull. Int. Fiscal Doc.*, Aug.–Sept. 1988, 42(8–9), pp. 365–67.

Zwick, Rami; Funk, Sandra G. and Rapoport, Amnon. Selection of Portfolios with Risky and Riskless Assets: Experimental Tests of Two Expected Utility Models. *J. Econ. Psych.*, June 1988, 9(2), pp. 169–94.

_____ **and Stein, William E.** Fuzzy Random Variables. In *Kacprzyk, J. and Fedrizzi, M., eds.*, 1988, pp. 66–74.

Zycher, Benjamin. Economic Efficiency and "Prudence" Analysis of Power Plant Investment. *Contemp. Policy Issues*, July 1988, 6(3), pp. 42–59.

van Zyl, J. and Groenewald, J. A. Effects of Protection on South African Commercial Agriculture. *J. Agr. Econ.*, September 1988, 39(3), pp. 387–401.

_____; **Vink, N. and Fenyes, T. I.** Structural Imbalances in South African Agriculture. *S. Afr. J. Econ.*, June–Sept. 1988, 56(2–3), pp. 181–95.

Zylberberg, André. L'économie mathématique chez les actuaires français au temps de Walras (1870–1914). (Mathematical Economics among the French Actuaries in Walras's Time [1870–1914]. With English summary.) *Écon. Soc.*, March 1988, 22(3), pp. 35–63.

Zysman, John and Cohen, Stephen. Muddling Through: American Interests in a Changing International Economy. In *Guerrieri, P. and Padoan, P. C., eds.*, 1988, pp. 162–94.

_____ **and Tyson, Laura D'Andrea.** Trade and Employment: An Overview of the Issues and Evidence. In *Tyson, L. D.; Dickens, W. T. and Zysman, J., eds.*, 1988, pp. 1–40.